The New College
FRENCH & ENGLISH
Dictionary

SECOND EDITION

ROGER J. STEINER
University of Delaware

AMSCO SCHOOL PUBLICATIONS, INC.
315 Hudson Street/New York, N.Y. 10013

THE NEW COLLEGE FRENCH & ENGLISH DICTIONARY, SECOND EDITION

When ordering this book, please specify:
either **R 504 P** or FRENCH DICTIONARY

ISBN 0-87720-493-4

Published by Amsco School Publications, Inc., by arrangement with the copyright owners.

The cover shows the Seine and the Conciergerie, Paris. Photo courtesy of French Government Tourist Office.

Printed in the United States of America

6   7   8   9   10

CONTENTS

PREFACE TO THE SECOND EDITION

A. *The New College French & English Dictionary* provides more grammatical help than any other French and English dictionary of its size. New features in the Second Edition show the user (1) which preposition to use after an adjective, (2) whether the adjective precedes the noun it modifies, and (3) which preposition follows a verb before a dependent infinitive. These new features are added to the unusually complete grammatical material already in the First Edition, such as the different meanings an adjective has when it precedes or when it follows a noun. As in the First Edition, a dictionary-grammar cross-referenced to the body of the Dictionary provides abundant information.

With the new additions on pronunciation, this Dictionary affords more help on pronunciation of French and English words than any other bilingual dictionary of its kind.

The inclusion of 5,200 new words and meanings is another major change in the Second Edition—terms that reflect recent scientific developments as well as current colloquial speech.

B. Inasmuch as the basic function of a bilingual dictionary is to provide semantic equivalences, syntactical constructions are shown in both the source and target languages on both sides of the Dictionary. In performing this function, a bilingual dictionary must fulfill six purposes. For example, a French and English bilingual dictionary must provide (1) French words that an English-speaking person wishes to use in speaking and writing (by means of the English-French part), (2) English meanings of French words that an English-speaking person encounters in listening and reading (by means of the French-English part), (3) the spelling, pronunciation, and inflection of French words and the gender of French nouns that an English-speaking person needs, to use French words correctly (by means of the French-English part), (4) English words that a French-speaking person wishes to use in speaking and writing (by means of the French-English part), (5) French meanings of English words that a French-speaking person encounters in listening and reading (by means of the English-French part), and (6) the spelling, pronunciation, and inflection of English words that a French-speaking person needs, to use English words correctly (by means of the English-French part).

It may seem logical to provide the pronunciation and inflection of English words and the pronunciation and inflection of French words and the gender of French nouns where these words appear as target words inasmuch as target words, according to (1) and (4) above, are sought for the purpose of speaking and writing. Thus the users would find not only the words they seek but all the information they need about them at one and the same place. But this technique is impractical because target words are not alphabetized and could, therefore, be found only by the roundabout and uncertain way of seeking them through their translations in the other part of the dictionary. And this would be particularly inconvenient for persons using the dictionary for purposes (2) and (5) above. It is much more convenient to provide immediate alphabetized access to pronunciation and inflection where the words appear as source words. Showing the gender of nouns takes so little space that this information is provided with both source and target words.

C. Prepositional phrases and expressions containing a verb and a noun are listed under the noun, e.g.,

channel [tʃænəl] *s* . . . ; **through channels** par la voie hiérarchique
sky [skaɪ] *s* (*pl* **skies**) ciel *m;* **to praise to the skies** porter aux nues
scrutin [skrytɛ̃] *m* . . . ; **dépouiller le scrutin** to count the votes

D. All subentries are listed alphabetically, e.g.,

    avis [avi] *m* . . . ; **à mon avis** . . . ; **avis au lecteur** . . . ; **changer d'avis** . . .

E. French expressions consisting of a noun and an adjective or a noun and an adjective phrase are listed under the noun, e.g.,

    scaphandre [skafɑ̃dr] *m* diving suit; spacesuit; **scaphandre autonome** aqualung
    portrait [portrɛ] *m* . . . ; **portrait à mi-corps** half-length portrait

F. All solid, hyphenated, and spaced compound English words are listed as separate entries, e.g.,

           mail′man′ *s* (*pl* **-men′**) facteur *m*
           point′-blank′ *adj & adv* . . . à bout portant
           tape′record′er *s* magnétophone *m*

G. All words are treated in a fixed order according to the parts of speech and the functions of verbs, as follows: article, adjective, substantive, pronoun, adverb, preposition, conjunction, transitive verb, intransitive verb, impersonal verb, auxiliary verb, reflexive verb, impersonal reflexive verb, interjection.

H. Meanings with subject and usage labels come after more general meanings. Subject and usage labels (printed in roman and in parentheses) refer to the preceding entry or phrase (printed in boldface). However, when labels come immediately, i.e., without any intervening punctuation mark, after a target word, they refer to that target word and the preceding word or words separated from it only by commas, e.g.,

    optometrist [ɑptɑmɪtrist] *s* opticien *m;* optométriste *mf* (Canad)

I. English adjectives are always translated by the French masculine form regardless of whether the translation of the exemplary noun modified would be masculine or feminine, e.g.,

    close [klos] *adj* . . . ; (*friendship*) étroit; (*room*) renfermé

J. In order to facilitate the finding of the meaning and use sought for, changes within a vocabulary entry in part of speech and function of verb, in irregular inflection, in the gender of French nouns, and in the pronunciation of French and English words are marked with parallels: ‖, instead of the usual semicolons.

K. Since vocabulary entries are not determined on the basis of etymology, homographs are included in a single entry. When the pronunciation of a homograph changes, this is shown in the proper place after parallels.

    Note, however, that plurals and words spelled with capitals are shown as run-on entries. They must be preceded by parallels only when there is a change in part of speech, in pronunciation, or in inflection.

L. Peculiarities in the pronunciation of the plural of French nouns and run-on entries are generally shown, e.g.,

        guet-apens [gɛtapɑ̃] *m* (*pl* **guets-apens** [gɛtapɑ̃])
        œil [œj] *m* . . . ; **entre quatre yeux** [ɑ̃trəkatzjø]

M. Periods are omitted after labels and grammatical abbreviations and at the end of vocabulary entries.

N.   Proper nouns and abbreviations are listed in their alphabetical position in the main body of the Dictionary. Thus **Algérie** and **algérien** or **Suède** and **suédois** do not have to be looked up in two different parts of the book. And all subentries are listed in strictly alphabetical order.

O.   The feminine form of a French adjective used as a noun (or a French feminine noun having identical spelling with the feminine form of an adjective) that falls alphabetically in a separate position from the adjective is treated in that position and is listed again as a cross reference under the adjective, e.g.,

> **cher chère** [ʃɛr] *adj* . . . ‖ *f* see **chère** ‖ . . .
> **chère** [ʃɛr] *f* fare, food and drink; . . .

P.   In French, the adjective most often follows the noun it modifies, and those adjectives that behave differently are identified in this Dictionary. In some cases the entry for the adjective includes the explanation "(precedes the noun it modifies)," e.g.,

> **jeune** [ʒœn] (precedes the noun it modifies) *adj* young . . .

In other cases the meaning of the adjective differs according to its position, and the indication "(when standing before noun)" is used, e.g.,

> **propre** [prɔpr] *adj* clean, neat; . . . ‖ (when standing before noun) *adj* own . . .

Note (1) that adjectives of color (e.g., **rouge**), nationality (e.g., **français**), and religion (e.g., **catholique**) always follow the modified noun; (2) that there is a literary and stylistic practice of setting any adjective before a modified noun: **d'excellentes récoltes, d'innocents touristes, l'impossible Français, un malhonnête homme, cette étonnante variété, un immonde marchandage.** In these last examples the sense of the adjective has been subdued and the importance of the noun has been increased.

Q.   The centered period is used in vocabulary entries of inflected words to mark off, according to standard orthographic principles in the two languages, the final syllable that has to be detached before the syllable showing the inflection is added, e.g.,

> **habi·tant** [abitɑ̃] **-tante** [tɑ̃t] *mf*
> **satis·fy** [sætɪsˌfaɪ] *v* (*pret & pp* **-fied**) *tr*

R.   Where the orthographic break, according to some authorities, is not permitted, for example, between a **y** and a following vowel, the centered period is not used, e.g.,

> **croyant** [krwajɑ̃] **croyante** [krwajɑ̃t]
> **moyen** [mwajɛ̃] **moyenne** [mwajɛn]

S.   If the two components of an English solid compound are not separated by an accent mark, a centered period is used to mark off the division between them, e.g., **la′dy·bird′.**

T.   Boldface numbers preceded by the paragraph sign § refer to the section on French Irregular Verbs (§1–§76) or to the section on French Grammatical References (§77–§102).

The author wishes to express his gratitude to the late Dr. Edwin B. Williams, whose efforts were unstinting in the attempt to make this a useful dictionary. The author wishes to thank his dear wife, Kathryn, whose patience carried through the ten years of research and compilation of the First Edition and the years of preparation of the Second Edition. Gratitude is due many persons who helped in the making of this book and in particular Walter D. Glanze; he has been a constant knowledgeable support. Among the many French informants who patiently answered inquiries, the author wishes to thank particularly Vital Komi Adjakey, Paul Barrette, Jean Béranger, Brigitte Calley, René Coulet du Gard, Jacques Dumestre, Paul Dumestre, Maurice Jonas, Marc Lampe, Philomena Lampe, Corinne Matrat, Daniel Pralus, Claud J. Pujoll, Paule Ready, Wayne Ready, Bruno Thibault, and André Vincent.

ROGER J. STEINER

LABELS AND ABBREVIATIONS

abbr abbreviation—abréviation
(acronym) word formed from the initial letters or syllables of a series of words—mot formé de la suite des lettres initiales ou des syllabes initiales d'une série de mots
adj adjective—adjectif
adv adverb—adverbe
(aer) aeronautics—aéronautique
(agr) agriculture—agriculture
(alg) algebra—algèbre
(anat) anatomy—anatomie
(archaic) archaïque
(archeol) archeology—archéologie
(archit) architecture—architecture
(arith) arithmetic—arithmétique
art article—article
(arti) artillery—artillerie
(astr) astronomy—astronomie
(astrol) astrology—astrologie
(aut) automobile—automobile
aux auxiliary verb—verbe auxiliaire
(bact) bacteriology—bactériologie
(baseball) base-ball
(bb) bookbinding—reliure
(Bib) Biblical—biblique
(billiards) billard
(biochem) biochemistry—biochimie
(biol) biology—biologie
(bk) bookkeeping—comptabilité
(bot) botany—botanique
(bowling) jeu de quilles, jeu de boules
(boxing) boxe
(Brit) British—britannique
(Canad) Canadian—canadien
(*cap*) capital—majuscule
(cards) cartes
(carpentry) charpenterie
(checkers) jeu de dames
(chem) chemistry—chimie
(chess) échecs
(coll) colloquial—familier
(com) commercial—commercial
comp comparative—comparatif
(comp) computers—ordinateurs
(complimentary close) formule de politesse
cond conditional—conditionnel
conj conjunction—conjonction; conjunctive—atone
(culin) cooking—cuisine

def definite—défini
dem demonstrative—démonstratif
(dentistry) art dentaire
(dial) dialectal—dialectal
(dipl) diplomacy—diplomatie
disj disjunctive—tonique
(eccl) ecclesiastical—ecclésiastique
(econ) economics—économique
(educ) education—éducation, pédagogie
e.g. par ex.
(elec) electricity—électricité
(electron) electronics—électronique
(embryol) embryology—embryologie
(eng) engineering—ingénierie, génie
(ent) entomology—entomologie
(equit) horseback riding—équitation
(escr) fencing—escrime
f feminine noun—nom féminin
(fa) fine arts—beaux-arts
fem feminine—féminin
(feudal) feudalism—féodalité
(fig) figurative—figuré
(fishing) pêche
fpl feminine noun plural—nom féminin pluriel
fut future—futur
(game) jeu
(geog) geography—géographie
(geol) geology—géologie
(geom) geometry—géométrie
ger gerund—gérondif
(govt) government—gouvernement
(gram) grammar—grammaire
(gymnastics) gymnastique
(heral) heraldry—héraldique, blason
(hist) history—histoire
(hort) horticulture—horticulture
(hum) humorous—humoristique
(hunting) chasse
(ichth) ichthyology—ichtyologie
i.e. c.-à-d.
imperf imperfect—imparfait
impers impersonal verb—verbe impersonnel
impv imperative—impératif
ind indicative—indicatif
indef indefinite—indéfini
inf infinitive—infinitif
(ins) insurance—assurance
interj interjection—interjection
interr interrogative—interrogatif

intr intransitive—intransitif
invar invariable—invariable
(ironical) ironique
(jewelry) bijouterie
(journ) journalism—journalisme
(Lat) Latin—latin
(law) droit
(*l.c.*) lower case—bas de casse
(letterword) word in the form of an abbreviation that is pronounced by sounding the names of its letters in succession and that functions as a part of speech—mot en forme d'abréviation qu'on prononce en faisant sonner le nom de chaque lettre consécutivement et qui fonctionne comme partie du discours
(lit) literary—littéraire
(logic) logique
m masculine noun—nom masculin
(mach) machinery—machinerie
(mas) masonry—maçonnerie
masc masculine—masculin
(Masonry) franc-maçonnerie
(math) mathematics—mathématiques
(mech) mechanics—mécanique
(med) medicine—médecine
(metallurgy) métallurgie
(meteo) meteorology—météorologie
mf masculine or feminine noun according to sex—nom masculin ou nom féminin selon le sexe
[for *m & f* see abbreviation following (mythol)]
(mil) military—militaire
(min) mining—travail des mines
(mineral) mineralogy—minéralogie
(mountaineering) alpinisme
(mov) moving pictures—cinéma
mpl masculine noun plural—nom masculin pluriel
(mus) music—musique
(mythol) mythology—mythologie
m & f masculine and feminine noun without regard to sex—nom masculin et féminin sans distinction de sexe
(naut) nautical—nautique
(nav) naval—naval
neut neuter—neutre
(nucl) nuclear physics—physique nucléaire
(obs) obsolete—vieilli, vieux
(obstet) obstetrics—obstétrique
(offensive) offensant, blessant
(opt) optics—optique
(orn) ornithology—ornithologie
(painting) peinture
(parl) parliamentary procedure—usages parlementaires
(pathol) pathology—pathologie
(pej) pejorative—péjoratif
perf perfect—parfait
pers personal—personnel; person—personne
(pharm) pharmacy—pharmacie
(phila) philately—philatélie
(philos) philosophy—philosophie
(phonet) phonetics—phonétique
(phot) photography—photographie

(phys) physics—physique
(physiol) physiology—physiologie
pl plural—pluriel
(poetic) poetical—poétique
(pol) politics—politique
poss possessive—possessif
pp past participle—participe passé
prep preposition—préposition
pres present—présent
pret preterit—prétérit, passé simple
pron pronoun—pronom
(pros) prosody—métrique, prosodie
(psychoanal) psychoanalytic—psychanalytique
(psychol) psychology—psychologie
(psychopathol) psychopathology—psychopathologie
(*public sign*) affiche, écriteau
q.ch. or *q.ch.* quelque chose—something
qn or *qn* quelqu'un—someone
(rad) radio—radio
ref reflexive verb—verbe pronominal, réfléchi ou réciproque
reflex reflexive—réfléchi
rel relative—relatif
(rel) religion—religion
(rhet) rhetoric—rhétorique
(rok) rocketry—fusées
(rowing) canotage
(rr) railroad—chemin de fer
s substantive—substantif
(sculp) sculpture—sculpture
(seismol) seismology—sismologie
(sewing) couture
sg singular—singulier
(slang) populaire, argotique
s.o. or *s.o.* someone—quelqu'un
spl substantive plural—substantif pluriel
(sports) sports
s.th. or *s.th.* something—quelque chose
subj subjunctive—subjonctif
super superlative—superlatif
(surg) surgery—chirurgie
(surv) surveying—topographie
(swimming) nage
(taur) bullfighting—tauromachie
(telg) telegraphy—télégraphie
(telp) telephony—téléphonie
(telv) television—télévision
(tennis) tennis
(tex) textile—textile
(theat) theater—théâtre
(theol) theology—théologie
tr transitive verb—verbe transitif
(trademark) marque déposée
(turf) horse racing—courses de chevaux
(typ) printing—imprimerie
(U.S.A.) U.S.A., E.-U.A.
v verb—verbe
var variant—variante
(vet) veterinary medicine—médecine vétérinaire
(vulg) vulgar—grossier
(weight lifting) haltérophilie
(wrestling) lutte, catch
(zool) zoology—zoologie

FRENCH REGULAR VERBS

The letters (a) to (f) before the names of the tenses in this table correspond to the letters (a) to (f) that designate the tenses in the section on French irregular verbs. The forms printed in boldface correspond to the key forms described there.

TENSE	FIRST CONJUGATION	SECOND CONJUGATION	THIRD CONJUGATION
inf	**DONNER**	**FINIR**	**VENDRE**
ger	donnant	finissant	vendant
pp	donné	fini	vendu
(*a*) *impv*	donne	finis	vends
	donnons	finissons	vendons
	donnez	finissez	vendez
(*b*) *pres ind*	**donne**	**finis**	**vends**
	donnes	finis	vends
	donne	finit	vend
	donnons	**finissons**	**vendons**
	donnez	finissez	vendez
	donnent	**finissent**	**vendent**
(*c*) *pres subj*	donne	finisse	vende
	donnes	finisses	vendes
	donne	finisse	vende
	donnions	finissions	vendions
	donniez	finissiez	vendiez
	donnent	finissent	vendent
(*d*) *imperf ind*	donnais	finissais	vendais
	donnais	finissais	vendais
	donnait	finissait	vendait
	donnions	finissions	vendions
	donniez	finissiez	vendiez
	donnaient	finissaient	vendaient
(*e*) *fut ind*	**donnerai**	**finirai**	**vendrai**
	donneras	finiras	vendras
	donnera	finira	vendra
	donnerons	finirons	vendrons
	donnerez	finirez	vendrez
	donneront	finiront	vendront
pres cond	donnerais	finirais	vendrais
	donnerais	finirais	vendrais
	donnerait	finirait	vendrait
	donnerions	finirions	vendrions
	donneriez	finiriez	vendriez
	donneraient	finiraient	vendraient
(*f*) *pret ind*	**donnai**	**finis**	**vendis**
	donnas	finis	vendis
	donna	finit	vendit
	donnâmes	finîmes	vendîmes
	donnâtes	finîtes	vendîtes
	donnèrent	finirent	vendirent
imperf subj	donnasse	finisse	vendisse
	donnasses	finisses	vendisses
	donnât	finît	vendît
	donnassions	finissions	vendissions
	donnassiez	finissiez	vendissiez
	donnassent	finissent	vendissent

FRENCH IRREGULAR VERBS

In addition to the infinitive, gerund, and past participle, all simple tenses are shown in these tables if they contain one irregular form or more, except the conditional (which can always be derived from the stem of the future indicative) and the imperfect subjunctive (which can always be derived from the preterit indicative). Those forms are considered irregular that deviate morphologically and/or orthographically in root, stem, or ending from the paradigms of regular verbs. The infinitive is printed in boldface capital letters. And the following forms are printed in boldface: (1) key forms (that is, irregular forms from which other irregular forms can be derived, but not the derived forms), e.g., **buvons,** (2) individual irregular forms that occupy the place of key forms but cannot function as key forms because other irregular forms cannot be derived from them, e.g., **sommes,** and (3) individual irregular forms that cannot be derived from key forms, e.g., **dites.** The names of the key forms and the forms derived from each of them are listed below.

The numbers are those that accompany the respective verbs and verbs of identical patterns where they are listed in their alphabetical places in this Dictionary. The letters (a) to (f) identify the tenses as follows:

(a)	imperative	(d)	imperfect indicative
(b)	present indicative	(e)	future indicative
(c)	present subjunctive	(f)	preterit indicative

KEY FORM	DERIVED FORMS
1st sg pres ind	*2d & 3d sg pres ind & 2d sg impv**
1st pl pres ind	*2d pl pres ind, 1st & 2d pl pres subj,* whole *imperf ind, 1st & 2d pl impv, &* ger
3d pl pres ind	whole *sg & 3d pl pres subj*
1st sg fut ind	rest of *fut ind & whole conditional*
1st sg pret ind	rest of *pret ind & whole imperf subj*
1st sg pres subj of **faire, pouvoir,** & **savoir**	rest of *pres subj*
1st sg pres subj of **aller, valoir,** & **vouloir**	*2d & 3d sg & 3d pl pres subj*

§1 ABRÉGER—abrégeant—abrégé Combination of §10 and §38
  (a) abrège, abrégeons, abrégez
  (b) **abrège,** abrèges, abrège, **abrégeons,** abrégez, **abrègent**
  (c) abrège, abrèges, abrège, abrégions, abrégiez, abrègent
  (d) abrégeais, abrégeais, abrégeait, abrégions, abrégiez, abrégeaient
  (f) **abrégeai,** abrégeas, abrégea, abrégeâmes, abrégeâtes, abrégèrent

§2 ACHETER—achetant—acheté
  (a) achète, achetons, achetez
  (b) **achète,** achètes, achète, achetons, achetez, **achètent**
  (c) achète, achètes, achète, achetions, achetiez, achètent
  (e) **achèterai,** achèteras, achètera, achèterons, achèterez, achèteront

§3 ACQUÉRIR—acquérant—**acquis**
  (a) acquiers, acquérons, acquérez
  (b) **acquiers,** acquiers, acquiert, **acquérons,** acquérez, **acquièrent**
  (c) acquière, acquières, acquière, acquérions, acquériez, acquièrent
  (d) acquérais, acquérais, acquérait, acquérions, acquériez, acquéraient
  (e) **acquerrai,** acquerras, acquerra, acquerrons, acquerrez, acquerront
  (f) **acquis,** acquis, acquit, acquîmes, acquîtes, acquirent

§4 ALLER—allant—allé

* Some irregular verbs of the third conjugation that end in **s,** not preceded by **d,** in the *1st sg pres ind,* end in **s** also in the *2d sg pres ind* and the *2d sg impv,* and in **t** in the *3d sg pres ind,* e.g., **crains, crains, craint** and **bois, bois, boit.** And three verbs, namely, **pouvoir, valoir,** and **vouloir,** which end in **x** in the *1st sg pres ind,* end in **x** also in the *2d sg pres ind* and the *2d sg impv,* and in **t** in the *3d sg pres ind,* e.g., **veux, veux, veut.**

(a) **va,** allons, allez
(b) **vais** [ve], **vas, va,** allons, allez, **vont**
(c) **aille** [aj], ailles, aille, allions, alliez, aillent
(e) **irai,** iras, ira, irons, irez, iront

§5A ASSEOIR—asseyant—**assis**
(a) assieds, asseyons, asseyez
(b) **assieds,** assieds, assied, **asseyons,** asseyez, **asseyent**
(c) asseye, asseyes, asseye, asseyions, asseyiez, asseyent
(d) asseyais, asseyais, asseyait, asseyions, asseyiez, asseyaient
(e) **assiérai,** assiéras, assiéra, assiérons, assiérez, assiéront
(f) **assis,** assis, assit, assîmes, assîtes, assirent

§5B ASSEOIR—assoyant—**assis**
(a) assois, assoyons, assoyez
(b) **assois,** assois, assoit, **assoyons,** assoyez, **assoient**
(c) assoie, assoies, assoie, assoyions, assoyiez, assoient
(d) assoyais, assoyais, assoyait, assoyions, assoyiez, assoyaient
(e) **assoirai,** assoiras, assoira, assoirons, assoirez, assoiront
(f) **assis,** assis, assit, assîmes, assîtes, assirent

§6 AVOIR—ayant—**eu** [y]
(a) **aie** [e], **ayons, ayez**
(b) **ai** [e], **as, a, avons,** avez, **ont**
(c) **aie, aies, ait, ayons, ayez, aient**
(d) avais, avais, avait, avions, aviez, avaient
(e) **aurai,** auras, aura, aurons, aurez, auront
(f) **eus** [y], eus, eut, eûmes, eûtes, eurent

§7 BATTRE—battant—**battu**
(a) bats, battons, battez
(b) **bats,** bats, bat, battons, battez, battent

§8 BOIRE—buvant—**bu**
(a) bois, buvons, buvez
(b) bois, bois, boit, **buvons,** buvez, **boivent**
(c) boive, boives, boive, buvions, buviez, boivent
(d) buvais, buvais, buvait, buvions, buviez, buvaient
(f) **bus,** bus, but, bûmes, bûtes, burent

§9 BOUILLIR—bouillant—**bouilli**
(a) bous, bouillons, bouillez
(b) **bous,** bous, bout, **bouillons,** bouillez, **bouillent**
(c) bouille, bouilles, bouille, bouillions, bouilliez, bouillent
(d) bouillais, bouillais, bouillait, bouillions, bouilliez, bouillaient

§10 CÉDER—cédant—cédé
(a) cède, cédons, cédez
(b) **cède,** cèdes, cède, cédons, cédez, **cèdent**
(c) cède, cèdes, cède, cédions, cédiez, cèdent

§11 CONCLURE—concluant—**conclu**
(f) **conclus,** conclus, conclut, conclûmes, conclûtes, conclurent

§12 CONNAÎTRE—connaissant—**connu**
(a) connais, connaissons, connaissez
(b) **connais,** connais, connaît, **connaissons,** connaissez, **connaissent**
(c) connaisse, connaisses, connaisse, connaissions, connaissiez, connaissent
(d) connaissais, connaissais, connaissait, connaissions, connaissiez, connaissaient
(f) **connus,** connus, connut, connûmes, connûtes, connurent

§13 COUDRE—cousant—**cousu**
(a) couds, cousons, cousez
(b) couds, couds, coud, **cousons,** cousez, **cousent**
(c) couse, couses, couse, cousions, cousiez, cousent
(d) cousais, cousais, cousait, cousions, cousiez, cousaient
(f) **cousis,** cousis, cousit, cousîmes, cousîtes, cousirent

§14   **COURIR**—courant—**couru**
- (a) cours, courons, courez
- (b) **cours,** cours, court, **courons,** courez, **courent**
- (c) coure, coures, coure, courions, couriez, courent
- (d) courais, courais, courait, courions, couriez, couraient
- (e) **courrai,** courras, courra, courrons, courrez, courront
- (f) **courus,** courus, courut, courûmes, courûtes, coururent

§15   **CRAINDRE**—craignant—**craint**
- (a) crains, craignons, craignez
- (b) **crains,** crains, craint, **craignons,** craignez, **craignent**
- (c) craigne, craignes, craigne, craignions, craigniez, craignent
- (d) craignais, craignais, craignait, craignions, craigniez, craignaient
- (f) **craignis,** craignis, craignit, craignîmes, craignîtes, craignirent

§16   **CROIRE**—croyant—**cru**
- (a) crois, croyons, croyez
- (b) crois, crois, croit, **croyons,** croyez, croient
- (c) croie, croies, croie, croyions, croyiez, croient
- (d) croyais, croyais, croyait, croyions, croyiez, croyaient
- (f) **crus,** crus, crut, crûmes, crûtes, crurent

§17   **CROÎTRE**—croissant—**crû, crue**
- (a) croîs, croissons, croissez
- (b) **croîs,** croîs, croît, **croissons,** croissez, **croissent**
- (c) croisse, croisses, croisse, croissions, croissiez, croissent
- (d) croissais, croissais, croissait, croissions, croissiez, croissaient
- (f) **crûs,** crûs, crût, crûmes, crûtes, crûrent

§18   **CUEILLIR**—cueillant—**cueilli**
- (a) cueille, cueillons, cueillez
- (b) **cueille,** cueilles, cueille, **cueillons,** cueillez, **cueillent**
- (c) cueille, cueilles, cueille, cueillions, cueilliez, cueillent
- (d) cueillais, cueillais, cueillait, cueillions, cueilliez, cueillaient
- (e) **cueillerai,** cueilleras, cueillera, cueillerons, cueillerez, cueilleront

§19   **CUIRE**—cuisant—**cuit**
- (a) cuis, cuisons, cuisez
- (b) cuis, cuis, cuit, **cuisons,** cuisez, **cuisent**
- (c) cuise, cuises, cuise, cuisions, cuisiez, cuisent
- (d) cuisais, cuisais, cuisait, cuisions, cuisiez, cuisaient
- (f) **cuisis,** cuisis, cuisit, cuisîmes, cuisîtes, cuisirent

§20   **DÉPECER**—dépeçant—dépecé Combination of §2 and §51
- (a) dépèce, dépeçons, dépecez
- (b) **dépèce,** dépèces, dépèce, **dépeçons,** dépecez, **dépècent**
- (c) dépèce, dépèces, dépèce, dépecions, dépeciez, dépècent
- (d) dépeçais, dépeçais, dépeçait, dépecions, dépeciez, dépeçaient
- (e) **dépècerai,** dépèceras, dépècera, dépècerons, dépècerez, dépèceront
- (f) **dépeçai,** dépeças, dépeça, dépeçâmes, dépeçâtes, dépecèrent

§21   **DEVOIR**—devant—**dû, due**
- (a) missing
- (b) **dois,** dois, doit, **devons,** devez, **doivent**
- (c) doive, doives, doive, devions, deviez, doivent
- (d) devais, devais, devait, devions, deviez, devaient
- (e) **devrai,** devras, devra, devrons, devrez, devront
- (f) **dus,** dus, dut, dûmes, dûtes, durent

§22   **DIRE**—disant—**dit**
- (a) dis, disons, **dites**
- (b) dis, dis, dit, **disons, dites, disent**
- (c) dise, dises, dise, disions, disiez, disent
- (d) disais, disais, disait, disions, disiez, disaient
- (f) **dis,** dis, dit, dîmes, dîtes, dirent

§23   **DORMIR**—dormant—dormi *invar*
- (a) dors, dormons, dormez

      (b) **dors,** dors, dort, **dormons,** dormez, **dorment**
      (c) dorme, dormes, dorme, dormions, dormiez, dorment
      (d) dormais, dormais, dormait, dormions, dormiez, dormaient

§24   **ÉCLORE**—éclosant—**éclos**
      (a) éclos
      (b) éclos, éclos, **éclôt, éclosent**
      (c) éclose, écloses, éclose, **éclosions, éclosiez,** éclosent
      (d) missing
      (f) missing

§25   **ÉCRIRE**—écrivant—**écrit**
      (a) écris, écrivons, écrivez
      (b) écris, écris, écrit, **écrivons,** écrivez, **écrivent**
      (c) écrive, écrives, écrive, écrivions, écriviez, écrivent
      (d) écrivais, écrivais, écrivait, écrivions, écriviez, écrivaient
      (f) **écrivis,** écrivis, écrivit, écrivîmes, écrivîtes, écrivirent

§26   **ENVOYER**—envoyant—envoyé
      (a) envoie, envoyons, envoyez
      (b) **envoie,** envoies, envoie, envoyons, envoyez, **envoient**
      (c) envoie, envoies, envoie, envoyions, envoyiez, envoient
      (e) **enverrai,** enverras, enverra, enverrons, enverrez, enverront

§27   **ESSUYER**—essuyant—essuyé
      (a) essuie, essuyons, essuyez
      (b) **essuie,** essuies, essuie, essuyons, essuyez, **essuient**
      (c) essuie, essuies, essuie, essuyions, essuyiez, essuient
      (e) **essuierai,** essuieras, essuiera, essuierons, essuierez, essuieront

§28   **ÊTRE**—étant—été *invar*
      (a) **sois, soyons, soyez**
      (b) **suis, es, est, sommes, êtes, sont**
      (c) **sois, sois, soit, soyons, soyez, soient**
      (d) **étais, étais, était, étions, étiez, étaient**
      (e) **serai,** seras, sera, serons, serez, seront
      (f) **fus,** fus, fut, fûmes, fûtes, furent

§29   **FAIRE**—faisant—**fait**
      (a) fais, faisons, **faites**
      (b) fais, fais, fait, **faisons, faites, font**
      (c) **fasse,** fasses, fasse, fassions, fassiez, fassent
      (d) faisais, faisais, faisait, faisions, faisiez, faisaient
      (e) **ferai,** feras, fera, ferons, ferez, feront
      (f) **fis,** fis, fit, fîmes, fîtes, firent

§30   **FALLOIR**—missing—**fallu** *invar*
      (a) missing
      (b) **faut**
      (c) **faille**
      (d) **fallait**
      (e) **faudra**
      (f) **fallut**

§31   **FUIR**—fuyant—fui
      (a) fuis, fuyons, fuyez
      (b) fuis, fuis, fuit, **fuyons,** fuyez, **fuient**
      (c) fuie, fuies, fuie, fuyions, fuyiez, fuient
      (d) fuyais, fuyais, fuyait, fuyions, fuyiez, fuyaient

§32   **GRASSEYER**—grasseyant—grasseyé
   (regular, unlike other verbs with stem ending in **y**)

§33   **HAÏR**—haïssant—**haï**
      (a) hais [ɛ], haïssons, haïssez
      (b) **hais** [ɛ], hais, hait, **haïssons,** haïssez, **haïssent**
      (c) haïsse, haïsses, haïsse, haïssions, haïssiez, haïssent
      (d) haïssais, haïssais, haïssait, haïssions, haïssiez, haïssaient
      (f) haïs, haïs, haït, **haïmes, haïtes,** haïrent

§34 **JETER**—jetant—jeté
(a) jette, jetons, jetez
(b) **jette,** jettes, jette, jetons, jetez, **jettent**
(c) **jette,** jettes, jette, jetions, jetiez, jettent
(e) **jetterai,** jetteras, jettera, jetterons, jetterez, jetteront

§35 **JOINDRE**—joignant—**joint**
(a) joins, joignons, joignez
(b) **joins,** joins, joint, **joignons,** joignez, **joignent**
(c) joigne, joignes, joigne, joignions, joigniez, joignent
(d) joignais, joignais, joignait, joignions, joigniez, joignaient
(f) **joignis,** joignis, joignit, joignîmes, joignîtes, joignirent

§36 **LIRE**—lisant—**lu**
(a) lis, lisons, lisez
(b) lis, lis, lit, **lisons,** lisez, **lisent**
(c) lise, lises, lise, lisions, lisiez, lisent
(d) lisais, lisais, lisait, lisions, lisiez, lisaient
(f) **lus,** lus, lut, lûmes, lûtes, lurent

§37 **LUIRE**—luisant—**lui**
(a) luis, luisons, luisez
(b) luis, luis, luit, **luisons,** luisez, **luisent**
(c) luise, luises, luise, luisions, luisiez, luisent
(d) luisais, luisais, luisait, luisions, luisiez, luisaient
(f) archaic

§38 **MANGER**—mangeant—mangé
(a) mange, mangeons, mangez
(b) mange, manges, mange, **mangeons,** mangez, mangent
(d) mangeais, mangeais, mangeait, mangions, mangiez, mangeaient
(f) **mangeai,** mangeas, mangea, mangeâmes, mangeâtes, mangèrent

§39 **MAUDIRE**—maudissant—**maudit**
(a) maudis, maudissons, maudissez
(b) maudis, maudis, maudit, **maudissons,** maudissez, **maudissent**
(c) maudisse, maudisses, maudisse, maudissions, maudissiez, maudissent
(d) maudissais, maudissais, maudissait, maudissions, maudissiez, maudis-
    saient
(f) **maudis,** maudis, maudit, maudîmes, maudîtes, maudirent

§40 **MÉDIRE**—médisant—**médit**
(a) médis, médisons, médisez
(b) médis, médis, médit, **médisons,** médisez, **médisent**
(c) médise, médises, médise, médisions, médisiez, médisent
(d) médisais, médisais, médisait, médisions, médisiez, médisaient
(f) **médis,** médis, médit, médîmes, médîtes, médirent

§41 **MENTIR**—mentant—menti
(a) mens, mentons, mentez
(b) **mens,** mens, ment, **mentons,** mentez, **mentent**
(c) mente, mentes, mente, mentions, mentiez, mentent
(d) mentais, mentais, mentait, mentions, mentiez, mentaient

§42 **METTRE**—mettant—**mis**
(a) mets, mettons, mettez
(b) **mets,** mets, met, mettons, mettez, mettent
(f) **mis,** mis, mit, mîmes, mîtes, mirent

§43 **MOUDRE**—moulant—**moulu**
(a) mouds, moulons, moulez
(b) mouds, mouds, moud, **moulons,** moulez, **moulent**
(c) moule, moules, moule, moulions, mouliez, moulent
(d) moulais, moulais, moulait, moulions, mouliez, moulaient
(f) **moulus,** moulus, moulut, moulûmes, moulûtes, moulurent

§44 **MOURIR**—mourant—**mort**
(a) meurs, mourons, mourez

(b) **meurs,** meurs, meurt, **mourons,** mourez, **meurent**
(c) meure, meures, meure, mourions, mouriez, meurent
(d) mourais, mourais, mourait, mourions, mouriez, mouraient
(e) **mourrai,** mourras, mourra, mourrons, mourrez, mourront
(f) **mourus,** mourus, mourut, mourûmes, mourûtes, moururent

§45 MOUVOIR—mouvant—**mû, mue, mus, mues**
(a) meus, mouvons, mouvez
(b) **meus,** meus, meut, **mouvons,** mouvez, **meuvent**
(c) meuve, meuves, meuve, mouvions, mouviez, meuvent
(d) mouvais, mouvais, mouvait, mouvions, mouviez, mouvaient
(e) **mouvrai,** mouvras, mouvra, mouvrons, mouvrez, mouvront
(f) **mus,** mus, mut, mûmes, mûtes, murent

§46 NAÎTRE—naissant—**né**
(a) nais, naissons, naissez
(b) **nais,** nais, naît, **naissons,** naissez, **naissent**
(c) naisse, naisses, naisse, naissions, naissiez, naissent
(d) naissais, naissais, naissait, naissions, naissiez, naissaient
(f) **naquis,** naquis, naquit, naquîmes, naquîtes, naquirent

§47 NETTOYER—nettoyant—nettoyé
(a) nettoie, nettoyons, nettoyez
(b) **nettoie,** nettoies, nettoie, nettoyons, nettoyez, **nettoient**
(c) nettoie, nettoies, nettoie, nettoyions, nettoyiez, nettoient
(e) **nettoierai,** nettoieras, nettoiera, nettoierons, nettoierez, nettoieront

§48 PAÎTRE—paissant—**pu** *invar*
(a) pais, paissez
(b) **pais,** pais, paît, **paissons,** paissez, **paissent**
(c) paisse, paisses, paisse, paissions, paissiez, paissent
(d) paissais, paissais, paissait, paissions, paissiez, paissaient
(f) missing

§49 PAYER—payant—payé
(a) paie or paye, payons, payez
(b) **paie,** paies, paie, payons, payez, **paient** or paye, payes, paye, payons, payez, payent
(c) paie, paies, paie, payions, payiez, paient or paye, payes, paye, payions, payiez, payent
(e) **paierai,** paieras, paiera, paierons, paierez, paieront or payerai, payeras, payera, payerons, payerez, payeront

§50 PEINDRE—peignant—**peint**
(a) peins, peignons, peignez
(b) **peins,** peins, peint, **peignons,** peignez, **peignent**
(c) peigne, peignes, peigne, peignions, peigniez, peignent
(d) peignais, peignais, peignait, paignions, peigniez, peignaient
(f) **peignis,** peignis, peignit, peignîmes, peignîtes, peignirent

§51 PLACER—plaçant—placé
(a) place, plaçons, placez
(b) place, places, place, **plaçons,** placez, placent
(d) plaçais, plaçais, plaçait, placions, placiez, plaçaient
(f) **plaçai,** plaças, plaça, plaçâmes, plaçâtes, placèrent

§52 PLAIRE—plaisant—**plu** *invar*
(a) plais, plaisons, plaisez
(b) plais, plais, **plaît, plaisons,** plaisez, **plaisent**
(c) plaise, plaises, plaise, plaisions, plaisiez, plaisent
(d) plaisais, plaisais, plaisait, plaisions, plaisiez, plaisaient
(f) **plus,** plus, plut, plûmes, plûtes, plurent

§53 PLEUVOIR—pleuvant—**plu** *invar*
(a) **pleus, pleuvons, pleuvez** (fig & rare)
(b) **pleut, pleuvent**
(c) pleuve, pleuvent
(d) **pleuvait, pleuvaient**

(e) **pleuvra, pleuvront**
(f) **plut, plurent**

§54 **POURVOIR**—pourvoyant—**pourvu**
(a) pourvois, pourvoyons, pourvoyez
(b) **pourvois,** pourvois, pourvoit, **pourvoyons,** pourvoyez, **pourvoient**
(c) pourvoie, pourvoies, pourvoie, pourvoyions, pourvoyiez, pourvoient
(d) pourvoyais, pourvoyais, pourvoyait, pourvoyions, pourvoyiez, pourvoyaient
(f) **pourvus,** pourvus, pourvut, pourvûmes, pourvûtes, pourvurent

§55 **POUVOIR**—pouvant—**pu** *invar*
(a) missing
(b) **peux** or **puis,** peux, peut, **pouvons,** pouvez, **peuvent**
(c) **puisse,** puisses, puisse, puissions, puissiez, puissent
(d) pouvais, pouvais, pouvait, pouvions, pouviez, pouvaient
(e) **pourrai,** pourras, pourra, pourrons, pourrez, pourront
(f) **pus,** pus, put, pûmes, pûtes, purent

§56 **PRENDRE**—prenant—**pris**
(a) prends, prenons, prenez
(b) prends, prends, prend, **prenons,** prenez, **prennent**
(c) prenne, prennes, prenne, prenions, preniez, prennent
(d) prenais, prenais, prenait, prenions, preniez, prenaient
(f) **pris,** pris, prit, prîmes, prîtes, prirent

§57 **PRÉVOIR**—prévoyant—**prévu**
(a) prévois, prévoyons, prévoyez
(b) **prévois,** prévois, prévoit, **prévoyons,** prévoyez, **prévoient**
(c) prévoie, prévoies, prévoie, prévoyions, prévoyiez, prévoient
(d) prévoyais, prévoyais, prévoyait, prévoyions, prévoyiez, prévoyaient
(f) **prévis,** prévis, prévit, prévîmes, prévîtes, prévirent

§58 **RAPIÉCER**—rapiéçant—rapiécé Combination of **§10** and **§51**
(a) rapièce, rapiéçons, rapiécez
(b) **rapièce,** rapièces, rapièce, **rapiéçons,** rapiécez, **rapiècent**
(c) rapièce, rapièces, rapièce, rapiécions, rapiéciez, rapiècent
(d) rapiéçais, rapiéçais, rapiéçait, rapiécions, rapiéciez, rapiéçaient
(f) **rapiéçai,** rapiéças, rapiéça, rapiéçâmes, rapiéçâtes, rapiécèrent

§59 **RECEVOIR**—recevant—**reçu**
(a) reçois, recevons, recevez
(b) **reçois,** reçois, reçoit, **recevons,** recevez, **reçoivent**
(c) reçoive, reçoives, reçoive, recevions, receviez, reçoivent
(d) recevais, recevais, recevait, recevions, receviez, recevaient
(e) **recevrai,** recevras, recevra, recevrons, recevrez, recevront
(f) **reçus,** reçus, reçut, reçûmes, reçûtes, reçurent

§60 **RÉSOUDRE**—résolvant—**résolu; résout** *invar*
(a) résous, résolvons, résolvez
(b) **résous,** résous, résout, **résolvons,** résolvez, **résolvent**
(c) résolve, résolves, résolve, résolvions, résolviez, résolvent
(d) résolvais, résolvais, résolvait, résolvions, résolviez, résolvaient
(f) **résolus,** résolus, résolut, résolûmes, résolûtes, résolurent

§61 **RIRE**—riant—**ri** *invar*
(f) **ris,** ris, rit, rîmes, rîtes, rirent

§62 **SAVOIR**—sachant—**su**
(a) **sache, sachons, sachez**
(b) **sais,** sais, sait, **savons,** savez, **savent**
(c) **sache,** saches, sache, sachions, sachiez, sachent
(d) savais, savais, savait, savions, saviez, savaient
(e) **saurai,** sauras, saura, saurons, saurez, sauront
(f) **sus,** sus, sut, sûmes, sûtes, surent

§63 **SERVIR**—servant—servi
(a) sers, servons, servez
(b) **sers,** sers, sert, **servons,** servez, **servent**

(c) serve, serves, serve, servions, serviez, servent
(d) servais, servais, servait, servions, serviez, servaient

§64 SORTIR—sortant—sorti
(a) sors, sortons, sortez
(b) **sors,** sors, sort, **sortons,** sortez, **sortent**
(c) sorte, sortes, sorte, sortions, sortiez, sortent
(d) sortais, sortais, sortait, sortions, sortiez, sortaient

§65 SOUFFRIR—souffrant—**souffert**
(a) souffre, souffrons, souffrez
(b) **souffre,** souffres, souffre, **souffrons,** souffrez, **souffrent**
(c) souffre, souffres, souffre, souffrions, souffriez, souffrent
(d) souffrais, souffrais, souffrait, souffrions, souffriez, souffraient

§66 SUFFIRE—suffisant—**suffi**
(a) suffis, suffisons, suffisez
(b) suffis, suffis, suffit, **suffisons,** suffisez, **suffisent**
(c) suffise, suffises, suffise, suffisions, suffisiez, suffisent
(d) suffisais, suffisais, suffisait, suffisions, suffisiez, suffisaient
(f) **suffis,** suffis, suffit, suffîmes, suffîtes, suffirent

§67 SUIVRE—suivant—**suivi**
(a) suis, suivons, suivez
(b) **suis,** suis, suit, suivons, suivez, suivent

§68 TRAIRE—trayant—**trait**
(a) trais, trayons, trayez
(b) trais, trais, trait, **trayons,** trayez, traient
(c) traie, traies, traie, trayions, trayiez, traient
(d) trayais, trayais, trayait, trayions, trayiez, trayaient
(f) missing

§69 TRESSAILLIR—tressaillant—tressailli
(a) tressaille, tressaillons, tressaillez
(b) **tressaille,** tressailles, tressaille, **tressaillons,** tressaillez, **tressaillent**
(c) tressaille, tressailles, tressaille, tressaillions, tressailliez, tressaillent
(d) tressaillais, tressaillais, tressaillait, tressaillions, tressailliez, tressaillaient
(e) **tressaillirai,** tressailliras, tressaillira, tressaillirons, tressaillirez, tressailliront, or **tressaillerai,** tressailleras, tressaillera, tressaillerons, tressaillerez, tressailleront

§70 VAINCRE—vainquant—vaincu
(a) vaincs [vɛ̃], vainquons, vainquez
(b) vaincs, vaincs, vainc, **vainquons,** vainquez, **vainquent**
(c) vainque, vainques, vainque, vainquions, vainquiez, vainquent
(d) vainquais, vainquais, vainquait, vainquions, vainquiez, vainquaient
(f) **vainquis,** vainquis, vainquit, vainquîmes, vainquîtes, vainquirent

§71 VALOIR—valant—**valu**
(a) vaux, valons, valez
(b) **vaux,** vaux, vaut, **valons,** valez, **valent**
(c) **vaille** [vaj], vailles, vaille, valions, valiez, vaillent
(d) valais, valais, valait, valions, valiez, valaient
(e) **vaudrai,** vaudras, vaudra, vaudrons, vaudrez, vaudront
(f) **valus,** valus, valut, valûmes, valûtes, valurent

§72 VENIR—venant—**venu**
(a) viens, venons, venez
(b) **viens,** viens, vient, **venons,** venez, **viennent**
(c) vienne, viennes, vienne, venions, veniez, viennent
(e) **viendrai,** viendras, viendra, viendrons, viendrez, viendront
(f) **vins,** vins, vint, vînmes [vɛ̃m], vîntes [vɛ̃t], vinrent [vɛ̃r]

§73 VÉTIR—vêtant—**vêtu**
(a) vêts, vêtons, vêtez
(b) **vêts,** vêts, vêt, **vêtons,** vêtez, **vêtent**
(c) vête, vêtes, vête, vêtions, vêtiez, vêtent
(d) vêtais, vêtais, vêtait, vêtions, vêtiez, vêtaient

§74 **VIVRE**—vivant—**vécu**
    (a) vis, vivons, vivez
    (b) **vis,** vis, vit, vivons, vivez, vivent
    (f) **vécus,** vécus, vécut, vécûmes, vécûtes, vécurent

§75 **VOIR**—voyant—**vu**
    (a) vois, voyons, voyez
    (b) **vois,** vois, voit, **voyons,** voyez, **voient**
    (c) voie, voies, voie, voyions, voyiez, voient
    (d) voyais, voyais, voyait, voyions, voyiez, voyaient
    (e) **verrai,** verras, verra, verrons, verrez, verront
    (f) **vis,** vis, vit, vîmes, vîtes, virent

§76 **VOULOIR**—voulant—**voulu**
    (a) veux, voulons, voulez
    (b) **veux,** veux, veut, **voulons,** voulez, **veulent**
    (c) **veuille,** veuilles, veuille, voulions, vouliez, veuillent
    (d) voulais, voulais, voulait, voulions, vouliez, voulaient
    (e) **voudrai,** voudras, voudra, voudrons, voudrez, voudront
    (f) **voulus,** voulus, voulut, voulûmes, voulûtes, voulurent

FRENCH GRAMMATICAL REFERENCES

This section contains grammatical information that is cross-referenced by paragraph numbers in the body of the Dictionary (continuing the references numbered §1 to §76 of the section on French irregular verbs).

§77 le *art def* the. The following table shows the forms of the definite article, the combination of **le** with **à** and **de,** and the combinations of **les** with **à, de,** and **en.**

	masc	*fem*
sg	**le; l'** before a vowel or mute **h**	**la; l'** before a vowel or mute **h**
pl	**les**	**les**
with **à** *sg*	**au; à l'** before a vowel or mute **h**	**à la; à l'** before a vowel or mute **h**
with **à** *pl*	**aux**	**aux**
with **de** *sg*	**du; de l'** before a vowel or mute **h**	**de la; de l'** before a vowel or mute **h**
with **de** *pl*	**des**	**des**
with **en** *pl*	**ès,** e.g., **maître ès arts**	**ès,** e.g., **docteur ès lettres**

un *art indef* a, an. The following table shows the forms of the indefinite article.

	masc	*fem*
sg	un	une

The indefinite article does not have a plural form in modern French. Vestiges of earlier plural forms are seen in **quelques-uns** and **quelques-unes** (see §81). The plural is also shown when **un** is a pronoun, e.g., **les uns et les autres** the ones and the others; **ni les unes ni les autres** neither the ones nor the others. Instead of an indefinite plural article, modern French uses the contraction **de** + **les** = **des** to express the partitive idea of "some":
   Je voudrais des carottes parce que je n'ai qu'une carotte.
   I would like some carrots because I have only one carrot.

Mass nouns and uncountables. The preposition **de** plus the definite article (**du, de la, de l', des**) is used to indicate the partitive idea with a mass noun, e.g., **de l'eau** "(some) water." English and French nouns sometimes differ in regard to uncountable features. For example, the English speaker cannot say "I have a furniture" but must say "I have a piece of furniture." The French speaker, on the other hand, can say *J'ai un meuble.* Differences of this type are often noted in the body of this Dictionary.

§78 lequel *pron rel* who, whom; which Ä *pron interr* which, which one. The following table shows all the forms of the word **lequel** and their combinations with the prepositions **à** and **de.**

	masc	*fem*
sg	**lequel**	**laquelle**
pl	**lesquels**	**lesquelles**
with **à** *sg*	**auquel**	**à laquelle**
with **à** *pl*	**auxquels**	**auxquelles**
with **de** *sg*	**duquel**	**de laquelle**
with **de** *pl*	**desquels**	**desquelles**

The forms combined with **de** and used as relative pronouns sometimes mean "whose," e.g., **l'étudiant avec la sœur duquel j'ai dansé** the student with whose sister I danced.

§79 dont *rel pron* of whom; of which; from which; with which; on which; at which; which; whose. The relative pronoun **dont** may be: (a) the complement of the subject of the dependent verb, e.g., **cette malheureuse dont la jambe droite était brisée** that wretched woman whose right leg was broken; (b) the complement of the object of the dependent verb, e.g., **sa grande chambre dont on avait fermé les volets** his large bedroom the shutters of which they had closed; (c) the complement of the verb itself, e.g., **les termes dont il se servait** the expressions (that) he used.

If the antecedent is one of point of origin, **d'où** is used, e.g., **la porte d'où il est sorti** the door from which he went out, unless the point of origin is one of ancestry or extraction having to do with a person, e.g., **la famille distinguée dont il sortait** the distinguished family from which he came.

The relative pronoun **dont** cannot be the complement of a noun that is the object of a preposition but must be replaced by a form of **lequel** combined with **de** (see §78), or by **de qui**, e.g., **l'étudiante avec le frère de laquelle** (or **de qui**) **j'ai dansé** the student with whose brother I danced.

§80 quel *adj* what; what sort of; which; what a, e.g., **quelle belle ville!** what a beautiful city!; **n'importe quel** any ‖ *adj interr* what, e.g., **quel est le but de la vie?** what is the purpose of life?; who, e.g., **quel est cet homme?** who is that man? ‖ *adj indef*—**quel que** whoever, e.g., **quel que soit l'homme** whoever the man may be; whatever, e.g., **quelles que soient les difficultés** whatever difficulties there may be; whichever, e.g., **quel que soit le pied sur lequel il s'appuie** whichever foot he leans on. The following table shows all the forms of the word **quel**.

	masc	*fem*
sg	quel	quelle
pl	quels	quelles

§81 quelqu'un *pron indef* someone, somebody; anyone, anybody; **quelques-uns** some; any, a few. The following table shows all the forms of the word **quelqu'un**.

	masc	*fem*
sg	quelqu'un	quelqu'une
pl	quelques-uns	quelques-unes

§82A ce *adj dem* this; that; **ces** these; those. The following table shows all the forms of this word.

	masc	*fem*
sg	ce; cet before a vowel or mute **h**	cette
pl	ces	ces

This word has two meanings as exemplified by the following example:

cet homme this man; that man

However, the particles **-ci** and **-là** are attached to the noun modified by the forms of **ce** to distinguish what is near the person speaking (i.e., the first person) from what is near the person spoken to (i.e., the second person) or what is remote from both (i.e., the third person), for example:

cet homme-ci this man (*not that man*)
cet homme-là that man (*not this man*)
cet homme-là that man (*yonder*)

§82B ce *pron dem*
it, e.g., **c'est un bon livre** it is a good book;
he, e.g., **c'est un bon professeur** he is a good professor;
she, e.g., **c'est une belle femme** she is a beautiful woman;
they, e.g., **ce sont des élèves** they are students

§83 celui *pron dem* this one; that one. The following table shows all the forms of the demonstrative pronoun with their translations into English.

	masc	*fem*
sg	celui this one; that one; he	celle this one; that one; she
pl	ceux these; those	celles these; those

This word in all its forms is generally used with a following **de** or the relative pronouns **que** and **qui**:

$$\left.\begin{array}{l} \textbf{celui de} \\ \textbf{celle de} \\ \textbf{ceux de} \\ \textbf{celles de} \end{array}\right\} \text{'s, e.g., } \textbf{celui de Marie} \text{ Mary's}$$

celui que	he whom; the one that; the one which	
celle que	she whom; the one that; the one which	whomever;
ceux que	those whom; the ones whom; the ones which	whichever
celles que	those whom; the ones whom; the ones which	

celui qui	he who; the one that; the one which	
celle qui	she who; the one that; the one which	whoever;
ceux qui	those who; the ones who; the ones which	whichever
celles qui	those who; the ones who; the ones which	

§84 celui-ci *pron dem* this one; he; the latter. The particles **-ci** and **-là** are attached to the forms of **celui** to distinguish what is near the person speaking (i.e., the first person) from what is near the person spoken to (i.e., the second person) or remote from both (i.e., the third person). The following table shows all the forms of this word with particles attached and with their translations into English.

	masc	*fem*
sg	**celui-ci** this one **celui-là** that one	**celle-ci** this one **celle-là** that one
pl	**ceux-ci** these **ceux-là** those	**celles-ci** these **celles-là** those

The forms of **celui-ci** also mean the latter; and the forms of **celui-là**, the former, e.g., **Henri était roi et Catherine était reine. Celle-ci était espagnole et celui-là anglais.** Henry was a king, and Catherine was a queen. The former was English and the latter Spanish. (The English word order requires the inversion.)

§85 Disjunctive personal and reflexive pronouns. The following table shows all the forms of the disjunctive personal and reflexive pronouns with their translations into English.

moi	me; myself; I	**nous**	we, us; ourselves
toi	you, thee; yourself	**vous**	you; yourselves
lui	he, him, it; himself	**eux**	they, them *masc;* themselves *masc*
elle	she, her, it; herself	**elles**	they, them *fem;* themselves *fem*
soi	oneself; himself, herself, itself	**soi**	themselves

A. The disjunctive personal pronouns are used:

(1) as the object of a preposition, e.g., **Jean a été invité chez elle** John was invited to her house; e.g., **il est très content de lui** he is very satisfied with himself. Disjunctive pronouns especially as objects of prepositions rarely stand for things. Prepositional phrases that would include them are generally expressed by **y** (see §87), e.g., **je m'y suis avancé** I walked up to it, as contrasted with **je me suis avancé vers lui** I walked up to him; or are expressed by one of the adverbs **là-dessus, là-dessous, là-dedans,** etc., e.g., **voilà mon nom; écrivez le vôtre là-dessous** there is my name; write yours under it, as contrasted with **il n'a pas d'argent sur lui** he has no money with him.

(2) after the preposition **à** in phrases that are used to clarify or to stress the meaning of a conjunctive personal pronoun, e.g., **il lui a parlé, à elle** he spoke to her (or, he spoke to *her*).

(3) after the preposition **à** in phrases that are used to clarify the meaning of a preceding possessive adjective, e.g., **son chapeau à elle** her hat.

(4) as predicate pronouns after the verb **être**, especially after **c'est** and **ce sont:**

c'est moi	it is I, it is me	**c'est nous**	it is we, it is us
c'est toi	it is you, it is thee	**c'est vous**	it is you
c'est lui	it is he, it is him	**ce sont eux**	it is they, it is them *masc*
c'est elle	it is she, it is her	**ce sont elles**	it is they, it is them *fem*

(5) after **que** (than, as) in comparisons, e.g., **nous y allons plus souvent qu'eux** we go there more often than they; e.g., **nous y allons aussi souvent que vous** we go there as often as you.

(6) when the verb is not expressed, e.g., **qui a fait cela? Lui** who did that? He did.

(7) to stress the subject or object of the sentence, e.g., **lui, il a raison** he is right.

(8) in compound subjects and objects, e.g., **lui et moi, nous sommes médecins** he and I are doctors.

(9) when an adverb separates the subject pronoun from the verb, e.g., **lui toujours arrive en retard** he always arrives late.

(10) after **être** + **à** to contrast ownership, e.g., **ce stylo est à lui mais ce papier est à elle** this pen is his, but this paper is hers.

B. The disjunctive indefinite reflexive pronoun **soi** corresponds to **on** and is used mainly as the object of a preposition, i.e., according to **A**, 1 above, e.g., **on doit parler rarement de soi** one should seldom talk about oneself. But it may also be used in the predicate after the verb **être**, according to **A**, 4 above, e.g., **on a plus confiance quand c'est soi qui conduit** one has more confidence when it is oneself who drives.

§86 Intensive personal pronouns. The following table shows all the forms of these pronouns. They are made by combining the disjunctive personal pronouns with the forms of **même**.

moi-même	myself; I myself	**nous-mêmes**	ourselves; we ourselves
toi-même	yourself, thyself; you yourself	**vous-même**	yourself; you yourself
		vous-mêmes	yourselves; you yourselves
lui-même	himself; he himself; itself		
elle-même	herself; she herself; itself	**eux-mêmes**	themselves; they themselves
soi-même	oneself; itself	**elles-mêmes**	themselves; they themselves

§87 SEE PAGES xxiv–xxv.

§88 Possessive adjectives. The following table shows all the forms of possessive adjectives with their translations into English.

masc sg	*fem sg*	*masc & fem pl*	
mon	**ma***	**mes**	my
ton	**ta***	**tes**	your, thy, thine
son	**sa***	**ses**	his, her, its
notre	**notre**	**nos**	our
votre	**votre**	**vos**	your
leur	**leur**	**leurs**	their

* The forms **mon, ton,** and **son** are used instead of **ma, ta,** and **sa** respectively before feminine nouns and adjectives beginning with a vowel or mute **h**, e.g., **Marie a fait un cadeau à son aïeule** Mary gave a present to her grandmother; **elle y est venue avec son aimable tante** she came with her nice aunt.

The possessive adjectives:
(1) agree in gender and number with the thing possessed rather than with the possessor, e.g., **Marie lit son livre** Mary is reading her book.
(2) must be repeated before each noun in a series, e.g., **Marie apporte son stylo et son crayon** Mary is bringing her pen and pencil.

§89 Possessive pronouns. The following table shows all the forms of possessive pronouns with their translations into English.

	sg	*pl*	

masc	le mien	les miens	mine
fem	la mienne	les miennes	
	sg	*pl*	
masc	le tien	les tiens	yours, thine
fem	la tienne	les tiennes	
masc	le sien	les siens	his, hers, its
fem	la sienne	les siennes	
masc	le nôtre	les nôtres	ours
fem	la nôtre		
masc	le vôtre	les vôtres	yours
fem	la vôtre		
masc	le leur	les leurs	theirs
fem	la leur		

The possessive pronouns:

(1) agree in gender and number with the thing possessed rather than with the possessor, e.g., **donnez votre livre à Marie, elle a perdu le sien** give your book to Mary; she has lost hers.

(2) are preceded by a definite article, e.g., **tu dois obéir à son ordre et au mien** you must obey his order and mine.

(3) are sometimes used without antecedent: (a) **le mien** mine, my own (*i.e., property*); **le sien** his, his own (*i.e., property*); hers, her own (*i.e., property*); etc.; (b) **les miens** my folks, my family; my friends; my men; **les siens** his folks, his family; his friends; his men; her folks, etc.; (c) **faire des siennes** (coll) to be up to one's (his, etc.) old tricks.

§90 The adverb **ne**. This is a conjunctive particle, i.e., it always precedes a verb and, like conjunctive pronouns, is unstressed. Because of its weakness, it is generally accompanied by another word, which follows the verb (or auxiliary) in most cases, is stressed, and gives force or added meaning to the negation, e.g., **il n'est pas ici** he is not here.

A. The following table shows **ne** with the various words with which it is associated. (For more detail, see each expression under the second word in the body of the Dictionary, e.g., s.v. **aucun**; s.v. **aucunement**.)

ne . . . aucun	no, none; no one, nobody	**ne . . . ni . . . ni**	neither . . . nor
		ne . . . nul	no, none
ne . . . aucunement	by no means	**ne . . . nullement**	not at all
ne . . . brin (archaic)	not a bit, not a single	**ne . . . pas**	not, no
		ne . . . pas que	not only
ne . . . davantage	no more	**ne . . . pas un**	not one
ne . . . goutte (archaic)	not a drop, nothing	**ne . . . personne**	no one, nobody
		ne . . . plus	no more, no longer
ne . . . guère	hardly, scarcely; hardly ever	**ne . . . plus jamais**	never any more
		ne . . . plus que	now only
ne . . . jamais	never	**ne . . . point**	not, no, not at all
ne . . . mie (archaic)	not a crumb, not	**ne . . . que**	only, but
ne . . . mot (archaic)	not a word, nothing	**ne . . . rien**	nothing

B. The position of **ne** in the sentence is that of column 2 of §87. The position of **pas** and all the other like words, with the exception of **aucun, ni . . . ni, nul, personne,** and **que** is that of column 9. The position of **aucun, nul, personne,** and **que** is that of column 11. And the position of the first **ni** of **ni . . . ni** is that of column 11 unless the past participle is one of the correlatives, in which case its position is that of column 9.

Aucun, nul, pas un, personne, and rien may be used as subjects of the verb; they then precede **ne** and the verb, e.g., **personne n'est ici** no one is here. And **aucun, nul,** and **pas un** may be used as adjectives in the same position, e.g., **nul péril ne l'arrête** no danger stops him.

Usually when an infinitive is in the negative, **pas** immediately follows **ne**, e.g., **il m'a dit de ne pas y aller** he told me not to go there; **il regrette de ne pas me l'avoir dit** he regrets not having told me it.

§87 Conjunctive personal and reflexive pronouns.

person	1 subject	2 negative	3 direct & indirect object	4 direct object	5 indirect object
1	je (j')—I		me (m')—me, to me; myself, to myself		
2	tu—you, thou		te (t')—you, to you; thee, to thee; thyself, to thyself		
3	il—he; it elle—she; it on—one, they	ne (n')—not §90B	se (s')—himself, herself, itself, oneself; to himself, to herself, to itself, to oneself	le (l')—him; it la (l')—her; it	lui—to him; to her
4	nous—we		nous—us, to us; ourselves, to ourselves		
5	vous—you		vous—you, to you; yourself, to yourself; yourselves, to yourselves		
6	ils—they elles—they		se (s')—themselves; to themselves	les—them	leur—to them

This table shows all the forms of the conjunctive personal and reflexive pronouns with their translations into English and their positions (reading horizontally, not vertically) with respect to each other and with respect to the verb; and in negative declarative sentences, with respect to **ne** and **pas** and **personne**. All of the elements in this table except the verb and **pas** and **personne** (and the other negative words listed in §90) are unstressed.

In affirmative and negative interrogative sentences, the subject pronouns in column 1 are placed after the verb or auxiliary in column 8 and attached to it with a hyphen. A **t**, preceded and followed by hyphens, is intercalated between third-singular forms ending in a vowel and the subject pronoun. The interrogative forms of the first singular present indicative whose final sound is a nasal vowel or a consonant are not used, while those whose final sound is an oral vowel are, e.g., **où vais-je?** where am I going?; e.g., **que dirai-je?** what shall I say? And the ending **-e** of the first singular present indicative of verbs of the first conjugation is changed to **-é**, e.g., **donné-je?** do I give?, but these forms are not in current use in prose. All the forms not used are replaced by the affirmative forms introduced by **est-ce que** in affirmative interrogative

sentences and by **n'est-ce pas que** in negative interrogative sentences. And **est-ce que** and **n'est-ce pas que** may be thus used in any person of any tense of the indicative. The ending **-e** of the first singular imperfect subjunctive of some verbs is likewise changed to **-é** in conditional clauses without **si** in literary usage, e.g., **dussé-je** if I should.

In affirmative imperative sentences, the subject pronouns are not expressed and the pronouns in columns 3, 4, 5, 6, and 7 are placed after the verb and attached to it and to each other with hyphens except where elision occurs, and the pronouns in column 4 precede those in column 3. And unless followed by **en** or **y**, **me** is replaced by **moi** and **te** is replaced by **toi**; and **moi** and **toi** are stressed.

In negative imperative sentences, the subject pronouns are not expressed either and columns 2, 3, 4, 5, 6, 7, 8, and 9 have the same order as in negative declarative sentences.

A pronoun of column 5 cannot be used with a pronoun of column 3 but is replaced by a disjunctive pronoun preceded by the preposition **à**.

	6	7	8	9	10	11
				negative		*negative*
person						
1						
2						
3						
	y—there, to it; to them	**en**—some; of it; of them	VERB or AUXILIARY	**pas**—not §90B	past participle	**personne**—no one §90B
4						
5						
6						

C. The adverb **ne** is often used without **pas** or a similar word with the verbs **bouger, cesser, oser, pouvoir,** and **savoir,** e.g., **je ne saurais vous le dire** I can't tell you. And it is not
translated (1) with a compound tense after **il y a . . . que, voilà . . . que,** and **depuis que,** e.g., **il y a trois jours que je ne l'ai vu** it is three days since I saw him or (2) with the verb of a clause introduced by (a) **à moins que, avant que, empêcher . . . que,** and **éviter . . . que,** e.g., **à moins que je ne sois retenu** unless I am detained; (b) **si** meaning unless, e.g., **si je ne me trompe** unless I am mistaken; (c) a comparative + **que,** e.g., **vous étiez plus occupé qu'il ne l'était** you were busier than he was; (d) a verb or expression of fear such as **avoir peur que, craindre que, redouter que,** e.g., **je crains qu'il ne soit malade** I am afraid that he is sick; (e) a negative verb or expression of doubt, denial, despair such as **ne pas désespérer que, ne pas disconvenir que, ne pas douter que, ne pas nier que,** e.g., **je ne doute pas qu'il ne vienne** I do not doubt that he will come.

§91 *adj & adv comp & super* The comparative of superiority of adjectives and adverbs is formed by placing **plus** before the positive, e.g., **heureux** happy, **plus heureux** happier. The superlative of superiority of adjectives and adverbs is the same as the comparative, e.g., **heureux** happy, **plus heureux** happier and happiest. It is to be observed that the superlative is generally used in both French and English with the definite article or the possessive pronoun, e.g., **le plus heureux** the happiest, **son plus heureux** his happiest.

Some adjectives and adverbs have irregular comparatives and superlatives:

ADJECTIVES		*ADVERBS*	
positive	*comp and super*	*positive*	*comp and super*
bon good	**meilleur** better; best	**beaucoup** much	**plus** more; most
mauvais bad	**pire** worse; worst	**bien** well	**mieux** better; best
petit small	**moindre** lesser, less; least	**mal** badly	**pis** worse; worst
		peu little	**moins** less; least

The formation of adverbs. The feminine form of an adjective + the suffix *ment* constitutes an adverb.

masculine form	*feminine form*	+ *ment*
affectueux	**affectueuse**	**affectueusement**
brusque	**brusque**	**brusquement**
certain	**certaine**	**certainement**

Some adverbs are irregular in form, such as **absolument** (*fem adj* **absolue**), **assidûment** (*fem adj* **assidue**), **constamment** (*fem adj* **constante**), **énormément** (*fem adj* **énorme**), and many others. When an adverb has an irregular form, it may be found in the body of this Dictionary. When an adverb has a regular form, it is found in the body of this Dictionary when it has a meaning different from that of the adjective.

§92 Adjectives followed by **à** before a complementary infinitive. Many common adjectives are followed by an infinitive governed by **à**:

C'est facile à faire. It is easy to do.

When **il est** is used instead of **c'est,** then **de** is used before the infinitive:

Il est facile de faire le travail. It is easy to do the work.

In the above example, the infinitive has an object, and in such a case **il est** is generally used.

Other adjectives in this category are **accoutumé, bon, dernier, difficile, disposé, facile, habitué, léger, lent, lourd, mauvais, premier, prêt, propre, résolu, seul, utile.**

§93 Adjectives followed by **de** before a complementary infinitive. Many common adjectives are followed by an infinitive governed by **de**:

Ils sont fatigués de travailler. They are tired of working.
Je suis heureux de faire votre connaissance. I am happy to meet you.
Robert est absolument sûr de réussir. Robert is absolutely sure to succeed.

Other adjectives in this category are **capable, certain, chargé, content, coupable, curieux, digne, fatigué, heureux, libre, ravi, sûr, tenu.**

§94 Numerals. There are idiomatic characteristics of both French and English numerals. The entries for **trois** and **three** may be used as models for the other numerals:

trois [trwɑ] *adj & pron* three; the Third, e.g., **Jean trois** John the Third; **trois heures** three o'clock ‖ *m* three; third (*in dates*)

troisième [trwɑzjɛm] *adj, pron* (*masc, fem*), *& m* third

three [θri] *adj & pron* trois ‖ *s* trois *m*; **three o'clock** trois heures; **three of a kind** (cards) un frédon

third [θʌrd] *adj & pron* troisième (*masc, fem*); **the Third** trois, e.g., **John the Third** Jean trois ‖ *s* troisième *m*; (*in fractions*) tiers *m*; **the third** (*in dates*) le trois

§95 Verbs not followed by a preposition before an infinitive. Some verbs take no preposition before a dependent infinitive, as the verb **vouloir** in the following example.

Je veux   **parler.**   I want to speak.

the verb   (no   the dependent
vouloir   *prep*)   infinitive

Here are five more examples:

Nous allons voir le film. We are going to see the film.
Henri doit respecter sa mère. Henry should respect his mother.
Elle ne sait pas jouer au tennis. She does not know how to play tennis.
Il faut manger. It is necessary to eat.
Ils pensent venir bientôt. They intend to come soon.

The most common of the verbs in this category are **accourir, affirmer, aimer, aimer mieux, aller, apercevoir, assurer, avoir beau, avouer, compter, confesser, courir, croire, daigner, déclarer, déposer, descendre, désirer, devoir, écouter, entendre, envoyer, espérer, être censé, faillir, faire, falloir, se figurer, s'imaginer, juger, jurer (or + de), laisser, mener, mettre, monter, oser, ouïr, paraître, penser, pouvoir, préférer, prétendre, se rappeler, reconnaître, regarder, rentrer, retourner, revenir, savoir, sembler, sentir, souhaiter, soutenir, supposer, témoigner, valoir mieux, venir, voir, voler, vouloir.**

§96 Verbs followed by the preposition **à** before an infinitive. Some verbs take **à** before a dependent infinitive as do **chercher** and **commencer** in these examples:

Vous cherchez à comprendre? You are trying to understand?
Marie commence à parler. Mary is beginning to speak.

There are almost two hundred verbs in this category. Note that some of these verbs are sometimes used with **de** by native speakers. (One of these verbs is **commencer.**)

§97 Verbs followed by the preposition **de** before an infinitive. Here are three examples:

Robert décide de parler. (compare §100) Robert decides to speak.
Jean essaie de parler. John is trying to speak.
Hélène refuse de parler. Helen refuses to speak.

There are hundreds of verbs in this category.

Some verbs in this category are more likely to be followed by a past infinitive, e.g., **avoir fait,** than by a present infinitive, e.g., **faire.** Examples:

Jean attend de l'avoir fait. Jean expects to have it done.
Jean regrette de ne pas m'avoir téléphoné. Jean regrets not to have telephoned me.
Jean trouve bon d'y avoir assisté. Jean thinks it right to have taken part in it.

Other verbs of this kind are **douter, enrager, gémir, mourir, nier, rire, rougir, souffrir, sourire, trembler.**

§98 When the object of the verb is also the logical subject of the dependent infinitive—pattern **à . . . de.** Examples:

Le professeur a demandé à Marie de se taire. The professor asked Marie to stop talking.
Marie a dit au professeur de lire les examens. Mary told the professor to read the tests.
Le directeur conseille à Marie de chercher un autre emploi. The director is advising Mary to look for another job.

In this pattern the preposition **à** is used before the person or acting agent and the preposition **de** is used before the infinitive that follows the verb.
The most important verbs of this type or pattern are **accorder, commander, conseiller, crier, défendre, demander, dire, écrire, expliquer, imposer, inspirer, interdire, jurer, offrir, ordonner, parler, persuader, prescrire, promettre, proposer, recommander, refuser, répondre, reprocher, suggérer.**

§99 When the object of the verb is also the logical subject of the dependent infinitive—pattern (no *prep*) . . . **de.** Examples:

Le directeur prie Georges de choisir un métier. The director is begging George to choose a trade.
Le soldat a empêché le voleur de sortir. The soldier prevented the thief from leaving.
Le père ne doit pas dissuader son fils de finir ses études. The father should not dissuade his son from finishing his studies.

In this pattern the preposition **de** is used before the infinitive and no preposition is used before the person or acting agent. Note that in the third example above the use of **devoir** (*ne doit pas*) is not a part of this pattern but refers to the pattern in **§95.**
Some important verbs of this kind or pattern are **arrêter, avertir, aviser, charger, convaincre, décourager, défier, dégoûter, détourner, dispenser, dissuader, empêcher, exempter, menacer, persuader, prier, supplier.**
Some verbs of this kind are more likely to be followed by a past infinitive, e.g., **avoir fait,** than by a present infinitive, e.g., **faire.** Examples:

Jean accuse Paul de l'avoir fait. John accuses Paul of having done it.
Robert félicite Henri d'y avoir réussi. Robert congratulates Henry on having succeeded.

Other verbs in this latter category are **admirer, blâmer, consoler, excuser, gronder, louer, punir, remercier, réprimander.**

§100 When the object of the verb is also the logical subject of the dependent infinitive—pattern (no *prep*) . . . **à.** Examples:

Henri aide sa sœur à travailler. Henry is helping his sister work.
Madame Durand invitera ses amis à chanter. Mrs. Durand will invite her friends to sing.
Son père a décidé mon ami à chercher un emploi. His father persuaded my friend to look for a job.

In this pattern the preposition **à** is used before the infinitive and no preposition is used before the person or acting agent. Note that in the third example above, **décider** does not take **de** as it does in **§97** because now it is set in a different pattern.
The most important verbs of this type or pattern are **accoutumer, aider, autoriser, condamner, décider, destiner, disposer, dresser, employer, engager, entraîner, exciter, exhorter, forcer, habituer, inciter, inviter, obliger, porter, pousser, préparer, réduire.**

§101 When the object of the verb is also the logical subject of the dependent infinitive—pattern **à . . . à.** Examples:

Marie enseigne à ses étudiants à prononcer correctement les voyelles. Mary is teaching her students to pronounce the vowels correctly.
Robert apprendra à son frère à écouter les instructions! (coll) Robert will teach his brother to listen to the directions!

In this pattern the preposition **à** is used both before the person or acting agent and before the infinitive.

There are only two verbs in this pattern, **enseigner** and **apprendre,** and they appear in the examples above.

§102 Plurals of nouns and adjectives. The general rule for plurals is to add an **s: la reine / les reines; joli / jolis**

The principal exception to the general rule is that nouns and adjectives ending in **-s, -x,** and **-z** remain unchanged in the plural: (*nouns*) **le bras / les bras; la voix / les voix; le nez / les nez;** (*adjectives*) singular: **frais, doux;** plural: **frais, doux**

Instead of referencing irregular plurals to the grammatical tables, this Dictionary gives that information in the body of the Dictionary. Nouns with two plural forms, foreign nouns, and compound nouns are also explained in the respective entry in the body of the Dictionary. However, a short summary of some irregularities follows here:

(1) Nouns in **-au** and **-eu** add an **-x** to form the plural: **château / châteaux; jeu / jeux.** But note these exceptions: **landau / landaus; pneu / pneus**

(2) Adjectives in **-eau** and **-eu** add an **-x** to form the plural: **beau / beaux; hébreu / hébreux.** But note these exceptions: **bleu / bleus; feu / feus**

(3) Nouns and adjectives in **-al** change the **-al** to **-au** and add an **-x** to form the plural: **cheval / chevaux; égal / égaux.** But note these exceptions: **fatals, finals, avals, bals, cals, carnavals, chacals, régals**

(4) Seven nouns ending in **-ou** do not take the **-s** of the general rule but add **-x** to form the plural; their plurals are **bijoux, cailloux, choux, genoux, hiboux, joujoux, poux.**

(5) The following are the plurals of seven nouns ending in **-ail:** **baux, coraux, soupiraux, travaux, vantaux, ventaux, vitraux.** But note, e.g.: **détail / détails; éventail / éventails**

FRENCH PRONUNCIATION

The following phonetic symbols represent all sounds of the French language.

VOWELS

SYMBOL	SOUND	EXAMPLE
[a]	A little more open than the **a** in English **hat.**	**patte** [pat]
[ɑ]	Like **a** in English **father.**	**pâte** [pɑt] **phase** [fɑz]
[ɛ]	Like **e** in English **met.** Native French pronunciation of this vowel in an open syllable is often somewhere between [ɛ] the **e** in **met** and [e] the **a** in **fate.**	**sec** [sɛk] **fer** [fɛr] **fête** [fɛt] **aile** [ɛl] **parallèle** [paralɛl]
[e]	Like **a** in English **fate,** but without the glide the English sound sometimes has.	**été** [ete] **fée** [fe] **et** [e] **créer** [kree]
[ə]	Like **a** in English **comma** or like **o** in English **pardon.**	**le** [lə] **petit** [pəti]
[i]	Like **i** in English **machine** or like **e** in English **she.**	**si** [si]
[ɔ]	A little more open and rounded than **aw** in English **law.**	**donne** [dɔn] **dormir** [dɔrmir]
[o]	Like **o** in English **note** but without the glide the English sound sometimes has.	**mot** [mo] **eau** [o] **faute** [fot]
[u]	Like **u** in English **rude.**	**sou** [su] **four** [fur]
[y]	The lips are rounded for [u] and held without moving while the sound [i] is pronounced.	**su** [sy] **sûr** [syr]
[ø]	The lips are rounded for [o] and held without moving while the sound [e] is pronounced	**peu** [pø] **eux** [ø] **feutre** [føtr]
[œ]	The lips are rounded for [ɔ] and held without moving while the sound [ɛ] is pronounced.	**peur** [pœr] **seul** [sœl]

NASAL VOWELS

To produce the nasal vowels, sound is emitted through both nose and mouth by means of a lowering of the velum. The orthographic **m** or **n** has no consonantal value.

SYMBOL	SOUND	EXAMPLE
[ɑ̃]	Like **a** in English **father** and nasalized.	**en** [ɑ̃] **tant** [tɑ̃] **temps** [tɑ̃] **paon** [pɑ̃]
[ɔ̃]	More close than **aw** in English **law** and nasalized.	**on** [ɔ̃] **pont** [pɔ̃] **comte** [kɔ̃t]
[ɛ̃]	Like **e** in English **met** and nasalized.	**pin** [pɛ̃] **pain** [pɛ̃] **faim** [fɛ̃] **teint** [tɛ̃]
[œ̃]	Like [œ] of French **bœuf** and nasalized. There has been a tendency in this century to assimilate the nasal sound [œ̃] to the nasal sound [ɛ̃], making **brun** [brœ̃] and **brin** [brɛ̃] sound much the same.	**un** [œ̃] **parfum** [parfœ̃]

DIPHTHONGS

The sounds [j], [ɥ], and [w] are used to form French diphthongs. In addition, [aɪ] and [aʊ] occur in some words of foreign origin.

SYMBOL	SOUND	EXAMPLE
[j]	Like **y** in English **year** or like **y** in English **toy.**	**hier** [jɛr] **ail** [aj]

SYMBOL	SOUND	EXAMPLE
[ɥ]	Like the letter **u** [y] pronounced with conso-nantal value preceding a vowel.	**lui** [lɥi] **situation** [sitɥasjɔ̃] **nuage** [nɥaʒ] **écuelle** [ekɥɛl]
[w]	Like **w** in English **water.**	**oie** [wa] **jouer** [ʒwe] **jouir** [ʒwir]
[aɪ]	Like **i** in English **fine.**	**sunlight** [sœnlaɪt]
[aʊ]	Like **ou** in English **house.**	**clubhouse**　[klybaʊs]

CONSONANTS

The speaker of French characteristically keeps the tip of the tongue down behind the lower teeth and arches the back of the tongue at the same time. Thus, sounds such as [t], [d], [n], [s], [z] and [r] must in French be articulated with the tongue tip and blade in the proximity of the back surface of the teeth.

SYMBOL	SOUND	EXAMPLE
[b]	Like **b** in English **baby.**	**basse** [bɑs]
[d]	Like **d** in English **dead.**	**doux** [du]
[f]	Like **f** in English **face.**	**fou** [fu]
[g]	Like **g** in English **go.**	**gare** [gar]
[k]	Like **k** in English **kill,** but without the aspira-tion that normally accompanies **k** in English.	**cas** [kɑ] **kiosque** [kjɔsk]
[l]	Like **l** in English **like** or in English **slip**—pronounced toward the front of the mouth. Not like **l** in **old.**	**lit** [li] **houle** [ul]
[m]	Like **m** in English **more.**	**masse** [mas]
[n]	Like **n** in English **nest.**	**nous** [nu]
[ɲ]	Like **ny** in English **canyon** or like **ni** in English **onion.**	**signe** [siɲ] **agneau** [aɲo]
[ŋ]	Like **ng** in English **parking.**	**parking** [parkiŋ]
[p]	Like **p** in English **pen,** but without the aspira-tion that normally accompanies **p** in English.	**passe** [pɑs]
[r]	Sometimes the uvular **r** but for some decades now usually a friction **r** with the point of articulation between the rounded back of the tongue and the hard palate. It resembles the Spanish aspirate in **jota,** the German aspirate in **ach,** and the **g** in modern Greek **gamma** more than it resembles the modern American retroflex **r.** The tip of the tongue must point down near the back of the lower teeth and must not move during the utterance of the French [r].	**rire** [rir] **caractère** [karaktɛr] **roi** [rwa] **roue** [ru]
[s]	Like **s** in English **send.**	**sot** [so] **leçon** [ləsɔ̃] **place** [plas] **lassitude** [lɑsityd] **attention** [atɑ̃sjɔ̃]
[ʃ]	Like **sh** in English **shall** or **ch** in English **machine.**	**cheval** [ʃval] **mèche** [mɛʃ]
[t]	Like **t** in English **ten,** but without the aspiration that normally accompanies **t** in English.	**toux** [tu] **thé** [te]
[v]	Like **v** in English **vest.**	**verre** [vɛr]
[z]	Like **z** in English **zeal.**	**zèle** [zɛl] **oser** [oze]

SYMBOL	SOUND	EXAMPLE
[ʒ]	Like s in English **pleasure**.	**joue** [ʒu] **rouge** [ruʒ] **mangeur** [mɑ̃ʒœr]

Note that truly French sounds are made by speaking in the front of the mouth, with vigorous movements of the lips (unlike English, which is spoken in the back, and with lazy lips).

LAW OF POSITION

In the modern French standard cultured pronunciation in France, the choice of the vowels [e] and [ɛ] (written variously as **e** + *cons,* **è, é, ai** + *cons,* **ais, ait, ei**) and the choice of the vowels [o] and [ɔ] (written variously as **o, ô, au, aux, eau, eaux**) follow what can be called the "law of position" (*la loi de position*). This is a rule of thumb that can be stated briefly as follows: Closed vowels are used in accented open syllables, and open vowels are used in closed syllables. The closed variants are [e] (**a** as in **fate**) and [o] (**o** as in **note**). An open syllable is one that does not end in a consonant sound. Examples: **est** [e], **allait** [ale], **été** [ete], **mot** [mo], **piano** [pjano], **ruisseau** [rɥiso]. In the examples just cited, the vowel is not followed by a consonant sound, and the closed variant is used. On the other hand, the open variants are [ɛ] (**e** as in **met**) and [ɔ] (**aw** as in **law**). A closed syllable is one that ends in a consonant sound. Examples: **père** [pɛr], **terre** [tɛr], **laisse** [lɛs], **donne** [dɔn], **encore** [ɑ̃kɔr]. In the examples just cited, the vowel is followed by a consonant sound, and the open variant is used. However, with the spellings **au** or **ô**, the closed variant is used even when followed by a pronounced consonant: **faute** [fot], **fausse** [fos], **hôte** [ot].

In this Dictionary the law of position is not used to explain pronunciation. For example, **très** [trɛ] is not presented with the pronunciation [tre] even though the latter pronunciation is frequently used today. Since the use of the law of position varies from speaker to speaker and from region to region, and the use of the law of position is inconsistent even in the same speaker (who might pronounce **est** as [e] but **paix** as [pɛ]), the notation of pronunciation in this Dictionary is traditional and conservative.

FRENCH STRESS

Stress is not shown on French words in this Dictionary because stress is not a fixed characteristic of the pronunciation of French words. It depends on the position of the word in the sentence and it falls on the last syllable of the word that terminates a rhythmic or sense grouping unless the vowel of that syllable is a mute **e** [ə], in which case it falls on the immediately preceding syllable.

VOWEL LENGTH

Vowel length is not shown in the phonetic transcription of French words in this Dictionary because it, like stress, is not a fixed characteristic of the pronunciation of French words.

Furthermore, vowel length in French is not phonemic: Whether the vowel is long or short does not make a difference in the meaning of the word. To take the word **maître** as an illustration, some reference sources use a colon [:] to indicate that the length of the preceding vowel has been increased: [mɛ:tr] / [mɛtr]. The meaning of the word has not been changed by the lengthening of the vowel, and so the change is stylistic, not phonemic. Only phonemes are afforded the user in the pronunciation in the body of this Dictionary, and therefore the length is not shown by a colon [:].

A third reason for not indicating length of vowel is pedagogical: The student's task should not be complicated by the idea that the number of vowels has doubled. Instead, the student should realize that the length of vowels in French depends upon the environment of the vowel—where it finds itself in the rhythmic grouping or which vowel and/or consonant sounds surround it. There are regular rules for vowel length. The student may follow these simple rules:

The following vowel sounds in the positions indicated are long when stressed: (1) all when followed by [r], [z], [v], [ʒ], or [vr]; (2) all spelled with a circumflex accent and followed by a consonant sound; and (3) [ɑ̃], [ɔ̃], [ɛ̃], [œ̃], [ɑ], [o], and [ø] followed by a consonant sound. When these conditions are not fulfilled, all vowel sounds are normal in length (or sometimes they may be short in length, even when stressed, if followed by [k], [p], [t], [kt], [rk], [rp], or [rt]).

ELISION AND LIAISON

Elision in French is the omission of the **a** in **la** and the **e** in words such as **le, de, que, se, me, te,** etc. Examples: **je + ai = j'ai, de + autres = d'autres.** Liaison is the pronunciation of a final written and usually silent consonant of a word as the first sound of the following word. Examples: **vous êtes, grand homme.** The **s** of **vous** is pronounced as a **z** and is the first sound of the following word as if that word were ''zêtes.'' The **d** of **grand** becomes a **t,** and the following word might be represented by ''tomme.'' Elision and liaison are usually made when the following word begins with a vowel or a mute **h.** Examples: **vous avez, beaux hommes.** Elision and liaison are made with some words beginning with **y,** such as: **yèbe, yeuse, yeux, Yonne,** and **York.**

However, there are words that begin with a vowel or an **h** with which elision and liaison are not made. Most of these words begin with **h,** called aspirate **h,** although it has not been pronounced for centuries. In this Dictionary these words are indicated by an asterisk placed before the opening bracket of the phonetic symbols, e.g., **hameau** *[amo], **onze** *[ɔ̃z], **a** *[ɑ], **s** *[ɛs].

Liaison is not always obligatory but depends upon level of speech. More liaison is used in formal speech than in informal speech. The standard cultured pronunciation of **ont attendu** takes the **t** of **ont** in liaison and sets it as the first sound of the word **attendu.** The informal pronunciation omits this liaison. There are some words that never make liaison, such as **et.** There are some combinations that always make liaison no matter what the level of speech, such as the pronouns and their following verbs, e.g., **nous avons, elles ont.**

LINKING

Linking (*enchaînement*) is the general term that refers to the final consonant of a word pronounced as the first sound of the following word. Thus, **autre ami** has three syllables: (1) **au,** (2) **tra,** (3) **mi.** This practice follows from the basic tendency of French pronunciation to end a syllable wherever possible with a vowel: consonant + vowel, consonant + vowel, etc. Note in these examples that the linked consonant need not be the last letter in the spelling of its word (**autre, quatre,** etc.). Examples:

Elle a quatre anges pour Anne. She has four angels for Ann.

Pronunciation division:

E	*lla*	*qua*	*tranges*	*pou*	*rAnne.*
V	CV	CV	CV	CV	CVC

Paul a mal au dents. Paul has a toothache.

Pronunciation division:

Pau	*la*	*ma*	*lau*	*dents.*
CV	CV	CV	CV	CV

Sometimes, of course, as in the case of a double consonant (**gouve*r*nement**) or a final position (**Anne,** above), the consonant must end the syllable.

Note that linking differs from liaison (see explanation above) in that liaison is a specialized type of linking that concerns a spelled but silent letter that would not otherwise be pronounced.

FRENCH-ENGLISH

A, a [ɑ], *[ɑ] *m invar* first letter of the French alphabet ‖ [a] *v* see **avoir**

à [a] *prep* to, into; at; by, e.g., **à l'année** by the year; from, e.g., **arracher à** to snatch from; in, e.g., **à l'italienne** in the Italian manner; on, e.g., **à temps** on time; with, e.g., **la jeune fille aux yeux bleus** the young woman with the blue eyes

abaisse-langue [abɛslɑ̃g] *m invar* tongue depressor

abaissement [abɛsmɑ̃] *m* lowering; drop; humbling

abaisser [abɛse] *tr* to lower; humble ‖ §96 *ref* to go down; humble oneself; to condescend

abandon [abɑ̃dɔ̃] *m* abandon; abandonment; desertion; neglect

abandonner [abɑ̃dɔne] §96 *tr* to abandon; forsake; give up ‖ *ref* to neglect oneself, become slovenly; **s'abandonner à** to give way to

abasourdir [abazurdir] *tr* to dumfound, flabbergast; deafen

abasourdis·sant [abazurdisɑ̃] **-sante** [sɑ̃t] *adj* astounding

abâtardir [abɑtardir] *tr* to debase ‖ *ref* to deteriorate, degenerate

abâtardissement [abɑtardismɑ̃] *m* debasement; deterioration, degeneration

abat·jour [abaʒur] *m invar* lampshade; eyeshade, sun visor; skylight

abats [aba] *mpl* giblets

abattage [abataʒ] *m* slaughtering (*of animals*); felling (*of trees*); demolition (*of a building*); bag, bagging (*of game*)

abattant [abatɑ̃] *m* drop leaf; toilet seat

abattement [abatmɑ̃] *m* dejection, despondency; prostration; tax deduction

abatteur [abatœr] *m* slaughterer; woodcutter; **abatteur de besogne** hard worker

abattis [abati] *m* felling (*of trees*); clearing (*of woods*); (mil) abatis; **abattis** *mpl* giblets; (slang) arms and legs

abattoir [abatwar] *m* slaughterhouse

abattre [abatr] §7 *tr* to pull down, demolish; fell; slaughter; overthrow; discourage; shoot down, bring down (*a bird, airplane, etc.*); lay (*dust*); (cards) to lay down (*one's hand*) ‖ *ref* to abate, subside; be dejected; swoop down; pounce; crash (*said of airplane*)

abat·tu -tue [abaty] *adj* dejected, downcast

abat·vent [abavɑ̃] *m invar* chimney pot

abbaye [abei] *f* abbey

abbé [abe] *m* abbot; abbé, father; **bonjour, monsieur l'abbé!** hello, father!

abbesse [abɛs] *f* abbess

a b c [abese] *m* (letterword) ABC's; speller

abcès [apsɛ] *m* abscess

abdiquer [abdike] *tr & intr* to abdicate

abdomen [abdɔmɛn] *m* abdomen

abécédaire [abesedɛr] *m* speller

abeille [abɛj] *f* bee

abêtir [abɛtir] *tr* to make stupid ‖ *intr & ref* to become stupid

abhorrer [abɔre] *tr* to abhor

abîme [abim] *m* abyss; depth

abîmer [abime] *tr* to spoil; damage ‖ *ref* to sink; be sunk; get spoiled

ab·ject -jecte [abʒɛkt] *adj* abject

abjurer [abʒyre] *tr* to abjure

abla·tif [ablatif] **-tive** [tiv] *adj & m* ablative

aboiement [abwamɑ̃] *m* barking; yelp, cry, outcry

abois [abwa] *mpl* desperate straits; **aux abois** at bay; hard pressed

abolir [abɔlir] *tr* to abolish; annul

abomination [abɔminasjɔ̃] *f* abomination

abondamment [abɔ̃damɑ̃] *adv* abundantly

abondance [abɔ̃dɑ̃s] *f* abundance, plenty; wealth; flow (*of words*); **parler d'abondance** to ad-lib

abon·dant [abɔ̃dɑ̃] **-dante** [dɑ̃t] *adj* abundant, plentiful; wordy

abon·né -née [abɔne] *mf* subscriber; season-ticket holder; consumer (*of gas, electricity, etc.*); commuter (*on railroad*)

abonnement [abɔnmɑ̃] *m* subscription

abonner [abɔne] *tr* to take out a subscription for (*s.o.*) ‖ *ref* to subscribe, take out a subscription

abord [abɔr] *m* approach; **abords** outskirts, surroundings; **d'abord** at first; **d'un abord facile** easy to approach; **tout d'abord** first of all

abordable [abɔrdabl] *adj* approachable, accessible; reasonable (*price*)

abordage [abɔrdaʒ] *m* (naut) boarding; (naut) collision

aborder [abɔrde] *tr* to approach, accost; board; collide with, run afoul of ‖ *intr* to land, go ashore

aborigène [abɔriʒɛn] *adj & m* native, aboriginal

abor·tif [abɔrtif] **-tive** [tiv] *adj* abortive

aboucher [abuʃe] *tr* to join; bring together ‖ *ref* to have an interview

aboutir [abutir] §96 *intr* to end; come to an end

aboutissement [abutismã] *m* outcome, result; success (*of a plan*)

aboyer [abwaje] §47 *intr* to bark; bay

abracada·brant [abrakadabrã] **-brante** [brãt] *adj* amazing, breath-taking

abra·sif [abrazif] **-sive** [ziv] *adj & m* abrasive

abrégé [abreʒe] *m* abridgment, summary; **en abrégé** in miniature; in brief, in an abbreviated form

abrégement [abreʒmã] *m* abridgment

abréger [abreʒe] §1 *tr* to abridge; shorten, curtail

abreuvage [abrœvaʒ] *m* watering

abreuver [abrœve] *tr* to water; soak; overwhelm, shower ‖ *ref* to drink

abreuvoir [abrœvwar] *m* drinking trough, watering trough, horsepond

abréviation [abrevjɑsjɔ̃] *f* abbreviation; abridgment, curtailment

abri [abri] *m* shelter, refuge, cover; air-raid shelter; carport; **à l'abri de** protected from

abribus [abribys] *m* bus shelter

abricot [abriko] *m* apricot

abricotier [abrikɔtje] *m* apricot tree

abri·promenade [abriprɔmnad] *m* hurricane deck, shelter deck

abriter [abrite] *tr* to shelter, protect, shield, screen ‖ *ref* to take shelter

abroger [abrɔʒe] §38 *tr* to abrogate, repeal

a·brupt -brupte [abrypt] *adj* abrupt, steep; rough, crude; blunt

abru·ti -tie [abryti] *adj* stunned, dazed, stupefied; idiotic ‖ *mf* idiot; sot

abrutir [abrytir] *tr* to brutalize; besot, deaden; overwhelm, exhaust

abrutis·sant [abrytisã] **-sante** [sãt] *adj* stupefying; deadening

absence [apsãs] *f* absence

ab·sent [apsã] **-sente** [sãt] *adj* absent; absent-minded ‖ *mf* absentee

absenter [apsãte] §97 *ref* to absent oneself, be absent, stay away

abside [apsid] *f* apse

absinthe [apsɛ̃t] *f* absinthe, wormwood; absinthe (*liqueur*)

abso·lu -lue [apsɔly] *adj* absolute

absolument [apsɔlymã] *adv* absolutely

absor·bant [apsɔrbã] **-bante** [bãt] *adj* absorbent; absorbing ‖ *m* absorbent

absorber [apsɔrbe] *tr* to absorb, soak up; eat up; drink ‖ *ref* to become absorbed, be deeply interested

absoudre [apsudr] §60, §97 (*pp* **absous, absoute;** no *pret* or *imperf subj*) *tr* to absolve; to forgive; to acquit

abstenir [apstǝnir] §72, §97, §99 *ref* to abstain, refrain

absti·nent [apstinã] **-nente** [nãt] *adj* abstinent; abstemious ‖ *mf* moderate eater or drinker

abstraction [apstraksjɔ̃] *f* abstraction; **faire abstraction de** to leave out, disregard

abstraire [apstrɛr] §68 (no *pret* or *imperf subj*) *tr* to abstract ‖ *ref* to become engrossed

abs·trait [apstrɛ] **-traite** [trɛt] *adj* abstract

abs·trus [apstry] **-truse** [tryz] *adj* abstruse

absurde [apsyrd] *adj* absurd

absurdité [apsyrdite] *f* absurdity

abus [aby] *m* abuse

abuser [abyze] *tr* to deceive ‖ *intr* to exaggerate; **abuser de** to take advantage of, impose upon; indulge unwisely in ‖ §96 *ref* to be mistaken

abu·sif [abyzif] **-sive** [ziv] *adj* abusive, wrong; excessive

acacia [akasja] *m* locust tree; **faux acacia** black locust tree

académicien [akademisjɛ̃] *m* academician

académie [akademi] *f* academy; (fa) nude

académique [akademik] *adj* academic

acagnarder [akaɲarde] *tr* to make lazy ‖ *ref* to grow lazy; lounge

acajou [akaʒu] *m* mahogany; mahogany tree; **acajou à pommes** (bot) cashew

acariâtre [akarjɑtr] *adj* grumpy

acca·blant [akablã] **-blante** [blãt] *adj* overwhelming

accabler [akable] *tr* to overwhelm; weigh down

accalmie [akalmi] *f* lull, standstill

accaparer [akapare] *tr* to corner (*the market*); monopolize

accéder [aksede] §10 *intr* to accede; acquiesce; have access

accéléra·teur [akseleratœr] **-trice** [tris] *adj* accelerating ‖ *m* accelerator

accéléré [akselere] *m* fast action; **en accéléré, à l'accéléré** (mov) speeded-up, high-speed

accélérer [akselere] §10 *tr, intr, & ref* to accelerate

accent [aksã] *m* accent; tone; stress, emphasis; **accent aigu** acute accent; **accent circonflexe** circumflex accent; **accent de hauteur** pitch accent; **accent d'insistance** emphasis; **accent d'intensité** stress accent; **accent grave** grave accent; **accent tonique** tonic accent; **mettre l'accent sur** to stress, emphasize

accentuer [aksãtɥe] *tr* to accent ‖ *ref* to become more marked

acceptable [aksɛptabl] *adj* acceptable

acceptation [aksɛptasjɔ̃] *f* acceptance

accepter [aksɛpte] §97 *tr* to accept ‖ *intr*—**accepter de** to agree to

acception [aksɛpsjɔ̃] *f* sense, meaning, preference, partiality

accès [aksɛ] *m* access; outburst; (pathol) attack, bout; **accès aléatoire, accès direct** (comp) random access; **accès aux quals** (public sign) to the docks

accessible [aksɛsibl] *adj* accessible; susceptible

accession [aksɛsjɔ̃] *f* accession

accessit [aksesit] *m* honorable mention

accessoire [aksɛswar] *adj* accessory ‖ *m* accessory; moonlighting job; (theat) prop; **accessoires** (theat) properties

accident [aksidɑ̃] *m* accident; unevenness (*of ground*); (mus) accidental

acciden·té -tée [aksidɑ̃te] *adj* rough, uneven; bumpy (*road*); eventful (*life*); (coll) wrecked (*car*) ‖ *mf* (coll) casualty, victim

acciden·tel -telle [aksidɑ̃tɛl] *adj* accidental

accidenter [aksidɑ̃te] *tr* to make uneven; vary; injure

accise [aksiz] *f* excise tax

acclamer [aklame] *tr* to acclaim

acclimater [aklimate] *tr* to acclimate ‖ *ref* to become acclimated

accolade [akɔlad] *f* embrace; accolade; (mus, typ) brace

accoler [akɔle] *tr* to hug; join side by side; couple (*names*); (typ) to brace

accommo·dant [akɔmɔdɑ̃] **-dante** [dɑ̃t] *adj* accommodating, obliging

accommodation [akɔmɔdɑsjɔ̃] *f* accommodation

accommodement [akɔmɔdmɑ̃] *m* settlement, compromise; arrangement

accommoder [akɔmɔde] *tr* to accommodate; conciliate; arrange (*furniture*); prepare (*food*) ‖ *ref* **s'accommoder à** to adapt oneself to; **s'accommoder de** to put up with

accompagna·teur [akɔ̃paɲatœr] **-trice** [tris] *mf* accompanist

accompagnement [akɔ̃paɲmɑ̃] *m* accompaniment

accompagner [akɔ̃paɲe] *tr* to accompany

accom·pli -plie [akɔ̃pli] *adj* completed; polished; accomplished

accomplir [akɔ̃plir] *tr* to accomplish; complete; fulfill (*a promise*) ‖ *ref* to come to pass

accomplissement [akɔ̃plismɑ̃] *m* accomplishment, performance

accord [akɔr] *m* accord, agreement, consent; harmony; settlement, bargain; (mus) chord; (mus) tuning; **accord global** package deal; **d'accord** in accord; **d'accord!** O.K.!, agreed!; check!; **d'un commun accord** by common consent

accordage [akɔrdaʒ] *m* tuning

accordéon [akɔrdeɔ̃] *m* accordion; **en accordéon** squashed; accordion-pleated

accorder [akɔrde] §97, §98 *tr* to grant; reconcile; (mus, rad) to tune ‖ *intr*—**accorder à qn de** to allow s.o. to ‖ §96 *ref* to harmonize; tally; agree

ac·cort [akɔr] **ac·corte** [akɔrt] *adj* sprightly, engaging (*e.g., young lady*)

accostage [akɔstaʒ] *m* (naut) coming alongside; (rok) docking

accoster [akɔste] *tr* to approach ‖ *intr* to dock, berth

accotement [akɔtmɑ̃] *m* shoulder (*of a road*); **accotement non-stabilisé** soft shoulder

accoter [akɔte] *tr* to shore up ‖ *ref* to lean

accouchement [akuʃmɑ̃] *m* childbirth

accoucher [akuʃe] *tr* to deliver ‖ *intr* (*aux:* ÊTRE) to be confined, be delivered ‖ *intr* (*aux:* AVOIR)—**accoucher de** to give birth to

accou·cheur [akuʃœr] **-cheuse** [ʃøz] *mf* obstetrician

accouder [akude] *ref* to lean on one's elbows

accoudoir [akudwar] *m* armrest

accouple [akupl] *f* leash

accouplement [akupləmɑ̃] *m* coupling; **accouplement consanguin** inbreeding

accoupler [akuple] *tr* to couple; yoke; bring together for breeding; link; (elec) to hook up ‖ *ref* to mate

accourir [akurir] §14, §95 *intr* (*aux:* AVOIR or ÊTRE) to run up; **accourir à** or **vers** to rush up to

accoutrement [akutrəmɑ̃] *m* togs, get-up

accoutrer [akutre] *tr* to rig out ‖ *ref* to dress ridiculously

accoutu·mé -mée [akutyme] §92 *adj* accustomed; **à l'accoutumée** as usual ‖ *mf* regular customer; frequent visitor

accoutumer [akutyme] §96, §100 *tr* to accustom ‖ *ref*—**s'accoutumer à** to get used to

accouvage [akuvaʒ] *m* artificial incubation

accouver [akuve] *tr* to set (*a hen*) ‖ *intr* to set (*said of a hen*) ‖ *ref* to begin to set

accréditer [akredite] *tr* to accredit; win a hearing for; **accrédité auprès de** accredited to ‖ *ref* to gain credence or favor

accréditeur [akreditœr] *m* bondsman

accroc [akro] *m* tear (*in a dress*); (fig) snag, hitch; **accroc à** blot on; breach of; **sans accroc** without a hitch

accrochage [akrɔʃaʒ] *m* hanging; hooking; clinch (*in boxing*); collision; (mil) encounter; (rad) receiving; (coll) squabble

accroche [akrɔʃ] *m* hanger

accrocher [akrɔʃe] *tr* to hang, hang up; hook; catch; (mil) to come to grips with; (rad) to pick up; (coll) to buttonhole ‖ *ref* (coll) to come to blows; cling; catch; get caught

accroire [akrwar] (used only in *inf* after *faire*) *tr*—**faire accroire à qn** to make s.o. believe ‖ *ref*—**s'en faire accroire** to get a swelled head

accroissement [akrwasmɑ̃] *m* growth; accumulation (*of capital*); increment

accroître [akrwɑtr] §17 (*pp* **accru;** *pres ind* **accrois;** *pret* **accrus,** etc.) *tr* & *ref* to increase

accroupir [akrupir] *ref* to squat, crouch

accu [aky] *m* storage battery

accueil [akœj] *m* reception, welcome

accueil·lant [akœjɑ̃] **-lante** [jɑ̃t] *adj* hospitable, gracious, welcoming, friendly

accueillir [akœjir] §18 *tr* to welcome; honor (*a bill*)

aculer [akyle] *tr* to corner

accumulateur [akymylatœr] *m* storage battery

accumuler [akymyle] *tr*, *intr*, & *ref* to accumulate

accusa·teur [akyzatœr] **-trice** [tris] *adj* incriminating ‖ *mf* accuser

accusatif [akyzatif] *m* accusative

accusation [akyzɑsjɔ̃] *f* accusation; charge

accu·sé -sée [akyze] *adj* marked; prominent (*features*) ‖ *mf* defendant ‖ *m* acknowledgment (*of receipt*)

accuser [akyze] §97, §99 *tr* to accuse; acknowledge (*receipt*)

acerbe [asɛrb] *adj* sour; sharp; caustic (*remark*)

acé·ré -rée [asere] *adj* keen (*edge*); sharp (*tongue*)

acétate [asetat] *m* acetate

acétique [asetik] *adj* acetic

acétone [asetɔn] *f* acetone

achalander [aʃalɑ̃de] *tr* to attract customers to ‖ *ref* to get customers

achar·né -née [aʃarne] *adj* fierce; relentless (*pursuit*); inveterate (*gambler*); bitter (*enemy*); **acharné à** bent on, set on

acharnement [aʃarnəmɑ̃] *m* fierceness, fury; stubbornness; eagerness

acharner [aʃarne] *tr* to set, sic (*dogs*); bait (*a trap*) ‖ §96 *ref* to fight bitterly; **s'acharner à** to work away at; be bent on, persist in; **s'acharner contre** to attack fiercely; **s'acharner sur** to light into; swoop down upon; bear down on; be dead set against

achat [aʃa] *m* purchase; **achat à terme** installment buying; **achat d'impulsion** impulse buying; **aller aux achats** to go shopping

ache [aʃ] *f* wild celery

acheminement [aʃminmɑ̃] *m* forwarding; progress

acheminer [aʃmine] *tr* to direct ‖ *ref* to proceed

acheter [aʃte] §2 *tr* to buy; **acheter à** to buy from; buy for; **acheter de** to buy from; **acheter pour** to buy for

achèvement [aʃɛvmɑ̃] *m* completion

achever [aʃve] §2, §97 *tr* to complete; finish off, kill ‖ *intr* to end; be just finishing ‖ *ref* to come to an end

Achille [aʃil] *m* Achilles

achoppement [aʃɔpmɑ̃] *m* obstacle; impact

achopper [aʃɔpe] *intr & ref* to stumble

achromatique [akrɔmatik] *adj* achromatic

acide [asid] *adj & m* acid; **acide phénique** carbolic acid

acidité [asidite] *f* acidity

acidu·lé -lée [asidyle] *adj* acid; fruit-flavored

aciduler [asidyle] *tr* to acidulate

acier [asje] *m* steel; (fig) sword; **acier inoxydable** stainless steel

aciérie [asjeri] *f* steelworks, steel mill

acmé [akme] *f* acme; (pathol) crisis

acné [akne] *f* acne

acolyte [akɔlit] *m* acolyte; accomplice

acompte [akɔ̃t] *m* installment; deposit; down payment; **acompte provisionnel** payment on estimated income tax

Açores [asɔr] *fpl* Azores

à·côté [akote] *m* (*pl* **-côtés**) sidelight; path (*beside road*); kickback

à·coup [aku] *m* (*pl* **-coups**) jerk; **par à-coups** by fits and starts

acoustique [akustik] *adj* acoustic, acoustical ‖ *f* acoustics

acquéreur [akerœr] *m* buyer

acquérir [akerir] §3 *tr* to acquire, get

acquiescement [akjɛsmɑ̃] *m* acquiescence

acquiescer [akjese] §51 *intr* to acquiesce

ac·quis [aki] **-quise** [kiz] *adj* established ‖ *m* know-how

acquisition [akizisjɔ̃] *f* acquisition

acquit [aki] *m* receipt; **pour acquit** paid in full

acquit-à-caution [akitakosjɔ̃] *m* (*pl* **acquits-à-caution**) permit to transport in bond

acquittement [akitmɑ̃] *m* acquittal

acquitter [akite] *tr* to acquit; receipt (*a bill*); pay, discharge ‖ *ref* to pay one's debts; **s'acquitter de** to fulfill, perform

acre [akr] *f* acre

âcre [ɑkr] *adj* acrid

acrylique [akrilik] *adj* acrylic

acrimo·nieux [akrimɔnjø] **-nieuse** [njøz] *adj* acrimonious

acrobate [akrɔbat] *mf* acrobat

acrobatie [akrɔbasi] *f* acrobatics

acropole [akrɔpɔl] *f* acropolis

acrostiche [akrɔstiʃ] *m* acrostic

acte [akt] *m* action; bill; act; certificate; deed; **acte de présence** personal appearance; **acte de vente** bill of sale; **actes** minutes; **faire acte** to make a declaration; **prendre acte** to take minutes

acteur [aktœr] *m* actor

ac·tif [aktif] **-tive** [tiv] *adj* active; live (*microphone*); full (*citizen*) ‖ *m* credit side (*of an account*); assets; (gram) active voice; **actifs corporels** tangible assets; **actifs incorporels** intangible assets

action [aksjɔ̃] *f* action; share (*of stock*); **action de grâces** thanksgiving; **action ordinaire** share of common stock; **action privilégiée** share of preferred stock; **action replay** (telv) replay (*of a play in a game*)

actionnaire [aksjɔnɛr] *mf* stockholder

actionner [aksjɔne] *tr* to actuate; drive; sue

activer [aktive] *tr* to activate; hasten ‖ *ref* to hasten

activité [aktivite] *f* activity; active service; **en pleine activité** in full swing

actrice [aktris] *f* actress

actuaire [aktɥɛr] *mf* actuary

actualisation [aktɥalizɑsjɔ̃] *f* modernization

actualiser [aktɥalize] *tr* to modernize, bring up to date

actualité [aktɥalite] *f* present condition; **actualités** current events; newsreel; **d'actualité** newsworthy

ac·tuel -tuelle [aktɥɛl] *adj* present, present-day, current

actuellement [aktɥɛlmɑ̃] *adv* now, at the present time

acuité [akɥite] *f* acuity

adage [adaʒ] *m* adage

Adam [adɑ̃] *m* Adam
adapta·teur [adaptatœr] **-trice** [tris] *mf* adapter ‖ *m* (mov) adapter
adaptation [adaptasjɔ̃] *f* adaptation
adapter [adapte] *tr & ref* to adapt
addenda [adɛ̃da] *m invar* addendum
addi·tif [aditif] **-tive** [tiv] *adj & m* additive
addition [adisjɔ̃] *f* addition; check (*for a restaurant meal*)
additionner [adisjɔne] *tr* to add up; add; dilute, mix
additionneuse [adisjɔnøz] *f* adding machine
adénoïde [adenɔid] *adj* adenoid
adent [adɑ̃] *m* dovetail
adepte [adɛpt] *mf* adept
adé·quat [adekwa] **-quate** [kwat] *adj* adequate
adhérence [aderɑ̃s] *f* adherence; traction; (pathol) adhesion
adhé·rent [aderɑ̃] **-rente** [rɑ̃t] *adj & mf* adherent
adhérer [adere] §10 *intr* to adhere; stick; **adhérer à la route** to hold the road
adhé·sif [adezif] **-sive** [ziv] *adj & m* adhesive
adhésion [adezjɔ̃] *f* adhesion
adieu [adjø] *m* (*pl* **adieux**) farewell ‖ *interj* adieu!, bon voyage!; good riddance!; **sans adieu!** see you later!
adja·cent [adʒasɑ̃] **-cente** [sɑ̃t] *adj* adjacent
adjec·tif [adʒɛktif] **-tive** [tiv] *adj & m* adjective
adjoindre [adʒwɛ̃dr] §35 *tr & ref* to join
ad·joint [adʒwɛ̃] **-jointe** [ʒwɛ̃t] *adj & mf* assistant, stand-by
adjudant [adʒydɑ̃] *m* warrant officer; sergeant major; (pej) martinet
adjudication [adʒydikɑsjɔ̃] *f* auction; awarding (*of a contract*)
adjuger [adʒyʒe] §38 *tr* to adjudge, award; knock down (*at auction*)
admettre [admɛtr] §42, §96 *tr* to admit
administra·teur [administratœr] **-trice** [tris] *mf* administrator, director
administration [administrasjɔ̃] *f* administration; **administration des ponts et chaussées** highway department
administrer [administre] *tr* to administer
admira·teur [admiratœr] **-trice** [tris] *mf* admirer
admira·tif [admiratif] **-tive** [tiv] *adj* admiring; amazed
admiration [admirɑsjɔ̃] *f* admiration; wonder
admirer [admire] §97, §99 *tr* to admire; wonder at
admissible [admisibl] *adj* admissible; eligible
admission [admisjɔ̃] *f* admission; (aut) intake
admonester [admɔnɛste] *tr* to admonish
adolescence [adɔlesɑ̃s] *f* adolescence
adoles·cent [adɔlesɑ̃] **-cente** [sɑ̃t] *adj & mf* adolescent
adonner [adɔne] §96 *ref* to devote oneself; **s'adonner à** to give oneself up to
adopter [adɔpte] *f* to adopt

adop·tif [adɔptif] **-tive** [tiv] *adj* adopted; adoptive
adoption [adɔpsjɔ̃] *f* adoption
adorable [adɔrabl] *adj* adorable
adora·teur [adɔratœr] **-trice** [tris] *mf* adorer; worshiper
adoration [adɔrɑsjɔ̃] *f* adoration
adorer [adɔre] *tr* to adore, worship
adosser [adɔse] *tr*—**adosser q.ch. à** to turn the back of s.th. against ‖ *ref*—**s'adosser à** to lean back against
adouber [adube] *tr* to dub
adoucir [adusir] *tr* to soften ‖ *ref* to soften; grow milder
adrénaline [adrenalin] *f* adrenalin
adressage [adrɛsaʒ] *m* mailing
adresse [adrɛs] *f* address; skill, dexterity; neatness; expertness, expertise; **adresse particulière** home address
adresser [adrɛse] *tr* to address ‖ *ref* to apply
Adriatique [adriatik] *adj & f* Adriatic
a·droit [adrwa] **-droite** [drwat] *adj* adroit, clever; neat
aduler [adyle] *tr* to adulate
adulte [adylt] *adj & mf* adult
adultère [adyltɛr] *adj* adulterous ‖ *m* adultery; adulterer ‖ *f* adulteress
adultérer [adyltere] §10 *tr* to adulterate; falsify (*a text*)
adulté·rin [adyltɛrɛ̃] **-rine** [rin] *adj* born in adultery
advenir [advənir] §72 (used only in *inf*; *pp*; 3d *pers sg & pl*) *intr* (*aux:* ÉTRE) to come to pass; **advienne que pourra** come what may
adventice [advɑ̃tis] *adj* adventitious
adverbe [advɛrb] *m* adverb
adversaire [advɛrsɛr] *mf* adversary
adverse [advɛrs] *adj* adverse; opposite (*side*)
adversité [advɛrsite] *f* adversity
aérer [aere] §10 *tr* to aerate; ventilate; to air
aé·rien [aerjɛ̃] **-rienne** [rjɛn] *adj* aerial ‖ *m* elevated railway
aéro [aero] *m* airplane
aérodynamique [aerɔdinamik] *adj* aerodynamic; streamlined ‖ *f* aerodynamics
aérogare [aerɔgar] *f* air terminal
aéroglisseur [aerɔglisœr] *m* hydrofoil
aérogramme [aerɔgram] *m* air letter
aérolite or **aérolithe** [aerɔlit] *m* meteorite, aerolite
aéronef [aerɔnɛf] *m* aircraft
aérophare [aerɔfar] *m* air beacon
aéroport [aerɔpɔr] *m* airport
aéropor·té -tée [aerɔpɔrte] *adj* airborne
aéropos·tal -tale [aerɔpɔstal] *adj* (*pl* **-taux** [to]) air-mail
aérosol [aerɔsɔl] *m* aerosol
aérospa·tial -tiale [aerɔspasjal] *adj* (*pl* **-tiaux** [sjo]) aerospace
A.F. *abbr* (**allocations familiales**) family (social-security) allotments
affable [afabl] *adj* affable
affadir [afadir] *tr & ref* to stale
affaiblir [afɛblir] *tr & ref* to weaken
affaire [afɛr] *f* affair; job; business; trouble; (law) case; (coll) belongings; **affaire à**

saisir bargain; **affaire d'or** (fig) gold mine; **affaire en instance** unfinished business; **affaires** business; **bonne affaire** bargain; **cela fait mon affaire** that is just what I want

affai·ré -rée [afɛre] *adj* busy, bustling

affairiste [afɛrist] *m* slicker, operator

affaissement [afɛsmɑ̃] *m* sagging; cave-in, collapse

affaisser [afɛse] *tr* to weigh down; depress ‖ *ref* to sag; cave in, collapse

affaler [afale] *tr* to haul down ‖ *ref* to drop, sink, flop

affa·mé -mée [afame] *adj* famished, starved

affamer [afame] *tr* to starve

affectable [afɛktabl] *adj* impressionable; mortgageable

affectation [afɛktɑsjɔ̃] *f* affectation; assignment; allotment

affec·té -tée [afɛkte] *adj* affected; §92 assigned

affecter [afɛkte] §97 *tr* to affect; assign; assume (*various shapes or manners*) ‖ *ref* to grieve

affec·tif -tive [tiv] *adj* affective, emotional

affection [afɛksjɔ̃] *f* affection; mental state; disease, affection

affection·né -née [afɛksjɔne] *adj* loving, fond, devoted

affectionner [afɛksjɔne] *tr* to be fond of ‖ *ref* to become attached

affectueusement [afɛktɥøzmɑ̃] *adv* affectionately

affec·tueux [afɛktɥø] **-tueuse** [tɥøz] *adj* affectionate

affé·rent [aferɑ̃] **-rente** [rɑ̃t] *adj* due, accruing

affermer [afɛrme] *tr* to lease, rent

affermir [afɛrmir] *tr* to strengthen, harden ‖ *ref* to become stronger, sounder

affichage [afiʃaʒ] *m* billposting

affiche [afiʃ] *f* poster, bill; (theat) playbill

afficher [afiʃe] *tr* to post, post up; display; (theat) to bill; (comp) to display (*on a screen*) ‖ *ref* to seek the limelight; **s'afficher avec** to hang around with

afficheur [afiʃœr] *m* billposter

affi·lé -lée [afile] *adj* sharpened; sharp (*tongue*) ‖ *adv*—**d'affilée** in a row

affiler [afile] *tr* to sharpen, whet; hone, strop; set (*a saw*)

affiliation [afiljɑsjɔ̃] *f* affiliation; franchising

affi·lié -liée [afilje] *adj* & *mf* affiliate; **affilié** franchise

affilier [afilje] *tr* & *ref* to affiliate

affiloir [afilwar] *m* sharpener; whetstone; hone, strop

affiner [afine] *tr* to improve; refine; sift ‖ *ref* to improve; mature, ripen

affinité [afinite] *f* affinity; in-law relationship

affirma·tif [afirmatif] **-tive** [tiv] *adj* & *f* affirmative

affirmer [afirme] *tr* §95 to affirm ‖ *ref* to assert oneself; **s'affirmer comme** to take one's place as

affixe [afiks] *m* affix

affleurer [aflœre] *tr* to level; come up to the level of ‖ *intr* to come to the surface

affliction [afliksjɔ̃] *f* affliction

affli·gé -gée [afliʒe] *adj* sorrowful

affli·geant [afliʒɑ̃] **-geante** [ʒɑ̃t] *adj* sorrowful (*news*)

affliger [afliʒe] §38 *tr* to afflict, distress ‖ §97 *ref*—**s'affliger de** to be distressed about

affluence [aflyɑ̃s] *f* crowd

af·fluent [aflyɑ̃] **-fluente** [flyɑ̃t] *adj* & *m* tributary

affluer [aflye] *intr* to flow; throng, crowd, flock

afflux [afly] *m* afflux, flow; rush

affo·lé -lée [afole] *adj* panic-stricken

affolement [afolmɑ̃] *m* distraction, panic; infatuation; unsteadiness (*of a compass*)

affoler [afole] *tr* to distract, panic; infatuate; disturb (*a compass*) ‖ *ref* to be distracted; stampede; become infatuated; spin (*as a compass*)

affran·chi -chie [afrɑ̃ʃi] *adj* emancipated; postpaid ‖ *mf* freethinker

affranchir [afrɑ̃ʃir] *tr* to emancipate, free; pay the postage for

affranchissement [afrɑ̃ʃismɑ̃] *m* emancipation; payment of postage; cancellation (*of mail*); **affranchissement insuffisant** postage due

affres [afr] *fpl* pangs

affrètement [afrɛtmɑ̃] *m* chartering (*of a boat*)

affréter [afrete] §10 *tr* to charter (*a boat*)

af·freux [afrø] **-freuse** [frøz] *adj* frightful

affront [afrɔ̃] *m* affront

affronter [afrɔ̃te] *tr* to confront; face

affubler [afyble] *tr* & *ref* to dress in a bizarre fashion

affût [afy] *m* hunting blind; mount (*for cannon*); **être à l'affût de** to lie in wait for

affûter [afyte] *tr* to sharpen

afin [afɛ̃] *adv*—**afin de** in order to; **afin que** + *subj* in order that, so that

afri·cain [afrikɛ̃] **-caine** [kɛn] *adj* African ‖ (*cap*) *mf* African

Afrique [afrik] *f* Africa; **l'Afrique** Africa

agacement [agasmɑ̃] *m* irritation, annoyance

agacer [agase] §51 *tr* to irritate, annoy; tease; set on edge

agape [agap] *f* agape; **agapes** banquet

âge [aʒ] *m* age; **d'un certain âge** middle-aged; **quel âge avez-vous?** how old are you?

â·gé -gée [aʒe] *adj* old, aged; old, e.g., **âgé de seize ans** sixteen years old

agence [aʒɑ̃s] *f* agency, office, service, bureau; **agence de location** rental service; real-estate office; **agence de recouvrement** collection agency; **agence de tourisme** travel agency; **agence de voyages** travel bureau; **agence immobilière** real-estate office

agencement [aʒɑ̃smɑ̃] *m* arrangement; furnishing (*of a house*); construction (*of a sentence*); **agencements** fixtures

agencer [aʒɑ̃se] §51 *tr* to arrange

agenda [aʒɛ̃da] *m* engagement book

agenouiller [aʒnuje] *ref* to kneel

agent [aʒɑ̃] *m* agent; policeman; **agent comptable** accountant; **agent de change** stockbroker; **agent de dépannage** (rad & telv) repairman; **agent de fret** cargo agent; **agent de la circulation** traffic cop; **agent de location** real-estate agent, Realtor; **pardon, monsieur l'agent** excuse me, officer

agglomeration [aglɔmerɑsjɔ̃] *f* agglomeration; metropolitan area; built-up area

agglomé·ré -rée [aglɔmere] *adj* compressed ‖ *m* briquette; adobe; composition board

agglomérer [aglɔmere] §10 *tr* & *ref* to agglomerate

aggraver [agrave] *tr* to aggravate ‖ *ref* to become more serious

agile [aʒil] *adj* agile, nimble

agilité [aʒilite] *f* agility

agio·teur [aʒjɔtœr] **-teuse** [tøz] *mf* speculator

agir [aʒir] *intr* to act; take action ‖ *ref*—**il s'agit de** it is a question of

agis·sant [aʒisɑ̃] **-sante** [sɑ̃t] *adj* active

agissements [aʒismɑ̃] *mpl* machinations

agita·teur [aʒitatœr] **-trice** [tris] *mf* agitator (*person*) ‖ *m* stirrer

agi·té -tée [aʒite] *adj* restless; rough (*sea*)

agiter [aʒite] *tr* to agitate; stir; wave; discuss ‖ *ref* to move about

a·gneau [aɲo] *m* (*pl* **-gneaux**) lamb

agnostique [agnɔstik] *adj* & *mf* agnostic

agonie [agɔni] *f* agony, death throes

agrafe [agraf] *f* clasp, pin; paper clip; staple (*for papers*); belt buckle; snap, hook; (med) clamp

agrafer [agrafe] *tr* to clasp, pin; buckle; snap; hook; fasten, clip; staple; (med) to clamp

agrafeuse [agraføz] *f* stapler

agraire [agrɛr] *adj* agrarian

agrandir [agrɑ̃dir] *tr* to enlarge ‖ *ref* to grow, become larger

agrandissement [agrɑ̃dismɑ̃] *m* enlargement

agréable [agreabl] *adj* agreeable, pleasant; neighborly

agréé agréée [agree] *adj* approved ‖ *m* attorney

agréer [agree] *tr* to accept, approve; **veuillez agréer l'expression de mes sentiments distingués** (complimentary close) sincerely yours ‖ *intr* —**agréer à** to agree with, please

agrégat [agrega] *m* aggregate

agrégation [agregɑsjɔ̃] *f* aggregation; admittance (*as a member of an organization*); competitive teacher's examination

agré·gé -gée [agreʒe] *adj* aggregate ‖ *mf* one who has passed his *agrégation*

agréger [agreʒe] §1 *tr* to attach, add ‖ *ref*—**s'agréger (à)** to join

agrément [agremɑ̃] *m* approval; pleasantness; pleasure, pastime; **agréments** adornments

agrès [agrɛ] *mpl* rigging; gym equipment

agresseur [agresœr] *adj* & *m* aggressor

agres·sif [agresif] **-sive** [siv] *adj* aggressive

agression [agresjɔ̃] *f* aggression; (law) assault

agreste [agrɛst] *adj* rustic, rural

agricole [agrikɔl] *adj* agricultural

agriculture [agrikyltyr] *f* agriculture

agrumes [agrym] *mpl* citrus fruit

aguerrir [agɛrir] §96 *tr* to season, inure ‖ *ref* to become seasoned, inured

aguets [agɛ] *mpl* watch, look-out; **être aux aguets** to be on the look-out

agui·chant [agiʃɑ̃] **-chante** [ʃɑ̃t] *adj* alluring ‖ *adj fem* sexy

ah [a] *interj* ah!; **ah çà!** now then!

ahu·ri -rie [ayri] *adj* dumfounded

ahurir [ayrir] *tr* to dumfound

ahurissement [ayrismɑ̃] *m* stupefaction

ai [e] *v* see **avoir**

aide [ɛd] *mf* aid, assistant, helper ‖ *f* aid, assistance, help; **aide à la navigation** instrument landing system; **aide sociale** welfare department

aider [ede] §96, §100 *tr* to aid, help; **aider à** + *inf* to help to + *inf* ‖ *intr* to help ‖ *ref*—**s'aider de** to use

aide-soignante [ɛdswaɲɑ̃t] *f* (*pl* **aides-soignante**) nurse's aid

aie [e] *v* (**aies, ait, aient**) see **avoir**

aïe [aj] *interj* ouch!

aïeul aïeule [ajœl] *mf* grandparent ‖ *m* grandfather ‖ *m* (*pl* **aieux** [ajø]) ancestor ‖ *f* grandmother

aigle [ɛgl] *mf* eagle; **aigle de mer** eagle ray; **aigle pêcheur grand aigle de mer** osprey, fish hawk; **grand aigle** spread eagle

aiglefin [ɛgləfɛ̃] *m* haddock

ai·glon [ɛglɔ̃] **-glonne** [glɔn] *mf* eaglet

aigre [ɛgr] *adj* sour, tart, bitter; harsh (*voice*)

aigre-doux [ɛgrədu] **-douce** [dus] *adj* bittersweet

aigrefin [ɛgrəfɛ̃] *m* crook

aigre·let [ɛgrəlɛ] **-lette** [lɛt] *adj* tart

aigrir [egrir] *tr* to turn (*s.th.*) sour ‖ *intr* & *ref* to turn sour

ai·gu -guë [egy] *adj* sharp; acute; shrill, high-pitched ‖ *m* (mus) treble

aigue-marine [ɛgmarin] *f* (*pl* **aigues-marines**) aquamarine

aiguille [egɥij] *f* needle; peak; spire (*of steeple*); hand (*of clock*); (rr) switch; **chercher une aiguille dans une botte de foin** to look for a needle in a haystack

aiguiller [egɥije] *tr* to switch, shunt ‖ *ref* to be switched, shunted

aiguilleur [egɥijœr] *m* (rr) tower man; (aer) air-traffic controller

aiguillon [egɥijɔ̃] *m* goad; sting

aiguiser [egɥize] *tr* to sharpen; whet (*appetite*)

ail [aj] *m* (*pl* **ails** or **aulx** [o]) garlic

aile [ɛl] *f* wing; flank (*of army*); fender (*of auto*); brim (*of hat*); blade (*of propeller*); vane, arm (*of windmill*); **aile en flèche** (aer) back-swept wing

aileron [ɛlrɔ̃] *m* aileron

aille [aj] *v* (**ailles, aillent**) see **avoir**

ailleurs [ajœr] *adv* elsewhere; **d'ailleurs** moreover, besides; from somewhere else; **par ailleurs** furthermore

aimable [ɛmabl] *adj* kind, likeable; **voulez-vous être assez aimable de** will you be good enough to

aimant [ɛmɑ̃] *m* magnet

aimanter [ɛmɑ̃te] *tr* to magnetize

aimer [eme], [ɛme] §95 *tr* to love; like; like to; **aimer à** to like to; **aimer bien** to like, be fond of; like to; **aimer mieux** to prefer; prefer to

aîne [ɛn] *f* groin

aî·né -née [ɛne] *adj* & *mf* elder, eldest, oldest; senior

aînesse [ɛnɛs] *f* seniority

ainsi [ɛ̃si] *adv* thus; **ainsi de suite** and so forth; **ainsi nommé** so-called; **ainsi que** as well as; **ainsi soit-il** amen

air [ɛr] *m* air; look, appearance; **air de famille** family resemblance; **avoir l'air de** to seem to; **en l'air** empty, idle (*threats, talk*)

airain [ɛrɛ̃] *m* brass; bronze

aire [ɛr] *f* area; threshing floor; eyrie; **aire d'attente** (aer) holding bay; **aire d'atterrissage** landing strip; **aire de lancement** launching pad; **aire de stationnement** parking area

airelle [ɛrɛl] *f*—**airelle coussinette** cranberry; **airelle myrtille, airelle noire** huckleberry, blueberry

aisance [ɛzɑ̃s] *f* ease, comfort

aise [ɛz] *adj*—**bien aise** glad, content ‖ *f* ease; **aises** comforts; **à son aise** well-to-do

ai·sé -sée [eze] *adj* easy; natural; well-to-do

aisément [ezemɑ̃] *adv* easily

aisselle [ɛsɛl] *f* armpit

ajonc [aʒɔ̃] *m* furze

ajou·ré -rée [aʒure] *adj* openwork, perforated

ajourer [aʒure] *tr* to cut openings in

ajournement [aʒurnəmɑ̃] *m* adjournment, postponement; subpoenaing; rejection (*of a candidate*)

ajourner [aʒurne] *tr* to postpone; to subpoena; to reject (*a candidate in an examination*)

ajouter [aʒute] *tr* & *intr* to add ‖ *ref* to be added

ajus·té -tée [aʒyste] *adj* tight-fitting

ajuster [aʒyste] *tr* to adjust; arrange; fit; aim at

ajusteur [aʒystœr] *m* fitter

alacrité [alakrite] *f* gaiety, vivacity

alambic [alɑ̃bik] *m* still

alambi·qué -quée [alɑ̃bike] *adj* fine-spun, far-fetched

alanguir [alɑ̃gir] *tr* to weaken ‖ *ref* to languish

alar·mant [alarmɑ̃] **-mante** [mɑ̃t] *adj* alarming

alarme [alarm] *f* alarm

alarmer [alarme] *tr* to alarm ‖ *ref* to be alarmed

alba·nais [albanɛ] **-naise** [nɛz] *adj* Albanian ‖ *m* Albanian (*language*) ‖ (*cap*) *mf* Albanian (*person*)

albâtre [albɑtr] *m* alabaster

albatros [albatros] *m* albatross

albi·geois [albiʒwa] **-geoise** [ʒwaz] *adj* Albigensian ‖ (*cap*) *mf* Albigensian

albinos [albinos] *adj* & *m* albino

album [albɔm] *m* album; scrapbook

albumen [albymɛn] *m* albumen

alcali [alkali] *m* alkali

alca·lin [alkalɛ̃] **-line** [lin] *adj* alkaline

alchimie [alʃimi] *f* alchemy

alcool [alkɔl] *m* alcohol; **alcool à friction** rubbing alcohol; **alcool dénaturé** denatured alcohol

alcoolique [alkɔɔlik], [alkɔlik] *adj* & *mf* alcoholic

alcoolisme [alkɔlism] *m* alcoholism; **alcoolisme au volant** drunken driving

alcotest [alkɔtɛst] *m* breath analyzer

alcôve [alkov] *f* alcove; **d'alcôve** amatory, gallant

ale [ɛl] *f* ale

aléa [alea] *m* risk

aléatoire [aleatwar] *adj* risky; aleatory

alène [alɛn] *f* awl

alentour [alɑ̃tur] *adv* round about ‖ **alentours** *mpl* neighborhood

alerte [alɛrt] *adj* & *f* alert; **alerte aérienne** air-raid alarm

alerter [alɛrte] *tr* to alert

alésage [alezaʒ] *m* bore (*of cylinder*)

aléser [aleze] §10 *tr* to ream; bore

ale·zan [alzɑ̃] **-zane** [zan] *adj* chestnut (*colored*)

algarade [algarad] *f* altercation

algèbre [alʒɛbr] *f* algebra

Alger [alʒe] *m* Algiers

Algérie [alʒeri] *f* Algeria

algé·rien [alʒerjɛ̃] **-rienne** [rjɛn] *adj* Algerian ‖ (*cap*) *mf* Algerian

algé·rois [alʒerwa] **-roise** [rwaz] *adj* of Algiers; Algerian ‖ (*cap*) *mf* native of Algiers; Algerian

algues [alg] *fpl* algae

alias [aljɑs] *adv* alias

alibi [alibi] *m* (law) alibi

alié·né -née [aljene] *adj* alienated; insane ‖ *mf* insane person

aliéner [aljene] §10 *tr* to transfer, alienate ‖ *ref* to alienate (*s.o.*); to lose (*e.g., s.o.'s sympathy*)

alignement [aliɲmɑ̃] *m* alignment

aligner [aliɲe] *tr* to align; **aligner ses phrases** to choose one's words with care ‖ *ref* to line up

aliment [alimɑ̃] *m* aliment, food; **aliments** (law) necessities; **aliments pour bébés (premier âge)** baby foods

alimentaire [alimɑ̃tɛr] *adj* alimentary; subsistence, e.g., **pension alimentaire** subsistence allowance

alimentation [alimɑ̃tasjɔ̃] *f* nourishment; supplying; feeding (*a fire, a machine*)

alimenter [alimɑ̃te] *tr* to nourish; supply; feed (*a fire, a machine*)

alinéa [alinea] *m* indentation (*of the first line of a paragraph*); paragraph

aliter [alite] *tr* to keep in bed ‖ *ref* to be confined to bed

alizés [alize] *mpl* trade winds

allaitement [alɛtmɑ̃] *m* feeding, nursing; **allaitement au biberon** bottle feeding; **allaitement maternel** breast feeding

allaiter [alɛte] *tr* to nurse

al·lant [alɑ̃] **-lante** [lɑ̃t] *adj* active ‖ *m*—**allants et venants** passers-by; **beaucoup d'allant** (coll) a lot of pep

allé·chant [aleʃɑ̃] **-chante** [ʃɑ̃t] *adj* enticing, tempting

allécher [aleʃe] §10 *tr* to allure

allée [ale] *f* walk, path; going; city street, boulevard; aisle (*of theater*)

allégeance [aleʒɑ̃s] *f* allegiance; lightening (*of care*); handicapping (*of a race*)

alléger [aleʒe] §1 *tr* to lighten; alleviate, mitigate, relieve

allégorie [alegɔri] *f* allegory

allègre [alɛgr] *adj* lively, cheerful

alléguer [allege] §10 *tr* to allege as an excuse; cite (*an authority*)

Allemagne [almaɲ] *f* Germany; **l'Allemagne** Germany

alle·mand [almɑ̃] **-mande** [mɑ̃d] *adj* German ‖ *m* German (*language*) ‖ (*cap*) *mf* German (*person*)

aller [ale] *m* going; go; **aller (et) retour** round trip; round-trip ticket; **au pis aller** at the worst ‖ §4, §95 *intr* (*aux:* ÊTRE) to go; work, function; **aller + inf** to be going to + *inf*, e.g., **je vais au magasin acheter des souliers** I am going to the store to buy some shoes; **aller à** to suit, fit, become, e.g., **la robe lui va bien** the dress beomes her; **allez!, allons!, allons donc!** well!, come on!, all right!; **allez-y doucement!** take it easy!; **ça va?, comment allez-vous?** how are you? ‖ *ref*—**s'en aller** to go away ‖ *aux*—**aller + inf** to be going to + *inf* (to express futurity), e.g., **il va se marier** he is going to get married

allergie [alɛrʒi] *f* allergy

aller·retour [alerətur] *m*—**faire l'aller-retour** to go and come back

alliage [aljaʒ] *m* alloy

alliance [aljɑ̃s] *f* alliance; marriage; wedding ring; **ancienne alliance** Old Covenant; **nouvelle alliance** New Covenant

al·lié -liée [alje] *adj* allied (*by treaty*); united (*in marriage*) ‖ *mf* ally; kin, in-law

allier [alje] *tr* to ally; to alloy ‖ *ref* to become allied, to ally oneself

alligator [alligatɔr] *m* alligator

allô [alo] *interj* hello!

allocation [allɔkɑsjɔ̃] *f* allocation, allotment; **allocation de chômage** unemployment insurance; **allocations familiales** family (social-security) allotments

allocution [allɔkysjɔ̃] *f* short speech

allonger [alɔ̃ʒe] §38 *tr, intr, & ref* to lengthen

allouer [alwe] *tr* to allow, allocate

allumage [alymaʒ] *m* lighting; switching on (*of a light*); kindling (*of a fire*); ignition; firing

allume-feu [alymfø] *m invar* kindling

allumer [alyme] *tr* to ignite; light (*a cigarette*); light up (*a room*); put on, switch on (*a light; a radio; a heater*); provoke (*anger*) ‖ *ref* to go on (*said of a light*); light up (*said of eyes*); catch fire

allumette [alymɛt] *f* match; **allumette de sûreté** safety match

allumette-gaz [alymɛtgaz] *m* pilot light

allumeur [alymœr] *m* ignition system; **allumeur de réverbères** lamplighter

allumeuse [alymøz] *f* (coll) vamp

allure [alyr] *f* speed, pace; gait, bearing, aspect; **à l'allure de l'escargot** at a snail's pace; **à toute allure** at top speed

allusion [allyzjɔ̃] *f* allusion

almanach [almana] *m* almanac; yearbook

aloès [alɔɛs] *m* aloe

aloi [alwa] *m* legal alloy; quality; **de bon aloi** genuine

alors [alɔr] *adv* then; **alors même que** even though; **alors que** whereas

alose [aloz] *f* shad

alouette [alwɛt] *f* lark, skylark; **alouette sans tête** rolled veal

alourdir [alurdir] *tr* to weigh down, make heavy ‖ *ref* to become heavy

aloyau [alwajo] *m* (*pl* **aloyaux**) sirloin

Alpes [alp] *fpl*—**les Alpes** the Alps

alphabet [alfabɛ] *m* alphabet

alpinisme [alpinism] *m* mountain climbing

alpiniste [alpinist] *mf* mountain climber

alpiste [alpist] *m* birdseed

alsa·cien [alzasjɛ̃] **-cienne** [sjɛn] *adj* Alsatian ‖ *m* Alsatian (*dialect*) ‖ (*cap*) *mf* Alsatian (*person*)

alté·rant [alterɑ̃] **-rante** [rɑ̃t] *adj* thirst-provoking

altération [alterasjɔ̃] *f* alteration, falsification; deterioration; heavy thirst; (mus) accidental

altérer [altere] §10 *tr* to alter, falsify; ruin (*one's health*); weaken, impair; make thirsty ‖ *ref* to undergo a change for the worse; become thirsty

alternance [altɛrnɑ̃s] *f* alternation; (agr) rotation

alterna·tif [altɛrnatif] **-tive** [tiv] *adj* alternative; alternating; alternate ‖ *f* alternative, dilemma; alternation

alterne [altɛrn] *adj* alternate (*angles*)

alterner [altɛrne] *tr* to rotate (*crops*) ‖ *intr* to alternate

al·tier [altje] **-tière** [tjɛr] *adj* haughty

altitude [altityd] *f* altitude

alto [alto] *m* alto; viola

altruiste [altrɥist] *adj & mf* altruist
aluminium [alyminjɔm] *m* aluminum
alun [alœ̃] *m* alum
alunir [alynir] *intr* to land on the moon
alunissage [alynisaʒ] *m* landing on the moon
alvéole [alveɔl] *m & f* alveolus; cavity; cell (*of honeycomb*); socket (*of tooth*)
amadou [amadu] *m* punk, tinder
amadouer [amadwe] *tr* to wheedle
amaigrir [amɛgrir] *tr* to emaciate; make thin ‖ *ref* to grow thin
amalgame [amalgam] *m* amalgam
amalgamer [amalgame] *tr & ref* to amalgamate
aman [amɑ̃] *m*—**demander l'aman** to give in
amande [amɑ̃d] *f* almond; kernel; **amande de Malaga** Jordan almond
amandier [amɑ̃dje] *m* almond tree
a·mant [amɑ̃] **-mante** [-mɑ̃t] *mf* lover
amareyeur [amarɛjœr] *m* oysterman
amariner [amarine] *tr* to season (*a crew*); impress (*a ship*)
amarre [amar] *f* hawser
amarrer [amare] *tr & ref* to moor
amas [ama] *m* mass; heap; cluster (*of stars*); **amas de neige** snowdrift
amasser [amase] *tr* to amass; gather ‖ *intr* to hoard ‖ *ref* to pile up, crowd
amateur [amatœr] *adj* amateur ‖ *m* amateur; (coll) prospective buyer
amatir [amatir] *tr* to mat, dull (*metal or glass*)
amazone [amazon] *f* amazon; horsewoman; riding habit; **monter en amazone** to ride sidesaddle ‖ (*cap*) *f* Amazon
ambages [ɑ̃baʒ] *fpl* circumlocutions; **sans ambages** without beating around the bush
ambassade [ɑ̃basad] *f* embassy
ambassadeur [ɑ̃basadœr] *m* ambassador
ambassadrice [ɑ̃basadris] *f* ambassadress; wife of an ambassador; emissary
ambiance [ɑ̃bjɑ̃s] *f* environment, milieu; atmosphere, tone
ambidextre [ɑ̃bidɛkstrə] *adj* ambidextrous ‖ *mf* ambidextrous person
ambi·gu -guë [ɑ̃bigy] *adj* ambiguous ‖ *m* ambiguousness; buffet lunch; odd mixture
ambiguïté [ɑ̃bigɥite] *f* ambiguity
ambi·tieux [ɑ̃bisjø] **-tieuse** [sjøz] *adj* ambitious
ambition [ɑ̃bisjɔ̃] *f* ambition
amble [ɑ̃bl] *m* amble; pacing
ambler [ɑ̃ble] *intr* (equit) to amble; pace
ambre [ɑ̃br] *m*—**ambre gris** ambergris; **ambre (jaune** or **succin)** amber
ambulance [ɑ̃bylɑ̃s] *f* ambulance
ambulan·cier [ɑ̃bylɑ̃sje] **-cière** [sjɛr] *mf* ambulance driver or attendant
ambu·lant [ɑ̃bylɑ̃] **-lante** [lɑ̃t] *adj* ambulant ‖ *m* railway mail clerk
ambulatoire [ɑ̃bylatwar] *adj* ambulatory; itinerant
âme [ɑm] *f* soul; spirit, heart, mind; core (*of cable*); bore (*of cannon*); web (*or rail*); sound post (*of violin*); **âme damnée** evil genius; **rendre l'âme** to give up the ghost

améliorer [ameljɔre] *tr & ref* to ameliorate, improve
amen [amɛn] *m invar* Amen
aménagement [amenaʒmɑ̃] *m* arrangement, equipping; preparation, development (*of land*); adjustment (*of taxes*); **aménagements** furnishings
aménager [amenaʒe] §38 *tr* to arrange, equip; remodel; parcel out; grade (*a road-bed*); feed (*a machine*); harness (*a water-fall*)
aménageur [amenaʒœr] *m* (land) developer
amende [amɑ̃d] *f* fine; forfeit (*in a game*); **faire amende honorable** (coll) to apologize
amendement [amɑ̃dmɑ̃] *m* amendment; fertilizer
amender [amɑ̃de] *tr* to amend; manure ‖ *ref* to mend one's ways, amend
amène [amɛn] *adj* pleasant
amener [amne] §2, §96 *tr* to bring; lead; bring on; furnish (*proof*); (naut) to lower; **amener pavillon** to surrender ‖ *ref* (coll) to arrive; **amenez-vous!** (slang) get a move on!
aménité [amenite] *f* amenity; **aménités** (ironical) cutting remarks
amenuiser [amənɥize] *tr* to whittle ‖ *ref* to be whittled down
a·mer -mère [amɛr] *adj* bitter ‖ *m* bitters; seamark; gall (*of animal*)
améri·cain [amerikɛ̃] **-caine** [kɛn] *adj* American ‖ *m* American English ‖ *f* phaeton; bicycle relay ‖ (*cap*) *mf* American (*person*)
américanisme [amerikanism] *m* Americanism; American studies
amérin·dieu [amerɛ̃djɛ̃] **-dienne** [djɛn] *adj* Amerindian ‖ (*cap*) *mf* Amerindian
Amérique [amerik] *f* America; **l'Amérique** America
amerrir [amerir] *intr* to land on water, alight on water
amerrissage [amerisaʒ] *m* landing (on water); (rok) splashdown; **amerrissage forcé** ditching; **faire un amerrisage forcé** to ditch
amertume [amɛrtym] *f* bitterness
améthyste [ametist] *f* amethyst
ameublement [amœbləmɑ̃] *m* furnishings; furniture, suite
ameublir [amœblir] *tr* (agr) to soften, mellow (*soil*)
ameuter [amøte] *tr* to rouse (*the pack*) ‖ *ref* to riot
a·mi -mie [ami] *adj* friendly ‖ *mf* friend ‖ *f* mistress
amiable [amjabl] *adj* amicable; **à l'amiable** privately, out of court
amiante [amjɑ̃t] *m* asbestos
amibe [amib] *f* amoeba
ami·bien [amibjɛ̃] **-bienne** [bjɛn] *adj* amoebic
ami·cal -cale [amikal] *adj* (*pl* **-caux** [ko]) amicable ‖ *f* professional club
amidon [amidɔ̃] *m* starch
amidonner [amidɔne] *tr* to starch

amincir [amɛ̃sir] *tr* to make more slender, attenuate ‖ *ref* to grow thinner
ami·ral [amiral] *m* (*pl* **-raux** [ro]) admiral
amirale [amiral] *f* admiral's wife
amirauté [amirote] *f* admiralty
amitié [amitje] *f* friendship; **amitiés** (complimentary close) cordially yours; **faites mes amitiés à** give my regards to; **faites-moi l'amitié de** do me the favor of
ammo·niac -niaque [amɔnjak] *adj* ammoniacal ‖ *m* ammonia (*gas*) ‖ *f* ammonia (*gas dissolved in water*)
amnésie [amnezi] *f* amnesia
amnistie [amnisti] *f* amnesty
amnistier [amnistje] *tr* to amnesty
amoindrir [amwɛ̃drir] *tr* to lessen ‖ *ref* to diminish
amollir [amɔlir] *tr & ref* to soften
amollissement [amɔlismɑ̃] *m* softening
amonceler [amɔ̃sle] §34 *tr* to pile up, gather ‖ *ref* to pile up, gather; drift (*said of snow*)
amont [amɔ̃] *m* upper waters; **en amont** upstream; **en amont de** above
amorçage [amɔrsaʒ] *m* baiting; priming
amorce [amɔrs] *f* bait, lure; fuse, percussion cap; beginning; leader (*of strip of film*); (mov) preview
amorcer [amɔrse] §51 *tr* to bait; prime; entice; begin
amorphe [amɔrf] *adj* amorphous; passive, apathetic (*student; spirit*)
amortir [amɔrtir] *tr* to absorb (*shock*); subdue (*color; pain; passions*); damp (*waves*); amortize
amortissement [amɔrtismɑ̃] *m* absorption (*of shock, sound, etc.*); amortization
amortisseur [amɔrtisœr] *m* shock absorber
amour [amur] *m* love; love affair; **premières amours** puppy love ‖ (*cap*) *m* Cupid
amou·reux [amurø] **-reuse** [røz] *adj* amorous; loving; fond, devoted; **amoureux de** in love with ‖ *m* lover ‖ *f* sweetheart
amour·propre [amurprɔpr] *m* (*pl* **amours-propres**) self-esteem; vanity
amovible [amɔvibl] *adj* removable; detachable; (jur) revocable
ampère [ɑ̃pɛr] *m* ampere
ampèremètre [ɑ̃pɛrmɛtr] *m* ammeter
amphibie [ɑ̃fibi] *adj* amphibious, amphibian ‖ *m* amphibian
amphibien [ɑ̃fibjɛ̃] *m* amphibian
amphithéâtre [ɑ̃fiteɑtr] *m* amphitheater; auditorium (*with raised seats*)
amphitryon [ɑ̃fitrijɔ̃] *m* host at dinner ‖ (*cap*) *m* Amphitryon
ample [ɑ̃pl] *adj* ample; long (*speech*); liberal (*reward*); full (*skirt; voice*)
amplifica·teur [ɑ̃plifikatœr] **-trice** [tris] *adj* amplifying ‖ *mf* exaggerator ‖ *m* amplifier; (phot) enlarger
amplifier [ɑ̃plifje] *tr* to amplify, enlarge
amplitude [ɑ̃plityd] *f* amplitude
ampoule [ɑ̃pul] *f* ampule; (elec) bulb; (pathol) blister
ampu·té -tée [ɑ̃pyte] *mf* amputee

amputer [ɑ̃pyte] *tr* to amputate; cut (*an article, speech*)
amuïr [amɥir] *ref* to become silent
amuïssement [amɥismɑ̃] *m* (phonet) silencing
amulette [amylɛt] *f* amulet
amure [amyr] *f* tack (*of sail*)
amuse-gueule [amyzgœl] *m* (*pl* **-gueule** or **-gueules**) (coll) appetizer, snack
amusement [amyzmɑ̃] *m* amusement
amuser [amyze] *tr* to amuse; to mislead ‖ §96 *ref* to have a good time; to sow one's wild oats; **s'amuser à** to pass the time by; **s'amuser de** to play with; to make fun of
amygdale [amigdal] *f* tonsil
an [ɑ̃] *m* year; **de six ans** six-year-old; **l'an de grâce** the year of Our Lord; **le nouvel an, le jour de l'an** New Year's Day
anacarde [anakard] *m* cashew nut
anachronisme [anakrɔnism] *m* anachronism
analogie [analɔʒi] *f* analogy
analogue [analɔg] *adj* analogous; similar
analphabète [analfabɛt] *adj & mf* illiterate
analphabétisme [analfabetism] *m* illiteracy
analyse [analiz] *f* analysis; **analyse des renseignements** data processing
analyser [analize] *tr* to analyze
analyseur [analizœr] *m* analyzer, tester; **analyseur d'haleine** breath tester
analyste [analist] *mf* analyst
analytique [analitik] *adj* analytic(al)
ananas [anana] *m* pineapple
anarchie [anarʃi] *f* anarchy
anarchiste [anarʃist] *mf* anarchist
anathème [anatɛm] *m* anathema
anatife [anatif] *m* barnacle
anatomie [anatɔmi] *f* anatomy
anatomique [anatɔmik] *adj* anatomic(al)
ances·tral -trale [ɑ̃sɛstral] *adj* (*pl* **-traux** [tro]) ancestral
ancêtre [ɑ̃sɛtr] *m* ancestor
anche [ɑ̃ʃ] *f* (mus) reed
anchois [ɑ̃ʃwa] *m* anchovy
an·cien [ɑ̃sjɛ̃] **-cienne** [sjɛn] *adj* ancient, old, long-standing; antiquated; antique ‖ (when standing before noun) *adj* former, previous, old; retired (*businessman*); ancient (*Greece, Rome*) ‖ *mf* senior (*in rank*); oldster; **les Anciens** the Ancients
anciennement [ɑ̃sjɛnmɑ̃] *adv* formerly
ancienneté [ɑ̃sjɛnte] *f* antiquity; seniority (*in rank*)
ancre [ɑ̃kr] *f* anchor; **ancres levées** anchors aweigh
ancrer [ɑ̃kre] *tr & intr* to anchor ‖ *ref* to become established
andain [ɑ̃dɛ̃] *m* swath; row of shocks
andouille [ɑ̃duj] *f* (coll) fool, sap
andouiller [ɑ̃duje] *m* antler
âne [ɑn] *m* ass, donkey
anéantir [aneɑ̃tir] *tr* to annihilate; prostrate ‖ *ref* to disappear; humble oneself (*before God*)
anéantissement [aneɑ̃tismɑ̃] *m* annihilation; prostration
anecdote [anɛgdɔt] *f* anecdote
anémie [anemi] *f* anemia

ânesse [anɛs] f she-ass
anesthésie [anɛstezi] f anesthesia
anesthésier [anɛstezje] tr to anesthetize
anesthésique [anɛstezik] adj abbr m anesthetic
anesthésiste [anɛstezist] mf anesthetist
anévrisme [anevrism] m aneurysm
anfractuosité [ɑ̃fraktɥozite] f rough outline (of coast); ruggedness, cragginess
ange [ɑ̃ʒ] m angel; ange gardien, ange tutélaire guardian angel; être aux anges to walk on air
angélique [ɑ̃ʒelik] adj angelic(al)
angélus [ɑ̃ʒelys] m Angelus
angine [ɑ̃ʒin] f tonsillitis, quinsy; angine de poitrine angina pectoris
an·glais [ɑ̃glɛ] -glaise [glɛz] adj English; à l'anglaise in the English manner; filer à l'anglaise to take French leave || m English (language) || (cap) m Englishman; les Anglais the English || f Englishwoman
angle [ɑ̃gl] m angle, corner
Angleterre [ɑ̃glətɛr] f England; l'Angleterre England
anglophone [ɑ̃glɔfɔn] adj English-speaking || mf English speaker
angois·sant [ɑ̃gwasɑ̃] -sante [sɑ̃t] adj agonizing
angoisse [ɑ̃gwas] f anguish
anguille [ɑ̃gij] f eel; anguille de mer conger eel
angulaire [ɑ̃gylɛr] adj angular
angu·leux [ɑ̃gylø] -leuse [løz] adj angular, sharp
anicroche [anikrɔʃ] f (coll) hitch, snag
ani·mal -male [animal] (pl -maux [mo]) adj animal || m animal, brute, beast; (coll) blockhead
anima·teur [animatœr] -trice [tris] adj animating || mf animator, moving spirit; master of ceremonies; DJ; animateur de théâtre theatrical producer
animation [animɑsjɔ̃] f animation
animer [anime] tr to animate; encourage || §96 ref to become alive, liven up
animosité [animozite] f animosity
anion [anjɔ̃] m anion
anis [ani] m anise
annales [anal] fpl annals
an·neau [ano] m (pl -neaux) ring
année [ane] f year; année bissextile leap year; année de lumière light-year; bonne année Happy New Year
année-lumière [anelymjɛr] f (pl années-lumière) light-year
annexe [anɛks] adj annexed || f annex
annexer [anɛkse] tr to annex
annexion [anɛksjɔ̃] f annexation
annihiler [aniile] tr to annihilate
anniversaire [anivɛrsɛr] adj & m anniversary; anniversaire de naissance birthday
annonce [anɔ̃s] f announcement; advertisement; (cards) bid; petites annonces classified ads
annoncer [anɔ̃se] §51 tr to announce; advertise; (cards) to bid, declare; annoncer

la couleur (fig) to lay one's cards on the table || ref to augur; promise to be
annonceur [anɔ̃sœr] m advertiser
annoncia·teur [anɔ̃sjatœr] -trice [tris] adj betokening, foreboding || m harbinger
annoter [anɔte] tr to annotate
annuaire [anɥɛr] m annual, yearbook, directory; catalog, bulletin (e.g., of a school)
an·nuel -nuelle [anɥɛl] adj annual
annuité [anɥite] f annuity
annuler [anyle] tr to cancel; invalidate (a contract); annul (a marriage)
ano·din [anɔdɛ̃] -dine [din] adj & m anodyne
ânon [anɔ̃] m foal of an ass
ânonner [anɔne] tr to recite in a stumbling manner
anonymat [anɔnima] m anonymity
anonyme [anɔnim] adj anonymous; incorporated; (fig) colorless, drab || mf unidentified person
anorak [anɔrak] m anorak; ski jacket, parka
anor·mal -male [anɔrmal] (pl -maux [mo]) adj abnormal || mf abnormal person
anse [ɑ̃s] f handle; cove; loop; faire danser l'anse du panier to pad the bill
antagonisme [ɑ̃tagɔnism] m antagonism
antan [ɑ̃tɑ̃] m yesteryear
Antarctique [ɑ̃tarktik] adj & m Antarctic || f Antarctic (region); l'Antarctique Antarctica
antécé·dent [ɑ̃tesedɑ̃] -dente [dɑ̃t] adj & m antecedent
antenne [ɑ̃tɛn] f antenna (feeler; aerial); outpost; (naut) lateen yard; porter à l'antenne to put on the air
antépénultième [ɑ̃tepenyltjɛm] adj antepenultimate || f antepenult
anté·rieur -rieure [ɑ̃terjœr] adj anterior; former; previous, preceding; earlier; front
antériorité [ɑ̃terjɔrite] f priority
anthologie [ɑ̃tɔlɔʒi] f anthology
anthropoïde [ɑ̃trɔpɔid] adj & m anthropoid
anthropophage [ɑ̃trɔpɔfaʒ] adj & mf cannibal
antiaé·rien [ɑ̃tiaerjɛ̃] -rienne [rjɛn] adj antiaircraft
antialcoolique [ɑ̃tialkɔɔlik] adj antialcoholic || mf teetotaler; temperance worker
antibiotique [ɑ̃tibjɔtik] adj & m antibiotic
antichambre [ɑ̃tiʃɑ̃br] f antechamber, anteroom
antichar [ɑ̃tiʃar] adj antitank
anticipation [ɑ̃tisipɑsjɔ̃] f anticipation; anticipations prophecies (of science fiction); d'anticipation science fiction (stories, films, etc.); par anticipation in advance
antici·pé -pée [ɑ̃tisipe] adj anticipated, advanced, ahead of time; premature (e.g., death)
anticiper [ɑ̃tisipe] tr to anticipate; advance || intr to act ahead of time; anticiper sur to encroach on; pay ahead of time; spend ahead of time
anticléri·cal -cale [ɑ̃tiklerikal] adj (pl -caux [ko]) anticlerical

anticonception·nel -nelle [ɑ̃tikɔ̃sɛpsjɔnɛl] *adj* contraceptive

anticorps [ɑ̃tikɔr] *m* antibody

antidéra·pant [ɑ̃tiderapɑ̃] **-pante** [pɑ̃t] *adj* nonskid ‖ *m* nonskid tire

antidéto·nant [ɑ̃tidetɔnɑ̃] **-nante** [nɑ̃t] *adj* & *m* antiknock

antidote [ɑ̃tidɔt] *m* antidote

antienne [ɑ̃tjɛn] *f* antiphon, anthem; **chanter toujours la même antienne** to harp on the same subject

antigel [ɑ̃tiʒɛl] *m* antifreeze

antigi·vrant [ɑ̃tiʒivrɑ̃] **-vrante** [vrɑ̃t] *adj* deicing, defrosting ‖ *m* deicer

antigivre [ɑ̃tiʒivr] *m* deicer, defroster

Antilles [ɑ̃tij] *fpl* West Indies

antilope [ɑ̃tilɔp] *f* antelope

antimite [ɑ̃timit] *adj* mothproof ‖ *m* moth killer

antimoine [ɑ̃timwan] *m* antimony

antiparasite [ɑ̃tiparazit] *adj* (rad) static-eliminating ‖ *m* (rad) static eliminator; insecticide

antipathie [ɑ̃tipati] *f* antipathy

antiquaire [ɑ̃tikɛr] *m* antique dealer

antique [ɑ̃tik] *adj* antique, classic; old-fashioned ‖ *m* antique

antiquité [ɑ̃tikite] *f* antiquity; **antiquités** antiques

antisèche [ɑ̃tisɛʃ] *m* & *f* (slang) crib (*for cheating during exams*)

antisémite [ɑ̃tisemit] *adj* anti-Semitic ‖ *mf* anti-Semite

antisémitique [ɑ̃tisemitik] *adj* anti-Semitic

antiseptique [ɑ̃tisɛptik] *adj* & *m* antiseptic

antiso·cial -ciale [ɑ̃tisɔsjal] *adj* (*pl* **-ciaux** [sjo]) antisocial

antispor·tif [ɑ̃tispɔrtif] **-tive** [tiv] *adj* unsportsmanlike

antithèse [ɑ̃titɛz] *f* antithesis

antitoxine [ɑ̃titɔksin] *f* antitoxin

antitranspirant [ɑ̃titrɑ̃spirɑ̃] *m* antiperspirant

antonyme [ɑ̃tɔnim] *m* antonym

antre [ɑ̃tr] *m* den, lair; cave

anxiété [ɑ̃ksjete] *f* anxiety

anxieux [ɑ̃ksjø] **anxieuse** [ɑ̃ksjøz] *adj* anxious, worried

aorte [aɔrt] *f* aorta

août [u], [ut] *m* August

A.P. *abbr* (**assistance publique**) welfare department

apache [apaʃ] *m* apache, hoodlum

apaisement [apɛzmɑ̃] *m* appeasement

apaiser [apɛze] *tr* to appease ‖ *ref* to quiet down

apanage [apanaʒ] *m* attribute

aparté [aparte] *m* stage whisper, aside; **en aparté** privately

apathie [apati] *f* apathy

apathique [apatik] *adj* apathetic

apatride [apatrid] *adj* stateless ‖ *mf* stateless person

apercevoir [apɛrsəvwar] §59, §95 *tr* to perceive ‖ §97 *ref* to notice; realize; **s'apercevoir de** to notice, realize, be aware of

aperçu [apɛrsy] *m* glimpse; view, look; outline

apéri·tif [aperitif] **-tive** [tiv] *adj* appetizing ‖ *m* apéritif

aperture [apɛrtyr] *f* (phonet) aperture

apesanteur [apəzɑ̃tœr] *f* weightlessness

à-peu-près [apøprɛ] *m invar* approximation, rough estimate

apeu·ré -rée [apœre] *adj* frightened

aphone [afɔn] *adj* voiceless, aphonic

aphorisme [afɔrism] *m* aphorism

aphrodisiaque [afrɔdizjak] *adj* & *m* aphrodisiac

aphte [aft] *m* mouth canker, cold sore

apiculteur [apikyltœr] *m* beekeeper

apiculture [apikyltyr] *f* beekeeping

apitoiement [apitwamɑ̃] *m* compassion

api·toyant [apitwajɑ̃] **-toyante** [twajɑ̃t] *adj* piteous, pitiful

apitoyer [apitwaje] §47 *tr* to move (*s.o.*) to pity ‖ *ref*—**s'apitoyer sur** to feel compassion for

ap. J.-C. *abbr* (**après Jésus-Christ**) A.D.

aplanir [aplanir] *tr* to even off; iron out (*difficulties*)

aplatir [aplatir] *tr* to flatten ‖ *ref* to go flat; grovel

aplomb [aplɔ̃] *m* aplomb; hang (*of gown*); (coll) cheek, rudeness; **aplombs** stand (*of horse*); **d'aplomb** plumb; steadily

apocalyptique [apɔkaliptik] *adj* apocalyptic

apocryphe [apɔkrif] *adj* apocryphal ‖ **Apocryphes** *mpl* Apocrypha

apogée [apɔʒe] *m* apogee

Apollon [apɔllɔ̃] *m* Apollo

apologie [apɔlɔʒi] *f* apology

apophonie [apɔfɔni] *f* ablaut

apoplectique [apɔplɛktik] *adj* & *mf* apoplectic

apoplexie [apɔplɛksi] *f* apoplexy

apostille [apɔstij] *f* endorsement

apostiller [apɔstije] *tr* to endorse

apostolat [apɔstɔla] *m* apostleship

apostrophe [apɔstrɔf] *f* apostrophe; sharp reprimand

apostropher [apɔstrɔfe] *tr* to apostrophize; reprimand sharply

apothicaire [apɔtikɛr] *m* apothecary

apôtre [apotr] *m* apostle; **faire le bon apôtre** to play the hypocrite

apparaître [aparɛtr] §12 *intr* (*aux:* AVOIR or ÊTRE) to appear, come into view; become evident

apparat [apara] *m* pomp, ostentation

apparaux [aparo] *mpl* rigging

appareil [aparɛj] *m* apparatus, machine, appliance; apparel; radio set; airplane; pomp, show, display; camera; telephone; (archit) bond; **à l'appareil!** speaking!; **appareil à sous** slot machine; **appareil auditif** hearing aid; **appareil photographique** camera; **appareil plâtré** plaster cast

appareillage [aparɛjaʒ] *m* equipment; (naut) getting under way

appareiller [apareje] *tr* to prepare; bond (*stones*); pair, match; (naut) to rig ‖ *intr* to set sail

apparemment [aparamɑ̃] *adv* apparently

apparence [aparɑ̃s] *f* appearance

appa·rent [aparɑ̃] **-rente** [rɑ̃t] *adj* apparent

apparenter [aparɑ̃te] *tr* to relate by marriage ‖ *ref* to become related

apparier [aparje] *tr* to pair off, match

apparition [aparisjɔ̃] *f* apparition; appearance

apparoir [aparwar] (used only in: *inf;* 3d *sg pres ind* **appert**) *impers*—**il appert de** it follows from; **il appert que** it is evident that

appartement [apartəmɑ̃] *m* apartment

appartenance [apartənɑ̃s] *f* membership, belonging, adherence

appartenir [apartənir] §72 *intr*—**appartenir à** to belong to; pertain to ‖ *impers*—**il appartient à qn de** it behooves s.o. to ‖ *ref* to be one's own master

appas [apɑ] *mpl* charms; bosom

appât [apɑ] *m* bait

appâter [apɑte] *tr* to lure; fatten up (*fowl*)

appauvrir [apovrir] *tr* to impoverish ‖ *ref* to become impoverished

ap·peau [apo] *m* (*pl* **-peaux**) decoy; bird call

appel [apɛl] *m* call; appeal; summons; roll call; ring (*on telephone*); (mil) draft; **appel interurbain** long-distance call; **appel nominal** roll call; **faire l'appel** to call the roll

appe·lant [aplɑ̃] **-lante** [lɑ̃t] *adj* appellant ‖ *mf* appellant ‖ *m* decoy

appelé [aple] *m* draftee; **appelé volontaire** volunteer

appeler [aple] §34 *tr* to call; name; summon; subpoena; require; call up, draft ‖ §96 *intr* to call; appeal (*in court*); **en appeler à** to appeal to ‖ *ref* to be named, e.g., **elle s'appelle Marie** she is named Mary, her name is Mary

appendice [apɛ̃dis] *m* appendix

appendicectomie [apɛ̃disɛktɔmi] *f* appendectomy

appendicite [apɛ̃disit] *f* appendicitis

appentis [apɑ̃ti] *m* lean-to

appesantir [apzɑ̃tir] *tr* to weigh down; slow down (*e.g., bodily activity*); make (*a burden*) heavier ‖ *ref* to be weighed down; **s'appesantir sur** to dwell on, expatiate on

appéstis·sant [apetisɑ̃] **-sante** [sɑ̃t] *adj* appetizing, tempting

appétit [apeti] *m* appetite

applaudir [aplodir] *tr* to applaud; **applaudir qn de** to commend, applaud s.o. for ‖ *intr* to applaud; **applaudir à** to approve, commend, applaud ‖ §97 *ref*—**s'applaudir de** to congratulate oneself on, pat oneself on the back for

applaudissement [aplodismɑ̃] *m* round of applause; **applaudissements** applause

applicable [aplikabl] *adj* applicable

application [aplikasjɔ̃] *f* application

applique [aplik] *f* appliqué; sconce

appli·qué -quée [aplike] *adj* industrious, studious; applied (*science*)

appliquer [aplike] *tr* to apply ‖ §96 *ref* to apply; apply oneself

appoint [apwɛ̃] *m* addition; balance; aid, help; **faire l'appoint** to have the right change

appointements [apwɛ̃tmɑ̃] *mpl* salary

appointer [apwɛ̃te] *tr* to point, sharpen; pay a salary to

appontage [apɔ̃taʒ] *m* deck-landing

appontement [apɔ̃tmɑ̃] *m* jetty (*landing pier*); wharf

apponter [apɔ̃te] *intr* to deck-land

apport [apɔr] *m* contribution

apporter [apɔrte] *tr* to bring; supply, provide, give; take, use, exercise (*care*)

apposer [apoze] *tr* to affix; insert (*a clause in a contract*)

appréciable [apresjabl] *adj* appreciable

appréciation [apresjɑsjɔ̃] *f* appreciation, appraisal

apprécier [apresje] *tr* to appreciate

appréhender [apreɑde] §97 *tr* to apprehend; be apprehensive about

appréhension [apreɑ̃sjɔ̃] *f* apprehension

apprendre [aprɑ̃dr] §56, §96, §101 *tr* to learn; **apprendre à vivre à qn** to teach s.o. manners; **apprendre q.ch. à qn** to inform s.o. of s.th.; teach s.o. s.th. ‖ *intr* to learn

appren·ti -tie [aprɑ̃ti] *mf* apprentice; beginner, learner

apprentissage [aprɑ̃tisaʒ] *m* apprenticeship

apprêt [aprɛ] *m* preparation, finishing touches; **sans apprêt** unaffectedly

apprêter [aprɛte] §96 *tr & ref* to prepare

apprivoi·sé -sée [aprivwaze] *adj* tame, domesticated

apprivoiser [aprivwaze] *tr* to tame; contain (*sorrow*) ‖ *ref* to become tame; become sociable

approba·teur [aprɔbatœr] **-trice** [tris] *adj* approving ‖ *m* (sl ang) yes man

approbation [aprɔbɑsjɔ̃] *f* approbation, approval, consent

appro·chant [aprɔʃɑ̃] **-chante** [ʃɑ̃t] *adj* similar ‖ **approchant** *adv* thereabouts

approche [aprɔʃ] *f* approach

approcher [aprɔʃe] *tr* to approach; draw up (*e.g., a chair*) ‖ *intr* to approach; **approcher de** to approach, approximate ‖ *ref* to approach, come near; **s'approcher de** to approach, come near to, go up to

approfon·di -die [aprɔfɔ̃di] *adj* thorough, deep

approfondir [aprɔfɔ̃dir] *tr* to deepen; go deep into, get to the bottom of

appropriation [aprɔprijɑsjɔ̃] *f* appropriation; adaptation

appro·prié -priée [aprɔprije] *adj* appropriate

approprier [aprɔprije] *tr* to fit, adapt ‖ *ref* to appropriate, preempt

approuver [apruve] *tr* to approve, approve of

approvisionnement [aprɔvizjɔnmɑ̃] *m* provisioning, stocking; **approvisionnements** supplies

approvisionner [aprɔvizjɔne] *tr* to provision, stock ‖ *ref* to lay in supplies

approxima·tif [aprɔksimatif] **-tive** [tiv] *adj* approximate

appui [apɥi] *m* support; endorsement

appui-bras [apɥibra] *m* (*pl* **appuis-bras**) armrest

appui-livres [apɥilivr] *m* (*pl* **appuis-livres**) book end

appui-main [apɥimɛ̃] *m* (*pl* **appuis-main**) maulstick

appui-tête [apɥitɛt] *m* (*pl* **appuis-tête**) headrest

appuyer [apɥije] §27 *tr* to support; prop; rest, lean; endorse (*a candidate*); **appuyer le doigt sur** to push (*a button, a lever, a switch*) with the finger ‖ *intr*—**appuyer sur** to lean on; press (*a button*); move (*a lever*); pull (*a trigger*); bear down on (*a pen or pencil*); stress (*a syllable*) ‖ *ref*—**s'appuyer sur** to lean on; be based on; rely on; (slang) to put up with

âpre [ɑpr] *adj* harsh, rough; bitter; greedy (*for gain*)

après [aprɛ] *adv* after, afterward; behind; **après que** after ‖ *prep* after; behind; **après Jésus-Christ** (**ap. J.-C.**) after Christ (**A.D.**); **d'après** after, from; by, according to

après-demain [aprɛdəmɛ̃] *adv* & *m* the day after tomorrow

après-guerre [aprɛgɛr] *m* & *f* (*pl* **-guerres**) postwar period

après-midi [aprɛmidi] *m* & *f* *invar* afternoon

âpreté [aprəte] *f* harshness; bitterness

à-propos [aprɔpo] *m* opportuneness, aptness

apte [apt] *adj* apt; **apte à** suitable for

aptitude [aptityd] *f* aptitude; proficiency

apurement [apyrmɑ̃] *m* audit, check

apurer [apyre] *tr* to audit, check

apyre [apir] *adj* fireproof

aquafortiste [akwafɔrtist] *mf* etcher

aquaplane [akwaplan] *m* aquaplane

aquarelle [akwarɛl] *f* watercolor

aquarium [akwarjɔm] *m* aquarium

aquatique [akwatik] *adj* aquatic

aqueduc [akdyk] *m* aqueduct

aquilin [akilɛ̃] *adj masc* aquiline

aquilon [akilɔ̃] *m* north wind

ara [ara] *m* (orn) macaw

arabe [arab] *adj* Arabian, Arab ‖ *m* Arabic; Arab (*horse*) ‖ (*cap*) *mf* Arabian, Arab

arachide [araʃid] *f* peanut

araignée [arɛɲe] *f* spider; grapnel; **araignée de mer** spider crab; **avoir une araignée dans le plafond** (coll) to have bats in the belfry

aratoire [aratwar] *adj* agricultural

arbalète [arbalɛt] *f* crossbow

arbitrage [arbitraʒ] *m* arbitration

arbitraire [arbitrɛr] *adj* arbitrary ‖ *m* arbitrariness, despotism

arbitre [arbitr] *m* arbiter; arbitrator; umpire, judge; **libre arbitre** free will

arbitrer [arbitre] *tr* & *intr* to arbitrate; umpire

arborer [arbɔre] *tr* to hoist (*a flag*); show off (*new clothes*)

arbouse [arbuz] *f* arbutus berry

arbousier [arbuzje] *m* arbutus

arbre [arbr] *m* tree; (mach) arbor, shaft; **arbre de Noël** Christmas tree; **arbre généalogique** family tree

arbris·seau [arbriso] *m* (*pl* **-seaux**) bushy tree

arbuste [arbyst] *m* shrub

arc [ark] *m* bow; arch; (elec, geom) arc

arcade [arkad] *f* arcade, archway

arcanes [arkan] *mpl* mysteries, secrets

arcanson [arkɑ̃sɔ̃] *m* rosin

arc-boutant [arkbutɑ̃] *m* (*pl* **arcs-boutants**) flying buttress

arc-en-ciel [arkɑ̃sjɛl] *m* (*pl* **arcs-en-ciel** [arkɑ̃sjɛl]) rainbow

archaïque [arkaik] *adj* archaic

archaïsme [arkaism] *m* archaism

archange [arkɑ̃ʒ] *m* archangel

arche [arʃ] *f* arch (*of bridge*); Ark

archéologie [arkeɔlɔʒi] *f* archaeology

archéologue [arkeɔlɔg] *mf* archaeologist

archer [arʃe] *m* archer, bowman

archet [arʃe] *m* bow

archétype [arketip] *m* archetype

archevêque [arʃəvɛk] *m* archbishop

archiduc [arʃidyk] *m* archduke

archipel [arʃipɛl] *m* archipelago

archiprêtre [arʃiprɛtr] *m* archpriest

architecte [arʃitɛkt] *m* architect

architecture [arʃitɛktyr] *f* architecture

archives [arʃiv] *fpl* archives

arçon [arsɔ̃] *m* saddletree

Arctique [arktik] *adj* & *m* Arctic ‖ *f* Arctic (*region*)

ardemment [ardamɑ̃] *adv* ardently

ar·dent [ardɑ̃] **-dente** [dɑ̃t] *adj* ardent; burning; bright-red (*hair*)

ardeur [ardœr] *f* ardor; intense heat

ardoise [ardwaz] *f* slate

ardoi·sier [ardwazje] **-sière** [zjɛr] *adj* slate ‖ *m* slate-quarry worker ‖ *f* slate quarry

ar·du -due [ardy] *adj* steep; arduous

arène [arɛn] *f* arena; sand; (fig) arena; **arènes** arena, coliseum, amphitheater

arête [arɛt] *f* fishbone; beard (*of wheat*); angle, ridge

argent [arʒɑ̃] *m* silver; money; **argent comptant** cash; **argent vif** cash flow

argenter [arʒɑ̃te] *tr* to silver ‖ *ref* to turn silvery (*i.e., gray*)

argenterie [arʒɑ̃tri] *f* silver plate, silverware

argentier [arʒɑ̃tje] *m* silverware cabinet; (hist) Treasurer

argen·tin [arʒɑ̃tɛ̃] **-tine** [tin] *adj* silvery (*voice*); Argentinian ‖ (*cap*) *mf* Argentinian (*person*) ‖ **l'Argentine** *f* Argentina

argile [arʒil] *f* clay

argot [argo] *m* slang; jargon, cant

argotique [argɔtik] *adj* slangy

arguer [argɥe] (many authorities write: **j'arguë, tu arguës,** etc.) *tr* to argue, imply; **arguer de faux** to doubt the authenticity of (*a document*) ‖ *intr* to draw a conclusion; **arguer de** to use as a pretext

argument [argymɑ̃] *m* argument

argumentation [argymɑ̃tɑsjɔ̃] *f* argument

argumenter [argymɑ̃te] *intr* to argue

argus [argys] *m* look-out, spy; price list, book (*e.g., for used cars*); **argus de la presse** clipping service

aria [arja] *m* (coll) fuss, bother ‖ *f* aria

aride [arid] *adj* arid; (*subject, speaker, etc.*) dry

aridité [aridite] *f* aridity; (fig) dryness, dullness

aristocrate [aristɔkrat] *adj* aristocratic ‖ *mf* aristocrat

aristocratie [aristɔkrasi] *f* aristocracy

Aristote [aristɔt] *m* Aristotle

arithméti·cien [aritmetisjɛ̃] **-cienne** [sjɛn] *mf* arithmetician

arithmétique [aritmetik] *f* arithmetic

arlequin [arləkɛ̃] *m* goulash; wrench ‖ (*cap*) *m* Harlequin

armateur [armatœr] *m* ship outfitter; shipowner

armature [armatyr] *f* framework; keeper (*of a horseshoe magnet*); (mus) key signature

arme [arm] *f* arm; weapon; **arme blanche** cold steel; steel blade; **armes portatives** small arms; **faire ses premières armes** to make one's début

armée [arme] *f* army

armement [armɑmɑ̃] *m* armament; fire power; (naut) outfitting

armé·nien [armenjɛ̃] **-nienne** [njɛn] *adj* Armenian ‖ *m* Armenian (*language*) ‖ (*cap*) *mf* Armenian (*person*)

armer [arme] *tr* to arm; cock (*a gun*); reinforce (*concrete*); **armer chevalier** to knight ‖ *ref* to arm oneself, arm

armistice [armistis] *m* armistice

armoire [armwar] *f* wardrobe, closet; **armoire à pharmacie** medicine cabinet; **armoire frigorifique** freezer

armoiries [armwari] *fpl* arms, coat of arms

armoise [armwaz] *f* sagebrush

armorier [armɔrje] *tr* to emblazon

armure [armyr] *f* armor; (tex) weave

arnaquer [arnake] *tr* (slang) to rip off

aromatique [arɔmatik] *adj* aromatic

arôme [arom] *m* aroma

aronde [arɔ̃d] *f* swallow

arpège [arpɛʒ] *m* arpeggio

arpent [arpɑ̃] *m* acre

arpentage [arpɑ̃taʒ] *m* surveying

arpenter [arpɑ̃te] *tr* to survey; (coll) to pace (*the floor*)

arpenteur [arpɑ̃tœr] *m* surveyor

ar·qué **-quée** [arke] *adj* arched, bowed; cambered (*beam*); hooked (*nose*)

arquer [arke] *tr* to arch, bow ‖ *ref* to arch, be bowed

arraché [araʃe] *m* (weight lifting) snatch

arrache-clou [araʃklu] *m* (*pl* **-clous**) claw hammer

arrache-pied [araʃpje] *adv*—**d'arrache-pied** at a stretch, without stopping

arracher [araʃe] *tr* to dig up, uproot, tear out, pull out; snatch; wheedle (*money; a confession*); **arracher q.ch. à qn** to take away, snatch, or pry s.th. from s.o.; **arracher q.ch. de q.ch.** to pull s.th. off, from, or out of s.th.; strip s.th. of s.th.; **arracher qn à** to deliver s.o. from (*evil; temptation; death*); **arracher qn de** to make s.o. get out of (*e.g., bed*) ‖ *ref* to tear oneself away

arra·cheur [araʃœr] **-cheuse** [ʃøz] *mf* puller ‖ *f* (mach) picker

arraisonnement [arɛzɔnmɑ̃] *m* port inspection

arraisonner [arɛzɔne] *tr* to inspect (*a ship*)

arrangement [arɑ̃ʒmɑ̃] *m* arrangement

arranger [arɑ̃ʒe] §38 *tr* to arrange; settle (*a difficulty*); fix (*repair; punish*) ‖ *ref* to be arranged; get ready; agree

arrérages [areraʒ] *mpl* arrears

arrestation [arɛstɑsjɔ̃] *f* arrest

arrêt [arɛ] *m* stop; stopping; arrest; decree; **arrêt complet** standstill; **arrêt de tabulateur** tabulator setting; **arrêt d'urgence** emergency shutdown; **arrêt facultatif** whistle stop; **arrêt par épuisement** burnout; **mettre aux arrêts** to keep in, confine to quarters

arrê·té **-tée** [arɛte] *adj* stopped, standing; decided, fixed ‖ *m* decree; authorization; (com) closing out (*of an account*); **arrêté de police** police ordinance; **prendre un arrêté** to pass a decree

arrêter [arɛte] §97, §99 *tr* to stop; arrest; fix (*one's gaze*); settle, decide upon; hire, engage; point (*game, as hunting dog does*) ‖ *intr* to stop; point (*said of hunting dog*) ‖ *ref* to stop; **s'arrêter à** to decide on; **s'arrêter de** + *inf* to stop + *ger*

arrhes [ar] *fpl* deposit, down payment

arriération [arjerɑsjɔ̃] *f* retardation

arrière [arjɛr] *adj invar* back, rear; tail (*wind*) ‖ *m* back, rear; stern; **à l'arrière** in back; astern; **en arrière** backward; **en arrière de** behind ‖ *adv* back

arrié·ré **-rée** [arjere] *adj* backward; delinquent (*in payment*); back (*pay, taxes, etc.*); old-fashioned ‖ *mf* backward child ‖ *m* arrears; back pay; back payment; backlog

arrière-boutique [arjɛrbutik] *f* (*pl* **-boutiques**) back room (*of a shop*)

arrière-cour [arjɛrkur] *f* (*pl* **-cours**) backyard

arrière-garde [arjɛrgard] *f* (*pl* **-gardes**) rear guard

arrière-goût [arjɛrgu] *m* (*pl* **-goûts**) aftertaste

arrière-grand-mère [arjɛrgrɑ̃mɛr] *f* (*pl* **-grands-mères**) great-grandmother

arrière-grand-père [arjɛrgrɑ̃pɛr] *m* (*pl* **-grands-pères**) great-grandfather

arrière-pays [arjɛrpei] *m invar* back country

arrière-pensée [arjɛrpɑ̃se] *f* (*pl* **-pensées**) mental reservation, ulterior motive

arrière-plan [arjɛrplɑ̃] *m* (*pl* **-plans**) background

arriérer [arjere] §10 *tr* to delay ‖ *ref* to fall behind (*in payment*)

arrière-train [arjɛrtrɛ̃] *m* (*pl* **-trains**) rear (*of a vehicle*); hindquarters

arrimage [arimaʒ] *m* stowage; docking (*of space vehicle*)

arrimer [arime] *tr* to stow; (aer) to dock

arrimeur [arimœr] *m* stevedore

arrivage [arivaʒ] *m* arrival (*of goods or ships*)

arrivée [arive] *f* arrival; intake; (sports) finish, goal; **arrivée en douceur** (rok) soft landing

arriver [arive] §96 *intr* (*aux:* ÉTRE) to arrive; succeed; happen; **arriver à** to attain, reach; **en arriver à** + *inf* to be reduced to + *ger*

arriviste [arivist] *mf* upstart, parvenu

arrogance [arɔgɑ̃s] *f* arrogance

arro·gant [arɔgɑ̃] **-gante** [gɑ̃t] *adj* arrogant

arroger [arɔʒe] §38 *ref* to arrogate to oneself

arrondir [arɔ̃dir] *tr* to round, round off, round out ‖ *ref* to become round

arrondissement [arɔ̃dismɑ̃] *m* district

arrosage [arozaʒ] *m* sprinkling; irrigation; (mil) heavy bombing

arroser [aroze] *tr* to sprinkle, water; irrigate; flow through (*e.g., a city*); wash down (*a meal*); (coll) to bribe; (coll) to drink to (*a success*)

arro·seur [arozœr] **-seuse** [zøz] *mf* sprinkler (*person*) ‖ *f* street sprinkler

arrosoir [arozwar] *m* sprinkling can

arse·nal [arsənal] *m* (*pl* **-naux** [no]) shipyard, navy yard; (fig) storehouse; (archaic) arsenal, armory

arsenic [arsənik] *m* arsenic

art [ar] *m* art; **arts d'agréments** music, drawing, dancing, etc.; **arts ménagers** home economics; **le huitième art** television; **les arts du spectacle** the performing arts; **le septième art** the cinema

artère [artɛr] *f* artery

arté·riel -rielle [arterjɛl] *adj* arterial

artérioscle·reux [arterjosklerø] **-reuse** [røz] *adj & mf* arteriosclerotic

arté·sien [artezjɛ̃] **-sienne** [zjɛn] *adj* of Artois; artesian (*well*)

arthrite [artrit] *f* arthritis

artichaut [artiʃo] *m* artichoke

article [artikl] *m* article; entry (*in a dictionary*); **à l'article de la mort** on the point of death; **article de fond** leader; editorial; **article de tête** front-page story; **articles divers** sundries

articuler [artikyle] *tr & ref* to articulate

artifice [artifis] *m* artifice; craftsmanship

artifi·ciel -cielle [artifisjɛl] *adj* artificial

artificier [artifisje] *m* fireworks maker; soldier in charge of ammunition supply

artifi·cieux [artifisjø] **-cieuse** [sjøz] *adj* artful, cunning

artillerie [artijəri] *f* artillery

artilleur [artijœr] *m* artilleryman

arti·san [artizɑ̃] **-sane** [zan] *mf* artisan, artificer ‖ *m* craftsman

artiste [artist] *adj* artistic; artist, of art, e.g., **le monde artiste** the world of art ‖ *mf* artist; actor

artistique [artistik] *adj* artistic

ar·yen [arjɛ̃] **-yenne** [jɛn] *adj* Aryan ‖ (*cap*) *mf* Aryan (*person*)

as [as] *m* ace; **as du volant** speed king ‖ [a] *v* see **avoir**

A.S. *abbr* (**assurances sociales**) social security

a/s *abbr* (**aux bons soins de**) c/o

asbeste [asbɛst] *m* asbestos

ascendance [asɑ̃dɑ̃s] *f* lineal ancestry; rising (*of air; of star*)

ascenseur [asɑ̃sœr] *m* elevator; **renvoyer l'ascenseur** to do a favor in return

ascension [asɑ̃sjɔ̃] *f* ascension; **Ascension** *f* Ascension Day

ascèse [asɛz] *f* asceticism

ascète [asɛt] *mf* ascetic

ascétique [asetik] *adj* ascetic

ascétisme [asetism] *m* asceticism

aseptique [asɛptik] *adj* aseptic

Asie [azi] *f* Asia; **Asie Mineure** Asia Minor; **l'Asie** Asia; **l'Asie Mineure** Asia Minor

asile [azil] *m* asylum, shelter, home

aspect [aspɛ] *m* aspect

asperge [aspɛrʒ] *f* asparagus; **des asperges** asparagus (*stalks and tips used as food*)

asperger [aspɛrʒe] §38 *tr* to sprinkle

aspérité [asperite] *f* roughness; harshness; gruffness

aspersion [aspɛrsjɔ̃] *f* sprinkling

asphalte [asfalt] *m* asphalt

asphyxier [asfiksje] *tr* to asphyxiate ‖ *ref* to be asphyxiated

aspic [aspik] *m* asp

aspi·rant [aspirɑ̃] **-rante** [rɑ̃t] *adj* aspirant, aspiring; suction (*pump*) ‖ *mf* candidate (*for a degree*) ‖ *m* midshipman

aspirateur [aspiratœr] *m* vacuum cleaner; **aspirateur de buée** kitchen fan

aspi·ré -rée [aspire] *adj & m* (phonet) aspirate

aspirer [aspire] *tr* to inhale; suck in ‖ §96 *intr*—**aspirer à** to aspire to

aspirine [aspirin] *f* aspirin

assagir [asaʒir] *tr* to make wiser ‖ *ref* to become wiser

assail·lant [asajɑ̃] **-lante** [jɑ̃t] *adj* attacking ‖ *mf* assailant

assaillir [asajir] §69 *tr* to assail, assault

assainir [asenir] *tr* to purify, clean up; drain (*a swamp*)

assainissement [asɛnismɑ̃] *m* purification; draining

assaisonnement [asɛzɔnmɑ̃] *m* seasoning

assaisonner [asɛzɔne] *tr* to season, flavor

assas·sin [asasɛ̃] **-sine** [sin] *adj* murderous ‖ *m* assassin

assassinat [asasina] *m* assassination

assassiner [asasine] *tr* to assassinate; (coll) to bore to death

assaut [aso] *m* assault, attack; match, bout

assèchement [asɛʃmɑ̃] *m* drainage, drying; dryness

assécher [aseʃe] §10 *tr* to drain, dry up

assemblage [asɑ̃blaʒ] *m* assemblage; assembling (*e.g., of printed pages*); (woodworking) joint, joining

assemblée [asɑ̃ble] *f* assembly, meeting

assembler [asɑ̃ble] *tr* to assemble ‖ *ref* to assemble, convene, meet

assener [asne] §2 *tr* to land (*a blow*)

assentiment [asɑ̃timɑ̃] *m* assent, consent

asseoir [aswar] §5 *tr* to seat, sit, place; base (*an opinion*) ‖ *ref* to sit down

assermen·té -tée [asɛrmɑ̃te] *adj* under oath

assertion [asɛrsjɔ̃] *f* assertion

asser·vi -vie [asɛrvi] *adj* subservient

asservir [asɛrvir] *tr* to enslave; to subdue (*e.g., passions*) ‖ *ref* to submit (*to convention; to tyranny*)

asservissement [asɛrvismɑ̃] *m* enslavement; subservience

assesseur [asɛsœr] *adj & m* assistant; associate (*judge*)

asseyez [aseje] *v* (**assieds** [asje]) see **asseoir**

assez [ase] *adv* enough; fairly, rather; **assez de** enough; **en voilà assez!** that's enough!, cut it out!, ‖ *interj* enough!, stop!

assi·du -due [asidy] *adj* assiduous; **assidu à** attentive to

assidûment [asidymɑ̃] *adv* assiduously

assié·geant [asjeʒɑ̃] **-geante** [ʒɑ̃t] *adj* besieging ‖ *mf* besieger

assiéger [asjeʒe] §1 *tr* to besiege

assiette [asjɛt] *f* plate, dish; plateful; seat (*of a rider on horseback*); position, condition; **assiette anglaise**, **assiette de viandes froides** cold cuts; **assiette au beurre** (fig) gravy train; **assiette creuse** soup plate; **assiette fiscale** tax basis; **je ne suis pas dans mon assiette** I'm in low spirits

assignation [asiɲasjɔ̃] *f* assignation; subpoena, summons

assi·gné -gnée [asiɲe] *mf* appointee; **assigné à résidence** permanent appointee; **assigné intérim** temporary appointee

assigner [asiɲe] §96 *tr* to assign, allot; fix (*a date*); subpoena, summon

assimilable [asimilabl] *adj* assimilable; comparable

assimilation [asimilɑsjɔ̃] *f* assimilation

assimiler [asimile] *tr* to assimilate; compare; identify with ‖ *ref* to assimilate

as·sis [asi] **-sise** [siz] *adj* seated, sitting; firmly established ‖ *f* foundation; stratum; **assises** assizes ‖ *v* see **asseoir**

assistance [asistɑ̃s] *f* assistance; audience, persons present; presence; **assistance judiciaire** public defender; **assistance publique** welfare department; **assistance sociale** social service

assis·tant [asistɑ̃] **-tante** [tɑ̃t] *adj* assistant ‖ *mf* assistant; bystander, spectator; **assistante sociale** public health nurse; social worker

assister [asiste] *tr* to assist, help ‖ *intr*—**assister à** to attend, be present at

association [asɔsjɑsjɔ̃] *f* association; (sports) soccer; **association des spectateurs** theater club; **association sans but lucratif** nonprofit organization

asso·cié -ciée [asɔsje] *adj & mf* associate

associer [asɔsje] *tr* to associate ‖ *ref* to go into partnership

assoif·fé -fée [aswafe] *adj* thirsty

assolement [asɔlmɑ̃] *m* rotation (*of crops*)

assombrir [asɔ̃brir] *tr & ref* to darken

assom·mant [asɔmɑ̃] **-mante** [mɑ̃t] *adj* (coll) boring, fatiguing

assommer [asɔme] *tr* to kill with a heavy blow; beat up; stun; (coll) to heckle; (coll) to bore

assommoir [asɔmwar] *m* bludgeon; (coll) gin mill, dive, clip joint

Assomption [asɔ̃psjɔ̃] *f* Assumption

assonance [asɔnɑ̃s] *f* assonance

assor·ti -tie [asɔrti] *adj* assorted (*e.g., cakes*); well-matched (*couple*); stocked, supplied (*store*); to match, e.g., **une cravate assortie** a necktie to match

assortiment [asɔrtimɑ̃] *m* assortment; matching (*of colors*); set (*of dishes*); platter (*of cold cuts*)

assortir [asɔrtir] *tr* to assort, match; stock ‖ *ref* to match; harmonize; **s'assortir de** to be accompanied with

assoupir [asupir] *tr* to make drowsy, lull; deaden (*pain*) ‖ *ref* to doze off; lessen (*with time*)

assoupissement [asupismɑ̃] *m* drowsiness; lethargy

assouplir [asuplir] *tr* to make supple, flexible; break in (*a horse*) ‖ *ref* to become supple, manageable

assouplissement [asuplismɑ̃] *m* suppleness, flexibility; limbering up; relaxation (*of a rule*)

assourdir [asurdir] *tr* to deafen; tone down, muffle

assouvir [asuvir] *tr* to assuage, appease, satiate; satisfy (*e.g., a thirst for vengeance*)

assouvissement [asuvismɑ̃] *m* assuagement, appeasement, satisfying

assujet·ti -tie [asyʒɛti] *adj* fastened; subject, liable ‖ *mf* taxpayer; contributor (*e.g., to social security*)

assujettir [asyʒɛtir] *tr* to subjugate; subject; fasten, secure ‖ §96 *ref* to submit

assujettis·sant [asyʒɛtisɑ̃] **-sante** [sɑ̃t] *adj* demanding

assujettissement [asyʒɛtismɑ̃] *m* subjugation, subduing; submission (*to a stronger force*); fastening, securing

assumer [asyme] *tr* to assume, take upon oneself

assurance [asyrɑ̃s] *f* assurance; insurance; **assurances sociales** social security; **assurance incendie** fire insurance; **assurance invalidité** disability insurance; **assurance maladie-sécurité** health insurance; **assurance multirisque** comprehensive insurance

assu·ré -rée [asyre] *adj* assured, satisfied; insured ‖ *mf* insured

assurément [asyremã] *adv* assuredly

assurer [asyre] §95 *tr* to assure; secure; insure ‖ *ref* to be assured; make sure; be insured

astate [astat] *m* astatine

aster [astɛr] *m* (bot) aster

astérie [asteri] *f* starfish

astérisque [asterisk] *m* asterisk

asthénie [asteni] *f* debility

asthme [asm] *m* asthma

asticot [astiko] *m* maggot

astiquer [astike] *tr* to polish

as·tral -trale [astral] *adj* (*pl* **-traux** [tro]) astral

astre [astrə] *m* star, heavenly body; leading light; **astre de la nuit** moon; **astre du jour** sun

astreindre [astrɛ̃dr] §50 *tr* to force, compel, subject ‖ §96 *ref* to force oneself; be subjected

astrologie [astrɔlɔʒi] *f* astrology

astrologue [astrɔlɔg] *m* astrologer

astronaute [astrɔnot] *mf* astronaut

astronautique [astrɔnotik] *f* astronautics

astronef [astrɔnɛf] *m* spaceship

astronome [astrɔnɔm] *mf* astronomer

astronomie [astrɔnɔmi] *f* astronomy

astronomique [astrɔnɔmik] *adj* astronomical

astuce [astys] *f* slyness, guile; tricks (*of a trade*)

astu·cieux [astysjø] **-cieuse** [sjøz] *adj* astute, crafty

atelier [atəlje] *m* studio; workshop

atermoiement [atɛrmwamã] *m* procrastination; extension of a loan

athée [ate] *adj* atheistic ‖ *mf* atheist

athéisme [ateism] *m* atheism

Athènes [atɛn] *f* Athens

athlète [atlɛt] *mf* athlete

athlétique [atletik] *adj* athletic

athlétisme [atletism] *m* athletics

Atlantique [atlãtik] *adj & m* Atlantic

atlas [atlɑs] *m* atlas ‖ (*cap*) *m* Atlas

atmosphère [atmɔsfɛr] *f* atmosphere

atome [atom] *m* atom

atomique [atɔmik] *adj* atomic

atomi·sé -sée [atɔmize] *adj* afflicted with radiation sickness

atomiser [atɔmize] *tr* to atomize

atomiseur [atomizœr] *m* spray; atomizer

atone [atɔn] *adj* dull, expressionless; drab (*life*); (phonet) unaccented

atours [atur] *mpl* finery

atout [atu] *m* trump; **sans atout** no-trump

atrabilaire [atrabilɛr] *adj & mf* hypochondriac

âtre [ɑtr] *m* hearth

atroce [atrɔs] *adj* atrocious

atrocité [atrɔsite] *f* atrocity

atrophie [atrɔfi] *f* atrophy

atrophier [atrɔfje] *tr & ref* to atrophy

atta·chant [ataʃã] **-chante** [ʃãt] *adj* appealing, attractive

attache [ataʃ] *f* attachment, tie; paper clip; (anat) joint; **attache parisienne** paper clip

attachement [ataʃmã] *m* attachment

attacher [ataʃe] *tr* to attach; tie up ‖ *intr* (culin) to stick ‖ §96 *ref* to be fastened, tied; **s'attacher à** to stick to; become devoted to.

attaque [atak] *f* attack; (pathol) stroke; **attaque brusque** or **attaque brusquée** surprise attack; **attaque de nerfs** case of nerves

attaquer [atake] *tr & intr* to attack ‖ *ref*—**s'attaquer à** to attack

attar·dé -dée [atarde] *adj* retarded; behind the times; belated, delayed ‖ *mf* mentally retarded person; lover of the past

attarder [atarde] *tr* to delay, retard ‖ *ref* to be delayed; stay, remain

atteindre [atɛ̃dr] §50 *tr* to attain; reach ‖ *intr*—**atteindre à** to attain; reach; attain to

at·teint [atɛ̃] **-teinte** [tɛ̃t] *adj* stricken ‖ *f* reaching; injury; **hors d'atteinte** out of reach; **porter atteinte à** to endanger; **premières atteintes** first signs (*of illness*)

attelage [atlaʒ] *m* harnessing; coupling

atteler [atle] §34 *tr* to harness; hitch; couple (*cars on a railroad*) ‖ *ref*—**s'atteler à** (coll) to buckle down to

attelle [atɛl] *m* splint; **attelles** hames

atte·nant [atənã] **-nante** [nãt] *adj* adjoining

attendre [atãdr] §97 *tr* to wait for, await; expect ‖ *intr* to wait ‖ §96 *ref*—**s'attendre à** to expect; rely on; **s'attendre à** + *inf* to expect to + *inf*; **s'attendre à ce que** + *subj* to expect (*s.o.*) to + *inf*, e.g., **il s'attend à ce que je lui raconte toute l'affaire** he expects me to tell him the whole story; **s'y attendre** to expect it or them

attendrir [atãdrir] *tr* to tenderize; soften ‖ *ref* to become tender; be deeply touched or moved

attendrissement [atãdrismã] *m* softening; compassion

atten·du -due [atãdy] *adj* expected ‖ **attendus** *mpl* (law) grounds ‖ *adv*—**attendu que** whereas, inasmuch as ‖ **attendu** *prep* in view of

attentat [atãta] *m* attempt, assault; outrage (*to decency*); offense (*against the state*)

attente [atãt] *f* wait; expectation; **en attente!** stand by!

attenter [atãte] *intr*—**attenter à** to attempt (*e.g., s.o.'s life*); **attenter à ses jours** to attempt suicide

atten·tif [atãtif] **-tive** [tiv] *adj* attentive

attention [atãsjɔ̃] *f* attention; **attentions** attention, care, consideration ‖ *interj* attention!, be careful!

attention·né -née [atãsjɔne] *adj* considerate

atténuation [atenɥasjɔ̃] *f* attenuation

atténuer [atenɥe] *tr* to subdue, soften (*color; pain; passions*); attenuate (*words;*

bacteria); extenuate (*a fault*) ‖ *ref* to soften; lessen

atterrer [atɛre] *tr* to dismay

atterrir [atɛrir] *intr* (*aux:* AVOIR or ÉTRE) to land

atterrissage [atɛrisaʒ] *m* landing; **atterrissage dur** hard landing; **atterrissage forcé** forced landing; **atterrissage sur le ventre** pancake landing

attestation [atɛstasjɔ̃] *f* attestation; **attestation d'études** transcript

attester [atɛste] *tr* to attest, attest to; **attester qn de q.ch.** to call s.o. to witness to s.th.

attiédir [atjedir] *tr & ref* to cool off; warm up

attifer [atife] *tr & ref* to spruce up

attirail [atiraj] *m* gear, tackle, outfit; (coll) paraphernalia

attirance [atirɑ̃s] *f* attraction, lure, attractiveness

atti·rant [atirɑ̃] **-rante** [rɑ̃t] *adj* appealing, attractive

attirer [atire] *tr* to attract ‖ *ref* to be attracted; attract each other; call forth (*criticism*)

attiser [atize] *tr* to stir, stir up, poke

atti·tré -trée [atitre] *adj* regular (*dealer*); **attitré de la cour** appointed by the court

attitude [atityd] *f* attitude

attrac·tif [atraktif] **-tive** [tiv] *adj* attractive (*force*)

attraction [atraksjɔ̃] *f* attraction; **les attractions** vaudeville

attrait [atrɛ] *m* attraction, attractiveness, appeal; **attraits** charms

attrape [atrap] *f* trap; (coll) trick, joke

attrape-mouche [atrapmuʃ] *m* (*pl* **-mouche** or **-mouches**) flypaper; Venus's-flytrap

attrape-nigaud [atrapnigo] *m* (*pl* **-nigauds**) booby trap

attraper [atrape] *tr* to catch; snare, trap; trick ‖ *ref* to trick each other; hang on

at·trayant [atrɛjɑ̃] **-trayante** [trɛjɑ̃t] *adj* attractive

attribuer [atribɥe] *tr* to ascribe, attribute; assign (*a share*) ‖ *ref* to claim, assume

attribut [atriby] *m* attribute; predicate

attribu·tif [atribytif] **-tive** [tiv] *adj* (gram) predicative

attribution [atribysjɔ̃] *f* attribution; assignment, assignation

attris·té -tée [atriste] *adj* sorrowful

attrister [atriste] *tr* to sadden ‖ §97 *ref* to become sad

attrition [atrisjɔ̃] *f* attrition

attroupement [atrupmɑ̃] *m* mob

attrouper [atrupe] *tr* to bring together in a mob ‖ *ref* to flock together in a mob

au [o] §77 to the

aubaine [obɛn] *f* windfall, godsend, bonanza

aube [ob] *f* dawn; (mach) paddle, blade, vane

aubépine [obepin] *f* hawthorn

auberge [obɛrʒ] *f* inn; **auberge de la jeunesse** youth hostel

aubergine [obɛrʒin] *f* eggplant; (Parisian slang) meter maid

aubergiste [obɛrʒist] *mf* innkeeper

auburn [obœrn] *adj invar* auburn

au·cun [okœ̃] **-cune** [kyn] *adj*—**aucun . . . ne** or **ne . . . aucun** §90 no, none, not any ‖ *pron indef*—**aucun ne** §90B no one, nobody; **d'aucuns** some, some people

aucunement [okynmɑ̃] §90 *adv*—**ne . . . aucunement** not at all, by no means

audace [odas] *f* audacity

auda·cieux [odasjø] **-cieuse** [sjøz] *adj* audacious

au-deçà [odəsa] *adv* (obs) on this side; **au-deçà de** (obs) on this side of

au-dedans [odədɑ̃] *adv* inside; **au-dedans de** inside, inside of

au-dehors [odəɔr] *adv* outside; **au-dehors de** outside, outside of

au-delà [odəla] *m*—**l'au-delà** the beyond ‖ *adv* beyond; **au-delà de** beyond

au-dessous [odəsu] *adv* below; **au-dessous de** under

au-dessus [odəsy] *adv* above; **au-dessus de** above

au-devant [odəvɑ̃] *adv*—**aller au devant de** to go to meet; anticipate (*s.o.'s wishes*); court (*defeat*)

audience [odjɑ̃s] *f* audience

audio-fréquence [odjɔfrekɑ̃s] *f* audio frequency

audiomètre [odjɔmɛtr] *m* audiometer

audio-vi·suel **-suelle** [odjɔvizɥɛl] *adj* audiovisual ‖ *m* audiovisual aids

audi·teur [oditœr] **-trice** [tris] *mf* listener; auditor (*in class*); **auditeur libre** auditor (*in class*)

audi·tif [oditif] **-tive** [tiv] *adj* auditory

audition [odisjɔ̃] *f* audition; public hearing; musical recital

auditionner [odisjɔne] *tr & intr* to audition

auditoire [oditwar] *m* audience; courtroom

auditorium [oditɔrjɔm] *m* auditorium; concert hall; projection room

auge [oʒ] *f* trough

augmentation [ɔgmɑ̃tasjɔ̃] *f* augmentation; raise (*in salary*)

augmenter [ɔgmɑ̃te] *tr* to augment; increase or supplement (*income*); raise (*prices*); raise the salary of (*an employee*) ‖ *intr* to augment, increase; **augmenter de** to increase by (*a stated amount*)

augure [ɔgyr] *m* augur; augury

augurer [ɔgyre] *tr & intr* to augur

auguste [ɔgyst] *adj* august

aujourd'hui [oʒurdɥi], [oʒordɥi] *m & adv* today; **d'aujourd'hui en huit** a week from today; **d'aujourd'hui en quinze** two weeks from today

aumône [omon] *f* alms; **faire l'aumône** to give alms; **faire l'aumône de** (fig) to hand out

aumônier [omonje] *m* chaplain

aune [on] *m* alder ‖ *f* ell

auprès [oprɛ] *adv* close by, in the neighborhood; **auprès de** near, close to; at the side of; to, at the side of; to (*a king, a government*); with; compared with

auquel [okɛl] (*pl* **auxquels**) §78

aurai [ɔre] *v* (**auras, aura, aurons,** etc.) see **avoir**

auréole [ɔreɔl] *f* aureole, halo

auréomycine [ɔreɔmisin] *f* aureomycin

auriculaire [ɔrikylɛr] *adj* firsthand (*witness*); auricular (*confession*) ‖ *m* little finger

auricule [ɔrikyl] *f* auricle

aurifier [orifje] *tr* to fill (*a tooth*) with gold

aurore [ɔrɔr] *f* aurora, dawn

ausculter [ɔskylte] *tr* to auscultate

auspice [ospis] *m* omen; **sous les auspices de** under the auspices of

aussi [osi] *adv* also, too; therefore, and so; so; **aussi . . . que** as . . . as

aussitôt [osito] *adv* right away, immediately; **aussitôt dit, aussitôt fait** no sooner said than done; **aussitôt que** as soon as

austère [ɔstɛr] *adj* austere

austérité [ɔsterite] *f* austerity

Australie [ɔstrali] *f* Australia; **l'Australie** Australia

austra·lien [ɔstraljɛ̃] **-lienne** [ljɛn] *adj* Australian ‖ (*cap*) *mf* Australian

autant [otɑ̃] *adv* as much, as many; as far, as long; **autant de** so many; **autant que** as much as, as far as; **d'autant** by so much; **d'autant plus** all the more; **d'autant plus** (or **moins**) **. . . que . . . plus** (or **moins**) all the more (*or* less) . . . as (*or* in proportion as) . . . more (*or* less); **d'autant que** inasmuch as

autel [otɛl], [otel] *m* altar

auteur [otœr] *adj*—**une femme auteur** an authoress ‖ *m* author

authentifier [otɑ̃tifje] *tr* to authenticate

authentique [otɑ̃tik] *adj* authentic; genuine (*antique*); notarized

authentiquer [otɑ̃tike] *tr* to notarize

autistique [ɔtistik] *adj* autistic

auto [ɔto], [oto] *f* auto

auto-allumage [ɔtoalymaʒ] *m* preignition

autobiographie [ɔtobjɔgrafi] *f* autobiography

auto-buffet [ɔtobyfɛ] *m* drive-in; curb service

autobus [ɔtobys] *m* bus, city bus

autocar [ɔtokar] *m* interurban bus

autochenille [ɔtoʃənij] *f* caterpillar (*tractor*)

autochtone [ɔtoktɔn] *adj & mf* native

autoclave [ɔtoklav] *m* pressure cooker; autoclave, sterilizer

autocollant [ɔtokɔlɑ̃] *m* bumpersticker

autocopie [ɔtokɔpi] *f* duplicating, multicopying; duplicated copy

autocopier [ɔtokɔpje] *tr* to run off, duplicate, ditto

auto-couchette [ɔtokuʃɛt] *f*—**en auto-couchette** piggyback

autocrate [ɔtokrat] *mf* autocrat

autocratique [ɔtokratik] *adj* autocratic

autocritique [ɔtokritik] *f* self-criticism

autocuiseur [ɔtokɥizœr] *m* pressure cooker

autodétermination [ɔtodetɛrminasjɔ̃] *f* self-determination

autodidacte [ɔtodidakt] *adj* self-taught ‖ *mf* self-taught person

autodrome [ɔtodrom] *m* race track; test strip

auto-école [ɔtoekɔl] *f* (*pl* **-écoles**) driving school

autogare [ɔtogar] *f* bus station

autographe [ɔtograf] *adj & m* autograph

autographie [ɔtografi] *f* multicopying

autographier [ɔtografje] *tr* to duplicate

autogreffe [ɔtogrɛf] *f* skin grafting

auto-grue [ɔtogry] *f* (*pl* **-grues**) tow truck

autoguidage [ɔtogidaʒ] *m* automatic piloting

auto-intoxication [ɔtoɛ̃tɔksikasjɔ̃] *f* autointoxication

automate [ɔtomat] *m* automaton

automation [ɔtomasjɔ̃] *f* automation

automatique [ɔtomatik] *adj* automatic ‖ *m* dial telephone

automatisation [ɔtomatizasjɔ̃] *f* automation

automatiser [ɔtomatize] *tr* to automate

automitrailleuse [ɔtomitrajøz] *f* armored car mounting machine guns

autom·nal -nale [ɔtomnal] *adj* (*pl* **-naux** [no]) autumnal

automne [ɔtɔn], [otɔn] *m* fall, autumn; **à l'automne, en automne** in the fall

automobile [ɔtomobil], [otomɔbil] *adj* automotive ‖ *f* automobile

automobilisme [ɔtomobilism] *m* driving, motoring

automobiliste [ɔtomobilist] *mf* motorist

automo·teur [ɔtomotœr] **-trice** [tris] *adj* self-propelling, automatic ‖ *m* self-propelled river barge ‖ *f* rail car

autonome [ɔtonɔm] *adj* autonomous, independent; (*comp*) off line

autonomie [ɔtonɔmi] *f* autonomy; cruising radius, range (*of ship, plane, or tank*)

autoplastie [ɔtoplasti] *f* plastic surgery

autoportrait [ɔtoportrɛ] *m* self-portrait

auto-propul·sé -sée [ɔtopropylse] *adj* self-propelled

autopsie [ɔtɔpsi] *f* autopsy

autopsier [ɔtɔpsje] *tr* to perform an autopsy on

autorail [ɔtoraj] *m* rail car

autorisation [ɔtorizasjɔ̃] *f* authorization

autoriser [ɔtorize] §96, §100 *tr* to authorize ‖ *ref*—**s'autoriser de** to take as authority, to base one's opinion on

autoritaire [ɔtoritɛr] *adj* authoritarian, bossy

autorité [ɔtorite] *f* authority

autoroute [ɔtorut] *f* superhighway; **autoroute à péage** turnpike

autosable [ɔtosabl] *m* dune buggy

auto-stop [ɔtostɔp] *m* hitchhiking; **faire de l'auto-stop** to hitchhike

auto-stop·peur [ɔtostɔpœr] **-peuse** [pøz] *mf* (*pl* **-peurs -peuses**) hitchhiker

autostrade [ɔtostrad] *f* superhighway

autour [otur] *m* goshawk ‖ *adv* around; **autour de** around; about

autre [otr] *adj indef* other; **autre chose** (coll) something else; **nous autres** we, e.g., **nous autres Américains** we Americans; **vous autres** you ‖ *pron indef* other; **d'autres** others; **j'en ai vu bien d'autres** I have seen worse than that; **l'un l'autre, les uns les autres** each other, one another; **l'un et l'autre** both; **l'un ou l'autre** either; **ni l'un ni l'autre** neither; **quelqu'un d'autre** someone else; **un autre** another

autrefois [otrəfwa] *adv* formerly, of old; **d'autrefois** of yore

autrement [otrəmɑ̃] *adv* otherwise

Autriche [otriʃ] *f* Austria; **l'Autriche** Austria

autri·chien [otriʃjɛ̃] **-chienne** [ʃjɛn] *adj* Austrian ‖ (*cap*) *mf* Austrian

autruche [otryʃ] *f* ostrich

autrui [otrɥi] *pron indef* others

auvent [ovɑ̃] *m* canopy (*over door*); flap (*of tent*)

aux [o] §77 to the

auxiliaire [oksiljɛr] *adj* auxiliary, stand-by; ancillary ‖ *m* (gram) auxiliary ‖ *f* noncombatant unit

aux·quels -quelles [okɛl] §78

avachir [avaʃir] *tr* to make limp, flabby ‖ *ref* to become limp, flabby

aval [aval] *m* lower waters; **en aval** downstream; **en aval de** below ‖ *m* (*pl* **avals**) endorsement

avalanche [avalɑ̃ʃ] *f* avalanche

avaler [avale] *tr* to swallow ‖ *intr* to go downstream

ava·leur [avalœr] **-leuse** [løz] *mf* swallower; **avaleur de sabres** sword swallower

avaliser [avalize] *tr* to endorse

avance [avɑ̃s] *f* advance; **en avance** fast (*clock*)

avan·cé -cée [avɑ̃se] *adj* advanced; overripe; tainted (*meat*)

avancement [avɑ̃smɑ̃] *m* advancement

avancer [avɑ̃se] §51 *tr, intr, & ref* to advance

avanie [avani] *f* snub, insult; **essuyer une avanie** to swallow an affront

avant [avɑ̃] *adj invar* front ‖ *m* front; (aer) nose; (naut) bow; **d'avant** previous; **en avant** forward; **en avant de** in front of, ahead of ‖ *adv* before; **avant de** (with *inf*) before; **avant que** + *subj* before; **bien** (or **très**) **avant dans** late into; far into; deep into; **plus avant** farther on ‖ *prep* before; **avant Jésus-Christ** (av. J.-C.) before Christ (B.C.)

avantage [avɑ̃taʒ] *m* advantage; (tennis) add; **avantages en nature** payment in kind; **avantages sociaux** fringe benefits

avanta·geux [avɑ̃taʒø] **-geuse** [ʒøz] *adj* advantageous; bargain (*price*); becoming (*e.g., hairdo*); conceited (*manner*)

avant-bras [avɑ̃bra] *m invar* forearm

avant-cour [avɑ̃kur] *f* (*pl* **-cours**) front yard

avant-coureur [avɑ̃kurœr] (*pl* **-coureurs**) *adj masc* presaging (*signs*) ‖ *m* forerunner, precursor, harbinger

avant-goût [avɑ̃gu] *m* (*pl* **-goûts**) foretaste

avant-guerre [avɑ̃gɛr] *m & f* (*pl* **-guerres**) prewar period

avant-hier [avɑ̃tjɛr], [avɑ̃jɛr] *adv & m* the day before yesterday

avant-port [avɑ̃pɔr] *m* (*pl* **-ports**) outer harbor

avant-poste [avɑ̃pɔst] *m* (*pl* **-postes**) outpost; **avant-postes** front lines

avant-première [avɑ̃prəmjɛr] *f* (*pl* **-premières**) review (*of a play*); premiere (*for the drama critics*); preview

avant-projet [avɑ̃prɔʒɛ] *m* (*pl* **-projets**) rough draft; draft (*of a law*)

avant-propos [avɑ̃prɔpo] *m invar* foreword

avant-scène [avɑ̃sɛn] *f* (*pl* **-scènes**) forestage, proscenium

avant-toit [avɑ̃twa] *m* (*pl* **-toits**) eave

avant-train [avɑ̃trɛ̃] *m* (*pl* **-trains**) front end, front assembly (*of vehicle*)

avant-veille [avɑ̃vɛj] *f* (*pl* **-veilles**) two days before

avare [avar] *adj* avaricious, miserly; saving, economical ‖ *mf* miser

avarice [avaris] *f* avarice

avari·cieux [avarisjø] **-cieuse** [sjøz] *adj* avaricious

avarie [avari] *f* damage; breakdown; spoilage; (naut) average

avarier [avarje] *tr* to damage; spoil ‖ *ref* to spoil

avatar [avatar] *m* avatar; **avatars** vicissitudes

avec [avɛk] *adv* (coll) with it; (coll) along, with me, etc. ‖ *prep* with

aveline [avlin] *f* filbert

ave·nant [avnɑ̃] **-nante** [nɑ̃t] *adj* gracious, charming; **à l'avenant** in keeping, to match; **à l'avenant de** in accord with ‖ *m* (ins) endorsement; codicil, rider

avènement [avɛnmɑ̃] *m* Advent; accession (*to the throne*)

avenir [avnir] *m* future; **à l'avenir** in the future

Avent [avɑ̃] *m* Advent

aventure [avɑ̃tyr] *f* adventure; **à l'aventure** at random; aimlessly; **d'aventure** by chance; **la bonne aventure** fortunetelling; **par aventure** by chance

aventurer [avɑ̃tyre] *tr* to venture ‖ *ref* to take a chance; **s'aventurer à** to venture to

aventu·reux [avɑ̃tyrø] **-reuse** [røz] *adj* adventurous

aventurier [avɑ̃tyrje] *m* adventurer

aventurière [avɑ̃tyrjɛr] *f* adventuress

avenue [avny] *f* avenue

avé·ré -rée [avere] *adj* established, authenticated

avérer [avere] §10 *tr* to aver ‖ *ref* to prove to be (*e.g., difficult*)

avers [avɛr] *m* heads (*of coin*), face (*of medal*)

averse [avɛrs] *f* shower

aversion [avɛrsjɔ̃] *f* aversion

avertir [avɛrtir] §97, §99 *tr* to warn; **avertir qn de** + *inf* to warn s.o. to + *inf*
avertissement [avɛrtismɑ̃] *m* warning; notification; foreword
avertisseur [avɛrtisœr] *adj masc* warning ‖ *m* alarm; (aut) horn; (theat) callboy; **avertisseur d'incendie** fire alarm
a·veu [avø] *m* (*pl* **-veux**) avowal, confession; consent; **sans aveu** unscrupulous
aveu·glant [avœglɑ̃] **-glante** [glɑ̃t] *adj* blinding
aveugle [avœgl] *adj* blind ‖ *mf* blind person; **en aveugle** without thinking
aveuglement [avœgləmɑ̃] *m* (fig) blindness
aveuglément [avœglemɑ̃] *adv* blindly
aveugler [avœgle] *tr* to blind; dazzle; stop up, plug; board up (*a window*) ‖ *ref*—**s'aveugler sur** to shut one's eyes to
aveuglette [avœglɛt] *adv*—**à l'aveuglette** blindly
aveulir [avølir] *tr* to enervate, deaden ‖ *ref* to become limp, enervated
aveulissement [avølismɑ̃] *m* enervation
aviateur [avjatœr] *m* aviator
aviation [avjasjɔ̃] *f* aviation
aviatrice [avjatris] *f* aviatrix
avide [avid] *adj* avid, eager; greedy; voracious; **avide de** avid for
avidité [avidite] *f* avidity, eagerness; greed; voracity
avilir [avilir] *tr* to debase, dishonor; (com) to lower the price of ‖ §96 *ref* to debase oneself; (com) to deteriorate
avilis·sant [avilisɑ̃] **-sante** [sɑ̃t] *adj* debasing
avilissement [avilismɑ̃] *m* debasement; (com) depreciation
avi·né -née [avine] *adj* drunk
aviner [avine] *tr* to soak (*a new barrel*) with wine ‖ *ref* (coll) to booze
avion [avjɔ̃] *m* airplane; **avion affété, avion nolisé, avion de transport à la demande** charter (air)plane; **avion à réaction** jet; **avion de chasse** fighter plane; **avion fugitif** spy plane; **avion long-courrier** long-range plane; **en avion** by plane; **par avion** air mail
avion-cargo [avjɔ̃kargo] *m* (*pl* **avions-cargos**) cargo liner, freighter
avion-géant [avjɔ̃ʒeɑ̃] *m* jumbo jet
avion-taxi [avjɔ̃taksi] *m* (*pl* **avions-taxis**) taxiplane
aviron [avirɔ̃] *m* oar; **aviron de couple** scull
avis [avi] *m* opinion; advice; notice, warning; decision; **à mon avis** in my opinion; **avis au lecteur** note to the reader; **changer d'avis** to change one's mind
avi·sé -sée [avize] *adj* prudent, shrewd; **bien avisé** well-advised

aviser [avize] §99 *tr* to glimpse, descry; advise, inform, warn ‖ *intr* to decide; **aviser à** to think of, look into; deal with ‖ §97 *ref*—**s'aviser de** to contrive, think up; be on the look-out for; **s'aviser de** + *inf* to take it into one's head to + *inf*
aviso [avizo] *m* dispatch boat, sloop
avivage [avivaʒ] *m* brightening; polishing
aviver [avive] *tr* to revive, stir up (*fire; passions*); brighten (*colors*); (med & fig) to open (*a wound*)
av. J.-C. *abbr* (**avant Jésus-Christ**) B.C.
avo·cat [avɔka] **-cate** [kat] *mf* lawyer; advocate; barrister (Brit); **avocat du diable** devil's advocate ‖ *m* avocado
avoine [avwan] *f* oats
avoir [avwar] *m* wealth; credit side (*of ledger*) ‖ §6 *tr* to have; get; **avoir . . . ans** to be . . . years old, e.g., **mon fils a dix ans** my son is ten years old; **avoir beau** + *inf* §95 no matter how (much) (s.o.) + *v* (*expressing futility*), e.g., **j'ai beau travailler** no matter how much I work; **avoir froid** to be cold; **avoir raison** to be right ‖ *intr*—**avoir à** to have to; **en avoir à** or **contre** to be angry with ‖ *impers*—**il y a** there is, there are, e.g., **il n'y a pas d'espoir** there is no hope ‖ *aux* to have, e.g., **j'ai couru trop vite** I have run too fast
avoisiner [avwazine] *tr* to neighbor, be near
avortement [avɔrtəmɑ̃] *m* abortion; miscarriage
avorter [avɔrte] *intr* to abort; miscarry
avorton [avɔrtɔ̃] *m* runt; (biol) stunt
avoué [avwe] *m* lawyer (*doing notarial work*); solicitor (Brit)
avouer [avwe] §95 *tr* to avow, admit; claim; acknowledge authorship of ‖ *ref* to be admitted; **s'avouer vaincu** to admit defeat
avril [avril] *m* April
axe [aks] *m* axis
axénique [aksenik] *adj* germ-free
axer [akse] *tr* to set on an axis; orient
axiomatique [aksjɔmatik] *adj* axiomatic
axiome [aksjom] *m* axiom
axonge [aksɔ̃ʒ] *f* lard
ayant-droit [ɛjɑ̃drwa] *m* (*pl* **ayants-droit**) claimant; beneficiary
ayez [eje] *v* (**ayons**) see **avoir**
azalée [azale] *f* azalea
azimut or **azimuth** [azimyt] *m* azimuth
azote [azɔt] *m* nitrogen
azo·té -tée [azɔte] *adj* nitrogenous
Aztèques [aztɛk] *mpl* Aztecs
azur [azyr] *adj* & *m* azure
azyme [azim] *adj* unleavened ‖ *m* unleavened bread

B, b [be] *m invar* second letter of the French alphabet

baba [baba] *adj* (coll) flabbergasted, wide-eyed ‖ *m* baba

babeurre [babœr] *m* buttermilk

babil [babil], [babi] *m* babble, chatter; **babil enfantin** baby talk

babillage [babijaʒ] *m* babbling

babil·lard [babijar] **-larde** [jard] *adj* babbling ‖ *mf* babbler ‖ *f* (slang) letter

babiller [babije] *intr* to babble, chatter

babine [babin] *f* chop (*mouth*); **s'essuyer les babines, se lécher les babines** to lick one's chops

babiole [babjɔl] *f* (coll) bauble

bâbord [babɔr] *m* (naut) port, portside; **à bâbord** port; **bâbord armures** port sail

babouche [babuʃ] *f* babouche, slipper

babouin [babwẽ] *m* baboon; pimple on the lips; brat

bac [bak] *m* ferryboat; tub, vat; box, bin; tray (*for ice cubes*); drawer (*of refrigerator*); case (*of battery*); (slang) baccalaureate

baccalauréat [bakalɔrea] *m* baccalaureate, bachelor's degree

bacchanale [bakanal] *f* bacchanal

bâche [baʃ] *f* tarpaulin; hot-water tank

bache·lier [baʃəlje] **-lière** [ljɛr] *mf* bachelor (*holder of degree*) ‖ *m* (hist) bachelor (*young knight*)

bâcher [baʃe] *tr* to cover with a tarpaulin

bachique [baʃik] *adj* bacchanalian, bacchic; drinking (*song*)

bachot [baʃo] *m* dinghy, punt; (coll) baccalaureate

bachotage [baʃotaʒ] *m* (coll) cramming (*for an exam*)

bachoter [baʃote] *intr* (coll) to cram

bacille [basil] *m* bacillus

bâclage [baklaʒ] *m* blocking up (*of harbor*); (slang) botching (*of work*)

bâcle [bakl] *f* bolt (*of door*)

bâcler [bakle] *tr* to bolt (*a door*); close up (*a harbor*); (coll) to botch, to hurry through carelessly

bâ·cleur [baklœr] **-cleuse** [kløz] *mf* (coll) botcher

bacon [bakɔ̃] *m* bacon

bactéricide [bakterisid] *adj* bactericidal ‖ *m* bactericide

bactérie [bakteri] *f* bacterium; **bactéries** bacteria

bactériologie [bakterjɔlɔʒi] *f* bacteriology

ba·daud [bado] **-daude** [dod] *mf* rubberneck, gawk, idler

badauder [badode] *intr* to stand and stare

badigeon [badiʒɔ̃] *m* whitewash

badigeonner [badiʒɔne] *tr* to whitewash; (med) to paint (*e.g., the throat*)

ba·din [badẽ] **-dine** [din] *adj* sprightly, playful, teasing ‖ *mf* tease ‖ *m* (aer) air-speed indicator ‖ *f* cane, switch

badinage [badinaʒ] *m* banter; **badinage amoureux** necking

badiner [badine] *intr* to joke, tease; trifle, be flippant

badinerie [badinri] *f* teasing; childishness

baffe [baf] *f* (coll) slap, blow, cuff

bafouer [bafwe] *tr* to heckle, humiliate

bafouiller [bafuje] *intr* (coll) to stammer, mumble, babble

bâfrer [bafre] *tr & intr* (slang) to guzzle

bagage [bagaʒ] *m* baggage; **bagages** baggage, luggage; **bagages à main** hand baggage; **bagages non accompagnés** baggage sent on ahead; **menus bagages** hand luggage; **plier bagage** to pack one's bags; (coll) to scram; (coll) to kick the bucket

bagarre [bagar] *f* brawl, row, riot; **chercher la bagarre** (coll) to be looking for a fight

bagarrer [bagare] *intr & ref* to riot; (coll) to brawl, scrap, scuffle

bagar·reur [bagarœr] **-reuse** [røz] *mf* (coll) rioter, brawler

bagatelle [bagatɛl] *f* trifle, bagatelle; frivolity ‖ *interj* nonsense!

bagnard [baɲar] *m* convict

bagne [baɲ] *m* penitentiary, penal colony; (nav) prison ship; (slang) sweatshop

bagnole [baɲɔl] *f* (slang) jalopy

bagou [bagu] *m* (coll) gift of gab

bague [bag] *f* ring; cigar band; (mach) collar, sleeve; **bague de fiançailles** engagement ring

baguenauder [bagnode] *intr* to waste time, fool around ‖ *ref* (coll) to wander about

baguer [bage] *tr* to band (*a tree*); baste (*cloth*)

baguette [bagɛt] *f* stick, switch, rod; baton; long thin loaf of bread; chopstick; **baguette de fée** fairy wand; **baguettes de tambour** drumsticks; **mener qn à la baguette** (coll) to lead s.o. by the nose; **passer par les baguettes** to run the gauntlet

baguier [bagje] *m* jewel box

bahut [bay] *m* trunk, chest; cupboard; (slang) high school

bai baie [bɛ] *adj* bay (*horse*) ‖ *m* bay; berry; bayberry; bay window

baignade [beɲad] *m* bathing, swimming; swimming hole, bathing spot

baigner [beɲe] *tr* to bathe; wash (*the coast*) ‖ *intr* to be immersed, soak ‖ *ref* to bathe; go bathing

bai·gneur [beɲœr] **-gneuse** [ɲøz] *mf* bather; vacationist at a spa or seaside resort; bathhouse attendant ‖ *m* doll

baignoire [beɲwar] *f* bathtub; (theat) orchestra box

bail [baj] *m* (*pl* **baux** [bo]) lease; **passer un bail** to sign a lease; **prendre à bail** to lease

bâillement [bajmã] *m* yawn

bailler [baje] *tr*—**vous me la baillez belle** (coll) you're pulling my leg

bâiller [baje] *intr* to yawn; be ajar, be half open

bail·leur [bajœr] **-leresse** [jərɛs] *mf* lessor; **bailleur de fonds** lender

bailli [baji] *m* bailiff

bailliage [baja3] *m* bailiwick

bâillon [bɑjɔ̃] *m* gag, muzzle

bâaillonner [bɑjɔne] *tr* to gag; (fig) to muzzle

bain [bɛ̃] *m* bath; **bain de soleil** sun bath; **bain de vapeur** steam bath; **bain moussant, bain de mousse** bubble bath; **bains** watering place, spa; bathing establishment; **être dans le bain** (coll) to be in hot water

bain·marie [bɛ̃mari] *m* (*pl* **bains-marie**) double boiler, bain-marie

baïonnette [bajɔnɛt] *f* bayonet

baiser [beze], [bɛze] *m* kiss ‖ *tr* (vulg) to have sex with; (archaic) to kiss

baisoter [bɛzɔte] *tr* (coll) to keep on kissing ‖ *ref* (coll) to bill and coo

baisse [bɛs] *f* fall; **jouer à la baisse** (com) to bear the market

baissement [bɛsmɑ̃] *m* lowering

baisser [bɛse] *m* lowering; **baisser du rideau** curtain fall ‖ *tr* to lower; take in (*sail*); dim (*headlights*) ‖ *intr* to fall, drop, sink ‖ *ref* to bend, stoop

baissier [bɛsje] *m* bear (*on the stock exchange*)

bajoue [ba3u] *f* jowl

bal [bal] *m* (*pl* **bals**) ball, dance; **bal travesti** fancy-dress ball

balade [balad] *f* stroll; **balade en auto** joy ride

balader [balade] *ref* to go for a stroll; **se balader en auto** to go joy-riding

bala·deur [baladœr] **-deuse** [døz] *adj* strolling ‖ *mf* stroller ‖ *m* gear; Walkman ‖ *f* cart (*of street vendor*); drop-cord light

baladin [baladɛ̃] *m* mountebank, showman; oaf

balafre [balɑfr] *f* gash, scar

balafrer [balafre] *tr* to gash, scar

balai [balɛ] *m* broom; **balai à laver** mop; **balai de sorcière** witches'-broom; **balai électrique** vacuum cleaner; **balai mécanique** carpet sweeper; **donner un coup de balai à** to make a clean sweep of (*s.th.*); to kick (*s.o.*) out

balai-éponge [balɛepɔ̃3] *m* (*pl* **balais-éponges**) mop

balance [balɑ̃s] *f* balance; scales; **faire la balance de** (bk) to balance; **la Balance** (astr, astrol) Libra

balancement [balɑ̃smɑ̃] *m* swaying, teetering; (fig) indecision, wavering; (fig) harmony (*of phrase*)

balancer [balɑ̃se] §51, §96 *tr* to balance; move (*arms or legs*) in order to balance; balance (*an account*); weigh (*the pros and cons*); swing, rock; (coll) to fire (*s.o.*); **elle est bien balancée** she is stacked (*well built*) ‖ *intr* to swing, rock; hesitate, waver ‖ *ref* to swing, seesaw; sway, rock; ride (*at anchor*)

balancier [balɑ̃sje] *m* pendulum; balance wheel; pole (*of tightrope walker*)

balançoire [balɑ̃swar] *f* swing; seesaw, teeter-totter; (slang) nonsense

balayage [balɛja3] *m* sweeping; (telv) scanning

balayer [balɛje], [baleje] §49 *tr* to sweep, sweep up; sweep out; scour (*the sea*); (telv) to scan

balayeur [balɛjœr] **balayeuse** [balɛjøz] *mf* sweeper, scavenger ‖ *f* street-cleaning truck

balayures [balɛjyr] *fpl* sweepings

balbutiement [balbysimɑ̃] *m* stammering, mumbling; initial effort

balbutier [balbysje] *tr* to stammer out ‖ *intr* to stammer, mumble

balbuzard [balbyzar] *m* osprey, bald buzzard, sea eagle

balcon [balkɔ̃] *m* balcony; (theat) dress circle

baldaquin [baldakɛ̃] *m* canopy, tester

Baléares [balear] *fpl* Balearic Islands

baleine [balɛn] *f* right whale, whalebone whale; whalebone; rib (*of umbrella*); stay (*of a corset*)

baleinier [balɛnje] *m* whaling vessel

baleinière [balɛnjɛr] *f* whaleboat; lifeboat

balisage [baliza3] *m* (aer) ground lights; (naut) buoys

balise [baliz] *f* buoy, marker; ground light, beacon; landing signal

baliser [balize] *tr* to furnish with markers, buoys, landing lights, beacons, or radio signals

balistique [balistik] *adj* ballistic ‖ *f* ballistics

baliverne [balivɛrn] *f* nonsense, humbug

balkanique [balkanik] *adj* Balkan

ballade [balad] *f* ballade

bal·lant [balɑ̃] **-lante** [lɑ̃t] *adj* waving, swinging, dangling ‖ *m* oscillation, shaking

balle [bal] *f* ball; bullet; hull, chaff; bale; (tennis) match point; **balle traçante** tracer bullet; **prendre** or **saisir la balle au bond** to seize time by the forelock

ballerine [balrin] *f* ballerina

ballet [balɛ] *m* ballet

ballon [balɔ̃] *m* balloon; ball; football, soccer ball; round-bottom flask; rounded mountaintop; **ballon d'essai** trial balloon

ballonner [balɔne] *tr, intr, & ref* to balloon

ballot [balo] *m* pack; bundle; (slang) blockhead, chump

ballottage [balɔta3] *m* tossing, shaking; second ballot

ballotter [balɔte] *tr & intr* to toss about

balnéaire [balneɛr] *adj* seaside

ba·lourd [balur] **-lourde** [lurd] *adj* awkward, lumpish ‖ *mf* blockhead, bumpkin ‖ *m* wobble

balte [balt] *adj* Baltic ‖ (*cap*) *mf* Balt

Baltique [baltik] *f* Baltic (*sea*)

balustrade [balystrad] *f* balustrade, banisters

balustre [balystr] *m* baluster, banister

bal·zan [balzɑ̃] **-zane** [zan] *adj* white-footed (*horse*) ‖ *f* white spot (*on horse's foot*)

bam·bin [bɑ̃bɛ̃] **-bine** [bin] *mf* (coll) babe
bambo·chard [bɑ̃bɔʃar] **-charde** [ʃard] *adj*
(coll) carousing ‖ *mf* (coll) carouser
bamboche [bɑ̃bɔʃ] *f* (slang) jag, bender
bambocher [bɑ̃bɔʃe] *intr* (coll) to carouse,
go on a spree
bambo·cheur [bɑ̃bɔʃœr] **-cheuse** [ʃøz] *adj*
(coll) carousing ‖ *mf* (coll) carouser
bambou [bɑ̃bu] *m* bamboo
ban [bɑ̃] *m* ban; cadenced applause; **ban de
mariage** banns; **convoquer le ban et
l'arrière-ban** to invite everyone and his
brother; **mettre au ban** to banish, ban
ba·nal -nale [banal] *adj* (*pl* **-nals -nales**)
banal, trite, commonplace ‖ *adj* (*pl* **-naux**
[no] **-nales**) (archaic) common, public, in
common
banaliser [banalize] *tr* to vulgarize, make
commonplace
banalité [banalite] *f* banality; triteness
banane [banan] *f* banana
bananier [bananje] *m* banana tree
banc [bɑ̃] *m* bench; shoal; school (*of fish*);
pew (*reserved for church officials*); (hist)
privy council; **banc de neige** snowbank;
être sur les bancs to go to high school
bancaire [bɑ̃kɛr] *adj* banking, of banks
ban·cal -cale [bɑ̃kal] *adj* (*pl* **-cals -cales**)
bowlegged, bandy-legged
bandage [bɑ̃daʒ] *m* bandage; bandaging;
truss; tire (*of metal or rubber*)
bande [bɑ̃d] *f* band; movie film; recording
tape; cushion (*in billiards*); wrapper (*of a
newspaper*); strip (*of stamps*); **bande dessinée** comic strip; **bande génératrice,
bande mère** master tape; **bande magnétique** recording tape; tape recording;
bande sonore or **parlante** sound track;
bande vidéo videotape; **donner de la
bande** to heel, to list; **faire bande à part**
to keep to oneself
bande-annonce [bɑ̃danɔ̃s] *f* (**bandes-
annonces**) film clip
ban·deau [bɑ̃do] *m* (*pl* **-deaux**) blindfold;
headband; bending (*of a bow*); **bandeau
royal** diadem; **bandeaux** hair parted in
the middle
bander [bɑ̃de] *tr* to band, put a band on;
bandage; blindfold; bend (*a bow*); put a
tire on; draw taut; (vulg) to have or get a
hard-on ‖ *ref* to band together; put up
resistance; **elle est bandante** (vulg) she is
a sexpot
banderole [bɑ̃derɔl] *f* pennant, streamer;
strap (*of gun*)
bandière [bɑ̃djɛr] *f* battle, e.g., **front de
bandière** battle front
bandit [bɑ̃di] *m* bandit
bandoulière [bɑ̃duljɛr] *f* shoulder strap,
sling; **en bandoulière** slung over the
shoulder
banlieue [bɑ̃ljø] *f* suburbs; **de banlieue**
suburban
banlieu·sard [bɑ̃ljøzar] **-sarde** [zard] *mf*
suburbanite (*especially of a Parisian suburb*)
banne [ban] *f* awning (*of store*)

ban·ni -nie [bani] *adj* banished, exiled ‖ *mf*
exile
bannière [banjɛr] *f* banner, flag
bannir [banir] *tr* to banish
bannissement [banismɑ̃] *m* banishment
banque [bɑ̃k] *f* bank; **banque de données**
(comp) data bank; **banque des yeux** eye
bank; **banque du sang** blood bank; **faire
sauter la banque** to break the bank
banqueroute [bɑ̃krut] *f* bankruptcy (*with
blame for negligence or fraud*)
banquerou·tier [bɑ̃krutje] **-tière** [tjɛr] *adj*
& *mf* bankrupt (*with culpability*)
banquet [bɑ̃kɛ] *m* banquet
banqueter [bɑ̃kte] §34 *intr* to banquet
banquette [bɑ̃kɛt] *f* seat (*in a train, bus,
automobile*); bank (*of earth or sand*); bunker (*in a golf course*); **banquette arrière**
back seat; **banquette de tir** (mil) emplacement for shooting; **jouer devant les
banquettes** to play to an empty house
ban·quier [bɑ̃kje] **-quière** [kjɛr] *mf* banker
banquise [bɑ̃kiz] *f* pack ice
banquiste [bɑ̃kist] *m* charlatan, quack
baptême [batɛm] *m* baptism; christening;
**baptême de la ligne, baptême des tro-
piques** or **du tropique** polliwog initiation
baptiser [batize] *tr* to baptize; christen;
(slang) to dilute (*wine*) with water
baptis·mal -male [batismal] *adj* (*pl* **-maux**
[mo]) baptismal
baptistaire [batistɛr] *adj* baptismal (*certificate*)
baptiste [batist] *mf* Baptist
baptistère [batistɛr] *m* baptistery
baquet [bakɛ] *m* wooden tub, bucket; (aut)
bucket seat
bar [bar] *m* bar; (ichth) bass, perch; **bar
payant** cash bar
baragouin [baragwɛ̃] *m* (slang) gibberish
baragouiner [baragwine] *tr* (coll) to murder
(*a language*); (coll) to stumble through (*a
speech*) ‖ *intr* (coll) to jabber
baraque [barak] *f* booth, stall; shanty, hovel
baraterie [baratri] *f* barratry
baratin [baratɛ̃] *m* (slang) blah-blah, hokum
baratte [barat] *f* churn
baratter [barate] *tr* to churn
Barbade [barbad] *f* Barbados; **la Barbade**
Barbados
barbare [barbar] *adj* barbarous, barbaric,
savage ‖ *mf* barbarian
barbaresque [barbarɛsk] *adj* of Barbary
barbarie [barbari] *f* barbarity, barbarism ‖
(*cap*) *f* Barbary
barbarisme [barbarism] *m* barbarism (*in
speech or writing*)
barbe [barb] *f* beard; bristle; whiskers (*of an
animal*); barbel; **barbes** vane (*of a
feather*); deckle edge; **faire q.ch. à la
barbe de qn** to do s.th. right under the
nose of s.o.; **rire dans sa barbe** to laugh
up one's sleeve; **se faire la barbe** to
shave ‖ *interj* **c'est la barbe!** what a
bore!; **la barbe!** shut up!
bar·beau [barbo] *m* (*pl* **-beaux**) cornflower;
(ichth) barbel; (slang) pimp

barbe·lé -lée [baʀbəle] *adj* barbed ‖ **barbelés** *mpl* barbed wire

bar·bet [baʀbɛ] **-bette** [bɛt] *mf* water spaniel

barbiche [baʀbiʃ] *f* goatee

barbier [baʀbje] *m* barber

barbillon [baʀbijɔ̃] *m* barb

barbiturique [baʀbityʀik] *m* barbiturate

barbon [baʀbɔ̃] *m* (pej) old fogy

barboter [baʀbɔte] *intr* to paddle (*like ducks*); wallow (*like pigs*); bubble (*like carbonated water*); (coll) to splutter; (slang) to steal

barbo·teur [baʀbɔtœʀ] **-teuse** [tøz] *mf* (slang) muddler ‖ *m* duck; wash bottle ‖ *f* rompers

barbouiller [baʀbuje] *tr* to smear, blur; daub; (coll) to scribble; **barbouiller le cœur à** to nauseate

barbouil·leur [baʀbujœʀ] **-leuse** [jøz] *mf* dauber; messy person; scribbler

barbouze [baʀbuz] *f* (slang) beard; (slang) secret agent; (slang) bodyguard

bar·bu -bue [baʀby] *adj* bearded

bard [baʀ] *m* handbarrow

bardage [baʀdaʒ] *m* siding (*of house*)

bardane [baʀdan] *f* burdock

barde [baʀd] *m* bard ‖ *f* blanket of bacon

bar·deau [baʀdo] *m* (*pl* **-deaux**) shingle; lath

barder [baʀde] *tr* to carry with a handbarrow; armor (*a horse*); blanket (*a roast*); **barder de** to cover with ‖ *intr* to rage

bardot [baʀdo] *m* hinny

barème [baʀɛm] *m* schedule (*of rates, taxes, etc.*)

baréter [baʀete] §10 *intr* to trumpet (*like an elephant*)

barge [baʀʒ] *f* barge; haystack; godwit, black-tailed godwit

barguigner [baʀgiɲe] *intr* to shilly-shally, have trouble deciding

bargui·gneur [baʀgiɲœʀ] **-gneuse** [ɲøz] *mf* shilly-shallyer, procrastinator

baricaut [baʀiko] *m* small cask, keg

baril [baʀil], [baʀi] *m* small barrel, cask, keg

barillet [baʀijɛ] *m* small barrel; revolver cylinder; spring case

bariolage [baʀjɔlaʒ] *m* (coll) motley, mixture of colors

bario·lé -lée [baʀjɔle] *adj* speckled, multicolored, variegated

barioler [baʀjɔle] *tr* to variegate

bariolure [baʀjɔlyʀ] *f* clashing colors, motley

bar·man [baʀman] *m* (*pl* **-men** [mɛn] or **-mans**) bartender

baromètre [baʀɔmɛtʀ] *m* barometer

barométrique [baʀɔmetʀik] *adj* barometric

baron [baʀɔ̃] *m* baron

baronne [baʀɔn] *f* baroness

baroque [baʀɔk] *adj* & *m* baroque

baroud [baʀud] *m* rumble (*gang war*); (mil) **baroud d'honneur** gallant last stand

barque [baʀk] *f* boat

barrage [baʀaʒ] *m* dam; barrage, cordon (*of police*); tollgate; barricade, roadblock, checkpoint; (sports) playoff

barre [baʀ], [baʀ] *f* bar; crossbar (*of a t*); tiller, helm; bore (*tidal flood*); **barre de contrôle** (nucl) control rod; **barre de dopage** (nucl) booster rod; **barre de justice** rod to hold shackles; **barre des témoins** witness stand; **barre du gouvernail** helm; **barres** (typ) parallels; **jouer aux barres** to play prisoner's base

bar·reau [baʀo] *m* (*pl* **-reaux**) bar, crossbar, rail; rung (*of ladder or chair*); (law) bar

barrer [baʀe] *tr* to cross out, strike out, cancel; cross (*a t; a check in a British bank*); bar (*the door; the way*); block off (*a street*); dam (*a stream*); steer (*a boat*)

barrette [baʀɛt], [baʀɛt] *f* biretta; bar; slide; pin; name tag

barreur [baʀœʀ] *m* helmsman

barricade [baʀikad] *f* barricade

barricader [baʀikade] *tr* to barricade

barrière [baʀjɛʀ] *f* barrier; gate (*of a town; of a grade crossing*); tollgate; neighborhood shopping district

barrique [baʀik] *f* cask; hogshead, large barrel

barrir [baʀiʀ] *intr* to trumpet (*like an elephant*)

barrot [baʀo] *m* beam (*of a ship*)

baryton [baʀitɔ̃] *m* baritone; alto (*saxhorn*)

baryum [baʀjɔm] *m* barium

bas [bɑ] **basse** [bɑs] *adj* low; base, vile; cloudy (*weather*) ‖ (when standing before noun) *adj* low; base, vile; early (*age*) ‖ *m* stocking; lower part, bottom; **à bas . . . !** down with . . . !; **bas de casse** (typ) lower case; **bas de laine** nest egg, savings; **en bas** at the bottom; downstairs ‖ *f* see **basse** ‖ **bas** *adv* softly; down, low

ba·sal -sale [bazal] *adj* (*pl* **-saux** [zo]) basic; basal (*metabolism*)

basalte [bazalt] *m* basalt

basa·né -née [bazane] *adj* tanned, sunburned

basaner [bazane] *tr* to tan, sunburn

bas-bleu [bablø] *m* (*pl* **-bleus**) bluestocking

bas-côté [bakote] *m* (*pl* **-côtés**) aisle (*of a church*); footpath (*beside a road*)

bascule [baskyl] *f* scale; rocker; seesaw

basculement [baskylmɑ̃] *m* rocking, seesawing, tipping; dimming

basculer [baskyle] *tr* to tip over ‖ *intr* to tip over; seesaw, rock, swing; **faire basculer** to dim (*the headlights*)

bas-dessus [badəsy] *m* mezzo-soprano

base [bɑz] *f* base; basis; **à la base** at heart, to the core; **base de données** (comp) data base; **de base** basic

base-ball [bɛzbol] *m* baseball

baser [bɑze] *tr* to base; ground, found (*an opinion*) ‖ *ref* to be based

bas-fond [bafɔ̃] *m* (*pl* **-fonds**) lowland; shallows; **bas-fonds** dregs, underworld; slums

basilic [bazilik] *m* basil

basilique [bazilik] *f* basilica

basin [bazɛ̃] *m* dimity

basique [bazik] *adj* basic, alkaline

basket [baskɛt] *m* basketball

basketteur [baskɛtœr] *m* basketball player

basoche [bazɔʃ] *f* law, legal profession

basque [bask] *adj* Basque ‖ *m* Basque (*language*) ‖ *f* coattail ‖ (*cap*) *mf* Basque (*person*)

basse [bɑs] *f* shoal; tuba; (mus) bass; **basse chiffrée** (mus) figured bass

basse-contre [bɑskɔ̃tr] *f* (*pl* **basses-contre**) basso profundo

basse-cour [bɑskur] *f* (*pl* **basses-cours**) barnyard, farmyard; barnyard animals; poultry yard

bassesse [bɑsɛs] *f* baseness; base act

bassin [basɛ̃] *m* basin; dock; artificial lake; collection plate; pelvis; **bassin à flot** tidal basin; **bassin de lit** bedpan; **bassin de radoub** dry dock; **bassin hygiénique** bedpan

bassine [basin] *f* dishpan

bassinoire [basinwar] *f* bedwarmer

basson [basɔ̃] *m* bassoon

baste [bast] *m* ace of clubs; saddle basket ‖ *interj* enough!

bastille [bastij] *f* small fortress

bastion [bastjɔ̃] *m* bastion

bastonnade [bastɔnad] *f* beating

bas-ventre [bɑvɑ̃tr] *m* abdomen, lower part of the belly

bât [bɑ] *m* packsaddle

bataclan [bataklɑ̃] *m*—**tout le bataclan** (slang) the whole caboodle

bataille [batɑj], [bataj] *f* battle, fight

batailler [batɑje], [bataje] *intr* to battle, fight

batail·leur [batɑjœr] **-leuse** [jøz] *adj* belligerent ‖ *mf* fighter

bataillon [batajɔ̃] *m* battalion

bâ·tard [bɑtar] **-tarde** [tard] *adj* & *mf* mongrel; bastard ‖ *m* one-pound loaf of short-length type of bread ‖ *f* cursive handwriting

bâtar·deau [bɑtardo] *m* (*pl* **-deaux**) cofferdam, caisson

ba·teau [bato] *m* (*pl* **-teaux**) boat; **bateau automobile** motorboat, motor launch; **bateau à vapeur** steamboat; **bateau à voiles** sailboat; **bateau de guerre** warship; **bateau de pêche** fishing boat; **bateau de sauvetage** lifeboat; **monter un bateau à qn** (slang) to pull s.o.'s leg; **par (le) bateau** by boat

bateau-citerne [batositɛrn] *m* (*pl* **bateaux-citernes**) tanker

bateau-feu [batofø] *m* (*pl* **bateaux-feux**) lightship

bateau-maison [batomezɔ̃] *m* (*pl* **bateaux-maisons**) houseboat

bateau-mouche [batomuʃ] *m* (*pl* **bateaux-mouches**) excursion boat

bateau-pompe [batopɔ̃p] *m* (*pl* **bateaux-pompes**) fireboat

batelage [batlaʒ] *m* lighterage; juggling; tumbling

batelée [batle] *f* boatload

bateler [batle] §34 *tr* to lighter ‖ *intr* to juggle; tumble

bateleur [batlœr] **-leuse** [løz] *mf* juggler; tumbler

bate·lier [batlje] **-lière** [ljɛr] *mf* skipper ‖ *m* boatman; ferryman

batellerie [batɛlri] *f* lighterage

bâter [bɑte] *tr* to packsaddle

bath [bat] *adj* (slang) A-one, swell

bâ·ti -tie [bɑti] *adj* built; **bien bâti** wellbuilt (*person*) ‖ *m* frame; basting (*thread*); basted garment

batifoler [batifɔle] *intr* (coll) to frolic

bâtiment [bɑtimɑ̃] *m* building; ship

bâtir [bɑtir] *tr* to build; baste, tack ‖ *ref* to be built

bâtisse [bɑtis] *f* masonry, construction; building, edifice; ramshackle house

bâtis·seur [bɑtisœr] **-seuse** [søz] *mf* builder

bâton [bɑtɔ̃] *m* stick; baton; staff, cane; rung (*of a chair*); stroke (*of a pen*); stick (*of gum*); **à bâtons rompus** by fits and starts; impromptu; (archit) with zigzag molding; **bâton de reprise** (mus) repeat bar; **bâton de rouge à lèvres** lipstick; **bâton de vieillesse** helper or nurse for the aged; **mettre des bâtons dans les roues** to throw a monkey wrench into the works

bâtonner [bɑtɔne] *tr* to cudgel; cross out

bâtonnet [bɑtɔnɛ] *m* rod (*in the retina*); chopstick

battage [bataʒ] *m* beating; threshing; churning; (slang) ballyhoo

bat·tant [batɑ̃] **-tante** [tɑ̃t] *adj* beating; pelting, driving; swinging (*door*) ‖ *m* flap; clapper (*of bell*); **à deux battants** double (*door*)

batte [bat] *f* mallet, beater; dasher, plunger; bench for beating clothes; wooden sword (*for slapstick comedy*); (sports) bat; **batte de l'or** goldbeating

battement [batmɑ̃] *m* beating, beat; throbbing, pulsing; clapping (*of hands*); dance step; wait (*e.g., between trains*)

batterie [batri] *f* (elec, mil, mus) battery; train service (*in one direction*); ruse, scheming; **batterie de cuisine** kitchen utensils

batteur [batœr] *m* beater; thresher; (sports) batter; **batteur de grève** beachcomber; **batteur de pieux** pile driver; **batteur électrique** electric mixer

batteuse [batøz] *f* threshing machine

battoir [batwar] *m* bat, beetle (*for washing clothes*); tennis racket

battre [batr] §7 *tr* to beat; clap (*one's hands*); flap, flutter; wink; bang; pound (*the sidewalk*); search; shuffle (*the cards*); **battre la mesure** to beat time; **battre monnaie** to mint money ‖ *intr* to beat ‖ *ref* to fight

bau [bo] *m* (*pl* **baux**) beam (*of a ship*)

baudet [bodɛ] *m* ass, donkey; stallion ass; sawhorse; (slang) jackass, idiot

baudrier [bodrije] *m* shoulder belt

bauge [boʒ] *f* lair, den; clay and straw mortar; (coll) pigsty

baume [bom] *m* balsam; (*consolation*) balm

ba·vard [bavar] **-varde** [vard] *adj* talkative, loquacious; tattletale ‖ *mf* chatterer; tattletale; gossip

bavardage [bavardaʒ] *m* chattering; gossiping

bavarder [bavarde] *intr* to chatter; gossip

bava·rois [bavarwa] **-roise** [rwaz] *adj* Bavarian ‖ (*cap*) *mf* Bavarian (*person*)

bave [bav] *f* dribble, froth, spittle; (fig) slander

baver [bave] *intr* to dribble, drool; run (*like a pen*); **baver sur** to besmirch

bavette [bavɛt] *f* bib

ba·veux [bavø] **-veuse** [vøz] *adj* drooling; tendentious, wordy; undercooked

Bavière [bavjɛr] *f* Bavaria; **la Bavière** Bavaria

bavocher [bavɔʃe] *intr* to smear

bavochure [bavɔʃyr] *f* smear

bavure [bavyr] *f* bur (*of metal*); smear

bayer [baje] §49 *intr*—**bayer aux corneilles** to gawk, stargaze

bazar [bazar] *m* bazaar; five-and-ten; **tout le bazar** (slang) the whole shebang

béant [beɑ̃] **béante** [beɑ̃t] *adj* gaping, wide-open

béat [bea] **béate** [beat] *adj* smug, complacent, sanctimonious

béatifier [beatifje] *tr* to beatify

béatitude [beatityd] *f* beatitude

beau [bo] (or **bel** [bɛl] before vowel or mute h) **belle** [bɛl] (*pl* **beaux belles**) *adj* beautiful; handsome; **bel et bien** truly, for sure; **de plus belle** more than ever; **il fait beau** it is nice out, we are having fair weather; **tout beau!** steady!, easy does it! ‖ (when standing before noun) *adj* beautiful; handsome; fine, good; considerable, large, long; fair (*weather*); odd-numbered or recto (*page*) ‖ *mf* fair one; **faire le beau**, **faire la belle** to strut, swagger; sit up and beg (*said of a dog*); **la belle** the deciding match; **la Belle au bois dormant** Sleeping Beauty ‖ **beau** *adv*—**il a beau parler** it is no use for him to speak ‖ **belle** *adv*—**la bailler belle** (slang) to tell a whopper; **l'échapper belle** to have a narrow escape

beaucoup [boku] §91 *adv* much, many; **beaucoup de** much, many; **de beaucoup** by far

beau-fils [bofis] *m* (*pl* **beaux-fils**) son-in-law; stepson

beau-frère [bofrɛr] *m* (*pl* **beaux-frères**) brother-in-law

beau-père [bopɛr] *m* (*pl* **beaux-pères**) father-in-law; stepfather

beau-petit-fils [bopətifis] *m* (*pl* **beaux-petits-fils**) son of a stepson or of a stepdaughter

beaupré [bopre] *m* bowsprit

beauté [bote] *f* beauty; **beauté du diable** (coll) bloom of youth; **se faire une beauté** (coll) to doll up

beaux-arts [bozar] *mpl* fine arts

beaux-parents [boparɑ̃] *mpl* in-laws

bébé [bebe] *m* baby; **bébé éprouvette** test-tube baby

bec [bɛk] *m* beak; nozzle, jet, burner; point (*of a pen*); (mus) mouthpiece; (slang) beak, face, mouth; **avoir bon bec** to be gossipy; **claquer du bec** (coll) to be hungry; **clore, clouer le bec à qn** (coll) to shut s.o. up; **tomber sur un bec** (coll) to encounter an unforeseen obstacle

bécane [bekan] *f* (coll) bike, bicycle

bécarre [bekar] *m* (mus) natural

bécasse [bekas] *f* woodcock; (slang) stupid woman

bécas·seau [bekaso] *m* (*pl* **bécas-seaux**) sandpiper

bec-de-cane [bɛkdəkan] *m* (*pl* **becs-de-cane**) door handle; flat-nosed pliers

bec-de-corbeau [bɛkdəkɔrbo] *m* (*pl* **becs-de-corbeau**) wire cutters

bec-de-corbin [bɛkdəkɔrbɛ̃] *m* (*pl* **becs-de-corbin**) crowbar

bec-de-lièvre [bɛkdəljɛvr] *m* (*pl* **becs-de-lièvre**) harelip

bêche [bɛʃ] *f* spade

bêcher [bɛʃe] *tr* to dig; (slang) to run (*s.th.*) down, to give (*s.o.*) a dig

bê·cheur [bɛʃœr] **-cheuse** [ʃøz] *mf* (coll) detractor, critic; (slang) stuffed shirt

bêchoir [bɛʃwar] *m* hoe

bécotage [bekɔtaʒ] *m* smooching, necking

bécoter [bekɔte] *tr* to give (*s.o.*) a peck or little kiss on the cheek

becqueter [bɛkte] §34 *tr* to peck at; (coll) to eat ‖ *ref* to bill and coo

bedaine [bədɛn] *f* paunch, beer belly

bédane [bedan] *m* cold chisel

be·deau [bədo] *m* (*pl* **-deaux**) beadle

bé·douin [bedwɛ̃] **-douine** [dwin] *adj* Bedouin ‖ (*cap*) *mf* Bedouin (*person*)

bée [be] *adj*—**bouche bée** mouth agape, flabbergasted ‖ *f* penstock

beffroi [befrwa] *m* belfry

bégaiement [begɛmɑ̃] *m* stammering, stuttering

bégayer [begeje] §49 *tr & intr* to stammer, stutter

bègue [bɛg] *adj* stammering, stuttering ‖ *mf* stammerer

bégueter [begte] §2 *intr* to bleat

bégueule [begœl] *adj* (coll) prudish ‖ *f* (coll) prudish woman

béguin [begɛ̃] *m* hood, cap; sweetheart; (coll) infatuation

béguine [begin] *f* Beguine; sanctimonious woman

beige [bɛʒ] *adj & m* beige

beignet [bɛɲɛ] *m* fritter

béjaune [beʒon] *m* nestling; greenhorn, novice, ninny

bel [bɛl] *adj* see **beau**

bêlement [bɛlmɑ̃] *m* bleat, bleating

bêler [bɛle] *intr* to bleat

belette [bəlɛt] *f* weasel

belge [bɛlʒ] *adj* Belgian ‖ (*cap*) *mf* Belgian (*person*)

Belgique [bɛlʒik] *f* Belgium; **la Belgique** Belgium

bélier [belje] *m* ram; battering ram; **le Bélier** (astr, astrol) Aries

bélière [beljɛr] *f* sheepbell

bélinogramme [belinɔgram] *m* Wirephoto (*trademark*)

bélinographe [belinɔgraf] *m* Wirephoto transmitter

bélitre [belitr] *m* scoundrel

belladone [bɛladɔn] *f* belladonna

bellâtre [bɛlɑtr] *adj* foppish ‖ *m* fop

belle [bɛl] *adj* see **beau**

belle-dame [bɛldam] *f* belladonna

belle-de-jour [bɛldəʒur] *f* (*pl* **belles-de-jour**) morning glory

belle-de-nuit [bɛldənɥi] *f* (*pl* **belles-de-nuit**) marvel-of-Peru

belle-d'un-jour [bɛldœ̃ʒur] *f* (*pl* **belles-d'un-jour**) day lily

belle-fille [bɛlfij] *f* (*pl* **belles-filles**) daughter-in-law; stepdaughter

belle-mère [bɛlmɛr] *f* (*pl* **belles-mères**) mother-in-law; stepmother

belle-petite-fille [bɛlpətitfij] *f* (*pl* **belles-petites-filles**) daughter of a stepson or of a stepdaughter

belles-lettres [bɛllɛtr] *fpl* belles-lettres, literature

belle-sœur [bɛlsœr] *f* (*pl* **belles-sœurs**) sister-in-law

belliciste [belisist] *mf* warmonger

belligé·rant [beliʒerɑ̃] **-rante** [rɑ̃t] *adj & m* belligerent

belli-queux [belikø] **-queuse** [køz] *adj* bellicose, warlike

bel·lot [bɛlo] **-lote** [lɔt] *adj* pretty, cute; dapper

bémol [bemɔl] *adj invar & m* (mus) flat

bémoliser [bemɔlize] *tr* to flat (*a note*); provide (*a key signature*) with flats

ben [bɛ̃] *interj* (slang) well!

bénédicité [benedisite] *m* grace (*before a meal*)

bénédic·tin [benediktɛ̃] **-tine** [tin] *adj & m* Benedictine ‖ (*cap*) *f* Benedictine (liqueur)

bénédiction [benediksjɔ̃] manna from heaven

bénéfice [benefis] *m* profit; benefit; benefice; parsonage, rectory; **à bénéfice** benefit (*performance*); **sous bénéfice d'inventaire** with grave reservations

bénéficiaire [benefisjɛr] *adj* profit, e.g., **marge bénéficiaire** profit margin ‖ *mf* beneficiary

bénéficier [benefisje] *intr* to profit, benefit

benêt [bənɛ] *adj masc* simple-minded ‖ *m* simpleton, numskull

bénévolement [benevɔlmɑ̃] *adv* voluntarily, free of charge, for nothing

bé·nin [benɛ̃] **-nigne** [niɲ] *adj* benign; mild, slight; benignant, accommodating

béni-oui-oui [beniwiwi] *mpl* yes men

bénir [benir] *tr* to bless, to consecrate

bé·nit [beni] **-nite** [nit] *adj* consecrated (*bread*); holy (*water*)

bénitier [benitje] *m* font (*for holy water*)

benja·min [bɛ̃ʒamɛ̃] **-mine** [min] *mf* baby (*the youngest child*) ‖ (*cap*) *m* Benjamin

benne [bɛn] *f* bucket, bin, hopper; dumper; cage (*in mine*); **benne preneuse** (mach) scoop, jaws (*of crane*)

be·noît [bənwa] **-noîte** [nwat] *adj* indulgent; sanctimonious ‖ (*cap*) *m* Benedict

benzène [bɛ̃zɛn] *m* (chem) benzene

benzine [bɛ̃zin] *f* benzine

béquille [bekij] *f* crutch

béquiller [bekije] *intr* to walk with a crutch or crutches

bercail [bɛrkaj] *m* fold, bosom (*of church or family*)

ber·ceau [bɛrso] *m* (*pl* **-ceaux**) cradle; bower; **berceau de verdure** or **de chèvre-feuille** arbor

bercelonnette [bɛrsəlɔnɛt] *f* bassinet

bercer [bɛrse] §51 *tr* to cradle, rock; beguile; assuage (*grief, pain*) ‖ *ref* to rock, swing; delude oneself (*with vain hopes*)

ber·ceur [bɛrsœr] **-ceuse** [søz] *adj* rocking, cradling ‖ *f* rocking chair; cradle song, lullaby

béret [bere] *m* beret

berge [bɛrʒ] *f* bank, steep bank

berger [bɛrʒe] *m* shepherd; shepherd dog

bergère [bɛrʒɛr] *f* shepherdess; wing chair

bergerie [bɛrʒəri] *f* sheepfold; pastoral poem

berle [bɛrl] *f* water parsnip

Berlin [bɛrlɛ̃] *m* Berlin; **Berlin-Est** East Berlin; **Berlin-Ouest** West Berlin

berline [bɛrlin] *f* sedan (*automobile*); berlin (*carriage*)

berlingot [bɛrlɛ̃go] *m* caramel candy; milk carton

berli·nois [bɛrlinwa] **-noise** [nwaz] *adj* Berlin ‖ *mf* Berliner (*person*)

berlue [bɛrly] *f*—**avoir la berlue** (coll) to be blind to what is going on

Bermudes [bɛrmyd] *fpl*—**les Bermudes** Bermuda

bernacle [bɛrnakl] *f* (orn) anatid; (zool) barnacle

berne [bɛrn] *f* hazing; **en berne** at half-mast

berner [bɛrne] *tr* to toss in a blanket; ridicule; fool

bernique [bɛrnik] *interj* (coll) shucks!, heck!, what a shame!

berthe [bɛrt] *f* corsage; cape

béryllium [beriljɔm] *m* beryllium

besace [bəzas] *f* beggar's bag; mendicancy

besicles [bəzikl] *fpl* (archaic) spectacles; **prenez donc vos besicles!** (coll) put your specs on!

besogne [bəzɔɲ] *f* work, task; **abattre de la besogne** to accomplish a great deal of work; **aller vite en besogne** to work too hastily

besogner [bəzɔɲe] *intr* to drudge, slave

beso·gneux [bəzɔɲø] **-gneuse** [ɲøz] *adj* needy ‖ *mf* needy person

besoin [bəzwɛ̃] *m* need; poverty, distress; **au besoin** if necessary; **avoir besoin de** to need; **si besoin est** if need be

bes·son [besɔ̃] **-sonne** [sɔn] *mf* (dial) twin

bestiaire [bɛstjɛr] *m* bestiary

bes·tial -tiale [bɛstjal] (*pl* **-tiaux** [tjo]) *adj* bestial ‖ *mpl* see **bestiaux**

bestialité [bɛstjalite] *f* bestiality

bestiaux [bɛstjo] *mpl* livestock, cattle and horses

bestiole [bɛstjɔl] *f* bug, vermin

bê·ta [bɛtɑ] **-tasse** [tɑs] *adj* (coll) silly ‖ *mf* (coll) sap, dolt

bétail [betaj] *m invar* grazing animals (*on a farm*); **gros bétail** cattle and horses; **menu bétail, petit bétail** sheep, goats, pigs, etc.

bête [bɛt] *adj* stupid, foolish ‖ *f* animal; beast; **bête à bon Dieu** (ent) ladybird; **bête de charge, bête de somme** pack animal; **bonne bête** harmless fool

bêtifier [betifje], [betifje] *tr* to make stupid ‖ *intr* to play the fool, talk foolishly

bêtise [betiz], [betiz] *f* foolishness, stupidity, nonsense; trifle; **faire des bêtises** to blunder, do stupid things; throw money around

béton [betɔ̃] *m* concrete; **béton armé** reinforced concrete; **béton précontraint** prestressed concrete

bétonner [betɔne] *tr* to make of concrete

bétonnière [betɔnjɛr] *f* cement mixer

bette [bɛt] *f* Swiss chard; **bette à carde** Swiss chard

betterave [bɛtrav] *f* beet; **betterave sucrière** sugar beet

beuglement [bøgləmɑ̃] *m* bellow, bellowing, lowing

beugler [bøgle], [bœgle] *tr* (slang) to bawl out (*a song*) ‖ *intr* to bellow (*like a bull*); low (*like cattle*)

beurre [bœr] *m* butter; (slang) dough; **faire son beurre** (coll) to feather one's nest

beurrée [bœre] *f* slice of bread and butter

beurrer [bœre] *tr* to butter

beur·rier [bœrje] **-rière** [jɛr] *adj* butter ‖ *m* butter dish

beuverie [bœvri] *f* drinking party

bévue [bevy] *f* blunder, slip, boner

biais [bjɛ] **biaise** [bjɛz] *adj* bias, oblique, slanting; skew (*arch*) ‖ *m* bias, slant; skew (*of an arch*); **de biais, en biais** aslant, askew

biaiser [bjɛze] *intr* to slant; (fig) to be evasive

bibelot [biblo] *m* curio, trinket, knickknack

bibeloter [biblɔte] *intr* to buy or collect curios

bibe·ron [bibrɔ̃] **-ronne** [rɔn] *adj* addicted to the bottle ‖ *mf* heavy drinker ‖ *m* nursing bottle

bibi [bibi] *m* (hum) me, yours truly

Bible [bibl] *f* Bible

bibliobus [bibliɔbys] *m* bookmobile

bibliographe [bibliɔgraf] *m* bibliographer

bibliographie [bibliɔgrafi] *f* bibliography

bibliomane [bibliɔman] *mf* book collector

bibliothécaire [bibliɔtekɛr] *mf* librarian

bibliothèque [bibliɔtɛk] *f* library; bookstand; **bibliothèque vivante** walking encyclopedia

biblique [biblik] *adj* Biblical

biceps [bisɛps] *m* biceps

biche [biʃ] *f* hind; doe; **ma biche** (coll) my darling

bicher [biʃe] *intr*—**ça biche!** (slang) fine!

bichlamar [biʃlamar] *m* pidgin

bichof [biʃɔf] *m* spiced wine

bi·chon [biʃɔ̃] **-chonne** [ʃɔn] *mf* lap dog

bichonner [biʃɔne] *tr* to curl (*one's hair*); doll up ‖ *ref* to doll up

bicoque [bikɔk] *f* shack, ramshackle house

bicorne [bikɔrn] *adj* two-cornered ‖ *m* cocked hat

bicot [biko] *m* (coll) kid (*goat*); (offensive) North African, Arab

bicyclette [bisiklɛt] *f* bicycle; **aller à bicyclette** to bicycle; **bicyclette d'entraînement** exercise bicycle; **faire de la bicyclette** to go bicycling

bident [bidɑ̃] *m* two-pronged fork

bidet [bidɛ] *m* bidet; nag (*horse*)

bidon [bidɔ̃] *m* drum (*for liquids*); canteen; water bottle

bidonville [bidɔ̃vil] *m* shantytown

bidule [bidyl] *m* (slang) gadget

bief [bjɛf] *m* millrace; reach, level (*of a stream or canal*)

bielle [bjɛl] *f* connecting rod, tie rod

bien [bjɛ̃] *m* good; welfare; estate, fortune; **biens** property, possessions; **biens consomptibles** consumer goods; **biens immeubles** real estate; **biens meubles** personal property ‖ *adv* §91 well; rightly, properly, quite; indeed, certainly; fine, e.g., **je vais bien** I'm fine; **bien de** + *art* much, e.g., **bien de l'eau** much water; many, e.g., **bien des gens** many people; **bien entendu** of course; **bien que** + *subj* although; **eh bien!** so!; **si bien que** so that; **tant bien que mal** so-so, as well as possible ‖ *interj* good!; all right!; that's enough!

bien-ai·mé -mée [bjɛ̃neme] *adj & mf* beloved, darling

bien·dire [bjɛ̃dir] *m* gracious speech, eloquent delivery; **être sur son bien-dire** to be on one's best behavior

bien-di·sant [bjɛ̃dizɑ̃] **-sante** [zɑ̃t] *adj* smooth-spoken, smooth-tongued

bien-être [bjɛ̃nɛtr] *m* well-being, welfare

bienfaisance [bjɛ̃fəzɑ̃s] *f* charity, beneficence

bienfai·sant [bjɛ̃fəzɑ̃] **-sante** [zɑ̃t] *adj* charitable, beneficent

bienfait [bjɛ̃fɛ] *m* good turn, good deed, favor; **bienfaits** benefits

bienfai·teur [bjɛ̃fɛtœr] **-trice** [tris] *mf* benefactor ‖ *f* benefactress

bien-fondé [bjɛ̃fɔ̃de] *m* cogency

bien-fonds [bjɛ̃fɔ̃] *m* (*pl* **biens-fonds**) real estate

bienheu·reux [bjɛ̃nœrø] **-reuse** [røz] *adj & mf* blessed

bien·nal -nale [bjɛnnal] adj (pl **-naux** [no]) biennial ‖ f biennial exposition

bienséance [bjẽseɑ̃s] f propriety

bien·séant [bjẽseɑ̃] **-séante** [seɑ̃t] adj fitting, proper, appropriate

bientôt [bjẽto] adv soon; **à bientôt!** so long!

bienveillance [bjẽvɛjɑ̃s] f benevolence, kindness

bienveil·lant [bjẽvɛjɑ̃] **-lante** [jɑ̃t] adj benevolent, kindly, kind

bienvenir [bjẽvnir] intr—**se faire bienvenir** to make oneself welcome

bienve·nu -nue [bjẽvny] adj welcome ‖ m—**soyez le bienvenu!** welcome! ‖ f welcome; **souhaiter la bienvenue à** to welcome

bière [bjɛr] f beer; coffin; **bière à la pression** draft beer

biffer [bife] tr to cross out, cancel, erase; (slang) to cut (class)

biffin [bifẽ] m (slang) ragman; (slang) doughboy, G.I. Joe

bifo·cal -cale [bifɔkal] adj (pl **-caux** [ko]) bifocal

bifteck [biftɛk] m beefsteak

bifurquer [bifyrke] tr to bifurcate, divide into two branches ‖ intr & ref to bifurcate, fork; branch off

bigame [bigam] adj bigamous ‖ mf bigamist

bigamie [bigami] f bigamy

bigar·ré -rée [bigare] adj mottled, variegated; motley (crowd)

bigar·reau [bigaro] m (pl **-reaux**) white-heart cherry

bigarrer [bigare] tr to mottle, variegate, streak

bigarrure [bigaryr] f variegation, medley, mixture

bigle [bigl] adj cross-eyed

bigler [bigle] intr to squint; be cross-eyed

bigorne [bigɔrn] f two-horn anvil

bigorner [bigɔrne] tr to form on the anvil; (slang) to smash

bi·got [bigo] **-gote** [gɔt] adj sanctimonious ‖ mf religious bigot

bigoterie [bigɔtri] f religious bigotry

bigoudi [bigudi] m hair curler, roller

bihebdomadaire [biɛbdɔmadɛr] adj semi-weekly

bi·jou [biʒu] m (pl **-joux**) jewel

bijouterie [biʒutri] f jewelry; jewelry shop; jewelry business

bijou·tier [biʒutje] **-tière** [tjɛr] mf jeweler

bilan [bilɑ̃] m balance sheet; balance; petition of bankruptcy; **bilan de santé** (med) checkup; **faire le bilan** to tabulate the results

bilboquet [bilbɔkɛ] m job printing

bile [bil] f bile; **se faire de la bile** (coll) to worry, fret

bi·lieux [biljø] **-lieuse** [ljøz] adj bilious; irascible, grouchy

bilingue [bilẽg] adj bilingual

billard [bijar] m billiards; billiard table; billiard room

bille [bij] f ball; ball bearing; billiard ball; marble; log; **à bille** ball-point (pen)

billet [bijɛ] m note; ticket; bill (currency); **billet à ordre** promissory note; **billet d'abonnement** season ticket; **billet d'aller et retour** round-trip ticket; **billet de banque** bank note; **billet de correspondance** transfer; **billet de faire-part** announcement, notification (of birth, wedding, death); **billet de logement** billet; **billet doux** love letter; **billet simple** one-way ticket

billette [bijɛt] f billet

billetterie [bijɛtri] f ticketing (at events)

billevesée [bijvəze], [bilvəze] f nonsense

billion [biljɔ̃] m trillion (U.S.A.); billion (Brit); (obs) billion, milliard

billot [bijo] m block, chopping block; executioner's block

biloquer [bilɔke] tr to plow deeply

bimen·suel -suelle [bimɑ̃sɥɛl] adj semi-monthly

bimes·triel -trielle [bimɛstriɛl] adj bimonthly (every two months)

bimoteur [bimɔtœr] adj twin-motor ‖ m twin-motor plane

binaire [binɛr] adj binary

biner [bine] tr to hoe; cultivate, work over (the soil) ‖ intr to say two masses the same day

binette [binɛt] f hoe; (hist) wig; (slang) phiz

bineur [binœr] m or **bineuse** [binøz] f cultivator (implement)

binocle [binɔkl] m pince-nez

binoculaire [binɔkylɛr] adj & f binocular

binôme [binom] adj & m binomial

binon [binɔ̃] m (comp) bit

biochimie [bjɔʃimi] f biochemistry

biographe [bjɔgraf] mf biographer

biographie [bjɔgrafi] f biography

biographique [bjɔgrafik] adj biographical

biologie [bjɔlɔʒi] f biology

biologiste [bjɔlɔʒist] mf biologist

biophysique [bjɔfizik] f biophysics

biopsie [bjɔpsi] f biopsy

bioxyde [bjɔksid] m dioxide

bip [bip] m (aer) blip

bipar·ti -tie [biparti] adj bipartite

bipartisme [bipartism] m bipartisanship

bipartite [bipartit] adj bipartite; bipartisan

bipède [bipɛd] adj & mf biped ‖ m pair of legs of a horse

biplan [biplɑ̃] m biplane

bique [bik] f nanny goat

bir·man [birmɑ̃] **-mane** [man] adj Burmese ‖ (cap) mf Burmese (person)

Birmanie [birmani] f Burma; **la Birmanie** Burma

bis [bi] **bise** [biz] adj gray-brown ‖ [bis] m—**un bis** an encore ‖ f see **bise** ‖ **bis** [bis] adv twice; (mus) repeat; **sept bis** seven A, seven and a half ‖ **bis** [bis] interj encore!

bisaïeul bisaïeule [bizajœl] mf great-grandparent ‖ m great-grandfather ‖ f great-grandmother

bisan·nuel -nuelle [bizanɥɛl] adj biennial

bisbille [bisbij] f (coll) squabble

biscaïen [biskajɛ̃] **biscaïenne** [biskajɛn] *adj* Biscayan ‖ (*cap*) *mf* Biscayan (*person*)

biscor·nu -nue [biskɔrny] *adj* misshapen, distorted

biscotin [biskɔtɛ̃] *m* hardtack

biscotte [biskɔt] *f* zwieback

biscuit [biskɥi] *m* hardtack; cracker; cookie; unglazed porcelain; **biscuit soda** soda cracker

bise [biz] *f* north wind; (fig) winter; (slang) kiss

bi·seau [bizo] *m* (*pl* **-seaux**) bevel, chamfer; **en biseau** beveled, chamfered

biseauter [bizote] *tr* to bevel, chamfer; to mark (*cards*)

biser [bize] *tr* to redye ‖ *intr* to blacken

bi·son [bizɔ̃] **-sonne** [zɔn] *mf* bison, buffalo

bisque [bisk] *f* bisque

bisquer [biske] *intr* (coll) to be resentful

bissac [bisak] *m* bag, sack

bisser [bise] *tr* to encore; repeat

bissextile [bisɛkstil] *adj* bissextile, leap, e.g., **année bissextile** leap year

bis·sexué -sexuée [bisɛksɥe] *adj* bisexual

bis·sexuel -sexuelle [bisɛksɥɛl] *adj* bisexual

bistouri [bisturi] *m* scalpel

bistournage [bisturnaʒ] *m* castration

bistre [bistr] *adj invar* soot-brown ‖ *m* bister, soot-brown

bis·tré -trée [bistre] *adj* swarthy

bisulfate [bisylfat] *m* bisulfate

bisulfite [bisylfit] *m* bisulfite

bitte [bit] *f* (vulg) penis

bitter [bitɛr] *m* bitters

bitume [bitym] *m* bitumen

bitumer [bityme] *tr* to asphalt

bitumi·neux [bityminø] **-neuse** [nøz] *adj* bituminous

bivouac [bivwak] *m* bivouac

bivouaquer [bivwake] *intr* to bivouac

bizarre [bizar] *adj* bizarre, strange

bizutage [bizytaʒ] *m* (slang) initiation, hazing

bizuth [bizyt] *m* (slang) freshman

blackbouler [blakbule] *tr* to blackball; (coll) to flunk

bla·fard -farde [blafar] **-farde** [fard] *adj* pallid, pale, wan; lambent (*flame*)

blague [blag] *f* tobacco pouch; (coll) yarn, tall story, blarney; **blague à part** (coll) all joking aside; **faire une blague** (coll) to play a trick; **sale blague** (coll) dirty trick; **sans blague!** (coll) no kidding!

blaguer [blage] *tr* (coll) to kid; **blaguer qn** (coll) to pull s.o.'s leg ‖ *intr* (coll) to kid, tell tall stories

bla·gueur [blagœr] **-gueuse** [gøz] *adj* (coll) kidding, tongue-in-cheek ‖ *mf* (coll) kidder, joker

blai·reau [blɛro] *m* (*pl* **-reaux**) badger; shaving brush

blâmable [blɑmabl] *adj* blameworthy

blâme [blɑm] *m* blame; **s'attirer un blâme** to receive a reprimand

blâmer [blɑme] §97, §99 *tr* to blame; disapprove of

blanc [blɑ̃] **blanche** [blɑ̃ʃ] *adj* white; blank; clean; sleepless (*night*); expressionless (*voice*); unconsummated (*marriage*); **blanc comme un linge** white as a sheet ‖ *m* white; blank; white meat; white man; white goods; chalk; bull's-eye; **blanc cassé** off-white; **blanc de baleine** spermaceti; **blanc de chaux** whitewash; **en blanc** blank; **en blanc et noir** in black and white ‖ *f* white woman

blanc-bec [blɑ̃bɛk] *m* (*pl* **blancs-bécs**) (coll) greenhorn, callow youth

blanchâtre [blɑ̃ʃɑtr] *adj* whitish

blancheur [blɑ̃ʃœr] *f* whiteness

blanchir [blɑ̃ʃir] *tr* to whiten; wash or bleach; whitewash; blanch (*almonds*) ‖ *intr* to blanch, whiten; grow old

blanchissage [blɑ̃ʃisaʒ] *m* laundering; sugar refining

blanchisserie [blɑ̃ʃisri] *f* laundry

blanchis·seur [blɑ̃ʃisœr] **-seuse** [søz] *mf* launderer ‖ *m* laundryman ‖ *f* laundress, washerwoman

blanc-manger [blɑ̃mɑ̃ʒe] *m* (*pl* **blancs-manger**) blancmange

blanc-seing [blɑ̃sɛ̃] *m* (*pl* **blancs-seings**) carte blanche

bla·sé -sée [blaze] *adj* blasé, jaded

blaser [blaze] *tr* to cloy, blunt

blason [blazɔ̃] *m* (heral) blazon

blasonner [blazɔne] *tr* (heral) to blazon

blasphéma·teur [blasfematœr] **-teuse** [tøz] *adj* blasphemous, blaspheming ‖ *mf* blasphemer

blasphématoire [blasfematwar] *adj* blasphemous

blasphème [blasfɛm] *m* blasphemy

blasphémer [blasfeme] §10 *tr* & *intr* to blaspheme

blatte [blat] *f* cockroach

blé [ble] *m* wheat; (slang) dough; **blé à moudre** grist; **blé de Turquie** corn; **blé froment** wheat; **blé noir** buckwheat; **manger son blé en herbe** to spend one's money before one has it

bled [blɛd] *m* (coll) backwoods, hinterland

blême [blɛm] *adj* pale; livid, sallow, wan; ghastly

blêmir [blemir] *intr* to turn pale or livid, blanch; grow dim

blennorragie [blɛnɔraʒi] *f* gonorrhea

blèse [blɛz] *adj* lisping ‖ *mf* lisper

blèsement [blɛzmɑ̃] *m* lisping

bléser [bleze] §10 *intr* to lisp

bles·sé -sée [blese] *adj* wounded ‖ *mf* injured person; victim; casualty

blesser [blese], [blɛse] *tr* to wound; injure; be disagreeable to

blessure [blɛsyr] *f* wound; injury

blet blette [blɛt] *adj* overripe ‖ *f* chard

blettir [blɛtir] *intr* to overripen

bleu bleue [blø] (*pl* **bleus bleues**) *adj* blue; fairy (*stories*); violent (*anger*); rare (*meat*) ‖ *m* blue; bluing; bruise; sauce for cooking fish; telegram or pneumatic letter; (coll) raw recruit, greenhorn; **bleu bar-**

beau light blue; **bleu marine** navy blue; **bleus** coveralls, dungarees; (mil) fatigues; **passer au bleu** to avoid, elude (*a question*); **petit bleu** bad wine

bleuâtre [bløɑtr] *adj* bluish

bleuet [bløɛ] *m* bachelor's-button

bleuir [bløir] *tr & intr* to turn blue

bleu·té -tée [bløte] *adj* bluish

blindage [blɛ̃daʒ] *m* armor plate; armor plating; (elec) shield

blin·dé -dée [blɛ̃de] *adj* armored; armor-plated; (elec) shielded ‖ *m* (mil) tank

blinder [blɛ̃de] *tr* to armor-plate; (elec) to shield

bloc [blɔk] *m* block; blocking; tablet, pad (*of paper*); (elec, mach) unit; brick (*of ice cream*); **à bloc** tight; **en bloc** all together, in a lump; **envoyer** or **mettre au bloc** (slang) to throw (*s.o.*) in the jug; **serrer le frein à bloc** to jam on the brakes

blocage [blɔkaʒ] *m* blockage, blocking; lumping together; rubble; freezing (*of prices; of wages*); application (*of brakes*)

blocaille [blɔkɑj] *f* rubble

bloc-diagramme [blɔkdjagram] *m* (*pl* **blocs-diagrammes**) cross section

bloc-moteur [blɔkmɔtœr] *m* (aut) motor and transmission system

bloc-notes [blɔknɔt] *m* (*pl* **blocs-notes**) scratch pad, note pad

blocus [blɔkys] *m* blockade

blond [blɔ̃] **blonde** [blɔ̃d] *adj* blond ‖ *m* blond ‖ *f* see **blonde**

blondasse [blɔ̃das] *adj* washed-out blond

blonde [blɔ̃d] *f* blonde; blond lace; **blonde platinée** platinum blonde

blon·din [blɔ̃dɛ̃] **-dine** [din] *adj* fair-haired ‖ *mf* blond ‖ *m* cableway; hopper for concrete; (obs) fop

blondir [blɔ̃dir] *tr* to bleach ‖ *intr* to turn yellow, become blond

bloquer [blɔke] *tr* to blockade; block up; fill with rubble; jam on (*the brakes*); stop (*a car*) by jamming on the brakes; pocket (*a billiard ball*); run on (*two paragraphs*); tighten (*a nut or bolt*) as much as possible; freeze (*wages*)

blottir [blɔtir] *ref* to cower; curl up

blouse [bluz] *f* smock; billiard pocket

blouser [bluze] *tr* to deceive, take in ‖ *intr* to pucker around the waist ‖ *ref* to be mistaken

blouson [bluzɔ̃] *m* jacket; windbreaker

blouson-noir [bluzɔ̃war] *m* (*pl* **blousons-noirs**) juvenile delinquent; hood

blue-jean [bludʒin] *m* blue jeans

bluet [blyɛ] *m* bachelor's-button; (Canad) blueberry

bluette [blyɛt] *f* piece of light fiction; spark, flash

bluffer [blyfe] *tr & intr* to bluff

bluf·feur [blyfœr] **-feuse** [føz] *mf* bluffer

blutage [blytaʒ] *m* bolting, sifting; boltings, siftings

bluter [blyte] *tr* to bolt, sift

blutoir [blytwar] *m* bolter, sifter

B.N. *abbr* (**Bibliothèque Nationale**) National Library

boa [bɔa] *m* boa

bobard [bɔbar] *m* (coll) fish story, tall tale

bobèche [bɔbɛʃ] *f* bobeche (*disk to catch drippings of candle*)

bobine [bɔbin] *f* bobbin; spool, reel; (elec) coil; **bobine d'allumage** (aut) ignition coil

bobiner [bɔbine] *tr* to spool, wind

bobo [bɔbo] *m* (*language used with children*) sore; cut; **avoir bobo** to have a pain

bocage [bɔkaʒ] *m* grove

boca·ger [bɔkaʒe] **-gère** [ʒɛr] *adj* wooded

bo·cal [bɔkal] *m* (*pl* **-caux** [ko]) jar, bottle, globe; fishbowl

boche [bɔʃ] *adj & mf* (slang & pej) German

bock [bɔk] *m* beer glass (*half pint*); glass of beer; enema; douche

boëte [bwɛt] *f* fish bait

bœuf [bœf] *m* (*pl* **bœufs** [bø]) beef; head of beef; steer; ox; **bœuf en conserve** corned beef

boggie [bɔʒi] *m* (rr) truck

bogue [bɔg] *f* chestnut bur; (comp) bug

Bohême [bɔɛm] *f* Bohemia; **la Bohême** Bohemia

bohème [bɔɛm] *adj & mf* Bohemian (*artist*) ‖ *f*—**la bohème** Bohemia (*of the artistic world*)

bohé·mien [bɔɛmjɛ̃] **-mienne** [mjɛn] *adj* Bohemian; gypsy ‖ (*cap*) *mf* Bohemian; gypsy

boire [bwar] *m* drink; drinking; **le boire et le manger** food and drink ‖ §8 *tr* to drink; swallow (*an affront*) ‖ *intr* to drink; **boire à la santé de** to drink to the health of; **boire à** (**même**) to drink out of (*a bottle*); **boire comme un trou** to drink like a fish; **boire dans** to drink out of (*a glass*)

bois [bwa] *m* wood; woods; horns; antlers; **bois de chauffage** firewood; **bois de lit** bedstead; **bois de placage** plywood; **bois flotté** driftwood; **bois fondu** plastic wood; **les bois** (mus) the woodwinds

boisage [bwazaʒ] *m* timbering

boi·sé -sée [bwaze] *adj* wooded; paneled

boiser [bwaze] *tr* to panel, wainscot; timber (*a mine*); reforest

boiserie [bwazri] *f* woodwork, paneling, wainscoting

bois·seau [bwaso] *m* (*pl* **-seaux**) bushel

boisson [bwasɔ̃] *f* drink, beverage; **boissons hygiéniques** light wines, beer, and soft drinks

boîte [bwat] *f* box; can; canister; (slang) joint, dump; **boîte aux lettres** mailbox; **boîte chaude** (rr) hotbox; **boîte de nuit** night club; **boîte d'essieu** (mach) journal box; **boîte de vitesses** transmission-gear box; **boîte postale** post-office box; **en boîte** boxed; canned; **ferme ta boîte!** (slang) shut up!, **mettre en boîte** to box; can; (slang) to make fun of

boiter [bwate] *intr* to limp

boi·teux [bwatø] **-teuse** [tøz] *adj* lame, limping; unsteady, wobbly (*chair*) ‖ *mf* lame person

boî·tier [bwatje] **-tière** [tjɛr] *mf* boxmaker; mail collector (*from mailboxes*) ‖ *m* box, case; kit; medicine kit; (mach) housing; **boîtier de montre** watchcase

boitte [bwat] *f* fish bait

bol [bɔl] *m* bowl, basin; cud; bolus, pellet

bolchevique [bɔlʃəvik] *adj* Bolshevik ‖ (*cap*) *mf* Bolshevik

bolcheviste [bɔlʃəvist] *adj* Bolshevik ‖ (*cap*) *mf* Bolshevik

bolduc [bɔldyk] *m* colored ribbon

bolée [bɔle] *f* bowlful

bolide [bɔlid] *m* meteorite, fireball; racing car

bombance [bɔ̃bɑ̃s] *f* (coll) feast; **faire bombance** (coll) to have a blowout

bombardement [bɔ̃bardəmɑ̃] *m* bombing; bombardment; **bombardement en tapis** saturation bombing

bombarder [bɔ̃barde] *tr* to bomb; bombard; (coll) to appoint at the last minute

bombardier [bɔ̃bardje] *m* bomber; bombardier

bombe [bɔ̃b] *f* bomb; **bombe à hydrogène** hydrogen bomb; **bombe atomique** atomic bomb; **bombe glacée** molded ice cream; **bombe volante** buzz bomb; **faire la bombe** (fig) to paint the town red

bom·bé -bée [bɔ̃be] *adj* convex, bulging

bomber [bɔ̃be] *tr* to bend, arch; stick out (*one's chest*); **bomber le torse** (fig) to stick one's nose up ‖ *intr & ref* to bulge

bon [bɔ̃] **bonne** [bɔn] §91, §92 *adj* good; **à quoi bon?** what's the use?; **sentir bon** to smell good; **tenir bon** to hold fast ‖ (when standing before noun) *adj* §91 good; fast (*color*) ‖ *m* coupon; **bon de change** voucher; **bon de commande** order blank; **bon de travail** work order; **pour (tout) de bon** for good, really ‖ *f* see **bonne** ‖ **bon** *interj* good!; what!

bonace [bɔnas] *f* calm (*of the sea*)

bonasse [bɔnas] *adj* simple, naïve

bon-bec [bɔ̃bɛk] *m* (*pl* **bons-becs**) fast talker

bonbon [bɔ̃bɔ̃] *m* bonbon, piece of candy

bonbonne [bɔ̃bɔn] *f* demijohn

bonbonnière [bɔ̃bɔnjɛr] *f* candy dish; candy box

bond [bɔ̃] *m* bound, bounce; leap, jump; **faire faux bond** to miss an appointment; **faux bond** misstep

bonde [bɔ̃d] *f* plug; bunghole; sluice gate

bon·dé -dée [bɔ̃de] *adj* crammed

bondir [bɔ̃dir] *intr* to bound, bounce; leap, jump; **faire bondir** to make (*s.o.*) hit the ceiling

bondissement [bɔ̃dismɑ̃] *m* bouncing, leaping

bondon [bɔ̃dɔ̃] *m* bung

bonheur [bɔnœr] *m* happiness; good luck; **au petit bonheur** by chance, at random; **par bonheur** luckily

bonheur-du-jour [bɔnœrdyʒur] *m* (*pl* **bonheurs-du-jour**) escritoire

bonhomie [bɔnɔmi] *f* good nature; credulity

bonhomme [bɔnɔm] *adj* good-natured, simple-minded ‖ *m* (*pl* **bonshommes** [bɔ̃zɔm]) fellow, guy; old fellow; **bonhomme de neige** snowman; **Bonhomme Hiver** Jack Frost; **faux bonhomme** humbug; **petit bonhomme** little man (*child*)

boni [bɔni] *m* bonus; discount coupon; surplus (*over estimated expenses*)

bonification [bɔnifikasjɔ̃] *f* improvement; discount; bonus; advantage

bonifier [bɔnifje] *tr* to improve; give a discount to

boniment [bɔnimɑ̃] *m* sales talk, smooth talk

bonimenteur [bɔnimɑ̃tœr] *m* huckster, charlatan

bonjour [bɔ̃ʒur] *m* good day, good morning, good afternoon, hello

bonne [bɔn] *f* maid; **bonne à tout faire** maid of all work ‖ *adj* see **bon**

bonne-maman [bɔnmamɑ̃] *f* (*pl* **bonnes-mamans**) grandma

bonnement [bɔnmɑ̃] *adv* honestly, plainly

bonnet [bɔnɛ] *m* bonnet; stocking cap; cup (*of a brassiere*); (mil) undress hat; **bonnet d'âne** dunce cap; **bonnet de nuit** nightcap; **gros bonnet** (coll) VIP

bonneterie [bɔnɛtri] *f* hosiery; knitwear

bon-papa [bɔ̃papa] *m* (*pl* **bons-papas**) grandpa

bonsoir [bɔ̃swar] *m* good evening; (coll) good night

bonté [bɔ̃te] *f* goodness; kindness

boomer [bumɛr] *m* (electron) boomer

booster [bustœr] *m* (rok) booster

borborygme [bɔrbɔrigm] *m* rumbling (*in the stomach*)

bord [bɔr] *m* edge, border; rim, brim; side (*of a ship*); ship, e.g., **les porteurs du bord** the ship's porters; e.g., **les hommes du bord** the ship's company; **à bord** on board; **à pleins bords** overflowing; without hindrance; **à ras bords** full to the brim; **être du (même) bord de** to be of the same mind as; **faux bord** list (*of ship*); **jeter par-dessus bord** to throw overboard

bordage [bɔrdaʒ] *m* edging (*of dress*); planking (*of ship*)

bordé [bɔrde] *m* border, edging

bordeaux [bɔrdo] *adj invar* maroon, burgundy ‖ *m* Bordeaux (wine); **bordeaux rouge** claret

bordée [bɔrde] *f* broadside, volley; (naut) tack; **bordée de bâbord** port watch; **bordée de tribord** starboard watch; **courir une bordée** to go skylarking on shore leave; **tirer une bordée** to jump ship

bordel [bɔrdɛl] *m* (vulgar) brothel

borde·lais [bɔrdəlɛ] **-laise** [lɛz] *adj* of Bordeaux ‖ *f* Bordeaux cask ‖ (*cap*) *mf* native or inhabitant of Bordeaux

border [bɔrde] *tr* to border; hem; sail along (*the coast*); **border un lit** to make a bed

borde·reau [bɔrdəro] *m* (*pl* **-reaux**) itemized account, memorandum

bordure [bɔrdyr] *f* border

bore [bɔr] *m* boron

boréal boréale [bɔreal] *adj* (*pl* **boréaux** [bɔreo] or **boréals**) boreal; northern

borgne [bɔrɲ] *adj* one-eyed; blind in one eye; disreputable (*bar, house, etc.*) ‖ *mf* one-eyed person

borne [bɔrn] *f* landmark; boundary stone; milestone; (elec) binding post, terminal; (slang) kilometer; **bornes** bounds, limits

bor·né -née [bɔrne] *adj* limited, narrow; dull (*mind*)

borner [bɔrne] *tr* to mark out the boundary of; set limits to ‖ §96 *ref* to restrain oneself

bosquet [bɔskɛ] *m* grove

bosse [bɔs] *f* hump; bump; (coll) flair

bosseler [bɔsle] §34 *tr* to emboss; to dent

bossoir [bɔswar] *m* davit; bow (*of ship*)

bos·su -sue [bɔsy] *adj* hunchbacked ‖ *mf* hunchback; **rire comme un bossu** to split one's sides laughing

botanique [bɔtanik] *adj* botanical ‖ *f* botany

botte [bɔt] *f* boot; bunch (*e.g., of radishes*); sword thrust; **lécher les bottes à qn** (coll) to lick s.o.'s boots

botteler [bɔtle] §34 *tr* to tie in bunches

botter [bɔte] *tr* to boot, boot out; **cela me botte** that suits me ‖ *ref* to put on one's boots

botteur [bɔtœr] *m* (sports) kicker

bottier [bɔtje] *m* custom shoemaker

Bottin [bɔtɛ̃] *m* business directory

bottine [bɔtin] *f* high button shoe

boubouler [bubule] *intr* to hoot like an owl

bouc [buk] *m* billy goat; goatee; **bouc émissaire** scapegoat

boucan [bukɑ̃] *m* smokehouse; (coll) uproar

boucaner [bukane] *tr* to smoke (*meat*)

boucanier [bukanje] *m* buccaneer

boucharde [buʃard] *f* bushhammer

bouche [buʃ] *f* mouth; muzzle (*of gun*); door (*of oven*); entrance (*to subway*); **bouche close!** mum's the word!; **bouche d'égout** catch basin; **bouche d'incendie** fire hydrant; **bouches** mouth (*of river*); **faire la petite bouche à, faire la fine bouche devant** to turn up one's nose at

bouchée [buʃe] *f* mouthful; patty; chocolate cream (*candy*)

boucher [buʃe] *m* butcher ‖ *tr* to stop up, plug; wall up; cut off (*the view*); bung (*a barrel*); cork (*a bottle*); **bouché à l'émeri** (coll) completely dumb ‖ *ref* to be stopped up

boucherie [buʃri] *f* butcher shop; **boucherie chevaline** horsemeat butcher shop

bouche-trou [buʃtru] *m* (*pl* **-trous**) stopgap

bouchon [buʃɔ̃] *m* cork, stopper; bob (*on a fishline*); **bouchon de circulation** traffic jam; **bouchon de vapeur** vapor lock

bouclage [buklaʒ] *m* closing of circuit; (mil) encirclement

boucle [bukl] *f* buckle; earring; curl; (aer) loop; **boucler la boucle** to loop the loop

boucler [bukle] *tr* to buckle; curl (*the hair*); lock up (*prisoners*); put a nose ring on (*a bull*); **boucler son budget** (coll) to make ends meet; **la boucler** (slang) to shut up, button one's lip ‖ *intr* to curl

bouclier [buklije] *m* shield; **bouclier antithermique** heat shield; **bouclier thermique** thermal cone

bouddhisme [budism] *m* Buddhism

bouddhiste [budist] *adj* (coll) *mf* Buddhist

bouder [bude] *tr* to be distant toward ‖ *intr* to pout, sulk

bou·deur -deuse [budœr] [døz] *adj* pouting ‖ *mf* sullen person

boudin [budɛ̃] *m* blood sausage; **à boudin** spiral

boudiner [budine] *tr* to twist

boue [bu] *f* mud

bouée [bwe] *f* buoy; **bouée de sauvetage** life preserver

boueur [bwœr] *m* garbage collector; scavenger

boueux [bwø] **boueuse** [bwøz] *adj* muddy; grimy; (typ) smeary

bouf·fant [bufɑ̃] **-fante** [fɑ̃t] *adj* puffed (*sleeves*); baggy (*trousers*)

bouffe [buf] *adj* comic (*opera*) ‖ *f* (slang) grub

bouffée [bufe] *f* puff, gust

bouffer [bufe] *tr* (slang) to gobble up ‖ *intr* to puff out

bouf·fi -fie [bufi] *adj* puffed up or out

bouffir [bufir] *tr & intr* to puff up

bouffissure [bufisyr] *f* swelling

bouf·fon [bufɔ̃] **-fonne** [fɔn] *adj & m* buffoon, comic

bouffonnerie [bufɔnri] *f* buffoonery

bouge [buʒ] *m* bulge; hovel, dive

bougeoir [buʒwar] *m* flat candlestick

bougeotte [buʒɔt] *f* (coll) wanderlust

bouger [buʒe] §38 *tr*—**ne bougez rien!** (coll) don't move a thing! ‖ *intr* to budge, stir; (ne) **bouge pas!** don't move!

bougie [buʒi] *f* candle; candlepower; spark plug; **bougies de gâteaux d'anniversaire** birthday candles

bou·gon [bugɔ̃] **-gonne** [gɔn] *adj* grumbling ‖ *mf* grumbler

bougran [bugrɑ̃] *m* buckram

bou·gre [bugr] **-gresse** [grɛs] *mf* (slang) customer; **bougre d'âne** (slang) perfect ass ‖ *m* (slang) guy; **bon bougre** (slang) swell guy ‖ *f* (slang) wench

bougrement [bugrəmɑ̃] *adv* (slang) awfully, darned

bouillabaisse [bujabɛs] *f* bouillabaisse, fish stew, chowder

bouil·lant [bujɑ̃] **-lante** [jɑ̃t] *adj* boiling; fiery, impetuous

bouilleur [bujœr] *m* distiller (*of brandy*); boiler tube; small nuclear reactor

bouilli [buji] *m* beef stew

bouillir [bujir] §9 *tr & intr* to boil; **faire bouillir la marmite** (coll) to bring home the bacon

bouilloire [bujwar] *f* kettle

bouillon [bujɔ̃] *m* broth, bouillon; bubble; bubbling; cheap restaurant; **à gros bouillons** gushing; **boire un bouillon** (coll) to gulp water; (coll) to suffer business losses; **bouillon de culture** (bact) broth; **bouillon d'onze heures** poisoned drink; **bouillons** unsold copies, remainders

bouillonnement [bujɔnmɑ̃] *m* boiling; effervescence

bouillonner [bujɔne] *tr* to put puffs in (*a dress*) ‖ *intr* to boil up; have copies left over

bouillotte [bujɔt] *f* hot-water bottle

boulan·ger [bulɑʒe] **-gère** [ʒɛr] *mf* baker ‖ §38 *intr* to bake bread

boulangerie [bulɑʒri] *f* bakery

boule [bul] *f* ball; (slang) nut, head; **boule d'eau chaude** hot-water bottle; **boule de neige** snowball; **boule noire** blackball; **boules** bowling; **en boule** (fig) tied in a knot, on edge; **perdre la boule** (slang) to go off one's rocker; **se mettre en boule** (coll) to get mad

bou·leau [bulo] *m* (*pl* **-leaux**) birch

boule-de-neige [buldənɛʒ] *f* (*pl* **boules-de-neige**) guelder-rose; meadow mushroom

bouledogue [buldɔg] *m* bulldog

bouler [bule] *tr* to pad (*a bull's horn*) ‖ *intr* to roll like a ball; **envoyer bouler** (slang) to send (*s.o.*) packing

boulet [bulɛ] *m* cannonball; (coll) cross to bear

boulette [bulɛt] *f* ball, pellet

boulevard [bulvar] *m* boulevard; **boulevard périphérique** belt road

boulevar·dier [bulvardje] **-dière** [djɛr] *adj* fashionable ‖ *m* boulevardier, man about town

bouleversement [bulvɛrsmɑ̃] *m* upset

bouleverser [bulvɛrse] *tr* to upset; overthrow

boulier [bulje] *m* abacus (*for scoring billiards*)

bouline [bulin] *f* (naut) bowline

boulingrin [bulɛ̃grɛ̃] *m* bowling green

bouliste [bulist] *mf* bowler

boulodrome [bulɔdrom] *m* bowling alley

boulon [bulɔ̃] *m* bolt; **boulon à œil** eyebolt

boulonner [bulɔne] *tr* to bolt ‖ *intr* (slang) to work

bou·lot [bulo] **-lotte** [lɔt] *adj* (coll) dumpy, squat ‖ *m* (slang) cylindrical loaf of bread; (slang) work

boulotter [bulɔte] *tr* (slang) to eat

boum [bum] *interj* boom!

bouquet [bukɛ] *m* bouquet; clump (*of trees*); prawn; jack rabbit; **c'est le bouquet** (coll) it's tops; (coll) that's the last straw

bouquetière [buktjɛr] *f* flower girl

bouquin [bukɛ̃] *m* (coll) book; (coll) old book

bouquiner [bukine] *intr* to shop around for old books; (coll) to read

bouquinerie [bukinri] *f* secondhand books; secondhand bookstore

bouqui·neur [bukinœr] **-neuse** [nøz] *mf* collector of old books; browser in bookstores

bouquiniste [bukinist] *mf* secondhand bookdealer

bourbe [burb] *f* mire

bour·beux [burbø] **-beuse** [bøz] *adj* miry, muddy

bourbier [burbje] *m* quagmire

bourbillon [burbijɔ̃] *m* core (*of boil*)

bourde [burd] *f* (coll) boner

bourdon [burdɔ̃] *m* bumblebee; big bell; (mus) bourdon; **avoir le bourdon** (slang) to have the blues; **faux bourdon** drone

bourdonnement [burdɔnmɑ̃] *m* buzzing

bourdonner [burdɔne] *tr* (coll) to hum (*a tune*) ‖ *intr* to buzz

bourg [bur] *m* market town

bourgade [burgad] *f* small town

bour·geois [burʒwa] **-geoise** [ʒwaz] *adj* bourgeois, middle-class ‖ *mf* commoner, middle-class person; Philistine; **gros bourgeois** solid citizen ‖ *m* businessman; **en bourgeois** in civies ‖ *f* (slang) old woman (*wife*)

bourgeoisie [burʒwazi] *f* middle class; **haute bourgeoisie** upper middle class; **petite bourgeoisie** lower middle class

bourgeon [burʒɔ̃] *m* bud; pimple

bourgeonnement [burʒɔnmɑ̃] *m* budding

bourgeonner [burʒɔne] *intr* to bud; break out in pimples

bourgeron [burʒərɔ̃] *m* jumper, overalls; sweat shirt

bourgogne [burgɔɲ] *m* Burgundy (wine) ‖ (*cap*) *f* Burgundy (*province*); **la Bourgogne** Burgundy

bourgui·gnon [burgiɲɔ̃] **-gnonne** [ɲɔn] *adj* Burgundian ‖ *m* Burgundian (*dialect*) ‖ (*cap*) *mf* Burgundian

bourlinguer [burlɛ̃ge] *intr* to labor (*in high seas*); (coll) to travel, venture forth

bourrade [burad] *f* sharp blow; poke

bourrage [buraʒ] *m* cramming; **bourrage de crâne** (coll) ballyhoo

bourre [bur] *f* stuffing, animal hair

bour·reau [buro] *m* (*pl* **-reaux**) executioner; torturer; **bourreau des cœurs** lady-killer; **bourreau de travail** workaholic

bourrée [bure] *f* fagot of twigs

bourreler [burle] §34 *tr* to torment

bourrelet [burlɛ] *m* weather stripping; roll (*of fat*); contour pillow

bourrer [bure] *tr* to stuff, cram; **bourrer de coups** to pummel, slug ‖ *ref* to stuff

bourriche [buriʃ] *f* hamper

bourrique [burik] *f* female donkey; (coll) ass

bour·ru **-rue** [bury] *adj* rough; grumpy; unfermented (*wine*)

bourse [burs] *f* purse; scholarship, fellowship; stock exchange, bourse; **bourse du travail** labor union hall; **bourses** scrotum

bourse-à-pasteur [bursapastœr] *f* (*pl* **bourses-à-pasteur** [bursapastœr]) (bot) shepherd's-purse

boursicaut or **boursicot** [bursiko] *m* little purse; nest egg

boursicoter [bursikɔte] *intr* to dabble in the stock market

bour·sier [bursje] **-sière** [sjɛr] *adj* scholarship (*student*); stock-market (*operation*) || *mf* scholar (*holder of scholarship*); speculator

boursoufler [bursufle] *tr* to puff up

bousculer [buskyle] *tr* to jostle

bouse [buz] *f*—**bouse de vache** cow dung

bouseux [buzø] *m* (slang) peasant

bousillage [buzijaʒ] *m* cob (*mixture of clay and straw*); (coll) botched job

bousiller [buzije] *tr* (coll) to bungle; (slang) to smash up || *intr* to build with cob

boussole [busɔl] *f* compass; **perdre la boussole** (coll) to go off one's rocker

boustifaille [bustifɑj] *f* (slang) feasting; (slang) good food

bout [bu] *m* end; piece, scrap, bit; head (*of a match; of a table*); **à bout** exhausted; **à bout de bras** at arm's length; **à bout portant** point-blank; **à tout bout de champ** at every turn, repeatedly; **au bout du compte** after all; **bout de fil** (telp) (coll) ring, call; **bout de l'an** watch night; **bout d'essai** screen test; **bout d'homme** wisp of a man; **bout filtre** filter tip; **de bout en bout** from start to finish; **haut bout** head (*of a table; of a lake*); **montrer le bout de l'oreille** to show one's true colors; **rire du bout des dents** to force a laugh; **sur le bout du doigt** at one's fingertips; **venir à bout de** to succeed in, to triumph over

boutade [butad] *f* sally, quip; whim

bout-dehors [budəɔr] *m* (*pl* **bouts-dehors**) (naut) boom

boute-en-train [butɑ̃trɛ̃] *m invar* life of the party, live wire

boute·feu [butfø] *m* (*pl* **-feux**) firebrand

bouteille [butɛj] *f* bottle; **bouteille isolante** vacuum bottle

bouteiller [buteje] *m* (hist) cupbearer

bouterolle [butrɔl] *f* ward (*of lock*); rivet snap

boute-selle [butsɛl] *m* boots and saddles (*trumpet call*)

bouteur [butœr] *m* bulldozer

boutique [butik] *f* shop; stock, goods; workshop; set of tools; **boutique cadeaux, boutique de souvenirs** gift shop; **boutique de modiste** millinery shop; **boutique franche** duty-free shop; **quelle boutique!** (coll) what a hellhole!, what an awful place!

boutiquier [butikje] *m* shopkeeper

bouton [butɔ̃] *m* button; pimple; doorknob; bud; **bouton de puissance** volume control

bouton-d'argent [butɔ̃darʒɑ̃] *m* (*pl* **boutons-d'argent**) sneezewort

bouton-d'or [butɔ̃dɔr] *m* (*pl* **boutons-d'or**) buttercup

boutonner [butɔne] *tr* to button || *intr* to bud

bouton·neux [butɔnø] **-neuse** [nøz] *adj* pimply

boutonnière [butɔnjɛr] *f* buttonhole

bouton-pression [butɔ̃prɛsjɔ̃] *m* (*pl* **boutons-pression**) snap (fastener)

bouture [butyr] *f* cutting (*from a plant*)

bouturer [butyre] *tr* to propagate (*plants*) by cuttings || *intr* to shoot suckers

bouverie [buvri] *f* cowshed

bou·vier [buvje] **-vière** [vjɛr] *mf* cowherd

bouvillon [buvijɔ̃] *m* steer, young bullock

bouvreuil [buvrœj] *m* bullfinch; **bouvreuil cramoisi** scarlet grosbeak

box [bɔks] *m* (*pl* **-boxes**) stall

boxe [bɔks] *f* boxing

boxer [bɔksœr] *m* boxer (*dog*) || [bɔkse] *tr* & *intr* to box

boxeur [bɔksœr] *m* (sports) boxer

boxon [bɔksɔ̃] *m* whorehouse

boy [bɔj] *m* houseboy; chorus boy

boyau [bwajo] *m* (*pl* **boyaux**) intestine, gut; inner tube; (mil) communication trench

boycottage [bɔjkɔtaʒ] *m* boycott

boycotter [bɔjkɔte] *tr* to boycott

boy-scout [bɔjskut] *m* (*pl* **-scouts**) boy scout

b. p. f. *abbr* (**bon pour francs**) value in francs

bracelet [braslɛ] *m* bracelet; wristband; **bracelet de caoutchouc** rubber band; **bracelet à breloques** charm bracelet; **bracelet de cheville** anklet

bracelet-montre [braslɛmɔ̃tr] *m* (*pl* **bracelets-montres**) wrist watch

braconnage [brakɔnaʒ] *m* poaching

braconner [brakɔne] *intr* to poach

bracon·nier [brakɔnje] **-nière** [njɛr] *mf* poacher

brader [brade] *tr* to sell off

braderie [bradəri] *f* clearance sale; garage sale

braguette [bragɛt] *f* fly (*of trousers*)

brahmane [braman] *m* Brahman

brai [brɛ] *m* resin, pitch

braille [brɑj] *m* braille

brailler [brɑje] *tr* & *intr* to bawl

brail·leur [brɑjœr] **-leuse** [jøz] *adj* loud-mouthed || *mf* loudmouth

braiment [brɛmɑ̃] *m* bray

braire [brɛr] §68 (usually used in: *inf; ger; pp;* 3d *sg* & *pl*) *intr* to bray

braise [brɛz] *f* embers, coals

braiser [brɛze] *tr* to braise

braisière [brɛzjɛr] *f* braising pan

bramer [brame] *intr* to bell

bran [brɑ̃] *m* bran; (slang) dung; **bran de scie** sawdust

brancard [brɑ̃kar] *m* stretcher; shaft (*of carriage*)

brancardier [brɑ̃kardje] *m* stretcher-bearer

branche [brɑ̃ʃ] *f* branch; blade (*of a scissors*); leg (*of a compass*); temple (*side-piece of a pair of glasses*)

brancher [brɑ̃ʃe] *tr* to branch, fork; hook up, connect; (elec) to plug in || *intr* to perch

brande [brɑ̃d] f heather; heath

brandir [brɑ̃dir] *tr* to brandish

brandon [brãdɔ̃] *m* torch; firebrand; **brandon de discorde** mischief-maker

bran·lant [brãlã] **-lante** [lãt] *adj* shaky, tottering, unsteady

branle [brãl] *m* oscillation; impetus; **mener le branle** to lead the dance; **mettre en branle** to set in motion

branle-bas [brãləba] *m invar* call to battle stations; bustle, commotion

branler [brãle] *tr* to shake (*the head*) ‖ *intr* to shake; oscillate; be loose (*said of tooth*); **branler dans le manche** to be about to fall

braque [brak] *adj* (coll) featherbrained ‖ *mf* (coll) featherbrain ‖ *m* pointer (*dog*)

braquer [brake] *tr* to aim, point; fix (*the eyes*); turn (*a steering wheel*); **braquer contre** to turn (e.g., *an audience*) against ‖ *intr* to steer

bras [bra] *m* arm; handle; shaft; **à bras raccourcis** violently; **bras de mer** sound (*passage of water*); **bras de pick-up** pickup arm, tone arm; **bras dessus bras dessous** arm in arm; **en bras de chemise** in shirt sleeves; **être resté sur les bras de** to be left on the hands of; **manquer de bras** to be short-handed

braser [braze] *tr* to braze

brasero [brazero] *m* brazier

brasier [brazje] *m* glowing coals; blaze

bras-le-corps [bralkɔr] *m*—**à bras-le-corps** around the waist

brassage [brasaʒ] *m* brewing

brasse [bras], [bras] *f* fathom; breast stroke

brassée [brase] *f* armful; stroke (*in swimming*)

brasser [brase] *tr* to brew

brasserie [brasri] *f* brewery; restaurant, lunchroom

bras·seur [brasœr] **-seuse** [søz] *mf* brewer; swimmer doing the breast stroke; **brasseur d'affaires** person with many irons in the fire

brassière [brasjɛr] *f* sleeved shirt (*for an infant*); shoulder strap; **brassière de sauvetage** life preserver

bravache [bravaʃ] *adj & m* braggart

bravade [bravad] *f* bravado

brave [brav] *adj* brave ‖ (when standing before noun) *adj* worthy, honest ‖ *m* brave man

braver [brave] *tr* to brave

bravoure [bravur] *f* bravery, gallantry

break [brɛk] *m* station wagon

brebis [brɛbi] *f* ewe; sheep, lamb; **brebis galeuse** black sheep

brèche [brɛʃ] *f* breach (*in a wall*); gap (*between mountains*); nick (e.g., *on china*); (fig) dent (*in a fortune*); **battre en brèche** to batter; (fig) to disparage; **mourir sur la brèche** to go down fighting

bredouille [brəduj]—**rentrer** or **revenir bredouille** to return empty-handed

bredouiller [brəduje] *tr* to stammer out (*an excuse*) ‖ *intr* to mumble

bref [brɛf] **brève** [brɛv] *adj* brief, short; curt ‖ *m* papal brief ‖ *f* short syllable;

brèves et longues dots and dashes ‖ **bref** *adv* briefly, in short

brelan [brəlã] *m* (cards) three of a kind

breloque [brəlɔk] *f* trinket, charm; **battre la breloque** to sound the all clear; keep irregular time; (coll) to have a screw loose somewhere

brème [brɛm] *f* (ichth) bream

Brésil [brezil] *m*—**le Brésil** Brazil

brési·lien [breziljɛ̃] **-lienne** [ljɛn] *adj* Brazilian ‖ (*cap*) *mf* Brazilian

Bretagne [brətaɲ] *f* Brittany; **la Bretagne** Brittany

bretelle [brətɛl] *f* strap, sling; access route; ramp; **bretelle de liaison** (aer) exit taxiway; **bretelles** suspenders

bre·ton [brətɔ̃] **-tonne** [tɔn] *adj* Breton ‖ *m* Breton (*language*) ‖ (*cap*) *mf* Breton (*person*)

bretteur [brɛtœr] *m* swashbuckler

bretzel [brɛtzɛl] *m* pretzel

breuvage [brœvaʒ] *m* beverage, drink

brevet [brəvɛ] *m* diploma; license; (mil) commission; **brevet d'invention** patent

breve·té -tée [brəvte] *adj* commissioned; patented; **non breveté** noncommissioned ‖ *m* commissioned officer

breveter [brəvte] §34 *tr* to patent

bréviaire [brevjɛr] *m* (eccl) breviary

bribe [brib] *f* hunk of bread; **bribes** scraps, leavings, fragments

bric [brik] *m*—**de bric et de broc** with odds and ends; somehow

bric-à-brac [brikabrak] *m invar* secondhand merchandise; junk shop

brick [brik] *m* brig (*kind of ship*)

bricolage [brikɔlaʒ] *m* do-it-yourself

bricole [brikɔl] *f* trifle

bricoler [brikɔle] *intr* to do odd jobs; putter around

brico·leur [brikɔlœr] **-leuse** [løz] *mf* jack-of-all-trades ‖ *m* handyman

bride [brid] *f* bridle; strap; clamp; **à toute bride** or **à bride abattue** full speed ahead

bridge [bridʒ] *m* (cards, dentistry) bridge

bridger [bridʒe] *intr* to play bridge

brid·geur [bridʒœr] **-geuse** [ʒøz] *mf* bridge player

briefing [brifiŋ] *m* briefing

brièvement [brijɛvmã] *adv* briefly

brièveté [brijɛvte] *f* brevity

brigade [brigad] *f* brigade

brigadier [brigadje] *m* corporal; police sergeant; noncom

brigand [brigã] *m* brigand

brigantin [brigãtɛ̃] *m* brigantine

brigue [brig] *f* intrigue, lobbying

briguer [brige] *tr* to influence underhandedly; lobby for (*s.th.*); court (*favor, votes*)

brigueur [brigœr] *m* schemer

bril·lant [brijã] **-lante** [jãt] *adj* brilliant, bright ‖ *m* brilliancy, luster; fingernail polish

briller [brije] *intr* to shine; sparkle; **faire briller** to show (*s.o.*) off

brimade [brimad] *f* hazing

brimborion [brɛ̃bɔrjɔ̃] *m* mere trifle

brimer [brime] *tr* to haze
brin [br̃ɛ] *m* blade; sprig, shoot; staple (*of hemp, linen*); strand (*of rope*); belt (*of pulley*); (coll) (little) bit, e.g., **un brin d'air** a (little) bit of air; **ne . . . brin** §90 (archaic) not a bit, not a single; **un beau brin de fille** (coll) a fine figure of a girl
brinde [br̃ɛd] *f* (archaic) toast
brindille [br̃ɛdij] *f* twig, sprig
brioche [brijɔʃ] *f* brioche, breakfast roll
brique [brik] *f* brick
briquer [brike] *tr* (coll) to polish up, scour
briquet [brikɛ] *m* lighter
briquetage [briktaʒ] *m* brickwork
briqueter [brikte] §34 *tr* to brick (up)
briqueterie [brikətri] *f* brickyard
briqueteur [briktœr] *m* bricklayer
brisant [brizɑ̃] *m* breakers; **brisants** surf
brise [briz] *f* breeze
bri·sé -sée [brize] *adj* broken; folding (*door*) ‖ *fpl* see **brisées**
brise-bise [brizbiz] *m invar* weather stripping; café curtain
brisées [brize] *fpl* track, footsteps
brise-glace [brizglas] *m invar* (naut) icebreaker
brise-jet [brizʒɛ] *m invar* (anti)splash attachment (*for water faucet*), spray filter
brise-lames [brizlam] *m invar* breakwater
brisement [brizmɑ̃] *m* breaking
briser [brize] *tr, intr, & ref* to break
brise-tout [briztu] *m invar* (coll) butterfingers, clumsy person
bri·seur [brizœr] **-seuse** [zøz] *mf* breaker (*person*); **briseur de grève** strikebreaker
brise-vent [brizvɑ̃] *m invar* windbreak
brisque [brisk] *f* service stripe
bristol [bristɔl] *m* Bristol board, pasteboard; visiting card
brisure [brizyr] *f* break; joint
britannique [britanik] *adj* British ‖ (*cap*) *mf* Briton
broc [bro] *m* pitcher, jug
brocanter [brɔkɑ̃te] *tr* to buy, sell, or trade (*secondhand articles*) ‖ *intr* to deal in secondhand articles
brocan·teur [brɔkɑ̃tœr] **-teuse** [tøz] *mf* secondhand dealer
brocard [brɔkar] *m* lampoon, brickbat; (zool) brocket; **lancer des brocards** to make sarcastic remarks, gibe
brocart [brɔkar] *m* brocade
broche [brɔʃ] *f* brooch; pin; (culin) spit, skewer
bro·ché -chée [brɔʃe] *adj* paperback, paperbound
brocher [brɔʃe] *tr* to brocade; sew (*book bindings*); (coll) to hurry through
brochet [brɔʃɛ] *m* (ichth) pike
brochette [brɔʃɛt] *f* skewer; skewerful; string (*of decorations*)
bro·cheur [brɔʃœr] **-cheuse** [ʃøz] *mf* bookbinder ‖ *f* stapler
brochure [brɔʃyr] *f* brochure, pamphlet
brocoli [brɔkɔli] *m* broccoli
brodequin [brɔdkɛ̃] *m* buskin
broder [brɔde] *tr & intr* to embroider

broderie [brɔdri] *f* embroidery
brome [brom] *m* (chem) bromine
bromure [brɔmyr] *m* bromide
bronche [brɔ̃ʃ] *f* bronchial tube
broncher [brɔ̃ʃe] *intr* to stumble; flinch; to grumble
bronchique [brɔ̃ʃik] *adj* bronchial
bronchite [brɔ̃ʃit] *f* bronchitis
bronze [brɔ̃z] *m* bronze
bron·zé -zée [brɔ̃ze] *adj* bronze; sun-tanned
bronzer [brɔ̃ze] *tr & ref* to bronze; sun-tan
brook [bruk] *m* (turf) water jump
broquette [brɔkɛt] *f* brad, tack
brossage [brɔsaʒ] *m* brushing
brosse [brɔs] *f* brush; **brosse à cheveux** hairbrush; **brosse à dents** toothbrush; **brosse à habits** clothesbrush; **brosse de chiendent** scrubbing brush; **brosses shrubs, bushes**
brosser [brɔse] *tr* to brush; paint the broad outlines of (*a picture*); (fig) to sketch; (slang) to beat, conquer ‖ *ref* to brush one's clothes; (coll) to skimp, to scrimp
brouet [bruɛ] *m* gruel, broth
brouette [bruɛt] *f* wheelbarrow
brouetter [bruɛte] *tr* to carry in a wheelbarrow
brouhaha [bruaa] *m* (coll) babel, hubbub
brouillage [brujaʒ] *m* (rad) jamming, jam
brouillamini [brujamini] *m* (coll) mess
brouillard [brujar] *adj masc* blotting (*paper*) ‖ *m* fog, mist; (com) daybook
brouillasse [brujas] *f* (coll) drizzle
brouillasser [brujase] *intr* (coll) to drizzle
brouille [bruj] *f* discord, misunderstanding
brouiller [bruje] *tr* to mix up; jam (*a broadcast*); scramble (*eggs*); **brouiller mes (ses, etc.) pistes** to cover my (his, etc.) tracks ‖ *ref* to quarrel; to cloud over
brouil·lon [brujɔ̃] **-lonne** [jɔn] *adj* crackpot; blundering; at loose ends ‖ *mf* crackpot ‖ *m* scratch pad; draft; outline
broussailles [brusaj] *fpl* underbrush, brushwood; **en broussailles** disheveled
broussail·leux [brusajø] **-leuse** [jøz] *adj* bushy
broussard [brusar] *m* (coll) bushman, colonist
brousse [brus] *f* veldt, bush
broutage [brutaʒ] *m* grazing (*of animal*); ratatat (*of a machine*)
brouter [brute] *intr* to browse, graze; jerk, grab (*said of clutch, cutting tool, brake*)
broutille [brutij] *f* twig; trifle, bauble
broyage [brwajaʒ] *m* grinding, crushing
broyer [brwaje] §47 *tr* to grind, crush; **broyer du noir** (coll) to be down in the dumps
broyeur [brwajœr] **broyeuse** [brwajøz] *adj* grinding, crushing ‖ *mf* grinder, crusher; **broyeur d'ordures** garbage disposal ‖ *f* (mach) grinder
bru [bry] *f* daughter-in-law
bruant [bryɑ̃] *m* (orn) bunting; **bruant jaune** yellowhammer
brucelles [brysɛl] *fpl* tweezers
brugnon [brynɔ̃] *m* nectarine

bruine [brɥin] *f* drizzle
bruiner [brɥine] *intr* to drizzle
bruire [brɥir] (usually used in: *inf;* 3d *sg pres ind* **bruit;** 3d *sg & pl imperf ind* **bruyait** or **bruissait, bruyaient** or **bruissaient**) *intr* to rustle; to hum, buzz; to splash
bruissement [brɥismɑ̃] *m* rustling
bruit [brɥi] *m* noise; stir, fuss; **le bruit court que** it is rumored that
bruitage [brɥitaʒ] *m* sound effects
brû·lant [brylɑ̃] **-lante** [lɑ̃t] *adj* burning; ardent; ticklish (*question*)
brû·lé -lée [bryle] *adj* burned ‖ *m* smell of burning; burned taste ‖ *f* (slang) beating
brûle-gueule [brylgœl] *m invar* (slang) short pipe (*for smoking*)
brûle-parfum [brylparfœ̃] *m invar* incense burner
brûle-pourpoint [brylpurpwɛ̃]—**à brûle-pourpoint** point-blank
brûler [bryle] §97 *tr* to burn; burn out (*a fuse*); go through (*a red light*); pass (*another car*); roast (*coffee*); distill (*liquor*); **brûler la cervelle à qn** to blow s.o.'s brains out ‖ *intr* to burn, burn up; **je brûle de vous voir** I long to see you ‖ *ref* to burn up, be burned
brû·leur [brylœr] **-leuse** [løz] *mf* arsonist; distiller ‖ *m* (mach) burner; **brûleur à café** coffee roaster
brûloir [brylwar] *m* roaster
brûlure [brylyr] *f* burn
brume [brym] *f* fog, mist
brumer [bryme] *intr* to be foggy
bru·meux [brymø] **-meuse** [møz] *adj* foggy, misty
brun [brœ̃] **brune** [bryn] *adj* brown, dark brown (*hair*); brown (*eyes; beer*); dusky, swarthy (*skin*); tanned, brown (*complexion*); dark (*tobacco*) ‖ *m* brown, dark brown; dark-haired man ‖ *f* see **brune**
brunâtre [brynɑtr] *adj* brownish
brune [bryn] *f* brunette; twilight; ale, stout
bru·net [brynɛ] **-nette** [nɛt] *adj* black-haired ‖ *m* dark-haired man, brunet ‖ *f* brunette
bru·ni -nie [bryni] *adj* burnished, polished ‖ *m* burnishment, polish
brunir [brynir] *tr* to brown; burnish, polish ‖ *intr* to turn brown
brunissoir [bryniswar] *m* (mach) buffer
brusque [brysk] *adj* brusque; sudden; surprise (*attack*); quick (*movements; decision*)
brusquement [bryskəmɑ̃] *adv* brusquely; abruptly, bluntly; suddenly, quickly
brusquer [bryske] *tr* to hurry, rush through; be blunt with
brusquerie [bryskri] *f* brusqueness; suddenness
brut [bryt] **brute** [bryt] *adj* crude, unpolished, unrefined, uncivilized; uncut (*diamond*); raw (*material*); dry (*champagne*); brown (*sugar*); gross (*weight*) ‖ *f* see **brute** ‖ **brut** *adv*—**peser brut** to have a gross weight of

bru·tal -tale [brytal] (*pl* **-taux** [to]) *adj* brutal, rough; outspoken; coarse, beastly ‖ *mf* brute, bully
brutaliser [brytalize] *tr* to bully; mistreat
brutalité [brytalite] *f* brutality; **brutalité policière** police brutality
brute [bryt] *f* brute
Bruxelles [brysɛl] *f* Brussels
bruxel·lois [brysɛlwa] **-loise** [lwaz] *adj* of Brussels ‖ (*cap*) *mf* native or inhabitant of Brussels
bruyamment [brɥijamɑ̃] *adv* noisily
bruyant [brɥijɑ̃] **bruyante** [brɥijɑ̃t] *adj* noisy
bruyère [brɥijɛr] *f* heather; heath
bu bue [by] *v* see **boire**
buanderie [bɥɑ̃dəri] *f* laundry room
buan·dier [bɥɑ̃dje] **-dière** [djɛr] *mf* laundry worker ‖ *f* laundress
bubonique [bybɔnik] *adj* bubonic
bûche [byʃ] *f* log; (slang) dunce; **bûche de Noël** yule log; cake decorated as a yule log; **ramasser une bûche** (slang) to take a tumble
bûcher [byʃe] *m* woodshed; pyre; stake (*e.g., for burning witches*) ‖ *tr* to rough-hew; (slang) to bone up on ‖ *intr* (slang) to keep on working; slave away ‖ *ref* (slang) to fight
bûche·ron [byʃrɔ̃] **-ronne** [rɔn] *mf* woodcutter ‖ *m* lumberjack
bûchette [byʃɛt] *f* stick of wood
bû·cheur [byʃœr] **-cheuse** [ʃøz] *mf* (coll) eager beaver
budget [bydʒɛ] *m* budget; **boucler son budget** (coll) to make ends meet
budgétaire [bydʒetɛr] *adj* budgetary
buée [bɥe] *f* steam, mist
buffet [byfɛ] *m* buffet; snack bar; station restaurant; **buffet de salades** salad bar; **danser devant le buffet** to miss a meal
buffle [byfl] *m* buffalo; Cape buffalo
bufflonne [byflɔn] *mf* water buffalo; Cape buffalo
bugle [bygl] *m* (mus) saxhorn; bugle ‖ *f* (bot) bugle
building [bildiŋ] *m* large office building, skyscraper
buire [bɥir] *f* ewer
buis [bɥi] *m* boxwood
buisson [bɥisɔ̃] *m* bush
buisson·neux [bɥisɔnø] **-neuse** [nøz] *adj* bushy
buisson·nier [bɥisɔnje] **-nière** [njɛr] *adj*—**faire l'école buissonnière** (coll) to play hooky
bulbe [bylb] *m* bulb
bul·beux [bylbø] **-beuse** [bøz] *adj* bulbous
bulgare [bylgar] *adj* Bulgarian ‖ *m* Bulgarian (*language*) ‖ (*cap*) *mf* Bulgarian (*person*)
Bulgarie [bylgari] *f* Bulgaria; **la Bulgarie** Bulgaria
bulle [byl] *m* wrapping paper ‖ *f* bubble; blister; (eccl) bull
bulletin [byltɛ̃] *m* bulletin; ballot; **bulletin d'adhésion** membership blank; **bulletin de bagages** baggage check; **bulletin de**

commande order blank; **bulletin de naiss-ance** birth certificate; **bulletin scolaire** report card

bul·leux [bylø] **-leuse** [løz] adj blistery

bure [byr] m mine shaft ‖ f drugget, sackcloth

bu·reau [byro] m (pl **-reaux**) desk; office; **bureau à cylindre** roll-top desk; **bureau ambulant** post-office car; **bureau d'aide sociale** welfare department; **bureau de dactylos** typing pool; **bureau de l'état civil** bureau of vital statistics; **bureau de location** box office; **bureau de placement** employment agency; **bureau de poste** post office; **bureau des objets trouvés** lost-and-found department; **bureau de tabac** tobacco shop; **bureau directoire** cabinet, committee; **deuxième bureau** intelligence division

bureaucrate [byrokrat] mf bureaucrat

bureaucratie [byrokrasi] f bureaucracy

bureaucratique [byrokratik] adj bureaucratic

burette [byrɛt] f cruet; oilcan

burin [byrɛ̃] m engraving; burin (tool)

burlesque [byrlɛsk] adj & m burlesque

bus [bys] m city bus

busard [byzar] m harrier, marsh hawk

busc [bysk] m whalebone

buse [byz] f buzzard

business [biznɛs] m (slang) work; (slang) complicated business

bus·qué -quée [byske] adj arched

buste [byst] m bust

but [by], [byt] m mark, goal, target; aim, end, purpose; point (scored in game);

aller droit au but to come straight to the point; **de but en blanc** point-blank

bu·té -tée [byte] adj obstinate, headstrong ‖ f abutment

buter [byte] tr to prop up; (slang) to bump off, kill ‖ intr—**buter contre** to bump into, stumble on ‖ ref—**se buter à** to butt up against; (fig) to be dead set on

buteur [bytœr] m scorer

butin [bytɛ̃] m booty; profits, savings

butiner [bytine] tr to pillage; gather honey from ‖ intr to pillage; gather honey (said of bees); **butiner dans** to browse among (books)

butoir [bytwar] m buffer, stop, catch

bu·tor [bytɔr] **-torde** [tɔrd] mf (slang) lout, good-for-nothing

butte [byt] f butte, knoll; **butte de tir** butt, mound (for target practice); **être en butte à** to be exposed to

butter [byte] tr to hill (plants)

buttoir [bytwar] m (agr) hiller

buty·reux [bytirø] **-reuse** [røz] adj buttery

buvable [byvabl] adj drinkable; (pharm) to be taken by mouth

buvard [byvar] adj blotting (paper) ‖ m blotter

buvette [byvɛt] f bar, fountain

buvette-buffet [byvɛtbyfɛ] f (coll) snack bar

bu·veur [byvœr] **-veuse** [vøz] mf drinker; **buveur d'eau** abstainer; vacationist at a spa

byzan·tin [bizɑ̃tɛ̃] **-tine** [tin] adj Byzantine

C

C, c [se] m invar third letter of the French alphabet

C / abbr (**compte**) account

ça [sa] pron indef (coll) that; **ah ça non!** no indeed!; **avec ça!** tell me another!; **ça y est** that's that; that's it, that's right; **comment ça!** how so?; **et avec ça?** what else?; **où ça,** where?

çà [sa] adv—**ah çà!** now then! **çà et là** here and there

cabale [kabal] f cabal, intrigue

cabaler [kabale] intr to cabal, intrigue

caban [kabɑ̃] m (naut) peacoat

cabane [kaban] f cabin, hut

cabanon [kabanɔ̃] m hut, padded cell

cabaret [kabarɛ] m tavern; cabaret, night club; liquor closet

cabas [kaba] m basket; shopping bag

cabestan [kabɛstɑ̃] m capstan

cabillaud [kabijo] m haddock; (coll) fresh cod

cabine [kabin] f cabin (of ship or airplane);

bathhouse; car (of elevator); cab (of locomotive or truck); **cabine téléphonique** telephone booth

cabinet [kabinɛ] m cabinet (small room; room for displaying collections; political committee; antique chest of drawers); toilet, rest room; storeroom closet; clientele, practice; office (of a professional person); study (of a scholar); staff (of a cabinet officer); **cabinet d'aisance** rest room; **cabinet de débarras** storeroom closet; **cabinet de toilette** powder room; **cabinets** rest rooms

câble [kɑbl] m cable; **câble de démarrage** jumper cable

câbler [kable] tr & intr to cable

câblier [kablije] m cable ship

câblodistribution [kablɔdistribysjɔ̃] f cable television

câblogramme [kablɔgram] m cablegram

cabo·chard [kabɔʃar] **-charde** [ʃard] adj obstinate, pigheaded

caboche [kabɔʃ] f hobnail; (coll) noodle (*head*)

cabochon [kabɔʃɔ̃] m uncut gem; stud, upholstery nail

cabot [kabo] m (ichth) miller's-thumb, bullhead; (coll) ham (actor)

cabotage [kabɔtaʒ] m coastal navigation, coasting trade

cabo·tin [kabɔtɛ̃] **-tine** [tin] mf barnstormer; (coll) ham (actor); **cabotin de la politique** (coll) corny politician, political orator given to histrionics

cabotinage [kabɔtinaʒ] m barnstorming; (coll) ham acting

cabotiner [kabɔtine] intr to barnstorm; (coll) to play to the grandstand

cabrer [kabre] tr to make (*a horse*) rear; nose up (*a plane*) || ref to rear; kick over the traces; (aer) to nose up

cabri [kabri] m (zool) kid

cabriole [kabrijɔl] f caper

cabrioler [kabrijɔle] intr to caper

caca [kaka] m—**caca d'oie** greenish-yellow; **faire caca** (*children's language*) to go potty

cacahouète or **cacahuète** [kakawɛt] f peanut

cacao [kakao] m cocoa; cocoa bean

cacaotier [kakaɔtje] m (bot) cacao

cacaoyer [kakaɔje] m (bot) cacao

cacarder [kakarde] intr to cackle

cacatoès [kakatɔɛs] or **cacatois** [kakatwa] m cockatoo

cachalot [kaʃalo] m sperm whale

cache [kaʃ] m masking tape || f hiding place

cache-cache [kaʃkaʃ] m invar hide-and-seek

cache-col [kaʃkɔl] m invar scarf

cachemire [kaʃmir] m cashmere

cache-nez [kaʃne] m invar muffler

cache-poussière [kaʃpusjɛr] m invar duster (*overgarment*)

cacher [kaʃe] tr to hide; **cacher q.ch. à qn** to hide s.th. from s.o. || ref to hide; **se cacher à** to hide from; **se cacher de q.ch.** to make a secret of s.th.

cache-radiateur [kaʃradjatœr] m invar radiator cover

cache-sexe [kaʃsɛks] m invar G-string; minimum (male) swimwear

cachet [kaʃɛ] m seal; postmark; fee; price of a lesson; meal ticket; (pharm, phila) cachet; (fig) seal; stylishness; **payer au cachet** to pay a set fee

cacheter [kaʃte] §34 tr to seal, seal up; seal with wax

cachette [kaʃɛt] f hiding place; **en cachette** secretly

cachot [kaʃo] m dungeon; prison

cacophonie [kakɔfɔni] f cacophony

cactier [kaktje] or **cactus** [kaktys] m cactus

c.-à-d. abbr (**c'est-à-dire**) that is

cadastre [kadastr] m land-survey register

cadavre [kadavr] m corpse, cadaver; (slang) dead soldier (*bottle*)

ca·deau [kado] m (*pl* **-deaux**) gift

cadenas [kadna] m padlock

cadenasser [kadnase] tr to padlock

cadence [kadɑ̃s] f cadence, rhythm, time; output (*of worker, of factory; etc.*); **cadence de tir** rate of firing

cadencer [kadɑ̃se] §51 tr to cadence || intr to call out cadence

ca·det [kadɛ] **-dette** [dɛt] adj younger || mf youngest; junior; (sports) player fifteen to eighteen years old; **le cadet de mes soucis** (coll) the least of my worries || m caddy; (mil) cadet; younger brother; younger son || f younger sister; younger daughter

cadmium [kadmjɔm] m cadmium

cadrage [kadraʒ] m (mov, telv) framing; (phot) centering

cadran [kadrɑ̃] m dial; **cadran d'appel** telephone dial; **cadran solaire** sundial; **faire le tour du cadran** to sleep around the clock

cadre [kadr] m frame; framework; setting; outline, framework (*of a literary work*); limits, scope (*of activities or duties*); (mil) cadre; (naut) cot; **cadres** officials; (mil) regulars; **cadres sociaux** memorable dates or events

cadrer [kadre] tr to frame (*film*) || intr to conform, tally

cadreur [kadrœr] m (mov) cameraman

ca·duc **-duque** [kadyk] adj decrepit, frail; outlived (*custom*); deciduous (*leaves*); lapsed (*insurance policy*); (law) null and void

caducée [kadyse] m caduceus

C.A.F. abbr (**coût, assurance, fret**) C.I.F. (*cost, insurance, and freight*)

ca·fard [kafar] **-farde** [fard] adj sanctimonious || mf hypocrite; (coll) squealer || m (coll) cockroach; (coll) blues

café [kafe] adj invar tan || m coffee; café; coffeehouse; **café au lait** coffee with hot milk; **café chantant** music hall (*with tables*); **café complet** coffee, hot milk, rolls, butter, and jam; **café crème** white coffee; **café décaféiné** decaffeinated coffee; **café en poudre** instant coffee; **café express** espresso coffee; **café filtre** drip coffee; **café instantané** instant coffee; **café liégeois** coffee ice cream topped with whipped cream; **café lyophilisé** freeze-dried coffee; **café nature, café noir** black coffee; **café vert** unroasted coffee; **café soluble** powdered coffee

café-concert [kafekɔ̃sɛr] m (*pl* **cafés-concerts**) music hall (*with tables*), cabaret

caféier [kafeje] m coffee plant

caféière [kafejɛr] f coffee plantation

caféine [kafein] f caffeine

cafétéria [kafeterja] f cafeteria

cafe·tier [kaftje] **-tière** [tjɛr] mf café owner || f coffeepot

cafouiller [kafuje] intr (slang) to miss (*said of engine*); (slang) to flounder around

cage [kaʒ] f cage; **cage d'un ascenseur** elevator shaft; **cage d'un escalier** stairwell; **cage thoracique** thoracic cavity; **en cage** (coll) in the clink, in the pen

cageot [kaʒo] m crate

ca·gnard [kaɲar] **-gnarde** [ɲard] *adj* indolent, lazy ‖ *m* (coll) sunny spot
ca·gneux [kaɲø] **-gneuse** [ɲøz] *adj* knock-kneed; pigeon-toed
cagnotte [kaɲɔt] *f* kitty, pool
ca·got [kago] **-gotte** [gɔt] *adj* hypocritical ‖ *mf* hypocrite
cagoule [kagul] *f* cowl; hood (*with eyeholes*)
cahier [kaje] *m* notebook; **cahier à feuilles mobiles** loose-leaf notebook; **cahier des charges** (com) specifications; **cahier (d'imprimerie)** (bb) signature, gathering
cahin-caha [kaẽkaa] *adv* (coll) so-so
cahot [kao] *m* jolt, bump
cahoter [kaɔte] *tr & intr* to jolt
caho·teux [kaɔtø] **-teuse** [tøz] *adj* bumpy (*road*)
cahute [kayt] *f* hut, shack
caille [kɑj] *f* quail
cail·lé -lée [kaje] *adj* curdled ‖ *m* curd
caillebotis [kajbɔti] *m* boardwalk; (mil) duckboard; (naut) grating
caillebotte [kajbɔt] *f* curds
caillebotter [kajbɔte] *tr & intr* to curdle
cailler [kaje] *tr & ref* to clot, curdle, curd
caillot [kajo] *m* clot; blood clot
cail·lou [kaju] *m* (*pl* **-loux**) pebble; (coll) bald head; **caillou du Rhin** rhinestone
caillou·teux [kajutø] **-teuse** [tøz] *adj* stony (*road*); pebbly (*beach*)
cailloutis [kajuti] *m* crushed stone, gravel
Caïn [kaẽ] *m* Cain
Caire [kɛr] *m*—**Le Caire** Cairo
caisse [kɛs] *f* chest, box; case (*for packing; of a clock or piano*); chestful, boxful; till, cash register, coffer, safe; cashier, cashier's window; desk (*in a hotel*); **caisse à eau** water tank; **caisse claire** snare drum; **caisse d'épargne** savings bank; **caisse des écoles** scholarship fund; **caisse de sortie** checkout counter; **grosse caisse** bass drum; bass drummer; **petite caisse** petty cash
caisson [kɛsɔ̃] *m* caisson; crate, box
cajoler [kaʒɔle] *tr* to cajole, wheedle
cajolerie [kaʒɔlri] *f* cajolery
cajou [kaʒu] *m* cashew nut
cake [kɛk] *m* fruit cake
cal [kal] *m* (*pl* **cals**) callus, callosity; **cal vicieux** badly knitted bone
calage [kalaʒ] *m* wedging, chocking; stalling (*of motor*)
calamité [kalamite] *f* calamity
calami·teux [kalamitø] **-teuse** [tøz] *adj* calamitous
calandre [kalɑ̃dr] *f* mangle (*for clothes*); calender (*for paper*); grill (*for car radiator*); (ent) weevil; (orn) lark
calandrer [kalɑ̃dre] *tr* to calender
calcaire [kalkɛr] *adj* calcareous; chalky; hard (*water*) ‖ *m* limestone
calcifier [kalsifje] *tr & ref* to calcify
calciner [kalsine] *tr & ref* to burn to a cinder
calcium [kalsjɔm] *m* calcium
calcul [kalkyl] *m* calculation; (math, pathol) calculus; **calcul biliaire** gallstone; **calcul**

mental mental arithmetic; **calcul rénal** kidney stone
calcula·teur [kalkylatœr] **-trice** [tris] *adj* calculating ‖ *mf* calculator (*person*) ‖ *m* (mach) calculator ‖ *f* adding machine; **calculatrice de poche** pocket calculator
calculer [kalkyle] *tr & intr* to calculate
calculette [kalkylɛt] *f* pocket calculator
cale [kal] *f* wedge, chock; hold (*of ship*); **cale de construction** stocks; **cale sèche** dry dock
ca·lé -lée [kale] *adj* stalled; (coll) well-informed; (slang) involved, difficult; **calé en** (coll) strong in, up on
calebasse [kalbas] *f* calabash
calèche [kalɛʃ] *f* open carriage
caleçon [kalsɔ̃] *m* drawers, shorts; **caleçon de bain** swimming trunks
calembour [kalɑ̃bur] *m* pun
calendes [kalɑ̃d] *fpl* calends; **aux calendes grecques** (coll) when pigs fly
calendrier [kalɑ̃drije] *m* calendar
calepin [kalpẽ] *m* notebook
caler [kale] *tr* to wedge, chock; jam; stall; lower (*sail*); (naut) to draw ‖ *intr* to stall (*said of motor*); (coll) to give in ‖ *ref* to stall; get nicely settled
calfater [kalfate] *tr* to caulk
calfeutrer [kalføtre] *tr* to stop up ‖ *ref* to shut oneself up
calibre [kalibr] *m* caliber
calibrer [kalibre] *tr* to calibrate
calice [kalis] *m* chalice; (bot) calyx
calicot [kaliko] *m* calico; sign, banner; (slang) sales clerk
califat [kalifa] *m* caliphate
calife [kalif] *m* caliph
Californie [kalifɔrni] *f* California; **la basse Californie** Lower California; **la Californie** California
califourchon [kalifurʃɔ̃]—**à califourchon** astride, astraddle; **s'asseoir à califourchon** to straddle
câ·lin [kɑlẽ] **-line** [lin] *adj* coaxing; caressing
câliner [kaline] *tr* to coax; caress
cal·leux [kalø] **-leuse** [løz] *adj* callous, calloused
callisthénie [kalisteni] *f* calisthenics
cal·mant [kalmɑ̃] **-mante** [mɑ̃t] *adj* calming ‖ *m* sedative
calmar [kalmar] *m* squid
calme [kalm] *adj & m* calm
calmement [kalməmɑ̃] *adv* calmly
calmer [kalme] *tr* to calm ‖ *ref* to become calm, calm down
calmir [kalmir] *intr* to abate
calomnie [kalɔmni] *f* calumny, slander
calomnier [kalɔmnje] *tr* to calumniate
calorie [kalɔri] *f* calory
calorifère [kalɔrifɛr] *adj* heating, heat-conducting ‖ *m* heater; **calorifère à air chaud** hot-air heater; **calorifère à eau chaude** hot-water heater
calorifuge [kalɔrifyʒ] *adj* insulating ‖ *m* insulator
calorifuger [kalɔrifyʒe] §38 *tr* to insulate

calorique [kalɔrik] *adj* caloric

calot [kalo] *m* policeman's hat, kepi

calotte [kalɔt] *f* skullcap; dome; (coll) box on the ear; (coll) clergy; **calotte des cieux** vault of heaven; **flanquer une calotte à** (coll) to box on the ear

calotter [kalɔte] *tr* (coll) to box on the ear, cuff; (slang) to snitch

calque [kalk] *m* tracing; decal; word-for-word correspondence (*between two languages*); slavish imitation; spitting image

calquer [kalke] *tr* to trace; imitate slavishly

calumet [kalymɛ] *m* calumet; **calumet de paix** peace pipe

calvados [kalvados] *m* applejack

calvaire [kalvɛr] *m* calvary

calviniste [kalvinist] *adj* & *mf* Calvinist

calvitie [kalvisi] *f* baldness

camarade [kamarad] *mf* comrade; **camarade de chambre** roommate; **camarade de travail** fellow worker; **camarade d'étude** schoolmate

camaraderie [kamaradri] *f* comradeship; camaraderie, fellowship

ca·mard [kamar] **-marde** [mard] *adj* snubnosed

cambouis [kābwi] *m* axle grease

cambrer [kābre] *tr* to curve, arch

cambrioler [kābrijɔle] *tr* to break into, burglarize

cambrio·leur [kābrijɔlœr] **-leuse** [løz] *mf* burglar

cambrure [kābryr] *f* curve, arch

cambuse [kābyz] *f* (naut) storeroom between decks

came [kam] *f* cam

ca·mé -mée [kame] *mf* drug user

camée [kame] *m* cameo

caméléon [kameleɔ̃] *m* chameleon

camélia [kamelja] *m* camellia

camelot [kamlo] *m* cheap woolen cloth; huckster; newsboy

camelote [kamlɔt] *f* shoddy merchandise, rubbish, junk; **camelote alimentaire** junk food

caméra [kamera] *f* (mov, telv) camera

camion [kamjɔ̃] *m* truck; paint bucket; **camion à remorque** trailer (truck); **camion à semi-remorque** semitrailer; **camion citerne** fuel truck; **camion de déménagement** moving van; **camion d'enregistrement** (mov) sound truck; **camion de remorquage** tow truck

camion-benne [kamjɔ̃bɛn] *m* (*pl* **camions-bennes**) dump truck

camion-citerne [kamjɔ̃sitɛrn] *m* (*pl* **camions-citernes**) tank truck

camion-grue [kamjɔ̃gry] *m* (*pl* **camions-grues**) tow truck

camionnage [kamjɔnaʒ] *m* trucking

camionner [kamjɔne] *tr* to truck

camionnette [kamjɔnɛt] *f* van; **camionnette de police** police wagon; **camionnette sanitaire** mobile health unit

camionneur [kamjɔnœr] *m* trucker; truckdriver, teamster

camisole [kamizɔl] *f* camisole; **camisole de force** strait jacket

camomille [kamɔmij] *f* camomile

camouflage [kamuflaʒ] *m* camouflage

camoufler [kamufle] *tr* to camouflage

camp [kā] *m* camp; **camp de base** base camp; **camp de concentration** concentration camp; **camp de vacances** resort; **changer de camp** to change sides

campa·gnard [kāpaɲar] **-gnarde** [ɲard] *adj* & *mf* rustic

campagne [kāpaɲ] *f* campaign; country

cam·pé -pée [kāpe] *adj* encamped; **bien campé** well-built (*man*); clearly presented (*story*); firmly fixed

campement [kāpmā] *m* encampment; camping

camper [kāpe] *tr* to camp; (coll) to clap (*e.g., one's hat on one's head*); **camper là qn** (coll) to run out on s.o. ‖ *intr* & *ref* to camp

cam·peur [kāpœr] **-peuse** [pøz] *mf* camper

camphre [kāfr] *m* camphor

camping [kāpiŋ] *m* campground; trailer; camping; **camping sauvage** wilderness camping

campos [kāpo] *m* (coll) vacation, day off

campus [kāpys] *m* campus

ca·mus [kamy] **-muse** [myz] *adj* snubnosed, pug-nosed, flat-nosed

Canada [kanada] *m*—**le Canada** Canada

cana·dien [kanadjɛ̃] **-dienne** [djɛn] *adj* Canadian ‖ *f* sheepskin jacket; station wagon ‖ (*cap*) *mf* Canadian

canaille [kanɑj] *adj* vulgar, coarse ‖ *f* rabble, riffraff; scoundrel

ca·nal [kanal] *m* (*pl* **-naux** [no]) canal; tube, pipe; ditch, drain; (rad, telv) channel; **canal de Panama** Panama Canal; **canal de Suez** [sɥɛz] Suez Canal; **par le canal de** through the good offices of

canapé [kanape] *m* sofa, davenport; (culin) canapé; **canapé à deux places** settee

canapé-lit [kanapeli] *m* (*pl* **canapés-lits**) sofa bed, day bed

canard [kanar] *m* duck; sugar soaked in coffee, brandy, etc.; (mus) false note; (coll) hoax; (coll) rag, paper; **canard mâle** drake; **canard publicitaire** publicity stunt; **canard sauvage** wild duck

canarder [kanarde] *tr* to snipe at ‖ *intr* to snipe

canari [kanari] *m* canary

cancan [kākā] *m* cancan (*dance*); (coll) gossip

cancaner [kākane] *intr* to quack; (coll) to gossip

canca·nier [kākanje] **-nière** [njɛr] *adj* (coll) catty ‖ *mf* (coll) gossip

cancer [kāsɛr] *m* cancer; **le Cancer** (astr, astrol) Cancer

cancé·reux [kāserø] **-reuse** [røz] *adj* cancerous

cancérigène [kāseriʒɛn] or **cancérogène** [kāserɔʒɛn] *adj* carcinogenic ‖ *m* carcinogen

cancre [kɑ̃kr] *m* (coll) dunce, lazy student; (coll) tightwad; (zool) crab

candélabre [kɑ̃delɑbr] *m* candelabrum; espaliered fruit tree; cactus; lamppost

candeur [kɑ̃dœr] *f* naïveté; guilelessness

candi [kɑ̃di] *adj* candied (*fruit*) ‖ *m* rock candy

candi·dat [kɑ̃dida] **-date** [dat] *mf* candidate; nominee

candidature [kɑ̃didatyr] *f* candidacy

candide [kɑ̃did] *adj* naïve; ingenuous

candir [kɑ̃dir] *intr*—**faire candir** to candy, crystallize (*sugar*) ‖ *ref* to candy, crystallize

cane [kan] *f* duck, female duck

caner [kane] *intr* (slang) to chicken out

caneton [kantɔ̃] *m* duckling

canette [kanɛt] *f* female duckling; beer bottle; **canette de bière** can of beer

canevas [kanva] *m* canvas (*cloth*); outline (*of novel, story, etc.*); embroidery netting; triangulation (*in artillery, in cartography*)

canezou [kanzu] *m* sleeveless lace blouse

caniche [kaniʃ] *m* poodle

canicule [kanikyl] *f* dog days

canif [kanif] *m* penknife, pocketknife

ca·nin [kanɛ̃] **-nine** [nin] *adj* canine ‖ *f* canine (*tooth*)

canitie [kanisi] *f* grayness (*of hair*)

cani·veau [kanivo] *m* (*pl* **-veaux**) gutter; (elec) conduit

cannaie [kanɛ] *f* sugar plantation

canne [kan] *f* cane; reed; cane, walking stick; **canne à pêche** fishing rod; **canne à sucre** sugar cane

canneberge [kanbɛrʒ] *f* cranberry

canneler [kanle] §34 *tr* to groove; corrugate; flute (*a column*)

cannelle [kanɛl] *f* cinnamon; spout

cannelure [kanlyr] *f* groove, channel; corrugation; fluting (*of column*)

canner [kane] *tr* to cane (*a chair*)

cannibale [kanibal] *adj & mf* cannibal

canoë [kanɔe] *m* canoe

canoéiste [kanɔeist] *mf* canoeist

canon [kanɔ̃] *m* canon; cannon; gun barrel; tube; nozzle, spout; **canon à électrons** electron gun

cañon [kaɲɔ̃] *m* canyon

cano·nial -niale [kanɔnjal] *adj* (*pl* **-niaux** [njo]) canonical

canonique [kanɔnik] *adj* canonical

canoniser [kanɔnize] *tr* to canonize

canonnade [kanɔnad] *f* cannonade

canonner [kanɔne] *tr* to cannonade

canonnier [kanɔnje] *m* cannoneer

canonnière [kanɔnjɛr] *f* gunboat; popgun

canot [kano] *m* rowboat, launch; **canot automobile** speedboat, motorboat; **canot de sauvetage** lifeboat

canotage [kanɔtaʒ] *m* boating

canoter [kanɔte] *intr* to go boating

canotier [kanɔtje] *m* rower; skimmer

cant [kɑ̃] *m* cant

cantaloup [kɑ̃talu] *m* cantaloupe

cantate [kɑ̃tat] *f* cantata

cantatrice [kɑ̃tatris] *f* singer

cantilever [kɑ̃tilevœr] *adj & m* cantilever

cantine [kɑ̃tin] *f* canteen (*restaurant*); **cantine d'officier** officer's kit

cantique [kɑ̃tik] *m* canticle, ode; **cantique de Noël** (eccl) Christmas carol; **Cantique des Cantiques** (Bib) Song of Songs

canton [kɑ̃tɔ̃] *m* canton, district; **Cantons de l'Est** Eastern Townships (*in Canada*)

cantonade [kɑ̃tɔnad] *f* (theat) wings; **à la cantonade** (theat) offstage; **crier à la cantonade** to yell out (*s.th.*); **parler à la cantonade** to seem to be talking to oneself; (theat) to speak toward the wings

cantonnement [kɑ̃tɔnmɑ̃] *m* billeting

cantonner [kɑ̃tɔne] *tr* to billet

cantonnier [kɑ̃tɔnje] *m* road laborer; (rr) section hand

canular [kanylar] *m* (coll) practical joke, hoax, canard

canule [kanyl] *f* nozzle (*of syringe or injection needle*)

canuler [kanyle] *tr* (slang) to bother

caoutchouc [kautʃu] *m* rubber; **caoutchouc mousse** foam rubber; **caoutchoucs** rubbers, overshoes

caoutchouter [kautʃute] *tr* to rubberize

caoutchou·teux [kautʃutø] **-teuse** [tøz] *adj* rubbery

cap [kap] *m* cape, headland; bow, head (*of ship*); **Cap de Bonne Espérance** Cape of Good Hope; **mettre le cap sur** (coll) to set a course for

capable [kapabl] §93 *adj* capable

capacité [kapasite] *f* capacity; ability

cape [kap] *f* cape; hood; derby; outer leaf, wrapper (*of cigar*); **à la cape** (naut) hove to; **de cape et d'épée** cloak-and-dagger (*novel, movie, etc.*); **rire sous cape** to laugh up one's sleeve; **vendre sous cape** (coll) to sell under the counter

C.A.P.E.S. [kapɛs] *m* (acronym) (**certificat d'aptitude au professorat de l'enseignement du second degré**) secondary-school teachers certificate

capillaire [kapilɛr] *adj* capillary ‖ *m* (bot) maidenhair (*fern*)

capitaine [kapitɛn] *m* captain; **capitaine des pompiers** fire chief

capi·tal -tale [kapital] (*pl* **-taux** [to] **-tales**) *adj* capital, principal, essential; capital (*city; punishment; crime; letter*); death (*sentence*); deadly (*sins*) ‖ *m* capital, assets; principal (*main sum*); **avec de minces capitaux** on a shoestring; **capital circulant, capital d'exploitation** working capital; **capital fixe** fixed assets; **capitaux** capital; **capitaux fébriles** (slang) hot money ‖ *f* capital (*city; letter*)

capitalisation [kapitalizɑsjɔ̃] *f* capitalization; hoarding (*of money*)

capitaliser [kapitalize] *tr* to capitalize (*an income*); compound (*interest*) ‖ *intr* to hoard

capitalisme [kapitalism] *m* capitalism

capitaliste [kapitalist] *adj* capitalist ‖ *mf* capitalist; investor

capi·teux [kapitø] **-teuse** [tøz] *adj* heady (*wine, champagne, etc.*); intoxicating, alluring (*beauty; woman*)

Capitole [kapitɔl] *m* Capitol

capitonner [kapitɔne] *tr* to upholster

capituler [kapityle] *intr* to capitulate; parley

ca·pon [kapɔ̃] **-ponne** [pɔn] *adj* cowardly ‖ *mf* coward; sneak; tattletale

capo·ral [kapɔral] *m* (*pl* **-raux** [ro]) corporal; shag, caporal (*tobacco*); **Caporal a dit . . .** Simon says . . .

caporalisme [kapɔralism] *m* militarism; dictatorial government

capot [kapo] *adj invar* speechless, confused; (cards) trickless ‖ *m* cover; hood (*of automobile*); (naut) hatch

capotage [kapɔtaʒ] *m* overturning

capote [kapɔt] *f* coat with a hood; hood (*of baby carriage*); **capote anglaise** condom, prophylactic; **capote rebattable** (aut) folding top

capoter [kapɔte] *intr* to capsize; overturn, upset

câpre [kɑpr] *f* (bot) caper

caprice [kapris] *m* caprice, whim

capri·cieux [kaprisjø] **-cieuse** [sjøz] *adj* capricious, whimsical

Capricorne [kaprikɔrn] *m*—**le Capricorne** (astr, astrol) Capricorn

capsule [kapsyl] *f* capsule; bottle cap; percussion cap; (bot) capsule, pod; (rok) capsule; **capsule spatiale** space capsule; **capsules surrénales** adrenal glands

capsuler [kapsyle] *tr* to cap

capter [kapte] *tr* to win over; harness (*a river*); tap (*electric current; a water supply*); (rad, telv) to receive, pick up

capteur [kaptœr] *m* (rok) sensor

cap·tieux [kapsjø] **-tieuse** [sjøz] *adj* captious, insidious; specious

cap·tif [kaptif] **-tive** [tiv] *adj & mf* captive

captiver [kaptive] *tr* to captivate

captivité [kaptivite] *f* captivity

capture [kaptyr] *f* capture

capturer [kaptyre] *tr* to capture

capuce [kapys] *m* (eccl) pointed hood

capuchon [kapyʃɔ̃] *m* hood (*of coat*); cap (*of pen*); (aut) valve cap; (eccl) cowl

capucine [kapysin] *f* nasturtium

caque [kak] *f* keg, barrel

caquet [kakɛ] *m* cackle

caqueter [kakte] §34 *intr* to cackle; gossip

car [kar] *m* bus, sightseeing bus, interurban; **car de police** patrol wagon; **car sonore** loudspeaker truck ‖ *conj* for, because

carabe [karab] *m* ground beetle

carabine [karabin] *f* carbine

carabi·né -née [karabine] *adj* (coll) violent (*wind, cold, criticism*)

caraco [karako] *m* loose blouse

caractère [karaktɛr] *m* character; **caractères gras** (typ) boldface; **caractères penchés** (typ) italics

caractériser [karakterize] *tr* to characterize

caractéristique [karakteristik] *adj & f* characteristic

carafe [karaf] *f* carafe; **rester en carafe** (slang) to be left out in the cold

carafon [karafɔ̃] *m* small carafe

caraïbe [karaib] *adj* Caribbean, Carib ‖ (*cap*) *mf* Carib (*person*)

carambolage [karɑ̃bɔlaʒ] *m* jostling; (coll) bumping (*e.g., of autos*)

caramboler [karɑ̃bɔle] *tr* (coll) to strike, bump into ‖ *intr* (billiards) to carom

caramel [karamɛl] *m* caramel

carapace [karapas] *f* turtle shell, carapace

carapater [karapate] *ref* (slang) to beat it

carat [kara] *m* carat

caravane [karavan] *f* caravan; house trailer; group (*of tourists*)

caravaning [karavaniŋ] *m* trailer camping

caravansérail [karavɑ̃seraj] *m* caravansary; (fig) world crossroads

caravelle [karavɛl] *f* caravel

carbonade [karbɔnad] *f* see **carbonnade**

carbone [karbɔn] *m* carbon

carbonique [karbɔnik] *adj* carbonic

carboniser [karbɔnize] *tr* to carbonize, char

carbonnade [karbɔnad] *f* charcoal-grilled steak (ham, etc.); beef and onion stew (*in northern France*); **à la carbonnade** charcoal-grilled

carburant [karbyrɑ̃] *m* motor fuel

carburateur [karbyratœr] *m* carburetor

carbure [karbyr] *m* carbide

carburéacteur [karbyreaktœr] *m* jet fuel

carcan [karkɑ̃] *m* pillory

carcasse [karkas] *f* skeleton; framework; (coll) carcass

cardan [kardɑ̃] *m* (mach) universal joint

carde [kard] *f* card; leaf rib; teasel head

carder [karde] *tr* to card

cardiaque [kardjak] *adj & mf* cardiac

cardi·nal -nale [kardinal] *adj & m* (*pl* **-naux** [no]) cardinal

cardiogramme [kardjɔgram] *m* cardiogram

carême [karɛm] *m* Lent; **de carême** Lenten; **faire carême** to fast during Lent

carême-prenant [karɛmprənɑ̃] *m* (*pl* **carêmes-prenants**) Shrovetide

carence [karɑ̃s] *f* lack, deficiency; failure

carène [karɛn] *f* hull

caréner [karene] §10 *tr* to streamline; (naut) to careen

caren·tiel -tielle [karɑ̃sjɛl] *adj* deficiency (*disease*)

cares·sant [karɛsɑ̃] **-sante** [sɑ̃t] *adj* caressing; lovable; nice to pet; soothing (*e.g., voice*)

caresse [karɛs] *f* caress; endearment

caresser [karɛse] *tr* to caress; pet; nourish (*a hope*)

cargaison [kargɛzɔ̃] *f* cargo

cargo [kargo] *m* freighter; **cargo mixte** freighter carrying passengers

cari [kari] *m* curry

caricature [karikatyr] *f* caricature; cartoon

caricaturer [karikatyre] *tr* to caricature

caricaturiste [karikatyrist] *mf* caricaturist; cartoonist

carie [kari] *f* caries; **carie sèche** dry rot

carillon [karijɔ̃] *m* carillon

carillonner [karijɔne] *tr & intr* to carillon, chime

carlingue [karlɛ̃g] *f* (aer) cockpit

carmin [karmɛ̃] *adj & m* carmine

carnage [karnaʒ] *m* carnage

carnas·sier [karnasje] **-sière** [sjɛr] *adj* carnivorous ‖ *m* carnivore ‖ *f* game bag

carnation [karnasjɔ̃] *f* flesh tint

carna·val [karnaval] *m* (*pl* **-vals**) carnival; parade dummy

car·né -née [karne] *adj* "flesh"-colored; meat (*diet*)

carnet [karnɛ] *m* notebook, address book; memo pad; book (*of tickets, checks, stamps, etc.*); **carnet à feuilles mobiles** loose-leaf notebook

carnier [karnje] *m* hunting bag

carotte [karɔt] *f* carrot; (min) core sample; **les carottes sont cuites** the die is cast; **tirer une carotte à** (coll) to cheat

carotter [karɔte] *tr* (coll) to cheat; chisel

carpe [karp] *m* (anat) wrist bones ‖ *f* carp; **être muet comme une carpe** to be still as a mouse

carpette [karpɛt] *f* rug, mat; **être une vraie carpette** to let s.o. walk all over one

carquois [karkwa] *m* quiver

carre [kar] *f* thickness (*of board*); crown (*of hat*); edge (*of ice skate*); square toe (*of shoe*); **d'une bonne carre** broad-shouldered (*man*)

car·ré -rée [kare] *adj* square; forthright ‖ *m* square; landing (*of staircase*); patch (*in garden*); (cards) four of a kind; (naut) wardroom ‖ *f* (slang) room, pad

car·reau [karo] *m* (*pl* **-reaux**) tile, flagstone; windowpane; stall (*in market*); pithead (*of mine*); goose (*of tailor*); quarrel (*square-headed arrow*); (cards) diamond; (cards) diamonds; **à carreaux** checked (*design*); **rester sur le carreaux** (coll) to be left out of the running; **se garder à carreau** (coll) to be on one's guard

carrefour [karfur] *m* crossroads; square (*in a city*)

carrelage [karlaʒ] *m* tiling

carreler [karle] §34 *tr* to tile

carrément [karemɑ̃] *adv* squarely; frankly

carrer [kare] *tr* to square ‖ *ref* (coll) to plunk oneself down; (coll) to strut

carrier [karje] *m* quarryman

carrière [karjɛr] *f* career; course (*e.g., of the sun*); quarry; **donner carrière à** to give free rein to

carriole [karjɔl] *f* light cart, trap; (coll) jalopy

carrossable [karɔsabl] *adj* passable

carrosse [karɔs] *m* carriage, coach

carrosserie [karɔsri] *f* (aut) body

carrossier [karɔsje] *m* coachmaker

carrousel [karuzɛl] *m* carrousel; parade ground; tiltyard

carrure [karyr] *f* width (*of shoulders, garment, etc.*); build; **d'une belle carrure** broad-shouldered (*man*)

cartable [kartabl] *m* briefcase

cartayer [karteje] §49 *intr* to avoid the ruts

carte [kart] *f* card; map, chart; bill (*to pay*); bill of fare, menu; **carte d'abonnement** commutation ticket; season ticket; **carte de crédit** credit card; **carte de Noël** Christmas card; **carte d'entrée** pass, ticket of admission; **carte des vins** wine list; **carte d'identité** identification card; **carte grise** automobile registration; **carte perforée** punch card; **carte postale** post card; **carte routière** road map; **cartes truquées** marked cards, stacked deck; **faire une carte de France** (slang) to have a wet dream; **manger à la carte** to eat a la carte; **tirer les cartes à qn** to tell s.o.'s fortunes with cards

cartel [kartɛl] *m* cartel; wall clock; challenge (*to a duel*)

carte-lettre [kartəlɛtr] *f* (*pl* **cartes-lettres**) gummed letter-envelope

carter [kartɛr] *m* housing; bicycle chain guard; (aut) crankcase

carte-retrait [kartərətrɛ] *f* (*pl* **cartes-retrait**) bank card

cartilage [kartilaʒ] *m* cartilage, gristle

cartographe [kartɔgraf] *m* cartographer

cartomancie [kartɔmɑ̃si] *f* fortunetelling with cards

carton [kartɔ̃] *m* pasteboard, cardboard; cardboard box, carton; carton (*of cigarettes*); cartoon (*preliminary sketch*); (typ) cancel; **carton à chapeau** hatbox; **carton à dessin** portfolio for drawings and plans; **carton ondulé** corrugated cardboard

carton-pâte [kartɔ̃pat] *m* papier-mâché

cartouche [kartuʃ] *m* (archit) cartouche, tablet; inset (*in a picture*) ‖ *f* cartridge; carton (*of cigarettes*); canister (*of gas mask*); refill (*of pen*); **cartouche à blanc** blank cartridge

cartouchière [kartuʃjɛr] *f* cartridge belt, cartridge case

carvi [karvi] *m* caraway

cas [ka] *m* case; **cas d'espèce** individual case; **cas limite** borderline case; **cas urgent** emergency; **en aucun cas** under no circumstances; **en cas de** in the event of, in a time of; **en cas d'imprévu** in case of emergency; **en cas que, au cas que, au cas où, dans le cas où** in the event that; **faire cas de** to esteem, to make much of; **le cas échéant** should the occasion arise, if necessary; **ne jamais faire aucun cas de** to never pay any attention to; **selon le cas** as the case may be

casa·nier [kazanje] **-nière** [njɛr] *adj* home-loving ‖ *mf* homebody

casaque [kazak] *f* jockey coat; blouse; **tourner casaque** to be a turncoat

cascade [kaskad] *f* cascade; jerk; spree; **faire une cascade** (mov) to do a stunt; **prendre à la cascade** to ad-lib

cascader [kaskade] *intr* to cascade; (slang) to lead a wild life

casca·deur [kaskadœr] **-deuse** [døz] *mf* (mov) double ‖ *m* stunt man ‖ *f* stunt girl

case [kaz] *f* compartment; pigeonhole; square (*e.g., of checkerboard or ledger*);

box (*to be filled out on a form*); hut, cabin; **case postale** post-office box; **cochez la case correspondante** check the appropriate box; **se retrouver à la case départ** (slang) to find oneself back on square one

caséine [kazein] *f* casein

caser [kaze] *tr* to put away (*e.g., in a drawer*); arrange (*e.g., a counter display in a store*); (coll) to place, find a job for || *ref* (coll) to get settled

caserne [kazɛrn] *f* barracks; **caserne de pompiers** firehouse; **de caserne** off-color (*jokes*); regimented

caserner [kazɛrne] *tr & intr* to barrack

ca·sher -shère [kaʃɛr] *adj* kosher

casier [kasje] *m* rack (*for papers, magazines, letters, bottles*); cabinet; locker; **casier à homards** lobster pot; **casier à tiroirs** music cabinet; **casier judiciaire** police record

casino [kazino] *m* casino

casque [kask] *m* helmet; earphones, headset; comb (*of rooster*); **casque à mèche** nightcap; **casque à pointe** spiked helmet; **casque blindé** crash helmet; **les Casques bleus** the U.N. peace-keeping force

casquer [kaske] *intr* to fall into a trap; (slang) to shell out

casquette [kaskɛt] *f* cap

cas·sant [kasɑ̃] **-sante** [sɑ̃t] *adj* brittle; abrupt, curt

casse [kɑs] *m* (slang) burglarizing || *f* breakage || [kas], [kɑs] *f* ladle, scoop; crucible; (bot) cassia; (pharm) senna; (typ) case; (coll) scrap heap, junk

cas·sé -sée [kɑse] *adj* broken-down; shaky, weak (*voice*)

casse-cou [kasku] *m invar* (coll) daredevil; (coll) stunt man; (coll) danger spot || *interj* look out!

casse-croûte [kaskrut] *m invar* snack

casse-gueule [kasgœl] *adj invar* (slang) risky || *m invar* (coll) risky business

casse-langue [kaslɑ̃g] *m invar* tongue twister

casse-noisettes [kasnwazɛt] *m invar* nutcracker

casse-noix [kasnwa], [kasnwa] *m invar* nutcracker

casse-pieds [kaspje] *m invar* (coll) pain in the neck

casser [kase] *tr* to break; crack, shatter; (law) to break (*a will*); (mil) to break, bust; (coll) to split (*one's eardrums*); **casser sa pipe** (coll) to kick the bucket || *ref* to break; (coll) to rack (*one's brains*); **se casser le nez** (coll) to fail

casserole [kasrɔl] *f* saucepan; (slang) jalopy; **passer à la casserole** (slang) to screw; bump off, kill

casse-tête [kastɛt] *m invar* truncheon; din; brain teaser, puzzler; **casse-tête chinois** jigsaw puzzle

cassette [kasɛt], [kasɛt] *f* strongbox, coffer; casket (*for jewels*); (phot, electron) cassette; **cassette magnétique** cassette

cassis [kasi], [kasis] *m* black currant; cassis (*liqueur*); gutter

cassolette [kasɔlɛt] *f* incense burner

cassonade [kasɔnad] *f* brown sugar

cassoulet [kasulɛ] *m* pork and beans

cassure [kasyr] *f* break; crease; rift

castagnettes [kastaɲɛt] *fpl* castanets

caste [kast] *f* caste; **hors caste** outcaste

castil·lan [kastijɑ̃] **-lane** [jan] *adj* Castilian || *m* Castilian (*language*) || (*cap*) *mf* Castilian (*person*)

Castille [kastij] *f* Castile; **la Castille** Castile

castor [kastɔr] *m* beaver

castrat [kastra] *m* castrato

castrer [kastre] *tr* to castrate

ca·suel -suelle [kazɥɛl] *adj* casual; (coll) brittle || *m* perquisites

cataclysme [kataklism] *m* cataclysm

catacombes [katakɔ̃b] *fpl* catacombs

catafalque [katafalk] *m* catafalque

cataire [katɛr] *f* catnip

Catalogne [katalɔɲ] *f* Catalonia; **la Catalogne** Catalonia

catalogue [katalɔg] *m* catalogue

cataloguer [katalɔge] *tr* to catalogue

catalyseur [katalizœr] *m* catalyst

cataplasme [kataplasm] *m* poultice

catapulte [katapylt] *f* catapult

catapulter [katapylte] *tr* to catapult

cataracte [katarakt] *f* cataract

catarrhe [katar] *m* catarrh; bad cold

catastrophe [katastrɔf] *f* catastrophe

catch [katʃ] *m* wrestling

catcheur [katʃœr] *m* wrestler

catéchiser [kateʃize] *tr* to catechize; reason with

catéchisme [kateʃism] *m* catechism

catégorie [kategɔri] *f* category

catégorique [kategɔrik] *adj* categorical

catgut [katgyt] *m* (surg) catgut

cathédrale [katedral] *f* cathedral

cathéter [katetɛr] *m* (med) catheter

cathode [katɔd] *f* cathode

catholicisme [katɔlisism] *m* Catholicism

catholicité [katɔlisite] *f* catholicity; Catholicism; Catholics

catholique [katɔlik] *adj* catholic; Catholic; orthodox; **pas très catholique** (coll) questionable || *mf* Catholic

cati [kati] *m* glaze, gloss

catimini [katimini]—**en catimini** (coll) on the sly

catir [katir] *tr* to glaze

cauca·sien [kɔkazjɛ̃] **-sienne** [zjɛn] *adj* Caucasian || (*cap*) *mf* Caucasian

caucasique [kɔkazik] *adj* Caucasian

cauchemar [koʃmar] *m* nightmare

cause [koz] *f* cause; (law) case; **à cause de** because of, on account of, for the sake of; **cause de décès** cause of death; **et pour cause** with good reason; **hors de cause** irrelevant, beside the point; **mettre q.ch. en cause** to question s.th.; **mettre qn en cause** to implicate s.o.

causer [koze] *tr* to cause || *intr* to chat

causerie [kozri] *f* chat; informal lecture

causette [kozɛt] *f*—**faire la causette** (coll) to chat

cau·seur [kozœr] **-seuse** [zøz] *adj* talkative, chatty ‖ *mf* speaker, conversationalist ‖ *f* love seat

caustique [kostik] *adj* caustic

caute·leux [kotlø] **-leuse** [løz] *adj* crafty, wily; cunning (*mind*)

cautériser [koterize] *tr* to cauterize

caution [kosjɔ̃] *f* security, collateral; guarantor, bondsman; **mettre en liberté sous caution** to let out on bail; **se porter caution pour qn** to put up bail for s.o.; **sujet à caution** unreliable; **verser une caution** to make a deposit

cautionnement [kosjɔnmɑ̃] *m* surety bond, guaranty; bail; deposit

cautionner [kosjɔne] *tr* to bail out; guarantee

cavalcade [kavalkad] *f* cavalcade

cavalerie [kavalri] *f* cavalry

cava·lier [kavalje] **-lière** [ljɛr] *adj* cavalier; bridle (*path*) ‖ *mf* horseback rider; dance partner ‖ *m* cavalier, horseman; escort; (chess) knight; **faire cavalier seul** to go it alone ‖ *f* horsewoman

cave [kav] *adj* hollow (*cheeks*) ‖ *f* cellar; liquor cabinet; liquor store; night club; bank (*in game of chance*); stake (*in gambling*); **cave à vin** wine cellar

ca·veau [kavo] *m* (*pl* **-veaux**) small cellar; vault, crypt; rathskeller

caver [kave] *tr* to hollow out ‖ *intr* to ante ‖ *ref* to become hollow (*said of eyes*); wager

caverne [kavɛrn] *f* cave, cavern; (pathol) cavity (*e.g., in lung*)

caver·neux [kavɛrnø] **-neuse** [nøz] *adj* cavernous; hollow (*voice*)

caviar [kavjar] *m* caviar; **caviar rouge** salmon roe; **passer au caviar** to bluepencil, censor

caviarder [kavjarde] *tr* to censor

cavité [kavite] *f* cavity, hollow

caw·cher -chère [kaʃɛr] *adj* kosher

Cayes [kaj] *fpl*—**Cayes de la Floride** Florida Keys

C.C.P. *abbr* (**Compte chèques postaux**) postal banking account

ce [sə] (or **cet** [sɛt] before vowel or mute **h**) **cette** [sɛt] *adj dem* (*pl* **ces** [se]) §82A ‖ **ce** *pron* §82B, §85A4

C.E.A. *abbr* (**Commissariat à l'Énergie atomique**) Atomic Energy Commission

céans [seɑ̃] *adv* herein

ceci [sesi] *pron dem indef* this, this thing, this matter

cécité [sesite] *f* blindness

céder [sede] §10 *tr* to cede, transfer; yield; give up; **ne le céder à personne** to be second to none ‖ *intr* to yield, succumb, give way

cédille [sedij] *f* cedilla

cédrat [sedra] *m* citron

cèdre [sɛdr] *m* cedar

cédule [sedyl] *f* rate, schedule; (law) notification

C.E.E. *abbr* (**Communauté économique européenne**) Common Market

cégétiste [seʒetist] *mf* unionist

ceindre [sɛ̃dr] §50 *tr* to buckle on, gird; encircle; wreathe (*one's head*); **ceindre la couronne** to assume the crown ‖ *ref*—**se ceindre de** to gird on

ceinture [sɛ̃tyr] *f* belt; waist, waistline; sash, waistband; girdle; **ceinture de chasteté** chastity belt; **ceinture de sauvetage** life belt; **ceinture de sécurité** safety belt; **ceinture herniaire** truss; **se mettre la ceinture** or **se serrer la ceinture** to tighten one's belt

ceinturer [sɛ̃tyre] *tr* to girdle, belt; encircle, belt; (wrestling) to grip around the waist

cela [səla] *pron dem indef* that, that thing; that matter; **à cela près** with that one exception; **et avec cela?** what else?

célébrant [selebrɑ̃] *m* (eccl) celebrant

célébration [selebrasjɔ̃] *f* celebration

célèbre [selebr] *adj* famous

célébrer [selebre] §10 *tr* to celebrate

célébrité [selebrite] *f* celebrity

celer [səle] §2 *tr* to hide, conceal

céleri [selri], [sɛlri] *m* celery

céleste [selɛst] *adj* celestial

célibat [seliba] *m* celibacy

célibataire [selibatɛr] *adj* single ‖ *mf* celibate ‖ *m* bachelor ‖ *f* spinster

celle [sɛl] §83

celle-ci [sɛlsi] §84

celle-là [sɛlla] §84

cellier [selje] *m* wine cellar; fruit cellar

cellophane [selɔfan] *f* cellophane

cellule [selyl], [sɛlyl] *f* cell

celluloïd [selylɔid] *m* celluloid

celte [sɛlt] *adj* Celtic ‖ (*cap*) *mf* Celt

celtique [sɛltik] *adj & m* Celtic

celui [səlɥi] **celle** [sɛl] (*pl* **ceux** [sø] **celles**) §83

celui-ci [səlɥisi] **celle-ci** [sɛlsi] (*pl* **ceux-ci** [søsi] **celles-ci**) §84

celui-là [səlɥila] **celle-là** [sɛlla] (*pl* **ceux-là** [søla] **celles-là**) §84

cémentation [semɑ̃tasjɔ̃] *f* casehardening

cendre [sɑ̃dr] *f* cinder; **cendres** ashes

cendrée [sɑ̃dre] *f* shot; buckshot; (sports) cinder track

cendrer [sɑ̃dre] *tr* to cinder

cendrier [sɑ̃drije] *m* ashtray

Cendrillon [sɑ̃drijɔ̃] *f*—**la Cendrillon** Cinderella

cène [sɛn] *f* (eccl) Holy Communion ‖ (*cap*) *f* (eccl) Last Supper

cens [sɑ̃s] *m* census; poll tax

cen·sé -sée [sɑ̃se] §95 *adj* supposed to, e.g., **je ne suis pas censé le savoir** I am not supposed to know it; reputed to be, e.g., **il est censé juge infaillible** he is reputed to be an infallible judge

censément [sɑ̃semɑ̃] *adv* supposedly, apparently, allegedly

censeur [sɑ̃sœr] *m* censor; census taker; critic; auditor; proctor

censure [sɑ̃syr] *f* censure; censorship; (psychoanal) censor

censurer [sɑ̃syre] §97 *tr* to censure; censor
cent [sɑ̃] §94 *adj & pron (pl* **cents** in
multiples when standing before modified
noun, e.g., **trois cents œufs** three hundred eggs) one hundred, a hundred, hundred; **cent pour cent** one hundred percent; **cent un** [sɑ̃œ̃] one hundred and one,
a hundred and one, hundred and one; **l'an
dix-neuf cent** the year nineteen hundred;
page deux cent page two hundred ‖ *m*
hundred, one hundred ‖ [sɑ̃t] *m* cent
centaine [sɑ̃tɛn] *f* hundred; **par centaines**
by the hundreds; **une centaine de** about a
hundred
centaure [sɑ̃tɔr] *m* centaur
centenaire [sɑ̃tnɛr] *adj* centenary ‖ *mf* centenarian ‖ *m* centennial
centen·nal -nale [sɑ̃tɛnnal] *adj (pl* **-naux**
[no]) centennial
centième [sɑ̃tjɛm] §94 *adj, pron (masc,
fem), & m* hundredth ‖ *f* hundredth performance
centigrade [sɑ̃tigrad] *adj & m* centigrade
centime [sɑ̃tim] *m* centime
centimètre [sɑ̃timɛtr] *m* centimeter; tape
measure
centrage [sɑ̃traʒ] *m* centering
cen·tral -trale [sɑ̃tral] *adj (pl* **-traux** [tro])
central; main *(office)* ‖ *m* (telp) central ‖ *f*
powerhouse; labor union; **centrale atomique** or **nucléaire** atomic generator
centralisation [sɑ̃tralizasjɔ̃] *f* centralization
centraliser [sɑ̃tralize] *tr & ref* to centralize
centre [sɑ̃tr] *m* center; **centre commercial**
shopping district; **centre commercial de
quartier** convenience store; **centre de
dépression** storm center; **centre de (la)
ville** center city; **centre de triage** (rr)
switchyard; **centre d'études** college; **centre de villégiature** resort; **centre social
des étudiants** student center, student
union
centrer [sɑ̃tre] *tr* to center
centrifuge [sɑ̃trifyʒ] *adj* centrifugal
centuple [sɑ̃typl] *adj & m* hundredfold; **au
centuple** hundredfold
cep [sɛp] *m* vine stock
cépage [sepaʒ] *m* (bot) vine
cèpe [sɛp] *f* cepe mushroom
cependant [səpɑ̃dɑ̃] *adv* meanwhile; however, but, still; **cependant que** while,
whereas; **et cependant** and yet
céramique [seramik] *adj* ceramic ‖ *f* (art of)
ceramics; ceramic piece; **céramiques** ceramics *(objects)*
cerbère [sɛrbɛr] *m* (coll) watchdog ‖ *(cap)
m* Cerberus
cer·ceau [sɛrso] *m (pl* **-ceaux**) hoop; **cer-
ceaux** pinfeathers
cercle [sɛrkl] *m* circle; circle, club, society;
clubhouse; hoop; **en cercle** in the cask
cercler [sɛrkle] *tr* to ring, encircle; to hoop
cercueil [sɛrkœj] *m* coffin
céréale [sereal] *adj & f* cereal
céré·bral -brale [serebral] *adj (pl* **-braux**
[bro]) cerebral

cérémo·nial -niale [seremɔnjal] *adj & m*
ceremonial
cérémonie [seremɔni] *f* ceremony; **faire des
cérémonies** to stand on ceremony
cérémo·niel -nielle [seremɔnjɛl] *adj* ceremonial
cérémo·nieux [seremɔnjø] **-nieuse** [njøz]
adj ceremonious, formal, stiff
cerf [sɛr] *m* deer, red deer; stag, buck
cerf-volant [sɛrvɔlɑ̃] *m (pl* **cerfs-volants**)
kite
cerisaie [sərize] *f* cherry orchard
cerise [səriz[*f* cherry
cerisier [sərizje] *m* cherry tree
cerne [sɛrn] *m* annual ring *(of tree)*; ring
(around moon, black eye, wound)
cer·neau [sɛrno] *m (pl* **-neaux**) unripe nut-
meat
cerner [sɛrne] *tr* to ring, encircle; hem in,
besiege; shell *(nuts)*
cer·tain [sɛrtɛ̃] **-taine** [tɛn] §93 *adj* certain,
sure ‖ (when standing before noun) *adj*
certain, some; **certain auteur** a certain
author; **depuis un certain temps** for some
time; **d'un certain âge** middle-aged ‖
certains *pron indef pl* certain people
certainement [sɛrtɛnmɑ̃] *adv* certainly
certes [sɛrt] *adv* indeed, certainly
certificat [sɛrtifika] *m* certificate; recommendation, attestation; **certificat d'aptitude au professorat de l'enseignement
du second degré (C.A.P.E.S.)** secondary-
school teachers certificate; **certificat
d'aptitude pédagogique (C.A.P.)** teachers license; **certificat d'urbanisation** zoning permit
certifier [sɛrtifje] *tr* to certify
certitude [sɛrtityd] *f* certainty
cérumen [serymɛn] *m* earwax
céruse [seryz] *f* white lead
cer·veau [sɛrvo] *m (pl* **-veaux**) brain; mind;
cerveau brûlé (coll) hothead; **laver le
cerveau à** (coll) to brainwash
cerveauté [sɛrvote] *f* brain trust
cervelas [sɛrvəla] *m* salami
cervelet [sɛrvəlɛ] *m* cerebellum
cervelle [sɛrvɛl] *f* brains; **brûler la cervelle
à qn** (coll) to shoot s.o.'s brains out; **sans
cervelle** brainless
ces [se] §82A
césa·rien [sezarjɛ̃] **-rienne** [rjɛn] *adj* Caesarean ‖ *f* Caesarean section
cesse [sɛs] *f* cessation, ceasing; **sans cesse**
unceasingly, incessantly
cesser [sɛse] §97 *tr* to stop, cease, leave off
(e.g., work) ‖ *intr* to cease, stop; **cesser
de** + *inf* to stop, cease, quit + *ger*
cessez-le-feu [sɛselfø] *m invar* cease-fire
cession [sɛsjɔ̃] *f* ceding, surrender; (law)
transfer
c'est-à-dire [sɛtadir] *conj* that is, namely
césure [sezyr] *f* caesura
cet [sɛt] §82A
cette [sɛt] §82A
ceux [sø] §83
ceux-ci [søsi] §84
ceux-là [søla] §84

Ceylan [sɛlɑ̃] *m* Ceylon

C.G.T. [seʒete] *f* (letterword) (**confédération générale du travail**) national labor union ‖ *abbr* (**C**^{ie} **Générale transatlantique**) French Line

cha·cal [ʃakal] *m* (*pl* **-cals**) jackal

cha·cun [ʃakœ̃] **-cune** [kyn] *pron indef* each, each one, every one; everybody, everyone; **chacun pour soi** every man for himself; **chacun son goût** every man to his own taste; **tout chacun** (coll) every Tom, Dick, and Harry

chadburn [tʃadbœrn] *m* (naut) public-address system

chadouf [ʃaduf] *m* well sweep

cha·grin [ʃagrɛ̃] **-grine** [grin] *adj* sad, downcast ‖ *m* grief, sorrow

chagriner [ʃagrine] *tr* to grieve, distress; make into shagreen leather ‖ *intr* to grieve, worry ‖ §97 *ref* to grieve

chah [ʃa] *m* shah

chahut [ʃay] *m* (coll) horseplay, row

chahuter [ʃayte] *tr* (coll) to upset; (coll) to boo, heckle ‖ *intr* (coll) to create a disturbance

chai [ʃɛ] *m* wine cellar

chaîne [ʃɛn] *f* chain; warp (*of fabric*); necklace; (archit) pier; (archit) tie; (naut) cable; (rad, telv) network; (telv) channel; **chaîne de fabrication, chaîne de montage** assembly line; **chaîne volontaire** franchise, franchising; **faire la chaîne** to form a bucket brigade; **travailler à la chaîne** to work on the assembly line

chaînon [ʃɛnɔ̃] *m* link

chair [ʃɛr] *f* flesh; pulp (*of fruits*); meat (*of animals*); **avoir la chair de poule** to have goose pimples; **chair à canon** cannon fodder; **chair de sa chair** one's flesh and blood; **chairs** (painting, sculpture) nude parts; **en chair et en os** in the flesh; **ni chair ni poisson** neither fish nor fowl

chaire [ʃɛr] *f* pulpit; lectern; chair (*held by university professor*)

chaise [ʃɛz] *f* chair; bowline knot; (mach) bracket; **chaise à bascule** rocking chair; **chaise à fond de paille** rush-bottomed chair; **chaise à porteurs** sedan chair; **chaise berceuse** rocking chair; **chaise brisée** folding chair; **chaise cannée** cane chair; **chaise d'enfant** high chair; **chaise électrique** electric chair; **chaise percée** commode, toilet; **chaise pliante** folding chair; **chaise roulante** wheelchair; **faire de la chaise longue** to relax in a deck chair; put one's feet up

cha·land [ʃalɑ̃] **-lande** [lɑ̃d] *mf* customer ‖ *m* barge; **chaland de débarquement** (mil) landing craft

châle [ʃɑl] *m* shawl

chalet [ʃalɛ] *m* chalet, cottage, summer home; **chalet de nécessité** public rest room

chaleur [ʃalœr] *f* heat; warmth; **les grandes chaleurs de l'été** the hot weather of summer

chaleu·reux [ʃalœrø] **-reuse** [røz] *adj* warm, heated

châlit [ʃali] *m* bedstead

chaloupe [ʃalup] *f* launch

chalu·meau [ʃalymo] *m* (*pl* **-meaux**) reed; blowtorch; (mus) pipe; **chalumeau oxhydrique, chalumeau oxyacétylénique** acetylene torch

chalut [ʃaly] *m* trawl

chalutier [ʃalytje] *m* trawler

chamade [ʃamad] *f*—**battre la chamade** to beat wildly (*said of the heart*)

chamailler [ʃamɑje] *ref* to squabble

chamarrer [ʃamare] *tr* to decorate, ornament; bedizen, bedeck; (slang) to cover (*s.o.*) with ridicule

chambarder [ʃɑ̃barde] *tr* (slang) to upset, turn upside down

chambellan [ʃɑ̃bɛllɑ̃] *m* chamberlain

chambouler [ʃɑ̃bule] *tr* (slang) to upset, turn topsy-turvy

chambranle [ʃɑ̃brɑl] *m* frame (*of a door or window*); mantelpiece

chambre [ʃɑ̃br] *f* chamber; room; **chambre à air** inner tube; **chambre à coucher** bedroom; **chambre d'ami** guest room; **chambre de compensation** clearing house; **chambre noire** darkroom; **chambre sourde** soundproof(ed) room

chambrée [ʃɑ̃bre] *f* dormitory, barracks; bunkmates

chambrer [ʃɑ̃bre] *tr* to keep under lock and key; keep (*wine*) at room temperature

cha·meau [ʃamo] **-melle** [mɛl] *mf* (*pl* **-meaux**) camel ‖ *m* (slang) bitch (*person*)

chamois [ʃamwa] *adj* & *m* chamois

champ [ʃɑ̃] *m* field; **aux champs** salute (*played on trumpet or drum*); **champ clos** lists, dueling field; **champ de courses** race track; **champ de foire** fairground; **champ de repos** cemetery; **champ de tir** firing range; **champ libre** clear field; **champs Élysées** Elysian Fields; **Champs Élysées** Champs Elysées (*street*); **en champ clos** behind closed doors

champagne [ʃɑ̃paɲ] *m* champagne; **champagne brut** extra dry champagne; **champagne d'origine** vintage champagne ‖ (*cap*) *f* Champagne; **la Champagne** Champagne

champe·nois [ʃɑ̃pənwa] **-noise** [nwaz] *adj* Champagne ‖ *m* Champagne dialect ‖ (*cap*) *mf* inhabitant of Champagne

champêtre [ʃɑ̃pɛtr] *adj* rustic, rural

champignon [ʃɑ̃piɲɔ̃] *m* mushroom; fungus; (slang) accelerator pedal; **champignon de couche** cultivated mushroom; **champignon vénéneux** toadstool

champignonner [ʃɑ̃piɲone] *intr* to mushroom

cham·pion [ʃɑ̃pjɔ̃] **-pionne** [pjɔn] *mf* champion; best seller ‖ *f* championess

championnat [ʃɑ̃pjona] *m* championship

champlever [ʃɑ̃lve] §2 *tr* to chase out, gouge out

chan·çard [ʃɑ̃sar] **-çarde** [sard] *adj* (slang) in luck ‖ *mf* (slang) lucky person

chance [ʃɑ̃s] *f* luck; good luck; **avoir de la chance** to be lucky; **bonne chance!** good luck!; **chance moyenne** off chance; **chances** chances, risks, probability, possibility

chance·lant [ʃɑ̃slɑ̃] **-lante** [lɑ̃t] *adj* shaky, unsteady, tottering; delicate (*health, constitution*)

chanceler [ʃɑ̃sle] §34 *intr* to stagger, totter, teeter; waver

chancelier [ʃɑ̃səlje] *m* chancellor

chancellerie [ʃɑ̃sɛlri] *f* chancellery

chan·ceux [ʃɑ̃sø] **-ceuse** [søz] *adj* lucky; risky

chanci [ʃɑ̃si] *m* manure pile for mushroom growing

chancir [ʃɑ̃sir] *intr* to grow moldy

chancre [ʃɑ̃kr] *m* chancre; ulcer, canker

chandail [ʃɑ̃daj] *m* sweater; **chandail à col roulé** turtleneck sweater

chandeleur [ʃɑ̃dlœr] *f*—**la chandeleur** Candlemas

chandelier [ʃɑ̃dəlje] *m* candlestick; chandler

chandelle [ʃɑ̃dɛl] *f* tallow candle; prop, stay (*used in construction*); **chandelle de glace** icicle; **en chandelle** vertically; **voir trente-six chandelles** to see stars (*on account of a blow*)

chanfrein [ʃɑ̃frɛ̃] *m* forehead (*of a horse*); chamfer, beveled edge

chanfreiner [ʃɑ̃frɛne] *tr* to chamfer, bevel

change [ʃɑ̃ʒ] *m* exchange; rate of exchange; **de change** in reserve, extra; **donner le change à** to throw off the trail; **prendre le change** to let one self be duped; **rendre le change à qn** to give s.o. a taste of his own medicine

changeable [ʃɑ̃ʒabl] *adj* changeable

chan·geant [ʃɑ̃ʒɑ̃] **-geante** [ʒɑ̃t] *adj* changeable, changing, fickle; iridescent

changement [ʃɑ̃ʒmɑ̃] *m* change; shift, shifting; **changement de propriétaire** under new ownership; **changement de vitesse** gearshift

changer [ʃɑ̃ʒe] §38 *tr* to change; **changer contre** to exchange for ‖ *intr* to change; **changer d'avis** to change one's mind; **changer de place** to change one's seat; **changer de ton** (coll) to change one's tune; **changer de visage** to blush; change color ‖ *ref* to change, change clothes

chanoine [ʃanwan] *m* (eccl) canon

chanson [ʃɑ̃sɔ̃] *f* song; **chanson bachique** drinking song; **chanson de geste** medieval epic; **chanson de Noël** Christmas carol; **chanson du terroir** folk song; **chanson sentimentale** torch song

chansonner [ʃɑ̃sɔne] *tr* to lampoon in a satirical song

chansonneur [ʃɑ̃sɔnœr] *m* lampooner (*who writes satirical songs*)

chanson·nier [ʃɑ̃sɔnje] **-nière** [njɛr] *mf* songwriter ‖ *m* chansonnier; song book

chant [ʃɑ̃] *m* singing; song, chant; canto; crowing (*of rooster*); side (*e.g., of a brick*); **chant du cygne** swan song; **chant de Noël** Christmas carol; **chant national** national anthem; **chants** poetry; **de chant** on end, edgewise

chantage [ʃɑ̃taʒ] *m* blackmail

chan·tant [ʃɑ̃tɑ̃] **-tante** [tɑ̃t] *adj* singable, melodious; singsong (*accent*); musical (*evening*)

chan·teau [ʃɑ̃to] *m* (*pl* **-teaux**) chunk (*of bread*); remnant

chantepleure [ʃɑ̃tplœr] *f* wine funnel; tap (*of cask*); sprinkler; weep hole

chanter [ʃɑ̃te] *tr* to sing ‖ *intr* to sing; crow (*as a rooster*); to pay blackmail; **chanter faux** to sing out of tune; **chanter juste** to sing in tune; **faire chanter** to blackmail

chanterelle [ʃɑ̃trɛl] *f* first string (*of violin*); decoy bird; mushroom; **appuyer sur la chanterelle** (coll) to rub it in

chan·teur [ʃɑ̃tœr] **-teuse** [tøz] *adj* singing; song (*bird*) ‖ *mf* singer; **chanteur de charme** crooner; **chanteur de rythme** jazz singer

chantier [ʃɑ̃tje] *m* shipyard; stocks, slip; workshop, yard; gantry, stand (*for barrels*); (public sign) men at work; **chantier de construction** building site; **chantier de démolition** junkyard, scrap heap; **mettre en** or **sur le chantier** to start work on

chantilly [ʃɑ̃tiji] *m* whipped cream

chantonner [ʃɑ̃tɔne] *tr & intr* to hum

chantoung [ʃɑ̃tuŋ] *m* shantung

chantourner [ʃɑ̃turne] *tr* to jigsaw

chantre [ʃɑ̃tr] *m* cantor, chanter; precentor; songster; bard, poet

chanvre [ʃɑ̃vr] *m* hemp; **en chanvre** hempen; flaxen (*color*)

chan·vrier [ʃɑ̃vrije] **-vrière** [vrijɛr] *adj* hemp (*industry*) ‖ *mf* dealer in hemp; hemp dresser

chaos [kao] *m* chaos

chaotique [kaɔtik] *adj* chaotic

chaparder [ʃaparde] *tr* (coll) to pilfer, filch; gyp

chape [ʃap] *f* cover, covering; tread (*of tire*); coping (*of bridge*); frame, shell (*of pulley block*); (eccl) cope

cha·peau [ʃapo] *m* (*pl* **-peaux**) hat; head (*of mushroom*); lead (*of magazine or newspaper article*); cap (*of fountain pen; of valve*); cowl (*of chimney*); **chapeau à cornes** cocked hat; **chapeau bas** hat in hand; **chapeau bas!** hats off!; **chapeau chinois** Chinese bells; **chapeau de cotillon** little hat for New Year's Eve; **chapeau de paille** straw hat; **chapeau de roue** hubcap; **chapeau haut de forme** top hat; **chapeau melon** derby; **chapeau mou** fedora

chapeau-cloche [ʃapoklɔʃ] *m* (*pl* **chapeaux-cloches**) cloche (hat)

chapeauter [ʃapote] *tr* (coll) to put a hat on (*e.g., a child*)

chapelain [ʃaplɛ̃] *m* chaplain (*of a private chapel*)

chapeler [ʃaple] §34 *tr* to scrape the crust off of (*bread*)

chapelet [ʃaplɛ] *m* chaplet, rosary; string (*of onions; of islands; of insults*); chain (*of events; of mountains*); series (*e.g., of attacks*); (mil) stick (*of bombs*); **chapelet hydraulique** bucket conveyor; **défiler son chapelet** (coll) to speak one's mind; **dire son chapelet** to tell one's beads; **en chapelet** (elec) in series

chape·lier [ʃapəlje]ˈ**-lière** [ljɛr] *mf* hatter ‖ *f* Saratoga trunk

chapelle [ʃapɛl] *f* chapel; clique, coterie; **chapelle ardente** mortuary chamber lighted by candles; hearse

chapellerie [ʃapɛlri] *f* hatmaking; millinery; hat shop; millinery shop

chapelure [ʃaplyr] *f* bread crumbs

chaperon [ʃaprɔ̃] *m* chaperon; hood; cape with a hood; coping (*of wall*); **le Petit Chaperon rouge** Little Red Ridinghood

chaperonner [ʃaprɔne] *tr* to chaperon

chapi·teau [ʃapito] *m* (*pl* **-teaux**) capital (*of column*); circus tent

chapitre [ʃapitr] *m* chapter; **commencer un nouveau chapitre** to turn over a new leaf

chapitrer [ʃapitre] *tr* to reprimand, admonish, lecture; divide into chapters

chapon [ʃapɔ̃] *m* capon; (culin) crust rubbed with garlic

chaque [ʃak] *adj indef* each, every ‖ *pron indef* (coll) each, each one

char [ʃar] *m* chariot; float (*in parade*); (mil) tank; **char d'assaut** or **char de combat** (mil) tank; **char funèbre** hearse

charabia [ʃarabja] *m* gibberish

charançon [ʃarɑ̃sɔ̃] *m* weevil

charbon [ʃarbɔ̃] *m* coal; soft coal; charcoal; carbon (*of an electric cell or arc*); cinder (*in the eye*); **charbon ardent** live coal; **charbon de bois** charcoal; **charbon de terre** coal; **être sur les charbons ardents** to be on pins and needles

charbonnage [ʃarbɔnaʒ] *m* coal mining; coal mine

charbonner [ʃarbɔne] *tr* to char; draw (*a picture*) with charcoal ‖ *intr & ref* to char, carbonize

charbon·neux [ʃarbɔnø] **-neuse** [nøz] *adj* sooty; anthrax-carrying

charbon·nier [ʃarbɔnje] **-nière** [njɛr] *adj* coal (*e.g., industry*) ‖ *mf* coal dealer ‖ *m* charcoal burner; coaler ‖ *f* coal scuttle; charcoal kiln; (orn) coal titmouse

charcuter [ʃarkyte] *tr* to butcher, mangle

charcuterie [ʃarkytri] *f* delicatessen; pork butcher shop

charcu·tier [ʃarkytje] **-tière** [tjɛr] *mf* pork butcher; (coll) sawbones

chardon [ʃardɔ̃] *m* thistle

chardonneret [ʃardɔnrɛ] *m* (orn) goldfinch

charge [ʃarʒ] *f* charge; load, burden; caricature; public office; **à charge de** on condition of, with the proviso of; **à charge de revanche** on condition of getting the same thing in return; **charges de famille** dependents; **charge utile** payload; **être à charge à** to be dependent upon; **être à la charge**

de to be supported by; **faire la charge de** to do a takeoff of

char·gé -gée [ʃarʒe] §93 *adj* loaded; full; overcast (*sky*); registered (*letter*) ‖ *m* assistant, deputy, envoy; **chargé de cours** assistant professor

chargement [ʃarʒəmɑ̃] *m* charging; loading; cargo

charger [ʃarʒe] §38, §97, §99 *tr* to charge; drive, take (*s.o. in one's car*) ‖ *intr* (mil) to charge; (naut) to load ‖ *ref* to be loaded; **se charger de** to take charge of; take up (*a question*)

chargeur [ʃarʒœr] *m* loader; stoker; shipper; clip (*of gun*); (elec) charger

chariot [ʃarjo] *m* wagon, cart; typewriter carriage; **chariot d'enfant** walker; **chariot élévateur** fork-lift truck; **Grand Chariot**, **Chariot de David** Big Dipper; **Petit Chariot** Little Dipper

charitable [ʃaritabl] *adj* charitable

charité [ʃarite] *f* charity; **faire la charité** to give alms; **faites la charité de**, **ayez la charité de** have the goodness to; **par charité** for charity's sake

charlatan [ʃarlatɑ̃] *m* charlatan

charlemagne [ʃarləmaɲ] *m* (cards) king of hearts; **faire charlemagne** to quit while winning

char·mant [ʃarmɑ̃] **-mante** [mɑ̃t] *adj* charming

charme [ʃarm] *m* charm; (*Carpinus betulus*) hornbeam; **se porter comme un charme** to be fit as a fiddle

charmer [ʃarme] *tr* to charm

char·meur [ʃarmœr] **-meuse** [møz] *adj* charming ‖ *mf* charmer

charmille [ʃarmij] *f* bower, arbor

char·nel -nelle [ʃarnɛl] *adj* carnal

charnière [ʃarnjɛr] *f* hinge

char·nu -nue [ʃarny] *adj* fleshy; plump; pulpy

charogne [ʃarɔɲ] *f* carrion

charpentage [ʃarpɑ̃taʒ] *m* carpentry

charpente [ʃarpɑ̃t] *f* framework; scaffolding; frame, build (*of body*)

charpenter [ʃarpɑ̃te] *tr* to square (*timber*); outline, map out, plan (*a novel, speech, etc.*); **être solidement charpenté** to be well built or well constructed ‖ *intr* to carpenter

charpenterie [ʃarpɑ̃tri] *f* carpentry; structure (*of building*)

charpentier [ʃarpɑ̃tje] *m* carpenter

charpei [ʃarpi] *f* lint; **en charpie** in shreds

charrée [ʃare] *f* lye

charre·tier [ʃartje] **-tière** [tjɛr] *mf* teamster; **jurer comme un charretier** to swear like a trooper

charrette [ʃarɛt] *f* cart

charriage [ʃarjaʒ] *m* cartage; drifting (*of ice*); (slang) exaggeration

charrier [ʃarje] *tr* to cart, transport; carry away (*sand, as the river does*); (slang) to poke fun at ‖ *intr* to be full of ice (*said of river*); (slang) to exaggerate

charroi [ʃarwɑ], [ʃarwa] *m* cartage

charron [ʃarɔ̃], [ʃarɔ̃] *m* wheelwright, cart-wright

charroyer [ʃarwaje] §47 *tr* to cart

charrue [ʃary] *f* plow; **mettre la charrue devant les bœufs** to put the cart before the horse

charte [ʃart] *f* charter; title deed; fundamental principle

chas [ʃa] *m* eye (*of needle*)

chasse [ʃas] *f* hunt, hunting; hunting song; chase; bag (*game caught*); **aller à la chasse** to go hunting; **chasse à courre** riding to the hounds; **chasse aux appartements** house hunting; **chasse aux fauves** big-game hunting; **chasse d'eau** flush; **chasse gardée** game preserve; **chasse réservée** (public sign) no shooting; **tirer la chasse** to pull the toilet chain

châsse [ʃas] *f* reliquary; frame (*e.g., for eyeglasses*) ‖ **châsses** *mpl* (slang) blinkers, eyes

chasse-ballon [ʃasbalɔ̃] *m invar* dodge ball

chasse-bestiaux [ʃasbɛstjo] *m invar* cow-catcher

chasse-clou [ʃasklu] *m* (*pl* **-clous**) punch, nail set; countersink

chassé-croisé [ʃasekrwaze] *m* (*pl* **chassés-croisées**) futile efforts; Double-Crostic

chasselas [ʃasla] *m* white table grape

chasse-mouches [ʃasmuʃ] *m invar* fly swatter; fly net

chasse-neige [ʃasnɛʒ] *m invar* snowplow; snowblower

chasse-pierres [ʃaspjɛr] *m invar* (rr) cow-catcher

chasser [ʃase] *tr* to hunt; chase; chase away, put to flight; drive (*e.g., a herd of cattle*); (coll) to fire (*e.g., a servant*) ‖ *intr* to hunt; skid; come, e.g., **le vent chasse du nord** the wind is coming from the north; **chasser de race** (coll) to be a chip off the old block

chasseresse [ʃasrɛs] *f* huntress

chas·seur [ʃasœr] **-seuse** [søz] *mf* hunter; bellhop ‖ *m* chasseur; fighter pilot; **chasseur à réaction** jet fighter; **chasseur d'assaut** fighter plane; **chasseur de chars** antitank tank; **chasseur de sous-marins** submarine chaser; **chasseur d'images** camera bug

chasseur-bombardier [ʃasœrbɔ̃bardje] *m* fighter-bomber

chassie [ʃasi] *f* gum (*on eyelids*)

chas·sieux [ʃasjø] **-sieuse** [søz] *adj* gummy (*eyelids*)

châssis [ʃasi] *m* chassis; window frame; chase (*for printing*); **châssis à demeure** or **dormant** sealed window frame; **châssis couche** (hort) hotbed; **châssis mobile** movable sash

châssis-presse [ʃasiprɛs] *m* (*pl* **-presses**) printing frame

chaste [ʃast] *adj* chaste

chasteté [ʃastəte] *f* chastity

chat [ʃa] **chatte** [ʃat] *mf* cat ‖ *m* tomcat; **à bon chat bon rat** tit for tat; **acheter chat en poche** (coll) to buy a pig in a poke;

appeler un chat un chat (coll) to call a spade a spade; **chat à neuf queues** cat-o'-nine-tails; **chat dans la gorge** (coll) frog in the throat; **chat de gouttière** alley cat; **chat fourré** (coll) judge; **chat sauvage** wildcat; **d'autres chats à fouetter** (coll) other fish to fry; **il ne faut pas réveiller le chat qui dort** let sleeping dogs lie; **le Chat botté** Puss in Boots; **mon petit chat!** darling!; **pas un chat** (coll) not a soul ‖ *f* see **chatte**

châtaigne [ʃatɛɲ] *f* chestnut

châtaignier [ʃatɛɲe] *m* chestnut tree

chataire [ʃatɛr] *f* catnip

châ·teau [ʃato] *m* (*pl* **-teaux**) chateau; palace; estate, manor; **château d'eau** water tower; **château de cartes** house of cards; **château fort** castle, fort, citadel; **château en Espagne** castles in the air; **mener une vie de château** to live like a prince

châteaubriand or **châteaubriant** [ʃatobriɑ̃] *m* filet mignon, fillet, tenderloin

châte·lain [ʃatlɛ̃] **-laine** [lɛn] *mf* proprietor of a country estate ‖ *f* wife of the lord of the manor; bracelet

châtelet [ʃatlɛ] *m* small chateau

chat-huant [ʃaɥɑ̃] *m* (*pl* **chats-huants** [ʃaɥɑ̃]) screech owl

châtier [ʃatje] *tr* to chasten, chastise; correct; purify (*style*)

chatière [ʃatjɛr] *f* ventilation hole; cathole

châtiment [ʃatimɑ̃] *m* punishment

chatoiement [ʃatwamɑ̃] *m* glisten, sparkle; sheen, shimmer; play of colors

chaton [ʃatɔ̃] *m* kitten; setting (*of ring*); (bot) catkin

chatonner [ʃatɔne] *tr* to set (*a gem*) ‖ *intr* to have kittens

chatouillement [ʃatujmɑ̃] *m* tickle; tickling sensation

chatouiller [ʃatuje] *tr* to tickle; (fig) to excite, arouse ‖ *intr* to tickle

chatouil·leux [ʃatujø] **-leuse** [jøz] *adj* ticklish; touchy

chatoyer [ʃatwaje] §47 *intr* to glisten, sparkle; shimmer

chat-pard [ʃapar] *m* (*pl* **chats-pards**) ocelot

châtrer [ʃatre] *tr* to castrate

chatte [ʃat] *adj fem* kittenish ‖ *f* cat, female cat

chatterie [ʃatri] *f* cajoling; sweets

chatterton [ʃatɛrtɔn] *m* friction tape

chaud [ʃo] **chaude** [ʃod] *adj* hot, warm; last-minute (*news flash*); **il fait chaud** it is warm (*weather*); **pleurer à chaudes larmes** to cry one's eyes out ‖ *m* heat, warmth; **à chaud** emergency (*operation*); (med) in the acute stage; **avoir chaud** to be warm, be hot (*said of person*); **il a eu chaud** (coll) he had a narrow escape ‖ *adv*—**coûter chaud** (coll) to cost a pretty penny; **servir chaud** to serve (*s.th.*) piping hot

chaude-pisse [ʃodpis] *f* (vulg) clap, gonorrhea

chaudière [ʃodjɛr] *f* boiler

chaudron [ʃodrɔ̃] *m* cauldron

chaudron·nier [ʃodrɔnje] **-nière** [njɛr] *mf* coppersmith; boilermaker

chauffage [ʃofaʒ] *m* heating; stoking; (coll) coaching

chauffard [ʃofar] *m* road hog, Sunday driver

chauffe [ʃof] *f* stoking; furnace

chauffe-assiettes [ʃofasjɛt] *m invar* hot plate

chauffe-bain [ʃofbɛ̃] *m* (*pl* **-bains**) bathroom water heater

chauffe-eau [ʃofo] *m invar* water heater

chauffe-lit [ʃofli] *m* (*pl* **-lits**) bed warmer

chauffe-pieds [ʃofpje] *m invar* foot warmer

chauffe-plats [ʃofpla] *m invar* chafing dish

chauffer [ʃofe] *tr* to heat; warm up; limber up; (coll) to coach; (slang) to snitch, filch || *intr* to heat up; get up steam; overheat; **ça va chauffer!** (coll) watch the fur fly! || *ref* to warm oneself; heat up

chaufferette [ʃofrɛt] *f* foot warmer; space heater; car heater

chauffeur [ʃofœr] *m* driver; chauffeur; (rr) stoker, fireman

chauffeuse [ʃoføz] *f* fireside chair

chaume [ʃom] *m* stubble; thatch

chaumière [ʃomjɛr] *f* thatched cottage

chaussée [ʃose] *f* pavement, road; causeway

chausse-pied [ʃospje] *m* (*pl* **-pieds**) shoehorn

chausser [ʃose] *tr* to put on (*shoes, skis, glasses, tires, etc.*); shoe; fit || *intr* to fit (*said of shoe*); **chausser de** to wear (*a certain size shoe*) || *ref* to put one's shoes on

chausses [ʃos] *fpl* hose (*in medieval dress*); **aux chausses de** on the heels of; **c'est elle qui porte les chausses** (coll) she wears the pants

chausse-trape [ʃostrap] *f* (*pl* **-trapes**) trap; booby trap

chaussette [ʃosɛt] *f* sock

chausseur [ʃosœr] *m* shoe salesman

chausson [ʃosɔ̃] *m* pump, slipper, savate; **chausson aux pommes** apple turnover

chaussure [ʃosyr] *f* footwear, shoes; shoe; **trouver chaussure à son pied** to find what one needs

chauve [ʃov] *adj* bald

chauve-souris [ʃovsuri] *f* (*pl* **chauves-souris**) (zool) bat

chau·vin [ʃovɛ̃] **-vine** [vin] *adj* chauvinistic || *mf* chauvinist

chauvir [ʃovir] *intr*—**chauvir de l'oreille, chauvir des oreilles** to prick up the ears (*said of horse, mule, donkey*)

chaux [ʃo] *f* lime

chavirement [ʃavirmɑ̃] *m* capsizing, overturning

chavirer [ʃavire] *tr & intr* to tip over, capsize

chef [ʃɛf] *m* head, chief, leader; boss; scoutmaster; **au premier chef** essentially; **chef de bande** ringleader, gang leader; **chef de cuisine** chef; **chef de file** leader, standard-bearer; **chef de gare** stationmaster; **chef de l'exécutif** chief executive; **chef de musique** bandmaster; **chef de rayon** floorwalker; **chef de tribu** chieftain; **chef d'orchestre** conductor; bandleader; **de son propre chef** by one's own authority, on one's own

chef-d'œuvre [ʃɛdœvr] *m* (*pl* **chefs-d'œuvre**) masterpiece

chef-lieu [ʃɛfljø] *m* (*pl* **chefs-lieux**) county seat, capital city

cheftaine [ʃɛftɛn] *f* Girl Scout unit leader

cheik [ʃɛk] *m* sheik

chelem [ʃlɛm] *m* slam (*at bridge*); **être chelem** (cards) to be shut out

chemin [ʃmɛ̃] *m* way; road; **chemin battu** beaten path; **chemin de la Croix** (eccl) Way of the Cross; **chemin de fer** railroad; **chemin de roulement** (aer) taxiway; **chemin des écoliers** (coll) long way around; **chemin de table** table runner; **chemin de traverse** side road; shortcut; **chemin de velours** primrose path; **n'y pas aller par quatre chemins** (coll) to come straight to the point

chemi·neau [ʃmino] *m* (*pl* **-neaux**) hobo, tramp; deadbeat

cheminée [ʃmine] *f* chimney, stack, smokestack; fireplace; (naut) funnel

cheminer [ʃmine] *intr* to trudge, tramp; make headway

cheminot [ʃmino] *m* railroader

chemise [ʃmiz] *f* shirt; dust jacket (*of book*); folder, file; jacket, shell, metal casing; **chemise classeur** folder; **chemise de mailles** coat of mail; **chemise de nuit** nightgown; **chemise polo** polo shirt

chemiser [ʃmize] *tr* (mach) to case, jacket

chemiserie [ʃmizri] *f* haberdashery

chemisette [ʃmizɛt] *f* short-sleeved shirt

chemi·sier [ʃmizje] **-sière** [zjɛr] *mf* haberdasher || *m* shirtwaist

che·nal [ʃnal] *m* (*pl* **-naux** [no]) channel; millrace

chenapan [ʃnapɑ̃] *m* rogue, scoundrel

chêne [ʃɛn] *m* oak

ché·neau [ʃeno] *m* (*pl* **-neaux**) rain spout

chêne-liège [ʃɛnljɛʒ] *m* (*pl* **chênes-lièges**) cork oak

chenet [ʃnɛ] *m* andiron

chènevis [ʃɛnvi] *m* hempseed, birdseed

chenil [ʃni] *m* kennel

chenille [ʃnij] *f* caterpillar; chenille; caterpillar tread

chenil·lé -lée [ʃnije] *adj* with a caterpillar tread

che·nu -nue [ʃny] *adj* hoary

cheptel [ʃɛptɛl], [ʃɛtɛl] *m* livestock; **cheptel mort** implements and buildings

chèque [ʃɛk] *m* check; **chèque certifié** certified check; **chèque de voyage** traveler's check; **chèque en blanc** blank check; **chèque en bois** bad check; **chèque prescrit** invalidated (*old*) check; **chèque sans provision** bad check

chéquier [ʃekje] *m* checkbook

cher chère [ʃɛr] *adj* expensive, dear || (when standing before noun) *adj* dear, beloved ‖ *f* see **chère** ‖ **cher** *adv* dear(ly); **coûter cher** to cost a great deal

chercher [ʃɛrʃe] §96 *tr* to look for, search for, seek, hunt; try to get; **aller chercher** to go and get; **envoyer chercher** to send for ‖ *intr* to search; **chercher à** to try to, endeavor to ‖ *intr* to look for each other; feel one's way

cher·cheur [ʃɛrʃœr] -**cheuse** [ʃøz] *adj* inquiring (*mind*); homing (*device*) ‖ *mf* seeker; researcher, scholar; investigator; prospector (*for gold, uranium, etc.*)

chère [ʃɛr] *f* fare, food and drink; **faire bonne chère** to live high

chèrement [ʃɛrmɑ̃] *adv* fondly, lovingly; dearly (*bought or won*)

ché·ri -rie [ʃeri] *adj & mf* darling

chérir [ʃerir] *tr* to cherish

cherry [ʃeri] *m* cherry cordial

cherté [ʃɛrte] *f* high price; **cherté de la vie** high cost of living

chérubin [ʃerybɛ̃] *m* cherub

ché·tif [ʃetif] -**tive** [tiv] *adj* puny, sickly; poor, wretched

che·val [ʃəval] *m* (*pl* -**vaux** [vo]) horse; metric or French horsepower (*735 watts*); **à cheval** on horseback; **à cheval sur** astride; insistent upon; **cheval à bascule** rocking horse; **cheval de bât** pack horse; **cheval de bataille** charger, warhorse; (fig) main issue (*in a political campaign*); **cheval de bois** or **cheval d'arçons** horse (*for vaulting*); **cheval de course** race horse; **cheval de race** thoroughbred; **cheval de retour** (coll) jailbird; **cheval de selle** saddle horse; **cheval de trait** draft horse; **cheval de Troie** Trojan horse; **cheval entier** stallion; **cheval vapeur** horsepower; **monter sur ses grands chevaux** (fig) to get up on one's high horse

chevalement [ʃvalmɑ̃] *m* support, shoring; (min) headframe

chevaler [ʃvale] *tr* to shore up

chevaleresque [ʃvalrɛsk] *adj* knightly, chivalrous

chevalerie [ʃvalri] *f* chivalry

chevalet [ʃvalɛ] *m* easel; sawhorse; stand, frame; bridge (*of violin*)

chevalier [ʃvalje] *m* knight; (orn) sandpiper; **chevalier d'industrie** manipulator, swindler; **chevalier errant** knight-errant; **Chevaliers du taste-vin** wine-tasting club

chevalière [ʃvaljɛr] *f* signet ring

cheva·lin [ʃvalɛ̃] -**line** [lin] *adj* equine

cheval-vapeur [ʃvalvapœr] *m* (*pl* **chevaux-vapeur**) metric or French horsepower (*735 watts*)

chevauchée [ʃəvoʃe] *f* ride

chevaucher [ʃəvoʃe] *tr* to straddle ‖ *intr* to ride horseback; overlap

cheve·lu -lue [ʃəvly] *adj* hairy; long-haired

chevelure [ʃəvlyr] *f* hair, head of hair; tail (*of a comet*)

chevet [ʃəvɛ] *m* headboard; bolster; **de chevet** bedside (*lamp, table, book*)

che·veu [ʃəvø] *m* (*pl* -**veux**) hair; **avoir mal aux cheveux** (coll) to have a hangover;

cheveux hair (*of the head*); hairs; **cheveux en brosse** crew cut; **couper les cheveux en quatre** (coll) to split hairs; **en cheveux** hatless; **faire dresser les cheveux** (coll) to make one's hair stand on end; **ne tenir qu'à un cheveu** (coll) to hang by a thread; **saisir l'occasion aux cheveux** (coll) to take time by the forelock; **se faire des cheveux** (coll) to worry oneself gray; **tiré par les cheveux** (coll) far-fetched

chevillard [ʃəvijar] *m* wholesale cattle dealer or jobber

cheville [ʃəvij] *f* ankle; peg; pin; bolt; padding (*of verse*); **cheville ouvrière** (mach) kingbolt; (fig) mainspring (*of an enterprise*); **être en cheville avec** (coll) to be in cahoots with; **ne pas arriver à la cheville de qn** (coll) not to hold a candle to s.o.

chèvre [ʃɛvr] *f* goat; nanny goat

che·vreau [ʃəvro] *m* (*pl* -**vreaux**) kid

chèvrefeuille [ʃɛvrəfœj] *m* honeysuckle

chevrette [ʃəvrɛt] *f* kid; doe (*roe deer*); shrimp; tripod

chevreuil [ʃəvrœj] *m* roe deer; roebuck

chevron [ʃəvrɔ̃] *m* rafter; chevron, hash mark; **en chevron** in a herringbone pattern

chevron·né -née [ʃəvrɔne] *adj* wearing chevrons; experienced, oldest

chevronner [ʃəvrɔne] *tr* to put rafters on; give chevrons to

chevroter [ʃəvrɔte] *intr* to bleat; sing or speak in a quavering voice

chewing-gum [ʃwingɔm], [tʃuwingɔm] *m* chewing gum

chez [ʃe] *prep* at the house, home, office, etc., of, e.g., **chez mes amis** at my friends' house; e.g., **chez le boulanger** at the baker's; in the country of, among, e.g., **chez les Français** among the French; in the time of, e.g., **chez les anciens Grecs** in the time of the ancient Greeks; in the work of, e.g., **chez Homère** in Homer's works; with, e.g., **c'est chez lui une habitude** it's a habit with him

chez-soi [ʃeswa] *m invar* home

chialer [ʃjale] *intr* (slang) to cry

chiasse [ʃjas] *f* flyspecks; (metallurgy) dross; (coll) loose bowels

chic [ʃik] *adj invar* stylish, chic; **un chic type** (coll) a good egg ‖ *m* style; skill, knack; (coll) smartness, elegance; (slang) ovation; **de chic** from memory ‖ *interj* (coll) fine!, grand!

chicane [ʃikan] *f* chicanery; shady lawsuit; baffle, baffle plate; **chercher chicane à** to engage in a petty quarrel with; **en chicane** staggered, zigzag; curved (*tube*)

chicaner [ʃikane] *tr* to pick a fight with; **chicaner q.ch. à qn** to quibble over s.th. with s.o. ‖ *intr* to quibble

chicanerie [ʃikanri] *f* chicanery

chiche [ʃiʃ] *adj* stingy; small, dwarf ‖ *interj* (coll) I dare you!

chichi [ʃiʃi] *m* fuss; **sans chichis** informally

chicon [ʃikɔ̃] *m* (coll) romaine

chicorée [ʃikɔre] *f* chicory; **chicorée frisée** endive

chicot [ʃiko] *m* stump (*of tree*); (coll) stump, stub (*of tooth*)

chien [ʃjɛ̃] **chienne** [ʃjɛn] *mf* dog ‖ *m* hammer (*of gun*); glamour; **à la chien** (coll) with bangs; **chien couchant** setter; (slang) apple polisher; **chien d'arrêt** pointer; **chien d'aveugle** Seeing Eye dog; **chien de** or **chienne de** (coll) dickens of a; **chien de garde** watchdog; **chien de traîneau** sled dog; **chien du jardinier** (coll) dog in the manger; **chien savant** performing dog; **de chien** (coll) miserable (*weather, life, etc.*); **en chien de fusil** (coll) curled up (*e.g., to sleep*); **entre chien et loup** (coll) at dusk; **les chiens écrasés** (slang) the accident page (*of newspaper*); **petit chien** pup; **se regarder en chiens de faïence** (coll) to glare at one another ‖ *f* see **chienne**

chiendent [ʃjɛ̃dɑ̃] *m* couch grass; (coll) trouble

chienlit [ʃjɑ̃li] *mf* (vulg) person who soils his bed ‖ *m* carnival mask; masquerade, fantastic costume ‖ *f* (vulg) crap (*rowdyness, havoc*), e.g., **réforme, oui! chienlit, non!** reform, yes! crap, no!

chien-loup [ʃjɛ̃lu] *m* (*pl* **chiens-loups**) wolfhound

chienne [ʃjɛn] *f* bitch

chienner [ʃjɛne] *intr* to whelp

chiennerie [ʃjɛnri] *f* stinginess, meanness

chier [ʃje] *tr & intr* (vulg) to crap, defecate; **tu me fais chier!** (vulg) you're a pain in the ass!

chiffe [ʃif] *f* rag; (coll) weakling

chiffon [ʃifɔ̃] *m* rag; scrap of paper; **chiffons** (coll) fashions

chiffonnade [ʃifɔnad] *f* salad greens

chiffonner [ʃifɔne] *tr* to rumple, crumple; make (*a dress*); (coll) to ruffle (*tempers*), bother ‖ *intr* to pick rags; make dresses

chiffon·nier [ʃifɔnje] **-nière** [njɛr] *mf* scavenger, ragpicker ‖ *m* chiffonier

chiffre [ʃifr] *m* figure, number; cipher, code; sum total; combination (*of lock*); monogram; **chiffre d'affaires** turnover; **chiffres romains** roman numerals

chiffrer [ʃifre] *tr* to number; monogram; figure the cost of; cipher, code ‖ *intr* to calculate; mount up; cipher, code ‖ *ref*—**se chiffrer par** to amount to

chignole [ʃiɲɔl] *f* breast drill, hand drill; (coll) jalopy

chignon [ʃiɲɔ̃] *m* chignon, bun, knot

Chili [ʃili] *m*—**le Chili** Chile

chimère [ʃimɛr] *f* chimera; **se forger des chimères** to indulge in wishful thinking

chimie [ʃimi] *f* chemistry

chimique [ʃimik] *adj* chemical

chimiste [ʃimist] *mf* chemist

chimpanzé [ʃɛ̃pɑ̃ze] *m* chimpanzee

Chine [ʃin] *f* China; **la Chine** China; **les deux Chine** the two Chinas

chi·né -née [ʃine] *adj* mottled, figured

chiner [ʃine] *tr* to mottle (*cloth*); (coll) to make fun of

chi·nois [ʃinwa] **-noise** [nwaz] *adj* Chinese ‖ *m* Chinese (*language*) ‖ (*cap*) *mf* Chinese (*person*)

chinoiserie [ʃinwazri] *f* Chinese curio; **chinoiseries administratives** (coll) red tape

chiot [ʃjo] *m* puppy

chiourme [ʃjurm] *f* chain gang

chip [ʃip] *m* (electron) chip

chiper [ʃipe] *tr* (slang) to swipe; gyp

chipie [ʃipi] *f* (coll) shrew

chipoter [ʃipɔte] *intr* to haggle; nibble, pick at one's food

chips [ʃips] *mpl* potato chips

chique [ʃik] *f* chew, quid (*of tobacco*); (ent) chigger

chiqué [ʃike] *m* (slang) sham, bluff

chiquenaude [ʃiknod] *f* fillip, flick

chiquer [ʃike] *tr* to chew (*tobacco*) ‖ *intr* to chew tobacco

chiromancie [kirɔmɑ̃si] *f* palmistry

chiroman·cien [kirɔmɑ̃sjɛ̃] **-cienne** [sjɛn] *mf* palm reader

chiropracteur [kirɔpraktœr] *m* chiropractor

chirurgi·cal -cale [ʃiryrʒikal] *adj* (*pl* **-caux** [ko]) surgical

chirurgie [ʃiryrʒi] *f* surgery

chirur·gien [ʃiryrʒjɛ̃] **-gienne** [ʒjɛn] *mf* surgeon

chirurgien-dentiste [ʃiryrʒjɛ̃dɑ̃tist] *m* (*pl* **chirurgiens-dentistes**) dental surgeon

chiure [ʃiyr] *f* flyspeck

chlamydiose [klamidjoz] *f* chlamydia

chlore [klɔr] *m* chlorine

chlo·ré -rée [klɔre] *adj* chlorinated

chlorhydrique [klɔridrik] *adj* hydrochloric

chloroforme [klɔrɔfɔrm] *m* chloroform

chloroformer [klɔrɔfɔrme] *tr* to chloroform

chlorophylle [klɔrɔfil] *f* chlorophyll

chlorure [klɔryr] *m* chloride; **chlorure de soude** sodium chloride

choc [ʃɔk] *m* shock; clash; bump; clink (*of glasses*)

chocolat [ʃɔkɔla] *adj invar & m* chocolate

chocolaterie [ʃɔkɔlatri] *f* chocolate factory

chœur [kœr] *m* choir, chorus

choir [ʃwar] (usually used only in *inf* and *pp* **chu**; sometimes used in *pres ind* **chois**, etc.; *pret* **chus**, etc; *fut* **choirai**, etc.) *intr* (*aux:* ꜰʀe or ᴀᴠᴏɪʀ) to fall; **se laisser choir** to drop, flop

choi·si -sie [ʃwazi] *adj* choice, select; chosen; selected (*works*)

choisir [ʃwazir] §97 *tr & intr* to choose

choix [ʃwa] *m* choice; **au choix** at one's discretion; **de choix** choice

choléra [kɔlera] *m* cholera

cholérique [kɔlerik] *mf* cholera victim

cholestérol [kɔlɛsterɔl] *m* cholesterol

chômage [ʃomaʒ] *m* unemployment; **en chômage** unemployed

chô·mé -mée [ʃome] *adj* closed for business, off, e.g., **jour chômé** day off

chômer [ʃome] *tr* to take (*a day*) off; observe (*a holiday*) ‖ *intr* to take off (*from work*); be unemployed

chô·meur [ʃomœr] -**meuse** [møz] *mf* unemployed worker

chope [ʃɔp] *f* stein, beer mug

choper [ʃɔpe] *tr* (coll) to catch

chopine [ʃɔpin] *f* half-liter measure; (slang) bottle

chopper [ʃɔpe] *intr* to stumble; blunder

choquer [ʃɔke] *tr* to shock; bump; clink (*glasses*); (elec) to shock ‖ *ref* to collide; take offense

cho·ral -**rale** [kɔral] *adj* (*pl* -**raux** [ro]) choral ‖ *m* (*pl* -**rals**) chorale ‖ *f* choral society, glee club

chorégraphie [kɔregrafi] *f* choreography

choriste [kɔrist] *mf* chorister

chorus [kɔrys] *m*—**faire chorus** to repeat in unison; chime in; approve unanimously

chose [ʃoz] *adj invar* (coll) odd; **être tout chose** (coll) to feel funny ‖ *m* thingamajig; **Monsieur Chose** (coll) Mr. what's-his-name ‖ *f* thing ‖ *pron indef masc*—**autre chose** something else; **quelque chose** something

chou [ʃu] **choute** [ʃut] *mf*—**ma choute, mon chou** (coll) sweetheart ‖ *m* (*pl* **choux**) cabbage; **chou à la crème** cream puff; **chou de Bruxelles** Brussels sprouts; **de chou** (coll) of little value; **faire chou blanc** (coll) to draw a blank; **finir dans le chou** (coll) to come in last

choucas [ʃukɑ] *m* jackdaw

choucroute [ʃukrut] *f* sauerkraut; **choucroute garnie** sauerkraut with ham or sausage

chouette [ʃwɛt] *adj* (coll) swell; **chouette alors!** (coll) oh boy! ‖ *f* owl; (coll) radio; **chouette épervière** hawk owl

chou-fleur [ʃuflœr] *m* (*pl* **choux-fleurs**) cauliflower

chou-rave [ʃurav] *m* (*pl* **choux-raves**) kohlrabi

chow-chow [ʃuʃu] *m* (*pl* -**chows**) chow (*dog*)

choyer [ʃwaje] §47 *tr* to pamper, coddle; cherish (*a hope*); entertain (*an idea*)

chrestomatie [krɛstɔmati], [krɛstɔmasi] *f* chrestomathy

chré·tien [kretjɛ̃] -**tienne** [tjɛn] *adj & mf* Christian

chrétiennement [kretjɛnmɑ̃] *adv* in the faith

chrétienté [kretjɛ̃te] *f* Christendom

christ [krist] *m* crucifix ‖ (*cap*) *m* Christ; **le Christ** Christ

christianiser [kristjanize] *tr* to Christianize

christianisme [kristjanism] *m* Christianity

chromatique [krɔmatik] *adj* chromatic

chrome [krom] *m* chrome, chromium

chromer [krome] *tr* to chrome

chromocodé [krɔmokɔde] *adj* (chem) color-coded

chromosome [krɔmozom] *m* chromosome

chronique [krɔnik] *adj* chronic ‖ *f* chronicle; column (*in newspaper*); **chronique financière** financial page; **chronique mondaine** society news; **chronique théâtrale** theater page

chroniqueur [krɔnikœr] *m* chronicler; columnist; **chroniqueur dramatique** drama critic

chrono [krɔno] *m*—**faire du 60 chrono** (coll) to do 60 by the clock

chronologie [krɔnɔlɔʒi] *f* chronology

chronologique [krɔnɔlɔʒik] *adj* chronological

chronomètre [krɔnɔmɛtr] *m* chronometer; stopwatch

chronométrer [krɔnɔmetre] §10 *tr* to clock, time

chronométreur [krɔnɔmetrœr] *m* timekeeper

chrysalide [krizalid] *f* chrysalis

chrysanthème [krizɑ̃tɛm] *m* chrysanthemum

chuchotement [ʃyʃɔtmɑ̃] *m* whisper, whispering

chuchoter [ʃyʃɔte] *tr & intr* to whisper

chuinter [ʃɥɛ̃te] *intr* to hoot (*said of owl*); make a swishing sound, hiss (*said of escaping gas*); pronounce [ʃ] instead of [s] and [ʒ] instead of [z]

chut [ʃyt] *interj* sh!

chute [ʃyt] *f* fall; downfall; drop (*in prices, voltage, etc.*); **chute d'eau** waterfall

chuter [ʃyte] *tr* to hush; hiss (*an actor*) ‖ *intr* (coll) to fail; (cards) to be down

Chypre [ʃipr] *f* Cyprus

ci [si] *pron indef*—**comme ci comme ça** so-so ‖ *adv*—**entre ci et là** between now and then

-ci [si] §82, §84

ci-après [siaprɛ] *adv* hereafter, below, further on

ci-bas [sibɑ] *adv* below

cible [sibl] *f* target

ciboule [sibul] *f* chive, scallion

ciboulette [sibulet] *f* chive, chives

cicatrice [sikatris] *f* scar

cicatriser [sikatrize] *tr* to heal; scar ‖ *ref* to heal

Cicéron [siserɔ̃] *m* Cicero

cicérone [siseron] *m* guide

ci-contre [sikɔ̃tr] *adv* opposite, on the opposite page; in the margin

ci-dessous [sidəsu] *adv* further on, below, hereunder

ci-dessus [sidəsy] *adv* above

ci-devant [sidəvɑ̃] *mf invar* (hist) aristocrat; (coll) back number ‖ *adv* previously, formerly

cidre [sidr] *m* cider

Cie *abbr* (**Compagnie**) Co.

ciel [sjɛl] *m* (*pl* **cieux** [sjø]) sky, heavens (*firmament*); heaven (*state of great happiness*) ‖ *m* (*pl* **ciels**) heaven (*abode of the blessed*); sky (*upper atmosphere, especially with reference to meteorological conditions; representation of sky in a painting*); canopy (*of a bed*) ‖ *m* (*pl* **cieux** or **ciels**) clime, sky

cierge [sjɛrʒ] *m* wax candle; cactus; **droit comme un cierge** straight as a ramrod; **en cierge** straight up

cigale [sigal] *f* cicada, grasshopper

cigare [sigar] *m* cigar
cigarette [sigarɛt] *f* cigarette
ci·gît [siʒi] see **gésir**
cigogne [sigɔɲ] *f* stork
ciguë [sigy] *f* hemlock (*herb and poison*)
ci-in·clus [siɛ̃kly] **-cluse** [klyz] *adj* enclosed ‖ **ci-inclus** *adv* enclosed
ci-joint [siʒwɛ̃] **-jointe** [jwɛt] *adj* enclosed ‖ **ci-joint** *adv* enclosed
cil [sil] *m* eyelash; **cils** eyelash (*fringe of hair*)
cilice [silis] *m* hair shirt
ciller [sije] *tr* & *intr* to blink
cime [sim] *f* summit, top
ciment [simɑ̃] *m* cement; **ciment armé** reinforced concrete
cimentation [simɑ̃tɑsjɔ̃] *f* cementing
cimenter [simɑ̃te] *tr* to cement
cimeterre [simtɛr] *m* scimitar
cimetière [simtjɛr] *m* cemetery
cinéaste [sineast] *mf* film producer; movie director; scenarist; movie technician
cinégraphiste [sinegrafist] *mf* scenarist
cinéma [sinema] *m* movies; moving-picture theater; cinema; **cinéma auto** drive-in movie; **cinéma d'essai** preview theater; **cinéma muet** silent movie
cinémathèque [sinematɛk] *f* film library
cinématographique [sinematɔgrafik] *adj* motion-picture, film
ciné-park [sinepark] *m* (*pl* **ciné-parks**) drive-in (movie) theater
cinéphile [sinefil] *mf* movie fan
cinéprojecteur [sineprɔʒɛktœr] *m* motion-picture projector
ciné-roman [sinerɔmɑ̃] *m* (*pl* **-romans**) novelization (*of a film*)
cinétique [sinetik] *adj* kinetic ‖ *f* kinetics
cin·glant [sɛ̃glɑ̃] **-glante** [glɑ̃t] *adj* scathing
cin·glé -glée [sɛ̃gle] *adj* (slang) screwy ‖ *mf* (slang) screwball
cingler [sɛ̃gle] *tr* to whip; cut to the quick ‖ *intr* to go full sail
cinq [sɛ̃(k)] §94 *adj* & *pron* five; the Fifth, e.g., **Jean cinq** John the Fifth; **cinq heures** five o'clock ‖ *m* five; fifth (*in dates*); **il était moins cinq** (coll) it was a close shave
cinquantaine [sɛ̃kɑ̃tɛn] *f* about fifty; age of fifty, fifty mark, fifties
cinquante [sɛ̃kɑ̃t] §94 *adj, pron,* & *m* fifty; **cinquante et un** fifty-one; **cinquante et unième** fifty-first
cinquantième [sɛ̃kɑ̃tjɛm] §94 *adj, pron* (*masc, fem*) & *m* fiftieth
cinquième [sɛ̃kjɛm] §94 *adj, pron* (*masc, fem*) & *m* fifth
cintre [sɛ̃tr] *m* arch; coat hanger; bend; **plein cintre** semicircular arch
cin·tré -trée [sɛ̃tre] *adj* (slang) crazy
cintrer [sɛ̃tre] *tr* to arch, bend
cirage [siraʒ] *m* waxing; shoe polish; **cirage automatique des chaussures** shoeshining in an automatic machine; **dans le cirage** (coll) in the dark
circoncire [sirkɔ̃sir] §66 (*pp* **circoncis**) *tr* to circumcise

circoncision [sirkɔ̃sizjɔ̃] *f* circumcision
circonférence [sirkɔ̃ferɑ̃s] *f* circumference
circonflexe [sirkɔ̃flɛks] *adj* & *m* circumflex
circonscription [sirkɔ̃skripsjɔ̃] *f* circumscription; ward, district
circonscrire [sirkɔ̃skrir] §25 *tr* to circumscribe
circons·pect [sirkɔ̃spɛ], [sirkɔ̃spɛk(t)] **-pecte** [pɛkt] *adj* circumspect
circonstance [sirkɔ̃stɑ̃s] *f* circumstance; **circonstances et dépendances** appurtenances; **de circonstance** proper for the occasion, topical; emergency (*measure*); guest, e.g., **orateur de circonstance** guest speaker
circonstan·cié -ciée [sirkɔ̃stɑ̃sje] *adj* circumstantial, in detail
circonstan·ciel -cielle [sirkɔ̃stɑ̃sjɛl] *adj* (gram) adverbial
circonvenir [sirkɔ̃vnir] §72 *tr* to circumvent
circonvoi·sin [sirkɔ̃vwazɛ̃] **-sine** [zin] *adj* nearby, neighboring
circuit [sirkɥi] *m* circuit; circumference; detour; tour; **circuit d'attente** (aer) holding point; **circuit imprimé** printed circuit
circulaire [sirkylɛr] *adj* & *f* circular
circulation [sirkylɑsjɔ̃] *f* circulation; traffic; **circulation interdite** (public sign) no thoroughfare
circuler [sirkyle] *intr* to circulate; go, move; **circulez au pas!** walk!
cire [sir] *f* wax; **cire à cacheter** sealing wax; **cire molle** (fig) wax in one's hands
ci·ré -rée [sire] *adj* waxed ‖ *m* waterproof garment; raincoat
cirer [sire] *tr* to wax; polish
ci·reur [sirœr] **-reuse** [røz] *mf* waxer, polisher (*person*); shoeblack, bootblack ‖ *f* floor waxer (*machine*)
ci·reux [sirø] **-reuse** [røz] *adj* waxy
ciron [sirɔ̃] *m* mite
cirque [sirk] *m* circus; amphitheater
cirrhose [siroz] *f* cirrhosis
cisaille [sizɑj] *f* metal clippings, scissel; paper cutter; **cisailles** clippers, shears; pruning shears; wire cutter
cisaillement [sizɑjmɑ̃] *m* cutting, clipping, pruning; shearing off; **cisaillement du vent** wind shear
cisailler [sizɑje] *tr* to shear
ci·seau [sizo] *m* (*pl* **-seaux**) chisel; **ciseau à froid** cold chisel; **ciseaux** scissors; **ciseaux à ongles** nail scissors; **ciseaux à raisin** pruning shears; **ciseaux à tondre** sheep shears
ciseler [sizle] §2 *tr* to chisel; chase; cut, shear; prune
ciseleur [sizlœr] *m* chaser, tooler
citadelle [sitadɛl] *f* citadel
cita·din [sitadɛ̃] **-dine** [din] *adj* urban ‖ *mf* city dweller
citation [sitɑsjɔ̃] *f* citation, quotation; citation, summons
cité [site] *f* housing development; (hist) fortified city, citadel; **cité ouvrière** low-cost housing development; **cité sainte** Holy City; **cité universitaire** university dormi-

tory complex; **la Cité** the City (*district within ancient boundaries*)

cité-jardin [siteʒardɛ̃] *f* (*pl* **cités-jardins**) landscaped housing development with parks

citer [site] *tr* to cite, quote; summon, subpoena

citerne [sitɛrn] *f* cistern; tank; **citerne flottante** tanker

cithare [sitar] *f* cither, zither

citoyen [sitwajɛ̃] **citoyenne** [sitwajɛn] *mf* citizen; (coll) individual, person; **citoyens** citizenry

citoyenneté [sitwajɛnte] *f* citizenship; citizenry

citrique [sitrik] *adj* citric

citron [sitrɔ̃] *adj* & *m* lemon

citronnade [sitrɔnad] *f* lemonade

citron·né -née [sitrɔne] *adj* lemon-flavored

citronnelle [sitrɔnɛl] *f* citronella

citronner [sitrɔne] *tr* to flavor with lemon

citronnier [sitrɔnje] *m* lemon tree

citrouille [sitruj] *f* pumpkin, gourd

cive [siv] *f* chive, scallion

civet [sivɛ] *m* stew

civette [sivɛt] *f* civet; civet cat; chive, chives

civière [sivjɛr] *f* stretcher, litter

ci·vil -vile [sivil] *adj* civil; civilian; secular ‖ *m* civilian; layman; **en civil** plainclothes (*person*); in civies

civilisation [sivilizɑsjɔ̃] *f* civilization

civiliser [sivilize] *tr* to civilize ‖ *ref* to become civilized

civilité [sivilite] *f* civility; **civilités** kind regards; amenities

civique [sivik] *adj* civic; civil (*rights*); national (*guard*)

civisme [sivism] *m* good citizenship

clabauder [klabode] *intr* to clamor

claie [klɛ] *f* wickerwork; trellis

clair claire [klɛr] *adj* clear, bright; evident, plain; light, pale ‖ *m* light, brightness; **clair de lune** moonlight; **clairs** highlights ‖ *f* oyster bed

clairance [klɛrɑ̃s] *f* (aer) clearance

clai·ret -rette [klɛrɛ] *adj* light-red; thin, high-pitched (*voice*) ‖ *m* light, red wine ‖ *f* light sparkling wine

claire-voie [klɛrvwa] *f* (*pl* **claires-voies**) latticework, slats; clerestory; **à claire-voie** with open spaces

clairière [klɛrjɛr] *f* clearing, glade

clairon [klɛrɔ̃] *m* bugle; bugler

claironner [klɛrɔne] *tr* to announce ‖ *intr* to sound the bugle

clairse·mé -mée [klɛrsəme] *adj* scattered, sparse; thin, thinned out

clairvoyance [klɛrvwajɑ̃s] *f* clear-sightedness, clairvoyance

clairvoyant [klɛrvwajɑ̃] **clairvoyante** [klɛrvwajɑ̃t] *adj* clear-sighted, clairvoyant

clamer [klame] *tr* & *intr* to cry out

clameur [klamœr] *f* clamor, outcry

clamp [klɑ̃] *m* (med) clamp

clampin [klɑ̃pɛ̃] *m* (mil) straggler

clan [klɑ̃] *m* clan, clique

clandes·tin [klɑ̃dɛstɛ̃] **-tine** [tin] *adj* clandestine

clapet [klapɛ] *m* valve; **ferme ton clapet!** (slang) shut your trap

clapier [klapje] *m* rabbit hutch

clapoter [klapɔte] *intr* to splash; be choppy

claque [klak] *m* opera hat ‖ *f* slap, smack; claque, paid applauders

cla·qué -quée [klake] *adj* dog-tired; sprained

claquement [klakmɑ̃] *m* clapping; slam (*of a door*); chattering (*of teeth*)

claquemurer [klakmyre] *tr* to shut in ‖ *ref* to shut oneself up at home

claquer [klake] *tr* to slap; clap; smack (*the lips*); slam (*the door*); crack (*the whip*); click (*the heels*); snap (*the fingers*); (coll) to tire out; (coll) to waste ‖ *intr* to clap, slap, slam; crack; (slang) to fail; (slang) to die ‖ *ref* to sprain; (slang) to work oneself to death

claquettes [klakɛt] *fpl* tap-dancing

claqueur [klakœr] *m* applauder, member of a claque

clarifier [klarifje] *tr* to clarify ‖ *ref* to become clear

clarine [klarin] *f* cowbell

clarinette [klarinɛt] *f* clarinet

clarté [klarte] *f* clarity; brightness; **clarté du soleil** sunshine

classe [klɑs] *f* class; classroom; **classe de rattrapage** refresher course (*for backward children*); **classe de travaux pratiques** lab class

clas·sé -sée [klɑse] *adj* pigeonholed, tabled; standard (*literary work*); listed; **non classé** (sports) also-ran

classer [klɑse] *tr* to class; sort out, file; pigeonhole, table ‖ *ref* to come in, rank, finish; **se classer premier** (sports) to come in first

classeur [klɑsœr] *m* file (*for letters, documents*); filing cabinet

classicisme [klasisism] *m* classicism

classification [klasifikɑsjɔ̃] *f* classification

classifier [klasifje] *tr* to classify; sort out

classique [klasik] *adj* classic, classical; standard (*author, work*) ‖ *mf* classicist ‖ *m* classic; standard work

claudication [klodikɑsjɔ̃] *f* limping

clause [kloz] *f* clause, stipulation, provision; **clause additionnelle** rider; **clause ambiguë** joker clause; **clause de style** unwritten provision; **clause d'indexation** escalator clause

claustration [klostrɑsjɔ̃] *f* confinement; cloistering

clavecin [klavsɛ̃] *m* harpsichord

claveciniste [klavsinist] *mf* harpsichordist

clavette [klavɛt] *f* pin, cotter pin; key

clavicule [klavikyl] *f* collarbone

clavier [klavje] *m* keyboard; key ring; range (*e.g., of the voice*); **clavier universel** standard keyboard

clayère [klɛjɛr] *f* oyster bed

clé [kle] *f* see **clef**

clef [klɛ] *adj invar* key ‖ *f* key; wrench; (mus) valve; (mus) clef; (wrestling) lock; **clef anglaise** monkey wrench; **clef à tube** socket wrench; **clef crocodile** alligator wrench; **clef d'allumage** ignition key; **clef de fa** bass clef; **clef des champs** vacation; **clef de sol** treble clef; **clef de voûte** keystone; **clef d'ut** tenor clef; **fausse clef** skeleton key; **sous clef** under lock and key

clémence [klemɑ̃s] *f* clemency

clé·ment [klemɑ̃] **-mente** [mɑ̃t] *adj* mild, clement

clenche [klɑ̃ʃ] *f* latch

cleptomane [klɛptɔman] *mf* kleptomaniac

clerc [klɛr] *m* cleric, clergyman; scholar; clerk

clergé [klɛrʒe] *m* clergy

clergie [klɛrʒi] *f* learning, scholarship; clergy

cléri·cal -cale [klerikal] *adj* & *mf* (*pl* **-caux** [ko]) clerical

cliché [kliʃe] *m* cliché; (phot) negative; (typ) plate, stereotype; **prendre un cliché** (phot) to make an exposure

clicher [kliʃe] *tr* (typ) to stereotype

client [klijɑ̃] **cliente** [kljɑ̃t] *mf* client; patient; customer; guest (*of a hotel*)

clientèle [klijɑ̃tɛl] *f* clientele; adherents

clignement [kliɲmɑ̃] *m* blinking

cligner [kliɲe] *tr* to squint (*one's eyes*) ‖ *intr* to squint, blink; **cligner de l'œil à** to wink at

cligno·tant [kliɲɔtɑ̃] **-tante** [tɑ̃t] *adj* blinking ‖ *m* (aut) directional signal

clignotement [kliɲɔtmɑ̃] *m* blinking; twinkling; flickering

clignoter [kliɲɔte] *intr* to blink; twinkle; flicker

clignoteur [kliɲɔtœr] *m* (aut) directional signal

climat [klima], [klimɑ] *m* climate

climatisation [klimatizɑsjɔ̃] *f* air conditioning

climati·sé -sée [klimatize] *adj* air-conditioned

climatiseur [klimatizœr] *m* air conditioner

clin [klɛ̃] *m*—**à clin** (carpentry) overlapping, covering; **clin d'œil** wink; **en un clin d'œil** in the twinkling of an eye

clinicien [klinisjɛ̃] *adj masc* clinical ‖ *m* clinician

clinique [klinik] *adj* clinical ‖ *f* clinic; private hospital

clinquant [klɛ̃kɑ̃] *m* foil, tinsel; flashiness, tawdriness

clip [klip] *m* clip, brooch

clique [klik] *f* drum and bugle corps; (coll) gang; **cliques** wooden shoes

cliquet [klikɛ] *m* (mach) pawl, catch

cliqueter [klikte] §34 *intr* to click, clink, clank, jangle

cliquetis [klikti] *m* click, clink, clank, jangle

cliquette [klikɛt] *f* castanets; (fishing) sinker

clisse [klis] *f* draining rack, wicker bottleholder

clitoris [klitɔris] *m* clitoris

clivage [klivaʒ] *m* cleavage

cliver [klive] *tr* to cleave; cut

cloaque [klɔak] *m* cesspool

clo·chard [klɔʃar] **-charde** [ʃard] *mf* beggar, tramp

cloche [klɔʃ] *adj* bell (*skirt*) ‖ *f* bell; bell; glass; blister (*on skin*); **cloche de plongeur** diving bell; **cloche de sauvetage** escape hatch (*on submarine*); **déménager à la cloche de bois** (coll) to skip out without paying; **la cloche** (slang) beggars

clochement [klɔʃmɑ̃] *m* limp, limping

cloche-pied [klɔʃpje]—**à cloche-pied** on one foot, hopping

clocher [klɔʃe] *m* steeple; belfry; parish, home town; **de clocher** local (*politics*) ‖ *intr* to limp; **quelque chose cloche** something jars, is not right

clocheton [klɔʃtɔ̃] *m* little steeple

clochette [klɔʃɛt] *f* little bell; (bot) bellflower

cloison [klwazɔ̃] *f* partition; division, barrier (*e.g., between classes*); (anat, bot) septum, dividing membrane; (naut) bulkhead; **cloison étanche** (naut) watertight compartment

cloisonner [klwazɔne] *tr* to partition

cloître [klwatr] *m* cloister

cloîtrer [klwatre] *tr* to cloister; confine

clonage [klɔnaʒ] *m* cloning; **faire du clonage** to clone

clone [klɔn] *m* clone

clopin-clopant [klɔpɛ̃klɔpɑ̃] *adv* (coll) so-so; **aller clopin-clopant** (coll) to go hobbling along

clopiner [klɔpine] *intr* to hobble

cloque [klɔk] *f* blister

cloquer [klɔke] *tr* & *intr* to blister

clore [klɔr] §24 *tr* & *intr* to close

clos [klo] **close** [kloz] *adj* closed ‖ *m* enclosure; **clos de vigne** vineyard

clôture [klotyr] *f* fence; wall; cloistered life; closing of an account

clôturer [klotyre] *tr* to enclose, wall in; close out (*an account*); conclude (*a discussion*)

clou [klu] *m* nail; (coll) boil; (coll) jalopy; (coll) feature attraction; (slang) pawnshop; **clou de girofle** clove; **clous** pedestrian crossing; **des clous!** (slang) nothing at all!

clouer [klue] *tr* to nail; immobilize, rivet; **clouer le bec à qn** (coll) to shut s.o.'s mouth

clouter [klute] *tr* to stud; trim or border with studs, e.g., **passage clouté** pedestrian crossing (bordered with studs)

clown [klun] *m* clown; **faire le clown** to clown (around)

clownerie [klunri] *f* high jinks, clowning

club [klyb] *m* (literary) society; (political) association ‖ [klœb] *m* club (*for social and athletic purposes, etc.*); clubhouse; (golf) club; armchair

club-house [klybbaus] *m* clubhouse

clubiste [klybist] *mf* (coll) club member; (coll) joiner

clubman [klœbman] *m* club member

coaccu·sé -sée [kɔakyze] *mf* codefendant

coaguler [koagyle] *tr & ref* to coagulate

coaliser [koalize] *tr* to form into a coalition ‖ *ref* to form a coalition

coalition [koalisjɔ̃] *f* coalition

coassement [kɔasmɑ̃] *m* croak, croaking

coasser [kɔase] *intr* to croak

coasso·cié -ciée [kɔasɔsje] *mf* copartner

coauteur [kɔotœr] *m* coauthor

cobalt [kɔbalt] *m* cobalt

cobaye [kɔbaj] *m* guinea pig

Coca-Cola [kɔkakɔla] *m* (trademark) Coca-Cola

cocaïne [kɔkain] *f* cocaine

cocarde [kɔkard] *f* cockade; rosette of ribbons; **avoir sa cocarde** (coll) to be tipsy; **prendre la cocarde** (coll) to enlist

cocar·dier [kɔkardje] **-dière** [djɛr] *mf* jingoist, chauvinist

cocasse [kɔkas] *adj* (coll) funny, ridiculous

coccinelle [kɔksinɛl] *f* ladybug

coche [kɔʃ] *m* coach, stagecoach; two-door sedan; barge ‖ *f* notch, score; (zool) sow

cocher [kɔʃe] *m* coachman, driver ‖ *tr* to notch, score; check off

cochère [kɔʃɛr] *adj* carriage (*entrance*)

co·chon [kɔʃɔ̃] **-chonne** [ʃɔn] *mf* (coll) skunk, slob ‖ *m* pig, hog; **chochon de lait** suckling pig; **cochon de mer** porpoise; **cochon de phallocrate** (slang) male chauvinist pig; **cochon d'Inde** guinea pig

cochonnerie [kɔʃɔnri] *f* (slang) dirty trick; (slang) filthy speech, smut

cocker [kɔkɛr] *m* cocker spaniel

cockpit [kɔkpit] *m* (aer) cockpit

cocktail [kɔktɛl] *m* cocktail; cocktail party

coco [kɔko], [koko] *m* coconut; licorice water; **mon coco** (coll) my darling; **un joli coco** (coll) a stinker ‖ *f* (slang) cocaine

cocon [kɔkɔ̃] *m* cocoon

cocorico [kɔkɔriko] *m* cockcrow ‖ *interj* cock-a-doodle-doo!

cocotier [kɔkɔtje] *m* coconut tree

cocotte [kɔkɔt] *f* saucepan; cocotte, floozy; **ma cocotte** (coll) my little chick, my baby doll

co·cu -cue [kɔky] *adj & m* cuckold

cocufier [kɔkyfje] *tr* (slang) to cuckold

code [kɔd] *m* code; **code de la route** traffic regulations; **code pénal** criminal code; **codes** (slang) dimmers; **se mettre en code** to dip one's headlights

codex [kɔdɛks] *m* pharmacopoeia

codicille [kɔdisil] *m* codicil

codifier [kɔdifje] *tr* to codify; **codifiez vos adresses postales!** use the zip code!

coéducation [kɔedykasjɔ̃] *f* coeducation

coefficient [koefisjɑ̃] *m* coefficient; **coefficient de sécurité** (aer) safety factor

coéqui·pier [kɔekipje] **-pière** [pjɛr] *mf* teammate; running mate (*of a political candidate*)

coercition [koɛrsisjɔ̃] *f* coercion

cœur [kœr] *m* heart; core; courage, spirit; bosom, breast; depth (*of winter*); (cards) heart; (cards) hearts; **à cœur joie** to one's heart's content; **avoir du cœur** to be kind-hearted; **avoir du cœur au ventre** (coll) to have guts; **avoir le cœur sur la main** (coll) to be open-handed; **avoir le cœur sur les lèvres** to wear one's heart on one's sleeve; **cœur de bronze** heart of stone; **de bon cœur** willingly, heartily; **de mauvais cœur** reluctantly; **en avoir le cœur net** to get to the bottom of it; **épancher son cœur** to open one's heart to; **fendre le cœur à** to break the heart of; **le cœur gros** with a heavy heart; **mal au cœur, mal de cœur** stomach ache; nausea; **par cœur** by heart; **prendre à cœur** to take to heart; **se ronger le cœur** to eat one's heart out; **soulever le cœur** to turn the stomach

coexistence [koegzistɑ̃s] *f* coexistence

coexister [koegziste] *intr* to coexist

coffre [kɔfr] *m* chest; coffer, bin; safe-deposit box; trunk (*of car*); buoy (*for mooring*); cofferdam

coffre-fort [kɔfrəfɔr] *m* (*pl* **coffres-forts**) safe, strongbox, vault

coffret [kɔfrɛ] *m* gift box

cognac [kɔɲnak] *m* cognac

cognat [kɔɲa] *m* blood kin

cognée [kɔɲe] *f* ax, hatchet

cogner [kɔɲe] *tr, intr, & ref* to knock, bump

cohabiter [kɔabite] *intr* to cohabit

cohé·rent [kɔerã] **-rente** [rãt] *adj* coherent

cohériter [kɔerite] *intr* to inherit jointly

cohéri·tier [kɔeritje] **-tière** [tjɛr] *mf* coheir

cohésion [kɔesjɔ̃] *f* cohesion

cohorte [kɔɔrt] *f* cohort

cohue [kɔy] *f* crowd, throng, mob

coi [kwa] **coite** [kwat] *adj* quiet; **demeurer coi, se tenir coi** to keep still

coiffe [kwaf] *f* cap; headdress; caul

coif·fé -fée [kwafe] *adj*—**coiffé de** wearing (*a hat*); (fig) crazy about (*a person*); **être coiffé** to be wearing a hairdo; **être né coiffé** (fig) to be lucky

coiffer [kwafe] *tr* to put a hat or cap on (*s.o.*); dress or do the hair of; to have overall responsibility for; (mil) to reach (*an objective*) ‖ *intr*—**coiffer de** to wear (*a certain size hat*) ‖ *ref* to do one's hair; **se coiffer de** (coll) to set one's cap for

coif·feur [kwafœr] **-feuse** [føz] *mf* hairdresser; barber; **coiffeur pour dames** coiffeur ‖ *f* dresser, dressing table

coiffure [kwafyr] *f* coiffure; headdress; **coiffure en brosse** crew cut

coin [kwɛ̃] *m* corner; angle; nook; wedge; coin; stamp, die (*for coining money*); (typ) quoin; **coin de détente, coin de retraite** den; **le petit coin** (coll) the powder room

coinçage [kwɛ̃saʒ] *m* wedging

coincer [kwɛ̃se] §51 *tr* to wedge, jam; (coll) to pinch, arrest ‖ *ref* to jam

coïncidence [kɔɛ̃sidɑ̃s] *f* coincidence

coïncider [kɔɛ̃side] *intr* to coincide

coin-coin [kwɛ̃kwɛ̃] *m invar* quack (*of duck*); toot (*of horn*)

coing [kwɛ̃] *m* quince

coït [kɔit] *m* coition, coitus

coke [kɔk] *m* coke (*coal*)

cokéfier [kɔkefje] *tr & ref* to coke

col [kɔl] *m* neck (*of bottle; of womb*); collar (*of dress*); mountain pass; (coll) head (*on beer*); **col blanc** white-collar worker; **col de fourrure** neckpiece; **col roulé** turtleneck; **faux col** detachable collar

colback [kɔlbak] *m* busby

colère [kɔlɛr] *f* anger; **en colère** angry; **se mettre en colère** to become angry

colé·reux [kɔlerø] **-reuse** [røz] *adj* irascible, choleric

colérique [kɔlerik] *adj* choleric

colibri [kɔlibri] *m* hummingbird

colifichet [kɔlifiʃɛ] *m* knickknack, trinket

colimaçon [kɔlimasɔ̃] *m* snail; **en colimaçon** spiral

colin [kɔlɛ̃] *m* hake

colin-maillard [kɔlɛ̃majar] *m* blindman's buff

colique [kɔlik] *f* colic

colis [kɔli] *m* piece of baggage, package, parcel; **colis postal** parcel post

colisée [kɔlize] *m* coliseum

colis·tier [kɔlistje] **-tière** [tjɛr] *mf* (pol) running mate

collabora·teur [kɔlabɔratœr] **-trice** [tris] *mf* collaborator; contributor

collaborationniste [kɔlabɔrasjɔnist] *mf* collaborationist

collaborer [kɔlabɔre] *intr* to collaborate; **collaborer à** to contribute to

collage [kɔlaʒ] *m* pasting, mounting; collage; sizing; clarifying (*of wine*); (coll) common-law marriage

col·lant [kɔlɑ̃] **-lante** [lɑ̃t] *adj* sticky; tight, close-fitting ‖ *m* tights; panty hose

collapsus [kɔlapsys] *m* (pathol) collapse

collaté·ral -rale [kɔllateral] (*pl* **-raux** [ro]) *adj* collateral; parallel; intermediate (*points of the compass*) ‖ *mf* collateral (*relative*) ‖ *m* side aisle of a church

collation [kɔllasjɔ̃] *f* conferring (*of titles, degrees, etc.*); collation (*of texts*) ‖ [kɔlasjɔ̃] *f* snack

collationner [kɔllasjɔne] *tr* to collate, to compare; **faire collationner un télégramme** to request a copy of a telegram ‖ *intr* to have a snack

colle [kɔl] *f* paste, glue; (coll) brain teaser, stickler; (slang) detention; (slang) oral exam; (slang) flunking; **colle forte** glue; **poser une colle** (slang) to ask a hard one

collecte [kɔlɛkt] *f* collection (*for charitable cause*); (eccl) collect

collecteur [kɔlɛktœr] *adj* main, e.g., **égout collecteur** main sewer ‖ *m* collector; commutator (*of motor or dynamo*); (aut) manifold; **collecteur d'ondes** aerial

collec·tif [kɔlɛktif] **-tive** [tiv] *adj* collective

collection [kɔlɛksjɔ̃] *f* collection

collectionner [kɔlɛksjɔne] *tr* to collect

collection·neur [kɔlɛksjɔnœr] **-neuse** [nøz] *mf* collector

collège [kɔlɛʒ] *m* high school; preparatory school; college (*of cardinals, electors, etc.*); **collège universitaire** junior college

collé·gial -giale [kɔleʒjal] (*pl* **-giaux** [ʒjo]) *adj* collegiate ‖ *f* collegiate church

collé·gien [kɔleʒjɛ̃] **-gienne** [ʒjɛn] *adj* highschool ‖ *m* schoolboy ‖ *f* schoolgirl; coed

collègue [kɔllɛg] *mf* colleague

coller [kɔle] *tr* to paste, stick, glue; clarify (*wine*); mat (*e.g., with blood*); (coll) to floor, stump; (coll) to punish (*a pupil*); (coll) to flunk; (coll) to sock (*e.g., on the jaw*) ‖ *intr* to cling, fit tightly (*said of dress*); (coll) to stick close; **ça colle!** (slang) O.K.! ‖ *ref* (slang) to have a common-law marriage; **se coller contre** to stand close to; cling to

collet [kɔlɛ] *m* collar; neck (*of person; of tooth*); neck, scrag (*e.g., of mutton*); cape; snare; stalk and roots; lasso, noose; **collet monté** (coll) stuffed shirt

colleter [kɔlte] §34 *tr* to collar; ‖ *ref* to fight, scuffle

collier [kɔlje] *m* necklace; collar; dog collar; horse collar; **à collier** ring-necked; **reprendre le collier** (coll) to get back into harness

colliger [kɔlliʒe] §38 *tr* to make a collection of

colline [kɔlin] *f* hill

collision [kɔllizjɔ̃] *f* collision; **collision manquée** near collision, near miss

colloï·dal -dale [kɔllɔidal] *adj* (*pl* **-daux** [do]) colloid, colloidal

colloïde [kɔllɔid] *m* colloid

colloque [kɔllɔk] *m* colloquy, symposium

colloquer [kɔllɔke] *tr* to classify (*creditors' claims*); **colloquer q.ch. à qn** (coll) to palm off s.th. on s.o.

collusion [kɔllyzjɔ̃] *f* collusion

collyre [kɔllir] *m* (med) eyewash

Cologne [kɔlɔɲ] *f* Cologne

Colomb [kɔlɔ̃] *m* Columbus

colombe [kɔlɔ̃b] *f* dove

Colombie [kɔlɔ̃bi] *f* Columbia; **la Colombie** Colombia

colombier [kɔlɔ̃bje] *m* dovecote; large-size paper

colom·bin [kɔlɔ̃bɛ̃] **-bine** [bin] *adj* columbine ‖ *m* stock dove; lead ore ‖ *f* bird droppings; (bot) columbine

colon [kɔlɔ̃] *m* colonist; tenant farmer; summer camper

côlon [kolɔ̃] *m* (anat) colon

colonel [kɔlɔnɛl] *m* colonel

colonelle [kɔlɔnɛl] *f* colonel's wife; (theat) performance for the press

colonie [kɔlɔni] *f* colony; **colonie de déportation** penal settlement; **colonie de vacances** summer camp

coloniser [kɔlɔnize] *tr* to colonize

colonnade [kɔlɔnad] *f* colonnade

colonne [kɔlɔn] *f* column; pillar; **cinquième colonne** fifth column; **colonne vertébrale** spinal column

colophane [kɔlɔfan] *f* rosin
colophon [kɔlɔfɔ̃] *m* colophon
colo·rant [kɔlɔrɑ̃] **-rante** [rɑ̃t] *adj* coloring ‖ *m* dye, stain
colorer [kɔlɔre] *tr* & *ref* to color
colorier [kɔlɔrje] *tr* to paint, color
coloris [kɔlɔri] *m* hue; brilliance
colos·sal -sale [kɔlɔsal] *adj* (*pl* **-saux** [so]) colossal
colosse [kɔlɔs] *m* colossus
colporter [kɔlpɔrte] *tr* to peddle
colporteur [kɔlpɔrtœr] *m* peddler
coltiner [kɔltine] *tr* to lug on one's back or on one's head
coma [kɔma] *m* (pathol) coma
coma·teux [kɔmatø] **-teuse** [tøz] *adj* comatose ‖ *mf* person in a coma
combat [kɔ̃ba] *m* combat; **combat tournoyant** (aer) dogfight; **combat rapproché** (mil) close combat; **hors de combat** disabled
comba·tif [kɔ̃batif] **-tive** [tiv] *adj* combative
combat·tant [kɔ̃batɑ̃] **-tante** [tɑ̃t] *adj* & *mf* combatant; **anciens combattants** veterans
combattre [kɔ̃batr] §7 *tr* & *intr* to combat
combien [kɔ̃bjɛ̃] *adv* how much, how many; how far; how long; how, e.g., **combien il était brave!** how brave he was! ‖ *m invar*—**du combien chaussez-vous?** what size shoes do you wear?; **du combien coiffez-vous?** what size hat do you wear?; **le combien?** which one (*in a series*)?; **le combien êtes-vous?** (coll) what rank do you have?; **le combien sommes-nous?** (coll) what day of the month is it?; **tous les combien?** how often?
combinaison [kɔ̃binɛzɔ̃] *f* combination; jump suit; coveralls; slip, undergarment
combi·né -née [kɔ̃bine] *adj* combined ‖ *m* French telephone, handset; radio phonograph
combiner [kɔ̃bine] *tr* to combine; arrange, group; concoct (*a scheme*) ‖ *ref* (chem) to combine
comble [kɔ̃bl] *adj* full, packed ‖ *m* summit; roof, coping; **au comble de** at the height of; **c'est le comble!, c'est un comble!** (coll) that's the limit!, that takes the cake!; **sous les combles** in the attic
combler [kɔ̃ble] *tr* to heap up; fill to the brim; overwhelm; **combler d'honneurs** to shower honors upon
combustible [kɔ̃bystibl] *adj* & *m* combustible, fuel
combustion [kɔ̃bystjɔ̃] *f* combustion
comédie [kɔmedi] *f* comedy; play; sham
comé·dien [kɔmedjɛ̃] **-dienne** [djɛn] *mf* comedian; actor; hypocrite; **comédien ambulant** strolling player ‖ *f* comedienne; actress
comédon [kɔmedɔ̃] *m* blackhead
comestible [kɔmɛstibl] *adj* edible ‖ **comestibles** *mpl* foodstuffs
comète [kɔmɛt] *f* comet

comique [kɔmik] *adj* comic ‖ *m* comedian, comic; humorist, writer of comedies; comic aspect of the situation
comité [kɔmite] *m* committee
commandant [kɔmɑ̃dɑ̃] *m* commandant, commander; major
commande [kɔmɑ̃d] *f* order (*for goods or services*); control, command; **à la commande** (paid) down; **commande à distance** remote control; **commande postale** mail order; **commandes de vol** flight controls; **de commande** operating; (**fait**) **sur commande** (made) to order
commandement [kɔmɑ̃dəmɑ̃] *m* command, order; commandment
commander [kɔmɑ̃de] §97, §98 *tr* to order (*goods or services*); command, order ‖ *intr* (mil) to command; **commander à** to control, have command over; **commander à qn de** + *inf* to order s.o. to + *inf* ‖ *ref* to control oneself
commanditaire [kɔmɑ̃diter] *adj* sponsoring ‖ *mf* (com) sponsor, backer
commandite [kɔmɑ̃dit] *f* joint-stock company
commanditer [kɔmɑ̃dite] *tr* to back, to finance; (rad, telv) to sponsor
comme [kɔm] *adv* as; how; **comme ci comme ça** so-so ‖ *prep* as, like ‖ *conj* as; since
commémoratifs [kɔmemɔratif] *mpl* (phila) commemoratives
commémorer [kɔmmemɔre] *tr* to commemorate
commen·çant [kɔmɑ̃sɑ̃] **-çante** [sɑ̃t] *mf* beginner
commencement [kɔmɑ̃smɑ̃] *m* beginning
commencer [kɔmɑ̃se] §51, §96, §97 *tr* & *intr* to begin; **commencer à** to begin to
comment [kɔmɑ̃] *m invar* how; wherefore ‖ *adv* how; why; **mais comment donc!** by all means!; **n'importe comment** any way ‖ *interj* what!; indeed!
commentaire [kɔmɑ̃ter] *m* commentary; unfriendly comment
commenta·teur [kɔmɑ̃tatœr] **-trice** [tris] *mf* commentator
commenter [kɔmɑ̃te] *tr* to comment on; make a commentary on; criticize
commérage [kɔmeraʒ] *m* (coll) gossip
commer·çant [kɔmɛrsɑ̃] **-çante** [sɑ̃t] *adj* commercial, business ‖ *mf* merchant, dealer
commerce [kɔmɛrs] *m* commerce, trade; business, store; merchants
commercer [kɔmɛrse] §51 *intr* to trade
commer·cial -ciale [kɔmɛrsjal] *adj* (*pl* **-ciaux** [sjo] **-ciales**) commercial ‖ *f* station wagon
commercialisation [kɔmɛrsjalizɑsjɔ̃] *f* marketing
commercialiser [kɔmɛrsjalize] *tr* to commercialize
commère [kɔmɛr] *f* (coll) busybody, gossip
commettre [kɔmɛtr] §42 *tr* to commit; compromise ‖ *ref* to compromise oneself

commis [kɔmi] *m* clerk; **commis voyageur** traveling salesman

commisération [kɔmizerɑsjɔ̃] *f* commiseration

commissaire [kɔmisɛr] *m* commissioner; commissary

commissaire-priseur [kɔmisɛrprizœr] *m* (*pl* **commissaires-priseurs**) appraiser; auctioneer

commissariat [kɔmisarja] *m* commissariat; **commissariat de police** police station

commission [kɔmisjɔ̃] *f* commission; errand; committee

commissionnaire [kɔmisjɔnɛr] *m* agent, broker; messenger

commissionner [kɔmisjɔne] *tr* to commission

commissure [kɔmisyr] *f* corner (*of lips*)

commode [kɔmɔd] *adj* convenient; comfortable; easygoing ‖ *f* chest of drawers, bureau

commodité [kɔmɔdite] *f* comfort, accommodation; **à votre commodité** at your convenience; **commodités** comfort station; utilities

commotion [kɔmosjɔ̃] *f* commotion; concussion; shock

commotionner [kɔmosjɔne] *tr* to shake up, injure, shock

commuer [kɔmɥe] *tr* (law) to commute

com·mun [kɔmœ̃] **com·mune** [kɔmyn] *adj* common ‖ *m* common run ‖ *f* see **commune**

commu·nal -nale [kɔmynal] (*pl* **-naux** [no]) *adj* communal, common ‖ *mpl* common property, commons

communautaire [kɔmynotɛr] *adj* communal

communauté [kɔmynote] *f* community; joint estate (*of husband and wife*); **Communauté économique européenne** Common Market; **communauté familiale** extended family

commune [kɔmyn] *f* commune; **communes** Commons

commu·niant [kɔmynjɑ̃] **-niante** [njɑ̃t] *mf* communicant

communicable [kɔmynikabl] *adj* communicable

communi·cant [kɔmynikɑ̃] **-cante** [kɑ̃t] *adj* communicating

communica·teur [kɔmynikatœr] **-trice** [tris] *adj* connecting (*wire*) ‖ *m* broadcaster

communica·tif [kɔmynikatif] **-tive** [tiv] *adj* communicative; infectious (*laughter*)

communication [kɔmynikɑsjɔ̃] *f* communication; telephone call; (telp) connection; **communication avec avis d'appel** (telp) messenger call; **communication avec préavis** person-to-person call; **communication payable à l'arrivée, communication P.C.V.** collect call; **en communication** in touch; **fausse communication** (telp) wrong number; **vous avez la communication!** (telp) go ahead!

communier [kɔmynje] *intr* to take communion; have a common bond of sympathy, be in accord

communion [kɔmynjɔ̃] *f* communion

communiqué [kɔmynike] *m* communiqué

communiquer [kɔmynike] *tr* & *intr* to communicate

communi·sant [kɔmynizɑ̃] **-sante** [zɑ̃t] *adj* fellow-traveling ‖ *mf* fellow traveler

communisme [kɔmynism] *m* communism

communiste [kɔmynist] *adj* & *mf* communist

commutateur [kɔmytatœr] *m* (elec) change-over switch, two-way switch

commutation [kɔmytɑsjɔ̃] *f* commutation

commutatrice [kɔmytatris] *f* (elec) rotary converter

com·pact -pacte [kɔ̃pakt] *adj* compact

compagne [kɔ̃paɲ] *f* companion; helpmate

compagnie [kɔ̃paɲi] *f* company; **compagnie aérienne de transport régulier** scheduled airline; **de compagnie, en compagnie** together; **fausser compagnie à** to give (*s.o.*) the slip; **tenir compagnie à** to keep (*s.o.*) company

compagnon [kɔ̃paɲɔ̃] *m* companion; journeyman; **compagnon d'armes** comrade in arms; **compagnon de jeu** playmate; **compagnon de route** fellow traveler; **compagnon d'infortune** fellow sufferer; **joyeux compagnon** good fellow

comparaison [kɔ̃parɛzɔ̃] *f* comparison; **en comparaison de** compared to; **par comparaison** in comparison; **sans comparaison** beyond comparison

comparaître [kɔ̃parɛtr] §12 *intr* (law) to appear (in court)

compara·tif [kɔ̃paratif] **-tive** [tiv] *adj* & *m* comparative

compa·ré -rée [kɔ̃pare] *adj* comparative

comparer [kɔ̃pare] *tr* to compare

comparoir [kɔ̃parwar] (used only in; *inf; ger* **comparant**) *intr* (law) to appear in court

comparse [kɔ̃pars] *mf* (theat) walk-on; (fig) nobody, unimportant person

compartiment [kɔ̃partimɑ̃] *m* compartment

comparution [kɔ̃parysjɔ̃] *f* appearance in court

compas [kɔ̃pa] *m* compasses (*for drawing circles*); calipers; (naut) compass; **avoir le compas dans l'œil** to have a sharp eye

compas·sé -sée [kɔ̃pase] *adj* stiff, studied

compasser [kɔ̃pase] *tr* to measure out, lay off; **compasser ses discours** to speak like a book

compassion [kɔ̃pɑsjɔ̃] *f* compassion

compatibilité [kɔ̃patibilite] *f* compatibility

compatir [kɔ̃patir] *intr*—**compatir à** to take pity on, feel for; be indulgent toward; share in (*s.o.'s bereavement*); **ne pouvoir compatir** to be unable to agree

compatis·sant [kɔ̃patisɑ̃] **-sante** [sɑ̃t] *adj* compassionate, sympathetic, indulgent

compatriote [kɔ̃patriɔt] *mf* compatriot

compensa·teur [kɔ̃pɑ̃satœr] **-trice** [tris] *adj* compensating, equalizing

compensation [kɔ̃pɑ̃sɑsjɔ̃] *f* compensation
compenser [kɔ̃pɑ̃se] *tr* to compensate; compensate for ‖ *ref* to balance each other
compérage [kɔ̃peraʒ] *m* complicity
compère [kɔ̃pɛr] *m* accomplice; comrade; stooge (*for a clown*)
compétence [kɔ̃petɑ̃s] *f* competence, proficiency; (law) jurisdiction
compé·tent [kɔ̃petɑ̃] **-tente** [tɑ̃t] *adj* competent, proficient; (law) having jurisdiction, expert
compéter [kɔ̃pete] §10 *intr*—**compéter à** to belong to by right; be within the competency of (*a court*)
compéti·teur [kɔ̃petitœr] **-trice** [tris] *mf* rival, competitor
compétition [kɔ̃petisjɔ̃] *f* competition
compila·teur [kɔ̃pilatœr] **-trice** [tris] *mf* plagiarist ‖ *m* (comp) compiler
compilation [kɔ̃pilɑsjɔ̃] *f* compilation
compiler [kɔ̃pile] *tr* to compile
complainte [kɔ̃plɛ̃t] *f* sad ballad; (law) complaint
complaire [kɔ̃plɛr] §52 *intr* to please, gratify; **complaire à** to please, gratify, e.g., **les fils complaisent au père** the sons (try to) please the father ‖ §96 *ref* (*pp* **complu** *invar*)—**se complaire à** to take pleasure in
complaisance [kɔ̃plɛzɑ̃s] *f* compliance; courtesy; complacency; **auriez-vous la complaisance de . . . ?** would you be so kind as to . . . ?; **de complaisance** out of kindness
complai·sant [kɔ̃plɛzɑ̃] **-sante** [zɑ̃t] *adj* complaisant, obliging; complacent
complément [kɔ̃plemɑ̃] *m* complement; (gram) object; **complément d'attribution** (gram) indirect object
com·plet [kɔ̃plɛ] **-plète** [plɛt] *adj* complete, full; **c'est complet!** that's the last straw! ‖ *m* suit (*of clothes*); **au complet** full (*house*); **au grand complet** at full strength
complètement [kɔ̃plɛtmɑ̃] *adv* completely; right through from cover to cover
compléter [kɔ̃plete] §10 *tr* to complete ‖ *ref* to be completed; complement one another
complet-veston [kɔ̃plɛvɛstɔ̃] *m* (*pl* **complets-veston**) man's suit
complexe [kɔ̃plɛks] *adj* & *m* complex; **complexe de culpabilité** guilt complex
complexé complexée [kɔ̃plɛkse] *adj* (coll) timid, withdrawn ‖ *mf* person with complexes
complexion [kɔ̃plɛksjɔ̃] *f* constitution, disposition
complication [kɔ̃plikɑsjɔ̃] *f* complication
complice [kɔ̃plis] *adj* accessory, abetting ‖ *mf* accomplice; **complice d'adultère** corespondent
complicité [kɔ̃plisite] *f* complicity
compliment [kɔ̃plimɑ̃] *m* compliment
complimenter [kɔ̃plimɑ̃te] *tr* to compliment; congratulate
complimen·teur [kɔ̃plimɑ̃tœr] **-teuse** [tøz] *adj* complimentary ‖ *mf* flatterer, yes man
compli·qué -quée [kɔ̃plike] *adj* complicated

compliquer [kɔ̃plike] *tr* to complicate ‖ *ref* to become complicated; have complications
complot [kɔ̃plo] *m* plot, conspiracy
comploter [kɔ̃plɔte] *tr* & *intr* to plot, conspire
comploteur [kɔ̃plɔtœr] *m* conspirator
comportement [kɔ̃pɔrtəmɑ̃] *m* behavior
comporter [kɔ̃pɔrte] *tr* to permit; include ‖ *ref* to behave
compo·sant [kɔ̃pozɑ̃] **-sante** [zɑ̃t] *adj* constituent ‖ *m* (chem) component ‖ *f* (mech) component
compo·sé -sée [kɔ̃poze] *adj* & *m* compound
composer [kɔ̃poze] *tr* to compose; compound; dial (*a telephone number*) ‖ *intr* to take an exam; come to terms ‖ *ref*—**se composer de** to be composed of
composi·teur [kɔ̃pozitœr] **-trice** [tris] *mf* composer; compositor; **amiable compositeur** (law) arbitrator
composition [kɔ̃pozisjɔ̃] *f* composition; compound; dialing (*of telephone number*); term paper; **composition programmée** (printing) computer composition; **de bonne composition** easygoing, reasonable; **entrer en composition** to reach an agreement
composteur [kɔ̃pɔstœr] *m* composing stick; dating and numbering machine, dating stamp
compote [kɔ̃pɔt] *f* compote; **compote de pommes** applesauce
compotier [kɔ̃pɔtje] *m* compote (*dish*)
compréhensible [kɔ̃preɑ̃sibl] *adj* comprehensible
compréhen·sif [kɔ̃preɑ̃sif] **-sive** [siv] *adj* understanding; comprehensive
compréhension [kɔ̃preɑ̃sjɔ̃] *f* comprehension, understanding
comprendre [kɔ̃prɑ̃dr] §56 *tr* to understand; comprehend, include, comprise ‖ *intr* to understand ‖ *ref* to be understood; be included
compresse [kɔ̃prɛs] *f* (med) compress
compresseur [kɔ̃presœr] *m* compressor
compression [kɔ̃presjɔ̃] *f* compression; repression; reduction
compri·mé -mée [kɔ̃prime] *adj* compressed ‖ *m* (pharm) tablet, lozenge
comprimer [kɔ̃prime] *tr* to compress; repress
com·pris [kɔ̃pri] **-prise** [priz] *adj* understood; included, including, e.g., **la ferme comprise** or **y compris la ferme** the farm included, including the farm
compromet·tant [kɔ̃prɔmetɑ̃] **-tante** [tɑ̃t] *adj* compromising, incriminating
compromettre [kɔ̃prɔmɛtr] §42 *tr* to compromise ‖ *intr* to submit to arbitration ‖ *ref* to compromise oneself
compromis [kɔ̃prɔmi] *m* compromise
comptabiliser [kɔ̃tabilize] *tr* (com) to enter into the books
comptabilité [kɔ̃tabilite] *f* bookkeeping, accounting; accounting department, accounts; **comptabilité à partie double**

double-entry bookkeeping; **comptabilité simple** single-entry bookkeeping; **tenir la comptabilité** to keep the books
comptable [kɔ̃tabl] *adj* accountable, responsible; accounting (*machine*) ‖ *mf* bookkeeper; **comptable agréé** or **expert comptable** certified public accountant; **comptable contrôleur** auditor
comp·tant [kɔ̃tɑ̃] **-tante** [tɑ̃t] *adj* spot (*cash*); down, e.g., **argent comptant** cash down ‖ *m*—**au comptant** cash, for cash ‖ **comptant** *adv* cash (down), e.g., **payer comptant** to pay cash
compte [kɔ̃t] *m* account; accounting; (sports) count; **à bon compte** cheap; **à ce compte** in that case; **à compte** on account; **au bout du compte** or **en fin de compte** when all is said and done; **compte à rebours** countdown; **compte courant** current account; charge account; **compte de couverture** margin account; **compte de dépôt** checking account; **compte de profits et pertes** profit and loss statement; **compte en banque** bank account; **compte rendu** report, review; **compte rond** round numbers; **donner son compte à** to give the final paycheck to, to discharge; **être en compte à demi** to go fifty-fifty; **loin de compte** wide of the mark; **rendre compte de** to review; **se rendre compte de** to realize, to be aware of; **tenir compte de** to bear in mind
compte-fils [kɔ̃tfil] *m invar* cloth prover
compte-gouttes [kɔ̃tgut] *m invar* dropper; **au compte-gouttes** in driblets
compte-minutes [kɔ̃tminyt] *m invar* timer
compter [kɔ̃te] §95 *tr* to count; number, have; **compter** + *inf* to count on + *ger*; **sans compter** not to mention ‖ *intr* to count; **à compter de** starting from; **compter avec** to reckon with; **compter sur** to count on
compte-tours [kɔ̃tatur] *m invar* tachometer, r.p.m. counter
comp·teur [kɔ̃tœr] **-teuse** [tøz] *mf* counter, checker (*person*) ‖ *m* meter; counter; speedometer; **compteur de gaz** gas meter; **compteur de Geiger** Geiger counter; **compteur de stationnement** parking meter; **relever le compteur** to read the meter
compteur-indicateur [kɔ̃tœrɛ̃dikatœr] *m* (*pl* **compteurs-indicateurs**) speedometer
comptine [kɔ̃tin] *f* counting-out rhyme
comptoir [kɔ̃twar] *m* counter; branch bank; bank; **comptoir postal** mail-order house
compulser [kɔ̃pylse] *tr* to go through, examine (*books, papers, etc.*)
computer [kɔ̃pyte] *tr* to compute
comte [kɔ̃t] *m* count
comté [kɔ̃te] *m* county
comtesse [kɔ̃tɛs] *f* countess
con [kɔ̃] *m* (vulg) vagina; (vulg) stupid and contemptible person
concasser [kɔ̃kase] *tr* to crush, pound
concasseur [kɔ̃kasœr] *adj masc* crushing ‖ *m* (mach) crusher

concave [kɔ̃kav] *adj* concave
concéder [kɔ̃sede] §10 *tr* & *intr* to concede
concentration [kɔ̃sɑ̃trɑsjɔ̃] *f* concentration
concentrationnaire [kɔ̃sɑ̃trɑsjɔnɛr] *adj* concentration-camp, in concentration camps
concen·tré -trée [kɔ̃sɑ̃tre] *adj* concentrated; condensed (*milk*); reserved (*person*)
concentrer [kɔ̃sɑ̃tre] *tr* to concentrate; re-press, hold back
concentrique [kɔ̃sɑ̃trik] *adj* concentric
concept [kɔ̃sɛpt] *m* concept
conception [kɔ̃sɛpsjɔ̃] *f* conception; **l'Immaculée Conception** (rel) the Immaculate Conception
concerner [kɔ̃sɛrne] *tr* to concern; **en ce qui concerne** concerning
concert [kɔ̃sɛr] *m* concert; **de concert** together, in concert
concer·tant [kɔ̃sɛrtɑ̃] **-tante** [tɑ̃t] *adj* performing together ‖ *mf* (mus) performer
concerter [kɔ̃sɛrte] *tr* & *ref* to concert, plan
concertiste [kɔ̃sɛrtist] *mf* concert performer
concession [kɔ̃sɛsjɔ̃] *f* concession
concessionnaire [kɔ̃sɛsjɔnɛr] *mf* grantee, licensee; dealer (*in automobiles*); agent (*for insurance*)
concetti [kɔ̃tʃɛti] *mpl* conceits
concevable [kɔ̃səvabl] *adj* conceivable
concevoir [kɔ̃səvwar] §59 *tr* to conceive; compose (*a letter, telegram*)
concierge [kɔ̃sjɛrʒ] *mf* concierge, building superintendent
concile [kɔ̃sil] *m* (eccl) council
concilia·teur [kɔ̃siljatœr] **-trice** [tris] *adj* conciliating ‖ *mf* conciliator
conciliatoire [kɔ̃siljatwar] *adj* conciliatory
concilier [kɔ̃silje] *tr* to reconcile (*two parties, two ideas, etc.*); win (*e.g., favor*) ‖ *ref* to win, gain (*friendship, esteem*)
con·cis [kɔ̃si] **-cise** [siz] *adj* concise
concitoyen [kɔ̃sitwajɛ̃] **concitoyenne** [kɔ̃sitwajɛn] *mf* fellow citizen
concluant [kɔ̃klyɑ̃] **concluante** [kɔ̃klyɑ̃t] *adj* conclusive
conclure [kɔ̃klyr] §11 *tr* to conclude ‖ *intr* to conclude; **conclure à** to decide on, decide in favor of
conclusion [kɔ̃klyzjɔ̃] *f* conclusion
concombre [kɔ̃kɔ̃br] *m* cucumber
concomi·tant [kɔ̃kɔmitɑ̃] **-tante** [tɑ̃t] *adj* concomitant
concordance [kɔ̃kɔrdɑ̃s] *f* agreement; concordance (*of Bible*)
concor·dant [kɔ̃kɔrdɑ̃] **-dante** [dɑ̃t] *adj* in agreement; supporting (*evidence*)
concorde [kɔ̃kɔrd] *f* concord
concorder [kɔ̃kɔrde] *intr* to agree
concourir [kɔ̃kurir] §14, §96 *intr* to compete; cooperate; converge, concur
concours [kɔ̃kur] *m* crowd; cooperation; contest, competition, meet; competitive examination; **concours de beauté** beauty contest; **concours de créanciers** meeting of creditors; **concours hippique** horse show; **hors concours** not competing; in a class by itself

con·cret [kɔ̃krɛ] **-crète** [krɛt] *adj & m* concrete

concrétiser [kɔ̃kretize] *tr* to put in concrete form

con·çu -çue [kɔ̃sy] *v* see **concevoir**

concubine [kɔ̃kybin] *f* concubine

concurrence [kɔ̃kyrɑ̃s] *f* competition; competitors; **jusqu'à concurrence de** to the amount of; **libre concurrence** free enterprise

concurrencer [kɔ̃kyrɑ̃se] §51 *tr* to rival, compete with

concur·rent [kɔ̃kyrɑ̃] **-rente** [rɑ̃t] *adj* competitive ‖ *mf* competitor; contestant

concurren·tiel -tielle [kɔ̃kyrɑ̃sjɛl] *adj* competitive

concussion [kɔ̃kysjɔ̃] *f* extortion; embezzlement

condamnable [kɔ̃dɑnabl] *adj* blameworthy

condamnation [kɔ̃dɑnɑsjɔ̃] *f* condemnation; conviction, sentence

condam·né -née [kɔ̃dɑne] *mf* convict

condamner [kɔ̃dɑne] §96, §100 *tr* to condemn; give up (*an incurable patient*); forbid the use of; board up (*a window*); batten down (*the hatches*)

condensateur [kɔ̃dɑ̃satœr] *m* (elec) condenser

condenser [kɔ̃dɑ̃se] *tr & ref* to condense

condenseur [kɔ̃dɑ̃sœr] *m* condenser

condescendance [kɔ̃desɑ̃dɑ̃s] *f* condescension

condescen·dant [kɔ̃desɑ̃dɑ̃] **-dante** [dɑ̃t] *adj* condescending

condescendre [kɔ̃desɑ̃dr] §96 *intr* to condescend; to yield, comply

condiment [kɔ̃dimɑ̃] *m* condiment

condisciple [kɔ̃disipl] *mf* classmate

condition [kɔ̃disjɔ̃] *f* condition; **à condition, sous condition** conditionally; on approval; **à condition de, à condition que** on condition that; **dans de bonnes conditions** in good condition; **sans conditions** unconditional

condition·nel -nelle [kɔ̃disjɔnɛl] *adj & m* conditional

conditionnement [kɔ̃disjɔnmɑ̃] *m* packaging; conditioning

conditionner [kɔ̃disjɔne] *tr* to condition; (com) to package

condoléances [kɔ̃dɔleɑ̃s] *fpl* condolence

condom [kɔ̃dɔm] *m* condom, prophylactic

conduc·teur [kɔ̃dyktœr] **-trice** [tris] *adj* conducting; driving; (elec) power (*line*); (elec) lead (*wire*) ‖ *adj masc* (elec, phys) (in predicate after **être**, it may be translated by a noun) conductor, e.g., **les métaux sont bons conducteurs de l'électricité** metals are good conductors of electricity ‖ *mf* guide; leader; driver; **conducteur qui prend la fuite** hit-and-run driver ‖ *m* motorman; foreman; pressman; (elec, phys) conductor

conduire [kɔ̃dɥir] §19, §95, §96 *tr* to conduct; to lead; drive; see (*s.o. to the door*) ‖ *intr* to drive ‖ *ref* to conduct oneself

conduit [kɔ̃dɥi] *m* conduit; **conduit auditif** auditory canal; **conduits lacrymaux** tear ducts

conduite [kɔ̃dɥit] *f* conduct, behavior; management, command; driving (*of a car; of cattle*); pipe line; duct, flue; **avoir de la conduite** to be well behaved; **conduite d'eau** water main; **conduite intérieure** closed car; **faire la conduite à** to escort; **faire une conduite de Grenoble à qn** (coll) to kick s.o. out

cône [kon] *m* cone

confection [kɔ̃fɛksjɔ̃] *f* manufacture; construction (*e.g., of a machine*); ready-made clothes; **de confection** ready-made (*suit, dress, etc.*)

confectionner [kɔ̃fɛksjɔne] *tr* to manufacture; prepare (*a dish*)

confection·neur [kɔ̃fɛksjɔnœr] **-neuse** [nøz] *mf* manufacturer (*esp. of ready-made clothes*)

confédération [kɔ̃federɑsjɔ̃] *f* confederation, confederacy

confédérer [kɔ̃federe] §10 *tr & ref* to confederate

conférence [kɔ̃ferɑ̃s] *f* conference; lecture, speech; **conférence au sommet** summit conference; **conférence de presse** press conference

conféren·cier [kɔ̃ferɑ̃sje] **-cière** [sjɛr] *mf* lecturer, speaker

conférer [kɔ̃fere] §10 *tr* to confer, award; administer (*a sacrament*); collate, compare ‖ *intr* to confer

confesse [kɔ̃fɛs] *f*—**à confesse** to confession; **de confesse** from confession

confesser [kɔ̃fɛse] §95 *tr* to confess; (coll) to pump (*s.o.*) ‖ *ref* to confess

confesseur [kɔ̃fɛsœr] *m* confessor

confession [kɔ̃fɛsjɔ̃] *f* confession; (eccl) denomination

confessionnal [kɔ̃fɛsjɔnal] *m* confessional

confession·nel -nelle [kɔ̃fɛsjɔnɛl] *adj* denominational

confiance [kɔ̃fjɑ̃s] *f* confidence; **confiance en soi** self-confidence; **de confiance** reliable; confidently; **en confiance** with confidence

con·fiant [kɔ̃fjɑ̃] **-fiante** [fjɑ̃t] *adj* confident; confiding, trusting

confidence [kɔ̃fidɑ̃s] *f* confidence, secret

confi·dent [kɔ̃fidɑ̃] **-dente** [dɑ̃t] *mf* confident

confiden·tiel -tielle [kɔ̃fidɑ̃sjɛl] *adj* confidential

confier [kɔ̃fje] *tr* to entrust; confide, disclose; commit (*to memory*); consign; **confier à** to put (*seed*) in (*the ground*) ‖ *ref*—**se confier à** to confide in, to trust; **se confier en** to put one's trust in

confinement [kɔ̃finmɑ̃] *m* imprisonment; (nucl) containment (*in a reactor*)

confiner [kɔ̃fine] *tr* to confine ‖ *intr*—**confiner à** to border on, verge on ‖ *ref* to confine oneself; **se confiner dans** to confine oneself to

confins [kɔ̃fɛ̃] *mpl* confines

confire [kɔ̃fir] §**66** (*pp* **confit**) *tr* to preserve; pickle; candy; can (*goose, chicken, etc.*); dip (*skins*) ‖ *ref* to become immersed (*in work, prayer, etc.*)

confirmer [kɔ̃firme] *tr* to confirm

confiscation [kɔ̃fiskɑsjɔ̃] *f* confiscation

confiserie [kɔ̃fizri] *f* confectionery

confi·seur [kɔ̃fizœr] **-seuse** [zøz] *mf* confectioner, candymaker

confisquer [kɔ̃fiske] *tr* to confiscate

con·fit [kɔ̃fi] **-fite** [fit] *adj* preserved; pickled; candied; steeped (*e.g., in piety*); incrusted (*in bigotry*) ‖ *m* canned chicken, goose, etc.

confiture [kɔ̃fityr] *f* preserves, jam

confitu·rier [kɔ̃fityrje] **-rière** [rjɛr] *mf* manufacturer of jams ‖ *m* jelly glass, jam jar

conflagration [kɔ̃flagrɑsjɔ̃] *f* conflagration, turmoil

conflit [kɔ̃fli] *m* conflict

confluer [kɔ̃flye] *intr* to meet, come together (*said of two rivers*)

confondre [kɔ̃fɔ̃dr] *tr* to confuse, mix up, mingle; confound ‖ *ref* to become bewildered, mixed up; **se confondre en excuses** to fall all over oneself apologizing

conforme [kɔ̃fɔrm] *adj* corresponding; certified, e.g., **pour copie conforme** certified copy; **conforme à** conformable to, consistent with; **conforme à l'échantillon** identical with sample; **conforme aux normes** according to specifications; **conforme aux règles** in order

confor·mé **-mée** [kɔ̃fɔrme] *adj* shaped, built; **bien conformé** well-built; **mal conformé** misshapen

conformément [kɔ̃fɔrmemɑ̃] *adv*—**conformément à** in compliance with

conformer [kɔ̃fɔrme] *tr* & *ref* to conform

conformiste [kɔ̃fɔrmist] *mf* conformist

conformité [kɔ̃fɔrmite] *f* conformity, conformance

confort [kɔ̃fɔr] *m* comfort; convenience

confortable [kɔ̃fɔrtabl] *adj* comfortable ‖ *m* comfort; easy chair

confrère [kɔ̃frɛr] *m* confrere, colleague

confrérie [kɔ̃freri] *f* brotherhood

confronter [kɔ̃frɔ̃te] *tr* to confront; compare, collate

con·fus [kɔ̃fy] **-fuse** [fyz] *adj* confused; vague, blurred; embarrassed

confusion [kɔ̃fyzjɔ̃] *f* confusion; embarrassment

congé [kɔ̃ʒe] *m* leave; vacation; dismissal; **congé libérable** military discharge; **congé payé** vacation with pay; **donner congé à** to lay off; **donner son congé à** to give notice to; **prendre congé de** to take leave of

congédiement [kɔ̃ʒedimɑ̃] *m* dismissal, discharge; paying off (*of crew*)

congédier [kɔ̃ʒedje] *tr* to dismiss

congélateur [kɔ̃ʒelatœr] *m* freezer (*for frozen foods*)

congélation [kɔ̃ʒelɑsjɔ̃] *f* freezing

congeler [kɔ̃ʒəle] §**2** *tr* & *ref* to freeze; congeal; **congeler à basse température** to deep-freeze

congénère [kɔ̃ʒenɛr] *adj* cognate (*words*); (biol) of the same species ‖ *mf* fellow creature; **lui et ses congénères** he and his like

congéni·tal **-tale** [kɔ̃ʒenital] *adj* (*pl* **-taux** [to]) congenital

congère [kɔ̃ʒer] *f* snowdrift

congestion [kɔ̃ʒɛstjɔ̃] *f* congestion; **congestion cérébrale** stroke; **congestion pulmonaire** pneumonia

congestionner [kɔ̃ʒɛstjɔne] *tr* & *ref* to congest

conglomération [kɔ̃glɔmerɑsjɔ̃] *f* conglomeration

conglomérer [kɔ̃glɔmere] §**10** *tr* & *ref* to conglomerate

congratulation [kɔ̃gratylɑsjɔ̃] *f* congratulation

congratuler [kɔ̃gratyle] *tr* to congratulate

congre [kɔ̃gr] *m* conger eel

congrégation [kɔ̃gregɑsjɔ̃] *f* (eccl) congregation

congrès [kɔ̃grɛ] *m* congress, convention, meeting, conference

congressiste [kɔ̃grɛsist] *mf* delegate ‖ *m* congressman ‖ *f* congresswoman

con·gru **-grue** [kɔ̃gry] *adj* precise, suitable; scanty; (math) congruent

conifère [kɔnifɛr] *adj* coniferous ‖ *m* conifer

conique [kɔnik] *adj* conical ‖ *f* conic section

conjecture [kɔ̃ʒɛktyr] *f* conjecture

conjecturer [kɔ̃ʒɛktyre] *tr* & *intr* to conjecture, surmise

conjoindre [kɔ̃ʒwɛ̃dr] §**35** *tr* to join in marriage

con·joint [kɔ̃ʒwɛ̃] **-jointe** [ʒwɛ̃t] *adj* united, joint ‖ *mf* spouse, consort

conjoncteur [kɔ̃ʒɔ̃ktœr] *m* automatic switch

conjonction [kɔ̃ʒɔ̃ksjɔ̃] *f* conjunction

conjoncture [kɔ̃ʒɔ̃ktyr] *f* juncture, situation; **de haute conjoncture** boom

conjugaison [kɔ̃ʒygɛzɔ̃] *f* conjugation

conju·gal **-gale** [kɔ̃ʒygal] *adj* (*pl* **-gaux** [go]) conjugal, connubial

conjuguer [kɔ̃ʒyge] *tr* to combine (*e.g., forces*); conjugate

conjuration [kɔ̃ʒyrɑsjɔ̃] *f* conjuration; conspiracy; **conjurations** entreaties

conju·ré **-rée** [kɔ̃ʒyre] *mf* conspirator

conjurer [kɔ̃ʒyre] §**97** *tr* to conjure; conjure away; conspire up; conspire for, plot; **conjurer qn de** + *inf* to entreat s.o. to + *inf* ‖ *intr* to hatch a plot ‖ *ref* to plot together, conspire

connaissance [kɔnɛsɑ̃s] *f* knowledge; acquaintance; consciousness; attention; **connaissance des temps** nautical almanac; **connaissances** knowledge; **en connaissance de** with full knowledge of; **faire connaissance avec** to become acquainted with; **faire la connaissance de** to meet; **parler en connaissance de cause** to know what one is talking about; **perdre con-**

naissance to lose consciousness; **sans connaissance** unconscious

connaissement [kɔnɛsmɑ̃] *m* bill of lading

connais·seur [kɔnɛsœr] **-seuse** [søz] *mf* connoisseur; expert

connaître [kɔnɛtr] §12 *tr* to know; be acquainted with ‖ *intr*—**connaître de** (law) to have jurisdiction over ‖ *ref* to be acquainted (with); become acquainted; **se connaître à** or **en** to know a lot about; **s'y connaître** to know what one is talking about; **s'y connaître en** to know a lot about

connecter [kɔnɛkte] *tr* to connect

connerie [kɔnri] *f* stupidity; (vulg) bullshit; **faire une connerie** to foul up

connétable [kɔnetabl] *m* constable

connexe [kɔnɛks] *adj* connected

connexion [kɔnɛksjɔ̃] *f* connection

connexité [kɔnɛksite] *f* connection

con·nu -nue [kɔny] *adj* well-known ‖ *m*—**le connu** the known ‖ *v* see **connaître**

conque [kɔk] *f* conch

conqué·rant [kɔkerɑ̃] **-rante** [rɑ̃t] *adj* (coll) swaggering ‖ *mf* conqueror

conquérir [kɔkerir] §3 *tr* to conquer

conquête [kɔkɛt] *f* conquest

consa·cré -crée [kɔsakre] *adj* accepted, time-honored, stock

consacrer [kɔsakre] §96 *tr* to consecrate; devote, dedicate (*time, energy, effort*); give, spare (*e.g., time*); to sanction, confirm ‖ *ref*—**se consacrer à** to devote or dedicate oneself to

consan·guin [kɔsɑ̃gɛ̃] **-guine** [gin] *adj* consanguineous; on the father's side ‖ *mf* blood relation

consciemment [kɔsjamɑ̃] *adv* consciously

conscience [kɔsjɑ̃s] *f* conscience; conscientiousness; consciousness; **avoir la conscience large** to be broad-minded; **en conscience** conscientiously

conscien·cieux [kɔsjɑ̃sjø] **-cieuse** [sjøz] *adj* conscientious

cons·cient [kɔsjɑ̃] **-ciente** [sjɑ̃t] §93 *adj* conscious, aware, knowing

conscription [kɔskripsjɔ̃] *f* draft, conscription

conscrit [kɔskri] *m* draftee, conscript

consécration [kɔsekrasjɔ̃] *f* consecration; confirmation

consécu·tif [kɔsekytif] **-tive** [tiv] *adj* consecutive; dependent (*clause*); **consécutif à** resulting from

conseil [kɔsɛj] *m* advice, counsel; counselor; council, board, committee; **conseil d'administration** board of directors; **conseil de guerre** court-martial; staff meeting of top brass; **conseil de prud'hommes** arbitration board; **conseil de révision** draft board; **conseils** advice; **un conseil** a piece of advice

conseil·ler [kɔseje] **-lère** [jɛr] *mf* councilor; counselor, adviser ‖ *f* councilor's wife; counselor's wife ‖ **conseiller** §97, §98 *tr* to advise, counsel (*s.o.* or *s.th.*); **conseiller q.ch. à qn** to recommend s.th. to

s.o. ‖ *intr* to advise, counsel; **conseiller à qn de** + *inf* to advise s.o. to + *inf*

conseil·leur [kɔsɛjɛr] **-leuse** [jøz] *mf* adviser; know-it-all

consensus [kɔsɛ̃sys] *m* consensus

consentement [kɔsɑ̃tmɑ̃] *m* consent

consentir [kɔsɑ̃tir] §41, §96 *tr* to grant, allow; accept, recognize; **consentir (à ce) que** + *subj* to permit (*s.o.*) to + *inf* ‖ *intr* to consent; **consentir à** to consent to, agree to, approve of

conséquemment [kɔsekamɑ̃] *adv* consequently; consistently; **conséquemment à** as a result of

conséquence [kɔsekɑ̃s] *f* consequence; consistency; **en conséquence** accordingly

consé·quent [kɔsekɑ̃] **-quente** [kɑ̃t] *adj* consequent; consistent; important ‖ *m* (logic, math) consequent; **par conséquent** consequently

conserva·teur [kɔsɛrvatœr] **-trice** [tris] *adj* conservative ‖ *mf* conservative; curator, keeper; warden, ranger; registrar

conservation [kɔsɛrvasjɔ̃] *f* conservation, preservation; curatorship; curator's office

conservatisme [kɔsɛrvatism] *m* conservatism

conservatoire [kɔsɛrvatwar] *m* conservatory (*of music*); museum, academy

conserve [kɔsɛrv] *f* canned food, preserves; escort, convoy; **conserves** dark glasses; **conserves au vinaigre** pickles; **mettre en conserve** to can; **voler de conserve avec** to fly alongside of

conserver [kɔsɛrve] *tr* to conserve; preserve; keep (*one's health; one's equanimity; a secret*); escort, convoy (*a ship*) ‖ *ref* to stay in good shape; take care of oneself

conserverie [kɔsɛrvəri] *f* canning factory; canning

considérable [kɔsiderabl] *adj* considerable; important; large, great

considérant [kɔsiderɑ̃] *m* motive, grounds; **considérant que** whereas

considération [kɔsiderasjɔ̃] *f* consideration

considé·ré -rée [kɔsidere] *adj* respected

considérer [kɔsidere] §10 *tr* to consider, examine; esteem, consider

consignataire [kɔsiɲatɛr] *m* consignee, trustee

consignation [kɔsiɲasjɔ̃] *f* consignment; **en consignation** on consignment

consigne [kɔsiɲ] *f* password; baggage room, checkroom; checking fee; confinement to barracks, detention; bottle deposit; (mil) orders, instructions; **consigne ordinaire** baggage check; **en consigne à la douane** held up in customs; **être de consigne** to be on duty; **manquer à la consigne** to disobey orders

consigner [kɔsiɲe] *tr* to consign; check (*baggage*); put down in writing, enter in the record; confine to barracks, keep (*a student*) in; put out of bounds (*e.g., for military personnel*); close (*a port*); **consigner sa** (or **la**) **porte** to be at home to no one

consistance [kɔ̃sistɑ̃s] *f* consistency; stability (*of character*); credit, reality, standing; **en consistance de** consisting of

consis·tant [kɔ̃sistɑ̃] **-tante** [tɑ̃t] *adj* consistent; stable (*character*); **consistant en** consisting of

consister [kɔ̃siste] §96 *intr*—**consister à** + *inf* to consist in + *ger;* **consister dans** or **en** to consist in; consist of

consistoire [kɔsistwar] *m* consistory

consola·teur [kɔ̃sɔlatœr] **-trice** [tris] *adj* consoling ‖ *mf* comforter

consolation [kɔ̃sɔlasjɔ̃] *f* consolation

console [kɔ̃sɔl] *f* console; console table; bracket

consoler [kɔ̃sɔle] §97, §99 *tr* to console

consolider [kɔ̃sɔlide] *tr* to consolidate; fund (*a debt*)

consomma·teur [kɔ̃sɔmatœr] **-trice** [tris] *mf* consumer; customer (*in a restaurant or bar*)

consommation [kɔ̃sɔmasjɔ̃] *f* consummation (*e.g., of a marriage*); perpetration (*e.g., of a crime*); consumption, use; drink (*e.g., in a café*)

consom·mé -mée [kɔ̃sɔme] *adj* consummate; skilled (*e.g., technician*); consumed, used up ‖ *m* consommé

consommer [kɔ̃sɔme] *tr* to consummate, complete; perpetrate (*e.g., a crime*); consume

consomp·tif [kɔ̃sɔ̃ptif] **-tive** [tiv] *adj* wasting away

consomption [kɔ̃sɔ̃psjɔ̃] *f* wasting away, decline

conso·nant [kɔ̃sɔnɑ̃] **-nante** [nɑ̃t] *adj* consonant, harmonious

consonne [kɔ̃sɔn] *f* consonant

consorts [kɔ̃sɔr] *mpl* partners, associates; (pej) confederates

conspira·teur [kɔ̃spiratœr] **-trice** [tris] *mf* conspirator

conspiration [kɔ̃spirasjɔ̃] *f* conspiracy

conspirer [kɔ̃spire] §96 *tr* & *intr* to conspire

conspuer [kɔ̃spɥe] *tr* to boo, hiss

constamment [kɔ̃stamɑ̃] *adv* constantly

constance [kɔ̃stɑ̃s] *f* constancy

cons·tant [kɔ̃stɑ̃] **-tante** [tɑ̃t] *adj* constant; true; established, evident ‖ *f* constant

constat [kɔ̃sta] *m* affidavit

constatation [kɔ̃statasjɔ̃] *f* authentication; declaration, claim

constater [kɔ̃state] *tr* to certify; find out; prove, establish

constellation [kɔ̃stɛllasjɔ̃] *f* constellation

consteller [kɔ̃stɛlle] *tr* to spangle

consterner [kɔ̃stɛrne] *tr* to dismay

constipation [kɔ̃stipasjɔ̃] *f* constipation

constiper [kɔ̃stipe] *tr* to constipate

consti·tuant [kɔ̃stitɥɑ̃] **-tuante** [tɥɑ̃t] *adj* & *m* constituent

constituer [kɔ̃stitɥe] *tr* to constitue; settle (*a dowry*); form (*a cabinet; a corporation*); empanel (*a jury*); appoint (*a lawyer*) ‖ *ref* to be formed; **se constituer prisonnier** to give oneself up

constitu·tif [kɔ̃stitytif] **-tive** [tiv] *adj* constituent

constitution [kɔ̃stitysjɔ̃] *f* constitution; settlement (*of a dowry*); **constitution en société** incorporation

construc·teur [kɔ̃stryktœr] **-trice** [tris] *adj* constructive, building ‖ *mf* constructor, builder

construc·tif [kɔ̃stryktif] **-tive** [tiv] *adj* constructive

construction [kɔ̃stryksjɔ̃] *f* construction; **construction mécanique** mechanical engineering

construire [kɔ̃strɥir] §19 *tr* to construct, build; draw (*e.g., a triangle*); (gram) to construe

consul [kɔ̃syl] *m* consul

consulaire [kɔ̃sylɛr] *adj* consular

consulat [kɔ̃syla] *m* consulate

consul·tant [kɔ̃syltɑ̃] **-tante** [tɑ̃t] *adj* consulting ‖ *mf* consultant

consulta·tif [kɔ̃syltatif] **-tive** [tiv] *adj* advisory

consultation [kɔ̃syltasjɔ̃] *f* consultation; **consultation externe** outpatient clinic; **consultation populaire** poll, referendum

consulte [kɔ̃sylt] *f* (eccl, law) consultation

consulter [kɔ̃sylte] *tr* to consult ‖ *intr* to consult, give consultations ‖ *ref* to deliberate

consumer [kɔ̃syme] *tr* to consume, use up, destroy ‖ §96 *ref* to burn out; waste away; fail

contact [kɔ̃takt] *m* contact; **mettre en contact** to put in touch, to connect; **prendre contact** to make contact

contacter [kɔ̃takte] *tr* (coll) to contact

conta·gieux [kɔ̃taʒiø] **-gieuse** [ʒjøz] *adj* contagious

contagion [kɔ̃taʒjɔ̃] *f* contagion

contamination [kɔ̃taminasjɔ̃] *f* contamination

contaminer [kɔ̃tamine] *tr* to contaminate

conte [kɔ̃t] *m* tale, story; **conte à dormir debout** cock-and-bull story, baloney; **conte de fées** fairy tale

contemplation [kɔ̃tɑ̃plasjɔ̃] *f* contemplation

contempler [kɔ̃tɑ̃ple] *tr* to contemplate

contempo·rain [kɔ̃tɑ̃pɔrɛ̃] **-raine** [rɛn] *adj* & *m* contemporary

contemp·teur [kɔ̃tɑ̃ptœr] **-trice** [tris] *mf* scoffer

contenance [kɔ̃tnɑ̃s] *f* capacity; area; countenance; **faire bonne contenance** to put up a bold front

conte·nant [kɔ̃tnɑ̃] **-nante** [nɑ̃t] *adj* containing ‖ *m* container

conteneur [kɔ̃tnœr] *m* container

conteneuriser [kɔ̃tnœrize] *tr* to containerize

contenir [kɔ̃tnir] §72 *tr* to contain; restrain ‖ *ref* to contain oneself, hold oneself back

con·tent [kɔ̃tɑ̃] **-tente** [tɑ̃t] §93 *adj* content; happy, glad, pleased; **content de** satisfied with ‖ *m* fill, e.g., **avoir son content** to have one's fill

contentement [kɔ̃tɑ̃tmɑ̃] *m* contentment

contenter [kɔ̃tɑ̃te] *tr* to content, satisfy ‖ §97, §99 *ref* to satisfy one's desires; **se contenter de** to be content or satisfied with

conten·tieux [kɔ̃tɑ̃sjø] **-tieuse** [sjøz] *adj* contentious ‖ *m* contention, litigation; claims department

contention [kɔ̃tɑ̃sjɔ̃] *f* application, intentness

conte·nu -nue [kɔ̃tny] *adj* contained, restrained, stifled ‖ *m* contents

conter [kɔ̃te] *tr* to relate, tell; **en conter à** (coll) to take (*s.o.*) in; **en conter (de belles)** (coll) to tell tall tales ‖ *intr* to narrate, tell a story

contestation [kɔ̃tɛstɑsjɔ̃] *f* argument, dispute; **sans contestation** without opposition

conteste [kɔ̃tɛst] *f*—**sans conteste** incontestably, unquestionably

contester [kɔ̃tɛste] *tr & intr* to contest

con·teur [kɔ̃tœr] **-teuse** [tøz] *mf* story teller, narrator

contexte [kɔ̃tɛkst] *m* context

contexture [kɔ̃tɛkstyr] *f* texture; structure, makeup

conti·gu -guë [kɔ̃tigy] *adj* contiguous; **contigue à** adjoining

continence [kɔ̃tinɑ̃s] *f* continence

conti·nent [kɔ̃tinɑ̃] **-nente** [nɑ̃t] *adj & m* continent

continen·tal -tale [kɔ̃tinɑ̃tal] *adj* (*pl* **-taux** [to]) continental

contingence [kɔtɛ̃ʒɑ̃s] *f* contingency

contin·gent [kɔtɛ̃ʒɑ̃] **-gente** [ʒɑ̃t] *adj* contingent ‖ *m* contingent; quota

conti·nu -nue [kɔ̃tiny] *adj* continuous; nonstop; direct (*current*) ‖ *m* continuum

continuation [kɔ̃tinɥɑsjɔ̃] *f* continuation

conti·nuel -nuelle [kɔ̃tinɥɛl] *adj* continual

continuer [kɔ̃tinɥe] §96, §97 *tr* to continue; carry on (with), go on with ‖ *intr & ref* to go on, continue

continuité [kɔ̃tinɥite] *f* continuity

continûment [kɔ̃tinymɑ̃] *adv* continuously

conton·dant [kɔ̃tɔ̃dɑ̃] **-dante** [dɑ̃t] *adj* blunt

contorsion [kɔ̃tɔrsjɔ̃] *f* contortion

contour [kɔ̃tur] *m* contour

contourner [kɔ̃turne] *tr* to contour; go around, skirt; get around (*the law*); twist, distort

contrac·tant [kɔ̃traktɑ̃] **-tante** [tɑ̃t] *adj* contracting (*parties*) ‖ *mf* contracting party

contracter [kɔ̃trakte] *tr* to contract; float (*a loan*) ‖ *ref* to contract; be contracted

contraction [kɔ̃traksjɔ̃] *f* contraction

contractuelle [kɔ̃traktɥɛl] *f* meter maid

contradiction [kɔ̃tradiksjɔ̃] *f* contradiction

contradictoire [kɔ̃tradiktwar] *adj* contradictory

contraindre [kɔ̃trɛ̃dr] §15, §97 *tr* to compel, force, constrain; restrain, curb ‖ *ref* to restrain oneself

con·traint [kɔ̃trɛ̃] **-trainte** [trɛ̃t] §93 *adj* constrained, forced; stiff (*person*) ‖ *f* con-

straint; restraint; exigencies (*e.g., of the rhyme*)

contraire [kɔ̃trɛr] *adj* contrary; opposite (*e.g., direction*); injurious (*e.g., to health*) ‖ *m* contrary, opposite; antonym; **au contraire** on the contrary

contrairement [kɔ̃trɛrmɑ̃] *adv* contrary

contrarier [kɔ̃trarje] *tr* to thwart; vex, annoy; contrast (*e.g., colors*)

contrariété [kɔ̃trarjete] vexation, annoyance; clashing (*e.g., of colors*)

contraste [kɔ̃trast] *m* contrast

contraster [kɔ̃traste] *tr & intr* to contrast

contrat [kɔ̃tra] *m* contract, agreement; **remplir son contrat** (bridge) to make one's contract

contravention [kɔ̃travɑ̃sjɔ̃] *f* infraction; **dresser une contravention** to write out a (traffic) ticket; **recevoir une contravention** to get a ticket

contre [kɔ̃tr] *m* opposite, con; (cards) double; **par contre** on the contrary ‖ *adv* against; nearby; **contre à contre** alongside ‖ *prep* against; contrary to; to, e.g., **dix contre un** ten to one; for, e.g., **échanger contre** to exchange for; e.g., **remède contre la toux** remedy for a cough; (sports) versus; **contre remboursement** (com) collect on delivery

contre-allée [kɔ̃trale] *f* (*pl* **-allées**) parallel walk

contre-amiral [kɔ̃tramiral] *m* (*pl* **-amiraux** [amiro]) rear admiral

contre-appel [kɔ̃trapɛl] *m* (*pl* **-appels**) second roll call; double-check

contre-attaque [kɔ̃tratak] *f* (*pl* **-attaques**) counterattack

contre-attaquer [kɔ̃tratake] *tr* to counterattack

contrebalancer [kɔ̃trəbalɑ̃se] §51 *tr* to counterbalance

contrebande [kɔ̃trəbɑ̃d] *f* contraband; smuggling; **faire la contrebande** to smuggle

contreban·dier [kɔ̃trəbɑ̃dje] **-dière** [djɛr] *adj* smuggled, contraband ‖ *mf* smuggler

contrebas [kɔ̃trəba]—**en contrebas** downwards

contrebasse [kɔ̃trəbas] *f* contrabass

contre-biais [kɔ̃trəbjɛ]—**à contre-biais** the wrong way, against the grain

contre-boutant [kɔ̃trəbutɑ̃] *m* (*pl* **-boutants**) shore

contrecarrer [kɔ̃trəkare] *tr* to stymie, thwart

contre-chant [kɔ̃trəʃɑ̃] *m* (*pl* **-chants**) counter melody

contrecœur [kɔ̃trəkœr] *m* smoke shelf; **à contrecœur** unwillingly

contrecoup [kɔ̃trəku] *m* rebound, recoil, backlash; repercussion

contre-courant [kɔ̃trəkurɑ̃] *m* (*pl* **courants**) countercurrent; **à contre-courant** upstream; behind the times

contredire [kɔ̃trədir] §40 *tr* to contradict ‖ *ref* to contradict oneself

contrée [kɔ̃tre] *f* region, countryside

contre-écrou [kɔ̃trekru] *m* (*pl* **-écrous**) lock nut

contre-espion [kɔ̃trɛspjɔ̃] *m* (*pl* **-espions**) counterspy

contre-espionnage [kɔ̃trɛspjɔnaʒ] *m* (*pl* **-espionnages**) counterespionage

contrefaçon [kɔ̃trəfasɔ̃] *f* infringement (*of patent or copyright*); forgery; counterfeit; plagiarism

contrefacteur [kɔ̃trəfaktœr] *m* forger; counterfeiter; plagiarist

contrefaction [kɔ̃trəfaksjɔ̃] *f* forgery; counterfeiting

contrefaire [kɔ̃trəfɛr] §29 *tr* to forge; counterfeit; imitate, mimic; disguise

contre·fait [kɔ̃trəfɛ] **-faite** [fɛt] *adj* counterfeit; deformed

contre-fenêtre [kɔ̃trəfnɛtr] *f* (*pl* **-fenêtres**) inner sash; storm window

contre-feu [kɔ̃trəfø] *m* (*pl* **-feux**) backfire (*in fire fighting*)

contreficher [kɔ̃trəfiʃe] *ref* (slang) to not give a rap

contre-fil [kɔ̃trəfil] *m* (*pl* **-fils**) opposite direction, wrong way; **à contre-fil** upstream; against the grain

contre-filet [kɔ̃trəfilɛ] *m* short loin (*club and porterhouse steaks*)

contrefort [kɔ̃trəfɔr] *m* buttress, abutment; foothills

contre-haut [kɔ̃trəo]—**en contre-haut** on a higher level; from top to bottom

contre-interrogatoire [kɔ̃trɛ̃tɛrɔgatwar] *m* cross-examination

contre-interroger [kɔ̃trɛ̃tɛrɔʒe] §38 *tr* to cross-examine

contre-jour [kɔ̃trəʒur] *m* *invar* backlighting; **à contre-jour** against the light

contremaî·tre [kɔ̃trəmɛtr] **-tresse** [trɛs] *mf* overseer ‖ *m* foreman; (naut) (hist) boatswain's mate; (nav) petty officer ‖ *f* forewoman

contremander [kɔ̃trəmɑ̃de] *tr* to countermand; call off

contremarche [kɔ̃trəmarʃ] *f* countermarch; riser (*of stair step*)

contremarque [kɔ̃trəmark] *f* countersign; pass-out check

contremarquer [kɔ̃trəmarke] *tr* to countersign

contre-mesure [kɔ̃trəmzyr] *f* (*pl* **-mesures**) countermeasure

contre-offensive [kɔ̃trɔfɑ̃siv] *f* (*pl* **-offensives**) counteroffensive

contrepartie [kɔ̃trəparti] *f* counterpart; (bk) duplicate entry; **en contrepartie** as against this

contre-pas [kɔ̃trəpɑ] *m* *invar* half step (*taken in order to get in step*)

contre-pente [kɔ̃trəpɑ̃t] *f* (*pl* **-pentes**) reverse slope

contre-performance [kɔ̃trəpɛrfɔrmɑ̃s] *f* (*pl* **-performances**) unexpected defeat

contrepèterie [kɔ̃trəpɛtri] *f* spoonerism

contre-pied [kɔ̃trəpje] *m* (*pl* **-pieds**) backtrack; opposite opinion; **à contre-pied** off balance

contre-plaqué [kɔ̃trəplake] *m* (*pl* **-plaqués**) plywood

contre-plaquer [kɔ̃trəplake] *tr* to laminate

contrepoids [kɔ̃trəpwa] *m* *invar* counterweight, counterbalance

contre-poil [kɔ̃trəpwal] *m* wrong way (*e.g.*, *of fur*); **à contre-poil** the wrong way; at the wrong end

contrepoint [kɔ̃trəpwɛ̃] *m* counterpoint

contre-pointe [kɔ̃trəpwɛ̃t] *f* (*pl* **-pointes**) false edge (*of sword*); tailstock (*of lathe*)

contre-pointer [kɔ̃trəpwɛ̃te] *tr* to quilt

contrepoison [kɔ̃trəpwazɔ̃] *m* antidote

contrer [kɔ̃tre] *tr* & *intr* (cards) to double; (coll) to counter

contreseing [kɔ̃trəsɛ̃] *m* countersignature

contresens [kɔ̃trəsɑ̃s] *m* *invar* misinterpretation; mistranslation; wrong way; **à contresens** in the wrong sense; in the wrong direction

contresigner [kɔ̃trəsiɲe] *tr* to countersign

contretemps [kɔ̃trətɑ̃] *m*—**à contre-temps** at the wrong moment; syncopated

contre-torpilleur [kɔ̃trətɔrpijœr] *m* (*pl* **-torpilleurs**) (nav) torpedo-boat destroyer

contreve·nant [kɔ̃trəvnɑ̃] **-nante** [nɑ̃t] *mf* lawbreaker, delinquent

contrevenir [kɔ̃trəvnir] §72 *intr*—**centrevenir à** to contravene, break (*a law*)

contrevent [kɔ̃trəvɑ̃] *m* shutter, window shutter

contre-voie [kɔ̃trəvwa] *f* (*pl* **-voies**) parallel route; **à contre-voie** in reverse (*of the usual direction*); on the side opposite the platform

contribuable [kɔ̃tribɥabl] *adj* taxpaying ‖ *mf* taxpayer

contribuer [kɔ̃tribɥe] §96 *intr* to contribute

contribution [kɔ̃tribysjɔ̃] *f* contribution; tax

contrister [kɔ̃triste] *tr* to sadden

con·trit [kɔ̃tri] **-trite** [trit] *adj* contrite

contrôlable [kɔ̃trolabl] *adj* verifiable

contrôle [kɔ̃trol] *m* inspection, verification, check; supervision, observation; auditing; inspection booth, ticket window; (mil) muster roll; **contrôle des naissances** birth control; **contrôle de soi** self-control; **contrôle par sondage** spot check

contrôler [kɔ̃trole] *tr* to inspect, verify, check; supervise, put under observation; audit; criticize ‖ *ref* to control oneself

contrô·leur [kɔ̃trolœr] **-leuse** [løz] *mf* inspector, checker; supervisor, observer; auditor, comptroller; conductor, ticket collector; **contrôleur de la navigation aérienne, contrôleur aérien** air-traffic controller ‖ *m* gauge; **contrôleur de vitesse** speedometer; **contrôleur de vol** flight indicator

controversable [kɔ̃trɔvɛrsabl] *adj* controversial

controverse [kɔ̃trɔvɛrs] *f* controversy

controverser [kɔ̃trɔvɛrse] *tr* to controvert

contumace [kɔ̃tymas] *f* contempt of court

con·tus [kɔ̃ty] **-tuse** [tyz] *adj* bruised

contusion [kɔ̃tyzjɔ̃] *f* contusion, bruise

contusionner [kɔ̃tyzjɔne] *tr* to bruise

convain·cant [kɔ̃vɛ̃kɑ̃] **-cante** [kɑ̃t] *adj* convincing

convaincre [kɔ̃vɛ̃kr] §70, §97, §99 *tr* to convince; to convict ‖ *ref* to be satisfied

convain·cu **-cue** [kɔ̃vɛ̃ky] *adj* convinced, dyed-in-the-wool; convicted

convalescence [kɔ̃valesɑ̃s] *f* convalescence

convales·cent [kɔ̃valesɑ̃] **-cente** [sɑ̃t] *adj* & *mf* convalescent

convenable [kɔ̃vnabl] *adj* suitable, proper; opportune (*moment*)

convenance [kɔ̃vnɑ̃s] *f* suitability, propriety; conformity; **convenances** conventions

convenir [kɔ̃vnir] §72, §97 *intr* to agree; **convenir à** to fit, suit, e.g., **ce travail lui convient** this work suits him; **convenir de** to admit, admit to, admit the truth of; agree on ‖ *ref* (*pp* **convenu** *invar*) to agree with one another ‖ *impers*—**il convient** it is fitting, it is appropriate

convention [kɔ̃vɑ̃sjɔ̃] *f* convention

convention·nel **-nelle** [kɔ̃vɑ̃sjɔnɛl] *adj* conventional

conve·nu **-nue** [kɔ̃vny] *adj* settled; stipulated (*price*); appointed (*time, place*); trite, stereotyped (*language*)

converger [kɔ̃vɛrʒe] §38 *intr* to converge

conversation [kɔ̃vɛrsasjɔ̃] *f* conversation

converser [kɔ̃vɛrse] *intr* to converse

conversion [kɔ̃vɛrsjɔ̃] *f* conversion; turning

conver·ti **-tie** [kɔ̃vɛrti] *adj* converted ‖ *mf* convert

convertible [kɔ̃vɛrtibl] *adj* convertible

convertir [kɔ̃vɛrtir] *tr* to convert ‖ *ref* to convert, be converted; change one's mind

convertissable [kɔ̃vɛrtisabl] *adj* convertible

convertisseur [kɔ̃vɛrtisœr] *m* converter; (elec) converter

convexe [kɔ̃vɛks] *adj* convex

conviction [kɔ̃viksjɔ̃] *f* conviction

convier [kɔ̃vje] §96 *tr* to invite

convive [kɔ̃viv] *mf* dinner guest; table companion

convocation [kɔ̃vɔkasjɔ̃] *f* convocation; summoning

convoi [kɔ̃vwa] *m* convoy; funeral procession

convoiter [kɔ̃vwate] *tr* to covet

convoi·teur [kɔ̃vwatœr] **-teuse** [tøz] *adj* covetous ‖ *mf* covetous person

convoitise [kɔ̃vwatiz] *f* covetousness, cupidity

covoquer [kɔ̃vɔke] *tr* to convoke; summon

convoyer [kɔ̃vwaje] §47 *tr* to convoy

convoyeur [kɔ̃vwajœr] *adj* convoying ‖ *m* (mach) conveyor; (nav) escort

convulser [kɔ̃vylse] *tr* to convulse

convulsion [kɔ̃vylsjɔ̃] *f* convulsion

convulsionner [kɔ̃vylsjɔne] *tr* to convulse

coopéra·tif [kɔɔperatif] **-tive** [tiv] cooperative ‖ *f*—**coopérative vinicole** cooperative winery

coopération [kɔɔperasjɔ̃] *f* cooperation

coopérer [kɔɔpere] *intr* to cooperate; **coopérer à** to cooperate in

coordination [kɔɔrdinasjɔ̃] *f* coordination

coordon·né **-née** [kɔɔrdɔne] *adj* & *f* coordinate; **coordonnées** address and telephone number

coordonner [kɔɔrdɔne] *tr* to coordinate

co·pain [kɔpɛ̃] **-pine** [pin] *mf* (coll) pal, chum

co·peau [kɔpo] *m* (*pl* **-peaux**) chip, shaving

copie [kɔpi] *f* copy; exercise, composition (*at school*); **copie au net** fair copy; **pour copie conforme** true copy

copier [kɔpje] *tr* & *intr* to copy

co·pieux [kɔpjø] **-pieuse** [pjøz] *adj* copious

copilote [kɔpilɔt] *m* copilot

copinisme [kɔpinism] *m* cronyism

copiste [kɔpist] *mf* copyist; copier

coposséder [kɔpɔsede] §10 *tr* to own jointly

copropriété [kɔprɔprijete] *f* joint ownership

copula·tif [kɔpylatif] **-tive** [tiv] *adj* (gram) coordinating

copulation [kɔpylasjɔ̃] *f* copulation

copule [kɔpyl] *f* (gram) copula

coq [kɔk] *adj* bantam ‖ *m* cock, rooster; (naut) cook

coq-à-l'âne [kɔkalɑn] *m invar* cock-and-bull story

coquart [kɔkar] *m* black eye, shiner

coque [kɔk] *f* shell; cocoon; hull; **à la coque** soft-boiled; **coque de noix** coconut

coquelicot [kɔkliko] *m* poppy

coqueluche [kɔklyʃ] *f* whooping cough; (coll) rage, vogue

coquemar [kɔkmar] *m* teakettle

coquerie [kɔkri] *f* (naut) galley

coqueriquer [kɔkrike] *intr* to crow

co·quet [kɔkɛ] **-quette** [kɛt] *adj* coquettish; stylish; considerable (*sum*)

coqueter [kɔkte] §34 *intr* to flirt

coquetier [kɔkɛtje] *m* eggcup; egg man

coquetterie [kɔkɛtri] *f* coquetry

coquillage [kɔkijaʒ] *m* shellfish; shell

coquille [kɔkij] *f* shell; typographical error (*of transposed letters*); pat (*of butter*); **coquille de noix** nutshell; **coquille Saint-Jacques** scallop

co·quin [kɔkɛ̃] **-quine** [kin] *adj* deceitful; roguish ‖ *mf* scoundrel; rogue

cor [kɔr] *m* horn; corn (*on foot*); prong (*of antler*); horn player; **à cor et à cri** with hue and cry; **cor anglais** English horn; **cor de chasse** hunting horn; **cor d'harmonie** French horn

co·rail [kɔraj] *m* (*pl* **-raux** [ro]) coral

cor·beau [kɔrbo] *m* (*pl* **-beaux**) crow, raven

corbeille [kɔrbɛj] *f* basket; flower bed; (theat) dress circle; **corbeille à papier** wastebasket; **corbeille de marriage** wedding present

corbillard [kɔrbijar] *m* hearse

corbillon [kɔrbijɔ̃] *m* small basket; word game

cordage [kɔrdaʒ] *m* cordage, rope; (naut) rigging

corde [kɔrd] *f* rope, cord; tightrope; thread (*of a carpet or cloth*); inside track; (geom) chord; (mus) string; **corde à** or **de boyau** catgut (*for, e.g., violin*); **corde à linge** wash line; **corde à nœuds** knotted rope;

corde à piano piano wire; **cordes vocales** vocal cords; **en double corde** on two strings; **être sur la corde raide** to be out on a limb; **les cordes** (mus) the strings; **toucher la corde sensible** to touch a sympathetic cord; **usé jusqu'à la corde** threadbare

cor·dé -dée [kɔrde] *adj* heart-shaped ‖ *f* cord (*of wood*); roped party (*of mountain climbers*)

cor·deau [kɔrdo] *m* (*pl* **-deaux**) tracing line; tracing thread; mine fuse; **tiré au cordeau** in a straight line

cordelier [kɔrdəlje] *m* Franciscan friar

corder [kɔrde] *tr* to twist; string (*a tennis racket*)

cor·dial -diale [kɔrdjal] *adj & m* (*pl* **-diaux** [djo]) cordial

cordialité [kɔrdjalite] *f* cordiality

cordier [kɔrdje] *m* ropemaker; tailpiece (*of violin*)

cordon [kɔrdɔ̃] *m* cordon; cord; latchstring; **cordon de sonnette** bellpull; **cordon de soulier** shoestring

cordon-bleu [kɔrdɔ̃blø] *m* (*pl* **cordons-bleus**) cordon bleu

cordonnerie [kɔrdɔnri] *f* shoemaking; shoe repairing; shoe store; shoemaker's

cordon·nier [kɔrdɔnje] **-nière** [njɛr] *mf* shoemaker

Corée [kɔre] *f* Korea; **la Corée** Korea

coréen [kɔreɛ̃] **coréenne** [kɔreɛn] *adj* Korean ‖ *m* Korean (*language*) ‖ (*cap*) *mf* Korean (*person*)

coriace [kɔrjas] *adj* tough, leathery; (coll) stubborn

coricide [kɔrisid] *m* corn remover

cormoran [kɔrmɔrɑ̃] *m* cormorant

cornac [kɔrnak] *m* mahout

cor·nard [kɔrnar] **-narde** [nard] *adj* horned; (slang) cuckold; wheezing (*of horse*) ‖ *m* (slang) cuckold

corne [kɔrn] *f* horn; dog-ear (*of page*); hoof; shoehorn; **corne d'abondance** horn of plenty; **faire les cornes à** (coll) to make a face at

cor·né -née [kɔrne] *adj* horny ‖ *f* cornea

corneille [kɔrnɛj] *f* crow, rook; **corneille d'église** jackdaw

cornemuse [kɔrnəmyz] *f* bagpipe

cornemuseur [kɔrnəmyzœr] *m* bagpiper

corner [kɔrne] *tr* to dog-ear; give (*s.o.*) the horn; (coll) to trumpet (*news*) about ‖ *intr* to blow the horn, honk; ring (*said of ears*); (mus) to blow a horn; **cornez!** sound your horn!

cornet [kɔrnɛ] *m* cornet; horn; dice-box; cornetist; mouthpiece (*of microphone*); receiver (*of telephone*); **cornet acoustique** ear trumpet; **cornet à pistons** cornet; **cornet de glace** ice-cream cone

cornette [kɔrnɛt] *m* (mil) cornet ‖ *f* (*headdress*) cornet

cornettiste [kɔrnetist] *mf* cornetist

corniche [kɔrniʃ] *f* cornice

cornichon [kɔrniʃɔ̃] *m* pickle, gherkin; (*fool*) (coll) dope, drip

cor·nier [kɔrnje] **-nière** [njɛr] *adj* corner ‖ *f* valley (*joining roofs*); angle iron

corniste [kɔrnist] *mf* horn player

Cornouailles [kɔrnwaj] *f* Cornwall

cornouiller [kɔrnuje] *m* dogwood

cor·nu -nue [kɔrny] *adj* horned; preposterous (*ideas*) ‖ *f* (chem) retort

corollaire [kɔrɔllɛr] *m* corollary

coronaire [kɔrɔnɛr] *adj* coronary

coroner [kɔrɔnœr] *m* coroner

corporation [kɔrpɔrasjɔ̃] *f* association, guild

corpo·rel -relle [kɔrpɔrɛl] *adj* corporal, bodily

corps [kɔr] *m* body; corps; **à corps perdu** without thinking; **à mon (ton,** etc.) **corps défendant** in self-defense; reluctantly; **corps à corps** hand-to-hand; in a clinch; **corps céleste** heavenly body; **corps composé** (chem) compound; **corps de garde** guardhouse, guardroom; **corps de logis** main part of the building; **corps du délit** corpus delicti; **corps enseignant** faculty; **corps noir** (phys) black body; **corps simple** (chem) simple substance; **prendre corps** to take shape; **saisir au corps** (law) to arrest

corps-à-corps [kɔrakɔr] *m* hand-to-hand combat; (boxing) infighting

corpulence [kɔrpylɑ̃s] *f* corpulence

corpuscule [kɔrpyskyl] *m* (phys) corpuscle

corral [kɔral] *m* corral

cor·rect -recte [kɔrrɛkt] *adj* correct

correc·teur [kɔrrɛktœr] **-trice** [tris] *mf* corrector; proofreader

correc·tif [kɔrrɛktif] **-tive** [tiv] *adj & m* corrective

correction [kɔrrɛksjɔ̃] *f* correction; correctness; proofreading; punishment; **correction en course** (aer) mid-course correction

corrélation [kɔrrelasjɔ̃] *f* correlation

correspondance [kɔrɛspɔ̃dɑ̃s] *f* correspondence; transfer, connection

correspon·dant [kɔrɛspɔ̃dɑ̃] **-dante** [dɑ̃t] *adj* corresponding, correspondent ‖ *mf* correspondent; party (*person who gets a telephone call*)

correspondre [kɔrɛspɔ̃dr] *intr* to correspond; **correspondre à** to correspond to, correlate with; **correspondre avec** to correspond with (*a letter writer*); connect with (*e.g., a train*)

corridor [kɔridɔr] *m* corridor

corrigé [kɔriʒe] *m* fair copy

corriger [kɔriʒe] §38 *tr* to correct; proofread ‖ *ref* to reform

corroborer [kɔrrɔbɔre] *tr* to corroborate

corroder [kɔrrɔde] *tr & ref* to corrode; erode

corrompre [kɔrɔ̃pr] (3d *sg pres ind* **corrompt**) *tr* to corrupt; rot; bribe; seduce; spoil

corro·sif -sive [kɔrrozif] **-sive** [ziv] *adj & m* corrosive

corrosion [kɔrrosjɔ̃] *f* corrosion; erosion

corroyer [kɔrwaje] §47 *tr* to weld; to plane (*wood*); to prepare (*leather*)

corruption [kɔrrypsjɔ̃] *f* corruption; bribery; seduction

corsage [kɔrsaʒ] *m* blouse; bodice, corsage, waist; (archaic) bust

corsaire [kɔrsɛr] *m* corsair; pedal pusher; **corsaire de finance** ruthless businessman, robber baron

corse [kɔrs] *adj* Corsican ‖ *m* Corsican (*language*) ‖ (*cap*) *f* Corsica; **la Corse** Corsica ‖ (*cap*) *mf* Corsican (*person*)

cor·sé -sée [kɔrse] *adj* full-bodied, heavy; spicy, racy

corser [kɔrse] *tr* to spike, give body to (*wine*); spice up (*a story*) ‖ *ref* to become serious; **ça se corse** the plot thickens

corset [kɔrsɛ] *m* corset

cortège [kɔrtɛʒ] *m* cortege; parade; **cortège funèbre** funeral procession

cortisone [kɔrtizɔn] *f* cortisone

corvée [kɔrve] *f* chore; forced labor; work party

coryphée [kɔrife] *m* coryphée; (fig) leader

cosaque [kɔzak] *adj* Cossack ‖ (*cap*) *mf* Cossack

cosmétique [kɔsmetik] *adj* cosmetic ‖ *m* cosmetic; hair set, hair spray ‖ *f* beauty culture

cosmique [kɔsmik] *adj* cosmic

cosmonaute [kɔsmɔnot] *mf* cosmonaut

cosmopolite [kɔsmɔpɔlit] *adj* & *mf* cosmopolitan

cosmos [kɔsmos], [kɔsmɔs] *m* cosmos; outer space

cosse [kɔs] *f* pod; **avoir la cosse** (slang) to be lazy

cos·su -sue [kɔsy] *adj* rich; well-to-do

cos·taud [kɔsto] **-taude** [tod] *adj* (slang) husky, strapping ‖ *m* (slang) muscleman

costume [kɔstym] *m* costume; suit; **costume sur mesure** custom-made or tailor-made suit; **costume tailleur** lady's tailor-made suit

costumer [kɔstyme] *tr* & *ref* to dress up (*for a fancy-dress ball*); **se costumer en** to come dressed as a

costu·mier [kɔstymje] **-mière** [mjɛr] *mf* costumer

cote [kɔt] *f* assessment, quota; identification mark, letter, or number; call number (*of book*); altitude (*above sea level*); bench mark; book value (*of, e.g., used cars*); racing odds; public-opinion poll; (telv) rating; **avoir la cote** (coll) to be highly thought of; **cote d'alerte** danger point; **cote d'amour** moral qualifications; **cote de la Bourse** stock-market quotations; **cote mal taillée** rough compromise

côte [kot] *f* rib; chop; coast; slope; **à côtes** ribbed, corded; **aller or se mettre à la côte, faire côte** to run aground; **avoir les côtes en long** (coll) to feel lazy; **côte à côte** side by side; **côte d'Azur** French Riviera; **côtes découvertes, plates côtes** spareribs; **en côte** uphill; **être à la côte** to be broke; **faire côte** to run aground

co·té -tée [kɔte] *adj* listed (*on the stock market*); (fig) esteemed

côté [kote] *m* side; **à côté** in the next room; near; **à côté!** a miss!; **à côté de** beside; **à côtés** fringe benefits; **côté cour** (theat) stage right; **côté jardin** (theat) stage left; **d'à côté** next-door; **de côté** sideways; sidelong; aside; **de mon côté** for my part; **donner, passer,** or **toucher à côté** to miss the mark; **du côté de** in the direction of, toward; on the side of; **d'un côté . . . de l'autre côté** or **d'un autre côté** on the one hand . . . on the other hand; **répondre à côté** to miss the point

co·teau [kɔto] *m* (*pl* **-teaux**) knoll; slope

Côte-de-l'Or [kotdəlɔr] *f* Gold Coast

côte·lé -lée [kotle] *adj* ribbed, corded

côtelette [kotlɛt] *f* cutlet, chop; **côtelettes découvertes** spareribs

coter [kɔte] *tr* to assess; mark; number; esteem; (com) to quote, give a quotation on; (geog) to mark the elevations on

coterie [kɔtri] *f* coterie, clique

cothurne [kɔtyrn] *m* buskin

cô·tier [kotje] **-tière** [tjɛr] *adj* coastal

cotir [kɔtir] *tr* to bruise (*fruit*)

cotisation [kɔtizasjɔ̃] *f* dues; assessment

cotiser [kɔtize] *tr* to assess (*each member of a group*) ‖ *intr* to pay one's dues ‖ *ref* to club together

coton [kɔtɔ̃] *m* cotton; **c'est coton** (slang) it's difficult; **coton de verre** glass wool; **coton hydrophile** absorbent cotton; cotton batting; **élever dans le coton** to coddle; **filer un mauvais coton** (coll) to be in a bad way

cotonnade [kɔtɔnad] *f* cotton cloth

cotonner [kɔtɔne] *tr* to pad or stuff with cotton ‖ *ref* to become fluffy; become spongy or mealy

cotonnerie [kɔtɔnri] *f* cotton field; cotton mill

coton·neux [kɔtɔnø] **-neuse** [nøz] *adj* cottony; spongy, mealy

coton·nier [kɔtɔnje] **-nière** [njɛr] *adj* cotton ‖ *mf* cotton picker ‖ *m* cotton plant

côtoyer [kotwaje] §47 *tr* to skirt (*the edge*); hug (*the shore*); border on (*the truth, the ridiculous, etc.*)

cotre [kɔtr] *m* (naut) cutter

cotte [kɔt] *f* petticoat; peasant skirt; overalls; **cotte de mailles** coat of mail

cou [ku] *m* neck; **sauter au cou de** to throw one's arms around

couard [kwar] **couarde** [kward] *adj mf* coward

couardise [kwardiz] *f* cowardice

couchage [kuʃaʒ] *m* bedding; bed for the night

cou·chant [kuʃɑ̃] **-chante** [ʃɑ̃t] *adj* setting ‖ *m* west; decline, old age

couche [kuʃ] *f* layer, stratum; coat (*of paint*); diaper; (hort) hotbed; **couche de fond** primer, prime coat; **couches strata**; childbirth, e.g., **une femme en couches** a woman in childbirth; **fausse couche** miscarriage

coucher [kuʃe] *m* setting (*of sun*); going to bed; **coucher du soleil** sunset; **le coucher et la nourriture** room and board ‖ *tr* to put to bed; put down, lay down; bend down, flatten; mention (*in one's will*); **coucher en joue** to aim at; **coucher par écrit** to set down in writing ‖ *intr* to spend the night; **coucher avec** to sleep with (*have sex with*); (naut) to heel over ‖ *ref* to go to bed, lie down; set (*said of sun*); bend; **allez vous coucher!** (coll) go to blazes! **une Marie-couche-toi-là** a promiscuous woman

couchette [kuʃɛt] *f* berth; crib

couci-couça [kusikusa] or **couci-couci** [kusikusi] *adv* so-so

coucou [kuku] *m* cuckoo; cuckoo clock; (coll) marsh marigold

coude [kud] *m* elbow; angle, bend, turn; **coude à coude** shoulder to shoulder; **jouer dés coudes à travers** to elbow one's way through (*a crowd*)

coudée [kude] *f* cubit; **avoir ses coudées franches** to have a free hand; to have elbowroom

cou-de-pied [kudpje] *m* (*pl* **cous-de-pied**) instep

couder [kude] *tr* to bend like an elbow

coudoiement [kudwamɑ̃] *m* elbowing

coudoyer [kudwaje] §47 *tr* to elbow, to jostle; to rub shoulders with

coudraie [kudrɛ] *f* hazel grove

coudre [kudr] §13 *tr & intr* to sew

coudrier [kudrije] *m* hazel tree

couenne [kwan] *f* pigskin; rind, crackling; mole, birthmark

couette [kwɛt] *f* feather bed; (little) tail; (mach) bearing; **couette de lapin** scut; **couettes** (naut) ship

cougouar or **couguar** [kugwar] *m* cougar

couiner [kwine] *intr* to send Morse code; (coll) to squeak (*said of animal*)

coulage [kulaʒ] *m* flow; leakage; casting (*of metal*); pouring (*of concrete*); (naut) scuttling; (coll) wasting

cou·lant [kulɑ̃] **-lante** [lɑ̃t] *adj* flowing, running; permissive; accommodating (*person*) ‖ *m* sliding ring; (bot) runner

coule [kul] *f* cowl; **être à la coule** (slang) to know the ropes

cou·lé -lée [kule] *adj* cast; sunken; (coll) sunk ‖ *m* (mus) slur ‖ *f* casting; run (*of wild beasts*); **coulée volcanique** outflow of lava

couler [kule] *tr* to pour; cast (*e.g., a statue*); scuttle; pass (*e.g., many happy hours*); (mus) to slur ‖ *intr* to flow; run; leak; sink; slip (away) ‖ *ref* to slip, slide; (coll) to be done for, be sunk; **se la couler douce** (coll) to take it easy

couleur [kulœr] *f* color; policy (*of newspaper*); (cards) suit; **de couleur** colored; **les trois couleurs** the tricolor; **sous couleur de** with the pretext of, with a show of

couleuvre [kulœvr] *f* snake; **avaler des couleuvres** (coll) to swallow insults; (coll) to be gullible; **couleuvre à collier** grass snake

coulis [kuli] *m*—**coulis de tomates** tomato sauce

coulisse [kulis] *f* groove; slide (*of trombone*); (com) curb exchange; (pol) lobby; **à coulisse** sliding; **coulisses** (theat) wings; (theat) backstage; **dans les coulisses** behind the scenes, out of sight; **travailler dans les coulisses** to pull strings

coulis·seau [kuliso] *m* (*pl* **-seaux**) slide, runner

couloir [kulwar] *m* corridor; hallway; lobby; **couloir de la mort** death row

couloire [kulwar] *f* strainer

coup [ku] *m* blow; stroke; blast (*of whistle*); jolt; move (*in a chess game*); **à coup de** with the aid of; **à coup sûr** certainly; **après coup** when it is too late; **à tout coup** each time; **boire à petits coups** to sip; **coup de bélier** water hammer (*in pipe*); **coup de chance** lucky hit; **coup de coude** nudge; **coup de dés** throw of the dice; risky business; **coup de fer** pressing, ironing; **coup de feu, coup de fusil** shot, gunshot; **coup de fion** (slang) finishing touch; **coup de foudre** thunderbolt; love at first sight; bolt from the blue; **coup de fouet** whiplash; stimulus; **coup de froid** cold snap; **coup de grâce** last straw; deathblow; **coup de Jarnac** [ʒarnak] stab in the back; **coup de patte** expert stroke (*e.g., of the brush*); (coll) dig, insult; **coup de pied** kick; **coup d'épingle** pinprick; **coup de poing** punch; **coup de pouce** final touch; help, little push; **coup de sang** (pathol) stroke; **coup de semonce** warning shot; **coup de sifflet** whistle, toot; **coup de soleil** sunburn; (coll) sunstroke; **coup de téléphone** telephone call; **coup de tête** butt; sudden impulse; **coup de théâtre** dramatic turn of events; **coup de tonnerre** thunderclap; **coup d'œil** glance, look; **coup manqué, coup raté** miss; **coup monté** put-up job, frame-up; **coups et blessures** assault and battery; **coup sur coup** one right after the other; **donner un coup de main** (à) to lend a helping hand (to); **encore un coup** once again; **en venir aux coups** to come to blows; **être dans le coup** (coll) to be in on it; **faire coup double** to kill two birds with one stone; **faire les quatre coups** (coll) to live it up, to dissipate; **faire un coup de main** to go on a raid; **manquer son coup** to miss one's chance; **se faire donner un coup de piston** (coll) to pull wires, to use influence; **sous le coup de** under the (immediate) influence of; **sur le coup** on the spot, outright; **tout à coup** suddenly; **tout d'un coup** at one shot, at once

coupable [kupabl] §93 *adj* guilty ‖ *mf* culprit

cou·pant [kupɑ̃] **-pante** [pɑ̃t] *adj* cutting, sharp ‖ *m* (cutting) edge

coup-de-poing [kudpwɛ̃] *m* (*pl* **coups-de-poing**) brass knuckles

coupe [kup] *f* champagne glass; loving cup, trophy; cup competition; cutting; cross section; wood acreage to be cut; cut (*of cloth; of clothes; of playing cards*); division (*of verse*); **coupe claire** cutover forest; **coupe de cheveux** haircut; **coupe sombre** harvested forest; **être sous la coupe de qn** (coll) to be under s.o.'s thumb; **il y a loin de la coupe aux lèvres** there is many a slip between the cup and the lip; **mettre en coupe réglée** (coll) to fleece

cou·pé -pée [kupe] *adj* cut, cut off; interrupted (*sleep*); diluted (*wine*) ‖ *m* coupé ‖ *f* gangway

coupe-circuit [kupsirkɥi] *m invar* (elec) fuse

coupe-coupe [kupkup] *m invar* machete

coupe-feu [kupfø] *m invar* firebreak

coupe-fil [kupfil] *m invar* wire cutter

coupe-file [kupfil] *m invar* police pass (*for emergency vehicles*)

coupe-gorge [kupgɔrʒ] *m invar* death trap, dangerous territory

coupe-jarret [kupʒarɛ] *m* (*pl* **-jarrets**) cut-throat

coupe-ongles [kupɔ̃gl] *m invar* nail clippers

coupe-papier [kuppapje] *m invar* paper knife, letter opener

couper [kupe] *tr* to cut; cut off; cut out; break off, interrupt; cut, water down; turn off; trump; castrate, geld; **ça te la coupe!** (coll) top that!; **couper en fin de ligne** to divide (*a word*) at the end of a line; **couper la file** (aut) to leave one's lane; **couper la parole à** to interrupt; **couper menu** to mince ‖ *intr* to cut; **couper court à** to cut (*s.o. or s.th.*) short ‖ *ref* to cut oneself; intersect; (coll) to contradict oneself; (coll) to give oneself away

couperet [kuprɛ] *m* cleaver; guillotine blade

couperose [kuproz] *f* (pathol) acne

cou·peur [kupœr] **-peuse** [pøz] *mf* cutter; **coupeur de bourses** (coll) purse snatcher; **coupeur d'oreilles** (coll) hatchet man, hired thug

couplage [kuplaʒ] *m* (mach) coupling

couple [kupl] *m* couple (*e.g., of friends, cronies, thieves, etc.; man and wife*); pair (*e.g., of pigeons*); (mech) couple, torque; **couple thermo-électrique** thermoelectric couple; **maître couple** (naut) midship frame ‖ *f* yoke (*of oxen*); couple; leash

coupler [kuple] *tr* to couple; pair

coupleur [kuplœr] *m* (mach) coupler

coupole [kupɔl] *f* cupola

coupon [kupɔ̃] *m* coupon; remnant (*of cloth*); theater ticket; **coupon date libre** open ticket

coupon-réponse [kupɔ̃repɔ̃s] *m*—**coupon-réponse international** international (postal) reply coupon; **coupon-réponse postal** return-reply post card or letter

coupure [kupyr] *f* cut, incision, slit; cut, deletion; newspaper clipping; small note;

interruption, break; drain (*e.g., through a marsh*); denomination

cour [kur] *f* court; courtyard; courtship; **bien en cour** in favor; **cour anglaise** courtyard or court (*of apartment building*); **cour d'appel** appellate court; **cour d'assises** criminal court; **cour de cassation** supreme court of appeals; **cour d'école** school playground; **faire la cour à** to court; **mal en cour** out of favor

courage [kuraʒ] *m* courage; **reprendre courage** to take heart; **travailler avec courage** to work hard ‖ *interj* buck up!, cheer up!

coura·geux [kuraʒø] **-geuse** [ʒøz] *adj* courageous; hard-working

courailler [kuraje] *intr* to gallivant

couramment [kuramɑ̃] *adv* currently; fluently, easily

cou·rant [kurɑ̃] **-rante** [rɑ̃t] *adj* current; running (*water*); present-day (*language, customs, etc.*) ‖ *m* current; flow; shift (*of opinion, population, etc.*); **courant alternatif** alternating current; **courant continu** direct current; **courant d'air** draft; **Courant du Golfe** Gulf Stream; **dans le courant du mois (de la semaine, etc.)** in the course of the month (of the week, etc.); **être au courant de** to be informed about

courant-jet [kurɑ̃ʒɛ] *m* (meteo) jet stream

courba·tu -tue [kurbaty] *adj* stiff in the joints, aching all over

courbature [kurbatyr] *f* stiffness, aching

courbaturer [kɔrbatyre] *tr* to make stiff; exhaust (*the body*)

courbe [kurb] *adj* curved ‖ *f* curve; **courbe de niveau** contour line

cour·bé -bée [kurbe] *adj* curved, bent, crooked

courber [kurbe] *tr* to bend, curve ‖ *intr & ref* to bend, curve; give in

courbure [kurbyr] *f* curve, curvature; **double courbure** S-curve

courette [kurɛt] *f* small courtyard

cou·reur [kurœr] **-reuse** [røz] *mf* runner; **coureur cycliste** bicycle racer; **coureur de cotillons** (coll) wolf; **coureur de dot** fortune hunter; **coureur de filles** Casanova, Don Juan; **coureur de girls** stage-door Johnny; **coureur de spectacles** playgoer; **coureur de vitesse** sprinter

courge [kurʒ] *f* gourd, squash

courir [kurir] §14, §95 *tr* to run; run after; roam; frequent ‖ *intr* to run; **le bruit court que** rumor has it that; **par le temps qui court** at the present time

courlis [kurli] *m* curlew

couronne [kurɔn] *f* crown; wreath; coronet; rim (*of atomic structures*)

couronnement [kurɔnmɑ̃] *m* crowning; coronation; coping

couronner [kurɔne] *tr* to crown; top, cap; reward ‖ *ref* to be crowned; be covered (*with flowers*)

courrier [kurje] *m* courier; mail; **courrier du cœur** advice to the lovelorn; **courrier**

mondain gossip column; **courrier théâtral** theater section
courriériste [kurjerist] *mf* columnist
courroie [kurwɑ] *f* strap; belt
courroucer [kuruse] §51 *tr* (lit) to anger
courroux [kuru] *m* (lit) wrath, anger
cours [kur] *m* course; current (*of river*); tree-lined walk; rate (*of exchange*); market quotation; style, vogue; **au cours de** in the course of; **avoir cours** to be in circulation; to be legal tender; to have classes; **cours d'eau** stream, river; **cours d'été** or **cours de vacances** summer school; **cours du soir** night school; **de cours** in length (*said of a river*); **de long cours** long-range; **suivre un cours** to take a course (*in school*) ‖ *v* see **courir**
course [kurs] *f* running; race; errand; trip; ride (*e.g., in a taxi*); course, path; privateering; stroke (*of a piston*); **course à pied** foot race; **course attelée** harness race; **course au trot** trotting race; **course aux armaments** arms race; **course de chevaux** horse race; **course de côte** hill climb; **course de taureaux** bullfight; **course de vitesse** sprint; **course d'obstacles** steeplechase; **courses sur route** road racing; **de course** at a run; racing (*car; track; crowd*); (mil) on the double; **en pleine course** in full swing; **faire des courses** to go shopping
cour·sier [kursje] **-sière** [sjɛr] *mf* messenger ‖ *m* errand boy; steed
coursive [kursiv] *f* (naut) alleyway, gangway (*connecting staterooms*)
court [kur] **courte** [kurt] *adj* short; brief; concise; choppy (*sea*); thick (*sauce, gravy*); close (*victory*); **à court** short; **de court** by surprise; **prendre le plus court** to take a shortcut; **tenir de court** to hold on a short leash ‖ (when standing before noun) *adj* short, brief (*interval, time, life*) ‖ *m* court (*for tennis*) ‖ **court** *adv* short; **demeurer court** to forget what one wanted to say; **tourner court** to turn sharp; to stop short, to change the subject; **tout court** simply, merely; plain ‖ **court** *v* see **courir**
courtage [kurtaʒ] *m* brokerage; broker's commission
cour·taud [kurto] **-taude** [tod] *adj* stocky, short and stocky
court-circuit [kursirkɥi] *m* (*pl* **courts-circuits**) short circuit
court-circuiter [kursirkɥite] *tr* to short-circuit
court-courrier [kurkurje] *s* (*pl* **courts-courriers**) short-range plane
courtepoint [kurtəpwɛ̃] *f* counterpane
cour·tier [kurtje] **-tière** [tjɛr] *mf* broker; agent; **courtier électoral** canvasser
courtisan [kurtizɑ̃] *m* courtier
courtisane [kurtizan] *f* courtesan
courtiser [kurtize] *tr* to court
cour·tois [kurtwɑ] **-toise** [twaz] *adj* courteous; courtly
courtoisie [kurtwazi] *f* courtesy

court-vê·tu -tue [kurvɛty] *adj* short-skirted
cou·ru -rue [kury] *adj* sought after, popular; **c'est couru** (coll) it's a sure thing ‖ *v* see **courir**
cou·seur [kuzœr] **-seuse** [zøz] *mf* sewer ‖ *f* seamstress; (mach) stitcher
cou·sin [kuzɛ̃] **-sine** [zin] *mf* cousin; **cousin germain** first cousin; **cousins issus de germains** first cousins once removed ‖ *m* mosquito
cousinage [kuzinaʒ] *m* cousinship; (coll) relatives
coussin [kusɛ̃] *m* cushion; **coussin gonflable** (aut) air bag
coussinet [kusinɛ] *m* little cushion; (mach) bearing
cou·su -sue [kusy] *v* see **coudre**
coût [ku] *m* cost; **coût de la vie** cost of living
cou·teau [kuto] *m* (*pl* **-teaux**) knife; **couteau à cran d'arrêt** clasp knife with safety catch; switchblade knife; **couteau à découper** carving knife; **couteau à ressort** switchblade knife; **couteau pliant, couteau de poche** jackknife
coutelas [kutlɑ] *m* cutlass; butcher knife
coutellerie [kutɛlri] *f* cutlery
coûter [kute] §96 *tr* to cost; **coûte que coûte** cost what it may; **il m'en coûte de** + *inf* it's hard for me to + *inf*
coû·teux [kutø] **-teuse** [tøz] *adj* costly, expensive
coutil [kuti] *m* duck (*cloth*); mattress ticking
coutume [kutym] *f* custom; habit; common law; **de coutume** ordinarily
coutu·mier [kutymje] **-mière** [mjɛr] *adj* customary; common (*law*); accustomed ‖ *m* book of common law
couture [kutyr] *f* needlework; sewing; seam; suture; scar; **battre qn à plate couture** (coll) to beat s.o. hollow; **examiner sur toutes les coutures** to examine inside and out or from every angle; **haute couture** fashion designing, haute couture; **sans couture** seamless
couturer [kutyre] *tr* to scar
coutu·rier [kutyrje] **-rière** [rjɛr] *mf* dressmaker ‖ *m* dress designer ‖ *f* seamstress
couvaison [kuvɛzɔ̃] *f* incubation period
couvée [kuve] *f* brood
couvent [kuvɑ̃] *m* convent; monastery; convent school
couver [kuve] *tr* to brood, hatch ‖ *intr* to brood; smolder
couvercle [kuvɛrkl] *m* cover, lid
cou·vert [kuvɛr] **-verte** [vɛrt] *adj* covered; dressed, clothed; cloudy (*weather*); wooded (*countryside*) ‖ *m* cover; setting (*of table*); service (*fork and spoon*); cover charge; room, lodging; authority (*given by a superior*); **à couvert** sheltered; **mettre le couvert** to set the table; **sous le couvert de** under cover of; **sous les couverts** under cover (*of trees*) ‖ *f* glaze
couverture [kuvɛrtyr] *f* cover; coverage; covering; wrapper; blanket; bedspread
couveuse [kuvøz] *f* brood hen; incubator

couvre-chef [kuvrəʃɛf] *m* (*pl* **-chefs**) (coll) headgear

couvre-feu [kuvrəfø] *m* (*pl* **-feux**) curfew

couvre-lit [kuvrəli] *m* (*pl* **-lits**) bedspread

couvre-livre [kuvrəlivr] *m* (*pl* **-livres**) dust jacket

couvre-oreille [kuvrɔrɛj] *m* (*pl* **-oreilles**) earmuff

couvre-pieds [kuvrəpje] *m invar* bedspread; quilt

couvre-plat [kuvrəpla] *m* (*pl* **-plats**) dish cover

couvre-théière [kuvrətejɛr] *m* (*pl* **-théières**) tea cozy

couvreur [kuvrœr] *m* roofer

couvrir [kuvrir] §65 *tr* to cover ‖ *ref* to cover; cover oneself; get cloudy; put one's hat on

co-voiturage [kɔvwatyraʒ] *m* car pool

cow-boy [kaubɔj], [kobɔj] *m* (*pl* **-boys**) cowboy

C.P. *abbr* (**case postale**) post-office box

C.R. [seɛr] *adv* (letterword) (**contre remboursement**) C.O.D.; **envoyez-le-moi C.R.** send it to me C.O.D.

crabe [krɑb] *m* crab; caterpillar (tractor)

crachat [kraʃa] *m* sputum, spit

cra·ché -chée [kraʃe] *adj* (coll) spitting (*image*)

cracher [kraʃe] *tr & intr* to spit

crachin [kraʃɛ̃] *m* light drizzle

crachoir [kraʃwar] *m* spittoon; **tenir le crachoir** (slang) to have the floor, speak

crachoter [kraʃɔte] *intr* to keep on spitting; sputter

crack [krak] *m* favorite (*the horse favored to win*); (coll) champion, ace; (coll) crackerjack

cracking [krakiŋ] *m* cracking (*of oil*)

craie [krɛ] *f* chalk; piece of chalk

craignez [krɛɲe] *v* (**craignons**) see **craindre**

crailler [krɑje] *intr* to caw

craindre [krɛ̃dr] §15, §97 *tr* to fear, be afraid of, dread; respect ‖ *intr* to be afraid

crainte [krɛ̃t] *f* fear, dread; **dans la crainte que** or **de crainte que** for fear that

crain·tif [krɛ̃tif] **-tive** [tiv] *adj* fearful; timid

cramoi·si -sie [kramwazi] *adj & m* crimson

crampe [krɑ̃p] *f* cramp (*in a muscle*)

crampon [krɑ̃pɔ̃] *m* clamp; cleat (*on a shoe*); (coll) pest, bore

cramponner [krɑ̃pɔne] *tr* to clamp together; (coll) to pester ‖ *ref* to hold fast, hang on, cling

cran [krɑ̃] *m* notch; cog, catch, tooth; **avoir du cran** (coll) to be game (*for anything*); **baisser un cran** to come down a peg; **être à cran** (coll) to be exasperated, cross

crâne [krɑn] *adj* bold, daring ‖ *m* skull, cranium; **bourrer le crâne à qn** (coll) to hand s.o. a line

crâner [krane] *intr* (coll) to swagger

cra·neur [krɑnœr] **-neuse** [nøz] *adj* (coll) *mf* (coll) braggart

crapaud [krapo] *m* toad; baby grand; flaw (*in diamond*); low armchair; (coll) brat;

avaler un crapaud (coll) to put up with a lot

crapule [krapyl] *f* underworld, scum; bum, punk; **vivre dans la crapule** to live in debauchery

crapu·leux [krapylø] **-leuse** [løz] *adj* debauched, lewd, filthy

craquage [krakaʒ] *m* cracking (*of petroleum*)

craquement [krakmɑ̃] *m* crack, crackle

craquer [krake] *intr* to crack; burst; (coll) to crash, fail

craqueter [krakte] §34 *intr* to crackle

crash [kraʃ] *m* crash landing

crasher [kraʃe] *intr* (aer) to crash

crasse [kras] *adj* gross; crass (*ignorance*) ‖ *f* filth, squalor; avarice; dross; **faire une crasse à qn** (slang) to play a dirty trick on s.o.

cras·seux [krasø] **-seuse** [søz] *adj* filthy, squalid; (coll) stingy

crassier [krasje] *m* slag heap

cratère [kratɛr] *m* crater; ewer

cravache [kravaʃ] *f* riding whip, horsewhip

cravacher [kravaʃe] *tr* to horsewhip

cravate [kravat] *f* necktie, cravat; scarf; sling (*for unloading goods*); **cravate de chanvre** (coll) noose; **cravate de drapeau** pennant; **derrière la cravate!** down the hatch!

cravater [kravate] *tr* to tie a necktie on (*s.o.*) ‖ *intr* (slang) to tell a fish story

crawl [krol] *m* crawl (*in swimming*)

crayeux [krɛjø] **crayeuse** [krɛjøz] *adj* chalky

crayon [krɛjɔ̃] *m* pencil; **crayon à bille** ball-point pen; **crayon de pastel** wax crayon; **crayon de rouge à lèvres** lipstick

crayon-feutre [krɛjɔ̃føtr] *m* (*pl* **crayons-feutres**) magic-marker pen

crayonnages [krɛjɔnaʒ] *mpl* doodles, doodling

crayonner [krɛjɔne] *tr* to crayon, pencil, sketch

créance [kreɑ̃s] *f* belief, credence; **créances gelées** frozen assets; **créances véreuses** bad debts

créan·cier [kreɑ̃sje] **-cière** [sjɛr] *mf* creditor; **créancier hypothécaire** mortgage holder

créa·teur [kreatœr] **-trice** [tris] *adj* creative ‖ *mf* creator; originator

création [kreasjɔ̃] *f* creation

créature [kreatyr] *f* creature

crécelle [kresɛl] *f* rattle; chatterbox; **de crécelle** rasping

crèche [krɛʃ] *f* manger; crèche; day nursery

crédence [kredɑ̃s] *f* buffet, sideboard, credenza

crédibilité [kredibilite] *f* credibility

crédit [kredi] *m* credit; (govt) appropriation; **crédit bail** leasing; **crédit croisé** swap

créditer [kredite] *tr* (com) to credit

crédi·teur [kreditœr] **-trice** [tris] *adj* credit (*side, account*) ‖ *mf* creditor

credo [kredo] *m invar* credo, creed

crédule [kredyl] *adj* credulous

créer [kree] *tr* to create

crémaillère [kremajɛr] *f* pothook; rack; rack rail; **crémaillère et pignon** rack and pinion; **pendre la crémaillère** to have a housewarming

crémation [kremɑsjɔ̃] *f* cremation

crématoire [krematwar] *adj & m* crematory

crème [krɛm] *f* cream; **crème chantilly** whipped cream; **crème de démaquillage** cleansing cream; **crème fouettée** whipped cream; **crème glacée** ice cream

crémer [kreme] §10 *intr* to cream

crémerie [krɛmri] *f* dairy; milkhouse (*on a farm*); dairy luncheonette

cré·meux [kremø] **-meuse** [møz] *adj* creamy

crémier [kremje] *m* dairyman

crémière [kremjɛr] *f* dairymaid; cream pitcher

crémone [kremɔn] *f* casement bolt

cré·neau [kreno] *m* (*pl* **-neaux**) crenel; loophole; marked lane (*on a highway*); extra passing lane; space between two cars; **créneau temporel** time slot; **créneaux** battlements

créneler [krɛnle] §34 *tr* to crenelate; tooth (*a wheel*); mill (*a coin*)

créole [kreɔl] *adj* Creole ‖ *m* Creole (*language*) ‖ (*cap*) *mf* Creole (*person*)

crêpe [krɛp] *m* crepe ‖ *f* pancake

crépitation [krepitɑsjɔ̃] *f* crackle

crépitement [krepitmɑ̃] *m* crackling

crépiter [krepite] *intr* to crackle

cré·pu -pue [krepy] *adj* crimped, frizzly, crinkled

crépuscule [krepyskyl] *m* twilight

cresson [krɛsɔ̃] *m* cress; **cresson de fontaine** watercress

crête [krɛt] *f* crest; **crête de coq** cockscomb

Crète [krɛt] *f* Crete; **la Crète** Crete

crête-de-coq [krɛtdəkɔk] *f* (*pl* **crêtes-de-coq**) (bot) cockscomb

cré·tin -tine [kretɛ̃] *mf* cretin; (coll) jackass, fathead

cré·tois -toise [kretwa] *adj* Cretan ‖ (*cap*) *mf* Cretan

creuser [krøze] *tr* to dig, excavate; hollow out; furrow; go into thoroughly ‖ *ref*—**se creuser la tête** (coll) to rack one's brains

creuset [krøzɛ] *m* crucible

creux [krø] **creuse** [krøz] *adj* hollow; concave; sunken, deep-set; empty (*stomach*); deep (*voice*); off-peak (*hours*); **songer creux** to dream idle dreams; **sonner creux** to sound hollow ‖ *m* hollow (*of hand*); hole (*in ground*); pit (*of stomach*); trough (*of wave*); **creux de l'aisselle** armpit; **creux des reins** small of the back

crevaison [krəvɛzɔ̃] *f* blowout

crevasse [krəvas] *f* crevice; crack (*in skin*); rift (*in clouds*); flaw (*in metal*)

crevasser [krəvase] *tr* to chap ‖ *intr & ref* to crack, chap

crève-cœur [krɛvkœr] *m invar* heartbreak, keen disappointment

crever [krəve] §2 *tr* to burst; work to death (*e.g., a horse*) ‖ *intr* to burst; split; burst;

go flat (*said of a tire*); (slang) to die, kick the bucket ‖ *ref* to work oneself to death

crevette [krəvɛt] *f* shrimp; **crevette grise** shrimp; **crevette rose, crevette bouquet** prawn

C.-R.F. *abbr* (**Croix-Rouge française**) French Red Cross

cri [kri] *m* cry; shout; whine, squeal; **dernier cri** last word, latest thing

criailler [kriɑje] *intr* to honk (*said of goose*); (coll) to whine, complain, grouse; **criailler après, criailler contre** (coll) to nag at

criaillerie [kriɑjri] *f* (coll) shouting; (coll) whining, complaining; (coll) nagging

criant [krijɑ̃] **criante** [krijɑ̃t] *adj* crying (*shame*); obvious (*truth*); flagrant (*injustice*)

criard [krijar] **criarde** [krijard] *adj* complaining; shrill (*voice*); loud (*color*); pressing (*debts*) ‖ *mf* complainer ‖ *f* scold, shrew

crible [kribl] *m* sieve; **crible à gravier** gravel screen; **crible à mineral** jig; **passer au crible** to sift or screen

cri·blé -blée [krible] *adj* riddled (*with, e.g., debts*); pitted (*by, e.g., smallpox*)

cribler [krible] *tr* to sift, screen; riddle; **cribler de ridicule** to cover with ridicule

cric [krik] *m* (aut) jack ‖ *interj* crack!, snap!

cricket [krikɛt] *m* (sports) cricket

cricri [krikri] *m* (ent) cricket

crier [krije] §97, §98 *tr* to cry; cry out; shout; cry for (*revenge*); **crier misère** to complain of being poor; cry poverty (*said of clothing, furniture, etc.*) ‖ *intr* to cry; cry out; shout; creak, squeak; squeal; **crier à** to cry out against (*scandal, injustice, etc.*); cry for (*help*); **crier après** to yell at, bawl out; **crier contre** to cry out against; to rail at

crieur [krijœr] **crieuse** [krijøz] *mf* crier; hawker, peddler; **crieur public** town crier

crime [krim] *m* crime; felony

crimi·nel -nelle [kriminɛl] *adj & mf* criminal

crin [krɛ̃] *m* horsehair (*on mane and tail*); **à tous crins** out-and-out, hard-core (*e.g., revolutionist*)

crinière [krinjɛr] *f* mane

crique [krik] *f* cove

criquet [krikɛ] *m* locust; weak wine; (coll) shrimp (*person*)

crise [kriz] *f* crisis; **crise d'appendicite** appendicitis attack; **crise de foi** shaken faith; **crise de main-d'œuvre** labor-shortage; **crise de nerfs** fit of hysterics; **crise du foie** liver upset; **crise du logement** housing shortage; **crise économique** (com) depression

cris·pant -pante [krispɑ̃] *adj* irritating, annoying

crispation [krispɑsjɔ̃] *f* contraction, shriveling up; (coll) fidgeting

cris·pé -pée [krispe] *adj* nervous, strained, tense

crisper [krispe] *tr* to contract, clench; (coll) to make fidgety ‖ *ref* to contract, curl up

crisser [krise] *tr* to grind or grit (*one's teeth*) ‖ *intr* to grate, crunch

cris·tal [kristal] *m* (*pl* -**taux** [to]) crystal; **cristal de roche** rock crystal; **cristal taillé** cut glass; **cristaux** glassware; **cristaux de soude** washing soda

cristal·lin [kristalɛ̃] -**line** [lin] *adj* crystalline ‖ *m* crystalline lens (*of the eye*)

cristalliser [kristalize] *tr, intr, & ref* to crystallize

critère [kritɛr] *m* criterion

critérium [kriterjɔm] *m* championship game

critiquable [kritikabl] *adj* open to criticism, questionable

critique [kritik] *adj* critical ‖ *mf* critic ‖ *f* criticism; critics; **critiques** censure

critiquer [kritike] *tr* to criticize, find fault with ‖ *intr* to find fault

critiqueur [kritikœr] *m* critic, fault-finder

croassement [krɔasmɑ̃] *m* croak, caw, croaking (*of raven*)

croasser [krɔase] *intr* to croak, caw

croate [krɔat] *adj* Croatian ‖ *m* Croat, Croatian (*language*) ‖ (*cap*) *mf* Croatian (*person*)

croc [kro] *m* hook; fang (*of dog*); tusk (*of walrus*)

croc-en-jambe [krɔkɑ̃jɑ̃b] *m* (*pl* **crocs-en-jambes** [krɔkɑ̃jɑ̃b])—**faire un croc-en-jambe à qn** to trip s.o. up

croche [krɔʃ] *f* (mus) quaver

crochet [krɔʃɛ] *m* hook; fang (*of snake*); crochet work; crochet needle; picklock; **crochet radiophonique** talent show; **crochets** (typ) brackets; **faire un crochet** to swerve; **vivre aux crochets de** to live on or at the expense of

crocheter [krɔʃte] §2 *tr* to pick (*a lock*)

crocheteur [krɔʃtœr] *m* picklock; porter

cro·chu -chue [krɔʃy] *adj* hooked (*e.g., nose*); crooked; **avoir les mains crochues** to be light-fingered

crocodile [krɔkɔdil] *m* crocodile

crocus [krɔkys] *m* crocus

croire [krwar] §16, §95 *tr* to believe; **croire** + *inf* to think that + *ind*; **croire qn** + *adj* to believe s.o. to be + *adj*; **croire que non** to think not; **croire que oui** to think so; **je crois bien** or **je le crois bien** I should say so ‖ *intr* to believe; **croire à** to believe in; **croire en Dieu** to believe in God; **j'y crois** I believe in it ‖ *ref* to believe oneself to be

croisade [krwazad] *f* crusade

croi·sé -sée [krwaze] *adj* crossed; twilled (*cloth*); double-breasted (*suit*); alternate (*rhymes*) ‖ *m* Crusader ‖ *f* crossing, crossroads

croisement [krwazmɑ̃] *m* crossing; intersection; meeting, passing (*of two vehicles*); cross-breeding; **croisement en trèfle** cloverleaf, cloverleaf intersection

croiser [krwaze] *tr* to cross; fold over; meet, pass ‖ *intr* to fold over, lap; cruise ‖ *ref* to cross, intersect; go on a crusade

croiseur [krwazœr] *m* cruiser; **croiseur de bataille** battle cruiser

croisière [krwazjɛr] *f* cruise; **en croisière** cruising

croissance [krwasɑ̃s] *f* growth

crois·sant [krwasɑ̃] -**sante** [sɑ̃t] *adj* growing, increasing, rising ‖ *m* crescent; crescent roll; billhook

croître [krwatr] §17 *intr* to grow; to increase, to rise

croix [krwa] *f* cross; (typ) dagger; **croix de bois, croix de fer, si je mens je vais en enfer** cross my heart and hope to die; **croix gammée** swastika; **en croix** crossed, crosswise

Croix-Rouge [krwaruʒ] *f* Red Cross

cro·quant [krɔkɑ̃] -**quante** [kɑ̃t] *adj* crisp, crunchy ‖ *m* wretch

croque-mitaine [krɔkmitɛn] *m* (*pl* -**mitaines**) bugaboo, bogeyman

croque-monsieur [krɔkməsjø] *m* *invar* grilled ham-and-cheese sandwich

croque-mort [krɔkmɔr] *m* (*pl* -**morts**) (coll) funeral attendant

croquer [krɔke] *tr* to munch; sketch; dissipate (*a fortune*) ‖ *intr* to crunch

croquet [krɔkɛ] *m* croquet; almond cookie

croquis [krɔki] *m* sketch; draft, outline; **croquis coté** diagram, sketch

crosse [krɔs] *f* crosier; butt (*of gun*); hockey stick; lacrosse stick; golf club; **chercher des crosses à** (slang) to pick a fight with; **mettre la crosse en l'air** to show the white flag, to surrender

crotale [krɔtal] *m* rattlesnake

crotte [krɔt] *f* dung; mud; **crotte de chocolat** chocolate cream (candy)

crotter [krɔte] *tr* to dirty ‖ *ref* to get dirty; commit a nuisance (*said of dog*)

crottin [krɔtɛ̃] *m* horse manure

crou·lant [krulɑ̃] -**lante** [lɑ̃t] *adj* crumbling ‖ *m* (slang) old fogy

crouler [krule] *intr* to collapse

croup [krup] *m* (pathol) croup

croupe [krup] *f* croup, rump; ridge, brow; **en croupe** behind the rider

croupetons [kruptɔ̃]—**à croupetons** squatting

crou·pi -pie [krupi] *adj* stagnant

croupier [krupje] *m* croupier; financial partner

croupière [krupjɛr] *f* crupper; **tailler des croupieres à** (coll) to make it hard for

croupion [krupjɔ̃] *m* rump

croupir [krupir] *intr* to stagnate; wallow (*in vice, filth*); remain (*e.g., in ignorance*)

croustil·lant [krustijɑ̃] -**lante** [jɑ̃t] *adj* crisp, crunchy; spicy (*story*)

croustille [krustij] *f* piece of crust; snack; **croustilles** potato chips

croustiller [krustije] *intr* to munch, nibble

croustil·leux [krustijø] -**leuse** [jøz] *adj* spicy (*story*)

croûte [krut] *f* crust; pastry shell (*of meat pie*); scab (*of wound*); (coll) daub, worthless painting; **casser la croûte** (coll) to have a snack

croû·teux [krutø] **-teuse** [tøz] *adj* scabby
croûton [krutɔ̃] *m* crouton; heel (*of bread*);
  vieux croûton (coll) old dodo
croyable [krwɑjabl], [krwajabl] *adj* believable
croyance [krwajɑ̃s] *f* belief
croyant [krwajɑ̃] **croyante** [krwajɑ̃t] *adj*
  believing ‖ *mf* believer
C.R.S. [seerɛs] *fpl* (letterword) (**Com-
  pagnies républicaines de sécurité**) state
  troopers
cru crue [kry] *adj* raw, uncooked; indigestible; crude (*language; art*); glaring, harsh
  (*light*); hard (*water*); plain (*terms*); **à cru**
  directly; bareback ‖ *m* region (*in which
  s.th. is grown*); vineyard; vintage; **de son
  cru** of his own intention; **du cru** local, at
  the vineyard ‖ *f* see **crue** ‖ *v* see **croire**
crû crue [kry] *v* see **croître**
cruaute [kryote] *f* cruelty
cruche [kryʃ] *f* pitcher, jug
cruchon [kryʃɔ̃] *m* small pitcher or jug
cru·cial -ciale [krysjal] *adj* (*pl* **-ciaux** [sjo])
  crucial; cross-shaped
crucifiement [krysifimɑ̃] *m* crucifixion
crucifier [krysifje] *tr* to crucify
crucifix [krysifi] *m* crucifix
crucifixion [krysifiksjɔ̃] *f* crucifixion
crudité [krydite] *f* crudity; indigestibility;
  rawness (*of food*); harshness (*of light*);
  hardness (*of water*); **crudités** raw fruits
  and vegetables; off-color remarks
crue [kry] *f* overflow (*of river*); growth
cruel cruelle [kryɛl] *adj* cruel
cruellement [kryɛlmɑ̃] *adv* cruelly; sorely
crû·ment [krymɑ̃] *adv* crudely; roughly
crustacé [krystase] *m* crustacean
crypte [kript] *f* crypt
CᵗᵉCᵗ *abbr* (**compte courant**) current account
cubage [kybaʒ] *m* volume
cu·bain [kybɛ̃] **-baine** [bɛn] *adj* Cuban ‖
  (*cap*) *mf* Cuban
cube [kyb] *adj* cubic ‖ *m* cube
cuber [kybe] *tr* to cube
cubique [kybik] *adj* cubic
cueillaison [kœjɛzɔ̃] *f* picking, gathering;
  harvest time
cueil·leur [kœjœr] **-leuse** [jøz] *mf* picker;
  fruit picker
cueillir [kœjir] §18 *tr* to pick; pluck; gather;
  win (*laurels*); steal (*a kiss*); (coll) to nab
  (*a thief*); (coll) to pick up (*a friend*)
cuiller or **cuillère** [kɥijɛr] *f* spoon; ladle (*for
  molten metal*); scoop (*of a dredger*);
  cuiller à bouche tablespoon; **cuiller à
  café** teaspoon; **cuiller à pot** ladle; **cuiller
  à soupe** soupspoon; **cuiller et fourchette**
  fork and spoon
cuillerée [kɥijre] *f* spoonful
cuilleron [kɥijrɔ̃] *m* bowl (*of spoon*)
cuir [kɥir] *m* leather; hide; **cuir chevelu**
  scalp; **cuir verni** patent leather; **cuir vert**
  rawhide; **faire des cuirs** to make mistakes
  in liaison
cuirasse [kɥiras] *f* cuirass, breastplate; armor

cuiras·sé -sée [kɥirase] *adj* armored ‖ *m*
  battleship
cuirasser [kɥirase] *tr* to armor ‖ *ref* to steel
  oneself
cuire [kɥir] §19 *tr* to cook; ripen; **c'est du
  tout cuit** (coll) it's in the bag ‖ *intr* to
  cook; to sting, smart; **faire cuire** to cook;
  il vous en cuira you'll suffer for it
cui·sant [kɥizɑ̃] **-sante** [zɑ̃t] *adj* stinging,
  smarting
cuisez [kɥize] *v* (**cuisons**) see **cuire**
cuisine [kɥizin] *f* kitchen; cooking; cuisine;
  (coll) skulduggery; **cuisine roulante**
  chuck wagon, field kitchen; **faire la cuisine** to cook
cuisiner [kɥizine] *tr* to cook; (coll) to grill
  (*a suspect*); (coll) to fix (*an election*) ‖
  intr to cook
cuisinette [kɥizinɛt] *f* kitchenette
cuisi·nier [kɥizinje] **-nière** [njɛr] *mf* cook ‖
  f kitchen stove, cookstove
cuissardes [kɥisard] *fpl* hip boots
cuisse [kɥis] *f* thigh; (culin) drumstick;
  cuisses de grenouille frogs' legs; **il se
  croit sorti de la cuisse de Jupiter** (coll)
  he thinks he is the Lord God Almighty
cuis·seau [kɥiso] *m* (*pl* **-seaux**) leg of veal
cuisson [kɥisɔ̃] *f* baking, cooking; (fig)
  burning sensation, smarting; **en cuisson**
  on the stove, on the grill, in the oven
cuissot [kɥiso] *m* leg (*of game*)
cuistre [kɥistr] *m* pedant, prig
cuit [kɥi] **cuite** [kɥit] *adj* cooked; **nous
  sommes cuits** (coll) our goose is cooked
  ‖ *f* firing (*in a kiln*); **prendre une cuite**
  (slang) to get soused ‖ *v* see **cuire**
cuivre [kɥivr] *m* copper; **cuivre jaune** brass;
  les cuivres (mus) the brasses
cui·vré -vrée [kɥivre] *adj* copper-colored,
  bronzed; brassy, metallic (*sound or voice*)
cuivrer [kɥivre] *tr* to copper; bronze, tan;
  make (*a sound or one's voice*) brassy or
  metallic ‖ *ref* to become copper-colored
cui·vreux [kɥivrø] **-vreuse** [vrøz] *adj*
  (chem) cuprous
cul [ky] *m* bottom (*of bottle, bag*); (slang)
  ass, hind end, rump; **bouche en cul de
  poule** (slang) pursed lips; **faire cul sec**
  (slang) to chug-a-lug
culasse [kylas] *f* breechblock; (mach) cylinder head
cul-blanc [kyblɑ̃] *m* (*pl* **culs-blancs**) wheat-
  ear, whitetail
culbute [kylbyt] *f* somersault; tumble, bad
  fall; (coll) failure; (coll) fall (*of a cabinet*); **faire la culbute** to sell at double the
  purchase price
culbuter [kylbyte] *tr* to overthrow; overwhelm (*the enemy*) ‖ *intr* to tumble, fall
  backwards; somersault
culbuteur [kylbytœr] *m* (mach) rocker arm
cul-de-basse-fosse [kydbɑsfos] *m* (*pl* **culs-
  de-basse-fosse**) dungeon
cul-de-jatte [kydəʒat] *mf* (*pl* **culs-de-jatte**)
  legless person
cul-de-sac [kydəsak] *m* (*pl* **culs-de-sac**)
  dead end; (public sign) no outlet

culée [kyle] *f* abutment
culer [kyle] *intr* to back water
culinaire [kylinɛr] *adj* culinary
culmi·nant [kylminɑ̃] **-nante** [nɑ̃t] *adj* culminating; highest (*point*)
culmination [kylminɑsjɔ̃] *f* (astr) culmination
culminer [kylmine] *intr* to rise high, tower; (astr) to culminate
culot [kylo] *m* base, bottom; (coll) baby of the family; **avoir du culot** (slang) to have a lot of nerve
culotte [kylɔt] *f* breeches, pants; forked pipe; panties (*feminine undergarment*); (culin) rump; **culotte de golf** plus fours; **culotte de peau** (slang) old soldier; **culotte de sport** shorts; **porter la culotte** (coll) to wear the pants; **prendre une culotte** (slang) to lose one's shirt; (slang) to have a jag on
culot·té -tée [kylɔte] *adj* (coll) nervy, fresh
culotter [kylɔte] *tr* to cure (*a pipe*) ‖ *ref* to put one's pants on
culte [kylt] *m* worship; cult; divine service, ritual; religion, creed; **avoir un culte pour** to worship, adore (*e.g., one's parents*)
cul-terreux [kytɛrø] *m* (*pl* **culs-terreux**) (coll) clodhopper, hayseed
cultivable [kyltivabl] *adj* arable, tillable
cultiva·teur [kyltivatœr] **-trice** [tris] *adj* farming ‖ *mf* farmer ‖ *m* (mach) cultivator
cultiver [kyltive] *tr* to cultivate; culture
cultu·ral -rale [kyltyral] *adj* (*pl* **-raux** [ro]) agricultural
culture [kyltyr] *f* culture; cultivation
cultu·rel -relle [kyltyrɛl] *adj* cultural
cumula·tif [kymylatif] **-tive** [tiv] *adj* cumulative
cumuler [kymyle] *intr* to moonlight
cunéiforme [kyneifɔrm] *adj* cuneiform
cupide [kypid] *adj* greedy
cupidité [kypidite] *f* cupidity
Cupidon [kypidɔ̃] *m* Cupid
curage [kyraʒ] *m* cleansing, cleaning out; unstopping (*of a drain*)
curatelle [kyratɛl] *f* guardianship, trusteeship
cura·teur [kyratœr] **-trice** [tris] *mf* guardian, trustee
cura·tif [kyratif] **-tive** [tiv] *adj* curative
cure [kyr] *f* treatment, cure; vicarage, rectory; parish; sun porch; **n'avoir cure de rien, n'en avoir cure** not to care
curé [kyre] *m* parish priest
cure-dent [kyrdɑ̃] *m* (*pl* **-dents**) toothpick

curée [kyre] *f* quarry (*given to the hounds*); scramble, mad race (*for gold, power, recognition, etc.*)
cure-oreille [kyrɔrɛj] *m* (*pl* **-oreilles**) earpick
cure-pipe [kyrpip] *m* (*pl* **-pipes**) pipe cleaner
curer [kyre] *tr* to clean out; dredge ‖ *ref* to pick (*one's nails, one's teeth, etc.*)
cu·rieux [kyrjø] **-rieuse** [rjøz] §93 *adj* curious
curiosité [kyrjozite] *f* curiosity; curio; connoisseurs, e.g., **le langage de la curiosité** the jargon of connoisseurs; **curiosités** sights; **visiter les curiosités** to go sightseeing
curseur [kyrsœr] *m* slide, runner
cur·sif [kyrsif] **-sive** [siv] *adj* cursory; cursive (*handwriting*) ‖ *f* cursive
cuta·né -née [kytane] *adj* cutaneous
cuticule [kytikyl] *f* cuticle
cuti-réaction [kytireaksjɔ̃] *f* skin test
cuve [kyv] *f* vat, tub, tank
cu·veau [kyvo] *m* (*pl* **-veaux**) small vat or tank
cuver [kyve] *tr* to leave to ferment; **cuver son vin** (coll) to sleep it off ‖ *intr* to ferment in a wine vat
cuvette [kyvɛt] *f* basin, pan; bulb (*of a thermometer*); (chem, phot) tray
cuvier [kyvje] *m* washtub
C.V. [seve] *m* (letterword) (**cheval-vapeur**) hp, horsepower
cyanamide [sjanamid] *f* cyanamide
cyanose [sjanoz] *f* cyanosis
cyanure [sjanyr] *m* cyanide
cyclable [siklabl] *adj* reserved for bicycles
cycle [sikl] *m* cycle
cyclique [siklik] *adj* cyclic(al)
cycliste [siklist] *mf* cyclist
cyclomoteur [siklɔmɔtœr] *m* motorbike
cyclone [siklon] *m* cyclone
cyclope [siklɔp] *m* cyclops
cyclotron [siklɔtrɔ̃] *m* cyclotron
cygne [siɲ] *m* swan
cylindrage [silɛ̃draʒ] *m* rolling (*of roads, gardens, etc.*); calendering, mangling
cylindre [silɛ̃dr] *m* cylinder; roller (*e.g., of rolling mill*); steam roller
cylindrée [silɛ̃dre] *f* piston displacement
cylindrer [silɛ̃dre] *tr* to roll (*a road, garden, etc.*); calender, mangle
cylindrique [silɛ̃drik] *adj* cylindrical
cymbale [sɛ̃bal] *f* cymbal
cynique [sinik] *adj & m* cynic
cynisme [sinism] *m* cynicism
cyprès [siprɛ] *m* cypress
cyrillique [sirilik] *adj* Cyrillic
cytoplasme [sitɔplasm] *m* cytoplasm
czar [ksar] *m* czar
czarine [ksarin] *f* czarina

D, d [de] *m invar* fourth letter of the French alphabet

d' = **de** before vowel or mute **h**

d'abord [dabɔr] see **abord**

dactylo [daktilo] *mf* (coll) typist

dactylographe [daktilɔgraf] *mf* typist

dactylographier [daktilɔgrafje] *tr* to type

dactyloscopie [daktilɔskɔpi] *f* fingerprinting

dada [dada] *m* hobby-horse; hobby, fad, pet subject; **enfourcher son dada** to ride one's hobby

dague [dag] *f* dagger; first antler; tusk

dahlia [dalja] *m* dahlia

daigner [deɲe] §95 *intr*—**daigner** + *inf* to deign to, condescend to + *inf;* **daignez please**

d'ailleurs [dajœr] see **ailleurs**

daim [dɛ̃] *m* fallow deer; suede

daine [dɛn] *f* doe

dais [dɛ] *m* canopy

dalle [dal] *f* flagstone, slab, paving block; **se rincer la dalle** (slang) to wet one's whistle

daller [dale] *tr* to pave with flagstones

dalto·nien [daltɔnjɛ̃] **-nienne** [njɛn] *adj* color-blind ‖ *mf* color-blind person

dam [dɑ̃] *m*—**au dam de** to the detriment of

damas [damɑ] *m* damask ‖ (*cap*) [damɑs] *f* Damascus

damasquiner [damaskine] *tr* to damascene

damas·sé -sée [damase] *adj* & *m* damask

dame [dam] *f* dame; lady; tamp, tamper; rowlock; (cards, chess) queen; (checkers) king; **aller à dame** (checkers) to crown a man king; (chess) to queen a pawn; **dame d'honneur** lady-in-waiting; **dame pipi** (slang) female toilet attendant; **dames** (public sign) ladies ‖ *interj* for heaven's sake!

damer [dame] *tr* to tamp (*the earth*); (checkers) to crown (*a checker*); (chess) to queen (*a pawn*); **damer le pion à qn** to outwit s.o.

damier [damje] *m* checkerboard

damnation [dɑnasjɔ̃] *f* damnation

dam·né -née [dane] *adj* & *mf* damned

damner [dane] *tr* to damn

damoi·seau [damwazo] **-selle** [zɛl] *mf* (*pl* **-seaux**) (archaic) young member of the nobility ‖ *m* lady's man ‖ *f* (archaic) damsel

dancing [dɑ̃siŋ] *m* dance hall

dandiner [dɑ̃dine] *tr* to dandle ‖ *ref* to waddle along

dandy [dɑ̃di] *m* dandy, fop

Danemark [danmark] *m*—**le Danemark** Denmark

danger [dɑ̃ʒe] *m* danger

dange·reux [dɑ̃ʒrø] **-reuse** [røz] *adj* dangerous

da·nois [danwa] **-noise** [nwaz] *adj* Danish ‖ *m* Danish (*language*) ‖ (*cap*) *mf* Dane

dans [dɑ̃] *prep* in; into; in (*at the end of*), e.g., **dans deux jours** in two days; **boire**

dans un verre to drink out of a glass; **dans la suite** later

danse [dɑ̃s] *f* dance; **danse de Saint Guy** St. Vitus's dance; **danse guerrière** war dance

danser [dɑ̃se] *tr* & *intr* to dance; **faire danser** to mistreat

dan·seur [dɑ̃sœr] **-seuse** [søz] *mf* dancer; **danseur de corde** tightrope walker; **en danseuse** in a standing position (*taken by cyclist*)

Danube [danyb] *m* Danube

d'après [dɑprɛ] see **après**

dard [dar] *m* dart; sting; snake's tongue; harpoon

darder [darde] *tr* to dart, hurl

dare-dare [dardar] *adv* (coll) on the double

darse [dars] *f* wet dock

date [dat] *f* date; **de fraîche date** recent; **de longue date** of long standing; **en date de** from; **faire date** to mark an epoch; **prendre date** to make an appointment

dater [date] *tr* & *intr* to date; **à dater de** dating from

datif [datif] *m* dative

datte [dat] *f* date

dattier [datje] *m* date palm

daube [dob] *f* braised meat; **en daube** braised

dauber [dobe] *tr* to braise; heckle; slander; (coll) to pummel ‖ *intr* **dauber sur qn** to heckle s.o., slander s.o.

dau·beur [dobœr] **-beuse** [bøz] *mf* heckler

dauphin [dofɛ̃] *m* dolphin; dauphin

dauphine [dofin] *f* dauphiness

dauphinelle [dofinɛl] *f* delphinium

davantage [davɑ̃taʒ] §90 *adv* more; any more; any longer; **ne . . . davantage** no more; **pas davantage** no longer

de [də] §77, §78, §79 *prep* of, from; with, e.g., **frapper d'une épée** to strike with a sword; (to indicate the agent with the passive voice) by, e.g., **ils sont aimés de tous** they are loved by all; (to indicate the point of departure) from, e.g., **de Paris à Madrid** from Paris to Madrid; (to indicate the point of arrival) for, e.g., **le train de Paris** the train for Paris; (with a following infinitive after certain verbs) to, e.g., **il essaie d'écrire la lettre** he is trying to write the letter; (with a following infinitive after an adjective used with the impersonal expression **il est**) to, e.g., **il est facile de chanter cette chanson** it is easy to sing that song; (after **changer, se souvenir, avoir besoin, etc.**), e.g., **changer de vêtements** to change clothes; (after a comparative and before a numeral) than, e.g., **plus de quarante** more than forty; (to express the indefinite plural or partitive idea), e.g., **de l'eau** water, some water; (to form prepositional phrases with some adverbs), e.g., **auprès de vous** near you; (with the historical infinitive), e.g., **et chacun de pleurer** and everyone cried

dé [de] *m* die (*singular of dice*); thimble; domino; golf tee; **dés** dice

dealer [dilœr] *m* (slang) drug dealer

déambulateur [deɑ̃bylatœr] *m* walker (*used by an infirm person*)

déambuler [deɑ̃byle] *intr* to stroll

débâcle [debakl] *f* debacle; breakup (*of ice*)

débâcler [debɑkle] *intr* to break up (*said of ice in a river*)

déballage [debalaʒ] *m* unpacking; cut-rate merchandise (*sold by street vendor*)

déballer [debale] *tr* to unpack (*merchandise*); display (*merchandise*)

débandade [debɑ̃dad] *f* rout, stampede; **à la débandade** in confusion, helter-skelter

débander [debɑ̃de] *tr* to rout, stampede; slacken (*s.th. under tension*); unwind; **débander les yeux à qn** to take the blindfold from s.o.'s eyes || *intr* to flee, stampede

débaptiser [debatize] *tr* to change the name of, rename

débarbouiller [debarbuje] *tr* to wash the face of

débarcadère [debarkadɛr] *m* wharf, dock, landing platform

débarder [debarde] *tr* to unload

débardeur [debardœr] *m* stevedore, longshoreman

débar·qué -quée [debarke] *adj* disembarking || *mf* new arrival || *m* disembarkment; **au débarqué** on arrival

débarquement [debarkmɑ̃] *m* disembarkation

débarquer [debarke] *m*—**au débarquer de qn** at the moment of s.o.'s arrival || *tr* to unload; lower (*a lifeboat, seaplane, etc.*); (coll) to sack (*s.o.*) || *intr* to disembark, get off

débarras [debara] *m* catchall

débarrasser [debarase] *tr* to disencumber, disentangle; clear (*the table*); rid || *ref*—**se débarrasser de** to get rid of

débarrasseur [debarasœr] *m* busboy

débarrer [debare] *tr* to unbar

débat [deba] *m* debate; dispute; **débats** discussion (*in a meeting*); proceedings (*in a court*)

débâter [debate] *tr* to unsaddle

débattre [debatr] §7 *tr* to debate, argue, discuss; haggle over (*a price*); question (*items in an account*) || *ref* to struggle; be debated

débauche [deboʃ] *f* debauch, debauchery; riot (*e.g., of colors*); overeating; striking, quitting work

débaucher [deboʃe] *tr* to debauch; induce (*a worker*) to strike; lay off (*workers*); steal (*a worker*) from another employer || *ref* to become debauched

débile [debil] *adj* weak || *mf* mental defective

débilité [debilite] *f* debility

débiliter [debilite] *tr* to debilitate

débiner [debine] *tr* (slang) to run (*s.o.*) down || *ref* (slang) to fly the coop

débit [debi] *m* debit; retail sale; shop; cutting up (*of wood*); output; way of speaking

débiter [debite] *tr* to debit; cut up in pieces; retail; produce; speak (*one's part*); repeat thoughtlessly

débi·teur [debitœr] **-trice** [tris] *adj* debit (*account, balance*); delivery (*spool*) || *mf* debtor || **-teur** [tœr] **-teuse** [tøz] *mf* gossip, talebearer; salesclerk

déblai [deblɛ] *m* excavation; **déblais** rubble, fill

déblaiement [deblɛmɑ̃] *m* clearing away

déblatérer [deblaterel] §10 *tr* to bluster or fling (*threats, abuse*) || *intr*—**déblatérer contre** to rail at

déblayer [debleje] §49 *tr* to clear, clear away

débloquer [debloke] *tr* to unblock; unfreeze (*funds, credits, etc.*)

déboguer [deboge] *tr* (comp) to debug

déboire [debwar] *m* unpleasant aftertaste; disappointment

déboisement [debwazmɑ̃] *m* deforestation

déboîter [debwate] *tr* to disconnect (*pipe*); dislocate (*a shoulder*) || *intr* to move into another lane (*said of automobile*); (naut) to haul (*out of line*)

débonder [debɔ̃de] *tr* to unbung

débonnaire [debonɛr] *adj* good-natured, easygoing; (Bib) meek

débor·dant [debordɑ̃] **-dante** [dɑ̃t] *adj* overflowing

débor·dé -dée [deborde] *adj* overwhelmed

débordement [debordmɑ̃] *m* overflowing; outburst; overlap; **débordements** excesses

déborder [deborde] *tr* to extend beyond, jut out over; trim the border from; overwhelm; untuck (*a bed*); (mil) to outflank || *intr* to overflow; (naut) to shove off

débotté [debote] *m*—**au débotté** immediately upon arrival, at once

débouché [debuʃe] *m* outlet; opening (*for trade; of an attack*)

déboucher [debuʃe] *tr* to free from obstruction; uncork || *intr*—**déboucher dans** to empty into (*said of river*); **déboucher sur** to open onto, to emerge into

débouchoir [debuʃwar] *m* plunger

déboucler [debukle] *tr* to unbuckle; take the curls out of

débouler [debule] *tr* to fly down (*e.g., a stairway*) || *intr* to run suddenly out of cover (*said of rabbits*); dash; **débouler dans** to roll down (*a stairway*)

déboulonner [debulone] *tr* to unbolt; (coll) to ruin, have fired; (coll) to debunk

débourber [deburbe] *tr* to clear of mud, clean

débourrer [debure] *tr* to unhair (*a hide*); remove the stuffing from (*a chair*); knock (*a pipe*) clean

débours [debur] *m* disbursement; **rentrer dans ses débours** to recover one's investment

déboursement [debursmɑ̃] *m* disbursing

débourser [deburse] *tr* to disburse

débousso·lé -lée [debusɔle] *adj* adrift, without direction, lost

debout [dəbu] *adv* upright, on end; standing; up (*out of bed*)

déboutonner [debutɔne] *tr* to unbutton; **à ventre déboutonné** immoderately ‖ *ref* (coll) to get something off one's chest

débrail·lé -lée [debrɑje] *adj* untidy, mussed up, unkempt; loose (*morals*); vulgar (*speech*) ‖ *m* untidiness

débrancher [debrɑ̃ʃe] *tr* to switch (*railroad cars*) to a siding; (elec) to disconnect

débrayage [debrɛjaʒ] *m* (aut) clutch release; (coll) walkout

débrayer [debrɛje] §49 *tr* to disengage, throw out (*the clutch*) ‖ *intr* to throw out the clutch; (coll) to walk out (*said of strikers*)

débri·dé -dée [debride] *adj* unbridled

débris [debri] *mpl* debris; remains

débrouil·lard [debrujar] **-larde** [jard] *adj* (coll) resourceful ‖ *mf* (coll) smart customer

débrouiller [debruje] *tr* to disentangle, unravel; clear up (*a mystery*); make out (*e.g., a signature*); (coll) to teach (*s.o.*) to be resourceful ‖ *ref* to clear (*said of sky*); (coll) to manage to get along, take care of oneself; (coll) to extricate oneself (*from a difficult situation*)

débucher [debyʃe] *tr* to flush out (*game*) ‖ *intr* to run out of cover (*said of game*)

débusquer [debyske] *tr* to flush out (*game; the enemy*)

début [deby] *m* debut; beginning, commencement; opening play

débu·tant [debytɑ̃] **-tante** [tɑ̃t] *adj* beginning ‖ *mf* beginner; newcomer (*e.g., to stage or screen*) ‖ *f* debutante

débuter [debyte] *intr* to make one's debut, begin; start up a business; make the opening play

deçà [dəsa] *adv*—**deçà delà** here and there; **en deçà de** on this side of

décacheter [dekaʃte] §34 *tr* to unseal

décade [dekad] *f* period of ten days; (hist, lit) decade

décadence [dekadɑ̃s] *f* decadence

déca·dent [dekadɑ̃] **-dente** [dɑ̃t] *adj & mf* decadent

décaféi·né -née [dekafeine] *adj* decaffeinated, caffeine-free

décagénaires [dekaʒenɛr] *mfpl* teenagers

décaisser [dekɛse] *tr* to uncrate; disburse, pay out

décalage [dekalaʒ] *m* unkeying; shift; slippage; (aer) stagger

décalcomanie [dekalkɔmani] *f* decal

décaler [dekale] *tr* to unkey; shift

décalquage [dekalkaʒ] or **décalque** [dekalk] *m* decal

décalquer [dekalke] *tr* to transfer (*a decal*) onto paper, canvas, metal, etc.; **décalquer sur** to transfer (*a decal*) onto (*e.g., paper*)

décamper [dekɑ̃pe] *intr* to decamp

décanat [dekana] *m* deanship

décanter [dekɑ̃te] *tr* to decant

décapant [dekapɑ̃] *m* scouring agent

décaper [dekape] *tr* to scour, scale

décapiter [dekapite] *tr* to behead, decapitate; top (*a tree*)

décapotable [dekapɔtabl] *adj & f* (aut) convertible

décapsuleur [dekapsylœr] *m* bottle opener

déca·ti -tie [dekati] *adj* haggard, worn-out, faded

décatir [dekatir] *tr* to steam (*cloth*)

décaver [dekave] *tr* (coll) to fleece

décéder [desede] §10 *intr* (*aux*: ÊTRE) to die (*said of human being*)

décèlement [desɛlmɑ̃] *m* disclosure

déceler [desle] §2 *tr* to uncover, detect; to betray (*confusion*)

décélération [deselerasjɔ̃] *f* deceleration

décembre [desɑ̃br] *m* December

décemment [desamɑ̃] *adv* decently

décennie [deseni] *f* decade

dé·cent [desɑ̃] **-cente** [sɑ̃t] *adj* decent

décentraliser [desɑ̃tralize] *tr* to decentralize

déception [desɛpsjɔ̃] *f* disappointment

décernement [desɛrnəmɑ̃] *m* awarding

décerner [desɛrne] *tr* to award (*a prize*); confer (*an honor*); issue (*a writ*)

décès [desɛ] *m* decease, demise

déce·vant [desvɑ̃] **-vante** [vɑ̃t] *adj* disappointing; deceptive

décevoir [desvwar] §59 *tr* to disappoint; deceive

déchaînement [deʃɛnmɑ̃] *m* unchaining, unleashing; outburst, wave

déchaîner [deʃɛne] *tr* to unchain, let loose ‖ *ref* to fly into a rage; break out (*said of storm*)

déchanter [deʃɑ̃te] *intr* (coll) to sing a different tune

décharge [deʃarʒ] *f* discharge; drain; rubbish heap; storeroom, shed; **à décharge** for the defense

déchargement [deʃarʒəmɑ̃] *m* unloading

décharger [deʃarʒe] §38 *tr* to discharge; unload; unburden; exculpate (*a defendant*) ‖ *ref* to vent one's anger; go off (*said of gun*); run down (*said of battery*); **se décharger de q.ch. sur qn** to shift the responsibility for s.th. on s.o.

déchargeur [deʃarʒœr] *m* porter (*e.g., in a market*); dock hand

déchar·né -née [deʃarne] *adj* emaciated, skinny, bony

décharner [deʃarne] *tr* to strip the flesh from; emaciate ‖ *ref* to waste away

déchaus·sé -sée [deʃose] *adj* barefoot

déchausser [deʃose] *tr* to take the shoes off of (*s.o.*); expose the roots of (*a tree, a tooth*) ‖ *ref* to take off one's shoes; shrink (*said of gums*)

déchéance [deʃeɑ̃s] *f* downfall; lapse, forfeiture (*of a right*); expiration, term (*of a note or loan*)

déchet [deʃɛ] *m* loss, decrease; **déchet de route** loss in transit; **déchets** waste products

décheveler [deʃəvle] §34 *tr* to dishevel, muss (*s.o.'s hair*)

déchiffonner [deʃifɔne] *tr* to iron (*wrinkled material*)

déchiffrable [deʃifrabl] *adj* legible; decipherable

déchiffrement [deʃifrəmɑ̃] *m* deciphering, decoding; sight-reading

déchiffrer [deʃifre] *tr* to decipher; sight-read (*music*)

déchif·freur [deʃifrœr] **-freuse** [frøz] *mf* decipherer, decoder; sight-reader

déchique·té -tée [deʃikte] *adj* jagged, torn

déchiqueter [deʃikte] §34 *tr* to cut into strips; shred; slash

déchi·rant [deʃirɑ̃] **-rante** [rɑ̃t] *adj* heart-rending

déchi·ré -rée [deʃire] *adj* torn; sorry

déchirer [deʃire] *tr* to tear, tear up; split (*a country; one's eardrums*); pick (*s.o.'s character*) to pieces ‖ *ref* to skin (*e.g., one's knee*)

déchirure [deʃiryr] *f* tear, rent; sprain

déchoir [deʃwar] (usually used only in: *inf; pp* **déchu**; sometimes used in: *pres ind* **déchois,** etc.; *fut* **déchoirai,** etc.; *cond* **déchoirais,** etc.) *intr* (*aux:* AVOIR or ÊTRE) to fall (*from high estate*); decline, fail

dé·chu -chue [deʃy] *adj* fallen; deprived (*of rights*); expired (*insurance policy*)

décibel [desibɛl] *m* decibel

décider [deside] §97, §100 *tr* to decide, decide on; **décider qn à** + *inf* to persuade s.o. to + *inf* ‖ *intr* to decide; **décider de** to decide, determine the outcome of, e.g., **le coup a décidé de la partie** the trick decided the (outcome of the) game; **décider de** + *inf* to decide to + *inf* ‖ §96, §97 *ref* to decide, make up one's mind, resolve; **se décider à** + *inf* to decide to + *inf*

déci·mal -male [desimal] *adj* (*pl* **-maux** [mo]) decimal ‖ *f* decimal

décimer [desime] *tr* to decimate

déci·sif [desizif] **-sive** [ziv] *adj* decisive

décision [desizjɔ̃] *f* decision; decisiveness

déclama·teur [deklamatœr] **-trice** [tris] *adj* bombastic ‖ *mf* declaimer

déclamatoire [deklamatwar] *adj* declamatory

déclamer [deklame] *tr* to declaim ‖ *intr* to rant; **déclamer contre** to inveigh against

déclara·tif [deklaratif] **-tive** [tiv] *adj* declarative

déclaration [deklarasjɔ̃] *f* declaration; **déclaration de revenus** income-tax return

déclarer [deklare] §95 *tr* & *intr* to declare ‖ *ref* to declare oneself; arise, break out, occur

déclassement [deklɑsmɑ̃] *m* disarrangement; drop in social status; transfer to another class (*on ship, train, etc.*); dismantling; demoting

déclasser [deklɑse] *tr* to disarrange; dismantle; demote

déclenchement [deklɑ̃ʃmɑ̃] *m* releasing; launching (*of an attack*)

déclencher [deklɑ̃ʃe] *tr* to unlatch, disengage; release (*the shutter*); open (*fire*); launch (*an attack*)

déclencheur [deklɑ̃ʃœr] *m* (mach, phot) release

déclic [deklik] *m* pawl, catch; hair trigger

déclin [deklɛ̃] *m* decline

déclinaison [deklinɛzɔ̃] *f* (astr) declination; (gram) declension

décliner [dekline] *tr* & *intr* to decline

déclive [dekliv] *adj* sloping ‖ *f* slope

déclivité [deklivite] *f* declivity

dé·clos -close [deklo] *adj* in bloom

décocher [dekɔʃe] *tr* to let fly; flash (*a smile*)

décoder [dekɔde] *tr* to decode

décoiffer [dekwafe] *tr* to loosen or muss the hair of; uncap (*a bottle*) ‖ *ref* to muss one's hair; take one's hair down

décoincer [dekwɛ̃se] §51 *tr* to unwedge, loosen (*a jammed part*)

décolérer [dekɔlere] §10 *intr* to calm down

décollage [dekɔlaʒ] *m* unsticking, ungluing; takeoff (*of airplane*)

décoller [dekɔle] *tr* to unstick, detach ‖ *intr* (aer) to take off

décolletage [dekɔltaʒ] *m* low-cut neck; screw cutting; topping

décolle·té -tée [dekɔlte] *adj* décolleté ‖ *m* low-cut neckline; bare neck and shoulders

décolleter [dekɔlte] §34 *tr* to cut the neck of (*a dress*) low; bare the neck and shoulders of ‖ *ref* to wear a low-necked dress

décoloration [dekɔlɔrasjɔ̃] *f* discoloration

décolorer [dekɔlɔre] *tr* & *ref* to bleach; fade

décombres [dekɔ̃br] *mpl* debris, ruins

décommander [dekɔmɑ̃de] *tr* to cancel an order for; call off (*a dinner*); cancel the invitation to (*a guest*) ‖ *ref* to cancel a meeting

décompléter [dekɔ̃plete] §10 *tr* to break up (*a set*)

décomposer [dekɔ̃poze] *tr* & *ref* to decompose

décomposition [dekɔ̃pozisjɔ̃] *f* decomposition

décompresser [dekɔ̃prese] *intr* to relax

décompression [dekɔ̃prɛsjɔ̃] *f* decompression

décomprimer [dekɔ̃prime] *tr* to decompress

décompte [dekɔ̃t] *m* itemized statement; discount (*to be deducted from total*); disappointment

décompter [dekɔ̃te] *tr* to deduct (*a sum from an account*) ‖ *intr* to strike the wrong hour

déconcerter [dekɔ̃sɛrte] *tr* to disconcert

décon·fit [dekɔ̃fi] **-fite** [fit] *adj* discomfited, baffled, confused

déconfiture [dekɔ̃fityr] *f* discomfiture; downfall, rout; business failure

décongeler [dekɔ̃ʒle] §2 *tr* to thaw; defrost

décongestionner [dekɔ̃ʒɛstjɔne] *tr* to relieve congestion in

déconseiller [dekɔ̃sɛje] *tr* to dissuade; **déconseiller q.ch. à qn** to advise s.o.

against s.th. ‖ *intr*—**déconseiller à qn de** + *inf* to advise s.o. against + *ger*

déconsidération [dekõsiderɑsjõ] *f* disrepute

déconsidérer [dekõsidere] §10 *tr* to bring into disrepute, discredit

déconsigner [dekõsiɲe] *tr* to take (*one's baggage*) out of the checkroom; free (*soldiers*) from detention

décontenancer [dekõtnɑ̃se] §51 *tr* to discountenance, abash ‖ *ref* to lose one's self-assurance

décontrac·té -tée [dekõtrakte] *adj* relaxed, at ease; indifferent

décontracter [dekõtrakte] *tr* to loosen up (*one's muscles*) ‖ *intr* to stretch one's muscles; relax

déconvenue [dekõvny] *f* disappointment, mortification

décor [dekɔr] *m* décor, decoration; (theat) setting; **décor découpé** cutout; **décors** (theat) set, stage setting

décora·teur [dekɔratœr] **-trice** [tris] *mf* interior decorator; stage designer

décora·tif [dekɔratif] **-tive** [tiv] *adj* decorative, ornamental

décoration [dekɔrɑsjõ] *f* decoration

décorum [dekɔrɔm] *m invar* decorum

découcher [dekuʃe] *intr* to sleep away from home

découdre [dekudr] §13 *tr* to unstitch, rip up; gore ‖ *intr*—**en découdre** to cross swords ‖ *ref* to come unsewn, rip at the seam

découler [dekule] *intr* to trickle; proceed, arise, be derived

découpage [dekupaʒ] *m* shooting script; **découpage des circonscriptions electorales** gerrymandering

découper [dekupe] *tr* to carve (*e.g., a turkey*); cut out (*a design*); indent (*the coast*) ‖ *ref*—**se découper sur** to stand out against (*the horizon*)

décou·plé -plée [dekuple] *adj* well-built, brawny

découpler [dekuple] *tr* to unleash

découpure [dekupyr] *f* cutting out; ornamental cutout; indentation (*in coast*)

découragement [dekuraʒmɑ̃] *m* discouragement

décourager [dekuraʒe] §38, §97, §99 *tr* to discourage ‖ *ref* to become discouraged

décours [dekur] *m* wane

décou·su -sue [dekuzy] *adj* unsewn; disjointed, unsystematic; incoherent (*words*); desultory (*remarks*) ‖ *v* see **découdre**

décou·vert [dekuvɛr] **-verte** [vɛrt] *adj* uncovered, open, exposed ‖ *m* deficit; overdraft ‖ *f* uncovering; discovery

décou·vreur [dekuvrœr] **-vreuse** [vrøz] *mf* discoverer

découvrir [dekuvrir] §65 *tr* to discover; discern (*in the distance*); pick out (*with a searchlight*); uncover ‖ *intr* to become visible (*said of rocks at low tide*) ‖ *ref* to take off one's hat; lower one's guard; clear up (*said of the sky*); say what one is thinking; come to light, be revealed

décrasser [dekrase] *tr* to clean; polish up; get the dirt out of

décré·pit [dekrepi] **-pite** [pit] *adj* decrepit

décret [dekrɛ] *m* decree; order

décrier [dekrije] *tr* to decry, disparage, run down

décrire [dekrir] §25 *tr* to describe

décrochage [dekrɔʃaʒ] *m* (aer) stall

décrocher [dekrɔʃe] *tr* to unhook, take down; (coll) to wangle; **décrocher la timbale** (coll) to hit the jackpot ‖ *intr* to withdraw, retire; (telp) to pick up the receiver ‖ *ref* to come unhooked

décrochez-moi-ça [dekrɔʃemwasa] *m invar* (coll) secondhand clothing store; (coll) hand-me-down

décroît [dekrwa] *m* last quarter (*of moon*)

décroître [dekrwatr] §17 (*pp* **décru;** *pres ind* **décrois,** etc.; *pret* **décrus,** etc.) *intr* to decrease; shorten (*said of days*); to fall (*said of river*)

décrotter [dekrɔte] *tr* to remove mud from; (coll) teach how to behave

décrotteur [dekrɔtœr] *m* shoeshine boy

décrottoir [dekrɔtwar] *m* doormat; scraper (*for shoes*)

décrue [dekry] *f* fall, drop, subsiding

décrypter [dekripte] *tr* to decipher

déculottage [dekylɔtaʒ] *m* undressing

déculotter [dekylɔte] *tr* to take the pants off of ‖ *ref* to take off one's pants

décuple [dekypl] *adj* & *m* tenfold

décupler [dekyple] *tr* & *intr* to increase tenfold

dédaigner [dedɛɲe] §97 *tr* to disdain; reject (*e.g., an offer*); **dédaigner de** + *inf* not to condescend to + *inf*

dédai·gneux [dedɛɲø] **-gneuse** [ɲøz] *adj* disdainful

dédain [dedɛ̃] *m* disdain

dédale [dedal] *s* maze, labyrinth

dedans [dədɑ̃] *m* inside; **en dedans** inside ‖ *adv* inside, within; **mettre dedans** (coll) to take in, to fool

dédicace [dedikas] *f* dedication

dédicacer [dedikase] §51 *tr* to dedicate, autograph

dédicatoire [dedikatwar] *adj* dedicatory

dédier [dedje] *tr* to dedicate; offer (*e.g., a collection to a museum*)

dédire [dedir] §40 *tr*—**dédire qn** to disavow s.o.'s words or actions ‖ *ref* to make a retraction, back down; **se dédire de** to go back on, fail to keep

dédit [dedi] *m* penalty (*for breaking a contract*); breach of contract

dédommagement [dedɔmaʒmɑ̃] *m* compensation, damages, indemnity

dédommager [dedɔmaʒe] §38 *tr* to compensate for a loss, indemnify

dédouaner [dedwane] *tr* to clear through customs; rehabilitate (*a politician, statesman, etc.*)

dédoublement [dedublɔmɑ̃] *m* splitting; subdivision; unfolding

dédoubler [deduble] *tr* to divide or split in two; remove the lining from; unfold; put on another section of (*a train*)

déduction [dedyksjɔ̃] *f* deduction; **déduction pour remplacement** deduction allowance (*on taxes*)

déduire [dedu̯ir] §19 *tr* to deduce; infer; (com) to deduct

déesse [deɛs] *f* goddess

défaillance [defajɑ̃s] *f* failure, failing; faint; lapse (*of memory*); nonappearance (*of witness*); **défaillance cardiaque** heart failure; **sans défaillance** unflinching

défail·lant [defajɑ̃] **-lante** [jɑ̃t] *adj* failing, faltering

défaillir [defajir] §69 *intr* to fail; falter, weaken, flag; faint

défaire [defɛr] §29 *tr* to undo; untie, unwrap, unpack; rearrange; let down (*one's hair*); rid; defeat, rout; wear (*s.o.*) down, tire (*s.o.*) out || *ref* to come undone; **se défaire de** to get rid of

dé·fait [defɛ] **-faite** [fɛt] *adj* undone, untied; loose; disheveled; drawn (*countenance*) || *f* defeat; disposal, turnover; (fig) loophole

défaitisme [defɛtism] *m* defeatism

défaitiste [defɛtist] *mf* defeatist

défalcation [defalkɑsjɔ̃] *f* deduction

défalquer [defalke] *tr* to deduct

défaufiler [defofile] *tr* to untack

défausser [defose] *tr* to straighten || *ref*—**se défausser (de)** to discard

défaut [defo] *m* defect, fault; lack (*of knowledge, memory, etc.*); flaw; chink (*in armor*); **à défaut de** in default of, lacking; **faire défaut à** to abandon, fail (*e.g., one's friends*); (law) to default; **mettre en défaut** to foil

défaveur [defavœr] *f* disfavor

défavorable [defavɔrabl] *adj* unfavorable

défavoriser [defavɔrize] *tr* to handicap, put at a disadvantage

défécation [defekɑsjɔ̃] *f* defecation

défec·tif [defɛktif] **-tive** [tiv] *adj* (gram) defective

défection [defɛksjɔ̃] *f* defection; **faire défection** to defect

défec·tueux [defɛktu̯ø] **-tueuse** [tu̯øz] *adj* defective, faulty

défectuosité [defɛktu̯ozite] *f* imperfection

défen·deur [defɑ̃dœr] **-deresse** [drɛs] *mf* defendant

défendre [defɑ̃dr] §97, §98 *tr* to defend; protect (*e.g., against the cold*); **à son corps défendant** in self-defense; against one's will; **défendre q.ch. à qn** to forbid s.o. s.th. || *intr*—**défendre à qn de** + *inf* to forbid, s.o. to + *inf* || *ref* to defend oneself; (coll) to hold one's own; **se défendre de** to deny (*e.g., having said s.th.*); refrain from, to keep from

défen·du -due [defɑ̃dy] *adj* forbidden

défense [defɑ̃s] *f* defense; tusk; **défense passive** civil defense (*against air raids*); (public signs): **défense d'afficher** post no bills; **défense de dépasser** no passing; **défense de déposer des ordures** no dumping, no littering; **défense de doubler** no passing; **défense de faire des ordures** commit no nuisance; **défense de fumer** no smoking; **défense d'entrer** private, keep out, no admittance

défenseur [defɑ̃sœr] *m* defender; lawyer for the defense; stand-by

défen·sif [defɑ̃sif] **-sive** [siv] *adj & f* defensive

déférence [deferɑ̃s] *f* deference

défé·rent [deferɑ̃] **-rente** [rɑ̃t] *adj* deferential

déférer [defere] §10 *tr* to confer; award; refer (*a case to a court*); **déférer en justice** to haul into court || *intr* to comply; **déférer à** to defer to, comply with

déferler [defɛrle] *tr* to unfurl; set (*the sails of a ship*) || *intr* to spread out (*said of a crowd*); break (*said of waves*)

défeuiller [defœje] *tr* to defoliate || *ref* to lose its leaves

défi [defi] *m* challenge, dare; **défi à l'autorité** defiance of authority; **porter un défi à** to defy; **relever un défi** to take a dare

défiance [defjɑ̃s] *f* distrust

dé·fiant [defjɑ̃] **-fiante** [fjɑ̃t] *adj* distrustful

déficeler [defisle] §34 *tr* to untie

déficience [defisjɑ̃s] *f* deficiency

défi·cient [defisjɑ̃] **-ciente** [sjɑ̃t] *adj* deficient

déficit [defisit] *m* deficit

déficitaire [defisitɛr] *adj* deficit; meager (*crop*); lean (*year*)

défier [defje] §97, §99 *tr* to challenge; defy (*death, time, etc.*); **défier qn de** to dare s.o. to || *ref*—**se défier de** to mistrust

défiger [defiʒe] §38 *tr* to liquefy

défiguration [defigyrɑsjɔ̃] *f* disfigurement; defacement

défigurer [defigyre] *tr* to disfigure; deface; distort

défilé [defile] *m* defile (*in mountains*); parade, procession, line of march; **défilé de modes** fashion parade

défilement [defilmɑ̃] *m* (mil) defilade, cover

défiler [defile] *tr* to unstring; (mil) to put under cover || *intr* to march by, parade, defile || *ref* to come unstrung; take cover; (coll) to gold-brick

défi·ni -nie [defini] *adj* definite; defined

définir [definir] *tr* to define || *ref* to be defined

définissable [definisabl] *adj* definable

défini·tif [definitif] **-tive** [tiv] *adj* definitive; standard (*edition*); **en définitive** in short, all things considered

définition [definisjɔ̃] *f* definition; **définition de fonction** job description

définitivement [definitivmɑ̃] *adv* definitively, for good, permanently

déflation [deflɑsjɔ̃] *f* deflation (*of currency*); sudden drop (*in wind*)

déflecteur [deflɛktœr] *m* vent window (*of an automobile*)

défleurir [deflœrir] *tr* to deflower, strip of flowers ‖ *intr* & *ref* to lose its flowers
déflexion [deflɛksjɔ̃] *f* deflection
défloraison [deflɔrɛzɔ̃] *f* dropping of petals
déflorer [deflɔre] *tr* to deflower
défon·cé -cée [defɔ̃se] *adj* battered, smashed, crumpled; bumpy
défoncer [defɔ̃se] §51 *tr* to batter in; stave in (*a cask*); remove the seat of (*a chair*); break up (*ground; a road*) ‖ *ref* to be broken up (*said of road*)
déformation [defɔrmasjɔ̃] *f* deformation, distortion; **déformation professionnelle** narrow professionalism
défor·mé -mée [defɔrme] *adj* out of shape; rough (*road*)
déformer [defɔrme] *tr* to deform, distort ‖ *ref* to become deformed
défoulement [defulmɑ̃] *m* (psychoanal) insight, recall; (coll) relief
défraî·chi -chie [defrɛʃi] *adj* dingy, faded
défraîchir [defrɛʃir] *tr* to make stale, fade
défrayer [defrɛje] §49 *tr* to defray the expenses of (*s.o.*); **défrayer la conversation** to be the subject of the conversation
défricher [defriʃe] *tr* to reclaim; clear up (*a puzzler*)
défricheur [defriʃœr] *m* pioneer, explorer
défriser [defrize] *tr* & *ref* to uncurl
défroncer [defrɔ̃se] §51 *tr* to remove the wrinkles from
défroque [defrɔk] *f* piece of discarded clothing
défroquer [defrɔke] *tr* to unfrock ‖ *ref* to give up the frock
dé·funt -funte [defœ̃] *adj* & *mf* deceased
déga·gé -gée [degaʒe] *adj* breezy, jaunty, nonchalant; free, detached
dégagement [degaʒmɑ̃] *m* disengagement; clearing, relieving of congestion; liberation (*e.g., of heat*); exit; retraction (*of promise*); redemption, taking out of hock
dégager [degaʒe] §38 *tr* to disengage; free, clear, release; draw, extract (*the moral or essential points*); give off, liberate; take back (*one's word*); redeem, take out of hock
dégaine [degɛn] *f* (coll) awkward bearing; ridiculous posture
dégainer [degɛne] *tr* to unsheathe ‖ *intr* to take up a sword
dégar·ni -nie [degarni] *adj* empty, depleted, stripped
dégarnir [degarnir] *tr* to clear (*a table*); withdraw soldiers from (*a sector*); prune ‖ *ref* to thin out
dégât [dega] *m* damage, havoc
dégauchir [degoʃir] *tr* to smooth out the rough edges of (*stone, wood; an inexperienced person*)
dégel [deʒɛl] *m* thaw
dégeler [deʒle] §2 *tr* to thaw, defrost; loosen up, relax ‖ *intr* to thaw out; **il dégèle** it it thawing
dégéné·ré -rée [deʒenere] *adj* & *mf* degenerate

dégénérer [deʒenere] §10 *intr* to degenerate
dégénérescence [deʒeneresɑ̃s] *f* degeneration
dégingan·dé -dée [deʒɛ̃gɑ̃de] *adj* gangling, ungainly
dégivrage [deʒivraʒ] *m* defrosting
dégivrer [deʒivre] *tr* to defrost, deice
dégivreur [deʒivrœr] *m* defroster, deicer
déglacer [deglase] §51 *tr* to deice; remove the glaze from (*paper*)
dégommer [degɔme] *tr* to ungum; (coll) to fire (s.o.)
dégon·flé -flée [degɔ̃fle] *adj* flat (*tire*)
dégonflement [degɔ̃fləmɑ̃] *m* deflation
dégonfler [degɔ̃fle] *tr* to deflate ‖ *ref* to go flat; go down, subside (*said of swelling*); (slang) to lose one's nerve
dégorger [degɔrʒe] §38 *tr* to disgorge; unstop, open (*a pipe*); scour (*e.g., wool*) ‖ *intr* to discharge, overflow
dégour·di -die [degurdi] *adj* limbered up, lively, sharp, adroit ‖ *mf* smart aleck
dégourdir [degurdir] *tr* to remove stiffness or numbness from (*e.g., legs*); stretch (*one's limbs*); take the chill off; teach (*s.o.*) the ropes, polish (*s.o.*) ‖ *ref* to limber up
dégoût [degu] *m* distaste, dislike
dégoû·tant -tante [degutɑ̃] *adj* disgusting, distasteful
dégoû·té -tée [degute] §93 *adj* fastidious, hard to please ‖ *mf* finicky person
dégoûter [degute] §97, §99 to disgust; **dégoûter qn de** to make s.o. dislike ‖ *ref* to become fed up
dégoutter [degute] *intr* to drip, trickle
dégradation [degradasjɔ̃] *f* degradation; defacement; shading off, graduation; worsening (*of a situation*); (mil) demotion; **dégradation civique** loss of civil rights
dégrader [degrade] *tr* to degrade, bring down; deface; shade off, graduate; (mil) to demote, break ‖ *ref* to debase oneself; become dilapidated
dégrafer [degrafe] *tr* to unhook, unclasp
dégraissage [degresaʒ] *m* dry cleaning
dégraisser [degrese] *tr* to remove grease from; dry-clean
dégrais·seur [degresœr] **-seuse** [søz] *mf* dry cleaner, cleaner and dyer
degré [dəgre] *m* degree; step (*of stairs*); **monter d'un degré** to take a step up (*on the ladder of success*)
dégringolade [degrɛ̃gɔlad] *f* (coll) tumble; (coll) comedown, collapse, downfall
dégringoler [degrɛ̃gɔle] *tr* to bring down (*a government*) ‖ *intr* (coll) to tumble, tumble down
dégriser [degrize] *tr* & *ref* to sober up
dégrossir [degrosir] *tr* to rough-hew; make the preliminary sketches of; refine, polish (*a hick*)
déguenil·lé -lée [degənije] *adj* ragged, in tatters ‖ *mf* ragamuffin
déguerpir [degɛrpir] *intr* (coll) to clear out, beat it; **fair déguerpir** to evict
déguisement [degizmɑ̃] *m* disguise

déguiser [degize] *tr* to disguise

dégusta·teur [degystatœr] **-trice** [tris] *mf* winetaster

dégustation [degystɑsjɔ̃] *f* tasting, art of tasting; consumption (*of beverages*)

déguster [degyste] *tr* to taste discriminatingly; sip, drink; consume

déhancher [deɑ̃/e] *tr* to dislocate the hip of ‖ *intr* to swing one's hips

déharnacher [dearnɑ/e] *tr* to unsaddle, unharness ‖ *ref* (coll) to throw off one's heavy clothing

dehors [dɔɔr] *m* outside; **dehors** *mpl* outward appearance; **du dehors** from without, foreign, external; **en dehors** outside; **en dehors de** outside of; beyond ‖ *adv* outside, out; out-of-doors

déification [deifikɑsjɔ̃] *f* deification

déifier [deifje] *tr* to deify

déiste [deist] *dj* & *mf* deist

déité [deite] *f* deity

déjà [deʒa] *adv* already; yet; before

déjanter [deʒɑ̃te] *tr* to take (*a tire*) off the rim ‖ *ref* to come off

déjection [deʒɛksjɔ̃] *f* excretion; volcanic debris

déjeter [deʒte] §34 *tr* & *ref* to warp, spring

déjeuner [deʒœne] *m* lunch; breakfast; breakfast set; **déjeuner d'affaires**, **déjeuner de travail** business lunch; **petit déjeuner** breakfast ‖ *intr* to have lunch; have breakfast

déjouer [deʒwe] *tr* to foil, thwart

déjucher [deʒy/e] *tr* to unroost ‖ *intr* to come off the roost (*said of fowl*)

déjuger [deʒyʒe] §38 *ref* to change one's mind

delà [dəla] *adv*—**au delà de** beyond; **par delà** beyond

délabrement [delɑbrəmɑ̃] *m* decay, dilapidation; impairment (*of health*)

délabrer [delɑbre] *tr* to ruin, wreck ‖ *ref* to become dilapidated

délacer [delase] §51 *tr* to unlace

délai [delɛ] *m* term, duration, period (*of time*); postponement, extension; **à bref délai** at short notice; **dans le plus bref délai** in the shortest possible time; **dans un délai de** within; **dans un délai record** in record time; **dernier délai** deadline; **sans délai** without delay

délais·sé -sée [delɛse] *adj* forsaken, forlorn, neglected

délaissement [delɛsmɑ̃] *m* abandonment

délaisser [delɛse] *tr* to abandon, desert; relinquish (*a right*)

délassement [delɑsmɑ̃] *m* relaxation

délasser [delɑse] *tr* to rest, refresh, relax ‖ *ref* to rest up

déla·teur [delatœr] **-trice** [tris] *mf* informer

délation [delɑsjɔ̃] *f* paid informing

déla·vé -vée [delave] *adj* washed-out, weak

délayer [delɛje] §49 *tr* to add water to, dilute; **délayer un discours** to stretch out a speech

deleatur [deleatyr] *m* dele

délébile [delebil] *adj* erasable

délectable [delɛktabl] *adj* delectable

délectation [delɛktɑsjɔ̃] *f* pleasure

délecter [delɛkte] *ref*—**se délecter à** to find pleasure in

délégation [delegɑsjɔ̃] *f* delegation

délé·gué -guée [delege] *adj* delegated ‖ *mf* delegate, spokesman

déléguer [delege] §10 *tr* to delegate

délester [delɛste] *tr* to unballast; unburden, relieve

délétère [deletɛr] *adj* deleterious

délibération [deliberɑsjɔ̃] *f* deliberation

délibé·ré -rée [delibere] *adj* deliberate, firm, decided

délibérer [delibere] §10, §97 *tr* & *intr* to deliberate

déli·cat -cate [delika] [kat] *adj* delicate; fine, sensitive (*ear, mind, taste*); touchy; tactful; scrupulous, honest

délicatesse [delikatɛs] *f* delicacy; refinement, fineness; fastidiousness; fragility, weakness

délice [delis] *m* great pleasure ‖ **délices** *f pl* delights, pleasures

déli·cieux [delisjø] **-cieuse** [sjøz] *adj* delicious; delightful, charming

dé·lié -liée [delje] *adj* slender (*figure*); nimble (*mind*); fine (*handwriting*); glib (*tongue*) ‖ *m* upstroke, thin stroke

délier [delje] *tr* to untie, loosen, release ‖ *ref* to come loose

délinéament [delineamɑ̃] *m* delineation

délinéer [delinee] *tr* to delineate

délinquance [delɛ̃kɑ̃s] *f* delinquency; **délinquance juvénile** juvenile delinquency

délin·quant [delɛ̃kɑ̃] **-quante** [kɑ̃t] *adj* & *mf* delinquent; **délinquant primaire** first offender

déli·rant [delirɑ̃] **-rante** [rɑ̃t] *adj* delirious, raving

délire [delir] *m* delirium; **en délire** delirious, in a frenzy

délirer [delire] *intr* to be delirious, rave

délit [deli] *m* offense, wrong, crime; **en flagrant délit** in the act

délivrance [delivrɑ̃s] *f* delivrance; delivery; rescue

délivre [delivr] *m* afterbirth, placenta

délivrer [delivre] *tr* to deliver; rescue

déloger [delɔʒe] §38 *tr* to dislodge; (coll) to oust, evict ‖ *intr* to move out (*of a house*)

déloyal -loyale [delwajal] *adj* (*pl* **déloyaux** [delwajo]) disloyal; unfair, dishonest

déloyauté [delwajote] *f* disloyalty; disloyal act; dishonesty

delta [dɛlta] *m* delta

deltaplane [dɛltaplan] *m* hang glider

déluge [delyʒ] *m* deluge, flood

délu·ré -rée [delyre] *adj* smart, clever; smart-alecky, forward

délurer [delyre] *tr* & *ref* to wise up

délustrer [delystre] *tr* to take the gloss off of

démagnétiser [demaɲetize] *tr* to demagnetize

démagogie [demagɔʒi] *f* demagogy

démagogique [demagɔʒik] *adj* demagogic

démagogue [demagɔg] *adj* demagogic ‖ *mf* demagogue

démaigrir [demɛgrir] *tr* to thin down

démailler [demaje] *tr* to unshackle (*a chain*); unravel (*e.g., a knitted sweater*); make a run in (*a stocking*) ‖ *ref* to run (*said of stocking*)

démailloter [demajɔte] *tr* to take the diaper off of

demain [dəmɛ̃] *adv* & *m* tomorrow; **à demain** until tomorrow; so long; **de demain en huit** a week from tomorrow; **de demain en quinze** two weeks from tomorrow; **demain matin** tomorrow morning

démancher [demɑ̃ʃe] *tr* to remove the handle of; (coll) to dislocate

demande [dəmɑ̃d] *f* request; application (*for a position*); inquiry; demand (*by buyers for goods*)

demander [dəmɑ̃de] §96, §97, §98 *tr* to ask (*a favor; one's way*); ask for (*a package; a porter*); require, need (*attention*); **demander q.ch. à qn** to ask s.o. for s.th. ‖ *intr*—**demander á** or **de** + *inf;* to ask permission to + *inf;* to insist upon + *ger;* **demander après** to ask about, ask for (*s.o.*); **demander à qn de** + *inf* to ask s.o. to + *inf;* **je ne demande pas mieux** I wish I could ‖ *ref* to be needed; wonder

deman·deur [dəmɑ̃dœr] **-deuse** [døz] *mf* asker; buyer ‖ **-deur** [dœr] **-deresse** [drɛs] *mf* plaintiff

démangeaison [demɑ̃ʒezɔ̃] *f* itch

démanger [demɑ̃ʒe] §38 *tr* & *intr* to itch ‖ *intr*—**démanger à** to itch, e.g., **l'épaule lui démange** his shoulder itches, **la langue lui démange** he is itching to speak

démanteler [demɑ̃tle] §2 *tr* to dismantle (*a fort or town*); uncover (*a spy ring*)

démaquillage [demakijaʒ] *m* removal of paint or make-up

démaquillant [demakijɑ̃] *m* cleansing cream, make-up remover

démaquiller [demakije] *tr* & *ref* to take the paint or make-up off

démarcation [demarkɑsjɔ̃] *f* demarcation

démarchage [demarʃaʒ] *m* door-to-door selling, house-to-house selling

démarche [demarʃ] *f* gait, step, bearing; method; step, move, action

démarier [demarje] *tr* to thin out (*plants*)

démarque [demark] *f* (com) markdown

démarquer [demarke] *tr* to remove the identification marks from; plagiarize; mark down

démarrage [demaraʒ] *m* start

démarrer [demare] *tr* to unmoor ‖ *intr* to cast off (*said of ship*); start (*said of train or car*); spurt (*said of racing contestant; said of economy*); **démarrer trop tôt** to jump the gun; **faire démarrer** to start (*a car*); **ne démarrez pas!** don't stir!

démarreur [demarœr] *m* starter (*of car*)

démasquer [demaske] *tr* & *ref* to unmask

démâter [demɑte] *tr* to dismast ‖ *intr* to lose her masts (*said of ship*)

démêlé [demɛle] *m* quarrel, dispute; **avoir des démêlés avec** to be at odds with, run afoul of

démêler [demɛle] *tr* to disentangle, unravel; bring to light, uncover (*a plot*); make out, discern

démembrement [demɑ̃brəmɑ̃] *m* dismemberment

déménagement [demenaʒmɑ̃] *m* moving

déménager [demenaʒe] §38 *tr* to move (*household effects*) to another residence; move the furniture from (*a house*) ‖ *intr* to move, change one's residence; (coll) to become childish; **tu déménages!** (coll) you're out of your mind!

déménageur [demenaʒœr] *m* mover

démence [demɑ̃s] *f* madness, insanity; **en démence** demented

démener [demne] §2 *ref* to struggle, be agitated; take great pains

dé·ment [demɑ̃] **-mente** [mɑ̃t] *adj* & *mf* lunatic

démenti [demɑ̃ti] *m* contradiction, denial; proof to the contrary; (coll) shame (*on account of a failure*)

démentir [demɑ̃tir] §41 *tr* to contradict, deny; give the lie to, belie ‖ *intr* to go back on one's word; be inconsistent

démerdard [demerdar] *m* (slang) shark, sharp customer; **petit démerdard** streetwise kid

démériter [demerite] *intr* to lose esteem, become unworthy

démesure [deməzyr] *f* lack of moderation, excess

démesu·ré -rée [deməzyre] *adj* measureless, immense; immoderate, excessive

démettre [demetr] §42 *tr* to dismiss (*from a job or position*); dislocate (*an arm*) ‖ *ref* to resign, retire

démeubler [demœble] *tr* to remove the furniture from

demeurant [dəmœrɑ̃]—**au demeurant** all things considered, after all

demeure [dəmœr] *f* home, abode, dwelling; **à demeure** permanently; **dernière demeure** final resting place; **en demeure** in arrears; **mettre qn en demeure de** to oblige s.o. to; **sans plus longue demeure** without further delay

demeurer [dəmœre] §96 *intr* to live, dwell ‖ *intr* (*aux:* ÊTRE) to stay, remain; **en demeurer** to leave off; **en demeurer là** to stop, rest there; leave it at that

demi [dəmi] *m* half; (sports) center; (sports) halfback; **à demi** half; **et demi** and a half, e.g., **un centimètre et demi** a centimeter and a half; (after **midi** or **minuit**) half past, e.g., **midi et demi** half past twelve

demi-bas [dəmibɑ] *m* half hose

demi-botte [dəmibɔt] *f* (*pl* **-bottes**) half boot

demi-cercle [dəmiserkl] *m* (*pl* **-cercles**) semicircle

demi-clef [dəmikle] *f* (*pl* **-clefs**) half hitch; **demi-clef à capeler** clove hitch; **deux demi-clefs** two half hitches

demi-congé [dəmikɔ̃ʒe] *m* (*pl* -**congés**) half-holiday

demi-deuil [dəmidœj] *m* (*pl* -**deuils**) half mourning

demi-dieu [dəmidjø] *m* (*pl* -**dieux**) demigod

demi-douzaine [dəmiduzɛn] *f* (*pl* - **douzaines**) half-dozen

demie [dəmi] *f* half hour; **et demie** half past, e.g., **deux heures et demie** half past two

demi-finale [dəmifinal] *f* (*pl* -**finales**) semifinal

demi-frère [dəmifrɛr] *m* (*pl* -**frères**) half brother; stepbrother

demi-heure [dəmiœr] *f* (*pl* -**heures**) half-hour; **toutes les demi-heures à la demi-heure juste** every half-hour on the half-hour

demi-interligne [dəmiɛ̃terliɲ] *m*—**demi-interligne de base** half-line space (*on typewriter*)

demi-jour [dəmiʒur] *m invar* twilight, half-light

demi-journée [dəmiʒurne] *f* (*pl* -**journées**) half-day; **à demi-journée** half-time

démilitariser [demilitarize] *tr* to demilitarize

demi-longueur [dəmilɔ̃gœr] *f* half-length

demi-lune [dəmilyn] *f* (*pl* -**lunes**) half-moon

demi-mondaine [dəmimɔ̃dɛn] *f* (*pl* - **mondaines**) demimondaine

demi-monde [dəmimɔ̃d] *m* demimonde

demi-mot [dəmimo] *m* (*pl* -**mots**) understatement, euphemism; **comprendre à demi-mot** to get the drift of; to take the hint

déminer [demine] *tr* to clear of mines

demi-pause [dəmipoz] *f* (*pl* -**pauses**) (mus) half rest

demi-pension [dəmipɑ̃sjɔ̃] *f* (*pl* -**pensions**) breakfast and one meal

demi-place [dəmiplas] *f* (*pl* -**places**) half fare; half-price seat

demi-reliure [dəmirəljyr] *f* (*pl* -**reliures**) quarter binding; **demi-reliure à petits coins** half binding

demi-saison [dəmisɛzɔ̃] *f* in-between season; **de demi-saison** spring-and-fall (*coat*)

demi-sang [dəmisɑ̃] *m invar* half-bred horse

demi-sœur [dəmisœr] *f* (*pl* -**sœurs**) half sister; stepsister

demi-solde [dəmisɔld] *m invar* pensioned officer ‖ *f* (*pl* -**soldes**) army pension, half pay

demi-soupir [dəmisupir] *m* (*pl* -**soupirs**) (mus) eighth rest

démission [demisjɔ̃] *f* resignation

démissionnaire [demisjɔnɛr] *adj* outgoing ‖ *mf* former incumbent

démissionner [demisjɔne] *tr* (coll) to fire ‖ *intr* to resign

demi-tasse [dəmitɑs] *f* (*pl* -**tasses**) half-cup; small cup, demitasse

demi-teinte [dəmitɛ̃t] *f* (*pl* -**teintes**) halftone

demi-ton [dəmitɔ̃] *m* (*pl* -**tons**) (mus) half tone

demi-tour [dəmitur] *m* (*pl* -**tours**) about-face; half turn; **demi-tour, (à) droite!** about face!, to the rear!; **donner un demi-tour** to make a half turn; **faire demi-tour** to do an about-face; to turn back

demi-volte [dəmivɔlt] *f* U-turn

démobiliser [demɔbilize] *tr* to demobilize

démocrate [demɔkrat] *mf* democrat

démocratie [demɔkrasi] *f* democracy

démocratique [demɔkratik] *adj* democratic

démo·dé -dée [demɔde] *adj* old-fashioned, out-of-date, outmoded

démoder [demɔde] *ref* to be outmoded

demoiselle [dəmwazɛl] *f* single woman, young woman, young lady, miss; dragonfly; (slang) girl; **demoiselle de magasin** saleswoman, female salesperson; **demoiselle d'honneur** maid of honor, bridesmaid; lady-in-waiting

démolir [demɔlir] *tr* to demolish; overturn (*a cabinet or government*)

démolition [demɔlisjɔ̃] *f* demolition; **démolitions** scrap, rubble

démon [demɔ̃] *m* demon

démoniaque [demɔnjak] *adj* demonic, demoniac(al) ‖ *mf* demoniac

démonstra·teur [demɔ̃stratœr] -**trice** [tris] *mf* demonstrator

démonstra·tif [demɔ̃stratif] -**tive** [tiv] *adj* & *m* demonstrative

démontable [demɔ̃tabl] *adj* collapsible, detachable; knockdown

démonte-pneu [demɔ̃tpnø] *m* (*pl* -**pneus**) tire iron

démonter [demɔ̃te] *tr* to dismount; dismantle ‖ *ref* to come apart; go to pieces (*while taking an exam*)

démontrable [demɔ̃trabl] *adj* demonstrable

démontrer [demɔ̃tre] *tr* to demonstrate

démoraliser [demɔralize] *tr* to demoralize

démouler [demule] *tr* to remove from a mold

démoustication [demustikasjɔ̃] *f* mosquito control

dému·ni -nie [demyni] *adj* out of money; **démuni de** out of; devoid of

démunir [demynir] *tr* to strip, deprive; deplete (*a garrison*) ‖ *ref* to deprive oneself

démystifier [demistifje] *tr* to debunk

dénationaliser [denasjɔnalize] *tr* to denationalize

dénaturaliser [denatyralize] *tr* to denaturalize

dénatu·ré -rée [denatyre] *adj* denatured; unnatural, perverse

dénaturer [denatyre] *tr* to denature; pervert; distort

dénébulation [denebylasjɔ̃] *f* defogging

dénégation [denegasjɔ̃] *f* denial

déneigement [denɛʒmɑ̃] *m* snow removal

déni [deni] *m* refusal; (law) denial

dénicher [deniʃe] *tr* to dislodge; take out of the nest; make (*s.o.*) move; search out ‖ *intr* to leave the nest

déni·cheur [deniʃœr] **-cheuse** [ʃøz] *mf* hunter (*of rare books, antiques, etc.*); **dénicheur de vedettes** talent scout

denier [dənje] *m* (fig) penny, farthing; **denier à Dieu** gratuity; **deniers** money, funds; **de ses deniers** with his own money

dénier [denje] *tr* to deny, refuse

dénigrer [denigre] *tr* to disparage

déniveler [denivle] §34 *tr* to make uneven, change the level of

dénivellation [denivɛllɑsjɔ̃] *f* or **dénivellement** [denivɛlmɑ̃] *m* unevenness; depression, settling

dénombrement [denɔ̃brəmɑ̃] *m* census, enumeration

dénombrer [denɔ̃bre] *tr* to take a census of, enumerate

dénomination [denɔminɑsjɔ̃] *f* denomination, appellation, designation

dénommer [denɔme] *tr* to denominate, name

dénoncer [denɔ̃se] §51 *tr* to renounce; indicate, reveal ‖ *ref* to give oneself up

dénonciation [denɔ̃sjɑsjɔ̃] *f* denunciation; declaration

dénoter [denɔte] *tr* to denote

dénouement [denumɑ̃] *m* outcome, denouement; untying

dénouer [denwe] *tr* to untie; unravel

dénoyer [denwaje] §47 *tr* to pump out

denrée [dɑ̃re] *f* commodity; **denrées** provisions, products

dense [dɑ̃s] *adj* dense

densité [dɑ̃site] *f* density

dent [dɑ̃] *f* tooth; cog; scallop (*of an edge*); **dent d'éléphant** tusk; **dents de lait** baby teeth; **dents de sagesse** wisdom teeth; **sur les dents** on one's toes

dentaire [dɑ̃tɛr] *adj* dental

den·tal -tale [dɑ̃tal] *adj* & *f* (*pl* **-taux** [to] **-tales**) dental

dent-de-chien [dɑ̃dəʃjɛ̃] *f* (*pl* **dents-de-chien**) dogtooth violet

dent-de-lion [dɑ̃dəljɔ̃] *f* (*pl* **dents-de-lion**) dandelion

denteler [dɑ̃tle] §34 *tr* to notch, indent; perforate (*stamps*)

dentelle [dɑ̃tɛl] *f* lace; lacework

dentelure [dɑ̃tlyr] *f* notching; serration; scalloping; (phila) perforation

denter [dɑ̃te] *tr* to furnish with cogs or teeth

dentier [dɑ̃tje] *m* false teeth, denture

dentifrice [dɑ̃tifris] *m* dentifrice

dentiste [dɑ̃tist] *mf* dentist

denture [dɑ̃tyr] *f* denture; **denture artificielle** false teeth

dénuder [denyde] *tr* to strip, denude

dé·nué -nué [denɥe] §93 *adj* stripped; **dénué de** devoid of, lacking in; **dénue de tout fondement** completely unfounded

dénuement [denymɑ̃] *m* destitution

dénuer [denɥe] *tr* to deprive, strip

déodorant [deɔdɔrɑ̃] *m* deodorant

déodoriser [deɔdɔrize] *tr* to deodorize

déontologie [deɔ̃tɔlɔʒi] *f* study of ethics; **déontologie médicale** (med) code of medical ethics

dépannage [depanaʒ] *m* emergency service, repairs

dépanner [depane] *tr* to give emergency service to; (coll) to get (*s.o.*) out of a scrape

dépan·neur [depanœr] **-neuse** [nøz] *adj* repairing ‖ *m* serviceman, repairman ‖ *f* tow truck, wrecker

dépaqueter [depakte] §34 *tr* to unpack, unwrap

dépareil·lé -lée [depareje] *adj* incomplete, broken (*set*); odd (*sock*)

dépareiller [depareje] *tr* to break (*a set*)

déparer [depare] *tr* to mar, spoil the beauty of; strip of ornaments

déparier [deparje] *tr* to break, split up the pair of

départ [depar] *m* departure; beginning; division; sorting out; **départ usine** F.O.B.; **faux départ** false start

département [departəmɑ̃] *m* department, section; (govt) department

départir [departir] §64 (or sometimes like **finir**) *tr* to divide up, distribute ‖ *ref*—**se départir de** to give up; depart from

dépassement [depasmɑ̃] *m* passing

dépasser [depase] *tr* to pass, overtake; go beyond; overshoot (*the mark*); exceed; extend beyond; be longer than; (coll) to surprise ‖ *intr* to pass; stick out, overlap, show

dépayser [depeize] *tr* to take out of one's familiar surroundings; bewilder ‖ *ref* to leave one's country

dépecer [depəse] §20 *tr* to carve, cut up

dépêche [depɛʃ] *f* dispatch; telegram

dépêcher [depɛʃe] *tr* to dispatch ‖ §97 *ref* to hurry

dépeigner [depeɲe] *tr* to tousle, muss up (*the hair*)

dépeindre [depɛ̃dr] §50 *tr* to depict

dépendance [depɑ̃dɑ̃s] *f* dependence; **dépendances** outbuildings, annex; dependencies, possessions

dépen·dant [depɑ̃dɑ̃] **-dante** [dɑ̃t] *adj* dependent

dépendre [depɑ̃dr] *tr* to take down ‖ *intr* to depend; **dépendre de** to depend on; belong to; **il dépend de vous de** it is for you to

dépens [depɑ̃] *mpl* expenses, costs; **aux dépens de** at the expense of

dépense [depɑ̃s] *f* expense; pantry; dispensary (*of hospital*); flow (*of water*); consumption (*of fuel*)

dépenser [depɑ̃se] §96 *tr* to spend, expend ‖ *ref* to exert oneself, spend one's energy

dépen·sier [depɑ̃sje] **-sière** [sjɛr] *adj* & *mf* spendthrift

déperdition [depɛrdisjɔ̃] *f* loss; **déperdition de chaleur due au vent** wind-chill factor

dépérir [deperir] *intr* to waste away, decline

dépêtrer [depɛtre] *tr* to get (*s.o.*) out of a jam

dépeupler [depœple] *tr* to depopulate; unstock (*a pond*)

dépha·sé -sée [defaze] *adj* out of phase; out of step, out of touch

dépiauter [depjote] *tr* to skin

dépiécer [depjese] §58 *tr* to dismember

dépiler [depile] *tr* to remove the hair from

dépistage [depistaʒ] *m* tracking down; (med) screening

dépister [depiste] *tr* to track down

dépit [depi] *m* spite, resentment; **en dépit de** in spite of

dépiter [depite] *tr* to spite, vex ‖ *ref* to take offense

dépla·cé -cée [deplase] *adj* displaced (*person*); misplaced, out of place

déplacement [deplasmɑ̃] *m* displacement; movement; travel; transfer (*of an official*); shift (*in votes*); change (*in schedule*); (naut) displacement

déplacer [deplase] §51 *tr* to displace; move; **déplacer la question** to stray from the subject ‖ *ref* to move

déplaire [depleʀ] §52 *intr* to displease, e.g., **la réplique déplaît à la jeune fille** the reply displeases the young woman; to dislike, e.g., **le lait lui déplaît** he dislikes milk; **ne vous en déplaise** if you have no objection, by your leave ‖ *ref* (*pp* **déplu** *invar*) to be displeased, e.g., **ils se sont déplu** they were displeased; **se déplaire à** not to like it in, e.g., **je me déplais à la campagne** I don't like it in the country

déplai·sant -sante [deplɛzɑ̃] -sante [zɑ̃t] *adj* unpleasant, disagreeable

déplaisir [deplɛziʀ] *m* displeasure

déplanter [deplɑ̃te] *tr* to dig up for transplanting

déplantoir [deplɑ̃twaʀ] *m* garden trowel

dépliant [deplijɑ̃] *m* folder, brochure

déplier [deplie] *tr* & *ref* to unfold

déplisser [deplise] *tr* to unpleat

déploiement [deplwamɑ̃] *m* unfolding, unfurling; display, array; (mil) deployment

déplorable [deplɔrabl] *adj* deplorable

déplorer [deplɔre] *tr* to deplore; grieve over

déployer [deplwaje] §47 *tr* to unfold, unfurl; display; (mil) to deploy ‖ *ref* (mil) to deploy

dé·plu -plue [deply] *v* see **déplaire**

déplumer [deplyme] *tr* to pluck (*a chicken*) ‖ *ref* (coll) to lose one's hair

dépoitrail·le -lée [depwatraje] *adj* with breast indecently exposed

dépolariser [depɔlarize] *tr* to depolarize

dépo·li -lie [depɔli] *adj* ground (*glass*)

dépolir [depɔliʀ] *tr* to remove the polish from; frost (*glass*)

déport [depɔʀ] *m* disqualifying of oneself; (com) commission; **sans déport** without delay

déportation [depɔʀtasjɔ̃] *f* deportation; internment in a concentration camp

dépor·té -tée [depɔʀte] *mf* deported criminal, convict; prisoner in a concentration camp

déportement [depɔʀtəmɑ̃] *m* swerve; **déportements** misconduct, immoral conduct, bad habits

déporter [depɔʀte] *tr* to deport; send to a concentration camp; make (*an automobile*) swerve; deflect (*an airplane*) from its course ‖ *intr* to swerve

dépo·sant -sante [depɔzɑ̃] -sante [zɑ̃t] *adj* testifying; depositing ‖ *mf* deponent, witness, depositor

dépose [depoz] *f* removal

déposer [depoze] §95 *tr* to deposit; depose; drop, leave off; register (*a trademark*); lodge (*a complaint*); file (*a petition*) ‖ *intr* & *ref* to depose; settle, form a deposit

dépositaire [depoziteʀ] *mf* trustee, holder; dealer

déposséder [depɔsede] §10 *tr* to dispossess

dépôt [depo] *m* deposit; depository, depot; warehouse; delivery, handing in; **dépôt d'autobus** carbarn; **dépôt de locomotives** roundhouse; **dépôt de mendicité** poorhouse; **dépôt d'épargne** savings account; **dépôt des bagages** baggage room; **dépôt d'essence** filling station; **dépôt de vivres** commissary; **dépôt d'ordures** dump

dépotoir [depɔtwaʀ] *m* landfill, dump; garbage can; storeroom

dépouille [depuj] *f* castoff skin; hide (*taken from animal*); **dépouille mortelle** mortal remains; **dépouilles** spoils (*of war*)

dépouillement [depujmɑ̃] *m* gathering, selection, sifting; despoilment; counting (*of votes*); **dépouillement volontaire** relinquishing

dépouiller [depuje] *tr* to skin; strip; gather, select, sift; count (*votes*) ‖ *ref* to shed one's skin (*said of insects and reptiles*); strip oneself, divest oneself

dépour·vu -vue [depurvy] *adj* destitute; **au dépourvu** unaware; **dépourvu de** devoid of, lacking in

dépoussiérer [depusjere] §10 *tr* to vacuum

dépravation [depravasjɔ̃] *f* depravity

dépraver [deprave] *tr* to deprave

déprécation [deprekasjɔ̃] *f* supplication

dépréciation [depresjasjɔ̃] *f* depreciation

déprécier [depresje] *tr* & *ref* to depreciate

déprédation [depredasjɔ̃] *f* depredation; embezzlement, misappropriation

déprendre [deprɑ̃dʀ] §56 *ref* to detach oneself; come loose; melt

dépres·sif -sive [deprɛsif] -sive [siv] *adj* depressive

dépression [depresjɔ̃] *f* depression

déprimer [deprime] *tr* to depress, lower ‖ *ref* to be depressed

dépriser [deprize] *tr* to undervalue

déprogrammer [deprɔgrame] *tr* to deprogram

depuis [dəpɥi] *adv* since; **depuis que** since ‖ *prep* since, for, e.g., **je suis à Paris depuis trois jours** I have been in Paris for three days; **depuis . . . jusqu'à** from . . . to

dépurer [depyre] *tr* to purify

députation [depytasjɔ̃] *f* deputation

député [depyte] *m* deputy

députer [depyte] *tr* to deputize

der [dɛr] *f*—**la der des der** (coll) the war to end all wars

déraci·né -née [derasine] *adj* uprooted ‖ *mf* uprooted person, wanderer

déraciner [derasine] *tr* to uproot, root out; eradicate

déraillement [derɑjmɑ̃] *m* derailment

dérailler [derɑje] *intr* to jump the track; (coll) to get off the track

déraison [derɛzɔ̃] *f* unreasonableness, irrationality

déraisonnable [derɛzɔnabl] *adj* unreasonable

déraisonner [derɛzɔne] *intr* to talk nonsense

dérangement [derɑ̃ʒmɑ̃] *m* derangement; breakdown; disturbance, bother; **en dérangement** out of order

déranger [derɑ̃ʒe] §38 *tr* to derange, put out of order; disturb, trouble ‖ *ref* to move, change jobs; become disordered, upset; **ne vous dérangez pas!** don't get up!; don't bother!

déraper [derape] *intr* to skid, sideslip; weigh anchor

dératé [derate] *m*—**courir comme un dératé** to run like a jack rabbit

dératiser [deratize] *tr* to derat

derby [dɛrbi] *m* derby (*race*)

derechef [dərəʃɛf] *adv* (lit) once again

déré·glé -glée [deregle] *adj* out of order, irregular (*pulse*); disorderly, excessive

dérégler [deregle] §10 *tr* to put out of order, upset ‖ *ref* to get out of order; run wild

déridage [deridaʒ] *m* face lift

dérider [deride] *tr* to smooth, unwrinkle; cheer up ‖ *ref* to cheer up

dérision [derizjɔ̃] *f* derision

dérisoire [derizwar] *adj* derisive

dériva·tif -tive [derivatif] [tiv] *adj* derivative ‖ *m* diversion, distraction

dérivation [derivasjɔ̃] *f* derivation; drift; by-pass; diversion (*of river, stream, etc.*); **en dérivation** shunted (*circuit*)

dérive [deriv] *f* drift; (aer) fin; (naut) centerboard; **à la dérive** adrift

déri·vé -vée [derive] *adj* drifting; shunted (*current*) ‖ *m* derivative

dériver [derive] *tr* to derive; divert (*e.g., a river*); unrivet ‖ *intr* to derive; be derived; result; drift

dermatologie [dɛrmatɔlɔʒi] *f* dermatology

der·nier -nière [dɛrnje] [njɛr] §92 *adj* last; latest; latter; final; last (*just elapsed*), e.g., **la semaine dernière** last week ‖ (when standing before noun) *adj* last (*in a series*), e.g., **la dernière semaine de la guerre** the last week of the war

dernièrement [dɛrnjɛrmɑ̃] *adv* lately

dernier-né [dɛrnjene] **dernière-née** [dɛrnjɛrne] *mf* (*pl* **-nés -nées**) last-born child

dérobade [derɔbad] *f* side-stepping; cop-out; (equit) refusal

déro·bé -bée [derɔbe] *adj* secret; **à la dérobée** stealthily, on the sly

dérober [derɔbe] *tr* to steal; hide; **dérober à** to steal from; rescue from (*e.g., death*) ‖ *ref* to steal away, disappear; hide; shy away, balk; shirk; give way (*said of knees or one's footing*); **se dérober à** to slip away from, escape from

dérogation [derɔgasjɔ̃] *f*—**dérogation à** departure from (*custom*); waiving of (*principle*); deviation from (*instructions*); release, exemption from; **par dérogation à** notwithstanding

déroger [derɔʒe] §38 *intr*—**déroger à** to depart from (*custom*); waive (*a principle*); derogate from (*dignity; one's rank*)

dérouiller [deruje] *tr* to remove the rust from; polish (*s.o.*); (coll) to limber up; (coll) to brush up on ‖ *ref* to lose its rust; brush up; limber up

dérouler [derule] *tr & ref* to unroll, unfold

dérou·tant -tante [derutɑ̃] [tɑ̃t] *adj* baffling, misleading

déroute [derut] *f* rout, downfall

dérouter [derute] *tr* to steer off the course; reroute; disconcert, baffle ‖ *ref* to go astray; become confused

derrick [dɛrik] *m* oil derrick

derrière [dɛrjɛr] *m* rear, backside ‖ *adv & prep* behind

derviche [dɛrviʃ] *m* dervish

des [de] §7

dès [dɛ] *prep* by (*a certain time*); from (*a certain place*); as early as, as far back as; from, beginning with; **dès lors** from that time, ever since; **dès lors que** since, inasmuch as; **dès que** as soon as

désabonner [dezabɔne] *tr* to cancel the subscription of ‖ *ref* to cancel one's subscription

désabu·sé -sée [dezabyze] *adj* disillusioned

désabuser [dezabyze] *tr* to disabuse, disillusion ‖ *ref* to have one's eyes opened

désaccord [dezakɔr] *m* disagreement, discord

désaccorder [dezakɔrde] *tr* to put (*an instrument*) out of tune ‖ *ref* to get out of tune

désaccoupler [dezakuple] *tr* to unpair; uncouple

désaccoutumer [dezakutyme] §97 *tr* to break (*s.o.*) of a habit ‖ *ref* to break oneself of a habit

désaffecter [dezafɛkte] *tr* to turn from its intended use

désagréable [dezagreabl] *adj* disagreeable; unpleasant

désagréger [dezagreʒe] §1 *tr* to break up, dissolve, disintegrate

désagrément [dezagremɑ̃] *m* unpleasantness, annoyance

désaimanter [dezɛmɑ̃te] *tr* to demagnetize

désalté·rant -rante [dezalterɑ̃] [rɑ̃t] *adj* thirst-quenching, refreshing

désaltérer [dezaltere] §10 *tr* to quench the thirst of; refresh with a drink ‖ *ref* to quench one's thirst

désamorcer [dezamɔrse] §51 *tr* to deactivate, disconnect the fuse of; unprime

désappointement [dezapwɛ̃tmɑ̃] *m* disappointment

désappointer [dezapwɛ̃te] *tr* to disappoint; break the point of, blunt

désapprendre [dezaprɑ̃dr] §56, §96, §97 *tr* to unlearn, forget

désapproba·teur [dezaprɔbatœr] **-trice** [tris] *adj* disapproving ‖ *mf* critic

désapprouver [dezapruve] *tr* to disapprove of, disapprove

désarçonner [dezarsɔne] *tr* to unhorse, buck off; (coll) to dumfound

désarmement [dezarmɔmɑ̃] *m* disarmament; disarming; dismantling (*of ship*)

désarmer [dezarme] *tr* to disarm; deactivate; dismantle; appease ‖ *intr* to disarm; slacken, let up (*said of hostility*)

désarroi [dezarwa] *m* disorder, disarray, confusion

désarticulation [dezartikylɑsjɔ̃] *f* dislocation

désassembler [dezasɑ̃ble] *tr* to disassemble

désastre [dezastr] *m* disaster

désas·treux [dezastrø] **-treuse** [trøz] *adj* disastrous

désavantage [dezavɑ̃taʒ] *m* disadvantage

désavantager [dezavɑ̃taʒe] §38 *tr* to put at a disadvantage, to handicap

désavanta·geux [dezavɑ̃taʒø] **-geuse** [ʒøz] *adj* disadvantageous

désa·veu [dezavø] *m* (*pl* **-veux**) disavowal, denial, repudiation

désavouer [dezavwe] *tr* to disavow, deny, repudiate, disown

désaxé désaxée [dezakse] *adj* unbalanced, out of joint

desceller [desɛle] *tr* to unseal

descendance [desɑ̃dɑ̃s] *f* descent

descendeur [desɑ̃dœr] *m* ski jumper

descendre [desɑ̃dr], [dɛsɑ̃dr] §95, §96 *tr* to descend, go down (*a hill, street, stairway*); take down, to lower (*a picture*); (coll) to bring down (*an airplane; luggage*); (coll) to drop off, let off at the door ‖ *intr* (*aux:* ÊTRE) to descend; go down, go downstairs; stay, stop (*at a hotel*); **descendre** + *inf* to go down to + *inf;* stop off to + *inf;* **descendre court** to undershoot (*said of airplane*); **descendre de** to come down from (*a mountain, ladder, tree*); be descended from

descente [desɑ̃t] *f* descent; invasion, raid; stay (*at a hotel*); stop (*en route*); **descente à terre** (nav) shore leave; **descente de lit** bedside rug

descriptible [dɛskriptibl] *adj* describable

descrip·tif [dɛskriptif] **-tive** [tiv] *adj* descriptive

description [dɛskripsjɔ̃] *f* description

déségrégation [desegregɑsjɔ̃] *f* desegregation

désembrouillage [dezɑ̃brujaʒ] *m* (electron) descrambling

désempa·ré -rée [dezɑ̃pare] *adj* disconcerted; disabled (*ship*)

désemparer [dezɑ̃pare] *tr* to disable (*a ship*) ‖ *intr*—**sans désemparer** continuously, without intermission

désemplir [dezɑ̃plir] *intr*—**ne pas désemplir** to be always full

désenchaîner [dezɑ̃ʃɛne] *tr* to unchain

désenchantement [dezɑ̃ʃɑ̃tmɑ̃] *m* disenchantment

désenchanter [dezɑ̃ʃɑ̃te] *tr* to disenchant

désencombrer [dezɑ̃kɔ̃bre] *tr* to disencumber, clear, free

désengager [dezɑ̃gaʒe] §34 *tr* to release from a promise

désengorger [dezɑ̃gɔrʒe] §38 *tr* to unstop

désengrener [dezɑ̃grɔne] §2 *tr* to disengage, throw out of gear

désenivrer [dezɑ̃nivre] *tr & intr* to sober up

désenlacer [dezɑ̃lase] §51 *tr* to unbind

désennuyer [dezɑ̃nɥije] §27 *tr* to divert, cheer up ‖ *ref* to find relief from boredom

désensabler [dezɑ̃sable] *tr* to free (*a ship*) from the sand; dredge the sand from (*a canal*)

désensibiliser [desɑ̃sibilize] *tr* to desensitize

désensorceler [dezɑ̃sɔrsəle] §34 *tr* to remove the spell from

désentortiller [dezɑ̃tɔrtije] *tr* to straighten out

désenvelopper [dezɑ̃vlɔpe] *tr* to unwrap

déséquilibre [dezekilibr] *m* mental instability

déséquili·bré -brée [dezekilibre] *adj* mentally unbalanced ‖ *mf* unbalanced person

déséquilibrer [dezekilibre] *tr* to unbalance

dé·sert [dezɛr] **-serte** [zɛrt] *adj & m* desert

déserter [dezɛrte] *tr & intr* to desert

déserteur [dezɛrtœr] *m* deserter

désertion [dezɛrsjɔ̃] *f* desertion

désespérance [dezɛsperɑ̃s] *f* despair

désespé·ré -rée [dezɛspere] *adj* desperate, hopeless ‖ *mf* desperate person

désespérer [dezɛspere] §10, §97 *tr* to be the despair of ‖ *ref* to lose hope

désespoir [dezɛspwar] *m* despair; **en désespoir de cause** as a last resort

déshabillage [dezabijaʒ] *m* striptease

déshabillé [dezabije] *m* morning wrap

déshabiller [dezabije] *tr & ref* to undress; **déshabiller saint Pierre pour habiller saint Paul** to rob Peter to pay Paul

déshabituer [dezabitɥe] §97 *tr* to break (*s.o.*) of a habit

déshéri·té -tée [dezerite] *adj* underprivileged; **les déshérités** the underprivileged

déshériter [dezerite] *tr* to disinherit; disadvantage

déshonnête [dezɔnɛt] *adj* improper, immodest

déshonnêteté [dezɔnɛtəte] *f* impropriety, immodesty, indecency

déshonneur [dezɔnœr] *m* dishonor

déshono·rant [dezɔnɔrɑ̃] **-rante** [rɑ̃t] *adj* dishonorable, discreditable

déshonorer [dezɔnɔre] *tr* to dishonor

déshydratation [dezidratɑsjɔ̃] *f* dehydration

déshydrater [dezidrate] *tr* to dehydrate

désignation [deziɲɑsjɔ̃] *f* designation; appointment, nomination

dési·gné -gnée [desiɲe] *mf* nominee

désigner [desiɲe] *tr* to designate; indicate, point out; appoint, nominate; signify, mean; set (*the hour of an appointment*) ‖ *ref*—**se désigner à l'attention de** to bring oneself to the attention of

désillusion [dezillyzjɔ̃] *f* disillusion; disappointment

désillusionner [dezillyzjɔne] *tr* to disillusion; disappoint

désinence [dezinɑ̃s] *f* (gram) ending

désinfecter [dezɛ̃fɛkte] *tr* to disinfect

désinformation [dezɛ̃fɔrmɑsjɔ̃] *f* disinformation

désintégration [dezɛ̃tegrɑsjɔ̃] *f* disintegration

désintégrer [dezɛ̃tegre] §10 *tr* & *ref* to disintegrate

désintéres·sé -sée [dezɛ̃terɛse] *adj* disinterested, impartial; unselfish

désintéressement [dezɛ̃terɛsmɑ̃] *m* disinterestedness, impartiality; payment, satisfaction (*of a debt*); paying off (*of a creditor*)

désintéresser [dezɛ̃terɛse] *tr* to pay off; buy out ‖ *ref*—**se désintéresser de** to lose interest in

désintoxication [dezɛ̃tɔksikɑsjɔ̃] *f* treatment for alcoholism, drug addiction, or poisoning; disintoxification

désinvolte [dezɛ̃vɔlt] *adj* free and easy, casual; offhanded, impertinent

désinvolture [dezɛ̃vɔltyr] *f* free and easy manner, offhandedness; impertinence

désir [dezir] *m* desire

désirable [dezirabl] *adj* desirable

désirer [dezire] §95, §96 *tr* to desire, wish

dési·reux -reuse [dezirø] **-reuse** [røz] *adj* desirous

désister [deziste] *ref* to desist; withdraw from a runoff election, **se désister de** to waive (*a claim*); drop (*a lawsuit*)

désobéir [dezɔbeir] *intr* to disobey; **désobéir à** to disobey, e.g., **le fils désobéira à son père** the son will disobey his father; **être désobéi** to be disobeyed

désobli·geant [dezɔbliʒɑ̃] **-geante** [ʒɑ̃t] *adj* disagreeable, ungracious

désobliger [dezɔbliʒe] §38 *tr* to offend, displease, disoblige

désodori·sant [dezɔdɔrizɑ̃] **-sante** [zɑ̃t] & *m* deodorant

désodoriser [dezɔdɔrize] *tr* to deodorize

désœu·vré -vrée [dezœvre] *adj* idle, unoccupied, out of work; **les désœuvrés** the unemployed

désœuvrement [dezœvrəmɑ̃] *m* idleness, unemployment

déso·lant [dezɔlɑ̃] **-lante** [lɑ̃t] *adj* distressing, sad

désolation [dezɔlɑsjɔ̃] *f* desolation; grief, distress

déso·lé -lée [dezɔle] *adj* desolate; distressed

désoler [dezɔle] *tr* to desolate, destroy; distress ‖ *ref* to be distressed

désopi·lant [dezɔpilɑ̃] **-lante** [lɑ̃t] *adj* hilarious, sidesplitting

désordon·né -née [dezɔrdɔne] *adj* disordered; untidy; disorderly

désordonner [dezɔrdɔne] *tr* to upset, confuse

désordre [dezɔrdr] *m* disorder, confusion, moral laxity

désorganisa·teur [dezɔrganizatœr] **-trice** [tris] *adj* disorganizing ‖ *mf* troublemaker

désorganisation [dezɔrganizɑsjɔ̃] *f* disorganization

désorganiser [dezɔrganize] *tr* to disorganize

désorien·té -tée [dezɔrjɑ̃te] *adj* disoriented, bewildered

désorienter [dezɔrjɑ̃te] *tr* to disorient; mislead; disconcert ‖ *ref* to become confused; lose one's bearings

désormais [dezɔrme] *adv* henceforth

désosser [dezɔse] *tr* to bone

despote [dɛspɔt] *m* despot

despotique [dɛspɔtik] *adj* despotic

despotisme [dɛspɔtism] *m* despotism

des·quels -quelles [dekɛl] §78

dessaisir [desezir] *tr* to dispossess; let go, release ‖ *ref*—**se dessaisir de** to relinquish

dessalement [desalmɑ̃] *m* desalinization

dessaler [desale] *tr* to desalt, desalinate ‖ *ref* (coll) to wise up

dessécher [deseʃe] §10 *tr* to dry up, wither; drain (*a pond*); dehydrate (*the body*); sear (*the heart*) ‖ *ref* to dry up; waste away

dessein [desɛ̃] *m* design, plan, intent; **à dessein** on purpose

desseller [desɛle] *tr* to unsaddle

desserrer [desɛre] *tr* to loosen; **ne pas desserrer les dents** to keep mum

dessert [desɛr] *m* dessert, last course

desserte [desɛrt] *f* buffet, sideboard; branch (*of railroad or bus line*); ministry (*of a substituting clergyman*)

dessertir [desɛrtir] *tr* to remove (*a gem*) from its setting

desservant [desɛrvɑ̃] *m* parish priest

desserveur [desɛrvœr] *m* busboy

desservir [desɛrvir] §63 *tr* to clear (*the table*); be of disservice to, harm; (aer, aut, rr) to stop at (*a town or station*); (aer, aut, eccl, rr) to serve (*a locality*); (elec) to supply (*a region*)

dessiller [desije] *tr*—**dessiller les yeux à qn** or **de qn** to open s.o.'s eyes, undeceive s.o.

dessin [desɛ̃] *m* drawing, sketch, design; profile (*of face*); **dessins animés** (mov) animated cartoons

dessina·teur [desinatœr] **-trice** [tris] *mf* designer; cartoonist

dessiner [desine] *tr* to draw, sketch, design; delineate, outline ‖ *ref* to stand out, be outlined

dessoûler or **dessouler** [desule] *tr* & *intr* to sober up

dessous [dəsu] *m* underpart; reverse side, wrong side; coaster (*underneath a glass*); seamy side, machinations behind the scenes; **au dessous de** below; **avoir le dessous** to get the short end of the deal;

du dessous below; **en dessous** underneath; **les dessous** lingerie, undergarments ‖ *adv & prep* under, underneath, below

dessous-de-bouteille [dəsudəbutɛj] *m invar* coaster

dessous-de-bras [dəsudəbra] *m invar* underarm pad

dessous-de-carafe [dəsudəkaraf] *m invar* coaster

dessous-de-plat [dəsudəpla] *m invar* hot pad

dessous-de-table [dəsudətabl] *m invar* under-the-counter money

dessus [dəsy] *m* upper part; back (*of the hand*); right side (*of material*); (mus) treble part; **au dessus de** beyond, above; **avoir le dessus** to have the upper hand; **le dessus du panier** the cream of the crop ‖ *adv* above ‖ *prep* on, above, over

dessus-de-cheminée [dəsydə/mine] *m invar* mantelpiece

dessus-de-lit [dəsydəli] *m invar* bedspread

dessus-de-porte [dəsydəpɔrt] *m invar* overdoor

dessus-de-table [dəsydətabl] *m invar* table cover

destin [dɛstɛ̃] *m* destiny, fate

destinataire [dɛstinatɛr] *mf* addressee; payee; **destinataire inconnu** or **absent** (formula stamped on envelope) not at this address

destination [dɛstinɑsjɔ̃] *f* destination; **à destination de** to, bound for

destinée [dɛstine] *f* destiny

destiner [dɛstine] §96, §100 *tr* to destine; set aside, reserve; **destiner q.ch. à qn** to mean or intend s.th. for s.o.

destituer [dɛstitɥe] *tr* to remove from office

destitution [dɛstitysjɔ̃] *f* dismissal, removal from office

destrier [dɛstrije] *m* (hist) steed, charger

destroyer [dɛstrɔjœr] *m* (nav) destroyer

destruc·teur [dɛstryktœr] **-trice** [tris] *adj* destroying, destructive ‖ *mf* destroyer

destruc·tif [dɛstryktif] **-tive** [tiv] *adj* destructive

destruction [dɛstryksjɔ̃] *f* destruction

dé·suet [dezɥɛ] **-suète** [zɥɛt] *adj* obsolete, antiquated, out-of-date

désuétude [dezɥetyd] *f* desuetude, disuse

désu·ni -nie [dezyni] *adj* at odds, divided against itself; uncoordinated

désunion [dezynjɔ̃] *f* dissension

désunir [dezynir] *tr* to disunite, divide; estrange

déta·ché -chée [deta/e] *adj* detached; clean; spare (*parts*); acting, temporary (*official*); staccato (*note*)

détachement [deta/mɑ̃] *m* detachment; (mil) detail

détacher [deta/e] *tr* to detach; let loose; clean; make (*s.th.*) stand out in relief ‖ *ref* to come loose; break loose; stand out in relief

détacheur [deta/œr] *m* spot remover

détail [detaj] *m* detail; retail; item (*of an account*); **au détail** at retail; **en détail** detailed

détail·lant [detajɑ̃] **-lante** [jɑ̃t] *adj* retail ‖ *mf* retailer

détailler [detaje] *tr* to detail; cut up into pieces; retail; itemize (*an account*)

détartrer [detartre] *tr* to remove the scale from (*a boiler*); remove the tartar from (*teeth*)

détaxation [detaksɑsjɔ̃] *f* lowering or removal of taxes

détaxer [detakse] *tr* to lower or remove the tax from

détecter [detɛkte] *tr* to detect

détecteur [detɛktœr] *m* detector; **détecteur de mines** mine detector

détection [detɛksjɔ̃] *f* detection

détective [detɛktiv] *m* detective, private detective; box camera

déteindre [detɛ̃dr] §50 *tr* to fade, bleach ‖ *intr* to fade, run

dételer [detle] §34 *tr* to unharness ‖ *intr* to let up; settle down

détendre [detɑ̃dr] *tr* to relax; stretch out (*one's legs*); lower (*the gas*) ‖ *ref* to relax, enjoy oneself

déten·du -due [detɑ̃dy] *adj* relaxed; slack ‖ *v* see **détendre**

détenir [detnir] §72 *tr* to detain (*in prison*); hold, withhold; own

détente [detɑ̃t] *f* trigger; relaxation, easing (*of tension*); relaxation of tension (*in international affairs*); spring, thrust, expansion

déten·teur [detɑ̃tœr] **-trice** [tris] *mf* holder (*of stock; of a record*); keeper (*of a secret*)

détention [detɑ̃sjɔ̃] *f* detention, custody; possession; **détention préventive** pretrial imprisonment, custody

déte·nu -nue [detny] *adj* detained, imprisoned ‖ *mf* prisoner

déter·gent [detɛrʒɑ̃] **-gente** [ʒɑ̃t] *adj & m* detergent

déterger [detɛrʒe] §38 *tr* to clean

détérioration [deterjorɑsjɔ̃] *f* deterioration

détériorer [deterjore] *tr* to damage ‖ *intr* to deteriorate

détermination [detɛrminɑsjɔ̃] *f* determination

déterminer [detɛrmine] §97, §100 *tr* to determine ‖ §96 *ref* to decide

déter·ré -rée [detɛre] *adj* disinterred ‖ *mf* (fig) corpse, ghost

déterrer [detɛre] *tr* to dig up; exhume

déter·sif [detɛrsif] **-sive** [siv] *adj & m* detergent

détester [detɛste] §95, §97 *tr* to detest, hate

déto·nant [detɔnɑ] **-nante** [nɑ̃t] *adj & m* explosive

détoner [detɔne] *intr* to detonate, explode

détonner [detɔne] *intr* to sing or play off key; clash (*said of colors*)

détordre [detɔrdr] *tr* to untwist

détortiller [detɔrtije] *tr* to untangle

détour [detur] *m* turn, curve, bend; roundabout way, detour; **sans détour** frankly, honestly

détour·né -née [deturne] *adj* off the beaten track, isolated; indirect, roundabout; twisted (*meaning*)

détournement [deturnəmɑ̃] *m* diversion, rerouting; embezzlement; hijacking (*of an airplane*); **détournement de mineur** child abuse

détourner [deturne] §97, §99 *tr* to divert; deter; embezzle; lead astray; distort, twist

détrac·teur [detraktœr] **-trice** [tris] *adj* disparaging || *mf* detractor

détra·qué -quée [detrake] *adj* out of order; broken (*in health*); unhinged, deranged || *mf* nervous wreck

détraquer [detrake] *tr* to put out of commission; (coll) to upset, unhinge || *ref* to break down

détrempe [detrɑ̃p] *f* distemper (*painting*); annealing (*of steel*)

détremper [detrɑ̃pe] *tr* to soak; dilute; anneal (*steel*)

détresse [detrɛs] *f* distress

détriment [detrimɑ̃] *m* detriment

détritus [detritys] *m* debris, rubbish, refuse

détroit [detrwa] *m* strait, sound

détromper [detrɔ̃pe] *tr* to undeceive, enlighten

détrôner [detrone] *tr* to dethrone

détrousser [detruse] *tr* to let down (*e.g., one's sleeves*); hold up (*s.o.*) in the street || *ref* to let down a garment

détrousseur [detrusœr] *m* highwayman

détruire [detrɥir] §19 *tr* to destroy; put an end to || *ref* (coll) to commit suicide

dette [dɛt] *f* debt; **dette active** asset; **dette passive** liability

deuil [dœj] *m* mourning; grief, sorrow; bereavement; funeral procession; **deuil de veuve** widow's weeds; **faire son deuil de** (coll) to say good-bye to

deux [dø] §94 *adj & pron* two; the Second, e.g., **Charles deux** Charles the Second; **deux heures** two o'clock || *m* two; second (*in dates*)

deuxième [døzjɛm] §94 *adj & m* second

deux-pièces [døpjɛs] *m invar* two-piece suit

deux-points [døpwɛ̃] *m invar* colon

deux-ponts [døpɔ̃] *m invar* (aer, naut) double-decker

dévaler [devale] *tr* to descend (*a slope*) || *intr* to descend quickly

dévaloriser [devalɔrize] *tr* to reduce the value of, devalue, devaluate; depreciate, underrate || *ref* to depreciate, fall in value

dévaluation [devalɥasjɔ̃] *f* devaluation

dévaluer [devalɥe] *tr* to devaluate

devancer [dəvɑ̃se] *tr* to get ahead; arrive ahead of; anticipate

devan·cier [dəvɑ̃sje] **-cière** [sjɛr] *mf* precursor, predecessor; **nos devanciers** those who have come before us, our forefathers

devant [dəvɑ̃] *m* front; **par devant** in front; **prendre les devants** to make the first move; to get ahead; to take precautions ||

adv before, in front || *prep* before, in front of

devanture [dəvɑ̃tyr] *f* show window; display; storefront

dévasta·teur [devastatœr] **-trice** [tris] *adj* devastating

dévastation [devastɑsjɔ̃] *f* devastation

dévaster [devaste] *tr* to devastate

déveine [devɛn] *f* bad luck

développé [devlɔpe] *m* press (*in weight lifting*)

développement [devlɔpmɑ̃] *m* development; unwrapping (*of package*); expansion; **développement urbain** urban development

développer [devlɔpe] *tr* to develop; unwrap (*a package*); reveal, show (*e.g., a card*); spread out, open out; expand (*an algebraic expression*) || *ref* to develop

devenir [dəvnir] §72 *intr* (*aux:* ÊTRE) to become; **qu'est devenu Robert?** what has become of Robert?

dévergondage [devɛrgɔ̃daʒ] *m* profligacy

dévergon·dé -dée [devɛrgɔ̃de] *adj & mf* profligate

dévergonder [devɛrgɔ̃de] *ref* to become dissolute

dévernir [devɛrnir] *tr* to remove the varnish from

déverrouiller [devɛruje] *tr* to unbolt

dé·vers [devɛr] **-verse** [vɛrs] *adj* warped; out of alignment || *m* inclination, slope; banking

déverser [devɛrse] *tr* to pour out; slope, bank || *intr* to pour out; lean, become lopsided || *ref* to empty, flow (*said of river*)

dévêtir [devɛtir] §73 *tr & ref* to undress

déviation [devjɑsjɔ̃] *f* deviation; detour

dévider [devide] *tr* to unwind, reel off

dévier [devje] *tr* deflect, by-pass || *intr* to deviate, swerve

de·vin [dəvɛ̃] **-vineresse** [vinrɛs] *mf* fortune-teller

deviner [dəvine] *tr* to guess

devinette [dəvinɛt] *f* riddle

dévirer [devire] *tr* to turn back; bend back; feather (*an oar*)

devis [dəvi] *m* estimate

dévisager [devizaʒe] §38 *tr* to stare at, stare down

devise [dəviz] *f* motto, slogan; heraldic device; name of a ship; currency; **devise forte** strong currency

deviser [dəvize] *intr* to chat

dévisser [devise] *tr* to unscrew

dévitaliser [devitalize] *tr* to kill the nerve of (*a tooth*)

dévoiler [devwale] *tr* to unveil; straighten (*e.g., a bent wheel*) || *ref* to unveil; come to light

devoir [dəvwar] *m* duty; exercise; homework; **devoirs** respects; homework || §21 *tr* §95 to owe || *aux* used to express 1) necessity, e.g., **il doit s'en aller** he must go away; **il devra s'en aller** he will have to go away; **il a dû s'en aller** he had to go away; 2) obligation, e.g., **il devrait s'en**

aller he ought to go away, he should go away; **il aurait dû s'en aller** he ought to have gone away, he should have gone away; 3) conjecture, e.g., **il doit être malade** he must be ill; **il a dû être malade** he must have been ill; 4) what is expected or scheduled, e.g., **que dois-je faire maintenant?** what am I to do now? **le train devait arriver à six heures** the train was to arrive at six o'clock

dévo·lu -lue [devɔly] *adj*—**dévolu à** devolving upon, vested in ‖ *m*—**jeter son dévolu sur** to fix one's choice upon

dévora·teur [devɔratœr] **-trice** [tris] *adj* devouring

dévorer [devɔre] *tr* to devour, eat up

dévo·reur [devɔrœr] **-reuse** [røz] *mf* devourer; (fig) glutton

dé·vot [devo] **-vote** [vɔt] *adj* devout, pious ‖ *mf* devout, pious person; devotee; **faux dévot** hypocrite

dévotion [devosjɔ̃] *f* devotion, devoutness; **à votre dévotion** at your service, at your disposal; **être à la dévotion de qn** to be at s.o.'s beck and call

dé·voué -vouée [devwe] *adj* devoted; **dévoué à vos ordres** (complimentary close) at your service; **votre dévoué** (complimentary close) yours truly

dévouement [devumɑ̃] *m* devotion

dévouer [devwe] *tr* §96 to sacrifice ‖ *ref*—**se dévouer à** to devote or dedicate oneself to

dévoyé dévoyée [devwaje] *adj* delinquent (*young person*) ‖ *mf* delinquent

dévoyer [devwaje] §47 *tr* to lead astray

dextérité [dɛksterite] *f* dexterity

dextrose [dɛkstroz] *m* dextrose

diabète [djabɛt] *m* diabetes

diabétique [djabetik] *adj & mf* diabetic

diable [djɑbl] *m* devil; hand truck, dolly; (coll) fellow; **à la diable** haphazardly; **au diable vauvert** miles from anywhere, far away; **c'est là le diable** (coll) there's the rub; **diable à ressort** jack-in-the-box; **du diable** extreme; **en diable** extremely; **faire le diable à quatre** (coll) to raise Cain; **tirer le diable par la queue** (coll) to be hard up

diablerie [djɑbləri] *f* deviltry

diabolique [djabɔlik] *adj* diabolic(al)

diaconesse [djakɔnɛs] *f* deaconess

diacre [djɑkr] *m* deacon

diacritique [djakritik] *adj* diacritical

diadème [djadɛm] *m* diadem; (*woman's headdress*) tiara, coronet

diagnose [djagnoz] *f* diagnostics, diagnosis

diagnostic [djagnɔstik] *m* diagnosis

diagnostiquer [djagnɔstike] *tr* to diagnose

diago·nal -nale [djagɔnal] *adj & f* (*pl* **-naux** [no] **-nales**) diagonal

diagonalement [djagɔnalmɑ̃] *adv* diagonally, cater-cornered

diagramme [djagram] *m* diagram

dialecte [djalɛkt] *m* dialect

dialogue [djalɔg] *m* dialogue; **de dialogue** (comp) conversational; **dialogue de sourds** irreconcilable argument

dialoguer [djalɔge] *tr* to dialogue, adapt (*a novel for the screen*) ‖ *intr* to carry on a dialogue

diamant [djamɑ̃] *m* diamond

diamantaire [djamɑ̃tɛr] *adj* diamond-bright ‖ *m* dealer in diamonds

diamé·tral -trale [djametral] *adj* (*pl* **-traux** [tro]) diametric(al)

diamètre [djamɛtr] *m* diameter

diane [djan] *f* reveille

diantre [djɑ̃tr] *interj* the dickens!

diapason [djapazɔ̃] *m* range (*of voice or instrument*); pitch, standard pitch; tuning fork; **être au diapason de** (fig) to be on the same wavelength as

diaphane [djafan] *adj* diaphanous

diaphragme [djafragm] *m* diaphragm

diapo [djapo] *f* (coll) slide

diapositive [djapozitiv] *f* (phot) transparency, slide

diaprer [djapre] *tr* to variegate

diarrhée [djare] *f* diarrhea

diastole [djastɔl] *f* diastole

diathermie [djatɛrmi] *f* diathermy

diatribe [djatrib] *f* diatribe

dichotomie [dikɔtɔmi] *f* dichotomy; split fee (*between physicians*)

dictaphone [diktafɔn] *m* dictaphone

dictateur [diktatœr] *m* dictator

dictature [diktatyr] *f* dictatorship

dictée [dikte] *f* dictation; **écrire sous la dictée de** to take dictation from

dicter [dikte] *tr & intr* to dictate

diction [diksjɔ̃] *f* diction

dictionnaire [diksjɔnɛr] *m* dictionary; **dictionnaire vivant** (coll) walking encyclopedia

dicton [diktɔ̃] *m* saying, proverb

didacticiel [didaktisjɛl] *m* (comp) instructional software

didactique [didaktik] *adj* didactic(al)

dièdre [diɛdr] *adj & m* dihedral

diérèse [djerɛz] *f* diaeresis

dièse [djɛz] *adj & m* (mus) sharp

diesel [dizɛl] *m* Diesel motor

diéser [djeze] §10 *tr* (mus) to sharp

diète [djɛt] *f* diet

diététi·cien [djetetisjɛ̃] **-cienne** [sjɛn] *mf* dietitian

diététique [djetetik] *adj* dietetic ‖ *f* dietetics

dieu [djø] *m* (*pl* **dieux**) god ‖ (*cap*) *m* God; **Dieu merci!** thank heavens!; **mon Dieu!** good gracious!

diffamation [difamɑsjɔ̃] *f* defamation

diffamer [difame] *tr* to defame

diffé·ré -rée [difere] *adj* deferred; delayed (*action*) ‖ *m* (rad, telv) prerecording; **en différé** (rad, telv) prerecorded

différemment [diferamɑ̃] *adv* differently

différence [diferɑ̃s] *f* difference; **à la différence de** unlike, contrary to

différencier [diferɑ̃sje] *tr & ref* to differentiate

différend [diferã] *m* dispute, disagreement, difference; **partager le différend** to split the difference

diffé·rent [diferã] **-rente** [rãt] *adj* different; **différent de** different from ‖ (when standing before noun) *adj* different, various

différen·tiel -tielle [diferãsjɛl] *adj* differential ‖ *m* (mach) differential ‖ *f* (math) differential

différer [difere] §10, §96, §97 *tr* to defer, put off ‖ *intr* to differ; disagree

difficile [difisil] §92 *adj* difficult, hard; hard to please, crotchety; **faire le difficile** to be hard to please

difficulté [difikylte] *f* difficulty

difforme [difɔrm] *adj* deformed

difformité [difɔrmite] *f* deformity

dif·fus [dify] **-fuse** [fyz] *adj* diffuse; verbose, windy

diffuser [difyze] *tr* to broadcast ‖ *ref* to diffuse

diffuseur [difyzœr] *m* spreader (*of news*); loudspeaker; nozzle

digérer [diʒere] §10 *tr* & *intr* to digest ‖ *ref* to be digested

digeste [diʒɛst] *adj* (coll) easy to digest ‖ *m* (law) digest

digestible [diʒɛstibl] *adj* digestible

diges·tif [diʒɛstif] **-tive** [tiv] *adj* digestive

digestion [diʒɛstjɔ̃] *f* digestion

digi·tal -tale [diʒital] *adj* (*pl* **-taux** [to]) digital ‖ *f* digitalis, foxglove

digitaline [diʒitalin] *f* (pharm) digitalis

digne [diɲ] §93 *adj* worthy; dignified; haughty, uppish; **digne d'éloges** praiseworthy, laudable

dignitaire [diɲitɛr] *mf* dignitary

dignité [diɲite] *f* dignity

digression [digresjɔ̃] *f* digression

digue [dig] *f* dike; breakwater; (fig) barrier

dilacérer [dilasere] §10 *tr* to lacerate

dilapider [dilapide] *tr* to squander; embezzle

dilater [dilate] *tr* & *ref* to dilate

dilatoire [dilatwar] *adj* dilatory

dilemme [dilɛm] *m* dilemma

dilettante [diletãt] *mf* dilettante

diligemment [diliʒamã] *adv* diligently

diligence [diliʒãs] *f* diligence; **à la diligence de** at the request of

dili·gent [diliʒã] **-gente** [ʒãt] *adj* diligent

diluer [dilɥe] *tr* to dilute

dilution [dilysjɔ̃] *f* dilution

dimanche [dimãʃ] *m* Sunday; **du dimanche** (coll) Sunday (*driver*); (coll) amateur (*painter*); **le dimanche des Rameaux** Palm Sunday

dîme [dim] *f* tithe

dimension [dimãsjɔ̃] *f* dimension

diminuer [diminɥe] *tr* to reduce, cut down, decrease ‖ *intr* to diminish, decrease

diminu·tif [diminytif] **-tive** [tiv] *adj* & *m* diminutive

diminution [diminysjɔ̃] *f* reduction; diminishing

dinde [dɛ̃d] *f* turkey; (culin) turkey; (coll) silly girl

dindon [dɛ̃dɔ̃] *m* turkey; (coll) dupe

dindonner [dɛ̃dɔne] *tr* to dupe, take in

dîner [dine] *m* dinner; **dîner de garçons** stag dinner; **dîner prié** formal dinner ‖ *intr* to dine

dînette [dinɛt] *f* family meal; children's playtime meal

dî·neur [dinœr] **-neuse** [nøz], *mf* diner, dinner guest

dingue [dɛ̃g] *adj* (slang) crazy, nuts, nutty, goffy ‖ *mf* nutty person, goof

dinosaure [dinɔzɔr] *m* dinosaur

diocèse [djɔsɛz] *m* diocese

diode [djɔd] *f* diode

dionée [djɔne] *f* Venus's-flytrap

diphtérie [difteri] *f* diphtheria

diphtongue [diftɔ̃g] *f* diphthong

diplomate [diplɔmat] *adj* diplomatic ‖ *mf* diplomat

diplomatie [diplɔmasi] *f* diplomacy

diplomatique [diplɔmatik] *adj* diplomatic

diplôme [diplom] *m* diploma

dire [dir] §95, §97, §98 *m* statement; **au dire de** according to ‖ §22 *tr* to say, tell, relate; **à l'heure dite** at the appointed time; **à qui le dites-vous?** (coll) you're telling me!; **autrement dit** in other words; **dire que . . .** to think that; **dites-lui bien des choses de ma part** say hello for me; **tu l'as dit!** (coll) you said it! ‖ *intr* to say; **à vrai dire** to tell the truth; **cela va sans dire** it goes without saying; **c'est beaucoup dire** (coll) that's going rather far; **c'est pas peu dire** (slang) that's saying a lot; **comme on dit** as the saying goes; **dites donc!** hey!, say!; **il n'y a pas à dire** make no mistake about it ‖ *ref* to be said; to say to oneself or to each other; to claim to be, to call oneself

di·rect -recte [dirɛkt] *adj* direct ‖ *m* (boxing) solid punch; **en direct** (rad, telv) live

direc·teur [dirɛktœr] **-trice** [tris] *adj* directing, guiding; principal; driving (*rod, wheel*) ‖ *mf* director; **directeur de jeu** referee; **directeur des services municipaux** city manager ‖ *f* directress

direction [dirɛksjɔ̃] *f* direction; administration, management, board; head office; (aut) steering

direction·nel -nelle [dirɛksjɔnɛl] *adj* directional

directive [dirɛktiv] *f* directive, order

directorat [dirɛktɔra] *m* directorship

dirigeable [diriʒabl] *adj* & *m* dirigible

diri·geant [diriʒã] **-geante** [ʒãt] *adj* governing, ruling ‖ *mf* ruler, leader, head, executive

diriger [diriʒe] §38 *tr* to direct, control, manage; steer ‖ *ref* to go; **se diriger vers** to head for

dirigisme [diriʒism] *m* government economic planning and control

dis [di] *v* (**disant, disons**) see **dire**

discernable [disɛrnabl] *adj* discernible

discernement [disɛrnəmã] *m* discernment, perception

discerner [disɛrne] *tr* to discern

disciple [displ] *m* disciple

disciplinaire [disiplinɛr] *adj* disciplinary ‖ *m* military policeman

discipline [disiplin] *f* discipline; scourge

discipliner [disipline] *tr* to discipline

disconti·nu -nue [diskɔ̃tiny] *adj* discontinuous

discontinuer [diskɔ̃tine] §97 *tr* to discontinue

disconvenir [diskɔ̃vnir] §72, §97 *tr* to deny ‖ *intr*—**disconvenir à** to not suit, displease ‖ *intr (aux:* ÊTRE)—**ne pas disconvenir de** to admit, not deny

discophile [diskɔfil] *mf* record collector

discord [diskɔr] *adj masc* out of tune ‖ *m* instrument out of tune

discordance [diskɔrdɑ̃s] *f* discordance

discor·dant [diskɔrdɑ̃] **-dante** [dɑ̃t] *adj* discordant

discorde [diskɔrd] *f* discord

discorder [diskɔrde] *intr* to be discordant, jar

discothèque [diskɔtɛk] *f* record cabinet; record library; discotheque

discourir [diskurir] §14 *intr* to discourse

discours [diskur] *m* discourse; speech

discour·tois [diskurtwa] **-toise** [twaz] *adj* discourteous

discourtoisie [diskurtwazi] *f* discourtesy

discrédit [diskredi] *m* discredit

discréditer [diskredite] *tr* to discredit

dis·cret [diskrɛ] **-crète** [krɛt] *adj* discreet; discrete

discrétion [diskresjɔ̃] *f* discretion; **à discrétion** as much as one wants

discrimination [diskriminɑsjɔ̃] *f* discrimination

discriminatoire [diskriminatwar] *adj* discriminatory

discriminer [diskrimine] *tr* to discriminate

disculper [diskylpe] §97 *tr* to clear, exonerate ‖ *ref* to clear oneself

discur·sif [diskyrsif] **-sive** [siv] *adj* discursive

discussion [diskysjɔ̃] *f* discussion

discuter [diskyte] *tr & intr* to discuss; question, debate

di·sert [dizɛr] **-serte** [zɛrt] *adj* eloquent, fluent

disertement [dizɛrtəmɑ̃] *adv* eloquently, fluently

disette [dizɛt] *f* shortage, scarcity; famine

di·seur [dizœr] **-seuse** [zøz] *mf* talker, speaker; monologuist; **diseuse de bonne aventure** fortuneteller

disgrâce [disgrɑs] *f* disfavor; misfortune; surliness, gruffness

disgra·cié -ciée [disgrɑsje] *adj* out of favor; ill-favored, homely; unfortunate

disgracier [disgrɑsje] *tr* to deprive of favor

disgra·cieux [disgrɑsjø] **-cieuse** [sjøz] *adj* awkward; homely, ugly; disagreeable

disjoindre [disʒwɛ̃dr] §35 *tr* to sever, separate

disjoncteur [disʒɔ̃ktœr] *m* circuit breaker

dislocation [dislɔkɑsjɔ̃] *f* dislocation; separation; dismemberment

disloquer [dislɔke] *tr* to dislocate; disperse; dismember ‖ *ref* to break up, disperse

disparaître [disparɛtr] §12 *intr* to disappear

disparate [disparat] *adj* incongruous ‖ *f* incongruity; clash *(of colors)*

disparité [disparite] *f* disparity

disparition [disparisjɔ̃] *f* disappearance

dispa·ru -rue [dispary] *adj* disappeared; missing *(in battle)* ‖ *mf* missing person; **le disparu** the deceased ‖ *v* see **disparaître**

dispen·dieux [dispɑ̃djø] **-dieuse** [djøz] *adj* expensive

dispensaire [dispɑ̃sɛr] *m* dispensary, outpatient clinic

dispensa·teur [dispɑ̃satœr] **-trice** [tris] *mf* dispenser

dispense [dispɑ̃s] *f* dispensation, exemption

dispenser [dispɑ̃se] §97, §99 *tr* to dispense; **dispensé du timbrage** (label on envelope) mailing permit

disperser [dispɛrse] *tr & ref* to disperse

dispersion [dispɛrsjɔ̃] *f* dispersion, dissipation

disponibilité [dispɔnibilite] *f* availability; **disponibilités** liquid assets; **en disponibilité** in the reserves

disponible [dispɔnibl] *adj* available; vacant *(seat)*; (govt, mil) subject to call

dis·pos [dispo] **-pose** [poz] *adj* alert, fit, in good condition

dispo·sé -sée [dispoze] §92 *adj* disposed; arranged; **disposé d'avance** predisposed; **peu disposé** reluctant

disposer [dispoze] §96, §100 *tr* to dispose ‖ *intr* to dispose; **disposer de** to dispose of, have use of; **disposer pour** to provide for *(e.g., the future)*; **vous pouvez disposer** you may leave ‖ *ref*—**se disposer à** to be disposed to; plan on

dispositif [dispozitif] *m* apparatus, device; (mil) disposition

disposition [dispozisjɔ̃] *f* disposition; disposal; **dispositions** arrangements; aptitude; provisions *(of a legal document)*

disproportion·né -née [disprɔpɔrsjɔne] *adj* disproportionate, incompatible

dispute [dispyt] *f* dispute

disputer [dispyte] *tr* to dispute; (coll) to bawl out ‖ *ref* to dispute

disquaire [diskɛr] *m* record dealer

disqualification [diskalifikɑsjɔ̃] *f* disqualification

disqualifier [diskalifje] *tr & ref* to disqualify

disque [disk] *m* disk; record, disk; (sports) discus; **changer de disque** (coll) to change the subject; **disque de longue durée** long-playing record; **disque volant** Frisbee

disquette [diskɛt] *f* (comp) floppy disk

dissection [disɛksjɔ̃] *f* dissection

dissemblable [disɑ̃blabl] *adj* dissimilar

dissemblance [disɑ̃blɑ̃s] *f* dissimilarity

disséminer [disemine] *tr* to disseminate

dissension [disɑ̃sjɔ̃] *f* dissension
dissentiment [disɑ̃timɑ̃] *m* dissent
disséquer [diseke] §10 *tr* to dissect
dissertation [disɛrtɑsjɔ̃] *f* dissertation; (*in school*) essay, term paper
dissidence [dysidɑ̃s] *f* dissent
dissi·dent [disidɑ̃] **-dente** [dɑ̃t] *adj* dissenting ‖ *mf* dissenter, dissident
dissimiler [disimile] *tr* (phonet) to dissimilate
dissimulation [disimylɑsjɔ̃] *f* dissemblance
dissimuler [disimyle] *tr* & *intr* to dissemble; **dissimuler q.ch. à qn** to conceal s.th. from s.o. ‖ *ref* to hide, skulk
dissipation [disipɑsjɔ̃] *f* dissipation
dissi·pé **-pée** [disipe] *adj* dissipated; pleasure-seeking; unruly (*schoolboy*)
dissiper [disipe] *tr* & *ref* to dissipate
dissocier [disɔsje] *tr* & *ref* to dissociate
disso·lu **-lue** [disɔly] *adj* dissolute ‖ *mf* profligate
dissolution [disɔlysjɔ̃] *f* dissolution; dissoluteness; rubber cement
dissol·vant [disɔlvɑ̃] **-vante** [vɑ̃t] *adj* & *m* solvent
dissonance [disɔnɑ̃s] *f* dissonance
dissoudre [disudr] §60 (*pp* **dissous, dissoute;** no *pret* or *imperf subj*) *tr* & *ref* to dissolve
dissuader [disɥade] §97, §99 *tr* to dissuade, deter
distance [distɑ̃s] *f* distance; **à distance** at a distance
distancer [distɑ̃se] §51 *tr* to outdistance, distance (*a race horse*)
dis·tant [distɑ̃] **-tante** [tɑ̃t] *adj* distant
distendre [distɑ̃dr] *tr* & *ref* to distend; strain (*a muscle*)
distillation [distilɑsjɔ̃] *f* distillation
distiller [distile] *tr* to distill
distillerie [distilri] *f* distillery; distilling industry
dis·tinct [distɛ̃], [distɛ̃kt] **-tincte** [tɛ̃kt] *adj* distinct
distinc·tif [distɛ̃ktif] **-tive** [tiv] *adj* distinctive
distinction [distɛ̃ksjɔ̃] *f* distinction
distin·gué **-guée** [distɛ̃ge] *adj* distinguished; famous; sincere, e.g., **veuillez accepter nos sentiments distingués** (complimentary close) please accept our sincere regards
distinguer [distɛ̃ge] *tr* to distinguish ‖ *ref* to be distinguished; distinguish oneself
distordre [distɔrdr] *tr* to twist, sprain
dis·tors [distɔr] **-torse** [tɔrs] *adj* twisted
distorsion [distɔrsjɔ̃] *f* sprain; convulsive twist; (electron, opt) distorsion
distraction [distraksjɔ̃] *f* distraction; heedlessness, lapse; embezzlement; appropriation (*of a sum of money*)
distraire [distrɛr] §68 *tr* to distract, amuse; separate, set aside (*e.g., part of one's savings*) ‖ *ref* to amuse oneself
dis·trait [distrɛ] **-traite** [trɛt] *adj* absentminded

distribuer [distribɥe] *tr* to distribute; arrange the furnishings of (*an apartment*)
distribu·teur [distribytœr] **-trice** [tris] *mf* distributor (*person*) ‖ *m* (mach) distributor; **distributeur automatique** vending machine; **distributeur de musique** jukebox
distribution [distribysjɔ̃] *f* distribution; mail delivery; supply system (*of gas, water, or electricity*); valve gear (*of steam engine*); timing gears (*of internal-combustion engine*); (theat) cast
district [distrik], [distrikt] *m* district
dit [di] **dite** [dit] *adj* agreed upon, stated ‖ *m* saying ‖ *v* see **dire**
dites [dit] *v* see **dire**
dito [dito] *adv* ditto
diva [diva] *f* diva
divaguer [divage] *intr* to ramble
divan [divɑ̃] *m* divan, sofa
diverger [divɛrʒe] §38 *intr* to diverge
di·vers [divɛr] **-verse** [vɛrs] *adj* changing, varied; miscellaneous (*expenses; remarks;* **faits divers** news items; **un fait divers** an incident ‖ **di·vers** **-verses** (when standing before or after noun) *adj pl* diverse, different, varied; various, several, e.g., **diverses personnes** several persons, **en diverses occasions** on various occasions
diversifier [divɛrsifje] *tr* & *ref* to diversify
diversion [divɛrsjɔ̃] *f* diversion
diversité [divɛrsite] *f* diversity
divertir [divɛrtir] §96 *tr* to divert, amuse ‖ *ref* to be diverted, amused
divertis·sant [divɛrtisɑ̃] **-sante** [sɑ̃t] *adj* entertaining, diverting, amusing
divertissement [divɛrtismɑ̃] *m* diversion, relaxation; entertainment, amusement; (mus) divertissement
dividende [dividɑ̃d] *m* dividend
di·vin [divɛ̃] **-vine** [vin] *adj* divine
divination [divinɑsjɔ̃] *f* divination
divinité [divinite] *f* divinity
diviser [divize] *tr* & *ref* to divide
diviseur [divizœr] *m* (math) divisor; (fig) troublemaker
divisible [divizibl] *adj* divisible
division [divizjɔ̃] *f* division
divisionnaire [divizjɔnɛr] *adj* divisional ‖ *m* division head
divorce [divɔrs] *m* divorce
divor·cé **-cée** [divɔrse] *mf* divorced person ‖ *f* divorcee
divorcer [divɔrse] §51 *tr* to divorce (*a married couple*) ‖ *intr* to divorce, get a divorce; **divorcer avec** to withdraw from (*the world*); **divorcer d'avec** to get a divorce from, be divorced from, divorce (*husband or wife*); withdraw from (*the world*)
divulguer [divylge] *tr* to divulge
dix [di(s)] §94 *adj* & *pron* ten; the Tenth, e.g., **Jean dix** John the Tenth; **dix heures** ten o'clock ‖ *m* ten; tenth (*in dates*)
dix-huit [dizɥi], [dizɥit] §94 *adj* & *pron* eighteen; the Eighteenth, e.g., **Jean dix-**

huit John the Eighteenth ‖ *m* eighteen; eighteenth (*in dates*)

dix-huitième [dizɥitjɛm] §94 *adj & m* eighteenth

dixième [dizjɛm] §94 *adj, pron* (*masc, fem*), *& m* tenth

dix-neuf [diznœf] §94 *adj & pron* nineteen; the Nineteenth, e.g., **Jean dix-neuf** John the Nineteenth ‖ *m* nineteen; nineteenth (*in dates*)

dix-neuvième [diznœvjɛm] §94 *adj & m* nineteenth

dix-sept [dissɛt] §94 *adj & pron* seventeen; the Seventeenth, e.g., **Jean dix-sept** John the Seventeenth ‖ *m* seventeen; seventeenth (*in dates*)

dix-septième [dissɛtjɛm] §94 *adj & m* seventeenth

djinn [dʒin] *m* jinn

d° *abbr* (**dito**) do. (ditto)

docile [dɔsil] *adj* docile

dock [dɔk] *m* dock; warehouse; **dock flottant** floating dry dock

docker [dɔkɛr] *m* dock worker

docte [dɔkt] *adj* learned, scholarly ‖ *mf* scholar ‖ *m* learned man

doc·teur [dɔktœr] **-toresse** [tɔrɛs] *mf* doctor; **le docteur Marie Dupont** Dr. Mary Dupont

docto·ral -rale [dɔktɔral] *adj* (*pl* **-raux** [ro]) doctoral

doctorat [dɔktɔra] *m* doctorate

doctrine [dɔktrin] *f* doctrine

document [dɔkymã] *m* document

documentaire [dɔkymãtɛr] *adj & m* documentary

documentation [dɔkymãtɑsjɔ̃sjɔ̃] *f* documentation; literature (*about a region, business, etc.*)

documenter [dɔkymãte] *tr* to document ‖ *ref* to gather documentary evidence

dodeliner [dɔdline] *tr & intr* to sway, rock

dodo [dodo] *m* (orn) dodo; **aller au dodo** (*baby talk*) to go to bed; **faire dodo** to sleep

do·du -due [dɔdy] *adj* (coll) plump

dogmatique [dɔgmatik] *adj* dogmatic ‖ *mf* dogmatic person ‖ *f* dogmatics

dogmatiser [dɔgmatize] *intr* to dogmatize

dogme [dɔgm] *m* dogma

dogue [dɔg] *m* bulldog

doigt [dwa] *m* finger; **à deux doigts de** a hairbreadth away from; **doigt annulaire** ring finger; **doigt de Dieu** hand of God; **doigt du pied** toe; **mettre le doigt dessus** to hit the nail on the head; **mon petit doigt m'a dit** (coll) a little bird told me; **montrer du doigt** to single out (*for ridicule*); to point at; **petit doigt** little finger; **se mettre le doigt dans l'œil** (coll) to fool oneself; **se mordre les doigts** to be sorry; **un doigt de vin** very little wine

doigté [dwate] *m* touch; adroitness, skillfulness; fingering

doigter [dwate] *m* fingering ‖ *tr & intr* to finger

doigtier [dwatje] *m* fingerstall

dois [dwa] *v* (**doit**) see **devoir**

doit [dwa] *m* debit

doléances [dɔleãs] *fpl* grievances; (pathol) symptoms

do·lent [dɔlã] **-lente** [lãt] *adj* doleful

dollar [dɔlar] *m* dollar

domaine [dɔmɛn] *m* domain

dôme [dom] *m* dome; cathedral

domestication [dɔmɛstikɑsjɔ̃] *f* domestication

domesticité [dɔmɛstisite] *f* domestication; staff of servants

domestique [dɔmɛstik] *adj & mf* domestic

domestiquer [dɔmɛstike] *tr* to domesticate

domicile [dɔmisil] *m* residence

domicilier [dɔmisilje] *tr* to domicile ‖ *ref* to take up residence

dominance [dɔminãs] *f* (genetics) dominance

domi·nant [dɔminã] **-nante** [nãt] *adj* dominant ‖ *f* dominating trait; (mus) dominant

domina·teur [dɔminatœr] **-trice** [tris] *adj* domineering, overbearing ‖ *mf* ruler, conqueror

domination [dɔminɑsjɔ̃] *f* domination

dominer [dɔmine] *tr & intr* to dominate ‖ *ref* to control oneself

domini·cal -cale [dɔminikal] *adj* (*pl* **-caux** [ko]) Sunday; dominical

domino [dɔmino] *m* domino

dommage [dɔmaʒ] *m* loss; injury; **c'est dommage!** that's too bad! **dommages et intérêts** (law) damages; **quel dommage!** what a pity!

dommageable [dɔmaʒabl] *adj* injurious

dommages-intérêts [dɔmaʒɛterɛ] *mpl* (law) damages

dompter [dɔ̃te] *tr* to tame; train (*animals*); subdue

domp·teur [dɔ̃tœr] **-teuse** [tøz] *mf* tamer, trainer; conqueror

don [dɔ̃] *m* gift; don (*Spanish title*)

donataire [dɔnatɛr] *mf* legatee

dona·teur [dɔnatœr] **-trice** [tris] *mf* (law) donor, legator

donation [dɔnɑsjɔ̃] *f* donation, gift, grant

donc [dɔ̃k], [dɔ̃] *adv* therefore, then; thus; now, of course; (often used for emphasis), e.g., **entrez donc!** do come in!

donjon [dɔ̃ʒɔ̃] *m* keep, donjon; (nav) turret

don·nant [dɔnã] **-nante** [nãt] *adj* generous, open-handed; **donnant donnant** tit for tat; cash down; **peu donnant** closefisted

donne [dɔn] *f* (cards) deal; doña (*Spanish title*); **fausse donne** misdeal

don·né -née [dɔne] *adj* given; **étant donné que** whereas, since ‖ *f* datum; **données** data, facts

donner [dɔne] §96 *tr* to give; (cards) to deal ‖ *intr* to give; **donner sur** to open onto, look out on; **donner sur les doigts** to rap one's knuckles

don·neur [dɔnœr] **-neuse** [nøz] *mf* donor; **donneur universel** type-O blood donor ‖ *m* (cards) dealer

dont [dɔ̃] §79

donzelle [dɔ̃zɛl] *f* woman of easy virtue

doper [dɔpe] *tr* to dope

doping [dɔpiŋ] *m* dope, pep pill

dorade [dɔrad] *f* gilthead

dorénavant [dɔrenavɑ̃] *adv* henceforth

dorer [dɔre] *tr* to gild; (fig) to sugar-coat

d'ores [dɔr] see **ores**

dorlotement [dɔrlɔtmɑ̃] *m* coddling

dorloter [dɔrlɔte] *tr* to coddle

dor·mant [dɔrmɑ̃] **-mante** [mɑ̃t] *adj* stagnant, immovable ‖ *m* doorframe

dor·meur [dɔrmœr] **-meuse** [møz] *adj* sleeping ‖ *mf* sleeper ‖ *f* earring

dormir [dɔrmir] §23 *intr* to sleep; lie dormant; **à dormir debout** boring, dull; **dormir debout** to sleep standing up; **dormir sur les deux oreilles** to feel secure

dors [dɔr] *v* (**dort**) see **dormir**

dortoir [dɔrtwar] *m* dormitory

dorure [dɔryr] *f* gilding; gilt; icing

dos [do] *m* back; bridge (*of nose*); **dans le dos de** behind the back of; **dos d'âne** (aut) speed bump; **en dos d'âne** saddlebacked, hog-backed; **se mettre qn à dos** to make an enemy of s.o.; **voir au dos** see other side

dosage [dozaʒ] *m* dosage

dose [doz] *f* dose; proportion, amount, share; (fig) tinge, suspicion; (slang) fix (*shot of a drug*)

doser [doze] *tr* to dose out, measure out, proportion

dossier [dosje] *m* chair back; dossier; case history

dot [dɔt] *f* dowry

dotation [dɔtasjɔ̃] *f* endowment

doter [dɔte] *tr* to endow; dower; give a dowry to

douaire [dwɛr] *m* dower

douairière [dwɛrjɛr] *f* dowager

douane [dwan] *f* customs, duty; customhouse

doua·nier [dwanje] **-nière** [njɛr] *adj* customs ‖ *m* customs officer

doublage [dublaʒ] *m* doubling; metal plating of a ship; lining (*act of lining*); dubbing (*on tape or film*)

double [dubl] *adj & adv* double; **à double face** two-faced; **se garer en double fil** to double-park ‖ *m* double; duplicate, copy; **au double** twice; **double au carbone** carbon copy; **en double** in duplicate

doublement [dubləmɑ̃] *m* doubling ‖ *adv* doubly

doubler [duble] *tr* to double; parallel, run alongside; pass (*s.o., s.th. going in the same direction*); line (*a coat*); dub (*a film*); copy, dub (*a sound tape*); replace (*an actor*); gain one lap on (*another contestant*); (coll) to cheat ‖ *intr* to double; pass (*on highway*)

doublure [dublyr] *f* lining; (theat) understudy, replacement

douce-amère [dusamɛr] *f* (*pl* **douces-amères**) (bot) bittersweet

douceâtre [dusɑtr] *adj* sweetish; mawkish

doucement [dusmɑ̃] *adv* softly; slowly ‖ *interj* easy now!, just a minute!

douce·reux [dusrø] **-reuse** [røz] *adj* unpleasantly sweet, cloying; mealy-mouthed

douceur [dusœr] *f* sweetness; softness, gentleness; **douceurs** sweets

douche [duʃ] *f* shower bath; douche; (coll) dressing down; (coll) shock, disappointment

doucher [duʃe] *tr* to give a shower bath to; (coll) reprimand; (coll) to disappoint ‖ *ref* to take a shower bath

doucir [dusir] *tr* to polish, rub

doué douée [dwe] *adj* gifted, endowed

douer [dwe] *tr* to endow; **douer de** to endow or gift (*s.o.*) with

douille [duj] *f* cartridge case; sconce (*of candlestick*); bushing; (elec) socket

douil·let [dujɛ] **-lette** [jɛt] *adj* soft, delicate; oversensitive ‖ *f* child's padded coat

douleur [dulœr] *f* pain; sorrow; soreness

doulou·reux [dulurø] **-reuse** [røz] *adj* painful; sad; sore

doute [dut] *m* doubt; **sans doute** no doubt

douter [dute] §97 *tr* to doubt, e.g., **je doute qu'il vienne** I doubt that he will come ‖ *intr* to doubt; **à n'en pas douter** beyond a doubt; **douter de** to doubt; distrust ‖ *ref*—**se douter de** to suspect; **se douter que** to suspect that

dou·teur [dutœr] **-teuse** [tøz] *adj* doubting ‖ *mf* doubter

dou·teux [dutø] **-teuse** [tøz] *adj* doubtful; dubious

Douvres [duvr] Dover

doux [du] **douce** [dus] *adj* sweet; soft; pleasing; suave; quiet; new (*wine*) fresh (*water*); gentle (*slope*); mild (*weather, climate*); **en douce** on the sly, on the q.t. ‖ **doux** *interj*—**tout doux!** easy there!

douzain [duzɛ̃] *m* twelve-line verse

douzaine [duzɛn] *f* dozen; **à la douzaine** by the dozen; **une douzaine de** a dozen

douze [duz] §94 *adj & pron* twelve; the Twelfth, e.g., **Jean douze** John the Twelfth ‖ *m* twelve; twelfth (*in dates*)

douzième [duzjɛm] §94 *adj, pron* (*masc, fem*), *& m* twelfth

doyen [dwajɛ̃] **doyenne** [dwajɛn] *mf* dean; **doyen d'âge** oldest member

doyenneté [dwajɛnte] *f* seniority

Dᵣ *abbr* (**Docteur**) Dr.

drachme [drakm] *m* drachma; dram

dragage [dragaʒ] *m* dredging

dragée [draʒe] *f* sugar-coated almond; (pharm) pill; (coll) bitter pill; **tenir la dragée haute à qn** to make s.o. pay through the nose; be high-handed with s.o.

drageon [draʒɔ̃] *m* (bot) sucker

dragon [dragɔ̃] *m* dragon; dragoon; shrew; **dragon de vertu** prude

dragonne [dragɔn] *f* tassel, sword knot

drague [drag] *f* dredge; minesweeping apparatus

draguer [drage] *tr* to dredge, drag; sweep for mines ‖ *intr* to be on the make

dragueur [dragœr] *adj* minesweeping ‖ *m* dredger; **dragueur de mines** minesweeper

drain [drɛ̃] *m* drainpipe; (med) drain

drainage [drɛnaʒ] *m* drainage

drainer [drɛne], [drene] *tr* to drain

draisine [drɛzin] *f* (rr) handcar

dramatique [dramatik] *adj* dramatic

dramatiser [dramatize] *tr* to dramatize

dramaturge [dramatyrʒ] *mf* playwright

dramaturgie [dramatyrʒi] *f* dramatics

drame [dram] *m* drama; tragic event

drap [dra] *m* cloth; sheet; **être dans de beaux draps** to be in a pretty pickle

dra·peau [drapo] *m* (*pl* **-peaux**) flag; **au drapeau!** colors (*bugle call*)!; **drapeau parlementaire** flag of truce; **être sous les drapeaux** to be a serviceman

draper [drape] *tr* to drape ‖ *ref* to drape oneself

draperie [drapəri] *f* drapery; drygoods business; textile industry

dra·pier [drapje] **-pière** [pjɛr] *mf* draper; textile manufacturer

drastique [drastik] *adj* (med) drastic

drêche [drɛʃ] *f* draff, residue of malt

drège [drɛʒ] *f* dragnet

drelin [drəlɛ̃] *m* ting-a-ling

drépanocytose [drepanɔsitoz] *f* sickle-cell anemia

dressage [drɛsaʒ] *m* training (*of animals*); erection

dresser [drɛse] §96, §100 *tr* to raise, hold erect; train; put up, erect; set (*the table; a trap*); draw up, draft; plane, smooth; **dresser l'oreille** to prick up one's ears ‖ *ref* to stand up straight, sit up straight; **se dresser contre** to be dead set against

dressoir [drɛswar] *m* sideboard, buffet, dish closet

dribble [dribl] *m* (sports) dribble

dribbler [drible] *tr & intr* (sports) to dribble

drille [drij] *m*—**joyeux drille** gay blade ‖ *f* jeweler's drill brace; **drilles** rags (*for papermaking*)

drisse [dris] *f* halyard, rope

drogue [drɔg] *f* drug; chemical; nostrum, concoction; narcotic; (coll) trash, rubbish; **drogues miracles** miracle drugs

dro·gué -guée [drɔge] *mf* drug addict; **drogué du travail** workaholic

droguer [drɔge] *tr* to drug or dope (*with too much medicine*) ‖ *intr* (coll) to cool one's heels ‖ *ref* to drug or dope oneself

droguerie [drɔgri] *f* drysaltery (Brit)

droguiste [drɔgist] *mf* drysalter (Brit)

droit [drwa], [drwa] **droite** [drwat], [drwat] *adj* right; honest, sincere; fair, just ‖ *m* law; right; justice; tax; right angle; **à bon droit** with reason; **de (plein) droit** rightfully, by rights, incontestably; **droit coutumier** common law; **droit de cité** key to the city; acceptability; **droits** duties, customs; rights; **droits civils** rights to manage property; **droits civiques**, **droits politiques** civil rights; **droits d'auteur** royalty; **droits de reproduction réservés** copyrighted; **tous droits réservés** all rights reserved, copyrighted ‖ *f* right, right-hand side; right hand; straight line; **à**

droite to or on the right ‖ **droit** *adv*—**droit au but** straight to the point; **tout droit** straight ahead

droit-fil [drwafil] *m* direct tradition

droi·tier [drwatje], [drwatje] **-tière** [tjɛr] *adj* right-handed ‖ *mf* right-handed person; rightist

droiture [drwatyr], [drwatyr] *f* integrity

drolatique [drɔlatik] *adj* droll, comic

drôle [drol] *adj* droll, funny, strange; **drôle de** funny, e.g., **une drôle d'idée** a funny idea; **drôle de guerre** phony war; **drôle d'homme, de corps, de pistolet**, or **de pierrot** (coll) queer duck ‖ *mf* (coll) queer duck, strange person

drôlerie [drolri] *f* drollery

drôlesse [droles] *f* wench, hussy

dromadaire [drɔmadɛr] *m* dromedary

dronte [drɔ̃t] *m* (orn) dodo

droppage [drɔpaʒ] *m* airdrop

drosser [drɔse] *tr* to drive, carry (*as the wind drives a ship ashore*)

dru drue [dry] *adj* thick, dense; fine (*rain*) ‖ **dru** *adv* thickly, heavily

druide [drɥid] *m* druid

du [dy] §77

dû due [dy] *adj & m* due ‖ *v* see **devoir**

duc [dyk] *m* duke; horned owl

ducat [dyka] *m* ducat

duché [dyʃe] *m* duchy, dukedom

duchesse [dyʃes] *f* duchess

duègne [dɥɛɲ] *f* duenna

duel [dɥɛl] *m* duel; dual number; **duel oratoire** verbal battle

duelliste [dɥelist] *m* duelist

dulcifier [dylsifje] *tr* to sweeten

dûment [dymɑ̃] *adv* duly

dune [dyn] *f* dune

dunette [dynɛt] *f* (naut) poop

Dunkerque [dœ̃kɛrk] *f* Dunkirk

duo [dɥo] *m* duet; duo; **duo d'injures** exchange of words, insults

duodénum [dɥɔdenɔm] *m* duodenum

dupe [dyp] *f* dupe

duper [dype] *tr* to dupe

duperie [dypri] *f* deception, trickery

duplex [dyplɛks] *adj* two-way ‖ *m* duplex apartment

duplicata [dyplikata] *m* duplicate

duplicateur [dyplikatœr] *m* duplicating machine

duplication [dyplikasjɔ̃] *f* duplication

duplicité [dyplisite] *f* duplicity

duquel [dykɛl] §78

dur dure [dyr] *adj* hard; tough; difficult; **coucher sur la dure** to sleep on the bare ground or floor; **dur à la détente** tightfisted; **dur d'oreille** hard of hearing; **élever un enfant à la dure** to give a child a strict upbringing ‖ *mf* (coll) tough customer ‖ *m* hard material, concrete ‖ **dur** *adv* hard, e.g., **travailler dur** to work hard

durable [dyrabl] *adj* durable

durant [dyrɑ̃] *prep* during; (sometimes stands after noun), e.g., **sa vie durant** during his life

durcir [dyrsir] *tr, intr* & *ref* to harden
durcissement [dyrsismɑ̃] *m* hardening
durée [dyre] *f* duration; wear
durer [dyre] *intr* to last, endure
dureté [dyrte] *f* hardness; cruelty
durillon [dyrijɔ̃] *m* callus, corn
duvet [dyvɛ] *m* down, fuzz; nap (*of cloth*)
duve·té -tée [dyvte] *adj* downy
duve·teux [dyvtø] **-teuse** [tøz] *adj* fuzzy
dynamique [dinamik] *adj* dynamic ‖

f dynamics
dynamiser [dinamize] *tr* (slang) to psych out
dynamite [dinamit] *f* dynamite
dynamiter [dinamite] *tr* to dynamite
dynamo [dinamo] *f* dynamo
dynaste [dinast] *m* dynast
dynastie [dinasti] *f* dynasty
dysenterie [disɑ̃tri] *f* dysentery
dyspepsie [dispɛpsi] *f* dyspepsia

E

E, e [ə], *[ə] *m invar* fifth letter of the French alphabet
E.A.O. [eao] *m* (letterword) (**enseignement assisté par ordinateur**) CAI (*computer-assisted instruction*)
eau [o] *f* (*pl* **eaux**) water; wake (*of ship*); à l'eau de rose maudlin; de la plus belle eau of the first water; eau calcaire hard water; eau de cale bilge water; eau de Javel bleach; eau dentifrice mouthwash; eau dormante still water; eau douce soft water; fresh water; eau dure hard water; eau lourde heavy water; eau oxygénée hydrogen peroxide; eau vive running water; eaux waters; waterworks; eaux d'égouts sewage; eaux juvéniles mineral waters; eaux thermales hot springs; eaux usées, eaux résiduelles polluted water; eaux vives swift current; être en eau to sweat; faire de l'eau to take in water; faire eau to leak; grandes eaux fountains; nager entre deux eaux to float under the surface; to play both sides of the street; pêcher en eau trouble to fish in troubled waters; porter de l'eau à la rivière or à la mer to carry coals to Newcastle; tomber à l'eau to fizzle out
eau-de-vie [odvi] *f* (*pl* **eaux-de-vie**) brandy; spirits
eau-forte [ofɔrt] *f* (*pl* **eaux-fortes**) aqua fortis; etching
éba·hi -hie [ebai] *adj* dumfounded
ébattre [ebatr] §7 *ref* to frolic, gambol, frisk about
ébauche [eboʃ] *f* rough sketch or draft; suspicion (*of a smile*)
ébaucher [eboʃe] *tr* to sketch, make a rough draft of
ébène [ebɛn] *f* ebony
ébénier [ebenje] *m* ebony (*tree*)
ébéniste [ebenist] *m* cabinetmaker
ébénisterie [ebenistri] *f* cabinetmaking
éberluer [ebɛrlɥe] *tr* to astonish
éblouir [ebluir] *tr* to dazzle, blind
éblouissement [ebluismɑ̃] *m* dazzle; glare; (pathol) dizziness
éboueur [ebwœr] *m* street cleaner, trash man; garbage collector
ébouillanter [ebujɑ̃te] *tr* to scald

éboulement [ebulmɑ̃] *m* cave-in, landslide
ébouler [ebule] *tr* & *ref* to cave in
ébourif·fant -fante [eburifɑ̃] **-fante** [fɑ̃t] *adj* (coll) astounding
ébouriffer [eburife] *tr* to ruffle; (coll) to astound
ébouter [ebute] *tr* to cut off the end of
ébranchage [ebrɑ̃ʃaʒ] *m* pruning
ébrancher [ebrɑ̃ʃe] *tr* to prune
ébranlement [ebrɑ̃lmɑ̃] *m* shaking; shock
ébranler [ebrɑ̃le] *tr* to shake, jar ‖ *ref* to start out; be shaken
ébrécher [ebreʃe] §10 *tr* to nick, chip; make a dent in (*e.g., a fortune*) ‖ *ref* to be nicked, chipped; break off (*a tooth*)
ébriété [ebrijete] *f* inebriation
ébrouer [ebrue] *ref* to snort (*said of horse*); splash about; shake the water off oneself
ébruiter [ebrɥite] *tr* to noise about, blab ‖ *ref* to get around (*said of news*); leak out (*said of secret*)
ébullition [ebylisjɔ̃] *f* boiling; ebullience, ferment
ébur·né -née [ebyrne] *adj* ivory
écaille [ekɑj] *f* scale (*of fish, snake*); shell; tortoise shell
écail·ler [ekɑje] **-lère** [jɛr] *mf* oyster opener ‖ *m* oysterman ‖ *f* oysterwoman ‖ **écailler** *tr* & *ref* to scale
écale [ekal] *f* shell, husk, hull
écaler [ekale] *tr* to shell, husk, hull
écarlate [ekarlat] *adj* & *f* scarlet
écarquiller [ekarkije] *tr* (coll) to open wide, spread apart
écart [ekar] *m* swerve, side step; digression, flight (*of imagination*); difference, gap, spread; error, (*in range*); lapse (*in good conduct*); (cards) discard; à l'écart aside; aloof; à l'écart de far from; faire le grand écart to do the splits; faire un écart to shy (*said of horse*) swerve (*said of car*); step aside (*said of person*)
écar·té -tée [ekarte] *adj* lonely, secluded; wide-apart
écartèlement [ekartɛlmɑ̃] *m* quartering
écarteler [ekartəle] §2 *tr* to quarter

écartement [ekartəmɑ̃] *m* removal, separation; spreading; space between; spark gap; gauge (*of rails*)

écarter [ekarte] *tr* to put aside; keep away; ward off; draw aside; spread; (cards) to discard ‖ *ref* to turn away; stray

ecchymose [ɛkimoz] *f* black-and-blue mark

ecclésiastique [eklezastik] *adj & m* ecclesiastic

écerve·lé -lée [esɛrvəle] *adj* scatterbrained ‖ *mf* scatterbrain

échafaud [eʃafo] *m* scaffold

échafaudage [eʃafodaʒ] *m* scaffolding

échafauder [eʃafode] *tr* to pile up; lay the ground work for ‖ *intr* to erect a scaffolding

échalasser [eʃalase] *tr* to stake

échalote [eʃalɔt] *f* shallot

échancrer [eʃɑ̃kre] *tr* to make a V-shaped cut in (*the neck of a dress*); cut (*a dress*) low in the neck; indent; to hollow out

échange [eʃɑ̃ʒ] *m* exchange

échanger [eʃɑ̃ʒe] §38 *tr* to exchange; **échanger pour** or **contre** to exchange (*s.th.*) for

échangeur [eʃɑ̃ʒœr] *m* interchange; **échangeur en trèfle** (aut) cloverleaf

échanson [eʃɑ̃sɔ̃] *m* cupbearer

échantillon [eʃɑ̃tijɔ̃] *m* sample; **comparer à l'échantillon** to spot-check

échantillonnage [eʃɑ̃tijɔnaʒ] *m* sampling; spot check

échantillonner [eʃɑ̃tijɔne] *tr* to cut samples of; spot-check; select (*a sampling to be polled*)

échappatoire [eʃapatwar] *f* loophole, way out

échap·pé -pée [eʃape] *mf* escapee ‖ *f* escape; short period; glimpse; (sports) spurt; **à l'échappée** stealthily

échappement [eʃapmɑ̃] *m* escape; leak; exhaust; escapement (*of watch*); **échappement libre** cutout

échapper [eʃape] *tr*—**l'échapper belle** to have a narrow escape ‖ *intr* to escape; **échapper à** to escape from; **échapper de** to slip out of ‖ *ref* to escape

écharde [eʃard] *f* splinter, sliver

écharpe [eʃarp] *f* scarf; sash; sling; **en écharpe** diagonally, crosswise; in a sling; across the shoulder

écharper [eʃarpe] *tr* to slash, cut up

échasse [eʃas] *f* stilt

échauder [eʃode] *tr* to scald; white-wash; gouge (*a customer*)

échauffement [eʃofmɑ̃] *m* heating; overexcitement

échauffer [eʃofe] *tr* to heat; warm; **échauffer les oreilles à qn** to get s.o.'s dander up ‖ *ref* to heat up; become excited

échauffourée [eʃofure] *f* skirmish; rash undertaking

èche [ɛʃ] *f* bait

échéance [eʃeɑ̃s] *f* due date, expiration; **à courte échéance** before long; **à longue échéance** in the long run

échec [eʃɛk] *m* check; chess piece, chessman; failure; **échec et mat** checkmate; **échecs** [eʃɛ] chess; chess set; **être échec** to be in check; **jouer aux échecs** to play chess; **voué à l'échec** doomed to failure

échelle [eʃɛl] *f* ladder; scale; **échelle coulisse** extension ladder; **échelle de sauvetage** fire escape; **échelle d'incendie** fire ladder; **échelle mobile** sliding scale; **échelle pliante** stepladder; **monter à l'échelle** (coll) to bite, be fooled

échelon [eʃlɔ̃] *m* echelon; rung (*of ladder*)

échelonner [eʃlɔne] *tr* to spread out, space out ‖ *ref* (aer) to stack

écheniller [eʃnije] *tr* to remove caterpillars from; exterminate (*pests*); eradicate (*corruption*)

éche·veau [eʃvo] *m* (*pl* **-veaux**) skein

écheve·lé -lée [eʃəvle] *adj* disheveled; wild (*dance, race*)

écheveler [eʃəvle] §34 *tr* to dishevel

échevin [eʃvɛ̃] *m* (hist) alderman

échine [eʃin] *f* spine, backbone; **avoir l'échine souple** (coll) to be a yes man

échiner [eʃine] *tr* to break the back of; beat, kill ‖ *ref* to tire oneself out

échiquier [eʃikje] *m* chessboard; exchequer

écho [eko] *m* echo; piece of gossip; **échos** gossip column; **faire écho** to echo

échoir [eʃwar] (usually used only in: *inf; ger* échéant; *pp* échu; 3d *sg: pres ind* échoit; *pret* échut; *fut* échoira; *cond* échoirait) *intr* (aux: AVOIR or ÊTRE) to fall, devolve; fall due

échoppe [eʃɔp] *f* burin; (com) stand, booth; workshop

échopper [eʃɔpe] *tr* to scoop out

échotier [ekɔrje] *m* gossip columnist, society editor

échouer [eʃwe] *tr* to ground, beach ‖ *intr* to sink; run aground; fail ‖ *ref* to run aground

é·chu -chue [eʃy] *adj* due, payable

écimer [esime] *tr* to top

éclaboussement [eklabusmɑ̃] *m* splash

éclabousser [eklabuse] *tr* to splash

éclair [eklɛr] *adj* lightning (*e.g., speed*); flash (*bulb*) ‖ *m* flash (*of light, of lightning, of the eyes, of wit*); (culin) éclair; **éclairs** lightning; **éclairs de chaleur** heat lightning; **éclairs en nappe** sheet lightning; **il fait des éclairs** it is lightening; **passer comme un éclair** to flash by

éclairage [eklɛraʒ] *m* lighting; **sous cet éclairage** (fig) in this light

éclaircie [eklɛrsi] *f* break, clearing; spell of good weather; glade

éclaircir [eklɛrsir] *tr* to lighten; clear up; solve; make thin ‖ *ref* to clear up; thin out

éclaircissement [eklɛrsismɑ̃] *m* explanation, clearing up

éclairement [eklɛrmɑ̃] *m* illumination

éclairer [eklɛre] *tr* to light; enlighten; **éclairer sa lanterne** (fig) to ring a bell for s.o. ‖ *intr* to light up, glitter; **il éclaire** it is lightening ‖ *ref* to be lighted

éclai·reur [eklɛrœr] **-reuse** [røz] *mf* scout ‖ *m* boy scout ‖ *f* girl scout

éclat [ekla] *m* splinter; ray (*of sunshine*); peal (*of thunder*); burst (*of laughter*); brightness, splendor

éclatement [eklatmɑ̃] *m* explosion; blowout (*of tire*); (fig) split

éclater [eklate] *intr* to splinter; sparkle, glitter; burst; break out; blow up, explode

éclateur [eklatœr] *m* spark gap (*of induction coil*)

éclectique [eklɛktik] *adj* eclectic

éclipse [eklips] *f* eclipse; **à éclipses** flashing, blinking

éclipser [eklipse] *tr* to eclipse ‖ *ref* to be eclipsed; (coll) to vanish; (coll) to sneak off

éclisse [eklis] *f* splinter; (med) splint; (rr) fishplate

éclisser [eklise] *tr* to splint

éclo·pé -pée [eklɔpe] *adj* lame ‖ *mf* cripple

éclore [eklɔr] §24 *intr* (*aux:* ÉTRE) to hatch; blossom out

éclosion [eklozjɔ̃] *f* hatching; blooming

écluse [eklyz] *f* lock (*of canal, river, etc.*); floodgate

écluser [eklyze] *tr* to close (*a canal*) by a lock; pass (*a boat*) through a lock

écœurer [ekœre] *tr* to sicken; dishearten

école [ekɔl] *f* school; **école à tir** artillery practice; **école d'application** model school; **école d'arts et métiers** trade school; **école dominicale, école du dimanche** Sunday School; **école libre** private school; **école maternelle** nursery school; **école mixte** co-educational school; **être à bonne école** to be in good hands; **faire école** to set a fashion; to form a school (*to set up a doctrine, gain adherents*); **faire l'école buissonnière** (coll) to play hooky

éco·lier [ekɔlje] **-lière** [ljɛr] *adj* schoolboy ‖ *mf* pupil, scholar; novice ‖ *m* schoolboy ‖ *f* schoolgirl

écologie [ekɔlɔʒi] *f* ecology

éconduire [ekɔ̃dɥir] §19 *tr* to show out

économat [ekɔnɔma] *m* comptroller's office; commissary, company or co-op store; **économats** chain stores

économe [ekɔnɔm] *adj* economical ‖ *mf* treasurer; housekeeper ‖ *m* bursar

économie [ekɔnɔmi] *f* economy; **économie de marché** free enterprise; **économie politique** economics; **économies** savings

économique [ekɔnɔmik] *adj* economic; economical ‖ *f* economics

économiser [ekɔnɔmize] *tr & intr* to economize, save

écope [ekɔp] *f* scoop (*for bailing*)

écoper [ekɔpe] *tr* to bail out ‖ *intr* (coll) to get a bawling out

écorce [ekɔrs] *f* bark (*of tree*); peel, rind; crust (*of earth*)

écorcer [ekɔrse] §51 *tr* to peel, strip off; to skin

écorcher [ekɔrʃe] *tr* to peel; chafe; fleece, overcharge; grate on (*the ears*); burn (*the throat*); murder (*a language*) ‖ *ref* to skin (*e.g., one's arm*)

écor·cheur [ekɔrʃœr] **-cheuse** [ʃøz] *mf* skinner; fleecer, swindler

écorchure [ekɔrʃyr] *f* scratch, abrasion

écorner [ekɔrne] *tr* to poll, break the horns of; dog-ear; to make a hole in (*e.g., a fortune*)

écornifler [ekɔrnifle] *tr* to cadge; **écornifler un dîner à qn** to bum a dinner off s.o.

écorni·fleur [ekɔrniflœr] **-fleuse** [fløz] *mf* sponger, moocher

écos·sais [ekɔse] **-saise** [sɛz] *adj* Scotch, Scottish ‖ *m* Scotch, Scottish (*language*); Scotch plaid ‖ (*cap*) *mf* Scot; **les Écossais** the Scotch ‖ *m* Scotchman

Écosse [ekɔs] *f* Scotland; **l'Écosse** Scotland

écosser [ekɔse] *tr* to shell, hull, husk

écot [eko] *m* share; tree stump; **payer son écot** to pay one's share

écoulement [ekulmɑ̃] *m* flow; (com) sale, turnover; (pathol) discharge; **écoulement d'eau** drainage

écouler [ekule] *tr* to sell, dispose of ‖ *ref* to run (*said, e.g., of water*); flow; drain; leak; elapse, go by

écourter [ekurte] *tr* to shorten (*a dress, coat, etc.*); crop (*the tail, ears, etc.*); cut short, curtail

écoute [ekut] *f* listening post; monitoring; (naut) sheet; **écoutes** wild boar's ears; **être aux écoutes** to eavesdrop, keep one's ears to the ground; **se mettre à l'écoute** to listen to the radio

écouter [ekute] §95 *tr* to listen to; **écouter parler** to listen to (*s.o.*) speaking ‖ *intr* to listen; **écouter aux portes** to eavesdrop ‖ *ref* to coddle oneself; **s'écouter parler** to be pleased with the sound of one's own voice

écou·teur [ekutœr] **-teuse** [tøz] *mf* listener; **écouteur aux portes** eavesdropper ‖ *m* telephone receiver; earphone

écoutille [ekutij] *f* hatchway

écouvillon [ekuvijɔ̃] *m* swab, mop

écrabouiller [ekrabuje] *tr* (coll) to squash

écran [ekrɑ̃] *m* screen; (photo) filter; **écran de cheminée** fire screen; **écran de protection aérienne** air umbrella; **écran en fil de fer** window screen; **le petit écran** television screen; **porter à l'écran** to put on the screen

écra·sant [ekrazɑ̃] **-sante** [zɑ̃t] *adj* crushing

écraser [ekraze] *tr* to crush; overwhelm; run over ‖ *ref* to be crushed; crash

écrémer [ekreme] §10 *tr* to skim; (fig) to skim the cream off

écrémeuse [ekremøz] *f* cream separator

écrevisse [ekrəvis] *f* crayfish

écrier [ekrije] *ref* to cry out, exclaim

écrin [ekrɛ̃] *m* jewel case

écrire [ekrir] §25, §97, §98 *tr* to write; spell ‖ *intr* to write ‖ *ref* to write to each other; be written; be spelled

é·crit [ekri] **-crite** [krit] *adj* written; **c'était écrit** it was fate ‖ *m* writing, written word; written examination; **écrits** writings, works; **par écrit** in writing

écri·teau [ekrito] *m* (*pl* -**teaux**) sign, placard

écritoire [ekritwar] *f* desk set

écriture [ekrityr] *f* handwriting; writing (*style of writing*); **écriture de chat** scrawl; **écritures** accounts; **Écritures** Scriptures; **écritures publiques** government documents

écrivailleur [ekrivɑjœr] *m* (coll) scribbler, hack writer

écrivain [ekrivɛ̃] *adj*—**femme écrivain** woman writer || *m* writer; **écrivain public** public letter writer

écrivasser [ekrivase] *intr* (coll) to scribble

écrou [ekru] *m* nut (*with internal thread*); register (*on police blotter*); **écrou à oreille** thumb nut

écrouer [ekrue] *tr* to jail, book

écrouler [ekrule] *ref* to collapse; crumble; flop (*in a chair*)

é·cru -crue [ekry] *adj* raw; unbleached

écu [eky] *m* shield; crown (*money*); **écus** money

écrubier [ekrybje] *m* (naut) hawsehole

écueil [ekœj] *m* reef, sandbank; stumbling block

écuelle [ekɥɛl] *f* bowl

éculer [ekyle] *tr* to wear down at the heel

écu·mant [ekymɑ̃] -**mante** [mɑ̃t] *adj* foaming; fuming (*with rage*)

écume [ekym] *f* foam; froth; lather; dross; scum (*on liquids; on metal; of society*); **écume de mer** meerschaum

écumer [ekyme] *tr* to skim, scum; pick up (*e.g., gossip*); scour (*the seas*) || *intr* to foam; scum; fume (*with anger*)

écu·meur [ekymœr] -**meuse** [møz] *mf* drifter; **écumeur de marmite** hanger-on; **écumeur de mer** pirate

écu·meux [ekymø] -**meuse** [møz] *adj* foamy, frothy

écumoire [ekymwar] *f* skimmer

écurage [ekyraʒ] *m* scouring; cleaning out

écurer [ekyre] *tr* to scour; clean out

écureuil [ekyrœj] *m* squirrel

écurie [ekyri] *f* stable (*for horses, mules, etc.*); string of horses

écusson [ekysɔ̃] *m* escutcheon; bud (*for grafting*); (mil) identification tag

écuyer [ekɥije] **écuyère** [ekɥijɛr] *mf* horseback rider || *m* horseman; squire; riding master || *f* horsewoman

eczéma [ɛkzema], [ɛgzema] *m* eczema

edelweiss [edəlvajs], [ɛdɛlvɛs] *m* edelweiss

éden [edɛn] *m* Eden || (*cap*) *m* Garden of Eden

éden·té -tée [edɑ̃te] *adj* toothless

E.D.F. *abbr* (**Électricité de France**) French national electric company

édicter [edikte] *tr* to decree, promulgate

édicule [edikyl] *m* kiosk; street urinal

édi·fiant [edifjɑ̃] -**fiante** [fjɑ̃t] *adj* edifying

édification [edifikɑsjɔ̃] *f* edification; construction, building

édifice [edifis] *m* edifice, building

édifier [edifje] *tr* to edify; inform, enlighten; construct, build; found

édit [edi] *m* edict

éditer [edite] *tr* to publish; edit (*a manuscript*)

édi·teur [editœr] -**trice** [tris] *mf* publisher; editor (*of a manuscript*)

édition [edisjɔ̃] *f* edition; publishing

edito·rial -**riale** [editɔrjal] *adj* & *m* (*pl* -**riaux** [rjo]) editorial

édredon [edrədɔ̃] *m* eiderdown

éduca·teur [edykatœr] -**trice** [tris] *adj* educational || *mf* educator

éduca·tif [edykatif] -**tive** [tiv] *adj* educational

éducation [edykɑsjɔ̃] *f* education, bringing-up, nurture

éduquer [edyke] *tr* to bring up (*children*); educate, train

éfaufiler [efofile] *tr* to unravel

effacement [efasmɑ̃] *m* effacement, erasing; self-effacement

effacer [efase] §51 *tr* to efface; erase || *ref* to efface oneself; stand aside

effarement [efarmɑ̃] *m* fright, scare

effaroucher [efaruʃe] *tr* to frighten, scare off

effec·tif [efɛktif] -**tive** [tiv] *adj* actual, real || *m* personnel, manpower; strength (*of military unit*); complement (*of ship*); size (*of class*)

effectivement [efɛktivmɑ̃] *adv* actually, really, sure enough, indeed

effectuer [efɛktɥe] *tr* to make, effect, perform, execute || *ref* to be made; take place, go off

effémi·né -née [efemine] *adj* effeminate

efféminer [efemine] *tr* to make a sissy of; unman || *ref* to become effeminate

effervescence [efɛrvesɑ̃s] *f* effervescence; excitement, ferment

efferves·cent [efɛrvesɑ̃] -**cente** [sɑ̃t] *adj* effervescent

effet [efɛ] *m* effect; (billiards) english; **à cet effet** for that purpose; **en effet** indeed, actually, sure enough; **effet de commerce** bill of exchange; **effet de serre** greenhouse effect; **effets publics** government bonds; **faire de l'effet** to be striking; **faire l'effet de** to give the impression of

effeuillage [efœjaʒ] *m* thinning of leaves; striptease

effeuillaison [efœjɛzɔ̃] *f* fall of leaves

effeuiller [efœje] *tr* to thin out the leaves of, pluck off the petals of || *ref* to shed its leaves

effeuilleuse [efœjøz] *f* (coll) stripteaser

efficace [efikas] *adj* effective

efficacement [efikasmɑ̃] *adv* effectively

efficacité [efikasite] *f* efficacy, efficiency

efficience [efisjɑ̃s] *f* efficiency

effi·cient [efisjɑ̃] -**ciente** [sjɑ̃t] *adj* efficient

effigie [efiʒi] *f* effigy

effiler [efile] *tr* to unravel; taper

effilocher [efilɔʃe] *tr* to unravel

efflan·qué -quée [eflɑ̃ke] *adj* skinny

effleurer [eflœre] *tr* to graze; touch on

effluve [eflyv] *m* effluvium, emanation

effondrement [efɔ̃drəmɑ̃] *m* collapse; (pathol) breakdown

effondrer [efɔ̃dre] *tr* to break open; break (*ground*) ‖ *ref* to collapse, cave in; sink

efforcer [efɔrse] §51, §96, §97 *ref*—**s'efforcer à** or **de** to try hard to, strive to

effort [efɔr] *m* effort; (med) hernia, rupture; **effort de rupture** breaking stress; **effort de tension** torque; **faire effort sur soi-même** to get a hold of oneself

effraction [efraksjɔ̃] *f* housebreaking

effraie [efrɛ] *f* screech owl

effranger [efrɑ̃ʒe] §38 *tr* & *ref* to fray

ef·frayant [efrɛjɑ̃] **-frayante** [frɛjɑ̃t] *adj* frightful, dreadful

effrayer [efrɛje] §49 *tr* to frighten ‖ §97 *ref* to be frightened

effré·né -née [efrene] *adj* unbridled

effritement [efritmɑ̃] *m* crumbling

effriter [efrite] *tr* & *ref* to crumble

effroi [efrwɑ] *m* fright

effron·té -tée [efrɔ̃te] *adj* impudent; shameless; (slang) saucy, sassy

effronterie [efrɔ̃tri] *f* effrontery

effroyable [efrwɑjabl] *adj* frightful

effusion [efyzjɔ̃] *f* effusion; shedding (*of blood*); (fig) gushing

égailler [egɑje] *ref* to scatter

é·gal -gale [egal] (*pl* **-gaux** [go]) *adj* equal; level; (coll) indifferent; **ça m'est égal** (coll) it's all the same to me, it's all right ‖ *mf* equal; **à l'égal de** as much as, no less than

également [egalmɑ̃] *adv* equally, likewise, also

égaler [egale] *tr* to equal, match

égaliser [egalize] *tr* to equalize; equate

égalitaire [egalitɛr] *adj* & *mf* equalitarian

égalité [egalite] *f* equality; evenness; **égalité des chances** equality of opportunity; **être à égalité** to be tied

égard [egar] *m* respect; **à l'égard de** with regard to; **à tous (les) égards** in all respects; **eu égard à** in consideration of

éga·ré -rée [egare] *adj* stray, lost

égarement [egarmɑ̃] *m* wandering (*of mind, senses, etc.*); frenzy (*of sorrow, anger, etc.*)

égarer [egare] *tr* to mislead; misplace; bewilder ‖ *ref* to get lost, stray; be on the wrong track

égayer [egeje] §49, §96 *tr* & *ref* to cheer up; brighten

égide [eʒid] *f* aegis

églefin [egləfɛ̃] *m* haddock

église [egliz] *f* church

églogue [eglɔg] *f* eclogue

égoïne [egɔin] *f* handsaw

égoïsme [egɔism] *m* egoism

égoïste [egɔist] *adj* selfish ‖ *mf* egoist

égorgement [egɔrʒəmɑ̃] *m* slaughter

égorger [egɔrʒe] §38 *tr* to cut the throat of; (coll) to overcharge

égosiller [egozije] *ref* to shout oneself hoarse

égotisme [egɔtism] *m* egotism

égotiste [egɔtist] *adj* egotistical ‖ *mf* egotist

égout [egu] *m* drainage; sewer; sink, cesspool (*e.g., of iniquity*)

égoutier [egutje] *m* sewer worker

égoutter [egute] *tr* to drain; let drip ‖ *ref* to drip

égouttoir [egutwar] *m* drainboard

égrapper [egrape] *tr* to pick off from the cluster

égratigner [egratiɲe] *tr* to scratch; take a dig at, to tease

égratignure [egratiɲyr] *f* scratch; gibe, dig

égrener [egrəne] §2 *tr* to shell (*e.g., peas*); gin (*cotton*); pick off (*grapes*); unstring (*pearls*); tell (*beads*) ‖ *ref* to drop one by one; be strung out

égril·lard [egrijar] **-larde** [jard] *adj* spicy, lewd ‖ *mf* shameless, unblushing person

égrugeoir [egryʒwar] *m* mortar (*for pounding or grinding*)

égruger [egryʒe] §38 *tr* to pound (*in a mortar*)

égueuler [egœle] *tr* to break the neck of (*e.g., a bottle*)

Égypte [eʒipt] *f* Egypt; **l'Égypte** Egypt

égyp·tien [eʒipsjɛ̃] **-tienne** [sjɛn] *adj* Egyptian ‖ (*cap*) *mf* Egyptian

eh [ɛ] *interj* well!; **en bien!** well, well!; very well!

éhon·té -tée [eɔ̃te] *adj* shameless

eider [ɛjdɛr] *m* eider duck

éjaculation [eʒakylɑsjɔ̃] *f* ejaculation; (eccl) short, fervent prayer

éjaculer [eʒakyle] *tr* & *intr* to ejaculate

éjecter [eʒɛkte] *tr* to eject; (coll) to oust

éjection [eʒɛksjɔ̃] *f* ejection

élabo·ré -rée [elabɔre] *adj* elaborated; prepared, elaborate

élaborer [elabɔre] *tr* to elaborate; work out, develop

élaguer [elage] *tr* to prune

élan [elɑ̃] *m* dash; impulse, outburst; spirit, glow; (zool) elk, moose; **avec élan** with enthusiasm

élan·cé -cée [elɑ̃se] *adj* slender, slim

élancement [elɑ̃smɑ̃] *m* throbbing, twinge; yearning (*e.g., for God*)

élancer [elɑ̃se] §51 *intr* to throb, twinge ‖ *ref* to rush, spring, dash; spurt out

élargir [elarʒir] *tr* to widen; broaden; release (*a prisoner*) ‖ *ref* to widen; become more lax

élasticité [elastisite] *f* elasticity

élastique [elastik] *adj* elastic ‖ *m* elastic; rubber band

élec·teur [elɛktœr] **-trice** [tris] *adj* voting ‖ *mf* voter, constituent; (hist) elector; **électeurs** electorate

élec·tif [elɛktif] **-tive** [tiv] *adj* elective

élection [elɛksjɔ̃] *f* election; choice; **élection blanche** election without a valid result

électorat [elɛktɔra] *m* right to vote; (hist) electorate

électri·cien [elɛktrisjɛ̃] **-cienne** [sjɛn] *adj* electrical (*worker*) ‖ *mf* electrician

électricité [elɛktrisite] *f* electricity

électrifier [elɛktrifje] *tr* to electrify

électrique [elɛktrik] *adj* electric(al)

électriser [elɛktrize] *tr* to electrify
électro [elɛktro] *m* electromagnet
électro-aimant [elɛktrɔɛmɑ̃] *m* (*pl -aimants*) electromagnet
électrochoc [elɛktrɔʃɔk] *m* (med) electric shock treatment
électro-culinaire [elɛktrɔkylinɛr] *adj* electric kitchen (*appliances*)
électrocuter [elɛktrɔkyte] *tr* to electrocute
électrode [elɛktrɔd] *f* electrode
électrolyse [elɛktrɔliz] *f* electrolysis
électrolyte [elɛktrɔlit] *m* electrolyte
électromagnétique [elɛktrɔmaɲetik] *adj* electromagnetic
électroména·ger [elɛktrɔmenaʒe] **-gère** [ʒɛr] *adj* household-electric
électromo·teur [elɛktrɔmɔtœr] **-trice** [tris] *adj* electromotive ‖ *m* electric motor
électron [elɛktrɔ̃] *m* electron
électronique [elɛktrɔnik] *adj* electronic ‖ *f* electronics
électron-volt [elɛktrɔ̃vɔlt] *m* (*pl* **électrons-volts**) electron-volt
électrophone [elɛktrɔfɔn] *m* electric phonograph
électrotype [elɛktrɔtip] *m* electrotype
électrotyper [elɛktrɔtipe] *tr* to electrotype
élégamment [elegamɑ̃] *adv* elegantly
élégance [elegɑ̃s] *f* elegance
élé·gant [elegɑ̃] **-gante** [gɑ̃t] *adj* elegant
élégiaque [eleʒjak] *adj* elegiac ‖ *mf* elegist
élégie [eleʒi] *f* elegy
élément [elemɑ̃] *m* element; (*of an electric battery*) cell, element; (elec, mach) unit; **élément standard** standard part
élémentaire [elemɑ̃tɛr] *adj* elementary
éléphant [elefɑ̃] *m* elephant
éléphantesque [elefɑ̃tɛsk] *adj* (coll) gigantic, elephantine
élevage [elvaʒ], [ɛlvaʒ] *m* rearing, raising, breeding; ranch
éléva·teur [elevatœr] **-trice** [tris] *adj* lifting ‖ *m* elevator; hoist
élévation [elevasjɔ̃] *f* elevation; promotion; increase; (rok) lift-off
élève [elɛv] *mf* pupil, student; **ancien élève** alumnus; **élève externe** day student; **élève interne** boarding student ‖ *f* breeder (*animal*); (hort) seedling
éle·vé -vée [elve] *adj* high, elevated; lofty, noble; **bien élevé** well-bred; **mal élevé** ill-bred
élever [elve] §2 *tr* to raise; raise, bring up, nurture; erect ‖ *ref* to rise; arise; be built, stand
éle·veur [ɛlvœr] **-veuse** [vøz] *mf* breeder, rancher
elfe [ɛlf] *m* elf
élider [elide] *tr* to elide
éligible [eliʒibl] *adj* eligible
élimer [elime] *tr & ref* to wear threadbare
éliminatoire [eliminatwar] *adj* (sports) preliminary ‖ *f* (sports) preliminaries
éliminer [elimine] *tr* to eliminate
élire [elir] §36 *tr* to elect
élision [elizjɔ̃] *f* elision
élite [elit] *f* elite

elle [ɛl] *pron disj* §85 her ‖ *pron conj* §87 she
elle-même [ɛlmɛm] §86 herself, itself
elles [ɛl] *pron disj* §85 them *pron conj* §87 they
ellipse [elips] *f* (gram) ellipsis; (math) ellipse
elliptique [eliptik] *adj* elliptic(al)
élocution [elɔkysjɔ̃] *f* elocution; choice and arrangement of words
éloge [elɔʒ] *m* eulogy; praise
élo·gieux [elɔʒjø] **-gieuse** [ʒjøz] *adj* full of praise
éloi·gné -gnée [elwaɲe] *adj* distant
éloignement [elwaɲəmɑ̃] *m* remoteness; aversion; postponement
éloigner [elwaɲe] *tr* to move away; remove; drive away; postpone ‖ *ref* to move away; digress, deviate; become estranged
élongation [elɔ̃gasjɔ̃] *f* stretching
élonger [elɔ̃ʒe] §38 *tr* to lay (*e.g., a cable*); **élonger la terre** to skirt the coast
éloquence [elɔkɑ̃s] *f* eloquence
élo·quent [elɔkɑ̃] **-quente** [kɑ̃t] *adj* eloquent
é·lu -lue [ely] *adj* elected ‖ *mf* chosen one; **les élus** the elect ‖ *v* see **élire**
élucider [elyside] *tr* to elucidate
éluder [elyde] *tr* to elude, avoid
éma·cié -ciée [emasje] *adj* emaciated
émacier [emasje] *ref* to become emaciated
é·mail [emaj] *m* (*pl* **-maux** [mo]) enamel ‖ *m* (*pl* **-mails**) nail polish; car or bicycle paint
émaillage [emajaʒ] *m* enameling
émailler [emaje] *tr* to enamel; sprinkle (*e.g., with quotations, metaphors, etc.*); dot (*e.g., the fields, as flowers do*)
émanation [emanasjɔ̃] *f* emanation; manifestation (*e.g., of authority*)
émanciper [emɑ̃sipe] *tr* to emancipate ‖ *ref* to be emancipated; (coll) to get out of hand
émaner [emane] *intr* to emanate
émarger [emarʒe] §38 *tr* to trim (*e.g., a book*); initial (*a document*) ‖ *intr* to get paid; **émarger à** to be paid from
émasculer [emaskyle] *tr* to emasculate
embâcle [ɑ̃bɑkl] *m* pack ice, ice floe
emballage [ɑ̃balaʒ] *m* packing, wrapping; **emballage consigné** returnable bottle; **emballage perdu** nonreturnable bottle
emballer [ɑ̃bale] *tr* to wrap up, pack; race (*a motor*); (coll) to thrill; (coll) to bawl out ‖ *ref* to bolt, run away; (mach) to race; (coll) to get worked up
embal·leur [ɑ̃balœr] **-leuse** [løz] *mf* packer
embarbouiller [ɑ̃barbuje] *tr* to besmear; (coll) to muddle, confuse ‖ *ref* (coll) to get tangled up
embarcadère [ɑ̃barkadɛr] *m* wharf; (rr) platform
embarcation [ɑ̃barkasjɔ̃] *f* small boat
embardée [ɑ̃barde] *f* lurch; (aut) swerve; (aer, naut) yaw
embarder [ɑ̃barde] *intr* (aut) to swerve; (aer, naut) to yaw

embargo [ãbargo] *m* embargo

embarquement [ãbarkəmã] *m* embarkation; shipping; loading

embarquer [ãbarke] *tr* to embark; ship (*a sea*); load (*in car, plane, etc.*); (coll) to put in the clink ‖ *ref* to embark; board; get into a car

embarras [ãbara] *m* embarrassment; trouble, inconvenience; encumbrance, obstruction; perplexity; financial difficulties; **embarras de voitures** traffic jam; **embarras du choix** too much to choose from; **faire des embarras** (coll) to put on airs

embarras·sé -sée [ãbarase] *adj* embarrassed; awkward, ill-at-ease; confused, muddled; upset (*stomach*)

embarrasser [ãbarase] *tr* to embarrass; hamper, obstruct; stump, perplex ‖ *ref*—**s'embarrasser de** to take an interest in; bother with

embaucher [ãboʃe] *tr* to hire, sign on; (coll) to entice (*soldiers*) to desert ‖ *intr* to hire; **on n'embauche pas** (*public sign*) no help wanted

embauchoir [ãboʃwar] *m* shoetree

embaumement [ãboməmã] *m* embalming; perfuming

embaumer [ãbome] *tr* to embalm; perfume ‖ *intr* to smell good

embaumeur [ãbomœr] *m* embalmer

embellir [ãbɛlir] *tr* to embellish ‖ *intr* to clear up (*said of weather*); improve in looks ‖ *ref* to grow more beautiful

embellissement [ãbɛlismã] *m* embellishment

embêtement [ãbɛtmã] *m* (coll) annoyance

embêter [ãbɛte], [ãbete] *tr* (coll) to annoy

emblave [ãblav] *f* grainfield

emblaver [ãblave] *tr* to sow

emblée [ãble]—**d'emblée** then and there, right off; without difficulty

emblématique [ãblematik] *adj* emblematic(al)

emblème [ãblɛm] *m* emblem

embobeliner [ãbɔbline] *tr* (coll) to bamboozle

embobiner [ãbɔbine] *tr* to wind up (*e.g., on a reel*); (coll) to bamboozle

emboîter [ãbwate] *tr* to encase; nest (*boxes, boats, etc.*); (mach) to interlock, joint; **emboîter le pas** to fall into step

embolie [ãbɔli] *f* (pathol) embolism

embonpoint [ãbɔ̃pwɛ̃] *m* portliness; **prendre de l'embonpoint** to put on flesh

embouche [ãbuʃ] *f* pasture

embou·ché -chée [ãbuʃe] *adj*—**mal embouché** foul-mouthed

emboucher [ãbuʃe] *tr* to blow, sound

embouchoir [ãbuʃwar] *m* mouthpiece

embouchure [ãbuʃyr] *f* mouth (*of a river*); mouthpiece

embourber [ãburbe] *tr* to stick in the mud; vilify, implicate

embout [ãbu] *m* tip, ferrule; rubber tip (*for chair*)

embouteillage [ãbutɛjaʒ] *m* bottling; bottleneck, traffic jam

emboutir [ãbutir] *tr* to stamp, emboss; smash (*e.g., a fender*) ‖ *ref* to bump

embranchement [ãbrãʃmã] *m* branching (off); branch; branch line; junction (*of roads, track, etc.*); **embranchement particulier** private siding

embrasement [ãbrazmã] *m* conflagration; illumination, glow

embraser [ãbraze] *tr* to set aflame or aglow ‖ *ref* to flame up; glow

embrassade [ãbrasad] *m* embrace; kissing

embrasse [ãbrɑs] *f* curtain tieback

embrassement [ãbrasmã] *m* embrace

embrasser [ãbrase] *tr* to embrace; kiss; join; undertake; take in (*at a glance*); take (*the opportunity*) ‖ *ref* to embrace; neck

embras·seur [ãbrasœr] **-seuse** [søz] *mf* smoocher

embrasure [ãbrazyr] *f* embrasure, loophole; opening (*for door or window*)

embrayage [ãbrɛjaʒ] *m* coupling engagement; (aut) clutch

embrayer [ãbrɛje], [ãbreje] §49 *tr* to engage, connect; throw into gear ‖ *intr* to throw the clutch in

embrocher [ãbrɔʃe] *tr* to put on a spit

embrouillage [ãbrujaz] *m* (electron) scrambling

embrouiller [ãbruje] *tr* to embroil ‖ *ref* to become embroiled

embroussail·lé -lée [ãbrusaje] *adj* bushy; tangled; complicated, complex

embru·mé -mée [ãbryme] *adj* foggy, misty

embruns [ãbrœ̃] *mpl* spray

embryologie [ãbrijɔlɔʒi] *f* embryology

embryon [ãbrijɔ̃] *m* embryo

embryonnaire [ãbrijɔnɛr] *adj* embryonic

em·bu -bue [ãby] *adj* lifeless, dull ‖ *m* dull tone (*of a painting*)

embûche [ãbyʃ] *f* snare, trap

embuer [ãbɥe] *tr* to cloud with steam; **embué de larmes** dimmed with tears

embuscade [ãbyskad] *f* ambush

embus·qué -quée [ãbyske] *adj* in ambush; **se tenir embusqué** to lie in ambush ‖ *m* (mil) goldbricker, shirker

embusquer [ãbyske] *tr* to ambush, trap ‖ *ref* to lie in ambush; (mil) to get a safe assignment

émé·ché -chée [emeʃe] *adj* (coll) tipsy, high

émender [emãde] *tr* to amend (*a sentence, decree, etc.*)

émeraude [ɛmrod] *f* emerald

émergence [emɛrʒãs] *f* emergence

émerger [emɛrʒe] §38 *intr* to emerge

émeri [ɛmri] *m* emery

émerillon [emrijɔ̃] *m* swivel; (orn) merlin

émerillon·né -née [emrijɔne] *adj* lively, gay

émérite [emerit] *adj* experienced; distinguished, remarkable; confirmed (*smoker*); (obs) retired, emeritus

émersion [emɛrsjɔ̃] *f* emersion

émerveillement [emɛrvɛjmɑ̃] *m* wonderment

émerveiller [emɛrvɛje] *tr* to astonish, amaze

émétique [emetik] *adj & m* emetic

émet·teur [emetœr] -trice [tris] *adj* issuing; transmitting ‖ *mf* maker (*of check, draft*); issuer ‖ *m* broadcasting station; (rad) transmitter

émetteur-récepteur [emɛtœrresɛptœr] *m* (*pl* émetteurs-récepteurs) (rad) walkie-talkie

émettre [emɛtr] §42 *tr* to emit; express (*an opinion*); issue (*stamps, bank notes, etc.*); transmit (*a radio signal*) ‖ *intr* to transmit, broadcast

é·meu [emø] *m* (*pl* -neus) (zool) emu

émeute [emøt] *f* riot

émeutier [emøtje] *m* rioter

émietter [emjete] *tr* to crumble; break up (*an estate*)

émi·grant [emigrɑ̃] -grante [grɑ̃t] *adj & mf* emigrant; migrant

émi·gré -grée [emigre] *adj* emigrating ‖ *mf* emigrant; émigré

émigrer [emigre] *intr* to emigrate; migrate

émincer [emɛ̃se] §51 *tr* to cut in thin slices

éminemment [eminamɑ̃] *adv* eminently

éminence [eminɑ̃s] *f* eminence

émi·nent [eminɑ̃] -nente [nɑ̃t] *adj* eminent

émissaire [emisɛr] *m* emissary; outlet (*of lake, basin, etc.*)

émission [emisjɔ̃] *f* emission; utterance; issue (*of stamps, bank notes, etc.*) (rad) transmission, broadcast

emmagasiner [ɑ̃magazine] *tr* to put in storage; store up; stockpile

emmailloter [ɑ̃majɔte] *tr* to swathe; bandage

emmancher [ɑ̃mɑ̃ʃe] *tr* to put a handle on ‖ *ref* (coll) to begin; s'emmancher bien (coll) to get off to a good start; s'emmancher mal (coll) to get off to a bad start

emmêler [ɑ̃mɛle], [ɑ̃mele] *tr* to tangle up; mix up

emménagement [ɑ̃menaʒmɑ̃] *m* moving in; installation

emménager [ɑ̃menaʒe] §38 *tr & intr* to move in

emmener [ɑ̃mne] §2 *tr* to take or lead away; take out (*e.g., to dinner*); take (*on a visit*)

emmenthal [emɛ̃tal], [emɛntal] *m* Swiss cheese

emmer·dant [ɑ̃mɛrdɑ̃] -dante [dɑ̃t] *adj* (slang) damned annoying, damned boring

emmerder [ɑ̃mɛrde] *tr* (slang) to annoy, bore, bug ‖ *ref* (slang) to be pissed off; (slang) to be bored stiff

emmiel·lé -lée [ɑ̃mjɛle], [ɑ̃mjele] *adj* honeyed (*e.g., words*)

emmitoufler [ɑ̃mitufle] *tr & ref* to bundle up (*in warm clothing*)

emmurer [ɑ̃myre] *tr* to wall in, immure

émoi [emwa] *m* agitation, alarm

émolument [emɔlymɑ̃] *m* share; émoluments emolument, fee, salary

émonder [emɔ̃de] *tr* to prune, trim

émo·tif [emɔtif] -tive [tiv] *adj* emotional ‖ *mf* emotional person

émotion [emosjɔ̃] *f* emotion; commotion

émotionnable [emosjɔnabl] *adj* emotional

émotion·nant [emosjɔnɑ̃] -nante [nɑ̃t] *adj* stirring, moving

émotionner [emosjɔne] *tr* to move deeply, thrill, affect ‖ *ref* to get excited, flustered

émoucher [emuʃe] *tr* to chase flies away from

émouchet [emuʃɛ] *m* sparrow hawk

émouchoir [emuʃwar] *m* whisk, fly swatter

émoudre [emudr] §43 *tr* to grind, sharpen

émoulage [emulaʒ] *m* grinding, sharpening

émou·lu -lue [emuly] *adj*—frais émoulu de (fig) fresh from, just back from

émous·sé -sée [emuse] *adj* blunt

émousser [emuse] *tr* to dull, blunt

émoustiller [emustije] *tr* (coll) to exhilarate, rouse; tantalize

émou·vant [emuvɑ̃] -vante [vɑ̃t] *adj* moving, touching, stirring

émouvoir [emuvwar] §45 (*pp* ému) *tr* to move; excite ‖ *ref* to be moved; be excited

empailler [ɑ̃pɑje] *tr* to stuff (*animals*); cane (*a chair*)

empail·leur [ɑ̃pɑjœr] -leuse [jøz] *mf* taxidermist; caner

empaler [ɑ̃pale] *tr* to impale

empan [ɑ̃pɑ̃] *m* span (*of hand*)

empanacher [ɑ̃panaʃe] *tr* to plume

empaquetage [ɑ̃paktaʒ] *m* packaging; package

empaqueter [ɑ̃pakte] §34 *tr* to package

emparer [ɑ̃pare] *ref*—s'emparer de to seize, take hold of

empâter [ɑ̃pate] *tr* to make sticky; fatten up (*chickens, turkeys, etc.*); coat (*the tongue*); (typ) to overlink ‖ *ref* to put on weight; become coated (*said of tongue*); become husky (*said of voice*)

empattement [ɑ̃patmɑ̃] *m* foundation, footing; (aut) wheelbase

empaumer [ɑ̃pome] *tr* to catch in the hand; hit with a racket; palm (*a card*); (coll) to hoodwink

empêchement [ɑ̃pɛʃmɑ̃] *m* impediment, bar; hindrance, obstacle

empêcher [ɑ̃pɛʃe] §97, §99 *tr* to hinder; empêcher qn de + *inf* to prevent or keep s.o. from + *ger;* n'empêche que all the same, e.g., n'empêche qu'il est très poli he's very polite all the same ‖ §97 *ref*—ne pouvoir s'empêcher de + *inf* not to be able to help + *ger*, e.g., je n'ai pu m'empêcher de rire I could not help laughing

empê·cheur [ɑ̃pɛʃœr] -cheuse [ʃøz] *mf*—empêcheur de danser en rond (coll) wet blanket

empeigne [ɑ̃pɛɲ] *f* upper (*of shoe*)

empennage [ɑ̃penaʒ] *m* feathers (*of arrow*); fins, vanes; (aer) empennage

empereur [ɑ̃prœr] *m* emperor

emperler [ɑ̃pɛrle] *tr* to ornament with pearls; cover with drops; la sueur emperlait son front his forehead was covered with beads of perspiration

empe·sé -sée [ɑ̃pəze] *adj* starched, stiff, wooden (*style*)

empeser [ɑ̃pəze] §2 *tr* to starch

empes·té -tée [ɑ̃pɛste] *adj* pestilential; stinking, reeking; depraved

empester [ɑ̃pɛste] *tr* to stink; corrupt ‖ *intr* to stink

empêtrer [ɑ̃pɛtre] *tr* to hamper; involve, entangle ‖ *ref* to become involved, entangled

emphase [ɑ̃fɑz] *f* overemphasis; bombast, pretentiousness

emphatique [ɑ̃fɑtik] *adj* overemphasized; bombastic, pretentious

emphysème [ɑ̃fizɛm] *m* emphysema

empiècement [ɑ̃pjɛsmɑ̃] *m* yoke (*of shirt, blouse, etc.*)

empierrer [ɑ̃pjɛre] *tr* to pave with stones; (rr) to ballast

empiètement [ɑ̃pjɛtmɑ̃] *m* encroachment, incursion

empiéter [ɑ̃pjete] §10 *intr* to encroach

empiffrer [ɑ̃pifre] *tr* (coll) to stuff, fatten ‖ *ref* (coll) to stuff oneself, guzzle

empiler [ɑ̃pile] *tr* to pile up, stack; (slang) to dupe ‖ *ref* to pile up; **se faire empiler** (slang) to be had

empire [ɑ̃pir] *m* empire; control, supremacy

empirer [ɑ̃pire] *tr* to make worse, aggravate ‖ *intr* (*aux:* AVOIR or ÊTRE) to grow worse

empirique [ɑ̃pirik] *adj* empiric(al) ‖ *m* empiricist; charlatan, quack

emplacement [ɑ̃plɑsmɑ̃] *m* emplacement; location, site

emplâtre [ɑ̃plɑtr] *m* patch (*on tire*); (med) plaster; (coll) boob

emplette [ɑ̃plɛt] *f* purchase; **aller faire des emplettes** to go shopping

emplir [ɑ̃plir] *tr & ref* to fill up

emploi [ɑ̃plwa] *m* employment, job; employment, use; (theat) type (*of role*); **double emploi** useless duplication; **emploi du temps** schedule

em·ployé -ployée [ɑ̃plwaje] *mf* employee; clerk

employer [ɑ̃plwaje] §47, §100 *tr* to employ; to use ‖ §96 *ref* to be employed; **s'employer à** to try to, do one's best to

em·ployeur [ɑ̃plwajœr] **-ployeuse** [plwajøz] *mf* employer

empocher [ɑ̃pɔʃe] *tr* (coll) to pocket

empoi·gnant [ɑ̃pwaɲɑ̃] **-gnante** [ɲɑ̃t] *adj* exciting, arresting, thrilling

empoigner [ɑ̃pwaɲe] *tr* to grasp; collar (*a crook*); grip, move (*an audience*)

empois [ɑ̃pwa] *m* starch

empoisonnement [ɑ̃pwazɔnmɑ̃] *m* poisoning; **avoir des empoisonnements** (coll) to be annoyed

empoisonner [ɑ̃pwazɔne] *tr* to poison; infect (*the air*); corrupt; (coll) to bother ‖ *intr* to reek ‖ *ref* to be poisoned

empoison·neur [ɑ̃pwazɔnœr] **-neuse** [nøz] *adj* poisoning ‖ *mf* poisoner; corrupter

empoissonner [ɑ̃pwasɔne] *tr* to stock with fish

empor·té -tée [ɑ̃pɔrte] *adj* quick-tempered, impetuous

emportement [ɑ̃pɔrtəmɑ̃] *m* anger, temper

emporte-pièce [ɑ̃pɔrtəpjɛs] *m* (*pl* **-pièces**) punch; **à l'emporte-pièce** trenchant, cutting, biting (*style, words, etc.*)

emporter [ɑ̃pɔrte] *tr* to take away; carry off; remove; **à emporter** to take out, to go (*e.g., said of food to take out of the restaurant*); **l'emporter sur** to have the upper hand over ‖ *ref* to be carried away; lose one's temper; run away

emporte-restes [ɑ̃pɔrtrɛst] *m invar* (coll) doggy bag

empo·té -tée [ɑ̃pɔte] *adj* (coll) clumsy ‖ *mf* (coll) butterfingers

empoter [ɑ̃pɔte] *tr* to pot (*a plant*)

empourprer [ɑ̃purpre] *tr* to set aglow ‖ *ref* to turn crimson; flush

empoussiérer [ɑ̃pusjere] §10 *tr* to cover with dust

empreindre [ɑ̃prɛ̃dr] §50 *tr* to imprint, stamp

empreinte [ɑ̃prɛt] *f* imprint, stamp; **empreinte des roues** wheel tracks; **empreinte digitale** fingerprint; **empreinte du pied** or **empreinte de pas** footprint

empres·sé -sée [ɑ̃prɛse] *adj* eager

empressement [ɑ̃prɛsmɑ̃] *m* haste, alacrity; eagerness, readiness

empresser [ɑ̃prɛse] §96, §97 *ref* to hasten; **s'empresser à** to be anxious to; **s'empresser auprès de** to be attentive to, make a fuss over; press around; **s'empresser de** to hasten to

emprise [ɑ̃priz] *f* expropriation; control, ascendancy

emprisonment [ɑ̃prizɔnmɑ̃] *m* imprisonment

emprisonner [ɑ̃prizɔne] *tr* to imprison

emprunt [ɑ̃prœ̃] *m* loan; loan word; **d'emprunt** feigned, assumed

emprun·té -tée [ɑ̃prœ̃te] *adj* timid, self-conscious, awkward; feigned, sham

emprunter [ɑ̃prœ̃te] *tr* to borrow; take (*a road, a route*); take on (*false appearances*); **emprunter q.ch. à** to borrow s.th. from; get s.th. from

empuantir [ɑ̃pɥɑtir] *tr* to stink up

empyème [ɑ̃pjɛm] *m* empyema

empyrée [ɑ̃pire] *m* empyrean

é·mu -mue [emy] *adj* moved, touched; tender (*memory*); **ému de** alarmed by ‖ *v see* **émouvoir**

émulation [emylɑsjɔ̃] *f* emulation, rivalry

émule [emyl] *mf* emulator, rival

émulsion [emylsjɔ̃] *f* emulsion

émulsionner [emylsjɔne] *tr* to emulsify

en [ɑ̃] *pron indef & adv* §87 ‖ *prep* in; into; to, e.g., **aller en France** to go to France; e.g., **de mal en pis** from bad to worse; at, e.g., **en mer** at sea; e.g., **en guerre** at war; on, e.g., **en congé** on leave; by, e.g., **en chemin de fer** by rail; of, made of, e.g., **en bois** (made) of wood; as, e.g., **il est mort en soldat** he died (as) a soldier

enamourer [ānamure] *ref* to become enamored, fall in love

énarque [enark] *mf* (fig) bureaucrat

encabaner [ākabane] *ref* (Canad) to hole up, dig in (*e.g., for the winter*)

encablure [ākablyr] *f* cable's length (*unit of measure*)

encadrement [ākɑdrəmā] *m* framing; frame: framework; window frame; doorframe; border, edge; staffing; officering (*furnishing with officers*)

encadrer [ākɑdre] *tr* to frame; staff (*an organization*); officer (*troops*); incorporate (*recruits*) into a unit; train, supervise

encadreur [ākɑdrœr] *m* framer (*person*)

encager [ākaʒe] §38 *tr* to cage

encaisse [ākɛs] *f* cash on hand, cash balance; **encaisse métallique** bullion

encais·sé -sée [ākɛse] *adj* deeply embanked, sunken

encaissement [ākɛsmā] *m* cashing (*e.g., of check*); boxing, crating; embankment

encaisser [ākɛse], [ākese] *tr* to cash; box, crate; receive (*a blow*); embank (*a river*); (coll) to put up with ‖ *ref* to be steeply embanked

encaisseur [ākɛsœr] *m* collector; payee; cashier

encan [ākā] *m* auction

encanailler [ākanaje] *tr* to debase ‖ *ref* to acquire bad habits; keep low company

encapuchonner [ākapyʃɔne] *tr* to hood

encaquer [ākake] *tr* to barrel; pack (*sardines*); (coll) to pack in like sardines

encart [ākar] *m* inset, insert

encarter [ākarte] *tr* to card (*buttons, pins, etc.*); (bb) to tip in

en-cas [āka] *m invar* snack; reserve, emergency supply

encasernement [ākazɛrnəmā] *m*—**encasernement de conscience** thought control, regimentation

encaserner [ākazɛrne] *tr* to quarter, barrack (*troops*)

encastrement [ākastrəmā] *m* groove; fitting

encas·tré -trée [ākastre] *adj* built-in

encastrer [ākastre] *tr & ref* to fit

encaustique [ākɔstik] *f* furniture polish; floor wax; encaustic painting

encaustiquer [ākɔstike] *tr* to wax

encaver [ākave] *tr* to cellar (*wine*)

enceindre [āsɛ̃dr] §50 *tr* to enclose, encircle

enceinte [āsɛ̃t] *adj fem* pregnant ‖ *f* enclosure; walls, ramparts; precinct, compass; (boxing) ring

encens [āsā] *m* incense; flattery

encenser [āsāse] *tr* to incense, perfume with incense; flatter

encensoir [āsāswar] *m* censer

encéphalite [āsefalit] *f* encephalitis

encercler [āsɛrkle] *tr* to encircle

enchaînement [āʃɛnmā] *m* chaining up; chain, sequence

enchaîner [āʃɛne], [āʃene], *tr* to chain; to connect ‖ *intr* to go on speaking ‖ *ref* to be connected

enchan·té -tée [āʃāte] §93 *adj* delighted, pleased

enchantement [āʃātmā] *m* enchantment

enchanter [āʃāte] *tr* to enchant

enchan·teur [āʃātœr] **-teresse** [trɛs] *adj* enchanting, bewitching ‖ *m* enchanter, magician ‖ *f* enchantress

enchâsser [āʃɑse] *tr* to enshrine; insert; set, chase (*a gem*)

enchère [āʃɛr] *f* bid, bidding; **folle enchère** bid that cannot be made good; folly

enchérir [āʃerir] *tr* to bid on; raise the price of ‖ *intr* to bid; rise in price; **enchérir sur** to improve on; outbid

enchérisseur [āʃerisœr] *m* bidder; **dernier enchérisseur** highest bidder

enchevêtrement [āʃvɛtrəmā] *m* entanglement; network; jumble

enchevêtrer [āʃvɛtre] *tr* to tangle up; halter (*a horse*) ‖ *ref* to become complicated or confused

enchifre·né -née [āʃifrəne] *adj* stuffed-up (*with a cold*)

enclave [āklav] *f* enclave

enclaver [āklave] *tr* to enclose; dovetail

enclencher [āklāʃe] *tr & ref* to interlock

en·clin [āklɛ̃] **-cline** [klin] *adj* inclined, prone

encliquetage [ākliktaʒ] *m* ratchet

encliqueter [āklikte] §34 *tr* to cog, mesh

enclitique [āklitik] *adj & m & f* enclitic

enclore [āklɔr] §24 (has also 1st & 2d *pl pres ind* **enclosons, enclosez**) *tr* to close in, wall in

enclos [āklo] *m* enclosure, close

enclume [āklym] *f* anvil; **se trouver entre l'enclume et le marteau** (coll) to be between the devil and the deep blue sea

encoche [ākɔʃ] *f* notch, nick; slot; thumb index

encocher [ākɔʃe] *tr* to notch, nick; slot

encoignure [ākɔɲyr] *f* corner; corner piece; corner cabinet

encollage [ākɔlaʒ] *m* gluing; sizing

encoller [ākɔle] *tr* to glue; size

encolure [ākɔlyr] *f* collar size; neck line; neck and withers (*of horse*); **gagner par une encolure** to win by a neck

encombre [ākɔ̃br] *m*—**sans encombre** without a hitch, without hindrance

encombrement [ākɔ̃brəmā] *m* encumbrance, congestion

encombrer [ākɔ̃bre] *tr* to encumber; crowd, congest; block up, jam; litter; load down ‖ *ref*—**s'encombrer de** (coll) to be saddled with

encontre [ākɔ̃tr]—**à l'encontre de** counter to, against; contrary to

encore [ākɔr] *adv* still, e.g., **il est encore ici** he is still here; yet, e.g., **encore mieux** better yet; e.g., **pas encore** not yet; only, e.g., **si encore vous m'en aviez parlé!** if only you had told me!; even, e.g., **il est encore plus intelligent**

que vous he is even more intelligent than you; **encore que** although; **encore une fois** once more, once again; **en voulez-vous encore?** do you want some more? ‖ *interj* again!, oh no, not again! (*expressing impatience or astonishment*)

encorner [ãkɔrne] *tr* to gore, toss

encouragement [ãkuraʒmã] *m* encouragement

encourager [ãkuraʒe] §38, §96, §100 *tr* to encourage

encourir [ãkurir] §14 *tr* to incur

encrasser [ãkrase] *tr* to soil, dirty; soot (*a chimney*); foul (*a gun*) ‖ *ref* to get dirty; stop up, clog; soot up

encre [ãkr] *f* ink; **encre de Chine** India ink; **encre de couleur** colored ink; **encre sympathique** invisibile ink

encrer [ãkre] *tr* to ink

encreur [ãkrœr] *adj* inking (*ribbon, roller*) ‖ *m* ink roller

encrier [ãkrije] *m* inkwell

encroûter [ãkrute] *tr* to encrust; plaster (*walls*) ‖ *ref* to become encrusted; get rusty; become hidebound, prejudiced

encyclique [ãsiklik] *adj & f* encyclical

encyclopédie [ãsiklɔpedi] *f* encyclopedia

encyclopédique [ãsiklɔpedik] *adj* encyclopedic

endauber [ãdobe] *tr* to braise

endémie [ãdemi] *f* endemic

endémique [ãdemik] *adj* endemic

endenter [ãdãte] *tr* to tooth, cog; mesh (*gears*); **bien endenté** (coll) with plenty of teeth; (coll) with a hearty appetite

endetter [ãdɛte] *tr & ref* to run into debt

endêver [ãdeve] *intr*—**faire endêver** to bedevil, drive wild

endia·blé -blée [ãdjable] *adj* devilish, reckless; full of pep

endiguement [ãdigmã] *m* damming up; embankment

endiguer [ãdige] *tr* to dam up

endimancher [ãdimãʃe] *tr & ref* to put on Sunday clothes, dress up

endive [ãdiv] *f* endive

endocrine [ãdɔkrin] *adj* endocrine

endoctriner [ãdɔktrine] *tr* to indoctrinate; win over

endolo·ri -rie [ãdɔlɔri] *adj* painful, sore

endommagement [ãdɔmaʒmã] *m* damage

endommager [ãdɔmaʒe] §38 *tr* to damage ‖ *ref* to suffer damage

endor·mi -mie [ãdɔrmi] *adj* asleep, sleeping; sluggish, apathetic; dormant; numb (*arm or leg*)

endormir [ãdɔrmir] §23 *tr* to put to sleep; lull, put off guard ‖ *ref* to go to sleep; slack off; let down one's guard

endos [ãdo] *m* endorsement

endosse [ãdos] *f* responsibility

endossement [ãdosmã] *m* endorsement

endosser [ãdose] *tr* to endorse; take on the responsibility of

endosseur [ãdosœr] *m* endorser

endroit [ãdrwa], [ãdrwa] *m* place, spot; right side (*of cloth*); **à l'endroit** right side

out; **à l'endroit de** with regard to; **le petit endroit** (coll) the toilet; **mettre à l'endroit** to put on right side out

enduire [ãdɥir] §19 *tr* to coat, smear

enduit [ãdɥi] *m* coat, coating

endurance [ãdyrãs] *f* endurance

endu·rant [ãdyrã] **-rante** [rãt] *adj* untiring; meek, patient

endur·ci -cie [ãdyrsi] *adj* hardened; tough, calloused; inveterate

endurcir [ãdyrsir] *tr* to harden; inure, toughen ‖ *ref* to harden; **s'endurcir à** to become accustomed to, become inured to

endurcissement [ãdyrsismã] *m* hardening

endurer [ãdyre] *tr* to endure

énergétique [enɛrʒetik] *adj* energy, energy-giving, energizing ‖ *f* energetics

énergie [enɛrʒi] *f* energy

énergique [enɛrʒik] *adj* energetic

énergumène [enɛrgymɛn] *mf* ranter, wild person, nut

éner·vant [enɛrvã] **-vante** [vãt] *adj* annoying, nerve-racking

énerver [enɛrve] *tr* to enervate; unnerve ‖ *ref* to get nervous; be exasperated

enfance [ãfãs] *f* childhood; infancy; dotage, second childhood; **c'est l'enfance de l'art** (coll) it's child's play; **enfance délinquante** juvenile delinquents; **première enfance** infancy

enfant [ãfã] *adj invar* childish, childlike; **bon enfant** good-natured ‖ *mf* child; **enfant de chœur** altar boy; **enfant de la balle** child who follows in his father's footsteps; **enfant en bas âge** infant; **enfant terrible** (fig) stormy petrel, troublemaker; **enfant trouvé** foundling; **mon enfant!** my boy!; **petit enfant** infant

enfantement [ãfãtmã] *m* childbirth

enfanter [ãfãte] *tr* to give birth to

enfantillage [ãfãtijaʒ] *m* childishness

enfan·tin [ãfãtɛ̃] **-tine** [tin] *adj* childish, infantile

enfari·né -née [ãfarine] *adj* smeared with flour

enfer [ãfɛr] *m* hell; erotica (*restricted section of a library*)

enfermer [ãfɛrme] *tr* to enclose; shut up, lock up ‖ *ref* to shut oneself in; closet oneself

enferrer [ãfɛre] *tr* to pierce, run through ‖ *ref* to run oneself through with a sword; bite (*said of fish*); (fig) to be caught in one's own trap

enfiévrer [ãfjevre] §10 *tr* to inflame, make feverish

enfilade [ãfilad] *f* row, string, series; (mil) enfilade; **en enfilade** connecting, e.g., **chambres en enfilade** connecting rooms

enfile-aiguille [ãfilegɥij] *m invar* threader, needle threader

enfiler [ãfile] *tr* to pierce; thread (*a needle*); string (*beads*); start down (*a street*); (coll) to put on (*clothes*)

enfin [ãfɛ̃] *adv* finally, at last; in short; after all, anyway

enflam·mé -mée [ãflɑme], [ãflame] *adj* flaming; bright red; inflamed

enflammer [ãflɑme], [ãflame] *tr* to inflame ‖ *ref* to be inflamed; flare up

enfler [ãfle] *tr* to swell; puff up or out; exaggerate ‖ *intr & ref* to swell, puff up

enflure [ãflyr] *f* swelling; (fig) exaggeration

enfon·cé -cée [ãfɔ̃se] *adj* sunken, deep; deep-set; broken (*ribs*); (coll) taken, had (*bested*)

enfoncement [ãfɔ̃smã] *m* driving in; breaking open; hollow, recess

enfoncer [ãfɔ̃se] §51 *tr* to drive in; push in, break open; (coll) to get the better of ‖ *intr* to sink to the bottom ‖ *ref* to sink, plunge; give way; disappear; penetrate (*said of root, bullet, etc.*)

enforcir [ãfɔrsir] *tr* to reinforce ‖ *intr & ref* to become stronger; grow

enfouir [ãfwir] *tr* to bury; hide ‖ *ref* to burrow; bury oneself (*e.g., in an out-of-the-way locality*)

enfourcher [ãfurʃe] *tr* to stick a pitchfork into; mount, straddle

enfourchure [ãfurʃyr] *f* crotch

enfourner [ãfurne] *tr* to put in the oven; (coll) to gobble down

enfreindre [ãfrɛ̃dr] §50 *tr* to violate, break (*e.g., a law*)

enfuir [ãfɥir] §31 *ref* to run away; escape; elope

enfu·mé -mée [ãfyme] *adj* blackened; smoky (*color*)

enfumer [ãfyme] *tr* to smoke up, blacken; smoke out

enfutailler [ãfytɑje] *tr* to cask, barrel

enga·gé -gée [ãgaʒe] *adj* committed; hocked ‖ *m* (mil) enlisted man

enga·geant [ãgaʒã] **-geante** [ʒãt] *adj* winsome, charming, engaging

engagement [ãgaʒmã] *m* engagement; hocking; obligation; promise; (mil) enlistment; (mil) engagement

engager [ãgaʒe] §38, §96, §97, §100 *tr* to engage; hock; enlist, urge, involve; open, begin (*negotiations, the conversation, etc.*) ‖ *ref* to commit oneself; promise, pledge; enter a contest; become engaged to be married; (mil) to enlist; **s'engager dans** to begin (*battle; a conversation*); plunge into; fit into

engainer [ãgɛne] *tr* to sheathe, envelop

engazonner [ãgazɔne] *tr* to sod

engeance [ãʒɑs] *f* (pej) breed, brood

engelure [ãʒlyr] *f* chilblain

engendrer [ãʒãdre] *tr* to engender

engin [ãʒɛ̃] *m* device; **engin balistique** ballistic missile; **engin guidé, engin spécial** guided missile; **engin non-identifié** unidentified flying object; **engins de pêche** fishing tackle

englober [ãglɔbe] *tr* to put together, unite; embrace, comprise

engloutir [ãglutir] *tr* to gobble down; swallow up, engulf

engluer [ãglye] *tr* to lime (*a trap*); catch; take in, hoodwink ‖ *ref* to be caught; fall into a trap, be taken in

engommer [ãgɔme] *tr* to gum

engon·cé -cée [ãgɔ̃se] *adj* awkward, stiff (*air*)

engoncer [ãgɔ̃se] §51 *tr* to bundle up; cramp

engorgement [ãgɔrʒəmã] *m* obstruction, blocking

engorger [ãgɔrʒe] §38 *tr* to obstruct, block

engouement [ãgumã] *m* infatuation; fad; (pathol) obstruction

engouer [ãgwe] *tr* to obstruct ‖ *ref*—**s'engouer de** (coll) to be infatuated with, be wild about

engouffrer [ãgufre] *tr* to engulf; gobble up; eat up (*e.g., a fortune*) ‖ *ref* to be swallowed up; dash; surge

engour·di -die [ãgurdi] *adj* numb

engourdir [ãgurdir] *tr* to numb; dull ‖ *ref* to grow numb

engourdissement [ãgurdismã] *m* numbness; dullness, torpidity

engrais [ãgrɛ] *m* fertilizer; manure; fodder; **mettre à l'engrais** to fatten

engraisser [ãgrɛse], [ãgrese] *tr* to fatten; fertilize; enrich ‖ *intr* (*aux:* AVOIR *or* ÊTRE) to fatten up, get fat ‖ *ref* to become fat; become rich

engranger [ãgrãʒe] §38 *tr* to garner; get in, put in the barn

engraver [ãgrave] *tr, intr, & ref* to silt up; (naut) to run aground

engrenage [ãgrənaʒ] *m* gear; gearing; (coll) mesh, toils; **engrenage à vis sans fin** worm gear; **engrenages de distribution** timing gears

engrener [ãgrəne] §2 *tr* to feed (*a hopper, a thresher; a fowl*); put into gear, mesh ‖ *intr & ref* (mach) to mesh, engage

engrenure [ãgrənyr] *f* engaging (*of toothed wheels*)

engrosser [ãgrose] *tr* (slang) to knock up, make pregnant

engrumeler [ãgrymle] §34 *tr & ref* to clot, curdle

engueuler [ãgœle] *tr* (slang) to bawl out, to give (*s.o.*) hell

enguirlander [ãgirlãde] *tr* to garland; adorn; (coll) to bawl out

enhardir [ãardir], §96, §97 *tr* to embolden ‖ *ref*—**s'enhardir à** to be so bold as to

énième [ɛnjɛm] *adj* nth

énigmatique [enigmatik] *adj* enigmatic(al), puzzling

énigme [enigm] *f* enigma, riddle, puzzle

enivrement [ãnivrəmã] *m* intoxication

enivrer [ãnivre] *tr* to intoxicate; elate ‖ *ref* to get drunk

enjambée [ãʒãbe] *f* stride

enjambement [ãʒãbmã] *m* enjambment

enjamber [ãʒãbe] *tr* to stride over, span ‖ *intr* to stride along; run on (*said of line of poetry*); **enjamber sur** to project over; encroach on

en·jeu [ãʒø] *m* (*pl* **-jeux**) stake, bet

enjoindre [ãʒwɛ̃dr] §35, §97 *tr* to enjoin

enjôler [ãʒole] *tr* (coll) to cajole

enjô·leur [ãʒolœr] **-leuse** [løz] *adj* cajoling ‖ *mf* cajoler, wheedler

enjoliver [ãʒɔlive] *tr* to embellish

enjoli·veur [ãʒɔlivœr] **-veuse** [vøz] *mf* embellisher ‖ *m* hubcap

en·joué -jouée [ãʒwe] *adj* sprightly

enjouement [ãʒumã] *m* playfulness

enlacement [ãlɑsmã] *m* embrace, hug; lacing, interweaving

enlacer [ãlɑse] §51 *tr & ref* to enlace, entwine; embrace

enlaidir [ãledir], [ãledir] *tr* to disfigure ‖ *intr* to grow ugly ‖ *ref* to disfigure oneself

enlèvement [ãlɛvmã] *m* removal; kidnaping, abduction; **enlèvement de bébé, enlèvement d'enfant** infant kidnaping

enlever [ãlve] §2 *tr* to take away, take off, remove; carry off; lift, lift up; send up (*a balloon*); (fig) to carry away (*an audience*); **enlever le couvert** to clear the table; **enlever q.ch. à** to take s.th. from, remove s.th. from ‖ *ref* to come off, wear off; rise; boil over; (fig) to flare up

enliasser [ãljase] *tr* to tie up in bundles

enliser [ãlize] *tr* to get (*s.th.*) stuck in the mud ‖ *ref* to get stuck

enluminer [ãlymine] *tr* to illuminate; make colorful

enluminure [ãlyminyr] *f* illuminated drawing; (painting) illumination

enneiger [ãneʒe], [ãneʒe] §38 *tr* to cover with snow

enne·mi -mie [ɛnmi] *adj* hostile, inimical; enemy, e.g., **en pays ennemi** in enemy country ‖ *mf* enemy

ennoblir [ãnɔblir] *tr* to ennoble

ennui [ãnɥi] *m* ennui, boredom; nuisance, bother; worry, trouble

ennuyer [ãnɥije] §27, §96, §97 *tr* to bore; bother ‖ *ref* to be bored

en·nuyeux [ãnɥijø] **-nuyeuse** [nɥijøz] *adj* boring, tedious; annoying, bothersome; sad, troublesome

énon·cé -cée [enõse] *m* statement; wording (*of a document*); terms (*of a theorem*)

énoncer [enõse] §51 *tr* to state, enunciate; utter

enorgueillir [ãnɔrgœjir] *tr* to make proud or boastful ‖ §97 *ref*—**s'enorgueillir de** to pride oneself on, boast of, glory in

énorme [enɔrm] *adj* enormous; (coll) shocking; (coll) outrageous

énormément [enɔrmemã] *adv* enormously, tremendously; (coll) awfully; **énormément de** lots of

énormité [enɔrmite] *f* enormity; (coll) nonsense; (coll) blunder

enquérir [ãkerir] §3 *ref*—**s'enquérir de** to ask or inquire about

enquête [ãkɛt] *f* investigation, inquiry; inquest; **enquête par sondage** public-opinion poll

enquêter [ãkɛte] *intr* to conduct an investigation

enraciner [ãrasine] *tr* to root; instill ‖ *ref* to take root

enra·gé -gée [ãraʒe] *adj* enraged, hot-headed; mad (*dog*); rabid (*communist*); out-and-out (*socialist*); inveterate (*gambler*); enthusiastic (*sportsman*) ‖ *mf* enthusiast, fan; fanatic, fiend

enrager [ãraʒe] §38, §97 *intr* to be mad; **faire enrager** to enrage

enrayer [ãrɛje], [ãreje] §49 *tr* to put spokes to; jam, lock; stem, halt ‖ *ref* to jam

enrayure [ãrɛjyr] *f* (mach) skid, shoe

enrégimenter [ãreʒimãte] *tr* to regiment

enregistrement [ãraʒistrəmã] *m* recording; registration; transcription; checking (*of baggage*); **enregistrement sur bande** or **sur ruban** tape recording

enregistrer [ãraʒistre] *tr* to record; register; transcribe; check (*baggage*)

enregis·treur [ãraʒistrœr] **-treuse** [trøz] *adj* recording ‖ *mf* recorder ‖ *m* recording machine; **enregistreur d'accident** crash recorder, black box; **enregistreur de vol** flight recorder

enrhumer [ãryme] *tr* to give a cold to ‖ *ref* to catch cold

enrichir [ãriʃir] *tr* to enrich ‖ *ref* to become rich

enrichissement [ãriʃismã] *m* enrichment

enrober [ãrɔbe] *tr* to coat; wrap

enrôlement [ãrolmã] *m* enrollment; enlistment

enrôler [ãrole] *tr & ref* to enroll, enlist

enrouement [ãrumã] *m* hoarseness, huskiness

enrouer [ãrwe] *tr* to make hoarse ‖ *ref* to become hoarse

enrouiller [ãruje] *tr & ref* to rust

enroulement [ãrulmã] *m* coil; (archit) volute; (elec) winding

enrouler [ãrule] *tr & ref* to wind, coil; roll up

ensabler [ãsɑble] *tr & ref* to run aground on the sand

ensacher [ãsaʃe] *tr* to bag

ensanglanter [ãsãglãte] *tr* to stain with blood; steep in blood

ensei·gnant [ãsɛɲã] **-gnante** [ɲãt] *adj* teaching ‖ *mf* teacher

enseigne [ãsɛɲ] *m* (nav) ensign ‖ *f* flag, ensign; sign (*on tavern, store*)

enseignement [ãsɛɲəmã] *m* teaching, instruction, education; **enseignement confessionnel** parochial school education; **enseignement libre** or **privé** private-school education; **enseignement mixte** coeducation; **enseignement par correspondance** correspondence courses; **enseignement programmé** computer programed courses; **enseignement public** public education; **enseignement secondaire** secondary education; **enseignement séquentiel** programed learning; **enseignement supérieur** higher education

enseigner [ãsɛɲe] §96, §101 *tr* to teach; show; **enseigner q.ch. à qn** to teach s.o. s.th. ‖ *intr* to teach; **enseigner à qn à + inf** to teach s.o. to + *inf*

ensemble [ãsãbl] *m* ensemble; **avec ensemble** in harmony, with one mind; **dans son ensemble** as a whole; **d'ensemble** general, comprehensive, overall; **ensemble immobilier** housing development; **grand ensemble** housing project ‖ *adv* together

ensemencement [ãsmãsmã] *m* sowing

ensemencer [ãsmãse] §51 *tr* to seed, sow; culture (*microorganisms*)

enserrer [ãsɛre] *tr* to enclose; squeeze, clasp

ensevelir [ãsəvlir] *tr* to bury; shroud

ensevelissement [ãsəvlismã] *m* burial; shrouding

ensilage [ãsilaʒ] *m* storing in a pit or silo

ensiler [ãsile] *tr* to ensilage

ensoleiller [ãsɔlɛje] *tr* to make sunny, brighten

ensommeil·lé -lée [ãsɔmɛje] *adj* drowsy

ensorceler [ãsɔrsəle] §34 *tr* to bewitch, enchant

ensorce·leur [ãsɔrsəlœr] **-leuse** [løz] *adj* bewitching, enchanting ‖ *m* sorcerer, wizard; charmer ‖ *f* witch; enchantress

ensorcellement [ãsɔrsɛlmã] *m* sorcery, enchantment; spell, charm

ensuite [ãsɥit] *adv* then, next; afterwards, after; **ensuite?** what then?, what next?; anything else?

ensuivre [ãsɥivr] §67 (used only in 3rd *sg* & *pl*) *ref* to ensue; **il s'ensuit que . . .** it follows that . . .

entacher [ãtaʃe] *tr* to blemish; **entaché de nullité** null and void

entaille [ãtaj] *f* notch, nick; gash

entailler [ãtaje] *tr* to notch, nick; gash

entame [ãtam] *f* top slice, first slice, end slice

entamer [ãtame] *tr* to cut the first slice of; begin; engage in, start (*a conversation*); make a break in (*the skin; a battle line*); cast a slur upon; open (*a bottle; negotiations; a card suit*); (coll) to make a dent in (*e.g., one's savings*)

entartrer [ãtartre] *tr* & *ref* to scale, fur

entassement [ãtasmã] *m* piling up

entasser [ãtase] *tr* & *ref* to pile up, accumulate; crowd

ente [ãt] *f* paintbrush handle; (hort) graft, scion

entendement [ãtãdmã] *m* understanding; consciousness

entendre [ãtãdr] §95 *tr* to hear; understand; mean; **entendre chanter** to hear (*s.o.*) singing, to hear (*s.o.*) sing; hear (*s.th.*) sung; **entendre dire que** to hear that; **entendre parler de** to hear of or about; **entendre raison** to listen to reason; **il entend que je le fasse** he expects me to do it, he insists that I do it ‖ *intr* to hear ‖ §96 *ref* to understand one another; get along; **s'entendre à** to be skilled in, know

enten·du -due [ãtãdy] *adj* agreed; **bien entendu** of course; **c'est entendu!** all right!

enténébrer [ãtenebre] §10 *tr* to plunge into darkness

entente [ãtãt] *f* understanding; agreement, pact; **à double entente** with a double meaning, e.g., **expression à double entente** expression with a double meaning, double entendre; **entente industrielle** (com) combine

enter [ãte] *tr* to graft; splice (*pieces of wood*)

entérinement [ãterinmã] *m* ratification

entériner [ãterine] *tr* to ratify

enterrement [ãtɛrmã] *m* burial, interment; funeral procession; funeral; funeral expenses; pigeonholing

enterrer [ãtɛre] *tr* to bury, inter; pigeonhole, sidetrack; (coll) to attend the funeral services of; **enterrer sa vie de garçon** (coll) to give a farewell stag party ‖ *ref* to bury oneself; (mil) to dig oneself in

en-tête [ãtɛt] *m* (*pl* -têtes) headline; chapter heading; letterhead

entê·té -tée [ãtɛte] *adj* obstinate, stubborn

entêtement [ãtɛtmã] *m* obstinacy, stubbornness

entêter [ãtɛte] *tr* to give a headache to; make giddy ‖ *intr* to go to one's head ‖ *ref* to persist

enthousiasme [ãtuzjasm] *m* enthusiasm

enthousiasmer [ãtuzjasme] *tr* & *ref* to enthuse

enthousiaste [ãtuzjast] *adj* enthusiastic ‖ *mf* enthusiast, fan, buff

entichement [ãtiʃmã] *m* infatuation

enticher [ãtiʃe] *tr* to infatuate ‖ *ref* to become infatuated

en·tier [ãtje] **-tière** [tjɛr] *adj* entire, whole, full, obstinate ‖ *m* whole, entirety; **en entier** in full

entièrement [ãtjɛrmã] *adv* entirely

entité [ãtite] *f* entity, being

entoiler [ãtwale] *tr* to put a backing on, mount

entomologie [ãtɔmɔlɔʒi] *f* entomology

entonner [ãtɔne] *tr* to barrel; intone, start off (*a song*); sing (*s.o.'s praises*) ‖ *ref* to rush up and down (*said of wind*)

entonnoir [ãtɔnwar] *m* funnel; shell hole

entorse [ãtɔrs] *f* sprain; infringement (*of a rule*); stretching (*of the truth*)

entortiller [ãtɔrtije] *tr* & *ref* to twist

entour [ãtur] *m*—**à l'entour** in the vicinity; **à l'entour de** around; **entours** surroundings

entourage [ãturaʒ] *m* setting, surroundings; entourage; (mach) casing

entourer [ãture] *tr* to surround ‖ *ref*—**s'entourer de** to surround oneself with

entourloupette [ãturlupɛt] *f* (coll) double cross; **faire une entourloupette à** (coll) to double-cross

entournure [ãturnyr] *f* armhole; **gêné dans les entournures** ill at ease

entraccuser [ãtrakyze] *ref* to accuse one another

entracte [ãtrakt] *m* intermission

entraide [ãtrɛd] *f* mutual assistance

entrailles [ãtraj] *fpl* entrails; tenderness, pity; bowels (*of the earth*); **sans entrailles** (fig) heartless

entr'aimer [ãtrɛme], [ãtreme] *ref* to love each other

entrain [ãtrɛ̃] *m* spirit, gusto, pep

entraînement [ãtrɛnmã] *m* training; enthusiasm

entraîner [ãtrɛne] §96, §100 *tr* to carry along or away, entrain; involve, entail; pull (*railroad cars*); work (*a pump*); train (*an athlete*) ‖ *ref* (sports) to train

entraîneur [ãtrɛnœr] *m* trainer, coach

entraîneuse [ãtrɛnøz] *f* B-girl

entr'apercevoir [ãtrapɛrsəvwar] §59 *tr* to catch a glimpse of

entrave [ãtrav] *f* shackle; hindrance

entra·vé -vée [ãtrave] *adj* impeded, hampered; checked (*vowel*)

entraver [ãtrave] *tr* to shackle; hinder, impede

entre [ãtr] *prep* between; among; in or into, e.g., **entre les mains de** in or into the hands of; **d'entre** among; from among, out of; of, e.g., **l'un d'entre eux** one of them; **entre deux eaux** under the surface of the water

entrebâillement [ãtrəbajmã] *m* chink, slit, crack

entrebâiller [ãtrəbaje] *tr* to leave ajar

entrechat [ãtrəʃfa] *m* caper; entrechat

entrechoquer [ãtrəʃɔke] *tr* to bump together ‖ *ref* to clash

entrecôte [ãtrəkot] *f* sirloin steak, loin of beef; top chuck roast

entrecouper [ãtrəkupe] *tr* to interrupt; intersect ‖ *ref* to intersect

entrecroiser [ãtrəkrwaze] *tr & ref* to interlace; intersect

entre-deux [ãtrədø] *m invar* space between; interval; partition; (sports) jump ball

entre-deux-guerres [ãtrədøgɛr] *m & f invar* period between the wars (*the First and Second World War*)

entrée [ãtre] *f* entrance, entry; admission, admittance; beginning; headword, entry word (*of a dictionary*); customs duty; (culin) first course; (culin) course before the main course; **avoir ses entrées à, chez,** or **dans** to have the entree into; **d'entrée** at the start, right off; **entrée de serrure** keyhole; **entrée d'un chapeau** hat size; **entrée en matière** introduction; **entrée en scène** (theat) entrance; **entrée interdite** (public sign) keep out, no admittance; **entrée libre** free admission; **entrée principale** main entrance

entrefaites [ãtrəfɛt] *fpl*—**sur ces entrefaites** meanwhile

entrefer [ãtrəfɛr] *m* (elec) air gap

entrefermer [ãtrəfɛrme] *tr* to close part way

entrefilet [ãtrəfilɛ] *m* short feature, special item

entregent [ãtrəʒã] *m* tact, diplomacy, savoir-faire; **avoir de l'entregent** to be a good mixer

entrejambe [ãtrəʒãb] *m* crotch

entrelacer [ãtrəlase] §51 *tr & ref* to interlace, entwine, intertwine

entrelarder [ãtrəlarde] *tr* to lard; interlard

entre-ligne [ãtrəliɲ] *m* (*pl* **-lignes**) space (*between the lines*); insertion (*written between the lines*); **à l'entre-ligne** double-spaced

entremêler [ãtrəmɛle] *tr* to mix, mingle; intersperse

entremets [ãtrəmɛ] *m* side dish; dessert

entremet·teur [ãtrəmɛtœr] **-teuse** [tøz] *mf* go-between ‖ *m* (pej) pimp

entremettre [ãtrəmɛtr] §42 *ref* to intervene, intercede

entremise [ãtrəmiz] *f* intervention; **par l'entremise de** through the medium of

entre-nuire [ãtrənɥir] §19 (*pp* **-nui** *invar*) to hurt each other

entrepont [ãtrəpɔ̃] *m* (naut) between-decks

entreposer [ãtrəpoze] *tr* to place in a warehouse, store; bond

entrepôt [ãtrəpo] *m* warehouse; **en entrepôt** in bond

entrepre·nant [ãtrəprənã] **-nante** [nãt] *adj* enterprising; bold, audacious; gallant

entreprendre [ãtrəprãdr] §56, §97 *tr* to undertake; contract for; enter upon; (coll) to try to win over ‖ *intr*—**entreprendre sur** to encroach upon

entrepre·neur [ãtrəprənœr] **-neuse** [nøz] *mf* contractor; **entrepreneur de camionnage** trucker; **entrepreneur de pompes funèbres** undertaker

entreprise [ãtrəpriz] *f* undertaking; business, firm; contract

entrer [ãtre] *tr* to introduce, bring in ‖ *intr* (*aux:* ÉTRE) to enter; go in, come in; **entrer à, dans,** or **en** to enter; enter into; begin; **entrer pour** to enter into, be an ingredient of

entre-rail [ãtrəraj] *m* (rr) gauge

entre-regarder [ãtrərəgarde] *ref* to exchange glances

entresol [ãtrəsɔl] *m* mezzanine

entre-temps [ãtrətã] *m invar* interval; **dans l'entre-temps** in the meantime ‖ *adv* meanwhile

entreteneur [ãtrətnœr] *m* keeper of a mistress

entretenir [ãtrətnir] §72 *tr* to maintain, keep up; carry on (*a conversation*); keep (*a mistress*); entertain, harbor ‖ *ref* to converse, talk

entrete·nu -nue [ãtrətny] *adj* kept (*woman*); continuous, undamped (*waves*)

entretien [ãtrətjɛ̃] *m* maintenance, upkeep; support (*of family, army, etc.*); interview; **entretien courant** servicing

entretoise [ãtrətwaz] *f* strut, brace, crosspiece

entre-tuer [ãtrətɥe] *ref* to kill each other, fight to the death

entre-voie [ãtrəvwa] *f* (rr) gauge

entrevoir [ãtrəvwar] §75 *tr* to glimpse; foresee

entre·vu -vue [ãtrəvy] adj half-seen; vaguely foreseen ‖ f interview
entrouvrir [ãtruvrir] §65 tr & ref to open part way
enture [ãtyr] f splice (of pieces of wood)
énumérer [enymere] §10 tr to enumerate
envahir [ãvair] tr to invade
envahissement [ãvaismã] m invasion
envaser [ãvɑze] tr to fill with mud; stick in the mud
enveloppe [ãvlɔp] f envelope; **enveloppe à fenêtre** window envelope
envelopper [ãvlɔpe] tr to envelop; wrap up
envenimer [ãvnime] tr to inflame, make sore; (fig) to envenom, embitter
envergure [ãvɛrgyr] f span; wingspread; spread of sail; span, scope
enverrai [ãvɛre] v (**enverras, enverra, enverrons,** etc.) see envoyer
envers [ãvɛr] m wrong side, reverse, back; **à l'envers** inside out; upside down; back to front; topsy-turvy; **mettre à l'envers** put on backwards ‖ prep towards; with regard to; **envers et contre tous** in spite of everyone else
envi [ãvi]—**à l'envi** vying with each other; **à l'envi de** vying with
enviable [ãvjabl] adj enviable
envie [ãvi] f desire, longing; envy; birthmark; hangnail; **avoir envie de** to feel like, to have a notion to
envier [ãvje] tr to envy; desire; **envier q.ch. à qn** to begrudge s.o. s.th.
en·vieux [ãvjø] **-vieuse** [vjøz] adj envious ‖ mf envious person
environ [ãvirɔ̃] m outlying section; **aux environs de** in the vicinity of; around, about; **environs** surroundings ‖ adv about, approximately
environnement [ãvirɔnmã] m environment
environner [ãvirɔne] tr to surround
envisager [ãvizaʒe] §38 tr to envisage ‖ intr—**envisager de** + inf to plan to + inf, to expect to + inf
envoi [ãvwa] m consignment; remittance; envoy (of ballad)
envol [ãvɔl] m flight; (aer) takeoff
envolée [ãvɔle] f flight; (aer) takeoff
envoler [ãvɔle] ref to fly (said of time); (aer) to take off
envoûtement [ãvutmã] m spell, voodoo
envoûter [ãvute] tr to cast a spell on
envoyé envoyée [ãvwaje] mf envoy; messenger; **envoyé spécial** special correspondent (of newspaper)
envoyer [ãvwaje] §26, §95 tr to send; send out; throw (e.g., a stone); give (a kick); **envoyer promener** to send (s.o.) about his business; **envoyer qn** + inf to send s.o. to + inf; **envoyer qn chercher q.ch.** or **qn** to send s.o. for s.th. or s.o. ‖ intr—**envoyer chercher** to send for (s.o. or s.th.) ‖ ref (coll) to gulp down
enzyme [ãzim] m & f enzyme
épa·gneul -gneule [epaɲœl] mf spaniel
épais [epɛ] **épaisse** [epɛs] adj thick ‖ **épais** adv thickly

épaisseur [epɛsœr] f thickness
épaissir [epɛsir] tr, intr, & ref to thicken
épanchement [epɑ̃ʃmã] m outpouring, effusion; (pathol) discharge
épancher [epɑ̃ʃe] tr to pour out; unburden (e.g., one's feelings) ‖ ref to pour out; **s'épancher auprès de** to unbosom oneself to; **s'épancher de q.ch.** to get s.th. off one's chest
épandre [epɑ̃dr] tr & ref to spread; scatter
épanouir [epanwir] tr to make (flowers) bloom; light up (the face) ‖ ref to bloom; beam (said of face)
épanouissement [epanwismã] m blossoming; brightening up (of a face)
épar·gnant [eparɲɑ̃] **-gnante** [ɲɑ̃t] adj thrifty ‖ mf depositor
épargne [eparɲ] f saving, thrift; **épargnes** savings
épargner [eparɲe] §97 tr to save; spare; husband
éparpillement [eparpijmã] m scattering
éparpiller [eparpije] tr to scatter; dissipate (e.g., one's efforts)
épars [epar] **éparse** [epars] adj scattered, sparse; in disorder
épa·tant [epatɑ̃] **-tante** [tɑ̃t] adj (coll) wonderful, terrific
épate [epat] f—**faire de l'épate** (slang) to make a big show, to splurge
épa·té -tée [epate] adj flattened; (slang) flabbergasted
épater [epate] tr (coll) to shock, amaze
épaulard [epolar] m killer whale
épaule [epol] f shoulder; **donner un coup d'épaule à qn** (coll) to give s.o. a hand; **par-dessus l'épaule** (fig) contemptuously
épaulé-jeté [epoleʒte] m clean and jerk (in weight lifting)
épaulement [epolmã] m breastworks
épauler [epole] tr to back, support ‖ intr to take aim
épaulette [epolɛt] f epaulet
épave [epav] f wreck; derelict, stray; **épaves** wreckage
épée [epe] f sword
épéiste [epeist] m swordsman
épeler [eple] §34 tr to spell, spell out; read letter by letter
épellation [epɛllasjɔ̃] f spelling
éper·du -due [epɛrdy] adj bewildered; desperate (resistance); mad (with pain); wild (with joy)
éperdument [epɛrdymã] adv desperately, madly, wildly
éperlan [epɛrlɑ̃] m smelt
éperon [eprɔ̃] m spur
éperonner [eprɔne] tr to spur
épervier [epɛrvje] m sparrow hawk; fish net; (pol & fig) hawk
éphémère [efemɛr] adj ephemeral ‖ m mayfly
épi [epi] m ear, cob, spike; cowlick; **épi de maïs** corncob
épice [epis] f spice
épicéa [episeɑ] m Norway spruce
épicer [epise] §51 tr to spice

épicerie [episri] *f* grocery store; canned goods; **épicerie de dépannage** convenience store

épi·cier [episje] **-cière** [sjɛr] *mf* grocer

épidémie [epidemi] *f* epidemic

épidémiologie [epidemjɔlɔʒi] *f* epidemiology

épidémique [epidemik] *adj* epidemic; contagious (*e.g., laughter*)

épiderme [epidɛrm] *m* epidermis

épier [epje] *tr* to spy upon; be on the lookout for ‖ *intr* to ear, head

épieu [epjø] *m* (*pl* **épieux**) pike

épiglotte [epiglɔt] *f* epiglottis

épigone [epigɔn] *m* imitator, follower

épigramme [epigram] *f* epigram

épigraphe [epigraf] *f* epigraph

épilepsie [epilɛpsi] *f* epilepsy

épileptique [epilɛptik] *adj* & *mf* epileptic

épiler [epile] *tr* to pluck (*one's eyebrows*); remove hair from

épilogue [epilɔg] *m* epilogue

épiloguer [epilɔge] *intr* to split hairs; **épiloguer sur** to carp at

épinard [epinar] *m* spinach; **des épinards** spinach (*leaves used as food*)

épine [epin] *f* thorn; **épine dorsale** backbone; **épine noire** blackthorn; **être sur les épines** to be on pins and needles

épinette [epinɛt] *f* spinet; hencoop

épi·neux [epinø] **-neuse** [nøz] *adj* thorny; ticklish (*question*)

épingle [epɛ̃gl] *f* pin; **épingle à chapeau** hatpin; **épingle à cheveux** hairpin; **épingle à linge** clothespin; **épingle anglaise** safety pin; **épingle dans une meule de foin** needle in a haystack; **épingle de cravate** stickpin; **épingle de nourrice, épingle de sûreté** safety pin; **monter en épingle** (coll) to make much of; **tiré à quatre épingles** (coll) spic-and-span; (coll) all dolled up; **tirer son épingle du jeu** (coll) to get out by the skin of one's teeth

épingler [epɛ̃gle] *tr* to pin; (coll) to pin down (*s.o.*)

épinière [epinjɛr] *adj fem* spinal (*cord*)

Épiphanie [epifani] *f* Epiphany, Twelfthnight

épique [epik] *adj* epic

épisco·pal -pale [episkɔpal] (*pl* **-paux** [po]) *adj* episcopal; Episcopalian ‖ *mf* Episcopalian

épiscope [episkɔp] *m* (mil) periscope of a tank

épisode [epizɔd] *m* episode

épisodique [epizɔdik] *adj* episodic

épisser [epise] *tr* to splice

épissure [episyr] *f* splice

épistémologie [epistemɔlɔʒi] *f* epistemology; theory of knowledge

épitaphe [epitaf] *f* epitaph

épithète [epitɛt] *f* epithet

épitoge [epitɔʒ] *f* shoulder band (*worn by French lawyers and holders of French degrees*)

épitomé [epitɔme] *m* epitome

épître [epitr] *f* epistle

éplo·ré -rée [eplɔre] *adj* in tears

épluchage [eplyʃaʒ] *m* peeling; examination

éplucher [eplyʃe] *tr* to peel, pare; clean, pick; (fig) to find fault with, pick holes in

éplu·cheur [eplyʃœr] **-cheuse** [ʃøz] *mf* (coll) faultfinder ‖ *m* potato peeler, orange peeler, peeling knife ‖ *f*—**éplucheuse électrique** electric peeler

épluchure [eplyʃyr] *f* peelings; **épluchure de maïs** cornhusks

épointer [epwɛ̃te] *tr* to dull the point of

éponge [epɔ̃ʒ] *f* sponge

éponger [epɔ̃ʒe] §38 *tr* to sponge off, mop up

épopée [epɔpe] *f* epic

époque [epɔk] *f* epoch; time; period; **à l'époque de** at the time of; **d'époque** a real antique; **faire époque** to be epoch-making

épouiller [epuje] *tr* to delouse

époumoner [epumɔne] *ref* to shout oneself out of breath

épousailles [epuzaj] *fpl* wedding

épouser [epuze] *tr* to marry; espouse; **épouser la forme de** to take the exact shape of

époussetage [epustaʒ] *m* dusting

épousseter [epuste] §34 *tr* to dust

époussette [epusɛt] *f* duster

épouvantable [epuvɑ̃tabl] *adj* frightful, terrible

épouvantail [epuvɑ̃taj] *m* scarecrow

épouvante [epuvɑ̃t] *f* fright, terror

épouvanter [epuvɑ̃te] *tr* to frighten, terrify

époux [epu] **épouse** [epuz] *mf* spouse ‖ *m* husband; **les époux** husband and wife ‖ *f* wife

éprendre [eprɑ̃dr] §56 *ref*—**s'éprendre de** to fall in love with; hold fast to (*liberty, justice, etc.*)

épreuve [eprœv] *f* proof, test, trial; ordeal; examination; (phot, typ) proof; **corriger les épreuves (de)** to proofread; **épreuve de mise en pages, épreuve de pages** page proof; **épreuve en placard, épreuve sous le galet** galley proof; **épreuves** (mov) rushes

épris [epri] **éprise** [epriz] *adj* infatuated; **épris de** in love with

éprouver [epruve] *tr* to prove, test, try; experience, feel; put to the test

éprouvette [epruvɛt] *f* test tube; specimen; (med) probe

epsomite [ɛpsɔmit] *f* Epsom salts

épucer [epyse] §51 *tr* to clean of fleas, delouse

épui·sé -sée [epɥize] *adj* exhausted, tired out; sold out

épuisement [epɥizmɑ̃] *m* exhaustion; diminution, draining off

épuiser [epɥize] *tr* to exhaust, use up; wear out; tire out ‖ *ref* to run out; wear out

épuration [epyrasjɔ̃] *f* purification; refining (*e.g., of petroleum*); (pol) purge

épure [epyr] *f* working drawing

épurement [epyrmɑ̃] *m* expurgation

épurer [epyre] *tr* to purify; expurgate; weed out, purge

équanimité [ekwanimite] *f* equanimity

équarrir [ekarir] *tr* to cut up, quarter (*an animal*); square off

équateur [ekwatœr] *m* equator; **l'Équateur** Ecuador

équation [ekwɑsjɔ̃] *f* equation

équato·rial -riale [ekwatɔrjal] *adj* (*pl* **-riaux** [rjo]) equatorial

équerrage [ekɛraʒ] *m* bevel; beveling

équerre [ekɛr] *f* square (*L- or T-shaped instrument*); **d'équerre** square, true; **mettre d'équerre** to square, to true

équerrer [ekɛre] *tr* to bevel

équestre [ekɛstr] *adj* equestrian

équilaté·ral -rale [ekɥilateral] *adj* (*pl* **-raux** [ro]) equilateral

équilibre [ekilibr] *m* equilibrium, balance; equipoise

équilibrer [ekilibre] *tr & ref* to balance

équilibriste [ekilibrist] *mf* balancer, rope-dancer

équinoxe [ekinɔks] *m* equinox

équipage [ekipaʒ] *m* crew; retinue, suite; attire

équipe [ekip] *f* team; crew; gang, work party; (naut) train of boats; **équipe de jour** day shift; **équipe de nuit** night shift; **équipe de secours** rescue squad

équipée [ekipe] *f* escapade, lark; crazy project

équipement [ekipmɑ̃] *m* equipment; **équipement de survie** survival kit

équiper [ekipe] *tr* to equip

équi·pier -pière [ekipje] [pjɛr] *mf* teammate; crew member

équitable [ekitabl] *adj* equitable

équitation [ekitɑsjɔ̃] *f* horseback riding

équité [ekite] *f* equity

équiva·lent -lente [ekivalɑ̃] [lɑ̃t] *adj & m* equivalent

équivaloir [ekivalwar] §71 *intr*—**équivaloir à** to be equivalent to; be tantamount to

équivoque [ekivɔk] *adj* equivocal; questionable (*e.g., reputation*) ‖ *f* double entendre; uncertainty; **sans équivoque** without equivocation

équivoquer [ekivɔke] *intr* to equivocate, quibble; pun

érable [erabl] *m* maple; **érable à sucre** sugar maple

érafler [erɑfle] *tr* to graze, scratch

éraflure [erɑflyr] *f* graze, scratch

érail·lé -lée [erɑje] *adj* bloodshot (*eyes*); hoarse (*voice*); frayed (*rope*)

érailler [erɑje] *tr* to fray

ère [ɛr] *f* era

érection [erɛksjɔ̃] *f* erection

érein·té -tée [erɛ̃te] *adj* all in, worn out, tired out

éreinter [erɛ̃te] *tr* to exhaust, tire out; (coll) to criticize unmercifully, run down (*an author, play, etc.*) ‖ *ref* to wear oneself out; drudge

erg [ɛrg] *m* erg

ergol [ɛrgɔl] *m* (rok) propellant

ergot [ɛrgo] *m* spur (*of rooster*); **monter or se dresser sur ses ergots** (fig) to get up on a high horse

ergotage [ɛrgɔtaʒ] *m* (coll) quibbling

ergoter [ɛrgɔte] *tr* (coll) to quibble

ériger [eriʒe] §38 *tr* to erect ‖ *ref*—**s'ériger en** to set oneself up as

ermitage [ɛrmitaʒ] *m* hermitage

ermite [ɛrmit] *m* hermit

éroder [erɔde] *tr* to erode

érosion [erozjɔ̃] *f* erosion

érotique [erɔtik] *adj* erotic

érotisme [erɔtism] *m* eroticism

érotothèque [erɔtɔtɛk] *f* adult book shop

er·rant -rante [ɛrɑ̃] [rɑ̃t] *adj* wandering, stray; errant

erratique [ɛratik] *adj* intermittent, irregular, erratic

erre [ɛr] *f* (naut) headway; **erres** track (*e.g., of deer*)

errements [ɛrmɑ̃] *mpl* ways, methods; (pej) erring ways, bad habits

errer [ɛre] *intr* to wander; err; play (*said of smile*)

erreur [ɛrœr] *f* error, mistake; **erreur de frappe** typing error

erro·né -née [ɛrɔne] *adj* erroneous

éructation [eryktɑsjɔ̃] *f* belch

éructer [erykte] *tr* (fig) to belch forth ‖ *intr* to belch

éru·dit -dite [erydi] [dit] *adj* erudite, learned ‖ *mf* scholar, erudite

érudition [erydisjɔ̃] *f* erudition

éruption [erypsjɔ̃] *f* eruption; blowout (*of an oil well*)

es [e] *v* see **être**

ès [ɛs] *prep* §77

esbroufe [ɛsbruf] *f* showing off; shoving

esc. *abbr* (**escompte**) discount

esca·beau [ɛskabo] *m* (*pl* **-beaux**) stool; stepladder

escadre [ɛskadr] *f* squadron; fleet

escadron [ɛskadrɔ̃] *m* (mil) squadron

escalade [ɛskalad] *f* scaling, climbing; escalation (*of a war*)

escalader [ɛskalade] *tr* to scale, climb; clamber over or up

escalator [ɛskalatɔr] *m* escalator

escale [ɛskal] *f* port of call, stop; **faire escale** to make a stop; **sans escale** nonstop

escalier [ɛskalje] *m* stairway; **escalier à vis** circular stairway; **escalier de sauvetage** fire escape; **escalier en colimaçon** spiral staircase; **escalier mécanique, escalier roulant** escalator

escalope [ɛskalɔp] *f* thin slice, escalope, scallop; **escalope de veau** veal cutlet

escamotable [ɛskamɔtabl] *adj* retractable (*e.g., landing gear*); concealable (*piece of furniture*)

escamotage [ɛskamɔtaʒ] *m* sleight of hand; side-stepping, avoiding; theft

escamoter [ɛskamɔte] *tr* to palm (*a card*); pick (*a wallet*); dodge (*a question*); slur (*a word*); hush up (*a scandal*); (aer) to retract (*landing gear*)

escamo·teur [ɛskamɔtœr] **-teuse** [tøz] *mf* prestidigitator; pickpocket

escapade [ɛskapad] *f* escapade, escape

escarbille [ɛskarbij] *f* cinder, clinker

escarbot [ɛskarbo] *m* beetle

escarboucle [ɛskarbukl] *f* (mineral) carbuncle

escargot [ɛskargo] *m* snail

escarmouche [ɛskarmuʃ] *f* skirmish

escarmoucher [ɛskarmuʃe] *intr* to skirmish

escarpe [ɛskarp] *m* ruffian, bandit ‖ *f* escarpment (*of a fort*)

escar·pé -pée [ɛskarpe] *adj* steep

escarpement [ɛskarpəmɑ̃] *m* escarpment

escarpin [ɛskarpɛ̃] *m* pump, dancing shoe

escarpolette [ɛskarpɔlɛt] *f* swing

escarre [ɛskar] *f* scab

escarrifier [ɛskarifje] *tr* to form a scab on

esche [ɛʃ] *f* bait

Eschyle [ɛʃil] [eʃil] *m* Aeschylus

escient [ɛsjɑ̃]—**à bon escient** knowingly, wittingly; **à mon (ton,** etc.) **escient** to my (your, etc.) certain knowledge

esclaffer [ɛsklafe] *ref* to burst out laughing

esclandre [ɛsklɑ̃dr] *m* scandal

esclavage [ɛsklavaʒ] *m* slavery

esclavagiste [ɛsklavaʒist] *adj* pro-slavery ‖ *mf* advocate of slavery

esclave [ɛsklav] *adv* & *mf* slave

escompte [ɛskɔ̃t] *m* discount, rebate; **escompte de caisse** cash discount; **escompte en dehors** bank discount; **prendre à l'escompte** to discount

escompter [ɛskɔ̃te] *tr* to discount (*a premature note*); anticipate

escompteur [ɛskɔ̃tœr] *adj* discounting (*banker*) ‖ *m* discount broker

escopette [ɛskɔpɛt] *f* blunderbuss

escorte [ɛskɔrt] *f* escort

escorter [ɛskɔrte] *tr* to escort

escouade [ɛskwad] *f* infantry section; gang (*of laborers*)

escrime [ɛskrim] *f* fencing

escrimer [ɛskrime] *intr* & *ref* to fence; **s'escrimer à** to work with might and main at; **s'escrimer contre** to fence with

escri·meur [ɛskrimœr] **-meuse** [møz] *mf* fencer

escroc [ɛskro] *m* crook, swindler

escroquer [ɛskrɔke] *tr* to swindle

escroquerie [ɛskrɔkri] *f* swindling, cheating; racket, swindle

ésotérique [ezɔterik] *adj* esoteric

espace [ɛspɑs] *m* space; room; **espace cosmique** outer space; **espace lointain** deep space ‖ *f* (typ) space

espacement [ɛspɑsmɑ̃] *m* spacing

espacer [ɛspɑse] §51 *tr* to space

espadon [ɛspadɔ̃] *m* swordfish

espadrille [ɛspadrij] *f* tennis shoe; beach sandal; esparto sandal

Espagne [ɛspaɲ] *f* Spain; **l'Espagne** Spain

espa·gnol -gnole [ɛspaɲɔl] *adj* Spanish ‖ *m* Spanish (*language*) ‖ (*cap*) *mf* Spaniard (*person*); **les Espagnols** the Spanish

espagnolette [ɛspaɲɔlɛt] *f* espagnolette (*door fastener for French casement window*)

espalier [ɛspalje] *m* espalier

espèce [ɛspɛs] *f* species; sort, kind; **en espèces** in specie; **en l'espèce** in the matter; **espèces sonnantes** hard cash; **sale espèce** cad, bounder ‖ *mf*—**espèce de** (coll) damn, e.g., **cet espèce d'idiot** that damn fool

espérance [ɛsperɑ̃s] *f* hope; **espérance de vie** life expectancy; **espérances** expectations; prospects

espéranto [ɛsperɑ̃to] *m* Esperanto

espérer [ɛspere] §10, §95 *tr* to hope, hope for; (coll) to wait for; **espérer** + *inf* to hope to + *inf* ‖ *intr* to trust; (coll) to wait

esperluète [ɛspɛrlɥɛt] *f* ampersand

espiègle [ɛspjɛgl] *adj* mischievous ‖ *mf* rogue

espièglerie [ɛspjɛgləri] *f* mischievousness; prank

es·pion [ɛspjɔ̃] **-pionne** [pjɔn] *mf* spy ‖ *m* concealed microphone; busybody (*mirror*)

espionnage [ɛspjɔnaʒ] *m* espionage

espionner [ɛspjɔne] *tr* to spy on

espoir [ɛspwar] *m* hope; promise

esprit [ɛspri] *m* spirit; mind; intelligence; wit; spirits (*of wine*); **à l'esprit clair** clearheaded; **avoir l'esprit de l'escalier** to think of what to say too late; **bel esprit** man of letters; **esprit d'équipe** teamwork; **esprit de système** love of order; (pej) pigheadedness; **esprit fort** freethinker; **rendre l'esprit** to give up the ghost

esquif [ɛskif] *m* skiff

esqui·mau [ɛskimo] **-maude** [mod] (*pl* **-maux**) *adj* Eskimo ‖ *m* husky, Eskimo dog; Eskimo (*language*) ‖ (*cap*) *mf* Eskimo (*person*)

esquinter [ɛskɛ̃te] *tr* (coll) to tire out; (coll) to wear out; (coll) to run down, knock, criticize

esquisse [ɛskis] *f* sketch; outline, draft; beginning (*e.g., of a smile*)

esquisser [ɛskise] *tr* to sketch; outline, draft; begin

esquiver [ɛskive] *tr* to dodge, side-step; **esquiver de la tête** to duck ‖ *ref* to sneak away

essai [ɛsɛ] *m* essay; trial, test; **à l'essai** on trial; **essais** first attempts (*of artist, writer, etc.*); **faire l'essai de** to try out

essaim [ɛsɛ̃] *m* swarm

essaimer [ɛsɛme] *intr* to swarm

essarter [ɛsarte] *tr* to clear (*brush*)

essarts [ɛsar] *mpl* clearings

essayage [ɛsɛjaʒ] *m* fitting, trying on

essayer [ɛsɛje], [eseje] §49, §96, §97 *tr* to try on, try out; assay (*ore*) ‖ *intr* to try; **essayer de** to try to ‖ §96 *ref*—**s'essayer à** to try one's skill at

essayeur [ɛsɛjœr] **essayeuse** [ɛsɛjøz] *mf* assayer

essayiste [ɛsɛjist] *mf* essayist

esse [ɛs] *f* S-hook; sound hole (*of violin*)

essence [esɑ̃s] *f* essence; gasoline; kind, species; **par essence** by definition

essen·tiel -tielle [esɑ̃sjɛl] *adj & m* essential

essentiellement [esɑ̃sjɛlmɑ̃] *adv* essentially

esseu·lé -lée [esœle] *adj* abandoned

es·sieu [esjø] *m* (*pl* **-sieux**) axle

essor [esɔr] *m* flight; development; boom (*in business*); **donner libre essor à** to give vent to; give full scope to; **prendre son essor** to take wing

essorer [esɔre] *tr* to spin-dry; wring; centrifuge

essoreuse [esɔrøz] *f* spin-drier; wringer; centrifuge

essouf·flé -flée [esufle] *adj* breathless, out of breath

essuie-glace [esɥiglas] *m* (*pl* **-glaces**) windshield wiper

essuie-mains [esɥimɛ̃] *m invar* towel; **essuie-mains en papier** paper toweling

essuie-plume [esɥiplym] *m* (*pl* **-plumes**) penwiper

essuyer [esɥije] §27 *tr* to wipe; wipe off; wipe away; suffer, endure; undergo; weather (*a storm*); **essuyer les plâtres** (coll) to be the first to occupy a house

est [ɛst] *adj invar* east, eastern ‖ *m* east; **de l'est** eastern; **faire l'est** to steer eastward; **vers l'est** eastward ‖ [e], [ɛ] *v* see **être**

estacade [ɛstakad] *f* breakwater; pier; boom (*barrier of floating logs*); railway trestle

estafette [ɛstafɛt] *f* messenger

estaminet [ɛstaminɛ] *m* bar, café

estampe [ɛstɑ̃p] *f* print, engraving; (*tool*) stamp

estamper [ɛstɑ̃pe] *tr* to stamp (*with a design*); engrave; overcharge, fleece

estampille [ɛstɑ̃pij] *f* identification mark; trademark; hallmark

est-ce que [ɛskə] see **être**

ester [ɛstɛr] *m* ester ‖ [ɛste] *intr*—**ester en justice** to go to law, to sue

esthète [ɛstɛt] *mf* aesthete

esthéti·cien [ɛstetisjɛ̃] **-cienne** [sjɛn] *mf* aesthetician ‖ *f* beautician

esthétique [ɛstetik] *adj* aesthetic; plastic (*surgery*); ‖ *f* aesthetics

estimable [ɛstimabl] *adj* estimable

estimateur [ɛstimatœr] *m* estimator, appraiser

estimation [ɛstimasjɔ̃] *f* estimation, appraisal

estime [ɛstim] *f* esteem; **à l'estime** by guesswork; (naut) by dead reckoning

estimer [ɛstime] §95 *tr* to esteem; estimate, assess; **estimer** + *inf* to think that + *inf*. e.g., **j'estime avoir fait mon devoir** I think that I did my duty

esti·val -vale [ɛstival] *adj* (*pl* **-vaux** [vol]) summer

esti·vant [ɛstivɑ̃] **-vante** [vɑ̃t] *mf* summer vacationist, summer resident

estiver [ɛstive] *intr* to summer

estocade [ɛstɔkad] *f* thrust (*in fencing*); unexpected attack

estomac [ɛstɔma] *m* stomach

estomaquer [ɛstɔmake] *tr* (coll) to astound ‖ *ref* (coll) to be angered

estomper [ɛstɔpe] *tr* to shade off, rub away (*a drawing*); blur ‖ *ref* to be blurred

estrade [ɛstrad] *f* platform

estragon [ɛstragɔ̃] *m* tarragon

estro·pié -piée [ɛstrɔpje] *adj* crippled ‖ *mf* cripple

estuaire [ɛstɥɛr] *m* estuary

estudian·tin [ɛstydjɑ̃tɛ̃] **-tine** [tin] *adj* student

esturgeon [ɛstyrʒɔ̃] *m* sturgeon

et [e] *conj* and; **et . . . et** both . . . and

Établ. *abbr* (**Établissement**) company, establishment

étable [etabl] *f* stable, cowshed

établer [etable] *tr* to stable

établi [etabli] *m* workbench

établir [etablir] *tr* to establish ‖ *ref* to settle down; set up headquarters

établissement [etablismɑ̃] *m* establishment; business; factory; **établissement d'enseignement**, **établissement scolaire** school; **établissements** company, firm, e.g., **les Établissements Martin** Martin & Co.

étage [etaʒ] *m* floor, story; tier, level; rank, social level; (rok) stage; **de bas étage** lower-class; **dernier étage** top floor; **premier étage** first floor above ground floor, second floor

étager [etaʒe] §38 *tr* to arrange in tiers; stagger; perform in stages

étagère [etaʒɛr] *f* rack, shelf

étai [etɛ] *m* prop, stay

étain [etɛ̃] *m* tin; pewter

étais [ete] *v* (**était, étions**) see **être**

étal [etal] *m* (*pl* **étals** or **étaux** [eto]) stall, stand; butcher's block

étalage [etalaʒ] *m* display

étalager [etalaʒe] §38 *tr* to display

étalagiste [etalaʒist] *mf* window dresser, display artist; demonstrator

étaler [etale] *tr* to display; spread out ‖ *ref* (coll) to sprawl

étalon [etalɔ̃] *m* stallion; monetary standard

étalonner [etalɔne] *tr* to verify, control; standardize; graduate, calibrate

étalon-or [etalɔ̃ɔr] *m* gold standard

étambot [etɑ̃bo] *m* (naut) sternpost

étamer [etame] *tr* to tin-plate; silver (*a mirror*)

étamine [etamin] *f.* stamen; sieve; cheesecloth

étampe [etɑ̃p] *f* stamp, die, punch

étamper [etɑ̃pe] *tr* to stamp, punch

étanche [etɑ̃ʃ] *adj* watertight, airtight

étancher [etɑ̃ʃe] *tr* to check, stanch the flow of; quench (*one's thirst*); make watertight or airtight

étang [etɑ̃] *m* pond

étape [etap] *f* stage; stop, halt; day's march; (sports) lap; **brûler les étapes** to go straight through

état [eta] *m* state; statement, record; trade, occupation; government; (hist) estate; **en tout état de cause** at all costs; in any case; **état civil** marital status, birth and death record; **état de la technique, état présent** state of the art; **état providence** welfare state; **état tampon** buffer state; **être dans tous ses états** to stew; **être en état de** to be in a position to; **faire état de** to take into account; expect to; **hors d'état** out of order, unfit; **tenir en état** to keep in shape, repair

étatisation [etatizɑsjɔ̃] *f* nationalization

étatiser [etatize] *tr* to nationalize

étatisme [etatism] *m* statism

état-major [etamaʒɔr] *m* (*pl* **états-majors**) headquarters, staff

état-providence [etaprɔvidɑ̃s] *m* welfare state

États-Unis [etazyni] *mpl* United States

étau [eto] *m* (*pl* **étaux**) vise

étayer [eteje] §49 *tr* to prop, stay

etc. [ɛtsetera] *abbr* (**et caetera, et cetera**) etc.

et Cⁱᵉ *abbr* (**et Compagnie**) & Co.

été [ete] *m* summer; **en été** in (the) summer ‖ *v* see **être**

éteignoir [etɛɲwar] *m* candle snuffer; (coll) kill-joy, wet blanket

éteindre [etɛ̃dr] §50 *tr* to extinguish, put out; turn off; wipe out; appease (*e.g., one's thirst*); dull (*a color*) ‖ *intr* to put out the light ‖ *ref* to go out; (fig) to die, pass away

éteint [etɛ̃] **éteinte** [etɛ̃t] *adj* extinguished; exinct; dull, dim

étendard [etɑ̃dar] *m* flag, banner

étendoir [etɑ̃dwar] *m* clothesline; drying rack

étendre [etɑ̃dr] *tr* to extend, spread out ‖ *ref* to stretch out; spread

éten·du -due [etɑ̃dy] *adj* outspread; extensive; vast; diluted, adulterated ‖ *f* stretch; range, scope

éter·nel -nelle [etɛrnɛl] *adj* eternal

éterniser [etɛrnize] *tr* to perpetuate (*a name*); drag out ‖ *ref* (coll) to drag on; **s'éterniser chez qn** (coll) to overstay an invitation

éternité [etɛrnite] *f* eternity

éternuement [etɛrnymɑ̃] *m* sneeze; sneezing

éternuer [etɛrnɥe] *intr* to sneeze

étes [ɛt] *v* see **être**

étêter [etete] *tr* to top (*a tree*); take the head off (*a fish, nail, etc.*)

éteule [etœl] *f* stubble

éther [etɛr] *m* ether

éthé·ré -rée [etere] *adj* ethereal

Éthiopie [etjɔpi] *f* Ethiopia; **l'Éthiopie** Ethiopia

éthio·pien [etjɔpjɛ̃] **-pienne** [pjɛn] *adj* Ethiopian ‖ *m* Ethiopian (*language*) ‖ (*cap*) *mf* Ethiopian (*person*)

éthique [etik] *adj* ethical ‖ *f* ethics

ethnique [ɛtnik] *adj* ethnic(al)

ethnographie [ɛtnɔgrafi] *f* ethnography

ethnologie [ɛtnɔlɔʒi] *f* ethnology

éthyle [etil] *m* ethyl

éthylène [etilɛn] *m* ethylene

étiage [etjaʒ] *m* low-water mark

étince·lant [etɛ̃slɑ̃] **-lante** [lɑ̃t] *adj* sparkling, glittering

étinceler [etɛ̃sle] §34 *intr* to sparkle, glitter

étincelle [etɛ̃sɛl] *f* spark; (fig) flash

étiolement [etjɔlmɑ̃] *m* wilting

étioler [etjɔle] *tr* & *ref* to wilt

étique [etik] *adj* lean, emaciated

étiquetage [etiktaʒ] *m* labeling

étiqueter [etikte] §34 *tr* to label

étiquette [etikɛt] *f* etiquette; label; **étiquette gommée** sticker

étirer [etire] *tr* to stretch, lengthen, elongate ‖ *ref* (coll) to stretch one's limbs

étoffe [etɔf] *f* stuff; material, fabric; quality, worth

étoffer [etɔfe] *tr* to fill out; enrich; stuff (*furniture*)

étoile [etwal] *f* star; traffic circle; **à la belle étoile** out of doors; **étoile de mer** starfish; **étoile filante** shooting or falling star; **étoile polaire** polestar

étoi·lé -lée [etwale] *adj* star-spangled, starry

étole [etɔl] *f* stole

éton·nant [etɔnɑ̃] **-nante** [nɑ̃t] *adj* astonishing

étonnement [etɔnmɑ̃] *m* surprise, astonishment; fissure, crack

étonner [etɔne] *tr* to surprise, astonish; shake or crack (*masonry*) ‖ §97 *ref* to be surprised

étouf·fant [etufɑ̃] **-fante** [fɑ̃t] *adj* suffocating; sweltering

étouffée [etufe] *f* braising; **cuire à l'étouffée** to braise

étouffer [etufe] *tr, intr,* & *ref* to suffocate; stifle; choke

étoupe [etup] *f* oakum, tow

étourderie [eturdri] *f* thoughtlessness

étour·di -die [eturdi] *adj* scatterbrained ‖ *mf* scatterbrain

étourdir [eturdir] *tr* to stun, daze; numb; deafen (*with loud noise*) ‖ *ref* to try to forget, get in a daze

étourdissement [eturdismɑ̃] *m* dizziness; numbing

étour·neau [eturno] *m* (*pl* **-neaux**) starling

étrange [etrɑ̃ʒ] *adj* strange

étran·ger [etrɑ̃ʒe] **-gère** [ʒɛr] *adj* foreign; irrelevant; unknown, strange; **être étranger à** to be unacquainted with ‖ *mf* foreigner; stranger; **à l'étranger** abroad, in a foreign country

étrangeté [etrɑ̃ʒte] *f* strangeness

étrangler [etrɑ̃gle] *tr* & *intr* to strangle ‖ *ref* to choke; narrow (*said of passageway, valley, etc.*)

étran·gleur [etrɑ̃glœr] **-gleuse** [gløz] *mf* strangler

étrave [etrav] *f* (naut) stempost; **de l'étrave à l'étambot** from stem to stern

être [ɛtr] *m* being ‖ §28, §95 *intr* to be; to go to + *inf* (usually in the past tense), e.g., **elle a été chanter à Paris** she went to sing in Paris, **où as-tu été passer tes vacances?** Where did you go for your vacation?; **en être pour sa peine** to have nothing for one's trouble; **est-ce que** (not translated in questions), e.g., **est-ce qu'ils sont riches?** are they rich?; **être à** + *pron disj* to be + *pron poss*, e.g., **le livre est à moi** the book is mine; **n'est-ce pas** see **ne**; **s'il en fut** it surely was, to be sure; **s'il en fut jamais** if ever there was one ‖ *aux* (used with some intransitive verbs and all reflexive verbs) to have, e.g., **elles sont arrivées** they have arrived; (used to form the passive voice) to be, e.g., **il est aimé de tout le monde** he is loved by everybody

étrécir [etresir] *tr* & *ref* to shrink

étreindre [etrɛ̃dr] §50 *tr* to embrace; grip, seize

étreinte [etrɛ̃t] *f* embrace; hold, grasp

étrenne [etrɛn] *f* first sale of the day; **avoir l'étrenne de** to have the first use of; **étrennes** New-Year gifts

étrenner [etrɛne] *tr* to put on for the first time; be the first to wear ‖ *intr* (coll) to be the first to catch it

étrier [etrije] *m* stirrup

étrille [etrij] *f* currycomb

étriller [etrije] *tr* to curry; (coll) to thrash, tan the hide of; (coll) to overcharge, fleece

étriper [etripe] *tr* to gut, disembowel

étri·qué -quée [etrike] *adj* skimpy, tight; narrow, cramped

étriquer [etrike] *tr* to make too tight; shorten (*e.g.*, *a speech*)

étroit [etrwa] **étroite** [etrwat] *adj* narrow; strict; tight; close; **à l'étroit** confined, cramped

étroitesse [etrwatɛs] *f* narrowness; **étroitesse d'esprit** narrow-mindedness

Ets. *abbr* **Établissements**

étude [etyd] *f* study; law office; law practice; spadework, planning; **à l'étude** under consideration; **étude de faisabilité** feasibility study; **étude des ovnis** UFOlogy; **étude sur dossier** case work; **mettre à l'étude** to study; **terminer ses études** to finish one's courses

étu·diant [etydjã] **-diante** [djãt] *mf* student

étu·dié -diée [etydje] *adj* studied; set (*speech*); artificial, affected

étudier [etydje] *tr* to study; practice, rehearse; learn by heart; design ‖ *intr* to study ‖ §96 *ref* to be overly introspective; **s'étudier à** to take pains to, make a point of

étui [etɥi] *m* case, box

étuve [etyv] *f* steam bath or room; drying room; steam sterilizer; incubator (*for breeding cultures*)

étuver [etyve] *tr* to stew; steam; dry

étymologie [etimɔlɔʒi] *f* etymology

étymon [etimɔ̃] *m* etymon

eucalyptus [økaliptys] *m* eucalyptus

Eucharistie [økaristi] *f* Eucharist

eunuque [ønyk] *m* eunuch

euphémique [øfemik] *adj* euphemistic

euphémisme [øfemism] *m* euphemism

euphonie [øfɔni] *f* euphony

euphonique [øfɔnik] *adj* euphonic

euphorie [øfɔri] *f* euphoria

Europe [ørɔp] *f* Europe; **l'Europe** Europe

euro·péen [ørɔpeɛ̃] **européenne** [ørɔpeɛn] *adj* European ‖ (*cap*) *mf* European

eus [y] *v* (**eut, eûmes**, etc.) see **avoir**

eux [ø] §85

eux-mêmes [ømɛm] §86

évacuer [evakɥe] *tr* & *ref* to evacuate

éva·dé -dée [evade] *mf* escapee

évader [evade] *ref* to escape, evade

évaluer [evalɥe] *tr* to evaluate, appraise; estimate

évanes·cent [evanesã] **-cente** [sãt] *adj* evanescent

évangélique [evãʒelik] *adj* evangelic(al)

évangéliste [evãʒelist] *m* evangelist

évangile [evãʒil] *m* gospel

évanouir [evanwir] *ref* to faint; lose consciousness; vanish; (rad) to fade

évanouissement [evanwismã] *m* fainting; disappearance; (rad, telv) fading

évapo·ré -rée [evapɔre] *adj* flighty, fickle, giddy

évaporer [evapɔre] *tr* & *ref* to evaporate

évaser [evaze] *tr* & *ref* to widen

éva·sif -sive [evazif] *adj* evasive

évasion [evɑzjɔ̃] *f* evasion; escape; **d'évasion** escapist (*literature*)

Ève [ɛv] *f* Eve; **je ne le connais ni d'Ève ni d'Adam** (coll) I don't know him from Adam

évêché [eveʃe] *m* bishopric

éveil [evɛj] *m* awakening; alarm, warning

éveil·lé -lée [eveje] *adj* alert, lively; sharp, intelligent

éveiller [eveje] *tr* & *ref* to wake up

événement [evenmã], [evɛnmã] *m* event; outcome, development; **faire événement** to cause quite a stir

évent [evã] *m* vent; staleness

éventail [evãtaj] *m* fan; range, spread; screen

éventaire [evãtɛr] *m* tray (*carried by flower girl, cigarette girl, etc.*); sidewalk display

éven·té -tée [evãte] *adj* stale, flat

éventer [evãte] *tr* to fan; ventilate; get wind of (*a secret*); **éventer la mèche** (coll) to let the cat out of the bag ‖ *ref* to fan oneself; fade away (*said of odor*); go stale or flat

éventrer [evãtre] *tr* to disembowel; smash open

éventualité [evãtɥalite] *f* eventuality, contingency; possibility

éven·tuel -tuelle [evãtɥel] *adj* possible; contingent; forthcoming ‖ *m* possibility; possibilities (*e.g.*, *of a job*)

éventuellement [evãtɥelmã] *adv* possibly; if need be

évêque [evɛk] *m* bishop

évertuer [evɛrtɥe] §96 *ref*—**s'évertuer à** or **pour** + *inf* to strive to + *inf*

éviction [eviksjɔ̃] *f* eviction, removal; **éviction scolaire** quarantine

évidement [evidmã] *m* hollowing out

évidemment [evidamã] *adv* evidently

évidence [evidãs] *f* evidence, obviousness; conspicuousness; **de toute évidence** by all appearances; **se mettre en évidence** to come to the fore

évi·dent [evidã] **-dente** [dãt] *adj* evident

évider [evide] *tr* to hollow out

évier [evje] *m* sink

évincer [evẽse] §51 *tr* to evict, oust; discriminate against

éviter [evite] §97 *tr* to avoid, escape

évoca·teur [evɔkatœr] **-trice** [tris] *adj* evocative, suggestive

évocation [evɔkasjɔ̃] *f* evocation

évoluer [evɔlɥe] *intr* to evolve; change one's mind

évolution [evɔlysjɔ̃] *f* evolution

évoquer [evɔke] *tr* to evoke; recall, call to mind

exact [ɛgza], [ɛgzakt] **exacte** [ɛgzakt] *adj* exact; punctual, on time

exactement [ɛgzaktəmã] *adv* exactly; on time

exactitude [ɛgzaktityd] *f* exactness; punctuality

exagération [ɛgzaʒerasjɔ̃] *f* exaggeration

exagérer [ɛgzaʒere] §10 *tr* to exaggerate; overdo

exal·té -tée [ɛgzalte] *adj* impassioned; high-strung, wrought-up ‖ *mf* hothead, fanatic

exalter [ɛgzalte] *tr* to exalt; excite (*e.g., the imagination*) ‖ *ref* to get excited

examen [ɛgzamɛ̃] *m* examination; **à l'examen** under consideration; on approval; **examen de fin d'études** or **examen de fin de classe** final examination; **examen de la vision** eye test; **examen de routine** routine examination; **examen probatoire** placement exam; **libre examen** free inquiry; **se présenter à, passer,** or **subir un examen** to take an examination

examina·teur [ɛgzaminatœr] **-trice** [tris] *mf* examiner

examiner [ɛgzamine] *tr* to examine

exaspération [ɛgzasperasjɔ̃] *f* exasperation; crisis, aggravation

exaspérer [ɛgzaspere] §10 *tr* to exasperate; make worse

exaucer [ɛgzose] §51 *tr* to answer the prayer of; fulfill (*a wish*)

excava·teur [ɛskavatœr] **-trice** [tris] *m & f* excavator, steam shovel

excaver [ɛskave] *tr* to excavate

excé·dant [ɛksedã] **-dante** [dãt] *adj* excess; tiresome

excédent [ɛksedã] *m* excess, surplus

excédentaire [ɛksedãtɛr] *adj* excess

excéder [ɛksede] §10 *tr* to exceed; tire out; overtax

excellence [ɛksɛlãs] *f* excellence; **Votre Excellence** Your Excellency

exceller [ɛksɛle] §96 *intr* to excel

excentricité [ɛksãtrisite] *f* eccentricity

excentrique [ɛksãtrik] *adj* eccentric; remote, outlying ‖ *mf* eccentric ‖ *m* (mach) eccentric

excep·té -tée [ɛksɛpte] *adj* excepted ‖ **excepté** *adv*—**excepté que** except that ‖ **excepté** *prep* except, except for

exception [ɛksɛpsjɔ̃] *f* exception; **à l'exception de** with the exception of

exception·nel -nelle [ɛksɛpsjɔnɛl] *adj* exceptional

exceptionnellement [ɛksɛpsjɔnɛlmã] *adv* exceptionally; as an exception

excès [ɛksɛ] *m* excess; **excès de pose** (phot) overexposure; **excès de vitesse** speeding

exces·sif [ɛksɛsif] **-sive** [siv] *adj* excessive

exciper [ɛksipe] *intr*—**exciper de** (law) to offer a plea of, allege

excitable [ɛksitabl] *adj* excitable

exci·tant [ɛksitã] **-tante** [tãt] *adj* stimulating ‖ *m* stimulant

exciter [ɛksite] §96, §100 *tr* to excite, stimulate; stir, incite; provoke (*e.g., laughter*) ‖ §96 *ref* to get excited; become (sexually) aroused

exclamation [ɛksklamasjɔ̃] *f* exclamation

exclamer [ɛksklame] *ref* to exclaim

exclure [ɛksklyr] §11 *tr* to exclude

exclu·sif [ɛksklyzif] **-sive** [ziv] *adj* exclusive

exclusion [ɛksklyzjɔ̃] *f* exclusion; **à l'exclusion de** exclusive of, excluding

exclusivité [ɛksklyzivite] *f* exclusiveness; exclusive rights; newsbeat; (journ) scoop; **en exclusivité** (public sign in front of a theater) exclusive showing

excommunication [ɛkskɔmynikasjɔ̃] *f* excommunication

excommunier [ɛkskɔmynje] *tr* to excommunicate

excorier [ɛkskɔrje] *tr* to scratch, skin

excrément [ɛkskremã] *m* excrement

excroissance [ɛkskrwasãs] *f* growth, tumor

excursion [ɛkskyrsjɔ̃] *f* excursion; tour, trip; outing

excursionner [ɛkskyrsjɔne] *intr* to go on an excursion

excusable [ɛkskyzabl] *adj* excusable

excuse [ɛkskyz] *f* excuse; **des excuses** apologies

excuser [ɛkskyze] §97, §99 *tr* to excuse ‖ *ref* to excuse oneself, apologize; **je m'excuse!** (coll) excuse me!

exécrer [ɛgzekre] §10 *tr* to execrate

exécu·tant [ɛgzekytã] **-tante** [tãt] *mf* performer

exécuter [ɛgzekyte] *tr* to execute; perform; make (*copies*) ‖ *ref* to comply

exécuteur [ɛgzekytœr] *m*—**exécuteur testamentaire** executor; **exécuteur des hautes œuvres** hangman

exécu·tif [ɛgzekytif] **-tive** [tiv] *adj & m* executive

exécution [ɛgzekysjɔ̃] *f* execution; performance; fulfillment; **mettre à exécution** to carry out

exécutrice [ɛgzekytris] *f* executrix

exemplaire [ɛgzãplɛr] *adj* exemplary ‖ *m* exemplar, model; sample, specimen; copy (*e.g., of book*); **en double exemplaire** with carbon copy; **exemplaire dédicacé**

autographed copy; **exemplaires de passe** extra copies

exemple [εgzɑ̃pl] *m* example; **à l'exemple de** after the example of; **par exemple** for example; **par exemple!** the idea!, well I never!; **prêcher d'exemple** to practice what one preaches; **sans exemple** unprecedented

exempt [εgzɑ̃] **exempte** [εgzɑ̃t] *adj* exempt ‖ *m* (hist) police officer

exempter [εgzɑ̃te] §97, §99 *tr* to exempt

exemption [εgzɑ̃psjɔ̃] *f* exemption

exer·cé -cée [εgzεrse] *adj* practiced, experienced

exercer [εgzεrse] §51 *tr* to exercise; exert; practice (*e.g., medicine*) ‖ §96 *ref* to exercise; practice, drill

exercice [εgzεrsis] *m* exercise; drill; practice; **exercice budgétaire** fiscal year

exergue [εgzεrg] *m* inscription; place on a medal for an inscription, **mettre en exergue** to inscribe (*e.g., a proverb*)

exhalaison [εgzalεzɔ̃] *f* exhalation (*of gas, vapors, etc.*)

exhalation [εgzalɑsjɔ̃] *f* exhalation (*of air from lungs*)

exhaler [εgzale] *tr, intr, & ref* to exhale

exhaure [εgzɔr] *f* pumping out (*of a mine*); drain pumps

exhaussement [εgzosmɑ̃] *m* raising; rise

exhausser [εgzose] *tr* to raise, increase the height of ‖ *ref* to rise

exhaus·tif [εgzostif] **-tive** [tiv] *adj* exhaustive

exhiber [εgzibe] *tr* to exhibit; show (*a ticket, passport, etc.*) ‖ *ref* to make an exhibition of oneself

exhibition [εgzibisjɔ̃] *f* exhibition

exhorter [εgzɔrte] §96, §100 *tr* to exhort

exhumer [εgzyme] *tr* to exhume

exi·geant [εgziʒɑ̃] **-geante** [ʒɑ̃t] *adj* exigent, exacting; unreasonable

exigence [εgziʒɑ̃s] *f* demand, claim; requirement; unreasonableness; **exigences** exigencies

exiger [εgziʒe] §38 *tr* to demand, require, exact

exigible [εgziʒibl] *adj* required; due, on demand

exi·gu -guë [εgzigy] *adj* tiny; insufficient

exiguïté [εgziguite] *f* smallness; insufficiency

exil [εgzil] *m* exile

exi·lé -lée [εgzile] *adj & mf* exile

exiler [εgzile] *tr* to exile

existence [εgzistɑ̃s] *f* existence

existentialisme [εgzistɑ̃sjalism] *m* existentialism

exister [εgziste] *intr* to exist

exode [εgzɔd] *m* exodus; flight (*of capital; of emigrants, refugees, etc.*)

exonération [εgzɔnerɑsjɔ̃] *f* exemption, exoneration

exonérer [εgzɔnere] §10 *tr* to exempt, exonerate ‖ *ref* to pay up a debt

exorbi·tant [εgzɔrbitɑ̃] **-tante** [tɑ̃t] *adj* exorbitant

exorciser [εgzorsize] *tr* to exorcise

exorde [εgzɔrd] *m* introduction

exotique [εgzɔtik] *adj* exotic

expan·sif [εkspɑ̃sif] **-sive** [siv] *adj* expansive

expansion [εkspɑ̃sjɔ̃] *f* expansion; expansiveness; spread (*of a belief*)

expa·trié -triée [εkspatrije] *adj & mf* expatriate

expatrier [εkspatrije] *tr* to expatriate

expectorer [εkspεktɔre] *tr & intr* to expectorate

expé·dient [εkspedjɑ̃] **-diente** [djɑ̃t] *adj* expedient ‖ *m* expedient; (coll) makeshift; **expédient provisoire** emergency measure; **vivre d'expédients** to live by one's wits

expédier [εkspedje] *tr* to expedite; ship; make a certified copy of; (coll) to dash off, do hurriedly

expédi·teur [εkspeditœr] **-trice** [tris] *adj* forwarding (*station, agency, etc.*) ‖ *mf* sender, shipper

expédi·tif [εkspeditif] **-tive** [tiv] *adj* expeditious

expédition [εkspedisjɔ̃] *f* expedition; shipping; shipment; certified copy

expéditionnaire [εkspedisjɔnεr] *adj* expeditionary ‖ *mf* sender; clerk

expérience [εksperjɑ̃s] *f* experience; experiment

expérimen·tal -tale [εksperimɑtal] *adj* (*pl* **-taux** [to]) experimental; tentative

expérimen·té -tée [εksperimɑ̃te] *adj* experienced

expérimenter [εksperimɑ̃te] *tr* to try out, test ‖ *intr* to conduct experiments

ex·pert [εkspεr] **-perte** [pεrt] *adj* expert ‖ *m* expert; connoisseur; appraiser

expert-comptable [εkspεrkɔ̃tabl] *m* (*pl* **experts-comptables**) certified public accountant

expertise [εkspεrtiz] *f* expert appraisal

expertiser [εkspεrtize] *tr* to appraise

expier [εkspje] *tr* to expiate, atone for

expiration [εkspirɑsjɔ̃] *f* expiration

expirer [εkspire] *tr & intr* to expire; exhale

explicable [εksplikabl] *adj* explicable, explainable

explica·tif [εksplikatif] **-tive** [tiv] *adj* explanatory

explication [εksplikɑsjɔ̃] *f* explanation; interpretation (*of a text*); **avoir une explication avec qn** to have it out with s.o.

explicite [εksplisit] *adj* explicit

expliciter [εksplisite] *tr* to make explicit

expliquer [εksplike] §98 *tr* to explain; give an interpretation of ‖ *ref* to explain oneself; understand

exploit [εksplwa] *m* exploit; **exploit d'ajournement** subpoena; **signifier un exploit** to serve a summons

exploi·tant [εksplwatɑ̃] **-tante** [tɑ̃t] *adj* operating, working ‖ *mf* operator (*of enterprise*); developer; cultivator; (mov) exhibitor

exploitation [ɛksplwatasjɔ̃] *f* exploitation; management, development, cultivation; land under cultivation

exploiter [ɛksplwate] *tr* to exploit; manage, develop, cultivate ‖ *intr* to serve summonses

explora·teur [ɛksplɔratœr] **-trice** [tris] *mf* explorer

exploration [ɛksplɔrasjɔ̃] *f* exploration

explorer [ɛksplɔre] *tr* to explore; (telv) to scan

exploser [ɛksploze] *intr* to explode

explosible [ɛksplozibl] *adj* explosive

explo·sif [ɛksplozif] **-sive** [ziv] *adj* & *m* explosive

explosion [ɛksplozjɔ̃] *f* explosion; **à explosion** internal-combustion (*engine*)

exporta·teur [ɛkspɔrtatœr] **-trice** [tris] *adj* exporting ‖ *mf* exporter

exportation [ɛkspɔrtasjɔ̃] *f* export; exportation

exporter [ɛkspɔrte] *tr* & *intr* to export

expo·sant [ɛkspozɑ̃] **-sante** [zɑ̃t] *mf* exhibitor; petitioner ‖ *m* (math) exponent

exposé [ɛkspoze] *m* exposition, account, statement; report (*given by a student in class*)

exposer [ɛkspoze] §96 *tr* to expose; explain, expound; exhibit, display

exposition [ɛkspozisjɔ̃] *f* exposition; exposure (*to one of the points of the compass*); introduction (*of a book*); lying in state; **exposition canine** dog show; **exposition d'horticulture** flower show; **exposition hippique** horse show; **exposition inter-professionelle** trade show

ex·près [ɛksprɛ] **-presse** [prɛs] *adj* express ‖ **exprès** *adj invar* special-delivery (*letter, package, etc.*) ‖ *m* express; **par exprès** by special delivery ‖ **exprès** *adv* expressly, on purpose

express [ɛksprɛs] *adj* & *m* express (*train*)

expressément [ɛksprɛsemɑ̃] *adv* expressly

expres·sif [ɛksprɛsif] **-sive** [siv] *adj* expressive

expression [ɛksprɛsjɔ̃] *f* expression; **d'expression française** native French-speaking

exprimer [ɛksprime] *tr* to express; squeeze out

exproprier [ɛksprɔprije] *tr* to expropriate

expul·sé -sée [ɛkspylse] *adj* deported ‖ *mf* deportee

expulser [ɛkspylse] *tr* to expel; evict; throw out

expulsion [ɛkspylsjɔ̃] *f* expulsion

expurger [ɛkspyrʒe] §38 *tr* to expurgate

ex·quis [ɛkski] **-quise** [kiz] *adj* exquisite; sharp (*pain*)

exsangue [ɛksɑ̃g] *adj* bloodless, anemic

exsuder [ɛksyde] *tr* & *intr* to exude

extase [ɛkstɑz] *f* ecstasy

exta·sié -siée [ɛkstɑzje] *adj* enraptured, ecstatic, in ecstasy

extasier [ɛkstɑzje] *ref* to be enraptured

extatique [ɛkstatik] *adj* & *mf* ecstatic

extempora·né -née [ɛkstɑ̃pɔrane] *adj* (law) unpremeditated; (pharm) ready for use

exten·sif [ɛkstɑ̃sif] **-sive** [siv] *adj* wide (*meaning*); (mech) tensile

extension [ɛkstɑ̃sjɔ̃] *f* extension

exténuer [ɛkstenɥe] *tr* to exhaust, tire out ‖ *ref* to tire oneself out

exté·rieur -rieure [ɛksterjœr] *adj* exterior; external; outer, outside; foreign (*policy*) ‖ *m* exterior; outside; (mov) location shot; **à l'extérieur** outside; abroad; **en extérieur** (mov) on location

extérieurement [ɛksterjœrmɑ̃] *adv* externally; superficially; on the outside

extérioriser [ɛksterjɔrize] *tr* to reveal, show ‖ *ref* to open one's heart

exterminer [ɛkstɛrmine] *tr* to exterminate

externat [ɛkstɛrna] *m* day school

externe [ɛkstɛrn] *adj* external ‖ *m* day student; outpatient; (med) nonresident intern

extinc·teur [ɛkstɛ̃ktœr] **-trice** [tris] *adj* extinguishing ‖ *m* fire extinguisher

extinction [ɛkstɛ̃ksjɔ̃] *f* exinction; extinguishing; loss (*of voice*); **extinction d'un traité** termination of a treaty; **l'extinction des feux** (mil) lights out, taps

extirper [ɛkstirpe] *tr* to extirpate

extorquer [ɛkstɔrke] *tr* to extort

extor·queur [ɛkstɔrkœr] **-queuse** [køz] *mf* extortionist

extorsion [ɛkstɔrsjɔ̃] *f* extortion

extra [ɛkstra] *adj invar* (coll) extraspecial, extra ‖ *m invar* extra

extraction [ɛkstraksjɔ̃] *f* extraction; descent, e.g., **d'extraction allemande** of German descent

extrader [ɛkstrade] *tr* to extradite

extradition [ɛkstradisjɔ̃] *f* extradition

extra·fin [ɛkstrafɛ̃] **-fine** [fin] *adj* high-quality

extraire [ɛkstrɛr] §68 *tr* to extract; excerpt; get out ‖ *ref* to extricate oneself

extrait [ɛkstrɛ] *m* extract; excerpt; abstract; certified copy; **extrait de baptême** baptismal certificate; **extrait de naissance** birth certificate; **extraits** selections (*e.g., in an anthology*)

extra-muros [ɛkstramyros] *adj invar* extramural; suburban ‖ *adv* outside the town

extraordinaire [ɛkstraɔrdinɛr], [ɛkstrɔrdinɛr] *adj* extraordinary

extrapoler [ɛkstrapole] *tr* to extrapolate

extra-sensoriel -sensorielle [ɛkstrasɑ̃sɔrjɛl] *adj* extrasensory

extravagance [ɛkstravagɑ̃s] *f* extravagance; excess; absurdity, wildness

extrava·gant [ɛkstravagɑ̃] **-gante** [gɑ̃t] *adj* excessive, extravagant; absurd, wild, eccentric ‖ *mf* eccentric, screwball

extraver·ti -tie [ɛkstravɛrti] *adj* & *mf* extrovert

extrême [ɛkstrɛm] *adj* & *m* extreme

extrêmement [ɛkstrɛməmɑ̃] *adv* extremely

extrême-onction [ɛkstrɛmɔ̃ksjɔ̃] *f* extreme unction

Extrême-Orient [ɛkstrɛmɔrjɑ̃] *m* Far East

extrémiste [ɛkstremist] *adj* & *mf* extremist

extrémité [ɛkstremite] f extremity; **en venir
à des extrémités** to resort to violence;
être à toute extrémité to be at death's
door
extrinsèque [ɛkstrɛ̃sɛk] adj extrinsic
exubé·rant [ɛgzyberɑ̃] **-rante** [rɑ̃t] adj

exuberant
exulter [ɛgzylte] intr to exult
exutoire [ɛgzytwar] m outlet; means of escape; (med) exutory
ex-voto [ɛksvɔto] m invar votive inscription
or tablet

F

F, f [ɛf], *[ɛf] m invar sixth letter of the
French alphabet
F (abbr) **(franc)** franc
fable [fɑbl] f fable; laughingstock
fabri·cant [fabrikɑ̃] **-cante** [kɑ̃t] mf manufacturer
fabrica·teur [fabrikatœr] **-trice** [tris] mf
fabricator (e.g., of lies); forger; counterfeiter
fabrication [fabrikɑsjɔ̃] f manufacture; forg-
ing; counterfeiting
fabrique [fabrik] f factory; factory workers;
mill hands; (obs) church trustees; (obs)
church revenue; **fabrique de papier** paper mill
fabriquer [fabrike] tr to manufacture; fabricate; forge; counterfeit; **fabriquer en
série** to mass-produce
fabu·leux [fabylø] **-leuse** [løz] adj fabulous
façade [fasad] f façade; frontage; **en façade
sur** facing, overlooking
face [fas] f face; side (of a diamond; of a
phonograph record); surface; heads (of
coin); **de face** full-faced (portrait); **en
face (de)** opposite, facing; **faire face à** to
face; face up to; meet (an obligation);
perdre la face to lose face; **sauver la
face** to save face
face-à-main [fasamɛ̃] m (pl **faces-à-main)**
lorgnette
facétie [fasesi] f off-color joke; practical
joke
facé·tieux [fasesjø] **-tieuse** [sjøz] adj droll,
funny ‖ mf wag
facette [fasɛt] f facet
fâ·ché **-chée** [fɑʃe] adj angry; sorry; **fâché
avec** at odds with; **fâché contre** angry
with (a person); **fâché de** angry at (a
thing); sorry for
fâcher [fɑʃe] tr to anger ‖ ref to get angry;
be sorry
fâ·cheux [fɑʃø] **-cheuse** [ʃøz] adj annoying, tiresome; unfortunate ‖ mf nuisance,
bore
fa·cial **-ciale** [fasjal] adj (pl **-ciaux** [sjo])
facial; face (value)
facile [fasil] §92 adj easy; easygoing; facile,
glib
facilité [fasilite] f facility; opportunity (e.g.,
to meet s.o.); **facilités de paiement** installments; easy terms
faciliter [fasilite] tr to facilitate

façon [fasɔ̃] f fashion; fashioning; way,
manner; fit (of clothes); **à façon** job (work;
workman); **à la façon de** like; **de façon à**
so as to; **de façon que** or **de telle façon
que** so that, e.g., **parlez de telle façon
qu'on vous comprenne** speak so that you
can be understood; **de toute façon** in any
event; **façons** manners; **faire des façons**
to stand on ceremony; **sans façon** informal
faconde [fakɔ̃d] f glibness, gift of gab
façonnage [fasɔnaʒ] m shaping; fashioning;
manufacturing; (comp) processing
façonner [fasɔne] tr to fashion, shape; work
(the land); accustom
façon·nier [fasɔnje] **-nière** [njɛr] adj job-
bing; fussy ‖ mf pieceworker; stuffed shirt
fac-sim [faksim] m (comp) hard copy
fac-similé [faksimile] m (pl **-similés)** facsimile
factage [faktaʒ] m delivery service; home
delivery
facteur [faktœr] m factor; mail carrier, mail-
man; expressman; auctioneer (at a market); maker (of musical instruments)
factice [faktis] adj imitation, artificial
fac·tieux [faksjø] **-tieuse** [sjøz] adj fac-
tious, seditious ‖ mf troublemaker, agitator
faction [faksjɔ̃] f faction; **être de faction** to
be on sentry duty
factionnaire [faksjɔnɛr] m sentry
factorerie [faktɔrəri] f trading post
factotum [faktɔtɔm] m factotum; meddler;
jack-of-all-trades
factrice [faktris] f woman letter carrier
factum [faktɔm] m political pamphlet; (law)
brief
facturation [faktyrɑsjɔ̃] f billing, invoicing
facture [faktyr] f invoice; bill; workmanship; **établir une facture** to make out an
invoice; **suivant facture** as per invoice
facturer [faktyre] tr to bill
factu·rier [faktyrje] **-rière** [rjɛr] mf billing
clerk ‖ m invoice book
faculta·tif [fakyltatif] **-tive** [tiv] adj optional
faculté [fakylte] f faculty; school, college
(of law, medicine, etc.); **la Faculté** medical men
fadaise [fadɛz] f piece of nonsense; **fadaises**
drivel

fade [fad] *adj* tasteless, flat; insipid, namby-pamby

fader [fade] *tr* (coll) to beat; (coll) to share the swag with; **il est fadé** (coll) he's done for

fadeur [fadœr] *f* insipidity; pointlessness; **fadeurs** platitudes

fagot [fago] *m* fagot (*bundle of sticks*); **fagot d'épines** ill-tempered person; **sentir le fagot** to smell of heresy

fagoter [fagɔte] *tr* to tie up in bundles; fagot; (coll) to dress like a scarecrow

faible [fɛbl] *adj* feeble, weak; low (*figure; moan*); poor (*harvest*); slight (*difference*) || *mf* weakling || *m* weakness; foible, weak spot; **faible d'esprit** feeble-minded person

faiblesse [fɛblɛs] *f* feebleness, weakness, frailty

faiblir [feblir] *intr* to weaken; diminish

faïence [fajãs] *f* earthenware, pottery

faille [faj] *f* (geol) fault; (tex) faille; (fig) defect; (fig) rift || *v* see **falloir**

fail·li -lie [faji] *adj* & *mf* bankrupt

faillible [fajibl] *adj* fallible

faillir [fajir] §95 *intr* to fail, go bankrupt || (used only in: *inf; ger* **faillant**; *pp* & compound tenses; *pret; fut; cond*) *intr* to fail; give way; **faillir à** to fail, let (*s.o.*) down; fail in (*a duty*); fail to keep (*a promise*); **faillir à** + *inf* to fail to + *inf*; **sans faillir** without fail || (used only in *pret* and *past indef*) *intr*—nearly, almost, e.g., **il a failli être écrasé** he was nearly run over

faillite [fajit] *f* bankruptcy; **faire faillite** to go bankrupt

faim [fɛ̃] *f* hunger; **avoir faim** to be hungry; **avoir une faim de loup** to be hungry as a bear; **manger à sa faim** to eat one's fill

fainéan [fɛneã] **fainéante** [fɛneãt] *adj* lazy || *mf* loafer, do-nothing

fainéanter [fɛneãte] *intr* (coll) to loaf

faire [fɛr] *m* making, doing || §29, §95 *tr* to make; do; give (*an order; a lecture; alms, a gift; thanks*); take (*a walk; a step*); pack (*a trunk*); clean (*the room, the shoes, etc.*); follow (*a trade*); keep (*silence*); perform (*a play; a miracle*); play the part of; charge for, e.g., **combien faites-vous ces souliers?** how much do you charge for these shoes?; to say, e.g., **oui, fit-il** yes, said he; (coll) to estimate the cost of; for expressions like **il fait chaud** it is warm, see the noun; **faire** + *inf* to have + *inf*, e.g., **je le ferai aller** I shall have him go; **faire** + *inf* to make + *inf*, e.g., **je le ferai parler** I will make him talk; **faire** + *inf* to have + *pp*, e.g., **je vais faire faire un complet** I am going to have a suit made; **il n'en fait pas d'autres** that's just like him; **ne faire que** + *inf* to keep on + *ger*, e.g., **il ne fait que crier** he keeps on yelling || *intr* to go, e.g., **la cravate fait bien avec la chemise** the tie goes well with the shirt; to act; **comment faire?**

what shall I do?; **faire dans** to make a mess in; **ne faire que de** + *inf* to have just + *pp*, e.g., **il ne fait que d'arriver** he has just arrived || *ref* to become (*a doctor, lawyer, etc.*); grow (*e.g., old*); improve; happen; pretend to be; **se faire à** to get accustomed to, adjust to; **s'en faire** to worry, e.g., **ne vous en faites pas!** don't worry!

faire-part [fɛrpar] *m invar* announcement (*of birth, marriage, death*)

faire-valoir [fɛrvalwar] *m invar* turning to account; **faire-valoir direct** farming by the owner

faisable [fəzabl] *adj* feasible

fai·san [fəzã] **-sane** [zan] or **-sande** [zãd] *mf* pheasant

faisander [fəzãde] *tr* to jerk (*game*) || *intr* to become gamy, get high

fais·ceau [fɛso] *m* (*pl* **-ceaux**) bundle, cluster; beam (*of light*); pencil (*of rays*); **faisceaux** fasces; **faisceaux de preuves** cumulative evidence; **former les faisceaux** to stack or pile arms

fai·seur [fəzœr] **-seuse** [zøz] *mf*—**bon faiseur** first-rate workman; **faiseur de mariages** matchmaker; **faiseur de vers** versifier, poetaster || *m* bluffer; schemer

fait [fɛ] **faite** [fɛt] *adj* well-built, shapely, full-grown; made-up (*with cosmetics*); **fait à la main** hand-made; **tout fait** ready-made || *m* deed, act; fact; **dire son fait à qn** (coll) to give s.o. a piece of one's mind; **prendre fait et cause pour** to take up the cudgels for; **si fait** yes, indeed; **sur le fait** redhanded, in the act; **tout à fait** entirely || [fɛt] *m*—**au fait** to the point; after all; **de fait** de facto; **du fait que** owing to the fact that; **en fait** as a matter of fact

faîtage [fɛtaʒ] *m* ridgepole; roofs; roofing

fait-divers [fɛdivɛr] *m* (*pl* **faits-divers**) news item

faîte [fɛt] *m* peak; top (*of tree*); ridge (*of roof*)

faîtière [fɛtjɛr] *adj fem* ridge || *f* ridge tile; skylight

fait-tout [fɛtu] *m invar* stewpan, casserole

faix [fɛ] *m* load, burden; (archit) settling; (physiol) fetus and placenta

falaise [falɛz] *f* cliff, bluff

falla·cieux [falasjø] **-cieuse** [sjøz] *adj* fallacious

fallait [fale] *v* see **falloir**

falloir [falwar] §30, §95 *impers* to be necessary; **c'est plus qu'il n'en faut** that's more than enough; **comme il faut** proper; properly; the right kind of, e.g., **un chapeau comme il faut** the right kind of hat; **il fallait le dire!** why didn't you say so!; **il faut** + *inf* it is necessary to + *inf*, one must + *inf*; **il faut qu'il** + *subj* it is necessary that he + *subj*, it is necessary for him to + *inf*; he must + *inf* (expressing conjecture), e.g., **il n'est pas venu, il faut qu'il soit malade** he did not come, he must be sick; **il faut qu'il ne** +

subj + **pas** he must not + *inf*, e.g., **il faut qu'il ne vienne pas** he must not come; **il faut une connaissance des affaires à ce travail** the work requires business experience; **il faut une heure** it takes an hour; **il leur a fallu trois jours** it took them three days; **il leur faut** + *inf* they have to + *inf*, they must + *inf*; **il leur faut du repos** they need rest; **il leur faut sept dollars** they need seven dollars; **il ne faut pas** + *inf* one must or should not + *inf*, e.g., **il ne faut pas se fier à ce garçon** one must not trust that boy; **il ne faut pas qu'il** + *subj* he must not + *inf*; **que leur faut-il?** what do they need?, what do they require?; **qu'il ne fallait pas** wrong, e.g., **la police a arrêté l'homme qu'il ne fallait pas** the police arrested the wrong man ‖ *ref*—**il s'en faut de beaucoup** not by a long shot, far from it, not by any means; **il s'en faut de dix dollars** there is a shortage of ten dollars; **peu m'en est fallu que . . .** it very nearly happened that . . . ; **peu s'en faut** very nearly; **tant s'en faut que** far from, e.g., **tant s'en faut qu'il soit artiste** he is far from being an artist

fallut [faly] *v* see **falloir**

fa·lot [falo] **-lotte** [lɔt] *adj* wan, colorless; quaint, droll ‖ *m* lantern

falsification [falsifikɑsjɔ̃] *f* falsification; adulteration; debasement (*of coin*)

falsifier [falsifje] *tr* to falsify; adulterate; debase (*coin*)

fa·mé -mée [fame] *adj*—**mal famé** disreputable

famélique [famelik] *adj* famished

fa·meux -meuse [famø] *adj* famous ‖ (when standing before noun) *adj* (coll) notorious; well-known

fami·lial -liale [familjal] *adj* (*pl* **-liaux** [ljo]) family, domestic ‖ *f* station wagon

familiariser [familjarize] *tr* to familiarize ‖ *ref* to become familiar

familiarité [familjarite] *f* familiarity

fami·lier -lière [familje] [ljɛr] *adj* familiar, intimate; household (*gods*); pet (*animal*) ‖ *mf* familiar, intimate; pet animal

famille [famij] *f* family; **en famille** in the family circle, at home; (Canad) pregnant

famine [famin] *f* famine

fa·nal [fanal] *m* (*pl* **-naux** [no]) lantern; (naut) running light

fanatique [fanatik] *adj* fanatic(al) ‖ *mf* fanatic; enthusiast, fan

fanatisme [fanatism] *m* fanaticism

faner [fane] *tr* & *ref* to fade

fanfare [fɑ̃far] *f* fanfare; brass band

fanfa·ron [fɑ̃farɔ̃] **-ronne** [rɔn] *adj* bragging ‖ *mf* braggart

fanfaronner [fɑ̃farɔne] *intr* to brag

fange [fɑ̃ʒ] *f* mire, mud; (fig) mire, gutter

fan·geux [fɑ̃ʒø] **-geuse** [ʒøz] *adj* muddy; (fig) dirty, soiled

fanion [fanjɔ̃] *m* pennant, flag

fanon [fanɔ̃] *m* dewlap (*of ox*); whalebone; fetlock; wattle

fantaisie [fɑ̃tezi] *f* imagination; fantasy; fancy, whim; **de fantaisie** fanciful; fancy, e.g., **pain de fantaisie** fancy bread

fantaisiste [fɑ̃tezist] *adj* fantastic, whimsical ‖ *mf* whimsical person; singing comedian

fantasque [fɑ̃task] *adj* fantastic; whimsical, temperamental

fantassin [fɑ̃tasɛ̃] *m* foot soldier

fantastique [fɑ̃tastik] *adj* fantastic

fantoche [fɑ̃tɔʃ] *m* puppet

fantôme [fɑ̃tom] *adj* shadow (*government*) ‖ *m* phantom, ghost

fanum [fanɔm] *m* hallowed ground

faon [fɑ̃] *m* fawn

faonner [fane] *intr* to bring forth young (*said especially of deer*)

faquin [fakɛ̃] *m* rascal

farami·neux [faraminø] **-neuse** [nøz] *adj* (coll) staggering, fantastic, astronomical

fa·raud [faro] **-raude** [rod] *adj* (coll) swanky ‖ *mf* (coll) fop, bumpkin; **faire le faraud** (coll) to show off

farce [fars] *f* farce; trick, joke; (culin) stuffing

far·ceur [farsœr] **-ceuse** [søz] *mf* practical joker; phony

farcir [farsir] *tr* to stuff

fard [far] *m* make-up; **fard à paupières** eye shadow; **parler sans fard** to speak plainly, to tell the unvarnished truth; **piquer un fard** (coll) to blush

far·deau [fardo] *m* (*pl* **-deaux**) load, burden; weight (*of years*)

farder [farde] *tr* to make up (*an actor*); disguise (*the truth*) ‖ *ref* to weigh heavily; (archit) to sink; (theat) to make up

fardier [fardje] *m* dray, cart

farfe·lu -lue [farfəly] *adj* (coll) harebrained, cockeyed, bizarre

farfouiller [farfuje] *tr* (coll) to rummage about in ‖ *intr* (coll) to rummage about; **farfouiller dans** (coll) to rummage about in

farine [farin] *f* flour, meal; **farine de froment** whole-wheat flour; **farine de riz** ground rice; **farine lactée** malted milk

fariner [farine] *tr* (culin) to flour

fari·neux [farinø] **-neuse** [nøz] *adj* white with flour; mealy; starchy

farouche [faruʃ] *adj* wild, savage; unsociable; shy; stubborn (*resistance*); fierce (*look*)

fart [fart] *m* ski wax

fascicule [fasikyl] *m* fascicle; **fascicule de mobilisation** marching orders

fascina·teur [fasinatœr] **-trice** [tris] *adj* fascinating ‖ *mf* spellbinder

fasciner [fasine] *tr* to fascinate; spellbind

fascisme [faʃism] *m* fascism

fasciste [faʃist] *adj* & *mf* fascist

fasse [fas] *v* (**fasses, fassions**, etc.) see **faire**

faste [fast] *adj* auspicious; feast (*day*) ‖ *m* pomp; **fastes** annals

fast food [fɛstfud] *m* fast food(s)

fasti·dieux [fastidjø] **-dieuse** [djøz] *adj* tedious, wearisome

fas·tueux [fastɥø] **-tueuse** [tɥøz] *adj* pompous, ostentatious
fat [fat] *adj masc* conceited, foppish ‖ *m* fop
fa·tal -tale [fatal] *adj* (*pl* -tals) fatal; fateful; inevitable
fatalement [fatalmã] *adv* inevitably
fatalisme [fatalism] *m* fatalism
fataliste [fatalist] *adj* fatalistic ‖ *mf* fatalist
fatalité [fatalite] *f* fatality; fatalism; fate; curse, misfortune
fatidique [fatidik] *adj* fateful; prophetic
fati·gant [fatigã] **-gante** [gãt] *adj* fatiguing; tiresome (*person*)
fatigue [fatig] *f* fatigue
fati·gué -guée [fatige] §93 *adj* fatigued; worn-out (*clothing*); well-thumbed (*book*)
fatiguer [fatige] *tr* to fatigue; wear out; weary ‖ *intr* to strain, labor; pull (*said of engine*); bear a heavy strain (*said of beam*) ‖ §96, §97 *ref* to get tired
fatras [fatra] *m* jumble, hodgepodge
fatuité [fatɥite] *f* conceit; foppishness
faubert [fobɛr] *m* (naut) swab
faubourg [fobur] *m* suburb; outskirts; quarter, district (*especially of Paris*)
faubou·rien [foburjẽ] **-rienne** [rjɛn] *adj* working-class, vulgar ‖ *mf* resident of the outskirts of a city; local inhabitant
fau·ché -chée [foʃe] *adj* (coll) broke (*without money*)
faucher [foʃe] *tr* to mow, reap; (coll) to swipe
fau·cheur [foʃœr] **-cheuse** [ʃøz] *mf* reaper ‖ *m* (ent) daddy-longlegs ‖ *f* (mach) reaper, mower
faucheux [foʃø] *m* (ent) daddy-longlegs
faucille [fosij] *f* sickle
faucon [fokõ] *m* falcon
fauconnier [fokɔnje] *m* falconer
faudra [fodra] *v* see **falloir**
faufil [fofil] *m* basting thread
faufiler [fofile] *tr* to baste ‖ *ref* to thread one's way, worm one's way
faune [fon] *m* faun ‖ *f* fauna
faunesse [fonɛs] *f* female faun
faussaire [fosɛr] *mf* forger
fausser [fose] *tr* to falsify, distort; bend, twist; warp (*the judgment*); force (*a lock*); strain (*the voice*); **fausser compagnie à qn** (coll) to give s.o. the slip ‖ *intr* to sing or play out of tune ‖ *ref* to bend, buckle; crack (*said of voice*)
fausset [fosɛ] *m* falsetto; plug (*for wine barrel*)
fausseté [foste] *f* falsity; double-dealing
faut [fo] *v* see **falloir**
faute [fot] *f* fault; mistake; blame; lack, need, want; (sports) foul; (sports) error; **faire faute** to be lacking; **faute de** for want of; **faute de copiste** clerical error; **faute de frappe** typing error; **faute d'impression** misprint; **sans faute** without fail
fauter [fote] *intr* (coll) to go wrong (*said of a woman*)
fauteuil [fotœj] *m* armchair, easy chair; seat (*of member of an academy*); chair (*of presiding officer*; presiding officer himself); **fauteuil à bascule** or **à balançoire** rocking chair; **fauteuil à oreilles** wing chair; **fauteuil d'orchestre** orchestra seat; **fauteuil pliant** folding chair; **fauteuil roulant pour malade** wheelchair; **siéger au fauteuil présidentiel** to preside
fau·teur [fotœr] **-trice** [tris] *mf* instigator, agitator
fau·tif [fotif] **-tive** [tiv] *adj* faulty
fautivement [fotivmã] *adv* by mistake, in error
fauve [fov] *adj* fawn (*color*); musky (*odor*); wild (*beast*) ‖ *m* fawn color; wild beast; **fauves** big game
fauvette [fovɛt] *f* warbler
faux [fo] **fausse** [fos] (usually stands before noun) *adj* false; counterfeit; wrong, e.g., **fausse date** wrong date; e.g., **fausse note** wrong note ‖ *m* imitation; forgery; **à faux** wrongly ‖ **faux** *f* scythe ‖ **faux** *adv* out of tune, off key
faux-bourdon [foburdõ] *m* (*pl* **-bourdons**) *m* (ent) drone
faux-col [fokɔl] *m* (*pl* **-cols**) collars, detachable collar
faux-filet [fofilɛ] *m* (*pl* **-filets**) sirloin
faux-fuyant [fofɥijã] *m* (*pl* **-fuyants**) subterfuge, pretext
faux-jour [foʒur] *m* (*pl* **-jours**) half-light
faux-monnayeur [fomɔnɛjœr] *m* (*pl* **-monnayeurs**) counterfeiter
faux-pas [fopɑ] *m invar* faux pas, slip, blunder
faux-semblant [fosãblã] *m* (*pl* **-semblants**) false pretense
faveur [favœr] *f* favor; **à la faveur de** under cover of; **en faveur de** in favor of; on behalf of
favorable [favɔrabl] *adj* favorable
favo·ri [favɔri] **-rite** [rit] *adj* & *mf* favorite ‖ **favoris** *mpl* sideburns ‖ *f* mistress
favoriser [favɔrize] *tr* to favor; encourage, promote
F^co or **fco** *abbr* (**franco**) postpaid
fébrile [febril] *adj* feverish
fèces [fɛs] *fpl* feces
fé·cond [fekõ] **-conde** [kõd] *adj* fecund, fertile
féconder [fekõde] *tr* to impregnate
fécondité [fekõdite] *f* fecundity, fertility
fécule [fekyl] *f* starch; **fécule de maïs** cornstarch
fécu·lent [fekylã] **-lente** [lãt] *adj* starchy ‖ *m* starchy food
fédé·ral -rale [federal] *adj* & *m* (*pl* **-raux** [ro]) federal
fédéra·tif [federatif] **-tive** [tiv] *adj* federated, federative
fédération [federasjõ] *f* federation
fédérer [federe] §10 *tr* & *ref* to federate
fée [fe] *f* fairy; **de fée** fairy; meticulous (*work*); **vieille fée** old hag
féerie [feri] *f* fairyland; fantasy
féerique [ferik] *adj* fairy, magic(al)
feindre [fẽdr] §50, §97 *tr* to feign ‖ *intr* to feign; limp (*said of horse*)
feinte [fẽt] *f* feint

feinter [fɛ̃te] *tr* (coll) to trick ‖ *intr* to feint
feldspath [fɛldspat], [fɛlspat] *m* feldspar
fê·lé -lée [fele] *adj* (coll) cracked, crazy
fêler [fele] *tr* to crack
félicitations [felisitɑsjɔ̃] *fpl* congratulations
féliciter [felisite] *tr* to congratulate; **féliciter qn de** + *inf* to congratulate s.o. for + *ger*; **féliciter qn de** or **pour** to congratulate s.o. for ‖ §97 *ref*—**se féliciter de** to congratulate oneself on, be pleased with oneself because of
fé·lon [felɔ̃] **-lonne** [lɔn] *adj* disloyal, treasonable
félonie [feloni] *f* disloyalty, treason
fêlure [felyr] *f* crack, chink
femelle [fəmɛl] *adj & f* female
fémi·nin [feminɛ̃] **-nine** [nin] *adj & m* feminine
féminisme [feminism] *m* feminism
femme [fam] *f* woman; wife; bride; **bonne femme** (coll) simple, good-natured woman; **femme agent** (*pl* **femmes agents**) policewoman; **femme auteur** (*pl* **femmes auteurs**), authoress; **femme de chambre** chambermaid; **femme de charge** housekeeper; **femme de journée** cleaning woman; **femme de ménage** cleaning woman; **femme d'intérieur** homebody; **femme docteur** woman doctor (*e.g., with Ph.D. degree*); **femme juge** woman judge; **femme médecin** woman doctor (*physician*); **femme pasteur** woman preacher; **femme porteuse** surrogate mother; **femme torero** woman bullfighter
fendiller [fɑ̃dije[*tr & ref* to crack
fendoir [fɑ̃dwar] *m* cleaver, chopper
fendre [fɑ̃dr] *tr* to crack; split (*e.g., wood*); cleave (*e.g., the air*); break (*one's heart*); elbow one's way through (*a crowd*) ‖ *ref* to crack; (escr) to lunge
fenêtre [fənɛtr] *f* window; **double fenêtre** storm window; **fenêtre à battants** casement window, French window; **fenêtre à guillotine** sash window; **fenêtre en saillie** bay window
fenil [fənil], [fəni] *m* hayloft
fenouil [fənuj] *m* fennel; **fenouil bâtard** dill
fente [fɑ̃t] *f* crack, split, fissure; notch; slot (*e.g., in a coin telephone*); (escr) lunge
féo·dal -dale [feodal] *adj* (*pl* **-daux** [do]) feudal
féodalisme [feodalism] *m* feudalism
fer [fɛr] *m* iron; head (*of tool*); point (*of weapon*); **croiser le fer avec** to cross swords with; **fer à cheval** horseshoe; **fer à friser** curling iron; **fer à marquer** or **flétrir** branding iron; **fer à repasser** iron, flatiron; **fer à souder** soldering iron; **fer de fonte** cast iron; **fer forgé** wrought iron; **fers irons**, chains, fetters; **marquer au fer** to brand; **remuer le fer dans la plaie** (coll) to rub it in
ferai [fəre], [fre] *v* see **faire**
ferblanterie [fɛrblɑ̃tri] *f* tinware; tinwork, sheet-metal work; tinsmith's shop
ferblantier [fɛrblɑ̃tje] *m* tinsmith
fé·rié -riée [ferje] *adj* feast (*day*)

férir [ferir] *tr*—**sans coup férir** without striking a blow
ferler [fɛrle] *tr* (naut) to furl
fermage [fɛrmaʒ] *m* tenant farming; rent
ferme [fɛrm] *adj* firm ‖ *f* farm, tenant farm; farmhouse ‖ *adv* firmly, fast; without parole
fer·mé -mée [fɛrme] *adj* exclusive, restricted; inscrutable (*countenance*)
ferment [fɛrmɑ̃] *m* ferment
fermenter [fɛrmɑ̃te] *intr* to ferment
fermer [fɛrme] *tr* to close, shut; turn off; **fermer à clef** to lock; **fermer au verrou** to bolt; **la ferme!** (slang) shut up!, shut your trap! ‖ *intr & ref* to close, shut
fermeté [fɛrməte] *f* firmness
fermeture [fɛrmətyr] *f* closing; fastening; **fermeture éclair**, **fermeture à glissière** zipper
fer·mier [fɛrmje] **-miere** [mjɛr] *adj* farming ‖ *m* farmer; tenant farmer; lessee ‖ *f* farmer's wife
fermoir [fɛrmwar] *m* snap, clasp
féroce [ferɔs] *adj* ferocious
férocité [ferɔsite] *f* ferocity
ferraille [fɛraj] *f* scrap iron; (coll) small change; **mettre à la ferraille** to junk
ferrailleur [fɛrajœr] *m* dealer in scrap iron; sword rattler
fer·ré -rée [fere] *adj* ironclad; hobnailed (*shoe*); paved (*road*); iron-tipped; **ferré sur** well versed in
ferrer [fere] *tr* to shoe (*a horse*)
ferret [fɛrɛ] *m* tag (*of shoelace*); (geol) hard core
ferronnerie [fɛrɔnri] *f* ironwork; hardware
ferron·nier [fɛrɔnje] **-nière** [njɛr] *mf* ironworker; hardware dealer
ferrotypie [fɛrɔtipi] *f* tintype
ferroviaire [fɛrɔvjɛr] *adj* railway
ferrure [fɛryr] *f* horseshoeing; **ferrures** hardware; metal trim
ferry-boat [fɛribot] *m* (*pl* **-boats**) train ferry
fertile [fɛrtil] *adj* fertile
fertiliser [fɛtilize] *tr* to fertilize
fertilité [fɛrtilite] *f* fertility
fé·ru -rue [fery] *adj*—**féru de** wrapped up in (*an idea, an interest*)
fer·vent -vente [vɑ̃t] *adj* fervent ‖ *mf* devotee
ferveur [fɛrvœr] *f* fervor
fesse [fɛs] *f* buttock
fessée [fɛse] *f* spanking
fesse-mathieu [fɛsmatjø] *m* (*pl* **-mathieux**) usurer; skinflint
fesser [fɛse] *tr* to spank
fes·su -sue [fɛsy] *adj* broad-bottomed
festin [fɛstɛ̃] *m* feast, banquet
festi·val [fɛstival] *m* (*pl* **-vals**) music festival
festivité [fɛstivite] *f* festivity
feston [fɛstɔ̃] *m* festoon
festonner [fɛstɔne] *tr* to festoon; scallop
festoyer [fɛstwaye] §47 *tr* to fete, regale ‖ *intr* to feast
fê·tard [fɛtar] **-tarde** [tard] *mf* merrymaker; boisterous drinker

fête [fɛt] *f* festival; feast day, holiday; name day; party, festivity; **être à la fête** (coll) to be very pleased or gratified; **faire fête à** to receive with open arms; **faire la fête** (coll) to carouse; **fête foraine** carnival; **fête légale** or **fête nationale** legal holiday; **la fête des Mères** Mother's Day; **fête des Morts** All Souls' Day; **la fête des Rois** Twelfth-night; **se faire une fête de** to look forward with pleasure to; **souhaiter une bonne fête à qn** to wish s.o. many happy returns

Fête-Dieu [fɛtdjø] *f* (*pl* **Fêtes-Dieu**)—**la Fête-Dieu** Corpus Christi

fêter [fɛte] *tr* to fete; celebrate (*a special event*)

fétiche [fetiʃ] *m* fetish

fétu [fety] *m* straw; trifle

feu feue [fø] *adj* (*pl* **feus**) (standing before noun) late, deceased, e.g., **la feue reine** the late queen ‖ **feu** *adj invar* (standing before article and noun) late, deceased, e.g., **feu la reine** the late queen ‖ *m* (*pl* **feux**) fire; flame; traffic light; burner (*of stove*); **à petit feu** by inches; **du feu** a light (*to ignite a cigar, etc.*); **être sous les feux de la rampe** to be in the limelight; **faire du feux** to light a fire; **faire long feu** to hang fire; to fail; (arti) to miss; **feu d'artifice** fireworks; **feu de joie** bonfire; **feu de paille** (fig) flash in the pan; **feu follet** will-o'-the-wisp; **feux de position, feux de stationnement** parking lights; **feux masqués** (mil) blackout; **mettre le feu à** to set on fire; **prendre feu** to catch fire ‖ **feu** *interj* fire! (*command to fire*); **au feu!** fire! (*warning*)

feuillage [fœjaʒ] *m* foliage; **feuillages** fallen branches

feuille [fœj] *f* leaf; sheet; form (*to be filled out*); **feuille de chou** (coll) rag (*newspaper of little value*); **feuille de présence** time sheet; **feuille d'étain** tin foil; **feuille de température** temperature chart; **feuille d'imposition, feuille d'impôt** income-tax form

feuil·lé -lée [fœje] *adj* leafy, foliaged ‖ *f* bower; **feuillées** (mil) camp latrine

feuiller [fœje] *intr* to leaf

feuille·té -tée [fœjte] *adj* foliated; in flaky layers

feuilleter [fœjte] §34 *tr* to leaf through; foliate; (culin) to roll into thin layers

feuilleton [fœjtɔ̃] *m* newspaper serial (*printed at bottom of page*); (rad, telv) serial

feuil·lu -lue [fœjy] *adj* leafy ‖ *m* foliage

feuillure [fœjyr] *f* groove

feuler [føle] *intr* to growl (*said of cat*)

feutre [føtr] *m* felt

feu·tré -trée [føtre] *adj* velvetlike; muffled (*steps*)

feutrer [føtre] *tr* to felt

fève [fɛv] *f* bean; **fève des Rois** bean or figurine baked in the Twelfth-night cake; **fèves au lard** pork and beans

février [fevrie] *m* February

fi [fi] *interj* fie!; **faire fi de** to scorn

fiabilité [fjabilite] *f* reliability

fiable [fjabl] *adj* reliable

fiacre [fjakr] *m* horse-drawn cab

fiançailles [fjɑ̃sɑj] *fpl* engagement, betrothal

fian·cé -cée [fjɑ̃se] *mf* betrothed ‖ *m* fiancé ‖ *f* fiancée

fiancer [fjɑ̃se] §51 *tr* to betroth ‖ *ref* to become engaged

fiasco [fjasko] *m* (coll) fiasco, failure; **faire fiasco** to flop, fail

fibre [fibr] *f* fiber; (fig) feeling, sensibility; **avoir la fibre sensible** to be easily moved

fi·breux [fibrø] **-breuse** [brøz] *adj* fibrous

ficeler [fisle] §34 *tr* to tie up

ficelle [fisɛl] *adj* (coll) knowing ‖ *f* string; **connaître les ficelles** (fig) to know the ropes; **tenir** or **tirer les ficelles** (fig) to pull strings; **vieille ficelle** (coll) old hand

fiche [fiʃ] *f* peg; slip, form, blank; filing card, index card; membership card; (cards) chip, counter; (elec) plug; **fiche de consolation** booby prize; **fiche femelle** (elec) jack; **fiche perforée** punch card; **fiche scolaire** report card

ficher [fiʃe] *tr* to drive in (*a stake*); take down (*information on a form*); fasten, fix, stick; **ficher qn à la porte** (coll) to kick s.o. out; **ficher une gifle à qn** (coll) to box s.o. on the ear; **fichez-moi le camp!** (slang) beat it!; **je m'en fiche!** I don't give a damn ‖ *ref*—**se ficher de** (slang) to make fun of

fichier [fiʃje] *m* card catalogue; cabinet, file (*for cards or papers*)

fichtre [fiʃtrə] *interj* (coll) gosh!

fi·chu -chue [fiʃy] *adj* (coll) wretched, ugly; **fichu de** capable of ‖ *m* scarf, shawl

fic·tif [fiktif] **-tive** [tiv] *adj* fictitious

fiction [fiksjɔ̃] *f* fiction

fidéicommis [fideikɔmi] *m* (law) trust

fidèle [fidɛl] *adj* faithful; regular ‖ *mf* supporter; **les fidèles** (eccl) the congregation, the faithful

fidèlement [fidɛlmɑ̃] *adv* faithfully; regularly

fidélité [fidelite] *f* fidelity, faithfulness; **haute fidélité** high fidelity

fief·fé [fjefe] *adj* (coll) downright, real, regular (*liar, coward, etc.*)

fiel [fjɛl] *m* bile; gall

fiel·leux [fjɛlø] **-leuse** [løz] *adj* galling

fiente [fjɑ̃t] *f* droppings

fier fière [fjɛr] §93 *adj* proud; haughty ‖ **fier** [fje] *tr* (archaic) to entrust ‖ *ref*—**se fier à** or **en** to trust, to have confidence in, to rely upon; **se fier à qn de** to entrust s.o. with; **s'y fier** to trust it

fier-à-bras [fjɛrabra] *m* (*pl* **fier-à-bras** or **fiers-à-bras** [fjɛrabra]) braggart

fierté [fjɛrte] *f* pride

fièvre [fjɛvr] *f* fever; **fièvre aphteuse** foot-and-mouth disease; **fièvre jaune** yellow fever

fifre [fifr] *m* fife; fife player

fi·gé -gée [fiʒe] *adj* curdled; fixed, set; frozen (*smile*); **figé sur place** rooted to the spot

figement [fiʒmã] *m* clotting, coagulation

figer [fiʒe] §38 *tr* to curdle; stop dead ‖ *ref* to curdle; set, freeze (*said, e.g., of smile*)

fignoler [fiɲɔle] *tr* to work carefully at ‖ *intr* to be finicky

figue [fig] *f* fig; **figue de Barbarie** prickly pear

figuier [figje] *m* fig tree

figu·rant [figyrã] **-rante** [rãt] *mf* (theat) supernumerary, extra

figura·tif [figyratif] **-tive** [tiv] *adj* figurative, emblematic

figure [figyr] *f* figure; face (*of a person*); face card; chess piece (other than a pawn); **faire figure** to cut a figure; **figure de proue** (naut) figurehead; **prendre figure** to take shape

figu·ré -rée [figyre] *adj* figurative; figured ‖ *m* figurative sense

figurer [figyre] *tr* to figure, take part; (theat) to walk on ‖ §95 *ref* to imagine, believe

fil [fil] *m* thread; wire; edge (*e.g., of knife*); grain (*of wood*); **au fil de l'eau** with the stream; **droit fil** with the grain; **elle lui a donné du fil à retordre** (fig) she gave him more than he bargained for; **fil à plomb** plumb line; **fil de fer barbelé** barbed wire; **fil de lin** yarn; **fil d'or** spun gold; **fils de la vierge** gossamer; **passer au fil de l'épée** to put to the sword; **plein de fils** stringy; **sans fil** wireless

filage [filaʒ] *m* spinning; (telv) ghost image

filament [filamã] *m* filament

filamen·teux [filamãtø] **-teuse** [tøz] *adj* stringy

filan·dreux [filãdrø] **-dreuse** [drøz] *adj* stringy (*meat*); long, drawn-out

fi·lant [filã] **-lante** [lãt] *adj* ropy (*liquid*); shooting (*star*)

filasse [filas] *f* tow, oakum

filature [filatyr] *f* manufacture of thread; spinning mill; shadowing (*of a suspect*)

fil-de-fériste [fildəferist] *mf* tightwire walker

file [fil] *f* file, row, lane; **à la file** one after another, in a row; **file d'attente** waiting line; (aer) stack; **marcher en file indienne** to walk Indian file

filer [file] *tr* to spin; pay out (*rope, cable*); prolong; shadow (*a suspect*) ‖ *intr* to ooze; smoke (*said of lamp*); (coll) to go fast; **filer à l'anglaise** (coll) to take French leave; **filer doux** (coll) to back down, to give in; **filez!** (coll) get out!

filet [filɛ] *m* net; trickle (*of water*); streak (*of light*); thread (*of screw or nut*); (culin) fillet; (typ) rule; **faux filet** sirloin; **filet à bagage** baggage rack; **filet à cheveux** hair net; **filet à provisions** string bag, mesh bag

fileter [filte] §2 *tr* to thread (*a screw*); draw (*wire*)

fi·leur [filœr] **-leuse** [løz] *mf* spinner

fi·lial -liale [filjal] *adj* (*pl* **-liaux** [ljo]) filial ‖ *f* (com) branch, subsidiary

filiation [filjɑsjɔ̃] *f* filiation

filière [filjɛr] *f* (mach) die; (mach) drawplate; **filière administrative** official channels; **passer par la filière** (coll) to go through channels; (coll) to work one's way up

filigrane [filigran] *m* filigree; watermark (*in paper*)

filigraner [filigrane] *tr* to filigree

filin [filɛ̃] *m* (naut) rope

fille [fij] *f* daughter; unmarried young woman or girl; servant; (pej) tart; **fille de joie, des rues,** or **de vie, fille publique** prostitute; **fille de salle** nurse's aid; **fille d'honneur** bridesmaid; **jeune fille** (unmarried) young woman; **petite fille** girl (under thirteen years of age); **vieille fille** old maid

fillette [fijɛt] *f* young girl, little lass

fil·leul -leule [fijœl] *mf* godchild ‖ *m* godson ‖ *f* goddaughter

film [film] *m* film; movie, film; (fig) train (*of events*); **film sonore** sound film

filmage [filmaʒ] *m* filming

filmer [filme] *tr* to film

filmique [filmik] *adj* film

filon [filɔ̃] *m* vein, lode; (coll) soft job; (coll) bonanza, strike; **filon guide** leader vein

filoselle [filozɛl] *f* floss silk

filou [filu] *m* sneak thief; cheat, sharper

filouter [filute] *tr* (coll) to swindle, cheat; **filouter q.ch. à qn** (coll) to do s.o. out of s.th. ‖ *intr* to cheat at cards

fils [fis] *m* son; (when following proper name) junior; **fils à papa** (coll) rich man's son, playboy; **fils de ses œuvres** (fig) self-made man

filtrage [filtraʒ] *m* filtering; screening; surveillance (*by the police*)

fil·trant [filtrã] **-trante** [trãt] *adj* filterable; filter, e.g., **papier filtrant** filter paper

filtre [filtrə] *m* filter

filtrer [filtre] *tr* & *intr* to filter

fin [fɛ̃] **fine** [fin] *adj* fine; thin; exquisite; keen, discriminating ‖ (when standing before noun) *adj* clever, sly, smart; secret, hidden; **au fin fond de** deep in the interior of; **le fin mot de l'histoire** the truth of the story ‖ *m* fine linen; smart person; **le fin du fin** the finest of the fine ‖ **fin** *f* end; **à la fin** at last; **à seule fin de** for the sole purpose of; **à toutes fins utiles** for your information; **c'est la fin des haricots** (slang) that takes the cake; **en fin de compte** in the end; to get to the point; **fin de semaine** weekend; **fins de série** (com) remnant, leftover article; **fin d'interdiction de dépasser** (*public sign*) end of no passing; **mettre fin à** to put an end to; **mot de la fin** clincher; **sans fin** endless ‖ **fin** *adv* absolutely; finely (*ground*); small, e.g., **écrire fin** to write small

fi·nal -nale [final] (*pl* **-nals** or **-naux** [no]) *adj* final ‖ *m* finale ‖ *f* last syllable or letter; (mus) keynote; (sports) finals

finalement [finalmɑ̃] *adv* finally

finaliste [finalist] *mf* finalist

finance [finɑ̃s] *f* finance

financement [finɑ̃smɑ̃] *m* financing

financer [finɑ̃se] §51 *tr* to finance

finan·cier [finɑ̃sje] **-cière** [sjɛr] *adj* financial; spicy (*sauce for vol-au-vent*) ‖ *m* financier

finasser [finase] *intr* (coll) to use finesse, finagle

finasserie [finasri] *f* shrewdness

fi·naud [fino] **-naude** [nod] *adj* wily, sly ‖ *mf* sly fox; smart aleck

finesse [finɛs] *f* finesse; fineness; **savoir les finesses** to know the fine points or niceties

fi·ni -nie [fini] *adj* finished; finite; ruined (*in health, financially, etc.*) arrant (*rogue*) ‖ *m* finish; finite

finir [finir] §97 *tr & intr* to finish; **en finir avec** to have done with; **finir de** + *inf* to finish + *ger;* **finir par** + *inf* to finish by + *inf*

finissage [finisaʒ] *m* finishing touch, final step

finition [finisjɔ̃] *f* finish; **finitions** finishing touches

finlan·dais [fɛ̃lɑ̃dɛ] **-daise** [dɛz] *adj* Finnish ‖ *m* Finnish (*language*) ‖ (*cap*) *mf* Finn

Finlande [fɛ̃lɑ̃d] *f* Finland; **la Finlande** Finland

fin·noise [finwa] **-noise** [nwaz] *adj* Finnish ‖ *m* Finnish (*language*); Finnic (*branch of Uralic*) ‖ (*cap*) *mf* Finn

fiole [fjɔl] *f* phial

fioriture [fjɔrityr] *f* flourish, curlicue

firmament [firmamɑ̃] *m* firmament

firme [firm] *f* firm, house, company

fis [fi] *v* (**fit, fîmes,** etc.) see **faire**

fisc [fisk] *m* bureau of internal revenue, tax-collection agency

fis·cal -cale [fiskal] *adj* (*pl* **-caux** [ko]) fiscal; revenue, taxation

fiscaliser [fiskalize] *tr* to subject to tax

fiscalité [fiskalite] *f* tax collections; fiscal policy

fissile [fisil] *adj* fissionable

fission [fisjɔ̃] *f* fission

fissure [fisyr] *f* fissure, crack

fissurer [fisyre] *tr & ref* to fissure

fiston [fistɔ̃] *m* (slang) sonny

fixa·teur [fiksatœr] **-trice** [tris] *adj* fixing, fixative ‖ *m* fixer; hair cream; (phot) fixing bath

fixation [fiksajsɔ̃] *f* fixation; fixing; **fixations** bindings (*on ski equipment*)

fixe [fiks] *adj* fixed; permanent (*ink*); glassy (*stare*); regular (*time*); set (*price*); standing (*rule*) ‖ *m* fixed income ‖*interj* (mil) eyes front!

fixe-chaussette [fiksəʃosɛt] *m* (*pl* **-chaussettes**) garter (*for men's socks*)

fixement [fiksəmɑ̃] *adv* fixedly

fixer [fikse] *tr* to fix; appoint; (coll) to stare at; **fixer son choix sur** to fix on; **pour fixer les idées** for the sake of argument ‖ *ref* to be fastened; establish residence; make up one's mind

flacon [flakɔ̃] *m* small bottle; flask

flagada [flagada] *adj* (slang) pooped

flageller [flaʒɛlle] *tr* to flagellate

flageoler [flaʒɔle] *intr* to quiver

flageolet [flaʒɔlɛ] *m* flageolet; kidney bean

flagorner [flagɔrne]*tr* to flatter

fla·grant [flagrɑ̃] **-grante** [grɑ̃t] *adj* flagrant, glaring, obvious

flair [flɛr] *m* scent, sense of smell; (*discernment*) flair, keen nose

flairer [flɛre] *tr* to smell, sniff; scent, smell out

fla·mand [flamɑ̃] **-mande** [mɑ̃d] *adj* Flemish ‖ *m* Flemish (*language*) ‖ (*cap*) *mf* Fleming (*person*)

flamant [flamɑ̃] *m* flamingo

flam·bant [flɑ̃bɑ̃] **-bante** [bɑ̃t] *adj* flaming; **flambant neuf** (coll) brand-new

flam·beau [flɑ̃bo] *m* (*pl* **-beaux**) torch; candlestick; large wax candle; (fig) light

flambée [flɑ̃be] *f* blaze; flare-up

flamber [flɑ̃be] *tr* to singe; sterilize; (culin) to flambé; **être flambé** (coll) to be all washed up, ruined ‖ *intr* to flame; burn

flamberge [flɑ̃bɛrʒ] *f* (archaic) sword, blade; **mettre flamberge au vent** to unsheathe the sword

flambeur [flɑ̃bœr] *m* high roller; big gambler

flamboiement [flɑ̃bwamɑ̃] *m* glow, flare

flamboyant [flɑ̃bwajɑ̃] **flamboyante** [flɑ̃bwajɑ̃t] *adj* flaming, blazing; (archit) flamboyant

flamboyer [flɑ̃bwaje] §47 *intr* to flame

flamme [flam], [flɑm] *f* flame; pennant

flammèche [flamɛʃ] *f* ember, large spark

flan [flɑ̃] *m* custard; blank (*coin, medal, record*); **à la flan** (slang) happy-go-lucky; botched (*job*); **c'est du flan** (slang) it's ridiculous

flanc [flɑ̃] *m* flank; side (*of ship, mountain, etc.*); **battre du flanc** to pant; **être sur le flanc** (coll) to be laid up; **flancs** (archaic) womb; bosom; **prêter le flanc à** to lay oneself open to; **se battre les flancs** to go to a lot of trouble for nothing; **tirer au flanc** (coll) to gold-brick, to malinger

flancher [flɑ̃ʃe] *intr* (coll) to give in; (coll) to weaken, give way

flanchet [flɑ̃ʃɛ] *m* flank (*of beef*)

Flandre [flɑ̃dr] *f* Flanders; **la Flandre** Flanders

flanelle [flanɛl] *f* flannel

flâner [flane] *intr* to stroll, saunter; loaf

flânerie [flɑnri] *f* strolling; loafing

flâ·neur [flɑnœr] **-neuse** [nøz] *mf* stroller; loafer

flanquer [flɑ̃ke] *tr* to flank; (coll) to throw, fling; **flanquer à la porte** (coll) to kick-out; **flanquer un coup à** (coll) to take a swing at

fla·pi -pie [flapi] *adj* (coll) tired out, fagged out

flaque [flak] *f* puddle, pool

flash [flaʃ] *m* (*pl* **flashes**) news flash; flash pictures; (phot) flash attachment; (phot) flash bulb

flasque [flask] *adj* flabby ‖ *m* metal trim ‖ *f* flask; powder horn

flatter [flate] *tr* to flatter; stroke; delight; cater to; delude ‖ *intr* to flatter ‖ §97 *ref*—**se flatter de** to flatter oneself on

flatterie [flatri] *f* flattery

flat·teur [flatœr] **-teuse** [tøz] *adj* flattering ‖ *mf* flatterer

flatulence [flatylɑs] *f* (pathol) flatulence

flatuosité [flatɥozite] *f* (pathol) flatulence

fléau [fleo] *m* (*pl* **fléaux**) flail; beam (*of balance*); (fig) scourge, plague

flèche [flɛʃ] *f* arrow; spire (*of church*); boom (*of crane*); flitch (*of bacon*); **en flèche** like an arrow; in tandem; **faire flèche de tout bois** to leave no stone unturned; **flèche d'eau** (bot) arrowhead

flèchette [fleʃɛt] *f* dart (*used in game*)

flèchir [fleʃir] *tr* to bend; move (*e.g., to pity*) ‖ *intr* to bend, give way; weaken, flag; go down, sag (*said of prices*)

flegmatique [flɛgmatik] *adj* phlegmatic, stolid

flegme [flɛgm] *m* phlegm

flemme [flɛm] *f* (slang) sluggishness; **tirer sa flemme** (slang) to not lift a finger

flet [flɛ] *m* flounder

flétan [fletɑ̃] *m* halibut

flétrir [fletrir] *tr & ref* to fade, wither; weaken

flétrissure [fletrisyr] *f* fading, withering; branding (*of criminals*); blot, stigma

fleur [flœr] *f* flower; blossom; **à fleur de** level with, even with; on the surface of; **à fleur de peau** skin-deep; **à fleur de tête** bulging (*eyes*); **elle est fleur bleue** (slang) she is a prude; **en fleur** in bloom; **en fleurs** in bloom (*said of group of different varieties*); **fleur de farine** fine white flour; **fleur de l'âge** prime of life; **fleur de lis** [flœrdəlis] fleur-de-lis; **fleur des pois** (coll) pick of the lot; **fleurs** mold (*on wine, cider, etc.*)

fleurer [flœre] *intr* to give off an odor; **fleurer bon** to smell good

fleuret [flœrɛ] *m* fencing foil

fleurette [flœrɛt] *f* little flower; **conter fleurette** to flirt

fleu·ri -rie [flœri] *adj* in bloom; flowery; florid (*complexion; style*)

fleurir [flœrir] *tr* to decorate with flowers ‖ *intr* to flower, bloom ‖ *intr* (*ger* **florissant;** *imperf* **florissais,** etc.) to flourish

fleuriste [flœrist] *mf* florist; floral gardener; maker or seller of artificial flowers

fleuron [flœrɔ̃] *m* floret; (archit) finial; **fleuron à sa couronne** feather in his cap

fleuve [flœv] *m* river (*flowing directly to the sea*); (fig) river (*of tears, blood, etc.*)

flexible [flɛksibl] *adj* flexible; (fig) pliant

flexion [flɛksjɔ̃] *f* bending, flexion; (gram) inflection

flibuster [flibyste] *tr* to rob, snitch ‖ *intr* to filibuster

flibustier [flibystje] *m* filibuster (*pirate*)

flic [flik] *m* (slang) copper, fuzz

flicaille [flikaj] *f* (slang) fuzz, cops

flic flac [flikflak] *interj* splash!

flingot [flɛ̃go] *m* (slang) rod, gat

flingue [flɛ̃g] *m* (slang) rod, gat

flipper [fliper] *m* pinball machine ‖ [flipe] *intr* (slang) to be high; (slang) to feel low

flirt [flœrt] *m* flirt; flirtation

flirter [flœrte] *intr* to flirt

flir·teur [flœrtœr] **-teuse** [tøz] *adj* flirtatious ‖ *mf* flirt

flocon [flɔkɔ̃] *m* flake; snowflake; tuft (*e.g., of wool*); **flocons d'avoine** oatmeal; **flocons de maïs** cornflakes; **flocons de neige** snowflakes

floconner [flɔkɔne] *intr* to form flakes; become fleecy

flocon·neux [flɔkɔnø] **-neuse** [nøz] *adj* flaky; fleecy

flopée [flɔpe] *f*—(slang) **une flopée de** loads of, lots of

floraison [flɔrɛzɔ̃] *f* flowering, blooming

flo·ral -rale [flɔral] *adj* (*pl* **-raux** [ro]) floral

floralies [flɔrali] *fpl* flower show

flore [flɔr] *f* flora

floren·tin [flɔrɑ̃tɛ̃] **-tine** [tin] *adj* Florentine; **à la florentine** with spinach ‖ (*cap*) *mf* Florentine (*native or inhabitant of Florence*)

Floride [flɔrid] *f* Florida; **la Floride** Florida

florilège [flɔrilɛʒ] *m* anthology

floris·sant [flɔrisɑ̃] **-sante** [sɑ̃t] *adj* flourishing

floss [flɔs] *m* (coll) dental floss

flot [flo] *m* wave; tide; flood, multitude; **à flot** afloat; **à flots** in torrents, abundantly; **flots** waters (*of a lake, the sea, etc.*); **flots de** lots of

flottabilité [flɔtabilite] *f* buoyancy

flottable [flɔtabl] *adj* buoyant; navigable (*for rafts*)

flottage [flɔtaʒ] *m* log driving

flottaison [flɔtɛzɔ̃] *f* water line

flot·tant [flɔtɑ̃] **-tante** [tɑ̃t] *adj* floating; vacillating, undecided

flotte [flɔt] *f* fleet buoy; float (*on fishline*); (slang) water, rain

flottement [flɔtmɑ̃] *m* floating; hesitation, vacillation; undulation

flotter [flɔte] *intr* to float; waver, hesitate; fly (*said of flag*); **il flotte** (slang) it is raining

flotteur [flɔtœr] *m* log driver; float (*of fishline, carburetor, etc.*); pontoon, float (*of seaplane*)

flottille [flɔtij] *f* flotilla; **flottille de pêche** fishing fleet

flou floue [flu] *adj* blurred, hazy; fluffy (*hair*); loose-fitting (*dress*); light and soft (*tones, lines in a painting*) ‖ *m* blur, fuzziness; dressmaking

flouer [flue] *tr* to dupe, swindle; **se faire flouer** to be had
fluctuation [flyktɥɑsjɔ̃] *f* fluctuation
fluctuer [flyktɥe] *intr* to fluctuate
fluet [flyɛ] **fluette** [flyɛt] *adj* thin, slender
fluide [flɥid] *adj & m* fluid
fluidifier [flɥidifje] *tr* to liquefy
fluor [flyɔr] *m* fluorine
fluores·cent [flyɔresɑ̃] **-cente** [sɑ̃t] *adj* fluorescent
fluoridation [flyɔridɑsjɔ̃] *f* fluoridation
fluorider [flyɔride] *tr & intr* to fluoridate
fluorure [flyɔryr] *m* fluoride
flûte [flyt] *f* flute; long thin loaf of French bread; tall champagne glass; **flûte à bec** recorder; **flûte de Pan** Pan's pipes; **flûtes** (slang) legs; **grande flûte** concert flute; **jouer** or **se tirer des flûtes** (slang) to run for it; **petite flûte** piccolo ‖ *interj* shucks! rats!
flûtiste [flytist] *mf* flutist
flux [fly] *m* flow; flood tide; (cards) flush; (chem, elec, med, metallurgy) flux; **flux de caisse** cash flow; **flux de sang** flush, blush; dysentery; **flux de ventre** diarrhea; **flux et reflux** ebb and flow
fluxion [flyksjɔ̃] *f* inflammation
foc [fɔk] *m* (naut) jib
fo·cal -cale [fɔkal] *adj* (*pl* **-caux** [ko]) focal
fœtus [fetys] *m* fetus
foi [fwa] *f* faith; word (*of a gentleman*); **ajouter foi à** to give credence to; **bonne foi** good faith, sincerity; **de bonne foi** sincere; sincerely; **de mauvaise foi** dishonest; dishonestly; **en foi de quoi** in witness whereof; **faire foi de** to be evidence of; **ma foi!** upon my word!; **manquer de foi à** to break faith with; **mauvaise foi** bad faith, insincerity; **sur la foi de** on the strength of
foie [fwa] *m* liver; **avoir les foies** (slang) to be scared stiff; **foie gras** goose liver
foin [fwɛ̃] *m* hay; **avoir du foin dans ses bottes** (coll) to be well heeled; **faire du foin** (slang) to kick up a fuss
foire [fwar] *f* fair; market; (coll) chaos, mess; **faire la foire** to raise hell; **foire d'empoigne** free-for-all
foirer [fware] *intr* (slang) to flop, fail; (slang) to hang fire; (slang) to be stripped (*said of screw, nut, etc.*)
fois [fwa] *f* time, e.g., **visiter trois fois par semaine** to visit three times a week; times, e.g., **deux fois deux font quatre** two times two is four; **à la fois** at the same time, together; **deux fois** twice; twofold; **encore une fois** once more, again; **il y avait une fois** once upon a time there was; **maintes et maintes fois** time and time again; **une fois** one time, once; **une fois pour toutes** or **une bonne fois** once and for all
foison [fwazɔ̃] *f*—**à foison** in abundance
foison·nant [fwazɔnɑ̃] **-nante** [nɑ̃t] *adj* abundant, plentiful
foisonner [fwazɔne] *intr* to abound
fol *adj* see **fou**

folâtre [fɔlɑtr] *adj* frisky, playful
folâtrer [fɔlɑtre] *intr* to frolic, romp
folie [fɔli] *f* madness, insanity; folly, piece of folly; country lodge, hideaway (*for romantic trysts*); **à la folie** madly, passionately; **faire une folie** to do something crazy; **folie de la persécution** persecution complex
folio [fɔljo] *m* folio
folioter [fɔljɔte] *tr* to folio
folle [fɔl] *f* crazy woman ‖ *adj* see **fou**
follement [fɔlmɑ̃] *adv* madly
fol·let [fɔlɛ] **-lette** [lɛt] *adj* merry, playful; elfish
follicule [fɔlikyl] *m* follicle
fomenta·teur [fɔmɑ̃tatœr] **-trice** [tris] *mf* agitator, troublemaker
fomenter [fɔmɑ̃te] *tr* to foment
fon·cé -cée [fɔ̃se] *adj* dark; deep
foncer [fɔ̃se] §51 *tr* to darken; dig (*a well*); fit a bottom to (*a cask*) ‖ *intr* to charge, rush
fon·cier [fɔ̃sje] **-cière** [sjɛr] *adj* landed (*property*); property (*tax*); fundamental, natural ‖ *m* real-estate tax
foncièrement [fɔ̃sjɛrmɑ̃] *adv* fundamentally, naturally
fonction [fɔ̃ksjɔ̃] *f* function; duty; **faire fonction de** to function as; **fonction publique** government work
fonctionnaire [fɔ̃ksjɔnɛr] *mf* civil servant; officeholder
fonctionnarisme [fɔ̃ksjɔnarism] *m* bureaucracy
fonction·nel -nelle [fɔ̃ksjɔnɛl] *adj* functional
fonctionnement [fɔ̃ksjɔnmɑ̃] *m* working, functioning, operation; **bon fonctionnement** good working order
fonctionner [fɔ̃ksjɔne] *intr* to function, work
fond [fɔ̃] *m* bottom; back, far end; background; foundation; dregs; core, inner meaning, main issue; **à fond** thoroughly; **à fond de train** at full speed; **au fond, dans le fond**, or **par le fond** actually, really, basically; **de fond** fundamental, main; **de fond en comble** from top to bottom; **faire fond sur** to rely on; **fond de tarte** bottom pie crust; **fonds de placement fermé** investment trust fund; **fond sonore** background noise; **râcler les fonds du tiroir** to scrape the bottom of the barrel; **sans fond** bottomless; **y aller au fond** to go the whole way ‖ see **fonds**
fondamen·tal -tale [fɔ̃damɑ̃tal] *adj* (*pl* **-taux** [to]) fundamental, basic
fon·dant [fɔ̃dɑ̃] **-dante** [dɑ̃t] *adj* melting; juicy, luscious ‖ *m* fondant (*candy*); (metallurgy) flux
fonda·teur [fɔ̃datœr] **-trice** [tris] *mf* founder
fondation [fɔ̃dɑsjɔ̃] *f* foundation; founding; endowment
fon·dé -dée [fɔ̃de] §92 *adj* founded; justified; authorized; **bien fondé** well-founded ‖ *m*—**fondé de pouvoir** proxy, authorized agent

fondement [fɔ̃dmɑ̃] *m* foundation, basis; (coll) behind; **sans fondement** unfounded

fonder [fɔ̃de] *tr* to found

fonderie [fɔ̃dri] *f* foundry; smelting

fondeur [fɔ̃dœr] *m* founder, smelter

fondre [fɔ̃dr] *tr* to melt, dissolve; smelt; cast (*metal*); blend (*colors*); merge (*companies*) ‖ *intr* to melt; (coll) to lose weight; **fondre en larmes** to burst into tears; **fondre sur** to pounce on

fondrière [fɔ̃drijɛr] *f* quagmire; mudhole, rut, pothole

fonds [fɔ̃] *m* land (*of an estate*); business, good will; fund; **bon fonds** good nature; **fonds** *mpl* capital; **fonds de commerce** business house; **fonds de prévoyance** reserve fund; **fonds d'État** *mpl* government bonds

fon·du -due [fɔ̃dy] *adj* melted; molten ‖ *m* blending (*of colors*); (mov, telv) dissolve, fade-out ‖ *f* fondue ‖ *v* see **fondre**

fongicide [fɔ̃ʒisid] *adj* fungicidal ‖ *m* fungicide

font [fɔ̃] *v* see **faire**

fontaine [fɔ̃tɛn] *f* fountain; spring; well; cistern; **fontaine de Jouvence** Fountain of Youth; **fontaines vivantes** dancing waters

fonte [fɔ̃t] *f* melting; casting; cast iron; holster; (typ) font; **venir de fonte avec** to be cast in one piece with

fonts [fɔ̃] *mpl*—**fonts baptismaux** baptismal font

football [futbol] *m* soccer; **football américain** football

footballeur [futbolœr] *m* soccer player

footing [futiŋ] *m* walking

for [fɔr] *m*—**dans son for intérieur** in his heart of hearts; **for intérieur** conscience

forage [fɔraʒ] *m* drilling; **forage d'exploration, forage sauvage** wildcat drilling

fo·rain [fɔrɛ̃] **-raine** [rɛn] *adj* traveling, itinerant ‖ **forains** *mpl* carnival people

forban [fɔrbɑ̃] *m* pirate

forçage [fɔrsaʒ] *m* (agr) forcing

forçat [fɔrsa] *m* convict; (hist) galley slave; (fig) drudge

force [fɔrs] *f* force; strength; **à force de** by dint of, as a result of; **à toute force** at all costs; **de première force** foremost (*musician, artist, scientist, etc.*) **de toutes ses forces** with all one's might; **force de frappe** striking force; **force m'est de . . .** (lit) I am obliged to . . .; **force majeure** (law) act of God; **forces** sheep shears; **force vive** (phys) kinetic energy; **la force de l'âge** the prime of life ‖ *adj invar* (archaic) many

forcément [fɔrsemɑ̃] *adv* inevitably, necessarily

force·né -née [fɔrsəne] *adj* frenzied, frantic ‖ *m* madman ‖ *f* crazy woman

forceps [fɔrsɛps] *m* (obstet) forceps

forcer [fɔrse] §51, §96, §97, §100 *tr* to force; do violence to; bring to bay; increase (*the dose*); strain (*a muscle*); mark up (*a receipt*); **forcer la main à qn** to

force s.o.'s hand; **forcer la note** (coll) to overdo it; **forcer le respect de qn** to compel respect from s.o.; **forcer qn à** or **de + inf** to force s.o. to + inf ‖ *ref* to overdo; do violence to one's feelings

forclore [fɔrklɔr] (used only in *inf* and *pp* **forclos**) *tr* to foreclose

forclusion [fɔrklyzjɔ̃] *f* foreclosure

forer [fɔre] *tr* to drill, bore

fores·tier [fɔrɛstje] **-tière** [tjɛr] *adj* forest ‖ *m* forester

foret [fɔrɛ] *m* drill

forêt [fɔrɛ] *f* forest

fo·reur [fɔrœr] **-reuse** [røz] *adj* drilling ‖ *mf* driller ‖ *f* drill, machine drill

forfaire [fɔrfɛr] §29 (used only in *inf;* 1st, 2d, & 3d *sg pres ind;* compound tenses) *intr*—**forfaire à** to forfeit (*one's honor*); fail in (*a duty*)

forfait [fɔrfɛ] *m* heinous crime; contract; package deal; (turf) forfeit; **à forfait** for a lump sum

forfaitaire [fɔrfɛtɛr] *adj* contractual

forfaiture [fɔrfɛtyr] *f* malfeasance

forfanterie [fɔrfɑ̃tri] *f* bragging

forge [fɔrʒ] *f* forge; steel mill

forger [fɔrʒe] §38 *tr* to forge

forgeron [fɔrʒərɔ̃] *m* blacksmith

forgeur [fɔrʒœr] *m* forger, smith; coiner (*e.g., of new expressions*); fabricator (*of false stories*)

formaldéhyde [fɔrmaldeid] *m* formaldehyde

formaliser [fɔrmalize] *ref* to take offense

formaliste [fɔrmalist] *adj* formalistic, conventional ‖ *mf* formalist

formalité [fɔrmalite] *f* formality, convention

format [fɔrma] *m* size, format

formation [fɔrmasjɔ̃] *f* formation; education, training

forme [fɔrm] *f* form; **en forme** fit, in shape; **en forme, en bonne forme,** or **en bonne et due forme** in order, in due form; **pour la forme** for appearances

for·mel -melle [fɔrmɛl] *adj* explicit; strict; formal, superficial

formellement [fɔrmɛlmɑ̃] *adv* absolutely, strictly

former [fɔrme] *tr & ref* to form; educate

formidable [fɔrmidabl] *adj* formidable; (coll) tremendous, terrific

formulaire [fɔrmylɛr] *m* formulary; form (*with spaces for answers*)

formule [fɔrmyl] *f* formula; form, blank; format; **formule de politesse** complimentary close

formuler [fɔrmyle] *tr* to formulate; draw up

fort [fɔr] **forte** [fɔrt] *adj* strong; fortified (*city*); **c'est fort!** it's hard to believe! ‖ (when standing before noun) *adj* high (*fever*); large (*sum*); hard (*task*) ‖ *m* fort; strong man; forte; height (*of summer*) ‖ **fort** *adv* exceedingly; loud; hard

fort-en-thème [fɔrɑ̃tɛm] *adj* (slang) grind (*student*)

forteresse [fɔrtərɛs] *f* fortress, fort

forti·fiant [fɔrtifjɑ̃] **-fiante** [fjɑ̃t] *adj & m* tonic

fortification [fɔrtifikasjɔ̃] *f* fortification

fortifier [fɔrtifje] *tr* to fortify; confirm (*one's opinions*)

fortin [fɔrtɛ̃] *m* small fort

for·tuit [fɔrtɥi] **-tuite** [tɥit] *adj* fortuitous, accidental

fortune [fɔrtyn] *f* fortune; **faire fortune** to make a fortune

fortu·né -née [fɔrtyne] *adj* fortunate; rich

fosse [fos] *f* pit; grave; **fosse aux lions** lions' den; **fosse commune** pauper's grave; **fosse d'aisances** cesspool; **fossse septique** septic tank

fossé [fose] *m* ditch, trench; moat; **fossé des générations** generation gap; **sauter le fossé** to take the plunge

fossette [fosɛt] *f* dimple

fossile [fosil] *adj & m* fossil ‖ *mf* fossil (*person*)

fossoyeur [foswajœr] *m* gravedigger

fosterage [fɔsteraʒ] *m* foster parenting

fou [fu] or **fol** [fɔl] **folle** [fɔl] (*pl* **fous folles**) *adj* mad, insane; foolish; extravagant; unsteady; loose (*pulley*); (coll) tremendous (*success*); **être fou à lier** to be raving mad; **être fou de** to be wild about; to be wild with (*joy, pain, etc.*) ‖ **fou** *m* madman; fool; jester; (cards) joker; (chess) bishop ‖ *f* see **folle**

foucade [fukad] *f* whim, impulse

foudre [fudr] *m* thunderbolt (*of Zeus*); large cask; **foudre de guerre** great captain; **foudre d'éloquence** powerful orator ‖ *f* lightning; **foudres** displeasure (*e.g., of a prince*); **foudres de l'Église** excommunication

foudroyant [fudrwajɑ̃] **foudroyante** [fudrwajɑ̃t] *adj* lightning-like; crushing, overwhelming

foudroyer [fudrwaje] §47 *tr* to strike with lightning; strike suddenly; dumfound; **foudroyer d'un regard** to cast a withering glance at ‖ *intr* to hurl thunderbolts

fouet [fwɛ] *m* whip; (culin) beater

fouetter [fwɛte] *tr & intr* to whip

fougère [fuʒɛr] *f* fern

fougue [fug] f spirit, ardor

fou·gueux [fugø] **-gueuse** [gøz] *adj* spirited, fiery, impetuous

fouille [fuj] *f* excavation; search

fouiller [fuje] *tr* to excavate; search, comb, inspect

fouillis [fuji] *m* jumble, disorder

fouine [fwin] *f* beech marten; pitchfork; harpoon

fouiner [fwine] *intr* (coll) to pry, meddle

fouir [fwir] *tr* to dig, burrow

foulard [fular] *m* scarf, neckerchief

foule [ful] *f* crowd, mob; **en foule** in great numbers

fouler [fule] *tr* to tread on, press; sprain ‖ *ref* to sprain; (slang) to put oneself out, to tire oneself out

foulque [fulk] *f* (zool) coot

foulure [fulyr] *f* sprain

four [fur] *m* oven; kiln, furnace; (coll) flop, turkey; **faire cuire au four** to bake; to roast; **faire four** (coll) to flop; **four à briques** brickkiln; **four à chaux** limekiln; **petit four** teacake

fourbe [furb] *adj* deceiving, cheating ‖ *mf* deceiver, cheat

fourberie [furbəri] *f* deceit, cheating

fourbir [furbir] *tr* to furbish, polish

fourbissage [furbisaʒ] *m* furnishing, polishing

four·bu -bue [furby] *adj* broken-down (*horse*); (coll) dead tired, all in

fourche [furʃ] *f* fork; pitchfork; **fourche avant** front fork (*of bicycle*); **fourches patibulaires** (hist) gallows

fourcher [furʃe] *tr & intr* to fork; **la langue lui a fourché** (coll) he made a slip of the tongue

fourchette [furʃɛt] *f* fork; wishbone; **posséder une bonne fourchette** to have a hearty appetite

four·chu -chue [furʃy] *adj* forked; cloven

fourgon [furgɔ̃] *m* truck; poker; (rr) baggage car; (rr) boxcar; **fourgon bancaire** armored car; **fourgon de queue** caboose; **fourgon funèbre** hearse

fourmi [furmi] *f* ant; (slang) pusher (*of drugs*); **fourmi blanche** white ant, termite

fourmilier [furmilje] *m* anteater

fourmilière [furmiljɛr] *f* ant hill

fourmiller [furmije] *intr* to swarm; tingle (*said, e.g., of foot*); **fourmiller de** to teem with

fournaise [furnɛz] *f* furnace; (fig) oven

four·neau [furno] *m* (*pl* **-neaux**) furnace; cooking stove; **haut fourneau** blast furnace

fournée [furne] *f* batch

four·ni -nie [furni] *adj* bushy, thick; **bien fourni** well-stocked

fourniment [furnimɑ̃] *m* (mil) kit

fournir [furnir] *tr* to furnish, supply, provide; play (*a card of the same suit that has been led*); **fournir q.ch. à qn** to supply or provide s.o. with s.th. ‖ *intr* to supply (*s.o.'s needs*), e.g., **ses parents fournissent à ses besoins** his parents supply his needs; defray (*expenses*); (cards) to follow suit, e.g., **fournir à trèfle** to follow suit in clubs ‖ *ref* to grow thick; be a customer

fournissement [furnismɑ̃] *m* contribution, holdings (*of each shareholder*); statement of holdings

fournisseur [furnisœr] *m* supplier, dealer

fourniture [furnityr] *f* furnishing, supplying; (culin) seasoning; **fournitures** supplies

fourrage [furaʒ] *m* fodder

fourrager [furaʒe] §38 *tr* to forage; rummage, rummage through ‖ *intr* to rummage (about), forage

fourragère [furaʒɛr] *f* lanyard; tailboard

four·ré -rée [fure] *adj* lined with fur; furred (*tongue*); stuffed (*dates*); filled (*candies*); sham, hollow (*peace*) ‖ *m* thicket

four·reau [furo] *m* (*pl* **-reaux**) sheath; scabbard; tight skirt; **coucher dans son fourreau** (coll) to sleep in one's clothes

fourrer [fure] *tr* to line with fur; (coll) to cram, stuff; (coll) to shut up (*in prison*); (coll) to stick, poke ‖ *ref* (coll) to turn, go; (coll) to curl up (*in bed*); **se fourrer dans** (coll) to stick one's nose in

fourre-tout [furtu] *m invar* catchall; duffel bag; tote bag

fourreur [furœr] *m* furrier

fourrier [furje] *m* quartermaster

fourrière [furjɛr] *f* pound (*for automobiles; for stray dogs*)

fourrure [furyr] *f* fur

fourvoyer [furvwaje] §47 *tr* to lead astray

foutre [futr] §7 (*pres* **je, tu fous; il fout**) *tr* (vulg) to have sex with; (vulg) to give; **fous-le dans ta poche!** shove it in your pocket!; **fous-moi la paix!** lay off!; **fous-moi le camp!** get the hell out!; **je t'en fous!** the hell with you!; **qu'est-ce qu'il fout?** what in hell is he doing?; *ref* (vulg) to be had; **je m'en fous!** to hell with it!; **se foutre de** not to give a damn about

fox [fɔks] *m* fox terrier

fox-terrier [fɔkstɛrje] *m* fox terrier

fox-trot [fɔkstrɔt] *m invar* fox trot

foyer [fwaje] *m* foyer, lobby; hearth, fireside; firebox; focus; home; greenroom; center (*of learning; of infection*); **à double foyer** bifocal; **foyer des étudiants** student center; **foyer du soldat** service club; **foyers** native land

frac [frak] *m* cutaway coat

fracas [fraka] *m* crash; roar (*of waves*); peal (*of thunder*)

fracasser [frakase] *tr & ref* to break; shatter, break to pieces

fraction [fraksjɔ̃] *f* fraction; breaking (*e.g., of bread*)

fractionnaire [fraksjɔnɛr] *adj* fractional

fractionnement [fraksjɔnmã] *m* cracking (*of petroleum*)

fractionner [fraksjɔne] *tr* to divide into fractions

fracture [fraktyr] *f* fracture; breaking open

fracturer [fraktyre] *tr* to fracture; break open

fragile [fraʒil] *adj* fragile

fragment [fragmã] *m* fragment

fragmenter [fragmãte] *tr* to fragment

frai [frɛ] *m* spawning; spawn, roe

fraîche [frɛʃ] *f* cool of the day

fraîchement [frɛʃmã] *adv* in the open air; recently; (coll) cordially

fraîcheur [frɛʃœr] *f* coolness; freshness; newness

fraîchir [fraʃir] *intr* to become cooler; freshen (*said of wind*)

frais [frɛ] **fraîche** [frɛʃ] *adj* cool; fresh; wet (*paint*); ready (*cash*); **frais et dispos**, **frais comme une rose** fresh as a daisy; **il**

fait frais it is cool out ‖ (when standing before noun) *adj* recent (*date*); latest (*news*) ‖ *m* cool place; fresh air; **aux frais de** at the expense of; **de frais** just, freshly; **faire les frais de la conversation** (coll) to take the lead in the conversation; be the subject of the conversation; **frais** *mpl* expenses; **frais généraux** overhead expenses; **se mettre en frais** (coll) to go to a great deal of expense or trouble ‖ *f* see **fraîche** ‖ **frais** *adv*—**boire frais** to have a cool drink ‖ **frais fraîche** *adv* (agrees with following *pp*) just, freshly, e.g., **garçon frais arrivé de l'école** boy just arrived from school; e.g., **roses fraîches cueillies** freshly gathered roses

fraise [frɛz] *f* strawberry; wattle (*of turkey*); (mach) countersink

fraiser [frɛze] *tr* (mach) to countersink

fraisier [frɛzje] *m* strawberry plant

framboise [frãbwaz] *f* raspberry

framboisier [frãbwazje] *m* raspberry bush

franc [frã] **franche** [frãʃ] *adj* free; frank, sincere; complete ‖ (when standing before noun) *adj* arrant (*knave*); downright (*fool*) ‖ **franc franque** [frãk] *adj* Frankish ‖ *m* franc (*unit of currency*) ‖ (*cap*) *m* Frank (*medieval German*) ‖ **franc** *adv* frankly

fran·çais [frasɛ] **-çaise** [sɛz] *adj* French ‖ *m* French (*language*); **en bon français** in correct French ‖ (*cap*) *m* Frenchman; **les Français** the French ‖ *f* Frenchwoman

franc-alleu [frãkalø] *m* (*pl* **francs-alleux** [frãkalø]) (hist) freehold

France [frãs] *f* France; **la France** France

franchement [frãʃmã] *adv* frankly, sincerely; without hesitation

franchir [frãʃir] *tr* to cross, go over or through; jump over; overcome (*an obstacle*)

franchise [frãʃiz] *f* exemption; frankness; freedom; **franchise postale** frank

francique [frãsik] *m* Frankish

franciser [frãsize] *tr* to make French

franc-maçon [frãmasɔ̃] *m* (*pl* **francs-maçons**) Freemason

franc-maçonnerie [frãmasɔnri] *f* Freemasonry

franco [frãko] *adv* free, without shipping costs; **franco de bord** free on board; **franco de port** postpaid

franco-cana·dien [frãkɔkanadjẽ] **-dienne** [djɛn] *adj* French-Canadian ‖ **Franco-Cana·dien -dienne** *mf* French Canadian

francophone [frãkɔfɔn] *adj* French-speaking ‖ *mf* French speaker

franc-parler [frãparle] *m*—**avoir son franc-parler** to be free-spoken

franc-tireur [frãtirœr] *m* (*pl* **francs-tireurs**) free lance; sniper

frange [frãʒ] *f* fringe; **à frange** fringed; **frange des dingues** lunatic fringe

franger [frãʒe] §38 *tr* to fringe

franglais [frãglɛ] *m* Franglais

franquette [frãkɛt] *f*—**à la bonne franquette** (coll) simply, without fuss

frap·pant [frapɑ̃] **-pante** [pɑ̃t] *adj* striking, surprising

frappe [frap] *f* minting, striking; stamp (*on coins, medals, etc.*); touch (*in typing*); space (*in typing*), e.g., **une ligne de 65 frappes** a 65-space line

frap·pé -pée [frape] *adj* struck; iced; (slang) crazy ‖ *m* (mus) downbeat

frapper [frape] *tr* to strike, hit, knock; mint (coin); stamp (*cloth*); ice (*e.g., champagne*) ‖ *intr* to strike, hit, knock ‖ *ref* (coll) to become panic-stricken

frasque [frask] *f* escapade

frater·nel -nelle [fratɛrnɛl] *adj* fraternal, brotherly

fraterniser [fratɛrnize] *intr* to fraternize

fraternité [fratɛrnite] *f* fraternity, brotherhood

fraude [frod] *f* fraud; smuggling; **en fraude** fraudulently; **faire la fraude** to smuggle; **fraude fiscale** tax evasion

fraudu·leux [frodylø] **-leuse** [løz] *adj* fraudulent

frayer [frɛje], [freje] §49 *tr* to mark out (*a path*) ‖ *intr* to spawn; **frayer avec** to associate with

frayeur [frɛjœr] *f* fright, scare

fredaine [frədɛn] *f* (coll) escapade, prank, spree

fredon [frədɔ̃] *m* (cards) three of a kind

fredonnement [frədɔnmɑ̃] *m* hum, humming

fredonner [frədɔne] *tr & intr* to hum

frégate [fregat] *f* frigate

frein [frɛ̃] *m* bit (*of bridle*); brake (*of car*); **frein à main** hand brake; **frein à pied** foot brake; **mettre le frein** to put the brake on; **mettre un frein à** to curb, check; **ronger son frein** to champ at the bit

freiner [frɛne] *tr & intr* to brake

frelater [frəlate] *tr* to adulterate

frêle [frɛl] *adj* frail

frelon [frəlɔ̃] *m* hornet

frémir [fremir] §97 *intr* to shudder

frémissement [fremismɑ̃] *m* shudder

frêne [frɛn] *m* ash tree

frénésie [frenezi] *f* frenzy

frénétique [frenetik] *adj* frenzied

fréquemment [frekamɑ̃] *adv* frequently

fréquence [frekɑ̃s] *f* frequency; **basse fréquence** low frequency; **fréquence du pouls** pulse rate; **haute fréquence** high frequency

fré·quent [frekɑ̃] **-quente** [kɑ̃t] *adj* frequent; rapid (*pulse*)

fréquenter [frekɑ̃te] *tr* to frequent; associate with; (coll) to go steady with (*a boy or girl*)

frère [frɛr] *m* brother; **frère consanguin** half brother (*by the father*); **frère convers** (eccl) lay brother; **frère de lait** foster brother; **frère germain** whole brother; **frère jumeau** twin brother; **frères siamois** Siamese twins; **frère utérin** half brother (*by the mother*)

fresque [frɛsk] *f* fresco

fret [frɛ] *m* freight; chartering; cargo

fréter [frete] §10 *tr* to charter (*a ship*); rent (*a car*)

fréteur [fretœr] *m* shipowner

frétiller [fretije] *intr* to wriggle; quiver; **frétiller de** to wag (*its tail*)

fretin [frətɛ̃] *m*—**le menu fretin** small fry

frette [frɛt] *f* hoop, iron ring

freudisme [frødism] *m* Freudianism

freux [frø] *m* rook, crow

friand [frijɑ̃] **friande** [frijɑ̃d] *adj* tasty; fond (*of food, praise, etc.*) ‖ *m* sausage roll

friandise [frijɑ̃diz] *f* candy, sweet; delicacy, tidbit

fric [frik] *m* (slang) jack, money

fricasser [frikase] *tr* to fricassee; squander

fric-frac [frikfrak] *m* (coll) break-in

friche [friʃ] *f* fallow land; **en friche** fallow

friction [friksjɔ̃] *f* friction; massage

frictionner [friksjɔne] *tr* to rub, massage

frigide [friʒid] *adj* frigid

frigidité [friʒidite] *f* frigidity

frigorifier [frigɔrifje] *tr* to refrigerate

frigorifique [frigɔrifik] *adj* refrigerating ‖ *m* cold-storage plant

fri·leux [frilø] **-leuse** [løz] *adj* chilly, shivery

frimas [frimɑ] *m* icy mist, rime

frime [frim] *f* (coll) sham, fake, hoax

frimousse [frimus] *f* (coll) little face, cute face

fringale [frɛ̃gal] *f* (coll) mad hunger

frin·gant [frɛ̃gɑ̃] **-gante** [gɑ̃t] *adj* dashing, spirited

fringuer [frɛ̃ge] *tr* (slang) to dress ‖ *intr* (obs) to frisk about

fringues [frɛ̃g] *fpl* (slang) duds

fri·pé -pée [fripe] *adj* rumpled, mussed; worn, tired (*face*)

friper [fripe] *tr* to wrinkle, rumple

friperie [fripri] *f* secondhand clothes; secondhand furniture

fri·pier [fripje] **-pière** [pjɛr] *mf* old-clothes dealer; junk dealer

fri·pon [fripɔ̃] **-ponne** [pɔn] *adj* roguish ‖ *mf* rogue, rascal

friponnerie [fripɔnri] *f* rascality, cheating

fripouille [fripuj] *f* (slang) scoundrel

frire [frir] §22 (used in *inf; pp;* 1st, 2d, 3d *sg pres ind; sg imperv;* rarely used in *fut; cond*) *tr* to fry; deep-fry; **être frit** (coll) to be done for ‖ *intr* to fry

frise [friz] *f* frieze

friselis [frizli] *m* soft rustling; gentle lapping (*of water*)

friser [frize] *tr* to curl; border on; graze ‖ *intr* to curl

frisoir [frizwar] *m* curling iron

fri·son [frizɔ̃] **-sonne** [zɔn] *adj* Frisian ‖ *m* wave, curl; Frisian (*language*) ‖ (*cap*) *mf* Frisian

fris·quet [friskɛ] **-quette** [kɛt] *adj* (coll) chilly

frisson [frisɔ̃] *m* shiver; shudder; thrill; **frissons** shivering

frissonner [frisɔne] *intr* to shiver

frisure [frizyr] *f* curling; curls

frit [fri] **frite** [frit] *v* see **frire**
frites [frit] *fpl* French fries
frittage [fritaʒ] *m* (metallurgy) sintering
friture [frityr] *f* frying; deep fat; fried fish; (rad, telv) static
frivole [frivɔl] *adj* frivolous, trifling
froc [frɔk] *m* (eccl) frock
froid [frwɑ] **froide** [frwɑd] *adj* cold; chilly (*manner*) ‖ *m* cold; coolness (*between persons*); **avoir froid** to be cold; **il fait froid** it is cold; **jeter un froid sur** (fig) to put a damper on
froideur [frwɑdœr] *f* coldness; coolness
froissement [frwɑsmɑ̃] *m* bruising; rumpling, crumpling; clash (*of interests*); ruffling (*of feelings*)
froisser [frwɑse] *tr* to bruise; rumple, crumple ‖ *ref* to take offense
frôlement [frolmɑ̃] *m* grazing; rustle
frôler [frole] *tr* to graze, brush against; (coll) to have a narrow escape from
fromage [frɔmaʒ] *m* cheese; (coll) soft job; **fromage blanc** cream cheese; **fromage de tête** headcheese
froma·ger [frɔmaʒe] **-gère** [ʒɛr] *adj* cheese (*industry*) ‖ *m* cheesemaker; (bot) silk-cotton tree
fromagerie [frɔmaʒri] *f* cheese factory; cheese store
froment [frɔmɑ̃] *m* wheat
fronce [frɔ̃s] *f* crease, fold; **à fronces** shirred
froncement [frɔ̃smɑ̃] *m* puckering; **froncement de sourcils** frown
froncer [frɔ̃se] §51 *tr* to pucker; **froncer les sourcils** to frown, wrinkle one's brow
frondaison [frɔ̃dɛzɔ̃] *f* foliation; foliage
fronde [frɔ̃d] *f* slingshot
fronder [frɔ̃de] *tr* to scoff at
fron·deur [frɔ̃dœr] **-deuse** [døz] *adj* bantering, irreverent ‖ *mf* scoffer
front [frɔ̃] *m* forehead; impudence; brow (*of hill*); (geog, mil, pol) front; **de front** abreast; frontal; at the same time; **faire front à** to face up to; **un front froid** (meteo) a cold front
fronta·lier [frɔ̃talje] **-lière** [ljɛr] *adj* frontier ‖ *m* frontiersman ‖ *f* frontier woman
frontière [frɔ̃tjɛr] *adj* & *f* frontier
frontispice [frɔ̃tispis] *m* frontispiece; title page
frottement [frɔtmɑ̃] *m* rubbing, friction
frotter [frɔte] *tr* to rub; polish; strike (*a match*); **frotter les oreilles à qn** (coll) to box s.o.'s ears ‖ *ref*—**se frotter à** (coll) to attack, challenge; (coll) to rub shoulders with
froufrou [frufru] *m* rustle, swish
frousse [frus] *f* (slang) jitters
fructifier [fryktifje] *intr* to bear fruit
fruc·tueux [fryktɥø] **-tueuse** [tɥøz] *adj* fruitful, profitable
fru·gal -gale [frygal] *adj* (*pl* **-gaux** [go]) temperate; frugal (*meal*)
fruit [frɥi] *m* fruit; **des fruits** fruit; **fruits civils** income (*from rent, interest, etc.*); **fruits de mer** seafood; **fruit sec** (fig) flop, failure

fruiterie [frɥitri] *f* fruit store
frui·tier [frɥitje] **-tière** [tjɛr] *adj* fruit; fruit-bearing ‖ *mf* fruit vendor
fruste [fryst] *adj* worn; rough, uncouth
frustrer [frystre] *tr* frustrate, disappoint; cheat, defraud
f.s. *abbr* (**faux sens**) mistranslation
fuel [fjul] *m* fuel oil
fuel-oil [fjulɔl] *m* fuel oil
fugace [fygas] *adj* fleeting, evanescent
fugi·tif [fyʒitif] **-tive** [tiv] *adj* & *mf* fugitive
fugue [fyg] *f* sudden disappearance; (mus) fugue
fuir [fɥir] §31 *tr* to flee, run away from ‖ *intr* to flee; leak; recede (*said of forehead*)
fuite [fɥit] *f* flight; leak
fulgu·rant [fylgyrɑ̃] **-rante** [rɑ̃t] *adj* flashing; vivid; stabbing (*pain*)
fulguration [fylgyrasjɔ̃] *f* sheet lightning
fulgurer [fylgyre] *intr* to flash
fuligi·neux [fyliʒinø] **-neuse** [nøz] *adj* sooty
fumage [fymaʒ] *m* smoking (*of meat*); manuring (*of fields*)
fume-cigare [fymsigar] *m invar* cigar holder
fume-cigarette [fymsigarɛt] *m invar* cigarette holder
fumée [fyme] *f* smoke; steam; **fumées** fumes
fumer [fyme] *tr* & *intr* to smoke; fume; manure
fumerie [fymri] *f* opium den; smoking room
fumet [fyme] *m* aroma; bouquet (*of wine*)
fu·meur [fymœr] **-meuse** [møz] *mf* smoker; **fumeur à la file** chain smoker
fu·meux [fymø] **-meuse** [møz] *adj* smoky; foggy, hazy (*ideas*)
fumier [fymje] *m* manure; dunghill; (slang) skunk, scoundrel
fumiger [fymiʒe] §38 *tr* to fumigate
fumillard [fymijar] *m* smog
fumiste [fymist] *m* heater man; (coll) practical joker
fumisterie [fymistri] *f* heater work; heater shop; (coll) hooey
fumoir [fymwar] *m* smoking room; smoke-house
funambule [fynɑ̃byl] *mf* tightrope walker
funèbre [fynɛbr] *adj* funereal; funeral (*march, procession, service*)
funérailles [fynerɑj] *fpl* funeral
funéraire [fynerɛr] *adj* funeral
funeste [fynɛst] *adj* baleful, fatal
funiculaire [fynikylɛr] *adj* & *m* funicular
fur [fyr] *m*—**au fur et à mesure** progressively, gradually; **au fur et à mesure de** in proportion to; **au fur et à mesure que** as, in proportion as
furet [fyrɛ] *m* ferret; snoop; ring-in-the-circle (*parlor game*)
fureter [fyrte] §2 *intr* to ferret
fureur [fyrœr] *f* fury; **à la fureur** passionately; **faire fureur** to be the rage
furi·bond [fyribɔ̃] **-bonde** [bɔ̃d] *adj* furious; withering (*look*) ‖ *mf* irascible individual
furie [fyri] *f* fury; termagant

fu·rieux [fyrjø] **-rieuse** [rjøz] *adj* furious; angry (*wind*)

furoncle [fyrɔ̃kl] *m* boil

fur·tif [fyrtif] **-tive** [tiv] *adj* furtive, stealthy

fus [fy] *v* (**fut, fûmes**, etc.) see **être**

fusain [fyzɛ̃] *m* charcoal; charcoal drawing; spindle tree

fu·seau [fyzo] *m* (*pl* **-seaux**) spindle; **à fuseau** tapering; **fuseau horaire** time zone (*between two meridians*)

fusée [fyze] *f* rocket; spindleful; spindle (*of axle*); (coll) ripple, burst (*of laughter*); **fusée à retard** delayed-action fuse; **fusée d'artifice** or **fusée volante** skyrocket; **fusée éclairante, fusée de signalisation** flare; **fusée engin** rocket engine; **fusée fusante** time fuse; **fusée percutante** percussion fuse

fuselage [fyzlaʒ] *m* fuselage

fuse·lé -lée [fyzle] *adj* spindle-shaped; tapering, slender (*fingers*); streamlined

fuseler [fyzle] §34 *tr* to taper; streamline

fuser [fyze] *intr* to melt; run (*said of colors*); fizz, spurt; stream in or out (*said of light*)

fusible [fyzibl] *adj* fusible ‖ *m* fuse

fusil [fyzi] *m* gun, rifle; whetstone rifleman; **fusil à canon scié** sawed-off shotgun; **fusil à deux coups** double-barreled gun; **fusil de chasse** shot gun; **fusil mitrailleur** light machine gun; **un bon fusil** a good shot (*person*)

fusillade [fyzijad] *f* fusillade

fusiller [fyzije] *tr* to shoot, execute by a firing squad

fusion [fyzjɔ̃] *f* fusion

fusionner [fyzjɔne] *tr* & *intr* to blend, fuse; (com) to merge

fustiger [fystiʒe] §38 *tr* to thrash, flog; castigate

fût [fy] *m* cask, keg; barrel (*of drum*); stock (*of gun*); trunk (*of tree*); shaft (*of column*); stem (*of candelabrum*)

futaie [fytɛ] *f* stand of timber; **de haute futaie** full-grown

futaille [fytaj] *f* cask, barrel

futaine [fytɛn] *f* fustian

fu·té -tée [fyte] *adj* (coll) cunning, shrewd ‖ *f* mastic, filler

futile [fytil] *adj* futile

futilité [fytilite] *f* futility; **futilités** trifles

fu·tur -ture [fytyr] *adj* future ‖ *m* future; husband-to-be ‖ *f* future wife

fuyant [fɥijɑ̃] **fuyante** [fɥijɑ̃t] *adj* fleeting; receding (*forehead*)

fuyard [fɥijar] **fuyarde** [fɥijard] *adj* & *mf* runaway

G

G, g [ʒe] *m invar* seventh letter of the French alphabet

garbardine [gabardin] *f* gabardine

gabare [gabar] *f* barge

gabarit [gabari] *m* templet; (rr) maximum structure; (coll) size

gabelle [gabɛl] *f* (hist) salt tax

gâche [gɑʃ] *f* catch (*at a door*); trowel; wooden spatula

gâcher [gɑʃe] *tr* to mix (*cement*); spoil, bungle, squander

gâchette [gɑʃɛt] *f* trigger; pawl, spring catch

gâ·cheur [gɑʃœr] **-cheuse** [ʃøz] *adj* bungling ‖ *f* bungler

gâchis [gɑʃi] *m* wet cement; mud, slush; (coll) mess, muddle

gaélique [gaelik] *adj* & *m* Gaelic

gaffe [gaf] *f* gaff; (coll) social blunder, faux pas

gaffer [gafe] *tr* to hook with a gaff ‖ *intr* (coll) to make a blunder

gaga [gaga] *adj* (coll) doddering ‖ *mf* (coll) dotard

gage [gaʒ] *m* pledge, pawn; forfeit (*in a game*); **gages** wage, wages; **prêter sur gages** to pawn

gager [gaʒe] §38, §97 *tr* to wager, bet; pay wages to

ga·geur [gaʒœr] **-geuse** [ʒøz] *mf* bettor

gageure [gaʒyr] *f* wager, bet

gagiste [gaʒist] *mf* pledger; wage earner; (theat) extra

ga·gnant [gaɲɑ̃] **-gnante** [ɲɑ̃t] *adj* winning ‖ *mf* winner

gagne-pain [gaɲpɛ̃] *m invar* breadwinner; livelihood, bread and butter

gagne-petit [gaɲpəti] *m invar* cheapjack, low-salaried worker

gagner [gaɲe] §96 *tr* to gain; win; earn; reach; save (*time*) ‖ *intr* to improve; gain; spread ‖ *ref* to be catching (*said of disease*)

ga·gneur [gaɲœr] **-gneuse** [ɲøz] *mf* winner; earner

gai gaie [ge] *adj* cheerful, merry, happy; (coll) tipsy

gaiement [gemɑ̃] *adv* gaily, cheerfully, merrily, happily

gaieté [gete] *f* gaiety; **de gaieté de cœur** of one's own free will

gail·lard [gajar] **-larde** [jard] *adj* healthy, hearty; merry; ribald, spicy ‖ *m* sturdy fellow; tricky fellow; **gaillard d'arrière** quarter-deck; **gaillard d'avant** forecastle ‖ *f* bold young lady; husky young woman

gaillardise [gajardiz] *f* cheerfulness; **gaillardises** spicy stories

gaîment [gemɑ̃] *adv* see **gaiement**

gain [gɛ̃] *m* gain; earnings; winning (*e.g., of bet*); **avoir gain de cause** to win one's case

gaine [gɛn] *f* sheath; case, covering; girdle (*corset*); **gaine d'aération** ventilation shaft

gainer [gɛne] *tr* to sheath, encase

gaîté [gete] *f* gaiety

gala [gala] *m* gala; state dinner

galamment [galamɑ̃] *adv* gallantly

ga·lant [galɑ̃] **-lante** [lɑ̃t] *adj* gallant; amorous; kept (*woman*) ‖ *m* gallant; **vert gallant** gay old blade

galanterie [galɑ̃tri] *f* gallantry; libertinism

galaxie [galaksi] *f* galaxy

galbe [galb] *m* curve, sweep, graceful outline

gale [gal] *f* mange; (coll) backbiter, cad

galée [gale] *f* (typ) galley

galéjade [galeʒad] *f* joke, far-fetched story

galère [galɛr] *f* galley; drudgery; mason's hand truck

galerie [galri] *f* gallery; cornice, rim; baggage rack; **galerie marchande** shopping center; shopping mall

galérien [galerjɛ̃] *m* galley slave

galet [galɛ] *m* pebble; (mach) roller

galetas [galta] *m* hovel

galette [galɛt] *f* cake; buckwheat pancake; hardtack; (slang) dough, money, **galette des Rois** twelfth-cake (*eaten at Epiphany*)

ga·leux [galø] **-leuse** [løz] *adj* mangy

galimatias [galimatja] *m* nonsense, gibberish

galion [galjɔ̃] *m* galleon

Galles [gal]—**le pays de Galles** Wales; **prince de Galles** Prince of Wales

gal·lois [galwa] **gal·loise** [galwaz] *adj* Welsh ‖ *m* Welsh (*language*) ‖ (*cap*) *m* Welshman; **les Gallois** the Welsh ‖ (*cap*) *f* Welshwoman

gallon [galɔ̃] *m* gallon (*imperial or American*)

galoche [galɔʃ] *f* clog (*shoe*); **de** or **en galoche** pointed (*chin*)

galon [galɔ̃] *m* galloon, braid; (mil) stripe, chevron; **prendre du galon** to move up

galonner [galɔne] *tr* to trim with braid

galop [galo] *m* gallop; **petit galop** canter

galoper [galɔpe] *tr & intr* to gallop

galopin [galɔpɛ̃] *m* (coll) urchin

galvaniser [galvanize] *tr* to galvanize

galvanoplastie [galvãnɔplasti] *f* electroplating

galvauder [galvode] *tr* (coll) to botch; (coll) to waste (*e.g., one's talent*); (coll) to sully (*a name*) ‖ *intr* (slang) to walk the streets ‖ *ref* (slang) to go bad

gambade [gɑ̃bad] *f* gambol

gambader [gɑ̃bade] *intr* to gambol

gambit [gɑ̃bi] *m* gambit

gamelle [gamɛl] *f* mess kit

ga·min [gamɛ̃] **-mine** [min] *mf* street urchin; youngster

gaminerie [gaminri] *f* mischievousness

gamme [gam] *f* gamut, range; set (*of tools*); (mus) scale, gamut; **haut de gamme** top-of-the-line

Gand [gɑ̃] *m* Ghent

ganglion [gɑ̃glijɔ̃] *m* ganglion

gangrène [gɑ̃grɛn] *f* gangrene

gangrener [gɑ̃grəne] §2 *tr & ref* to gangrene

ganse [gɑ̃s] *f* braid, piping

gant [gɑ̃] *m* glove; **gant à laver** glove washcloth; **jeter le gant** to throw down the gauntlet; **prendre des gants pour** to put on kid gloves to; **relever le gant** to take up the gauntlet; **se donner des gants** to take all the credit

gantelet [gɑ̃tlɛ] *m* protective glove

ganter [gɑ̃te] *tr* to put gloves on (*s.o.*); fit, become (*s.o.; said of gloves*); **cela me gante** (coll) that suits me ‖ *intr*—**ganter de** to wear, take (*a certain size of glove*) ‖ *ref* to put on one's gloves

garage [garaʒ] *m* garage; turnout, passing place; service station, repair shop; used-car lot; **garage d'autobus** bus depot; **garage d'avions** hangar

garagiste [garaʒist] *m* garageman, mechanic; car dealer

ga·rant [garɑ̃] **-rante** [rɑ̃t] *adj* guaranteeing ‖ *mf* guarantor, warrantor; **se porter garant de** to guarantee ‖ *m* guarantee, warranty

garantie [garɑ̃ti] *f* guarantee, warranty

garantir [garɑ̃tir] *tr* to guarantee; vouch for; shelter, protect

garce [gars] *f* (coll) wench; (coll) bitch

garçon [garsɔ̃] *m* boy; young man; bachelor; apprentice; waiter; **être bon garçon** to be nice; **garçon de café** café waiter; **garçon de courses** errand boy; **garçon de recette** bank messenger; **garçon de salle** orderly; **garçon d'honneur** best man; **garçon manqué** tomboy; **petit garçon** boy (*two to thirteen years of age*); **vieux garçon** old bachelor

garçonne [garsɔn] *f* bachelor woman, female bachelor

garçonnet [garsɔnɛ] *m* little boy

garçon·nier [garsɔnje] **-nière** [njɛr] *adj* bachelor; tomboyish ‖ *f* bachelor apartment; tomboy

garde [gard] *m* guard, guardsman; keeper, custodian; **garde champêtre** constable; **garde de nuit** night watchman; **garde forestier** ranger ‖ *f* guard; custody; nurse; flyleaf; **de garde** on duty; **garde à vous!** (mil) attention!; **garde civique** national guard; **monter la garde** to go on guard duty; **prendre garde à** to look out for, to take notice of; **prendre garde de** to take care not to; to be careful to; **prendre garde que** to notice that; **prendre garde que . . . ne** + *subj* to be careful lest, to be careful that . . . not; **sur ses gardes** on one's guard

garde-à-vous [gardavu] *m invar* attention (*military position*)

garde-à-vue [gardavy] *f* custody, imprisonment

garde-barrière [gardəbarjɛr] *mf* (*pl* **gardes-barrière** or **gardes-barrières**) crossing guard

garde-bébé [gardəbebe] *mf* (*pl* **-bébés**) babysitter

garde-boue [gardəbu] *m invar* mudguard

garde-chasse [gardəʃas] *m* (*pl* **gardes-chasse** or **gardes-chasses**) gamekeeper

garde-corps [gardəkɔr] *m invar* guardrail; (naut) life line

garde-côte [gardəkot] *m* (*pl* **-côtes**) coastguard cutter ‖ *m* (*pl* **gardes-côtes**) (obs) coastguardsman; (obs) coast guard

garde-feu [gardəfø] *m invar* fire screen

garde-fou [gardəfu] *m* (*pl* **-fous**) guardrail

garde-frein [gardəfrɛ̃] *m* (*pl* **gardes-frein** or **gardes-freins**) brakeman

garde-magasin [gardəmagazɛ̃] *m* (*pl* **gardes-magasin** or **gardes-magasins**) warehouseman

garde-malade [gardəmalad] *mf* (*pl* **gardes-malades**) nurse

garde-manger [gardəmɑ̃ʒe] *m invar* icebox; larder

garde-meuble [gardəmœbl] *m* (*pl* **-meuble** or **meubles**) furniture warehouse

garde-nappe [gardənap] *m* (*pl* **-nappe** or **nappes**) table mat, place mat

garde-pêche [gardəpɛʃ] *m* (*pl* **gardes-pêche**) fish warden ‖ *m invar* fishery service boat

garder [garde] §97 *tr* to guard; keep; **garder à vue** to hold in custody; **garder jusqu'à l'arrivée** (formula on envelope) hold for arrival; **garder la chambre** to stay in one's room; **garder la ligne** to keep one's figure ‖ *ref* to keep (*to stay free of deterioration*); **se garder de** to protect oneself from; watch out for; take care not to

garde-rats [gardəra] *m invar* rat guard

garderie [gardəri] *f* nursery; forest reserve

garde-robe [gardərɔb] *f* (*pl* **-robes**) wardrobe

gar·deur [gardœr] **-deuse** [døz] *mf* keeper, herder

garde-voie [gardəvwa] *m* (*pl* **gardes-voie** or **gardes-voies**) trackwalker

garde-vue [gardəvy] *m invar* eyeshade, visor

gar·dien [gardjɛ̃] **-dienne** [djɛn] *adj* guardian (*angel*) ‖ *mf* guard, guardian; keeper; caretaker; attendant (*at a garage*); **gardien de but** goalkeeper; **gardien de la paix** policeman

gardiennage [gardjɛnaʒ] *m* baby-sitting

gare [gar], [gar] *f* station; **gare aérienne** airport; **gare de fret** cargo terminal; **gare de triage** switchyard; **gare maritime** port, dock; **gare routière** or **gare d'autobus** bus station ‖ [gar] *interj* look out!; **sans crier gare** without warning

garer [gare] *tr* to park; put in the garage; (naut) to dock; (rr) to shunt; (coll) to secure (*e.g., a fortune*) ‖ *ref* to get out of

the way; park, park one's car; **se garer de** to look out for

gargariser [gargarize] *ref* to gargle

gargarisme [gargarism] *m* gargle

gargote [gargɔt] *f* (coll) hash house, beanery

gargouille [garguj] *f* gargoyle

gargouillement [gargujmɑ̃] *m* gurgling; rumbling (*in stomach*)

gargouiller [garguje] *intr* to gurgle

garnement [garnəmɑ̃] *m* scamp, bad boy

gar·ni -nie [garni] *adj* furnished (*room*) ‖ *m* furnished room; furnished house

garnir [garnir] *tr* to garnish, adorn; furnish; strengthen; line (*a brake*) ‖ *ref* to fill up (*said of crowded room, theater seats, etc.*)

garnison [garnizɔ̃] *f* garrison

garniture [garnityr] *f* garniture, decoration; fittings; accessories; complete set; (culin) garnish; **garniture de feu** fire irons; **garniture de lit** bedding

garrot [garo] *m* garrote (*instrument of torture*); (med) tourniquet; (zool) withers

garrotte [garɔt] *f* garrotte (*torture*)

garrotter [garɔte] *tr* to garrote; pinion

gars [gɑ] *m* (coll) lad; **c'est un gars!** (coll) he's a brave young man!

Gascogne [gaskɔɲ] *f* Gascony; **la Gascogne** Gascony

gasconnade [gaskɔnad] *f* gasconade; insincere invitation

gas-oil [gazwal] *m* diesel oil

Gaspésie [gaspezi] *f* Gaspé Peninsula

gaspiller [gaspije] *tr* to waste, squander

gastrique [gastrik] *adj* gastric

gastronomie [gastrɔnɔmi] *f* gastronomy

gâ·teau [gato] *adj invar* (coll) fond (*papa*); (coll) fairy (*godmother*) ‖ *m* (*pl* **-teaux**) cake; (coll) booty, loot; **gâteau de miel** honeycomb; **gâteau des Rois** twelfthcake

gâte-métier [gatmetje] *m invar* undercutter

gâte-papier [gatpapje] *m invar* hack writer

gâter [gate] *tr* & *ref* to spoil

gâte-sauce [gatsos] *m invar* poor cook; kitchen boy

gâ·teux [gatø] **-teuse** [tøz] *adj* (coll) senile ‖ *mf* (coll) dotard

gâtisme [gatism] *m* senility

gauche [goʃ] *adj* left; left-hand; crooked; awkward ‖ *f* left hand; left side; (pol) left wing; **à gauche** to the left; **à gauche,** **gauche!** (mil) left, face!

gauchement [goʃmɑ̃] *adv* clumsily, awkwardly

gau·cher [goʃe] **-chère** [ʃɛr] *adj* left-handed ‖ *mf* left-hander

gauchir [goʃir] *tr* & *intr* to warp

gauchiste [goʃist] *adj* & *mf* leftist

gaudriole [godrijɔl] *f* broad joke

gaufre [gofr] *f* waffle; **gaufre de miel** honeycomb

gaufrer [gofre] *tr* to emboss, figure; flute; corrugate

gaufrette [gofrɛt] *f* wafer

gaufrier [gofrije] *m* waffle iron

gaule [gol] *f* pole; **la Gaule** Gaul
gauler [gole] *tr* to bring down (*e.g.*, *fruit*) with a pole
gau·lois [golwa] **-loise** [lwaz] *adj* Gaulish, Gallic; broad (*humor*) ‖ *m* Gaulish (*language*) ‖ (*cap*) *mf* Gaul ‖ (*cap*) *f* gauloise (*cigarette*)
gauloiserie [golwazri] *f* racy joking
gaulthèrie [goteri] *f* (bot) wintergreen
gausser [gose] *ref*—**se gausser de** (coll) to poke fun at
gaver [gave] *tr* & *ref* to cram
gavroche [gavrɔʃ] *mf* street urchin
gaz [gɑz] *m* gas; gaslight; gas company; **gaz d'échappement** exhaust; **gaz d'éclairage** illuminating gas; **gaz de combat** poison gas; **gaz en cylindre** bottled gas; **gaz hilarant** laughing gas; **gaz lacrimogène** tear gas; **mettre les gaz** (aut) to step on the gas
gaze [gɑz] *f* gauze; cheesecloth
ga·zé -zée [gɑze] *adj* gassed ‖ *mf* gas casualty
gazéifier [gɑzeifje] *tr* to gasify; carbonate, charge
gazelle [gɑzɛl] *f* gazelle
gazer [gɑze] *tr* to gas; cover with gauze; tone down ‖ *intr* (coll) to go full steam ahead; **ça gaze?** (coll) how goes it?
ga·zeux [gɑzø] **-zeuse** [zøz] *adj* gaseous; carbonated
ga·zier [gɑzje] **-zière** [zjɛr] *adj* gas ‖ *m* gasman; gas fitter
gazoduc [gɑzɔdyk] *m* gas pipe line
gazogène [gɑzɔʒɛn] *m* gas producer
gazoline [gɑzɔlin] *f* petroleum ether
gazomètre [gɑzɔmɛtr] *m* gasholder, gas tank
gazon [gɑzɔ̃] *m* lawn; turf, sod
gazonner [gɑzɔne] *tr* to sod
gazouiller [gɑzuje] *intr* to chirp, twitter; warble; babble
gazouillis [gɑzuji] *m* chirping, warbling; babbling
geai [ʒɛ] *m* jay
géant [ʒeɑ̃] **-géante** [ʒeɑ̃t] *adj* gigantic ‖ *m* giant ‖ *f* giantess
Gédéon [ʒedeɔ̃] *m* (Bib) Gideon
gei·gnard [ʒɛɲar] **-gnard** [ɲard] *adj* (coll) whining ‖ *mf* (coll) whiner
geignement [ʒɛɲmɑ̃] *m* whining, whimper
geindre [ʒɛ̃dr] §50 *intr* to whine, whimper; (coll) to complain
gel [ʒɛl] *m* frost, freezing; (chem) gel
gélatine [ʒelatin] *f* gelatin
gelée [ʒəle] *f* frost; (culin) jelly; **gelée blanche** hoarfrost
geler [ʒəle] §2 *tr*, *intr*, & *ref* to freeze; to congeal
gelure [ʒəlyr] *f* frostbite
Gémeaux [ʒemo] *mpl*—**les Gémeaux** (astr, astrol) Gemini
gémi·né -née [ʒemine] *adj* twin; coeducational (*school*)
gémir [ʒemir] §97 *intr* to groan, moan
gémissement [ʒemismɑ̃] *m* groaning, moaning

gemme [ʒɛm] *f* gem; bud; pine resin
gemmer [ʒɛmme] *tr* to tap for resin ‖ *intr* to bud
gê·nant [ʒenɑ̃] **-nante** [nɑ̃t] *adj* troublesome, embarrassing
gencive [ʒɑ̃siv] *f* (anat) gum
gendarme [ʒɑ̃darm] *m* policeman; military policeman; rock pinnacle; flaw (*of gem*); (coll) virago; (slang) red herring
gendarmerie [ʒɑ̃darmri] *f* police headquarters
gendre [ʒɑ̃dr] *m* son-in-law
gêne [ʒɛn] *f* discomfort, embarrassment; **être dans la gêne** to be hard up; **être sans gêne** (coll) to be rude, casual
gène [ʒɛn] *m* (biol) gene
généalogie [ʒenealɔʒi] *f* genealogy
gêner [ʒene] §97 *tr* to embarrass; inconvenience; hinder; embarrass financially; pinch (*the feet*) ‖ *ref* to put oneself out, be inconvenienced; **ne vous gênez pas!** don't be disturbed; make yourself at home!
géné·ral -rale [ʒeneral] *adj* & *m* (*pl* **-raux** [ro]) general; **en général** in general; **général de brigade** brigadier general; **général de corps d'armée** lieutenant general; **général de division** major general ‖ *f* general's wife; (theat) opening night; **battre la générale** (mil) to sound the alarm
généralat [ʒenerala] *m* generalship
généralement [ʒeneralmɑ̃] *adv* generally
généraliser [ʒeneralize] *tr* & *intr* to generalize
généralissime [ʒeneralisim] *m* generalissimo
généraliste [ʒeneralist] *m* (med) general practitioner, family doctor
généralité [ʒeneralite] *f* generality; **la généralité de** the general run of
généra·teur [ʒeneratœr] **-trice** [tris] *adj* generating ‖ *m* boiler ‖ *f* generator
génération [ʒenerasjɔ̃] *f* generation; **les générations montantes** the generations to come
générer [ʒenere] §10 *tr* to generate
géné·reux [ʒenerø] **-reuse** [røz] *adj* generous; full (*bosom*); rich, full (*wine*)
générique [ʒenerik] *adj* generic ‖ *m* (mov) credit line
générosité [ʒenerozite] *f* generosity; **générosités** acts of generosity
Gênes [ʒɛn] *f* Genoa
genèse [ʒənɛz] *f* genesis
genet [ʒənɛ] *m* jennet (*horse*)
genêt [ʒənɛ] *m* (bot) broom; **genêt pineux** furze
génétique [ʒenetik] *adj* genetic ‖ *f* genetics
gê·neur [ʒenœr] **-neuse** [nøz] *mf* intruder, spoilsport
Genève [ʒənɛv] *f* Geneva
gene·vois [ʒənvwa], [ʒɛnvwa] **-voise** [vwaz] *adj* Genevan ‖ (*cap*) *mf* Genevan (*person*)
genévrier [ʒənevrije] *m* juniper
gé·nial -niale [ʒenjal] *adj* (*pl* **-niaux** [njo]) brilliant, ingenious; geniuslike, of genius

génie [ʒeni] *m* genius; bent, inclination; genie; engineer corps; **génie civil** civil engineering; **génie industriel** industrial engineering; **génie logiciel** software engineering; **génie maritime** naval construction

genièvre [ʒenjɛvr] *m* juniper; juniper berry; gin

génisse [ʒenis] *f* heifer

géni·tal -tale [ʒenital] *adj* (*pl* **-taux** [to]) genital

géni·teur [ʒenitœr] **-trice** [tris] *adj* engendering‖ *m* sire ‖ *f* genetrix

géni·tif [ʒenitif] **-tive** [tiv] *adj & m* genitive

génocide [ʒenɔsid] *m* genocide

gé·nois [ʒenwa] **-noise** [nwaz] *adj* Genoese ‖ (*cap*) *mf* Genoese

ge·nou [ʒənu] *m* (*pl* **-noux**) knee; (mach) joint

genouillère [ʒənujɛr] *f* kneecap; kneepad

genre [ʒɑr] *m* genre; genus; kind, sort; manner, way; fashion, taste; (gram) gender; **dans votre genre** like you; **de genre** (fa) genre; **faire du genre** (coll) to put on airs; **genre humain** humankind

gens [ʒɑ̃] (an immediately preceding adjective that varies in its feminine form is put in that form, and so are **certain, quel, tel,** and **tout** that precede that preceding adjective, but the noun remains masculine for pronouns that stand for it, for past participles that agree with it, and for adjectives in all other positions, e.g., **toutes ces vieilles gens sont intéressants** all these old people are interesting) *mpl* people; nations, e.g., **droit des gens** law of nations; men, e.g., **gens de lettres** men of letters; **gens d'affaires** businesspeople, businessmen; **gens d'Église** clergy; **gens de la presse** news persons, newsmen; **gens de mer** seamen; **gens de robe** bar; **jeunes gens** young people (*men and women*); young men

gent [ʒɑ̃] *f* (obs) nation, race

gentiane [ʒɑ̃sjan] *f* gentian

gen·til [ʒɑ̃ti] **-tille** [tij] *adj* nice, kind ‖ (*cap*) *m* pagan, gentile

gentilhomme [ʒɑ̃tijɔm] *m* (*pl* **gentils-hommes** [ʒɑ̃tizɔm]) nobleman

gentillesse [ʒɑ̃tijɛs] *f* niceness, kindness; **gentillesses** nice things, kind words

gentil·let [ʒɑ̃tijɛ] **-lette** [jɛt] *adj* rather nice

gentiment [ʒɑ̃timɑ̃] *adv* nicely; gracefully

gentleman [ʒɛntləman] *m* (*pl* **gentlemen** [ʒɛntləmɛn]) (nineteenth-century) gentleman

géographie [ʒeɔgrafi] *f* geography

geôle [ʒol] *f* jail

geô·lier [ʒolje] **-lière** [ljɛr] *mf* jailer

géologie [ʒeɔlɔʒi] *f* geology

géologique [ʒeɔlɔʒik] *adj* geologic(al)

géomé·tral -trale [ʒeɔmetral] *adj* (*pl* **-traux** [tro]) flat (*projection*)

géométrie [ʒeɔmetri] *f* geometry

géométrique [ʒeɔmetrik] *adj* geometric(al)

géophysique [ʒeɔfizik] *f* geophysics

géopolitique [ʒeɔpɔlitik] *f* geopolitics

Georges [ʒɔrʒ] *m* George

gérance [ʒerɑ̃s] *f* management; board of directors

géranium [ʒeranjɔm] *m* geranium

gé·rant [ʒerɑ̃] **-rante** [rɑ̃t] *mf* manager; **gérant d'une publication** managing editor

gerbe [ʒɛrb] *f* sheaf; spray (*of flowers; of water; of bullets*); shower (*of sparks*)

gerbée [ʒɛrbe] *f* straw

gerber [ʒɛrbe] *tr* to sheave; stack

gerce [ʒɛrs] *f* crack, split; clothes moth

gercer [ʒɛrse] §51 *tr, intr, & ref* to crack, chap

gerçure [ʒɛrsyr] *f* crack, chap

gérer [ʒere] §10 *tr* to manage, run

gériatrie [ʒerjatri] *f* geriatrics

ger·main [ʒɛrmɛ̃] **-maine** [mɛn] *adj* german, first (*cousin*)

germe [ʒɛrm] *m* germ

germer [ʒɛrme] *intr* to germinate

germicide [ʒɛrmisid] *adj* germicidal ‖ *m* germicide

gérondif [ʒerɔ̃dif] *m* gerund

gérontologie [ʒerɔ̃tɔlɔʒi] *f* gerontology

gésier [ʒesje] *m* gizzard

gésir [ʒezir] (used only in *inf; ger* **gisant;** 3d *sg pres ind* **git;** 1st, 2d, 3d *pl pres ind* **gisons, gisez, gisent;** *imperf ind* **gisais, gisait, gisions, gisiez, gisaient**) *intr* to lie; **ci-gît** here lies (*buried*)

gesse [ʒɛs] *f* vetch; **gesse odorante** sweet pea

gestation [ʒɛstasjɔ̃] *f* gestation

geste [ʒɛst] *m* gesture ‖ *f* medieval epic poem

gesticuler [ʒɛstikyle] *intr* to gesticulate

gestion [ʒɛstjɔ̃] *f* management, administration

gestionnaire [ʒɛstjɔnɛr] *adj* managing ‖ *mf* manager, administrator

geyser [ʒɛzɛr], [ʒejzɛr] *m* geyser

ghetto [geto], [getto] *m* ghetto

gib·beux [ʒibø] **-beuse** [bøz] *adj* humped, hunchbacked

gibecière [ʒibsjɛr] *f* game bag; sack (*for papers, books, etc.*)

gibelotte [ʒiblɔt] *f* rabbit stew

gibet [ʒibɛ] *m* gibbet, gallows

gibier [ʒibje] *m* game; **gibier à plume** feathered game; **gibier de potence** gallows bird

gibloulée [ʒibule] *f* shower; hailstorm

gibo·yeux [ʒibwajø] **giboyeuse** [ʒibwajøz] *adj* full of game

gibus [ʒibys] *m* opera hat

giclée [ʒikle] *f* spurt

gicler [ʒikle] *intr* to spurt

gicleur [ʒiklœr] *m* atomizer; (aut) spray nozzle (*of carburetor*)

gifle [ʒifl] *f* slap in the face

gifler [ʒifle] *tr* to slap in the face

gigantesque [ʒigɑ̃tɛsk] *adj* gigantic

gigogne [ʒigɔɲ] *adj*—**table gigogne** nest of tables ‖ (*cap*) *f*—**la mère Gigogne** the old woman who lived in a shoe

gigolo [ʒigɔlo] *m* (coll) gigolo

gigot [ʒigo] *m* leg of lamb, leg of mutton; **à gigot** leg-of-mutton (*sleeve*)

gigue [ʒig] *f* jig; haunch (*of venison*); (coll) leg; (slang) long-legged gawky girl

gilet [ʒilɛ] *m* vest; **gilet de sauvetage** life jacket; **gilet pare-balles** bulletproof vest; **pleurer dans le gilet de qn** (coll) to cry on s.o.'s shoulder

gimmick [gimik] *m* gadget

gingembre [ʒɛ̃ʒɑ̃br] *m* ginger

girafe [ʒiraf] *f* giraffe

giration [ʒirɑsjɔ̃] *f* gyration

girl [gœrl] *f* chorus girl

girofle [ʒirɔfl] *m* clove

giroflée [ʒirɔfle] *f* gillyflower

giron [ʒirɔ̃] *m* lap; bosom (*of the Church*)

girouette [ʒirwɛt] *f* weather vane

gisement [ʒizmɑ̃] *m* deposit; lode, seam; (naut) bearing; **gisement de pétrole** oil field

gi·tan [ʒitɑ̃] **-tane** [tan] *adj & mf* gypsy

gîte [ʒit] *m* lodging; lair, cover; deposit (*of ore*); **gîte à la noix** round steak ‖ *f* (naut) list; **donner de la gîte** to heel

gîter [ʒite] *intr* to lodge; lie, couch; perch; (naut) to list, heel ‖ *ref* to find shelter

givre [ʒivr] *m* rime, hoarfrost

givrer [ʒivre] *tr* to frost

glabre [glɑbr] *adj* beardless

glaçage [glasaʒ] *m* icing (*on cake*)

glace [glas] *f* ice; ice cream; mirror; plate glass; car window; glaze, icing; flaw (*of gem*); **être de glace** (fig) to be hard as stone; **glace au sirop** sundae; **glace panachée** Neapolitan ice cream; **rompre la glace** (fig) to break the ice

gla·cé -cée [glase] *adj* frozen; iced, chilled; icy, frosty; glazed, glossy

glacer [glase] §51 *tr* to freeze; chill; glaze; ice (*a cake*)

glacerie [glasri] *f* glass factory

glaciaire [glasjɛr] *adj* glacial

gla·cial -ciale [glasjal] *adj* (*pl* **-cials**) glacial

glacier [glasje] *m* glacier; ice-cream man

glacière [glasjɛr] *f* icehouse; icebox; freezer

glacis [glasi] *m* slope; ramp; (mil) glacis; (painting) glaze; (pol) buffer states

glaçon [glasɔ̃] *m* icicle; ice cube; ice floe; (fig) cold fish, iceberg

glaçure [glasyr] *f* (ceramics) glaze

gladiateur [gladjatœr] *m* gladiator

glaïeul [glajœl] *m* gladiola

glaire [glɛr] *f* white of egg; mucus

glaise [glɛz] *f* clay, loam

glaisière [glɛzjɛr] *f* clay pit

glaive [glɛv] *m* (lit) sword

gland [glɑ̃] *m* acorn; tassel

glande [glɑ̃d] *f* gland

glane [glan] *f* gleaning; cluster

glaner [glane] *tr* to glean

glanure [glanyr] *f* gleaning

glapir [glapir] *intr* to yelp, yap

glas [glɑ] *m* knell, tolling

glasnost [glasnɔst] *m* glasnost

glauque [glok] *adj & m* blue-green

glèbe [glɛb] *f* clod (*sod*); soil (*land*)

glène [glɛn] *f* (anat) socket; (naut) coil of rope

glissade [glisad] *f* slip; sliding; (dancing) glide; **glissade de terre** landslide; **glissade sur l'aile** (aer) sideslip; **glissade sur la queue** (aer) tail dive

glis·sant [glisɑ̃] **-sante** [sɑ̃t] *adj* slippery

glissement [glismɑ̃] *m* sliding; gliding; **glissement de terrain** landslide

glisser [glise] *tr* to slip; drop (*a word into s.o.'s ear*) ‖ *intr* to slip; slide; skid; glide ‖ *ref* to slip

glissière [glisjɛr] *f* slide, groove; **à glissière** sliding; zippered; **glissière de sécurité** guard rail

glissoire [gliswar] *f* slide (*on ice or snow*)

glo·bal -bale [glɔbal] *adj* (*pl* **-baux** [bo]) global; lump (*sum*)

globe [glɔb] *m* globe; **globe de feu** fireball; **globe de l'œil** eyeball

globule [glɔbyl] *m* globule; (physiol) corpuscle

gloire [glwar] *f* glory; pride; halo; **pour la gloire** for fun, for nothing; **se faire gloire de** to glory in

gloriette [glɔrjɛt] *f* arbor, summerhouse

glo·rieux [glɔrjø] **-rieuse** [rjøz] *adj* glorious; blessed; vain

glorifier [glɔrifje] *tr* to glorify ‖ §97 *ref*—**se glorifier de** to glory in

gloriole [glɔrjɔl] *f* vainglory

glose [gloz] *f* gloss; (coll) gossip

gloser [gloze] *intr* (coll) to gossip

glossaire [glɔsɛr] *m* glossary

glotte [glɔt] *f* glottis

glouglou [gluglu] *m* gurgle, glug; gobble-gobble; coo (*of dove*)

glouglouter [gluglute] *intr* to gurgle; gobble (*said of turkey*)

glousser [gluse] *intr* to cluck; chuckle

glou·ton [glutɔ̃] **-tonne** [tɔn] *adj* gluttonous ‖ *mf* glutton ‖ *m* (zool) glutton, wolverine

gloutonnerie [glutɔnri] *f* gluttony

glu [gly] *f* birdlime; (coll) trap

gluant [glyɑ̃] **gluante** [glyɑ̃t] *adj* sticky, gummy; (fig) tenacious

glucose [glykoz] *m* glucose

glycérine [gliserin] *f* glycerine

gnognote [ɲɔɲɔt] *f* (coll) junk

gnome [gnom] *m* gnome

gnomon [gnɔmɔ̃] *m* sundial

gnon [ɲɔ̃] *m* (slang) blow, punch

go [go]—**tout de go** (coll) straight off, at once

goal [gol] *m* goalkeeper

gobelet [gɔblɛ] *m* cup, tumbler, mug; **gobelets utilisés** (public sign) used paper drinking cups

gobe-mouches [gɔbmuʃ] *m invar* (zool) flycatcher; (fig) sucker, gull

gober [gɔbe] *tr* to gulp down, gobble; suck (*an egg*); (coll) to swallow, be a sucker for

goberger [gɔbɛrʒe] §38 *ref* (coll) to guzzle; (coll) to live in comfort

gobeter [gɔbte] §34 *tr* to plaster, fill in the cracks of

go·beur [gɔbœr] **-beuse** [bøz] *mf* (coll) sucker, gullible person

godet [gɔdɛ] *m* cup; basin; bucket (*of water wheel*); (bot) calyx; **à godets** flared

godille [gɔdij] *f* scull, oar; **à la godille** without rhyme or reason, erratically

godiller [gɔdije] *intr* to scull

godillot [gɔdijo] *m* (slang) clodhopper (*shoe*)

goéland [gɔelɑ̃] *m* seal gull

goélette [gɔelɛt] *f* (naut) schooner

goémon [gɔemɔ̃] *m* seaweed

gogo [gɔgo] *m* (coll) sucker, gull; **à gogo** (coll) galore

gogue·nard [gɔgnar] **-narde** [nard] *adj* jeering, mocking

goguenarder [gɔgnarde] *intr* to jeer

goguette [gɔgɛt] *f*—**en goguette** (coll) tipsy

goinfre [gwɛ̃fr] *m* glutton, guzzler

goitre [gwatr] *m* goiter

golf [gɔlf] *m* golf

golfe [gɔlf] *m* gulf

golfeur [gɔlfœr] *m* golfer

gomme [gɔm] *f* gum; eraser; **gomme à claquer** bubble gum; **gomme à mâcher** chewing gum; **gomme d'épinette** spruce gum; **gomme de sapin** balsam; **gomme élastique** India rubber; **mettre la gomme** (slang) to speed it up

gomme-laque [gɔmlak] *f* (*pl* **gommes-laques**) shellac

gommelaquer [gɔmlake] *tr* to shellac

gommer [gɔme] *tr* to gum; erase ‖ *intr* to stick, gum up

gond [gɔ̃] *m* hinge; **sortir de ses gonds** (coll) to fly off the handle

gondole [gɔ̃dɔl] *f* gondola

gondoler [gɔ̃dɔle] *intr & ref* to buckle up

gondolier [gɔ̃dɔlje] *m* gondolier

gonfalon [gɔ̃falɔ̃] *m* pennant

gonflement [gɔ̃fləmɑ̃] *m* swelling

gonfler [gɔ̃fle] *tr* to swell, inflate ‖ *intr* to swell up, puff up ‖ *ref* to become inflated; (coll) to swell up with pride

gonfleur [gɔ̃flœr] *m* tire pump

gong [gɔ̃g] *m* gong

gonococcie [gɔnokɔksi] *f* gonorrhea

goret [gɔrɛ] *m* piglet; (coll) slob

gorge [gɔrʒ] *f* throat; bust, breasts (*of woman*); gorge; **à pleine gorge** or **à gorge déployée** at the top of one's voice; **avoir la gorge serrée** to have a lump in one's throat; **faire des gorges chaudes de** (coll) to scoff at; to gloat over; **rendre gorge** to make restitution

gorger [gɔrʒe] §38 tr & ref to gorge, stuff

gorille [gɔrij] *m* gorilla; (slang) strong-arm man, bodyguard; (slang) bouncer (*in a night club*)

gosier [gozje] *m* throat, gullet; **à plein gosier** loudly, lustily; **gosier serré** with one's heart in one's mouth; **s'humecter** or **se rincer le gosier** (slang) to wet one's whistle

gosse [gɔs] *mf* (coll) kid, youngster

gothique [gɔtik] *adj* Gothic ‖ *m* Gothic (*language*); Gothic art ‖ *f* black letter, Old English

gouailler [gwɑje] *tr* to jeer at ‖ *intr* to jeer

gouape [gwap] *f* (slang) hoodlum, blackguard

gouaper [gwape] *intr* (slang) to lead a disreputable life

goudron [gudrɔ̃] *m* tar; **goudron de houille** coal tar

goudronner [gudrɔne] *tr* to tar

gouffre [gufr] *m* gulf, abyss; whirlpool

gouge [guʒ] *f* gouge; harlot

gouger [guʒe] §38 *tr* to gouge

gouine [gwin] *f* (slang) dyke (*homosexual woman*)

goujat [guʒa] *m* boor, cad

goujon [guʒɔ̃] *m* gudgeon, pin; pintle (*of hinge*); dowel; (ichth) gudgeon; **taquiner le goujon** to go fishing

goulasch [gulaʃ] *m & f* goulash

goule [gul] *f* ghoul

goulet [gulɛ] *m* narrows, sound; **goulet d'étranglement** bottleneck

goulot [gulo] *m* neck (*of bottle*); **boire au goulot** to drink right out of the bottle

gou·lu -lue [guly] *adj* gluttonous

goupil [gupi] *m* (obs) fox

goupille [gupij] *f* pin; **goupille fendue** cotter pin

goupiller [gupije] *tr* to cotter; (slang) to contrive, wangle

goupillon [gupijɔ̃] *m* bottle brush; sprinkler (*for holy water*); **goupillon nettoie-pipes** pipe cleaner

gourd [gur] **gourde** [gurd] *adj* numb (*with cold*) ‖ *adj fem* (coll) dumb ‖ *f* gourd; canteen, metal flask; (coll) dumbbell

gourdin [gurdɛ̃] *m* cudgel

gourgandine [gurgɑ̃din] *f* (hist) low-necked bodice; (coll) trollop

gour·mand [gurmɑ̃] **-mande** [mɑ̃d] *adj & mf* gourmand, gourmet

gourmander [gurmɑ̃de] *tr* to bawl out

gourmandise [gurmɑ̃diz] *f* gluttony; love of good food; **gourmandises** delicacies

gourme [gurm] *f* impetigo; **jeter sa gourme** (coll) to sow one's wild oats

gour·mé -mée [gurme] *adj* stiff, stuckup

gourmet [gurmɛ] *m* gourmet

gourmette [gurmɛt] *f* curb (*of harness*); curb watch chain

gousse [gus] *f* pod; clove (*of garlic*)

gousset [gusɛ] *m* vest pocket; fob, watch pocket (*in trousers*)

goût [gu] *m* taste; flavor; sense of taste; **au goût du jour** up to date

goûter [gute] *m* afternoon snack ‖ *tr* to taste; sample; relish, enjoy ‖ *intr* to have a bite to eat; **goûter à** to sample, try; **goûter de** (coll) to try out (*e.g., a trade*)

goutte [gut] *f* drop, drip; (pathol) gout; **boire la goutte** (coll) to take a nip of brandy; **la goutte d'eau qui a fait déborder le vase** the straw which broke the camel's back; **ne . . . goutte** §90 (used

only with **comprendre, connaître, entendre,** and **voir**) (archaic & hum) not at all, e.g., **je n'y vois goutte** I don't see at all; **tomber goutte à goutte** to drip
goutte-à-goutte [gutagut] *m invar* (med) dropping bottle (*for intravenous drip*); (med) I.V. stand
gouttelette [gutlɛt] *f* droplet
goutter [gute] *intr* to drip
gouttière [gutjɛr] *f* eavestrough, gutter; (med) splint
gouvernail [guvɛrnɑj] *m* rudder, helm; **gouvernail de profondeur** (aer) elevator
gouver·nant [guvɛrnɑ̃] **-nante** [nɑ̃t] *adj* governing ‖ **gouvernants** *mpl* powers that be, rulers ‖ *f* governess; housekeeper
gouverne [guvɛrn] *f* guidance; **gouvernes** (aer) controls; **pour votre gouverne** for your guidance
gouvernement [guvɛrnəmɑ̃] *m* government; **gouvernement fantoche** puppet government
gouvernemen·tal -tale [guvɛrnəmɑ̃tal] *adj* (*pl* **-taux** [to]) governmental
gouverner [guvɛrne] *tr* to govern, control; steer; manage with care ‖ *intr* to govern; (naut) to answer to the helm
gouverneur [guvɛrnœr] *m* governor; tutor; director (*e.g., of a bank*)
goyave [gɔjav] *f* guava
goyavier [gɔjavje] *m* guava tree
Graal [gral] *m* Grail
grabat [grabɑ] *m* pallet, straw bed
grâce [grɑs] *f* grace; **de bonne grâce** willingly; **de grâce** for mercy's sake; **de mauvaise grâce** unwillingly; **faire grâce à** to pardon; to spare; **faites-moi la grâce de** be kind enough to; **grâce!** mercy!; **grâce à** thanks to
gracier [grasje] *tr* to reprieve
gra·cieux [grasjø] **-cieuse** [sjøz] *adj* gracious; graceful
gracile [grasil] *adj* slender, slim
gradation [gradɑsjɔ̃] *f* gradation
grade [grad] *m* grade; rank; degree (*in school*); **en prendre pour son grade** (coll) to get called down
gra·dé -dée [grade] *adj* noncommissioned ‖ *mf* noncommissioned officer
gradient [gradjɑ̃] *m* gradient
gradin [gradɛ̃] *m* tier
graduation [gradɥasjɔ̃] *f* graduation
gra·dué -uée [gradɥe] *adj* graduated (*scale*); graded (*lessons*) ‖ *mf* graduate
gra·duel -duelle [gradɥɛl] *adj & m* gradual
graduer [gradɥe] *tr* to graduate
grailler [grɑje] *intr* to speak hoarsely; sound the horn to recall the dogs
grain [grɛ̃] *m* grain; particle, speck; bean; squall; **grain de beauté** beauty spot, mole; **grain de raisin** grape; **grains** grain, cereals; **veiller au grain** (fig) to be on one's guard
graine [grɛn] *f* seed; **graine d'anis** aniseed; **mauvaise graine** (coll) incorrigible youth; **monter en graine** to run to seed; to soon be on the shelf (*said of young girl*); (coll)

to grow; **prendre de la graine de** (coll) to follow the example of
graissage [grɛsaʒ] *m* (aut) lubrication
graisse [grɛs] *f* grease; fat; mother (*of wine*)
graisser [grɛse], [grese] *tr* to grease; lubricate; get grease stains on; **graisser la patte à qn** (coll) to grease s.o.'s palm
grais·seux [grɛsø] **-seuse** [søz] *adj* greasy
grammaire [gramɛr] *f* grammar
grammai·rien [gramɛrjɛ̃] **-rienne** [rjɛn] *mf* grammarian
grammati·cal -cale [gramatikal] *adj* (*pl* **-caux** [ko]) grammatical
gramme [gram] *m* gram
grand [grɑ̃] **grande** [grɑ̃d] *adj* tall, e.g., **un homme grand** a tall man ‖ (when standing before noun) *adj* large; great; important; tall; high (*priest; mass; society; explosive*), vain, empty (*words*); broad (*daylight*); grand (*dignitary; officer; lady*); main (*road*); long (*arms or legs*); greater, e.g., **le Grand Londres** Greater London; (fig) big (*heart*) ‖ *m* adult, grownup; grandee, noble; **en grand** life-size; on a grand scale; enlarged (*copy*); wide (*open*); **grands et petits** young and old ‖ **grand** *adv*—**voir grand** to see big, to envisage great projects
grand-chose [grɑ̃ʃoz] *mf invar*—**pas grand-chose** (coll) nobody, person of no importance ‖ *adv*—**pas grand-chose** not much
grand-duc [grɑ̃dyk] *m* (*pl* **grands-ducs**) grand duke
grand-duché [grɑ̃dyʃe] *m* (*pl* **grands-duchés**) grand duchy
Grande-Bretagne [grɑ̃dbrətaɲ] *f* Great Britain; **la Grande-Bretagne** Great Britain
grande-duchesse [grɑ̃dədyʃɛs] *f* (*pl* **grandes-duchesses**) grand duchess
grande·let -lette [grɑ̃dlɛ] *adj* tall for his or her age
grandement [grɑ̃dmɑ̃] *adv* highly; handsomely; **se tromper grandement** to be very mistaken
grand-erre [grɑ̃tɛr] *adv* at full speed
gran·det [grɑ̃dɛ] **-dette** [dɛt] *adj* rather big; rather tall
grandeur [grɑ̃dœr] *f* size; height; greatness; (astr) magnitude
grandiose [grɑ̃djoz] *adj* grandiose
grandir [grɑ̃dir] *tr* to enlarge; increase ‖ *intr* to grow; grow up
grandissement [grɑ̃dismɑ̃] *m* magnification, enlargement; growth
grand-livre [grɑ̃livr] *m* (*pl* **grands-livres**) ledger
grand-maman [grɑ̃mamɑ̃] *f* (*pl* **-mamans**) grandma
grand-mère [grɑ̃mɛr] *f* (*pl* **-mères** or **grands-mères**) grandmother; (coll) old lady
grand-messe [grɑ̃mɛs] *f* (pl **-messes**) high mass
grand-oncle [grɑ̃tɔ̃kl] *m* (*pl* **grands-oncles**) granduncle
Grand-Orient [grɑ̃tɔrjɑ̃] *m* grand lodge

grand-papa [grɑ̃papa] m (pl **grands-papas**) grandpa

grand-peine [grɑ̃pɛn]—**à grand-peine** with great difficulty

grand-père [grɑ̃pɛr] m (pl **grands-pères**) grandfather

grand-route [grɑ̃rut] f (pl **-routes**) highway

grand-rue [grɑ̃ry] f (pl **-rues**) main street

Grands Lacs [grɑ̃lak] mpl Great Lakes

grands-parents [grɑ̃parɑ̃] mpl grandparents

grand-tante [grɑ̃tɑ̃t] f (pl **-tantes**) grandaunt

grange [grɑ̃ʒ] f barn

granit [grani], [granit] m granite

granite [granit] m granite

granulaire [granylɛr] adj granular

granule [granyl] m granule

granu·lé -lée [granyle] adj granulated ‖ m little pill; medicine in granulated form

granuler [granyle] tr & ref to granulate

graphie [grafi] f spelling

graphique [grafik] adj graphic(al) ‖ m graph

graphite [grafit] m graphite

grappe [grap] f bunch, cluster; string (of onions); **une grappe humaine** a bunch of people

grappillage [grapijaʒ] m gleaning; (coll) graft

grappiller [grapije] tr & intr (in vineyard) to glean; (coll) to pilfer

grappillon [grapijɔ̃] m little bunch

grappin [grapɛ̃] m grapnel; **jeter** or **mettre le grappin sur qn** (coll) to get one's hooks into s.o.

gras [grɑ] **grasse** [grɑs] adj fat; greasy; rich (soil); carnival (days); smutty (stories); (typ) bold-faced ‖ m fatty part; calf (of leg); foggy weather; **au gras** with meat sauce; **faire gras** to eat meat ‖ **gras** adv—**parler gras** to speak with uvular r; to tell smutty stories

gras-double [grɑdubl] m (pl **-doubles**) tripe

grassement [grɑsmɑ̃] adv comfortably; generously, handsomely

grasseyer [grɑseje] §32 tr to make (one's r's) uvular ‖ intr to speak with uvular r

grassouil·let -lette [grɑsujɛ] **-lette** [jɛt] adj (coll) plump, chubby

gratification [gratifikasjɔ̃] f tip, gratuity

gratifier [gratifje] tr to favor, reward; **gratifier qn de q.ch.** to bestow s.th. upon s.o.

gratin [gratɛ̃] m cooking au gratin; dish of food prepared au gratin; friction surface (of a matchbox); (culin) crust; (coll) upper crust; **au gratin** au gratin (breaded and/or with grated cheese)

gratiner [gratine] tr to cook au gratin ‖ intr to brown, crisp

gratis [gratis] adv gratis

gratitude [gratityd] f gratitude

gratte [grat] f scraper; (coll) graft

gratte-ciel [gratsjɛl] m invar skyscraper

gratte-cul [gratky] m invar (bot) hip

gratte-dos [gratdo] m invar back scratcher

gratte-papier [gratpapje] m invar (coll) pencil pusher, office drudge

gratte-pieds [gratpje] m invar shoe scraper

gratter [grate] tr to scratch; scratch out; scrape up, scrape together; itch; (coll) to pocket ‖ intr to knock gently ‖ ref to scratch

grattoir [gratwar] m scraper; knife eraser

gra·tuit [gratɥi] **-tuite** [tɥit] adj free of charge; gratuitous; unfounded

gratuité [gratɥite] f gratuity

grave [grav], [grɑv] adj grave; low (frequency); (mus) bass; (mus) flat

grave·leux [gravlə] **-leuse** [ləz] adj gravelly, gritty; smutty, licentious

gravelle [gravɛl] f (pathol) gravel

graver [grave] tr to engrave; cut (a phonograph record)

graveur [gravœr] m engraver; etcher

gravier [gravje] m gravel

gravillons [gravijɔ̃] mpl gravel (on roadway)

gravir [gravir] tr to climb, climb up

gravitation [gravitasjɔ̃] f gravitation

gravité [gravite] f gravity

graviter [gravite] intr to gravitate

gravure [gravyr] f engraving; etching; cutting (of phonograph record)

gré [gre] m will; **à son gré** to one's liking; **bon gré mal gré** willy-nilly; **de bon gré** willingly; **de gré à gré** by mutual consent; **de gré ou de force** willy-nilly; **savoir (bon) gré de** to be grateful for; **savoir mauvais gré de** to be displeased with

grec grecque [grɛk] adj Greek; classic (profile) ‖ m Greek (language) ‖ f Greek fret ‖ (cap) mf Greek

Grèce [grɛs] f Greece; **la Grèce** Greece

gre·din [grədɛ̃] **-dine** [din] mf scoundrel

gréement [gremɑ̃] m (naut) rigging

gréer [gree] tr (naut) to rig

greffe [grɛf] m (jur) office of the court clerk ‖ f grafting; (hort, med) graft; **greffe du cœur** heart transplant; **greffe du rein** kidney transplant

greffer [grɛfe] tr to graft; add ‖ ref to be added

greffier [grɛfje] m clerk of court, recorder; court reporter

greffon [grɛfɔ̃] m (hort) graft; (surg) transplant

grégaire [gregɛr] adj gregarious

grège [grɛʒ] adj raw (silk) ‖ f raw silk

grégo·rien [gregɔrjɛ̃] **-rienne** [rjɛn] adj Gregorian

grêle [grɛl] adj slender, slim; thin, high-pitched ‖ f hail; (fig) shower

grê·lé -lée [grɛle] adj pockmarked

grêler [grɛle] tr to damage by hail; pockmark ‖ intr (fig) to rain down thick; **il grêle** it is hailing

grêlon [grɛlɔ̃] m hailstone

grelot [grəlo] m sleigh bell

grelottement [grəlɔtmɑ̃] m shivering, trembling; jingle, jingling

grelotter [grəlɔte] intr to shiver, tremble; jingle

grenade [grənad] _f_ grenade; (bot) pomegranate; **grenade à main** hand grenade; **grenade éclairante** flare; **grenade lacrymogène** tear bomb; **grenade sous-marine** depth charge

grenadier [grənadje] _m_ pomegranate tree; (mil) grenadier

grenadine [grənadin] _f_ grenadine

grenaille [grənɑj] _f_ shot; **grenaille de plomb** buckshot

grenailler [grənɑje] _tr_ to granulate

grenat [grəna] _adj invar & m_ garnet

grenier [grənje] _m_ attic, loft; granary

grenouille [grənuj] _f_ frog; **grenouille mugissante** or **taureau** bullfrog; **manger la grenouille** (coll) to make off with the money, to abscond

grenouillère [grənujɛr] _f_ marsh

gre·nu -nue [grəny] _adj_ full of grain; grainy (_leather_); granular (_marble_) ‖ _m_ graininess; granularity

grès [grɛ] _m_ gritstone, sandstone; stoneware; terra cotta (_for drainpipes_)

grésil [grezil] _m_ sleet

grésillement [grezijmɑ̃] _m_ sizzling; chirping (_of cricket_)

grésiller [grezije] _tr_ to scorch, shrivel up ‖ _intr_ to sizzle, sputter; **il grésille** it is sleeting

grève [grɛv] _f_ beach; strike; (_armor_) greave; **faire (la) grève** to strike; **faire la grève de la faim** to go on a hunger strike; **grève avec occupation de l'usine, grève avec occupation des locaux** sitdown strike; **grève de solidarité** sympathy strike; **grève du zèle** work-to-rule action, job action (_rigid application of rules_); **grève improvisée, grève inattendue, grève surprise** walkout; **grève perlée** slowdown; **grève sauvage, grève spontanée** wildcat strike; **grève sur le tas** sitdown strike; **grève tournante** strike in one industry at a time or for several hours at a time; **se mettre en grève** to go on strike

grever [grəve] §2 _tr_ to burden; assess (_property_); **grever de** to burden with

gréviste [grevist] _mf_ striker

gribouillage [gribujaʒ] _m_ (coll) scribble, scrawl; (coll) daub (_in painting_)

gribouiller [gribuje] _tr_ (coll) to scribble off (_a note_) ‖ _intr_ (coll) to scribble, scrawl; (coll) to daub

grief [grijɛf] _m_ grievance, complaint; **faire grief de q.ch. à qn** to complain to s.o. about s.th.

grièvement [grijɛvmɑ̃] _adv_ seriously, badly

griffe [grif] _f_ claw, talon; signature stamp; (bot) tendril; (mach) hook, grip; **faire ses griffes** to sharpen its claws (_said of cat_); **griffe à papiers** paper clip; **porter la griffe de** to carry the stamp of; **tomber sous la griffe de** (coll) to fall into the clutches of

griffer [grife] _tr_ to claw, scratch

griffon [grifɔ̃] _m_ griffin

griffonner [grifɔne] _tr_ to scrawl; (coll) to scribble off (_a letter_)

grignoter [griɲɔte] _tr_ to nibble on or at; wear down (_e.g., the enemy_) ‖ _intr_ (coll) to make a little profit, get a cut

gril [gril] _m_ gridiron, grid, grill; (theat) upper flies; **être sur le gril** (coll) to be on tenterhooks

grillade [grijad] _f_ grilled meat; broiling

grillage [grijaʒ] _m_ grating, latticework, trellis; broiling; roasting; toasting; burning out (_of a light bulb_); (tex) singeing

grille [grij] _f_ grille; grate, grating; bars; railing; gate; squares (_of crossword puzzle_); grid (_of storage battery and vacuum tube_); **grille d'entrée** iron gate; **grille des salaires** salary schedule

grille-pain [grijpɛ̃] _m invar_ toaster

grille-pain-four [grijpɛ̃fur] _m_ toaster oven

griller [grije] _tr_ to grill, broil; put a grill on; roast (_coffee_); toast (_bread_); burn out (_a fuse, lamp, electric iron, etc._); singe; scorch; nip (_a bud, as the frost does_) ‖ _intr_ to grill; toast; burn out; **griller de** to long to

grilloir [grijwar] _m_ roaster; (culin) broiler

grillon [grijɔ̃] _m_ cricket

grimace [grimas] _f_ grimace; **faire des grimaces** to make faces; smirk, simper; be full of wrinkles

grimacer [grimase] §51 _intr_ to grimace; make wrong creases

grime [grim] _m_ dotard, old fogey

grimer [grime] _tr_ to make up (_an actor_) ‖ _ref_ to make up

grimper [grɛ̃pe] _tr_ to climb ‖ _intr_ to climb; **grimper à** or **sur** to climb up on

grimpe·reau [grɛ̃pro] _m_ (_pl_ **-reaux**) (orn) tree creeper

grim·peur [grɛ̃pœr] **-peuse** [pøz] _adj_ climbing ‖ _m_ climber

grincement [grɛ̃smɑ̃] _m_ grating

grincer [grɛ̃se] §51 _tr_ to gnash, grit (_the teeth_) ‖ _intr_ to grate, grind, creak; scratch (_said of pen_)

grin·cheux [grɛ̃ʃø] **-cheuse** [ʃøz] _adj_ grumpy ‖ _mf_ grumbler, sorehead

ginga·let [grɛ̃gale] **-lette** [lɛt] _adj_ weak, puny ‖ _m_ (coll) weakling, shrimp

griot [grijo] **griotte** [grijɔt] _mf_ witch doctor ‖ _m_ seconds (_in milling grain_) ‖ _f_ sour cherry

grippe [grip] _f_ grippe; **prendre en grippe** to take a dislike to

grippeminaud [gripmino] _m_ (coll) smoothly, hypocrite

gripper [gripe] _tr_ to snatch; (slang) to steal ‖ _intr_ (mach) to jam ‖ _ref_ to get stuck

grippe-sou [gripsu] _m_ (_pl_ **-sou** or **-sous**) (coll) tightwad, skinflint

gris [gri] **grise** [griz] _adj_ gray; cloudy; brown (_paper_); (coll) tipsy

grisailler [grizaje] _tr_ to paint gray ‖ _intr_ to turn gray

grisâtre [grizɑtr] _adj_ grayish

griser [grize] _tr_ to paint gray; (coll) to intoxicate; **les succès l'ont grisé** (coll) success has gone to his head ‖ _ref_ to get tipsy; **se griser de** (coll) to revel in

griserie [grizri] *f* intoxication

grisette [grizɛt] *f* gay working girl

gris-gris [grigri] *m* lucky charm

grisonner [grizɔne] *intr* to turn gray

grisotte [grizɔt] *f* clock (*in stocking*)

grisou [grizu] *m* firedamp

grive [griv] *f* thrush; **grive mauvis** song thrush; **grive migratoire** (*Turdus migratorius*) robin

grive·lé -lée [grivle] *adj* speckled

grivèlerie [grivɛlri] *f* sneaking out without paying the check

gri·vois [grivwa] **-voise** [vwaz] *adj* spicy, off-color

grizzly [grizli] *m* grizzly bear

Groënland [grɔɛnlɑ̃d] *m*—**le Groënland** Greenland

grog [grɔg] *m* grog

gro·gnard [grɔɲar] **-gnarde** [ɲard] *adj* grumbling ‖ *mf* grumbler

grogner [grɔɲe] *intr* to grunt, growl; grumble, grouch

gro·gnon [grɔɲɔ̃] **-gnonne** [ɲɔn] *adj* grouchy, grumbling ‖ *mf* grouch, grumbler

grognonner [grɔɲɔne] *intr* to grunt; be a complainer, whine

groin [grwɛ̃] *m* snout; (coll) ugly mug

grommeler [grɔmle] §34 *tr* & *intr* to mutter, grumble; growl

grondement [grɔ̃dmɑ̃] *m* growl; rumble

gronder [grɔ̃de] §97 *tr* to scold ‖ *intr* to scold; growl; grumble

gron·deur [grɔ̃dœr] **-deuse** [døz] *adj* scolding; grumbling ‖ *mf* grumbler

groom [grum] *m* bellhop, pageboy

gros [gro] **grosse** [gros] *adj* big (*with child*); heavy (*heart*) ‖ (when standing before noun) *adj* big, large, bulky; coarse; plain (*common sense*); main (*walls*); high (*stakes*); rich (*merchant*); booming (*voice*); bad (*weather*); heavy, rough (*sea*); swear (words) ‖ *m* bulk, main part; **en gros** wholesale; roughly, without going into detail; **faire le gros et le détail** to deal in wholesale and retail ‖ *f* see **grosse** ‖ **gros** *adv* much, a great deal; (fig) probably

gros-bec [grobɛk] *m* (*pl* **-becs**) grosbeak

groseille [grozɛj] *f* currant; **groseille à maquereau** gooseberry

groseillier [grozeje] *m* currant bush

Gros-Jean [grozɑ̃] *m*—**être Gros-Jean comme devant** to be in the same fix again

gros-porteur [groportœr] *m* (*pl* **-porteurs**) (aer) jumbo jet

grosse [gros] *f* fat woman; (com) gross; (law) engrossed copy

grosserie [grosri] *f* silver dishes

grossesse [grosɛs] *f* pregnancy

grosseur [grosœr] *f* size; swelling, tumor

gros·sier [grosje] **-sière** [sjɛr] *adj* coarse; crude, rude; vulgar, ribald; glaring (*error*)

grossièrement [grosjɛrmɑ̃] *adv* grossly

grossièreté [grosjɛrte] *f* coarseness, grossness, vulgarity

grossir [grosir] *tr* to enlarge; increase ‖ *intr* to grow larger; put on weight

grossis·sant [grosisɑ̃] **-sante** [sɑ̃t] *adj* swelling; magnifying (*glasses*)

grossiste [grosist] *m* wholesaler, jobber

grotesque [grɔtɛsk] *adj* grotesque ‖ *mf* grotesque person ‖ *m* grotesque ‖ *f* grotesque (*ornament*)

grotte [grɔt] *f* grotto

grouillement [grujmɑ̃] *m* swarming; rumbling

grouiller [gruje] *intr* to swarm; **grouiller de** to teem with ‖ *ref* (slang) to get a move on

grouillot [grujo] *m* (coll) gofer, errand boy

groupe [grup] *m* group; (mach & mil) unit; **groupe de pression** lobby; **groupe d'experts** think tank; **groupe franc** (mil) commando; **groupe sanguin** blood type

groupement [grupmɑ̃] *m* grouping; organization

grouper [grupe] *tr* & *ref* to group

gruau [gryo] *m* (*pl* **gruaux**) groats; (culin) gruel; (orn) small crane

grue [gry] *f* crane; (orn) crane; (coll) tart

gruger [gryʒe] §38 *tr* to sponge on, exploit; crunch

grume [grym] *f* bark; **en grume** rough (*timber*)

gru·meau [grymo] *m* (*pl* **-meaux**) gob; curd

grumeler [grymle] §34 *intr* to curdle, clot

gruyère [gryjɛr] *m* Gruyère cheese

guatémaltèque [gwatemaltɛk] *adj* Guatemalan ‖ (*cap*) *mf* Guatemalan

gué [ge] *m* ford, crossing; **sonder le gué** (coll) to see how the land lies ‖ *interj* hurrah!

guéable [geabl] *adj* fordable

guéer [gee] *tr* to ford; water (*a horse*)

guelte [gɛlt] *f* commission, percentage

guenille [gənij] *f* ragged garment; **en guenilles** in tatters

guenon [gənɔ̃] *f* female monkey; long-tailed monkey; (coll) hag, old bag

guépard [gepar] *m* cheetah

guêpe [gɛp] *f* wasp

guère [gɛr] §90 *adv* hardly ever; **ne . . . guère** hardly, scarcely; hardly ever; not very; **ne . . . guère de** hardly any; **ne . . . guère que** hardly any but; hardly anyone but; **ne . . . plus guère** hardly ever any more; not much longer

guères [gɛr] *adv* (poetic) var of **guère**

guéret [gerɛ] *m* fallow land

guéridon [geridɔ̃] *m* pedestal table

guérilla [gerija] *f* guerrilla warfare

guérillero [gerijero] *m* guerrilla

guérir [gerir] *tr* to cure ‖ *intr* to get well; get better; heal ‖ *ref* to cure oneself; recover

guérison [gerizɔ̃] *f* cure, healing; recovery

guérissable [gerisabl] *adj* curable

guéris·seur [gerisœr] **-seuse** [søz] *mf* healer; quack

guérite [gerit] *f* sentry box; (rr) signal box; **guérite téléphonique** call box

guerre [gɛr] *f* war; **de guerre lasse** for the sake of peace and quiet; **être de bonne guerre** to be fair, to be cricket; **guerre à outrance** all-out war; **Guerre de Troie** Trojan War; **guerre d'usure** war of attrition; **guerre éclair** blitzkrieg; **guerre froide** cold war; **guerre presse-bouton** push-button war

guer·rier [gɛrje] **-rière** [rjɛr] *adj* warlike, martial ‖ *m* warrior ‖ *f* amazon

guerroyant [gɛrwajɑ̃] **guerroyante** [gɛrwajɑ̃t] *adj* warlike, bellicose

guerroyer [gɛrwaje] §47 *intr* to make war

guer·royeur [gɛrwajœr] **-royeuse** [wajøz] *adj* fighting (*spirit*) ‖ *mf* fighter

guet [gɛ] *m* watch, lookout

guet-apens [gɛtapɑ̃] *m* (*pl* **guets-apens** [gɛtapɑ̃]) ambush, trap

guêtre [gɛtr] *f* gaiter, legging

guêtrer [gɛtre] *tr & ref* to put gaiters on

guetter [gɛte] *tr* to watch; watch for; (coll) to lie in wait for

guetteur [gɛtœr] *m* lookout, sentinel

gueu·lard [gœlar] **-larde** [lard] *adj* (slang) loud-mouthed; (slang) fond of good eating ‖ *mf* gourmet; (slang) loud-mouth ‖ *m* mouth (*of blast furnace; of cannon*); (naut) megaphone

gueule [gœl] *f* mouth (*of animal; of furnace, cannon, etc.*); (slang) mouth, mug (*of person*); **avoir de la gueule** (coll) to have a certain air; **avoir la gueule de bois** (coll) to have a hangover; **fine gueule** (coll) gourmet; **gueule cassée** (coll) disabled veteran; **gueule noire** (coll) miner; **ta gueule!** (slang) shut up!

gueule-de-loup [gœldəlu] *f* (*pl* **gueules-de-loup**) (bot) snapdragon

gueuler [gœle] *tr & intr* (slang) to bellow

gueuleton [gœltɔ̃] *m* (slang) big feed

gueux [gø] **gueuse** [gøz] *adj* beggarly, wretched ‖ *mf* beggar; scamp ‖ *f* pig iron; pig (*mold*); woolen jacket; (coll) whore; **courir la gueuse** (coll) to go whoring

gugusse [gygys] *m* clown

gui [gi] *m* mistletoe; (naut) boom

guichet [giʃe] *m* window (*in post office, bank, box office, etc.*); counter (*e.g., in bank*); wicket; **guichet libre-service** automated teller

guidage [gidaʒ] *m* (rok) guidance

guide [gid] *m* guide; guidebook ‖ *f* rein; **mener la vie à grandes guides** to live extravagantly

guide-âne [gidɑn] *m* (*pl* **-âne** or **-ânes**) manual, guide

guider [gide] *tr* to guide

guidon [gidɔ̃] *m* handlebars; sight, bead (*of gun*); (naut) pennant

guigne [giɲ] *f* heart cherry; (coll) jinx

guigner [giɲe] *tr* to steal a glance at; (coll) to covet ‖ *intr* to peep

guignol [giɲɔl] *m* Punch (*puppet*); Punch and Judy show; (aer) king post

guignolet [giɲɔlɛ] *m* cherry brandy

guillaume [gijom] *m* rabbet plane; **Guillaume** William

guilledou [gijdu] *m*—**courir le guilledou** (coll) to make the rounds

guillemet [gijmɛ] *m* quotation mark; **fermer les guillemets** to close quotes; **ouvrir les guillemets** to quote

guillemeter [gijmøte] §34 *tr* to put in quotes

guiller [gije] *intr* to ferment

guille·ret [gijrɛ] **-rette** [rɛt] *adj* chipper, lively, cheerful

guillotine [gijɔtin] *f* guillotine; **à guillotine** sliding; sash (*window*)

guillotiner [gijɔtine] *tr* to guillotine

guimauve [gimov] *f* (bot) marshmallow

guimbarde [gɛ̃bard] *f* (mus) jew's-harp; (coll) jalopy

guimpe [gɛ̃p] *f* wimple

guin·dé -dée [gɛ̃de] *adj* affected, stiff

guin·deau [gɛ̃do] *m* (*pl* **-deaux**) windlass

guinder [gɛ̃de] *tr* to hoist ‖ *ref* to put on airs

guinée [gine] *f* guinea (*coin*); **Guinée** Guinea (*the region*); **la Guinée** Guinea (*the region*)

guingan [gɛ̃gɑ̃] *m* gingham

guingois [gɛ̃gwa] *m*—**de guingois** askew; lopsidedly

guinguette [gɛ̃gɛt] *f* roadside inn, roadside park

guipage [gipaʒ] *m* wrapping, lapping

guiper [gipe] *tr* to wind; cover (*a wire*)

guipure [gipyr] *f* pillow lace

guirlande [girlɑ̃d] *f* garland, wreath

guirlander [girlɑ̃de] *tr* to garland

guise [giz] *f* manner; **à sa guise** as one pleases; **en guise de** by way of

guitare [gitar] *f* guitar

guitariste [gitarist] *mf* guitarist

guppy [gypi] *m* guppy

gustation [gystasjɔ̃] *f* tasting; drinking

guttu·ral -rale [gytyral] (*pl* **-raux** [ro] **-rales**) *adj & f* guttural

Guyane [gɥijan] *f* Guyana; **la Guyane** Guyana

gymnase [ʒimnɑz] *m* gymnasium

gymnaste [ʒimnast] *mf* gymnast

gymnote [ʒimnɔt] *m* electric eel

gynécologie [ʒinekɔlɔʒi] *f* gynecology

gypse [ʒips] *m* gypsum

gyrocompas [ʒirɔkɔ̃pa] *m* gyrocompass

gyrophare [ʒirɔfar] *m* (aut) emergency light, dome light (*flashing, revolving*)

gyroscope [ʒirɔskɔp] *m* gyroscope

H, h [aʃ], *[aʃ] m invar eighth letter of the French alphabet
habile [abil] *adj* skillful; clever
habileté [abilte] *f* skill; cleverness
habiliter [abilite] *tr* to qualify, entitle
habillage [abijaʒ] *m* preparation; dressing; cover, outside surface; assembly; packaging and presentation; labeling and sealing; (mach) casing
habillement [abijmɑ̃] *m* clothing; clothes
habiller [abije] *tr* to dress; clothe; put together ‖ *intr* to be becoming, e.g., **robe qui habille bien** becoming dress ‖ *ref* to dress; get dressed; **s'habiller chez** to buy one's clothes at or from
habit [abi] *m* dress suit; habit, frock; **habit de cérémonie** or **soirée**, **habit à queue** de **pie, habit à queue de morue** tails; **habits** clothes
habitacle [abitakl] *m* (aer) cockpit; (naut) binnacle; (poetic) dwelling
habi·tant [abitɑ̃] **-tante** [tɑ̃t] *mf* inhabitant
habitat [abita] *m* habitat; living conditions, housing
habitation [abitasjɔ̃] *f* habitation; dwelling; residence; **habitation à bon marché** or **à loyer modéré** low-rent apartment
habi·té -tée [abite] *adj* inhabited; (rok) manned
habiter [abite] *tr* to live in, inhabit ‖ *intr* to live, reside
habitude [abityd] *f* habit, custom; **comme d'habitude** as usual; **d'habitude** usually
habi·tuel -tuelle [abityɛl] *adj* habitual
habituer [abitɥe] §96, §100 *tr* to accustom *ref*—**s'habituer à** to get used to
hâbler *[ɑble] *intr* to brag, to boast
hâblerie *[ɑbləri] *f* bragging
hâ·bleur *[ɑblœr] **-bleuse** [bløz] *adj* boastful ‖ *mf* braggart, boaster
hache *[aʃ] *f* ax, hatchet
ha·ché -chée *[aʃe] *adj* ground, chopped; hachured; choppy (*sea*); jerky (*style*); dotted (*line*)
hacher *[aʃe] *tr* to hack; grind, chop up; **hacher menu** to mince
hache·reau *[aʃro] *m* (*pl* **-reaux**) hatchet
hachette *[aʃɛt] *f* hatchet
hachis *[aʃi] *m* hash, forcemeat; chopped vegetables
hachisch *[aʃiʃ] *m* hashish
hachoir *[aʃwar] *m* cleaver; chopping board
hachure *[aʃyr] *f* shading
hachurer *[aʃyre] *tr* to shade, hatch
haddock *[adɔk] *m* finnan haddie
ha·gard *[agar] **-garde** [gard] *adj* haggard
haie *[ɛ] *f* hedge; hurdle; line, row
haïe *[aj] *interj* giddap!
haillon *[ajɔ̃] *m* old piece of clothing; **en haillons** in rags and tatters
haillon·neux *[ajɔnø] **-neuse** [nøz] *adj* ragged, tattered
haine *[ɛn] *f* hate
hai·neux *[ɛnø] **-neuse** [nøz] *adj* full of hate, spiteful, malevolent

haïr *[air] §33, §96, §97 *tr* to hate, detest ‖ *intr*—**haïr de** to hate to
haire *[ɛr] *f* hair shirt
haïssable *[aisabl] *adj* hateful
Haïti [aiti] *f* Haiti
haï·tien [aisjɛ̃] **-tienne** [sjɛn] *adj* Haitian ‖ (*cap*) *mf* Haitian
halcyon [alsjɔ̃] *m* (orn) kingfisher
hâle *[ɑl] *m* sun tan
haleine [alɛn] *f* breath; **avoir l'haleine courte** to be short-winded; (fig) to have little inspiration; **de longue haleine** hard, arduous (*work*); **en haleine** in good form; **hors d'haleine** out of breath; **perdre haleine** to get out of breath; **reprendre haleine** to catch one's breath; **tenir en haleine** to hold (*an audience*) breathless
halenée [alne] *f* whiff; strong breath
haler *[ale] *tr* to haul, tow
hâler *[ale] *tr* to tan
hale·tant *[altɑ̃] **-tante** [tɑ̃t] *adj* breathless, panting
haleter *[alte] §2 *intr* to pant, puff
hall *[ol] *m* lobby; hall, auditorium
halle *[al] *f* market, marketplace; exchange
hallebarde *[albard] *f* halberd; **il pleut des hallebardes** (coll) it's raining cats and dogs
hallebardier [albardje] *m* halberdier
hallier *[alje] *m* thicket
halluci·nant [allysinɑ̃[**-nante** [nɑ̃t] *adj* staggering, incredible
hallucination [allysinasjɔ̃] *f* hallucination
halo *[alo] *m* halo
halogène [alɔʒɛn] *m* halogen
halte *[alt] *f* halt; stop; (rr) flag stop, way station; **faire faire halte à** to halt ‖ *interj* halt!
halte-là *[altla] *interj* (mil) halt!
haltère [altɛr] *m* dumbbell
haltérophile [alterɔfil] *m* weight lifter
haltérophilie [alterɔfili] *f* weight lifting
hamac *[amak] *m* hammock
hamburger *[ɑburgœr], [ɑburʒe] *m* hamburger
ha·meau *[amo] *m* (*pl* **-meaux**) hamlet
hameçon [amsɔ̃] *m* hook, fishhook; (fig) bait
hammam *[ammam] *m* Turkish bath
hampe *[ɑ̃p] *f* staff, pole; shaft; downstroke; (culin) flank
hamster *[amstɛr] *m* hamster
han *[ɑ̃], [hɑ̃] *m* grunt
hanap *[anap] *m* hanap, goblet
hanche *[ɑ̃ʃ] *f* hip; haunch
hancher *[ɑ̃ʃe] *intr* to lean on one leg ‖ *ref* (mil) to stand at ease
handball *[ɑbol] *m* handball
handicap *[ɑdikap] *m* handicap
handicaper *[ɑdikape] *tr* to handicap
hangar *[ɑgar] *m* hangar; shed
hanneton *[antɔ̃] *m* June bug, chafer
hanter *[ɑte] *tr* to haunt
hantise *[ɑtiz] *f* obsession

happe *[ap] f crucible tongs; (carp) cramp, staple
happer *[ape] tr to snap up; (coll) to nab ‖ intr to stick
haquenée *[akne] f palfrey
haquet *[akɛ] m dray; **haquet à main** push-cart
harangue *[arɑ̃g] f harangue
haranguer *[arɑ̃ge] tr & intr to harangue
haras *[arɑ] m stud farm
harasser *[arase] tr to tire out
harceler *[arsəle] §2 or §34 tr to harass, harry; pester; dun
harde *[ard] f herd; leash; set (of dogs); **hardes** old clothes
har·di -die *[ardi] adj bold, daring; audacious, brazen ‖ **hardi** interj up and at them!
hardiesse *[ardjɛs] f boldness
hardiment *[ardimɑ̃] adv boldly; audaciously, brazenly
harem *[arɛm] m harem
hareng *[arɑ̃] m herring; **hareng fumé** kipper; **hareng saur** red herring; **sec comme un hareng** (coll) long and thin; **serrés comme des harengs** (coll) packed like sardines
harengère *[arɑ̃ʒɛr] f fishwife; (coll) shrew
harenguet *[arɑ̃gɛ] m sprat
hargne *[arɲ] f bad temper
har·gneux *[arɲø] **-gneuse** [ɲøz] adj bad-tempered, peevish, surly
haricot *[ariko] m bean; **haricot beurre** lima bean, butter bean; **haricot de Lima** lima bean; **haricot de mouton** haricot (stew); **haricot de Soissons** kidney bean; **haricot vert** string bean
harmonica [armɔnika] m mouth organ
harmonie [armɔni] f harmony; (mus) band
harmo·nieux [armɔnjø] **-nieuse** [njøz] adj harmonious
harmonique [armɔnik] adj harmonic
harmoniser [armɔnize] tr & ref to harmonize
harnachement *[arnaʃmɑ̃] m harness; harnessing
harnacher *[arnaʃe] tr to harness; rig out
harnais *[arnɛ] m harness
haro *[aro] m—**crier haro sur** (coll) to make a hue and cry against
harpagon [arpagɔ̃] m scrooge
harpe *[arp] f harp
harpie *[arpi] f harpy
harpiste *[arpist] mf harpist
harpon *[arpɔ̃] m harpoon
harponner *[arpɔne] tr to harpoon; (coll) to nab (e.g., a thief)
hart *[ar] f noose
hasard *[azar] m hazard, chance; **à tout hasard** just in case, come what may; **au hasard** at random; **par hasard** by chance
hasar·dé -dée *[azarde] adj hazardous
hasarder *[azarde] §96, §97 tr to risk, hazard, gamble ‖ §96 ref to venture, risk
hasar·deux *[azardø] **-deuse** [døz] adj risky, uncertain
hase *[ɑz] f doe hare

hâte *[ɑt] f haste; **à la hâte** hastily; **avoir hâte de** to be eager to; **en hâte, en toute hâte** posthaste
hâter *[ɑte] §97 tr & ref to hasten
hâ·tif *[ɑtif] **-tive** [tiv] adj premature; (hort) early
hauban *[obɑ̃] m (naut) shroud; (naut) guy
haubert *[obɛr] m coat of mail
hausse *[os] f rise, increase; block, wedge, prop; (mil) elevation, range; **jouer à la hausse** to bull the market
haussement *[osmɑ̃] m shrug
hausser *[ose] tr to raise, lift; shrug (one's shoulders) ‖ intr to rise
haussier *[osje] m bull (on the stock exchange)
haussière *[osjɛr] f (naut) hawser
haut *[o] **haute** *[ot] adj high; loud; high and mighty ‖ (when standing before noun) adj high; loud; upper, higher; extra (pay); early (antiquity, Middle Ages, etc.) ‖ m top; height; **de haut en bas** from top to bottom; **en haut** up; upstairs; **haut de casse** (typ) upper case; **haut des côtes** sparerib; **le prendre de haut** to get on one's high horse; **traiter de haut en bas** to high-hat ‖ f see **haute** ‖ **haut** adv high; up high; loudly; **haut les bras!** start working!; **haut les cœurs!** lift up your hearts!; **haut les mains!** hands up!
hau·tain *[otɛ̃] **-taine** [tɛn] adj haughty
hautbois *[obwa] m oboe
haut-de-chausses *[odəʃos] m (pl **hauts-de-chausses**) trunk hose, breeches
haut-de-forme *[odəfɔrm] m (pl **hauts-de-forme**) top hat
haute *[ot] f high society
haute-fidélité [otfidelite] f high fidelity, hi-fi
hautement *[otmɑ̃] adv loudly; openly, clearly; highly (qualified); proudly
hauteur *[otœr] f height; hill, upland; altitude; nobility; haughtiness; (phys) pitch (of sound); **à la hauteur de** equal to, up to; (naut) off
haut-fond *[ofɔ̃] m (pl **hauts-fonds**) shoal, shallows
haut-le-cœur *[oləkœr] m invar nausea
haut-le-corps *[oləkɔr] m invar jump, sudden start
haut-parleur *[oparlœr] m (pl **haut-parleurs**) loudspeaker
hautu·rier *[otyrje] **-rière** [rjɛr] adj deep-sea
havage *[avaʒ] m (min) cutting
havane *[avan] adj invar tan, brown ‖ m Havana cigar ‖ (cap) f—**La Havane** Havana
hâve *[ɑv] adj haggard, peaked
havir *[avir] tr (culin) to sear
havre *[ɑvr] m haven, harbor
havresac *[ɑvrəsak] m haversack, knapsack; tool bag
hawaïen or **hawaiien** [awajɛ̃], [avajɛ̃] **ha-waïenne** or **hawaiienne** [awajɛn], [avajɛn] adj Hawaiian ‖ (cap) mf Hawaiian

Hawaii [awai], [awaji] **l'île Hawaii** Hawaii; **les îles Hawaii** the Hawaiian Islands
Haye *[ɛ] f—**La Haye** The Hague
hayon *[ajɔ̃] m (aut) hatchback
H.B.M. [aʃbeɛm] f (letterword) **(habitation à bon marché)** low-rent apartment
he *[e], [he] interj hey!
heaume *[om] m helmet
hebdomadaire [ɛbdɔmadɛr] adj & m weekly
héberger [ebɛrʒe] §38 tr to lodge
hébé·té -tée [ebete] adj dazed
hébéter [ebete] §10 tr to daze, stupefy
hébraïque [ebraik] adj Hebrew
hébraï·sant [ebraizɑ̃] **-sante** [zɑ̃t] mf Hebraist
hébraïser [ebraize] tr & intr to Hebraize
hé·breu [ebrø] (pl **-breux**) adj masc Hebrew ‖ m Hebrew (language); **c'est de l'hébreu pour moi** it's Greek to me ‖ (cap) m Hebrew (man)
hécatombe [ekatɔ̃b] f hecatomb
hégire [eʒir] f Hegira
hein *[ɛ̃] interj (coll) eh!, what!
hélas [elɑs] interj alas!
Hélène [elɛn] f Helen
héler *[ele] §10 tr to hail, call
hélice [elis] f (aer) propeller; (math) helix, spiral; (naut) screw
hélicoptère [elikɔptɛr] m helicopter
héliport [elipɔr] m heliport
hélistation [elistasjɔ̃] f helicopter landing
hélium [eljɔm] m helium
hélix [eliks] m helix
hellène [ɛlɛn] adj Hellenic ‖ (cap) mf Hellene
helvétique [ɛlvetik] adj Swiss
hématie [emati] f red blood corpuscle
hémisphere [emisfɛr] m hemisphere
hémistiche [emistiʃ] m hemistich
hémoglobine [emɔglɔbin] f hemoglobin
hémophile [emɔfil] adj hemophilic ‖ mf hemophiliac
hémophilie [emɔfili] f hemophilia
hémorragie [emɔraʒi] f hemorrhage
hémorroïdes [emɔrɔid] fpl hemorrhoids
hémostatique [emɔstatik] adj hemostatic ‖ m hemostatic, hemostat
henné *[ɛnne] m henna
hennir *[enir] intr to neigh, whinny
hennissement *[enismɑ̃] m neigh, whinny
Henri [ɑ̃ri], *[ɑ̃ri] m Henry
hépatite [epatit] f hepatitis
héraldique [eraldik] adj heraldic
héraut *[ero] m herald
herbe [ɛrb] f grass; lawn; herb; **couper l'herbe sous le pied de qn** (coll) to pull the rug from under s.o.'s feet; **en herbe** unripe; budding; **fines herbes** herbs for seasoning; **herbe à la puce** (Canad) poison ivy; **herbe aux chats** catnip; **herbes médicinales** or **officinales** (pharm) herbs; **herbes potagères** potherbs; **mauvaise herbe** weed
her·beux [ɛrbø] **-beuse** [bøz] adj grassy
herbicide [ɛrbisid] adj herbicidal ‖ m weed killer

herboristerie [ɛrbɔristri] f herb shop
her·bu -bue [ɛrby] adj grassy
her·culéen [ɛrkyleɛ̃] **-culéenne** [kyleɛn] adj herculean
hère *[ɛr] m wretch
héréditaire [ereditɛr] adj hereditary
hérédité [eredite] f heredity
hérésie [erezi] f heresy
hérétique [eretik] adj & mf heretic
héris·sé -sée *[erise] adj bristly; shaggy; prickly; surly
hérisser *[erise] tr & intr to bristle
hérisson *[erisɔ̃] m hedgehog
héritage [eritaʒ] m heritage; inheritance
hériter [erite] tr to inherit ‖ intr to inherit; **hériter de** to become the heir of; inherit, come into
héri·tier [eritje] **-tière** [tjɛr] mf heir ‖ f heiress
hermétique [ɛrmetik] adj hermetic(al), airtight; (fig) obscure
hermine [ɛrmin] f ermine
herminette [ɛrminɛt] f adze
hernie *[ɛrni] f hernia
her·nieux *[ɛrnjø] **-nieuse** [njøz] adj ruptured
héroïne [erɔin] f heroine; (drug) heroin
héroïque [erɔik] adj heroic
héroïsme [erɔism] m heroism
héron *[erɔ̃] m heron
héros *[ero] m hero
herpès [ɛrpɛs] m herpes
herse [ɛrs] f harrow; portcullis; **les herses** (theat) stage lights
herser *[ɛrse] tr to harrow
hési·tant [ezitɑ̃] **-tante** [tɑ̃t] adj hesitant
hésitation [ezitasjɔ̃] f hesitation
hésiter [ezite] §96 intr to hesitate
hétéroclite [eterɔklit] adj unusual, odd
hétérodoxe [eterɔdɔks] adj heterodox
hétérodyne [eterɔdin] adj heterodyne
hétérogène [eterɔʒɛn] adj heterogeneous
hêtre *[ɛtr] m beech, beech tree
heur [œr] m pleasure; **heur et malheur** joys and sorrows
heure [œr] f hour; time (of day); o'clock; **à la bonne heure!** fine!; **à l'heure** on time; by the hour, per hour; **à l'heure juste, à l'heure sonnante** on the hour; **à tout à l'heure!** see you later!; **à toute heure** at any time; **de bonne heure** early; **heure d'été** daylight-saving time; **heure H** zero hour; **heure légale** twelve-month daylight time (standard time); **heure militaire** sharp, e.g., **huit heures, heure militaire** eight sharp; **heures d'affluence** rush hours; **heures de consultation** office hours; **heures de pointe** rush hours; **heures d'ouverture** business hours; **heure semestrielle** semester hour; **heures supplémentaires** overtime; **l'heure du déjeuner** lunch hour; **tout à l'heure** in a little while; a little while ago
heu·reux [œrø], [ørø] **-reuse** [røz] §93 adj happy, pleased; lucky, fortunate
heurt *[œr] m knock, bump; clash; bruise; **sans heurt** without a hitch

heur·té -tée *[œrte] *adj* clashing (*colors*); abrupt (*style*)

heurter *[œrte] *tr* to knock against, bump into; antagonize ‖ *intr*—**heurter contre** to bump into ‖ *ref* to clash, collide; **se heurter à** to come up against

heurtoir *[œrtwar] *m* door knocker; (rr) buffer

hexagone [ɛgzagɔn] *m* hexagon; **l'Hexagone (national)** (fig) France

hi *[i] *m invar*—**hi hi hi!** ho ho ho!; **pousser des hi et des ha** to sputter in amazement

hiatus [jatys], *[jatys] *m* hiatus

hiberner [ibɛrne] *intr* to hibernate

hibiscus [ibiskys] *m* hibiscus

hi·bou *[ibu] *m* (*pl* **-boux**) owl

hic *[ik] *m*—**violà le hic!** (coll) there's the rub!

hi·deux *[idø] **-deuse** [døz] *adj* hideous

hie *[i] *f* pile driver

hièble [jɛbl] *f* (bot) elder

hié·mal -male [jemal] *adj* (*pl* **-maux** [mo]) winter

hier [jɛr] *adv & m* yesterday; **hier soir** last evening, last night

hiérarchie *[jerarʃi] *f* hierarchy

hiéroglyphe [jerɔglif] *m* hieroglyphic

hiéroglyphique [jerɔglifik] *adj* hieroglyphic

hi-han *[iɑ̃] *interj* heehaw

hila·rant [ilarɑ̃] **-rante** [rɑ̃t] *adj* hilarious; laughing (*gas*)

hilare [ilar] *adj* hilarious

hin·dou -doue [ɛ̃du] *adj* Hindu ‖ (*cap*) *mf* Hindu

hippique [ipik] *adj* horse (*race, show*)

hippisme [ipism] *m* horse racing

hippodrome [ipɔdrom] *m* hippodrome, race track

hippopotame [ipɔpɔtam] *m* hippopotamus

hirondelle [irɔ̃dɛl] *f* (orn) swallow; (coll) bicycle cop

hispanique [ispanik] *adj* Hispanic

hispani·sant [ispanizɑ̃] **-sante** [zɑ̃t] *mf* Hispanist

hisser *[ise] *tr* to hoist, to raise

histoire [istwar] *f* history; story; **faire des histoires à** (coll) to make trouble for; **histoire à dormir debout** (coll) tall tale; **histoire de rire** (coll) just for fun; **histoire de s'informer** (coll) out of curiosity; **pas d'histoires** (coll) no fuss

histologie [istɔlɔʒi] *f* histology

histo·rien [istɔrjɛ̃] **-rienne** [rjɛn] *mf* historian

historier [istɔrje] *tr* to illustrate, adorn

historique [istɔrik] *adj* historic(al) ‖ *m* historical account

histrion [istrijɔ̃] *m* ham actor

hiver [ivɛr] *m* winter

hiveriser [ivɛrize] *tr* (aut) to winterize

hiver·nal -nale [ivɛrnal] *adj* (*pl* **-naux** [no]) winter

hiverner [ivɛrne] *intr* to winter

H.L.M. [aʃɛlɛm] *m* (letterword) (**habitation à loyer modéré**) low-rent apartment

ho *[o], [ho] *interj* hey there!; what!

hobe·reau *[ɔbro] *m* (*pl* **-reaux**) (orn) hobby; (coll) squire

hoche *[ɔʃ] *f* nick on a blade

hochement *[ɔʃmɑ̃] *m* shake, toss

hochepot *[ɔʃpo] *m* (culin) hotchpotch

hochequeue *[ɔʃkø] *m* (orn) wagtail

hocher *[ɔʃe] *tr* to shake; nod

hochet *[ɔʃɛ] *m* rattle (*toy*); bauble

hockey *[ɔkɛ] *m* hockey; **hockey sur glace** ice hockey

hockeyeur [ɔkɛjœr] *m* hockey player

hoirie [wari] *f* legacy

holà *[ɔla], [hɔla] *m invar*—**mettre le holà à** (coll) to put a stop to ‖ *interj* hey!; stop!

holding *[ɔldiŋ] *m* holding company

hold-up *[ɔldœp] *m invar* holdup

hollan·dais *[ɔlɑ̃dɛ] **-daise** [dɛz] *adj* Dutch ‖ *m* Dutch (*language*) ‖ (*cap*) *mf* Hollander (*person*)

hollande *[ɔlɑ̃d] *m* Edam cheese ‖ *f* Holland (*linen*) ‖ (*cap*) *f* Holland; **la Hollande** Holland

holocauste [ɔlɔkost] *m* holocaust

homard *[ɔmar] *m* lobster

home *[om] *m* home

homélie [ɔmeli] *f* homily

homéopathie [ɔmeɔpati] *f* homeopathy

home-trainer [omtrɛnœr] *m* exercise bicycle

homicide [ɔmisid] *adj* homicidal ‖ *mf* homicide (*person*) ‖ *m* homicide, murder; **homicide involontaire, homicide par imprudence** manslaughter

hommage [ɔmaʒ] *m* homage; **hommage de l'auteur** (formula in presenting complimentary copies) with the compliments of the author; **hommages** respects, compliments

hommasse [ɔmas] *adj* mannish (*woman*)

homme [ɔm] *m* man; **brave homme** fine man, honest man; **être homme à** to be the man to, to be capable of; **homme à tout faire** jack-of-all-trades; handyman; **homme d'affaires** businessman; **homme d'armes** man-at-arms; **homme de droite** rightist; **homme de gauche** leftist; **homme d'église** churchman; **homme de guerre** or **d'épée** military man; **homme de la rue** man in the street, first comer; **homme de l'espace** spaceman; **homme de lettres** man of lettrs; **homme de paille** figurehead, stooge; **homme de peine** workingman; **homme des bois** orang-utan; **homme d'État** statesman; **homme de troupe** (*pl* **hommes des troupes**) (mil) enlisted man, private; **homme d'expédition** go-getter; **homme d'intérieur** homebody; **homme du monde** man of the world; **homme galant** ladies' man; **homme orchestra** one-man band; **hommes de bien** men of good will; **honnête homme** upright man; man of culture, gentleman; **jeune homme** young man; teen-age boy; **le vieil homme** (Bib) the old Adam; **un homme à la mer!** man overboard!

homme-grenouille [ɔmgrənuj] *m* (*pl* **hommes-grenouilles**) frogman
homme-sandwich[ɔmsɑ̃dwitʃ],[ɔmsɑ̃dwiʃ] *m* (*pl* **hommes-sandwichs**) sandwich man
homogène [ɔmɔʒɛn] *adj* homogeneous
homogénéiser [ɔmɔʒeneize] *tr* to homogenize
homologation [ɔmɔlɔgɑsjɔ̃] *f* validation
homologue [ɔmɔlɔg] *adj* homologous ‖ *mf* (fig) opposite number
homologuer [ɔmɔlɔge] *tr* to confirm, endorse; probate (*e.g., a will*)
homonyme [ɔmɔnim] *adj* homonymous ‖ *m* homonym; namesake
homosexualité [ɔmɔsɛksɥalite] *f* homosexuality
homo·sexuel -sexuelle [ɔmɔsɛksɥɛl] *adj* & *mf* homosexual
hongre *[ɔ̃gr] *adj* gelded ‖ *m* gelding
hongrer *[ɔ̃gre] *tr* to geld
Hongrie *[ɔ̃gri] *f* Hungary; **la Hongrie** Hungary
hon·grois *[ɔ̃grwa] **-groise** [grwaz] *adj* Hungarian ‖ *m* Hungarian (*language*) ‖ (*cap*) *mf* Hungarian (*person*)
honnête [ɔnɛt] *adj* honest, honorable
honnêteté [ɔnɛtəte] *f* honesty, uprightness
honneur [ɔnœr] *m* honor; **faire honneur à sa parole** to keep one's word
honnir *[ɔnir] *tr* to shame
honorabilité [ɔnɔrabilite] *f* respectability
honorable [ɔnɔrabl] *adj* honorable
honoraire [ɔnɔrɛr] *adj* honorary, emeritus ‖ **honoraires** *mpl* honorarium, fee
honorer [ɔnɔre] *tr* to honor ‖ *ref*—**s'honorer de** to pride oneself on
honorifique [ɔnɔrifik] *adj* honorific
honte *[ɔ̃t] *f* shame; **avoir honte** to be ashamed; **faire honte à qn** to make s.o. ashamed; **faire honte à ses parents** to be a disgrace to one's parents; **fausse honte** bashfulness; **sans honte** unashamedly
hon·teux *[ɔ̃tø], **-teuse** [tøz] *adj* ashamed; shameful; sheepish, shamefaced, bashful; venereal (*diseases*)
hop *[ɔp] *interj* go!, off with you!
hôpi·tal [ɔpital] *m* (*pl* **-taux** [to]) hospital; charity hospital
hoquet *[ɔkɛ] *m* hiccough
hoqueter *[ɔkte] §34 *intr* to hiccough
horaire [ɔrɛr] *adj* hourly, by hour ‖ *m* timetable; schedule; **horaire flottant** flex(i)time
horde *[ɔrd] *f* horde
horion *[ɔrjɔ̃] *m* punch, clout
horizon [ɔrizɔ̃] *m* horizon
horizon·tal -tale [ɔrizɔ̃tal] (*pl* **-taux** [to] **-tales**) *adj* & *f* horizontal
horloge [ɔrlɔʒ] *f* clock; **horloge à eau, horloge d'eau** water clock; **horloge à sable, horloge de sable** hourglass; **horloge atomique, horloge moléculaire** atomic clock; **horloge comtoise, horloge normande, horloge parquet** grandfather's clock; **horloge solaire** sundial

horlo·ger [ɔrlɔʒe] **-gère** [ʒɛr] *adj* clockmaking, watchmaking ‖ *mf* clockmaker, watchmaker
horlogerie [ɔrlɔʒri] *f* clockmaking, watchmaking; **d'horlogerie** clockwork
hormis *[ɔrmi] *prep* (lit) except for
hormone [ɔrmɔn] *f* hormone
horoda·té -tée [ɔrɔdate] *adj* stamped with the hour and date
horoscope [ɔrɔskɔp] *m* horoscope; **tirer l'horoscope de qn** to cast s.o.'s horoscope
horreur [ɔrœr] *f* horror; **avoir horreur de** to have a horror of; **commettre des horreurs** to commit atrocities; **dire des horreurs** to say obscene things; **dire des horreurs de** to say shocking things about
horrible [ɔribl] *adj* horrible
horrifier [ɔrifje] *tr* to horrify
horripi·lant [ɔrripilɑ̃] **-lante** [lɑ̃t] (coll) *adj* hair-raising
horripilation [ɔrripilɑsjɔ̃] *f* gooseflesh; (coll) exasperation
horripiler [ɔrripile] *tr* to give gooseflesh to; (coll) to exasperate
hors *[ɔr] *prep* out, beyond, outside; except, except for, save; **hors de** out of, outside of; **hors de soi** beside oneself, frantic; **hors d'ici!** get out!; **hors tout** overall
hors-bord *[ɔrbɔr] *m invar* outboard (*motor or motorboat*)
hors-caste *[ɔrkast] *mf invar* outcaste
hors-concours *[ɔrkɔ̃kur] *adj invar* excluded from competition ‖ *m invar* contestant excluded from competition
hors-d'œuvre *[ɔrdœvr] *m invar* hors d'œuvre; **le déjeuner commence par des hors-d'œuvre** the dinner begins with the hors d'œuvres
hors-jeu *[ɔrjø] *m invar* offside position
hors-la-loi *[ɔrlalwa] *m invar* outlaw
hors-ligne *[ɔrliɲ] *adj invar* (coll) exceptional ‖ *m invar* roadside
hors-texte *[ɔrtɛks] *m invar* (bb) insert
hortensia [ɔrtɑ̃sja] *m* hydrangea
horticole [ɔrtikɔl] *adj* horticultural
horticulture [ɔrtikyltyr] *f* horticulture
hospice [ɔspis] *m* hospice; home (*for the old, infirm, orphaned, etc.*)
hospita·lier [ɔspitalje] **-lière** [ljɛr] *adj* hospitable; hospital ‖ *mf* hospital employee
hospitaliser [ɔspitalize] *tr* to hospitalize
hospitalité [ɔspitalite] *f* hospitality
hostie [ɔsti] *f* (eccl) Host
hostile [ɔstil] *adj* hostile
hostilité [ɔstilite] *f* hostility
hôte [ot] *mf* guest ‖ *m* host
hôtel [otɛl], [ɔtɛl] *m* hotel; mansion; **hôtel des Monnaies** mint; **hôtel des Postes** main post office; **hôtel de ville** city hall; **hôtel meublé** rooming house, residential hotel; **hôtel particulier** mansion
hôtel-Dieu [otɛldjø], [ɔtɛldjø] *m* (*pl* **hôtels-Dieu**) city hospital
hôte·lier [otəlje], [ɔtəlje] **-lière** [ljɛr] *adj* hotel (*business*) ‖ *mf* hotel manager

hôtellerie [otɛlri], [ɔtɛlri] *f* hotel business; fine restaurant; hostelry, hostel

hôtesse [otɛs] *f* hostess; **hôtesse de l'air** air hostess, stewardess

hotte *[ɔt] *f* basket (*carried on back*); hod (*of mason*); hood (*of chimney*); **hotte aspirante** exhaust hood

hou *[u] *interj* oh no!

houache *[waʃ] *f* wake (*of ship*)

houblon *[ublɔ̃] *m* hop (*vine*); hops (*dried flowers*)

houe *[u] *f* hoe

houer *[we] *tr* to hoe

houille *[uj] *f* coal; **houille blanche** water power; **houille bleue** tide power; **houille d'or** energy from the sun; **houille grasse** or **collante** soft coal; **houille incolore** wind power; **houille maigre** or **éclatante** hard coal; **houille rouge** energy from the heat of the earth

houil·ler *[uje] **houil·lère** *[ujɛr] *adj* coal-bearing, carboniferous; coal (*industry*) ‖ *f* coal mine

houilleur *[ujœr] *m* coal miner

houle *[ul] *f* swell

houlette *[ulɛt] *f* crook (*of shepherd*); (hort) trowel

hou·leux *[ulø] **-leuse** [løz] *adj* swelling (*sea*); (fig) stormy, turbulent

houp *[up], [hup] *interj* go to it!

houppe *[up] *f* tuft; crest; tassel; **houppe à poudre** powder puff

houppelande *[uplɑ̃d] *f* greatcoat

houppette *[upɛt] *f* tuft; powder puff

hourra *[ura], [hura] *m*—**pousser trois hourras** to give three cheers ‖ *interj* hurrah!

hourvari *[urvari] *m* call to the hounds; (coll) uproar

houspiller *[uspije] *tr* to jostle, knock around; to rake over the coals, to tell off

housse *[us] *f* slipcover; cover (*e.g., for typewriter*); garment bag; housing, horse-cloth; (aut) seat cover

housser *[use] *tr* to dust (*with feather duster*)

houssine *[usin] *f* rug beater; switch

houssoir *[uswar] *m* feather duster; whisk broom

houx *[u] *m* holly

hoyau *[wajo] *m* (*pl* **hoyaux**) mattock; pickax

hublot *[yblo] *m* porthole

huche *[yʃ] *f* hutch; bin

hucher *[yʃe] *tr* to call, shout to

hue *[y] *interj* gee!; gee up! **tirer à hue et à dia** (fig) to pull in opposite directions

huée *[ɥe] *f* hoot, boo

huer *[ɥe] *tr & intr* to hoot, boo

hugue·not *[ygno] **-note** [nɔt] *adj* Huguenot ‖ *f* pipkin ‖ (*cap*) *mf* Huguenot (*person*)

huile *[ɥil] *f* oil; big shot; **ça baigne dans l'huile** (coll) everything is going smoothly; **d'huile** calm, e.g., **mer d'huile** calm sea; **huile de coude** elbow grease; **huile de foie de morue** cod-liver

oil; **huile de freins** brake fluid; **huile de ricin** castor oil; **huile lourde** disel fuel; **huile solaire** suntan oil; **les huiles** (coll) the VIP's; **sentir l'huile** (fig) to smell of midnight oil; **verser de l'huile sur le feu** (fig) to add fuel to the fire

huiler [ɥile] *tr* to oil; grease

hui·leux [ɥilø] **-leuse** [løz] *adj* oily; greasy

huilier [ɥilje] *m* oil-and-vinegar cruet

huis [ɥi] *m* (archaic) door; **à huis clos** behind closed doors; (law) in camera; **à huis ouvert** spectators admitted ‖ *[ɥi] *m*—**demander le huis clos** to request a closed-door session

huisserie [ɥisri] *f* doorframe

huissier [ɥisje] *m* doorman; usher (*before a person of rank*); **huissier audiencier** bailiff; **huissier exploitant** process server

huit *[ɥi(t)] §94 *adj & pron* eight; the Eighth, e.g., **Jean huit** John the Eighth; **huit heures** eight o'clock ‖ *m* eight; eighth (*in dates*); **faire des huit** to cut figures of eight (*in figure skating*)

huitain *[ɥitɛ̃] *m* eight-line verse

huitaine *[ɥitɛn] *f* (grouping of) eight; week; **à huitaine** the same day next week; **une huitaine de** about eight

huitième *[ɥitjɛm] §94 *adj, pron* (*masc, fem*), & *m* eighth

huître [ɥitr] *f* oyster

huit-reflets *[ɥirəflɛ] *m invar* top hat

huî·trier [ɥitrije] **-trière** [trijɛr] *adj* oyster (*industry*) ‖ *m* (orn) oystercatcher ‖ *f* oyster bed

hulotte *[ylɔt] *f* hoot owl

hululer *[ylyle] *intr* to hoot

hum *[œm], [hœm] *interj* hum!

hu·main [ymɛ̃] **-maine** [mɛn] *adj* human; humane

humaniste [ymanist] *adj & m* humanist

humanitaire [ymanitɛr] *adj & mf* humanitarian

humanité [ymanite] *f* humanity; **humanités** (**classiques**) humanities (*Greek & Latin classics*); **humanités modernes** humanities, belles-letters; **humanités scientifiques** liberal studies (*concerned with the observation and classification of facts*)

humble [œ̃bl] *adj* humble

humecter [ymɛkte] *tr* to moisten ‖ *ref* to become damp; **s'humecter le gosier** (slang) to wet one's whistle

humer *[yme] *tr* to suck, suck up; sip; inhale, breathe in

humérus [ymerys] *m* humerus

humeur [ymœr] *f* humor, body fluid; humor, mood, spirits; **avec humeur** testily; **avoir de l'humeur** to be in a bad mood; **être de bonne humeur** to be in a good humor

humide [ymid] *adj* humid, damp; wet

humidifier [ymidifje] *tr* to humidify

humidité [ymidite] *f* humidity

humi·liant [ymiljɑ̃] **-liante** [ljɑ̃t] *adj* humiliating

humiliation [ymiljɑsjɔ̃] *f* humiliation

humilier [ymilje] *tr* to humiliate, humble ‖ *ref* to humble oneself
humilité [ymilite] *f* humility
humoriste [ymɔrist] *adj* humorous (*writer*) ‖ *mf* humorist
humoristique [ymɔristik] *adj* humorous
humour [ymur] *m* humor; **humour noir** macabre humor, sick humor
humus [ymys] *m* humus
hune *[yn] f* (naut) top; **hune de vigie** (naut) crow's-nest
huppe *[yp] f* tuft, crest (*of bird*); (orn) hoopoe
hup·pé -pée *[ype] adj* tufted, crested; (coll) smart, stylish
hure *[yr] f* head (*of boar, salmon, etc.*); (culin) headcheese
hurlement *[yrlmã] m* howl, roar; howling, roaring (*e.g., of wind*)
hurler *[yrle] tr* to cry out, yell ‖ *intr* to howl, roar
hur·leur *[yrlœr] -leuse* [løz] *adj* howling ‖ *mf* howler ‖ *m* (zool) howler
hurluberlu [yrlyberly] *m* (coll) scatterbrain
hu·ron *[yrɔ̃] -ronne* [rɔn] *adj* (coll) boorish, uncouth ‖ *mf* (coll) boor
hurricane *[urikan]*, *[œrikɛn] m* hurricane
hutte *[yt] f* hut, cabin
hyacinthe [jasɛ̃t] *f* hyacinth (*stone*)
hya·lin [jalɛ̃] *-line* [lin] *adj* glassy
hybride [ibrid] *adj & m* hybrid
hydrate [idrat] *m* hydrate
hydrater [idrate] *tr & ref* to hydrate
hydraulique [idrolik] *adj* hydraulic ‖ *f* hydraulics
hydravion [idravjɔ̃] *m* hydroplane
hydre [idr] *f* hydra
hydrocarbure [idrɔkarbyr] *m* hydrocarbon
hydro-électrique [idrɔelɛktrik] *adj* hydroelectric
hydrofoil [idrɔfɔjl] *m* hydrofoil
hydrofuge [idrɔfyʒ] *adj* waterproof
hydrofuger [idrɔfyʒe] §38 *tr* to waterproof
hydrogène [idrɔʒɛn] *m* hydrogen
hydroglisseur [idrɔglisœr] *m* speedboat
hydromètre [idrɔmɛtr] *m* hydrometer ‖ *f* (ent) water spider
hydrophile [idrɔfil] *adj* absorbent ‖ *m*—**hydrophile brun** (ent) water devil

hydrophobie [idrɔfɔbi] *f* hydrophobia
hydropisie [idrɔpizi] *f* dropsy
hydroptère [idrɔptɛr] *m* hydrofoil
hydroscope [idrɔskɔp] *m* dowser
hydroxyde [idrɔksid] *m* hydroxide
hyène [jɛn] *f* hyena
hygiène [iʒjɛn] *f* hygiene
hygiénique [iʒjenik] *adj* hygienic
hymnaire [imnɛr] *m* hymnal
hymne [imnə], [im] *m* hymn, ode, anthem; **hymne national** national anthem ‖ *f* (eccl) hymn, canticle
hyperacidité [iperasidite] *f* hyperacidity
hyperbole [ipɛrbɔl] *f* (math) hyperbola; (rhet) hyperbole
hypersensible [ipɛrsãsibl] *adj* hypersensitive, supersensitive
hypersensi·tif [ipɛrsãsitif] *-tive* [tiv] *adj* hypersensitive, supersensitive
hyper·sexué -sexuée [ipɛrsɛksɥe] *adj* oversexed
hypertension [ipɛrtãsjɔ̃] *f* high blood pressure, hypertension
hypnose [ipnoz] *f* hypnosis
hypnotique [ipnɔtik] *adj & m* hypnotic
hypnotiser [ipnɔtize] *tr* to hypnotize ‖ *ref*—**s'hypnotiser sur** (fig) to be hypnotized by
hypnoti·seur [ipnɔtizœr] *-seuse* [zøz] *mf* hypnotist
hypnotisme [ipnɔtism] *m* hypnotism
hypocondriaque [ipɔkɔ̃drijak] *adj & mf* hypochondriac
hypocrisie [ipɔkrizi] *f* hypocrisy
hypocrite [ipɔkrit] *adj* hypocritical ‖ *mf* hypocrite
hypodermique [ipɔdɛrmik] *adj* hypodermic
hyposulfite [ipɔsylfit] *m* hyposulfite
hypotension [ipɔtãsjɔ̃] *f* low blood pressure
hypoténuse [ipɔtenyz] *f* hypotenuse
hypothèque [ipɔtɛk] *f* mortgage; **prendre une hypothèque sur** to put a mortgage on; **purger une hypothèque** to pay off a mortgage
hypothéquer [ipɔteke] §10 *tr* to mortgage
hypothèse [ipɔtɛz] *f* hypothesis
hypothétique [ipɔtetik] *adj* hypothetic(al)
hystérie [isteri] *f* hysteria
hystérique [isterik] *adj* hysteric(al)

I

I, i [i], *[i] m invar* ninth letter of the French alphabet
ïambique [jãbik] *adj* iambic
ibé·rien [iberjɛ̃] *-rienne* [rjɛn] *adj* Iberian ‖ (*cap*) *mf* Iberian
ibérique [iberik] *adj* Iberian
iceberg [isbɛrg] *m* iceberg
ichtyologie [iktjɔlɔʒi] *f* ichthyology
ici [isi] *adv* here; this is, e.g., **ici Paris** (rad,

telv) this is Paris; e.g., **ici Robert** (telp) this is Robert; **d'ici** hereabouts; from today; **d'ici demain** before tomorrow; **d'ici là** between now and then, in the meantime; **d'ici peu** before long; **jusqu'ici** up to now, hitherto; **par ici** this way, through here
ici-bas [isiba] *adv* here below, on earth
icône [ikon] *f* icon

iconoclaste [ikɔnɔklast] *adj* iconoclastic || *mf* iconoclast

iconographie [ikɔnɔgrafi] *f* iconography; pictures, pictorial material

iconoscope [ikɔnɔskɔp] *m* iconoscope

ictère [iktɛr] *m* jaundice

ictérique [ikterik] *adj* jaundiced

idéal idéale [ideal] *adj* & *m* (*pl* **idéaux** [ideo] or **idéals**) ideal

idéaliser [idealize] *tr* to idealize

idéaliste [idealist] *adj* & *mf* idealist

idée [ide] *f* idea; mind, head; opinion, esteem; (coll) shade, touch; **changer d'idée** to change one's mind

idem [idɛm] *adv* idem, the same, ditto

identification [idɑ̃tifikasjɔ̃] *f* identification

identifier [idɑ̃tifje] *tr* to identify

identique [idɑ̃tik] *adj* identic(al)

identité [idɑ̃tite] *f* identity

idéologie [ideɔlɔʒi] *f* ideology; (pej) utopianism

idéologique [ideɔlɔʒik] *adj* ideologic(al); conceptual

ides [id] *fpl* ides

idiomatique [idjɔmatik] *adj* idiomatic

idiome [idjɔm] *m* idiom, language

idiosyncrasie [idjɔsɛ̃krazi] *f* idiosyncrasy

i·diot [idjo] **-diote** [djɔt] *adj* idiotic || *mf* idiot

idiotie [idjɔsi] *f* idiocy

idiotisme [idjɔtism] *m* idiom, idiomatic expression

idolâtrer [idɔlatre] *tr* to idolize

idolâtrie [idɔlatri] *f* idolatry

idole [idɔl] *f* idol

idylle [idil] *f* idyll; romance, love affair

idyllique [idilik] *adj* idyllic

if [if] *m* yew

IGAME [igam] *m* (acronym) (**Inspecteur Général de l'Administration en Mission Extraordinaire**) head prefect

igname [iɲam], [ignam] *f* yam

ignare [iɲar] *adj* ignorant

ig·né -née [igne] *adj* igneous

ignifuge [ignifyʒ] *adj* fireproof || *m* fireproofing

ignifuger [ignifyʒe] §38 *tr* to fireproof

ignition [ignisjɔ̃] *f* ignition; red heat (*of metal*)

ignoble [iɲɔbl] *adj* ignoble; disgusting

ignomi·nieux [iɲɔminjø] **-nieuse** [njøz] *adj* ignominious

ignorance [iɲɔrɑ̃s] *f* ignorance

igno·rant [iɲɔrɑ̃] **-rante** [rɑ̃t] *adj* ignorant || *mf* ignoramus

ignorer [iɲɔre] *tr* not to know, be ignorant of; be unacquainted with

il [il] §87, §92 *pron* he, it

île [il] *f* island, isle; **les îles Normandes** the Channel Islands

illé·gal -gale [illegal] *adj* (*pl* **-gaux** [go]) illegal

illégitime [illeʒitim] *adj* illegitimate; unjustified

illet·tré -trée [illetre] *adj* & *mf* illiterate

illicite [illisit] *adj* illicit; foul (*blow*)

illimi·té -tée [illimite] *adj* unlimited

illisible [illizibl] *adj* illegible; unreadable (*book*)

illogique [illɔʒik] *adj* illogical

illumination [illyminasjɔ̃] *f* illumination

illumi·né -née [illymine] *adj* & *mf* fanatic, visionary

illuminer [illymine] *tr* to illuminate

illusion [illyzjɔ̃] *f* illusion; **illusion de la vue** optical illusion; **se faire des illusions** to indulge in wishful thinking

illusionner [illyzjɔne] *tr* to delude || *ref* to delude oneself

illusionniste [illyzjɔnist] *mf* magician

illusoire [illyzwar] *adj* illusory, illusive

illustra·teur [illystratœr] *m* illustrator

illustration [illystrasjɔ̃] *f* illustration; glorification; glory; celebrity

illustre [illystr] *adj* illustrious, renowned

illus·tré -trée [illystre] *adj* illustrated || *m* illustrated magazine

illustrer [illystre] *tr* to illustrate || *ref* to distinguish oneself

îlot [ilo] *m* small island, isle; block (*of houses*)

ils [il] §87 *pron* they

image [imaʒ] *f* image; picture; **images** imagery; **image de marque** name brand; **images** imagery; **images d'archives** file film; **une image vaut mieux que dix mille mots** a picture is worth a thousand words

imager [imaʒe] §38 *tr* to embellish with metaphors, to color

imagerie [imaʒri] *f*—**imagerie d'Épinal** cardboard cutouts

imaginaire [imaʒinɛr] *adj* imaginary

imagination [imaʒinasjɔ̃] *f* imagination

imaginer [imaʒine] §97 *tr* to imagine; invent || *intr* to imagine; imagine **+ inf** to have the idea of **+ ger** || §95 *ref* to imagine oneself; **imaginez-vous!** imagine!

imbattable [ɛ̃batabl] *adj* unbeatable

imbat·tu -tue [ɛ̃baty] *adj* unbeaten

imbécile [ɛ̃besil] *adj* & *mf* imbecile

imbécillité [ɛ̃besilite] *f* imbecility

imberbe [ɛ̃bɛrb] *adj* beardless

imbi·bé -bée [ɛ̃bibe] *adj* (coll) drunk, tipsy; **imbibé de** soaked with; steeped in

imbiber [ɛ̃bibe] *tr* & *ref* to soak; **s'imbiber de** to soak up; be imbued with; (coll) to imbibe (*liquor*)

imbrication [ɛ̃brikasjɔ̃] *f* overlapping

imbriquer [ɛ̃brike] *tr* to overlap; interweave; fit (*s.th.*) into || *ref* to overlap; be interwoven; **ça s'imbrique l'un dans l'autre** they fit into each other; they are linked

imbrisable [ɛ̃brizabl] *adj* unbreakable

imbrûlable [ɛ̃brylabl] *adj* fireproof

im·bu -bue [ɛ̃by] *adj*—**imbu de** imbued with, steeped in

imbuvable [ɛ̃byvabl] *adj* undrinkable; unbearable, insufferable, awful

imita·teur [imitatœr] **-trice** [tris] *mf* imitator

imitation [imitasjɔ̃] *f* imitation

imiter [imite] *tr* to imitate
immacu·lé -lée [immakyle] *adj* immaculate
immangeable [ɛ̃mɑ̃ʒabl] *adj* inedible
immanquable [ɛ̃mɑ̃kabl] *adj* infallible; inevitable
immaté·riel -rielle [immaterjɛl] *adj* immaterial
immatriculation [immatrikylɑsjɔ̃] *f* registration; enrollment; **immatriculation de livraison** dealer's plate
immatriculer [immatrikyle] *tr* to register
immature [immatyr] *adj* unmatured
immé·diat [immedja] **-diate** [djat] *adj* immediate
immédiatement [immedjatmɑ̃] *adv* immediately
immémo·rial -riale [immemɔrjal] *adj* (*pl* **-riaux** [rjo]) immemorial
immense [immɑ̃s] *adj* immense
immensurable [immɑ̃syrabl] *adj* immeasurable, immensurable
immerger [immɛrʒe] §38 *tr* to immerse, dip; throw overboard; lay (*a cable*)
imméri·té -tée [immerite] *adj* undeserved
immersion [immɛrsjɔ̃] *f* immersion
immettable [ɛ̃mɛtabl] *adj* unwearable
immeuble [immœbl] *adj* real, e.g., **biens immeubles** real estate ‖ *m* building, apartment building; **immeuble à copropriété** condominium
immi·grant [immigrɑ̃] **-grante** [grɑ̃t] *adj* & *mf* immigrant
immigration [immigrɑsjɔ̃] *f* immigration
immi·gré -grée [immigre] *adj* & *mf* immigrant
immigrer [immigre] *intr* to immigrate
immi·nent [imminɑ̃] **-nente** [nɑ̃t] *adj* imminent, impending
immiscer [immise] §51 *ref*—**s'immiscer dans** to interfere with, meddle with
immixtion [immiksjɔ̃] *f* interference; **immixtions** intrusions upon privacy (*e.g.*, *wiretapping*)
immobile [immɔbil] *adj* motionless; immobile (*resolute*); dead (*typewriter key*)
immobi·lier [immɔbilje] **-lière** [ljɛr] *adj* real-estate, property; real, e.g., **biens immobiliers** real estate
immobiliser [immɔbilize] *tr* to immobilize; tie up ‖ *ref* to come to a stop
immodé·ré -rée [immɔdere] *adj* immoderate
immonde [immɔ̃d] *adj* foul, filthy; (eccl) unclean
immondices [immɔ̃dis] *fpl* garbage, refuse
immo·ral -rale [immɔral] *adj* (*pl* **-raux** [ro]) immoral
immortaliser [immɔrtalize] *tr* to immortalize
immor·tel -telle [immɔrtɛl] *adj* & *mf* immortal ‖ *f* (bot) everlasting
immoti·vé -vée [immɔtive] *adj* groundless
immuable [immɥabl] *adj* changeless
immuniser [immynize] *tr* to immunize
immunité [immynite] *f* immunity
immunologie [imynɔlɔʒi] *f* immunology

impact [ɛ̃pakt] *m* impact; **impact résistant** unbreakable (*e.g.*, *glasses*)
im·pair -paire [ɛ̃pɛr] *adj* odd, uneven ‖ *m* (coll) blunder
impardonnable [ɛ̃pardɔnabl] *adj* unpardonable
impar·fait [ɛ̃parfɛ] **-faite** [fɛt] *adj* & *m* imperfect
imparité [ɛ̃parite] *f* inequality, disparity
impar·tial -tiale [ɛ̃parsjal] *adj* (*pl* **-tiaux** [sjo]) impartial
impartir [ɛ̃partir] *tr* to grant
impasse [ɛ̃pɑs] *f* blind alley, dead-end street; impasse, deadlock; (cards) finesse; **faire l'impasse à** (cards) to finesse
impassible [ɛ̃pasibl] *adj* impassible; impassive (*look*, *face*, *etc.*)
impatiemment [ɛ̃pasjamɑ̃] *adv* impatiently
impatience [ɛ̃pasjɑ̃s] *f* impatience; **impatiences** (coll) attack of nerves
impa·tient [ɛ̃pasjɑ̃] **-tiente** [sjɑ̃t] *adj* impatient
impatienter [ɛ̃pasjɑ̃te] *tr* to make impatient ‖ §97 *ref* to lose patience
impatroniser [ɛ̃patrɔnize] *ref* to take charge; take hold
impavide [ɛ̃pavid] *adj* fearless
impayable [ɛ̃pɛjabl] *adj* (coll) priceless, very funny
im·payé -payée [ɛ̃peje] *adj* unpaid
impec [ɛ̃pɛk] *adj* (coll) impeccable
impeccable [ɛ̃pɛkabl] *adj* impeccable
impénétrable [ɛ̃penetrabl] *adj* impenetrable
impéni·tent [ɛ̃penitɑ̃] **-tente** [tɑ̃t] *adj* impenitent, obdurate, inveterate
impensable [ɛ̃pɑ̃sabl] *adj* unthinkable
imper [ɛ̃pɛr] *m* (coll) raincoat
impéra·tif [ɛ̃peratif] **-tive** [tiv] *adj* & *m* imperative
impératrice [ɛ̃peratris] *f* empress
imperceptible [ɛ̃pɛrsɛptibl] *adj* imperceptible; negligible
imperdable [ɛ̃pɛrdabl] *adj* unlosable
imperfection [ɛ̃pɛrfɛksjɔ̃] *f* imperfection, defect
impé·rial -riale [ɛ̃perjal] *adj* (*pl* **-riaux** [rjo]) imperial ‖ *f* goatee; upper deck (*of bus*, *coach*, *etc.*)
impérialiste [ɛ̃perjalist] *adj* & *mf* imperialist
impé·rieux [ɛ̃perjø] **-rieuse** [rjøz] *adj* imperious, haughty; imperative, urgent
impérissable [ɛ̃perisabl] *adj* imperishable
impéritie [ɛ̃perisi] *f* incompetence
imperméabiliser [ɛ̃pɛrmeabilize] *tr* to waterproof
imperméable [ɛ̃pɛrmeabl] *adj* waterproof; impervious ‖ *m* raincoat
imperson·nel -nelle [ɛ̃pɛrsɔnɛl] *adj* impersonal; commonplace; ordinary
imperti·nent [ɛ̃pɛrtinɑ̃] **-nente** [nɑ̃t] *adj* impertinent ‖ *mf* impertinent person
impesanteur [ɛ̃pəzɑ̃tœr] *f* weightlessness
impé·trant [ɛ̃petrɑ̃] **-trante** [trɑ̃t] *mf* holder (*of a title or degree*)
impé·tueux [ɛ̃petɥø] **-tueuse** [tɥøz] *adj* impetuous

impie [ɛ̃pi] *adj* impious, ungodly; blasphemous ‖ *mf* unbeliever; blasphemer

impiété [ɛ̃pjete] *f* impiety; disrespect

impitoyable [ɛ̃pitwajabl] *adj* unmerciful

implacable [ɛ̃plakabl] *adj* implacable

implanter [ɛ̃plɑ̃te] *tr* to implant; introduce ‖ *ref* to take root; **s'implanter chez** (coll) to thrust oneself upon

implication [ɛ̃plikɑsjɔ̃] *f* implication

implicite [ɛ̃plisit] *adj* implicit

impliquer [ɛ̃plike] *tr* to implicate; imply

implorer [ɛ̃plɔre] *tr* to implore

imployable [ɛ̃plwajabl] *adj* pitiless; inflexible

impo·li -lie [ɛ̃pɔli] *adj* impolite

impolitique [ɛ̃pɔlitik] *adj* ill-advised

impondérable [ɛ̃pɔ̃derabl] *adj & m* imponderable

impopulaire [ɛ̃pɔpylɛr] *adj* unpopular

impopularité [ɛ̃pɔpylarite] *f* unpopularity

importance [ɛ̃pɔrtɑ̃s] *f* importance; size; **d'importance** large, of consequence; thoroughly, very hard

impor·tant [ɛ̃pɔrtɑ̃] **-tante** [tɑ̃t] *adj* important; large, considerable ‖ *m* main thing; **faire l'important** (coll) to act big

importa·teur [ɛ̃pɔrtatœr] **-trice** [tris] *adj* importing ‖ *mf* importer

importation [ɛ̃pɔrtɑsjɔ̃] *f* importation

importer [ɛ̃pɔrte] *tr* to import ‖ *intr* to matter; be important; **n'importe** no matter, never mind; **n'importe comment** any way; **n'importe où** anywhere; **n'importe quand** anytime; **n'importe quel . . .** any . . . ; **n'importe qui** anybody; **n'importe quoi** anything; **peu m'importe** it doesn't matter to me; **qu'importe?** what does it matter?

impor·tun [ɛ̃pɔrtœ̃] **-tune** [tyn] *adj* bothersome ‖ *mf* pest, nuisance

importuner [ɛ̃pɔrtyne] *tr* to importune

imposable [ɛ̃pozabl] *adj* taxable

impo·sant [ɛ̃pozɑ̃] **-sante** [zɑ̃t] *adj* imposing

impo·sé -sée [ɛ̃poze] *adj* taxed; fixed (*price*) ‖ *mf* taxpayer

imposer [ɛ̃poze] §97, §98 *tr* to impose; levy a tax on ‖ *intr*—**en imposer à** to make an impression on; impose on ‖ *ref* to assert oneself; be indispensable; **s'imposer à** to force itself upon; **s'imposer chez** to foist oneself upon

imposition [ɛ̃pozisjɔ̃] *f* imposition; taxation; laying on, levying; **niveau d'imposition** tax bracket

impossibilité [ɛ̃pɔsibilite] *f* impossibility; **être dans l'impossibilité de** to be unable to

impossible [ɛ̃pɔsibl] *adj* impossible

imposte [ɛ̃pɔst] *f* transom; (archit) impost

imposteur [ɛ̃pɔstœr] *m* impostor

imposture [ɛ̃pɔstyr] *f* imposture

impôt [ɛ̃po] *m* tax; **impôt du sang** military duty; **impôt foncier** property tax; **impôt indirecte** sales tax; **impôt retenu à la source** withholding tax; **impôt sur le revenu** income tax

impotence [ɛ̃pɔtɑ̃s] *f* lameness, infirmity

impo·tent [ɛ̃pɔtɑ̃] **-tente** [tɑ̃t] *adj* crippled; bedridden ‖ *mf* cripple

impraticable [ɛ̃pratikabl] *adj* impracticable; impassable (*e.g., road*)

impré·cis [ɛ̃presi] **-cise** [siz] *adj* vague, hazy

imprégner [ɛ̃preɲe] §10 *tr* to impregnate

imprenable [ɛ̃prənabl] *adj* impregnable

impréparation [ɛ̃preparɑsjɔ̃] *f* unpreparedness

imprésario [ɛ̃presarjo] *m* impresario

impression [ɛ̃prɛsjɔ̃] *f* impression; printing; (phot) print

impression·nant [ɛ̃prɛsjɔnɑ̃] **-nante** [nɑ̃t] *adj* impressive

impressionner [ɛ̃prɛsjɔne] *tr* to impress, affect; (phot) to expose

impressionnisme [ɛ̃prɛsjɔnism] *m* (painting) impressionism

imprévisible [ɛ̃previzibl] *adj* unforeseeable

imprévision [ɛ̃previzjɔ̃] *f* lack of foresight

im·prévoyant [ɛ̃prevwajɑ̃] **-prévoyante** [prevwajɑ̃t] *adj* improvident, short-sighted

impré·vu -vue [ɛ̃prevy] *adj & m* unforeseen, unexpected; **sauf imprévu** unless something unforeseen happens

impri·mé -mée [ɛ̃prime] *adj* printed ‖ *m* print, calico; printed work, book; printing (*as opposed to script*); **imprimés** printed matter

imprimer [ɛ̃prime] *tr* to print; imprint; impress; impart (*e.g., movement*)

imprimerie [ɛ̃primri] *f* printing; printing office, print shop

imprimeur [ɛ̃primœr] *m* printer

imprimeur-éditeur [ɛ̃primœreditœr] *m* (*pl* **imprimeurs-éditeurs**) printer and publisher

imprimeur-libraire [ɛ̃primœrlibrɛr] *m* (*pl* **imprimeurs-libraires**) printer and publisher

imprimeuse [ɛ̃primøz] *f* printing press

improbable [ɛ̃prɔbabl] *adj* improbable

improba·tif [ɛ̃prɔbatif] **-tive** [tiv] *adj* disapproving

improbité [ɛ̃prɔbite] *f* dishonesty

improduc·tif [ɛ̃prɔdyktif] **-tive** [tiv] *adj* unproductive

impromp·tu -tue [ɛ̃prɔ̃pty] *adj* impromptu ‖ *m* impromptu play; (mus) impromptu ‖ **impromptu** *adv* impromptu

impropre [ɛ̃prɔpr] *adj* improper (*not right*); **impropre à** unfit for

impropriété [ɛ̃prɔprijete] *f* incorrectness

improviser [ɛ̃prɔvize] *tr & intr* to improvise

improviste [ɛ̃prɔvist]—**à l'improviste** unexpectedly, impromptu; **prendre à l'improviste** to catch napping

impru·dent [ɛ̃prydɑ̃] **-dente** [dɑ̃t] *adj* imprudent

impubère [ɛ̃pybɛr] *adj* under the age of puberty

impubliable [ɛ̃pybljabl] *adj* unpublishable, not fit to print

impu·dent [ɛ̃pydɑ̃] **-dente** [dɑ̃t] *adj* impudent

impudeur [ɛ̃pydœr] *f* immodesty

impudicité [ɛ̃pydisite] *f* indecency

impudique [ɛ̃pydik] *adj* immodest

impuissance [ɛ̃pɥisɑ̃s] *f* powerlessness, helplessness; ineffectiveness; (pathol) impotence: **être dans l'impuissance de faire q.ch.** to be incapable of doing s.th.

impuis·sant [ɛ̃pɥisɑ̃] **-sante** [sɑ̃t] *adj* impotent, powerless, helpless; (pathol) impotent

impul·sif [ɛ̃pylsif] **-sive** [siv] *adj* impulsive ‖ *mf* impulsive person

impulsion [ɛ̃pylsjɔ̃] *f* impulse; **donner l'impulsion à** to give an impetus to; **sous l'impulsion du moment** on the spur of the moment

impunément [ɛ̃pynemɑ̃] *adv* with impunity

impu·ni -nie [ɛ̃pyni] *adj* unpunished

impunité [ɛ̃pynite] *f* impunity

im·pur -pure [ɛ̃pyr] *adj* impure

impureté [ɛ̃pyrte] *f* impurity; unchastity

imputation [ɛ̃pytɑsjɔ̃] *f* imputation; (com) charge; (com) deduction

imputer [ɛ̃pyte] §97, §98 *tr* to impute, ascribe; (com) **imputer q.ch. à** to charge s.th. to

inabordable [inabɔrdabl] *adj* unapproachable, inaccessible; prohibitive (*price*)

inaccessible [inaksɛsibl] *adj* inaccessible

inaccoutu·mé -mée [inakutyme] *adj* unusual; **inaccoutumé à** unaccustomed to, unused to

inache·vé -vée [inaʃve] *adj* unfinished, uncompleted

inac·tif [inaktif] **-tive** [tiv] *adj* inactive

inaction [inaksjɔ̃] *f* inaction

inactivité [inaktivite] *f* inactivity

inadaptation [inadaptɑsjɔ̃] *f* maladjustment

inadap·té -tée [inadapte] *adj* maladjusted ‖ *mf* misfit

inadvertance [inadvɛrtɑ̃s] *f*—**par inadvertance** inadvertently

inalté·ré -rée [inaltere] *adj* unspoiled

inamovible [inamɔvibl] *adj* fixed, unmovable; not removable

inani·mé -mée [inanime] *adj* inanimate

inappréciable [inapresjabl] *adj* inappreciable, imperceptible; invaluable

inapte [inapt] *adj* inept; **inapte à** unfit for, unsuitable for ‖ *mf* dropout, washout; **les inaptes** the unfit; the unemployable

inaptitude [inaptityd] *f* unfitness

inarticu·lé -lée [inartikyle] *adj* inarticulate

inassou·vi -vie [inasuvi] *adj* unsatisfied

inattaquable [inatakabl] *adj* unquestionable; unassailable; **inattaquable par** unaffected by, resistant to

inatten·du -due [inatɑ̃dy] *adj* unexpected

inatten·tif [inatɑ̃tif] **-tive** [tiv] *adj* inattentive; careless

inattention [inatɑ̃sjɔ̃] *f* inattentiveness, carelessness

inaudible [inodibl] *adj* inaudible

inaugu·ral -rale [inogyral] *adj* (*pl* **-raux** [ro]) inaugural

inauguration [inogyrɑsjɔ̃] *f* inauguration

inaugurer [inogyre] *tr* to inaugurate; unveil (*a statue*)

inauthentique [inotɑ̃tik] *adj* unauthentic

inavouable [inavuabl] *adj* shameful

ina·voué -vouée [inavwe] *adj* unacknowledged

inca [ɛ̃ka] *adj invar* Inca ‖ (*cap*) *m* Inca

incandes·cent [ɛ̃kɑ̃desɑ̃] **-cente** [sɑ̃t] *adj* incandescent; wild, stirred up (*crowd*)

incapable [ɛ̃kapabl] §93 *adj* incapable; (law) incompetent ‖ *mf* (law) incompetent person

incapacité [ɛ̃kapasite] *f* incapacity; disability

incarcérer [ɛ̃karsere] §10 *tr* to incarcerate

incar·nat [ɛ̃karna] **-nate** [nat] *adj* "flesh"-colored; rosy ‖ *m* "flesh" color

incarnation [ɛ̃karnɑsjɔ̃] *f* incarnation

incar·né -née [ɛ̃karne] *adj* incarnate; ingrowing (*nail*)

incarner [ɛ̃karne] *tr* to incarnate, embody ‖ *ref* to become incarnate; (pathol) to become ingrown; **s'incarner dans** to become the embodiment of

incartade [ɛ̃kartad] *f* indiscretion; prank

incassable [ɛ̃kasabl] *adj* unbreakable

incendiaire [ɛ̃sɑ̃djɛr] *adj & mf* incendiary

incendie [ɛ̃sɑ̃di] *m* fire, conflagration; **incendie volontaire** arson

incen·dié -diée [ɛ̃sɑ̃dje] *adj* burnt down ‖ *mf* fire victim

incendier [ɛ̃sɑ̃dje] *tr* to set on fire; burn down; (fig) to fire, inflame; (slang) to give a tongue-lashing to

incer·tain [ɛ̃sɛrtɛ̃] **-taine** [tɛn] *adj* uncertain; indistinct; unsettled (*weather*)

incertitude [ɛ̃sɛrtityd] *f* incertitude, uncertainty; **dans l'incertitude** in doubt

incessamment [ɛ̃sɛsamɑ̃] *adv* incessantly; without delay, at any moment

inces·sant [ɛ̃sɛsɑ̃] **-sante** [sɑ̃t] *adj* incessant

inceste [ɛ̃sɛst] *m* incest

inces·tueux [ɛ̃sɛstɥø] **-tueuse** [tɥøz] *adj* incestuous

inchan·gé -gée [ɛ̃ʃɑ̃ʒe] *adj* unchanged

incidemment [ɛ̃sidamɑ̃] *adv* incidentally

incidence [ɛ̃sidɑ̃s] *f* incidence

inci·dent [ɛ̃sidɑ̃] **-dente** [dɑ̃t] *adj & m* incident

incinérer [ɛ̃sinere] §10 *tr* to incinerate; cremate

incirconcis [ɛ̃sirkɔ̃si] *adj masc* uncircumcised

inciser [ɛ̃size] *tr* to make an incision in; tap (*a tree*); (med) to lance

inci·sif [ɛ̃sizif] **-sive** [ziv] *adj* incisive ‖ *f* incisor

incision [ɛ̃sizjɔ̃] *f* incision

incitation [ɛ̃sitɑsjɔ̃] *f* incitement

inciter [ɛ̃site] §96, §100 *tr* to incite

inci·vil -vile [ɛ̃sivil] *adj* uncivil

incivili·sé -sée [ɛ̃sivilize] *adj* uncivilized

inclassable [ɛ̃klɑsabl] *adj* unclassifiable

inclé·ment [ɛ̃klemã] **-mente** [mãt] *adj* inclement

inclinaison [ɛ̃klinɛzɔ̃] *f* inclination; slope

inclination [ɛ̃klinɑsjɔ̃] *f* inclination; bow; love, affection

incliner [ɛ̃kline] §96 *tr & ref* to incline; bend; bow; obey

inclure [ɛ̃klyr] §11 (*pp* **inclus**) *tr* to include; enclose

in·clus [ɛ̃kly] **-cluse** [klyz] *adj* including, e.g., **jusqu'à la page dix incluse** up to and including page ten; inclusive, e.g., **de mercredi à samedi inclus** from Wednesday to Saturday inclusive

inclu·sif [ɛ̃klyzif] **-sive** [ziv] *adj* inclusive

inclusivement [ɛ̃klyzivmã] *adv* inclusively, inclusive

incognito [ɛ̃kɔɲito] *m & adv* incognito

incohé·rent [ɛ̃kɔerã] **-rente** [rãt] *adj* incoherent; inconsistent, illogical

incollable [ɛ̃kɔlabl] *adj* (coll) knowing all the answers, not to be stumped

incolore [ɛ̃kɔlɔr] *adj* colorless

incomber [ɛ̃kɔ̃be] *intr*—**incomber à** to devolve on, fall upon; **il incombe à qn de** it behooves s.o. to

incombustible [ɛ̃kɔ̃bystibl] *adj* incombustible; fireproof

incommode [ɛ̃kɔmɔd] *adj* inconvenient; unwieldy

incommoder [ɛ̃kɔmɔde] *tr* to inconvenience

incommodité [ɛ̃kɔmɔdite] *f* inconvenience

incomparable [ɛ̃kɔ̃parabl] *adj* incomparable

incompatible [ɛ̃kɔ̃patibl] *adj* incompatible; conflicting

incompétence [ɛ̃kɔ̃petɑ̃s] *f* incompetence; lack of jurisdiction

incompé·tent [ɛ̃kɔ̃petã] **-tente** [tãt] *adj* incompetent; lacking jurisdiction

incom·plet [ɛ̃kɔ̃plɛ] **-plète** [plɛt] *adj* incomplete

incompréhensible [ɛ̃kɔ̃preãsibl] *adj* incomprehensible

incom·pris [kɔ̃pri] **-prise** [priz] *adj* misunderstood

inconcevable [ɛ̃kɔ̃svabl] *adj* inconceivable

inconciliable [ɛ̃kɔ̃siljabl] *adj* irreconcilable

incondition·nel -nelle [ɛ̃kɔ̃disjɔnɛl] *adj* unconditional

inconduite [ɛ̃kɔ̃dɥit] *f* misconduct

inconfort [ɛ̃kɔ̃fɔr] *m* discomfort

incon·gru -grue [ɛ̃kɔ̃gry] *adj* incongruous

incon·nu -nue [ɛ̃kɔny] *adj* unknown; **inconnu à cette adresse** address unknown ‖ *mf* unknown (*person*) ‖ *m* unknown (*what is not known*) ‖ *f* (math) unknown

inconsciemment [ɛ̃kɔ̃sjamã] *adv* subconsciously; unconsciously

inconscience [ɛ̃kɔ̃sjɑ̃s] *f* unconsciousness; unawareness

incons·cient [ɛ̃kɔ̃sjã] **-ciente** [sjãt] *adj* unconscious, unaware, oblivious; thoughtless; subconscious ‖ *mf* dazed person ‖ *m* unconscious

inconséquence [ɛ̃kɔ̃sekɑ̃s] *f* inconsistency; thoughtlessness, inconsiderateness

inconsé·quent [ɛ̃kɔ̃sekã] **-quente** [kãt] *adj* inconsistent; thoughtless, inconsiderate

inconsidé·ré -rée [ɛ̃kɔ̃sidere] *adj* inconsiderate

inconsistance [ɛ̃kɔ̃sistɑ̃s] *f* inconsistency; flimsiness, instability

inconsis·tant [ɛ̃kɔ̃sistã] **-tante** [tãt] *adj* inconsistent; flimsy, unstable

inconsolable [ɛ̃kɔ̃sɔlabl] *adj* inconsolable

incons·tant [ɛ̃kɔ̃stã] **-tante** [tãt] *adj* inconstant

inconstitution·nel -nelle [ɛ̃kɔ̃stitysjɔnɛl] *adj* unconstitutional

incontestable [ɛ̃kɔ̃tɛstabl] *adj* incontestable, unquestionable, indisputable

inconti·nent [ɛ̃kɔ̃tinã] **-nente** [nãt] *adj* incontinent ‖ **incontinent** *adv* at once, forthwith

incontrôlable [ɛ̃kɔ̃trolabl] *adj* unverifiable

incontrô·lé -lée [ɛ̃kɔ̃trole] *adj* unverified; unchecked, uncontrollable

inconvenance [ɛ̃kɔ̃vnɑ̃s] *f* impropriety

inconve·nant [ɛ̃kɔ̃vnã] **-nante** [nãt] *adj* improper, indecent

inconvénient [ɛ̃kɔ̃venjã] *m* inconvenience, disadvantage; **voir un inconvénient à** to have an objection to

incorporation [ɛ̃kɔrpɔrɑsjɔ̃] *f* incorporation; (mil) induction

incorpo·ré -rée [ɛ̃kɔrpɔre] *adj* built-in

incorpo·rel -relle [ɛ̃kɔrpɔrɛl] *adj* incorporeal; intangible (*property*)

incorporer [ɛ̃kɔrpɔre] *tr* to incorporate; (mil) to induct ‖ *ref* to incorporate

incor·rect -recte [ɛ̃kɔrɛkt] *adj* incorrect; unfair; improper; discourteous; indecent

incorrectement [ɛ̃kɔrɛktəmã] *adv* incorrectly; improperly; discourteously; in an underhand way

incorrection [ɛ̃kɔrɛksjɔ̃] *f* impropriety; incorrectness; impolite behavior; dishonesty

incrédule [ɛ̃kredyl] *adj* incredulous; unbelieving ‖ *mf* unbeliever, freethinker

incrédulité [ɛ̃kredylite] *f* incredulity; disbelief

incrément [ɛ̃kremã] *m* (comp) increment

incrémenter [ɛ̃kremãte] *tr* (comp) to increment

increvable [ɛ̃krəvabl] *adj* punctureproof; (slang) untiring

incriminer [ɛ̃krimine] *tr* to incriminate

incrochetable [ɛ̃krɔʃtabl] *adj* burglarproof (*lock*)

incroyable [ɛ̃krwajabl] *adj* unbelievable

in·croyant [ɛ̃krwajã] **-croyante** [krwajãt] *adj* unbelieving ‖ *mf* unbeliever

incrustation [ɛ̃krystɑsjɔ̃] *f* incrustation; inlay; (sewing) insert

incruster [ɛ̃kryste] *tr* to incrust; inlay ‖ *ref* to take root, become ingrained

incubateur [ɛ̃kybatœr] *m* incubator

incuber [ɛ̃kybe] *tr* to incubate

inculpation [ɛ̃kylpɑsjɔ̃] *f* indictment; **sous l'inculpation de** on a charge of

incul·pé -pée [ɛ̃kylpe] *adj* indicted; **inculpé de** charged with, accused of ‖ *mf* accused, defendant

inculper [ɛ̃kylpe] *tr* to indict, charge
inculquer [ɛ̃kylke] *tr* to inculcate
inculte [ɛ̃kylt] *adj* uncultivated; uncouth
incunables [ɛ̃kynabl] *mpl* incunabula
incurable [ɛ̃kyrabl] *adj* & *mf* incurable
incurie [ɛ̃kyri] *f* carelessness
incursion [ɛ̃kyrsjɔ̃] *f* incursion, foray
Inde [ɛ̃d] *f* India; **Indes Occidentales** West Indies; **l'Inde** India
indébrouillable [ɛ̃debrujabl] *adj* inextricable, hopelessly involved
indécence [ɛ̃desɑ̃s] *f* indecency
indé·cent [ɛ̃desɑ̃] **-cente** [sɑ̃t] *adj* indecent
indéchiffrable [ɛ̃deʃifrabl] *adj* undecipherable; incomprehensible; illegible
indé·cis [ɛ̃desi] **-cise** [siz] *adj* indecisive; uncertain, undecided; blurred
indéclinable [ɛ̃deklinabl] *adj* indeclinable
indécrottable [ɛ̃dekrɔtabl] *adj* (coll) incorrigible, hopeless
indéfectible [ɛ̃defɛktibl] *adj* everlasting; unfailing
indéfendable [ɛ̃defɑ̃dabl] *adj* indefensible
indéfi·ni -nie [ɛ̃defini] *adj* indefinite
indéfinissable [ɛ̃definisabl] *adj* indefinable
indéfrisable [ɛ̃defrizabl] *adj* permanent (*wave*) ‖ *f* permanent wave
indélébile [ɛ̃delebil] *adj* indelible
indéli·cat [ɛ̃delika] **-cate** [kat] *adj* indelicate; dishonest
indémaillable [ɛ̃demajabl] *adj* runproof
indemne [ɛ̃dɛmn] *adj* undamaged, unharmed
indemnisation [ɛ̃dɛmnizɑj5] *f* indemnification, compensation
indemniser [ɛ̃dɛmnize] *tr* to compensate
indemnité [ɛ̃dɛmnite] *f* indemnity; allowance, grant; compensation; **indemnité journalière** workmen's compensation; **indemnité parlementaire** salary of members (*of parliamentary body*)
indéniable [ɛ̃denjabl] *adj* undeniable
indépendamment [ɛ̃depɑ̃damɑ̃] *adv* independently; **indépendamment de** apart from; regardless of
indépendance [ɛ̃depɑ̃dɑ̃s] *f* independence
indépen·dant [ɛ̃depɑ̃dɑ̃] **-dante** [dɑ̃t] *adj* & *mf* independent
indéréglable [ɛ̃dereglabl] *adj* foolproof
indescriptible [ɛ̃dɛskriptibl] *adj* indescribable
indésirable [ɛ̃dezirabl] *adj* undesirable
indestructible [ɛ̃dɛstryktibl] *adj* indestructible
indétermi·né -née [ɛ̃detɛrmine] *adj* indeterminate
indétraquable [ɛ̃detrakabl] *adj* foolproof
index [ɛ̃dɛks] *m* index; forefinger; index number; **Index** (eccl) Index
indexation [ɛ̃dɛksɑsj5] *f*—**indexation des traitements sur le coût de la vie** consumer price index, CPI
indica·teur [ɛ̃dikatœr] **-trice** [tris] *adj* indicating ‖ *mf* informer ‖ *m* gauge; indicator, pointer; timetable; road sign; guidebook; street guide

indica·tif [ɛ̃dikatif] **-tive** [tiv] *adj* indicative, suggestive ‖ *m* (gram) indicative; (rad) station identification; **indicatif d'appel** (rad, telg) call letters or number; **indicatif postal** zip code
indication [ɛ̃dikɑsj5] *f* indication; **fausse indication** wrong piece of information; **indications** directions; **sauf indication contraire** unless otherwise directed; **sur l'indication de** at the suggestion of
indice [ɛ̃dis] *m* indication, sign; clue; **indice de pose** exposure index; **indice de refroidissement** chill factor; **indice des prix** price index; **indice d'octane** octane number; **indice du coût de la vie** cost-of-living index
indicible [ɛ̃disibl] *adj* inexpressible
in·dien [ɛ̃djɛ̃] **-dienne** [djɛn] *adj* Indian ‖ *f* calico, chintz ‖ (cap) *mf* Indian
indifféremment [ɛ̃diferamɑ̃] *adv* indiscriminately
indiffé·rent [ɛ̃diferɑ̃] **-rente** [rɑ̃t] *adj* indifferent; unimportant; **cela m'est indifférent** it's all the same to me
indigence [ɛ̃diʒɑ̃s] *f* indigence, poverty
indigène [ɛ̃diʒɛn] *adj* indigenous, native ‖ *mf* native
indi·gent [ɛ̃diʒɑ̃] **-gente** [ʒɑ̃t] *adj* indigent ‖ *mf* pauper; **les indigents** the poor
indigeste [ɛ̃diʒɛst] *adj* indigestible; heavy, stodgy; undigested, mixed up
indigestion [ɛ̃diʒɛstjɔ̃] *f* indigestion
indignation [ɛ̃diɲɑsjɔ̃] *f* indignation
indigne [ɛ̃diɲ] *adj* unworthy; shameful
indi·gné -gnée [ɛ̃diɲe] *adj* indignant
indigner [ɛ̃diɲe] *tr* to outrage ‖ §97 *ref* to be indignant
indignité [ɛ̃diɲite] *f* unworthiness; indignity, outrage
indigo [ɛ̃digo] *adj invar* & *m* indigo
indi·qué -quée [ɛ̃dike] *adj* advisable, appropriate; **être tout indiqué pour** to be just the thing for; be just the man for
indiquer [ɛ̃dike] *tr* to indicate; name; **indiquer du doigt** to point to, point out
indi·rect -recte [ɛ̃dirɛkt] *adj* indirect
indisciplinable [ɛ̃disiplinabl] *adj* unruly
indiscipline [ɛ̃disiplin] *f* lack of discipline, disobedience
indiscipli·né -née [ɛ̃disipline] *adj* undisciplined
indis·cret [ɛ̃diskrɛ] **-crète** [krɛt] *adj* indiscreet
indiscrétion [ɛ̃diskresjɔ̃] *f* indiscretion; **sans indiscrétion . . .** if I may ask . . .
indiscutable [ɛ̃diskytabl] *adj* unquestionable
indiscu·té -tée [ɛ̃diskyte] *adj* unquestioned
indispensable [ɛ̃dispɑ̃sabl] *adj* & *m* indispensable, essential
indisponible [ɛ̃dispɔnibl] *adj* unavailable; out of commission (*said of car, machine, etc.*)
indispo·sé -sée [ɛ̃dispoze] *adj* indisposed (*slightly ill*); ill-disposed
indisposer [ɛ̃dispoze] *tr* to indispose
indissoluble [ɛ̃disɔlybl] *adj* indissoluble

indis·tinct [ɛ̃distɛ̃], [ɛ̃distɛ̃kt] **-tincte** [tɛ̃kt] *adj* indistinct

indistinctement [ɛ̃distɛ̃ktəmɑ̃] *adv* indistinctly; indiscriminately

individu [ɛ̃dividy] *m* individual; (coll) fellow, guy

individualiser [ɛ̃dividɥalize] *tr* to individualize

individualité [ɛ̃dividɥalite] *f* individuality

indivi·duel -duelle [ɛ̃dividɥɛl] *adj* individual; separate

indi·vis [ɛ̃divi] **-vise** [viz] *adj* joint; **par indivis** jointly

indivisible [ɛ̃divizibl] *adj* indivisible

Indochine [ɛ̃doʃin] *f* Indochina; **l'Indochine** Indochina

indocile [ɛ̃dɔsil] *adj* rebellious, unruly

indo-européen [ɛ̃dɔørɔpeɛ̃] **-européenne** [ørɔpeɛn] *adj* Indo-European ‖ *m* Indo-European (*language*) ‖ (*cap*) *mf* Indo-European

indolemment [ɛ̃dɔlamɑ̃] *adv* indolently

indo·lent [ɛ̃dɔlɑ̃] **-lente** [lɑ̃t] *adj* indolent; apathetic; painless (*e.g., tumor*) ‖ *mf* idler

indolore [ɛ̃dɔlɔr] *adj* painless

indomptable [ɛ̃dɔ̃tabl] *adj* indomitable

indomp·té -tée [ɛ̃dɔ̃te] *adj* untamed

Indonésie [ɛ̃dɔnezi] *f* Indonesia; **l'Indonésie** Indonesia

indoné·sien [ɛ̃dɔnezjɛ̃] **-sienne** [zjɛn] *adj* Indonesian ‖ *m* Indonesian (*language*) ‖ (*cap*) *mf* Indonesian (*person*)

in-douze [ɛ̃duz] *adj invar & m invar* duodecimo

in·du -due [ɛ̃dy] *adj* unseemly (*e.g., hour*); undue (*haste*); unwarranted (*remark*) ‖ *m* something not due

indubitable [ɛ̃dybitabl] *adj* indubitable; **c'est indubitable** there's no doubt about it

inducteur [ɛ̃dyktœr] *m* (elec) field

induction [ɛ̃dyksjɔ̃] *f* (elec, logic) induction

induire [ɛ̃dɥir] §19, §96 *tr* to induce; **induire en** to lead into (*temptation, error, etc.*)

in·duit [ɛ̃dɥi] **-duite** [dɥit] *adj* induced ‖ *m* (elec) armature

indulgence [ɛ̃dylʒɑ̃s] *f* indulgence

indul·gent [ɛ̃dylʒɑ̃] **-gente** [ʒɑ̃t] *adj* indulgent

indûment [ɛ̃dymɑ̃] *adv* unduly

indurer [ɛ̃dyre] *tr & ref* to harden

industrialiser [ɛ̃dystrijalize] *tr* to industrialize ‖ *ref* to become industrialized

industrie [ɛ̃dystri] *f* industry; trickery; (obs) occupation, trade; **industrie du bâtiment** building industry, construction; **l'industrie du spectacle** show business

industrie-clef [ɛ̃dystrikle] *f* (*pl* **industries-clefs**) key industry

indus·triel -trielle [ɛ̃dystrijɛl] *adj* industrial ‖ *m* industrialist

indus·trieux -trieuse [trijøz] *adj* industrious; skilled

inébranlable [inebrɑ̃labl] *adj* unshakable

inéchangeable [ineʃɑ̃ʒabl] *adj* unexchangeable

iné·dit [inedi] **-dite** [dit] *adj* unpublished; new, novel

inéducable [inedykabl] *adj* unteachable

ineffable [inɛfabl] *adj* ineffable

ineffaçable [inɛfasabl] *adj* indelible

inefficace [inɛfikas] *adj* ineffective, inefficient

inefficacité [inefikasite] *f* ineffectiveness, inefficiency

iné·gal -gale [inegal] *adj* (*pl* **-gaux** [go]) unequal; uneven

inégalité [inegalite] *f* inequality; unevenness

inélégamment [inelegamɑ̃] *adv* inelegantly

inéligible [ineliʒibl] *adj* ineligible

inéluctable [inelyktabl] *adj* unavoidable

inem·ployé -ployée [inɑ̃plwaje] *adj* unused

inénarrable [inenarabl] *adj* beyond words, too funny for words

inepte [inɛpt] *adj* inept, inane

ineptie [inɛpsi] *f* ineptitude, inanity; inane remark

inépuisable [inepɥizabl] *adj* inexhaustible

inerme [inɛrm] *adj* thornless

inertie [inɛrsi] *f* inertia

inescomptable [inɛskɔ̃tabl] *adj* not subject to discount

inespé·ré -rée [inɛspere] *adj* unhoped-for, unexpected

inestimable [inɛstimabl] *adj* inestimable, invaluable, priceless

inévitable [inevitabl] *adj* inevitable

inexact inexacte [inɛgzakt] *adj* inexact, inaccurate; unpunctual

inexactitude [inɛgzaktityd] *f* inexactness, inaccuracy; unpunctuality

inexau·cé -cée [inɛgzose] *adj* unfulfilled, unanswered

inexcitable [inɛksitabl] *adj* unexcitable

inexcusable [inɛkskyzabl] *adj* inexcusable

inexécutable [inɛgzekytabl] *adj* impracticable

inexécution [inɛgzekysjɔ̃] *f* nonfulfillment

inexer·cé -cée [inɛgzɛrse] *adj* untried; untrained

inexhaustible [inɛgzostibl] *adj* inexhaustible

inexigible [inɛgziʒibl] *adj* uncollectable

inexis·tant [inɛksistɑ̃] **-tante** [tɑ̃t] *adj* nonexistent

inexorable [inɛgzɔrabl] *adj* inexorable

inexpérience [inɛksperjɑ̃s] *f* inexperience

inexpérimen·té -tée [inɛksperimɑ̃te] *adj* inexperienced; untried; unskilled

inex·pié -piée [inɛkspje] *adj* unexpiated

inexplicable [inɛksplikabl] *adj* inexplicable, unexplainable

inexpli·qué -quée [inɛksplike] *adj* unexplained

inexploi·té -tée [inɛksplwate] *adj* untapped

inexplo·ré -rée [inɛksplɔre] *adj* unexplored

inexpres·sif [inɛksprɛsif] **-sive** [siv] *adj* expressionless

inexprimable [inɛksprimabl] *adj* inexpressible

inexpri·mé -mée [inɛksprime] *adj* unexpressed

inexpugnable [inɛkspygnabl] *adj* impregnable

inextinguible [inɛkstɛ̃gibl], [inɛkstɛ̃gɥibl] *adj* inextinguishable; uncontrollable; unquenchable

infaillible [ɛ̃fajibl] *adj* infallible

infaisable [ɛ̃fəzabl] *adj* unfeasible

infa·mant [ɛ̃famɑ̃] **-mante** [mɑ̃t] *adj* opprobrious

infâme [ɛ̃fɑm] *adj* infamous; squalid

infamie [ɛ̃fami] *f* infamy; **dire des infamies à** to hurl insults at; **noter d'infamie** to brand as infamous

infant [ɛ̃fɑ̃] *m* infante

infante [ɛ̃fɑ̃t] *f* infanta

infanterie [ɛ̃fɑ̃tri] *f* infantry; **infanterie de l'air, infanterie aéroportée** parachute troops; **infanterie de marine** overseas troops; **infanterie portée, infanterie motorisée** motorized troops

infantile [ɛ̃fɑ̃til] *adj* infantile

infarctus [ɛ̃farktys] *m* (pathol) infarct, infarction; **infarctus du myocarde** coronary thrombosis

infatigable [ɛ̃fatigabl] *adj* indefatigable

infatuation [ɛ̃fatɥɑsjɔ̃] *f* conceit, false pride

infa·tué -tuée [ɛ̃fatɥe] *adj* infatuated with oneself, conceited

infé·cond [ɛ̃fekɔ̃] **-conde** [kɔ̃d] *adj* sterile, barren

in·fect -fecte [ɛ̃fɛkt] *adj* stinking; foul, vile

infecter [ɛ̃fɛkte] *tr* to infect; pollute; stink up

infec·tieux [ɛ̃fɛksjø] **-tieuse** [sjøz] *adj* infectious

infection [ɛ̃fɛksjɔ̃] *f* infection; stench

inférer [ɛ̃fere] §10 *tr* to infer, conclude

infé·rieur -rieure [ɛ̃ferjœr] *adj* lower; inferior; **inférieur à** below; less than ‖ *mf* subordinate, inferior

infériorité [ɛ̃ferjɔrite] *f* inferiority

infer·nal -nale [ɛ̃fɛrnal] *adj* (*pl* **-naux** [no]) infernal

infester [ɛ̃fɛste] *tr* to infest

infidèle [ɛ̃fidɛl] *adj* infidel; unfaithful ‖ *mf* infidel ‖ *m* unfaithful husband ‖ *f* unfaithful wife

infidélité [ɛ̃fidelite] *f* infidelity; inaccuracy, unfaithfulness

infiltration [ɛ̃filtrɑsjɔ̃] *f* infiltration

infiltrer [ɛ̃filtre] *ref* to infiltrate; seep, percolate; **s'infiltrer à travers** or **dans** to infiltrate

infime [ɛ̃fim] *adj* very small, infinitesimal; very low; trifling, negligible

infi·ni -nie [ɛ̃fini] *adj* infinite ‖ *m* infinite; (math) infinity; **à l'infini** infinitely

infiniment [ɛ̃finimɑ̃] *adv* infinitely; (coll) greatly, deeply, terribly

infinité [ɛ̃finite] *f* infinity

infini·tif [ɛ̃finitif] **-tive** [tiv] *adj & m* infinitive

infirme [ɛ̃firm] *adj* infirm, crippled, disabled ‖ *mf* invalid, cripple

infirmer [ɛ̃firme] *tr* (law) to invalidate

infirmerie [ɛ̃firməri] *f* infirmary; (nav) sick bay

infir·mier [ɛ̃firmje] **-mière** [mjɛr] *mf* nurse; **infirmière bénévole** volunteer nurse; **infirmière diplômée** registered nurse ‖ *m* male nurse; orderly, attendant

infirmière-major [ɛ̃firmjɛrmaʒɔr] *f* head nurse

infirmité [ɛ̃firmite] *f* infirmity

infixe [ɛ̃fiks] *m* infix

inflammable [ɛ̃flamabl] *adj* inflammable

inflammation [ɛ̃flamɑsjɔ̃] *f* inflammation

inflammatoire [ɛ̃flamatwar] *adj* inflammatory

inflation [ɛ̃flɑsjɔ̃] *f* inflation

inflationniste [ɛ̃flɑsjɔnist] *adj* inflationary

infléchir [ɛ̃fleʃir] *tr* to inflect, bend ‖ *ref* to bend, curve

inflexible [ɛ̃flɛksibl] *adj* inflexible

inflexion [ɛ̃flɛksjɔ̃] *f* inflection; change; bend, curve; metaphony

infliger [ɛ̃fliʒe] §38 *tr* to inflict; **infliger q.ch. à** to inflict s.th. on

influence [ɛ̃flyɑ̃s] *f* influence

influencer [ɛ̃flyɑ̃se] §51 *tr* to influence

in·fluent [ɛ̃flyɑ̃] **-fluente** [flyɑ̃t] *adj* influential

influenza [ɛ̃flyɑ̃za] *f* influenza

influer [ɛ̃flye] *intr*—**influer sur** to influence

in-folio [ɛ̃fɔljo] *adj & m* (*pl* **-folio** or **-folios**) folio

informa·teur [ɛ̃fɔrmatœr] **-trice** [tris] *mf* informant; informer

informati·cien [ɛ̃fɔrmatisjɛ̃] **-cienne** [sjɛn] *mf* informant; computer specialist

information [ɛ̃fɔrmɑsjɔ̃] *f* information; piece of information; (law) investigation; **aller aux informations** to make inquiries; **information génétique** genetic characteristics; **informations** news; information; **information de presse** press reports

informatique [ɛ̃fɔrmatik] *adj* informational; computer ‖ *f* computer science; data processing; information storage; **faire de l'informatique** to operate a computer

informatisation [ɛ̃fɔrmatizɑsjɔ̃] *f* computerization

informatiser [ɛ̃fɔrmatize] *tr* to computerize

informe [ɛ̃fɔrm] *adj* formless, shapeless

informer [ɛ̃fɔrme] *tr* to inform, advise ‖ *intr*—**informer contre** to inform on ‖ *ref* to inquire, keep oneself informed

infortune [ɛ̃fɔrtyn] *f* misfortune

infortu·né -née [ɛ̃fɔrtyne] *adj* unfortunate

infraction [ɛ̃fraksjɔ̃] *f* infraction

infranchissable [ɛ̃frɑ̃ʃisabl] *adj* insuperable; impassable (*e.g.*, *mountain*)

infrarouge [ɛ̃fraruʒ] *adj & m* infrared

infrason [ɛ̃frasɔ̃] *m* infrasonic vibration

infrastructure [ɛ̃frastryktyr] *f* infrastructure; (rr) roadbed

infroissable [ɛ̃frwasabl] *adj* creaseless, wrinkleproof

infruc·tueux [ɛ̃fryktɥø] **-tueuse** [tɥøz] *adj* unfruitful, fruitless

in·fus -fuse [ɛ̃fy] *adj* inborn, innate, intuitive

infuser [ɛ̃fyze] *tr* to infuse; brew; **infuser un sang nouveau à** to put new blood or life into ‖ *intr* to steep

infusion [ɛ̃fyzjɔ̃] *f* steeping; brew

ingambe [ɛ̃gɑ̃b] *adj* spry, nimble, alert

ingénier [ɛ̃ʒenje] §96 *ref* to strive hard

ingénierie [ɛ̃ʒeniri] or **ingéniérie** [ɛ̃ʒenjeri] *f* engineering

ingénieur [ɛ̃ʒenjœr] *m* engineer; **ingénieur des ponts et chaussées** civil engineer

ingé·nieux [ɛ̃ʒenjø] **-nieuse** [njøz] *adj* ingenious

ingéniosité [ɛ̃ʒenjozite] *f* ingenuity

ingé·nu -nue [ɛ̃ʒeny] *adj* ingenuous, artless ‖ *mf* naïve person ‖ *f* ingénue

ingénuité [ɛ̃ʒenɥite] *f* ingenuousness

ingérer [ɛ̃ʒere] §10 *tr* to ingest ‖ §97 *ref* to meddle

ingouvernable [ɛ̃guvɛrnabl] *adj* unruly, unmanageable

in·grat [ɛ̃gra] **-grate** [grat] *adj* ungrateful; disagreeable; thankless (*task*); unprofitable (*work*); barren (*soil*); awkward (*age*) ‖ *mf* ingrate

ingratitude [ɛ̃gratityd] *f* ingratitude

ingrédient [ɛ̃gredjɑ̃] *m* ingredient

inguérissable [ɛ̃gerisabl] *adj & mf* incurable

ingurgiter [ɛ̃gyrʒite] *tr* to swallow; gulp down

inhabile [inabil] §92 *adj* unfitted, unqualified; incompetent; clumsy; incapable, inefficient

inhabileté [inabilte] *f* unfitness, inability; incompetence; clumsiness; lack of skill; (law) incompetency, legal incapacity

inhabitable [inabitabl] *adj* uninhabitable

inhabi·té -tée [inabite] *adj* uninhabited

inhabi·tuel -tuelle [inabitɥel] *adj* unusual

inhaler [inale] *tr & intr* to inhale, breathe in

inhé·rent [inerɑ̃] **-rente** [rɑ̃t] *adj* inherent

inhiber [inibe] *tr* to inhibit

inhibition [inibisjɔ̃] *f* inhibition

inhospita·lier [inɔspitalje] **-lière** [ljɛr] *adj* inhospitable

inhu·main [inymɛ̃] **-maine** [mɛn] *adj* inhuman

inhumanité [inymanite] *f* inhumanity

inhumation [inymɑsjɔ̃] *f* burial

inhumer [inyme] *tr* to bury, inter

inimitable [inimitabl] *adj* inimitable

inimitié [inimitje] *f* enmity

ininflammable [inɛ̃flamabl] *adj* nonflammable, non-inflammable

inintelli·gent [inɛ̃teliʒɑ̃] **-gente** [ʒɑ̃t] *adj* unintelligent

inintéres·sant [inɛ̃teresɑ̃] **-sante** [sɑ̃t] *adj* uninteresting

ininterrom·pu -pue [inɛ̃terɔ̃py] *adj* uninterrupted

inique [inik] *adj* iniquitous, unjust, unfair

iniquité [inikite] *f* iniquity; unjustness, unfairness

ini·tial -tiale [inisjal] (*pl* **-tiaux** [sjo] **-tiales**) *adj & f* initial

initia·teur [inisjatœr] **-trice** [tris] *adj* initiating ‖ *mf* initiator

initiation [inisjɑsjɔ̃] *f* initiation

initiative [inisjativ] *f* initiative

initier [inisje] *tr* to initiate; introduce ‖ *ref* to become initiated

injecter [ɛ̃ʒɛkte] *tr* to inject; impregnate ‖ *ref* to become bloodshot

injec·teur [ɛ̃ʒɛktœr] **-trice** [tris] *adj* injecting ‖ *m* injector; nozzle (*in motor*)

injection [ɛ̃ʒɛksjɔ̃] *f* injection; impregnation; redness (*of eyes*); (geog) intrusion; **injection de rappel** booster shot

injonction [ɛ̃ʒɔ̃ksjɔ̃] *f* injunction, order

injouable [ɛ̃ʒwabl] *adj* unplayable

injure [ɛ̃ʒyr] *f* insult; wrong; **l'injure des ans** the ravages of time

injurier [ɛ̃ʒyrje] *tr* to insult, abuse

inju·rieux [ɛ̃ʒyrijø] **-rieuse** [rjøz] *adj* insulting, abusive; harmful, offensive

injuste [ɛ̃ʒyst] *adj* unjust

injustice [ɛ̃ʒystis] *f* injustice

injusti·fié -fiée [ɛ̃ʒystifje] *adj* unjustified

inlassable [ɛ̃lɑsabl] *adj* untiring

in·né -née [inne] *adj* innate, inborn

innocemment [inɔsamɑ̃] *adv* innocently

innocence [inɔsɑ̃s] *f* innocence

inno·cent [inɔsɑ̃] **-cente** [sɑ̃t] *adj & mf* innocent

innocenter [inɔsɑ̃te] *tr* to exonerate

innocuité [inɔkɥite] *f* innocuousness

innombrable [inɔ̃brabl] *adj* innumerable

innova·teur [inɔvatœr] **-trice** [tris] *adj* innovating ‖ *mf* innovator

innovation [inɔvɑsjɔ̃] *f* innovation

innover [inɔve] *tr & intr* to innovate

innocu·pé -pée [inɔkype] *adj* unoccupied; unemployed, idle ‖ *mf* idler

in-octavo [inɔktavo] *adj & m* (*pl* **-octavo** or **-octavos**) octavo

inoculation [inɔkylɑsjɔ̃] *f* inoculation

inoculer [inɔkyle] *tr* to inoculate

inodore [inɔdɔr] *adj* odorless

inoffen·sif [inɔfɑ̃sif] **-sive** [siv] *adj* inoffensive

inondation [inɔ̃dɑsjɔ̃] *f* flood

inonder [inɔ̃de] *tr* to flood

inopi·né -née [inɔpine] *adj* unexpected

inoppor·tun [inɔpɔrtœ̃] **-tune** [tyn] *adj* untimely, inconvenient

inopportunité [inɔpɔrtynite] *f* untimeliness

inorganique [inɔrganik] *adj* inorganic

inorgani·sé -sée [inɔrganize] *adj* unorganized (*workers*), nonunion

inoubliable [inublijabl] *adj* unforgettable

inouï inouïe [inwi] *adj* unheard-of

inoxydable [inɔksidabl] *adj* inoxidizable, stainless, rustproof

inqualifiable [ɛ̃kalifjabl] *adj* unspeakable

in·quiet [ɛ̃kjɛ] **-quiète** [kjɛt] *adj* anxious, worried, uneasy; restless

inquié·tant [ɛ̃kjetɑ̃] **-tante** [tɑ̃t] *adj* disquieting, worrisome

inquiéter [ɛ̃kjete] §10 *tr & intr* to worry

inquiétude [ɛ̃kjetyd] *f* uneasiness, worry

inquisi·teur [ɛ̃kizitœr] **-trice** [tris] *adj* inquisitorial; searching (*e.g., look*) ‖ *m* inquisitor; investigator

inquisition [ɛ̃kizisjɔ̃] *f* inquisition; investigation

inracontable [ɛ̃rakɔ̃tabl] *adj* untellable
insaisissable [ɛ̃sezisabl] *adj* hard to catch; elusive
insalubre [ɛ̃salybr] *adj* unhealthy
insane [ɛ̃san] *adj* insane, crazy
insanité [ɛ̃sanite] *f* insanity; piece of folly
insatiable [ɛ̃sasjabl] *adj* insatiable
insatisfaction [ɛ̃satisfaksjɔ̃] *f* dissatisfaction
inscription [ɛ̃skripsjɔ̃] *f* inscription; registration, enrollment; **inscription de** or **en faux** (law) plea of forgery; **prendre ses inscriptions** to register at a university
inscrire [ɛ̃skrir] §25 *tr* to inscribe; register; record ‖ *ref* to register, enroll; **s'inscrire à** to join; **s'inscrire en faux contre** to deny; **s'inscrire pour** to sign up for
ins·crit [ɛ̃skri] **-crite** [krit] *adj* inscribed; registered, enrolled ‖ *mf* registered student; (sports) entry; **inscrit maritime** naval recruit
insecte [ɛ̃sɛkt] *m* insect, bug
insecticide [ɛ̃sɛktisid] *adj* insecticidal ‖ *m* insecticide
insen·sé -sée [ɛ̃sɑ̃se] *adj* senseless, insane, crazy ‖ *m* madman ‖ *f* madwoman
insensible [ɛ̃sɑ̃sibl] *adj* insensitive; imperceptible
inséparable [ɛ̃separabl] *adj* inseparable ‖ *m* lovebird
insérer [ɛ̃sere] §10 *tr* to insert
insertion [ɛ̃sɛrsjɔ̃] *f* insertion
insi·dieux [ɛ̃sidjø] **-dieuse** [djøz] *adj* insidious
insigne [ɛ̃siɲ] *adj* signal, noteworthy; notorious ‖ *m* badge, mark; **insignes** insignia
insigni·fiant [ɛ̃siɲifjɑ̃] **-fiante** [fjɑ̃t] *adj* insignificant
insincère [ɛ̃sɛ̃sɛr] *adj* insincere
insinuation [ɛ̃sinɥasjɔ̃] *f* insinuation
insinuer [ɛ̃sinɥe] *tr* to insinuate; hint, hint at; work in, introduce ‖ *ref*—**s'insinuer dans** to worm one's way into
insipide [ɛ̃sipid] *adj* insipid, tasteless; insipid, dull
insister [ɛ̃siste] *intr* to insist; (coll) to continue, persevere; **insister pour** to insist on; **insister sur** to stress, emphasize
insociable [ɛ̃sɔsjabl] *adj* unsociable
insolateur [ɛ̃sɔlatœr] *m* solar heater
insolation [ɛ̃sɔlasjɔ̃] *f* exposure to the sun; sunstroke
insolence [ɛ̃sɔlɑ̃s] *f* insolence
inso·lent [ɛ̃sɔlɑ̃] **-lente** [lɑ̃t] *adj* insolent; extraordinary, unexpected
insolite [ɛ̃sɔlit] *adj* bizarre
insoluble [ɛ̃sɔlybl] *adj* insoluble
insolvabilité [ɛ̃sɔlvabilite] *f* insolvency
insolvable [ɛ̃sɔlvabl] *adj* insolvent
insomnie [ɛ̃sɔmni] *f* insomnia
insondable [ɛ̃sɔ̃dabl] *adj* unfathomable
insonore [ɛ̃sɔnɔr] *adj* soundproof; noiseless
insonoriser [ɛ̃sɔnɔrize] *tr* to soundproof
insouciance [ɛ̃susjɑ̃s] *f* carefreeness; indifference, carelessness
insou·ciant [ɛ̃susjɑ̃] **-ciante** [sjɑ̃t] *adj* carefree, unconcerned

insou·cieux [ɛ̃susjø] **-cieuse** [sjøz] *adj* carefree, unmindful
insou·mis [ɛ̃sumi] **-mise** [miz] *adj* unruly; unsubjugated ‖ *mf* rebel ‖ *m* (mil) A.W.O.L.
insoumission [ɛ̃sumisjɔ̃] *f* insubordination, rebellion; (mil) absence without leave
insoupçonnable [ɛ̃supsɔnabl] *adj* above suspicion
insoupçon·né -née [ɛ̃supsɔne] *adj* unsuspected
insoutenable [ɛ̃sutnabl] *adj* untenable; unbearable
inspecter [ɛ̃spɛkte] *tr* to inspect
inspec·teur [ɛ̃spɛktœr] **-trice** [tris] *mf* inspector
inspection [ɛ̃spɛksjɔ̃] *f* inspection; inspectorship
inspiration [ɛ̃spirasjɔ̃] *f* inspiration
inspirer [ɛ̃spire] §97, §98 *tr* to inspire; breathe in; **inspirer à qn de** to inspire s.o. to; **inspirer q.ch. à qn** to inspire s.o. with s.th. ‖ *ref*—**s'inspirer de** to be inspired by
instable [ɛ̃stabl] *adj* unstable
installateur [ɛ̃stalatœr] *m* heater man; fitter, plumber
installation [ɛ̃stalasjɔ̃] *f* installation; equipment, outfit; appointments, fittings
installer [ɛ̃stale] *tr* to install; equip, furnish; **être bien installé** to be comfortably settled ‖ *ref* to settle down, set up shop; **s'installer chez** to foist oneself on
instamment [ɛ̃stamɑ̃] *adv* urgently, earnestly
instance [ɛ̃stɑ̃s] *f* insistence; **avec instance** earnestly; **en instance** pending; **en instance de** on the point of; **en seconde instance** on appeal; **instances** entreaties; **introduire une instance** to start proceedings
ins·tant [ɛ̃stɑ̃] **-tante** [tɑ̃t] *adj* urgent, pressing ‖ *m* instant, moment, **à chaque instant**, **à tout instant** continually; **à l'instant** at once, right away; just now; at the moment; **par instants** from time to time
instanta·né -née [ɛ̃stɑ̃tane] *adj* instantaneous ‖ *m* snapshot
instantanément [ɛ̃stɑ̃tanemɑ̃] *adv* instantaneously; instantly
instar [ɛ̃star]—**à l'instar de** in the manner of
instauration [ɛ̃stɔrasjɔ̃] *f* establishment
instaurer [ɛ̃stɔre] *tr* to establish
instigation [ɛ̃stigasjɔ̃] *f* instigation
instiller [ɛ̃stile] *tr* to instill
instinct [ɛ̃stɛ̃] *m* instinct; **d'instinct, par instinct** by instinct
instinc·tif [ɛ̃stɛ̃ktif] **-tive** [tiv] *adj* instinctive
instituer [ɛ̃stitɥe] *tr* to found; institute (*e.g., proceedings*)
institut [ɛ̃stity] *m* institute; **institut de beauté** beauty parlor; **institut de coupe** tonsorial parlor; **institut dentaire** dental school

institu·teur [ɛ̃stitytœr] **-trice** [tris] *mf* schoolteacher; founder

institution [ɛ̃stitysjɔ̃] *f* institution

instructeur [ɛ̃stryktœr] *m* instructor

instruc·tif [ɛ̃stryktif] **-tive** [tiv] *adj* instructive

instruction [ɛ̃stryksjɔ̃] *f* instruction; directive; education; (comp) statement; **instruction judiciaire** (law) preliminary investigation; **instructions** directions (*for use*); **instructions permanentes** standing orders

instruire [ɛ̃strɥir] §19, §96 *tr* to instruct; (law) to conduct the investigation of; **instruire qn de** to inform s.o. of ‖ *ref* to improve one's mind

instrument [ɛ̃strymɑ̃] *m* instrument; **instrument à anche** reed instrument; **instrument à cordes** stringed instrument; **instrument à vent** wind instrument; **instrument en bois** woodwind; **instrument en cuivre** brass

instrumen·tal -tale [ɛ̃strymɑ̃tal] *adj* (*pl* **-taux** [to]) instrumental

instrumenter [ɛ̃strymɑ̃te] *tr* to instrument

instrumentiste [ɛ̃strymɑ̃tist] *mf* instrumentalist

insu [ɛ̃sy] *m*—**à l'insu de** unknown to; **à mon insu** unknown to me

insubmersible [ɛ̃sybmɛrsibl] *adj* unsinkable

insubordon·né -née [ɛ̃sybɔrdɔne] *adj* insubordinate

insuccès [ɛ̃syksɛ] *m* failure

insuffisamment [ɛ̃syfizamɑ̃] *adv* insufficiently

insuffi·sant [ɛ̃syfizɑ̃] **-sante** [zɑ̃t] *adj* insufficient

insulaire [ɛ̃sylɛr] *adj* insular ‖ *mf* islander

insuline [ɛ̃sylin] *f* insulin

insulte [ɛ̃sylt] *f* insult

insulter [ɛ̃sylte] *tr* to insult ‖ *intr*—**insulter à** to offend, outrage

insupportable [ɛ̃sypɔrtabl] *adj* unbearable

insur·gé -gée [ɛ̃syrʒe] *adj & mf* insurgent

insurger [ɛ̃syrʒe] §38 *ref* to revolt, rebel

insurmontable [ɛ̃syrmɔ̃tabl] *adj* insurmountable

insurrection [ɛ̃syrɛksjɔ̃] *f* insurrection

in·tact -tacte [ɛ̃takt] *adj* intact, untouched

intangible [ɛ̃tɑ̃ʒibl] *adj* intangible

intarissable [ɛ̃tarisabl] *adj* inexhaustible

inté·gral -grale [ɛ̃tegral] *adj* (*pl* **-graux** [gro]) integral; complete (*e.g., edition*); full (*e.g., payment*) ‖ *f* complete works; (math) integral

inté·grant -grante [ɛ̃tegrɑ̃] *adj* integral

intégration [ɛ̃tegrasjɔ̃] *f* integration

intègre [ɛ̃tegr] *adj* honest, upright

intégrer [ɛ̃tegre] §10 *tr* to integrate ‖ *ref* to form an integral part; (slang) to be accepted (*at an exclusive school*)

intégrité [ɛ̃tegrite] *f* integrity

intellect [ɛ̃telɛkt] *m* intellect

intellec·tuel -tuelle [ɛ̃telɛktɥɛl] *adj & mf* intellectual

intelligemment [ɛ̃teliʒamɑ̃] *adv* intelligently

intelligence [ɛ̃teliʒɑ̃s] *f* intelligence; intellect (*person*); **en bonne intelligence avec** on good terms with; **être d'intelligence** to be in collusion

intelli·gent [ɛ̃teliʒɑ̃] **-gente** [ʒɑ̃t] *adj* intelligent

intelligible [ɛ̃teliʒibl] *adj* intelligible

intempé·rant [ɛ̃tɑ̃perɑ̃] **-rante** [rɑ̃t] *adj* intemperate

intempéries [ɛ̃tɑ̃peri] *fpl* bad weather

intempes·tif [ɛ̃tɑ̃pɛstif] **-tive** [tiv] *adj* untimely

intenable [ɛ̃tnabl] *adj* untenable

intendance [ɛ̃tɑ̃dɑ̃s] *f* stewardship; controllership, office of bursar; **Intendance** (mil) Quartermaster Corps

inten·dant [ɛ̃tɑ̃dɑ̃] **-dante** [dɑ̃t] *mf* steward, superintendent; controller, bursar; **intendant militaire** quartermaster

intense [ɛ̃tɑ̃s] *adj* intense

inten·sif [ɛ̃tɑ̃sif] **-sive** [siv] *adj* intensive

intensifier [ɛ̃tɑ̃sifje] *tr & ref* to intensify

intensité [ɛ̃tɑ̃site] *f* intensity

intenter [ɛ̃tɑ̃te] *tr* to start (*a suit*); bring (*an action*)

intention [ɛ̃tɑ̃sjɔ̃] *f* intention, intent; **à l'intention de** for (the sake of)

intention·né -née [ɛ̃tɑ̃sjɔne] *adj* motivated; **bien intentionné** well-meaning; **mal intentionné** ill-disposed

intention·nel -nelle [ɛ̃tɑ̃sjɔnɛl] *adj* intentional

inter [ɛ̃tɛr] *m* (coll) long distance

interaction [ɛ̃tɛraksjɔ̃] *f* interaction, interplay

intercaler [ɛ̃tɛrkale] *tr* to intercalate; insert, sandwich

intercéder [ɛ̃tɛrsede] §10 *intr* to intercede

intercepter [ɛ̃tɛrsɛpte] *tr* to intercept

intercepteur [ɛ̃tɛrsɛptœr] *m* interceptor

interchangeable [ɛ̃tɛrʃɑ̃ʒabl] *adj* interchangeable

interclasse [ɛ̃tɛrklɑs] *m* (educ) break between classes

intercontinen·tal -tale [ɛ̃tɛrkɔ̃tinɑ̃tal] (*pl* **-taux** [to]) *adj* intercontinental

intercourse [ɛ̃tɛrkurs] *f* (naut) free entry

interdépen·dant [ɛ̃tɛrdepɑ̃dɑ̃] **-dante** [dɑ̃t] *adj* interdependent

interdiction [ɛ̃tɛrdiksjɔ̃] *f* interdiction; suspension; **interdiction de séjour** forbidden entry

interdire [ɛ̃tɛrdir] §40, §97, §98 *tr* to prohibit, forbid; confound, abash; interdict; suspend; **interdire q.ch. à qn** to forbid s.o. s.th.

interdisciplinaire [ɛ̃tɛrdisiplinɛr] *adj* interdisciplinary

inter·dit [ɛ̃tɛrdi] **-dite** [dit] *adj* prohibited, forbidden; dumfounded, abashed; deprived of rights; (mil) off limits ‖ *m* interdict

intéres·sant [ɛ̃terɛsɑ̃] **-sante** [sɑ̃t] *adj* interesting; attractive (*offer*)

intéres·sé -sée [ɛ̃terese] *adj* interested; self-seeking ‖ *mf* interested party

intéresser [ɛ̃terese] *tr* to interest; involve ‖ **§96** *ref*—**s'intéresser à** or **dans** to be interested in

intérêt [ɛ̃terɛ] *m* interest; **intérêts composés** compound interest

interface [ɛ̃tɛrfas] *f* (comp) interface

interférence [ɛ̃tɛrferɑ̃s] *f* interference

interférer [ɛ̃tɛrfere] **§10** *intr* (phys) to interfere ‖ *ref* to interfere with each other

inté·rieur -rieure [ɛ̃terjœr] *adj* interior; inner, inside ‖ *m* interior; inside; house, home; **à l'intérieur (de)** inside

intérieurement [ɛ̃terjœrmɑ̃] *adv* inwardly, internally; to oneself

intérim [ɛ̃terim] *m invar* interim; **dans l'intérim** in the meantime; **par intérim** acting, pro tem, interim

intérimaire [ɛ̃terimɛr] *adj* temporary, acting

interjection [ɛ̃tɛrʒɛksjɔ̃] *f* interjection

interligne [ɛ̃tɛrliɲ] *m* space between the lines; writing in the space between the lines; **à double interligne** double-spaced; **à simple interligne** single-spaced ‖ *f* lead

interligner [ɛ̃tɛrliɲe] *tr* to interline; (typ) to lead out

interlocu·teur [ɛ̃tɛrlɔkytœr] **-trice** [tris] *mf* interlocutor; intermediary; party (*with whom one is conversing*)

interlope [ɛ̃tɛrlɔp] *adj* illegal, shady ‖ *m* (naut) smuggling vessel

interloquer [ɛ̃tɛrlɔke] *tr* to disconcert

interlude [ɛ̃tɛrlyd] *m* interlude

intermède [ɛ̃tɛrmɛd] *m* (theat & fig) interlude

intermédiaire [ɛ̃tɛrmedjɛr] *adj* intermediate, intermediary ‖ *mf* intermediary ‖ *m* (com) middleman; **par l'intermédiaire de** by means of, by the medium of

interminable [ɛ̃tɛrminabl] *adj* interminable

intermit·tent [ɛ̃tɛrmitɑ̃] **-tente** [tɑ̃t] *adj* intermittent

internat [ɛ̃tɛrna] *m* boarding school; boarding-school life; (med) internship

internatio·nal -nale [ɛ̃tɛrnasjɔnal] *adj* (*pl* **-naux** [no]) international

interne [ɛ̃tɛrn] *adj* inner; (math) interior ‖ *mf* boarder (*at a school*); (med) intern

inter·né -née [ɛ̃tɛrne] *mf* internee

internement [ɛ̃tɛrnəmɑ̃] *m* internment; confinement (*of a mental patient*)

interner [ɛ̃tɛrne] *tr* to intern

interpeller [ɛ̃tɛrpele] *tr* to question, interrogate; yell at; heckle

interphone [ɛ̃tɛrfɔn] *m* intercom

interplanétaire [ɛ̃tɛrplanetɛr] *adj* interplanetary

interpoler [ɛ̃tɛrpɔle] *tr* to interpolate

interposer [ɛ̃tɛrpoze] *tr* to interpose

interprétation [ɛ̃tɛrpretasjɔ̃] *f* interpretation

interprète [ɛ̃tɛrprɛt] *mf* interpreter; spokesperson; intermediary, go-between, agent, helper; (theat) performer; **les interprètes** (theat) the cast

interpréter [ɛ̃tɛrprete] **§10** *tr* to interpret; **mal interpréter** to misinterpret

interrogation [ɛ̃tɛrɔgasjɔ̃] *f* interrogation

interroger [ɛ̃tɛrɔʒe] **§38** *tr* to interrogate, question

interrompre [ɛ̃tɛrɔ̃pr] (3d *sg pres ind* **interrompt** [ɛ̃tɛrɔ̃]) *tr* to interrupt; heckle ‖ **§97** *ref* to break off, be interrupted

interrup·teur [ɛ̃tɛryptœr] **-trice** [tris] *adj* interrupting; circuit-breaking ‖ *m* switch; **interrupteur à couteau** knife switch; **interrupteur à culbuteur** or **à bascule** toggle switch; **interrupteur d'escalier** two-way switch; **interrupteur encastré** flush switch; **interrupteur olive** pear switch

interruption [ɛ̃tɛrypsjɔ̃] *f* interruption

intersection [ɛ̃tɛrsɛksjɔ̃] *f* intersection

intersigne [ɛ̃tɛrsiɲ] *m* omen, portent

interstellaire [ɛ̃tɛrstelɛr] *adj* interstellar

interstice [ɛ̃tɛrstis] *m* interstice

interur·bain [ɛ̃tɛryrbɛ̃] **-baine** [bɛn] *adj* interurban; (telp) long-distance ‖ *m* (telp) long distance

intervalle [ɛ̃tɛrval] *m* interval

intervenir [ɛ̃tɛrvnir] **§72** (*aux:* ÊTRE) *intr* to intervene; take place, happen; (med) to operate; **faire intervenir** to call in

intervention [ɛ̃tɛrvɑ̃sjɔ̃] *f* intervention; (med) operation

intervertir [ɛ̃tɛrvɛrtir] *tr* to invert, transpose

interview [ɛ̃tɛrvju] *f* (journ) interview

interviewer [ɛ̃tɛrvjuvœr] *m* interviewer ‖ [ɛ̃tɛrvjuve] *tr* to interview

intervox [ɛ̃tɛrvɔks] *m* intercom

intestat [ɛ̃tɛsta] *adj & mf invar* intestate

intes·tin [ɛ̃tɛstɛ̃] **-tine** [tin] *adj* intestine, internal ‖ *m* intestine; **gros intestin** large intestine; **intestin grêle** small intestine

intimation [ɛ̃timasjɔ̃] *f* (law) summons

intime [ɛ̃tim] *adj & mf* intimate

inti·mé -mée [ɛ̃time] *mf* (law) defendant

intimer [ɛ̃time] *tr* to notify; give (*an order*)

intimider [ɛ̃timide] *tr* to intimidate

intimité [ɛ̃timite] *f* intimacy; privacy; depths (*of one's being*)

intituler [ɛ̃tityle] *tr* to entitle

intolérable [ɛ̃tɔlerabl] *adj* intolerable

intolé·rant [ɛ̃tɔlerɑ̃] **-rante** [rɑ̃t] *adj* intolerant

intonation [ɛ̃tɔnasjɔ̃] *f* intonation

intouchable [ɛ̃tuʃabl] *adj & mf* untouchable

intoxication [ɛ̃tɔksikasjɔ̃] *f* poisoning

intoxiquer [ɛ̃tɔkside] *tr* to poison

intraduisible [ɛ̃tradɥizibl] *adj* untranslatable

intraitable [ɛ̃trɛtabl] *adj* intractable

intransi·geant [ɛ̃trɑ̃ziʒɑ̃] **-geante** [ʒɑ̃t] *adj* intransigent ‖ *mf* diehard, standpatter

intransi·tif [ɛ̃trɑ̃zitif] **-tive** [tiv] *adj* intransitive

intrant [ɛ̃trɑ̃] *m* input

intravei·neux [ɛ̃travɛnø] **-neuse** [nøz] *adj* intravenous

intrépide [ɛ̃trepid] *adj* intrepid; persistent

intri·gant [ɛ̃trigɑ̃] **-gante** [gɑ̃t] *adj* intriguing ‖ *mf* plotter, schemer

intrigue [ɛ̃trig] *f* intrigue, plot; love affair; **intrigues de couloir** lobbying

intriguer [ɛ̃trige] *tr & intr* to intrigue

intrinsèque [ɛ̃trɛ̃sɛk] *adj* intrinsic

introduction [ɛ̃trɔdyksjɔ̃] *f* introduction; admission

introduire [ɛ̃trɔdɥir] §19 *tr* to introduce, bring in; show in; interject (*e.g.*, *a remark*); insert (*a coin*) ‖ *ref* to be introduced; **s'introduire dans** to slip in

intronisation [ɛ̃trɔnizasjɔ̃] *f* investiture, inauguration

introniser [ɛ̃trɔnize] *tr* to enthrone

introspec·tif [ɛ̃trɔspɛktif] **-tive** [tiv] *adj* introspective

introuvable [ɛ̃truvabl] *adj* unfindable

introver·ti -tie [ɛ̃trɔvɛrti] *adj & mf* introvert

in·trus [ɛ̃try] **-truse** [tryz] *adj* intruding ‖ *mf* intruder

intrusion [ɛ̃tryzjɔ̃] *f* intrusion

intuition [ɛ̃tɥisjɔ̃] *f* intuition

inusable [inyzabl] *adj* durable, wearproof

inusi·té -tée [inyzite] *adj* obsolete

inutile [inytil] *adj* useless, unnecessary

inutilement [inytilmɑ̃] *adv* in vain, uselessly; unnecessarily

inutilité [inytilite] *f* uselessness

invain·cu -cue [ɛ̃vɛ̃ky] *adj* unconquered

invalide [ɛ̃valid] *adj* invalid ‖ *mf* invalid, cripple; **invalide de guerre** disabled veteran

invalider [ɛ̃valide] *tr* to invalidate

invalidité [ɛ̃validite] *f* invalidity; disability

invariable [ɛ̃varjabl] *adj* invariable

invasion [ɛ̃vɑzjɔ̃] *f* invasion

invective [ɛ̃vɛktiv] *f* invective

invectiver [ɛ̃vɛktive] *tr* to rail at ‖ *intr* to inveigh

invendable [ɛ̃vɑ̃dabl] *adj* unsalable

inven·du -due [ɛ̃vɑ̃dy] *adj* unsold ‖ *m*—**les invendus** the unsold copies; the unsold articles

inventaire [ɛ̃vɑ̃tɛr] *m* inventory

inventer [ɛ̃vɑ̃te] *tr* to invent

inven·teur [ɛ̃vɑ̃tœr] **-trice** [tris] *mf* inventor; (law) finder

inven·tif [ɛ̃vɑ̃tif] **-tive** [tiv] *adj* inventive

invention [ɛ̃vɑ̃sjɔ̃] *f* invention

inventorier [ɛ̃vɑ̃tɔrje] *tr* to inventory

inversable [ɛ̃vɛrsabl] *adj* untippable, uncapsizable

inverse [ɛ̃vɛrs] *adj & m* inverse; **faire l'inverse de** to do the opposite of

inverser [ɛ̃vɛrse] *tr* to invert, reverse ‖ *intr* (elec) to reverse

inverseur [ɛ̃vɛrsœr] *m* reversing device; **inverseur des phares** (aut) dimmer

inversion [ɛ̃vɛrsjɔ̃] *f* inversion

inverté·bré -brée [ɛ̃vɛrtebre] *adj & m* invertebrate

inver·ti -tie [ɛ̃vɛrti] *mf* invert

invertir [ɛ̃vɛrtir] *tr* to invert, reverse

investiga·teur [ɛ̃vɛstigatœr] **-trice** [tris] *adj* investigative; searching ‖ *mf* investigator

investigation [ɛ̃vɛstigasjɔ̃] *f* investigation

investir [ɛ̃vɛstir] *tr* to invest; vest; **investir qn de sa confiance** to place one's confidence in s.o.

investissement [ɛ̃vɛstismɑ̃] *m* investment

investiture [ɛ̃vɛstityr] *f* investiture; nomination (*as a candidate for election*); primary election

invété·ré -rée [ɛ̃vetere] *adj* inveterate

invétérer [ɛ̃vetere] *ref* to become inveterate

invincible [ɛ̃vɛ̃sibl] *adj* invincible

invisible [ɛ̃vizibl] *adj* invisible; (coll) hiding, keeping out of sight

invitation [ɛ̃vitasjɔ̃] *f* invitation

invite [ɛ̃vit] *f* invitation, inducement; **répondre à l'invite de qn** (cards) to return s.o.'s lead; (fig) to respond to s.o.'s advances

invi·té -tée [ɛ̃vite] §92 *adj* invited ‖ *mf* guest

inviter [ɛ̃vite] §96, §100 *tr* to invite

involontaire [ɛ̃vɔlɔ̃tɛr] *adj* involuntary

invoquer [ɛ̃vɔke] *tr* to invoke

invraisemblable [ɛ̃vrɛsɑ̃blabl] *adj* improbable, unlikely, hard to believe; (coll) strange, weird

invraisemblance [ɛ̃vrɛsɑ̃blɑ̃s] *f* improbability, unlikelihood; (coll) queerness

invulnérable [ɛ̃vylnerabl] *adj* invulnerable

iode [jɔd] *m* iodine

iodure [jɔdyr] *m* iodide

ion [jɔ̃] *m* ion

ioniser [jɔnize] *tr* to ionize

iota [jɔta] *m* iota

irai [ire] *v* see **aller**

Irak [irak] *m*—**l'Irak** Iraq

ira·kien [irakjɛ̃] **-kienne** [kjɛn] *adj* Iraqi ‖ (cap) *mf* Iraqi

Iran [irɑ̃] *m*—**l'Iran** Iran

ira·nien [iranjɛ̃] **-nienne** [njɛn] *adj* Iranian ‖ *m* Iranian (*language*) ‖ (cap) *mf* Iranian (*person*)

iras [ira] *v* (**ira, irez**) see **aller**

iris [iris] *m* iris

irlan·dais [irlɑ̃dɛ] **-daise** [dɛz] *adj* Irish ‖ *m* Irish (*language*) ‖ (cap) *m* Irishman; **les Irlandais** the Irish ‖ (cap) *f* Irishwoman

Irlande [irlɑ̃d] *f* Ireland; **l'Irlande** Ireland

ironie [irɔni] *f* irony

ironique [irɔnik] *adj* ironic(al)

ironiser [irɔnize] *tr* to say ironically ‖ *intr* to speak ironically, jeer

irons [irɔ̃] *v* (**iront**) see **aller**

irradier [iradje] *tr & ref* to irradiate

irraison·nable [irɛzɔne] *adj* unreasoning

irration·nel -nelle [irasjɔnɛl] *adj* irrational

irréalisable [irealizabl] *adj* impractical, unattainable

irréalité [irealite] *f* unreality

irrecevable [irəsvable] *adj* inadmissable (*evidence*); unacceptable (*demand*)

irrécouvrable [irekuvrabl] *adj* uncollectible

irrécupérable [irekyperabl] *adj* irretrievable

irrécusable [irekyzabl] *adj* unimpeachable, incontestable, indisputable

ir·réel -réelle [ireɛl] *adj* unreal

irréflé·chi -chie [irefleʃi] *adj* rash, thoughtless

irréfutable [irefytabl] *adj* irrefutable

irrégu·lier [iregylje] **-lière** [ljɛr] *adj & m* irregular

irréli·gieux [ireliʒjø] **-gieuse** [ʒjøz] *adj* irreligious

irrémédiable [iremedjabl] *adj* irremediable

irremplaçable [irɑ̃plasabl] *adj* irreplaceable

irréparable [ireparabl] *adj* irreparable; irretrievable (*loss, mistake, etc.*)

irrépressible [irepresibl] *adj* irrepressible

irréprochable [ireproʃabl] *adj* irreproachable

irrésistible [irezistibl] *adj* irresistible

irréso·lu -lue [irezɔly] *adj* irresolute

irrespect [irɛspɛ] *m* disrespect

irrespec·tueux [irɛspɛktɥø] **-tueuse** [tɥøz] *adj* disrespectful

irrespirable [irɛspirabl] *adj* unbreathable

irresponsable [irɛspɔ̃sabl] *adj* irresponsible

irrétrécissable [iretresisabl] *adj* preshrunk, unshrinkable

irrévéren·cieux [ireverɑ̃sjø] **-cieuse** [sjøz] *adj* irreverent

irréversible [ireversibl] *adj* irreversible

irrévocable [irevɔkabl] *adj* irrevocable

irrigation [irigɑsjɔ̃] *f* irrigation

irriguer [irige] *tr* to irrigate

irri·tant [iritɑ̃] **-tante** [tɑ̃t] *adj* irritating ‖ *m* irritant

irritation [iritɑsjɔ̃] *f* irritation

irriter [irite] *tr* to irritate ‖ *ref* to become irritated

irruption [irypsjɔ̃] *f* irruption; invasion; **faire irruption** to burst in

isabelle [izabɛl] *m* dun or light-bay horse ‖ (*cap*) *f* Isabel

Isaïe [izai] *m* Isaiah

Islam [islam] *m*—**l'Islam** Islam

islamique [islamik] *adj* Islamic

islan·dais [islɑ̃dɛ] **-daise** [dɛz] *adj* Icelandic ‖ *m* Icelandic (*language*) ‖ (*cap*) *mf* Icelander

Islande [islɑ̃d] *f* Iceland; **l'Islande** Iceland

isocèle [izɔsɛl] *adj* isosceles

iso·lant [izɔlɑ̃] **-lante** [lɑ̃t] *adj* insulating ‖ *m* insulator

isolation [izɔlɑsjɔ̃] *f* insulation; **isolation phonique** soundproofing

isolationniste [izɔlɑsjɔnist] *adj & mf* isolationist

iso·lé -lée [izɔle] *adj* isolated; independent; insulated

isolement [izɔlmɑ̃] *m* isolation; insulation

isolément [izɔlemɑ̃] *adv* separately, independently

isoler [izɔle] *tr* to isolate; insulate ‖ *ref* to cut oneself off

isoloir [izɔlwar] *m* polling booth

isotope [izɔtɔp] *m* isotope

Israël [israɛl] *m* Israel; **à Israël** (*to give*) to Israel; **d'Israël** of Israel, e.g., **l'état d'Israël** the state of Israel; **en Israël** in Israel; (*to go*) to Israel

israé·lien [israeljɛ̃] **-lienne** [ljɛn] *adj* Israeli ‖ (*cap*) *mf* Israeli

israélite [israelit], [izraelit] *adj* Israelite ‖ (*cap*) *mf* Israelite

is·su -sue [isy] *adj*—**issu de** descended from, born of ‖ *f* exit, way out; outlet; outcome, issue; **à l'issue de** on the way out from; at the end of; **issues** sharps, middlings (*in milling flour*); offal (*in butchering*); **sans issue** without exit; without any way out

isthme [ism] *m* isthmus

Italie [itali] *f* Italy; **l'Italie** Italy

ita·lien [italjɛ̃] **-lienne** [ljɛn] *adj* Italian ‖ *m* Italian (*language*) ‖ (*cap*) *mf* Italian (*person*)

italique [italik] *adj* Italic; (*typ*) italic ‖ *m* (*typ*) italics

item [itɛm] *m* question (*in a test*) ‖ *adv* ditto

itinéraire [itinerɛr] *adj & m* itinerary

itiné·rant [itinerɑ̃] **-rante** [rɑ̃t] *adj & mf* itinerant

itou [itu] *adv* (slang) also, likewise

I.V.G. [iveʒe] *f* (letterword) (**interruption volontaire de grossesse**) abortion

ivoire [ivwar] *m* ivory

ivraie [ivrɛ] *f* darnel, cockle; (Bib) tares

ivre [ivr] *adj* drunk, intoxicated

ivresse [ivrɛs] *f* drunkenness; ecstasy, rapture

ivrogne [ivrɔɲ] *adj* hard-drinking ‖ *m* drunkard

ivrognerie [ivrɔɲri] *f* drunkenness

ivrognesse [ivrɔɲɛs] *f* drinking woman

J

J, j [ʒi] *m invar* tenth letter of the French alphabet

jabot [ʒabo] *m* jabot; crop (*of bird*)

jabotage [ʒabɔtaʒ] *m* jabbering

jaboter [ʒabɔte] *tr & intr* to jabber

jacasse [ʒakas] *f* magpie; chatterbox

jacasser [ʒakase] *intr* to chatter, jabber

jacasserie [ʒakasri] *f* chatter, jabber

jachère [ʒaʃɛr] *f* fallow ground

jacinthe [ʒasɛ̃t] *f* hyacinth; **jacinthe des bois** bluebell

Jacques [ʒak] *m* James, Jacob; **Jacques Bonhomme** the typical Frenchman

jactance [ʒaktɑ̃s] *f* bragging

jade [ʒad] *m* jade

jadis [ʒadis] *adv* formerly of yore

jaguar [ʒagwar] *m* jaguar

jaillir [ʒajir] *intr* to gush, burst forth

jaillissement [ʒajismɑ̃] *m* gush
jais [ʒɛ] *m* jet
jalon [ʒalɔ̃] *m* stake; landmark; surveying staff
jalonner [ʒalɔne] *tr* to stake out; mark (*a way, a channel*)
jalousie [ʒaluzi] *f* jealousy; awning; Venetian blind
ja·loux [ʒalu] **-louse** [luz] *adj* jealous
jamais [ʒamɛ] *adv* ever; never; **jamais de la vie!** not on your life! **jamais plus** never again; **ne . . . jamais** §90 never; **pour jamais** forever
jambe [ʒɑ̃b] *f* leg; **à toutes jambes** as fast as possible; **prendre ses jambes à son cou** to take to one's heels
jambon [ʒɑ̃bɔ̃] *m* ham; **jambon d'York** boiled ham
jambon·neau [ʒɑ̃bɔno] *m* (*pl* **-neaux**) ham knuckle
jamboree [ʒɑ̃bɔre], [dʒɑ̃bɔri] *m* jamboree
jante [ʒɑ̃t] *f* felloe; rim (*of auto wheel*)
janvier [ʒɑ̃vje] *m* January
Japon [ʒapɔ̃] *m*—**le Japon** Japan
japo·nais [ʒapɔnɛ] **-naise** [nɛz] *adj* Japanese ‖ *m* Japanese (*language*) ‖ (*cap*) *mf* Japanese (*person*)
japper [ʒape] *intr* to yap, yelp
jaquemart [ʒakmar] *m* jack (*figurine striking the time on a bell*)
jaquette [ʒakɛt] *f* coat, jacket; cut-away coat, morning coat; book jacket
jardin [ʒardɛ̃] *m* garden; **jardin d'acclimatation** zoo; **jardin d'enfants** kindergarten; **jardin d'hiver** greenhouse
jardiner [ʒardine] *tr* to clear out, trim ‖ *intr* to garden
jardi·nier [ʒardinje] **-nière** [njɛr] *adj* garden ‖ *mf* gardener ‖ *m* flower stand; mixed vegetables; spring wagon ‖ *f* kindergartner (*teacher*)
jargon [ʒargɔ̃] *m* jargon
jarre [ʒar] *f* earthenware jar
jarret [ʒarɛ] *m* hock, gambrel; shin (*of beef or veal*); back of the knee
jarretelle [ʒartɛl] *f* garter
jarretière [ʒartjɛr] *f* garter
jars [ʒar] *m* gander
jaser [ʒɑze] *intr* to babble; prattle; blab, gossip
jasmin [ʒasmɛ̃] *m* jasmine
jaspe [ʒasp] *m* jasper; (bb) marbling
jasper [ʒaspe] *tr* to marble, speckle
jatte [ʒat] *f* bowl
jauge [ʒoʒ] *f* gauge; (agr) trench; (naut) tonnage; **jauge d'huile, jauge à tige** dipstick
jauger [ʒoʒe] §38 *tr* to gauge, measure; (naut) to draw
jaunâtre [ʒonɑtr] *adj* yellowish, sallow
jaune [ʒon] *adj* yellow ‖ *mf* yellow person (*Oriental*) ‖ *m* yellow; yolk (*of egg*); scab, strikebreaker
jaunir [ʒonir] *tr* & *intr* to yellow
jaunisse [ʒonis] *f* jaundice
Javel [ʒavɛl] *f*—**eau de Javel** bleach

javelle [ʒavɛl] *f* swath (*of grain*); bunch (*of twigs*)
javelliser [ʒavɛlize] *tr* to chlorinate (*water*)
javelot [ʒavlo] *m* javelin
jazz [dʒaz] *m* jazz
je [ʒə] §87 I
Jean [ʒɑ̃] *m* John
Jeanne [ʒɑn] *f* Jane, Jean, Joan
jeannette [ʒanɛt] *f* gold cross (*ornament*); sleeveboard
Jeannot [ʒano] *m* (coll) Johnny, Jack
jeep [dʒip] *f* jeep
Jéhovah [ʒeɔva] *m* Jehovah
je-m'en-fichisme [ʒmɑ̃fiʃism] *m* (slang) what-the-hell attitude
je-ne-sais-quoi [ʒɛnsekwa] *m invar* what-you-call-it
Jérôme [ʒerom] *m* Jerome
jerrycan [dʒɛrikan] *m* gasoline can
jersey [ʒɛrsɛ] *m* jersey, sweater
Jérusalem [ʒeryzalɛm] *f* Jerusalem
jésuite [ʒezɥit] *adj* Jesuit; (pej) hypocritical ‖ (*cap*) *m* Jesuit; (pej) hypocrite
Jésus [ʒezy] *m* Jesus
Jésus-Christ [ʒezykri] *m* Jesus Christ
jet [ʒɛ] *m* throw, cast; jet; spurt, gush; flash (*of light*); **du premier jet** at the first try; **jet à la mer** jettison; **jet d'eau** fountain; **jet dentaire** water pick; **jet de pierre** stone's throw
jetable [ʒɛtabl] *adj* disposable
jetée [ʒəte] *f* breakwater, jetty
jeter [ʒəte] §34 *tr* to throw; throw away; throw down; hurl, fling; toss; cast (*a glance*); shed (*the skin*); pour forth; utter; to drop (*anchor*); lay (*the foundations*) ‖ *intr* to sprout ‖ *ref* to throw oneself; rush; empty (*said of a river*)
jeton [ʒətɔ̃] *m* token, counter; slug
jeu [ʒø] *m* (*pl* **jeux**) play; game, sport; gambling; pack, deck (*of cards*); set (*of chess pieces; of tools*); playing, acting; execution, performance; **en jeu** in gear; at stake; **franc jeu** fair play; **gros jeu** high stakes; **jeu d'eau** dancing waters; **jeu de dames** checkers; **jeu de hasard** game of chance; **jeu de massacre** hit-the-baby (*game at fair*); **jeu de mots** pun, play on words; **jeu d'enfant** child's play; **jeu de patience** jigsaw puzzle; **jeu de puce** tiddlywinks; **jeu de société** parlor game; **jeu d'orgue** organ stop; **jouer un jeu d'enfer** to play for high stakes; **vieux jeu** old hat
jeudi [ʒødi] *m* Thursday; **jeudi saint** Maundy Thursday
jeun [ʒœ̃]—**à jeun** fasting; on an empty stomach
jeune [ʒœn] (precedes the noun it modifies) *adj* young; youthful; junior, younger ‖ *m* young man; **jeunes délinquants** juvenile delinquents; **les jeunes** young people; the young (*of an animal*)
jeûne [ʒøn] *m* fast, fasting
jeûner [ʒøne] *intr* to fast; abstain; eat sparingly

jeunesse [ʒœnɛs] *f* youth; youthfulness; boyhood, girlhood; **jeunesse dorée** young people of wealth and fashion

jeu·net [ʒœnɛ] **-nette** [nɛt] *adj* youngish

jeû·neur [ʒønœr] **-neuse** [nøz] *mf* faster

jex [ʒɛks] *m* steel wool

joaillerie [ʒɔɑjri] *f* jewelry; jewelry business; jewelry shop

joail·lier [ʒɔɑje] **-lière** [jɛr] *mf* jeweler

jobard [ʒɔbar] *m* (coll) dupe

jobarderie [ʒɔbardri] *f* gullibility

jockey [ʒɔkɛ] *m* jockey

jodler [ʒɔdle] *tr & intr* to yodel

joie [ʒwa] *f* joy; **joies** pleasures

joindre [ʒwɛ̃dr] §35 *tr* to join; add; adjoin; catch up with; **joindre les deux bouts** to make both ends meet ‖ *intr* to join ‖ *ref* to join, unite; be adjacent, come together

joint [ʒwɛ̃] **jointe** [ʒwɛ̃t] *adj* joined; joint (*effort*); **joint à** added to ‖ *m* joint; **joint de cardan** (mach) universal joint; **joint de culasse** (aut) gasket (*of cylinder head*); **joint de dilatation thermique** expansion joint; **trouver le joint** (coll) to hit on the solution ‖ *v* see **joindre**

jointure [ʒwɛ̃tyr] *f* knuckle; joint

joker [ʒɔkɛr] *m* joker

jo·li -lie [ʒɔli], [ʒɔli] (precedes the noun it modifies) *adj* pretty; tidy (*income*)

joliment [ʒɔlimɑ̃] *adv* nicely; (coll) extremely, awfully

Jonas [ʒɔnɑs], [ʒɔnɑ] *m* Jonah

jonc [ʒɔ̃] *m* rush; **jonc d'Inde** rattan

jonchée [ʒɔ̃ʃe] *f* litter (*things strewn about*); cottage cheese

joncher [ʒɔ̃ʃe] *tr* to strew; litter

jonction [ʒɔ̃ksjɔ̃] *f* junction

jongler [ʒɔ̃gle] *intr* to juggle

jonglerie [ʒɔ̃gləri] *f* jugglery

jongleur [ʒɔ̃glœr] *m* juggler; jongleur

jonque [ʒɔ̃k] *f* (naut) junk

jonquille [ʒɔ̃kij] *adj invar* pale-yellow ‖ *m* pale yellow ‖ *f* jonquil

Jordanie [ʒɔrdani] *f* Jordan; **la Jordanie** Jordan

joue [ʒu] *f* cheek; **se caler les joues** (slang) to stuff oneself

jouer [ʒwe] §96 *tr* to play; gamble away; feign; act (*a part*) ‖ *intr* to play; gamble; feign; **faire jouer** to spring (*a lock*); **jouer à** to play (*a game*); **jouer à la baisse** to bear the market; **jouer à la hausse** to bull the market; **jouer de** to play (*a musical instrument*) ‖ *ref* to frolic; **se jouer de** to make fun of; be independent of; make light of

jouet [ʒwɛ] *m* toy, plaything

joueur [ʒwœr] **joueuse** [ʒwøz] *mf* player (*of games; of musical instruments*); gambler; **beau joueur** good sport; **joueur à la baisse** bear; **joueur à la hausse** bull; **mauvais joueur** poor sport

jouf·flu -flue [ʒufly] *adj* chubby

joug [ʒu] *m* yoke

jouir [ʒwir] §97 *intr* to enjoy oneself, enjoy life; come (*have an orgasm*); **jouir de** to enjoy

jouissance [ʒwisɑ̃s] *f* enjoyment; use, possession

jouis·seur [ʒwisœr] **-seuse** [søz] *adj* pleasure-loving ‖ *mf* pleasure lover

jou·jou [ʒuʒu] *m* (*pl* **-joux**) toy, plaything

jour [ʒur] *m* day; daylight; light, window, opening; **à jour** openwork; up to date; **de nos jours** nowadays; **du jour au lendemain** overnight, suddenly; **grand jour** broad daylight; **huit jours** a week; **il fait jour** it is getting light; **jour chômé** day off; **jour de ma fête** my birthday; **jour férié** legal holiday; **jour ouvrable** workday; **le jour de l'An** New Year's day; **le jour J** D-Day; **quinze jours** two weeks; **sous un faux jour** in a false light; **vivre au jour le jour** to live from hand to mouth

Jourdain [ʒurdɛ̃] *m* Jordan (*river*)

jour·nal [ʒurnal] *m* (*pl* **-naux** [no]) newspaper; journal; diary; (naut) logbook, journal; **journal parlé** newscast; **journal télévisé** telecast

journa·lier [ʒurnalje] **-lière** [ljɛr] *adj* daily ‖ *m* day laborer

journalisme [ʒurnalism] *m* journalism

journaliste [ʒurnalist] *mf* journalist

journée [ʒurne] *f* day; day's journey; day's pay; day's work; **journée d'accueil** open house; **toute la journée** all day long

journellement [ʒurnɛlmɑ̃] *adv* daily

joute [ʒut] *f* joust

jouter [ʒute] *intr* to joust

jo·vial -viale [ʒɔvjal] *adj* (*pl* **-vials** or **-viaux** [vjo] **-viales**) jovial, jocose

joyau [ʒwajo] *m* (*pl* **joyaux**) jewel

joyeux [ʒwajø] **joyeuse** [ʒwajøz] *adj* joyful, cheerful; jocose

jubi·lant [ʒybilɑ̃] **-lante** [lɑ̃t] *adj* jubilant

jubilé [ʒybile] *m* jubilee; golden-wedding anniversary

jucher [ʒyʃe] *tr & intr* to perch ‖ *ref* to go to roost

judaïque [ʒydaik] *adj* Jewish

judaïsme [ʒydaism] *m* Judaism

judas [ʒyda] *m* peephole ‖ (*cap*) *m* Judas

judicature [ʒydikatyr] *f* judiciary

judiciaire [ʒydisjɛr] *adj* legal, judicial

judi·cieux [ʒydisjø] **-cieuse** [sjøz] *adj* judicious, judicial

juge [ʒyʒ] *m* judge; umpire; **juge arbitre** umpire; **juge assesseur** associate judge

jugement [ʒyʒmɑ̃] *m* judgment

juger [ʒyʒe] §38, §95 *tr & intr* to judge; **juger bon de** to consider it a good thing to; **jugez de ma surprise!** imagine my surprise!; **si j'en juge par mon expérience** judging by my experience

jugulaire [ʒygylɛr] *adj* jugular ‖ *f* chin strap

juif [ʒɥif] **juive** [ʒɥiv] *adj* Jewish ‖ (*cap*) *mf* Jew

juillet [ʒɥije] *m* July

juin [ʒɥɛ̃] *m* June

Jules [ʒyl] *m* Julius; (coll) Mack; (slang) pimp; (slang) chamber pot

ju·lien [ʒyljɛ̃] **-lienne** [ljɛn] *adj* Julian || *f* (*soup*) julienne; (bot) rocket

ju·meau [ʒymo] **-melle** [mɛl] (*pl* **-meaux -melles**) *adj* & *mf* twin || *f* see **jumelles**

jumelage [ʒymlaʒ] *m* twinning

jume·lé -lée [ʒymle] *adj* double; twin (*cities*); semidetached (*house*); bilingual (*text*)

jumeler [ʒymle] §34 *tr* to couple, join; pair

jumelles [ʒymɛl] *fpl* opera glasses; field glasses; **jumelles de manchettes** cuff links

jument [ʒymɑ̃] *f* mare

jungle [ʒɔ̃gl] *f* jungle

jupe [ʒyp] *f* skirt; **jupe portefeuille** wraparound skirt

jupe-culotte [ʒypkylɔt] *f* split skirt

jupon [ʒypɔ̃] *m* petticoat

juré [ʒyre] *m* juror; member of an examining board

jurer [ʒyre] §95, §97, §98 *tr* to swear || *intr* to swear; clash

juridiction [ʒyridiksjɔ̃] *f* jurisdiction

juridique [ʒyridik] *adj* legal, judicial

juriste [ʒyrist] *m* writer on legal matters

juron [ʒyrɔ̃] *m* oath

jury [ʒyri] *m* jury; examining board

jus [ʒy] *m* juice; gravy; (slang) drink (*body of water*)

jusqu'au-boutiste [ʒyskobutist] *mf* (coll) bitterender, diehard

jusque [ʒysk(ə)] *adv* even; **jusqu'à** as far as, down to, up to; until; even; **jusqu'à ce que** until; **jusqu'après** until after; **jusqu'à quand** how long || *prep* as far as; until; **jusques et y compris** [ʒyskəzeikɔ̃pri] up to and including; **jusqu'ici** this far; until now; **jusqu'où** how far

jusque-là [ʒyskəla] *adv* that far, until then

jusquiame [ʒyskjam] *f* henbane

juste [ʒyst] *adj* just, righteous; accurate; just enough; sharp, e.g., **à six heures justes** at six o'clock sharp; (mus) in tune, on key || *adv* justly; correctly, exactly

justement [ʒystəmɑ̃] *adv* just; justly; exactly; as it happens

juste-milieu [ʒystəmiljø] *m* happy medium, golden mean

justesse [ʒystɛs] *f* justness; precision, accuracy; **de justesse** barely

justice [ʒystis] *f* justice; **faire justice de** to mete out just punishment to; to make short work of

justiciable [ʒystisjabl] *adj*—**justiciable de** accountable to; subject to

justifier [ʒystifje] *tr* to justify || *intr*—**justifier de** to account for, prove || *ref* to clear oneself

jute [ʒyt] *m* jute

ju·teux [ʒytø] **-teuse** [tøz] *adj* juicy

juvénile [ʒyvenil] *adj* juvenile, youthful

juxtaposer [ʒykstapoze] *tr* to juxtapose

K

K, k [kɑ] *m invar* eleventh letter of the French alphabet

kakatoès [kakatɔɛs] *m* cockatoo

kaki [kaki] *adj invar* & *m* khaki

kaléidoscope [kaleidɔskɔp] *m* kaleidoscope

kamikaze [kamikaze] *m* kamikaze

kangourou [kɑ̃guru] *m* kangaroo

karaté [karate] *m* karate

kascher or **kasher** [kaʃɛr] *adj* kosher; **c'est kascher** it's kosher

kayak [kajak] *m* kayak; **faire du kayak** to go canoeing

keepsake [kipsɛk] *m* giftbook, keepsake

képi [kepi] *m* kepi

kermesse [kɛrmɛs] *f* charity bazaar

kérosène [kerozɛn] *m* kerosene; **kérosène aviation** jet fuel; rocket fuel

ketchup [kɛtʃœp] *m* ketchup

khan [kɑ̃] *m* khan

kidnapper [kidnape] *tr* to kidnap

kidnap·peur [kidnapœr] **-peuse** [pøz] *mf* kidnaper

kif [kif] *m* (coll) pot, marijuana

kif-kif [kifkif] *adj invar* (coll) all the same; **c'est kif-kif** (coll) it's fifty-fifty

kilo [kilo] *m* kilo, kilogram

kilocycle [kilɔsikl] *m* kilocycle

kilogramme [kilɔgram] *m* kilogram

kilomètre [kilɔmɛtr] *m* kilometer, kilo

kilowatt [kilɔwat] *m* kilowatt

kilowatt-heure [kilɔwatœr] *m* (*pl* **kilowatts-heures**) kilowatt-hour

kilt [kilt] *m* kilt

kimono [kimɔno] *m* kimono

kinescope [kinɛskɔp] *m* kinescope

kiosque [kjɔsk] *m* newsstand; bandstand; summerhouse

kipper [kipœr], [kipɛr] *m* kipper

klaxon [klaksɔn] *m* (aut) horn

klaxonner [klaksɔne] *intr* to sound the horn

kleptomane [klɛptɔman] *adj* & *mf* kleptomaniac

km/h *abbr* (**kilomètres-heure, kilomètres à l'heure**) kilometers per hour

knock-out [nɔkaut], [nɔkut] *adj invar* (boxing) knocked out, groggy || *m* (boxing) knockout

k.o. [kao] *adj* (letterword) (**knock-out**) k.o., knocked out; **mettre k.o.** to knock out || *m* k.o., knockout

krach [krak] *m* crash (*e.g., on the stock market*)
kraft [kraft] *m* strong wrapping paper
krak [krak] *m* medieval castle

Kremlin [krɛmlɛ̃] *m*—**le Kremlin** the Kremlin
kyrielle [kirjɛl] *f* rigmarole, string
kyste [kist] *m* cyst

L

L, l [ɛl], *[ɛl] *m invar* twelfth letter of the French alphabet
l' = **le** or **la** before a vowel or mute *h* ‖ often untranslated, e.g., **plus que je ne l'ai fait** more than I did; never translated when used for euphony, e.g., **comme l'on** as one, **que l'on** that one, **si l'on** if one
la [la] *art* §77 the ‖ *m* (mus) la ‖ *pron* §87 her; it
là [la] *adv* there; here, e.g., **je suis là** I am here; in, e.g., **est-il là?** is he in?; **il n'était pas là** he was out; **là, là!** there, there! (*it's not as bad as that!*)
-là [la] § 82, §84
là-bas [laba] *adv* yonder, over there
label [labɛl] *m* union label
labeur [labœr] *m* labor, toil
la·bial -biale [labjal] (*pl* **-biaux** [bjo] **-biales**) *adj & f* labial
laboran·tin [labɔrɑ̃tɛ̃] **-tine** [tin] *mf* laboratory assistant
laboratoire [labɔratwar] *m* laboratory; **laboratoire d'analyses** pathology laboratory; **laboratoire de langues** language laboratory; **laboratoire de prothèse dentaire** dental laboratory; **laboratoire du ciel** Skylab; **laboratoire nucléaire** nuclear research laboratory
labo·rieux [labɔrjø] **-rieuse** [rjøz] *adj* laborious; arduous; industrious; working (*classes*); **c'est laborieux!** (coll) it's endless!
labour [labur] *m* tilling, plowing
labourable [laburabl] *adj* arable, tillable
labourer [labure] *tr* to till, plow; furrow (*the brow*); scratch
laboureur [laburœr] *m* farm hand, plowman
Labrador [labradɔr] *m*—**le Labrador** Labrador
labyrinthe [labirɛ̃t] *m* labyrinth, maze
lac [lak] *m* lake; **Grands Lacs** Great Lakes
lacer [lase] §51 *tr* to lace; tie (*one's shoes*)
lacération [laserɑsjɔ̃] *f* tearing
lacérer [lasere] §10 *tr* to lacerate; tear up one
lacet [lasɛ] *m* lace; snare, noose; bowstring (*for strangling*); **en lacet** winding (*road*); **lacet de soulier** shoelace
lâche [laʃ] *adj* slack, loose; lax, careless; cowardly ‖ *mf* coward
lâcher [laʃe] *tr* to loosen; let go, release; turn loose; blurt out (*a word*); fire (*a shot*); (coll) to drop (*one's friends*); **lâcher pied** to give ground; **lâcher prise** to let go
lâcheté [laʃte] *f* cowardice

lâ·cheur [laʃœr] **-cheuse** [ʃøz] *mf* fickle friend, turncoat
lacis [lasi] *m* network (*of threads, nerves*)
laconique [lakɔnik] *adj* laconic
lacrymogène [lakrimɔʒɛn] *adj* tear (*gas*)
lacs [la] *m* noose, snare; **lacs d'amour** love knot
lac·té -tée [lakte] *adj* milky, milk (*diet*)
lacune [lakyn] *f* lacuna, gap, blank
lad [lad] *m* stableboy
là-dedans [ladədɑ̃] §85A *adv* in it, within, in that, in there
là-dessous [ladəsu] §85A *adv* under it, under that, under there
là-dessus [ladəsy] §85A *adv* on it, on that; thereupon
ladre [ladr] *adj* stingy, niggardly ‖ *mf* miser
ladrerie [ladrəri] *f* miserliness
lagon [lagɔ̃] *m* lagoon
lagune [lagyn] *f* lagoon
lai laie [lɛ] *adj* lay ‖ *m* lay (*poem*) ‖ *f* see **laie**
laïc laïque [laik] *adj* lay, secular ‖ *mf* layman ‖ *f* laywoman
laiche [lɛʃ] *f* (bot) sedge, reed grass
laïcisation [laisizɑsjɔ̃] *f* secularization
laïciser [laisize] *tr* to secularize
laid [lɛ] **laide** [lɛd] *adj* ugly; plain, homely; mean, low-down
laide·ron [lɛdrɔ̃] **-ronne** [rɔn] *adj* homely, ugly ‖ **laideron** *m* or *f* ugly wench
laideur [lɛdœr] *f* ugliness; meanness
laie [lɛ] *f* (zool) wild sow
lainage [lɛnaʒ] *m* woolens
laine [lɛn] *f* wool; **laine d'acier** steel wool; **manger** or **tondre la laine sur le dos à** (fig) to fleece
lainer [lɛne] *tr* to teasel, nap
lai·neux [lɛnø] **-neuse** [nøz] *adj* wooly; downy
lai·nier [lɛnje] **-nière** [njɛr] *adj* wool (*industry*) ‖ *mf* dealer in wool; worker in wool
laïque [laik] *adj* lay, secular ‖ *mf* layman ‖ *f* laywoman
laisse [lɛs] *f* leash; foreshore
laissé-pour-compte laissée-pour-compte [lesepurkɔ̃t] *adj* returned (*merchandise*) ‖ *m* (*pl* **laissés-pour-compte**) reject; left-over merchandise
laisser [lɛse], [lese] §95, §96, §97 *tr* to leave, quit; let, allow; let go (*at a low price*); let have, e.g., **il me l'a laissé pour trois dollars** he let me have it for three dollars; **laisser** + *inf* + **qn** to let

s.o. + *inf*, e.g., **il a laissé Marie aller au théâtre** he let Mary go to the theater; e.g., **il me l'a laissé peindre** or **il m'a laissé le peindre** he let me paint it ‖ *intr*—**ne pas laisser de** to not fail to, to not stop ‖ *ref* to let oneself, e.g., **se laisser aller** to let oneself go; **se laisser aller à** to give way to

laisser-aller [leseale] *m* abandon, easygoingness; slovenliness, negligence

laisser-passer [lesepɑse] *m invar* permit, pass

lait [lɛ] *m* milk; **lait de chaux** whitewash; **lait de poule** eggnog; **lait écrémé** skim milk; **se mettre au lait** to go on a milk diet

laitage [lɛtaʒ] *m* dairy products

laitance [lɛtɑ̃s] *f* milt

laiterie [lɛtri] *f* dairy, creamery; dairy farming

lai·tier [letje] **-tière** [tjɛr] *adj* dairy; milch (*cow*) ‖ *m* milkman; (metallurgy) slag, dross ‖ *f* dairymaid; milch cow

laiton [lɛtɔ̃] *m* brass; brass wire

laitonner [lɛtɔne] *tr* to plate with brass

laitue [lety] *f* lettuce; **laitue romaine** romaine

laïus [lajys] *m* (coll) speech, impromptu remarks; (coll) hot air

laïus·seur [lajyscœr] **-seuse** [søz] *mf* (coll) windbag

laize [lɛz] *f* width (*of cloth*)

lamanage [lamanaʒ] *m* harborage

lamaneur [lamancœr] *m* harbor pilot

lam·beau [lɑ̃bo] *m* (*pl* **-beaux**) scrap, bit; rag; **en lambeaux** in tatters, in shreds

lam·bin [lɑ̃bɛ̃] **-bine** [bin] *adj* (coll) slow ‖ *mf* (coll) slowpoke

lambiner [lɑ̃bine] *intr* (coll) to dawdle

lambris [lɑ̃bri] *m* paneling, wainscoting; plaster (*of ceiling*); **lambris dorés** (fig) palatial home

lambrisser [lɑ̃brise] *tr* to panel, wainscot; plaster

lame [lam] *f* blade; slat (*of blinds*); runner (*of skate*); wave; lamina, thin plate, sword; (fig) swordsman; **lame de fond** ground swell

la·mé -mée [lame] *adj* gold-trimmed, silver-trimmed, spangled ‖ *m*—**de lamé**, e.g., **une robe de lamé** a spangled dress

lamelle [lamɛl] *f* lamella, thin strip; slide (*of microscope*)

lamentable [lamɑ̃tabl] *adj* lamentable

lamentation [lamɑ̃tɑsjɔ̃] *f* lamentation, lament

lamenter [lamɑ̃te] *intr & ref* to lament

laminer [lamine] *tr* to laminate; roll (*a metal*)

laminoir [laminwar] *m* rolling mill; calender

lampadaire [lɑ̃padɛr] *m* lamppost; floor lamp

lampe [lɑ̃p] *f* lamp; (electron) tube; **lampe à pétrole** kerosene lamp; **lampe à rayons ultraviolets** sun lamp; **lampe à souder** blowtorch; **lampe au néon** neon light; **lampe de chevet** bedlamp; **lampe de poche** flashlight; **lampe survoltée** photoflood bulb; **s'en mettre plein la lampe** (slang) to stuff one's face

lampée [lɑ̃pe] *f* (coll) gulp, swig

lamper [lɑ̃pe] *tr* (coll) to gulp down, guzzle

lampe-tempête [lɑ̃ptɑ̃pɛt] *f* (*pl* **lampes-tempête**) hurricane lamp

lampion [lɑ̃pjɔ̃] *m* Chinese lantern; **les lampions** rhythmical call or rhythmical stamping of feet to denote impatience

lampiste [lɑ̃pist] *m* lightman; (coll) scapegoat; (coll) underling

lamproie [lɑ̃prwa] *f* lamprey

lampyre [lɑ̃pir] *m* glowworm

lance [lɑ̃s] *f* lance; nozzle (*of hose*); **rompre une lance avec** to cross swords with

lan·cé -cée [lɑ̃se] *adj* flying (*start*); in the swim

lance-bombes [lɑ̃sbɔ̃b] *m invar* trench mortar; (aer) bomb release

lancée [lɑ̃se] *f* impetus

lance-flammes [lɑ̃sflam] *m invar* flamethrower

lance-fusées [lɑ̃sfyze] *m invar* rocket launcher

lancement [lɑ̃smɑ̃] *m* launching, throwing; launching (*of ship; of new product on the market*); (aer) airdrop; (aer) release; (baseball) pitching

lance-mines [lɑ̃smin] *m invar* minelayer

lance-pierres [lɑ̃spjɛr] *m invar* slingshot

lancer [lɑ̃se] §51 *tr* to throw, fling, cast; launch (*e.g., a ship, a new product*); issue (*e.g., an appeal*); (baseball) to pitch ‖ *ref* to rush, dash; **se lancer dans** to launch out into, take up

lance-roquettes [lɑ̃srɔkɛt] *m invar* (arti) bazooka

lance-torpilles [lɑ̃stɔrpij] *m invar* torpedo tube

lancette [lɑ̃sɛt] *f* (surg) lancet

lan·ceur [lɑ̃scœr] **-ceuse** [søz] *mf* promoter; (baseball) pitcher; (sports) hurler, thrower ‖ *m* (rok) booster

lanci·nant [lɑ̃sinɑ̃] **-nante** [nɑ̃t] *adj* shooting, throbbing (*pain*); gnawing (*regret*)

lanciner [lɑ̃sine] *tr* to torment ‖ *intr* to shoot; throb

lan·dau [lɑ̃do] *m* (*pl* **-daus**) landau; baby carriage

lande [lɑ̃d] *f* moor, heath

landier [lɑ̃dje] *m* kitchen firedog with pothangers

langage [lɑ̃gaʒ] *m* language, speech; **langage de programmation** computer language

lange [lɑ̃ʒ] *m* diaper

langer [lɑ̃ʒe] §38 *tr* to swaddle, diaper

langou·reux [lɑ̃gurø] **-reuse** [røz] *adj* languorous

langouste [lɑ̃gust] *f* spiny lobster, crayfish

langous·tier [lɑ̃gustje] **-tière** [tjɛr] *m & f* lobster net ‖ *m* lobster boat

langoustine [lɑ̃gustin] *f* prawn

langue [lɑ̃g] *f* tongue; language, speech; **avoir la langue bien pendue** (coll) to have the gift of gab; **donner sa langue au**

chat (coll) to give up; **langue cible** target language; **langue d'arrivée** target language; **langue de départ** source language; **langue de terre** tongue (*neck or narrow strip*) of land; **langue source** source language; **langue verte** racy underworld slang; **langues vivantes** modern languages; **langue verte** slang; **mauvaise langue** backbiter, gossip; **prendre langue avec** to open up a conversation with; **tirer la langue à** to stick out one's tongue at

langue-de-chat [lãgdǝʃa] *f* (*pl* **langues-de-chat**) (culin) ladyfinger

languette [lãgɛt] *f* tongue (*e.g.*, *of shoe*); pointer (*of scale*); flap, strip

langueur [lãgœr] *f* languor

languir [lãgir] *intr* to languish; to pine away

languis·sant [lãgisã] **-sante** [sãt] *adj* languid; languishing; long-drawn-out, tiresome

lanière [lanjɛr] *f* strap, strip, thong

lanoline [lanɔlin] *f* lanolin

lanterne [lãtɛrn] *f* lantern; (aut) parking light; (obs) street lamp; **conter des lanternes** (coll) to talk nonsense; **lanterne d'agrandissement** (phot) enlarger; **lanterne de projection, lanterne à projections** slide projector, filmstrip projector; **lanterne rouge** (slang) tail end, last to arrive; **lanterne sourde** dark lantern; **lanterne vénitienne** Japanese lantern; **oublier d'éclairer** or **d'allumer sa lanterne** (coll) to leave out the most important point

lanterner [lãtɛrne] *tr* (coll) to string along, put off ‖ *intr* to loaf around, dawdle; **faire lanterner qn** to keep s.o. waiting

lapider [lapide] *tr* to stone; vilify

la·pin [lapɛ̃] **-pine** [pin] *mf* rabbit; **lapin de garenne** wild rabbit; **lapin russe** albino rabbit; **poser un lapin à qn** (coll) to stand s.o. up

la·pon [lapɔ̃] **-pone** [pɔn] *adj* Lappish ‖ *m* Lapp, Lappish (*language*) ‖ (*cap*) *mf* Lapp, Laplander (*person*)

Laponie [lapɔni] *f* Lapland; **la Laponie** Lapland

lapsus [lapsys] *m* slip (*of tongue, pen, etc.*)

laquais [lakɛ] *m* lackey, footman

laque [lak] *m & f* lacquer ‖ *m* lacquer ware ‖ *f* lac; shellac; hair spray

laquelle [lakɛl] §78

laquer [kake] *tr* to shellac; lacquer

larcin [larsɛ̃] *m* petty larceny; plagiarism

lard [lar] *m* bacon, side prok; (coll) fat (*of a person*); (slang) fat slob; **se faire du lard** (coll) to get fat

larder [larde] *tr* to lard; pierce, riddle

large [larʒ] *adj* wide, broad; generous; ample; loose-fitting ‖ (when standing before noun) *adj* wide, broad; generous; ample; large, e.g., **pour une large part** to a large extent ‖ *m* width, breadth; open sea; room, e.g. **donner du large à qn** to give s.o. room; **au large** within sight of shore; **au large de** off, e.g. **au large du Havre** off Le Havre; **de large** wide, e.g., **trois**

mètres de large three meters wide; **je suis au large dans cet habit** this suit is roomy for me; **passer au large de** to give a wide berth to; **prendre le large** (coll) to shove off ‖ *adv* boldly; **calculer large** to figure roughly; **habiller large** to dress in loose-fitting clothes; **il n'en mène pas large** (fig) he gets rattled in a tight spot; **voir large** (fig) to think big

largement [larʒǝmã] *adv* widely; abundantly; fully; plenty, e.g., **vous avez largement le temps** you have plenty of time

largesse [larʒɛs] *f* largess

largeur [larʒœr] *f* width, breadth; (naut) beam; **dans les grandes largeurs** (coll) in a big way; **grande largeur** double-width (*cloth*); **largeur d'esprit** broadmindedness

larguer [large] *tr* to let go, release

larme [larm] *f* tear; (coll) drop; **fondre en larmes** to burst into tears; **pleurer à chaudes larmes** to shed bitter tears

lar·moyant [larmwajã] **-moyante** [mwajãt] *adj* tearful; watery (*eyes*)

larmoyer [larmwaje] §47 *intr* to water (*said of eyes*); snivel, blubber

lar·ron [larɔ̃] **lar·ronnesse** [larɔnɛs] *mf* thief; **s'entendre comme larrons en foire** to be as thick as thieves

larve [larv] *f* larva

laryn·gé -gée [larɛ̃ʒe] *adj* laryngeal

laryn·gien [larɛ̃ʒjɛ̃] **-gienne** [ʒjɛn] *adj* laryngeal

laryngite [larɛ̃ʒit] *f* laryngitis

laryngoscope [larɛ̃gɔskɔp] *m* laryngoscope

larynx [larɛ̃ks] *m* larynx

las [lɑ] **lasse** [lɑs] *adj* weary ‖ **las** [lɑs], [lɑ] *interj* alas!

lascar [laskar] *m* character, rogue

las·cif [lasif] **las-cive** [lasiv] *adj* lascivious

lasciveté [lasivte] *f* lasciviousness

laser [lazɛr] *m* laser

las·sant [lɑsã] **-sante** [sãt] *adj* tiring, tedious

lasser [lɑse] § **96**, §97 *tr* to tire, weary; wear out (*s.o.'s patience*) ‖ *ref*—**sans se lasser** unceasingly; **se lasser de** + *inf* to tire of + *ger*; to tire oneself out + *ger*

lassitude [lɑsityd] *f* lassitude, weariness

lasso [lɑso] *m* lasso

latence [latɑ̃s] *f* latency

la·tent [latɑ̃] **-tente** [tɑ̃t] *adj* latent

laté·ral -rale [lateral] *adj* (*pl* **-raux**) lateral

la·tin [latɛ̃] **-tine** [tin] *adj* Latin ‖ *m* Latin (*language*); **latin vulgaire** Vulgar Latin ‖ (*cap*) *mf* Latin (*person*)

latino-améri·cain [latinɔamerikɛ̃] **-caine** [kɛn] (*pl* **-américains**) *adj* Latin-American ‖ (*cap*) *mf* Latin American

latitude [latityd] *f* latitude

latrines [latrin] *fpl* latrine

latte [lat] *f* lath; broadsword

latter [late] *tr* to lath

lattis [lati] *m* lathing, laths

laudanum [lodanɔm] *m* laudanum

lauda·tif [lodatif] **-tive** [tiv] *adj* laudatory

lau·réat [lɔrea] **-réate** [reat] *adj* laureate ‖ *mf* winner, laureate

laurier [lɔrje] *m* laurel, sweet bay; **laurier rose** rosebay; **s'endormir sur ses lauriers** to rest on one's laurels

lavable [lavabl] *adj* washable

lavabo [lavabo] *m* washbowl; washroom; **lavabos** toilet, lavatory

lavage [lavaʒ] *m* washing; **lavage de cerveau** (coll) brainwashing; **lavage des titres** wash sale; **lavage de tête** (coll) dressing down, scolding

lavallière [lavaljɛr] *f* loosely tied bow

lavande [lavɑ̃d] *f* lavender

lavandière [lavɑ̃djɛr] *f* washerwoman

lavasse [lavas] *f* (coll) dishwater

lave [lav] *f* lava

lave-glace [lavglas] *m* (*pl* **-glaces**) (aut) windshield washer

lavement [lavmɑ̃] *m* enema

laver [lave] *tr* to wash; **laver la tête à qn** (coll) to haul s.o. over the coals; **laver le cerveau à** (coll) to brainwash ‖ *intr* to wash ‖ *ref* to wash oneself, wash; **elle s'en est lavé les mains** (fig) she washed her hands of it

laverie [lavri] *f* (min) washery; **laverie automatique, laverie libre-service** self-service laundry

lavette [lavɛt] *f* dishcloth

la·veur [lavœr] **-veuse** [vøz] *mf* washer; **laveur de vaisselle** dishwasher (*person*); **laveur de vitres** window washer (*person*) ‖ *f* washerwoman; washing machine

lavoir [lavwar] *m* place for washing clothes

lavure [lavyr] *f* dishwater; (coll) swill, hogwash

laxa·tif [laksatif] **-tive** [tiv] *adj & m* laxative

layer [leje] §49 *tr* to blaze a trail through; blaze (*trees to mark a trail*)

layette [lɛjɛt] *f* layette; packing case

lazzi [lazi] *mpl* jeers

le [lə] *art* §77 the ‖ *pron* §87 him; it

leader [lidœr] *m* leader

lèche [lɛʃ] *f* (coll) thin slice (*e.g., of bread*); **faire de la lèche à qn** (slang) to lick s.o.'s boots

lèche-carreaux [lɛʃkaro] *m invar* (slang) window-shopping

lèchefrite [lɛʃfrit] *f* dripping pan

lècher [leʃe] §10 *tr* to lick; over-polish (*one's style*)

lé·cheur [leʃœr] **-cheuse** [ʃøz] *mf* (coll) bootlicker, flatterer

lèche-vitrines [lɛʃvitrin] *m invar* window-shopping; **faire du lèche-vitrines** to go window-shopping

leçon [ləsɔ̃] *f* lesson; reading (*of manuscript*); **faire la leçon à** to lecture, sermonize; prime on what to say

lec·teur [lɛktœr] **-trice** [tris] *mf* reader; lecturer (*of university rank*) ‖ *m* playback

lecture [lɛktyr] *f* reading; playback; **lecture sur les lèvres** lip reading

ledit [lədi] **ladite** [ladit] *adj* (*pl* **lesdits** [ledi] **lesdites** [ledit]) the aforesaid

lé·gal -gale [legal] *adj* (*pl* **-gaux** [go]) legal; statutory

légaliser [legalize] *tr* to legalize

légalité [legalite] *f* legality

légat [lega] *m* papal legate

légataire [legatɛr] *mf* legatee; **légataire universel** residual heir

légation [legasjɔ̃] *f* legation

légendaire [leʒɑ̃dɛr] *adj* legendary

légende [leʒɑ̃d] *f* legend; caption

lé·ger [leʒe] **-gère** [ʒɛr] §92 *adj* light; slight (*accent, difference, pain, mistake, etc.*); faint (*sound, tint, etc.*); delicate (*odor, perfume, etc.*); mild, weak (*drink*); scanty (*dress*); graceful (*figure*); empty (*stomach*); agile, active; frivolous, carefree; **à la légère** lightly; without due consideration

légèrement [leʒɛrmɑ̃] *adv* lightly; slightly; flippantly, thoughtlessly

légèreté [leʒɛrte] *f* lightness; gracefulness, frivolity; fickleness

leggings [legiŋs] *mpl & fpl* leggings

leghorn [legɔrn] *f* leghorn (*chicken*)

légiférer [leʒifere] §10 *intr* to legislate

légion [leʒjɔ̃] *f* legion

législa·teur [leʒislatœr] **-trice** [tris] *mf* legislator

législa·tif [leʒislatif] **-tive** [tiv] *adj* legislative

législation [leʒislasjɔ̃] *f* legislation

législature [leʒislatyr] *f* legislative session; legislature

légiste [leʒist] *m* jurist

légitime [leʒitim] *adj* legitimate ‖ *f* (slang) lawful spouse; **ma légitime** (slang) my better half

légitimer [leʒitime] *tr* to legitimate; justify

légitimité [leʒitimite] *f* legitimacy

legs [lɛ], [lɛg] *m* legacy

léguer [lege] §10 *tr* to bequeath

légume [legym] *m* vegetable; legume (*pod*) ‖ *f*—**grosse légume** (slang) bigwig, big wheel

légu·mier [legymje] **-mière** [mjɛr] *adj* vegetable (*garden, farming, etc.*) ‖ *m* vegetable dish

lemme [lɛm] *m* lemma

lendemain [lɑ̃dmɛ̃] *m* next day; results, outcome, e.g., **avoir d'heureux lendemains** to have happy results or a happy outcome; **au lendemain de** the day after; **le lendemain matin** the next morning; **sans lendemain** short-lived

lénifier [lenifje] *tr* (med) to soothe

lent [lɑ̃] **lente** [lɑ̃t] §92 *adj* slow ‖ *f* nit

lentement [lɑ̃tmɑ̃] *adv* slowly; deliberately

lenteur [lɑ̃tœr] *f* slowness, sluggishness; **lenteurs** delays, dilatoriness

lentille [lɑ̃tij] *f* lens; (bot) lentil; **lentilles** freckles; **lentilles cornéennes** contact lenses

léopard [leɔpar] *m* leopard

lèpre [lɛpr] *f* leprosy

lé·preux [leprø] **-preuse** [prøz] *adj* leprous ‖ *mf* leper

lequel [ləkɛl] §78

les [le] *art* §77 the ‖ *pron* §87 them ‖ *prep* near (*in place names*)
les·bien [lɛsbjɛ̃] **-bienne** [bjɛn] *adj* Lesbian ‖ *f* lesbian ‖ (*cap*) *mf* Lesbian
lèse-majesté [lɛzmaʒɛste] *f*—**crime de lèse-majesté** lese majesty, high treason
léser [leze] §10 *tr* to injure
lésine [lezin] *f* stinginess
lésiner [lezine] *intr* to haggle, be stingy
lésion [lezjɔ̃] *f* lesion; wrong, damage
les·quels -quelles [lekɛl] §78
lessivage [lesivaʒ] *m* washing; **lessivage de crâne** (coll) brainwashing
lessive [lesiv] *f* washing (*of clothes*); wash; washing soda, lye; **faire la lessive** to do the wash
lessiver [lesive] *tr* to wash; scrub (*with a cleaning agent*); (slang) to clean out (*e.g., another poker player*); **être lessivé** (slang) to be exhausted
lessiveuse [lesivøz] *f* washing machine
lest [lɛst] *m* ballast
leste [lɛst] *adj* nimble, quick; suggestive, broad; flippant
lestement [lɛstəmɑ̃] *adv* nimbly, deftly
lester [lɛste] *tr* to ballast; (coll) to fill (*one's stomach, pockets, etc.*) ‖ *ref* (coll) to stuff oneself
léthargie [letarʒi] *f* lethargy
léthargique [letarʒik] *adj* lethargic ‖ *mf* lethargic person
lettrage [lɛtraʒ] *m* lettering
lettre [lɛtr] *f* letter; **à la lettre, au pied de la lettre** to the letter; **avant la lettre** before complete development; **en toutes lettres** in full; in so many words; **lettre de change** bill of exchange; **lettre de faire-part** announcement; **lettre de voiture** bill of lading; **lettre d'imprimerie** printed letter; **lettre majuscule** capital letter; **lettre recommandée** registered letter; **lettres** letters (*literature*); **lettres numérales** roman numerals; **mettre une lettre à la poste** to mail a letter
let·tré -trée [lɛtre] *adj* lettered, literate ‖ *mf* learned person
lettre-morte [lɛtrəmɔrt] *f* letter returned to sender
lettrine [letrin] *f* catchword; initial letter
leu [lø] *m*—**à la queue leu leu** in single file
leucémie [løsemi] *f* leukemia
leucorrhée [løkɔre] *f* leucorrhea
leur [lœr] *adj poss* §88 their ‖ *pron poss* §89 theirs *pron pers* §87 them; to them
leurre [lœr] *m* lure; delusion
leurrer [lœre] *tr* to lure; trick, delude ‖ *ref* to be deceived
levain [ləvɛ̃] *m* leaven
levant [ləvɑ̃] *adj masc* rising (*sun*) ‖ *m* east ‖ (*cap*) *m* Levant
levan·tin [ləvɑ̃tɛ̃] **-tine** [tin] *adj* **Levantine** ‖ (*cap*) *mf* Levantine
le·vé -vée [ləve] *adj* rising (*sun*); raised (*e.g., hand*); up, e.g., **le soleil est levé** the sun is up ‖ *m* (mus) upbeat; (surv) survey ‖ *f* levee, embankment; collection (*of mail*); levying (*of troops, taxes, etc.*);

raising (*of siege*); lifting (*of embargo*); striking (*of camp*); breaking (*of seals*); upstroke (*of piston*); **faire une levée** (cards) to take a trick; **levée de boucliers** public protest, outcry; **levée d'écrou** discharge (*from prison*); **levée de séance** adjournment; **levée du corps** removal of the body; funeral service (*in front of the coffin*); **levées manquantes** (cards) undertricks
lever [ləve] *m* rising; (surv) survey; **lever du rideau** rise of the curtain; curtain raiser; **lever du soleil** sunrise ‖ §2 *tr* to lift; raise; collect, pick up (*the mail*); levy (*troops, taxes, etc.*); strike (*camp*); adjourn (*a meeting*); weigh (*anchor*); relieve (*a guard*); remit (*a punishment*); flush (*e.g., a partridge*); effect (*a survey*); break (*the seals*) ‖ *intr* to come up (*said of plants*); rise (*said of dough*) ‖ *ref* to get up; stand up; rise; heave (*said of sea*); clear up (*said of weather*)
léviathan [levjatɑ̃] *m* leviathan
levier [ləvje] *m* lever, crowbar; **être aux leviers de commande** (aer) to be at the controls; (fig) to be in control; **levier de changement de vitesse** gearshift lever; **levier d'interligne et de retour du chariot** return lever (*of a typewriter*)
lévitation [levitasjɔ̃] *f* levitation
levraut [ləvro] *m* young hare, leveret
lèvre [levr] *f* lip; rim; **du bout des lèvres** half-heartedly, guardedly; **embrasser sur les lèvres** to kiss; **serrer les lèvres** to purse one's lips
lévrier [levrije] *m* greyhound
levure [ləvyr] *f* yeast, **levure anglaise** or **chimique** baking powder; **levure de bière** brewer's yeast
lexi·cal -cale [lɛksikal] *adj* (*pl* **-caux** [ko]) lexical
lexicographe [lɛksikɔgraf] *mf* lexicographer
lexicographie [lɛksikɔgrafi] *f* lexicography
lexicographique [lɛksikɔgrafik] *adj* lexicographic(al)
lexicologie [lɛksikɔlɔʒi] *f* lexicology
lexique [lɛksik] *m* lexicon, vocabulary; abridged dictionary
lez [le] *prep* near (*in place names*)
lézard [lezar] *m* lizard; **faire le lézard** (coll) to sun oneself, loaf
lézarde [lezard] *f* crack, split, crevice; gimp (*of furniture*); braid; (mil) gold braid
lézarder [lezarde] *tr* & *ref* to crack, split ‖ *intr* (coll) to bask in the sun
liaison [ljɛzɔ̃] *f* liaison
liant [ljɑ̃] **liante** [ljɑ̃t] *adj* flexible, supple; sociable, affable ‖ *m* flexibility; sociability; binder, binding material; **avoir du liant** to be a good mixer
liard [ljar] *m* (fig) farthing
liasse [ljas] *f* packet, bundle (*e.g., of letters*); wad (*of bank notes*)
Liban [libɑ̃] *m*—**le Liban** Lebanon
liba·nais [libanɛ] **-naise** [nɛz] *adj* Lebanese ‖ (*cap*) *mf* Lebanese
libation [libasjɔ̃] *f* libation

libelle [libɛl] *m* lampoon

libellé [libɛlle] *m* wording

libeller [libele], [libɛlle] *tr* to word; draw up (*e.g.*, *a contract*); make out (*a check*)

libellule [libɛlyl] *f* dragonfly

libé·ral -rale [liberal] *adj* & *mf* (*pl* **-raux** [ro]) liberal

libéralisme [liberalism] *m* liberalism

libéralité [liberalite] *f* liberality

libéra·teur [liberatœr] **-trice** [tris] *adj* liberating ‖ *mf* liberator

libération [liberɑsjɔ̃] *f* liberation; freeing; **libération conditionnelle** release on parole; **libération sous caution** release on bail

libérer [libere] §10 *tr* to liberate ‖ *ref* to free oneself; pay up

liberté [libɛrte] *f* liberty, freedom; **liberté d'association** or **liberté de réunion** right of assembly; **liberté de langage** freedom of speech; **liberté de la presse** freedom of the press; **liberté de la propriété** right to own private property; **liberté du commerce et de l'industrie** free enterprise; **liberté du culte** freedom of worship

liber·tin [libɛrtɛ̃] **-tine** [tin] *adj* libertine; (archaic) freethinking ‖ *mf* libertine; (archaic) freethinker

libidi·neux [libidinø] **-neuse** [nøz] *adj* libidinous

libido [libido] *f* libido

libraire [librɛr] *mf* bookseller; publisher

libraire-éditeur [librɛreditœr] *m* (*pl* **libraires-éditeurs**) publisher and bookseller

librairie [libreri] *f* bookstore; book trade; publishing house

libre [libr] §93 *adj* free; vacant; available; (*public sign*) not in use, empty; for hire; **je suis libre de mon temps** my time is my own; **libre arbitre** free will; **libre de** free to, at liberty to

libre-échange [libreʃɑ̃ʒ] *m* free trade

libre-échangiste [libreʃɑ̃ʒist] *m* (*pl* **-échangistes**) free trader

libre-pen·seur [librəpɑ̃sœr] **-seuse** [søz] *mf* (*pl* **libres-penseurs**) freethinker

libre-service [librəsɛrvis] *m* (*pl* **libres-services**) self-service; self-service store

lice [lis] *f* enclosure or fence (*of race track, fairground, tiltyard, etc.*); (zool) hound bitch; **de basse lice** (tex) low-warp; **de haute lice** (tex) high-warp; **entrer en lice** to enter the lists

licence [lisɑ̃s] *f* license; **licence ès lettres** advanced liberal-arts degree, master of arts; **prendre des licences avec** to take liberties with

licen·cié -ciée [lisɑ̃sje] *mf* holder of a master's degree

licenciement [lisɑ̃simɑ̃] *m* discharge, layoff

licencier [lisɑ̃sje] *tr* to discharge, lay off

licen·cieux [lisɑ̃sjø] **-cieuse** [sjøz] *adj* licentious

lichen [likɛn] *m* lichen

licher [liʃe] *tr* (slang) to gulp down

licite [lisit] *adj* lawful, licit

licorne [likɔrn] *f* unicorn

licou [liku] *m* halter

lie [li] *f* dregs, lees; (fig) dregs, scum

lie-de-vin [lidvɛ̃] *adj invar* maroon

liège [ljɛʒ] *m* cork

lien [ljɛ̃] *m* tie, bond, link

lier [lje] *tr* to tie, bind, link ‖ *ref* to bind together; make friends; **lier conversation avec** to fall into conversation with; **se lier d'amitié avec** to become friends with

lierre [ljɛr] *m* ivy

liesse [ljɛs] *f*—**en liesse** in festive mood, gay

lieu [ljø] *m* (*pl* **lieux**) place; **au lieu de** instead of, in lieu of; **avoir lieu** to take place; **avoir lieu de** to have reason to; **donner lieu à** to give rise to; **en aucun lieu** nowhere; **en dernier lieu** finally; **en haut lieu** high up, in responsible circles; **en premier lieu** first of all; **en quelque lieu que** wherever; **en tous lieux** everywhere; **il y a lieu à** there is room for; **lieu commun** commonplace; platitude; **lieu de villégiature** resort; **lieu géométrique** locus; **lieux** premises; **lieux d'aisances** rest rooms; **lieux payants** comfort station, public lavatory; **sur les lieux** on the spot; on the premises; **tenir lieu** to take place; **tenir lieu de** to take the place of

lieu-dit [ljødi] *m* (*pl* **lieux-dits**)—**le lieu-dit** . . . the place called . . .

lieue [ljø] *f* league (*unit of distance*)

lieur [ljœr] **lieuse** [ljøz] *mf* binder ‖ *f* (mach) binder

lieutenant [ljøtnɑ̃] *m* lieutenant; (merchant marine) mate; **lieutenant de port** harbor master; **lieutenant de vaisseau** (nav) lieutenant commander

lieutenant-colonel [ljøtnɑ̃kɔlɔnɛl] *m* (*pl* **lieutenants-colonels**) lieutenant colonel

lièvre [ljɛvr] *m* hare; **c'est là que gît le lièvre** there's the rub; **lever un lièvre** (fig) to raise an embarrassing question; **prendre le lièvre au gîte** (fig) to catch s.o. napping

ligament [ligamɑ̃] *m* ligament

ligature [ligatyr] *f* ligature

ligaturer [ligatyre] *tr* to tie up

lignage [liɲaʒ] *m* lineage

ligne [liɲ] *f* line; figure, waistline; (*of an automobile*) lines; **aller à la ligne** to begin a new paragraph; **avoir de la ligne** to have a good figure; **en ligne** (comp) on line; **en première ligne** of the first importance; on the firing line; **entrer en ligne de compte** to be under consideration; **garder sa ligne** to keep one's figure; **grande ligne** (rr) main line; **grandes lignes** broad outline; **hors ligne** unrivaled, outstanding; **la ligne est occupée** the line is busy, I hear the busy signal; **ligne à postes groupés** (telp) party line; **ligne brisée** dotted line; **ligne de but** goal line; **ligne de changement de date** international date line; **ligne de faille** fault line; **ligne de flottaison** water line; **ligne de mire, ligne de visée** (arti) line of sight;

ligne de partage des eaux, ligne de faîte watershed; **ligne des arbres** timber line; **ligne d'horizon** skyline; **ligne droite** straight line; **ligne partagée** (telp) party line; **ligne pointillée** or **hachée** dotted line

ligne-bloc [liɲblɔk] (*pl* **lignes-blocs**) *m* linotype slug

lignée [liɲe] *f* lineage, offspring

li·gneux [liɲø] **-gneuse** [ɲøz] *adj* woody

lignifier [liɲifje] *tr & ref* to turn into wood

ligot [ligo] *m* firewood (*in tied bundle*)

ligoter [ligɔte] *tr* to tie up, bind

ligue [lig] *f* league

liguer [lige] *tr & ref* to league

lilas [lila] *adj invar & m* lilac

li·lial -liale [liljal] *adj* (*pl* **-liaux** [ljo]) lily-white, lily-like

lillipu·tien [lilipysjɛ̃] **-tienne** [sjɛn] *adj & mf* Lilliputian

limace [limas] *f* (zool) slug; (coll) slowpoke; (slang) shirt

limaçon [limasɔ̃] *m* snail; **en limaçon** spiral

limaille [limɑj] *f* filings

limbe [lɛ̃b] *m* (astr, bot) limb; **limbes** limbo

lime [lim] *f* file; (*Citrus limetta*) sweet lime; **dernier coup de lime** finishing touches; **enlever à la lime** to file off; **lime à ongles** nail file; **lime émeri** emery board

limer [lime] *tr* to file; fray; (fig) to polish

limette [limɛt] *f* (*Citrus limetta*) sweet lime

limier [limje] *m* bloodhound; (coll) sleuth

liminaire [liminɛr] *adj* preliminary

limitation [limitɑsjɔ̃] *f* limitation

limite [limit] *f* limit; maximum, e.g., **vitesse limite** maximum speed; **dernière limite** deadline

limiter [limite] *tr* to limit ‖ *ref* to be limited; limit oneself

limitrophe [limitrɔf] *adj* frontier; **limitrophe de** adjacent to

limogeage [limɔʒaʒ] *m* (coll) removal from office

limoger [limɔʒe] §38 *tr* (coll) to remove from office, relieve of a command

limon [limɔ̃] *m* silt; clay; mud; shaft (*of wagon*)

limonade [limɔnad] *f* lemon soda

limona·dier [limɔnadje] **-dière** [djɛr] *mf* soft-drink manufacturer; café manager

limo·neux [limɔnø] **-neuse** [nøz] *adj* silty; muddy

limousine [limuzin] *f* heavy cloak; (aut) limousine

limpide [lɛ̃pid] *adj* limpid

lin [lɛ̃] *m* flax; linen

linceul [lɛ̃sœl] *m* shroud; cover (*of snow*)

linéaire [lineɛr] *adj* linear

linéament [lineamɑ̃] *m* lineament

linge [lɛ̃ʒ] *m* linen (*sheets, tablecloths, underclothes, etc.*); piece of linen; **il faut laver son linge sale en famille** one must wash one's dirty linen in private; **laver le linge** to do the wash; **linge de corps** underclothes

lingère [lɛ̃ʒɛr] *f* linen maid; linen closet

lingerie [lɛ̃ʒri] *f* linen (*sheets, tablecloths, underclothes, etc.*); linen closet; **lingerie de dame** lingerie; **lingerie d'homme** men's underwear

lingot [lɛ̃go] *m* ingot

lin·gual -guale [lɛ̃gwal] (*pl* **-guaux** [gwo] **-guales**) *adj & f* lingual

linguiste [lɛ̃gɥist] *mf* linguist

linguistique [lɛ̃gɥistik] *adj* linguistic ‖ *f* linguistics

liniment [linimɑ̃] *m* liniment

linoléum [linɔleɔm] *m* linoleum

linon [linɔ̃] *m* lawn (*sheer linen*)

linotte [linɔt] *f* (orn) linnet

linotype [linɔtip] *f* linotype

linotypiste [linɔtipist] *mf* linotype operator

lin·teau [lɛ̃to] *m* (*pl* **-teaux**) lintel

lion [ljɔ̃] **lionne** [ljɔn] *mf* lion ‖ *m*—**le Lion** (astr, astrol) Leo ‖ *f* lioness

lion·ceau [ljɔ̃so] *m* (*pl* **-ceaux**) lion cub

lippe [lip] *f* thick lower lip, blubber lip

lip·pu -pue [lipy] *adj* thick-lipped

liquéfier [likefje] *tr* to liquefy

liqueur [likœr] *f* liqueur; liquid; (chem, pharm) liquor

liquidation [likidɑsjɔ̃] *f* liquidation; settlement; clearance sale

liquide [likid] *adj & m* liquid ‖ *f* liquid (*consonant*)

liquider [likide] *tr* to liquidate; settle (*a score*); wind up (*a piece of business*); (coll) to get rid of; put an end to

liquidité [likidite] *f* liquidity

liquo·reux [likɔrø] **-reuse** [røz] *adj* sweet, syrupy

lire [lir] §36 *tr & intr* to read; **lire à haute voix** to read aloud; **lire à vue** to sight-read; **lire sur les lèvres** to lip-read ‖ *ref* to read; show, e.g., **la surprise se lit sur votre visage** your face shows surprise

lis [lis] *m* lily; **lis blanc** lily; **lis jaune** day lily

Lisbonne [lizbɔn] *f* Lisbon

liseré [lizre] or **liséré** [lizere] *m* braid, border, strip

li·seur [lizœr] **-seuse** [zøz] *mf* reader ‖ *f* bookmark; reading lamp; book jacket; bed jacket

lisibilité [lizibilite] *f* legibility

lisible [lizibl] *adj* legible; readable

lisière [lisjɛr] *f* edge, border, list, selvage; **tenir en lisières** to keep in leading strings

lissage [lisaʒ] *m* face-lift

lisse [lis] *adj* smooth, polished, sleek ‖ *f* (naut) handrail

lissé [lise] *m* smoothness

lisser [lise] *tr* to smooth, polish, sleek; glaze (*paper*) ‖ *ref* to become smooth; **se lisser les plumes** to preen its feathers

lisseuse [lisøz] *f* ice resurfacer

listage [listaʒ] *m* (comp) listing

liste [list] *f* list; (comp) listing; **liste de vérification** check list

lister [liste] *tr* (comp) to list

lit [li] *m* bed; layer; stratum; **dans le lit de la marée** in the tideway; **dans le lit du vent** in the wind's eye; **du premier lit** by or of the first marriage; **lit de mort** deathbed; **lit d'époque** period bed; **lit de repos** day bed; **lit de sangle, lit de camp** folding cot, camp bed; **lit en portefeuille** applepie bed; **lit pliant, lit escamotable, lit à rabattement** foldaway bed; **lits jumeaux** twin beds; **lits superposés** bunk beds

litanie [litani] *f* litany; tale of woe

lit-cage [likaʒ] *m* (*pl* **lits-cages**) foldaway bed

lit-canapé [likanape] *m* (*pl* **lits-canapés**) sofa bed

litée [lite] *f* litter (*of animals*)

literie [litri] *f* bedding, bedclothes

lithine [litin] *f* lithia

lithium [litjɔm] *m* lithium

lithographe [litɔgraf] *mf* lithographer

lithographie [litɔgrafi] *f* lithography; lithograph

lithographier [litɔgrafje] *tr* to lithograph

litière [litjɛr] *f* litter (*bedding for animals*); **faire litière de** to trample

litige [litiʒ] *m* litigation

liti·gieux [litiʒjø] **-gieuse** [ʒjøz] *adj* litigious

litre [litr] *m* liter

littéraire [literɛr] *adj* literary ‖ *mf* teacher of literature; belletrist

litté·ral -rale [literal] *adj* (*pl* **-raux** [ro]) literal; literary, written

littérature [literatyr] *f* literature

litto·ral -rale [litɔral] (*pl* **-raux** [ro]) *adj* littoral, coastal ‖ *m* coast, coastline

liturgie [lityrʒi] *f* liturgy

liturgique [lityrʒik] *adj* liturgic(al)

livid [livid] *adj* livid

living [liviŋ] *m* living room; all-purpose room in a studio apartment

Livourne [livurn] *f* Leghorn

livrable [livrabl] *adj* ready for delivery

livraison [livrɛzɔ̃] *f* delivery; installment; **livraison contre remboursement** cash on delivery

livre [livr] *m* book; **à livre ouvert** at sight; **faire un livre** to write a book; (*racing*) to make book; **feuilleter un livre** to glance through a book; **grand livre** (bk) ledger; **livre broché, livre de poche** paperback; **livre de bord** (aer, naut) logbook; **livre de classe** textbook; **livre de cuisine, livre de recettes** cookbook; **livre d'or** blue book; testimonial volume; guest book; **livre jaune** white book; **petit livre** (bk) journal, day book; **porter au grand livre** (bk) to post ‖ *f* pound (*weight; currency*)

livrée [livre] *f* livery; appearances; coat (*of horse, deer, etc.*)

livrer [livre] *tr* to deliver; surrender; betray ‖ *ref*—**se livrer à** to surrender oneself to; give way to, indulge in

livresque [livrɛsk] *adj* bookish

livret [livre] *m* booklet; (mus) libretto; **livret de caisse d'épargne** bankbook; **livret de famille** marriage certificate; **livret d'instruction** instruction manual; **livret militaire** military record; **livret scolaire** transcript (*of grades*)

li·vreur [livrœr] **-vreuse** [vrøz] *mf* deliverer (*of parcels, packages, etc.*) ‖ *m* deliveryman ‖ *f* woman who makes deliveries; delivery truck

lobby [lɔbi] (*pl* **lobbies**) *m* lobby; **lobby environnementaliste** environmental-protection lobby; **lobby des marchands de revolvers** gun lobby

lobe [lɔb] *m* lobe; **lobe de l'oreille** ear lobe

lo·cal -cale [lɔkal] (*pl* **-caux** [ko]) *adj* local ‖ *m* place, premises, quarters; headquarters; **locaux** (sports) home team; **locaux commerciaux** office space

localiser [lɔkalize] *tr* to locate; localize

localité [lɔkalite] *f* locality

locataire [lɔkatɛr] *mf* tenant, renter

location [lɔkasjɔ̃] *f* rental; reservation

loch [lɔk] *m* (naut) log (*to determine speed*)

lock-out [lɔkaut] *m invar* lockout

locomotive [lɔkɔmɔtiv] *f* locomotive; (fig) mover; (fig) price leader

locuste [lɔkyst] *f* (ent) locust

locu·teur [lɔkytœr] **-trice** [tris] *mf* speaker

locution [lɔkysjɔ̃] *f* locution; phrase

lof [lɔf] *m* windward side; **aller** or **venir au lof** to sail into the wind

logarithme [lɔgaritm] *m* logarithm

loge [lɔʒ] *f* lodge; circus cage; concierge's room; chamber, cell; (theat) dressing room; (theat) box

logeabilité [lɔʒabilite] *f* spaciousness

logeable [lɔʒabl] *adj* livable, inhabitable

logement [lɔʒmɑ̃] *m* lodging, lodgings

loger [lɔʒe] §38 *tr, intr, & ref* to lodge

lo·geur [lɔʒœr] **-geuse** [ʒøz] *mf* proprietor of a boardinghouse ‖ *m* landlord ‖ *f* landlady

logiciel [lɔʒisjɛl] *m* (comp) software

logi·cien [lɔʒisjɛ̃] **-cienne** [sjɛn] *mf* logician

logique [lɔʒik] *adj* logical ‖ *f* logic

logis [lɔʒi] *m* abode

logistique [lɔʒistik] *adj* logistic(al) ‖ *f* logistics

loi [lwa] *f* law; **faire des lois** to legislate; **faire la loi** to lay down the law; **loi exceptionnelle** emergency legislation; **loi sélective du plus fort, loi du mieux adapté** survival of the fittest

loin [lwɛ̃] *adv* far; far away, far off; **au loin** in the distance; **d'aussi loin que, du plus loin que** as soon as; as far back as; **de loin** from afar; far from; far be it from (*e.g., me*); **de loin en loin** now and then; **il y a loin de** it is a far cry from; **loin des yeux, loin du cœur** out of sight, out of mind

loin·tain [lwɛ̃tɛ̃] **-taine** [tɛn] *adj* faraway, distant, remote; early (*e.g., memories*) ‖ *m* distance, background; **le lointain** (theat) upstage

loir [lwar] *m* dormouse; **dormir comme un loir** to sleep like a log

loisible [lwazibl] *adj*—**il m'est (lui est, etc.) loisible de** I am (he is, etc.) free to or entitled to, it is open for me (him, etc.) to

loisir [lwazir] *m* leisure, spare time; **à loisir** at one's convenience; **loisirs** diversions

lolo [lolo] *m* (coll) milk (*in baby talk*)

lombes [lɔ̃b] *mpl* loins

londo·nien [lɔ̃dɔnjɛ̃] **-nienne** [njɛn] *adj* London ‖ (*cap*) *mf* Londoner

Londres [lɔ̃dr] *m* London

londrès [lɔ̃drɛs] *m* Havana cigar

long [lɔ̃] **longue** [lɔ̃g] *adj* long; lengthy (*speech*); long (*syllable, vowel*); thin, weak (*sauce, gravy*); slow (*to understand, to decide*) ‖ (when standing before noun) *adj* long; **de longue main** of long standing ‖ *m* length; extent; **au long** at length; **de long** lengthwise; **de long en large** up and down, back and forth; **le long de** along; **tout au long** without forgetting anything ‖ *f* see **longue** ‖ **long** *adv* much; **en dire long** to talk a long time; to speak volumes; **en savoir long sur** to know a great deal about; **en savoir plus long** to know more about it

longanimité [lɔ̃ganimite] *f* long-suffering

long-courrier [lɔ̃kurje] (*pl* **-courriers**) *adj* long-range ‖ *m* airliner; liner, ocean liner

longe [lɔ̃ʒ] *f* tether, leash; (culin) loin

longer [lɔ̃ʒe] §38 *tr* to walk along, go beside; extend along, skirt

longeron [lɔ̃ʒrɔ̃] *m* crossbeam, girder

longévité [lɔ̃ʒevite] *f* longevity

longitude [lɔ̃ʒityd] *f* longitude

longtemps [lɔ̃tɑ̃] *m* a long time; **avant longtemps** before long; **depuis longtemps** for a long time; long since; **ne . . . plus longtemps** no . . . longer ‖ *adv* long; for a long time

longue [lɔ̃g] *f* long syllable; long vowel; long suit (*in cards*); **à la longue** in the long run

longuement [lɔ̃gmɑ̃] *adv* at length, a long time

lon·guet [lɔ̃gɛ] **-guette** [gɛt] *adj* (coll) longish, rather long

longueur [lɔ̃gœr] *f* length; lengthiness; **à longueur de journée** all day long; **de longueur, dans la longueur** lengthwise; **d'une longueur** by a length, by a head; **longueur d'onde** wavelength; **longueurs** slowness, delays; tedious passages (*e.g., of a book*); **traîner en longueur** to drag on

longue-vue [lɔ̃gvy] *f* (*pl* **longues-vues**) telescope, spyglass

looping [lupiŋ] *m* loop-the-loop

lopin [lɔpɛ̃] *m* patch of ground, plot

loquace [lɔkwas], [lɔkas] *adj* loquacious

loque [lɔk] *f* rag; **être comme une loque** to feel like a dishrag; **être en loques** to be in tatters

loquet [lɔkɛ] *m* latch

loque·teux [lɔktø] **-teuse** [tøz] *adj* in tatters ‖ *mf* tatterdemalion

lorgner [lɔrɲe] *tr* to cast a sidelong glance at; ogle; have one's eyes on (*a job, an inheritance, etc.*)

lorgnette [lɔrɲɛt] *f* opera glasses

lorgnon [lɔrɲɔ̃] *m* pince-nez; lorgnette

loriot [lɔrjo] *m* golden oriole

lorry [lɔri] *m* lorry, small flatcar

lors [lɔr] *adv*—**lors de** at the time of; **lors même que** even if

lorsque [lɔrsk] *conj* when

losange [lozɑ̃ʒ] *m* (geom) lozenge; **en losange** diamond-shaped; oval-shaped

lot [lo] *m* lot; prize (*e.g., in lottery*); **gagner le gros lot** to hit the jackpot

loterie [lɔtri] *f* lottery

lo·ti -tie [lɔti] *adj* built-up (*area*); **bien loti** well off; **mal loti** badly off

lotion [losjɔ̃] *f* lotion; **lotion capillaire** hair tonic

lotionner [losjɔne] *tr* to bathe (*a wound*)

lotir [lɔtir] *tr* to parcel out; **lotir qn de q.ch.** to allot s.th. to s.o.

lotissement [lɔtismɑ̃] *m* allotment, apportionment; building lot; (building) development

louable [lwabl] *adj* praiseworthy; for hire

louage [lwaʒ] *m* hire

louange [lwɑ̃ʒ] *f* praise; **à la louange de** in praise of

louanger [lwɑ̃ʒe] §38 *tr* to praise, extol

louan·geur [lwɑ̃ʒœr] **-geuse** [ʒøz] *adj* laudatory, flattering

loubard [lubar] *m* hood (*gangster*); punk

louche [luʃ] *adj* ambiguous; suspicious; shady; cross-eyed; cloudy (*e.g., wine*) ‖ *f* ladle; basting spoon

loucher [luʃe] *intr* to be cross-eyed, squint; **faire loucher qn de jalousie** (coll) to turn s.o. green with envy; **loucher sur** (coll) to cast longing eyes at

louchet [luʃɛ] *m* spade (*for digging*)

louer [lwe] §97 *tr* to rent, hire; to reserve (*a seat*); praise ‖ *ref* to be rented; hire oneself out; **se louer de** to be satisfied with

loueur [lwœr] **loueuse** [lwøz] *mf* operator of a rental service; flatterer

loufoque [lufɔk] *adj* (slang) cracked ‖ *m* (slang) crackpot

lougre [lugr] *m* (naut) lugger

Louisiane [lwizjan] *f* Louisiana; **la Louisiane** Louisiana

lou·lou [lulu] **-loute** [lut] *mf* (coll) darling, pet ‖ *m*—**loulou de Poméranie** Pomeranian, spitz

loup [lu] *m* wolf; mask; flaw; **avoir vu le loup** to have lost one's innocence; **crier au loup** to cry wolf; **loup de mer** (ichth) wolf eel; (coll) old salt; **mon petit loup** (coll) my pet ‖ see **louve**

loup-cervier [lusɛrvje] *m* (*pl* **loups-cerviers**) lynx

loupe [lup] *f* magnifying glass; gnarl (*on tree*); (pathol) wen

lou·pé -pée [lupe] *adj* bungled; defective ‖ *m* defect

louper [lupe] *tr* (coll) to goof up, muff; (coll) to miss (*e.g., one's train*) ‖ *intr* (coll) to fail, goof

loup-garou [lugaru] *m* (*pl* **loups-garous**) werewolf

lou·piot [lupjo] **-piotte** [pjɔt] *mf* (coll) kid, child; **loupiots** (coll) small fry

lourd [lur] **lourde** [lurd] §92 *adj* heavy; hefty; clumsy; sultry (*weather*); off-color (*joke*); dull (*mind*); (agr) hard to cultivate ‖ (when standing before noun) *adj* heavy; grave; clumsy (*e.g., compliments*); off-color (*joke*) ‖ **lourd** *adv* heavy, heavily

lour·daud [lurdo] **-daude** [dod] *adj* clumsy, loutish, dull ‖ *mf* lout, oaf

lourdement [lurdəmɑ̃] *adv* heavily; clumsily; **avancer** or **rouler lourdement** to lumber along

lourdeur [lurdœr] *f* heaviness; clumsiness; sultriness; dullness

loustic [lustik] *m* wag, clown; (coll) screwball, character

loutre [lutr] *f* otter

louve [luv] *f* she-wolf

louve·teau [luvto] *m* (*pl* **-teaux**) wolf cub; cub scout

louvoyer [luvwaje] §47 *intr* to be evasive; (naut) to tack

lovelace [lɔvlas] *m* seducer, Don Juan

lover [lɔve] *tr & ref* to coil

loyal loyale [lwajal] *adj* (*pl* **loyaux** [lwajo]) loyal; honest; fair, just

loyaliste [lwajalist] *mf* loyalist

loyauté [lwajote] *f* loyalty; honesty; fairness

loyer [lwaje] *m* rent

lu lue [ly] *v* see **lire**

lubie [lybi] *f* whim; fad

lubricité [lybrisite] *f* lubricity, lewdness

lubri·fiant [lybrifjɑ̃] **-fiante** [fjɑ̃t] *adj & m* lubricant

lubrifier [lybrifje] *tr* to lubricate

lubrique [lybrik] *adj* lecherous, lustful, lewd

lucarne [lykarn] *f* dormer window; skylight

lucide [lysid] *adj* lucid

luciole [lysjɔl] *f* firefly

lucra·tif [lykratif] **-tive** [tiv] *adj* lucrative; **sans but lucratif** nonprofit

lucre [lykr] *m* lucre

ludiciel [lydisjɛl] *m* games software

luette [lɥet] *f* uvula

lueur [lɥœr] *f* glimmer, gleam; flash, blink

luge [lyʒ] *f* sled

lugubre [lygybr] *adj* gloomy

lui [lɥi] *pron disj* §85 him ‖ *pron conj* §87 him; her; it; to him; to her; to it

lui-même [lɥimɛm] §86 himself; itself

luire [lɥir] §37 *intr* to shine; to gleam, glow, glisten; to dawn

lui·sant [lɥizɑ̃] **-sante** [zɑ̃t] *adj* shining

lulu [lyly] *m* (orn) tree pipit

lumbago [lɔ̃bago] *m* lumbago

lumière [lymjɛr] *f* light; aperture; (*person*) luminary; **avoir des lumières de** to have knowledge of; **lumière ultraviolette** ultraviolet light

lumignon [lymiɲɔ̃] *m* feeble light

luminaire [lyminɛr] *m* luminary

lumines·cent [lyminɛsɑ̃] **-cente** [sɑ̃t] *adj* luminescent

lumi·neux [lyminø] **-neuse** [nøz] *adj* luminous; light (*e.g., spot*); bright (*idea*)

lunaire [lynɛr] *adj* lunar ‖ *f* (bot) honesty

lunatique [lynatik] *adj* whimsical, eccentric ‖ *mf* whimsical person, eccentric

lunch [lœntʃ], [lœ̃ʃ] *m* buffet lunch

lundi [lœ̃di] *m* Monday

lune [lyn] *f* moon; **être dans la lune** to be daydreaming; **lune de miel** honeymoon; **lune des moissons** harvest moon; **vieilles lunes** good old days, bygone days

lu·né -née [lyne] *adj* moon-shaped; **bien luné** in a good mood; **mal luné** in a bad mood

lune·tier [lyntje] **-tière** [tjɛr] *mf* optician

lunette [lynɛt] *f* telescope, spyglass; toilet seat; hole (*in toilet seat*); wishbone (*of turkey, chicken*); (archit) lunette; (aut) rear window; **lunettes** eyeglasses, spectacles; goggles; **lunettes auditives** eyeglass hearing aid; **lunettes de lecture, lunettes pour lire** reading glasses; **lunettes de soleil** sunglasses; **lunettes noires** dark glasses

lurette [lyrɛt] *f*—**il y a belle lurette** (coll) ages ago

luron [lyrɔ̃] *m* (coll) playboy

luronne [lyrɔn] *f* (coll) hussy

lustre [lystr] *m* luster; five-year period; chandelier

lus·tré -trée [lystre] *adj* glossy, shiny

lustrine [lystrin] *f* cotton satin

lut [lyt] *m* (chem) lute

luth [lyt] *m* (mus) lute

lutherie [lytri] *f* violin making

luthé·rien [lyterjɛ̃] **-rienne** [rjɛn] *adj* Lutheran ‖ (*cap*) *mf* Lutheran

luthier [lytje] *m* violin maker

lu·tin [lytɛ̃] **-tine** [tin] *adj* impish ‖ *m* imp

lutiner [lytine] *tr* to tease

lutrin [lytrɛ̃] *m* lectern

lutte [lyt] *f* struggle, fight; wrestling; **de bonne lutte** aboveboard; **de haute lutte** by force; in open competition; hard-won; **lutte à la corde de traction** tug of war; **lutte libre** catch-as-catch-can

lutter [lyte] *intr* to fight, struggle; wrestle

lut·teur [lytœr] **-teuse** [tøz] *mf* wrestler; (fig) fighter

luxation [lyksasjɔ̃] *f* dislocation

luxe [lyks] *m* luxury; **avec un trés grand luxe** luxury (*e.g., apartment*)

Luxembourg [lyksɑ̃bur] *m*—**le Luxembourg** Luxembourg

luxer [lykse] *tr* to dislocate

lu·xueux [lyksɥø] **-xueuse** [ksɥøz] *adj* luxurious

luxure [lyksyr] *f* lechery, lust

luxu·riant [lyksyrjɑ̃] **-riante** [rjɑ̃t] *adj* luxuriant

luxu·rieux [lyksyrjø] **-rieuse** [rjøz] *adj* lecherous, lustful

luzerne [lyzɛrn] *f* alfalfa

lycée [lise] *m* high school (with academic courses); lyceum

ly·céen [liseɛ̃] **-céenne** [seɛn] *mf* secondary-school student

lymphatique [lɛ̃fatik] *adj* lymphatic

lymphe [lɛ̃f] *f* lymph

lynchage [lɛ̃ʃaʒ] *m* lynching

lyncher [lɛ̃ʃe] *tr* to lynch
lynx [lɛ̃ks] *m* lynx
Lyon [ljɔ̃] *m* Lyons
lyon·nais [liɔnɛ] **-naise** [nɛz] *adj* Lyonese;
  à la lyonnaise lyonnaise
lyophilisation [ljɔfilizasjɔ̃] *f* freeze drying
lyophiliser [ljɔfilize] *tr* to freeze-dry

lyre [lir] *f* lyre
lyrique [lirik] *adj* lyric(al) ‖ *m* lyric poet ‖ *f*
  lyric poetry
lyrisme [lirism] *m* lyricism
lys [lis] *m* lily; **lys blanc** lily; **lys jaune** day
  lily
lysimaque [lizimak] *f* loosestrife

M

M, m [ɛm], *[ɛm] *m invar* thirteenth letter
  of the French alphabet
M. *abbr* (**Monsieur**) Mr.
m' = **me** before vowel or mute **h**
ma [ma] §88 my
ma·boul -boule [mabul] *adj* (slang) nuts,
  balmy ‖ *mf* (slang) nut
macabre [makɑbr] *adj* macabre
macadam [makadam] *m* macadam
macadamiser [makadamize] *tr* to macadamize
macaron [makarɔ̃] *m* macaroon; (coll) bumpersticker
macchabée [makabe] *m* (slang) stiff (*corpse*)
macédoine [masedwan] *f* macédoine, medley; **macédoine de fruits** fruit salad; **macédoine de légumes** mixed vegetables
macérer [masere] §10 *tr* to macerate; mortify (*the flesh*); soak, steep ‖ *intr* to soak,
  steep
mâchefer [mɑʃfɛr] *m* clinker
mâcher [mɑʃe] *tr* to chew; **mâcher la besogne à qn** to do all one's work for one;
  ne pas mâcher ses mots to not mince
  words
machin [maʃɛ̃] *m* (coll) what-do-you-call-it;
  (coll) what's-his-name, so-and-so
machi·nal -nale [maʃinal] *adj* (*pl* **-naux**
  [no]) mechanical
machination [maʃinɑsjɔ̃] *f* machination
machine [maʃin] *f* machine; engine; **faire
  machine arrière** to go into reverse; **ma-
  chine à calculer** adding machine; **ma-
  chine à coudre** sewing machine; **ma-
  chine à écrire** typewriter; **machine à
  écrire portative** portable typewriter; **machine à laver** washing machine; **machine
  à laver la vaisselle** dishwasher; **machine
  à sous** slot machine; **machine à vapeur**
  steam engine; **machine de télégestion
  bancaire** automatic teller; **machines** machinery
machine-outil [maʃinuti] *f* (*pl* **machines-
  outils**) machine tool
machinerie [maʃinri] *f* machinery; engine
  room
machiniste [maʃinist] *m* (theat) stagehand
mâchoire [mɑʃwar] *f* jaw; jawbone; lower
  jaw
mâchonner [mɑʃɔne] *tr* to chew, munch;
  mumble (*e.g., the end of a sentence*)
mâchurer [mɑʃyre] *tr* to crush; smudge

maçon [masɔ̃] *m* mason
maçonner [masɔne] *tr* to mason, wall up
maçonnerie [masɔnri] *f* masonry
macule [makyl] *f* spot, blotch; inkblot;
  birthmark
maculer [makyle] *tr* to soil, spot; (typ) to
  smear
madame [madam] *f* (*pl* **mesdames** [me-
  dam]) madam; Mrs.; (not translated),
  e.g., **madame votre femme** your wife
Madeleine [madlɛn] *f* Madeleine, Magdalen; sponge cake; **pleurer comme une
  Madeleine** to weep bitterly
mademoiselle [madmwazɛl] *f* (*pl* **mesdemoiselles** [medmwazɛl]) Miss; eldest
  daughter; (not translated), e.g., **mademoiselle votre fille** your daughter
Madone [madɔn] *f* Madonna
ma·dré -drée [madre] *adj* sly, cagey ‖ *mf*
  sly one
madrier [madrije] *m* beam
mafia or **maffia** [mafja] *f* Mafia, Maffia; **la
  Maf(f)ia** the Mafia
maf·flu -flue [mafly] *adj* heavy-jowled
magasin [magazɛ̃] *m* store; warehouse;
  magazine (*of gun or camera; for munitions or powder*); **avoir en magasin** to
  have in stock; **grands magasins** department store; **magasin à libre service** self-
  service store; **magasin à prix unique**
  variety store; **magasin à succursales
  multiples** chain store; **magasin d'antiquités** antique shop; **magasin de modes**
  dress shop; **magasin de rabais** discount
  store; **magasin entrepôt** no-frills store
magasinage [magazinaʒ] *m* storage, ware-
  housing; storage charges; (Canad) shopping
magasinier [magazinje] *m* warehouseman
magazine [magazin] *m* magazine; (mov,
  telv) hour, program, e.g., **magazine féminin** woman's hour
mages [maʒ] *mpl* Magi
magi·cien [maʒisjɛ̃] **-cienne** [sjɛn] *mf* magician
magie [maʒi] *f* magic
magique [maʒik] *adj* magic
magis·tral -trale [maʒistral] *adj* (*pl* **-traux**
  [tro]) masterful, masterly; magisterial;
  (pharm) magistral
magistrat [maʒistra] *m* magistrate
magnanime [maɲanim] *adj* magnanimous

magnat [magna] *m* magnate

magnésium [maɲezjɔm] *m* magnesium

magnétique [maɲetik] *adj* magnetic; hypnotic

magnétiser [maɲetize] *tr* to magnetize; hypnotize; spellbind

magnétisme [maɲetism] *m* magnetism

magnéto [maɲeto] *f* magneto

magnétophone [maɲetofɔn] *m* tape recorder; **magnétophone à fil d'acier** wire recorder

magnétoscope [maɲetɔskɔp] *m* videotape recorder; videocassette recorder

magnétoscopie [maɲetɔskɔpi] *f* videotape recording, videocassette recording

magnifier [magnifje] *tr* to extol, glorify

magnifique [maɲifik] *adj* magnificent; lavishly generous

magnitude [magnityd] *f* (astr) magnitude

magot [mago] *m* Barbary ape; figurine; (coll) hoard, pile (*of money*)

Mahomet [maɔmɛ] *m* Mohammad

mahomé·tan [maɔmetɑ̃] **-tane** [tan] *adj* & *m* Mohammedan

mai [mɛ] *m* May; Maypole

maie [mɛ] *f* bread bin; kneading trough

maigre [mɛgr] *adj* lean; thin; meager; meatless (*day*); **faire maigre** to abstain from meat

maigreur [mɛgrœr] *f* leanness; meagerness

maigri·chon [megriʃɔ̃] **-chonne** [ʃɔn] *adj* (coll) skinny

maigrir [megrir] *tr* to slim; make (*s.o.*) look thinner ‖ *intr* to lose weight

mail [maj] *m* mall

maille [mɑj] *f* link; stitch; mesh, loop; **avoir maille à partir avec qn** to have a bone to pick with s.o.; **mailles** mail

maillet [majɛ] *m* mallet

maillon [mɑjɔ̃] *m* link (*of a chain*)

maillot [majo] *m* swimming suit; jersey; **maillot de bain** swimming suit; **maillot de corps** undershirt; **maillot de danseur** tights; **maillot des acrobates** tights

main [mɛ̃] *f* hand; quire; **à la main** by hand; **à main levée** by show of hands; in one stroke; **avoir la haute main sur** to control; **avoir la main, être la main** (cards) to be the dealer; **battre des mains** to applaud; **de la main à la main** privately; **de longue main** carefully; for a long time; **de main à main** from one person to another; **de première main** firsthand; **donner les mains à q.ch.** to be in favor of s.th.; **en venir aux mains** to come to blows; **faire main basse sur** to grab, to steal; **haut les mains!** hands up!; **main dans la main** hand in hand; **passer la main dans le dos à qn** to soft-soap s.o.; **serrer la main à** to shake hands with; **sous main** secretly; **tout main** handmade

main-d'œuvre [mɛ̃dœvr] *f* (*pl* **mains-d'œuvre**) labor; laborers; manpower

maint [mɛ̃] **mainte** [mɛ̃t] *adj* many a; **à maintes reprises** time and again

maintenant [mɛ̃tenɑ̃] *adv* now

maintenir [mɛ̃tnir] §72 *intr* to maintain; hold up ‖ *ref* to keep on; keep up

maintien [mɛ̃tjɛ̃] *m* maintenance; bearing

maire [mɛr] *m* mayor

mairesse [mɛrɛs] *f* (coll) mayor's wife

mairie [meri] *f* town hall, city hall

mais [mɛ] *m* but ‖ *adv* why, well; **mais non** certainly not ‖ *conj* but

maïs [mais] *m* corn, maize; **maïs en épi** corn on the cob; **maïs explosé** popcorn

maison [mɛzɔ̃] *f* house; home; household, family; house, firm, business; **à la maison** at home, home; **fait à la maison** homemade; **la Maison Blanche** the White House; **maison centrale** state or federal prison; **maison close, borgne, publique, mal famée, de débauche, de passe, de rendez-vous, de tolérance** house of ill fame; **maison d'accouchement** lying-in hospital; **maison d'antiquités, de meubles d'époque,** or **d'originaux** antique shop; **maison de commerce** firm; **maison de confiance** (com) trustworthy firm; **maison de correction** reform school; **maison de couture** dressmaking establishment; **maison de fous** madhouse; **maison de jeux** gambling house; **maison de plaisance** or **de campagne** cottage, summer home; **maison de rapport** apartment house; **maison de repos** rest home; **maison de retraite** old-people's home; **maison de santé** nursing home; **maison jumelée** semi-detached house; **maison mère** head office; **maison mortuaire** home of the deceased; **maison religieuse** convent

maisonnée [mɛzɔne] *f* household

maisonnette [mɛzɔnɛt] *f* little house, cottage

maî·tre [mɛtr] **-tresse** [trɛs] *adj* expert, capable; basic, key; main (*beam, girder*); utter (*fool*); arrant (*knave*); high (*card*) ‖ *m* master; Mr. (*when addressing a lawyer*); (naut) mate; (naut) petty officer; **être passé maître en** to be a past master of or in; **maître chanteur** blackmailer; **maître d'armes** fencing master; **maître de chapelle** choirmaster; **maître d'école** schoolmaster; **maître de conférences** associate professor; **maître de forges** ironmaster; **maître de maison** man of the house, householder; **maître d'équipage** boatswain; **maître d'études** monitor, supervisor; **maître d'hôtel** headwaiter; butler; **maître d'œuvre** foreman; **maître Jacques** jack-of-all-trades; **maître mécanicien** chief engineer; **maître mineur** mine foreman; **maître queue** chef; **passer maître** to know one's trade ‖ *f see* **maîtresse**

maître-autel [mɛtrotɛl] *m* (*pl* **maîtres-autels**) high altar

maîtresse [mɛtrɛs] *f* mistress; **maîtresse d'école** schoolmistress; **maîtresse de maison** lady of the house

maîtrise [metriz] *f* mastery, command; master's degree; **maîtrise de soi** self-control

maîtriser [metrize] *tr* to master, control; subdue

maj. *abbr* (**majuscule**) cap.

majesté [maʒɛste] *f* majesty

majes·tueux [maʒɛstɥø] **-tueuse** [tɥøz] *adj* majestic

ma·jeur -jeure [maʒœr] *adj & m* major

major [maʒɔr] *m* regimental quartermaster; army doctor; **être le major de sa promotion** to be at the head of one's class

majordome [maʒɔrdɔm] *m* major-domo

majorer [maʒɔre] *tr* to increase the price of; overprice; raise (*the price*)

majoritaire [maʒɔritɛr] *adj* majority

majorité [maʒɔrite] *f* majority; time of being of full legal age

Majorque [maʒɔrk] *f* Majorca

major·quin [maʒɔrkɛ̃] **-quine** [kin] *adj* Majorcan ‖ (*cap*) *mf* Majorcan

majuscule [maʒyskyl] *adj* capital (*letter*) ‖ *f* capital letter

mal [mal] *adj*—**de mal** bad, e.g., **dire q.ch. de mal** to say s.th. bad; **pas mal** not bad, quite good-looking ‖ *m* (*pl* **maux** [mo]) evil; trouble; hurt; pain; wrong; **avoir du mal à** + *inf* to have a hard time + *ger* to have difficulty in + *ger;* **avoir mal à la tête** to have a headache; **avoir mal au cœur** to be nauseated; **avoir mal aux dents** to have a toothache; **avoir mal de gorge** to have a sore throat; **dire du mal de qn** to speak ill of s.o.; **faire mal à, faire du mal à** to hurt, to harm; **le Mal** Evil; **mal aux reins** backache; **mal blanc** whitlow; **mal de l'air** airsickness; **mal de la route** carsickness; **mal de mer** seasickness; **mal des rayons** radiation sickness; **mal du pays** homesickness; **mal du siècle** Weltschmerz, romantic melancholy; **se donner du mal** to take pains ‖ *adv* §91 badly, bad; **de mal en pis** from bad to worse; **être mal avec qn** to be on bad terms with s.o.; **pas mal** not bad; **pas mal de** a lot of, quite a few

malade [malad] *adj* sick, ill ‖ *mf* patient, sick person

maladie [maladi] *f* disease, sickness; distemper; **elle va en faire une maladie** (coll) she'll be terribly upset over it; **maladie de carence** or **par carence** deficiency disease; **maladie de cœur** heart trouble; **maladie des caissons** bends; **maladie diplomatique** malingering; **maladie sexuellement transmissible** sexually transmitted disease; **revenir de maladie** to convalesce

mala·dif [maladif] **-dive** [div] *adj* sickly; morbid

maladresse [maladrɛs] *f* awkwardness; blunder

mala·droit [maladrwa] **-droite** [drwat] *adj* clumsy, awkward

ma·lais [malɛ] **-laise** [lɛz] *adj* Malay ‖ *m* Malay (*language*) ‖ see **malaise** *m* ‖ (*cap*) *mf* Malay (*person*)

malaise [malɛz] *m* malaise, discomfort

malai·sé -sée [maleze] *adj* difficult

malap·pris [malapri] **-prise** [priz] *adj* uncouth, ill-bred ‖ *mf* ill-bred person

malard [malar] *m* (orn) mallard

malaria [malarja] *f* malaria

malavi·sé -sée [malavize] *adj* ill-advised, indiscreet

malaxer [malakse] *tr* to knead; churn (*butter*); massage

malaxeur [malaksœr] *m* churn; (mach) mixer

malchance [malʃɑ̃s] *f* bad luck; **par malchance** unluckily; **une malchance** a piece of bad luck

malchan·ceux [malʃɑ̃sø] **-ceuse** [søz] *adj* unlucky

malcommode [malkɔmɔd] *adj* inconvenient; unsuitable, impracticable

maldonne [maldɔn] *f* misdeal

mâle [mɑl] *adj* male; energetic, virile ‖ *m* male

malédiction [malediksjɔ̃] *f* curse

maléfice [malefis] *m* evil spell

maléfique [malefik] *adj* baleful

malencon·treux [malɑ̃kɔ̃trø] **-treuse** [trøz] *adj* untimely, unfortunate

malentendu [malɑ̃tɑ̃dy] *m* misunderstanding

malfaçon [malfasɔ̃] *f* defect

malfai·sant [malfəzɑ̃] **-sante** [zɑ̃t] *adj* mischievous, harmful

malfaiteur [malfɛtœr] *m* malefactor

malfa·mé -mée [malfame] *adj* ill-famed

malgra·cieux [malgrasjø] **-cieuse** [sjøz] *adj* ungracious

malgré [malgre] *prep* in spite of; **malgré que** in spite of the fact that, although

malhabile [malabil] *adj* inexperienced, clumsy

malheur [malœr] *m* misfortune; unhappiness; bad luck; **faire un malheur** to commit an act of violence; (theat) to be a howling success; **jouer de malheur** to be unlucky

malheureusement [malœrøzmɑ̃] *adv* unfortunately

malheu·reux [malœrø] **-reuse** [røz] *adj* unfortunate; unhappy; unlucky; paltry ‖ *m* poor man, wretch; **les malheureux** the unfortunate ‖ *f* poor woman, wretch

malhonnête [malɔnɛt] *adj* dishonest; (slang) rude, uncivil

malhonnêteté [malɔnɛtte] *f* dishonesty

malice [malis] *f* mischievousness; malice; trick

mali·cieux [malisjø] **-cieuse** [sjøz] *adj* malicious, mischievous

malignité [maliɲite] *f* malignancy

ma·lin [malɛ̃] **-ligne** [liɲ] *adj* cunning, sly, smart; mischievous; malignant; **ce n'est pas malin** (coll) it's easy ‖ *mf* sly one; **Le Malin** the Evil One

malingre [malɛ̃gr] *adj* weakly, puny

malintention·né -née [malɛ̃tɑ̃sjɔne] *adj* evil-minded, ill-disposed

mal-jugé [malʒyʒe] *m* miscarriage (*of justice*)

malle [mal] *f* trunk; mailboat; **faire ses malles** to pack

malléable [maleabl] *adj* malleable; compliant, pliable

mallette [malɛt] *f* valise; case

malmener [malməne] §2 *tr* to rough up

malodo·rant [malɔdɔrɑ̃] **-rante** [rɑ̃t] *adj* malodorous; bad (*breath*)

malo·tru -true [malɔtry] *adj* coarse, uncouth ‖ *mf* ill-bred person, oaf

malpropre [malprɔpr] *adj* dirty; improper; crude, clumsy (*workmanship*)

mal·sain [malsɛ̃] **-saine** [sɛn] *adj* unhealthy

mal·séant [malseɑ̃] **-séante** [seɑ̃t] *adj* improper

malson·nant [malsɔnɑ̃] **-nante** [nɑ̃t] *adj* offensive, objectionable

malt [malt] *m* malt

maltraiter [maltrete] *tr* to mistreat

malveil·lant [malvɛjɑ̃] **-lante** [jɑ̃t] *adj* malevolent

malve·nu -nue [malvəny] *adj* ill-advised, out of place; poorly developed

malversation [malvɛrsasjɔ̃] *f* embezzlement

maman [mamɑ̃] *f* mamma

mamelle [mamɛl] *f* breast; udder

mamelon [mamlɔ̃] *m* nipple, teat; knoll

mamie [mami] *f* (coll) my dear

mammifère [mamifɛr] *adj* mammalian ‖ *m* mammal

mammouth [mamut] *m* mammoth

mamours [mamur] *mpl* (coll) caresses

mam'selle or **mam'zelle** [mamzɛl] *f* (coll) Miss

manant [manɑ̃] *m* hick, yokel

manche [mɑ̃ʃ] *m* handle; stick, stock; neck (*of violin*); (culin) knuckle; **branler au manche** or **dans le manche** to be shaky; **manche à balai** broomstick; (aer) joy stick; **manche à gigot** holder (*for carving*) ‖ *f* sleeve; hose; channel; game, heat, round; shaft, chute; (baseball) inning; (bridge) game; (tennis) set; **en manches de chemise** in shirt sleeves; **la Manche** the English Channel; **manche à air** windsock; **manche à manche** neck and neck, even up; **manches à gigot** leg-of-mutton sleeves

manchette [mɑ̃ʃɛt] *f* cuff; (journ) headline

manchon [mɑ̃ʃɔ̃] *m* muff; mantle (*of gaslight*); (mach) casing, sleeve

man·chot [mɑ̃ʃo] **-chote** [ʃɔt] *adj* one-armed; one-handed; (coll) clumsy ‖ *mf* one-armed person; one-handed person ‖ *m* (orn) penguin

mandarine [mɑ̃darin] *f* mandarin orange

mandat [mɑ̃da] *m* mandate; term of office; money order; power of attorney; proxy; **mandat d'arrêt** warrant; **mandat de perquisition** search warrant

mandataire [mɑ̃datɛr] *mf* representative; proxy; defender

mandat-carte [mɑ̃dakart] *m* (*pl* **mandats-carte**) postal-card money order

mandat-poste [mɑ̃dapɔst] *m* (*pl* **mandats-poste**) postal money order

Mandchourie [mɑ̃tʃuri] *f* Manchuria; **la Mandchourie** Manchuria

mander [mɑ̃de] §97 *tr* to summon

mandoline [mɑ̃dɔlin] *f* mandolin

mandragore [mɑ̃dragɔr] *f* mandrake

mandrin [mɑ̃drɛ̃] *m* (mach) punch; (mach) chuck

manécanterie [manekɑ̃tri] *f* choir school

manège [manɛʒ] *m* horsemanship; riding school; trick, little game; **manège de chevaux de bois** merry-go-round

mânes [mɑn] *mpl* shades, spirits (*of ancestors*)

maneton [mantɔ̃] *m* crank handle; pin (*of crankshaft*)

manette [manɛt] *f* lever, switch

manganèse [mɑ̃ganɛz] *m* manganese

mangeable [mɑ̃ʒabl] *adj* edible; barely fit to eat

mangeaille [mɑ̃ʒaj] *f* swill; (coll) grub, chow

mangeotter [mɑ̃ʒɔte] *tr* to pick at (*one's food*)

manger [mɑ̃ʒe] *m* food, e.g., **le boire et le manger** food and drink; (slang) meal ‖ §38 *tr* to eat; eat up; mumble (*one's words*); **manger du bout des lèvres** to nibble at ‖ *intr* to eat; **manger à la fortune du pot** to take potluck

mangerie [mɑ̃ʒri] *f* (coll) big meal

mange-tout [mɑ̃ʒtu] *m invar* sugar pea

man·geur [mɑ̃ʒœr] **-geuse** [ʒøz] *mf* eater; wastrel, spendthrift; **mangeur d'hommes** man-eater

mangouste [mɑ̃gust] *f* mongoose

maniable [manjabl] *adj* maneuverable, easy to handle, supple

maniaque [manjak] *adj & mf* maniac

manie [mani] *f* mania

maniement [manimɑ̃] *m* handling

manier [manje] *tr* to handle ‖ *ref* (coll) to get a move on

manière [manjɛr] *f* manner; **à la manière de** in the manner of; **de manière à** so as to; **de manière que** so that; **de toute manière** in any case; **d'une manière ou d'une autre** one way or another; **en aucune manière** by no means; **faire des manières** to pretend to be indifferent, to want to be coaxed; **manière de voir** point of view; **manières** manners

manié·ré -rée [manjere] *adj* mannered, affected

maniérisme [manjerism] *m* mannerism

ma·nieur [manjœr] **-nieuse** [njøz] *mf* handler; **grand manieur d'argent** tycoon

manifes·tant [manifɛstɑ̃] **-tante** [tɑ̃t] *mf* demonstrator

manifestation [manifɛstasjɔ̃] *f* demonstration, manifestation

manifeste [manifɛst] *adj* manifest ‖ *m* manifesto; (naut) manifest

manifester [manifɛste] *tr* to manifest ‖ *intr* to demonstrate ‖ *ref* to reveal oneself

manigance [manigɑ̃s] *f* trick, intrigue

manipuler [manipyle] *tr* to manipulate; handle (*e.g.*, *packages*); arrange (*equipment*) for an experiment

manitou [manitu] *m* manitou; (coll) bigwig

manivelle [manivɛl] *f* crank

manne [man] *f* manna

mannequin [mankɛ̃] *m* model; mannequin, dummy; scarecrow

manœuvre [manœvr] *m* hand, laborer ‖ *f* maneuver; (naut) handling, maneuvering; (rr) shifting; **fausse manœuvre** wrong move; **manœuvres** rigging

manœuvrer [manœvre] *tr* & *intr* to maneuver; (rr) to shift

manoir [manwar] *m* manor, manor house

man·quant [mɑ̃kɑ̃] **-quante** [kɑ̃t] *adj* missing ‖ *mf* absentee ‖ *m* missing article; **manquants** shortages

manque [mɑ̃k] *m* lack; shortage; insufficiency; **manque à gagner** lost opportunity; **manque de parole** breach of faith; **par manque de** for lack of ‖ *f*—**à la manque** (coll) rotten, poor, dud

man·qué -quée [mɑ̃ke] *adj* missed, unsuccessful; broken (*engagement*); (with abilities which were not professionally developed), e.g., **le docteur est un cuisinier manqué** the doctor could have been a cook by profession

manquement [mɑ̃kmɑ̃] *m* breach, lapse

manquer [mɑ̃ke] §96, §97 *tr* to miss; flunk ‖ *intr* to misfire; be missing, e.g., **il en manque trois** three are missing; be missed, e.g., **vous lui manquez beaucoup** you are very much missed by him, he misses you very much; be short, e.g., **il lui manque cinq francs** he is five francs short; **manquer à** to break (*one's word*); disobey (*an order*); fail to observe (*a rule*); fail, e.g., **le cœur lui a manqué** his heart failed him; **manquer de** to lack, be short of, to run out of; **manquer de** + *inf* to nearly + *inf*, e.g., **il a manqué de se noyer** he nearly drowned; **sans manquer** without fail ‖ *ref* to miss each other; to fail

mansarde [mɑ̃sard] *f* mansard roof; mansard

manse [mɑ̃s] *m* & *f* (hist) small manor

mante [mɑ̃t] *f* mantle; **mante religieuse** (ent) praying mantis

man·teau [mɑ̃to] *m* (*pl* **-teaux** [to]) overcoat; mantle, cloak; mantelpiece; **sous le manteau** sub rosa

mantille [mɑ̃tij] *f* mantilla

manucure [manykyr] *mf* manicurist

ma·nuel -nuelle [manɥɛl] *adj* manual ‖ *mf* laborer, blue-collar worker ‖ *m* manual, handbook

manufacture [manyfaktyr] *f* factory, plant

manufacturer [manyfaktyre] *tr* to manufacture

manus·crit [manyskri] **-crite** [krit] *adj* & *m* manuscript

manutention [manytɑ̃sjɔ̃] *f* handling (*of goods*); stopping for unloading

manutentionner [manytɑ̃sjɔne] *tr* to handle (*merchandise*)

mappemonde [mapmɔ̃d] *f* world map; **mappemonde céleste** map of the heavens

maque·reau [makro] **-relle** [rɛl] (*pl* **-reaux -relles**) *mf* (slang) procurer ‖ *m* mackerel; (slang) pimp ‖ *f* (slang) madam (*of a brothel*)

maquette [makɛt] *f* maquette, model; dummy (*of book*); rough sketch

maquignon [makiɲɔ̃] *m* horse trader; wholesale cattle dealer; (coll) go-between

maquignonnage [makiɲɔnaʒ] *m* horse trading

maquignonner [makiɲɔne] *intr* to horse-trade

maquillage [makijaʒ] *m* make-up; fakery

maquiller [makije] *tr* to make up; fake, distort ‖ *ref* to make up

maquil·leur [makijœr] **-leuse** [jøz] *mf* make-up artist ‖ *m* make-up man

maquis [maki] *m* bush; maquis; **prendre le maquis** to go underground

maraî·cher [mareʃe] **-chère** [ʃɛr] *adj* truck-farming ‖ *mf* truck farmer

marais [mare] *m* marsh; truck farm; **marais salant** saltern

marasme [marasm] *m* depression; doldrums, standstill

marathon [maratɔ̃] *m* marathon

marâtre [marɑtr] *f* stepmother; cruel mother

maraude [marod] *f* marauding; **en maraude** cruising (*taxi*)

marauder [marode] *intr* to maraud; cruise (*said of taxi*)

marau·deur [marodœr] **-deuse** [døz] *adj* marauding ‖ *mf* marauder

marbre [marbr] *m* marble; (typ) stone

marbrer [marbre] *tr* to marble; mottle, vein; bruise, blotch

marc [mar] *m* mark (*old coin*); marc, pulp; **marc de café** coffee grounds; **marc de thé** tea leaves ‖ [mark] (*cap*) *m* Mark

marcassin [markasɛ̃] *m* young wild boar

mar·chand [marʃɑ̃] **-chande** [ʃɑ̃d] *adj* marketable; sale (*value*); trading (*center*); wholesale (*price*); merchant (*marine*) ‖ *mf* merchant; **marchand ambulant** peddler; **marchand clandestin** fence (*seller of stolen goods*); **marchand de canons** munitions maker; **marchand de couleurs** paint dealer, dealer in household articles; **marchand de ferraille** junk dealer; **marchand de journaux** newsdealer; **marchand des quatre-saisons** fruit vendor; **marchand en gros** wholesaler; **marchand forain** hawker ‖ *f*—**marchande d'amour** or **de plaisir** prostitute

marchandage [marʃɑ̃daʒ] *m* bargaining; haggling; deal, underhanded arrangement

marchander [marʃɑ̃de] *tr* to bargain over; haggle over; be stingy with (*e.g., one's compliments*) ‖ *intr* to haggle

marchan·deur [marʃɑ̃dœr] **-deuse** [døz] *mf* bargainer; haggler

marchandisage [marʃɑ̃dizaʒ] *m* merchandising

marchandise [marʃɑ̃diz] *f* merchandise; **marchandises** goods

mar·chant [marʃɑ̃] **-chante** [ʃɑ̃t] *adj* marching; militant (*wing of political party*); (mil) wheeling (*flank*)

marche [marʃ] *f* march; step (*of stairway*); walking; movement; progress, course; (aut) gear; **à dix minutes de marche** ten minutes' walk from here; **attention à la marche!** watch your step!; **en marche** in motion, running, operating; **faire marche arrière** to back up; to reverse; **fermer la marche** to bring up the rear; **marche funèbre** funeral march; **ouvrir la marche** to lead off the procession

marché [marʃe] *m* market; marketing, shopping; deal, bargain; **à bon marché** cheap; cheaply; **à meilleur marché** cheaper; more cheaply; **bon marché** cheapness; cheap; cheaply; **faire bon marché de** to set little store by; **faire son marché** to do the marketing; **lancer, mettre,** or **vendre sur le marché** to market; **marché noir** black market; **par-dessus le marché** into the bargain

marchepied [marʃəpje] *m* footstool; little stepladder; running board; (fig) stepping stone

marcher [marʃe] *intr* to walk; run, operate; march; **faire marcher qn** to pull someone's leg; **marcher à grands pas** to stride; **marcher au pas** to walk in step; **marcher dans l'espace** to take a space walk; **marcher sur** to tread on, walk on; **marchez au pas** (*public sign*) drive slowly

mar·cheur [marʃœr] **-cheuse** [ʃøz] *mf* walker

mardi [mardi] *m* Tuesday; **mardi gras** Shrove Tuesday; Mardi gras

mare [mar] *f* pool, pond

marécage [mareka3] *m* marsh, swamp

maréca·geux [mareka3ø] **-geuse** [3øz] *adj* marshy, swampy

maré·chal [mareʃal] *m* (*pl* **-chaux** [ʃo]) marshal; blacksmith; **maréchal des logis** artillery or cavalry sergeant

maréchale [mareʃal] *f* marshal's wife

maréchal-ferrant [mareʃalferɑ̃] *m* (*pl* **maréchaux-ferrants**) blacksmith, farrier

marée [mare] *f* tide; fresh seafood; **marée descendante** ebb tide; **marée montante** flood tide

marelle [marɛl] *f* hopscotch

marémo·teur [maremɔtœr] **-trice** [tris] *adj* tide-driven

margarine [margarin] *f* margarine

marge [mar3] *f* margin; border, edge; leeway, room; **en marge de** on the fringe of; a footnote to; **marge bénéficiaire** margin of profit; **marge brute d'autofinancement (MBA)** cash flow; **marge de sécurité** margin of safety

margelle [mar3ɛl] *f* curb, edge (*of well, fountain, etc.*)

margeur [mar3œr] *m* margin stop

margi·nal -nale [mar3inal] *adj* (*pl* **-naux** [no]) marginal

margot [margo] *f* (coll) magpie; (coll) chatterbox; **Margot** (coll) Maggie

margotin [margɔtɛ̃] *m* kindling

margouillis [marguji] *m* (coll) rotten stinking mess

margou·lin [margulɛ̃] **-line** [lin] *mf* sharpster, shyster

marguerite [margərit] *f* daisy; **Marguerite** Margaret

marguillier [margije] *m* churchwarden

mari [mari] *m* husband

mariable [marjabl] *adj* marriageable

mariage [marja3] *m* marriage; wedding; blend, combination

Marianne [marjan] *f* Marian; Marianne (*symbol of the French Republic*)

ma·rié -riée [marje] *adj* married ‖ *m* bridegroom; **jeunes mariés** newlyweds; **les mariés** the bride and groom ‖ *f* bride

marier [marje] *tr* to marry, join in wedlock; marry off; blend, harmonize ‖ *ref* to get married; **se marier avec** to marry

marie-salope [marisalɔp] *f* (*pl* **maries-salopes**) dredger; (slang) slut

ma·rieur [marjœr] **-rieuse** [rjøz] *mf* (coll) matchmaker

marihuana [mariɥana] or **marijuana** [mari3ɥana] *f* marijuana

ma·rin [marɛ̃] **-rine** [rin] *adj* marine; seagoing; sea, e.g., **brise marine** sea breeze ‖ *m* sailor, seaman; sailor suit ‖ *f* navy; seascape; **marine marchande** merchant marine

mariner [marine] *tr & intr* to marinate

mari·nier [marinje] **-nière** [njɛr] *adj* naval; petty (*officer*); **à la marinière** cooked in gravy with onions ‖ *m* waterman ‖ *f* blouse; (swimming) sidestroke

marionnette [marjɔnɛt] *f* marionette; (fig) puppet

mari·tal -tale [marital] *adj* (*pl* **-taux** [to]) of the husband

maritime [maritim] *adj* maritime

maritorne [maritɔrn] *f* slut

marivaudage [marivoda3] *m* playful flirting; sophisticated conversation

marjolaine [mar3olɛn] *f* marjoram

marlou [marlu] *m* (slang) pimp

marmaille [marmɑj] *f* (coll) brats

marmelade [marmələad] *f* marmalade; (coll) mess

marmite [marmit] *f* pot, pan; (geol) pothole; (mil) shell, heavy shell; **marmite autoclave, marmite sous pression** pressure cooker; **marmite norvégienne** double boiler

marmiton [marmitɔ̃] *m* cook's helper

marmonner [marmɔne] *tr & intr* to mumble

marmot [marmo] *m* (coll) lad; (coll) grotesque figurine (*on knocker*); **croquer le marmot** (coll) to cool one's heels; **marmots** (coll) urchins, kids

marmotte [marmɔt] *f* woodchuck; **dormir comme une marmotte** to sleep like a log; **marmotte d'Amérique** groundhog; **mar-**

motte de commis voyageur traveling salesman's sample case

marmouset [marmuzɛ] *m* grotesque figurine; little man

marner [marne] *tr* to marl ‖ *intr* (naut) to flow, rise; (coll) to drudge

Maroc [marɔk] *m*—**le Maroc** Morocco

maro·cain [marɔkɛ̃] **-caine** [kɛn] *adj* Moroccan ‖ (*cap*) *mf* Moroccan

maronner [marɔne] *intr* (coll) to grumble

maroquin [marɔkɛ̃] *m* morocco leather

maroquinerie [marɔkinri] *f* leather goods

marotte [marɔt] *f* fad; whim; dummy head (*of milliner*); jester's staff

mar·quant [markɑ̃] **-quante** [kɑ̃t] *adj* remarkable, outstanding; purple (*passages*)

marque [mark] *f* mark; brand, make; hallmark; token, sign; **à vos marques!** on your mark(s)!; **de marque** distinguished; **marque déposée** trademark

marquer [marke] *tr* to mark; brand; score; indicate, show ‖ *intr* to make a mark, leave an impression

marqueterie [markətri], [markɛtri] *f* marquetry, inlay

mar·queur [markœr] **-queuse** [køz] *mf* marker ‖ *m* scorekeeper; scorer ‖ *f* (mach) stenciler

marquis [marki] *m* marquis

marquise [markiz] *f* marchioness, marquise; marquee, awning; (rr) roof (*over platform*)

marraine [marɛn] *f* godmother, sponsor; christener; **marraine de guerre** war mother

mar·rant [marɑ̃] **-rante** [rɑ̃t] *adj* (slang) sidesplitting; (slang) funny, queer

marre [mar] *adv*—**en avoir marre** (coll) to be fed up

marrer [mare] *ref* (slang) to have a good laugh

mar·ron [marɔ̃] **-ronne** [rɔn] *adj* quack (*doctor*); shyster (*lawyer*) ‖ **marron** *adj invar* brown ‖ *m* chestnut; **marron d'Inde** horse chestnut

marronnier [marɔnje] *m* chestnut tree; **marronnier d'Inde** horse-chestnut tree

mars [mars] *m* March; **Mars** Mars

Marseille [marsɛj] *f* Marseilles

marsouin [marswɛ̃] *m* porpoise

marte [mart] *f* (zool) marten

mar·teau [marto] *m* (*pl* **-teaux**) *adj* (coll) cracked; balmy ‖ *m* hammer; (ichth) hammerhead; **marteau de porte** knocker

marteau-pilon [martopilɔ̃] *m* (*pl* **marteaux-pilons**) drop hammer

marteau-piqueur [martopikœr] *m* (*pl* **marteaux-piqueurs**) pneumatic drill

marteler [martəle] §2 *tr* to hammer; hammer at; hammer out

Marthe [mart] *f* Martha

mar·tial -tiale [marsjal] *adj* (*pl* **-tiaux** [sjo]) martial

martinet [martinɛ] *m* triphammer; scourge, cat-o'-nine-tails; (orn) martin, swift

martin-pêcheur [martɛ̃pɛʃœr] *m* (*pl* **martins-pêcheurs**) (orn) kingfisher

martre [martr] *f* (zool) marten

mar·tyr -tyre [martir] *adj* & *mf* martyr ‖ **martyre** *m* martyrdom

martyriser [martirize] *tr* to martyr

marxiste [marksist] *adj* & *mf* Marxist

maryland [marilɑ̃] *m* choice tobacco ‖ (*cap*) *m*—**le Maryland** Maryland

mas [mɑ], [mɑs] *m* farmhouse or farm (*in Provence*)

mascarade [maskarad] *f* masquerade

mascaret [maskarɛ] *m* bore

mascaron [maskarɔ̃] *m* mask, mascaron

mascotte [maskɔt] *f* mascot

mascu·lin [maskylɛ̃] **-line** [lin] *adj* & *m* masculine

masque [mask] *m* mask; **masque à gaz** gas mask; **masque mortuaire** death mask

masquer [maske] *tr* & *ref* to mask

massacre [masakr] *m* massacre; botched job

massacrer [masakre] *tr* to massacre; to botch

massage [masaʒ] *m* massage

masse [mas] *f* mass; sledgehammer; mace; pool, common fund; (elec) ground (*e.g., of an automobile*); **masse d'air froid** cold front; **mettre à la masse** (elec) to ground; **une masse de** (coll) a lot of

massepain [maspɛ̃] *m* marzipan

masser [mase] *tr* to mass; massage ‖ *ref* to mass; massage oneself

massette [masɛt] *f* sledge hammer (*of stonemason*); (bot) bulrush

mas·seur [masœr] **-seuse** [søz] *mf* masseur ‖ *m* massager (*instrument*)

mas·sif [masif] **-sive** [siv] *adj* massive; heavyset; solid (*e.g., gold*) ‖ *m* massif, high plateau; clump (*of flowers, trees, etc.*)

massue [masy] *f* club, bludgeon

mastic [mastik] *m* putty

mastiquer [mastike] *tr* to masticate; putty

mastoc [mastɔk] *adj invar* heavy, massive

masturber [mastyrbe] *tr* & *ref* to masturbate

m'as-tu-vu -vue [matyvy] (*pl* **-vu -vue**) *adj* (coll) stuck-up ‖ *mf* (coll) show-off, smart aleck; (coll) bragging actor

masure [mɑzyr] *f* hovel, shack, shanty

mat mate [mat] *adj* dull, flat ‖ **mat** *adj invar* checkmated ‖ *m* checkmate ‖ **mat** *adv* dull

mât [mɑ] *m* mast; pole

matamore [matamɔr] *m* braggart

match [matʃ] *m* match, contest, game

matelas [matla] *m* mattress; (coll) roll (*of bills*); **matelas à eau** water bed

matelasser [matlase] *tr* to pad, cushion

matelot [matlo] *m* sailor, seaman

matelote [matlɔt] *f* fish stew in wine

mater [mate] *tr* to dull; checkmate; subdue

matérialiser [materjalize] *ref* to materialize

matérialiste [materjalist] *adj* materialistic ‖ *mf* materialist

maté·riau [materjo] *m* (*pl* **-riaux**) material

maté·riel -rielle [materjɛl] *adj* material; materialistic ‖ *m* material; equipment; (comp) hardware; (mil) material; **matériel**

roulant (rr) rolling stock ‖ *f* (slang) living
maternage [maternaʒ] *m* nursing; mothering
mater·nel -nelle [maternɛl] *adj* maternal ‖ *f* nursery school
maternité [maternite] *f* maternity; maternity hospital
math or **maths** [mat] *fpl* (coll) math
mathémati·cien [matematisjɛ̃] **-cienne** [sjɛn] *mf* mathematician
mathématique [matematik] *adj* mathematical ‖ **mathématiques** *fpl* mathematics
matière [matjɛr] *f* matter; subject matter; material; **matière première** raw material
matin [matɛ̃] *m* morning; early part of the morning; **au petit matin** in the wee hours of the morning; **de bon matin, de grand matin** very early; **du matin** in the morning, A.M., e.g., **onze heures du matin** eleven o'clock in the morning, eleven

...) sly one ‖
tv indeed!,

-naux [no])

crossbred; red with tinée; **faire**

dj sly, cun-

club, billy , bludgeon rchy

(*person*) ‖

(*number*) ‖ ter

al] *adj* (*pl* rital

triarch; old

damn arsed nble, gripe p) *m* Moor h ‖ (*cap*) *f*

n loomy vez] (pre-1, §92 *adj* auvais the is to smell auvais the

ot) mallow (coll) mil-

maxillaire [maksillɛr] *m* jawbone
maxime [maksim] *f* maxim
maximum [maksimɔm] *adj & m* maximum
mayonnaise [majɔnɛz] *f* mayonnaise
mazette [mazɛt] *f* duffer ‖ *interj* gosh!
mazout [mazut] *m* fuel oil
mazouter [mazute] *intr* to fuel up
Mᵉ *abbr* (**Maître**) Mr.
me [mə] §87 me, to me
méandre [meɑ̃dr] *m* meander
mec [mɛk] *m* (slang) guy; (slang) tough egg
mécanicien [mekanisjɛ̃] *m* mechanic; machinist; engineer (*of locomotive*)
mécanicienne [mekanisjɛn] *f* sewing-machine operator
mécanique [mekanik] *adj* mechanical ‖ *f* mechanism; mechanics
mécaniser [mekanize] *tr* to mechanize
mécanisme [mekanism] *m* mechanism
mécano [mekano] *m* (coll) mechanic
mécène [mesɛn] *m* patron, Maecenas
méchamment [meʃamɑ̃] *adv* maliciously, nastily; (coll) fantastically
méchanceté [meʃɑ̃ste] *f* malice, wickedness; nastiness
mé·chant [meʃɑ̃] **-chante** [ʃɑ̃t] *adj* malicious, wicked; nasty; naughty (*child*) ‖ *mf* mean person; **faire le méchant** to threaten; (coll) to strike back; **les méchants** the wicked; **méchant!** naughty boy!
mèche [mɛʃ] *f* wick; fuse; lock (*of hair*); bit (*of drill*); **être de mèche avec** (coll) to be in cahoots with; **éventer** or **découvrir la mèche** to discover the plot; **il n'y a pas mèche** (coll) it's no go, nothing doing; **vendre la mèche** (coll) to let the cat out of the bag
mécompte [mekɔ̃t] *m* miscalculation; disappointment
méconnaissable [mekɔnɛsabl] *adj* unrecognizable
méconnaître [mekɔnɛtr] §12 *tr* to ignore; underestimate
mécon·nu -nue [mekɔny] *adj* underestimated, misunderstood
mécon·tent [mekɔ̃tɑ̃] **-tente** [tɑ̃t] *adj* dissatisfied, displeased ‖ *mf* grumbler
mécontentement [mekɔ̃tɑ̃tmɑ̃] *m* dissatisfaction, displeasure
mécontenter [mekɔ̃tɑ̃te] *tr* to displease
Mecque [mɛk] *f*—**La Mecque** Mecca
mécréant [mekreɑ̃] **mécréante** [mekreɑ̃t] *adj* unbelieving ‖ *mf* unbeliever
médaille [medaj] *f* medal
médaillon [medajɔ̃] *m* medallion; locket; thin round slice (*e.g., of meat*); pat (*of butter*)
médecin [medsɛ̃], [mɛtsɛ̃] *m* doctor; **femme médecin** woman doctor
médecine [medsin], [mɛtsin] *f* medicine (*science and art*)
média [medja] *m* mass media
mé·dian [medjɑ̃] **-diane** [djan] *adj & f* median
média·teur [medjatœr] **-trice** [tris] *mf* mediator, arbitrator

médiation [medjɑsjɔ̃] *f* mediation
médi·cal -cale [medikal] *adj* (*pl* **-caux** [ko]) medical
médicament [medikamɑ̃] *m* (pharm) medicine; **médicament miracle** wonder drug
médicamenter [medikamɑ̃te] *tr* to dose
médicamen·teux [medikamɑ̃tø] **-teuse** [tøz] *adj* medicinal
médici·nal -nale [medisinal] *adj* (*pl* **-naux** [no]) medicinal
médié·val -vale [medjeval] *adj* (*pl* **-vaux** [vo]) medieval
médiéviste [medjevist] *mf* medievalist
médiocre [medjɔkr] *adj* mediocre, poor, inferior, second-rate
médiocrité [medjɔkrite] *f* mediocrity
médire [medir] §40 *intr* to backbite; **médire de** to run down, to disparage
médisance [medizɑ̃s] *f* disparagement, backbiting
médi·sant [medizɑ̃] **-sante** [zɑ̃t] *adj* disparaging, backbiting ‖ *mf* slanderer
méditation [meditɑsjɔ̃] *f* meditation
méditer [medite] §97 *tr* & *intr* to meditate
méditerra·né -née [mediterane] *adj* Mediterranean; inland ‖ (*cap*) *f* Mediterranean (Sea)
méditerranéen [mediteraneɛ̃] **méditerranéenne** [mediteraneɛn] *adj* Mediterranean
médium [medjɔm] *m* medium (*in spiritualism*); range (*of voice*)
médiumnique [medjɔmnik] *adj* psychic
médius [medjys] *m* middle finger
méduse [medyz] *f* jellyfish, medusa ‖ (*cap*) *f* Medusa
méduser [medyze] *tr* to petrify (*with terror*)
meeting [mitiŋ] *m* rally, meet, meeting
méfait [mefɛ] *m* misdeed; **méfaits** ravages
méfiance [mefjɑ̃s] *f* mistrust
mé·fiant [mefjɑ̃] **-fiante** [fjɑ̃t] *adj* mistrustful
méfier [mefje] *ref* to beware; **se méfier de** to guard against, to mistrust
mégacycle [megasikl] *m* megacycle
mégaphone [megafɔn] *m* megaphone
mégarde [megard] *f*—**par mégarde** inadvertently
mégère [meʒɛr] *f* shrew
mégohm [megom] *m* megohm
mégot [mego] *m* butt (*of cigarette or cigar*)
meil·leur -leure [mɛjœr] (precedes the noun it modifies) §91 *adj comp* & *super* better; best; **meilleur marché** cheaper
mélancolie [melɑ̃kɔli] *f* melancholy, melancholia
mélancolique [melɑ̃kɔlik] *adj* melancholy
mélange [melɑ̃ʒ] *m* mixing, blending; mixture, blend; **mélanges** homage volume, Festschrift
mélanger [melɑ̃ʒe] §38 *tr* to mix, blend
mélan·geur [melɑ̃ʒœr] **-geuse** [ʒøz] *m* & *f* mixer
mélasse [melas] *f* molasses; **dans la mélasse** (coll) in the soup
mê·lé -lée [mele] *adj* mixed ‖ *f* melee
mêler [mele] §97 *tr* to mix; tangle; shuffle (*the cards*) ‖ *ref* to mix; **se mêler à** to

mingle with; join in; **se mêler de** to meddle with, interfere with
mélèze [melɛz] *m* (bot) larch
méli-mélo [melimelo] *m* mishmash
mélodie [melɔdi] *f* melody
mélo·dieux [melɔdjø] **-dieuse** [djøz] *adj* melodious
mélodique [melɔdik] *adj* melodic
mélodramatique [melɔdramatik] *adj* melodramatic
mélomane [melɔman] *adj* music-loving ‖ *mf* music lover
melon [məlɔ̃] *m* melon; derby; **melon d'eau** watermelon
mélopée [melɔpe] *f* singsong, chant
membrane [mɑ̃bran] *f* membrane; **membrane vibrante** (elec) diaphragm
membre [mɑ̃br] *m* member; limb, member; **membre actif** active member; **membre bienfaiteur** sustaining member; **membre de phrase** clause; **membre donateur** contributing member; **membre perpétuel** life member
membrure [mɑ̃bryr] *f* frame, limbs
même [mɛm] *adj indef* very, e.g., **le jour même** on that very day ‖ (when standing before noun) *adj indef* same, e.g., **en même temps** at the same time ‖ *pron indef* same, same one; **à même de** + *inf* up to + *ger*, in a position to + *inf*; **à même le** (**la,** etc.) straight out of the (*e.g., bottle*); flush with the (*e.g., pavement*); next to one's (*e.g., skin*); on the bare (*ground, sand, etc.*) **cela revient au même** that amounts to the same thing; **de même** likewise; **de même que** in the same way as; **tout de même** nevertheless ‖ *adv* even; **même quand** even when; **même si** even if
-même [mɛm] §86
mémé [meme] *f* (*children's language*) granny
mémento [memɛ̃to] *m* memento; memo book
mémère [memɛr] *f* (coll) granny; (coll) blowsy dame
mémoire [memwar] *m* memorandum; statement, account; term paper; treatise; petition; **mémoires** memoirs ‖ *f* memory; **de mémoire** from memory; **de mémoire d'homme** within memory; **mémoire morte** (comp) read-only memory, ROM; **mémoire vive** (comp) random-access memory, RAM; **pour mémoire** for the record
mémorandum [memɔrɑ̃dɔm] *m* memorandum; **mémorandum de combat** battle orders
mémo·rial [memɔrjal] *m* (*pl* **-riaux** [rjo]) memorial; (dipl) memorandum; memoirs
mena·çant [mənasɑ̃] **-çante** [sɑ̃t] *adj* menacing
menace [mənas] *f* menace, threat
menacer [mənase] § 51, §97, §99 *tr* & *intr* to menace, threaten
ménage [menaʒ] *m* household; family; married couple; furniture; **de ménage** home-

made; **faire bon ménage** to get along well; **faire des ménages** to do housework (*for hire*); **faire le ménage** to do the housework; **se mettre en ménage** to set up housekeeping; (coll) to live together (*without being married*)

ménagement [menaʒmɑ̃] *m* discretion; consideration

ména·ger [menaʒe] **-gère** [ʒɛr] *adj* household; **ménager de** thrifty with ‖ *f* housewife, homemaker; silverware; silverware case ‖ **ménager** §38 *tr* to be careful with, spare; save (*money; one's strength*); husband (*one's resources, one's strength*); be considerate of, handle with kid gloves; arrange, bring about; install, provide; make (*e.g., a hole*); **ménager un espace pour** leave a space for ‖ *intr* to save ‖ *ref* to take good care of oneself

ménagerie [menaʒri] *f* menagerie

men·diant [mɑ̃djɑ̃] **-diante** [djɑ̃t] *adj & mf* beggar; **des mendiants** dessert (*of dried fruits and nuts*)

mendier [mɑ̃dje] *tr & intr* to beg

menées [məne] *fpl* intrigues, schemes

mener [məne] §2, §95 *tr* to lead; take; manage; draw (*e.g., a line*) ‖ *intr* to lead

ménestrel [menɛstrɛl] *m* wandering minstrel

ménétrier [menetrije] *m* fiddler

me·neur [mənœr] **-neuse** [nøz] *mf* leader; ringleader; **meneur de jeu** master of ceremonies; narrator; moving spirit

menotte [mənɔt] *f* tiny hand; **menottes** handcuffs; **mettre** or **passer les menottes à** to handcuff

mens [mɑ̃] *v* (**ment**) see **mentir**

mensonge [mɑ̃sɔ̃ʒ] *m* lie; **pieux mensonge** white lie

mensonger [mɑ̃sɔ̃ʒe] **-gère** [ʒɛr] *adj* lying, false; illusory, deceptive

men·struel -struelle [mɑ̃stryɛl] *adj* menstrual

menstrues [mɑ̃stry] *fpl* menses

mensualité [mɑ̃syalite] *f* monthly installment; monthly salary

men·suel -suelle [mɑ̃sɥɛl] *adj* monthly

men·tal -tale [mɑ̃tal] *adj* (*pl* **-taux** [to]) mental

mentalité [mɑ̃talite] *f* mentality

men·teur [mɑ̃tœr] **-teuse** [tøz] *adj* lying ‖ *mf* liar

menthe [mɑ̃t] *f* mint; **menthe poivrée** peppermint; **menthe verte** spearmint

mention [mɑ̃sjɔ̃] *f* mention; **avec mention** with honors; **biffer les mentions inutiles** to cross out the questions which do not apply; **être reçu sans mention** to receive just a passing grade

mentionner [mɑ̃sjɔne] *tr* to mention

mentir [mɑ̃tir] §41 *intr* to lie

menton [mɑ̃tɔ̃] *m* chin

mentonnière [mɑ̃tɔnjɛr] *f* chin rest; chin strap

me·nu -nue [məny] *adj* small, little; tiny, fine ‖ *m* menu; minute detail

menuet [mənɥɛ] *m* minuet

menuiserie [mənɥizri] *f* carpentry; woodwork

menuisier [mənɥizje] *m* carpenter

méprendre [meprɑ̃dr] §56 *ref* to be mistaken; **à s'y méprendre** enough to take one for the other; **il n'y a pas à s'y méprendre** there's no mistake about it

mépris [mepri] *m* contempt, scorn

méprisable [meprizabl] *adj* contemptible, despicable

mépri·sant [meprizɑ̃] **-sante** [zɑ̃t] *adj* contemptuous, scornful

méprise [mepriz] *f* mistake

mépriser [meprize] *tr* to despise, scorn

mer [mɛr] *f* sea; **basse mer** low tide; **de haute mer** seagoing; **haute mer, pleine mer** high seas; high tide; **mer des Indes** Indian Ocean; **sur mer** afloat

mercanti [mɛrkɑ̃ti] *m* profiteer

mercantile [mɛrkɑ̃til] *adj* profiteering, mercenary

mercenaire [mɛrsənɛr] *adj & mf* mercenary

mercerie [mɛrsəri] *f* notions

merci [mɛrsi] *m* thanks, thank you; **merci de** + *inf* thank you for + *ger;* **merci de** or **pour** thank you for ‖ *f*—**à la merci de** at the mercy of; **Dieu merci!** thank heavens! ‖ *interj* thanks!, thank you!; no thanks!, no thank you!

mercredi [mɛrkrədi] *m* Wednesday; **mercredi des Cendres** Ash Wednesday

mercure [mɛrkyr] *m* mercury

mercuriale [mɛrkyrjal] *f* reprimand; market quotations; mercury (*weed*)

merde [mɛrd] *f* excrement; **merde alors!** (coll) well I'll be!

mère [mɛr] *f* mother; **la mère Gigogne** the old woman who lived in a shoe

méri·dien [meridjɛ̃] **-dienne** [djɛn] *adj & m* meridian ‖ *f* meridian line; couch, sofa; siesta

méridio·nal -nale [meridjɔnal] (*pl* **-naux** [no]) *adj* meridional, southern ‖ (*cap*) *mf* inhabitant of the Midi

meringue [mərɛ̃g] *f* meringue

merise [məriz] *f* wild cherry

merisier [mərizje] *m* wild cherry (tree)

méri·tant [meritɑ̃] **-tante** [tɑ̃t] *adj* deserving, worthy

mérite [merit] *m* merit

mériter [merite] §7 *tr* to merit, deserve; win, earn ‖ *intr*—**mériter bien de** to deserve the gratitude of

méritoire [meritwar] *adj* deserving, meritorious

merlan [mɛrlɑ̃] *m* (ichth) whiting

merle [mɛrl] *m* (orn) blackbird; **merle blanc** (fig) rara avis; **vilain merle** (fig) dirty dog

merlin [mɛrlɛ̃] *m* ax; poleax; (naut) marline

merluche [mɛrlyʃ] *f* (ichth) hake, cod

merveille [mɛrvɛj] *f* marvel, wonder; **à merveille** marvelously, wonderfully

merveil·leux [mɛrvɛjø] **-leuse** [jøz] *adj* marvelous, wonderful

mes [me] §88 my

mésalliance [mezaljɑ̃s] *f* misalliance, mismatch

mésallier [mezalje] *tr* to misally ‖ *ref* to marry beneath one's station

mésange [mezɑ̃ʒ] *f* (orn) chickadee, titmouse

mésaventure [mezavɑ̃tyr] *f* misadventure

mesdames *fpl* see **madame**

mesdemoiselles *fpl* see **mademoiselle**

mésentente [mezɑ̃tɑ̃t] *f* misunderstanding

mésestimer [mezɛstime] *tr* to underestimate

mésintelligence [mezɛ̃teliʒɑ̃s] *f* misunderstanding, discord

mes·quin [mɛskɛ̃] **-quine** [kin] *adj* mean; stingy; petty

mess [mɛs] *m* officer's mess

message [mesaʒ] *m* message

messa·ger [mesaʒe] **-gère** [ʒɛr] *mf* messenger

messagerie [mesaʒri] *f* express; **messageries** express company; **messageries aériennes** air freight

messe [mɛs] *f* (eccl) Mass; **dire** or **faire des messes basses** (coll) to speak in an undertone; **messe basse, petite messe** Low Mass; **première messe, messe du début** early Mass

Messie [mesi] *m* Messiah

messieurs *mpl* see **monsieur**

messieurs-dames [mɛsjødam] *interj* ladies and gentlemen!

mesure [məzyr] *f* measure; measurement; (mus, poetic) measure; **à mesure** successively, one by one; **à mesure que** as; according to, proportionately as; **battre la mesure** to keep time; **dans la mesure de** insofar as; **dans une certaine mesure** to a certain extent; **être en mesure de** to be in a position to; **faire sur mesure** to make (*clothing*) to order; (fig) to tailor-make; **mesure de circonstance** emergency measure; **mesure en ruban** tape measure; **prendre des mesures de** to take measures to; **prendre la mesure de** to size up; **prendre les mesures de** to measure

mesurer [məzyre] *tr* to measure; measure off or out ‖ *ref* to measure; **se mesurer avec** to measure swords with

métairie [metɛri] *f* farm (*of a sharecropper*)

mé·tal [metal] *m* (*pl* **-taux** [to]) metal

métallique [metalik] *adj* metallic

métalloïde [metalɔid] *m* nonmetal

métallurgie [metalyrʒi] *f* metallurgy

métamorphose [metamɔrfoz] *f* metamorphosis

métaphore [metafɔr] *f* metaphor

métaphorique [metafɔrik] *adj* metaphorical

métathèse [metatɛz] *f* metathesis

métayage [metɛjaʒ] *m* sharecropping, tenant farming

mé·tayer [meteje] **-tayère** [tejɛr] *mf* sharecropper

méteil [metɛj] *m* wheat and rye

météo [meteo] *adj invar* meteorological ‖ *m* weatherman ‖ *f* meteorology; weather bureau; weather report

météore [meteɔr] *m* meteor (*atmospheric phenomenon*)

météorite [meteɔrit] *m* & *f* meteorite

météorologie [meteɔrɔlɔʒi] *f* meteorology; weather bureau; weather report

métèque [metɛk] *m* (pej) foreigner

méthane [metan] *m* methane

méthode [metɔd] *f* method; **méthode insufflatoire bouche à bouche** mouth-to-mouth resuscitation

méthodique [metɔdik] *adj* methodic(al)

méthodiste [metɔdist] *adj* & *mf* Methodist

méticu·leux [metikylø] **-leuse** [løz] *adj* meticulous

métier [metje] *m* trade, craft; loom; **faites votre métier!** mind your own business!; **sur le métier** on the stocks

mé·tis -tisse [metis] *adj* & *mf* half-breed

métisser [metise] *tr* to crossbreed

métrage [metraʒ] *m* length in meters; length (*of remnant, film, etc.*); (mov) length of film in meters (*in English:* footage, *i.e., length of film in feet*); **court métrage** (mov) short subject, short; **long métrage** (mov) full-length movie, feature

mètre [mɛtr] *m* meter; **mètre à ruban** tape measure; **mètre pliant** folding rule

métrer [metre] §10 *tr* to measure out by the meter

métrique [metrik] *adj* metric(al) ‖ *f* metrics

métro [metro] *m* subway

métronome [metrɔnɔm] *m* metronome

métropole [metrɔpɔl] *f* metropolis; mother country

métropoli·tain [metrɔpɔlitɛ̃] **-taine** [tɛn] *adj* metropolitan ‖ *m* subway; (eccl) metropolitan

mets [mɛ] *m* dish, food

mettable [mɛtabl] *adj* wearable

met·teur [metœr] **-teuse** [tøz]) *mf*—**metteur au point** mechanic; **metteur en œuvre** setter; (fig) promoter; **metteur en ondes** (rad) director, producer; **metteur en pages** (typ) make-up man; **metteur en scène** (mov, theat) director, producer

mettre [mɛtr] §42, §95, §96 *tr* to put, lay, place; put on (*clothes*); set (*the table*); take (*time*); **mettre à feu** (rok) to fire; **mettre au point** to carry out, complete; tune up, adjust; (opt) to focus; (rad) to tune; **mettre au rancart** to pigeonhole; **mettre en accusation** to indict; **mettre en marche** to start; **mettre en œuvre** to put into action; **mettre en valeur** to develop, improve; set off, enhance; **mettre en vigueur** to enforce; **mettre feu à** to set fire to; **mettre que** (coll) to suppose that ‖ *intr*—**mettre bas** (zool) to litter ‖ §96 *ref* to sit or stand; go; set; **se mettre à** to begin to; **se mettre à table** to sit down to eat; (slang) to confess; **se mettre en colère** to get angry; **se mettre en route** to set out; **se mettre mal avec** to quarrel with

meuble [mœbl] *adj* uncemented; loose (*ground*); personal (*property*) ‖ *m* piece of furniture; **meubles** furniture; **meubles d'occasion** secondhand furniture

meubler [mœble] *tr* to furnish

meuglement [møɡləmɑ̃] *m* lowing (*of cow*)

meugler [møgle] *intr* to low
meuh! meuh! [mœmœ] *interj* moo! moo!
meule [møl] *f* millstone; grindstone; stack (*e.g., of hay*)
meuler [møle] *tr* to grind
meu·nier [mønje] **-nière** [njɛr] *adj* milling (*e.g., industry*) ‖ *m* miller ‖ *f* miller's wife; **à la meunière** sautéed in butter
meurs [mœr] *v* (**meurt**) see **mourir**
meurt-de-faim [mœrdəfɛ̃] *mf invar* starveling; **de meurt-de-faim** starvation (*wages*)
meurtre [mœrtr] *m* manslaughter; (fig) shame, crime; **meurtre commis avec préméditation** murder
meur·trier [mœrtrije] **-trière** [trijɛr] *adj* murderous; deadly ‖ *m* murderer ‖ *f* murderess; gun slit, loophole
meurtrir [mœrtrir] *tr* to bruise
meurtrissure [mœrtrisyr] *f* bruise
meute [møt] *f* pack, band
mévente [mevɑ̃t] *f* slump (*in sales*)
mexi·cain [mɛksikɛ̃] **-caine** [kɛn] *adj* Mexican ‖ (*cap*) *mf* Mexican
Mexico [mɛksiko] Mexico City
Mexique [mɛksik] *m*—**le Mexique** Mexico
mezzanine [mɛdzanin] *m & f* (theat) mezzanine ‖ *f* mezzanine; mezzanine window
miam! miam! [mjɑ̃mjɑ̃] *interj* purr! purr!
miaou [mjau] *m* meow
miaulement [mjolmɑ̃] *m* meow; caterwauling; catcall
miauler [mjole] *intr* to meow
mi-bas [miba] *m invar* half hose
mica [mika] *m* mica
miche [miʃ] *f* round loaf of bread
mi-chemin [miʃmɛ̃] *m*—**à mi-chemin** halfway
micheton [miʃtɔ̃] *m* (slang) john (*prostitute's customer*)
mi-clos [miklo] **-close** [kloz] *adj* (*pl* **-clos -closes**) half-shut
micmac [mikmak] *m* (coll) underhand dealing
mi-corps [mikɔr]—**à mi-corps** to the waist
mi-côte [mikot]—**à mi-côte** halfway up the hill
microbe [mikrɔb] *m* microbe
microbicide [mikrɔbisid] *adj & m* germicide
microbiologie [mikrɔbjɔlɔʒi] *f* microbiology
microfilm [mikrɔfilm] *m* microfilm
microfilmer [mikrɔfilme] *tr* to microfilm
micro-onde [mikrɔɔ̃d] *f* (*pl* **-ondes**) microwave
micro-ordinateur [mikrɔɔrdinatœr] *m* (*pl* **-ordinateurs**) microcomputer
microphone [mikrɔfɔn] *m* microphone
micro-plastron [mikrɔplastrɔ̃] *m* chest microphone
microscope [mikrɔskɔp] *m* microscope; **microscope électronique** electron microscope
microscopique [mikrɔskɔpik] *adj* microscopic
microsillon [mikrɔsijɔ̃] *adj & m* microgroove

midi [midi] *m* noon; south; twelve, e.g., **midi dix** ten minutes after twelve; **chercher midi à quatorze heures** (fig) to look for difficulties where there are none; **Midi** south of France
midinette [midinɛt] *f* dressmaker's assistant; working girl
mie [mi] *f* soft part, crumb; female friend; **ne . . . mie** §90 (archaic) not a crumb, not, e.g., **je n'en veux mie** I don't want any
miel [mjɛl] *m* honey
miel·leux [mjɛlø] **-leuse** [løz] *adj* honeyed, unctuous
mien [mjɛ̃] **mienne** [mjɛn] §89 mine
miette [mjɛt] *f* crumb
mieux [mjø] §91 *adv comp & super* better; **aimer mieux** to prefer; **à qui mieux mieux** trying to outdo each other; **de mieux en mieux** better and better; **être mieux, aller mieux** to feel better; **tant mieux** so much the better; **valoir mieux** to be better
mieux-être [mjøzɛtr] *m* improved well-being
mièvre [mjɛvr] *adj* dainty, affected
mi-figue [mifig] *f*—**mi-figue mi-raisin** half one way half the other; half in jest half in earnest
mi·gnard [miɲar] **-gnarde** [ɲard] *adj* affected, mincing
mi·gnon [miɲɔ̃] **-gnonne** [ɲɔn] *adj* cute, darling ‖ *mf* darling
mignon·net [miɲɔnɛ] **-nette** [nɛt] *adj* dainty ‖ *f* fine lace; pepper; (bot) pink
mignoter [miɲɔte] *tr* (coll) to pet (*a child*)
migraine [migrɛn] *f* migraine; headache
migratoire [migratwar] *adj* migratory
mi-jambe [miʒɑ̃b] *f*—**à mi-jambe** up to one's knee
mijoter [miʒɔte] *tr* to simmer; (coll) to cook up, brew ‖ *intr* to simmer
mijoteuse [miʒɔtøz] *f* crockpot
mil [mil] *adj* one thousand, e.g., **mil neuf cent quatorze** nineteen fourteen (*year*) ‖ *m* Indian club; millet
milan [milɑ̃] *m* (orn) kite
milice [milis] *f* militia
mi·lieu [miljø] *m* (*pl* **-lieux**) middle; milieu; **milieu de table** centerpiece
militaire [militɛr] *adj* military ‖ *m* soldier; **le militaire** the military
mili·tant [militɑ̃] **-tante** [tɑ̃t] *adj & mf* militant
militariser [militarize] *tr* to militarize
militarisme [militarism] *m* militarism
militer [milite] *intr* to militate
mille [mil] *adj & pron* thousand ‖ *m* thousand; mile; **mettre dans le mille** to hit the bull's-eye; **mille marin** international nautical mile
millefeuille [milfœj] *m* napoleon (*pastry*)
mille-feuille [milfœj] *f* (*pl* **-feuilles**) (bot) yarrow
millénaire [milenɛr] *adj* millennial ‖ *m* millennium
mille-pattes [milpat] *m invar* centipede

millésime [milezim] *m* date, vintage; year of issue
millet [mijɛ] *m* millet; birdseed
milliard [miljar] *m* billion
milliardaire [miljardɛr] *mf* billionaire
millième [miljɛm] *adj, pron (masc, fem)* thousandth ‖ *m* thousandth; mill *(thousandth part of a dollar)*
millier [milje] *m* thousand; about a thousand; **par milliers** by the thousands; **un millier de** a thousand
milligramme [miligram] *m* milligram
millimètre [milimɛtr] *m* millimeter
million [miljɔ̃] *m* million; **un million de** a million
millionième [miljɔnjɛm] *adj, pron (masc, fem)*, & *m* millionth
millionnaire [miljɔnɛr] *adj* & *m* millionaire
mime [mim] *mf* mime; mimic
mimer [mime] *tr* & *intr* to mime; mimic
mimique [mimik] *adj* sign *(language)* ‖ *f* mimicry
mi-moyen [mimwajɛ̃] *m (pl -moyens)* welterweight
minable [minabl] *adj* wretched, shabby; (coll) pitiful *(performance, existence, etc.)* ‖ *mf* unfortunate
minaret [minarɛ] *m* minaret
minauder [minode] *intr* to simper, smirk
minau·dier [minodje] **-dière** [djɛr] *adj* mincing
mince [mɛ̃s] *adj* thin, slim, slight; **mince!** or **mince alors!** golly!
mine [min] *f* mine; lead *(of pencil)*; look, face; looks; (fig) mine *(of information)*; **avoir bonne mine** to look well; **avoir la mine d'être** to look to be; **avoir mauvaise mine** to look badly; **faire bonne mine à** to be nice to; **faire des mines to** simper; **faire la mine à** to pout at; **faire mauvaise mine à** to be unpleasant to; **faire mine de** to make as if to
miner [mine] *tr* to mine; undermine; wear away
minerai [minrɛ] *m* ore
miné·ral -rale [mineral] *(pl -raux* [ro]*) adj* & *m* mineral
minéralogie [mineralɔʒi] *f* mineralogy
mi·net [minɛ] **-nette** [nɛt] *mf* (coll) kitty, pussy; (coll) darling
mi·neur -neure [minœr] *adj* & *mf* minor ‖ *m* miner
miniature [minjatyr] *f* miniature
miniaturisation [minjatyrizɑsjɔ̃] *f* miniaturization
miniaturiser [minjatyrize] *tr* to miniaturize
minijupe [miniʒyp] *f* miniskirt
mini·mal -male [minimal] *adj (pl -maux* [mo]*)* minimum *(temperature)*
minimarge [minimarʒ] *f* discount house
minime [minim] *adj* tiny; derisory *(salary)*
minimiser [minimize] *tr* to minimize
minimum [minimɔm] *adj* & *m* minimum; **minimum vital** minimum wage
ministère [ministɛr] *m* ministry; **ministère des affaires étrangères** ministry of foreign affairs (department of state)

ministé·riel -rielle [ministerjɛl] *adj* ministerial
ministre [ministr] *m* minister; **ministre des affaires étrangères** minister of foreign affairs (secretary of state); **premier ministre** premier, prime minister
minium [minjɔm] *m* red lead
minois [minwa] *m* (coll) pretty little face
minoritaire [minɔritɛr] *adj* minority
minorité [minɔrite] *f* minority; time of being under legal age
Minorque [minɔrk] *f* Minorca
minoterie [minɔtri] *f* flour mill; flour industry
minotier [minɔtje] *m* miller
minuit [minɥi] *m* midnight; twelve, e.g. **minuit et demi** twelve-thirty
minuscule [minyskyl] *adj* tiny; small *(letter)* ‖ *f* small letter
minus habens [minysabɛ̃s] *mf invar* (coll) moron, idiot
minutage [minytaʒ] *m* timing
minute [minyt] *f* minute; moment, instant; **à la minute** that very moment ‖ *interj* (coll) just a minute!
minuter [minyte] *tr* to itemize; time
minuterie [minytri] *f* delayed-action switch; (mach) timing mechanism
minutie [minysi] *f* minute detail; great care; **minuties** minutiae
minu·tieux [minysjø] **-tieuse** [sjøz] *adj* meticulous, thorough
mioche [mjɔʃ] *mf* (coll) brat
mi-pente [mipɑ̃t]—**à mi-pente** halfway up or halfway down
mirabilis [mirabilis] *m* (bot) marvel-of-Peru
miracle [mirakl] *m* miracle; wonder, marvel; miracle play; **crier au miracle** to go into ecstasies
miracu·leux [mirakylø] **-leuse** [løz] *adj* miraculous; wonderful, marvelous
mirador [miradɔr] *m* watchtower
mirage [miraʒ] *m* mirage
mire [mir] *f* sight *(of gun)*; surveyor's pole; (telv) test pattern
mire-œufs [mirø] *m invar* candler
mirer [mire] *tr* to candle *(eggs)* ‖ *ref* to look at oneself; be reflected
mirifique [mirifik] *adj* (coll) marvelous
mirobo·lant [mirɔbɔlɑ̃] **-lante** [lɑ̃t] *adj* (coll) astounding
miroir [mirwar] *m* mirror; **miroir à alouettes** decoy
miroiter [mirwate] *intr* to sparkle, gleam; **faire miroiter q.ch. à qn** to lure s.o. with s.th.
miroton [mirɔtɔ̃] *m* Irish stew
mis [mi] **mise** [miz] *v* see **mettre**
misaine [mizɛn] *f* foresail
misanthrope [mizɑ̃trɔp] *mf* misanthrope
miscellanées [miselane], [misɛllane] *fpl* miscellany
mise [miz] *f* placing, putting; dress, attire; (cards) stake, ante; **de mise** acceptable, proper; **mise à feu** firing *(e.g., of missile)*; **mise à l'eau** launching; **mise à prix** opening bid; **mise au point** carrying out,

completion; tuning up, adjustment; (opt) focusing; (rad) tuning; **mise au rancart** pigeonholding; **mise bas** delivery (*of litter*); **mise de fonds** investment; **mise en accusation** indictment; **mise(s) en chantier** construction start(s); **mise en demeure** (law) injunction; **mise en marche** starting; **mise en œuvre** putting into action; **mise en plis** set; **mise en scène** (theat) direction; (theat & fig) staging; **mise en valeur** development, improvement; **mise en vigueur** enforcement; **mise sur ordinateur** computerization

miser [mize] *tr & intr* to ante; stake, bet; bid (*e.g., at auction*)

misérable [mizerabl] *adj* miserable ‖ *mf* wretch

misère [mizɛr] *f* misery, wretchedness; poverty; worry; (coll) trifle; **crier misère** to make a poor mouth; to look forsaken; **faire des misères à** to pester; **misères** woes, misfortunes

misé·reux [mizerø] **-reuse** [røz] *adj* destitute, wretched ‖ *mf* pauper

miséricorde [mizerikɔrd] *f* mercy

miséricor·dieux [mizerikɔrdjø] **-dieuse** [djøz] *adj* merciful

missel [misɛl] *m* missal

missile [misil] *m* guided missile

mission [misjɔ̃] *f* mission

missionnaire [misjɔnɛr] *adj & m* missionary

missive [misiv] *adj & f* missive

mitaine [mitɛn] *f* mitt

mite [mit] *f* (ent) mite; (ent) clothes moth

mi·té -tée [mite] *adj* moth-eaten; (coll) shabby

mi-temps [mitɑ̃] *f invar* (sports) half time; **à mi-temps** half time

miter [mite] *ref* to become moth-eaten

mi·teux [mitø] **-teuse** [tøz] *adj* shabby ‖ *mf* (coll) shabby-looking person

mitiger [mitiʒe] §38 *tr* to mitigate

mitonner [mitɔne] *tr* to simmer; pamper; (coll) to contrive, devise ‖ *intr* to simmer

mitoyen [mitwajɛ̃] **mitoyenne** [mitwajɛn] *adj* midway, intermediate, dividing; jointly owned, common

mitraille [mitrɑj] *f* scrap iron; grapeshot; artillery fire

mitrailler [mitrɑje] *tr* to machine-gun; pepper (*with gunfire, flash bulbs, etc.*)

mitraillette [mitrɑjɛt] *f* submachine gun, Tommy gun

mitrail·leur [mitrɑjœr] **-leuse** [jøz] *adj* repeating, automatic (*firearm*) ‖ *m* machine gunner ‖ *f* machine gun

mitre [mitr] *f* miter; chimney pot

mitron [mitrɔ̃] *m* baker's boy

mi-voix [mivwa]—**à mi-voix** in a low voice, under one's breath

mixer or **mixeur** [miksœr] *m* electric food mixer

mixte [mikst] *adj* mixed; coeducational; composite; joint (*e.g., commission*); (rr) freight-and-passenger

mixtion [mikstjɔ̃] *f* mixing; mixture

mixture [mikstyr] *f* mixture

M.L.F. [ɛmɛlɛf] *m* (letterword) (**mouvement de libération de la femme**) women's lib(eration movement)

Mlle *abbr* (**Mademoiselle**) Miss

MM. *abbr* (**Messieurs**) Messrs.

Mme *abbr* (**Madame**) Mrs.; Mme.

mobile [mɔbil] *adj* mobile ‖ *m* motive; (fa) mobile

mobi·lier [mɔbilje] **-lière** [ljɛr] *adj* personal ‖ *m* furniture

mobilisable [mɔbilizabl] *adj* (mil) subject to call

mobilisation [mɔbilizɑsjɔ̃] *f* mobilization

mobiliser [mɔbilize] *tr & intr* to mobilize

mobilité [mɔbilite] *f* mobility

moche [mɔʃ] *adj* (coll) ugly; (coll) lousy

modalité [mɔdalite] *f* modality, manner, method; **modalités** terms

mode [mɔd] *m* kind, method, mode; (gram) mood; (mus) mode; **mode d'emploi** directions for use; **mode dialogué** (comp) conversational mode ‖ *f* fashion; **à la mode** in style, fashionable; **à la mode de** in the manner of; **modes** fashions; millinery

modèle [mɔdɛl] *adj & m* model; sample, e.g., **villa modèle** sample home

modeler [mɔdle] §2 *tr* to model; shape, mold ‖ *ref*—**se modeler sur** to take as a model

modéliste [mɔdelist] *mf* model-airplane designer, etc.; dress designer

modéra·teur [mɔderatœr] **-trice** [tris] *adj* moderating ‖ *mf* moderator; regulator; moderator (*for slowing down neutrons*); **modérateur de son** volume control

modé·ré -rée [mɔdere] *adj* moderate

modérer [mɔdere] §10 *tr & ref* to moderate

moderne [mɔdɛrn] *adj* modern

moderniser [mɔdɛrnize] *tr* to modernize

modeste [mɔdɛst] *adj* modest

modestie [mɔdɛsti] *f* modesty

modicité [mɔdisite] *f* paucity (*of resources*); lowness (*of price*)

modifica·teur [mɔdifikatœr] **-trice** [tris] *adj* modifying ‖ *m* modifier

modifier [mɔdifje] *tr* to modify

modique [mɔdik] *adj* moderate, reasonable

modiste [mɔdist] *f* milliner

modulation [mɔdylɑsjɔ̃] *f* modulation; **modulation d'amplitude** amplitude modulation; **modulation de fréquence** frequency modulation

module [mɔdyl] *m* module; **module lunaire** (rok) lunar module

moduler [mɔdyle] *tr & intr* to modulate

moelle [mwal] *f* marrow; (bot) pith; **moelle épinière** spinal cord

moel·leux [mwalø] **-leuse** [løz] *adj* soft; mellow; flowing (*brush stroke*)

moellon [mwalɔ̃] *m* building stone

mœurs [mœr], [mœrs] *fpl* customs, habits; morals; **mœurs spéciales** (coll) homosexual life-style

mohair [mɔɛr] *m* mohair

moi [mwa] §85, §87 me

moignon [mwaɲɔ̃] *m* stump

moi-même [mwamɛm] §86 myself

moindre [mwɛ̃dr] (precedes the noun it modifies) §91 *adj comp* & *super* less; lesser; least, slightest

moine [mwan] *m* monk

moi·neau [mwano] *m* (*pl* **-neaux**) sparrow

moins [mwɛ̃] *m* less; minus; **au moins** or **du moins** at least; **(le) moins** (the) least; **moins de** fewer ‖ *adv comp* & *super* §91 less; fewer; **à moins de** + *inf* without + *ger*, unless + *ind;* **à moins que** unless; **de moins en moins** less and less; **en moins de rien** in no time at all; **moins de** (followed by numeral) less than; **moins que** less than; **rien moins que** anything but ‖ *prep* minus; to, e.g., **dix heures moins le quart** a quarter to ten

moire [mwar] *f* moire; **moire de soie watered silk**

moi·ré -rée [mware] *adj* watered (*silk*) ‖ *m* wavy sheen

mois [mwa] *m* month

Moïse [mɔiz] *m* Moses

moi·si -sie [mwazi] *adj* moldy ‖ *m* mold; **sentir le moisi** to have a musty smell

moisir [mwazir] *tr* to mold ‖ *intr* to become moldy, mold; (fig) to vegetate ‖ *ref* to mold

moisissure [mwazisyr] *f* mold

moisson [mwasɔ̃] *f* harvest

moissonner [mwasɔne] *tr* to harvest, reap

moisson·neur [mwasɔnœr] **-neuse** [nøz] *mf* reaper ‖ *f* (mach) reaper

moite [mwat] *adj* moist, damp; clammy

moiteur [mwatœr] *f* moistness, dampness; **moiteur froide** clamminess

moitié [mwatje] *f* half; (coll) better half (*wife*); **à moitié**, **la moitié** half; **à moitié chemin** halfway; **à moitié prix** at half price; **de moitié** by half ‖ *adv* half

moka [mɔka] *m* mocha coffee; mocha cake

mol *adj* see **mou**

molaire [mɔlɛr] *adj* & *f* molar

môle [mol] *m* mole, breakwater ‖ *f* (ichth) sunfish

molécule [mɔlekyl] *f* molecule

moleskine [mɔlɛskin] *f* (*fabric*) moleskin; imitation leather

molester [mɔlɛste] *tr* to molest

moleter [mɔlte] §34 *tr* to knurl, mill

mollas·son [mɔlasɔ̃] **-sonne** [sɔn] *mf* (coll) softy

molle *adj* see **mou**

mollement [mɔlmɑ̃] *adv* flabbily; listlessly

mollesse [mɔlɛs] *f* flabbiness; apathy; permissiveness; softness (*of contour*); mildness (*of climate*)

mol·let [mɔlɛ] **-lette** [lɛt] *adj* soft, downy; soft-boiled (*egg*) ‖ *m* (anat) calf

molletière [mɔltjɛr] *f* puttee, legging

molleton [mɔltɔ̃] *m* flannel

mollir [mɔlir] *intr* to weaken

mollusque [mɔlysk] *m* mollusk

molosse [mɔlɔs] *m* watchdog

molybdène [mɔlibdɛn] *m* molybdenum

môme [mom] *adj* (slang) little ‖ *mf* (coll) kid ‖ *f* (slang) babe

moment [mɔmɑ̃] *m* moment; **à aucun moment** at no time; **à ce moment-là**, **en ce moment-là** then, at that time; **à tout moment**, **à tous moments** continually; **au moment où** just when; **c'est le moment** now is the time; **d'un moment à l'autre** at any moment; **en ce moment** now; at this moment; **par moments** now and then; **sur le moment** at the very moment; **un petit moment** a little while

momenta·né -née [mɔmɑ̃tane] *adj* momentary

momerie [mɔmri] *f* mummery

momie [mɔmi] *f* mummy

mon [mɔ̃] §88 my

M[on] *abbr* (**Maison**) (com) House

mona·cal -cale [mɔnakal] *adj* (*pl* **-caux** [ko]) monastic, monkish

monachisme [mɔnaʃism], [mɔnakism] *m* monasticism

monarchique [mɔnarʃik] *adj* monarchic

monarque [mɔnark] *m* monarch

monastère [mɔnastɛr] *m* monastery

monastique [mɔnastik] *adj* monastic

mon·ceau [mɔ̃so] *m* (*pl* **-ceaux**) heap, pile

mon·dain [mɔ̃dɛ̃] **-daine** [dɛn] *adj* worldly; social (*life, functions, etc.*); sophisticated ‖ *mf* worldly-minded person; socialite

mondanité [mɔ̃danite] *f* worldliness; **mondanités** social events; (journ) social news

monde [mɔ̃d] *m* world; people; **avoir du monde chez soi** to have company; **il y a du monde, il y a un monde fou** there is a big crowd; **le beau monde, le grand monde** high society, fashionable society; **mettre au monde** to give birth to; **tout le monde** everybody, everyone

monder [mɔ̃de] *tr* to hull; blanch; stone

mon·dial -diale [mɔ̃djal] *adj* (*pl* **-diaux** [djo]) world; world-wide

monétaire [mɔnetɛr] *adj* monetary

mon·gol -gole [mɔ̃gɔl] *adj* Mongol ‖ *m* Mongol (*language*) ‖ (*cap*) *mf* Mongol (*person*)

moni·teur [mɔnitœr] **-trice** [tris] *mf* coach, trainer, instructor; monitor (*at school*)

monnaie [mɔnɛ] *f* change, small change; money (*legal tender of a country*); **fausse monnaie** counterfeit money; **la Monnaie** the Mint; **monnaie forte** hard currency; **payer en monnaie de singe** to give lip service to

monnayer [mɔneje] §49 *tr* to mint, coin; convert into cash; cash in on

monnayeur [mɔnɛjœr] *m*—**faux monnayeur** counterfeiter

monocle [mɔnɔkl] *m* monocle

monogamie [mɔnɔgami] *f* monogamy

monogramme [mɔnɔgram] *m* monogram

monographie [mɔnɔgrafi] *f* monograph

monokini [mɔnɔkini] *m* topless swimsuit

monolithique [mɔnɔlitik] *adj* monolithic

monolingue [mɔnɔlɛ̃g] *adj* monolingual

monologue [mɔnɔlɔg] *m* monologue

monologuer [mɔnɔlɔge] *tr* to soliloquize

monologuiste [mɔnɔlɔgist] *mf*—**monologuiste comique** stand-up comedian

monomanie [mɔnɔmani] *f* monomania

monôme [mɔnom] *m* single file (*of students*); (math) monomial

monoplan [mɔnɔplɑ̃] *m* monoplane

monopole [mɔnɔpɔl] *m* monopoly

monopoliser [mɔnɔpɔlize] *tr* to monopolize

monorail [mɔnɔrɑj] *m* monorail

monosyllabe [mɔnɔsilab] *m* monosyllable

monothéiste [mɔnɔteist] *adj & mf* monotheist

monotone [mɔnɔtɔn] *adj* monotonous

monotonie [mɔnɔtɔni] *f* monotony

monotype [mɔnɔtip] *adj* monotypic ‖ *m* monotype ‖ *f* Monotype (*machine to set type*)

monseigneur [mɔ̃sɛɲœr] *m* (*pl* **messeigneurs** [mesɛɲœr]) monseigneur

monsieur [məsjø] *m* (*pl* **messieurs** [mesjø]) gentleman; sir; mister; Mr.; (often untranslated) e.g., **oui, monsieur!** yes, of course!, yes, I will!, etc. (*instead of "yes, Sir!"*)

monstre [mɔ̃str] *adj* huge, monster ‖ *m* monster; freak; **monstres sacrés** (fig) sacred cows, idols

mons·trueux [mɔ̃stryø] **-trueuse** [tryøz] *adj* monstrous

mont [mɔ̃] *m* mount; mountain; **par monts et par vaux** over hill and dale; **passer les monts** to cross the Alps

montage [mɔ̃taʒ] *m* hoisting; setting up (*of a machine*); (elec) hookup; (mov) cutting, editing

monta·gnard [mɔ̃taɲar] **-gnarde** [ɲard] *adj* mountain ‖ *mf* mountaineer

montagne [mɔ̃taɲ] *f* mountain; **montagnes russes** roller coaster

monta·gneux [mɔ̃taɲø] **-gneuse** [ɲøz] *adj* mountainous

mon·tant [mɔ̃tɑ̃] **-tante** [tɑ̃t] *adj* rising, ascending; uphill; vertical; high-necked (*dress*) ‖ *m* upright, riser; gatepost; total (*sum*); allure; (culin) tang; **montants** goal posts; (slang) pair of trousers

mont-de-piété [mɔ̃dpjete] *m* (*pl* **monts-de-piété**) pawnshop

mon·té -tée [mɔ̃te] *adj* mounted; organized; equipped, well-provided; worked-up, angry ‖ *f* climb; slope

monte-charge [mɔ̃tʃarʒ] *m invar* freight elevator

monte-plats [mɔ̃tpla] *m invar* dumbwaiter

monter [mɔ̃te] §95, §96 *tr* to go up, climb; mount; set up; carry up, take up, bring up ‖ *intr* (*aux:* ÊTRE) to go up, come up; come upstairs; rise; come in (*said of tide*); **monter** + *inf* to go up to + *inf;* **monter à** or **en** to go up, climb, ascend, mount; **monter sur** to go up, climb (*the throne*); go on (*the stage*) ‖ *ref*—**se monter à** to amount to; **se monter en** to lay in a supply of; **se monter la tête** to get excited

montre [mɔ̃tr] *f* show, display; watch; **en montre** in the window, on display; **faire montre de** to show off, parade; **montre à** **affichage numérique** digital watch; **montre à remontoir** stem-winder; **montre à répétition** repeater

montre-bracelet [mɔ̃trəbraslɛ] *f* (*pl* **montres-bracelets**) wristwatch

montrer [mɔ̃tre] §96 *tr* to show; **montrer du doigt** to point out or at ‖ *ref* to appear; show oneself to be (*e.g., patient*)

mon·treur [mɔ̃trœr] **-treuse** [trøz] *mf* showman, exhibitor

mon·tueux [mɔ̃tɥø] **-tueuse** [tɥøz] *adj* rolling, hilly

monture [mɔ̃tyr] *f* mounting; assembling; mount (*e.g., horse*)

monument [mɔnymɑ̃] *m* monument; **monument aux morts** memorial monument

moquer [mɔke] §97 *tr & ref* to mock; **se moquer de** to make fun of, laugh at

moquerie [mɔkri] *f* mockery

moquette [mɔkɛt] *f* pile carpet; wall-to-wall carpeting

mo·ral -rale [mɔral] *adj* (*pl* **-raux** [ro]) *adj* moral ‖ *m* morale ‖ *f* ethics; moral (*of a fable*); **faire la morale à qn** to lecture s.o.

moralité [mɔralite] *f* morality; moral (*e.g., of a fable*)

morasse [mɔras] *f* final proof (*of newspaper*)

moratoire [mɔratwar] *m* moratorium

moratorium [mɔratɔrjɔm] *m* moratorium

morbide [mɔrbid] *adj* morbid

morbleu [mɔrblø] *interj* (obs) zounds!

mor·ceau [mɔrso] *m* (*pl* **-ceaux**) piece, bit; morsel; **bas morceaux** (culin) cheap cuts; **en morceaux** in cubes (*of sugar*); **morceaux choisis** selected passages

morceler [mɔrsəle] §34 *tr* to parcel out

morcellement [mɔrsɛlmɑ̃] *m* parceling out, division

mordancer [mɔrdɑ̃se] §51 *tr* to size

mor·dant [mɔrdɑ̃] **-dante** [dɑ̃t] *adj* mordant, caustic ‖ *m* mordant; cutting edge; fighting spirit; (mus) mordent

mordicus [mɔrdikys] *adv* (coll) stoutly, tenaciously

mordiller [mɔrdije] *tr & intr* to nibble; nip

mordo·ré -rée [mɔrdɔre] *adj* golden-brown, bronze-colored

mordre [mɔrdr] *tr* to bite ‖ *intr* to bite; **mordre à** to bite on; take to, find easy; **mordre dans** to bite into; **mordre sur** to encroach upon ‖ *ref* to bite; **s'en mordre la langue** to feel like biting off one's tongue because of it

mor·du -due [mɔrdy] *adj* bitten; smitten ‖ *mf* (coll) fan (*person*)

morelle [mɔrɛl] *f* nightshade

morfondre [mɔrfɔ̃dr] *tr* to chill to the bone ‖ *ref* to be bored waiting

morgue [mɔrg] *f* morgue; haughtiness

mori·caud [mɔriko] **-caude** [kod] *adj* (coll) dark-skinned, dusky

morigéner [mɔriʒene] §10 *tr* to scold

morillon [mɔrijɔ̃] *m* rough emerald; duck; **morillon à dos blanc** canvasback

mor·mon [mɔrmɔ̃] -**mone** [mɔn] *adj* & *mf* Mormon

morne [mɔrn] *adj* dismal, gloomy ‖ *m* hillock, knoll

mornifle [mɔrnifl] *f* (coll) slap

morose [mɔroz] *adj* morose

morphine [mɔrfin] *f* morphine

morphologie [mɔrfɔlɔʒi] *f* morphology

morpion [mɔrpjɔ̃] *m* tick-tack-toe; (*youngster*) (slang) squirt; (*Phthirus pubis*) (slang) crab louse

mors [mɔr] *m* bit; jaw (*of vise*)

morse [mɔrs] *m* Morse code; walrus

morsure [mɔrsyr] *f* bite

mort [mɔr] **morte** [mɔrt] *adj* dead; spent (*bullet*); (aut) neutral; motionless, e.g., **au point mort** at a standstill ‖ *mf* dead person, corpse ‖ *m* (bridge) dummy; **faire le mort** to play dead ‖ **mort** *f* death; **attraper la mort** to catch one's death of cold ‖ *v* see **mourir**

mortadelle [mɔrtadɛl] *f* bologna

mortaise [mɔrtɛz] *f* mortise

mortaiser [mɔrteze] *tr* to mortise

mortalité [mɔrtalite] *f* mortality

mort-aux-rats [mɔrtora], [mɔrora] *f invar* rat poison

mort-bois [mɔrbwa] *m* deadwood

morte-eau [mɔrto] *f* (*pl* **mortes-eaux** [mɔrtəzo]) low tide

mor·tel -telle [mɔrtɛl] *adj* & *mf* mortal

morte-saison [mɔrtəsɛzɔ̃] *f* (*pl* **mortes-saisons**) off-season

mortier [mɔrtje] *m* mortar; round judicial cap

mortifier [mɔrtifje] *tr* to mortify; tenderize (*meat*)

mort-né -née [mɔrne] (*pl* **-nés**) *adj* stillborn ‖ *mf* stillborn child

mortuaire [mɔrtɥɛr] *adj* mortuary; funeral (*e.g., service*); death (*notice*)

morue [mɔry] *f* cod

morve [mɔrv] *f* snot

mor·veux [mɔrvø] -**veuse** [vøz] *adj* snotty ‖ *mf* (coll) young snot, brat, whippersnapper

mosaïque [mɔzaik] *adj* mosaic; Mosaic ‖ *f* mosaic

Moscou [mɔsku] *m* Moscow

mosquée [mɔske] *f* mosque

mot [mo] *m* word; answer (*to riddle*); **à mots couverts** guardedly; **au bas mot** at least; **avoir toujours le mot pour rire** to be always cracking jokes; **bon mot** witticism; **gros mots** foul words; **le mot à mot** the word-for-word translation; **mot à double sens** double entendre; **mot d'entrée** headword, entry word (*of a dictionary*); **mot de passe** password; **mot d'ordre** slogan; **mot pour mot** word for word; **mots croisés** crossword puzzle; **ne . . . mot** §90 (archaic) not a word, nothing; **placer un mot** to put in a word; **prendre qn au mot** to take s.o. at his word; **sans mot dire** without a word

motard [mɔtar] *m* (coll) motorcyclist; (coll) motorcycle cop

mot-clé [mokle] *m* (*pl* **mots-clés**) key word

motel [mɔtɛl] *m* motel

mo·teur [mɔtœr] -**trice** [tris] *adj* driving (*wheel*); drive (*shaft*); motive (*power*); power (*brake*); motor (*nerve*) ‖ *m* motor, engine; prime mover; instigator; **moteur à deux temps** two-cycle engine; **moteur à explosion** internal-combustion engine; **moteur à quatre temps** four-cycle engine; **moteur à réaction** jet engine; **moteur hors bord** outboard motor

moteur-fusée *m* (*pl* **moteurs-fusées**) rocket engine

motif [mɔtif] *m* motive; (fa, mus) motif

motion [mosjɔ̃] *f* (parl) motion

motiver [mɔtive] *tr* to state the reason for, account for, explain, justify; motivate; warrant; **motiver une décision sur** to base a decision on

moto [mɔto] *f* motorcycle

motoneige [mɔtɔnɛʒ] *f* snowmobile

motoriser [mɔtɔrize] *tr* to motorize

mot-outil [mouti] *m* (*pl* **mots-outils**) link word

mot-piège [mɔpjɛʒ] *m* (*pl* **mots-pièges**) tricky word

mots-croisés [mokrwaze] *mpl* crossword puzzle

mot-souche [mosuʃ] *m* (*pl* **mots-souches**) headword, entry word; (typ) catchword

motte [mɔt] *f* clod, lump; slab (*of butter*); **motte de gazon** turf, divot

motus [mɔtys] *interj* mum's the word!

mou [mu] (or **mol** [mɔl] before vowel or mute h) **molle** [mɔl] (*pl* **mous molles**) *adj* soft; limp, flabby, slack; spineless, listless ‖ *m* slack; lights, lungs; (coll) softy; **bourrer le mou à qn** to hand s.o. a line

mou·chard [muʃar] -**charde** [ʃard] *mf* (coll) stool pigeon, squealer

moucharder [muʃarde] *tr* (coll) to spy on; (coll) to squeal on ‖ *intr* (coll) to squeal

mouche [muʃ] *f* fly; beauty spot; **faire d'une mouche un éléphant** to make a mountain out of a molehill; **faire la mouche** to fly into a rage; **faire mouche** to hit the bull's-eye; **fine mouche** sly, cagey person; **mouche à miel** honeybee; **mouche d'Espagne** (pharm) Spanish fly; **mouche du coche** busybody

moucher [muʃe] *tr* to blow (*one's nose*); to snuff, trim; (coll) to scold ‖ *ref* to blow one's nose

moucherolle [muʃrɔl] *f* (orn) flycatcher

moucheron [muʃrɔ̃] *m* gnat; snuff (*of candle*)

moucheter [muʃte] §34 *tr* to speckle

mouchoir [muʃwar] *m* handkerchief; **mouchoirs à jeter** disposable tissues; **mouchoirs en papier** paper handkerchiefs

moudre [mudr] §43 *tr* to grind

moue [mu] *f* wry face; **faire la moue** to pout

mouette [mwɛt] *f* gull, sea gull; **mouette rieuse** black-headed gull

mouffette [mufɛt] *f* skunk

moufle [mufl] *m* & *f* pulley block ‖ *f* mitten

mouillage [mujaʒ] *m* anchorage; wetting; watering, diluting

mouil·lé -lée [muje] *adj* wet; at anchor; palatalized; liquid (*l*)

mouiller [muje] *tr* to wet; water, dilute; palatalize; drop (*anchor*) ‖ *intr* to drop anchor ‖ *ref* to get wet; water; (coll) to become involved

moulage [mulaʒ] *m* molding, casting; mold, cast; grinding, milling

moule [mul] *m* mold, form; **moule à gaufre** waffle iron ‖ *f* mussel; (slang) fleabrain; (slang) jellyfish

mouler [mule] *tr* to mold; outline, e.g., **corsage qui moule le buste** blouse which outlines the bosom

moulin [mulɛ̃] *m* mill; **moulin à paroles** (coll) windbag; **moulin à vent** windmill

moulinet [mulinɛ] *m* winch; reel (*of casting rod*); turnstile; pinwheel (*child's toy*); **faire le moulinet avec** to twirl

moult [mult] *adv* (obs) much, many

mou·lu -lue [muly] *adj* ground; (coll) done in ‖ *v* see **moudre**

moulure [mulyr] *f* molding

mou·rant [murɑ̃] **-rante** [rɑ̃t] *adj* dying ‖ *mf* dying person

mourir [murir] §44, §97 *intr* (*aux:* ÊTRE) to die ‖ *ref* to be dying

mouron [murɔ̃] *m* (bot) starwort, stitchwort; (bot) pimpernel

mousquetaire [muskətɛr] *m* musketeer

mousse [mus] *adj* dull ‖ *m* cabin boy ‖ *f* moss; froth, foam; lather, suds; whipped cream; (culin) mousse

mousseline [muslin] *f* muslin; **mousseline de soie** chiffon

mousser [muse] *intr* to froth, foam; lather; **faire mousser** (coll) to crack up, build up; (slang) to enrage

mous·seux [musø] **-seuse** [søz] *adj* mossy; frothy, foamy; sudsy; sparkling (*wine*)

mousson [musɔ̃] *f* monsoon

moustache [mustaʃ] *f* mustache; **moustaches** whiskers (*of, e.g., cat*); **moustaches en croc** handle-bar mustache

moustiquaire [mustikɛr] *f* mosquito net

moustique [mustik] *m* mosquito

moût [mu] *m* must; wort

moutard [mutar] *m* (slang) kid

moutarde [mutard] *f* mustard

moutier [mutje] *m* (obs) monastery

mouton [mutɔ̃] *m* sheep; mutton; (slang) stool pigeon; **doux comme un mouton** gentle as a lamb; **moutons** whitecaps; **moutons de Panurge** (fig) chameleons, yes men; **revenons à nos moutons** let's get back to our subject

mouton·né -née [mutɔne] *adj* fleecy; frothy (*sea*); mackerel (*sky*)

moutonner [mutɔne] *tr* to curl ‖ *intr* to break into whitecaps

mouton·neux [mutɔnø] **-neuse** [nøz] *adj* frothy; fleecy (*e.g., cloud*)

mouture [mutyr] *f* grinding; mixture of wheat, rye, and barley; (fig) reworking

mouvement [muvmɑ̃] *m* movement; motion; **mouvement d'horlogerie** clockwork; **mouvement d'humeur** fit of bad temper; **mouvement ondulatoire** wave motion

mouvemen·té -tée [muvmɑ̃te] *adj* lively; eventful; hilly, broken (*terrain*)

mouvementer [muvmɑ̃te] *tr* to enliven

mouvoir [muvwar] §45 *tr* to move; set in motion, drive ‖ *ref* to move, stir

moyen [mwajɛ̃] **moyenne** [mwajɛn] *adj* average; ordinary; middle, intermediate; medium ‖ *m* way, manner; **au moyen de** by means of; **moyens** means ‖ *f* average; mean; passing mark; **en moyenne** on an average

moyen-âge [mwajɛnɑʒ] *m* Middle Ages

moyenâ·geux [mwajɛnɑʒø] **-geuse** [ʒøz] *adj* medieval; outdated

moyen-courrier [mwajɛ̃kurje] *m* (*pl* **moyens-courriers**) medium-range plane

moyennant [mwajɛnɑ̃] *prep* in exchange for ‖ *conj* provided that

Moyen-Orient [mwajɛnɔrjɑ̃] *m* Middle East

moyeu [mwajø] *m* (*pl* **moyeux**) hub

MST [ɛmɛste] *f* (letterword) (**maladie sexuellement transmissible**) STD (*sexually transmitted disease*)

mû mue [my] *adj* (*pl* **mus mues** [my]) *adj* driven, propelled ‖ *f* see **mue** ‖ *v* see **mouvoir**

mucosité [mykozite] *f* mucus

mucus [mykys] *m* mucus

mue [my] *f* molt, shedding

muer [mɥe] *intr* to molt; shed; (*said of voice*) to break, change

muet [mɥɛ] **muette** [mɥɛt] *adj* mute; silent; non-speaking (*rôle*); blank; dead (*key*) ‖ *mf* mute ‖ *m* silent movie

mufle [myfl] *m* muzzle, snout; (coll) cad, skunk

mugir [myʒir] *intr* to bellow

mugissement [myʒismɑ̃] *m* bellow

muguet [mygɛ] *m* lily of the valley

mulâ·tre [mylɑtr] **-tresse** [trɛs] *mf* mulatto

mule [myl] *f* mule

mulet [mylɛ] *m* mule; (ichth) mullet

mule·tier [myltje] **-tière** [tjɛr] *adj* mule (*e.g., trail*) ‖ *mf* muleteer

mulette [mylɛt] *f* fresh-water clam

mulot [mylo] *m* field mouse

multilaté·ral -rale [myltilateral] *adj* (*pl* **-raux** [ro]) multilateral

multiple [myltipl] *adj & m* multiple

multiplet [myltiplɛ] *m* (comp) byte

multiplicité [myltiplisite] *f* multiplicity

multiplier [myltiplije] *tr & ref* to multiply

multiprocesseur [myltiprɔsɛsœr] *m* (comp) multiprocessor

multitraitement [myltitrɛtmɑ̃] *m* (comp) multiprocessing

multitude [myltityd] *f* multitude

munici·pal -pale [mynisipal] *adj* (*pl* **-paux** [po]) municipal

municipalité [mynisipalite] *f* municipality; city officials; city hall

munifi·cent [mynifisɑ̃] **-cente** [sɑ̃t] *adj* munificent

munir [mynir] *tr* to provide, equip ‖ *ref—se munir de* to provide oneself with

munitions [mynisjɔ̃] *fpl* munitions

mu·queux [mykø] **-queuse** [køz] *adj* mucous ‖ *f* mucous membrane

mur [myr] *m* wall; **mettre au pied du mur** to corner; **mur de soutènement** retaining wall; **mur sonique, mur du son** sound barrier

mûr mûre [myr] *adj* ripe, mature ‖ *f* see **mûre**

muraille [myrɑj] *f* wall, rampart

mu·ral -rale [myral] *adj* (*pl* **-raux** [ro]) mural

mûre [myr] *f* mulberry; blackberry

murer [myre] *tr* to wall up or in ‖ *ref* to shut oneself up

mûrier [myrje] *m* mulberry tree

mûrir [myrir] *tr & intr* to ripen, mature

murmure [myrmyr] *m* murmur

murmurer [myrmyre] *tr & intr* to murmur

musaraigne [myzarɛɲ] *f* (zool) shrew

musarder [myzarde] *intr* to dawdle

musc [mysk] *m* musk

muscade [myskad] *f* nutmeg; **passez muscade!** presto!

muscardin [myskardɛ̃] *m* dormouse

muscat [myska] *m* muscatel

muscle [myskl] *m* muscle

mus·clé -clée [myskle] *adj* muscular; (coll) powerful (*e.g., drama*); (slang) difficult

musculaire [myskylɛr] *adj* muscular

muscu·leux [myskylø] **-leuse** [løz] *adj* muscular

muse [myz] *f* muse; **les Muses** the Muses

mu·seau [myzo] *m* (*pl* **-seaux**) snout; (coll) mug, face

musée [myze] *m* museum

museler [myzle] §34 *tr* to muzzle

muselière [myzəljɛr] *f* muzzle

muser [myze] *intr* to dawdle

musette [myzɛt] *f* feed bag; kit bag; haversack; (mus) musette

muséum [myzeɔm] *m* museum of natural history

musi·cal -cale [myzikal] *adj* (*pl* **-caux** [ko]) musical

music-hall [myzikol] *m* (*pl* **-halls**) vaudeville; vaudeville house; music hall (Brit)

musi·cien [myzisjɛ̃] **-cienne** [sjɛn] *mf* musician

musicologie [myzikɔlɔʒi] *f* musicology

musique [myzik] *f* music; band; **musique rustique** country music; **toujours la même musique** (coll) the same old song

mus·qué -quée [myske] *adj* musk-scented

musul·man [myzylmɑ̃] **-mane** [man] *adj & mf* Muslim

mutation [mytɑsjɔ̃] *f* mutation; transfer; (biol) mutation, sport

muter [myte] *tr* to transfer

muti·lé -lée [mytile] *mf* disabled veteran

mutiler [mytile] *tr* to mutilate; deface; disable; garble (*e.g., the truth*)

mu·tin [mytɛ̃] **-tine** [tin] *adj* roguish ‖ *mf* mutineer

muti·né -née [mytine] *adj* mutinous ‖ *mf* mutineer

mutiner [mytine] *ref* to mutiny

mutualité [mytɥalite] *f* mutual insurance

mu·tuel -tuelle [mytɥɛl] *adj* mutual ‖ *f* mutual benefit association

myope [mjɔp] *adj* near-sighted ‖ *mf* near-sighted person

myriade [mirjad] *f* myriad

myrrhe [mir] *f* myrrh

myrte [mirt] *m* myrtle

myrtille [mirtij] *f* blueberry

mystère [mistɛr] *m* mystery

mysté·rieux [misterjø] **-rieuse** [rjøz] *adj* mysterious

mysticisme [mistisism] *m* mysticism

mystification [mistifikɑsjɔ̃] *f* mystification; hoax

mystifier [mistifje] *tr* to mystify; hoax

mystique [mistik] *adj & mf* mystic

mythe [mit] *m* myth

mythique [mitik] *adj* mythical

mythologie [mitɔlɔʒi] *f* mythology

mythologique [mitɔlɔʒik] *adj* mythological

N

N, n [ɛn], *[ɛn] *m invar* fourteenth letter of the French alphabet

n' = **ne** before vowel or mute **h**

na·bot [nabo] **-bote** [bɔt] *adj* dwarfish ‖ *mf* dwarf, midget

nacelle [nasɛl] *f* (aer) nacelle; (naut) wherry, skiff; (fig) boat

nacre [nakr] *f* mother-of-pearl

na·cré -crée [nakre] *adj* pearly

nage [naʒ] *f* swimming; rowing, paddling; **être (tout) en nage** to be wet with sweat; **nage à la pagaie** paddling; **nage de côté**

sidestroke; **nage en couple** sculling; **nage en grenouille** breaststroke

nagée [naʒe] *f* swimming stroke

nageoire [naʒwar] *f* fin; flipper (*of seal*); float (*for swimmers*)

nager [naʒe] §38 *intr* to swim; float; row; **nager à culer** (naut) to back water; **nager debout** to tread water; to row standing up; **nager entre deux eaux** to swim under water; (fig) to carry water on both shoulders

na·geur [naʒœr] **-geuse** [ʒøz] *adj* swimming; floating ‖ *mf* swimmer; rower

naguère or **naguères** [nagɛr] *adv* lately, just now
naïf [naif] **naïve** [naiv] *adj* naïve ‖ *mf* simple-minded person
nain [nɛ̃] **naine** [nɛn] *adj* & *mf* dwarf
naissain [nɛsɛ̃] *m* seed oysters
naissance [nɛsɑ̃s] *f* birth; lineage; descent; beginning; (archit) springing line; **de basse naissance** lowborn; **de haute naissance** highborn; **de naissance** by birth; **donner naissance à** to give birth to; to give rise to; **naissance de la gorge** bosom, throat; **naissance des cheveux** hairline; **naissance du jour** daybreak; **prendre naissance** to arise, originate
nais·sant [nɛsɑ̃] **-sante** [sɑ̃t] *adj* nascent, rising, budding
naître [nɛtr] §46 *intr* (*aux:*ÊTRE) to be born; bud; arise, originate; dawn; **faire naître** to give birth to; give rise to
naïveté [naivte] *f* naïveté; artlessness
nana [nana] *f* (slang) chick (*girl*)
nanan [nanɑ̃], [nãnɑ̃] *m* (coll) goody; **du nanan** (coll) nice
nantir [nɑ̃tir] *tr* to give security or a pledge to; **nantir de** to provide with ‖ *intr* to stock up; feather one's nest ‖ *ref*—**se nantir de** to provide oneself with
nantissement [nɑ̃tismɑ̃] *m* security
napée [nape] *f* wood nymph
napel [napɛl] *m* monkshood, wolfsbane
naphte [naft] *m* naphtha
napoléo·nien [napɔleɔnjɛ̃] **-nienne** [njɛn] *adj* Napoleonic
nappage [napaʒ] *m* table linen
nappe [nap] *f* tablecloth; sheet (*of water, flame*); net (*for fishing; for bird catching*); **mettre la nappe** to set the table; **nappe d'autel** altar cloth; **ôter la nappe** to clear the table
napperon [naprɔ̃] *m* tablecloth cover; **petit napperon** doily
narcisse [narsis] *m* narcissus; **narcisse des bois** daffodil; **Narcisse** Narcissus
narcotique [narkɔtik] *adj* & *m* narcotic
narcotiser [narkɔtize] *tr* to dope
nargue [narg] *f* scorn, contempt; **faire nargue de** to defy; **nargue de ...!** fie on ...!
narguer [narge] *tr* to flout, snap one's fingers at
narguilé [nargile] *m* hookah
narine [narin] *f* nostril
nar·quois [narkwa] **-quoise** [kwaz] *adj* sly, cunning; sneering
narra·teur [naratœr] **-trice** [tris] *mf* narrator, storyteller
narra·tif [naratif] **-tive** [tiv] *adj* narrative
narration [narasjɔ̃] *f* narration; narrative
narrer [nare] *tr* to narrate, relate
na·sal -sale [nazal] *adj* (*pl* **-saux** [zo]) nasal ‖ *f* nasal (*vowel*)
nasaliser [nazalize] *tr* & *intr* to nasalize
nasarde [nazard] *f* fillip on one's nose (*in contempt*); snub, insult
na·seau [nazo] *m* (*pl* **-seaux**) nostril (*of horse, etc.*); **naseaux** (coll) snout

nasil·lard [nazijar] **-larde** [jard] *adj* nasal
nasiller [nazije] *intr* to talk through one's nose; squawk, quack
nasse [nas] *f* fish trap; (sports) basket
na·tal -tale [natal] *adj* (*pl* **-tals**) natal, of birth, native
nataliste [natalist] *mf* right-to-lifer
natalité [natalite] *f* birth rate; **natalité dirigée** birth control
natation [natasjɔ̃] *f* swimming
na·tif [natif] **-tive** [tiv] *adj* & *mf* native
nation [nasjɔ̃] *f* nation; **Nations Unies** United Nations
natio·nal -nale [nasjɔnal] *adj* & *mf* (*pl* **-naux** [no] **-nales**) national
nationaliser [nasjɔnalize] *tr* to nationalize
nationalité [nasjɔnalite] *f* nationality
nativité [nativite] *f* nativity; nativity scene; **Nativité** Nativity
natte [nat] *f* mat, matting; braid
natter [nate] *tr* to weave; braid
naturalisation [natyralizasjɔ̃] *f* naturalization
naturaliser [natyralize] *tr* to naturalize
naturalisme [natyralism] *m* naturalism
naturaliste [natyralist] *adj* & *mf* naturalist
nature [natyr] *adj invar* raw; black (*coffee*) ‖ *f* nature; **nature morte** (painting) still life
natu·rel -relle [natyrɛl] *adj* natural; native ‖ *m* naturalness; native, citizen
naturellement [natyrɛlmɑ̃] *adv* naturally; of course
naufrage [nofraʒ] *m* shipwreck
naufra·gé -gée [nofraʒe] *adj* shipwrecked ‖ *mf* shipwrecked person; **naufragés de l'espace** persons lost in space
nauséa·bond [nozeabɔ̃] **-bonde** [bɔ̃d] *adj* nauseating
nausée [noze] *f* nausea
nau·séeux [nozeø] **-séeuse** [zeøz] *adj* nauseous
nautique [notik] *adj* nautical
nautisme [notism] *m* yachting
nauto·nier [notɔnje] **-nière** [njɛr] *mf* pilot
na·val -vale [naval] *adj* (*pl* **-vals**) naval; nautical, maritime
navel [navɛl] *f* navel orange
navet [navɛ] *m* turnip
navette [navɛt] *f* shuttle; shuttle train; **faire la navette** to shuttle, to ply back and forth; **navette spatiale** space shuttle
navigable [navigabl] *adj* navigable (*river*); seaworthy (*ship*)
naviga·teur [navigatœr] **-trice** [tris] *adj* seafaring ‖ *m* navigator
navigation [navigasjɔ̃] *f* navigation; sailing; **navigation de plaisance** (sports) sailing
naviguer [navige] *intr* to navigate, sail; **naviguer sur** to navigate, sail (*the sea*)
navire [navir] *m* ship; **navire de débarquement** landing craft; **navire marchand** merchantman
navire-citerne [navirsitɛrn] *m* (*pl* **navires-citernes**) tanker
navire-école [navirekɔl] *m* (*pl* **navires-écoles**) training ship

navire-jumeau [navirʒymo] *m* (*pl* navires-jumeaux) sister ship

na·vrant [navrɑ̃] -**vrante** [vrɑ̃t] *adj* distressing, heartrending

na·vré -**vrée** [navre] *adj* sorry, grieved

navrer [navre] *tr* to distress, grieve

nazaréen [nazareɛ̃] **nazaréenne** [nazareɛn] *adj* Nazarene ‖ (*cap*) *mf* Nazarene

na·zi -**zie** [nazi] *adj* & *mf* Nazi

N.-D. *abbr* (**Notre-Dame**) Our Lady

ne [nə] §87, §90; **n'est-ce pas?** isn't that so? La traduction précédente est généralement remplacée par diverses locutions. Si l'énoncé est négatif, la question qui équivaut à **n'est-ce pas?** sera affirmative, par ex., **Vous ne travaillez pas. N'est-ce pas?** You are not working. Are you? Si l'énoncé est affirmatif, la question sera négative, par ex., **Vous travaillez. N'est-ce pas?** You are working. Are you not? ou Aren't you? Si l'énoncé contient un auxiliaire, la question contiendra cet auxiliaire moins l'infinitif ou moins le participe passé, par ex., **Il arrivera demain. N'est-ce pas?** He will arrive tomorrow. Won't he?; par ex., **Paul est déjà arrivé. N'est-ce pas?** Paul has already arrived. Hasn't he? Si l'énoncé ne contient ni auxiliaire ni forme de la copule "to be," la question contiendra l'auxiliaire "do" ou "did" moins l'infinitif, par ex., **Marie parle anglais. N'est-ce pas?** Mary speaks English. Doesn't she?

né née [ne] *adj* born; by birth; **bien né** highborn; **né pour** cut out for

néanmoins [neɑ̃mwɛ̃] *adv* nevertheless

néant [neɑ̃] *m* nothing, nothingness; worthlessness; obscurity; none (*as a response on the appropriate blank of an official form*)

nébu·leux [nebylø] -**leuse** [løz] *adj* nebulous; gloomy (*facial expression*); worried (*brow*) ‖ *f* nebula

nécessaire [neseser] *adj* necessary, needful; **nécessaire à** required for ‖ *m* necessities; kit, dressing case

nécessairement [nesesermɑ̃] *adv* necessarily

nécessité [nesesite] *f* necessity; need; **nécessité préalable** prerequisite

nécessiter [nesesite] §96 *tr* to necessitate

nécessi·teux [nesesitø] -**teuse** [tøz] *adj* needy ‖ *mf* needy person; **les nécessiteux** the needy

nécrologie [nekrɔlɔʒi] *f* necrology, obituary

nectar [nɛktar] *m* nectar

néerlan·dais [neerlɑ̃dɛ] -**daise** [dɛz] *adj* Dutch ‖ *m* Dutch (*language*) ‖ (*cap*) *mf* Netherlander

nef [nɛf] *f* nave; (archaic) ship; **nef latérale** aisle

néfaste [nefast] *adj* ill-starred, unlucky

nèfle [nɛfl] *f* medlar

néflier [neflije] *m* medlar tree

néga·teur [negatœr] -**trice** [tris] *adj* negative

néga·tif [negatif] -**tive** [tiv] *adj* negative ‖ *m* (phot) negative ‖ *f* negative (*side of a question*)

négation [negɑsjɔ̃] *f* negation; (gram) negative

négli·gé -**gée** [negliʒe] *adj* careless; unadorned, unstudied ‖ *m* carelessness; negligee, dressing gown

négligeable [negliʒabl] *adj* negligible

négligence [negliʒɑ̃s] *f* negligence; (med) malpractice; **avec négligence** slovenly

négli·gent [negliʒɑ̃] -**gente** [ʒɑ̃t] *adj* negligent ‖ *mf* careless person

négliger [negliʒe] §38, §97 *tr* to neglect ‖ *ref* to neglect oneself

négoce [negɔs] *m* trade, commerce; (com) company

négociable [negɔsjabl] *adj* negotiable

négo·ciant [negɔsjɑ̃] -**ciante** [sjɑ̃t] *mf* wholesaler, dealer

négocia·teur [negɔsjatœr] -**trice** [tris] *mf* negotiator

négociation [negɔsjɑsjɔ̃] *f* negotiation

négocier [negɔsje] *tr* to negotiate ‖ *intr* to negotiate; deal

nègre [nɛgr] *adj* black (*ethnic*); dark brown ‖ *m* black (*ethnic*); ghost writer; **petit nègre** pidgin, Creole

négrerie [negrəri] *f* slave quarters

négrier [negrije] *adj masc* slave ‖ *m* slave driver; slave ship

neige [nɛʒ] *f* snow

neiger [neʒe] §38 *intr* to snow

Némésis [nemezis] *f* Nemesis

nenni [nani], [neni], [nɛni] *adv* (archaic) no, not

nénuphar [nenyfar] *m* water lily

néologisme [neɔlɔʒism] *m* neologism

néon [neɔ̃] *m* neon

néophyte [neɔfit] *mf* neophyte, convert; beginner

neptunium [nɛptynjɔm] *m* neptunium

nerf [nɛr] *m* nerve; tendon, sinew; (archit, bb) rib; (fig) backbone, sinew; **avoir du nerf** to have nerves of steel; **avoir les nerfs à fleur de peau** to be on edge; **nerf de bœuf** scourge; **porter sur les nerfs à qn** to get on s.o.'s nerves

Néron [nerɔ̃] *m* Nero

ner·veux [nɛrvø] -**veuse** [vøz] *adj* nervous; nerve; jittery; sinewy; muscular; forceful (*style*)

nervosité [nɛrvozite] *f* nervousness; irritability; agitation

nervure [nɛrvyr] *f* rib; vein, nervure

net nette [nɛt] *adj* clean; clear, sharp, distinct; net; **net d'impôt** tax-exempt ‖ *m*—**mettre au net** to make a fair copy of ‖ *adv* flatly, point-blank; outright

netteté [nɛtəte] *f* neatness; clearness, sharpness

nettoiement [nɛtwamɑ̃] *m* cleaning

nettoyage [nɛtwajaʒ] *m* cleaning; **nettoyage à sec** dry cleaning

nettoyant [nɛtwajɑ̃] *m* cleaning product

nettoyer [nɛtwaje] §47 *tr* to clean; wash up or out; **nettoyer à sec** to dry-clean ‖ *ref* to wash up, clean oneself
net·toyeur [nɛtwajœr] **-toyeuse** [twajøz] *mf* cleaner
neuf [nœf] **neuve** [nœv] §94 *adj* new; **flambant neuf, tout neuf** brand-new ‖ **neuf** *adj & pron* nine; the Ninth, e.g., **Jean neuf** John the Ninth; **neuf heures** nine o'clock ‖ *m* nine; ninth (*in dates*)
neutraliser [nøtralize] *tr* to neutralize
neutralité [nøtralite] *f* neutrality
neutre [nøtr] *adj & m* neuter; neutral
neuvième [nœvjɛm] §94 *adj, pron* (*masc, fem*), *& m* ninth
névasse [nevɑs] *f* slush
ne·veu [nəvø] *m* (*pl* **-veux**) nephew; **nos neveux** our posterity
névralgie [nevralʒi] *f* neuralgia
névrose [nevroz] *f* neurosis
névro·sé -sée [nevroze] *adj & mf* neurotic
New York [nujɔrk], [nœjɔrk] *m* New York
newyor·kais [nœjɔrke] **-kaise** [kez] *adj* New York ‖ (*cap*) *mf* New Yorker
nez [ne] *m* nose; cape, headland; **à plein nez** entirely, really; **nez à nez** face to face; **parler du nez** to talk through one's nose
ni [ni] §90 *conj*—**ne . . . ni . . . ni** neither . . . nor, e.g., **elle n'a ni papier ni stylo** she has neither paper nor pen; **ni . . . ni** neither . . . nor; **ni . . . non plus** nor . . . either
niable [njabl] *adj* deniable
niais [njɛ] **niaise** [njɛz] *adj* foolish, silly, simple-minded ‖ *mf* fool, simpleton
niaiserie [njɛzəri] *f* foolishness, silliness, simpleness
niche [niʃ] *f* niche; alcove; prank; **niche à chien** doghouse
nichée [niʃe] *f* brood
nicher [niʃe] *tr* to niche, lodge ‖ *intr* to nestle; nest; hide ‖ *ref* to nest
nickel [nikɛl] *adj* (slang) spic and span ‖ *m* nickel
nickeler [nikle] §34 *tr* to nickel-plate
nickelure [niklyr] *f* nickel plate
nicotine [nikɔtin] *f* nicotine
nid [ni] *m* nest; **en nid d'abeilles** honey-combed; **nid de pie** crow's-nest
nid-à-feu [nidafø] *m* (*pl* **nids-à-feu**) fire trap
nid-de-poule [nidəpul] *m* (*pl* **nids-de-poule**) pothole
nièce [njɛs] *f* niece
nième [njɛm] *adj* nth
nier [nje] §97 *tr* to deny ‖ *intr* to plead not guilty
ni·gaud [nigo] **-gaude** [god] *adj* silly ‖ *mf* nincompoop
nigauderie [nigodri] *f* silliness
nihilisme [niilism] *m* nihilism
Nil [nil] *m* Nile
nimbe [nɛ̃b] *m* halo, nimbus
nimber [nɛ̃be] *tr* to halo
nimbus [nɛ̃bys] *m* (meteo) nimbus
nipper [nipe] *tr* (coll) to tog ‖ *ref* (coll) to tog oneself out

nippes [nip] *fpl* (coll) worn-out clothes; (slang) duds
nique [nik] *f*—**faire la nique à** to turn up one's nose at
nitouche [nituʃ] *f*—**de sainte nitouche** hypocritically pious
nitrate [nitrat] *m* nitrate
nitre [nitr] *m* niter, nitrate
ni·treux [nitrø] **-treuse** [trøz] *adj* nitrous
nitrière [nitrijɛr] *f* saltpeter bed
nitrique [nitrik] *adj* nitric
nitrogène [nitrɔʒɛn] *m* nitrogen
nitroglycérine [nitrɔgliserin] *f* nitroglycerin
ni·veau [nivo] *m* (*pl* **-veaux**) level; **au niveau de** on a par with; **niveau à bulle d'air** spirit level; **niveau à lunettes** surveyor's level; **niveau d'essence** gasoline gauge; **niveau de vie** standard of living; **niveau d'huile** oil gauge; **niveau mental** I.Q.
niveler [nivle] §34 *tr* to level; survey
nive·leur [nivlœr] **-leuse** [løz] *mf* leveler ‖ *m* harrow ‖ *f* (agr) leveler
nivellement [nivɛlmɑ̃] *m* leveling; surveying
N°, n° *abbr* (**numéro**) no.
noble [nɔbl] *adj & mf* noble
noblesse [nɔblɛs] *f* nobility; nobleness
noce [nɔs] *f* wedding; wedding party; **faire la noce** to go on a spree; **ne pas être à la noce** to be in trouble; **noces** wedding
no·ceur [nɔsœr] **-ceuse** [søz] *adj* (coll) bacchanalian, reveling ‖ *mf* (coll) reveler, debauchee
no·cif [nɔsif] **-cive** [siv] *adj* noxious
noctambule [nɔktɑ̃byl] *mf* nighthawk; sleepwalker
nocturne [nɔktyrn] *adj* nocturnal; night; nightly ‖ *m* (mus) nocturne ‖ *f* open night (*of store*)
nodosité [nɔdozite] *f* nodule (*of root*); node, wart
Noé [nɔe] *m* Noah
noël [nɔel] *m* Christmas carol; (coll) Christmas present; **Noël** Christmas
nœud [nø] *m* knot; rosette; finger joint; Adam's apple; tie, alliance; crux (*of question, plot, crisis*); node; (naut) knot; **nœud de vache** granny knot; **nœud plat** square knot; **nœuds** coils (*of snake*); **nœud vital** nerve center
noir noire [nwar] *adj* black; **noir comme poix** pitch-black ‖ *mf* black (*ethnic*) ‖ *m* black; bruise; **broyer du noir** to be blue, down in the dumps; **noir de fumée** lamp-black ‖ *f* (mus) quarter note
noirâtre [nwarɑtr] *adj* blackish
noi·raud [nwaro] **-raude** [rod] *adj* swarthy
noirceur [nwarsœr] *f* blackness; black spot
noircir [nwarsir] *tr* to blacken ‖ *intr & ref* to burn black; turn dark
noircissure [nwarsisyr] *f* black spot, smudge
noise [nwaz] *f* squabble; **chercher noise à** to pick a quarrel with
noisetier [nwaztje] *m* hazelnut tree
noisette [nwazɛt] *adj invar* reddish-brown ‖ *f* hazelnut

noix [nwɑ], [nwa] *f* walnut; nut; **à la noix** (slang) trifling; **noix d'acajou, noix de cajou** cashew nut; **noix du Brésil** Brazil nut; **noix de coco** coconut; **noix de galle** nutgall; **noix de muscade** nutmeg; **noix de veau** round of veal

nolis [nɔli] *m* freight

noliser [nɔlize] *tr* to charter (*a ship*)

nom [nɔ̃] *m* name; noun; **de nom** by name; **nom à rallonges, nom à tiroirs** (coll) word made up of several parts; **nom commercial** trade name; **nom de baptême** baptismal name, Christian name; **nom de demoiselle** maiden name; **nom de Dieu!** God damn!, for Chrissakes!; **nom de famille** surname; **nom de guerre** fictitious name, assumed name; **nom de jeune fille** maiden name; **nom d'emprunt** assumed name; **nom de nom!** God damn!; **nom de théâtre** stage name; **nom marchand** trade name; **petit nom d'amitié** pet name; **sans nom** nameless; **sous le nom de** by the name of

nomade [nɔmad] *adj & mf* nomad

nombre [nɔ̃br] *m* number, quantity

nombrer [nɔ̃bre] *tr* to number

nom·breux [nɔ̃brø] **-breuse** [brøz] *adj* numerous; rhythmic, harmonious (*e.g., prose*)

nombril [nɔ̃bri] *m* navel

nomenclature [nɔmɑ̃klatyr] *f* nomenclature; vocabulary; body (*of dictionary*)

nomi·nal -nale [nɔminal] *adj* (*pl* **-naux** [no]) nominal; **appel nominal** roll call

nomina·tif [nɔminatif] **-tive** [tiv] *adj* nominative; registered (*stocks, bonds, etc.*) ‖ *m* nominative

nomination [nɔminasjɔ̃] *f* appointment

nom·mé -mée [nɔme] *adj* named; appointed; called ‖ *m*—**le nommé . . .** the man called . . .

nommément [nɔmenɑ̃] *adv* namely, particularly

nommer [nɔme] *tr* to name, call; appoint ‖ *ref* to be named, e.g., **je me nomme . . .** my name is . . .

non [nɔ̃] *m invar* no ‖ *adv* no, not; **non pas** not so; **non plus** neither, not, nor . . . either, e.g., **moi non plus** nor I either; **non point!** by no means!; **que non!** no indeed!

non-belligé·rant [nɔ̃beliʒerɑ̃] **-rante** [rɑ̃t] *adj & mf* nonbelligerent

nonce [nɔ̃s] *m* nuncio

nonchalamment [nɔ̃ʃalamɑ̃] *adv* nonchalantly

noncha·lant [nɔ̃ʃalɑ̃] **-lante** [lɑ̃t] *adj* nonchalant

non-combat·tant [nɔ̃kɔ̃batɑ̃] **-tante** [tɑ̃t] *adj & mf* noncombatant

non-conformiste [nɔ̃kɔ̃fɔrmist] *adj & mf* nonconformist

non-enga·gé -gée [nɔ̃nɑ̃gaʒe] *adj* unaligned, uncommitted

non-ingérence [nɔ̃ɛ̃ʒerɑ̃s] *f* noninterference

nonnain [nɔnɛ̃] *f* (pej) nun

nonne [nɔn] *f* nun

nonobstant [nɔnɔpstɑ̃] *adv* notwithstanding; **nonobstant que** although ‖ *prep* in spite of

non-pesanteur [nɔ̃pəzɑ̃tœr] *f* weightlessness

non-rési·dent [nɔ̃rezidɑ̃] **-dente** [dɑ̃t] *adj & mf* nonresident

non-réussite [nɔ̃reysit] *f* failure

non-sens [nɔ̃sɑ̃s] *m* absurdity, nonsense

non-usage [nɔnyzaʒ] *m* disuse

non-violence [nɔ̃vjɔlɑ̃s] *f* nonviolence

nord [nɔr] *adj invar* north, northern ‖ *m* north; **du nord** northern; **faire le nord** to steer northward; **perdre le nord** to become disoriented, not to know one's way; **vers le nord** northward

nord-est [nɔrɛst] *adj invar & m* northeast

nord-ouest [nɔrwɛst] *adj invar & m* northwest

nor·mal -male [nɔrmal] *adj* (*pl* **-maux** [mo]) normal; regular, standard; perpendicular ‖ *f* normal; perpendicular; normalcy

norma·lien [nɔrmaljɛ̃] **-lienne** [ljɛn] *mf* student at a teachers college

nor·mand [nɔrmɑ̃] **-mande** [mɑ̃d] *adj* Norman ‖ *m* Norman (*dialect*) ‖ (*cap*) *mf* Norman (*person*)

Normandie [nɔrmɑ̃di] *f* Normandy; **la Normandie** Normandy

norme [nɔrm] *f* norm; specifications

nor·rois [nɔrwa] **nor·roise** [nɔrwaz] *adj* Norse ‖ *m* Norse (*language*) ‖ (*cap*) *m* Norseman

Norvège [nɔrvɛʒ] *f* Norway; **la Norvège** Norway

norvé·gien [nɔrveʒjɛ̃] **-gienne** [ʒjɛn] *adj* Norwegian ‖ *m* Norwegian (*language*) ‖ *f* round-stemmed rowboat ‖ (*cap*) *mf* Norwegian (*person*)

nos [no] §88 our

nostalgie [nɔstalʒi] *f* nostalgia, homesickness

nostalgique [nɔstalʒik] *adj* nostalgic, homesick

nota bene [nɔtabene] *m invar* memo (*preceded by "N.B."*)

notable [nɔtabl] *adj* notable, noteworthy ‖ *m* notable

notaire [nɔtɛr] *m* notary; lawyer

notamment [nɔtamɑ̃] *adv* especially

notation [nɔtasjɔ̃] *f* notation

note [nɔt] *f* note; bill (*to be paid*); grade, mark (*in school*); footnote; **être dans la note** to be in the swing of things; **note de rappel** reminder; **prendre note de** to note down

noter [nɔte] *tr* to note; note down; notice; mark (*a student*); write down (*a tune*)

notice [nɔtis] *f* notice; instructions, directions; instruction manual; preface; **notice d'un livre** review of a book

notification [nɔtifikasjɔ̃] *f* notification, notice

notifier [nɔtifje] §97 *tr* to report on; serve (*a summons*)

notion [nosjɔ̃] *f* notion

notoire [nɔtwar] *adj* well-known
notoriété [nɔtɔrjete] *f* fame
notre [nɔtr] §88 our
nôtre [notr] §89 ours; **serez-vous des nôtres?** will you join us?
noue [nu] *f* pasture land; roof gutter
noué nouée [nwe] *adj* afflicted with rickets
nouer [nwe] *tr* to knot; tie; form; cook up (*a plot*) ‖ *ref* to form knots; be tied; (hort) to set
noueux [nwø] **noueuse** [nwøz] *adj* knotty, gnarled
nouille [nuj] *f* noodle
nounou [nunu] *f* nanny
nour·ri -rie [nuri] *adj* heavy, sustained; rich (*style*)
nourrice [nuris] *f* wet nurse; can; (aut) reserve tank
nourricerie [nurisri] *f* baby farm; stock farm; silkworm farm
nourri·cier [nurisje] **-cière** [sjɛr] *adj* nutritive; nourishing; foster
nourrir [nurir] *tr* to nourish; suckle; to feed (*a fire*); nurse (*plants; hopes*) ‖ *intr* to be nourishing ‖ *ref* to feed; thrive
nourrisseur [nurisœr] *m* stock raiser, dairyman
nourrisson [nurisɔ̃] *m* nursling, suckling; foster child
nourriture [nurityr] *f* nourishment, food; nourishing; nursing, breastfeeding; **nourriture du feu** firewood
nous [nu] §85, §87 we; us; to us; **nous autres Américains** we Americans
nous-mêmes [numɛm] §86 ourselves
nou·veau [nuvo] (or **-vel** [vɛl] before vowel or mute **h**) **-velle** [vɛl] (*pl* **-veaux -velles**) *adj* new (*recent*) ‖ (when standing before noun) *adj* new (*other, additional, different*) ‖ *m* freshman; **à nouveau** anew; **de nouveau** again; **du nouveau** something new; **le nouveau** the new ‖ *f* see **nouvelle**
nouveau-né -née [nuvone] *adj & mf* (*pl* **nés**) newborn
nouveauté [nuvote] *f* newness, novelty
nouvelle [nuvɛl] *f* piece of news; novelette, short story; **donnez-moi de vos nouvelles** let me hear from you; **nouvelles news** ‖ *adj* see **nouveau**
Nouvelle-Angleterre [nuvɛlɑ̃glətɛr] *f* New England; **la Nouvelle-Angleterre** New England
Nouvelle-Écosse [nuvɛlekos] *f* Nova Scotia; **la Nouvelle-Écosse** Nova Scotia
Nouvelle-Orléans [nuvɛlɔrleɑ̃] *f*—**la Nouvelle-Orléans** New Orleans
Nouvelle-Zélande [nuvɛlzelɑ̃d] *f* New Zealand; **la Nouvelle-Zélande** New Zealand
nouvelliste [nuvelist] *mf* short-story writer
nova·teur [nɔvatœr] **-trice** [tris] *adj* innovating ‖ *mf* innovator
novembre [nɔvɑ̃br] *m* November
novice [nɔvis] *adj* inexperienced, new ‖ *mf* novice, neophyte
noviciat [nɔvisja] *m* novitiate
novocaïne [nɔvɔkain] *f* novocaine
noyade [nwajad] *f* drowning

noyau [nwajo] *m* (*pl* **noyaux**) nucleus; stone, kernel; pit (*of fruit*); core (*of electromagnet*); newel; hub; (fig) cell (*of conspirators*); (fig) bunch (*of card players*), **noyau d'atome** atomic nucleus
noyautage [nwajotaʒ] *m* infiltration (*e.g., of communists*)
noyer [nwaje] *m* walnut tree; **en noyer** in walnut (*wood*) ‖ §47 *tr & ref* to drown
nu nue [ny] *adj* naked, nude; bare; barren; uncarpeted; unharnessed, unsaddled (*horse*); (aut) stripped ‖ *m* nude; **à nu** exposed; bareback ‖ *f* see **nue**
nuage [nɥaʒ] *m* cloud
nua·geux [nɥaʒø] **-geuse** [ʒøz] *adj* cloudy
nuance [nɥɑ̃s] *f* hue, shade, tone, nuance
nucléaire [nykleɛr] *adj* nuclear
nucléole [nykleɔl] *m* nucleolus
nucléon [nykleɔ̃] *m* nucleon
nudiste [nydist] *adj & mf* nudist
nudité [nydite] *f* nakedness; nudity; plainness (*of style*); nude
nue [ny] *f* clouds; sky; **mettre** or **porter aux nues** to praise to the skies
nuée [nɥe] *f* cloud, storm cloud; flock
nuire [nɥir] §19 (*pp* **nui** *invar*) *intr*—**nuire à** to harm, injure, e.g., **cette accusation lui a beaucoup nui** that accusation hurt him very much
nuisible [nɥizibl] *adj* harmful
nuit [nɥi] *f* night; **à la nuit close** after dark; **bonne nuit** good night; **cette nuit** last night; **nuit blanche** sleepless night
nuitamment [nɥitamɑ̃] *adv* at night
nu-jambes [nyʒɑ̃b] *adj invar* bare-legged
nul nulle [nyl] *adj indef* no; **ne . . . nul** or **nul . . . ne** §90 no; **nul et non avenu, nulle et non avenue** [nylenɔ̃navny] null and void ‖ *f* dummy word or letter ‖ **nul** *pron indef*—**nul ne** §90B no one, nobody
nullement [nylmɑ̃] §90 *adv* not at all
nullité [nylite] *f* nonentity, nobody; invalidity
nûment [nymɑ̃] *adv* candidly, frankly
numéraire [nymerɛr] *m* specie; **payer en numéraire** to pay in cash
numé·ral -rale [nymeral] *adj & m* (*pl* **-raux** [ro]) numeral
numération [nymerɑsjɔ̃] *f* numeration; **numération globulaire** blood count
numérique [nymerik] *adj* numerical; digital
numéro [nymero] *m* numeral; number; issue, number (*of a periodical*), e.g., **dernier numéro** current issue; e.g., **numéro ancien** back number; (slang) queer duck; **faire un numéro** to dial; **numéro de vestiaire** check (*of checkroom*); **numéro d'ordre** serial number
numéroter [nymerɔte] *tr* to number
numismatique [nymismatik] *adj* numismatic ‖ *f* numismatics
nu-pieds [nypje] *adj invar* barefooted
nup·tial -tiale [nypsjal] *adj* (*pl* **-tiaux** [sjo]) nuptial
nuque [nyk] *f* nape, scruff
nurse [nœrs] *f* children's nurse
nu-tête [nytɛt] *adj invar* bareheaded

nutri·tif [nytritif] **-tive** [tiv] *adj* nutritive; nutritious
nutrition [nytrisjɔ̃] *f* nutrition

nylon [nilɔ̃] *m* nylon
nymphe [nɛ̃f] *f* nymph; (Ent) nympha, chrysalis, pupa

O

O, o [o], *[o] *m invar* fifteenth letter of the French alphabet
oasis [ɔazis] *f* oasis
obéir [ɔbeir] *intr* to obey; yield to; be subject to; **obéir à** to obey, e.g., **je leur obéis** I obey them, **j'obéis à la loi** I obey the law; **obéir au doigt et à l'œil** to obey blindly; **vous êtes obéi** you are obeyed
obéissance [ɔbeisɑ̃s] *f* obedience
obéis·sant [ɔbeisɑ̃] **-sante** [sɑ̃t] *adj* obedient
obélisque [ɔbelisk] *m* obelisk
obérer [ɔbere] §10 *tr* to burden with debt ‖ *ref* to run into debt
obèse [ɔbez] *adj* obese
obésité [ɔbezite] *f* obesity
objecter [ɔbʒɛkte] *tr* to object, e.g., **objecter que . . .** to object that . . . ; to bring up, e.g., **objecter q.ch. à qn** to bring up s.th. against s.o.; put forward (*in opposition*), e.g., **objecter de bonnes raisons à** or **contre un argument** to put forward good reasons against an argument
objecteur [ɔbʒɛktœr] *m*—**objecteur de conscience** conscientious objector
objec·tif [ɔbʒɛktif] **-tive** [tiv] *adj* objective ‖ *m* objective; object lens; (mil) target
objection [ɔbʒɛksjɔ̃] *f* objection; **faire des objections** to object
objectivité [ɔbʒɛktivite] *f* objectivity
objet [ɔbʒɛ] *m* object; **menus objets** notions; **objet d'art** work of art; **objet de risée** laughingstock; **objets de première nécessité** articles of everyday use; **objet volant non-identifié** unidentified flying object; **remplir son objet** to attain one's end
obligation [ɔbligasjɔ̃] *f* obligation; (com) bond, debenture; **être dans l'obligation de** to be obliged to
obligatoire [ɔbligatwar] *adj* required, obligatory; (coll) inevitable
obli·gé -gée [ɔbliʒe] §93 *adj* obliged, compelled; necessary, indispensable; **bien obligé** much obliged; **c'est obligé** (coll) it has to be; **être obligé de** to be obliged to
obli·geant [ɔbliʒɑ̃] **-geante** [ʒɑ̃t] *adj* obliging
obliger [ɔbliʒe] §38, §96, §97, §100 *tr* to oblige ‖ §96 *ref*—**s'obliger à** + *inf* to undertake to + *inf*; **s'obliger pour qn** to stand surety for s.o.
oblique [ɔblik] *adj* oblique
oblitération [ɔbliterasjɔ̃] *f* obliteration; cancellation (*of postage stamp*); (pathol) occlusion

oblitérer [ɔblitere] §10 to obliterate; cancel (*a postage stamp*); obstruct (*e.g., a vein*)
o·blong [ɔblɔ̃] **-blongue** [blɔ̃g] *adj* oblong
obnubiler [ɔbnybile] *tr* to cloud, befog
obole [ɔbɔl] *f* widow's mite
obscène [ɔpsɛn] *adj* obscene
obscénité [ɔpsenite] *f* obscenity
obs·cur -cure [ɔpskyr] *adj* obscure
obscurcir [ɔpskyrsir] *tr* to obscure; dim ‖ *ref* to grow dark; grow dim
obscurité [ɔpskyrite] *f* obscurity
obséder [ɔpsede] §10 *tr* to obsess; importune, harass
obsèques [ɔpsɛk] *fpl* obsequies, funeral rites
obsé·quieux [ɔpsekjø] **-quieuse** [kjøz] *adj* obsequious
observance [ɔpsɛrvɑ̃s] *f* observance
observa·teur [ɔpsɛrvatœr] **-trice** [tris] *adj* observant ‖ *mf* observer
observation [ɔpsɛrvasjɔ̃] *f* observation
observatoire [ɔpsɛrvatwar] *m* observatory
observer [ɔpsɛrve] *tr* to observe ‖ *ref* to watch oneself; watch each other
obsession [ɔpsesjɔ̃] *f* obsession
obsolète [ɔpsɔlɛt] *adj* obsolete
obstacle [ɔpstakl] *m* obstacle
obstétrique [ɔpstetrik] *adj* obstetrical ‖ *f* obstetrics
obstination [ɔpstinasjɔ̃] *f* obstinacy
obsti·né -née [ɔpstine] *adj* obstinate
obstruction [ɔpstryksjɔ̃] *f* obstruction; (sports) blocking; **faire de l'obstruction** (pol) to filibuster; **obstruction systématique** filibustering
obstruer [ɔpstrye] *tr* to obstruct
obtempérer [ɔptɑ̃pere] §10 *intr*—**obtempérer à**) to comply with, obey
obtenir [ɔptənir] §72, §97 *tr* to obtain, get
obtention [ɔptɑ̃sjɔ̃] *f* obtaining
obtura·teur [ɔptyratœr] **-trice** [tris] *adj* stopping, closing ‖ *m* (mach) stopcock; (phot) shutter
obturation [ɔptyrasjɔ̃] *f* stopping up; filling (*of tooth*); **obturation des lumières** blackout
obturer [ɔptyre] *tr* to stop up; fill (*a tooth*)
ob·tus [ɔpty] **-tuse** [tyz] *adj* obtuse
obus [ɔby] *m* (mil) shell; plunger (*of tire valve*); **obus à balles** shrapnel; **obus à mitraille** shrapnel; **obus de rupture** armor-piercing shell
obvier [ɔbvje] *intr*—**obvier à** to obviate, prevent
oc [ɔk] *adv* (Old Provençal) yes
occasion [ɔkazjɔ̃], [ɔkɑzjɔ̃] *f* occasion; opportunity; bargain; **à l'occasion** on

occasion; **à l'occasion de** for (*e.g.*, *s.o.'s birthday*); **d'occasion** secondhand (*clothing*); used (*car*); **venez me voir à votre première occasion** come to see me at your first opportunity

occasion·nel -nelle [ɔkazjɔnɛl] *adj* occasional; chance (*meeting*); determining (*cause*)

occasionnellement [ɔkazjɔnɛlmã] *adv* occasionally; by chance, accidentally

occasionner [ɔkazjɔne] *tr* to occasion

occident [ɔksidã] *m* occident, west

occiden·tal -tale [ɔdsidãtal] *adj & mf* (*pl* **-taux** [to]) occidental

occlu·sif [ɔklyzif] **-sive** [ziv] *adj & f* occlusive

occlusion [ɔklyzjɔ̃] *f* occlusion

occulte [ɔkylt] *adj* occult

occu·pant [ɔkypã] **-pante** [pãt] *adj* occupying ‖ *mf* occupant

occupation [ɔkypasjɔ̃] *f* occupation; **occupation sauvage** sit-in

occu·pé -pée [ɔkype] *adj* occupied; **occupé** (public sign) in use

occuper [ɔkype] *tr* to occupy ‖ §96, §97 *ref* to find something to do; **s'occuper de** to be occupied with, be busy with; take care of, handle

occurrence [ɔkyrãs] *f* occurrence; **en l'occurrence** under the circumstances; **être en occurrence** to occur; **selon l'occurrence** as the case may be

océan [ɔseã] *m* ocean; **océan glacial arctique** Arctic Ocean; **océan Indien** Indian Ocean

océanique [ɔseanik] *adj* oceanic

ocre [ɔkr] *f* ochre

octane [ɔktan] *m* octane

octave [ɔktav] *f* octave

octa·von [ɔktavɔ̃] **-vonne** [vɔn] *mf* octoroon

octet [ɔktɛ] *m* (comp) byte (of eight bits)

octobre [ɔktɔbr] *m* October

octroi [ɔktrwa] *m* granting (*of a favor*); tax on provisions being brought into town

octroyer [ɔktrwaje] §47 *tr* to grant, concede; bestow

oculaire [ɔkylɛr] *adj* ocular, eye ‖ *m* ocular, eyepiece

oculariste [ɔkylarist] *mf* optician (*who specializes in glass eyes*)

oculiste [ɔkylist] *mf* oculist

ode [ɔd] *f* ode

odeur [ɔdœr] *f* odor, scent

o·dieux [ɔdjø] **-dieuse** [djøz] *adj* odious ‖ *m* odium, odiousness

odo·rant [ɔdɔrã] **-rante** [rãt] *adj* fragrant

odorat [ɔdɔra] *m* (sense of) smell

Odyssée [ɔdise] *f* Odyssey

œcuménique [ekymenik] *adj* ecumenical

œdème [edɛm] *m* (pathol) edema

Œdipe [edip] *m* Oedipus

œil [œj] *m* (*pl* **yeux** [jø] **les yeux** [lezjø]) eye; typeface, font; bud; **avoir l'œil (américain)** (coll) to be observant; **coûter les yeux de la tête** (coll) to cost a fortune; **donner de l'œil à** to give a better appearance to; **entre quatre yeux** [ãtrəkatzjø]

(coll) between you and me; **faire les gros yeux à** (coll) to glare at; **faire les yeux doux à** to make eyes at; **ne pas avoir les yeux dans la poche** (coll) to keep one's eyes peeled; (coll) to be no shrinking violet; **œil au beurre noir** (coll) black eye; **œil de pie** (naut) eyelet; **œil de verre** glass eye; **œil électrique** electric eye; **pocher un œil à qn** to give s.o. a black eye; **sale œil** disapproving or dirty look; **sauter aux yeux, crever les yeux** to be obvious; **se mettre le doigt dans l'œil** (coll) to put one's foot in one's mouth; **se rincer l'œil** (slang) to get an eyeful; **taper dans l'œil à** or **de qn** (coll) to take s.o.'s fancy; **voir d'un mauvais œil** to take a dim view of

œil-de-bœuf [œjdəbœf] *m* (*pl* **œils-de-bœuf**) bull's-eye, small oval window

œil-de-chat [œjdəʃa] *m* (*pl* **œils-de-chat**) cat's-eye (*gem*)

œil-de-perdrix [œjdəpɛrdri] *m* (*pl* **œils-de-perdrix**) (pathol) soft corn

œillade [œjad] *f* glance, leer, wink; **lancer, jeter,** or **décocher une œillade à** to ogle

œillère [œjɛr] *f* eyecup; blinker; **avoir des œillères** to be biased

œillet [œjɛ] *m* eyelet; eyelet hole; carnation, clove pink; **œillet d'Inde** (*Tagetes*) marigold

œilleton [œjtɔ̃] *m* eye, bud; eyepiece; sight (*of rifle, camera, etc.*)

œillette [œjɛt] *f* opium poppy

œnologie [enɔlɔʒi] *f* science of viniculture, oenology

œsophage [ezɔfaʒ] *m* esophagus

œstres [ɛstr] *mpl* botflies, nose flies

œuf [œf] *m* (*pl* **œufs** [ø]) egg; **marcher sur des œufs** to walk on thin ice; **œuf à la coque** soft-boiled egg; **œuf à repriser** darning egg; **œuf de Colomb** ingenious, though obvious, solution to a problem; **œuf de Pâques** or **œuf rouge** Easter egg; **œuf dur** hard-boiled egg; **œuf mollet** soft-boiled egg; **œuf poché** poached egg; **œufs** spawn, roe; **œufs au lait** custard; **œufs au miroir** fried eggs; **œufs brouillés** scrambled eggs; **œuf sur le plat** fried egg; **plein comme un œuf** chock-full; **tondre un œuf** to squeeze blood out of a turnip; **tuer, écraser,** or **étouffer dans l'œuf** to nip in the bud

œuvre [œvr] *m* works (*of a painter*); **dans œuvre** inside (*measurements*); **hors d'œuvre** out of alignment; **le grand œuvre** the philosopher's stone; **le gros œuvre** (archit) the foundation, walls, and roof ‖ *f* work; piece of work; **bonnes œuvres** good works; **mettre en œuvre** to implement, to use; **mettre qn à l'œuvre** to set s.o. to work; **mettre tout en œuvre** to leave no stone unturned; **œuvres complètes** collected works; **œuvres mortes** (naut) topsides; **œuvre pie** good deed, good work; **œuvres vives** (naut) hull below water line; **se mettre à l'œuvre** to get to work

offen·sant [ɔfɑ̃sɑ̃] **-sante** [sɑ̃t] *adj* offensive

offense [ɔfɑ̃s] *f* offense; **faire offense à qn** to offend s.o.; **soit dit sans offense** with all due respect

offenser [ɔfɑ̃se] *tr* to offend ‖ *ref* to be offended

offen·sif [ɔfɑ̃sif] **-sive** [siv] *adj & f* offensive

of·fert [ɔfɛr] **-ferte** [fɛrt] *v* see **offrir**

office [ɔfis] *m* office; (eccl) office, service; **d'office** ex officio; **faire l'office de** to act as; **office d'ami** friendly turn; **remplir son office** (fig) to do its job ‖ *f* pantry

offi·ciel -cielle [ɔfisjɛl] *adj & mf* official

officier [ɔfisje] *m* officier; (naut) mate; **officier de service** (mil) officier of the day; **officier ministériel** notary public; **officier supérieur** (mil) field officer ‖ *intr* to officiate

offi·cieux [ɔfisjø] **-cieuse** [sjøz] *adj* unofficial, off-the-cuff; zealous; well-meant (*lie*); **faire l'officieux** to be officious

officine [ɔfisin] *f* pharmacy; den (*of thieves*); **officine d'intrigue** hotbed of intrigue

offrant [ɔfrɑ̃] *m*—**le plus offrant** the highest bidder

offre [ɔfr] *f* offer; **l'offre et la demande** supply and demand; **offres d'emploi** (formula in want ads) help wanted

offrir [ɔfrir] §65, §97, §98 *tr* to offer ‖ §96 *ref* to offer oneself; offer itself, occur

offset [ɔfsɛt] *m invar* offset

offusquer [ɔfyske] *tr* to obfuscate, obscure; irritate, displease ‖ *ref*—**s'offusquer de** to take offense at

ogive [ɔʒiv] *f* ogive; (rok) nose cone

ogre [ɔgr] **ogresse** [ɔgrɛs] *mf* ogre; **manger comme un ogre** (coll) to eat like a horse

ohé [ɔe] *interj* hey!; **ohé du navire!** ship ahoy!

ohm [om] *m* ohm

oie [wa] *f* goose; simpleton; **oie blanche** simple little goose (*naïve girl*); **oie sauvage** wild goose

oignon [ɔɲɔ̃] *m* onion; (hort) bulb; (pathol) bunion; (coll) turnip, pocket watch; **aux petits oignons** (coll) perfect; **ce ne sont pas mes oignons** it's no business of mine; **occupe-toi de tes oignons** (coll) mind your own business

oïl [ɔil], [ɔj] *adv* (Old French) yes

oindre [wɛ̃dr] §35 *tr* to anoint

oi·seau [wazo] *m* (*pl* -**seaux**) bird; hod (*of mason*); (coll) character; **être comme l'oiseau sur la branche** to be here today and gone tomorrow; **oiseau de paradis, oiseau des îles** bird of paradise; **oiseau des tempêtes** stormy petrel; **oiseaux domestiques, oiseaux de basse-cour** poultry

oiseau-mouche [wazomuʃ] *m* (*pl* -**mouches**) hummingbird

oiseler [wazle] §34 *tr* to train (*hawks*) ‖ *intr* to trap birds

oiselet [wazlɛ] *m* little bird

oiseleur [wazlœr] *m* fowler

oise·lier [wazəlje] **-lière** [ljɛr] *mf* bird fancier

oi·seux [wazø] **-seuse** [zøz] *adj* useless

oi·sif [wazif] **-sive** [ziv] *adj* idle ‖ *mf* idler

oisillon [wazijɔ̃] *m* fledgling

oisiveté [wazivte] *f* idleness

oison [wazɔ̃] *m* gosling; (coll) ninny

O.K. [oke] *interj* (letterword) O.K.!

oléagi·neux [ɔleaʒinø] **-neuse** [nøz] *adj* oily

oléoduc [ɔleɔdyk] *m* oil pipeline

olfac·tif [ɔlfaktif] **-tive** [tiv] *adj* olfactory

olibrius [ɔlibrijys] *m* pedant; pest; braggart (*in medieval plays*)

oligarchie [ɔligarʃi] *f* oligarchy

olivaie [ɔlivɛ] *f* olive grove

olivâtre [ɔlivɑtr] *adj* olive (*complexion*)

olive [ɔliv] *adj invar & f* olive

olivette [ɔlivɛt] *f* olive grove; plum tomato

olivier [ɔlivje] *m* olive tree; olive wood; Olivier Oliver

O.L.P. [ɔɛlpe] *f* (letterword) (**Organisation de la libération de la Palestine**) PLO

olympiade [ɔlɛ̃pjad] *f* olympiad

olym·pien [ɔlɛ̃pjɛ̃] **-pienne** [pjɛn] *adj* Olympian

olympique [ɔlɛ̃pik] *adj* Olympic

ombilic [ɔ̃bilik] *m* umbilicus

ombili·cal -cale [ɔ̃bilikal] *adj* (*pl* -**caux** [ko]) umbilical

ombrage [ɔ̃braʒ] *m* shade; **porter ombrage à** to offend; **prendre ombrage (de)** to take offense (at)

ombrager [ɔ̃braʒe] §38 *tr* to shade

ombra·geux [ɔ̃braʒø] **-geuse** [ʒøz] *adj* shy, skittish; touchy; distrustful

ombre [ɔ̃br] *f* shadow; shade; **ombres (chinoises)** shadow play, shadowgraph; **une ombre au tableau** (coll) a fly in the ointment

ombrelle [ɔ̃brɛl] *f* parasol; (aer) umbrella

ombrer [ɔ̃bre] *tr* to shade; apply eye shadow to

om·breux [ɔ̃brø] **-breuse** [brøz] *adj* shady

omelette [ɔmlɛt] *f* omelet

omettre [ɔmɛtr] §42, §97 *tr* to omit

omission [ɔmisjɔ̃] *f* omission

omnibus [ɔmnibys] *adj* omnibus; local (*train*) ‖ *m* omnibus; local (train)

omnipo·tent [ɔmnipɔtɑ̃] **-tente** [tɑ̃t] *adj* omnipotent

omnis·cient [ɔmnisjɑ̃] **-ciente** [sjɑ̃t] *adj* omniscient

omnium [ɔmnjɔm] *m* (com) holding company, general trading company; (sports) open race

omnivore [ɔmnivɔr] *adj* omnivorous

omoplate [ɔmɔplat] *f* shoulder blade

on [ɔ̃] §87 *pron indef* one, they, people; (coll) we, e.g., **y va-t-on?** are we going there?; (coll) I, e.g., **on est fatigué** I am tired; (often translated by passive forms), e.g., **on sait que** it is generally known that

once [ɔ̃s] *f* ounce

oncle [ɔ̃kl] *m* uncle

onction [ɔ̃ksjɔ̃] *f* unction; eloquence

onc·tueux [ɔ̃ktɥø] **-tueuse** [tɥøz] *adj* unctuous; greasy; bland

onde [ɔ̃d] *f* wave; watering (*of silk*); (poetic) water; **les petites ondes** (rad) shortwave; **mettre en ondes** to put on the air; **onde de choc** (aer) shock wave; **onde porteuse** (rad) carrier wave; **ondes amorties** (rad) damped waves; **ondes entretenues** (rad) continuous waves; **ondes radiophoniques** airwaves; **onde sonore** sound wave

ondée [ɔ̃de] *f* shower

on·dit [ɔ̃di] *m invar* gossip, scuttlebutt

on·doyant [ɔ̃dwajɑ̃] **-doyante** [dwajɑ̃t] *adj* undulating, wavy; wavering (*person*)

ondoyer [ɔ̃dwaje] §47 *tr* to baptize in an emergency ‖ *intr* to undulate, wave

ondulation [ɔ̃dylɑsjɔ̃] *f* undulation, waving; flowing (*e.g.,* *of drapery*); wave (*of hair*); **à ondulations** rolling (*ground*); **ondulation permanente** permanent wave

ondu·lé -lée [ɔ̃dyle] *adj* wavy; corrugated

onduler [ɔ̃dyle] *tr* to wave (*hair*) ‖ *intr* to wave, undulate

oné·reux [ɔnerø] **-reuse** [røz] *adj* onerous

ongle [ɔ̃gl] *m* nail, fingernail; **jusqu'au bout des ongles** to or at one's fingertips; **ongle des pieds** toenail

onglée [ɔ̃gle] *f* numbness in the fingertips

onglet [ɔ̃glɛ] *m* nail hole, groove (*in blade*); thimble; **à onglets** thumb-indexed; **monter sur onglet** (bb) to insert (*a page*)

onguent [ɔ̃gɑ̃] *m* ointment, salve

ont [ɔ̃] *v* see **avoir**

O.N.U. [ɔny] (acronym) or [ɔɛny] (letter-word) *f* (**Organisation des Nations Unies**) UN

onu·sien [ɔnyzjɛ̃] **-sienne** [zjɛn] *adj* UN

onyx [ɔniks] *m* onyx

onzain *[ɔ̃zɛ̃] m* eleven-line verse

onze *[ɔ̃z]* §94 *adj & pron* eleven; the Eleventh, e.g., **Jean onze** John the Eleventh; **onze heures** eleven o'clock ‖ *m* eleven; eleventh (*in dates*); e.g., **le onze mai** the eleventh of May

onzième *[ɔ̃zjɛm]* §94 *adj, pron* (*masc, fem*), *& m* eleventh

opale [ɔpal] *f* opal

opaque [ɔpak] *adj* opaque

O.P.E.P. [ɔpɛp] *f* (acronym) (**organisation des pays exportateurs de pétrole**) OPEC

opéra [ɔpera] *m* opera; opera house; **grand opéra, opéra sérieux** grand opera; **opéra bouffe** comic opera, opéra bouffe

opéra-comique [ɔperakɔmik] *m* (*pl* **opéras-comiques**) light opera

opéra·teur [ɔperatœr] **-trice** [tris] *mf* operator; **opérateur de permanence** operator on duty ‖ *m* cameraman

opération [ɔperɑsjɔ̃] *f* operation; **opérations à terme** (com) futures; **opération test** exploratory operation

opé·ré -rée [ɔpere] *mf* surgical patient

opérer [ɔpere] §10 *tr* to operate on; **opérer à chaud** to perform an emergency operation on (*s.o.*); **opérer qn de qch.** (med) to operate on s.o. for s.th. ‖ *intr* to operate; work ‖ *ref* to occur, take place

opérette [ɔperɛt] *f* operetta, musical comedy

opia·cé -cée [ɔpjase] *adj* opiate

opiner [ɔpine] *intr* to opine; **opiner du bonnet** (coll) to be a yes man

opiniâtre [ɔpinjɑtr] *adj* stubborn

opiniâtreté [ɔpinjɑtrəte] *f* stubbornness

opinion [ɔpinjɔ̃] *f* opinion; public opinion; **avoir bonne opinion de** to think highly of; **avoir une piètre opinion de** to take a dim view of

opium [ɔpjɔm] *m* opium

oponce [ɔpɔ̃s] *m* prickly pear

opossum [ɔpɔsɔm] *m* opossum

oppor·tun [ɔpɔrtœ̃] **-tune** [tyn] *adj* opportune, timely, expedient

opportuniste [ɔpɔrtynist] *adj* opportunistic *mf* opportunist

opportunité [ɔpɔrtynite] *f* opportuneness, timeliness; appropriateness

oppo·sant [ɔpozɑ̃] **-sante** [zɑ̃t] *adj* opposing ‖ *mf* opponent

oppo·sé -sée [ɔpoze] §92 *adj & m* opposite, contrary; **à l'opposé de** contrary to

opposer [ɔpoze] *tr* to raise (*an objection*); **opposer q.ch. à** to set up s.th. against; place s.th. opposite; contrast s.th. with ‖ *ref—s'opposer à* to oppose, object to

opposite [ɔpozit] *m—à l'opposite (de)* opposite

opposition [ɔpozisjɔ̃] *f* opposition; contrast

oppresser [ɔprese] *tr* to oppress; impede (*respiration*); weigh upon (*one's heart*)

oppresseur [ɔprescœr] *m* oppressor

oppres·sif [ɔpresif] **-sive** [siv] *adj* oppressive

oppression [ɔpresjɔ̃] *f* oppression; difficulty in breathing

opprimer [ɔprime] *tr* to oppress

opprobre [ɔprɔbr] *m* opprobrium, shame

opter [ɔpte] *intr* to opt, choose

opticien [ɔptisjɛ̃] *m* optician

optimisme [ɔptimism] *m* optimism

optimiste [ɔptimist] *adj* optimistic ‖ *mf* optimist

option [ɔpsjɔ̃] *f* option

optique [ɔptik] *adj* optic(al) ‖ *f* optics; perspective; **sous cette optique** from that point of view

opu·lent [ɔpylɑ̃] **-lente** [lɑ̃t] *adj* opulent

opuscule [ɔpyskyl] *m* opuscule, treatise; brochure, pamphlet

or [ɔr] *m* gold; **rouler sur l'or** to be rolling in money ‖ *adv* now; therefore

oracle [ɔrakl] *m* oracle

orage [ɔraʒ] *m* storm

ora·geux [ɔraʒø] **-geuse** [ʒøz] *adj* stormy

oraison [ɔrɛzɔ̃] *f* prayer; **oraison dominicale** Lord's Prayer; **oraison funèbre** funeral oration; **prononcer l'oraison funèbre de** (coll) to write off (*a custom, institution, etc.*)

o·ral -rale [ɔral] *adj* (*pl* **-raux** [ro]) oral

orange [ɔrɑ̃ʒ] *adj invar* orange (*color*) ‖ *m* orange (*color*) ‖ *f* orange (*fruit*)

oran·gé -gée [ɔrɑ̃ʒe] *adj & m* orange (*color*)

orangeade [ɔrɑ̃ʒad] *f* orangeade

oranger [ɔrɑ̃ʒe] *m* orange tree
orangeraie [ɔrɑ̃ʒrɛ] *f* orange grove
orangerie [ɔrɑ̃ʒri] *f* orangery; orange grove
orang-outan [ɔrɑ̃utɑ̃] *m* (*pl* **orangs-outans**) orang-outan
ora·teur [ɔratœr] **-trice** [tris] *mf* orator; speaker
oratoire [ɔratwar] *adj* oratorical ‖ *m* (eccl) oratory
oratorio [ɔratɔrjo] *m* oratorio
orbite [ɔrbit] *f* orbit; socket (*of eye*); **placer sur son orbite, mettre en orbite** to orbit; **sur orbite** in orbit
orchestre [ɔrkɛstr] *m* orchestra; band; **orchestre de typique** rumba band
orchestrer [ɔrkɛstre] *tr* to orchestrate
orchidée [ɔrkide] *f* orchid
ordalie [ɔrdali] *f* (hist) ordeal
ordinaire [ɔrdinɛr] *adj* ordinary ‖ *m* ordinary; regular bill of fare; (mil) mess; **d'ordinaire, à l'ordinaire** ordinarily
ordi·nal -nale [ɔrdinal] *adj* & *m* (*pl* **-naux** [no]) ordinal
ordinateur [ɔrdinatœr] *m* (comp) computer; **fait à l'ordinateur** computerized; **mettre sur ordinateur** to computerize; **mise sur ordinateur** computerization; **ordinateur de poche** pocket computer; **ordinateur domestique, ordinateur familial, ordinateur maison** home computer
ordination [ɔrdinasjɔ̃] *f* ordination
ordonnance [ɔrdɔnɑ̃s] *f* ordinance; order, arrangement; (pharm) prescription
ordonna·teur [ɔrdɔnatœr] **-trice** [tris] *mf* organizer; marshal; **ordonnateur des pompes funèbres** funeral director
ordon·né -née [ɔrdɔne] *adj* orderly
ordonner [ɔrdɔne] §97, §98 *tr* to arrange, put in order; order; prescribe (*e.g., medicine*); (eccl) to ordain; **ordonner à qn de + *inf*** to order s.o. to + *inf*; **ordonner q.ch. à qn** to order s.o. to do s.th.
ordre [ɔrdr] *m* order; **avoir de l'ordre** to be neat, orderly; **à vos ordres** at your service; **dans l'ordre d'entrée en scène** (theat) in order of appearance; **en ordre** in order; **jusqu'à nouvel ordre** until further notice; as things stand; **les ordres** (eccl) orders; **ordre du jour** (mil) order of the day; (parl) agenda; **ordre public** law and order; **payez à l'ordre de** (com) pay to the order of; **sous les ordres de** under the command of
ordure [ɔrdyr] *f* rubbish, filth; **ordures ménagères** garbage
ordu·rier [ɔrdyrje] **-rière** [rjɛr] *adj* lewd, filthy
orée [ɔre] *f* edge (*of a forest*)
oreille [ɔrɛj] *f* ear; **avoir l'oreille basse** to be humiliated; **dormir sur les deux oreilles** to sleep soundly; **dresser** or **tendre l'oreille** to prick up one's ears; **échauffer les oreilles à qn** to rile s.o. up; **faire la sourde oreille** to turn a deaf ear; **rompre les oreilles à qn** (coll) to talk s.o.'s head off; **se faire tirer l'oreille** (coll) to play hard to get

oreiller [ɔreje] *m* pillow
oreillette [ɔrɛjɛt] *f* earflap (*of cap*); (anat) auricle
oreillons [ɔrɛjɔ̃] *mpl* mumps
ores [ɔr] *adv*—**d'ores et déjà** [dɔrzedeʒa] from now on
Orfée [ɔrfe] *m* Orpheus
orfèvre [ɔrfɛvr] *m* goldsmith; silversmith; **être orfèvre en la matière** (coll) to know one's onions
orfèvrerie [ɔrfɛvrəri] *f* goldsmith's shop; goldsmith's trade; gold plate; gold or silver jewelry
orfraie [ɔrfrɛ] *f* osprey, fish hawk
organdi [ɔrgɑ̃di] *m* organdy
organe [ɔrgan] *m* organ; part (*of a machine*)
organique [ɔrganik] *adj* organic
organisa·teur [ɔrganizatœr] **-trice** [tris] *adj* organizing ‖ *mf* organizer
organisation [ɔrganizɑsjɔ̃] *f* organization
organiser [ɔrganize] *tr* to organize
organisme [ɔrganism] *m* organism; organization
organiste [ɔrganist] *mf* organist
orgasme [ɔrgasm] *m* orgasm
orge [ɔrʒ] *f* barley
orgelet [ɔrʒəlɛ] *m* (pathol) sty
orgie [ɔrʒi] *f* orgy
orgue [ɔrg] *m* organ; **orgue de Barbarie** hand organ; **orgue de cinéma** theater organ ‖ *f*—**les grandes orgues** the pipe organ
orgueil [ɔrgœj] *m* pride, conceit; **avoir l'orgueil de** to take pride in
orgueil·leux [ɔrgœjø] **-leuse** [jøz] *adj* proud, haughty
orient [ɔrjɑ̃] *m* orient; east; **Orient** Orient, East
orien·tal -tale [ɔrjɑ̃tal] (*pl* **-taux** [to]) *adj* oriental; eastern, east ‖ (cap) *mf* Oriental (*person*)
orientation [ɔrjɑ̃tɑsjɔ̃] *f* orientation; **orientation professionnelle** vocational guidance
orienter [ɔrjɑ̃te] *tr* to orient; guide ‖ *ref* to take one's bearings
orien·teur [ɔrjɑ̃tœr] **-teuse** [tøz] *mf* guidance counselor
orifice [ɔrifis] *m* orifice, hole, opening
origan [ɔrigɑ̃] *m* marjoram
originaire [ɔriʒinɛr] *adj* native; original, first
origi·nal -nale [ɔriʒinal] *adj* (*pl* **-naux** [no]) original; eccentric, peculiar ‖ *m* antique (*piece of furniture*); eccentric, card (*person*); (typ) copy, original
originalité [ɔriʒinalite] *f* originality; eccentricity
origine [ɔriʒin] *f* origin
origi·nel -nelle [ɔriʒinɛl] *adj* original (*sin; meaning*); primitive, early
ori·gnal [ɔriɲal] *m* (*pl* **-gnaux** [ɲo]) moose, elk
orillon [ɔrijɔ̃] *m* ear, handle; (archit) projection
ori·peau [ɔripo] *m* (*pl* **-peaux**) tinsel; **oripeaux** cheap finery

Orléans [ɔrleɑ̃] *f* Orléans; **la Nouvelle Or-léans** New Orleans

orme [ɔrm] *m* elm; **attendez-moi sous l'orme** (coll) I won't be there

or·né -née [ɔrne] *adj* ornate

ornement [ɔrnəmɑ̃] *m* ornament

ornemen·tal -tale [ɔrnəmɑ̃tal] *adj* (*pl* **-taux** [to]) ornamental

orner [ɔrne] *tr* to ornament, adorn

ornière [ɔrnjɛr] *f* rut, groove

ornithologie [ɔrnitɔlɔʒi] *f* ornithology

orphe·lin [ɔrfəlɛ̃] **-line** [lin] *adj & mf* orphan

orphelinat [ɔrfəlina] *m* orphanage (*asylum*)

orphéon [ɔrfeɔ̃] *m* male choir, glee club; brass band

orteil [ɔrtɛj] *m* toe; **big toe**; **gros orteil** big toe

O.R.T.F. [oɛrteɛf] *m* (letterword) (**Office de radio-télévision française**) French radio and television system

orthodoxe [ɔrtɔdɔks] *adj* orthodox

orthographe [ɔrtɔgraf] *f* spelling, orthography

orthographier [ɔrtɔgrafje] *tr* to spell

ortie [ɔrti] *f* nettle

orviétan [ɔrvjetɑ̃] *m* nostrum

O.S. [oɛs] *f* (letterword) (**ouvrière spécialisée**) specialist

os [ɔs] *m* (*pl* **os** [o]) bone; **à gros os** big-boned; **os à moelle** marrowbone; **tomber sur un os** (coll) to meet up with a problem; **trempé jusqu'aux os** soaked to the skin

osciller [ɔsile] *intr* to oscillate; waver, hesitate

o·sé -sée [oze] *adj* daring, bold; risqué, off-color

oseille [ozɛj] *f* sorrel; (slang) dough

oser [oze] §95 *tr & intr* to dare

osier [ozje] *m* osier; **d'osier** wicker

osmose [ɔsmoz] *f* osmosis

ossature [ɔsatyr] *f* bone structure; framework, skeleton

ossements [ɔsmɑ̃] *mpl* bones, remains

os·seux -seuse [ɔsø] [søz] *adj* bony

ossifier [ɔsifje] *tr & ref* to ossify

os·su -sue [ɔsy] *adj* bony; big-boned

ostensible [ɔstɑ̃sibl] *adj* conspicuous, ostensible; ostentatious

ostensoir [ɔstɑ̃swar] *m* monstrance

ostentatoire [ɔstɑ̃tatwar] *adj* ostentatious

ostracisme [ɔstrasism] *m* ostracism

otage [ɔtaʒ] *m* hostage

otalgie [ɔtalʒi] *f* earache

O.T.A.N. or **OTAN** [ɔtan], [otan], [otɑ̃] *f* (acronym) (**Organisation du traité de l'Atlantique Nord**)—l'**O.T.A.N.** NATO

otarie [ɔtari] *f* sea lion

OTASE [ɔtɑz] *f* (acronym) (**Organisation du traité de l'Asie du Sud-Est**)—l'**OTASE** SEATO

ôter [ote] *tr* to remove, take away; take off; tip (*one's hat*); **ôter q.ch. à qn** to remove or take away s.th. from s.o.; **ôter q.ch.**

de q.ch. to take s.th. away from s.th. ‖ *ref* to withdraw, get out of the way

otto·man [ɔtɔmɑ̃] **-mane** [man] *adj* Ottoman ‖ *m* ottoman (*corded fabric*) ‖ *f* ottoman (*divan*) ‖ (*cap*) *mf* Ottoman (*person*)

ou [u] *conj* or; **ou . . . ou** either . . . or

où [u] *adv* where; **d'où** from where, whence; **où que** wherever; **par où** which way ‖ *conj* where; when; **d'où** from where, whence; **par où** through which; **partout où** wherever

ouailles [waj] *fpl* (eccl) flock

ouais [wɛ] *interj* (coll) oh yeah!

ouate *[wat]* *f* cotton batting, wadding

ouater *[wate]* *tr* to pad, wad

oubli [ubli] *m* forgetfulness; omission, oversight; **tomber dans l'oubli** to fall into oblivion

oublier [ublije] §97 *tr & intr* to forget ‖ *ref* to forget oneself; be forgotten

oubliettes [ublijɛt] *fpl* dungeon of oblivion

ou·blieux [ublijø] **-blieuse** [blijøz] *adj* forgetful, oblivious, unmindful

ouche [uʃ] *f* orchard; vegetable garden

ouest [wɛst] *adj invar* west, western ‖ *m* west; **de l'ouest** western; **faire l'ouest** to steer westward; **vers l'ouest** westward

ouest-alle·mand [wɛstalmɑ̃] **-mande** [mɑ̃d] *adj* West German ‖ (*cap*) *mf* West German

ouf *[uf]* *interj* whew!

oui *[wi]* *m invar* yes; **les oui l'emportent** the ayes have it ‖ *adv* yes; **je crois que oui** I think so; **oui madame** yes ma'am; **oui monsieur** yes sir; **oui mon capitaine** (**mon général,** etc.) yes sir

ouï-dire [widir] *m invar* hearsay; **simples ouï-dire** (law) hearsay evidence

ouïe [wi] *f* hearing; **être tout ouïe** [tutwi] to be all ears; **ouïs** gills; sound holes (*of violin*) ‖ *interj* oh my!

ouïr [wir] §95 (used only in: *inf,* compound tenses with *pp* **ouï,** and 2d *pl impv* **oyez**) *tr* to hear; **oyez . . . !** hear ye . . . !

ouragan [uragɑ̃] *m* hurricane

ourdir [urdir] *tr* to warp (*cloth before weaving*); hatch (*e.g., a plot*)

ourler [urle] *tr* to hem; **ourler à jour** to hemstitch

ourlet [urlɛ] *m* hem; **ourlet de la jupe** hemline

ours [urs] *m* bear; (fig) lone wolf; **ours en peluche** teddy bear; **ours mal léché** unmannerly boor; **ours marin** (zool) seal; **vendre la peau de l'ours avant de l'avoir tué** to count one's chickens before they are hatched

ourse [urs] *f* she-bear; **la Grande Ourse** the Great Bear; **la Petite Ourse** the Little Bear

oursin [ursɛ̃] *m* sea urchin

ourson [ursɔ̃] *m* bear cub

ouste [ust] *interj* (coll) out!, out you go!

outarde [utard] *f* (orn) bustard

outil [uti] *m* tool, implement

outillage [utijaʒ] *m* tools; equipment

outil·lé -lée [utije] *adj* equipped with tools; tooled-up (*factory*)

outiller [utije] *tr* to equip with tools; tool up (*a factory*) ‖ *ref* to supply oneself with equipment; tool up

outilleur [utijœr] *m* toolmaker

outrage [utraʒ] *m* outrage, affront; ravages (*of time*); contempt of court; **faire outrage à qn** to outrage s.o.; **outrage aux bonnes mœurs** traffic in pornography; **outrage public à la pudeur** indecent exposure

outrager [utraʒe] §38 *tr* to outrage, affront

outra·geux [utraʒø] **-geuse** [ʒøz] *adj* outrageous, insulting

outrance [utrɑ̃s] *f* excess; exaggeration; **à outrance** to the limit

outran·cier [utrɑ̃sje] **-cière** [sjɛr] *adj* extreme, excessive, out-and-out ‖ *mf* extremist, out-and-outer

outre [utr] *f* goatskin canteen ‖ *adv* further; **d'outre en d'outre** right through; **en outre** besides, moreover; **passer outre à** to ignore (*e.g., an order*) ‖ *prep* in addition to, apart from; beyond

ou·tré -trée [utre] *adj* overdone, exaggerated; exasperated

outrecui·dant [utrəkɥidɑ̃] **-dante** [dɑ̃t] *adj* self-satisfied; insolent, presumptuous

outre-Manche [utrəmɑ̃ʃ] *adv* across the Channel

outremer [utrəmɛr] *m* ultramarine, lapis lazuli (*color*)

outre-mer [utrəmɛr] *adv* overseas

outre-monts [utrəmɔ̃] *adv* over the mountains (*i.e., the Alps*)

outrepasser [utrəpɑse] *tr* to go beyond, to exceed

outrer [utre] *tr* to overdo, exaggerate; exasperate

outre-tombe [utrətɔ̃b] *adv*—**d'outre-tombe** posthumous

ou·vert [uvɛr] **-verte** [vɛrt] *adj* open; exposed; frank, candid; on (*said of meter, gas, etc.*); ‖ *v* see **ouvrir**

ouverture [uvɛrtyr] *f* opening; hole, gap; (mus) overture; (phot) aperture; **ouverture en fondu** (mov) fade-in

ouvrable [uvrabl] *adj* working, e.g., **jour ouvrable** working day

ouvrage [uvraʒ] *m* work, handiwork; piece of work; work, treatise

ouvrager [uvraʒe] §38 *tr* to work (*e.g., iron*); turn (*wood*)

ou·vré -vrée [uvre] *adj* worked, wrought; finished (*product*)

ouvre-boîtes [uvrəbwat] *m invar* can opener

ouvre-bouteilles [uvrəbutɛj] *m invar* bottle opener

ouvreur [uvrœr] *m* opener (*in poker*)

ouvreuse [uvrøz] *f* usher

ou·vrier [uvrije] **-vrière** [vrijɛr] *adj* working, worker; worker's, workingman's ‖ *mf* worker ‖ *m* workman, laborer; workingman ‖ *f* workingwoman

ouvrir [uvrir] §65 *tr* to open; turn on (*the light; the radio or television; the gas*); **ouvrir boutique** to set up shop ‖ *intr* to be open; open (*said of store, school, etc.; said of card player*) ‖ *ref* to open; be opened; **s'ouvrir à** to open up to, confide in

ouvroir [uvrwar] *m* workroom

ovaire [ɔvɛr] *m* ovary

ovale [ɔval] *adj* & *m* oval

ovation [ɔvasjɔ̃] *f* ovation

ovationner [ɔvasjɔne] *tr* to give an ovation to

Ovide [ɔvid] *m* Ovid

O.V.N.I. [ɔvni] *m* (acronym) (**objet volant non-identifié**) UFO

oxford [ɔksfɔr] *m* oxford cloth

oxycarbonisme [ɔksikarbɔnism] *m* carbon-monoxide poisoning

oxyde [ɔksid] *m* oxide

oxyder [ɔkside] *tr* & *ref* to oxidize

oxygène [ɔksiʒɛn] *m* oxygen

oxygéner [ɔksiʒene] §10 *tr* to oxygenate; bleach (*hair*) ‖ *ref*—**s'oxygéner les poumons** (coll) to fill one's lungs full of ozone

oxyton [ɔksitɔ̃] *adj* & *m* oxytone

ozone [ozɔn] *m* ozone

P

P, p [pe] *m invar* sixteenth letter of the French alphabet

pacage [pakaʒ] *m* pasture

pacifica·teur [pasifikatœr] **-trice** [tris] *mf* pacifier

pacifier [pasifje] *tr* to pacify

pacifique [pasifik] *adj* pacific ‖ **Pacifique** *adj* & *m* Pacific

pacifisme [pasifism] *m* pacifism

pacifiste [pasifist] *mf* pacifist

pacotille [pakɔtij] *f* junk; **de pacotille** shoddy; junky

pacte [pakt] *m* pact, covenant

pactiser [paktize] *intr* to compromise; traffic (*with the enemy*)

paf [paf] *adj* (slang) tipsy, tight ‖ *interj* bang!

pagaie [pagɛ] *f* paddle

pagaïe or **pagaille** [pagaj] *f* disorder; **en**

pagaïe (coll) in great quantity; (coll) in a mess

paganisme [paganism] *m* paganism

pagayer [pageje] §49 *tr & intr* to paddle

page [paʒ] *m* page ‖ *f* page (*of a book*); **être à la page** to be up to date

paginer [paʒine] *tr* to page

pagne [paɲ] *m* loincloth

paie [pɛ] *f* pay, wages

paiement [pɛmɑ̃] *m* payment

païen [pajɛ̃] **païenne** [pajɛn] *adj & mf* pagan

pail·lard [pajar] **-larde** [jard] *adj* ribald ‖ *mf* debauchee

paillasse [pajas] *m* buffoon ‖ *f* straw mattress; (slang) whore

paillasson [pɑjasɔ̃] *m* doormat

paille [pɑj] *f* straw; flaw; (Bib) mote; **paille de fer** iron shavings

pail·lé -lée [pɑje] *adj* rush-bottomed (*chair*)

pailler [pɑje] *m* straw stack ‖ *tr* to bottom (*a chair*) with straw; mulch

pailleter [pajte] §34 *tr* to spangle

paillette [pajɛt] *f* spangle; flake (*of mica; of soap*); grain (*of gold*); flaw (*in a diamond*)

pain [pɛ̃] *m* bread; loaf (*of bread, of sugar*); cake (*of soap*); pat (*of butter*); **avoir du pain sur la planche** (coll) to have a lot to do; **pain à cacheter** sealing wafer; **pain aux raisins** raisin roll; **pain bis** brown bread; **pain complet** whole-wheat bread; **pain de fantaisie** bread sold by the loaf (*instead of by weight*); **pain de mie** sandwich bread; **pain d'épice** gingerbread; **pain grillé** toast; **pain perdu** French toast; **petit pain** roll; **se vendre comme des petits pains** (coll) to sell like hot cakes

pair paire [pɛr] *adj* even (*number*) ‖ *m* peer; equal; (com) par; **hors de pair, hors pair** unrivaled; **marcher de pair avec** to keep abreast of; **travailler au pair** (coll) to work for one's keep; **au pair** at par ‖ *f* pair; couple; brace (*of dogs, pistols, etc.*); yoke (*of oxen*)

pairesse [pɛrɛs] *f* peeress

pairie [pɛri], [peri] *f* peerage

pais [pe] *v* (**paît**) see **paître**

paisible [pezibl] *adj* peaceful

paître [pɛtr] §48 *tr & intr* to graze; **envoyer paître** (coll) to send packing

paix [pɛ] *f* peace

Pakistan [pakistɑ̃] *m*—**le Pakistan** Pakistan

pakista·nais [pakistanɛ] **-naise** [nɛz] *adj* Pakistani ‖ (*cap*) *mf* Pakistani

pal [pal] *m* (*pl* **paux** [po] or **pals**) pale, stake

palabre [palabr] *m & f* palaver

palace [palas] *m* luxury hotel

palais [palɛ] *m* palace; palate; courthouse, law courts

palan [palɑ̃] *m* block and tackle

palanque [palɑ̃k] *f* stockade

pala·tal -tale [palatal] (*pl* **-taux** [to] **-tales**) *adj & f* palatal

pale [pal] *f* blade (*of, e.g., oar*); stake; sluice gate; (eccl) pall

pâle [pɑl] *adj* pale

palefrenier [palfrənje] *m* groom; (coll) hick, oaf

palefroi [palfrwa] *m* palfrey

paleron [palrɔ̃] *m* bottom chuck roast

palet [palɛ] *m* disk, flat stone; puck

paletot [palto] *m* topcoat

palette [palɛt] *f* palette; paddle

pâleur [pɑlœr] *f* pallor; paleness

palier [palje] *m* landing (*of stairs*); plateau (*of curve of a graph*); (mach) bearing; **en palier** on the level; **palier à billes** ball bearing; **par paliers** graduated (*e.g., tax*); in stages

pâlir [pɑlir] *tr & intr* to pale, turn pale

palis [pali] *m* picket fence

palissade [palisad] *f* palisade; fence

palissandre [palisɑ̃dr] *m* rosewood

pallier [palje] *tr* to palliate ‖ *intr*—**pallier à** to mitigate

palmarès [palmarɛs] *m* list of winners; hit parade

palme [palm] *f* (bot) palm; **palmes** fins (*for swimming*)

palmeraie [palmərɛ] *f* palm grove

palmier [palmje] *m* palm tree

palmipède [palmipɛd] *adj* webfooted ‖ *m* webfoot

palombe [palɔ̃b] *f* ringdove

palourde [palurd] *f* clam

palpable [palpabl] *adj* palpable; plain, obvious

palper [palpe] *tr* to feel; palpate; (coll) to pocket (*money*)

palpiter [palpite] *intr* to palpitate

palsambleu [palsɑ̃blø] *interj* zounds!

paltoquet [paltɔkɛ] *m* nonentity

palu·déen [palydeɛ̃] **-déenne** [deɛn] *adj* marsh (*plant*); swamp (*fever*)

paludisme [palydism] *m* malaria

pâmer [pɑme] *ref* to swoon

pâmoison [pɑmwazɔ̃] *f* swoon

pamphlet [pɑ̃flɛ] *m* lampoon

pamplemousse [pɑ̃pləmus] *m & f* grapefruit

pan [pɑ̃] *m* tail (*of shirt or coat*); section; side, face; patch (*of sky*); **Pan** Pan ‖ *interj* bang!

panacée [panase] *f* panacea

panachage [panaʃaʒ] *m* mixing; **faire du panachage** to split one's vote

panache [panaʃ] *m* plume; wreath (*of smoke*); **aimer le panache** to be fond of show; **avoir son panache** (coll) to be tipsy; **faire panache** to somersault, turn over

pana·ché -chée [panaʃe] *adj* variegated; mixed (*salad*); motley (*crowd*)

panacher [panaʃe] *tr* to variegate; plume; split (*one's vote*) ‖ *ref* to become variegated

panais [panɛ] *m* parsnip

panama [panama] *m* panama hat; **le Panama** Panama; **Panama** Panama City

panaris [panari] *m* (pathol) whitlow, felon

pancarte [pɑ̃kart] *f* placard; poster, sign

panchromatique [pɑ̃krɔmatik] *adj* panchromatic

pancréas [pɑ̃kreɑs] *m* pancreas

pandémonium [pãdemɔnjɔm] *m* den of iniquity; pandemonium
pa·né -née [pane] *adj* breaded
panetière [pantjɛr] *f* breadbox
panier [panje] *m* basket; hoop (*of skirt*); creel (*trap*); **être dans le même panier** to be in the same boat; **panier à ouvrage** work basket; **panier à papier** wastepaper basket; **panier à provisions** shopping basket; **panier à salade** wire salad washer; (coll) paddy wagon; **panier percé** spendthrift
panier-repas [panjerəpɑ] *m* (*pl* **paniers-repas**) box lunch
panique [panik] *adj & f* panic
panne [pan] *f* breakdown, trouble; plush; fat (*of pig*); peen (*of hammer*); tip (*of soldering iron*); bank (*of clouds*); purlin (*of roof*); daub; (theat) small part; **(en) panne sèche** (*public sign*) out of gas; **être dans la panne** (coll) to be hard up; **être en panne** (coll) to be unable to continue; **être en panne de** (coll) to be deprived of; **laisser en panne** to leave in the lurch; **mettre en panne** (naut) to heave to; **panne fendue** claw (*of hammer*); **rester en panne** to come to a standstill; **tomber en panne** to have a breakdown
pan·né -née [pane] *adj* (slang) hard up
pan·neau [pano] *m* (*pl* **-neaux**) panel; snare, net; **condamner les panneaux** (naut) to batten down the hatches; **donner dans le panneau** to walk into the trap; **panneau d'affichage** billboard; **panneau de tête** headboard (*of bed*); **panneaux** paneling; **panneaux de signalisation** traffic signs; **tomber** or **donner dans le panneau** to be taken in, to fall into a trap
panoplie [panɔpli] *f* panoply
panorama [panɔrama] *m* panorama
panoramiquer [panɔramike] *intr* (mov, telv) to pan
panse [pãs] *f* belly; rumen, first stomach
pansement [pãsmã] *m* (surg) dressing
panser [pãse] *tr* to dress, bandage; groom (*an animal*)
pan·su -sue [pãsy] *adj* potbellied
pantalon [pãtalɔ̃] *m* trousers, pair of trousers; panties; slacks; **pantalon à pattes d'éléphant** bell-bottomed trousers; **pantalon corsaire** pedal pushers; **pantalon de coutil** ducks; blue jeans; **pantalon de golf** knickers; **pantalon de ski** ski pants
pante [pãt] *m* (slang) guy
panteler [pãtle] §34 *intr* to pant
panthéisme [pãteism] *m* pantheism
panthéon [pãteɔ̃] *m* pantheon
panthère [pãtɛr] *f* panther
pantin [pãtɛ̃] *m* puppet; jumping jack; **pantin articulé** string puppet
pantois [pãtwa] *adj* flabbergasted
pantomime [pãtɔmim] *f* pantomime
pantou·flard -flarde [flard] *mf* (coll) homebody
pantoufle [pãtufl] *f* slipper
pantoufler [pãtufle] *intr* to leave government service

paon [pã] *m* peacock, peafowl; peacock butterfly
paonne [pan] *f* peahen
papa [papa] *m* papa; **à la papa** (coll) cautiously; **de papa** (coll) outmoded; **papa gâteau** (coll) sugar daddy
papas [papɑs] *m* pope (*in Orthodox Church*)
papauté [papote] *f* papacy
pape [pap] *m* pope
pape·lard [paplar] **-larde** [lard] *adj* hypocritical ‖ *mf* hypocrite ‖ *m* scrap of paper
paperasse [papras] *f* old paper
paperasserie [paprasri] *f* red tape
paperas·sier [paprasje] **-sière** [sjɛr] *adj* fond of red tape ‖ *mf* bureaucrat
papeterie [paptri] *f* paper mill; stationery store
pape·tier [paptje] **-tière** [tjɛr] *mf* stationer
papier [papje] *m* paper; newspaper article; document; piece of paper; **être dans les petits papiers de** (coll) to be in the good graces of; **gratter du papier** to scribble; **papier à calquer, papier végétal** tracing paper; **papier à en-tête** letterhead (stationery); **papier à lettres** writing paper; **papier alu** aluminum foil; **papier à machine** typewriter paper; **papier à musique** staff paper; **papier bible, indien,** or **pelure** Bible paper, onionskin; **papier buvard** blotting paper; **papier carbone** carbon paper; **papier collant** Scotch tape; **papier d'emballage** wrapping paper; **papier de soie** tissue paper; **papier d'étain** tin foil; **papier de verre** sandpaper; **papier fort** cardboard; **papier hygiénique** toilet paper; **papier journal** newsprint; **papier kraft** cardboard (*for packing*); **papier mâché** papier-mâché; **papier ministre** foolscap; **papier paraffiné** wax paper; **papier peint** wallpaper; **papier rayé** lined paper; **papiers** (*public sign*) waste paper; **papier sensible** photographic paper; **papier tue-mouches** flypaper; **rayez cela de vos papiers!** (coll) don't count on it!
papier-filtre [papjefiltrə] *m* filter paper
papier-monnaie [papjemɔnɛ] *m* paper money
papier-pierre [papjepjɛr] *m* (*pl* **papiers-pierre**) papier-mâché
papille [papij], [papil] *f* papilla; **papille gustative** taste bud
papillon [papijɔ̃] *m* butterfly; flier, handbill; inset; form, application; thumbscrew, wing nut; butterfly valve; rider (*to document*); (coll) parking ticket; **papillon de nuit** moth; **papillons noirs** gloomy thoughts
papillonner [papijɔne] *intr* to flit about
papillote [papijɔt] *f* curlpaper; (culin) paper wrapper
papilloter [papijɔte] *intr* to blink; to flicker
papoter [papote] *intr* to chitchat
paprika [paprika] *m* paprika
papyrus [papirys] *m* papyrus
pâque [pɑk] *f* Passover; **la pâque russe** Russian Easter; **Pâque** Passover
paquebot [pakbo] *m* liner

pâquerette [pakrɛt] *f* white daisy

Pâques [pɑk] *m* Easter ‖ *fpl* Easter; **faire ses pâques** or **Pâques** to take Easter Communion; **Pâques fleuries** Palm Sunday

paquet [pakɛ] *m* packet, bundle; package; parcel; pack (*of cigarettes*); dressing down; **être un paquet d'os** [dɔs] to be nothing but skin and bones; **faire son paquet** (coll) to pack up; **mettre le paquet** (coll) to shoot the works; **paquet de mer** heavy sea; **petit paquet** parcel (*under a kilogram*); **petits paquets** parcel post; **un paquet de** a lot of

paquetage [pakta3] (comp) batch

par [par] *prep* by; through; out of, e.g., **par la fenêtre** out of the window; per, a, e.g., **huit dollars par jour** eight dollars per day, eight dollars a day; on, e.g., **par une belle matinée** on a beautiful morning; in, e.g., **par temps de brume** in foggy weather; **de par la loi** in the name of the law; **par avion** (*formula on envelope*) air mail; **par delà** beyond; **par derrière** at the back, the back way; **par devant** in front, before; **par exemple** for example; **par ici** this way; **par là** that way; **par où?** which way?

para [para] *m* (coll) paratrooper

parabole [parabɔl] *f* parable; (*curve*) parabola

parachever [paraʃve] §2 *tr* to finish off

parachutage [paraʃyta3] *m* airdrop, airdropping

parachute [paraʃyt] *m* parachute

parachuter [paraʃyte] *tr* to airdrop; (coll) to appoint in haste

parachutisme [paraʃytism] *m* parachuting; (sports) skydiving

parachutiste [paraʃytist] *mf* parachutist; (sports) skydiver ‖ *m* paratrooper

parade [parad] *f* show; parry; sudden stop (*of horse*); come-on (*in front of sideshow*); (mil) inspection, parade; **à la parade** on parade; **faire parade de** to show off, to display

parader [parade] *intr* to show off

paradis [paradi] *m* paradise; (theat) peanut gallery

parado·xal -xale [paradɔksal] *adj* (*pl* -**xaux** [kso]) paradoxical

paradoxe [paradɔks] *m* paradox

parafe [paraf] *m* flourish; initials

parafer [parafe] *tr* to initial

paraffine [parafin] *f* paraffin

paraffiner [parafine] *tr* to paraffin

parages [para3] *mpl* region, vicinity; **dans ces parages** in these parts

paragraphe [paragraf] *m* paragraph

Paraguay [paragɛ] *m*—**le Paraguay** Paraguay

para·guayen [paragɛjɛ̃] -**guayenne** [gɛjɛn] *adj* Paraguayan ‖ (*cap*) *mf* Paraguayan

paraître [parɛtr] §12, §95 *intr* to appear; seem; come out; show off; **à ce qu'il paraît** from all appearances; **faire paraître** to publish; **vient de paraître** just out

parallèle [paralɛl] *adj* parallel ‖ *m* parallel, comparison; (geog) parallel ‖ *f* (geom) parallel

paralyser [paralize] *tr* to paralyze

paralysie [paralizi] *f* paralysis

paralytique [paralitik] *adj* & *mf* paralytic

parangon [parɑ̃gɔ̃] *m* paragon

paranoïaque [paranɔjak] *adj* & *mf* paranoiac

parapet [parapɛ] *m* railing, parapet; (mil) parapet

paraphe [paraf] *m* flourish; initials

parapher [parafe] *tr* to initial

paraphrase [parafrɑz] *f* circumlocution, paraphrase; commentary

paraphraser [parafrɑze] *tr* to paraphrase

parapluie [paraplɥi] *m* umbrella; cover, front

parasite [parazit] *adj* parasitic(al) ‖ *m* parasite; **parasites** (rad) static

parasiter [parazite] *tr* to live as a parasite on or in (*a host*); (fig) to sponge on

parasol [parasɔl] *m* parasol; beach umbrella

paratonnerre [paratɔnɛr] *m* lightning rod

parâtre [parɑtr] *m* stepfather; cruel father

paravent [paravɑ̃] *m* folding screen

parbleu [parblø] *interj* rather!, by Jove!, you bet!

parc [park] *m* park; sheepfold; corral, pen; playpen; grounds, property; (mil) supply depot; (rr) rolling stock; **parc à huîtres** oyster bed; **parc automobile** motor pool; **parc d'attractions** amusement park; **parc de stationnement (payant)** parking lot

parcage [parka3] *m* parking

parcelle [parsɛl] *f* particle; plot

parce que [pars(ə)kə] *conj* because

parchemin [parʃəmɛ̃] *m* parchment; (coll) sheepskin (*diploma*)

parchemi·né -née [parʃəmine] *adj* wrinkled

parcheminer [parʃəmine] *tr* to parchmentize ‖ *ref* to shrivel up

par-ci [parsi] *adv*—**par-ci par-là** here and there

parcimo·nieux [parsimɔnjø] -**nieuse** [njøz] *adj* parsimonious

parcomètre [parkɔmɛtr] *m* parking meter

parcourir [parkurir] §14 *tr* to travel through, tour; wander about; cover (*a distance*); scour (*the country*); glance through

parcours [parkur] *m* run, trip; route, distance covered; round (*e.g., of golf*); stroke (*of piston*)

par-delà [pardəla] *adv* & *prep* beyond

par-derrière [pardɛrjɛr] *adv* & *prep* behind

par-dessous [pardəsu] *adv* & *prep* underneath

pardessus [pardəsy] *m* overcoat

par-dessus [pardəsy] *adv* on top, over ‖ *prep* on top of, over

par-devant [pardəvɑ̃] *adv* in front ‖ *prep* in front of, before

par-devers [pardəvɛr] *prep* in the presence of; **par-devers soi** in one's own possession

pardi [pardi] *interj* (coll) of course!

pardon [pardɔ̃] *m* pardon; Breton pilgrimage ‖ *adv* (to contradict a negative statement or question) yes, e.g., **Vous ne parlez pas français, n'est-ce pas? Pardon, je le parle très bien** You don't speak French, do you? Yes, I speak it very well ‖ *interj* pardon me!; (slang) oh boy!

pardonnable [pardɔnabl] *adj* pardonable

pardonner [pardɔne] §98 *tr* to pardon, forgive, excuse, e.g., **Marie pardonne à Robert d'avoir manqué le rendez-vous** Mary forgives Robert for missing the date; **pardonnez-moi de vous avoir dérangé** excuse me for disturbing you; **pardonnez-moi, mais . . . excuse** me, but . . . ; **pardonner q.ch. à qn** to pardon s.o. for s.th. ‖ *intr* (**à qn**) to pardon, forgive, e.g., **Marie pardonnera à Robert** Mary will forgive Robert; **ne pas pardonner** to be fatal (*said of illness, mistake, etc.*)

pare-balles [parbal] *adj invar* bulletproof

pare-boue [parbu] *m invar* mudguard

pare-brise [parbriz] *m invar* windshield

pare-chocs [parʃɔk] *m invar* (aut) bumper; **pare-chocs contre pare-chocs** bumper to bumper

pare-étincelles [paretẽsɛl] *m invar* fire screen

pa·reil -reille [parɛj] *adj* identical, the same; such, such a ‖ *mf* equal, match; **sans pareil, sans pareille** without parallel, unequaled ‖ *m*—**c'est du pareil au même** (coll) it's six of one and half dozen of the other ‖ *f* same (thing); **rendre la pareille à qn** to pay s.o. back in his own coin

pareillement [parɛjmɑ̃] *adv* likewise

parement [parmɑ̃] *m* cuff; facing; trimming; (eccl) parament

pa·rent [parɑ̃] **-rente** [rɑ̃t] *adj* like ‖ *mf* relative; **parents** parents; relatives; ancestors; **plus proche parent** next of kin

parenté [parɑ̃te] *f* relationship; relations

parenthèse [parɑ̃tɛz] *f* parenthesis; **entre parenthèses** in parentheses

parer [pare] *tr* to adorn; parry; prepare ‖ *intr*—**parer à** to provide for ‖ *ref* to show off

pare-soleil [parsɔlɛj] *m invar* sun visor

paresse [parɛs] *f* laziness

paresser [parese] *intr* (coll) to loaf

pares·seux [parɛsø] **-seuse** [søz] *adj* lazy ‖ *mf* lazy person, lazybones; malingerer ‖ *m* (zool) sloth

par ex. *abbr* (**par exemple**) e.g.

parfaire [parfɛr] §29 *tr* to perfect; make up (*e.g., a sum of money*)

par·fait [parfɛ] **-faite** [fɛt] *adj & m* perfect ‖ **parfait** *interj* fine!, excellent!

parfaitement [parfɛtmɑ̃] *adv* perfectly; completely; certainly, of course

parfois [parfwa] *adv* sometimes

parfum [parfœ̃] *m* perfume; aroma; bouquet (*of wines*); flavor (*of ice cream*); **au parfum** in the know

parfumer [parfyme] *tr* to perfume; flavor ‖ *ref* to use perfume

parfumerie [parfymri] *f* perfume shop; perfumery

pari [pari] *m* bet, wager

paria [parja] *m* pariah

parier [parje] §97 *tr & intr* to bet, wager

Paris [pari] *m* Paris

pari·sien [parizjẽ] **-sienne** [zjɛn] *adj* Parisian ‖ (*cap*) *mf* Parisian

parité [parite] *f* parity; likeness; evenness (*of numbers*)

parjure [parʒyr] *adj* perjured ‖ *mf* perjurer ‖ *m* perjury

parking [parkiŋ] *m* parking lot

par·lant [parlɑ̃] **-lante** [lɑ̃t] *adj* speaking; talking (*e.g., picture*); eloquent, expressive

parlement [parləmɑ̃] *m* parliament

parlementaire [parləmɑ̃tɛr] *adj* parliamentary ‖ *mf* peace envoy; member of a parliament, legislator

parlementer [parləmɑ̃te] *intr* to parley

parler [parle] *m* speech, way of speaking; dialect ‖ §97, §98 *tr & intr* to speak, talk; **tu parles Charles!** you don't say!

par·leur [parlœr] **-leuse** [løz] *mf*—**beau parleur** good talker; windbag

parloir [parlwar] *m* reception room

parlote [parlɔt] *f* (coll) talk, gossip, rumor

parmi [parmi] *prep* among

Parnasse [parnɑs] *m*—**le Parnasse** Parnassus (*poetry*); Mount Parnassus

parodie [parɔdi] *f* parody, travesty

parodier [parɔdje] *tr* to parody, travesty

paroi [parwa] *f* partition, wall; inner side; (anat) wall

paroisse [parwas] *f* parish

parois·sial -siale [parwasjal] *adj* (*pl* **-siaux** [sjo]) parochial, parish

parois·sien [parwasjẽ] **-sienne** [sjɛn] *mf* parishioner ‖ *m* prayer book; (coll) fellow

parole [parɔl] *f* word; speech; word, promise; **avoir la parole** to have the floor; **donner la parole à** to recognize, to give the floor to; **sur parole** on one's word

paro·lier [parɔlje] **-lière** [ljɛr] *mf* lyricist; librettist

parpaing [parpẽ] *m* concrete block; building block

parquer [parke] *tr* to park; pen in ‖ *intr* to be penned in ‖ *ref* to park

Parque [park] *f* (lit) destiny, death; **les Parques** (myth) the Fates

parquet [parkɛ] *m* parquet, floor; floor (*of stock exchange*); public prosecutor's office

parqueter [parkəte] §34 *tr* to parquet, floor

parrain [parẽ] *m* godfather; sponsor

parrainer [parene] *tr* to sponsor

parricide [parisid] *mf* parricide, patricide (*person*) ‖ *m* parricide, patricide (*act*)

parsemer [parsəme] §2 *tr* to sprinkle; spangle

part [par] *m* newborn child; dropping (*of young by animal in labor*) ‖ *f* part, share; **aller quelque part** (coll) to go to the toilet; **à part** aside; aside from; **à part entière** with full privileges; **autre part** elsewhere; **avoir part au gâteau** (coll) to have a slice of the pie; **d'autre part** besides; **de la part de** on the part of, from; **de part en part** through and through; **de toutes parts** on all sides; **d'une part . . . d'autre part** on the one hand . . . on the other hand; **faire la part de** to make allowance for; **faire part de** to announce; **faire part de q.ch. à qn** to inform s.o. of s.th.; **nulle part** nowhere; **nulle part ailleurs** nowhere else; **pour ma part** as for me, for my part; **prendre en bonne part** to take good-naturedly; **prendre en mauvaise part** to take offense at; **prendre part à** to take part in; **quelque part** somewhere

partage [partaʒ] *m* division, partition; sharing; share; tie vote; **échoir en partage à qn** to fall to s.o.'s lot; **partage de temps** (comp) time sharing

partager [partaʒe] §38 *tr* to share; divide

partance [partɑ̃s] *f* departure; **en partance** leaving; **en partance pour** bound for

partant [partɑ̃] *m* (sports) starter; **partants** departing guests, departing travelers, etc. ‖ *adv* (lit) consequently

partenaire [partənɛr] *mf* partner; sparring partner

parterre [partɛr] *m* orchestra circle; flower bed

parti [parti] *m* party; side; match, good catch; **faire un mauvais parti à** to rough up; to mistreat; **parti pris** fixed opinion; prejudice; **prendre le parti de** to decide to; **prendre le parti de qn** to take s.o.'s side; **prendre parti** to take sides; **prendre son parti** to make up one's mind; **prendre son parti de** to resign oneself to; **tirer parti de** to take advantage of

par·tial -tiale [parsjal] *adj* (*pl* -tiaux [sjo]) partial, biased

partici·pant [partisipɑ̃] -pante [pɑ̃t] *adj & mf* participant

participation [partisipasjɔ̃] *f* participation

participe [partisip] *m* participle

participer [partisipe] *intr*—**participer à** to participate in; **participer de** to partake of

particulariser [partikylarize] *tr* to specify ‖ *ref* to make oneself conspicuous

particularité [partikylarite] *f* peculiarity; detail

particule [partikyl] *f* particle

particu·lier [partikylje] -lière [ljɛr] *adj* particular; special; private ‖ *mf* private citizen; (coll) odd person ‖ *m* particular

particulièrement [partikyljɛrmɑ̃] *adv* particularly

partie [parti] *f* part; line, specialty; game; winning score; contest; party (*diversion*); (law) party; **avoir partie liée avec** to be in league with; **faire partie de** to belong to; **faire partie intégrante de** to be part

and parcel of; **partie civile** plaintiff; **partie de chasse** hunting party; **partie de plaisir** outing, picnic; **partie nulle** tie game; **prendre à partie** to take to task

par·tiel -tielle [parsjɛl] *adj* partial

partir [partir] (used only in *inf*) *tr*—**avoir maille à partir** to have a bone to pick ‖ §64, §95, §96 *intr* (*aux:* ÊTRE) to leave; go off (*said of firearm*); begin; **à partir de** from; from . . . on, e.g., **à partir de maintenant** from now on; **faire partir** to send off; remove (*a spot*); set off (*an explosive*); fire (*a gun*); **partir + inf** to leave in order to + *inf;* **partir de** to come from; start with; **partir pour** or **à** to leave for

parti·san [partizɑ̃] -sane [zan] *adj & mf* partisan

partition [partisjɔ̃] *f* (mus) score

partout [partu] *adv* everywhere; **partout ailleurs** anywhere else; everywhere else; **partout où** wherever; everywhere

parure [paryr] *f* ornament; set; finery; necklace

parution [parysjɔ̃] *f* appearance, publication

parvenir [parvənir] §72, §96 *intr* (*aux:* ÊTRE)—**parvenir à** to reach; **parvenir à** + *inf* to succeed in + *ger*

parve·nu -nue [parvəny] *adj & mf* upstart

parvis [parvi] *m* square (*in front of a church*)

pas [pɑ] *m* step; pace; footprint; footfall; pass; straits; pitch (*of screw*); **allonger le pas** to quicken one's pace; to put one's best foot forward; **à pas comptés** with measured tread; **à pas de loup, à pas feutrés** stealthily; **à pas de tortue** at a snail's pace; **à quatre pas** nearby; **au pas** at a walk; **céder le pas (à)** to stand aside (for); to keep clear (*in front of a driveway*); **de ce pas** at once; **être au pas** to be in step; **faire le premier pas** to make the first move; **faire les cent pas** to come and go; **faux pas** misstep; blunder; **marcher sur les pas de** to follow in the footsteps of; **marquer le pas** to mark time; **mauvais pas** tight squeeze, fix; **pas à pas** little by little, cautiously; **pas d'armes** passage at arms; **Pas de Calais** Straits of Dover; **pas de cheval** hoofbeat; **pas de clerc** blunder; **pas de deux** two-step; **pas de la porte** doorstep; **pas de l'oie** goosestep; **pas de porte** (com) price paid for good will; **prendre le pas sur** to get ahead of ‖ *adv*—**ne . . . pas** §90 not, e.g., **je ne sais pas** I do not know; e.g., **ne pas signer** to not sign; (used with **non**), e.g., **non pas** no; (used without **ne**) (slang) not, e.g., **je fais pas de politique** I don't meddle in politics; **n'est-ce pas?** see **ne; pas?** (coll) not so?; **pas de** no; **pas du tout** not at all; **pas encore** not yet

pas·cal -cale [paskal] *adj* (*pl* -caux [ko]) Passover; Easter

passable [pɑsabl] *adj* passable, fair; mediocre, so-so

passade [pɑsad] *f* passing fancy

passage [pɑsaʒ] *m* passage; crossing; pass; **barrer le passage** to block the way; **du passage** in passing, in parentheses; **livrer passage à** to let through; **passage à niveau** grade crossing; **passage au-dessous de la voie, passage souterrain** underpass; **passage au-dessus de la voie** overpass; **passage clouté, passage zébré** pedestrian crossing; **passage de vitesses** gear shifting; **passage interdit** (*public sign*) do not enter; (*public sign*) no thoroughfare; **passage protégé** arterial crossing (*vehicles intersecting highway must stop*)

passa·ger [pɑsaʒe] **-gère** [ʒɛr] *adj* passing, fleeting; migratory; busy (*road*) ‖ *mf* passenger; **passager clandestin, passager de cale** stowaway; **passager d'entrepont** steerage passenger

pas·sant [pɑsɑ̃] **-sante** [sɑ̃t] *adj* busy (*street*) ‖ *mf* passer-by

passation [pɑsasjɔ̃] *f* handing over

passavant [pɑsavɑ̃] *m* permit; (naut) gangway

passe [pɑs] *m* master key ‖ *f* pass; channel; **être en bonne passe de** to be in a fair way to; **être en passe de** to be about to; **mauvaise passe** tight spot

pas·sé -sée [pɑse] *adj* past; faded; overripe; last (*week*) ‖ *m* past; past tense ‖ **passé** *prep* past, beyond, after

passe-bouillon [pɑsbujɔ̃] *m invar* soup strainer

passe-droit [pɑsdrwa] *m* (*pl* **-droits**) illegal favor; injustice

passe-lacet [pɑslasɛ] *m* (*pl* **-lacets**) bodkin

passe-lait [pɑslɛ] *m invar* milk strainer

passe-lettres [pɑslɛtr] *m* (*pl* **-lettres**) letter drop

passement [pɑsmɑ̃] *m* braid, trimming

passementer [pɑsmɑ̃te] *tr* to trim

passementerie [pɑsmɑ̃tri] *f* trimmings

passe-montagne [pɑsmɔ̃taɲ] *m* (*pl* **-montagnes**) storm hood, ski mask

passe-partout [pɑspartu] *m invar* master key; slip mount

passe-passe [pɑspɑs] *m invar* legerdemain; sleight of hand

passepoil [pɑspwal] *m* piping, braid

passeport [pɑspɔr] *m* passport

passer [pɑse] §96 *tr* to pass; ferry; get across (*e.g., a river*); spend, pass (*e.g., the evening*); take (*an exam*); slip on (*e.g., a dressing gown*); show (*a film*); make (*a telephone call*); go on (*one's way*); **passer q.ch. à qn** to hand or lend s.o. s.th.; forgive s.o. s.th. ‖ *intr* (*aux:* AVOIR or ÊTRE) to pass; pass away; become; **en passer par là** to knuckle under; **faire passer** to get (*e.g., a message*) through; while away (*the time*); **passer à** to pass over to; **passer chez** or **passer voir** to drop in on; **passer outre à** to override; **passer par** to pass through, go through; **passer pour** to pass for or as; **passons!** let's skip it! ‖ §97 *ref* to happen, take place; **se passer de** to do without

passe·reau [pɑsro] *m* (*pl* **-reaux**) sparrow

passerelle [pɑsrɛl] *f* footbridge; gangplank; (naut) bridge; **passerelle couverte extensible** (aer) enclosed swinging gangplank; **passerelle télescopique** telescopic corridor

passe-temps [pɑstɑ̃] *m invar* pastime, hobby

passe-thé [pɑste] *m invar* tea strainer

pas·seur [pɑsœr] **-seuse** [søz] *mf* smuggler ‖ *m* ferryman

passible [pɑsibl] *adj*—**passible de** liable for, subject to

pas·sif [pɑsif] **-sive** [siv] *adj* passive ‖ *m* passive; debts, liabilities

passiflore [pɑsiflɔr] *f* passionflower

passion [pɑsjɔ̃], [pɑsjɔ̃] *f* passion

passion·nant [pɑsjɔnɑ̃] **-nante** [nɑ̃t] *adj* thrilling, fascinating

passion·né -née [pɑsjɔne] *adj* passionate; impassioned; **passionné de** or **pour** passionately fond of ‖ *mf* enthusiast, fan

passion·nel -nelle [pɑsjɔnɛl] *adj* of passion, of jealousy

passionner [pɑsjɔne] *tr* to excite the interest of, arouse ‖ *ref*—**se passionner pour** or **à** to be passionately fond of

passoire [pɑswar] *f* colander; strainer; (fig) sieve

pastel [pɑstɛl] *m* pastel; (bot) woad

pastèque [pɑstɛk] *f* watermelon

pasteur [pɑstœr] *m* pastor, minister; shepherd

pasteuriser [pɑstœrize] *tr* to pasteurize

pastiche [pɑstiʃ] *m* pastiche; parody

pastille [pɑstij] *f* lozenge, drop; tire patch; polka dot; (comp) chip; **pastille pectorale** cough drop

pasto·ral -rale [pɑstɔral] (*pl* **-raux** [ro] **-rales**) *adj & f* pastoral

pastorat [pɑstɔra] *m* pastorate

pat [pat] *adj invar* (chess) in stalemate; **faire pat** to stalemate ‖ *m* (chess) stalemate

patache [pataʃ] *f* police boat; (coll) rattletrap

patachon [pataʃɔ̃] *m*—**mener une vie de patachon** to lead a wild life

patapouf [patapuf] *m* (coll) roly-poly ‖ *interj* flop!

pataquès [patakɛs] *m* faulty liaison; blooper, goof

patate [patat] *f* sweet potato; (coll) spud

patati [patati]—**et patati et patata** (coll) and so on and on

patatras [patatra] *interj* bang!, crash!

pa·taud [pato] **-taude** [tod] *adj* clumsy, loutish ‖ *mf* lout

pataugeoire [patoʒwar] *f* wading pool

patauger [patoʒe] §38 *intr* to splash; to wade; (coll) to flounder

pâte [pat] *f* paste; dough, batter; **en pâte** (typ) pied; **mettre la main à la pâte** to put one's shoulder to the wheel; **pâte à papier** wood pulp; **pâte brisée, pâte feuilletée** puff paste; **pâte dentifrice** toothpaste; **pâte molle** spineless person; **pâtes alimentaires** pastas (*macaroni,*

noodles, spaghetti, etc.); **peindre à la pâte** to paint with a full brush; **une bonne pâte d'homme** (coll) a good sort
pâté [pɑte] *m* blot, splotch; (typ) pi; **pâté de foie gras** minced goose livers; **pâté de maisons** block of houses; **pâté en croûte** meat or fish pie; **pâté maison** chef's-special pâté
pâtée [pɑte] *f* dog food, cat food; chicken feed
pate·lin [patlɛ̃] **-line** [lin] *adj* fawning, wheedling ‖ *m* wheedler; (coll) native village
patenôtre [patnotr] *f* prayer; (archaic) mumbo jumbo
pa·tent [patɑ̃] **-tente** [tɑ̃t] *adj* patent ‖ *f* license; tax; **patente (de santé)** (naut) bill of health
paten·té -tée [patɑ̃te] *adj* licensed ‖ *mf* licensed dealer
patenter [patɑ̃te] *tr* to license
Pater [patɛr] *m invar* Lord's Prayer
patère [patɛr] *f* clothes hook; curtain hook
paterne [patɛrn] *adj* mawkish, mealy-mouthed
pater·nel -nelle [patɛrnɛl] *adj* paternal; fatherly ‖ *m* (slang) pop, dad
paternité [patɛrnite] *f* paternity; fatherhood; authorship
pâ·teux [patø] **-teuse** [tøz] *adj* pasty; thick; coated (*tongue*)
pathétique [patetik] *adj* pathetic ‖ *m* pathos
pathologie [patɔlɔʒi] *f* pathology
pathos [patos] *m* bathos
patibulaire [patibylɛr] *adj* hangdog (*look*)
patience [pasjɑ̃s] *f* patience
pa·tient [pasjɑ̃] **-tiente** [sjɑ̃t] *adj & mf* patient
patienter [pasjɑ̃te] *intr* to be patient
patin [patɛ̃] *m* skate; runner; sill, sleeper; (*sole*) patten; (aer) skid; (rr) base, flange (*of rails*); **patin à glace** ice skate; **patin à roulettes** roller skate; **patin de frein** brake shoe
patiner [patine] *intr* to skate; slide; skid
patinette [patinɛt] *f* scooter
pati·neur [patinœr] **-neuse** [nøz] *mf* skater
patinoire [patinwar] *f* skating rink
patio [patjo], [pasjo] *m* patio
pâtir [pɑtir] *intr*—**pâtir de** to suffer from
pâtisserie [pɑtisri] *f* pastry; pastry shop; pastry making
pâtis·sier [pɑtisje] **-sière** [sjɛr] *mf* pastry cook; proprietor of a pastry shop
patoche [patɔʃ] *f* (coll) hand, paw
patois [patwa] *m* patois; jargon, lingo
patouiller [patuje] *tr* (coll) to paw, maul ‖ *intr* (coll) to splash
patraque [patrak] *adj* in bad shape ‖ *f* (coll) turnip (*old watch*)
pâtre [pɑtr] *m* herdsman
patriarche [patrijarʃ] *m* patriarch
patrice [patris] *m* patrician; **Patrice** Patrick
patri·cien [patrisjɛ̃] **-cienne** [sjɛn] *adj & mf* patrician
patrie [patri] *f* native land, fatherland
patrimoine [patrimwan] *m* patrimony

patrio·tard [patrijɔtar] **-tarde** [tard] *adj* flag-waving, chauvinistic
patriote [patrijɔt] *adj* patriotic ‖ *mf* patriot
patriotique [patrijɔtik] *adj* patriotic
patriotisme [patrijɔtism] *m* patriotism
pa·tron [patrɔ̃] **-tronne** [trɔn] *mf* patron saint; proprietor; boss; sponsor ‖ *m* pattern, model; captain, skipper; coxswain; master, lord; medium size; **grand patron** large size; **patron à jours** stencil; **patron de thèse** thesis sponsor ‖ *f* mistress of the house; (slang) better half
patronage [patrɔnaʒ] *m* patronage, protection; sponsorship; (eccl) social center
patronat [patrɔna] *m* management
patronner [patrɔne] *tr* to patronize, protect; sponsor; stencil
patrouille [patruj] *f* patrol
patrouiller [patruje] *intr* to patrol
patte [pat] *f* paw; foot (*of bird*); leg (*of insect*); flap, tab; hook; (coll) hand, foot, or leg (*of person*); **à pattes d'éléphant** bell-bottom (*trousers*); **à quatre pattes** on all fours; **faire patte de velours** (coll) to pull in one's claws; **graisser la patte à** (coll) to grease the palm of; **patte d'épaule** shoulder strap; **pattes de mouche** (coll) scrawl
patte-d'oie [patdwa] *f* (*pl* **pattes-d'oie**) crow's-foot; crossroads; (bot) goosefoot
pattemouille [patmuj] *f* damp cloth
pâturage [pɑtyraʒ] *m* pasture; pasturage; pasture rights
pâture [pɑtyr] *f* fodder; pasture; (fig) food
paume [pom] *f* palm; (archaic) tennis
pau·mé -mée [pome] *adj* (coll) lost
paupière [popjɛr] *f* eyelid
pause [poz] *f* pause; (mus) full rest; **pause café** coffee break
pauvre [povr] *adj* poor; **pauvre de moi!** woe is me!; **pauvre d'esprit** (coll) dimwitted ‖ (when standing before noun) *adj* poor, wretched; late (*deceased*) ‖ *mf* pauper; **les pauvres** the poor
pauvreté [povrəte] *f* poverty
P.A.V. [peave] *adj* (letterword) (**payable avec préavis**) person-to-person (*telephone call*)
pavaner [pavane] *ref* to strut
pavé [pave] *m* pavement, street; paving stone; paving block; (culin) slab; **sur le pavé** pounding the streets, out of work
pavement [pavmɑ̃] *m* paving (*act*); mosaic or marble flooring
paver [pave] *tr* to pave
pavillon [pavijɔ̃] *m* pavilion; tent, canopy; lodge, one-story house; wing, pavilion; hospital ward; flag; bell (*of trumpet*); **amener son pavillon** to strike one's colors; **baisser pavillon** to knuckle under; **pavillon de chasse** hunting lodge; **pavillon des sports** field house; **pavillon noir** Jolly Roger
pavois [pavwa] *m* shield; **élever sur le pavois** to extol
pavoiser [pavwaze] *tr* to deck out with bunting, decorate

pavot [pavo] *m* poppy
payable [pɛjabl] *adj* payable
payant [pɛjɑ̃] **payante** [pɛjɑ̃t] *adj* paying
paye [pɛj] *f* pay, wages
payement [pɛjmɑ̃] *m* payment
payer [peje] §49 *tr* to pay; pay for; **payer comptant** to pay cash for; **payer de retour** to pay back; **payer q.ch. à qn** to pay s.o. for s.th.; pay for s.th. for s.o.; **payer qn de q.ch.** to pay s.o. for s.th.; **payer rubis sur l'ongle** to pay down on the nail ‖ *intr* to pay; **paye et prends** cash and carry ‖ *ref* to treat oneself to; take what is due; **pouvoir se payer** to be able to afford; **se payer de** to be satisfied with
pays [pei] *m* country; region; town; (coll) fellow countryman; **du pays** local; **le pays de** the land of; **pays de cocagne** land of milk and honey
paysage [peizaʒ] *m* landscape, scenery; (painting) landscape
paysagiste [peizaʒist] *m* landscape painter
pay·san [peizɑ̃] **-sane** [zan] *adj & mf* peasant
Pays-Bas [peibɑ], [pɛibɑ] *mpl*—**les Pays-Bas** The Netherlands
payse [peiz] *f* countrywoman
P.C. [pese] *m* (letterword) (**parti communiste**) Communist party; (**poste de commandement**) command post
P.c.c. *abbr* (**pour copie conforme**) certified copy
p.c.v. or **P.C.V.** [peseve] *m* (letterword) (**payable chez vous**) or (**à percevoir**)—**téléphoner en p.c.v.** to telephone collect
péage [peaʒ] *m* toll
peau [po] *f* (*pl* **peaux**) skin; pelt; hide; film (*on milk*); (slang) bag, whore; **entrer dans la peau d'un personnage** (theat) to get right inside a part; **faire peau neuve** to turn over a new leaf; **la peau!** (slang) nothing doing!; **peau d'âne** (coll) sheepskin; **peau de tambour** drumhead; **vendre la peau de l'ours avant de l'avoir tué** to count one's chickens before they are hatched
peau-rouge [poruʒ] *mf* (*pl* **peaux-rouges**) redskin
pêche [pɛʃ] *f* peach; fishing; **pêche à la mouche noyée** fly casting; **pêche au coup** fishing with hook, line, and pole; **pêche au lancer** casting; **pêche sous-marine** deep-sea fishing; **pêche sportive** fishing with a fly rod or casting rod
péché [peʃe] *m* sin
pécher [peʃe] §10 *intr* to sin
pêcher [peʃe] *m* peach tree ‖ *tr* to fish, fish for; (coll) to get ‖ *intr* to fish; **pêcher à la mouche** to fly-fish
pêcherie [pɛʃri] *f* fishery
pé·cheur [peʃœr] **-cheresse** [ʃrɛs] *mf* sinner
pê·cheur [pɛʃœr] **-cheuse** [ʃøz] *mf* fisher; **pêcheur de perles** pearl diver ‖ *m* fisherman
pécore [pekɔr] *f* (coll) silly goose
pecque [pɛk] *f* (coll) silly affected woman
péculat [pekyla] *m* embezzlement

pécule [pekyl] *m* nest egg
pédagogie [pedagoʒi] *f* pedagogy, education
pédagogue [pedagɔg] *adj* pedagogical ‖ *mf* pedagogue; teacher
pédale [pedal] *f* pedal; treadle; (slang) pederast; **de la pédale** gay, homosexual; **pédale d'embrayage** (aut) clutch pedal
pédaler [pedale] *intr* to pedal; **pédaler dans la choucroute** (slang) to be mixed up
pédalier [pedalje] *m* pedal keyboard; pedal and sprocket-wheel assembly
pédalo [pedalo] *m* water bicycle
pé·dant [pedɑ̃] **-dante** [dɑ̃t] *adj* pedantic ‖ *mf* pedant
pédanterie [pedɑ̃tri] *f* pedantry
pédantesque [pedɑ̃tɛsk] *adj* pedantic
pédé [pede] *m* (slang) queer (*homosexual*)
pédéraste [pederast] *m* pederast, male homosexual
pédestre [pedɛstr] *adj* on foot
pédiatrie [pedjatri] *f* pediatrics
pédicure [pedikyr] *mf* chiropodist
pedigree [pedigri] *m* pedigree
Pégase [pegɑz] *m* Pegasus
pègre [pɛgr] *f* underworld
peigne [pɛɲ] *m* comb; card (*for wool*); reed (*of loom*); (zool) scallop
peigner [peɲe] *tr* to comb; to card ‖ *ref* to comb one's hair
peignez [peɲe] *v* (**peignons**) see **peindre**; see **peigner**
peignoir [peɲwar] *m* bathrobe; dressing gown, peignoir
peindre [pɛ̃dr] §50 *tr & intr* to paint
peine [pɛn] *f* pain; trouble; difficulty; penalty; **à peine** hardly, scarcely; **en être pour sa peine** to have nothing to show for one's trouble; **faire (de la) peine à** to grieve; **faire peine à voir** to be pathetic; **peine capitale** capital punishment; **peine de cœur** heartache; **peine de mort** death penalty; **peine pécuniaire** financial distress; **purger sa peine** to serve one's sentence; **valoir la peine** to be worth while; **veuillez vous donner la peine de** please be so kind as to
peiner [pene] *tr* to pain, grieve; fatigue ‖ *intr* to labor
peint [pɛ̃] **peinte** [pɛ̃t] *v* see **peindre**
peintre [pɛ̃tr] *m* painter
peinture [pɛ̃tyr] *f* paint; painting; **attention à la peinture** (*public sign*) wet paint; **je ne peux pas le voir en peinture** (coll) I can't stand him
peinturer [pɛ̃tyre] *tr* to lay a coat of paint on; to daub
peinturlurer [pɛ̃tyrlyre] *tr* (coll) to paint in all the colors of the rainbow
péjora·tif [peʒɔratif] **-tive** [tiv] *adj & m* pejorative
pékin [pekɛ̃] *m* pekin; **en pékin** (slang) in civies; **Pékin** Peking
péki·nois [pekinwa] **-noise** [nwaz] *adj* Pekingese ‖ *m* Pekingese (*language; dog*) ‖ (*cap*) *mf* Pekingese (*inhabitant*)
pelage [pəlaʒ] *m* coat (*of animal*)
pe·lé **-lée** [pəle] *adj* bald; bare

pêle-mêle [pɛlmɛl] *m invar* jumble ‖ *adv* pell-mell

peler [pəle] §2 *tr, intr,* & *ref* to peel, peel off

pèle·rin [pɛlrɛ̃] **-rine** [rin] *mf* pilgrim ‖ *m* peregrine falcon; basking shark ‖ *f* see **pèlerine**

pèlerinage [pɛlrinaʒ] *m* pilgrimage

pèlerine [pɛlrin] *f* pelerine, cape; hooded cape

péliade [peljad] *f* adder

pélican [pelikɑ̃] *m* pelican

pellagre [pelagr] *f* pellagra

pelle [pɛl] *f* shovel; scoop; **pelle à poussière** dustpan; **pelle à vapeur** steam shovel; **pelle mécanique** power shovel; **ramasser à la pelle** to shovel, to shovel up

pelletée [pɛlte] *f* shovelful

pelleter [pɛlte] §34 *tr* to shovel

pelleterie [pɛltri] *f* fur trade; skin, pelt

pelleteuse [pɛltøz] *f* power shovel

pellicule [pelikyl] *f* film; pellicle; speck of dandruff; (phot) film; **pellicules** dandruff

pelote [plɔt] *f* ball (*of string, of snow, etc.*); **faire sa pelote** (coll) to make one's pile; **pelote basque** pelota; **pelote d'épingles** pincushion

peloter [plɔte] *tr* to wind into a ball; (fig) to flatter; (slang) to feel up, to paw ‖ *intr* to bat the ball back and forth

pelo·teur [plɔtœr] **-teuse** [tøz] *adj* flattering, ingratiating; (coll) fresh, amorous, spoony ‖ *mf* (coll) masher, spooner

peloton [plɔtɔ̃] *m* little ball (*e.g., of wool*); group (*of racers*); (mil) platoon, troop, detachment; **peloton d'exécution** firing squad

pelotonner [plɔtɔne] *tr* to wind into a ball ‖ *ref* to curl up, snuggle

pelouse [pluz] *f* lawn; (golf) green

peluche [plyʃ] *f* plush; lint

pelure [plyr] *f* peel, peeling, skin; rind; (coll) coat

pénaliser [penalize] *tr* to penalize

pénalité [penalite] *f* penalty

pe·naud [pəno] **-naude** [nod] *adj* bashful, shy; shamefaced; crestfallen

penchant [pɑ̃ʃɑ̃] *m* penchant, bent

pen·ché -chée [pɑ̃ʃe] *adj* leaning; stooping; bent over

pencher [pɑ̃ʃe] §96 *tr, intr,* & *ref* to lean, bend, incline; **se pencher sur** to make a close study of

pendable [pɑ̃dabl] *adj* outrageous; (archaic) hangable

pendaison [pɑ̃dɛzɔ̃] *f* hanging

pen·dant [pɑ̃dɑ̃] **-dante** [dɑ̃t] *adj* hanging; pending ‖ *m* pendant; counterpart; **pendant d'oreille** eardrop; **se faire pendant** to make a pair ‖ **pendant** *adv*—**pendant que** while ‖ **pendant** *prep* during

pendeloque [pɑ̃dlɔk] *f* pendant; jewel (*of eardrop*)

pendentif [pɑ̃dɑ̃tif] *m* pendant; eardrop; lavaliere

penderie [pɑ̃dri] *f* clothes closet

pendoir [pɑ̃dwar] *m* meat hook

pendre [pɑ̃dr] *tr* to hang; hang up; **être pendu à** to hang on (*e.g., the telephone*) ‖ *intr* to hang; hang down; sag; **ça lui pend au nez** he's got it coming to him ‖ *ref* to hang oneself; **se pendre à** to hang on to

pen·du -due [pɑ̃dy] *adj* hanging; hanged ‖ *mf* hanged person

pendule [pɑ̃dyl] *m* pendulum ‖ *f* clock; **pendule à pile** battery clock

pêne [pɛn] *m* bolt; latch

pénétration [penetrasjɔ̃] *f* penetration; permeation

pénétrer [penetre] §10 *tr* to penetrate, permeate ‖ *intr* to penetrate; enter ‖ *ref* to mix; **se pénétrer de** to become imbued with

pénible [penibl] *adj* hard, painful

péniche [peniʃ] *f* barge; houseboat; **péniche de débarquement** landing craft

pénicilline [penisilin] *f* penicillin

pé·nien [penjɛ̃] **-nienne** [njɛn] *adj* penile, penis

péninsulaire [penɛ̃sylɛr] *adj* peninsular

péninsule [penɛ̃syl] *f* large peninsula

pénis [penis] *m* penis

pénitence [penitɑ̃s] *f* penitence; penalty (*in games*); punishment; **en pénitence** in disgrace; **faire pénitence** to do penance

pénitencier [penitɑ̃sje] *m* penitentiary; penal colony

péni·tent [penitɑ̃] **-tente** [tɑ̃t] *adj* & *mf* penitent

penne [pɛn] *f* quill, feather

Pennsylvanie [pɛnsilvani] *f* Pennsylvania; **la Pennsylvanie** Pennsylvania

pénombre [penɔ̃br] *f* penumbra; half-light; **dans la pénombre** out of the limelight

pense-bête [pɑ̃sbɛt] *m* (*pl* **-bêtes**) (coll) reminder

pensée [pɑ̃se] *f* thought; thinking; (bot) pansy

penser [pɑ̃se] §95 *tr* to think; **penser de** to think of (*to have as an opinion of*); **penser + inf** to intend to + *inf* ‖ *intr* to think; **penser à** to think of (*to direct one's thoughts toward*); **y penser** to think of it, e.g., **pendant que j'y pense** while I think of it

penseur [pɑ̃sœr] *m* thinker

pen·sif [pɑ̃sif] **-sive** [siv] *adj* pensive; absentminded

pension [pɑ̃sjɔ̃] *f* pension (*annuity; room and board; boardinghouse*); **avec pension complète** with three meals; **pension alimentaire** alimony; **pension de famille** residential hotel; **pension de retraite, pension viagère** annuity; **prendre pension** to board; **sans pension** without meals

pensionnaire [pɑ̃sjɔnɛr] *mf* boarder; guest (*in hotel*); resident student ‖ *f* naïve woman or girl

pensionnat [pɑ̃sjɔna] *m* boarding school

pension·né -née [pɑ̃sjɔne] *adj* pensioned ‖ *mf* pensioner

pensionner [pɑ̃sjɔne] *tr* to pension

pensum [pɛ̃sɔm] *m* thankless task

Pentagone [pɛ̃tagɔn] *m* Pentagon

pente [pɑ̃t] *f* slope; inclination, bent; fall (*of river*); **en pente** sloping
Pentecôte [pɑ̃tkot] *f*—**la Pentecôte** Pentecost, Whitsunday
pénultième [penyltjɛm] *adj* next to the last ‖ *f* penult
pénurie [penyri] *f* lack, shortage
pépé [pepe] *m* (slang) grandpa
pépée [pepe] *f* doll; (slang) doll
pépère [pepɛr] *adj* (coll) easygoing ‖ *m* grandpa; (coll) old duffer; (coll) overgrown boy
pépètes [pepɛt] *fpl* (slang) dough
pépie [pepi] *f* (vet) pip; **avoir le pépie** (coll) to be thirsty
pépiement [pepimɑ̃] *m* chirp
pépier [pepje] *intr* to chirp
pépin [pepɛ̃] *m* pip, seed; (coll) umbrella; **avoir un pépin** (coll) to strike a snag
pépinière [pepinjɛr] *f* (hort) nursery; (fig) training school; (fig) hotbed
pépiniériste [pepinjerist] *m* nurseryman
pépite [pepit] *f* nugget
péque·naud [pɛkno] **-naude** [nod] *adj & mf* (slang) peasant
péquenot [pɛkno] *m* (slang) peasant
perçage [pɛrsaʒ] *m* drilling, boring
per·çant [pɛrsɑ̃] **-çante** [sɑ̃t] *adj* piercing, penetrating
perce [pɛrs] *f* drill, bore; **en perce** on tap
percée [pɛrse] *f* opening, gap; clearing; breakthrough; discovery
perce-neige [pɛrsənɛʒ] *m invar* (bot) snowdrop
percepteur [pɛrsɛptœr] *m* tax collector
perceptible [pɛrsɛptibl] *adj* perceptible; collectable, payable
perception [pɛrsɛpsjɔ̃] *f* perception; tax collection; tax; tax department, bureau of internal revenue
percer [pɛrse] §51 *tr* to pierce; drill; tap (*a barrel*); break through ‖ *intr* to come through or out; burst (*said, e.g., of abscess*); to make a name for oneself
perceuse [pɛrsøz] *f* drill; machine drill
percevoir [pɛrsəvwar] §59 *tr* to perceive; collect
perche [pɛrʃ] *f* pole; (ichth) perch; (sports) pole vaulting; (coll) beanpole; **perche à sauter** vaulting pole; **perche à son** microphone stand; **tendre la perche à** to lend a helping hand to
percher [pɛrʃe] *tr* to perch ‖ *intr* to perch, roost
perchoir [pɛrʃwar] *m* perch
per·clus [pɛrkly] **-cluse** [klyz] *adj* crippled, paralyzed
percolateur [pɛrkɔlatœr] *m* large coffee maker
percuter [pɛrkyte] *tr* to strike; crash into; percuss ‖ *intr* to crash
percuteur [pɛrkytœr] *m* firing pin
per·dant [pɛrdɑ̃] **-dante** [dɑ̃t] *adj* losing ‖ *mf* loser
perdition [pɛrdisjɔ̃] *f* perdition; **en perdition** (naut) in distress

perdre [pɛrdrə] §96 *tr* to lose; ruin ‖ *intr* to lose; leak; deterioriate ‖ *ref* to get lost; disappear
per·dreau [pɛrdro] *m* (*pl* **-dreaux**) young partridge
perdrix [pɛrdri] *f* partridge
per·du -due [pɛrdy] *adj* lost; spare (*time*); stray (*bullet*); remote (*locality*); advance (*sentry*)
père [pɛr] *m* father; senior, e.g., **M. Martin père** Mr. Martin, senior; **père de famille** head of the household; **père spirituel** father confessor
péremptoire [perɑ̃ptwar] *adj* peremptory
péréquation [perekwasjɔ̃] *f* equalizing
perfection [pɛrfɛksjɔ̃] *f* perfection
perfectionner [pɛrfɛksjɔne] *tr* to perfect ‖ *ref* to improve
perfide [pɛrfid] *adj* perfidious ‖ *mf* treacherous person
perfidie [pɛrfidi] *f* perfidy
perforation [pɛrfɔrasjɔ̃] *f* perforation; puncture
perforatrice [pɛrfɔratris] *f* pneumatic drill; perforator; keypunch (machine)
perforer [pɛrfɔre] *tr* to perforate; drill, bore; punch (*a card*)
performance [pɛrfɔrmɑ̃s] *f* (sports) performance
pergélisol [pɛrʒelisɔl] *m* permafrost
péricliter [periklite] *intr* to fail
péril [peril] *m* peril
péril·leux [perijø] **-leuse** [jøz] *adj* perilous
péri·mé -mée [perime] *adj* expired, elapsed; out-of-date
périmer [perime] *intr & ref* to lapse
période [perjɔd] *f* period; (phys) cycle; (phys) half-life
périodique [perjɔdik] *adj* periodic(al)
péripétie [peripesi] *f* vicissitude
périphérie [periferi] *f* periphery
périphérique [periferik] *adj* peripheral
périple [peripl] *m* journey
périr [perir] *intr* to perish
périscope [periskɔp] *m* periscope
périssable [perisabl] *adj* perishable
perle [pɛrl] *f* pearl; bead
perler [pɛrle] *tr* to pearl; do to perfection ‖ *intr* to form beads
permanence [pɛrmanɑ̃s] *f* permanence; headquarters, station; **en permanence** at all hours
perma·nent [pɛrmanɑ̃] **-nente** [nɑ̃t] *adj* permanent; standing; continuous, nonstop ‖ *f* permanent
perme [pɛrm] *f* (coll) furlough
permettre [pɛrmɛtr] §42, §97, §98 *tr* to permit; **permettre q.ch. à qn** to allow s.o. s.th. ‖ *intr*—**permettez!** excuse me!; **permettre à qn de** + *inf* to permit s.o. to or let s.o. + *inf*; **vous permettez?** may I? ‖ *ref*—**se permettre de** to take the liberty of
permis [pɛrmi] *m* permit, license; **permis de conduire** driver's license; **permis de construire** construction permit

permission [pɛrmisjɔ̃] *f* permission; (mil) furlough, leave

permissionnaire [pɛrmisjɔnɛr] *m* soldier on leave

permutation [pɛrmytɑsjɔ̃] *f* permutation; exchange of posts; transposition

permuter [pɛrmyte] *tr* to permute; exchange || *intr* to change places

perni·cieux [pɛrnisjø] **-cieuse** [sjøz] *adj* pernicious

péroné [pɛrɔne] *m* (anat) fibula

pérorer [pɛrɔre] *intr* to hold forth

Pérou [peru] *m*—**le Pérou** Peru

peroxyde [pɛrɔksid] *m* peroxide

perpendiculaire [pɛrpɑ̃dikylɛr] *adj & f* perpendicular

perpète [pɛrpɛt]—**à perpète** (slang) forever

perpétrer [pɛrpetre] §10 *tr* to perpetrate

perpé·tuel -tuelle [pɛrpetɥɛl] *adj* perpetual; life (*imprisonment*); constant, continual

perpétuer [pɛrpetɥe] *tr* to perpetuate || *ref* to be perpetuated

perpétuité [pɛrpetɥite] *f* perpetuity; **à perpétuité** forever; for life

perplexe [pɛrplɛks] *adj* perplexed; **rendre perplexe** to perplex

perplexité [pɛrplɛksite] *f* perplexity

perquisition [pɛrkizisjɔ̃] *f* search

perquisitionner [pɛrkizisjɔne] *intr* to make a search

perron [pɛrɔ̃] *m* front-entrance stone steps

perroquet [pɛrɔkɛ] *m* parrot

perruche [peryʃ] *f* parakeet; hen parrot

perruque [peryk] *f* wig; **vieille perruque** (coll) old fogey

per·san [pɛrsɑ̃] **-sane** [san] *adj* Persian || *m* Persian (*language*) || (*cap*) *mf* Persian (*person*)

perse [pɛrs] *adj* Persian || (*cap*) *mf* Persian || (*cap*) *f* Persia; **la Perse** Persia

persécuter [pɛrsekyte] *tr* to persecute

persécution [pɛrsekysjɔ̃] *f* persecution

persévérer [pɛrsevere] §10, §96 *intr* to persevere

persienne [pɛrsjɛn] *f* Persian blind, slatted shutter

persil [pɛrsi] *m* parsley

persis·tant [pɛrsistɑ̃] **-tante** [tɑ̃t] *adj* persistent

persister [pɛrsiste] §96 *intr* to persist; **persister à** to persist in

personnage [pɛrsɔnaʒ] *m* personage; (theat) character

personnalité [pɛrsɔnalite] *f* personality

personne [pɛrsɔn] *f* person; self; appearance; lady, e.g., **belle personne** beautiful lady; e.g., **jolie personne** pretty lady; **grande personne** grown-up; **par personne** per person; **payer de sa personne** to not spare one's efforts; **s'assurer de la personne de** to arrest; **une tierce personne** a third party || *pron indef* no one, nobody; **personne ne** or **ne ... personne** §90B no one, nobody, not anyone

person·nel -nelle [pɛrsɔnɛl] *adj* personal || *m* personnel; **personnel navigant** (aer) flying personnel; **personnel de route (rr)** train crew

personnifier [pɛrsɔnifje] *tr* to personify

perspective [pɛrspɛktiv] *f* perspective; outlook; **en perspective** in view

perspicace [pɛrspikas] *adj* perspicacious

persuader [pɛrsɥade] §97, §99 *tr* to persuade; **persuader q.ch. à qn** or **persuader qn de q.ch** to persuade s.o. of s.th. || §98 *intr*—**persuader à qn de** to persuade s.o. to || *ref* to be convinced

persuasion [pɛrsɥazjɔ̃] *f* persuasion

perte [pɛrt] *f* loss; ruin, downfall; **à perte de vue** as far as the eye can see; **en pure perte** uselessly

perti·nent [pɛrtinɑ̃] **-nente** [nɑ̃t] *adj* pertinent

perturba·teur [pɛrtyrbatœr] **-trice** [tris] *adj* disturbing || *mf* troublemaker

perturbation [pɛrtyrbɑsjɔ̃] *f* disruption; perturbation; **perturbation atmosphérique** atmospheric disturbance

perturber [pɛrtyrbe] *tr* to perturb; disturb

péru·vien [peryvjɛ̃] **-vienne** [vjɛn] *adj* Peruvian || (*cap*) *mf* Peruvian

pervenche [pɛrvɑ̃ʃ] *f* periwinkle

per·vers [pɛrvɛr] **-verse** [vɛrs] *adj* perverted || *mf* pervert

perversion [pɛrvɛrsjɔ̃] *f* perversion

perversité [pɛrvɛrsite] *f* perversity, depravity

pervertir [pɛrvɛrtir] *tr* to pervert

pesage [pəzaʒ] *m* weigh-in; paddock

pesamment [pəzamɑ̃] *adv* heavily

pe·sant [pəzɑ̃] **-sante** [zɑ̃t] *adj* heavy || *m*—**valoir son pesant d'or** to be worth one's weight in gold

pesanteur [pəzɑ̃tœr] *f* heaviness; weight; (phys) gravity

pèse-bébé [pezbebe] *m* (*pl* **-bébés**) baby scale

pesée [pəze] *f* weighing; leverage

pèse-lettre [pɛzlɛtr] *m* (*pl* **-lettres**) letter scale

pèse-personne [pɛzpɛrsɔn] *m* (*pl* **-personnes**) bathroom scale

peser [pəze] §2 *tr* to weigh || *intr* to weigh; **peser à** to hang heavy on; **peser sur** to bear down on; lie down on; lie heavy on; stress || *ref* to weigh oneself; weigh in

peson [pəzɔ̃] *m* spring scale

pessimisme [pesimism] *m* pessimism

pessimiste [pesimist] *adj* pessimistic || *mf* pessimist

peste [pɛst] *f* plague; pest, nuisance || *interj* gosh!

pester [pɛste] *intr* to grouse; **pester contre** to rail at

pestifé·ré -rée [pɛstifere] *adj* plague-ridden || *mf* victim of the plague

pestilence [pɛstilɑ̃s] *f* pestilence

pet [pɛ] *m* (slang) scandal; (vulg) wind; **ça ne vaut pas un pet (de lapin)** (coll) it's not worth a wooden nickel || *interj* (coll) look out!

pétale [petal] *m* petal

pétanque [petɑ̃k] *f* petanque

pétarade [petarad] *f* series of explosions; backfire; (vulg) making wind

pétard [petar] *m* firecracker; blast; (slang) gat, revolver; (slang) backside; **faire du pétard** (coll) to kick up a fuss; **lancer un pétard** (coll) to drop a bombshell

pet-de-loup [pɛdlu] *m* (*pl* **pets-de-loup**) absent-minded professor

pet-de-nonne [pɛdnɔn] *m* (*pl* **pets-de-nonne**) fritter

pet-en-l'air [pɛtɑ̃lɛr] *m invar* short jacket

péter [pete] §10 *tr*—**péter du feu** (coll) to be a live wire ‖ *intr* (coll) to go bang; (vulg) to break wind, fart

pètesec [pɛtsɛk] *adj invar* (coll) bossy, despotic ‖ *m invar* (coll) martinet, bossy fellow

pétil·lant [petijɑ̃] **-lante** [jɑ̃t] *adj* crackling; sparkling

pétiller [petije] *intr* to crackle; to sparkle

pe·tiot [pətjo] **-tiote** [tjɔt] *adj* (coll) tiny, wee ‖ *mf* (coll) tot

pe·tit [pəti] **-tite** [tit] (precedes the noun it modifies) §91 *adj* small, little; short; minor, lower; **en petit** shortened; miniature; **petit à petit** little by little, bit by bit ‖ *mf* youngster; young (*of an animal*); poor little thing ‖ *m* little boy ‖ *f* little girl

petit-beurre [pətibœr] *m* (*pl* **petits-beurre**) cookie

petit-cou·sin [pətikuzɛ̃] **-sine** [zin] *mf* (*pl* **petits-cousins**) second cousin

petite-fille [pətitfij] *f* (*pl* **petites-filles**) granddaughter

petite-nièce [pətitnjɛs] *f* (*pl* **petites-nièces**) great-niece

petitesse [pətitɛs] *f* smallness

petit-fils [pətifis] *m* (*pl* **petits-fils**) grandson; grandchild

petit-gris [pətigri] *m* (*pl* **petits-gris**) miniver; snail

pétition [petisjɔ̃] *f* petition; **faire une pétition de principe** to beg the question

petit-lait [pətilɛ] *m* (*pl* **petits-laits**) whey

petit-neveu [pətinvø] *m* (*pl* **petits-neveux**) great-nephew

petits-enfants [pətizɑ̃fɑ̃] *mpl* grandchildren

petit-suisse [pətisɥis] *m* (*pl* **petits-suisses**) cream cheese

peton [pətɔ̃] *m* (coll) tiny foot

pétoncle [petɔ̃kl] *m* scallop

Pétrarque [petrark] *m* Petrarch

pétrifier [petrifje] *tr* & *ref* to petrify

pétrin [petrɛ̃] *m* kneading trough; (coll) mess, jam

pétrir [petrir] *tr* to knead; mold

pétrochimique [petroʃimik] *adj* petrochemical

pétrole [petrɔl] *m* petroleum; **à pétrole** kerosene (*lamp*); **pétrole brut** crude oil; **pétrole lampant** kerosene

pétro·lier [petrɔlje] **-lière** [ljɛr] *adj* oil ‖ *m* tanker; oil baron

P et T [peete] *fpl* (letterword) (**Postes et télécommunications**) post office, telephone, and telegraph

pétu·lant [petylɑ̃] **-lante** [lɑ̃t] *adj* lively, frisky

peu [pø] *m* bit, little; **peu de** few; not much; not many; **peu de chose** not much ‖ *adv* §91 little; not very; **à peu près** about, practically; **depuis peu** of late; **peu ou prou** more or less; **peu probable** improbable; **peu s'en faut** very nearly; **pour peu que, si peu que** however little; **quelque peu** somewhat; **sous peu** before long; **tant soit peu** ever so little

peuplade [pœplad] *f* tribe

peuple [pœpl] *adj* plebeian, common ‖ *m* people

peuplement [pœpləmɑ̃] *m* populating; planting; stocking (*e.g., with fish*)

peupler [pœple] *tr* to people; plant; stock ‖ *intr* to multiply, breed

peuplier [pøplje] *m* poplar

peur [pœr] *f* fear; **avoir peur (de)** to be afraid (of); **de peur que** lest, for fear that; **une peur bleue** (coll) an awful fright

peu·reux [pœrø] **-reuse** [røz] *adj* fearful, timid

peux [pø] (*v* **peut, peuvent**) see **pourvoir**

peut-être [pøtɛtr] *adv* perhaps; **peut-être que non** perhaps not

p. ex. *abbr* (**par exemple**) e.g.

phalange [falɑ̃ʒ] *f* phalanx

phalène [falɛn] *m* & *f* moth

phallique [falik] *adj* phallic

phallus [falys] *m* phallus, penis

Pharaon [faraɔ̃] *m* Pharaoh

phare [far] *m* lighthouse; beacon; (aut) headlight; **phares code** dimmers

phari·sien [farizjɛ̃] **-sienne** [zjɛn] *adj* pharisaic ‖ *mf* pharisee

pharmaceutique [farmasøtik] *adj* pharmaceutical ‖ *f* pharmaceutics

pharmacie [farmasi] *f* drugstore, pharmacy; medicine chest; drugs

pharma·cien [farmasjɛ̃] **-cienne** [sjɛn] *mf* pharmacist

pharynx [farɛ̃ks] *m* pharynx

phase [fɑz] *f* phase

Phébé [febe] *f* Phoebe

Phénicie [fenisi] *f* Phoenicia; **la Phénicie** Phoenicia

phéni·cien [fenisjɛ̃] **-cienne** [sjɛn] *adj* Phoenician ‖ (*cap*) *mf* Phoenician

phénix [feniks] *m* phoenix

phénomé·nal **-nale** [fenɔmenal] *adj* (*pl* **-naux** [no]) phenomenal

phénomène [fenɔmɛn] *m* phenomenon; (coll) monster, freak

philanthrope [filɑ̃trɔp] *mf* philanthropist

philanthropie [filɑ̃trɔpi] *f* philanthropy

philatélie [filateli] *f* philately

philatéliste [filatelist] *mf* philatelist

philip·pin [filipɛ̃] **-pine** [pin] *adj* Philippine ‖ (*cap*) *mf* Filipino

Philippines [filipin] *fpl* Philippines

philistin [filistɛ̃] *adj masc* & *m* Philistine

philologie [filɔlɔʒi] *f* philology

philologue [filɔlɔg] *mf* philologist

philosophe [filɔzɔf] *adj* philosophic ‖ *mf* philosopher

philosophie [filɔzɔfi] *f* philosophy
philosophique [filɔzɔfik] *adj* philosophic(al)
philtre [filtr] *m* philter
phlébite [flebit] *f* phlebitis
phobie [fɔbi] *f* phobia
phonétique [fɔnetik] *adj* phonetic ‖ *f* phonetics
phoniatrie [fɔnjatri] *f* speech therapy
phono [fɔno] *m* (coll) phonograph
phonographe [fɔnograf] *m* phonograph
phonologie [fɔnɔlɔʒi] *f* phonology
phonothèque [fɔnɔtɛk] *f* record library
phoque [fɔk] *m* seal
phosphate [fɔsfat] *m* phosphate
phosphore [fɔsfɔr] *m* phosphorus
phosphores·cent [fɔsfɔresã] **-cente** [sãt] *adj* phosphorescent
photo [fɔtɔ] *f* photo, snapshot
photocopier [fɔtɔkɔpje] *tr* to photocopy, to photostat
photocopieur [fɔtɔkɔpjœr] *m* photocopier
photogénique [fɔtɔʒenik] *adj* photogenic
photographe [fɔtɔgraf] *mf* photographer
photographie [fɔtɔgrafi] *f* photography; photograph
photographier [fɔtɔgrafje] *tr* to photograph
photogravure [fɔtɔgravyr] *f* photoengraving
photostat [fɔtɔsta] *m* photostat
photothèque [fɔtɔtɛk] *f* photograph library
phrase [frɑz] *f* sentence; (mus) phrase; **phrase de choc** punch line
phrénologie [frenɔlɔʒi] *f* phrenology
physi·cien [fizisjɛ̃] **-cienne** [sjɛn] *mf* physicist
physiologie [fizjɔlɔʒi] *f* physiology
physiologique [fizjɔlɔʒik] *adj* physiological
physionomie [fizjɔnɔmi] *f* physiognomy
physique [fizik] *adj* physical; material ‖ *m* physique; appearance ‖ *f* physics
piaffer [pjafe] *intr* to paw the ground; fidget, fume
piailler [pjɑje] *intr* (coll) to cheep; (coll) to squeal
pianiste [pjanist] *mf* pianist
piano [pjano] *m* piano; **piano à queue** grand piano; **piano droit** upright piano ‖ *adv* (coll) quietly
pianoter [pjanɔte] *intr* to strum; to drum, to thrum; to rattle away
piastre [pjastr] *f* (Canad) dollar
piaule [pjol] *f* (slang) pad (*one's home*)
piauler [pjole] *intr* to peep; screech (*said of pulley*); (coll) to whine
pic [pik] *m* peak; (*tool*) pick; (orn) woodpecker; **à pic** sheer, steep; (coll) in the nick of time; **couler à pic** to sink like a stone
picaillons [pikajɔ̃] *mpl* (slang) dough
picaresque [pikarɛsk] *adj* picaresque
piccolo [pikɔlo] *m* piccolo
pichet [piʃɛ] *m* pitcher, jug
pick-up [pikœp] *m invar* pickup; record player; pickup truck
picoler [pikɔle] *intr* (slang) to get pickled
picorer [pikɔre] *tr & intr* to peck

picoter [pikɔte] *tr* to prick; peck at; sting
picotin [pikɔtɛ̃] *m* peck (*measure*)
pictu·ral -rale [piktyral] *adj* (*pl* **-raux** [ro]) pictorial
pie [pi] *adj invar* piebald ‖ *f* magpie
pièce [pjɛs] *f* piece; patch; room; play; document; coin; wine barrel; **à la pièce** separately; **donner la pièce** to tip; **faire pièce à** to play a trick on; to put a check on; **inventé de toutes pièces** made up out of the whole cloth; **la pièce** apiece; **pièce à conviction** (law) exhibit; **pièce comptable** voucher; **pièce d'eau** ornamental pond; **pièce de rechange, pièce détachée** spare part; **pièce de résistance** pièce de résistance; (culin) entree; **pièce rapportée** in-law; **pièces rendues** change; **reprenez alors votre pièce au retour de monnaies** take your change from the coin return; **tout d'une pièce** in one piece; (coll) rigid; (coll) stiffly ‖ *adv* apiece
pied [pje] *m* foot; foothold; **à pied** on foot; **à pied d'œuvre** on the site, on the spot, where the work is being done; **au pied de la lettre** literally; **au pied levé** offhand; **c'est des pieds!** (slang) that's cool!, that's fresh!; **de pied en cap** from head to toe; **faire le pied de grue** (coll) to cool one's heels, to stand around waiting; **faire les pieds à** (coll) to give what's coming to; **faire un pied de nez** (coll) to thumb one's nose; **lever le pied** to abscond; **mettre à pied** to dismiss, fire; **mettre les pieds dans le plat** (coll) to put one's foot in one's mouth; **mettre pied à terre** to dismount; **mettre qn au pied du mur** to corner s.o.; force s.o. to a showdown; **pied d'athlète** (pathol) athlete's foot; **pied équin** clubfoot; **travailler comme un pied** (coll) to botch one's work; **vous avez pied?** can you touch bottom?
pied-à-terre [pjetatɛr] *m invar* hangout, temporary base
pied-bot [pjebo] *m* (*pl* **pieds-bots**) club-footed person
pied-d'alouette [pjedalwɛt] *m* (*pl* **pieds-d'alouette**) delphinium
pied-de-poule [pjedəpul] *adj invar* hound's-tooth (*design or pattern*)
pied-droit [pjedrwa] *m* (*pl* **pieds-droits**) (archit) pier
piédes·tal -tale [pjedɛstal] *m* (*pl* **-taux** [to]) pedestal
pied-noir [pjenwar] *m* (*pl* **pieds-noirs**) Algerian of European descent
piège [pjɛʒ] *m* trap, snare
piéger [pjeʒe] §1 *tr* to trap, snare; booby-trap
pie-grièche [pigrijɛʃ] *f* (*pl* **pies-grièches**) shrike; shrew
pierraille [pjɛrɑj] *f* rubble
pierre [pjɛr] *f* stone; **faire d'une pierre deux coups** to kill two birds with one stone; **Pierre** Peter; **pierre à aiguiser** whetstone; **pierre à briquet** flint; **pierre à chaux, pierre à plâtre** gypsum; **pierre à feu, pierre à fusil** gunflint;

pierre angulaire cornerstone; **pierre à rasoir** hone; **pierre calcaire** limestone; **pierre d'achoppement** stumbling block; **pierre de gué** stepping stone; **pierre de touche** touchstone; **pierre tombale** tombstone

pierreries [pjɛri] *fpl* precious stones

pier·reux [pjɛrø] **-reuse** [røz] *adj* stony ‖ *f* (coll) streetwalker

pierrot [pjɛro] *m* clown; sparrow; (coll) oddball; (coll) greenhorn

piété [pjete] *f* piety; devotion

piéter [pjete] §10 *intr* to toe the line ‖ *ref* to stand firm

piétiner [pjetine] *tr* to trample on ‖ *intr* to stamp; mark time

piéton [pjetɔ̃] *m* pedestrian

piètre [pjɛtr] *adj* poor, wretched

pieu [pjø] *m* (*pl* **pieux**) post, stake; (archit) pile

pieuvre [pjœvr] *f* octopus; (coll) leech

pieux [pjø] **pieuse** [pjøz] *adj* pious; dutiful; white (*lie*)

pif [pif] *m* (slang) snout (*nose*) ‖ *interj* bang!

pige [piʒ] *f* (slang) year; **à la pige** (journ) so much a line; on a free-lance basis; **faire la pige à** (slang) to outdo

pigeon [piʒɔ̃] *m* pigeon; **pigeon voyageur** homing pigeon

pigeonner [piʒɔne] *tr* (coll) to dupe

pigeonnier [piʒɔnje] *m* dovecote

piger [piʒe] §38 *tr* (slang) to look at; (slang) to get ‖ *intr*—**tu piges?** (slang) do you get it?

pigment [pigmɑ̃] *m* pigment

pignocher [piɲɔʃe] *intr* to pick at one's food

pignon [piɲɔ̃] *m* gable; (mach) pinion; **avoir pignon sur rue** (coll) to have a home of one's own; (coll) to be well off; **pignon de chaîne** sprocket wheel

pile [pil] *f* stack, pile; pier; (elec) battery (*primary cell*); (coll) thrashing; **pile atomique** atomic pile; **pile ou face** heads or tails; **pile sèche** dry cell ‖ *adv* (coll) short; (coll) exactly; **tomber pile** (coll) to happen at the right moment

piler [pile] *tr* to grind, crush

pilier [pilje] *m* pillar; **pilier de cabaret** barfly

pillage [pijaʒ] *m* looting

pil·lard [pijar] **-larde** [jard] *adj* looting ‖ *mf* looter

piller [pije] *tr & intr* to loot; plagiarize

pil·leur [pijœr] **-leuse** [jøz] *mf* pillager

pilon [pilɔ̃] *m* pestle; (coll) drumstick (*of chicken*); (coll) wooden leg; **pilon à vapeur** steam hammer

pilonnage [pilɔnaʒ] *m* crushing; **pilonnage aérien** saturation bombing

pilonner [pilɔne] *tr* to crush; bomb

pilori [pilɔri] *m* pillory

pilot [pilo] *m* pile (*in piling*); rags (*for paper*)

pilotage [pilotaʒ] *m* piloting; **pilotage sans visibilité** blind flying

pilote [pilɔt] *m* pilot; **pilote de ligne** airline pilot; **pilote d'émission** (telv) anchor man; **pilote d'essai** test pilot

piloter [pilɔte] *tr* to pilot; guide; drive piles into ‖ *intr* to pilot; be a guide

pilotis [pilɔti] *m* piles

pilule [pilyl] *f* pill; (coll) bitter pill; **dorer la pilule** to gild the lily

piment [pimɑ̃] *m* allspice (*berry*); (fig) spice; **piment doux** sweet pepper; **piment rouge** red or hot pepper

pimenter [pimɑ̃te] *tr* to season with red pepper; (fig) to spice

pim·pant [pɛ̃pɑ̃] **-pante** [pɑ̃t] *adj* smart, spruce

pin [pɛ̃] *m* pine; **pin de Weymouth** (*Pinus strobus*) white pine; **pin sylvestre** (*Pinus sylvestris*) Scotch pine

pinacle [pinakl] *m* pinnacle

pince [pɛ̃s] *f* tongs; pliers; forceps; crowbar; gripper; grip; pleat; claw (*of crab*); **aller à pinces** (slang) to hoof it; **petites pinces, pince à épiler** tweezers; **pince à linge** clothespin; **pince à sucre** sugar tongs; **pince hémostatique** hemostat; **pinces** tongs; pincers; pliers; **pinces de cycliste** bicycle clips; **serrer la pince à** (slang) to shake hands with

pin·cé **-cée** [pɛ̃se] *adj* prim, tight-lipped; thin, pinched ‖ *f* see **pincée**

pin·ceau [pɛ̃so] *m* (*pl* **-ceaux**) paintbrush; pencil (*of light*)

pincée [pɛ̃se] *f* pinch

pincement [pɛ̃smɑ̃] *m* pinching; plucking

pince-monseigneur [pɛ̃smɔ̃sɛɲœr] *f* (*pl* **pinces-monseigneur**) jimmy

pince-nez [pɛ̃sne] *m invar* nose glasses

pincer [pɛ̃se] §51 *tr* to pinch; grip; nip off; pluck; top (*plants*); purse (*the lips*); pleat; (coll) to nab, to catch ‖ *intr* to bite (*said of cold*); **en pincer pour** (slang) to have a crush on; **pincer de** (mus) to strum on

pince-sans-rire [pɛ̃ssɑ̃rir] *adj invar* deadpan ‖ *mf invar* deadpan comic

pincette [pɛ̃sɛt] *f* tweezers; **pincettes** tweezers; fire tongs

pinçon [pɛ̃sɔ̃] *m* bruise (*from pinch*)

pinède [pinɛd] *f* pine grove

pingouin [pɛ̃gwɛ̃] *m* (*family:* Alcidae) auk

ping-pong [piŋpɔ̃g] *m* table tennis, Ping-Pong

pingre [pɛ̃gr] *adj* (coll) stingy ‖ *mf* (coll) tightwad

pinson [pɛ̃sɔ̃] *m* (orn) finch

pintade [pɛ̃tad] *f* guinea fowl

pin up [pinœp] *f invar* (coll) pinup girl

pioche [pjɔʃ] *f* pickax

piocher [pjɔʃe] *tr & intr* to dig, pick; (coll) to cram

pio·cheur [pjɔʃœr] **-cheuse** [ʃøz] *mf* digger; (coll) grind ‖ *f* (mach) cultivator

piolet [pjɔlɛ] *m* ice ax

pion [pjɔ̃] *m* (checkers) man; (chess & fig) pawn; (slang) proctor; **damer le pion à** (coll) to get the better of

pionnier [pjɔnje] *m* pioneer; young student chess player

pipe [pip] *f* pipe; **casser sa pipe** (slang) to kick the bucket

pi·peau [pipo] *m* (*pl* **-peaux**) bird call; shepherd's pipe; lime twig

piper [pipe] *tr* to snare, catch; load (*the dice*); mark (*the cards*) ‖ *intr*—**ne pipe pas!** (coll) not a peep out of you!

pi·quant [pikɑ̃] **-quante** [kɑ̃t] *adj* piquant, intriguing; racy, spicy ‖ *m* sting; prickle; quill (*of porcupine*); piquancy, pungency; point (*of story*); (fig) bite

pique [pik] *m* (cards) spade; (cards) spades ‖ *f* pike; pique

pi·qué -quée [pike] *adj* stung; sour; (mus) staccato; (coll) batty; **ne pas être piqué des vers** (slang) to be first rate; **piqué de** studded with ‖ *m* quilt; **descendre en piqué** to nose-dive

pique-assiette [pikasjɛt] *mf* (*pl* **-assiettes**) (coll) sponger

pique-feu [pikfø] *m invar* poker

pique-fleurs [pikflœr] *m invar* flower holder

pique-nique [piknik] *m* (*pl* **-niques**) picnic

pique-niquer [piknike] *intr* to picnic

piquer [pike] *tr* to sting; prick; pique; stimulate; quilt; spur; give a shot to; (mus) to play staccato; (slang) to filch; (slang) to pinch, nab ‖ *intr* to turn sour; (aer) to nose-dive ‖ §97 *ref* to be piqued; spot; give oneself a shot; **se piquer de** to take pride in; **se piquer pour** to take a fancy to

piquet [pikɛ] *m* peg, stake; picket; **piquet de grève** picket line

piqueter [pikte] §34 *tr* to stake out; spot, dot

piquette [pikɛt] *f* poor wine; (coll) crushing defeat

pi·queur [pikœr] **-queuse** [køz] *mf* stitcher ‖ *m* huntsman; outrider

piqûre [pikyr] *f* sting, bite; prick; injection, shot; stitching; puncture; **piqûre de ver** moth hole

pirate [pirat] *m* pirate; **pirate de l'air** hijacker

pirater [pirate] *intr* to pirate

piraterie [piratri] *f* piracy; **piraterie aérienne** hijacking

pire [pir] (precedes the noun it modifies) §91 *adj comp & super* worse; worst ‖ *m* (the) worst

pirouette [pirwɛt] *f* pirouette

pirouetter [pirwete] *intr* to pirouette

pis [pi] *adj comp & super* worse; worst ‖ *m* udder; **au pis aller** at worst; **de pis en pis** worse and worse; **(le) pis** (the) worst; **qui pis est** what's worse; **tant pis** so much the worse ‖ *adv comp & super* §91 worse; worst

pis-aller [pizale] *m invar* makeshift

piscine [pisin] *f* swimming pool

pissenlit [pisɑ̃li] *m* dandelion

pisser [pise] *tr* (coll) to spout (*water*); (coll) to leak; (slang) to pass (*e.g., blood*); **pisser de la copie** (slang) to be a hack writer ‖ *intr* (slang) to urinate

pisse-vinaigre [pisvinɛgr] *m invar* (coll) skinflint

pissoir [piswar] *m* (coll) urinal

pissotière [pisɔtjɛr] *f* (coll) street urinal

pistache [pistaʃ] *f* pistachio

pistage [pistaʒ] *m* tracking

piste [pist] *f* track; trail; ring (*of, e.g., circus*); rink; lane (*of highway*); **à double piste** four-lane (*highway*); runway; **piste cavalière** bridle path; **piste cyclable** bicycle path; **piste d'atterrissage** landing strip; **piste de danse** dance floor; **piste d'envol** runway; **piste pour skieurs** ski run; **piste sonore** sound track

pister [piste] *tr* to track, trail

pistolet [pistɔlɛ] *m* pistol; spray gun; (coll) card; **pistolet à bouchon** popgun; **pistolet à souder** welding gun; **pistolet d'arçon** horse pistol; **pistolet mitrailleur** submachine gun

piston [pistɔ̃] *m* piston; (coll) pull

pistonner [pistɔne] *tr* (coll) to push, back

pitance [pitɑ̃s] *f* ration; food

pi·teux [pitø] **-teuse** [tøz] *adj* pitiful, sorry, sad

pitié [pitje] *f* pity; **à faire pitié** (coll) very badly; **par pitié!** for pity's sake!; **quelle pitié!** how awful!

piton [pitɔ̃] *m* screw eye; peak

pitou [pitu] *m* (Canad) dog; (Canad) tyke

pitoyable [pitwajabl] *adj* pitiful

pitre [pitr] *m* clown

pittoresque [pitɔrɛsk] *adj* picturesque

pivoine [pivwan] *f* peony

pivot [pivo] *m* pivot

pivoter [pivɔte] *intr* to pivot

P.J. [peʒi] *f* (letterword) (**police judiciaire**) (coll) police (*dealing with criminal cases*)

placage [plakaʒ] *m* veneering; plating

placard [plakar] *m* cupboard; closet; placard, poster; (typ) galley; **placards de presse** press passes

placarder [plakarde] *tr* to placard; (typ) to print in galleys

place [plas] *f* place; city square; room; seat; job, position; fare; **places debout** standing room; **sur place** on the spot

placement [plasmɑ̃] *m* placement; investment; **de placement** employment (*agency*)

placer [plase] §51 *tr* to place; invest; slip in ‖ *ref* to seat oneself; rank; get a job; take place

pla·ceur [plasœr] **-ceuse** [søz] *mf* employment agent ‖ *m* usher

placide [plasid] *adj* placid

pla·cier [plasje] **-cière** [sjɛr] *mf* agent, representative

placoplâtre [plakɔplɑtr] *m* plasterboard

plafond [plafɔ̃] *m* ceiling

plafonner [plafɔne] *intr*—**plafonner (à)** to hit the top (at)

plafonnier [plafɔnje] *m* ceiling light; (aut) dome light

plage [plaʒ] *f* beach; band (*of record*); (poetic) clime

plagiaire [plaʒjɛr] *mf* plagiarist

plagiat [plaʒja] *m* plagiarism

plagier [plaʒje] *tr & intr* to plagiarize

plagiste [plaʒist] *mf* beach concessionaire
plaider [plede] *tr* to argue (*a case*); plead (*e.g., ignorance*) ‖ *intr* to plead; go to law
plai·deur [plɛdœr] **-deuse** [døz] *mf* litigant
plaidoirie [plɛdwari] *f* pleading
plaidoyer [plɛdwaje] *m* appeal (*of lawyer to judge or jury*)
plaie [plɛ] *f* wound, sore; plague; **plaie en séton** flesh wound
plai·gnant [plɛɲɑ̃] **-gnante** [ɲɑ̃t] *mf* plaintiff
plain [plɛ̃] *m* high tide
plaindre [plɛ̃dr] §15, §97 *tr* to pity ‖ *ref* to complain
plaine [plɛn] *f* plain
plain-pied [plɛ̃pje] *m*—**de plain-pied** on the same floor; (fig) on an equal footing
plainte [plɛ̃t] *f* complaint; moan
plain·tif [plɛ̃tif] **-tive** [tiv] *adj* plaintive
plaire [plɛr] §52 *intr* to please; **plaire à** to be pleasing to, appeal to, e.g., **cette musique leur plaît** that music appeals to them; to inspire liking in, e.g., **le lait lui plaît** he likes milk, **le dîner m'a plu** I liked the dinner; to be suitable for, e.g., **ce plan lui plaît** that plan suits her; **s'il vous plaît** please ‖ §96 *ref* (*pp* **plu** *invar*) to be pleased; enjoy oneself; like one another; **se plaire à** to like it in, e.g., **je me plais à la campagne** I like it in the country
plaisance [plɛzɑ̃s] *f*—**de plaisance** pleasure (*e.g., boat*)
plai·sant [plɛzɑ̃] **-sante** [zɑ̃t] *adj* pleasant; funny ‖ *m*—**mauvais plaisant** practical joker
plaisanter [plɛzɑ̃te] *tr* to poke fun at ‖ *intr* to joke
plaisanterie [plɛzɑ̃tri] *f* joke; joking
plaisantin [plɛzɑ̃tɛ̃] *adj masc* roguish, waggish ‖ *m* wag, kidder
plaisent [plɛz] *v* (**plaisons**) see **plaire**
plaisir [plezir] *m* pleasure; **à plaisir** without cause; at one's pleasure; **au plaisir (de vous revoir)** good-by; **faire plaisir à** to please, give pleasure to
plaît [ple] *v* see **plaire**
plan [plɑ̃] **plane** [plan] *adj* even, flat; plane (*angle*) ‖ *m* plan; design; (geom) plane; **au deuxième plan** in the background; **au premier plan** in the foreground; downstage; **au troisième plan** far in the background; **gros plan** (mov) close-up; **laisser en plan** (coll) to leave stranded; (coll) to put off, delay; **lever un plan** to survey; **plan de paix** peace plan; **plan de travail** work schedule; **plan d'occupation des sols (P.O.S.)** zoning code; **rester en plan** (coll) to remain in suspense; **sur le plan de** from the point of view of ‖ *f* see **plane**
planche [plɑ̃ʃ] *f* board; plank; (hort) bed; (typ) plate; (slang) blackboard; **faire de la planche à voile** to go wind surfing; **faire la planche** to float on one's back; **planche à pain** breadboard; (slang) flatchested woman; **planche à repasser** iron-

ing board; **planche à roulettes** skateboard; **planche de bord** instrument panel; **planche de débarquement** gangplank; **planche de salut** sheet anchor; last hope; **planche pourrie** (slang) dubious character
planchéier [plɑ̃ʃeje] *tr* to floor; board
plancher [plɑ̃ʃe] *m* floor; **le plancher des vaches** (coll) terra firma
plane [plan] *f* drawknife
planer [plane] *tr* to plane ‖ *intr* to hover; glide; float; **planer sur** to overlook, sweep (*e.g., a landscape with one's eyes*); (fig) to hover over
planète [planɛt] *f* planet
planeur [planœr] *m* glider
planeuse [planøz] *f* planing machine
planification [planifikɑsjɔ̃] *f* planning; **planification des naissances** family planning
planifier [planifje] *tr* to plan
planisme [planism] *m*—**planisme familial** family planning
planning [planiŋ] *m* detailed plan; **planning familial** birth control
plan-plan [plɑ̃plɑ̃] *adv* (coll) quietly, without hurrying
planque [plɑ̃k] *f* (coll) soft job; (slang) hideout
planquer [plɑ̃ke] *tr* to hide ‖ *ref* (mil) to take cover; (slang) to hide out
plant [plɑ̃] *m* planting; bed, patch; seedling, sapling
plantation [plɑ̃tɑsjɔ̃] *f* planting; plantation; **plantation de cheveux** hairline; head of hair
plante [plɑ̃t] *f* plant; sole
plan·té-tée [plɑ̃te] *adj* set, situated
planter [plɑ̃te] *tr* to plant; set; **planter là** to give the slip to ‖ *ref* to stand
planteur [plɑ̃tœr] *m* planter
plantoir [plɑ̃twar] *m* (hort) dibble
planton [plɑ̃tɔ̃] *m* (mil) orderly
plantu·reux [plɑ̃tyrø] **-reuse** [røz] *adj* abundant; fertile; (coll) buxom
plaque [plak] *f* plate; plaque; splotch; **plaque à crêpes** pancake griddle; **plaque croûteuse** scab; **plaque d'immatriculation, plaque minéralogique** (aut) license plate; **plaque tournante** (rr) turntable; (fig) hub (*of a city*)
plaquer [plake] *tr* to plate; veneer; plaster down (*one's hair*); strike (*a chord*); (football) to tackle; (coll) to jilt; **plaquer à l'électricité** to electroplate ‖ *ref* to lie flat; (aer) to pancake
plaquette [plakɛt] *f* plaque; pamphlet; (histology) platelet
plastic [plastik] *m* plastic bomb
plastique [plastik] *adj* plastic ‖ *m* plastics ‖ *f* plastic art
plastron [plastrɔ̃] *m* shirt front; breastplate; hostile contingent (*in war games*)
plastronner [plastrɔne] *intr* (fig) to throw out one's chest
plat [pla] **plate** [plat] *adj* flat; even; smooth (*sea*); dead; (*calm*); corny (*joke*); **à plat**

run-down; flat; **tomber plat** (coll) to fall unluckily ‖ *m* dish; platter; course (*of meal*); flat (*of hand*); blade (*of oar*); face (*of hammer*); **plat cuisiné** platter, short-order meal; **plat de côtes** sparerib; **plat du jour** today's special, chef's special; **plat principal, plat de résistance** entree; **plats** (bb) boards

platane [platan] *m* plane tree; **faux platane** sycamore

pla·teau [plato] *m* (*pl* -teaux) plateau; tray; shelf; platform; plate; pan (*of scale*); (mov, telv) set; (rr) flatcar; (theat) stage; **plateau porte-disque** turntable (*of phonograph*); **pleateau repas congelé** frozen dinner; **plateau tournant** revolving stage; lazy Susan

plate-bande [platbɑ̃d] *f* (*pl* **plates-bandes**) flower bed

plate-forme [platfɔrm] *f* (*pl* **plates-formes**) platform; (rr) flatcar

platine [platin] *m* platinum ‖ *f* plate; platen; lock (*of gun*); stage (*of microscope*)

plati·né -née [platine] *adj* platinum-plated; platinum

platitude [platityd] *f* platitude; flatness; obsequiousness

Platon [platɔ̃] *m* Plato

plâtre [platr] *m* plaster; plaster cast; **essuyer les plâtres** to be the first occupant of a new house; **plâtre à mouler** plaster of Paris

plâtrer [platre] *tr* to plaster; put in a cast; fertilize ‖ *ref* (coll) to pile on the make-up or face powder

plausible [plozibl] *adj* plausible

plé·béien [plebejɛ̃] **-béienne** [bejɛn] *adj* & *mf* plebeian

plein [plɛ̃] **pleine** [plɛn] *adj* full; round, plump; solid (*bar, wheel, wire, etc.*); continuous (*line*); heavy (*heart*); in foal, with calf, etc.; (coll) drunk; **plein aux as** (coll) well-heeled; **plein de** full of; covered with; preoccupied with; **plein de soi** self-centered ‖ (when standing before noun) *adj* full; high (*tide*); **en plein** + *noun* in the midst of the + *noun*, right in the + *noun;* at the height of the (*season*); in the open (*air*); out at (*sea*), on the high (*seas*); in broad (*daylight*); in the dead of (*winter*) ‖ *m* full (*of the moon*); bull's-eye; downstroke; **battre son plein** to be in full swing; **en plein** plumb, plump, squarely; **faire le plein (de)** to fill up the tank (with) ‖ **plein** *adv* full; **tout plein** very much

plein-emploi [plɛ̃ɑ̃plwa] *m* full employment

pleu·rard [plœrar] **-rarde** [rard] *adj* (coll) whimpering ‖ *mf* (coll) whimperer

pleurer [plœre] *tr* to weep over; shed (*tears*); **pleurer misère** to complain of being poor ‖ *intr* to cry, weep; **pleurer à chaudes larmes** to weep bitterly; **pleurer dans le gilet de qn** (coll) to cry on s.o.'s shoulder

pleurésie [plœrezi] *f* pleurisy

pleu·reur [plœrœr] **-reuse** [røz] *adj* weeping ‖ *f* paid mourner

pleurnicher [plœrniʃe] *intr* to whimper, snivel

pleurs [plœr] *mpl* tears

pleutre [pløtr] *adj* (coll) cowardly ‖ *m* (coll) coward

pleuvasser [pløvase] *intr* (coll) to drizzle

pleuvoir [pløvwar] §53 *intr* & *impers* to rain; **pleuvoir à verse, à flots,** or **à seaux** to rain buckets

pli [pli] *m* fold; pleat; bend (*of arm or leg*); hollow (*of knee*); letter; envelope; undulation (*of ground*); (cards) trick; **faux pli** crease, wrinkle; **petit pli** tuck; **sous ce pli** enclosed, herewith; **sous pli cacheté** in a sealed envelope; **sous pli distinct** or **séparé** under separate cover; **sous pli fermé** in a sealed envelope

pliage [plijaʒ] *m* folding

pliant [plijɑ̃] **pliante** [plijɑ̃t] *adj* folding; collapsible; pliant ‖ *m* campstool, folding chair

plier [plije] *tr* to fold; bend; force; **plier bagage** to leave ‖ *intr* to fold; bend; yield; **ne pas plier, s.v.p.** (*formula on envelope*) please do not bend ‖ §96 *ref* to fold; yield; fall back (*said of army*)

plinthe [plɛ̃t] *f* baseboard

plisser [plise] *tr* to pleat; crease; wrinkle; squint (*the eyes*) ‖ *intr* to fold ‖ *ref* to wrinkle; pucker up (*said of mouth*)

plomb [plɔ̃] *m* lead; shot; seal; plumb; sinker (*of fishline*); (elec) fuse; **à plomb** plumb, vertical; straight down, directly; **faire sauter un plomb** to burn or blow out a fuse

plombage [plɔ̃baʒ] *m* filing (*of tooth*); sealing (*e.g., at customs*)

plombagine [plɔ̃baʒin] *f* graphite

plom·bé -bée [plɔ̃be] *adj* leaden; in bond, sealed; filled (*tooth*); livid (*hue*)

plomber [plɔ̃be] *tr* to cover with lead; seal; plumb; fill (*a tooth*); make livid; roll (*the ground*)

plomberie [plɔ̃bri] *f* plumbing; plumbing-supply store; leadwork

plombeur [plɔ̃bœr] *m* (mach) roller

plombier [plɔ̃bje] *m* plumber; worker in lead

plonge [plɔ̃ʒ] *f* dishwashing

plon·geant [plɔ̃ʒɑ̃] **-geante** [ʒɑ̃t] *adj* plunging; from above

plongée [plɔ̃ʒe] *f* plunge; dive; dip, slope; **en plongée** submerged

plongeoir [plɔ̃ʒwar] *m* diving board

plongeon [plɔ̃ʒɔ̃] *m* plunge; dive; (football) tackle; **plongeon de haut vol** high dive

plonger [plɔ̃ʒe] §38 *tr* to plunge; thrust, stick ‖ *intr* to plunge; dive; (coll) to have a good view; **plonger raide** to crash-dive ‖ *ref*—**se plonger dans** to immerse oneself in; give oneself over to

plon·geur [plɔ̃ʒœr] **-geuse** [ʒøz] *adj* diving ‖ *mf* diver; dishwasher (*in restaurant*) ‖ *m* (mach) plunger; (orn) diver

plot [plo] *m* (elec) contact point

plouc [pluk] *m* (coll) peasant, hick

ployer [plwaje] §47 *tr & intr* to bend

plu [ply] *v* see **plaire**; see **pleuvoir**

pluches [plyʃ] *fpl* (mil) K.P.

pluie [plɥi] *f* rain; shower; **pluie acide** acid rain; **pluies radioactives** fallout

plumage [plymaʒ] *m* plumage

plumard [plymar] *m*—**aller au plumard** (slang) to hit the hay

plume [plym] *f* feather; pen; penpoint

plu·meau [plymo] *m* (*pl* **-meaux**) feather duster

plumer [plyme] *tr* to pluck; (coll) to fleece ‖ *intr* to feather one's oar

plumet [plymɛ] *m* plume

plu·meux [plymø] **-meuse** [møz] *adj* feathery

plumier [plymje] *m* pencil box

plupart [plypar] *f*—**la plupart** most; the most; for the most part; **la plupart de** most; the most; most of, the majority of; **la plupart d'entre nous (eux)** most of us (them); **pour la plupart** for the most part

plu·riel -rielle [plyrjɛl] *adj & m* plural; **au pluriel** in the plural

plus [ply] ([plyz] before vowel; [plys] in final position) *m* plus; **au plus, tout au plus** at the most, at best; at the latest; at the outside; **d'autant plus** all the more so; **de plus** more; moreover, besides; **de plus en plus** more and more; **en plus** extra; **en plus de** in addition to, besides; **le plus, la plus, les plus** (the) most; **le plus de** the most; **le plus que** as much as, as fast as; **ni . . . non plus** nor . . . either, e.g., **ni moi non plus** nor I either; **ni plus ni moins** neither more nor less; **non plus** neither, not . . . either; **plus de** more, e.g., **plus de chaleur** more heat; no more, e.g., **plus de potage** no more soup; **qui plus est** what is more, moreover ‖ *adv comp & super* §91 more; **des plus** + *adj* most + *adj*, extremely + *adj*; **(le) plus . . .** (the) most . . . , e.g., **ce que j'aime le plus** what I like (the) most; **le** (or **son**, etc.) **plus** + *adj* the (or his, etc.) most; **ne . . . plus** §90 no more, no longer; **ne . . . plus que** §90 now only, e.g., **il n'y a plus que mon oncle** there is now only my uncle; **on ne peut plus** + *adj* or *adv* extremely + *adj* or *adv*; **plus de** (followed by numeral) more than; **plus jamais** never more; **plus . . . plus** (or **moins**) the more . . . the more (or the less); **plus que** more than; **plus tôt** sooner ‖ *prep* plus

plusieurs [plyzjœr] *adj & pron indef* several

plus-que-parfait [plyskəparfɛ] *m* pluperfect

plus-value [plyvaly] *f* (*pl* **-values**) appreciation; increase; surplus; extra cost; surplus value (*in Marxian economics*)

Plutarque [plytark] *m* Plutarch

Pluton [plytɔ̃] *m* Pluto

plutonium [plytɔnjɔm] *m* plutonium

plutôt [plyto] *adv* rather; instead; **plutôt . . . que** rather . . . than

pluvier [plyvje] *m* (orn) plover

plu·vieux [plyvjø] **-vieuse** [vjøz] *adj* rainy

P.N.B. [peɛnbe] *m* (letterword) (**produit national brut**) G.N.P. (*gross national product*)

pneu [pnø] *m* (*pl* **pneus**) tire; express letter (*by Parisian tube*); **pneu ballon** or **confort** balloon tire; **pneu de secours** spare tire; **pneu radial** radial tire; **pneus à clous** studded tires; **pneus neiges** snow tires

pneumatique [pnømatik] *adj* pneumatic ‖ *m* tire; express letter (*by Parisian tube*); **pneumatiques à carcasse radiale** radial tires

pneumonie [pnømɔni] *f* pneumonia

pochade [pɔʃad] *f* sketch

po·chard [pɔʃar] **-charde** [ʃard] *mf* (coll) boozer, guzzler

poche [pɔʃ] *f* pocket; bag, pouch; crop (*of bird*)

po·ché -chée [pɔʃe] *adj* poached; black (*eye*)

pocher [pɔʃe] *tr* to poach; dash off (*a sketch*)

pochette [pɔʃɛt] *f* folder; book (*of matches*); kit; fancy handkerchief; **pochette à disque** record jacket; **pochette surprise** surprise package

pocheuse [pɔʃøz] *f* egg poacher

pochoir [pɔʃwar] *m* stencil

poêle [pwɑl] *m* stove; pall; canopy ‖ *f* frying pan

poêlon [pwɑlɔ̃] *m* saucepan

poème [pɔɛm] *m* poem; **poème symphonique** tone poem

poésie [pɔezi] *f* poetry; poem

poète [pɔɛt] *mf* poet

poétesse [pɔetɛs] *f* poetess

poétique [pɔetik] *adj* poetic(al) ‖ *f* poetics

pogrom [pɔgrɔm] *m* pogrom

poids [pwa], [pwɑ] *m* weight; **deux poids deux mesures** double standard; **poids brut, poids total** gross weight; **poids coq** bantamweight; **poids et haltères** weightlifting; weights; **poids léger** lightweight; **poids lourd** heavy truck; (boxing) heavyweight; **poids mort** (& fig) dead weight; **poids moyen** middleweight; **poids net** net weight; **poids plume, poids mouche** featherweight; **poids welter** welterweight

poi·gnant [pwaɲɑ̃] **-gnante** [ɲɑ̃t] *adj* poignant

poignard [pwaɲar] *m* dagger

poignarder [pwaɲarde] *tr* to stab

poigne [pwaɲ] *f* grip, grasp; **à poigne** strong, energetic

poignée [pwaɲe] *f* handful; handle; grip; hilt; **poignée de main** handshake

poignet [pwaɲɛ] *m* wrist; cuff; **poignet mousquetaire** French cuff

poil [pwal] *m* hair; bristle; nap, pile; coat (*of animals*); **à long poil** shaggy; **à poil** naked; bareback; (coll) peachy; **avoir un poil dans la main** (coll) to be lazy; **de mauvais poil** (coll) in a bad mood; **de tout poil** (coll) of every shade and hue; **poil follet** down; **reprendre du poil de la bête** (coll) to be one's own self again; **se mettre à poil** to strip to the skin

poi·lu -lue [pwaly] *adj* hairy ‖ *m* (mil) doughboy

poinçon [pwɛ̃sɔ̃] *m* punch; stamp; hallmark; **poinçon à glace** ice pick

poinçonner [pwɛ̃sɔne] *tr* to punch; stamp; prick; hallmark

poinçonneuse [pwɛ̃sɔnøz] *f* stamping machine; ticket punch

poindre [pwɛ̃dr] §35 *intr* to dawn; sprout

poing [pwɛ̃] *m* fist; **dormir à poings fermés** to sleep like a log

point [pwɛ̃] *m* point; stitch; period (*used also in French to mark the divisions of whole numbers*); hole (*in a strap*); mark (*on a test*); (aer, naut) position; (typ) point; **à point** at the right moment; to a turn, medium; **à point nommé** in the nick of time; **à tel point que** to such a degree that; **au dernier point** to the utmost degree; **de point en point** exactly to the letter; **de tout point, en tout point** entirely; **deux points** colon; **faire le point** to take stock, get one's bearings; **mettre au point** to focus; adjust, tune up; develop, perfect; **mettre les points sur les i** to dot one's i's; **point d'appui** fulcrum; base of operations; **point de bâti** (sewing) tack; **point de coupure** cut-off; **point de départ** starting point; **point de mire** target; **point de repère** point of reference, guide; (surv) bench mark; (fig) landmark; **point d'estime** dead reckoning; **point de vue** viewpoint; **point d'exclamation** exclamation point; **point d'interrogation** question mark; **point d'orgue** (mus) pause; **point du jour** break of day; **point et virgule** semicolon; **point mort** dead center; (aut) neutral; **point noir** construction (*on highway*); **points et traits** dots and dashes ‖ *adv*—**ne . . . point** §90 not; not at all

pointage [pwɛ̃taʒ] *m* checking; check mark; aiming

pointe [pwɛ̃t] *f* point; tip; peak; head (*of arrow*); nose (*e.g., of bullet*); toe (*of shoe*); twinge (*of pain*); dash (*of, e.g., vanilla*); suggestion, touch; witty phrase, quip; (geog) cape, point; (mil) spearhead; **à pointes** spiked (*shoes*); **de pointe** peak (*e.g., hours*); **discuter sur les pointes d'épingle** to split hairs; **en pointe** tapering; **faire des pointes** to toe-dance; **pointe d'aiguille** needlepoint; **pointe de Paris** wire nail; **pointe de vitesse** spurt; **pointe du jour** daybreak; **sur la pointe des pieds** on tiptoe

poin·teau [pwɛ̃to] *m* (*pl* **-teaux**) checker; needle

pointer [pwɛ̃tœr] *m* pointer (*dog*) ‖ [pwɛ̃te] *tr* to check off; check in; prick up (*the ears*); dot ‖ *intr* to rise, soar skywards; stand out; sprout; **pointer sur** (coll) zero in on ‖ *ref* to check in, show up

poin·teur [pwɛ̃tœr] **-teuse** [tøz] *mf* checker; scorer; timekeeper; gunner; (*dog*) pointer

pointillé [pwɛ̃tije] *m* perforated line

pointil·leux [pwɛ̃tijø] **-leuse** [jøz] *adj* punctilious; touchy; captious

poin·tu -tue [pwɛ̃ty] *adj* pointed; shrill; (fig) touchy

pointure [pwɛ̃tyr] *f* size

poire [pwar] *f* pear; bulb (*of camera, syringe, horn, etc.*); (slang) mug; (slang) sucker, sap; **couper la poire en deux** to split the difference; **garder une poire pour la soif** to put something aside for a rainy day; **poire à poudre** powder flask; **poire électrique** pear-shaped switch

poi·reau [pwaro] *m* (*pl* **-reaux**) (bot) leek; **faire le poireau** (slang) to cool one's heels

poirée [pware] *f* (bot) Swiss chard

poirier [pwarje] *m* pear tree

pois [pwa] *m* pea; polka dot; **petits pois, pois verts** peas; **petit pois sauteur** jumping bean; **pois cassés** split peas; **pois chiche** chickpea; **pois de senteur** sweet pea

poison [pwazɔ̃] *m* poison

pois·sard -sarde [pwasar] [sard] *adj* vulgar ‖ *f* fishwife

poisser [pwase] *tr* to coat with wax or pitch ‖ *intr* to be sticky

pois·seux -seuse [pwasø] [søz] *adj* sticky

poisson [pwasɔ̃] *m* fish; **les Poissons** (astr, astrol) Pisces; **poisson d'avril** April Fool (*joke, trick*); **poisson rouge** goldfish

poisson-chat [pwasɔ̃ʃa] *m* (*pl* **poissons-chats**) catfish

poissonnerie [pwasɔnri] *f* fish market

poisson·nier [pwasɔnje] **-nière** [njɛr] *mf* dealer in fish ‖ *f* fishwife; fish kettle

poitrail [pwatraj] *m* breast

poitrinaire [pwatrinɛr] *adj & mf* (pathol) consumptive

poitrine [pwatrin] *f* chest; breast; bosom

poivre [pwavr] *m* pepper

poivrer [pwavre] *tr* to pepper

poivrier [pwavrije] *m* pepper plant; pepper shaker

poivrière [pwavrijɛr] *f* pepper shaker; pepper plantation; **en poivrière** bulblike, turreted

poivron [pwavrɔ̃] *m* pepper; sweet pepper plant

poix [pwa] [pwɑ] *f* pitch; **poix sèche** resin

poker [pɔkɛr] *m* poker; four of a kind

polaire [pɔlɛr] *adj* pole, polar

polariser [pɔlarize] *tr* to polarize

pôle [pol] *m* pole

po·li -lie [pɔli] *adj* polished; polite ‖ *m* polish, gloss

police [pɔlis] *f* police; policy; **police d'assurance** insurance policy

policer [pɔlise] §51 *tr* to civilize; (obs) to police

Polichinelle [pɔliʃinɛl] *m* Punch; **de polichinelle** open (*secret*)

poli·cier [pɔlisje] **-cière** [sjɛr] *adj* police (*investigation, dog, etc.*); detective (*e.g., story*) ‖ *m* plain-clothes man, detective

polio [pɔljo] *mf* (coll) polio victim || *f* (coll) polio

polir [pɔlir] *tr* to polish

polissoir [pɔliswar] *m* polisher

polis·son [pɔlisɔ̃] **-sonne** [sɔn] *adj* smutty || *mf* scamp, rascal

politesse [pɔlitɛs] *f* politeness; **politesses** civilities, compliments

politicard [pɔlitikar] *m* unscrupulous politician

politi·cien [pɔlitisjɛ̃] **-cienne** [sjɛn] *adj* short-sighted; insincere || *mf* (often pej) politician

politique [pɔlitik] *adj* political; prudent, wise || *m* politician; statesman || *f* politics; policy; cunning, shrewdness; **politique du place-sous** patronage

pollen [pɔlɛn] *m* pollen

pol·luant [pɔlɥɑ̃] **-luante** [lɥɑ̃t] *adj* polluting

polluer [pɔlɥe] *tr* to pollute

pollution [pɔlysjɔ̃] *f* pollution; **pollutions nocturnes** wet dreams

polo [pɔlo] *m* polo

poloéiste [pɔlɔeist] *mf* polo player

Pologne [pɔlɔɲ] *f* Poland; **la Pologne** Poland

polo·nais [pɔlɔnɛ] **-naise** [nɛz] *adj* Polish || *m* Polish (*language*) || (*cap*) *mf* Pole

polonium [pɔlɔnjɔm] *m* polonium

pol·tron [pɔltrɔ̃] **-tronne** [trɔn] *adj* cowardly || *mf* coward

polycopie [pɔlikɔpi] *f* mimeographing; **tiré à la polycopie** mimeographed

polycopié [pɔlikɔpje] *m* mimeographed university lectures

polycopier [pɔlikɔpje] *tr* to mimeograph

polygame [pɔligam] *adj* polygamous || *mf* polygamist

polyglotte [pɔliglɔt] *adj* polyglot || *mf* polyglot, linguist

polygone [pɔligɔn] *m* polygon; shooting range

polynôme [pɔlinom] *m* polynomial

polype [pɔlip] *m* polyp

polythéiste [pɔliteist] *adj* polytheistic || *mf* polytheist

pom [pɔ̃] *interj* bang!

pommade [pɔmad] *f* pomade; **passer de la pommade à** (coll) to soft-soap

pomme [pɔm] *f* apple; ball, knob; head (*of lettuce*); **pomme à couteau** eating apple; **pomme de discorde** bone of contention; **pomme de pin** pine cone; **pomme de terre** potato; **pommes chips** potato chips; **pommes de terre au four** baked potatoes; scalloped potatoes; **pommes de terre en robe de chambre, en robe des champs,** or **en chemise** potatoes in their jackets; **pommes de terre sautées** fried potatoes; **pommes frites** French fried potatoes; **pommes soufflées** potato puffs; **pommes vapeur** boiled potatoes; steamed potatoes

pom·meau [pɔmo] *m* (*pl* **-meaux**) pommel; butt (*of fishing pole*)

pomme·lé -lée [pɔmle] *adj* dappled; fleecy (*clouds*); mackerel (*sky*)

pommette [pɔmɛt] *f* cheekbone

pommier [pɔmje] *m* apple tree

pompe [pɔ̃p] *f* pomp; pump; **à la pompe** on draught; **aller à toute pompe** (slang) to go lickety-split; **être en dehors de ses pompes** (slang) to be absent-minded; **pompe à incendie** fire engine; **pompe aspirante** suction pump; **pompe à vélo** bicycle pump; **pompe de chaleur** heat pump; **pompes funèbres** funeral

pomper [pɔ̃pe] *tr* to pump; suck in

pompette [pɔ̃pɛt] *adj* (coll) tipsy

pom·peux [pɔ̃pø] **-peuse** [pøz] *adj* pompous; high-flown

pom·pier [pɔ̃pje] **-pière** [pjɛr] *adj* conventional; pretentious || *mf* fitter || *m* fireman

pompiste [pɔ̃pist] *mf* filling-station attendant

pomponner [pɔ̃pɔne] *tr & ref* to dress up

ponçage [pɔ̃saʒ] *m* sandpapering; pumicing

ponce [pɔ̃s] *f* pumice stone

pon·ceau [pɔ̃so] (*pl* **-ceaux**) *adj* poppy-red || *m* rude bridge; culvert

poncer [pɔ̃se] §51 *tr* to sandpaper; pumice

ponceuse [pɔ̃søz] *f* sander

poncho [pɔ̃tʃo] *m* poncho

poncif [pɔ̃sif] *m* banality

ponctualité [pɔ̃ktɥalite] *f* punctuality

ponctuation [pɔ̃ktɥasjɔ̃] *f* punctuation

ponc·tuel -tuelle [pɔ̃ktɥɛl] *adj* punctual

ponctuer [pɔ̃ktɥe] *tr* to punctuate

pondération [pɔ̃derasjɔ̃] *f* balance; weighting

pondé·ré -rée [pɔ̃dere] *adj* moderate, well-balanced; weighted

pondérer [pɔ̃dere] §10 *tr* to balance; weight

pondeuse [pɔ̃døz] *f* layer (*hen*); (coll) prolific woman

pondre [pɔ̃dr] *tr* to lay (*an egg*); (coll) to turn out (*a book*); (slang) to bear (*a child*) || *intr* to lay

poney [pɔnɛ] *m* pony

pongiste [pɔ̃ʒist] *mf* table-tennis player, Ping-Pong player

pont [pɔ̃] *m* bridge; (naut) deck; **faire le pont** (coll) to take the intervening day or days off; **pont aérien** airlift; **pont arrière** (aut) rear-axle assembly; **pont cantilever,** **pont à consoles** cantilever bridge; **ponts et chaussées** [pɔ̃zeʃose] highway department; **ponts restaurants** turnpike restaurants; **pont suspendu** suspension bridge

ponte [pɔ̃t] *f* egg laying; eggs

pontet [pɔ̃tɛ] *m* trigger guard

pontife [pɔ̃tif] *m* pontiff

pont-levis [pɔ̃lvi] *m* (*pl* **ponts-levis**) drawbridge

ponton [pɔ̃tɔ̃] *m* pontoon; landing stage

pont-promenade [pɔ̃prɔmnad] *m* (*pl* **ponts-promenades**) promenade deck

pool [pul] *m* pool (*combine*)

pope [pɔp] *m* Orthodox priest

popeline [pɔplin] *f* poplin

popote [pɔpɔt] *adj invar* (coll) stay-at-home || *f* (mil) mess; (coll) cooking; **faire la**

popote (coll) to do the cooking oneself
populace [pɔpylas] *f* populace, rabble
populaire [pɔpylɛr] *adj* popular; vulgar, common
populariser [pɔpylarize] *tr* to popularize
popularité [pɔpylarite] *f* popularity
population [pɔpylɑsjɔ̃] *f* population
popu·leux [pɔpylø] **-leuse** [løz] *adj* populous; crowded
populo [pɔpylo] *m* (coll) rabble
porc [pɔr] *m* pig, hog; pork
porcelaine [pɔrsəlɛn] *f* porcelain; china
porcelet [pɔrsəle] *m* piglet
porc-épic [pɔrkepik] *m* (*pl* **porcs-épics** [pɔrkepik] porcupine
porche [pɔrʃ] *m* porch, portico
porcher [pɔrʃe] *m* swineherd
porcherie [pɔrʃəri] *f* pigpen
pore [pɔr] *m* pore
po·reux [pɔrø] **-reuse** [røz] *adj* porous
porno [pɔrno] *m & f* (coll) porn
pornographie [pɔrnɔgrafi] *f* pornography
porphyre [pɔrfir] *m* porphyry
port [pɔr] *m* port; carryings; wearing; bearing; shipping charges; **arriver à bon port** to arrive safe; **port d'attache** home port; **port d'escale** port of call; **port franc** duty-free; free port; **port payé** postpaid
portable [pɔrtabl] *adj* portable; wearable
portail [pɔrtaj] *m* portal, gate
por·tant [pɔrtɑ̃] **-tante** [tɑ̃t] *adj* bearing; lifting; **être bien portant** to be in good health ‖ *m* handle
porta·tif [pɔrtatif] **-tive** [tiv] *adj* portable
porte [pɔrt] *f* door; doorway; gate; **fausse porte** blind door; **porte à deux battants** double door; **porte à porte** door to door (*selling*); **porte à tambour** revolving door; **porte battante** swinging door; **porte cochère** covered carriage entrance
porte-à-faux [pɔrtafo] *m invar*—**en porte-à-faux** out of line; (fig) in an untenable position
porte-aiguilles [pɔrtegɥi] *m invar* needle case
porte-allumettes [pɔrtalymɛt] *m invar* matchbox
porte-assiette [pɔrtasjɛt] *m* (*pl* **-assiette** or **-assiettes**) place mat
porte-avions [pɔrtavjɔ̃] *m invar* aircraft carrier
porte-bagages [pɔrtbagaʒ] *m invar* baggage rack
porte-bannière [pɔrtbanjɛr] *mf* (*pl* **-bannière** or **-bannières**) colorbearer
porte-bonheur [pɔrtbɔnœr] *m invar* good-luck charm
porte-carte [pɔrtəkart] *m* (*pl* **-carte** or **-cartes**) card case
porte-chapeaux [pɔrtʃapo] *m invar* hatrack
porte-cigarette [pɔrtsigarɛt] *m invar* cigarette holder
porte-cigarettes [pɔrtsigarɛt] *m invar* cigarette case
porte-clés or **porte-clefs** [pɔrtəkle] *m invar* key ring
porte-disques [pɔrtdisk] *m invar* record case

porte-documents [pɔrtdɔkymɑ̃] *m invar* letter case, portfolio
porte-drapeau [pɔrtdrapo] *m* (*pl* **-drapeau** or **-drapeaux**) standard-bearer
portée [pɔrte] *f* range, reach; import, significance; litter; (mus) staff; **à la portée de** within reach of; **à portée de la voix** within speaking distance; **à portée de l'oreille** within hearing distance; **hors de la portée de** out of reach of
portefaix [pɔrtəfɛ] *m* porter; dock hand
porte-fenêtre [pɔrtfənɛtr], [pɔrtəfnɛtr] *f* (*pl* **portes-fenêtres**) French window, French door
portefeuille [pɔrtəfœj] *m* portfolio; wallet, billfold
porteman·teau [pɔrtmɑ̃to] *m* (*pl* **-teaux**) clothes tree; **en portemanteau** square (*shoulders*)
porte-mine [pɔrtəmin] *m* (*pl* **-mine** or **mines**) mechanical pencil
porte-monnaie [pɔrtmɔnɛ] *m invar* change purse
porte-parapluies [pɔrtparaplɥi] *m invar* umbrella stand
porte-parole [pɔrtparɔl] *m invar* spokesperson, spokesman, mouthpiece
porte-plume [pɔrtəplym] *m invar* penholder; **porte-plume réservoir** fountain pen
porter [pɔrte] §96, §100 *tr* to carry; bear; wear; propose (*a toast*); **être porté à** to be inclined to; **être porté sur** to have a weakness for; **porter à l'écran** (mov) to put on the screen; **porter qn sur son testament** to put s.o. in one's will; **portez . . . arme!** present . . . arms! ‖ *intr* to carry; **porter sur** to bear down on, emphasize; be aimed at ‖ *ref* to be worn; proceed, go; to be, e.g., **comment vous portez-vous?** how are you?; **se porter à** to indulge in; **se porter candidat** to run as a candidate
porte-savon [pɔrtsavɔ̃] *m* (*pl* **-savon** or **-savons**) soap dish
porte-serviettes [pɔrtsɛrvjɛt] *m invar* towel rack
por·teur [pɔrtœr] **-teuse** [tøz] *mf* porter; bearer; holder
porte-vêtement [pɔrtəvɛtmɑ̃] *m invar* clothes hanger
porte-voix [pɔrtəvwa] *m invar* megaphone; **mettre les mains en porte-voix** to cup one's hands
por·tier [pɔrtje] **-tière** [tjɛr] *mf* concierge ‖ *m* doorman ‖ *f* door (*of car*); portiere
portillon [pɔrtijɔ̃] *m* gate; (rr) side gate (*at crossing*); **refouler du portillon** (slang) to have bad breath
portion [pɔrsjɔ̃] *f* portion; share
portique [pɔrtik] *m* portico
porto [pɔrto] *m* port wine
portori·cain [pɔrtorikɛ̃] **-caine** [kɛn] *adj* Puerto Rican ‖ (*cap*) *mf* Puerto Rican
Porto Rico [pɔrtoriko] *f* Puerto Rico
portrait [pɔrtrɛ] *m* portrait; **être tout le portrait de** to be the very image of;

portrait à mi-corps half-length portrait; **portrait de face** full-faced portrait

portraitiste [pɔrtretist] *mf* portrait painter

portu·gais [pɔrtygɛ] **-gaise** [gɛz] *adj* Portuguese ‖ *m* Portuguese (*language*) ‖ (*cap*) *mf* Portuguese (*person*)

Portugal [pɔrtygal] *m*—**le Portugal** Portugal

P.O.S. [peoɛs] *m* (letterword) (**plan d'occupation des sols**) zoning code

pose [poz] *f* pose; laying, setting in place; (phot) exposure

po·sé -sée [poze] *adj* poised, steady; trained (*voice*)

pose-marge [pozmarʒ] *f invar* margin setter (*on a typewriter*)

posément [pozemɑ̃] *adv* calmly, steadily, carefully

posemètre [pozmɛtr] *m* (phot) light meter, exposure meter

poser [poze] *tr* to place; arrange; ask (*a question*); set up (*a principle*) ‖ *intr* to pose ‖ *ref* to pose; alight; land; **se poser en** to set oneself up as

po·seur [pozœr] **-seuse** [zøz] *mf* layer; poseur; phony; **poseur d'affiches** billposter

posi·tif [pozitif] **-tive** [tiv] *adj & m* positive

position [pozisjɔ̃] *f* position

posologie [pɔsɔlɔʒi] *f* dosage

posséder [pɔsede] §10 *tr* to possess, own; have a command of, know perfectly ‖ *ref* to control oneself

possession [pɔsesjɔ̃] *f* possession

possibilité [pɔsibilite] *f* possibility

possible [pɔsibl] *adj & m* possible

postage [pɔstaʒ] *m* mailing

pos·tal -tale [pɔstal] *adj* (*pl* **-taux** [to]) postal

postalage [pɔstalaʒ] *m* selling by mail

postdate [pɔstdat] *f* postdate

postdater [pɔstdate] *tr* to postdate

poste [pɔst] *m* post; station; set; position, job; **poste de douane** port of entry; **poste d'émetteur** broadcasting station; **poste de pilotage** cockpit; **poste de radio** radio set; **poste de repérage** tracking station; **poste de secours** first-aid station; **poste des malades** (nav) sick bay; **poste d'essence** gas station; **poste d'incendie** fire station; **poste supplémentaire** (telp) extension ‖ *f* post, mail; **mettre à la poste** to mail; **poste restante** general delivery; **postes** post office department

poster [pɔste] *tr* to post ‖ *ref* to lie in wait

postérité [pɔsterite] *f* posterity

posthume [pɔstym] *adj* posthumous

postiche [pɔstiʃ] *adj* false; detachable ‖ *m* toupee; switch, false hair

pos·tier [pɔstje] **-tière** [tjɛr] *mf* postal clerk

postscolaire [pɔstskɔlɛr] *adj* adult (*education*); extension (*courses*)

post-scriptum [pɔstskriptɔm] *m invar* postscript

postu·lant [pɔstylɑ̃] **-lante** [lɑ̃t] *mf* applicant, candidate; postulant

postuler [pɔstyle] *tr* to apply for ‖ *intr* to apply; **postuler pour** to represent (*a client*)

posture [pɔstyr] *f* posture; situation

pot [po] *m* pot; pitcher; jug; jar; can; **avoir du pot** (coll) to be lucky; **découvrir le pot aux roses** (coll) to discover the secret; **payer les pots cassés** (coll) to pay the piper; **pot à bière** beer mug; **pot à fleurs** flowerpot; **pot de café** coffee mug; **pot d'échappement** (aut) muffler; **pot de noir** cloudy weather; **pot d'étain** pewter tankard; **tourner autour du pot** (coll) to beat about the bush

potable [pɔtabl] *adj* drinkable; (coll) acceptable, passable

potache [pɔtaʃ] *m* (coll) schoolboy

potage [pɔtaʒ] *m* soup; **potage de maïs** hominy; **pour tout potage** (lit) all told

pota·ger [pɔtaʒe] **-gère** [ʒɛr] *adj* vegetable ‖ *m* vegetable garden; dinner pail

potasse [pɔtas] *f* potash

potasser [pɔtase] *tr* (coll) to bone up on ‖ *intr* (coll) to grind away

potas·seur [pɔtasœr] **-seuse** [søz] *mf* (coll) grind

potassium [pɔtasjɔm] *m* potassium

pot-au-feu [pɔtofø] *adj invar* (coll) homeloving ‖ *m invar* beef stew

pot-de-vin [podvɛ̃] *m* (*pl* **pots-de-vin**) bribe, money under the table

po·teau [pɔto] *m* (*pl* **-teaux**) post, pole; **franchir le poteau** to reach the goal (*to succeed*); **poteau de but** goal post; **poteau indicateur** signpost

pote·lé -lée [pɔtle] *adj* chubby

potence [pɔtɑ̃s] *f* gallows; bracket

potentat [pɔtɑ̃ta] *m* potentate

poten·tiel -tielle [pɔtɑ̃sjɛl] *adj & m* potential

poterie [pɔtri] *f* pottery; metalware; **poterie mordorée** lusterware

poterne [pɔtɛrn] *f* postern

potiche [pɔtiʃ] *f* large Oriental vase; (fig) figurehead

potin [pɔtɛ̃] *m* piece of gossip; racket; **faire du potin** (coll) to raise a row; **potins** gossip

potiner [pɔtine] *intr* to gossip

potion [posjɔ̃] *f* potion

potiron [pɔtirɔ̃] *m* pumpkin; **potiron lumineux** jack-o'-lantern

pou [pu] *m* (*pl* **poux**) louse

poubelle [pubɛl] *f* garbage can

pouce [pus] *m* thumb; big toe; inch; **manger sur le pouce** (coll) to eat on the run

poudre [pudr] *f* powder; face powder; **en poudre** powdered; granulated (*sugar*); **il n'a pas inventé la poudre** (coll) he's not so smart; **jeter de la poudre aux yeux de** to deceive; **poudre à pâte** baking powder; **poudre dentifrice** tooth powder; **se mettre de la poudre** to powder one's nose

poudrer [pudre] *tr* to powder

poudrerie [pudrəri] *f* powder mill

pou·dreux [pudrø] **-dreuse** [drøz] *adj* powdery; dusty ‖ *f* sugar shaker

poudrier [pudrije] *m* compact
poudrière [pudrijɛr] *f* powder magazine; (fig) powder keg
poudroyer [pudrwaje] §47 *intr* to raise the dust; shine through the dust
pouf [puf] *m* hassock, pouf ‖ *interj* plop!; **faire pouf** (slang) to flop
pouffer [pufe] *intr* to burst out laughing
pouil·leux [pujø] **-leuse** [jøz] *adj* lousy; sordid ‖ *mf* person covered with lice
pouillot [pujo] *m* (orn) warbler
poulailler [pulaje] *m* henhouse; (theat) peanut gallery
poulain [pulɛ̃] *m* colt, foal
poule [pul] *f* hen; chicken; (*in games*) pool; jackpot; (turf) sweepstakes; (coll) skirt, dame; (slang) tart, mistress; **ma poule** (coll) my pet; **poule au pot** chicken stew; **poule de luxe** (slang) high-class prostitute; call girl; **poule d'Inde** turkey hen; **poule mouillée** (coll) milksop, coward; **tuer la poule aux œufs d'or** to kill the goose that lays the golden eggs
poulet [pulɛ] *m* chicken; (coll) love letter; (slang) cop; **mon petit poulet** (coll) my pet; **poulet d'Inde** turkey cock
poulette [pulɛt] *f* pullet; (coll) gal; **ma poulette** (coll) darling
pouliche [puliʃ] *f* filly
poulie [puli] *f* pulley; block
pou·lot [pulo] **-lotte** [lɔt] *mf* child, kid, lovie, baby (*term of affection*); **attention aux petits poulots** (*public sign*) watch children
poulpe [pulp] *m* octopus
pouls [pu] *m* pulse; **tâter le pouls à** to feel the pulse of
poumon [pumɔ̃] *m* lung
poupe [pup] *f* (naut) stern, poop
poupée [pupe] *f* doll; dummy; sore finger; (mach) headstock
pou·pon [pupɔ̃] **-ponne** [pɔn] *mf* baby; chubby-faced youngster
pouponnière [pupɔnjɛr] *f* nursery
pour [pur] *m*—**le pour et le contre** the pros and the cons ‖ *adv*—**pour lors** then; **pour peu que** however little; **pour que** in order that; **pour . . . que** however, e.g., **pour charmante qu'elle soit** however charming she may be ‖ *prep* for; in order to; **pour ainsi dire** so to speak; **pour cent** per cent
pourboire [purbwar] *m* tip
pour·ceau [purso] *m* (*pl* **-ceaux**) swine, hog, pig
pourcentage [pursɑ̃taʒ] *m* percentage
pourchasser [purʃase] *tr* to hound
pourlécher [purleʃe] §10 *ref* to smack one's lips
pourparlers [purparle] *mpl* talks, parley, conference
pourpoint [purpwɛ̃] *m* doublet
pourpre [purpr] *adj* purple ‖ *m* purple (*violescent*) ‖ *f* purple (*deep red, crimson*)
pourquoi [purkwa] *m* why; **le pourquoi et le comment** the why and the wherefore ‖

adv & *conj* why; **pourquoi pas?** why not?
pour·ri -rie [puri] *adj* rotten; spoiled ‖ *m* rotten part
pourrir [purir] *tr, intr, & ref* to rot; spoil; corrupt
pourriture [purityr] *f* rot; decay; corruption
poursuite [pursɥit] *f* pursuit; (aer) tracking; (law) action, suit; (coll) spotlight
poursui·vant [pursɥivɑ̃] **-vante** [vɑ̃t] *mf* pursuer; (law) plaintiff
poursuivre [pursɥivr] §67 *tr* to pursue, chase; proceed with; persecute; sue ‖ *intr* to continue ‖ *ref* to be continued
pourtant [purtɑ̃] *adv* however, nevertheless, yet
pourtour [purtur] *m* circumference
pourvoi [purvwa] *m* (law) appeal
pourvoir [purvwar] §54, §95 *tr*—**pourvoir de** to supply with, provide with; favor with ‖ *intr*—**pourvoir à** to provide for, attend to ‖ *ref* (law) to appeal
pour·voyeur [purvwajœr] **-voyeuse** [vwajøz] *mf* provider, supplier; caterer; **pourvoyeurs** gun crew
pourvu que [purvykə] *conj* provided that
pousse [pus] *f* shoot, sprout
pous·sé -sée [puse] *adj* elaborate; searching, exhaustive ‖ *f* push, shove; thrust; rise; pressure; (rok) thrust
pousse-café [puskafe] *m invar* liqueur
pousser [puse] §96, §100 *tr* to push, shove, egg on, urge; utter (*a cry*); heave (*a sigh*); **pousser plus loin** to carry further ‖ *intr* to push, shove; grow; push on ‖ *ref* to push oneself forward
poussette [pusɛt] *f* baby carriage
poussier [pusje] *m* coal dust
poussière [pusjɛr] *f* dust; powder; **poussière d'eau** spray; **une poussière a** trifle; **une poussière de** a lot of
poussié·reux [pusjerø] **-reuse** [røz] *adj* dusty; powdery
pous·sif [pusif] **-sive** [siv] *adj* wheezy
poussin [pusɛ̃] *m* chick
poussoir [puswar] *m* push button
poutre [putr] *f* beam; joist; girder
poutrelle [putrɛl] *f* small girder
pouvoir [puvwar] *m* power; **pouvoir d'achat** purchasing power ‖ §55, §95 *tr* to be able to do; **je n'y puis rien** I can't or cannot help it, I can do nothing about it ‖ *intr* to be able; **on ne peut mieux** couldn't be better; **on ne peut plus** I (we, they, etc.) can do no more; I'm (we're, they're, etc.) all in ‖ *aux* used to express 1) ability, e.g., **elle peut prédire l'avenir** she is able to predict the future, she can predict the future; 2) permission, e.g., **vous pouvez partir** you may go; e.g., **puis-je partir?** may I go?; 3) possibility, e.g., **il peut pleuvoir** it may rain; e.g., **il a pu oublier son parapluie** he may have forgotten his umbrella; 4) optative, e.g., **puisse-t-il venir!** may he come! ‖ *impers ref*—**il se peut que** it is possible that, e.g., **il se peut qu'il vienne ce soir** it is

possible that he may come this evening, he may come this evening; **il se pourrait bien que** it might well be that, e.g., **il se pourrait bien qu'il vînt ce soir** it might well be that he will come this evening, he might come this evening ‖ *ref* to be possible; **cela ne se peut pas** that is not possible

pragmatique [pragmatik] *adj* pragmatic(al)

prairie [prɛri], [preri] *f* meadow; **les Prairies** the prairie

praticable [pratikabl] *adj* practicable; passable ‖ *m* practicable stage property; (mov, telv) camera platform

prati·cien [pratisjɛ̃] **-cienne** [sjɛn] *mf* practitioner

prati·quant [pratikɑ̃] **-quante** [kɑ̃t] *adj* practicing (*e.g., Catholic*); churchy ‖ *mf* churchgoer

pratique [pratik] *adj* practical ‖ *f* practice; contact, company; customer; **libre pratique** freedom of worship; (naut) freedom from quarantine

pratiquement [pratikmɑ̃] *adv* practically, in practice

pratiquer [pratike] *tr* to practice; cut, make (*e.g., a hole*); frequent; read a great deal of ‖ *intr* to practice (*said, e.g., of doctor*); practice one's religion ‖ *ref* to be practiced, done; rule, prevail (*said of prices*)

pré [pre] *m* meadow; **pré et marée** surf and turf; **sur le pré** on the field of honor (*dueling ground*)

préalable [prealabl] *adj* previous; preliminary ‖ *m* prerequisite; **au préalable** before, in advance

préambule [preɑ̃byl] *m* preamble

préau [preo] *m* (*pl* **préaux**) yard

préavis [preavi] *m* advance warning; **avec préavis** person-to-person (*telephone call*)

précaire [prekɛr] *adj* precarious

précaution [prekosjɔ̃] *f* precaution

précautionner [prekosjone] *tr* to caution ‖ *intr* to be on one's guard

précaution·neux [prekosjɔnø] **-neuse** [nøz] *adj* precautious

précédemment [presedamɑ̃] *adv* before, previously

précé·dent [presedɑ̃] **-dente** [dɑ̃t] *adj* preceding ‖ *m* precedent

précéder [presede] §10 *tr & intr* to precede

précepte [presɛpt] *m* precept

précep·teur [preseptœr] **-trice** [tris] *mf* tutor

prêche [prɛʃ] *m* sermon

prêcher [preʃe] *tr* to preach; preach to ‖ *intr* to preach; **prêcher d'exemple** to practice what one preaches

prê·cheur [prɛʃœr] **-cheuse** [ʃøz] *adj* preaching ‖ *mf* sermonizer

pré·cieux [presjø] **-cieuse** [sjøz] *adj* precious; valuable; affected

préciosité [presjozite] *f* preciosity (*French literary style corresponding to English euphuism*)

précipice [presipis] *m* precipice

précipi·té **-tée** [presipite] *adj* hurried, precipitious ‖ *m* precipitate

précipiter [presipite] *tr* to hurl ‖ *ref* to hurl oneself; precipitate; hurry, rush

pré·cis [presi] **-cise** [siz] *adj* precise; sharp, e.g., **trois heures précises** three o'clock sharp ‖ *m* abstract, summary

précisément [presizemɑ̃] *adv* precisely, exactly; clearly, accurately

préciser [presize] *tr* to specify ‖ *intr* to be precise ‖ *ref* to become clear; take shape, jell

précision [presizjɔ̃] *f* precision; **précisions** data

préci·té **-tée** [presite] *adj* aforementioned

précoce [prekɔs] *adj* precocious; (bot) early

précon·çu **-çue** [prekɔ̃sy] *adj* preconceived

préconiser [prekɔnize] *tr* to advocate, recommend

précurseur [prekyrsœr] *adj masc* precursory ‖ *m* forerunner, harbinger

prédateur [predatœr] *adj masc* predatory ‖ *m* predatory animal

prédécesseur [predesesœr] *m* predecessor

prédicateur [predikatœr] *m* preacher

prédiction [prediksjɔ̃] *f* prediction

prédire [predir] §40 *tr* to predict

prédisposer [predispoze] *tr* to predispose

prédomi·nant **-nante** [predɔminɑ̃] [nɑ̃t] *adj* predominant

préémi·nent **-nente** [preeminɑ̃] [nɑ̃t] *adj* preeminent

préfabri·qué **-quée** [prefabrike] *adj* prefabricated

préface [prefas] *f* preface

préfacer [prefase] §51 *tr* to preface

préfecture [prefɛktyr] *f* prefecture; **préfecture de police** police headquarters

préférable [preferabl] *adj* preferable

préférence [preferɑ̃s] *f* preference

préférer [prefere] §10, §95 *tr* to prefer

préfet [prefɛ] *m* prefect; **préfet de police** police commissioner

préfixe [prefiks] *m* prefix

préfixer [prefikse] *tr* to prefix

préhistorique [preistorik] *adj* prehistoric

préjudice [preʒydis] *m* prejudice, detriment; **porter préjudice à** to injure, to harm; **sans préjudice de** without affecting

préjudiciable [preʒydisjabl] *adj* detrimental

préjudicier [preʒydisje] *intr—***préjudicier à** to harm, damage

préjugé [preʒyʒe] *m* prejudice

préjuger [preʒyʒe] §38 *tr* to foresee ‖ *intr—***préjuger de** to prejudge

prélart [prelar] *m* tarpaulin

prélasser [prelase] *ref* to lounge

prélat [prela] *m* prelate

prélèvement [prelɛvmɑ̃] *m* deduction; sample; levy

prélever [prelve] §2 *tr* to set aside, deduct; take (*a sample*); levy; **prélever à** to take from

préliminaire [preliminɛr] *adj & m* preliminary

prélude [prelyd] *m* prelude

préluder [prelyde] *intr* to warm up (*said of singer, musician, etc.*); **préluder à** to prelude

prématu·ré -rée [prematyre] *adj* premature

préméditer [premedite] *tr* to premeditate

prémices [premis] *fpl* first fruits; beginning

pre·mier [prəmje] **-mière** [mjɛr] §92 *adj* first; raw (*materials*); prime (*number*); the First, e.g., **Jean premier** John the First ‖ (when standing before noun) *adj* first; prime (*minister*); maiden (*voyage*); early (*infancy*) ‖ *m* first; **jeune premier** leading man; **premier de cordée** leader ‖ *f* first; first class; (*theat*) première; **jeune première** leading lady ‖ *pron* (*masc & fem*) first

premièrement [prəmjɛrmɑ̃] *adv* firstly, first, in the first place, to begin with

premier-né [prəmjene] **-née** [ne] (*pl* **premiers-nés**) *adj & mf* first-born

prémisse [premis] *f* premise

prémonition [premɔnisjɔ̃] *f* premonition

prémunir [premynir] *tr* to forewarn ‖ *ref*—**se prémunir contre** to protect oneself against

pre·nant [prənɑ̃] **-nante** [nɑ̃t] *adj* sticky; winning, pleasing

prendre [prɑ̃dr] §56 *tr* to take; take on; take up; catch; get (*to obtain and bring*); steal (*a kiss*); buy (*a ticket*); make (*an appointment*); **à tout prendre** all things considered; **prendre de l'âge** to be getting old; **prendre la mer** to take to sea; **prendre l'eau** to leak; **prendre le large** to take to the open sea; **prendre q.ch. à qn** to take s.th. from s.o.; charge s.o. s.th. (*i.e., a certain sum of money*); **prendre son temps** to take one's time ‖ *intr* to catch (*said of fire*); take root; form (*said of ice*); set (*said of mortar*); stick (*to a pan or dish*); catch on (*said of a style*); to turn (*right or left*); to bear to the right; **qu'est-ce qui lui prend?** what's come over him? ‖ §96 *ref* to get caught, catch (*e.g., on a nail*); congeal; clot; curdle; jam; take from each other; **pour qui se prend-il?** who does he think he is?; **s'en prendre à qn de q.ch.** to blame s.o. for s.th.; **se prendre à** to begin to; **se prendre d'amitié** to strike up a friendship; **se prendre de vin** to get drunk; **s'y prendre** to go about it

pre·neur [prənœr] **-neuse** [nøz] *mf* taker; buyer; payee; lessee

prenne [prɛn] *v* (**prennes, prennent**) see **prendre**

prénom [prenɔ̃] *m* first name

prénommer [prenɔme] *tr* to name ‖ *ref*—**il** (**elle,** etc.) **se prénomme** his (her, etc.) first name is

préoccupation [preɔkypɑsjɔ̃] *f* preoccupation

préoccuper [preɔkype] *tr* to preoccupy ‖ *ref*—**se préoccuper de** to pay attention to; be concerned about

prépara·teur [preparatœr] **-trice** [tris] *mf* laboratory assistant

préparatifs [preparatif] *mpl* preparations

préparation [preparɑsjɔ̃] *f* preparation; notice, warning

préparatoire [preparatwar] *adj* preparatory

préparer [prepare] §96, §100 *tr, intr, & ref* to prepare

prépondé·rant [prepɔ̃derɑ̃] **-rante** [rɑ̃t] *adj* preponderant

prépo·sé -sée [prepoze] *mf* employee, clerk; mail carrier, postman; **préposé de la douane** customs officer; **préposée au vestiaire** hatcheck person, hatcheck girl

préposer [prepoze] *tr*—**préposer qn à q.ch.** to put s.o. in charge of s.th.

préposition [prepozisjɔ̃] *f* preposition

prérogative [prerɔgativ] *f* prerogative

près [prɛ] *adv* near; **à beaucoup près** by far; **à cela près** except for that; **à peu d'exceptions près** with few exceptions; **à peu près** about, practically; **à . . . près** except for; within, e.g., **je peux vous dire l'heure à cinq minutes près** I can tell you what time it is within five minutes; **au plus près** to the nearest point; **de près** close; closely; **ici près** near here; **près de** near; nearly, about; alongside, at the side of; **près de** + *inf* about to + *inf*; **tout près** nearby, right here ‖ *prep* near; to, at

présage [prezaʒ] *m* presage, foreboding

présager [prezaʒe] §38 *tr* to presage, forebode; anticipate

pré-salé [presale] *m* (*pl* **prés-salés**) salt-meadow sheep; salt-meadow mutton

presbyte [prɛsbit] *adj* far-sighted ‖ *mf* far-sighted person

presbytère [prɛsbitɛr] *m* presbytery

presbyté·rien [prɛsbiterjɛ̃] **-rienne** [rjɛn] *adj & mf* Presbyterian

presbytie [prɛsbisi] *f* far-sightedness

prescription [prɛskripsjɔ̃] *f* prescription

prescrire [prɛskrir] §25, §97, §98 *tr* to prescribe ‖ *ref* to be prescribed

préséance [preseɑ̃s] *f* precedence

présélection [preselɛksjɔ̃] *f*—**présélection des candidats** screening of candidates

présence [prezɑ̃s] *f* presence; attendance; **en présence** face to face; under consideration

pré·sent [prezɑ̃] **-sente** [zɑ̃t] *adj* present ‖ *m* present, gift; (*gram*) present; **les présents** those present

présentable [prezɑ̃tabl] *adj* presentable

présenta·teur [prezɑ̃tatœr] **-trice** [tris] *mf* (*rad*) announcer; **présentateur de disques** disk jockey

présentateur-tronc [prezɑ̃tatœrtrɔ̃] *m* (*telv*) anchor man

présentation [prezɑ̃tɑsjɔ̃] *f* presentation; introduction; appearance; look, form (*of a new product*)

présentement [prezɑ̃tmɑ̃] *adv* right now

présenter [prezɑ̃te] *tr* to present; introduce; offer; pay (*one's respects*) ‖ *ref* to present oneself; present itself; **se présenter à** to be a candidate for

présérie [preseri] *f* (com) trial run, sample run

préservatif [prezɛrvatif] *m* preventive; condom, prophylactic

préserver [prezɛrve] *tr* to preserve

présidence [prezidɑ̃s] *f* presidency; chairmanship; presidential mansion

prési·dent [prezidɑ̃] **-dente** [dɑ̃t] *mf* president; chairperson; chairman; presiding judge ‖ *f* president's wife; chairwoman; **madame la présidente** madam chairman

présiden·tiel -tielle [prezidɑ̃sjɛl] *adj* presidential

présider [prezide] *tr* to preside over ‖ *intr* to preside; **présider à** to preside over

présomp·tif [prezɔ̃ptif] **-tive** [tiv] *adj* presumptive, presumed

présomption [prezɔ̃psjɔ̃] *f* presumption

présomp·tueux [prezɔ̃ptɥø] **-tueuse** [tɥøz] *adj* presumptuous

présonorisation [presɔnɔrizasjɔ̃] *f* playback

presque [prɛsk(ə)] *adv* almost, nearly; **presque jamais** hardly ever; **presque personne** scarcely anybody

presqu'île [prɛskil] *f* peninsula

pres·sant [prɛsɑ̃] **-sante** [sɑ̃t] *adj* pressing, urgent

presse [prɛs] *f* press; hurry, rush; crowd; hand screw, clamp; **mettre sous presse** to go to press

pres·sé -sée [prese] §93 *adj* pressed; pressing, urgent; squeezed

presse-bouton [prɛsbutɔ̃] *adj invar* push-button (*warfare*)

presse-citron [prɛssitrɔ̃] *m invar* lemon squeezer

pressentiment [presɑ̃timɑ̃] *m* presentiment, foreboding

pressentir [presɑ̃tir] §41 *tr* to have a foreboding of; sound out

presse-papiers [prɛspapje] *m invar* paperweight

presse-purée [prɛspyre] *m invar* potato masher

presser [prese], [prɛse] §97 *tr* to press; squeeze; hurry, hasten ‖ *intr* to be urgent ‖ *ref* to hurry; **se presser à** to crowd around

pressing [presiŋ] *m* dry cleaner's

pression [presjɔ̃] *f* pressure; snap fastener; **à la pression** on draught; **pression artérielle** blood pressure

pressoir [preswar] *m* press

pressurer [presyre] *tr* to press, squeeze; bleed white, wring money out of

pressuriser [presyrize] *tr* to pressurize

prestance [prestɑ̃s] *f* commanding appearance, dignified bearing

prestation [prestasjɔ̃] *f* taking (*of oath*); tax; allotment, allowance, benefit

preste [prɛst] *adj* nimble

prestidigita·teur [prɛstidiʒitatœr] **-trice** [tris] *mf* magician

prestidigitation [prɛstidiʒitasjɔ̃] *f* sleight of hand, legerdemain

prestige [prɛstiʒ] *m* prestige; illusion, magic

presti·gieux [prɛstiʒjø] **-gieuse** [ʒjøz] *adj* prestigious, famous; marvelous

présumer [prezyme] §95, §97 *tr* to presume; presume to be ‖ *intr* to presume; **présumer de** to presume upon

présupposer [presypoze] *tr* to presuppose

présure [prezyr] *f* rennet

prêt [prɛ] **prête** [prɛt] §92 *adj* ready; **prêt à porter** ready-to-wear, ready-made; **prêt à tout** ready for anything ‖ *m* loan

prêt-à-monter [prɛtamɔ̃te] *m* (*pl* **prets-à-monter** [prɛzamɔ̃te]) kit

prêt-à-porter [prɛtapɔrte] *m* (*pl* **prêts-à-porter** [prɛtapɔrte]) ready-to-wear, ready-made clothes

prêt-bail [prɛbaj] *m invar* lend-lease

préten·dant [pretɑ̃dɑ̃] **-dante** [dɑ̃t] *mf* pretender ‖ *m* suitor

prétendre [pretɑ̃dr] §95, §96 *tr* to claim; require ‖ *intr*—**prétendre à** to aspire to; lay claim to

préten·du -due [pretɑ̃dy] *adj* so-called, alleged ‖ *m* fiancé ‖ *f* fiancée

prête-nom [prɛtnɔ̃] *m* (*pl* **-noms**) dummy, figurehead, straw man

prétentaine [pretɑ̃tɛn] *f*—**courir la prétentaine** (coll) to be on the loose; (coll) to have many love affairs

préten·tieux [pretɑ̃sjø] **-tieuse** [sjøz] *adj* pretentious

prétention [pretɑ̃sjɔ̃] *f* pretention, pretense; claim, pretensions

prêter [prete], [prɛte] *tr* to lend; give (*e.g., help*); pay (*attention*); take (*an oath*); impart (*e.g., luster*); attribute, ascribe ‖ *intr* to lend; stretch; **prêter à** to lend itself to ‖ *ref*—**se prêter à** to lend itself to; be a party to; countenance; indulge in

prê·teur [pretœr] **-teuse** [tøz] *mf* lender; **prêteur sur gages** pawnbroker

prétexte [pretɛkst] *m* pretext

prétexter [pretɛkste] *tr* to give as a pretext

prétonique [pretɔnik] *adj* pretonic

prêtre [prɛtr] *m* priest

prêtresse [prɛtrɛs] *f* priestess

prêtrise [pretriz] *f* priesthood

preuve [prœv] *f* proof, evidence

preux [prø] *adj masc* valiant ‖ *m* doughty knight

prévaloir [prevalwar] §71 (*subj* **prévale,** etc.) *intr* to prevail ‖ *ref*—**se prévaloir de** to avail oneself of; pride oneself on

prévarication [prevarikasjɔ̃] *f* breach of trust

prévariquer [prevarike] *intr* to betray one's trust

prévenance [prevnɑ̃s] *f* kindness, thoughtfulness

préve·nant [prevnɑ̃] **-nante** [nɑ̃t] *adj* attentive, considerate; prepossessing

prévenir [prevnir] §72 *tr* to anticipate; avert, forestall; ward off, prevent; notify, inform; bias, prejudice

préven·tif [prevɑ̃tif] **-tive** [tiv] *adj* preventive; pretrial (*detention*)

prévention [prevɑ̃sjɔ̃] *f* bias, prejudice; predisposition; custody, imprisonment; prevention (*of accidents*); **prévention rou-tière** traffic police; road safety

préve·nu -nue [prɛvny] *adj* biased, preju-diced; forewarned; accused ‖ *mf* prisoner, accused, defendant

prévision [previzjɔ̃] *f* anticipation, estimate; **prévision du temps** weather forecast; **prévisions** expectations

prévoir [prevwar] §57 *tr* to foresee, antici-pate; forecast

prévoyance [prevwajɑ̃s] *f* foresight

pré·voyant [prevwajɑ̃] **-voyante** [vwajɑ̃t] *adj* far-sighted, provident

prie-dieu [pridjø] *m invar* prie-dieu ‖ *f* praying mantis

prier [prije] §96, §97, §99 *tr* to ask, beg; pray (*God*); **je vous en prie!** I beg your pardon!; by all means!; you are welcome!; please have some!; **je vous prie!** please!; **prier qn de** + *inf* to ask, beg s.o. to + *inf* ‖ *intr* to pray

prière [prijɛr] *f* prayer; **prière de . . .** please . . .; **prière de faire suivre** please for-ward; **prière de garder jusqu'à l'arrivée** please hold until arrival; **prière d'insérer** publisher's insert for reviewers

primaire [primɛr] *adj* primary; first (*offender*); (coll) narrow-minded ‖ *m* (elec) primary; (coll) primitive

primat [prima] *m* (eccl) primate

primate [primat] *m* (zool) primate

primauté [primote] *f* supremacy

prime [prim] *adj* early (*youth*); (math) prime ‖ *f* premium; bonus; free gift; (eccl) prime; **prime de transport** traveling expenses

primer [prime] *tr* to excel; take priority over; award a prize to

primerose [primroz] *f* hollyhock

primesau·tier [primsotje] **-tière** [tjɛr] *adj* impulsive, quick

primeur [primœr] *f* freshness; first fruit; early vegetable; (journ) beat, scoop; **pri-meurs** fruits and vegetables out of season

primevère [primvɛr] *f* primrose

primi·tif [primitif] **-tive** [tiv] *adj* primitive; original, early; primary (*colors; tense*) ‖ *mf* primitive

primo [primo] *adv* firstly

primor·dial -diale [primɔrdjal] *adj* (*pl* **-diaux** [djo]) primordial, fundamental, prime, primary

prince [prɛ̃s] *m* prince; **prince de Galles** Prince of Wales

princesse [prɛ̃sɛs] *f* princess

prin·cier [prɛ̃sje] **-cière** [sjɛr] *adj* princely

princi·pal -pale [prɛ̃sipal] *adj & m* (*pl* **-paux** [po]) principal, chief

principauté [prɛ̃sipote] *f* principality

principe [prɛ̃sip] *m* principle; beginning; source

printa·nier [prɛ̃tanje] **-nière** [njɛr] *adj* spring; springlike

printemps [prɛ̃tɑ̃] *m* spring; springtime; **au printemps** in the spring

priorité [prijɔrite] *f* priority; right of way; **de priorité** preferred (*stock*); main (*road*); **priorité à droite, priorité à gauche**

(*public sign*) yield; **priorité piétons** pe-destrian right of way

pris [pri] **prise** [priz] *adj* set, frozen; **être pris** to be busy; **pris de vin** drunk ‖ *f* capture, seizure; taking; hold; setting; tap, faucet; (med) dose; (naut) prize; **donner prise à** to lay oneself open to; **être aux prises avec** to be struggling with; **hors de prise** out of gear; **lâcher prise** to let go; **mettre en prise** (aut) to put into gear; **prise d'air** ventilator; **prise d'antenne** (rad) lead-in; **prise d'armes** military pa-rade; **prise d'eau** water faucet; hydrant; **prise de bec** (coll) quarrel; **prise de con-science** awakening, awareness; **prise de courant** (elec) plug; (elec) tap, outlet; **prise de position** statement of opinion; **prise de sang** blood specimen; **prise de son** recording; **prise de tabac** pinch of snuff; **prise de terre** (elec) ground con-nection; **prise de vue(s)** (phot) shot, pic-ture taking; **prise de vue directe** (telv) live broadcast; **prise directe** high gear ‖ *v* see **prendre**

prisée [prize] *f* appraisal

priser [prize] *tr* to value; snuff up ‖ *intr* to take snuff

pri·seur [prizœr] **-seuse** [zøz] *mf* snuffer ‖ *m* appraiser

prisme [prism] *m* prism

prison [prizɔ̃] *f* prison

prison·nier [prizɔnje] **-nière** [njɛr] *mf* pris-oner

privautés [privote] *fpl* liberties

pri·vé -vée [prive] *adj* private; tame, pet ‖ *m* private life ‖ *v* see **priver**

priver [prive] §97 *tr* to deprive ‖ *ref* to deprive oneself; **se priver de** to do with-out, abstain from

privilège [privilɛʒ] *m* privilege

privilé·gié -giée [privileʒje] *adj* privileged; preferred (*stock*)

prix [pri] *m* price; prize; value; **à aucun prix** not at any price; by no means; **à tout prix** at all costs; **au prix de** at the price of; at the rate of; compared with; **dans mes prix** within my means; **grand prix** championship race; **hors de prix** at a prohibitive cost; **prix courant** list price; **prix de départ** upset price; **prix de détail** retail price; **prix de fabrique** factory price; **prix de gros** wholesale price; **prix de lancement** introductory offer; **prix de la vie** cost of living; **prix de location** rent; **prix de revient** cost price; **prix de vente** selling price; **prix fixe** table d'hôte; **prix unique** variety store

probabilité [prɔbabilite] *f* probability

probable [prɔbabl] *adj* probable, likely

probablement [prɔbabləmɑ̃] *adv* probably

pro·bant [prɔbɑ̃] **-bante** [bɑ̃t] *adj* convinc-ing; conclusive (*evidence*)

probatoire [prɔbatwar] *adj* experimental, preliminary

probe [prɔb] *adj* honest, upright

problème [prɔblɛm] *m* problem

procédé [prɔsede] *m* process; procedure; tip (*of cue*); **procédés** proceedings; behavior

procéder [prɔsede] §10, §96 *intr* to proceed; **procéder à** to carry out, conduct, undertake, perform; **procéder de** to arise from

procédure [prɔsedyr] *f* procedure; proceedings

procès [prɔsɛ] *m* lawsuit, case; trial; **intenter un procès à** to sue; to prosecute; **sans autre forme de procès** then and there, without appeal

proces·sif [prɔsesif] **-sive** [siv] *adj* litigious

procession [prɔsesjɔ̃] *f* procession

processus [prɔsesys] *m* process

procès-verbal [prɔsɛvɛrbal] *m* (*pl* **-verbaux** [vɛrbo]) report; minutes; ticket (*e.g., for speeding*)

pro·chain [prɔʃɛ̃] **-chaine** [ʃɛn] *adj* next; impending; (lit) nearest, immediate; **la prochaine semaine** the next week; **la semaine prochaine** next week ‖ *m* neighbor, fellow-man ‖ *f*—**à la prochaine!** (coll) so long!

prochainement [prɔʃɛnmɑ̃] *adv* shortly

proche [prɔʃ] *adj* near; nearby; close (*relative*) ‖ **proches** *mpl* close relatives ‖ *adv*—**de proche en proche** little by little

proclamer [prɔklame] *tr* to proclaim

proclitique [prɔklitik] *adj & m* proclitic

procuration [prɔkyrɑsjɔ̃] *f* power of attorney; **par procuration** by proxy

procurer [prɔkyre] *tr & ref* to procure, get

procureur [prɔkyrœr] *m* attorney; **procureur de la république** district attorney; **procureur général** attorney general

prodige [prɔdiʒ] *m* prodigy; wonder

prodi·gieux [prɔdiʒjø] **-gieuse** [ʒjøz] *adj* prodigious, wonderful; terrific

prodigue [prɔdig] *adj* prodigal, lavish ‖ *mf* prodigal, spendthrift

prodiguer [prɔdige] *tr* to squander, waste; lavish ‖ *ref* to not spare oneself; show off

prodrome [prɔdrom] *m* harbinger; introduction

produc·teur [prɔdyktœr] **-trice** [tris] *adj* productive ‖ *mf* producer

produc·tif [prɔdyktif] **-tive** [tiv] *adj* productive; producing

production [prɔdyksjɔ̃] *f* production

produire [prɔdɥir] §19 *tr* to produce; create; introduce ‖ *ref* to take place; be produced; show up

produit [prɔdɥi] *m* product; proceeds; offspring; **produit de luxe** luxury item; **produit pharmaceutique** patent medicine, drug; **produits agricoles** agricultural produce; **produits de beauté** cosmetics

proémi·nent [prɔeminɑ̃] **-nente** [nɑ̃t] *adj* prominent, protuberant

profane [prɔfan] *adj* profane; lay, uninformed ‖ *mf* profane; layman

profaner [prɔfane] *tr* to profane; (fig) to prostitute

proférer [prɔfere] §10 *tr* to utter

professer [prɔfese] *tr* to profess; teach ‖ *intr* to teach

professeur [prɔfɛsœr] *m* teacher; professor

profession [prɔfɛsjɔ̃] *f* profession; occupation, trade

profession·nel -nelle [prɔfɛsjɔnɛl] *adj & mf* professional

profil [prɔfil] *m* profile; pattern; side face; cross section; skyline (*of city*)

profi·lé -lée [prɔfile] *adj* streamlined, aerodynamic

profiler [prɔfile] *tr* to profile ‖ *ref*—**se profiler sur** to stand out against

profit [prɔfi] *m* profit; **mettre à profit** to take advantage of; **profits et pertes** profit and loss

profitable [prɔfitabl] *adj* profitable

profiter [prɔfite] *intr* to profit; to thrive, grow; **profiter à qn** to benefit s.o.; **profiter de** to profit from, take advantage of

profi·teur [prɔfitœr] **-teuse** [tøz] *mf* profiteer

pro·fond [prɔfɔ̃] **-fonde** [fɔ̃d] *adj* profound; deep; low (*bow; voice*); **peu profond** shallow ‖ *m* depths ‖ *f* (slang) pocket ‖ **profond** *adv* deep

profondément [prɔfɔ̃demɑ̃] *adv* profoundly, deeply; soundly; deep

profondeur [prɔfɔ̃dœr] *f* depth

progéniture [prɔʒenityr] *f* progeny; offspring, child

programma·teur [prɔgramatœr] **-trice** [tris] *mf* (mov, rad, telv) programer

programmation [prɔgramɑsjɔ̃] *f* programing

programme [prɔgram] *m* program; **programme de prévoyance** retirement program; **programme des études** curriculum

programmer [prɔgrame] *tr* to program

programmerie [prɔgramri] *f* (comp) software

program·meur [prɔgramœr] **-meuse** [møz] *mf* (comp) programer

progrès [prɔgrɛ] *m* progress; **faire des progrès** to make progress

progresser [prɔgrese] *intr* to progress

progres·sif [prɔgresif] **-sive** [siv] *adj* progressive

progressiste [prɔgresist] *adj & mf* progressive

prohiber [prɔibe] *tr* to prohibit

prohibition [prɔibisjɔ̃] *f* prohibition

proie [prwa], [prwɑ] *f* prey; **de proie** predatory; **en proie à** a prey to

projecteur [prɔʒɛktœr] *m* projector; searchlight; (mov) projection machine

projectile [prɔʒɛktil] *m* projectile; **projectile téléguidé** guided missile

projection [prɔʒɛksjɔ̃] *f* projection; **projection en boucle fermée** endless strip

projet [prɔʒɛ] *m* project; draft; sketch, plan; **faire des projets** to make plans; **projet de loi** bill

projeter [prɔʒte] §34, §97 *tr* to project; pour fourth (*smoke*); cast (*a shadow*); plan ‖ *intr* to plan

prolétaire [prɔletɛr] *m* proletarian

prolétariat [prɔletarja] *m* proletariat

proléta·rien [prɔletarjɛ̃] **-rienne** [rjɛn] *adj* proletarian

proliférer [prɔlifere] §10 *intr* to proliferate

prolifique [prɔlifik] *adj* prolific

prolixe [prɔliks] *adj* prolix

prologue [prɔlɔg] *m* prologue; preface

prolongateur [prɔlɔ̃gatœr] *m* extension cord

prolongation [prɔlɔ̃gasjɔ̃] *f* extension (*of time*); overtime period

prolonger [prɔlɔ̃ʒe] §38 *tr* to prolong; extend ‖ *ref* to be prolonged; continue, extend

promenade [prɔmnad] *f* promenade; walk; ride; drive; sail; **faire une promenade (en auto, à cheval, à motocyclette, en bateau,** etc.) to take a ride

promener [prɔmne] §2 *tr* to take for a walk; take for a ride; walk (*e.g., a dog*); take along; **envoyer promener qn** (coll) to send s.o. packing; **promener . . . sur** to run (*e.g., one's hand, eyes*) over ‖ *ref* to stroll; go for a walk, ride, drive, or sail; **allez vous promener!** get out of here!

prome·neur [prɔmnœr] **-neuse** [nøz] *mf* walker, stroller

promenoir [prɔmnwar] *m* ambulatory, cloister; (theat) standing room

promesse [prɔmɛs] *f* promise

promettre [prɔmɛtr] §42, §98 *tr* to promise; **promettre q.ch. à qn** to promise s.th. to s.o. ‖ *intr* to look promising; **promettre à qn de** + *inf* to promise s.o. to + *inf* ‖ §97 *ref* to promise oneself; **se promettre de** to resolve to

pro·mis [prɔmi] **-mise** [miz] *adj* promised; **promis** is headed for

promiscuité [prɔmiskɥite] *f* indiscriminate mixture; lack of privacy

promontoire [prɔmɔ̃twar] *m* promontory

promo·teur [prɔmɔtœr] **-trice** [tris] *mf* promoter; originator; **promoteur immobilier** housing developer

promotion [prɔmosjɔ̃] *f* promotion; uplift; class (*in school*)

promouvoir [prɔmuvwar] §45 (*pp* **promu**) *tr* to promote

prompt [prɔ̃] **prompte** [prɔ̃t] *adj* prompt, ready, quick

promptitude [prɔ̃tityd] *f* promptness

promulguer [prɔmylge] *tr* to promulgate

prône [pron] *m* homily

prôner [prone] *tr* to extol

pronom [prɔnɔ̃] *m* pronoun

pronomi·nal -nale [prɔnɔminal] *adj* (*pl* **-naux** [no]) pronominal; reflexive (*verb*)

pronon·cé -cée [prɔnɔ̃se] *adj* marked; sharp (*curve*); prominent (*nose*)

prononcer [prɔnɔ̃se] §51 *tr* to pronounce; utter; deliver (*a speech*); pass (*judgment*) ‖ *intr* to decide ‖ *ref* to be pronounced; express an opinion

prononciation [prɔnɔ̃sjɑsjɔ̃] *f* pronunciation

pronostic [prɔnɔstik] *m* prognosis

pronostiquer [prɔnɔstike] *tr* to prognosticate

propagande [prɔpagɑ̃d] *f* propaganda; publicity, advertising

propager [prɔpaʒe] §38 *tr* to propagate; spread ‖ *ref* to be propagated; spread

propédeutique [prɔpedøtik] *f* (educ) preliminary study

propension [prɔpɑ̃sjɔ̃] *f* propensity

prophète [prɔfɛt] *m* prophet

prophétesse [prɔfetɛs] *f* prophetess

prophétie [prɔfesi] *f* prophecy

prophétiser [prɔfetize] *tr* to prophesy

prophylactique [prɔfilaktik] *adj* prophylactic

propice [prɔpis] *adj* propitious; lucky (*star*)

proportion [prɔpɔrsjɔ̃] *f* proportion; **en proportion de** in proportion to

proportion·né -née [prɔpɔrsjɔne] *adj* proportionate

proportion·nel -nelle [prɔpɔrsjɔnɛl] *adj* proportional

proportionner [prɔpɔrsjɔne] *tr* to proportion

propos [prɔpo] *m* remark; purpose; **à ce propos** in this connection; **à propos** by the way; timely, fitting; at the right moment; **à propos de** with regard to, concerning; **à tout propos** at every turn; **changer de propos** to change the subject; **de propos délibéré** on purpose; **des propos en l'air** idle talk; **hors de propos** out of place; irrelevant

proposer [prɔpoze] §97, §98 *tr* to propose; nominate; recommend (*s.o.*) ‖ *ref* to have in mind; apply (*for a job*); **se proposer de** to intend to

proposition [prɔpozisjɔ̃] *f* proposition; proposal; clause

propre [prɔpr] *adj* clean, neat; original (*meaning*); proper (*name*); literal (*meaning*); **propre à** fit for, suited to ‖ (when standing before noun) *adj* own ‖ *m* characteristic; **au propre** in the literal sense; **c'est du propre!** (coll) what a dirty trick! **en propre** in one's own right

proprement [prɔprəmɑ̃] *adv* neatly; cleanly; properly; exactly, literally; strictly

pro·pret [prɔprɛ] **-prette** [prɛt] *adj* (coll) clean, bright

propreté [prɔprəte] *f* cleanliness, neatness

propriétaire [prɔprijetɛr] *mf* proprietor, owner; landowner ‖ *m* landlord ‖ *f* proprietress; landlady

propriété [prɔprijete] *f* property; propriety, appropriateness

propulseur [prɔpylsœr] *m* engine, motor; outboard motor; (rok) booster

propulsion [prɔpylsjɔ̃] *f* propulsion; **propulsion à réaction** jet propulsion

prorata [prɔrata] *m invar*—**au prorata de** in proportion to

proroger [prɔrɔʒe] §38 *tr* to postpone; extend; adjourn ‖ *ref* to be adjourned

prosaïque [prozaik] *adj* prosaic

prosateur [prozatœr] *m* prose writer

proscrire [prɔskrir] §25 *tr* to proscribe; banish, outlaw

pros·crit [prɔskri] **-crite** [krit] *adj* banished ‖ *mf* outlaw

prose [proz] *f* prose; (coll) style (*of writing*)

prosélyte [prɔzelit] *mf* proselyte
prosodie [prɔzɔdi] *f* prosody
prospecter [prɔspɛkte] *tr & intr* to prospect
prospec·teur [prɔspɛktœr] **-trice** [tris] *mf* prospector
prospecteur-placier [prɔspɛktœrplasje] *m* head hunter (*for employment*)
prospectus [prɔspɛktys] *m* prospectus; handbill
prospère [prɔspɛr] *adj* prosperous
prospérer [prɔspere] §10 *intr* to prosper, thrive
prospérité [prɔsperite] *f* prosperity
prostate [prɔstat] *f* prostate (gland)
prosternation [prɔstɛrnɑsjɔ̃] *f* prostration; groveling
prosterner [prɔstɛrne] *tr* to bend over ‖ *ref* to prostrate oneself; grovel
prostituée [prɔstitɥe] *f* prostitute
prostituer [prɔstitɥe] *tr* to prostitute
prostration [prɔstrɑsjɔ̃] *f* prostration
pros·tré -trée [prɔstre] *adj* prostrate
protagoniste [prɔtagɔnist] *m* protagonist
prote [prɔt] *m* (typ) foreman
protection [prɔtɛksjɔ̃] *f* protection; **protection civile** civil defense
proté·gé -gée [prɔteʒe] *adj* guarded; arterial (*crossing*); **automatiquement protégé** fail-safe ‖ *mf* protégé, dependent; pet
protège-cahier [prɔtɛʒkaje] *m* (*pl* **-cahiers**) notebook cover
protège-livre [prɔtɛʒlivr] *m* (*pl* **-livres**) dust jacket
protège-slip [prɔtɛʒslip] *m* (*pl* **-slips** [slip]) panty liner
protéger [prɔteʒe] §1 *tr* to protect; be a patron of
protéine [prɔtein] *f* protein
protes·tant [prɔtɛstɑ̃] **-tante** [tɑ̃t] *adj & mf* Protestant; protestant
protestation [prɔtɛstɑsjɔ̃] *f* protest
protester [prɔtɛste] §97 *tr & intr* to protest; **protester de** to protest
protêt [prɔtɛ] *m* (com) protest
protocole [prɔtɔkɔl] *m* protocol
proton [prɔtɔ̃] *m* proton
protoplasme [prɔtɔplasm] *m* protoplasm
prototype [prɔtɔtip] *m* prototype
protozoaire [prɔtɔzɔɛr] *m* protozoan
protubérance [prɔtyberɑ̃s] *f* protuberance
proue [pru] *f* prow, bow
prouesse [prɥɛs] *f* prowess
prouver [pruve] *tr* to prove
provenance [prɔvnɑ̃s] *f* origin; **en provenance de** from
proven·çal -çale [prɔvɑ̃sal] (*pl* **-çaux** [so]) *adj* Provençal ‖ *m* Provençal (*language*) ‖ (*cap*) *mf* Provençal (*person*)
provenir [prɔvnir] §72 *intr* (*aux*: ÊTRE) —**provenir de** to come from
proverbe [prɔvɛrb] *m* proverb
providence [prɔvidɑ̃s] *f* providence
providen·tiel -tielle [prɔvidɑ̃sjɛl] *adj* providential
province [prɔvɛ̃s] *adj invar* (coll) provincial ‖ *f* province; **la province** the provinces (*all of France outside of Paris*)

proviseur [prɔvizœr] *m* headmaster
provision [prɔvizjɔ̃] *f* stock, store; deposit; **aller aux provisions** to go shopping; **faire provision de** to stock up on; **provisions**, foodstuffs; **sans provision** bad (*check*)
provisoire [prɔvizwar] *adj* provisional, temporary; emergency
provo·cant [prɔvɔkɑ̃] **-cante** [kɑ̃t] *adj* provocative
provoquer [prɔvɔke] §96 *tr* to provoke; cause, bring about; arouse
proxénète [prɔksenɛt] *mf* procurer ‖ *m* pimp
proximité [prɔksimite] *f* proximity; **à proximité de** near
prude [pryd] *adj* prudish ‖ *f* prude
prudemment [prydamɑ̃] *adv* carefully, prudently
prudence [prydɑ̃s] *f* prudence
pru·dent [prydɑ̃] **-dente** [dɑ̃t] *adj* prudent
pruderie [prydri] *f* prudery
prud'homme [prydɔm] *m* arbitrator; (obs) solid citizen
prudhommesque [prydɔmɛsk] *adj* pompous
pruine [prɥin] *f* bloom
prune [pryn] *f* plum; **des prunes!** (slang) nuts!; **pour des prunes** (coll) for nothing
pru·neau [pryno] *m* (*pl* **-neaux**) prune; (slang) bullet
prunelle [prynɛl] *f* pupil (*of eye*); sloe; sloe gin; **jouer de la prunelle** (coll) to ogle; **prunelle de ses yeux** apple of his (one's, etc.) eye
prunellier [prynelje] *m* sloe, blackthorn
prunier [prynje] *m* plum tree
prus·sien [prysjɛ̃] **-sienne** [sjɛn] *adj* Prussian ‖ (*cap*) *mf* Prussian
P.-S. [peɛs] *m* (letterword) (**post-scriptum**) P.S.
psalmodier [psalmɔdje] *tr & intr* to speak in a singsong
psaume [psom] *m* psalm
psautier [psotje] *m* psalter
pseudonyme [psødɔnim] *adj* pseudonymous ‖ *m* pseudonym; nom de plume
psitt [psit] *interj* (coll) hist!
P.S.V. [peɛsve] *m* (letterword) (**pilotage sans visibilité**) blind flying
psychanalyse [psikanaliz] *f* psychoanalysis
psychanalyser [psikanalize] *tr* to psychoanalyze
psyché [psiʃe] *f* psyche; cheval glass
psychiatre [psikjatr] *mf* psychiatrist
psychiatrie [psikjatri] *f* psychiatry
psychique [psiʃik] *adj* psychic
psychologie [psikɔlɔʒi] *f* psychology
psychologique [psikɔlɔʒik] *adj* psychologic(al)
psychologue [psikɔlɔg] *mf* psychologist
psychopathe [psikɔpat] *mf* psychopath
psychose [psikoz] *f* psychosis
psychotique [psikɔtik] *adj & mf* psychotic
ptomaïne [ptɔmain] *f* ptomaine
P.T.T. [petete] *fpl* (letterword) (**Postes, télégraphes et téléphones**) post office, telephone, and telegraph

pu [py] *v* see **pouvoir;** see **paître**
puant [pɥɑ̃] **puante** [pɥɑ̃t] *adj* stinking
puanteur [pɥɑ̃tœr] *f* stench, stink
pub [pyb] *abbr* (**publicité**) publicity
puberté [pybɛrte] *f* puberty
pu·blic -blique [pyblik] *adj* public; notorious ‖ *m* public; audience
publication [pyblikɑsjɔ̃] *f* publication; proclamation
publiciste [pyblisist] *mf* public-relations expert
publicitaire [pyblisitɛr] *adj* advertising ‖ *m* advertising specialist
publicité [pyblisite] *f* publicity; advertising; **publicité aérienne** skywriting
publier [pyblije] *tr* to publish; publicize, proclaim
puce [pys] *f* flea; (comp) chip; **mettre la puce à l'oreille à qn** (fig) to put a bug in s.o.'s ear
pu·ceau [pyso] **-celle** [sɛl] (*pl* **-ceaux**) *adj* & *mf* (coll) virgin ‖ *f* maid
puceron [pysrɔ̃] *m* plant louse
pudding [pudiŋ] *m* plum pudding
puddler [pydle] *tr* to puddle
pudeur [pydœr] *f* modesty
pudi·bond [pydibɔ̃] **-bonde** [bɔ̃d] *adj* prudish
pudibonderie [pydibɔ̃dri] *f* false modesty
pudique [pydik] *adj* modest, chaste
puer [pɥe] *tr* to reek of ‖ *intr* to stink
pué·ril -rile [pɥeril] *adj* puerile
puérilité [pɥerilite] *f* puerility
pugilat [pyʒila] *m* fight, brawl
pugiliste [pyʒilist] *m* pugilist
pugnace [pygnas] *adj* pugnacious
pui·né -née [pɥine] *adj* younger ‖ *mf* younger child
puis [pɥi] *adv* then; next; **et puis** besides; **et puis aprés?** (coll) what next? ‖ *v* see **pouvoir**
puisard [pɥizar] *m* drain, cesspool; sump
puisatier [pɥizatje] *m* well digger
puiser [pɥize] *tr* to draw (*water*); **puiser à** or **dans** to draw (*s.th.*) from ‖ *intr*—**puiser à** or **dans** to draw from or on; dip or reach into
puisque [pɥisk(ə)] *conj* since, as, seeing that
puissamment [pɥisamɑ̃] *adv* powerfully; exceedingly
puissance [pɥisɑ̃s] *f* power
puis·sant [pɥisɑ̃] **-sante** [sɑ̃t] *adj* powerful
puisse [pɥis] *v* (**puisses, puissions,** etc.) see **pouvoir**
puits [pɥi] *m* well; pit; (min) shaft; (naut) locker; **puits absorbant, puits perdu** cesspool; **puits de pétrole** oil well; **puits de science** fountain of knowledge
pull-over [pulɔvœr], [pylɔvɛr] *m* (*pl* **-overs**) sweater, pullover
pulluler [pylyle] *intr* to swarm, to teem
pulmonaire [pylmɔnɛr] *adj* pulmonary ‖ *f* (bot) lungwort
pulpe [pylp] *f* pulp
pulsation [pylsɑsjɔ̃] *f* pulsation, beat; pulse

pulsion [pylsjɔ̃] *f* (psychoanal) impulse
pulvérisateur [pylverizatœr] *m* spray, atomizer
pulvérisation [pylverisɑsjɔ̃] *f* (med) spray (*for nose or throat*)
pulvériser [pylverize] *tr* to pulverize; spray
punaise [pynɛz] *f* bug; bedbug; thumbtack
punch [pɔ̃ʃ] *m* punch (*drink*) ‖ [pœnʃ] *m* (boxing) punch
punching-ball [pœnʃiŋbol] *m* punching bag
punir [pynir] §97 *tr* & *intr* to punish
punition [pynisjɔ̃] *f* punishment
pupille [pypil], [pypij] *mf* ward ‖ *f* pupil (*of eye*)
pupitre [pypitr] *m* desk; stand, rack; lectern; console, controls; **pupitre à musique** music stand
pur pure [pyr] *adj* pure ‖ *mf* diehard; **les purs** the pure in heart
purée [pyre] *f* purée; mashed potatoes; (coll) wretch; **être dans la purée** (coll) to be broke; **purée de pois** (culin, fig) pea soup ‖ *interj* (slang) how awful!
pureté [pyrte] *f* purity
purga·tif [pyrgatif] **-tive** [tiv] *adj* & *m* purgative
purgatoire [pyrgatwar] *m* purgatory
purge [pyrʒ] *f* purge
purger [pyrʒe] §38 *tr* to purge; pay off (*e.g., a mortgage*); serve (*a sentence*)
purifier [pyrifje] *tr* to purify
puri·tain [pyritɛ̃] **-taine** [tɛn] *adj* & *mf* puritan; Puritan
pur-sang [pyrsɑ̃] *adj* & *m invar* thoroughbred
pus [py] *m* pus ‖ *v* (**put, pûmes,** etc.) see **pouvoir**
pusillanime [pyzilanim] *adj* pusillanimous
pustule [pystyl] *f* pimple
putain [pytɛ̃] *adj invar* (coll) amiable, agreeable ‖ *f* (vulg) whore
putois [pytwa] *m* skunk, polecat
putréfier [pytrefje] *tr* & *ref* to decompose, rot
putride [pytrid] *adj* putrid
puy [pɥi] *m* volcanic peak
puzzle [pœzl] *m* jigsaw puzzle
p.-v. [peve] *m* (letterword) (**procès-verbal**) (coll) ticket, e.g., **attraper un p.-v.** to get a ticket
pygargue [pigarg] *m* osprey, fish hawk
pygmée [pigme] *m* pygmy
pygméen [pigmeɛ̃] **pygméenne** [pigmeɛn] *adj* pygmy
pyjama [piʒama] *m* pajamas; **un pyjama** a pair of pajamas
pylône [pilon] *m* pylon; tower
pyramide [piramid] *f* pyramid
Pyrénées [pirene] *fpl* Pyrenees
pyrite [pirit] *f* pyrites
pyrotechnie [pirɔtɛkni] *f* pyrotechnics
pyrotechnique [pirɔtɛknik] *adj* pyrotechnical
python [pitɔ̃] *m* python
pythonisse [pitɔnis] *f* pythoness
pyxide [piksid] *f* pyx

Q, q [ky] *m invar* seventeenth letter of the French alphabet

Q.I. [kyi] *m* (letterword) (**quotient intellectuel**) I.Q.

quadrant [kwadrɑ̃], [kadrɑ̃] *m* (math) quadrant

quadrilatère [kwadrilatɛr] *m* quadrilateral

quadrupède [kwadrypɛd] *m* quadruped

quadruple [kwadrypl] *adj & m* quadruple

quadrupler [kwadryple] *tr & intr* to quadruple

quadru·plés -plées [kwadryple] *mfpl* quadruplets

quai [ke] *m* quay, wharf; platform (*e.g., in a railroad station*); embankment, levee; **amener à quai** to berth; **le Quai d'Orsay** the French foreign office

qua·ker [kwɛkœr], [kwakɛr] **-keresse** [krɛs] *mf* Quaker

qualifiable [kalifjabl] *adj* describable

quali·fié -fiée [kalifje] *adj* qualified; qualifying; aggravated (*crime*)

qualifier [kalifje] *tr & intr* to qualify

qualité [kalite] *f* quality; title, capacity; **avoir qualité pour** to be authorized to; **en qualité de** in the capacity of

quand [kɑ̃] *adv* when; how soon; **n'importe quand** anytime; **quand même** though, just the same ‖ *conj* when; **quand même** even if

quant [kɑ̃] *adv*—**quant à** as for, as to, as far as; **quant à cela** for that matter

quant-à-soi [kɑ̃taswa] *m* dignity, reserve; **rester** or **se tenir sur son quant-à-soi** to keep one's distance

quantique [kwɑ̃tik] *adj* quantum

quantité [kɑ̃tite] *f* quantity

quan·tum [kwɑ̃tɔm] *m* (*pl* **-ta** [ta]) quantum

quarantaine [karɑ̃tɛn] *f* age of forty, forty mark, forties; quarantine; **une quarantaine de** about forty

quarante [karɑ̃t] §94 *adj, pron, & m* forty; **quarante et un** forty-one; **quarante et unième** forty-first

quarante-deux [karɑ̃tdø] §94 *adj, pron, & m* forty-two

quarante-deuxième [karɑ̃tdøzjɛm] §94 *adj, pron (masc, fem), & m* forty-second

quarantième [karɑ̃tjɛm] §94 *adj, pron (masc, fem), & m* fortieth

quart [kar] *m* quarter; fourth (*in fractions*); quarter of a pound; quarter of a liter; **au quart de tour** immediately; **bon quart!** (naut) all's well!; **passer un mauvais quart d'heure** to have a trying time; **petit quart** (naut) dogwatch; **prendre le quart** (naut) to come on watch; **quart de cercle** quadrant; **quart de soupir** (mus) sixteenth-note rest; **quart d'heure de Rabelais** day of reckoning; **tous les quarts d'heure au quart d'heure juste** every quarter-hour on the quarter-hour; **un petit quart d'heure** a quarter of an hour or so

quarte [kart] *adj* quartan (*fever*) ‖ *f* half-gallon; (escr) quarte; (mus) fourth

quarte·ron [kartərɔ̃] **-ronne** [rɔn] *mf* quadroon ‖ *m* handful (*e.g., of people*)

quartette [kwartɛt] *m* combo (*foursome*)

quartier [kartje] *m* quarter; neighborhood; section (*of orange*); portion; **à quartier** aloof; apart; **avoir quartier libre** (mil) to have a pass; to be off duty; **les beaux quartiers** the upper-class residential district; **mettre en quartiers** to dismember; **quartier d'affaires** business district; **quartier général** (mil) headquarters; **quartier réservé** red-light district; **quartiers** quarters, barracks

quartier-maître [kartjemɛtr] *m* (*pl* **quartiers-maîtres**) quartermaster

quartz [kwarts] *m* quartz

quasar [kwazar], [kazar] *m* quasar

quasi [kazi] *m* butt (*of a loin cut*) ‖ *adv* almost

quasi-collision [kazikɔlisjɔ̃] *f* (aer) near collision, near miss

quasiment [kazimɑ̃] *adv* (coll) almost

quatorze [katɔrz] §94 *adj & pron* fourteen; the Fourteenth, e.g., **Jean quatorze** John the Fourteenth; **c'est parti comme en quatorze** (slang) it's off to a good start ‖ *m* fourteen; fourteenth (*in dates*)

quatorzième [katɔrzjɛm] §94 *adj, pron (mas, fem), & m* fourteenth

quatrain [katrɛ̃] *m* quatrain

quatre [katr] §94 *adj & pron* four; the Fourth, e.g., **Jean quatre** John the Fourth; **quatre à quatre** four at a time; **quatre heures** four o'clock ‖ *m* four; fourth (*in dates*); **se mettre en quatre pour** to fall all over oneself for; **se tenir à quatre** to keep oneself under control

quatre-épices [katrepis] *m & f invar* allspice (*plant*); **des quatre-épices** allspice (*spice*)

quatre-saisons [katrəsɛzɔ̃], [katsɛzɔ̃] *f invar* everbearing small strawberry

quatre-temps [katrətɑ̃] *mpl* Ember days

quatre-vingt-deux [katrəvɛ̃dø] *adj, pron, & m* eighty-two

quatre-vingt-deuxième [katrəvɛ̃døzjɛm] *adj, pron (masc, fem), & m* eighty-second

quatre-vingt-dix [katrəvɛ̃di(s)] §94 *adj, pron, & m* ninety

quatre-vingt-dixième [katrəvɛ̃dizjɛm] §94 *adj, pron (masc, fem), & m* ninetieth

quatre-vingtième [katrəvɛ̃tjɛm] §94 *adj, pron (masc, fem), & m* eightieth

quatre-vingt-onze [katrəvɛ̃ɔ̃z] §94 *adj, pron, & m* ninety-one

quatre-vingt-onzième [katrəvɛ̃ɔ̃zjɛm] §94 *adj, pron (masc, fem), & m* ninety-first

quatre-vingts [katrəvɛ̃] §94 *adj & pron* eighty; **quatre-vingt** eighty, e.g., **page quatre-vingt** page eighty ‖ *m* eighty

quatre-vingt-un [katrəvɛ̃œ̃] §94 *adj, pron, & m* eighty-one

quatre-vingt-unième [katrəvɛ̃ynjɛm] §94 *adj, pron (masc, fem), & m* eighty-first

quatrième [katrijɛm] §94 *adj, pron (masc, fem),* & *m* fourth

quatuor [kwatɥɔr] *m (mus)* quartet

que [kə] (or **qu'** [k] before a vowel or mute h) *pron rel* whom; which, that; **ce que** that which, what ‖ *pron interr* what; **qu'est-ce que . . . ?** what (as direct object) . . . ?; **qu'est-ce qui . . . ?** what (as subject) . . . ? ‖ *adv* why, e.g., **qu'avez-vous besoin de tant de livres?** why do you need so many books?; how!, e.g., **que cette femme est belle!** how beautiful that woman is!; **que de** what a lot of, e.g., **que de difficultés!** what a lot of difficulties! ‖ *conj* that; when, e.g., **un jour que je suis allé chez le dentiste** once when I went to the dentist; since, e.g., **il y a trois jours qu'il est arrivé** it is three days since he came; until, e.g., **attendez qu'il vienne** wait until he comes; than, e.g., **plus grand que moi** taller than I; as, e.g., **aussi grand que moi** as tall as I; but, e.g., **personne que vous** no one but you; whether, e.g., **qu'il parte ou qu'il reste** whether he leaves or stays; (in a conditional sentence without **si,** to introduce the conditional in a dependent clause which represents the main clause of the corresponding sentence in English), e.g., **il ferait faillite que cela ne m'étonnerait pas** if he went bankrupt it would not surprise me; (as a repetition of another conjunction), e.g., **si elle chante et que la salle soit comble** if she sings and there is a full house; e.g., **comme il avait soif et que le vin était bon** as he was thirsty and the wine was good; (in a prayer or exhortation), e.g., **que Dieu vous bénisse!** may God bless you!, God bless you!; (in a command), e.g., **qu'il parle (aille, parte,** etc.**)** let him speak (go, leave, etc.); **ne . . . que** §90 only, but

quel quelle [kɛl] §80

quelconque [kɛlkɔ̃k] *adj indef* any; any, whatever; any at all, some kind of ‖ (when standing before noun) *adj indef* some, some sort of ‖ *adj* ordinary, nondescript, mediocre

quelque [kɛlkə] *adj indef* some, any; **quelque chose** (always *masc*) something; **quelque chose de bon** something good; **quelque part** somewhere; **quelque . . . qui** or **quelque . . . que** whatever . . . ; whichever . . . ; **quelques** a few ‖ *adv* some, about; **quelque peu** somewhat; **quelque** + *adj* or *adv* . . . **que** however + *adj* or *adv*

quelquefois [kɛlkəfwa] *adv* sometimes

quel·qu'un [kɛlkœ̃] **-qu'une** [kyn] §81

quémander [kemɑ̃de] *tr* to beg for ‖ *intr* to beg

qu'en-dira-t-on [kɑ̃diratɔ̃] *m invar* what other people will say, gossip

quenotte [kənɔt] *f* (coll) baby tooth

quenouille [kənuj] *f* distaff; distaff side

querelle [kərɛl] *f* quarrel; **chercher querelle à** to pick a quarrel with; **une querelle d'Allemand, une mauvaise querelle** a groundless quarrel

quereller [kərɛle] *tr* to nag, scold ‖ *ref* to quarrel

querel·leur [kərɛlœr] **-leuse** [løz] *adj* quarrelsome ‖ *mf* wrangler ‖ *f* shrew

quérir [kerir] (used only in *inf*) *tr* to go for, to fetch

question [kɛstjɔ̃] *f* question; **question discutable** moot point

questionnaire [kɛstijɔner] *m* questionnaire

questionner [kɛstjɔne] *tr* to question

question·neur [kɛstjɔnœr] **-neuse** [nøz] *adj* inquisitive ‖ *mf* inquisitive person ‖ *m* (rad, telv) quizmaster

quête [kɛt] *f* quest; **faire la quête** to take up the collection

quêter [kete] *tr* to beg or fish for (*votes, praise, etc.*); hunt for (*game*); collect (*contributions*) ‖ *intr* to take up a collection

quetsche [kwɛtʃ] *f* quetsch

queue [kø] *f* tail; queue; billiard cue; train (*of dress*); handle (*of pan*); bottom (*of class*); stem, stalk; **à la queue leu leu** in single file; **en queue** at the back; **faire la queue** to line up, to queue up; **fausse queue** miscue; **queue de cheval** (bot) horsetail; **queue de loup** (bot) purple foxglove; **queue de poisson** (aut) fishtail; **queue de vache** cat's-tail (*cirrus*); **sans queue ni tête** without head or tail; **venir en queue** to bring up the rear

queue-d'aronde [kødarɔ̃d] *f* (*pl* **queues-d'aronde**) dovetail; **assembler à queue-d'aronde** to dovetail

queue-de-cheval [kødʃval] *f* (*pl* **queues-de-cheval**) ponytail

queue-de-morue [kødmɔry] *f* (*pl* **queues-de-morue**) tails, swallow-tailed coat; (painting) flat brush

queue-de-rat [kødəra] *f* (*pl* **queues-de-rat**) rat-tail file; taper

qui [ki] *pron rel* who, whom; which; that; **ce qui** that which, what; **n'importe qui** anyone; **qui que** anyone, no one; whoever, e.g., **qui que vous soyez** whoever you are ‖ *pron interr* who, whom; **qui est-ce que . . . ?** whom . . . ?; **qui est-ce qui . . . ?** who . . . ?

quia [kɥija]—**mettre** or **réduire qn à quia** (obs) to stump or floor s.o.

quiconque [kikɔ̃k] *pron indef* whoever, whosoever; whomever; anyone

quidam [kɥidam], [kidam] *m* individual, person

quiétude [kɥijetyd], [kjetyd] *f* peace of mind; quiet, calm

quignon [kiɲɔ̃] *m* hunk (*of bread*)

quille [kij] *f* keel; pin (*for bowling*); **quilles** ninepins

quincaillerie [kɛ̃kɑjri] *f* hardware; hardware store

quincail·lier [kɛ̃kɑje] **-lière** [jɛr] *mf* hardware dealer

quinconce [kɛ̃kɔ̃s] *m* quincunx; **en quinconce** quincuncially
quinine [kinin] *f* quinine
quinquen·nal **-nale** [kɥɛ̃kɥɛnal] *adj* (*pl* **-naux** [no]) five-year
quinquet [kɛ̃ke] *m*—**allume tes quinquets!** (slang) open your eyes!
quinquina [kɛ̃kina] *m* cinchona
quin·tal [kɛ̃tal] *m* (*pl* **-taux** [to]) hundredweight; one hundred kilograms
quinte [kɛ̃t] *f* whim; (cards) sequence of five; (mus) fifth; **quinte de toux** fit of coughing
quintessence [kɛ̃tesɑ̃s] *f* quintessence
quintette [kɥɛ̃tɛt], [kɛ̃tɛt] *m* (mus) quintet; (coll) five-piece combo; **quintette à cordes** string quintet
quin·teux [kɛ̃tø] **-teuse** [tøz] *adj* crotchety, fitful, restive
quintu·plés **-plées** [kɛ̃typle] *mfpl* quintuplets
quinzaine [kɛ̃zɛn] *f* (group of) fifteen; two weeks, fortnight; **une quinzaine de** about fifteen
quinze [kɛ̃z] §94 *adj* & *pron* fifteen; the Fifteenth, e.g., **Jean quinze** John the Fifteenth ‖ *m* fifteen; fifteenth (*in dates*)
quinzième [kɛ̃zjɛm] §94 *adj, pron* (*masc, fem*), & *m* fifteenth
quiproquo [kiprɔko] *m* mistaken identity, misunderstanding
quiscale [kɥiskal] *m* (orn) purple grackle

quittance [kitɑ̃s] *f* receipt
quitte [kit] *adj* free (*from obligation*); clear (*of debts*); (en) **être quitte pour** to get off with; **être quitte** to be quits; **tenir qn quitte de** to release s.o. from ‖ *m*—**jouer** (à) **quitte ou double** to play double or nothing ‖ *adv*—**quitte à** even if it means
quitter [kite] *tr* to leave; take off (*e.g., a coat*) ‖ *intr* to leave, go away; **ne quittez pas!** (telp) hold the line! ‖ *ref* to part, separate
quitus [kɥitys] *m* discharge, acquittance
qui-vive [kiviv] *m invar*—**sur le quivive** on the qui vive ‖ *interj* (mil) who goes there?
quoi [kwa] *pron indef* what, which; **à quoi bon?** what's the use?; **de quoi** enough; **moyennant quoi** in exchange for which; **n'importe quoi** anything; **quoi que** whatever; **quoi qu'il en soit** be that as it may; **sans quoi** otherwise
quoique [kwakə] *conj* although, though
quolibet [kɔlibɛ] *m* gibe, quip
quorum [kwɔrɔm], [kɔrɔm] *m* quorum
quota [kwɔta], [kɔta] *m* quota
quote-part [kɔtpar] *f invar* quota, share
quoti·dien [kɔtidjɛ̃] **-dienne** [djɛn] *adj* daily ‖ *m* daily newspaper
quotient [kɔsjɑ̃] *m* quotient; **quotient cours-bénéficié** price-earnings ratio; **quotient intellectuel** intelligence quotient
quotité [kɔtite] *f* share, amount

R

R, r [ɛr], *[ɛr] *m invar* eighteenth letter of the French alphabet
rabâcher [rabɑʃe] *tr* to harp on ‖ *intr* to harp on the same thing
rabais [rabɛ] *m* reduction, discount
rabaisser [rabese] *tr* to lower; to disparage
rabat [raba] *m* flap (*vestment*)
rabat-joie [rabaʒwa] *m invar* kill-joy
rabattre [rabatr] §7 *tr* to lower; discount; turn down; fold up; pull down; cut back; flush (*game*) ‖ *intr* to turn; **en rabattre** to come down a peg or two; **rabattre de** to reduce (*a price*) ‖ *ref* to fold; drop down; turn the other way; **se rabattre sur** to fall back on
rabat·tu **-tue** [rabaty] *adj* turndown
rabbin [rabɛ̃] *m* rabbi
rabibocher [rabibɔʃe] *tr* (coll) to patch up ‖ *ref* (coll) to make up
rabiot [rabjo] *m* overtime; extra bit; (mil) extra service; (coll) graft
rabioter [rabjɔte] *tr* & *intr* to graft
râ·blé **-blée** [rɑble] *adj* husky
rabot [rabo] *m* plane
raboter [rabɔte] *tr* to plane

rabo·teux **-teuse** [rabɔtø] *adj* rough, uneven ‖ *f* (mach) planer
rabou·gri **-grie** [rabugri] *adj* scrub, scrawny
rabrouer [rabrue] *tr* to snub
racaille [rakɑj] *f* riffraff
raccommodage [rakɔmɔdaʒ] *m* mending; darning; patching
raccommodement [rakɔmɔdmɑ̃] *m* (coll) reconciliation
raccommoder [rakɔmɔde] *tr* to mend; darn; patch; (coll) to patch up
raccompagner [rakɔ̃paɲe] *tr* to see back, see home
raccord [rakɔr] *m* connection; coupling; joint; adapter; **faire un raccord à** to touch up
raccordement [rakɔrdəmɑ̃] *m* connecting, linking, joining
raccorder [rakɔrde] *tr* & *ref* to connect
raccour·ci **-cie** [rakursi] *adj* shortened; abridged; squat, dumpy; bobbed (*hair*) ‖ *m* abridgment; shortcut, cutoff; foreshortening; **en raccourci** in miniature; in a nutshell

raccourcir [rakursir] *tr* to shorten; abridge; foreshorten ‖ *intr* to grow shorter
raccourcissement [rakursismɑ̃] *m* shortening; abridgment; shrinking
raccroc [rakro] *m* (billiards) fluke
raccrocher [rakrɔʃe] *tr & intr* to hang up ‖ *ref*—se raccrocher à to hang on to
race [ras] *f* race; **de race** thoroughbred
ra·cé -cée [rase] *adj* thoroughbred
rachat [raʃa] *m* repurchase; redemption; ransom
racheter [raʃte] §2 *tr* to buy back; redeem; ransom
rachitique [raʃitik] *adj* rickety
rachitisme [raʃitism] *m* rickets
ra·cial -ciale [rasjal] *adj* (*pl* -ciaux [sjo]) race, racial
racine [rasin] *f* root; **racine carrée** square root; **racine cubique** cube root
racisme [rasism] *m* racism
raciste [rasist] *adj & mf* racist
racket [rakɛt] *m* (coll) racket
racketter or **racketteur** [rakɛtœr] *m* racketeer
raclée [rakle] *f* beating
racler [rakle] *tr* to scrape
raclette [raklɛt] *f* scraper; hoe; (phot) squeegee
racloir [raklwar] *m* scraper
raclure [raklyr] *f* scrapings
racolage [rakɔlaʒ] *m* soliciting
racoler [rakɔle] *tr* (coll) to solicit; (archaic) to shanghai
raco·leur [rakɔlœr] **-leuse** [løz] *mf* recruiter ‖ *f* (coll) hustler, streetwalker
racontar [rakɔ̃tar] *m* (coll) gossip
raconter [rakɔ̃te] *tr* to tell, narrate; describe
racon·teur [rakɔ̃tœr] **-teuse** [tøz] *mf* storyteller
racornir [rakɔrnir] *tr & intr* to harden; shrivel
radar [radar] *m* radar
rade [rad] *f* roadstead; **en rade** (coll) abandoned
ra·deau [rado] *m* (*pl* -deaux) raft
ra·diant [radjɑ̃] **-diante** [djɑ̃t] *adj* (astr, phys) radiant
radiateur [radjatœr] *m* radiator
radiation [radjɑsjɔ̃] *f* radiation; striking off
radi·cal -cale [radikal] *adj & mf* (*pl* -caux [ko]) radical ‖ *m* (chem, gram, math) radical
radier [radje] *tr* to cross out, strike out or off
ra·dieux [radjø] **-dieuse** [djøz] *adj* radiant
radin [radɛ̃] *adj masc & fem* (slang) stingy
radio [radjo] *m* radiogram; radio operator ‖ *f* radio; radio set; X-ray
radioac·tif [radjoaktif] **-tive** [tiv] *adj* radioactive
radio-crochet [radjokrɔʃɛ] *m* (*pl* -crochets) talent show
radiodiffuser [radjodifyze] *tr* to broadcast
radiodiffusion [radjodifyzjɔ̃] *f* broadcasting
radiofréquence [radjofrekɑ̃s] *f* radiofrequency
radiogramme [radjogram] *m* radiogram

radiographier [radjografje] *tr* to X-ray
radioguidage [radjogidaʒ] *m* radio control; radio guidance; **radioguidage d'aérodrome** instrument-landing system
radiogui·dé -dée [radjogide] *adj* radio-controlled; guided (*missile*)
radio-journal [radjoʒurnal] *m* (*pl* -journaux [ʒurno]) radio newscast
radiologie [radjolɔʒi] *f* radiology
radiophare [radjofar] *m* radio beacon
radioreportage [radjorəpɔrtaʒ] *m* news broadcast; sports broadcast
radioscopie [radjoskɔpi] *f* radioscopy, fluoroscopy
radio-taxi [radjotaksi] *m* (*pl* -taxis) radio taxi
radiotéléphone [radjotelefɔn] *m* radiophone, car telephone
radiotélévi·sé -sée [radjotelevize] *adj* broadcast over radio and television
radis [radi] *m* radish
radium [radjɔm] *m* radium
radius [radjys] *m* (anat) radius
radotage [radotaʒ] *m* drivel, twaddle
radoter [radote] *intr* to talk nonsense, ramble
radoub [radu] *m* (naut) graving
radouber [radube] *tr* (naut) to grave
radoucir [radusir] *tr & ref* to calm down
rafale [rafal] *f* squall, gust; burst of gunfire
raffermir [rafɛrmir] *tr & ref* to harden
raffinage [rafinaʒ] *m* refining
raffinement [rafinmɑ̃] *m* refinement
raffiner [rafine] *tr* to refine ‖ *intr* to be subtle; **raffiner sur** to overdo
raffinerie [rafinri] *f* refinery
raffoler [rafole] *intr*—raffoler de to dote on, to be wild about
raffut [rafy] *m* (coll) uproar
rafistolage [rafistolaʒ] *m* (coll) patching up
rafistoler [rafistole] *tr* (coll) to patch up
rafle [rafl] *f* raid, mass arrest; stalk; corncob
rafler [rɑfle] *tr* (coll) to carry away, make a clean sweep of
rafraîchir [rafreʃir] *tr* to cool; refresh; freshen up; trim (*the hair*) ‖ *intr* to cool ‖ *ref* to cool off; refresh oneself
rafraîchissement [rafreʃismɑ̃] *m* refreshment; cooling off
ragaillardir [ragajardir] *tr* to cheer up
rage [raʒ] *f* rage; rabies; **à la rage** madly, **faire rage** to rage
rager [raʒe] §38 *intr* (coll) to be enraged
ra·geur [raʒœr] **-geuse** [ʒøz] *adj* bad-tempered
ragot [rago] *m* (coll) gossip
ragoût [ragu] *m* stew, ragout; (obs) spice, relish
ragoû·tant [ragutɑ̃] **-tante** [tɑ̃t] *adj* tempting, inviting; pleasing; **peu ragoûtant** not very appetizing
rai [rɛ] *m* ray; spoke
raid [rɛd] *m* raid; air raid; endurance test
raide [rɛd] *adj* stiff; tight, taut; steep; (coll) incredible ‖ *adv* suddenly
raideur [rɛdœr] *f* stiffness
raidillon [rɛdijɔ̃] *m* short steep path

raidir [redir] *tr & ref* to stiffen
raie [rɛ] *f* stripe, streak; stroke; line (*of spectrum*); part (*of hair*); (ichth) ray, skate
raifort [rɛfɔr] *m* horseradish
rail [rɑj] *m* rail; **rail conducteur** third rail; **remettre sur les rails** (fig) to put back on the track; **sortir des rails** to jump the track
railler [rɑje] *tr* to make fun of ‖ *intr* to joke ‖ *ref*—**se railler de** to make fun of
raillerie [rɑjri] *f* raillery, banter
rail·leur [rɑjœr] **-leuse** [jøz] *adj* teasing, bantering ‖ *mf* teaser
rainette [rɛnɛt] *f* tree frog
rainure [renyr] *f* groove
raisin [rɛzɛ̃] *m* grapes; grape; **raisin d'ours** (bot) bearberry; **raisins de Corinthe** currants; **raisins de mer** cuttlefish eggs; **raisins de Smyrne** seedless raisins; **raisins secs** raisins
raisiné [rɛzine] *m* grape jelly; (slang) blood
raison [rɛzɔ̃] *f* reason; ratio, rate; **à raison de** at the rate of; **avoir raison** to be right; **avoir raison de** to get the better of; **donner raison à** to back, support; **en raison de** because of; **raison sociale** trade name; **se faire une raison** to resign oneself
raisonnable [rɛzɔnabl] *adj* reasonable; rational
raison·né -née [rɛzɔne] *adj* rational; detailed
raisonnement [rɛzɔnmɑ̃] *m* reasoning; argument
raisonner [rɛzɔne] *tr* to reason out; reason with ‖ *intr* to reason; argue ‖ *ref* to reason with oneself
raison·neur [rɛzɔnœr] **-neuse** [nøz] *adj* rational; argumentative ‖ *mf* reasoner; arguer
rajeunir [raʒœnir] *tr* to rejuvenate ‖ *intr* to grow young again ‖ *ref* to pretend to be younger than one is
rajeunissement [raʒœnismɑ̃] *m* rejuvenation
rajouter [raʒute] *tr* to add again; (coll) to add more
rajuster [raʒyste] *tr* to readjust; adjust ‖ *ref* to adjust one's clothes
râle [rɑl] *m* rale; death rattle; (orn) rail
ralen·ti -tie [ralɑ̃ti] *adj* slow ‖ *m* slowdown; **au ralenti** slowdown (*work*); go-slow (*policy*); slow-motion (*moving picture*); idling (*motor*); **tourner au ralenti** (aut) to idle
ralentir [ralɑ̃tir] *tr, intr, & ref* to slow down; **ralentir** (*public sign*) slow
ralliement [ralimɑ̃] *m* rally
rallier [ralje] *tr & ref* to rally
rallonge [ralɔ̃ʒ] *f* extra piece; extension cord; extra (*in building a new house*); (coll) raise (*in pay*); leaf (*of table*); (coll) under-the-table payment; **à rallonges** extension (*table*)
rallonger [ralɔ̃ʒe] §38 *tr & intr* to lengthen ‖ *ref* to grow longer

rallumer [ralyme] *tr* to relight; (fig) to rekindle ‖ *intr* to put on the lights again ‖ *ref* to be rekindled
rallye [rali] *m* rallye
ramage [ramaʒ] *m* floral design; warbling
ramas [ramɑ] *m* heap; pack (*e.g., of thieves*)
ramassage [ramɑsaʒ] *m* gathering; **ramassage scolaire** school-bus service
ramas·sé -sée [ramɑse] *adj* stocky; compact (*style*)
ramasse-poussière [ramaspusjɛr] *m invar* dustpan
ramasser [ramɑse] *tr* to gather; gather together; pick up; (coll) to catch (*a scolding; a cold*) ‖ *ref* to gather; gather oneself together
rambarde [rɑ̃bard] *f* handrail
rame [ram] *f* prop, stick; oar, pole; ream (*of paper*); string (*e.g., of barges*); (rr) train, section; **rame de métro** subway train
ra·meau [ramo] *m* (*pl* **-meaux**) branch; sprig
ramée [rame] *f* boughs
ramener [ramne] §2 *tr* to lead back; bring back; reduce; restore
ramer [rame] *tr* to stake (*a plant*) ‖ *intr* to row
ra·meur [ramœr] **-meuse** [møz] *mf* rower
ramier [ramje] *m* wood pigeon
ramifier [ramifje] *tr & ref* to ramify, branch out
ramol·li -lie [ramɔli] *adj* sodden; (coll) half-witted ‖ *mf* (coll) half-wit
ramollir [ramɔlir] *tr & ref* to soften
ramoner [ramɔne] *tr* to sweep (*a chimney*)
ramoneur [ramɔnœr] *m* chimney sweep
ram·pant [rɑ̃pɑ̃] **-pante** [pɑ̃t] *adj* crawling, creeping; (hum) ground (*crew*)
rampe [rɑ̃p] *f* ramp; grade, gradient; banister; flight (*of stairs*); (aer) runway lights; (theat) footlights; **rampe de lancement** launching pad
ramper [rɑ̃pe] *intr* to crawl; grovel; (bot) to creep
ramure [ramyr] *f* branches; antlers
rancart [rɑ̃kar] *m* (slang) rendezvous; **mettre au rancart** (coll) to scrap, to shelve
rance [rɑ̃s] *adj* rancid
ranch [rɑ̃tʃ] *m* ranch
rancir [rɑ̃sir] *intr & ref* to turn rancid
rancœur [rɑ̃kœr] *f* rancor
rançon [rɑ̃sɔ̃] *f* ransom; price (*e.g., of fame*); **mettre à rançon** to hold for ransom
rançonner [rɑ̃sɔne] *tr* to ransom, to hold for ransom; extort money from; steal from; to overcharge, e.g., **cet hôtelier rançonne ses clients** that hotel manager overcharges his guests
rancune [rɑ̃kyn] *f* grudge
rancu·nier [rɑ̃kynje] **-nière** [njɛr] *adj* vindictive, spiteful, rancorous
randonnée [rɑ̃dɔne] *f* long walk; long ride
rang [rɑ̃] *m* rank; **au premier rang** in the first row; ranking; **en rang d'oignons** in a line

ran·gé -gée [rɑ̃ʒe] *adj* orderly; pitched (*battle*); steady (*person*)

ranger [rɑ̃ʒe] §38 *tr* to range; rank ‖ *ref* to take one's place; get out of the way; mend one's ways; **se ranger à** to adopt, take (*e.g., a suggestion*)

ranimer [ranime] *tr & ref* to revive

raout [raut] *m* reception

rapace [rapas] *adj* rapacious ‖ *m* bird of prey

rapatriement [rapatrimɑ̃] *m* repatriation

rapatrier [rapatrije] *tr* to repatriate

râpe [rɑp] *f* rasp; grater

râ·pé -pée [rɑpe] *adj* grated; threadbare ‖ *m* (coll) grated cheese

râper [rɑpe] *tr* to rasp, grate

rapetasser [raptase] *tr* (coll) to patch up

rapetisser [raptise] *tr, intr, & ref* to shrink, shorten

râ·peux [rɑpø] **-peuse** [pøz] *adj* raspy, grating

ra·piat [rapja] **-piate** [pjat] *adj* (coll) stingy ‖ *mf* (coll) skinflint

rapide [rapid] *adj* rapid; steep ‖ *m* rapids; (rr) express; **rapides** rapids

rapidement [rapidmɑ̃] *adv* rapidly

rapidité [rapidite] *f* rapidity; steepness

rapiéçage [rapjesaʒ] *m* patching

rapiécer [rapjese] §58 *tr* to patch

rapière [rapjɛr] *f* rapier

rapin [rapɛ̃] *m* dauber; (coll) art student

rapine [rapin] *f* rapine, pillage

rappel [rapɛl] *m* recall; reminder; call-up; recurrence; booster (*shot*); (*public sign*) end of speed limit, resume speed; (theat) curtain call; **battre le rappel** to call to arms; **rappel au règlement** point of order; **rappel de chariot** backspacer

rappeler [raple] §34 *tr* to recall; remind; call back; call up ‖ §95, §97 *ref* to remember

rapport [rapɔr] *m* yield; return; report; connection, bearing; (math) ratio; **avoir de bons rapports avec** to be on good terms with; **en rapport avec** in touch with; in keeping with; **par rapport à** in comparison with; **rapports** relations; sexual relations; **sous le rapport de** from the standpoint of; **sous tous les rapports** in all respects

rapporter [rapɔrte] *tr* to bring back; yield; report; relate; repeal, call off; attach; retrieve (*game*); (bk) to post ‖ *intr* to yield; (coll) to squeal ‖ *ref*—**s'en rapporter à** to leave it up to; **se rapporter à** to be related to, refer to, have to do with

rappor·teur [rapɔrtœr] **-teuse** [tøz] *mf* tattletale ‖ *m* recorder; (geom) protractor

rapprochement [raprɔʃmɑ̃] *m* bringing together; parallel; rapprochement

rapprocher [raprɔʃe] *tr* to bring closer; reconcile; compare ‖ *ref* to draw closer, approach; **se rapprocher de** to approximate, resemble

rapt [rapt] *m* kidnaping

raquette [rakɛt] *f* racket; snowshoe; tennis player; (bot) prickly pear

rare [rar] *adj* rare; scarce; sparse, thin (*hair*)

rarement [rarmɑ̃] *adv* rarely, seldom

rareté [rarte] *f* rarity; scarcity; rareness

R.A.S. [ɛraɛs] (letterword) (**rien à signaler**) nothing worth talking about

ras [rɑ] **rase** [rɑz] *adj* short (*hair, nap, etc.*); level; close-cropped; close-shaven; open (*country*) ‖ *m*—**à ras de, au ras de** flush with; **ras d'eau** water line; **ras du cou** crew neck; **voler au ras du sol** to skim along the ground

rasade [rɑzad] *f* bumper, glassful

rasage [rɑzaʒ] *m* shearing; shaving

ra·sant [rɑzɑ̃] **-sante** [zɑ̃t] *adj* level; grazing; close to the ground; (coll) boring

rase-mottes [rɑzmɔt] *m invar* hedgehopper; **faire du rase-mottes** or **voler en rase-mottes** to hedgehop

raser [rɑze] *tr* to shave; raze; graze ‖ *ref* to shave

ra·seur [rɑzœr] **-seuse** [zøz] *adj* (coll) boring ‖ *mf* (coll) bore

rasoir [rɑzwar] *adj invar* (slang) boring ‖ *m* razor; (slang) bore; **rasoir à manche** straight razor; **rasoir de sûreté** safety razor

rassasiement [rasazimɑ̃] *m* satiation

rassasier [rasazje] *tr* to satisfy; satiate ‖ *ref* to have one's fill

rassemblement [rasɑ̃bləmɑ̃] *m* assembling; crowd; muster; (*trumpet call*) assembly; **rassemblement!** (mil) fall in!

rassembler [rasɑ̃ble] *tr & ref* to gather together

rasseoir [raswar] §5 *tr* to reseat; set in place again ‖ *ref* to sit down again

rasséréner [raserene] §10 *tr & ref* to calm down

rassir [rasir] *intr & ref* (coll) to get stale

ras·sis [rasi] **-sise** [siz] *adj* level-headed; stale (*bread*)

rassortir [rasɔrtir] *tr* to restock ‖ *ref* to lay in a new stock

rassurer [rasyre] *tr* to reassure ‖ *ref* to be reassured

rastaquouère [rastakwɛr] *m* (coll) flashy stranger

rat [ra] *m* rat; (coll) tightwad; **fait comme un rat** caught like a rat in a trap; **mon rat** (coll) my turtledove; **rat à bourse** gopher; **rat de bibliothèque** bookworm; **rat de cale** stowaway; **rat de cave** thin candle; tax collector; **rat d'égout** sewer rat; **rat des champs** field mouse; **rat d'hôtel** hotel thief; **rat d'Opéra** ballet girl; **rat musqué** muskrat

ratatiner [ratatine] *ref* to shrivel up

ratatouille [ratatuj] *f* ratatouille; (coll) stew; (coll) bad cooking; (coll) blows

rate [rat] *f* spleen; female rat

ra·té -tée [rate] *adj* miscarried; bad (*shot, landing, etc.*) ‖ *mf* failure, dropout

râ·teau [rɑto] *m* (*pl* **-teaux**) rake

râteler [rɑtle] §34 *tr* to rake

râtelier [rɑtəlje] *m* rack; set of false teeth; **manger à deux râteliers** (coll) to play both sides of the street; **râtelier d'armes** gun rack

rater [rate] *tr* to miss ‖ *intr* to miss, misfire; fail

ratiboiser [ratibwaze] *tr* (coll) to take to the cleaners; **ratiboiser q.ch. à qn** (coll) to clean s.o. out of s.th.

ratière [ratjɛr] *f* rattrap

ratifier [ratifje] *tr* to ratify

ration [rɑsjɔ̃] *f* ration

ration·nel -nelle [rasjɔnɛl] *adj* rational

rationnement [rasjɔnmɑ̃] *m* rationing

rationner [rasjɔne] *tr* to ration

ratisser [ratise] *tr* to rake; rake in; search with a fine-tooth comb; (coll) to fleece

ratissoire [ratiswar] *f* hoe

raton [ratɔ̃] *m* little rat; **raton laveur** raccoon

rattacher [rataʃe] *tr* to tie again; link; unite ‖ *ref* to be connected

rattrapage [ratrapaʒ] *m* catch-up; (typ) catchword

rattraper [ratrape] *tr* to catch up to; recover; recapture ‖ *ref* to catch up; **se rattraper à** to catch hold of; **se rattraper de** to make good, recoup

rature [ratyr] *f* erasure

raturer [ratyre] *tr* to cross out

rauque [rok] *adj* hoarse, raucous

ravage [ravaʒ] *m* ravage

ravager [ravaʒe] §38 *tr* to ravage

ravalement [ravalmɑ̃] *m* trimming down; resurfacing; disparagement

ravaler [ravale] *tr* to choke down; disparage; drag down; resurface; eat (*one's words*) ‖ *ref* to lower oneself

ravaudage [ravodaʒ] *m* mending; darning; (fig) patchwork

ravauder [ravode] *tr* to mend; darn

ra·vi -vie [ravi] §93 *adj* delighted, happy, charmed

ravier [ravje] *m* hors-d'oeuvre dish

ravigoter [ravigɔte] *tr* (coll) to revive

ravilir [ravilir] *tr* to debase

ravin [ravɛ̃] *m* ravine

ravine [ravin] *f* mountain torrent

raviner [ravine] *tr* to furrow

ravir [ravir] *tr* to ravish; kidnap, abduct; delight, entrance; **ravir q.ch. à qn** to snatch, take s.th. from s.o. ‖ *intr*—**à ravir** marvelously

raviser [ravize] *ref* to change one's mind

ravis·sant [ravisɑ̃] **-sante** [sɑ̃t] *adj* ravishing, entrancing

ravis·seur [ravisœr] **-seuse** [søz] *mf* kidnaper

ravitaillement [ravitajmɑ̃] *m* supplying; supplies

ravitailler [ravitaje] *tr* to supply; fill up the gas tank of (*a vehicle*) ‖ *ref* to lay in supplies; fill up (*to get gas*)

raviver [ravive] *tr* to revive; brighten up; reopen (*an old wound*) ‖ *ref* to revive; break out again

ravoir [ravwar] (used only in *inf*) *tr* to get back again

rayer [reje] §49 *tr* to cross out, strike out; rule, line; stripe, pinstripe; rifle (*a gun*)

rayon [rɛjɔ̃] *m* ray; radius; spoke; shelf; honeycomb; department (*in a store*); point (*of star*); **ce n'est pas mon rayon** (coll) that's not in my line; **rayon de lune** moonbeam; **rayons X** X rays; **rayon visuel** line of sight

rayonnage [rɛjɔnaʒ] *m* set of shelves, shelving

rayon·nant [rɛjɔnɑ̃] **-nante** [nɑ̃t] *adj* radiant; radiating; radioactive; (rad) transmitting

rayonne [rɛjɔn] *f* rayon

rayonnement [rɛjɔnmɑ̃] *m* radiance; influence, diffusion; (phys) radiation; **rayonnement de faible (grande) énergie** low-level (high-level) radiation; **rayonnement diffusé** scattered radiation; **rayonnement ionisant** ionizing radiation; **rayonnement parasite** stray radiation; **rayonnement solaire** solar radiation

rayonner [rɛjɔne] *intr* to radiate

rayure [rejyr] *f* stripe; scratch; rifling

raz [rɑ] *m* race (*channel and current of water*); **raz de marée** tidal wave; landslide (*in an election*)

razzia [razja] *f* raid

razzier [razje] *tr* to raid

réacteur [reaktœr] *m* reactor; **réacteur nucléaire** nuclear reactor

réactif [reaktif] *m* (chem) reagent

réaction [reaksjɔ̃] *f* reaction; kick (*of rifle*); **à réaction** jet; **réaction en chaîne** chain reaction

réactionnaire [reaksjɔnɛr] *adj & mf* reactionary

réactiver [reaktive] *tr* to reactivate

réadaptation [readaptɑsjɔ̃] *f* rehabilitation; readjustment; **réadaptation fonctionnelle** occupational therapy

réadapter [readapte] *tr* to rehabilitate; readjust ‖ *ref* to be rehabilitated

réaffirmer [reafirme] *tr* to reaffirm

réagir [reaʒir] *intr* to react

réalisable [realizabl] *adj* feasible; (com) saleable

réalisa·teur [realizatœr] **-trice** [tris] *adj* producing ‖ *mf* achiever; producer ‖ *m* (mov, rad, telv) director

réalisation [realizɑsjɔ̃] *f* accomplishment; work; (mov, rad, telv) production; (com) liquidation

réaliser [realize] *tr* to accomplish; realize; sell out; (mov) to produce ‖ *ref* to come to pass, be realized

réalisme [realism] *m* realism

réaliste [realist] *adj* realistic ‖ *mf* realist

réalité [realite] *f* reality; **en réalité** in reality, really, in actual fact

réanimer [reanime] *tr* to revive

réapparaître [reaparɛtr] §12 *intr* to reappear

réapparition [reaparisjɔ̃] *f* reappearance

réarmement [rearməmɑ̃] *m* rearmament

réassortir [reasɔrtir] *tr* to restock ‖ *ref* to lay in a new stock

réassurer [reasyre] *tr* to reinsure
rébarba·tif [rebarbatif] **-tive** [tiv] *adj* forbidding, repulsive
rebâtir [rəbɑtir] *tr* to rebuild
rebattre [rəbatr] §7 *tr* to beat; reshuffle; repeat over and over again
rebat·tu -tue [rəbaty] *adj* hackneyed
rebelle [rəbɛl] *adj* rebellious ‖ *mf* rebel
rebeller [rəbele], [rəbɛlle] *ref* to rebel
rébellion [rebelj5] *f* rebellion
rebiffer [rɛbife] *ref* to kick over the traces
reboisement [rəbwazmɑ̃] *m* reforestation
rebond [rəb5] *m* rebound
rebon·di -die [rəb5di] *adj* plump, buxom; paunchy
rebondir [rəb5dir] *intr* to bounce; (fig) to come up again
rebord [rəbɔr] *m* edge, border; sill, ledge; hem; brim (*of hat*); rim (*of saucer*); lip (*of cup*)
reboucher [rəbuʃe] *tr* to recork; stop up ‖ *ref* to be stopped up
rebours [rəbur] *m*—à **rebours** backwards; against the grain; the wrong way; backhanded (*compliment*); à or **au rebours de** contrary to
rebouter [rəbute] *tr* to set (*a bone*)
rebrousse-poil [rəbruspwal]—à **rebrousse-poil** against the grain, the wrong way
rebrousser [rəbruse] *tr* to brush up; **rebrousser chemin** to turn back; **rebrousser qn** (coll) to rub s.o. the wrong way ‖ *ref* to turn up, bend back
rebuffade [rəbyfad] *f* rebuff; **essuyer une rebuffade** to be snubbed
rebut [rəby] *m* castoff; waste; scum (*of society*); rebuff; **de rebut** castoff; waste; unclaimed (*letter*); **mettre au rebut** to discard
rebu·tant [rəbytɑ̃] **-tante** [tɑ̃t] *adj* dull, tedious; repugnant
rebuter [rəbyte] *tr* to rebuff; bore; be repulsive to
recaler [rəkale] *tr* (coll) to flunk
récapitulation [rekapitylasj5] *f* recapitulation
recéder [rəsede] §10 *tr* to give back; sell back; resell
recel [rəsɛl] *m* concealment (*of stolen goods; of criminals*)
receler [rəsle] §2 or **recéler** [rəsele] §10 *tr* to conceal; receive (*stolen goods*); harbor (*a criminal*) ‖ *intr* to hide
rece·leur [rəslœr] **-leuse** [løz] *mf* fence, receiver of stolen goods
récemment [resamɑ̃] *adv* recently, lately
recensement [rəsɑ̃smɑ̃] *m* census; **recensement du contingent** draft registration
recenser [rəsɑ̃se] *tr* to take the census of; take a count of
recenseur [rəsɑ̃sœr] *m* census taker
ré·cent [resɑ̃] **-cente** [sɑ̃t] *adj* recent
récépissé [resepise] *m* receipt; certificate, permit
réceptacle [resɛptakl] *m* receptacle
récep·teur [resɛptœr] **-trice** [tris] *adj* receiving ‖ *m* receiver

récep·tif [resɛptif] **-tive** [tiv] *adj* receptive
réception [resɛpsj5] *f* reception; receipt; approval; admission (*to a club*); registration desk (*of hotel*); landing (*of, e.g., a parachutist*); (sports) catch; **accuser réception de** to acknowledge receipt of
réceptionnaire [resɛpsjɔnɛr] *mf* consignee; chief receptionist
récession [resesj5] *f* recession
recette [rəsɛt] *f* receipt; collection (*of debts, taxes, etc.*); (culin) recipe; **faire recette** to be a box-office attraction; **recettes de métier** tricks of the trade
recevable [rəsvabl] *adj* acceptable; admissible
rece·veur [rəsvœr] **-veuse** [vøz] *mf* collector; conductor (*of bus, streetcar, etc.*); blood recipient; **receveur des postes** postmaster; **receveur universel** recipient of blood from a universal donor
recevoir [rəsvwar] §59 *tr* to receive; accommodate; admit (*to a school, club, etc.*); **être reçu** to be admitted; pass ‖ *intr* to receive
rechange [rəʃɑ̃ʒ] *m* replacement, change; **de rechange** spare (*e.g., parts*)
rechaper [rəʃape] *tr* to recap, retread
réchapper [reʃape] *intr*—**en réchapper** to get away with it; to get well; **réchapper à** or **de** to escape from
recharge [rəʃarʒ] *f* refill; recharging; reloading
recharger [rəʃarʒe] §38 *tr* to recharge; refill; reload; ballast (*a roadbed*)
réchaud [reʃo] *m* hot plate
réchauffer [reʃofe] *tr* & *ref* to warm up
rêche [rɛʃ] *adj* rough, harsh
recherche [rəʃɛrʃ] *f* search; quest; investigation, piece of research; refinement; **recherches** research
recher·ché -chée [rəʃɛrʃe] *adj* sought-after, in demand; elaborate; studied, affected
rechercher [rəʃɛrʃe] *tr* to seek, look for
rechigner [rəʃiɲe] *intr*—**rechigner à** to balk at
rechute [rəʃyt] *f* relapse
rechuter [rəʃyte] *intr* to relapse
récidive [residiv] *f* recurrence; second offense
récidiver [residive] *intr* to recur; relapse
récif [resif] *m* reef
récipiendaire [resipjɑ̃dɛr] *m* new member, inductee; recipient
récipient [resipjɑ̃] *m* container, receptacle, recipient
réciprocité [resiprɔsite] *f* reciprocity
réciproque [resiprɔk] *adj* reciprocal ‖ *f* converse
récit [resi] *m* recital, account
réci·tal [resital] *m* (*pl* **-tals**) recital
récitation [resitasj5] *f* recitation
réciter [resite] *tr* to recite
récla·mant [reklamɑ̃] **-mante** [mɑ̃t] *mf* claimant
réclamation [reklamasj5] *f* complaint; demand

réclame [reklam] *f* advertising; advertisement; (theat) cue; (typ) catchword; **faire de la réclame** to advertise, to ballyhoo; **réclame à éclipse** flashing sign; **réclame lumineuse** illuminated sign

réclamer [reklame] *tr* to claim; clamor for; demand ‖ *intr* to lodge a complaint; intercede ‖ *ref*—**se réclamer de** to appeal to; claim kinship with; **se réclamer de qn** to use s.o.'s name as a reference

reclassement [rəklɑsmɑ̃] *m* reclassification

reclasser [rəklɑse] *tr* to reclassify

re·clus [rəkly] **-cluse** [klyz] *adj* & *mf* recluse

recoin [rəkwɛ̃] *m* nook, cranny

récollection [rekɔlɛksjɔ̃] *f* religious meditation

recoller [rəkɔle] *tr* to paste again

récolte [rekɔlt] *f* harvest

récolter [rekɔlte] *tr* to harvest

recommander [rəkɔmɑ̃de] §97, §98 *tr* to recommend; register (*a letter*) ‖ *ref*—**se recommander à** to seek the protection of; **se recommander de** to ask (*s.o.*) for a reference

recommencer [rəkɔmɑ̃se] §51, §96, §97 *tr* & *intr* to begin again

récompense [rekɔ̃pɑ̃s] *f* recompense, reward; award

récompenser [rekɔ̃pɑ̃se] *tr* to recompense

réconcilier [rekɔ̃silje] *tr* to reconcile

reconduction [rəkɔ̃dyksjɔ̃] or **réconduction** [rekɔ̃dyksjɔ̃] *f* continuation; renewal (*of a lease*)

reconduire [rəkɔ̃dɥir] §19 *tr* to escort; (coll) to kick out, to send packing

réconfort [rekɔ̃fɔr] *m* comfort

réconfor·tant [rekɔ̃fɔrtɑ̃] **-tante** [tɑ̃t] *adj* consoling; stimulating

réconforter [rekɔ̃fɔrte] *tr* to comfort; revive ‖ *ref* to recuperate; cheer up

reconnaissance [rəkɔnɛsɑ̃s] *f* recognition; gratitude; (mil) reconnaissance; **aller en reconnaissance** to reconnoiter; **reconnaissance de** or **pour** gratitude for

reconnais·sant [rəkɔnɛsɑ̃] **-sante** [sɑ̃t] *adj* grateful; **être reconnaissant de** + *inf* to be grateful for + *ger;* **être reconnaissant de** or **pour** to be grateful for

reconnaître [rəkɔnɛtr] §12, §95 *tr* to recognize; (mil) to reconnoiter ‖ *ref* to recognize oneself; know where one is; acknowledge oneself (*e.g., guilty*); **s'y reconnaître** to know where one is

reconquérir [rəkɔ̃kerir] §3 *tr* to reconquer

reconquête [rəkɔ̃kɛt] *f* reconquest

reconsidérer [rəkɔ̃sidere] §10 *tr* to reconsider

reconstituant [rəkɔ̃stitɥɑ̃] *m* tonic

reconstituer [rəkɔ̃stitɥe] *tr* to reconstruct; restore

reconstruire [rəkɔ̃strɥir] §19 *tr* to reconstruct

record [rəkɔr] *adj invar* & *m* record

recordman [rəkɔrdman] *m* record holder

recoudre [rəkudr] §13 *tr* to sew up

recoupement [rəkupmɑ̃] *m* cross-check, cross-checking; **faire un recoupement** to cross-check

recouper [rəkupe] *tr* to cut again; blend (*wines*)

recourir [rəkurir] §14 *intr* to run again; **recourir à** to resort to; appeal to

recours [rəkur] *m* recourse; **avoir recours à** to resort to; call on for help; **en dernier recours** as a last resort; **recours en grâce** petition for pardon

recouvrement [rəkuvrəmɑ̃] *m* recovery

recouvrer [rəkuvre] *tr* to recover

recouvrir [rəkuvrir] §65 *tr* to cover; cover up; mask; resurface (*e.g., a road*) ‖ *ref* to overlap

récréation [rekreɑsjɔ̃] *f* recreation; recess (*at school*)

recréer [rəkree] *tr* to re-create

récréer [rekree] *tr* & *ref* to relax

récrier [rekrije] *ref* to cry out

récrire [rekrir] §25 *tr* to rewrite; write again

recroquevil·lé -lée [rəkrɔkvije] *adj* shriveled up, curled up; huddled up

recroqueviller [rəkrɔkvije] *tr* & *ref* to shrivel up, curl up

re·cru -crue [rəkry] *adj* exhausted

recrue [rəkry] *f* recruit

recruter [rəkryte] *tr* to recruit; **recrutons** (*public sign for job openings*) help wanted ‖ *ref* to be recruited

rectangle [rɛktɑ̃gl] *m* rectangle

rectificateur [rɛktifikatœr] *m* rectifier

rectifier [rɛktifje] *tr* to rectify; true up; grind (*a cylinder*)

rectum [rɛktɔm] *m* rectum

re·çu -çue [rəsy] *adj* received; accepted; recognized; successful ‖ *m* receipt ‖ *v* see **recevoir**

recueil [rəkœj] *m* collection; compilation

recueillement [rəkœjmɑ̃] *m* meditation

recueillir [rəkœjir] §18 *tr* to collect, gather; take in (*a needy person*); receive (*a legacy*) ‖ *ref* to collect oneself, meditate

recuire [rəkɥir] §19 *tr* to anneal, temper; cook over again ‖ *intr* (fig) to stew

recul [rəkyl] *m* backing, backward movement; kick, recoil; **être en recul** to be losing ground; **prendre du recul** to consider in perspective

reculer [rəkyle] *tr* to move back; put off (*e.g., a decision*) ‖ *intr* to move back; back out; recoil; **reculer devant** to shrink from ‖ *ref* to move back

reculons [rəkylɔ̃]—**à reculons** backwards

récupération [rekyperɑsjɔ̃] *f* recovery

récurer [rekypere] §10 *tr* to salvage, recover; recuperate; make up (*e.g., lost hours*); find another job for ‖ *intr* to recuperate

récurer [rekyre] *tr* to scour

récur·rent [rekyrɑ̃] **-rente** [rɑ̃t] *adj* recurrent

récusable [rekysabl] *adj* (law) untrustworthy, unreliable

récuser [rekyze] *tr* to take exception to ‖ *ref* to refuse to give one's opinion

recyclage [rəsiklaʒ] *m* recycling; retraining, reorientation

recycler [rəsikle] *tr* to recycle; retrain, reorient

rédac·teur [redaktœr] **-trice** [tris] *mf* editor; **rédacteur en chef** editor in chief; **rédacteur gérant** managing editor; **rédacteur publicitaire** copywriter; **rédacteur sportif** sports editor

rédaction [redaksjɔ̃] *f* editorial staff; editorial office; edition; editing

reddition [redisjɔ̃] *f* surrender

redécouvrir [rədekuvrir] §65 *tr* to rediscover

rédemp·teur [redɑ̃ptœr] **-trice** [tris] *adj* redemptive ‖ *mf* redeemer

rédemption [redɑ̃psjɔ̃] *f* redemption

redevable [rədvabl] *adj* indebted

redevance [rədvɑ̃s] *f* dues, fees; rent; tax (*on radio sets*); royalty

rédiger [rediʒe] §38 *tr* to edit; draft; write up

redingote [rədɛ̃gɔt] *f* frock coat

redire [rədir] §22 *tr* to repeat; give away (*a secret*) ‖ *intr*—**trouver à redire à** to find fault with

redon·dant [redɔ̃dɑ̃] **-dante** [dɑ̃t] *adj* redundant

redoublement [rədubləmɑ̃] *m* redoubling; repeating (*of a course*)

redoutable [rədutabl] *adj* frightening

redoute [rədut] *f* redoubt

redouter [rədute] §97 *tr* to dread

redressement [rədrɛsmɑ̃] *m* straightening out; redress; (elec) rectifying

redresser [rədrese] *tr* to straighten; hold up (*e.g., the head*); redress; (elec) to rectify ‖ *ref* to straighten up

redresseur [rədrɛsœr] *m* (elec) rectifier; **redresseur de torts** knight-errant; (coll) reformer

réduction [redyksjɔ̃] *f* reduction; **réduction des effectifs** reduction in force

réduire [redɥir] §19, §96, §100 *tr* to reduce; set (*a bone*) ‖ §96 *ref* to boil down; **se réduire à** to amount to; **se réduire en** to be reduced to

réduit [redɥi] *m* retreat, nook; redoubt

rééditer [reedite] *tr* to reedit

réel réelle [reɛl] *adj & m* real, actual

réélection [reelɛksjɔ̃] *f* reelection

réellement [reɛlmɑ̃] *adv* really

réémetteur [reemɛtœr] *m* (electron) relay transmitter

réescompte [reɛskɔ̃t] *m* rediscount

réexamen [reɛgzamɛ̃] *m* reexamination

réexpédier [reɛkspedje] *tr* to reship; return to sender

réexpédition [reɛkspedisjɔ̃] *f* reshipment; return

refaire [rəfɛr] §29 *tr* to redo ‖ *intr*—**à refaire** to be done over; be dealt over ‖ *ref* to recover; make good one's losses

réfection [refɛksjɔ̃] *f* repairing, rebuilding, remaking

référence [referɑ̃s] *f* reference

référendum or **referendum** [referɛ̃dɔm] *m* referendum

référer [refere] §10 *intr*—**en référer à** to appeal to ‖ *ref*—**s'en référer à** to leave it up to; **se référer à** to refer to

refermer [rəfɛrme] *tr & ref* to close again, to close

refiler [rəfile] *tr*—**refiler à qn** (slang) to palm off on s.o.

réflé·chi -chie [refleʃi] *adj* thoughtful; well-thought-out; (gram) reflexive ‖ *m* (gram) reflexive

réfléchir [refleʃir] *tr & intr* to reflect; **réfléchir à, réfléchir sur** to think about, ponder ‖ *ref* to be reflected

réflec·teur [reflɛktœr] **-trice** [tris] *adj* reflecting ‖ *m* reflector

reflet [rəflɛ] *m* reflection; glint, gleam

refléter [rəflete] §10 *tr* to reflect, mirror ‖ *ref* to be mirrored

réflexe [reflɛks] *adj & m* reflex

réflexion [reflɛksjɔ̃] *f* reflection

refluer [rəflye] *intr* to ebb

reflux [rəfly] *m* ebb

refonte [rəfɔ̃t] *f* recasting

réforma·teur [reformatœr] **-trice** [tris] *mf* reformer

réformation [reformasjɔ̃] *f* reformation

réforme [refɔrm] *f* reform; **la Réforme** the Reformation

réfor·mé -mée [reforme] *adj* (eccl) Reformed; (mil) disabled

reformer [rəfɔrme] *tr & ref* to regroup

réformer [reforme] *tr* to reform; (mil) to discharge ‖ *ref* to reform

refou·lé -lée [rəfule] *adj* (coll) inhibited

refoulement [rəfulmɑ̃] *m* driving back; (psychoanal) repression

refouler [rəfule] *tr* to drive back; choke back (*a sob*); sail against (*the current*); compress, stem; (psychoanal) to repress ‖ *intr* to flow back

réfractaire [refraktɛr] *adj* refractory; rebellious ‖ *mf* insubordinate; draft dodger

réfraction [refraksjɔ̃] *f* refraction

refrain [rəfrɛ̃] *m* refrain; hum; **le même refrain** the same old tune; **refrain publicitaire** (advertising) jingle

refréner [rəfrene] §10 *tr* to curb

réfrigérateur [refriʒeratœr] *m* refrigerator

réfrigérer [refriʒere] §10 *tr* to refrigerate; (coll) to chill to the bone

refroidir [rəfrwadir] *tr* to cool; (slang) to rub out ‖ *intr* to cool ‖ *ref* to cool; catch cold

refroidissement [rəfrwadismɑ̃] *m* cooling

refuge [rəfyʒ] *m* refuge; shelter; safety zone

réfu·gié -giée [refyʒje] *mf* refugee

réfugier [refyʒje] *ref* to take refuge

refus [rəfy] *m* refusal; **refus seulement** regrets only (*to invitation*)

refuser [rəfyze] §96, §97, §98 *tr* to refuse; refuse; recognize; flunk; decline ‖ *intr* to refuse; **refuser de** or **à** to refuse to ‖ §96 *ref* to be refused; **se refuser à** to refuse to accept

réfuter [refyte] *tr* to refute

regagner [rəgaɲe] *tr* to regain
regain [rəgɛ̃] *m* second growth; (fig) aftermath; **regain de** new lease on
ré·gal [regal] *m* (*pl* **-gals**) treat
régaler [regale] *tr* to treat; level ‖ *intr* to treat
regard [rəgar] *m* look, glance; **couver du regard** to gloat over; look fondly at; look greedily at; **en regard** facing, opposite
regar·dant [rəgardɑ̃] **-dante** [dɑ̃t] *adj* (coll) penny-pinching
regarder [rəgarde] §95 *tr* to look at; face; concern ‖ *intr* to look; **regarder à** to pay attention to; watch (*one's money*); mind (*the price*); **y regarder à deux fois** to watch one's step, think twice ‖ *ref* to face each other
régate [regat] *f* regatta
régence [reʒɑ̃s] *f* regency
régénérer [reʒenere] §10 *tr* & *ref* to regenerate
ré·gent [reʒɑ̃] **-gente** [ʒɑ̃t] *mf* regent
régenter [reʒɑ̃te] *tr* & *intr* to boss
régicide [reʒisid] *mf* regicide (*person*) ‖ *m* regicide (*act*)
régie [reʒi] *f* commission, administration; excise tax; stage management; **en régie** state-owned or -operated
regimber [rəʒɛ̃be] *intr* & *ref* to revolt; balk
régime [reʒim] *m* government, form of government; administration; system; diet; performance, working conditions; rate (*of speed; of flow; of charge or discharge of a storage battery*); bunch, cluster; stem (*of bananas*); (gram) complement; (gram) government; **en régime permanent** under steady working conditions
régiment [reʒimɑ̃] *m* regiment
régimentaire [reʒimɑ̃tɛr] *adj* regimental
région [reʒjɔ̃] *f* region, area
régir [reʒir] *tr* to govern
régisseur [reʒisœr] *m* manager; stage manager
registre [rəʒistr] *m* register; damper; throttle valve
réglable [reglabl] *adj* adjustable
réglage [reglaʒ] *m* setting, adjusting; lines (*on paper*); (mach, rad, telv) tuning
règle [rɛgl] *f* rule; ruler; **en règle** in order; **en règle générale** as a general rule; **règle à calcul** slide rule; **règles** menstrual period
ré·glé -glée [regle] *adj* regulated; adjusted, tuned; well-behaved, orderly; ruled (*paper*); finished, decided
règlement [rɛgləmɑ̃] *m* regulation, rule; settlement; **en règlement judiciaire** in bankruptcy proceedings; **règlement intérieur** bylaws
réglementaire [reglɑmɑ̃tɛr] *adj* regular; regulation
réglementer [reglɑmɑ̃te] *tr* to regulate, control
régler [regle] §10 *tr* to regulate, put in order; set (*a watch*); settle (*an account*); rule (*paper*); (aut, rad, telv) to tune ‖ *intr* to pay

réglisse [reglis] *m* & *f* licorice
ré·gnant [reɲɑ̃] **-gnante** [ɲɑ̃t] *adj* reigning; ruling; prevailing, prevalent
règne [rɛɲ] *m* reign; (biol) kingdom
régner [reɲe] §10 *intr* to reign
regorger [rəgɔrʒe] §38 *intr* to overflow; **regorger de** to abound in
regratter [rəgrate] *tr* to scrape ‖ *intr* to pinch pennies
regret [rəgrɛ] *m* regret; **à regret** regretfully
regrettable [rəgrɛtabl] *adj* regrettable
regretter [rəgrete] *tr* to regret; long for, miss; **regretter** + *subj* to be sorry that + *ind* ‖ §97 *intr* to be sorry, regret, e.g., **je regrette d'avoir fait cela** I regret having done that
régulariser [regylarize] *tr* to regularize; adjust, regulate
régularité [regylarite] *f* regularity
régula·teur [regylatœr] **-trice** [tris] *adj* regulating ‖ *m* (mach) governor
régulation [regylasjɔ̃] *f* regulation
régu·lier [regylje] **-lière** [ljɛr] *adj* regular; scheduled; exact, prompt; legitimate; honest, aboveboard, on the level ‖ *m* (mil, rel) regular ‖ *f*—**ma régulière** (slang) my woman
réhabiliter [reabilite] *tr* to rehabilitate
rehausser [rəose] *tr* to heighten; enhance
Reims [rɛ̃s] *m* Rheims
rein [rɛ̃] *m* kidney
réincarnation [reɛ̃karnɑsjɔ̃] *f* reincarnation
reine [rɛn] *f* queen
reine-claude [rɛnklod] *f* (*pl* **-claudes** or **reines-claudes**) greengage
reine-des-prés [rɛndepre] *f* (*pl* **reines-des-prés**) meadowsweet
reine-marguerite [rɛnmargərit] *f* (*pl* **reines-marguerites**) aster
réintégrer [reɛ̃tegre] §10 *tr* to reinstate; return to
réitérer [reitere] §10 *tr* reiterate
rejaillir [rəʒajir] *intr* to spurt out; bounce; splash; **rejaillir sur** to reflect on
rejet [rəʒɛ] *m* casting up; rejection; enjambment; (bot) shoot
rejeter [rəʒte] §34 *tr* to reject; throw back; throw up; shift (*responsibility*) ‖ *ref* to fall back
rejeton [rəʒtɔ̃] *m* shoot; offshoot, offspring; (coll) child
rejeu [rəʒø] *m* (electron) playback
rejoindre [rəʒwɛ̃dr] §35 *tr* to rejoin; overtake ‖ *ref* to meet
réjouir [reʒwir] *tr* to gladden, cheer ‖ §97 *ref* to rejoice, be delighted
réjouissance [reʒwisɑ̃s] *f* rejoicing; **réjouissances** festivities
réjouis·sant [reʒwisɑ̃] **-sante** [sɑ̃t] *adj* cheery; amusing
relâche [rəlɑʃ] *m* & *f* respite, letup ‖ *f* (naut) stop; **faire relâche** (naut) to make a call; (theat) to close (*for a day or two*); **relâche** (*public sign*) no performance today
relâ·ché -chée [rəlɑʃe] *adj* lax; loose

relâchement [rəlɑʃmɑ̃] *m* relaxation; letting up

relâcher [rəlɑʃe] *tr* to loosen; relax; release ‖ *intr* (naut) to make a call ‖ *ref* to loosen; become lax

relais [rəlɛ] *m* relay; shift; **prendre le relais** (slang) to take up the slack; **relais routier** service stop (*on a superhighway*)

relance [rəlɑ̃s] *f* raise (*e.g., in poker*); outbreak

relancer [rəlɑ̃se] §51 *tr* to start up again; harass, hound; return (*the ball*); raise (*the ante*) ‖ *intr* (cards) to raise

re·laps -lapse [rəlaps] *mf* backslider

relater [rəlate] *tr* to relate

rela·tif [rəlatif] **-tive** [tiv] *adj* relative

relation [rəlɑsjɔ̃] *f* relation; **en relation avec, en relations avec** in touch with; **relations** connections

relativité [rəlativite] *f* relativity

relaxation [rəlaksɑsjɔ̃] *f* relaxation

relaxer [rəlakse] *tr* to relax; free ‖ *ref* to relax

relayer [rəleje] §49 *tr* to relay; relieve ‖ *ref* to work in relays or shifts

reléguer [rəlege] §10 *tr* to relegate

relent [rəlɑ̃] *m* musty smell

relève [rəlɛv] *f* relief; change (*of the guard*); **prendre la relève** to take over

rele·vé -vée [rəlve] *adj* lofty, elevated; turned up; graded (*curve*); spicy ‖ *m* check list; tuck (*in dress*); (culin) next course; **faire le relevé de** to survey; to check off; **relevé de compte** bank statement; **relevé de compteur** meter reading; **relevé de notes des écoles** transcript of grades

relèvement [rəlɛvmɑ̃] *m* raising; recovery, improvement; picking up (*e.g., of wounded*); (naut) bearing

relever [rəlve] §2 *tr* to raise; turn up; restore; relieve, enhance; pick out; take a reading of; season; (mil) to relieve ‖ *intr*—**relever de** to recover from; depend on ‖ *ref* to rise; recover; right itself; take turns

re·lié -liée [rəlje] *adj* (bb) hardbound, hardcover; **relié cuir** leather-bound; **relié plein chagrin** entirely bound in grained leather

relief [rəljɛf] *m* relief; **en relief** in relief; **reliefs** leavings

relier [rəlje] *tr* to bind; to link

re·lieur [rəljœr] **-lieuse** [ljøz] *mf* bookbinder

reli·gieux [rəliʒjø] **-gieuse** [ʒjøz] *adj* religious ‖ *m* monk ‖ *f* nun; cream puff

religion [rəliʒjɔ̃] *f* religion

reliquat [rəlika] *m* remainder

relique [rəlik] *f* relic

relire [rəlir] §36 *tr* to read again; read over again

reliure [rəljyr] *f* binding; bookbinding

reloger [rələʒe] §38 *tr* to find a new home for, relocate

reluire [rəlɥir] §37 *intr* to shine, gleam, sparkle

relui·sant [rəlɥizɑ̃] **-sante** [zɑ̃t] *adj* shiny, gleaming; **peu reluisant** unpromising, not brilliant

reluquer [rəlyke] *tr* to have an eye on

remâcher [rəmɑʃe] *tr* (coll) to stew over

remailler [rəmɑje] *tr* to mend the meshes of

remanier [rəmanje] *tr* to revise, revamp; to reshuffle

remarier [rəmarje] *tr* & *ref* to remarry

remarquable [rəmarkabl] *adj* remarkable

remarque [rəmark] *f* remark; **accompagner de remarques** to annotate; **des remarques?** any comments?; **faire une remarque** to make a remark; remark, make a critical observation

remarquer [rəmarke] *tr* & *intr* to remark, notice; **faire remarquer** to point out ‖ *ref*—**se fair remarquer** to make oneself conspicuous

remballer [rɑ̃bale] *tr* to repack

rembarquer [rɑ̃barke] *tr, intr,* & *ref* to reembark

rembarrer [rɑ̃bare] *tr* to snub, rebuff

remblai [rɑ̃blɛ] *m* fill; embankment

remblayer [rɑ̃bleje] §49 *tr* to fill; bank up

rembobiner [rɑ̃bɔbine] *tr* to rewind

remboîter [rɑ̃bwate] *tr* to reset (*a bone*); recase (*a book*)

rembourrer [rɑ̃bure] *tr* to upholster; stuff; pad

rembourrure [rɑ̃buryr] *f* stuffing

remboursement [rɑ̃bursəmɑ̃] *m* reimbursement; **contre remboursement** C.O.D.; with cash, e.g., **envoi contre remboursement** cash with order; **remboursement dans le bas de l'appareil** coin return

rembourser [rɑ̃burse] *tr* to reimburse

rembrunir [rɑ̃brynir] *tr* to darken; sadden ‖ *ref* to cloud over

remède [rəmɛd] *m* remedy

remédier [rəmedje] *intr*—**remédier à** to remedy

remembrement [rəmɑ̃brəmɑ̃] *m* regrouping

remémorer [rəmemɔre] *tr*—**remémorer q.ch. à qn** to remind s.o. of s.th. ‖ *ref* to remember

remerciement [rəmɛrsimɑ̃] *m* thanking; **remerciements** thanks; **mille remerciements de** or **pour** a thousand thanks for

remercier [rəmɛrsje] §97 *tr* to thank; dismiss (*an employee*); refuse with thanks; **remercier qn de** + *inf* to thank s.o. for + *ger;* **remercier qn de** or **pour** to thank s.o. for

remettre [rəmɛtr] §42 *tr* to remit, deliver; put back; put back on; give back; put off; reset ‖ *ref* to resume; recover; pull oneself together; (*said of weather*) clear; **s'en remettre à** to leave it up to, depend on

remise [rəmiz] *f* remittance; discount; delivery; postponement; surrender, return; garage; cover (*for game*); **de remise** rented (*car*)

remiser [rəmize] *tr* to put away; park ‖ *ref* to take cover

rémission [remisjɔ̃] *f* remission

remmailler [rɑ̃mɑje] *tr* to darn

remmener [rɑ̃mne] §2 *tr* to take back

remodelage [rəmɔdlaʒ] *m* remodeling; plastic surgery

remon·tant [rəmɔ̃tɑ̃] **-tante** [tɑ̃t] *adj* fortifying; remontant (*rose*) ‖ *m* tonic

remonte [rəmɔ̃t] *f* ascent

remontée [rəmɔ̃te] *f* climb; surfacing; comeback

remonte-pente [rəmɔ̃tpɑ̃t] *m* (*pl* **-pentes**); ski lift

remonter [rəmɔ̃te] *tr* to remount; pull up; wind (*a clock*); pep up; (theat) to put on again ‖ *intr* (*aux:* ÉTRE) to go up again; date back ‖ *ref* to pep up

remontoir [rəmɔ̃twar] *m* knob (*of stemwinder*); key, winder

remontrance [rəmɔ̃trɑ̃s] *f* remonstrance

remontrer [rəmɔ̃tre] *tr* to show again; point out ‖ *intr*—**en remontrer à** to outdo, best

remords [rəmɔr] *m* remorse

remorque [rəmɔrk] *f* tow rope; trailer; **à la remorque** in tow

remorquer [rəmɔrke] *tr* to tow; haul

remorqueur [rəmɔrkœr] *m* tugboat

rémouleur [remulœr] *m* knife grinder, scissors grinder

remous [rəmu] *m* eddy; wash (*of boat*); agitation

rempailler [rɑ̃pɑje] *tr* to cane

rempart [rɑ̃par] *m* rampart

remplaçable [rɑ̃plasabl] *adj* replaceable

rempla·çant [rɑ̃plasɑ̃] **-çante** [sɑ̃t] *mf* replacement, substitute

remplacement [rɑ̃plasmɑ̃] *m* replacement

remplacer [rɑ̃plase] §51 *tr* to replace; take the place of; **remplacer par** to replace with

rem·pli -plie [rɑ̃pli] *adj* full ‖ *m* tuck

remplir [rɑ̃plir] *tr* to fill; fill up; fill out or in; fulfill ‖ *ref* to fill up

remplissage [rɑ̃plisaʒ] *m* filling up

remplumer [rɑ̃plyme] *ref* (coll) to put on flesh again; (coll) to make a comeback

remporter [rɑ̃pɔrte] *tr* to take back; carry off; win

remue-ménage [rəmymenaʒ] *m invar* stir, bustle, to-do

remue-méninges [rəmymenɛ̃ʒ] *f invar* (slang) brainstorming

remuer [rəmɥe] *tr* to move; stir; remove (*e.g., a piece of furniture*) ‖ *intr* to move ‖ *ref* to move; hustle

rémunération [remynerɑsjɔ̃] *f* remuneration

renâcler [rənɑkle] *intr* to snort; **renâcler à** (coll) to shrink from, bridle at

renaissance [rənɛsɑ̃s] *f* renascence, rebirth; renaissance

renais·sant [rənɛsɑ̃] **-sante** [sɑ̃t] *adj* renascent, reviving; Renaissance

renaître [rənɛtr] §46 *tr* to be reborn; revive; grow again

re·nard [rənar] **-narde** [nard] *mf* fox

renché·ri -rie [rɑ̃ʃeri] *adj* fastidious

renchérir [rɑ̃ʃerir] *tr* to make more expensive ‖ *intr* to go up in price; **renchérir sur** to improve on

rencontre [rɑ̃kɔ̃tr] *f* meeting, encounter; clash; collision; **aller à la rencontre de** to go to meet; **de rencontre** chance (*e.g., acquaintance*)

rencontrer [rɑ̃kɔ̃tre] *tr* to meet, encounter ‖ *ref* to meet; collide; occur

rendement [rɑ̃dmɑ̃] *m* yield; (mech) output, efficiency

rendez-vous [rɑ̃devu] *m* appointment, date; rendezvous; **donner (un) rendez-vous à,** **fixer (un) rendez-vous à** to make an appointment with; **sur rendez-vous** by appointment

rendre [rɑ̃dr] *tr* to render; yield; surrender; make; translate; vomit ‖ *intr* to bring in, yield ‖ *ref* to surrender; **se rendre à** to go to; **se rendre compte de** to realize

ren·du -due [rɑ̃dy] *adj* arrived; translated; all in, exhausted ‖ *m* rendering; returned article

rêne [rɛn] *f* rein

réné·gat [renega] **-gate** [gat] *mf* renegade

renfer·mé -mée [rɑ̃fɛrme] *adj* closemouthed, stand-offish ‖ *m* close smell; **sentir le renfermé** to smell stuffy

renfermer [rɑ̃fɛrme] *tr* to contain; include ‖ *ref*—**se renfermer dans** to withdraw into; confine oneself to

renfler [rɑ̃fle] *ref* to swell up

renflouer [rɑ̃flue] *tr* to keep afloat; salvage

renfoncement [rɑ̃fɔ̃smɑ̃] *m* recess; hollow; dent

renfoncer [rɑ̃fɔ̃se] §51 *tr* to recess; dent; pull down (*e.g., one's hat*) ‖ *ref* to recede; draw back

renforcement [rɑ̃fɔrsəmɑ̃] *m* reinforcement

renforcer [rɑ̃fɔrse] §51 *tr* to reinforce

renforcir [rɑ̃fɔrsir] *tr* (slang) to strengthen ‖ *intr* (slang) to grow stronger

renfort [rɑ̃fɔr] *m* reinforcement

renfro·gné -gnée [rɑ̃frɔɲe] *adj* sullen, glum

renfrogner [rɑ̃frɔɲe] *ref* to scowl

rengager [rɑ̃gaʒe] §38 *tr* to rehire ‖ *intr* & *ref* to reenlist

rengaine [rɑ̃gɛn] *f*—**la même rengaine** the same old story; **vieille rengaine** old refrain

rengorger [rɑ̃gɔrʒe] §38 *ref* to strut

reniement [rənimɑ̃] *m* denial

renier [rənje] *tr* to deny; repudiate

renifler [rənifle] *tr* & *intr* to sniff

renne [rɛn] *m* reindeer

renom [rənɔ̃] *m* renown, fame

renom·mé -mée [rənɔme] *adj* renowned, well-known ‖ *f* fame; reputation

renommer [rənɔme] *tr* to reelect; reappoint

renoncement [rənɔ̃smɑ̃] *m* renunciation

renoncer [rənɔ̃se] §51, §96 *tr* to renounce, repudiate ‖ *intr* to give up; (cards) to renege; **renoncer à** to renounce; give up, abandon, e.g., **lui renoncer** to abandon her (or him); **y renoncer** to give it up

renonciation [rənɔ̃sjɑsjɔ̃] *f* renunciation; waiver

renoncule [rənɔ̃kyl] *f* buttercup; **renoncule double** bachelor's-button; **renoncule langue** spearwort

renouer [rənwe] *tr* to tie again; resume (*e.g., a conversation*) ‖ *intr* to renew a friendship

renou·veau [rənuvo] *m* (*pl* **-veaux**) springtime; revival

renouvelable [rənuvlabl] *adj* renewable

renouveler [rənuvle] §34 *tr* & *ref* to renew

renouvellement [rənuvɛlmã] *m* renewal

rénover [renɔve] *tr* to renew; renovate

renseignement [rãsɛɲmã] *m* piece of information; **de renseignements** (mil) intelligence; **renseignements** information

renseigner [rãsɛɲe] *tr* to inform ‖ *ref* to find out; **se renseigner auprès de qn** to inquire of s.o.

rentable [rãtabl] *adj* profitable

rente [rãt] *f* revenue, income; annuity; dividend, return; **rente viagère** life annuity

ren·té -tée [rãte] *adj* well-off

renter [rãte] *tr* to endow

ren·tier [rãtje] **-tière** [tjɛr] *mf* person of independent means

ren·tré -trée [rãtre] *adj* sunken (*eyes*); suppressed (*feelings*) ‖ *f* return; reopening (*of school*); yield, income; (comp) reentry

rentrer [rãtre] §95 *tr* to bring in or back; put in; hold back (*e.g., one's tears*); draw in (*claws*) ‖ *intr* (*aux:* ÊTRE) to return, reenter; go or come home; be paid or collected; **rentrer dans** to fit into; come back to; get back, recover; **rentrer en soi-même** to take stock of oneself

renverse [rãvɛrs] *f* shift, turn; **à la renverse** backwards

renversement [rãvɛrsəmã] *m* reversal, shift; upset, overturn; overthrow

renverser [rãvɛrse] *tr* to reverse; overthrow; bowl over, astonish ‖ *intr* & *ref* to capsize

renvoi [rãvwa] *m* dismissal; postponement; reference; return; belch

renvoyer [rãvwaje] §26 *tr* to dismiss; fire (*an employee*); postpone; refer; send back

réorganiser [reɔrganize] *tr* & *ref* to reorganize

réouverture [reuvɛrtyr] *f* reopening

repaire [rəpɛr] *m* den

repaître [rəpɛtr] §12 *tr* to graze; **repaître de** to feast (*e.g., one's eyes*) on ‖ *ref* to eat one's fill (*said of only animals*); **se repaître de** to indulge in, to wallow in

répandre [repãdr] *tr* to spread; strew, scatter; spill; shed ‖ *ref* to spread; **se répandre en** to be profuse in

répan·du -due [repãdy] *adj* widespread; widely known

reparaître [rəparɛtr] §12 *intr* to reappear

répara·teur [reparatœr] **-trice** [tris] *adj* restorative ‖ *m* repairman

réparation [reparasjõ] *f* repair; reparation; restoration

réparer [repare] *tr* to repair, fix; mend, patch; make up (*a loss*); redress (*a wrong*); restore (*one's strength*)

repartie [rəparti], [reparti] *f* repartee

repartir [rəpartir] §64 *tr* to retort ‖ *intr* (*aux:* ÊTRE) to start again; leave again; **repartir à zéro** to go back to square one

répartir [repartir] *tr* to distribute

répartiteur [repartitœr] *m* distributor; assessor; dispatcher

répartition [repartisjõ] *f* distribution; apportionment; range (*of words*)

repas [rəpɑ] *m* meal, repast; **dernier repas** (rel) last supper; **repas champêtre** picnic; **repas de noce** wedding breakfast; **repas froid** cold snack; **repas principal** main meal; **repas sur le pouce** takeout meal; **repas tiré du sac** brown-bag lunch

repassage [rəpɑsaʒ] *m* recrossing; ironing; stropping; whetting

repasser [rəpɑse] *tr* to pass again; go over, review; iron; strop; whet ‖ *intr* to pass by again; drop in again

repêcher [rəpɛʃe] *tr* to fish out; give another chance to; (coll) to get (*s.o.*) out of a scrape

repentance [rəpãtãs] *f* repentance

repen·tant [rəpãtã] **-tante** [tãt] *adj* repentant

repen·ti -tie [rəpãti] *adj* repentant

repentir [rəpãtir] *m* repentance ‖ §41, §97 *ref* to repent; **se repentir de** to be sorry for, to repent

repérage [reperaʒ] *m* spotting, locating; tracking; marking with a reference mark; (mov) synchronization

répercussion [repɛrkysjõ] *f* repercussion; reverberation

répercuter [repɛrkyte] *tr* to reflect ‖ *ref* to reverberate; have repercussions

repère [rəpɛr] *m* mark, reference

repérer [rəpere] §10 *tr* to locate, spot; mark with a reference mark; (mov) to synchronize

répertoire [repɛrtwar] *m* repertory; index; **répertoire à onglets** thumb index; **répertoire d'adresses** address book; **répertoire vivant** walking encyclopedia

répéter [repete] §10 *tr* & *ref* to repeat

répéti·teur [repetitœr] **-trice** [tris] *mf* assistant teacher; coach, tutor

répétition [repetisjõ] *f* repetition; private lesson; tutoring; rehearsal; **répétition des couturières** next-to-last dress rehearsal; **répétition générale** final dress rehearsal

repeupler [rəpœple] *tr* to repeople; restock

repiquer [rəpike] *tr* to plant out (*seedlings*); repave; restitch; rerecord; (phot) to retouch ‖ *intr*—**repiquer à** (slang) to come back to

répit [repi] *m* respite, letup

replacement [rəplasmã] *m* replacement; reinvestment

replacer [rəplase] §51 *tr* to replace; find a new job for; reinvest ‖ *ref* to find a new job

replâtrage [rəplɑtraʒ] *m* replastering; makeshift; (fig) patchwork

re·plet [rəplɛ] **-plète** [plɛt] *adj* fat, plump

repli [rəpli] *m* crease, fold; dip, depression; (mil) falling back

replier [rəplije] *tr* to refold; turn up; close (*e.g., an umbrella*) ‖ *ref* to curl up, coil up; (mil) to fall back

réplique [replik] *f* reply, retort; replica; **donner la réplique à qn** to answer s.o.; (theat) to give s.o. his cue; (theat) to play the straight man or stooge for s.o.

répliquer [replike] *tr & intr* to reply

replonger [rəplɔ̃ʒe] §38 *tr* to plunge again ‖ *intr* to dive again ‖ *ref*—**se replonger dans** to get back into

répon·dant [repɔ̃dɑ̃] **-dante** [dɑ̃t] *mf* guarantor; (eccl) server; **avoir du répondant** (coll) to have money behind one

répon·deur [repɔ̃dœr] **-deuse** [døz] *adj* (coll) back-talking ‖ *m*—**répondeur automatique, répondeur téléphonique** (telephone) answering machine

répondre [repɔ̃dr] §98 *tr* to answer (*e.g., yes or no*); assure ‖ *intr* to answer, reply; answer back, be saucy; reecho; **répondre à** to answer (*e.g., a question, a letter*); correspond to; **répondre de** to answer for (*a person*); guarantee (*a thing*) ‖ *ref* to answer each other; correspond to each other; be in harmony

réponse [repɔ̃s] *f* answer, response; **réponse normande** evasive answer

report [rəpɔr] *m* carrying forward or over; carry-over

reportage [rəpɔrtaʒ] *m* reporting

reporter [rəpɔrtɛr] *m* reporter; **reporter d'images** news cameraman ‖ [rəpɔrte] *tr* to carry back; to postpone; (math) to carry forward ‖ *intr* (com) to carry stock; **à reporter** carried forward ‖ *ref*—**se reporter à** to be carried back to (*e.g., childhood days*); refer to

reporteur [rəpɔrtœr] *m* broker

repos [rəpo] *m* rest, repose; **au repos** not running, still; **de tout repos** reliable; **en repos** at rest; **repos!** (mil) at ease!

repo·sé -sée [rəpoze] *adj* refreshed, relaxed

reposer [rəpoze] *tr* to rest ‖ *intr* to rest; **ici repose** . . . here lies . . . ‖ *ref* to rest; **s'en reposer sur** to rely on

repous·sant [rəpusɑ̃] **-sante** [sɑ̃t] *adj* repulsive

repousser [rəpuse] *tr* to push, shove; repulse, repel; reject, refuse; postpone; emboss ‖ *intr* to grow again; be offensive; (arti) to recoil

repoussoir [rəpuswar] *m* foil; contrast; (mach) driving bolt

reprendre [rəprɑ̃dr] §56, §97 *tr* to take back; resume; regain (*consciousness*); find fault with; take in (*e.g., a dress*); catch (*one's breath*); (theat) to put on again ‖ *intr* to start again; pick up, improve; criticize ‖ *ref* to pull oneself together; correct oneself in speaking

représailles [rəprezaj] *fpl* reprisal

représen·tant [rəprezɑ̃tɑ̃] **-tante** [tɑ̃t] *adj & mf* representative; **représentant de commerce** traveling salesman

représenta·tif [rəprezɑ̃tatif] **-tive** [tiv] *adj* representative

représentation [rəprezɑ̃tasjɔ̃] *f* representation; performance; remonstrance

représenter [rəprezɑ̃te] *tr* to represent; put on, perform ‖ *intr* to make a good showing

répression [represjɔ̃] *f* repression

réprimande [reprimɑ̃d] *f* reprimand

réprimander [reprimɑ̃de] §97 *tr* to reprimand

réprimer [reprime] *tr* to repress

re·pris [rəpri] **-prise** [priz] *adj* recaptured; **être repris de** to suffer from a recurrence of ‖ *m*—**repris de justice** hardened criminal, habitual offender ‖ *f* see **reprise**

reprisage [rəprizaʒ] *m* darning

reprise [rəpriz] *f* recapture; resumption; darning; pickup (*acceleration of motor*); (mov) rerun; (theat) revival; **à plusieurs reprises** several times; **faire une reprise à** to darn; **par reprises** a little at a time

repriser [rəprize] *tr* to darn; mend

réproba·teur [reprɔbatœr] **-trice** [tris] *adj* reproving

reproche [rəprɔʃ] *m* reproach

reprocher [rəprɔʃe] §98 *tr* to reproach; begrudge; (law) to take exception to (*a witness*); **reprocher q.ch. à qn** to reproach s.o. for s.th.; begrudge s.o. s.th.; remind s.o. reproachfully of s.th.

reproduction [rəprɔdyksjɔ̃] *f* reproduction

reproduire [rəprɔdɥir] §19 *tr & ref* to reproduce

reprographieur [rəprɔgrafjœr] *m* copying machine

réprou·vé -vée [repruve] *adj & mf* outcast; damned

réprouver [repruve] *tr* to disapprove

reptile [rɛptil] *m* reptile

re·pu -pue [rəpy] *adj* satiated

républi·cain [repyblikɛ̃] **-caine** [kɛn] *adj & mf* republican

république [repyblik] *f* republic

répudier [repydje] *tr* to repudiate

répu·gnant [repyɲɑ̃] **-gnante** [ɲɑ̃t] *adj* repugnant

répugner [repyɲe] §96, §97 *intr*—**répugner à** to be repugnant to, disgust, repel, e.g., **cette odeur leur répugne** that odor disgusts them; **il me (te, lui,** etc.) **répugne de** it is distasteful for me (you, him, etc.) to; **répugner à** or **de** + *inf* to be reluctant or loath to + *inf*, balk at + *ger*

répul·sif [repylsif] **-sive** [siv] *adj* repulsive

réputation [repytasjɔ̃] *f* reputation

répu·té -tée [repyte] *adj* of high repute; **être réputé** to be reputed to be

requérir [rəkerir] §3 *tr* to demand; ask; require; summon

requête [rəkɛt] *f* petition, appeal

requiem [rekɥijɛm] *m* requiem

requin [rəkɛ̃] *m* shark

re·quis [rəki] **-quise** [kiz] *adj* required, requisite ‖ *mf* conscript ‖ *v* see **requérir**

réquisition [rekizisjɔ̃] *f* requisition

réquisitionner [rekizisjɔne] *tr* to requisition

réquisitoire [rekizitwar] *m* indictment

res·capé -capée [rɛskape] *adj* rescued ‖ *mf* survivor

rescinder [resɛ̃de] *tr* to rescind
rescousse [rɛskus] *f* rescue
ré·seau [rezo] *m* (*pl* **-seaux**) net; network, system; **réseau de barbelés** barbed wire entanglement
réséda [rezeda] *m* mignonette
réservation [rezɛrvɑsjɔ̃] *f* reservation; booking
réserve [rezɛrv] *f* reserve; reservation; reserve room (*in a library*); **de réserve** emergency, reserve (*rations, fund, etc.*); **réserve des imprimés** periodical room (*in a library*); **sous réserve que** on condition that; **sous toutes réserves** without committing oneself
réserver [rezɛrve] §97 *tr* to reserve; set aside ‖ *ref* to set aside for oneself; wait and see, hold off
réserviste [rezɛrvist] *m* reservist
réservoir [rezɛrvwar] *m* reservoir, tank; **réservoir de bombes** bomb bay
résidanat [rezidana] *m* (med) residency
résidence [rezidɑ̃s] *f* residence
rési·dent [rezidɑ̃] **-dente** [dɑ̃t] *mf* alien, foreigner; (dipl) resident
résiden·tiel -tielle [rezidɑ̃sjɛl] *adj* residential
résider [rezide] *intr* to reside
résidu [rezidy] *m* residue; refuse
resi·duel -duelle [rezidɥɛl] *adj* residual
résignation [reziɲɑsjɔ̃] *f* resignation
résigner [reziɲe] *tr* to resign ‖ §96 *ref* to be or become resigned
résilier [rezilje] *tr* to cancel
résille [rezij] *f* hair net
résine [rezin] *f* resin
résistance [rezistɑ̃s] *f* resistance
résis·tant [rezistɑ̃] **-tante** [tɑ̃t] *adj* resistant; strong; fast (*color*) ‖ *mf* (hist) Resistance fighter
résister [reziste] §96 *intr* to be fast, not run (*said of colors or dyes*); **résister à** to weather (*e.g., a storm*); resist, hold out against, withstand, e.g., **inutile de lui résister** useless to resist him; **résister à +** *inf* to resist + *ger*
réso·lu -lue [rezɔly] §92 *adj* resolute, resolved ‖ *v* see **résoudre**
résolution [rezɔlysjɔ̃] *f* resolution; canceling
résonance [rezɔnɑ̃s] *f* resonance
résonner [rezɔne] *intr* to resound; to re-echo, ring, clank; twang
résorber [rezɔrbe] *tr* to absorb ‖ *ref* to become absorbed
résoudre [rezudr] §60, §96, §97 *tr* to resolve; decide; solve; persuade; cancel; **être résolu à** to be resolved to ‖ *intr*—**résoudre de** to decide to ‖ §96—*ref*—**se résoudre à** to decide to; reconcile oneself to; **se résoudre en** to turn into
résout [rezu] *v* see **résoudre**
respect [rɛspɛ] *m* respect; **présenter ses respects (à)** to pay one's respects (to); **respect de soi** or **soi-même** self-respect; **respect humain** [rɛspɛkymɛ̃] fear of what people might say; **sauf votre (mon,** etc.) **respect** with all due respect; pardon the language; **tenir en respect** to keep at a respectful distance
respectable [rɛspɛktabl] *adj* respectable
respecter [rɛspɛkte] *tr* to respect; **respecter les fleurs** (*public sign*) keep off the flowers ‖ *ref* to keep one's self-respect
respec·tif [rɛspɛktif] **-tive** [tiv] *adj* respective
respec·tueux [rɛspɛktɥø] **-tueuse** [tɥøz] *adj* respectful
respirer [rɛspire] *tr* to breathe ‖ *intr* to breathe; catch one's breath
resplendis·sant [rɛsplɑ̃disɑ̃] **-sante** [sɑ̃t] *adj* radiant, beaming, shining, aglow, resplendent
responsabilité [rɛspɔ̃sabilite] *f* responsibility
responsable [rɛspɔ̃sabl] *adj* responsible; **responsable de** responsible for; **responsable envers** accountable to; **solidairement responsable** jointly liable ‖ *mf* person responsible, person in charge
resquiller [rɛskije] *tr* (coll) to obtain by fraud ‖ *intr* (coll) to crash the gate
resquil·leur [rɛskijœr] **-leuse** [jøz] *mf* (coll) gate-crasher
ressac [rəsak] *m* surf; undertow
ressaisir [rəsezir] *tr* to recapture ‖ *ref* to regain one's self-control
ressasser [rəsase] *tr* to go over and over again
ressaut [rəso] *m* projection; sharp rise
ressemblance [rəsɑ̃blɑ̃s] *f* resemblance
ressembler [rəsɑ̃ble] *intr*—**ressembler à** to look like, resemble, e.g., **le fils lui ressemble** the son looks like him ‖ *ref* (*pp* **ressemblé** *invar*) to resemble one another; be alike, look alike
ressemeler [rəsəmle] §34 *tr* to resole
ressentiment [rəsɑ̃timɑ̃] *m* resentment
ressentir [rəsɑ̃tir] §41 *tr* to feel keenly, be hurt by (*an insult*); experience (*joy, pain, surprise*) ‖ *ref*—**se ressentir de** to feel the aftereffects of
resserre [rəsɛr] *f* shed, storeroom
resserrer [rəsere] *tr* to tighten; contract; close; lock up (*e.g., valuables*) again ‖ *ref* to tighten; contract
ressort [rəsɔr] *m* spring; springiness; motive; **du ressort de** within the jurisdiction of; **en dernier ressort** without appeal; as a last resort; **ressort à boudin** coil spring; **sans ressort** slack
ressortir [rəsɔrtir] *intr*—**ressortir à** to come under the jurisdiction of; fall under the head of ‖ §64 *intr* (*aux:* ÊTRE) to go out again; stand out, be evident; **faire ressortir** to set off; bring out de it follows from; **il ressort que** it follows that
ressortis·sant [rəsɔrtisɑ̃] **-sante** [sɑ̃t] *adj*—**ressortissant à** under the jurisdiction of ‖ *mf* national
ressource [rəsurs] *f* resource; **de ressource** resourceful; **sans ressources** without resources
ressouvenir [rəsuvnir] §72, §97 *ref* to reminisce; **se ressouvenir de** to recall

ressusciter [resysite] *tr* to resuscitate; to resurrect ‖ *intr* (*aux:* ÉTRE) to rise from the dead; get well

res·tant [rɛstɑ̃] **-tante** [tɑ̃t] *adj* remaining ‖ *m* remainder

restaupouce [rɛstɔpus] *m* fast-food restaurant

restaurant [rɛstɔrɑ̃] *m* restaurant; **restaurant libre-service** self-service restaurant

restauration [rɛstɔrɑsjɔ̃] *f* restoration; restaurant business; **restauration rapide** fast food

restaurer [rɛstɔre] *tr* to restore ‖ *ref* (coll) to take some nourishment

reste [rɛst] *m* rest, remainder; remnant; relic; **au reste, du reste** moreover; **de reste** spare; **restes** remains; leftovers

rester [rɛste] §96 *intr* (*aux:* ÉTRE) to remain, stay; be left over; **en rester** to stop, leave off; **en rester là** to stop right there; **il me (te, leur,** etc.) **reste q.ch.** I (you, they, etc.) have s.th. left

restituer [rɛstitɥe] *tr* to restore; give back; (comp) to print out

restitution [rɛstitysjɔ̃] *f* restitution; restoration

restoroute [rɛstɔrut] *m* drive-in restaurant; service stop (*on a superhighway*)

restreindre [rɛstrɛ̃dr] §50 *tr* to restrict; curtail ‖ *ref* to become limited; cut down expenses

res·treint [rɛstrɛ̃] **-treinte** [trɛ̃t] *adj* limited

restriction [rɛstriksjɔ̃] *f* restriction; **restriction mentale** mental reservation

résultat [rezylta] *m* result; **résultat financier** bottom line

résulter [rezylte] *intr* to result; **il en résulte que** it follows that

résumé [rezyme] *m* summary, recapitulation; **en résumé** in short, in a word

résumer [rezyme] *tr* to summarize ‖ *ref* to be summed up

résurrection [rezyrɛksjɔ̃] *f* resurrection

rétablir [retablir] *tr* to restore ‖ *ref* to recover

rétablissement [retablismɑ̃] *m* restoration; recovery

retailler [rɔtaje] *tr* to resharpen

retape [rɔtap] *f* (slang) streetwalking

retaper [rɔtape] *tr* (coll) to straighten up; (coll) to give a lick and a promise to ‖ *ref* (coll) to perk up

retard [rɔtar] *m* delay; **en retard** late; slow (*clock*); **en retard sur** behind

retardataire [rɔtardatɛr] *adj* tardy; retarded ‖ *mf* latecomer, straggler

retarder [rɔtarde] *tr* to delay; put off; set back ‖ *intr* to go slow, be behind

retenir [rɔtnir] §72 *tr* to hold back, keep back; detain; remember, note; reserve; retain (*a lawyer*); carry (*a number*) ‖ §97 *ref*—**se retenir à** to cling to; **se retenir de** to refrain from

retentir [rɔtɑ̃tir] *intr* to resound

rete·nu **-nue** [rɔtny] *adj* reserved; held back ‖ *f* withholding; reserve; **retenue à la source** withholding tax

réticence [retisɑ̃s] *f* evasiveness, concealment; hesitation; reservation, misgiving

réti·cent [retisɑ̃] **-cente** [sɑ̃t] *adj* evasive; hesitant; reserved, withdrawn

réticule [retikyl] *m* handbag

ré·tif [retif] **-tive** [tiv] *adj* restive

rétine [retin] *f* retina

reti·ré **-rée** [rɔtire] *adj* remote, out-of-the-way; retired

retirement [rɔtirmɑ̃] *m* contraction

retirer [rɔtire] *tr* to withdraw; take off; fire again ‖ *intr* to fire again ‖ *ref* to withdraw; retire

retombée [rɔtɔ̃be] *f* fall; hang (*of cloth*); **retombées radioactives** fallout

retomber [rɔtɔ̃be] *intr* (*aux:* ÉTRE) to fall again; fall; fall back; hang, hang down; relapse

retordre [rɔtɔrdrə] *tr* to twist; wring out

rétorquer [retɔrke] *tr* to retort

re·tors [rɔtɔr] **-torse** [tɔrs] *adj* twisted; wily; curved (*beak*) ‖ *mf* rascal

retouche [rɔtuʃ] *f* retouch; (phot) retouching; **retouches** alterations

retoucher [rɔtuʃe] *tr* to retouch; make alterations on

retour [rɔtur] *m* return; turn, bend; reversal (*e.g., of opinion*); **de retour** in return; **en retour d'équerre** at right angles; **être de retour** to be back; **par retour du courrier** by return mail; **retour à la masse** (elec) ground (*on chassis of auto, radio, etc.*); **retour à la terre** (elec) ground; **retour à l'envoyeur** return to sender (*on letter*); **retour d'âge** change of life; **retour de flamme** backfire; **retour de manivelle** kick (of the crank); (fig) backlash; **retour de monnaie** coin return; **retour en arrière** flashback

retourner [rɔturne] §95 *tr* to send back, return; upset; turn over (*e.g., the soil*); turn inside out ‖ *intr* (*aux:* ÉTRE) to go back, return ‖ *ref* to turn around, look back; turn over; (fig) to veer, shift; **s'en retourner** to go back; **se retourner contre** to turn against

retracer [rɔtrase] §51 *tr* to retrace; bring to mind, recall ‖ *ref* to recall

rétracter [retrakte] *tr* & *ref* to retract

rétraction [retraksjɔ̃] *f* contraction

retrait [rɔtrɛ] *m* withdrawal; shrinkage; running out (*of tide*); **en retrait** set back, recessed; (typ) indented; **retrait de permis** suspension of driver's license

retraite [rɔtrɛt] *f* retreat; retirement; pension; **battre en retraite** to retreat; **en retraite** retired; **prendre sa retraite** to retire; **retraite anticipée** early retirement; **toucher sa retraite** to draw one's pension

retrai·té **-tée** [rɔtrete] *adj* pensioned, retired ‖ *mf* pensioner

retranchement [rɔtrɑ̃ʃmɑ̃] *m* retrenchment; cutting out

retrancher [rɔtrɑ̃ʃe] *tr* to cut off or out, retrench ‖ *ref* to become entrenched

retransmettre [rɔtrɑ̃smɛtr] §42 *tr* to retransmit; rebroadcast

retransmission [rətrɑ̃smisjɔ̃] *f* retransmission; rebroadcast

rétré·ci -cie [retresi] *adj* narrow; shrunk

rétrécir [retresir] *tr* to shrink; take in (*a garment*) ‖ *intr* & *ref* to shrink; narrow

retremper [rətrɑ̃pe] *tr* to soak again; retemper; give new strength to ‖ *ref* to take another dip; get new vigor

rétribuer [retribɥe] *tr* to remunerate

rétribution [retribysjɔ̃] *f* retribution; salary, fee

rétro [retro] *adj invar*—**le style rétro** (coll) the style of the twenties ‖ *m* recoil; rearview mirror

rétroaction [retrɔaksjɔ̃] *f* feedback; retroaction

rétrofusée [retrɔfyze] *f* retrorocket

rétrograder [retrɔgrade] *intr* to retrogress

rétroprojecteur [retrɔprɔʒɛktœr] *m* overhead projector

rétrospec·tif [retrɔspɛktif] **-tive** [tiv] *adj* retrospective ‖ *m* flashback

rétrospection [retrɔspɛksjɔ̃] *f* restrospection

retrousser [rətruse] *tr* to roll up, turn up; curl up (*one's lip*) ‖ *ref* to turn up or pull up one's clothes

retrouve [rətruv] *f* (comp) retrieval

retrouver [rətruve] *tr* to find again; recover ‖ *ref* to be back again; meet again; get one's bearings

rétroviseur [retrɔvizœr] *m* rear-view mirror

rets [rɛ] *m*—**prendre dans des rets** to snare

réunification [reynifikasjɔ̃] *f* reunification

réunion [reynjɔ̃] *f* reunion; meeting; **réunion de service** staff meeting

réunir [reynir] *tr* to unite, join; reunite; call together, convene ‖ *ref* to meet; reunite

réus·si -sie [resyi] *adj* successful

réussir [reysir] **§96** *tr* to make a success of, be good at; accomplish ‖ *intr* to succeed; **réussir à** to succeed in; pass (*an exam*)

réussite [reysit] *f* success; **faire une réussite** (cards) to play solitaire

réutilisable [reytilizabl] *adj* reusable

revaloir [rəvalwar] **§71** *tr*—**revaloir q.ch à qn** to pay s.o. back for s.th.

revaloriser [rəvalɔrize] *tr* to revalue, reassert the value of; raise (*a salary*)

revan·chard [rəvɑ̃ʃar] **-charde** [ʃard] *adj* (coll) vengeful ‖ *mf* (coll) avenger

revanche [rəvɑ̃ʃ] *f* revenge; return bout or engagement, return match; **en revanche** on the other hand; **prendre sa revanche sur** to get even with

revancher [rəvɑ̃ʃe] *ref* to get even

rêvasser [rɛvase] *intr* to daydream

rêvasserie [rɛvasri] *f* fitful dreaming; daydreaming

rêve [rɛv] *m* dream

revêche [rəvɛʃ] *adj* sullen, crabbed

réveil [revɛj] *m* awakening; recovery; alarm clock; (mil) reveille

réveille-matin [revɛjmatɛ̃] *m invar* alarm clock

réveiller [reveje] *tr* & *ref* to wake up

réveillon [revɛjɔ̃] *m* Christmas Eve supper; New Year's Eve party

réveillonner [revɛjɔne] *intr* to celebrate Christmas Eve or New Year's Eve

révéla·teur [revelatœr] **-trice** [tris] *adj* revealing; telltale ‖ *mf* informer ‖ *m* (phot) developer

révélation [revelasjɔ̃] *f* revelation

révéler [revele] **§10** *tr* to reveal; (phot) to develop

revenant [rəvnɑ̃] *m* ghost

reven·deur [rəvɑ̃dœr] **-deuse** [døz] *mf* retailer; secondhand dealer

revendication [rəvɑ̃dikasjɔ̃] *f* claim

revendiquer [rəvɑ̃dike] *tr* to claim; insist upon; assume (*a responsibility*)

revendre [rəvɑ̃dr] *tr* to resell

revenez-y [rəvnezi] *m invar* (coll) return; **un goût de revenez-y** (coll) a taste like more

revenir [rəvnir] **§72, §95** *intr* (*aux:* ÊTRE) to return, come back; **en revenir** to have a narrow escape; **faire revenir** (culin) to brown; **n'en pas revenir** to not get over it; **revenir à** to come to, amount to; come to (*e.g., mind*); **revenir à soi** to come to; **revenir bredouille** to come back empty-handed; **revenir de** to recover from; realize (*a mistake*); **revenir de loin** to have been at death's door; **revenir sur** to go back on (*e.g., one's word*) ‖ *ref* —**s'en revenir** to come back

revente [rəvɑ̃t] *f* resale

revenu [rəvny] *m* revenue, income

revenue [rəvny] *f* new growth (*of trees*)

rêver [rɛve] *tr* to dream ‖ *intr* to dream; **rêver à** to dream of (*think about*); **rêver de** to dream of (*in sleep*); to long to + *inf*

réverbère [revɛrbɛr] *m* streetlight

réverbérer [revɛrbere] **§10** *tr* to reflect (*light, heat, etc.*); re-echo, reverberate ‖ *ref* to be reflected

reverdir [rəvɛrdir] *tr* to make green ‖ *intr* to grow green; become young again

révérence [reverɑ̃s] *f* reverence; curtsy; **révérence parler** (coll) pardon the language; **tirer sa révérence** to bow out

révéren·cieux [reverɑ̃sjø] **-cieuse** [sjøz] *adj* obsequious

révé·rend [reverɑ̃] **-rende** [rɑ̃d] *adj* & *m* reverend

révérer [revere] **§10** *tr* to revere

rêverie [rɛvri] *f* reverie

revers [rəvɛr] *m* reverse; lapel; (tennis) backhand; **à revers** from behind; **revers de main** slap with the back of the hand

reverser [rəvɛrse] *tr* to pour back; pour out again

réversible [revɛrsibl] *adj* reversible

revêtement [rəvɛtmɑ̃] *m* surfacing; facing; lining; casing

revêtir [rəvɛtir] **§73** *tr* to put on; clothe, dress up; invest; surface; line; face; assume (*a form; an aspect*)

rê·veur [rɛvœr] **-veuse** [vøz] *adj* dreamy ‖ *mf* dreamer; **cela me laisse rêveur** that leaves me puzzled

revirement [rəvirmɑ̃] *m* sudden reversal; (naut) tack

réviser [revize] *tr* to revise; review; overhaul; recondition

réviseur [revizœr] *m* proofreader

révision [revizjɔ̃] *f* revision; review; overhauling; proofreading

révisionniste [revizjɔnist] *adj & mf* revisionist

revivre [rəvivr] §74 *tr* to live again, relive ‖ *intr* to live again

révocation [revɔkɑsjɔ̃] *f* dismissal; revocation

revoici [rəvwasi] *prep*—**me (vous,** etc.) **revoici** (coll) here I am (you are, etc.) again

revoilà [rəvwala] *prep*—**le (la,** etc.) **voilà** (coll) there it, he (she, etc.) is again

revoir [rəvwar] *m*—**au revoir** good-by ‖ §75 *tr* to see again; review; revise ‖ *ref* to meet again

révol·tant [revɔltɑ̃] **-tante** [tɑ̃t] *adj* revolting

révolte [revɔlt] *f* revolt, rebellion

révol·té -tée [revɔlte] *adj & mf* rebel

révolter [revɔlte] *tr & ref* to revolt; **se révolter devant** to be revolted by

révo·lu -lue [revɔly] *adj* completed; elapsed; bygone

révolution [revɔlysjɔ̃] *f* revolution

révolutionnaire [revɔlysjɔnɛr] *adj & mf* revolutionary

revolver [revɔlvɛr] *m* revolver

révoquer [revɔke] *tr* to revoke; countermand; dismiss; recall

re·vu -vue [rəvy] *adj* revised ‖ *f* see **revue**

revue [rəvy] *f* review; magazine, journal; (theat) revue; **passer en revue** to review *(past events; troops)*

rez-de-chaussée [redʃose] *m invar* first floor, ground floor

R.F. *abbr* (**République Française**) French Republic

rhabiller [rabije] *tr* to repair; dress again; refurbish ‖ *ref* to change one's clothes; **va te rhabiller!** (pej) get out!

rhapsodie [rapsɔdi] *f* rhapsody

Rhénanie [renani] *f* Rhineland

rhéostat [reɔsta] *m* rheostat

rhétorique [retɔrik] *adj* rhetorical ‖ *f* rhetoric

Rhin [rɛ̃] *m* Rhine

rhinocéros [rinɔserɔs] *m* rhinoceros

rhubarbe [rybarb] *f* rhubarb

rhum [rɔm] *m* rum

rhumati·sant [rymatizɑ̃] **-sante** [zɑ̃t] *adj & mf* rheumatic

rhumatis·mal -male [rymatismal] *adj (pl* **-maux** [mo]) rheumatic

rhumatisme [rymatism] *m* rheumatism

rhume [rym] *m* cold; **rhume des foins** hay fever

ri [ri] *v* see **rire**

riant [rjɑ̃] **riante** [rjɑ̃t] *adj* smiling; cheerful, pleasant

ribambelle [ribɑ̃bɛl] *f* (coll) long string, swarm, lot

ri·baud [ribo] **-baude** [bod] *adj* licentious ‖ *mf* camp follower; debauchee

ricanement [rikanmɑ̃] *m* snicker

ricane [rikane] *intr* to snicker

ri·chard [riʃar] **-charde** [ʃard] *mf* (coll) moneybags

riche [riʃ] *adj* rich ‖ *m* rich man; **nouveaux riches** newly rich

riche·lieu [riʃəljø] *m (pl* **-lieu** or **-lieus**) oxford

richesse [riʃɛs] *f* wealth; richness; **richesses** riches; **richesses naturelles** natural resources

ricin [risɛ̃] *m* castor-oil plant; castor bean

ricocher [rikɔʃe] *intr* to ricochet, rebound

ricochet [rikɔʃɛ] *m* ricochet; **faire des ricochets** to play ducks and drakes; **par ricochet** indirectly

rictus [riktys] *m* rictus; grin

ride [rid] *f* wrinkle; ripple

ri·dé -dée [ride] *adj* wrinkled; corrugated

ri·deau [rido] *m (pl* **-deaux**) curtain; **rideau d'arbres** line of trees; **rideau de fer** iron curtain; safety blind *(of a store)*; (theat) fire curtain; **rideau de feu** (mil) cover of artillery fire; **rideau de fumée** smoke screen

ridectomie [ridɛktɔmi] *f* face-lift

ridelle [ridɛl] *f* rave, side rails *(of wagon)*

rider [ride] *tr* to wrinkle; ripple

ridicule [ridikyl] *adj* ridiculous ‖ *m* ridicule

ridiculiser [ridikylize] *tr* to ridicule

rien [rjɛ̃] *m* trifle; **comme un rien** with no trouble at all; **un rien de** just a little (bit) of; **un rien de temps** no time at all ‖ *pron indef*—**de rien** don't mention it, you're welcome; of no importance; **il n'en est rien** such is not the case; **rien ne** or **ne . . . rien** §90B nothing, not anything; **rien de moins (que)** nothing less (than); **rien que** nothing but

rieur [rjœr] **rieuse** [rjøz] *adj* laughing ‖ *mf* laugher, mocker ‖ *f* (orn) black-headed gull

riflard [riflar] *m* coarse file; jack plane; paring chisel

rigide [riʒid] *adj* rigid; stiff; strict

rigolade [rigɔlad] *f* (coll) good time; fun; (coll) big joke

rigole [rigɔl] *f* drain; ditch

rigoler [rigɔle] *intr* (slang) to laugh, joke

rigo·lo [rigɔlo] **-lote** [lɔt] *adj* (coll) comical; (coll) queer, funny ‖ *mf* (coll) card ‖ *m* (slang) rod, gat

rigou·reux [rigurø] **-reuse** [røz] *adj* rigorous; severe

rigueur [rigœr] *f* rigor, strictness; **à la rigueur** to the letter; as a last resort; **de rigueur** compulsory, de rigueur

rillons [rijɔ̃] *mpl* cracklings

rimail·leur [rimɑjœr] **-leuse** [jøz] *mf* (coll) rhymester

rime [rim] *f* rhyme; **rimes croisées** alternate rhymes; **rimes plates** couplets of alternate masculine and feminine rhymes

rimer [rime] *tr & intr* to rhyme

rimmel [rimɛl] *m* mascara

rinçage [rɛ̃saʒ] *m* rinse

rince-bouche [rɛ̃sbuʃ] *m invar* mouthwash

rince-bouteilles [rɛ̃sbutɛj] *m invar* (mach) bottle-washing machine

rince-doigts [rɛ̃sdwa] *m invar* fingerbowl

rincer [rɛ̃se] §51 *tr* to rinse; (slang) to ruin, take to the cleaners

rinçure [rɛ̃syr] *f* rinsing water

ring [riŋ] *m* ring (*for, e.g., boxing*)

ringard [rɛ̃gar] *m* poker (*for fire*)

ripaille [ripɑj] *f* (coll) blowout; **faire ripaille** (coll) to carouse

ripe [rip] *f* scraper

riper [ripe] *tr* to scrape; (naut) to slip ‖ *intr* to slip; skid

riposte [ripɔst] *f* riposte, retort

riposter [ripɔste] *tr* to riposte, retort

rire [rir] *m* laugh; laughter; laughing; **rire** uncontrollable laughter; **gros rire** guffaw; **rire jaune** forced laugh ‖ §61 (*pp* **ri** *invar*) *intr* to laugh, joke, smile; **pour rire** for fun, in jest; **rire dans sa barbe, rire sous cape** to laugh up one's sleeve; **rire de** to laugh at or over; **rire du bout des lèvres, rire du bout des dents** to titter; **rire jaune** to force a laugh ‖ §97 *ref*—**se rire de** to laugh at

ris [ri] *m* (naut) reef; (obs) laughter; **ris d'agneau** or **de veau** sweetbread

risée [rize] *f* scorn; laughingstock; light squall

risible [rizibl] *adj* laughable

risque [risk] *m* risk

ris·qué -quée [riske] *adj* risky; risqué

risquer [riske] §97 *tr* to risk; hasard (*e.g., a remark*) ‖ *intr*—**risquer de** + *inf* to risk + *ger;* have a good chance of + *ger*

risque-tout [riskətu] *mf invar* daredevil

rissoler [risɔle] *tr & intr* to brown

ristourne [risturn] *f* rebate, refund; dividend

ristourner [risturne] *tr* to refund

ritournelle [riturnɛl] *f*—**c'est toujours la même ritournelle** it's always the same old story; **ritournelle publicitaire** advertising jingle or slogan

ri·tuel -tuelle [ritɥɛl] *adj & m* ritual

rivage [rivaʒ] *m* shore; bank

ri·val -vale [rival] (*pl* **-vaux** [vo] **-vales**) *adj & mf* rival

rivaliser [rivalize] *intr* to compete; **rivaliser avec** to compete with, rival

rivalité [rivalite] *f* rivalry

rive [riv] *f* shore; bank; **rive droite** Right Bank; **rive gauche** Left Bank

river [rive] *tr* to rivet

rive·rain -raine [rivrɛ̃] **-raine** [rɛn] *adj* waterfront; bordering ‖ *mf* riversider; dweller along a street or road

riveraineté [rivrɛnte] *f* riparian rights

rivet [rivɛ] *m* rivet

rivière [rivjɛr] *f* river, stream, tributary; (turf) water jump; **rivière de diamants** diamond necklace

rixe [riks] *f* brawl

riz [ri] *m* rice; **riz au lait** rice pudding; **riz glacé** polished rice; **riz précuit** minute rice

rizière [rizjɛr] *f* rice field

robe [rɔb] *f* dress; gown; robe; wrapper (*of cigar*); skin (*of onion, sausage, etc.*); husk (*of, e.g., bean*); **robe de chambre** dressing gown; **robe de cocktail** cocktail dress; **robe de grossesse** maternity dress; **robe de mariée** wedding dress; **robe d'intérieur** housecoat; **robe du soir** evening gown; **robe tunique** smock

rober [rɔbe] *tr* to husk, skin; wrap (*a cigar*)

roberts [rɔbɛr] *mpl* (slang) breasts

robin [rɔbɛ̃] *m* (coll) judge; (pej) shyster

robinet [rɔbinɛ] *m* faucet, tap; cock; **robinet d'eau tiède** (coll) bore; **robinet mélangeur** mixing faucet

robinier [rɔbinje] *m* (bot) locust tree

robot [rɔbo] *m* robot; pilotless (*airplane*); **robot cireur** automatic shoeshiner

robotiser [rɔbɔtize] *tr* to robotize

robre [rɔbr] *m* rubber (*in bridge*)

robuste [rɔbyst] *adj* robust; firm

roc [rɔk] *m* rock

rocade [rɔkad] *f* bypass (*of a road*)

rocaille [rɔkɑj] *adj* rococo ‖ *f* stones; rocky ground; stonework

rocail·leux [rɔkɑjø] **-leuse** [jøz] *adj* rocky, stony; harsh

roche [rɔʃ] *f* rock; boulder

rocher [rɔʃe] *m* rock; crag

rochet [rɔʃɛ] *m* ratchet; bobbin

ro·cheux [rɔʃø] **-cheuse** [ʃøz] *adj* rocky

rodage [rɔdaʒ] *m* grinding; breaking in; **en rodage** being broken in, new

roder [rɔde] *tr* to grind (*a valve*); break in (*a new car*); polish up (*a new play*)

rôder [rode] *intr* to prowl

rô·deur [rodœr] **-deuse** [døz] *adj* prowling ‖ *mf* prowler

rogatons [rɔgatɔ̃] *mpl* (coll) scraps

rogne [rɔɲ] *f* (coll) anger; **mettre qn èn rogne** (coll) to make s.o. see red

rogner [rɔɲe] *tr* to pare, trim

rognon [rɔɲɔ̃] *m* kidney

rogomme [rɔgɔm] *m*—**de rogomme** (coll) husky, beery (*voice*)

rogue [rɔg] *adj* arrogant

roi [rwa], [rwɑ] *m* king; **tirer les rois** to gather to eat the Twelfth-night cake

roitelet [rwatlɛ] *m* kinglet; (orn) kinglet

rôle [rol] *m* role; roll, muster

ro·main [rɔmɛ̃] **-maine** [mɛn] *adj* Roman; roman (*type*); romaine (*lettuce*) ‖ *m* (typ) roman ‖ *f* romaine (lettuce); **bon comme la romaine** (slang) done for ‖ (*cap*) *mf* Roman (*person*)

ro·man [rɔmɑ̃] **-mane** [man] *adj* Romance (*language*); (archit) Romanesque ‖ *m* novel; **roman à l'eau de rose** romance; **roman d'anticipation, roman de science fiction** science-fiction novel; **roman de série noire** thriller; **roman noir** whodunit; Gothic novel; **roman policier** detective story

romance [rɔmɑ̃s] *f* ballad

romanche [rɔmɑ̃ʃ] *m* Romansh

roman·cier [rɔmɑ̃sje] **-cière** [sjɛr] *mf* novelist; **romancier d'anticipation** science-fiction writer

ro·mand [rɔmɑ̃] **-mande** [mɑ̃d] *adj* French-speaking (*Switzerland*)

romanesque [rɔmanɛsk] *adj* romanesque, romantic, fabulous

roman-feuilleton [rɔmɑ̃fœjtɔ̃] *m* (*pl* **romans-feuilletons**) newspaper serial

roman-fleuve [rɔmɑ̃flœv] *m* (*pl* **romans-fleuves**) saga novel

romani·chel -chelle [rɔmaniʃɛl] *mf* gypsy, vagrant

romantique [rɔmɑ̃tik] *adj & mf* romantic

romantisme [rɔmɑ̃tism] *m* romanticism

romarin [rɔmarɛ̃] *m* (bot) rosemary

Rome [rɔm] *f* Rome

rompre [rɔ̃pr] (3d *sg pres ind* **rompt** [rɔ̃]) *tr* to break; burst; break in, train; break off ‖ *intr & ref* to break

rom·pu -pue [rɔ̃py] *adj*—**rompu à** accustomed to, experienced in; **rompu de** tired out from or by, exhausted with

romsteck [rɔmstɛk] *m* rump steak

ronce [rɔ̃s] *f* bramble; curly grain (*of wood*); **en ronces artificielles** barbed-wire (*fence*)

ronchonner [rɔ̃ʃɔne] *intr* (coll) to belly-ache, grumble

rond [rɔ̃] **ronde** [rɔ̃d] *adj* round; rounded; plump; straightforward; (slang) tight, drunk ‖ *m* ring, circle; round slice; (coll) dough, money; **en rond** in a circle; **faire les ronds de jambes** (slang) to bow and scrape; **rond comme une queue de pelle** (slang) soused, stoned, dead drunk; **rond de fumée** smoke ring; **rond de serviette** napkin ring ‖ *f* round; beat, round; round dance; radius; round hand; (mus) whole note; **à la ronde** around; **s'amuser à la ronde, faire la ronde** to go ring-around-a-rosy ‖ **rond** *adv*—**tourner rond** to work or go smoothly

rond-de-cuir [rɔ̃dkɥir] *m* (*pl* **ronds-de-cuir**) leather seat; (pej) bureaucrat

ron·deau [rɔ̃do] *m* (*pl* **-deaux**) rondeau; field roller

ronde·let -lette [rɔ̃dlɛ] *adj* plump; tidy (*sum*)

rondelle [rɔ̃dɛl] *f* disk; slice; washer (*of faucet, bolt, etc.*)

rondement [rɔ̃dmɑ̃] *adv* briskly; **mener rondement** to make short work of; **parler rondement** to be blunt

rondeur [rɔ̃dœr] *f* roundness; plumpness; frankness

rond-point [rɔ̃pwɛ̃] *m* (*pl* **ronds-points**) intersection, crossroads; traffic circle; circus, roundabout (Brit)

ronéo [rɔneo] *f* Mimeograph machine

ronéotyper [rɔneotipe] *tr* to mimeograph

ron·flant [rɔ̃flɑ̃] **-flante** [flɑ̃t] *adj* snoring; roaring; whirring; humming; (pej) high-sounding, pretentious

ronflement [rɔ̃fləmɑ̃] *m* snore; roar; whirr, hum

ronfler [rɔ̃fle] *intr* to snore; roar; whirr, hum

ron·fleur [rɔ̃flœr] **-fleuse** [fløz] *mf* snorer ‖ *m* vibrator (*replacing bell*)

ronger [rɔ̃ʒe] §38 *tr* to gnaw, nibble; eat away; bite (*one's nails*); corrode; torment ‖ *ref* to be worn away; be eaten away; eat one's heart out, fret

ron·geur [rɔ̃ʒœr] **-geuse** [ʒøz] *adj* gnawing ‖ *m* rodent

ronron [rɔ̃rɔ̃] *m* purr; drone

ronronnement [rɔ̃rɔnmɑ̃] *m* purring

ronronner [rɔ̃rɔne] *intr* to purr

roquer [rɔke] *intr* (chess) to castle

roquet [rɔkɛ] *m* cur, yapper; (*breed of dog*) pug

roquette [rɔkɛt] *f* (*plant; missile*) rocket

rosace [rozas] *f* rose window; (archit) rosette

rosa·cé -cée [rozase] *adj* roselike ‖ *f* skin eruption

rosaire [rozɛr] *m* rosary

rosâtre [rozɑtr] *adj* dusty-pink

rosbif [rɔsbif] *m* roast beef

rose [roz] *adj & m* rose, pink (*color*) ‖ *f* rose; rose window; **dire la rose** to box the compass; **rose des vents** compass card; **rose d'Inde** (*Tagetes*) marigold

ro·sé -sée [roze] *adj* rose, rose-colored ‖ *m* rosé wine ‖ *f* see **rosée**

ro·seau [rozo] *m* (*pl* **-seaux**) reed

rosée [roze] *f* dew

roséole [rozeɔl] *f* rash; rose rash

roseraie [rozrɛ] *f* rose garden

rosette [rozɛt] *f* bowknot; rosette; red ink; red chalk

rosier [rozje] *m* rosebush; **rosier églantier** sweetbrier

rosse [rɔs] *adj* nasty, mean; strict, stern; cynical ‖ *f* (coll) beast, stinker; (coll) nag; **sale rosse** (coll) dirty bitch

rossée [rose] *f* (coll) thrashing

rosser [rose] *tr* to beat up, thrash; (coll) to beat, beat

rossignol [rosiɲɔl] *m* skeleton key; (orn) nightingale; (coll) piece of junk, drug on the market

rot [ro] *m* (slang) burp, belch

rota·tif [rɔtatif] **-tive** [tiv] *adj* rotary ‖ *f* rotary press

rotation [rɔtasjɔ̃] *f* rotation; turnover (*of merchandise*)

rotatoire [rɔtatwar] *adj* rotary

roter [rɔte] *intr* (slang) to burp

rô·ti -tie [roti] *adj* roasted ‖ *m* roast ‖ *f* piece of toast; **rôtie à l'anglaise** Welsh rarebit

rotin [rɔtɛ̃] *m* rattan; **de** or **en rotin** cane (*chair*); **pas un rotin!** not a penny!

rôtir [rotir] *tr, intr, & ref* to roast; toast; scorch

rôtisserie [rotisri] *f* rotisserie shop (*where roasted fowl is sold*); grillroom (*restaurant*)

rôtissoire [rotiswar] *f* rotisserie

rotogravure [rɔtogravyr] *f* rotogravure

rotonde [rɔtɔ̃d] *f* rotunda; (rr) roundhouse

rotor [rɔtɔr] *m* rotor

rotule [rɔtyl] *f* kneecap

roture [rɔtyr] *f* common people

rotu·rier [rɔtyrje] **-rière** [rjɛr] *adj* plebeian, of the common people ‖ *mf* commoner

rouage [rwaʒ] *m* cog; **rouages** movement (*of a watch*)

rou·blard [rublar] **-blarde** [blard] *adj* (coll) wily ‖ *mf* (coll) schemer

roublardise [rublardiz] *f* (coll) cunning

roucoulement [rukulmɑ̃] *m* cooing; billing and cooing

roucouler [rukule] *tr & intr* to coo

roue [ru] *f* wheel; **faire la roue** to turn cartwheels; to strut; **roue de secours** spare wheel (*with tire*)

roué rouée [rwe] *adj* slick; knocked out ‖ *mf* slicker ‖ *m* rake

rouelle [rwɛl] *f* fillet (*of veal*)

rouer [rwe] *tr* to break upon the wheel; **rouer de coups** to thrash, beat up

rouerie [ruri] *f* trickery; trick

rouet [rwɛ] *m* spinning wheel

rouge [ruʒ] *adj* red ‖ *m* red; rouge; blush; **porter au rouge** to heat red-hot; **rouge à lèvres** lipstick ‖ *adv* red

rou·geaud [ruʒo] **-geaude** [ʒod] *adj* ruddy ‖ *mf* ruddy-faced person

rouge-gorge [ruʒgɔrʒ] *m* (*pl* **rouges-gorges**) robin (*Erithacus rubecula*)

rougeole [ruʒɔl] *f* measles

rougeoyer [ruʒwaje] §47 *intr* to glow red; turn red

rougeur [ruʒœr] *f* redness; blush; **rougeurs** red spots

rougir [ruʒir] §97 *tr* to redden ‖ *intr* to turn red; blush

rouille [ruj] *f* rust

rouil·lé -lée [ruje] *adj* rusty; (*out of practice; blighted*) rusty

rouiller [ruje] *tr, intr, & ref* to rust

roulade [rulad] *f* trill; (mus) run

rou·lant [rulɑ̃] **-lante** [lɑ̃t] *adj* rolling; (coll) funny

rou·leau [rulo] *m* (*pl* **-leaux**) roller; roll; spool; rolling pin; **rouleau compresseur** road roller; **rouleau du printemps** egg roll

roulement [rulmɑ̃] *m* roll; rotation; rattle; clatter; exchange; **par roulement** in rotation; **roulement à billes** ball bearing

rouler [rule] *tr* to roll; (coll) to take in, cheat ‖ *intr* to roll; roll along; **rouler sur** to roll in (*wealth*); turn on ‖ *ref* to roll; roll up; toss and turn; to twiddle (*one's thumbs*); **se les rouler** (coll) to not turn a hand

roule-ta-bille [rultabij] *m invar* (coll) rolling stone

roulette [rulɛt] *f* small wheel; castor; roulette; **aller comme sur des roulettes** to go well, to work smoothly

rou·leur [rulœr] **-leuse** [løz] *mf* drifter (*from one job to another*) ‖ *m* freight handler ‖ *f* streetwalker

roulis [ruli] *m* (naut) roll

roulotte [rulɔt] *f* trailer; gypsy wagon

rou·main [rumɛ̃] **-maine** [mɛn] *adj* Rumanian ‖ *m* Rumanian (*language*) ‖ (*cap*) *mf* Rumanian (*person*)

roupiller [rupije] *intr* to take a snooze

rou·quin [rukɛ̃] **-quine** [kin] *adj* (coll) red-headed; ‖ *mf* (coll) redhead ‖ *m* (slang) red wine; **Rouquin** Red (*nickname*)

rouspéter [ruspete] §10 *intr* (coll) to bellyache, complain, kick

rouspé·teur [ruspetœr] **-teuse** [tøz] *mf* (coll) bellyacher, complainer

roussâtre [rusatr] *adj* auburn

rousse [rus] *f* redhead, auburn-haired woman; (slang) cops

rousseur [rusœr] *f* reddishness; freckle

roussir [rusir] *tr* to scorch; singe ‖ *intr* to become brown; **faire roussir** (culin) to brown

route [rut] *f* road; route, itinerary; **bonne route!** happy motoring!; **en route!** let's go!; **faire fausse route** to take the wrong road; (fig) to be on the wrong track; **mettre en route** to start; **route déformée** rough road; **route déviée** detour; **route express** expressway

rou·tier [rutje] **-tière** [tjɛr] *adj* road (*e.g., map*) ‖ *m* trucker; bicycle racer; Explorer, Rover (*boy scout*); (naut) track chart; **vieux routier** veteran, old hand

routine [rutin] *f* routine

routi·nier [rutinje] **-nière** [njɛr] *adj* routine; one-track (*mind*)

rouvieux [ruvjø] *adj masc* mangy ‖ *m* mange

rouvrir [ruvrir] §65 *tr & intr* to reopen

roux [ru] **rousse** [rus] *adj* russet, reddish; red, auburn (*hair*); browned (*butter*) ‖ *mf* redhead ‖ *m* russet, reddish brown, auburn (*color*); brown sauce ‖ *f* see **rousse**

royal royale [rwajal] *adj* (*pl* **royaux** [rwajo]) royal ‖ *f* imperial, goatee

royaliste [rwajalist] *adj & mf* royalist

royaume [rwajom] *m* kingdom

royauté [rwajote] *f* royalty

R.S.V.P. [ɛrɛsvepe] *m* (letterword) (**répondez, s'il vous plaît**) R.S.V.P.

R.T.F. [ɛrteɛf] *f* (letterword) (**radio-diffusion-télévision française**) French radio and television

ruade [ryad] *f* kick, buck

ruban [rybɑ̃] *m* ribbon; tape; **ruban adhésif** adhesive tape; **ruban adhésif transparent** transparent tape; **ruban cache** masking tape; **ruban de chapeau** hatband; **ruban de frein** brake lining; **ruban encreur** typewriter ribbon; **ruban magnétique** recording tape

rubéole [rybeɔl] *f* German measles

rubis [rybi] *m* ruby; jewel (*of watch*); **payer rubis sur l'ongle** to pay down on the nail

rubrique [rybrik] *f* rubric; caption, heading; label (*in a dictionary*)

ruche [ryʃ] *f* beehive

rude [ryd] *adj* rude, rough; rugged; hard; steep; (coll) amazing

rudement [rydmɑ̃] *adv* roughly; (coll) awfully, mighty

rudesse [rydɛs] *f* rudeness, roughness; harshness

rudiment [rydimɑ̃] *m* rudiment

rudoyer [rydwaje] §47 *tr* to bully, browbeat; abuse, treat roughly

rue [ry] *f* street; **rue barrée** (*public sign*) no thoroughfare; (*public sign*) closed for repairs; **rue piétonne** pedestrian mall; **rue sans issue** (*public sign*) no outlet

ruée [rɥe] *f* rush; **ruée vers l'or** gold rush

ruelle [rɥɛl] *f* alley, lane; space between bed and wall

ruer [rɥe] *intr* to kick, buck; **ruer dans les brancards** to kick over the traces ‖ *ref*—**se ruer sur** to rush at

rugir [ryʒir] *intr* to roar, bellow

rugissement [ryʒismɑ̃] *m* roar

rugosité [rygozite] *f* roughness; ruggedness, bumpiness; coarseness

ru·gueux [rygø] **-gueuse** [gøz] *adj* rough, rugged; coarse; gnarled (*tree*)

ruine [rɥin] *f* ruin

ruiner [rɥine] *tr* to ruin ‖ *ref* to ruin oneself; fall into ruins

ruis·seau [rɥiso] *m* (*pl* **-seaux**) stream, brook; (fig) gutter

ruisseler [rɥisle] §34 *intr* to stream; drip, trickle

ruisselet [rɥislɛ] *m* little stream

ruissellement [rɥisɛlmɑ̃] *m* streaming; (*e.g., of light*) flood

rumeur [rymœr] *f* rumor; hum (*e.g., of voices*); roar (*of the sea*); **rumeur publique** public opinion

ruminer [rymine] *tr* & *intr* to ruminate; ruminate on or over

ru·pin [rypɛ̃] **-pine** [pin] *adj* (slang) rich ‖ *mf* (slang) swell

rupiner [rypine] *tr* & *intr* (coll) to do well

rupteur [ryptœr] *m* (elec) contact breaker

rupture [ryptyr] *f* rupture; breach; break; breaking off

ru·ral -rale [ryral] (*pl* **-raux** [ro]) *adj* rural ‖ *mf* farmer; **ruraux** country people

ruse [ryz] *f* ruse

ru·sé -sée [ryze] *adj* cunning, crafty ‖ *mf* sly one

russe [rys] *adj* Russian ‖ *m* Russian (*language*) ‖ (*cap*) *mf* Russian (*person*)

Russie [rysi] *f* Russia; **la Russie** Russia

rus·taud [rysto] **-taude** [tod] *adj* rustic, clumsy ‖ *mf* bumpkin

rustique [rystik] *adj* rustic; hardy

rustre [rystr] *adj* oafish ‖ *m* bumpkin, oaf; (obs) peasant

rut [ryt] *m* (zool) rut

ruti·lant [rytilɑ̃] **-lante** [lɑ̃t] *adj* bright-red; gleaming

rutiler [rytile] *intr* to gleam, glow

rythme [ritm] *m* rhythm; rate (*of production*)

ryth·mé -mée [ritme] *adj* rhythmic(al); cadenced

rythmer [ritme] *tr* to cadence; mark with a rhythm

rythmique [ritmik] *adj* rhythmic(al)

S

S, s [ɛs], *[ɛs] *m invar* nineteenth letter of the French alphabet

S. *abbr* (**saint**) St.

s' = **se** before vowel or mute **h**

sa [sa] §88 his, her, its

S.A. [ɛsɑ] *f* (letterword) (**société anonyme**) Inc.

sabbat [saba] *m* Sabbath; witches' Sabbath; racket, uproarious gaiety; **sabbat des chats** caterwauling

sabir [sabir] *m* pidgin

sable [sɑbl] *m* sand; sable; **sable mouvant** quicksand

sabler [sɑble] *tr* to sandblast; drink in one gulp; toss off (*some champagne*)

sa·bleux [sɑblø] **-bleuse** [bløz] *adj* sandy ‖ *f* sandblast; sandblaster

sablier [sɑblije] *m* hourglass; (*for drying ink*) sandbox; dealer in sand

sablière [sɑblijɛr] *f* sandpit; wall plate; (rr) sandbox

sablon·neux [sɑblɔnø] **-neuse** [nøz] *adj* sandy

sablonnière [sɑblɔnjɛr] *f* sandpit

sabord [sabɔr] *m* porthole

saborder [sabɔrde] *tr* to scuttle

sabot [sabo] *m* wooden shoe; hoof; whipping top; bungled work; ferrule; caster cup; **dormir comme un sabot** to sleep like a top; **sabot de frein** brake shoe; **sabot d'enrayage** wedge, block, scotch

sabotage [sabotaʒ] *m* sabotage

saboter [sabote] *tr* to sabotage; bungle ‖ *intr* (coll) to make one's wooden shoes clatter

sabo·teur [sabotœr] **-teuse** [tøz] *mf* saboteur; bungler

sabo·tier [sabotje] **-tière** [tjɛr] *mf* maker and seller of wooden shoes ‖ *f* clog dance

sabre [sɑbr] *m* saber

sabrer [sɑbre] *tr* to saber; (coll) to botch; (coll) to cut, condense

sac [sak] *m* sack, bag; **être un sac d'os** [dos] to be nothing but skin and bones; **mettre à sac** (coll) to rifle; **sac à main** handbag; **sac à malice** bag of tricks; **sac à provisions** shopping bag; **sac de couchage** sleeping bag; **sac de nœuds** (slang) can of worms; **sac de voyage** traveling bag, overnight suitcase; **vider son sac** (slang) to get something off one's chest

saccade [sakad] *f* jerk

sacca·dé -dée [sakade] *adj* jerky

saccager [sakaʒe] §38 *tr* to sack; (coll) to upset, turn topsy-turvy

saccha·rin [sakarɛ̃] **-rine** [rin] *adj* saccharine ‖ *f* saccharin

saccharose [sakaroz] *m* sucrose

sacerdoce [sasɛrdɔs] *m* priesthood

sacerdo·tal -tale [sasɛrdɔtal] *adj* (*pl* **-taux** [to]) sacerdotal, priestly

sache [saʃ] *v* (**saches, sachions,** etc.) see **savoir**

sachet [saʃɛ] *m* sachet; packet (*of needles, medicine, etc.*); powder charge

sacoche [sakɔʃ] *f* satchel

sacramen·tel -telle [sakramɑ̃tɛl] *adj* sacramental

sacre [sakr] *m* crowning, consecration

sa·cré -crée [sakre] *adj* sacred; (anat) sacral ‖ (when standing before noun) *adj* (coll) darned, blasted

sacrement [sakrəmɑ̃] *m* sacrament

sacrer [sakre] *tr* to crown, consecrate ‖ *intr* to curse

sacrifice [sakrifis] *m* sacrifice

sacrifier [sakrifje] *tr* to sacrifice

sacrilège [sakrilɛʒ] *adj* sacrilegious ‖ *mf* sacrilegious person ‖ *m* sacrilege

sacristain [sakristɛ̃] *m* sexton

sadique [sadik] *adj* sadistic ‖ *mf* sadist

safran [safrɑ̃] *m* saffron

sagace [sagas] *adj* sagacious, shrewd

sage [saʒ] *adj* wise; well-behaved; modest (*woman*); good (*child*); **soyez sage!** be good! ‖ *mf* sage

safe-femme [saʒfam] *f* (*pl* **sages-femmes**) midwife

sagesse [saʒɛs] *f* wisdom; good behavior

Sagittaire [saʒitɛr] *m*—**le Sagittaire** (astr, astrol) Sagittarius

sai·gnant [seɲɑ̃] **-gnante** [ɲɑ̃t] *adj* bleeding; (*wound*) fresh; (*meat*) rare

saignée [seɲe] *f* bloodletting; bend of the arm, small of the arm; (fig) drain on the purse

saignement [seɲmɑ̃] *m* bleeding; **saignement de nez** nosebleed

saigner [seɲe], [seɲe] *tr & intr* to bleed; **saigner à blanc, saigner aux quatre veines** to bleed white

sail·lant [sajɑ̃] **-lante** [jɑ̃t] *adj* prominent, salient; projecting; high (*cheekbones*)

saillie [saji] *f* projection; spurt; sally, outburst; **faire saillie** to jut out, project

saillir [sajir] (used only in *inf, ger, & 3d sg & pl*) *tr* (agr) to cover ‖ §69 *intr* to protrude, project; spurt

sain [sɛ̃] **saine** [sɛn] *adj* healthy; **sain d'esprit** sane; **sain et sauf, saine et sauve** safe and sound

saindoux [sɛ̃du] *m* lard

sainement [sɛnmɑ̃] *adv* soundly

sais [se] *v* (**sait**) see **savoir**

saint [sɛ̃] **sainte** [sɛ̃t] *adj* saintly; sacred, holy ‖ *mf* saint

Saint-Esprit [sɛ̃tɛspri] *m* (rel) Holy Spirit

sainteté [sɛ̃təte] *f* holiness

Saint-Siège [sɛ̃sjɛʒ] *m* Holy See

saisie [sezi] *f* seizure; foreclosure

saisie-arrêt [seziarɛ] *f* (*pl* **-arrêts**) attachment, garnishment

saisir [sezir] *tr* to seize; sear (*meat*); grasp (*to understand*); strike, startle; overcome; **saisir un tribunal de** to lay before a court ‖ *ref*—**se saisir de** to take possession of

saisissement [sezismɑ̃] *m* chill; shock

saison [sɛzɔ̃] *f* season

salace [salas] *adj* salacious

salade [salad] *f* salad; (fig) mess; **raconter des salades** (slang) to tell fish stories; **salade de fruits** fruit salad

saladier [saladje] *m* salad bowl

salaire [salɛr] *m* salary, wage; recompense, punishment

salariat [salarja] *m* salaried workers, employees; salary (*fixed wage*)

sala·rié -riée [salarje] *adj* salaried, hired ‖ *mf* wage earner; employee

sa·laud [salo] **-laude** [lod] *adj* (coll) slovenly ‖ *mf* (slang) skunk, scoundrel

sale [sal] *adj* dirty; dull (*color*) ‖ *mf* dirty person

sa·lé -lée [sale] *adj* salty, salted; dirty (*joke*); padded (*bill*); (slang) exaggerated ‖ *m* salt pork

saler [sale] *tr* to salt

saleté [salte] *f* dirtiness; piece of dirt; (slang) dirty trick; (slang) dirt

saleuse [saløz] *f* road-salting truck

salière [saljɛr] *f* saltcellar

salir [salir] *tr & ref* to soil

salive [saliv] *f* saliva

salle [sal] *f* room; hall; auditorium; ward (*in a hospital*); (theat) audience, house; **salle à manger** dining room; **salle d'armes** fencing room; **salle d'attente** waiting room; **salle de bains** bathroom; **salle d'écoute** language laboratory; **salle de détente** rec room; **salle de jeux électroniques** amusement arcade; **salle d'embarquement** (aer) gate; **salle de la réserve** rare-book room; **salle de police** (mil) guardhouse; **salle de réveil, salle de réanimation** (med) recovery room; **salle de rédaction** city room; **salle des accouchées** maternity ward; **salle de séjour** living room; **salle de services du prêt** reserve-book room; **salle des fêtes** hall, auditorium; **salle des machines** engine room; **salle des pas perdus** lobby, waiting room; **salle de spectacle** movie house; **salle des ventes** salesroom, showroom; **salle de travail** delivery room; **salle d'exposition** showroom

salmigondis [salmigɔ̃di] *m* hodgepodge

salon [salɔ̃] *m* living room, parlor; exposition; saloon (*ship's lounge*); **salon de beauté** beauty parlor; **salon de l'automobile** automobile show; **salon de thé** tearoom

salon·nard [salɔnar] **-narde** [nard] *mf* sycophant

saloperie [salɔpri] *f* (slang) trash

salopette [salɔpɛt] *f* coveralls, overalls; bib; smock

salpêtre [salpɛtr] *m* saltpeter

salsepareille [salsəparɛj] *f* sarsaparilla

saltimbanque [saltēbãk] *mf* tumbler; mountebank, charlatan

salubre [salybr] *adj* salubrious, healthful

saluer [salɥe] *tr* to salute; greet, bow to, wave to

salut [saly] *m* health; safety; salvation; salute; greeting, bow; nod; **salut!** (coll) hi!, howdy!; **salut les gars!, salut les copains!** hi, fellows!

salutaire [salytɛr] *adj* healthy, salutary, beneficial

salutation [salytɑsjɔ̃] *f* greeting; **salutations distinguées** or **sincères salutations** (complimentary close) yours truly

salve [salv] *f* salvo, salute

samari·tain [samaritē] **-taine** [tɛn] *adj* Samaritan ‖ (*cap*) *mf* Samaritan

samedi [samdi] *m* Saturday

sanatorium [sanatɔrjɔm] *m* sanitarium

sanctifier [sãktifje] *tr* to sanctify

sanction [sãksjɔ̃] *f* sanction; penalty

sanctionner [sãksjɔne] *tr* to sanction; penalize

sanctuaire [sãktɥɛr] *m* sanctuary

sandale [sãdal] *f* sandal; gym shoe

sandwich [sãdwitʃ], [sãdviʃ] *m* (*pl* **sandwiches, sandwichs**) sandwich

sang [sã] *m* blood; **avoir le sang chaud** (coll) to be a go-getter; **bon sang!** (coll) darn it!; **sang et tripes** blood and guts; **se faire du bon sang** to enjoy oneself; **se faire du mauvais sang** to get all stewed up

sang-froid [sãfrwa] *m* self-control

san·glant [sãglã] **-glante** [glãt] *adj* bloody; cruel

sangle [sãgl] *f* cinch

sanglier [sãglije] *m* wild boar; **tirer sur un sanglier de carton** (coll) to tear down a straw man

sanglot [sãglo] *m* sob

sangloter [sãglɔte] *intr* to sob

sang-mêlé [sãmɛle] *m invar* half-breed

sangsue [sãsy] *f* bloodsucker, leech

san·guin [sãgē] **-guine** [gin] *adj* sanguine ‖ *f* (fa) sanguine

sanitaire [sanitɛr] *adj* sanitary; hospital, e.g., **avion sanitaire** hospital plane

sans [sã] *adv*—**sans que** without; **sans quoi** or else ‖ *prep* without; **sans cesse** ceaselessly; **sans façon** informally; **sans fil** wireless

sans-abri [sãzabri] *mf invar* homeless person

sans-cœur [sãkœr] *mf invar* heartless person

sans-filiste [sãfilist] *mf* (*pl* **-filistes**) radio operator; radio amateur

sans-gêne [sãʒɛn] *adj invar* offhanded ‖ *mf invar* offhanded person ‖ *m* offhandedness

sansonnet [sãsɔnɛ] *m* starling; blackbird

sans-travail [sãtravaj] *mf invar* unemployed worker

san·tal [sãtal] *m* (*pl* **-taux** [to]) (bot) sandalwood

santé [sãte] *f* health; sanity; **santé publique** public-health service

sape [sap] *f* sap (*undermining*)

saper [sape] *tr* to sap, undermine

sapeur [sapœr] *m* (mil) sapper; **fumer comme un sapeur** (coll) to smoke like a chimney

sapeur-pompier [sapœrpɔ̃pje] *m* (*pl* **sapeurs-pompiers**) fireman; **sapeurs-pompiers** fire department

saphir [safir] *m* sapphire; sapphire needle

sapin [sapē] *m* fir

sapristi [sapristi] *interj* hang it!

saquer [sake] *tr* (slang) to fire, sack

sarbacane [sarbakan] *f* blowgun

sarcasme [sarkasm] *m* sarcasm

sarcler [sarkle] *tr* to weed, root out

sarcloir [sarklwar] *m* hoe

Sardaigne [sardɛɲ] *f* Sardinia; **la Sardaigne** Sardinia

sarde [sard] *adj* Sardinian ‖ *m* Sardinian (*language*) ‖ (*cap*) *mf* Sardinian (*person*)

sardine [sardin] *f* sardine

S.A.R.L. *abbr* (**société à responsabilité limitée**) corporation

sarment [sarmã] *m* vine; vine shoot

sarra·sin [sarazē] **-sine** [zin] *adj* Saracen ‖ *m* buckwheat ‖ *f* portcullis ‖ (*cap*) *mf* Saracen

sar·rau [saro] *m* (*pl* **-raus**) smock

sarriette [sarjɛt] *f* (bot) savory

sas [sɑ], [sɑs] *m* sieve; lock (*of canal, submarine, etc.*); air lock (*of caisson, spaceship, etc.*); **sas d'évacuation** (aer) escape hatch

sasser [sɑse] *tr* to sift, screen; pass through a lock

satanique [satanik] *adj* satanic; fiendish, wicked

satelliser [satelize] *tr* to make a satellite of; (rok) to put into orbit

satellite [satelit] *adj* & *m* satellite; **satellite de relais** relay satellite

satin [satē] *m* satin

satinette [satinɛt] *f* sateen

satire [satir] *f* satire

satirique [satirik] *adj* satiric(al)

satiriser [satirize] *tr* to satirize

satisfaction [satisfaksjɔ̃] *f* satisfaction

satisfaire [satisfɛr] §29 *tr* to satisfy ‖ *intr*—**satisfaire à** to satisfy, fulfill, meet, e.g., **avez-vous satisfait à tous les besoins?** have you met all the needs? ‖ *ref* to be satisfied

satisfai·sant [satisfəzã] **-sante** [zãt] *adj* satisfactory; satisfying

saturer [satyre] *tr* to saturate

Saturne [satyrn] *m* Saturn

saturnisme [satyrnism] *m* lead poisoning

sauce [sos] *f* sauce; gravy; drawing pencil; (tech) solution

saucer [sose] §51 *tr* to dip in sauce or gravy; (coll) to soak to the skin; (coll) to reprimand severely

saucière [sosjɛr] *f* gravy bowl

saucisse [sosis] *f* sausage; frankfurter

saucisson [sosisɔ̃] *m* bologna, sausage

sauf [sof] **sauve** [sov] *adj* safe ‖ **sauf** *prep* save, except; barring; subject to (*e.g., correction*)

sauf-conduit [sofkɔ̃dᶁi] *m* (*pl* **-conduits**) safe-conduct

sauge [soʒ] *f* (bot) sage, salvia

saugre·nu -nue [sogrəny] *adj* absurd, silly

saule [sol] *m* willow

saumâtre [somɑtr] *adj* brackish

saumon [somɔ̃] *m* salmon; pig (*of crude metal*)

saumure [somyr] *f* brine

sauner [sone] *intr* to make salt

saupoudrer [sopudre] *tr* to sprinkle (*with powder, sugar; citations*)

saurai [sɔre] *v* (**sauras, saura, saurons,** etc.) see **savoir**

saurer [sɔre] *tr* to kipper

saut [so] *m* leap, jump; falls, waterfall; **au saut du lit** on getting out of bed; **faire le saut** to take the fatal step; **faire un saut chez** to drop in on; **par sauts et par bonds** by fits and starts; **saut à la perche** pole vault; **saut de carpe** jackknife; **saut de l'ange** swan dive; **saut en chute libre** skydiving; **saut en hauteur** high jump; **saut en longueur** long jump; **saut périlleux** somersault

saut-de-lit [sodli] *m invar* wrap

saut-de-mouton [sodmutɔ̃] *m* (*pl* **sauts-de-mouton**) overpass

saute [sot] *f* change in direction, shift

saute-mouton [sotmutɔ̃] *m* leapfrog

sauter [sote] *tr* to leap over; skip ‖ *intr* to leap, jump; blow up; **faire sauter** to sauté; flip (*a pancake*); fire (*an employee*); **sauter à cloche-pied** to hop on one foot; **sauter à pieds joints** to do a standing jump; **sauter aux nues** to get mad

sauterelle [sotrɛl] *f* grasshopper

sauterie [sotri] *f* (coll) hop (*dancing party*)

sau·teur [sotœr] **-teuse** [tøz] *adj* jumping ‖ *mf* jumper; **sauteur (sauteuse) en hauteur** high jumper; ‖ *m* jumper, jumping horse ‖ *f* frying pan

sautiller [sotije] *intr* to hop

sautoir [sotwar] *m* St. Andrew's cross; **en sautoir** crossways

sauvage [sovaʒ] *adj* savage; wild; shy ‖ *mf* savage

sauvagerie [sovaʒri] *f* savagery; wildness; shyness

sauvegarde [sovgard] *f* safeguard

sauvegarder [sovgarde] *tr* to safeguard

sauve-qui-peut [sovkipø] *m invar* panic, stampede, rout

sauver [sove] *tr* to save; rescue ‖ *intr*—**sauve qui peut!** every man for himself! ‖ *ref* to run away; escape; (theat) to exit; **sauve-toi!** (coll) scram!

sauvetage [sovtaʒ] *m* salvage; lifesaving, rescue

sauveteur [sovtœr] *adj masc* lifesaving ‖ *m* lifesaver

sauveur [sovœr] *adj masc* Saviour ‖ *m* savior; **Le Sauveur** the Saviour

savamment [savamɑ̃] *adv* knowingly; skillfully

savane [savan] *f* prairie, savanna

sa·vant [savɑ̃] **-vante** [vɑ̃t] *adj* scholarly, learned ‖ *mf* scientist, scholar, savant; **savant atomiste** nuclear physicist

savate [savat] *f* old slipper; foot boxing; (coll) butterfingers; **traîner la savate** to be down at the heel

saveur [savœr] *f* savor, taste

savoir [savwar] *m* learning ‖ §62, §95 *tr & intr* to know; know how to; **à savoir** namely, to wit; **à savoir que** with the understanding that; **en savoir long** to know all about it; **pas que je sache** not that I know of

savoir-faire [savwarfɛr] *m invar* know-how

savon [savɔ̃] *m* soap; (slang) sharp reprimand; **savon à barbe** shaving soap; **passer un savon à** (slang) to shout at; **savon en paillettes** soap flakes

savonnage [savɔnaʒ] *m* soaping

savonner [savɔne] *tr* to soap

savonnerie [savɔnri] *f* soap factory

savonnette [savɔnɛt] *f* toilet soap

savon·neux [savɔnø] **-neuse** [nøz] *adj* soapy

savourer [savure] *tr* to savor

savou·reux [savurø] **-reuse** [røz] *adj* savory, tasty

saxon [saksɔ̃] **saxonne** [saksɔn] *adj* Saxon ‖ *m* Saxon (*language*) ‖ (*cap*) *mf* Saxon (*person*)

saxophone [saksɔfɔn] *m* saxophone

saynète [sɛnɛt] *f* sketch, playlet

sca·bieux [skabjø] **-bieuse** [bjøz] *adj* scabby ‖ *f* scabious

sca·breux [skɑbrø] **-breuse** [brøz] *adj* rough (*road*); risky (*business*); scabrous (*remark*)

scalpel [skalpɛl] *m* scalpel

scalper [skalpe] *tr* to scalp

scandale [skɑdal] *m* scandal; disturbance

scanda·leux [skɑdalø] **-leuse** [løz] *adj* scandalous

scandaliser [skɑdalize] *tr* to lead astray; scandalize ‖ *ref* to take offense

scander [skɑde] *tr* to scan (*verses*)

scandinave [skɑdinav] *adj* Scandinavian ‖ *m* Scandinavian (*language*) ‖ (*cap*) *mf* Scandinavian (*person*); **Scandinaves** Scandinavian countries

scanographe [skanɔgraf] *m* (med) CAT scanner

scaphandre [skafɑdr] *m* diving suit; spacesuit; **scaphandre autonome** aqualung; **scaphandre spatial** spacesuit

scaphandrier [skafɑdrije] *m* diver

scarlatine [skarlatin] *f* scarlet fever

scarole [skarɔl] *f* escarole

sceau [so] *m* (*pl* **-seaux**) seal

scélé·rat [selera] **-rate** [rat] *adj* villainous ‖ *mf* villain

scellé [sɛle] *m* seal

sceller [sɛle] *tr* to seal

scénario [senarjo] *m* scenario

scène [sɛn] *f* scene; stage; theater

scénique [senik] *adj* scenic
scepticisme [sɛptisism] *m* skepticism
sceptique [sɛptik] *adj & mf* skeptic
sceptre [sɛptr] *m* scepter
schah [ʃa] *m* shah
schelem [ʃlɛm] *m* slam (at bridge)
schéma [ʃema] *m* diagram, sketch; outline; pattern
schisme [ʃism] *m* schism
schiste [ʃist] *m* schist, shale
schizophrène [skizɔfrɛn] *adj & mf* schizophrenic
schlague [ʃlag] *f* flogging
schooner [skunœr], [ʃunœr] *m* schooner
sciatique [sjatik] *adj* sciatic ‖ *f* (pathol) sciatica
scie [si] *f* saw; (coll) bore, nuisance; **scie à découper, scie sauteuse** jig saw
sciemment [sjamɑ̃] *adv* knowingly
science [sjɑ̃s] *f* science; learning, knowledge; **science de l'information** computer science
science-fiction [sjɑ̃sfiksjɔ̃] *f* science fiction
scientifique [sjɑ̃tifik] *adj* scientific ‖ *mf* scientist
scier [sje] *tr* to saw; (coll) to bore ‖ *intr* (naut) to row backwards
scierie [siri] *f* sawmill
scieur [sjœr] *m* sawyer
scinder [sɛ̃de] *tr* to divide ‖ *ref* to be divided
scintil·lant [sɛ̃tijɑ̃] **-lante** [jɑ̃t] *adj* scintillating; twinkling
scintillation [sɛ̃tijɑsjɔ̃] *f* twinkling, twinkle; (phys) scintillation
scintillement [sɛ̃tijmɑ̃] *m* twinkling
scintiller [sɛ̃tije] *intr* to scintillate; twinkle
scion [sjɔ̃] *m* scion; tip (of fishing rod)
scission [sisjɔ̃] *f* schism; (biol & phys) fission
sciure [sjyr] *f* sawdust
sclérose [skleroz] *f* sclerosis
scolaire [skɔlɛr] *adj* school
scolastique [skɔlastik] *adj & m* scholastic ‖ *f* scholasticism
sconse [skɔ̃s] *m* skunk fur; skunk
scories [skɔri] *fpl* slag, dross
scorpion [skɔrpjɔ̃] *m* scorpion; **le Scorpion** (astr, astrol) Scorpion
scout scoute [skut] *adj & m* scout
scoutisme [skutism] *m* scouting
scribe [skrib] *m* scribe
script [skript] *m* scrip; (typ) script
scripturaire [skriptyrɛr] *adj* Scriptural ‖ *m* fundamentalist
scrofule [skrɔfyl] *f* scrofula
scrotum [skrɔtɔm] *m* scrotum
scrupule [skrypyl] *m* scruple
scrupu·leux [skrypylø] **-leuse** [løz] *adj* scrupulous
scruter [skryte] *tr* to scrutinize
scrutin [skrytɛ̃] *m* ballot; balloting, voting, poll; **dépouiller le scrutin** to count the votes; **scrutin de ballottage** runoff election
scrutiner [skrytine] *intr* to ballot

sculpter [skylte] *tr* to sculpture; carve (wood)
sculpteur [skyltœr] *m* sculptor
sculpture [skyltyr] *f* sculpture
s.d. *abbr* (**sans date**) n.d.
S.D.E.C. [ɛsdeəse] *m* (letterword) (**Service de documentation extérieure et de contre-espionnage**) foreign-intelligence agency (equivalent of the C.I.A.)
S.D.N. [ɛsdeɛn] *f* (letterword) (**Société des Nations**) League of Nations
se [sə] §87 *ref pron*
séance [seɑ̃s] *f* session, sitting; seat (in an assembly); performance, showing; séance; **séance tenante** on the spot
séant [seɑ̃] **séante** [seɑ̃t] *adj* fitting, decent; sitting (as a king or a court in session) ‖ *m* buttocks, bottom; **se mettre sur son séant** to sit up (in bed)
seau [so] *m* (pl **seaux**) bucket, pail; **il pleut à seaux** it's raining cats and dogs; **seau à charbon** coal scuttle
sébile [sebil] *f* wooden bowl; (telp) coin return
sec [sɛk] **sèche** [sɛʃ] *adj* dry; sharp; rude; unguarded (card); total (loss); **en cinq sec** in a jiffy; **sec comme un hareng** (coll) long and thin; **tout sec** and nothing more ‖ *m* dryness; à **sec** dry; (coll) broke ‖ *f see* **sèche** ‖ **sec** *adv*—**aussi sec** (slang) on the spot; **boire sec** to drink one's liquor straight; **frapper sec** to land a hard fast punch; **parler sec** to talk tough
sécession [sesesjɔ̃] *f* secession
sèche [sɛʃ] *f* (slang) fag, cigarette
sèche-cheveux [sɛʃʃəvø] *m invar* hair drier
sèche-linge [sɛʃlɛ̃ʒ] *m invar* clothes drier
sécher [seʃe] §10 *tr* to dry; season; cut (a class) ‖ *intr* to become dry
sécheresse [sɛʃrɛs] *f* dryness; drought; baldness (of style); curtness (fig) coldness
séchoir [seʃwar] *m* drier; drying room; clotheshorse
se·cond [səgɔ̃] **-conde** [gɔ̃d] *adj & pron* second; **en second** next in rank ‖ *m* second ‖ *f see* **seconde**
secondaire [səgɔ̃dɛr] *adj & m* secondary
seconde [səgɔ̃d] *f* second (in time; musical interval; of angle); second class
seconder [səgɔ̃de] *tr* to help, second
se·coué -couée [səkwe] *adj* (slang) nuts, crazy
secouer [səkwe] *tr* to shake; shake off or down ‖ *ref* to pull oneself together
secourable [səkurabl] *adj* helpful
secourir [səkurir] §14 *tr* to help, aid
secourisme [səkurism] *m* first aid
secouriste [səkurist] *mf* first-aider; first-aid worker
secours [səkur] *m* help, aid; **au secours!** help!; **de secours** emergency; spare (tire); **des secours** supplies, relief
secousse [səkus] *f* shake, jolt; (elec) shock
se·cret [səkrɛ] **-crète** [krɛt] *adj* secret; secretive ‖ *m* secret; secrecy; **au secret** in solitary confinement ‖ *f see* **secrète**

secrétaire [səkretɛr] *mf* secretary ‖ *m* secretary (*desk*)

secrète [səkrɛt] *f* central intelligence

sécréter [sekrete] §10 *tr* to secrete

sectaire [sɛktɛr] *adj & mf* sectarian

secte [sɛkt] *f* sect

secteur [sɛktœr] *m* sector; (elec) house current, local supply circuit; **secteur postal** postal zone; (mil) A.P.O. number

section [sɛksjɔ̃] *f* section; cross section

sectionner [sɛksjɔne] *tr* to section; cut ‖ *ref* to break apart

séculaire [sekylɛr] *adj* secular

sécu·lier [sekylje] **-lière** [ljɛr] *adj & m* secular

sécurité [sekyrite] *f* security

séda·tif [sedatif] **-tive** [tiv] *adj & m* sedative

sédation [sedasjɔ̃] *f* sedation

sédentaire [sedɑ̃tɛr] *adj* sedentary

sédiment [sedimɑ̃] *m* sediment

sédi·tieux [sedisjø] **-tieuse** [sjøz] *adj* seditious

sédition [sedisjɔ̃] *f* sedition

séduc·teur [sedyktœr] **-trice** [tris] *adj* seducing, bewitching ‖ *mf* seducer ‖ *f* vamp

séduction [sedyksjɔ̃] *f* seduction

séduire [sedɥir] §19 *tr* to seduce; charm, bewitch; bribe

sédui·sant [sedɥizɑ̃] **-sante** [zɑ̃t] *adj* seductive, tempting

segment [sɛgmɑ̃] *m* segment; **segment de piston** piston ring

ségrégation [segregasjɔ̃] *f* segregation

ségrégationniste [segregasjɔnist] *adj* segregationist

seiche [sɛʃ] *f* cuttlefish; tidal wave; **chasser la seiche** (slang) to look for the end of the rainbow

séide [seid] *m* henchman

seigle [sɛgl] *m* rye

seigneur [sɛɲœr] *m* lord

sein [sɛ̃] *m* breast; bosom; womb; **au sein de** in the heart of

seine [sɛn] *f* dragnet

seing [sɛ̃] *m* signature; **sous seing privé** privately witnessed

seize [sɛz] §94 *adj & pron* sixteen; the Sixteenth, e.g., **Jean seize** John the Sixteenth ‖ *m* sixteen; sixteenth (*in dates*)

seizième [sɛzjɛm] §94 *adj, pron* (*masc, fem*), *& m* sixteenth

séjour [seʒur] *m* stay, visit

séjourner [seʒurne] *intr* to reside; stay, visit

sel [sɛl] *m* salt; **gros sel** coarse salt; (fig) dirty joke; **sel ammoniac** sal ammoniac; **sel fin, sel de table** table salt; **sel gemme** rock salt

sélec·tif [selɛktif] **-tive** [tiv] *adj* selective

sélection [selɛksjɔ̃] *f* selection

sélectionner [selɛksjɔne] *tr* to select

self [sɛlf] *f* (elec) coil, spark coil

self-service [sɛlfsɛrvis] *m* self-service

selle [sɛl] *f* saddle; seat (*of bicycle, motorcycle, etc.*); sculptor's tripod; stool, movement; (culin) saddle; **aller à la selle** to go to the toilet

seller [sɛle] *tr* to saddle

sellier [sɛlje] *m* saddler

selon [səlɔ̃] *adv*—**c'est selon** that depends; **selon que** according as ‖ *prep* according to; after (*e.g., my own heart*)

semailles [səmɑj] *fpl* sowing, seeding

semaine [səmɛn] *f* week; week's wages; set of seven; **à la petite semaine** day-to-day, hand-to-mouth; short-sighted; **de semaine** on duty during the week; **la semaine des quatre jeudis** (coll) never; **semaine anglaise** five-day workweek

semai·nier [səmenje] **-nière** [njɛr] *mf* week worker ‖ *m* highboy; office calendar

sémantique [semɑ̃tik] *adj* semantic ‖ *f* semantics

sémaphore [semafɔr] *m* semaphore

semblable [sɑ̃blabl] *adj* similar, like ‖ *m* fellow-man, equal

semblant [sɑ̃blɑ̃] *m* semblance, appearance; **faire semblant** to pretend

sembler [sɑ̃ble] §95 *intr* to seem; seem to

semelle [səmɛl] *f* sole; foot (*of stocking*); tread (*of tire*); bed (*of concrete*); **battre la semelle** to stamp one's feet

semence [səmɑ̃s] *f* seed; semen; brad; **semence de perles** seed pearls

semer [səme] §2 *tr* to seed, sow; scatter, strew; lay (*mines*); (slang) to outdistance; (slang) to drop (*an acquaintance*)

semestre [səmɛstr] *m* semester; six-month period

semes·triel **-trielle** [səmɛstrijɛl] *adj* six-month; semester

se·meur [səmœr] **-meuse** [møz] *mf* sower; spreader of gossip ‖ *f* seeder, drill

semi-chenillé [səmiʃnije] *m* half-track

semi-conduc·teur [səmikɔ̃dyktœr] **-trice** [tris] *adj* semiconductive ‖ *m* semiconductor

semifi·ni **-nie** [səmifini] *adj* unfinished

sémil·lant [semijɑ̃] **-lante** [jɑ̃t] *adj* sprightly, lively

séminaire [seminɛr] *m* seminary; seminar; conference

semi-remorque [səmirəmɔrk] *f* (*pl* -remorques*) semitrailer

semis [səmi] *m* sowing; seedling; seedbed

sémite [semit] *adj* Semitic ‖ (*cap*) *mf* Semite

sémitique [semitik] *adj* Semitic

semoir [səmwar] *m* seeder, drill

semonce [səmɔ̃s] *f* reprimand; (naut) order to heave to

semoncer [səmɔ̃se] §51 *tr* to reprimand; (naut) to order to heave to

semoule [səmul] *f* (culin) semolina

sénat [sena] *m* senate

sénateur [senatœr] *m* senator

sénile [senil] *adj* senile

sens [sɑ̃s] *m* sense, meaning; opinion; direction; **à double sens** ambiguous, e.g., **mot à double sens** double entendre; **en sens inverse** in the opposite direction; **sens antihoraire** counterclockwise; **sens dessus dessous** [sɑ̃dəsydəsu] upside down; **sens devant derrière** [sɑ̃dəvɑ̃dɛrjɛr] back to front; **sens interdit** (*public sign*) no entry; **sens obligatoire** (*public sign*) right way, this way; **sens unique** (*public sign*) one way

sensation [sɑ̃sasjɔ̃] *f* sensation

sensation·nel -nelle [sɑ̃sasjɔnɛl] *adj* sensational

sen·sé -sée [sɑ̃se] *adj* sensible

sensibiliser [sɑ̃sibilize] *tr* to sensitize

sensibilité [sɑ̃sibilite] *f* sensitivity, sensitiveness; compassion, feeling

sensible [sɑ̃sibl] *adj* sensitive; considerable, appreciable; perceptible; (mus) leading (*note*)

sensiblement [sɑ̃siblǝmɑ̃] *adv* approximately; appreciably, noticeably; acutely, keenly

sensi·tif [sɑ̃sitif] **-tive** [tiv] *adj* sensory; sensitive, touchy

senso·riel -rielle [sɑ̃sɔrjɛl] *adj* sensory

sen·suel -suelle [sɑ̃sɥɛl] *adj* sensual

sent-bon [sɑ̃bɔ̃] *m invar* odor, perfume

sentence [sɑ̃tɑ̃s] *f* proverb; (law) sentence

senteur [sɑ̃tœr] *f* odor, perfume

sentier [sɑ̃tje] *m* path; **hors des sentiers battus** off the beaten track

sentiment [sɑ̃timɑ̃] *m* feeling; opinion; **nos meilleurs sentiments** (*formula in letter writing*) our best wishes

sentimen·tal -tale [sɑ̃timɑ̃tal] *adj* (*pl* **-taux** [to]) sentimental

sentine [sɑ̃tin] *f* bilge

sentinelle [sɑ̃tinɛl] *f* sentinel

sentir [sɑ̃tir] §41, §95 *tr* to feel; smell; smell like, smell of; taste of; have all the earmarks of; show the effects of; **ne pas pouvoir sentir qn** to be unable to stand s.o. ‖ *intr* to smell; smell bad ‖ *ref* to feel; be felt; **se sentir de** to feel the effects of

seoir [swar] §5A (3d *pl pres ind* **siéent**; used only in 3d *sg & pl* of most simple tenses) *intr*—**seoir à** to be fitting for, proper to; be suitable to, suit, become, e.g., **cette robe lui sied** that dress suits her, that dress becomes her ‖ (used only in *inf* and 2d *sg & pl* and 1st *pl impv*) *ref* (coll & poetic) to sit down, have a seat

séparation [separasjɔ̃] *f* separation

séparer [separe] *tr & ref* to separate, divide

sept [sɛt] §94 *adj & pron* seven; the Seventh, e.g., **Jean sept** John the Seventh; **sept heures** seven o'clock ‖ *m* seven; seventh (*in dates*)

septembre [sɛptɑ̃br] *m* September

septentrio·nal -nale [sɛptɑ̃trijɔnal] (*pl* **-naux** [no]) *adj* northern

septième [sɛtjɛm] §94 *adj, pron* (*masc, fem*), & *m* seventh

septique [sɛptik] *adj* septic

sépulcre [sepylkr] *m* sepulcher

sépulture [sepyltyr] *f* grave, tomb, burial place; burial

séquelle [sekɛl] *f* gang; (pathol) complications; **séquelles** aftermath

séquence [sekɑ̃s] *f* sequence; (*in poker*) straight

séquestrer [sekɛstre] *tr* to sequester

serai [sǝre], [sre] *v* (**seras, sera, serons,** etc.) see **être**

sérail [seraj] *m* (*pl* **sérails**) seraglio

séraphin [serafɛ̃] *m* seraph; (coll) angel

serbe [sɛrb] *adj* Serb ‖ (*cap*) *mf* Serb

se·rein -reine [sǝrɛ̃] *adj* serene ‖ *m* night dew

sérénade [serenad] *f* serenade

sérénité [serenite] *f* serenity

serf [sɛr], [sɛrf] **serve** [sɛrv] *mf* serf

serge [sɛrʒ] *f* serge

sergent [sɛrʒɑ̃] *m* sergeant

série [seri] *f* series, string, set; (elec) series; **de série** standard; stock (*car*); **en série** in (a) series; mass, e.g., **fabrication en série** mass production; **hors série** outsize (*wearing apparel*); discontinued (*as an item of manufacture*); custom-built; almost unheard of; **série noire** run of bad luck

sé·rieux -rieuse [serjø] **-rieuse** [rjøz] *adj* serious

serin [sǝrɛ̃] *m* canary; (coll) simpleton

seringa [sǝrɛ̃ga] *m* mock orange

seringue [sǝrɛ̃g] *f* syringe; (hort) spray gun; **seringue à graisse** grease gun; **seringue à injections** hypodermic syringe; **seringue à instillations** nasal spray

serment [sɛrmɑ̃] *m* oath; **prêter serment** to take oath

sermon [sɛrmɔ̃] *m* sermon

sermonner [sɛrmɔne] *tr* to sermonize

serpe [sɛrp] *f* billhook

serpent [sɛrpɑ̃] *m* snake, serpent; **serpent à sonnettes** rattlesnake; **serpent caché sous les fleurs** snake in the grass

serpenter [sɛrpɑ̃te] *intr* to wind

serpen·tin [sɛrpɑ̃tɛ̃] **-tine** [tin] *adj* serpentine ‖ *m* coil; worm (*of still*); paper streamer

serpillière [sɛrpijɛr] *f* floorcloth; sacking, burlap

serpolet [sɛrpɔlɛ] *m* thyme

serre [sɛr] *f* greenhouse; **serres** claws, talons

ser·ré -rée [sɛre] *adj* tight; narrow; compact; close ‖ **serré** *adv* —**jouer serré** to play it close to the vest

serre-fils [sɛrfil] *m invar* (elec) binding post

serre-freins [sɛrfrɛ̃] *m invar* brakeman

serre-livres [sɛrlivr] *m invar* book end

serrement [sɛrmɑ̃] *m* squeezing, pressing; (min) partition (*to keep out water*); (pathol) pang; **serrement de cœur** heaviness of heart; **serrement de main** handshake

serrer [sɛre] *tr* to press; squeeze; wring; tighten; close up (*ranks*); clasp, shake, e.g., **serrer la main à** to shake hands with; grit (*one's teeth*); put on (*the brakes*) ‖ *intr*—**serrez à droite** (*public sign*) squeeze to right ‖ *ref* to squeeze together, be close together

serre-tête [sɛrtɛt] *m invar* headband; kerchief; crash helmet; (telp) headset

serrure [sɛryr] *f* lock; **serrure de sûreté** safety lock

serrurier [seryrje] *m* locksmith

sers [sɛr] *v* (**sert**) see **servir**

sertir [sɛrtir] *tr* to set (*a stone*)

sérum [serɔm] *m* serum

servage [sɛrvaʒ] *m* serfdom

ser·veur [sɛrvœr] **-veuse** [vøz] *mf* (tennis) server ‖ *m* waiter; barman ‖ *f* waitress; barmaid; extra maid; (mach) coffee maker

serviable [sɛrvjabl] *adj* obliging

service [sɛrvis] *m* service; agency; **service après vente** warranty service; **être de service** to be on duty; **service compris** tip included; **service de déménage** bomb squad; **service de garde** twenty-four-hour service; **service des abonnés absents** telephone answering service; **service des renseignements téléphoniques** information; **service sanitaire** ambulance corps

serviette [sɛrvjɛt] *f* napkin; towel; brief case; **serviette de bain** bath towel; **serviette de table** table napkin; **serviette de toilette en papier** paper towel; **serviette en papier** paper napkin; **serviette éponge** washcloth; Turkish towel; **serviette hygiénique** sanitary napkin

servile [sɛrvil] *adj* servile

servir [sɛrvir] §63, §96 *tr* to serve; deal (*cards*) ‖ *intr* to serve; **servir à** to be useful for, to serve as; **servir à qn de** to serve s.o. as; **servir de** to serve as, to function as ‖ *ref* to help oneself; **se servir chez** to patronize; **se servir de** to use

serviteur [sɛrvitœr] *m* servant

servitude [sɛrvityd] *f* servitude; (law) easement

servofrein [sɛrvɔfrɛ̃] *m* power brake

ses [se] §88

sésame [sezam] *m* sesame

session [sesjɔ̃] *f* session

seuil [sœj] *m* threshold

seul seule [sœl] §92 *adj* alone; lonely ‖ (when standing before noun) *adj* sole, single, only ‖ *pron indef* single one, only one; single person, only person ‖ **seul** *adv* alone

seulement [sœlmɑ̃] *adv* only, even ‖ *conj* but

sève [sɛv] *f* sap; vim

sévère [sevɛr] *adj* severe; stern; strict

sévices [sevis] *mpl* cruelty, brutality

sévir [sevir] *intr* to rage

sevrage [səvraʒ] *m* weaning

sevrer [səvre] §2 *tr* to wean

sexe [sɛks] *m* sex; **le beau sexe** the fair sex; **le sexe fort** the sterner sex

sexisme [sɛksism] *m* sexism

sexiste [sɛksist] *adj & mf* sexist

sextant [sɛkstɑ̃] *m* sextant

sextuor [sɛkstɥɔr] *m* (mus) sextet

sexuel sexuelle [sɛksɥɛl] *adj* sexual

seyant [sɛjɑ̃] **seyante** [sɛjɑ̃t] *adj* becoming

shampooing [ʃɑ̃pwɛ̃] *m* shampoo

shérif [ʃerif] *m* sheriff

shooter [ʃute] *ref* (slang) to shoot up (*intravenously*)

short [ʃɔrt] *m* shorts

si [si] *m invar* if; **des si et des cars** ifs and buts ‖ *adv* so; as; (to contradict a negative statement or question) yes, e.g., **Vous ne le saviez pas. Si!** You didn't know. Yes, I did!; **si bien que** so that, with the result that; **si peu que** so little that; **si peu que ce soit** however little it may be; **si + *adj* or *adv* + que + *subj*** however + *adj* or *adv* + *ind*, e.g., **si vite qu'il s'en aille** however fast he goes away ‖ *conj* if; whether; **si . . . ne** unless, e.g., **si je ne me trompe** unless I am mistaken; **si ce n'est** unless; **si tant est que** if it is true that

sia·mois [sjamwa] **-moise** [mwaz] *adj* Siamese ‖ (*cap*) *mf* Siamese

sibé·rien [siberjɛ̃] **-rienne** [rjɛn] *adj* Siberian ‖ (*cap*) *mf* Siberian

sibylle [sibil] *f* sibyl

Sicile [sisil] *f* Sicily; **la Sicile** Sicily

sici·lien [sisiljɛ̃] **-lienne** [ljɛn] *adj* Sicilian ‖ (*cap*) *mf* Sicilian

SIDA [sida] *m* (acronym) (**syndrome d'immunodéficience acquise**)—**le SIDA** AIDS (*acquired immune-deficiency syndrome*)

sidé·ral -rale [sideral] *adj* (*pl* **-raux** [ro]) sidereal

sidérer [sidere] §10 *tr* (coll) to flabbergast

sidérurgie [sideryrʒi] *f* iron-and-steel industry

sidérurgique [sideryrʒik] *adj* iron-and-steel

siècle [sjɛkl] *m* century; age; (eccl) world

siège [sjɛʒ] *m* seat; headquarters; (eccl) see; (mil) siege; **siège à glissière** glider; **siège arrière** back seat; **siège avant** front seat; **siège baquet** (*pl* **sièges baquets**) bucket seat; **siège billes** bean-bag chair; **siège éjectable** ejection seat

siéger [sjeʒe] §1 *intr* to sit, be in session; (*said of malady*) be seated

sien [sjɛ̃] **sienne** [sjɛn] §89

sieste [sjɛst] *f* siesta; **faire le sieste** to take a siesta; (coll) to be caught napping

sifflement [sifləmɑ̃] *m* whistle; hiss; swish; whiz; wheezing

siffler [sifle] *tr* to whistle (*e.g., a tune*); to hiss, boo; whistle to ‖ *intr* to whistle; hiss; swish, whiz

sifflet [siflɛ] *m* whistle; **sifflet à gaz** protective whistle in a woman's handbag

sif·fleur [siflœr] **-fleuse** [fløz] *mf* whistler

siffloter [siflɔte] *tr & intr* to whistle (a tune)

sigle [sigl] *m* abbreviation; word formed by literation; acronym

si·gnal [siɲal] *m* (*pl* **-gnaux** [ɲo]) signal; sign; (telp) busy signal

signa·lé -lée [siɲale] *adj* signal, noteworthy

signalement [siɲalmɑ̃] *m* description

signaler [siɲale] *tr* to signal; point out ‖ *ref* to distinguish oneself

signalisation [siɲalizasjɔ̃] *f* signs

signataire [siɲatɛr] *adj & mf* signatory

signature [siɲatyr] *f* signature; signing

signe [siɲ] *m* sign; **faire signe à** to motion to, to signal; **signe de ponctuation** punctuation mark; **signe de tête** nod

signer [siɲe] *tr* to sign ‖ *ref* to cross oneself

signet [siɲɛ], [sinɛ] *m* bookmark

significa·tif [siɲifikatif] **-tive** [tiv] *adj* significant

signifier [siɲifje] §**97** *tr* to signify; mean

silence [silɑ̃s] *m* silence

silen·cieux [silɑ̃sjø] **-cieuse** [sjøz] *adj* silent ‖ *m* silencer (*of a gun*); (aut) muffler

silex [silɛks] *m* flint

silhouette [silwɛt] *f* silhouette

silhouetter [silwete] *tr* to silhouette

silicium [silisjɔm] *m* silicon

silicone [silikon] *f* silicone

sillage [sijaʒ] *m* wake

sillet [sijɛ] *m* (mus) nut

sillon [sijɔ̃] *m* furrow; groove; **sillon sonore** sound track

sillonner [sijɔne] *tr* to furrow; groove; cross, streak

silo [silo] *m* silo

silure [silyr] *m* catfish

simagrée [simagre] *f* pretense

similaire [similɛr] *adj* similar

similigravure [similigravyr] *f* halftone

similitude [similityd] *f* similarity

similor [similɔr] *m* ormolu

simple [sɛ̃pl] *adj* simple; one-way (*ticket*); **à simple interligne** (typ) single-spaced; **passer en simple police** to go to police court; **simple particulier** private citizen; **simple soldat** private ‖ *mf* simple-minded person ‖ *m* simple (*herb*); (tennis) singles

simplement [sɛ̃pləmɑ̃] *adv* simply, plainly, naturally; simply, merely, just; **with a simple mind**

sim·plet [sɛ̃plɛ] **-plette** [plɛt] *adj* artless

simplicité [sɛ̃plisite] *f* simplicity; simpleness; simple-mindedness; **en toute simplicité** naturally, without affectation; **venez en toute simplicité** come as you are

simplifier [sɛ̃plifje] *tr* to simplify

simpliste [sɛ̃plist] *adj* oversimple

simulacre [simylakr] *m* sham; **simulacre de combat** sham battle

simuler [simyle] *tr* to simulate

simulta·né -née [simyltane] *adj* simultaneous; **en simultané** simultaneous (*translation*)

sinapisme [sinapism] *m* mustard plaster

sincère [sɛ̃sɛr] *adj* sincere

sincérité [sɛ̃serite] *f* sincerity

sinécure [sinekyr] *f* sinecure

singe [sɛ̃ʒ] *m* monkey; (slang) boss; **grimacer comme un vieux singe** to grin like a Cheshire cat

singer [sɛ̃ʒe] §**38** *tr* to ape

singerie [sɛ̃ʒri] *f* monkeyshine; grimace; monkey cage

singulariser [sɛ̃gylarize] *tr* to draw attention to ‖ *ref* to stand out

singu·lier [sɛ̃gylje] **-lière** [ljɛr] *adj & m* singular

sinistre [sinistr] *adj* sinister ‖ *m* disaster

sinis·tré -trée [sinistre] *adj* damaged, ruined; homeless; shipwrecked ‖ *mf* victim

sinon [sinɔ̃] *adv* if not; perhaps even; **sinon que** except for the fact that ‖ *prep* except for, except to ‖ *conj* except, unless; or else, else, otherwise

si·nueux [sinɥø] **-nueuse** [nɥøz] *adj* sinuous, winding

sinus [sinys] *m* sinus; (trig) sine

sionisme [sjɔnism] *m* Zionism

siphon [sifɔ̃] *m* siphon; siphon bottle; trap (*double-curved pipe*)

siphonner [sifɔne] *tr* to siphon

sire [sir] *m* sire; (archaic) sir; **un triste sire** a miserable wretch

sirène [sirɛn] *f* siren; foghorn; mermaid

sirop [siro] *m* syrup; **sirop pectoral** cough syrup

siroter [sirɔte] *tr & intr* (coll) to sip

sis [si] **sise** [siz] *adj* located

sismique [sismik] *adj* seismic

sismographe [sismɔgraf] *m* seismograph

sismologie [sismɔlɔʒi] *f* seismology

site [sit] *m* site; lay of the land

sitôt [sito] *adv* immediately; **sitôt dit, sitôt fait** no sooner said than done; **sitôt que** as soon as

sittelle [sitɛl] *f* (orn) nuthatch

situation [sitɥasjɔ̃] *f* situation; **situation sans issue** deadlock, impasse

situer [sitɥe] *tr* to situate, locate

six [si(s)] §**94** *adj & pron* six; the Sixth, e.g., **Jean six** John the Sixth; **six heures** six o'clock ‖ *m* six; sixth (*in dates*)

sixième [sizjɛm] §**94** *adj, pron* (*masc, fem*), *& m* sixth

six-quatre-deux [siskatdø]—**à la six-quatre-deux** (coll) slapdash

sizain [sizɛ̃] *m* six-line verse; pack (*of cub scouts*)

sizerin [sizrɛ̃] *m* (orn) redpoll

ski [ski] *m* ski; skiing; **faire du ski** to go skiing; **ski de fond** cross-country ski; **ski nautique** water-skiing

skier [skje] *intr* to ski

skieur [skjœr] **skieuse** [skjøz] *mf* skier

slalom [slalɔm] *m* slalom

slave [slav] *adj* Slav; Slavic ‖ *m* Slavic (*language*) ‖ (*cap*) *mf* Slav (*person*)

slip [slip] *m* supporter; swimming trunks; (women's) panties; **slip de soutien**, **slip coquille** supporter, jockstrap; **slip minimum** bikini

s.l.n.d. *abbr* (**sans lieu ni date**) n.p. & n.d.

slogan [slɔgɑ̃] *m* (com) slogan

slovaque [slɔvak] *adj* Slovak ‖ *m* Slovak (*language*) ‖ (*cap*) *mf* Slovak (*person*)

smicard [smikar] *m* (coll) minimum-wage earner

smoking [smɔkiŋ] *m* tuxedo

smurf [smyrf] *m* break dancing

snack [snak] *m* snack bar

S.N.C.F. [ɛsɛnseɛf] *f* (letterword) (**Société nationale des chemins de fer français**) French railroad

snob [snɔb] *adj invar* snobbish ‖ *mf* (*pl* **snob** or **snobs**) snob

snober [snɔbe] *tr* to snub

snobisme [snɔbism] *m* snobbery

sobre [sɔbr] *adj* sober, moderate; simple (*ornamentation*)

sobriété [sɔbrijete] *f* sobriety; moderation (*in eating, speaking*)

sobriquet [sɔbrikɛ] *m* nickname

soc [sɔk] *m* plowshare

sociable [sɔsjabl] *adj* sociable, neighborly; social (*creature*)

so·cial -ciale [sɔsjal] *adj* (*pl* **-ciaux** [sjo]) social

sociali·sant [sɔsjalizɑ̃] **-sante** [zɑ̃t] *adj* socialistic ‖ *mf* socialist sympathizer

socialiser [sɔsjalize] *tr* to socialize

socialisme [sɔsjalism] *m* socialism

socialiste [sɔsjalist] *adj* & *mf* socialist

sociétaire [sɔsjetɛr] *mf* stockholder; member (*e.g., of an acting company*)

société [sɔsjete] *f* society; company; firm, partnership; **société anonyme** stock company, corporation; **société de gardiennage** security-systems company; **société de prévoyance** benefit society; **Société des Nations** League of Nations; **société d'investissement à capital variable** mutual-fund society

sociologie [sɔsjɔlɔʒi] *f* sociology

socle [sɔkl] *m* pedestal; footing, socle; **socle roulant** portable stand (*e.g., for a television set*)

socque [sɔk] *m* clog, sabot; (theat) comedy

socquette [sɔkɛt] *f* anklet

Socrate [sɔkrat] *m* Socrates

soda [sɔda] *m* soda water

sodium [sɔdjɔm] *m* sodium

sodomie [sɔdɔmi] *f* sodomy

sœur [sœr] *f* sister; **et ta sœur!** (slang) knock it off!; **ma sœur** (eccl) sister

sofa [sɔfa] *m* sofa

soi [swa] §85, §85B; **à part soi** to oneself (himself, etc.); **de soi, en soi** in itself

soi-disant [swadizɑ̃] *adj invar* so-called, self-styled ‖ *adv* supposedly

soie [swa] *f* silk; bristle

soierie [swari] *f* silk goods; silk factory

soif [swaf] *f* thirst; **avoir soif** to be thirsty

soi·gné -gnée [swaɲe] *adj* well-groomed, trim; polished (*speech*)

soigner [swaɲe] *tr* to nurse, take care of; groom; polish (*one's style*)

soigneur [swaɲœr] *m* (sports) trainer

soi·gneux [swaɲø] **-gneuse** [ɲøz] *adj* careful, meticulous

soi-même [swamɛm] §86

soin [swɛ̃] *m* care, attention; treatment; **aux bons soins de** in care of (*c/o*); **être aux petits soins auprès de** to wait on (*s.o.*) hand and foot; **premiers soins** first aid; **soins à domicile** home-care nursing; **soins d'urgence** first aid; **soins infirmière** nursing

soir [swar] *m* evening, night; **hier soir** last night; **le soir** in the evening, at night

soirée [sware] *f* evening; evening party; **en soirée** evening (*performance*); **soirée dansante** dance; **soirée-hébergement** pajama party

sois [swa] *v* (**soit, soient**) see **être**

soit [swa], [swat] *conj* take for instance, e.g., **soit quatre multiplié par deux** take for instance four multiplied by two; say, e.g., **bien des hommes étaient perdus,**

soit un million many men were lost, say a million; **soit . . . soit** either . . . or, whether . . . or; **soit que . . . soit que** whether . . . or ‖ [swat] *interj* so be it!, all right!

soixante [swasɑ̃t] §94 *adj, pron,* & *m* sixty; **soixante et onze** seventy-one; **soixante et onzième** seventy-first; **soixante et un** sixty-one; **soixante et unième** sixty-first

soixante-dix [swasɑ̃tdi(s)] §94 *adj, pron,* & *m* seventy

soixante-dixième [swasɑ̃tdizjɛm] §94 *adj, pron* (*masc, fem*), & *m* seventieth

soixante-douze [swasɑ̃tduz] §94 *adj, pron,* & *m* seventy-two

soixante-douzième [swasɑ̃tduzjɛm] §94 *adj, pron* (*masc, fem*), & *m* seventy-second

soixantième [swasɑ̃tjɛm] §94 *adj, pron* (*masc, fem*), & *m* sixtieth

soja [sɔʒa] *m* soybean

sol [sɔl] *m* soil; ground; floor

solaire [sɔlɛr] *adj* solar

soldat [sɔlda] *m* soldier

soldatesque [sɔldatɛsk] *adj* barrack-room (*humor; manners*) ‖ *f* rowdies

solde [sɔld] *m* balance (*of an account*); remnant; clearance sale; **en solde** reduced (*in price*) ‖ *f* (mil) pay

solder [sɔlde] *tr* to settle (*an account*); to sell out; (mil) to pay ‖ *intr* to sell out

sol·deur [sɔldœr] **-deuse** [døz] *mf* dealer in seconds and remnants

sole [sɔl] *f* sole (*fish*); field (*used for crop rotation*)

soleil [sɔlɛj] *m* sun; sunshine, sunlight; sunflower; pinwheel; **il fait (du) soleil** it is sunny

solen·nel -nelle [sɔlanɛl] *adj* solemn

solenniser [sɔlanize] *tr* to solemnize

solénoïde [sɔlenɔid] *m* solenoid

solfège [sɔlfɛʒ] *m* sol-fa

solidage [sɔlidaʒ] *f* goldenrod

solidaire [sɔlidɛr] *adj* interdependent; jointly binding; **solidaire de** responsible for; answerable to; integral with, in one piece with

solidariser [sɔlidarize] *ref* to join together

solidarité [sɔlidarite] *f* solidarity, interdependence

solide [sɔlid] *adj* & *m* solid

solidité [sɔlidite] *f* solidity; soundness; strength (*e.g., of a fabric*)

soliloque [sɔlilɔk] *m* soliloquy

soliste [sɔlist] *mf* soloist

solitaire [sɔlitɛr] *adj* solitary; lonely ‖ *m* solitary, anchorite; old wild boar; solitaire

solitude [sɔlityd] *f* solitude

solive [sɔliv] *f* joist

soli·veau [sɔlivo] *m* (*pl* **-veaux**) small joist; (coll) nobody

solliciter [sɔllisite] *tr* to solicit; apply for; incite; attract (*attention; iron*); induce ‖ *intr* to seek favors

sollici·teur [sɔllisitœr] **-teuse** [tøz] *mf* solicitor, office seeker, petitioner, lobbyist

solo [sɔlo] *adj invar* & *m* solo

solstice [sɔlstis] *m* solstice
soluble [sɔlybl] *adj* soluble; solvable
solution [sɔlysjɔ̃] *f* solution
solutionner [sɔlysjɔne] *tr* to solve
solvabilité [sɔlvabilite] *f* solvency
solvable [sɔlvabl] *adj* solvent
solvant [sɔlvɑ̃] *m* solvent
sombre [sɔ̃br] *adj* somber; sullen
sombrer [sɔ̃bre] *intr* to sink; vanish (*as a fortune*)
sommaire [sɔmɛr] *adj & m* summary
sommation [sɔmɑsjɔ̃] *f* summons; sentry challenge; **faire les trois sommations** to read the riot act
somme [sɔm] *m* nap ‖ *f* sum; **en somme, somme toute** in short, when all is said and done
sommeil [sɔmɛj] *m* sleep; **avoir sommeil** to be sleepy
sommeiller [sɔmeje] *intr* to doze; lie dormant
sommelier [sɔməlje] *m* wine steward
sommer [sɔme] §97 *tr* to add up; summon, issue a legal writ to
sommes [sɔm] *v* see **être**
sommet [sɔme] *m* summit, top; apex (*of a triangle*); vertex (*of an angle*); (fig) acme
sommier [sɔmje] *m* bedspring; ledger; crossbeam; (archaic) pack animal; **sommier élastique** spring mattress
sommité [sɔmite] *f* pinnacle, crest; leader, authority
somnambule [sɔmnɑ̃byl] *adj* sleepwalking ‖ *mf* sleepwalker
somnifère [sɔmnifɛr] *adj* sleep-inducing, soporific ‖ *m* sleeping pill
somnolence [sɔmnɔlɑ̃s] *f* drowsiness; indolence, laziness
somno·lent [sɔmnɔlɑ̃] **-lente** [lɑ̃t] *adj* somnolent, drowsy; indolent
somnoler [sɔmnɔle] *intr* to doze
somptuaire [sɔ̃ptɥɛr] *adj* luxury (*tax*)
somp·tueux [sɔ̃ptɥø] **-tueuse** [tɥøz] *adj* sumptuous
son [sɔ̃] *adj poss* §88 his, her, its ‖ *m* sound; bran
sonal [sɔnal] *m* (advertising) jingle
sonate [sɔnat] *f* sonata
sondage [sɔ̃daʒ] *m* sounding, probing; **sondage de l'opinion** public-opinion poll; **sondage d'exploration** wildcat (*well*); **sondage isoloir** exit poll
sonde [sɔ̃d] *f* lead, probe; borer, drill; **sonde spatiale** space probe
sonder [sɔ̃de] *tr* to sound, probe, bore, fathom; explore, reconnoiter; poll (*e.g., public opinion*); sound out (*s.o.*)
son·deur [sɔ̃dœr] **-deuse** [døz] *mf* prober, sounder
songe [sɔ̃ʒ] *m* dream
songe-creux [sɔ̃ʒkrø] *m invar* visionary, pipe dreamer
songer [sɔ̃ʒe] §38, §96 *tr* to dream up ‖ *intr* to dream; think; intend to; **songer à** to think of; imagine, dream of; **songez-y!** think it over!
songerie [sɔ̃ʒri] *f* reverie, daydreaming

son·geur [sɔ̃ʒœr] **-geuse** [ʒøz] *adj* dreamy, preoccupied ‖ *mf* daydreamer
sonique [sɔnik] *adj* sonic, of sound
sonnaille [sɔnɑj] *f* cowbell, sheepbell
sonnailler [sɔnɑje] *m* bellwether ‖ *intr* to ring often and without cause
son·nant [sɔnɑ̃] **-nante** [nɑ̃t] *adj* striking (*clock*); metal (*money*); at the stroke of, e.g., **à huit heures sonnantes** at the stroke of eight
son·né -née [sɔne] *adj* past, e.g., **deux heures sonnées** past two o'clock; over, e.g., **il a soixante ans sonnés** he is over sixty; (slang) cuckoo, nuts; (slang) stunned; **être sonné** (slang) to be knocked out
sonner [sɔne] *tr* to ring; ring for; sound ‖ *intr* to ring; strike; sound
sonnerie [sɔnri] *f* chimes, chiming; set of bells, carillon; fanfare; ring (*of a telephone, doorbell, etc.*); alarm or striking mechanism (*of clock*)
sonnet [sɔnɛ] *m* sonnet
sonnette [sɔnɛt] *f* doorbell; pile driver
sonneur [sɔnœr] *m* bellringer; trumpeter
sonore [sɔnɔr] *adj* sonorous; sound (*wave, track*); echoing (*hall, cathedral, etc.*); (phonet) voiced ‖ *f* voiced consonant
sonorisation [sɔnɔrizɑsjɔ̃] *f* public-address system; (mov) sound track
sonoriser [sɔnɔrize] *tr* to record sound effects on (*a film*); equip (*an auditorium*) with loudspeakers
sonorité [sɔnɔrite] *f* sonority, resonance
sonotone [sɔnɔtɔn] *m* hearing aid
sont [sɔ̃] *v* see **être**
sophistication [sɔfistikɑsjɔ̃] *f* adulteration
sophisti·qué -quée [sɔfistike] *adj* adulterated; artificial, counterfeit; (comp) sophisticated
sophistiquer [sɔfistike] *tr* to adulterate; subtilize
Sophocle [sɔfɔkl] *m* Sophocles
sopraniste [sɔpranist] *m* male soprano
sopra·no [sɔprano] *mf* (*pl* **-ni** [ni] or **-nos**) soprano ‖ *m* soprano (*voice*)
sorbet [sɔrbɛ] *m* sherbet
sorbetière [sɔrbətjɛr] *f* ice-cream freezer
sorbon·nard [sɔrbɔnar] **-narde** [nard] *mf* (coll) Sorbonne student; (coll) Sorbonne professor
sorcellerie [sɔrsɛlri] *f* sorcery
sor·cier [sɔrsje] **-cière** [sjɛr] *adj* sorcerer's; **cela n'est pas sorcier** there's no trick to that ‖ *m* sorcerer, wizard ‖ *f* sorceress, witch; **vieille sorcière** old hag
sordide [sɔrdid] *adj* sordid
sornette [sɔrnɛt] *f* nonsense
sors [sɔr] *v* (**sort**) see **sortir**
sort [sɔr] *m* fate, destiny; fortune, lot; spell, charm
sortable [sɔrtabl] *adj* suitable, acceptable; presentable
sor·tant [sɔrtɑ̃] **-tante** [tɑ̃t] *adj* retiring (*congressman*); winning (*number*) ‖ *mf* person leaving

sorte [sɔrt] *f* sort, kind; state, condition; way, manner; **de la sorte** this way, thus; **de sorte que** so that, with the result that; **en quelque sorte** in a certain way; **en sorte que** in such a way that

sortie [sɔrti] *f* exit, way out; outing, jaunt; quitting time; outburst, tirade; (mil) sortie; **faire une sortie à** (slang) to bawl out; **sortie de bain** bathrobe; **sortie de bal** evening wrap; **sortie de secours** emergency exit; **sortie de voiture(s)** driveway

sortilège [sɔrtilɛʒ] *m* spell, charm

sortir [sɔrtir] §64 *tr* to take out, bring out; publish ‖ *intr* (*aux:* ÊTRE) to go out, come out; come forth; stand out; **au sortir de** on coming out of; **sortir de** + *inf* (coll) to have just + *pp*

S.O.S. [ɛsoɛs] *m* (letterword) S.O.S.

sosie [sozi] *m* double

sot [so] **sotte** [sɔt] (precedes the noun it modifies) *adj* stupid, silly ‖ *mf* fool, simpleton

sottise [sɔtiz] *f* stupidity, silliness, foolishness

sou [su] *m* sou; (fig) penny, farthing; **sans le sou** penniless; **sou à sou** or **sou par sou** a penny at a time

soubassement [subɑsmɑ̃] *m* subfoundation, infrastructure

soubresaut [subrəso] *m* sudden start, jerk; palpitation, jump (*of the heart*)

soubrette [subrɛt] *f* (theat) soubrette; (coll) attractive chambermaid

souche [suʃ] *f* stump; stock; stack (*of fireplace*); strain (*of virus*); (coll) dolt; **de pure souche** full-blooded

souci [susi] *m* care; marigold; **sans souci** carefree

soucier [susje] §97 *ref* to care, concern oneself

soucieusement [susjøzmɑ̃] *adv* uneasily, anxiously; with concern

sou·cieux [susjø] **-cieuse** [sjøz] *adj* solicitous, concerned; uneasy, anxious

soucoupe [sukup] *f* saucer; **soucoupe volante** flying saucer

soudage [sudaʒ] *m* soldering; welding

sou·dain [sudɛ̃] **-daine** [dɛn] *adj* sudden ‖ **soudain** *adv* suddenly

soudainement [sudɛnmɑ̃] *adv* suddenly

soudaineté [sudɛnte] *f* suddenness

souda·nais [sudanɛ] **-naise** [nɛz] *adj* Sudanic ‖ *m* Sudanic (*language*) ‖ (*cap*) *mf* Sudanese (*person*)

soude [sud] *f* (chem) soda

souder [sude] *tr* to solder; weld ‖ *ref* to knit (*as bones do*)

soudeur [sudœr] *m* welder

soudoyer [sudwaje] §47 *tr* to bribe; hire (*assassins*)

soudure [sudyr] *f* solder; soldering; soldered joint; knitting (*of bones*); **faire la soudure** to bridge the gap; **soudure autogène** welding

soue [su] *f* pigsty

soufflage [suflaʒ] *m* blowing; glass blowing

souf·fert [sufɛr] **-ferte** [fɛrt] *v* see **souffrir**

souffle [sufl] *m* breath; breathing; **second souffle** second wind

souf·flé -flée [sufle] *adj* puffed up ‖ *m* soufflé

souffler [sufle] *tr* to blow; blow out (*a candle*); blow up (*a balloon*); prompt (*an actor*); huff (*a checker*); suggest (*an idea*); **ne pas souffler mot** to not breathe a word; **souffler à l'oreille** to whisper; **souffler q.ch. à qn** to take s.th. from s.o. ‖ *intr* to blow; pant, puff; take a breather, catch one's breath

soufflerie [sufləri] *f* bellows; wind tunnel

soufflet [suflɛ] *m* slap in the face; affront, insult; bellows; gore (*of dress*); (rr) flexible cover (*between two cars*)

souffleter [sufləte] §34 *tr* to slap in the face; affront

souf·fleur [suflœr] **-fleuse** [fløz] *mf* (theat) prompter ‖ *m* glass blower ‖ *f* (mach) blower

soufflure [suflyr] *f* blister, bubble

souffrance [sufrɑ̃s] *f* suffering; **en souffrance** unfinished (*business*); outstanding (*bill*); unclaimed (*parcel*); at a standstill, suspended

souf·frant [sufrɑ̃] **-frante** [frɑ̃t] *adj* suffering; sick, ailing

souffre-douleur [sufrədulœr] *m invar* butt (*of a joke*), laughingstock

souffre·teux [sufrətø] **-teuse** [tøz] *adj* sickly; destitute, half-starved

souffrir [sufrir] §65, §96, §97 *tr* to suffer; stand, bear, tolerate; permit ‖ *intr* to suffer ‖ *ref* to put up with each other

soufre [sufr] *m* sulfur

soufrer [sufre] *tr* to sulfurate

souhait [swɛ] *m* wish; **à souhait** to one's liking, to perfection; **à vos souhaits!** (salutation) gesundheit!; **souhaits** good wishes; **souhaits de bonne année** New Year's greetings

souhaitable [swɛtabl] *adj* desirable

souhaiter [swɛte] §95, §97 *tr* to wish; wish for; wish to; **je vous la souhaite bonne et heureuse** I wish you a happy New Year

souille [suj] *f* wallow

souiller [suje] *tr* to dirty, spot, stain, soil, sully

souillon [sujɔ̃] *f* (coll) scullery maid

souillure [sujyr] *f* spot, stain

soûl [su] **soûle** [sul] *adj* drunk; sottish ‖ *m* fill, e.g., **manger son soûl** to eat one's fill

soulagement [sulaʒmɑ̃] *m* relief; comfort

soulager [sulaʒe] §38 *tr* to relieve; comfort

soûler [sule] *tr* (slang) to cram down one's throat; (slang) to get (*s.o.*) drunk ‖ *ref* (fig) to have one's fill; (slang) to get drunk

soulèvement [sulɛvmɑ̃] *m* upheaval; uprising; surge; **soulèvement de cœur** nausea

soulever [sulve] §2 *tr* to raise, heave, lift (up); stir up ‖ *ref* to rise; raise oneself; revolt

soulier [sulje] *m* shoe; **être dans ses petits souliers** (coll) to feel awkward; **souliers à**

talons hauts high-heeled shoes; souliers
bas low-heeled shoes; souliers compensés elevator shoes; souliers de marche walking shoes; souliers montants
boots; souliers richelieu oxfords
soulignement [suliɲəmɑ̃] m underlining
souligner [suliɲe] tr to underline; emphasize
soulte [sult] f balance due
soumettre [sumɛtr] §42 tr to submit; subject; overcome, subdue ‖ ref to submit, surrender
sou·mis [sumi] -mise [miz] adj submissive, subservient; subject; amenable (to a law)
soumission [sumisjɔ̃] f submission, surrender; bid (to perform a service); guarantee
soumissionnaire [sumisjɔnɛr] mf bidder
soupape [supap] f valve; soupape à réglage or à papillon damper; soupape de sûreté safety valve; soupape électrique rectifier
soupçon [supsɔ̃] m suspicion; misgiving; dash, touch (small amount)
soupçonner [supsɔne] §97 tr & intr to suspect
soupçon·neux [supsɔnø] -neuse [nøz] adj suspicious
soupe [sup] f vegetable soup; sop (bread); (mil) mess; de soupe on K.P.; soupe au lait (coll) mean-tempered person; soupe populaire soup kitchen; trempé comme une soupe soaking wet
soupente [supɑ̃t] f attic
souper [supe] m supper ‖ intr to have supper
soupeser [supəze] §2 tr to heft, weigh (e.g., a package) in one's hand
soupière [supjɛr] f soup tureen
soupir [supir] m sigh; breath; (mus) quarter rest
soupi·rail [supiraj] m (pl -raux [ro]) cellar window
soupirant [supirɑ̃] m suitor
soupirer [supire] intr to sigh; soupirer après or pour to long for
souple [supl] adj supple; flexible, pliant; versatile, adaptable
souplesse [suplɛs] f suppleness, flexibility
souquer [suke] tr to haul taut ‖ intr to pull hard (on the oars)
source [surs] f source; spring, fountain; source de pétrole oil well; source jaillissante gusher
sourcier [sursje] m dowser
sourcil [surci] m eyebrow
sourciller [sursije] intr to knit one's brows; sans sourciller without batting an eye
sourcil·leux [sursijø] -leuse [jøz] adj supercilious
sourd [sur] sourde [surd] adj deaf; quiet; dull (sound, color); deep (voice); undeclared (war); (phonet) unvoiced; sourd comme un pot (coll) stone-deaf ‖ mf deaf person ‖ f unvoiced consonant
sourdement [surdəmɑ̃] adv secretly; heavily; dully
sourdine [surdin] f (mus) mute; à la sourdine muted; en sourdine on the sly

sourd-muet [surmɥɛ] sourde-muette [surdəmɥɛt] (pl sourds-muets) adj deaf and dumb, deaf-mute ‖ mf deaf-mute
sourdre [surdr] (used in: inf; 3d sg & pl pres ind sourd, sourdent) intr to spring, well up
souricier [surisje] m mouser
souricière [surisjɛr] f mousetrap; (fig) trap
sourire [surir] m smile ‖ §61, §97 intr to smile; sourire à to smile at; smile on; look good to
souris [suri] m (obs) smile ‖ f mouse
sour-nois [surnwa] -noise [nwaz] adj sly, cunning, artful
sous [su] prep under; on (a certain day; certain conditions); sous caoutchouc rubber-covered; sous clef under lock and key; sous la main at hand; sous les drapeaux in the army; sous main underhandedly; sous peu shortly; sous un certain angle from a certain point of view
sous-alimentation [suzalimɑ̃tasjɔ̃] f undernourishment
sous-bois [subwa] m underbrush, undergrowth
sous-chef [suʃɛf] m (pl -chefs) assistant (to the head person), deputy, second-in-command
souscripteur [suskriptœr] m subscriber (to a loan or charity); signer (of a commercial paper)
souscription [suskripsjɔ̃] f signature; subscription; souscription de soutien sustaining membership
souscrire [suskrir] §25 tr & intr to subscribe
sous-cuta·né -née [sukytane] adj subcutaneous
sous-dévelop·pé -pée [sudɛvlɔpe] adj underdeveloped
sous-diacre [sudjakr] m subdeacon
sous-direc·teur [sudirɛktœr] -trice [tris] mf (pl -directeurs) second-in-command
sous-entendre [suzɑ̃tɑ̃dr] tr to understand (what is not expressed); to imply
sous-entendu [suzɑ̃tɑ̃dy] m inference, implication, innuendo, double meaning, double entendre
sous-entente [suzɑ̃tɑ̃t] f mental reservation; hidden, cryptic meaning
sous-entrepreneur [suzɑ̃trəprənœr] m (pl -entrepreneurs) subcontractor
sous-estimer [suzɛstime] tr to underestimate
sous-fifre [sufifr] m (pl -fifres) (coll) underling
sous-garde [sugard] f trigger guard
sous-lieutenant [suljøtnɑ̃] m (pl -lieutenants) second lieutenant
sous-location [sulɔkasjɔ̃] f sublease
sous-louer [sulwe] tr to sublet, sublease
sous-main [sumɛ̃] m invar desk blotter; en sous-main underhandedly
sous-marin [sumarɛ̃] -marine [marin] adj & m (pl -marins) submarine
sous-marinier [sumarinje] m (pl -mariniers) submarine crewman

sous-mentonnière [sumɑ̃tɔnjər] *f* (*pl* **-mentonnières**) chin strap

sous-nappe [sunap] *f* (*pl* **-nappes**) table pad

sous-off [suzɔf] *m* (*pl* **-offs**) noncom

sous-officier [suzɔfisje] *m* (*pl* **-officiers**) noncommissioned officer

sous-ordre [suzɔrdr] *m* (*pl* **-ordres**) underling, subordinate; (biol) suborder; **en sous-ordre** subordinate; subordinately

sous-production [suprɔdyksjɔ̃] *f* underproduction

sous-produit [suprɔdɥi] *m* (*pl* **-produits**) by-product

sous-secrétaire [suskretɛr] *m* (*pl* **-secrétaires**) undersecretary

sous-secrétariat [suskretarja] *m* undersecretaryship

sous-seing [susɛ̃] *m invar* privately witnessed document

soussi·gné -gnée [sisiɲe] *adj* & *mf* undersigned

sous-sol [susɔl] *m* (*pl* **-sols**) subsoil; basement

sous-titre [sutitr] *m* (*pl* **-titres**) subtitle

sous-titrer [sutitre] *tr* to subtitle

soustraction [sustraksjɔ̃] *f* subtraction; (law) purloining

soustraire [sustrɛr] §68 *tr* to remove; take away; subtract; deduct; **soustraire de** to subtract from; **soustraire q.ch. à qn** to take s.th. away from s.o.; steal s.th. from s.o. || *ref* to withdraw; **se soustraire à** to escape from

sous-traitant [sutrɛtɑ̃] *m* (*pl* **-traitants**) subcontractor; sublessee

sous-traité [sutrɛte] *m* (*pl* **-traités**) subcontract

sous-traiter [sutrɛte] *tr* & *intr* to subcontract

sous-ventrière [suvɑ̃trijɛr] *f* (*pl* **-ventrières**) girth

sous-verre [suvɛr] *m invar* passe-partout; coaster

sous-vêtement [suvɛtmɑ̃] *m* (*pl* **-vêtements**) undergarment

soutache [sutaʃ] *f* braid

soutacher [sutaʃe] *tr* to trim with braid

soutane [sutan] *f* soutane, cassock

soutanelle [sutanɛl] *f* frock coat; choir robe

soute [sut] *f* (naut) storeroom; **soute à charbon** coal bunker

soutenable [sutnabl] *adj* supportable, tenable

soutenance [sutnɑ̃s] *f* defense (*of an academic thesis*)

soutènement [sutɛnmɑ̃] *m* support

souteneur [sutnœr] *m* pimp

soutenir [sutnir] §72, §95 *tr* to support, bear; sustain; insist, claim; defend (*a thesis*) || *ref* to stand up; keep afloat

soute·nu -nue [sutny] *adj* sustained; elevated (*style*); steady (*market*); true (*colors*)

souter·rain [sutɛrɛ̃] **-raine** [rɛn] *adj* subterranean, underground; underhanded || *m* tunnel, subway (*for pedestrians*)

soutien [sutjɛ̃] *m* support; stand-by

soutien-gorge [sutjɛ̃gɔrʒ] *m* (*pl* **soutiens-gorge**) brassiere

soutirage [sutiraʒ] *m* racking

soutirer [sutire] *tr* to rack (*wine*); **soutirer q.ch. à qn** to get s.th. out of s.o., sponge on s.o. for s.th.

souvenir [suvnir] *m* memory, remembrance; souvenir; **en souvenir de** in remembrance of || §72 *intr*—**faire souvenir qn de q.ch.** to remind s.o. of s.th. || §97 *ref* to remember; **se souvenir de** to remember

souvent [suvɑ̃] *adv* often

souve·rain [suvrɛ̃] **-raine** [rɛn] *adj* & *mf* sovereign || *m* sovereign (*coin*)

souveraineté [suvrɛnte] *f* sovereignty

soviet [sɔvjɛt] *m* soviet

soviétique [sɔvjetik] *adj* Soviet || (*cap*) *mf* Soviet Russian

soya [sɔja] *m* soybean

soyeux [swajø] **soyeuse** [swajøz] *adj* silky

soyez [swaje] *v* (**soyons**) see **être**

S.P. *abbr* (**sapeurs-pompiers**) fire department

spa·cieux [sapsjø] **-cieuse** [sjøz] *adj* spacious, roomy

spadassin [spadasɛ̃] *m* hatchet man, hired thug

spaghetti [spageti] *mpl* spaghetti

sparadrap [sparadra] *m* adhesive tape

spartiate [sparsjat] *adj* Spartan || (*cap*) *mf* Spartan

spasme [spasm] *m* spasm

spasmodique [spasmɔdik] *adj* spasmodic; (pathol) spastic

spath [spat] *m* (mineral) spar

spa·tial -tiale [spasjal] *adj* (*pl* **-tiaux** [sjo]) spatial

spatiocarte [spasjɔkart] *f* maps drawn from satellite pictures

spationef [spasjɔnɛf] *m* space vehicle

spatule [spatyl] *f* spatula; (orn) spoon-bill

spea·ker [spikœr] **-kerine** [krin] *mf* (rad, telv) announcer || *m* speaker (*presiding officer*)

spé·cial -ciale [spesjal] *adj* (*pl* **-ciaux** [sjo]) special, especial, particular; specialized; peculiar, odd

spécialiser [spesjalize] *tr* & *ref* to specialize

spécialiste [spesjalist] *mf* specialist; expert

spécialité [spesjalite] *f* specialty; specialization; patent medicine

spécialement [spesjalmɑ̃] *adv* specially, especially, particularly

spé·cieux [spesjø] **-cieuse** [sjøz] *adj* specious

spécifier [spesifje] *tr* to specify

spécifique [spesifik] *adj* & *m* specific

spécimen [spesimɛn] *m* specimen; sample copy

spectacle [spɛktakl] *m* spectacle, sight; show; play; **à grand spectacle** spectacular (*production*); **spectacle solo** one-man show

specta·teur [spɛktatœr] **-trice** [tris] *mf* spectator

spectre [spɛktr] *m* ghost; spectrum; (fig) specter

spécula·teur [spekylatœr] **-trice** [tris] *mf* speculator

spéculer [spekyle] *tr* to speculate

spéléologie [speleɔlɔʒi] *f* speleology

sperme [spɛrm] *m* sperm

sphère [sfɛr] *f* sphere

sphérique [sferik] *adj* spherical

sphinx [sfɛ̃ks] *m* sphinx

spider [spider] *m* (aut) rumble seat

spi·nal -nale [spinal] *adj* (*pl* **-naux** [no]) spinal

spi·ral -rale [spiral] (*pl* **-raux** [ro]) *adj* spiral ‖ *m* hairspring (*of watch*) ‖ *f* spiral; **en spirale** spiral

spire [spir] *f* turn (*in a wire*); whorl (*of a shell*)

spirée [spire] *f* (bot) spirea

spirite [spirit] *adj* & *mf* spiritualist

spiri·tuel -tuelle [spirityɛl] *adj* spiritual; sacred (*music*); witty ‖ *m* ecclesiastical power

spiri·tueux [spirityø] **-tueuse** [tyøz] *adj* spirituous ‖ *m* spirituous liquor

spleen [splin] *m* boredom, melancholy

splendeur [splɑ̃dœr] *f* splendor

splendide [splɑ̃did] *adj* splendid; bright, brilliant

spolia·teur [spɔljatœr] **-trice** [tris] *adj* despoiling ‖ *mf* despoiler

spolier [spɔlje] *tr* to despoil

spon·gieux [spɔ̃ʒjø] **-gieuse** [ʒjøz] *adj* spongy

sponta·né -née [spɔ̃tane] *adj* spontaneous

sporadique [spɔradik] *adj* sporadic(al)

sport [spɔr] *adj invar* sport, sporting; sportsmanlike ‖ *m* sport

spor·tif -tive [spɔrtif] *adj* sport, sporting ‖ *mf* athlete, player ‖ *m* sportsman

spot [spɔt] *m* spotlight; (radar) blip

spoutnik [sputnik] *m* sputnik

spu·meux [spymø] **-meuse** [møz] *adj* frothy, foamy

squale [skwal] *m* (ichth) dogfish

squelette [skəlɛt] *m* skeleton

squelettique [skəletik] *adj* skeletal

S.R. *abbr* (**service de renseignements**) information desk or bureau

stabiliser [stabilize] *tr* to stabilize

stabilité [stabilite] *f* stability

stable [stabl] *adj* stable

stade [stad] *m* stadium; (fig) stage (*of development*)

stage [staʒ] *m* probationary period, apprenticeship; training period

stagiaire [staʒjɛr] *adj* apprentice ‖ *mf* trainee, apprentice; student teacher

stag·nant [stagnɑ̃] **-nante** [nɑ̃t] *adj* stagnant

stalle [stal] *f* stall; parking spot

stance [stɑ̃s] *f* stanza

stand [stɑ̃d] *m* stands; shooting gallery; pit (*for motor racing*)

standard [stɑ̃dar] *adj invar* standard ‖ *m* standard; switchboard

standardiser [stɑ̃dardize] *tr* to standardize

standardiste [stɑ̃dardist] *mf* switchboard operator, telephone operator

standing [stɑ̃diŋ] *m* status, standing; standard of living; **de grand standing** luxury (*apartments*)

star [star] *f* (mov, theat) star

starter [startɛr], [startœr] *m* (aut) choke; (sports) starter

station [stasjɔ̃] *f* station; resort; (rr) flag station; **station balnéaire** beach resort; **station d'autobus** bus stop; **station d'écoute** monitoring station; **station d'émission** broadcasting station; **station de repérage** tracking station; **station de taxis** taxi stand; **station libre-service** self-service station; **station orbitale** space station; **stations de la Croix** (rel) Stations of the Cross

stationnaire [stasjɔnɛr] *adj* stationary ‖ *m* gunboat

stationnement [stasjɔnmɑ̃] *m* parking; **stationnement interdit** (*public sign*) no parking

stationner [stasjɔne] *intr* to stop; park

station-service [stasjɔ̃sɛrvis] *f* (*pl* **stations-service**) service station

statique [statik] *adj* static

statisti·cien [statistisjɛ̃] **-cienne** [sjɛn] *mf* statistician

statistique [statistik] *adj* statistical ‖ *f* statistics

statuaire [statyɛr] *adj* statuary ‖ *mf* sculptor ‖ *f* statuary

statue [staty] *f* statue

statuer [statye] *tr* to hand down (*a ruling*) ‖ *intr* to hand down a ruling

statu quo [statykwo], [statuko] *m* status quo

stature [statyr] *f* stature

statut [staty] *m* statute; legal status; **le statut de** the status of

statutaire [statytɛr] *adj* statutory

Ste *abbr* (**Sainte**) St. (*female saint*)

Sté *abbr* (**Société**) Inc.

sténo [steno] *f* stenographer; stenography

sténodactylo [stenɔdaktilo] *f* shorthand typist; shorthand typing

sténogramme [stenɔgram] *m* shorthand notes

sténographe [stenɔgraf] *mf* stenographer

sténographie [stenɔgrafi] *f* stenography

sténographier [stenɔgrafje] *tr* to take down in shorthand

stéréo [stereo] *adj invar* stereo ‖ *f*—**en stéréo** (electron) in stereo

stéréophonie [stereɔfɔni] *f* stereophonic sound system; **en stéréophonie** stereophonic (*e.g., broadcast*)

stéréoscopique [stereɔskɔpik] *adj* stereo, stereoscopic

stéréoty·pé -pée [stereɔtipe] *adj* stereotyped

stérile [steril] *adj* sterile

stériliser [sterilize] *tr* to sterilize

stérilité [sterilite] *f* sterility

sterling [stɛrliŋ] *adj invar* sterling

stéthoscope [stetɔskɔp] *m* stethoscope

stick [stik] *m* walking stick

stigmate [stigmat] *m* stigma

stigmatiser [stigmatize] *tr* to stigmatize

stimu·lant [stimylɑ̃] **-lante** [lɑ̃t] *adj & m* stimulant

stimulateur [stimylatœr] *m* pacemaker

stimuler [stimyle] *tr* to stimulate

stimu·lus [stimylys] *m* (*pl* **-li** [li]) (physiol) stimulus

stipendier [stipɑ̃dje] *tr* to hire (*e.g., an assassin*); bribe

stipuler [stipyle] *tr* to stipulate

stock [stɔk] *m* goods, stock; hoard

stocker [stɔke] *tr & intr* to stockpile

stockiste [stɔkist] *m* authorized dealer (*carrying parts, motors, etc.*)

stoï·cien [stɔisjɛ̃] **-cienne** [sjɛn] *adj & mf* Stoic

stoïque [stɔik] *adj* stoical ‖ *mf* stoic

stop [stɔp] *m* stop; stoplight; **du stop** (coll) hitchhiking ‖ *interj* stop!

stoppage [stɔpaʒ] *m* reweaving, invisible mending

stopper [stɔpe] *tr* to reweave; stop ‖ *intr* to stop

store [stɔr] *m* blind; window awning; outside window shade

strabique [strabik] *adj* squint-eyed

strabisme [strabism] *m* squint

strapontin [strapɔ̃tɛ̃] *m* jump seat; (theat) attached folding seat

strass [stras] *m* paste (*jewelry*)

stratagème [strataʒɛm] *m* stratagem

strate [strat] *f* (geol) stratum

stratège [strateʒ] *m* strategist

stratégie [strateʒi] *f* strategy

stratégique [strateʒik] *adj* strategic(al)

stratégiste [strateʒist] *m* strategist

stratifier [stratifje] *tr & ref* to stratify

stratosphère [stratɔsfɛr] *f* stratosphere

strict stricte [strikt] *adj* strict

stri·dent [stridɑ̃] **-dente** [dɑ̃t] *adj* strident

strie [stri] *f* streak; stripe

strier [strije] *tr* to streak; score, groove

strip-teaseuse [striptisøz] *f* (*pl* **-teaseuses**) stripteaser

strontium [strɔ̃sjɔm] *m* strontium

strophe [strɔf] *f* verse, stanza; strophe

structu·ral -rale [stryktyral] *adj* (*pl* **-raux** [ro]) structural

structure [stryktyr] *f* structure

strychnine [striknin] *f* strychnine

stuc [styk] *m* stucco; **enduire de stuc** to stucco

stu·dieux [stydjø] **-dieuse** [djøz] *adj* studious

studio [stydjo] *m* studio

stupé·fait [stypefɛ] **-faite** [fɛt] *adj* dumfounded, amazed

stupé·fiant [stypefjɑ̃] **-fiante** [fjɑ̃t] *adj* astounding ‖ *m* drug, narcotic

stupéfier [stypefje] *tr* to astound; stupefy (*as with a drug*)

stupeur [stypœr] *f* stupor; amazement

stupide [stypid] *adj* stupid

stupidité [stypidite] *f* stupidity

stuquer [styke] *tr* to stucco

style [stil] *m* style; stylus

styler [stile] *tr* to train

stylet [stilɛ] *m* stiletto

styliser [stilize] *tr* to stylize

stylo [stilo] *m* pen, fountain pen; **stylo à bille** ball-point pen; **stylo à réservoir** fountain pen

stylo-bille [stilobij] *m* (*pl* **stylos-billes**) ball-point pen

stylo-feutre [stiloføtr] *m* (*pl* **stylos-feutres**) felt-tip pen

styptique [stiptik] *adj & m* styptic

suaire [sɥɛr] *m* shroud, winding sheet

suave [sɥav] *adj* sweet (*perfume, music, etc.*); bland (*food*); suave

subcons·cient [sypkɔ̃sjɑ̃] **-ciente** [sjɑ̃t] *& m* subconscious

subdiviser [sybdivize] *tr* to subdivide

subir [sybir] *tr* to submit to; undergo; feel, experience; take (*an exam*); serve (*a sentence*)

su·bit [sybi] **-bite** [bit] *adj* sudden

subjec·tif [sybʒɛktif] **-tive** [tiv] *adj* subjective

subjonc·tif [sybʒɔ̃ktif] **-tive** [tiv] *adj & m* subjunctive

subjuguer [sybʒyge] *tr* to dominate; spellbind

sublime [syblim] *adj* sublime

sublimer [syblime] *tr* to sublimate

submerger [sybmɛrʒe] §38 *tr* to submerge

submersible [sybmɛrsibl] *adj & m* submersible

submersion [sybmɛrsjɔ̃] *f* submersion

subodorer [sybodore] *tr* to scent (*game*); (fig) to scent (*a plot*)

subordon·né -née [sybɔrdɔne] *adj & mf* subordinate

subordonner [sybɔrdɔne] *tr* to subordinate

suborner [sybɔrne] *tr* to bribe

subrécargue [sybrekarg] *m* supercargo

subreptice [sybrɛptis] *adj* surreptitious

subsé·quent [sypsekɑ̃] **-quente** [kɑ̃t] *adj* subsequent

subside [sypsid], [sybzid] *m* subsidy

subsidiaire [sypsidjɛr] *adj* subsidiary

subsistance [sybzistɑ̃s], [sypsistɑ̃s] *f* subsistence; (mil) rations

subsister [sybziste], [sypsiste] *intr* to subsist

substance [sypstɑ̃s] *f* substance; **en substance** briefly

substan·tiel -tielle [sypstɑ̃sjɛl] *adj* substantial

substan·tif [sypstɑ̃tif] **-tive** [tiv] *adj & m* substantive

substituer [sypstitɥe] *tr*—**substituer qn or q.ch. à** to substitute s.o. or s.th. for, e.g., **une biche fut substituée à Iphigénie** a hind was substituted for Iphigenia ‖ *ref*—**se substituer à** to take the place of

substitut [sypstity] *m* substitute

substitution [sypstitysjɔ̃] *f* substitution

substrat [sypstra] *m* substratum

subterfuge [syptɛrfyʒ] *m* subterfuge

sub·til -tile [syptil] *adj* subtle; fine (*powder, dust, etc.*); quick (*poison*); delicate (*scent*); clever (*crook*)

subtiliser [syptilize] *tr* to pick (*a purse*) ‖ *intr* to split hairs

subtilité [syptilite] *f* subtlety

subur·bain [sybyrbɛ̃] **-baine** [bɛn] *adj* suburban

subvenir [sybvənir] §72 *intr* to supply, provide, satisfy

subvention [sybvãsjɔ̃] *f* subsidy, subvention

subventionner [sybvãsjɔne] *tr* to subsidize

subver·sif [sybvɛrsif] **-sive** [siv] *adj* subversive

subvertir [sybvɛrtir] *tr* to subvert

suc [syk] *m* juice; sap; (fig) essence

succéda·né -née [syksedane] *adj* & *m* substitute

succéder [syksede] §10 *intr* to happen; **succéder à** to succeed, follow, e.g., **son fils lui succédera** his son will succeed him ‖ *ref* (*pp* **succédé** *invar*) to follow one another, follow one after the other

succès [syksɛ] *m* success; outcome; **avoir du succès** to be a success

succes·sif [syksɛsif] **-sive** [siv] *adj* successive

succession [syksɛsjɔ̃] *f* succession; inheritance; heirs

suc·cinct [syksɛ̃] **-cincte** [sɛ̃t] *adj* succinct; scanty; meager

succion [syksjɔ̃] *f* suction

succomber [sykɔ̃be] *intr* to succumb

succursale [sykyrsal] *f* branch

sucer [syse] §51 *tr* to suck

sucette [sysɛt] *f* pacifier; lollipop, sucker

su·ceur [sysœr] **-ceuse** [søz] *adj* sucking ‖ *m* nozzle

suçon [sysɔ̃] *m* (coll) hickie

suçoter [sysɔte] *tr* to suck away at

sucre [sykr] *m* sugar; **sucre brut** brown sugar; **sucre candi** rock candy; **sucre de canne** cane sugar; **sucre d'érable** maple sugar; **sucre en morceaux** cube sugar, lump sugar; **sucre glace** confectioners' sugar; **sucre semoule** granulated sugar

su·cré -crée [sykre] *adj* sugary; with sugar, e.g., **du café sucré** coffee with sugar ‖ *f*—**faire la sucrée** to be mealy-mouthed

sucrer [sykre] *tr* to sugar; (slang) to take away, cut out ‖ *ref* (slang) to grab the lion's share

sucrerie [sykrəri] *f* sugar refinery; **sucreries** candy

su·crier [sykrije] **-crière** [krijɛr] *adj* sugar ‖ *m* sugar bowl

sud [syd] *adj invar* south, southern ‖ *m* south; **du sud** southern; **faire le sud** to steer southward; **vers le sud** southward

sud-améri·cain [sydamerikɛ̃] **-caine** [kɛn] *adj* South American ‖ (*cap*) *mf* (*pl* **Sud-Américains**) South American

sudation [sydasjɔ̃] *f* sweating

sud-est [sydɛst] *adj invar* & *m* southeast

sudiste [sydist] *mf* Southerner (*in U.S.A.*)

sud-ouest [sydwɛst] *adj invar* & *m* southwest

suède [sɥɛd] *m* suede ‖ (*cap*) *f* Sweden; **la Suède** Sweden

sué·dois [sɥedwa] **-doise** [dwaz] *adj* Swedish ‖ *m* Swedish (*language*) ‖ (*cap*) *mf* Swede

suée [sɥe] *f* sweating

suer [sɥe] *tr* & *intr* to sweat

sueur [sɥœr] *f* sweat

suffire [syfir] §66, §96 *intr* to suffice; **il suffit de** + *inf* it suffices to + *inf;* **suffire à** to be sufficient for, be adequate to, meet, satisfy, e.g., **suffire à mes besoins** to meet my needs; **suffire à** + *inf* to suffice to + *inf;* **suffit!** enough! ‖ *ref* (*pp* **suffi** *invar*) to be self-sufficient

suffisamment [syfizamã] *adv* sufficiently, adequately

suffisance [syfizãs] *f* sufficiency; self-sufficiency, smugness

suffi·sant [syfizã] **-sante** [zãt] *adj* sufficient; smug, sophomoric; impudent ‖ *mf* prig

suffixe [syfiks] *m* suffix

suffo·cant [syfɔkã] **-cante** [kãt] *adj* suffocating, stifling; astonishing, stunning

suffoquer [syfɔke] *tr* & *intr* to suffocate, choke, stifle, smother

suffrage [syfraʒ] *m* suffrage, vote; public approval; **au suffrage universel** by popular vote; **suffrage capacitaire** suffrage contingent upon literacy tests; **suffrage censitaire** suffrage upon payment of taxes

suggérer [sygʒere] §10, §97, §98 *tr* to suggest

sugges·tif [sygʒɛstif] **-tive** [tiv] *adj* suggestive

suggestion [sygʒɛstjɔ̃] *f* suggestion

suggestionner [sygʒɛstjɔne] *tr* to influence by means of suggestion

suicide [sɥisid] *adj* suicidal ‖ *m* suicide (*act*)

suici·dé -dée [sɥiside] *adj* dead by suicide ‖ *mf* suicide (*person*)

suicider [sɥiside] *ref* to commit suicide

suie [sɥi] *f* soot

suif [sɥif] *m* tallow

suint [sɥɛ̃] *m* wool fat, wool grease

suinter [sɥɛ̃te] *intr* to seep, ooze; sweat (*said of wall*); run (*said of wound*)

suis [sɥi] *v* see **être;** see **suivre**

suisse [sɥis] *adj* Swiss; **faire suisse** to eat or drink by oneself; to go Dutch ‖ *m* Swiss guard; uniformed usher; **petit suisse** cream cheese ‖ (*cap*) *f* Switzerland; **la Suisse** Switzerland ‖ **Suisse Suissesse** [sɥises] *mf* Swiss (*person*)

suite [sɥit] *f* suite; consequence; continuation, sequel (*of literary work*); sequence, series; **à la suite de** after; **de suite** in succession; in a row; **par la suite** later on; **par suite** consequently; **par suite de** because of

sui·vant [sɥivã] **-vante** [vãt] *adj* next, following, subsequent ‖ *mf* follower; next (person) ‖ *f* servant, confidante ‖ **suivant** *adv*—**suivant que** according as ‖ **suivant** *prep* according to

sui·veur [sɥivœr] **-veuse** [vøz] *adj* follow-up (*e.g., car*) ‖ *mf* follower

sui·vi -vie [sɥivi] *adj* connected, coherent; popular

suivre [sɥivr] §67 *tr* to follow; take (*a course in school*); **suivre la mode** (fig) to follow suit ‖ *intr* to follow; **à suivre** to be continued ‖ *ref* to follow in succession; follow one after the other

su·jet [syʒɛ] **-jette** [ʒɛt] *adj* subject; apt, liable; inclined ‖ *mf* subject (*of a government*); **mauvais sujet** ne'er-do-well ‖ *m* subject, topic; (gram) subject; **au sujet de** about, concerning

sujétion [syʒesjɔ̃] *f* subjection

sulfamide [sylfamid] *m* sulfa drug

sulfate [sylfat] *m* sulphate

sulfure [sylfyr] *m* sulfide

sulfurique [sylfyrik] *adj* sulfuric

sultan [syltɑ̃] *m* sultan

sumac [symak] *m* sumac; **sumac vénéneux** poison ivy

sunlight [sœnlaɪt] *m invar* (mov, telv) projector

super [sypɛr] *m* (coll) high-test gas

superbe [sypɛrb] *adj* superb; proud ‖ *m* proud person ‖ *f* pride

supercarburant [sypɛrkarbyrɑ̃] *m* high-test gasoline

supercherie [sypɛrʃəri] *f* hoax, swindle

superdécrochage [sypɛrdekrɔʃaʒ] *m* (aer) deep stall

superfétatoire [sypɛrfetatwar] *adj* redundant

superficie [sypɛrfisi] *f* surface, area

superfi·ciel -cielle [sypɛrfisjɛl] *adj* superficial

super·flu -flue [sypɛrfly] *adj* superfluous ‖ *m* superfluity, excess

supé·rieur -rieure [syperjœr] *adj* superior; higher; upper (*e.g., story*); **supérieur à** above; more than ‖ *mf* superior

supérieurement [syperjœrmɑ̃] *adv* superlatively, exceptionally

supériorité [syperjɔrite] *f* superiority

superla·tif [sypɛrlatif] **-tive** [tiv] *adj & m* superlative; **au superlatif** superlatively; in the superlative

supermarché [sypɛrmarʃe] *m* supermarket

superposer [sypɛrpoze] *tr* to superimpose ‖ *ref* to intervene

supersonique [sypɛrsɔnik] *adj* supersonic

supersti·tieux [sypɛrstisjø] **-tieuse** [sjøz] *adj* superstitious

superstition [sypɛrstisjɔ̃] *f* superstition

superstrat [sypɛrstra] *m* superstratum

superviser [sypɛrvize] *tr* to inspect; revise; correct; supervise

supplanter [syplɑ̃te] *tr* to supplant

suppléance [sypleɑ̃s] *f* substituting; temporary post

sup·pléant [sypleɑ̃] **-pléante** [pleɑ̃t] *adj* substituting ‖ *mf* substitute (*e.g., a teacher, judge*)

suppléer [syplee] *tr* to supply; take the place of; make up for (*what is lacking*); fill in (*the gaps*); substitute for (*s.o.*); fill (*a vacancy*) ‖ *intr*—**suppléer à** to make up for (*s.th.*)

supplément [syplemɑ̃] *m* supplement; extra charge

supplémentaire [syplemɑ̃tɛr] *adj* supplementary, additional, extra; supplemental

supplé·tif [sypletif] **-tive** [tiv] *adj & m* (mil) auxiliary

sup·pliant [syplijɑ̃] **-pliante** [plijɑ̃t] *adj & mf* suppliant, supplicant

supplice [syplis] *m* torture; punishment; **être au supplice** to be in agony

supplicier [syplisje] *tr* to torture to death; torment

supplier [syplije] §97, §99 *tr* to beseech, implore, supplicate; **je vous en supplie** I beg you; **supplier qn de** to implore s.o. to

supplique [syplik] *f* petition

support [sypɔr] *m* support, prop, pillar, bracket, strut; standard (*e.g., for a lamp*)

support-chaussette [sypɔrʃosɛt] *m* (*pl* **supports-chaussette**) garter (*for men*)

supporter [sypɔrtœr] *m* fan, devotee, supporter, partisan ‖ [sypɔrte] *tr* to support, prop up; bear, endure; stand, tolerate, put up with ‖ *intr*—**supporter de** + *inf* to tolerate or stand for + *ger* ‖ *ref* to be tolerated; put up with each other

suppo·sé -sée [sypoze] *adj* supposed, admitted; spurious, assumed ‖ **supposé** *prep* supposing, admitting, granting

supposer [sypoze] §95 *tr* to suppose; imply; **à supposer que . . .** suppose that . . . ; **supposer un testament** to palm off a forged will

supposition [sypozisjɔ̃] *f* supposition; forgery, fraudulent substitution or alteration; **supposition de part** or **supposition d'enfant** false claim of maternity and maternal rights

suppositoire [sypozitwar] *m* suppository

suppôt [sypo] *m* henchman, tool, agitator, hireling; **suppôt de Bacchus** drunkard; **suppôt du diable** imp

suppression [sypresjɔ̃] *f* suppression; elimination (*of a job*); discontinuance (*of a festival*); killing (*of a person*); **suppression de part** or **suppression d'enfant** concealment of a child's birth or death

supprimer [syprime] *tr* to suppress, cancel, abolish; cut out, omit; (slang) to eliminate, liquidate ‖ *ref* to kill oneself

suppurer [sypyre] *intr* to suppurate

supputation [sypytasjɔ̃] *f* calculation, evaluation, reckoning

supputer [sypyte] *tr* to calculate (*e.g., forthcoming profits, expenses*)

suprématie [sypremasi] *f* supremacy

suprême [syprɛm] *adj* supreme; last

sur sure [syr] *adj* sour ‖ **sur** *prep* on, over; about, concerning; with (*on the person of*); out of, in, e.g., **un jour sur quatre** one day out of four, one day in four; after, e.g., **page sur page** page after page; **sur ce, sur quoi** whereupon; **sur le fait** in the act

sûr sûre [syr] §93 *adj* sure; trustworthy; safe; certain; **à coup sûr, pour sûr** for sure, without fail

surabon·dant [syrabɔ̃dɑ̃] **-dante** [dɑ̃t] *adj* superabundant

surabonder [syrabɔ̃de] *intr* to superabound; **surabonder de** or **en** to be glutted with
surajouter [syraʒute] *tr* to add on
suralimentation [syralimɑ̃tasjɔ̃] *f* forced feeding; (aut) supercharging
suran·né -née [syrane] *adj* outmoded, out-of-date, superannuated; expired (*driver's license, passport, etc.*)
surboum [syrbum] *f* (slang) dance, hop
surcharge [syrʃarʒ] *f* surcharge; overwriting; (sports) handicap (*of weight on a horse*); (comp) overload(ing)
surcharger [syrʃarʒe] §38 *tr* to surcharge; write a word over (*another word*); write a word over a crossed-out word on (*a document*)
surchauffe [syrʃof] *f* superheating; overheating (*of the economy*)
surchauffer [syrʃofe] *tr* to superheat (*steam; an oven*); overheat (*an oven, iron, etc.*)
surchoix [syrʃwa] *m* finest quality
surclasser [syrklase] *tr* to outclass
surcompo·sé -sée [syrkɔ̃poze] *adj* (gram) double-compound
surcompression [syrkɔ̃presjɔ̃] *f* pressurization, high compression
surcompri·mé -mée [syrkɔ̃prime] *adj* high-compression (*engine*)
surcomprimer [syrkɔ̃prime] *tr* to supercharge; pressurize
surcontrer [syrkɔ̃tre] *tr* (cards) to redouble
surcouper [syrkupe] *tr* (cards) to overtrump
surcroît [syrkrwɑ], [syrkrwa] *m* addition, increase; **de surcroît** or **par sucroît** in addition, extra
surdi-mutité [syrdimytite] *f* deaf-muteness
surdité [syrdite] *f* deafness
surdosage [syrdosaʒ] *m* overdose
su·reau [syro] *m* (*pl* **-reaux**) elderberry
surélévation [syrelevasjɔ̃] *f* escalation, excessive increase; extra story (*added to a building*)
surélever [syrelve] §2 *tr* to raise, raise up; drive up; jack up
sûrement [syrmɑ̃] *adv* surely, certainly; safely; steadily, confidently
surenchère [syrɑ̃ʃɛr] *f* higher bid; **surenchère électorale** campaign promise, political outbidding
surenchérir [syrɑ̃ʃerir] *intr* to make a higher bid; **surenchérir sur qn** to outbid s.o.
surestimer [syrɛstime] *tr* to overestimate
su·ret [syrɛ] **-rette** [rɛt] *adj* tart
sûreté [syrte] *f* safety, security; sureness (*of touch; of taste*); surety; **à sûreté intégrée** fail-safe; **en sûreté** out of harm's way; in custody, confined (*e.g., in prison*); **sûreté individuelle** legal protection (*e.g., against arbitrary arrest*); **Sûreté nationale** or **la Sûreté** central intelligence; **sûretés** precautions; guarantees, security (*for a loan*)
surévaluer [syrevalɥe] *tr* to overvalue
surexciter [syrɛksite] *tr* to overexcite

surexposer [syrɛkspoze] *tr* (phot) to overexpose
surexposition [syrɛkspozisjɔ̃] *f* (phot) overexposure
surface [syrfas] *f* surface; financial backing; **faire surface** to surface (*said of a submarine*)
surfaire [syrfɛr] §29 *tr* & *intr* to overprice; to overrate
sur·fin [syrfɛ̃] **-fine** [fin] *adj* superfine
surgélation [syrʒelasjɔ̃] *f* deep freezing
surge·lé -lée [syrʒəle] *adj* frozen (*foods*)
surgeon [syrʒɔ̃] *m* offshoot, sucker
surgir [syrʒir] *intr* to spring up; arise, appear; arrive, reach port
surglacer [syrglase] §51 *tr* to glaze; ice (*cake*)
surhaussement [syrosmɑ̃] *m* heightening, raising; banking (*of road*)
surhausser [syrose] *tr* to heighten, raise; force up (*prices*); force up the price of (*s.th.*); bank (*a road*)
surhomme [syrɔm] *m* superman
surhu·main [syrymɛ̃] **-maine** [mɛn] *adj* superhuman
surimpression [syrɛ̃presjɔ̃] *f* superimposition; (mov) montage
surintendant [syrɛ̃tɑ̃dɑ̃] *m* superintendent, administrator
surir [syrir] *intr* to turn sour
surjeu [syrʒø] *m* playback
sur-le-champ [syrlʃɑ̃] *adv* on the spot, immediately
surlendemain [syrlɑ̃dmɛ̃] *m*—**le surlendemain** the second day after, two days later
surlier [syrlje] *tr* to whip (*a rope*)
surliure [syrljyr] *f* whipping (*of rope*)
surmédicaliser [syrmedikalize] *intr* (med) to overprescribe, overmedicate
surmenage [syrmənaʒ] *m* overworking, fatigue
surmener [syrməne] §2 *tr* & *ref* to overwork
sur·moi [syrmwa] *m* superego
surmonter [syrmɔ̃te] *tr* to surmount ‖ *intr* to come to the top (*said of oil in water*)
surmouler [syrmule] *tr* to cast from another mold
surmultiplication [syrmyltiplikasjɔ̃] *f* (aut) overdrive
surnager [syrnaʒe] §38 *intr* to float; survive
surnatu·rel -relle [syrnatyrɛl] *adj* & *m* supernatural
surnom [syrnɔ̃] *m* nickname, sobriquet
surnombre [syrnɔ̃br] *m* excess number; **en surnombre** supernumerary; spare; **rester en surnombre** to be odd man; **surnombre des habitants** overpopulation
surnommer [syrnɔme] *tr* to name, call, nickname
surnuméraire [syrnymerɛr] *adj* supernumerary, extra ‖ *mf* substitute, supernumerary
suroffre [syrɔfr] *f* better or higher offer
suroît [syrwa] *m* southwest wind
surpasser [syrpɑse] *tr* to surpass; astonish ‖ *ref* to outdo oneself

surpaye [syrpɛj] *f* extra pay

surpayer [syrpɛje] §49 *tr* to pay too much to; pay too much for

surpeu·plé -plée [syrpœple] *adj* overpopulated

surpeuplement [syrpœpləmɑ̃] *m* overpopulation

surplis [syrpli] *m* surplice

surplomber [syrplɔ̃be] *tr* & *intr* to overhang; to look down upon

surplus [syrply] *m* surplus; **au surplus** moreover

surpopulation [syrpɔpylɑsjɔ̃] *f* overpopulation

surprendre [syrprɑ̃dr] §56, §96 *tr* to surprise; come upon by chance; detect; overtake, catch

surprise [syrpriz] *f* surprise

surprise-party or **surprise-partie** [syrprizparti] *f* (*pl* **surprises-parties**) private dancing party

surproduction [syrprɔdyksjɔ̃] *f* overproduction

surréalisme [syrealism] *m* surrealism

surrégénérateur [syreʒeneratœr] **-trice** [tris] *adj* (nucl) breeder (reactor)

surréservation [syresɛrvɑsjɔ̃] *f* overbooking

sursaut [syrso] *m* sudden start; **en sursaut** with a start

sursauter [syrsote] *intr* to give a jump, start, jerk

surseoir [syrswar] §5B (*fut* **surseoirai**, etc.) *intr*—**surseoir à** (law) to defer, postpone, stay, e.g., **surseoir à une exécution** to stay an execution

sursis [syrsi] *m* suspension (*of penalty*); postponement, deferment, stay; **en sursis, avec sursis** suspended (*sentence*)

surtaxe [syrtaks] *f* surtax, surcharge; **surtaxe postale** postage due

surtaxer [syrtakse] *tr* to surtax

surtension [syrtɑ̃sjɔ̃] *f* (elec) surge

surtout [syrtu] *m* topcoat; centerpiece, epergne ‖ *adv* especially, particularly

surveillance [syrvɛjɑ̃s] *f* supervision; (*by the police*) surveillance

surveil·lant [syrvɛjɑ̃] **-lante** [jɑ̃t] *mf* supervisor, superintendent, overseer; **surveillant d'études** study-hall proctor

surveiller [syrvɛje] *tr* to inspect, put under surveillance; supervise, watch over, monitor

survenir [syrvənir] §72 *intr* (*aux:* ÊTRE) to arrive unexpectedly, happen suddenly, crop up

survenue [syrvəny] *f* unexpected arrival

survêtement [syrvɛtmɑ̃] *m* track suit, sweat shirt

survie [syrvi] *f* survival; afterlife; (law) survivorship; **survie du plus apte** survival of the fittest

survivance [syrvivɑ̃s] *f* survival

survi·vant [syrvivɑ̃] **-vante** [vɑ̃t] *adj* surviving ‖ *mf* survivor

survivre [syrvivr] §74 *intr* to survive; **survivre à** to survive, outlive, e.g., **elle lui**

survécut she survived him ‖ *ref* (*pp* **survécu** *invar*) (fig) to outlive one's time; **se survivre dans** to live on in

survoler [syrvɔle] *tr* to fly over; skim over (*e.g., a problem*)

survol·té -tée [syrvɔlte] *adj* electrified, charged with emotion

sus [sys], [sy] *adv*—**en sus de** in addition to ‖ *interj* up and at it (them)!

susceptible [sysɛptibl] *adj* sensitive, touchy; **susceptible de** capable of, liable to, susceptible of

susciter [sysite] *tr* to stir up, evoke, rouse; (lit) to raise up

sus·dit [sysdi] **-dite** [dit] *adj* aforesaid

susmention·né -née [sysmɑ̃sjɔne] *adj* aforementioned

sus·pect [syspɛ], [syspɛkt] **-pecte** [pɛkt] *adj* suspect, suspicious ‖ *mf* suspect

suspecter [syspɛkte] *tr* to suspect

suspendre [syspɑ̃dr] *tr* to suspend; hang, hang up; **être suspendu aux lèvres de qn** to hang on s.o.'s every word ‖ *ref* to be hung; hang on

suspen·du -due [syspɑ̃dy] *adj* suspended; hanging

suspens [syspɑ̃] *m* suspense; **en suspens** suspended; in abeyance; outstanding; in suspense

suspension [syspɑ̃sjɔ̃] *f* suspension

suspi·cieux [syspisjø] **-cieuse** [sjøz] *adj* suspicious

suspicion [syspisjɔ̃] *f* suspicion

sustenter [systɑ̃te] *tr* to sustain ‖ *ref* to sustain oneself

susurrer [sysyre] *tr* & *intr* to murmur, whisper

susvi·sé -sée [sysvize] *adj* above-mentioned

suture [sytyr] *f* suture

suturer [sytyre] *tr* to suture

suze·rain [syzrɛ̃] **-raine** [rɛn] *adj* & *mf* suzerain

svastika [svastika] *m* swastika

svelte [svɛlt] *adj* slender, lithe, willowy

S.V.P. [ɛsvepe] *m* (letterword) (**s'il vous plaît**) if you please, please

sweater [switœr] *m* sweater; **sweater à col roulé** turtleneck sweater

sycophante [sikɔfɑ̃t] *m* informer

syllabe [silab] *f* syllable

syllogisme [silɔʒism] *m* syllogism

sylphe [silf] *m* sylph

sylvestre [silvɛstr] *adj* sylvan

symbole [sɛ̃bɔl] *m* symbol; **Symbole des apôtres** Apostles' Creed

symbolique [sɛ̃bɔlik] *adj* symbolic(al)

symboliser [sɛ̃bɔlize] *tr* to symbolize

symbolisme [sɛ̃bɔlism] *m* symbolism

symétrie [simetri] *f* symmetry

symétrique [simetrik] *adj* symmetric(al)

sympa [sɛ̃pa] *adj* (coll) likable, attractive

sympathie [sɛ̃pati] *f* fondness, liking; sympathy

sympathique [sɛ̃patik] *adj* likable, attractive; sympathetic

sympathi·sant [sɛ̃patizɑ̃] **-sante** [zɑ̃t] *adj* sympathetic ‖ *mf* sympathizer

sympathiser [sɛ̃patize] *intr* to get along well; **sympathiser avec** to be drawn toward; support

symphonie [sɛ̃fɔni] *f* symphony

symptôme [sɛ̃ptom] *m* symptom

synagogue [sinagɔg] *f* synagogue

synchrone [sɛ̃krɔn] *adj* synchronous

synchroniser [sɛ̃krɔnize] *tr* to synchronize

syncope [sɛ̃kɔp] *f* faint, swoon, syncope; syncopation

syndicat [sɛ̃dika] *m* labor union; **syndicat de distribution** (journ) syndicate; **syndicat d'initiative** chamber of commerce; **syndicat patronal** employers' association

syndicats-patrons [sɛ̃dikapatrɔ̃] *adj invar* labor-management

syndi·qué -quée [sɛ̃dike] *adj* union ‖ *mf* union member

syndiquer [sɛ̃dike] *tr & ref* to unionize

syndrome [sɛ̃drom] *m* syndrome; **syndrome de l'usure au travail** burnout; **syndrome d'immunodéficience acquise** acquired immune-deficiency syndrome, AIDS

synonyme [sinɔnim] *adj* synonymous ‖ *m* synonym

synopsis [sinɔpsis] *m & f* (mov) synopsis

syntaxe [sɛ̃taks] *f* syntax

synthèse [sɛ̃tɛz] *f* synthesis

synthétique [sɛ̃tetik] *adj* synthetic

synthétiser [sɛ̃tetize] *tr* to synthesize

syntonisation [sɛ̃tɔnizɑsjɔ̃] *f* tuning (*of radio*)

syntoniser [sɛ̃tɔnize] *tr* to tune in

syphilis [sifilis] *f* syphilis

Syrie [siri] *f* Syria; **la Syrie** Syria

sy·rien [sirjɛ̃] **-rienne** [rjɛn] *adj* Syrian ‖ (*cap*) *mf* Syrian (*person*)

systématique [sistematik] *adj* systematic; routine

systématiser [sistematize] *tr* to systematize

système [sistɛm] *m* system; **courir, porter,** or **taper sur le système à qn** (slang) to get on s.o.'s nerves; **système D** (coll) resourcefulness; **système d'exploitation** (comp) operating system

systole [sistɔl] *f* systole

T

T, t [te] *m invar* twentieth letter of the French alphabet

t. *abbr* (**tome**) vol.

t' = **te** before vowel or mute **h**

ta [ta] §88 your

tabac [taba] *m* tobacco; tobacco shop; **avoir le gros tabac** (slang) to be a hit; **passer qn à tabac** (coll) to give s.o. the third degree; **tabac à chiquer** chewing tobacco; **tabac à priser** snuff

tabagie [tabaʒi] *f* smoke-filled room

tabasser [tabase] *tr* (slang) to give a licking to, shellac

tabatière [tabatjɛr] *f* snuffbox; skylight, dormer window

tabernacle [tabɛrnakl] *m* tabernacle

table [tabl] *f* table; **aimer la table** to like good food; **à table!** dinner is served!; **dresser** or **mettre la table** to set the table; **faire table rase** to make a clean sweep; **sainte table** altar rail; **se mettre à table** (slang) to tell all, to confess, to squeal; **table à abattants** gate-leg table; **table à ouvrage** worktable; **table à rallonges** extension table; **table à salade** salad bar; **table de chevet, table de nuit** bedside table; **table d'écoute** wiretap; **table de jeu** card table; **table des matières** table of contents; **table de toilette** dressing table; **table d'hôte** table d'hôte; chef's special; **table d'opération** operating table; **table du téléphone** telephone table; **table gigogne** nest of tables; **table interurbaine** long-distance switchboard; **table roulante**

serving cart; **tenir table ouverte** to keep open house

ta·bleau [tablo] *m* (*pl* **-bleaux**) painting, picture; scoreboard; board; table, catalogue; panel (*of jurors*); **former un tableau** (law) to empanel a jury; **jouer sur les deux tableaux** (slang) to play both sides of the street; **tableau d'affichage** bulletin board; **tableau d'avancement** seniority list; **tableau de bord** dashboard; instrument panel; **tableau de distribution** switchboard; **tableau d'honneur** honor roll; **tableau noir** blackboard; **tableau vivant** tableau

tableautier [tablotje] *m* tabulator (*of typewriter*)

tabler [table] *intr*—**tabler sur** to count on; use as a base

tablette [tablɛt] *f* shelf; mantelpiece; bar (*e.g., of chocolate*); **rayez cela de vos tablettes** don't count on it; **tablettes** pocket notebook

table-valise [tabləvaliz] *f* (*pl* **tables-valises**) folding table

tablier [tablije] *m* apron; roadway (*of bridge*); hood (*of chimney*); **tablier de fer** protective shutter (*on store window*)

ta·bou -bou or **-boue** [tabu] *adj & m* taboo

tabouret [taburɛ] *m* stool; footstool

tabulaire [tabylɛr] *adj* tabular

tabulateur [tabylatœr] *m* tabulator

tac [tak] *m* click, clack; **du tac au tac** tit for tat; **tac tac tac!** rat-a-tat-tat!

tache [taʃ] *f* spot, stain; blemish, flaw; blot, smear; speck; **faire tache** to be out of place; **faire tache d'huile** to spread; **sans tache** spotless, unblemished; **tache de rousseur, tache de son** freckle; **tache de vin** birthmark; **tache originelle** original sin; **tache solaire** sunspot

tâche [tɑʃ] *f* task, job; **prendre à tâche de** to try to; **travailler à la tâche** to do piecework

tacher [taʃe] *tr* & *ref* to spot, stain

tâcher [tɑʃe] §96, §97 *tr*—**tâcher que** to see to it that ‖ *intr*—**tâcher de** to try to; **y tâcher** to try

tâcheron [tɑʃrɔ̃] *m* small jobber; pieceworker; hard worker; wage slave

tacheter [taʃte] §34 *tr* to spot, speckle

tacite [tasit] *adj* tacit

taciturne [tasityrn] *adj* taciturn

tacot [tako] *m* (coll) jalopy

tact [takt] *m* tact; sense of touch

tacticien [taktisjɛ̃] *m* tactician

tactique [taktik] *adj* tactical ‖ *f* tactics

taffetas [tafta] *m* taffeta; **taffetas gommé** adhesive tape

Tage [taʒ] *m* Tagus

taïaut [tajo] *interj* tallyho!

taie [tɛ] *f* (pathol) leukoma; **avoir une taie sur l'œil** (fig) to be blinded by prejudice; **taie d'oreiller** pillowcase

taillader [tɑjade] *tr* & *ref* to slash, cut

taille [tɑj] *f* cutting (*e.g., of diamond*); trimming (*e.g., of hedge*); height, stature; waist, waistline; size; cut (*of garment*); **à la taille de, de la taille de** to the measure of, suitable for; **avoir la taille fine** to have a slim waist; **de taille** big enough, strong enough; (coll) big; **être de taille à** to be up to, to be big enough to; **taille de guêpe** wasp waist; **taille en dessous** next size smaller; **taille en dessus** next size larger

tail·lé -lée [tɑje] *adj* cut; trimmed; **bien taillé** well-built; **taillé pour** cut out for

taille-crayon [tɑjkrɛjɔ̃] *m* (*pl* **-crayon** or **-crayons**) pencil sharpener

taille-douce [tɑjdus] *f* (*pl* **tailles-douces**) copperplate

taille-haies [tɑj-ɛ] *m invar* hedge cutter

taille-pain [tɑjpɛ̃] *m invar* bread knife; bread slicer

tailler [tɑje] *tr* to cut; sharpen (*a pencil*); prune, trim (*a tree*); carve (*stone*); clip (*hair*) ‖ *intr* (cards) to deal ‖ *ref* to carve out (*a path; a career*); (coll) to beat it

tailleur [tɑjœr] *m* tailor; woman's suit; (cards) dealer; **en tailleur** squatting (*while tailoring*); **tailleur de diamants** diamond cutter; **tailleur de pierre** stonecutter; **tailleur sur mesure** lady's tailor-made suit

taillis [tɑji] *m* thicket, copse

tain [tɛ̃] *m* silvering (*of mirror*)

taire [tɛr] §52 (3d *sg pres ind* **tait**) *tr* to hush up, hide; **la tairas-tu?** (slang) will you shut your trap?; **taire q.ch. à qn** to keep s.th. from s.o. ‖ *intr*—**faire taire** to silence ‖ *ref* to keep quiet, keep still; **se taire sur** to say nothing about; **tais-toi!** shut up!

talent [talɑ̃] *m* talent

talen·tueux [talɑ̃tɥø] **-tueuse** [tɥøz] *adj* talented

talkie-walkie [tɔkiwɔki] *m* (*pl* **talkies-walkies**) walkie-talkie

taloche [talɔʃ] *f* plastering trowel; (coll) clout, smack

talon [talɔ̃] *m* heel; stub

talonnage [talɔnaʒ] *m* tailgating

talonner [talɔne] *tr* to tail; tailgate; harass; dig one's spurs into ‖ *intr* to bump

talus [taly] *m* slope; embankment; **talus de neige** snowbank

tambour [tɑ̃bur] *m* drum; drummer; entryway; spool (*of reel*); **tambour battant** (coll) roughly; (coll) quickly; **tambour cylindrique** revolving door; **tambour de basque** tambourine; **tambour de freins** brake drum; **tambour de ville** town crier

tambouriner [tɑ̃burine] *tr* to drum; broadcast far and wide ‖ *intr* to beat a tattoo; drum

tambour-major [tɑ̃burmaʒɔr] *m* (*pl* **tambours-majors**) drum major

tamis [tami] *m* sieve; **passer au tamis** to sift; **tamis à farine** flour sifter

Tamise [tamiz] *f* Thames

tamiser [tamize] *tr* & *intr* to sift

tampon [tɑ̃pɔ̃] *m* plug; bung; swab; rubber stamp; buffer; cancellation, postmark; (surg) tampon; **tampon buvard** hand blotter; **tampon encreur** stamp pad

tamponner [tɑ̃pɔne] *tr* to swag, dab; bump, bump into; (surg) to tampon

tan [tɑ̃] *adj invar* tan ‖ *m* tanbark

tancer [tɑ̃se] §51 *tr* to scold

tandem [tɑ̃dɛm] *m* tandem; **en tandem** tandem

tandis que [tɑ̃dikǝ], [tɑ̃diskǝ] *conj* while; whereas

tangage [tɑ̃gaʒ] *m* (naut) pitching

Tanger [tɑ̃ʒe] *m* Tangier

tangible [tɑ̃ʒibl] *adj* tangible

tanguer [tɑ̃ge] *intr* to pitch (*said of ship*)

tanière [tanjɛr] *f* den, lair

tanker [tɑ̃kɛr] *m* oil tanker

tan·nant [tanɑ̃] **-nante** [nɑ̃t] *adj* (coll) boring

tanne [tan] *f* spot (*on leather*); blackhead

tanner [tane] *tr* to tan; (coll) to pester

tannerie [tanri] *f* tannery

tanneur [tanœr] *m* tanner

tan-sad [tɑ̃sad] *m* (*pl* **-sads**) rear seat (*of motorcycle*)

tant [tɑ̃] *adv* so, so much; so long; **en tant que** as; in so far as; **si tant est que** if it is true that; **tant bien que mal** somehow or other; **tant de** so many; so much; **tant mieux** so much the better; **tant pis** so much the worse; never mind; **tant qu'à faire** while we're (you're, etc.) at it; **tant que** as well as; as long as; **tant s'en faut** far from it; **tant soit peu** ever so little; **vous m'en direz tant** (coll) you've just said a mouthful

tante [tɑ̃t] *f* aunt; (slang) fairy; **ma tante** (coll) the hockshop

tantième [tãtjɛm] *m* percentage

tantine [tãtin] *f* (coll) auntie

tantôt [tãto] *m* (coll) afternoon ‖ *adv* in a little while; a little while ago; (coll) in the afternoon; **à tantôt** see you soon; **tantôt . . . tantôt** sometimes . . . sometimes

taon [tã] *m* horsefly

tapage [tapaʒ] *m* uproar

tapa·geur [tapaʒœr] **-geuse** [ʒøz] *adj* loud

tape [tap] *f* tap, slap

ta·pé -pée [tape] *adj* dried (*fruit*); rotten in spots; (coll) crazy; (slang) worn (*with age or fatigue*); **bien tapé** (coll) well done; (coll) nicely served; (coll) to the point

tape-à-l'œil [tapalœj] *adj* gaudy, showy ‖ *m invar* mere show

taper [tape] *tr* to tap, slap; type; (coll) to hit (*s.o. for money*) ‖ *intr* to tap, slap; type; (coll) to go to the head (*said of wine*); **ça tape ici** (slang) it hurts here; **taper dans** (coll) to use; **taper dans le mille** (coll) to succeed; **taper dans l'œil de qn** (coll) to make a hit with s.o.; **taper de** to hit (*e.g., 100 m.p.h.*); **taper des pieds** to stamp one's feet; **taper sur** (coll) to get on (*s.o.'s nerves*); **taper sur le ventre de qn** (coll) to give s.o. a poke in the ribs; **taper sur qn** (coll) to run down s.o., give s.o. a going-over

tapette [tapɛt] *f* carpet beater; fly swatter; handball; (slang) homo, fruit (*homosexual*); **avoir une fière tapette** (coll) to be a chatterbox; **tapette tue-mouche** fly swatter

tapin [tapɛ̃] *m* (coll) drummer boy; (slang) solicitation (*by a prostitute*)

tapinois [tapinwa]—**en tapinois** stealthily

tapir [tapir] *ref* to crouch, squat; hide

tapis [tapi] *m* carpet; rug; game of chance; **mettre sur le tapis** to bring up for discussion; **tapis de bain** bath mat; **tapis de sol** ground cloth; **tapis de table** table covering; **tapis d'orient** oriental rug; **tapis mur à mur** wall-to-wall carpeting; **tapis roulant** conveyor belt; moving sidewalk

tapis-brosse [tapibrɔs] *m* (*pl* **-brosses**) doormat

tapisser [tapise] *tr* to upholster; tapestry; wallpaper

tapisserie [tapisri] *f* upholstery; tapestry; **faire tapisserie** to be a wallflower

tapis·sier [tapisje] **-sière** [sjɛr] *mf* upholsterer; tapestry maker; paperhanger

tapoter [tapɔte] *tr & intr* to tap

taquet [takɛ] *m* wedge, peg; (mach) tappet; (naut) cleat; **taquet d'arrêt** (rr) scotch, wedge

ta·quin [takɛ̃] **-quine** [kin] *adj* teasing ‖ *mf* tease

taquiner [takine] *tr* to tease

taquinerie [takinri] *f* teasing

taraud [taro] *m* (mach) tap

tarauder [tarode] *tr* (mach) to tap; (coll) to pester

taraudeuse [tarodøz] *f* tap wrench

tard [tar] *m*—**sur le tard** late in the day; late in life ‖ *adv* late; **pas plus tard que** no later than; **plus tard** later on

tarder [tarde] §96, §97 *intr* to delay; **tarder à** to be long in ‖ *impers*—**il me** (**te**, etc.) **tarde de** + *inf* **I** (you, etc.) long to + *inf*, e.g., **il lui tarde de vous voir** he longs to see you

tar·dif [tardif] **-dive** [div] *adj* late; backward; tardy

tardivement [tardivmã] *adv* belatedly

tare [tar] *f* defect, blemish; taint; loss in value; tare (*weight*)

tarer [tare] *tr* to damage; taint; tare ‖ *ref* to spoil

targette [tarʒɛt] *f* latch

targuer [targe] *ref*—**se targuer de** to pride oneself on

tarière [tarjɛr] *f* auger, drill

tarif [tarif] *m* price list; rate, tariff; **plein tarif** full fare; **tarifs postaux** postal rates

tarifaire [tarifɛr] *adj* tariff

tarifer [tarife] *tr* to price; rate

tarir [tarir] *tr* to drain, exhaust, dry up ‖ *intr* to dry up, run dry; **ne pas tarir** to never run out ‖ *ref* to dry up; be exhausted

tarse [tars] *m* tarsus; instep

tartare [tartar] *adj* tartar (*sauce*); **Tartar** ‖ (*cap*) *mf* Tartar

tarte [tart] *adj* (coll) silly, stupid; (coll) ugly ‖ *f* pie, tart; (slang) slap; **c'est pas de la tarte** (slang) it's no easy matter; **tarte à la crème** custard pie; (slang) slapstick comedy; **tarte mousseline** chiffon pie

tartine [tartin] *f* slice of bread and butter or jam; (coll) long-winded speech; (coll) rambling article

tartiner [tartine] *tr* to spread

tartre [tartr] *m* tartar; scale

tartuferie [tartyfri] *f* hypocrisy

tas [tɑ] *m* heap, pile; **mettre en tas** to pile up; **prendre sur le tas** to catch redhanded; **tas de foin** haystack; **un tas de** (coll) a lot of

tasse [tɑs] *f* cup; **tasse à café** coffee cup; **tasse à thé** teacup; **tasse de café** cup of coffee

tas·sé -sée [tɑse] *adj* squat, dumpy; shrunk; curled up, slumped; complete; well-filled; packed tight; stiff (*drink*)

tas·seau [tɑso] *m* (*pl* **-seaux**) bracket; cleat; lug (*on casting*)

tasser [tɑse] *tr* to cram; tamp, pack down ‖ *intr* to grow thick ‖ *ref* to settle; huddle; (coll) to go back to normal

taste-vin [tastəvɛ̃] *m invar* wine taster (*cup*); sampling tube

tata [tata] *f* (slang) auntie

tâter [tɑte] *tr* to feel, touch; test, feel out; **tâter le pouls à qn** to feel s.o.'s pulse ‖ *intr*—**tâter de** to taste; experience; try one's hand at ‖ *ref* to stop to think, ponder

tâte-vin [tɑtvɛ̃] *m invar* wine taster (*cup*); sampling tube

tatil·lon [tatijɔ̃] **-lonne** [jɔn] *adj* fussy, hairsplitting ‖ *mf* hairsplitter
tâtonner [tɑtɔne] *intr* to grope
tâtons [tɑtɔ̃]—**à tâtons** gropingly
tatouage [tatwaʒ] *m* tattoo
tatouer [tatwe] *tr* to tattoo
taudis [todi] *m* hovel; **taudis** *mpl* slums
taule [tol] *f* (slang) fleabag; (slang) jug, clink; **faire de la taule** (slang) to do a stretch
taupe [top] *f* mole; moleskin
taupin [topɛ̃] *m* (mil) sapper; (coll) engineering student
taupinière [topinjɛr] *f* molehill
tau·reau [toro] *m* (*pl* **-reaux**) bull; **le Taureau** (astr, astrol) Taurus
taux [to] *m* rate; ratio; degree (*of disability*); **taut de base** prime rate; **taux de change** exchange rate; **taux d'escompte** discount rate; **taux d'intérêt** interest rate
taveler [tavle] §34 *tr* to spot ‖ *ref* to become spotted
taverne [tavɛrn] *f* inn, tavern
taxation [taksɑsjɔ̃] *f* fixing (*of prices, wages, etc.*); assessment; taxation
taxe [taks] *f* fixed price; rate; tax; **taxe à la valeur ajoutée** value-added tax; **taxe de luxe** luxury tax; **taxe de séjour** nonresident tax; **taxe directe** sales tax; **taxe perçue** postage paid; **taxe supplémentaire** postage due; **taxe sur les spectacles** entertainment tax
taxer [takse] *tr* to fix the price of; regulate the rate of; assess; tax; **taxer qn de** to tax or charge s.o. with ‖ *ref* to set an offering price; **se taxer de** to accuse oneself of
taxi [taksi] *m* taxi; (coll) cabdriving; **hep taxi!** taxi! ‖ *mf* (coll) cabdriver
taxidermie [taksidɛrmi] *f* taxidermy
taxiphone [taksifɔn] *m* pay phone
Tchécoslovaquie [tʃekɔslɔvaki] *f* Czechoslovakia; **la Tchécoslovaquie** Czechoslovakia
tchèque [tʃɛk] *adj* Czech ‖ *m* Czech (*language*) ‖ (*cap*) *mf* Czech (*person*)
te [tə] §87 you, to you
techni·cien [tɛknisjɛ̃] **-cienne** [sjɛn] *mf* technician; engineer
technique [tɛknik] *adj* technical ‖ *f* technique; engineering
teck [tɛk] *m* teak
teckel [tɛkɛl] *m* dachshund
teigne [tɛɲ] *f* moth; ringworm; (fig) pest, nuisance
teindre [tɛ̃dr] §50 *tr* to dye; tint ‖ *ref* to be tinted; dye or tint (*one's hair*)
teint [tɛ̃] **teinte** [tɛ̃t] *adj* dyed; with dyed hair ‖ *m* dye; complexion; **bon teint** fast color ‖ *f* tint, shade; (fig) tinge
teinter [tɛ̃te] *tr* to tint; tinge
teinture [tɛ̃tyr] *f* dye; dyeing; tincture; (fig) smattering; **teinture d'iode** (pharm) iodine
teinturerie [tɛ̃tyrri] *f* dry cleaner's; dyer's; dyeing
teintu·rier [tɛ̃tyrje] **-rière** [rjɛr] *mf* dry cleaner; dyer

tel telle [tɛl] *adj* such; like, e.g., **tel père tel fils** like father like son; **de telle sorte que** so that; **tel ou tel** such and such a; **tel que** such as, the same as, as; **tel quel** as is ‖ *mf*—**un tel** or **une telle** so-and-so ‖ *pron* such a one, such
télé [tele] *f* (coll) TV; (coll) TV set
télécommander [telekɔmɑ̃de] *tr* to operate by remote control; (fig) to inspire, influence
télécommunications [telekɔmynikɑsjɔ̃] *fpl* telecommunications
téléenseignement [teleɑ̃sɛɲmɑ̃] *m* educational television
téléférique [teleferik] *m* skyride, cableway
télégramme [telegram] *m* telegram
télégraphe [telegraf] *m* telegraph
télégraphier [telegrafje] *tr* & *intr* to telegraph
télégraphiste [telegrafist] *mf* telegrapher
téléguider [telegide] *tr* to guide (*e.g., a missile*); (coll) to influence
téléimprimeur [teleɛ̃primœr] *m* teletype, teleprinter
télémètre [telemɛtr] *m* telemeter; range finder
téléobjectif [teleɔbʒɛktif] *m* telephoto lens
télépathie [telepati] *f* telepathy
téléphérique [teleferik] *m* skyride, cableway
téléphone [telefɔn] *m* telephone; **téléphone à clavier** tone telephone, digital telephone, push-button telephone; **téléphone non sur la liste rouge** unlisted telephone; **téléphone public** public telephone; **téléphone payant** coin telephone; **téléphone rouge** (pol) hot line
téléphoner [telefɔne] *tr* & *intr* to telephone
téléphoniste [telefɔnist] *mf* telephone operator ‖ *m* lineman
télescope [telɛskɔp] *m* telescope
télescoper [telɛskɔpe] *intr* & *ref* to telescope
télescopique [telɛskɔpik] *adj* telescopic
téléscripteur [teleskriptœr] *m* teletype, teletypewriter
télésiège [telesjɛʒ] *m* chair lift
téléski [teleski] *m* ski lift
télésouffleur [telesuflœr] *m* teleprompter
téléspecta·teur [telespɛktatœr] **-trice** [tris] *mf* (television) viewer
télétraitement [teletrɛtmɑ̃] *m* (comp) processing by modem
télétype [teletip] *m* teletype
téléviser [televize] *tr* to televise
téléviseur [televizœr] *m* television set; **téléviseur à servo-réglage** remote-control television set
télévision [televizjɔ̃] *f* television; (coll) television set; **télévision payante** pay television
télévi·suel **-suelle** [televizɥɛl] *adj* television
tellement [tɛlmɑ̃] *adv* so much; so; **tellement de** so much, so many; **tellement que** to such an extent that
téméraire [temerɛr] *adj* rash, reckless, foolhardy

témérité [temerite] *f* temerity, rashness

témoignage [temwaɲaʒ] *m* testimony, witness; **en témoignage de quoi** in witness whereof; **rendre témoignage à** or **pour** to testify in favor of

témoigner [temwaɲe] §95 *tr* to show; testify ‖ *intr* to testify; **témoigner de** to give evidence of; bear witness to

témoin [temwɛ̃] *adj invar* type, model; pilot; sample, model (*home or apartment*) ‖ *m* witness; control (*in scientific experiment*); second (*in duel*); **prendre à témoin** to call to witness; **témoin à charge** witness for the prosecution; **témoin à décharge** witness for the defense; **témoin oculaire** eyewitness; **Témoins de Jéhovah** Jehovah's Witnesses

tempe [tɑ̃p] *f* (anat) temple

tempérament [tɑ̃peramɑ̃] *m* temperament; amorous nature; **à tempérament** on the installment plan

tempérance [tɑ̃perɑ̃s] *f* temperance

tempé·rant [tɑ̃perɑ̃] **-rante** [rɑ̃t] *adj* temperate

température [tɑ̃peratyr] *f* temperature

tempé·ré -rée [tɑ̃pere] *adj* temperate; tempered; restrained

tempérer [tɑ̃pere] §10 *tr* to temper ‖ *ref* to moderate

tempête [tɑ̃pɛt] *f* tempest, storm; **affronter la tempête** (fig) to face the music; **tempête dans un verre d'eau** tempest in a teapot; **tempête de neige** blizzard; **tempête de poussière** dust storm; **tempête de sable** sandstorm

tempêter [tɑ̃pɛte] *intr* to storm

tempé·tueux [tɑ̃petɥø] **-tueuse** [tɥøz] *adj* tempestuous

temple [tɑ̃pl] *m* temple; chapel, church

tempo [tɛmpo], [tɛ̃po] *m* tempo

temporaire [tɑ̃pɔrɛr] *adj* temporary

tempo·ral -rale [tɑ̃pɔral] *adj* (*pl* **-raux** [ro]) (anat) temporal

tempo·rel -relle [tɑ̃pɔrɛl] *adj* temporal

temporiser [tɑ̃pɔrize] *intr* to temporize, stall

temps [tɑ̃] *m* time; times; cycle (*of internal-combustion engine*); position, movement (*in gymnastics, fencing, carrying of arms*); weather, e.g., **quel temps fait-il?** what is the weather like?; (gram) tense; (mus) beat, measure; **à temps** in time; **au temps de** in the time of; **avoir fait son temps** to have seen better days; **dans le bon vieux temps, en le bon vieux temps** in the good old days; **dans le temps** formerly; **de temps en temps** from time to time; **en même temps** at the same time; **en temps de crise** in the time of crisis; **en temps et lieu** in due course; **en temps partagé** (comp) time-sharing; **en temps utile** in due course; **faire son temps** to do time (*in prison*); **gagner du temps** to save time; **le bon vieux temps** the good old days; **Le Temps** Father Time; **temps atomique** atomic era; **temps d'arrêt** pause, halt; **temps de chien** (slang) lousy weather; **temps mort** (sports) time-out;

temps partagé (comp) time sharing; **temps réel** (comp) real time

tenable [tənabl] *adj*—**pas tenable** untenable; unbearable

tenace [tənas] *adj* tenacious

ténacité [tenasite] *f* tenacity

tenailler [tənaje] *tr* to torture

tenailles [tənaj] *fpl* pliers, pincers

tenan·cier [tənɑ̃sje] **-cière** [sjɛr] *mf* sharecropper; lessee; keeper (*e.g., of a dive*)

te·nant [tənɑ̃] **-nante** [nɑ̃t] *adj* attached (*collar*) ‖ *mf* (sports) holder (*of a title*) ‖ *m* champion, supporter; **connaître les tenants et les aboutissants** to know the ins and outs; **d'un seul tenant** in one piece

tendance [tɑ̃dɑ̃s] *f* tendency

tendan·cieux [tɑ̃dɑ̃sjø] **-cieuse** [sjøz] *adj* tendentious, slanted

ten·deur [tɑ̃dœr] **-deuse** [døz] *mf* paperhanger; layer (*of traps*) ‖ *m* stretcher

tendoir [tɑ̃dwar] *m* clothesline

tendon [tɑ̃dɔ̃] *m* tendon

tendre [tɑ̃dr] *adj* tender ‖ §96 *tr* to stretch; hang; bend (*a bow*); lay (*a trap*); strain (*one's ear*); hold out, reach out ‖ *intr*—**tendre à** to aim at; tend toward ‖ *ref* to become strained

tendresse [tɑ̃drɛs] *f* tenderness, love, affection; (coll) partiality; **mille tendresses** (*closing of letter*) fondly

tendreté [tɑ̃drəte] *f* tenderness

ten·du-due [tɑ̃dy] *adj* tense, taut; strained; stretched out; **tendu de** hung with

ténèbres [tenɛbr] *fpl* darkness

téné·breux [tenebrø] **-breuse** [brøz] *adj* dark; somber (*person*); shady (*deal*); obscure (*style*)

te·neur [tənœr] **-neuse** [nøz] *mf* holder; **teneur de livres** bookkeeper ‖ **teneur** *f* tenor, gist; text; grade (*e.g., of ore*)

ténia [tenja] *m* tapeworm

tenir [tənir] §72, §96 *tr* to hold; keep; take up (*space*); **être tenu à** to be obliged to; **être tenu de** to be responsible for ‖ *intr* to hold; **il ne tient qu'à vous** it's up to you; **tenez!** here!; **tenir à** to insist upon; care for, value; be caused by; **tenir dans** to fit in; **tenir de** to take after, resemble; **tenir debout** (fig) to hold water, ring true; **tenir q.ch. de qn** to have s.th. from s.o., learn s.th. from s.o.; **tiens!** well!, hey! ‖ *ref* to stay, remain; sit up; stand up; behave; contain oneself; **à quoi s'en tenir** what to believe; **s'en tenir à** to limit oneself to; abide by

tennis [tenis] *m* tennis; tennis court; **tennis de table** table tennis, Ping-Pong

ténor [tenɔr] *adj masc* tenor ‖ *m* tenor; star performer

tension [tɑ̃sjɔ̃] *f* tension; blood pressure; pressure; voltage; **avoir de la tension** to have high blood pressure; **haute tension** (elec) high tension; **tension artérielle, tension du sang** blood pressure

tentacule [tɑ̃takyl] *m* tentacle

tenta·teur [tɑ̃tatœr] **-trice** [tris] *mf* tempter

tentation [tɑ̃tɑsjɔ̃] *f* temptation
tentative [tɑ̃tativ] *f* attempt
tente [tɑ̃t] *f* tent; awning
tente-abri [tɑ̃tabri] *f* (*pl* **tentes-abris** [tɑ̃tabri]) pup tent
tenter [tɑ̃te] §97 *tr* to tempt; attempt ‖ *intr*—**tenter de** to attempt to
tenture [tɑ̃tyr] *f* drape; hangings; wallpaper
te·nu -nue [təny] §93 *adj* firm (*securities, market, etc.*); **bien tenu** well-kept ‖ *f* see **tenue** ‖ *v* see **tenir**
té·nu -nue [teny] *adj* tenuous; thin
tenue [təny] *f* holding; managing; upkeep, maintenance; behavior; bearing; dress, costume; uniform; session; (mus) hold; **avoir de la tenue** to have good manners; **avoir une bonne tenue** (equit) to have a good seat; **en bonne tenue physique** in good shape physically; **en tenue** in uniform; **grande tenue** (mil) full dress; **petite tenue** (mil) undress; **tenue des livres** bookkeeping; **tenue de soirée** evening clothes; **tenue de ville** street clothes
térébenthine [terebɑ̃tin] *f* turpentine
tergiverser [tɛrʒivɛrse] *intr* to duck, equivocate, vacillate
terme [tɛrm] *m* term; end, limit; quarterly payment; **avant terme** prematurely; **terme fatal** last day of grace
terminaison [tɛrminɛzɔ̃] *f* ending, termination
termi·nal -nale [tɛrminal] *adj* & *m* (*pl* **-naux** [no]) terminal
terminer [tɛrmine] *tr* & *ref* to terminate; **se terminer par** to end with ‖ *interj*—**terminé** over (*in CB language*)
terminus [tɛrminys] *m* terminal ‖ *interj* the end has come!
termite [tɛrmit] *m* termite
terne [tɛrn] *adj* dull, drab
ternir [tɛrnir] *tr* & *ref* to tarnish
terrain [tɛrɛ̃] *m* ground; terrain; playing field; dueling field; **ne pas être sur son terrain** to be out of one's depth; **tâter le terrain** to find out the lay of the land; **terrain à bâtir** or **à lotir** building plot; **terrain brûlant** (fig) unsafe ground; **terrain d'atterrissage** landing field; **terrain d'aviation** airfield; **terrain de courses** race track; **terrain de jeux** playground; **terrain de manœuvres** parade ground; **terrain vague** vacant lot; **tout terrain** all-surface (vehicle)
terrasse [tɛras] *f* terrace; sidewalk café; **terrasse en plein air** outdoor café
terrasser [tɛrase] *tr* to embank; floor, knock down
terre [tɛr] *f* earth; land; (elec) ground; **descendre à terre** to go ashore; **la Terre Sainte** the Holy Land; **mettre pied à terre** to dismount; **par terre** on the floor; on the ground; **terre cuite** terra cotta; **Terre de Feu** Tierra del Fuego; **terre ferme** terra firma; **terre franche** loam
ter·reau [tɛro] *m* (*pl* **-reaux**) compost

terre-neuve [tɛrnœv] *m invar* Newfoundland dog ‖ *f*—**Terre-Neuve** Newfoundland
terre-plein [tɛrplɛ̃] *m* (*pl* **-pleins**) median, divider (*of road*); fill, embankment; earthwork, rampart; terrace; (rr) roadbed
terrer [tɛre] *tr* to earth up (*e.g., a tree*); earth over (*seed*) ‖ *ref* to burrow; entrench oneself
terrestre [tɛrɛstr] *adj* land; terrestrial
terreur [tɛrœr] *f* terror; **la Terreur** the Reign of Terror
ter·reux -reuse [tɛrø] *adj* earthy; dirty; sallow (*complexion*)
terrible [tɛribl] *adj* terrible; terrific
ter·rien -rienne [tɛrjɛ̃] *adj* landed (*gentry*) ‖ *mf* landowner; landlubber ‖ *m* earthman
terrier [tɛrje] *m* hole, burrow; (*dog*) terrier
terrifier [tɛrifje] *tr* to terrify
terrir [tɛrir] *intr* to come close to shore (*said of fish*)
territoire [tɛritwar] *m* territory
terroir [tɛrwar] *m* soil; homeland
terroriser [tɛrɔrize] *tr* to terrorize
tertiaire [tɛrsjɛr] *adj* tertiary
tertre [tɛrtr] *m* mound, knoll
tes [te] §88 your
tesson [tɛsɔ̃] *m* shard; broken glass
test [tɛst] *m* test; (zool) shell; **test de capacité intellectuelle** intelligence test; **test de la descendance** paternity test; **test de niveau** placement test; **test d'intelligence pratique**, **test de talent** aptitude test; **test nucléaire** nuclear test
testament [tɛstamɑ̃] *m* testament; will
testa·teur -trice [tɛstatœr] [tris] *mf* testator
tester [tɛste] *tr* to test ‖ *intr* to make one's will
testicule [tɛstikyl] *m* testicle
tétanos [tetanos] *m* tetanus
têtard [tɛtar] *m* tadpole; (bot) pollard
tête [tɛt] *f* head; heading (*e.g., of chapter*); **à la tête de** in charge of, at the head of; **à tête reposée** at (one's) leisure; **avoir la tête près du bonnet** (coll) to be quick-tempered; **avoir une bonne tête** to have a pleasant look or expression; **de tête** in one's mind's eye, mentally; capable, e.g., **une femme de tête** a capable woman; **en avoir par-dessus la tête** (coll) to be fed up with it; **en tête** foremost, at the front, leading; **en tête à tête avec** alone with; **faire la tête à** to frown at, give a dirty look to; **faire une tête** to wear a long face; **forte tête** strong-minded person; **jeter à la tête à qn** (fig) to cast in s.o.'s face; **la tête en bas** head downwards, upside down; **la tête la première** headfirst, headlong; **laver la tête à qn** (coll) to give s.o. a dressing down; **mauvaise tête** troublemaker; **monter à la tête de qn** to go to s.o.'s head; **n'en faire qu'à sa tête** to be a law unto oneself; **par tête** per capita, per head; **piquer une tête** to take a header, dive; **saluer de la tête** to nod; **se mettre en tête de** to take it into

one's head to; **se payer la tête de qn** (coll) to pull s.o.'s leg; **tenir tête à** to face up to, to stand up to; **tête baissée** headlong, heedless; **tête bêche** from top to bottom; head to foot; **tête brûlée** daredevil; **tête chercheuse** homing head (*of missile*); **tête d'affiche** (theat) headliner; **tête de bois** blockhead; **tête de cuvée** choice wine; **tête de lecture** (elec) playback head; **tête de ligne** truck terminal; railhead; **tête de linotte** scatterbrain; **tête de pont** (mil) bridgehead, beachhead; **tête de Turc** butt, scapegoat, fall guy; **tête montée** excitable person; **tête morte et tibias** skull and crossbones; **tomber sur la tête** (coll) to be off one's rocker

tête-à-queue [tɛtakø] *m invar* about-face, slue

tétée [tete] *f* sucking; feeding time

téter [tete] §10 *tr & intr* to suck

tétine [tetin] *f* nipple; teat

téton [tetɔ̃] *m* (coll) tit

tétras [tetrɑ] *m* grouse

tette [tɛt] *f* (coll) tit

tê·tu -tue [tety] *adj* stubborn

teuf-teuf [tœftœf] *m* (*pl* **teuf-teuf** or **teufs-teufs**) (coll) jalopy ‖ *interj* chug! chug!

tévé [teve] *f* (acronym) (**télévision**) TV

texte [tɛkst] *m* text; (mov, telv) script; **apprendre son texte** (theat) to learn one's lines

textile [tɛkstil] *adj & m* textile

tex·tuel -tuelle [tɛkstɥɛl] *adj* textual; verbatim

texture [tɛkstyr] *f* texture

thaï [tai] *adj invar & m* Thai

thaïlan·dais [tajlɑ̃dɛ] **-daise** [dɛz] *adj* Thai ‖ (*cap*) *mf* Thai

Thaïlande [tajlɑ̃d] *f* Thailand

thaumaturge [tomatyrʒ] *m* miracle worker, magician

thé [te] *m* tea

théâ·tral -trale [teɑtral] *adj* (*pl* **-traux** [tro]) theatrical

théâtre [teɑtr] *m* theater; stage, boards; scene (*e.g., of the crime*)

théier [teje] **théière** [tejɛr] *adj* tea ‖ *m* tea (*shrub*) ‖ *f* see **théière**

théière [tejɛr] *f* teapot

thème [tɛm] *m* theme; translation (*into a foreign language*)

théologie [teɔlɔʒi] *f* theology

théorème [teɔrɛm] *m* theorem

théorie [teɔri] *f* theory; procession

théorique [teɔrik] *adj* theoretical

thérapeutique [terapøtik] *adj* therapeutic ‖ *f* therapeutics

thérapie [terapi] *f* therapy

Thérèse [terɛz] *f* Theresa

ther·mal -male [tɛrmal] *adj* (*pl* **-maux** [mo]) thermal

thermique [tɛrmik] *adj* thermal

thermocouple [tɛrmɔkupl] *m* thermocouple

thermodynamique [tɛrmɔdinamik] *adj* thermodynamic ‖ *f* thermodynamics

thermomètre [tɛrmɔmɛtr] *m* thermometer

thermonucléaire [tɛrmɔnykleɛr] *adj* thermonuclear

Thermopyles [tɛrmɔpil] *fpl*—**les Thermopyles** Thermopylae

thermos [tɛrmɔs] *f* thermos bottle

thermosiphon [tɛrmɔsifɔ̃] *m* hot-water heater

thermostat [tɛrmɔsta] *m* thermostat

thésauriser [tezorize] *tr & intr* to hoard

thésauri·seur [tezorizœr] **-seuse** [zøz] *mf* hoarder

thèse [tɛz] *f* thesis; viewpoint, idea, position

thon [tɔ̃] *m* tuna

thorax [tɔraks] *m* thorax

thrène [trɛn] *m* threnody

thuriféraire [tyriferɛr] *m* incense bearer; flatterer

thym [tɛ̃] *m* thyme

thyroïde [tirɔid] *adj & f* thyroid

tiare [tjar] *f* tiara (*papal miter*); papacy

tibia [tibja] *m* tibia; shin; **tibias croisés et tête de mort** skull and crossbones

tic [tik] *m* (pathol) tic; **tic tac** ticktock

ticket [tikɛ] *m* ticket (*of bus, subway, etc.*); check (*for article in baggage room*); ration stamp; **sans tickets** unrationed; **ticket de quai** platform ticket

tic-tac [tiktak] *m invar* tick

tiède [tjɛd] *adj* lukewarm; mild

tiédeur [tjedœr] *f* lukewarmness; mildness

tiédir [tjedir] *tr* to take the chill off ‖ *intr* to become lukewarm

tien [tjɛ̃] **tienne** [tjɛn] §89 yours

tiens [tjɛ̃] *interj* well!, hey! ‖ *v* see **tenir**; **un "tiens" vaux mieux que deux "tu l'auras"** a bird in the hand is worth two in the bush

tiers [tjɛr] **tierce** [tjɛrs] *adj* third; tertian (*fever*) ‖ *m* third (*in fractions*); **le tiers a** third; the third party; **le tiers et le quart** (coll) everybody and anybody; **le Tiers Monde** the Third World ‖ *f* (typ) press proof

tige [tiʒ] *f* stem; trunk; shaft; shank; piston rod; leg (*of boot*); stock (*of genealogy*)

tignasse [tiɲas] *f* shock, mop (*of hair*)

tigre [tigr] *m* tiger

ti·gré -grée [tigre] *adj* striped; speckled, spotted

tigresse [tigrɛs] *f* tigress

tillac [tijak] *m* top deck (*of old-time ships*)

tilleul [tijœl] *m* linden

tilt [tilt] *m*—**faire tilt** to give an out-of-order signal; (slang) to strike home

timbale [tɛ̃bal] *f* metal cup, mug; (culin) mold; (mus) kettledrum; **décrocher la timbale** (coll) to carry off the prize

timbalier [tɛ̃balje] *m* kettledrummer

timbrage [tɛ̃braʒ] *m* stamping; cancellation (*of mail*)

timbre [tɛ̃br] *m* bell; doorbell; buzzer; seal, stamp; postage stamp; postmark; snare (*of drum*); (phonet, phys) timbre

tim·bré -brée [tɛ̃bre] *adj* stamped; ringing (*voice*); (coll) cracked, crazy

timbre-poste [tɛ̃brəpɔst] *m* (*pl* **timbres-poste**) postage stamp

timbrer [tɛ̃bre] *tr* to stamp; postmark
timbres-prime [tɛ̃mbrəprim] *mpl* trading stamps
timide [timid] *adj* timid, shy
timon [timɔ̃] *m* pole (*of carriage*); beam (*of plow*); (naut) helm
timonier [timɔnje] *m* helmsman; wheel horse
timo·ré -rée [timɔre] *adj* timorous
tin [tɛ̃] *m* chock
tinette [tinɛt] *f* firkin (*tub*); bucket (*for fecal matter*)
tintamarre [tɛ̃tamar] *m* uproar
tintement [tɛ̃tmɑ̃] *m* tolling (*of bell*); tinkle (*of bell*); ringing (*in ears*)
tinter [tɛ̃te] *tr* to toll ‖ *intr* to toll; tinkle; jingle, clink; ring (*said of ears*)
tintin [tɛ̃tɛ̃] *m*—**faire tintin** (slang) to do without ‖ *interj* (slang) nothing doing!
tintouin [tɛ̃twɛ̃] *m* (coll) trouble
tique [tik] *f* (ent) tick
tiquer [tike] *intr* to twitch; (coll) to wince; **sans tiquer** (coll) without turning a hair
tir [tir] *m* shooting; firing; aim; shooting gallery; **tir à la cible** target practice; **tir à l'arc** archery; **tir au fusil** gunnery; **tir au pigeon** trapshooting
tirade [tirad] *f* (theat) long speech
tirage [tiraʒ] *m* drawing; towing; draft (*of chimney*); printing; circulation (*of newspaper*); (coll) tension, friction; **tirage à part** offprint; **tirage au sort** lottery drawing; **tirage de luxe** deluxe edition
tiraillement [tirɑjmɑ̃] *m* pain, cramp; conflict, tension
tirailler [tirɑje] *tr* to pull about, tug at; pester ‖ *intr* to blaze away; **tirailler sur** to snipe at ‖ *ref* to have a misunderstanding
tirailleur [tirɑjœr] *m* sharpshooter; sniper; (fig) free lance
tirant [tirɑ̃] *m* string; strap; **tirant d'eau** draft (*of ship*)
tire [tir] *f* (heral) row (*of vair*); (slang) car, auto; (Canad) taffy pull
ti·ré -rée [tire] *adj* drawn; printed ‖ *m* shooting preserve; payee; **tiré à part** offprint
tire-au-flanc [tiroflɑ̃] *m invar* (coll) malingerer, shirker, goof-off
tire-botte [tirbɔt] *m* (*pl* **-bottes**) bootjack
tire-bouchon [tirbuʃɔ̃] *m* (*pl* **-bouchons**) corkscrew; corkscrew curl
tire-bouchonner [tirbuʃɔne] *tr* to twist in a spiral
tire-bouton [tirbutɔ̃] *m* (*pl* **-boutons**) buttonhook
tire-clou [tirklu] *m* (*pl* **-clous**) nail puller
tire-d'aile [tirdɛl]—**à tire-d'aile** with wings outspread, swiftly
tire-fond [tirfɔ̃] *m invar* spike; screw eye
tire-larigot [tirlarigo]—**boire à tire-larigot** to drink like a fish
tire-ligne [tirliɲ] *m* (*pl* **-lignes**) ruling pen
tirelire [tirlir] *f* piggy bank; (*face*) (coll) mug; (*head*) (coll) noggin; (slang) belly
tire-l'œil [tirlœj] *m invar* eye catcher

tirer [tire] *tr* to draw; pull, tug; shoot, fire; run off, print; take out; take, get; stick out (*one's tongue*); **tirer au clair** to bring out into the open; **tirer parti de** to turn to account ‖ *intr* to pull; shoot; draw (*e.g., to a close*); draw (*said of chimney*); **tirer à, vers,** or **sur** to border on ‖ *ref* to extricate oneself; **s'en tirer** to manage; get off (*get out of a difficulty*); **se tirer d'affaire** to pull through, get along
tiret [tirɛ] *m* dash; blank (*on an exam*)
tirette [tirɛt] *f* slide (*of desk*); damper (*of chimney*)
tireur [tirœr] *m* marksman; drawer, payer (*of check*); printer; **tireur de bois flotté** log driver; **tireur d'élite** sharpshooter; **tireur d'épée** fencer; **tireur isolé** sniper
tireuse [tirøz] *f* markswoman; **tireuse de cartes** fortuneteller
tiroir [tirwar] *m* drawer; (mach) slide valve; **à tiroirs** episodic (*play, novel, etc.*)
tiroir-caisse [tirwarkɛs] *m* (*pl* **tiroirs-caisses**) cash register
tisane [tizan] *f* tea, infusion; (coll) bad champagne; (slang) slap
tison [tizɔ̃] *m* ember; (fig) firebrand
tisonner [tizɔne] *tr* to poke
tisonnier [tizɔnje] *m* poker
tissage [tisaʒ] *m* weaving
tisser [tise] *tr* & *intr* to weave
tisse·rand [tisrɑ̃] **-rande** [rɑ̃d] *mf* weaver
tis·seur [tisœr] **-seuse** [søz] *mf* weaver
tissu [tisy] *m* tissue; cloth; fabric, material; pack (*of lies*)
tissu-éponge [tisyepɔ̃ʒ] *m* (*pl* **tissus-éponges**) toweling, terry cloth
tissure [tisyr] *f* texture; (fig) framework
titane [titan] *m* titanium
titi [titi] *m* (slang) street urchin
Titien [tisjɛ̃] *m*—**le Titien** Titian
titre [titr] *m* title; title page; heading; headline; fineness (*of coinage*); claim, right; concentration (*of a solution*); **à juste titre** rightly so; **à titre de** in the capacity of; by virtue of; **à titre d'emprunt** as a loan; **à titre d'essai** on trial; **à titre expérimental** as an experiment; **à titre gratuit** or **gracieux** free of charge; **titres** qualifications; (com) securities
titrer [titre] *tr* to title; subtitle (*films*)
tituber [titybe] *intr* to stagger
titulaire [titylɛr] *adj* titular ‖ *mf* incumbent; holder (*of passport, license, degree, post, lock box, etc.*)
titulariser [titylarize] *tr* to confirm the appointment of
toast [tost] *m* toast; **porter un toast à** to toast
toboggan [tɔbɔgɑ̃] *m* toboggan; toboggan run; slide, chute
toc [tɔk] *adj invar* (coll) worthless; (coll) crazy ‖ *m* (mach) chuck; (coll) imitation; **en toc** (coll) worthless; **toc, toc!** knock, knock!
tohu-bohu [tɔybɔy] *m* hubbub
toi [twa] §85, §87 you

toile [twal] *f* cloth; linen; canvas, painting; (theat) curtain; **toile à coton** calico; **toile à laver** dishrag; **toile à matelas** ticking; **toile à voile** sailcloth; **toile cirée** oilcloth; **toile d'araignée** cobweb; **toile de fond** backdrop

toilette [twalɛt] *f* toilet; dressing table; dress, outfit (*of a woman*); **aimer la toilette** to be fond of clothing; **faire la toilette de** to lay out (*a corpse*)

toi-même [twamɛm] §86 yourself

toise [twaz] *f* fathom; **passer à la toise** to measure the height of

toiser [twaze] *tr* to size up

toison [twazɔ̃] *f* fleece; mop (*of hair*); **Toison d'or** Golden Fleece

toit [twa] *m* roof; rooftop; home, house; **crier sur les toits** to shout from the housetops

toiture [twatyr] *f* roofing

tôle [tol] *f* sheet metal; tole (*decorative metalware*); **tôle de blindage** armor plate; **tôle étamée** tin plate; **tôle galvanisée** galvanized iron; **tôle noire** sheet iron; **tôle ondulée** corrugated iron

tolérable [tɔlerabl] *adj* tolerable, bearable

tolérance [tɔlerɑ̃s] *f* tolerance

tolérer [tɔlere] §10 *tr* to tolerate

tôlerie [tolri] *f* sheet metal; rolling mill

tolet [tɔlɛ] *m* oarlock

tollé [tɔle] *m* outcry, protest

tomaison [tɔmɛzɔ̃] *f* volume number

tomate [tɔmat] *f* tomato

tombe [tɔ̃b] *f* tomb; grave; tombstone

tom·beau [tɔ̃bo] *m* (*pl* **-beaux**) tomb; **à tombeau couvert** lickety-split

tombée [tɔ̃be] *f* fall (*of rain, snow, etc.*); **tombée de la nuit** nightfall

tomber [tɔ̃be] *tr* to throw (*a wrestler*); (coll) to remove (*a piece of clothing*); (slang) to seduce (*a woman*) ‖ *intr* (*aux:* ÉTRE) to fall, drop; **tomber amoureux** to fall in love; **tomber bien** to happen just in time; **tomber en panne** to have a breakdown; **tomber sur** to run into, chance upon; turn to (*said of conversation*)

tombe·reau [tɔ̃bro] *m* (*pl* **-reaux**) dump truck; dumpcart; load

tombola [tɔ̃bɔla] *m* raffle

tome [tɔm] *m* tome, volume

ton [tɔ̃] *adj poss* §88 your ‖ *m* tone; (mus) key

to·nal -nale [tɔnal] *adj* (*pl* **-nals**) tonal

tonalité [tɔnalite] *f* tonality; (telp) dial tone; **tonalité continue** dial tone; **tonalité d'appel** ring; **tonalité insolite** warning tone; out-of-order signal

ton·deur [tɔ̃dœr] **-deuse** [døz] *mf* shearer ‖ *f* shears; **tondeuse à cheveux** hair clippers; **tondeuse à gazon** lawn mower; **tondeuse (à gazon) à moteur** power mower; **tondeuse auto-portée** riding mower; **tondeuse électrique** electric clippers; **tondeuse mécanique** cropper; power mower

tondre [tɔ̃dr] *tr* to clip; shear; mow

toni·fiant [tɔnifjɑ̃] **-fiante** [fjɑ̃t] *adj & m* tonic

tonifier [tɔnifje] *tr* to tone up

tonique [tɔnik] *adj & m* tonic

toni·truant [tɔnitryɑ̃] **-truante** [tryɑ̃t] *adj* (coll) thunderous

tonne [tɔn] *f* ton; tun

ton·neau [tɔno] *m* (*pl* **-neaux**) barrel; cart; roll (*of automobile, airplane, etc.*); (naut) ton; **au tonneau** on draught; **tonneau de poudre** powder keg

tonnelet [tɔnlɛ] *m* keg

tonnelier [tɔnəlje] *m* cooper

tonnelle [tɔnɛl] *f* arbor

tonner [tɔne] *intr* to thunder

tonnerre [tɔnɛr] *m* thunder

tonte [tɔ̃t] *f* clipping; shearing; mowing

tonton [tɔ̃tɔ̃] *m* (slang) uncle

top [tɔp] *m* beep

topaze [tɔpaz] *f* topaz

toper [tɔpe] *intr* to shake hands on it; **tope là!** it's a deal!

topinambour [tɔpinɑ̃bur] *m* Jerusalem artichoke

topique [tɔpik] *adj* local, regional

topographie [tɔpɔgrafi] *f* topography

toquade [tɔkad] *f* (coll) infatuation

toquante [tɔkɑ̃t] *f* (coll) ticker (*watch*)

toque [tɔk] *f* toque; cap (*of chef; of judge*)

to·qué -quée [tɔke] *adj* (coll) crazy, cracked ‖ *mf* (coll) nut

toquer [tɔke] *tr* to infatuate ‖ *intr* (coll) to rap, tap ‖ *ref*—**se toquer de** to be infatuated with

torche [tɔrʃ] *f* torch; **se mettre en torche** to fail to open (*said of parachute*); **torche électrique** flashlight

torcher [tɔrʃe] *tr* to wipe clean; rush through, botch; daub with clay and straw; (vulg) **je m'en torche!** to hell with it!

torchère [tɔrʃɛr] *f* candelabrum; floor lamp

torchis [tɔrʃi] *m* adobe

torchon [tɔrʃɔ̃] *m* dishcloth; rag; (coll) scribble; **le torchon brûle** they're squabbling

torchonner [tɔrʃɔne] *tr* (coll) to botch

tor·dant [tɔrdɑ̃] **-dante** [dɑ̃t] *adj* (coll) sidesplitting

tord-boyaux [tɔrbwajo] *m invar* (coll) rotgut

tordeuse [tɔrdøz] *f* moth

tordoir [tɔrdwar] *m* wringer; rope-making machine

tordre [tɔrdr] *tr* to twist; wring ‖ *ref* to twist; writhe; **se tordre de rire** to split one's sides laughing

toréador [tɔreadɔr] *m* (obs) toreador

tornade [tɔrnad] *f* tornado

toron [tɔrɔ̃] *m* strand (*of rope*)

torpédo [tɔrpedo] *f* (archaic) open touring car

torpeur [tɔrpœr] *f* torpor

torpille [tɔrpij] *f* torpedo; (arti) mine

torpiller [tɔrpije] *tr* to torpedo

torpilleur [tɔrpijœr] *m* torpedo boat; torpedoman

torque [tɔrk] *f* coil of wire; twist (*of to-bacco*)

torréfaction [tɔrefaksjɔ̃] *f* roasting

torréfier [tɔrefje] *tr* to roast

torrent [tɔrɑ̃] *m* torrent

torride [tɔrid] *adj* torrid

tors [tɔr] **torse** [tɔrs] *adj* twisted; crooked || *m* twist || see **torse** *m*

torsade [tɔrsad] *f* twisted cord; coil (*of hair*); à **torsades** fringed

torsader [tɔrsade] *tr* to twist

torse [tɔrs] *m* torso, trunk

torsion [tɔrsjɔ̃] *f* twisting, torsion

tort [tɔr] *m* wrong; harm; à **tort** wrongly; à **tort et à travers** at random, wildly; carelessly, inconsiderately; à **tort ou à raison** rightly or wrongly; **avoir tort** to be wrong; **donner tort** à to lay the blame on; **faire tort** à to wrong

torticolis [tɔrtikɔli] *m* stiff neck

tortillard [tɔrtijar] *adj masc* knotty || *m* (coll) jerkwater train

tortiller [tɔrtije] *tr* to twist, twirl; (slang) to gulp down || *intr* to wriggle; (coll) to beat about the bush || *ref* to wriggle, squirm; writhe, twist

tor·tu -tue [tɔrty] *adj* crooked || *f* turtle, tortoise

tor·tueux [tɔrtɥø] **-tueuse** [tɥøz] *adj* winding; devious, underhanded

torture [tɔrtyr] *f* torture

torturer [tɔrtyre] *tr* to torture

torve [tɔrv] *adj* menacing

tos·can [tɔskɑ̃] **-cane** [kan] *adj* Tuscan || *m* Tuscan (*dialect*) || (*cap*) *mf* Tuscan (*person*)

tôt [to] *adv* soon; early; **au plus tôt** as soon as possible; at the earliest; **le plus tôt possible** as soon as possible; **pas de si tôt** not soon; **tôt ou tard** sooner or later

to·tal -tale [tɔtal] *adj & m* (*pl* **-taux** [to]) total

totaliser [tɔtalize] *tr* to total

totalitaire [tɔtalitɛr] *adj* totalitarian

totem [tɔtɛm] *m* totem

toton [tɔtɔ̃] *m* teetotum

toubib [tubib] *m* (coll) medical officer; (coll) doctor, physician

tou·chant [tuʃɑ̃] **-chante** [ʃɑ̃t] *adj* touching || **touchant** *prep* touching, concerning

touche [tuʃ] *f* touch; key (*of piano or type-writer*); stop (*of organ*); fret (*of guitar*); fingerboard (*of violin*); hit (*in fencing*); bite (*on fishline*); goad (*for cattle*); tab (*of file index*); thumb index; (elec) contact; (coll) look, appearance; **touche de blocage** shift lock; **touche de manœuvre** shift key; **touche de recul** backspacer; **touche marge libre, touche passe-marge** margin release

touche-à-tout [tuʃatu] *m invar* (coll) busybody

toucher [tuʃe] *m* touch, sense of touch || *tr* to touch; concern; cash (*a check*); draw out (*money*); goad (*cattle*); (mus) to pluck (*the strings*) || *intr* to touch; **toucher à** to touch (*one's food, capital, etc.*); touch

on; call at (*a port*); be about to achieve (*one's aim*); **toucher de** to play (*e.g., the piano*) || *ref* to touch

touer [twe] *tr* to warp, kedge

touffe [tuf] *f* tuft; clump (*of trees*)

touffeur [tufœr] *f* suffocating heat

touf·fu -fue [tufy] *adj* bushy; (fig) dense

touille [tuj] *m* dogfish, shark

touiller [tuje] *tr* (coll) to stir; (coll) to mix; (coll) to shuffle

toujours [tuʒur] *adv* always; still; anyhow; **M. Toujours** (coll) yes man; **pour toujours** forever

toupet [tupɛ] *m* tuft (*of hair*); forelock (*of horse*); (coll) nerve, brass

toupie [tupi] *f* top; molding board; silly woman

tour [tur] *m* turn; tour; trick; lathe; à **tour de bras** with all one's might; à **tour de rôle** in turn; **en un tour de main** in a jiffy, in a flash; **faire le tour de** to tour, to visit; to walk or ride around; **faire un tour de** to take a walk or ride in; **faire un tour de cochon à** (slang) to play a dirty trick on; **fermer à double tour** to double-lock; **tour à tour** by turns; **tour de bâton** (coll) rake-off; killing; **tour de main, tour d'adresse** sleight of hand; **tour de poitrine** chest size; **tour de reins** sudden back pain; **tour de taille** waist measurement; **tour de tête** hat size; **tours et retours** twists and turns; **tours mn.** revolutions per minute || *f* tower; (chess) castle, rook; (mil) turret; **tour de contrôle** control tower; **tour de forage** oil rig, derrick; **tour de guet** lookout tower

tourbe [turb] *f* peat; mob

tourbillon [turbijɔ̃] *m* whirl; whirlpool; whirlwind

tourbillonner [turbijɔne] *intr* to whirl, to swirl

tourelle [turɛl] *f* turret

tourillon [turijɔ̃] *m* axle; trunnion

tourisme [turism] *m* tourism; tourist industry; sightseeing; **de tourisme** tourist; **faire du tourisme** to do some sightseeing

touriste [turist] *adj & mf* tourist

tourment [turmɑ̃] *m* torment

tourmente [turmɑ̃t] *f* storm

tourmenter [turmɑ̃te] *tr* to torment || *ref* to fret

tour·nant [turnɑ̃] **-nante** [nɑ̃t] *adj* turning, revolving || *m* turn; turning point; water wheel

tourne-à-gauche [turnagoʃ] *m invar* wrench; saw set; diestock

tournebroche [turnəbrɔʃ] *m* roasting jack, turnspit

tourne-disque [turnədisk] *m* (*pl* **-disques**) record player

tournedos [turnədo] *m* filet mignon

tournée [turne] *f* round; **en tournée** (theat) on tour; **faire une tournée** to take a trip; **offrir la tournée générale** (coll) to treat everyone to a round of drinks; **tournée électorale** political campaign

tournemain [turnəmɛ̃]—**en un tournemain** in a split second

tourne-pierre [turnɛpjɛr] *m* (*pl* **-pierres**) (orn) turnstone

tourner [turne] *tr* to turn; turn over; shoot (*a moving picture; a scene*); outflank; **tourner et retourner** to turn over and over ‖ *intr* to turn; (mov) to shoot a picture; (theat) to tour; **la tête me (lui,** etc.**) tourne** my (his, etc.) head is turning, I feel (he feels, etc.) dizzy; **silence, on tourne!** quiet on the set!; **tourner à** or **en** to turn into; **tourner autour du pot** (coll) to beat about the bush; **tourner bien** to turn out well; **tourner court** to make a sharp turn; **tourner en rond** to go around in circles, spin; **tourner mal** to go bad ‖ *ref* to turn

tournesol [turnəsɔl] *m* litmus; sunflower

tournevis [turnəvis] *m* screwdriver

tourniquet [turnikɛ] *m* turnstile; revolving door; revolving display stand; (surg) tourniquet; **passer au tourniquet** (slang) to be court-martialed

tournoi [turnwa] *m* tournament

tournoyer [turnwaje] §47 *intr* to turn, wheel; twirl; tourney

tournure [turnyr] *f* turn, course (*of events*); wording, phrasing, turn (*of phrase*); expression; shape, figure; **prendre tournure** to take shape

tourte [turt] *adj* (slang) stupid ‖ *f* (coll) dolt; **tourte à la viande** meat pie

tour·teau [turto] *m* (*pl* **-teaux**) oil cake; crab

tourte·reau [turtəro] *m* (*pl* **-reaux**) turtledove, young lover

tourterelle [turtərɛl] *f* turtledove

tourtière [turtjɛr] *f* pie pan

toussailler [tusaje] *intr* to keep on coughing

Toussaint [tusɛ̃] *f* All Saints' Day; **la Toussaint** All Saints' Day

tousser [tuse] *intr* to cough; clear one's throat

tousserie [tusri] *f* constant coughing

toussotement [tusɔtmɑ̃] *m* slight coughing

toussoter [tusɔte] *intr* to cough slightly

tout [tu] **toute** [tut] (*pl* **tous toutes**) *adj* any, every, all; all of, e.g., **tous les hommes** all men, all of the men; whole, entire, e.g., **toute la journeé** the whole day; **à tout coup** every time; **à toute heure** at any time; **tous les deux** both; **tout le monde** everybody, everyone ‖ *m* (*pl* **touts**) whole, all; everything; sum; **du tout** (coll) not at all; **en tout** wholly, in all; **jouer le tout pour le tout** (slang) to shoot the works; **pas du tout** not at all ‖ **tout toute** (*pl* **tous** [tus] **toutes**) *pron* all, everything, anything; **à tout prendre** on the whole; **tout compté** all things considered ‖ *tout adv* all, quite, completely; very, e.g., **un des tout premiers** one of the very foremost; **tout à côté de** right next to; **tout à coup** suddenly; **tout à fait** quite; **tout à l'heure** in a little while; a little while ago; **tout au plus** at most; **tout**

de même however, all the same; **tout de suite** at once, immediately; **tout d'un coup** all at once; **tout en** while, e.g., **tout en parlant** while talking; **tout éveillé** wide awake; **tout fait** ready-made; **tout haut** aloud; **tout neuf** brand-new; **tout nu** stark-naked; **tout près** nearby; **tout . . . que** despite the fact that, e.g., **tout vieux qu'il était** despite the fact that he was old ‖ **toute toutes** *adv* (before a feminine word beginning with a consonant or an aspirate **h**) all, quite, completely, e.g., **elles sont toutes seules** they are all (or quite or completely) alone

tout-à-l'égout [tutalegu] *m invar* sewerage

toute-épice [tutepis] *f* (*pl* **toutes-épices** [tutepis]) allspice (*berry*)

toutefois [tutfwa] *adv* however

toute-puissance [tutpµisɑ̃s] *f* omnipotence

toutou [tutu] *m* (coll) doggie

Tout-Paris [tupari] *m invar* high society, smart set (*in Paris*)

tout-petit [tupəti] *m* (*pl* **-petits**) toddler

tout-puissant [tupµisɑ̃] **toute-puissante** [tutpµisɑ̃t] (*pl* **tout-puissants toutes-puissantes**) *adj* almighty ‖ **le Tout-Puissant** the Almighty

tout-venant [tuvnɑ̃] *m invar* all comers; run-of-the-mine coal; run-of-the-mill product; ordinary run of people

toux [tu] *f* cough

toxicomane [tɔksikɔman] *adj* addicted ‖ *mf* drug addict, junkie

toxicomanie [tɔksikɔmani] *f* drug addiction

toxique [tɔksik] *adj* toxic ‖ *m* poison

tph *abbr* (**telephone**) tel.

trac [trak] *m* (coll) stage fright; **avoir le trac** (coll) to lose one's nerve; **tout à trac** without thinking

tracas [traka] *m* worry, trouble

tracasser [trakase] *tr & ref* to worry

tracasserie [trakasri] *f* bother; **tracasseries** interference

tracassin [trakasɛ̃] *m* (coll) worry

trace [tras] *f* trace; track, trail; sketch; footprint; **marcher sur les traces de** to follow in the footsteps of

tracé [trase] *m* tracing; **faire le tracé de** to lay out; (math) to plot

tracer [trase] §51 *tr* to trace, draw

tra·ceur [trasœr] **-ceuse** [søz] *mf* tracer ‖ *m* tracer (*radioactive substance*)

trachée [traʃe] *f* trachea, windpipe

trachée-artère [traʃeartɛr] *f* (*pl* **trachées-artères**) windpipe

tract [trakt] *m* tract

tractation [traktɑsjɔ̃] *f* underhanded deal

tracteur [traktœr] *m* tractor

traction [traksjɔ̃] *f* traction; **faire des tractions** to do chin-ups; **traction avant** front-wheel drive

tradition [tradisjɔ̃] *f* tradition

tradition·nel -nelle [tradisjɔnɛl] *adj* traditional

traduc·teur [tradyktœr] **-trice** [tris] *mf* translator

traduction [tradyksjɔ̃] *f* translation

traduire [tradɥir] §19 *tr* to translate; **traduire en justice** to haul into court

trafic [trafik] *m* traffic, trade; **trafic d'influence** influence peddling; **trafic routier** highway traffic

trafi·quant [trafikã] **-quante** [kãt] *mf* racketeer; **trafiquant en stupéfiants** dope peddler

trafiquer [trafike] *tr* to traffic in ‖ *intr* to traffic; **trafiquer de** to traffic in or on

trafi·queur [trafikœr] **-queuse** [køz] *mf* racketeer

tragédie [traʒedi] *f* tragedy

tragé·dien [traʒedjɛ̃] **-dienne** [djɛn] *mf* tragedian

tragique [traʒik] *adj* tragic

trahir [trair] *tr* to betray

trahison [traizɔ̃] *f* betrayal; treason

train [trɛ̃] *m* pace, speed; manner, way; series; raft (*of logs*); (rr) train; (coll) row, racket; (slang) hind end; **aller son petit train** to go along nicely; **être en train de** + *inf* to be in the act or process of + *ger*; (translated by a progressive form of the verb), e.g., **je suis en train d'écrire** I am writing; **mettre en train** to start; **se magner le train** (slang) to get a move on; **train arrière** (aut) rear-axle assembly; (rr) rear car; **train avant** (aut) front-axle assembly; **train d'atterrissage** landing gear; **train de banlieue** suburban train; **train de marchandises** freight train; **train d'enfer** furious pace; **train de vie** way of life; standard of living; **train de voyageurs** passenger train; **train direct** express train; **train omnibus** local train; **train sanitaire** military hospital train

traî·nant [trɛnã] **-nante** [nãt] *adj* trailing; creeping; drawling; languid

traî·nard [trɛnar] **-narde** [nard] *mf* straggler

traîne [trɛn] *f* train (*of dress*); dragnet; **à la traîne** dragging; straggling; in tow

traî·neau [trɛno] *m* (*pl* **-neaux**) sleigh; sled; sledge; dragnet

traînée [trene] *f* trail, train; streak; (aer) drag; (coll) streetwalker

traîner [trene] *tr* to drag, lug; drawl; shuffle (*the feet*) ‖ *intr* to drag; straggle; lie around ‖ *ref* to crawl; creep; limp

traî·neur [trɛnœr] **-neuse** [nøz] *mf* straggler; loiterer

train-train [trɛ̃trɛ̃] *m* routine

traire [trɛr] §68 *tr* to milk

trait [trɛ] *m* arrow, dart; dash; stroke; feature (*of face*); trait, characteristic; trace (*of harness*); **avoir trait à** to refer to; **de trait** draft (*horse*); **d'un trait** in one gulp; **partir comme un trait** to be off like a shot; **tracer à grands traits** to trace in broad outlines; **trait d'esprit** witticism; **trait d'héroïsme** heroic deed; **trait d'union** hyphen; **trait pour trait** exactly ‖ *f* see **traite** ‖ **trait** [trɛ] **traite** [trɛt] *v* see **traire**

traitable [trɛtabl] *adj* tractable

traite [trɛt] *f* trade, traffic; milking; (com) draft; **tout d'une traite** at a single stretch ‖ *v* see **traire**

traité [trete] *m* treatise; treaty

traitement [trɛtmã] *m* treatment; salary; (comp) processing; **mauvais traitements** affront, mistreatment; **traitement des données**, **traitement de l'information** information processing; **traitement de texte** word processing

traiter [trete] *tr* to treat; receive; **traiter qn de** to call s.o. (*a name*) ‖ *intr* to negotiate; **traiter de** to deal with

traiteur [trɛtœr] *m* caterer; (obs) restaurateur

traî·tre [trɛtr] **-tresse** [trɛs] *adj* traitorous; treacherous; (coll) single ‖ *mf* traitor; (theat) villain ‖ *f* traitress

traîtrise [tretriz] *f* treachery

trajectoire [traʒɛktwar] *f* trajectory; **trajectoire d'attente** (aer) holding pattern

trajet [traʒɛ] *m* distance, trip, passage; (aer) flight

tralala [tralala] *m* (coll) fuss

trame [tram] *f* weft; web (*of life*); conspiracy

tramer [trame] *tr* to weave; hatch (*a plot*) ‖ *ref* to be plotted

traminot [tramino] *m* traction-company employee

tramontane [tramɔ̃tan] *f* north wind; **perdre la tramontane** to lose one's bearings

tramp [trãp] *m* tramp steamer

tramway [tramwɛ] *m* streetcar

tran·chant [trãʃã] **-chante** [ʃãt] *adj* cutting; glaring; trenchant ‖ *m* cutting edge; knife; side (*of hand*); **à double tranchant** or **à deux tranchants** two-edged

tranche [trãʃ] *f* slice; section; portion, installment; group (*of figures*); cross section; tax bracket; **doré sur tranches** gilt-edged; (coll) gilded (*e.g., youth*); **une tranche de vie** a slice of life

tranchée [trãʃe] *f* trench; **tranchées** colic

trancher [trãʃe] *tr* to cut off; slice; decide, settle ‖ *intr* to decide once and for all; stand out; **trancher avec** to contrast with; **trancher dans le vif** to cut to the quick; (fig) to take drastic measures; **trancher de** (lit) to affect the manners of

trancheuse [trãʃøz] *f* food slicer

tranquille [trãkil] *adj* quiet, tranquil; **laissez-moi tranquille** leave me alone; **soyez tranquille** don't worry

tranquillement [trãkilmã] *adv* quietly, tranquilly

tranquilli·sant [trãkilizã] **-sante** [zãt] *adj* tranquilizing ‖ *m* tranquilizer

tranquilliser [trãkilize] *tr* to tranquilize; to reassure ‖ *ref* to calm down

tranquillité [trãkilite] *f* tranquillity

transaction [trãzaksjɔ̃] *f* transaction; compromise

transat [trãzat] *m* (coll) transatlantic liner; (coll) deck chair ‖ **la Transat** (coll) the French Line

transatlantique [trɑ̃zatlɑ̃tik] *adj* transatlantic ‖ *m* transatlantic liner; deck chair
transbordement [trɑ̃sbɔrdəmɑ̃] *m* transshipment, transfer
transborder [trɑ̃sbɔrde] *tr* to transship, transfer
transbordeur [trɑ̃sbɔrdœr] *m* transporter bridge
transcender [trɑ̃sɑ̃de] *tr & ref* to transcend
transcription [trɑ̃skripsjɔ̃] *f* transcription
transcrire [trɑ̃skrir] §25 *tr* to transcribe; **transcrire en clair** to decode
transe [trɑ̃s] *f* apprehension, anxiety; trance; **être dans des transes** to be quaking in one's boots
transept [trɑ̃sɛpt] *m* transept
transférer [trɑ̃sfere] §10 *tr* to transfer; convey
transfert [trɑ̃sfɛr] *m* transfer, transference
transfo [trɑ̃sfo] *m* (coll) transformer
transforma·teur [trɑ̃sfɔrmatœr] **-trice** [tris] *adj* (elec) transforming ‖ *m* (elec) transformer; **transformateur abaisseur (de tension)** step-down transformer; **transformateur de sonnerie** doorbell transformer; **transformateur élévateur (de tension)** step-up transformer
transformer [trɑ̃sfɔrme] *tr & ref* to transform
transfuge [trɑ̃sfyʒ] *m* turncoat
transfuser [trɑ̃sfyze] *tr* to transfuse; instill
transfusion [trɑ̃sfyzjɔ̃] *f* transfusion
transgresser [trɑ̃sgrese] *tr* to transgress
transgression [trɑ̃sgresjɔ̃] *f* transgression
transhumer [trɑ̃zyme] *tr & intr* to move from winter to summer pasture
tran·si -sie [trɑ̃zi], [trɑ̃si] *adj* chilled to the bone; numb, transfixed (*with fright*)
transiger [trɑ̃ziʒe] §38 *intr* to compromise
transistor [trɑ̃zistɔr] *m* transistor
transit [trɑ̃zit] *m* transit
transi·tif [trɑ̃zitif] **-tive** [tiv] *adj* transitive
transition [trɑ̃zisjɔ̃] *f* transition
transitoire [trɑ̃zitwar] *adj* transitory; transitional
translation [trɑ̃slɑsjɔ̃] *f* transfer, translation
translitérer [trɑ̃slitere] §10 *tr* to transliterate
translucide [trɑ̃slysid] *adj* translucent
transmetteur [trɑ̃smɛtœr] *adj masc* transmitting ‖ *m* (telg, telp) transmitter; **transmetteur d'ordres** (naut) engine-room telegraph
transmettre [trɑ̃smɛtr] §42 *tr* to transmit; transfer; (sports) to pass
transmission [trɑ̃smisjɔ̃] *f* transmission; broadcast; **transmission en différé** recorded broadcast; **transmission en direct** live broadcast; **transmissions** (mil) signal corps
transmuer [trɑ̃smɥe] *tr* to transmute
transmuter [trɑ̃smyte] *tr* to transmute
transparaître [trɑ̃sparɛtr] §12 *intr* to show through
transparence [trɑ̃sparɑ̃s] *f* transparency; (mov) back projection

transpa·rent [trɑ̃sparɑ̃] **-rente** [rɑ̃t] *adj* transparent ‖ *m* transparent screen; transparency
transpercer [trɑ̃sperse] §51 *tr* to transfix
transpiration [trɑ̃spirɑsjɔ̃] *f* perspiration
transpirer [trɑ̃spire] *tr* to sweat ‖ *intr* to sweat, perspire; leak out (*said of news*)
transplanter [trɑ̃splɑ̃te] *tr* to transplant
transport [trɑ̃spɔr] *m* transport; transportation; **transport au cerveau** cerebral hemorrhage; **transport en commun** public transportation
transpor·té -tée [trɑ̃spɔrte] *adj* enraptured, carried away
transporter [trɑ̃spɔrte] *tr* to transport
transposer [trɑ̃spoze] *tr* to transpose
transver·sal -sale [trɑ̃svɛrsal] *adj* (*pl* **-saux** [so]) transversal; cross (*street*)
trapèze [trapɛz] *m* trapeze; trapezoid
trappe [trap] *f* trap door; pitfall, trap; Trappist monastery; **Trappe** Trappist order
trappeur [trapœr] *m* trapper
tra·pu -pue [trapy] *adj* stocky, squat
traque [trak] *f* driving of game
traquenard [traknar] *m* trap, booby trap, pitfall
traquer [trake] *tr* to hem in, bring to bay
traumatique [tromatik] *adj* traumatic
tra·vail [travaj] *m* (*pl* **-vaux** [vo]) work; workmanship; **en travail** in labor; **Travail** Labor; **travail à la pièce, travail à la tâche** piecework; **travail d'équipe** teamwork; **travail de Romain** herculean task; **travaux forcés** hard labor; **travaux ménagers** housework ‖ *m* (*pl* **-vails**) stocks (*for horses*)
travail·lé -lée [travaje] *adj* finely wrought, elaborate; labored
travailler [travaje] §96 *tr* to work; worry ‖ *intr* to work; warp (*said of wood*); **travailler à son compte, travailler pour son compte, travailler à la pige** to freelance; **travailler d'arrache-pied** (coll) to work like a beaver
travail·leur [travajœr] **-leuse** [jøz] *adj* hardworking ‖ *mf* worker, toiler
travailliste [travajist] *adj & mf* Labourite (Brit)
travaillomane [travajɔman] *mf* (coll) workaholic
travée [trave] *f* span (*of bridge*); row of seats; (archit) bay
traveling [travliŋ] *m* (mov, telv) dolly (*for camera*)
travers [traver] *m* breadth; fault, failing; **à travers** across, through; **de travers** awry; **en travers de** across; **par le travers de** abreast of
traverse [travɛrs] *f* crossbeam; cross street; setback; rung (*of ladder*); (rr) tie; **de traverse** cross (*e.g., street*); **mettre à la traverse de** to oppose
traversée [traverse] *f* crossing
traverser [traverse] *tr* to cross; cut across
traver·sier [traversje] **-sière** [sjɛr] *adj* cross, crossing

traversin [travɛrsɛ̃] *m* bolster (*of bed*)
traves·ti -tie [travɛsti] *adj* disguised; costume (*ball*) ‖ *m* fancy costume, disguise; transvestite; female impersonator
travestir [travɛstir] *tr* to travesty; disguise
travestissement [travɛstismɑ̃] *m* travesty; disguise
trébucher [trebyʃe] *intr* to stumble
tréfiler [trefile] *tr* to wiredraw
trèfle [trɛfl] *m* clover; trefoil; cloverleaf (*intersection*); (cards) club; (cards) clubs
tréfonds [trefɔ̃] *m* secret depths
treillage [trɛjaʒ] *m* trellis
treillager [trɛjaʒe] §38 *tr* to trellis
treille [trɛj] *f* grape arbor
treillis [trɛji] *m* latticework; iron grating; denim; **treillis métallique** wire netting
treilliser [trɛjize] *tr* to trellis
treize [trɛz] §94 *adj & pron* thirteen; the Thirteenth, e.g., **Jean treize** John the Thirteenth ‖ *m* thirteen; thirteenth (*in dates*); **treize à la douzaine** baker's dozen
treizième [trɛzjɛm] §94 *adj, pron (masc, fem), & m* thirteenth
tréma [trema] *m* dieresis
tremble [trɑ̃bl] *m* aspen (*tree*)
tremblement [trɑ̃bləmɑ̃] *m* trembling; **tremblement de terre** earthquake
trembler [trɑ̃ble] §96, §97 *intr* to tremble
trembleur [trɑ̃blœr] *m* vibrator, buzzer; (rel) Shaker; (rel) Quaker
trembloter [trɑ̃blɔte] *intr* to quiver; quaver
trémie [tremi] *f* hopper
trémolo [tremɔlo] *m* tremolo
trémoussement [tremusmɑ̃] *m* fluttering, flutter; jiggling, jiggle
trémousser [tremuse] *ref* to flutter; jiggle; (coll) to bustle
trempage [trɑ̃paʒ] *m* soaking
trempe [trɑ̃p] *f* temper; soaking; (slang) scolding
trempée [trɑ̃pe] *f* tempering
tremper [trɑ̃pe] *tr* to temper; dilute; dunk ‖ *intr* to soak; become involved (*in, e.g., a crime*)
trempette [trɑ̃pɛt] *f*—**faire la trempette, faire une trempette** to dunk; **faire trempette** to take a dip
tremplin [trɑ̃plɛ̃] *m* springboard, diving board; trampoline; ski jump; (fig) springboard
trentaine [trɑ̃tɛn] *f* age of thirty; **une trentaine de** about thirty
trente [trɑ̃t] §94 *adj & pron* thirty; **sur son trente et un** (coll) all spruced up; **trente et un** thirty-one; **trente et unième** thirty-first ‖ *m* thirty; thirtieth (*in dates*); **trente et un** thirty-one; thirty-first (*in dates*); **trente et unième** thirty-first
trente-deux [trɑ̃tdø] §94 *adj, pron, & m* thirty-two
trente-deuxième [trɑ̃tdøzjɛm] §94 *adj, pron (masc, fem), & m* thirty-second
trente-six [trɑ̃tsi(s)] §94 *adj, pron, & m* thirty-six; **tous les trente-six du mois** (coll) once in a blue moon

trentième [trɑ̃tjɛm] §94 *adj, pron (masc, fem), & m* thirtieth
trépas [trepɑ] *m* (lit) death; **passer de vie à trépas** (lit) to pass away
trépasser [trepɑse] *intr* (lit) to die
trépied [trepje] *m* tripod
trépigner [trepiɲe] *intr* to stamp one's feet
très [trɛ] *adv* very; **le très honorable** the Right Honorable
trésor [trezɔr] *m* treasure; **Trésor** Treasury
trésorerie [trezɔrri] *f* treasury
tréso·rier [trezɔrje] **-rière** [rjɛr] *mf* treasurer
tressaillement [tresajmɑ̃] *m* start, quiver
tressaillir [tresajir] §69 *intr* to give a start, quiver
tressauter [tresote] *intr* to start
tresse [trɛs] *f* tress
tresser [trɛse] *tr* to braid, plait; weave (*e.g., a basket*)
tré·teau [treto] *m* (*pl* **-teaux**) trestle; **sur les tréteaux** (theat) on the boards
treuil [trœj] *m* windlass; winch
trêve [trɛv] *f* truce; respite; **faire trève à q.ch.** to interrupt or suspend s.th.; **trève de . . .** that's enough . . .
tri [tri] *m* sorting
triage [trijaʒ] *m* sorting, selection; classification; (rr) shifting
triangle [trijɑ̃gl] *m* triangle
tribord [tribɔr] *m* starboard
tribu [triby] *f* tribe
tribu·nal [tribynal] *m* (*pl* **-naux** [no]) tribunal, court; **en plein tribunal** in open court; **tribunal de police** police court; **tribunaux pour enfants** juvenile courts
tribune [tribyn] *f* rostrum, tribune; gallery; grandstand; **monter à la tribune** to take the floor; **tribune des journalistes** press box; **tribune d'orgue** organ loft; **tribune libre** open forum; **tribune téléphonique** phone-in show
tribut [triby] *m* tribute
tributaire [tribytɛr] *adj & m* tributary; **être tributaire de** to be dependent upon
tricher [triʃe] *tr & intr* to cheat
tricherie [triʃri] *f* cheating
tri·cheur [triʃœr] **-cheuse** [ʃøz] *mf* cheater; **tricheur professionnel** cardsharper
tricolore [trikɔlɔr] *adj & m* tricolor
tricot [triko] *m* knitting; knitted garment; **tricot de corps, tricot de peau** undershirt
tricotage [trikɔtaʒ] *m* knitting
tricoter [trikɔte] *tr & intr* to knit
trictrac [triktrak] *m* backgammon; backgammon board
trier [trije] *tr* to pick out, screen; **trier sur le volet** to hand-pick
trieur [trijœr] **trieuse** [trijøz] *mf* sorter ‖ *m & f* (mach) sorter
trigonométrie [trigɔnɔmetri] *f* trigonometry
trille [trij] *m* trill
triller [trije] *tr & intr* to trill
trillion [triljɔ̃] *m* quintillion (U.S.A.); trillion (Brit)
trilogie [trilɔʒi] *f* trilogy
trimbaler [trɛ̃bale] *tr* to cart around

trimer [trime] *intr* to slave

trimestre [trimɛstr] *m* quarter (*of a year*); quarter's salary; quarter's rent; (educ) term

tringle [trɛ̃gl] *f* rod; **tringle de rideau** curtain rod

trinité [trinite] *f* trinity

trinquer [trɛ̃ke] *intr* to clink glasses, toast; (slang) to drink; **trinquer avec** to hobnob with

trio [trijo] *m* trio

triom·phant [trijɔ̃fɑ̃] **-phante** [fɑ̃t] *adj* triumphant

triomphe [trijɔ̃f] *m* triumph; **faire triomphe à** to welcome in triumph

tripar·ti -tie [triparti] *adj* tripartite

tripartite [tripartit] *adj* tripartite

tripatouiller [tripatuje] *tr* (coll) to tamper with

tripette [tripɛt] *f*—**ça ne vaut pas tripette** it's not worth a wooden nickel

triple [tripl] *adj & m* triple

tri·plé -plée [triple] *mf* triplet

tripler [triple] *tr & intr* to triple

triplicata [triplikata] *m invar* triplicate

tripot [tripo] *m* gambling den; house of ill repute

tripoter [tripɔte] *tr* to finger, toy with ‖ *intr* to dabble, potter around; rummage

trique [trik] *f* (coll) cudgel

triste [trist] *adj* sad

tristesse [tristɛs] *f* sadness, sorrow

triturer [trityre] *tr* to pulverize, grind ‖ *ref*—**se triturer la cervelle** to rack one's brain

tri·vial -viale [trivjal] *adj* (*pl* **-viaux** [vjo]) trivial; vulgar, coarse

trivialité [trivjalite] *f* triviality; vulgarity, coarseness

tr/mn *abbr* (**tours par minute**) r.p.m.

troc [trɔk] *m* barter; swap; **troc pour troc** even up

troglodyte [trɔglɔdit] *m* cave dweller; (orn) wren

trognon [trɔɲɔ̃] *m* core; (slang) darling, pet

Troie [trwa], [trwa] *f* Troy

trois [trwa] §94 *adj & pron* three; the Third, e.g., **Jean trois** John the Third; **trois heures** three o'clock ‖ *m* three; third (*in dates*)

troisième [trwazjɛm] §94 *adj, pron* (*masc, fem*), *& m* third

trolley [trɔlɛ] *m* trolley

trolleybus [trɔlɛbys] *m* trackless trolley

trombe [trɔ̃b] *f* waterspout; **entrer en trombe** to dash in; **trombe d'eau** deluge

trombone [trɔ̃bɔn] *m* trombone; paper clip

trompe [trɔ̃p] *f* horn; trunk (*of elephant*); beak (*of insect*); **trompe d'Eustache** Eustachian tube

trompe-la-mort [trɔ̃plamɔr] *mf invar* daredevil

trompe-l'œil [trɔ̃plœj] *m invar* dummy effect; (coll) bluff, fake; **en trompe-l'œil** in perspective

tromper [trɔ̃pe] *tr* to deceive, cheat ‖ *ref* to be wrong; **se tromper de** to be mistaken about

tromperie [trɔ̃pri] *f* deceit; fraud; illusion

trompeter [trɔ̃pte] §34 *tr & intr* to trumpet

trompette [trɔ̃pɛt] *m* trumpeter ‖ *f* trumpet; **en trompette** turned up

trom·peur [trɔ̃pœr] **-peuse** [pøz] *adj* false, lying ‖ *mf* deceiver

tronc [trɔ̃] *m* trunk; (slang) head; **tronc des pauvres** poor box

tronche [trɔ̃ʃ] *f* (slang) noodle

tronçon [trɔ̃sɔ̃] *m* stump; section (*e.g., of track*)

tronçonneuse [trɔ̃sɔnøz] *f* chain saw

trône [tron] *m* throne

trôner [trone] *intr* to sit in state ‖ *ref*—**se trôner sur** to lord it over

tronquer [trɔ̃ke] *tr* to truncate, cut off; mutilate

trop [tro] *m* excess; too much; **de trop** too much; to excess; in the way, e.g., **il est de trop ici** he is in the way here; **par trop** altogether, excessively; **trop de . . .** too much . . . ; too many . . . ‖ *adv* too; too much; **trop lourd** overweight

trophée [trɔfe] *m* trophy

tropi·cal -cale [trɔpikal] *adj* (*pl* **-caux** [ko]) tropical

trop-plein [trɔplɛ̃] *m* (*pl* **-pleins**) overflow

troquer [trɔke] *tr* to barter; **troquer contre** to swap for

trot [tro] *m* trot; **au trot** at a trot; (coll) on the double, quickly

trotte [trɔt] *f* (coll) quite a distance to walk

trotter [trɔte] *intr* to trot

trot·teur [trɔtœr] **-teuse** [tøz] *mf* (turf) trotter ‖ *f* second hand; **trotteuse centrale** sweep-second

trottin [trɔtɛ̃] *m* errand girl

trottinette [trɔtinɛt] *f* scooter

trottoir [trɔtwar] *m* sidewalk; **faire le trottoir** to walk the streets (*said of prostitute*); **trottoir roulant** moving walkway, moving sidewalk

trou [tru] *m* hole; pothole; eye (*of needle*); gap; jerkwater town; **boire comme un trou** to drink like a fish; **faire son trou** to feather one's nest; **faire un trou à la lune** to fly the coop; **trou d'air** air pocket; **trou de balle, trou du cul** (vulg) asshole; (fig) asshole; **trou de clef** keyhole (*of clock*); **trou de la serrure** keyhole; **trou de souris** mousehole; **trou d'homme** manhole; **trou d'obus** shell hole; **trou du souffleur** prompter's box; **trou individuel** (mil) foxhole; **trou noir** (astr) black hole

trouble [trubl] *adj* muddy, cloudy, turbid (*liquid*); murky (*sky*); misty (*glass*); blurred (*image; sight*); dim (*light*); vague, disquieting ‖ *m* disquiet; unrest; trouble (*illness*); **troubles dûs au décalage horaire** jet lag

trouble-fête [trubləfɛt] *mf invar* wet blanket, kill-joy

troubler [truble] *tr* to upset, trouble; make muddy; disturb; make cloudy; blur ‖ *ref* to become muddy or cloudy; lose one's composure

trouée [true] *f* gap, breach; (mil) breakthrough

trouille [truj] *f*—**avoir la trouille** (slang) to get cold feet

troupe [trup] *f* troop; band, party; (theat) troupe

trou·peau [trupo] *m* (*pl* -**peaux**) flock; herd; **attention aux troupeaux** (*public sign*) cattle crossing

troupier [trupje] *m* (coll) soldier; **jurer comme un troupier** to swear like a trooper

trousse [trus] *f* case, kit; **avoir qn à ses trousses** to have s.o. at one's heels; **trousse de première urgence** first-aid kit

trous·seau [truso] *m* (*pl* -**seaux**) trousseau; outfit; bunch (*of keys*)

troussequin [truskɛ̃] *m* cantle

trousser [truse] *tr* to turn up; tuck up; polish off; (culin) to truss ‖ *ref* to lift one's skirts

trouvaille [truvɑj] *f* find

trouver [truve] §96 *tr* to find ‖ §95 *ref* to be found; find oneself; to be, e.g., **où se trouve-t-il?** where is he?; **il se trouve que . . .** it happens that . . . ; **se trouver mal** to feel ill

troyen [trwajɛ̃] **troyenne** [trwajɛn] *adj* Trojan ‖ (*cap*) *mf* Trojan

truand [tryɑ̃] **truande** [tryɑ̃d] *adj & m* good-for-nothing

truc [tryk] *m* gadget, device; (coll) trick, gimmick; (coll) thing; (coll) what's-his-name

truchement [tryʃmɑ̃] *m* spokesman; interpreter; **par le truchement de** thanks to, through

trucu·lent [trykylɑ̃] -**lente** [lɑ̃t] *adj* truculent

truelle [tryɛl] *f* trowel

truffe [tryf] *f* truffle

truie [trɥi] *f* sow

truisme [tryism] *m* truism

truite [trɥit] *f* trout; **truite arc-en-ciel** rainbow trout; **truite saumonée** salmon trout

tru·meau [trymo] *m* (*pl* -**meaux**) trumeau (*mirror with painting above in same frame*)

truquage [trykaʒ] *m* faking

truquer [tryke] *tr* to fake; cook (*the accounts*); stack (*the deck*); load (*the dice*); fix (*the outcome of a fight*) ‖ *intr* to resort to fakery

trust [trœst] *m* trust, holding company

T.S.F. [teɛsɛf] *f* (letterword) (**télégraphie sans fil**) wireless; radio

t.s.v.p. *abbr* (**tournez s'il vous plaît**) over (*please turn the page*)

tu [ty] §87 you; **être à tu et à toi avec** to hobnob with

T.U. [tey] *m* (letterword) (**temps universel**) universal time, Greenwich Mean Time

tube [tyb] *m* tube; pipe; (anat) duct; (slang) hit

tubercule [tybɛrkyl] *m* tubercle; tuber

tuberculose [tybɛrkyloz] *f* tuberculosis

tue-mouches [tymuʃ] *m invar* flypaper

tuer [tɥe] *tr* to kill ‖ §96 *ref* to be killed; kill oneself

tuerie [tyri] *f* slaughter

tue-tête [tytɛt]—**à tue-tête** at the top of one's voice

tuile [tɥil] *f* tile; (coll) nasty blow

tuilerie [tɥilri] *f* tileworks

tulipe [tylip] *f* tulip

tumeur [tymœr] *f* tumor

tumulte [tymylt] *m* tumult, hubbub

tungstène [tœ̃kstɛn] *m* tungsten

tunique [tynik] *f* tunic; membrane; (bot) coat, envelope, skin

tunnel [tynɛl] *m* tunnel; **passer sous un tunnel** to go through a tunnel; **tunnel aérodynamique** wind tunnel

turban [tyrbɑ̃] *m* turban

turbine [tyrbin] *f* turbine

turbopropulseur [tyrbɔprɔopylsœr] *m* turboprop

turboréacteur [tyrbɔreaktœr] *m* turbojet

turbu·lent [tyrbylɑ̃] -**lente** [lɑ̃t] *adj* turbulent

turc turque [tyrk] *adj* Turkish ‖ *m* Turkish (*language*) ‖ (*cap*) *mf* Turk (*person*)

turf [tyrf] *m*—**le turf** the turf, the track

turfiste [tyrfist] *m* turfman, racegoer

turlututu [tyrlytyty] *interj* fiddlesticks!, nonsense!

Turquie [tyrki] *f* Turkey; **la Turquie** Turkey

turquoise [tyrkwaz] *m* turquoise (*color*) ‖ *f* turquoise (*stone*)

tutelle [tytɛl] f guardianship, tutelage; trusteeship

tu·teur [tytœr] -**trice** [tris] *mf* guardian ‖ *m* (hort) stake, prop

tutoyer [tytwaje] §47 *tr* to address familiarly; use familiar grammatical forms (**toi, tu,** etc.) in speaking to an intimate, an inferior, or (if a Protestant) to God (*to "thou"*) ‖ *ref* to be on a first-name basis

tuyau [tɥijo], [tyjo] *m* (*pl* **tuyaux**) pipe; tube; fluting; (coll) tip; **tuyau d'arrosage** garden hose; **tuyau d'échappement** exhaust; **tuyau d'incendie** fire hose

tuyauter [tɥijote], [tyjote] *tr* to flute; (coll) to tip off ‖ *intr* (coll) to crib

tuyauterie [tɥijotri] *f* pipe mill; piping; (aut) manifold; **tuyauterie d'admission** intake manifold; **tuyauterie d'échappement** exhaust manifold

tympan [tɛ̃pɑ̃] *m* eardrum; (archit, mus) tympanum

type [tip] *m* type; (coll) fellow, character

typer [tipe] *tr* to type, mark, stamp; characterize

typesse [tipɛs] *f* (slang) dame, broad, gal

typhoïde [tifɔid] *adj & f* typhoid

typhon [tifɔ̃] *m* typhoon

typique [tipik] *adj* typical; South American (*music*)

typographie [tipɔgrafi] *f* typography

typographique [tipɔgrafik] *adj* typograph-
  ic(al)
typon [tipɔ̃] *m* offset film

tyran [tirɑ̃] *m* tyrant; (orn) kingbird
tyrannie [tirani] *f* tyranny
tyrannique [tiranik] *adj* tyrannic(al)

U

U, u [y], *[y] *m invar* twenty-first letter of
  the French alphabet
Ukraine [ykrɛn] *f* Ukraine
ukrai·nien [ykrɛnjɛ̃] **-nienne** [njɛn] *adj*
  Ukrainian ‖ *m* Ukrainian (*language*) ‖
  (*cap*) *mf* Ukrainian (*person*)
ulcère [ylsɛr] *m* ulcer, sore
ulcérer [ylsere] §10 *tr* to ulcerate; embitter
  ‖ *ref* to ulcerate; fester
ulté·rieur -rieure [ylterjœr] *adj* ulterior;
  subsequent
ultimatum [yltimatɔm] *m* ultimatum
ultime [yltim] *adj* ultimate, final
ultra [yltra] *m* (pol) extremist
ultra-court [yltrakur] **-courte** [kurt] *adj*
  (electron) ultrashort
ultravio·let [yltravjɔlɛ] **-lette** [lɛt] *adj & m*
  ultraviolet
ululer [ylyle] *intr* to hoot
un [œ̃] **une** [yn] §77 *adj & pron* one; **l'un à**
  l'autre to each other, to one another; **l'un**
  et l'autre both; **l'un l'autre** each other,
  one another; **ni l'un ni l'autre** neither,
  neither one; **un à un** one by one; **une**
  heure one o'clock ‖ *art indef* a ‖ *m* one ‖
  f—**il était moins une** it was a narrow
  escape; **la une** the front page
unanime [ynanim] *adj* unanimous
unanimité [ynanimite] *f* unanimity
Unesco [ynɛsko] *f* (acronym) (**Organisation**
  des Nations Unies pour l'Éducation, la
  Science et la Culture)—l'Unesco UNE-
  SCO
u·ni -nie [yni] *adj* united; smooth, level;
  uneventful; plain; solid (*color*); together
  (*said, e.g., of the hands of a clock*) ‖ *m*
  plain cloth
unicorne [ynikɔrn] *m* unicorn
unième [ynjɛm] *adj* first, e.g., **vingt et**
  unième twenty-first
unification [ynifikɑsjɔ̃] *f* unification
unifier [ynifje] *tr* to unify ‖ *ref* to consolidate, merge; become unified
uniforme [ynifɔrm] *adj & m* uniform
uniformément [ynifɔrmemɑ̃] *adv* uni-
  formly; regularly; steadily
uniformiser [ynifɔrmize] *tr* to make uniform
uniformité [ynifɔrmite] *f* uniformity
unijambiste [yniʒɑ̃bist] *adj* one-legged ‖ *mf*
  one-legged person
unilaté·ral -rale [ynilateral] *adj* (*pl* **-raux**
  [ro]) unilateral
union [ynjɔ̃] *f* union; **union libre** common-
  law marriage
unique [ynik] *adj* only, single; unique

unir [ynir] *tr & ref* to unite
unisson [ynisɔ̃] *m* unison
unitaire [yniter] *adj* unit
unité [ynite] *f* unity; unit; battleship; (coll)
  one million old francs; **unités de valeur**
  (educ) hours of credit
univers [yniver] *m* universe
univer·sel -selle [yniversɛl] *adj & m* universal
universitaire [yniversiter] *adj* university;
  academic ‖ *mf* academic
université [yniversite] *f* university
Untel [œ̃tɛl] *mf* so-and-so, e.g., **Monsieur/**
  Madame Untel Mr. and Mrs. So-and-so
uranium [yranjɔm] *m* uranium
ur·bain -baine [yrbɛ̃] **-baine** [bɛn] *adj* urban; urbane
urbaniser [yrbanize] *tr* to urbanize
urbanisme [yrbanism] *m* city planning
urbaniste [yrbanist] *adj* zoning (*ordinance*)
  ‖ *mf* city planner
urbanité [yrbanite] *f* urbanity
urètre [yrɛtr] *m* urethra
urgence [yrʒɑ̃s] *f* urgency; emergency;
  emergency case; **d'urgence** emergency
  (*e.g., hospital ward*); right away, without
  delay
ur·gent [yrʒɑ̃] **-gente** [ʒɑ̃t] *adj* urgent;
  emergency (*case*); (formula on letter or
  envelope) rush ‖ *m* urgent matter
urinaire [yriner] *adj* urinary
uri·nal [yrinal] *m* (*pl* **-naux** [no]) urinal (*for*
  use in bed)
urine [yrin] *f* urine
uriner [yrine] *tr & intr* to urinate
urinoir [yrinwar] *m* urinal (*place*)
urne [yrn] *f* urn; ballot box; **aller aux urnes**
  to go to the polls
urologie [yrɔlɔʒi] *f* urology
U.R.S.S. [yɛrɛsɛs] *f* (letterword) (**Union**
  des Républiques Socialistes Soviétiques)
  U.S.S.R.
Ursse [yrs] *f* (acronym) (**Union des Ré-**
  publiques Socialistes Soviétiques)
  U.S.S.R.
urticaire [yrtiker] *f* hives
urubu [yryby] *m* turkey vulture
us [ys] *mpl*—**les us et (les) coutumes** the
  manners and customs
U.S. [yɛs] *adj* (letterword) (**United States**)
  U.S., e.g., **l'aviation U.S.** U.S. aviation
U.S.A. [yɛsa] *mpl* (letterword) (**United**
  States of America) U.S.A.
usage [yzaʒ] *m* usage; custom; use; **faire**
  de l'usage to wear well; **hors d'usage**
  outmoded; (gram) obsolete; **manquer**

d'usage to lack good breeding; **usage du monde** good breeding, savoir-vivre

usa·gé -gée [yzaʒe] *adj* secondhand; worn-out, used

usa·ger [yzaʒe] **-gère** [ʒɛr] *mf* user

usant [yzɑ̃] **usante** [yzɑ̃t] *adj* exhausting, wearing

u·sé -sée [yze] *adj* worn-out; trite, commonplace

user [yze] *tr* to wear out; wear away; ruin (*e.g., health*) ‖ *intr*—**en user bien avec** to treat well; **user de** to use ‖ *ref* to wear out

usine [yzin] *f* factory, mill, plant; **usine à gaz** gasworks

usiner [yzine] *tr* to machine, tool

usi·nier [yzinje] **-nière** [njɛr] *adj* manufacturing; factory (*town*) ‖ *m* manufacturer

usi·té -tée [yzite] *adj* used, in use; **peu usité** out of use, rare

ustensile [ystɑ̃sil] *m* utensil, implement

u·suel -suelle [yzɥɛl] *adj* usual

usure [yzyr] *f* usury; wear and tear

usurper [yzyrpe] *tr* to usurp

utérus [yterys] *m* uterus, womb

utile [ytil] §92 *adj* useful, helpful; **puis-je vous être utile?** can I be of help?

utilisable [ytilazabl] *adj* usable

utilisa·teur [ytilizatœr] **-trice** [tris] *mf* user

utilitaire [ytilitɛr] *adj* utilitarian; utility (*vehicle, goods, etc.*)

utilité [ytilite] *f* utility, usefulness, use; (*theat*) support; (*theat*) supporting rôle; **jouer les utilités** (*fig*) to play second fiddle; **utilités** (*theat*) small parts

utopique [ytɔpik] *adj* utopian

utopiste [ytɔpist] *mf* utopian

V

V, v [ve] *m invar* twenty-second letter of the French alphabet

v. *abbr* (**voir**) see; (**volume**) vol.

va [va] *v* see **aller**

vacance [vakɑ̃s] *f* vacancy, opening; **vacances** vacation

vacancier [vakɑ̃sje] *m* vacationist

va·cant [vakɑ̃] **-cante** [kɑ̃t] *adj* vacant

vacarme [vakarm] *m* din, racket

vacation [vakɑsjɔ̃] *f* investigation; **vacations** fee; recess

vaccin [vaksɛ̃] *m* vaccine

vaccination [vaksinɑsjɔ̃] *f* vaccination

vaccine [vaksin] *f* cowpox

vacciner [vaksine] *tr* to vaccinate

vache [vaʃ] *adj* embarrassing (*question*); cantankerous (*person*) ‖ *f* cow; cowhide; (*woman*) (slang) bitch; (*man*) (slang) swine, rat; (*policeman*) (slang) flatfoot, bull; **en vache** leather (*e.g., suitcase*); **manger de la vache enragée** (coll) not to have a red cent to one's name; **oh, la vache!** damn it!; **parler français comme une vache espagnole** (coll) to murder the French language; **vache à eau** canvas bucket (*for camping*); **vache à lait** milch cow; (coll) gull, sucker

vachement [vaʃmɑ̃] *adv* (slang) tremendously

va·cher [vaʃe] **-chère** [ʃɛr] *mf* cowherd

vacherie [vaʃri] *f* cowshed; dairy farm; (coll) dirty trick

vachette [vaʃɛt] *f* young calf; calf (*leather*)

vaciller [vasije] *intr* to vacillate, waver; flicker; totter

vacuité [vakɥite] *f* vacuity, emptiness

vacuum [vakɥɔm] *m* vacuum

vade-mecum [vademekɔm] *m invar* handbook, vade mecum

vadrouille [vadruj] *f* (naut) mop, swab; plunger (*plumber's*); (slang) bender, spree

vadrouiller [vadruje] *intr* (slang) to ramble around, gad about

vadrouil·leur [vadrujœr] **-leuse** [jøz] *mf* (slang) rounder

va-et-vient [vaevjɛ̃] *m invar* backward-and-forward motion; hurrying to and fro; comings and goings; ferryboat; (elec) two-way switch

vaga·bond [vagabɔ̃] **-bonde** [bɔ̃d] *adj* vagabond ‖ *mf* vagabond, tramp

vagabondage [vagabɔ̃daʒ] *m* vagrancy; **vagabondage interdit** (*public sign*) no loitering, no begging

vagabonder [vagabɔ̃de] *intr* to wander about, roam, tramp

vagin [vaʒɛ̃] *m* vagina

vagi·nal -nale [vaʒinal] (*pl* **-naux** [no]) *adj* vaginal

vagir [vaʒir] *intr* to cry, wail

vague [vag] *adj* vague; vacant (*look; lot*); waste (*land*) ‖ *m* vagueness; (fig) space, thin air; **vague à l'âme** uneasy sadness ‖ *f* wave; **la nouvelle vague** the wave of the future; **vague de fond** ground swell

vaguemestre [vagmɛstr] *m* (mil, nav) mail clerk

vaguer [vage] *intr* to wander

vaillance [vajɑ̃s] *f* valor

vail·lant [vajɑ̃] **-lante** [jɑ̃t] *adj* valiant; up to scratch

vaille [vaj] *v* (**vailles, vaillent**) see **valoir**

vain [vɛ̃] **vaine** [vɛn] *adj* vein; **en vain** in vain

vaincre [vɛ̃kr] §70 *tr* to defeat, conquer; overcome (*fear, instinct, etc.*) ‖ *intr* to conquer ‖ *ref* to control oneself

vaincs [vɛ̃] *v* (**vainc**) see **vaincre**

vain·cu -cue [vɛ̃ky] *adj* defeated, beaten, conquered ‖ *mf* loser ‖ *v* see **vaincre**

vainquant [vɛ̃kɑ̃] *v* (**vainquez, vainquons**) see **vaincre**

vainqueur [vɛ̃kœr] *adj masc* victorious ‖ *m* victor, winner

vairon [verɔ̃] *adj masc* whitish (*eye*); **vairons** of different colors (*said of eyes*) ‖ *m* (ichth) minnow

vais [vɛ] *v* see **aller**

vais·seau [vɛso] *m* (*pl* **-seaux**) vessel; nave (*of church*); **vaisseau amiral** flagship; **vaisseau sanguin** blood vessel; **vaisseau spatial** spaceship

vaisseau-école [vɛsoekɔl] *m* (*pl* **vaisseaux-écoles**) (nav) training ship

vaisselier [vɛsəlje] *m* china closet

vaisselle [vɛsɛl] *f* dishes; **faire la vaisselle** to wash the dishes; **vaisselle plate** plate (*of gold or silver*)

val [val] *m* (*pl* **vaux** [vo] or **vals**) (obs) valley; **à val** going down the valley; **à val de** (obs) down from

valable [valabl] *adj* valid; worthwhile (*e.g., experience*)

valence [valɑ̃s] *f* (chem) valence

valen·tin [valɑ̃tɛ̃] **-tine** [tin] *mf* valentine (*sweetheart*)

valet [vale] *m* valet; holdfast, clamp; (cards) jack; **valet de chambre** valet; **valet de ferme** hired man; **valet de pied** footman

valeur [valœr] *f* value, worth, merit; valor; (*person, thing, or quality worth having*) asset; (com) security, stock; **de valeur** able; valuable; (Canad) too bad, unfortunate; **envoyer en valeur déclarée** to insure (*a package*); **mettre en valeur** to develop (*e.g., a region*); set off, enhance; **valeur d'avenir** growth stock; **valeur de père de famille** blue chips

valeu·reux [valœrø] **-reuse** [røz] *adj* valorous, brave

validation [validɑsjɔ̃] *f* validation

valide [valid] *adj* valid; fit, able-bodied

valider [valide] *tr* to validate

validité [validite] *f* validity

valise [valiz] *f* suitcase; **faire ses valises** to pack, pack one's bags; **valise diplomatique** diplomatic pouch

vallée [vale] *f* valley

vallon [valɔ̃] *m* vale, dell

valoir [valwar] §71, §95 *tr* to equal; **un service en vaut un autre** one good turn deserves another; **valoir q.ch. à qn** to get or bring s.o. s.th., e.g., **cela lui a valu une amélioration** that got him a raise; e.g., **la condamnation lui a valu cinq ans de prison** the verdict brought him five years in prison ‖ *intr* to be worth; **autant vaut y renoncer** might as well give up; **cela ne vaut rien** it's worth nothing; **faire valoir** to set off to advantage; use to advantage; develop (*one's land*); invest (*funds, capital*); put forward (*one's reasons*); **faire valoir que . . .** to argue that . . . ; **vaille que vaille** somehow or other ‖ *impers*—**il vaut mieux** it

would be better to, e.g., **il vaut mieux attendre** it would be better to wait; **mieux vaut tard que jamais** better late than never ‖ *ref*—**les deux se valent** one is as good as the other

valse [vals] *f* waltz

valser [valse] *tr & intr* to waltz

va·lu -lue [valy] *v* see **valoir**

valve [valv] *f* (aut, bot, zool) valve; (elec) vacuum tube

valvule [valvyl] *f* valve

vamp [vɑ̃p] *f* vamp

vamper [vɑ̃pe] *tr* (coll) to vamp

vampire [vɑ̃pir] *m* vampire

van [vɑ̃] *m* van (*for moving horses*)

vandale [vɑ̃dal] *adj* vandal; Vandal ‖ *m* vandal ‖ (*cap*) *mf* Vandal

vandalisme [vɑ̃dalism] *m* vandalism

vanille [vanij] *f* vanilla

vani·teux [vanitø] **-teuse** [tøz] *adj* vain, conceited

vanne [van] *f* sluice gate, floodgate; butterfly valve; (slang) gibe

van·neau [vano] *m* (*pl* **-neaux**) (orn) lapwing

vanner [vane] *tr* to winnow; tire out

vannerie [vanri] *f* basketry

vannier [vanje] *m* basket maker

van·tail [vɑ̃taj] *m* (*pl* **-taux** [to]) leaf (*of door, shutter, sluice gate, etc.*)

van·tard [vɑ̃tar] **-tarde** [tard] *adj* bragging, boastful ‖ *mf* braggart

vantardise [vɑ̃tardiz] *f* bragging, boasting

vanter [vɑ̃te] §97 *tr* to praise; boost, push (*a product on the market*) ‖ *ref* to brag, boast

va-nu-pieds [vanypje] *mf invar* (coll) tramp

vapeur [vapœr] *m* steamship ‖ *f* steam; vapor, mist; **à la vapeur** steamed (*e.g., potatoes*); under steam; (coll) at full speed; **à vapeur** steam (*e.g., engine*); **vapeur d'eau** water vapor; **vapeurs** low spirits

vaporisateur [vapɔrizatœr] *m* atomizer, spray

vaporiser [vapɔrize] *tr & ref* to vaporize; spray

vaquer [vake] *intr* to take a recess; **vaquer à** to attend to ‖ *impers*—**il vaque** there is vacant

varappe [varap] *f* cliff; rock climbing

varech [varɛk] *m* wrack, seaweed

vareuse [varøz] *f* (mil) blouse; (nav) peacoat

variable [varjabl] *adj & f* variable

va·riant [varjɑ̃] **-riante** [rjɑ̃t] *adj & f* variant

variation [varjɑsjɔ̃] *f* variation

varice [varis] *f* varicose veins

varicelle [varisɛl] *f* chicken pox

va·rié -riée [varje] *adj* varied

varier [varje] *tr & intr* to vary

variété [varjete] *f* varity; **variétés** selections (*from literary works*); vaudeville

variole [varjɔl] *f* smallpox

vari·queux [varikø] **-queuse** [køz] *adj* varicose

Varsovie [varsɔvi] *f* Warsaw
vase [vɑs] *m* vase; vessel; **en vase clos** shut up; in an airtight chamber; **vase de nuit** chamber pot ‖ *f* mud, slime
vas [va] *v* see **aller**
vaseline [vazlin] *f* petroleum jelly, Vaseline
va·seux [vazø] **-seuse** [zøz] *adj* muddy, slimy; (coll) all in, tired; (coll) fuzzy, obscure
vasistas [vazistɑs] *m* transom
vasouiller [vazuje] *tr* (coll) to make a mess of ‖ *intr* (coll) to go badly
vasque [vask] *f* basin (*of fountain*)
vas·sal -sale [vasal] (*pl* **-saux** [so] **-sales**) *adj & mf* vassal
vaste [vast] *adj* vast
vastement [vastəmɑ̃] *adv* (coll) very
Vatican [vatikɑ̃] *m* Vatican
vaticane [vatikan] *adj fem* Vatican
va-tout [vatu] *m*—**jouer son va-tout** to stake one's all, play one's last card
vaudeville [vodvil] *m* vaudeville (*light theatrical piece interspersed with songs*); (obs) satirical song
vaudou [vodu] *adj invar & m* voodoo
vaudrai [vodre] *v* (**vaudras, vaudra, vaudrons,** etc.) see **valoir**
vau-l'eau [volo]—**à vau-l'eau** downstream; **s'en aller à vau-l'eau** (fig) to go to pot
vau·rien [vorjɛ̃] **-rienne** [rjɛn] *mf* good-for-nothing
vautour [votur] *m* vulture
vautrer [votre] *ref* to wallow
vaux [vo] *v* (**vaut**) see **valoir**
veau [vo] *m* (*pl* **veaux**) calf; veal; calfskin; (coll) lazybones, dope; **pleurer comme un veau** to cry like a baby; **veau marin** seal
vé·cu -cue [veky] *adj* true to life ‖ *v* see **vivre**
vedette [vədɛt] *f* patrol boat; scout; lead, star; **en vedette** in the limelight; **mettre en vedette** to headline, to highlight; **vedette de l'écran** movie star; **vedette du petit écran** television star
végé·tal -tale [veʒetal] (*pl* **-taux** [to]) *adj* vegetable, vegetal ‖ *m* vegetable
végéta·rien [veʒetarjɛ̃] **-rienne** [rjɛn] *adj & mf* vegetarian
végétation [veʒetasjɔ̃] *f* vegetation; **végétations (adénoïdes)** adenoids
végéter [veʒete] §10 *intr* to vegetate
véhémence [veemɑ̃s] *f* vehemence
véhé·ment [veemɑ̃] **-mente** [mɑ̃t] *adj* vehement
véhicule [veikyl] *m* vehicle
veille [vɛj] *f* watch, vigil; wakefulness; **à la veille de** on the eve of; just before; on the verge or point of; **la veille de** the eve of; the day before; **la Veille de Noël** Christmas Eve; **la Veille du jour de l'An** New Year's Eve; **veilles** sleepless nights, late nights; night work
veillée [veje] *f* evening; social evening; **veillée funèbre, veillée du corps** wake

veiller [veje] *tr* to sit up with, watch over ‖ *intr* to sit up, stay up; keep watch; **veiller à** to look after, see to
veil·leur [vɛjœr] **-leuse** [jøz] *mf* watcher ‖ *m* watchman; **veilleur de nuit** night watchman ‖ *f* see **veilleuse**
veilleuse [vɛjøz] *f* night light; rushlight; pilot light; **mettre en veilleuse** to turn down low; to dim (*the headlights*); to slow down (*production in a factory*)
vei·nard [vɛnar] **-narde** [nard] *adj* (coll) lucky ‖ *mf* (coll) lucky person
veine [vɛn] *f* vein; luck; **veine alors!** (coll) swell!
veiner [vene] *tr* to vein
vei·neux [vɛnø] **-neuse** [nøz] *adj* veined; venous
vélaire [velɛr] *adj & f* v·lar
vêler [vele] *intr* to calve
vélin [velɛ̃] *m* vellum
velléitaire [veleitɛr] *adj & mf* erratic
velléité [veleite] *f* stray impulse, fancy; **velléité de sourire** slight smile
vélo [velo] *m* bike; **faire du vélo** to go bicycle riding
vélocité [velɔsite] *f* velocity; speed; agility
vélomoteur [velɔmɔtœr] *m* motorbike
velours [vəlur] *m* velvet; **velours côtelé** corduroy
velou·té -tée [vəlute] *adj* velvety ‖ *m* velvetiness
velouter [vəlute] *tr* to make velvety
ve·lu -lue [vəly] *adj* hairy
vélum [velɔm] *m* awning
velvet [vɛlvɛt] *m* velveteen
venaison [vənɛzɔ̃] *f* venison
ve·nant [vənɑ̃] **-nante** [nɑ̃t] *adj* coming; thriving ‖ *mf* comer; **à tout venant** to all comers
vendange [vɑ̃dɑ̃ʒ] *f* grape harvest; vintage
vendanger [vɑ̃dɑ̃ʒe] §38 *tr* to pick (*the grapes*) ‖ *intr* to harvest grapes
ven·deur [vɑ̃dœr] **-deuse** [døz] *mf* seller, vendor; salesclerk; **vendeur ambulant** peddler ‖ *m* salesman ‖ *f* salesgirl, saleslady
vendre [vɑ̃dr] *tr* to sell; sell out, betray; **à vendre** for sale; **vendre à découvert** to sell short; **vendre au détail** to retail; **vendre aux enchères** to auction off; **vendre en gros** to wholesale ‖ *ref* to sell; sell oneself, sell out
vendredi [vɑ̃drədi] *m* Friday; **vendredi saint** Good Friday
ven·du -due [vɑ̃dy] *adj* sold; corrupt ‖ *mf* traitor
véné·neux [venenø] **-neuse** [nøz] *adj* poisonous
vénérable [venerabl] *adj* venerable
vénérer [venere] §10 *tr* to venerate
véné·rien [venerjɛ̃] **-rienne** [rjɛn] *adj* venereal ‖ *mf* person with venereal disease
vengeance [vɑ̃ʒɑ̃s] *f* vengeance, revenge
venger [vɑ̃ʒe] §38 *tr* to avenge ‖ *ref* to get revenge
ven·geur [vɑ̃ʒœr] **-geuse** [ʒøz] *adj* avenging ‖ *mf* avenger

veni·meux [vənimø] -**meuse** [møz] *adj* venomous

venin [vənɛ̃] *m* venom

venir [vənir] §72, §95, §96, §97 *intr (aux:* ÊTRE) to come; **à venir** forthcoming; **faire venir** to send for; **où voulez-vous en venir?** what are you getting at?; **venez avec** (coll) come along; **venir de** to have just, e.g., **il vient de partir** he has just left || *impers*—**il me** (**nous**, etc.) **vient à l'esprit que** it occurs to me (to us, etc.) that

Venise [vəniz] *f* Venice

véni·tien [venisjɛ̃] -**tienne** [sjɛn] *adj* Venetian || *(cap) mf* Venetian

vent [vɑ̃] *m* wind; **avoir le vent en poupe** to be in luck; **avoir vent de** to get wind of; **contre vents et marées** through thick and thin; **en plein vent** in the open air; **être dans le vent** to be up to date; **il fait du vent** it is windy; **les vents** (mus) the woodwinds; **vent arrière** tailwind; **vent coulis** draft; **vent debout** headwind; **vent en poupe** (naut) tailwind

vente [vɑ̃t] *f* sale; felling (*of timber*); **en vente** on sale; **en vente libre** (pharm) on sale without a prescription; **jeunes ventes** new overgrowth; **vente à l'éventaire** sidewalk sale; **vente amiable** private sale; **vente à tempérament** installment selling; **vente à terme** sale on time; **vente au détail** retailing; **vente aux enchères** auction; **vente en gros** wholesaling; **vente par correspondance** mail-order business

ventilateur [vɑ̃tilatœr] *m* ventilator; fan; electric fan

ventiler [vɑ̃tile] *tr* to ventilate; to value separately; (bk) to apportion

ventouse [vɑ̃tuz] *f* sucker; suction cup; suction grip; nozzle (*of vacuum cleaner*); vent; plunger (*for clogged drain*)

ventre [vɑ̃tr] *m* belly; stomach; womb; **à plat ventre** prostrate; **à ventre déboutonné** (coll) excessively; (coll) with all one's might; **q.ch. dans le ventre** (coll) to have s.th. on the ball; **bas ventre** (fig) genitals; **ventre à terre** (coll) lickety-split

ventricule [vɑ̃trikyl] *m* ventricle

ventriloque [vɑ̃trilɔk] *mf* ventriloquist

ventriloquie [vɑ̃trilɔki] *f* ventriloquism

ventripo·tent [vɑ̃tripɔtɑ̃] -**tente** [tɑ̃t] *adj* (coll) potbellied

ven·tru -true [vɑ̃try] *adj* potbellied

ve·nu -nue [vəny] *adj*—**bien venu** successful; welcome || *mf*—**le premier venu** the first comer; just anyone; **les nouveaux venus** the newcomers || *f* coming, advent || *v* see **venir**

Vénus [venys] *f* Venus

vénusté [venyste] *f* charm, grace

vêpres [vɛpr] *fpl* vespers

ver [vɛr] *m* worm; **tirer les vers du nez à** to worm secrets out of, to pump; **ver à soie** silkworm; **ver de terre** earthworm; **ver luisant** glowworm

véracité [verasite] *f* veracity

véranda [verɑ̃da] *f* veranda

ver·bal -bale [vɛrbal] *adj (pl* -**baux** [bo]) verbal; (gram) verb

verbaliser [vɛrbalize] *intr* to write out a report or summons; **verbaliser contre qn** to give s.o. a ticket (*e.g., for speeding*)

verbe [vɛrb] *m* verb; **avoir le verbe haut** to talk loud; **Verbe** (eccl) Word

ver·beux [vɛrbø] -**beuse** [bøz] *adj* verbose, wordy

verbiage [vɛrbjaʒ] *m* verbiage

verdâtre [vɛrdɑtr] *adj* greenish

verdeur [vɛrdœr] *f* greenness; vigor, spryness; crudeness (*of speech*)

verdict [vɛrdik], [vɛrdikt] *m* verdict

verdir [vɛrdir] *tr & intr* to turn green

verdoyer [vɛrdwaje] §47 *intr* to become green

verdure [vɛrdyr] *f* verdure; greens

vé·reux [verø] -**reuse** [røz] *adj* wormy

verge [vɛrʒ] *f* rod; shank (*of anchor*); penis

verger [vɛrʒe] *m* orchard

verglas [vɛrgla] *m* glare ice; sleet

vergogne [vɛrgɔɲ] *f*—**sans vergogne** immodest, brazen; immodestly, brazenly

véridique [veridik] *adj* veracious

vérifica·teur [verifikatœr] -**trice** [tris] *mf* inspector, examiner; **vérificateur comptable** auditor

vérification [verifikasjɔ̃] *f* verification; auditing; ascertainment

vérifier [verifje] *tr* to verify; audit; ascertain

vérin [verɛ̃] *m* jack; (aer) control; **vérin hydraulique** hydraulic lift, hydraulic jack

véritable [veritabl] *adj* veritable; real, genuine

vérité [verite] *f* truth; **à la vérité** to tell the truth; **dire à qn ses quatre vérités** (coll) to give s.o. a piece of one's mind; **en vérité** truly, in truth

ver·meil -meille [vɛrmɛj] *adj* rosy

vermillon [vɛrmijɔ̃] *adj invar & m* vermillion

vermine [vɛrmin] *f* vermin

vermou·lu -lue [vɛrmuly] *adj* worm-eaten

vermout or **vermouth** [vɛrmut] *m* vermouth

vernaculaire [vɛrnakylɛr] *adj* vernacular

vernir [vɛrnir] *tr* to varnish; **être verni** (coll) to be lucky

vernis [vɛrni] *m* varnish; (fig) veneer

vernissage [vɛrnisaʒ] *m* varnishing; private viewing (*of pictures*)

vernisser [vɛrnise] *tr* to glaze

vérole [verɔl] *f* (slang) syphilis; **petite vérole** smallpox

verrai [vɛre] *v* (**verras, verra, verrons,** etc.) see **voir**

verre [vɛr] *m* glass; crystal (*of watch*); **verre à vitre** windowpane; **verre consigné** bottle with deposit; **verre de contact** contact lens; **verre de lampe** lamp chimney; **verre dépoli** frosted glass; **verre perdu** disposable bottle (*no deposit*); **verres** eyeglasses; **verres de soleil** sunglasses; **verres grossissants** magnifying glasses; **verre taillé** cut glass

verrière [vɛrjɛr] *f* stained-glass window

verrou [vɛru] *m* bolt; **être sous les verrous** to be locked up

verrouiller [vɛruje] *tr* to bolt; lock up ‖ *ref* to lock oneself in

verrue [vɛry] *f* wart

vers [vɛr] *m* verse; **les vers** verse, poetry ‖ *prep* toward; about, e.g., **vers les cinq heures** about five o'clock

Versailles [vɛrsaj] *f* Versailles

versant [vɛrsɑ̃] *m* slope, side

versatile [vɛrsatil] *adj* fickle

verse [vɛrs] *f*—**pleuvoir à verse** to pour

ver·sé -sée [vɛrse] *adj*—**versé dans** versed in

Verseau [vɛrso] *m*—**le Verseau** (astr, astrol) Aquarius

versement [vɛrsəmɑ̃] *m* deposit; installment; **versement anticipé** payment in advance

verser [vɛrse] *tr* to pour; upset; tip over; deposit ‖ *intr* to overturn

verset [vɛrsɛ] *m* (Bib) verse

versification [vɛrsifikɑsjɔ̃] *f* versification

versifier [vɛrsifje] *tr & intr* to versify

version [vɛrsjɔ̃] *f* version; translation from a foreign language

verso [vɛrso] *m* verso; **au verso** on the back

vert [vɛr] **verte** [vɛrt] *adj* green; verdant; vigorous (*person*); new (*wine*); raw (*leather*); sharp (*scolding*); spicy (*story*); **ils sont trop verts!** sour grapes! ‖ *m* green; greenery; **mettre au vert** to put out to pasture; **se mettre au vert** to take a rest in the country

vert-de-gris [vɛrdəgri] *m invar* verdigris

vertèbre [vɛrtɛbr] *f* vertebra

verté·bré -brée [vɛrtebre] *adj & m* vertebrate

verti·cal -cale [vɛrtikal] (*pl* **-caux** [ko] **-cales**) *adj* vertical ‖ *m* (astr) vertical circle ‖ *f* vertical

vertige [vɛrtiʒ] *m* vertigo, dizziness

vertigo [vɛrtigo] *m* staggers (*of horse*); caprice

vertu [vɛrty] *f* virtue

ver·tueux [vɛrtɥø] **-tueuse** [tɥøz] *adj* virtuous

verve [vɛrv] *f* verve

ver·veux [vɛrvø] **-veuse** [vøz] *adj* lively, animated ‖ *m* fishnet

vésanie [vezani] *f* madness

vesce [vɛs] *f* vetch

vésicule [vezikyl] *f* vesicle; blister; **vésicule bilaire** gall bladder

vespasienne [vɛspazjɛn] *f* street urinal

vessie [vesi] *f* bladder; **vessie à glace** ice bag

veste [vɛst] *f* coat, suit coat; **remporter une veste** (coll) to suffer a setback; **retourner sa veste** (coll) to do an about-face; **veste croisée** double-breasted coat; **veste de pyjama** pajama top; **veste de sport** sport coat; **veste d'intérieur, veste d'appartement** lounging robe; **veste droite** single-breasted coat

vestiaire [vɛstjɛr] *m* checkroom, cloakroom; dressing room

vestibule [vɛstibyl] *m* vestibule

vestige [vɛstiʒ] *m* vestige; footprint

veston [vɛstɔ̃] *m* coat

Vésuve [vezyv] *m*—**le Vésuve** Vesuvius

vêtement [vɛtmɑ̃] *m* garment; **vêtements assortis, vêtements coordonnés** mix-and-match clothes; **vêtements de bébé** baby clothes; **vêtements de travail** working clothes

vétéran [veterɑ̃] *m* veteran

vétérinaire [veterinɛr] *adj & mf* veterinary

vétille [vetij] *f* trifle

vétiller [vetije] *intr* to split hairs

vêtir [vɛtir] §73 *tr & ref* to dress

veto [veto] *m* veto; **mettre** or **opposer son veto à** to veto

vê·tu -tue [vɛty] *v* see **vêtir**

vétuste [vetyst] *adj* decrepit, rickety

veuf [vœf] **veuve** [vœv] *adj* widowed ‖ *m* widower ‖ *f* see **veuve**

veuille [vœj] *v* (**veuilles, veuillent**) see **vouloir**

veule [vøl] *adj* (coll) feeble, weak

veuvage [vœvaʒ] *m* widowhood; widowerhood

veuve [vœv] *adv* widow

veux [vø] *v* (**veut**) see **vouloir; en veux-tu en voilà** (slang) as many as you want

vexation [vɛksasjɔ̃] *f* vexation

vexer [vɛkse] *tr* to vex

via [vja] *prep* via

viaduc [vjadyk] *m* viaduct

via·ger [vjaʒe] **-gère** [ʒɛr] *adj* life, for life ‖ *m* life annuity

viande [vjɑ̃d] *f* meat; **amène ta viande!** (slang) get over here!

vibration [vibrɑsjɔ̃] *f* vibration

vibrer [vibre] *intr* to vibrate

vicaire [vikɛr] *m* vicar

vice [vis] *m* vice; defect; **vice de conformation** physical defect; **vice de forme** (law) irregularity, flaw; **vice versa** vice versa

vice-amiral [visamiral] *m* (*pl* **-amiraux** (amiro)) vice-admiral

vice-président [visprezidɑ̃] **-présidente** [prezidɑ̃t] *mf* (*pl* **-présidents**) vice-president

vice-roi [visrwa] *m* (*pl* **-rois**) viceroy

vice-versa [viseversa], [visvɛrsa] *adv* vice versa

vi·cié -ciée [visje] *adj* foul, polluted; poor, thin (*blood*)

vicier [visje] *tr* to foul, pollute; taint, spoil

vi·cieux [visjø] **-cieuse** [sjøz] *adj* vicious; wrong (*use*); libertine; balky

vici·nal -nale [visinal] *adj* (*pl* **-naux** [no]) local, side (*road*)

vicissitude [visisityd] *f* vicissitude

vicomte [vikɔ̃t] *m* viscount

victime [viktim] *f* victim

victoire [viktwar] *f* victory

victo·rieux [viktɔrjø] **-rieuse** [rjøz] *adj* victorious

victuailles [viktɥaj] *fpl* victuals, foods

vidange [vidɑ̃ʒ] *f* draining; night soil; drain (*of pipe, sink, etc.*)

vidanger [vidɑ̃ʒe] §38 *tr* to drain

vide [vid] *adj* empty; blank; vacant ‖ *m* emptiness, void; vacuum; **emballé sous vide** vacuum packed; **vide d'air** air space

vi·dé -dée [vide] *adj* cleaned (*fish, fowl, etc.*); played out, exhausted

vide-bouteille [vidbutɛj] *m* (*pl* -**bouteilles**) siphon

vide-cave [vidkav] *m invar* sump pump

vide-citron [vidsitrɔ̃] *m* (*pl* -**citrons**) lemon squeezer

vide-gousset [vidgusɛ] *m* (*pl* -**goussets**) (hum) thief

vidéocâble [videokɑbl] *m* cable television

vidéocassette [videokasɛt] *f* videocassette, videotape

vidéogramme [videogram] *m* videorecording, videotape

vide-ordures [vidɔrdyr] *m invar* garbage shoot

vide-poches [vidpɔʃ] *m invar* dresser; pin tray; (aut) glove compartment

vider [vide] *tr* to empty; drain; clean (*fish, fowl, etc.*); settle (*a question*); **se faire vider de** (coll) to get thrown out of; be fired from; be expelled from

vi·deur [vidœr] -**deuse** [døz] *mf* (coll) bouncer (*in a night club*)

viduité [vidɥite] *f* widowhood

vidure [vidyr] *f* guts (*e.g., of cleaned fish*); **vidures de poubelle** garbage

vie [vi] *f* life; livelihood, living; **à vie** for life; **de ma (sa, etc.) vie** in my (his, etc.) life, e.g., **je ne l'ai jamais vu de ma vie** I have never seen it in my life; **jamais de la vie!** not on your life!; **vie de bâton de chaise** disorderly life; **vie de château** life of ease

vieil [vjɛj] *adj* see **vieux**

vieillard [vjɛjar] *m* old man; **les vieillards** old people

vieille [vjɛj] *f* old woman ‖ *adj* see **vieux**

vieilleries [vjɛjri] *fpl* old things; old ideas

vieillesse [vjɛjɛs] *f* old age

vieil·li -lie [vjeji] *adj* aged; out-of-date, antiquated

vieillir [vjejir] *tr* to age; make (*s.o.*) look older ‖ *intr* to age, grow old ‖ *ref* to make oneself look older

vieil·lot [vjejo] -**lotte** [jɔt] *adj* (coll) oldish, quaint

vielle [vjɛl] *f* (hist) hurdy-gurdy

viendrai [vjɛ̃dre] *v* (**viendras, viendra, viendrons,** etc.) see **venir**

Vienne [vjɛn] *f* Vienna; Vienne (*city in France*)

vien·nois [vjɛnwa] -**noise** [nwaz] *adj* Viennese ‖ (*cap*) *mf* Viennese

viens [vjɛ̃] *v* (**vient**) see **venir**

vierge [vjɛrʒ] *adj* virginal; virgin; blank; unexposed (*film*) ‖ *f* virgin; **la Vierge** (astr, astrol) Virgo

Vietnam [vjɛtnam] *m*—**le Vietnam** Vietnam

vietna·mien [vjɛtnamjɛ̃] -**mienne** [mjɛn] *adj* Vietnamese ‖ (*cap*) *mf* Vietnamese

vieux [vjø] (or **vieil** [vjɛj] before vowel or mute h) **vieille** [vjɛj] *adj* old (*wine*) ‖ (when standing before noun) *adj* old; old-fashioned; obsolete (*word, meaning, etc.*) ‖ *mf* old person ‖ *m* old man; **les vieux** old people; **mon vieux** (coll) my boy ‖ *f* see **vieille**

vif [vif] **vive** [viv] *adj* alive, living; lively, quick; bright, intense; hearty, heartfelt; sharp (*criticism*); keen (*pleasure*); spring (*water*) ‖ *m* quick; **couper dans le vif** to take drastic measures; **entrer dans le vif de** to get to the heart of; **peindre au vif** to paint from life; **piqué au vif** stung to the quick

vif-argent [vifarʒɑ̃] *m* quicksilver; (*person*) live wire

vigie [viʒi] *f* lookout

vigilance [viʒilɑ̃s] *f* vigilance

vigi·lant [viʒilɑ̃] -**lante** [lɑ̃t] *adj* vigilant ‖ *m* night watchman

vigile [viʒil] *m* night watchman ‖ *f* (eccl) vigil

vigne [viɲ] *f* vine; vineyard; **vigne blanche** clematis; **vigne de Judas** bittersweet; **vigne vierge** Virginia creeper

vigne·ron [viɲrɔ̃] -**ronne** [rɔn] *mf* winegrower; vintner

vignette [viɲɛt] *f* vignette; tax stamp; gummed tab

vignoble [viɲɔbl] *m* vineyard

vigou·reux [vigurø] -**reuse** [røz] *adj* vigorous

vigueur [vigœr] *f* vigor; **entrer en vigueur** to go into effect

vil vile [vil] *adj* vile; cheap

vi·lain [vilɛ̃] -**laine** [lɛn] (precedes the noun it modifies) *adj* nasty; ugly; naughty ‖ *mf* nasty person

vilebrequin [vilbrəkɛ̃] *m* brace (*of brace and bit*); crankshaft

vilenie [vilni] *f* villainy; abuse

villa [villa] *f* villa; cottage; small one-story home

village [vilaʒ] *m* village

villa·geois [vilaʒwa] -**geoise** [ʒwaz] *mf* villager

ville [vil] *f* city; town; **aller en ville** to go downtown; **la Ville Lumière** the City of Light (*Paris*); **ville champignon** boom town; **ville satellite** suburban town; **villes jumelées, villes réunies** twin cities

villégiature [vileʒjatyr] *f* vacation

vin [vɛ̃] *m* wine; **avoir le vin gai** to be hilariously drunk; **être entre deux vins** to be tipsy; **vin d'honneur** reception (*at which toasts are offered*); **vin d'orange** sangaree; **vin mousseux** sparkling wine; **vin ordinaire** table wine

vinaigre [vinɛgr] *m* vinegar

vinaigrette [vinɛgrɛt] *f* French dressing, vinaigrette sauce

vindica·tif [vɛ̃dikatif] -**tive** [tiv] *adj* vindictive

vingt [vɛ̃] §94 *adj & pron* twenty; the Twentieth, e.g., **Jean vingt** John the Twentieth; **vingt et un** [vɛ̃teœ̃] twenty-one; Twenty-first, e.g., **Jean vingt et un** John the Twenty-first; **vingt et unième**

twenty-first ‖ *m* twenty; twentieth (*in dates*); **vingt et un** twenty-one; twenty-first (*in dates*); **vingt et unième** twenty-first

vingtaine [vɛ̃tɛn] *f* score; **une vingtaine de** about twenty

vingt-deux [vɛ̃tdø] §94 *adj & pron* twenty-two; the Twenty-second, e.g., **Jean vingt-deux** John the Twenty-second ‖ *m* twenty-two; twenty-second (*in dates*) ‖ *interj* (slang) watch out!, cheese it!

vingt-deuxième [vɛ̃tdøzjɛm] §94 *adj, pron* (*masc, fem*), *& m* twenty-second

vingt-et-un [vɛ̃teœ̃] *m* (cards) twenty-one

vingtième [vɛ̃tjɛm] §94 *adj, pron* (*masc, fem*), *& m* twentieth

vinyle [vinil] *m* vinyl

viol [vjɔl] *m* rape; **viol collectif** gang rape

violation [vjɔlɑsjɔ̃] *f* violation

violence [vjɔlɑ̃s] *f* violence

vio·lent [vjɔlɑ̃] **-lente** [lɑ̃t] *adj* violent

violenter [vjɔlɑ̃te] *tr* to do violence to

violer [vjɔle] *tr* to violate; break (*the faith*); rape, ravish

vio·let [vjɔlɛ] **-lette** [lɛt] *adj & m* violet (*color*) ‖ *f* (bot) violet

violon [vjɔlɔ̃] *m* violin; (slang) calaboose, jug; **payer les violons** (coll) to pay the piper; **violon d'Ingres** hobby

violoncelle [vjɔlɔ̃sɛl] *m* violoncello

violoniste [vjɔlɔnist] *mf* violinist

vipère [vipɛr] *f* viper

virage [viraʒ] *m* turning; turn, e.g., **pas de virage à gauche** no left turn; (aer) bank; (phot) toning; **virage en épingle à cheveux** hairpin curve; **virages** (*public sign*) winding road; **virage sur place** U-turn

virago [virago] *f* mannish woman

virée [vire] *f* (coll) spin (*in a car*); (coll) round (*of bars*)

virement [virmɑ̃] *m* transfer (*of funds*); (naut) tacking

virer [vire] *tr* to transfer (*funds*); (phot) to tone ‖ *intr* to turn; (aer) to bank; **virer à** to turn (*sour, red, etc.*); **virer de bord** (naut) to tack

virevolte [virvɔlt] *f* turn; about-face

virevolter [virvɔlte] *intr* to make an about-face; go hither and thither

virginité [virʒinite] *f* virginity, maidenhood

virgule [virgyl] *f* (gram) comma; (*used in French to set off the decimal fraction from the integer*) decimal point

virilité [virilite] *f* virility

virole [virɔl] *f* ferrule

virologie [virɔlɔʒi] *f* virology

vir·tuel -tuelle [virtɥɛl] *adj* potential; (mech, opt, phys) virtual

virtuose [virtɥoz] *mf* virtuoso

virtuosité [virtɥozite] *f* virtuosity

virulence [virylɑ̃s] *f* virulence

viru·lent [virylɑ̃] **-lente** [lɑ̃t] *adj* virulent

virus [virys] *m* virus

vis [vis] *f* screw; thread (*of screw*); spiral staircase; **fermer à vis** to screw shut; **serrer la vis à** (fig) to put the screws on; **vis à ailettes** wing nut; **vis à bois** wood

screw; **vis à métaux, vis à tôle** machine screw; **vis à tête plate** flat-headed screw; **vis à tête ronde** round-headed screw; **vis de blocage** setscrew ‖ [vi] *v* (**vit**) see **vivre**; see **voir**

visa [viza] *m* visa; (fig) approval

visage [vizaʒ] *m* face; **à deux visages** two-faced; **faire bon visage à** to pretend to be friendly to; **trouver visage de bois** to find the door closed; **visages pâles** palefaces; **voir qn sous son vrai visage** to see s.o. in his true colors

visagiste [vizaʒist] *mf* beautician

vis-à-vis [vizavi] *adv* vis-à-vis; **vis-à-vis de** vis-à-vis; towards; in the presence of ‖ *m* vis-à-vis; **en vis-à-vis** facing

viscère [visɛr] *m* organ; **viscères** viscera

visée [vize] *f* aim

viser [vize] §96 *tr* to aim; aim at; concern; visa ‖ *intr* to aim; **viser à** to aim at; aim to

viseur [vizœr] *m* viewfinder; sight (*of gun*); **viseur de lancement** bombsight

visibilité [vizibilite] *f* visibility; **sans visibilité** blind (*flying*)

visible [vizibl] *adj* visible; obvious; (coll) at home, free; (coll) open to the public

visière [vizjɛr] *f* visor; sight (*of gun*); **rompre en visière à** to take a stand against

vision [vizjɔ̃] *f* vision

visionnaire [vizjɔnɛr] *adj & mf* visionary

visionner [vizjɔne] *tr* to view, inspect

visionneuse [vizjɔnøz] *f* viewer

visite [vizit] *f* visit; inspection; **en** or **de visite** visiting; **faire** or **rendre visite à** to visit

visiter [vizite] *tr* to visit; inspect

visi·teur [vizitœr] **-teuse** [tøz] *adj* visiting (*e.g., nurse*) ‖ *mf* visitor; inspector

vison [vizɔ̃] *m* mink

vis·queux [viskø] **-queuse** [køz] *adj* viscous

visser [vise] *tr* to screw; screw on; (coll) to put the screws on

visualiser [vizɥalize] *tr* to visualize

vi·suel -suelle [vizɥɛl] *adj* visual

vi·tal -tale [vital] *adj* (*pl* **-taux** [to]) vital

vitaliser [vitalize] *tr* to vitalize

vitalité [vitalite] *f* vitality

vitamine [vitamin] *f* vitamin

vite [vit] *adj* fast, swift ‖ *adv* fast, quickly; **faites vite!** hurry up!

vitesse [vitɛs] *f* speed, velocity; rate; **à toute vitesse** at full speed; **changer de vitesse** (aut) to shift gears; **en grande vitesse** (rr) by express; **en petite vitesse** (rr) by freight; **en première (seconde, etc.) vitesse** (aut) in first (second, etc.) gear; **vitesse acquise** momentum

viticole [vitikɔl] *adj* wine

viticulteur [vitikyltœr] *m* winegrower

vitrage [vitraʒ] *m* glasswork; small window curtain; sash; glazing

vi·trail [vitraj] *m* (*pl* **-traux** [tro]) stained-glass window

vitre [vitr] *f* windowpane, pane; (aut) window; **casser les vitres** (coll) to kick up a fuss

vi·tré -trée [vitre] *adj* glazed; vitreous (*humor*); glassed-in

vi·treux [vitrø] **-treuse** [trøz] *adj* glassy; vitreous

vitrier [vitrije] *m* glazier

vitrine [vitrin] *f* show window; showcase; glass cabinet; **lécher les vitrines** (coll) to go window-shopping

vitupérer [vitypere] §10 *tr* to vituperate, abuse ‖ *intr*—**vitupérer contre** (coll) to vituperate

vivace [vivas] *adj* hardy, vigorous; long-lived; (bot) perennial

vivacité [vivasite] *f* vivacity

vivan·dier [vivãdje] **-dière** [djɛr] *mf* sutler ‖ *f* camp follower

vi·vant [vivã] **-vante** [vãt] *adj* living, alive; lively; modern, spoken (*language*) ‖ *m*—**bon vivant** high liver, jolly companion; **du vivant de** during the lifetime of; **les vivants et les morts** the quick and the dead

vivat [viva] *m* viva ‖ *interj* viva!

vivement [vivmã] *adv* quickly, warmly; deeply; sharply, briskly

viveur [vivœr] *m* pleasure seeker, rounder

vivier [vivje] *m* fish preserve, fishpond

vivifier [vivifje] *tr* to vivify, vitalize

vivisection [vivisɛksjɔ̃] *f* vivisection

vivoir [vivwar] *m* (Canad) living room

vivoter [vivɔte] *intr* (coll) to live from hand to mouth

vivre [vivr] *m*—**le vivre et le couvert** room and board; **le vivre et le vêtement** food and clothing; **vivres** provisions; (mil) rations, supplies ‖ §74 *tr* to live (*one's life, faith, art*); live through, experience ‖ *intr* to live; **être difficile à vivre** to be difficult to live with; **qui vive?** (mil) who is there?; **qui vivra verra** time will tell; **vive!**, **vivent!** viva!, long live!; **vivre au jour le jour** to live from hand to mouth; **vivre de** to live on

vizir [vizir] *m* vizier

vlan [vlã] *interj* whack!

vocable [vɔkabl] *m* word

vocabulaire [vɔkabylɛr] *m* vocabulary

vo·cal -cale [vɔkal] *adj* (*pl* **-caux** [ko]) vocal

vocaliser [vɔkalize] *tr, intr, & ref* to vocalize

vocatif [vɔkatif] *m* vocative

vocation [vɔkɑsjɔ̃] *f* vocation, calling; **vocation pédagogique** teaching career

vociférer [vɔsifere] §10 *tr* to shout (*e.g., insults*) ‖ *intr* to vociferate

vœu [vø] *m* (*pl* **vœux**) vow; wish; resolution; **meilleurs vœux!** best wishes!; **tous mes vœux!** my best wishes!

vogue [vɔg] *f* vogue, fashion; **en vogue** in vogue, in fashion

voguer [vɔge] *intr* to sail; **vogue la galère!** let's chance it, here goes!

voici [vwasi] *prep* here is, here are; for, e.g., **voici quatre jours qu'elle est partie** she has been gone for four days; **le voici** here he is; **nous voici** here we are;

que voici here, e.g., **mon frère que voici va vous accompagner** my brother here is going to accompany you

voie [vwa] *f* way; road; lane (*of highway*); (anat) tract; (rr) track; **en voie de** on the road to, nearing; **être en bonne voie** to be doing well; **voie d'eau** leak; **voie de garage** driveway; **voie d'évitement** siding; **voie lactée** Milky Way; **voie maritime** seaway; **voie(s) de fait** (law) assault and battery; **voie surface** surface mail

voilà [vwala] *prep* there is, there are; here is, here are; that's, e.g., **voilà pourquoi** that's why; ago, e.g., **voilà quatre jours qu'elle est partie** she left four days ago; **voilà, monsieur** there you are, sir

voile [vwal] *m* veil; (phot) fog (*on negative*); **voile du palais** soft palate; **voile noir** (pathol) blackout ‖ *f* sail; sailboat; **faire voile sur** to set sail for

voi·lé -lée [vwale] *adj* veiled; overcast; muffled; warped; husky (*voice*); (phot) fogged; **peu voilé** thinly veiled, broad (*e.g., hint*)

voiler [vwale] *tr* to veil; (phot) to fog ‖ *ref* to cloud over; become warped

voi·lier [vwalje] **-lière** [ljɛr] *adj* sailing ‖ *m* sailboat; sailmaker; migratory bird

voilure [vwalyr] *f* sails; warping

voir [vwar] §75, §95 *tr* to see; **faire voir** to show; **voir jouer** to see (*s.o.*) playing, to see (*s.o.*) play; to see (*s.th.*) played; **voir qn qui vient** to see s.o. coming, see s.o. come; **voir venir qn** to see s.o. coming, see s.o. come; (fig) to see through s.o. ‖ *intr* to see; **faites voir!** let's see it!, let me see it!; **j'en ai vu bien d'autres** I have seen worse than that; **n'avoir rien à voir avec, à,** or **dans** to have nothing to do with; **voir à** + *inf* to see that + *ind*, e.g., **voir à nous loger** to see that we are housed; **voir au dos** see other side, turn the page; **voyons!** see here!, come now! ‖ *ref* to see oneself; see one another; be obvious; be seen, be found

voire [vwar] *adv* nay, indeed; **voire même** or even, and even

voirie [vwari] *f* highway department; garbage collection; dump

voi·sé -sée [vwaze] *adj* voiced

voi·sin [vwazɛ̃] **-sine** [zin] *adj* neighboring; adjoining; **voisin de** near ‖ *mf* neighbor

voisinage [vwazinaʒ] *m* neighborhood; neighborliness

voisiner [vwazine] *intr* to visit one's neighbors; **voisiner avec** to be placed next to

voiture [vwatyr] *f* vehicle; carriage; (aut, rr) car; **en voiture!** all aboard!; **petite voiture** (coll) wheelchair; **voiture à bras** handcart; **voiture banalisée** unmarked police car; **voiture de location** rented car; **voiture d'enfant** baby carriage; **voiture de pompier** fire engine; **voiture de remise** rented car; **voiture de ronde** patrol car; **voiture de série** stock car; **voiture de tourisme** pleasure car; **voiture d'infirme** wheelchair; **voiture d'occasion** used car

voiture-bar [vwatyrbar] *f* (*pl* **voitures-bars**) club car

voiturette [vwatyrɛt] *f*—**voiturette de golf** golf cart

voiture-lit [vwatyrli] *f* (*pl* **voitures-lits**) sleeping car

voiturer [vwatyre] *tr* to transport, convey

voiture-restaurant [vwatyrrɛstorɑ̃] *f* (*pl* **voitures-restaurants**) dining car

voiture-salon [vwatyrsalɔ̃] *f* (*pl* **voitures-salons**) parlor car

voix [vwa], [vwɑ] *f* voice; vote; **à haute voix** aloud; in a loud voice; **à pleine voix** at the top of one's voice; **avoir voix au chapitre** (coll) to have a say in the matter; **à voix basse** in a low voice; **à voix haute** in a loud voice; **de vive voix** by word of mouth; **voix de tête, voix de fausset** falsetto

vol [vɔl] *m* theft, robbery; flight; flock; **au vol** in flight; in passing; **à vol d'oiseau** as the crow flies; **de haut vol** high-flying; big-time (*crook*); **vol à la demande** charter flight; **vol à la tire** purse snatching; **vol à l'étalage** shoplifting; **vol avec effraction** burglary; **vol à voile** gliding; **vol cosmique** space flight; **vol plané** volplane; **vol sans visibilité** blind flying; **vol sur aile delta, vol libre** hang gliding

volage [vɔlaʒ] *adj* fickle, changeable

volaille [vɔlɑj] *f* fowl; (slang) hens (*women*); (slang) gal

vo·lant [vɔlɑ̃] **-lante** [lɑ̃t] *adj* flying ‖ *m* steering wheel; flywheel; shuttlecock; sail (*of windmill*); flounce (*of dress*); leaf (*attached to stub*); **volant de sécurité** safety margin, reserve

vola·til -tile [vɔlatil] *adj* volatile ‖ *m* bird; fowl

volatiliser [vɔlatilize] *tr & ref* to volatilize

volcan [vɔlkɑ̃] *m* volcano

volcanique [vɔlkanik] *adj* volcanic

vole [vɔl] *f*—**faire la vole** to take all the tricks

volée [vɔle] *f* volley; flight (*of birds; of stairs*); flock; **à la volée** on the wing; at random; **à toute volée** loud and clear; **de haute volée** upper-class; **de la première volée** first-class, crack; **sonner à toute volée** to peal out

voler [vɔle] §95 *tr* to rob; steal; fly at; **ne l'avoir pas volé** to deserve all that is coming; **voler à** to steal from ‖ *intr* to rob; steal; fly

volet [vɔlɛ] *m* shutter; inside flap; end paper; (aer) flap; **trier sur le volet** to choose with care

voleter [vɔlte] §34 *intr* to flutter

vo·leur [vɔlœr] **-leuse** [løz] *adj* thievish ‖ *mf* thief; **au voleur!** stop thief!; **voleur à la tire** pickpocket; **voleur à l'étalage** shoplifter; **voleur de grand chemin** highwayman

volition [vɔlisjɔ̃] *f* volition

volley-ball [vɔlɛbol] *m* volleyball

vol·leyeur [vɔlɛjœr] **-leyeuse** [lɛjøz] *mf* volleyball player

volontaire [vɔlɔ̃tɛr] *adj* voluntary; headstrong, willful; determined (*chin*) ‖ *mf* volunteer

volonté [vɔlɔ̃te] *f* will; wishes; **à volonté** at will; **bonne volonté** good will; **faire ses quatre volontés** (coll) to do just as one pleases; **mauvaise volonté** ill will

volontiers [vɔlɔ̃tje] *adv* gladly, willingly

volt [vɔlt] *m* volt

voltage [vɔltaʒ] *m* voltage

volte-face [vɔltəfas] *f invar* volte-face

voltige [vɔltiʒ] *f* acrobatics

voltiger [vɔltiʒe] §38 *intr* to flit about; flutter

voltmètre [vɔltmɛtr] *m* voltmeter

volubile [vɔlybil] *adj* voluble

volume [vɔlym] *m* volume; **faire du volume** (coll) to put on airs

volumi·neux [vɔlyminø] **-neuse** [nøz] *adj* voluminous

volupté [vɔlypte] *f* voluptuousness, ecstasy

volup·tueux [vɔlyptɥø] **-tueuse** [tɥøz] *adj* voluptuous ‖ *mf* voluptuary

vomir [vɔmir] *tr & intr* to vomit

vomissure [vɔmisyr] *f* vomit

vont [vɔ̃] *v* see **aller**

vorace [vɔras] *adj* voracious

voracité [vɔrasite] *f* voracity

vos [vo] §88 your

vo·tant [vɔtɑ̃] **-tante** [tɑ̃t] *mf* voter

vote [vɔt] *m* vote; **passer au vote** to vote on; **vote affirmatif** yea; **vote négatif** nay; **vote par correspondance** absentee ballot; **vote par procuration** proxy

voter [vɔte] *tr* to vote; vote for ‖ *intr* to vote; **voter à mains levées** to vote by show of hands; **voter par assis et levé** to give one's vote by standing or by remaining seated

vo·tif [vɔtif] **-tive** [tiv] *adj* votive

votre [vɔtr] §88 your

vôtre [votr] §89 yours

voudrai [vudre] *v* (**voudras, voudra, voudrons,** etc.) see **vouloir**

vouer [vwe] *tr* to vow, dedicate; doom, condemn; vous é headed for; doomed to ‖ §96 *ref*—**se vouer à** to dedicate oneself to

vouloir [vulwar] *m* will ‖ §76, §95 *tr* to want, wish; require; **je voudrais** I would like; I would like to; **veuillez** + *inf* please + *inf;* **voulez-vous vous taire?** will you be quiet?; **vouloir bien** to be glad to, be willing to; **vouloir dire** to mean ‖ *intr*—**en vouloir à** to bear a grudge against; **je veux!** (slang) and how!; **je veux bien** I'm quite willing; **si vous voulez bien** if you don't mind ‖ *ref*—**s'en vouloir** to have it in for each other

vou·lu -lue [vuly] *adj* required; deliberate ‖ *v* see **vouloir**

vous [vu] §85, §87 you, to you; **vous autres Américains** you Americans

vous-même [vumɛm] §86 yourself

voussoir [vuswar] *m* (archit) arch stone

voussure [vusyr] *f* arch, arching

voûte [vut] *f* vault; **voûte céleste** canopy of heaven

voûter [vute] *tr* to vault; bend ‖ *ref* to become round-shouldered

vouvoyer [vuvwaje] §47 *tr* to address with formality; use formal grammatical forms (**vous**, etc.) in speaking to a stranger, a superior, or, often (if a Catholic), to God ‖ *ref* to use **vous** and corresponding verbal forms in speaking with one another

voy. *abbr* (**voyez**) see

voyage [vwaja3] *m* trip, journey, voyage; ride (*in car, train, plane, etc.*); **voyage à forfait** all-expense tour; **voyage aller et retour** round trip; **voyage de noces** honeymoon

voyager [vwaja3e] §38 *intr* to travel

voya·geur [vwaja3œr] **-geuse** [3øz] *mf* traveler; passenger

voyance [vwajɑ̃s] *f* clairvoyance

voyant [vwajɑ̃] **voyante** [vwajɑ̃t] *adj* loud, gaudy ‖ *mf* clairvoyant ‖ *m* signal; (aut) gauge ‖ *f* fortuneteller

voyelle [vwajɛl] *f* vowel

voyeur [vwajœr] **voyeuse** [vwajøz] *mf* voyeur ‖ *m* Peeping Tom

voyez [vwaje] *v* (**voyons**) see **voir**

voyou [vwaju] **voyoute** [vwajut] *adj* gutter (*e.g., language*) ‖ *mf* guttersnipe; brat; hoodlum

vrac [vrak]—**en vrac** unpacked, loose; in bulk; in disorder

vrai vraie [vrɛ], [vre] *adj* true, real, genuine ‖ *m* truth; **à vrai dire** to tell the truth; **pour vrai** (coll) for good

vraiment [vrɛmɑ̃] *adv* truly, really

vraisemblable [vrɛsɑ̃blabl] *adj* probable, likely; true to life, realistic (*play, novel*)

vraisemblance [vrɛsɑ̃blɑ̃s] *f* probability, likelihood; realism

vrille [vrij] *f* drill; (aer) spin; (bot) tendril

vriller [vrije] *tr* to bore ‖ *intr* to go into a tailspin

vrombir [vrɔ̃bir] *intr* to throb; buzz; hum, purr (*said of motor*)

vu vue [vy] *adj* seen, regarded; **bien vu de** in favor with; **mal vu de** out of favor with ‖ *m*—**au vu de** upon presentation of; **au vu et au su de tout le monde** openly ‖ *f* view; sight; eyesight; **avoir à vue** to have in mind; **à vue** in sight; (com) on demand; **à vue de nez** at first sight; at a rough estimate; **à vue d'œil** visibly, quickly; **de vue** by sight; **en vue** in evidence; in sight; **en vue de** in order to; **garder à vue** to keep under observation, keep locked up; **perdre qn de vue** to lose sight of s.o.; get out of touch with s.o.; **vue à vol d'oiseau** bird's-eye view; **vues sur** designs on ‖ *vu prep* considering, in view of; **vu que** whereas ‖ *v* see **voir**

vulcaniser [vylkanize] *tr* to vulcanize

vulgaire [vylgɛr] *adj* common, vulgar; ordinary, everyday; vernacular ‖ *m* common herd; vernacular

vulgariser [vylgarize] *tr* to popularize; make vulgar

vulgarité [vylgarite] *f* vulgarity

vulnérable [vylnerabl] *adj* vulnerable

Vve *abbr* (**veuve**) widow

W

W, w [dublǝve] *m invar* twenty-third letter of the French alphabet

wagon [vagɔ̃] *m* (rr) car, coach; (coll) big car; **un wagon** (coll) a lot; **wagon à bagages** baggage car; **wagon à bestiaux** cattle car; **wagon couvert** boxcar; **wagon de marchandises** freight car; **wagon de voyageurs** passenger car; **wagon frigorifique** or **réfrigérant** refrigerator car; **wagon plat** flat car

wagon-bar [vagɔ̃bar] *m* (*pl* **wagons-bars**) club car

wagon-citerne [vagɔ̃sitɛrn] *m* (*pl* **wagons-citernes**) tank car

wagon-lit [vagɔ̃li] *m* (*pl* **wagons-lits**) sleeping car

wagon-poste [vagɔ̃pɔst] *m* (*pl* **wagons-poste**) mail car

wagon-réservoir [vagɔ̃rezɛrvwar] *m* (*pl* **wagons-réservoirs**) tank car

wagon-restaurant [vagɔ̃rɛstɔrɑ̃] *m* (*pl* **wagons-restaurants**) dining car

wagon-salon [vagɔ̃salɔ̃] *m* (*pl* **wagons-salons**) parlor car

wagon-tombereau [vagɔ̃tɔ̃bro] *m* (*pl* **wagons-tombereaux**) dump truck

walkman [wɔkman] *m* walkman (*portable earphones*)

wallace [valas] *f* drinking fountain

wal·lon [walɔ̃] **-lonne** [lɔn] *adj* Walloon ‖ *m* Walloon (*dialect*) ‖ (*cap*) *mf* Walloon

warrant [warɑ̃], [varɑ̃] *m* receipt

water-polo [waterpɔlo] *m* water polo

waterproof [waterpruf] *adj invar* waterproof ‖ *m invar* raincoat

waters [water], [vater] *mpl* toilet

watt [wat] *m* watt

watt-heure [watœr] *m* (*pl* **watts-heures**) watt-hour

wattman [watman] *m* motorman

wattmètre [watmɛtr] *m* wattmeter

week-end [wikɛnd] *m* (*pl* **-ends**) weekend

whisky [wiski] *m* whiskey; **whisky écossais** Scotch

wolfram [vɔlfram] *m* wolfram

X

X, x [iks], *[iks] *m invar* twenty-fourth letter of the French alphabet
Xavier [gzavje] *m* Xavier
xénon [ksenɔ̃] *m* xenon
xénophobe [ksenɔfɔb] *adj* xenophobic ‖ *mf* xenophobe

Xérès [kerɛs], [gzerɛs] *m* Jerez; sherry
xérographie [kserɔgrafi] *f* xerography
xérographier [kserɔgrafje] *tr* to xerograph
Xerxès [gzɛrsɛs] *m* Xerxes
xylophone [ksilɔfɔn] *m* xylophone

Y

Y, y [igrɛk], *[igrɛk] *m invar* twenty-fifth letter of the French alphabet
y [i] *pron pers* §87 to it, to them; at it, at them; in it, in them; by it, by them; of it, of them, e.g., **j'y pense** I am thinking of it or them; (untranslated with certain verbs), e.g., **je n'y vois pas** I don't see; e.g., **il s'y connaît** (coll) he's an expert, he knows what he's talking about; him, her, e.g., **je m'y fie** I trust him; **allez-y!** go ahead!, start!; **ça y est!** that's it!; **je n'y suis pour personne** I am not at home for anybody; **je n'y suis pour rien** I have nothing to do with it; **j'y suis!** I've got it! ‖ *adv* there; here, in, e.g., **Monsieur votre père y est-il?** is your father here?, is your father in?
yacht [jɔt], [jak] *m* yacht; **yacht à glace** iceboat

yacht-club [jɔtklœb] *m* yacht club
yankee [jãki] *adj masc* Yankee ‖ (*cap*) *mf* Yankee
yèble [jɛbl] *f* (bot) elder; **l'yèble** the elder
yeoman [jɔman] *m* yeoman
yeuse [jøz] *f* holm oak; **l'yeuse** the holm oak
yeux [jø] *mpl* see **œil**
yé-yé [jeje] (*pl* -**yés**) *adj & mf* jitterbug
yi·dich -diche [jidiʃ] *adj & m* Yiddish
yiddish [jidiʃ] *adj invar & m* Yiddish
yogourt [jɔgur] *m* yogurt
yole [jɔl] *f* yawl
Yonne [jɔn] *f* Yonne; **l'Yonne** the Yonne
yougoslave [jugɔslav] *adj* Yugoslav ‖ (*cap*) *mf* Yugoslav
Yougoslavie [jugɔslavi] *f* Yugoslavia; **la Yougoslavie** Yugoslavia
youyou [juju] *m* dinghy

Z

Z, z [sɛd] *m invar* twenty-sixth letter of the French alphabet
za·zou -zoue [zazu] *adj* (coll) jazzy ‖ *m* (coll) zoot suiter
zèbre [zɛbr] *m* zebra; (slang) guy
zébrer [zebre] §10 *tr* to stripe; **le soleil zèbre** the sun casts streaks of light on
zébrure [zebryr] *f* stripe
zéla·teur [zelatœr] -**trice** [tris] *mf* zealot
zèle [zɛl] *m* zeal
zénith [zenit] *m* zenith
zéphyr [zefir] *m* zephyr
zeppelin [zɛplɛ̃] *m* zeppelin
zéro [zero] *m* zero; **les avoir à zéro** (slang) to be scared stiff
zest [zɛst] *m*—**entre le zist et le zest** (coll) betwixt and between ‖ *interj* tush!
zeste [zɛst] *m* peel (*of citrus fruit*); dividing membrane (*of nut*); **pas un zeste** (fig) not a particle of difference
Zeus [zøs] *m* Zeus
zézaiement [zezɛmã] *m* lisp

zézayer [zezeje] §49 *intr* to lisp
zibeline [ziblin] *f* sable
zieuter [zjøte] *tr* (slang) to get a load of
zigzag [zigzag] *m* zigzag; gypsy moth
zigzaguer [zigzage] *intr* to zigzag
zinc [zɛ̃g] *m* zinc; (coll) bar
zizanie [zizani] *f* wild rice; tare; **semer la zizanie** to sow discord
zodiaque [zɔdjak] *m* zodiac
zonage [zɔnaʒ] *m* zoning
zone [zon] *f* zone; **zone bleue** center city with limited parking; **zone chic** fashionable neighborhood
zoning [zoniŋ] *m* zoning
zoo [zɔo] *m* zoo
zoologie [zɔɔlɔʒi] *f* zoology
zoologique [zɔɔlɔʒik] *adj* zoologic(al)
zoom [zum] *m* zoom; zoom lens
zouave [zwav] *m* Zouave; **faire le zouave** (coll) to play the fool
zut [zyt] *interj* heck!; hang it!
zygote [zigɔt] *m* zygote

ANGLAIS–FRANÇAIS

A, a [e] *s* Iière lettre de l'alphabet

a *art indef* un

aback [ə'bæk] *adv* avec le vent dessus; **taken aback** déconcerté

abandon [ə'bændən] *s* abandon *m* ‖ *tr* abandonner

abase [ə'bes] *tr* abaisser, humilier

abasement [ə'besmənt] *s* abaissement *m*

abash [ə'bæʃ] *tr* décontenancer

abashed *adj* confus, confondu

abate [ə'bet] *tr* (*to reduce*) diminuer, réduire; (*part of price*) rabattre ‖ *intr* se calmer; (*said of wind*) tomber

abbess ['æbɪs] *s* abbesse *f*

abbey ['æbi] abbaye *f*

abbot ['æbət] *s* abbé *m*

abbreviate [ə'brivɪˌet] *tr* abréger

abbreviation [əˌbrivɪ'eʃən] *s* abréviation *f*

A B C's [ˌeˌbi'siz] *spl* (letterword) a b c *m*

abdicate ['æbdɪˌket] *tr & intr* abdiquer

abdomen ['æbdəmən], [æb'domən] *s* abdomen *m*

abduct [æb'dʌkt] *tr* enlever, ravir

abet [ə'bɛt] *v* (*pret & pp* **abetted;** *ger* **abetting**) *tr* encourager

abettor [ə'bɛtər] *s* complice *mf*

abeyance [ə'be·əns] *s* suspension *f;* **in abeyance** en suspens

ab·hor [æb'hɔr] *v* (*pret & pp* **-horred;** *ger* **-horring**) *tr* abhorrer, détester

abhorrent [æb'hɔrənt] *adj* détestable, répugnant

abide [ə'baɪd] *v* (*pret & pp* **abode** or **abided**) *tr* attendre‖ *intr* demeurer, continuer, persister; **to abide by** s'en tenir à; rester fidèle à

abili·ty [ə'bɪlɪti] *s* (*pl* **-ties**) (*power to perform*) capacité *f*, compétence *f;* (*proficiency*) aptitude *f;* (*cleverness*) habileté *f*, talent *m*

abject [æb'dʒɛkt] *adj* abject

ablative ['æblətɪv] *adj & s* ablatif *m*

ablaut ['æblaʊt] *s* apophonie *f*

ablaze [ə'blez] *adj* (*on fire*) enflammé; (*colorful*) replendissant ‖ *adv* en feu

able ['ebəl] *adj* capable, habile; **to be able to** pouvoir

a'ble-bod'ied *adj* robuste, vigoureux; (*seaman*) breveté

abloom [ə'blum] *adj & adv* en fleur

abnormal [æb'nɔrməl] *adj* anormal

abnormali·ty [ˌæbnɔr'mælɪti] *s* (*pl* **-ties**) anomalie *f*, irrégularité *f;* (*of body*) difformité *f*

aboard [ə'bord] *adv* à bord; **all aboard!** en voiture!; **to go aboard** s'embarquer ‖ *prep* à bord de

abode [ə'bod] *s* demeure *f*, résidence *f*

abolish [ə'balɪʃ] *tr* abolir

A-bomb ['eˌbam] *s* bombe *f* atomique

abomination [əˌbamɪ'neʃən] *s* abomination *f*

aborigines [ˌæbə'rɪdʒɪˌniz] *spl* aborigènes *mpl*

abort [ə'bɔrt] *intr* avorter

abortion [ə'bɔrʃən] *s* avortement *m*, I.V.G. *f*

abound [ə'baʊnd] *intr* abonder

about [ə'baʊt] *adv* (*all round*) à la ronde, tout autour; (*almost*) presque; (*here and there*) çà et là; **to be about to** être sur le point de ‖ *prep* (*around*) autour de, aux environs de; (*approximately*) environ; vers, e.g., **about six o'clock** vers six heures; (*concerning*) au sujet de; **it is about** (*it concerns*) . . . il s'agit de . . .

about'-face' or **about'-face'** *s* volte-face *f;* (mil) demi-tour *m* ‖ **about'-face'** *intr* faire volte-face

above [ə'bʌv] *adv* (*overhead*) en haut, audessus; (*earlier*) ci-dessus ‖ *prep* audessus de; (*more than*) plus que, outre; (*another point on the river*) en amont de; **above all** surtout

above'-men'tioned *adj* susmentionné

abrasive [ə'bresiv] *adj & s* abrasif *m*

abreast [ə'brɛst] *adj & adv* de front; **three abreast** par rangs de trois; **to be abreast of** or **with** être en ligne avec; **to keep abreast of** se tenir au courant de

abridge [ə'brɪdʒ] *tr* abréger

abridgment [ə'brɪdʒmənt] *s* (*shortened version*) abrégé *m*, résumé *m*; (*shortening*) diminution *f*, réduction *f*

abroad [ə'brɔd] *adv* au loin; (*in foreign parts*) à l'étranger

abrogate ['æbrəˌget] *tr* abroger

abrupt [ə'brʌpt] *adj* (*steep; impolite*) abrupt; (*hasty*) brusque, précipité

abscess ['æbsɛs] *s* abcès *m*

abscond [æb'skand] *intr* s'enfuir, déguerpir; **to abscond with** lever le pied avec

absence ['æbsəns] *s* absence *f*

absent ['æbsənt] *adj* absent ‖ [æb'sɛnt] *tr*—**to absent oneself** s'absenter

absentee [ˌæbsən'ti] *s* absent *m*

ab'sentee bal'lot *s* vote *m* par correspondance

ab'sent-mind'ed *adj* absent, distrait

absolute ['æbsəˌlut] *adj & s* absolu *m*

absolutely [ˌæbsə'lutli] *adv* absolument

absolve [æb'salv] *tr* absoudre

absorb [æb'sɔrb] *tr* absorber; **to be** or **become absorbed in** s'absorber dans

absorbent [æb'sɔrbənt] *adj* absorbant; (*cotton*) hydrophile ‖ *s* absorbant *m*

absorbing [æb'sɔbɪŋ] *adj* absorbant

abstain [æb'sten] *intr* s'abstenir

abstemious [æb'stimi·əs] *adj* abstinent, sobre

abstinent ['æbstɪnənt] *adj* abstinent

abstract ['æbstrækt] *adj* abstrait ‖ *s* abrégé *m*, résumé *m* ‖ *tr* résumer ‖ [æb'strækt] *tr* abstraire; (*to remove*) soustraire

abstractedly [æb'stræktɪdli] *adv* d'un œil distrait

abstruse [æb'strus] *adj* abstrus

absurd [æb'sʌrd] *adj* absurde

absurdi·ty [æb'sʌrdɪti] *s* (*pl* **-ties**) absurdité *f*

abundance [ə'bʌndəns] s abondance *f*
abundant [ə'bʌndənt] *adj* abondant
abuse [ə'bjus] s abus *m*; (*mistreatment*) maltraitement *m*; (*insulting words*) insultes *fpl* ‖ [ə'bjuz] *tr* abuser de; maltraiter; insulter
abusive [ə'bjusɪv] *adj* (*insulting*) injurieux; (*wrong*) abusif
abut [ə'bʌt] *v* (*pret & pp* **abutted;** *ger* **abutting**) *intr*—**to abut on** border, confiner
abutment [ə'bʌtmənt] s (*of wall*) contrefort *m*; (*of bridge*) culée *f*; (*of arch*) pied-droit *m*
abyss [ə'bɪs] s abîme *m*
A.C. ['e'si] s (letterword) (**alternating current**) courant *m* alternatif
academic [,ækə'dɛmɪk] *adj* (*of a college*) universitaire; (*of an academy*) académique; (*theoretical*) théorique ‖ s étudiant *m* or professeur *m* de l'université
academician [ə,kædə'mɪʃən] s académicien *m*
acade·my [ə'kædəmi] s (*pl* **-mies**) académie *f*; (*preparatory school*) collège *m*
accede [æk'sid] *intr* acquiescer; **to accede to** accéder à; (*the throne*) monter sur
accelerate [æk'sɛlə,ret] *tr & intr* accélérer
accelerator [æk'sɛlə,retər] s accélérateur *m*
accent ['æksɛnt] s accent *m* ‖ ['æksɛnt], [æk'sɛnt] *tr* accentuer
accentuate [æk'sɛntʃu,et] *tr* accentuer
accept [æk'sɛpt] *tr* accepter
acceptable [æk'sɛptəbəl] *adj* acceptable
acceptance [æk'sɛptəns] s acceptation *f*; (*approval*) approbation *f*
acceptation [,æksɛp'teʃən] s acceptation *f*; (*meaning*) acception *f*
access ['æksɛs] s accès *m*
accessible [æk'sɛsɪbəl] *adj* accessible
accession [æk'sɛʃən] s accession *f*
accesso·ry [æk'sɛsəri] *adj* accessoire ‖ s (*pl* **-ries**) accessoire *m*; (*to a crime*) complice *mf*
acc'ess route' s voie *f* de raccordement, bretelle *f*
accident ['æksɪdənt] s accident *m;* **by accident** par accident
accidental [,æksɪ'dɛntəl] *adj* accidentel ‖ s (mus) accident *m*
ac'cident-prone' *adj* prédisposé aux accidents
acclaim [ə'klem] *tr* acclamer
acclimate ['æklɪ,met] *tr* acclimater
accommodate [ə'kɑmə,det] *tr* accommoder; (*to oblige*) rendre service à; (*to lodge*) loger
accommodating [ə'kɑmə,detɪŋ] *adj* accommodant, serviable
accommodation [ə,kɑmə'deʃən] s accommodation *f;* **accommodations** commoditiés *fpl*; (*in a train*) place *f*; (*in a hotel*) chambre *f*; (*room and board*) le vivre et le couvert
accompaniment [ə'kʌmpənɪmənt] s accompagnement *m*

accompanist [ə'kʌmpənist] s accompagnateur *m*
accompa·ny [ə'kʌmpəni] *v* (*pret & pp* **-nied**) *tr* accompagner
accomplice [ə'kɑmplɪs] s complice *mf*
accomplish [ə'kɑmplɪʃ] *tr* accomplir
accomplishment [ə'kɑmplɪʃmənt] s accomplissement *m*, réalisation *f*; (*thing itself*) œuvre *f* accomplie; **accomplishments** arts *mpl* d'agrément, talents *mpl*
accord [ə'kɔrd] s accord *m*; **in accord** d'accord; **of one's own accord** de son plein gré ‖ *tr* accorder ‖ *intr* se mettre d'accord
accordance [ə'kɔrdəns] s accord *m*; **in accordance with** conformément à
according [ə'kɔrdɪŋ] *adj*—**according as** selon que; **according to** selon, d'après, suivant; **according to expert advice** au dire d'experts
accordingly [ə'kɔrdɪŋli] *adv* en conséquence
accordion [ə'kɔrdɪ·ən] s accordéon *m*
accost [ə'kɔst] *tr* accoster
account [ə'kaunt] s (*calculation; bill; bank account; report*) compte *m*; (*benefit*) profit *m*, avantage *m*; (*narration*) récit *m*; (*report*) compte rendu; (*explanation*) explication *f*; **of no account** sans importance; **on account of** à cause de; **on no account** en aucune façon; **to call to account** demander des comptes à ‖ *intr*—**to account for** expliquer; (*money*) rendre compte de
accountable [ə'kauntəbəl] *adj* responsable; (*explainable*) explicable
accountant [ə'kauntənt] s comptable *mf*
account' book' s registre *m* de comptabilité
accounting [ə'kauntɪŋ] s (*profession*) comptabilité *f*
accouterments [ə'kutərmənts] *spl* équipement *m*
accredit [ə'krɛdɪt] *tr* accréditer
accretion [ə'kriʃən] s accroissement *m*
accrue [ə'kru] *intr* s'accroître; **to accrue from** dériver de; **to accrue to** échoir à
accumulate [ə'kjumjə,let] *tr* accumuler ‖ *intr* s'accumuler
accuracy ['ækjərəsi] s exactitude *f*
accurate ['ækjərɪt] *adj* exact; (*aim*) juste; (*translation*) fidèle
accursed [ə'kʌrsɪd], [ə'kʌrst] *adj* maudit
accusation [,ækjə'zeʃən] s accusation *f*
accusative [ə'kjuzətɪv] *adj & s* accusatif *m*
accuse [ə'kjuz] *tr* accuser
accused s accusé *m*, inculpé *m*
accustom [ə'kʌstəm] *tr* accoutumer; **to become accustomed** s'accoutumer
ace [es] s as *m*; **to have an ace up one's sleeve** avoir un atout dans la manche
acetate ['æsɪ,tet] s acétate *m*
ace'tic ac'id [ə'sitɪk] s acide *m* acétique
acetone ['æsɪ,ton] s acétone *f*
acet'ylene torch' [ə'sɛtɪ,lin] s chalumeau *m* oxyacétylénique
ache [ek] s douleur *f* ‖ *intr* faire mal; **my head aches** j'ai mal à la tête; **to be aching to** (coll) brûler de

achieve [ə'tʃiv] *tr* (*a task*) accomplir; (*an aim*) atteindre; (*success*) obtenir; (*a victory*) remporter

achievement [ə'tʃivmənt] *s* (*completion*) accomplissement *m*, réalisation *f*; (*thing itself*) œuvre *f* remarquable, réussite *f*; (*heroic deed*) exploit *m*

Achil'les' heel' [ə'kɪliz] *s* talon *m* d'Achille

acid ['æsɪd] *adj & s* acide *m*

acidi·ty [ə'sɪdɪti] *s* (*pl* **-ties**) acidité *f*

ac'id rain' *s* pluie *f* acide

ac'id test' *s* (fig) épreuve *f* définitive

acknowledge [æk'nɑlɪdʒ] *tr* reconnaître; **to acknowledge receipt of** accuser réception de

acknowledgment [æk'nɑlɪdʒmənt] *s* (*recognition*) reconnaissance *f*; (*of an error*) aveu *m*; (*of a letter*) accusé *m* de réception; (*receipt*) récépissé *m*

acme ['ækmi] *s* comble *m*, sommet *m*

acne ['ækni] *s* acné *f*

acolyte ['ækə,laɪt] *s* enfant *m* de chœur; (*priest*) acolyte *m*; assistant *m*

acorn ['ekɔrn] *s* gland *m*

acoustic [ə'kustɪk] *adj* acoustique ‖ **acoustics** *s & spl* acoustique *f*

acquaint [ə'kwent] *tr* informer; **to be acquainted** se connaître; **to be acquainted with** connaître

acquaintance [ə'kwentəns] *s* connaissance *f*

acquiesce [,ækwɪ'ɛs] *intr* acquiescer

acquiescence [,ækwɪ'ɛsəns] *s* acquiescement *m*, contentement *m*

acquire [ə'kwaɪr] *tr* acquérir; (*friends; a reputation*) s'acquérir

acquired' immune'-defi'ciency syn'drome [ə'kwaɪrd] *s* syndrome *m* d'immuno-déficience acquise (le SIDA)

acquirement [ə'kwaɪrmənt] *s* acquisition *f*

acquisition [,ækwɪ'zɪʃən] *s* acquisition *f*

acquisitive [ə'kwɪzɪtɪv] *adj* âpre au gain, avide

acquit [ə'kwɪt] *v* (*pret & pp* **acquitted**; *ger* **acquitting**) *tr* acquitter; **to acquit oneself** se comporter

acquittal [ə'kwɪtəl] *s* acquittement *m*

acre ['ekər] *s* acre *f*

acrid ['ækrɪd] *adj* âcre

acrimonious [,ækrɪ'moni·əs] *adj* acrimonieux

acrobat ['ækrə,bæt] *s* acrobate *mf*

acrobatic [,ækrə'bætɪk] *adj* acrobatique ‖ **acrobatics** *s* (*profession*) acrobatie *f*; **acrobatics** *spl* (*stunts*) acrobaties

acronym ['ækrənɪm] *s* sigle *m*

acropolis [ə'krɑpəlɪs] *s* acropole *f*

across [ə'krɔs] *adv* en travers, à travers; (*sidewise*) en largeur ‖ *prep* en travers de; (*e.g., the street*) de l'autre côté de; **across country** à travers champs; **to come across** rencontrer par hasard; **to go across** traverser

acrostic [ə'krɔstɪk] *s* acrostiche *m*

acrylic [ə'krɪlɪk] *adj* acrylique

act [ækt] *s* action *f*, acte *m*; (circus, rad, telv) numéro *m*; (govt) loi *f*; (law, theat) acte; (coll) allure *f* affectée, comédie *f*; **in the act** sur le fait, en flagrant délit ‖ *tr* jouer; **to act the fool** faire le pitre ‖ *intr* agir; se conduire; (theat) jouer; **to act as** servir de; **to act on** influer sur

acting ['æktɪŋ] *adj* intérimaire, par intérim ‖ *s* (*actor's art*) jeu *m*; (*profession*) théâtre *m*

action ['ækʃən] *s* action *f*; (law) acte *m*; (mach) jeu *m*; (theat) intrigue *f*; **out of action** hors de service; **to go into action** (mil) aller au feu; **to suit the action to the word** joindre le geste à la parole; **to take action** prendre des mesures

activate ['æktɪ,vet] *tr* activer, actionner

active ['æktɪv] *adj* actif

activi·ty [æk'tɪvɪti] *s* (*pl* **-ties**) activité *f*

actor [æktər] *s* acteur *m*

actress ['æktrɪs] *s* actrice *f*

actual ['æktʃʊ·əl] *adj* véritable, réel, effectif

actually ['æktʃʊ·əli] *adv* réellement, en réalité, effectivement

actuar·y ['æktʃʊ,ɛri] *s* (*pl* **-ies**) actuaire *m*

actuate ['æktʃʊ,et] *tr* (*to turn on*) actionner; (*to motivate*) animer

acuity [ə'kju·ɪti] *s* acuité *f*

acumen [ə'kjumən] *s* finesse *f*

acupuncture ['ækjʊpʌnktʃər] *s* acupuncture *f*, acuponcture *f*

acute [ə'kjut] *adj* aigu; (fig) avisé

acutely [ə'kjutli] *adv* profondément

A.D. ['e'di] *adj* (letterword) (**Anno Domini**) ap. **J.-C.**

ad [æd] *s* (coll) annonce *f*

adage ['ædɪdʒ] *s* adage *m*

Adam ['ædəm] *s* Adam *m*; **I don't know him from Adam** (coll) je ne le connais ni d'Ève ni d'Adam

adamant ['ædəmənt] *adj* inflexible

Ad'am's ap'ple *s* pomme *f* d'Adam

adapt [ə'dæpt] *tr* adapter

adaptation [,ædæp'teʃən] *s* adaptation *f*

adapter [ə'dæptər] *s* adaptateur *m*; (phot) bague *f* porte-objectif

add [æd] *tr* ajouter; **to add up** additionner ‖ *intr* additionner; **to add up to** s'élever à

adder ['ædər] *s* (zool) vipère *f*

addict ['ædɪkt] *s* (pathol) toxicomane *mf*; (sports) fanatique *mf* ‖ [ə'dɪkt] *tr* atteindre de toxicomanie; **to be addicted to** (*to enjoy*) s'adonner à

addiction [ə'dɪkʃən] *s* toxicomanie *f*; **addiction to** penchant *m* pour

add'ing machine' *s* machine *f* à calculer, additionneuse *f*, calculatrice *f*

addition [ə'dɪʃən] *s* addition *f*; **in addition to** en plus de

additive ['ædɪtɪv] *adj & s* additif *m*

addle ['ædəl] *tr* brouiller

address [ə'drɛs], ['ædrɛs] *s* adresse *f* ‖ [ə'drɛs] *s* discours *m*; **to deliver an address** prononcer un discours ‖ *tr* adresser; s'adresser à; (*an audience*) faire un discours à

address' book' *s* carnet *m* d'adresses

addressee [,ædrɛ'si] *s* destinataire *mf*

adduce [ə'd(j)us] *tr* alléguer; (*proof*) fournir

adenoids ['ædə,nɔɪdz] *spl* végétations *fpl* adénoïdes

adept [ə'dɛpt] *adj* habile ‖ *s* adepte *mf*

adequate ['ædɪkwɪt] *adj* suffisant, adéquat; adequate to à la hauteur de, proportionné à

adhere [æd'hɪr] *intr* adhérer

adherence [æd'hɪrəns] *s* adhérence *f*

adherent [æd'hɪrənt] *adj* & *s* adhérent *m*

adhesion [æd'hiʒən] *s* adhésion *f*; (pathol) adhérence *f*

adhesive [æd'hisɪv] *adj* & *s* adhésif *m*

adhe'sive hook' *s* piton *m* adhésif

adhe'sive tape' *s* sparadrap *m*

adieu [ə'd(j)u] *s* (*pl* adieus or adieux) adieu *m* ‖ *interj* adieu!

ad infinitum [,æd,ɪnfɪ'naɪtəm] *adv* sans fin

adjacent [ə'dʒesənt] *adj* adjacent

adjective ['ædʒɪktɪv] *adj* & *s* adjectif *m*

adjoin [ə'dʒɔɪn] *tr* avoisiner ‖ *intr* être contigus

adjoining [ə'dʒɔɪnɪŋ] *adj* contigu

adjourn [ə'dʒʌrn] *tr* (*to postpone*) remettre, reporter; (*a meeting, a session*) lever; (*sine die; for resumption at another time or place*) ajourner ‖ *intr* s'ajourner; lever la séance

adjournment [ə'dʒʌrnmənt] *s* suspension *f* de séance

adjudge [ə'dʒʌdʒ] *tr* adjuger; (*a criminal*) condamner

adjudicate [ə'dʒudɪ,ket] *tr* & *intr* juger

adjunct ['ædʒʌŋkt] *adj* & *s* adjoint *m*; adjuncts accessoires *mpl*

adjust [ə'dʒʌst] *tr* ajuster ‖ *intr* s'adapter

adjustable [ə'dʒʌstəbəl] *adj* réglable; (*antenna*) orientable

adjustment [ə'dʒʌstmənt] *s* (*act of adjusting*) ajustage *m*, réglage *m*; (*wages, prices*) rajustement *m*; (*arrangement*) ajustement *m*, règlement *m*; (telv) mise *f* au point

adjutant ['ædʒətənt] *s* adjutant *m*

ad-lib [,æd'lɪb] *adj* improvisé ‖ *v* (*pret & pp* -libbed; *ger* -libbing) *tr* & *intr* improviser (en cascade)

administer [æd'mɪnɪstər] *tr* administrer; to administer an oath faire prêter serment ‖ *intr*—to administer to pourvoir à, aider, assister

administration [æd,mɪnɪs'treʃən] *s* (*management*) administration *f*; (*government*) gouvernement *m*

administrator [æd'mɪnɪs,tretər] *s* administrateur *m*

admiral ['ædmɪrəl] *s* amiral *m*

admiration [,ædmɪ'reʃən] *s* admiration *f*

admire [æd'maɪr] *tr* admirer

admirer [æd'maɪrər] *s* admirateur *m*; (*suitor*) soupirant *m*

admission [æd'mɪʃən] *s* (*entry*) admission *f*; (*price*) entrée *f*; (*confession*) aveu *m*

ad·mit [æd'mɪt] *v* (*pret & pp* -mitted; *ger* -mitting) *tr* admettre; (*e.g., a mistake*) avouer; admit bearer laisser passer

admittance [æd'mɪtəns] *s* entrée *f*

admittedly [æd'mɪtɪdli] *adv* manifestement

admonish [æd'mɑnɪʃ] *tr* admonester

ad nauseam [æd'nɔʃɪ·əm], [æd'nɔsɪ·əm] *adv* jusqu'au dégoût

ado [ə'du] *s* agitation *f*; much ado about nothing beaucoup de bruit pour rien; without further ado sans plus de façons

adolescence [,ædə'lɛsəns] *s* adolescence *f*

adolescent [,ædə'lɛsənt] *adj* & *s* adolescent *m*

adopt [ə'dɑpt] *tr* adopter

adoption [ə'dɑpʃən] *s* adoption *f*

adoptive [ə'dɑptɪv] *adj* adoptif

adorable [ə'dorəbəl] *adj* adorable

adoration [,ædə'reʃən] *s* adoration *f*

adore [ə'dor] *tr* adorer

adorn [ə'dɔrn] *tr* orner, parer

adornment [ə'dɔrnmənt] *s* parure *f*

adre'nal glands' [æd'rinəl] *spl* (capsules) surrénales *fpl*

adrenaline [ə'drɛnəlɪn] *s* adrénaline *f*

Adriatic [,edrɪ'ætɪk] *adj* & *s* Adriatique *f*

adrift [ə'drɪft] *ad* & *adv* à la dérive

adroit [ə'drɔɪt] *adj* adroit, habile

adulate ['ædʒə,let] *tr* aduler

adult [ə'dʌlt] *adj* & *s* adulte *mf*

adult' book' shop *s* érotothèque *f*

adulterate [ə'dʌltə,ret] *tr* frelater

adulteration [ə,dʌltə'reʃən] *s* frelatage *m*

adulterer [ə'dʌltərər] *s* adultère *m*

adulteress [ə'dʌltərɪs] *s* adultère *f*

adulterous [ə'dʌltərəs] *adj* adultère

adulter·y [ə'dʌltəri] *s* (*pl* -ies) adultère *m*

adumbrate ['ædəm,bret] *tr* ébaucher; (*to foreshadow*) présager

advance [æd'væns] *s* avance *f*; advances propositions *fpl*; propositions malhonnêtes; in advance d'avance; en avance ‖ *tr* avancer ‖ *intr* avancer, s'avancer; (*said of prices*) augmenter; (*said of stocks*) monter

advancement [æd'vænsmənt] *s* avancement *m*

advance' pay'ment *s* versement *m* anticipé

advantage [æd'væntɪdʒ] *s* avantage *m*; to take advantage of profiter de

advent ['ædvɛnt] *s* venue *f*; Advent (eccl) Avent *m*

adventitious [,ædvɛn'tɪʃəs] *adj* adventice

adventure [æd'vɛntʃər] *s* aventure *f*

adventurer [æd'vɛntʃərər] *s* aventurier *m*

adventuress [æd'vɛntʃərɪs] *s* aventurière *f*

adventurous [æd'vɛntʃərəs] *adj* aventureux

adverb ['ædvʌrb] *s* adverbe *m*

adversar·y ['ædvər,sɛri] *s* (*pl* -ies) adversaire *mf*

adverse [æd'vʌrs] *adj* adverse

adversi·ty [æd'vʌrsɪti] *s* (*pl* -ties) adversité *f*

advertise ['ædvər,taɪz] *tr* & *intr* annoncer

advertisement [æd'vʌrtɪzmənt] *s* annonce *f*

advertiser ['ædvər,taɪzər] *s* annonceur *m*

advertising ['ædvər,taɪzɪŋ] *s* réclame *f*

ad'vertising a'gency *s* agence *f* de publicité

ad'vertising spe'cialist *s* publicitaire *mf*, entrepreneur *m* de publicité

advice [æd'vaɪs] *s* conseil *m*; conseils; **a piece of advice** un conseil

advisable [æd'vaɪzəbəl] *adj* opportun, recommandable

advise [æd'vaɪz] *tr* (*to counsel*) conseiller; (*to inform*) aviser; **to advise against** déconseiller; **to advise s.o. to** + *inf* conseiller à qn de + *inf*

advisedly [æd'vaɪzɪdli] *adv* en connaissance de cause

advisement [æd'vaɪzmənt] *s* conseils *mpl*; **to take under advisement** mettre en délibération

adviser [æd'vaɪzər] *s* conseiller *m*

advisory [æd'vaɪzəri] *adj* consultatif

advocacy ['ædvəkəsi] *s* plaidoyer *m*

advocate ['ædvə,ket] *s* partisan *m*; (*lawyer*) avocat *m* ‖ *tr* préconiser

Aege'an Sea' [ɪ'dʒi·ən] *s* mer *f* Égée, mer de l'Archipel

aegis ['idʒɪs] *s* égide *f*

aerate ['ɛret] *tr* aérer

aerial ['ɛrɪ·əl] *adj* aérien ‖ *s* antenne *f*

aerodynamic [,ɛrodaɪ'næmɪk] *adj* aérodynamique ‖ **aerodynamics** *s* aérodynamique *f*

aeronautic [,ɛro'nɔtɪk] *adj* aéronautique ‖ **aeronautics** *s* aéronautique *f*

aerosol ['ɛrə,sol] *s* aérosol *m*

aerospace ['ɛrə,spes] *adj* aérospatial

Aeschylus ['ɛskɪləs] *s* Eschyle *m*

aesthete ['ɛsθit] *s* esthète *mf*

aesthetic [ɛs'θɛtɪk] *adj* esthétique ‖ **aesthetics** *s* esthétique *f*

afar [ə'fɑr] *adv* au loin

affable ['æfəbəl] *adj* affable

affair [ə'fɛr] *s* affaire *f*; (*of lovers*) affaire de cœur

affect [ə'fɛkt] *tr* affecter

affectation [,æfɛk'teʃən] *s* affectation *f*

affected *adj* affecté, maniéré

affection [ə'fɛkʃən] *s* affection *f*

affectionate [ə'fɛkʃənɪt] *adj* affectueux

affidavit [,æfɪ'devɪt] *s* déclaration *f* sous serment

affiliate [ə'fɪlɪ,et] *s* (com) société *f* affiliée ‖ *tr* affilier ‖ *intr* s'affilier

affini·ty [ə'fɪnɪti] *s* (*pl* **-ties**) affinité *f*; (*connection, resemblance*) rapport *m*, ressemblance *f*; (*liking*) attrait *m*, attraction *f*

affirm [ə'fʌrm] *tr* & *intr* affirmer

affirmative [ə'fʌrmətɪv] *adj* affirmatif ‖ *s* affirmative *f*

affix ['æfɪks] *s* affixe *m* ‖ [ə'fɪks] *tr* (*a signature*) apposer; (*guilt*) attribuer; (*a stamp*) coller

afflict [ə'flɪkt] *tr* affliger

affliction [ə'flɪkʃən] *s* (*sorrow*) affliction *f*; (*disorder*) infirmité *f*

affluence ['æflu·əns] *s* affluence *f* de biens, richesse *f*

afford [ə'ford] *tr* (*to provide*) fournir; (*to be able to pay for*) se permettre, avoir de quoi payer, avoir les moyens d'acheter

affront [ə'frʌnt] *s* affront *m* ‖ *tr* insulter

Afghanistan [æf'gænɪ,stæn] *s* l'Afghanistan *m*

afire [ə'faɪr] *adj* & *adv* en feu

aflame [ə'flem] *adj* & *adv* en flammes

afloat [ə'flot] *adj* & *adv* à flot; (*rumor*) en circulation; **to keep afloat on the water** se tenir sur l'eau

afoot [ə'fʊt] *adj* & *adv* à pied; (*underway*) en œuvre

aforesaid [ə'for,sɛd] *adj* susdit, susmentionné, précité

afraid [ə'fred] *adj* effrayé; **to be afraid** avoir peur

afresh [ə'frɛʃ] *adv* à nouveau

Africa ['æfrɪkə] *s* Afrique *f*; l'Afrique

African ['æfrɪkən] *adj* africain ‖ *s* Africain *m*

after ['æftər] *adj* suivant, postérieur ‖ *adv* après, plus tard ‖ *prep* après, à la suite de; (*in the manner or style of*) d'après; (not translated in expressions of time), e.g., **eight minutes after ten** dix heures huit ‖ *conj* après que

af'ter-din'ner *adj* d'après dîner

af'ter-ef·fect' *s* contrecoup *m*; **after-effects** (pathol) séquelles *fpl*

af'ter-glow' *s* lueur *f* du coucher

af'ter-im'age *s* image *f* consécutive

af'ter-life' *s* survie *f*

aftermath ['æftər,mæθ] *s* conséquences *fpl* sérieuses, suites *fpl*; (agr) regain *m*

af'ter-noon' *s* après-midi *m* & *f*; **good afternoon!** bonjour!

af'ter-shav'ing lo'tion *s* eau *f* de Cologne pour la barbe

af'ter·taste' *s* arrière-goût *m*

af'ter-thought' *s* réflexion *f* après coup

afterward ['æftərwərd] *adv* après, ensuite

again [ə'gɛn] *adv* encore; (*besides, moreover*) de plus, d'ailleurs, en outre; (*once more*) de nouveau, encore une fois; **as much again** deux fois autant; **not again** ne . . . plus, e.g., **I won't do it again** je ne le ferai plus; **now and again** de temps en temps

against [ə'gɛnst] *prep* contre; **against the grain** à rebrousse-poil; **over against** en face de; par contraste avec

age [edʒ] *s* âge *m*; (*about a hundred years*) siècle *m*; **for ages** depuis longtemps; **of age** majeur; **to come of age** atteindre sa majorité; **under age** mineur ‖ *tr* & *intr* vieillir

age' brack'et *s* tranche *f* d'âge

aged [edʒd] *adj* (*wine, cheese, etc.*) vieilli; (*of the age of*) âgé de ‖ ['edʒɪd] *adj* âgé, vieux

agen·cy ['edʒənsi] *s* (*pl* **-cies**) agence *f*; (*means*) action *f*

agenda [ə'dʒɛndə] *s* ordre *m* du jour

agent ['edʒənt] *s* agent *m*; (*means*) moyen *m*; (com) commissionnaire *m*

agglomeration [ə,glɑmə'reʃən] *s* agglomération *f*

aggrandizement [ə'grændɪzmənt] *f* agrandissement *m*

aggravate ['ægrə,vet] *tr* aggraver; (coll) exaspérer

aggregate [ˈægrɪˌget] *adj* global ‖ *s* agrégat *m* ‖ *tr* rassembler; (coll) s'élever à

aggression [əˈgrɛʃən] *s* agression *f*

aggressive [əˈgrɛsɪv] *adj* agressif; (*live-wire*) entreprenant

aggressor [əˈgrɛsər] *s* agresseur *m*

aghast [əˈgæst] *adj* abasourdi

agile [ˈædʒɪl] *adj* agile

agility [əˈdʒɪlɪti] *s* agilité *f*

agitate [ˈædʒɪˌtet] *tr* agiter

agitator [ˈædʒɪˌtetər] *s* agitateur *m*

aglow [əˈglo] *adj* & *adv* rougeoyant

agnostic [ægˈnɑstɪk] *adj* & *s* agnostique *mf*

ago [əˈgo] *adv* il y a, e.g., **two days ago** il y a deux jours

agog [əˈgɑg] *adj* & *adv* en émoi

agonizing [ˈægəˌnaɪzɪŋ] *adj* angoissant

ago·ny [ˈægəni] *s* (*pl* **-nies**) (*physical pain*) douleur *f* atroce; (*mental pain*) angoisse *f*; (*death struggle*) agonie *f*

agrarian [əˈgrɛrɪ·ən] *adj* agraire; (law) agrairien ‖ *s* agrairien *m*

agree [əˈgri] *intr* être d'accord, s'accorder; **agreed!** d'accord!; **to agree to** consentir à

agreeable [əˈgri·əbəl] *adj* agréable, sympathique; (*consenting*) d'accord

agreement [əˈgrimənt] *s* accord *m*

agriculture [ˈægrɪˌkʌltʃər] *s* agriculture *f*

aground [əˈgraʊnd] *adj* (naut) échoué ‖ *adv*—**to run aground** échouer

ahead [əˈhɛd] *adj* & *adv* en avant; **ahead of** avant; devant; **straight ahead** tout droit; **to get ahead of** devancer

ahem [əˈhɛm] *interj* hum!

ahoy [əˈhɔɪ] *interj*—**ship ahoy!** ohé du navire!

aid [ed] *s* (*assistance*) aide *f*; (*assistant*) aide *mf* ‖ *tr* aider

aide-de-camp [ˈeddəˈkæmp] *s* (*pl* **aides-de-camp**) officier *m* d'ordonnance, aide *m* de camp

AIDS [edz] *s* (acronym) (**acquired immune-deficiency syndrome**) le SIDA (syndrome d'immuno-déficience acquise)

ail [el] *tr* affliger; **what ails you?** qu'avez-vous? ‖ *intr* être souffrant

ailment [ˈelmənt] *s* indisposition *f*, maladie *f*

aim [em] *s* (*purpose*) but *m*, objectif *m*; (*of gun*) pointage *m* ‖ *tr* diriger; (*a blow*) allonger; (*a telescope, cannon, etc.*) pointer, viser ‖ *intr* viser

air [ɛr] *s* air *m*; **on the air** à la radio, à la télévision, à l'antenne; **to put on airs** prendre des airs; **to put on the air** radiodiffuser; **to walk on air** ne pas toucher terre; **up in the air** confondu, sidéré; (*angry*) très monté ‖ *tr* aérer; (*a question*) ventiler; (*feelings*) donner libre cours à

air′ bag′ *s* (aut) coussin *m* gonflable

air-borne [ˈɛrˌborn] *adj* aéroporté

air′ brake′ *s* frein *m* à air comprimé

air′-condi′tion *tr* climatiser

air′ condi′tioner *s* climatiseur *m*

air′ condi′tioning *s* climatisation *f*

air′craft′ *s* aéronef *m*, appareil *m* d'aviation

air′craft car′rier *s* porte-avions *m*

air′drop′ *s* parachutage *m* ‖ *tr* parachuter

air′field′ *s* terrain *m* d'aviation, aérodrome *m*

air′foil′ *s* voilure *f*

air′ force′ *s* forces *fpl* aériennes

air′ freight′ *s* (*parcels*) transport *m* par avion, fret *m* par avion; (*company*) messageries *fpl* aériennes

air′ gap′ *s* (elec) entrefer *m*

air′ let′ter *s* aérogramme *m*

air′lift′ *s* pont *m* aérien

air′line′ *s* ligne *f* aérienne

air′line pi′lot *s* pilote *m* de ligne

air′lin′er *s* avion *m* de transport

air′mail′ *adj* aéropostal ‖ *s* poste *f* aérienne; **by airmail** par avion

air′ mat′tress *s* matelas *m* pneumatique

air′plane′ *s* avion *m*

air′ pock′et *s* trou *m* d'air

air′ pollu′tion *s* pollution *f* de l'air

air′port′ *s* aéroport *m*

air′port police′ *s* police *f* de l'air

air′ raid′ *s* attaque *f* aérienne

air′-raid drill′ *s* exercice *m* d'alerte aérienne

air′-raid shel′ter *s* abri *m*

air′-raid ward′en *s* chef *m* d'îlot

air′-raid warn′ing *s* alarme *f* aérienne

air′sick′ *adj* atteint du mal de l'air

air′sick′ness *s* mal *m* de l'air

air′ sleeve′ or **sock′** *s* manche *f* à air

air′strip′ *s* piste *f*

air′ term′inal *s* aérogare *f*

air′tight′ *adj* hermétique

air′ (traf′fic) control′ler *s* contrôleur *m* aérien, aiguilleur *m* (du ciel), contrôleur de la navigation aérienne

air′waves′ *spl* ondes *fpl* radiophoniques

air′way′ *s* route *f* aérienne

air·y [ˈɛri] *adj* (*comp* **-ier**; *super* **-iest**) (*room*) bien aéré; (*casual, light*) léger; (*graceful*) gracieux; (coll) maniéré

aisle [aɪl] *s* (*through rows of seats*) passage *m* central, allée *f*; (*in a train*) couloir *m*; (*long passageway in a church*) nef *f* latérale

ajar [əˈdʒɑr] *adj* entrebâillé

akimbo [əˈkɪmbo] *adj* & *adv*—**with arms akimbo** les poings sur les hanches

akin [əˈkɪn] *adj* apparenté

alabaster [ˈælɑˌbæstər] *s* albâtre *m*

alacrity [əˈlækrɪti] *s* vivacité *f*, empressement *m*

alarm [əˈlɑrm] *s* alarme *f*; (*of clock*) sonnerie *f* ‖ *tr* alarmer

alarm′ clock′ *s* réveille-matin *m*, réveil *m*

alarming [əˈlɑrmɪŋ] *adj* alarmant

alas [əˈlæs] *interj* hélas!

Albanian [ælˈbenɪ·ən] *adj* albanais ‖ *s* (*language*) albanais *m*; (*person*) Albanais

albatross [ˈælbəˌtrɔs] *s* albatros *m*

albi·no [ælˈbaɪno] *adj* albinos ‖ *s* (*pl* **-nos**) albinos *m*

album [ˈælbəm] *s* album *m*

albumen [ælˈbjumən] *s* albumen *m*

alchemy [ˈælkɪmi] *s* alchimie *f*

alcohol [ˈælkəˌhɔl] *s* alcool *m*

alcoholic [,ælkə'hɔlɪk] *adj & s* alcoolique *mf*

alcove ['ælkov] *s* niche *f*; (*for a bed*) alcôve *f*

alder ['ɔldər] *s* aune *m*

alder·man ['ɔldərmən] *s* (*pl* **-men**) conseiller *m* municipal

ale [el] *s* ale *f*

alembic [ə'lɛmbɪk] *s* alambic *m*; (fig) creuset *m*

alert [ə'lʌrt] *adj & s* alerte *f* ‖ *tr* alerter

alfalfa [æl'fælfə] *s* luzerne *f*

algebra ['ældʒɪbrə] *s* algèbre *f*

Algeria [æl'dʒɪrɪ·ə] *s* Algérie *f*

Algerian [æl'dʒɪrɪ·ən] *adj* (*of Algeria*) algérien; (*of Algiers, the Barbary state*) algérois ‖ *s* Algérien *m*; Algérois *m*

Algiers [æl'dʒɪrz] *s* Alger *m*

alias ['elɪ·əs] *s* nom *m* d'emprunt ‖ *adv* alias, autrement dit

ali·bi ['ælɪ,baɪ] *s* (*pl* **-bis**) excuse *f*; (law) alibi *m*

alien ['eljən] *adj & s* étranger *m*

alienate ['eljə,net] *tr* aliéner, s'aliéner

alight [ə'laɪt] *adj* allumé ‖ *v* (*pret & pp* **alighted** or **alit** [ə'lɪt]) *intr* descendre, se poser; (aer) (*on land*) atterrir; (aer) (*on sea*) amerrir

align [ə'laɪn] *tr* aligner ‖ *intr* s'aligner

alike [ə'laɪk] *adj* pareils, e.g., **these books are alike** ces livres sont pareils; **to look alike** se ressembler ‖ *adv* de la même façon

alimony ['ælɪ,moni] *s* pension *f* alimentaire après divorce

alive [ə'laɪv] *adj* vivant; vif; **alive to** sensible à

alka·li ['ælkə,laɪ] *s* (*pl* **-lis** or **-lies**) alcali *m*

alkaline ['ælkə,laɪn] *adj* alcalin

all [ɔl] *adj indef* tout; tout le ‖ *s* tout *m* ‖ *pron indef* tout; tous; **all of** tout le; **first of all** tout d'abord; **is that all?** c'est tout?; (*ironically*) ce n'est que ça?; **not at all** pas du tout ‖ *adv* tout; **all at once** tout à coup; **all but** presque; **all in** (coll) éreinté; **all in all** à tout prendre; **all off** (slang) abandonné; **all right** bon, ça va, très bien; **all's well!** (naut) bon quart!; **all the better** tant mieux; **all told** en tout; **fifteen (thirty,** etc.) **all** (tennis) égalité à quinze (trente, etc.); partout, e.g., **thirty all** trente partout; **to be all for** ne demander mieux que

allay [ə'le] *tr* apaiser

all'-clear' *s* fin *f* d'alerte

allege [ə'lɛdʒ] *tr* (*to assert*) alléguer; (*to assert without proof*) affirmer sans preuve; (law) déclarer sous serment

alleged *adj* présumé, prétendu, censé

allegedly [ə'lɛdʒɪdli] *adv* prétendument, censément

allegiance [ə'lidʒəns] *s* allégeance *f*

allegoric(al) [,ælɪ'gɔrɪk(əl)] *adj* allégorique

allego·ry ['ælɪ,gori] *s* (*pl* **-ries**) allégorie *f*

aller·gy ['ælərdʒi] *s* (*pl* **-gies**) allergie *f*

alleviate [ə'livɪ,et] *tr* soulager, alléger

alley ['æli] *s* ruelle *f*; **that is up my alley** (slang) cela est dans mes cordes

al'ley cat' *s* chat *m* de gouttière

alliance [ə'laɪ·əns] *s* alliance *f*

alligator ['ælɪ,getər] *s* alligator *m*

al'ligator clip' *s* pince *f* crocodile

al'ligator pear' *s* poire *f* d'avocat

al'ligator wrench' *s* clef *f* crocodile

alliteration [ə,lɪtə'reʃən] *s* allitération *f*

all'-know'ing *adj* omniscient

allocate ['ælə,ket] *tr* allouer, assigner

allot [ə'lɑt] *v* (*pret & pp* **allotted;** *ger* **allotting**) *tr* répartir

allotment [ə'lɑtmənt] *s* allocation *f*

all'-out' *adj* total

allow [ə'laʊ] *tr* (*to permit*) permettre, tolérer; (*to concede*) admettre; (*as a grant*) allouer, accorder ‖ *intr*—**to allow for** tenir compte de

allowance [ə'laʊ·əns] *s* (*money*) allocation *f*, indemnité *f*; (com) réduction *f*, rabais *m*, concession *f*; **to make allowances for** tenir compte de

alloy ['ælɔɪ] *s* alliage *m* ‖ [ə'lɔɪ] *tr* allier

all' right' *interj* bon!, très bien!, ça va!; (*agreed!*) c'est entendu!, d'accord!

all'-round' *adj* (*athlete*) complet; (*man*) universel; total, global

All' Saints'' Day' *s* la Toussaint

All' Souls'' Day' *s* la fête des Morts

all'spice' *s* (*plant*) quatre-épices *f*; (*berry*) toute-épice *f*; piment *m*

all'-time' *adj* record

allude [ə'lud] *intr*—**to allude to** faire allusion à

allure [ə'lur] *tr* séduire, tenter

allurement [ə'lurmənt] *s* charme *m*

alluring [ə'lurɪŋ] *adj* séduisant

all' wet' *adj* (coll) fichu, erroné

al·ly ['ælaɪ] *s* (*pl* **-lies**) allié *m* ‖ [ə'laɪ] *v* (*pret & pp* **-lied**) *tr* allier

almanac ['ɔlmə,næk] *s* almanach *m*

almighty [ɔl'maɪti] *adj* omnipotent

almond ['ɑmənd], ['æmənd] *s* amande *f*

al'mond tree' *s* amandier *m*

almost ['ɔlmost] *adv* presque; **I almost fell** j'ai failli tomber

alms [ɑmz] *s & spl* aumône *f*

alms'house' *s* hospice *m*

aloe ['ælo] *s* aloès *m*

aloft [ə'lɔft] *adv* en l'air, en haut; (aer) en vol; (naut) en haut

alone [ə'lon] *adj* seul, e.g., **my arm alone suffices** mon bras seul suffit; e.g., **the metropolis alone** la seule métropole; **let alone . . .** sans compter . . . ; **to leave alone** laisser tranquille ‖ *adv* seulement

along [ə'lɔŋ] *adv* avec; **all along** tout le temps; **come along!** venez donc!; **to get along** s'en aller; se porter, faire des progrès ‖ *prep* le long de; sur

along'side' *adv* à côté ‖ *prep* à côté de

aloof [ə'luf] *adj* isolé, peu abordable ‖ *adv* à l'écart, à distance

aloud [ə'laud] *adv* à haute voix

alpenstock ['ælpən,stɑk] *s* bâton *m* ferré

alphabet ['ælfə,bɛt] *s* alphabet *m*

alpine [ˈælpaɪn] *adj* alpin

Alps [ælps] *spl*—**the Alps** les Alpes *fpl*

already [ɔlˈrɛdi] *adv* déjà

Alsatian [ælˈseʃən] *adj* alsacien ‖ *s* (*dialect*) alsacien *m*; (*person*) Alsacien *m*

also [ˈɔlso] *adv* aussi, également

altar [ˈɔltər] *s* autel *m*

al′tar boy′ *s* enfant *m* de chœur

al′tar cloth′ *s* nappe *f* d'autel

al′tar-piece′ *s* rétable *m*

al′tar rail′ *s* grille *f* du chœur, grille de l'autel

alter [ˈɔltər] *tr* (*to transform*) changer, modifier; (*to date; evidence*) falsifier, fausser; (*a text*) altérer; (*a suit of clothes*) retoucher, faire des retouches à; (*an animal*) châtrer ‖ *intr* changer, se modifier

alteration [ˌɔltəˈreʃən] *s* (*transformation*) changement *m*; (*falsification*) altération *f*; (*in a building*) modification *f*; **alterations** (*in clothing*) retouches *fpl*

alternate [ˈɔltərnɪt] *adj* alternatif; (*angle*) alterne; (*rhyme*) croisé ‖ [ˈɔltər,net] *tr* faire alternance à ‖ *intr* alterner

al′ternating cur′rent *s* courant *m* alternatif

alternative [ɔlˈtʌrnətɪv] *adj* alternatif ‖ *s* alternative *f*

although [ɔlˈðo] *conj* bien que, quoique

altitude [ˈæltɪ,t(j)ud] *s* altitude *f*

al-to [ˈælto] *s* (*pl* **-tos**) alto *m*

altogether [ˌɔltəˈgɛðər] *adv* (*wholly*) entièrement, tout à fait; (*on the whole*) somme toute, tout compte fait; (*with everything included*) en tout, tout compris

altruist [ˈæltrʊ·ɪst] *adj & s* altruiste *mf*

alum [ˈæləm] *s* alun *m*

aluminum [əˈlumɪnəm] *s* aluminium *m*

alu′minum foil′ *s* papier *m* alu

alum·nus [əˈlʌmnəs] *s* (*pl* **-ni** [naɪ]) diplômé *m*, ancien étudiant *m*

alveo·lus [ælˈvi·ələs] *s* (*pl* **-li** [,laɪ]) alvéole *m*

always [ˈɔlwɪz], [ˈɔlwez] *adv* toujours

AM [ˈeˈɛm] *s* (letterword) (**amplitude modulation**) modulation *f* d'amplitude

A.M. [ˈeˈɛm] *adv* (letterword) (**ante meridiem**) du matin, a.m.

amalgam [əˈmælgəm] *s* amalgame *m*

amalgamate [əˈmælgə,met] *tr* amalgamer ‖ *intr* s'amalgamer

amass [əˈmæs] *tr* amasser

amateur [ˈæmətʃər] *adj & s* amateur *m*

amaze [əˈmez] *tr* étonner

amazing [əˈmezɪŋ] *adj* étonnant

amazon [ˈæmə,zɑn] *s* amazone *f*; **Amazon** Amazone *f*; (*river*) fleuve *m* des Amazones

ambassador [æmˈbæsədər] *s* ambassadeur *m*

ambassadress [æmˈbæsədrɪs] *s* ambassadrice *f*, ambassadeur *m*

amber [ˈæmbər] *adj* ambré ‖ *s* ambre *m* jaune, ambre succin

ambidextrous [ˌæmbɪˈdɛkstrəs] *adj* ambidextre

ambigui·ty [ˌæmbɪˈgju·ɪti] *s* (*pl* **-ties**) ambiguïté *f*

ambition [æmˈbɪʃən] *s* ambition *f*

ambitious [æmˈbɪʃəs] *adj* ambitieux

amble [ˈæmbəl] *s* amble *m* ‖ *intr* (*to stroll*) déambuler; (*equit*) ambler

ambulance [ˈæmbjələns] *s* ambulance *f*

am′bulance corps′ *s* service *m* sanitaire

am′bulance driv′er *s* ambulancier *m*

ambulatory [ˈæmbjələ,tori] *adj* ambulatoire

ambush [ˈæmbʊʃ] *s* embuscade *f* ‖ *tr* embusquer

ameliorate [əˈmiljə,ret] *tr* améliorer ‖ *intr* s'améliorer

amen [ˈeˈmɛn], [ˈɑˈmɛn] *s* amen *m* ‖ *interj* ainsi soit-il!

amenable [əˈminəbəl] *adj* docile; **amenable to** (*a court*) justiciable de; (*a fine*) passible de; (*a law*) soumis à; (*persuasion*) disposé à; (*a superior*) responsable envers

amend [əˈmɛnd] *tr* amender ‖ *intr* s'amender

amendment [əˈmɛndmənt] *s* amendement *m*

amends [əˈmɛndz] *spl* dédommagement *m*; **to make amends to** dédommager

ameni·ty [əˈmɛnɪti] *s* (*pl* **-ties**) aménité *f*; **amenities** agréments *mpl*; civilités *fpl*

America [əˈmɛrɪkə] *s* Amérique *f*; l'Amérique

American [əˈmɛrɪkən] *adj* américain ‖ *s* Américain *m*

Amer′ican Eng′lish *s* anglais *m* d'Amérique, américain *m*

Amer′ican In′dian *s* amérindien *m*

Americanism [əˈmɛrɪkə,nɪzəm] *s* (*word*) américanisme *m*; patriotisme *m* américain

Amer′ican plan′ *s* pension *f* complète

Amer′ican way of life′ *s* mode *m* de vie américain

Amerindian [ˌæməˈrɪndi·ən] *adj* amérindien ‖ *s* Amérindien *m*

amethyst [ˈæmɪθɪst] *s* améthyste *f*

amiable [ˈemi·əbəl] *adj* aimable

amicable [ˈæmɪkəbəl] *adj* amical

amid [əˈmɪd] *prep* au milieu de

amid′ships *adv* au milieu du navire

amidst [əˈmɪdst] *prep* au milieu de

amiss [əˈmɪs] *adj* détraqué; **not amiss** pas mal; **something amiss** quelque chose qui manque, quelque chose qui cloche ‖ *adv* de travers; **to take amiss** prendre en mauvaise part

ami·ty [ˈæmɪti] *s* (*pl* **-ties**) amitié *f*

ammeter [ˈæm,mitər] *s* ampèremètre *m*

ammonia [əˈmoni·ə] *s* (*gas*) ammoniac *m*; (*gas dissolved in water*) ammoniaque *f*

ammunition [ˌæmjəˈnɪʃən] *s* munitions *fpl*

amnesia [æmˈniʒə] *s* amnésie *f*

amnes·ty [ˈæmnɪsti] *s* (*pl* **-ties**) amnistie *f* ‖ *v* (*pret & pp* **-tied**) *tr* amnistier

amoeba [əˈmibə] *s* amibe *f*

among [əˈmʌŋ] *prep* entre, parmi

amorous [ˈæmərəs] *adj* amoureux

amorphous [əˈmɔrfəs] *adj* amorphe

amortize [ˈæmər,taɪz] *tr* amortir

amount [əˈmaunt] *s* montant *m*, quantité *f* ‖ *intr*—**to amount to** s'élever à

ampere [ˈæmpɪr] *s* ampère *m*

ampersand ['æmpər,sænd] s esperluète f
amphibian [æm'fɪbɪ·ən] adj & s amphibie mf; amphibien m
amphibious [æm'fɪbɪ·əs] adj amphibie
amphitheater ['æmfɪ,θi·ətər] s amphithéâtre m
ample ['æmpəl] adj ample; (speech) satisfaisant; (reward) suffisant
amplifier ['æmplɪ,faɪ·ər] s amplificateur m
ampli·fy ['æmplɪ,faɪ] v (pret & pp -fied) tr amplifier
amplitude ['æmplɪ,t(j)ud] s amplitude f
am'plitude modula'tion s modulation f d'amplitude
amputate ['æmpjə,tet] tr amputer
amputee [,æmpjə'ti] s amputé m
amuck [ə'mʌk] adv—**to run amuck** s'emballer
amulet ['æmjəlɪt] s amulette f
amuse [ə'mjuz] tr amuser
amusement [ə'mjuzmənt] s amusement m
amuse'ment arcade' s salle f de jeux électroniques
amuse'ment park' s parc m d'attractions
amusing [ə'mjuzɪŋ] adj amusant
an [æn], [ən] art indef (devant un son vocalique) un
anachronism [ə'nækrə,nɪzəm] s anachronisme m
analogous [ə'næləgəs] adj analogue
analo·gy [ə'nælədʒi] s (pl -gies) analogie f
analy·sis [ə'nælɪsɪs] s (pl -ses) [,siz]) analyse f
analyst ['ænəlɪst] s analyste mf
analytic(al) [,ænə'lɪtɪk(əl)] adj analytique
analyze ['ænə,laɪz] tr analyser
anarchist ['ænərkɪst] s anarchiste mf
anarchy ['ænərki] s anarchie f
anathema [ə'næθɪmə] s anathème m
anatomic(al) [,ænə'tɑmɪk(əl)] adj anatomique
anato·my [ə'nætəmi] s (pl -mies) anatomie f
ancestor ['ænsɛstər] s ancêtre m
ances·try ['ænsɛstri] s (pl -tries) ancêtres mpl, aïeux mpl; (line) ascendance f
anchor ['æŋkər] s ancre f; **anchors aweigh!** ancres levées!; **to cast anchor** jeter l'ancre, mouiller l'ancre; **to weigh anchor** lever l'ancre || tr & intr ancrer
an'chor man' s (telv) présentateur-tronc m, pilote m d'émission
ancho·vy ['æntʃovi] s (pl -vies) anchois m
ancient ['enʃənt] adj ancien
and [ænd] conj et; **and/or** et/ou; **and so forth** et ainsi de suite
andiron ['ænd,aɪ·ərn] s chenet m
anecdote ['ænɪk,dot] s anecdote f
anemia [ə'nimɪ·ə] s anémie f
anesthesia [,ænɪs'θiʒə] s anesthésie f
anesthetic [,ænɪs'θɛtɪk] adj & s anesthésique m
anesthetist [æ'nɛsθɪtɪst] s anesthésiste mf
anesthetize [æ'nɛsθɪ,taɪz] tr anesthésier
aneurysm ['ænjə,rɪzəm] s anévrisme m
anew [ə'n(j)u] adv à (or de) nouveau

angel ['endʒəl] s ange m (financial backer) (coll) bailleur m de fonds
angelic(al) [æn'dʒɛlɪk(əl)] adj angélique
anger ['æŋgər] s colère f || tr mettre en colère, fâcher
angina pectoris [æn'dʒaɪnə'pɛktərɪs] s angine f de poitrine
angle ['æŋgəl] s angle m || tr (journ) présenter sous un certain angle || intr pêcher à la ligne; **to angle for** essayer d'attraper; (a compliment) quêter
angler ['æŋglər] s (fisherman) pêcheur m à la ligne; (schemer) intrigant m
an·gry ['æŋgri] adj (comp -grier; super -griest) fâché; **angry at** fâché de; **angry with** fâché contre; **to become angry** se mettre en colère
anguish ['æŋgwɪʃ] s angoisse f
angular ['æŋgjələr] adj angulaire; (features) anguleux
animal ['ænɪməl] adj & s animal m
animate ['ænɪmɪt] adj animé || ['ænɪ,met] tr animer
an'imated cartoon' s dessins mpl animés
animation [,ænɪ'meʃən] s animation f
animosi·ty [,ænɪ'mɑsɪti] s (pl -ties) animosité f
animus ['ænɪməs] s animosité f; intention f
anion ['æn,aɪ·ən] s anion m
anise ['ænɪs] s anis m
aniseed ['ænɪ,sid] s graine f d'anis
ankle ['æŋkəl] s cheville f
anklet ['æŋklɪt] s (sock) socquette f; (ornamental circlet) bracelet m de cheville
annals ['ænəlz] spl annales fpl
anneal [ə'nil] tr recuire, détremper
annex ['ænɛks] s annexe f || [ə'nɛks] tr annexer, rattacher
annexation [,ænɛks'eʃən] s annexion f, rattachement m
annihilate [ə'naɪ·ɪ,let] tr annihiler
annihilation [ə,naɪ·ɪ'leʃən] s anéantissement m
anniversa·ry [,ænɪ'vʌrsəri] adj anniversaire || s (pl -ries) anniversaire m
annotate ['ænə,tet] tr annoter
announce [ə'naʊns] tr annoncer
announcement [ə'naʊnsmənt] s annonce f, avis m
announcer [ə'naʊnsər] s annonceur m; (rad) présentateur m, speaker m
annoy [ə'nɔɪ] tr ennuyer, tourmenter
annoyance [ə'nɔɪ·əns] s ennui m
annoying [ə'nɔɪ·ɪŋ] adj ennuyeux
annual ['ænju·əl] adj annuel || s annuaire m; plante f annuelle
annui·ty [ə'n(j)u·ɪti] s (pl -ties) (annual payment) annuité f; (of a retired person) pension f de retraite, pension viagère
an·nul [ə'nʌl] v (pret & pp -nulled; ger -nulling) tr annuler; abolir
anode ['ænod] s anode f
anodyne ['ænə,daɪn] adj & s anodin m
anoint [ə'nɔɪnt] tr oindre
anon [ə'nɑn] adv tout à l'heure
anonymity [,ænə'nɪmɪti] s anonymat m
anonymous [ə'nɑnɪməs] adj anonyme

another [ə'nʌðər] *adj* & *pron indef* un autre; *(an additional)* encore un; **many another** beaucoup d'autres

answer ['ænsər] *s* réponse *f*; (math) solution *f* ‖ *tr (e.g., yes or no)* répondre; *(a question, a letter)* répondre à ‖ *intr* répondre; **to answer for** répondre de

an'swer book' *s* livre *m* du maître

an'swering machine' *s* répondeur *m* automatique

an'swering ser'vice *s* (telp) service *m* des abonnés absents

ant [ænt] *s* fourmi *f*

antagonism [æn'tægə,nɪzəm] *s* antagonisme *m*

antagonize [æn'tægə,naɪz] *tr* contrarier; *(a friend)* s'aliéner

Antarctic [ænt'arktɪk] *adj* & *s* Antarctique *f*

Antarctica [ænt'arktɪkə] *s* l'Antarctique *f*

Antarc'tic O'cean *s* Océan *m* glacial antarctique

ante ['ænti] *s* mise *f* ‖ *tr* miser ‖ *intr* miser, caver; **ante up!** misez!

anteater ['ænt,itər] *s* fourmilier *m*

antecedent [,æntɪ'sidənt] *adj* & *s* antécédent *m*

antechamber ['ænti,tʃembər] *s* antichambre *f*

antelope ['ænti,lop] *s* antilope *f*

anten·na [æn'tɛnə] *s* (*pl* **-nae** [ni]) (ent) antenne *f* ‖ *s* (*pl* **-nas**) (rad) antenne *f*

antepenult [,ænti'pinʌlt] *s* antépénultième *f*

anterior [æn'tɪrɪ·ər] *adj* antérieur

anthem ['ænθəm] *s* hymne *m*; (eccl) antienne *f*, hymne *f*

ant' hill' *s* fourmilière *f*

antholo·gy [æn'θalədʒi] *s* (*pl* **-gies**) anthologie *f*

anthropoid ['ænθro,pɔɪd] *adj* & *s* anthropoïde *m*

antiaircraft [,æntɪ'ɛr,kræft] *adj* antiaérien, contre-avions

antibiotic [,æntɪbaɪ'atɪk] *adj* & *s* antibiotique *m*

antibod·y ['ænti,badi] *s* (*pl* **-ies**) anticorps *m*

anticipate [æn'tɪsɪ,pet] *tr* anticiper; *(to expect)* s'attendre à

anticipation [æn,tɪsɪ'peʃən] *s* anticipation *f*

anticlimax [,ænti'klaɪmæks] *s* chute *f* dans le trivial, désillusion *f*

antics ['æntɪks] *spl* bouffonnerie *f*

antidote ['ænti,dot] *s* antidote *m*

antifreeze [,ænti'friz] *s* antigel *m*

antiglare [,ænti'glɛr] *adj* antiaveuglant

antiknock [,ænti'nak] *adj* & *s* antidétonant *m*

an'timis'sile mis'sile [,ænti'mɪsəl] *s* missile *m* antimissile

antimony ['ænti,moni] *s* antimoine *m*

antipa·thy [æn'tɪpəθi] *s* (*pl* **-thies**) antipathie *f*

antiperspirant [,æntɪ'pʌrspərənt] *s* antitranspirant *m*

antiphon ['ænti,fan] *s* antienne *f*

antiquated ['ænti,kwetɪd] *adj* vieilli, démodé

antique [æn'tik] *adj* antique; ancien ‖ *s* *(piece of furniture)* original *m*; **antiques** meubles *mpl* d'époque

antique' **deal'er** *s* antiquaire *m*

antique' **shop'** *s* magasin *m* d'antiquités, maison *f* de meubles d'époque

antiqui·ty [æn'tɪkwɪti] *s* (*pl* **-ties**) antiquité *f*; *(oldness)* ancienneté *f*

anti-Semitic [,æntɪsɪ'mɪtɪk] *adj* antisémite, antisémitique

antiseptic [,æntɪ'sɛptɪk] *adj* & *s* antiseptique *m*

an'titank' gun' [,æntɪ'tæŋk] *s* canon *m* antichar

antithe·sis [æn'tɪθɪsɪs] *s* (*pl* **-ses** [,siz]) antithèse *f*

antitoxin [,æntɪ'taksɪn] *s* antitoxine *f*

antiwar [,ænti'wɔr] *adj* antimilitariste

antler ['æntlər] *s* andouiller *m*

antonym ['æntənɪm] *s* antonyme *m*

anvil ['ænvɪl] *s* enclume *f*

anxie·ty [æŋ'zaɪ·əti] *s* (*pl* **-ties**) anxiété *f*, inquiétude *f*

anxious ['æŋkʃəs] *adj* inquiet, soucieux; **to be anxious to** avoir envie de, tenir beaucoup à

any ['ɛni] *adj indef* quelque; du, e.g., **do you have any butter?** avez-vous du beurre?; aucun, e.g., **he reads more than any other child** il lit plus qu'aucun autre enfant; **any day** n'importe quel jour; **any place** n'importe où; **any time** n'importe quand, à tout moment; **any way** n'importe comment, de toute façon ‖ *pron indef* quiconque; quelques-uns §81; **not . . . any** ne . . . aucun §90; ne . . . en . . . pas, e.g., **I will not give him any** je ne lui en donnerai pas ‖ *adv* un peu

an'y·bod'y *pron indef* quelqu'un §81; n'importe qui; **not . . . anybody** ne . . . personne

an'y·how' *adv* en tout cas

an'y·one' *pron indef* quelqu'un §81; n'importe qui; quiconque; **not . . . anyone** ne . . . personne, e.g., **I don't see anyone** je ne vois personne

an'y·thing' *pron indef* quelque chose; n'importe quoi, e.g., **say anything (at all)** dites n'importe quoi; **anything at all** quoi que ce soit, si peu que ce soit; **anything but** rien moins que; **anything else?** et avec ça?, ensuite?; **not . . . anything** ne . . . rien

an'y·way' *adv* en tout cas

an'y·where' *adv* n'importe où; **not . . . anywhere** ne . . . nulle part

aor·ta [e'ɔrtə] *s* (*pl* **-tas** or **-tae** [ti]) aorte *f*

apace [ə'pes] *adv* vite, rapidement

apache [ə'pæʃ] *s* apache *m* ‖ **Apache** [ə'pætʃi] *s* apache *m*

apart [ə'part] *adj* séparé ‖ *adv* à part, à l'écart; **apart from** en dehors de

apartment [ə'partmənt] *s* appartement *m*

apart'ment house' *s* maison *f* de rapport, immeuble *m* d'habitation

apathetic [,æpə'θɛtɪk] *adj* apathique, amorphe

apa·thy ['æpəθi] s (pl **-thies**) apathie f
ape [ep] s singe m ‖ tr singer
aperture ['æpərtʃər] s ouverture f; (phonet) aperture f
apex ['epɛks] s (pl **apexes** or **apices** ['æpɪ,siz]) sommet m; (astr) apex m
aphid ['æfɪd] s puceron m
aphorism ['æfə,rɪzəm] s aphorisme m
aphrodisiac [,æfrə'dɪzɪ,æk] adj & s aphrodisiaque m
apiar·y ['epɪ,ɛri] s (pl **-ies**) rucher m
apiece [ə'pis] adv la pièce, chacun
apish ['epɪʃ] adj simiesque; (fig) imitateur
aplomb [ə'plɑm] s aplomb m
apocalyptic(al) [ə,pɑkə'lɪptɪk(əl)] adj apocalyptique
Apocrypha [ə'pɑkrɪfə] s apocryphes mpl
apogee ['æpə,dʒi] s apogée m
Apollo [ə'pɑlo] s Apollon m
apologetic [ə,pɑlə'dʒɛtɪk] adj prêt à s'excuser, humble, penaud
apologize [ə'pɑlə,dʒaɪz] intr faire des excuses, s'excuser
apolo·gy [ə'pɑlədʒi] s (pl **-gies**) excuse f; (makeshift) semblant, m, prétexte m; (apologia) apologie f
A.P.O. number ['e'pi'nʌmbər] s (letterword) (**Army Post Office**) secteur m postal
apoplectic [,æpə'plɛktɪk] adj & s apoplectique mf
apoplexy ['æpə,plɛksi] s apoplexie f
apostle [ə'pɑsəl] s apôtre m
Apos'tles' Creed' s symbole m des apôtres
apos'tle·ship' s apostolat m
apostrophe [ə'pɑstrəfi] s apostrophe f
apothecar·y [ə'pɑθɪ,kɛri] s (pl **-ies**) apothicaire m
appall [ə'pɔl] tr épouvanter, effrayer, consterner
appalling [ə'pɔlɪŋ] adj épouvantable
appara·tus [,æpə'rætəs] s (pl **-tus** or **tuses**) appareil m, dispositif m
appar·el [ə'pærəl] s (equipment; clothes) appareil m; (clothes) habillement m ‖ v (pret & pp **-eled** or **-elled**; ger **-eling** or **elling**) tr habiller, vêtir; parer
apparent [ə'pærənt] adj apparent; (heir) présomptif
apparition [,æpə'rɪʃən] s apparition f
appeal [ə'pil] s (call) appel m; (attraction) charme m, attrait m; (law) pourvoi m, appel ‖ tr (a case) faire appeler ‖ intr (to request publicly) lancer un appel; (to beg) faire appel; (law) pouvoir en appel; **to appeal to** (to attract) séduire, charmer
appealing [ə'pilɪŋ] adj séduisant, attrayant, sympathique
appear [ə'pɪr] intr (to come into view; to be published; to seem) paraître; (to come into view) apparaître
appearance [ə'pɪrəns] s (look) apparence f, aspect m; (act of showing up) apparition f; (in print) parution f; **to all appearances** selon toute vraisemblance; **to make one's appearance** faire acte de présence
appease [ə'piz] tr apaiser

appeasement [ə'pizmənt] s apaisement m
appeaser [ə'pizər] s conciliateur m, pacificateur m
appel'late court' [ə'pɛlet] s tribunal m d'appel; **highest appellate court** cour f de cassation
append [ə'pɛnd] tr apposer, ajouter
appendage [ə'pɛndɪdʒ] s dépendance f, accessoire m
appendecto·my [,æpən'dɛktəmi] s (pl **-mies**) appendicectomie f
appendicitis [ə,pɛndɪ'saɪtɪs] s appendicite f
appen·dix [ə'pɛndɪks] s (pl **-dixes** or **dices** [dɪ,siz]) appendice m
appertain [,æpər'ten] intr se rapporter
appetite ['æpɪ,taɪt] s appétit m
appetizer ['æpɪ,taɪzər] s stimulant m, tonique m; (culin) premier plat m
appetizing ['æpɪ,taɪzɪŋ] adj appétissant
applaud [ə'plɔd] tr (to give applause to) applaudir; (to approve) applaudir à; **to applaud s.o. for** applaudir qn de ‖ intr applaudir
applause [ə'plɔz] s applaudissements mpl
apple ['æpəl] s pomme f; (tree) pommier m
ap'ple·jack' s calvados m
ap'ple of the eye' s prunelle f des yeux
ap'ple or'chard s pommeraie f, verger m à pommes
ap'ple pie' s tarte f aux pommes
ap'ple pol'isher s (coll) chien m couchant, flagorneur m
ap'ple·sauce' s compote f de pommes; (slang) balivernes fpl
ap'ple tree' s pommier m
ap'ple turn'over s chausson m (aux pommes)
appliance [ə'plaɪ·əns] s (machine or instrument) appareil m; (act of applying) application f; **appliances** accessoires mpl
applicable ['æplɪkəbəl] adj applicable
applicant ['æplɪkənt] s candidat m, postulant m
application [,æplɪ'keʃən] s (putting into effect) application f; (for a job) demande f, sollicitation f
applica'tion blank' s formule f
applied' arts' spl arts mpl industriels
ap·ply [ə'plaɪ] v (pret & pp **-plied**) tr appliquer ‖ intr s'appliquer; **to apply for** solliciter, postuler; **to apply to s.o.** s'adresser à qn
appoint [ə'pɔɪnt] tr nommer, désigner; (obs) équiper
appointed adj (person) nommé, désigné; (time) convenu, dit
appointment [ə'pɔɪntmənt] s (engagement) rendez-vous m; (to a position) désignation f, nomination f; **appointments** (of a room) aménagements mpl; **by appointment** sur rendez-vous
apportion [ə'pɔrʃən] tr répartir; (com) ventiler
appraisal [ə'prezəl] s appréciation f, estimation f, évaluation f
appraise [ə'prez] tr estimer, évaluer

appraiser [ə'prezər] *s* estimateur *m*, évaluateur *m*

appreciable [ə'priʃɪ·əbəl] *adj* appréciable, sensible

appreciate [ə'priʃɪ,et] *tr* (*to value, esteem*) apprécier; (*to be grateful for*) reconnaître; (*to be aware of*) être sensible à, s'apercevoir de ‖ *intr* augmenter, hausser

appreciation [ə,priʃɪ'eʃən] *s* (*judgment, estimation*) appréciation *f*; (*gratitude*) reconnaissance *f*; (*rise in value*) plus-value *f*

appreciative [ə'priʃɪ,etɪv] *adj* reconnaissant

apprehend [,æprɪ'hɛnd] *tr* (*to understand*) comprendre; (*to seize; fear*) apprehender

apprehension [,æprɪ'hɛnʃən] *s* appréhension *f*

apprehensive [,æprɪ'hɛnsɪv] *adj* craintif

apprentice [ə'prɛntɪs] *s* apprenti *m*, stagiaire *mf*

appren'tice·ship' *s* apprentissage *m*, stage *m*

apprise [ə'praɪz] *tr* prévenir, informer, mettre au courant

approach [ə'protʃ] *s* approche *f*; **to make approaches to** faire des avances à ‖ *tr* approcher, approcher de, s'approcher de ‖ *intr* approcher, s'approcher

approachable [ə'protʃəbəl] *adj* abordable, accessible

approbation [,æprə'beʃən] *s* approbation *f*

appropriate [ə'propri·ɪt] *adj* approprié ‖ [ə'propri,et] *tr* (*to take for oneself*) s'approprier; (*to assign*) affecter

appropriation [ə,propri'eʃən] *s* appropriation *f*; (*assigning*) affectation *f*; (govt) crédit *m* budgétaire

approval [ə'pruvəl] *s* approbation *f*, consentement *m*; **on approval** à l'essai, à condition

approve [ə'pruv] *tr* approuver ‖ *intr* être d'accord; **to approve of** approuver

approximate [ə'praksɪmɪt] *adj* approximatif ‖ [ə'praksɪ,met] *tr* se rapprocher de

apricot ['æprɪ,kɑt] *s* abricot *m*; (*tree*) abricotier *m*

April ['eprɪl] *s* avril *m*

A'pril fool' *s* (*joke*) poisson *m* d'avril; (*victim*) dupe *f*, dindon *m*

A'pril Fools'' Day' *s* le jour du poisson d'avril

apron ['eprən] *s* tablier *m*; (aer) aire *f* de manœuvre

apropos [,æprə'po] *adj* opportun ‖ *adv* opportunément; **apropos of** quant à, à l'égard de

apse [æps] *s* abside *f*

apt [æpt] *adj* apte; bien à propos; **apt to** enclin à, porté à

aptitude ['æptɪ,t(j)ud] *s* aptitude *f*

ap'titude test' *s* test *m* d'intelligence pratique, test de talent

aquacade ['ækwə,ked] *s* féerie *f* sur l'eau, spectacle *m* aquatique

aqualung ['ækwə,lʌŋ] *s* scaphandre *m* autonome

aquamarine [,ækwəmə'rin] *s* aiguemarine *f*

aquaplane ['ækwə,plen] *s* aquaplane *m*

aquari·um [ə'kwɛrɪ·əm] *s* (*pl* **-ums** or **-a** [ə]) aquarium *m*

Aquarius [ə'kwɛrɪ·əs] *s* (astr, astrol) le Verseau

aquatic [ə'kwætɪk] *adj* aquatique ‖ **aquatics** *spl* sports *mpl* nautiques

aqueduct ['ækwə,dʌkt] *s* aqueduc *m*

aquiline ['ækwɪ,laɪn] *adj* aquilin

Arab ['ærəb] *adj* arabe ‖ *s* (*horse*) arabe *m*; (*person*) Arabe *mf*

Arabian [ə'rebɪ·ən] *adj* arabe ‖ *s* Arabe *mf*

Arabic ['ærəbɪk] *adj* arabique ‖ *s* (*language*) arabe *m*

Ar'abic nu'meral *s* chiffre *m* arabe

arbiter ['ɑrbɪtər] *s* arbitre *m*

arbitrary ['ɑrbɪ,trɛri] *adj* arbitraire

arbitrate ['ɑrbɪ,tret] *tr* & *intr* arbitrer

arbitration [,ɑrbɪ'treʃən] *s* arbitrage *m*

arbitrator ['ɑrbɪ,tretər] *s* arbitre *m*, médiateur *m*; (law) amiable compositeur *m*

arbor ['ɑrbər] *s* (*shady recess*) berceau *m*, charmille *f*; (mach) arbre *m*

arbore·tum [,ɑrbə'ritəm] *s* (*pl* **-tums** or **-ta** [tə]) jardin *m* botanique d'arbres

arbutus [ɑr'bjutəs] *s* arbousier *m*

arc [ɑrk] *s* (elec, geom) arc *m*

arcade [ɑr'ked] *s* (*for shopping*) galerie *f* marchande; (archit) arcade *f*

arcane [ɑr'ken] *adj* mystérieux

arch [ɑrtʃ] *adj* insigne; espiègle ‖ *s* (*of a building, cathedral, etc.*) arc *m*; (*of bridge*) arche *f*; (*of vault*) voûte *f* ‖ *tr* (*the back*) arquer; (archit) voûter ‖ *intr* s'arquer; se voûter

archaic [ɑr'ke·ɪk] *adj* archaïque

archaism ['ɑrke,ɪzəm] *s* archaïsme *m*

archangel ['ɑrk,endʒəl] *s* archange *m*

arch'bish'op *s* archevêque *m*

arch'duke' *s* archiduc *m*

arched [ɑrtʃt] *adj* voûté, courbé, arqué

archeologist [,ɑrkɪ'ɑlədʒɪst] *s* archéologue *mf*

archeology [,ɑrkɪ'ɑlɪdʒi] *s* archéologie *f*

archer ['ɑrtʃər] *s* archer *m*

archery ['ɑrtʃəri] *s* tir *m* à l'arc

archetype ['ɑrkɪ,taɪp] *s* archétype *m*

archipela·go [,ɑrkɪ'pɛləgo] *s* (*pl* **-gos** or **-goes**) archipel *m*

architect ['ɑrkɪ,tɛkt] *s* architecte *m*

architecture ['ɑrkɪ,tɛktʃər] *s* architecture *f*

archives ['ɑrkaɪvz] *spl* archives *fpl*

arch'priest' *s* archiprêtre *m*

arch'way' *s* voûte *f*, arcade *f*

Arctic ['ɑrktɪk] *adj* & *s* (*ocean*) Arctique *m*; (*region*) Arctique *f*

arc' weld'ing *s* soudure *f* à l'arc

ardent ['ɑrdənt] *adj* ardent

ardor ['ɑdər] *s* ardeur *f*

arduous ['ɑrdjʊ·əs] *adj* ardu, difficile

area ['ɛrɪ·ə] *s* région *f*, e.g., **the New York area** la région de New York; (*surface measure*) aire *f*, superficie *f*, e.g., **area of a triangle** aire d'un triangle; (*of knowledge; field*) domaine *m*, champ *m*; (geog; pol) territoire *m*; (mil) secteur *m*, zone *f*; **in this area** (*on this subject*) à ce propos

arena [ə'rinə] *s* arène *f*

Argentina [,ɑrdʒən'tinə] *s* Argentine *f*; l'Argentine

argue ['ɑrgju] *tr* (*a question*) discuter; (*a case*) plaider; (*a point*) soutenir; (*to imply*) arguer; **to argue s.o. into** + *ger* persuader à qn de + *inf* ‖ *intr* discuter, argumenter; plaider

argument ['ɑrgjəmənt] *s* (*proof; reason; theme*) argument *m*; (*debate*) discussion *f*, dispute *f*

argumentative [,ɑrgjə'mɛntətɪv] *adj* disposé à argumenter, raisonneur

aria ['ɑrɪ·ə] *s* aria *f*

arid ['ærɪd] *adj* aride

aridity [ə'rɪdɪti] *s* aridité *f*

Aries ['ɛriz] *s* (astr, astrol) le Bélier

arise [ə'raɪz] *v* (*pret* **arose** [ə'roz]; *pp* **arisen** [ə'rɪzən]) *intr* (*to rise*) se lever; (*to originate*) provenir, prendre naissance; (*to occur*) se produire; (*to be raised, as objections*) s'élever

aristocra·cy [,ærɪs'tɑkrəsi] *s* (*pl* **-cies**) aristocratie *f*

aristocrat [ə'rɪstə,kræt] *s* aristocrate *mf*

aristocratic [ə,rɪstə'krætɪk] *adj* aristocrate

Aristotle ['ærɪ,stɑtəl] *s* Aristote *m*

arithmetic [ə'rɪθmətɪk] *s* arithmétique *f*

arithmetician [ə,rɪθmə'tɪʃən] *s* arithméticien *m*

ark [ɑrk] *s* arche *f*

arm [ɑrm] *s* bras *m*; (mil) arme *f*; **arm in arm** bras dessus bras dessous; **at arm's length** à bout de bras; **under my (your, etc.) arm** sous mon (ton, etc.) aisselle; **up in arms** en rébellion ouverte ‖ *tr* armer ‖ *intr* s'armer

armada [ɑr'mɑdə] *s* armada *f*, grande flotte *f*

armadil·lo [,ɑrmə'dɪlo] *s* (*pl* **-los**) tatou *m*

armament ['ɑrməmənt] *s* armement *m*

armature ['ɑrmə,tʃər] *f* (elec) induit *m*

arm'band' *s* brassard *m*

arm'chair' *s* fauteuil *m*, chaise *f* à bras

Armenian [ɑr'minɪ·ən] *adj* arménien ‖ *s* (*language*) arménien *m*; (*person*) Arménien

armful ['ɑrm,fʊl] *s* brassée *f*

arm'hole' *s* emmanchure *f*, entournure *f*

armistice ['ɑrmɪstɪs] *s* armistice *m*

armor ['ɑrmər] *s* (*personal*) armure *f*; (*on ships, tanks, etc.*) cuirasse *f*, blindage *m* ‖ *tr* cuirasser, blinder ‖ *intr* se mettre l'armure

ar'mored car' *s* fourgon *m* blindé

ar'mor plate' *s* plaque *f* de blindage

ar'mor-plate' *tr* cuirasser, blinder

armor·y ['ɑrməri] *s* (*pl* **-ies**) ateliers *mpl* d'armes, salle *f* d'armes

arm'pit' *s* aisselle *f*

arm'rest' *s* appui-bras *m*, accoudoir *m*

arms' race' *s* course *f* aux armements

arms' reduc'tion *s* contrôle *m* des armes

arm'wres'tle *intr* faire le bras de fer

ar·my ['ɑrmi] *adj* militaire ‖ *s* (*pl* **-mies**) armée *f*

aroma [ə'romə] *s* arôme *m*

aromatic [,ærə'mætɪk] *adj* aromatique

around [ə'raʊnd] *adv* (*nearby*) autour, alentour; **all around** de tous côtés ‖ *prep* autour de; (*approximately*) environ, à peu près; **around 1950** (coll) vers 1950

arouse [ə'raʊz] *tr* éveiller; (*from sleep*) réveiller

arpeg'gio [ɑr'pɛdʒo] *s* (*pl* **-gios**) arpège *m*

arraign [ə'ren] *tr* accuser; (law) mettre en accusation

arrange [ə'rendʒ] *tr* arranger ‖ *intr* s'arranger

arrangement [ə'rendʒmənt] *s* arrangement *m*

array [ə're] *s* (*display*) étalage *m*; (*adornment*) parure *f*; (mil) ordre *m*, rang *m* ‖ *tr* ranger, disposer; (*to adorn*) parer

arrearage [ə'rɪrɪdʒ] *s* arriéré *m*

arrears [ə'rɪrz] *spl* arriéré *m*; **in arrears** arriéré

arrest [ə'rɛst] *s* (*capture*) arrestation *f*; (*halt*) arrêt *m* ‖ *tr* arrêter; fixer; (*attention*) retenir

arrival [ə'raɪvəl] *s* arrivée *f*; (*of goods or ships*) arrivage *m*

arrive [ə'raɪv] *intr* arriver

arrogance ['ærəgəns] *s* arrogance *f*

arrogant ['ærəgənt] *adj* arrogant

arrogate ['ærə,get] *tr*—**to arrogate to oneself** s'arroger

arrow ['æro] *s* flèche *f*

ar'row·head' *s* (*point*) tête *f* de flèche; (bot) sagittaire *m*

arsenal ['ɑrsənəl] *s* (*stock*) arsenal *m*; (*factory*) manufacture *f* d'armes

arsenic ['ɑrsɪnɪk] *s* arsenic *m*

arson ['ɑrsən] *s* incendie *m* volontaire

arsonist ['ɑrsənɪst] *s* incendiaire *mf*

art [ɑrt] *s* art *m*

arterial [ɑr'tɪrɪ·əl] *adj* artériel

arteriosclerotic [ɑr,tɪrɪ·osklɪ'rɑtɪk] *adj* artérioscléreux

arter·y ['ɑrtəri] *s* (*pl* **-ies**) artère *f*

arte'sian well' [ɑr'tiʒən] *s* puits *m* artésien

artful ['ɑrtfəl] *adj* (*skillful*) ingénieux; (*crafty*) artificieux, sournois; artificiel

arthritis [ɑr'θraɪtɪs] *s* arthrite *f*

artichoke ['ɑrtɪ,tʃok] *s* artichaut *m*

article ['ɑrtɪkəl] *s* article; **article of clothing** objet *m* d'habillement

articulate [ɑr'tɪkjəlɪt] *adj* articulé; (*expressing oneself clearly*) clair, expressif; (*speech*) intelligible; (*creature*) doué de la parole ‖ [ɑr'tɪkjə,let] *tr* articuler ‖ *intr* s'articuler

artifact ['ɑrtɪ,fækt] *s* objet *m* fabriqué; (biol) artefact *m*

artifice ['ɑrtɪfɪs] *s* artifice *m*

artificial [,ɑrtɪ'fɪʃəl] *adj* artificiel

artifi'cial insem'ina'tion *s* fécondation *f* artificielle

artificiali·ty [,ɑrtɪ,fɪʃɪ'ælɪti] *s* (*pl* **-ties**) manque *m* de naturel

artifi'cial respira'tion *s* respiration *f* artificielle

artillery [ɑr'tɪləri] *s* artillerie *f*

artil'lery·man *s* (*pl* **-men**) artilleur *m*

artisan [ˈɑrtɪzən] s artisan m
artist [ˈɑrtɪst] s artiste mf
artistic [ɑrˈtɪstɪk] adj artistique, artiste
artistry [ˈɑrtɪstri] s art m, habileté f
artless [ˈɑrtlɪs] adj (uncontrived) naturel; (ingenuous) ingénu, naïf; (lacking art) sans art
arts' and crafts' spl arts et métiers mpl
Aryan [ˈɛrɪ·ən] adj aryen ‖ s (person) Aryen m
as [æz], [əz] pron rel que, e.g., **the same as** le même que ‖ adv aussi, e.g., **as . . . as** aussi . . . que; **as for** quant à; **as is** tel quel; **as of** (a certain date) en date du; **as regards** en ce qui concerne; **as soon as** aussitôt que; **as though** comme si; **as yet** jusqu'ici ‖ prep comme; (in the capacity of) en tant que, en qualité de, à titre de; (in such a way as) en manière de; (such as) tel que; (considered as) considéré comme; (insofar as) dans la mesure où; (at the same time as and to the same degree as) au fur et à mesure que ‖ conj puisque; comme; que
asbestos [æsˈbɛstəs] s amiante m, asbeste m
ascend [əˈsɛnd] tr (a ladder) monter à; (a mountain) gravir; (a river) remonter ‖ intr monter, s'élever
ascendancy [əˈsɛndənsi] s supériorité f, domination f
ascension [əˈsɛnʃən] s ascension f
Ascen'sion Day' s Ascension f
ascent [əˈsɛnt] s ascension f
ascertain [ˌæsərˈten] tr vérifier
ascertainment [ˌæsərˈtenmənt] s constatation f
ascetic [əˈsɛtɪk] adj ascétique ‖ s ascéte mf
asceticism [əˈsɛtɪˌsɪzəm] s ascétisme m, ascése f
ascor'bic ac'id [əˈskɔrbɪk] s acide m ascorbique
ascribe [əˈskraɪb] tr attribuer, imputer
aseptic [eˈsɛptɪk] adj aseptique
ash [æʃ] s cendre f; (tree) frêne m
ashamed [əˈʃemd] adj honteux; **to be ashamed** avoir honte
ash'can' s poubelle f
ashen [ˈæʃən] adj cendré
ashore [əˈʃor] adv à terre; **to go ashore** débarquer
ash'tray' s cendrier m
Ash' Wednes'day s le mercredi des Cendres
Asia [ˈeʒə] s Asie f; l'Asie
A'sia Mi'nor s Asie f Mineure; l'Asie Mineure
aside [əˈsaɪd] s aparté m ‖ adv de côté, à part; (aloof, at a distance) à l'écart; **aside from** en dehors de, à part; **to step aside** s'écarter; (fig) quitter la partie
asinine [ˈæsɪˌnaɪn] adj stupide
ask [æsk] tr (a favor; one's way) demander; (a question) poser; **to ask s.o. about s.th.** interroger qn au sujet q.ch.; **to ask s.o. for s.th.** demander q.ch. à qn; **to ask s.o. to + inf** demander à qn de + inf, prier qn de + inf ‖ intr—**to ask about** s'enquérir

de; **to ask for** (a package; a porter) demander; (to inquire about) demander après; **you asked for it** (you're in for it) (coll) c'est bien fait pour vous
askance [əˈskæns] adv de côté; **to look askance at** regarder de travers
askew [əˈskju] adj & adv de travers, en biais, de biais
asleep [əˈslip] adj endormi; **to fall asleep** s'endormir
asp [æsp] s aspic m
asparagus [əˈspærəgəs] s asperge f; (stalks and tips used as food) des asperges
aspect [ˈæspɛkt] s aspect m
aspen [ˈæspən] s tremble m
aspersion [əˈspʌrʒən] s (sprinkling) aspersion f; (slander) calomnie f
asphalt [ˈæsfɔlt] s asphalte m
asphyxiate [æsˈfɪksɪˌet] tr asphyxier
aspirate [ˈæspɪrɪt] adj & s (phonet) aspiré m ‖ [ˈæspɪˌret] tr aspirer
aspire [əˈspaɪr] intr—**to aspire to** aspirer à
aspirin [ˈæspɪrɪn] s aspirine f
ass [æs] s âne m; (anat & vulg) cul m; (person) (vulg) imbécile mf, crétin m, âne m
assail [əˈsel] tr assaillir
assailant [əˈselənt] s assaillant m
assassin [əˈsæsɪn] s assassin m
assassinate [əˈsæsɪˌnet] tr assassiner
assassination [ə,sæsɪˈneʃən] s assassinat m
assault [əˈsɔlt] s (military attack) assaut m; (unlawful physical attack) agression f; (rape) viol m; (law) voie f de fait ‖ tr assaillir
assault' and bat'tery s (law) voies fpl de fait
assay [əˈse], [ˈæse] s essai m; métal m titré ‖ [əˈse] t essayer; titrer
assayer [əˈse·ər] s essayeur m
as'say val'ue s teneur f
assemblage [əˈsɛmblɪdʒ] s assemblage m
assemble [əˈsɛmbəl] tr assembler ‖ intr s'assembler, se réunir
assem·bly [əˈsɛmbli] s (pl -blies) (meeting) assemblée f, réunion f; (assembling) assemblage m, montage m
assem'bly hall' s salle f de conférences; (educ) grand amphithéâtre m
assem'bly line' s chaîne f de fabrication, chaîne de montage
assem'bly room' s salle f de réunion; (mach) atelier m de montage
assent [əˈsɛnt] s assentiment m ‖ intr assentir
assert [əˈsʌrt] tr affirmer; (one's rights) revendiquer; **to assert oneself** imposer le respect, s'imposer
assertion [əˈsʌrʃən] s assertion f
assess [əˈsɛs] tr (damages, taxes, etc.) évaluer; (value of property) coter; (property for tax purposes) grever
assessment [əˈsɛsmənt] s (estimation) évaluation f; (of real estate) calcul m (de la valeur imposable); (amount of tax) charge f, taxe f
assessor [əˈsɛsər] s répartiteur m d'impôts

asset ['æsɛt] s (*advantage*) avantage *m*, atout *m*; **assets** biens *mpl*, avoirs, *mpl*, actif *m*
ass'hole' s (anat, fig, vulg) trou *m* de cul, trou de balle
assiduous [ə'sɪdjʊ·əs] *adj* assidu
assign [ə'saɪn] *tr* (*task, date, etc.*) assigner; (mil) affecter
assignation [ˌæsɪg'neʃən] s attribution *f*, allocation *f*, affectation *f*; (*lovers' tryst*) rendez-vous *m* illicite
assignment [ə'saɪnmənt] s (*allocation*) attribution *f*; (*schoolwork*) devoirs *mpl*; (law) assignation *f*, transfer *m*; (mil) affectation *f*
assimilate [ə'sɪmɪˌlet] *tr* assimiler ‖ *intr* s'assimiler
assimilation [əˌsɪmɪ'leʃən] s assimilation *f*
assist [ə'sɪst] *tr* assister, aider, secourir ‖ *intr* être assistant
assistance [ə'sɪstəns] s assistance *f*, aide *f*, secours *m*
assistant [ə'sɪstənt] *adj & s* assistant *m*, adjoint *m*
assizes [ə'saɪzɪz] *spl* assises *fpl*
associate [ə'soʃɪ·ɪt] *adj* associé ‖ s associé *m* ‖ [ə'soʃɪˌet] *tr* associer ‖ *intr* s'associer
association [əˌsoʃɪ'eʃən] s association *f*
assonance ['æsənəns] s assonance *f*
assort [ə'sɔrt] *tr* assortir ‖ *intr* s'associer
assorted *adj* assorti
assortment [ə'sɔrtmənt] s assortiment *m*
assuage [ə'swedʒ] *tr* assouvir; soulager, apaiser
assume [ə's(j)um] *tr* (*to suppose*) supposer; (*various forms*) affecter; (*a fact*) présumer; (*a name*) emprunter; (*duties*) assumer, se charger de
assumed *adj* (*supposed*) supposé; (*borrowed*) d'emprunt, emprunté; (*feigned*) feint
assumed' name' s nom *m* d'emprunt, nom de guerre
assuming [ə's(j)umɪŋ] *adj* prétentieux
assumption [ə'sʌmpʃən] s (*supposition*) présomption *f*, hypothèse *f*; (*of virtue*) affectation *f*; (*of power*) appropriation *f*; **Assumption** (eccl) Assomption *f*
assurance [ə'ʃurəns] s (*certainty; self-confidence*) assurance *f*; (*guarantee*) promesse *f*
assure [ə'ʃur] *tr* assurer, garantir
astatine ['æstəˌtin] s astate *m*
aster ['æstər] s aster *m*; (*China aster*) reine-marguerite *f*
asterisk ['æstəˌrɪsk] s astérisque *m*
astern [ə'stʌrn] *adv* à l'arrière
asthma ['æzmə] s asthme *m*
astonish [ə'stɑnɪʃ] *tr* étonner
astonishing [ə'stɑnɪʃɪŋ] *adj* étonnant
astonishment [ə'stɑnɪʃmənt] s étonnement *m*
astound [ə'staʊnd] *tr* stupéfier, ahurir, étonner
astounding [ə'staʊndɪŋ] *adj* étonnant, stupéfiant, abasourdissant
astraddle [ə'strædəl] *adv* à califourchon

astray [ə'stre] *adv*—**to go astray** s'égarer; **to lead astray** égarer
astride [ə'straɪd] *adv* à califourchon ‖ *prep* à califourchon sur
astrologer [ə'strɑlədʒər] s astrologue *m*
astrology [ə'strɑlədʒi] s astrologie *f*
astronaut ['æstrəˌnɔt] s astronaute *mf*
astronautics [ˌæstrə'nɔtɪks] s astronautique *f*
astronomer [ə'strɑnəmər] s astronome *m*
astronomic(al) [ˌæstrə'nɑmɪk(əl)] *adj* astronomique
as'tronom'ical year' s année *f* solaire, année tropique
astronomy [ə'strɑnəmi] s astronomie *f*
astute [ə'st(j)ut] *adj* astucieux, fin
asunder [ə'sʌndər] *adj* séparé ‖ *adv* en deux
asylum [ə'saɪləm] s asile *m*
at [æt], [ət] *prep* à, e.g., **at Paris** à Paris; chez, e.g., **at John's** chez Jean; en, e.g., **at the same time** en même temps
atheism ['eθiˌɪzəm] s athéisme *m*
atheist ['eθi·ɪst] s athée *mf*
atheistic [ˌeθi'ɪstɪk] *adj* athée
Athens ['æθɪnz] s Athènes *f*
athlete ['æθlit] s athlète *m*, sportif *m*
ath'lete's foot' s pied *m* d'athlète
athletic [æθ'lɛtɪk] *adj* athlétique ‖ **athletics** s athlétisme *m*
athwart [ə'θwɔrt] *adv* par le travers
Atlantic [æt'læntɪk] *adj & s* Atlantique *m*
atlas ['ætləs] s atlas *m*
atmosphere ['ætməsˌfɪr] s atmosphère *f*
atmospheric [ˌætməs'fɛrɪk] *adj* atmosphérique ‖ **atmospherics** *spl* parasites *mpl* atmosphériques
atom ['ætəm] s atome *m*
atomic [ə'tɑmɪk] *adj* atomique
atom'ic bomb' s bombe *f* atomique
atom'ic nuc'leus s noyau *m* d'atome
atom'ic pile' s pile *f* atomique
atom'ic struc'ture s édifice *m* atomique
atom'ic weight' s poids *m* atomique, masse *f* atomique
atomize ['ætəˌmaɪz] *tr* atomiser
atomizer ['ætəˌmaɪzər] s atomiseur *m*, vaporisateur *m*; (*e.g., of hair spray*) bombe *f*
atone [ə'ton] *intr*—**to atone for** expier
atonement [ə'tonmənt] s expiation *f*
atrocious [ə'troʃəs] *adj* atroce
atroci·ty [ə'trɑsɪti] s (*pl* -**ties**) atrocité *f*
atro·phy ['ætrəfi] s atrophie *f* ‖ *v* (*pret & pp* -**phied**) *tr* atrophier ‖ *intr* s'atrophier
attach [ə'tætʃ] *tr* (*to join; attribute*) attacher; (*property*) saisir; (*salary*) mettre opposition sur; **to be attached to** s'attacher à
attachment [ə'tætʃmənt] s (*fastener*) attache *f*; (*of the sentiments*) attachement *m*; (*supplementary device*) accessoire *m*; (law) opposition *f*, saisie-arrêt *f*
attack [ə'tæk] s attaque *f* ‖ *tr* attaquer; s'attaquer à ‖ *intr* attaquer
attacker [ə'tækər] s assaillant *m*
attain [ə'ten] *tr* atteindre

attainment [ə'tenmənt] s acquisition f, réalisation f; **attainments** connaissances fpl

attar ['ætər] s essence f

attempt [ə'tɛmpt] s tentative f, effort m; (try) essai m; (assault) attentat m ‖ tr tenter; (s.o.'s life) attenter à

attend [ə'tɛnd] tr (a performance) assister à; (a sick person) soigner; (a person) servir; **to attend classes** suivre des cours ‖ intr—**to attend to** vaquer à, s'occuper de

attendance [ə'tɛndəns] s (number of people present) assistance f; (being present) présence f; (med) soins mpl

attendant [ə'tɛndənt] adj concomitant ‖ s assistant m; (to royalty) serviteur m; **attendants** suite f

attention [ə'tɛnʃən] s attention f; **attention: Mr. Doe** à l'attention de M. Dupont; **attentions** égards mpl ‖ interj attention!; (mil) garde à vous!

attentive [ə'tɛntɪv] adj attentif

attenuate [ə'tɛnju,et] tr (to make thin) amincir; (words; bacteria) atténuer

attest [ə'tɛst] tr attester ‖ intr—**to attest to** attester

Attic ['ætɪk] adj attique ‖ (l.c.) s mansarde f, grenier m, soupente f

attire [ə'taɪr] s vêtement m, parure f ‖ tr habiller, vêtir, parer

attitude ['ætɪ,t(j)ud] s attitude f

attorney [ə'tʌrni] s avoué m, avocat m

attor'ney gen'eral s procureur m général, ministre m de la justice

attract [ə'trækt] tr attirer

attraction [ə'trækʃən] s attraction f

attractive [ə'træktɪv] adj (person, manner) attirant, attrayant; (said, e.g., of a force) attractif; (price, offer; idea) intéressant

attribute ['ætrɪ,bjut] s attribut m ‖ [ə'trɪbjut] tr attribuer

attrition [ə'trɪʃən] s attrition f, usure f

attune [ə't(j)un] tr accorder

auburn ['ɔbərn] adj auburn, brun rougeâtre

auction ['ɔkʃən] s vente f aux enchères ‖ tr vendre aux enchères

auctioneer [,ɔkʃən'ɪr] s adjudicateur m, commissaire-priseur m ‖ tr & intr vendre aux enchères

audacious [ɔ'deʃəs] adj audacieux

audacity [ɔ'dæsɪti] s audace f

audience ['ɔdɪ,əns] s (hearing; formal interview) audience f; (assembly of hearers or spectators) assistance f, salle f, auditoire m; (those who follow what one says or writes) public m

au'dio fre'quency ['ɔdɪ,o] s audio-fréquence f

audiometer [,ɔdɪ'ɑmɪtər] s audiomètre m

audiovisual [,ɔdɪ·o·'vɪʒu·əl] adj audiovisuel

au'dio·visual aids' spl support m audiovisuel, moyens mpl audio-visuels

audit ['ɔdɪt] s apurement m ‖ tr apurer; **to audit a class** assister à la classe en auditeur libre

audition [ɔ'dɪʃən] s audition f ‖ tr & intr auditionner

auditor ['ɔdɪtər] s (com) comptable m agréé, expert comptable m; (educ) auditeur m libre

auditorium [,ɔdɪ'tori·əm] s auditorium m, salle f, amphithéâtre m

auditory ['ɔdɪ,tori] adj auditif

auger ['ɔgər] s tarière f

aught [ɔt] s zéro m ‖ pron indef—**for aught I know** autant que je sache ‖ adv du tout

augment [ɔg'mɛnt] tr & intr augmenter

augur ['ɔgər] s augure m ‖ tr & intr augurer; **to augur well** être de bon augure

augu·ry ['ɔgjəri] s (pl -ries) augure m

august [ɔ'gʌst] adj auguste ‖ **August** ['ɔgəst] s août m

auk [ɔk] s guillemot m

aunt [ænt], [ɑnt] s tante f

aureomycin [,ɔri·o'maɪsɪn] s (pharm) auréomycine f

auricle ['ɔrɪkəl] s auricule f, oreillette f

aurora [ə'rorə] s aurore f

auscultate ['ɔskəl,tet] tr ausculter

auspices ['ɔspɪsɪz] spl auspices mpl

auspicious [ɔs'pɪʃəs] adj propice, favorable

austere [ɔs'tɪr] adj austère

Australia [ɔ'streljə] s Australie f; l'Australie

Australian [ɔ'streljən] adj australien ‖ s (person) Australien m

Austria ['ɔstri·ə] s Autriche f; l'Autriche

Austrian ['ɔstri·ən] adj autrichien ‖ s (person) Autrichien m

authentic [ɔ'θɛntɪk] adj authentique

authenticate [ɔ'θɛntɪ,ket] tr authentifier, constater l'authenticité de

author ['ɔθər] s auteur m

authoress ['ɔθərɪs] s femme f auteur

authoritarian [ɔ,θɑrɪ'tɛri·ən], [ɔ,θɔrɪ'tɛri·ən] adj autoritaire ‖ s homme m autoritaire

authoritative [ɔ'θɑrɪ,tetɪv] adj autorisé; (dictatorial) autoritaire

authority [ɔ'θɔrɪti] s (pl -ties) autorité f; **on good authority** de bonne part

authorize ['ɔθə,raɪz] tr autoriser

au'thor·ship' s paternité f

autistic [ɔ'tɪstɪk] adj autistique

au·to ['ɔto] s (pl -tos) (coll) auto f, voiture f

autobiogra·phy [,ɔtobaɪ'ɑgrəfi] s (pl -phies) autobiographie f

autocrat ['ɔtə,kræt] s autocrate mf

autocratic(al) [,ɔtə'krætɪk(əl)] adj autocratique

autograph ['ɔtə,græf] s autographe m ‖ tr écrire l'autographe sur, dédicacer

au'tographed cop'y s exemplaire m dédicacé

au'to·intox'ica'tion s auto-intoxication f

automat ['ɔtə,mæt] s restaurant m libre service

automate ['ɔtə,met] tr automatiser

automatic [,ɔtə'mætɪk] adj automatique ‖ s revolver m

automat′ed tell′er s (com) machine f de télégestion bancaire, guichet m libre service

automat′ic transmis′sion s changement m de vitesse automatique

automation [‚ɔtə′meʃən] s automatisation f, automation f

automa‧ton [ɔ′tɑmə‚tɑn] s (pl -tons or -ta) [tə] automate m

automobile [‚ɔtəmo′bil] s automobile f

automobile′ show′ s salon m de l'automobile

automotive [‚ɔtə′motɪv] adj automobile; automoteur

autonomous [ɔ′tɑnəməs] adj autonome

autonomy [ɔ′tɑnəmi] s autonomie f

autop‧sy [′ɔtɑpsi] s (pl -sies) autopsie f

autumn [′ɔtəm] s automne m

autumnal [ɔ′tʌmnəl] adj automnal, d'automne

auxilia‧ry [ɔg′zɪljəri] adj auxiliaire ‖ s (pl -ries) auxiliaire mf; **auxiliaries** (mil) troupes fpl auxiliaires

avail [ə′vel] s utilité f ‖ tr profiter à; **to avail oneself of** avoir recours à, profiter de ‖ intr être utile, servir

available [ə′veləbəl] adj disponible; (e.g., train) accessible; **to make available to** mettre à la disposition de

avalanche [′ævə‚læntʃ] s avalanche f

avarice [′ævərɪs] s avarice f

avaricious [‚ævə′rɪʃəs] adj avaricieux

avenge [ə′vɛndʒ] tr venger

avenger [ə′vɛndʒər] s vengeur m

avenue [′ævə‚n(j)u] s avenue f

aver [ə′vʌr] v (pret & pp **averred;** ger **averring**) tr avérer, affirmer

average [′ævərɪdʒ] adj moyen ‖ s moyenne f; **on the average** en moyenne ‖ tr prendre la moyenne de ‖ intr atteindre une moyenne

averse [ə′vʌis] adj—**averse to** hostile à, opposé à, ennemi de

aversion [ə′vʌrʒən] s aversion f

avert [ə′vʌrt] tr (one's eyes; a blow) détourner, écarter; (an accident) éviter

aviar‧y [′evɪ‚ɛri] s (pl -ies) volière f

aviation [‚evɪ′eʃən] s aviation f

aviator [′evɪ‚etər] s aviateur m

avid [′ævɪd] adj avide; **avid for** avide de

avidity [ə′vɪdɪti] s avidité f

avoca‧do [‚ævo′kɑdo] s (pl -dos) avocat m

avocation [‚ævə′keʃən] s occcupation f, profession f; (hobby) distraction f

avoid [ə′vɔɪd] tr éviter

avoidable [ə′vɔɪdəbəl] adj évitable

avoidance [ə′vɔɪdəns] s dérobade f

avow [ə′vaʊ] tr avouer

avowal [ə′vaʊ‧əl] s aveu m

avowedly [ə′vaʊ‧ɪdli] adv ouvertement, franchement

await [ə′wet] tr attendre

awake [ə′wek] adj éveillé ‖ v (pret & pp **awoke** [ə′wok] or **awaked**) tr éveiller ‖ intr s'éveiller

awaken [ə′wekən] tr éveiller, réveiller ‖ intr se réveiller

awakening [ə′wekənɪŋ] s réveil m

award [ə′wɔrd] s (prize) prix m; (law) dommages et intérêts mpl ‖ tr (a prize) décerner; (a sum of money) allouer; (damages) accorder

aware [ə′wɛr] adj conscient; **to become aware of** se rendre compte de

awareness [ə′wɛrnɪs] s conscience f

away [ə′we] adj absent ‖ adv au loin, loin; **away from** éloigné de, loin de; **to do away with** abolir; **to get away** s'absenter; (to escape) échapper; **to go away** s'en aller; **to make away with** (to steal) dérober; **to run away** se sauver; **to send away** renvoyer; **to take away** enlever ‖ interj hors d'ici!; **away with!** à bas!

awe [ɔ] s crainte f révérentielle ‖ tr inspirer de la crainte à

awesome [′ɔsəm] adj impressionnant

awful [′ɔfəl] adj terrible; (coll) terrible, affreux

awfully [′ɔfəli] adv terriblement; (coll) joliment, rudement

awhile [ə′hwaɪl] adv quelque temps, un peu, un moment

awkward [′ɔkwərd] adj (clumsy) gauche, maladroit; (moment) embarrassant; (problem, situation) délicat

awl [ɔl] s alène f

awning [′ɔnɪŋ] s (over a window) tente f; (in front of store) banne f

A.W.O.L. [′ewɔl] s (acronym) (**absent without leave**) absence f illégale; **to be A.W.O.L.** être absent sans permission

awry [ə′raɪ] adv de travers

ax [æks] s hache f

axiom [′æksɪ‚əm] s axiome m

axiomatic [‚æksɪ‧ə′mætɪk] adj axiomatique

axis [′æksɪs] s (pl **axes** [′æksiz]) axe m

axle [′æksəl] s essieu m

ax′le grease′ s cambouis m

ay or **aye** [aj] s oui m; **aye, aye, sir!** oui, commandant!, bien, capitaine!; **the ayes have it** les oui l'emportent ‖ [e] adv toujours

azalea [ə′zeljə] s azalée f

azimuth [′æzɪmə̸θ] s azimut m

Azores [ə′zorz] spl Açores fpl

Aztecs [′æztɛks] spl Aztèques mpl

azure [′eʒər] adj azuré, d'azur ‖ s azur m ‖ tr azurer

B, b [bi] *s* **II**ᵉ lettre de l'alphabet

babble ['bæbəl] *s* babil *m* ‖ *tr* (*secrets*) dire à tort et à travers ‖ *intr* babiller; (*said of birds*) jaser; (*said of brook*) murmurer

babbling ['bæblɪŋ] *adj* (*gossiper*) babillard; (*brook*) murmurant ‖ *s* babillage *m*

babe [beb] *s* bébé *m*, bambin *m*; (*naive person*) (coll) enfant *mf*; (*pretty girl*) (coll) pépée *f*, môme *f*

babel ['bebəl] *s* brouhaha *m*, vacarme *m*

baboon [bæ'bun] *s* babouin *m*

ba·by ['bebi] *s* (*pl* -**bies**) bébé *m*; (*youngest child*) cadet *m*, benjamin *m*; **baby!** (*honey!*) (coll) ma choute! ‖ *v* (*pret & pp* -**bied**) *tr* traiter en bébé, dorloter; (*e.g., a machine*) traiter avec soin

ba'by car'riage *s* voiture *f* d'enfant, poussette *f*; (*with hood*) landau *m*

ba'by foods' *spl* aliments *mpl* pour bébés premier âge, nourriture *f* pour enfants premier âge, la diététique infantile

ba'by grand' *s* piano *m* demi-queue

ba'by-sit'ter *s* gardienne *f* d'enfants, garde-bébé *mf*

ba·by-sit'ting *s* gardiennage *m* d'enfants

ba·by talk' *s* babil *m* enfantin

ba'by teeth' *spl* dents *fpl* de lait

baccalaureate [,bækə'lɔrɪ·ɪt] *s* baccalauréat *m*

bacchanal ['bækənəl] *adj* bachique ‖ *s* bacchanale *f*; (*person*) noceur *m*

bachelor ['bætʃələr] *s* (*single person*) célibataire *m*; (*graduate*) bachelier *m*

bach'elor apart'ment *s* garçonnière *f*

bach'elor girl' *s* garçonne *f*

bach'elor's degree' *s* baccalauréat *m*

bacil·lus [bə'sɪləs]*s* (*pl* -**li** [laɪ]) bacille *m*

back [bæk] *adj* postérieur ‖ *s* (*part of the body; of a living being, hand, tongue, garment, chair, page*) dos *m*; (*of house; of head or body*) derrière *m*; (*of house; of car*) arrière *m*; (*of room*) fond *m*; (*of fabric*) envers *m*; (*of seat*) dossier *m*; (*of medal; of hand*) revers *m*; (*of page*) verso *m*; (sports) arrière; **at the back** en queue; **back to back** dos à dos; **with one's back to the wall** poussé au pied du mur, aux abois ‖ *adv* en arrière, à l'arrière; **as far back as** déjà en, dès, **back and forth** de long en large; **back of** derrière; **back to front** sens devant derrière; **in back** par derrière; **some weeks back** il y a quelques semaines; **to be back** être de retour; **to come back** revenir; **to go back** retourner; **to go back home** rentrer; **to go back on** (coll) abandonner; **to go back to** (*to hark back to*) remonter à; **to make one's way back** s'en retourner ‖ *tr* faire faire marche arrière à; (*e.g., a car*) faire reculer; (*to support*) appuyer, soutenir; (*to reinforce*) renforcer; (*e.g. a racehorse*) parier pour; **to back s.o. up** soutenir qn; **to back water** nager à culer ‖ *intr* reculer; faire marche arrière; **to back down** (fig) se rétracter, se retirer; **to back out of** (*e.g.,*

an agreement) se dédire de, se soustraire à; **to back up** reculer

back'ache' *s* mal *m* de dos

back'bite' *v* (*pret* -**bit**; *pp* -**bitten** or **bit**) *tr* médire de ‖ *intr* médire

back'bit'er *s* médisant *m*

back'bone' *s* (*spinal column*) colonne *f* vertébrale, épine *f* dorsale, échine *f*; (*of a fish*) grande arête *f*; (*of an enterprise*) colonne *f*, appui *m*; (fig) caractère *m*, cran *m*; **to have no backbone** (fig) avoir l'échine souple

back'break'ing *adj* éreintant, dur

back'door' *adj* (fig) secret, clandestin

back' door' *s* porte *f* de derrière; (fig) petite porte

back'down' *s* (coll) palinodie *f*

back'drop' *s* toile *f* de fond

backer ['bækər] *s* (*of team, party, etc.*) supporter *m*; (com) bailleur *m* de fonds, commanditaire *m*

back'fire' *s* retour *m* de flamme, pétarade *f*; (*for firefighting*) contre-feu *m*; (mach) contre-allumage *m* ‖ *intr* donner des retours de flamme; (fig) produire un résultat imprévu

backgammon ['bæk,gæmən] *s* trictrac *m*, jacquet *m*

back'ground' *s* fond *m*; (*of person*) origines *fpl*, éducation *f*; (*music, sound effects, etc.*) fond sonore

back'hand' *s* (tennis) revers *m*

back'hand'ed *adj* de revers; (*compliment*) à rebours, équivoque

backing ['bækɪŋ] *s* (*support*) appui *m*, soutien *m*; (*reinforcement*) renforcement *m*; (*backing up*) recul *m*

back' in'terest *s* arrérages *mpl*

back'lash' *s* contrecoup *m*

back'light'ing *s* contre-jour *m*

back'log' *s* arriéré *m*, accumulation *f*

back' num'ber *s* (*of newspaper, magazine*) vieux numéro *m*; (coll) vieux jeu *m*

back'pain *s* tour *m* de reins

back' pay' *s* salaire *m* arriéré; (mil) arriéré *m* de solde

back' pay'ment *s* arriéré *m*

back' scratch'er *s* gratte-dos *m*; (slang) lèche-bottes *m*

back' seat' *s* banquette *f* arrière; **to take a back seat** (fig) aller au second plan

back'side' *s* derrière *m*, postérieur *m*

back'slide' *intr* récidiver

back'slid'er *s* récidiviste *mf*, relaps *m*

back'spac'er *s* touche *f* d'espace arrière, touche de recul

back'spin' *s* (*of ball*) coup *m* en bas, effet *m*

back'stage' *adv* dans les coulisses

back'stairs' *adj* caché, indirect

back' stairs' *spl* escalier *m* de service

back'stitch' *s* point *m* arrière

back'stop' *s* (*baseball*) attrapeur *m* ‖ *v* (*pret & pp* -**stopped**; *ger* -**stopping**) *tr* (coll) soutenir

back′stroke′ s (of piston) course f de retour; (swimming) brasse f sur le dos

back′swept wing′ s aile f en flèche

back′ talk′ s réplique f impertinente

back′tax′es spl impôts mpl arriérés

back′track′ intr rebrousser chemin

back′up′ s appui m, soutien m

back′up light′ s phare m de recul

backward ['bækwərd] adj (in direction) en arrière, rétrograde; (in time) en retard; (in development) arriéré, attardé ‖ adv en arrière; (opposite to the normal) à rebours; (walking) à reculons; (flowing) à contre-courant; (stroking of the hair) à contre-poil; **backward and forward** de long en large; **to go backward and forward** aller et venir

back′ward-and-for′ward mo′tion s va-et-vient m

backwardness ['bækwərdnɪs] s retard m, lenteur f

backwards ['bækwərdz] adv var of **backward**

back′wash′ s remous m

back′wa′ter s (of river) bras m mort; (e.g., of water wheel) remous m; (fig) endroit m isolé, trou m

back′ wheel′ s roue f arrière

back′woods′ spl forêts fpl de l'intérieur; (godforsaken place) bled m, brousse f

back′woods′man s (pl -men) défricheur m de forêts, coureur m des bois

back′yard′ s derrière m (de la maison)

bacon ['bekən] s lard m, bacon m; (slang) butin m; **bacon and eggs** œufs au bacon; **to bring home the bacon** (coll) remporter la timbale

bacteria [bæk'tɪrɪ·ə] spl bactéries fpl

bacteriology [bæk,tɪrɪ'ɑlədʒi] s bactériologie f

bacteri·um [bæk'tɪrɪ·əm] s (pl -a [ə]) bactérie f

bad [bæd] adj mauvais §91; (wicked) méchant; (serious) grave; **from bad to worse** de mal en pis; **too bad!** c'est dommage!

bad′ breath′ s haleine f forte

bad′ check′ s chèque m en bois, chèque sans provision

bad′ com′pany s mauvaises fréquentations fpl

bad′ debt′ s mauvaise créance f

bad′ egg′ s (slang) mauvais sujet m

bad′ exam′ple s exemple m pernicieux

badge [bædʒ] s insigne m, plaque f

badger ['bædʒər] s blaireau m ‖ tr harceler, ennuyer

bad′ lot′ s voyous mpl, racaille f

badly ['bædli] adv mal §91; (seriously) gravement; **to want badly** avoir grande envie de

bad′man′ s (pl -men′) bandit m

badness ['bædnɪs] s mauvaise qualité f; (of character) méchanceté f

bad′-tem′pered adj susceptible, méchant; (e.g., horse) vicieux, rétif

bad′ trip′ s (slang) (on drugs) voyage m trop poussé

baffle ['bæfəl] s déflecteur m, chicane f ‖ tr déconcerter, confondre

baffling ['bæflɪŋ] adj déconcertant

bag [bæg] s sac m; (suitcase) valise f; (of game) chasse f; **it's in the bag** (coll) c'est du tout cuit ‖ v (pret & pp **bagged**; ger **bagging**) tr ensacher, mettre en sac; (game) abattre, tuer ‖ intr (said of clothing) faire poche

bagful ['bæg,ful] s sachée f

baggage ['bægɪdʒ] s bagage m, bagages

bag′gage car′ s (rr) fourgon m à bagages

bag′gage check′ s (receipt) bulletin m de bagages; (checking) consigne f ordinaire

bag′gage rack′ s (aer) casier m à bagages; (rr) porte-bagages m invar, filet m

bag′gage room′ s bureau m de gare expéditeur; (checkroom) consigne f

bag′gage truck′ s chariot m à bagages; (hand truck) diable m

bag·gy ['bægi] adj (comp **-gier**; super **-giest**) bouffant

bag′ of tricks′ s sac m à malice

bag′pipe′ s cornemuse f

bail [bel] s caution f; **to be out on bail** être libre sous caution; **to put up bail** se porter caution ‖ tr cautionner; **to bail out** se porter caution pour; (a boat) écoper ‖ intr—**to bail out** (aer) sauter en parachute

bailiff ['belɪf] s (of a court) huissier m, bailli m; (on a farm) régisseur m

bailiwick ['belɪwɪk] s bailliage m, rayon m; (fig) domaine m

bait [bet] s appât m, amorce f ‖ tr appâter, amorcer; (to harass) harceler

bake [bek] tr faire cuire au four; **to bake bread** boulanger, faire le pain ‖ intr cuire au four

baked′ pota′toes spl pommes fpl de terre au four

bakelite ['bekə,laɪt] s bakélite f

baker ['bekər] s boulanger m

bak′er's doz′en s treize m à la douzaine

baker·y ['bekəri] s (pl **-ies**) boulangerie f

baking ['bekɪŋ] s cuisson f au four

bak′ing pow′der s levure f anglaise, poudre f à pâte

bak′ing so′da s bicarbonate m de soude

balance ['bæləns] s balance f, équilibre m; (scales) balance f; (what is left) reste m; (com) solde m, report m ‖ tr balancer; (an account) solder ‖ intr se balancer; se solder

bal′ance of pay′ments s balance f des comptes

bal′ance of pow′er s équilibre m politique

bal′ance of trade′ s balance f du commerce

bal′ance sheet′ s bilan m

bal′ance wheel′ s balancier m

balancing ['bælənsɪŋ] s (oscillation) balancement m; (evening up) équilibrage m, ajustement m; (com) règlement m des comptes

balco·ny ['bælkəni] s (pl **-nies**) balcon m; (in a theater) galerie f

bald [bɔld] adj chauve; (fact, statement, etc.) simple, net, carré

baldness ['bɔldnɪs] *s* calvitie *f*

bale [bɔl] *s* balle *f* ‖ *tr* emballer

baleful ['belfəl] *adj* funeste, fatal; triste

balk [bɔk] *s* (*disappointment*) déception *f*, contretemps *m*; (*beam*) poutre *f*; (agr) billon *m* ‖ *tr* frustrer ‖ *intr* regimber

Balkan ['bɔlkən] *adj* balkanique

balk·y ['bɔki] *adj* (*comp* **-ier;** *super* **-iest**) regimbé, rétif

ball [bɔl] *s* balle *f*; (*in billiards; in bearings*) bille *f*; (*spherical body*) boule *f*; (*dance*) bal *m*; **balls** (vulg) couilles *fpl* **to be on the ball** (slang) être toujours là pour le coup; **to have s.th. on the ball** (slang) avoir q.ch. dans le ventre; **to play ball** jouer à la balle, jouer au ballon; (slang) coopérer; (*to be in cahoots*) (slang) être en tandem ‖ *tr*—**to ball up** (slang) bousiller, embrouiller

ballad ['bæləd] *s* (*song*) romance *f*, complainte *f*; (*poem*) ballade *f*

ball′ and chain′ *s* boulet *m*; (slang) femme *f*, épouse *f*

ball′-and-sock′et joint′ *s* joint *m* à rotule

ballast ['bæləst] *s* (aer, naut) lest *m*; (rr) ballast *m* ‖ *tr* lester; ballaster

ball′ bear′ing *s* bille *f*, roulement *m* à billes

ball′ cock′ *s* robinet *m* à flotteur

ballerina [,bælə'rinə] *s* ballerine *f*

ballet ['bæle] *s* ballet *m*

ballistic [bə'lɪstɪk] *adj* balistique ‖ **ballistics** *s* balistique *f*

ballis′tic mis′sile *s* engin *m* balistique

balloon [bə'lun] *s* ballon *m* ‖ *tr* ballonner ‖ *intr* ballonner, se ballonner

ballot ['bælət] *s* (*balloting*) scrutin *m*; (*individual ballot*) bulletin *m* (de vote) ‖ *intr* scrutiner, voter

bal′lot box′ *s* urne *f*; **to stuff the ballot boxes** bourrer les urnes

balloting ['bælətɪŋ] *s* scrutin *m*

ball′-point pen′ *s* stylo *m* à bille, crayon *m* à bille

ball′room′ *s* salon *m* de bal, salle *f* de danse

ballyhoo ['bælɪ,hu] *s* publicité *f* tapageuse ‖ *tr* faire de la réclame pour

balm [bɑm] *s* baume *m* ‖ *tr* parfumer

balm·y ['bɑmi] *adj* (*comp* **-ier;** *super* **-iest**) embaumé; (slang) toqué

baloney [bə'loni] *s* (culin) mortadelle *f*; (slang) fadaises *fpl*

balsam ['bɔlsəm] *s* baume *m*

bal′sam fir′ *s* sapin *m* baumier

bal′sam pop′lar *s* peuplier *m* baumier

Balt [bɔlt] *s* Balte *mf*

Bal′timore o′riole ['bɔltɪ,mor] *s* loriot *m* de Baltimore

baluster ['bæləstər] *s* balustre *m*

balustrade [,bæləs'tred] *s* balustrade *f*, rampe *f*

bamboo [bæm'bu] *s* bambou *m*

bamboozle [bæm'buzəl] *tr* (slang) mystifier

ban [bæn] *s* ban *m*, interdiction *f*; **bans** bans *mpl* ‖ *v* (*pret & pp* **banned;** *ger* **banning**) *tr* mettre au ban

banal ['bænəl], [bə'næl] *adj* banal

banali·ty [bə'nælɪti] *s* (*pl* **-ties**) banalité *f*

banana [bə'nænə] *s* banane *f*

banan′a tree′ *s* bananier *m*

band [bænd] *s* (*strap, connection*) bande *f*, lien *m*; (*group*) bande, troupe *f*; (*brass band*) musique *f*, fanfare *f*; (*dance band*) orchestre *m*; (*strip of color*) raie *f*; **to beat the band** (slang) sans pareille; (*hastily*) vivement ‖ *tr* entourer de bandes; (*a bird*) marquer de bandes ‖ *intr*—**to band together** se grouper

bandage ['bændɪdʒ] *s* (*dressing*) pansement *m*; (*holding the dressing in place*) bandage *m* ‖ *tr* panser; bander

band′box′ *s* carton *m* de modiste

bandit ['bændɪt] *s* bandit *m*

band′mas′ter *s* chef *m* de musique

band′saw′ *s* scie *f* à ruban

band′stand′ *s* kiosque *m*

band′wag′on *s* char *m* de la victoire; **to jump on the bandwagon** suivre la majorité victorieuse

ban·dy ['bændi] *adj* tortu ‖ *v* (*pret & pp* **-died**) *tr* renvoyer, échanger; **to bandy words** se renvoyer des paroles ‖ *intr* se disputer

ban′dy-leg′ged *adj* bancal

bane [ben] *s* poison *m*; ruine *f*

baneful 'benfəl] *adj* funeste, nuisible

bang [bæŋ] *s* coup *m*; (*of a door*) claquement *m*; (*of fireworks; of a gun*) détonation *f*; **bangs** frange *f*; **to go off with a bang** détoner; (slang) réussir ‖ *tr* frapper; (*a door*) faire claquer; **to bang down** (*e.g., a lid*) abattre violemment; **to bang up** (slang) rosser, cogner ‖ *intr* claquer avec fracas; **to bang against** cogner; **to bang on** frapper à ‖ *interj* pan!; pom!

bang′-up′ *adj* (slang) de premier ordre, à la hauteur

banish ['bænɪʃ] *tr* bannir, exiler

banishment ['bænɪʃmənt] *s* bannissement *m*

banister ['bænɪstər] *s* balustre *m*; **banisters** balustrade *f*, rampe *f*

bank [bæŋk] *s* (*for money, blood, data, etc.*) banque *f*; (*of river*) rive *f*, bord *m*; (*shoal*) banc *m*; (*slope*) talus *m*, terrasse *f*; (*in a gambling game*) cave *f*; (aer) virage *m* incliné; **to break the bank** faire sauter la banque ‖ *tr* terrasser; (*money*) déposer; (*an airplane*) incliner ‖ *intr* (aer) virer, virer sur l'aile, s'incliner; **to bank on** compter sur

bank′ account′ *s* compte *m* en banque

bank′book′ *s* carnet *m* de banque

bank′ card′ *s* carte-retrait *f*

banked *adj* incliné

banker ['bæŋkər] *s* banquier *m*

banking ['bæŋkɪŋ] *adj* bancaire

bank′ note′ *s* billet *m* de banque

bank′roll′ *s* paquet *m* de billets, liasse *f* de billets

bankrupt ['bæŋkrʌpt] *adj & s* failli *m*; (*with guilt*) banqueroutier *m*; **to go bankrupt** faire banqueroute ‖ *tr* mettre en faillite

bankrupt·cy [ˈbæŋkrʌptsi] s (pl **-cies**) faillite f, banqueroute f; (fig) ruine f
bank' vault' s chambre f forte
banner [ˈbænər] s bannière f
ban'ner cry' s cri m de guerre
ban'ner year' s année f record
banquet [ˈbæŋkwɪt] s banquet m ‖ intr banqueter
bantam [ˈbæntəm] adj nain ‖ s poulet m nain, poulet de bantam
ban'tam·weight' s poids m bantam; (boxing) poids bantam, poids coq
banter [ˈbæntər] s badinage m ‖ tr & intr badiner
bantering [ˈbæntərɪŋ] adj railleur, goguenard
baptism [ˈbæptɪzəm] s baptême m
baptismal [bæpˈtizməl] adj baptismal
baptis'mal certif'icate s extrait m de baptême
baptis'mal font' s fonts mpl baptismaux
Baptist [ˈbæptɪst] s baptiste mf
baptister·y [ˈbæptɪstəri] s (pl **-ies**) baptistère m
baptize [ˈbæptaɪz] tr baptiser
bar [bɑr] s barre f, barreau m; (obstacle) barrière f, empêchement m; (barroom; counter) bar m; (profession of law) barreau; (of public opinion) tribunal m; (of chocolate) tablette f, plaquette f; (mus) mesure f; (phys) bar; **behind bars** sous les barreaux ‖ prep—**bar none** sans exception ‖ v (pret & pp **barred**; ger **barring**) tr barrer
barb [bɑrb] s (of a fishhook, arrow, feather) barbillon m; (arrowhead) dent f d'une flèche; (in metalwork) barbe f ‖ tr garnir de barbillons
Barbados [bɑrˈbedoz] s la Barbade
barbarian [bɑrˈbɛrɪ·ən] adj & s barbare mf
barbaric [bɑrˈbærɪk] adj barbare
barbarism [ˈbɑrbə‚rɪzəm] s barbarie f; (in speech or writing) barbarisme m
barbari·ty [bɑrˈbærɪti] s (pl **-ties**) barbarie f
barbarous [ˈbɑrbərəs] adj barbare
barbecue [ˈbɑrbɪ‚kju] s grillade f en plein air ‖ tr griller à la sauce piquante et au charbon de bois
bar'becue pit' s rôtisserie f en plein air
barbed adj barbelé, pointu
barbed' wire' s fil m de fer barbelé
barbed'-wire entan'glement s réseau m de barbelés
barber [ˈbɑrbər] s coiffeur m; (who shaves) barbier m
bar'ber pole' s enseigne f de barbier
bar'ber·shop' s salon m de coiffeur
bar'ber·shop quartet' s ensemble m harmonique de chanteurs amateurs
barbiturate [bɑrˈbɪtʃə‚ret], [‚bɑrbɪˈtjʊret] adj & s barbiturique m
bard [bɑrd] s barde m
bare [bɛr] adj nu; (uncovered) découvert; (wire) dénudé, à nu; (necessities) simple, strict; (ace, king, queen) sec ‖ tr mettre à nu
bare'back' adv à nu

bare'faced' adj éhonté, effronté
bare'foot' adj nu-pieds
bare'head'ed adj nu-tête
bare'leg'ged adj nu-jambes
barely [ˈbɛrli] adv à peine
bareness [ˈbɛrnɪs] s nudité f, dénuement m; (of style) pauvreté f
bar'fly' s (pl **-flies**) (slang) pilier m de cabaret
bargain [ˈbɑrgɪn] s (deal) marché m, affaire f; (cheap purchase) solde m, occasion f; **into the bargain** par-dessus le marché ‖ tr—**to bargain away** vendre à perte ‖ intr entrer en négociations; **she gave him more than he bargained for** (fig) elle lui a donné du fil à retordre; **to bargain over** marchander; **to bargain with** traiter avec
bar'gain coun'ter s rayon m des soldes
bar'gain sale' s vente f de soldes
barge [bɑrdʒ] s barge f, chaland m, péniche f ‖ intr—**to barge into** entrer sans façons
baritone [ˈbærɪ‚ton] adj de baryton ‖ s baryton m
barium [ˈbɛ‚rɪ·əm] s baryum m
bark [bɑrk] s (of tree) écorce f; (of dog) aboiement m; (boat) trois-mâts m; **his bark is worse than his bite** il fait plus de bruit que de mal ‖ tr—**to bark out** dire d'un ton sec ‖ intr aboyer; **to bark up the wrong tree** suivre une mauvaise piste
bar'keep'er s barman m
barker [ˈbɑrkər] (coll) s bonimenteur m, barnum m
barley [ˈbɑrli] s orge f
bar'maid' s fille f comptoir, demoiselle f de comptoir, serveuse f
barn [bɑrn] s (for grain) grange f; (for horses) écurie f; (for livestock) étable f
barnacle [ˈbɑrnəkəl] s (on a ship) anatife m, patelle f; (goose) bernacle f
barn' owl' s (Tyto alba) effraie f
barn'storm' intr aller en tournée
barn'yard' s basse-cour f
barometer [bəˈrɑmɪtər] s baromètre m
barometric [‚bærəˈmɛtrɪk] adj barométrique
baron [ˈbærən] s baron m; (of steel, coal, lumber) (coll) magnat m
baroness [ˈbærənɪs] s baronne f
baroque [bəˈrok] adj & s baroque m
barracks [ˈbærəks] spl caserne f
barrage [bəˈrɑʒ] s barrage m
barred adj barré; (excluded) exclu
barrel [ˈbærəl] s tonneau m, fût m; **large barrel** barrique f, baricaut m, barillet m
bar'rel or'gan s orgue m de Barbarie
barren [ˈbærən] adj stérile; (bare) nu; (of style) aride, sec
barricade [‚bærɪˈked] s barricade f ‖ tr barricader
barrier [ˈbærɪ·ər] s barrière f
bar'rier reef' s récif-barrière m
barring [ˈbɑrɪŋ] prep sauf
barrister [ˈbærɪstər] s (Brit) avocat m
bar'room' s cabaret m, bar m, bistrot m
bar'tend'er s barman m

barter ['bɑrtər] *s* échange *m*, troc *m* ‖ *tr* échanger

ba′sal metab′olism ['besəl] *s* métabolisme *m* basal

basalt [bə'sɔlt], ['bæsɔlt] *s* basalte *m*

base [bes] *adj* bas, vil ‖ *s* (*main ingredient; starting point; lowest part*) base *f*; (*fundamental, principal*) fondement *m*, ligne *f* d'appui, principe *m*; (*pedestal*) socle *m* ‖ *tr* baser; fonder

base′ball′ *s* base-ball *m*

base′board′ *s* plinthe *f*

basement ['besmənt] *s* sous-sol *m*, cave *f*

base′ment win′dow *s* soupirail *m*

bash [bæʃ] *tr* cogner, assommer

bashful ['bæʃfəl] *adj* timide

basic ['besɪk] *adj* fondamental, de base, essentiel; (*alkaline*) basique

basil ['bæzəl] *s* basilic *m*

basilica [bə'sɪlɪkə] *s* basilique *f*

ba·sis ['besɪs] *s* (*pl* **-ses** [siz]) base *f*, fondement *m*; **on the basis of** sur la base de, par suite de

bask [bæsk] *intr* se chauffer

basket ['bæskɪt] *s* panier *m*; (*with a handle*) corbeille *f*; (*carried on the back*) hotte *f*

bas′ket·ball′ *s* basket-ball *m*, basket *m*

bas′ket·ball play′er *s* basketteur *m*

bas′ket lunch′ *s* panier-repas *m*

bas′ket·mak′er *s* vannier *m*

bas′ket·work′ *s* vannerie *f*

Basque [bæsk] *adj* basque ‖ *s* (*language*) basque *m*; (*person*) Basque *mf*

bass [bes] *adj* grave, bas ‖ *s* (mus) basse *f* ‖ [bæs] *s* (ichth) bar *m*

bass′ clef′ *s* clef *f* de fa

bass′ drum′ [bes] *s* grosse caisse *f*

bassinet [,bæsɪ'nɛt] *s* bercelonnette *f*

bassoon [bə'sun] *s* basson *m*

bass viol ['bes'vaɪ·əl] *s* basse *f* de viole

basswood ['bæs,wʊd] *s* tilleul *m*

bastard ['bæstərd] *adj* bâtard ‖ *s* bâtard *m*; (vulg) salaud *m*, saligaud *m*

baste [best] *tr* (*to thrash*) rosser; (*to scold*) éreinter; (culin) arroser; (sewing) faufiler, baguer, bâtir

bastion ['bæstʃən] *s* bastion *m*

bat [bæt] *s* (*cudgel*) bâton *m*; (*for cricket*) bat *m*; (sports) batte *f*; (zool) chauve-souris *f*; (*blow*) (coll) coup *m*; **right off the bat** sur-le-champ; **to be at bat** tenir la batte; **to go to bat for** (coll) intervenir au profit de; **to have bats in the belfry** (coll) avoir une araignée dans le plafond ‖ *v* (*pret & pp* **batted**; *ger* **batting**) *tr* battre

batch [bætʃ] *s* (*of papers*) liasse *f*; (comp) paquetage *m*; (coll) fournée *f*, lot *m*

batch′ proc′essing (comp) traitement *m* par lots

bated ['betɪd] *adj*—**with bated breath** en baissant la voix, dans un souffle

bath [bæθ] *s* bain *m*; (*bathroom*) salle *f* de bains; **to take a bath** prendre un bain, se baigner

bathe [beð] *tr* baigner ‖ *intr* se baigner

bather ['beðər] *s* baigneur *m*

bath′house′ *s* établissement *m* de bains; (*at the seashore*) cabine *f*

bath′ing suit′ *s* costume *m* de bain

bath′ing trunks′ *s* slip *m* de bain

bath′ mat′ *s* tapis *m* de bain

bath′robe′ *s* peignoir *m*

bath′room′ *s* salle *f* de bains

bath′room fix′tures *spl* appareils *mpl* sanitaires

bath′room scale′ *s* pèse-personne *m*

bath′ tow′el *s* serviette *f* de bain

bath′tub′ *s* baignoire *f*

baton [bæ'tan] (*scepter*) bâton *m*; (mus) baguette *f*, bâton de chef d'orchestre; (sports) bâton de relais, témoin *m*

battalion [bə'tæljən] *s* bataillon *m*

batten ['bætən] *tr*—**to batten down the hatches** condamner les panneaux

batter ['bætər] *s* (culin) pâte *f*; (sports) batteur *m* ‖ *tr* battre

bat′tering ram′ *s* bélier *m*

batter·y ['bætəri] *s* (*pl* **-ies**) (elec, mil, mus) batterie *f*; (*primary cell*) pile *f*; (*secondary cell or cells*) accumulateur *m*, accu *m*

battle ['bætəl] *s* bataille *f*; **to do battle** livrer combat ‖ *tr & intr* combattre

bat′tle·ax′ *s* hache *f* d'armes; (*shrew*) (slang) harpie *f*, mégère *f*

bat′tle cruis′er *s* croiseur *m* de bataille

bat′tle cry′ *s* cri *m* de guerre

bat′tle·field′ *s* champ *m* de bataille

bat′tle·front′ *s* front *m* de bataille

bat′tle line′ *s* ligne *f* de feu

battlement ['bætəlmənt] *s* créneau *m*; **battlements** parapet *m*, rempart *m*

bat′tle roy′al *s* mêlée *f* générale

bat′tle·ship′ *s* cuirassé *m*, navire *m* de guerre

bat·ty ['bæti] *adj* (*comp* **-tier**; *super* **-tiest**) (slang) dingo, maboul, braque

bauble ['bɔbəl] *s* babiole *f*, bagatelle *f*; (*of jester*) marotte *f*

Bavaria [bə'vɛrɪ·ə] *s* la Bavière

Bavarian [bə'vɛrɪ·ən] *adj* bavarois ‖ *s* Bavarois *m*

bawd·y ['bɔdi] *adj* (*comp* **-ier**; *super* **-iest**) obscène, impudique

bawl [bɔl] *tr*—**to bawl out** (slang) faire une sortie à, engueuler ‖ *intr* gueuler; (*to cry*) sangloter

bawl′ing out′ *s* (slang) engueulade *f*

bay [be] *adj & s* baie *f*; **at bay** aux abois ‖ *intr* aboyer, hurler

bay′ber′ry *s* (*pl* **-ries**) baie *f*

bay′berry tree′ *s* laurier *m*

bayonet ['be·ənɪt] *s* baïonnette *f* ‖ *tr* percer d'un coup de baïonnette

bayou ['baɪ·u] *s* anse *f*

bay′ rum′ *s* eau *f* de toilette au laurier

bay′ win′dow *s* fenêtre *f* en saillie; (slang) bedaine *f*, gros ventre *m*

bazaar [bə'zɑr] *s* bazar *m*; (*social event*) kermesse *f*

B.C. ['bi'si] *adv* (letterword) (**before Christ**) av. J.-C.

be [bi] *v* (*pres am* [æm], **is** [ɪz], **are** [ɑr]; *pret* **was** [wɑz] or [wʌz], **were** [wʌr]; *pp* **been** [bɪn]) *intr* être; avoir, e.g., **to be five years old** avoir cinq ans; e.g., **to be ten feet long** avoir dix pieds de long; e.g., **what is the matter with you?** qu'a-vez-vous?; **here is** or **here are** voici; **how are you?** comment allez-vous?, ça va?, comment vous portez-vous?; **how much is that?** combien coûte cela?, c'est com-bien ça?; **so be it** ainsi soit-il; **there is** or **there are** il y a; (in directing the atten-tion) voilà; for expressions like **it is warm** il fait chaud or **I am cold** j'ai froid, see the noun ‖ *aux* (to form the passive voice) être, e.g., **he is loved by everybody** il est aimé de tout le monde; (progressive not expressed in French), e.g., **he is eating** il mange; **to be to** + *inf* devoir + *inf*, e.g., **I am to give a speech** je dois prononcer un discours

beach [bitʃ] *s* plage *f*, bord *m* de la mer; grève *f*, rivage *m* ‖ *tr & intr* échouer

beach′ ball′ *s* ballon *m* de plage

beach′ bug′gy *s* buggy *m*

beach′comb′er *s* batteur *m* de grève

beach′head′ *s* (mil) tête *f* de pont

beach′ resort′ *s* station *f* balnéaire

beach′ robe′ *s* sortie *f* de bain, peignoir *m* de bain

beach′ shoe′ *s* claquette *f*

beach′ umbrel′la *s* parasol *m* de plage

beach′ wear′ *s* tenue *f* de plage

beacon [ˈbikən] *s* signal *m*, phare *m* ‖ *tr* éclairer ‖ *intr* briller

bead [bid] *s* perle *f*, grain *m*; (*of a gun*) guidon *m*; **beads** collier *m*; (*of sweat*) gouttes *fpl*; (eccl) chapelet *m*; **to draw a bead on** viser; **to tell one's beads** égrener son chapelet

beagle [ˈbigəl] *s* beagle *m*, briquet *m*

beak [bik] *s* bec *m*; (*nose*) (slang) pif *m*; grand nez *m* crochu

beaker [ˈbikər] *s* coupe *f*, vase *m* à bec, verre *m* à expérience

beam [bim] *s* (*girder*) poutre *f*; (*plank*) madrier *m*; (*of roof*) solive *f*; (*of ship*) bau *m*, barrot *m*; (*of light; of hope*) rayon *m*; (rad) faisceau *m*; **on the beam** (slang) sur la bonne piste; **to be off the beam** (slang) faire fausse route ‖ *tr* (*light, waves, etc.*) émettre; **to beam a broadcast** faire une émission ‖ *intr* rayonner

bean [bin] *s* haricot *m*; (*broad bean*) fève *f*; (slang) caboche *f*; **to spill the beans** (coll) vendre la mèche

bean′-bag chair′ *s* siège-billes *m*

bean′ pole′ *s* perche *f* à fèves; (*person*) (slang) asperge *f*

bean′stalk′ *s* tige *f* de fève, tige de haricot

bear [bɛr] *s* ours *m*; (*in the stock market*) baissier *m* ‖ *v* (*pret* **bore** [bor]; *pp* **borne** [born]) *tr* porter; (*a child*) enfanter; (*in-terest on money*) rapporter; (*to put up with*) souffrir, supporter; **to bear the market** jouer à la baisse ‖ *intr* porter; **to bear down** appuyer; **to bear up against**

résister à; **to bear upon** avoir du rapport à; **to bring to bear** mettre en jeu

bearable [ˈbɛrəbəl] *adj* supportable

bear′ cub′ *s* ourson *m*

beard [bɪrd] *s* barbe *f* ‖ *tr* braver, narguer

bearded *adj* barbu

beardless [ˈbɪrdlɪs] *adj* imberbe, sans barbe

bearer [ˈbɛrər] *s* porteur *m*

bearing [ˈbɛrɪŋ] *s* (*posture; behavior*) port *m*, maintien *m*; (mach) roulement *m*, coussinet *m*; (naut) relèvement *m*; **to get one's bearings** se retrouver; **to have a bearing on** s'appliquer à; **to take bear-ings** (naut) faire le point

bear′ mar′ket *s* marché *m* à la baisse

bear′skin′ *s* peau *f* d'ours; colback *m*

beast [bist] *s* bête *f*, animal *m*; (*person*) brute *f*, animal *m*

beast·ly [ˈbistli] *adj* (*comp* **-lier**; *super* **-liest**) brutal, bestial; (coll) abominable, détestable

beast′ of bur′den *s* bête *f* de somme, bête de charge

beat [bit] *s* (*of heart, pulse, drums*) batte-ment *m*; (*of policeman*) ronde *f*; (mus) mesure *f*, temps *m* ‖ *v* (*pret* **beat**; *pp* **beat** or **beaten**) *tr* battre; (*to defeat*) vaincre, battre; **that beats me!** (slang) ça me dépasse!; **to beat back** or **down** rabattre; **to beat in** enfoncer; **to beat it** (slang) filer, décamper; **to beat s.o. hollow** (coll) battre qn à plate couture; **to beat s.o. out of money** (slang) escroquer qn; **to beat time** battre la mesure; **to beat up** (slang) rosser ‖ *intr* battre; **to beat around the bush** (coll) tourner autour du pot

beater [ˈbitər] *s* batteur *m*; (culin) fouet *m*

beati·fy [bɪˈæti,faɪ] *v* (*pret & pp* **-fied**) *tr* béatifier

beating [ˈbitɪŋ] *s* (*of wings, heart, pulse, drums*) battement *m*; (*thrashing*) correc-tion *f*, rossée *f*, raclée *f*; (*defeat*) défaite *f*, raclée; **to take a beating** se faire battre à plate couture

beatitude [bɪˈæti,t(j)ud] *s* béatitude *f*

beau [bo] *s* (*pl* **beaus** or **beaux** [boz]) beau *m*, galant *m*

beautician [bjuˈtɪʃən] *s* coiffeur *m*, coif-feuse *f*, esthéticienne *f*

beautiful [ˈbjutɪfəl] *adj* beau

beautifully [ˈbjutɪfəli] *adv* admirablement

beauti·fy [ˈbjuti,faɪ] *v* (*pret & pp* **-fied**) *tr* embellir

beau·ty [ˈbjuti] *s* (*pl* **-ties**) beauté *f*

beau′ty con′test *s* concours *m* de beauté

beau′ty par′lor or **beau′ty shop′** *s* salon *m* de beauté, institut *m* de beauté

beau′ty queen′ *s* reine *f* de beauté

beau′ty sleep′ *s* sommeil *m* avant minuit

beau′ty spot′ *s* (*place*) coin *m* délicieux; (*on face*) grain *m* de beauté

beaver [ˈbivər] *s* castor *m*

becalm [bɪˈkɑm] *tr* calmer, apaiser; (naut) abriter

because [bɪˈkɔz] *conj* parce que; **because of** à cause de, par suite de

beck [bɛk] *s*—**to be at s.o.'s beck and call** obéir à qn au doigt et à l'œil

beckon ['bɛkən] *tr* faire signe à, appeler ‖ *intr* appeler

be·come [bɪ'kʌm] *v* (*pret* **-came;** *pp* **-come**) *tr* convenir à, aller à, seoir à ‖ *intr* devenir; se faire, e.g., **to become a doctor** se faire médecin; e.g., **to become known** se faire connaître; **to become accustomed** s'accoutumer; **to become old** vieillir; **what has become of him?** qu'est-ce qu'il est devenu?

becoming [bɪ'kʌmɪŋ] *adj* convenable, seyant

bed [bɛd] *s* lit *m*; couche *f*; **to go to bed** se coucher; **to put to bed** coucher

bed' and board' *s* le vivre et le couvert

bed' and break'fast *s* (Brit) chambre *f* avec petit déjeuner

bed'bug' *s* punaise *f* (des lits)

bed'clothes' *spl* couvertures *fpl* et draps *mpl*

bedding ['bɛdɪŋ] *s* literie *f*

bedeck [bɪ'dɛk] *tr* parer, orner, chamarrer; **to bedeck oneself** s'attifer

bed'fast' *adj* cloué au lit

bed'fel'low *s* camarade *m* de lit

bed'jack'et *s* liseuse *f*

bedlam ['bɛdləm] *s* pétaudière *f*, tumulte *m*

bed'lamp' *s* lampe *f* de chevet

bed' lin'en *s* literie *f*, draps *mpl* en toile de fil

bed'pan' *s* bassin *m* (de lit)

bed'post' *s* pied *m* de lit

bedraggled [bɪ'drægəld] *adj* crotté, échevelé

bedridden ['bɛd,rɪdən] *adj* alité, cloué au lit

bed'rock' *s* roche *f* de fond; (geol) soubassement *m*; (fig) fondement *m*, base *f*

bed'room' *s* chambre *f* à coucher

bed'room lamp' *s* lampe *f* de chevet

bed'side' *s* bord *m* du lit, chevet *m*

bed'side book' *s* livre *m* de chevet

bed'sore' *s* escarre *f*

bed'spread' *s* dessus-de-lit *m invar*

bed'spring' *s* sommier *m*

bed'stead' *s* bois *m* de lit

bed' tick' *s* coutil *m*

bed'time' *s* l'heure *f* du coucher

bed' warm'er *s* chauffe-lit *m*

bed'wet'ting *s* énurésie *f*

bee [bi] *s* abeille *f*; (*get-together*) réunion *f*; (*contest*) concours *m*

beech [bitʃ] *s* hêtre *m*

beech' mar'ten *s* (zool) fouine *f*

beech'nut' *s* faîne *f*

beef [bif] *s* bœuf *m* ‖ *tr*—**to beef up** (coll) renforcer ‖ *intr* (slang) rouspéter

beef' cat'tle *s* bœufs *mpl* de boucherie

beef'steak' *s* bifteck *m*

beef' stew' *s* ragoût *m* de bœuf

bee'hive' *s* ruche *f*

bee'keep'er *s* apiculteur *m*

bee'keep'ing *s* apiculture *f*

bee'line' *s*—**to make a beeline for** aller en droite ligne à

beeper ['bipər] *s* bip-bip *m*

beer [bɪr] *s* bière *f*

beer' bot'tle or **beer' can** *s* canette *f* (de bière)

bees'wax' *s* circe *f* d'abeille

beet *s* betterave *f*

beetle ['bitəl] *s* scarabée *m*, escarbot *m*

bee'tle-browed' *adj* à sourcils épais, à sourcils fournis

be·fall [bɪ'fɔl] *v* (*pret* **-fell;** *pp* **-fallen**) *tr* arriver à ‖ *intr* arriver

befitting [bɪ'fɪtɪŋ] *adj* convenable, seyant

before [bɪ'for] *adv* avant, auparavant ‖ *prep* avant; (*in front of*) devant; **before** + *ger* avant de + *inf* ‖ *conj* avant que

before'hand' *adv* d'avance, préalablement, auparavant

befriend [bɪ'frɛnd] *tr* venir en aide à

befuddle [bɪ'fʌdəl] *tr* embrouiller

beg [bɛg] *v* (*pret* & *pp* **begged;** *ger* **begging**) *tr* mendier; (*to entreat*) supplier ‖ *intr* mendier; (*said of dog*) faire le beau; **I beg of you** je vous en prie; **to beg for** solliciter; **to beg off** s'excuser; **to beg off from** se faire excuser de; **to go begging** (fig) rester pour compte

be·get [bɪ'gɛt] *v* (*pret* **-got;** *pp* **-gotten** or **-got;** *ger* **-getting**) *tr* engendrer

beggar ['bɛgər] *s* mendiant *m*

beggarly ['bɛgərli] *adj* chétif, misérable

be·gin [bɪ'gɪn] *v* (*pret* **-gan** ['gæn]; *pp* **-gun** ['gʌn]; *ger* **-ginning**) *tr* & *intr* commencer; **beginning with** à partir de; **to begin to** commencer à

beginner [bɪ'gɪnər] *s* débutant *m*, commençant *m*; (*tyro*) blanc-bec *m*, novice *m*, béjaune *m*; (mil) bleu *m*

beginning [bɪ'gɪnɪŋ] *s* commencement *m*, début *m*

begrudge [bɪ'grʌdʒ] *tr* donner à contre-cœur; **to begrudge s.o. s.th.** envier q.ch. à qn

beguile [bɪ'gaɪl] *tr* charmer, tromper

behalf [bɪ'hæf] *s*—**on behalf of** de la part de, au nom de

behave [bɪ'hev] *intr* se comporter, se conduire; (*to behave well*) se comporter bien

behavior [bɪ'hevjər] *s* comportement *m*, conduite *f*; (mach) fonctionnement *m*

behaviorism [bɪ'hevjərɪzəm] *s* behaviorisme *m*

behead [bɪ'hɛd] *tr* décapiter

beheading [bɪ'hɛdɪŋ] *s* décapitation *f*

behest [bɪ'hɛst] *s* ordre *m*, demande *f*

behind [bɪ'haɪnd] *s* derrière *m* ‖ *adv* derrière, par derrière; **to be behind** être en retard; **to fall behind** traîner en arrière ‖ *prep* derrière; en arrière de; **behind the back of** dans le dos de; **behind time** en retard

be·hold [bɪ'hold] *v* (*pret* & *pp* **-held** ['hɛld]) *tr* contempler ‖ *interj* voyez!, voici!

behoove [bɪ'huv] *impers*—**it behooves him to** il lui appartient de; **it does not behoove him to** mal lui sied de

being ['bi·ɪŋ] *adj*—**for the time being** pour le moment ‖ *s* être *m*

belabor [bɪˈlebər] *tr* rosser; (fig) trop insister sur

belated [bɪˈletɪd] *adj* attardé, tardif

belch [bɛltʃ] *s* éructation *f*; rot *m* (slang) ‖ *tr* & *intr* éructer

bel·fry [ˈbɛlfri] *s* (*pl* **-fries**) beffroi *m*, clocher *m*

Belgian [ˈbɛldʒən] *adj* belge ‖ *s* Belge *mf*

Belgium [ˈbɛldʒəm] *s* Belgique *f*; la Belgique

be·lie [bɪˈlaɪ] *v* (*pret* & *pp* **-lied** [ˈlaɪd]; *ger* **-lying** [ˈlaɪɪŋ]) *tr* démentir

belief [bɪˈlif] *s* croyance *f*

believable [bɪˈlivəbəl] *adj* croyable

believe [bɪˈliv] *tr* & *intr* croire; **to believe in** croire à or en; **to make believe** faire semblant, feindre

believer [bɪˈlivər] *s* croyant *m*

belittle [bɪˈlɪtəl] *tr* rabaisser

bell [bɛl] *s* (*hollow instrument*) cloche *f*; (*of a clock or gong*) timbre *m*; (*small bell*) sonnette *f*; clochette *f*; (*big bell*) bourdon *m*; (*on animals*) grelot *m*, clarine *f*, sonnaille *f*; (*of a trumpet*) pavillon *m*; **bells** sonnerie *f* ‖ *tr* attacher un grelot à

belladonna [ˌbɛləˈdɑnə] *s* belladone *f*

bell'-bot'tom trou'sers *spl* pantalon *m* à pattes d'éléphant

bell'boy' *s* chasseur *m*, garçon *m* d'hôtel

bell' glass' *s* globe *m*, garde-poussière *m*

bell'hop' *s* chasseur *m*, garçon *m* d'hôtel

bellicose [ˈbɛlɪ,kos] *adj* belliqueux

belligerent [bəˈlɪdʒərənt] *adj* & *s* belligérant *m*

bell' jar' *s* var of **bell glass**

bellow [ˈbɛlo] *s* mugissement *m*; **bellows** (*of camera*; *of fireplace*) soufflet *m*; (*of organ*; *of forge*) soufflerie *f* ‖ *intr* mugir, beugler

bell'pull' *s* cordon *m* de sonnette

bell' ring'er *s* sonneur *m*; carillonneur *m*

bell'-shaped' *adj* en forme de cloche

bell' tow'er *s* clocher *m*, campanile *m*

bellwether [ˈbɛl,wɛðər] *s* sonnailler *m*

bel·ly [ˈbɛli] *s* (*pl* **-lies**) ventre *m* ‖ *v* (*pret* & *pp* **-lied**) *intr*—**to belly out** s'enfler

bel'ly·ache' *s* (coll) mal *m* de ventre ‖ *intr* (slang) rouspéter

bel'ly·but'ton *s* (coll) nombril *m*

bel'ly dance' *s* (coll) danse *f* du ventre

bel'ly flop' *s* plat ventre *m* (acrobatique)

bellyful [ˈbɛli,fʊl] *s* (slang) ventrée *f*

bel'ly-land' *intr* (aer) aterrir sur le ventre

belong [bɪˈlɔŋ] *intr* (*to have the proper qualities*) aller bien; **to belong in** devoir être dans, e.g., **this chair belongs in that corner** cette chaise doit être dans ce coin-là; **to belong to** appartenir à; **to belong together** aller ensemble

belongings [bɪˈlɔŋɪŋz] *spl* biens *mpl*, effets *mpl*

beloved [bɪˈlʌvɪd], [bɪˈlʌvd] *adj* & *s* bien-aimé *m*

below [bɪˈlo] *adv* dessous, au-dessous, en bas; (*as follows, following*) ci-dessous, ci-après ‖ *prep* sous, au-dessous de; (*another point on the river*) en aval de

belt [bɛlt] *s* (*encircling band or strip*) ceinture *f*; (*tract of land, region*) zone *f*; (*blow*) coup *m*; (*of a machine*) courroie *f*; **to tighten one's belt** se serrer la ceinture ‖ *tr* ceindre; (slang) cogner

belt' buck'le *s* boucle *f* de ceinturon

belt' convey'or *s* tapis *m* roulant

belted *adj* à ceinture

belt'way' *s* route *f* de ceinture, boulevard *m* périphérique

bemoan [bɪˈmon] *tr* déplorer

bemuse [bɪˈmjuz] *tr* stupéfier, hébéter

bench [bɛntʃ] *s* banc *m*; (law) siège *m*

bench' mark' *s* repère *m*

bend [bɛnd] *s* (*curvature*) courbure *f*; (*of river, tube, road*) coude *m*; (*of arm, knee*) pli *m*; **bends** mal *m* des caissons ‖ *v* (*pret* & *pp* **bent** [bɛnt]) *tr* courber; (*the elbow*; *a person to one's will*) plier; (*the knee*) fléchir ‖ *intr* courber; plier; **do not bend** (label) ne pas plier; **to bend down** se courber

bender [ˈbɛndər] *s*—**to go on a bender** (slang) faire la bombe

beneath [bɪˈniθ] *adv* dessous, au-dessous, en bas ‖ *prep* sous, au-dessous de

benediction [ˌbɛnɪˈdɪkʃən] *s* bénédiction *f*

benefactor [ˈbɛnɪ,fæktər] *s* bienfaiteur *m*

beneficence [bɪˈnɛfɪsəns] *s* bienfaisance *f*

beneficent [bɪˈnɛfɪsənt] *adj* bienfaisant

beneficial [ˌbɛnɪˈfɪʃəl] *adj* profitable, avantageux; (*remedy*) salutaire

beneficiar·y [ˌbɛnɪˈfɪʃɪ,ɛri] *s* (*pl* **-ies**) bénéficiaire *mf*, ayant droit *m*

benefit [ˈbɛnɪfɪt] *s* profit *m*; (theat) bénéfice *m*; **benefits** bienfaits *mpl*, avantages *mpl*; **for the benefit of** au profit de ‖ *tr* profiter à ‖ *intr* se trouver bien, gagner

ben'efit soci'ety *s* société *f* de prévoyance

benevolent [bɪˈnɛvələnt] *adj* bienveillant, bienfaisant, bénévole

benign [bɪˈnaɪn] *adj* bénin

bent [bɛnt] *adj* courbé, plié; (*person's back*) voûté; (*determined*) résolu; **bent over** (*shoulders*) voûté; (*figure, person*) courbé; **to be bent on** être acharné à ‖ *s* penchant *m*; **to have a bent for** avoir du goût pour

benzene [bɛnˈzin] *s* (chem) benzène *m*

benzine [bɛnˈzin] *s* benzine *f*

bequeath [bɪˈkwið] *tr* léguer

bequest [bɪˈkwɛst] *s* legs *m*

berate [bɪˈret] *tr* gronder

be·reave [bɪˈriv] *v* (*pret* & *pp* **-reaved** or **-reft** [ˈrɛft]) *tr* priver; (*to cause sorrow to*) affliger

bereavement [bɪˈrivmənt] *s* (*loss*) privation *f*; (*sorrow*) deuil *m*, affliction *f*

Berlin [bərˈlɪn] *adj* berlinois ‖ *s* Berlin *m*

Berliner [bərˈlɪnər] *s* berlinois *m*

Bermuda [bərˈmjudə] *s* les Bermudes *fpl*

ber·ry [ˈbɛri] *s* (*pl* **-ries**) baie *f*; (*seed*) grain *m*

berserk [bərˈzʌrk] *adv* frénétiquement; **to go berserk** frapper à tort et à travers

berth [bʌrθ] *s* (*sleeping space*) couchette *f*; (*at a dock*) emplacement *m*; (*space to* move *about*) évitage *m*; (fig) poste *m*, situation *f* ‖ *tr* (*a ship*) acoster

beryllium [bə'rɪlɪ·əm] *s* béryllium *m*

be·seech [bɪ'sitʃ] *v* (*pret & pp* **-sought** ['sɔt] or **-seeched**) *tr* supplier

be·set [bɪ'sɛt] *v* (*pret & pp* **-set;** *ger* **-setting**) *tr* assiéger, assaillir

beside [bɪ'saɪd] *prep* à côté de, auprès de; **to be beside oneself** être hors de soi; **to be beside oneself with** (*e.g., joy*) être transporté de

besides [bɪ'saɪdz] *adv* (*in addition*) en outre, de plus; (*otherwise*) d'ailleurs ‖ *prep* en sus de, en plus de, outre

besiege [bɪ'sidʒ] *tr* assiéger

besmear [bɪ'smɪr] *tr* barbouiller

besmirch [bɪ'smʌrtʃ] *tr* souiller

best [bɛst] *adj super* (le) meilleur §91 ‖ *s* (le) meilleur *m*; **at best** au mieux; **to do one's best** faire de son mieux; **to get the best of it** avoir le dessus; **to make the best of** s'accommoder de ‖ *adv super* (le) mieux §91 ‖ *tr* l'emporter sur

best′ girl′ *s* (coll) petite amie *f*, atitrée *f*

bestial ['bɛstjəl] *adj* bestial, brutal

best′ man′ *s* garçon *m* d'honneur

bestow [bɪ'sto] *tr* accorder, conférer

bestowal [bɪ'sto·əl] *s* don *m*, dispensation *f*

best′ sel′ler *s* livre *m* à succès, succès *m* de librairie, champion *m*

bet [bɛt] *s* pari *m*, gageure *f*; **make your bets!** faites vos jeux! ‖ *v* (*pret & pp* **bet** or **betted;** *ger* **betting**) *tr & intr* parier; **you bet!** (slang) je vous crois!, tu parles!

be·take [bɪ'tek] *v* (*pret* **-took;** *pp* **-taken**) *tr*—**to betake oneself** se rendre

betray [bɪ'tre] *tr* trahir

betrayal [bɪ'tre·əl] *s* trahison *f*

betrayer [bɪ'tre·ər] *s* traître *m*

betrothal [bɪ'troðəl] *s* fiançailles *fpl*

better ['bɛtər] *adj comp* meilleur §91; **better than** meilleur que ‖ *adv comp* mieux §91; **better than** mieux que; (followed by numeral) plus de; **it is better to** il vaut mieux de; **so much the better** tant mieux; **to be better** (*in better health*) aller mieux; **to be better to** valoir mieux; **to get better** s'améliorer; **to get the better of** l'emporter sur; **to think better** se raviser ‖ *tr* améliorer ‖ *intr* s'améliorer

bet′ter half′ *s* (coll) chère moitié *f*

bet′ting odds′ *spl* cote *f* (des paris)

bettor ['bɛtər] *s* parieur *m*, gageur *m*

between [bɪ'twin] *adv* au milieu, dans l'intervalle ‖ *prep* entre; **between friends** dans l'intimité

between′-decks′ *s* (naut) entrepont *m*

bev·el ['bɛvəl] *adj* biseauté, taillé en biseau ‖ *s* (*instrument*) équerre *f*; (*sloping part*) biseau *m* ‖ *v* (*pret & pp* **-eled** or **-elled;** *ger* **-eling** or **-elling**) *tr* biseauter, chanfreiner, équerrer

beverage ['bɛvərɪdʒ] *s* boisson *f*

bev·y ['bɛvi] *s* (*pl* **-ies**) bande *f*

bewail [bɪ'wel] *tr* lamenter, pleurer

beware [bɪ'wɛr] *tr* se bien garder de ‖ *intr* prendre garde; **to beware of** prendre garde à ‖ *interj* gare!, prenez garde!

bewilder [bɪ'wɪldər] *tr* confondre, ahurir

bewilderment [bɪ'wɪldərmənt] *s* confusion *f*, ahurissement *m*

bewitch [bɪ'wɪtʃ] *tr* ensorceler

bewitching [bɪ'wɪtʃɪŋ] *adj* enchanteur

beyond [bɪ'jɑnd] *s*—**the beyond** l'au-delà *m* ‖ *adv* au-delà ‖ *prep* au-delà de; **beyond a doubt** hors de doute; **it's beyond me** (coll) je n'y comprends rien; **to go beyond** dépasser

biannual [baɪ'ænju·əl] *adj* semi-annuel

bias ['baɪ·əs] *adj* biais ‖ *s* biais *m*; (fig) prévention *f*, préjugé *m* ‖ *tr* prédisposer, prévenir, rendre partial

bib [bɪb] *s* bavette *f*

Bible ['baɪbəl] *s* Bible *f*

Biblical ['bɪblɪkəl] *adj* biblique

bibliographer [,bɪblɪ'ɑgrəfər] *s* bibliographe *m*

bibliogra·phy [,bɪblɪ'ɑgrəfi] *s* (*pl* **-phies**) bibliographie *f*

biceps ['baɪsɛps] *s* biceps *m*

bicker ['bɪkər] *intr* se quereller, se chamailler

bickering ['bɪkərɪŋ] *s* bisbille *f*

bicuspid [baɪ'kʌspɪd] *s* prémolaire *f*

bicycle ['baɪsɪkəl] *s* bicyclette *f*, vélo *m* ‖ *intr* faire de la bicyclette, aller à bicyclette

bi′cycle path′ *s* piste *f* cyclable

bi′cycle pump′ *s* pompe *f* à vélo

bicyclist ['baɪsɪklɪst] *s* cycliste *mf*

bid [bɪd] *s* (*offer*) enchère *f*, offre *f*, mise *f*; (*e.g., to build a school*) soumission *f*; (cards) demande *f* ‖ *v* (*pret* **bade** [bæd] or **bid;** *ger* **bidden** ['bɪdən]) *tr* inviter; (*to order*) commander; (cards) demander; **to bid ten thousand on** mettre une enchère de dix mille sur ‖ *intr*—**to bid on** mettre une enchère sur

bidder ['bɪdər] *s* enchérisseur *m*, offrant *m*; (*person who submits an estimate*) soumissionnaire *mf*

bidding ['bɪdɪŋ] *s* enchères *fpl*; **at s.o.'s bidding** aux ordres de qn

bide [baɪd] *tr*—**to bide one's time** attendre l'heure or le bon moment

biennial [baɪ'ɛnɪ·əl] *adj* biennal

bier [bɪr] *s* (*frame or stand*) catafalque *m*; (*coffin*) cercueil *m*

biff [bɪf] *s* (slang) gnon *m*, beigne *f* ‖ *tr* (slang) gifler, cogner

bifocal [baɪ'fokəl] *adj* bifocal ‖ **bifocals** *spl* lunettes *fpl* bifocales

big [bɪg] *adj* (*comp* **bigger;** *super* **biggest**) gros, grand; (*man*) de grande taille ‖ *adv*—**to grow big** grossir, grandir; **to talk big** (slang) se vanter

bigamist ['bɪgəmɪst] *s* bigame *mf*

bigamous ['bɪgəməs] *adj* bigame

bigamy ['bɪgəmi] *s* bigamie *f*

big′ boned′ *adj* ossu, à gros os

big′ broth′er *s* grand frère *m*

big′ busi′ness *s* (pej) les grosses affaires *fpl*

Big′ Dip′per s Grand Chariot m
big′ game′ s fauves mpl, gros gibier m
big′-heart′ed adj généreux, cordial
big′mouth′ s (slang) gueulard m
bigot [ˈbɪgət] s bigot m
bigoted [ˈbɪgətɪd] adj bigot
bigot·ry [ˈbɪgətri] s (pl -ries) bigoterie f
big′ shot′ s (slang) grand manitou m, gros bonnet m, grand caïd m, grosse légume f
big′ sis′ter s grande sœur f
big′ splash′ s (slang) sensation f à tout casser
big′ stiff′ s (slang) personnage m guindé
big′ talk′ s (slang) vantardise f
big′ toe′ s orteil m, gros orteil
big′ top′ s (circus tent) chapiteau m
big′ wheel′ s (slang) gros bonnet m, grand manitou m, grosse légume f
big′wig′ s (coll) gros bonnet m, grand manitou m, grosse légume f
bike [baɪk] s (coll) bécane f, vélo m
bikini [bɪˈkini] s slip m minimum
bile [baɪl] s bile f
bilge [bɪldʒ] s sentine f, cale f
bilge′ wa′ter s eau f de cale
bilingual [baɪˈlɪŋgwəl] adj bilingue
bilious [ˈbɪljəs] adj bilieux
bilk [bɪlk] s tromperie f, escroquerie f ‖ tr tromper, escroquer
bill [bɪl] s (invoice) facture f, mémoire m; (in a hotel) note f; (in a restaurant) addition f; (currency) billet m; (of a bird) bec m; (posted) affiche f, placard m, écriteau m; (in a legislature) projet m de loi; **post no bills** (public sign) défense d'afficher; **to head the bill** (theat) avoir la vedette ‖ tr facturer
bill′board′ s tableau m d'affichage, panneau m d'affichage
billet [ˈbɪlɪt] s (order) billet m de logement; (of metal or wood) billette f ‖ tr loger, cantonner
bill′fold′ s portefeuille m
bil′liard ball′ s bille f
billiards [ˈbɪljərdz] s & spl billard m
bil′liard ta′ble s billard m
billion [ˈbɪljən] s (U.S.A.) milliard m; (Brit) billion m
billionaire [ˌbɪljənˈɛr] s milliardaire mf
bill′ of exchange′ s lettre f de change, traite f
bill′ of fare′ s carte f du jour
bill′ of health′ s patente f de santé
bill′ of lad′ing s connaissement m
bill′ of rights′ s déclaration f des droits de l'homme
bill′ of sale′ s acte m de vente
billow [ˈbɪlo] s flot m, grosse vague f ‖ intr ondoyer
billowy [ˈbɪlo·i] adj onduleux, ondoyant
bill′post′er s colleur m d'affiches, afficheur m
bil·ly [ˈbɪli] s (pl -lies) bâton m
bil′ly goat′ s (coll) bouc m
bimonthly [baɪˈmʌnθli] adj bimestriel
bin [bɪn] s huche f, coffre m
binary [ˈbaɪnəri] adj binaire

binaural [baɪˈnɔrəl] adj stéréophonique; à deux oreilles
bind [baɪnd] v (pret & pp bound [baʊnd] tr (to fasten) lier, attacher; (a book) relier; (s.o. to an agreement) obliger; **to bind with** (to encircle) entourer de ‖ intr (to be obligatory) être obligatoire; (to cohere) adhérer
binder [ˈbaɪndər] s (person) lieur m; (of books) relieur m; (agreement) conventions fpl; (mach) lieuse f
binder·y [ˈbaɪndəri] s (pl -ies) atelier m de reliure
binding [ˈbaɪndɪŋ] adj obligatoire; (med) astringent; **binding on all concerned** solidaire ‖ s reliure f
bind′ing post′ s (elec) borne f
binge [bɪndʒ] s (coll) noce f, bombe f
bingo [ˈbɪŋgo] s loto m
binocular [bɪˈnɑkjələr] adj & s binoculaire m; **binoculars** jumelles fpl
binomial [baɪˈnomɪ·əl] adj & s binôme m
biochemistry [ˌbaɪ·oˈkɛmɪstri] s biochimie f
biodegradable [ˈbaɪ·odɪˈgredəbəl] adj biodégradable
biographer [baɪˈɑgrəfər] s biographe mf
biographic(al) [ˌbaɪ·əˈgræfɪk(əl)] adj biographique
biogra·phy [baɪˈɑgrəfi] s (pl -phies) biographie f
biologist [baɪˈɑlədʒɪst] s biologiste mf
biology [baɪˈɑlədʒi] s biologie f
biophysics [ˌbaɪ·əˈfɪzɪks] s biophysique f
biop·sy [ˈbaɪ·ɑpsi] s (pl -sies) biopsie f
bipartisan [baɪˈpɑrtɪzən] adj bipartite
bipartite [baɪˈpɑrtaɪt] adj biparti
biped [ˈbaɪpɛd] adj & s bipède m
biplane [ˈbaɪˌplen] s biplan m
birch [bʌrtʃ] s bouleau m; (for whipping) verges fpl ‖ tr battre à coups de verges
birch′ rod s verges fpl
bird [bʌrd] s oiseau m; (slang) type m, individu m; **a bird in the hand is worth two in the bush** un ''tiens'' vaut mieux que deux ''tu l'auras''; **to give s.o. the bird** (slang) envoyer qn promener; **to kill two birds with one stone** faire d'une pierre deux coups
bird′ bath′ s bain m pour oiseaux
bird′cage′ s cage f d'oiseau
bird′ call′ s appeau m, pipeau m
bird′ dog′ s chien m pour la plume
bird′ fan′cier s oiselier m
birdie [ˈbʌrdi] s oiselet m, oisillon m
bird′lime′ s glu f
bird′ of pas′sage s oiseau m de passage
bird′ of prey′ s oiseau m de proie
bird′seed′ s alpiste m, chènevis m
bird's′-eye′ s (pattern) œil-de-perdrix m
bird's′-eye view′ s vue f à vol d'oiseau, tour m d'horizon, vue d'ensemble
biretta [bɪˈrɛtə] s barette f
birth [bʌrθ] s naissance f; **by birth** de naissance; **to give birth to** donner naissance à

birth′ certif′icate *s* acte *m* de naissance, extrait *m* de naissance, bulletin *m* de naissance

birth′ control′ *s* contrôle *m* des naissances, natalité *f* dirigée

birth′day′ *s* anniversaire *m*; **happy birthday!** heureux anniversaire!

birth′day cake′ *s* gâteau *m* d'anniversaire

birth′day can′dles *spl* bougies *fpl* de gâteaux d'anniversaire

birth′day pres′ent *s* cadeau *m* d'anniversaire

birth′mark′ *s* tache *f*, envie *f*

birth′place′ *s* lieu *m* de naissance

birth′ rate′ *s* natalité *f*, taux *m* de natalité

birth′right′ *s* droit *m* de naissance

biscuit [′bɪskɪt] *s* petit pain *m*, crêpe *f* au beurre, gâteau *m* feuilleté

bisect [baɪ′sɛkt] *tr* couper en deux, diviser en deux

bisexual [baɪ′sɛkʃʊ·əl] *adj* bissexuel

bishop [′bɪʃəp] *s* évêque *m*; (chess) fou *m*

bishopric [′bɪʃəprɪk] *f* évêché *m*

bison [′baɪzən] *s* bison *m*

bisulfate [baɪ′sʌlfet] *s* bisulfate *m*

bisulfite [baɪ′sʌlfaɪt] *s* bisulfite *m*

bit [bɪt] *s* (*morsel*) morceau *m*, bout *m*, brin *m*; (*of a bridle*) mors *m*; (*of a drill*) mèche *f*; (comp) binon *m*, bit *m*; **bit by bit** petit à petit

bitch [bɪtʃ] *s* (*dog*) chienne *f*; (*fox*) renarde *f*; (*wolf*) louve *f*; (vulg) vache *f*, salope *f*, ordure *f*

bite [baɪt] *s* (*of food*) bouchée *f*; (*by an animal*) morsure *f*; (*by an insect*) piqûre *f*; (*by a fish on a hook*) touche *f* ‖ *v* (*pret* bit [bɪt]; *pp* bit or bitten [′bɪtən]) *tr* mordre; (*said of an insect or snake*) piquer; **to bite off** mordre d'un coup de dent; **to feel like biting off one's tongue because of it** s'en mordre la langue

biting [′baɪtɪŋ] *adj* mordant; (*cold*) piquant; (*wind*) coupant

bit′ play′er *s* figurant *m*

bitter [′bɪtər] *adj* amer; (*cold*) âpre noir, (*flight*) acharné; (*style*) mordant ‖ **bitters** *spl* bitter *m*

bit′ter end′ *s*—**to the bitter end** jusqu'au bout

bit′ter-end′er *s* (coll) intransigeant *m*, jusqu'au-boutiste *mf*

bitterness [′bɪtərnɪs] *s* amertume *f*; (*of winter*) âpreté *f*; (fig) aigreur *f*

bit′ter·sweet′ *adj* aigre-doux ‖ *s* douce-amère *f*

bitumen [bɪ′t(j)umən] *s* bitume *m*

bivou·ac [′bɪvʊˌæk] *s* bivouac *m*, cantonnement *m* ‖ *v* (*pret* & *pp* **-acked**; *ger* **-acking**) *intr* bivouaquer

biweekly [baɪ′wikli] *adj* bimensuel ‖ *adv* bimensuellement

biyearly [baɪ′jɪrli] *adj* semestriel ‖ *adv* semestriellement

bizarre [bɪ′zɑr] *adj* bizarre

blab [blæb] *v* (*pret* & *pp* **blabbed**; *ger* **blabbing**) *tr* ébruiter ‖ *intr* jaser

blabber [′blæbər] *intr* jaser

blab′ber·mouth′ *s* (slang) jaseur *m*

black [blæk] *adj* & *s* noir *m*; **black is beautiful** nous sommes fiers d'être noirs ‖ *tr* noircir; **to black out** faire le black-out dans

black′-and-blue′ *adj* couvert de bleus

black′-and-white′ *adj* en blanc et noir

black′ball′ *tr* blackbouler

black′ber′ry *s* (*pl* **-ries**) mûre *f*, mûre de ronce

black′bird′ *s* (*Turdus merula*) merle *m*

black′board′ *s* tableau *m* noir

black′board eras′er *s* éponge *f*, chiffon *m*

black′ bod′y *s* (phys) corps *m* noir

black′ box′ *s* (aer) enregistreur *m* d'accident

black′ cur′rant *s* cassis *m*

black′ damp′ *s* mofette *f*

blacken [′blækən] *tr* noircir

black′ eye′ *s* œil *m* poché; (*shiner*) coquart *m*; **to give s.o. a black eye** pocher l'œil à qn; (fig) ruiner la réputation de qn

black′-eyed Su′san [′suzən] *s* marguerite *f* américaine

blackguard [′blægard] *s* vaurien *m*, salaud *m*

black′head′ *s* comédon *m*, tanne *f*

black′-headed gull′ *s* mouette *f* rieuse

black′ hole′ *s* (astr) trou *m* noir

blacking [′blækɪŋ] *s* cirage *m* noir

blackish [′blækɪʃ] *adj* noirâtre

black′jack′ *s* assommoir *m*; (cards) vingt-et-un *m* ‖ *tr* assommer

black′ lead′ [lɛd] *s* mine *f* de plomb

black′ let′ter *s* caractère *m* gothique

black′ list′ *s* liste *f* noire

black′-list′ *tr* mettre à l'index, mettre en quarantaine

black′ lo′cust *s* (bot) faux acacia *m*

black′ mag′ic *s* magie *f* noire

black′mail′ *s* chantage *m* ‖ *tr* faire chanter ‖ *intr* faire du chantage

blackmailer [′blækˌmelər] *s* maître *m* chanteur

black′ mark′ *s* (*of censure*) tache *f*

black′ mar′ket *s* marché *m* noir

black′ marketeer′ [ˌmarkɪ′tir] *s* trafiquant *m* du marché noir

black′out′ *s* (*accidental*) panne *f* d'électricité; (*planned for protection*) feux *mpl* masqués, black-out *m*; (*of aviator*) cécité *f* temporaire

black′ pep′per *s* poivre *m* noir

black′ sheep′ *s* (fig) brebis *f* galeuse

black′smith′ *s* forgeron *m*, maréchal-ferrant *m*

bladder [′blædər] *s* vessie *f*

bladderwort [′blædərˌwʌrt] *s* utriculaire *f*

blade [bled] *s* (*of knife, tool, weapon, razor*) lame *f*; (*of scissors*) branche *f*; (*of grass*) brin *m*; (*of propeller*) aile *f*, pale *f*; (*of oar; of tongue*) plat *m*; (*of guillotine*) couperet *m*; (*of windshield wiper*) caoutchouc *m*; (*young man*) gaillard *m*; (mach) ailette *f*, palette *f*, aube *f*

blah [blɑ] *s* (slang) sornettes *fpl*, fadaises *fpl*, bêtises *fpl* ‖ *interj* patati-patata!

blah-blah [ˈblɑˈblɑ] *s* baratin *m*

blamable [ˈblemǝbǝl] *adj* blâmable, coupable

blame [blem] *s* (*censure*) blâme *m*, reproches *mpl*; (*responsibility*) faute *f* ‖ *tr* blâmer; reprocher; s'en prendre à

blameless [ˈblemlɪs] *adj* sans reproche

blame′wor′thy *adj* blâmable

blanch [blæntʃ] *tr & intr* blanchir

bland [blænd] *adj* doux, suave; (*with dissimulation*) narquois

blandish [ˈblændɪʃ] *tr* flatter, cajoler

blandishment [ˈblændɪʃmǝnt] *s* flatterie

blank [blæŋk] *adj* blanc; (*check; form*) en blanc; (*mind*) confondu, déconcerté ‖ *s* (*void*) blanc *m*; (*gap*) trou *m*, vide *m*, lacune *f*; (*metal mold*) flan *m*; (*form to be filled out*) fiche *f*, formule *f*, feuille *f*; (*space to be filled in*) tiret *m* ‖ *tr*—**to blank out** effacer ‖ *intr*—**to blank out** (coll) s'évanouir

blank′ check′ *s* chèque *m* en blanc; (fig) chèque *m* en blanc

blanket [ˈblæŋkɪt] *adj* général ‖ *s* couverture *f* ‖ *tr* envelopper

blank′ verse′ *s* vers *mpl* blancs

blare [blɛr] *s* bruit *m* strident; (*of trumpet*) sonnerie *f* ‖ *tr* faire retentir; (*like a trumpet*) sonner ‖ *intr* retentir

blarney [ˈblɑrni] *s* (coll) flagornerie *f* ‖ *tr* (coll) flagorner

blaspheme [blæsˈfim] *tr & intr* blasphémer

blasphemous [ˈblæsfɪmǝs] *adj* blasphématoire, blasphémateur

blasphe·my [ˈblæsfɪmi] *s* (*pl* **-mies**) blasphème *m*

blast [blæst] *s* (*gust*) rafale *f*, souffle *m*; (*of bomb*) explosion *f*; (*of dynamite*) charge *f*; (*of whistle*) coup *m*; (*of trumpet*) sonnerie *f*; **at full blast** à toute allure ‖ *tr* (*to blow up*) faire sauter; (*hopes*) ruiner; (*a plant*) flétrir ‖ *intr* (*said of plant*) se faner; **to blast off** (*said of rocket*) se mettre à feu

blast′ fur′nace *s* haut fourneau *m*

blasting [ˈblæstɪŋ] *s* abattage *m* à la poudre; (*of hopes*) anéantissement *m*; (coll) abattage *m*, verte semonce *f*

blast′ing cap′ *s* capsule *f* fulminante

blast′off′ *s* mise *f* à feu, lancement *m*

blatant [ˈbletǝnt] *adj* criard; (*injustice*) criant

blaze [blez] *s* (*fire*) flamme *f*, flambée *f*; (*e.g., blazing house*) incendie *m*; **to run like blazes** (slang) courir furieusement ‖ *tr*—**to blaze the trail** frayer la piste ‖ *intr* flamboyer, s'embraser

blazing [ˈblezɪŋ] *adj* (*building, etc.*) embrasé, en feu; (*sun*) flamboyant

blazon [ˈblezǝn] *s* (heral) blason *m* ‖ *tr* célébrer; exalter; (heral) blasonner

bleach [blitʃ] *s* (*for washing clothes*) décolorant *m*, eau *f* de Javel; (*for hair*) eau oxygénée *f* ‖ *tr* blanchir, décolorer

bleachers [ˈblitʃǝrz] *spl* grandins *mpl*, tribune *f*

bleak [blik] *adj* froid, morne, nu

blear-eyed [ˈblɪrˈaɪd] *adj* (*teary*) chassieux, larmoyant; (*dull*) d'un esprit épais

blear·y [ˈblɪri] *adj* (*comp* **-ier**; *super* **-iest**) (*eyes*) chassieux; (*prospect*) voilé, incertain

bleat [blit] *s* bêlement *m* ‖ *intr* bêler, bégueter

bleed [blid] *v* (*pret & pp* **bled** [blɛd]) *tr & intr* saigner; **to bleed white** saigner à blanc

bleeding [ˈblidɪŋ] *adj* saignant ‖ *s* saignement *m*; (*bloodletting*) saignée *f*

blemish [ˈblemɪʃ] *s* défaut *m*, tache *f* ‖ *tr* défigurer; (*a reputation*) tacher

blench [blentʃ] *intr* (*to turn pale*) pâlir; (*to draw back*) broncher

blend [blɛnd] *s* mélange *m* ‖ *v* (*pret & pp* **blended** or **blent** [blɛnt]) *tr* mêler, mélanger; fondre, marier ‖ *intr* se fondre, se marier

bless [blɛs] *tr* bénir

blessed [ˈblɛsɪd] *adj* (*holy*) béni, saint; (*happy*) bienheureux

blessing [ˈblɛsɪŋ] *s* bénédiction *f*; (*at meals*) bénédicité *m*

blight [blaɪt] *s* (*of cereals, plants*) rouille *f*, nielle *f*; (*of peaches*) cloque *f*; (*of potatoes; of vines*) brunissure *f*; (fig) flétrissure *f* ‖ *tr* rouiller, nieller; (*hopes, aspirations*) flétrir, frustrer

blimp [blɪmp] *s* vedette *f* (aérienne)

blind [blaɪnd] *adj* aveugle; **blind by birth** aveugle-né; **blind in one eye** borgne; **blind person** aveugle *m* ‖ *s* store *m*; (*for hunting*) guet-apens *m*; (fig) feinte *f*; (cards) talon *m* ‖ *tr* aveugler; (*by dazzling*) éblouir

blind′ al′ley *s* cul-de-sac *m*, impasse *f*

blinder [ˈblaɪndǝr] *s* œillère *f*

blind′ flight′ *s* vol *m* à l'aveuglette

blind′ fly′ing *s* (aer) pilotage *m* sans visibilité

blind′fold′ *adj* les yeux bandés ‖ *s* bandeau *m* ‖ *tr* bander les yeux de

blindly [ˈblaɪndli] *adv* aveuglément

blind′ man′ *s* aveugle *m*

blind′man's bluff′ *s* colin-maillard *m*

blindness [ˈblaɪndnɪs] *s* cécité *f*; (fig) aveuglement *m*

blind′ spot′ *s* côté *m* faible

blink [blɪŋk] *s* clignotement *m* ‖ *tr* faire clignoter ‖ *intr* clignoter

blinker [ˈblɪŋkǝr] *s* (*signal*) feu *m* clignotant; (*for horses*) œillère *f*; (*for signals*) projecteur *m* clignotant

blink′er light′ *s* feu *m* à éclipses

blinking [ˈblɪŋkɪŋ] *s* clignement *m*

blip [blɪp] *s* spot *m*, bip *m*

bliss [blɪs] *s* félicité *f*, béatitude *f*

blissful [ˈblɪsfǝl] *adj* bienheureux

blister [ˈblɪstǝr] *s* ampoule *f*, bulle *f* ‖ *tr* couvrir d'ampoules; (*paint*) boursoufler ‖ *intr* se couvrir d'ampoules; se boursoufler

blithe [blaɪθ] *adj* gai, joyeux

blitzkrieg [ˈblɪts,krig] *s* guerre *f* éclair

blizzard [ˈblɪzǝrd] *s* tempête *f* de neige

bloat [blot] *tr* boursoufler, enfler ‖ *intr* se boursoufler, enfler

blob [blɑb] *s* motte *f*; (*of color*) tache *f*; (*of ink*) pâté *m*

block [blɑk] *s* (*stone*) bloc *m*; (*toy*) cube *m*; (*of shares*) tranche *f*; (*of houses*) pâté *m*, îlot *m* ‖ *tr* (*a project*) contrecarrer; (*a wall*) condamner, murer; **to block up** boucher, bloquer

blockade [blɑˈked] *s* blocus *m*; **to run the blockade** forcer le blocus ‖ *tr* bloquer

block′ and tac′kle *s* palan *m*

block′head′ *s* sot *m*, niais *m*

blond [blɑnd] *adj & s* blond *m*

blonde [blɑnd] *adj & s* blonde *f*

blood [blʌd] *s* sang *m*; **in cold blood** de sang-froid; **to put new blood into** infuser un sang nouveau à

blood′ and guts′ *spl* sang *m* et tripes

blood′bank′ *s* banque *f* du sang

blood′ count′ *s* numération *f* globulaire

blood′curd′ling *adj* horripilant

blood′ don′or *s* donneur *m* de sang

blood′hound′ *s* limier *m*

bloodless [ˈblʌdlɪs] *adj* (*without blood*) exsangue; (*revolution*) sans effusion de sang

bloodletting [ˈblʌdˌlɛtɪŋ] *s* saignée *f*; (fig) effusion *f* de sang

blood′ plas′ma *s* plasma *m* sanguin

blood′ poi′soning *s* septicémie *f*, empoisonnement *m* du sang

blood′ pres′sure *s* tension *f* artérielle

blood′ sam′ple *s* échantillon *m* de sang

blood′shed′ *s* effusion *f* de sang

blood′shot′ *adj* injecté, éraillé

blood′ spec′imen *s* prise *f* de sang

blood′stained′ *adj* taché de sang

blood′stream′ *s* circulation *f* du sang

blood′suck′er *s* sangsue *f*

blood′ test′ *s* examen *m* du sang, analyse *f* de sang

blood′thirst′y *adj* sanguinaire

blood′ transfu′sion *s* transfusion *f* de sang, transfusion sanguine

blood′ type′ *s* groupe *m* de sang

blood′ ves′sel *s* vaisseau *m* sanguin

blood·y [ˈblʌdi] *adj* (*comp* **-ier**; *super* **-iest**) sanglant

bloom [blum] *s* fleur *f*; (*of a fruit*) velouté *m*, duvet *m*; **in bloom** en fleur; **in full bloom** en pleine floraison ‖ *intr* fleurir

bloomers [ˈblumərz] *spl* culotte *f* de femme

blooper [ˈblupər] *s* (coll) gaffe *f*, bévue *f*; (rad) poste *m* brouilleur

blossom [ˈblɑsəm] *s* fleur *f*; **in blossom** en fleur ‖ *intr* fleurir; **to blossom out** s'épanouir

blot [blɑt] *s* (& fig) tache *f*, pâté *m* ‖ *v* (*pret & pp* **blotted**; *ger* **blotting**) *tr* tacher, barbouiller; (*ink*) sécher; **to blot out** rayer ‖ *intr* (*said of ink*) boire

blotch [blɑtʃ] *s* tache ‖ *tr* couvrir de taches; (*the skin*) marbrer

blotch·y [ˈblɑtʃi] *adj* (*comp* **-ier**; *super* **-iest**) brouillé, tacheté

blotter [ˈblɑtər] *s* buvard *m*

blot′ting pa′per *s* papier *m* buvard

blouse [blaʊs] *s* (*women's wear*) corsage *m*; (*children's*) chemise *f*; (mil) vareuse *f*

blow [blo] *s* coup *m*; **to come to blows** en venir aux coups ‖ *v* (*pret* **blew** [blu]; *pp* **blown**) *tr* souffler; **to blow one's nose** se moucher; **to blow out** (*a candle*) éteindre; **to blow up** faire sauter; (*a photograph*) agrandir; (*a balloon*) gonfler ‖ *intr* souffler; (slang) décamper en vitesse; **to blow out** (*said of a tire*) éclater; **to blow over** passer; **to blow up** éclater; (slang) se mettre en colère

blower [ˈblo·ər] *s* soufflerie *f*; (mach) ventilateur *m*

blow′fly′ *s* (*pl* **-flies**) mouche *f* à viande

blow′gun′ *s* sarbacane *f*

blow′hard′ *s* (slang) hâbleur *m*

blow′hole′ *s* (*of tunnel*) ventilateur *m*; (*of whale*) évent *m*

blowing [ˈblo·ɪŋ] *s* soufflage *m*; (*of the wind*) soufflement *m*

blow′out′ *s* (*of a tire*) éclatement *m*; (*of an oil well*) éruption *f*; (*orgy*) (slang) gueuleton *m*

blow′pipe′ *s* chalumeau *m*

blow′torch′ *s* lampe *f* à souder

blubber [ˈblʌbər] *s* graisse *f* de baleine ‖ *tr* bredouiller ‖ *intr* pleurer comme un veau

bludgeon [ˈblʌdʒən] *s* matraque *f* ‖ *tr* assommer

blue [blu] *adj* bleu; **to be blue** (coll) broyer du noir, avoir le cafard ‖ *s* bleu *m*; **from out of the blue** du ciel, à l'improviste; **the blues** le cafard, l'humeur *f* noire ‖ *tr* bleuir

blue′bell′ *s* jacinthe *f* des bois

blue′ber′ry *s* (*pl* **-ries**) myrtille *f*

blue′bird′ *s* oiseau *m* bleu

blue′-black′ *adj* noir tirant sur le bleu

blue′ blood′ *s* sang *m* royal, sang noble

blue′bot′tle *s* bluet *m*, barbeau *m*

blue′ cheese′ *s* roquefort *m* américain

blue′ chip′ *s* valeur-vedette *f*, valeur *f* de tout repos, valeur de père de famille

blue′-gray′ *adj* gris bleuté, gris-bleu

blue′jay′ *s* geai *m* bleu

blue′ jeans′ *spl* blue-jean *m*

blue′ moon′ *s*—**once in a blue moon** tous les trente-six du mois

blue′nose′ *s* puritain *m*, collet *m* monté

blue′-pen′cil *v* (*pret & pp* **-ciled** or **-cilled**; *ger* **-ciling** or **-cilling**) *tr* (*to make corrections*) corriger au crayon bleu; (*to censure*) couper, censurer

blue′print′ *s* dessin *m* négatif, photocalque *m*; (fig) plan *m*, schéma *m* ‖ *tr* planifier

blue′stock′ing *s* (coll) bas-bleu *m*

bluff [blʌf] *adj* (*steep*) abrupt; (*cliff*) accore, escarpé; (*person*) brusque ‖ *s* (*cliff*) falaise *f*, cap *m* à pic; (*deception*) bluff *m*; **to call s.o.'s bluff** relever un défi ‖ *tr & intr* bluffer

bluffer [ˈblʌfər] *s* bluffeur *m*

bluish [ˈblu·ɪʃ] *adj* bleuté, bleuâtre

blunder [ˈblʌndər] *s* bévue *f*, gaffe *f* ‖ *intr* faire une bévue, gaffer; **to blunder into**

se heurter contre; **to blunder upon** découvrir par hasard; tomber sur

blunt [blʌnt] *adj* (*blade*) émoussé; (*point*) épointé; (*person*) brusque ‖ *tr* émousser; épointer

bluntly [ˈblʌntli] *adv* (*rudely*) brusquement, sans façons; (*frankly*) carrément, sans ménagements

blur [blʌr] *s* barbouillage *m* ‖ *v* (*pret & pp* **blurred**; *ger* **blurring**) *tr* embrouiller, voiler

blurb [blʌrb] *s* (*ad*) baratin *m* publicitaire; (*on book cover*) publicité *f* au protège-livre

blurt [blʌrt] *tr*—**to blurt out** laisser échapper, lâcher

blush [blʌʃ] *s* rougeur *f*; **at first blush** au premier abord ‖ *intr* rougir

bluster [ˈblʌstər] *s* rodomontade *f*, fanfaronnade *f* ‖ *intr* (*of wind*) souffler en rafales; (*of person*) faire du fracas

blustery [ˈblʌstəri] *adj* (*wind*) orageux; (*person*) bravache, fanfaron

boar [bor] *s* (*male swine*) verrat *m*; (*wild hog*) sanglier *m*

board [bord] *s* (*piece of wood*) planche *f*; (*e.g., of directors*) conseil *m*, commission *f*; (*meals*) le couvert; **above board** cartes sur table; **on board** à bord ‖ *tr* (*a ship*) monter à bord de; (*paying guests*) nourrir ‖ *intr* monter à bord; (*said of paying guest*) prendre pension

board′ and room′ *s* pension *f* et chambre *f*

boarder [ˈbordər] *s* pensionnaire *mf*; (*student*) interne *mf*

board′ing·house′ *s* pension *f* (de famille)

board′ of direc′tors *s* conseil *m* d'administration, gérance *f*

board′ of trade′ *s* association *f* des industriels et commerçants

board′ of trustees′ *s* comité *m* administrateur (*e.g., of a university*)

board′walk′ *s* promenade *f* planchéiée au bord de la mer; (*over mud*) caillebotis *m*

boast [bost] *s* vanterie *f* ‖ *intr* se vanter

boastful [ˈbostfəl] *adj* vantard

boasting [ˈbostɪŋ] *s* jactance *f*

boat [bot] *s* bateau *m*; (*small boat*) embarcation *f*; **to miss the boat** (coll) manquer le coche

boat′ hook′ *s* gaffe *f*

boat′house′ *s* hangar *m* à bateaux or à canots

boating [ˈbotɪŋ] *s* canotage *m*; **to go boating** faire du canotage

boat′load′ *s* batelée *f*

boat′man *s* (*pl* **-men**) batelier *m*

boat′ race′ *s* régate *f*

boatswain [ˈbosən], [ˈbot‚swen] *s* maître *m* d'équipage

bob [bab] *s* (*hair style*) coiffure *f* courte ‖ *v* (*pret & pp* **bobbed**; *ger* **bobbing**) *intr* s'agiter, danser

bobbin [ˈbabɪn] *s* bobine *f*

bob′by pin′ *s* épingle *f* à cheveux

bob′by·socks′ *spl* (coll) socquettes *fpl*, chaussettes *fpl* basses

bobbysoxer [ˈbabɪ‚saksər] *s* (coll) zazou *m*, jeune lycéenne *f*

bob′sled′ *s* bobsleigh *m*

bob′tail′ *adj* à queue écartée ‖ *tr* couper court

bode [bod] *tr & intr* présager

bodily [ˈbadɪli] *adj* corporel, physique ‖ *adv* corporellement, en corps

bod·y [ˈbadi] *s* (*pl* **-ies**) corps *m*; (*dead body*) cadavre *m*; (*solidity*) consistance *f*; (*flavor of wine*) sève *f*, générosité *f*; (aer) fuselage *m*; (aut) carrosserie *f*; **to come in a body** venir en corps

bod′y·guard′ *s* garde *m* du corps; (*group*) garde *f* du corps

bog [bag] *s* marécage *m*, fondrière *f* ‖ *v* (*pret & pp* **bogged**; *ger* **bogging**) *intr*—**to bog down** s'enliser

bogey·man [ˈbogi‚mæn] *s* (*pl* **-men**) croquemitaine *m*

bogus [ˈbogəs] *adj* faux, simulé

Bohemia [boˈhimɪ·ə] *s* (*country*) Bohême *f*, la Bohême; (*of artistic world*) la bohème

Bohemian [boˈhimɪ·ən] *adj* (*of Bohemia*) bohémien; (*unconventional, arty*) bohème, de bohème ‖ *s* (*person living in the country of Bohemia*) Bohémien *m*; (*artist*) bohème *mf*

boil [bɔɪl] *s* (*boiling*) ébullition *f*; (*on the skin*) furoncle *m*, clou *m* ‖ *tr* faire bouillir ‖ *intr* bouillir

boiled′ din′ner *s* pot-au-feu *m*

boiled′ ham′ *s* jambon *m* d'York

boiled′ pota′toes *spl* pommes *fpl* bouillies, pommes vapeur

boiler [ˈbɔɪlər] *s* chaudière *f*

boi′ler·mak′er *s* chaudronnier *m*

boiling [ˈbɔɪlɪŋ] *adj* bouillonnant ‖ *s* ébullition *f*, bouillonnement *m*

boil′ing point′ *s* point *m* d'ébullition

boisterous [ˈbɔɪstərəs] *adj* bruyant

bold [bold] *adj* hardi, osé, intrépide; (*forward*) effronté, impudent; (*cliff*) abrupt

bold′face′ *s* (typ) caractères *mpl* gras

bold′-faced′ *adj* (*forward*) effronté

boldness [ˈboldnɪs] *s* hardiesse *f*; effronterie *f*

boll′ wee′vil [bol] *s* anthonome *m* du cotonnier, charançon *m* du coton

bologna [bəˈlonə], [bəˈlonjə] *s* mortadelle *f*, gros saucisson *m*

bolster [ˈbolstər] *s* traversin *m* ‖ *tr* soutenir

bolt [bolt] *s* (*of door or window*) verrou *m*; (*of lock*) pêne *m*; (*with a thread at one end*) boulon *m*; (*of cloth*) rouleau *m* ‖ *tr* verrouiller; (*food*) gober; (*e.g., a political party*) lâcher ‖ *intr* décamper

bomb [bam] *s* bombe *f* ‖ *tr* bombarder

bombard [bamˈbard] *tr* bombarder

bombardier [‚bambərˈdɪr] *s* bombardier *m*

bombardment [bamˈbardmənt] *s* bombardement *m*

bombast [ˈbambæst] *s* boursouflure *f*

bombastic [bamˈbæstɪk] *adj* boursouflé

bomb′ bay′ *s* (aer) soute *f* à bombes

bomb′ cra′ter *s* entonnoir *m*, trou *m* d'obus

bomber ['bɑmər] *s* avion *m* de bombardement, bombardier *m*

bombing ['bɑmɪŋ] *s* bombardement *m*

bomb'proof' *adj* à l'épreuve des bombes

bomb'shell' *s* obus *m*; **to fall like a bombshell** tomber comme une bombe

bomb' shel'ter *s* abri *m* à l'épreuve des bombes

bomb'sight' *s* viseur *m* de lancement

bomb' service *m* de déminage

bona fide ['bonə,faɪdə] *adj & adv* de bonne foi

bonanza [bo'nænzə] *s* aubaine *f*, filon *m*

bonbon ['bɑn,bɑn] *s* bonbon *m*

bond [bɑnd] *s* (*link*) lien *m*; (com) obligation *f*; **in bond** en entrepôt ‖ *tr* (com) entreposer, mettre en entrepôt

bondage ['bɑndɪdʒ] *s* esclavage *m*

bond'hold'er *s* obligataire *mf*

bone [bon] *s* os *m*; (*of a fish*) arête *f*; **to have a bone to pick** avoir maille à partir ‖ *tr* (*meat or fish*) désosser ‖ *intr*—**to bone up on** (*a subject*) (slang) potasser, piocher

bone'head' *s* (slang) ignorant *m*

boneless ['bonlɪs] *adj* sans os; sans arêtes

bone' of conten'tion *s* pomme *f* de discorde

boner ['bonər] *s* (coll) bourde *f*

bonfire ['bɑn,faɪr] *s* feu *m* de joie; (*for burning trash*) feu de jardin

bonnet ['bɑnɪt] *s* bonnet *m*; chapeau *m* à brides; (fig) chapeau

bonus ['bonəs] *s* boni *m*, prime *f*

bon·y ['boni] *adj* (*comp* **-ier**; *super* **-iest**) osseux; (*thin*) décharné

boo [bu] *s* huée *f*, sifflement *m*; **not to say boo** ne pas souffler mot ‖ *tr & intr* huer, siffler

boob [bub] *s* (coll) emplâtre *m*

boo·by ['bubi] *s* (*pl* **-bies**) (coll) nigaud *m*

boo'by hatch' *s* (slang) asile *m* d'aliénés; (*prison*) (slang) violon *m*

boo'by prize' *s* fiche *f* de consolation

boo'by trap' *s* engin *m* piégé; (fig) attrape-nigaud *m*, traquenard *m*

boo'by-trap' *v* (*pret & pp* **-trapped**; *ger* **-trapping**) *tr* piéger

book [buk] *s* livre *m*; (*of tickets*) carnet *m*; (*libretto*) livret *m*; **by the book** d'après le texte, selon les règles; **to make book** (sports) inscrire les paris ‖ *tr* (*a seat or room*) retenir, réserver

book'bind'er *s* relieur *m*

book'bind'er·y *s* (*pl* **-ies**) atelier *m* de reliure

book'bind'ing *s* reliure *f*

book'case' *s* bibliothèque *f*, étagère *f*

book' end' *s* serre-livres *m*, appui-livres *m*

booking ['bukɪŋ] *s* réservation *f*; (theat) location *f*

bookish ['bukɪʃ] *adj* livresque; (*person*) studieux

book'keep'er *s* comptable *mf*, teneur *m* de livres

book'keep'ing *s* comptabilité *f*

book' learn'ing *s* science *f* livresque

booklet ['buklɪt] *s* livret *m*; (*notebook*) cahier *m*; (*pamphlet*) brochure *f*

book'lov'er *s* bibliophile *mf*

book'mark' *s* signet *m*

bookmobile ['bukmo,bil] *s* bibliobus *m*

book'plate' *s* ex-libris *m*

book'rack' *s* étagère *f*

book' review' *s* compte *m* rendu

book'sel'ler *s* libraire *mf*

book'shelf' *s* (*pl* **-shelves**) rayon *m*, étagère *f*

books' in print' *s* livres *mpl* disponibles

book'stand' *s* étalage *m* de livres; (*in a station*) bibliothèque *f*

book'store' *s* librairie *f*

book' val'ue *s* (com) valeur *f* comptable

book'worm' *s* ciron *m*; (fig) rat *m* de bibliothèque

boom [bum] *s* retentissement *m*, grondement *m*; (*rapid rise or growth*) vague *f* de prospérité, boom *m*; (naut) bout-dehors *m* ‖ *intr* retentir; (com) prospérer ‖ *interj* boum!

boomer ['bumər] *s* (electron) boomer *m*

boomerang ['bumə,ræŋ] *s* boomerang *m*

boom' town' *s* ville *f* champignon

boon [bun] *s* bienfait *m*, avantage *m*; (*archaic*) don *m*, faveur *f*

boor [bur] *s* rustre *m*, goujat *m*

boost [bust] *s* relèvement *m*; (*help*) aide *f* ‖ *tr* soulever par derrière; (*prices*) hausser; (*to praise*) faire la réclame pour

booster ['bustər] *s* (*enthusiastic backer*) réclamiste *mf*; (*go-getter*) homme *m* d'expédition, lanceur *m* d'affaires; (aut) suramplificateur *m*; (elec) survolteur *m*; (rok) booster *m*, propulseur *m*

boost'er rock'et *s* fusée *f* de lancement

boost'er rod' *s* (nucl) barre *f* de dopage

boost'er shot' *s* piqûre *f* de rappel

boot [but] *s* botte *f*, bottine *f*; **to boot** en sus; **to lick s.o.'s boots** (coll) lécher les bottes à qn ‖ *tr* botter

boot'black' *s* cireur *m* de bottes

booth [buθ] *s* (*at fair*) baraque *f*; (*e.g., for telephoning*) cabine *f*

boot'leg' *adj* (slang) clandestin, de contrebande ‖ *v* (*pret & pp* **-legged**; *ger* **-legging**) *tr* (slang) faire la contrebande de ‖ *intr* (slang) faire la contrebande

bootlegger ['but,lɛgər] *s* (slang) contrebandier *m*; (slang) contrebandier *m* d'alcool, bootlegger *m*

boot'leg'ging *s* contrebande *f*

boot'lick' *tr* (coll) lécher les bottes à

boo·ty ['buti] *s* (*pl* **-ties**) butin *m*

booze [buz] *s* (coll) boisson *f* alcoolique ‖ *intr* (coll) s'adonner à la boisson

border ['bɔrdər] *s* (*edge*) bord *m*, bordure *f*; (*of field and forest; of a piece of cloth*) lisière *f*; (*of a road*) marge *f*; (*of a country*) frontière *f*; (*edging*) galon *m*, bord *m* ‖ *tr* border; (*a handkerchief*) lisérer ‖ *intr*—**to border on** confiner à, toucher à; (*a color*) tirer sur

bor·der·line' *adj* indéterminé ‖ *s* ligne *f* de démarcation

bor′der·line case′ *s* cas *m* limite
bore [bor] *s* (*hole*) trou *m*; (*of gun*) calibre *m*; (*of cannon*) âme *f*; (*of cylinder*) alésage *m*; (*nuisance*) ennui *m*; (*person*) raseur *m*; **what a bore!** c'est la barbe!, ô rasoir! ‖ *tr* percer; (*a cylinder*) aléser; (*to annoy*) ennuyer
boreal [′borı·əl] *adj* boréal
boredom [′bordəm] *s* ennui *m*
boring [′borıŋ] *adj* ennuyeux, rasant, rasoir ‖ *s* perçage *m*, percement *m*
born [bɔrn] *adj* né; **to be born** naître
borrow [′baro], [′bɔro] *tr* emprunter; **to borrow from** emprunter à
borrower [′baro·ər], [′bɔro·ər] *s* emprunteur *m*
bor′rower's card′ *s* bulletin *m* de prêt
borrowing [′baro·ıŋ] *s* emprunt *m*
borzoi [′bɔrzɔı] *s* lévrier *m* russe
bosom [′buzəm] *s* sein *m*, poitrine *f*; (*of the Church*) giron *m*
boss [bɔs] *s* patron *m*, chef *m*; (*foreman*) contremaître *m* ‖ *tr* mener, régenter
boss·y [′bɔsi] *adj* (*comp* **-ier**; *super* **-iest**) autoritaire, tyrannique
botanical [bə′tænıkəl] *adj* botanique
botanist [′batənıst] *s* botaniste *mf*
botany [′batəni] *s* botanique *f*
botch [batʃ] *tr*—**to botch up** bousiller, saloper
both [boθ] *adj* deux, e.g., **with both hands** à deux mains; les deux, e.g., **both books** les deux livres ‖ *pron* les deux, tous les deux ‖ *conj* à la fois; **both . . . and** aussi bien . . . que, e.g., **both in England and France** aussi bien en Angleterre qu'en France
bother [′baðər] *s* ennui *m* ‖ *tr* ennuyer, déranger ‖ *intr* se déranger
bothersome [′baðərsəm] *adj* importun
bottle [′batəl] *s* bouteille *f* ‖ *tr* mettre en bouteille, embouteiller
bot′tle cap′ *s* capsule *f*
bot′tle depos′it *s* consigne *f*
bot′tled gas′ *s* gaz *m* en cylindre
bot′tle·neck′ *s* goulot *m*; (*fig*) embouteillage *m*, goulot *m* d'étranglement
bot′tle o′pener *s* ouvre-bouteilles *m*, décapsuleur *m*
bottler [′batlər] *s* metteur *m* en bouteilles
bottling [′batlıŋ] *s* mise *f* en bouteilles
bottom [′batəm] *s* fond *m*; **at the bottom of** au fond de; (*the page*) en bas de; **to reach the bottom of the barrel** (coll) être à fond de cale
bot′tom dol′lar *s* dernier sou *m*
bottomless [′batəmlıs] *adj* sans fond
bot′tom line′ *s* (com) résultat *m* financier; (*fig*) conclusion *f*; point *m* essentiel
bough [bau] *s* rameau *m*
boulder [′boldər] *s* bloc *m*, rocher *m*
boulevard [′bulə‚vard] *s* boulevard *m*
bounce [bauns] *s* (*elasticity*) bond *m*; (*of a ball*) rebond *m* ‖ *tr* faire rebondir; (slang) flanquer à la porte ‖ *intr* rebondir
bouncer [′baunsər] *s* (*in night club*) (coll) videur *m*, gorille *m*

bound [baund] *adj* (*tied*) lié; (*obliged*) obligé, tenu; **bound for** en partance pour ‖ *s* bond *m*, saut *m*; **bounds** bornes *fpl*, limites *fpl*; **out of bounds** hors jeu; (*prohibited*) défendu ‖ *tr* borner, limiter ‖ *intr* bondir
bounda·ry [′baundəri] *s* (*pl* **-ries**) borne *f*, limite *f*
boun′dary stone′ *s* borne *f*
boundless [′baundlıs] *adj* sans bornes
boun·ty [′baunti] *s* (*pl* **-ties**) largesse *f*; (*award*) prime *f*
bouquet [bu′ke] *s* bouquet *m*
bout [baut] *s* (*time*) période *f*; (*of fever*) accès *m*, attaque *f*; (sports) combat *m*, rencontre *f*
bow [bau] *s* (*greeting*) inclination *f*, révérence *f*; (*of ship*) avant *m*, proue *f* ‖ *tr* incliner, courber ‖ *intr* s'incliner, se courber; **to bow down** se prosterner; **to bow out** se retirer; **to bow to** saluer ‖ [bo] *s* (*weapon*) arc *m*; (*bowknot*) nœud *m*; (*of violin*) archet *m* ‖ *intr* (mus) tirer l'archet
bowdlerize [′baudlə‚raız] *tr* expurger
bowel [′bau·əl] *s* intestin *m*, boyau *m*; **bowels** entrailles *fpl*
bower [′bau·ər] *s* berceau *m*, tonnelle *f*
bow′ie knife′ [′bo·ı] *s* couteau-poignard *m*
bowknot [′bo‚nat] *s* nœud *m* en forme de rose, rosette *f*
bowl [bol] *s* (*container*) bol *m*, jatte *f*; (*of pipe*) fourneau *m*; (*of spoon*) cuilleron *m*; **bowls** (sports) boules *fpl* ‖ *tr* rouler, lancer; **to bowl over** (*to overturn*) (coll) renverser; (slang) déconcerter ‖ *intr*—**to bowl along** rouler rapidement
bowlegged [′bo‚lɛgd], [′bo‚lɛgıd] *adj* aux jambes arquées
bowler [′bolər] *s* (*hat*) chapeau *m* melon; (*in cricket*) lanceur *m*; (*in bowling*) joueur *m* de boules
bowling [′bolıŋ] *s* bowling *m*; (*lawn bowling*) jeu *m* de boules; (*skittles*) jeu de quilles
bowl′ing al′ley *s* boulodrome *m*, bowling *m*
bowl′ing green′ *s* boulingrin *m*
bowl′ing pin′ *s* quille *f*
bowsprit [′bausprıt] *s* beaupré *m*
bow′ tie′ [bo] *s* nœud *m* papillon
box [baks] *s* boîte *f*; (*in a questionnaire*) case *f*; (*law*) barre *f*; (*theat*) loge *f*, baignoire *f*; **box on the ear** claque *f* ‖ *tr* emboîter; (*to hit*) boxer; **to box the compass** réciter la rose des vents ‖ *intr* (sports) boxer
box′car′ *s* (rr) wagon *m* couvert
boxer [′baksər] *s* (*person*) boxeur *m*; (*dog*) boxer *m*
boxing [′baksıŋ] *s* emboîtage *m*; (sports) boxe *f*
box′ of′fice *s* bureau *m* de location
box′-office flop′ *s* (slang) four *m*
box′-office hit′ *s* pièce *f* à succès
box′wood′ *s* buis *m*
boy [bɔı] *s* garçon *m*; (*little boy*) garçonnet *m*

boycott ['bɔɪkɑt] s boycottage m ‖ tr boycotter

boy' friend' s ami m, camarade m; (of a girl) bon ami m

boyhood ['bɔɪhʊd] s enfance f, jeunesse f, adolescence f

boyish ['bɔɪ·ɪʃ] adj de garçon

boy' scout' s boy-scout m

bra [brɑ] (coll) soutien-gorge m

brace [bres] s (support) attache f, lien m; (of game birds) couple f; (of pistols) paire f; (to impart a rotary movement to a bit) vilebrequin m; (aer, aut) entretoise f; (dentistry) appareil m; (med) appareil orthopédique; (mus, typ) accolade f ‖ tr ancrer, entretoiser; (to tone up) fortifier, remonter ‖ intr—**to brace up** prendre courage

brace' and bit' s vilebrequin m

bracelet ['breslɪt] s bracelet m

bracer ['bresər] s tonique m

bracing ['bresɪŋ] adj tonique, fortifiant

bracket ['brækɪt] s (angled support) support m, console f; (grouping) group m, classe f, tranche f; (level) niveau m; (mach) chaise f; (typ) crochet m ‖ tr grouper; (typ) mettre entre crochets

brackish ['brækɪʃ] adj saumâtre

brad [bræd] s semence f, clou m (sans tête)

brag [bræg] s (pret & pp bragged; ger bragging) intr se vanter, se targuer

braggadoci·o [,brægə'doʃɪ,o] s (pl -os) fanfaronnade f; (person) fanfaron m

braggart ['brægərt] s vantard m

bragging ['brægɪŋ] s vanterie f

Brah·man ['brɑmən] s (pl -mans) brahmane m

braid [bred] s tresse f, passement m; (mil) galon m; **to trim with braid** soutacher ‖ tr passementer; (the hair) tresser

braille [brel] s braille m

brain [bren] s cerveau m; **brains** cervelle f; (fig) intelligence f, cerveau; **to rack one's brains** se creuser la cervelle ‖ tr casser la tête à

brain' child' s idée f de génie

brain' drain' s évasion f de(s) cerveaux, fuite f de(s) cerveaux

brainless ['brenlɪs] adj sans cervelle

brain'storm' s accès m de folie; (coll) confusion f mentale; (coll) trouvaille f, bonne idée f

brain' storm'ing s remue-méninges m

brain' trust' s cerveauté f, projéticiens mpl

brain'wash' tr faire un lavage de cerveau à

brain'wash'ing s lavage m de cerveau

brain'work' s travail m intellectuel

brain·y ['breni] adj (comp -ier; super -iest) (coll) intelligent à l'esprit vif

braise [brez] tr braiser, endauber

brais'ing pan' s braisière f

brake [brek] s frein m; **to put on the brakes** serrer les freins ‖ tr & intr freiner

brake' drum' s tambour m de frein

brake' light' s (aut) feu m de freinage

brake' lin'ing s garniture f de frein

brake'man s (pl -men) serre-freins m

brake' ped'al s pédale f de frein

brake' shoe' s sabot m de frein

bramble ['bræmbəl] s ronce f

bran [bræn] s son m, bran m

branch [bræntʃ] s branche f; (of tree) rameau m, branche; (of a business) succursale, filiale ‖ intr—**to branch off** s'embrancher, se bifurquer; **to branch out** se ramifier

branch' line' s embranchement m

branch' of'fice s succursale f

branch' road' s embranchement m

brand [brænd] s (trademark) marque f; (torch) brandon m; (coal) tison m; (on a criminal) flétrissure f; (on cattle) marque ‖ tr marquer au fer rouge, flétrir

brand'ing i'ron s fer m à flétrir

brandish ['brændɪʃ] tr brandir

brand'-new' adj tout neuf, flambant neuf

bran·dy ['brændi] s (pl -dies) eau-de-vie f

brash [bræʃ] adj impertinent

brass [bræs] s (metal) laiton m; (mil) (coll) officiers mpl supérieurs, galonnard m; (slang) toupet m, culot m; **big brass** (slang) grosses légumes fpl; **the brasses** (mus) les cuivres

brass' band' s fanfare f, musique f

brassiere [brə'zɪr] s soutien-gorge m

brass' knuck'les spl coup-de-poing m

brass' tack' s semence f (de tapissier); **to get down to brass tacks** (coll) en venir aux faits

brat [bræt] s (coll) gamin m, gosse mf

brava·do [brə'vɑdo] s (pl -does or -dos) bravade f

brave [brev] adj brave ‖ s guerrier m peau-rouge ‖ tr braver

bravery ['brevəri] s bravoure f

bra·vo ['brɑvo] (pl -vos) bravo m ‖ interj bravo!

brawl [brɔl] s bagarre f, querelle f ‖ intr se bagarrer, se quereller

brawler ['brɔlər] s bagarreur m

brawn [brɔn] s (strength) muscle m; (muscles) muscles bien développés; (culin) fromage m de cochon

brawn·y ['brɔni] adj (comp -ier; super -iest) bien découplé, musclé

bray [bre] s braiment m ‖ intr braire

braze [brez] tr braser

brazen ['brezən] adj effronté, hardi ‖ tr—**to brazen through** mener à bonne fin avec une effronterie audacieuse

Brazil [brə'zɪl] s le Brésil

Brazilian [brə'zɪljən] adj brésilien ‖ s (person) Brésilien m

Brazil' nut' s noix f du Brésil

breach [britʃ] s (in a wall) brèche f; (violation) infraction f ‖ tr ouvrir une brèche dans

breach' of con'tract s rupture f de contrat

breach' of prom'ise s rupture f de fiançailles

breach' of the peace' s attentat m contre l'ordre public

breach' of trust' s abus m de confiance

bread [brɛd] s pain m ‖ tr paner, gratiner

bread′ and but′ter s (fig) gagne-pain m
bread′bas′ket s corbeille f à pain
bread′board′ s planche f à pain
bread′ crumbs′ spl chapelure f
breaded adj (culin) au gratin
bread′ed veal′ cut′let s escalope f panée de veau
bread′fruit′ s fruit m à pain; (tree) arbre m à pain, jacquier m
bread′ knife′ s couteau m à pain
breadth [brɛdθ] s largeur f
bread′win′ner s soutien m de famille
break [brek] s (fracture) rupture f; (of an object) brisure f, cassure f; (in time or space) trou m, pause f; (slang) chance f || v (pret **broke** [brok]; pp **broken**) tr rompre, briser, casser; (a law) violer; (the heart) fendre; (one's word) manquer à; (a will; a soldier by reducing his rank) casser; **to break bread** rompre le pain; **to break down** (for analysis) analyser; **to break in** (a door) enfoncer; (a new car) roder || intr rompre, briser, se briser; (said of clouds) se dissiper; (said of waves) déferler; **to break down** avoir une panne
breakable [′brekəbəl] adj fragile
breakage [′brekɪdʒ] s casse f
break′ danc′ing s smurf m
break′down′ s (stoppage) arrêt m; (disaster) débâcle f; (of health) effondrement m, dépression f; (of negotiations) rupture f; (for analysis) analyse f, ventilation f; (mach) panne f
breaker [′brekər] s brisant m
breakfast [′brɛkfəst] s petit déjeuner m || intr prendre le petit déjeuner
break′fast food′ s céréales fpl (pour le petit déjeuner)
break′ing point′ s point m limite zéro
break′neck′ adj vertigineux; **at breakneck speed** à tombeau ouvert
break′ of day′ s point m du jour
break′through′ s (mil) percée f; (fig) découverte f sensationnelle
break′up′ s (splitting up) dissolution f; (of ice) débâcle f; (of friendship) rupture f
break′wa′ter s digue f, brise-lames m
breast [brɛst] s sein m; (of cooked chicken) blanc m; **to make a clean breast of it** se déboutonner
breast′bone′ s sternum m; (of fowl) bréchet m
breast′ feed′ing s allaitement m maternel
breast′ opera′tion s remodelage m
breast′plate′ s (of high priest) pectoral m; (of armor) plastron m
breast′stroke′ s brasse f
breast′work′ s (mil) parapet m
breath [brɛθ] s haleine f, souffle m; **last breath** dernier soupir m; **out of breath** hors d'haleine
breathalyzer [′brɛθə,laɪzər] s alcotest m, prise f d'haleine
breathe [brið] tr & intr respirer, souffler; **not to breathe a word** ne pas souffler mot

breathing [′briðɪŋ] s souffle m
breath′ing space′ s répit m
breathless [′brɛθlɪs] adj haletant, hors d'haleine; (silence) ému; (lifeless) inanimé
breath′tak′ing adj émouvant, sensationnel
breech [britʃ] s culasse f
breech′es bu′oy s (naut) bouée-culotte f
breed [brid] s race f || v (pret & pp **bred** [brɛd]) tr engendrer; (e.g., cattle) élever || intr se reproduire
breeder [′bridər] s éleveur m
breed′er reac′tor s (nucl) réacteur m surrégénérateur
breeding [′bridɪŋ] s (of animals) élevage m; **good breeding** savoir-vivre m
breeze [briz] s brise f
breez·y [′brizi] adj (comp **-ier**; super **-iest**) aéré; (coll) désinvolte, dégagé
brethren [′brɛðrɪn] spl frères mpl
Breton [′brɛtən] adj breton || s (language) breton m; (person) Breton m
breviar·y [′brɛvɪ,ɛri] s (pl **-ies**) (eccl) bréviaire m
brevi·ty [′brɛvɪti] s (pl **-ties**) brièveté f
brew [bru] s breuvage m, infusion f || tr infuser; (beer) brasser || intr s'infuser
brewer [′bru·ər] s brasseur m
brew′er's yeast′ s levure f de bière
brewer·y [′bru·əri] s (pl **-ies**) brasserie f
brewing [′bru·ɪŋ] s brassage m
bribe [braɪb] s pot-de-vin m || tr corrompre, suborner, soudoyer
briber·y [′braɪbəri] f (pl **-ies**) corruption f, subornation f
brick [brɪk] s brique f; (of ice cream) bloc m || tr briqueter
brick′bat′ s brocard m; **to hurl brickbats** lancer des brocards
brick′lay′er s briqueteur m
brick′work′ s briquetage m
brick′yard′ s briqueterie f
bridal [′braɪdəl] adj nuptial
bride [braɪd] s (nouvelle) mariée f
bride′groom′ s (nouveau) marié m
brides′maid′ s demoiselle f d'honneur
bride′-to-be′ s future femme f
bridge [brɪdʒ] s pont m; (naut) passerelle f; **to burn one's bridges** couper les ponts || tr construire un pont sur; **to bridge a gap** combler une lacune
bridge′head′ s (mil) tête f de pont
bridle [′braɪdəl] s bride f; (fig) frein m || tr brider; (fig) freiner || intr se raidir
bri′dle path′ s piste f cavalière
brief [brif] adj bref || s résumé m; (law) dossier m; **briefs** slip m; **to hold a brief for** plaider pour || tr mettre au courant
brief′ case′ s serviette f
briefing [′brifɪŋ] s briefing m, renseignements mpl tactiques
briefly [′brifli] adv bref, brièvement, en substance
brier [′braɪ·ər] s ronce f
brig [brɪg] s prison f navale; (ship) brick m
brigade [brɪ′ged] s brigade f

brigadier [,brɪgə'dɪr] *s* général *m* de brigade

brigand ['brɪgənd] *s* brigand *m*

brigantine ['brɪgən,tin] *s* brigantin *m*

bright [braɪt] *adj* brillant; (*day*) clair; (*color*) vif; (*person*) (fig) brillant

brighten ['braɪtən] *tr* faire briller; égayer, réjouir ‖ *intr* s'éclaircir

bright' ide'a *s* (coll) idée *f* lumineuse

brightness ['braɪtnɪs] *s* éclat *m*, clarté *f*; (*of mind*) vivacité *f*

brilliance ['brɪljəns] or **brilliancy** ['brɪljənsi] *s* brillant *m*, éclat *m*

brilliant ['brɪljənt] *adj & s* brillant *m*

brim [brɪm] *s* bord *m* ‖ *v* (*pret & pp* **brimmed**; *ger* **brimming**) *intr*—**to brim over (with)** déborder (de)

brimful ['brɪm,fʊl] *adj* à ras bords

brim'stone' *s* soufre *m*

brine [braɪn] *s* saumure *f*

bring [brɪŋ] *v* (*pret & pp* **brought** [brɔt]) *tr* apporter; (*a person*) amener, conduire; **to bring back** rapporter; (*a person*) ramener; **to bring down** (*baggage*) descendre; (*with a gun*) abbatre; **to bring in** entrer, introduire; **to bring out** faire ressortir; (*e.g., a book*) publier; **to bring together** réunir; **to bring to pass** causer, opérer; **to bring up** éduquer, élever; (*baggage*) monter

bring'ing-up' *s* éducation *f*

brink [brɪŋk] *s* bord *m*

brisk [brɪsk] *adj* vif, actif, animé

brisket ['brɪskɪt] *s* (culin) poitrine *f*

bristle ['brɪsəl] *s* soie *f*; (*of brush*) poil *m* ‖ *tr* hérisser ‖ *intr* se hérisser

bristling ['brɪslɪŋ] *adj* hérissé

Bris'tol board' ['brɪstəl] *s* bristol *m*

Britain ['brɪtən] *s* Grande-Bretagne *f*; la Grande-Bretagne

British ['brɪtɪʃ] *adj* britannique ‖ **the British** les Britanniques

Britisher ['brɪtɪʃər] *s* Britannique *mf*

Briton ['brɪtən] *s* Britannique *mf*

Brittany ['brɪtəni] *s* Bretagne *f*; la Bretagne

brittle ['brɪtəl] *adj* fragile, cassant

broach [brotʃ] *s* (*spit*) broche *f*; (*for tapping casks*) mèche *f* à percer, perçoir *m*, foret *m* ‖ *tr* (*e.g., a keg of beer*) mettre en perce; (*a subject*) entamer

broad [brɔd] *adj* (*wide*) large; (*immense*) vaste; (*mind, views*) libéral, tolérant; (*accent*) fort, prononcé; (*use, sense*) répandu, général; (*daylight*) plein; (*joke, story*) grossier, salé

broad'-backed' *adj* d'une belle carrure

broad'brimmed' *adj* à larges bords

broad'cast' *adj* diffusé; (rad) radiodiffusé ‖ *s* (rad) radiodiffusion *f*, émission *f* ‖ *v* (*pret & pp* **-cast**) *tr* diffuser, répandre ‖ (*pret & pp* **-cast** or **-casted**) *tr* radiodiffuser ‖ *intr* (rad) émettre

broad'cast'er *s* communicateur *m*

broad'casting sta'tion *s* station *f* d'émission

broad'cloth' *s* popeline *f*

broaden ['brɔdən] *tr* élargir ‖ *intr* s'élargir

broad'-gauge' *adj* à voie large

broad' jump' *s* saut *m* en longueur

broad'-mind'ed *adj* évolué, à l'esprit large

broad'side' *s* bordée *f*; (typ) placard *m*

brocade [bro'ked] *s* brocart *m* ‖ *tr* brocher

broccoli ['brakəli] *s* brocoli *m*

brochure [bro'ʃʊr] *s* brochure *f*

brogue [brog] *s* accent *m* irlandais; (*shoe*) soulier *m* grossier

broil [brɔil] *s* grillade *f*; (*quarrel*) rixe *f* ‖ *tr & intr* griller

broiler ['brɔilər] *s* gril *m*

broke [brok] *adj* (slang) fauché

broken ['brokən] *adj* brisé, cassé; (*promise; ranks; beam*) rompu

bro'ken-down' *adj* délabré; en panne

bro'ken-heart'ed *adj* au cœur brisé

broker ['brokər] *s* courtier *m*

brokerage ['brokərɪdʒ] *s* courtage *m*

bro'kerage fee' *s* (frais *mpl* de) courtage *m*

bromide ['bromaɪd] *s* bromure *m*; (coll) platitude *f*

bromine ['bromin] *s* brome *m*

bronchial ['braŋkɪ·əl] *adj* bronchique

bron'chial tube' *s* bronche *f*

bronchitis [braŋ'kaɪtɪs] *s* bronchite *f*

bron·co ['braŋko] *s* (*pl* **-cos**) cheval *m* sauvage

bronze [branz] *adj* bronzé ‖ *s* bronze *m* ‖ *tr* bronzer ‖ *intr* se bronzer

brooch [brotʃ], [brutʃ] *s* broche *f*

brood [brud] *s* couvée *f*; (*of children*) nichée *f* ‖ *intr* couver; (*to sulk*) broyer du noir; **to brood over** songer sombrement à

brood' hen' *s* couveuse *f*

brood'mare' *s* poulinière *f*

brook [brʊk] *s* ruisseau *m* ‖ *tr*—**to brook no ne pas** tolérer

brooklet ['brʊklɪt] *s* ruisseau *m*

broom [brum] *s* balai *m*; (bot) genêt *m*

broom'stick' *s* manche *m* à balai

broth [brɔθ] *s* bouillon *m*, consommé *m*

brothel ['brɛðəl] *s* bordel *m*

brother ['brʌðər] *s* frère *m*

broth'er·hood' *s* fraternité *f*

broth'er-in-law' *s* (*pl* **brothers-in-law**) beau-frère *m*

brotherly ['brʌðərli] *adj* fraternel ‖ *adv* fraternellement

brow [braʊ] *s* (*forehead*) front *m*; (*eyebrow*) sourcil *m*; **to knit one's brow** froncer le sourcil

brow'beat' *v* (*pret* **-beat**; *pp* **-beaten**) *tr* rabrouer, brusquer

brown [braʊn] *adj* marron; (*eyes*) brun; (*hair*) brun, châtain; (*shoes*) marron; (*ale*) brune; (*bread*) bis; (*sugar*) brun; (*butter*) roux, noir; (*bear*) brun; (*tanned*) bronzé, bruni; (*dark-complexioned*) brun de peau; **brown wrapping paper** papier *m* d'emballage ‖ *s* marron *m*, brun *m* ‖ *tr* (*skin*) bronzer, brunir; (culin) faire dorer, rissoler ‖ *intr* (*sauce; leaves*) roussir; (*skin*) brunir; (culin) dorer, rissoler

brown' bag' lunch *s* repas *m* tiré du sac

brownish ['braʊnɪʃ] *adj* brunâtre

brown' out' s (*shortage of power*) panne f partielle; (mil) camouflage m partiel des lumières

brown' stone' s (*brownstone front*) bâtiment m de grès brun; (mineral) grès m brun

brown' stud'y s—**in a brown study** absorbé dans des méditations

brown' sug'ar s cassonade f, sucre m brut

browse [brauz] intr (*said of animals*) brouter; (*said of booklovers*) butiner; (*said of customers for secondhand books*) bouquiner

bruise [bruz] s (*on body or fruit*) meurtrissure f; (*on body*) contusion f ‖ tr meurtrir, contusionner

bruiser ['bruzər] s (coll) costaud m

bruit [brut] tr ébruiter; **to bruit about** répandre

brunette [bru'nɛt] adj & s brune f, brunette f

brunt [brʌnt] s choc m, assaut m; **to bear the brunt of** (fig) faire tous les frais de

brush [brʌʃ] s brosse f; (*countryside*) brousse f; (elec) balai m ‖ tr brosser; **to brush aside** écarter ‖ intr—**to brush against** frôler; **to brush up on** repasser, rafraîchir

brush'-off' s (slang) affront m; **to give a brush-off to** (slang) expédier avec rudesse

brush'wood' s broussailles fpl, brindilles fpl

brusque [brʌsk] adj brusque

Brussels ['brʌsəlz] s Bruxelles f

Brus'sels sprouts' mpl chou m de Bruxelles

brutal ['brutəl] adj brutal

brutali·ty [bru'tælɪti] s (pl **-ties**) brutalité f

brute [brut] adj brutal ‖ s bête f, animal m; (*person*) brute f, animal m

brutish ['brutɪʃ] adj grossier, brut, brutal

bubble ['bʌbəl] s bulle f ‖ intr bouillonner; (*said of drink*) pétiller; **to bubble over** déborder

bub'ble bath' s bain m moussant, bain de mousse

bub'ble gum' s gomme f à claquer

bub·bly ['bʌbli] adj (comp **-blier**; super **-bliest**) bouillonnant, gazeux

bubon'ic plague' [bju'bɑnɪk] s peste f bubonique

buccaneer [,bʌkə'nɪr] s boucanier m

buck [bʌk] s (*red deer*) cerf m; (*fallow deer*) daim m; (*roebuck*) chevreuil m; (slang) dollar m; the male of many animals such as: (*goat*) bouc m; (*rabbit*) lapin m; (*hare*) lièvre m; **to pass the buck** (coll) renvoyer la balle ‖ tr—**to buck off** (*a rider*) désarçonner; **to buck up** (coll) remonter le courage de ‖ intr—**to buck up** (coll) reprendre courage

bucket ['bʌkɪt] s seau m; **to kick the bucket** (slang) casser sa pipe, claquer, crever

buck'et seat' s siège m baquet

buckle ['bʌkəl] s boucle f ‖ tr boucler ‖ intr arquer, gauchir; **to buckle down** s'appliquer

buck' pri'vate s simple soldat m

buckram ['bʌkrəm] s bougran m

buck'saw' s scie f à bûches

buck'shot' s gros plomb m

buck'tooth' s (pl **-teeth**) dent f saillante

buck'wheat' s sarrasin m

buck'wheat cake' s crêpe f de sarrasin

bud [bʌd] s bouton m, bourgeon m ‖ v (pret & pp **budded**; ger **budding**) intr boutonner, bourgeonner

Buddhism ['budɪzəm] s bouddhisme m

Buddhist ['budɪst] adj & s bouddhiste mf

budding ['bʌdɪŋ] adj en bouton; (*beginning*) en germe, naissant

bud·dy ['bʌdi] s (pl **-dies**) (coll) copain m

budge [bʌdʒ] tr faire bouger ‖ intr bouger

budget ['bʌdʒɪt] s budget m ‖ tr comptabiliser, inscrire au budget

budgetary ['bʌdʒɪ,tɛri] adj budgétaire

buff [bʌf] adj (*color*) chamois ‖ s (coll) fanatique mf, enthousiaste mf ‖ tr polir, émeuler

buffa·lo ['bʌfə,lo] s (pl **-loes** or **-los**) bison m; (*water buffalo; Cape buffalo*) buffle m

buffer ['bʌfər] s (mach) brunissoir m; (rr) (*on cars*) tampon m; (rr) (*at end of track*) butoir m

buff'er state' s état m tampon

buff'er zone' s zone f tampon

buffet [bu'fe] s buffet m ‖ ['bʌfɪt] tr frapper (violemment)

buffet' lunch' [bu'fe] s lunch m

buffet' sup'per s buffet m

buffoon [bə'fun] s bouffon m

buffooner·y [bə'funəri] s (pl **-ies**) bouffonnerie f

bug [bʌg] s insecte m; (germ) microbe m; (*in a mechanical device*) vice m, défaut m; (*hidden microphone*) micro m; (comp) bogue f; (coll) idée f fixe, lutin m; (Brit) punaise f; **he's a bug for . . .** (coll) il est fou de . . . ‖ v (pret & pp **bugged**; ger **bugging**) tr (slang) installer une table d'écoute dans; installer un microphone dans; (*to annoy*) (slang) embêter, emmerder

bug'bear' s (*scare*) épouvantail m, croquemitaine m; (*pet peeve*) bête f noire

bug'-eyed' adj (slang) aux yeux saillants

bug·gy ['bʌgi] adj (comp **-gier**; super **-giest**) infesté d'insectes; infesté; (slang) fou ‖ s (pl **-gies**) buggy m à quatre roues; (*two-wheeled*) buggy, boguet m

bug'house' s (slang) cabanon m

bugle ['bjugəl] s (bot) bugle f; (mus) clairon m ‖ tr & intr claironner

bu'gle call' s sonnerie f de clairon

bugler ['bjuglər] s clairon m

build [bɪld] s (*of human body*) taille f, charpente f, carrure f ‖ v (pret & pp **built** [bɪlt]) tr bâtir, construire

builder ['bɪldər] s constructeur m; (*of bridges, roads, etc.*) entrepreneur m

building ['bɪldɪŋ] s immeuble m, bâtiment m, édifice m; (*erection*) construction f

build'ing and loan' associa'tion s société f de prêt à la construction

build′ing lot′ *s* terrain *m* à bâtir

build′ing per′mit *s* permis *m* de construire

build′ing site′ *s* chantier *m* de construction; lotissement *m* à bâtir

build′-up *s* (*of excitement*) montée *f*; (*of pressure*) intensification *f*; (*of gas*) accumulation *f*; (fig) présentation *f* publicitaire, battage *m*

built′-in′ *adj* incorporé, encastré

built′-up′ *adj* aggloméré; (*heel*) renforcé; (*land*) bâti, loti

bulb [bʌlb] *s* bulbe *m*; (*of vaporizer*) poire *f*; (bot) oignon *m*; (elec) ampoule *f*

bulbous [′bʌlbəs] *adj* bulbeux

Bulgaria [bʌl′gɛrɪ·ə] *s* Bulgarie *f*; la Bulgarie

Bulgarian [bʌl′gɛrɪ·ən] *adj* bulgare ‖ *s* (*language*) bulgare *m*; (*person*) Bulgare *mf*

bulge [bʌldʒ] *s* bosse *f*, bombement *m*; (mil) saillant *m* ‖ *tr* bourrer, gonfler ‖ *intr* faire une bosse, bomber

bulk [bʌlk] *s* masse *f*, volume *m*; **in bulk** en bloc; (com) en vrac ‖ *tr* entasser (en vrac) ‖ *intr* tenir de la place; **to bulk large** devenir important

bulk′head′ *s* (naut) cloison *f*

bulk·y [′bʌlki] *adj* (*comp* -ier; *super* -iest) volumineux

bull [bʊl] *s* taureau *m*; (*on the stock exchange*) haussier *m*, spéculateur *m* à la hausse; (eccl) bulle *f*; (*policeman*) (slang) flic *m*, vache *f*; (*exaggeration*) (slang) blague *f*, boniment *m*, chiqué *m*; **like a bull in a china shop** comme un éléphant dans un magasin de porcelaine; **to take the bull by the horns** (fig) prendre le taureau par les cornes ‖ *tr*—**to bull the market** jouer à la hausse

bull′dog′ *s* bouledogue *m*

bull′doze′ *tr* passer au bulldozer; (coll) intimider

bulldozer [′bʊl,dozər] *s* chasse-terre *m*, bouteur *m*, bouldozeur *m*

bullet [′bʊlɪt] *s* balle *f*

bulletin [′bʊlətɪn] *s* bulletin *m*; (*e.g., of a university*) annuaire *m*

bul′letin board′ *s* tableau *m* d'affichage

bul′let·proof′ *adj* à l'épreuve des balles ‖ *tr* blinder

bul′let·proof vest′ *s* gilet *m* pare-balles

bull′fight′ *s* course *f* de taureaux

bull′fight′er *s* torero *m*

bull′fight′ing *s* tauromachie *f*

bull′finch′ *s* bouvreuil *m*

bull′frog′ *s* grenouille *f* d'Amérique

bull′head′ *s* (ichth) chabot *m*, cabot *m*; (*miller′s-thumb*) meunier *m*, cabot

bull′head′ed *adj* entêté

bullion [′bʊljən] *s* (*of gold*) or *m*; (*of silver*) argent *m*; encaisse *f* métallique, lingots *mpl* d'or, lingots d'argent; (*on uniform*) cordonnet *m* d'or, cordonnet d'argent

bull′ mar′ket *s* marché *m* à la hausse

bullock [′bʊlək] *s* bœuf *m*

bull′ pen′ *s* toril *m*; (*jail*) poste *m* de détention préventive

bull′ring′ *s* arène *f*, arène pour les courses de taureaux

bull′s-eye′ *s* mouche *f*; **to hit the bull′s-eye** faire mouche

bull′s′-eye win′dow *s* œil-de-bœuf *m*

bul·ly [′bʊli] *adj* (coll) épatant ‖ *s* (*pl* -lies) brute *f*, brutal *m*; (*at school*) tyranneau *m* ‖ *v* (*pret & pp* -lied) *tr* brutaliser, malmener; (*at school*) brimer, tyranniser

bulrush [′bʊl,rʌʃ] *s* jonc *m* des marais

bulwark [′bʊlwərk] *s* rempart *m*; (naut) pavois *m* ‖ *tr* garnir de remparts; (fig) protéger

bum [bʌm] *adj* (slang) moche, de camelote ‖ *s* (slang) clochard *m* ‖ *v* (*pret & pp* bummed; *ger* bumming) *tr & intr* (slang) écornifler

bumble [′bʌmbəl] *tr* bâcler ‖ *intr* (*to stumble*) trébucher; (*in speaking*) bafouiller; (*said of bee*) bourdonner

bum′ble·bee′ *s* bourdon *m*

bump [bʌmp] *s* (*blow*) choc *m*; (*protuberance*) bosse *f*; (*of car on rough road*) cahot *m* ‖ *tr* cogner, tamponner, heurter; **to bump off** (*to kill*) (slang) buter ‖ *intr* se cogner; **to bump along** (*said of car*) cahoter; **to bump into** buter contre, choquer

bumper [′bʌmpər] *adj* exceptionnel ‖ *s* (aut) pare-chocs *m*; (rr) tampon *m*; **bumper to bumper** pare-chocs contre pare-chocs

bump′er car′ *s* (*at a carnival*) auto *f* tamponneuse

bump′er stick′er *s* autocollant *m*, macaron *m*

bumpkin [′bʌmpkɪn] *s* péquenot *m*, rustre *m*

bumptious [′bʌmpʃəs] *adj* outrecuidant

bump·y [′bʌmpi] *adj* (*comp* -ier; *super* -iest) bosselé; (*road*) cahoteux

bun [bʌn] *s* brioche *f*, petit pain *m*; (*hair*) chignon *m*

bunch [bʌntʃ] *s* (*of vegetables*) botte *f*; (*of bananas*) régime *m*; (*of flowers*) bouquet *m*; (*of grapes*) grappe *f*; (*of keys*) trousseau *m*; (*of people*) groupe *m*, bande *f*; (*of ribbons*) flot *m*; (*of feathers, hair*) touffe *f*; (*of twigs*) paquet *m*; (*on body*) bosse *f* ‖ *tr* grouper ‖ *intr* se serrer

buncombe [′bʌŋkəm] *s* (coll) balivernes *fpl*, sornettes *fpl*

bundle [′bʌndəl] *s* paquet *m*; (*of banknotes, papers, etc.*) liasse *f* ‖ *tr* empaqueter, mattre en paquet; **to bundle up** (*in warm clothing*) emmitoufler ‖ *intr*—**to bundle up** s'emmitoufler

bung [bʌŋ] *s* bonde *f* ‖ *tr* mettre une bonde à

bungalow [′bʌŋgə,lo] *s* bungalow *m*

bung′hole′ *s* bonde *f*

bungle [′bʌŋgəl] *s* gâchis *m*, bousillage *m* ‖ *tr* saboter, bousiller ‖ *intr* saboter

bungler [′bʌŋglər] *s* gâcheur *m*, bousilleur *m*

bungling ['bʌŋglɪŋ] *adj* gauche, maladroit ‖ *s* maladresse *f*

bunion ['bʌnjən] *s* oignon *m* (au pied)

bunk [bʌŋk] *s* (*bed*) couchette *f*; (slang) balivernes *fpl*, sornettes *fpl* ‖ *intr* (coll) se coucher

bunk′ bed′ *s* lit *m* superposé; (naut) cadre *m*

bunker ['bʌŋkər] *s* (golf) banquette *f*; (naut) soute *f*; (mil) blockhaus *m*, bunker *m*

bun·ny ['bʌni] *s* (*pl* **-nies**) petit lapin *m*

bunting ['bʌntɪŋ] *s* (*flags*) drapeaux *mpl*; (*cloth*) étamine *f*; (orn) bruant *m*

buoy [bɔɪ], ['bu·i] *s* bouée *f* ‖ *tr*—**to buoy up** faire flotter; (fig) soutenir

buoyancy ['bɔɪ·ənsi] *s* flottabilité *f*

buoyant ['bɔɪ·ənt] *adj* flottant; (*cheerful*) plein d'allant, plein de ressort

bur [bʌr] *s* (*of chestnut*) bogue *f*; (*ragged metal edge*) bavure *f*, barbe *f*

burble ['bʌrbəl] *s* murmure *m* ‖ *intr* murmurer

burden ['bʌrdən] *s* fardeau *m*, charge *f*; (mus) refrain *m* ‖ *tr* charger

bur′den of proof′ *s* fardeau *m* de la preuve

burdensome ['bʌrdənsəm] *adj* onéreux

burdock ['bʌrdɑk] *s* bardane *f*

bureau ['bjʊro] *s* (*piece of furniture*) commode *f*, chiffonier *m*; (*office*) bureau *m*

bureaucra·cy [bjʊ'rɑkrəsi] *s* (*pl* **-cies**) bureaucratie *f*, énarchie *f*

bureaucrat ['bjʊrə,kræt] *s* bureaucrate *mf*, rond-de-cuir *m*, énarque *mf*

bureaucratic [,bjʊrə'krætɪk] *adj* bureaucratique

bur′eau of vi′tal statis′tics *s* bureau *m* de l'état civil

burglar ['bʌrglər] *s* cambrioleur *m*

bur′glar alarm′ *s* signalisateur *m* anti-vol, sonnette *f* d'alarme

burglarize ['bʌrglə,raɪz] *tr* cambrioler

bur′glar·proof′ *adj* incrochetable

burglar·y ['bʌrgləri] *s* (*pl* **-ies**) cambriolage *m*

Burgundian [bər'gʌndɪ·ən] *adj* bourguignon ‖ *s* (*dialect*) bourguignon *m*; (*person*) Bourguignon *m*

Burgundy ['bʌrgəndi] *s* Bourgogne *f*; la Bourgogne ‖ **burgun·dy** *s* (**-dies**) (*wine*) bourgogne *m*

burial ['bɛrɪ·əl] *s* enterrement *m*, inhumation *f*

bur′ial ground′ *s* cimetière *m*

burlap ['bʌrlæp] *s* toile *f* d'emballage, serpillière *f*

burlesque [bər'lɛsk] *adj* & *s* burlesque *m* ‖ *tr* parodier

burlesque′ show′ *s* striptease *m*

bur·ly ['bʌrli] *adj* (*comp* **-lier**; *super* **-liest**) solide, costaud

Burma ['bʌrmə] *s* Birmanie *f*; la Birmanie

Bur·mese [bər'miz] *adj* birman ‖ *s* (*pl* **-mese**) (*language*) birman *m*; (*person*) Birman *m*

burn [bʌrn] *s* brûlure *f* ‖ *v* (*pret* & *pp* **burned** or **burnt** [bʌrnt]) *tr* & *intr* brûler; **to burn out** (elec) griller

burner ['bʌrnər] *s* (*on which to cook*) brûleur *m*; (*using gas*) bec *m*; (*of a stove*) feu *m*

burning ['bʌrnɪŋ] *adj* brûlant; (*in flames*) en feu ‖ *s* brûlure *f*; (*fire*) incendie *m*

burnish ['bʌrnɪʃ] *tr* brunir, polir

burn′-out *s* arrêt *m* par épuisement; (*emotional breakdown*) syndrome *m* de l'usure au travail

burrow ['bʌro] *s* terrier *m* ‖ *tr* creuser ‖ *intr* se terrer

bursar ['bʌrsər] *s* économe *m*

burst [bʌrst] *s* éclat *m*, explosion *f* ‖ *v* (*pret* & *pp* **burst**) (*a balloon*) crever; (*a boiler; one's buttons*) faire sauter ‖ *intr* éclater, exploser; (*said of tire*) crever; **to burst into tears** fondre en larmes; **to burst out laughing** éclater de rire

bur·y ['bɛri] *v* (*pret* & *pp* **-ied**) *tr* enterrer, ensevelir; (*e.g., pirate treasure*) enfouir

bus [bʌs] *s* (*pl* **busses** or **buses**) (*city*) autobus *m*, bus *m*; (*interurban or sightseeing*) car *m*, autocar *m*; **to miss the bus** (fig) manquer le coche ‖ *v* (*pret* & *pp* **bused** or **bussed**; *ger* **busing** or **bussing**) *tr* transporter en autobus

bus′boy′ *s* aide-serveur *m*, desserveur *m*, débarrasseur *m*

bush [bʊʃ] *s* (*shrub*) buisson *m*; (*small shrub*) arbuste *m*; (*in Africa and Australia*) brousse *f*; **to beat around the bush** tourner autour du pot, tortiller

bushed [bʊʃt] *adj* (coll) éreinté

bushel ['bʊʃəl] *s* boisseau *m*

bushing ['bʊʃɪŋ] *s* manchon *m*, douille *f*, bague *f*, coussinet *m*

bush·y ['bʊʃi] *adj* (*comp* **-ier**; *super* **-iest**) (*countryside*) buissonneux; (*hair*) touffu; (*eyebrows*) broussailleux

business ['bɪznɪs] *adj* commercial ‖ *s* affaires *fpl*, les affaires; (*subject*) sujet *m*; (*store*) commerce *m*; (*company*) établissement *m*; (theat) jeux *mpl* de scène; **it's none of your business** cela ne vous regarde pas; **mind your own business!** occupez-vous de vos affaires!, faites votre métier!; **to mean business** (coll) ne pas plaisanter; **to send about one's business** envoyer paître

busi′ness dis′trict *s* quartier *m* commerçant

busi′ness hours′ *s* heures *fpl* d'ouverture

busi′ness house′ *s* maison *f* de commerce

busi′ness·like′ *adj* pratique; (*manner, transaction*) sérieux

busi′ness lunch′ *s* déjeuner *m* d'affaires, déjeuner de travail

busi′ness·man′ *s* (*pl* **-men′**) homme *m* d'affaires; **big businessman** grand industriel *m*, chef *m* d'industrie

busi′ness man′ager *s* directeur *m* commercial

busi′ness reply′ card′ *s* carte *f* postale avec réponse payée

busi′ness suit′ *s* complet *m* veston

busi′ness·wom′an *s* (*pl* **-wom′en**) femme *f* d'affaires

busing [ˈbʌsɪŋ] s busing m, ramassage m scolaire
bus′ shel′ter s abribus m
buskin [ˈbʌskɪn] s brodequin m
bus′ sta′tion s gare f routière
bus′ stop′ s arrêt m d'autobus
bust [bʌst] s (statue) buste m; (of woman) gorge f, buste; (slang) faillite f ‖ tr (mil) limoger; (slang) casser ‖ intr (slang) échouer
busting [ˈbʌstɪŋ] s (mil) cassation f
bustle [ˈbʌsəl] s remue-ménage m, affairement m, branle-bas m ‖ intr se remuer, s'affairer
bustling [ˈbʌslɪŋ] adj affairé
bus·y [ˈbɪzi] adj (comp -ier; super -iest) occupé ‖ v (pret & pp -ied) tr—**to busy oneself with** s'occuper de
bus′y·bod′y s (pl -ies) officieux m
bus′y sig′nal s (telp) signal m d'occupation, tonalité f occupée; **there's a busy signal** la ligne est occupée
but [bʌt] adv seulement; ne . . . que, e.g., **to have nothing but trouble** n'avoir que des ennuis; **but for** sans; **but for that** à part cela ‖ prep sauf, excepté; **all but** presque ‖ conj mais
butcher [ˈbʊtʃər] s boucher m ‖ tr (an animal for meat) abattre, dépecer; (to massacre; to bungle) massacrer
butch′er knife′ s couperet m, coutelas m (de boucher)
butch′er shop′ s boucherie f
butler [ˈbʌtlər] s maître m d'hôtel, intendant m
butt [bʌt] s (end) bout m; (cask) futaille f; (of a gun) crosse f; (of a cigarette) mégot m; (of a joke) souffre-douleur m, plastron m; (blow) coup m de tête, coup de corne; (slang) postérieur m, derrière m ‖ tr (like a goat) donner un coup de corne à ‖ intr—**to butt up against** buter contre; **to butt in** (coll) intervenir sans façon
butte [bjut] s butte f, tertre m, puy m
butt′ end′ s gros bout m
butter [ˈbʌtər] s beurre m ‖ tr beurrer; **to butter up** (coll) passer de la pommade à, pateliner
but′ter·cup′ s renoncule f, bouton-d'or m
but′ter dish′ s beurrier m, beurrière f
but′ter·fat′ s crème f
but′ter·fin′gered adj maladroit
but′ter·fin′gers s brise-tout mf
but′ter·fly′ s (pl -flies) papillon m
but′ter knife′ s couteau m à beurre
but′ter·milk′ s babeurre m
but′ter·scotch′ s caramel m au beurre
buttocks [ˈbʌtəks] spl fesses fpl

button [ˈbʌtən] s bouton m ‖ tr boutonner
but′ton cell′ s (battery) pile-bouton f
but′ton·hole′ s boutonnière f ‖ tr (coll) retenir (qqn) par le pan de sa veste
but′ton·hook′ s tire-bouton m
buttress [ˈbʌtrɪs] s contrefort m ‖ tr arc-bouter; (fig) étayer
buxom [ˈbʌksəm] adj plantureuse
buy [baɪ] s—**a good buy** (coll) une bonne affaire ‖ v (pret & pp **bought** [bɔt]) tr acheter; (a ticket) prendre; **to buy a drink for** payer un verre à; **to buy back** racheter; **to buy from** acheter à or de; **to buy out** (a partner) désintéresser; **to buy s.o. off** se débarrasser de qn, racheter qn; **to buy up** accaparer
buyer [ˈbaɪ·ər] s acheteur m
buzz [bʌz] s bourdonnement m; **to give s.o. a buzz** (on the telephone) (coll) passer un coup de fil à ‖ tr (aer) survoler à basse altitude ‖ intr bourdonner
buzzard [ˈbʌzərd] s buse f
buzz′ bomb′ s bombe f volante
buzzer [ˈbʌzər] s vibreur m sonore, trembleur m
buzz′ saw′ s scie f circulaire
buzz′ word′ s grand mot m, mot résonnant et emphatique
by [baɪ] adv près, auprès; (aside) de côté; **by and by** tout à l'heure, sous peu; **by and large** généralement parlant ‖ prep par; (near) près de; **by a head** (taller) d'une tête; **by day** pendant la journée; **by far** de beaucoup; **by Monday** d'ici à lundi; **by 1944** déjà en 1944, en 1944 au plus tard; **by profession** de profession; **by the way** à propos; **to be followed (loved, etc.) by** être suivi (aimé, etc.) de
by-and-by [ˈbaɪ·ən′baɪ] s proche avenir m; **in the sweet by-and-by** à la Saint-Glinglin
by′gone′ adj d'autrefois, passé
by′law′ s ordonnance f, règlement m
by′-line′ s signature f de journaliste
by′-pass′ s (road) bretelle f de contournement, rocade f; (elec, med) dérivation f ‖ tr éviter, contourner; (mach) amener or placer en dérivation
by′-play′ s (theat) jeu m en aparté
by′-prod′uct s sous-produit m
by′-road′ s chemin m détourné
bystander [ˈbaɪ,stændər] s spectateur m, assistant m
byte [baɪt] s (comp) multiplet m; (of eight bits) octet m
by′way′ s chemin m écarté, voie f indirecte
by′word′ s dicton m, proverbe m; objet m de dérision
Byzantine [ˈbɪzən,tin] adj & s byzantin m

C, c [si] *s* IIIe lettre de l'alphabet
cab [kæb] *s* taxi *m; (of locomotive or truck)* cabine *f; (hansom)* fiacre *m*, cab *m*
cabaret [ˌkæbə're] *s* boîte *f* de nuit, cabaret *m*
cabbage ['kæbidʒ] *s* chou *m*
cab'driv'er *s* chauffeur *m* de taxi
cabin ['kæbin] *s (hut)* case *f*, cabane *f; (of ship or airplane)* cabine *f*
cab'in boy' *s* (naut) mousse *m*
cabinet ['kæbinit] *s (small room; room for displaying art; political committee)* cabinet *m; (piece of furniture)* meuble *m* à tiroirs, cabinet; *(wall cupboard)* placard *m*, armoire *f* fixe
cab'inet-mak'er *s* ébéniste *m*, menuisier *m*
cab'inet mem'ber *s* ministre *m*
cable ['kebəl] *s* câble *m* ‖ *tr & intr* câbler
ca'ble car' *s* funiculaire *m*, téléférique *m*, tramway *m* funiculaire
ca'ble-gram' *s* câblogramme *m*
ca'ble ship' *s* câblier *m*
ca'ble's length' *s* encablure *f*
ca'ble tel'evision *s* câblodistribution *f*, vidéocâble *m*
caboose [kə'bus] *s* (naut) coquerie *f; (rr)* fourgon *m* de queue, wagon *m* du personnel
cab'stand' *s* station *f* de taxi
cache [kæʃ] *s* cachette *f*, cache *f* ‖ *tr* mettre dans une cachette, cacher
cachet [kæ'ʃe] *s* cachet *m*
cackle ['kækəl] *s* caquet *m* ‖ *intr* caqueter; *(said of goose)* cacarder
cacopho·ny [kə'kɑfəni] *s (pl* -nies*)* cacophonie *f*
cac·tus ['kæktəs] *s (pl* -tuses *or* -ti [taɪ]*)* cactus *m*
cad [kæd] *s* malotru *m*
cadaver [kə'dævər] *s* cadavre *m*
cad·dy ['kædi] *s (pl* -dies*)* boîte *f* à thé; *(person)* cadet *m*, caddie *m*
cadence ['kedəns] *s* cadence *f*
cadet [kə'dɛt] *s* cadet *m*
cadmium ['kædmɪ·əm] *s* cadmium *m*
Caesar'ean opera'tion [sɪ'zɛrɪ·ən] *s* césarienne *f*
café [kæ'fe] *s* cabaret *m*; café-restaurant *m*
ca'fé soci'ety *s* gens *mpl* chic des cabarets à la mode
cafeteria [ˌkæfə'tɪrɪ·ə] *s* cafétéria *f*, restaurant *m* de libre-service
caffeine [kæ'fin], ['kæfi·ɪn] *s* caféine *f*
cage [kedʒ] *s* cage *f* ‖ *tr* mettre en cage
ca·gey ['kedʒi] *adj (comp* -gier; *super* -giest*)* prudent, peu communicatif; *(secretive)* dissimulé; (coll) rusé, fin
cahoots [kə'huts] *s*—**in cahoots** (slang) de mèche
CAI ['si'e'aɪ] *s* (letterword) **(computer-assisted instruction)** E.A.O. (enseignement assisté par ordinateur)
Cain [ken] *s* Caïn *m;* **to raise Cain** (coll) faire le diable à quatre
Cairo ['kaɪro] *s* Le Caire

caisson ['kesən] *s* caisson *m*
cais'son disease' *s* maladie *f* des caissons
cajole [kə'dʒol] *tr* cajoler, enjôler
cajoler·y [kə'dʒoləri] *s (pl* -ies*)* cajolerie *f*, enjôlement *m*
cake [kek] *s (dessert; shaped like a cake)* gâteau *m; (one-layer cake)* galette *f; (pastry)* pâtisserie *f; (of soap, wax)* pain *m; (of ice)* bloc *m; (crust)* croûte *f;* **to sell like hot cakes** (coll) se vendre comme des petits pains; **to take the cake** (coll) être la fin des haricots ‖ *tr* couvrir d'une croûte ‖ *intr* s'agglutiner, faire croûte
calabash ['kælə,bæʃ] *s* calebasse *f; (tree)* calebassier *m*
calaboose ['kælə,bus] *s* (coll) violon *m*, tôle *f*
calamitous [kə'læmɪtəs] *adj* calamiteux
calami·ty [kə'læmɪti] *s (pl* -ties*)* calamité *f*
calci·fy ['kælsɪ,faɪ] *v (pret & pp* -fied*) tr* calcifier ‖ *intr* se calcifier
calcium ['kælsɪ·əm] *s* calcium *m*
calculate ['kælkjə,let] *tr & intr* calculer
calculating ['kælkjə,letɪŋ] *adj* calculateur
calculation [ˌkælkjə'leʃən] *s* calcul *m*
calcu·lus ['kælkjələs] *s (pl* -luses *or* -li [,laɪ]*)* (math, pathol) calcul *m*
caldron ['kɔldrən] *s* (culin) chaudron *m; (mach)* chaudière *f*
calendar ['kæləndər] *s* calendrier *m*
cal'endar year' *s* année *f* civile
calender ['kæləndər] *s* calandre *f* ‖ *tr* calandrer, cylindrer
calf [kæf] *s (pl* **calves** [kævz]*)* veau *m; (of leg)* mollet *m*
calf'skin' *s* veau *m*, peau *f* de veau
calf's' liv'er *s* foie *m* de veau
caliber ['kælɪbər] *s* calibre *m*, ‖ *tr* graduer, jauger
calibrate ['kælɪ,bret] *tr* calibrer
cali·co ['kælɪ,ko] *s (pl* -coes *or* -cos*)* calicot *m*, indienne *f*
California [ˌkælɪ'fɔrnɪ·ə] *s* Californie *f;* la Californie
calipers ['kælɪpərz] *spl* compas *m* à calibrer
caliph ['kelɪf], ['kælɪf] *s* calife *m*
caliphate ['kælɪfet] *s* califat *m*
calisthenic ['kælɪs'θenɪk] *adj* callisthénique ‖ **calisthenics** *spl* callisthénie *f*
calk [kɔk] *s* crampon *m* à glace ‖ *tr* calfater
call [kɔl]*s (signal; summons; naming)* appel *m; (cry)* cri *m; (visit)* visite *f; (at a port)* escale *f;* (telp) appel téléphonique; **to have no call to** n'avoir aucune raison de ‖ *tr* appeler; *(e.g., the doctor)* faire venir; *(a meeting)* convoquer; **to call aside** prendre à part; **to call back** rappeler; **to call down** *(from upstairs)* faire descendre; *(the wrath of the gods)* invoquer; *(to scold)* (coll) gronder; **to call off** *(a dog)* rappeler; (coll) annuler, décommander; **to call the roll** faire l'appel; **to call to mind** rappeler; **to call to order** rappeler à l'ordre; **to call up** (coll) passer un coup de fil à; (mil) mobiliser ‖ *intr* appeler, crier; *(to*

visit) faire une visite; (*naut*) faire escale; **to call upon** faire appel à; **to call upon s.o. to speak** inviter qn à prendre la parole

call′ bell′ s sonnette f

call′ box′ s guérite f téléphonique

call′ boy′ s (*in a hotel*) chasseur m; (*theat*) avertisseur m

caller [′kɔlər] s visiteur m

call′ girl′ s call-girl f

calling [′kɔlɪŋ] s (*occupation*) métier m, vocation f; (*of a meeting*) convocation f

call′ing card′ s carte f de visite

call′ let′ter s (telg, rad) indicatif m d'appel

call′ mon′ey s prêts mpl au jour le jour

callous [′kæləs] adj (*foot, hand, etc.*) calleux; (*unfeeling*) endurci, insensible

callow [′kælo] adj inexpérimenté, novice

cal′low youth′ s blanc-bec m

callus [′kæləs] s (*on skin*) cal m, durillon m, callosité f; (bot) cal m

calm [kɑm] adj & s calme m ‖ tr calmer; **to calm down** pacifier ‖ intr—**to calm down** se calmer; (*said of wind or sea*) calmir

calorie [′kæləri] s calorie f

calum·ny [′kæləmni] s (*pl* **-nies**) calomnie f

calva·ry [′kælvəri] s (*pl* **-ries**) calvaire m; **Calvary** le Calvaire

calve [kæv], [kɑv] intr vêler

cam [kæm] s came f

cambric [′kembrɪk] s batiste f

camel [′kæməl] s chameau m

camellia [kə′mɪljə] s camélia m

cameo [′kæmi,o] s (*pl* **-os**) camée m

camera [′kæmərə] s appareil m (photographique)

cam′era bug′ s chasseur m d'images

cam′era·man′ s (*pl* **-men′**) photographe m; (mov) cadreur m

camomile [′kæmə,maɪl] s camomille f

camouflage [′kæmə,flɑʒ] s camouflage m ‖ tr camoufler

camp [kæmp] s camp m ‖ intr camper; **to go camping** faire du camping

campaign [kæm′pen] s campagne f ‖ intr faire campagne

campaigner [kæm′penər] s propagandiste mf; vétéran m

camp′ bed′ s lit m de camp, lit de sangle

camp′ chair′ s chaise f pliante

camper [′kæmpər] s campeur m; (aut) camping-car m

camp′fire′ s feu m de camp

camp′ground′ s camping m

camphor [′kæmfər] s camphre m

camping [′kæmpɪŋ] s camping m

camp′stool′ s pliant m

campus [′kæmpəs] s campus m, terrain m universitaire

cam′shaft′ s arbre m à cames

can [kæn] s (*of food, beer, film, garbage, etc.*) boîte f; (*e.g., for gasoline*) bidon m ‖ v (*pret & pp* **canned**; *ger* **canning**) tr mettre en boîte, conserver; (*to dismiss*) (slang) dégommer ‖ v (*pret & cond* **could** [kʊd]) aux—**Albert can't do it** Albert ne

peut (pas) le faire; **can he swim?** sait-il nager?

Canada [′kænədə] s le Canada

Canadian [kə′nedɪ·ən] adj canadien ‖ s (*person*) Canadien m

canal [kə′næl] s canal m

canar·y [kə′nɛri] s (*pl* **-ies**) canari m, serin m

can·cel [′kænsəl] v (*pret & pp* **-celed** or **-celled**; *ger* **-celing** or **-celling**) tr annuler; (*a word*) biffer, rayer; (*a contract*) résilier; (*a postage stamp*) oblitérer; **to cancel an invitation** décommander les invités; **to cancel each other out** s'annuler, se détruire

cancellation [,kænsə′leʃən] s annulation f; (*of postage stamp*) oblitération f; (*of contract*) résiliation f

cancer [′kænsər] s cancer m; **Cancer** (astr, astrol) le Cancer

cancerous [′kænsərəs] adj cancéreux

candela·brum [,kændə′lebrəm] s (*pl* **-bra** [brə] or **-brums**) candélabre m

candid [′kændɪd] adj franc

candida·cy [′kændɪdəsi] s (*pl* **-cies**) candidature f

candidate [′kændɪ,det] s candidat m

can′did cam′era s caméra f invisible

candied adj candi

candied′ fruit′ s fruit m candi

candle [′kændəl] s bougie f; (*of tallow*) chandelle f; (eccl) cierge m

can′dle·hold′er s bougeoir m

can′dle·light′ s lumière f de bougie

can′dle·pow′er s (phys) bougie f

can′dle·stick′ s chandelier m, bougeoir m

can′dle ta′ble s guéridon m

candor [′kændər] s franchise f, loyauté f

can·dy [′kændi] s (*pl* **-dies**) confiserie f, bonbons mpl; **candies** douceurs fpl; **piece of candy** bonbon ‖ v (*pret & pp* **-died**) tr glacer, faire candir ‖ intr se candir

can′dy box′ s boîte f à bonbons

can′dy corn′ s grains mpl de maïs soufflés et sucrés

can′dy dish′ s bonbonnière

can′dy machine′ s distributeur m de friandises

can′dy store′ s confiserie f

cane [ken] s canne f; (bot) canne ‖ tr canner, rempailler

cane′ chair′ s chaise f cannée

cane′ sug′ar s sucre m de canne

canine [′kenaɪn] adj canin ‖ s (*tooth*) canine f

canister [′kænɪstər] s boîte f métallique; (mil) boîte à mitraille

canker [′kæŋkər] s chancre m; (*in fruit; in society*) ver m rongeur ‖ tr ronger; (*society*) corrompre

canned [kænd] adj (*food*) en boîte, en conserve; (*drunk*) (slang) rétamé, rond; (*fired*) (slang) flanqué à la porte, vidé

canned′ goods′ spl conserves fpl, aliments mpl conservés

canned′ mu′sic s (coll) musique f enregistrée, musique en conserve

canner·y [ˈkænəri] *s* (*pl* **-ies**) conserverie *f*
cannibal [ˈkænɪbəl] *adj* & *s* cannibale *mf*
canning [ˈkænɪŋ] *s* conservation *f*
can′ning fac′tory *s* conserverie *f*
cannon [ˈkænən] *s* canon *m*
cannonade [ˌkænəˈned] *s* canonnade *f* ‖ *tr* canonner
can′non·ball′ *s* boulet *m* (de canon)
can′non fod′der *s* chair *f* à canon
can·ny [ˈkæni] *adj* (*comp* **-nier**; *super* **-niest**) prudent, circonspect; rusé, malin
canoe [kəˈnu] *s* canoë *m*
canoeist [kəˈnu·ɪst] *s* canoéiste *mf*
canon [ˈkænən] *s* canon *m*
canonical [kəˈnɑnɪkəl] *adj* canonique, canonial ‖ **canonicals** *spl* vêtements *mpl* sacerdotaux
canonize [ˈkænəˌnaɪz] *tr* canoniser
can′ o′pener *s* ouvre-boîtes *m*
canopy [ˈkænəpi] *s* (*pl* **-pies**) dais *m*; (*over an entrance*) marquise *f*
cant [kænt] *s* (*insincere conventional expression*) l'affectation *f* de pruderie, des phrases *fpl* toute faites; (*argot*) jargon *m* ‖ *tr* (*to tip*) incliner ‖ *intr* (*to tip*) s'incliner; (*to be hypocritical*) papelarder
cantaloupe [ˈkæntəˌlop] *s* cantaloup *m*
cantankerous [kænˈtæŋkərəs] *adj* revêche, acariâtre
cantata [kənˈtɑtə] *s* cantate *f*
canteen [kænˈtin] *s* (*shop*) cantine *f*; (*water flask*) bidon *m*; (*service club*) foyer *m* du soldat, du marin, etc.
canter [ˈkæntər] *s* petit galop *m* ‖ *intr* aller au petit galop
canticle [ˈkæntɪkəl] *s* cantique *m*, hymne *f*
cantilever [ˈkæntɪˌlivər] *adj* & *s* cantilever *m*
can′tilever bridge′ *s* pont *m* cantilever, pont à consoles
canton [ˈkæntɑn] *s* canton *m*
canvas [ˈkænvəs] *s* (*cloth*) canevas *m*; (*picture*) toile *f*
canvass [ˈkænvəs] *s* (*scrutiny*) enquête *f*; (*campaign*) tournée *f* électorale ‖ *tr* (*a voter*) solliciter la voix de; (*a district*) faire une tournée électorale dans; (com) prospecter ‖ *intr* (com) faire la place; **to canvass for** (*a candidate*) faire une campagne électorale en faveur de
canyon [ˈkænjən] *s* cañon *m*
cap [kæp] *s* (*with visor*) casquette *f*; (*without brim*) bonnet *m*; (*to wear with academic gown*) toque *f*, mortier *m*; (*of bottle*) capsule *f*; (*of cartridge*) amorce *f*, capsule; (*of fountain pen*) capuchon *m*, chapeau *m*; (*of valve*; *to cover photographic lens*) chapeau; **to set one's cap for** chercher à captiver ‖ *v* (*pret* & *pp* **capped**; *ger* **capping**) *tr* coiffer; (*a bottle*) capsuler; (*a cartridge*) amorcer; (*a success*) couronner; (*to outdo*) (coll) surpasser
cap. *abbr* (**capital letter**) maj.
capable [ˈkepəbəl] *adj* capable
capacious [kəˈpeʃəs] *adj* spacieux, vaste, ample

capaci·ty [kəˈpæsɪti] *s* (*pl* **-ties**) capacité *f*; **filled to capacity** comble; **in the capacity of** en tant que, en qualité de, à titre de
cap′ and gown′ *s* costume *m* académique, toge *f* et mortier *m*; **in cap and gown** en toque et en toge
cape [kep] *s* (*clothing*) cape *f*, pèlerine *f*; (geog) cap *m*, promontoire *m*
Cape′ of Good Hope′ *s* Cap *m* de Bonne Espérance
caper [ˈkepər] *s* cabriole *f*, gambade *f*; (bot) câpre *f* ‖ *tr* cabrioler, gambader
Cape′town′ *s* Le Cap
capital [ˈkæpɪtəl] *adj* capital; excellent ‖ *s* (*city*) capitale *f*; (archit) chapiteau *m*; (com) capital *m*; (typ) majuscule *f*, capitale; **small capital** petite capitale
cap′ital and la′bor *spl* le capital et le travail
capitalism [ˈkæpɪtəˌlɪzəm] *s* capitalisme *m*
capitalist [ˈkæpɪtəlɪst] *adj* & *s* capitaliste *mf*
capitalize [ˈkæpɪtəˌlaɪz] *tr* & *intr* capitaliser; (typ) écrire avec une majuscule; **to capitalize on** miser sur, tourner à son profit, tirer parti de
cap′ital let′ter *s* majuscule *f*
cap′ital pun′ishment *s* peine *f* capitale
capitol [ˈkæpɪtəl] *s* capitole *m*
capitulate [kəˈpɪtʃəˌlet] *intr* capituler
capon [ˈkepɑn] *s* chapon *m*
caprice [kəˈpris] *s* caprice *m*
capricious [kəˈprɪʃəs] *adj* capricieux
Capricorn [ˈkæprɪˌkɔrn] *s* (astr, astrol) le Capricorne
capsize [ˈkæpsaɪz] *tr* faire chavirer ‖ *intr* chavirer, capoter
capstan [ˈkæpstən] *s* cabestan *m*
capsule [ˈkæpsəl] *s* capsule *f*; (bot, rok) capsule
captain [ˈkæptən] *s* (*head*) chef *m*, capitaine *m*; (mil) capitaine; (naut) commandant *m*; (sports) chef d'équipe ‖ *tr* commander, diriger
captain·cy [ˈkæptənsi] *s* (*pl* **-cies**) direction *f*, commandement *m*; grade *m* de capitaine
caption [ˈkæpʃən] *s* légende *f*; (mov) sous-titre *m* ‖ *tr* intituler, donner un sous-titre à
captious [ˈkæpʃəs] *adj* pointilleux, chicaneux; (*insidious*) captieux
captivate [ˈkæptɪˌvet] *tr* captiver
captive [ˈkæptɪv] *adj* & *s* captif *m*
captivi·ty [kæpˈtɪvɪti] *s* (*pl* **-ties**) captivité *f*
captor [ˈkæptər] *s* ravisseur *m*; (naut) auteur *m* d'une prise
capture [ˈkæptʃər] *s* capture *f*, prise *f* ‖ *tr* capturer
car [kɑr] *s* (*automobile*) auto *f*, voiture *f*; (*of elevator*) cabine *f*; (rr) wagon *m*, voiture; (*for mail, baggage, etc.*) (rr) fourgon *m*
carafe [kəˈræf] *s* carafe *f*
caramel [ˈkærəməl] *s* caramel *m*
carat [ˈkærət] *s* carat *m*
caravan [ˈkærəˌvæn] *s* caravane *f*
caravansa·ry [ˌkærəˈvænsəri] *s* (*pl* **-ries**) caravansérail *m*
caraway [ˈkærəˌwe] *s* carvi *m*
car′away seed′ *s* graine *f* de carvi

car′barn′ s dépôt m de tramways

carbide [′kɑrbaɪd] s carbure m

carbine [′kɑrbaɪn] s carabine f

carbol′ic ac′id [kɑr′bɑlɪk] s acide m phénique

car′ bomb′ s voiture f piégée

carbon [′kɑrbən] s (chemical element) carbone m; (part of arc light or battery) charbon m; (in auto cylinder) calamine f; papier m carbone

car′bonated wa′ter [′kɑrbə,netɪd] s eau f gazeuse, soda m

car′bon cop′y s double m au carbone; (fig) calque m; (person) (fig) sosie m

car′bon diox′ide s gaz m carbonique

car′bon monox′ide s oxyde m de carbone

car′bon monox′ide poi′soning s oxycarbonisme m

car′bon pa′per s papier m carbone

carbuncle [′kɑrbʌŋkəl] s furoncle m

carburetor [′kɑrbə,retər] s carburateur m

carcass [′kɑrkəs] s (dead body) cadavre m; (without offal) carcasse f

carcinogenic [,kɑrsəno′ʒɛnɪk] adj cancérigène, cancérogène

carcinoma [,kɑrsɪ′nomə] s carcinome m

card [kɑrd] s carte f; (for filing) fiche f; (for carding) carde f; (coll) original m, numéro m, type m; **to have a card up one's sleeve** avoir un atout dans sa manche; **to put one's cards on the table** jouer cartes sur table ‖ tr carder, peigner

card′board′ s carton m, papier m fort

card′ case′ s porte-cartes m

card′ cat′alogue s fichier m

cardiac [′kɑrdɪ,æk] adj cardiaque ‖ s (patient) (coll) cardiaque mf

cardinal [′kɑrdɪnəl] adj & s cardinal m

card′ in′dex s fichier m

cardiogram [′kɑrdɪ·o,græm] s cardiogramme m

card′ par′ty s soirée f bridge, soirée poker, soirée whist (etc.)

card′sharp′ s tricheur m

card′ ta′ble s table f de jeu

card′ trick′ s tour m de cartes

care [kɛr] s (attention) soin m; (anxiety) souci m; (responsibility) charge f; (upkeep) entretien m; **in care of** aux bons soins de, à l'attention de; **take care!** faites attention!; **to take care not to** se garder de; **to take care of** se charger de; (a sick person) soigner; **to take care to** avoir soin de ‖ intr—**I don't care** ça m'est égal; **to care about** se soucier de, se préoccuper de; **to care for** (s.o.) avoir de la sympathie pour; (s.th.) trouver plaisir à; (a sick person) soigner; **to care to** désirer, vouloir

careen [kə′rin] tr faire coucher sur le côté ‖ intr donner de la bande, s'incliner

career [kə′rɪr] s carrière f

care′free′ adj sans souci, insouciant

careful [′kɛrfəl] adj soigneux, attentif; **be careful!** soyez prudent!

careless [′kɛrlɪs] adj (neglectful) négligent; (nonchalant) insouciant

carelessness [′kɛrlɪsnɪs] s négligence f

caress [kə′rɛs] s caresse f ‖ tr caresser

caret [′kærət] s guidon m de renvoi

care′tak′er s concierge mf, gardien m

care′taker gov′ernment s gouvernement m intérimaire

care′worn′ adj rongé par les soucis

car′fare′ s prix m du trajet, place f; **to pay carfare** payer le parcours

car·go [′kɑrgo] s (pl -goes or -gos) cargaison f

car′go ter′minal s gare f de fret

car′ heat′er s chauffage m de voiture

car′ hop′ s serveur m (qui apporte à manger aux automobilistes dans leur voiture)

Car′ibbe′an Sea [,kærɪ′bi·ən], [kə′rɪbɪ·ən] s Mer f des Caraïbes, Mer des Antilles

caricature [′kærɪkətʃər] s caricature f ‖ tr caricaturer

caricaturist [′kærɪkətʃərɪst] s caricaturiste mf

car′load′ s voiturée f

carnage [′kɑrnɪdʒ] s carnage m

carnal [′kɑrnəl] adj charnel; sexuel

car′nal sin′ s péché m de la chair

carnation [kɑr′neʃən] s œillet m

carnival [′kɑrnɪvəl] s carnaval m; fête f

car·ol [′kærəl] s chanson f, cantique m; (Christmas carol) noël m ‖ v (pret & pp -oled or -olled; ger -oling or -olling) tr & intr chanter

carom [′kærəm] s carambolage m ‖ intr caramboler

carouse [kə′raʊz] intr faire la bombe

carp [kɑrp] s carpe f ‖ intr se plaindre

carpenter [′kɑrpəntər] s charpentier m; (joiner) menuisier m

carpentry [′kɑrpəntri] s charpenterie f

carpet [′kɑrpɪt] s tapis m ‖ tr recouvrir d'un tapis

car′pet sweep′er s balai m mécanique

car′ pool′ s co-voiturage m

car′port′ s abri m pour auto

car′-rent′al serv′ice s entreprise f de location de voitures

carriage [′kærɪdʒ] s (horse-drawn) voiture f, équipage m; (used to transport royalty) carrosse m; (bearing) port m, maintien m; (cost of transport) frais mpl de port; (of typewriter; of rocket) chariot m; (of gun) affût m

carrier [′kærɪ·ər] s (person) porteur m; (e.g., a teamster) camionneur m, voiturier m; (vehicle) transporteur m

car′rier pig′eon s pigeon m voyageur

car′rier wave′ s onde f porteuse

carrion [′kærɪ·ən] s charogne f

carrot [′kærət] s carotte f

carrousel [,kærə′zɛl] s (merry-go-round) manège m de chevaux de bois; (hist) carrousel m

car·ry [′kæri] v (pret & pp -ried) tr porter; (in adding numbers) retenir; **to be carried** (parl) être voté, être adopté; **to be carried**

away (*e.g., with enthusiasm*) être entraîné, s'importer; **to carry away** or **off** emporter, enlever; **to carry back** rapporter; **to carry down** descendre; **to carry forward** avancer; (bk) reporter; **to carry on** continuer; (*e.g., a conversation*) soutenir; **to carry oneself straight** se tenir droit; **to carry out** (*a plan*) exécuter; **to carry over** (bk) reporter; **to carry through** mener à bonne fin; **to carry up** monter; **to carry with one** (*e.g., an audience*) entraîner ‖ *intr* (*said of voice or sound*) porter; **to carry on** continuer; (*in a ridiculous manner*) (coll) faire des espiègleries; (*angrily*) (coll) s'emporter

car′ sick′ness *s* mal *m* de la route

cart [kɑrt] *s* charrette *f*; (*in a supermarket*) poussette *f*; **to put the cart before the horse** mettre la charrue devant les bœufs ‖ *tr* charrier; (*to truck*) camionner

cartel [kɑr′tɛl] *s* cartel *m*

car′ tel′ephone *s* radiotéléphone *m*

cartilage [′kɑrtɪlɪdʒ] *s* cartilage *m*

cartographer [kɑr′tɑgrəfər] *s* cartographe *m*

carton [′kɑrtən] *s* carton *m*, boîte *f*

cartoon [kɑr′tun] *s* dessin *m* humoristique; caricature *f*; (*comic strip*) bande *f* dessinée; (fa) carton *m*; (mov) dessin animé *‖ tr* caricaturer, ridiculiser

cartoonist [kɑr′tunɪst] *s* caricaturiste *mf*

cartridge [′kɑrtrɪdʒ] *s* cartouche *f*; capsule *f* enregistreuse de pick-up

car′tridge belt′ *s* cartouchière *f*

car′tridge case′ *s* cartouchière *f*

cart′wheel′ *s* roue *f*; **to turn cartwheels** faire la roue

carve [kɑrv] *tr & intr* sculpter; (culin) découper

carver [′kɑrvər] *s* sculpteur *m*; (culin) découpeur *m*

carv′ing knife′ *s* couteau *m* à découper

car′ wash′ *s* (*place of business*) lave-auto *m*, tunnel *m* de lavage; (*car washing*) lavage *m* de voitures

car′ wax′ *s* crème *f* pour auto

cascade [kæs′ked] *s* cascade *f* ‖ *intr* cascader

case [kes] *s* (*instance, example*) cas *m*; (*for packing; of clock or piano*) caisse *f*; (*for cigarettes, eyeglasses, cartridges*) étui *m*; (*for jewels, silver, etc.*) écrin *m*; (*for watch*) boîtier *m*; (*for pillow*) taie *f*; (*for surgical instruments*) trousse *f*; (*for sausage*) peau *f*; (*showcase*) vitrine *f*; (*covering*) enveloppe *f*, couverture *f*; (*law*) cause *f*; (typ) casse *f*; **as the case may be** selon le cas; **in any case** en tout cas; **in case** au cas où; **in case of emergency** en cas d'imprévu; **in no case** en aucun cas; **just in case** à tout hasard; **to win one's case** avoir gain de cause ‖ *tr* (*to put into a case*) encaisser; (*to package*) envelopper; (*to observe*) (slang) observer, épier

case′hard′en *tr* aciérer, cémenter; (fig) endurcir

casein [′kesi·ɪn] *s* caséine *f*

casement [′kesmənt] *s* croisée *f*

case′ work′ *s* étude *f* sur dossier

cash [kæʃ] *s* espèces *fpl*; **cash down** argent comptant; **cash offer** offre *f* réelle; **cash on delivery** livraison contre remboursement; **cash on hand** fonds *mpl* en caisse; **in cash** en numéraire ‖ *tr* toucher, encaisser ‖ *intr*—**to cash in on** (coll) tirer parti de

cash′ and car′ry *s* achat *m* au comptant et à emporter, paye et prends

cash′ bal′ance *s* solde *m* de caisse

cash′ bar′ *s* bar *m* payant

cash′ dis′count *s* escompte *m* au comptant

cash′ flow′ *s* argent *m* vif, flux *m* de caisse

cashew [′kæʃu] *s* noix *f* d'acajou, anacarde *m*, cajou *m*; (*tree*) anacardier *m*

cash′ew nut′ *s* noix *f* d'acajou, cajou *m*

cashier [kæ′ʃɪr] *s* caissier *m*

cashmere [′kæʃmɪr] *s* cachemire *m*

cash′ reg′ister *s* caisse *f* enregistreuse

casing [′kesɪŋ] *s* enveloppe *f*, chemise *f*, coffrage *m*; (*of door or window*) chambranle *m*

cask [kæsk] *s* tonneau *m*, fût *m*

casket [′kæskɪt] *s* (*for jewels*) écrin *m*, cassette *f*; (*for interment*) cercueil *m*

casserole [′kæsə,rol] *s* terrine *f*

cassette [kə′sɛt] *s* cassette *f*

cassette′ deck′ *s* platine *f* à cassettes

cassette′ play′er *s* lecteur *m* de cassettes

cassock [′kæsək] *s* soutane *f*

cast [kæst] *s* (*mold*) moule *m*; (*of metal*) fonte *f*; (*of fish line*) lancer *m*; (*throw*) jet *m*; (*for broken limb*) plâtre *m*; (*squint*) léger strabisme *m*; (theat) distribution *f* ‖ *v* (*pret & pp* cast) *tr* fondre, jeter en moule; (*to throw*) lancer; (*a glance*) jeter; (*a play*) distribuer les rôles de; **to be cast in one piece with** venir de fonte avec; **to cast aside** mettre de côté; **to cast lots** tirer au sort; **to cast off** rejeter; **to cast out** mettre à la porte; (*a spell*) exorciser ‖ *intr* (fishing) lancer la canne; **to cast about for** chercher; **to cast off** (naut) larguer les amarres

castanets [,kæstə′nɛts] *spl* castagnettes *fpl*

cast′away′ *adj & s* naufragé *m*

caste [kæst] *s* caste *f*

caster [′kæstər] *s* (*wheel*) roulette *f*; (*cruet stand*) huilier *m*; (*shaker*) saupoudreuse *f*

castigate [′kæstɪ,get] *tr* châtier, corriger

Castile [kæs′til] *s* Castille *f*; **la Castille**

Castilian [kæs′tɪljən] *adj* castillan ‖ *s* (*language*) castillan *m*; (*person*) Castillan *m*

casting [′kæstɪŋ] *s* (*act or process*) fonte *f*; (*thing cast*) pièce *f* fondue; (*act*) lancement *m*; (fishing) pêche *f* au lancer; (theat) distribution *f*

cast′ing rod′ *s* canne *f* à lancer

cast′ i′ron *s* fonte *f*

cast′-i′ron *adj* en fonte

cast′-iron stom′ach *s* estomac *m* d'autruche

castle [′kæsəl] *s* (*palace*) château *m*; (*fortified castle*) château fort; (*chess*) tour *f* ‖ *tr & intr* (chess) roquer

cast'off' *adj* & *s* rejeté *m*

cas'tor oil' ['kæstər] *s* huile *f* de ricin

castrate ['kæstret] *tr* castrer

casual ['kæʒʊ·əl] *adj* casuel; (*indifferent*) insouciant, désinvolte

casually ['kæʒʊ·əli] *adv* nonchalamment, avec désinvolture; (*by chance*) fortuitement

casual·ty ['kæʒʊ·əlti] *s* (*pl* **-ties**) accident *m*; (*person*) accidenté *m*; **casualties** (mil) pertes *fpl*

cas'ualty list' *s* état *m* des pertes

cat [kæt] *s* (*tomcat*) chat *m*; (*female cat*) chatte *f*; (naut) capon *m*; (*shrew*) (coll) cancanière *f*, chipie *f*; **a cat may look at a queen** un chien regarde bien un évêque; **to let the cat out of the bag** (coll) vendre or éventer la mèche; **to rain cats and dogs** (coll) pleuvoir à seaux

CAT [kæt] *s* (acronym) (**computerized axial tomography**) scanographie *f*

CAT' scan'ner *s* (med) scanographe *m*

cataclysm ['kætə,klɪzəm] *s* cataclysme *m*

catacombs ['kætə,komz] *spl* catacombes *fpl*

catalogue ['kætə,ləg] *s* catalogue *m*; (*of university*) annuaire *m* ‖ *tr* cataloguer, classer

Catalonia [,kætə'lonɪ·ə] *s* Catalogne *f*; la Catalogne

catalyst ['kætəlɪst] *s* catalyseur *m*

catapult ['kætə,pʌlt] *s* catapulte *f* ‖ *tr* catapulter

cataract ['kætə,rækt] *s* cataracte *f*

catarrh [kə'tɑr] *s* catarrhe *m*

catastrophe [kə'tæstrəfi] *s* catastrophe *f*

cat'call' *s* huée *f*; (theat) coup *m* de sifflet ‖ *tr* & *intr* (theat) siffler

catch [kætʃ] *s* (*catching and thing caught*) prise *f*, capture *f*; (*on door*) loquet *m*; (*on buckle*) ardillon *m*; (*caught by fisherman*) pêche *f*; (mach) cliquet *m*, chien *m*; **good catch!** (sports) bien rattrapé! **there's a catch to it** (coll) c'est une attrape ‖ *v* (*pret* & *pp* **caught** [kɔt]) *tr* attraper; (*a train; a fish; fire*) prendre; (*a word or sound*) saisir; (*e.g., one's coat*) accrocher; **caught like a rat in a trap** fait comme un rat; **to catch hold of** saisir, s'accrocher à; **to catch s.o. in the act** prendre qn sur le fait; **to catch up** (*in a mistake*) surprendre ‖ *intr* prendre; (*said of fire*) s'allumer, s'enflammer, se prendre; **to catch on** (*a nail, thorn, etc.*) s'accrocher à; (*to understand*) (coll) comprendre; (*to become popular*) (coll) devenir célèbre, devenir populaire; **to catch up** se rattraper; **to catch up with** rattraper

catch'all' *s* débarras *m*, fourre-tout *m*

catch' ba'sin *s* bouche *f* d'égout

catching ['kætʃɪŋ] *adj* contagieux; (*e.g., smile*) communicatif

catch' ques'tion *s* (coll) colle *f*

catch'word' *s* mot *m* de ralliement, slogan *m*; (*cliché*) rengaine *f*, scie *f*; (*at the bottom of page*) réclame *f*; (theat) réplique *f*; (typ) mot-souche *m*

catch·y ['kætʃi] *adj* (*comp* **-ier;** *super* **-iest**) (*tune*) facile à retenir, entraînant; (*question*) insidieux, à traquenard

catechism ['kætɪ,kɪzəm] *s* catéchisme *m*

categorical [,kætɪ'gɔrɪkəl] *adj* catégorique

catego·ry ['kætɪ,gori] *s* (*pl* **-ries**) catégorie *f*

cater ['ketər] *tr* (*e.g., a wedding*) fournir le buffet de ‖ *intr* être fournisseur; **to cater to** pourvoir à; (*to favor*) entourer de prévenances

cat'er-cor'nered ['kætər,kɔrnərd] *adj* diagonal ‖ *adv* diagonalement

caterer ['ketərər] *s* fournisseur *m*, traiteur *m*

caterpillar ['kætər,pɪlər] *s* chenille *f*

cat'erpillar trac'tor *s* autochenille *f*

cat'fish' *s* poisson-chat *m*

cat'gut' *s* boyau *m* de chat; (*string*) corde *f* à boyau, boyau; (surg) catgut *m*

cathedral [kə'θidrəl] *s* cathédrale *f*

catheter ['kæθɪtər] *s* (med) cathéter *m*

catheterization [,kæθɪtərɪ'zeʃən] *s* (surg) cathétérisme *m*

cathode ['kæθod] *s* cathode *m*

catholic ['kæθəlɪk] *adj* (*universal*) catholique; tolérant, large, e.g., **he has a catholic mind** il a l'esprit large, il est fort tolérant ‖ (*cap*) *adj* & *s* catholique *mf*

Catholicism [kə'θɑlɪ'sɪzəm] *s* catholicisme *m*

catholicity [,kæθə'lɪsɪti] *s* catholicité *f*, universalité *f*; (*tolerance*) largeur *f* d'esprit, tolérance *f*

catkin ['kætkɪn] *s* (bot) chaton *m*

cat'nap' *s* petit somme *m*

cat'nip' *s* herbe-aux-chats *f*, cataire *f*

cat-o'-nine-tails [,kætə'naɪn,telz] *s* chat *m* à neuf queues

cat's'-paw' *s* (naut) risée *f*; (coll) dupe *f*

catsup ['kætsəp] *s* = **ketchup**

cattle ['kætəl] *s* bœufs *mpl*; (*including horses*) gros bétail *m*, bestiaux *mpl*

cat'tle car' *s* fourgon *m* à bestiaux

cat'tle cross'ing *s* passage *m* de troupeaux

cat'tle·man *s* (*pl* **-men**) éleveur *m* de bétail

cat'tle thief' *s* voleur *m* de bétail

cat·ty ['kæti] *adj* (*comp* **-tier;** *super* **-tiest**) (coll) cancanier, méchant

cat'ty-cor'ner *adj* (coll) diagonal ‖ *adv* (coll) diagonalement

cat'walk' *s* passerelle *f*

Caucasian [kɔ'keʃən] *adj* caucasien ‖ *s* Caucasien *m*

caucus ['kɔkəs] *s* comité *m* électoral ‖ *intr* se grouper en comité électoral

cauliflower ['kɔlɪ,flaʊ·ər] *s* chou-fleur *m*

caulk [kɔk] *tr* calfater

cause [kɔz] *s* cause *f*; **to have cause to** avoir lieu de ‖ *tr* causer; **to cause to** + *inf* faire + *inf*, e.g., **he caused him to stumble** il l'a fait trébucher

cause'way' *s* chaussée *f*

caustic ['kɔstɪk] *adj* caustique

cauterize ['kɔtə,raɪz] *tr* cautériser

caution ['kɔʃən] *s* prudence *f*, précaution *f*; (*warning*) avertissement *m* ‖ *tr* mettre en garde, avertir

cautious ['kɔʃəs] *adj* prudent, circonspect

cavalcade [,kævəl'ked] s cavalcade f
cavalier [,kævə'lɪr] adj & s cavalier m
caval·ry ['kævəlri] s (pl -ries) cavalerie f
cav'alry·man or **cav'alry·man** s (pl -men' or -men) cavalier m
cave [kev] s caverne f ‖ intr—**to cave in** s'effondrer
cave'-in' s effondrement m
cave' man' s homme m des cavernes; (coll) rustre m, ours m
cavern ['kævərn] s caverne f
caviar ['kævɪ,ɑr] s caviar m
cav·il ['kævɪl] v (pret & pp -iled or -illed; ger -iling or -illing) intr ergoter, chicaner
cavi·ty ['kævɪti] s (pl -ties) cavité f
cavort [kə'vɔrt] intr gambader, caracoler
caw [kɔ] s croassement m ‖ intr croasser, crailler
C.B. ['si'bi] s (letterword) (**citizen band**) bande f publique
C.B. ra'dio s appareil m de radio émetteur-récepteur multicanaux
cease [sis] s cessation f; **without cease** sans cesse ‖ tr & intr cesser; **to cease fire** cesser le feu
cease'-fire' s cessez-le-feu m
ceaseless ['sislɪs] adj incessant, continuel
cedar ['sidər] s cèdre m
cede [sid] tr & intr céder
cedilla [sɪ'dɪlə] s cédille f
ceiling ['silɪŋ] s plafond m; **to hit the ceiling** (coll) sortir de ses gonds
ceil'ing lamp' s plafonnier m
ceil'ing price' s prix m maximum
celebrant ['sɛlɪbrənt] s (eccl) célébrant m
celebrate ['sɛlɪ,bret] tr célébrer
celebrated adj célèbre
celebration [,sɛlɪ'breʃən] s célébration f, fête f
celebri·ty [sɪ'lɛbrɪti] s (pl -ties) célébrité f; (e.g., movie star) vedette f
celery ['sɛləri] m céleri m
celestial [sɪ'lɛstʃəl] adj céleste
celiba·cy ['sɛlibəsi] s (pl -cies) célibat m
celibate ['sɛli,bet] adj & s célibataire mf
cell [sɛl] s cellule f; (of electric battery) élément m
cellar ['sɛlər] s (basement; wine cellar) cave f; (often partly above ground) sous-sol m
cellist or **'cellist** ['tʃɛlɪst] s violoncelliste mf
cel·lo or **'cel·lo** ['tʃɛlo] s (pl -los) violoncelle m
cellophane ['sɛlə,fen] s cellophane f
celluloid ['sɛljə,lɔɪd] s celluloïd m
Celt [sɛlt], [kɛlt] s Celte mf
Celtic ['sɛltɪk], ['kɛltɪk] adj celte, celtique ‖ s celtique m
cement' [sɪ'mɛnt] s ciment m ‖ tr cimenter
cement' mix'er s bétonnière f
cemeter·y ['sɛmɪ,tɛri] s (pl -ies) cimetière m
censer ['sɛnsər] s encensoir m
censor ['sɛnsər] s censeur m ‖ tr censurer
cen'sor·ship' s censure f
censure ['sɛnʃər] s blâme m ‖ tr blâmer

census ['sɛnsəs] s recensement m, dénombrement m; (in Roman Empire) cens m
cen'sus tak'er s recenseur m; (in ancient Rome) censeur m
cent [sɛnt] s cent m; **not to have a red cent to one's name** n'avoir pas un sou vaillant
centaur ['sɛntɔr] s centaure m
centenarian [,sɛntɪ'nɛrɪ·ən] s centenaire mf
centennial [sɛn'tɛnɪ·əl] adj centennal ‖ s centenaire m
center ['sɛntər] adj central ‖ s centre m; (middle) milieu m ‖ tr centrer ‖ intr—**to center on** concentrer sur
cen'ter cit'y s centre m de (la) ville
cen'ter fold' s double page f
centering ['sɛntərɪŋ] s centrage m; (phot) cadrage m
cen'ter·piece' s milieu m de table, surtout m
centigrade ['sɛntɪ,gred] adj & s centigrade m
centimeter ['sɛntɪ,mitər] s centimètre m
centipede ['sɛntɪ,pid] s mille-pattes m, myriapodes mpl
central ['sɛntrəl] adj & s central m
Cen'tral Amer'ica s l'Amérique f centrale
Cen'tral Intel'ligence s la Sûreté, la Sûreté nationale
centralize ['sɛntrə,laɪz] tr centraliser ‖ intr se centraliser
centrifugal [sɛn'trɪfjʊgəl] adj centrifuge
centrifuge ['sɛntrɪ,fjudʒ] s essoreuse f ‖ tr essorer
centu·ry ['sɛntʃəri] s (pl -ries) siècle m
cen'tury-old' adj séculaire
ceramic [sɪ'ræmɪk] adj céramique ‖ **ceramics** s (art) céramique f; spl (objects) céramiques
cereal ['sɪrɪ·əl] adj céréalier ‖ s (grain) céréale f; (oatmeal) flocons mpl d'avoine; (cornflakes) flocons de maïs; (cooked cereal) bouillie f, gruau m
cerebral ['sɛrɪbrəl] adj cérébral
ceremonial [,sɛrɪ'monɪ·əl] adj cérémonial; (e.g., tribal rites) cérémoniel ‖ s cérémonial m
ceremonious [,sɛrɪ'monɪ·əs] adj cérémonieux
ceremo·ny ['sɛrɪ,moni] s (pl -nies) cérémonie f; **to stand on ceremony** faire des cérémonies
certain ['sɜrtən] adj certain; **a certain** certain; **certain people** certains; **for certain** pour sûr, à coup sûr; **to make certain of** s'assurer de
certainly ['sɜrtənli] adv certainement
certain·ty ['sɜrtənti] s (pl -ties) certitude f
certificate [sər'tɪfɪkɪt] s certificat m, acte m; (of birth, of marriage, etc.) bulletin m, acte m, extrait m; (proof) attestation f; (educ) diplôme m
cer'tified cop'y s extrait m; (formula used on documents) pour copie conforme
cer'tified pub'lic account'ant s expert-comptable m, comptable m agréé
certi·fy ['sɜrtɪ,faɪ] v (pret & pp -fied) tr certifier

cervix ['sʌrvɪks] *s* (*pl* **cervices** [sər'vaɪsiz]) nuque *f*

cessation [sɛ'seʃən] *s* cessation *f*, cesse *f*

cesspool ['sɛs,pul] *s* fosse *f* d'aisance, cloaque *m*

Ceylon [sɪ'lɑn] *s* Ceylan *m*

Ceylo·nese [,silə'niz] *adj* cingalais ‖ *s* (*pl* **-nese**) Cingalais *m*

chafe [tʃef] *tr* écorcher, irriter ‖ *intr* s'écorcher, s'irriter

chaff [tʃæf] *s* balle *f*; (*banter*) raillerie *f* ‖ *tr* railler, persifler

chaf'ing dish' *s* réchaud *m* de table, chauffe-plats *m*

chagrin [ʃə'grɪn] *s* mortification *f*, humiliation *f* ‖ *tr* mortifier, humilier

chain [tʃen] *s* chaîne *f* ‖ *tr* enchaîner

chain' gang' *s* forçats *mpl* à la chaîne

chain' reac'tion *s* (phys) réaction *f* en chaîne

chain' saw' *s* tronçonneuse *f*

chain' smok'er *s* fumeur *m* à la file

chain'stitch' *s* point *m* de chaînette

chain' store' *s* magasin *m* à succursales multiples, économat *m*

chair [tʃɛr] *s* (*seat*) chaise *f*; (*held by university professor*) chaire *f*; (*of presiding officer; presiding officer himself*) fauteuil *m*; (*of a committee, department, etc.*) chef *m*; **to take a chair** prendre un siège, s'asseoir; **to take the chair** occuper le fauteuil, présider une assemblée ‖ *tr* présider

chair' lift' *s* télésiège *m*

chair'man *s* (*pl* **-men**) président *m*

chair'man·ship' *s* présidence *f*

chair'wom'an *s* (*pl* **-wom'en**) présidente *f*

chalice ['tʃælɪs] *s* calice *m*

chalk [tʃɔk] *s* craie *f*; **a piece of chalk** une craie, un morceau de craie ‖ *tr* marquer avec de la craie, écrire à la craie

chalk·y ['tʃɔki] *adj* (*comp* **-ier**; *super* **-iest**) crayeux

challenge ['tʃælɪndʒ] *s* (*call, summons*) défi *m*; (*objection*) contestation *f*; (mil) qui-vive *m*; (sports) challenge *m* ‖ *tr* défier; (*to question*) mettre en question, contester; (mil) crier qui-vive à

chamber ['tʃembər] *s* chambre *f*

chamberlain ['tʃembərlɪn] *s* chambellan *m*

cham'ber·maid' *s* femme *f* de chambre

cham·ber mu'sic *s* musique *f* de chambre

Cham'ber of Com'merce *s* syndicat *m* d'initiative

chameleon [kə'milɪ·ən] *s* caméléon *m*

chamfer ['tʃæmfər] *s* chanfrein *m* ‖ *tr* chanfreiner

cham·ois ['ʃæmi] *s* (*pl* **-ois**) chamois *m*

champ [tʃæmp] *s* mâchonnement *m* ‖ *tr* mâcher bruyamment; **to champ at the bit** ronger son frein

champagne [ʃæm'pen] *s* champagne *m* ‖ (*cap*) *adj* champenois ‖ (*cap*) *s* Champagne *f*; la Champagne

champion ['tʃæmpɪ·ən] *s* champion *m* ‖ *tr* se faire le champion de, défendre

cham'pion·ship' *s* championnat *m*

chance [tʃæns] *adj* fortuit, de rencontre ‖ *s* (*luck*) hasard *m*; (*good luck*) chance *f*, coup *m* de chance; (*possibility*) chance, possibilité *f*, e.g., **one chance in four** une chance sur quatre; (*opportunity*) occasion *f*, chance; **by chance** par hasard, fortuitement; **chances** chances *fpl*, sort *m*; **to take a chance** encourir un risque; acheter un billet de loterie; **to take chances** jouer gros jeu ‖ *tr* hasarder, risquer ‖ *intr*—**to chance to** venir à, avoir l'occasion de; **to chance upon** rencontrer par hasard

chance' acquaint'ance *s* connaissance *f* de rencontre

chancel ['tʃænsəl] *s* chœur *m*, sanctuaire *m*

chancellor·y ['tʃænsələri] *s* (*pl* **-ies**) chancellerie *f*

chancellor ['tʃænsələr] *s* chancelier *m*, ministre *m*

chancre ['ʃæŋkər] *s* chancre *m*

chandelier [,ʃændə'lɪr] *s* lustre *m*

change [tʃendʒ] *s* changement *m*; (*coins*) pièces *fpl* rendues, monnaie *f*; **change in the wind** saute *f* de vent; **change of address** changement de domicile; **change of clothes** vêtements *mpl* de rechange; **for a change** comme distraction; pour changer ‖ *tr* changer; changer de, e.g., **to change religions** changer de culte; **to change sides** tourner casaque ‖ *intr* changer; (*said of voice at puberty*) muer; **to change over** (*e.g., from one system to another*) passer

changeable ['tʃendʒəbəl] *adj* changeable; (*weather*) variable; (*character*) changeant, mobile

changeless ['tʃendʒlɪs] *adj* immuable

change' of life' *s* retour *m* d'âge

change' of voice' *s* mue *f*

change'o'ver *s* changement *m*, renversement *m*, relève *f*

change' purse' *s* porte-monnaie *m*

change' return' *s* remboursement *m* dans le bas de l'appareil, retour *m* de monnaies

chan·nel ['tʃænəl] *s* (*body of water joining two others*) canal *m*; (*bed of river*) chenal *m*; (*means of communication*) voie *f*, canal; (*passage*) conduit *m*; (*groove*) cannelure *f*; (*strait*) bras *m* de mer; (*for trade*) débouché *m*; (rad) canal; (rad, telv) chaîne *f*; (telv) canal (Canad); **through channels** par la voie hiérarchique, par la filière ‖ *v* (*pret & pp* **-neled** *or* **-nelled**; *ger* **-neling** *or* **-nelling**) *tr* creuser, canneler

Chan'nel Is'lands *spl* îles *fpl* Anglo-Normandes

chant [tʃænt] *s* (*song; singing*) chant *m*; (*monotonous chant*) mélopée *f*; (*chanted by demonstrators*) chant scandé; (mus) psalmodie *f*, plain-chant *m* ‖ *tr & intr* psalmodier

chanter ['tʃæntər] *s* chantre *m*

chantey ['ʃænti] *s* chanson *f* de bord

chaos ['ke·ɑs] *s* chaos *m*

chaotic [ke'ɑtɪk] *adj* chaotique

chap [tʃæp] *s* (*fissure, crack*) crevasse *f*, gerçure *f*; (coll) type *m*, individu *m*; **poor**

chap (coll) pauvre vieux *m*; pauvre garçon *m* ‖ *v* (*pret & pp* **chapped**; *ger* **chapping**) *tr* crevasser, gercer ‖ *intr* se crevasser, se gercer

chapel [ˈtʃæpəl] *s* chapelle *f*; (*in a house*) oratoire *m*; (*Protestant chapel*) temple *m*

chaperon [ˈʃæpə‚rɔn] *s* chaperon *m*, duègne *f* ‖ *tr* chaperonner

chaplain [ˈtʃæplɪn] *s* aumônier *m*

chaplet [ˈtʃæplɪt] *s* chapelet *m*

chapter [ˈtʃæptər] *s* chapitre *m*; (*of an association*) bureau *m* régional

char [tʃɑr] *v* (*pret & pp* **charred**; *ger* **charring**) *tr & intr* charbonner; **to become charred** se charbonner, se carboniser

character [ˈkærɪktər] *s* caractère *m*; (*theat*) personnage *m*; (*typ*) signe *m*; (*coll*) type *m*, sujet *m*, numéro *m*, phénomène *m*

char′acter ac′tor *s* acteur *m* de genre

characteristic [‚kærɪktəˈrɪstɪk] *adj & s* caractéristique *f*

characterize [ˈkærɪktə‚raɪz] *tr* caractériser, typer

char′acter ref′erence *s* certificat *m* de moralité, certificat de bonne vie et mœurs

char′coal′ *s* charbon *m* de bois

char′coal burn′er *s* charbonnier *m*

char′coal pen′cil *s* charbon *m*, crayon *m* de fusain

charge [tʃɑrdʒ] *s* (*responsibility*) charge *f*; (*cost*) prix *m*; (*person cared for*) personne *f* à charge; (*thing cared for*) chose *f* à charge; (*accusing*) accusation *f*; (*against a defendant*) chef *m* d'accusation; (*made to a jury*) résumé *m*; (*mil*) charge; **on a charge of** sous l'inculpation de; **to reverse the charges** téléphoner en p.c.v.; **to take charge of** se charger de; **without charge** gratis ‖ *tr* charger; **to charge s.o. s.th. for s.th.** prendre *or* demander q.ch. à qn pour q.ch.; **to charge to s.o.'s account** mettre sur le compte de qn ‖ *intr* (mil) charger; **to charge down on** foncer sur

charge′ account′ *s* compte *m* courant

charger [ˈtʃɑrdʒər] *s* cheval *m* de bataille; (elec) chargeur *m*

chariot [ˈtʃærɪ‚ət] *s* char *m*

charisma [kəˈrɪzmə] *s* charme *m*, don *m* de plaire; (theol) charisme *m*

charitable [ˈtʃærɪtəbəl] *adj* charitable

chari·ty [ˈtʃærɪti] *s* (*pl* **-ties**) (*kindness*) charité *f*; (*action*) acte *m* de charité; (*alms*) bienfaisance *f*, aumônes *fpl*, charité; (*institution*) société *f or* œuvre *f* de bienfaisance; **for charity's sake** par charité

charlatan [ˈʃɑrlətən] *s* charlatan *m*

charm [tʃɑrm] *s* charme *m*; (*e.g., on a bracelet*) breloque *f*, porte-bonheur *m* ‖ *tr* charmer

charming [ˈtʃɑrmɪŋ] *adj* charmeur, charmant

charnel [ˈtʃɑrnəl] *adj* de charnier ‖ *s* charnier *m*, ossuaire *m*

chart [tʃɑrt] *s* (*map*) carte *f*; (*graph*) dessin *m* graphique; (*diagram*) diagramme *m*;

(*table*) tableau *m* ‖ *tr* inscrire sur un dessin graphique; (naut) porter sur une carte, dresser la carte de

charter [ˈtʃɑrtər] *s* (*document*) charte *f*; (*authorization*) statuts *mpl*; (*of a bank*) privilège; (*chartering of a boat, bus, plane, etc.*) affrètement *m* ‖ *tr* accorder une charte à; (*a ship*) affréter, noliser; (*a bus*) louer

char′ter flight′ *s* vol *m* en charter, vol *m* à la demande

char′ter mem′ber *s* membre *m* fondateur

char′ter plane′ *s* charter *m*, avion *m* affété, avion nolisé

char′wom′an *s* (*pl* **-wom′en**) nettoyeuse *f*

chase [tʃes] *s* chasse *f*, poursuite *f*; (*for printing*) châssis *m* ‖ *tr* chasser; (*a gem*) enchâsser; (*gold*) ciseler; (*metal*) repousser; **to chase away** chasser ‖ *intr*—**to chase after** pourchasser, poursuivre

chaser [ˈtʃesər] *s* chasseur *m*; (*of women*) (coll) coureur *m*; (*taken after an alcoholic drink*) (coll) rince-gueule *m*

chasm [ˈkæzəm] *s* abîme *m*

chas·sis [ˈtʃæsi] *s* (*pl* **-sis** [siz]) châssis *m*

chaste [tʃest] *adj* chaste

chasten [ˈtʃesən] *tr* châtier

chastise [tʃæsˈtaɪz] *tr* châtier, corriger

chastisement [tʃæsˈtaɪzmənt] *s* châtiment *m*

chastity [ˈtʃæstɪti] *s* chasteté *f*

chat [tʃæt] *s* causerie *f*, causette *f* ‖ *v* (*pret & pp* **chatted**; *ger* **chatting**) *intr* causer, bavarder

château [ʃæto] *s* château *m*, manoir *m*, castel *m*

chattel [ˈtʃætəl] *s* bien *m* meuble, objet *m* mobilier

chatter [ˈtʃætər] *s* bavardage *m*, caquetage *m* ‖ *intr* bavarder, caqueter; (*said of teeth*) claquer

chat′ter·box′ *s* bavard *m*, babillard *m*

chauffeur [ˈʃofər] *s* chauffeur *m*

chauvinistic [‚ʃovɪˈnɪstɪk] *adj* chauvin

cheap [tʃip] *adj* bon marché; (coll) honteux; **to get off cheap** (coll) en être quitte à bon compte

cheapen [ˈtʃipən] *tr* baisser le prix de; diminuer la valeur de

cheap′skate′ *s* (slang) rat *m*

cheat [tʃit] *s* tricheur *m*, fraudeur *m* ‖ *tr* tricher, frauder ‖ *intr* (*e.g., at cards*) tricher; (*e.g., in an examination*) frauder

cheating [ˈtʃitɪŋ] *s* tricherie *f*, fraude *f*

check [tʃɛk] *s* (*stopping*) arrêt *m*; (*brake*) frein *m*; (*supervision*) contrôle *m*, vérification *f*; (*in a restaurant*) addition *f*; (*drawn on a bank*) chèque *m*; (*e.g., of a chessboard*) carreau *m*; (*of the king in chess*) échec *m*; (*for baggage*) bulletin *m*; (*pass-out check*) contremarque *f*; (*chip, counter*) jeton *m*; **in check** en échec ‖ *tr* arrêter, freiner; contrôler, vérifier; (*baggage*) faire enregistrer; (*e.g., one's coat*) mettre au vestiaire; (*the king in chess*) faire échec à; **to check off** pointer, cocher ‖ *intr* s'arrêter; **to check in** (*at a hotel*) s'inscrire sur le registre; **to check out** (*of* *a hotel)* régler sa note; **to check up on** contrôler, examiner

check′book′ *s* carnet *m* de chèques, chéquier *m*

checked *adj (checkered)* à carreaux; *(syllable)* entravé

checker [′tʃɛkər] *s (inspector)* contrôleur *m; (piece used in game)* pion *m; (square of checkerboard)* carreau *m;* **checkers** jeu *m* de dames ‖ *tr (to divide in squares)* quadriller; *(to scatter here and there)* diaprer

check′er·board′ *s* damier *m*

checkered *adj (divided into squares)* quadrillé, à carreaux; *(varied)* varié, accidenté; *(career, life)* plein de vicissitudes, mouvementé

check′girl′ *s* préposée *f* au vestiaire

check′ing account′ *s* compte *m* en banque

check′ list′ *s* liste *f* de contrôle, liste de vérification

check′ mark′ *s* trait *m* de repère, repère *m,* coche *f*

check′mate′ *s* échec et mat *m;* (fig) échec *m* ‖ *tr* faire échec et mat à, mater ‖ *intr* faire échec et mat, mater ‖ *interj* échec et mat!

check′-out count′er *s* caisse *f* de sortie; *(in supermarket)* caisse de supermarché

check′point′ *s* contrôle *m* de police

check′room′ *s (cloakroom)* vestiaire *m; (baggage room)* consigne *f*

check′up′ *s* vérification *f,* examen *m* complet; (med) bilan *m* de santé

cheek [tʃik] *s* joue *f;* (coll) aplomb *m,* toupet *m*

cheek′bone′ *s* pommette *f*

cheep [tʃip] *intr* piauler

cheer [tʃɪr] *s* bonne humeur *f,* gaieté *f;* encouragement *m,* e.g., **word of cheer** parole *f* d'encouragement; **cheers** acclamations *fpl,* bravos *mpl,* vivats *mpl;* **three cheers for . . .!** vive . . .!; **to give three cheers** pousser trois hourras ‖ *tr (to cheer up)* encourager, égayer; *(to applaud)* acclamer, applaudir ‖ *intr* pousser des vivats, applaudir; **cheer up!** courage!

cheerful [′tʃɪrfəl] *adj* de bonne humeur, gai; *(place)* d'aspect agréable

cheerfully [′tʃɪrfəli] *adv* gaiement; *(willingly)* de bon cœur

cheer′lead′er *s* chef *m* de claque

cheerless [′tʃɪrlɪs] *adj* morne, triste

cheese [tʃiz] *s* fromage *m*

cheese′cake′ *s* (slang) les pin up *fpl*

cheese′ cake′ *s* soufflé *m* au fromage, tarte *f* au fromage

cheese′cloth′ *s* gaze *f*

chees·y [′tʃizi] *adj (comp* -ier; *super* -iest) caséeux; *(slang)* miteux

cheetah [′tʃitə] *s* guépard *m*

chef [ʃɛf] *s* chef *m* de cuisine, maître queux *m*

chemical [′kɛmɪkəl] *adj* chimique ‖ *s* produit *m* chimique

chemist [′kɛmɪst] *s* chimiste *mf*

chemistry [′kɛmɪstri] *s* chimie *f*

cherish [′tʃɛrɪʃ] *tr* chérir; *(an idea)* nourrir; *(a hope)* caresser

cher·ry [′tʃɛri] *s (pl* -ries) cerise *f; (tree)* cerisier *m*

cher′ry or′chard *s* cerisaie *f*

cher′ry tree′ *s* cerisier *m*

cher·ub [′tʃɛrəb] *s (pl* -ubim [əbɪm]) chérubin *m* ‖ *s (pl* -ubs) (fig) chérubin *m*

chess [tʃɛs] *s* échecs *mpl;* **to play chess** jouer aux échecs

chess′board′ *s* échiquier *m*

chess′ piece′ *s* pièce *f* du jeu d'échecs; *(other than pawn)* figure *f*

chess′ set′ *s* échecs *mpl*

chest [tʃɛst] *s* caisse *f; (of drawers)* commode *f;* (anat) poitrine *f;* **to get s.th. off one's chest** (coll) se déboutonner, dire ce qu'on a sur le cœur

chest′ mic′rophone *s* micro-plastron *m*

chestnut [′tʃɛsnət] *adj (color)* châtain ‖ *s (color)* châtain *m; (nut)* châtaigne *f,* marron *m; (tree)* châtaignier *m*

chest′ of drawers′ *s* commode *f,* chiffonnier *m*

cheval′ glass′ [ʃə′væl] *s* psyché *f*

chevron [′ʃɛvrən] *s* chevron *m*

chew [tʃu] *tr* mâcher; *(tobacco)* chiquer

chewing [′tʃu·ɪŋ] *s* mastication *f*

chew′ing gum′ *s* gomme *f* à mâcher, chewing-gum *m*

chicaner·y [ʃɪ′kɛnəri] *s (pl* -ies) truc *m,* ruse *f,* artifice *m*

chick [tʃɪk] *s* poussin *m; (girl)* (slang) tendron *m,* nana *f*

chickadee [′tʃɪkə‚di] *s (Parus atricapillus)* mésange *f* boréale

chicken [′tʃɪkən] *s* poulet *m;* **to be chicken** (slang) avoir la frousse ‖ *intr*—**to chicken out** (slang) caner

chick′en coop′ *s* poulailler *m*

chick′en-heart′ed *adj* froussard, poltron

chick′en pox′ *s* varicelle *f*

chick′en stew′ *s* poule-au-pot *m*

chick′en wire′ *s* treillis *m* métallique

chick′pea′ *s* pois *m* chiche

chico·ry [′tʃɪkəri] *s (pl* -ries) chicorée *f*

chide [tʃaɪd] *v (pret* **chided** or **chid** [tʃɪd]; *pp* **chided, chid,** or **chidden** [′tʃɪdən]) *tr & intr* gronder

chief [tʃif] *adj* principal, en chef ‖ *s* chef *m; (boss)* (coll) patron *m*

chief′ exec′utive *s* chef *m* de l'exécutif

chief′ jus′tice *s* président *m* de la Cour suprême

chiefly [′tʃifli] *adv* principalement

chief′ of police′ *s* préfet *m* de police

chief′ of staff′ *s* chef *m* d'état-major

chief′ of state′ *s* chef *m* d'État

chieftain [′tʃiftən] *s* chef *m*

chiffon [ʃɪ′fɑn] *s* mousseline *f* de soie

chiffonier [‚ʃɪfə′nɪr] *s* chiffonnier *m*

chilblain [′tʃɪl‚blen] *s* engelure *f*

child [tʃaɪld] *s (pl* **children** [′tʃɪldrən]) enfant *mf;* **with child** enceinte

child′ molest′ing [mo′lɛstɪŋ] *s* détournement *m* de mineur

child′birth′ *s* accouchement *m*

child'hood s enfance f
childish [ˈtʃaɪldɪʃ] adj enfantin, puéril
child' la'bor s travail m des enfants
child'like' adj enfantin, d'enfant
child's' play' s jeu m d'enfant; **it's child's play** c'est l'enfance de l'art
child' wel'fare s protection f de l'enfance
Chile [ˈtʃɪli] s le Chili
chil'i pep'per [ˈtʃɪli] s piment m
chill [tʃɪl] adj & s froid m; **sudden chill** saisissement m, coup m de froid; **to take the chill off** faire tiédir ‖ tr refroidir; (a person) transir, faire frisonner; (wine) frapper
chill' fac'tor s indice m de refroidissement
chill·y [ˈtʃɪli] adj (comp -ier; super -iest) froid; (sensitive to cold) frileux; **it is chilly** il fait frisquet, il fait frais
chime [tʃaɪm] s coup m de son; **chimes** (at doorway) sonnerie f; (in bell tower) carillon m ‖ tr & intr carillonner; **to chime in** faire chorus
chimera [kaɪˈmɪrə] s chimère f
chiming [ˈtʃaɪmɪŋ] s carillonnement m, sonnerie f
chimney [ˈtʃɪmni] s cheminée f; (of lamp) verre m
chim'ney pot' s abat-vent m, mitre f
chim'ney sweep' s ramoneur m
chimpanzee [tʃɪmˈpænzi] s chimpanzé m
chin [tʃɪn] s menton m
china [ˈtʃaɪnə] s porcelaine f de Chine; **China** Chine f; la Chine
chi'na clos'et s vitrine f
chi'na·ware' s porcelaine f
Chi·nese [tʃaɪˈniz] adj chinois ‖ s (language) chinois m ‖ s (pl -nese) Chinois m (person)
Chi'nese lan'tern s lanterne f vénitienne, lampion m
chink [tʃɪŋk] s fente f, crevasse f; **chink in one's armor** (coll) défaut m de la cuirasse
chin' strap' s sous-mentonnière f, jugulaire f
chip [tʃɪp] s fragment m; (of wood) copeau m, éclat m; (in gambling) jeton m; (electron) microplaquette f, pastille f, chip m; **chips** (potato chips) pommes fpl chips; (Brit) frites fpl; **to be a chip off the old block** (coll) chasser de race, être un rejeton de la vieille souche ‖ v (pret & pp **chipped**; ger **chipping**) tr enlever un copeau à ‖ intr s'écailler; **to chip in** contribuer
chipmunk [ˈtʃɪp,mʌŋk] s tamias m rayé
chipper [ˈtʃɪpər] adj (coll) en forme, guilleret
chiropodist [kaɪˈrɑpədɪst] s pédicure mf
chiropractor [ˈkaɪrə,præktər] s chiropracteur m
chirp [tʃʌrp] s gazouillis m, pépiement m ‖ intr gazouiller, pépier
chis·el [ˈtʃɪzəl] s ciseau m ‖ v (pret & pp **-eled** or **-elled**; ger **-eling** or **-elling**) tr ciseler; (a person) (slang) escroquer, carotter; **to chisel s.o. out of s.th.** (slang) escroquer q.ch. à qn

chiseler [ˈtʃɪzələr] s ciseleur m; (slang) escroc m
chit [tʃɪt] s note f, ticket m; (coll) gamin m
chit'-chat' s bavardage m
chivalrous [ˈʃɪvəlrəs] adj honorable, courtois; (lit) chevaleresque
chivalry [ˈʃɪvəlri] s (of Middle Ages) chevalerie f; (politeness) courtoisie f, galanterie f
chive [tʃaɪv] s ciboulette f, civette f
chloride [ˈklɔraɪd] s chlorure m
chlorinate [ˈklɔrɪ,net] tr (water) verduniser
chlorination [,klɔrɪˈneʃən] s verdunisation f
chlorine [ˈklɔrin] s chlore m
chloroform [ˈklɔrə,fɔrm] s chloroforme m ‖ tr chloroformer
chlorophyll [ˈklɔrəfɪl] s chlorophylle f
chock [tʃɑk] s cale f; (naut) poulie f ‖ tr caler
chock'-full' adj bondé, comble, bourré
chocolate [ˈtʃɔkəlɪt] adj & s chocolat m
choc'olate bar' s tablette f de chocolat
choice [tʃɔɪs] adj de choix, choisi ‖ m choix m; **by choice** par goût, volontairement
choir [kwaɪr] s chœur m
choir'boy' s enfant m de chœur
choir'mas'ter s chef m de chœur; (eccl) maître m de chapelle
choir' robe' s soutanelle f
choke [tʃok] s (aut) starter m ‖ tr étouffer; (to obstruct) obstruer, boucher; **to choke back, down,** or **off** étouffer; **to choke up** obstruer, engorger ‖ intr étouffer; **to choke up** (e.g., with tears) étouffer
choke' coil' s (elec) bobine f de réactance
choker [ˈtʃokər] s (scarf) foulard m; (necklace) collier m court
choking [ˈtʃokɪŋ] s étouffement m
cholera [ˈkɑlərə] s choléra m
choleric [ˈkɑlərɪk] adj coléreux
cholesterol [kəˈlɛstə,rol] s cholestérol m
choose [tʃuz] v (pret **chose** [tʃoz]; pp **chosen** [ˈtʃozən]) tr & intr choisir
choos·y [ˈtʃuzi] adj (comp -ier; super -iest) (coll) difficile à plaire, chipoteur
chop [tʃɑp] s (blow) coup m de hache; (culin) côtelette f; **to lick one's chops** (coll) se lécher ou s'essuyer les babines ‖ v (pret & pp **chopped**; ger **chopping**) tr hacher, couper; **to chop down** abattre; **to chop off** trancher, couper; **to chop up** couper en morceaux, hacher ‖ intr (said of waves) clapoter
chopper [ˈtʃɑpər] s (of butcher) couperet m; (coll) hélicoptère m; **choppers** (slang) les dents fpl
chop'ping block' s billot m, hachoir m
chop·py [ˈtʃɑpi] adj (comp -pier; ger -piest) agité; (waves) clapoteux
chop'stick' s baguette f, bâtonnet m
choral [ˈkɔrəl] adj choral
chorale [koˈrɑl] s choral m
cho'ral soci'ety s chorale f
chord [kɔrd] s accord m; (geom) corde f
chore [tʃor] s devoir m; (burdensome chore) corvée f, besogne f

choreography [ˌkorɪˈɑgrəfi] s chorégraphie f

chorister [ˈkɔrɪstər] s choriste mf

chortle [ˈtʃɔrtəl] intr glousser

chorus [ˈkorəs] s (group) chœur m, chorale f; (of song) refrain m; (of protest) concert m ‖ tr répéter en chœur, faire chorus

cho′rus boy′ s boy m

cho′rus girl′ s girl f

cho′sen few′ [ˈtʃozən] s élite f

chow [tʃaʊ] s (dog) chow-chow m; (mil) boustifaille f, mangeaille f

chow′-chow′ s (culin) macédoine f assaisonnée

chowder [ˈtʃaʊdər] s soupe f au poisson

Christ [kraɪst] s Christ m; le Christ

christen [ˈkrɪsən] tr baptiser

Christendom [ˈkrɪsəndəm] s chrétienté f

christening [ˈkrɪsənɪŋ] s baptême m

Christian [ˈkrɪstʃən] adj & s chrétien m

Christianity [ˌkrɪstʃɪˈænɪti] s christianisme m

Christianize [ˈkrɪstʃəˈnaɪz] tr christianiser

Christ′ian name′ s nom m de baptême

Christmas [ˈkrɪsməs] adj de Noël ‖ s Noël m; **Merry Christmas!** Joyeux Noël!

Christ′mas card′ s carte f de Noël

Christ′mas car′ol s chanson f de Noël, chant m de Noël; (eccl) cantique m de Noël

Christ′mas Day′ s le jour de Noël

Christ′mas Eve′ s la veille de Noël

Christ′mas gift′ s cadeau m de Noël

Christ′mas tree′ s arbre m de Noël

Christ′mas tree lights′ spl guirlandes fpl

chromatic [kroˈmætɪk] adj chromatique

chrome [krom] adj chromé ‖ s acier m chromé; (color) jaune m; (chem) chrome m ‖ tr chromer

chromium [ˈkromɪ·əm] s chrome m

chromosome [ˈkromə‚som] s chromosome m

chronic [ˈkranɪk] adj chronique

chronicle [ˈkranɪkəl] s chronique f ‖ tr faire la chronique de

chronicler [ˈkranɪklər] s chroniqueur m

chronologic(al) [ˌkranəˈladʒɪk(əl)] adj chronologique

chronolo·gy [krəˈnalədʒi] s (pl **-gies**) chronologie f

chronometer [krəˈnamɪtər] s chronomètre m

chrysanthemum [krɪˈsænθɪməm] s chrysanthème m

chub·by [ˈtʃʌbi] adj (comp **-bier**; super **-biest**) joufflu, potelé, dodu

chuck [tʃʌk] s (tap, blow, etc.) petite tape f; (under the chin) caresse f sous le menton; (of lathe) mandrin m; (bottom chuck and chuck rib) paleron m; (top chuck roast and chuck rib) entrecôte f ‖ tr tapoter; **to chuck away** jeter

chuckle [ˈtʃʌkəl] s gloussement m, petit rire m ‖ intr glousser, rire tout bas

chum [tʃʌm] s (coll) copain m ‖ v (pret & pp **chummed**; ger **chumming**) intr—**to chum around with** (coll) fraterniser avec

chum·my [ˈtʃʌmi] adj (comp **-mier**; super **-miest**) intime, familier

chump [tʃʌmp] s (slang) ballot m, lourdaud m

chunk [tʃʌŋk] s gros morceau m; (e.g., of wood) bloc m

church [tʃʌrtʃ] s église f

church′go′er s pratiquant m

church′man s (pl **-men**) (clergyman) ecclésiastique m; (layman) membre m d'une église, fidèle mf, paroissien m

church′ mem′ber s fidèle mf

church′ ser′vice s office m, culte m

church′yard′ s cimetière m

churlish [ˈtʃʌrlɪʃ] adj rustre, grossier; (out of sorts) grincheux

churn [tʃʌrn] s baratte f ‖ tr (cream) baratter; (e.g., water) agiter; **to churn butter** battre le beurre ‖ intr bouillonner

chute [ʃut] s (inclined channel or trough) glissière f; (of river) rapide m, chute f d'eau; (aer) parachute m

CIA [ˈsiˈaɪˈe] s (letterword) (central intelligence agency) (equivalent French agency) S.D.E.C. (service de documentation extérieure et de contre-espionnage)

Cicero [ˈsisə‚ro] s Cicéron m

cider [ˈsaɪdər] s cidre m

cigar [sɪˈgɑr] s cigare m

cigarette [ˌsɪgəˈret] s cigarette f

cigarette′ butt′ s mégot m

cigarette′ case′ s étui m à cigarettes

cigarette′ fiend′ s fumeur m enragé

cigarette′ hold′er s fume-cigarette m

cigarette′ light′er s briquet m

cigar′ hold′er s fume-cigare m

cigar′ store′ s bureau m de tabac

cinch [sɪntʃ] s (of saddle) sangle f; **it's a cinch** (coll) c'est couru d'avance ‖ tr sangler; (to make sure of) (slang) assurer

cinder [ˈsɪndər] s cendre f ‖ tr cendrer

Cinderella [ˌsɪndəˈrɛlə] s la Cendrillon f

cin′der track′ s piste f cendrée

cinema [ˈsɪnəmə] s cinéma m

cinnamon [ˈsɪnəmən] s cannelle f

cipher [ˈsaɪfər] s zéro m; (code) chiffre m; **in cipher** en chiffres ‖ tr & intr chiffrer

circle [ˈsʌrkəl] s cercle m; (coterie) milieu m, monde m; **to have circles around the eyes** avoir les yeux cernés ‖ tr ceindre, entourer; (to travel around) faire le tour de

circuit [ˈsʌrkɪt] s circuit m; (of judge) tournée f

cir′cuit break′er s (elec) disjoncteur m

cir′cuit court′ s cour f d'assises

circuitous [sərˈkju·ɪtəs] adj détourné, indirect

circular [ˈsʌrkjələr] adj & s circulaire f

circulate [ˈsʌrkjə‚let] tr faire circuler ‖ intr circuler

circulation [ˌsʌrkjəˈleʃən] s circulation f; (of newspaper) tirage m

circumcise [ˈsʌrkəm‚saɪz] tr circoncire

circumcision [ˌsʌrkəmˈsɪʒən] s circoncision f

circumference [sər'kʌmfərəns] *s* circonférence *f*

circumflex ['sʌrkəm,flɛks] *adj & s* circonflexe *m*

circumlocution [,sʌrkəmlo'kjuʃən] *s* circonlocution *f*

circumscribe [,sʌrkəm'skraɪb] *tr* circonscrire

circumspect ['sʌrkəm,spɛkt] *adv* circonspect

circumstance ['sʌrkəm,stæns] *s* circonstance *f*; (*pomp*) cérémonie *f*; **in easy circumstances** aisé; **under no circumstance** sous aucun prétexte; **under the circumstances** dans ces conditions

circumstantial [,sʌrkəm'stænʃəl] *adj* (*derived from circumstances*) circonstanciel; (*detailed*) circonstancié

cir'cumstan'tial ev'idence *s* preuves *fpl* indirectes

circumvent [,sʌrkəm'vɛnt] *tr* circonvenir

circus ['sʌrkəs] *s* cirque *m*; (Brit) rond-point *m*

cirrhosis [sɪ'rosɪs] *s* cirrhose *f*

cistern ['sɪstərn] *s* citerne *f*

citadel ['sɪtədəl] *s* citadelle *f*

citation [saɪ'teʃən] *s* citation *f*; (*award*) présentation *f*, mention *f*

cite [saɪt] *tr* citer

cither ['sɪθər] *s* cithare *f*

citified ['sɪtɪ,faɪd] *adj* urbain

citizen ['sɪtɪzən] *s* citoyen *m*

citizen·ry ['sɪtɪzənri] *s* (*pl* **-ries**) citoyens *mpl*

cit'izen·ship' *s* citoyenneté *f*

citric ['sɪtrɪk] *adj* citrique

citron ['sɪtrən] *s* cédrat *m*; (*tree*) cédratier *m*

citronella [,sɪtrə'nɛlə] *s* citronnelle *f*

cit'rus fruit' ['sɪtrəs] *s* agrumes *mpl*

cit·y ['sɪti] *s* (*pl* **-ies**) ville *f*; **the City** (*district within ancient boundaries*) la Cité

cit'y coun'cil *s* conseil *m* municipal

cit'y hall' *s* hôtel *m* de ville

cit'y plan'ner *s* urbaniste *mf*

cit'y plan'ning *s* urbanisme *m*

cit'y room' *s* (journ) salle *f* de rédaction

civ'et cat' ['sɪvɪt] *s* civette *f*

civic ['sɪvɪk] *adj* civique; **civics** instruction *f* civique

civies ['sɪviz] *spl* (coll) vêtements *mpl* civils; **in civies** en civil, en bourgeois

civil ['sɪvɪl] *adj* civil; (*courteous*) poli

civ'il defense' *s* protection *f* civile

civ'il engineer'ing *s* génie *m* civil

civilian [sɪ'vɪljən] *adj & s* civil *m*

civ'ilian life' *s* vie *f* civile

civili·ty [sɪ'vɪlɪti] *s* (*pl* **-ties**) civilité *f*

civilization [,sɪvɪlɪ'zeʃən] *s* civilisation *f*

civilize ['sɪvɪ,laɪz] *tr* civiliser

civ'il rights' *spl* droits *mpl* civiques, droits politiques

civ'il ser'vant *s* fonctionnaire *mf*

civ'il serv'ice *s* fonction *f* publique

civ'il war' *s* guerre *f* civile; **Civil War** (*of the United States*) Guerre de Sécession

clack [klæk] *s* claquement *m* ‖ *intr* claquer

clad [klæd] *adj* vêtu, habillé

claim [klem] *s* (*request*) demande *f*; (*to a right*) revendication *f*; (*assertion*) affirmation *f*; (*right*) droit *m*, titre *m*; (*insurance claim*) déclaration de sinistre, demande d'indemnité; (*in prospecting*) concession *f* ‖ *tr* (*a right*) réclamer, revendiquer; (*to require*) exiger, demander; **to claim that . . .** prétendre que . . .; **to claim to** prétendre

claimant ['klemənt] *s* prétendant *m*, ayant droit *m*

clairvoyance [klɛr'vɔɪ·əns] *s* voyance *f*, seconde vue *f*; (*keen insight*) clairvoyance *f*

clairvoyant [klɛr'vɔɪ·ənt] *adj* clairvoyant ‖ *s* voyante *f*; voyant *m* ·

clam [klæm] *s* palourde *f* ‖ *v* (*pret & pp* **clammed**; *ger* **clamming**) *intr*—**to clam up** (slang) se taire

clam'bake' *s* pique-nique *m* aux palourdes

clamber ['klæmbər] *intr* grimper; **to clamber over** or **up** escalader

clam·my ['klæmi] *adj* (*comp* **-mier**; *super* **-miest**) moite; (*clinging*) collant

clamor ['klæmər] *s* clameur *f* ‖ *intr* vociférer; **to clamor for** réclamer

clamorous ['klæmərəs] *adj* bruyant

clamp [klæmp] *s* crampon *m*, agrafe *f*; (med) clamp *m* ‖ *tr* fixer, attacher; **to clamp together** cramponner ‖ *intr*—**to clamp down on** (coll) visser

clan [klæn] *s* clan *m*

clandestine [klæn'dɛstɪn] *adj* clandestin

clang [klæŋ] *s* bruit *m* métallique, choc *m* retentissant, cliquetis *m* ‖ *tr* faire résonner ‖ *intr* résonner

clank [klæŋk] *s* bruit *m* sec, bruit métallique, cliquetis *m* ‖ *tr* faire résonner ‖ *intr* résonner

clannish ['klænɪʃ] *adj* partisan

clap [klæp] *s* (*sound*) bruit *m* sec, claquement *m*; (*action*) tape *f*; (*with the hands*) battement *m* ‖ *v* (*pret & pp* **clapped**; *ger* **clapping**) *tr* battre; (*into jail*) (coll) fourrer; **to clap the hands** claquer or battre les mains ‖ *intr* applaudir, claquer

clapper ['klæpər] *s* (*person*) applaudisseur *m*; (*of bell*) battant *m*

clapping ['klæpɪŋ] *s* (*applause*) applaudissements *mpl*

claque [klæk] *s* (*paid clappers*) claque *f*; (*crush hat*) claque *m*

claret ['klærɪt] *s* bordeaux *m*

clari·fy ['klærɪ,faɪ] *v* (*pret & pp* **-fied**) *tr* clarifier

clarinet [,klærɪ'nɛt] *s* clarinette *f*

clarity ['klærɪti] *s* clarté *f*

clash [klæʃ] *s* (*sound*) choc *m* métallique; (*conflict*) dispute *f*, heurt *m*, choc; (*between people; with police*) accrochage *m*; (*of colors*) disparate *f* ‖ *intr* se heurter, s'entre-choquer; (*said of colors*) former une disparate

clasp [klæsp] *s* (*on brooch, necklace, purse*) agrafe *f*, fermoir *m*; (*embrace*) étreinte *f* ‖ *tr* agrafer; (*to embrace*) étreindre

clasp' knife' *s* couteau *m* pliant

class [klæs] *s* classe *f* ‖ *tr* classer
classic [ˈklæsɪk] *adj* & *s* classique *m*
classical [ˈklæsɪkəl] *adj* classique
classicism [ˈklæsɪˌsɪzəm] *s* classicisme *m*
classicist [ˈklæsɪsɪst] *s* classique *mf*
classification [ˌklæsɪfɪˈkeʃən] *s* classification *f*, classement *m*
classified *adj* classifié, classé; (*documents*) secret, confidentiel
clas′sified adver′tise′ments *spl* petites annonces *fpl*
classi·fy [ˈklæsɪˌfaɪ] *v* (*pret* & *pp* -fied) *tr* classifier
class′mate *s* camarade *mf* de classe
class′room′ *s* salle *f* de classe, classe *f*
class·y [ˈklæsi] *adj* (*comp* -ier; *super* -iest) (slang) chic
clatter [ˈklætər] *s* fracas *m* ‖ *intr* faire un fracas
clause [klɔz] *s* clause *f*, article *m*; (gram) proposition *f*
clavicle [ˈklævɪkəl] *s* clavicule *f*
claw [klɔ] *s* (*of animal*) griffe *f*; (*of crab*) pince *f*; (*of hammer*) panne *f* fendue ‖ *tr* griffer, déchirer
clay [kle] *s* argile *f*, glaise *f*
clay′ pig′eon *s* pigeon *m* d'argile, pigeon de tir
clay′ pipe′ *s* pipe *f* en terre
clay′ pit′ *s* argilière *f*, glaisière *f*
clean [klin] *adj* propre; (*precise*) net ‖ *adv* net; tout à fait ‖ *tr* nettoyer; (*fish*) vider; (*streets*) balayer; **to clean out** curer; (*a person*) (slang) mettre à sec, décaver; **to clean up** nettoyer ‖ *intr* faire le nettoyage
clean′ and jerk′ *s* (weightlifting) épaulé-jeté *m*
clean′-cut′ *adj* bien délimité, net; (*e.g., athlete*) bien découplé
cleaner [ˈklinər] *s* (*person*) nettoyeur *m*, dégraisseur *m*; (*cleaning agent*) nettoyant *m*; **to be taken to the cleaners** (slang) se faire rincer
cleaning [ˈklinɪŋ] *s* nettoyage *m*
clean′ing wom′an *s* femme *f* de ménage
cleanliness [ˈklɛnlɪnɪs] *s* propreté *f*, netteté *f*
cleanse [klɛnz] *tr* nettoyer, écurer; (*e.g., a wound*) assainir; (*e.g., one's thoughts*) purifier
cleanser [ˈklɛnzər] *s* produit *m* de nettoyage; (*soap*) détersif *m*
clean′-shav′en *adj* rasé de frais
cleans′ing cream′ *s* crème *f* de démaquillage
clean′up′ *s* nettoiement *m*
clear [klɪr] *adj* clair; (*sharp*) net; (*free*) dégagé, libre; (*unmortgaged*) franc d'hypothèque; **to become clear** s'éclaircir; **to keep clear of** éviter ‖ *tr* (*to brighten*) éclaircir; (*e.g., a fence*) franchir; (*obstacles*) dégager; (*land*) défricher; (*goods in customs*) dédouaner; (*an account*) solder; **to clear away** écarter, enlever; **to clear oneself** se disculper; **to clear out** (*e.g., a garden*) jardiner; **to clear the table** desservir, enlever le couvert, ôter la nappe; **to clear up** éclaircir ‖ *intr* (*said of*

weather) s'éclaircir; **to clear out** (coll) filer, se sauver
clearance [ˈklɪrəns] *s* (*permission*) permis *m*, laissez-passer *m*, autorisation *f*; (*between two objects*) espace *m* libre; (aer) clairance *f*; (com) compensation *f*; (mach) espace *m* mort, jeu *m*
clear′ance sale′ *s* vente *f* de soldes
clear′-cut′ *adj* net, tranché; (*case*) absolu
clear′-head′ed *adj* lucide, perspicace
clearing [ˈklɪrɪŋ] *s* (*in clouds*) éclaircie *f*; (*in forest*) clairière *f*, trouée *f*
clear′ing house′ *s* (com) comptoir *m* de règlement, chambre *f* de compensation
clearness [ˈklɪrnɪs] *s* clarté *f*, netteté *f*
clear′-sight′ed *adj* perspicace, clairvoyant
cleat [klit] *s* taquet *m*
cleavage [ˈklivɪdʒ] *s* clivage *m*
cleave [kliv] *v* (*pret* & *pp* **cleft** [klɛft] or **cleaved**) *tr* fendre ‖ *intr* se fendre; **to cleave to** s'attacher à, adhérer à
cleaver [ˈklivər] *s* couperet *m*, hachoir *m*
clef [klɛf] *s* (mus) clef *f*
cleft [klɛft] *adj* fendu ‖ *s* fente *f*, crevasse *f*
cleft′ pal′ate *s* palais *m* fendu, fissure *f* palatine
clemen·cy [ˈklɛmənsi] *s* (*pl* -cies) clémence *f*
clement [ˈklɛmənt] *adj* clément
clench [klɛntʃ] *tr* serrer, crisper
cler·gy [ˈklʌrdʒi] *s* (*pl* -gies) (*members*) clergé *m*; (*profession*) clergie *f*
cler′gy·man *s* (*pl* -men) ecclésiastique *m*, clerc *m*
cleric [ˈklɛrɪk] *s* clerc *m*, ecclésiastique *m*
clerical [ˈklɛrɪkəl] *adj* clerical; de bureau ‖ *s*—**clericals** habit *m* ecclésiastique
cler′ical er′ror *s* faute *f* de copiste, faute de sténographe
cler′ical work′ *s* travail *m* de bureau
clerk [klʌrk] *s* (*clerical worker*) employé *m* de bureau, commis *m*; (*in lawyer's office*) clerc *m*; (*in store*) vendeur *m*; (*in bank*) comptable *mf*; (*of court*) greffier *m*; (eccl) clerc
clever [ˈklɛvər] *adj* habile, adroit
cliché [kliˈʃe] *s* cliché *m*, expression *f* consacrée
click [klɪk] *s* cliquetis *m*, clic *m*; (*of heels*) bruit *m* sec; (*of tongue*) claquement *m*; (*of a machine*) déclic *m* ‖ *intr* cliqueter, faire un déclic; (*to succeed*) (coll) réussir; (*to get along well*) (coll) s'entendre à merveille
client [ˈklaɪ·ənt] *s* client *m*
clientele [ˌklaɪ·ənˈtɛl] *s* clientèle *f*
cliff [klɪf] *s* falaise *f*, talus *m* raide
climate [ˈklaɪmɪt] *s* climat *m*
climax [ˈklaɪmæks] *s* point *m* culminant, comble *m*
climb [klaɪm] *s* montée *f*, ascension *f* ‖ *tr* & *intr* monter, gravir; grimper; **to climb down** descendre
climber [ˈklaɪmər] *s* grimpeur *m*; (bot) plante *f* grimpante; (*social climber*) parvenu *m*, arriviste *mf*
climbing [ˈklaɪmɪŋ] *s* montée *f*, escalade *f*

clinch [klɪntʃ] s (*act*) rivetage *m*; (*fastener*) crampon *m*, rivet *m*; (boxing) corps-à-corps *m* ‖ *tr* (*a nail*) river; (*a bargain*) boucler ‖ *intr* se prendre corps à corps

clincher ['klɪntʃər] s (coll) argument *m* sans réplique

cling [klɪŋ] *v* (*pret* & *pp* **clung** [klʌŋ]) *intr* s'accrocher, se cramponner; **to cling to** (*a person*) se serrer contre; (*a belief*) adhérer à

cling'stone peach' s alberge *f*

clinic ['klɪnɪk] s clinique *f*

clinical ['klɪnɪkəl] *adj* clinique

clinician [klɪ'nɪʃən] s clinicien *m*

clink [klɪŋk] s cliquetis *m*; (*e.g., of glasses*) tintement *m*, choc *m*; (*jail*) (slang) taule *f*, bloc *m* ‖ *tr* (*glasses, in a toast*) choquer; **to clink glasses with** trinquer avec ‖ *intr* tinter, cliqueter

clip [klɪp] s (*for papers*) attache *f*; (*brooch*) agrafe *f*, clip *m*; (*of gun*) chargeur *m*; (*blow*) (coll) taloche *f*; (*fast pace*) (coll) pas *m* rapide ‖ *v* (*pret* & *pp* **clipped**; *ger* **clipping**) *tr* (*to fasten*) attacher; (*hair*) rafraîchir; (*sheep*) tondre; (*one's words*) avaler

clipper ['klɪpər] s (aer) clipper *m*; (naut) voilier *m* de course; **clippers** tondeuse *f*

clipping ['klɪpɪŋ] s tondage *m*; (*of sheep*) tonte *f*; (*of one's hair*) taille *f*; (*of newspaper*) coupure *f* (de presse); **clippings** (*cuttings, shavings, etc.*) rognures *fpl*, chutes *fpl*

clip'ping ser'vice s argus *m*

clique [klik] s coterie *f*, clan *m*, chapelle *f*

clitoris ['klɪtərɪs] s clitoris *m*

cloak [klok] s manteau *m* ‖ *tr* masquer

cloak'-and-dag'ger *adj* (*e.g., story*) de cape et d'épée

cloak'room' s vestiaire *m*; (rr) consigne *f*

clock [klɑk] s (*larger type of clock*) horloge *f*; (*smaller type of clock*) pendule *f*; (*e.g., in a tower*) horloge; **to turn back the clock** retarder l'horloge; (fig) revenir en arrière ‖ *tr* chronométrer

clock'mak'er s horloger *m*

clock'tow'er s tour *f* de l'horloge

clock'wise' *adj* & *adv* dans le sens des aiguilles d'une montre

clock'work' s mouvement *m* d'horlogerie; **like clockwork** (coll) comme une horloge

clod [klɑd] s motte *f*; (*person*) rustre *mf*

clod'hop'per s cul-terreux *m*; (*shoe*) godillot *m*

clog [klɑg] s (*shoe*) galoche *f*, socque *m*; (*hindrance*) entrave *f* ‖ *v* (*pret* & *pp* **clogged**; *ger* **clogging**) *tr* (*e.g., a pipe*) boucher; (*e.g., traffic*) entraver ‖ *intr* se boucher

cloister ['klɔɪstər] s cloître *m* ‖ *tr* cloîtrer

clone [klon] s clone *m* ‖ *tr* faire du clonage à ‖ *intr* faire du clonage

cloning ['klonɪŋ] s clonage *m*

close [klos] *adj* proche, tout près; (*game; weave; formation, order*) serré; (*friend*) intime; (*friendship*) étroit; (*room*) renfermé, étouffant; (*translation*) fidèle; **close**

to près de ‖ *adv* près, de près ‖ [kloz] s (*enclosure*) clos *m*; (*end*) fin *f*; (*closing*) fermeture *f* ‖ *tr* fermer; (*to end*) conclure, terminer; (*an account*) régler, clôturer; (*ranks*) serrer, resserrer; (*a meeting*) lever; **close quotes** fermez les guillemets; **to close in** enfermer; **to close out** (com) liquider, solder ‖ *intr* se fermer; finir, se terminer; (*on certain days*) (theat) faire relâche; **to close in on** (*the enemy*) aborder

close' call' [klos] s—**to have a close call** (coll) l'échapper belle

close-cropped ['klos'krɑpt] *adj* coupé ras

closed [klozd] *adj* fermé; (*road*) barré; (*e.g., pipe*) obturé, bouché; (*ranks*) serré; (public sign in front of theater) relâche; **with closed eyes** les yeux clos

closed' car' s conduite *f* intérieure

closed'-cir'cuit tel'evision s télévision *f* en circuit fermé

closed' sea'son s fermeture *f* de la chasse, fermeture de la pêche

closefisted ['klos'fɪstəd] *adj* ladre, avare

close-fitting ['klos'fɪtɪŋ] *adj* collant, ajusté, qui moule le corps

close-grained ['klos'grend] *adj* serré

closely ['klosli] *adv* (*near*) de près, étroitement; (*exactly*) exactement

close-mouthed ['klos'mauðd] *adj* peu communicatif, économe de mots

closeness ['klosnɪs] s (*nearness*) proximité *f*; (*accuracy*) exactitude *f*; (*stinginess*) avarice *f*; (*of weather*) lourdeur *f*; (*of air*) manque *m* d'air

close'out' s fin *f* de série

close' shave' [klos] s—**to have a close shave** se faire raser de près; (coll) échapper à un cheveu près

closet ['klɑzɪt] s placard *m*

clos'et dra'ma s spectacle *m* dans un fauteuil

close-up ['klos,ʌp] s premier plan *m*, gros plan, plan serré, plan rapproché

closing ['klozɪŋ] *adj* dernier, final ‖ s fermeture *f*; (*of account; of meeting*) clôture *f*

clos'ing-out' sale' s soldes *mpl* des fins de séries

clos'ing price' s dernier cours *m*

clot [klɑt] s caillot *m* ‖ *v* (*pret* & *pp* **clotted**; *ger* **clotting**) *tr* cailler ‖ *intr* se cailler

cloth [klɔθ] s étoffe *f*; (*fabric*) tissu *m*; (*of wool*) drap *m*; (*of cotton or linen*) toile *f*; **cloths** (*for cleaning*) chiffons *mpl*, torchons *mpl*, linge *m*; **the cloth** le clergé

clothe [kloð] *v* (*pret* & *pp* **clothed** or **clad** [klæd]) *tr* habiller, vêtir; (*e.g., with authority*) revêtir, investir

clothes [kloz] *spl* vêtements *mpl*, habits *mpl*; (*underclothes, shirts, etc.; wash*) linge *m*; **in plain clothes** en civil; **to put on one's clothes** s'habiller; **to take off one's clothes** se déshabiller

clothes'bas'ket s panier *m* à linge

clothes'brush' s brosse *f* à habits

clothes'clos'et s garde-robe *f*, penderie *f*, placard *m*

clothes′ dry′er *s* séchoir *m* à linge
clothes′ hang′er *s* cintre *m*
clothes′horse′ *s* séchoir-chevalet *m*
clothes′line′ *s* corde *f* à linge, étendoir *m*
clothes′ moth′ *s* gerce *f*
clothes′pin′ *s* pince *f* à linge
clothes′ rack′ *s* patère *f*
clothier ['kloðjər] *s* confectionneur *m*, marchand *m* de confections
clothing ['kloðɪŋ] *s* vêtements *mpl*
cloud [klaʊd] *s* nuage *m*; (*heavy cloud; multitude*) nuée *f*; **in the clouds** dans les nues ‖ *tr* couvrir de nuages; (phot) voiler ‖ *intr* (phot) se voiler; **to cloud over** or **up** se couvrir de nuages
cloud′burst′ *s* averse *f*, rafale *f* de pluie
cloud′ cham′ber *s* (phys) chambre *f* d'ionisation
cloudless ['klaʊdlɪs] *adj* sans nuages
cloud·y ['klaʊdi] *adj* (*comp* **-ier**; *super* **-iest**) nuageux; (phot) voilé
clout [klaʊt] *s* (coll) gifle *f* ‖ *tr* (coll) gifler
clove [klov] *s* (*spice*) clou *m* de girofle, girofle *m*; (*of garlic*) gousse *f*; (bot) giroflier *m*
clove′ hitch′ *s* demi-clef *f* à capeler
clo′ven hoof′ ['klovən] *s* pied *m* fourchu; **to show the cloven hoof** (coll) montrer le bout de l'oreille
clover ['klovər] *s* trèfle *m*; **to be in clover** (coll) être sur le velours
clo′ver-leaf′ *s* (*pl* **-leaves**) (*leaf*) feuille *f* de trèfle; (*intersection*) croisement *m* en trèfle, échangeur *m* en trèfle
clown [klaʊn] *s* clown *m*, pitre *m*, bouffon *m* ‖ *intr* faire le pitre
clownish ['klaʊnɪʃ] *adj* bouffon; (*clumsy*) empoté, rustre
cloy [klɔɪ] *tr* rassasier
club [klʌb] *s* (*weapon*) massue *f*, gourdin *m*, assommoir *m*; (*group*) cercle *m*, amicale *f*, club *m*; (cards) trèfle *m*; (golf) crosse *f*, club *m* ‖ *v* (*pret & pp* **clubbed**; *ger* **clubbing**) *tr* (*to strike*) assommer; (*to pool*) mettre en commun ‖ *intr*—**to club together** s'associer; se cotiser
club′ car′ *s* voiture-salon *f*
club′foot′ *s* (*pl* **-feet**) pied *m* équin, pied bot
club′foot′ed *adj*—**to be clubfooted** avoir le pied bot, être pied-bot
club′house′ *s* club *m*, club-house *m*
club′man *s* (*pl* **-men**) clubman *m*
club′room′ *s* salle *f* de réunion
club′ steak′ *s* aloyau *m* de bœuf
club′wom′an *s* (*pl* **-wom′en**) cercleuse *f*
cluck [klʌk] *s* gloussement *m* ‖ *intr* glousser
clue [klu] *s* indice *m*, indication *f*; **to find the clue** trouver la clef; **to give s.o. a clue** mettre qn sur la piste; **to have the clue** tenir le bout du fil
clump [klʌmp] *s* (*of earth*) bloc *m*, masse *f*; (*of trees*) bouquet *m*; (*of shrubs or flowers*) massif *m*; (*gait*) pas *m* lourd ‖ *intr*—**to clump along** marcher lourdement

clum·sy ['klʌmzi] *adj* (*comp* **-sier**; *super* **-siest**) (*worker*) maladroit, gauche; (*work*) bâclé, grossier
cluster ['klʌstər] *s* (*of people*) groupe *m*, rassemblement *m*; (*of trees*) bouquet *m*; (*of grapes, fruit, blossoms, flowers*) grappe *f*; (*of pears*) glane *f*; (*of bananas*) régime *m*; (*of diamonds*) épi *m*, nœud *m*; (*of stars*) amas *m* ‖ *tr* grouper ‖ *intr*—**to cluster around** se rassembler; **to cluster together** se conglomérer
clutch [klʌtʃ] *s* (*grasp, grip*) griffe *f*, serre *f*; (aut) embrayage *m*; (aut) pédale *f* d'embrayage; **to fall into the clutches of** tomber sous la patte de; **to let in the clutch** embrayer; **to throw out the clutch** débrayer ‖ *tr* saisir, empoigner ‖ *intr*—**to clutch at** se raccrocher à
clutter ['klʌtər] *s* encombrement *m* ‖ *tr*—**to clutter up** encombrer
Co. *abbr* (**Company**) Cⁱᵉ
c/o *abbr* (**in care of**) a/s (aux soins de)
coach [kotʃ] *s* (*drawn by horses*) coche *m*, carrosse *f*; (*bus*) autocar *m*, car *m*; (*two-door sedan*) coche *m*; (rr) voiture *f*; (sports) entraîneur *m*, moniteur *m* ‖ *tr* donner des leçons particulières à; entraîner; (*for an exam*) préparer à un examen, chauffer; (*an actor*) faire répéter
coach′-and-four′ *s* carrosse *f* à quatre chevaux
coach′ box′ *s* siège *m* du cocher
coach′ house′ *s* remise *f*
coaching ['kotʃɪŋ] *s* leçons *fpl* particulières, chauffage *m*, répétitions *fpl*; (sport) entraînement *m*
coach′man *s* (*pl* **-men**) cocher *m*
coagulate [ko'ægjə,let] *tr* coaguler ‖ *intr* se coaguler
coal [kol] *adj* charbonnier, houiller ‖ *s* houille *f*, charbon *m*; **coals** (*embers*) tisons *mpl*, charbons ardents; **to carry coals to Newcastle** porter de l'eau à la rivière
coal′bin′ *s* coffre *m* à charbon
coal′ bunk′er *s* soute *f* à charbon
coal′ car′ *s* wagon-tombereau *m*
coal′deal′er *s* charbonnier *m*
coalesce [,ko·ə'lɛs] *intr* s'unir, se combiner, fusionner
coal′ field′ *s* bassin *m* houiller
coalition [,ko·ə'lɪʃən] *s* coalition *f*; **to form a coalition** se coaliser
coal′ mine′ *s* houillère *f*
coal′ oil′ *s* pétrole *m* lampant
coal′ scut′tle *s* seau *m* à charbon
coal′ tar′ *s* goudron *m* de houille
coal′yard′ *s* charbonnerie *f*
coarse [kors] *adj* (*in manners*) grossier; (*composed of large particles*) gros; (*hair, skin*) rude
coarse′-grained′ *adj* à gros grain; (*wood*) à gros fil
coarseness ['korsnɪs] *s* (*in manners*) grossièreté *f*; (*of hair, skin*) rudesse *f*
coast [kost] *s* côte *f*; **the coast is clear** la route est libre ‖ *intr* caboter; (*said of automobile*) aller au débrayé; (*said of*

bicycle) aller en roue libre; **to coast along** continuer sur sa lancée

coastal ['kostəl] *adj* côtier

coaster ['kostər] *s* (*under a glass*) dessous-de-verre *m*, sous-verre *m*; (naut) caboteur *m*

coast'er brake' *s* frein *m* à contrepédalage

coast' guard' *s* service *m* de guet le long des côtes

coast'-guard cut'ter *s* garde-côte *m*

coast'guards'man *s* (*pl* **-men**) soldat *m* chargé de la garde des côtes

coasting ['kostɪŋ] *s* (*e.g.*, *on a cycle*) descente *f* en roue libre

coast'ing trade' *s* cabotage *m*

coast'line' *s* littoral *m*

coast'wise' *adj* côtier ‖ *adv* le long de la côte

coat [kot] *s* (*jacket*) veste *f*; (*suitcoat*) veston *m*; (*topcoat*) manteau *m*; (*of an animal*) robe *f*, pelage *m*, livrée *f*; (*of paint*) couche *f* ‖ *tr* enduire; (*with chocolate*) enrober; (*a pill*) dragéifier

coat' hang'er *s* cintre *m*, portemanteau *m*

coating ['kotɪŋ] *s* enduit *m*, couche *f*

coat' of arms' *s* écu *m* armorial; (*bearings*) blason *m*, armoiries *fpl*

coat' of mail' *s* cotte *f* de mailles

coat'rack' *s* portemanteau *m*

coat'room' *s* vestiaire *m*

coat'tail' *s* basque *f*

coauthor [ko'ɔθər] *s* coauteur *m*

coax [koks] *tr* cajoler, amadouer

cob [kab] *s* (*of corn*) épi *m* de maïs; (*horse*) cob *m*; (*swan*) cygne *m* mâle

cobalt ['kobɔlt] *s* cobalt *m*

cobbler ['kablər] *s* (*shoemaker*) cordonnier *m*; (*cake*) tourte *f* aux fruits; (*drink*) boisson *f* glacée

cobblestone ['kabəl,ston] *s* pavé *m*

cob'web' *s* toile *f* d'araignée

cocaine [ko'ken] *s* cocaïne *f*

cock [kak] *s* (*rooster*) coq *m*; (*faucet*) robinet *m*; (*of gun*) chien *m* ‖ *tr* (*one's ears*) dresser, redresser; (*one's hat*) mettre sur l'oreille, retrousser; (*a rifle*) armer

cockade [ka'ked] *s* cocarde *f*

cock-a-doodle-doo ['kakə,dudəl'du] *interj* cocorico!

cock'-and-bull' sto'ry *s* coq-à-l'âne *m*

cock'crow' *s* cocorico *m*

cocked' hat' *s* chapeau *m* à cornes; **to knock into a cocked hat** (slang) démolir, aplatir

cock'er span'iel ['kakər] *s* cocker *m*

cock'eyed' *adj* (coll) de travers, de biais; (slang) insensé

cock'fight' *s* combat *m* de coqs

cockle ['kakəl] *s* (bot) nielle *f*; (zool) bucarde *f*, clovisse *f*

cock'pit' *s* (aer) cockpit *m*, carlingue *f*, poste *m* de pilotage, habitacle *m*

cock'roach' *s* blatte *f*, cafard *m*

cockscomb ['kaks,kom] *s* crête *f* de coq; (bot) crête-de-coq *f*

cock'sure' *adj* (coll) sûr et certain

cock'tail' *s* cocktail *m*

cock'tail dress' *s* robe *f* de cocktail

cock'tail par'ty *s* cocktail *m*

cock'tail shak'er *s* shaker *m*

cock·y ['kaki] *adj* (*comp* **-ier**; *super* **-iest**) (coll) effronté, suffisant

cocoa ['koko] *s* cacao *m*

co'coa bean' *s* cacao *m*

coconut ['kokə,nʌt] *s* noix *f* de coco, coco *m*

co'conut palm' *s* cocotier *m*

cocoon [kə'kun] *s* cocon *m*

cod [kad] *s* (ichth) morue *f*

C.O.D. ['si'o'di] *s* (letterword) (**Collect on Delivery**) C.R., contre remboursement, e.g., **send it to me C.O.D.** envoyez-le-moi C.R.

coddle ['kadəl] *tr* dorloter, gâter

code [kod] *s* code *m*; (*secret code*) chiffre *m* ‖ *tr* chiffrer

code' word' *s* mot *m* convenu

codex ['kodɛks] *s* (*pl* **codices** ['kadɪ,siz]) manuscrit *m* ancien

cod'fish' *s* morue *f*

codger ['kadʒər] *s*—**old codger** (coll) vieux bonhomme *m*

codicil ['kadɪsɪl] *s* (*of will*) codicille *m*; (*of contract, treaty, etc.*) avenant *m*

codi·fy ['kadɪ,faɪ] *v* (*pret & pp* **-fied**) *tr* codifier

cod'-liver oil' *s* huile *f* de foie de morue

coed ['ko,ɛd] *s* collégienne *f*, étudiante *f* universitaire

coeducation [,ko·ɛdʒə'keʃən] *s* coéducation *f*, enseignement *m* mixte

co'educa'tional school' [,ko·ɛdʒə'keʃənəl] *s* école *f* mixte

coefficient [,ko·ɪ'fɪʃənt] *s* coefficient *m*

coerce [ko'ʌrs] *tr* contraindre, forcer

coercion [ko'ʌrʃən] *s* coercition *f*

coexist [,ko·ɪg'zɪst] *intr* coexister

coexistence [,ko·ɪg'zɪstəns] *s* coexistence *f*

coffee ['kɔfi] *s* café *m*; **black coffee** café noir, café nature; **ground coffee** café moulu; **roasted coffee** café brûlé, café torréfié

cof'fee and rolls' *s* café *m* complet

cof'fee bean' *s* grain *m* de café

cof'fee break' *s* pause-café *f*, pause café

cof'fee·cake' *s* gimblette *f* (qui se prend avec le café)

cof'fee cup' *s* tasse *f* à café

cof'fee grind'er *s* moulin *m* à café

cof'fee grounds' *spl* marc *m* de café

cof'fee mak'er *s* percolateur *m*

cof'fee mill' *s* moulin *m* à café

cof'fee mug' *s* pot *m* de café

cof'fee planta'tion *s* caféière *f*

cof'fee·pot' *s* cafetière *f*; (*for pouring*) verseuse *f*

cof'fee roast'er *s* brûloir *m*

cof'fee shop' *s* (*of hotel*) hôtel-restaurant *m*; (*in station*) buffet *m*

cof'fee tree' *s* caféier *m*

coffer ['kɔfər] *s* coffre *m*, caisse *f*; (archit) caisson *m*; **coffers** trésor *m*, fonds *mpl*

cof'fer·dam' *s* coffre *m*, bâtardeau *m*

coffin ['kɔfɪn] *s* cercueil *m*, bière *f*

cog [kɑg] *s* dent *f*; (*cogwheel*) roue *f* dentée; **to slip a cog** (coll) avoir des absences

cogency [ˈkodʒənsi] *s* force *f* (de persuasion)

cogent [ˈkodʒənt] *adj* puissant, convaincant

cogitate [ˈkɑdʒɪˌtet] *tr & intr* méditer

cognac [ˈkonjæk] *s* cognac *m*

cognate [ˈkɑgnet] *adj* congénère, apparenté ‖ *s* congénère *mf*; (*word*) mot *m* apparenté

cognizance [ˈkɑgnɪzəns] *s* connaissance *f*

cognizant [ˈkɑgnɪzənt] *adj* informé

cog′wheel *s* roue *f* dentée

cohabit [koˈhæbɪt] *intr* cohabiter

coheir [koˈɛr] *s* cohéritier

cohere [koˈhɪr] *intr* s'agglomérer, adhérer; (*said of reasoning or style*) se suivre logiquement, correspondre

coherent [koˈhɪrənt] *adj* cohérent

cohesion [koˈhiʒən] *s* cohésion *f*

coiffeur [kwɑˈfʌr] *s* coiffeur *m* pour dames

coiffure [kwɑˈfjʊr] *s* coiffure *f* ‖ *tr* coiffer

coil [kɔɪl] *s* (*something wound in a spiral*) rouleau *m*; (*single turn of spiral*) tour *m*; (*of a still*) serpentin *m*; (*of hair*) boucle *f*; (elec) bobine *f*; **coils** (*of snake*) nœuds *mpl* ‖ *tr* enrouler; (naut) lover, gléner ‖ *intr* s'enrouler; (*said of snake or stream*) serpenter

coil′ spring′ *s* ressort *m* en spirale, ressort à boudin

coin [kɔɪn] *s* monnaie *f*; (*single coin*) pièce *f* de monnaie; (*wedge*) coin *m*; **in coin** en espèces, en numéraire; **to pay back s.o. in his own coin** rendre à qn la monnaie de sa pièce; **to toss a coin** jouer à pile ou face ‖ *tr* (*a new word; a story or lie*) forger, inventer; **to coin money** frapper de la monnaie; (coll) faire des affaires d'or, s'enrichir à vue d'œil

coinage [ˈkɔɪnɪdʒ] *s* monnayage *m*; (fig) invention *f*

coincide [ˌkoˈɪnˈsaɪd] *intr* coïncider

coincidence [koˈɪnsɪdəns] *s* coïncidence *f*

coin′ lock′er *s* consigne *f* automatique

coin′ return′ *s* retour *m* de monnaie; (*receptacle*) sébile *f*

coition [koˈɪʃən] *or* **coitus** [ˈkoˈɪtəs] *s* coït *m*

coke [kok] *s* coke *m* ‖ *tr* cokéfier ‖ *intr* se cokéfier

colander [ˈkʌləndər] *s* passoire *f*

cold [kold] *adj* froid; **it is cold** (*said of weather*) il fait froid; **to be cold** (*said of person*) avoir froid ‖ *s* froid *m*; (*indisposition*) rhume *m*; **to be left out in the cold** (slang) rester en carafe; **to catch a cold** attraper un rhume, s'enrhumer

cold′ blood′ *s*—**in cold blood** de sang-froid

cold′-blood′ed *adj* insensible; (*sensitive to cold*) frileux; (zool) à sang froid

cold′ chis′el *s* ciseau *m* à froid

cold′ com′fort *s* maigre consolation *f*

cold′ cream′ *s* cold-cream *m*

cold′ cuts′ *spl* viandes *fpl* froides, assiette *f* anglaise

cold′ feet′ [fit] *spl*—**to have cold feet** (coll) avoir froid aux yeux

cold′ front′ *s* front *m* froid

cold′-heart′ed *adj* au cœur dur, insensible

coldness [ˈkoldnɪs] *s* froideur *f*; (*in the air*) froidure *f*

cold′ should′er *s*—**to give s.o. the cold shoulder** (coll) battre froid à qn

cold′ snap′ *s* coup *m* de froid

cold′ stor′age *s* entrepôt *m* frigorifique; **in cold storage** en glacière

cold′-stor′age *adj* frigorifique

cold′ war′ *s* guerre *f* froide

cold′ wave′ *s* vague *f* de froid

coleslaw [ˈkolˌslɔ] *s* salade *f* de chou

colic [ˈkɑlɪk] *s* colique *f*

coliseum [ˌkɑlɪˈsiˑəm] *s* colisée *m*

colitis [koˈlaɪtɪs] *s* colite *f*

collaborate [kəˈlæbəˌret] *intr* collaborer

collaborationist [kəˌlæbəˈreʃənɪst] *s* collaborationniste *mf*

collaborator [kəˈlæbəˌretər] *s* collaborateur *m*

collapse [kəˈlæps] *s* écroulement *m*, effondrement *m*; (*of prices, of government*) chute *f*; (*of a beam*) fléchissement *m*; (pathol) collapsus *m* ‖ *intr* s'écrouler, s'effondrer; (*said of government*) tomber; (*said of structure or prices*) s'effondrer; (*said of balloon*) se dégonfler

collapsible [kəˈlæpsɪbəl] *adj* démontable, rabattable, pliant

collar [ˈkɑlər] *s* (*of dress, shirt*) collet *m*, col *m*; (*worn by dog; on pigeon*) collier *m*; (mach) collier ‖ *tr* colleter; (coll) empoigner

col′lar·band′ *s* pied *m* de col (d'une chemise)

col′lar·bone′ *s* clavicule *f*

collate [kəˈlet] *tr* collationner, conférer

collateral [kəˈlætərəl] *adj* (*fact*) correspondant, concomitant; (*parallel*) parallèle; (*subordinate*) accessoire; (*kin*) collatéral ‖ *s* (*kin*) collatéral *m*; (com) nantissement *m*

collation [kəˈleʃən] *s* collation *f*

colleague [ˈkɑlig] *s* collègue *mf*

collect [ˈkɑlɛkt] *s* (eccl) collecte *f* ‖ [kəˈlɛkt] *tr* rassembler; (*taxes*) percevoir, lever; (*stamps, antiques*) collectionner; (*eggs; classroom papers; tickets*) ramasser; (*mail*) faire la levée de; (*debts*) recouvrer; (*gifts, money*) collecter; (*one's thoughts; anecdotes*) recueillir; **to collect oneself** se reprendre, se remettre ‖ *intr* (*for the poor*) quêter; (*to gather together*) se rassembler, se réunir; (*to pile up*) s'amasser ‖ *adv* en p.c.v., e.g., **to telephone collect** téléphoner en p.c.v.

collect′ call′ *s* (telp) communication *f* P.C.V.

collected *adj* recueilli, maître de soi

collection [kəˈlɛkʃən] *s* collection *f*; (*of taxes*) perception *f*, levée *f*, recouvrement *m*; (*of mail*) levée; (*of verses*) recueil *m*

collec′tion a′gency *s* agence *f* de recouvrement

collec′tion plate′ *s* plateau *m* de quête

collective [kə'lɛktɪv] *adj* collectif
collector [kə'lɛktər] *s (of stamps, antiques)* collectionneur *m*; *(of taxes)* percepteur *m*, receveur *m*, collecteur *m*; *(of tickets)* contrôleur *m*
college ['kalɪdʒ] *s (of cardinals, electors, etc.)* collège *m*; *(school in a university)* faculté *f*; (U.S.A.) école *f* des arts et sciences
collegian [kə'lidʒɪ·ən] *s* étudiant *m*
collegiate [kə'lidʒɪ·ɪt] *adj* collégial, de l'université, universitaire
collide [kə'laɪd] *intr* se heurter, se tamponner; **to collide with** se heurter à or contre, heurter contre
collier ['kaljər] *s* houilleur *m*; *(ship)* charbonnier *m*
collier·y ['kaljəri] *s (pl -ies)* houillère *f*
collision [kə'lɪʒən] *s* collision *f*
collocate ['kalo,ket] *tr* disposer en rapport; *(creditors)* colloquer
colloid ['kalɔɪd] *adj* colloïdal ‖ *s* colloïde *m*
colloquial [kə'lokwɪ·əl] *adj* familier
colloquialism [kə'lokwɪ·ə,lɪzəm] *s* expression *f* familière
collo·quy ['kaləkwi] *s (pl -quies)* colloque *m*
collusion [kə'luʒən] *s* collusion *f*; **to be in collusion with** être d'intelligence avec
cologne [kə'lon] *s* eau *f* de Cologne
Colombia [kə'lʌmbɪ·ə] *s* Colombie *f*; la Colombie
colon ['kolən] *s* (anat) côlon *m*; (gram) deux points *mpl*
colonel ['kʌrnəl] *s* colonel *m*
colonial [kə'lonɪ·əl] *adj & s* colonial *m*
colonist ['kalənɪst] *s* colon *m*
colonize ['kalə,naɪz] *tr & intr* coloniser
colonnade [,kalə'ned] *s* colonnade *f*
colo·ny ['kaləni] *s (pl -nies)* colonie *f*
colophon ['kalə,fan] *s* colophon *m*
color ['kʌlər] *s* couleur *f*; **the colors** les couleurs, le drapeau; **to call to the colors** appeler sous les drapeaux; **to give** or **lend color to** colorer; (fig) rendre vraisemblable; **to show one's true colors** se révéler sous son vrai jour; **under color of** sous couleur de; **with flying colors** enseignes déployées ‖ *tr* colorer; *(e.g., a drawing)* colorier; *(to exaggerate)* donner de l'éclat à, imager; *(to dye)* teindre ‖ *intr* se colorer; *(to blush)* rougir
col'or·bear'er *s* porte-drapeau *m*
col'or·blind' *adj* daltonien, aveugle des couleurs
col'or-cod'ed *adj* (chem) chromocodé
colored *adj* coloré; *(ink)* de couleur; *(person; usually offensive)* de couleur; *(drawing)* colorié
colorful ['kʌlərfəl] *adj (striking)* coloré; *(unusual)* pittoresque
col'or guard' *s* garde *f* d'honneur du drapeau
coloring ['kʌlərɪŋ] *adj* colorant ‖ *s* colorant *m*; *(of painting, complexion, style)* coloris *m*
colorless ['kʌlərlɪs] *adj* incolore

col'or photog'raphy *s* photographie *f* en couleurs
col'or salute' *s* (mil) salut *m* au drapeau, salut aux couleurs
col'or ser'geant *s* sergent-chef *m*, sergent-major *m*
col'or tel'evision *s* télévision *f* en couleurs
colossal [kə'lasəl] *adj* colossal
colossus [kə'lasəs] *s* colosse *m*
colt [kolt] *s* poulain *m*
Columbus [kə'lʌmbəs] *s* Colomb *m*
column ['kaləm] *s* colonne *f*; (journ) rubrique *f*, chronique *f*, courrier *m*; (mil) colonne
columnar [kə'lʌmnər] *adj* en colonne
columnist ['kaləmɪst] *s* chroniqueur *m*, courriériste *mf*
coma ['komə] *s* (pathol) coma *m*
comb [kom] *s (for hair)* peigne *m*; *(currycomb)* étrille *f*; *(of rooster; of wave)* crête *f*; *(filled with honey)* rayon *m* ‖ *tr* peigner; explorer minutieusement, fouiller; **to comb out** démêler ‖ *intr (said of waves)* déferler
com·bat ['kambæt] *s* combat *m* ‖ ['kambæt], [kəm'bæt] *v (pret & pp -bated* or **-batted**; *ger -bating* or **-batting**) *tr & intr* combattre
combatant ['kambətənt] *adj & s* combattant *m*
com'bat du'ty *s* service *m* de combat, service au front
combination [,kambɪ'neʃən] *s* combinaison *f*
combine ['kambaɪn] *s* (com) trust *m*, combinaison *f* financière, entente *f* industrielle; (agr) moissonneuse-batteuse *f* ‖ [kəm'baɪn] *tr* combiner ‖ *intr* se liguer, fusionner; (chem) se combiner
combin'ing form' *s* élément *m* de composition
combo ['kambo] *s (of four musicians)* quartette *f*
combustible [kəm'bʌstɪbəl] *adj & s* combustible *m*
combustion [kəm'bʌstʃən] *s* combustion *f*
come [kʌm] *v (pret* **came** [kem]; *pp* **come)** *intr* venir; **come in!** entrez!; **to come after** succéder à, suivre; *(to come to get)* venir chercher; **to come apart** se séparer, se défaire; **to come around** *(to snap back)* se rétablir; *(to give in)* céder; **to come at** *(to attack)* se jeter sur; **to come back** revenir; (coll) revenir en vogue; **to come before** précéder; *(e.g., a legislature)* se mettre devant; **to come between** s'interposer entre; **to come by** *(to get)* obtenir; *(to pass)* passer; **to come down** descendre; **to come downstairs** descendre (en bas); **to come down with** tomber malade avec; **to come for** venir chercher; **to come from** provenir de, dériver de; *(said of wind)* chasser de; **to come in** entrer; entrer dans; *(said of tide)* monter; *(said of style)* entrer en vogue; **to come in for** avoir part à; *(e.g., an inheritance)* succéder à; *(e.g., sympathy)* s'attirer; **to**

come off se détacher; (*to take place*) avoir lieu; en sortir, e.g., **to come off victori-ous** en sortir vainqueur; **to come out** sortir; (*said of sun, stars; said of book*) paraître; (*said of buds*) éclore; (*said of news*) se divulguer; (*said of debutante*) débuter; **to come out for** se prononcer pour; **to come over** se laisser persuader; arriver, e.g., **what's come over him?** qu'est-ce qui lui est arrivé?; **to come through** (*e.g., fields*) passer par, passer à travers; (*e.g., a wall*) pénétrer; (*an ill-ness*) surmonter; se tirer indemne; **to come to** revenir à soi; **to come together** s'as-sembler, se réunir; **to come true** se réa-liser; **to come up** monter; (*to occur*) se présenter; **to come upstairs** monter (en haut); **to come up to** monter jusqu'à, venir à; **to come up with** proposer

come′-and-go′ s va-et-vient *m*

come′back′ s (*of style*) (coll) retour *m* en vogue; (*of statesman*) (coll) retour *m* au pouvoir; (*slang*) réplique *f*, riposte *f*; **to stage a comeback** (coll) se réhabiliter, faire une belle remontée

comedian [kə′midɪ·ən] s (*comic*) comique *m*; (*on the legitimate stage*) comédien *m*; (*author*) auteur *m* comique

comedienne [kə,midɪ′ɛn] s comédienne *f*

come′down′ s humiliation *f*, déchéance *f*

come·dy [′kɑmədi] s (*pl* **-dies**) comédie *f*

come·ly [′kʌmli] adj (*comp* **-lier;** *super* **-liest**) (*attractive*) avenant, gracieux; (*dec-orous*) convenable, bienséant

come′-on′ s (slang) leurre *m*, attrape *f*

comet [′kɑmɪt] s comète *f*

comfort [′kʌmfərt] s (*well-being*) confort *m*; (*sympathy*) consolation *f*; (*person*) consolateur *m*; **comforts** commodités *fpl* ‖ *tr* consoler, réconforter

comfortable [′kʌmfərtəbəl] adj confortable; (*in a state of comfort*) bien; (*well-off*) à l'aise

comforter [′kʌmfərtər] s (*person*) consola-teur *m*; (*bedcover*) couvre-pieds *m* piqué; (*of wool*) cache-nez *m*; (*for baby*) tétine *f*, sucette *f*

comforting [′kʌmfərtɪŋ] adj consolateur, réconfortant

com′fort sta′tion s châlet *m* de nécessité, lieux *mpl* d'aisances, toilette *f*

comic [′kɑmɪk] adj & s comique *m*; **comics** (*cartoons*) dessins *mpl* humoristiques

com′ic op′era s opéra *m* bouffe

com′ic strip′ s bande *f* humoristique, bande dessinée

coming [′kʌmɪŋ] adj qui vient; (*future*) d'avenir, de demain ‖ s arrivée *f*, venue *f*; **comings and goings** allées et venues

com′ing out′ s (*of stocks, bonds, etc.*) émission *f*; (*of a book*) parution *f*; (*of a young lady*) début *m*

comma [′kɑmə] s virgule *f*; (*in French a period or sometimes a small space is used to mark the divisions of whole numbers*) point *m*

command [kə′mænd] s (*leadership*) gouver-nement *m*; (*order, direction*) commande-ment *m*, ordre *m*; (*e.g., of a foreign language*) maîtrise *f*; **to be at s.o.'s com-mand** être aux ordres de qn; **to have a command of** (*a language*) posséder; **to have at one's command** avoir à sa dispo-sition ‖ *tr* commander, ordonner; (*re-spect*) inspirer; (*to look out over*) do-miner; (*a language*) connaître ‖ *intr* (mil) commander, donner les ordres

commandant [,kɑmən′dænt] s commandant *m*

commandeer [,kɑmən′dɪr] *tr* réquisitionner

commander [kə′mændər] s commandant *m*

comman′der in chief′ s commandant *m* en chef

commanding [kə′mændɪŋ] adj imposant; (*in charge*) d'autorité

commemorate [kə′mɛməret] *tr* commé-morer, célébrer

commence [kə′mɛns] *tr & intr* commencer

commencement [kə′mɛnsmənt] s com-mencement *m*; (educ) jour *m* de la distri-bution des prix, jour de la collation des grades

commence′ment ex′ercise s cérémonie *f* de remise des diplômes

commend [kə′mɛnd] *tr* (*to praise*) louer; (*to entrust*) confier, recommander

commendable [kə′mɛndəbəl] adj louable

commendation [,kɑmən′deʃən] s louange *f*, éloge *m*; (mil) citation *f*

comment [′kɑmənt] s remarque *f*, observa-tion *f*, commentaire *m* ‖ *intr* faire des observations; **to comment on** commenter

commentar·y [′kɑmən,tɛri] s (*pl* **-ies**) com-mentaire *m*

commentator [′kɑmən,tetər] s commenta-teur *m*

commerce [′kɑmərs] s commerce *m*, négoce *m*

commercial [kə′mʌrʃəl] adj commercial, commerçant ‖ s annonce *f* publicitaire

commercialize [kə′mʌrʃə,laɪz] *tr* commer-cialiser

commiserate [kə′mɪzə,ret] *intr*—**to com-miserate with** compatir aux malheurs de

commiseration [kə,mɪzə′reʃən] s commisé-ration *f*

commissar [,kɑmɪ′sɑr] s commissaire *m*

commissar·y [′kɑmɪ,sɛri] s (*pl* **-ies**) (*person*) commissaire *m*; (*canteen*) can-tine *f*

commission [kə′mɪʃən] s commission *f*; (*board, council*) conseil *m*; (com) guelte *f*; (mil) brevet *m*; **out of commission** hors de service; (naut) désarmé ‖ *tr* commis-sionner; (mil) promouvoir

commis′sioned of′ficer s breveté *m*

commissioner [kə′mɪʃənər] s commissaire *m*

com·mit [kə′mɪt] *v* (*pret & pp* **-mitted;** *ger* **-mitting**) *tr* (*an error, crime, etc.*) com-mettre; (*one's soul, one's money, etc.*) confier; (*one's word*) engager; (*to a men-tal hospital*) interner; **to commit to mem-**

ory apprendre par cœur; **to commit to prison** envoyer en prison; **to commit to writing** coucher par écrit

commitment [kə'mɪtmənt] *s* (*act of committing*) perpétration *f*; (*to a mental institution*) internement *m*; (*to prison*) emprisonnement *m*; (*to a cause*) engagement *m*

committal [kə'mɪtəl] *s* (*of a crime*) perpétration *f*; (*of a task*) délégation *f*; **committal to prison** mise *f* en prison

commit'tal ser'vice *s* (eccl) prières *fpl* au bord de la tombe

committee [kə'mɪti] *s* comité *m*, commission *f*

commode [kə'mod] *s* (*toilet*) chaise *f* percée; (*dressing table*) grande table *f* de nuit

commodious [kə'modɪ·əs] *adj* spacieux, confortable

commodi·ty [kə'madɪti] *s* (*pl* -**ties**) denrée *f*, marchandise *f*

common ['kamən] *adj* commun ‖ *s* terrain *m* communal; **commons** communaux *mpl*; (*of school*) réfectoire *m*; **the Commons** (Brit) les communes *fpl*

com'mon car'rier *s* entreprise *f* de transports en commun

commoner ['kamənər] *s* homme *m* du peuple, roturier *m*; (Brit) membre *m* de la Chambre des communes

com'mon law' *s* droit *m* coutumier, coutume *f*

com'mon-law mar'riage *s* union *f* libre, collage *m*

Com'mon Mar'ket *s* Marché *m* Commun

com'mon noun' *s* nom *m* commun

com'mon·place' *adj* banal ‖ *s* banalité *f*

com'mon sense' *s* sens *m* commun

com'mon-sense' *adj* sensé

com'mon stock' *s* action *f* ordinaire, actions ordinaires

commonweal ['kamən,wil] *s* bien *m* public

com'mon·wealth' *s* état *m*, république *f*

commotion [kə'moʃən] *s* commotion *f*

commune [kə'mjun] *intr* s'entretenir; (eccl) communier

communicant [kə'mjunɪkənt] *s* informateur *m*; (eccl) communiant *m*

communicate [kə'mjunɪ,ket] *tr & intr* communiquer

communicating [kə'mjunɪ,ketɪŋ] *adj* communicant

communication [kə,mjunɪ'keʃən] *s* communication *f*

communica'tions sat'ellite *s* satellite *m* de transmission

communicative [kə'mjunɪ,ketɪv] *adj* communicatif

communion [kə'mjunjən] *s* communion *f*; **to take communion** communier

communism ['kamjə,nɪzəm] *s* communisme *m*

communist ['kamjənɪst] *adj & s* communiste *mf*

communi·ty [kə'mjunɪti] *s* (*pl* -**ties**) (*locality*) voisinage *m*; (*group of people living together*) communauté *f*

commu'nity chest' *s* caisse *f* de secours

commutation [,kamjə'teʃən] *s* commutation *f*

commuta'tion tick'et *s* carte *f* d'abonnement

commutator ['kamjə,tetər] *s* (elec) collecteur *m*

commute [kə'mjut] *tr* échanger; (*e.g.*, *a prison term*) commuer ‖ *intr* s'abonner au chemin de fer; voyager avec carte d'abonnement

commuter [kə'mjutər] *s* abonné *m* au chemin de fer

commut'er air'line *s* transporteur *m* d'appoint

compact [kəm'pækt] *adj* compact ‖ ['kampækt] *s* (*agreement*) pacte *m*; (*for cosmetics*) poudrier *m*, boîte *f* à poudre

companion [kəm'pænjən] *s* compagnon *m*; (*female companion*) compagne *f*

companionable [kəm'pænjənəbəl] *adj* sociable

compan'ion·ship' *s* camaraderie *f*

compan'ion·way' *s* escalier *m* des cabines

compa·ny ['kʌmpəni] *s* (*pl* -**nies**) compagnie *f*; (com) société *f*, compagnie; (naut) équipage *m*; (theat) troupe *f*; **to have company** avoir du monde; **to keep bad company** fréquenter la mauvaise compagnie; **to keep company** sortir ensemble; **to keep s.o. company** tenir compagnie à qn; **to part company** se séparer

comparative [kəm'pærətɪv] *adj* comparatif; (*anatomy, literature, etc.*) comparé ‖ *s* comparatif *m*

compare [kəm'pɛr] *s*—**beyond compare** incomparablement, sans égal ‖ *tr* comparer; **compared to** en comparaison de; **to be compared to** se comparer à

comparison [kəm'pærɪsən] *s* comparaison *f*

compartment [kəm'partmənt] *s* compartiment *m*

compass ['kʌmpəs] *s* (*for showing direction*) boussole *f*; (*range, reach*) portée *f*; (*for drawing circles*) compas *m*; **to box the compass** réciter la rose des vents ‖ *tr*—**to compass about** entourer

com'pass card' *s* rose *f* des vents

compassion [kəm'pæʃən] *s* compassion *f*

compassionate [kəm'pæʃənɪt] *adj* compatissant

compatibility [kəm,pætɪ'bɪlɪti] *s* compatibilité *f*, convenance *f*

com·pel [kəm'pɛl] *v* (*pret & pp* -**pelled**; *ger* -**pelling**) *tr* contraindre, obliger; (*respect, silence*) imposer

compelling [kəm'pɛlɪŋ] *adj* irrésistible; (*motive*) impérieux

compendious [kəm'pɛndɪ·əs] *adj* abrégé, succinct

compensate ['kampən,set] *tr* compenser; **to compensate s.o. for** dédommager qn de ‖ *intr*—**to compensate for** compenser

compensation [,kampən'seʃən] *s* compensation *f*

compete [kəm'pit] *intr* concourir

competence ['kampɪtəns] *or* **competency** ['kampɪtənsi] *s* compétence *f*

competent [ˈkɑmpɪtənt] *adj* compétent
competition [ˌkɑmpɪˈtɪʃən] *s* concurrence *f*, compétition *f*; (*contest*) concours *m*; (sports) compétition, épreuve *f*
competitive [kəmˈpɛtɪtɪv] *adj* compétitif
compet′itive exam′ination *s* concours *m*
competitiveness [kəmˈpɛtɪtɪvnɪs] *s* compétitivité *f*
competitor [kəmˈpɛtɪtər] *s* concurrent *m*
compilation [ˌkɑmpɪˈleʃən] *s* compilation *f*
compile [kəmˈpaɪl] *tr* compiler
compiler [kəmˈpaɪlər] *s* compilateur *m*, rédacteur *m*; (comp) compilateur
complacency [kəmˈplesənsi] *s* complaisance *f*; (*self-satisfaction*) suffisance *f*
complacent [kəmˈplesənt] *adj* complaisant; content de soi, suffisant
complain [kəmˈplen] *intr* se plaindre
complainant [kəmˈplenənt] *s* plaignant *m*
complaint [kəmˈplent] *s* plainte *f*; (*grievance*) grief *m*; (*illness*) maladie *f*, mal *m*, symptômes *mpl*, doléances *fpl*
complaisant [kəmˈplezənt] *adj* complaisant
complement [ˈkɑmplɪmənt] *s* complément *m*; (mil) effectif *m* ‖ [ˈkɑmplɪˌmɛnt] *tr* compléter
complete [kəmˈplit] *adj* complet ‖ *tr* compléter
complex [kəmˈplɛks] *adj* complexe ‖ [ˈkɑmplɛks] *s* complexe *m*
complexion [kəmˈplɛkʃən] *s* (*texture of skin, especially of face*) teint *m*; (*general aspect*) caractère *m*; (*constitution*) complexion *f*
compliance [kəmˈplaɪ·əns] *s* complaisance *f*, soumission *f*, conformité *f*; **in compliance with** conformément à
complicate [ˈkɑmplɪˌket] *tr* compliquer
complicated *adj* compliqué
complication [ˌkɑmplɪˈkeʃən] *s* complication *f*
complici·ty [kəmˈplɪsɪti] *s* (*pl* -ties) complicité *f*
compliment [ˈkɑmplɪmənt] *s* compliment *m*; **compliments** (*kind regards*) civilités *fpl*; **to pay a compliment to** faire un compliment à; **with the compliments of the author** hommage de l'auteur ‖ *tr* complimenter
com′plimen′tary cop′y [ˌkɑmplɪˈmɛntəri] *s* exemplaire *m* en hommage; **to give a complimentary copy of a book** faire hommage d'un livre
com′plimen′tary tick′et *s* billet *m* de faveur
com·ply [kəmˈplaɪ] *v* (*pret & pp* -plied) *intr*—**to comply with** se conformer à, acquiescer à
component [kəmˈponənt] *adj* composant ‖ *s* (chem) composant *m*; (mech, math) composante *f*
comportment [kəmˈportmənt] *s* comportement *m*
compose [kəmˈpoz] *tr* composer; **to be composed of** se composer de; **to compose oneself** se calmer
composed *adj* paisible, tranquille

composer [kəmˈpozər] *s* compositeur *m*
compos′ing stick′ *s* composteur *m*
composite [kəmˈpazɪt] *adj & s* composé *m*
composition [ˌkɑmpəˈzɪʃən] *s* composition *f*
compositor [kəmˈpazɪtər] *s* compositeur *m*
compost [ˈkɑmpost] *s* compost *m*
composure [kəmˈpoʒər] *s* calme *m*, sangfroid *m*
compote [ˈkɑmpot] *s* (*stewed fruits*) compote *f*; (*dish*) compotier *m*
compound [ˈkɑmpaʊnd] *adj* composé ‖ *s* (*mixture*) composé *m*; (gram) mot *m* composé; (math) complexe *m*; (mil) enceinte *f* ‖ [kɑmˈpaʊnd] *tr* composer, combiner; (*interest*) capitaliser
comprehend [ˌkɑmprɪˈhɛnd] *tr* comprendre
comprehensible [ˌkɑmprɪˈhɛnsɪbəl] *adj* compréhensible
comprehension [ˌkɑmprɪˈhɛnʃən] *s* compréhension *f*
comprehensive [ˌkɑmprɪˈhɛnsɪv] *adj* compréhensif, étendu; (*study, view, measure*) d'ensemble
comprehen′sive insur′ance *s* assurance *f* multirisque
compress [ˈkɑmprɛs] *s* (med) compresse *f* ‖ [kəmˈprɛs] *tr* comprimer
compression [kəmˈprɛʃən] *s* compression *f*
comprise [kəmˈpraɪz] *tr* comprendre, renfermer
compromise [ˈkɑmprəˌmaɪz] *s* compromis *m*; (*with one's conscience*) transaction *f*; **rough compromise** cote *f* mal taillée ‖ *tr* (*e.g., one's honor*) compromettre ‖ *intr* (*to make concessions*) transiger
comptroller [kənˈtrolər] *s* vérificateur *m*, contrôleur *m*
compulsive [kəmˈpʌlsɪv] *adj* obligatoire; (psychol) compulsif
compulsory [kəmˈpʌlsəri] *adj* obligatoire, forcé
compute [kəmˈpjut] *tr* computer, calculer, supputer ‖ *intr* calculer
computer [kəmˈpjutər] *adj* informatique ‖ *s* ordinateur *m*; **to operate a computer** faire de l'informatique
comput′er composi′tion *s* (typ) composition *f* programmée
computerization [kəmˌpjutəraɪˈzeʃən] *s* informatisation *f*, mise *f* sur ordinateur
computerize [kəmˈpjutəraɪz] *tr* informatiser, mettre sur ordinateur
computerized *adj* fait à l'ordinateur
comput′er lan′guage *s* langage *m* de programmation
comput′er pro′gramer *s* programmeur *m*
comput′er pro′graming *s* programmation *f*
comput′er sci′ence *s* informatique *f*, science *f* de l'information
comrade [ˈkɑmræd] *s* camarade *mf*
com′rade in arms′ *s* compagnon *m* d'armes
com′rade·ship′ *s* camaraderie *f*
con [kɑn] *s* contre *m* ‖ *v* (*pret & pp* **conned**; *ger* **conning**) *tr* étudier; (naut) gouverner; (slang) escroquer
concave [kɑnˈkev] *adj* concave

conceal [kən'sil] *tr* dissimuler
concealment [kən'silmənt] *s* (*hiding*) dissimulation *f*; (*place*) cachette *f*
concede [kən'sid] *tr* & *intr* concéder
conceit [kən'sit] *s* (*vanity*) vanité *f*; (*witty expression*) saillie *f*, mot *m*; **conceits** concetti *mpl*
conceited *adj* vaniteux, vain
conceivable [kən'sivəbəl] *adj* concevable
conceive [kən'siv] *tr* & *intr* concevoir
concentrate ['kɑnsən,tret] *tr* concentrer || *intr* se concentrer
concentra'tion camp' [,kɑnsən'treʃən] *s* camp *m* de concentration
concentric [kən'sɛntrɪk] *adj* concentrique
concept ['kɑnsɛpt] *s* concept *m*
conception [kən'sɛpʃən] *s* conception *f*
concern [kən'sʌrn] *s* (*business establishment*) maison *f*, compagnie *f*; (*worry*) inquiétude *f*; (*relation, reference*) intérêt *m*; (*matter*) affaire *f* || *tr* concerner; **as concerns** quant à; **my book concerns** . . . mon livre traite de . . ., il s'agit dans mon livre de . . .; **persons concerned** intéressés *mpl*; **to be concerned** être inquiet; **to be concerned about** se préoccuper de; **to concern oneself with** s'intéresser à; **to whom it may concern** à qui de droit
concerning [kən'sʌrnɪŋ] *prep* concernant, en ce qui concerne, touchant
concert ['kɑnsərt] *s* concert *m*; **in concert** de concert || [kən'sʌrt] *tr* concerter || *intr* se concerter
con'cert·mas'ter *s* premier violon *m* soliste
concer·to [kən'tʃɛrto] *s* (*pl* **-tos** or **-ti** [ti]) concerto *m*
concession [kən'sɛʃən] *s* concession *f*
conciliate [kən'sɪlɪ,et] *tr* concilier
conciliatory [kən'sɪlɪ·ə,tori] *adj* conciliatoire
concise [kən'saɪs] *adj* concis
conclude [kən'klud] *tr* & *intr* conclure
conclusion [kən'kluʒən] *s* conclusion *f*
conclusive [kən'klusɪv] *adj* concluant
concoct [kən'kɑkt] *tr* confectionner; (*a story*) inventer; (*a plan*) machiner
concoction [kən'kɑkʃən] *s* confection *f*; (*mixture*) mélange *m*; (*pej*) drogue *f*
concomitant [kən'kɑmɪtənt] *adj* concomitant || *s* accompagnement *m*
concord ['kɑŋkɔrd] *s* concorde *f*; (*gram*) concordance *f*; (*mus*) accord *m*
concordance [kən'kɔrdəns] *s* concordance *f*
concourse ['kɑŋkors] *s* (*of people*) concours *m*, foule *f*; (*road*) boulevard *m*; (*of railroad station*) hall *m*, salle *f* des pas perdus
concrete ['kɑnkrit] *adj* concret; de béton || *s* concret *m*; (*for construction*) béton *m* || *tr* (*a sidewalk*) bétonner
con'crete block' *s* parpaing *m*
con'crete mix'er *s* bétonnière *f*
concubine ['kɑŋkjə,baɪn] *s* concubine *f*
con·cur [kən'kʌr] *v* (*pret* & *pp* **-curred**; *ger* **-curring**) *intr* (*said of events*) concourir; (*said of persons*) s'accorder

concurrence [kən'kʌrəns] *s* concours *m*
concurrent [kən'kʌrənt] *adj* concourant
concussion [kən'kʌʃən] *s* secousse *f*, ébranlement *m*; (*pathol*) commotion *f*
condemn [kən'dɛm] *tr* condamner
condemnation [,kɑndɛm'neʃən] *s* condamnation *f*
condense [kən'dɛns] *tr* condenser || *intr* se condenser
condenser [kən'dɛnsər] *s* condenseur *m*; (*elec*) condensateur *m*
condescend [,kɑndɪ'sɛnd] *intr* condescendre
condescending [,kɑndɪ'sɛndɪŋ] *adj* condescendant
condescension [,kɑndɪ'sɛnʃən] *s* condescendance *f*
condiment ['kɑndɪmənt] *s* condiment *m*
condition [kən'dɪʃən] *s* condition *f*; **on condition that** à condition que || *tr* conditionner
conditional [kən'dɪʃənəl] *adj* & *s* conditionnel *m*
condi'tioned re'flex *s* réflexe *m* conditionné
conditioning [kən'dɪʃənɪŋ] *s* conditionnement *m*
condo ['kɑndo] *s* (coll) immeuble *m* à copropriété
condole [kən'dol] *intr*—**to condole with** offrir ses condoléances à
condolence [kən'doləns] *s* condoléances *fpl*
condom ['kɑndəm] *s* préservatif *m*, capote *f* anglaise
condominium [,kɑndə'mɪni·əm] *s* immeuble *m* à copropriété
condone [kən'don] *tr* pardonner, tolérer
conducive [kən'd(j)usɪv] *adj* favorable
conduct ['kɑndʌkt] *s* conduite *f*, comportement *m* || [kən'dʌkt] *tr* conduire
conductor [kən'dʌktər] *s* (*on bus or streetcar*) receveur *m*; (*mus*) chef *m* d'orchestre; (rr) chef de train; (*elec, phys*) conducteur *m*; (*elec, phys*) (in predicate after **to be**, it may be translated by an adjective) conducteur, e.g., **metals are good conductors of electricity** les métaux sont bons conducteurs de l'électricité
conduit ['kɑndɪt], ['kɑndu·ɪt] *s* (*pipe*) conduit *m*, tuyau *m*; (*elec*) caniveau *m*, tube *m*
cone [kon] *s* cône *m*; (*for popcorn, ice cream*) cornet *m*, plaisir *m*
confection [kən'fɛkʃən] *s* confiserie *f*
confectioner [kən'fɛkʃənər] *s* confiseur *m*
confec'tioners' sug'ar *s* sucre *m* glace
confectioner·y [kən'fɛkʃə,nɛri] *s* (*pl* **-ies**) confiserie *f*
confedera·cy [kən'fədərəsi] *s* (*pl* **-cies**) confédération *f*; (*for unlawful purposes*) conspiration *f*, entente *f*
confederate [kən'fɛdərɪt] *adj* confédéré || *s* complice *mf*; **Confederate** (hist) Confédéré *m* || [kən'fɛdə,ret] *tr* confédérer || *intr* se confédérer
con·fer [kən'fʌr] *v* (*pret* & *pp* **-ferred**; *ger* **-ferring**) *tr* & *intr* conférer

conference ['kɑnfərəns] s conférence f; (*interview*) entretien m; (sports) groupement m (d'équipes); **to be in conference** être en conférence
con'ference room' s salle f de conférences
con'ference ta'ble s table f de conférence
conferment [kən'fʌrmənt] s (*of degrees*) collation f
confess [kən'fɛs] tr confesser ‖ intr se confesser
confession [kən'fɛʃən] s confession f
confessional [kən'fɛʃənəl] s confessional m
confessor [kən'fɛsər] s confesseur m
confidant [,kɑnfɪ'dænt] s confident m
confide [kən'faɪd] tr confier ‖ intr—**to confide in** se confier à
confidence ['kɑnfɪdəns] s confiance f; (*secret*) confidence f; **in strict confidence** sous toute réserve; **to have confidence in** se confier à
confident ['kɑnfɪdənt] adj confiant ‖ s confident m
confidential [,kɑnfɪ'dɛnʃəl] adj confidentiel
confiden'tial sec'retary s secrétaire m particulier, secrétaire f particulière
confine ['kɑnfaɪn] s (obs) confinement m; **the confines** les confins mpl ‖ [kən'faɪn] tr confiner, enfermer; (*to keep within limits*) limiter; **to be confined** (*said of woman*) accoucher; **to be confined to bed** être alité
confinement [kən'faɪnmənt] s limitation f; (*in prison*) emprisonnement m; (*in childbirth*) accouchement m
confirm [kən'fʌrm] tr confirmer
confirmed adj (*reassured*) confirmé; (*bachelor*) endurci; (*drunkard*) fieffé; (*drinker*) invétéré; (*smoker*) émérite
confiscate ['kɑnfɪs,ket] tr confisquer
conflagration [,kɑnflə'greʃən] s conflagration f, incendie m
conflict ['kɑnflɪkt] s conflit m ‖ [kən'flɪkt] intr être en contradiction, se heurter
conflicting [kən'flɪktɪŋ] adj contradictoire; (*events, class hours, etc.*) incompatible
con'flict of in'terest s conflit m d'intérêts, conflit des intérêts
conform [kən'fɔrm] tr conformer ‖ intr se conformer, s'accommoder
conformist [kən'fɔrmɪst] s conformiste mf
conformi·ty [kən'fɔrmɪti] s (pl **-ties**) conformité f; **in conformity with** conformément à
confound [kɑn'faʊnd] tr confondre ‖ ['kɑn'faʊnd] tr maudire; **confound it!** diable!
confounded adj confus; (*damned*) sacré
confrere ['kɑnfrɛr] s confrère m
confront [kən'frʌnt] tr (*to face boldly*) affronter, faire face à; (*witnesses; documents*) confronter; **to be confronted by** se trouver en face de
confuse [kən'fjuz] tr confondre
confused adj confus, embarrassé
confusing [kən'fjuzɪŋ] adj déroutant, embrouillant
confusion [kən'fjuʒən] s confusion f

confute [kən'fjut] tr réfuter
congeal [kən'dʒil] tr congeler ‖ intr se congeler
congenial [kən'dʒinjəl] adj sympathique, agréable; compatible; **congenial to** or **with** apparenté à, conformer au tempérament de
congenital [kən'dʒɛnɪtəl] adj congénital
con'ger eel' ['kɑŋgər] s congre m, anguille f de mer
congest [kən'dʒɛst] tr congestionner ‖ intr se congestionner
congestion [kən'dʒɛstʃən] s congestion f
conglomeration [kən,glɑmə'reʃən] s conglomération f
congratulate [kən'grætʃə,let] tr féliciter, congratuler; **to congratulate s.o. for** féliciter qn de or pour; **to congratulate s.o. for** + *ger* féliciter qn de + *inf*
congratulations [kən,grætʃə'leʃənz] spl félicitations fpl
congregate ['kɑŋgrɪ,get] tr rassembler ‖ intr se rassembler
congregation [,kɑŋgrɪ'geʃən] s (*grouping*) rassemblement m; (*parishioners*) fidèles mfpl; (*Protestant parishioners; committee of Roman Catholic prelates*) congrégation f
congress ['kɑŋgrɪs] s congrès m
congressional [kən'grɛʃənəl] adj parlementaire
con'gress·man s (pl **-men**) congressiste m, parlementaire m
con'gress·wom'an s (pl **-wom'en**) congressiste f, parlementaire f
congruent ['kɑŋgru·ənt] adj (math) congru
conical ['kɑnɪkəl] adj conique
conjecture [kən'dʒɛktʃər] s conjecture f ‖ tr & intr conjecturer
conjugal ['kɑndʒəgəl] adj conjugal
conjugate ['kɑndʒə,get] tr conjuguer
conjugation [,kɑndʒə'geʃən] s conjugaison f
conjunction [kən'dʒʌŋkʃən] s conjonction f
conjuration [,kɑndʒə'reʃən] s conjuration f
conjure [kən'dʒʊr] tr (*to appeal to solemnly*) conjurer ‖ ['kɑndʒər], ['kʌndʒər] tr (*to exorcise, drive away*) conjurer; **conjure up** évoquer ‖ intr faire de la sorcellerie
con' man' s escroc m
connect [kə'nɛkt] tr (*to join*) relier, joindre; (*e.g., two parties on the telephone*) mettre en communication; (*a pipe, an electrical device*) brancher, connecter ‖ intr se lier, se joindre; **to connect with** (*said of train*) correspondre avec
connected adj (*related*) connexe; (*logical*) suivi
connecting [kə'nɛktɪŋ] adj de liaison; (*wire*) de connexion; (*pipe*) de raccord; (*street*) communiquant
connect'ing flight' s vol m en transit
connect'ing rod' s bielle f
connection [kə'nɛkʃən] s connexion f, liaison f; (*between two causes*) connexité f;

(*in families*) parenté *f*, parent *m*; (*by telephone*) communication *f*; (*of trains*) correspondance *f*; (elec) connexion; **connections** (*in the business world*) clientèle *f*, relations *fpl*; (*in families*) alliés *mpl*, consanguins *mpl*; **in connection with** à propos de

con′ning tow′er [ˈkɑnɪŋ] *s* (*e.g.*, *on battleship*) poste *m* or tourelle *f* de commandement; (*on sub*) kiosque *m*

conniption [kəˈnɪpʃən] *s* (*coll*) rogne *f*

connive [kəˈnaɪv] *intr* être de connivence, être complice

connote [kəˈnot] *tr* (*to signify*) signifier, vouloir dire; (*to imply*) suggérer, sous-entendre

connubial [kəˈn(j)ubɪ·əl] *adj* conjugal

conquer [ˈkɑŋkər] *tr* conquérir

conqueror [ˈkɑŋkərər] *s* conquérant

conquest [ˈkɑŋkwɛst] *s* conquête *f*

conscience [ˈkɑnʃəns] *s* conscience *f*; **in all conscience** en conscience; **to have on one's conscience** avoir sur la conscience

conscientious [ˌkɑnʃɪˈɛnʃəs] *adj* consciencieux

conscien′tious objec′tor [əbˈdʒɛktər] *s* objecteur *m* de conscience

conscious [ˈkɑnʃəs] *adj* conscient; **to be conscious** (*not unconscious*) avoir connaissance; **to be conscious of** avoir conscience de

consciousness [ˈkɑnʃəsnɪs] *s* (*not sleep or coma*) connaissance *f*; (*awareness*) conscience *f*

conscript [ˈkɑnskrɪpt] *s* (mil) conscrit *m*; (nav) inscrit *m* maritime ‖ [kənˈskrɪpt] *tr* (mil) enrôler; (nav) inscrire

conscription [kənˈskrɪpʃən] *s* conscription *f*

consecrate [ˈkɑnsɪˌkret] *tr* consacrer; (*e.g., bread*) bénir; (*a king or bishop*) sacrer

consecration [ˌkɑnsɪˈkreʃən] *s* consécration *f*; (*to a task*) dévouement *m*; (*of a king or bishop*) sacre *m*

consecutive [kənˈsɛkjətɪv] *adj* de suite, consécutif

consensus [kənˈsɛnsəs] *s* consensus *m*

consent [kənˈsɛnt] *s* consentement *m*; **by common consent** d'un commun accord ‖ *intr* consentir

consequence [ˈkɑnsɪˌkwɛns] *s* conséquence *f*

consequential [ˌkɑnsɪˈkwɛnʃəl] *adj* conséquent, logique

consequently [ˈkɑnsɪˌkwɛntli] *adv* conséquemment, par conséquent

conservation [ˌkɑnsərˈveʃən] *s* conservation *f*

conservatism [kənˈsɑrvəˌtɪzəm] *s* conservatisme *m*

conservative [kənˈsɑrvətɪv] *adj & s* conservateur *m*; **at a conservative estimate** au bas mot, au moins

conservato·ry [kənˈsɑrvəˌtori] *s* (*pl* **-ries**) (*of music*) conservatoire *m*; (*greenhouse*) serre *f*

conserve [kənˈsɑrv] *tr* conserver

consider [kənˈsɪdər] *tr* considérer

considerable [kənˈsɪdərəbəl] *adj* considérable

considerate [kənˈsɪdərɪt] *adj* prévenant, plein d'égards

consideration [kənˌsɪdəˈreʃən] *s* (*thoughtfulness; careful thought; fact*) considération *f*; (*remuneration*) rétribution *f*; (*favor*) indulgence *f*; **to take into consideration** tenir compte de; **under consideration** à l'étude, en ligne de compte, en présence

considering [kənˈsɪdərɪŋ] *prep* eu égard à; **considering that** vu que

consign [kənˈsaɪn] *tr* consigner

consignee [ˌkɑnsaɪˈni] *s* consignataire *m*

consignment [kənˈsaɪnmənt] *s* consignation *f*, livraison *f*

consist [kənˈsɪst] *intr*—**to consist in** consister dans or en; **to consist in** + *ger* consister à + *inf*; **to consist of** consister dans or en

consisten·cy [kənˈsɪstənsi] *s* (*pl* **-cies**) (*logical connection*) conséquence *f*; (*firmness, amount of firmness*) consistance *f*

consistent [kənˈsɪstənt] *adj* (*agreeing with itself or oneself*) conséquent; (*holding firmly together*) consistant; **consistent with** compatible avec

consisto·ry [kənˈsɪstəri] *s* (*pl* **-ries**) consistoire *m*

consolation [ˌkɑnsəˈleʃən] *s* consolation *f*

console [ˈkɑnsol] *s* console *f* ‖ [kənˈsol] *tr* consoler

con′sole ta′ble *s* console *f*

consolidate [kənˈsɑlɪˌdet] *tr* consolider

consonant [ˈkɑnsənənt] *adj* (*in sound*) consonant; **consonant with** d'accord avec ‖ *s* consonne *f*

consort [ˈkɑnsɔrt] *s* (*husband*) conjoint *m*; (*wife*) conjointe *f*; prince *m* consort; (*convoy*) conserve *f* ‖ [kənˈsɔrt] *tr* unir ‖ *intr* s'associer; (*to harmonize*) s'accorder; **to consort with** s'associer à or avec

conspicuous [kənˈspɪkju·əs] *adj* (*difference*) apparent, frappant; (*attracting special attention*) voyant; **to make oneself conspicuous** se faire remarquer

conspira·cy [kənˈspɪrəsi] *s* (*pl* **-cies**) conspiration *f*, conjuration *f*

conspirator [kənˈspɪrətər] *s* conspirateur *m*, conjuré *m*

conspire [kənˈspaɪr] *intr* conspirer

constancy [ˈkɑnstænsi] *s* constance *f*

constant [ˈkɑnstənt] *adj* constant ‖ *s* constante *f*

constantly [ˈkɑnstəntli] *adv* constamment

constellation [ˌkɑnstəˈleʃən] *s* constellation *f*

constipate [ˈkɑnstɪˌpet] *tr* constiper

constipation [ˌkɑnstɪˈpeʃən] *s* constipation *f*

constituen·cy [kənˈstɪtʃu·ənsi] *s* (*pl* **-cies**) (*persons*) électeurs *mpl*, mandants *mpl*; (*place*) circonscription *f* électorale

constituent [kənˈstɪtʃu·ənt] *adj* constituant, constitutif ‖ *s* élément *m*, constituant *m*; (*voter, client*) électeur *m*, commettant *m*

constitute [ˈkɑnstɪˌt(j)ut] *tr* constituer

constitution [,kɑnstɪ't(j)uʃən] *s* constitution *f*

constrain [kən'stren] *tr* contraindre

constraint [kən'strent] *s* contrainte *f*; (*restraint*) retenue *f*; (*uneasiness*) gêne *f*

constrict [kən'strɪkt] *tr* resserrer

construct [kən'strʌkt] *tr* construire

construction [kən'strʌkʃən] *s* construction *f*; interprétation *f*

construc′tion per′mit *s* permis *m* de construire

construc′tion start′ *s* mise *f* en chantier

constructive [kən'strʌktɪv] *adj* constructif, constructeur

construe [kən'stru] *tr* expliquer, interpréter; (gram) construire

consul ['kɑnsəl] *s* consul *m*

consular ['kɑns(j)ələr] *adj* consulaire

consulate ['kɑns(j)əlɪt] *s* consulat *m*

consult [kən'sʌlt] *tr* consulter ‖ *intr* consulter; se consulter

consultant [kən'sʌltənt] *s* conseiller *m*, consultant *m*

consultation [kɑn,səl'teʃən] *s* consultation *f*; (eccl, law) consulte *f*

consume [kən's(j)um] *tr* (*to make use of, use up*) consommer; (*to use up entirely; to destroy*) consumer, épuiser

consumer [kən's(j)umər] *s* consommateur *m*; (*of gas, electricity, etc.*) abonné *m*

consum′er goods′ *spl* denrées *fpl* de consommation

consummate [kən'sʌmɪt] *adj* consommé ‖ ['kɑnsə,met] *tr* consommer

consumption [kən'sʌmpʃən] *s* consommation *f*; (pathol) tuberculose *f* pulmonaire

contact ['kɑntækt] *s* contact *m*; **to put in contact** mettre en contact ‖ *tr* (coll) prendre contact avec, contacter ‖ *intr* prendre contact

con′tact lens′ *s* verre *m* de contact, lentille *f* de contact, lentille cornéenne

contagion [kən'tedʒən] *s* contagion *f*

contagious [kən'tedʒəs] *adj* contagieux

contain [kən'ten] *tr* contenir; (*one's sorrow*) apprivoiser

container [kən'tenər] *s* boîte *f*, contenant *m*, récipient *m*; (*to ship goods*) conteneur *m*

containment [kən'tenmənt] *s* refoulement *m*, retenue *f*; (*in a nuclear reactor*) confinement *m*

contaminate [kən'tæmɪ,net] *tr* contaminer

contamination [kən,tæmɪ'neʃən] *s* contamination *f*

contemplate ['kɑntəm,plet] *tr* & *intr* contempler; (*e.g., a trip*) projeter; **to contemplate** + *ger* penser + *inf*

contemplation [,kɑntəm'pleʃən] *s* contemplation *f*

contemporaneous [kən,tɛmpə'renɪ·əs] *adj* contemporain

contemporar·y [kən'tɛmpə,rɛri] *adj* contemporain ‖ *s* (*pl* -ies) contemporain *m*

contempt [kən'tɛmpt] *s* mépris *m*, nargue *f*; (law) contumace *f*; **to hold in contempt** mépriser

contemptible [kən'tɛmptɪbəl] *adj* méprisable

contempt′ of court′ *s* outrage *m* à la justice

contemptuous [kən'tɛmptʃu·əs] *adj* méprisant

contend [kən'tɛnd] *tr* prétendre ‖ *intr* combattre; **to contend with** lutter contre

contender [kən'tɛndər] *s* concurrent *m*, compétiteur *m*

content [kən'tɛnt] *adj* & *s* content *m* ‖ ['kɑntɛnt] *s* contenu *m*; **contents** contenu; (*of table of contents*) matières *fpl* ‖ [kən'tɛnt] *tr* contenter

contented [kən'tɛntɪd] *adj* content, satisfait

contention [kən'tɛnʃən] *s* (*strife*) dispute *f*, différend *m*; (*point argued for*) point *m* discuté, argument *m*; (law) contentieux *m*

contentious [kən'tɛnʃəs] *adj* contentieux

contentment [kən'tɛntmənt] *s* contentement *m*

contest ['kɑntɛst] *s* (*struggle, fight*) lutte *f*, dispute *f*; (*competition*) concours *m*, compétition *f* ‖ [kən'tɛst] *tr* & *intr* contester

contestant [kən'tɛstənt] *s* concurrent *m*

context ['kɑntɛkst] *s* contexte *m*

contiguous [kən'tɪgju·əs] *adj* contigu

continence ['kɑntɪnəns] *s* continence *f*

continent ['kɑntɪnənt] *adj* & *s* continent *m*

continental [,kɑntɪ'nɛntəl] *adj* continental

contingen·cy [kən'tɪndʒənsi] *s* (*pl* -cies) contingence *f*, éventualité *f*

contingent [kən'tɪndʒənt] *adj* & *s* contingent *m*

continual [kən'tɪnju·əl] *adj* continuel

continuation [kən,tɪnju'eʃən] *s* continuation *f*; (*e.g., of a story*) suite *f*

continue [kən'tɪnju] *tr* & *intr* continuer; **continued on page two (three, etc.)** suite page deux (trois, etc.); **to be continued** à suivre

continui·ty [,kɑntɪ'n(j)u·ɪti] *s* (*pl* -ties) continuité *f*; (mov, rad, telv) découpage *m*, scénario *m*

continuous [kən'tɪnju·əs] *adj* continu

contin′uous show′ing *s* (mov) spectacle *m* permanent

contin′uous waves′ *spl* ondes *fpl* entretenues

contortion [kən'tɔrʃən] *s* contorsion *f*

contour ['kɑntʊr] *s* contour *m* ‖ *tr* contourner

con′tour line′ *s* courbe *f* de niveau

contraband ['kɑntrə,bænd] *adj* contrebandier ‖ *s* contrebande *f*

contrabass ['kɑntrə,bes] *s* contrebasse *f*

contraceptive [,kɑntrə'sɛptɪv] *adj* & *s* contraceptif *m*

contract ['kɑntrækt] *s* contrat *m* ‖ *tr* contracter ‖ *intr* se contracter

contraction [kən'trækʃən] *s* contraction *f*

contractor [kən'træktər], [kɑntræktər] *s* entrepreneur *m* du bâtiment

contradict [,kɑntrə'dɪkt] *tr* contredire

contradiction [,kɑntrə'dɪkʃən] *s* contradiction *f*

contradictory [,kɑntrə'dɪktəri] *adj* contradictoire

contral·to [kən'trælto] *s* (*pl* **-tos**) contralto *m*

contraption [kən'træpʃən] *s* (coll) machin *m*, truc *m*

contra·ry ['kɑntrɛri] *adj* contraire ‖ *adv* contrairement ‖ [kən'trɛri] *adj* (coll) obstiné, têtu ‖ ['kɑntrɛri] *s* (*pl* **-ries**) contraire *m*; **on the contrary** au contraire, par contre

contrast ['kɑntræst] *s* contraste *m* ‖ [kən'træst] *tr* & *intr* contraster

contravene [,kɑntrə'vin] *tr* contredire; (*a law*) contrevenir

contribute [kən'trɪbjut] *tr* (*e.g.*, *a sum of money*) contribuer pour ‖ *intr* contribuer; (*to a newspaper, conference, etc.*) collaborer

contribution [,kɑntrɪ'bjuʃən] *s* contribution *f*, apport *m*; (*e.g.*, *for charity*) souscription *f*; (*to a newspaper, conference, etc.*) collaboration *f*

contributor [kən'trɪbjutər] *s* (*donor*) donneur *m*; (*e.g.*, *to a charitable cause*) souscripteur *m*; (*to a newspaper, conference, etc.*) collaborateur *m*

contrite [kən'traɪt] *adj* contrit

contrition [kən'trɪʃən] *s* contrition *f*

contrivance [kən'traɪvəns] *s* invention *f*, expédient *m*; (*gadget*) dispositif *m*

contrive [kən'traɪv] *tr* inventer ‖ *intr* s'arranger; **to contrive to** trouver moyen de

con·trol [kən'trol] *s* (*authority*) direction *f*, autorité *f*; (*mastery*) maîtrise *f*; (*surveillance*) contrôle *m*; **controls** commandes *fpl* ‖ *v* (*pret* & *pp* **-trolled**; *ger* **-trolling**) *tr* diriger; maîtriser; (*to give surveillance to*) contrôler; (*to handle the controls of*) commander; **to control oneself** se contrôler

controller [kən'trolər] *s* contrôleur *m*, appareil *m* de contrôle; (elec) controller *m*

control' pan'el *s* (aer) planche *f* de bord, tableau *m* de bord

control' rod' *s* (nucl) barre *f* de contrôle

control' stick' *s* (aer) manche *m* à balai

control' tow'er *s* poste-vigie *m*, tourelle *f* de commandement

controversial [,kɑntrə'vʌrʃəl] *adj* controversable

controver·sy ['kɑntrə,vʌrsi] *s* (*pl* **-sies**) controverse *f*; dispute *f*, querelle *f*

controvert ['kɑntrə,vʌrt] *tr* controverser; contredire

contumacious [,kɑnt(j)u'meʃəs] *adj* rebelle, récalcitrant

contume·ly ['kɑnt(j)umɪli] *s* (*pl* **-lies**) injure *f*, outrage *m*, mépris *m*

contusion [kən't(j)uʒən] *s* contusion *f*

conundrum [kə'nʌndrəm] *s* devinette *f*, énigme *f*

convalesce [,kɑnvə'lɛs] *intr* guérir, se remettre, se rétablir

convalescence [,kɑnvə'lɛsəns] *s* convalescence *f*

convalescent [,kɑnvə'lɛsənt] *adj* & *s* convalescent *m*

convales'cent home' *s* maison *f* de repos

convene [kən'vin] *tr* assembler, convoquer ‖ *intr* s'assembler

convenience [kən'vinjəns] *s* commodité *f*, confort *m*; **at your convenience** quand cela vous conviendra; **at your earliest convenience** (com) dans les meilleurs délais; **for my own convenience** pour mon utilité personnelle

conven'ience store' *s* centre *m* commercial de quartier, épicerie *f* de dépannage

convent ['kɑnvɛnt] *s* couvent *m* (de religieuses)

convention [kən'vɛnʃən] *s* (*meeting*) assemblée *f*, congrès *m*; (*agreement*) convention *f*; (*accepted usage*) convention sociale; **conventions** convenances *fpl*, bienséances *fpl*

conventional [kən'vɛnʃənəl] *adj* conventionnel; (*in conduct*) respectueux des convenances; (*everyday*) usuel; (*model, type*) traditionnel

converge [kən'vʌrdʒ] *intr* converger

conversant [kən'vʌrsənt] *adj* familier, versé

conversation [,kɑnvər'seʃən] *s* conversation *f*

conversational [,kɑnvər'seʃənəl] *adj* de conversation; (comp) de dialogue

conversa'tional mode' *s* (comp) mode *m* dialogué

converse ['kɑnvʌrs] *adj* & *s* contraire *m*, inverse *m*, réciproque *f* ‖ [kən'vʌrs] *intr* converser

conversion [kən'vʌrʒən] *s* conversion *f*

convert ['kɑnvʌrt] *s* converti *m* ‖ [kən'vʌrt] *tr* convertir ‖ *intr* se convertir

converter [kən'vʌrtər] *s* convertisseur *m*

convertible [kən'vʌrtɪbəl] *adj* (*person*) convertissable; (*thing; security*) convertible; (*sofa*) transformable; (aut) décapotable ‖ *s* (aut) décapotable *f*

convex [kɑn'vɛks] *adj* convexe, bombé

convey [kən've] *tr* (*goods, passengers*) transporter; (*e.g.*, *a message*) communiquer; (*e.g.*, *property*) transmettre; (law) céder

conveyance [kən've·əns] *s* (*of goods, passengers*) transport *m*; (*vehicle*) moyen *m* de transport, voiture *f*; (*of message*) communication *f*; (*transfer*) transmission *f*; (law) transfert *m*, cession *f*

conveyor [kən've·ər] *s* transporteur *m*, convoyeur *m*

convey'or belt' *s* tapis *m* roulant

convict ['kɑnvɪkt] *s* condamné *m*, forçat *m* ‖ [kən'vɪkt] *tr* condamner, convaincre

conviction [kən'vɪkʃən] *s* (*sentencing*) condamnation *f*; (*certainty*) conviction *f*

convince [kən'vɪns] *tr* convaincre

convincing [kən'vɪnsɪŋ] *adj* convaincant

convivial [kən'vɪvɪ·əl] *adj* jovial, plein d'entrain

convocation [,kɑnvə'keʃən] *s* (*calling together*) convocation *f*; (*meeting*) assemblée *f*

convoke [kən'vok] *tr* convoquer

convolution [,kɑnvə'luʃən] *s* (*of brain*) circonvolution *f*

convoy [ˈkɑnvɔɪ] s convoi m, conserve f, e.g., **to sail in convoy** naviguer de conserve ‖ tr convoyer

convulse [kənˈvʌls] tr convulsionner, convulser; **to be convulsed with laughter** se tordre de rire

coo [ku] intr roucouler

cooing [ˈku·ɪŋ] s roucoulement m

cook [kʊk] s cuisinier m, chef m; (female cook) cuisinière f ‖ tr cuisiner, faire cuire; **to cook up** (a plot) machiner, tramer ‖ intr faire la cuisine, cuisiner; (said of food) cuire

cook'book' s livre m de cuisine

cooker [ˈkʊkər] s réchaud m, cuisinière f

cookery [ˈkʊkəri] s cuisine f

cookie [ˈkʊki] s var of **cooky**

cooking [ˈkʊkɪŋ] s cuisine f; (e.g., of meat) cuisson f

cook'ing uten'sils spl batterie f de cuisine

cook'stove' s cuisinière f

cook·y [ˈkʊki] s (pl -ies) biscuit m, gâteau m sec

cool [kul] adj frais; (e.g., to an idea) indifférent; **it is cool out** il fait frais; **to keep cool** tenir au frais; se tenir tranquille ‖ s fraîcheur f ‖ tr rafraîchir, refroidir; **to cool one's heels** (coll) se morfondre ‖ intr se refroidir, se rafraîchir; **to cool down** se calmer; **to cool off** se refroidir

cooler [ˈkulər] s frigorifique m; (prison) (slang) violon m, tôle f

cool'-head'ed adj imperturbable, de sang-froid

coolness [ˈkulnɪs] s fraîcheur f; (of disposition) sang-froid m, calme m; (standoffishness) froideur f

coon [kun] s raton m laveur

coop [kup] s poulailler m; **to fly the coop** (slang) débiner, décamper ‖ tr enfermer dans un poulailler; **to coop up** claquemurer

co-op [ˈko·ɑp] s entreprise f coopérative

cooper [ˈkupər] s tonnelier m

cooperate [koˈɑpə,ret] intr coopérer; (to be helpful) faire preuve de bonne volonté

cooperation [ko,ɑpəˈreʃən] s coopération f

cooperative [koˈɑpə,retɪv] adj coopératif ‖ s coopérative f

coordinate [koˈɔrdɪnɪt] adj coordonné ‖ s coordonnée f ‖ [koˈɔrdɪ,net] tr coordonner

coordination [ko,ɔrdəˈneʃən] s coordination f

coot [kut] s foulque f; **old coot** (coll) vieille baderne f

cootie [ˈkuti] s (slang) pou m

cop [kɑp] s (coll) agent m ‖ v (pret & pp **copped**; ger **copping**) tr (slang) dérober

copartner [koˈpɑrtnər] s coassocié m, coparticipant m; (in crime) complice mf

cope [kop] intr—**to cope with** faire face à, tenir tête à

cope'stone' s couronnement m

copier [ˈkɑpi·ər] s (person who copies) copiste mf, imitateur m; (apparatus) appareil m à copier; (making photocopies)

machine f à photocopier, reprographieur m

copilot [ˈko,paɪlət] s copilote m

coping [ˈkopɪŋ] s faîte m, comble m; (of bridge) chape f

copious [ˈkopi·əs] adj copieux

cop'-out' s (slang) démission f, dérobade f

copper [ˈkɑpər] adj de cuivre, en cuivre; (color) cuivré ‖ s cuivre m; (coin) petite monnaie f; (slang) flic m

cop'per·smith' s chaudronnier m

coppery [ˈkɑpəri] adj cuivreux

coppice [ˈkɑpɪs] s taillis m

copulate [ˈkɑpjə,let] intr s'accoupler

copulation [,kɑpjəˈleʃən] s copulation f, accouplement m

cop·y [ˈkɑpi] s (pl -ies) copie f; (of a book) exemplaire m; (of a magazine) numéro m; (for printer) original m; **to make copies** exécuter des doubles ‖ v (pret & pp -ied) tr & intr copier

cop'y·book' s cahier m

cop'y·cat' s (coll) imitateur m, singe m

cop'ying machine' [ˈkɑpi·ɪŋ] s machine f à photocopier, reprographieur m

cop'y·right' s propriété f artistique or littéraire, droit m de l'artiste or de l'auteur, copyright m; (formula on printed matter) dépôt m légal ‖ tr réserver les droits de publication de

cop'y·right'ed adj (formula used on printed material) droits de reproduction réservés

cop'y·writ'er s rédacteur m d'annonces publicitaires

co·quet [koˈkɛt] v (pret & pp **-quetted**; ger **-quetting**) intr coqueter

coquet·ry [ˈkokətri] s (pl -ries) coquetterie f

coquette [koˈkɛt] s coquette f ‖ intr coqueter

coquettish [koˈkɛtɪʃ] adj coquet

coral [ˈkɔrəl] adj de corail, en corail ‖ s corail m

cor'al reef' s récif m de corail

cord [kɔrd] s corde f; (string) ficelle f; (attached to a bell) cordon m; (elec) fil m ‖ tr corder

cordage [ˈkɔrdɪdʒ] s cordage m

cordial [ˈkɔrdʒəl] adj & s cordial m

cordiali·ty [kɔrˈdʒælɪti] s (pl -ties) cordialité f

corduroy [ˈkɔrdə,rɔɪ] s velours m côtelé; **corduroys** pantalon en velours côtelé

core [kor] s (of fruit) trognon m, cœur m; (of magnet, cable, earth, atom) noyau m; (nucl) cœur m; **rotten to the core** pourri à la base ‖ tr vider

corespondent [,kɔrɪsˈpɑndənt] s complice mf d'adultère

cork [kɔrk] s liège m; (of bottle) bouchon m; **to take the cork out of** déboucher ‖ tr boucher

corking [ˈkɔrkɪŋ] adj (coll) épatant

cork'oak' s chêne-liège m

cork'screw' s tire-bouchon m

cork'-tipped' adj à bout de liège

cormorant [ˈkɔrmərənt] s cormoran m

corn [kɔrn] s (in U.S.A.) maïs m; (in England) blé m; (in Scotland) avoine f; (single seed) grain m; (on foot) cor m, durillon m; (whiskey) (coll) eau-de-vie f de grain; (slang) platitude f, banalité f
corn' bread' s pain m de maïs
corn'cob' s épi m de maïs; (without the grain) rafle f
corn'cob pipe' s pipe f en rafle de maïs
corn'crib' s dépôt m de maïs
cornea ['kɔrnɪ·ə] s cornée f
corned' beef' s bœuf m salé
corner ['kɔrnər] adj cornier || s coin m, angle m; (of room) encoignure f; (of lips) commissure f; (on the market) prise f de contrôle; **around the corner** au tournant; **in a corner** (fig) au pied du mur, à l'accul; **to cut a corner close** prendre un virage à la corde; **to cut corners** (in spending) rogner les dépenses; (in work) bâcler un travail || tr coincer, acculer; (the market) accaparer
cor'ner cup'board s encoignure f
cor'ner room' s pièce f d'angle
cor'ner·stone' s pierre f angulaire
cornet [kɔr'nɛt] s cornet m; (headdress) cornette f; (mil) cornette m; (mus) cornet à pistons
corn' exchange' s bourse f des céréales
corn'field' s (in U.S.A.) champ m de maïs; (in England) champ de blé; (in Scotland) champ d'avoine
corn'flakes' spl paillettes fpl de maïs
corn' flour' s farine f de maïs
corn'flow'er s bluet m, barbeau m
corn' frit'ter s crêpes fpl de maïs
corn'husk' s enveloppe f de l'épi de maïs
cornice ['kɔrnɪs] s corniche f
corn' meal' s farine f de maïs
corn' on the cob' s maïs m en épi
corn' pad' s bourrelet m coricide
corn' pone' s pain m de maïs
corn' pop'per s appareil m pour faire éclater le maïs
corn' remov'er s coricide m
corn' silk' s barbe f de maïs
corn'stalk' s tige f de maïs
corn'starch' s fécule f de maïs
cornucopia [,kɔrnə'kopɪ·ə] s corne f d'abondance
Cornwall ['kɔrn,wɔl] s la Cornouailles
corn·y ['kɔrni] adj (comp -ier; super -iest) (slang) banal, trivial, fade
corollar·y ['kɔrə,lɛri] s (pl -ies) corollaire m
coronary ['kɔrə,nɛri] adj coronaire
cor'onary thrombo'sis s (pathol) infarctus m du myocarde
coronation [,kɔrə'neʃən] s couronnement m, sacre m
cor'oner's in'quest ['kɔrənərz] s enquête f judiciaire par-devant jury (en cas de mort violente ou suspecte)
coronet ['kɔrə,nɛt] s (worn by lady) diadème m; (worn by members of nobility) couronne f; (worn by earl or baron) tortil m

corporal ['kɔrpərəl] adj corporel || s (mil) caporal m
corporate ['kɔrpərɪt] adj incorporé
corporation [,kɔrpə'reʃən] s société f anonyme, compagnie f anonyme
corporeal [kɔr'porɪ·əl] adj corporel, matériel
corps [kor] s (pl corps [korz]) corps m; (mil) corps d'armée
corpse [kɔrps] s cadavre m
corps'man s (pl -men) (mil) infirmier m
corpulent ['kɔrpjələnt] adj corpulent
corpuscle ['kɔrpəsəl] s (phys) corpuscule m; (physiol) globule m
corpus delicti ['kɔrpəsdɪ'lɪktaɪ] s (law) corps m du délit
cor·ral [kə'ræl] s corral m, enclos m || v (pret & pp -ralled; ger -ralling) tr enfermer dans un corral; (fig) saisir
correct [kə'rɛkt] adj correct || tr corriger
correction [kə'rɛkʃən] s correction f
corrective [kə'rɛktɪv] adj & s correctif m
correc'tive lens'es spl verres mpl correcteurs
correctness [kə'rɛktnɪs] s correction f
correlate ['kɔrə,let] tr mettre en corrélation || intr correspondre; **to correlate with** correspondre à
correlation [,kɔrɪ'leʃən] s corrélation f
correspond [,kɔrɪ'spand] intr correspondre
correspondence [,kɔrɪ'spandəns] s correspondance f
correspond'ence course' s cours m de l'enseignement par correspondance
correspondent [,kɔrɪ'spandənt] adj & s correspondant m
corresponding [,kɔrɪ'spandɪŋ] adj correspondant
corridor ['kɔrɪdər] s corridor m, couloir m
corroborate [kə'rabə,ret] tr corroborer
corrode [kə'rod] tr corroder || intr se corroder
corrosion [kə'roʒən] s corrosion f
corrosive [kə'rosɪv] adj & s corrosif m
corrugated ['kɔrə,getɪd] adj ondulé
corrupt [kə'rʌpt] adj corrompu || tr corrompre
corruption [kə'rʌpʃən] s corruption f
corsage [kɔr'saʒ] s bouquet m porté or fleur f portée à l'épaule ou à la ceinture; (waist) corsage m
corsair ['kɔr,sɛr] s corsaire m
corset ['kɔrsɪt] s corset m
Corsica ['kɔrsɪkə] s Corse f; la Corse
Corsican ['kɔrsɪkən] adj corse || s (dialect) corse m; (person) Corse mf
cortege [kɔr'teʒ] s cortège m
cor·tex ['kɔr,tɛks] s (pl -tices [tɪ,siz]) cortex m
cortisone ['kɔrtɪ,son] s cortisone f
coruscate ['kɔrəs,ket] intr scintiller
cosmetic [kaz'mɛtɪk] adj & s cosmétique m
cosmic ['kazmɪk] adj cosmique
cosmonaut ['kazmə,nɔt] s cosmonaute mf
cosmopolitan [,kazmə'palɪtən] adj & s cosmopolite mf
cosmos ['kazməs] s cosmos m

Cossack ['kɑ,sæk] *adj* cosaque ‖ *s* Cosaque *mf*

cost [kɔst] *s* coût *m*; (*price*) prix *m*; **at all costs** à tout prix, coûte que coûte; **at cost** au prix coûtant; **costs** frais *mpl*; (law) dépens *mpl* ‖ *v* (*pret & pp* **cost**) *intr* coûter

cost' account'ing *s* comptabilité *f* industrielle

costliness ['kɔstlɪnɪs] *s* cherté *f*, haut prix *m*

cost·ly ['kɔstli] *adj* (*comp* **-lier**; *super* **-liest**) coûteux, cher

cost' of liv'ing *s* coût *m* de la vie

cost' price' *s* prix *m* coûtant; (*net price*) prix de revient

costume ['kɑst(j)um] *s* costume *m*

cos'tume ball' *s* bal *m* costumé

cos'tume jew'elry *s* bijoux *mpl* en toc

costumer [kɑs't(j)umər] *s* costumier *m*

cot [kɑt] *s* lit *m* de sangle

coterie ['kotəri] *s* coterie *f*

cottage ['kɑtɪdʒ] *s* chalet *m*, cabanon *m*, villa *f*; (*with a thatched roof*) chaumière *f*

cot'tage cheese' *s* lait *m* caillé, caillé *m*, jonchée *f*

cot'ter pin' ['kɑtər] *s* goupille *f* fendue, clavette *f*

cotton ['kɑtən] *adj* cotonnier, de coton ‖ *s* coton *m* ‖ *intr*—**to cotton up to** (coll) éprouver de la sympathie pour

cot'ton bat'ting *s* coton *m* or ouate *f* hydrophile

cot'ton field' *s* cotonnerie *f*

cot'ton gin' *s* égreneuse *f*

cot'ton mill' *s* filature *f* de coton, cotonnerie *f*

cot'ton pick'er *s* cotonnier *m*

cot'ton pick'ing *s* récolte *f* du coton

cot'ton·seed' *s* graine *f* de coton

cot'tonseed oil' *s* huile *f* de coton

cot'ton waste' *s* déchets *mpl* or bourre *f* de coton

cot'ton·wood' *s* peuplier *m* de Virginie

cottony ['kɑtəni] *adj* cotonneux

couch [kaʊtʃ] *s* (*without back*) divan *m*; (*with back*) sofa *m*, canapé *m* ‖ *tr* (*a demand, a letter*) rédiger ‖ *intr* (*to lie in wait*) se tapir

cougar ['kugər] *s* couguar *m*, cougouar *m*

cough [kɔf], [kɑf] *s* toux *f* ‖ *tr*—**to cough up** cracher en toussant; (slang) (*money*) cracher ‖ *intr* tousser

cough' drop' *s* pastille *f* pectorale, pastille pour la toux

cough' syr'up *s* sirop *m* pectoral, sirop contre la toux

could [kʊd] *aux*—**he could not come** il ne pouvait pas venir; **he couldn't do it** il n'a (pas) pu le faire; **he couldn't do it if he wanted to** il ne pourrait (pas) le faire s'il le voulait, il ne saurait (pas) le faire s'il le voulait

council ['kaʊnsəl] *s* conseil *m*; (eccl) concile *m*

coun'cil·man *s* (*pl* **-men**) conseiller *m* municipal

councilor ['kaʊnsələr] *s* conseiller *m*

coun·sel ['kaʊnsəl] *s* conseil *m*, avis *m*; (*lawyer*) avocat *m* ‖ *v* (*pret & pp* **-seled** or **-selled**; *ger* **-seling** or **-selling**) *tr & intr* conseiller; **to counsel s.o. to** + *inf* conseiller à qn de + *inf*

counselor ['kaʊnsələr] *s* conseiller *m*, conseil *m*; (*lawyer*) avocat *m*

count [kaʊnt] *s* (*counting*) compte *m*; (*nobleman*) comte *m* ‖ *tr* compter; **to count the votes** dépouiller le scrutin ‖ *intr* compter; **count off!** (mil) comptez-vous!; **count for** valoir; **to count on** (*to have confidence in*) compter sur (*s.o. or s.th.*); **to count on** + *ger* compter + *inf*

countable ['kaʊntəbəl] *adj* comptable

count'down' *s* compte *m* à rebours

countenance ['kaʊntɪnəns] *s* mine *f*, contenance *f*; **to give countenance to** appuyer; **to keep one's countenance** garder son sérieux; **to lose countenance** perdre contenance ‖ *tr* soutenir, approver

counter ['kaʊntər] *adj* contraire ‖ *s* (*counting agent or machine*) compteur *m*; (*piece of wood or metal for keeping score*) jeton *m*; (*board in shop over which business is transacted*) comptoir *m*; (*in a bar or café*) zinc *m*; **over the counter** (com) hors bourse, hors cote; **under the counter** en dessous de table, sous le comptoir, sous cape ‖ *adv* contrairement, en sens inverse; **to run counter to** aller à l'encontre de ‖ *tr* contrarier, contrecarrer; (*a move, e.g., in chess*) contrer; (*an opinion*) prendre le contre-pied de ‖ *intr* parer le coup, parer un coup; **to counter with** riposter par

coun'ter·act' *tr* contrebalancer

coun'ter·attack' *s* contre-attaque *f* ‖ **coun'ter·attack'** *tr* contre-attaquer

coun'ter·bal'ance *s* contrepoids *m* ‖ **coun'ter·bal'ance** *tr* contrebalancer

coun'ter·clock'wise' *adj & adv* en sens inverse des aiguilles d'une montre, en sens antihoraire

coun'ter·cul'ture *s* contre-culture *f*

coun'ter·cur'rent *s* contre-courant *m*

coun'ter·es'pionage *s* contre-espionnage *m*

counterfeit ['kaʊntərfɪt] *adj* contrefait; (*beauty*) sophistiqué ‖ *s* contrefaction *f*, contrefaçon *f*; (*money*) fausse monnaie *f* ‖ *tr* contrefaire; (*e.g., an illness*) feindre

counterfeiter ['kaʊntər,fɪtər] *s* contrefacteur *m*; (*of money*) faux-monnayeur *m*

coun'terfeit mon'ey *s* fausse monnaie *f*, faux billets *mpl*

coun'ter·ir'ritant *adj & s* révulsif *m*

countermand ['kaʊntər,mænd] *s* contre-ordre *m* ‖ *tr* contremander

coun'ter·march' *s* contremarche *f* ‖ *intr* faire une contremarche

coun'ter·meas'ure *s* contre-mesure *f*

coun'ter·offen'sive *s* contre-offensive *f*

coun'ter·pane' *s* courtepoint *f*

coun'ter·part' *s* contrepartie *f*, homologue *m*

coun'ter·point' *s* contrepoint *m*

coun'ter·poise' s contrepoids m ‖ tr faire équilibre à

coun'ter·rev'olu'tionar·y adj contrerévolutionnaire ‖ s (pl **-ies**) contrerévolutionnaire mf

coun'ter·sign' s contremarque f; (signature) contreseing m; (mil) mot m d'ordre ‖ tr contresigner

coun'ter·sig'nature s contreseing m

coun'ter·sink' s fraise f, chasse-clou m ‖ v (pret & pp **-sunk**) tr fraiser

coun'ter·spy' s (pl **-spies**) contre-espion m

coun'ter·stroke' s contrecoup m

coun'ter·weight' s contrepoids m

countess ['kauntis] s comtesse f

countless ['kauntls] adj innombrable

countrified ['kʌntrɪ,faɪd] adj provincial, compagnard

coun·try ['kʌntri] s (pl **-tries**) (territory of a nation) pays m; (land of one's birth) patrie f; (region) contrée f; (not the city) campagne f

coun'try club' s club m privé situé hors des agglomérations

coun'try estate' s domaine m

coun'try·folk' s campagnards mpl

coun'try gen'tleman s châtelain m, propriétaire m d'un château

coun'try house' s maison f de campagne

coun'try·man s (pl **-men**) (of the same country) compatriote mf; (rural) compagnard m

coun'try mu'sic s musique f rustique

coun'try·side' s paysage m, campagne f

coun'try town' s petite ville f de province

coun'try·wide' adj national

coun'try·wom'an s (pl **-wom'en**) (of the same country) compatriote f; (rural) campagnarde f

coun·ty ['kaunti] s (pl **-ties**) comté m

coun'ty seat' s chef-lieu m de comté

coupé [kupe] s coupé m

couple ['kʌpəl] s (man and wife; male and female; friends) couple m, paire f; (of eggs, cakes, etc.) couple f; (elec, mech) couple m ‖ tr coupler, accoupler; (mach) embrayer ‖ intr s'accoupler

coupler ['kʌplər] s (mach) coupleur m

coupling ['kʌplɪŋ] s accouplement m; (mach) couplage m

coupon ['k(j)upɑn] s coupon m, bon m

courage ['kʌrɪdʒ] s courage m

courageous [kəˈredʒəs] adj courageux

courier ['kurɪ·ər] s courrier m; (on horseback) estafette f

course [kors] s (duration, process; course in school) cours m; (of a meal) service m, plat m; (of a stream) parcours m, cours m; (direction) route f, chemin m; **course before the main course** (culin) entrée f; **first course** (culin) premier plat, entrée en matière; **in due course** en temps voulu; **in the course of** au cours de; **in the course of time** avec le temps; **main course** (culin) plat principal, pièce f de résistance; **of course!** naturellement!, bien entendu!; **to give a course** faire un cours; **to set a**

course for (naut) mettre le cap sur; **to take a course** suivre un cours ‖ tr & intr courir

court [kort] s cour f; (of law) tribunal m, cour; (sports) terrain m, court m; **out of court** à l'amiable ‖ tr courtiser, faire la cour à; (favor, votes) briguer, solliciter; (danger) aller au-devant de

courteous ['kʌrtɪ·əs] adj poli, courtois

courtesan ['kɔrtɪzən] s courtisane f

courte·sy ['kʌrtɪsi] s (pl **-sies**) politesse f, courtoisie f; **through the courtesy of** avec la gracieuse permission de

court'house' s palais m de justice

courtier ['kɔrtɪ·ər] s courtisan m

court' jest'er s bouffon m du roi

court·ly ['kortli] adj (comp **-lier**; super **-liest**) courtois, élégant

court'-mar'tial s (pl **courts-martial**) conseil m de guerre ‖ v (pret & pp **-tialed** or **-tialled**; ger **-tialing** or **-tialling**) tr traduire en conseil de guerre; **to be court-martialed** passer en conseil de guerre

court' plas'ter s taffetas m gommé, sparadrap m

court'room' s salle f du tribunal

court'ship s cour f

court'yard' s cour f

cousin ['kʌzɪn] s cousin m

cove [kov] s anse f, crique f

covenant ['kʌvənənt] s contrat m, accord m, pacte m; (Bib) alliance f

cover ['kʌvər] s (blanket; military protection; book cover) couverture f; (lid) couvercle m; (for furniture) housse f; (of wild game) remise f, gîte m; (com) couverture f, provision f, marge f; (mach) chape f; (phila) enveloppe f; **from cover to cover** de la première page à la dernière; **to take cover** se mettre à l'abri; **under cover** (e.g., of trees) sous les couverts; (safe from harm) à couvert; **under cover of** sous le couvert de, dissimulé dans; **under separate cover** sous pli distinct ‖ tr couvrir; (a certain distance) parcourir; (a newspaper story) faire le reportage de; (one's tracks) brouiller; (with, e.g., chocolate) enrober; **to cover up** recouvrir ‖ intr se couvrir; (to brood) couver

coverage ['kʌvərɪdʒ] s (amount or space covered) portée f; (of news) reportage m; (insurance) assurance f, couverture f d'assurance

co'ver·alls' spl salopette f, bleus mpl

cov'er charge' s couvert m

cov'ered wag'on s chariot m couvert

cov'er girl' s cover-girl f, pin up f

covering ['kʌvərɪŋ] s couverture f, recouvrement m

covert ['kʌvərt] adj couvert, caché

cov'er-up' s subterfuge m; (reply) réponse f évasive

covet ['kʌvɪt] tr convoiter

covetous ['kʌvɪtɪs] adj cupide, avide

covetousness ['kʌvɪtəsnɪs] s convoitise f, cupidité f

covey ['kʌvi] s couvée f; (in flight) volée f

cow [kaʊ] *s* vache *f*; (*of seal, elephant*) femelle *f* ‖ *tr* (coll) intimider

coward [`kaʊ·ərd] *s* lâche *mf*

cowardice [`kaʊ·ərdɪs] *s* lâcheté *f*

cowardly [`kaʊ·ərdli] *adj* lâche ‖ *adv* lâchement, peureusement

cow′bell′ *s* grelot *m*, clarine *f*

cow′boy′ *s* cow-boy *m*

cow′catch′er *s* (rr) chasse-bestiaux *m*

cower [`kaʊ·ər] *intr* se tapir

cow′herd′ *s* vacher *m*, bouvier *m*

cow′hide′ *s* vache *f*, peau *f* de vache; fouet *m* ‖ *tr* fouetter

cowl [kaʊl] *s* (*religious dress*) capuchon *m*, cagoule *f*; (*of chimney*) chapeau *m*; (aer, aut) capot *m*

cow′lick′ *s* mèche *f* rebelle

cow′pox′ *s* (pathol) vaccine *f*

coxcomb [`kɑks,kom] *s* (*conceited person*) petit-maître *m*; fat *m*; (bot) crête-de-coq *f*

coxswain [`kɑksən], [`kɑk,swen] *s* (naut) patron *m* de chaloupe; (rowing) barreur *m*

coy [kɔɪ] *adj* réservé, modeste

co·zy [`kozi] *adj* (*comp* **-zier**; *super* **-ziest**) douillet, intime ‖ *s* (*pl* **-zies**) couvre-théière *m*

C.P.A. [`si`pi`e] *s* (letterword) (**certified public accountant**) expert-comptable *m*, comptable *m* agréé

CPI [`si`pi`aɪ] *s* (letterword) (**consumer price index**) indexation *f* des traitements sur le coût de la vie

crab [kræb] *s* crabe *m*; (*grouch*) grincheux *m* ‖ *v* (*pret & pp* **crabbed**; *ger* **crabbing**) *intr* (coll) se plaindre

crab′ ap′ple *s* pomme *f* sauvage

crabbed [`kræbɪd] *adj* acariâtre; (*handwriting*) de chat; (*author*) hermétique; (*style*) entortillé

crab·by [`kræbi] *adj* (*comp* **-bier**; *super* **-biest**) (coll) revêche, grognon

crack [kræk] *adj* (*troops*) d'élite; (coll) expert, de premier ordre ‖ *s* (*noise*) bruit *m* sec, craquement *m*; (*of whip*) claquement *m*; (*fissure*) fente *f*; (*e.g., in a dish*) fêlure *f*; (*e.g., in a wall*) lézarde *f*; (*in skin*) gerçure *f*; (*joke*) bon mot *m*; **crack of dawn** pointe *f* du jour ‖ *tr* (*one's fingers; petroleum*) faire craquer; (*a whip*) claquer; (*to split*) fendre; (*e.g., a dish*) fêler; (*e.g., a wall*) lézarder; (*the skin*) gercer; (*nuts*) casser; **to crack a joke** (slang) faire or lâcher une plaisanterie; **to crack up** (*to praise*) (coll) vanter, prôner; (*to crash*) (coll) écraser ‖ *intr* (*to make a noise*) craquer; (*said of whip*) claquer; (*to be split*) se fendre; (*said of dish*) se fêler; (*said of wall*) se lézarder; (*said of skin*) se gercer; **to crack up** (*to crash*) (coll) s'écraser; (*to break down*) (coll) craquer, s'effondrer

crack′-brained′ *adj* timbré; **to be crack-brained** avoir le cerveau fêlé

crack′down′ *s* (coll) répression *f*

cracked *adj* (*split*) fendu, fêlé; (*foolish*) (coll) timbré, toqué, cinglé

cracker [`krækər] *s* biscuit *m* sec

crack′er-bar′rel *adj* (coll) en chambre, au petit pied

crack′er·jack′ *adj* (slang) expérimenté, remarquable ‖ *s* (slang) crack *m*

cracking [`krækɪŋ] *s* (*of petroleum*) cracking *m*

crackle [`krækəl] *s* crépitation *f* ‖ *intr* crépiter, pétiller

crack′le·ware′ *s* porcelaine *f* craquelée

crackling [`kræklɪŋ] *s* crépitement *m*, pétillement *m*; (culin) couenne *f* rissolée;

cracklings cretons *mpl*

crack′pot′ *adj & s* (slang) original *m*, excentrique *mf*

crack′ shot′ *s* (coll) fin tireur *m*

crack′-up′ *s* (*collision*) (coll) écrasement *m*; (*breakdown*) (coll) effondrement *m*

cradle [`kredəl] *s* berceau *m* ‖ *tr* bercer

cra′dle·song′ *s* berceuse *f*

craft [kræft] *s* (*profession*) métier *m*; (*trickery*) artifice *m*; (naut) embarcation *f*, barque *f*

craftiness [`kræftɪnɪs] *s* ruse *f*, astuce *f*

crafts′man *s* (*pl* **-men**) artisan *m*

crafts′man·ship′ *s* habileté *f* technique; exécution *f*

craft·y [`kræfti] *adj* (*comp* **-ier**; *super* **-iest**) rusé

crag [kræg] *s* rocher *m* escarpé

cram [kræm] *v* (*pret & pp* **crammed**; *ger* **cramming**) *tr* (*with food*) bourrer, gaver; (*with people*) bonder; (*for an exam*) (coll) chauffer ‖ *intr* se bourrer, se gaver; (*for an exam*) (coll) potasser

cramp [kræmp] *s* (*metal bar; clamp*) crampon *m*; (*in a muscle*) crampe *f*; (carpentry) serre-joint *m* ‖ *tr* cramponner, agrafer; presser, serrer; (*one's movements, style, or manner of living*) gêner

cranber·ry [`kræn,bɛri] *s* (*pl* **-ries**) (Vaccinium oxycoccus or V. uliginosum) canneberge *f*, airelle *f* coussinette

crane [kren] *s* (mach, orn) grue *f* ‖ *tr* (*one's neck*) allonger, tendre ‖ *intr* allonger le cou

crani·um [`kreni·əm] *s* (*pl* **-a** [ə]) crâne *m*

crank [kræŋk] *s* (*which turns*) manivelle *f*; (*person*) (coll) excentrique *mf* ‖ *tr* (*a motor*) faire partir à la manivelle

crank′case′ *s* carter *m*

crank′shaft′ *s* vilebrequin *m*

crank·y [`kræŋki] *adj* (*comp* **-ier**; *super* **-iest**) (*person*) revêche, grincheux; (*not working well*) détraqué; (*queer*) excentrique

cran·ny [`kræni] *s* (*pl* **-nies**) fente *f*, crevasse *f*; (*corner*) coin *m*

crape [krep] *s* crêpe *m*

crape′hang′er *s* (slang) rabat-joie *m*

craps [kræps] *s* (slang) jeu *m* de dés; **to shoot craps** (slang) jouer aux dés

crash [kræʃ] *s* (*noise*) fracas *m*, écroulement *m*; (*of thunder*) coup *m*; (*e.g., of airplane*) écrasement *m*; (*e.g., on stock market*) krach *m* ‖ *tr* briser, fracasser; (*e.g., an airplane*) écraser ‖ *intr* retentir; (*said of airplane*) s'écraser; (*to fail*)

craquer; **to crash into** emboutir, tamponner; **to crash through** enfoncer
crash′ dive′ s brusque plongée f
crash′ hel′met s casque m
crash′-land′ing s crash m, atterrissage m violent
crash′ record′er s (aer) enregistreur m d'accident
crass [kræs] adj grossier; (ignorance) crasse
crate [kret] s caisse f à claire-voie, cageot m, caisson m ‖ tr emballer dans une caisse à claire-voie
crater [′kretər] s cratère m
cravat [krə′væt] s cravate f
crave [krev] tr (drink, tobacco, etc.) avoir un besoin maladif de; (affection) avoir grand besoin de; (attention) solliciter; **to crave s.o.'s pardon** implorer le pardon de qn ‖ intr—**to crave for** désirer ardemment; implorer
craven [′krevən] adj & s poltron m
craving [′krevɪŋ] s désir m ardent, désir obsédant
craw [krɔ] s jabot m
crawl [krɔl] s (snail's pace) allure f très ralentie; (swimming) crawl m ‖ intr ramper; (to go slowly) avancer au pas; **to be crawling with** fourmiller de, grouiller de; **to crawl along** se traîner; **to crawl on one's hands and knees** aller à quatre pattes; **to crawl over** escalader; **to crawl up** grimper
crayon [′kre·ən] s crayon m de pastel, pastel m ‖ tr crayonner
craze [krez] s manie f, toquade f ‖ tr rendre fou
cra·zy [′krezi] adj (comp -zier; super -ziest) fou; (rickety) délabré; (coll) dingue, fou; **to be crazy about** (coll) être fou de, être toqué de; **to drive crazy** rendre fou, affoler; **to go crazy** perdre la boule
cra′zy bone′ s nerf m du coude
cra′zy quilt′ s courtepointe f multicolore
creak [krik] s cri m, grincement m ‖ intr crier, grincer
creak·y [′kriki] adj (comp -ier; super -iest) criard
cream [krim] s crème f; **creams** (with chocolate coating) chocolats mpl fourrés ‖ tr écrémer; (butter and sugar together) mélanger ‖ intr crémer
cream′ cheese′ s fromage m à la crème, fromage blanc, petit suisse m
creamer·y [′kriməri] s (pl -ies) laiterie f; compagnie f laitière
cream′ of tar′tar s crème f de tartre
cream′ pitch′er s crémière f
cream′ puff′ s chou m à la crème
cream′ sep′arator [′sɛpə,retər] s écrémeuse f
cream·y [′krimi] adj (comp -ier; super -iest) crémeux
crease [kris] s pli m, faux pli m ‖ tr & intr plisser
create [kri′et] tr créer
creation [kri′eʃən] s création f
creative [kri′etɪv] adj créateur, inventif

creator [kri′etər] s créateur m
creature [′kritʃər] s créature f
credence [′kridəns] s créance f, croyance f, foi f
credentials [krɪ′dɛnʃəlz] spl papiers mpl, pièces fpl justificatives, lettres fpl de créance
credibility [,krɛdɪ′bɪlɪti] s crédibilité f
credible [′krɛdɪbəl] adj croyable, digne de foi
credit [′krɛdɪt] s crédit m; **on credit** à crédit; **to be a credit to** faire honneur à; **to take credit for** s'attribuer le mérite de ‖ tr croire, ajouter foi à; (com) créditer, porter au crédit
creditable [′krɛdɪtəbəl] adj estimable, honorable
cred′it card′ s carte f de crédit
creditor [′krɛdɪtər] s créditeur m, créancier m
cre·do [′krido] s (pl -dos) credo m
credulous [′krɛdʒələs] adj crédule
creed [krid] s credo m; (denomination) foi f
creek [krik] s ruisseau m
creep [krip] v (pret & pp crept [krɛpt]) intr (to crawl) ramper; (stealthily) se glisser; (slowly) se traîner, se couler; (to climb) grimper; (with a sensation of insects) fourmiller; **to creep up on s.o.** s'approcher de qn à pas lents
creeper [′kripər] s plante f rampante
creeping [′kripɪŋ] adj (lagging) lent, traînant; (plant) rampant ‖ s rampement m
creep·y [′kripi] adj (comp -ier; super -iest) (coll) mystérieux, terrifiant; **to feel creepy** fourmiller
cremate [′krimet] tr incinérer
cremation [krɪ′meʃən] s crémation f, incinération f
cremato·ry [′krimə,tori] adj crématoire ‖ s (pl -ries) crématoire m, four m crématoire
Creole [′kri·ol] adj créole ‖ s (language) créole m; (person) Créole mf
crepe [krep] s (paper) crêpe m; (pancake) crêpe f
crepe′ pa′per s papier m crêpe
crescent [′krɛsənt] s croissant m
cress [krɛs] s cresson m
crest [krɛst] s crête f
crested [′krɛstɪd] adj à crête; (with feathers) huppé
crest′fall′en adj abattu, découragé
Cretan [′kritən] adj crétois ‖ s Crétois m
Crete [krit] s Crète f; la Crète
cretin [′kritən] s crétin m
crevice [′krɛvɪs] s crevasse f, fente f
crew [kru] s (rowing; group working together) équipe f; (of a ship) équipage m; (group, especially of armed men) bande f, troupe f
crew′ cut′ s cheveux mpl en brosse
crew′ mem′ber s équipier m
crib [krɪb] s lit m d'enfant; (manger) crèche f, mangeoire f; (for grain) coffre m; (student's pony) antisèche m & f ‖ v (pret & pp cribbed; ger cribbing) tr & intr (coll) copier à la dérobée

cricket ['krɪkɪt] *s* (ent) grillon *m*; (sports) cricket *m*; (coll) franc jeu *m*, jeu loyal; **to be cricket** être de bonne guerre

crier ['kraɪ·ər] *s* crieur *m*

crime [kraɪm] *s* crime *m*; (*misdemeanor*) délit *m*

criminal ['krɪmɪnəl] *adj* & *s* criminel *m*

crim′inal code′ *s* code *m* pénal

crim′inal court′ *s* cour *f* d'assises

crim′inal law′ *s* loi *f* pénale

crimp [krɪmp] *s* (*in cloth*) pli *m*; (*in hair*) frisure *f*; (*recruiter*) racoleur *m*; **to put a crimp in** (coll) mettre obstacle à ‖ *tr* (*cloth*) plisser; (*hair*) friser, crêper; (*metal*) onduler

crimson ['krɪmzən] *adj* & *s* cramoisi *m*

cringe [krɪndʒ] *intr* s'humilier, s'abaisser

cringing ['krɪndʒɪŋ] *adj* craintif, servile ‖ *s* crainte *f*, servilité *f*

crinkle ['krɪŋkəl] *s* pli *m*, ride *f* ‖ *tr* froisser, plisser ‖ *intr* se froisser

cripple ['krɪpəl] *s* estropié *m*, boiteux *m*; (*disabled*) infirme, invalide ‖ *tr* estropier; (*a machine*) disloquer; (*business or industry*) paralyser; (*a ship*) désemparer

cri·sis ['kraɪsɪs] *s* (*pl* **-ses** [siz]) crise *f*

crisp [krɪsp] *adj* (*crackers, bread, etc.*) croustillant; (*tone*) tranchant, brusque; (*air*) vif, frais

crisscross ['krɪs,krɔs] *adj* entrecroisé, treillissé ‖ *s* entrecroisement *m*; (*e.g., of wires*) enchevêtrement *m* ‖ *adv* en forme de croix ‖ *tr* entrecroiser ‖ *intr* s'entrecroiser

criteri·on [kraɪ'tɪrɪ·ən] *s* (*pl* **-a** [ə] or **-ons**) critère *m*

critic ['krɪtɪk] *s* (*of books, music, films, etc.*) critique *mf*; (*fault-finder*) critiqueur *m*, désapprobateur *m*

critical ['krɪtɪkəl] *adj* critique

critically ['krɪtɪkəli] *adv* en critique; **critically ill** gravement malade

criticism ['krɪtɪ,sɪzəm] *s* critique *f*

criticize ['krɪtɪ,saɪz] *tr* & *intr* critiquer

croak [krok] *s* (*of raven*) croassement *m*; (*of frog*) coassement *m* ‖ *intr* (*said of raven*) croasser; (*said of frog*) coasser; (*to die*) (slang) mourir

Croat ['kro·æt] *s* (*language*) croate *m*; (*person*) Croate *mf*

Croatian [kro'eʃən] *adj* croate ‖ *s* (*language*) croate *m*; (*person*) Croate *mf*

cro·chet [kro'ʃe] *s* crochet *m* ‖ *v* (*pret* & *pp* **-cheted** ['ʃed]; *ger* **-cheting** ['ʃe·ɪŋ]) *tr* & *intr* tricoter au crochet

crochet′ nee′dle *s* crochet *m*

crock [krɑk] *s* pot *m* de terre

crock′pot *s* mijoteuse *f*

crockery ['krɑkəri] *s* faïence *f*, poterie *f*

crocodile ['krɑkə,daɪl] *s* crocodile *m*

croc′odile tears′ *spl* larmes *fpl* de crocodile

crocus ['krokəs] *s* crocus *m*

crone [kron] *s* vieille ratatinée *f*, vieille bique *f*

cro·ny ['kroni] *s* (*pl* **-nies**) copain *m*

cronyism ['kroni·ɪzəm] *s* copinisme *m*

crook [kruk] *s* (*hook*) croc *m*; (*of shepherd*) houlette *f*; (*of bishop*) crosse *f*; (*in road*) courbure *f*; (*person*) (coll) escroc *m* ‖ *tr* courber ‖ *intr* se courber

crooked ['krukɪd] *adj* (*stick*) courbé, crochu; (*path; conduct*) tortueux; (*tree; nose; legs*) tortu; (*person*) (coll) malhonnête, fourbe

croon [krun] *intr* chanter des chansons sentimentales

crooner ['krunər] *s* chanteur *m* de charme

crop [krɑp] *s* (*produce*) produit *m* agricole; (*amount produced*) récolte *f*; (*head of hair*) cheveux *mpl* ras; (*of bird*) jabot *m*; (*whip*) fouet *m*; (*of whip*) manche *m*; (*appointments, promotions, heroes, discoveries*) moisson *f* ‖ *v* (*pret* & *pp* **cropped**; *ger* **cropping**) *tr* tondre; (*head of hair*) couper, tailler; (*ears of animal*) essoriller ‖ *intr*—**to crop up** (coll) surgir, s'élever brusquement

crop′ dust′ing *s* pulvérisation *f* des cultures

croquet [kro'ke] *s* croquet *m*

crosier ['kroʒər] *s* crosse *f*

cross [krɔs] *adj* (*diagonal*) transversal, oblique; (*breed*) croisé; (*ill-humored*) maussade ‖ *s* croix *f*; (*of races or breeds; of roads*) croisement *m* ‖ *tr* (*e.g., one's arms or legs*) croiser; (*the sea; a street*) traverser; (*breeds*) croiser, métisser; (*the threshold*) franchir; (*said of one road with respect to another*) couper; (*the letter t*) barrer; (*e.g., s.o.'s plans*) (coll) contrecarrer; **to cross oneself** (eccl) se signer; **to cross out** biffer, rayer ‖ *intr* se croiser, passer; **to cross over** passer de l'autre côté

cross′bones′ *spl* tibias *mpl* croisés

cross′bow′ *s* arbalète *f*

cross′breed′ *v* (*pret* & *pp* **-bred**) *tr* croiser, métisser

cross′-check′ *s* recoupement *m* ‖ *tr* faire un recoupement de

cross′-coun′try *adj* à travers champs

cross′-country ski′ing *s* ski *m* de fonds

cross′cur′rent *s* contre-courant *m*; tendance *f* contraire

cross′-examina′tion *s* contre-interrogatoire *m*

cross′-exam′ine *tr* contre-interroger, contre-examiner

cross′-eyed′ *adj* louche

crossing ['krɔsɪŋ], ['krɑsɪŋ] *s* (*road junction*) croisement *m*; (*of ocean*) traversée *f*; (*of river, mountain, etc.*) passage *m*; (rr) passage *m* à niveau; (*for pedestrians*) passage *m* clouté

cross′ing gate′ *s* barrière *f* d'un passage à niveau

cross′patch′ *s* (coll) grincheux *m*, grognon *m*

cross′piece′ *s* entretoise *f*

cross′ ref′erence *s* renvoi *m*

cross′road′ *s* voie *f* transversale, chemin *m* de traverse; **crossroads** carrefour *m*, croisement *m*

cross′ sec′tion *s* (*cut*) coupe *f* transversale; (*e.g., of building*) section *f*; (*of opinion*) sondage *m*, groupe *m* représentatif, échantillon *m*

cross′-sec′tion *tr* couper transversalement

cross′ street′ *s* rue *f* de traverse, rue transversale

cross′wise′ *adv* en croix, en sautoir

cross′word puz′zle *s* mots *mpl* croisés

crotch [krɑtʃ] *s* (*forked piece*) fourche *f*; (*between legs*) entrejambe *f*, enfourchure *f*

crotchet [′krɑtʃɪt] *s* (mus) noire *f*; (coll) lubie *f*

crotchety [′krɑtʃɪti] *adj* capricieux, fantasque

crouch [krɑʊtʃ] *s* accroupissement *m* ‖ *intr* s'accroupir, se blottir

croup [krup] *s* (*of horse*) croupe *f*; (pathol) croup *m*

croupier [′krupɪ·ər] *s* croupier *m*

crouton [′krutɑn] *s* croûton *m*

crow [kro] *s* corbeau *m*; (*rook*) corneille *f*, freux *m*; **as the crow flies** à vol d'oiseau; **to eat crow** (coll) avaler des couleuvres ‖ *intr* (*said of cock*) chanter; (*said of babies*) gazouiller; **to crow over** chanter victoire sur, triompher bruyamment de

crow′bar′ *s* levier *m*; (*for forcing doors*) pince-monseigneur *f*

crowd [krɑʊd] *s* foule *f*; (*clique, set*) bande *f*, monde *m*; **a crowd** (*of people*) du monde, beaucoup de monde ‖ *tr* serrer, entasser; (*to push*) pousser; (*a debtor*) presser; **to crowd out** ne pas laisser de place à ‖ *intr* affluer, s'amasser; **to crowd around** se presser autour de; **to crowd in** s'attrouper

crowded *adj* encombré, bondé

crow′foot′ *s* renoncule *f*, bouton *m* d'or

crowing [′kro·ɪŋ] *s* chant *m* de coq, cocorico *m*; (*of babies*) gazouillement *m*

crown [krɑʊn] *s* couronne *f*; (*of hat*) calotte *f* ‖ *tr* couronner, sacrer; (checkers) damer; **to crown s.o.** (slang) flanquer un coup sur la tête à qn

crowning [′krɑʊnɪŋ] *s* couronnement *m*

crown′ prince′ *s* prince *m* héritier

crown′ prin′cess *s* princesse *f* héritière

crow′s′-foot′ *s* (*pl* **-feet**) patte-d'oie *f*

crow′s′-nest *s* (naut) nid *m* de pie, tonneau *m* de vigie

crucial [′kruʃəl] *adj* crucial

crucible [′krusɪbəl] *s* creuset *m*

crucifix [′krusɪfɪks] *s* crucifix *m*, christ *m*

crucifixion [,krusɪ′fɪkʃən] *s* crucifixion *f*

cruci·fy [′krusɪ,faɪ] *v* (*pret & pp* **-fied**) *tr* crucifier

crude [krud] *adj* (*raw, unrefined*) cru, brut; (*lacking culture*) fruste, grossier; (*unfinished*) informe, grossier, mal développé; (*oil*) brut

crudi·ty [′krudɪti] *s* (*pl* **-ties**) crudité *f*; (*of person*) grossièreté *f*

cruel [′kru·əl] *adj* cruel

cruel·ty [′kru·əlti] *s* (*pl* **-ties**) cruauté *f*

cruet [′kru·ɪt] *s* burette *f*

cru′et stand′ *s* huilier *m*

cruise [kruz] *s* croisière *f* ‖ *intr* croiser

cruiser [′kruzər] *s* croiseur *m*

cruising [′kruzɪŋ] *adj* en croisière; (*taxi*) en maraude

cruis′ing range′ *s* autonomie *f*

cruis′ing speed′ *s* vitesse *f* de route

cruller [′krʌlər] *s* beignet *m*

crumb [krʌm] *s* miette *f*; (*soft part of bread*) mie *f* ‖ *tr* (*cutlets, etc.*) paner

crumble [′krʌmbəl] *tr* émietter, réduire en miettes; (*e.g., stone*) effriter ‖ *intr* s'émietter; s'effriter; (*to fall to pieces*) s'écrouler

crum·my [′krʌmi] *adj* (*comp* **-mier**; *super* **-miest**) (slang) sale, minable

crumple [′krʌmpəl] *tr* friper, froisser; (*a fender*) mettre en accordéon ‖ *intr* se friper, se froisser

crunch [krʌnʃ] *tr* croquer, broyer ‖ *intr* (*said of snow*) craquer

crupper [′krʌpər] *s* croupière *f*

crusade [kru′sed] *s* croisade *f* ‖ *intr* se croiser, prendre part à une croisade

crush [krʌʃ] *s* (*crushing*) écrasement *m*; (*of people*) presse *f*, foule *f*; **to have a crush on** (slang) avoir un béguin pour ‖ *tr* écraser; (*e.g., stone*) broyer, concasser; (*to oppress, grieve*) accabler, aplatir

crush′ hat′ *s* claque *m*, gibus *m*

crust [krʌst] *s* croûte *f*

crustacean [krʌs′teʃən] *s* crustacé *m*

crust·y [′krʌsti] *adj* (*comp* **-ier**; *super* **-iest**) croustillant; (*said of person*) bourru, hargneux

crutch [krʌtʃ] *s* béquille *f*

crux [krʌks] *s* nœud *m*

cry [kraɪ] *s* (*pl* **cries**) (*loud shout*) cri *m*; (*of wolf*) hurlement *m*; (*of bull*) mugissement *m*; **to cry one's eyes out** pleurer à chaudes larmes; **to have a good cry** donner libre cours aux larmes ‖ *v* (*pret & pp* **cried**) *tr* crier; **to cry out** crier ‖ *intr* crier; (*to weep*) pleurer; **to cry for** crier à; **to cry for joy** pleurer de joie; **to cry out** pousser des cris, s'écrier; **to cry out against** crier à

cry′ba′by *s* (*pl* **-bies**) pleurard *m*

crying [′kraɪ·ɪŋ] *adj* pleurant; (*need*) pressant; **for crying out loud!** (coll) il ne manquait plus que ça!; **a crying shame** une honte ‖ *s* larmes *fpl*, pleurs *mpl*

crypt [krɪpt] *s* crypte *f*

cryptic(al) [′krɪptɪk(əl)] *adj* secret, occulte; (*silence*) énigmatique

crystal [′krɪstəl] *s* cristal *m*

crys′tal ball′ *s* boule *f* de cristal

crystalline [′krɪstəlɪn] *adj* cristallin

crystallize [′krɪstə,laɪz] *tr* cristalliser; (*sugar*) candir ‖ *intr* cristalliser; (*said of sugar*) se candir; (*said of one's thoughts*) (fig) se cristalliser

cub [kʌb] *s* (*of animal*) petit *m*; (*of bear*) ourson *m*; (*of fox*) renardeau *m*; (*of lion*) lionceau *m*; (*of wolf*) louveteau *m*

Cuban [′kjubən] *adj* cubain ‖ *s* Cubain *m*

cubbyhole [′kʌbɪ,hol] *s* (*room*) retraite *f*; (*in wall*) placard *m*; (*in furniture*) case *f*

cube [kjub] *adj & s* cube *m*; **in cubes** (*said of sugar*) en morceaux ‖ *tr* cuber
cube' root' *s* racine *f* cubique
cube' sug'ar *s* sucre *m* en morceaux
cubic ['kjubɪk] *adj* cubique, cube
cu'bic me'ter *s* mètre *m* cube
cub' report'er *s* reporter *m* débutant
cub' scout' *s* louveteau *m*
cuckold ['kʌkəld] *adj & s* cocu *m*, cornard *m* ‖ *tr* cocufier
cuckoo ['kuku] *adj* (slang) niais, benêt ‖ *s* coucou *m*
cuck'oo clock' *s* coucou *m*
cucumber ['kjukəmbər] *s* concombre *m*
cud [kʌd] *s* bol *m* alimentaire; **to chew the cud** ruminer
cuddle ['kʌdəl] *tr* serrer doucement dans les bras ‖ *intr* (*said of lovers*) s'étreindre; **to cuddle up** se pelotonner
cudg·el ['kʌdʒəl] *s* gourdin *m*, trique *f*; **to take up the cudgels for** prendre fait et cause pour ‖ *v* (*pret & pp* **-eled** or **-elled**; *ger* **-eling** or **-elling**) *tr* bâtonner, rosser
cue [kju] *s* (*notice*) signal *m*; (*hint*) mot *m*; (*rod used in billiards; persons in line*) queue *f*; (*mus*) indication *f* de rentrée; (*theat*) réclame *f*; **to give s.o. the cue** faire la leçon à qn, donner le mot à qn; **to take one's cue from** se conformer à
cuff [kʌf] *s* (*of shirt*) poignet *m*, manchette *f*; (*of coat or trousers*) parement *m*; (*blow*) taloche *f*, manchette *f* ‖ *tr* talocher, flanquer une taloche à
cuff' link' *s* bouton *m* de manchette
cuirass [kwɪ'ræs] *s* cuirasse *f*
cuisine [kwɪ'zin] *s* cuisine *f*
culinary ['kjulɪˌneri] *adj* culinaire
cull [kʌl] *tr* (*to select*) choisir; (*to gather, pluck*) cueillir; **to cull from** recueillir dans
culm [kʌlm] *s* chaume *m*; (*coal dust*) charbonnaille *f*
culminate ['kʌlmɪˌnet] *intr* (astr) culminer; **to culminate in** finir par, se terminer en
culmination [ˌkʌlmɪ'neʃən] *s* point *m* culminant; (astr) culmination *f*
culottes [k(j)u'lɑts] *spl* pantalon *m* de plage
culpable ['kʌlpəbəl] *adj* coupable
culprit ['kʌlprɪt] *s* (*guilty one*) coupable *mf*; (*accused*) accusé *m*, prévenu *m*
cult [kʌlt] *s* culte *m*
cultivate ['kʌltɪˌvet] *tr* cultiver
cultivation [ˌkʌltɪ'veʃən] *s* culture *f*
cultivator ['kʌltɪˌvetər] *s* (*person*) cultivateur *m*, exploitant *m* agricole; (mach) cultivateur *m*, scarificateur *m*
cultural ['kʌltʃərəl] *adj* culturel
culture ['kʌltʃər] *s* culture *f* ‖ *tr* cultiver
cultured adj (*learned*) cultivé, lettré
cul'tured pearl' *s* perle *f* de culture
culvert ['kʌlvərt] *s* ponceau *m*, cassis *m*
cumbersome ['kʌmbərsəm] *adj* incommode, encombrant; (*clumsy*) lourd, difficile à manier
cummerbund ['kʌmərˌbʌnd] *s* ceinture *f* d'étoffe

cumulative ['kjumjəˌletɪv] *adj* croissant, cumulatif
cunning ['kʌnɪŋ] *adj* (*sly*) astucieux, rusé; (*clever*) habile, fin; (*attractive*) gentil ‖ *s* (*slyness*) astuce *f*, ruse *f*; (*cleverness*) habileté *f*, finesse *f*
cup [kʌp] *s* (*for coffee or tea; cupful*) tasse *f*; (*of metal*) gobelet *m*, timbale *f*; (bot, eccl) calice *m*; (mach) godet *m* graisseur; (sports) coupe *f* ‖ *v* (*pret & pp* **cupped**; *ger* **cupping**) *tr* (surg) ventouser
cupboard ['kʌbərd] *s* armoire *f*; (*in wall*) placard *m*
Cupid ['kjupɪd] *s* Cupidon *m*
cupidity [kju'pɪdɪti] *s* cupidité *f*
cupola ['kjupələ] *s* coupole *f*
cur [kʌr] *s* (*mongrel dog*) chien *m* métis, roquet *m*; (*despicable person*) mufle *m*
curate ['kjurɪt] *s* vicaire *m*
curative ['kjurətɪv] *adj* curatif
curator [kju'retər] *s* conservateur *m*
curb [kʌrb] *s* (*edge of road*) bordure *f* de pavés, bord *m* de trottoir; (*of well*) margelle *f*; (*of bit*) gourmette *f*; (*market*) coulisse *f*; (*check, restraint*) frein *m* ‖ *tr* (*a horse*) gourmer; (*passions, anger, desires*) réprimer, refréner; **curb your dog** (*public sign*) faites faire votre chien dans le ruisseau
curb' serv'ice *s* restoroute *m*
curb'stone' *s* garde-pavé *m*; **curbstones** bordure *f* de pavés
curd [kʌrd] *s* caillé *m*; **curds** caillebotte *f* ‖ *tr* cailler, caillebotter ‖ *intr* se cailler, se caillebotter
curdle ['kʌrdəl] *tr* (*milk*) cailler; (*the blood*) figer ‖ *intr* se cailler; se figer
curds' and whey' *spl* lait *m* caillé sucré
cure [kjur] *s* (*recovery*) guérison *f*; (*treatment*) cure *f*; (*remedy*) remède *m* ‖ *tr* guérir; (*meat; leather*) saler; (*a pipe*) culotter
cure'-all' *s* panacée *f*
curfew ['kʌrfju] *s* couvre-feu *m*
curi·o ['kjurɪˌo] *s* (*pl* **-os**) bibelot *m*
curiosi·ty [ˌkjurɪ'ɑsiti] *s* (*pl* **-ties**) curiosité *f*
curious ['kjurɪˌəs] *adj* curieux
curl [kʌrl] *s* (*of hair*) boucle *f*, frisure *f*; (*spiral-shaped*) volute *f*; (*of smoke*) spirale *f* ‖ *tr* boucler, friser; (*to coil, to roll up*) enrouler, tire-bouchonner; **to curl one's lip** faire la moue ‖ *intr* boucler, friser; (*said of smoke*) s'élever en spirales; (*said of waves*) onduler, déferler; **to curl up** (*said of leaves, paper, etc.*) se recroqueviller; (*in bed*) se rouler en boule
curlew ['kʌrl(j)u] *s* courlis *m*
curlicue ['kʌrliˌkju] *s* paraphe *m*
curl'ing i'ron *s* fer *m* à friser
curl'pa'per *s* papillote *f*
curl·y ['kʌrli] *adj* (*comp* **-ier**; *super* **-iest**) bouclé, frisé
curmudgeon [kər'mʌdʒən] *s* (*crosspatch*) bourru *m*, sale bougre *m*; (*miser*) ladre *mf*
currant ['kʌrənt] *s* groseille *f*

curren·cy [ˈkʌrənsi] s (pl **-cies**) circulation f; (legal tender) monnaie f, devises fpl; **to give currency to** donner cours à

current [ˈkʌrənt] adj (opinion, price, word, etc.) courant; (month) en cours; (accepted) admis, reçu; (present-day) actuel ‖ s courant m; (stream) courant, cours m

cur′rent account′ s compte m courant

cur′rent events′ spl actualités fpl

cur′rent fail′ure s panne f de secteur

cur′rent is′sue s dernier numéro m

curricu·lum [kəˈrɪkjələm] s (pl **-lums** or **-la** [lə]) programme m scolaire, plan m d'études

cur·ry [ˈkʌri] s (pl **-ries**) cari m ‖ v (pret & pp **-ried**) tr (a horse) étriller; (culin) apprêter au cari; **to curry favor with** faire la cour à

cur′ry-comb′ s étrille f ‖ tr étriller

cur′ry pow′der s cari m

curse [kʌrs] s (imprecation) malédiction f; (swearword) juron m; (bane) fléau m, malheur m ‖ tr maudire ‖ intr jurer, sacrer

cursed [ˈkʌrsɪd], [kʌrst] adj maudit, exécrable, sacré

cursive [ˈkʌrsɪv] adj cursif ‖ s cursive f

cursory [ˈkʌrsəri] adj superficiel, précipité

curt [kʌrt] adj brusque, court

curtail [kərˈtel] tr (to reduce) raccourcir, diminuer; (expenses) restreindre; (rights) enlever

curtailment [kʌrˈtelmənt] s (reduction) diminution f; (of expenses) restriction f; (of rights) privation f

curtain [ˈkʌrtən] s rideau m ‖ tr garnir de rideaux; (to hide) cacher sous des rideaux; **to curtain off** séparer par un rideau

cur′tain call′ s rappel m

cur′tain rais′er s (play) lever m de rideau

cur′tain ring′ s anneau m de rideau

cur′tain rod′ s tringle f de rideau

curt·sy [ˈkʌrtsi] s (pl **-sies**) révérence f ‖ v (pret & pp **-sied**) intr faire la révérence

curvature [ˈkʌrvətʃər] s courbure f; (of spine) déviation f

curve [kʌrv] s courbe f; (of road) virage m; (curvature) courbure f ‖ tr courber ‖ intr se courber

curved adj courbe, courbé

cushion [ˈkuʃən] s coussin m ‖ tr (a chair) rembourrer; (a shock) amortir

cuspidor [ˈkʌspɪˌdɔr] s crachoir m

cuss [kʌs] s (person) (coll) vaurien m, chenapan m ‖ tr (coll) maudire ‖ intr (coll) jurer, sacrer

cuss′word′ s (coll) juron m

custard [ˈkʌstərd] s flan m, œufs mpl au lait, crème f caramel

custodian [kəsˈtodɪ·ən] s gardien m; concierge mf

custo·dy [ˈkʌstədi] s (pl **-dies**) (care) garde f; (imprisonment) emprisonnement m; **in custody** en sûreté; **to take into custody** mettre en état d'arrestation

custom [ˈkʌstəm] s coutume f; (customers) clientèle f; **customs** douane f; (duties) droits mpl de douane

customary [ˈkʌstəˌmɛri] adj coutumier, ordinaire, habituel

custom-built [ˈkʌstəmˈbɪlt] adj hors série, fait sur commande

customer [ˈkʌstəmər] s (buyer) client m, chaland m; (coll) individu m, type m; **customers** clientèle f, achalandage m

cus′tom-house′ adj douanier ‖ s douane f

custom-made [ˈkʌstəmˈmed] adj fait sur commande; (clothes) sur mesure

cus′toms clear′ance s expédition f douanière

cus′toms of′ficer s douanier m

cus′toms un′ion s union f douanière

cus′tom tai′lor s tailleur m à façon

cut [kʌt] adj coupé; **cut out** taillé, e.g., **he is not cut out for that** il n'est pas taillé pour cela; e.g., **your work is cut out for you** voilà votre besogne taillée ‖ s (of a garment; of cards; haircut; act of cutting) coupe f; (piece cut off) tranche f, morceau m; (slash) coupure f; (with knife, whip, etc.) coup m; (in prices, wages, etc.) réduction f, baisse f; (typ) gravure f, planche f; (absence from school) (coll) séchage m; (in winnings, earnings, etc.) (slang) part f; **the cheap cuts** les bas morceaux mpl ‖ v (pret & pp **cut**; ger **cutting**) tr couper; (meat, bread) trancher; (prices) réduire, baisser; (e.g., a hole) pratiquer; (glass, diamonds) tailler; (fingernails) rogner; (an article, play, speech) sabrer, faire des coupures à; (a phonograph record) enregistrer; (a class) (coll) sécher; **to cut down** faucher, abattre; (expenses) réduire; **to cut off, out,** or **up** découper, couper; **to cut short** couper court à ‖ intr couper; trancher; **to cut in** (a conversation) s'immiscer dans; (coll) enlever la danseuse d'un autre; **to cut off** (debate) clore; **to cut up** (slang) faire le pitre

cut′-and-dried′ adj décidé d'avance, tout fait; monotone, rasoir

cutaneous [kjuˈteni·əs] adj cutané

cut′away′ s frac m

cut′back′ s réduction f; (mov) retour m en arrière

cute [kjut] adj (coll) mignon; (shrewd) (coll) rusé

cut′ flowers′ spl fleurs fpl coupées

cut′ glass′ s cristal m taillé

cuticle [ˈkjutɪkəl] s cuticule f

cutlass [ˈkʌtləs] s coutelas m

cutlery [ˈkʌtləri] s coutellerie f

cutlet [ˈkʌtlɪt] s (slice of meat) côtelette f; (without bone) escalope f; (croquette of minced chicken, etc.) croquette f

cut′off′ s point m de coupure; (road) raccourci m; (of river) bras m mort; (of cylinder) obturateur m

cut′out′ s (aut) échappement m libre; (elec) coupe-circuit m; (mov) décor m découpé

cut′-rate′ adj à prix réduit

cutter [ˈkʌtər] s (naut) cotre m

cut′throat′ s coup-jarret m

cutting [ˈkʌtɪŋ] adj tranchant; (tone, remark) mordant, cinglant ‖ s (action) coupe *f*; (*from a newspaper*) coupure *f*; (*e.g., of prices*) réduction *f*; (hort) bouture *f*; (mov) découpage *m*

cuttlefish ['kʌtəl,fɪʃ] *s* seiche *f*

cut'wa'ter *s* (naut) étrave *f*; (*of bridge*) bec *m*

cyanamide [saɪ'ænə,maɪd] *s* cyanamide *f*

cyanide ['saɪ·ə,naɪd] *s* cyanure *m*

cyanosis [,saɪ·ə'nosɪs] *s* cyanose *f*

cycle ['saɪkəl] *s* cycle *m*; (*of internal-combustion engine*) temps *m*; (phys) période *f* ‖ *intr* faire de la bicyclette

cyclic(al) ['sɪklɪk(əl)] *adj* cyclique

cyclist ['saɪklɪst] *s* cycliste *mf*

cyclone ['saɪklon] *s* cyclone *m*

cyclops ['saɪklɑps] *s* cyclope *m*

cyclotron ['saɪklo,trɑn] *s* cyclotron *m*

cylinder ['sɪlɪndər] *s* cylindre *m*; (*of revolver*) barillet *m*

cyl'inder block' *s* cylindre *m*

cyl'inder bore' *s* alésage *m*

cyl'inder head' *s* culasse *f*

cylindric(al) [sɪ'lɪndrɪk(əl)] *adj* cylindrique

cymbal ['sɪmbəl] *s* cymbale *f*

cynic ['sɪnɪk] *adj & s* cynique *m*

cynical ['sɪnɪkəl] *adj* cynique

cynicism ['sɪnɪ,sɪzəm] *s* cynisme *m*

cynosure ['saɪnə,ʃʊr] *s* guide *m*, exemple *m*, norme *f*; (*center of attention*) clou *m*; (astr) cynosure *f*

cypress ['saɪprəs] *s* cyprès *m*

Cyprus ['saɪprəs] *s* Chypre *f*

Cyrillic [sɪ'rɪlɪk] *adj* cyrillique

cyst [sɪst] *s* kyste *m*; (*on the skin*) vésicule *f*

czar [zɑr] *s* tsar *m*, czar *m*

czarina [zɑ'rinə] *s* tsarine *f*, czarine *f*

Czech [tʃɛk] *adj* tchèque ‖ *s* (*language*) tchèque *m*; (*person*) Tchèque *mf*

Czecho-Slovak ['tʃɛko'slovæk] *adj* tchéco-slovaque ‖ *s* Tchécoslovaque *mf*

Czecho-Slovakia [,tʃɛkoslo'vækɪ·ə] *s* Tchécoslovaquie *f*; la Tchécoslovaquie

D

D, d [di] *s* IVe lettre de l'alphabet

dab [dæb] *s* touche *f*; (*of ink*) tache *f*; (*of butter*) petit morceau *m* ‖ *v* (*pret & pp* **dabbed**; *ger* **dabbing**) *tr* essuyer légèrement; (*to pat*) tapoter

dabble ['dæbəl] *tr* humecter ‖ *intr* barboter; **to dabble in** se mêler de; **to dabble in the stock market** boursicoter

dachshund ['dɑks,hund] *s* teckel *m*

dad [dæd] *s* (coll) papa *m*

dad·dy ['dædi] *s* (*pl* **-dies**) papa *m*

dad'dy-long'legs' *s* (*pl* **-legs**) faucheux *m*

daffodil ['dæfədɪl] *s* jonquille *f* des prés, narcisse *m* des bois

daff·y ['dæfi] *adj* (*comp* **-ier**; *super* **-iest**) (coll) timbré, toqué

dagger ['dægər] *s* poignard *m*, dague *f*; (typ) croix *f*, obel *m*; **to look daggers at** foudroyer du regard

dahlia ['dæljə] *s* dahlia *m*

dai·ly ['deli] *adj* quotidien, journalier ‖ *s* (*pl* **-lies**) quotidien *m* ‖ *adv* journellement

dain·ty ['denti] *adj* (*comp* **-tier**; *super* **-tiest**) délicat ‖ *s* (*pl* **-ties**) friandise *f*

dair·y ['dɛri] *s* (*pl* **-ies**) laiterie *f*; (*shop*) crémerie *f*; (*farm*) vacherie *f*

dair'y farm' *s* vacherie *f*

dair'y·man *s* (*pl* **-men**) laitier *m*

dais ['de·ɪs] *s* estrade *f*

dai·sy ['dezi] *s* (*pl* **-sies**) marguerite *f*

dal·ly ['dæli] *v* (*pret & pp* **-lied**) *intr* (*to tease*) badiner; (*to delay*) s'attarder

dam [dæm] *s* (*obstruction*) barrage *m*; (*female quadruped*) mère *f* ‖ *v* (*pret & pp* **dammed**; *ger* **damming**) *tr* contenir, endiguer

damage ['dæmɪdʒ] *s* dommage *m*, dégâts *mpl*; (*to engine, ship, etc.*) avaries *fpl*; (*to one's reputation*) tort *m*; **damages** (law) dommages-intérêts *mpl* ‖ *tr* endommager; (*merchandise; a machine*) avarier; (*a reputation*) faire du tort à

damaging ['dæmɪdʒɪŋ] *adj* dommageable, préjudiciable

damascene ['dæmə,sin], [,dæmə'sin] *adj* damasquiné ‖ *s* damasquinage *m* ‖ *tr* damasquiner

Damascus [də'mæskəs] *s* Damas *f*

dame [dem] *s* dame *f*; (coll) jupon *m*, typesse *f*, gonzesse *f*

damn [dæm] *s* juron *m*, gros mot *m*; **I don't give a damn** (slang) je m'en fiche; **that's not worth a damn** (slang) ça ne vaut pas un pet de lapin, ça ne vaut pas chipette ‖ *tr* condamner; (*to criticize harshly*) éreinter; (*to curse*) maudire; **damn him!** qu'il aille au diable!; **damn it!** merde!, nom de Dieu!, oh, la vache!; **I'll be damned if . . .** que le diable m'emporte si . . . ; **to damn with faint praise** assommer avec des fleurs; **well, I'll be damned!** ça c'est trop fort! ‖ *intr* maudire

damnation [dæm'neʃən] *s* damnation *f*

damned [dæmd] *adj* damné *m* ‖ *s*—**the damned** les damnés ‖ [dæm] *adv* (slang) diablement, bigrement

damp [dæmp] *adj* humide, moite ‖ *s* humidité *f*; (*firedamp*) grisou *m* ‖ *tr* (*to dampen*) humecter, mouiller; (*a furnace*) étouffer; (*sound; electromagnetic waves*) amortir

dampen ['dæmpən] *tr* (*to moisten*) humecter; (*enthusiasm*) refroidir; (*to muffle*) amortir

damper [ˈdæmpər] *s* (*of chimney*) registre *m*; (*of stovepipe*) soupage *f* de réglage; (*of piano*) étouffoir *m*; **to put a damper on** (fig) jeter un froid sur

damsel [ˈdæmzəl] *s* demoiselle *f*

dance [dæns] *s* danse *f*; bal *m*, soirée *f* dansante ‖ *tr* & *intr* danser

dance′ band′ *s* orchestre *m* de danse

dance′ floor′ *s* piste *f* de danse

dance′ hall′ *s* dancing *m*, salle *f* de danse

dance′ pro′gram *s* carnet *m* de bal

dancer [ˈdænsər] *s* danseur *m*

danc′ing part′ner *s* danseur *m*

danc′ing wa′ters *spl* fontaines *fpl* vivantes

dandelion [ˈdændɪˌlaɪ·ən] *s* pissenlit *m*

dandruff [ˈdændrəf] *s* pellicules *fpl*

dan·dy [ˈdændi] *adj* (*comp* **-dier**; *super* **-diest**) (coll) chic, chouette ‖ *s* (*pl* **-dies**) dandy *m*, élégant *m*

Dane [den] *s* Danois *m*

danger [ˈdendʒər] *s* danger *m*

dangerous [ˈdendʒərəs] *adj* dangereux

dangle [ˈdæŋgəl] *tr* faire pendiller ‖ *intr* pendiller

Danish [ˈdenɪʃ] *adj* & *s* danois *m*

dank [dæŋk] *adj* humide, moite

Danube [ˈdænjʊb] *s* Danube *m*

dapper [ˈdæpər] *adj* fringant, élégant

dappled [ˈdæpəld] *adj* (*mottled*) tacheté; (*sky*) pommelé; (*horse*) moucheté, miroité

dare [dɛr] *s* défi *m*; **to take a dare** relever un défi ‖ *tr* défier; oser; **to dare s.o. to** + *inf* défier qn de + *inf* ‖ *intr* oser; **to dare** + *inf* oser + *inf*

dare′dev′il *s* risque-tout *mf*

daring [ˈdɛrɪŋ] *adj* audacieux, hardi ‖ *s* audace *f*, hardiesse *f*

dark [dɑrk] *adj* sombre, obscur; (*color*) foncé; (*complexion*) basané, brun; **it is dark** il fait noir, il fait nuit ‖ *s* obscurité *f*, ténèbres *fpl*

Dark′ Ag′es *spl* âge *m* des ténèbres

dark′ brown′ *adj* brun, brun foncé, chocolat

dark′ choc′olate *s* chocolat *m* à croquer

dark′-complex′ioned *adj* brun, basané, brun de peau

darken [ˈdɑrkən] *tr* assombrir; (*the complexion*) brunir; (*a color*) foncer ‖ *intr* s'assombrir; (*said of forehead*) se rembrunir

dark′ glass′es *spl* lunettes *fpl* noires, verres *mpl* fumés

dark′ horse′ *s* (pol) candidat *m* obscur; (sports) outsider *m*

darkly [ˈdɑrkli] *adv* obscurément; (*mysteriously*) ténébreusement; (*threateningly*) d'un air menaçant

dark′ meat′ *s* viande *f* brune; (*of game*) viande noire

darkness [ˈdɑrknɪs] *s* obscurité *f*

dark′room′ *s* (phot) chambre *f* noire

darling [ˈdɑrlɪŋ] *adj* & *s* chéri *m*, bien-aimé *m*; **my darling** mon chou

darn [dɑrn] *s* reprise *f*, raccommodage *m* ‖ *tr* repriser, raccommoder ‖ *interj* zut!

darn′ing egg′ *s* œuf *m* à repriser

darn′ing nee′dle *s* aiguille *f* à repriser

dart [dɑrt] *s* dard *m*; (*small missile used in a game*) fléchette *f* ‖ *intr* se précipiter, aller comme une flèche

dash [dæʃ] *s* (*sudden rush*) mouvement *m* brusque; (*small amount*) soupçon *m*, petit brin *m*; (*of color*) pointe *f*, touche *f*; (*splash*) choc *m*, floc *m*; (*spirit*) élan *m*, fougue *f*; (*in printing, writing*) tiret *m*; (*in telegraphy*) trait *m*, longue *f*; (sports) sprint *m* ‖ *tr* (*quickly*) précipiter; (*violently*) heurter; (*hopes*) abattre; **to dash off** écrire d'un trait, esquisser; **to dash to pieces** fracasser ‖ *intr* se précipiter; **to dash against** se heurter contre; **to dash by** filer à grand train; **to dash in** entrer en trombe; **to dash off** or **out** s'élancer, s'élancer dehors

dash′board′ *s* tableau *m* de bord

dashing [ˈdæʃɪŋ] *adj* impétueux, fougueux; (*elegant*) fringant

dastard [ˈdæstərd] *adj* & *s* lâche *mf*

data [ˈdetə], [ˈdætə] *spl* données *fpl*

da′ta bank′ *s* banque *f* de données

da′ta base′ *s* base *f* de données

da′ta proc′essing *s* analyse *f* des renseignements, étude *f* des données, (l') informatique *f*

date [det] *s* (*time*) date *f*; (*on books, on coins*) millésime *m*; (*palm*) dattier *m*; (*fruit*) datte *f*; (*of note, of loan*) terme *m*, échéance *f*; (*appointment*) rendez-vous *m*; **out of date** suranné, périmé; **to date** à ce jour; **up to date** à la page, au courant ‖ *tr* dater; (*e.g., a work of art*) assigner une date à; (coll) fixer un rendez-vous avec ‖ *intr* (*to be outmoded*) dater; **to date from** dater de, remonter à

date′ line′ *s* ligne *f* de changement de date

date′ palm′ *s* dattier *m*

dative [ˈdetɪv] *s* datif *m*

daub [dɔb] *s* barbouillage *m* ‖ *tr* barbouiller

daughter [ˈdɔtər] *s* fille *f*

daugh′ter-in-law′ *s* (*pl* **daughters-in-law**) belle-fille *f*, bru *f*

daunt [dɔnt] *tr* intimider, abattre

dauntless [ˈdɔntlɪs] *adj* intrépide

dauphin [ˈdɔfɪn] *s* dauphin *m*

davenport [ˈdævənˌpɔrt] *s* canapé-lit *m*

daw [dɔ] *s* choucas *m*

dawdle [ˈdɔdəl] *intr* flâner, muser

dawn [dɔn] *s* aube *f*, aurore *f* ‖ *intr* poindre; **to dawn on** venir à l'esprit à

day [de] *adj* (*work*) diurne; (*worker*) de journée ‖ *s* jour *m*; (*of travel, work, worry*) journée *f*; (*of the month*) quantième *m*; **a day** (*per day*) par jour; **by the day** à la journée; **day by day** au jour le jour, jour par jour; **every day** tous les jours; **every other day** tous les deux jours; **from day to day** de jour en jour; **good old days** bon vieux temps; **in less than a day** du jour au lendemain; **in these days** de nos jours; **in those days**

à ce moment-là, à cette époque; **one fine day** un beau jour; **the day after** le lendemain; le lendemain de; **the day after tomorrow** après-demain; l'après-demain *m*; **the day before** la veille; la veille de; **the day before yesterday** avant-hier; l'avant-hier *m*; **to have had its day** avoir fait son temps

day′ bed′ *s* canapé-lit *m*, petit lit *m* de repos

day′break′ *s* pointe *f* du jour, lever *m* du jour; **at daybreak** au jour levant

day′ coach′ *s* (rr) voiture *f*

day′dream′ *s* rêvasserie *f*, rêverie *f* ‖ *intr* rêvasser, rêver creux

day′dream′er *s* songe-creux *m*, songeur *m*

day′dream′ing *s* rêvasserie *f*

day′ la′borer *s* journalier *m*

day′light′ *s* jour *m*; **in broad daylight** en plein jour; **to see daylight** (coll) comprendre; (coll) voir la fin d'une tâche difficile

day′light-sav′ing time′ *s* heure *f* d'été

day′ lil′y *s* lis *m* jaune, belle-d'un-jour *f*

day′ nurs′ery *s* garderie *f* d'enfants, crèche *f*

day′ off′ *s* jour *m* de congé, jour chômé

day′ of reck′oning *s* jour *m* de règlement; (*last judgment*) jour d'expiation

day′ shift′ *s* équipe *f* de jour

day′ stu′dent *s* externe *mf*

day′time′ *s* jour *m*, journée *f*

daze [dez] *s* étourdissement *m*; **in a daze** hébété ‖ *tr* étourdir

dazzle [′dæzəl] *s* éblouissement *m* ‖ *tr* éblouir

dazzling [′dæzlɪŋ] *adj* éblouissant

D.C. [′di′si] *s* (letterword) (**District of Columbia**) le district de Columbia; (**direct current**) le courant continu

D′-day′ *s* le jour J

deacon [′dikən] *s* diacre *m*

deaconess [′dikənɪs] *s* diaconesse *f*

dead [dɛd] *adj* mort; (*tired*) épuisé; (*color*) terne; (*business*) stagnant; (*sleep*) profond; (*calm*) plat; (*loss*) sec; (*typewriter key*) immobile; **on a dead level** à franc niveau ‖ *s*—**in the dead of night** au milieu de la nuit; **the dead** les morts; **the dead of winter** le cœur de l'hiver ‖ *adv* absolument; **to stop dead** s'arrêter net

dead′beat′ *s* (slang) écornifleur *m*

dead′ bolt′ *s* pêne *m* dormant

dead′ calm′ *s* calme *m* plat

dead′ cen′ter *s* point *m* mort

dead′-drunk′ *adj* ivre mort

deaden [′dɛdən] *tr* amortir; (*sound*) assourdir

dead′ end′ *s* cul-de-sac *m*, impasse *f*

dead′latch′ *s* pêne *m* dormant

dead′-let′ter of′fice *s* bureau *m* des rebuts

dead′line′ *s* dernier délai *m*, date *f* limite, terme *m* de rigueur

dead′lock′ *s* serrure *f* à pêne dormant; (fig) impasse *f* ‖ *tr* faire aboutir à une impasse

dead·ly [′dɛdli] *adj* (*comp* **-lier**; *super* **-liest**) mortel; (*sin*) capital

dead′ pan′ *s* (slang) visage *m* sans expression

dead′ reck′oning *s* estime *f*; (*position*) point *m* d'estime

dead′ ring′er *s* (coll) portrait *m* vivant

dead′ sol′dier *s* (*bottle*) (slang) cadavre *m*

dead′ weight′ *s* poids *m* mort

dead′wood′ *s* bois *m* mort; (fig) objet *m* or individu *m* inutile

deaf [dɛf] *adj* sourd; **to turn a deaf ear** faire la sourde oreille

deaf′-and-dumb′ *adj* sourd-muet

deafen [′dɛfən] *tr* assourdir

deafening [′dɛfənɪŋ] *adj* assourdissant

deaf′-mute′ *adj* & *s* sourd-muet *m*

deafness [′dɛfnɪs] *s* surdité *f*

deal [dil] *s* (*bargain*) affaire *f*; (cards) main *f*, donne *f*; **a good deal (of)** or **a great deal (of)** beaucoup (de); **to think a great deal of s.o.** estimer qn ‖ *v* (*pret* & *pp* **dealt** [dɛlt]) *tr* (*a blow*) donner, porter; (cards) donner, distribuer; **to deal out** (*e.g., gifts*) distribuer, répartir; (*alms*) dispenser; (*justice*) rendre ‖ *intr* négocier; (cards) faire la donne; **to deal in** faire le commerce de; **to deal with** (*a person*) traiter avec; (*a subject*) traiter de

dealer [′dilər] *s* marchand *m*, négociant *m*, revendeur *m*; (*of cards*) donneur *m*; (*middleman, e.g., in selling automobiles*) concessionnaire *m*, stockiste *m*

deal′er's plate′ *s* (aut) immatriculation *f* de livraison

dean [din] *s* doyen *m*; (educ) chef *m* de branche

dean′ship *s* doyenné *m*, décanat *m*

dear [dɪr] *adj* cher; **dear me!** mon Dieu!; **Dear Sir** (*salutation in a letter*) Monsieur ‖ *s* chéri *m*, chérie *f*

dearie [′dɪri] *s* (coll) chérie *f*, chéri *m*

dearth [dʌrθ] *s* disette *f*, pénurie *f*

death [dɛθ] *s* mort *f*; **at death's door** à deux doigts de la mort; **to bore to death** raser; **to put to death** mettre à mort; **to starve to death** mourir de faim; faire mourir de faim

death′bed′ *s* lit *m* de mort

death′blow′ *s* coup *m* mortel

death′ certif′icate *s* constatation *f* de décès, extrait *m* mortuaire

death′ house′ *s* quartier *m* de la mort

death′ knell′ *s* glas *m* funèbre

deathless [′dɛθlɪs] *adj* immortel

deathly [′dɛθli] *adj* mortel ‖ *adv* mortellement, comme la mort

death′ mask′ *s* masque *m* mortuaire

death′ pen′alty *s* peine *f* capitale, peine de mort

death′ rate′ *s* mortalité *f*, taux *m* de mortalité

death′ rat′tle *s* râle *m* de la mort

death′ row′ *s* couloir *m* de la mort

death′ war′rant *s* ordre *m* d'exécution

death′watch′ *s* veillée *f* funèbre

deb [dɛb] *s* (slang) débutante *f*

debacle [də′bakəl] *s* débâcle *f*

de·bar [dɪ′bar] *v* (*pret* & *pp* **-barred**; *ger* **-barring**) *tr* exclure; empêcher

debark [dɪ′bark] *tr* & *intr* débarquer

debarkation [‚dɪbɑr'keʃən] s débarquement *m*

debase [dɪ'bes] *tr* avilir, abaisser; (*e.g., money*) altérer

debatable [dɪ'betəbəl] *adj* discutable

debate [dɪ'bet] s débat *m*; **under debate** en discussion || *tr* & *intr* discuter

debauch [dɪ'bɔtʃ] s débauche *f* || *tr* débaucher, corrompre

debauchee [‚dɛbə'ʃi] s débauché *m*

debaucher·y [dɪ'bɔtʃəri] s (*pl* **-ies**) débauche *f*

debenture [dɪ'bɛntʃər] s (*bond*) obligation *f*; (*voucher*) reçu *m*

debilitate [dɪ'bɪlɪ,tet] *tr* débiliter

debili·ty [dɪ'bɪlɪti] s (*pl* **-ties**) débilité *f*

debit ['dɛbɪt] s débit *m*; (*entry on debit side*) article *m* au débit || *tr* débiter, porter au débit

deb'it bal'ance s solde *m* débiteur

debonair [‚dɛbə'nɛr] *adj* gai, jovial; élégant, charmant

debris [də'bri] s débris *mpl*, détritus *m*; (*from ruined buildings*) décombres *mpl*

debt [dɛt] s dette *f*; **to run into debt** s'endetter

debtor ['dɛtər] s débiteur *m*

debug [di'bʌg] *tr* (*an activity*) enlever les défauts de; (*a room*) enlever des micros de; (*comp*) déboguer

debut [de'bju] s début *m* || *intr* débuter

debutante ['dɛbjə,tænt] s débutante *f*

decade ['dɛked] s décennie *f*, décade *f*

decadence [dɪ'kedəns] s décadence *f*

decadent [dɪ'kedənt] *adj* & s décadent *m*

decaffeinated [di'kæfənetɪd] *adj* décaféiné

decal ['dikæl] s décalcomanie *f*

decamp [dɪ'kæmp] *intr* décamper

decanter [dɪ'kæntər] s carafe *f*

decapitate [dɪ'kæpɪ,tet] *tr* décapiter

decay [dɪ'ke] s (*rotting*) pourriture *f*; (*decline*) décadence *f*; (*falling to pieces*) délabrement *m*; (*of teeth*) carie *f* || *tr* pourrir; (*teeth*) carier || *intr* pourrir, se gâter; (*said of teeth*) se carier; tomber en décadence or ruine; délabrer

decease [dɪ'sis] s décès *m* || *intr* décéder

deceit [dɪ'sit] s tromperie *f*

deceitful [dɪ'sitfəl] *adj* trompeur

deceive [dɪ'siv] *tr* & *intr* tromper

decelerate [dɪ'sɛlə,ret] *tr* & *intr* ralentir

December [dɪ'sɛmbər] s décembre *m*

decen·cy ['disənsi] s (*pl* **-cies**) décence *f*; **decencies** convenances *fpl*

decent ['disənt] *adj* décent

decently ['disəntli] *adv* décemment

decentralize [dɪ'sɛntrə,laɪz] *tr* décentraliser

deception [dɪ'sɛpʃən] s tromperie *f*

deceptive [dɪ'sɛptɪv] *adj* trompeur

decibel ['dɛsəbɛl] s décibel *m*

decide [dɪ'saɪd] *tr* décider; (*the outcome*) décider de || *intr* décider, se décider; **to decide to** + *inf* décider de + *inf*, se décider à + *inf*; **to decide upon a day** fixer un jour

deciduous [dɪ'sɪdʒʊ·əs] *adj* caduc

decimal ['dɛsɪməl] *adj* décimal || s décimale *f*

dec'imal point' s (*in French the comma is used to separate the decimal fraction from the integer*) virgule *f*

decimate ['dɛsɪ,met] *tr* décimer

decipher [dɪ'saɪfər] *tr* déchiffrer

decision [dɪ'sɪʒən] s décision *f*

decisive [dɪ'saɪsɪv] *adj* décisif

deck [dɛk] s (*of cards*) jeu *m*, paquet *m*; (*of ship*) pont *m*; **between decks** (naut) dans l'entrepont || *tr*—**to deck out** parer, orner

deck' chair' s transatlantique *m*, transat *m*, chaise *f* longue de bord

deck' hand' s matelot *m* de pont

deck'-land' *intr* apponter

deck'-land'ing s appontage *m*

deck'le edge' ['dɛkəl] s barbes *fpl*, bords *mpl* baveux

declaim [dɪ'klem] *tr* & *intr* déclamer

declaration [‚dɛklə'reʃən] s déclaration *f*

declarative [dɪ'klærətɪv] *adj* déclaratif

declare [dɪ'klɛr] *tr* & *intr* déclarer

declension [dɪ'klɛnʃən] s (gram) déclinaison *f*

declination [‚dɛklɪ'neʃən] s (astr, geog) déclinaison *f*

decline [dɪ'klaɪn] s déclin *m*, décadence *f*; (*in prices*) baisse *f* || *tr* & *intr* décliner

declivi·ty [dɪ'klɪvɪti] s (*pl* **-ties**) déclivité *f*, pente *f*

decode [dɪ'kod] *tr* décoder, déchiffrer

decompose [‚dikəm'poz] *tr* décomposer || *intr* se décomposer

decomposition [‚dikɑmpə'zɪʃən] s décomposition *f*

decompression [‚dikəm'prɛʃən] s décompression *f*

decontamination [‚dikən,tæmɪ'neʃən] s décontamination *f*

decontrol [‚dikən'trol] *tr* lever les contrôles gouvernementaux de

decorate ['dɛkə,ret] *tr* décorer

decoration [‚dɛkə'reʃən] s décoration *f*

decorator ['dɛkə,retər] s décorateur *m*

decorous ['dɛkərəs], [dɪ'korəs] *adj* convenable, correct, bienséant

decorum [dɪ'korəm] s décorum *m*

decoy ['dikɔɪ] s leurre *m*, appât *m*; (*bird*) appeau *m* || *tr* [dɪ'kɔɪ] *tr* leurrer

decrease ['dikris] s diminution *f* || [dɪ'kris] *tr* & *intr* diminuer

decree [dɪ'kri] s décret *m*, arrêté *m*; (*of divorce*) ordonnance *f* || *tr* décréter, arrêter, ordonner

decrepit [dɪ'krɛpɪt] *adj* décrépit

de·cry [dɪ'kraɪ] *v* (*pret* & *pp* **-cried**) *tr* décrier, dénigrer

dedicate ['dɛdɪ,ket] *tr* dédier

dedication [‚dɛdɪ'keʃən] s consécration *f*; (*e.g., in a book*) dédicace *f*

dedicatory ['dɛdɪkə,tori] *adj* dédicatoire

deduce [dɪ'd(j)us] *tr* déduire, inférer

deduct [dɪ'dʌkt] *tr* déduire

deduction [dɪ'dʌkʃən] s déduction *f*

deed [did] s action *f*, acte *m*; (law) acte, titre *m*, contrat *m*; **deed of valor** haut fait *m*;

good deed bonne action; **in deed** dans le fait ‖ *tr* transférer par un acte

deem [dim] *tr* estimer, juger, croire ‖ *intr* penser

deep [dip] *adj* profond; (*sound*) grave; (*color*) foncé; de profondeur, e.g., **to be twenty feet deep** avoir vingt pieds de profondeur; **deep in debt** criblé de dettes; **deep in thought** plongé dans la méditation ‖ *adv* profondément; **deep into the night** très avant dans la nuit

deepen ['dipən] *tr* approfondir ‖ *intr* s'approfondir

deep'-freeze' *v* (*pret* **-froze**; *pp* **-frozen** or *pret* & *pp* **-freezed**) *tr* surgeler

deep' freez'er *s* congélateur *m*

deep' freez'ing *s* surgélation *f*

deep'-fry' *v* (*pret* & *pp* **-fried**) *tr* faire frire (en friteuse)

deep' fry'er *s* friteuse *f*

deep'-laid' *adj* habilement ourdi

deep' mourn'ing *s* grand deuil *m*

deep'-root'ed *adj* profondément enraciné, indéracinable

deep'-sea fish'ing *s* grande pêche *f* au large, pêche maritime

deep' space' *s* espace *m* lointain

deep' stall' *s* (aer) superdécrochage *m*

deer [dɪr] *s* (*red deer*) cerf *m*; (*fallow deer*) daim *m*; (*roe deer*) chevreuil *m*

deer'skin' *s* peau *f* de daim

deface [dɪ'fes] *tr* défigurer

de facto [di'fækto] *adv* de fait, de facto

defamation [,dɛfə'meʃən] *s* diffamation *f*, injures *fpl*

defame [dɪ'fem] *tr* diffamer

default [dɪ,fɔlt] *s* manque *m*, défaut *m*; (*on an obligation*) carence *f*; **by default** par défaut; (sports) par forfait; **in default of** à défaut de ‖ *tr* (*a debt*) manquer de s'acquitter de ‖ *intr* ne pas tenir ses engagements; (sports) perdre par forfait

defeat [dɪ'fit] *s* défaite *f*; **unexpected defeat** contre-performance *f* ‖ *tr* vaincre, battre, défaire

defeatism [dɪ'fitɪzəm] *s* défaitisme *m*

defeatist [dɪ'fitɪst] *adj* & *s* défaitiste *mf*

defecate ['dɛfɪ,ket] *intr* déféquer

defect ['difɛkt] *s* défaut *m*, imperfection *f*, vice *m* ‖ [dɪ'fɛkt] *intr* faire défection, déserter

defection [dɪ'fɛkʃən] *s* défection *f*

defective [dɪ'fɛktɪv] *adj* défectueux, vicieux; (gram) défectif

defend [dɪ'fɛnd] *tr* défendre

defendant [dɪ'fɛndənt] *s* (law) défendeur *m*, intimé *m*

defense [dɪ'fɛns] *s* défense *f*

defenseless [dɪ'fɛnslɪs] *adj* sans défense

defensive [dɪ'fɛnsɪv] *adj* défensif ‖ *s* défensive *f*

de·fer [dɪ'fʌr] *v* (*pret* & *pp* **-ferred**; *ger* **-ferring**) *tr* (*to postpone*) différer; (mil) mettre en sursis ‖ *intr*—**to defer to** (*to yield to*) déférer à

deference ['dɛfərəns] *s* déférence *f*

deferential [,dɛfə'rɛnʃəl] *adj* déférent

deferment [dɪ'fʌrmənt] *s* (*postponement*) ajournement *m*, remise *f*; (*extension of time*) délai *m*; (mil) sursis *m* d'appel, sursis d'incorporation

defiance [dɪ'faɪ·əns] *s* défi *m*, provocation *f*, nargue *f*; **in defiance of** au mépris de, en dépit de

defiant [dɪ'faɪ·ənt] *adj* provocant, hostile, de défi

deficien·cy [dɪ'fɪʃənsi] *s* (*pl* **-cies**) déficience *f*, insuffisance *f*; (*of vitamins or minerals*) carence *f*; (com) déficit *m*

deficient [dɪ'fɪʃənt] *adj* déficient, insuffisant

deficit ['dɛfɪsɪt] *adj* déficitaire ‖ *s* déficit *m*

defile [dɪ'faɪl], ['dɪfaɪl] *s* défilé *m* ‖ [dɪ'faɪl] *tr* souiller ‖ *intr* défiler

defilement [dɪ'faɪlmənt] *s* souillure *f*

define [dɪ'faɪn] *tr* définir

definite ['dɛfɪnɪt] *adj* défini; (*opinions, viewpoints*) viewpoints) défini

definitely ['dɛfɪnɪtli] *adv* décidément, nettement

definition [,dɛfɪ'nɪʃən] *s* définition *f*

definitive [dɪ'fɪnɪtɪv] *adj* définitif

deflate [dɪ'flet] *tr* dégonfler; (*currency*) amener la déflation de ‖ *intr* se dégonfler

deflation [dɪ'fleʃən] *s* dégonflement *m*; (*of prices*) déflation *f*

deflect [dɪ'flɛkt] *tr* & *intr* dévier

deflower [di'flau·ər] *tr* déflorer; (*to strip of flowers*) défleurir

defogging [dɪ'fɔgɪŋ] *s* dénébulation *f*

deforest [di'fɔrɪst] *tr* déboiser

deform [dɪ'fɔrm] *tr* déformer

deformed *adj* contrefait, difforme

deformi·ty [dɪ'fɔrmɪti] *s* (*pl* **-ties**) difformité *f*

defraud [dɪ'frɔd] *tr* frauder

defray [dɪ'fre] *tr* payer, supporter

defrost [di'frɔst] *tr* décongeler, dégivrer

defroster [di'frɔstər] *s* déglaceur *m*, dégivreur *m*

defrosting [di'frɔstɪŋ] *s* dégèlement *m*, dégivrage *m*

deft [dɛft] *adj* adroit, habile; (*hand*) exercé, preste

defunct [dɪ'fʌŋkt] *adj* défunt; (*practice, style, etc.*) tombé en désuétude

de·fy [dɪ'faɪ] *v* (*pret* & *pp* **-fied**) *tr* défier, braver, porter un défi à

degeneracy [dɪ'dʒɛnərəsi] *s* dégénérescence *f*

degenerate [dɪ'dʒɛnərɪt] *adj* & *s* dégénéré *m* ‖ [dɪ'dʒɛnə,ret] *intr* dégénérer

degrade [dɪ'gred] *tr* dégrader

degrading [dɪ'gredɪŋ] *adj* dégradant

degree [dɪ'gri] *s* degré *m*; (*from a university*) grade *m*; (*of humidity*) titre *m*; **to take a degree** obtenir ses diplômes, obtenir ses titres universitaires

dehumidi·fy [,dihju'mɪdɪ,faɪ] *v* (*pret* & *pp* **-fied**) *tr* déshumidifier

dehydrate [di'haɪdret] *tr* déshydrater; (*the body*) dessécher

deice [di'aɪs] *tr* déglacer, dégivrer

deicer [di'aɪsər] *s* dégivreur *m*, antigivrant *m*

dei·fy ['di·ɪ,faɪ] v (pret & pp **-fied**) tr déifier

deign [den] intr—**to deign to** daigner

dei·ty ['di·ɪti] s (pl **-ties**) divinité f; (mythol) déité f; **the Deity** Dieu m

dejected [dɪ'dʒɛktɪd] adj abattu, découragé

dejection [dɪ'dʒɛkʃən] s abattement m

delay [dɪ'le] s retard m; (postponement) sursis m, remise f; **without delay** sans délai; **without further delay** sans plus tarder ‖ tr retarder; (to put off) remettre, différer ‖ intr tarder, s'attarder

delayed'-ac'tion adj à action différée

delayed'-ac'tion switch' s minuterie f d'escalier

delayed' record'ing s différé m

delayed'-time' switch' s coupe-circuit m à action différée

dele ['dili] s (typ) deleatur m

delectable [dɪ'lɛktəbəl] adj délectable

delegate ['dɛlɪ,get] s délégué m; (at a convention) congressiste mf, délégué ‖ tr déléguer

delegation [,dɛlɪ'geʃən] s délégation f

delete [dɪ'lit] tr supprimer

deletion [dɪ'liʃən] s suppression f; (the deleted part) passage m supprimé

deliberate [dɪ'lɪbərɪt] adj (premeditated) délibéré, réfléchi; (cautious) circonspect; (slow) lent ‖ [dɪ'lɪbə,ret] tr & intr délibérer

deliberately [dɪ'lɪbərɪtli] adv (on purpose) exprès, de propos délibéré; (without hurrying) posément, sans hâte

deliberation [dɪ,lɪbə'reʃən] s délibération f; (slowness) lenteur f

delica·cy ['dɛlɪkəsi] s (pl **-cies**) délicatesse f; (choice food) friandise f, gourmandise f

delicate ['dɛlɪkɪt] adj délicat

delicatessen [,dɛlɪkə'tɛsən] s charcuterie f

delicious [dɪ'lɪʃəs] adj délicieux

delight [dɪ'laɪt] s délice m, délices fpl, plaisir m ‖ tr enchanter, ravir ‖ intr—**to delight in** se délecter à

delighted adj enchanté, ravi, content

delightful [dɪ'laɪtfəl] adj délicieux, ravissant, enchanteur

delineate [dɪ'lɪnɪ,et] tr esquisser

delinquen·cy [dɪ'lɪŋkwənsi] s (pl **-cies**) délit m, faute f; (e.g., of juveniles) délinquance f

delinquent [dɪ'lɪŋkwənt] adj négligent, coupable; (in payment) arriéré; (in guilt) délinquant ‖ s délinquant m; créancier m en retard

delirious [dɪ'lɪrɪ·əs] adj délirant

deliri·um [dɪ'lɪrɪ·əm] s (pl **-ums** or **-a** [ə]) délire m

deliver [dɪ'lɪvər] tr délivrer; (e.g., laundry) livrer; (mail) distribuer; (a blow) asséner; (an opinion) exprimer; (a speech) prononcer; (energy) débiter, fournir; **to be delivered of a child** accoucher d'un enfant

deliver·y [dɪ'lɪvəri] s (pl **-ies**) s remise f; (e.g., of a package) livraison f; (of mail) distribution f; (of a speech; of electricity)

débit m; (of a woman in childbirth) accouchement m, délivrance f; **free delivery** livraison franco

deliv'ery·man s (pl **-men**) livreur m

deliv'ery room' s salle f d'accouchement, salle de travail

deliv'ery truck' s fourgon m à livraison

dell [dɛl] s vallon m

delouse [di'laʊs] tr épouiller

delphinium [dɛl'fɪnɪ·əm] s dauphinelle f, pied-d'alouette m

delta ['dɛltə] s delta m

delude [dɪ'lud] tr duper, tromper

deluge ['dɛljudʒ] s déluge m ‖ tr inonder

delusion [dɪ'luʒən] s illusion f, tromperie f; **delusions** (psychopathol) hallucinations fpl; **delusions of grandeur** folie f des grandeurs

delusive [dɪ'lusɪv] or **delusory** [dɪ'lusəri] adj trompeur

de luxe [dɪ'lʌks] adj & adv de luxe

delve [dɛlv] intr—**to delve into** fouiller dans, approfondir

demagnetize [di'mægnɪ,taɪz] tr démagnétiser, désaimanter

demagogue ['dɛmə,gag] s démagogue mf

demand [dɪ'mænd] s exigence f; (of the buying public) demande f; **demands** exigences; **in great demand** très recherché; **on demand** sur demande ‖ tr exiger

demanding [dɪ'mændɪŋ] adj exigeant

demarcate ['dimar,ket] tr délimiter

demean [dɪ'min] tr dégrader; **to demean oneself** se conduire

demeanor [dɪ'minər] s conduite f, tenue f

demented [dɪ'mɛntɪd] adj aliéné, fou

demerit [dɪ'mɛrɪt] s démérite m

demigod ['dɛmɪ,gad] s demi-dieu m

demijohn ['dɛmɪ,dʒan] s dame-jeanne f

demilitarize [di'mɪlɪtə,raɪz] tr démilitariser

demise [dɪ'maɪz] s décès m

demitasse ['dɛmɪ,tæs] s petite tasse f à café; (contents) café m noir

demobilize [di'mobɪ,laɪz] tr démobiliser

democra·cy [dɪ'makrəsi] s (pl **-cies**) démocratie f

democrat ['dɛmə,kræt] s démocrate mf

democratic [,dɛmə'krætɪk] adj démocratique

demolish [dɪ'malɪʃ] tr démolir

demolition [,dɛmə'lɪʃən] s démolition f

demon ['dimən] s démon m

demoniac [dɪ'monɪ,æk] adj & s démoniaque mf

demonic [dɪ'manɪk] adj démoniaque

demonstrate ['dɛmən,stret] tr démontrer ‖ intr (to show feelings in public gatherings) manifester

demonstration [,dɛmən'streʃən] s démonstration f; (public show of feeling) manifestation f

demonstrative [dɪ'manstrətɪv] adj démonstratif

demonstrator ['dɛmən,stretər] s (salesman) démonstrateur m; (agitator) manifestant m

demoralize [dɪ'mɔrə,laɪz] tr démoraliser

demote [dɪ'mot] tr rétrograder

demotion [dɪ'moʃən] s rétrogradation f

de·mur [dɪ'mʌr] v (pret & pp **-murred**; ger **-murring**) intr faire des objections

demure [dɪ'mjʊr] adj modeste, posé

demurrage [dɪ'mʌrɪdʒ] s (naut) surestarie f

den [dɛn] s (of animals; of thieves) repaire m, retraite f, officine f; (of wild beasts) antre m; (of lions) tanière f; (room in a house) cabinet m de travail, fumoir m, coin m de détente, coin de retraite; (Cub Scouts) sizaine f

denaturalize [di'nætʃərə,laɪz] tr dénaturaliser

denial [dɪ'naɪ·əl] s (contradiction) dénégation f, démenti m; (refusal) refus m, déni m

denim ['dɛnɪm] s coutil m

denizen ['dɛnɪzən] s habitant m

Denmark ['dɛnmɑrk] s le Danemark

denomination [dɪ'nɑmɪ'neʃən] s dénomination f; (of coin or stamp) valeur f; (eccl) secte f, confession f, communion f

denote [dɪ'not] tr dénoter

denounce [dɪ'nauns] tr dénoncer

dense [dɛns] adj dense; (stupid) bête

densi·ty ['dɛnsɪti] s (pl **-ties**) densité f

dent [dɛnt] s (depression) marque f de coup, creux m; (in a knife; in a fortune) brèche f; **to make a dent in** faire une brèche à ‖ tr ébrécher

dental ['dɛntəl] adj dentaire; (phonet) dental ‖ s dentale f

den'tal brac'es spl appareil m dentaire

den'tal floss' s fil m dentaire, soie f dentaire

den'tal lab'oratory s laboratoire m de prothèse dentaire

den'tal sur'geon s chirurgien-dentiste m

dentifrice ['dɛntɪfrɪs] s dentifrice m

dentist ['dɛntɪst] s dentiste mf

dentistry ['dɛntɪstri] s odontologie f

denture ['dɛntʃər] s (set of teeth) denture f; (set of artificial teeth) dentier m, râtelier m, prothèse f dentaire

denunciation [dɪ,nʌnsɪ'eʃən] s dénonciation f

de·ny [dɪ'naɪ] v (pret & pp **-nied**) tr nier, démentir; **to deny oneself** se refuser, se priver

deodorant [di'odərənt] adj & s désodorisant m

deodorize [di'odə,raɪz] tr désodoriser

depart [dɪ'pɑrt] intr partir; **to depart from** se départir de

departed adj (dead) mort, défunt

department [dɪ'pɑrtmənt] s département m; (of hospital) service m; (of agency) bureau m; (of store) rayon m, comptoir m; (of university) section f

Depart'ment of State' s ministère m des affaires étrangères

depart'ment store' s grands magasins mpl, galerie f

departure [dɪ'pɑrtʃər] s départ m

depend [dɪ'pɛnd] intr dépendre; **to depend on** or **upon** dépendre de

dependable [dɪ'pɛndəbəl] adj sûr; (person) digne de confiance

dependence [dɪ'pɛndəns] s dépendance f; **dependence on** dépendance de; (trust in) confiance en

dependen·cy [dɪ'pɛndənsi] s (pl **-cies**) dépendance f; (country, territory) possession f, colonie f

dependent [dɪ'pɛndənt] adj dépendant; **dependent on** dépendant de; (s.o. for family support) à la charge de ‖ s charge f de famille

depend'ent clause' s proposition f subordonnée

depict [dɪ'pɪkt] tr dépeindre, décrire

depiction [dɪ'pɪkʃən] s peinture f

deplete [dɪ'plit] tr épuiser

depletion [dɪ'pliʃən] s épuisement m

deple'tion allow'ance s déduction f pour remplacement

deplorable [dɪ'plorəbəl] adj déplorable

deplore [dɪ'plor] tr déplorer

deploy [dɪ'plɔɪ] tr (mil) déployer ‖ intr (mil) se déployer

deployment [dɪ'plɔɪmənt] s (mil) déploiement m

depolarize [di'polə,raɪz] tr dépolariser

depopulate [di'pɑpjə,let] tr & intr dépeupler

deport [dɪ'port] tr déporter; **to deport oneself** se comporter

deportation [,dipor'teʃən] s déportation f

deportee [,dipor'ti] s déporté m

deportment [dɪ'portmənt] s comportement m, tenue f, manières fpl

depose [dɪ'poz] tr & intr déposer

deposit [dɪ'pɑzɪt] s dépôt m; (as pledge) cautionnement m, arrhes fpl, gage m; **no deposit** (bottle) perdu; **to pay a deposit** verser une provision, un acompte, or une caution; **with deposit** (on a bottle) consigné ‖ tr déposer; laisser comme provision

depos'it account' s compte m courant

depositor [dɪ'pɑzɪtər] s déposant m

deposito·ry [dɪ'pɑzɪ,tori] s (pl **-ries**) dépôt m; (person) dépositaire mf

depot ['dipo] s dépôt m; (rr) gare f

depraved [dɪ'prevd] adj dépravé

depravi·ty [dɪ'prævɪti] s (pl **-ties**) dépravation f

deprecate ['dɛprɪ,ket] tr désapprouver

depreciate [dɪ'priʃɪ,et] tr déprécier ‖ intr se déprécier

depreciation [dɪ,priʃɪ'eʃən] s dépréciation f

depredation [,dɛprɪ'deʃən] s déprédation f

depress [dɪ'prɛs] tr déprimer; (prices) abaisser

depressing [dɪ'prɛsɪŋ] adj attristant

depression [dɪ'prɛʃən] s dépression f

deprive [dɪ'praɪv] tr priver

deprogram [di'progræm] tr déprogrammer

depth [dɛpθ] s profondeur f; (in sound) gravité f; **depths** abîme m; **in the depth of winter** en plein hiver; **to go beyond one's depth** perdre pied; sortir de sa compétence

depth' bomb' s bombe f sous-marine

depth' charge' s grenade f sous-marine

deputation [,dɛpjə'teʃən] s députation f

deputize ['dɛpjə,taɪz] *tr* députer

depu·ty ['dɛpjəti] *s* (*pl* **-ties**) député *m*

derail [dɪ'rel] *tr* faire dérailler ‖ *intr* dérailler

derailment [dɪ'relmənt] *s* déraillement *m*

derange [dɪ'rendʒ] *tr* déranger

derangement [dɪ'rendʒmənt] *s* dérangement *m*; (*of mind*) aliénation *f*

der·by ['dʌrbi] *s* (*pl* **-bies**) (*race*) derby *m*; (*hat*) chapeau *m* melon

deregulate [dɪ'rɛgjə,let] *tr* déréglementer

derelict ['dɛrɪlɪkt] *adj* abandonné, délaissé; (*in one's duty*) négligent ‖ *s* épave *f*

dereliction [,dɛrɪ'lɪkʃən] *s* abandon *m*, renoncement *m*

deride [dɪ'raɪd] *tr* tourner en dérision, ridiculiser

derision [dɪ'rɪʒən] *s* dérision *f*

derisive [dɪ'raɪsɪv] *adj* dérisoire

derivation [,dɛrɪ'veʃən] *s* dérivation *f*

derivative [dɪ'rɪvətɪv] *adj & s* dérivé *m*

derive [dɪ'raɪv] *tr & intr* dériver

dermatitis [,dɛrmə'taɪtɪs] *s* dermatite *f*, dermite *f*

dermatology [,dʌrmə'tɑlədʒi] *s* dermatologie *f*

derogatory [dɪ'rɑgə,tori] *adj* péjoratif

derrick ['dɛrɪk] *s* (*crane*) grue *f*; (*for extracting oil*) derrick *m*, tour *f* (de forage)

dervish ['dʌrvɪʃ] *s* derviche *m*

desalinization [di,selɪnɪ'zeʃən] *s* dessalement *m*

desalt [di'sɔlt] *tr* dessaler

descend [dɪ'sɛnd] *tr* descendre ‖ *intr* descendre; (*said of rain*) tomber; **to be descended from** descendre de; **to be directly descended from** (*e.g., an idea*) être dans le droit-fil de; **to descend on** s'abattre sur

descendant [dɪ'sɛndənt] *adj & s* descendant *m*

descendent [dɪ'sɛndənt] *adj* descendant

descent [dɪ'sɛnt] *s* descente *f*; (*drop in temperature*) chute *f*; (*lineage*) descendance *f*, naissance *f*; **of German descent** d'extraction allemande

descrambling [di'skræmblɪŋ] *s* (electron) désembrouillage *m*

describe [dɪ'skraɪb] *tr* décrire

description [dɪ'skrɪpʃən] *s* description *f*

descriptive [dɪ'skrɪptɪv] *adj* descriptif

de·scry [dɪ'skraɪ] *v* (*pret & pp* **-scried**) *tr* découvrir, apercevoir

desecrate ['dɛsɪ,kret] *tr* profaner

desegregate [di'sɛgrɪ,get] *intr* supprimer la ségrégation raciale

desegregation [di,sɛgrɪ'geʃən] *s* déségrégation *f*

desensitize [di'sɛnsɪ,taɪz] *tr* désensibiliser

desert ['dɛzərt] *adj & s* désert *m* ‖ [dɪ'zʌrt] *s* mérite *m*; **to get one's just deserts** recevoir son salaire, recevoir sa juste punition ‖ *tr & intr* déserter

deserted *adj* (*person*) abandonné; (*place*) désert, nu

deserter [dɪ'zʌrtər] *s* déserteur *m*

desertion [dɪ'zʌrʃən] *s* désertion *f*

deserve [dɪ'zʌrv] *tr & intr* mériter

deservedly [dɪ'zʌrvɪdli] *adv* à juste titre, dignement

deserving [dɪ'zʌrvɪŋ] *adj* méritoire, digne

design [dɪ'zaɪn] *s* (*combination of details; art of designing; work of art*) dessin *m*; (*plan, scheme*) dessein *m*, projet *m*, plan *m*; (*model, outline*) modèle *m*, type *m*, grandes lignes *fpl*; **to have designs on** avoir des desseins sur ‖ *tr* inventer, projeter; (*e.g., a dress*) dessiner; (*a secret plan*) combiner; **designed for** destiné à

designate ['dɛzɪg,net] *tr* désigner

designer [dɪ'zaɪnər] *s* dessinateur *m*; (com) concepteur-projecteur *m*; (mov, theat) décorateur *m*

designing [dɪ'zaɪnɪŋ] *adj* artificieux, intrigant ‖ *s* dessin *m*

desirable [dɪ'zaɪrəbəl] *adj* désirable

desire [dɪ'zaɪr] *s* désir *m* ‖ *tr* désirer

desirous [dɪ'zaɪrəs] *adj* désireux

desist [dɪ'zɪst] *intr* cesser

desk [dɛsk] *s* (*in office*) bureau *m*; (*in schoolroom*) pupitre *m*; (*of cashier*) caisse *f*

desk' blot'ter *s* sous-main *m*

desk' clerk' *s* réceptionnaire *mf*, réceptionniste *mf*

desk' set' *s* écritoire *f*

desolate ['dɛsəlɪt] *adj* désert; (*sad*) désolé; (*alone*) abandonné ‖ ['dɛsə,let] *tr* désoler

desolation [,dɛsə'leʃən] *s* désolation *f*

despair [dɪ'spɛr] *s* désespoir *m*, désespérance *f* ‖ *intr* désespérer

despairing [dɪ'spɛrɪŋ] *adj* désespéré

despera·do [,dɛspə'rɑdo] *s* (*pl* **-does** or **-dos**) hors-la-loi *m*

desperate ['dɛspərɪt] *adj* capable de tout, poussé à bout; (*bitter, excessive*) acharné, à outrance; (*hopeless*) désespéré; (*remedy*) héroïque

desperation [,dɛspə'reʃən] *s* (*despair*) désespoir *m*; (*recklessness*) témérité *f*

despicable ['dɛspɪkəbəl] *adj* méprisable, mesquin

despise [dɪ'spaɪz] *tr* mépriser, dédaigner

despite [dɪ'spaɪt] *prep* en dépit de, malgré

despoil [dɪ'spɔɪl] *tr* dépouiller

desponden·cy [dɪ'spɑndənsi] *s* (*pl* **-cies**) abattement *m*, accablement *m*

despondent [dɪ'spɑndənt] *adj* abattu, accablé, déprimé

despot ['dɛspɑt] *s* despote *m*, tyran *m*

despotic [dɛs'pɑtɪk] *adj* despotique

despotism ['dɛspə,tɪzəm] *s* despotisme *m*

dessert [dɪ'zʌrt] *s* dessert *m*

dessert' spoon' *s* cuiller *f* à dessert

destination [,dɛstɪ'neʃən] *s* destination *f*

destine ['dɛstɪn] *tr* destiner

desti·ny ['dɛstɪni] *s* (*pl* **-nies**) destin *m*, destinée *f*

destitute ['dɛstɪ,t(j)ut] *adj* (*poverty-stricken*) indigent; (*lacking*) dépourvu, dénué

destitution [,dɛstɪ't(j)uʃən] *s* dénuement *m*, indigence *f*

destroy [dɪ'strɔɪ] *tr* détruire

destroyer [dɪˈstrɔɪ·ər] *s* destructeur *m*; (nav) destroyer *m*

destruction [dɪˈstrʌkʃən] *s* destruction *f*

destructive [dɪˈstrʌktɪv] *adj* destructeur, destructif

desultory [ˈdɛsəl,tori] *adj* décousu, sans suite; (*conversation*) à bâtons rompus

detach [dɪˈtætʃ] *tr* détacher

detachable [dɪˈtætʃəbəl] *adj* détachable, démontable; (*collar*) faux

detached *adj* détaché

detachment [dɪˈtætʃmənt] *s* détachement *m*

detail [dɪˈtel] (*ˈditel*) *s* détail *m*; (mil) extrait *m* de l'ordre du jour; (mil) détachement *m* ‖ [dɪˈtel] *tr* détailler

detailed' state'ment *s* bordereau *m*

detain [dɪˈten] *tr* retenir, retarder; (*in prison*) détenir

detect [dɪˈtɛkt] *tr* déceler, détecter

detection [dɪˈtɛkʃən] *s* détection *f*

detective [dɪˈtɛktɪv] *adj* (*device*) détecteur; (*film, novel*) policier ‖ *s* détective *m*, agent *m* de la sûreté

detec'tive sto'ry *s* roman *m* policier

detector [dɪˈtɛktər] *s* détecteur *m*

detention [dɪˈtɛnʃən] *s* détention *f*

de·ter [dɪˈtʌr] *v* (*pret & pp* **-terred**; *ger* **-terring**) *tr* dissuader, détourner

detergent [dɪˈtʌrdʒənt] *adj & s* détersif *m*, détergent *m*

deteriorate [dɪˈtɪrɪ·ə,ret] *tr* détériorer ‖ *intr* se détériorer

determination [di,tʌrmɪˈneʃən] *s* détermination *f*

determine [dɪˈtʌrmɪn] *tr* déterminer

determined *adj* déterminé, résolu

deterrent [dɪˈtʌrənt] *adj & s* préventif *m*

detest [dɪˈtɛst] *tr* détester

dethrone [dɪˈθron] *tr* détrôner

detonate [ˈdɛtə,net] *tr* faire détoner, faire éclater ‖ *intr* détoner

detour [ˈditʊr] *s* déviation *f*; (*indirect manner*) détour *m* ‖ *tr & intr* dévier

detract [dɪˈtrækt] *tr* diminuer ‖ *intr*—**to detract from** amoindrir

detractor [dɪˈtræktər] *s* détracteur *m*

detriment [ˈdɛtrɪmənt] *s* détriment *m*

detrimental [,dɛtrɪˈmɛntəl] *adj* préjudiciable, nuisible

deuce [d(j)us] *s* deux *m*; (*score*) égalité *f*; **what the deuce!** (coll) diantre!, que diable!

devaluate [diˈvæljʊ,et] *tr* dévaluer

devaluation [di,væljʊˈeʃən] *s* dévaluation *f*

devastate [ˈdɛvəs,tet] *tr* dévaster

devastating [ˈdɛvəs,tetɪŋ] *adj* dévastateur; (coll) écrasant, accablant

devastation [,dɛvəsˈteʃən] *s* dévastation *f*

develop [dɪˈvɛləp] *tr* développer; (*a mine*) exploiter; (*to perfect*) mettre au point, réaliser, étudier; (*e.g., a fever*) contracter, être atteint de; (phot) révéler, développer ‖ *intr* se développer; (*to become evident*) se produire, se manifester

developer [dɪˈvɛləpər] *s* entrepreneur *m*, aménager *m*; (*of houses*) promoteur *m* de

construction, lotisseur *m*; (*builder*) maître *m* d'œuvre; (phot) révélateur *m*

development [dɪˈvɛləpmənt] *s* développement *m*; (*event*) événement *m* récent; (*of housing*) aménagement *m*, lotissement *m*, grand ensemble *m*

deviate [ˈdivɪ,et] *s* perverti *m* ‖ *tr* faire dévier ‖ *intr* dévier

deviation [,divɪˈeʃən] *s* déviation *f*

device [dɪˈvaɪs] *s* appareil *m*, dispositif *m*; (*trick*) stratagème *m*, ruse *f*; emblème *m*, devise *f*; **to leave s.o. to his own devices** abandonner qn à ses propres moyens

dev·il [ˈdɛvəl] *s* diable *m*; **speak of the devil!** (coll) je vois un loup!; **to be between the devil and the deep blue sea** (coll) se trouver entre l'enclume et le marteau; **to raise the devil** (slang) faire le diable à quatre ‖ *v* (*pret & pp* **-iled** or **-illed**; *ger* **-iling** or **-illing**) *tr* épicer fortement; (coll) tourmenter

devilish [ˈdɛvəlɪʃ] *adj* diabolique; (*roguish*) coquin

dev'il-may-care' *adj* insouciant, étourdi

devilment [ˈdɛvəlmənt] *s* (*mischief*) diablerie *f*; (*evil*) méchanceté *f*

devil·try [ˈdɛvəltri] *s* (*pl* **-tries**) méchanceté *f*, cruauté *f*; (*mischief*) espièglerie *f*

devious [ˈdivɪ·əs] *adj* (*straying*) détourné, dévié; (*roundabout; shifty*) tortueux

devise [dɪˈvaɪz] *tr* combiner, inventer; (law) léguer

devoid [dɪˈvɔɪd] *adj* dépourvu, vide, dénué

devolve [dɪˈvalv] *intr*—**to devolve on, to,** or **upon** échoir à

devote [dɪˈvot] *tr* consacrer

devoted *adj* dévoué; **devoted to** voué à, dévoué à, attaché à

devotee [,dɛvəˈti] *s* dévot *m*, adepte *mf*; (sports) fervent *m*, fanatique *mf*

devotion [dɪˈvoʃən] *s* dévotion *f*; (*to study, work, etc.*) dévouement *m*; **devotions** dévotions, prières *fpl*

devour [dɪˈvaʊr] *tr* dévorer

devout [dɪˈvaʊt] *adj* dévot, pieux

dew [d(j)u] *s* rosée *f*

dew'drop' *s* goutte *f* de rosée

dew'lap' *s* fanon *m*, double menton *m*

dew' point' *s* point *m* de rosée

dew·y [ˈd(j)u·i] *adj* (*comp* **-ier**; *super* **-iest**) couvert de rosée

dexterity [dɛksˈtɛrɪti] *s* dextérité *f*, adresse *f*

diabetes [,daɪ·əˈbitiz] *s* diabète *m*

diabetic [,daɪ·əˈbɛtɪk] *adj & s* diabétique *mf*

diabolic(al) [,daɪ·əˈbɑlɪk(əl)] *adj* diabolique

diacritical [,daɪ·əˈkrɪtɪkəl] *adj* diacritique

diadem [ˈdaɪ·ə,dɛm] *s* diadème *m*

diaeresis = **dieresis**

diagnose [,daɪ·əgˈnos] *tr* diagnostiquer

diagnosis [,daɪ·əgˈnosɪs] *s* (*pl* **-ses** [siz]) diagnostic *m*

diagonal [daɪˈægənəl] *adj* diagonal ‖ *s* diagonale *f*

dia·gram [ˈdaɪ·ə,græm] *s* diagramme *m*, croquis *m* coté ‖ *v* (*pret & pp* **-gramed** or

-grammed; *ger* -graming or -gramming)
tr représenter schématiquement

di·al [ˈdaɪ·əl] *s* cadran *m* ‖ *v* (*pret & pp*
-aled or -alled; *ger* -aling or -alling) *tr* (*a*
telephone number) composer ‖ *intr* faire
un numéro

dialect [ˈdaɪ·ə,lɛkt] *s* dialecte *m*

dialing [ˈdaɪ·əlɪŋ] *s* (telp) composition *f* du
numéro

dialogue [ˈdaɪ·ə,lɔg] *s* dialogue *m*; **to carry
on a dialogue** dialoguer

di·al tel·ephone *s* téléphone *m* automatique,
automatique *m*

di·al tone *s* (telp) tonalité *f*

diameter [daɪˈæmɪtər] *s* diamètre *m*

diametric(al) [,daɪ·əˈmɛtrɪk(əl)] *adj* dia-
mètral

diamond [ˈdaɪmənd] *s* (*gem*) diamant *m*;
(*figure of a rhombus*) losange *m*; (baseball) petit champ *m*; (cards) carreau *m*

diaper [ˈdaɪ·əpər] *s* lange *m*, couche *f* ‖ *tr*
(*to variegate*) diaprer

diaphanous [daɪˈæfənəs] *adj* diaphane

diaphragm [ˈdaɪ·ə,fræm] *s* diaphragme *m*

diarrhea [,daɪ·əˈri·ə] *s* diarrhée *f*

dia·ry [ˈdaɪ·əri] *s* (*pl* -ries) journal *m*

diastole [daɪˈæstəli] *s* diastole *f*

diathermy [ˈdaɪ·ə,θʌrmi] *s* diathermie *f*

diatribe [ˈdaɪ·ə,traɪb] *s* diatribe *f*

dice [daɪs] *spl* dés *mpl*; **no dice!** (slang) pas
moyen!; **to load the dice** piper les dés ‖ *tr*
couper en cubes

dice·box *s* cornet *m* à dés

dichoto·my [daɪˈkɑtəmi] *s* (*pl* -mies) dichotomie *f*

Dictaphone [ˈdɪktə,fon] *s* (trademark) dictaphone *m*

dictate [ˈdɪktet] *s* précepte *m*, règle *f* ‖ *tr &
intr* dicter

dictation [dɪkˈteʃən] *s* dictée *f*; **to take
dictation from** écrire sous la dictée de

dictator [dɪkˈtetər] *s* dictateur *m*

dic·tator·ship *s* dictature *f*

diction [ˈdɪkʃən] *s* diction *f*

dictionar·y [ˈdɪkʃən,ɛri] *s* (*pl* -ies) dictionnaire *m*

dic·tum [ˈdɪktəm] *s* (*pl* -ta [tə]) dicton *m*;
(law) opinion *f*, arrêt *m*

didactic(al) [dɪˈdæktɪk(əl)] *adj* didactique

die [daɪ] *s* (*pl* dice [daɪs]) dé *m*; **the die is
cast** le dé en est jeté ‖ *s* (*pl* dies) (*for
stamping coins, medals, etc.*) coin *m*; (*for
cutting threads*) filière *f*; (*key pattern*) jeu
m ‖ *v* (*pret & pp* died; *ger* dying) *intr*
mourir; **to be dying** se mourir; **to be
dying to** (coll) mourir d'envie de; **to die
away** s'éteindre; **to die laughing** (coll)
mourir de rire

die·hard *adj* intransigeant ‖ *s* intransigeant
m, jusqu'au-boutiste *mf*

diere·sis [daɪˈɛrɪsɪs] *s* (*pl* -ses [,siz]) (*separation*) diérèse *f*; (*mark*) tréma *m*

die·sel en·gine [ˈdizəl] *s* diesel *m*, moteur *m*
diesel

die·sel oil *s* gas-oil *m*, gasoil *m*, gazole *m*

die·stock *s* porte-filière *m*

diet [ˈdaɪ·ət] *s* (*food and drink*) nourriture *f*;
(*congress; abstention from food*) diète *f*;
(*special menu*) régime *m* ‖ *intr* être or se
mettre au régime, suivre un régime

dietetic [,daɪ·əˈtɛtɪk] *adj* diététique ‖ **dietetics** *s* diététique *f*

dietician [,daɪ·əˈtɪʃən] *s* diététicien *m*

differ [ˈdɪfər] *intr* différer; **to differ with**
être en désaccord avec

difference [ˈdɪfərəns] *s* différence *f*; (*controversy*) différend *m*; **to make no difference** ne rien faire; **to split the difference**
partager le différend

different [ˈdɪfərənt] *adj* différent

differential [,dɪfəˈrɛnʃəl] *adj* différentiel ‖
s (mach) différentiel *m*; (math) différen-
tielle *f*

differentiate [,dɪfəˈrɛnʃɪ,et] *tr* différencier
‖ *intr* se différencier

difficult [ˈdɪfɪ,kʌlt] *adj* difficile

difficul·ty [ˈdɪfɪ,kʌlti] *s* (*pl* -ties) difficulté *f*

diffident [ˈdɪfɪdənt] *adj* défiant, timide

diffuse [dɪˈfjus] *adj* diffus ‖ [dɪˈfjuz] *tr*
diffuser ‖ *intr* se diffuser

dig [dɪg] *s*—**to give s.o. a dig** (coll) lancer
un trait à qn ‖ *v* (*pret & pp* dug [dʌg];
ger digging) *tr* bêcher, creuser; **to dig up**
déterrer ‖ *intr* bêcher

digest [ˈdaɪdʒɛst] *s* abrégé *m*, résumé *m*;
(*publication*) digest *m*, sélection *f*; (law)
digeste *m* ‖ [dɪˈdʒɛst] *tr & intr* digérer

digestible [dɪˈdʒɛstɪbəl] *adj* digestible

digestion [dɪˈdʒɛstʃən] *s* digestion *f*

digestive [dɪˈdʒɛstɪv] *adj* digestif

diges·tive tract *s* appareil *m* digestif

digit [ˈdɪdʒɪt] *s* (*numeral*) chiffre *m*; (*finger*)
doigt *m*; (*toe*) doigt du pied

digital [ˈdɪdʒɪtəl] *adj* (*numerical*) numérique; (anat) digital

dig·ital comput·er *s* calculateur *m* numérique

digitalis [,dɪgɪˈtælɪs] *s* (bot) digitale *f*;
(pharm) digitaline *f*

dig·ital watch *s* montre *f* à affichage numérique

dignified *adj* distingué; (*air*) digne

digni·fy [ˈdɪgnɪ,faɪ] *v* (*pret & pp* -fied) *tr*
glorifier, honorer

dignitar·y [ˈdɪgnɪ,tɛri] *s* (*pl* -ies) dignitaire
mf

digni·ty [ˈdɪgnɪti] *s* (*pl* -ties) dignité *f*; **to
stand on one's dignity** rester sur son
quant-à-soi, le prendre de haut

digress [dɪˈgrɛs] *intr* faire une digression

digression [dɪˈgrɛʃən] *s* digression *f*

dihedral [daɪˈhidrəl] *adj & s* dièdre *m*

dike [daɪk] *s* digue *f*

dilapidated [dɪˈlæpɪ,detɪd] *adj* délabré, dé-
glingué

dilate [daɪˈlet] *tr* dilater ‖ *intr* se dilater

dilatory [ˈdɪlə,tori] *adj* lent, tardif;
(*strategy, answer*) dilatoire

dilemma [dɪˈlɛmə] *s* dilemme *m*

dilettan·te [,dɪləˈtænti] *adj* dilettante ‖ *s* (*pl*
-tes or -ti [ti]) dilettante *mf*

diligence [ˈdɪlɪdʒəns] *s* diligence *f*

diligent [ˈdɪlɪdʒənt] *adj* diligent

dill [dɪl] *s* fenouil *m* bâtard, aneth *m*

dillydal·ly ['dɪlɪ,dælɪ] *v* (*pret & pp* **-lied**) *intr* traînasser

dilute [dɪ'lut] *adj* dilué ‖ *tr* diluer, délayer

dilution [dɪ'luʃən] *s* dilution *f*

dim [dɪm] *adj* faible, indistinct; (*forebodings*) obscur; (*memory*) effacé; (*color*) terne; (*idea of what is going on*) obtus, confus; **to take a dim view of** envisager sans enthousiasme ‖ *v* (*pret & pp* **dimmed**; *ger* **dimming**) *tr* affaiblir, obscurcir; (*beauty*) ternir; (*the headlights*) baisser, mettre en code ‖ *intr* s'affaiblir, s'obscurcir; (*said of color, beauty, etc.*) se ternir

dime [daɪm] *s* monnaie *f* de dix cents américains

dimension [dɪ'mɛnʃən] *s* dimension *f*

diminish [dɪ'mɪnɪʃ] *tr & intr* diminuer

diminutive [dɪ'mɪnjətɪv] *adj & s* diminutif *m*

dimi·ty ['dɪmɪtɪ] *s* (*pl* **-ties**) basin *m*, brillanté *m*

dimly ['dɪmlɪ] *adv* indistinctement

dimmers ['dɪmərz] *spl* (aut) feux *mpl* code, feux de croisement; **to put on the dimmers** se mettre en code

dimple ['dɪmpəl] *s* fossette *f*

dim'wit' *s* (slang) sot *m*, niais *m*

din [dɪn] *s* tapage *m*, fracas *m* ‖ *v* (*pret & pp* **dinned**; *ger* **dinning**) *tr* assourdir; répéter sans cesse ‖ *intr* sonner bruyamment

dine [daɪn] *tr* fêter par un dîner ‖ *intr* dîner; **to dine out** dîner en ville

diner ['daɪnər] *s* (*eater*) dîneur *m*; (*short-order restaurant*) plats-cuisinés *m*; (rr) wagon-restaurant *m*

dinette [daɪ'nɛt] *s* coin-repas *m*

ding-dong ['dɪŋ,dɔŋ] *s* tintement *m*, digue-din-don *m*

din·ghy ['dɪŋgɪ] *s* (*pl* **-ghies**) canot *m*, youyou *m*

din·gy ['dɪndʒɪ] *adj* (*comp* **-gier**; *super* **-giest**) défraîchi, terne

din'ing car' *s* wagon-restaurant *m*

din'ing hall' *s* salle *f* à manger; (*of university*) réfectoire *m*

din'ing room' *s* salle *f* à manger

din'ing-room suite' *s* salle *f* à manger

dinner ['dɪnər] *s* dîner *m*

din'ner coat' *s* smoking *m*

din'ner dance' *s* dîner *m* suivi de bal

din'ner guest' *s* convive *mf*, invité *m*

din'ner jack'et *s* smoking *m*

din'ner pail' *s* potager *m*

din'ner set' *s* service *m* de table

din'ner time' *s* heure *f* du dîner

dinosaur ['daɪnə,sɔr] *s* dinosaure *m*

dint [dɪnt] *s*—**by dint of** à force de

diocese ['daɪ·ə,sɪs] *s* diocèse *m*

diode ['daɪ·od] *s* diode *f*

dioxide [daɪ'aksaɪd] *s* bioxyde *m*

dip [dɪp] *s* (*immersion*) plongeon *m*; (*swim*) baignade *f*; (*slope*) pente *f*; (*of magnetic needle*) inclinaison *f* ‖ *v* (*pret & pp* **dipped**; *ger* **dipping**) *tr* plonger; (*a flag*) marquer ‖ *intr* plonger; (*said of magnetic needle*) incliner; (*said of scale*) pencher; **to dip into** (*a book*) feuilleter; (*one's capital*) prendre dans

diphtheria [dɪf'θɪrɪ·ə] *s* diphtérie *f*

diphthong ['dɪfθɔŋ] *s* diphtongue *f*

diphthongize ['dɪfθɔŋ,gaɪz] *tr* diphtonguer ‖ *intr* se diphtonguer

diploma [dɪ'plomə] *s* diplôme *m*

diploma·cy [dɪ'ploməsɪ] *s* (*pl* **-cies**) diplomatie *f*

diplomat ['dɪplə,mæt] *s* diplomate *mf*

diplomatic [,dɪplə'mætɪk] *adj* diplomatique, diplomate

dip'lomat'ic pouch' *s* valise *f* diplomatique

dipper ['dɪpər] *s* louche *f*, cuiller *f* à pot

dip'stick' *s* jauge *f* d'huile, jauge à tige

dire [daɪr] *adj* affreux, terrible

direct [dɪ'rɛkt] *adj* direct; franc, sincère ‖ *tr* diriger; (*to order*) ordonner; (*a letter, question, etc.*) adresser; (*to point out*) indiquer; (theat) mettre en scène

direct' cur'rent *s* courant *m* continu

direct' di'aling *s* (telp) automatique *m* interurbain

direct' hit' *s* coup *m* or tir *m* direct

direction [dɪ'rɛkʃən] *s* direction *f*; (*e.g., a street*) sens *m*; (theat) mise *f* en scène; **directions** (*orders*) instructions *fpl*; (*for use*) mode *m* d'emploi, instructions

directional [dɪ'rɛkʃənəl] *adj* directionnel

direc'tional sig'nal *s* clignotant *m*

directive [dɪ'rɛktɪv] *s* ordre *m*, avis *m*, directive *f*

direct' ob'ject *s* (gram) complément *m* direct

director [dɪ'rɛktər] *s* directeur *m*, administrateur *m*, chef *m*; (*of a board*) membre *m* du conseil, votant *m*; (theat) metteur *m* en scène

direc'tor·ship' *s* direction *f*, directorat *m*

directo·ry [dɪ'rɛktərɪ] *s* (*pl* **-ries**) (*board of directors*) conseil *m* d'administration; (*e.g., of telephone*) annuaire *m*; (*e.g., of genealogy*) almanach *m*; (eccl) directoire *m*

dirge [dʌrdʒ] *s* hymne *f* or chant *m* funèbre

dirigible ['dɪrɪdʒɪbəl] *adj & s* dirigeable *m*

dirt [dʌrt] *s* saleté *f*, ordure *f*; (*on clothes, skin, etc.*) crasse *f*; (*mire*) crotte *f*, boue *f*; (*earth*) terre *f*; **to get the dirt out of** décrasser

dirt'-cheap' *adj* vendu à vil prix

dirt' road' *s* chemin *m* de terre

dirt·y ['dʌrtɪ] *adj* (*comp* **-ier**; *super* **-iest**) sale, malpropre; (*clothes, skin, etc.*) crasseux; (*muddy*) crotté, boueux; (*mean*) méchant, vilain

dir'ty lin'en *s* linge *m* sale; **don't wash your dirty linen in public** il faut laver son linge sale en famille

dir'ty trick' *s* (slang) sale tour *m*; **to play a dirty trick on** (slang) faire un tour de cochon à

disabili·ty [,dɪsə'bɪlɪtɪ] *s* (*pl* **-ties**) incapacité *f*, invalidité *f*

disabil'ity insur'ance *s* assurance *f* invalidité

disabil′ity pen′sion s pension f d'invalidité
disable [dɪs'ebəl] tr rendre incapable, mettre hors de combat; (to hurt the limbs of) estropier, mutiler
disabled adj (serviceman) invalide; (ship) désemparé
disa′bled vet′eran s invalide m, réformé m
disabuse [,dɪsə'bjuz] tr désabuser
disadvantage [,dɪsəd'væntɪdʒ] s désavantage m ‖ tr désavantager
disadvantaged adj défavorisé, désavantagé
disadvantageous [dɪs,ædvən'tedʒəs] adj désavantageux
disagree [,dɪsə'gri] intr différer; **to disagree with** (to cause discomfort to) ne pas convenir à; (to dissent from) donner tort à
disagreeable [,dɪsə'gri·əbəl] adj désagréable; (mood, weather, etc.) maussade
disagreement [,dɪsə'grimənt] s désaccord m, différend m
disallow [,dɪsə'lau] tr désapprouver, rejeter
disappear [,dɪsə'pɪr] intr disparaître; (phonet) s'amuïr
disappearance [,dɪsə'pɪrəns] s disparition f; (phonet) amuïssement m
disappoint [,dɪsə'pɔɪnt] tr décevoir, désappointer
disappointed adj déçu
disappointment [,dɪsə'pɔɪntmənt] s déception f, désappointement m
disapproval [,dɪsə'pruvəl] s désapprobation f
disapprove [,dɪsə'pruv] tr & intr désapprouver
disarm [dɪs'arm] tr & intr désarmer
disarmament [dɪs'arməmənt] s désarmement m
disarming [dɪs'armɪŋ] adj désarmant
disarray [,dɪsə're] s désarroi m, désordre m; **in disarray** (said of apparel) à demi vêtu ‖ tr mettre en désarroi
disassemble [,dɪsə'sɛmbəl] tr démonter, désassembler
disassociate [,dɪsə'soʃɪ,et] tr dissocier
disaster [dɪ'zæstər] s désastre m
disas′ter ar′ea s région f sinistrée
disastrous [dɪ'zæstrəs] adj désastreux
disavow [,dɪsə'vau] tr désavouer
disavowal [,dɪsə'vau·əl] s désaveu m
disband [dɪs'bænd] tr licencier, congédier ‖ intr se débander, se disperser
dis·bar [dɪs'bar] v (pret & pp **-barred**; ger **-barring**) tr (law) rayer du barreau
disbelief [,dɪsbɪ'lif] s incroyance f
disbelieve [,dɪsbɪ'liv] tr & intr ne pas croire
disburse [dɪs'bʌrs] tr débourser
disbursement [dɪs'bʌrsmənt] s déboursement m; **disbursements** débours mpl
disc [dɪsk] s disque m
discard [dɪs'kard] s rebut m; (cards) écart m; **discards** marchandises fpl de rebut ‖ tr mettre de côté, jeter; (cards) écarter ‖ intr (cards) se défausser
discern [dɪ'sʌrn] tr discerner, percevoir
discernible [dɪ'sʌrnɪbəl] adj discernable
discerning [dɪ'sʌrnɪŋ] adj judicieux, pénétrant, éclairé

discernment [dɪ'sʌrnmənt] s discernement m
discharge [dɪs't ʃardʒ] (of a gun; of a battery) décharge f; (of a prisoner) élargissement m; (from a job) congé m, renvoi m; (from the armed forces) libération f; (from the armed forces for unfitness) réforme f; (from a wound) suppuration f ‖ tr décharger; (a prisoner) élargir; (an employee) congédier, renvoyer, licencier; (a soldier) libérer, réformer ‖ intr se décharger; (pathol) suppurer
disciple [dɪ'saɪpəl] s disciple m
disciplinarian [,dɪsɪplɪ'nɛrɪ·ən] s partisan m d'une forte discipline; personne f qui impose une forte discipline
disciplinary ['dɪsɪplɪ,nɛri] adj disciplinaire
discipline ['dɪsɪplɪn] s discipline f ‖ tr discipliner
disclaim [dɪs'klem] tr désavouer, renier
disclaimer [dɪs'klemər] s désaveu m
disclose [dɪs'kloz] tr découvrir, révéler
disclosure [dɪs'kloʒər] s découverte f, révélation f
disco ['dɪsko] s discothèque f
discolor [dɪs'kʌlər] tr décolorer ‖ intr se décolorer
discoloration [dɪs,kʌlə're ʃən] s décoloration f
discomfit [dɪs'kʌmfɪt] tr décontenancer, bafouer
discomfiture [dɪs'kʌmfɪt ʃər] s déconfiture f, déconvenue f
discomfort [dɪs'kʌmfərt] s (uneasiness, mild pain) malaise f; (inconvenience) gêne f ‖ tr gêner
disconcert [,dɪskən'sʌrt] tr déconcerter
disconnect [,dɪskə'nɛkt] tr (to separate) désunir, séparer; (a mechanism) débrayer; (a plug) débrancher; (current) couper
disconsolate [dɪs'kansəlɪt] adj désolé, inconsolable
discontent [,dɪskən'tɛnt] adj mécontent ‖ s mécontentement m ‖ tr mécontenter
discontented adj mécontent
discontinue [,dɪskən'tɪnju] tr discontinuer
discontinuous [,dɪskən'tɪnju·əs] adj discontinu
discord ['dɪskɔrd] s discorde f, désaccord m; (mus) discordance f
discordance [dɪs'kɔrdəns] s discordance f
discotheque ['dɪsko,tɛk] s discothèque f
discount ['dɪskaunt] s escompte m, remise f, rabais m ‖ [dɪs'kaunt] tr escompter, rabattre
dis′count rate′ s taux m d'escompte
dis′count store′ s magasin m de rabais, minimarge f
discourage [dɪs'kʌrɪdʒ] tr décourager
discouragement [dɪs'kʌrɪdʒmənt] s découragement m
discourse ['dɪskɔrs] s discours m ‖ [dɪs'kɔrs] intr discourir
discourteous [dɪs'kʌrtɪ·əs] adj impoli, discourtois
discourte·sy [dɪs'kʌrtəsi] s (pl **-sies**) impolitesse f, discourtoisie f

discover [dɪs'kʌvər] *tr* découvrir
discoverer [dɪs'kʌvərər] *s* découvreur *m*
discover·y [dɪs'kʌvəri] *s* (*pl* **-ies**) découverte *f*
discredit [dɪs'krɛdɪt] *s* discrédit *m* ‖ *tr* discréditer
discreditable [dɪs'krɛdɪtəbəl] *adj* déshonorant, peu honorable
discreet [dɪs'krit] *adj* discret
discrepan·cy [dɪs'krɛpənsi] *s* (*pl* **-cies**) désaccord *m*, différence *f*
discretion [dɪs'krɛʃən] *s* discrétion *f*
discriminate [dɪs'krɪmɪ,net] *tr & intr* discriminer; **to discriminate against** défavoriser
discrimination [dɪs,krɪmɪ'neʃən] *s* discrimination *f*
discriminatory [dɪs'krɪmɪnə,tori] *adj* discriminatoire
discus ['dɪskəs] *s* (sports) disque, *m*, palet *m*
discuss [dɪs'kʌs] *tr & intr* discuter
discussion [dɪs'kʌʃən] *s* discussion *f*
disdain [dɪs'den] *s* dédain *m* ‖ *tr* dédaigner
disdainful [dɪs'denfəl] *adj* dédaigneux
disease [dɪ'ziz] *s* maladie *f*
diseased *adj* malade
disembark [,dɪsɛm'bark] *tr & intr* débarquer
disembarkation [dɪs,ɛmbar'keʃən] *s* débarquement *m*
disembow·el [,dɪsɛm'bau·əl] *v* (*pret & pp* **-eled** or **-elled**; *ger* **-eling** or **-elling**) *tr* éventrer
disenchant [,dɪsɛn'tʃænt] *tr* désenchanter
disenchantment [,dɪsɛn'tʃæntmənt] *s* désenchantement *m*
disengage [,dɪsɛn'gedʒ] *tr* dégager; (*toothed wheels*) désengrener; (*a motor*) débrayer ‖ *intr* se dégager
disengagement [,dɪsɛn'gedʒmənt] *s* dégagement *m*, détachement *m*
disentangle [,dɪsɛn'tæŋgəl] *tr* démêler, débrouiller
disentanglement [,dɪsɛn'tæŋgəlmənt] *s* démêlage *m*, débrouillement *m*
disestablish [,dɪsɛs'tæblɪʃ] *tr* (*the Church*) séparer de l'État
disfavor [dɪs'fevər] *s* défaveur *f* ‖ *tr* défavoriser
disfigure [dɪs'fɪgjər] *tr* défigurer, enlaidir
disfigurement [dɪs'fɪgjərmənt] *s* défiguration *f*
disfranchise [dɪs'fræntʃaɪz] *tr* priver de ses droits civiques
disgorge [dɪs'gɔrdʒ] *tr & intr* dégorger
disgrace [dɪs'gres] *s* déshonneur *m* ‖ *tr* déshonorer; (*to deprive of favor*) disgracier; **to disgrace oneself** se déshonorer
disgraceful [dɪs'gresfəl] *adj* déshonorant, honteux
disgruntled [dɪs'grʌntəld] *adj* contrarié, de mauvaise humeur
disguise [dɪs'gaɪz] *s* déguisement *m* ‖ *tr* déguiser
disgust [dɪs'gʌst] *s* dégoût *m* ‖ *tr* dégoûter
disgusting [dɪs'gʌstɪŋ] *adj* dégoûtant

dish [dɪʃ] *s* plat *m*; (*food*) mets *m*, plat; **to wash the dishes** faire la vaisselle ‖ *tr—to dish up** servir
dish' clos'et *s* étagère *f* à vaisselle
dish'cloth' *s* lavette *f*
dishearten [dɪs'hartən] *tr* décourager
dishev·el [dɪ'ʃɛvəl] *v* (*pret & pp* **-eled** or **-elled**; *ger* **-eling** or **-elling**) *tr* écheveler
dishonest [dɪs'anɪst] *adj* malhonnête, déloyal
dishones·ty [dɪs'anɪsti] *s* (*pl* **-ties**) malhonnêteté *f*, déloyauté *f*, improbité *f*
dishonor [dɪs'anər] *s* déshonneur *m* ‖ *tr* déshonorer
dishonorable [dɪs'anərəbəl] *adj* déshonorant
dish'pan' *s* bassine *f*
dish' rack' *s* égouttoir *m*
dish'rag' *s* lavette *f*
dish'tow'el *s* torchon *m*
dish'wash'er *s* machine *f* à laver la vaisselle, lave-vaisselle *f*; (*person*) plongeur *m*
dish'wa'ter *s* eau *f* de vaisselle
disillusion [,dɪsɪ'luʒən] *s* désillusion *f* ‖ *tr* désillusionner
disillusionment [,dɪsɪ'luʒənmənt] *s* désillusionnement *m*
disinclination [dɪs,ɪnklɪ'neʃən] *s* répugnance *f*, aversion *f*
disinclined [,dɪsɪn'klaɪnd] *adj* indisposé
disinfect [,dɪsɪn'fɛkt] *tr* désinfecter
disinfectant [,dɪsɪn'fɛktənt] *adj & s* désinfectant *m*
disinformation [dɪs,ɪnfər'meʃən] *s* désinformation *f*
disingenuous [,dɪsɪn'dʒɛnju·əs] *adj* insincère, sans franchise
disinherit [,dɪsɪn'hɛrɪt] *tr* déshériter
disintegrate [dɪs'ɪntɪ,gret] *tr* désagréger; (nucl) désintégrer ‖ *intr* se désagréger; (nucl) se désintégrer
disintegration [dɪs,ɪntɪ'greʃən] *s* désagrégation *f*; (nucl) désintégration *f*
disin·ter [,dɪsɪn'tʌr] *v* (*pret & pp* **-terred**; *ger* **-terring**) *tr* déterrer
disinterested [dɪs'ɪntə,rɛstɪd] *adj* désintéressé
disjointed [dɪs'dʒɔɪntɪd] *adj* désarticulé; (*e.g., style*) décousu
disjunctive [dɪs'dʒʌŋktɪv] *adj* disjonctif; (*pronoun*) tonique
disk [dɪsk] *s* disque *m*
diskette [dɪs'kɛt] *s* (comp) disquette *f*
disk' jock'ey *s* présentateur *m* de disques, animateur *m*
dislike [dɪs'laɪk] *s* aversion *f*; **to take a dislike for** prendre en aversion ‖ *tr* ne pas aimer
dislocate ['dɪslo,ket] *tr* disloquer; (*a joint*) luxer
dislodge [dɪs'ladʒ] *tr* déplacer; (*e.g., the enemy*) déloger
disloyal [dɪs'lɔɪ·əl] *adj* déloyal
disloyal·ty [dɪs'lɔɪ·əlti] *s* (*pl* **-ties**) déloyauté *f*
dismal ['dɪzməl] *adj* sombre, triste

dismantle [dɪs'mæntəl] *tr* démanteler; (*a machine*) démonter; (*a ship*) désarmer

dismay [dɪs'me] *s* consternation *f* ‖ *tr* consterner

dismember [dɪs'mɛmbər] *tr* démembrer

dismiss [dɪs'mɪs] *tr* (*a thought, suggestion, or subject*) écarter; (*an employee*) congédier, renvoyer, licencier; (*an official, an officer*) destituer, casser; terminer; (*an appeal*) (law) rejeter; (*a class in school*) laisser partir, congédier; **class dismissed!** partez!

dismissal [dɪs'mɪsəl] *s* congédiement *m*, renvoi *m*, destitution *f*; (*of an idea*) abandon *m*; (*of an appeal*) (law) rejet *m*

dismount [dɪs'maʊnt] *tr* démonter ‖ *intr* descendre

disobedience [,dɪsə'bidɪ·əns] *s* désobéissance *f*

disobedient [,dɪsə'bidɪ·ənt] *adj* désobéissant

disobey [,dɪsə'be] *tr* désobéir à; **to be disobeyed** être désobéi ‖ *intr* désobéir

disorder [dɪs'ɔrdər] *s* désordre *m* ‖ *tr* désordonner

disorderly [dɪs'ɔrdərli] *adj* désordonné, déréglé; (*crowd*) turbulent, effervescent

disor'derly con'duct *s* conduite *f* désordonnée

disorganize [dɪs'ɔrgə,naɪz] *tr* désorganiser

disoriented [dɪs'ɔrɪ,ɛntɪd] *adj* désorienté; **to become disoriented** perdre le nord

disown [dɪs'on] *tr* désavouer, renier

disparage [dɪ'spærɪdʒ] *tr* dénigrer, déprécier

disparagement [dɪ'spærɪdʒmənt] *s* dénigrement *m*, dépréciation *f*

disparate ['dɪspərɪt] *adj* disparate

dispari·ty [dɪ'spærɪti] *s* (*pl* -ties) disparité *f*

dispassionate [dɪs'pæʃənɪt] *adj* calme; impartial

dispatch [dɪ'spætʃ] *s* envoi *m*, expédition *f*; (*govt, journ, mil*) dépêche *f*; (*promptness*) promptitude *f* ‖ *tr* dépêcher, expédier, envoyer; (coll & fig) expédier

dis·pel [dɪ'spɛl] *v* (*pret* & *pp* **-pelled**; *ger* **-pelling**) *tr* dissiper, disperser

dispensa·ry [dɪ'spɛnsəri] *s* (*pl* -ries) dispensaire *m*

dispensation *s* [,dɪspɛn'seʃən] (*dispensing*) dispensation *f*; (*exemption*) dispense *f*

dispense [dɪ'spɛns] *tr* dispenser, distribuer ‖ *intr*—**to dispense with** se passer de; se défaire de

dispenser [dɪ'spɛnsər] *s* dispensateur *m*; (*automatic*) distributeur *m*

disperse [dɪ'spʌrs] *tr* disperser ‖ *intr* se disperser

dispersion [dɪ'spʌrʒən] *s* dispersion *f*

dispirit [dɪ'spɪrɪt] *tr* décourager

displace [dɪs'ples] *tr* déplacer; (*to take the place of*) remplacer

displaced' per'son *s* personne *f* déplacée

displacement [dɪs'plesmənt] *s* déplacement *m*; (*substitution*) remplacement *m*

display [dɪ'sple] *s* exposition *f*, étalage *m*; (*of emotion*) manifestation *f*; (comp) vi-suel ‖ *tr* exposer, étaler; (*anger, courage, etc.*) manifester; (*ignorance*) révéler; (comp) afficher, visualiser

display' cab'inet *s* vitrine *f*

display' win'dow *s* vitrine *f*, devanture *f*

displease [dɪs'pliz] *tr* déplaire à

displeasing [dɪs'plizɪŋ] *adj* déplaisant

displeasure [dɪs'plɛʒər] *s* déplaisir *m*, mécontentement *m*

disposable [dɪ'spozəbəl] *adj* (*available*) disponible; (*made to be disposed of*) jetable, à jeter; (*container*) perdu, e.g., **disposable bottle** verre perdu

disposal [dɪ'spozəl] *s* disposition *f*; (*of a question*) résolution *f*; (*of trash, garbage, etc.*) destruction *f*

dispos'able tis'sues *spl* mouchoirs *mpl* à jeter

dispose [dɪ'spoz] *tr* disposer ‖ *intr* disposer; **to dispose of** disposer de; (*to get rid of*) se défaire de; (*a question*) résoudre, trancher

disposed *adj*—**to be disposed to** se disposer à, être porté à

disposition [,dɪspə'zɪʃən] *s* disposition *f*; (*mental outlook*) naturel *m*; (mil) dispositif *m*

dispossess [,dɪspə'zɛs] *tr* déposséder; expulser

disproof [dɪs'pruf] *s* réfutation *f*

disproportionate [,dɪsprə'porʃənɪt] *adj* disproportionné

disprove [dɪs'pruv] *tr* réfuter

dispute [dɪs'pjut] *s* dispute *f*; **beyond dispute** incontestable ‖ *tr* disputer ‖ *intr* se disputer

disquali·fy [dɪs'kwɑlɪ,faɪ] *v* (*pret* & *pp* -fied) *tr* disqualifier

disquiet [dɪs'kwaɪ·ət] *s* inquiétude *f* ‖ *tr* inquiéter

disquisition [,dɪskwɪ'zɪʃən] *s* essai *m*, traité *m* considérable

disregard [,dɪsrɪ'gɑrd] *s* indifférence *f*; **disregard for** manque *m* d'égards envers ‖ *tr* ne pas faire cas de, passer sous silence

disrepair [,dɪsrɪ'pɛr] *s* délabrement *m*

disreputable [dɪs'rɛpjətəbəl] *adj* déshonorant, suspect; (*shabby*) débraillé, râpé

disrepute [,dɪsrɪ'pjut] *s* discrédit *m*

disrespect [,dɪsrɪ'spɛkt] *s* irrévérence *f*, manque *m* de respect, irrespect *m*

disrespectful [,dɪsrɪ'spɛktfəl] *adj* irrévérencieux, irrespectueux; **to be disrespectful to** manquer de respect à

disrobe [dɪs'rob] *tr* déshabiller ‖ *intr* se déshabiller

disrupt [dɪs'rʌpt] *tr* rompre; (*to throw into disorder*) bouleverser

disruption [dɪs'rʌpʃən] *s* bouleversement *m*, perturbation *f*, interruption *f*

dissatisfaction [,dɪssætɪs'fækʃən] *s* mécontentement *m*

dissatisfied *adj* mécontent

dissatis·fy [dɪs'sætɪs,faɪ] *v* (*pret* & *pp* -fied) *tr* mécontenter

dissect [dɪ'sɛkt] *tr* disséquer

dissection [dɪ'sɛkʃən] *s* dissection *f*

dissemble [dɪ'sɛmbəl] *tr* & *intr* dissimuler
disseminate [dɪ'sɛmɪ,net] *tr* disséminer
dissension [dɪ'sɛnʃən] *s* dissension *f*
dissent [dɪ'sɛnt] *s* dissentiment *m*; *(nonconformity)* dissidence *f* ‖ *intr* différer
dissenter [dɪ'sɛntər] *s* dissident *m*
dissertation [,dɪsər'teʃən] *s* dissertation *f*; *(for a degree)* thèse *f*; *(speech)* discours *m*
disservice [dɪ'sʌrvɪs] *s* mauvais service *m*, tort *m*
dissidence ['dɪsɪdəns] *s* dissidence *f*
dissident ['dɪsɪdənt] *adj* & *s* dissident *m*
dissimilar [dɪ'sɪmɪlər] *adj* dissemblable
dissimilate [dɪ'sɪmɪ,let] *tr* (phonet) dissimiler
dissimulate [dɪ'sɪmjə,let] *tr* & *intr* dissimuler
dissipate ['dɪsɪ,pet] *tr* dissiper; *(energy, heat, etc.)* disperser ‖ *intr* se dissiper
dissipated *adj* dissipé; débauché
dissipation [,dɪsɪ'peʃən] *s* dissipation *f*; *(of energy, heat, etc.)* dispersion *f*
dissociate [dɪ'soʃɪ,et] *tr* dissocier ‖ *intr* se dissocier
dissolute ['dɪsə,lut] *adj* dissolu
dissolution [,dɪsə'luʃən] *s* dissolution *f*
dissolve [dɪ'zɑlv] *tr* dissoudre ‖ *intr* se dissoudre
dissonance ['dɪsənəns] *s* dissonance *f*
dissuade [dɪ'swed] *tr* dissuader
distaff ['dɪstæf] *s* quenouille *f*
dis'taff side' *s* côté *m* maternel
distance ['dɪstəns] *s* distance *f*; **at a distance** à distance; **in the distance** au loin, dans le lointain ‖ *tr* distancer
distant ['dɪstənt] *adj* distant; *(uncle, cousin, etc.)* éloigné
distaste [dɪs'test] *s* dégoût *m*, aversion *f*
distasteful [dɪs'testfəl] *adj* dégoûtant, répugnant
distemper [dɪs'tɛmpər] *s* *(of dog)* roupie *f*; (painting) détrempe *f* ‖ *tr* peindre en détrempe
distend [dɪs'tɛnd] *tr* distendre ‖ *intr* se distendre
distension [dɪs'tɛnʃən] *s* distension *f*
distill [dɪs'tɪl] *tr* distiller
distillation [,dɪstɪ'leʃən] *s* distillation *f*
distiller·y [dɪs'tɪləri] *s* (*pl* **-ies**) distillerie *f*
distinct [dɪs'tɪŋkt] *adj* distinct; *(unusual)* insigne
distinction [dɪs'tɪŋkʃən] *s* distinction *f*
distinctive [dɪs'tɪŋktɪv] *adj* distinctif
distinguish [dɪs'tɪŋgwɪʃ] *tr* distinguer; **to distinguish oneself** se distinguer, se faire remarquer
distinguished *adj* distingué
distort [dɪs'tɔrt] *tr* déformer
distortion [dɪs'tɔrʃən] *s* déformation *f*; *(of meaning)* sens *m* forcé; (phot, rad) distorsion *f*
distract [dɪ'strækt] *tr* *(to amuse)* distraire; *(to bewilder)* bouleverser
distracted *adj* bouleversé, éperdu
distraction [dɪ'strækʃən] *s* *(amusement)* distraction *f*; *(madness)* folie *f*
distraught [dɪ'strɔt] *adj* bouleversé

distress [dɪ'strɛs] *s* détresse *f* ‖ *tr* affliger
distress' call' *s* signal *m* de détresse
distressing [dɪ'strɛsɪŋ] *adj* affligeant, pénible
distribute [dɪ'strɪbjut] *tr* distribuer
distribution [,dɪstrə'bjuʃən] *s* distribution *f*
distributor [dɪ'strɪbjətər] *s* distributeur *m*; *(for a product)* concessionnaire *mf*
district ['dɪstrɪkt] *s* contrée *f*, région *f*; *(of a city)* quartier *m*; *(administrative division)* district *m*, circonscription *f* ‖ *tr* diviser en districts
dis'trict attor'ney *s* procureur *m* de la République, procureur général
distrust [dɪs'trʌst] *s* défiance *f*, méfiance *f* ‖ *tr* se défier de, se méfier de
distrustful [dɪs'trʌstfəl] *adj* défiant
disturb [dɪ'stʌrb] *tr* déranger, troubler; *(the peace)* perturber
disturbance [dɪ'stʌrbəns] *s* dérangement *m*, trouble *m*; *(riot)* bagarre *f*, émeute *f*; *(in the atmosphere or magnetic field)* perturbation *f*
disuse [dɪs'jus] *s* désuétude *f*
ditch [dɪtʃ] *s* fossé *m*; **to the last ditch** jusqu'à la dernière extrémité ‖ *tr* fossoyer; (slang) se défaire de ‖ *intr* (aer) faire un amerrissage forcé
ditch' reed' *s* (bot) laîche *f*
dither ['dɪðər] *s* agitation *f*; **to be in a dither** (coll) s'agiter sans but
dit·to ['dɪto] *s* (*pl* **-tos**) le même; *(on a duplicating machine)* copie *f*, duplicata *m* ‖ *adv* dito, de même, idem ‖ *tr* copier, reproduire
dit·ty ['dɪti] *s* (*pl* **-ties**) chansonnette *f*; **old ditty** (coll) vieux refrain *m*
diva ['divɑ] *s* diva *f*
divan ['daɪvæn], [dɪ'væn] *s* divan *m*
dive [daɪv] *s* *(of a swimmer)* plongeon *m*; *(of a submarine)* plongée *f*; (aer) piqué *m*; (coll) gargote *f*, cabaret *m* borgne ‖ *v* *(pret & pp* **dived** or **dove** [dov]) *intr* plonger; *(said of submarine)* plonger, effectuer une plongée; (aer) piquer; **to dive for** *(e.g., pearls)* pêcher; **to dive into** (coll) piquer une tête dans
dive'-bomb' *tr* & *intr* bombarder en piqué
dive' bomb'er *s* bombardier *m* à piqué
dive' bomb'ing *s* bombardement *m* en piqué, piqué *m*
diver ['daɪvər] *s* plongeur *m*; *(person who works under water)* scaphandrier *m*; (orn) plongeon *m*
diverge [dɪ'vʌrdʒ] *intr* diverger
divers ['daɪvərz] or **diverse** [dɪ'vʌrs] *adj* divers
diversi·fy [dɪ'vʌrsɪ,faɪ] *v* *(pret & pp* **-fied**) *tr* diversifier ‖ *intr* se diversifier
diversion [dɪ'vʌrʒən] *s* *(relaxation)* distraction *f*, dérivatif *m*, diversion *f*; *(of traffic)* déviation *f*; *(rerouting)* dérivation *f*, détournement *m*; (mil) diversion
diversi·ty [dɪ'vʌrsɪti] *s* (*pl* **-ties**) diversité *f*
divert [dɪ'vʌrt] *tr* détourner; *(to entertain)* distraire, divertir
diverting [dɪ'vʌrtɪŋ] *adj* divertissant

divest [dɪ'vɛst] *tr* dépouiller; **to divest one-self of** se défaire de; (*property, holdings*) se déposséder de

divestment [dɪ'vɛstmənt] *s* dépossession *f*

divide [dɪ'vaɪd] *s* (geog) ligne *f* de partage ‖ *tr* diviser ‖ *intr* se diviser

dividend ['dɪvɪ,dɛnd] *s* dividende *m*

dividers [dɪ'vaɪdərz] *spl* compas *m* de mesure

dividing [dɪ'vaɪdɪŋ] *s* division *f*; **dividing up** répartition *f*, partage *m*

divination [,dɪvɪ'neʃən] *s* divination *f*

divine [dɪ'vaɪn] *adj* divin ‖ *s* ecclésiastique *mf* ‖ *tr* deviner

diviner [dɪ'vaɪnər] *s* devin *m*

diving ['daɪvɪŋ] *s* plongeon *m*

div'ing bell' *s* cloche *f* à plongeur

div'ing board' *s* plongeoir *m*, tremplin *m*

div'ing suit' *s* scaphandre *m*

divin'ing rod' [dɪ'vaɪnɪŋ] *s* baguette *f* divinatoire

divin·i·ty [dɪ'vɪnɪti] *s* (*pl* -ties) divinité *f*; (*subject of study*) théologie *f*; **the Divinity** Dieu *m*

divisible [dɪ'vɪzɪbəl] *adj* divisible

division [dɪ'vɪʒən] *s* division *f*

divisor [dɪ'vaɪzər] *s* diviseur *m*

divorce [di'vors] *s* divorce *m*; **to get a divorce** divorcer; **to get a divorce from** (*husband or wife*) divorcer d'avec ‖ *tr* (*the married couple*) divorcer; (*husband or wife*) divorcer d'avec ‖ *intr* divorcer

divorcee [dɪvor'si] *s* divorcée *f*

divulge [dɪ'vʌldʒ] *tr* divulguer

dizziness ['dɪzɪnɪs] *s* vertige *m*

diz·zy ['dɪzi] *adj* (*comp* -zier; *super* -ziest) vertigineux; (coll) étourdi, farfelu; **to feel dizzy** avoir le vertige; **to make dizzy** étourdir

do [du] *v* (3d *pers* **does** [dʌz]; *pret* **did** [dɪd]; *pp* **done** [dʌn]; *ger* **doing** ['du·ɪŋ]) *tr* faire; (*homage; justice; a good turn*) rendre; **to do over** refaire; **to do up** emballer, envelopper ‖ *intr* faire; **how do you do?** enchanté de faire votre connaissance; **that will do** c'est bien; en voilà assez; **that will never do** cela n'ira jamais; **to do away with** supprimer; **to do without** se passer de; **will I do?** suis-je bien comme ça?; **will it do?** ça va-t-il comme ça? ‖ *aux* used in English but not specifically expressed in French: 1) in questions, e.g., **do you speak French?** parlez-vous français?; 2) in negative sentences, e.g., **I do not speak French** je ne parle pas français; 3) as a substitute for another verb in an elliptical question, e.g., **I saw him. Did you?** je l'ai vu. L'avez-vous vu?; 4) for emphasis, e.g., **I do believe what you told me** je crois bien ce que vous m'avez dit; 5) in inversions after certain adverbs, e.g., **hardly did we finish when . . .** à peine avions-nous fini que . . .; 6) in an imperative entreaty, e.g., **do come in!** entrez donc!

do. *abbr* (ditto) d°

docile ['dasɪl] *adj* docile

dock [dak] *s* embarcadère *m*, quai *m*; (*area including piers and waterways*) bassin *m*, dock *m*; (bot) oseille *f*, patience *f*; (law) banc *m* des prévenus ‖ *tr* faire entrer au bassin; (*an animal*) couper la queue à; (*s.o.'s salary*) retrancher ‖ *intr* (naut) s'amarrer au quai

docket ['dakɪt] *s* (law) rôle *m*; **on the docket** pendant, non jugé; **to put on the docket** (coll) prendre en main

dock' hand' *s* docker *m*

docking ['dakɪŋ] *s* (rok) arrimage *m*, accostage *m*

dock' work'er *s* docker *m*

dock'yard' *s* chantier *m*

doctor ['daktər] *s* docteur *m*; (*woman*) femme *f* docteur; (med) docteur, médecin *m*; (med) doctoresse *f*; **Doctor Curie** (*professor, Ph.D., etc.*) Monsieur Curie; Madame Curie ‖ *tr* soigner; (*e.g., a chipped vase*) réparer; (*e.g., the facts*) falsifier ‖ *intr* pratiquer la médecine; (coll) être en traitement; (coll) prendre des médicaments

doctorate ['daktərɪt] *s* doctorat *m*

Doc'tor of Laws' *s* docteur *m* en droit

doctrine ['daktrɪn] *s* doctrine *f*

document ['dakjəmənt] *s* document *m* ‖ ['dakjə,mɛnt] *tr* documenter

documenta·ry [,dakjə'mɛntəri] *adj* documentaire ‖ *s* (*pl* -ries) documentaire *m*

documentation [,dakjəmɛn'teʃən] *s* documentation *f*

doddering ['dadərɪŋ] *adj* tremblotant, gâteux

dodge [dadʒ] *s* écart *m*, esquive *f*; (coll) ruse *f*, truc *m* ‖ *tr* esquiver; (*a question*) éluder ‖ *intr* s'esquiver

dodge' ball' *s* chasse-ballon *m invar*

do·do ['dodo] *s* (*pl* -dos *or* -does) (orn) dronte *m*, dodo *m*; (coll) vieux fossile *m*, innocent *m*

doe [do] *s* (*of fallow deer*) daine *f*; (*hind*) biche *f*; (*roe doe*) chevrette *f*; (*of hare*) hase *f*; (*of rabbit*) lapine *f*

doe'skin' *s* peau *f* de daim

doff [daf] *tr* ôter

dog [dɔg] *s* chien *m*; **let sleeping dogs lie** il ne faut pas réveiller le chat qui dort; **to go to the dogs** (coll) se débaucher; (*said of business*) (coll) aller à vau-l'eau; **to put on the dog** (coll) faire de l'épate ‖ *v* (*pret & pp* **dogged**; *ger* **dogging**) *tr* poursuivre

dog'catch'er *s* employé *m* de la fourière

dog' days' *spl* canicule *f*

doge [dodʒ] *s* doge *m*

dog'face' *s* (slang) troufion *m*

dog'fight' *s* (aer) combat *m* aérien tournoyant et violent; (coll) bagarre *f*

dogged ['dɔgɪd] *adj* tenace, obstiné

doggerel ['dɔgərəl] *s* vers *mpl* de mirliton

dog·gy ['dɔgi] *adj* (*comp* -gier; *super* -giest) canin, de chien ‖ *s* (*pl* -gies) toutou *m*

dog'gy bag' *s* emporte-restes *m*

dog'house' *s* niche *f* à chien; **in the doghouse** (slang) en disgrâce

dog′ in the man′ger s chien m du jardinier
dog′ Lat′in s latin m de cuisine
dogma [′dɔgmə] s dogme m
dogmatic [dɔg′mætɪk] adj dogmatique ‖ **dogmatics** s dogmatique f
dog′ pound′ s fourrière f
dog′ rac′ing s courses fpl de lévriers
dog′ rose′ s rose f des haies
dog's′-ear′ s corne f ‖ tr corner
dog′ show′ s exposition f canine
dog′ sled′ or **dog′ sledge′** s traîneau m à chiens
dog's′ life′ s vie f de chien
Dog′ Star′ s Canicule f
dog′ tag′ s (mil) plaque f d'identité
dog′-tired′ adj éreinté, fourbu
dog′tooth′ s (pl **-teeth**) dent f de chien, canine f; (archit, bot, mach) dent-de-chien f
dog′tooth vi′olet s dent-de-chien f
dog′trot′ s petit-trot m
dog′watch′ s (naut) petit quart m
dog′wood′ s cornouiller m
doi·ly [′dɔɪli] s (pl **-lies**) napperon m; (underplate) garde-nappe m
doings [′du·ɪŋz] spl actions fpl, œuvres fpl, faits et gestes mpl
do-it-yourself [,du·ɪtʃər′sɛlf] adj de bricolage ‖ s bricolage m
doldrums [′dɔldrəmz] spl marasme m; (naut) zone f des calmes
dole [dol] s aumône f; indemnité f de chômage ‖ tr—**to dole out** distribuer parcimonieusement
doleful [′dolfəl] adj dolent
doll [dɑl] s poupée f ‖ tr—**to be dolled up** (coll) être tiré à quatre épingles ‖ intr—**to doll up** (coll) se parer, s'endimancher
dollar [′dɑlər] s dollar m
dol·ly [′dɑli] s (pl **-lies**) (low movable frame) chariot m; (hand truck) diable m; (child's doll) poupée f; (mov, telv) travelling m
dolphin [′dɑlfɪn] s dauphin m
dolt [dolt] s nigaud m, lourdaud m
doltish [′doltɪʃ] adj nigaud, lourdaud
domain [do′men] s domaine m; (private estate) terres fpl, propriété f
dome [dom] s dôme m, coupole f
dome′ light′ s (aut) plafonnier m; (aut) (flashing, revolving outside light) gyrophare m
domestic [də′mɛstɪk] adj & s domestique mf
domesticate [də′mɛstɪ,ket] tr domestiquer
domesticity [,domɛs′tɪsɪti] s caractère m casanier; vie f familiale
domicile [′dɑmɪsɪl] s domicile m ‖ tr domicilier
dominance [′dɑmɪnəns] s prédominance f; (genetics) dominance f
dominant [′dɑmɪnənt] adj prédominant, dominant ‖ s (mus) dominante f
dominate [′dɑmɪ,net] tr & intr dominer
dominating [′dɑmɪ,netɪŋ] adj dominateur
domination [,dɑmɪ′neʃən] s domination f

domineer [,dɑmɪ′nɪr] intr se montrer tyrannique
domineering [,dɑmɪ′nɪrɪŋ] adj tyrannique, autoritaire
dominion [də′mɪnjən] s domination f; (of British Commonwealth) dominion m
domi·no [′dɑmɪ,no] s (pl **-noes** or **-nos**) domino m; **dominoes** sg (game) les dominos
don [dɑn] s (tutor) précepteur m ‖ v (pret & pp **donned**; ger **donning**) tr mettre, enfiler
donate [′donet] tr faire un don de
donation [do′neʃən] s don m, cadeau m
done [dʌn] adj fait; **are you done?** en avez-vous fini?; **it is done** (it is finished) c'en est fait; **to be done** (e.g., beefsteak) être cuit; **to have done with** en finir avec; **well done!** très bien!, bravo!, à la bonne heure!
done′ for′ adj (tired out) (coll) fourbu; (ruined) (coll) abattu; (out of the running) (coll) hors de combat; (dead) (coll) estourbi
donkey [′dɑŋki] s âne m, baudet m
donor [′donər] s donneur m; (law) donateur m
doodle [′dudəl] s (doodling) crayonnages mpl ‖ tr & intr griffonner
doom [dum] s condamnation f; destin m funeste ‖ tr condamner
dooms′day′ s jugement m dernier
door [dor] s porte f; (of a carriage or automobile) portière f; (one part of a double door) battant m; **behind closed doors** à huis clos; **to see to the door** conduire à la porte; **to show s.o. the door** éconduire qn, mettre qn à la porte
door′bell′ s timbre m, sonnette f
door′bell transform′er s transformateur m de sonnerie
door′bell wire′ s fil m sonnerie
door′ check′ s arrêt m de porte
door′frame′ s chambranle m, huisserie f, dormant m
door′head′ s linteau m
door′jamb′ s jambage m
door′knob′ s bouton m de porte
door′knock′er s heurtoir m, marteau m de porte
door′ latch′ s loquet m
door′man s (pl **-men**) portier m
door′mat′ s essuie-pieds m, paillasson m
door′nail′ s clou m de porte; **dead as a doornail** (coll) bien mort
door′post′ s montant m de porte
door′ scrap′er [′skrepər] s décrottoir m, grattepieds m
door′sill′ s seuil m, traverse f
door′step′ s seuil m, pas m
door′stop′ s entrebâilleur m, butoir m
door′-to-door′ adj porte-à-porte
door′-to-door′ sell′ing s démarchage m
door′way′ s porte f, portail m
dope [dop] s (varnish) enduit m; (slang) narcotique m, stupéfiant m; (information) (slang) renseignements mpl; (fool) (slang)

cornichon *m* ‖ *tr* enduire; (slang) doper, stupéfier; **to dope out** (slang) deviner, déchiffrer

dope′ fiend′ *s* (slang) toxicomane *mf*

dope′ ped′dler *s* trafiquant *m* de stupéfiants

dormant [′dɔrmənt] *adj* endormi, assoupi; latent; **to lie dormant** dormir

dor′mer win′dow [′dɔrmər] *s* lucarne *f*

dormito·ry [′dɔrmɪ,tori] *s* (*pl* **-ries**) (*room*) dortoir *m*; (*building*) pavillon *m* des étudiants, maison *f* de résidence, foyer *m* d'étudiants

dor′mitory com′plex *s* cité *f* universitaire

dor·mouse [′dɔr,maʊs] *s* (*pl* **-mice**) loir *m*

dosage [′dosɪdʒ] *s* (*administration*) dosage *m*; (*amount*) dose *f*; (*information on medicine bottle*) posologie *f*

dose [dos] *s* dose *f* ‖ *tr* donner en doses; donner un médicament à

dossier [′dɑsɪ,e] *s* dossier *m*

dot [dɑt] *s* point *m*; **on the dot** (coll) à l'heure tapante; pile, e.g., **at noon on the dot** à midi pile ‖ *v* (*pret & pp* **dotted**; *ger* **dotting**) *tr* (*to make with dots*) pointiller; **to dot one's i's** mettre les points sur les i

dotage [′dotɪdʒ] *s* radotage *m*

dotard [′dotərd] *s* gâteux *m*, gaga *m*

dote [dot] *intr* radoter; **to dote on** raffoler de

doting [′dotɪŋ] *adj* radoteur; (*loving to excess*) qui aime follement

dots′ and dash′es *spl* (telg) points et traits *mpl*

dot′ted line′ *s* ligne *f* pointillée, ligne hachée, pointillé *m*; **to sign on the dotted line** signer en bonne et due forme

double [′dʌbəl] *adj & adv* double, en deux, deux fois ‖ *s* double *m*; (cards) contre *m*; (*stunt man*) (mov) cascadeur *m*; **doubles** (tennis) double; **on the double!** (coll) dare-dare!, au trot!; **to play double or nothing** jouer à quitte ou double ‖ *tr* doubler; (cards) contrer; **to double up** plier en deux ‖ *intr* doubler; (cards) contrer; **to double back** faire un crochet; **to double up** se plier, se tordre

dou′ble-act′ing *adj* à double effet

dou′ble-bar′reled *adj* (*gun*) à deux coups

dou′ble bass′ [bes] *s* contrebasse *f*

dou′ble bed′ *s* grand lit *m*, lit à deux places

dou′ble broil′er *s* bain-marie *m*

dou′ble-breast′ed *adj* croisé

dou′ble chin′ *s* double menton *m*

dou′ble cross′ *s* (slang) entourloupette *f*, double jeu *m*

dou′ble-cross′ *tr* (coll) doubler, rouler, faire une entourloupette à

dou′ble-cross′er *s* (slang) personne *f* double, faux jeton *m*

Dou′ble-Cros′tic [′krɔstɪk] *s* (trademark) chassé-croisé *m*

dou′ble date′ *s* partie *f* carrée, sortie à quatre

dou′ble-deal′er *s* personne *f* double, homme *m* à deux visages

dou′ble-deal′ing *adj* hypocrite ‖ *s* duplicité *f*

dou′ble-deck′er *s* (*bed*) lits *mpl* superposés, lit gigognes, lit à deux étages; (*bus*) autobus *m* à deux étages; (*sandwich*) double sandwich *m*; (aer, naut) deux-ponts *m*

dou′ble-edged′ *adj* à deux tranchants, à double tranchant

double entendre [′dubələn′tandrə] *s* expression *f* à double entente, mot *m* à double sens

dou′ble-en′try *adj* en partie double

dou′ble-faced′ *adj* à double face

dou′ble fea′ture *s* (mov) deux grands films *mpl*, double programme *m*

dou′ble-joint′ed *adj* désarticulé

dou′ble-lock′ *tr* fermer à double tour

dou′ble-park′ *tr* faire stationner en double file ‖ *intr* stationner en double file, se garer en double file

dou′ble room′ *s* chambre *f* à deux lits

dou′ble-spaced′ *adj* à l'interligne double, à double interligne

dou′ble stand′ard *s* code *m* de morale à deux aspects; **to have a double standard** avoir deux poids et deux mesures

doublet [′dʌblɪt] *s* (*close-fitting jacket*) pourpoint *m*; (*counterfeit stone; each of two words having the same origin*) doublet *m*

dou′ble-talk′ *s* (coll) non-sens *m*; (coll) paroles *fpl* creuses or ambiguës, mots *mpl* couverts

dou′ble time′ *s* (*for work*) salaire *m* double; (mil) pas *m* redoublé

doubleton [′dʌbəltən] *s* deux cartes *fpl* d'une couleur

dou′ble track′ *s* double piste *f*

doubling [′dʌblɪŋ] *s* doublement *m*

doubly [′dʌbli] *adv* doublement

doubt [daʊt] *s* doute *m*; **beyond a doubt** à n'en pas douter; **no doubt** sans doute ‖ *tr* douter de; **to doubt that** douter que; **to doubt whether** douter si ‖ *intr* douter

doubter [′daʊtər] *s* douteur *m*

doubtful [′daʊtfəl] *adj* douteux; indécis, hésitant

doubtless [′daʊtlɪs] *adv* sans doute

douche [duʃ] *s* douche *f*; (*instrument*) seringue *f* à lavement ‖ *tr* doucher ‖ *intr* se doucher

dough [do] *s* pâte *f*; (slang) fric *m*, blé *m*, beurre *m*; **big dough** (slang) grosse galette *f*

dough′boy′ *s* (coll) troufion *m*, biffin *m*; (*in the First World War*) poilu *m*

dough′nut′ *s* beignet *m*

dough·ty [′daʊti] *adj* (*comp* **-tier**; *super* **-tiest**) vaillant, preux

dough·y [′do·i] *adj* (*comp* **-ier**; *super* **-iest**) pâteux

dour [daʊr] *adj* (*severe*) austère; (*obstinate*) buté; (*gloomy*) mélancolique

douse [daʊs] *tr* tremper, arroser; (slang) éteindre

dove [dʌv] *s* colombe *f*

dovecote [′dʌv,kot] *s* pigeonnier *m*, colombier *m*

Dover ['dovər] s Douvres
dove'tail' s queue-d'aronde f, adent m ‖ tr assembler à queue-d'aronde, adenter; (fig) raccorder, opérer le raccord entre ‖ intr se raccorder
dove'tailed' adj à queue-d'aronde
dowager ['dau·ədʒər] s douairière f
dow·dy ['daudi] adj (comp **-dier**; super **-diest**) gauche, fagoté, mal habillé
dow·el ['dau·əl] s goujon m ‖ v (pret & pp **-eled** or **-elled**; ger **-eling** or **-elling**) tr goujonner
dower ['dau·ər] s (widow's portion) douaire m; (marriage portion) dot f; (natural gift) don m ‖ tr assigner un douaire à; doter
down [daun] adj bas; (train) descendant; (storage battery) épuisé; (tire) à plat; (sun) couché; (wind, sea, etc.) calmé; (blinds; prices) baissé; (stocks) en moins-value; (sad) abattu, triste ‖ s (on a bird) duvet m; (sand hill) dune f ‖ adv en bas, au bas, vers les bas; à terre; (south) au sud; **down!** (in elevator) on descend!, pour la descente!; **down from** du haut de; **down there** là-bas; **down to** jusqu'à; **down under** aux antipodes; **down with . . . !** à bas . . . !; for expressions like **to go down** descendre or **to pay down** payer comptant, see the verb ‖ prep en bas de; (along) le long de; (a stream) en descendant ‖ tr descendre, abattre; (to swallow) (coll) avaler
down'-and-out' adj décavé
down'beat' s (mus) temps m fort, frappé m, premier accent m
down'cast' adj abattu, baissé
down'fall' s chute f, ruine f
down'grade' adj (coll) descendant ‖ s descente f; **to be on the downgrade** déchoir ‖ adv en déclin ‖ tr déclasser
down'heart'ed adj abattu, découragé
down'hill' adj descendant ‖ adv—**to go downhill** aller en descendant; (fig) décliner
down' pay'ment s acompte m
down'pour' s déluge m, averse f
down'right' adj absolu, véritable ‖ adv tout à fait, absolument
down'stairs' s rez-de-chaussée m ‖ adv en bas; **to go downstairs** descendre
down'stream' adv en aval
down'stroke' s (of piston) course f descendante; (in writing) jambage m
down'-to-earth' adj terre-à-terre
down'town' adj du centre ‖ s centre m ‖ adv en ville
down'trend' s tendance f à la baisse
downtrodden ['daun,trɑdən] adj opprimé
downward ['daunwərd] adj descendant ‖ adv en bas, en descendant
downwards ['daunwərdz] adv en bas, en descendant
down'wash' s (aer) air m déplacé
down·y ['dauni] adj (comp **-ier**; super **-iest**) duveteux; (velvety) velouté; (soft) mou, moelleux
dow·ry ['dauri] s (pl **-ries**) dot f

dowser ['dauzər] s sourcier m, hydroscope m
doze [doz] s petit somme m ‖ intr sommeiller; **to doze off** s'assoupir
dozen ['dʌzən] s douzaine f; **a dozen** . . . une douzaine de · · . ; **by the dozen** à la douzaine
D.P. abbr (displaced person) personne f déplacée
Dr. abbr (Doctor) Dʳ
drab [dræb] adj (comp **drabber**; super **drabbest**) gris ‖ s gris m
drach·ma ['drækmə] s (pl **-mas** or **-mae** [mi]) drachme f
draft [dræft] s (air current) courant m d'air; (pulling; current of air in chimney) tirage m; (sketch, outline) ébauche f; (of a letter, novel, etc.) brouillon m, premier jet m; (of a bill in Congress) projet m; (of a law) avant-projet m; (drink) trait m, gorgée f; (com) mandat m, traite f; (mil) conscription f; (naut) tirant m d'eau; **drafts** (game) dames fpl; **on draft** à la pression; **to be exempted from the draft** être exempté du service militaire ‖ tr (a document) rédiger, faire le brouillon de; (a bill in Congress) dresser; (a recruit) appeler sous les drapeaux; **to be drafted** être appelé sous les drapeaux
draft' beer' s bière f pression
draft' board' s conseil m de révision; commission f locale des conscriptions
draft' call' s appel m sous les drapeaux
draft' dodg'er ['dɑdʒər] s embusqué m, réfractaire mf
draftee [,dræf'ti] s appelé m (sous les drapeaux), conscrit m
draft' horse' s cheval m de trait
drafting ['dræftɪŋ] s dessin m industriel
draft'ing room' s bureau m d'études
drafts'man s (pl **-men**) dessinateur m; (man who draws up documents) rédacteur m
draft·y ['dræfti] adj (comp **-ier**; super **-iest**) plein de courants d'air
drag [dræg] s (net) drège f; (sledge or sled) traîneau m; (stone drag) fardier m; (brake) enrayure f; (impediment) entrave f; (aer) traînée f ‖ v (pret & pp **dragged**; ger **dragging**) tr traîner; (one's feet) traînasser; (a net) draguer; (a field) herser; **to drag down** entraîner; **to drag in** introduire de force; **to drag on** traîner en longueur; **to drag out** faire sortir de force ‖ intr traîner à terre; se traîner
drag'net' s traîneau m, chalut m
dragon ['drægən] s dragon m
drag'on·fly' s (pl **-flies**) demoiselle f, libellule f
dragoon [drə'gun] s dragon m ‖ tr tyranniser; forcer, contraindre
drain [dren] s (sewer) égout m; (pipe) tuyau m d'égout; (ditch) tranchée f d'écoulement; (source of continual expense) saignée f; (med) drain m ‖ tr (wet ground) drainer; (a glass or cup) vider entièrement; (a crankcase) vidanger; (s.o. of

strength) épuiser; (med) drainer ‖ *intr* s'égoutter, s'écouler

drainage ['dreɪnɪdʒ] *s* drainage *m*

drain'board' *s* égouttoir *m*

drain' cock' *s* purgeur *m*

drain'pipe' *s* tuyau *m* d'écoulement, drain *m*

drain' plug' *s* bouchon *m* de vidange

drake [drek] *s* canard *m* mâle

dram [dræm] *s (weight)* drachme *m*; (drink) petit verre *f*, goutte *f*

drama ['drɑmə], ['dræmə] *s* drame *m*

dra'ma crit'ic *s* chroniqueur *m* dramatique

dra'ma review' *s* avant-première *f*

dramatic [drə'mætɪk] *adj* dramatique ‖ **dramatics** *s* dramaturgie *f*, art *m* dramatique

dramatist ['dræmətɪst] *s* auteur *m* dramatique, dramaturge *mf*

dramatize ['dræmə,taɪz] *tr* dramatiser

drape [drep] *s (curtain)* rideau *m*; *(hang of a curtain, skirt, etc.)* drapement *m* ‖ *tr* draper, tendre; se draper dans

draper·y ['drepəri] *s (pl* **-ies)** draperie *f*; **draperies** rideaux *mpl*, tentures *fpl*

drastic ['dræstɪk] *adj* énergique, radical; *(laxative)* drastique

draught [dræft] *s (of fish)* coup *m* de filet; *(drink)* trait *m*, gorgée *f*; (naut) tirant *m* d'eau; **draughts** *(game)* dames *fpl*; **on draught** à la pression

draught' beer' *s* bière *f* pression

draught'board' *s* damier *m*

draw [drɔ] *s (taking, drawing, pulling; in a fireplace)* tirage *m*; *(in a game or other contest)* partie *f* nulle, match *m* nul ‖ *v (pret* **drew** [dru]; *pp* **drawn** [drɔn]) *tr* tirer; *(a crowd)* attirer; *(a design)* dessiner; *(a card)* tirer; *(trumps)* faire tomber; *(a bow)* bander, tendre; *(water)* puiser; **to draw a conclusion** tirer une conséquence; **to draw aside** prendre à l'écart; **to draw blood** faire saigner; **to draw interest** porter intérêt; **to draw lots** tirer au sort; **to draw off** *(e.g., a liquid)* soutirer; **to draw out** *(a person)* faire parler; *(an activity)* prolonger, traîner; **to draw up** *(a list)* dresser; *(a plan)* rédiger; (naut) jauger ‖ *intr* tirer; dessiner; faire partie nulle, faire match nul; **to draw away** s'éloigner; **to draw back** reculer, se retirer; **to draw near** approcher; s'approcher de

draw'back' *s* désavantage *m*, inconvénient *m*

draw'bridge' *s* pont-levis *m*

drawee [,drɔ'i] *s* tiré *m*, accepteur *m*

drawer ['drɔ·ər] *s* dessinateur *m*; (com) tireur *m* ‖ [drɔr] *s* tiroir *m*; **drawers** caleçon *m*

drawing ['drɔ·ɪŋ] *s (sketch)* dessin *m*; *(in a lottery)* tirage *m*; **drawing off** tirage *m*

draw'ing board' *s* planche *f* à dessin

draw'ing card' *s* attrait *m*, attraction *f*

draw'ing room' *s* salon *m*

draw'knife' *s (pl* **-knives)** plane *f*

drawl [drɔl] *s* voix *f* traînante ‖ *tr* dire d'une voix traînante ‖ *intr* traîner la voix en parlant

drawn' but'ter [drɔn] *s* beurre *m* fondu; sauce *f* blanche

drawn' work' *s* broderie *f* à fils tirés

dray [dre] *s* haquet *m*, charrette *f*; *(sledge)* fardier *m*, schlitte *f*

drayage ['dre·ɪdʒ] *s* charriage *m*, charroi *m*; frais *mpl* de transport

dray' horse' *s* cheval *m* de trait

dray'man *s (pl* **-men)** haquetier *m*

dread [drɛd] *adj* redoutable, terrible ‖ *s* terreur *f*, crainte *f* ‖ *tr & intr* redouter, craindre

dreadful ['drɛdfəl] *adj* épouvantable

dream [drim] *s* rêve *m*, songe *m*; *(fancy, illusion)* rêverie *f*, songerie *f* ‖ *v (pret & pp* **dreamed** or **dreamt** [drɛmt]) *tr*—**to dream up** rêver ‖ *intr* rêver, songer; **to dream of** *(future plans)* rêver à; *(s.o.)* rêver de

dreamer ['drimər] *s* rêveur *m*

dream'land' *s* pays *m* des songes

dream' world' *s* monde *m* des rêves

dream·y ['drimi] *adj (comp* **-ier**; *super* **-iest)** rêveur; (slang) épatant

drear·y ['drɪri] *adj (comp* **-ier**; *super* **-iest)** triste, morne, monotone

dredge [drɛdʒ] *s* drague *f* ‖ *tr* draguer

dredger ['drɛdʒər] *s* dragueur *m*; (mach) drague *f*

dredging ['drɛdʒɪŋ] *s* dragage *m*

dregs [drɛgz] *spl* lie *f*

drench [drɛntʃ] *tr* tremper, inonder

dress [drɛs] *s* habillement *m*, costume *m*; *(woman's attire)* toilette *f*, mise *f*; *(woman's dress)* robe *f* ‖ *tr* habiller, vêtir; *(to apply a dressing to)* panser; (culin) garnir; **to dress down** (coll) passer un savon à, chapitrer; **to dress up** parer; *(ranks)* (mil) aligner; **to get dressed** s'habiller ‖ *intr* s'habiller, se vêtir; (mil) s'aligner; **to be dressing** être à sa toilette; **to dress up** se parer

dress' ball' *s* bal *m* paré

dress' cir'cle *s* corbeille *f*, premier balcon *m*

dress' coat' *s* frac *m*

dresser ['drɛsər] *s* coiffeuse *f*; commode *f* à miroir; *(sideboard)* dressoir *m*; **to be a good dresser** être recherché dans sa mise

dress' form' *s* mannequin *m*

dress' goods' *spl* étoffes *fpl* pour costumes

dressing ['drɛsɪŋ] *s (providing with clothes)* habillement *m*; *(for food)* assaisonnement *m*, sauce *f*; *(stuffing for fowl)* farce *f*; *(fertilizer)* engrais *m*; *(for a wound)* pansement *m*

dress'ing down' *s* (coll) savon *m*, verte réprimande *f*, algarade *f*

dress'ing gown' *s* peignoir *m*, robe *f* de chambre

dress'ing room' *s* cabinet *m* de toilette, vestiaire *m*; (theat) loge *f*

dress'ing sta'tion *s* poste *m* de secours

dress'ing ta'ble *s* coiffeuse *f*, toilette *f*

dress'mak'er s couturière f
dress'mak'ing s couture f
dress'making estab'lishment s maison f de couture
dress' rehear'sal s répétition f en costume; **final dress rehearsal** répétition générale
dress' shield' s dessous-de-bras m
dress' shirt' s chemise f à plastron
dress' shop' s magasin m de modes
dress' suit' s habit m de cérémonie, tenue f de soirée
dress' tie' s cravate f de smoking, cravate-plastron f
dress' u'niform s (mil) grande tenue f
dress·y ['drɛsi] adj (comp **-ier;** super **-iest**) (coll) élégant, chic
dribble ['drɪbəl] s dégouttement m; (of child) bave f; (sports) dribble m || tr (sports) dribbler || intr dégoutter; (said of child) baver; (sports) dribbler
driblet ['drɪblɪt] s chiquet m; **in driblets** au compte-gouttes
dried' ap'ple [draɪd] s pomme f tapée
dried' beef' s viande f boucanée
dried' fig' s figue f sèche
dried' fruit' s fruit m sec
dried' pear' s poire f tapée
drier ['draɪ·ər] s (for clothes) séchoir m, sécheuse f; (for paint) siccatif m; (mach) sécheur m
drift [drɪft] s mouvement m, force f, poussée f; (of sand, snow) amoncellement m; (of meaning) sens m, direction f; (aer & naut) dérive f, dérivation f || intr aller à la dérive; (said of snow) s'amonceler; (aer, naut) dériver; (fig) se laisser aller, flotter
drift' ice' s glaces fpl flottantes
drift'wood' s bois m flotté
drill [drɪl] s (for metal, wood) foret m, mèche f; (machine) perforatrice f; (fabric) coutil m, treillis m; (furrow) sillon m; (agricultural implement) semoir m; (in school; on the drill ground) exercice m || tr instruire; (e.g., students) former, entraîner; (mach) forer; (mil) faire faire l'exercice à; **to drill s.th. into s.o.** seriner q.ch. à qn || intr faire l'exercice; forer
driller ['drɪlər] s foreur m
drill' field' or **drill' ground'** s terrain m d'exercice
drilling ['drɪlɪŋ] s (of metal; of an oil well) forage m; (dentistry) fraisage m
drill'mas'ter s moniteur m; (mil) instructeur m
drill' press' s foreuse f à colonnes
drink [drɪŋk] s boisson f, breuvage m; boire m, e.g., **food and drink** le boire et le manger || v (pret **drank** [dræŋk]; pp **drunk** [drʌŋk]) tr boire; (e.g., with a meal) prendre; **to drink down** boire d'un trait || intr boire; **to drink out of** (a glass) boire dans; (a bottle) boire à; **to drink to the health of** boire à la santé de
drinkable ['drɪŋkəbəl] adj buvable, potable
drinker ['drɪŋkər] s buveur m
drink'ing cup' s tasse f à boire, gobelet m

drink'ing foun'tain s fontaine f à boire, borne-fontaine f
drink'ing song' s chanson f à boire
drink'ing trough' s abreuvoir m
drink'ing wa'ter s eau f potable
drip [drɪp] s (drop) goutte f; (dripping) égout m, dégouttement m; (person) (slang) cornichon m || v (pret & pp **dripped**; ger **dripping**) intr dégoutter, goutter
drip' cof'fee s café-filtre m
drip' cof'fee mak'er s cafetière f à filtre
drip'-dry' adj à séchage rapide; (label on shirt) repassage inutile
dripolator ['drɪpə,letər] s filtre m à café
drip' pan' s égouttoir m
dripping ['drɪpɪŋ] s ruissellement m; **drip-pings** graisse f de rôti
drive [draɪv] s (in an automobile) prome-nade f; (road) chaussée f; (vigor) énergie f, initiative f; (fund-raising) campagne f; (push forward) propulsion f; (aut) (point of power application to roadway) traction f; (golf) crossée f; (mach) transmission f; **to go for a drive** faire une promenade en auto || v (pret **drove** [drov]; pp **driven** ['drɪvən]) tr (an automobile, locomotive, etc.; an animal; a person in an automo-bile) conduire; (a nail) enfoncer; (a bar-gain) conclure; (the ball in a game) ren-voyer, chasser; (to push, force) pousser, forcer; (to overwork) surmener; **to drive away** chasser; **to drive back** repousser; (e.g., in a car) reconduire; **to drive crazy** rendre fou; **to drive in** enfoncer; **to drive out** chasser; **to drive to despair** conduire au désespoir || intr conduire; **drive slowly** (public sign) marcher au pas; **to drive away** partir, démarrer; **to drive back** rentrer en auto; **to drive on** continuer sa route; **to drive out** sortir
drive'-in' s (motion-picture theater) cinéma m auto, ciné-park m; (restaurant) resto-route m
driv·el ['drɪvəl] s (slobber) bave f; (non-sense) bêtises fpl || v (pret **-eled** or **-elled**; ger **-eling** or **-elling**) intr baver; (to talk nonsense) radoter
driver ['draɪvər] s chauffeur m, conducteur m; (of a carriage) cocher m; (of a locomo-tive) mécanicien m; (of pack animals) toucheur m
driv'er's li'cense s permis m de conduire
drive' shaft' s arbre m d'entraînement
drive'way' s voie f de garage, sortie f de voiture
drive' wheel' s roue f motrice, roue de transmission
driv'ing school' s auto-école f
drizzle ['drɪzəl] s pluie f fine, bruine f || intr bruiner, brouillasser
droll [drol] adj drôle, drolatique
dromedar·y ['drɑmə,dɛri] s (pl **-ies**) dro-madaire m
drone [dron] s (humming) bourdonnement m; (of plane or engine) vrombissement m, ronron m; (do-nothing) fainéant m; (aer) avion m téléguidé, avion sans pilote; (ent)

faux bourdon *m* ‖ *intr* bourdonner, ronronner

drool [drul] *intr* baver

droop [drup] *s* inclinaison *f* ‖ *intr* se baisser; (*to lose one's pep*) s'alanguir; (bot) languir

drooping ['drupɪŋ] *adj* languissant

drop [drɑp] *s* (*e.g., of water*) goutte *f*; (*fall*) chute *f*; (*slope*) précipice *m*; (*depth of drop*) hauteur *f* de chute; (*in price; in temperature*) baisse *f*; (*lozenge*) pastille *f*; (*of supplies from an airplane*) droppage *m*; **a drop in the bucket** une goutte d'eau dans la mer ‖ *v* (*pret & pp* **dropped**; *ger* **dropping**) *tr* laisser tomber; (*a curtain; the eyes, voice*) baisser; (*from an airplane*) lâcher; (*e.g., a name from a list*) omettre, supprimer; (*a remark*) glisser; (*a conversation; relations; negotiations*) cesser; (*anchor*) jeter, mouiller; (*an idea, a habit, etc.*) renoncer à; **to drop off** déposer ‖ *intr* tomber; se laisser tomber; baisser; cesser; **to drop in** entrer en passant; **to drop in on** faire un saut chez; **to drop off** se détacher; s'endormir; **to drop out of** (*to quit*) renoncer à, abandonner

drop' cur'tain *s* rideau *m* d'entracte

drop'-cord light' *s* baladeuse *f*

drop' ham'mer *s* marteau-pilon *m*

drop' kick' *s* coup *m* tombé

drop' leaf' *s* abattant *m*

drop'light' *s* lampe *f* suspendue

drop'out' *s* raté *m*; **to become a dropout** abandonner les études

dropper ['drɑpər] *s* compte-gouttes *m*

dropsy ['drɑpsi] *s* hydropisie *f*

drop' ta'ble *s* table *f* à abattants

dross [drɔs] *s* scories *mpl*, écume *f*

drought [draʊt] *s* sécheresse *f*

drove [drov] *s* (*of animals*) troupeau *m*; (*multitude*) foule *f*, flots *mpl*; **in droves** par bandes

drover ['drovər] *s* bouvier *m*

drown [draʊn] *tr* noyer; **to drown out** couvrir ‖ *intr* se noyer

drowse [draʊz] *intr* somnoler, s'assoupir

drow·sy ['draʊzi] *adj* (*comp* **-sier**; *super* **-siest**) somnolent

drub [drʌb] *v* (*pret & pp* **drubbed**; *ger* **drubbing**) *tr* flanquer une raclée à, rosser

drudge [drʌdʒ] *s* homme *m* de peine, piocheur *m*; **harmless drudge** (*e.g., who compiles dictionaries*) gratte-papier *m* inoffensif

drudger·y ['drʌdʒəri] *s* (*pl* **-ies**) corvée *f*, travail *m* pénible

drug [drʌg] *s* (*medicine*) produit *m* pharmaceutique, drogue *f*; (*narcotic*) stupéfiant *m*, drogue; **drug on the market** rossignol *m* ‖ *v* (*pret & pp* **drugged**; *ger* **drugging**) *tr* (*a person*) donner un stupéfiant à, stupéfier; (*food or drink*) ajouter un stupéfiant à

drug' ad'dict *s* toxicomane *mf*, drogué *m*, intoxiqué *m*, camé *m*

drug' addic'tion *s* toxicomanie *f*

drug' deal'er *s* ravitailleur *m* en drogues; (slang) dealer *m*, vendeur *m* de mort, fourmi *f*

druggist ['drʌgɪst] *s* pharmacien *m*

drug' hab'it *s* toxicomanie *f*, vice *m* des stupéfiants

drug' push'er *s* revendeur *m* (de drogues); (slang) dealer *m*, vendeur *m* de mort, fourmi *f*

drug'store *s* pharmacie-bazar *f*, pharmacie *f*

drug' traf'fic *s* trafic *m* des stupéfiants

druid ['dru·ɪd] *s* druide *m*

drum [drʌm] *s* (*cylinder; instrument of percussion*) tambour *m*; (*container for oil, gasoline, etc.*) bidon *m*; **to play the drum** battre du tambour ‖ *v* (*pret & pp* **drummed**; *ger* **drumming**) *tr* (*e.g., a march*) tambouriner; rassembler au son du tambour; **to drum into** fourrer dans; **to drum up customers** racoler des clients ‖ *intr* jouer du tambour; (*with the fingers*) tambouriner; (*on the piano*) pianoter

drum' and bu'gle corps' *s* clairons et tambours *mpl*, clique *f*

drum'beat' *s* coup *m* de tambour

drum'fire' *s* (mil) tir *m* nourri, feu *m* roulant

drum'head' *s* peau *f* de tambour; (naut) noix *f*

drum' ma'jor *s* tambour-major *m*

drummer ['drʌmər] *s* tambour *m*; (*salesman*) (coll) commis *m* voyageur

drum'stick' *s* baguette *f* de tambour; (*of chicken*) (coll) cuisse *f*, pilon *m*

drunk [drʌŋk] *adj* ivre, soûl; **to get drunk** s'enivrer; **to get s.o. drunk** enivrer qn ‖ *s* (*person*) (coll) ivrogne *m*; (*state*) ivresse *f*; **to go on a drunk** (coll) se soûler

drunkard ['drʌŋkərd] *s* ivrogne *m*

drunken ['drʌŋkən] *adj* enivré

drunk'en driv'er *s* chauffeur *m* en état d'ivresse

drunk'en driv'ing *s* conduite *f* en état d'ivresse, ivresse *f* au volant, alcoolisme *m* au volant

drunkenness ['drʌŋkənnɪs] *s* ivresse *f*

dry [draɪ] *adj* (*comp* **drier**; *super* **driest**) sec; (*thirsty*) assoiffé; (*boring*) aride ‖ *s* (*pl* **drys**) (*prohibitionist*) antialcoolique *mf* ‖ *v* (*pret & pp* **dried**) *tr* sécher; (*the dishes*) essuyer ‖ *intr* sécher; **to dry up se** dessécher; (slang) se taire

dry' bat'tery *s* pile *f* sèche; (*number of dry cells*) batterie *f* de piles

dry' cell' *s* pile *f* sèche

dry'-clean' *tr* nettoyer à sec

dry' clean'er *s* nettoyeur *m* à sec, teinturier *m*

dry' clean'er's *s* teinturerie *f*

dry' clean'ing *s* nettoyage *m* à sec

dry' dock' *s* cale *f* sèche, bassin *m* de radoub

dry'-eyed' *adj* d'un œil sec

dry' goods' *spl* tissus *mpl*, étoffes *fpl*

dry' ice' *s* glace *f* sèche

dry' land' *s* terre *f* ferme

dry′ meas′ure s mesure f à grains

dryness ['draɪnɪs] s sécheresse f; (e.g., of a speaker) aridité f

dry′ nurse′ s nourrice f sèche

dry′ rot′ s carie f sèche

dry′ run′ s exercice m simulé, répétition f, examen m blanc

dry′ sea′son s saison f sèche

dry′ wash′ s blanchissage m sans repassage

dual ['d(j)u·əl] adj double ‖ s duel m

dub [dʌb] s (slang) balourd m ‖ v (pret & pp **dubbed**; ger **dubbing**) tr (to nickname) donner un sobriquet à; (to knight) donner l'accolade à, adouber; (a tape recording or movie film) doubler

dubbing ['dʌbɪŋ] s (mov) doublage m

dubious ['d(j)ubɪ·əs] adj (undecided) hésitant; (questionable) douteux

ducat ['dʌkət] s ducat m

duchess ['dʌtʃɪs] s duchesse f

duch·y ['dʌtʃi] s (pl **-ies**) duché m

duck [dʌk] s canard m; (female) cane f; (motion) esquive f; **ducks** (trousers) pantalon m de coutil ‖ tr (the head) baisser ‖ intr se baisser; **to duck out** (coll) s'esquiver

ducking ['dʌkɪŋ] s plongeon m, bain m forcé

duckling ['dʌklɪŋ] s caneton m; (female) canette f

ducks′ and drakes′ s—**to play at ducks and drakes** faire des ricochets sur l'eau; (fig) jeter son argent par les fenêtres

duck′-toed′ adj qui marche en canard

duct [dʌkt] s conduit m, canal m

duct′less glands′ ['dʌktlɪs] spl glandes fpl closes

duct′work′ s tuyauterie f, canalisation f

dud [dʌd] s (slang) obus m qui a raté, fusée f mouillée; (slang) raté m, navet m; **duds** (clothes) (coll) frusques fpl, nippes fpl

dude [d(j)ud] s poseur m, gommeux m

dude′ ranch′ s ranch m d'opérette

due [d(j)u] adj dû; (note) échéant; (bill) exigible; (train, bus, person) attendu; **due to** par suite de; **in due (and proper) form** en bonne forme, en règle, en bonne et due forme; **to fall due** venir à l'échéance; **when is the train due?** à quelle heure doit arriver le train? ‖ s dû m; **dues** cotisation f; **to pay one's dues** cotiser ‖ adv droit vers, e.g., **due north** droit vers le nord

due′ date′ s échéance f

duel ['d(j)u·əl] s duel m; **to fight a duel** se battre en duel ‖ v (pret & pp **dueled** or **duelled**; ger **dueling** or **duelling**) intr se battre en duel

duelist or **duellist** ['d(j)u·əlɪst] s duelliste m

duenna [d(j)u'ɛnə] s duègne f

dues′-pay′ing adj cotisant

duet [d(j)u'ɛt] s duo m

duke [d(j)uk] s duc m

dukedom ['d(j)ukdəm] s duché m

dull [dʌl] adj (not sharp) émoussé; (color) terne; (sound; pain) sourd; (stupid) lourd; (business) lent; (boring) ennuyeux; (flat) fade, insipide; **to become dull** s'émousser; (said of senses) s'engourdir ‖ tr (a knife) émousser; (color) ternir; (sound; pain) amortir; (spirits) hébéter, engourdir ‖ intr s'émousser; se ternir; s'amortir; s'engourdir

dullard ['dʌlərd] s lourdaud m, hébété m

dullness ['dʌlnɪs] s (of knife) émoussement m; (e.g., of wits) lenteur f

duly ['d(j)uli] adv dûment, justement

dumb [dʌm] adj (lacking the power to speak) muet; (coll) gourde, imbécile; **completely dumb** (coll) bouché à l'émeri; **to play dumb** (coll) feindre l'innocence

dumb′bell′ s (sports) haltère m; (slang) gourde f, imbécile mf

dumb′ crea′ture s animal m, brute f

dumb′wait′er s monte-plats m; (serving table) table f roulante

dumfound ['dʌm,faʊnd] tr abasourdir, ébahir

dum·my ['dʌmi] adj faux, factice ‖ s (pl **-mies**) (dress form) mannequin; (in card games) mort m; (figurehead, straw man) prête-nom m, homme m de paille; (skeleton copy of a book or magazine) maquette f; (object put in place of the real thing) simulacre m; (slang) bêta m, ballot m

dump [dʌmp] s (pile of rubbish) amas m, tas m; (place) dépotoir m; (mil) dépôt m; (slang) taudis m; **to be down in the dumps** (coll) avoir le cafard ‖ tr décharger, déverser; (on rubbish pile) jeter au rebut; (com) vendre en faisant du dumping

dumping ['dʌmpɪŋ] s (com) dumping m

dumpling ['dʌmplɪŋ] s dumpling m, boulette f

dump′ truck′ s tombereau m

dump·y ['dʌmpi] adj (comp **-ier**; super **-iest**) (short and fat) courtaud, trapu, tassé; (shabby) râpé, minable

dun [dʌn] adj isabelle ‖ s créancier m importun; (demand for payment) demande f pressante ‖ v (pret & pp **dunned**; ger **dunning**) tr (for payment) importuner, poursuivre

dunce [dʌns] s âne m, cancre m

dunce′ cap′ s bonnet m d'âne

dune [d(j)un] s dune f

dune′ bug′gy s autosable m

dung [dʌŋ] s fumier m

dungarees [,dʌŋgə'riz] spl pantalon m de treillis, treillis m, bleu m

dungeon ['dʌndʒən] s cachot m, cul-de-basse-fosse m; (keep of castle) donjon m

dung′hill′ s tas m de fumier

dunk [dʌŋk] tr & intr tremper

du·o ['d(j)u·o] s (pl **-os**) duo m

duode·num [,d(j)u·ə'dinəm] s (pl **-na** [nə]) duodénum m

dupe [d(j)up] s dupe f, dindon m de la farce ‖ tr duper, flouer, faire marcher

duplex ['d(j)uplɛks] adj double, duplex ‖ s (apartment) appartement m sur deux

étages, duplex *m*; (*house*) maison *f* double
du'plex house' *s* maison *f* double
duplicate ['d(j)uplɪkɪt] *adj* double ‖ *s* duplicata *m*, polycopie *f*; **in duplicate** en double, en duplicata ‖ ['d(j)uplɪ,ket] *tr* faire le double de, reproduire; (*on a machine*) polycopier, ronéocopier
du'plicating machine' *s* duplicateur *m*
duplici·ty [d(j)u'plɪsɪti] *s* (*pl* **-ties**) duplicité *f*
durable ['d(j)Urəbəl] *adj* durable
duration [d(j)U'reʃən] *s* durée *f*
duress [d(j)U'rɛs] *s* contrainte *f*; emprisonnement *m*
during ['d(j)Urɪŋ] *prep* pendant
dusk [dʌsk] *s* crépuscule *m*; **at dusk** entre chien et loup
dust [dʌst] *s* poussière *f* ‖ *tr* (*to free of dust*) épousseter; (*to sprinkle with dust*) saupoudrer; **to dust off** épousseter
dust' bowl' *s* région *f* dénudée
dust'cloth' *s* chiffon *m* à épousseter
dust' cloud' *s* nuage *m* de poussière
duster ['dʌstər] *s* (*made of feathers*) plumeau *m*; (*made of cloth*) chiffon *m*; (*overgarment*) cache-poussière *m*
dust' jack'et *s* protège-livre *m*, couvre-livre *m*, liseuse *f*
dust'pan' *s* pelle *f* à poussière, ramasse-poussière *m invar*
dust' rag' *s* chiffon *m* à épousseter
dust' storm' *s* tempête *f* de poussière
dust·y ['dʌsti] *adj* (*comp* **-ier**; *super* **-iest**) poussiéreux; (*color*) cendré
Dutch [dʌtʃ] *adj* hollandais, néerlandais; (*slang*) allemand ‖ *s* (*language*) hollandais *m*, néerlandais *m*; (*slang*) allemand *m*; **in Dutch** (*slang*) en disgrâce; **the Dutch** les Hollandais *mpl*, les Néerlandais *mpl*; (*slang*) les Allemands *mpl*; **we will**

go Dutch (*coll*) chacun paiera son écot
Dutch'man *s* (*pl* **-men**) Hollandais *m*, Néerlandais *m*; (*slang*) Allemand *m*
Dutch' treat' *s* —**to have a Dutch treat** (*coll*) faire suisse, payer son écot
dutiable ['d(j)Utɪ·əbəl] *adj* soumis aux droits de douane
dutiful ['d(j)Utɪfəl] *adj* respectueux, soumis, plein d'égards
du·ty ['d(j)Uti] *s* (*pl* **-ties**) devoir *m*; **duties** fonctions *fpl*; (*taxes, customs*) droits *mpl*; **to be off duty** ne pas être de service, avoir quartier libre; **to be on duty** être de service, être de garde; **to have the duty to** avoir pour devoir de
du'ty-free' *adj* exempt de droits
du'ty-free shop' *s* boutique *f* franche
dwarf [dwɔrf] *adj* & *s* nain *m* ‖ *tr* & *intr* rapetisser
dwell [dwɛl] *v* (*pret* & *pp* **dwelled** or **dwelt** [dwɛlt]) *intr* demeurer; **to dwell on** appuyer sur
dwelling ['dwɛlɪŋ] *s* demeure *f*, habitation *f*
dwell'ing house' *s* maison *f* d'habitation
dwindle ['dwɪndəl] *intr* diminuer; **to dwindle away** s'affaiblir
dye [daɪ] *s* teinture *f* ‖ *v* (*pret* & *pp* **dyed**; *ger* **dyeing**) *tr* teindre
dyed'-in-the-wool' *adj* intransigeant
dyeing ['daɪ·ɪŋ] *s* teinture *f*
dyer ['daɪ·ər] *s* teinturier *m*
dying ['daɪ·ɪŋ] *adj* mourant, moribond
dynamic [daɪ'næmɪk], [dɪ'næmɪk] *adj* dynamique ‖ **dynamics** *s* dynamique *f*
dynamite ['daɪnə,maɪt] *s* dynamite *f* ‖ *tr* dynamiter
dyna·mo ['daɪnə,mo] *s* (*pl* **-mos**) dynamo *f*
dynas·ty ['daɪnəsti] *s* (*pl* **-ties**) dynastie *f*
dysentery ['dɪsən,tɛri] *s* dysenterie *f*
dyspepsia [dɪs'pɛpsɪ·ə] *s* dyspepsie *f*

E

E, e [i] *s* Vᵉ lettre de l'alphabet
each [itʃ] *adj indef* chaque ‖ *pron indef* chacun; **each other** nous, se; l'un l'autre; **to each other** l'un à l'autre ‖ *adv* chacun; (*apiece*) pièce, la pièce
eager ['igər] *adj* ardent, empressé; **eager for** avide de; **to be eager to** brûler de, désirer ardemment
ea'ger bea'ver *s* bûcheur *m*, mouche *f* du coche
eagerness ['igərnɪs] *s* ardeur *f*, empressement *m*
eagle ['igəl] *s* aigle *m*
ea'gle-eyed' *adj* à l'œil d'aigle
ea'gle ray' *s* (ichth) aigle *m* de mer
eaglet ['iglɪt] *s* aiglon *m*
ear [ɪr] *s* oreille *f*; (*of corn or wheat*) épi *m*; **to box s.o.'s ears** frotter les oreilles à qn;

to prick up one's ears dresser l'oreille; **to turn a deaf ear** faire la sourde oreille ‖ *intr* (*said of grain*) épier
ear'ache' *s* douleur *m* d'oreille
ear'drop' *s* pendant *m* d'oreille
ear'drum' *s* tympan *m*
ear'flap' *s* lobe *m* de l'oreille; (*on a cap*) protège-oreilles *m*
earl [ʌrl] *s* comte *m*
earldom ['ʌrldəm] *s* comté *m*
ear·ly ['ʌrli] (*comp* **-lier**; *super* **-liest**) *adj* primitif; (*first in a series*) premier; (*occurring in the near future*) prochain; (*in the morning*) matinal; (*ahead of time*) en avance; **at an early age** dès l'enfance ‖ *adv* de bonne heure, tôt; anciennement; **as early as** dès; **earlier** plus tôt, de meilleure heure

ear'ly bird' *s* matinal *m*
ear'ly mass' *s* première messe *f*
ear'ly-morn'ing *adj* matinal
ear'ly retire'ment *s* retraite *f* anticipée
ear'ly ris'er *s* matinal *m*
ear'ly-ris'ing *adj* matineux, matinal
ear'mark' *s* marque *f*, cachet *m* ‖ *tr (animals)* marquer à l'oreille; (*e.g., money*) spécialiser; **to earmark for** affecter à, assigner à
ear'muff' *s* couvre-oreille *m*
earn [ʌrn] *tr* gagner; (*to get as one's due*) mériter; (*interest*) rapporter
earnest [ˈʌrnɪst] *adj* sérieux; **in earnest** sérieusement ‖ *s* gage *m*; (com) arrhes *fpl*
earn'ing pow'er *s* (*person*) capacité *f* de gain; (*stock*) rentabilité *f*
earnings [ˈʌrnɪŋz] *spl* (*wages*) gages *mpl*; (*profits*) profit *m*, bénéfices *mpl*
ear'phone' *s* écouteur *m*; **earphones** casque *m*, écouteurs *m*
ear'ring' *s* boucle *f* d'oreille
ear'split'ting *adj* assourdissant
earth [ʌrθ] *s* terre *f*; **to come down to earth** retomber des nues; **where on earth . . .?** où diable . . .?
earthen [ˈʌrθən] *adj* de terre, en terre
ear'then·ware' *s* faïence *f*
earthly [ˈʌrθli] *adj* terrestre
earth'man' *s* (*pl* **men**) terrien *m*
earth'quake' *s* tremblement *m* de terre
earth'work' *s* terrassement *m*
earth'worm' *s* lombric *m*, ver *m* de terre
earth·y [ˈʌrθi] *adj* (*comp* **-ier**; *super* **-iest**) terreux; (*worldly*) mondain; (*unrefined*) grossier, terre à terre
ear'trum'pet *s* cornet *m* acoustique
ease [iz] *s* aise *f*; (*readiness, naturalness*) désinvolture *f*; (*comfort, well-being*) bien-être *m*, tranquillité *f*; **at ease** tranquille; (mil) au repos; **to take one's ease** prendre ses aises; **with ease** facilement ‖ *tr* faciliter; (*a burden*) alléger; (*e.g., one's mind*) calmer, apaiser; (*to let up on*) ralentir ‖ *intr* se calmer, s'apaiser
easel [ˈizəl] *s* chevalet *m*
easement [ˈizmənt] *s* (law) servitude *f*
easily [ˈizɪli] *adv* facilement, aisément; (*certainly*) sans doute
easiness [ˈizɪnɪs] *s* facilité *f*; (*of manner*) désinvolture *f*, insouciance *f*
east [ist] *adj* & *s* est *m* ‖ *adv* à l'est, vers l'est
Easter [ˈistər] *s* Pâques *m*; **Happy Easter!** Joyeuses Pâques!
East'er egg' *s* œuf *m* de Pâques
East'er Mon'day *s* lundi *m* de Pâques
eastern [ˈistərn] *adj* oriental, de l'est
East'ern Stan'dard Time' *s* l'heure *f* de l'Est
East'ern Town'ships *spl* (*in Canada*) Cantons *mpl* de l'Est
eastward [ˈistwərd] *adv* vers l'est
eas·y [ˈizi] *adj* (*comp* **-ier**; *super* **-iest**) facile; (*easygoing*) aisé, désinvolte; **it's not easy to** + *inf* ce n'est pas commode à + *inf* ‖ *adv* (coll) facilement; (coll) lente-

ment; **to take it easy** (coll) en prendre à son aise
eas'y chair' *s* fauteuil *m*, bergère *f*
eas'y·go'ing *adj* insouciant, nonchalant, commode à vivre
eas'y mark' *s* jobard *m*
eas'y pay'ments *spl* facilités *fpl* de paiement
eat [it] *v* (*pret* **ate** [et]; *pp* **eaten** [ˈitən]) *tr* manger; **to eat away** ronger ‖ *intr* manger
eatable [ˈitəbəl] *adj* comestible
eat'ing ap'ple *s* pomme *f* à couteau
eaves [ivz] *spl* avant-toits *mpl*
eaves'drop' *v* (*pret* & *pp* **-dropped**; *ger* **-dropping**) *intr* écouter à la porte
ebb [ɛb] *s* reflux *m*, baisse *f* ‖ *intr* refluer, baisser; **to ebb and flow** monter et baisser, fluer et refluer
ebb' and flow' *s* flux et reflux *m*
ebb' tide' *s* marée *f* descendante, jusant *m*
ebon·y [ˈɛbəni] *s* (*pl* **-ies**) ébène *f*; (*tree*) ébénier *m*
ebullient [ɪˈbʌljənt] *adj* bouillonnant; (fig) enthousiaste, exubérant
eccentric [ɛkˈsɛntrɪk] *adj* excentrique ‖ *s* (*odd person*) excentrique *mf*; (*device*) excentrique *m*
eccentrici·ty [ˌɛksɛnˈtrɪsɪti] *s* (*pl* **-ties**) excentricité *f*
ecclesiastic [ɪˌkliziˈæstɪk] *adj* & *s* ecclésiastique *m*
echelon [ˈɛʃəˌlɑn] *s* échelon *m* ‖ *tr* (mil) échelonner
ech·o [ˈɛko] *s* (*pl* **-oes**) écho *m* ‖ *tr* répéter ‖ *intr* faire écho
eclectic [ɛkˈlɛktɪk] *adj* & *s* éclectique *mf*
eclipse [ɪˈklɪps] *s* éclipse *f* ‖ *tr* éclipser
eclogue [ˈɛklɔg] *s* églogue *f*
ecology [ɪˈkɑlədʒi] *s* écologie *f*
economic [ˌikəˈnɑmɪk] *adj* économique ‖ **economics** *s* économique *f*
economical [ˌikəˈnɑmɪkəl] *adj* économe
economize [ɪˈkɑnəˌmaɪz] *tr* & *intr* économiser
econo·my [ɪˈkɑnəmi] *s* (*pl* **-mies**) économie *f*
ecsta·sy [ˈɛkstəsi] *s* (*pl* **-sies**) extase *f*
ecstatic [ɛkˈstætɪk] *adj* & *s* extatique *mf*
Ecuador [ˈɛkwəˌdɔr] *s* l'Équateur *m*
ecumenic(al) [ˌɛkjəˈmɛnɪk(əl)] *adj* œcuménique
eczema [ˈɛksɪmə] *s* eczéma *m*
edema [ɪˈdimə] *s* (pathol) œdème *m*
ed·dy [ˈɛdi] *s* (*pl* **-dies**) tourbillon *m* ‖ *v* (*pret* & *pp* **-died**) *intr* tourbillonner
edelweiss [ˈedəlˌvaɪs] *s* edelweiss *m*, fleur *f* de neige
Eden [ˈidən] *s* (fig) éden *m*
edge [ɛdʒ] *s* bord *m*; (*of a knife, sword, etc.*) fil *m*, tranchant *m*; (*of a field, forest, etc.; of a strip of cloth*) lisière *f*; (slang) avantage *m*; **on edge** de chant; (*nervous*) énervé, crispé; **to be on edge** avoir les nerfs à fleur de peau; **to have the edge on** (coll) enfoncer; **to set the teeth on edge** agacer les dents ‖ *tr* border; (*to sharpen*) affiler, aiguiser ‖ *intr* s'avancer de biais;

to edge away s'écarter peu à peu; **to edge in** se glisser parmi or dans
edge′ways′ *adv* de côté, de biais
edging [ˈɛdʒɪŋ] *s* bordure *f*
edg·y [ˈɛdʒi] *adj* (*comp* **-ier**; *super* **-iest**) (*nervous*) crispé, irritable
edible [ˈɛdɪbəl] *adj* comestible
edict [ˈidɪkt] *s* édit *m*
edification [ˌɛdɪfɪˈkeʃən] *s* édification *f*
edifice [ˈɛdɪfɪs] *s* édifice *m*
edi·fy [ˈɛdɪˌfaɪ] *v* (*pret* & *pp* **-fied**) *tr* édifier
edifying [ˈɛdɪˌfaɪ·ɪŋ] *adj* édifiant
edit [ˈɛdɪt] *tr* préparer la publication de; (*e.g., a newspaper*) diriger, rédiger; (*a text*) éditer
edition [ɪˈdɪʃən] *s* édition *f*
editor [ˈɛdɪtər] *s* (*of newspaper or magazine*) rédacteur *m*; (*of manuscript*) éditeur *m*; (*of feature or column*) chroniqueur *m*, courriériste *mf*
editorial [ˌɛdɪˈtorɪ·əl] *adj* & *s* éditorial *m*
edito′rial of′fice *s* rédaction *f*
edito′rial pol′icy *s* ligne *f* politique
edito′rial staff′ *s* rédaction *f*
ed′itor in chief′ *s* rédacteur *m* en chef
educate [ˈɛdʒʊˌket] *tr* instruire, éduquer
educated *adj* cultivé, instruit
education [ˌɛdʒʊˈkeʃən] *s* éducation *f*, instruction *f*
educational [ˌɛdʒʊˈkeʃənəl] *adj* éducatif, éducateur
educa′tional tel′evision *s* télé-enseignement *m*, télévision *f* éducative, télévision scolaire
educator [ˈɛdʒʊˌketər] *s* éducateur *m*
eel [il] *s* anguille *f*
ee·rie or **ee·ry** [ˈɪri] *adj* (*comp* **-rier**; *super* **-riest**) mystérieux, spectral
efface [ɪˈfes] *tr* effacer
effect [ɪˈfɛkt] *s* effet *m*; **in effect** en fait, effectivement; **to be in effect** être en vigueur; **to feel the effects of** se ressentir de; **to go into effect, to take effect** prendre effet; (*said of law*) entrer en vigueur ‖ *tr* effectuer, mettre à exécution
effective [ɪˈfɛktɪv] *adj* efficace; (*actually in effect*) en vigueur; (*striking*) impressionnant; **to become effective** produire son effet; (*to go into effect*) entrer en vigueur
effectual [ɪˈfɛktʃʊ·əl] *adj* efficace
effectuate [ɪˈfɛktʃʊˌet] *tr* effectuer
effeminacy [ɪˈfɛmɪnəsi] *s* effémination *f*
effeminate [ɪˈfɛmɪnɪt] *adj* efféminé; **to become effeminate** s'efféminer
effervesce [ˌɛfərˈvɛs] *intr* être en effervescence
effervescent [ˌɛfərˈvɛsənt] *adj* effervescent
effete [ɪˈfit] *adj* stérile, épuisé
efficacious [ˌɛfɪˈkeʃəs] *adj* efficace
efficacy [ˈɛfɪkəsi] *s* efficacité *f*
efficien·cy [ɪˈfɪʃənsi] *s* (*pl* **-cies**) efficacité *f*; (*of business*) efficience *f*; (*of machine*) rendement *m*; (*of person*) compétence *f*
effi′ciency ex′pert *s* ingénieur *m* en organisation

efficient [ɪˈfɪʃənt] *adj* efficace; (*of machine*) efficient, de bon rendement; (*of person*) efficient, compétent
effi·gy [ˈɛfɪdʒi] *s* (*pl* **-gies**) effigie *f*
effort [ˈɛfərt] *s* effort *m*
effronter·y [ɪˈfrʌntəri] *s* (*pl* **-ies**) effronterie *f*
effusion [ɪˈfjuʒən] *s* effusion *f*
effusive [ɪˈfjusɪv] *adj* démonstratif; **to be effusive in** se répandre en
e.g. *abbr* (Lat: **exempli gratia** for example) par ex., ex.
egg [ɛg] *s* œuf *m*; **eggs and bacon** œufs *mpl* au bacon; **good (bad) egg** (*person*) (slang) brave (sale) type; **to put all one's eggs in one basket** mettre tous ses œufs dans le même panier ‖ *tr*—**to egg on** (coll) pousser, inciter
egg′beat′er *s* fouet *m*, batteur *m* à œufs
egg′cup′ *s* coquetier *m*
egg′head′ *s* (slang) intellectuel *m*
eggnog [ˈɛgˌnɑg] *s* lait *m* de poule
egg′plant′ *s* aubergine *f*
egg′ poach′er *s* pocheuse *f*
egg′shell′ *s* coquille *f* d'œuf
egg′ white′ *s* blanc *m* d'œuf
egoism [ˈigoˌɪzəm] *s* égoïsme *m*
egoist [ˈigo·ɪst] *s* égoïste *mf*
egotism [ˈigoˌtɪzəm] *s* égotisme *m*
egotist [ˈigotɪst] *s* égotiste *mf*
egregious [ɪˈgridʒəs] *adj* insigne, notoire
egress [ˈigrɛs] *s* sortie *f*, issue *f*
egret [ˈigrɛt] *s* aigrette *f*
Egypt [ˈidʒɪpt] *s* Égypte *f*; l'Égypte
Egyptian [ɪˈdʒɪpʃən] *adj* égyptien ‖ *s* Égyptien *m*
ei′der down′ [ˈaɪdər] *s* édredon *m*
ei′der duck′ *s* eider *m*
eight [et] *adj* & *pron* huit ‖ *s* huit *m*; (*group of eight*) huitaine *f*; **about eight** une huitaine de; **eight o′clock** huit heures
eight′ball′ *s*—**behind the eightball** (coll) dans le pétrin
eighteen [ˈetˈtin] *adj, pron,* & *s* dix-huit *m*
eighteenth [ˈetˈtinθ] *adj* & *pron* dix-huitième (*masc, fem*); **the Eighteenth** dix-huit, e.g., **John the Eighteenth** Jean dix-huit ‖ *s* dix-huitième *m*; **the eighteenth** (*in dates*) le dix-huit
eighth [etθ] *adj* & *pron* huitième (*masc, fem*); **the Eighth** huit, e.g., **John the Eighth** Jean huit ‖ *s* huitième *m*; **the eighth** (*in dates*) le huit
eightieth [ˈetɪ·ɪθ] *adj* & *pron* quatre-vingtième (*masc, fem*) ‖ *s* quatre-vingtième *m*
eigh·ty [ˈeti] *adj* & *pron* quatre-vingts ‖ *s* (*pl* **-ties**) quatre-vingts *m*
eight′y-first′ *adj* & *pron* quatre-vingt-unième (*masc, fem*) ‖ *s* quatre-vingt-unième *m*
eight′y-one′ *adj, pron,* & *s* quatre-vingt-un *m*
either [ˈiðər], [ˈaɪðər] *adj* & *pron indef* l'un ou l'autre; l'un et l'autre; **on either side** de chaque côté ‖ *adv*—**not either** non plus ‖ *conj*—**either . . . or** ou

. . . ou, soit . . . soit, ou bien . . . ou bien

ejaculate [ɪ'dʒækjə,let] *tr & intr* crier; (physiol) éjaculer

eject [ɪ'dʒɛkt] *tr* éjecter; (*to evict*) expulser, chasser

ejection [ɪ'dʒɛkʃən] *s* éjection *f*; (*eviction*) expulsion *f*

ejec'tion seat' *s* (aer) siège *m* éjectable

eke [ik] *tr*—**to eke out** gagner avec difficulté

elaborate [ɪ'læbərɪt] *adj* élaboré, soigné; (*ornate*) orné, travaillé; (*involved*) compliqué, recherché ‖ [ɪ'læbə,ret] *tr* élaborer ‖ *intr*—**to elaborate on** or **upon** donner des détails sur

elapse [ɪ'læps] *intr* s'écouler

elastic [ɪ'læstɪk] *adj & s* élastique *m*

elasticity [,ilæs'tɪsɪti] *s* élasticité *f*

elated [ɪ'letɪd] *adj* transporté, exalté

elation [ɪ'leʃən] *s* transport *m*, exultation *f*

elbow ['ɛlbo] *s* coude *m*; **at one's elbow** à portée de la main; **to rub elbows with** coudoyer ‖ *tr* coudoyer; **to elbow one's way** se frayer un chemin à coups de coude ‖ *intr* jouer des coudes

el'bow grease' *s* (coll) huile *f* de coude

el'bow·room' *s* espace *m*; **to have elbowroom** avoir ses coudées franches

elder ['ɛldər] *adj* aîné, plus âgé ‖ *s* aîné *m*; (*senior*) doyen *m*; (bot) sureau *m*; (eccl) ancien *m*

el'der·ber'ry *s* (*pl* **-ries**) sureau *m*; (*berry*) baie *f* de sureau

elderly ['ɛldərli] *adj* vieux, âgé

eld'er states'man *s* vétéran *m* de la politique

eldest ['ɛldɪst] *adj* (l')aîné, (le) plus âgé

elect [ɪ'lɛkt] *adj* élu ‖ *s*—**the elect** les élus *mpl* ‖ *tr* élire

election [ɪ'lɛkʃən] *s* élection *f*

electioneer [ɪ,lɛkʃə'nɪr] *intr* faire la campagne électorale, solliciter des voix

elective [ɪ'lɛktɪv] *adj* électif; (*optional*) facultatif ‖ *s* matière *f* à option

elec'toral col'lege [ɪ'lɛktərəl] *s* collège *m* électoral

electorate [ɪ'lɛktərɪt] *s* corps *m* électoral, électeurs *mpl*, votants *mpl*

electric(al) [ɪ'lɛktrɪk(əl)] *adj* électrique

elec'trical engineer' *s* ingénieur *m* électricien

elec'trical engineer'ing *s* technique *f* électrique

elec'tric blan'ket *s* couverture *f* chauffante

elec'tric chair' *s* chaise *f* électrique

elec'tric clothes' dri'er *s* séchoir *m* électrique

elec'tric eel' *s* gymnote *m*

elec'tric eye' *s* cellule *f* photo-électrique

elec'tric fan' *s* ventilateur *m* électrique

elec'tric heat'er *s* radiateur *m* électrique

electrician [,ɛlɛk'trɪʃən] *s* électricien *m*

electricity [,ɛlɛk'trɪsɪti] *s* électricité *f*

elec'tric light' *s* lampe *f* électrique

elec'tric me'ter *s* compteur *m* de courant

elec'tric mix'er *s* batteur *m* électrique

elec'tric per'colator *s* cafetière *f* électrique

elec'tric range' *s* cuisinière *f* électrique

elec'tric shav'er *s* rasoir *m* électrique

elec'tric shock' treat'ment *s* (méd) électrochoc *m*

elec'tric tim'er *s* prise *f* de courant programmatrice

electri·fy [ɪ'lɛktrɪ,faɪ] *v* (*pret & pp* **-fied**) *tr* (*to provide with electric power*) électrifier; (*to communicate electricity to; to thrill*) électriser

elec·tro [ɪ'lɛktro] *s* (*pl* **-tros**) électrotype *m*

electrocute [ɪ'lɛktrə,kjut] *tr* électrocuter

electrode [ɪ'lɛktrod] *s* électrode *f*

electrolysis [,ɛlɛk'trɑlɪsɪs] *s* électrolyse *f*

electrolyte [ɪ'lɛktrə,laɪt] *s* électrolyte *m*

elec'tro·mag'net *s* électro-aimant *m*

elec'tro·magnet'ic *adj* électromagnétique

electron [ɪ'lɛktrɑn] *s* électron *m*

elec'tron gun' *s* canon *m* à électrons

electronic [,ɛlɛk'trɑnɪk] *adj* électronique ‖ **electronics** *s* électronique *f*

elec'tron mi'croscope *s* microscope *m* électronique

electroplate [ɪ'lɛktrə,plet] *tr* galvaniser

elec'tro·type' *s* électrotype *m* ‖ *tr* électrotyper

elegance ['ɛlɪgəns] *s* élégance *f*

elegant ['ɛlɪgənt] *adj* élégant

elegiac [,ɛlɪ'dʒaɪ·æk] *adj* élégiaque

ele·gy ['ɛlɪdʒi] *s* (*pl* **-gies**) élégie *f*

element ['ɛlɪmənt] *s* élément *m*

elementary [,ɛlɪ'mɛntəri] *adj* élémentaire

elephant ['ɛlɪfənt] *s* éléphant *m*

elevate ['ɛlɪ,vet] *tr* élever

elevated *adj* élevé; (*style*) soutenu; (*train, railway, etc*) aérien

el'evated rail'way *s* métro *m* aérien

elevation [,ɛlɪ've ʃən] *s* élévation *f*

elevator ['ɛlɪ,vetər] *s* ascenseur *m*; (*for freight*) monte-charge *m*; (*for hoisting grain*) élévateur *m*; (*warehouse for storing grain*) silo *m* à céréales, (aer) gouvernail *m* d'altitude, gouvernail de profondeur

el'evator shoes' *spl* souliers *mpl* compensés

eleven [ɪ'lɛvən] *adj & pron* onze ‖ *s* onze *m*; **eleven o'clock** onze heures

eleventh [ɪ'lɛvənθ] *adj & pron* onzième (*masc, fem*); **the Eleventh** onze, e.g., **John the Eleventh** Jean onze ‖ *s* onzième *m*; **the eleventh** (*in dates*) le onze

elev'enth hour' *s* dernier moment *m*

elf [ɛlf] *s* (*pl* **elves** [ɛlvz]) elfe *m*

elicit [ɪ'lɪsɪt] *tr* (*e.g., a smile*) provoquer, faire sortir; (*e.g., help*) obtenir

elide [ɪ'laɪd] *tr* élider

eligible ['ɛlɪdʒɪbəl] *adj* éligible; (*e.g., bachelor*) sortable

eliminate [ɪ'lɪmɪ,net] *tr* éliminer

elision [ɪ'lɪʒən] *s* élision *f*

elite [e'lit] *s* élite *f*

elk [ɛlk] *s* élan *m*

ellipse [ɪ'lɪps] *s* (geom) ellipse *f*

ellip·sis [ɪ'lɪpsɪs] *s* (*pl* **-ses** [siz]) ellipse *f*; (*punctuation*) points *mpl* de suspension

elliptic(al) [ɪ'lɪptɪk(əl)] *adj* elliptique

elm [ɛlm] *s* orme *m*

elongate [ɪ'lɔŋget] *tr* allonger, prolonger

elope [ɪ'lop] *intr* s'enfuir avec un amant

elopement [ɪ'lopmənt] *s* enlèvement *m* consenti

eloquence ['ɛləkwəns] *s* éloquence *f*

eloquent ['ɛləkwənt] *adj* éloquent

else [ɛls] *adj*—**nobody else** personne d'autre; **nothing else** rien d'autre; **somebody else** quelqu'un d'autre; **something else** autre chose; **what else** quoi encore; **who else** qui encore; **who's else** de qui d'autre ‖ *adv* d'une autre façon, autrement; **how(ever) else** de toute autre façon; **nowhere else** nulle part ailleurs; **or else** sinon, ou bien, sans quoi; **somewhere else** ailleurs, autre part; **when else** quand encore; **where else** où encore

else'where' *adv* ailleurs, autre part

elucidate [ɪ'lusɪ,det] *tr* élucider

elude [ɪ'lud] *tr* éluder, se soustraire à; (*a pursuer*) échapper à

elusive [ɪ'lusɪv] *adj* évasif, fuyant; (*baffling*) insaisissable, déconcertant

emaciated [ɪ'meʃɪ,etɪd] *adj* émacié; **to become emaciated** s'émacier

emanate ['ɛmə,net] *intr* émaner

emancipate [ɪ'mænsɪ,pet] *tr* émanciper

embalm [ɛm'bɑm] *tr* embaumer

embalming [ɛm'bɑmɪŋ] *s* embaumement *m*

embankment [ɛm'bæŋkmənt] *s* (*of river*) digue *f*; (*of road*) remblai *m*

embar·go [ɛm'bɑrgo] *s* (*pl* **-goes**) embargo *m* ‖ *tr* mettre un embargo sur

embark [ɛm'bɑrk] *intr* s'embarquer

embarkation [,ɛmbɑr'keʃən] *s* embarquement *m*

embarrass [ɛm'bærəs] *tr* faire honte à; (*to make difficult*) embarrasser

embarrassment [ɛm'bærəsmənt] *s* honte *f*, confusion *f*, gêne *f*; (*difficulty*) embarras *m*

embas·sy ['ɛmbəsi] *s* (*pl* **-sies**) ambassade *f*

em·bed [ɛm'bɛd] *v* (*pret* & *pp* **-bedded**; *ger* **-bedding**) *tr* encastrer

embellish [ɛm'bɛlɪʃ] *tr* embellir

embellishment [ɛm'bɛlɪʃmənt] *s* embellissement *m*

ember ['ɛmbər] *s* tison *m*; **embers** braise *f*

Em'ber days' *spl* quatre-temps *mpl*

embezzle [ɛm'bɛzəl] *tr* détourner, s'approprier ‖ *intr* commettre des détournements

embezzler [ɛm'bɛzlər] *s* détourneur *m* de fonds

embitter [ɛm'bɪtər] *tr* aigrir

emblazon [ɛm'blezən] *tr* embellir; exalter, célébrer

emblem ['ɛmbləm] *s* emblème *m*

emblematic(al) [,ɛmblə'mætɪk(əl)] *adj* emblématique

embodiment [ɛm'bɑdɪmənt] *s* personnification *f*, incarnation *f*

embod·y [ɛm'bɑdi] *v* (*pret* & *pp* **-ied**) *tr* personnifier, incarner; (*to include*) incorporer

embolden [ɛm'boldən] *tr* enhardir

embolism ['ɛmbə,lɪzəm] *s* embolie *f*

emboss [ɛm'bɔs] *tr* (*to raise in relief*) graver en relief; (*metal*) bosseler; (*e.g., leather*) gaufrer, repousser

embouchure [,ɑmbu'ʃur] *s* embouchure *f*; (*mus*) position *f* des lèvres

embrace [ɛm'bres] *s* étreinte *f*, embrassement *m* ‖ *tr* étreindre, embrasser ‖ *intr* s'étreindre, s'embrasser

embroider [ɛm'brɔɪdər] *tr* broder

embroider·y [ɛm'brɔɪdəri] *s* (*pl* **-ies**) broderie *f*

embroil [ɛm'brɔɪl] *tr* (*to throw into confusion*) embrouiller; (*to involve in contention*) brouiller

embroilment [ɛm'brɔɪlmənt] *s* embrouillage *m*, brouillamini *m*, imbroglio *m*

embry·o ['ɛmbrɪ,o] *s* (*pl* **-os**) embryon *m*

embryology [,ɛmbrɪ'ɑlədʒi] *s* embryologie *f*

embryonic [,ɛmbrɪ'ɑnɪk] *adj* embryonnaire

emend [ɪ'mɛnd] *tr* corriger

emendation [,imɛn'deʃən] *s* correction *f*

emerald ['ɛmərəld] *s* émeraude *f*

emerge [ɪ'mʌrdʒ] *intr* émerger

emergence [ɪ'mʌrdʒəns] *s* émergence *f*

emergen·cy [ɪ'mʌrdʒənsi] *adj* urgent, d'urgence; (*exit*) de secours ‖ *s* (*pl* **-cies**) cas *m* urgent

emer'gency brake' *s* frein *m* de secours

emer'gency ex'it *s* sortie *f* de secours

emer'gency land'ing *s* atterrissage *m* forcé

emer'gency opera'tion *s* (med) opération *f* à chaud

emer'gency ra'tions *spls* vivres *mpl* de réserve

emer'gency shut'down *s* arrêt *m* d'urgence

emer'gency ward' *s* salle *f* d'urgence

emeritus [ɪ'mɛrɪtəs] *adj* honoraire, d'honneur

emersion [ɪ'mʌrʒən] *s* émersion *f*

emery ['ɛməri] *s* émeri *m*

em'ery cloth' *s* toile *f* d'émeri

em'ery wheel' *s* meule *f* en émeri

emetic [ɪ'mɛtɪk] *adj* & *s* émétique *m*

emigrant ['ɛmɪgrənt] *adj* & *s* émigrant *m*

emigrate ['ɛmɪ,gret] *intr* émigrer

eminence ['ɛmɪnəns] *s* éminence *f*

eminent ['ɛmɪnənt] *adj* éminent; **most eminent** (eccl) éminentissime

emissar·y ['ɛmɪ,sɛri] *s* (*pl* **-ies**) émissaire *m*

emit [ɪ'mɪt] *v* (*pret* & *pp* **emitted**; *ger* **emitting**) *tr* émettre; (*a gas, an odor, etc.*) exhaler

emolument [ɪ'mɑljəmənt] *s* émoluments *mpl*

emotion [ɪ'moʃən] *s* émotion *f*

emotional [ɪ'moʃənəl] *adj* émotif, émotionnable

emperor ['ɛmpərər] *s* empereur *m*

empha·sis ['ɛmfəsɪs] *s* (*pl* **-ses** [,siz]) (*on an idea, event, project, etc.*) importance *f* accordée, mise *f* en relief, insistance *f*; (*on a word or phrase*) accent *m* d'insistance, accentuation *f*; **to place emphasis on** insister vivement sur, souligner; (*a word or syllable*) mettre l'accent sur; **with**

emphasis on en insistant particulièrement sur

emphasize ['ɛmfə,saɪz] *tr* appuyer sur, insister sur, mettre en relief, faire ressortir, souligner; (*a word or syllable*) mettre l'accent sur

emphatic [ɛm'fætɪk] *adj* accentué, énergique; (*denial*) catégorique

emphysema [,ɛmfɪ'simə] *s* emphysème *m*

empire ['ɛmpaɪr] *s* empire *m*

empiric(al) [ɛm'pɪrɪk(əl)] *adj* empirique

empiricist [ɛm'pɪrɪsɪst] *s* empirique *m*

emplacement [ɛm'plesmənt] *s* emplacement *m*

employ [ɛm'plɔɪ] *s* service *m* ‖ *tr* employer

employee [,ɛmplɔɪ'i] *s* employé *m*

employer [ɛm'plɔɪ·ər] *s* employeur *m*, patron *m*, chef *m*

employment [ɛm'plɔɪmənt] *s* emploi *m*

employ'ment a'gency *s* bureau *m* de placement

empower [ɛm'paʊ·ər] *tr* autoriser

empress ['ɛmprɪs] *s* impératrice *f*

emptiness ['ɛmptɪnɪs] *s* vide *m*

emp·ty ['ɛmpti] *adj* (*comp* **-tier;** *super* **-tiest**) vide; (*hollow*) creux, vain; (coll) affamé ‖ *v* (*pret & pp* **-tied**) *tr* vider ‖ *intr* se vider; (*said of river*) se jeter; (*said of auditorium*) se dégarnir

emp'ty-hand'ed *adj & adv* les mains vides

emp'ty-head'ed *adj* écervelé

empye·ma [,ɛmpɪ'imə] *s* (*pl* **-mata** [mətə]) empyème *m*

empyrean [,ɛmpɪ'ri·ən] *s* empyrée *m*

emu ['imju] *s* (zool) émeu *m*

emulate ['ɛmjə,let] *tr* chercher à égaler, imiter ‖ *intr* rivaliser

emulator ['ɛmjə,letər] *s* émule *mf*

emulsi·fy [ɪ'mʌlsɪ,faɪ] *v* (*pret & pp* **-fied**) *tr* émulsionner

emulsion [ɪ'mʌlʃən] *s* émulsion *f*

enable [ɛn'ebəl] *tr*—**to enable to** rendre capable de, mettre à même de

enact [ɛn'ækt] *tr* (*to decree*) décréter, arrêter; (theat) représenter

enactment [ɛn'æktmənt] *s* (*establishing*) établissement *m*; (govt) promulgation *f*; (law) décret *m*, arrêté *m*; (theat) représentation *f*

enam·el [ɪ'næməl] *s* émail *m* ‖ *v* (*pret & pp* **-eled** or **-elled;** *ger* **-eling** or **-elling**) *tr* émailler

enameling [ɪ'næməlɪŋ] *s* émaillage *m*

enam'el·ware' *s* ustensiles *mpl* en fer émaillé

enamor [ɛn'æmər] *tr* rendre amoureux; **to become enamored with** s'énamourer de

encamp [ɛn'kæmp] *tr & intr* camper

encampment [ɛn'kæmpmənt] *s* campement *m*

encase [ɛn'kes] *tr* mettre en caisse; enfermer, envelopper

encephalitis [ɛn,sɛfə'laɪtɪs] *s* encéphalite *f*

enchain [ɛn'tʃen] *tr* enchaîner

enchant [ɛn'tʃænt] *tr* enchanter

enchanting [ɛn'tʃæntɪŋ] *adj* charmant, ravissant; (*casting a spell*) enchanteur

enchantment [ɛn'tʃæntmənt] *s* enchantement *m*

enchantress [ɛn'tʃæntrɪs] *s* enchanteresse *f*

encircle [ɛn'sʌrkəl] *tr* encercler, cerner; (*a word*) entourer d'un cercle

enclitic [ɛn'klɪtɪk] *adj & s* enclitique *m*

enclose [ɛn'kloz] *tr* enclore, entourer; (*in a letter*) inclure, joindre

enclosed *adj* (*surrounded*) entouré; (*fenced in*) clôturé; (*covered*) couvert; (*with a letter*) ci-joint, ci-inclus

enclosure [ɛn'kloʒər] *s* clôture *f*, enceinte *f*, enclos *m*; (*e.g., in a letter*) pièce *f* jointe, pièce annexée

encomi·um [ɛn'komi·əm] *s* (*pl* **-ums** or **-a** [ə]) panégyrique *m*, éloge *m*

encompass [ɛn'kʌmpəs] *tr* entourer, renfermer

encore ['ankor] *s* rappel *m*, bis *m* ‖ *tr* bisser ‖ *interj* bis!

encounter [ɛn'kaʊntər] *s* rencontre *f* ‖ *tr* rencontrer ‖ *intr* se rencontrer, combattre

encourage [ɛn'kʌrɪdʒ] *tr* encourager

encouragement [ɛn'kʌrɪdʒmənt] *s* encouragement *m*

encroach [ɛn'krotʃ] *intr*—**to encroach on** or **upon** empiéter sur; abuser de

encumber [ɛn'kʌmbər] *tr* encombrer, embarrasser; (*with debts*) grever

encumbrance [ɛn'kʌmbrəns] *s* encombrement *m*, embarras *m*; (law) charge *f*

encyclical [ɛn'sɪklɪkəl] *adj & s* encyclique *f*

encyclopedia [ɛn,saɪklə'pidɪ·ə] *s* encyclopédie *f*

encyclopedic [ɛn,saɪklə'pidɪk] *adj* encyclopédique

end [ɛnd] *s* (*in time*) fin *f*; (*in space; small piece*) bout *m*; (*purpose*) but *m*; (*end of set period of time*) terme *m*; **at loose ends** en pagaille; **at the end, in the end** à la fin; **to be at the end of one's rope** être au bout de son rouleau; **to bring to an end** mettre fin à; **to come to an end** prendre fin; **to make both ends meet** joindre les deux bouts; **to stand on end** (*said of hair*) se dresser; **to this end** à cet effet ‖ *tr* achever, terminer ‖ *intr* s'achever, se terminer; **to end up by** finir par; **to end with** (or in) se terminer par

endanger [ɛn'dendʒər] *tr* mettre en danger

endear [ɛn'dɪr] *tr* faire aimer; **to endear oneself to** se faire aimer de

endeavor [ɛn'dɛvər] *s* effort *m*, tentative *f* ‖ *intr*—**to endeavor to** s'efforcer de, tâcher de

endemic [ɛn'dɛmɪk] *adj* endémique

ending ['ɛndɪŋ] *s* fin *f*, terminaison *f*; (gram) désinence *f*

endive ['ɛndaɪv] *s* (*blanched type*) endive *f*; (*Cichorium endivia*) chicorée *f* frisée

endless ['ɛndlɪs] *adj* sans fin

end'most' *adj* extrême

endocrine ['ɛndokrɪn] *adj* endocrine

endorse [ɛn'dɔrs] *tr* endosser; (*a candidate*) appuyer; (*a plan*) souscrire à

endorsement [ɛn'dɔrsmənt] *s* endos *m*, endossement *m*; (*approval*) appui *m*, approbation *f*
endorser [ɛn'dɔrsər] *s* endosseur *m*
endow [ɛn'dau] *tr* doter, fonder
endowment [ɛn'daumənt] *s* dotation *f*, fondation *f*; (*talent*) don *m*
endow'ment fund' *s* caisse *f* de dotation
end' pa'per *s* pages *fpl* de garde
endurance [ɛn'd(j)urəns] *s* endurance *f*
endur'ance test' *s* épreuve *f* d'endurance
endure [ɛn'd(j)ur] *tr* endurer ‖ *intr* durer
enduring [ɛn'd(j)urɪŋ] *adj* durable
enema ['ɛnəmə] *s* lavement *m*
ene·my ['ɛnəmi] *adj* ennemi ‖ *s* (*pl* -mies) ennemi *m*
en'emy al'ien *s* étranger *m* ennemi
energetic [,ɛnər'dʒɛtɪk] *adj* énergique
energizing ['ɛnər,dʒaɪzɪŋ] *adj* énergétique
ener·gy ['ɛnərdʒi] *s* (*pl* -gies) énergie *f*
en'ergy bal'ance *s* (nucl) bilan *m* énergétique
enervate ['ɛnər,vet] *tr* énerver
enfeeble [ɛn'fibəl] *tr* affaiblir
enfold [ɛn'fold] *tr* envelopper, enrouler; (*to embrace*) embrasser
enforce [ɛn'fors] *tr* (*a law*) faire exécuter, mettre en vigueur; (*one's rights, one's point of view*) faire valoir, appuyer; (*e.g., obedience*) imposer
enforcement [ɛn'forsmənt] *s* contrainte *f*; (*of a law*) exécution *f*, mise *f* en vigueur
enfranchise [ɛn'fræntʃaɪz] *tr* affranchir; donner le droit de vote à
engage [ɛn'gedʒ] *tr* engager; (*to hire*) engager, embaucher; (*to reserve*) retenir, réserver, louer; (*s.o.'s attention*) fixer, attirer; (*the clutch*) embrayer; (*toothed wheels*) engrener; **to be engaged in** s'occuper de; **to be engaged to be married** être fiancé; **to engage s.o. in conversation** entamer une conversation avec qn ‖ *intr* s'engager; (mach) engrener; **to engage in** s'embarquer dans, entrer en or dans
engaged *adj* (*to be married*) fiancé; (*busy*) occupé, pris; (mach) en prise; (mil) aux prises, aux mains
engagement [ɛn'gedʒmənt] *s* engagement *m*; (*betrothal*) fiançailles *fpl*; (*appointment*) rendez-vous *m*; (mach) embrayage *m*, engrenage *m*; (mil) engagement, combat *m*
engage'ment ring' *s* bague *f* or anneau *m* de fiançailles
engaging [ɛn'gedʒɪŋ] *adj* engageant, attirant
engender [ɛn'dʒɛndər] *tr* engendrer
engine ['ɛndʒɪn] *s* machine *f*; (*of automobile*) moteur *m*
engineer [,ɛndʒə'nɪr] *s* ingénieur *m*; (*engine driver*) mécanicien *m* ‖ *tr* diriger or construire en qualité d'ingénieur; (coll) manigancer, machiner
engineer' corps' *s* génie *m*
engineering [,ɛndʒə'nɪrɪŋ] *s* ingénierie *f*

en'gine house' *s* dépôt *m* de pompes à incendie
en'gine·man' *s* (*pl* -men') mécanicien *m*
en'gine room' *s* chambre *f* des machines
en'gine-room tel'egraph *s* (naut) transmetteur *m* d'ordres
en'gine trou'ble *s* panne *f* de moteur
England ['ɪŋglənd] *s* Angleterre *f*; l'Angleterre
English ['ɪŋglɪʃ] *adj* anglais ‖ *s* (*language*) anglais *m*; (billiards) effet *m*; **the English** les Anglais
Eng'lish Chan'nel *s* Manche *f*
Eng'lish dai'sy *s* marguerite *f* des champs
Eng'lish horn' *s* cor *m* anglais
Eng'lish·man *s* (*pl* -men) Anglais *m*
Eng'lish-speak'ing *adj* anglophone, d'expression anglaise; (*country*) de langue anglaise
Eng'lish·wom'an *s* (*pl* -wom'en) Anglaise *f*
engraft [ɛn'græft] *tr* greffer; (fig) implanter
engrave [ɛn'grev] *tr* graver
engraver [ɛn'grevər] *s* graveur *m*
engraving [ɛn'grevɪŋ] *s* gravure *f*
engross [ɛn'gros] *tr* absorber, occuper; (*a document*) grossoyer
engrossing [ɛn'grosɪŋ] *adj* absorbant
engulf [ɛn'gʌlf] *tr* engouffrer, engloutir
enhance [ɛn'hæns] *tr* rehausser, relever
enhancement [ɛn'hænsmənt] *s* rehaussement *m*
enigma [ɪ'nɪgmə] *s* énigme *f*
enigmatic(al) [,ɪnɪg'mætɪk(əl)] *adj* énigmatique
enjoin [ɛn'dʒɔɪn] *tr* enjoindre; (*to forbid*) interdire
enjoy [ɛn'dʒɔɪ] *tr* jouir de; **to enjoy +** *ger* prendre plaisir à + *inf*; **to enjoy oneself** s'amuser, se divertir
enjoyable [ɛn'dʒɔɪ·əbəl] *adj* agréable, plaisant; (*show, party, etc.*) divertissant
enjoyment [ɛn'dʒɔɪmənt] *s* (*pleasure*) plaisir *m*; (*pleasurable use*) jouissance *f*
enkindle [ɛn'kɪndəl] *tr* allumer
enlarge [ɛn'lardʒ] *tr* agrandir, élargir; (phot) agrandir ‖ *intr* s'agrandir, s'élargir; **to enlarge on** or **upon** discourir longuement sur, amplifier
enlargement [ɛn'lardʒmənt] *s* agrandissement *m*
enlighten [ɛn'laɪtən] *tr* éclairer
enlightenment [ɛn'laɪtənmənt] *s* éclaircissements *mpl*; **the Enlightenment** le siècle des lumières
enlist [ɛn'lɪst] *tr* enrôler ‖ *intr* s'enrôler, s'engager
enlist'ed man' *s* homme *m* de troupe
enlistment [ɛn'lɪstmənt] *s* enrôlement *m*, engagement *m*
enliven [ɛn'laɪvən] *tr* animer, égayer
enmesh [ɛn'mɛʃ] *tr* prendre dans les rets; (*e.g., in an evil design*) empêtrer; (mach) engrener
enmi·ty ['ɛnmɪti] *s* (*pl* -ties) inimitié *f*
ennoble [ɛn'nobəl] *tr* ennoblir; (*to confer a title of nobility upon*) anoblir

ennui [ˈɑnwi] *s* ennui *m*

enormous [ɪˈnɔrməs] *adj* énorme

enormously [ɪˈnɔrməsli] *adv* énormément

enough [ɪˈnʌf] *adj, s, & adv* assez; **more than enough** plus qu'il n'en faut; **that's enough!** en voilà assez!; **to be intelligent enough** être assez intelligent; **to have enough to live on** avoir de quoi vivre ‖ *interj* assez!, ça suffit!

enounce [ɪˈnaʊns] *tr* énoncer

enrage [ɛnˈredʒ] *tr* faire enrager, rendre furieux; **to be enraged** enrager

enrapture [ɛnˈræptʃər] *tr* ravir, transporter

enrich [ɛnˈrɪtʃ] *tr* enrichir

enrichment [ɛnˈrɪtʃmənt] *s* enrichissement *m*

enroll [ɛnˈrol] *tr* enrôler; (*a student*) inscrire; (*to wrap up*) enrouler ‖ *intr* s'enrôler; (*said of student*) prendre ses inscriptions, se faire inscrire

enrollment [ɛnˈrolmənt] *s* enrôlement *m*; (*of a student*) inscription *f*; (*wrapping up*) enroulement *m*

ensconce [ɛnˈskɑns] *tr* cacher; **to ensconce oneself** s'installer

ensemble [ɑnˈsɑmbəl] *s* ensemble *m*

ensign [ˈɛnsaɪn] *s* enseigne *f* ‖ [ˈɛnsən] *s* (nav) enseigne *m* de deuxième classe

ensilage [ˈɛnsɪlɪdʒ] *s* fourrage *m* d'un silo américain ‖ *tr* ensiler

enslave [ɛnˈslev] *tr* asservir, réduire en esclavage

enslavement [ɛnˈslevmənt] *s* asservissement *m*

ensnare [ɛnˈsnɛr] *tr* prendre au piège, attraper

ensue [ɛnˈs(j)u] *intr* s'ensuivre, résulter

ensuing [ɛnˈs(j)u·ɪŋ] *adj* suivant

ensure [ɛnˈʃʊr] *tr* assurer, garantir

entail [ɛnˈtel] *tr* occasionner, entraîner

entangle [ɛnˈtæŋgəl] *tr* embrouiller

entanglement [ɛnˈtæŋgəlmənt] *s* embrouillement *m*, embarras *m*

enter [ˈɛntər] *tr* (*a room, a house, etc.*) entrer dans; (*a school, the army, etc.*) entrer à; (*e.g., a period of convalescence*) entrer en; (*a highway, a public square, etc.*) déboucher sur; (*e.g., a club*) devenir membre de; (*a request*) enregistrer, consigner par écrit; (*a student, a contestant, etc.*) admettre, faire inscrire; (*in the customhouse*) déclarer; (*to make a record of*) inscrire, porter; **to enter one's name for** se faire inscrire à or pour ‖ *intr* entrer; (theat) entrer en scène; **to enter into** entrer à, dans, or en; (*to be an ingredient of*) entrer pour; **to enter on** or **upon** entreprendre, débuter dans

enterprise [ˈɛntər‚praɪz] *s* (*undertaking*) entreprise *f*; (*spirit, push*) esprit *m* d'entreprise, allant *m*, entrain *m*

enterprising [ˈɛntər‚praɪzɪŋ] *adj* entreprenant

entertain [‚ɛntərˈten] *tr* (*to distract*) amuser, divertir; (*to show hospitality to*) recevoir; (*at a meal*) régaler; (*a hope*) entretenir,

nourrir; (*an idea*) concevoir ‖ *intr* recevoir

entertainer [‚ɛntərˈtenər] *s* (*host*) hôte *m*, amphitryon *m*; amuseur *m*; (*comedian*) comique *mf*

entertaining [‚ɛntərˈtenɪŋ] *adj* amusant, divertissant

entertainment [‚ɛntərˈtenmənt] *s* (*distraction*) amusement *m*, divertissement *m*; (*show*) spectacle *m*; (*as a guest*) accueil *m*, hospitalité *f*

enˈterˈtainˈment tax' *s* taxe *f* sur les spectacles

enthrall [ɛnˈθrɔl] *tr* (*to charm*) captiver, charmer; (*to enslave*) asservir, rendre esclave

enthrone [ɛnˈθron] *tr* introniser

enthuse [ɛnˈθ(j)uz] *tr* (coll) enthousiasmer ‖ *intr* (coll) s'enthousiasmer

enthusiasm [ɛnˈθ(j)uzɪ‚æzəm] *s* enthousiasme *m*

enthusiast [ɛnˈθ(j)uzɪ‚æst] *s* enthousiaste *mf*; (*camera fiend, sports fan, etc.*) fanatique *mf*, enragé *m*

enthusiastic [ɛn‚θ(j)uzɪˈæstɪk] *adj* enthousiaste; (*for sports, music, a hobby*) fanatique, enragé

entice [ɛnˈtaɪs] *tr* attirer, séduire; (*to evil*) tenter, chercher à séduire

enticement [ɛnˈtaɪsmənt] *s* attrait *m*, appât *m*; tentation *f*, séduction *f*

entire [ɛnˈtaɪr] *adj* entier

entirely [ɛnˈtaɪrli] *adv* entièrement, en entier; (*absolutely*) tout à fait, absolument

entire·ty [ɛnˈtaɪrti] *s* (*pl* **-ties**) totalité *f*, entier *m*; **in its entirety** dans sa totalité

entitle [ɛnˈtaɪtəl] *tr* (*to name*) intituler; (*to qualify*) donner le droit à; **to be entitled to** avoir droit à

enti·ty [ˈɛntɪti] *s* (*pl* **-ties**) entité *f*

entomb [ɛnˈtum] *tr* ensevelir

entombment [ɛnˈtummənt] *s* ensevelissement *m*

entomology [‚ɛntəˈmɑlədʒi] *s* entomologie *f*

entourage [‚ɑntuˈrɑʒ] *s* entourage *m*

entrails [ˈɛntrelz] *spl* entrailles *fpl*

entrain [ɛnˈtren] *tr* faire prendre le train, embarquer; (*to carry along*) entraîner ‖ *intr* embarquer, s'embarquer

entrance [ˈɛntrəns] *s* entrée *f*; (theat) entrée en scène; **entrance to . . .** (public sign) accès à . . . ‖ [ɛnˈtræns], [ɛnˈtrɑns] *tr* enchanter, ensorceler; **to be entranced** s'extasier

enˈtrance examinaˈtion *s* examen *m* d'entrée

enˈtrance fee' *s* prix *m* d'entrée, droit *m* d'entrée

entrancing [ɛnˈtrænsɪŋ] *adj* enchanteur, ensorceleur

entrant [ˈɛntrənt] *s* inscrit *m*; (*in a competition*) concurrent *m*, participant *m*

en·trap [ɛnˈtræp] *v* (*pret & pp* **-trapped**; *ger* **-trapping**) *tr* attraper

entreat [ɛnˈtrit] *tr* supplier, prier, conjurer

entreat·y [ɛnˈtriti] *s* (*pl* **-ies**) supplication *f*, prière *f*

entree [ˈɑntre] *s* (*entrance; course preceding the roast*) entrée *f*; (*main dish*) plat *m* de résistance

entrench [ɛnˈtrɛntʃ] *tr* retrancher; **to be entrenched** se retrancher ‖ *intr*—**to entrench on** or **upon** empiéter sur

entrust [ɛnˈtrʌst] *tr*—**to entrust s.o. with s.th., to entrust s.th. to s.o.** confier q.ch. à qn

en·try [ˈɛntri] *s* (*pl* **-tries**) entrée *f*; (*in a dictionary*) article *m*, entrée; (*on a register*) inscription *f*; (*in a competition*) concurrent *m*, participant *m*; (*thing entered for judging in a competition*) objet *m* exposé

en'try blank' *s* feuille *f* d'inscription

en'try vi'sa *s* visa *m* d'entrée

en'try word' *s* (*of a dictionary*) mot *m* d'entrée, mot-souche *m*, entrée *f*, adresse *f*

entwine [ɛnˈtwaɪn] *tr* entrelacer, enlacer ‖ *intr* s'entrelacer, s'enlacer

enumerate [ɪˈn(j)uməˌret] *tr* énumérer

enunciate [ɪˈnʌnsɪˌet] *tr* énoncer, déclarer; (*to articulate*) articuler, prononcer

envelop [ɛnˈvɛləp] *tr* envelopper

envelope [ˈɛnvəˌlop], [ˈɑnvəˌlop] *s* enveloppe *f*; **in an envelope** sous enveloppe, sous pli

envenom [ɛnˈvɛnəm] *tr* envenimer, empoisonner

enviable [ˈɛnvɪ·əbəl] *adj* enviable, digne d'envie

envious [ˈɛnvɪ·əs] *adj* envieux

environment [ɛnˈvaɪrənmənt] *s* environnement *m*, milieu *m*

environmental [ɛnˌvaɪrənˈmɛntəl] *adj* écologique, du milieu

environs [ɛnˈvaɪrənz] *spl* environs *mpl*

envisage [ɛnˈvɪzɪdʒ] *tr* envisager

envoi [ˈɛnvɔɪ] *s* envoi *m*

envoy [ˈɛnvɔɪ] *s* envoyé *m*, émissaire *m*; (*of poem*) envoi *m*

en·vy [ˈɛnvi] *s* (*pl* **-vies**) envie *f* ‖ *v* (*pret & pp* **-vied**) *tr* envier

enzyme [ˈɛnzaɪm] *s* enzyme *m & f*

epaulet [ˈɛpəˌlɛt] *s* épaulette *f*

epergne [ɪˈpʌrn], [eˈpɛrn] *s* surtout *m*

ephemeral [ɪˈfɛmərəl] *adj* éphémère

epic [ˈɛpɪk] *adj* épique ‖ *s* épopée *f*

epicure [ˈɛpɪˌkjʊr] *s* gourmet *m*, gastronome *m*

epidemic [ˌɛpɪˈdɛmɪk] *adj* épidémique ‖ *s* épidémie *f*

epidemiology [ˌɛpɪˌdimɪˈɑlədʒi] *s* épidémiologie *f*

epidermis [ˌɛpɪˈdʌrmɪs] *s* épiderme *m*

epiglottis [ˌɛpɪˈglɑtɪs] *s* épiglotte *f*

epigram [ˈɛpɪˌgræm] *s* épigramme *f*

epilepsy [ˈɛpɪˌlɛpsi] *s* épilepsie *f*

epileptic [ˌɛpɪˈlɛptɪk] *adj & s* épileptique *mf*

epilogue [ˈɛpɪˌlɔg] *s* épilogue *m*

episcopal [ɪˈpɪskəpəl] *adj* épiscopal

Episcopalian [ɪˌpɪskəˈpelɪ·ən] *adj* épiscopal ‖ *s* épiscopal *m*

episode [ˈɛpɪˌsod] *s* épisode *m*

episodic [ˌɛpɪˈsɑdɪk] *adj* épisodique

epistle [ɪˈpɪsəl] *s* épître *f*

epitaph [ˈɛpɪˌtæf] *s* épitaphe *f*

epithet [ˈɛpɪˌθɛt] *s* épithète *f*

epitome [ɪˈpɪtəmi] *s* (*abridgment*) épitomé *m*; (*representative of a class*) modèle *m*, personnification *f*

epitomize [ɪˈpɪtəˌmaɪz] *tr* abréger; personnifier

epoch [ˈipɑk] *s* époque *f*

epochal [ˈɛpəkəl] *adj* mémorable

ep'och-mak'ing *adj* qui fait époque

epoxy [ɪˈpɑksi] *s* résine *f* époxyde

Ep'som salts' [ˈɛpsəm] *spl* epsomite *f*, sels *mpl* d'Epsom

equable [ˈɛkwəbəl], [ˈikwəbəl] *adj* uniforme, égal; tranquille

equal [ˈikwəl] *adj* égal; **to be equal to** égaler, valoir; (*e.g., the occasion*) être à la hauteur de; **to be equal to** + *ger* être de force à + *inf*, être à même de + *inf*; **to get equal with** (coll) se venger de ‖ *s* égal *m*, pareil *m* ‖ *v* (*pret & pp* **equaled** or **equalled**; *ger* **equaling** or **equalling**) *tr* égaler

equali·ty [ɪˈkwɑlɪti] *s* (*pl* **-ties**) égalité *f*

equalize [ˈikwəˌlaɪz] *tr* égaliser

equally [ˈikwəli] *adv* également

e'qual opportu'nity *s* chances *fpl* égales

equanimity [ˌikwəˈnɪmɪti] *s* équanimité *f*, égalité *f* d'âme

equate [iˈkwet] *tr* égaliser, mettre en équation

equation [iˈkweʒən] *s* équation *f*

equator [iˈkwetər] *s* équateur *m*

equatorial [ˌikwəˈtorɪ·əl] *adj* équatorial

equestrian [ɪˈkwɛstrɪ·ən] *adj* équestre ‖ *s* cavalier *m*, écuyer *m*

equilateral [ˌikwɪˈlætərəl] *adj* équilatéral

equilibrium [ˌikwɪˈlɪbrɪ·əm] *s* équilibre *m*

equinoctial [ˌikwɪˈnɑkʃəl] *adj* équinoxial

equinox [ˈikwɪˌnɑks] *s* équinoxe *m*

equip [ɪˈkwɪp] *v* (*pret & pp* **equipped**; *ger* **equipping**) *tr* équiper, outiller; **to equip with** munir de

equipment [ɪˈkwɪpmənt] *s* équipement *m*, matériel *m*, appareillage *m*

equipoise [ˈikwɪˌpɔɪz], [ˈɛkwɪˌpɔɪz] *s* équilibre *m* ‖ *tr* équilibrer

equitable [ˈɛkwɪtəbəl] *adj* équitable

equi·ty [ˈɛkwɪti] *s* (*pl* **-ties**) équité *f*; (com) part *f* résiduaire

equivalent [ɪˈkwɪvələnt] *adj & s* équivalent *m*

equivocal [ɪˈkwɪvəkəl] *adj* équivoque

equivocate [ɪˈkwɪvəˌket] *intr* équivoquer

equivocation [ɪˌkwɪvəˈkeʃən] *s* tergiversation *f*, équivoque *f*

era [ˈɪrə] *s* ère *f*, époque *f*

eradicate [ɪˈrædɪˌket] *tr* déraciner, extirper

erase [ɪˈres] *tr* effacer, biffer

eraser [ɪˈresər] *s* gomme *f* à effacer; brosse *f*

erasure [ɪˈreʃər] *s* effacement *m*, rature *f*

ere [ɛr] *prep* (poetic) avant ‖ *conj* (poetic) avant que

erect [ɪˈrɛkt] *adj* droit, debout ‖ *tr* (*to set in an upright position*) dresser, élever; (*a* *building*) ériger, édifier; (*a machine*) monter

erection [ɪˈrɛkʃən] *s* érection *f*

erg [ʌrg] *s* erg *m*

ermine [ˈʌrmɪn] *s* hermine *f*

erode [ɪˈrod] *tr* éroder

erosion [ɪˈroʒən] *s* érosion *f*

erotic [ɪˈrɑtɪk] *adj* érotique

err [ʌr] *intr* se tromper, faire erreur, errer; (*to do wrong*) s'égarer, pécher

errand [ˈɛrənd] *s* commission *f*, course *f*; **to go on** or **to run an errand** faire une course

er'rand boy' *s* coursier *m*, garçon *m* de courses

erratic [ɪˈrætɪk] *adj* variable; capricieux, excentrique

erroneous [ɪˈronɪ·əs] *adj* erroné

error [ˈɛrər] *s* erreur *f*

erudite [ˈɛr(j)ʊˌdaɪt] *adj* érudit

erudition [ˌɛr(j)ʊˈdɪʃən] *s* érudition *f*

erupt [ɪˈrʌpt] *intr* faire éruption

eruption [ɪˈrʌpʃən] *s* éruption *f*

escalate [ˈɛskəˌlet] *tr* escalader

escalation [ˌɛskəˈleʃən] *s* escalade *f*

escalator [ˈɛskəˌletər] *s* escalator *m*, escalier *m* mécanique or roulant

es'calator clause' *s* clause *f* d'indexation

escallop [ɛsˈkæləp] *s* (*seafood*) coquille *f* Saint-Jacques, peigne *m*, pétoncle *m*; (*culin*) coquille au gratin ‖ *tr* (culin) gratiner et cuire au four et à la crème; (culin) servir en coquille

escapade [ˌɛskəˈped] *s* fredaine *f*, frasque *f*; (*getting away*) escapade *f*

escape [ɛsˈkep] *s* (*getaway*) évasion *f*, fuite *f*; (*from responsibilities, duties, etc.*) évasion, escapade *f*; (*of gas, liquid, etc.*) échappement *m*, fuite *f*; (*of a clock*) échappement; **to have a narrow escape** l'échapper belle; **to make one's escape** se sauver, s'échapper ‖ *tr* échapper à, éviter ‖ *intr* échapper, s'échapper, s'évader; **to escape from** échapper à

escape' clause' *s* échappatoire *f*

escapee [ˌɛskəˈpi] *s* évadé *m*, échappé *m*

escape' hatch' *s* (aer) sas *m* d'évacuation

escapement [ɛsˈkepmənt] *s* issue *f*, débouché *m*; (mach) échappement *m*

escape' wheel' *s* roue *f* de rencontre

escarole [ˈɛskəˌrol] *s* scarole *f*

escarpment [ɛsˈkɑrpmənt] *s* escarpement *m*

eschew [ɛsˈtʃu] *tr* éviter, s'abstenir de

escort [ˈɛskɔrt] *s* escorte *f*; (*gentleman escort*) cavalier *m* ‖ [ɛsˈkɔrt] *tr* escorter

escutcheon [ɛsˈkʌtʃən] *s* écusson *m*

Eski·mo [ˈɛskɪˌmo] *adj* eskimo, esquimau ‖ *s* (*pl* **-mos** or **-mo**) (*language; dog*) esquimau *m*; (*person*) Eskimo *m*, Esquimau *m*

Es'kimo wom'an *s* Esquimaude *f*, femme *f* esquimau

esopha·gus [iˈsɑfəgəs] *s* (*pl* **-gi** [ˌdʒaɪ]) œsophage *m*

esoteric [ˌɛsoˈtɛrɪk] *adj* ésotérique

especial [ɛsˈpɛʃəl] *adj* spécial

especially [ɛsˈpɛʃəli] *adv* surtout, particulièrement

Esperanto [ˌɛspəˈrɑnto] *s* espéranto *m*

espionage [ˌɛspɪ·əˈnɑʒ] *s* espionnage *m*

espousal [ɛsˈpauzəl] *s* épousailles *f*; **espousal of** (*a cause*) adoption de, adhésion à

espouse [ɛsˈpauz] *tr* épouser; (*to advocate, adopt*) adopter, embrasser

Esq. *abbr* (**Esquire**)—**John Smith, Esq.** Monsieur Jean Smith

esquire [ˈɛskwaɪr] *s* (hist) écuyer *m*

essay [ˈɛse] *s* essai *m* ‖ *tr* essayer

essayist [ˈɛse·ɪst] *s* essayiste *mf*

essence [ˈɛsəns] *s* essence *f*

essential [ɛˈsɛnʃəl] *adj & s* essentiel *m*

essentially [əˈsɛnʃəli] *adv* essentiellement, avant tout, au premier chef

establish [ɛsˈtæblɪʃ] *tr* établir

establishment [ɛsˈtæblɪʃmənt] *s* établissement *m*; **the Establishment** (pol) les pouvoirs *mpl* établis, les milieux *mpl* dirigeants

estate [ɛsˈtet] *s* (*landed property*) domaine *m*, propriété *f*, terres *fpl*; (*a person's possessions*) biens *mpl*, possessions *fpl*; (*left by a decedent*) héritage *m*, succession *f*; (*social status*) rang *m*, condition *f*; (hist) état *m*

esteem [ɛsˈtim] *s* estime *f* ‖ *tr* estimer

esthete [ˈɛsθit] *s* esthète *mf*

esthetic [ɛsˈθɛtɪk] *adj* esthétique ‖ **esthetics** *s* esthétique *f*

estimable [ˈɛstɪməbəl] *adj* estimable

estimate [ˈɛstɪˌmet] *s* évaluation *f*, appréciation *f*; (*appraisal*) estimation *f* ‖ *tr* (*to judge, deem*) apprécier, estimer; (*the cost*) estimer, évaluer

estimation [ˌɛstɪˈmeʃən] *s* (*opinion*) jugement *m*; (*esteem*) estime *f*; (*appraisal*) estimation *f*; **in my estimation** à mon avis

estrangement [ɛsˈtrendʒmənt] *s* éloignement *m*; (*a becoming unfriendly*) désaffection *f*

estuar·y [ˈɛstʃu·ˌɛri] *s* (*pl* **-ies**) estuaire *m*

etc. *abbr* (Lat **et cetera** and so on) et c., et ainsi de suite

etch [ɛtʃ] *tr & intr* graver à l'eau-forte

etcher [ˈɛtʃər] *s* aquafortiste *m*

etching [ˈɛtʃɪŋ] *s* eau-forte *f*

eternal [ɪˈtʌrnəl] *adj* éternel

eterni·ty [ɪˈtʌrnɪti] *s* (*pl* **-ties**) éternité *f*

ether [ˈiθər] *s* éther *m*

ethereal [ɪˈθɪrɪ·əl] *adj* éthéré

ethical [ˈɛθɪkəl] *adj* éthique

ethics [ˈɛθɪks] *s* (*branch of philosophy*) étique *f*, morale *f*; spl (*one's conduct, one's moral principles*) morale

Ethiopia [ˌiθɪˈopɪ·ə] *s* Éthiopie *f*; l'Éthiopie

Ethiopian [ˌiθɪˈopɪ·ən] *adj* éthiopien ‖ *s* (*language*) éthiopien *m*; (*person*) Éthiopien *m*

ethnic(al) [ˈɛθnɪk(əl)] *adj* ethnique

ethnography [ɛθˈnɑgrəfi] *s* ethnographie *f*

ethnology [ɛθˈnɑlədʒi] *s* ethnologie *f*

ethyl [ˈɛθɪl] *s* éthyle *m*

ethylene [ˈɛθɪˌlin] *s* éthylène *m*

etiquette [ˈɛtɪˌkɛt] *s* étiquette *f*

etymolo·gy [ˌɛtɪˈmɑlədʒi] *s* (*pl* **-gies**) étymologie *f*

ety·mon [ˈɛtɪˌmɑn] *s* (*pl* **-mons** or **-ma** [mə]) étymon *m*

eucalyp·tus [ˌjukəˈlɪptəs] *s* (*pl* **-tuses** or **-ti** [taɪ]) eucalyptus *m*

Eucharist [ˈjukərɪst] *s* Eucharistie *f*

euchre [ˈjukər] *s* euchre *m* ‖ *tr* (coll) l'emporter sur

eulogize [ˈjuləˌdʒaɪz] *tr* faire l'éloge de

eulo·gy [ˈjulədʒi] *s* (*pl* **-gies**) éloge *m*

eunuch [ˈjunək] *s* eunuque *m*

euphemism [ˈjufɪˌmɪzəm] *s* euphémisme *m*

euphemistic [ˌjufɪˈmɪstɪk] *adj* euphémique

euphonic [juˈfɑnɪk] *adj* euphonique

eupho·ny [ˈjufəni] *s* (*pl* **-nies**) euphonie *f*

euphoria [juˈforɪ·ə] *s* euphorie *f*

euphuism [ˈjufjuˌɪzəm] *s* euphuisme *m*; préciosité *f*

Europe [ˈjurəp] *s* Europe *f*; l'Europe

European [ˌjurəˈpi·ən] *adj* européen ‖ *s* Européen *m*

euthanasia [ˌjuθəˈneʒə] *s* euthanasie *f*

evacuate [ɪˈvækjuˌet] *tr* évacuer ‖ *intr* s'évacuer

evade [ɪˈved] *tr* échapper à, éviter, esquiver ‖ *intr* s'évader

evaluate [ɪˈvæljuˌet] *tr* évaluer

Evangel [ɪˈvændʒəl] *s* évangile *m*

evangelic(al) [ˌɛvənˈdʒɛlɪk(əl)] *adj* évangélique

evangelist [ɪˈvændʒəlɪst] *s* évangéliste *m*

evaporate [ɪˈvæpəˌret] *tr* évaporer ‖ *intr* s'évaporer

evasion [ɪˈveʒən] *s* évasion *f*; subterfuge *m*, détour *m*

evasive [ɪˈvesɪv] *adj* évasif

eve [iv] *s* veille *f*; (poetic) soir *m*; **on the eve of** à la veille de; **Eve** Ève *f*

even [ˈivən] *adj* (smooth) uni; (number) pair; (equal, uniform) égal; (temperament) calme, rassis, égal; **even with** à fleur de; **to be even** être quitte; (cards, sports) être manche à manche or point à point; **to get even with** (coll) rendre la pareille à ‖ *adv* même; **even** + *comp* encore + *comp*, e.g., **even better** encore mieux; **even so** quand même ‖ *tr* aplanir, égaliser

evening [ˈivnɪŋ] *adj* du soir ‖ *s* soir *m*; **all evening** toute la soirée; **every evening** tous les soirs; **in the evening** le soir; **the evening before** la veille au soir

eve′ning clothes′ *s* tenue *f* de soirée; (for women) toilette *f* de soirée; (for men) habit *m* de soirée

eve′ning damp′ *s* serein *m*

eve′ning gown′ *s* robe *f* du soir

eve′ning prim′rose *s* onagraire *f*

eve′ning star′ *s* étoile *f* du soir, étoile du berger

eve′ning wrap′ *s* sortie *f* de bal

e′ven·song′ *s* (eccl) vêpres *fpl*

event [ɪˈvɛnt] *s* événement *m*; **at all events** or **in any event** en tout cas; **in the event that** dans le cas où

eventful [ɪˈvɛntfəl] *adj* mouvementé; mémorable

eventual [ɪˈvɛntʃu·əl] *adj* final

eventuali·ty [ɪˌvɛntʃuˈælɪti] *s* (*pl* **-ties**) éventualité *f*

eventually [ɪˈvɛntʃu·əli] *adv* finalement, à la longue, en fin de compte

eventuate [ɪˈvɛntʃuˌet] *intr*—**to eventuate in** se terminer par, aboutir à

ever [ˈɛvər] *adv* (at all times) toujours; (at any time) jamais; **ever since** dès lors, depuis; **for ever and ever** à tout jamais; **hardly ever** presque jamais

ev′er·glade′ *s* région *f* marécageuse

ev′er·green′ *adj* toujours vert ‖ *s* arbre *m* vert; **evergreens** plantes *fpl* vertes, verdure *f* décorative

ev′er·last′ing *adj* éternel; (continual) sempiternel, perpétuel

ev′er·more′ *adv* toujours; **for evermore** à jamais

every [ˈɛvri] *adj* tous les; (each) chaque, tout; (coll) tout, e.g., **every bit as good as** tout aussi bon que; **every man for himself** sauve qui peut; **every now and then** de temps en temps; **every once in a while** de temps à autre; **every other day** tous les deux jours; **every other one** un sur deux; **every which way** (coll) de tous côtés; (coll) en désordre

ev′ery·bod′y *pron indef* tout le monde

ev′ery·day′ *adj* de tous les jours

ev′ery·man′ *s* Monsieur Tout-le-monde

ev′ery·one′ or **ev′ery one′** *pron indef* chacun, tous, tout le monde

ev′ery·thing′ *pron indef* tout

ev′ery·where′ *adv* partout, de toutes parts; partout où; **everywhere else** partout ailleurs

evict [ɪˈvɪkt] *tr* évincer, expulser

eviction [ɪˈvɪkʃən] *s* éviction *f*

evidence [ˈɛvɪdəns] *s* évidence *f*; (proof) preuve *f*, témoignage *m* ‖ *tr* manifester, démontrer

evident [ˈɛvɪdənt] *adj* évident

evidently [ˈɛvɪdəntli] *adv* évidemment

evil [ˈivəl] *adj* mauvais, méchant ‖ *s* mal *m*, méchanceté *f*

evildoer [ˈivəlˌdu·ər] *s* malfaisant *m*, méchant *m*

e′vil-do′ing *s* malfaisance *f*

e′vil eye′ *s* mauvais œil *m*

e′vil-mind′ed *adj* malintentionné, malin

E′vil One′ *s* Esprit *m* malin

evince [ɪˈvɪns] *tr* montrer, manifester

evocative [ɪˈvakətɪv] *adj* évocateur

evoke [ɪˈvok] *tr* évoquer

evolution [ˌɛvəˈluʃən] *s* évolution *f*

evolve [ɪˈvalv] *tr* développer, élaborer ‖ *intr* évoluer

ewe [ju] *s* brebis *f*

ewer [ˈju·ər] *s* aiguière *f*

exact [ɛgˈzækt] *adj* exact ‖ *tr* exiger

exacting [ɛgˈzæktɪŋ] *adj* exigeant

exactly [ɛgˈzæktli] *adv* exactement; (sharp, on the dot) précisément, justement

exactness [ɛgˈzæktnɪs] *s* exactitude *f*

exaggerate [ɛg`zædʒə,ret] *tr* exagérer

exalt [ɛg`zɔlt] *tr* exalter

exam [ɛg`zæm] *s* (coll) examen *m*

examination [ɛg,zæmɪ`neʃən] *s* examen *m*; **to take an examination** se présenter à, passer, or subir un examen

examine [ɛg`zæmɪn] *tr* examiner

examiner [ɛg`zæmɪnər] *s* inspecteur *m*, vérificateur *m*; (*in a school*) examinateur *m*

example [ɛg`zæmpəl] *s* exemple *m*; **for example** par exemple

exasperate [ɛg`zæspə,ret] *tr* exaspérer

exasperation [ɛg,zæspə`reʃən] *s* exaspération *f*

excavate [`ɛkskə,vet] *tr* excaver

exceed [ɛk`sid] *tr* excéder

exceedingly [ɛk`sidɪŋli] *adv* extrêmement

ex·cel [ɛk`sɛl] *v* (*pret & pp* -**celled**; *ger* -**celling**) *tr* surpasser ‖ *intr* exceller; **to excel in** exceller dans; **to excel in** + *ger* exceller à + *inf*

excellence [`ɛksələns] *s* excellence *f*

excellen·cy [`ɛksələnsi] *s* (*pl* -**cies**) excellence *f*; **Your Excellency** Votre Excellence

excelsior [ɛk`sɛlsɪ·ər] *s* copeaux *mpl* d'emballage

except [ɛk`sɛpt] *adv*—**except for** excepté; **except that** excepté que ‖ *prep* excepté ‖ *tr* excepter

exception [ɛk`sɛpʃən] *s* exception *f*; **to take exception to** trouver à redire à; **with the exception of** à l'exception de

exceptional [ɛk`sɛpʃənəl] *adj* exceptionnel

excerpt [`ɛksʌrpt] *s* extrait *m*, citation *f* ‖ [ɛk`sʌrpt] *tr* extraire

excess [`ɛksɛs] *adj* excédentaire ‖ [ɛk`sɛs] *s* (*amount or degree*) excédent *m*, excès *m*; (*excessive amount; immoderate indulgence*) excès *m*; **in excess of** en plus de

ex'cess bag'gage *s* excédent *m* de bagages

ex'cess fare' *s* supplément *m*

excessive [ɛk`sɛsɪv] *adj* excessif

ex'cess-prof'its tax' *s* contribution *f* sur les bénéfices extraordinaires

ex'cess weight' *s* excédent *m* de poids

exchange [ɛks`tʃendʒ] *s* échange *m*; (*barter*) troc *m*; (com) bourse *f*; (telp) central *m*; **in exchange for** en contrepartie de ‖ *tr* échanger; (*to barter*) troquer; **to exchange compliments** échanger des politesses; **to exchange for** échanger contre, échanger pour

exchange' rate' *s* taux *m* de change

exchequer [`ɛkstʃɛkər] *s* trésor *m* public; ministère *m* des finances; (hist) échiquier *m*

excise [`ɛksaɪz] *s* contributions *fpl* indirectes ‖ *tr* effacer, rayer; (surg) exciser

excitable [ɛk`saɪtəbəl] *adj* excitable

excite [ɛk`saɪt] *tr* exciter

excited *adj* agité, surexcité; **don't get excited!** ne vous énervez pas!; **to get excited** s'emballer; **to get excited about** se passionner de or pour

excitement [ɛk`saɪtmənt] *m* agitation *f*, excitation *f*

exciting [ɛk`saɪtɪŋ] *adj* émotionnant, entraînant, passionnant

exclaim [ɛks`klem] *tr* s'écrier, e.g., **"All is lost!" he exclaimed** "Tout est perdu!" s'écria-t-il ‖ *intr* s'exclamer, se récrier

exclamation [,ɛksklə`meʃən] *s* exclamation *f*

exclama'tion mark' *s* point *m* d'exclamation

exclude [ɛks`klud] *tr* exclure

excluding [ɛks`kludɪŋ] *prep* à l'exclusion de, sans compter

exclusion [ɛks`kluʒən] *s* exclusion *f*

exclusive [ɛks`klusɪv] *adj* exclusif; (*expensive; fashionable*) (coll) choisi, select; **exclusive of** à l'exclusion de

exclu'sive rights' *spl* exclusivité *f*

exclu'sive show'ing *s* (public sign in front of a theater) en exclusivité

excommunicate [,ɛkskə`mjunɪ,ket] *tr* excommunier

excommunication [,ɛkskə,mjunɪ`keʃən] *s* excommunication *f*

excoriate [ɛks`korɪ,et] *tr* (fig) vitupérer

excrement [`ɛkskrəmənt] *s* excrément *m*

excruciating [ɛks`kruʃɪ,etɪŋ] *adj* affreux, atroce

exculpate [`ɛkskʌl,pet] *tr* disculper

excursion [ɛks`kʌrʒən] *s* excursion *f*

excusable [ɛks`kjuzəbəl] *adj* excusable

excuse [ɛks`kjus] *s* excuse *f* ‖ [ɛks`kjuz] *tr* excuser; **excuse me!** pardon!, je m'excuse!, **to excuse oneself** s'excuser

execrate [`ɛksɪ,kret] *tr* exécrer; (*to curse*) maudire

execute [`ɛksɪ,kjut] *tr* exécuter

execution [,ɛksɪ`kjuʃən] *s* exécution *f*

executioner [,ɛksɪ`kjuʃənər] *s* bourreau *m*

executive [ɛg`zɛkjətɪv] *adj* (*powers*) exécutif; (*position*) administratif ‖ *s* exécutif *m*; (*of school, business, etc.*) directeur *m*, administrateur *m*

Exec'utive Man'sion *s* (U.S.A.) demeure *f* du Président

executor [ɛg`zɛkjətər] *s* exécuteur *m* testamentaire

executrix [ɛg`zɛkjətrɪks] *s* exécutrice *f* testamentaire

exemplary [`ɛgzəm,plɛri] *adj* exemplaire

exempli·fy [ɛg`zɛmplɪ,faɪ] *v* (*pret & pp* -**fied**) *tr* démontrer par des exemples; (*to be a model of*) servir d'exemple à

exempt [ɛg`zɛmpt] *adj* exempt ‖ *tr* exempter

exemption [ɛg`zɛmpʃən] *s* exemption *f*; **exemptions** (*from taxes*) déductions *fpl*

exercise [`ɛksər,saɪz] *s* exercice *m*; **exercises** cérémonies *fpl* ‖ *tr* exercer ‖ *intr* s'exercer, s'entraîner

ex'ercise bi'cycle *s* bicyclette *f* d'entraînement, home-trainer *m*

exert [ɛg`zʌrt] *tr* exercer; **to exert oneself** faire des efforts

exertion [ɛg`zʌrʃən] *s* effort *m*; (*e.g., of power*) exercice *m*

exhalation [,ɛks·hə`leʃən] *s* (*of air*) expiration *f*; (*of gas, vapors, etc.*) exhalaison *f*

exhale [ɛks'hel] *tr* (*air from lungs*) expirer; (*gas, vapor*) exhaler ‖ *intr* expirer; s'exhaler

exhaust [ɛg'zɔst] *s* (*system*) échappement *m*; (*fumes*) gaz *mpl* d'échappement ‖ *tr* épuiser; faire le vide dans

exhaust′ fan′ *s* ventilateur *m* aspirant

exhaust′ hood′ *s* hotte *f* aspirante

exhaustion [ɛg'zɔstʃən] *s* épuisement *m*

exhaustive [ɛg'zɔstɪv] *adj* exhaustif

exhaust′ man′ifold *s* tuyauterie *f* or collecteur *m* d'échappement

exhaust′ pipe′ *s* tuyau *m* d'échappement

exhaust′ valve′ *s* soupape *f* d'échappement

exhibit [ɛg'zɪbɪt] *s* exhibition *f*; (*of art*) exposition *f*; (law) document *m* à l'appui, pièce *f* à conviction ‖ *tr* exhiber; (*e.g., pictures*) exposer ‖ *intr* faire une exposition

exhibition [,ɛksɪ'bɪʃən] *s* exhibition *f*

ex′hibi′tion game′ *s* (sports) match *m* amical

exhibitor [ɛg'zɪbɪtər] *s* exposant *m*

exhilarate [ɛg'zɪlə,ret] *tr* égayer, animer

exhort [ɛg'zɔrt] *tr* exhorter

exhume [ɛks'hjum] *tr* exhumer

exigen·cy [′ɛksɪdʒənsi] *s* (*pl* **-cies**) exigence *f*

exigent [′ɛksɪdʒənt] *adj* exigeant

exile [′ɛgzaɪl] *s* exil *m*; (*person*) exilé *m* ‖ *tr* exiler

exist [ɛg'zɪst] *intr* exister

existence [ɛg'zɪstəns] *s* existence *f*

exit [′ɛksɪt] *s* sortie *f* ‖ *intr* sortir

ex′it poll′ *s* (pol) sondage *m* isoloir

ex′it tax′i·way *s* (aer) bretelle *f* de liaison

exodus [′ɛksədəs] *s* exode *m*

exonerate [ɛg'zɑnə,ret] *tr* (*to free from blame*) disculper; (*to free from an obligation*) exonérer, dispenser

exorbitant [ɛg'zɔrbɪtənt] *adj* exorbitant

exorcize [′ɛksɔr,saɪz] *tr* exorciser

exotic [ɛg'zɑtɪk] *adj* exotique

expand [ɛks'pænd] *tr* (*a gas, metal, etc.*) dilater; (*to enlarge, develop*) élargir, développer; (*to unfold, stretch out*) étendre, déployer; (*the chest*) gonfler; (math) développer ‖ *intr* se dilater; s'élargir, se développer; s'étendre, se déployer; se gonfler

expanse [ɛks'pæns] *s* étendue *f*

expansion [ɛks'pænʃən] *s* expansion *f*

expan′sion joint′ *s* joint *m* de dilatation thermique

expansive [ɛks'pænsɪv] *adj* expansif; (*broad*) large, étendu

expatiate [ɛks'peʃɪ,et] *intr* discourir, s'étendre

expatriate [ɛks'petrɪ·ɪt] *adj* & *s* expatrié *m* ‖ [ɛks'petrɪ,et] *tr* expatrier

expect [ɛks'pɛkt] *tr* (*to await the coming of*) attendre; (*to look for as likely*) s'attendre à; **to expect it** s'y attendre; **to expect s.o. to** + *inf* s'attendre à ce que qn + *subj*; **to expect to** + *inf* s'attendre à + *inf*

expectan·cy [ɛks'pɛktənsi] *s* (*pl* **-cies**) attente *f*, expectative *f*

expect′ant moth′er [ɛks'pɛktənt] *s* future mère *f*

expectation [,ɛkspɛk,teʃən] *s* expectative *f*, espérance *f*

expectorate [ɛks'pɛktə,ret] *tr* & *intr* expectorer

expedien·cy [ɛks'pidɪ·ənsi] *s* (*pl* **-cies**) convenance *f*, opportunité *f*; opportunisme *m*, débrouillage *m*

expedient [ɛks'pidɪ·ənt] *adj* expédient; (*looking out for oneself*) débrouillard ‖ *s* expédient *m*

expedite [′ɛkspɪ,daɪt] *tr* expédier

expedition [,ɛkspɪ'dɪʃən] *s* expédition *f*; célérité *f*, promptitude *f*

expeditionary [,ɛkspɪ'dɪʃən,ɛri] *adj* expéditionnaire

expeditious [,ɛkspɪ'dɪʃəs] *adj* expéditif

ex·pel [ɛks'pɛl] *v* (*pret & pp* **-pelled**; *ger* **-pelling**) *tr* expulser; (*from school*) renvoyer

expend [ɛks'pɛnd] *tr* (*to pay out*) dépenser; (*to use up*) consommer

expendable [ɛks'pɛndəbəl] *adj* non récupérable; (*soldier*) sacrifiable

expenditure [ɛks'pɛndɪtʃər] *s* dépense *f*, consommation *f*

expense [ɛks'pɛns] *s* dépense *f*; **at the expense of** aux dépens de; **expenses** frais *mpl*; (*for which a person will be reimbursed*) indemnité *f*; **to meet expenses** faire face aux dépenses

expense′ account′ *s* état *m* de frais, note *f* de frais

expensive [ɛks'pɛnsɪv] *adj* cher, couteux; (*tastes*) dispendieux

experience [ɛks'pɪrɪ·əns] *s* expérience *f* ‖ *tr* éprouver

experienced *adj* expérimenté

experiment [ɛks'pɛrɪmənt] *s* expérience *f* ‖ *intr* faire des expériences, expérimenter

experimental [ɪk,spɛrə,mɛntəl] *adj* expérimental, probatoire

expert [′ɛkspərt] *adj* & *s* expert *m*

expertise [,ɛkspər'tiz] *s* maîtrise *f*

expiate [′ɛkspɪ,et] *tr* expier

expiration [,ɛkspə'reʃən] *s* expiration *f*

expire [ɛks'paɪr] *tr* & *intr* expirer

expired *adj* (*lease; passport*) expiré; (*note; permit*) périmé; (*e.g., driver's license*) suranné; (*insurance policy*) déchu

explain [ɛks'plen] *tr* expliquer; **to explain oneself** s'expliquer ‖ *intr* expliquer

explainable [ɛks'plenəbəl] *adj* explicable

explanation [,ɛksplə'neʃən] *s* explication *f*

explanatory [ɛks'plænə,tori] *adj* explicatif

explicit [ɛks'plɪsɪt] *adj* explicite

explode [ɛks'plod] *tr* faire sauter; (*a theory, opinion, etc.*) discréditer ‖ *intr* exploser, éclater, sauter

exploit [′ɛksplɔɪt] *s* exploit *m* ‖ [ɛks'plɔɪt] *tr* exploiter

exploitation [,ɛksplɔɪ'teʃən] *s* exploitation *f*

exploration [,ɛksplə're ʃən] *s* exploration *f*

explore [ɛks'plor] *tr* explorer

explorer [ɛks'plorər] *s* explorateur *m*; (*boy*

scout) routier *m*

explosion [ɛks'ploʒən] *s* explosion *f*

explosive [ɛks'plosɪv] *adj* explosif; (*mixture*) explosible ‖ *s* explosif *m*

exponent [ɛks'ponənt] *s* interprète *mf*; (math) exposant *m*

export ['ɛksport] *s* exportation *f* ‖ *tr & intr* exporter

exportation [,ɛkspɔr'teʃən] *s* exportation *f*

exporter ['ɛksportər] *s* exportateur *m*

expose [ɛks'poz] *tr* exposer; (*to unmask*) démasquer, dévoiler; (phot) impressionner

exposé [,ɛkspo'ze] *s* dévoilement *m*, révélation *f*, mise *f* en lumière

exposition [,ɛkspə'zɪʃən] *s* exposition *f*

expostulate [ɛks'pɑstʃə,let] *intr* faire des remontrances; **to expostulate with** faire des remontrances à

exposure [ɛks'poʒər] *s* exposition *f*; (*unmasking*) dévoilement *m*; (phot) exposition *f*, prise *f* de vue(s); (phot) durée *f* d'exposition, indice *m* de pose

expound [ɛks'paʊnd] *tr* exposer

express [ɛks'prɛs] *adj* exprès, formel; (*train*; *gun*) express ‖ *s* (*merchandise*) messagerie *f*, (*train*) express *m*, rapide *m*, train *m* direct; **by express** (rr) en grande vitesse ‖ *adv* (rr) en grande vitesse ‖ *tr* exprimer; (*merchandise*) envoyer en grande vitesse; (*through the express company*) expédier par les messageries; **to express oneself** s'exprimer

express' com'pany *s* messageries *fpl*

express' high'way *s* autoroute *f*

expression [ɛks'prɛʃən] *s* expression *f*

expressive [ɛks'prɛsɪv] *adj* expressif

expressly [ɛks'prɛsli] *adv* exprès

express'man *s* (*pl* **-men**) entrepreneur *m* de messageries; facteur *m*, agent *m* d'un service de messageries

express' train' *s* train *m* express

express'way' *s* autoroute, route *f* express

expropriate [ɛks'propri,et] *tr* exproprier

expulsion [ɛks'pʌlʃən] *s* expulsion *f*; (*from schools*) renvoi *m*

expunge [ɛks'pʌndʒ] *tr* effacer, supprimer, rayer

expurgate ['ɛkspər,get] *tr* expurger

exquisite ['ɛkskwɪzɪt] *adj* exquis

ex-service-man [,ɛks'sʌrvɪs,mæn] *s* (*pl* **-men'**) ancien combattant *m*

extant ['ɛkstənt], [ɛks'tænt] *adj* existant, subsistant

extemporaneous [ɛks,tɛmpə'renɪ·əs] *adj* improvisé, impromptu

extemporaneously [ɛks,tɛmpə'renɪ·əsli] *adv* à l'impromptu, d'abondance

extempore [ɛks'tɛmpəri] *adj* improvisé ‖ *adv* d'abondance, à l'impromptu

extemporize [ɛks'tɛmpə,raɪz] *tr & intr* improviser

extend [ɛks'tɛnd] *tr* (*to stretch out*) étendre; (*a period of time; a street; a line*) prolonger; (*a treaty; a session; a right; a due date*) proroger; (*a helping hand*) tendre ‖ *intr* s'étendre

extended *adj* étendu, prolongé

extend'ed fam'ily *s* communauté *f* familiale, famille *f* étendue

extension [ɛks'tɛnʃən] *s* extension *f*; prolongation *f*; (*board for a table*) rallonge *f*; (*to building*) annexe *f*; (telp) poste *m*

exten'sion cord' *s* cordon *m* prolongateur, prolongateur *m*, rallonge *f*

exten'sion lad'der *s* échelle *f* à coulisse

exten'sion ta'ble *s* table *f* à rallonges

extensive [ɛks'tɛnsɪv] *adj* vaste, étendu

extent [ɛks'tɛnt] *s* étendue *f*; **to a certain extent** dans une certaine mesure; **to a great extent** en grande partie, considérablement; **to the full extent** dans toute la mesure

extenuate [ɛks'tɛnju,et] *tr* atténuer; minimiser

exterior [ɛks'tɪrɪ·ər] *adj & s* extérieur *m*

exterminate [ɛks'tʌrmɪ,net] *tr* exterminer

external [ɛks'tʌrnəl] *adj* extérieur; (pharm, med) externe ‖ **externals** *spl* dehors *mpl*, apparences *fpl*; (*superficialities*) choses *fpl* secondaires

extinct [ɛks'tɪŋkt] *adj* (*volcano*) éteint; disparu; tombé en désuétude

extinction [ɛks'tɪŋkʃən] *s* extinction *f*

extinguish [ɛks'tɪŋgwɪʃ] *tr* éteindre

extinguisher [ɛks'tɪŋgwɪʃər] *s* (*for candles*) éteignoir *m*; (*for fires*) extincteur *m*

extirpate ['ɛkstər,pet] *tr* extirper

ex·tol [ɛks'tol] *v* (*pret & pp* **-tolled**; *ger* **-tolling**) *tr* exalter, vanter

extort [ɛks'tɔrt] *tr* extorquer

extortion [ɛks'tɔrʃən] *s* extorsion *f*

extortionist [ɛks'tɔrʃənɪst] *s* extorqueur *m*

extra ['ɛkstrə] *adj* supplémentaire; (*of high quality*) extra, extra-fin; (*spare*) de rechange ‖ *s* extra *m*; (*of a newspaper*) édition *f* spéciale; (*in building a new house*) rallonge *f*; (mov, theat) figurant *m* ‖ *adv* en plus, en sus; (*not on the bill*) non compris

ex'tra board' *s* (*for extension table*) rallonge *f*

ex'tra charge' *s* supplément *m*

extract ['ɛkstrækt] *s* extrait *m* ‖ [ɛks'trækt] *tr* extraire

extraction [ɛks'trækʃən] *s* extraction *f*

extracurricular [,ɛkstrəkə'rɪkjələr] *adj* extra-scolaire

extradite ['ɛkstrə,daɪt] *tr* extrader

extradition [,ɛkstrə'dɪʃən] *s* extradition *f*

ex'tra-dry' *adj* (*champagne*) très sec

ex'tra fare' *s* supplément *m* de billet

ex'tra·galac'tic *adj* extragalactique

ex'tra·mu'ral *adj* à l'extérieur de la ville; à l'extérieur de l'université

extraneous [ɛks'trenɪ·əs] *adj* étranger

extraordinary [ɛks'trɔrdɪ,nɛri] *adj* extraordinaire

extrapolate [ɛks'træpə,let] *tr & intr* extrapoler

ex'tra·sen'sory *adj* extrasensoriel

ex'tra-spe'cial *adj* extra

ex'tra·terres'trial *adj* extraterrestre

extravagance [ɛks'trævəgəns] *s* (*lavishness*)

prodigalité *f*, gaspillage *m*; (*folly*) extravagance *f*

extravagant [ɛks'trævəgənt] *adj* (*person*) dépensier, prodigue; (*price*) exorbitant; (*e.g., praise*) outré; (*e.g., claims*) exagéré, extravagant

extreme [ɛks'trim] *adj* & *s* extrême *m*; **in the extreme, to extremes** à l'extrême

extremely [ɛks'trimli] *adv* extrêmement

extreme' unc'tion *s* extrême-onction *f*

extremist [ɛks'trimɪst] *adj* & *s* extrémiste *mf*, ultra *mf*

extremi·ty [ɛks'trɛmɪti] *s* (*pl* **-ties**) extrémité *f*; **extremities** extrémités

extricate ['ɛkstrɪ,ket] *tr* dégager; (*a gas*) libérer; **to extricate oneself from** se tirer de, se dépêtrer de

extrinsic [ɛks'trɪnsɪk] *adj* extrinsèque

extrovert ['ɛkstrə,vʌrt] *adj* & *s* extraverti *m*

extrude [ɛks'trud] *intr* faire saillie, dépasser

exuberant [ɛg'z(j)ubərənt] *adj* exubérant

exude [ɛg'zud] *tr* & *intr* exsuder

exult [ɛg'zʌlt] *intr* exulter

exultant [ɛg'zʌltənt] *adj* triomphant

eye [aɪ] *s* œil *m*; (*of needle*) chas *m*, trou *m*; (*of hook and eye*) porte *f*; **eyes** *pl* yeux *mpl*; **to catch s.o.'s eye** tirer l'œil à qn; **to lay eyes on** jeter les yeux sur; **to make eyes at** (coll) faire les yeux doux à; **to see eye to eye with s.o.** voir les choses du même œil que qn; **with an eye to** en vue de; **without batting an eye** (coll) sans sourciller ‖ *v* (*pret* & *pp* **eyed**; *ger* **eying** or **eyeing**) *tr* toiser, reluquer

eye'ball' *s* globe *m* oculaire

eye' bank' *s* banque *f* des yeux

eye'bolt' *s* boulon *m* à œil

eye'brow' *s* sourcil *m*

eye'cup' *s* œillère *f*

eye' drops' *spl* collyre *m*

eye,' ear,' nose,' and throat' (*public sign*) yeux, nez, gorge, oreilles

eyeful ['aɪful] *s* vue *f*, coup *m* d'œil; **to get an eyeful** (coll) s'en mettre plein la vue, se rincer l'œil

eye'glass' *s* (*of optical instrument*) oculaire *m*; (*eyecup*) œillère *f*; **eyeglasses** lunettes *fpl*

eye'lash' *s* cil *m*; (*fringe of hair*) cils

eyelet ['aɪlɪt] *s* œillet *m*; (*of sail*) œil *m* de pie

eye'lid' *s* paupière *f*

eye' of the morn'ing *s* astre *m* du jour

eye' o'pener ['opənər] *s* révélation *f*; (coll) goutte *f* de bonne heure

eye'piece' *s* oculaire *m*

eye'shade' *s* visière *f*, abat-jour *m*

eye' shad'ow *s* fard *m* à paupières

eye'shot' *s* portée *f* de la vue

eye'sight' *s* vue *f*; (*eyeshot*) portée *f* de la vue

eye' sock'et *s* orbite *f* de l'œil

eye'sore' *s* objet *m* déplaisant

eye'strain' *s* fatigue *f* des yeux; **to suffer from eyestrain** avoir les yeux fatigués

eye' test' *s* examen *m* de la vision

eye'-test chart' *s* tableau *m* de lecture pour la vision

eye'tooth' *s* (*pl* **-teeth**) dent *f* œillère or canine; **to cut one's eyeteeth** (coll) ne pas être un blanc-bec; **to give one's eyeteeth for** (coll) donner la prunelle de ses yeux pour

eye'wash' *s* collyre *m*; (slang) de l'eau bénite de cour, de la poudre aux yeux

eye'wit'ness *s* témoin *m* oculaire

ey·rie or **ey·ry** ['ɛri] *s* (*pl* **-ries**) aire *f* (de l'aigle); (fig) nid *m* d'aigle

F

F, f [ɛf] *s* VIe lettre de l'alphabet

fable ['febəl] *s* fable *f*

fabric ['fæbrɪk] *s* tissu *m*, étoffe *f*

fabricate ['fæbrɪ,ket] *tr* fabriquer

fabrication [,fæbrɪ'keʃən] *s* fabrication *f*; (*lie*) mensonge *m*

fabulous ['fæbjələs] *adj* fabuleux

façade [fə'sɑd] *s* façade *f*

face [fes] *s* visage *m*, figure *f*; (*side*) face *f*; (*of the earth*) surface *f*; (*appearance, expression*) mine *f*, physionomie *f*; **about face!** (mil) demi-tour! **to keep a straight face** montrer un front sérieux; **to lose face** perdre la face; **to make a face** faire une grimace; **to set one's face against** faire front à ‖ *tr* faire face à; (*a wall*) revêtir; (*a garment*) mettre un revers à ‖ *intr*—**to face about** faire demi-tour; **to face up to** faire face à, affronter

face' card' *s* figure *f*

face' lift' or **face' lift'ing** *s* ridectomie *f*, déridage *m*, lissage *m*

face' pow'der *s* poudre *f* de riz

facet ['fæsɪt] *s* facette *f*

facetious [fə'siʃəs] *adj* plaisant

face' tow'el *s* serviette *f* de toilette

face' val'ue *s* valeur *f* faciale, valeur nominale

facial ['feʃəl] *adj* facial ‖ *s* massage *m* esthétique

fa'cial tis'sue *s* serviette *f* à démaquiller

facilitate [fə'sɪlɪ,tet] *tr* faciliter

facili·ty [fə'sɪlɪti] *s* (*pl* **-ties**) facilité *f*; **facilities** installations *fpl*

facing ['fesɪŋ] *s* revêtement *m*; (*of garment*) revers *m*

facsimile [fæk'sɪmɪli] *s* fac-similé *m*

fact [fækt] *s* fait *m*; **in fact** en fait, de fait; **the fact is that** c'est que

faction ['fækʃən] *s* faction *f*; (*strife*) discorde *f*

factor ['fæktər] *s* facteur *m* ‖ *tr* résoudre or décomposer en facteurs

facto·ry ['fæktəri] *s* (*pl* **-ries**) usine *f*, fabrique *f*

fac'tory price' *s* prix *m* de facture, prix usine

factual ['fæktʃu·əl] *adj* vrai, réel

facul·ty ['fækəlti] *s* (*pl* **-ties**) faculté *f*; (*teaching staff*) corps *m* enseignant

fad [fæd] *s* mode *f*, marotte *f*, lubie *f*; **latest fad** dernier cri *m*

fade [fed] *tr* déteindre, décolorer ‖ *intr* déteindre, se décolorer; (*to lose vigor, freshness*) se faner; **to fade in** apparaître graduellement; **to fade out** disparaître graduellement

fade'-in' *s* (mov) apparition *f* en fondu

fade'-out' *s* (mov) fondu *m*

fag [fæg] *s* (slang) cibiche *f* ‖ *v* (*pret & pp* **fagged**; *ger* **fagging**) *tr*—**to fag out** éreinter

fagot ['fægət] *s* fagot *m*; (*for filling up trenches*) fascine *f* ‖ *tr* fagoter

fail [fel] *s*—**without fail** sans faute ‖ *tr* manquer à; (*a student*) refuser; (*an examination*) échouer à or dans ‖ *intr* manquer, faire défaut, (*to not succeed*) échouer, rater; (*said of motor*) tomber en panne; (*to weaken*) baisser, faiblir; **to fail completely** faire chou blanc; **to fail in** faillir à; **to fail to** manquer de, faillir à; **to fail to do** or **to keep** faillir à

failing ['felɪŋ] *adj* défaillant ‖ *s* défaut *m* ‖ *prep* à défaut de

fail'-safe' *adj* automatiquement protégé, à sûreté intégrée

failure ['feljər] *s* insuccès *m*, échec *m*; (*lack*) manque *m*, défaut *m*; (*person*) raté *m*; (com) faillite *f*

faint [fent] *adj* faible; **to feel faint** se sentir mal ‖ *s* évanouissement *m* ‖ *intr* s'évanouir

faint'-heart'ed *adj* timide, peureux

fair [fɛr] *adj* juste, équitable; (*honest*) loyal, honnête, (*average*) moyen, passable; (*clear*) clair; (*beautiful*) beau; (*pleasing*) agréable, plaisant; (*of hair*) blond; (*complexion*) blanc; **to be fair** (*to be just*) être de bonne guerre ‖ *s* foire *f*, fête *f*; (*bazaar*) kermesse *f* ‖ *adv* impartialement; **to bid fair to** avoir des chances de; **to play fair** jouer franc jeu

fair' cop'y *s* copie *f* au net

fair'ground' *s* champ *m* de foire

fairly ['fɛrli] *adv* impartialement, loyalement; assez

fair'-mind'ed *adj* impartial

fairness ['fɛrnɪs] *s* impartialité *f*, justice *f*; (*of complexion*) clarté *f*

fair' play' *s* franc jeu *m*

fair' sex' *s* beau sexe *m*

fair'way' *s* (golf) parcours *m* normal; (naut) chenal *m*

fair'-weath'er *adj* (*e.g., friend*) des beaux jours

fair·y ['fɛri] *adj* féerique ‖ *s* (*pl* **-ies**) fée *f*; (*homosexual*) (pej) tapette *f*, tante *f*

fair'y god'mother *s* marraine *f* fée; (coll) marraine gâteau

fair'y·land' *s* royaume *m* des fées

fair'y tale' *s* conte *m* de fées

faith [feθ] *s* foi *f*; **to break faith with** manquer de foi à; **to keep faith with** tenir ses engagements envers; **to pin one's faith on** mettre tout son espoir en

faithful ['feθfəl] *adj* fidèle ‖ *s*—**the faithful** les fidèles *mpl*

faithless ['feθlɪs] *adj* infidèle

fake [fek] *adj* (coll) faux ‖ *s* faux *m*, article *m* truqué ‖ *tr* truquer

faker ['fekər] *s* truqueur *m*

falcon ['fɔkən], ['fɔlkən] *s* faucon *m*

falconer ['fɔkənər] *s* fauconnier *m*

fall [fɔl] *adj* automnal ‖ *s* chute *f*; (*of prices*) baisse *f*; (*season*) automne *m & f*; **falls** chute d'eau ‖ *v* (*pret* **fell** [fɛl]; *pp* **fallen** ['fɔlən]) *intr* tomber; (*said of prices*) baisser; **fall in!** (mil) rassemblement!; **fall out!** (mil) rompez les rangs!; **to fall down** (*said of person*) tomber par terre; (*said of building*) s'écrouler; **to fall for** (coll) se laisser prendre à; (*to fall in love with*) (coll) tomber amoureux de; **to fall in** s'effondrer; (mil) former des rangs; **to fall into the trap** donner dans le piège; **to fall off** tomber de; (*to decline*) baisser, diminuer; **to fall out** (*to disagree*) se brouiller; **to fall over oneself to** (coll) se mettre en quatre pour

fallacious [fə'leʃəs] *adj* fallacieux

falla·cy ['fæləsi] *s* (*pl* **-cies**) erreur *f*, fausseté *f*

fall' guy' *s* (slang) tête *f* de Turc

fallible ['fælɪbəl] *adj* faillible

fall'ing star' *s* étoile *f* filante

fall'out' *s* pluies *fpl* radioactives, retombées *fpl* radioactives

fall'out shel'ter *s* abri *m* antiatomique

fallow ['fælo] *adj* en friche, en jachère ‖ *s* friche *f*, jachère *f* ‖ *tr* laisser en friche or en jachère

false [fɔls] *adj* faux; artificiel, simulé; (*hair*) postiche ‖ *adv* faussement; **to play false** tromper

false' alarm' *s* fausse alerte *f*

false' bot'tom *s* double fond *m*

false' cog'nate *s* faux ami *m*

false' eye'lashes *spl* cils *mpl* postiches

false' face' *s* masque *m*

false'-heart'ed *adj* perfide, traître

false'hood *s* mensonge *m*

false' pretens'es *spl* faux-semblants *mpl*

false' return' *s* fausse déclaration *f* d'impôts

false' step' *s* faux-pas *m*

false' teeth' ['tiθ] *spl* fausses dents *fpl*

falset·to [fɔl'sɛto] *s* (*pl* **-tos**) fausset *m*, voix *f* de tête; (*person*) fausset *m*

falsi·fy ['fɔlsɪ‚faɪ] *v* (*pret & pp* **-fied**) *tr* falsifier, fausser

falsi·ty ['fɔlsɪtɪ] s (pl **-ties**) fausseté f
falter ['fɔltər] s vacillation f, hésitation f; (of speech) balbutiement m ‖ intr vaciller, hésiter; balbutier
fame [fem] s renom m, renommée f
famed adj renommé, célèbre
familiar [fə'mɪljər] adj & s familier m; **to become familiar with** se familiariser avec
familiari·ty [fə,mɪlɪ'ærɪtɪ] s (pl **-ties**) familiarité f
familiarize [fə'mɪljə,raɪz] tr familiariser
fami·ly ['fæmɪlɪ] adj familial; **in a** or **the family way** (coll) dans une position intéressante; (coll) en famille (Canad) ‖ s (pl **-lies**) famille f
fam'ily man' s (pl **men'**) père m de famille; (stay-at-home) homme m casanier, pantouflard m
fam'ily name' s nom m de famille
fam'ily physi'cian s médecin m de famille
fam'ily plan'ning s planisme m familial
fam'ily tree' s arbre m généalogique
famine ['fæmɪn] s famine f
famish ['fæmɪʃ] tr affamer, priver de vivres ‖ intr souffrir de la faim
famished adj affamé, famélique; **to be famished** (coll) mourir de faim
famous ['feməs] adj renommé, célèbre
fan [fæn] s éventail m; (mach) ventilateur m; (coll) fanatique mf, enragé m ‖ v (pret & pp **fanned**; ger **fanning**) tr éventer; (to winnow) vanner; (e.g., passions) exciter ‖ intr—**to fan out** se déployer en éventail
fanatic [fə'nætɪk] adj & s fanatique mf
fanatical [fə'nætɪkəl] adj fanatique
fanaticism [fə'nætɪ,sɪzəm] s fanatisme m
fan' belt' s (aut) courroie f de ventilateur
fancied adj imaginaire, supposé
fanciful ['fænsɪfəl] adj fantaisiste, capricieux
fan·cy ['fænsɪ] adj (comp **-cier**; super **-ciest**) ornemental; (goods, clothes, bread) de fantaisie; (high-quality) fin, extra, de luxe ‖ s (pl **-cies**) fantaisie f, caprice m; **to take a fancy to** prendre du goût pour; (a loved one) prendre en affection ‖ v (pret & pp **-cied**) tr s'imaginer, se figurer; **to fancy oneself** s'imaginer; **to fancy that** imaginer que
fan'cy dress' s costume m de fantaisie, travesti m
fan'cy dress' ball' s bal m costumé, bal travesti
fan'cy foods' spl comestibles mpl de fantaisie
fan'cy-free' adj libre, gai, sans amour
fan'cy jew'elry s bijouterie f de fantaisie
fan'cy skat'ing s patinage m de fantaisie
fan'cy·work' s broderie f, ouvrage m d'agrément
fanfare ['fænfɛr] s fanfare f
fang [fæŋ] s croc m; (of snake) crochet m
fantastic(al) [fæn'tæstɪk(əl)] adj fantastique
fanta·sy ['fæntəsɪ] s (pl **-sies**) fantaisie f
far [fɑr] adj lointain; **on the far side of** à l'autre côté de ‖ adv loin; **as far as** autant que; (up to) jusqu'à; **as far as I am** concerned quant à moi; **as far as I know** pour autant que je sache; **by far** de beaucoup; **far and wide** partout; **far away** au loin; **far from** loin de; **far from it** tant s'en faut; **far into the night** fort avant dans la nuit; **far into the woods** avant dans le bois; **far off** au loin; **how far?** jusqu'où?; **how far is it from . . .?** combien y a-t-il de . . .?; **in so far as** dans la mesure où; **so far** or **thus far** jusqu'ici; **to go far to** contribuer pour beaucoup à
far'away' adj éloigné, distant
farce [fɑrs] s farce f
farcical ['fɑrsɪkəl] adj grotesque, ridicule
fare [fɛr] s prix m, tarif m; (cost of taxi) course f; (passenger in taxi) client m; (passenger in bus) voyageur m; (culin) chère f, ordinaire m; **fares, please!** vos places, s'il vous plaît! ‖ intr se porter; **how did you fare?** comment ça s'est-il passé?
Far' East' s Extrême-Orient m
fare'well' s adieu m; **to bid s.o. farewell** dire adieu à qn
far'-fetched' adj tiré par les cheveux
far-flung ['fɑr'flʌŋ] adj étendu, vaste, d'une grande envergure
farm [fɑrm] s ferme f; (sharecropper's farm) métairie f ‖ tr cultiver, exploiter; **to farm out** donner à ferme; (work) donner en exploitation à l'extérieur ‖ intr faire de la culture
farmer ['fɑrmər] s fermier m
farm' hand' s valet m de ferme
farm'house' s ferme f, maison f de ferme
farming ['fɑrmɪŋ] s agriculture f, exploitation f agricole
farm'yard' s cour f de ferme
Far' North' s Grand Nord m
far'-off' adj lointain, éloigné
far'-reach'ing adj à longue portée
far'sight'ed adj prévoyant; (physiol) presbyte
farther ['fɑrðər] adj plus éloigné ‖ adv plus loin
farthest ['fɑrðɪst] adj (le) plus éloigné ‖ adv le plus loin; au plus
farthing ['fɑrðɪŋ] s liard m
fascinate ['fæsɪ,net] tr fasciner
fascinating ['fæsɪ,netɪŋ] adj fascinateur, fascinant
fascism ['fæʃɪzəm] s fascisme m
fascist ['fæʃɪst] adj & s fasciste mf
fashion ['fæʃən] s mode f, vogue f; (manner) façon f, manière f; **after a fashion** tant bien que mal; **in fashion** à la mode, en vogue; **out of fashion** démodé ‖ tr façonner
fashionable ['fæʃənəbəl] adj à la mode, élégant, chic
fash'ion design'ing s haute couture f
fash'ion parade' s défilé m de modes
fash'ion plate' s gravure f de mode; (person) (coll) élégant m
fash'ion show' s présentation f de collection, présentation de modèles

fast [fæst], [fɑst] *adj* rapide; (*fixed*) solide, fixe; (*clock*) en avance; (*friend*) fidèle; (*color*) grand, bon, e.g., **fast color** grand teint, bon teint; (*person*) (slang) dévergondé; **to make fast** fixer, fermer ‖ *s* jeûne *m*; **to break one's fast** rompre le jeûne ‖ *adv* vite, rapidement; (*firmly*) solidement, ferme; (*asleep*) profondément; **to hold fast** tenir bon; **to live fast** (coll) faire la noce, mener la vie à grandes guides; **to stand fast against** tenir tête à ‖ *intr* jeûner

fast' day' *s* jour *m* de jeûne, jour maigre

fasten ['fæsən] *tr* attacher, fixer; (*e.g., a belt*) ajuster ‖ *intr* s'attacher, se fixer

fastener ['fæsənər] *s* attache *f*, agrafe *f*

fast' food' *s* or **fast foods** *spl* fast food *m*; (*type of business*) restauration *f* rapide

fast'-food res'taurant *s* restaupouce *m*

fastidious [fæs'tɪdɪ·əs] *adj* délicat, dégoûté, difficile

fasting ['fæstɪŋ] *s* jeûne *m*

fat [fæt] *adj* (*comp* **fatter**; *super* **fattest**) (*plump; greasy*) gras; (*large*) gros; (*soil*) riche; (*spark*) nourri; **to get fat** engraisser ‖ *s* graisse *f*; (*of meat*) gras *m*

fatal ['fetəl] *adj* fatal

fatalism ['fetə,lɪzəm] *s* fatalisme *m*

fatalist ['fetəlɪst] *s* fataliste *mf*

fatali·ty [fə'tælɪti] *s* (*pl* **-ties**) fatalité *f*; (*in accidents, war, etc.*) mort *f*, accident *m* mortel

fate [fet] *s* sort *m*, destin *m*; **the Fates** les Parques *fpl*

fated *adj* destiné, voué

fateful ['fetfəl] *adj* fatal; (*prophetic*) fatidique

fat'head' *s* (coll) crétin *m*, sot *m*

father ['fɑðər] *s* père *m*; **Father** (*salutation given a priest*) Monsieur l'abbé ‖ *tr* servir de père à; (*to beget*) engendrer; (*an idea, project*) inventer

fa'ther·hood' *s* paternité *f*

fa'ther-in-law' *s* (*pl* **fathers-in-law**) beau-père *m*

fa'ther·land' *s* patrie *f*

fatherless ['fɑðərlɪs] *adj* sans père, orphelin de père

fatherly ['fɑðərli] *adj* paternel

Fa'ther Time' *s* le Temps

fathom ['fæðəm] *s* brasse *f* ‖ *tr* sonder

fathomless ['fæðəmlɪs] *adj* insondable

fatigue [fə'tig] *s* fatigue *f*; **fatigues** (mil) bleus *mpl*

fatigue' clothes' *spl* tenue *f* de corvée

fatigue' du'ty *s* (mil) corvée *f*

fatten ['fætən] *tr* & *intr* engraisser

fat·ty ['fæti] *adj* (*comp* **-tier**; *super* **-tiest**) gras, grasseux; (*tissue*) adipeux; (*chubby*) (coll) potelé, dodu ‖ *s* (*pl* **-ties**) (coll) bon gros *m*

fatuous ['fætʃu·əs] *adj* sot, idiot

faucet ['fɔsɪt] *s* robinet *m*

fault [fɔlt] *s* faute *f*; (geol) faille *f*; **to a fault** à l'excès; **to find fault with** trouver à redire à

fault'find'er *s* critiqueur *m*, éplucheur *m*

fault'find'ing *adj* chicaneur ‖ *s* chicanerie *f*, critique *f*

faultless ['fɔltlɪs] *adj* sans défaut

fault·y ['fɔlti] *adj* (*comp* **-ier**; *super* **-iest**) fautif, défectueux

faun [fɔn] *s* faune *m*

fauna ['fɔnə] *s* faune *f*

favor ['fevər] *s* faveur *f*; **do me the favor to** faites-moi le plaisir de; **to be in favor of** être partisan de; **to be in favor with** jouir de la faveur de; **to decide in s.o.'s favor** donner gain de cause à qn; **to do a favor in return** renvoyer l'ascenseur ‖ *tr* favoriser; (*to look like*) (coll) tenir de; (*e.g., a sore leg*) (coll) ménager

favorable ['fevərəbəl] *adj* favorable

favorite ['fevərɪt] *adj* & *s* favori *m*

fawn [fɔn] *s* (*color*) fauve ‖ *s* faon *m* ‖ *intr*—**to fawn upon** (*said of dog*) faire des caresses à; (*said of person*) faire le chien couchant auprès de

faze [fez] *tr* (coll) affecter, troubler

FBI [,ɛf,bi'aɪ] *s* (letterword) (**Federal Bureau of Investigation**) Sûreté *f* nationale, Sûreté (*the French equivalent*)

fear [fɪr] *s* crainte *f*, peur *f* ‖ *tr* craindre, avoir peur de ‖ *intr* craindre, avoir peur

fearful ['fɪrfəl] *adj* (*frightened*) peureux, effrayé; (*frightful*) effrayant; (coll) énorme, effrayant

fearless ['fɪrlɪs] *adj* sans peur

feasible ['fɪzɪbəl] *adj* faisable

feast [fist] *s* festin *m*, régal *m* ‖ *tr* régaler ‖ *intr* faire bonne chère; **to feast on** se régaler de

feast' day' *s* fête *f*, jour *m* de fête

feat [fit] *s* exploit *m*, haut fait *m*

feather ['fɛðər] *s* plume *f*; **feather in one's cap** (coll) fleuron *m* sa couronne; **in fine feather** (coll) plein d'entrain ‖ *tr* emplumer; (*an oar*) ramener à plat; **to feather one's nest** (coll) faire son beurre

feath'er bed' *s* lit *m* de plumes, couette *f*

feath'er·bed'ding *s* emploi *m* de plus d'ouvriers qu'il n'en faut

feath'er·brained' *adj* braque, étourdi

feath'er dust'er *s* plumeau *m*

feath'er·edge' *s* (*of board*) biseau *m*; (*of tool*) morfil *m*

feath'er·weight' *s* (boxing) poids *m* plume, poids mouche

feathery ['fɛðəri] *adj* plumeux

feature ['fitʃər] *s* trait *m*, caractéristique *f*; (mov) long métrage *m*, grand film *m* ‖ *tr* caractériser; offrir comme attraction principale

fea'ture writ'er *s* rédacteur *m*

February ['fɛbru,ɛri] *s* février *m*

feces ['fisiz] *spl* fèces *fpl*

feckless ['fɛklɪs] *adj* veule, faible

federal ['fɛdərəl] *adj* & *s* fédéral *m*

federate ['fɛdə,ret] *adj* fédéré ‖ *tr* fédérer ‖ *intr* se fédérer

federation [,fɛdə'reʃən] *s* fédération *f*

fedora [fɪ'dorə] *s* chapeau *m* mou

fed′ up′ [fɛd] *adj*—**to be fed up** (coll) en avoir marre; **to be fed up with** (coll) avoir plein le dos de

fee [fi] *s* honoraires *mpl*, cachet *m*; **for a nominal fee** pour une somme symbolique

feeble [ˈfibəl] *adj* faible

fee′ble·mind′ed *adj* imbécile; obtus, à l'esprit lourd

feed [fid] *s* nourriture *f*, pâture *f*; (mach) alimentation *f*; (slang) grand repas *m* ‖ *v* (*pret & pp* **fed** [fɛd]) *tr* nourrir, donner à manger à; (*a machine*) alimenter ‖ *intr* manger; **to feed upon** se nourrir de

feed′back′ *s* réalimentation *f*, régénération *f*, contre-réaction *f*, réaction *f*

feed′ bag′ *s* musette-mangeoire *f*; **to put on the feed bag** (slang) casser la croûte

feeder [ˈfidər] *s* alimenteur *m*; (elec) canal *m* d'amenée

feed′ pump′ *s* pompe *f* d'alimentation

feed′ trough′ *s* mangeoire *f*, auge *f*

feed′ wire′ *s* (elec) fil *m* d'amenée

feel [fil] *s* sensation *f* ‖ *v* (*pret & pp* **felt** [fɛlt]) *tr* sentir, éprouver; (*the pulse*) tâter; (*to examine*) palper; **to feel one's way** avancer à tâtons ‖ *intr* (*sick, tired, etc.*) se sentir; **I feel as if . . .** il me semble que . . .; **not to feel well** être mal en point; **to feel for** tâtonner, chercher à tâtons; (*to sympathize with*) (coll) être plein de pitié pour; **to feel like** avoir envie de

feeler [ˈfilər] *s* (ent) antenne *f*; **to put out a feeler** (coll) tâter le terrain

feeling [ˈfilɪŋ] *s* (*with senses*) toucher *m*, tact *m*; (*with hands*) tâtage *m*; (*impression, emotion*) sentiment *m*; **feelings** sensibilité *f*

feign [fen] *tr & intr* feindre

feint [fent] *s* feinte *f* ‖ *intr* feinter

feldspar [ˈfɛld,spar] *s* feldspath *m*

felicitate [fəˈlɪsɪ,tet] *tr* féliciter

felicitous [fəˈlɪsɪtəs] *adj* heureux, à propos

fell [fɛl] *adj* cruel, féroce ‖ *tr* abattre

felloe [ˈfɛlo] *s* jante *f*

fellow [ˈfɛlo] *s* (*of a society*) membre *m*; (*holder of a fellowship*) boursier *m*; (*friend, neighbor, etc.*) homme *m*, compagnon *m*; (coll) type *m*, bonhomme *m*, gars *m*; **poor fellow!** (coll) pauvre garçon!

fel′low cit′izen *s* concitoyen *m*

fel′low coun′tryman *s* compatriote *mf*

fel′low crea′ture *s* semblable *mf*

fel′low-man′ *s* (*pl* -**men′**) semblable *m*, prochain *m*

fel′low mem′ber *s* confrère *m*

fel′low·ship′ *s* camaraderie *f*; (*scholarship*) bourse *f*; (*organization*) association *f*

fel′low stu′dent *s* condisciple *m*

fel′low trav′eler *s* compagnon *m* de voyage; (pol) compagnon de route

felon [ˈfɛlən] *s* criminel *m*; (pathol) panaris *m*

felo·ny [ˈfɛləni] *s* (*pl* -**nies**) crime *m*

felt [fɛlt] *s* feutre *m* ‖ *tr* feutrer

felt′-tip pen′ *s* stylo-feutre *m*

female [ˈfimel] *adj* (*sex*) féminin *m*; (*animal, plant, piece of a device*) femelle ‖ *s* (*person*) femme *f*; (*plant, animal*) femelle *f*

feminine [ˈfɛmɪnɪn] *adj & s* féminin *m*

feminism [ˈfɛmɪ,nɪzəm] *s* féminisme *m*

fen [fɛn] *s* marécage *m*

fence [fɛns] *s* barrière *f*, clôture *f*; palissade *f*; (*for stolen goods*) receleur *m*, marchand *m* clandestin; **on the fence** (coll) indécis, en balance ‖ *tr* clôturer ‖ *intr* faire de l'escrime

fencing [ˈfɛnsɪŋ] *s* (*enclosure*) clôture *f*; (sports) escrime *f*

fenc′ing acad′emy *s* salle *f* d'armes

fenc′ing mas′ter *s* maître *m* d'armes

fenc′ing match′ *s* assaut *m* d'armes

fend [fɛnd] *tr*—**to fend off** parer ‖ *intr*—**to fend for oneself** (coll) se débrouiller, se tirer d'affaire

fender [ˈfɛndər] *s* (*mudguard*) aile *f*, garde-boue *m*; (*of locomotive*) chasse-pierres *m*; (*of fireplace*) garde-feu *m*

fennel [ˈfɛnəl] *s* fenouil *m*

ferment [ˈfʌrmɛnt] *s* ferment *m* ‖ [fərˈmɛnt] *tr* faire fermenter; (*wine*) cuver ‖ *intr* fermenter

fern [fʌrn] *s* fougère *f*

ferocious [fəˈroʃəs] *adj* féroce

feroci·ty [fəˈrasɪti] *s* (*pl* -**ties**) férocité *f*

ferret [ˈfɛrɪt] *s* furet *m* ‖ *tr*—**to ferret out** dénicher ‖ *intr* fureter

Fer′ris wheel′ [ˈfɛrɪs] *s* grande roue *f*

fer·ry [ˈfɛri] *s* (*pl* -**ries**) bac *m*; (*to transport trains*) ferry-boat *m* ‖ *v* (*pret & pp* -**ried**) *tr & intr* passer en bac

fer′ry·boat′ *s* bac *m*; (*to transport trains*) ferry-boat *m*

fer′ry·man *s* (*pl* -**men**) passeur *m*

fertile [ˈfʌrtɪl] *adj* fertile, fécond

fertilize [ˈfʌrtɪ,laɪz] *tr* fertiliser; (*to impregnate*) féconder

fertilizer [ˈfʌrtɪ,laɪzər] *s* engrais *m*, amendement *m*; (bot) fécondateur *m*

fervent [ˈfʌrvənt] *adj* fervent

fervid [ˈfʌrvɪd] *adj* fervent

fervor [ˈfʌrvər] *s* ferveur *f*

fester [ˈfɛstər] *s* ulcère *m* ‖ *tr* ulcérer ‖ *intr* s'ulcérer

festival [ˈfɛstɪvəl] *adj* de fête ‖ *s* fête *f*; (mov, mus) festival *m*

festive [ˈfɛstɪv] *adj* de fête, gai

festivi·ty [fɛsˈtɪvɪti] *s* (*pl* -**ties**) festivité *f*

festoon [fɛsˈtun] *s* feston *m* ‖ *tr* festonner

fetch [fɛtʃ] *tr* aller chercher; (*a certain price*) se vendre à

fetching [ˈfɛtʃɪŋ] *adj* (coll) séduisant

fete [fet] *s* fête *f* ‖ *tr* fêter

fetish [ˈfɛtɪʃ] *s* fétiche *m*

fetlock [ˈfɛtlak] *s* boulet *m*; (*tuft of hair*) fanon *m*

fetter [ˈfɛtər] *s* lien *m*; **fetters** fers *mpl*, chaînes *fpl* ‖ *tr* enchaîner, entraver

fettle [ˈfɛtəl] *s* condition *f*, état *m*; **in fine fettle** en pleine forme

fetus [ˈfitəs] *s* fœtus *m*

feud [fjud] *s* querelle *f*, vendetta *f* ‖ *intr* se quereller, être à couteaux tirés

feudal [ˈfjudəl] *adj* féodal

feudalism ['fjudə,lɪzəm] s féodalisme m

fever ['fivər] s fièvre f

fe'ver blis'ter s bouton m de fièvre

feverish ['fivərɪʃ] adj fiévreux

few [fju] adj peu de; **a few . . .** quelques
. . .; **quite a few** pas mal de; **the few . . .**
les rares . . . ‖ pron indef peu; **a few**
quelques-uns §81; **quite a few** beaucoup

ff. abbr et seq., et suivantes; see p. 21 ff.
voir à partir de la page 21

fiancé [,fi·ɑn'se] s fiancé m

fiancée [,fi·ɑn'se] s fiancée f

fias·co [fɪ'æsko] s (pl **-cos** or **-coes**) fiasco
m, échec m

fiat ['faɪ·æt] s ordonnance f, autorisation f

fib [fɪb] s (coll) petit mensonge m, blague f
‖ v (pret & pp **fibbed**; ger **fibbing**) intr
(coll) blaguer

fiber ['faɪbər] s fibre f

fibrous ['faɪbrəs] adj fibreux

fickle ['fɪkəl] adj inconstant, volage

fiction ['fɪkʃən] s fiction f; (branch of literature) ouvrages mpl d'imagination, ro-
mans mpl

fictional ['fɪkʃənəl] adj romanesque, d'imagination

fictionalize ['fɪkʃənə,laɪz] tr romancer

fictitious [fɪk'tɪʃəs] adj fictif

fiddle ['fɪdəl] s violon m ‖ tr—**to fiddle
away** (coll) gaspiller ‖ intr jouer du violon; **to fiddle around** or **with** (coll) tripoter

fiddler ['fɪdlər] s (coll) violoneux m

fid'dle·stick' s (coll) archet m; **fiddlesticks!**
(coll) quelle blague!

fiddling ['fɪdlɪŋ] adj (coll) musard

fideli·ty [fɪ'dɛlɪti] s (pl **-ties**) fidélité f

fidget ['fɪdʒɪt] intr se trémousser; **to fidget
with** tripoter

fidgety ['fɪdʒɪti] adj nerveux

fiduciar·y [fɪ'd(j)uʃɪ,ɛri] adj fiduciaire ‖ s
(pl **-ies**) fiduciaire m

fie [faɪ] interj fi!; **fie on . . .!** nargue
de . . .!

field [fild] s (piece of land) champ m; (area,
activity) domaine m, aire f; (aer, sports)
terrain m; (elec) champ; (of motor or
dynamo) (elec) inducteur m; (mil) aire f,
théâtre m

field' day' s (cleanup) (mil) manœuvres fpl
de garnison; (sports) manifestation f sportive

fielder ['fildər] s (baseball) chasseur m,
homme m de champ

field' glass'es spl jumelles fpl

field' hock'ey s hockey m sur gazon

field' hos'pital s ambulance f, formation f
sanitaire

field' house' s complexe m sportif

field' mag'net s aimant m inducteur

field' mar'shal s maréchal m

field' mouse' s mulot m

field'piece' s pièce f de campagne

fiend [find] s démon m; (mischiefmaker)
(coll) espiègle mf; (enthusiast) (coll)
mordu m; (addict) (coll) toxicomane mf

fiendish ['findɪʃ] adj diabolique

fierce [fɪrs] adj féroce, farouche; (wind)
furieux; (coll) très mauvais

fierceness ['fɪrsnɪs] s férocité f

fier·y ['faɪri] adj (comp **-ier**; super **-iest**)
(coals, sun) ardent; (heat, sand) brûlant;
(speech) fougueux, enflammé; (horse,
person, etc.) fougueux, ardent

fife [faɪf] s fifre m

fifteen ['fɪf'tin] adj, pron, & s quinze m;
about fifteen une quinzaine de

fifteenth ['fɪf'tinθ] adj & pron quinzième
(masc, fem); **the Fifteenth** quinze, e.g.,
John the Fifteenth Jean quinze ‖ s quinzième m; **the fifteenth** (in dates) le quinze

fifth [fɪfθ] adj & pron cinquième (masc,
fem); **the Fifth** cinq, e.g., **John the Fifth**
Jean cinq ‖ s cinquième; (mus) quinte f;
the fifth (in dates) le cinq

fifth' col'umn s cinquième colonne f

fiftieth ['fɪftɪ·ɪθ] adj & pron cinquantième
(masc, fem) ‖ s cinquantième m

fif·ty ['fɪfti] adj & pron cinquante ‖ s (pl
-ties) cinquante m; **about fifty** une cinquantaine f; **fifties** (years of the decade)
années fpl cinquante

fif'ty-fif'ty adv—**to go fifty-fifty** (coll) être
de moitié, être en compte à demi

fig [fɪg] s figue f; (tree) figuier m; **a fig for
. . .!** (coll) nargue de . . .!

fight [faɪt] s combat m, bataille f; (spirit)
cœur m; **to pick a fight with** chercher
querelle à ‖ v (pret & pp **fought** [fɔt]) tr
combattre, se battre contre; **to fight off**
repousser ‖ intr combattre, se battre; **to
fight shy of** se défier de

fighter ['faɪtər] s combattant m; (game person) batailleur m; (aer) chasseur m, avion
m de chasse

fight'er pi'lot s chasseur m

fig' leaf' s feuille f de figuier; (on statues)
feuille de vigne

figment ['fɪgmənt] s fiction f, invention f

figurative ['fɪgjərətɪv] adj figuratif; (meaning) figuré

figure ['fɪgjər] s (diagram, drawing, image;
important person; in skating, dancing)
figure f; (silhouette) forme f; (bodily form)
taille f; (math) chiffre m; **to be good at
figures** être bon en calcul; **to have a good
figure** avoir de la ligne; **to keep one's
figure** garder sa ligne ‖ tr figurer; (to
embellish) orner de motifs; (to imagine)
se figurer, s'imaginer; **to figure out** calculer; (coll) déchiffrer ‖ intr figurer; **to
figure on** compter sur

fig'ured bass' [bes] s (mus) basse f chiffrée

fig'ured silk' s soie f à dessin

fig'ure·head' s prête-nom m, homme m de
paille; (naut) figure f de proue

fig'ure of speech' s figure f de rhétorique;
(fig) façon f de parler

fig'ure skat'ing s patinage m de fantaisie

filament ['fɪləmənt] s filament m

filbert ['fɪlbərt] s noisette f, aveline f; (tree)
noisetier m, avelinier m

filch [fɪltʃ] tr chaparder, chiper

file [faɪl] s (*tool*) lime *f*; (*for papers*) classeur *m*; (*for cards*) fichier *m*; (*personal record*) dossier *m*; (*line*) file *f*; **in single file** en file indienne, à la queue leu leu; **to form single file** dédoubler les rangs ‖ *tr* limer; classer, ranger; (*a petition*) déposer; **to file down** enlever à la lime ‖ *intr*—**to file off** défiler; **to file out** sortir un à un

file′ case′ s fichier *m*

file′ clerk′ s employé *m*, commis *m*

file′ film′ s images *fpl* d'archives

file′ num′ber s (*e.g.*, *used in answering a letter*) référence *f*

filial [′fɪlɪ-əl] *adj* filial

filiation [,fɪlɪ′eʃən] s filiation *f*

filibuster [′fɪlɪ,bʌstər] s (*use of delaying tactics*) obstruction *f*; (*legislator*) obstructionnaire *mf*; (*pirate*) flibustier *m* ‖ *tr* (*legislation*) obstruer ‖ *intr* faire de l'obstruction

filigree [′fɪlɪ,gri] *adj* filigrané ‖ s filigrane *m* ‖ *tr* filigraner

filing [′faɪlɪŋ] s (*of documents*) classement *m*; (*with a tool*) limage *m*; **filings** limaille *f*, grains *mpl* de limaille

fil′ing cab′inet s classeur *m*

fil′ing card′ s fiche *f*

Filipi·no [,fɪlɪ′pino] *adj* philippin ‖ s (*pl* -nos) Philippin *m*

fill [fɪl] s (*earth, stones, etc.*) remblai *m*; **I've had my fill!** j'en ai assez!; **to eat one's fill** manger à sa faim, manger tout son content; **to have one's fill of** avoir tout son soûl de ‖ *tr* remplir; (*a prescription*) exécuter; (*a tooth*) plomber; (*a cylinder with gas*) charger; (*a hollow or gap*) combler; (*a job*) occuper; **to fill in** remblayer, combler; **to fill out** (*a questionnaire*) remplir ‖ *intr* se remplir; **to fill out** se gonfler; (*said of sail*) s'enfler; **to fill up** se combler; (*to fill the tank full*) faire le plein

filler [′fɪlər] s remplissage *m*; (*of cigar*) tripe *f*; (*sizing*) apprêt *m*, mastic *m*; (*in notebook*) papier *m*; (journ) pesée *f*

fillet [′fɪlɪt] s bande *f*; (*for hair*) bandeau *m*; (archit) moulure *f* ‖ [′fɪle], [′fɪlɪt] s (culin) filet *m* ‖ *tr* couper en filets

filling [′fɪlɪŋ] *adj* (*food*) rassasiant ‖ s (*of job*) occupation *f*; (*of tooth*) plombage *m*; (*e.g.*, *of turkey*) farce *f*; (*of cigar*) tripe *f*

fill′ing sta′tion s poste *m* d'essence

fill′ing-station attend′ant s pompiste *mf*

fillip [′fɪlɪp] s tonique *m*, stimulant *m*; (*with finger*) chiquenaude *f* ‖ *tr* donner une chiquenaude à

fil·ly [′fɪli] s (*pl* -lies) pouliche *f*; (coll) fillette *f*

film [fɪlm] s film *m*; (*in a roll*) pellicule *f*, film *m* ‖ *tr* filmer

film′ clip′ s bande-annonce *f*

filming [′fɪlmɪŋ] s filmage *m*

film′ li′brary s cinémathèque *f*

film′ mak′er s cinéaste *mf*

film′ star′ s vedette *f* du cinéma

film′strip′ s film *m* fixe

film·y [′fɪlmi] *adj* (*comp* -ier; *super* -iest) diaphane, voilé

filter [′fɪltər] s filtre *m* ‖ *tr* & *intr* filtrer

filtering [′fɪltərɪŋ] s filtrage *m*; (*of water*) filtration *f*

fil′ter pa′per s papier-filtre *m*

fil′ter tip′ *adj* à bout-filtre ‖ s bout-filtre *m*, bout-filtrant *m*

filth [fɪlθ] s saleté *f*, ordure *f*; (fig) obscénité *f*

filth·y [′fɪlθi] *adj* (*comp* -ier; *super* -iest) sale, immonde

filth′y lu′cre [′lukər] s (coll) lucre *m*

fin [fɪn] s nageoire *f*; **fins** (*for swimming*) palmes *fpl*

final [′faɪnəl] *adj* final; (*last in a series*) ultime, définitif ‖ s examen *m* final; (sports) finale *f*

finale [fɪ′nɑli] s (mus) final *m*

finalist [′faɪnəlɪst] s finaliste *mf*

finally [′faɪnəli] *adv* finalement, enfin

fi′nal touch′ s coup *m* de pouce

finance [′faɪnæns] s finance *f* ‖ *tr* financer

fi′nance com′pany s entreprise *f* de prêt, caisse *f* de prévoyance

financial [faɪ′nænʃəl] *adj* financier; (*interest; distress*) pécuniaire

financier [,faɪnən′sɪr] s financier *m*

financing [′faɪnænsɪŋ] s financement *m*

finch [fɪntʃ] s pinson *m*

find [faɪnd] s trouvaille *f* ‖ *v* (*pret* & *pp* **found** [faund]) *tr* trouver; **to find out** apprendre ‖ *intr* (law) déclarer; **to find out (about)** se renseigner (sur), se mettre au courant (de); **find out!** à vous de trouver!

finder [′faɪndər] s (*of camera*) viseur *m*; (*of optical instrument*) chercheur *m*

finding [′faɪndɪŋ] s découverte *f*; (law) décision *f*; **findings** conclusions *fpl*

fine [faɪn] *adj* fin; (*weather*) beau; (*person, manners, etc.*) distingué, excellent; **that's fine!** bien!, parfait! ‖ s amende *f* ‖ *tr* mettre à l'amende

fine′ arts′ *spl* beaux-arts *mpl*

fineness [′faɪnɪs] s finesse *f*; (*of metal*) titre *m*

fine′ print′ s petits caractères *mpl*; (*of a contract*) petites lignes *fpl* (illisibles)

finer·y [′faɪnəri] s (*pl* -ies) parure *f*

finespun [′faɪn,spʌn] *adj* ténu; (fig) subtil

finesse [fɪ′nɛs] s finesse *f*; (*in bridge*) impasse *f*; **to use finesse** finasser ‖ *tr* faire l'impasse à

fine′-toothed comb′ s peigne *m* aux dents fines, peigne fin

finger [′fɪŋgər] s doigt *m*; (slang) mouchard *m*, indicateur *m*; **not to lift a finger** (fig) ne pas remuer le petit doigt; **to burn one's fingers** (fig) se faire échauder; **to put one's finger on the spot** (fig) mettre le doigt dessus; **to slip between the fingers** glisser entre les doigts; **to snap one's fingers at** (fig) faire la figue à, narguer; **to twist around one's little finger** (coll) mener par le bout du nez, faire tourner comme un toton ‖ *tr* toucher du doigt, manier; (mus) doigter; (slang) espionner; (slang) identifier

fin′ger board′ s (of guitar) touche f; (of piano) clavier m

fin′ger bowl′ s rince-doigts m

fin′ger dexter′ity s (mus) doigté m

fingering [′fɪŋgərɪŋ] s maniement m; (mus) doigté m

fin′ger-nail′ s ongle m

fin′gernail pol′ish s brillant m

fin′ger·print′ s empreinte f digitale ‖ tr prendre les empreintes digitales de

fin′ger·tip′ s bout m du doigt; **to have at one's fingertips** tenir sur le bout du doigt

finicky [′fɪnɪki] adj méticuleux

finish [′fɪnɪʃ] s (perfection) achevé m, fini m; (elegance) finesse f; (conclusion) fin f; (gloss, coating, etc.) fini m ‖ tr & intr finir; **to finish** + ger finir de + inf; **to finish by** + ger finir par + inf

fin′ishing touch′ s dernière main f

finite [′faɪnaɪt] adj & s fini m

Finland [′fɪnlənd] s Finlande f; la Finlande

Finlander [′fɪnləndər] s Finlandais m

Finn [fɪn] s (member of a Finnish-speaking group of people) Finnois m; (native or inhabitant of Finland) Finlandais m

Finnish [′fɪnɪʃ] adj & s finnois m

fir [fʌr] s sapin m

fire [faɪr] s feu m; (destructive burning) incendie m; **to catch fire** prendre feu; **to set on fire** mettre le feu à ‖ tr mettre le feu à; (e.g., passions) enflammer; (a weapon) tirer; (a rocket) lancer; (an employee) (coll) renvoyer ‖ interj (warning) au feu!; (command to fire) feu!

fire′ alarm′ s avertisseur m d'incendie; (box) poste m avertisseur d'incendie

fire′arm′ s arme f à feu

fire′ball′ s globe m de feu; (mil) grenade f incendiaire

fire′bird′ s loriot m d'Amérique

fire′boat′ s bateau-pompe m

fire′box′ s boîte f à feu; (rr) foyer m

fire′brand′ s tison m; (coll) brandon m de discorde

fire′break′ s tranchée f garde-feu, pare-feu m

fire′brick′ s brique f réfractaire

fire′ brigade′ s corps m de sapeurs-pompiers

fire′bug′ s (coll) incendiaire mf

fire′ chief′ s capitaine m des pompiers

fire′ com′pany s corps m de sapeurs-pompiers; (insurance company) compagnie f d'assurance contre l'incendie

fire′crack′er s pétard m

fire′damp′ s grisou m

fire′ depart′ment s service m des incendies, sapeurs-pompiers mpl

fire′dog′ s chenet m, landier m

fire′ drill′ s exercices mpl de sauvetage en cas d'incendie

fire′ en′gine s pompe f à incendie

fire′ escape′ s échelle f de sauvetage, escalier m de secours

fire′ extin′guisher s extincteur m

fire′fly′ s (pl -flies) luciole f

fire′guard′ s (before hearth) pare-étincelles m; (in forest) pare-feu m

fire′ hose′ s manche f d'incendie

fire′house′ s caserne f de pompiers, poste m de pompiers

fire′ hy′drant s bouche f d'incendie

fire′ insur′ance s assurance f contre l'incendie

fire′ i′rons spl garniture f de foyer

fire′less cook′er [′faɪrlɪs] s marmite f norvégienne

fire′man s (pl -men) (man who stokes fires) chauffeur m; (man who extinguishes fires) sapeur-pompier m, pompier m

fire′place′ s cheminée f, foyer m

fire′plug′ s bouche f d'incendie

fire′ pow′er s puissance f de feu

fire′proof′ adj ignifuge; (dish) apyre ‖ tr ignifuger

fire′ sale′ s vente f après incendie

fire′ screen′ s écran m de cheminée, garde-feu m

fire′ ship′ s brûlot m

fire′ shov′el s pelle f à feu

fire′side′ s coin m du feu

fire′side chat′ s (pol) causerie f télévisée au coin du feu

fire′trap′ s nid-à-feu m

fire′ wall′ s coupe-feu m

fire′ward′en s garde m forestier, vigie f

fire′ wa′ter s (slang) gnole f, whisky m

fire′wood′ s bois m de chauffage

fire′works′ spl feu m d'artifice

firing [′faɪrɪŋ] s (of furnace) chauffe f; (of bricks, ceramics, etc.) cuite f; (of gun) tir m, feu m; (by a group of soldiers) fusillade f; (of an internal-combustion engine) allumage m; (of an employee) (coll) renvoi m

fir′ing line′ s ligne f de feu, chaîne f de combat

fir′ing or′der s rythme m d'allumage

fir′ing pin′ s percuteur m, aiguille f

fir′ing squad′ s peloton m d'exécution; (for ceremonies) piquet m d'honneurs funèbres

firm [fʌrm] adj & adv ferme; **to stand firm** tenir bon ‖ s maison f de commerce, firme f

firmament [′fʌrməmənt] s firmament m

firm′ name′ s nom m commercial

firmness [′fʌrmnɪs] s fermeté f

firm′ware′ s (comp) programmerie f particulière

first [fʌrst] adj, pron, & s premier m; **a first** (a record) une première; **at first** au commencement, au début; **first come first served** les premiers vont devant; **from the first** depuis le premier jour; **John the First** Jean premier ‖ adv premièrement, d'abord; **first and last** en tout et pour tout; **first of all, first off** tout d'abord, de prime abord, premièrement

first′ aid′ s premiers soins mpl, premiers secours mpl

first'-aid' kit' s boîte f à pansements, trousse f de première urgence

first'-aid' sta'tion s poste m de secours

first'-born' adj & s premier-né m

first'-class' adj de première classe, de premier ordre ‖ adv en première classe

first' cous'in s cousin m germain

first' draft' s brouillon m, premier jet m

first' fin'ger s index m

first' floor' s rez-de-chaussée m; (first floor above the ground floor) (Brit) premier étage m

first' fruits' spl prémices fpl

first'hand' adj & adv de première main

first' lieuten'ant s lieutenant m en premier

firstly ['fʌrstli] adv en premier lieu, d'abord

first' mate' s (naut) second m

first' name' s prénom m, petit nom m

first' night' s (theat) première f

first-nighter [,fʌrst'naɪtər] s (theat) habitué m des premières

first' offend'er s délinquant m primaire

first' of'ficer s (naut) officier m en second

first' prize' s (in a lottery) gros lot m; **to win first prize** remporter le prix

first' quar'ter s (of the moon) premier quartier m

first'-rate' adj de premier ordre, de première qualité; (coll) excellent ‖ adv (coll) très bien, à merveille

first'-run mov'ie s film m en exclusivité

first' try' s coup m d'essai

fiscal ['fɪskəl] adj fiscal

fis'cal year' s exercice m budgétaire

fish [fɪʃ] s poisson m; **to be like a fish out of water** être comme un poisson sur la paille; **to be neither fish nor fowl** être ni chair ni poisson; **to drink like a fish** boire comme un trou; **to have other fish to fry** avoir d'autres chiens à fouetter ‖ tr pêcher; (rr) éclisser; **to fish out** or **up** repêcher ‖ intr pêcher; **to fish for compliments** quêter des compliments; **to go fishing** aller à la pêche; **to take fishing** emmener à la pêche

fish'bone' s arête f

fish'bowl' s bocal m

fisher ['fɪʃər] s pêcheur m; (zool) martre f

fish'er·man s (pl -men) pêcheur m

fisher·y ['fɪʃəri] s (pl -ies) (activity; business) pêche f; (grounds) pêcherie f

fish' hawk' s aigle m pêcheur

fish'hook' s hameçon m

fishing ['fɪʃɪŋ] adj pêcheur, de pêche ‖ s pêche f

fish'ing ground' s pêcherie f

fish'ing reel' s moulinet m

fish'ing rod' s canne f à pêche

fish'ing tack'le s attirail m de pêche

fish'line' s ligne f de pêche

fish' mar'ket s poissonnerie f

fish'net stock'ings spl bas mpl en résille

fish'plate' s (rr) éclisse f

fish'pool' s vivier m

fish' spear' s foëne f, fouëne f

fish' sto'ry s hâblerie f, blague f

fish'tail' s queue f de poisson; (aer) embardée f ‖ intr (aer) embarder

fish'wife' s (pl **-wives'**) poissonnière f; (foul-mouthed woman) poissarde f

fish'worm' s asticot m

fish·y ['fɪʃi] adj (comp **-ier**; super **-iest**) (eyes) (coll) vitreux; (coll) véreux, louche, pas franc du collier

fission ['fɪʃən] s (biol) scission f; (nucl) fission f

fissionable ['fɪʃənəbəl] adj fissible, fissile

fissure ['fɪʃər] s fissure f, fente f ‖ tr fissurer ‖ intr se fissurer

fist [fɪst] s poing m; (typ) petite main f; **to shake one's fist at** menacer du poing

fist'fight' s combat m à coup de poings

fistful ['fɪstfʊl] s poignée f

fisticuffs ['fɪstɪ,kʌfs] spl empoignade f or rixe f à coups de poing; (sports) boxe f

fit [fɪt] adj (comp **fitter**; super **fittest**) bon, convenable; capable, digne; (in good health) en forme, sain; **fit to be tied** (coll) en colère; **fit to drink** buvable; **fit to eat** mangeable; **to feel fit** être frais et dispos ‖ s ajustement m; (of clothes) coupe f, façon f; (of fever, rage, coughing) accès m; **by fits and starts** par accès; **fit of coughing** quinte f de toux ‖ v (pret & pp **fitted**; ger **fitting**) tr ajuster; (s.th. in s.th.) emboîter; **to fit for** (e.g., a task) préparer à; **to fit out** or **up** aménager; **to fit out with** garnir de ‖ intr s'emboîter; **to fit in** tenir dans; **to fit in with** s'accorder avec, convenir à

fitful ['fɪtfəl] adj intermittent

fitness ['fɪtnɪs] s convenance f; (for a task) aptitude f; (good shape) bonne forme f

fitter ['fɪtər] s ajusteur m; (of machinery) monteur m; (of clothing) essayeur m

fitting ['fɪtɪŋ] adj convenable, approprié, à propos ‖ s ajustage m; (of a garment) essayage m; **fittings** aménagements mpl; (of metal) ferrures fpl

five [faɪv] adj & pron cinq ‖ s cinq m; **five o'clock** cinq heures

five'-year plan' s plan m quinquennal

fix [fɪks] s (aer, naut) position f; (coll) mauvais pas m; (injection) (slang) piqûre f, piquouse f, dose f; **to be in a fix** (coll) être dans le pétrin; **to give oneself a fix** (slang) se shooter, se piquer ‖ tr réparer; (e.g., a date; a photographic image; prices; one's eyes) fixer; (slang) donner son compte à

fixed' as'sets spl capital m fixe

fixedly ['fɪksɪdli] adv fixement

fixed'-price' con'tract s marché m à forfait

fixing ['fɪksɪŋ] s fixation f; (phot) fixage m; **fixings** (slang) collation f, des mets mpl

fix'ing bath' s bain m de fixage, fixateur m

fixture ['fɪkstʃər] s accessoire m, garniture f; **fixtures** meubles mpl à demeure

fizz [fɪz] s pétillement m ‖ intr pétiller

fizzle ['fɪzəl] s (coll) avortement m ‖ intr (coll) avorter; **to fizzle out** (coll) tomber à l'eau, échouer

flabbergasted ['flæbər,gæstɪd] adj (coll) éberlué, épaté

flab·by [ˈflæbi] *adj* (*comp* **-bier**; *super* **-biest**) mou, flasque; **to become flabby** s'avachir

flag [flæg] *s* drapeau *m* ‖ *v* (*pret* & *pp* **flagged**; *ger* **flagging**) *tr*—**to flag s.o.** transmettre des signaux à qn en agitant un fanion ‖ *intr* faiblir, se relâcher

flag′ cap′tain *s* (nav) capitaine *m* de pavillon

flag′man *s* (*pl* **-men**) signaleur *m*; (rr) garde-voie *m*

flag′ of truce′ *s* drapeau *m* parlementaire

flag′pole′ *s* hampe *f* de drapeau; (naut) mât *m* de pavillon; (surv) jalon *m*

flagrant [ˈflegrənt] *adj* scandaleux; (*e.g., injustice*) flagrant

flag′ship′ *s* (nav) vaisseau *m* amiral

flag′staff′ *s* hampe *f* de drapeau

flag′stone′ *s* dalle *f*

flag′ stop′ *s* (rr) halte *f*, arrêt *m* facultatif

flag′-wav′ing *adj* cocardier ‖ *s* patriotisme *m* de façade

flail [flel] *s* fléau *m* ‖ *tr* (agr) battre au fléau; (fig) éreinter

flair [flɛr] *s* flair *m*; aptitude *f*

flak [flæk] *s* tir *m* contre-avions

flake [flek] *s* (*of snow; of cereal*) flocon *m*; (*of soap; of mica*) paillette *f*; (*of paint*) écaille *f* ‖ *intr* tomber en flocons; **to flake off** s'écailler

flak·y [ˈfleki] *adj* (*comp* **-ier**; *super* **-iest**) floconneux, lamelleux

flamboyant [flæmˈbɔɪ·ənt] *adj* fleuri, orné, coloré; (archit) flamboyant

flame [flem] *s* flamme *f*; (coll) amant *m*, amante *f* ‖ *tr* flamber ‖ *intr* flamber, flamboyer

flamethrower [ˈflem,θro·ər] *s* lance-flammes *m*

flaming [ˈflemɪŋ] *adj* flambant

flamin·go [fləˈmɪŋgo] *s* (*pl* **-gos** or **-goes**) flamant *m*

flammable [ˈflæməbəl] *adj* inflammable

Flanders [ˈflændərz] *s* Flandre *f*; la Flandre

flange [flændʒ] *s* rebord *m*, saillie *f*; (*of wheel*) jante *f*; (*of rail*) patin *m*

flank [flæŋk] *s* flanc *m* ‖ *tr* flanquer

flannel [ˈflænəl] *s* flanelle *f*

flap [flæp] *s* (*part that can be folded under*) rabat *m*; (*fold in clothing*) pan *m*; (*of a cap*) couvre-nuque *m*; (*of a pocket; of an envelope*) patte *f*; (*of wings*) coup *m*, battement *m*; (*of a table*) battant *m*; (*of a sail, flag, etc.*) claquement *m*; (*slap*) tape *f*; (aer) volet *m* ‖ *v* (*pret* & *pp* **flapped**; *ger* **flapping**) *tr* (*wings, arms, etc.*) battre; (*to slap*) taper ‖ *intr* battre; (*said of sail, flag, etc.*) claquer; (*said of curtain*) voltiger; (*to hang down*) pendre

flap′jack′ *s* (coll) crêpe *f*

flare [flɛr] *s* (*of light or fire*) éclat *m* vif; (*e.g., of skirt; of pipe or funnel*) évasement *m*; (*for signaling*) fusée *f* éclairante ‖ *tr* évaser ‖ *intr* flamboyer; (*to spread outward*) s'évaser; **to flare up** s'enflammer; (*to reappear*) se produire de nouveau; (*to become angry*) s'emporter

flare′-up′ *s* flambée *f* soudaine; (*of illness*) recrudescence *f*; (*of anger*) accès *m* de colère

flash [flæʃ] *s* (*of lightning*) éclair *m*; (*of flame, jewels*) éclat *m*; (*of hope*) lueur *f*, rayon *m*; (*of wit*) trait *m*; (*of genius*) éclair; (*brief moment*) instant *m*; (phot) flash *m*; (*ostentation*) (coll) tape-à-l'œil *m*; (*last-minute news*) (coll) nouvelle *f* éclair; **flash in the pan** (coll) feu *m* de paille; **in a flash** en un clin d'œil ‖ *tr* projeter; (*a gem*) faire étinceler; (*to show off*) faire parade de; (*a message*) répandre, transmettre ‖ *intr* jeter des éclairs; (*said of gem, eyes, etc.*) étinceler; **to flash by** passer comme un éclair

flash′back′ *s* (mov) retour *m* en arrière, rappel *m*, rétrospectif *m*

flash′bulb′ *s* ampoule *f* flash, flash *m*

flash′ flood′ *s* crue *f* subite

flashing [ˈflæʃɪŋ] *adj* éclatant; (*light*) à éclats; (*signal*) clignotant ‖ *s* bande *f* de solin

flash′light′ *s* lampe *f* torche, lampe de poche; (phot) lampe éclair

flash′light bat′tery *s* pile *f* torche

flash·y [ˈflæʃi] *adj* (*comp* **-ier**; *super* **-iest**) (coll) tapageur, criard

flask [flæsk] *s* flacon *m*, gourde *f*; (*in lab*) ballon *m*, flacon

flat [flæt] *adj* (*comp* **flatter**; *super* **flattest**) (*level*) plat, uni; (*nose*) aplati; (*refusal*) net; (*beer*) éventé; (*tire*) dégonflé; (*dull, tasteless*) fade, terne; (mus) bémol ‖ *s* appartement *m*; (flat tire) crevaison *f*; (*of sword*) plat *m*; (mus) bémol *m*; (theat) châssis *m* ‖ *adv* (*outright*) (coll) nettement, carrément; **to fall flat** tomber à plat; (fig) manquer son effet; **to sing flat** chanter faux

flat′boat′ *s* plate *f*

flat-broke [ˈflætˈbrok] *adj* (coll) complètement fauché, à la côte

flat′car′ *s* plate-forme *f*

flat′foot′ *s* (*police*) (slang) flic *m*, vache *f*

flat′-foot′ed *adj* aux pieds plats; (coll) franc, brutal

flat′i′ron *s* fer *m* à repasser

flatly [ˈflætli] *adv* net, platement

flat′-nosed′ *adj* camard, camus

flatten [ˈflætən] *tr* aplatir, aplanir; (metallurgy) laminer ‖ *intr* s'aplatir, s'aplanir; **to flatten out** (aer) se redresser

flatter [ˈflætər] *tr* & *intr* flatter

flatterer [ˈflætərər] *s* flatteur *m*

flattering [ˈflætərɪŋ] *adj* flatteur

flatter·y [ˈflætəri] *s* (*pl* **-ies**) flatterie *f*

flat′ tire′ *s* pneu *m* dégonflé, à plat, or crevé, crevaison *f*

flat′top′ *s* (nav) porte-avions *m*

flatulence [ˈflætʃələns] *s* boursouflure *f*; (pathol) flatulence *f*

flat′ware′ *s* couverts *mpl*; (*plates*) assiettes *fpl*

flaunt [flɔnt] *tr* faire étalage de

flautist [ˈflɔtɪst] *s* flûtiste *mf*

flavor ['flevər] *s* saveur *f*, goût *m*; (*of ice cream*) parfum *m* ‖ *tr* assaisonner, parfumer

flavoring ['flevərɪŋ] *s* assaisonnement *m*; (*lemon, rum, etc.*) parfum *m*

flaw [flɔ] *s* (*defect*) défaut *m*, tache *f*, vice *m*; (*crack*) fêlure *f*; (*in metal*) paille *f*; (*in diamond*) crapaud *m*

flawless ['flɔlɪs] *adj* sans défaut, sans tache

flax [flæks] *s* lin *m*

flaxen ['flæksən] *adj* de lin, blond

flax′seed′ *s* graine *f* de lin

flay [fle] *tr* écorcher; (*to criticize*) rosser, fustiger

flea [fli] *s* puce *f*

flea′ and tick′ col′lar *s* collier *m* antiparasitaire

flea′bite′ *s* piqûre *f* de puce; (*trifle*) vétille *f*

fleck [flɛk] *s* tache *f*; (*particle*) particule *f* ‖ *tr* tacheter

fledgling ['flɛdʒlɪŋ] *adj* (*lawyer, teacher*) en herbe, débutant ‖ *s* oisillon *m*; (*novice*) débutant *m*, béjaune *m*

flee [fli] *v* (*pret & pp* **fled** [flɛd]) *tr & intr* fuir

fleece [flis] *s* toison *f* ‖ *tr* tondre; (*to strip of money*) (coll) écorcher, plumer

fleec·y ['flisi] *adj* (*comp* **-ier**; *super* **-iest**) laineux; (*snow, wool*) floconneux; (*hair*) moutonneux; (*clouds*) moutonné

fleet [flit] *adj* rapide ‖ *s* flotte *f*

fleet′-foot′ed *adj* au pied léger

fleeting ['flitɪŋ] *adj* passager, fugitif

Fleming ['flemɪŋ] *s* Flamand *m*

Flemish ['flɛmɪʃ] *adj & s* flamand *m*

flesh [flɛʃ] *s* chair *f*; **in the flesh** en chair et en os; **to lose flesh** perdre de l'embonpoint; **to put on flesh** prendre de l'embonpoint, s'empâter

flesh′ and blood′ *s* nature *f* humaine; (*relatives*) famille *f*, parenté *f*

flesh′-col′ored *adj* couleur *f* de chair, carné, incarnat

flesh′pot′ *s* (*pot for cooking meat*) pot-au-feu *m*; **fleshpots** (*high living*) luxe *m*, grande chère *f*; (*evil places*) maisons *fpl* de débauche, mauvais lieux *mpl*

flesh′ wound′ [wund] *s* blessure *f* en séton, blessure superficielle

flesh·y ['flɛʃi] *adj* (*comp* **-ier**; *super* **-iest**) charnu

flex [flɛks] *tr & intr* fléchir

flexible ['flɛksɪbəl] *adj* flexible

flex(i)time ['flɛks(ə),taɪm] *s* horaire *m* flottant

flick [flɪk] *s* (*with finger*) chiquenaude *f*; (*with whip*) petit coup *m*; **flicks** (coll) ciné *m* ‖ *tr* faire une chiquenaude à; (*a whip*) faire claquer

flicker ['flɪkər] *s* petite lueur *f* vacillante; (*of eyelids*) battement *m*; (*of emotion*) frisson *m* ‖ *intr* trembloter, vaciller; (*said of eyelids*) ciller

flier ['flaɪ·ər] *s* aviateur *m*; (coll) spéculation *f* au hasard; (rr) rapide *m*; (*handbill*) (coll) prospectus *m*

flight [flaɪt] *s* fuite *f*; (*of airplane*) vol *m*; (*of birds*) volée *f*; (*of stairs*) volée; (*of fancy*) élan *m*; **to put to flight** mettre en fuite; **to take flight** prendre la fuite

flight′ attend′ant *s* membre *m* d'un service de vol, stewart *m*; (*air hostess*) stewardess *f*, hôtesse *f* de l'aire

flight′ controls′ *spl* commandes *fpl* de vol

flight′ deck′ *s* (nav) pont *m* d'envol

flight′ record′er *s* enregistreur *m* de vol

flight·y ['flaɪti] *adj* (*comp* **-ier**; *super* **-iest**) volage, léger; braque, écervelé

flim·flam ['flɪm,flæm] *s* (coll) baliverne *f*; (*fraud*) (coll) escroquerie *f* ‖ *v* (*pret & pp* **-flammed**; *ger* **-flamming**) *tr* (coll) escroquer

flim·sy ['flɪmzi] *adj* (*comp* **-sier**; *super* **-siest**) léger; (*e.g., cloth*) fragile; (*e.g., excuse*) frivole

flinch [flɪntʃ] *intr* reculer, fléchir; **without flinching** sans broncher, sans hésiter

fling [flɪŋ] *s* jet *m*; **to go on a fling** faire la noce; **to have a fling at** tenter; **to have one's fling** jeter sa gourme ‖ *v* (*pret & pp* **flung** [flʌŋ]) *tr* lancer; (*on the floor, out the window; in jail*) jeter; **to fling open** ouvrir brusquement

flint [flɪnt] *s* silex *m*; (*of lighter*) pierre *f*

flint′lock′ *s* fusil *m* à pierre

flint·y ['flɪnti] *adj* (*comp* **-ier**; *super* **-iest**) siliceux; (*heart*) de pierre, insensible

flip [flɪp] *adj* (*comp* **flipper**; *super* **flippest**) (coll) mutin, moqueur ‖ *s* (*flick*) chiquenaude *f*; (*somersault*) culbute *f*; (aer) petit tour *m* de vol ‖ *v* (*pret & pp* **flipped**; *ger* **flipping**) *tr* donner une chiquenaude à; (*a page*) tourner rapidement; **to flip a coin** jouer à pile ou face; **to flip over** (*a phonograph record*) retourner

flippancy ['flɪpənsi] *s* désinvolture *f*

flippant ['flɪpənt] *adj* désinvolte

flipper ['flɪpər] *s* nageoire *f*

flip′ side′ *s* autre face *f* (d'un disque)

flirt [flʌrt] *s* flirteur *m*, flirt *m* ‖ *intr* flirter; (*said only of a man*) conter fleurette

flit [flɪt] *v* (*pret & pp* **flitted**; *ger* **flitting**) *intr* voleter; **to flit away** passer rapidement; **to flit here and there** voltiger

float [flot] *s* (*raft*) radeau *m*; (*on fish line; on seaplane*) flotteur *m*; (*on fish line or net*) flotte *f*; (*of mason*) aplanissoire *f*; (*in parade*) char *m* de cavalcade, char de Carnaval ‖ *tr* faire flotter; (*a loan*) émettre, contracter ‖ *intr* flotter, nager; (*on one's back*) faire la planche

floater ['flotər] *s* (*tramp*) vagabond *m*; (*illegal voter*) faux électeur *m*

floating ['flotɪŋ] *adj* flottant; (*free*) libre ‖ *s* flottement *m*; (*of loan*) émission *f*

float′ing is′land *s* (culin) œufs *mpl* à la neige

flock [flɑk] *s* (*of birds*) volée *f*; (*of sheep*) troupeau *m*; (*of people*) foule *f*, bande *f*; (*of nonsense*) tas *m*; (*of faithful*) ouailles *fpl* ‖ *intr* s'assembler; **to flock in** entrer en foule; **to flock together** s'attrouper

floe [flo] *s* banquise *f*; (*floating piece of ice*) glaçon *m* flottant

flog [flɑg] *v* (*pret & pp* **flogged**; *ger* **flogging**) *tr* fouetter, flageller

flogging [`flɑgɪŋ] *s* fouet *m*

flood [flʌd] *s* inondation *f*; (*caused by heavy rain*) déluge *m*; (*sudden rise of river*) crue *f*; (*of tide*) flot *m*; (*of words, tears, light*) flots *mpl*, déluge ‖ *tr* inonder; (*to overwhelm*) submerger, inonder; (*a carburetor*) noyer ‖ *intr* (*said of river*) déborder; (aut) se noyer

flood′gate′ *s* (*of a dam*) vanne *f*; (*of a canal*) porte *f* d'écluse

flood′light′ *s* phare *m* d'éclairage, projecteur *m* de lumière ‖ *tr* illuminer par projecteurs

flood′tide′ *s* marée *f* montante, flux *m*

floor [flor] *s* (*inside bottom surface of room*) plancher *m*, parquet *m*; (*story of building*) étage *m*; (*of swimming pool, the sea, etc.*) fond *m*; (*of assembly hall*) enceinte *f*, parquet; (*of the court*) prétoire *m*, parquet; (naut) varangue *f*; **to ask for the floor** réclamer la parole; **to give s.o. the floor** donner la parole à qn; **to have the floor** avoir la parole; **to take the floor** prendre la parole ‖ *tr* parqueter; (*an opponent*) terrasser; (*to disconcert*) (coll) désarçonner

flooring [`florɪŋ] *s* planchéiage *m*, parquetage *m*

floor′ lamp′ *s* lampe *f* à pied, lampadaire *m*

floor′ mop′ *s* brosse *f* à parquet

floor′ sam′ple *s* article *m* de démonstration, article de montre

floor′ show′ *s* spectacle *m* de cabaret

floor′ tim′ber *s* (naut) varangue *f*

floor′walk′er *s* chef *m* de rayon

floor′ wax′ *s* cire *f* à parquet, encaustique *f*

flop [flɑp] *s* (coll) insuccès *m*, échec *m*; (*literary work or painting*) (coll) navet *m*; (*play*) (coll) four *m*; **to take a flop** (coll) faire patapouf ‖ *v* (*pret & pp* **flopped**; *ger* **flopping**) *intr* tomber lourdement; (*to fail*) (coll) échouer, rater

floppy [`flɑpi] *adj* lâche, flottant

flop′py disk′ *s* (comp) disquette *f*

flora [`florə] *s* flore *f*

floral [`florəl] *adj* floral

florescence [flo′rɛsəns] *s* floraison *f*

florid [`florɪd] *adj* fleuri, flamboyant; (*complexion*) rubicond

Florida [`florɪdə] *s* Floride *f*; la Floride

Flor′ida Keys′ *spl* Cayes *fpl* de la Floride

floss [flɔs] *s* bourre *f*; (*of corn*) barbe *f*

floss′ silk′ *s* bourre *f* de soie, filoselle *f*

flossy [`flɔsi] *adj* (*comp* **-ier**; *super* **-iest**) soyeux; (slang) pimpant, tapageur

flotsam [`flɑtsəm] *s* épave *f*

flot′sam and jet′sam *s* choses *fpl* de flot et de mer, épaves *fpl*

flounce [flaʊns] *s* volant *m* ‖ *tr* garnir de volants ‖ *intr* s'élancer avec emportement

flounder [`flaʊndər] *s* flet *m*; (*plaice*) carrelet *m*, plie *f* ‖ *intr* patauger

flour [flaʊr] *s* farine *f* ‖ *tr* fariner

flourish [`flʌrɪʃ] *s* fioriture *f*; (*on a signature*) paraphe *m*; (*of trumpets*) fanfare *m*; (*brandishing*) brandissement *m* ‖ *tr* brandir; (*to wave*) agiter ‖ *intr* fleurir, prospérer

flourishing [`flʌrɪʃɪŋ] *adj* florissant

flour′ mill′ *s* moulin *m*, minoterie *f*

floury [`flaʊri] *adj* farineux

flout [flaʊt] *tr* se moquer de, narguer ‖ *intr* se moquer

flow [flo] *s* (*running*) écoulement *m*; (*of tide, blood, words*) flot *m*, flux *m*; (*of blood to the head*) afflux *m*; (*rate of flow*) débit *m*; (*current*) courant *m* ‖ *intr* écouler; (*said of tide*) monter; (*said of blood in the body*) circuler; (fig) couler; **to flow into** déboucher dans, se verser dans; **to flow over** déborder

flow′chart′ *s* organigramme *m*, ordinogramme *m*

flower [`flaʊ·ər] *s* fleur *f* ‖ *tr & intr* fleurir

flow′er bed′ *s* plate-bande *f*, parterre *m*; (*round flower bed*) corbeille *f*

flow′er gar′den *s* jardin *m* de fleurs, jardin d'agrément

flow′er girl′ *s* bouquetière *f*; (*at a wedding*) fille *f* d'honneur

flow′er·pot′ *s* pot *m* à fleurs

flow′er shop′ *s* boutique *f* de fleuriste

flow′er show′ *s* exposition *f* horticole, floralies *fpl*

flow′er stand′ *s* jardinière *f*

flowery [`flaʊ·əri] *adj* fleuri

flu [flu] *s* (coll) grippe *f*

fluctuate [`flʌktʃʊ,et] *intr* fluctuer

flue [flu] *s* tuyau *m*

fluency [`flu·ənsi] *s* facilité *f*

fluent [`flu·ənt] *adj* disert, facile; (*flowing*) coulant

fluently [`flu·əntli] *adv* couramment

fluff [flʌf] *s* (*velvety cloth*) peluche *f*; (*tuft of fur, dust, etc.*) duvet *m*; (*boner made by actor*) (coll) loup *m* ‖ *tr* lainer, rendre pelucheux; (*one's entrance*) (coll) louper; (*one's lines*) (coll) bouler ‖ *intr* pelucher

fluff·y [`flʌfi] *adj* (*comp* **-ier**; *super* **-iest**) duveteux; (*hair*) flou

fluid [`flu·ɪd] *adj & s* fluide *m*

fluke [fluk] *s* (*of anchor*) patte *f*; (billiards) raccroc *m*, coup *m* de veine

flume [flum] *s* canalisation *f*, ravin *m*

flunk [flʌŋk] *tr* (*a student*) (coll) recaler, coller; (*an exam*) rater ‖ *intr* être recalé, se faire coller

flunk·y [`flʌŋki] *s* (*pl* **-ies**) laquais *m*

fluorescent [,flu·ə′rɛsənt] *adj* fluorescent

fluoridate [`florɪ,det] *tr & intr* fluorider

fluoridation [,florɪ′deʃən] *s* fluoridation *f*

fluoride [`flu·ə,raɪd] *s* fluorure *m*

fluorine [`flu·ə,rin] *s* fluor *m*

fluoroscopy [,flu·ə′rɑskəpi] *s* radioscopie *f*

fluorspar [`flu·ər,spɑr] *s* spath *m* fluor

flur·ry [`flʌri] *s* (*pl* **-ries**) agitation *f*; (*of wind, snow, etc.*) rafale *f* ‖ *v* (*pret & pp* **-ried**) *tr* agiter

flush [flʌʃ] *adj* (*level*) à ras; (*well-provided*) bien pourvu; (*healthy*) vigoureux; **flush**

with au ras de, au niveau de ‖ *s* (*of light*) éclat *m*; (*in the cheeks*) rougeur *f*; (*of joy*) transport *m*; (*of toilet*) chasse *f* d'eau; (*in poker*) flush *m*; **in the first flush of** dans l'ivresse or le premier éclat de ‖ *adv* à ras, de niveau; (*directly*) droit ‖ *tr* (*a bird*) lever; **to flush a toilet** tirer la chasse d'eau; **to flush out** (*e.g., a drain*) laver à grande eau ‖ *intr* (*to blush*) rougir

flush′ switch′ *s* interrupteur *m* encastré

flush′ tank′ *s* réservoir *m* de chasse

flush′ toi′let *s* water-closet *m* à chasse d'eau

fluster [′flʌstər] *s* agitation *f*; **in a fluster** en émoi ‖ *tr* agiter

flute [flut] *s* flûte *f* ‖ *tr* (*a column*) canneler; (*a dress*) tuyauter

flutist [′flutɪst] *s* flûtiste *mf*

flutter [′flʌtər] *s* battement *m*; **all of a flutter** (coll) tout agité ‖ *intr* voleter; (*said of pulse*) battre fébrilement; (*said of heart*) palpiter

flux [flʌks] *s* flux *m*; (*for fusing metals*) acide *m* à souder; **to be in flux** être dans un état indécis

fly [flaɪ] *s* (*pl* **-flies**) mouche *f*; (*for fishing*) mouche artificielle; (*of trousers*) braguette *f*; (*of tent*) auvent *m*; **flies** (theat) cintres *mpl*; **fly in the ointment** (fig) ombre *f* au tableau; **on the fly** au vol ‖ *v* (*pret* **flew** [flu]; *pp* **flown** [flon]) *tr* (*a kite*) faire voler; (*an airplane*) piloter; (*freight or passengers*) transporter en avion; (*e.g., the Atlantic*) survoler; (*to flee from*) fuir ‖ *intr* voler; (*to flee*) fuir; (*said of flag*) flotter; **to fly blind** voler à l'aveuglette; **to fly by** voler; **to fly in the face of** porter un défi à; **to fly off** s'envoler; **to fly off the handle** (coll) sortir de ses gonds; **to fly open** s'ouvrir brusquement; **to fly over** survoler

fly′blow′ *s* œufs *mpl* de mouche

fly′-by-night′ *adj* mal financé, indigne de confiance ‖ *s* financier *m* qui lève le pied

fly′ cast′ing *s* pêche *f* à la mouche noyée

fly′catch′er *s* attrape-mouches *m*; (bot) dionée *f*, attrape-mouches; (orn) gobe-mouches *m*

fly′-fish′ *intr* pêcher à la mouche

flying [′flaɪɪŋ] *adj* volant; rapide; court, passager ‖ *s* aviation *f*; vol *m*

fly′ing but′tress *s* arc-boutant *m*

fly′ing col′ors—with flying colors drapeau *m* déployé; brillamment

fly′ing field′ *s* champ *m* d'aviation

fly′ing-fish′ *s* poisson *m* volant

fly′ing sau′cer *s* soucoupe *f* volante

fly′ing start′ *s* départ *m* lancé

fly′ing time′ *s* heures *fpl* de vol

fly′leaf′ *s* (*pl* **-leaves**) feuille *f* de garde, garde *f*

fly′ net′ *s* (*for a bed*) moustiquaire *f*; (*for a horse*) chasse-mouches *m*

fly′pa′per *s* papier *m* tue-mouches

fly′rod′ *s* canne *f* à mouche

fly′speck′ *s* chiure *f*, chiasse *f*

fly′ swat′ter [‚swɑtər] *s* chasse-mouches *m*, émouchoir *m*, tapette *f* tue-mouche

fly′trap′ *s* attrape-mouches *m*

fly′wheel′ *s* volant *m*

FM [′ɛf′ɛm] *s* (letterword) (**frequency modulation**) modulation *f* de fréquence

foal [fol] *s* poulain *m* ‖ *intr* mettre bas

foam [fom] *s* écume *f*; (*on beer*) mousse *f* ‖ *intr* écumer, mousser

foam′ rub′ber *s* caoutchouc *m* mousse

foam·y [′fomi] *adj* (*comp* **-ier**; *super* **-iest**) écumeux, mousseux

fob [fɑb] *s* (*pocket*) gousset *m*; (*ornament*) breloque *f* ‖ *v* (*pret & pp* **fobbed**; *ger* **fobbing**) *tr*—**to fob off s.th. on s.o.** refiler q.ch. à qn

f.o.b. or **F.O.B.** [‚ɛf‚o′bi] *adv* (letterword) (**free on board**) franco de bord, départ usine

focal [′fokəl] *adj* focal

fo·cus [′fokəs] *s* (*pl* **-cuses** or **-ci** [saɪ]) foyer *m*; **in focus** au point; **out of focus** non réglé, hors du point focal ‖ *v* (*pret & pp* **-cused** or **-cussed**; *ger* **-cusing** or **-cussing**) *tr* mettre au point, faire converger; (*a beam of electrons*) focaliser; (*e.g., attention*) concentrer ‖ *intr* converger; **to focus on** se concentrer sur

fodder [′fɑdər] *s* fourrage *m*

foe [fo] *s* ennemi *m*, adversaire *mf*

fog [fɔg] *s* brouillard *m*; (naut) brume *f*; (phot) voile *m* ‖ *v* (*pret & pp* **fogged**; *ger* **fogging**) *tr* embrumer; (phot) voiler ‖ *intr* s'embrumer; (phot) se voiler

fog′ bank′ *s* banc *m* de brume

fog′ bell′ *s* cloche *f* de brume

fog′bound′ *adj* arrêté par le brouillard, pris dans le brouillard

fog·gy [′fɔgi] *adj* (*comp* **-gier**; *super* **-giest**) brumeux; (phot) voilé; (fig) confus, flou; **it is foggy** il fait du brouillard

fog′horn′ *s* sirène *f*, corne *f*, or trompe *f* de brume

fogy [′fogi] *s* (slang) croulant *m*

foible [′fɔɪbəl] *s* faible *m*, marotte *f*

foil [fɔɪl] *s* (*thin sheet of metal*) feuille *f*, lame *f*; (*of mirror*) tain *m*; (*sword*) fleuret *m*; (*person whose personality sets off another's*) repoussoir *m* ‖ *tr* déjouer, frustrer

foil′-wrapped′ *adj* ceint de papier d'argent

foist [fɔɪst] *tr*—**to foist oneself upon** s'imposer chez; **to foist s.th. on s.o.** imposer q.ch. à qn

fold [fold] *s* (*crease*) pli *m*, repli *m*; (*for sheep*) parc *m*, bergerie *f*; (*of fat*) bourrelet *m*; (*of the faithful*) bercail *m* ‖ *tr* plier, replier; (*one's arms*) se croiser; **to fold in** (culin) incorporer; **to fold up** replier ‖ *intr* se replier; **to fold up** (theat) faire four; (coll) s'effondrer

folder [′foldər] *s* (*covers for holding papers*) chemise *f*, chemise classeur; (*pamphlet*) dépliant *m*; (*person folding newspapers*) plieur *m*

folderol [′fɑldə‚rɑl] *s* sottise *f*; (*piece of foolishness*) bagatelle *f*

folding [ˈfoldɪŋ] *adj* pliant, repliant, rabat-table

fold′ing cam′era *s* appareil *m* pliant

fold′ing chair′ *s* chaise *f* pliante, chaise brisée

fold′ing cot′ *s* lit *m* pliant or escamotable

fold′ing door′ *s* porte *f* à deux battants

fold′ing rule′ *s* mètre *m* pliant

fold′ing screen′ *s* paravent *m*

fold′ing seat′ *s* strapontin *m*

foliage [ˈfolɪ·ɪdʒ] *s* feuillage *m*, feuillu *m*

foli·o [ˈfolɪ,o] *adj* in-folio ‖ *s* (*pl* -os) (*sheet*) folio *m*; (*book*) in-folio *m* ‖ *tr* folioter, paginer

folk [fok] *adj* populaire, traditionnel, du peuple ‖ *s* (*pl* **folk** or **folks**) peuple *m*, race *f*; **folks** (coll) gens *mpl*, personnes *fpl*; **my folks** (coll) les miens *mpl*, ma famille

folk′ dance′ *s* danse *f* folklorique

folk′lore′ *s* folklore *m*

folk′ mu′sic *s* musique *f* populaire

folk′ song′ *s* chanson *f* du terroir

folk·sy [ˈfoksi] *adj* (*comp* -sier; *super* -siest) (coll) sociable, liant; (*like common people*) (coll) du terroir

folk′ways′ *spl* coutumes *fpl* traditionnelles

follicle [ˈfalɪkəl] *s* follicule *m*

follow [ˈfalo] *tr* suivre; (*to come after*) succéder; (*to understand*) comprendre; (*a profession*) embrasser; **to follow up** pour-suivre; (*e.g., a success*) exploiter ‖ *intr* suivre; (*one after the other*) se suivre; **as follows** comme suit; **it follows that** il s'ensuit que

follower [ˈfalo·ər] *s* suivant *m*; partisan *m*, disciple *m*, épigone *m*

following [ˈfalo·ɪŋ] *adj* suivant ‖ *s* (*of a prince*) suite *f*; (*followers*) partisans *mpl*, disciples *mpl*

fol′low the lead′er *s* jeu *m* de la queue leu leu

fol′low-up′ *adj* de continuation, complé-mentaire; (*car*) suiveur ‖ *s* soins *mpl* post-hospitaliers

fol·ly [ˈfali] *s* (*pl* -lies) sottise *f*; (*madness*) folie *f*; **follies** spectacle *m* de music-hall, folies *fpl*

foment [foˈmɛnt] *tr* fomenter

fond [fand] *adj* affectueux, tendre; **to be-come fond of** s'attacher à

fondle [ˈfandəl] *tr* caresser

fondness [ˈfandnɪs] *s* affection *f*, tendresse *f*; (*appetite*) goût *m*, penchant *m*

font [fant] *s* source *f*; (*for holy water*) bénitier *m*; (*for baptism*) fonts *mpl*; (typ) fonte *f*

food [fud] *adj* alimentaire ‖ *s* nourriture *f*, aliments *mpl*; **food for thought** matière *f* à réflexion; **good food** bonne cuisine *f*

food′ and cloth′ing *s* le vivre et le vê-tement

food′ and drink′ *s* le boire et le manger

food′ proc′essor *s* robot *m* multifonctions

food′ slic′er *s* trancheuse *f*

food′stuffs′ *spl* denrées *fpl* alimentaires, vivres *mpl*

fool [ful] *s* sot *m*; (*jester*) fou *m*; (*person imposed on*) innocent *m*, niais *m*; **to make a fool of** se moquer de; **to play the fool** faire le pitre ‖ *tr* mystifier, abuser; **to fool away** gaspiller sottement ‖ *intr* faire la bête; **to fool around** (coll) gâcher son temps; **to fool with** (coll) tripoter

fooler·y [ˈfuləri] *s* (*pl* -ies) sottise *f*, ânerie *f*

fool′har′dy *adj* (*comp* -dier; *super* -diest) téméraire

fooling [ˈfulɪŋ] *s* tromperie *f*; **no fooling!** sans blague!

foolish [ˈfulɪʃ] *adj* sot, niais; ridicule, ab-surde

fool′proof′ *adj* à toute épreuve; infaillible

fools′cap′ *s* papier *m* ministre

fool's′ er′rand *s*—**to go on a fool's er-rand** y aller pour des prunes

foot [fut] *s* (*pl* **feet** [fit]) pied *m*; (*of cat, dog, bird*) patte *f*; **on foot** à pied; **to drag one's feet** aller à pas de tortue; **to have one foot in the grave** avoir un pied dans la tombe; **to put one's best foot forward** (coll) partir du bon pied; **to put one's foot down** faire acte d'autorité; **to put one's foot in one's mouth** (coll) mettre les pieds dans le plat; **to stand on one's own feet** voler de ses propres ailes; **to tread under foot** fouler aux pieds ‖ *tr* (*the bill*) payer; **to foot it** aller à pied

footage [ˈfutɪdʒ] *s* (mov, telv) (*in French* métrage *m*, *i.e., length of film in meters*) longueur *f* d'un film en pieds

foot′-and-mouth′ disease′ *s* (vet) fièvre *f* aphteuse

foot′ball′ *s* football *m* américain; (*ball*) bal-lon *m*

foot′ brake′ *s* frein *m* à pédale

foot′bridge′ *s* passerelle *f*

foot′fall′ *s* pas *m* léger, bruit *m* de pas

foot′hills′ *spl* contreforts *mpl*, collines *fpl* basses

foot′hold′ *s*—**to gain a foothold** prendre pied

footing [ˈfutɪŋ] *s* équilibre *m*; (archit) em-pattement *m*, base *f*, socle *m*; **to be on a friendly footing** être en bons termes; **to be on an equal footing** être sur un pied d'égalité; **to lose one's footing** perdre pied

foot′lights′ *spl* (theat) rampe *f*

foot′lock′er *s* (mil) cantine *f*

foot′loose′ *adj* libre, sans entraves

foot′man *s* (*pl* -men) valet *m* de pied

foot′mark′ *s* empreinte *f* de pied

foot′note′ *s* note *f* au bas de la page

foot′pad′ *s* voleur *m* de grand chemin

foot′path′ *s* sentier *m* pour piétons

foot′print′ *s* empreinte *f* de pas, trace *f*

foot′ race′ *s* course *f* à pied

foot′rest′ *s* cale-pied *m*, repose-pied *m*

foot′ sol′dier *s* fantassin *m*

foot′sore′ *adj* aux pieds endoloris, éclopé

foot′step′ *s* pas *m*; **to follow in s.o.'s footsteps** suivre les traces de qn

foot′stone′ *s* pierre *f* tumulaire (au pied d'une tombe); (archit) première pierre

foot′stool′ *s* tabouret *m*

foot′ warm′er *s* chauffe-pieds *m*

foot′wear′ *s* chaussures *fpl*

foot′work′ *s* jeu *m* de jambes

foot′worn′ *adj* usé; (*person*) aux pieds endoloris

fop [fɑp] *s* petit-maître *m*, bellâtre *m*

for [fɔr], [fər] *prep* pour; de, e.g., **to thank s.o. for** remercier qn de; e.g., **time for dinner** l'heure du dîner; e.g., **to cry for joy** pleurer de joie; e.g., **request for money** demande d'argent; à, e.g., **for sale** à vendre; e.g., **to sell for a high price** vendre à un prix élevé; e.g., **it is for you to decide** c'est à vous de décider; par, e.g., **famous for** célèbre par; e.g., **for example** par exemple; e.g., **for pity's sake** par pitié; contre, e.g., **a remedy for** un remède contre; **as for** quant à; **for** + *ger* pour + *perf inf*, e.g., **he was punished for stealing** il fut puni pour avoir volé; **for all that** malgré tout cela; **for short** en abrégé; **he has been in Paris for a week** il est à Paris depuis une semaine, il y a une semaine qu'il est à Paris; **he was in Paris for a week** il était à Paris pendant une semaine; **to be for** (*to be in favor of*) être en faveur de, être partisan de or pour; **to use s.th. for s.th.** employer q.ch. comme q.ch.; e.g., **to use coal for fuel** employer le charbon comme combustible ‖ *conj* car, parce que

forage [′fɔrɪdʒ] *s* fourrage *m* ‖ *tr & intr* fourrager

foray [′fɔre] *s* incursion *f* ‖ *tr* saccager, fourrager ‖ *intr* faire une incursion

for·bear′ [fɔr′bɛr] *s* (*pret* **-bore**; *pp* **-borne**) *tr* s'abstenir de ‖ *intr* se montrer patient

forbearance [fɔr′bɛrəns] *s* abstention *f*; patience *f*

for·bid [fɔr′bɪd] *v* (*pret* **-bade** or **-bad** [′bæd]; *pp* **-bidden**; *ger* **-bidding**) *tr* défendre, interdire; **God forbid!** qu'à Dieu ne plaise!; **to forbid s.o. s.th.** défendre q.ch. à qn; **to forbid s.o. to** défendre à qn de

forbidden [fɔr′bɪdən] *adj* défendu

forbidding [fɔr′bɪdɪŋ] *adj* rebutant, rébarbatif, sinistre

force [fɔrs] *s* force *f*; (*of a word*) signification *f*, valeur *f*; **in force** en vigueur; **in full force** en force; **the allied forces** les puissances alliées ‖ *tr* forcer; **to force back** repousser; (*air; water*) refouler; **to force in** (*e.g., a door*) enfoncer; **to force one's way into** (*e.g., a house*) pénétrer de force dans; **to force s.o.'s hand** forcer la main à qn; **to force s.o. to** + *inf* forcer qn à or de + *inf*; **to force s.th. into s.th.** faire entrer q.ch. dans q.ch.; **to force up** (*e.g., prices*) faire monter

forced′ draft′ *s* tirage *m* forcé

forced′ land′ing *s* atterrissage *m* forcé

forced′ march′ *s* marche *f* forcée

force′-feed′ *tr* (*pret & pp* **-fed**) gaver, suralimenter

force′-feed′ing *s* suralimentation *f*

forceful [′fɔrsfəl] *adj* énergique

for·ceps [′fɔrsɛps] *s* (*pl* **-ceps** or **-cipes** [sɪ‚piz]) (dent, surg) pince *f*; (obstet) forceps *m*

force′ pump′ *s* pompe *f* foulante

forcible [′fɔrsɪbəl] *adj* énergique, vigoureux; (*convincing*) convaincant; (*imposed*) forcé

ford [fɔrd] *s* gué *m* ‖ *tr* franchir à gué

fore [fɔr] *adj* antérieur; (naut) de l'avant ‖ *s* (naut) avant *m*; **to the fore** en vue, en vedette ‖ *adv* à l'avant ‖ *interj* (golf) gare devant!

fore′ and aft′ *adv* de l'avant à l'arrière

fore′arm′ *s* avant-bras *m* ‖ **fore·arm′** *tr* prémunir; (*to warn*) avertir

fore′bear′ *s* ancêtre *m*

foreboding [fɔr′bodɪŋ] *s* (*sign*) présage *m*; (*feeling*) pressentiment *m*

fore′cast′ *s* prévision *f* ‖ *v* (*pret & pp* **-cast** or **-casted**) *tr* pronostiquer

forecastle [′foksəl], [′fɔr‚kæsəl] *s* gaillard *m* d'avant

fore·close′ *tr* exclure; (law) forclore; **to foreclose the mortgage** saisir l'immeuble hypothéqué

foreclosure [fɔr′kloʒər] *s* saisie *f*, forclusion *f*

fore·doom′ *tr* condamner par avance

fore′ edge′ *s* (bb) tranche *f*

fore′fa′ther *s* aïeul *m*, ancêtre *m*

fore′fin′ger *s* index *m*

fore′foot′ *s* (*pl* **-feet**) patte *f* de devant

fore′front′ *s* premier rang *m*; **in the forefront** en première ligne

fore·go′ *v* (*pret* **-went**; *pp* **-gone**) *tr* (*to give up*) renoncer à

foregoing [fɔr′go·ɪŋ] *adj* précédent, antérieur; (*facts, text, etc., already cited*) déjà cité, ci-dessus

fore′gone′ *adj* inévitable; (*anticipated*) décidé d'avance, prévu

fore′ground′ *s* premier plan *m*

fore′hand′ed *adj* prévoyant; (*thrifty*) ménager

forehead [′fɔrɪd] *s* front *m*

foreign [′fɔrɪn] *adj* étranger

for′eign affairs′ *spl* affaires *fpl* étrangères

foreigner [′fɔrɪnər] *s* étranger *m*

for′eign exchange′ *s* change *m* étranger; (*currency*) devises *fpl*

for′eign min′ister *s* ministre *m* des affaires étrangères

for′eign of′fice *s* ministère *m* des affaires étrangères

for′eign serv′ice *s* (dipl) service *m* diplomatique; (mil) service *m* à l'étranger

for′eign trade′ *s* commerce *m* extérieur

fore′leg′ *s* jambe *f* de devant

fore′lock′ *s* mèche *f* sur le front; (*of horse*) toupet *m*; **to take time by the forelock** saisir l'occasion par les cheveux

fore′man *s* (*pl* **-men**) chef *m* d'équipe; (*in machine shop, factory*) contremaître *m*; (*of jury*) premier juré *m*

foremast [′fɔrməst], [′fɔr‚mæst] *s* mât *m* de misaine

fore′most′ *adj* premier, principal ‖ *adv* au premier rang

fore′noon′ *s* matinée *f*

fore′part′ *s* avant *m*, devant *m*, partie *f* avant

fore′paw′ *s* patte *f* de devant

fore′quar′ter *s* quartier *m* de devant

fore′run′ner *s* précurseur *m*, avant-coureur *m*; (*sign*) signe *m* avant-coureur

foresail [′fɔrsəl], [′fɔr,sel] *s* misaine *f*, voile *f* de misaine

fore·see′ *v* (*pret* **-saw**; *pp* **-seen**) *tr* prévoir

foreseeable [fɔr′si·əbəl] *adj* prévisible

fore·shad′ow *tr* présager, préfigurer

fore·short′en *tr* dessiner en raccourci

fore·short′ening *s* raccourci *m*

fore′sight′ *s* prévision *f*, prévoyance *f*

fore′sight′ed *adj* prévoyant

fore′skin′ *s* prépuce *m*

forest [′fɔrɪst] *adj* forestier ‖ *s* forêt *f*

fore′stage′ *s* (theat) avant-scène *f*

fore·stall′ *tr* anticiper, devancer

for′est rang′er *s* garde *m* forestier

forestry [′fɔrɪstri] *s* sylviculture *f*

fore′taste′ *s* avant-goût *m*

fore·tell′ *v* (*pret* & *pp* **-told**) *tr* prédire

fore′thought′ *s* prévoyance *f*; (law) préméditation *f*

for·ev′er *adv* pour toujours, à jamais

fore·warn′ *tr* avertir, prévenir

fore′word′ *s* avant-propos *m*, avis *m* au lecteur

forfeit [′fɔrfɪt] *adj* perdu ‖ *s* (*pledge*) dédit *m*, gage *m*; (*fine*) amende *f*; **to play at forfeits** jouer aux gages ‖ *tr* être déchu de, être privé de

forfeiture [′fɔrfɪtʃər] *s* perte *f*; (*fine*) amende *f*, confiscation *f*

forge [fɔrdʒ] *s* forge *f* ‖ *tr* forger; (*e.g., documents*) contrefaire, falsifier

forger [′fɔrdʒər] *s* forgeur *m*; (*e.g., of documents*) faussaire *mf*

forger·y [′fɔrdʒəri] *s* (*pl* **-ies**) contrefaçon *f*; (*of a document, a painting, etc.*) faux *m*

for·get [fɔr′gɛt] *v* (*pret* **-got**; *pp* **-got** or **-gotten**; *ger* **-getting**) *tr* & *intr* oublier; **forget it!** n'y pensez plus!; **to forget to** + *inf* oublier de + *inf*

forgetful [fɔr′gɛtfəl] *adj* oublieux

forget′-me-not′ *s* myosotis *m*, ne-m'oubliez-pas *m*

forgivable [fɔr′gɪvəbəl] *adj* pardonnable

for·give [fɔr′gɪv] *v* (*pret* **-gave**; *pp* **-given**) *tr* & *intr* pardonner

forgiveness [fɔr′gɪvnɪs] *s* pardon *m*

forgiving [fɔr′gɪvɪŋ] *adj* indulgent, miséricordieux

for·go [fɔr′go] *v* (*pret* **-went**; *pp* **-gone**) *tr* renoncer à, s'abstenir de

fork [fɔrk] *s* fourche *f*; (*of road, tree, stem*) fourche *f*, bifurcation *f*; (*at table*) fourchette *f* ‖ *tr* & *intr* fourcher, bifurquer

forked *adj* fourchu

forked′ light′ning *s* éclairs *mpl* en zigzag

fork′lift truck′ *s* chariot *m* élévateur

forlorn [fɔr′lɔrn] *adj* (*destitute*) abandonné; (*hopeless*) désespéré; (*wretched*) misérable

forlorn′ hope′ *s* tentative *f* désespérée

form [fɔrm] *s* forme *f*; (*paper to be filled out*) formule *f*, fiche *f*, feuille f; (*construction to give shape to cement*) coffrage *m* ‖ *tr* former ‖ *intr* se former

formal [′fɔrməl] *adj* cérémonieux, officiel; (*formalistic*) formaliste; (*superficial*) formel, de pure forme

for′mal attire′ *s* tenue *f* de cérémonie

for′mal call′ *s* visite *f* de politesse

formaldehyde [fɔr′mældə,haɪd] *s* formaldéhyde

for′mal din′ner *s* dîner *m* de cérémonie, dîner prié

formali·ty [fɔr′mælɪti] *s* (*pl* **-ties**) formalité *f*; (*stiffness*) raideur *f*; (*polite conventions*) cérémonie *f*, étiquette *f*

for′mal par′ty *s* soirée *f* de gala

for′mal speech′ *s* discours *m* d'apparat

format [′fɔrmæt] *s* format *m*

formation [fɔr′meʃən] *s* formation *f*

former [′fɔrmər] *adj* antérieur, précédent; (*long past*) ancien; (*first of two things mentioned*) premier ‖ *pron*—**the former** celui-là §84; le premier

formerly [′fɔrmərli] *adv* autrefois, anciennement, jadis

form′fit′ting *adj* ajusté, moulant

formidable [′fɔrmɪdəbəl] *adj* formidable

formless [′fɔrmlɪs] *adj* informe

form′ let′ter *s* lettre *f* circulaire

formu·la [′fɔrmjələ] *s* (*pl* **-las** or **-lae** [,li]) formule *f*

formulate [′fɔrmjə,let] *tr* formuler

for·sake [fɔr′sek] *v* (*pret* **-sook** [′sʊk]; *pp* **-saken** [′sekən]) *tr* abandonner, délaisser

fort [fɔrt] *s* fort *m*, forteresse *f*; **hold the fort!** (coll) je vous confie la maison!

forte [fɔrt] *s* fort *m*

forth [fɔrθ] *adv* en avant; **and so forth** et ainsi de suite; **from this day forth** à partir de ce jour; **to go forth** sortir, se mettre en route

forth′com′ing *adj* à venir, à paraître, prochain

forth′right′ *adj* net, direct ‖ *adv* droit, carrément; (*immediately*) tout de suite

forth′with′ *adv* sur-le-champ

fortieth [′fɔrtɪ·ɪθ] *adj* & *pron* quarantième (*masc, fem*) ‖ *s* quarantième *m*

fortification [,fɔrtɪfɪ′keʃən] *s* fortification *f*

forti·fy [′fɔrtɪ,faɪ] *v* (*pret* & *pp* **-fied**) *tr* fortifier; (*wine*) viner

fortitude [′fɔrtɪ,t(j)ud] *s* force *f* d'âme

fortnight [′fɔrt,naɪt] *s* quinze jours *mpl*, quinzaine *f*

fortress [′fɔrtrɪs] *s* forteresse *f*

fortuitous [fɔr′t(j)u·ɪtəs] *adj* (*accidental*) fortuit; (*lucky*) heureux

fortunate [′fɔrtʃənɪt] *adj* heureux

fortune [′fɔrtʃən] *s* fortune *f*; **to cost a fortune** coûter les yeux de la tête; **to make a fortune** faire fortune; **to tell s.o. his fortune** dire la bonne aventure à qn

for'tune hunt'er s coureur m de dots
for'tune·tel'ler s diseuse f de bonne aventure
for·ty ['fɔrti] adj & pron quarante ‖ s (pl **-ties**) quarante m; **about forty** une quarantaine
fo·rum ['forəm] s (pl **-rums** or **-ra** [rə]) forum m; (e.g., of public opinion) tribunal m; **open forum** tribune f libre
forward ['fɔrwərd] adj de devant; (precocious) avancé, précoce; (bold) audacieux, effronté ‖ s (sports) avant m ‖ adv en avant; **to bring forward** (bk) reporter; **to come forward** s'avancer; **to look forward to** compter sur, se faire une fête de ‖ tr envoyer, expédier; (a letter) faire suivre; (a project) avancer, favoriser; **please forward** prière de faire suivre
for'warding address' s adresse f d'expédition, adresse d'envoi
fossil ['fɑsɪl] adj & s fossile m
foster ['fɔstər] adj de lait, nourricier ‖ tr encourager, entretenir
fos'ter fa'ther s père m adoptif
fos'ter moth'er s mère f adoptive
fos'ter par'enting s fosterage m
foul [faul] adj immonde; (air) vicié; (wind) contraire; (weather) gros, sale; (breath) fétide; (language) ordurier; (water) bourbeux; (ball) hors jeu ‖ s (baseball) faute f; (boxing) coup m bas ‖ adv déloyalement ‖ tr (sports) commettre une faute contre ‖ intr (said of anchor, propeller, rope, etc.) s'engager
foul-mouthed ['faul'mauðd] adj mal embouché
foul' play' s malveillance f; (sports) jeu m déloyal
found [faund] tr fonder, établir; (metal) fondre
foundation [faun'deʃən] s (basis; masonry support) fondement m; (act of endowing) dotation f; (endowment) fondation f
founder ['faundər] s fondateur m; (in foundry) fondeur m ‖ intr (said of horse) boiter bas; (said of building) s'effondrer; (naut) sombrer
foundling ['faundlɪŋ] s enfant m trouvé
found'ling hos'pital s hospice m des enfants trouvés
found·ry ['faundri] s (pl **-ries**) fonderie f
found'ry·man s (pl **-men**) fondeur m
fount [faunt] s source f
fountain ['fauntən] s fontaine f
foun'tain·head' s source f, origine f
Foun'tain of Youth' s fontaine f de Jouvence
foun'tain pen' s stylo m (à réservoir)
four [for] adj & pron quatre ‖ s quatre m; **four o'clock** quatre heures; **on all fours** à quatre pattes
four'-cy'cle adj (mach) à quatre temps
four'-cyl'inder adj (mach) à quatre cylindres
four'-flush' intr (coll) bluffer, faire le fanfaron
fourflusher ['for‚flʌʃər] s (coll) bluffeur m

four'-foot'ed adj quadrupède
four' hun'dred adj & pron quatre cents ‖ s quatre cents m; **the Four Hundred** la haute société; le Tout Paris
four'-in-hand' s (tie) cravate-plastron f; (team) attelage m à quatre
four'-lane' adj à quatre voies
four'-leaf clo'ver s trèfle m à quatre feuilles
four'-motor plane' s quadrimoteur m
four'-o'clock' s (Mirabilis jalapa) belle-de-nuit f
four' of a kind' s (cards) un carré
four'-post'er s lit m à colonnes
four'score' adj quatre-vingts
foursome ['forsəm] s partie f double
fourteen ['for'tin] adj, pron, & s quatorze m
fourteenth ['for'tinθ] adj & pron quatorzième (masc, fem); **the Fourteenth** quatorze, e.g., **John the Fourteenth** Jean quatorze ‖ s quatorze m; **the fourteenth** (in dates) le quatorze
fourth [forθ] adj & pron quatrième (masc, fem); **the Fourth** quatre, e.g., **John the Fourth** Jean quatre ‖ s quatrième m; (in fractions) quart m; **the fourth** (in dates) le quatre
fourth' estate' s quatrième pouvoir m
fowl [faul] s volaille f
fox [faks] s renard m ‖ tr (coll) mystifier
fox'glove' s digitale f
fox'hole' s renardière f; (mil) gourbi m, abri m de tranchée
fox'hound' s fox-hound m
fox' hunt' s chasse f au renard
fox' ter'rier s fox-terrier m
fox' trot' s (of animal) petit trot m; (dance) fox-trot m
fox·y ['faksi] adj (comp **-ier**; super **-iest**) rusé, madré
foyer ['fɔɪ·ər] s (lobby) foyer m; (entrance hall) vestibule m
fracas ['frekəs] s bagarre f, rixe f
fraction ['frækʃən] s fraction f
fractional ['frækʃənəl] adj fractionnaire
frac'tional cur'rency s monnaie f divisionnaire
fracture ['fræktʃər] s fracture f; **to set a fracture** réduire une fracture ‖ tr fracturer
fragile ['frædʒɪl] adj fragile
fragment ['frægmənt] s fragment m ‖ tr fragmenter
fragrance ['fregrəns] s parfum m
fragrant ['fregrənt] adj parfumé
frail [frel] adj frêle; (e.g., virtue) fragile, faible ‖ s (basket) couffe f
frail·ty ['frelti] s (pl **-ties**) fragilité f; (weakness) faiblesse f
frame [frem] s (of picture, mirror) cadre m; (of glasses) monture f; (of window, car) châssis m; (of window, motor) bâti m; (support, stand) armature f; (structure) charpente f; (for embroidering) métier m; (of comic strip) cadre, dessin m; (mov, telv) image f ‖ tr former, charpenter; (a picture) encadrer; (film) cadrer; (an answer) formuler; (slang) monter une accusation contre

frame' house' s maison f en bois
frame' of mind' s disposition f d'esprit
frame'-up' s (slang) coup m monté
frame'work' s charpente f, squelette m
framing ['fremɪŋ] s (mov, phot) cadrage m
France [fræns] s France f; la France
franchise ['fræntʃaɪz] s concession f, privilège m; (com) chaîne f volontaire; (pol) droit m de vote
frank [fræŋk] adj franc ‖ s franchise f postale; **Frank** (medieval German person) Franc m; (masculine name) François m ‖ tr affranchir
frankfurter ['fræŋkfərtər] s saucisse f de Francfort
frankincense ['fræŋkɪn,sɛns] s oliban m
Frankish ['fræŋkɪʃ] adj franc ‖ s francique m
frankness ['fræŋknɪs] s franchise f
frantic ['fræntɪk] adj frénétique
fraternal [frə'tʌrnəl] adj fraternel
fraterni·ty [frə'tʌrnɪti] s (pl -ties) fraternité f; (association) confrérie f; (at a university) club m d'étudiants, amicale f estudiantine
fraternize ['frætər,naɪz] intr fraterniser
fraud [frɔd] s fraude f; (person) imposteur m, fourbe mf
fraudulent ['frɔdjələnt] adj frauduleux, en fraude
fraught [frɔt] adj—**fraught with** chargé de
fray [fre] s bagarre f ‖ tr érailler ‖ intr s'érailler
freak [frik] s (sudden fancy) caprice m; (anomaly) curiosité f; (person, animal) monstre m
freakish ['frikɪʃ] adj capricieux; bizarre; (grotesque) monstrueux
freckle ['frɛkəl] s tache f de rousseur, éphélide f
freckly ['frɛkli] adj couvert de taches de rousseur
free [fri] adj (comp **freer** ['fri·ər]; super **freest** ['fri·ɪst]) libre; (without charge) gratuit; (without extra charge) franc, exempt; (e.g., end of a rope) dégagé; (with money, advice, etc.) libéral, généreux; (manner, speech, etc.) franc, ouvert; **to set free** libérer, affranchir ‖ adv franco, gratis, gratuitement; (naut) largue, e.g., **running free** courant largue ‖ v (pret & pp **freed** [frid]; ger **freeing** ['fri·ɪŋ]) tr libérer; (a prisoner) affranchir, élargir; (to disengage) dégager; (from an obligation) exempter
free' admis'sion s entrée f libre, entrée gratuite
free' and eas'y adj désinvolte, dégagé
freebooter ['fri,butər] s flibustier m, maraudeur m
free' com'peti'tion s libre concurrence f
freedom ['fridəm] s liberté f
free'dom of speech' s liberté f de la parole
free'dom of the press' s liberté f de la presse
free'dom of the seas' s liberté f des mers

free'dom of thought' s liberté f de la pensée
free'dom of wor'ship s liberté f du culte, libre pratique f
free'-for-all' s foire f d'empoigne, mêlée f
free' hand' s carte f blanche
free'-hand draw'ing s dessin m à main levée
free'hand'ed adj libéral, généreux
free'hold' s (law) propriété f foncière perpétuelle; (hist) franc-alleu m
free' lance' s franc-tireur m
free'-lance' intr travailler à la pige, travailler à (or pour) son compte
free'man s (pl -men) homme m libre; (citizen) citoyen m
Free'ma'son s franc-maçon m
Free'ma'sonry s franc-maçonnerie f
free' of charge' adj & adv gratis, exempt de frais, gratuit, bénévolement
free' on board' adv franco de bord, départ usine
free' port' s port m franc
free' speech' s liberté f de la parole
free'-spo'ken adj franc; **to be free-spoken** avoir son franc-parler
free'stone' adj (bot) à noyau non-adhérent ‖ s (mas) pierre f de taille
free'think'er s libre penseur m
free' thought' s libre pensée f
free' throw' s (sports) lancer m franc
free' tick'et s billet m de faveur
free' trade' s libre-échange m
free'way' s autoroute f
free'will' adj volontaire, de plein gré
free' will' s libre arbitre m; **of one's own free will** de son propre gré
freeze [friz] s congélation f ‖ v (pret **froze** [froz]; pp **frozen**) tr geler, congeler; (e.g., wages) geler, bloquer; (foods) surgeler ‖ intr geler; **it is freezing** il gèle
freeze'-dry' v (pret & pp -**dried**) tr lyophiliser
freeze' dry'ing s lyophilisation f
freezer ['frizər] s (for making ice cream) sorbetière f; (for foods) congélateur m
freez'er bag' s sac m congélateur
freight [fret] s fret m, chargement m; (cost) fret, prix m du transport; **by freight** (rr) en petite vitesse ‖ tr transporter; (a ship, truck, etc.) charger
freight' car' s wagon m de marchandises, wagon à caisse
freighter ['fretər] s cargo m
freight' plat'form s quai m de déchargement
freight' sta'tion s gare f de marchandises
freight' train' s train m de marchandises
freight' yard' s (rr) cour f de marchandises
French [frɛntʃ] adj français ‖ s (language) français m; **the French** les Français
French' Cana'dian s Franco-Canadien m
French'-Cana'dian adj franco-canadien
French' chalk' s craie f de tailleur, stéatite f
French' cuff' s poignet m mousquetaire
French' door' s porte-fenêtre f

French′ dress′ing s vinaigrette f

French′ fries′ spl frites fpl

French′ horn′ s (mus) cor m d'harmonie

French′ horse′power s (735 watts) cheval-vapeur m, cheval m

French′ leave′ s—**to take French leave** filer à l'anglaise

French′man s (pl **-men**) Français m

French′ roll′ s petit pain m

French′-speak′ing adj francophone; (country) de langue française

French′ tel′ephone s combiné m

French′ toast′ s pain m perdu

French′ win′dow s porte-fenêtre f

French′wom′an s (pl **-wom′en**) Française f

frenzied [′frɛnzid] adj frénétique

fren·zy [′frɛnzi] s (pl **-zies**) frénésie f

frequen·cy [′frikwənsi] s (pl **-cies**) fréquence f

fre′quency modula′tion s modulation f de fréquence

frequent [′frikwənt] adj fréquent ‖ [frɪ′kwɛnt] tr fréquenter

frequently [′frikwəntli] adv fréquemment

fres·co [′frɛsko] s (pl **-coes** or **-cos**) fresque f ‖ tr peindre à fresque

fresh [frɛʃ] adj frais; (water) doux; (e.g., idea) nouveau; (wound) saignant; (cheeky) (coll) osé, impertinent; **fresh paint!** (public sign) attention, peinture fraîche! ‖ adv nouvellement; **fresh in** (coll) récemment arrivé; **fresh out** (coll) récemment épuisé

freshen [′frɛʃən] tr rafraîchir ‖ intr se rafraîchir; (said of wind) fraîchir

freshet [′frɛʃɪt] s crue f

fresh′man s (pl **-men**) étudiant m de première année, bizut m

freshness [′frɛʃnɪs] s fraîcheur f; (sauciness) impudence f, impertinence f

fresh′-wa′ter adj d'eau douce

fret [frɛt] s (interlaced design) frette f; (uneasiness) inquiétude f; (mus) touchette f ‖ v (pret & pp **fretted**; ger **fretting**) tr ajourer ‖ intr s'inquiéter, geindre

fretful [′frɛtfəl] adj irritable, boudeur

fret′work′ s ajour m, ornementation f ajourée

Freudianism [′frɔɪdɪ·ə‚nɪzəm] s freudisme m

friar [′fraɪ·ər] s moine m

fricassee [‚frɪkə′si] s fricassé f

friction [′frɪkʃən] s friction f

fric′tion tape′ s chatterton m, ruban m isolant

Friday [′fraɪdi] s vendredi m

fried [fraɪd] adj frit

fried′ egg′ s œuf m sur le plat

friend [frɛnd] s ami m; **to make friends with** se lier d'amitié avec

friend·ly [′frɛndli] adj (comp **-lier;** super **-liest**) amical, sympathique

friendship [′frɛndʃɪp] s amitié f

frieze [friz] s (archit) frise f

frigate [′frɪgɪt] s frégate f

fright [fraɪt] s frayeur f, effroi m; (grotesque or ridiculous person) (coll) épouvantail m; **to take fright at** s'effrayer de

frighten [′fraɪtən] tr effrayer; **to frighten away** effaroucher, faire fuir

frightful [′fraɪtfəl] adj effroyable; (coll) affreux; (coll) énorme

frigid [′frɪdʒɪd] adj frigide; (zone) glacial

frigidity [frɪ′dʒɪdɪti] s frigidité f

frill [frɪl] s (on shirt front) jabot m; (frippery) falbala m

fringe [frɪndʒ] s frange f; (border) bordure f; (opt) frange; **on the fringe of** en marge de ‖ tr franger

fringe′ ben′efits spl supplément m de solde, bénéfices mpl marginaux, avantages mpl sociaux

fripper·y [′frɪpəri] s (pl **-ies**) (flashiness) clinquant m; (inferior goods) camelote f

Frisbee [′frɪzbi] s (trademark) disque m volant

frisk [frɪsk] tr (slang) fouiller, palper ‖ intr—**to frisk about** gambader, folâtrer

frisk·y [′frɪski] adj (comp **-ier;** super **-iest**) vif, folâtre; (horse) fringant

fritter [′frɪtər] s beignet m ‖ tr—**to fritter away** gaspiller

frivolous [′frɪvələs] adj frivole

frizzle [′frɪzəl] s frisure f ‖ tr frisotter; (culin) faire frire ‖ intr frisotter; (culin) grésiller

friz·zly [′frɪzli] adj (comp **-zlier;** super **-zliest**) crépu, crépelu

fro [fro] adv—**to and fro** de long en large; **to go to and fro** aller et venir

frock [frɑk] s robe f; (overalls, smock) blouse f; (eccl) froc m

frock′ coat′ s redingote f

frog [frɑg], [frɔg] s grenouille f; (in throat) chat m

frog′man′ s (pl **-men′**) homme-grenouille m

frogs′′ legs′ spl cuisses fpl de grenouille

frol·ic [′frɑlɪk] s gaieté f, ébats mpl ‖ v (pret & pp **-icked;** ger **-icking**) intr s'ébattre, folâtrer

frolicsome [′frɑlɪksəm] adj folâtre

from [frʌm], [frɑm], [frəm] prep de; de la part de, e.g., **greetings from your friend** compliments de la part de votre ami; contre, e.g., **a shelter from the rain** un abri contre la pluie; **from a certain angle** sous un certain angle; **from . . . to** depuis . . . jusqu'à; **from what I hear** d'après ce que j'apprends; **the flight from** le vol en provenance de; **to drink from** (a glass) boire dans; (a bottle) boire à; **to learn from a book** apprendre dans un livre; **to steal from** voler à

front [frʌnt] adj antérieur, de devant ‖ s devant m; (first place) premier rang m; (aut) avant m; (geog, mil, pol) front m; (figurehead) (coll) prête-nom m; **in front** par devant; **in front of** en tête de, devant; **to put up a bold front** (coll) faire bonne contenance ‖ tr (to face) donner sur; (to *confront*) affronter ‖ *intr*—**to front on** donner sur

frontage [ˈfrʌntɪdʒ] *s* façade *f*; (*along a street, lake, etc.*) largeur *f*

front' door' *s* porte *f* d'entrée

front' drive' *s* (aut) traction *f* avant

frontier [frʌnˈtɪr] *adj* frontalier ‖ *s* frontière *f*; (hist) front *m* de colonisation, front pionnier

frontiers'man *s* (*pl* **-men**) frontalier *m*, broussard *m*

frontispiece [ˈfrʌntɪs͵pis] *s* frontispice *m*; (archit) façade *f* principale

front' lines' *s* avant-postes *mpl*

front' mat'ter *s* (*of book*) feuilles *fpl* liminaires

front' of'fice *s* direction *f*

front' page' *s*—**the front page** la première page, la une

front' porch' *s* porche *m*

front' room' *s* chambre *f* sur la rue

front' row' *s* premier rang *m*

front' seat' *s* siège *m* avant; (aut) banquette *f* avant

front' steps' *spl* perron *m*

front' view' *s* vue *f* de face

front'-wheel drive' *s* traction *f* avant

front'yard' *s* devant *m* de la maison

frost [frɔst] *s* (*freezing*) gelée *f*; (*frozen dew*) givre *m* ‖ *tr* (*to freeze*) geler; (*to cover with frost*) givrer; (culin) glacer

frost'bite' *s* engelure *f*

frost'ed glass' *s* verre *m* dépoli

frosting [ˈfrɔstɪŋ] *s* (*on glass*) dépolissage *m*; (culin) fondant *m*

frost·y [ˈfrɔsti] *adj* (*comp* **-ier**; *super* **-iest**) couvert de givre; (*reception, welcome*) glacé, glacial

froth [frɔθ] *s* écume *f*; (*on soap, beer, chocolate*) mousse *f*; (*frivolity*) futilité *f* ‖ *intr* mousser; (*at the mouth*) écumer

froth·y [ˈfrɔθi] *adj* (*comp* **-ier**; *super* **-iest**) écumeux; (*soap, beer, chocolate*) mousseux; (*frivolous*) creux, futile

froward [ˈfrowərd] *adj* obstiné, revêche

frown [fraʊn] *s* froncement *m* de sourcils ‖ *intr* froncer les sourcils; **to frown at** or **on** être contraire à, désapprouver

frows·y or **frowz·y** [ˈfraʊzi] *adj* (*comp* **-ier**; *super* **-iest**) malpropre, négligé, peu soigné; (*smelling bad*) malodorant

fro'zen as'sets [ˈfrozən] *spl* fonds *mpl* gelés

fro'zen din'ner *s* plateau *m* repas congelé

fro'zen foods' *spl* aliments *mpl* surgelés

frugal [ˈfrugəl] *adj* sobre, modéré; (*meal*) frugal

fruit [frut] *adj* fruitier ‖ *s* fruit *m*; les fruits, e.g., **I like fruit** j'aime les fruits; (*homosexual*) (pej) tapette *f*, pédé *m*

fruit' cake' *s* cake *m*

fruit' cup' *s* coupe *f* de fruits

fruit' fly' *s* mouche *f* du vinaigre

fruitful [ˈfrutfəl] *adj* fructueux, fécond

fruition [fruˈɪʃən] *s* réalisation *f*; **to come to fruition** fructifier

fruit' juice' *s* jus *m* de fruits

fruitless [ˈfrutlɪs] *adj* stérile, vain

fruit' sal'ad *s* macédoine *f* de fruits, salade *f* de fruits

fruit' stand' *s* étalage *m* de fruits

fruit' store' *s* fruiterie *f*

frumpish [ˈfrʌmpɪʃ] *adj* fagoté, négligé

frustrate [ˈfrʌstret] *tr* frustrer

fry [fraɪ] *s* (*pl* **-fries**) (culin) friture *f*; (ichth) fretin *m* ‖ *v* (*pret* & *pp* **fried**) *tr* faire frire; (*to sauté*) faire sauter ‖ *intr* frire

fry'ing pan' *s* poêle *f* à frire; **to jump from the frying pan into the fire** sauter de la poêle dans le feu

fudge [fʌdʒ] *s* fondant *m* de chocolat; (*humbug*) blague *f*

fuel [ˈfju·əl] *s* combustible *m*; (aut) carburant *m*; (fig) aliment *m* ‖ *v* (*pret* & *pp* **fueled** or **fuelled**; *ger* **fueling** or **fuelling**) *tr* pourvoir en combustible

fu'el gauge' *s* jauge *f* de combustible

fu'el line' *s* conduite *f* de combustible

fu'el oil' *s* mazout *m*, fuel-oil *m*, fuel *m*

fu'el tank' *s* réservoir *m* de carburant; (aut) réservoir à essence

fu'el truck' *s* camion *m* citerne

fugitive [ˈfjudʒɪtɪv] *adj* & *s* fugitif *m*

ful·crum [ˈfʌlkrəm] *s* (*pl* **-crums** or **-cra** [krə]) point *m* d'appui

fulfill [fʊlˈfɪl] *tr* accomplir; (*an obligation*) s'acquitter de, remplir

fulfillment [fʊlˈfɪlmənt] *s* accomplissement *m*

full [fʊl] *adj* plein; (*dress, garment*) ample, bouffant; (*schedule*) chargé; (*lips*) gros, fort; (*brother, sister*) germain; (*having no more room*) complet; **full to overflowing** plein à déborder ‖ *s* plein *m*; **in full** intégralement, entièrement; (*to spell in full*) en toutes lettres; **to the full** complètement ‖ *adv* complètement; **full in the face** en pleine figure; **full many a** bien des; **full well** parfaitement ‖ *tr* (*cloth*) fouler

full' blast' *adv* (coll) en pleine activité

full'-blood'ed *adj* robuste; (*thoroughbred*) pur sang, de pure souche

full-blown [ˈfʊlˈblon] *adj* achevé, développé; en pleine fleur

full'-bod'ied *adj* (*e.g., wine*) corsé

full' dress' *s* grande tenue *f*

full'-dress coat' *s* frac *m*

full'-faced' *adj* (*portrait*) de face

full-fledged [ˈfʊlˈflɛdʒd] *adj* véritable, rien moins que

full-grown [ˈfʊlˈgron] *adj* (*plant*) mûr; (*tree*) de haute futaie; (*person*) adulte

full' house' *s* (poker) main *f* pleine; (theat) salle *f* comble

full'-length' *adj* (*portrait*) en pied

full'-length mir'ror *s* psyché *f*

full'-length mov'ie *s* long métrage *m*

full' load' *s* plein chargement *m*

full' meas'ure *s* mesure *f* comble

full' moon' *s* pleine lune *f*

full' name' *s* nom *m* et prénoms *mpl*

full' pow'ers *spl* pleins pouvoirs *mpl*

full' rest' *s* (mus) pause *f*

full' sail' *adv* toutes voiles dehors

full' ses'sion *s* assemblée *f* plénière

full′-sized′ *adj* de grandeur nature
full′ speed′ *s* toute vitesse *f*
full′ stop′ *s* (gram) point *m* final; **to come to a full stop** s'arrêter net
full′ swing′ *s*—**in full swing** en pleine activité, en train
full′ tilt′ *adv* à toute vitesse
full′ time′ *adv* à pleines journées
full′-time′ *adj* à temps plein
full′ view′ *s*—**in full view** à la vue de tous
full′ weight′ *s* poids *m* juste
fully [ˈfʊli] *adv* entièrement, pleinement
fulsome [ˈfʊlsəm] *adj* écœurant, bas, servile
fumble [ˈfʌmbəl] *tr* manier maladroitement; (*the ball*) ne pas attraper, laisser tomber ‖ *intr* tâtonner
fume [fjum] *s* (*bad humor*) rage *f*; **fumes** fumées *fpl*, vapeurs *fpl* ‖ *tr & intr* fumer
fumigate [ˈfjumɪˌget] *tr* fumiger
fun [fʌn] *s* amusement *m*, gaieté *f*; (*badinage*) plaisanterie *f*; **in fun** pour rire; **to have fun** s'amuser; **to make fun of** se moquer de
function [ˈfʌŋkʃən] *s* fonction *f*; (*meeting*) cérémonie *f* ‖ *intr* fonctionner; **to function as** faire fonction de
functional [ˈfʌŋkʃənəl] *adj* fonctionnel
functionar·y [ˈfʌŋkʃəˌnɛri] *s* (*pl* **-ies**) fonctionnaire *mf*
fund [fʌnd] *s* fonds *m*; **funds** fonds *mpl* ‖ *tr* (*a debt*) consolider
fundamental [ˌfʌndəˈmɛntəl] *adj* fondamental ‖ *s* principe *m*, base *f*
fundamentalist [ˌfʌndəˈmɛntəlɪst] *s* (rel) scripturaire *m*
funeral [ˈfjunərəl] *adj* (*march, procession, ceremony*) funèbre; (*expenses*) funéraire ‖ *s* funérailles *fpl*
fu′neral direc′tor *s* entrepreneur *m* de pompes funèbres
fu′neral home′ or **par′lor** *s* chapelle *f* mortuaire; salon *m* mortuaire (Canad); (*business*) entreprise *f* de pompes funèbres
fu′neral proces′sion *s* convoi *m* funèbre, enterrement *m*, deuil *m*
fu′neral serv′ice *s* office *m* des morts
funereal [fjuˈnɪrɪ·əl] *adj* funèbre
fungicide [ˈfʌndʒɪˌsaɪd] *s* fongicide *m*
fungus [ˈfʌŋgəs] *s* (*pl* **funguses** or **fungi** [ˈfʌndʒaɪ]) (bot) champignon *m*; (pathol) fongus *m*
funicular [fjuˈnɪkjələr] *adj & s* funiculaire *m*
funk [fʌŋk] *s* (coll) frousse *f*
fun·nel [ˈfʌnəl] *s* (*for pouring through*) entonnoir *m*; (*smokestack*) cheminée *f*; (*tube for ventilation*) tuyau *m* ‖ *v* (*pret & pp* **-neled** or **-nelled**; *ger* **-neling** or **-nelling**) *tr* verser avec un entonnoir; (*to channel*) concentrer
funnies [ˈfʌniz] *spl* pages *fpl* comiques
fun·ny [ˈfʌni] *adj* (*comp* **-nier**; *super* **-niest**) comique; amusant, drôle; (coll) bizarre, curieux; **to strike s.o. as funny** paraître drôle à qn
fun′ny pa′per *s* pages *fpl* comiques

fur [fʌr] *s* fourrure *f*; (*on tongue*) empâtement *m*; **furs** pelleteries *fpl*
furbish [ˈfʌrbɪʃ] *tr* fourbir; **to furbish up** remettre à neuf
furious [ˈfjʊrɪ·əs] *adj* furieux
furl [fʌrl] *tr* (naut) ferler
fur′-lined′ *adj* doublé de fourrure
furlough [ˈfʌrlo] *s* permission *f*; **on furlough** en permission ‖ *tr* donner une permission à
furnace [ˈfʌrnɪs] *s* (*to heat a house*) calorifère *m*; (*to produce steam*) chaudière *f*; (*e.g., to smelt ores*) fourneau *m*; (rr) foyer *m*; (fig) fournaise *f*
furnish [ˈfʌrnɪʃ] *tr* fournir; (*a house*) meubler
fur′nished apart′ment *s* garni *m*, appartement *m* meublé
furnishings [ˈfʌrnɪʃɪŋz] *spl* (*of a house*) ameublement *m*; (*things to wear*) articles *mpl* d'habillement
furniture [ˈfʌrnɪtʃər] *s* meubles *mpl*; **a piece of furniture** un meuble; **a suite of furniture** un mobilier
fur′niture deal′er *s* marchand *m* de meubles
fur′niture pol′ish *s* encaustique *f*
fur′niture store′ *s* maison *f* d'ameublement
fur′niture ware′house *s* garde-meuble *m*
furor [ˈfjʊrɔr] *s* fureur *f*
furrier [ˈfʌrɪ·ər] *s* fourreur *m*, pelletier *m*
furrow [ˈfʌro] *s* sillon *m* ‖ *tr* sillonner
fur·ry [ˈfʌri] *adj* (*comp* **-rier**; *super* **-riest**) fourré, à fourrure
further [ˈfʌrðər] *adj* additional, supplémentaire ‖ *adv* plus loin; (*besides*) en outre, de plus ‖ *tr* avancer, favoriser
furtherance [ˈfʌrðərəns] *s* avancement *m*
fur′ther·more′ *adv* de plus, d'ailleurs
furthest [ˈfʌrðɪst] *adj* (le) plus éloigné ‖ *adv* le plus loin
furtive [ˈfʌrtɪv] *adj* furtif
fu·ry [ˈfjʊri] *s* (*pl* **-ries**) furie *f*
furze [fʌrz] *s* genêt *m* épineux, ajonc *m* d'Europe
fuse [fjuz] *s* (*tube or wick filled with explosive material*) étoupille *f*, mèche *f*; (*device for exploding a bomb or projectile*) fusée *f*; (elec) fusible *m*, plomb *m* de sûreté, plomb fusible; **to burn** or **blow out a fuse** faire sauter un plomb ‖ *tr* fondre; étoupiller ‖ *intr* se fondre
fuse′ box′ *s* boîte *f* à fusibles
fuselage [ˈfjuzəlɪdʒ] *s* fuselage *m*
fusible [ˈfjuzɪbəl] *adj* fusible
fusillade [ˌfjuzɪˈled] *s* fusillade *f*
fusion [ˈfjuʒən] *s* fusion *f*
fuss [fʌs] *s* (*excitement*) tapage *m*, agitation *f*; (*attention*) façons *fpl*, chichi *m*; (*dispute*) bagarre *f*; **to kick up a fuss** (coll) faire un tas d'histoires; **to make a fuss over** faire grand cas de ‖ *intr* faire des embarras, simagrées, or chichis; **to fuss over** être aux petits soins auprès de
fuss·y [ˈfʌsi] *adj* (*comp* **-ier**; *super* **-iest**) tracassier, tatillon; (*in dress*) pomponné

fustian ['fʌstʃən] s (*cloth*) futaine f; (*bombast*) grandiloquence f
futile ['fjutɪl] adj futile
future ['fjutʃər] adj futur, d'avenir ‖ s avenir m; (gram) futur m; **futures** (com) valeurs fpl négociées à terme; **in the**

future à l'avenir; **in the near future** à brève échéance
fuzz [fʌz] s (*on a peach*) duvet m; (*on a blanket*) peluche f; (*in pockets and corners*) bourre f
fuzz·y ['fʌzi] adj (*comp* **-ier**; *super* **-iest**) pelucheux; (*hair*) crêpelu; (*indistinct*) flou

G

G, g [dʒi] s VIIᵉ lettre de l'alphabet
gab [gæb] s (coll) bavardage m, langue f ‖ v (*pret & pp* **gabbed**; *ger* **gabbing**) intr (coll) bavarder
gabardine ['gæbər,din] s gabardine f
gabble ['gæbəl] s jacasserie f ‖ intr jacasser
gable ['gebəl] s (*of roof*) pignon m; (*over a door or window*) gable m
ga′ble end′ s pignon m
ga′ble roof′ s comble m sur pignon, toit m à deux pentes
gad [gæd] v (*pret & pp* **gadded**; *ger* **gadding**) intr—**to gad about** courir la prétantaine, vadrouiller
gad′about′ s vadrouilleur m
gad′fly′ s (*pl* **-flies**) taon m
gadget ['gædʒɪt] s dispositif m; (*unnamed article*) machin m, truc m, gimmick m
Gaelic ['gelɪk] adj & s gaélique m
gaff [gæf] s gaffe f; **to stand the gaff** (slang) ne pas broncher
gaffer ['gæfər] s (coll) vieux bonhomme m
gag [gæg] s bâillon m; (*interpolation by an actor*) gag m; (*joke*) blague f ‖ v (*pret & pp* **gagged**; *ger* **gagging**) tr bâillonner ‖ intr avoir des haut-le-cœur
gage [gedʒ] s (*pledge*) gage m; (*challenge*) défi m
gaie·ty ['ge·ɪti] s (*pl* **-ties**) gaieté f
gaily ['geli] adv gaiement
gain [gen] s gain m; (*increase*) accroissement m ‖ tr gagner; (*to reach*) atteindre, gagner ‖ intr gagner du terrain; (*said of invalid*) s'améliorer; (*said of watch*) avancer; **to gain on** prendre de l'avance sur
gainful ['genfəl] adj profitable
gain′say′ v (*pret & pp* **-said** [,sed], [,sɛd]) tr (*to deny*) nier; (*to contradict*) contredire; **not to gainsay** ne pas disconvenir de
gait [get] s démarche f, allure f
gaiter ['getər] s guêtre f
gala ['gælə] adj de gala ‖ s gala m
galax·y ['gæləksi] s (*pl* **-ies**) galaxie f
gale [gel] s gros vent m; **gales of laughter** éclats mpl de rire; **to weather a gale** étaler un coup de vent
gall [gɔl] s bile f, fiel m; (*something bitter*) (fig) fiel m, amertume f; (*audacity*) (coll) toupet m ‖ tr écorcher par le frottement; (fig) irriter

gallant ['gælənt] adj (*spirited, daring*) vaillant, brave; (*stately, grand*) fier, noble; (*showy, gay*) élégant, superbe, de fête ‖ adj galant ‖ s galant m; vaillant m ‖ [gə'lænt] intr faire le galant
gallant·ry ['gæləntri] s (*pl* **-ries**) galanterie f; (*bravery*) vaillance f
gall′ blad′der s vésicule f biliaire
gall′ duct′ s conduit m biliaire
galleon ['gælɪ·ən] s (naut) galion m
galler·y ['gæləri] s (*pl* **-ies**) galerie f; (*cheapest seats in theater*) poulailler m; **to play to the gallery** poser pour la galerie
galley ['gæli] s (*ship*) galère f; (*ship's kitchen*) coquerie f; (typ) galée f, placard m
gal′ley proof′ s épreuve f en placard, épreuve sous le galet
gal′ley slave′ s galérien m
Gallic ['gælɪk] adj gaulois
Gal′lic wit′ s esprit m gaulois
galling ['gɔlɪŋ] adj irritant, blessant
gallivant ['gælɪ,vænt] intr courailler
gall′nut′ s noix f de galle
gallon ['gælən] s gallon m américain
galloon [gə'lun] s galon m
gallop ['gæləp] s galop m ‖ tr faire galoper ‖ intr galoper
gal·lows ['gæloz] s (*pl* **-lows** or **-lowses**) gibet m, potence f
gal′lows bird′ s (coll) gibier m de potence
gall′stone′ s calcul m biliaire
galore [gə'lor] adv à foison, à gogo
galoshes [gə'lɑʃɪz] spl caoutchoucs mpl
galvanize ['gælvə,naɪz] tr galvaniser
gal′vanized i′ron s tôle f galvanisée
gambit ['gæmbɪt] s gambit m
gamble ['gæmbəl] s risque m, affaire f de chance ‖ tr jouer; **to gamble away** perdre au jeu ‖ intr jouer; jouer à la Bourse; (fig) prendre des risques
gambler ['gæmblər] s joueur m
gambling ['gæmblɪŋ] s jeu m
gam′bling den′ s tripot m
gam′bling house′ s maison f de jeu
gam′bling ta′ble s table f de jeu
gam·bol ['gæmbəl] s gambade f ‖ v (*pret & pp* **-boled** or **-bolled**; *ger* **-boling** or **-bolling**) intr gambader
gambrel ['gæmbrəl] s (*hock*) jarret m; (*in butcher shop*) jambier m
gam′brel roof′ s toit m en croupe

game [gem] *adj* (*plucky*) crâne, résolu; (*leg*) boiteux ‖ *s* jeu *m*; (*contest*) match *m*; (*score necessary to win*) partie *f*; (*animal or bird*) gibier *m*; **to make game of** tourner en dérision

game'bag' *s* carnassière *f*, gibecière *f*

game' bird' *s* oiseau *m* que l'on chasse

game'cock' *s* coq *m* de combat

game'keep'er *s* garde-chasse *m*

game' of chance' *s* jeu *m* de hasard

game' preserve' *s* chasse *f* gardée

game' war'den *s* garde-chasse *m*

gamut ['gæmət] *s* gamme *f*

gam·y ['gemi] *adj* (*comp* **-ier**; *super* **-iest**) (*having flavor of uncooked game*) faisandé; (*plucky*) crâne

gander ['gændər] *s* jars *m*

gang [gæŋ] *adj* multiple ‖ *s* (*of workmen*) équipe *f*, brigade *f*; (*of thugs*) bande *f*; (*of wrongdoers*) séquelle *f*, clique *f* ‖ *intr*—**to gang up** se concerter; **to gang up on** se liguer contre

gangling ['gæŋglɪŋ] *adj* dégingandé

gangli·on ['gæŋglɪ·ən] *s* (*pl* **-ons** or **-a** [ə]) ganglion *m*

gang'plank' *s* passerelle *f*, planche *f* de débarquement

gang' rape' *s* viol *m* collectif

gangrene ['gæŋgrin] *s* gangrène *f* ‖ *tr* gangrener ‖ *intr* se gangrener

gangster ['gæŋstər] *s* bandit *m*, gangster *m*

gang'way' *s* (*passageway*) passage *m*, coursive *f*; (*gangplank*) planche *f* de débarquement; (*in ship's side*) coupée *f* ‖ *interj* rangez-vous!, dégagez!

gan·try ['gæntri] *s* (*pl* **-tries**) (*for barrels*) chantier *m*; (*for crane*) portique *m*; (rr) pont *m* à signaux

gan'try crane' *s* grue *f* à portique

gap [gæp] *s* (*blank*) lacune *f*; (*in wall*) brèche *f*; (*between mountains*) col *m*, gorge *f*; (*between two points of view*) abîme *m*, gouffre *m*

gape [gep] *s* (*gap*) ouverture *f*, brèche *f*; (*yawn*) bâillement *m*; (*look of astonishment*) badauderie *f* ‖ *intr* (*to yawn*) bâiller; (*to look with astonishment*) badauder; **to gape at** regarder bouche bée

garage [gə'rɑʒ] *s* garage *m*

garage' sale' *s* braderie *f*, vente *f* bric-à-brac

garb [gɑrb] *s* costume *m* ‖ *tr* vêtir

garbage ['gɑrbɪdʒ] *s* ordures *fpl*

gar'bage can' *s* poubelle *f*, dépotoir *m* (d'ordures)

gar'bage collec'tion *s* voirie *f*

gar'bage collec'tor *s* boueur *m*

gar'bage dispos'al *s* broyeur *m* d'ordures

gar'bage truck' *s* benne *f* à ordures

garble ['gɑrbəl] *tr* mutiler, tronquer

garden ['gɑrdən] *s* jardin *m*; (*of vegetables*) potager *m*; (*of flowers*) parterre *m* ‖ *intr* jardiner

gar'den cit'y *s* cité-jardin *f*

gardener ['gɑrdnər] *s* jardinier *m*

gardening ['gɑrdnɪŋ] *s* jardinage *m*

gar'den par'ty *s* garden-party *f*

gargle ['gɑrgəl] *s* gargarisme *m* ‖ *intr* se gargariser

gargoyle ['gɑrgɔɪl] *s* gargouille *f*

garish ['gærɪʃ] *adj* cru, rutilant, criard

garland ['gɑrlənd] *s* guirlande *f* ‖ *tr* guirlander

garlic ['gɑrlɪk] *s* ail *m*

garment ['gɑrmənt] *s* vêtement *m*

gar'ment bag' *s* housse *f* à vêtements

garner ['gɑrnər] *tr* (*to gather, collect*) amasser; (*cereals*) engranger

garnet ['gɑrnɪt] *adj* & *s* grenat *m*

garnish ['gɑrnɪʃ] *s* garniture *f* ‖ *tr* garnir; (law) effectuer une saisie-arrêt sur

garret ['gærɪt] *s* grenier *m*; (*dormer room*) mansarde *f*

garrison ['gærɪsən] *s* garnison *f* ‖ *tr* (*troops*) mettre en garnison; (*a city*) mettre des troupes en garnison dans

garrote [gə'rɑt], [gə'rot] *s* (*method of execution*) garrotte *f*; (*iron collar used for such an execution*) garrot *m* ‖ *tr* garrotter

garrulous ['gær(j)ələs] *adj* bavard

garter ['gɑrtər] *s* jarretelle *f*, jarretière *f*; (*for men's socks*) support-chaussette *m*, fixe-chaussette *m*

garth [gɑrθ] *s* cour *f* intérieure d'un cloître

gas [gæs] *s* gaz *m*; (coll) essence *f*; (*empty talk*) (coll) bavardage *m*; **out of gas** en panne sèche; **to step on the gas** (coll) appuyer sur le champignon ‖ *v* (*pret & pp* **gassed**; *ger* **gassing**) *tr* gazer, asphyxier ‖ *intr* dégager des gaz; (mil) gazer; (*to talk nonsense*) (coll) bavarder

gas'bag' *s* enveloppe *f* à gaz; (coll) blagueur *m*, baratineur *m*

gas' burn'er *s* bec *m* de gaz

gas' cham'ber *s* chambre *f* à gaz

Gascony ['gæskəni] *s* Gascogne *f*; la Gascogne

gas' en'gine *s* moteur *m* à gaz

gaseous ['gæsɪ·əs] *adj* gazeux

gas' gen'erator *s* gazogène *m*

gash [gæʃ] *s* entaille *f*; (*on face*) balafre *f* ‖ *tr* entailler; balafrer

gas' heat' *s* chauffage *m* au gaz

gas' heat'er *s* (*for hot water*) chauffe-eau *m* à gaz; (*for house heat*) calorifère *m* à gaz

gas'hold'er *s* gazomètre *m*

gasi·fy ['gæsɪ,faɪ] *v* (*pret & pp* **-fied**) *tr* gazéifier ‖ *intr* se gazéifier

gas' jet' *s* bec *m* de gaz

gasket ['gæskɪt] *s* joint *m*

gas'light' *s* éclairage *m* au gaz

gas' main' *s* conduite *f* de gaz

gas' mask' *s* masque *m* à gaz

gas' me'ter *s* compteur *m* à gaz

gasoline ['gæsə,lin] *s* essence *f*

gas'oline can' *s* bidon *m* d'essence

gas'oline gauge' *s* voyant *m* d'essence

gas'oline pump' *s* pompe *f* à essence

gasp [gæsp] *s* halètement *m*; (*of surprise; of death*) hoquet *m* ‖ *tr*—**to gasp out** (*a word*) dire dans un souffle ‖ *intr* haleter

gas' pipe' *s* conduite *f* de gaz

gas' produc'er *s* gazogène *m*

gas' range' *s* fourneau *m* à gaz, cuisinière *f* à gaz

gassed *adj* (*in warfare*) gasé

gas' sta'tion *s* poste *m* d'essence

gas' stove' *s* cuisinière *f* à gaz, réchaud *m* à gaz

gas' tank' *s* gazomètre *m*; (aut) réservoir *m* d'essence

gastric ['gæstrɪk] *adj* gastrique

gastronomy [gæs'trɑnəmi] *s* gastronomie *f*

gas' works' *spl* usine *f* à gaz

gat [gæt] *s* (gun) (slang) flingue *f*

gate [get] *s* porte *f*; (*in fence or wall*) grille *f*; (*main gate*) portail *m*; (*of sluice*) vanne *f*; (*number paying admission; amount paid*) entrée *f*; (*waiting area*) (aer) salle *f* d'embarquement; (rr) barrière *f*; **to crash the gate** resquiller

gate-crasher ['get,kræʃər] *s* (coll) resquilleur *m*

gate' keep'er *s* portier *m*; (rr) garde-barrière *mf*

gate'-leg ta'ble *s* table *f* à abattants

gate' post' *s* montant *m*

gate' way' *s* passage *m*, entrée *f*; (*main entrance*) portail *m*

gather ['gæðər] *tr* amasser, rassembler; (*the harvest*) rentrer; (*fruits, flowers, etc.*) cueillir, ramasser; (*one's thoughts*) recueillir; (bb) rassembler; (sewing) froncer; (*to deduce*) (fig) conclure; **to gather dust** s'encrasser; **to gather oneself together** se ramasser ‖ *intr* se réunir, s'assembler; (*said of clouds*) s'amonceler

gathering ['gæðərɪŋ] *s* réunion *f*, rassemblement *m*; (*of harvest*) récolte *f*; (*of fruits, flowers, etc.*) cueillette *f*; (bb) assemblage *m*, cahier *m* (d'imprimerie); (sewing) froncis *m*

gaud·y ['gɔdi] *adj* (*comp* **-ier;** *super* **-iest**) criard, voyant

gauge [gedʒ] *s* jauge *f*, calibre *m*; (*of liquid in a container*) niveau *m*; (*of gasoline, oil, etc.*) indicateur *m*; (*of carpenter*) trusquin *m*; (rr) écartement *m* ‖ *tr* jauger, calibrer; (*a person; s.o.'s capacities; a distance*) juger de, jauger

gauge' glass' *s* indicateur *m* de niveau

Gaul [gɔl] *s* Gaule *f*; la Gaule

Gaulish ['gɔlɪʃ] *adj* & *s* gaulois *m*

gaunt [gɔnt] *adj* décharné, étique, efflanqué

gauntlet ['gɔntlɪt] *s* gantelet *m*; **to run the gauntlet** passer par les baguettes; **to take up the gauntlet** relever le gant; **to throw down the gauntlet** jeter le gant

gauze [gɔz] *s* gaze *f*

gavel ['gævəl] *s* marteau *m*

gawk [gɔk] *s* (coll) godiche *mf* ‖ *intr* (coll) bayer aux corneilles; **to gawk at** (coll) regarder bouche bée

gawk·y ['gɔki] *adj* (*comp* **-ier;** *super* **-iest**) godiche

gay [ge] *adj* de la pédale, homosexuel; (obs) gai

gay' blade' *s* (coll) joyeux drille *m*

gaze [gez] *s* regard *m* fixe ‖ *intr* regarder fixement

gazelle [gə'zɛl] *s* gazelle *f*

gazette [gə'zɛt] *s* gazette *f*; journal *m* officiel

gazetteer [,gæzə'tɪr] *s* dictionnaire *m* géographique

gear [gɪr] *s* (*paraphernalia*) attirail *m*, appareil *m*; (*of transmission, steering, etc.*) mécanisme *m*; (*adjustment of automobile transmission*) marche *f*, vitesse *f*; (*two or more toothed wheels meshed together*) engrenage *m*; **out of gear** débrayé; **to throw into gear** embrayer; **to throw out of gear** débrayer; (fig) disloquer ‖ *tr* & *intr* engrener

gear' box' *s* (aut) boîte *f* de vitesses

gear' shift' *s* changement *m* de vitesse

gear' shift lev'er *s* levier *m* de changement de vitesse

gear' wheel' roue *f* d'engrenage

gee [dʒi] *interj* sapristi!; (*to the right*) hue!; **gee up!** hue!

Gei'ger count'er ['gaɪgər] *s* compteur *m* de Geiger

gel [dʒɛl] *s* (chem) gel *m*

gelatine ['dʒɛlətɪn] *s* gélatine *f*

geld [gɛld] *v* (*pret* & *pp* **gelded** or **gelt** [gɛlt]) *tr* châtrer

gelding ['gɛldɪŋ] *s* hongre *m*

gem [dʒɛm] *s* gemme *f*; (fig) bijou *m*

Gemini ['dʒɛmə,naɪ] *s* (astr, astrol) les Gémeaux *mpl*

gender ['dʒɛndər] *s* (gram) genre *m*; (coll) sexe *m*

gene [dʒin] *s* (biol) gène *m*

genealo·gy [,dʒɛni'ælədʒi] *s* (*pl* **-gies**) généalogie *f*

general ['dʒɛnərəl] *adj* & *s* général *m*; **in general** en général

gen'eral deliv'ery *s* poste *f* restante

generalissi·mo [,dʒɛnərə'lɪsɪmo] *s* (*pl* **-mos**) généralissime *m*

generali·ty [,dʒɛnə'rælɪti] *s* (*pl* **-ties**) généralité *f*

generalize ['dʒɛnərə,laɪz] *tr* & *intr* généraliser

generally ['dʒɛnərəli] *adj* généralement

gen'eral practi'tioner *s* (med) généraliste *m*

gen'eral·ship' *s* tactique *f*; (*office*) généralat *m*

gen'eral staff' *s* état-major *m*

generate ['dʒɛnə,ret] *tr* générer; (*to beget*) engendrer; (geom) engendrer

gen'erating sta'tion *s* usine *f* génératrice, centrale *f*

generation [,dʒɛnə'reʃən] *s* génération *f*

genera'tion gap' *s* fossé *m* des générations

generator ['dʒɛnə,retər] *s* (chem) gazogène *m*; (elec) génératrice *f*

generic [dʒɪ'nɛrɪk] *adj* générique

generosi·ty [,dʒɛnə'rɑsɪti] *s* (*pl* **-ties**) générosité *f*

generous ['dʒɛnərəs] *adj* (*action, quantity*) généreux; (*supply; harvest*) abondant; (*size*) ample

gene·sis ['dʒɛnɪsɪs] *s* (*pl* **-ses** [,siz]) genèse *f*; **Genesis** (Bib) La Genèse

genetic [dʒɪˈnɛtɪk] *adj* génétique ‖ **genetics** *s* génétique *f*

genet'ic en'gineer'ing *s* sélection *f* eugénique

Geneva [dʒɪˈnivə] *s* Genève *f*

genial [ˈdʒinɪ·əl] *adj* affable

genie [ˈdʒini] *s* génie *m*

genital [ˈdʒɛnɪtəl] *adj* génital ‖ **genitals** *spl* organes *mpl* génitaux

genitive [ˈdʒɛnɪtɪv] *s* génitif *m*

genius [ˈdʒinjəs] *s* (*pl* **geniuses**) génie *m* ‖ *s* (*pl* **genii** [ˈdʒinɪ,aɪ]) génie *m*

Genoa [ˈdʒɛno·ə] *s* Gênes *f*

genocide [ˈdʒɛnə,saɪd] *s* génocide *m*

genteel [dʒɛnˈtil] *adj* distingué, de bon ton, élégant

gentian [ˈdʒɛnʃən] *s* gentiane *f*

gentile [ˈdʒɛntaɪl] *s* non-juif *m*, chrétien *m*

gentili·ty [dʒɛnˈtɪlɪti] *s* (*pl* **-ties**) (*birth*) naissance *f* distinguée; (*breeding*) politesse *f*

gentle [ˈdʒɛntəl] *adj* doux; (*in birth*) noble, bien né; (*e.g., tap on the shoulder*) léger

gen'tle·folk' *s* gens *mpl* de bonne naissance

gen'tle·man *s* (*pl* **-men**) monsieur *m*; (*polite person*) homme *m* bien élevé; (*man of independent means*) rentier *m*; (hist) gentilhomme *m*

gentlemanly [ˈdʒɛntəlmənli] *adj* bien élevé, de bon ton

gen'tleman's agree'ment *s* engagement *m* sur parole, contrat *m* verbal

gen'tle sex' *s* sexe *m* faible

gentry [ˈdʒɛntri] *s* gens *mpl* de bonne naissance; (Brit) petite noblesse *f*

genuine [ˈdʒɛnju·ɪn] *adj* véritable, authentique; (*person*) sincère, franc

genus [ˈdʒinəs] *s* (*pl* **genera** [ˈdʒɛnərə] or **genuses**) genre *m*

geogra·phy [dʒɪˈɑgrəfi] *s* (*pl* **-phies**) géographie *f*

geologic(al) [,dʒi·əˈlɑdʒɪk(əl)] *adj* géologique

geolo·gy [dʒɪˈɑlədʒi] *s* (*pl* **-gies**) géologie *f*

geometric(al) [,dʒi·əˈmɛtrɪk(əl)] *adj* géométrique

geome·try [dʒɪˈɑmɪtri] *s* (*pl* **-tries**) géométrie *f*

geophysics [,dʒi·əˈfɪzɪks] *s* géophysique *f*

geopolitics [,dʒi·əˈpɑlɪtɪks] *s* géopolitique *f*

George [dʒɔrdʒ] *s* Georges *m*

geranium [dʒɪˈreni·əm] *s* géranium *m*

geriatrics [,dʒɛrɪˈætrɪks] *s* gériatrie *f*

germ [dʒʌrm] *s* germe *m*

German [ˈdʒʌrmən] *adj* allemand ‖ *s* (*language*) allemand *m*; (*person*) Allemand *m*

germane [dʒɛrˈmen] *adj* à propos, pertinent; **germane to** se rapportant à

Ger'man mea'sles *s* rubéole *f*

Ger'man sil'ver *s* maillechort *m*, argentan *m*

Germa·ny [ˈdʒʌrməni] *s* (*pl* **-nies**) Allemagne *f*; l'Allemagne

germ'-free' *adj* axénique

germicidal [,dʒʌrmɪˈsaɪdəl] *adj* germicide

germicide [ˈdʒʌrmɪ,saɪd] *s* germicide *m*

germinate [ˈdʒʌrmɪ,net] *intr* germer

germ' war'fare *s* guerre *f* bactériologique

gerontology [,dʒɛrɑnˈtɑlədʒi] *s* gérontologie *f*

gerrymander [ˈgɛrɪ,mændər] *s* découpage *m* des circonscriptions électorales

gerund [ˈdʒɛrənd] *s* gérondif *m*

gestation [dʒɛsˈteʃən] *s* gestation *f*

gesticulate [dʒɛsˈtɪkjə,let] *intr* gesticuler

gesture [ˈdʒɛstʃər] *s* geste *m* ‖ *intr* faire des gestes; **to gesture to** faire signe à

get [gɛt] *v* (*pret* **got** [gɑt]; *pp* **got** or **gotten** [ˈgɑtən]; *ger* **getting**) *tr* obtenir, procurer; (*to receive*) avoir, recevoir; (*to catch*) attraper; (*to seek*) chercher, aller chercher; (*to reach*) atteindre; (*to find*) trouver, rencontrer; (*to obtain and bring*) prendre; (*e.g., dinner*) faire; (rad) avoir, prendre, accrocher; (*to understand*) (coll) comprendre; **to get across** faire accepter; faire comprendre; **to get a kick out of** (coll) prendre plaisir à; **to get back** ravoir, se faire rendre; **to get down** descendre; (*to swallow*) avaler; **to get in** rentrer; **to get out the trump** purger les atouts; **to get s.o. to** + *inf* persuader à qn de + *inf*; **to get s.th. done** faire faire q.ch. ‖ *intr* (*to become*) devenir, se faire; (*to arrive*) arriver, parvenir; **get up!** (*said to an animal*) hue!; **to get about** (*said of news*) se répandre; (*said of convalescent*) être de nouveau sur pied; (*to move about*) circuler; **to get accustomed to** se faire à; **to get across** traverser; **to get along** (coll) circuler; (*to succeed*) se tirer d'affaire; **to get along with** faire bon ménage avec; **to get along without** se passer de; **to get angry** se fâcher; **to get away** s'évader; **to get away with** s'en aller avec; (coll) s'en tirer avec; **to get back** reculer; (*to return*) rentrer; **to get back at** (coll) rendre la pareille à, se venger sur; **to get by** passer; (*to manage, to shift*) (coll) s'en tirer sans peine; **to get dark** faire nuit; **to get down** descendre; **to get going** se mettre en marche; **to get in** or **into** entrer dans; **to get off** (*to go free*) s'en tirer; **to get off (of)** (*a bus, a horse, etc.*) descendre de; (*a chair, the floor*) se lever de; **to get off with** en être quitte pour; **to get on** monter sur; (*a car*) monter dans; continuer; (*to succeed*) faire des progrès; **to get out** sortir; **to get rid of** se défaire de; **to get to** arriver à; (*to have an opportunity to*) avoir l'occasion de; **to get up** se lever; **to not get over it** (coll) ne pas en revenir

get'away' *s* démarrage *m*; (*flight*) fuite *f*

get'-togeth'er *s* réunion *f*

get'up' *s* (*style*) (coll) présentation *f*; (*outfit*) (coll) affublement *m*

geyser [ˈgaɪzər] *s* geyser *m*

ghast·ly [ˈgæstli] *adj* (*comp* **-lier**; *super* **-liest**) livide, blême; horrible, affreux

Ghent [gɛnt] *s* Gand *m*

gherkin [ˈgʌrkɪn] *s* cornichon *m*

ghet·to [ˈgɛto] *s* (*pl* **-tos**) ghetto *m*

ghost [gost] *s* revenant *m*, spectre *m*; (*shade, semblance*) ombre *f*; **not the ghost of a**

chance pas la moindre chance; **to give up the ghost** rendre l'âme, rendre l'esprit

ghost′ im′age s filage m

ghost·ly ['gostli] adj (comp **-lier**; super **-liest**) spectral, fantomatique

ghost′ sto′ry s histoire f de revenants

ghost′ town′ s ville f morte

ghost′ writ′er s rédacteur m anonyme

ghoul [gul] s goule f; (body snatcher) déterreur m de cadavres

ghoulish ['gulɪʃ] adj vampirique

GI ['dʒi'aɪ] (letterword) (**General Issue**) adj fourni par l'armée ‖ s (pl **GI's**) soldat m américain, simple soldat

giant ['dʒaɪ·ənt] adj & s géant m

giantess ['dʒaɪ·əntɪs] s géante f

gibberish ['dʒɪbərɪʃ] s baragouin m

gibbet ['dʒɪbɪt] s gibet m, potence f

gibe [dʒaɪb] s raillerie f, moquerie f ‖ tr & intr railler; **to gibe at** se moquer de, railler

giblets ['dʒɪblɪts] spl abattis m, abats mpl

gid·dy ['gɪdi] adj (comp **-dier**; super **-diest**) étourdi; (height) vertigineux; (foolish) léger, frivole

Gideon ['gɪdɪ·ən] s (Bib) Gédéon m

gift [gɪft] s cadeau m; (natural ability) don m, talent m ‖ tr douer

gifted adj doué

gift′ horse′ s—**never look a gift horse in the mouth** à cheval donné on ne regarde pas à la bride

gift′ of gab′ s (coll) bagou m, faconde f

gift′ shop′ s boutique f de souvenirs, magasin m de nouveautés

gift′-wrap v (pret & pp **-wrapped**; ger **-wrapping**) tr faire un paquet cadeau de

gigantic [dʒaɪ'gæntɪk] adj gigantesque

giggle ['gɪgəl] s petit rire m ‖ intr pousser des petits rires, glousser

gigo·lo ['dʒɪgə,lo] s (pl **-los**) gigolo m

GI Joe [,dʒi,aɪ'dʒo] s le troufion

gild [gɪld] v (pret & pp **gilded** or **gilt** [gɪlt]) tr dorer

gilding ['gɪldɪŋ] s dorure f

gill [gɪl] s (of cock) fanon m; **gills** (of fish) ouïes fpl, branchies fpl

gilt [gɪlt] adj & s doré m

gilt′-edged′ adj (e.g., book) doré sur tranche; (securities) de premier ordre, de tout repos

gimcrack ['dʒɪm,kræk] adj de pacotille, de camelote ‖ s babiole f

gimlet ['gɪmlɪt] s vrille f, perçoir m

gimmick ['gɪmɪk] s (coll) truc m, machin m; (trick) tour m

gin [dʒɪn] s (alcoholic liquor) gin m, genièvre m; (for cotton, corn, etc.) égreneuse f; (snare) trébuchet m ‖ v (pret & pp **ginned**; ger **ginning**) tr égrener

ginger ['dʒɪndʒər] s gingembre m; (fig) entrain m, allant m

gin′ger ale′ s boisson f gazeuse au gingembre

gin′ger·bread′ s pain m d'épice; ornement m de mauvais goût

gingerly ['dʒɪndʒərli] adj précautionneux ‖ adv tout doux, avec précaution

gin′ger·snap′ s gâteau m sec au gingembre

gingham ['gɪŋəm] s guingan m

giraffe [dʒɪ'ræf] s girafe f

gird [gʌrd] v (pret & pp **girt** [gʌrt] or **girded**) tr ceindre; **to gird on** se ceindre de; **to gird oneself for** se préparer à

girder ['gʌrdər] s poutre f

girdle ['gʌrdəl] s ceinture f ‖ tr ceindre, entourer

girl [gʌrl] s jeune fille f; (little girl) petite fille; (servant) bonne f

girl′ friend′ s (sweetheart) petite amie f, bonne amie f; (female friend) amie f, camarade f

girl′hood s enfance f, jeunesse f d'une femme

girlish ['gʌrlɪʃ] adj de jeune fille, de petite fille

girl′ scout′ s éclaireuse f, guide f

girls′′ school′ s école f de filles

girth [gʌrθ] s (band) sangle f; (measure around) circonférence f; (of person) tour m de taille

gist [dʒɪst] s fond m, essence f

give [gɪv] s élasticité f ‖ v (pret **gave** [gev]; pp **given** ['gɪvən]) tr donner; (a speech, a lecture, a class; a smile) faire; **to give away** donner, distribuer; révéler; **to give back** rendre, remettre; **to give forth** or **off** émettre; **to give oneself up** se rendre; **to give up** renoncer à, abandonner ‖ intr donner; **to give in** se rendre; **to give out** manquer; (to become exhausted) s'épuiser; **to give way** faire place, reculer

give′-and-take′ s compromis m; échange m de propos plaisants

give′away′ s (coll) révélation f involontaire; (coll) trahison f; **to play giveaway** jouer à qui perd gagne

given ['gɪvən] adj donné; **given that** vu que, étant donné que

giv′en name′ s prénom m

giver ['gɪvər] s donneur m, donateur m

gizzard ['gɪzərd] s gésier m

glacial ['gleʃəl] adj glacial; (chem) en cristaux; (geol) glaciaire

glacier ['gleʃər] s glacier m

glad [glæd] adj (comp **gladder**; super **gladdest**) content, heureux; **to be glad to** être content or heureux de

gladden ['glædən] tr réjouir

glade [gled] s clairière f, éclaircie f, percée f

glad′ hand′ s (coll) accueil m chaleureux

gladiator ['glædɪ,etər] s gladiateur m

gladiola [,glædɪ'olə] s glaïeul m

gladly ['glædli] adv volontiers, avec plaisir

gladness ['glædnɪs] s joie f, plaisir m

glad′ rags′ spl (slang) frusques fpl des grands jours

glamorous ['glæmərəs] adj ravissant, éclatant

glamour ['glæmər] s charme m, éclat m

glam′our girl′ s ensorceleuse f

glance [glæns] s coup m d'œil; **at a glance** d'un seul coup d'œil; **at first glance** à première vue ‖ *intr* jeter un regard; **to glance at** jeter un coup d'œil sur; **to glance off** ricocher, dévier; **to glance through a book** feuilleter un livre; **to glance up** lever les yeux

gland [glænd] *s* glande *f*

glanders ['glændərz] *spl* (vet) morve *f*

glare [glɛr] *s* (*light*) lumière *f* éblouissante; (*look*) regard *m* irrité ‖ *intr* éblouir, briller; **to glare at** lancer un regard méchant à, foudroyer du regard

glare′ ice′ *s* verglas *m*

glaring ['glɛrɪŋ] *adj* (*shining*) éblouissant; (*mistake, fact*) évident, qui saute aux yeux; (*blunder, abuse*) grossier, scandaleux

glasnost ['glas,nɑst] *s* transparence *f*, glasnost *m*

glass [glæs] *s* verre *m*; (*mirror*) glace *f*; **glasses** lunettes *fpl*

glass′ blow′er ['blo·ər] *s* verrier-souffleur *m*

glass′ case′ *s* vitrine *f*

glass′ cut′ter *s* (*tool*) diamant *m*; (*workman*) vitrier *m*

glass′ door′ *s* porte *f* vitrée

glassful ['glæsful] *s* verre *m*

glass′ house′ *s* serre *f*; (fig) maison *f* de verre

glass′ware′ *s* verrerie *f*

glass′ wool′ *s* laine *f* de verre

glass′works′ *s* verrerie *f*, glacerie *f*

glass·y ['glæsi] *adj* (*comp* **-ier**; *super* **-iest**) vitreux; (*smooth*) lisse

glaze [glez] *s* (*ceramics*) vernis *m*; (culin) glace *f*; (tex) lustre *m* ‖ *tr* (*to cover with a glossy coating*) glacer; (*to fit with glass*) vitrer

glazier ['glezər] *s* vitrier *m*

gleam [glim] *s* rayon *m*; (*of hope*) lueur *f* ‖ *intr* rayonner, reluire

glean [glin] *tr* glaner

glee [gli] *s* allégresse *f*, joie *f*

glee′ club′ *s* orphéon *m*, société *f* chorale

glen [glɛn] *s* vallon *m*, ravin *m*

glib [glɪb] *adj* (*comp* **glibber**; *super* **glibbest**) facile; (*tongue*) délié

glide [glaɪd] *s* glissement *m*; (aer) vol *m* plané; (mus) port *m* de voix; (phonet) son *m* transitoire ‖ *intr* glisser, se glisser; (aer) planer

glider ['glaɪdər] *s* (*porch seat*) siège *m* à glissière; (aer) planeur *m*

gliding ['glaɪdɪŋ] *s* vol *m* à voile

glimmer ['glɪmər] *s* faible lueur *f* ‖ *intr* jeter une faible lueur

glimmering ['glɪmərɪŋ] *adj* faible, vacillant ‖ *s* faible lueur *f*, miroitement *m*; soupçon *m*, indice *m*

glimpse [glɪmps] *s* aperçu *m*; **to catch a glimpse of** entrevoir, aviser ‖ *tr* entrevoir

glint [glɪnt] *s* reflet *m*, éclair *m* ‖ *intr* jeter un reflet, étinceler

glisten ['glɪsən] *s* scintillement *m* ‖ *intr* scintiller

glitter ['glɪtər] *s* éclat *m*, étincellement *m* ‖ *intr* étinceler

gloaming ['glomɪŋ] *s* crépuscule *m*, jour *m* crépusculaire

gloat [glot] *intr* éprouver un malin plaisir; **to gloat over** faire des gorges chaudes de; (*e.g., one's victim*) couver du regard

global ['globəl] *adj* sphérique; mondial

globe [glob] *s* globe *m*

globe′-trot′ter *s* globe-trotter *m*

globule ['globjul] *s* globule *m*

gloom [glum] *s* obscurité *f*, ténèbres *fpl*; tristesse *f*

gloom·y ['glumi] *adj* (*comp* **-ier**; *super* **-iest**) sombre, lugubre; (*ideas*) noir

glori·fy ['glorɪ,faɪ] *v* (*pret & pp* **-fied**) *tr* glorifier

glorious ['glorɪ·əs] *adj* glorieux

glo·ry ['glori] *s* (*pl* **-ries**) gloire *f*; **to be in one's glory** être aux anges; **to go to glory** (slang) aller à la ruine ‖ *v* (*pret & pp* **-ried**) *intr*—**to glory in** se glorifier de

gloss [glɔs] *s* lustre *m*; (*on cloth*) cati *m*; (*on floor*) brillant *m*; (*note, commentary*) glose *f*; **to take off the gloss from** décatir ‖ *tr* lustrer; **to gloss over** maquiller, farder

glossa·ry ['glɑsəri] *s* (*pl* **-ries**) glossaire *m*

gloss·y ['glɑsi] *adj* (*comp* **-ier**; *super* **-iest**) lustré, brillant

glot′tal stop′ ['glɑtəl] *s* coup *m* de glotte

glottis ['glɑtɪs] *s* glotte *f*

glove [glʌv] *s* gant *m* ‖ *tr* ganter

glove′ compart′ment *s* boîte *f* à gants

glove′ wash′cloth *s* gant *m* à laver

glow [glo] *s* rougeoiement *m* ‖ *intr* rougeoyer

glower ['glau·ər] *s* grise mine *f* ‖ *intr* avoir l'air renfrogné

glowing ['glo·ɪŋ] *adj* rougeoyant, incandescent; (*healthy*) rayonnant; (*cheeks*) vermeil; (*reports*) enthousiaste, élogieux

glow′worm′ *s* ver *m* luisant

glucose ['glukos] *s* glucose *m*

glue [glu] *s* colle *f* ‖ *tr* coller

glue′ pot′ *s* pot *m* à colle

gluey ['glu·i] *adj* (*comp* **gluier**; *super* **gluiest**) gluant

glum [glʌm] *adj* (*comp* **glummer**; *super* **glummest**) maussade, renfrogné

glut [glʌt] *s* (*excess*) surabondance *f*, excès *m*; (*on the market*) engorgement *m*, surplus *m* ‖ *v* (*pret & pp* **glutted**; *ger* **glutting**) *tr* (*with food*) rassasier; (*the market*) inonder, engorger

glutton ['glʌtən] *s* glouton *m*

gluttonous ['glʌtənəs] *adj* glouton

glutton·y ['glʌtəni] *s* (*pl* **-ies**) gloutonnerie *f*

glycerine ['glɪsərɪn] *s* glycérine *f*

G.M.T. *abbr* (**Greenwich mean time** temps moyen de Greenwich) T.U., temps *m* universel

gnarl [nɑrl] *s* (bot) nœud *m* ‖ *tr* tordre ‖ *intr* grogner

gnarled *adj* noueux

gnash [næʃ] *tr*—**to gnash the teeth** grincer des dents ou les dents

gnat [næt] *s* moucheron *m*, moustique *m*

gnaw [nɔ] *tr* ronger

gnome [nom] s gnome m

G.N.P. [ˈdʒiˈɛnˈpi] s (letterword) (**gross national product**) R.N.P. (revenu national brut), P.N.B. (produit national brut)

go [go] s (pl **goes**) aller m; **a lot of go** (slang) beaucoup d'allant; **it's no go** (coll) ça ne marche pas, pas mèche; **to have a go at** (coll) essayer; **to make a go of** (coll) réussir à ‖ v (pret **went** [wɛnt]; pp **gone** [gɔn], [gɑn] tr—**to go it alone** le faire tout seul, faire cavalier seul ‖ intr aller; (to work, operate) marcher; y aller, e.g., **did you go?** y êtes-vous allé?; devenir, y ça, **to go crazy** devenir fou; faire, e.g., **to go quack-quack** faire couin-couin; **going, going, gone!** une fois, deux fois, adjugé!; **go to it!** allez-y!; **to be going to** or **to go to** + inf aller + inf, e.g., **I am going to the store to buy some shoes** je vais au magasin acheter des souliers; (to express futurity from the point of view of the present or past) aller + inf, e.g., **he is going to get married** il va se marier; e.g., **he was going to get married** il allait se marier; **to go** (to take out) (coll) à emporter; **to go against** contrarier; **to go ahead of** dépasser; **to go away** s'en aller; **to go back** retourner; (to return home) rentrer; (to back up) reculer; (to date back) remonter; **to go by** passer; (a rule, model, etc.) agir selon; **to go down** descendre; (said of sun) se coucher; (said of ship) sombrer; (cards) chuter; **to go fishing** aller à la pêche; **to go for** or **to go get** aller chercher; **to go in** entrer; entrer dans; (to fit into) tenir dans; **to go in for** se consacrer à; **to go in with** s'associer à or avec, se joindre à; **to go off** (said of bomb, gun, etc.) partir; **to go on** + ger continuer à + inf; **to go out** sortir; (said of light, fire, etc.) s'éteindre; **to go over** (to examine) parcourir, repasser; **to go through** (e.g., a door) passer par; (e.g., a city) traverser; (a fortune) dissiper, dilapider; **to go together** (said, e.g., of colors) s'assortir; (said of lovers) être très liés; **to go under** succomber; (said, e.g., of submarine) plonger; (a false name) être connu sous; **to go up** monter; **to go with** accompagner; (a color, dress, etc.) s'assortir avec; **to go without** se passer de; **to let go of** lâcher

goad [god] s aiguillon m ‖ tr aiguillonner

go'-ahead' adj (coll) entreprenant ‖ s (coll) signal m d'aller en avant

goal [gol] s but m

goal'keep'er s goal m, gardien m de but

goal' line' s ligne f de but

goal' post' s montant m, poteau m de but

goat [got] s chèvre f; (male goat) bouc m; (coll) dindon m; **to get the goat of** (slang) exaspérer, irriter

goatee [goˈti] s barbiche f

goat'herd' s chevrier m

goat'skin' s peau f de chèvre

goat'suck'er s (orn) engoulevent m

gob [gɑb] s (lump) (coll) grumeau m; (sailor) (slang) mataf m

gobble [ˈgɑbəl] s glouglou m ‖ tr engloutir, bâfrer ‖ intr bâfrer; (said of turkey) glouglouter

gobbledegook [ˈgɑbəldɪˌguk] s (coll) palabre m & f, charabia m

go'-between' s intermédiaire mf; (in shady love affairs) entremetteur m

goblet [ˈgɑblɪt] s verre m à pied

goblin [ˈgɑblɪn] s lutin m

go'-by' s (coll) affront m; **to give s.o. the go-by** (coll) brûler la politesse à qn

go'cart' s chariot m; (baby carriage) poussette f; (handcart) charrette f à bras

god [gɑd] s dieu m; **God damn!** (pej) nom m de Dieu!, nom de nom!; **God forbid** qu'à Dieu ne plaise; **God grant** plût à Dieu; **my God!** bon Dieu!; **God willing** s'il plaît à Dieu

god'child' s (pl **-chil'dren**) filleul m

god'damn'it interj nom d'une pipe!, nom d'un chien!, nom d'un petit bonhomme!, cré nom de Dieu!

god'daugh'ter s filleule f

goddess [ˈgɑdɪs] s déesse f

god'fa'ther s parrain m

God'-fear'ing adj dévot, pieux

God'forsak'en adj abandonné de Dieu; (coll) perdu, misérable

god'head' s divinité f; **Godhead** Dieu m

godless [ˈgɑdlɪs] adj athée, impie

god·ly [ˈgɑdli] adj (comp **-lier**; super **-liest**) dévot, pieux

God's' a'cre s le champ de repos

god'send' s aubaine f

god'son' s filleul m

God'speed' s bonne chance f, bon voyage m

go-getter [ˈgoˌgɛtər] s (coll) homme m d'expédition, lanceur m d'affaires

goggle [ˈgɑgəl] intr (to open the eyes wide) écarquiller les yeux, rouler de gros yeux ronds

gog'gle-eyed' adj aux yeux saillants

goggles [ˈgɑgəlz] spl lunettes fpl protectrices

going [ˈgoɪŋ] adj en marche; **going on two o'clock** presque deux heures ‖ s départ m; **good going!** bien joué!

go'ing concern' s maison f en pleine activité

go'ings on' spl (coll) chahut m, tapage m; (coll) événements mpl

goiter [ˈgɔɪtər] s goitre m

gold [gold] adj d'or, en or ‖ s or m

gold'beat'er s batteur m d'or

gold'beater's skin' s baudruche f

gold'crest' s roitelet m à tête dorée

golden [ˈgoldən] adj d'or; (gilt) doré; (hair) d'or, d'un blond doré; (opportunity) favorable, magnifique

gold'en age' s âge m d'or

gold'en calf' s veau m d'or

Gold'en Fleece' s Toison f d'or

gold'en mean' s juste-milieu m

gold´en plov´er s pluvier m doré
gold´en·rod´ s solidage f, gerbe f d'or
gold´en rule´ s règle f de la charité chrétienne
gold´en wed´ding s noces fpl d'or, jubilé m
gold´-filled´ adj (tooth) aurifié
gold´finch´ s chardonneret m
gold´fish´ s poisson m rouge
goldilocks [ˈgoldɪˌlɑks] s jeune fille f aux cheveux d'or
gold´ leaf´ s feuille f d'or
gold´ mine´ s mine f d'or; **to strike a gold mine** (fig) dénicher le bon filon, faire des affaires d'or
gold´ plate´ s vaisselle f d'or
gold´-plate´ tr plaquer d'or
gold´ rush´ s ruée f vers l'or
gold´smith´ s orfèvre m
gold´ stan´dard s étalon-or m
golf [gɑlf] s golf m ‖ intr jouer au golf
golf´ ball´ s balle f de golf
golf´ cart´ s voiturette f de golf
golf´ club´ s crosse f de golf, club m; (association) club m de golf
golfer [ˈgɑlfər] s joueur m de golf, golfeur m
golf´ links´ spl terrain m de golf
gondola [ˈgɑndələ] s gondole f
gondolier [ˌgɑndəˈlɪr] s gondolier m
gone [gɑn] adj parti, disparu; (used up) épuisé; (ruined) ruiné, fichu; (dead) mort; **far gone** avancé; **gone on** (in love with) (coll) entiché de, épris de
gong [gɔŋ] s gong m
gonorrhea [ˌgɑnəˈri·ə] s blennorragie f, gonococcie f
goo [gu] s (slang) matière f collante
good [gʊd] adj (comp **better**; super **best**) bon §91; (child) sage; (meals) soigné; **good for you!** bien joué!; **to be good at** être fort en, être expert à; **to make good** prospérer; (a loss) compenser; (a promise) tenir; **will you be good enough to** voulez-vous être assez aimable de ‖ s bien m; **for good** pour de bon, définitivement; **goods** biens mpl; (com) marchandises fpl; **to catch with the goods** (slang) prendre la main dans le sac; **to the good** de gagné, e.g., **all** or **so much to the good** autant de gagné ‖ interj bon!, bien!, à la bonne heure!; **very good!** parfait!
good´ afternoon´ s bonjour m
good´-by´ or **good´-bye´** s adieu m ‖ interj au revoir!; (before a long journey) adieu!
good´ cit´izenship s civisme m
good´ day´ s bonjour m
good´ deed´ s bonne action f
good´ egg´ s (slang) chic type m
good´ eve´ning s bonsoir m
good´ faith´ s la bonne volonté
good´ fel´low s brave garçon m, brave type m
good´ fel´lowship s camaraderie f
good´-for-noth´ing adj inutile m ‖ s bon m à rien
Good´ Fri´day s le Vendredi saint
good´ grac´es spl bonnes grâces fpl

good´-heart´ed adj au cœur généreux
good´-hu´mored adj de bonne humeur
good´-look´ing adj beau, joli
good´ looks´ spl belle mine f
good´ luck´ s bonne chance f
good·ly [ˈgʊdli] adj (comp **-lier**; super **-liest**) considérable, important; (quality) bon; (appearance) beau
good´ morn´ing s bonjour m
good´-na´tured adj aimable, accommodant
goodness [ˈgʊdnɪs] s bonté f; **for goodness' sake!** pour l'amour de Dieu!; **goodness knows** Dieu seul sait ‖ interj mon Dieu!
good´ night´ s bonne nuit f
good´ sense´ s bon sens m
good´-sized´ adj de grandeur moyenne, assez grand
good´ speed´ s succès m, bonne chance f
good´-tem´pered adj de caractère facile, d'humeur égale
good´ time´ s bon temps m; **to have a good time** prendre du bon temps, bien s'amuser; **to make good time** arriver en peu de temps
good´ turn´ s bienfait m, service m
good´ will´ s bonne volonté f; (com) achalandage m
good´ works´ spl bonnes œuvres fpl
good·y [ˈgʊdi] adj (coll) d'une piété affectée ‖ s (pl **-ies**) (coll) petit saint m; **goodies** friandises fpl ‖ interj chouette!; chic!
gooey [ˈgu·i] adj (comp **gooier**; super **gooiest**) (slang) gluant; (sentimental) (slang) à l'eau de rose
goof [guf] s (slang) toqué m ‖ intr—**to goof off** (slang) tirer au flanc
goof·y [ˈgufi] adj (comp **-ier**; super **-iest**) (slang) toqué, maboul
goon [gun] s (roughneck) (coll) dur m; (coll) terroriste m professionnel; (slang) niais m
goose [gus] s (pl **geese** [gis]) oie f; **to kill the goose that lays the golden eggs** tuer la poule aux œufs d'or ‖ s (pl **gooses**) (of tailor) carreau m
goose´ber´ry s (pl **-ries**) groseille f verte
goose´ egg´ s œuf m d'oie; (slang) zéro m
goose´ flesh´ s chair f de poule
goose´neck´ s col m de cygne
goose´ pim´ples spl chair f de poule
goose´ step´ s (mil) pas m de l'oie
goose´-step´ v (pret & pp **-stepped**; ger **-stepping**) intr marcher au pas de l'oie
gopher [ˈgofər] s citelle m
gore [gor] s (blood) sang m caillé; (sewing) soufflet m ‖ tr percer d'un coup de corne; (sewing) tailler en pointe
gorge [gɔrdʒ] s gorge f ‖ tr gorger ‖ intr se gorger
gorgeous [ˈgɔrdʒəs] adj magnifique
gorilla [gəˈrɪlə] s gorille m
gorse [gɔrs] s (bot) genêt m épineux
gor·y [ˈgori] adj (comp **-ier**; super **-iest**) ensanglanté, sanglant
gosh [gɑʃ] interj (coll) sapristi!, mon Dieu!
goshawk [ˈgɑsˌhɔk] s autour m

gospel [ˈgɑspəl] *s* évangile *m*; **Gospel** Évangile

gos'pel truth' *s* parole *f* d'Évangile

gossamer [ˈgɑsəmər] *adj* ténu ‖ *s* toile *f* d'araignée, fils *mpl* de la Vierge; (*gauze*) gaze *f*

gossip [ˈgɑsɪp] *s* commérage *m*, cancan *m*; (*person*) commère *f*; **piece of gossip** potin *m*, racontar *m* ‖ *intr* cancaner

gos'sip col'umnist *s* échotier *m*

Gothic [ˈgɑθɪk] *adj & s* gothique *m*

gouge [gaʊdʒ] *s* gouge *f* ‖ *tr* gouger; (*to swindle*) empiler

goulash [ˈgulɑʃ] *s* goulasch *m & f*

gourd [gʊrd] *s* gourde *f*

gourmand [ˈgʊrmənd] *s* gourmand *m*; (*glutton*) glouton *m*

gourmet [ˈgʊrme] *s* gourmet *m*

gout [gaʊt] *s* goutte *f*

govern [ˈgʌvərn] *tr* gouverner; (gram) régir ‖ *intr* gouverner

governess [ˈgʌvərnɪs] *s* institutrice *f*, gouvernante *f*

government [ˈgʌvərnmənt] *s* gouvernement *m*

governmental [ˌgʌvərnˈmɛntəl] *adj* gouvernemental

governor [ˈgʌvərnər] *s* gouverneur *m*; (mach) régulateur *m*

gown [gaʊn] *s* robe *f*

grab [græb] *s* prise *f*; (coll) vol *m*, coup *m* ‖ *v* (*pret & pp* **grabbed**; *ger* **grabbing**) *tr* empoigner, saisir ‖ *intr*—**to grab at** s'agripper à

grab' bag' *s* sac *m* à surprises

grace [gres] *s* grâce *f*; (*prayer at table before meals*) bénédicité *m*; (*prayer at table after meals*) grâces; (*extension of time*) délai *m* de grâce; **in someone's good graces** en odeur de sainteté auprès de qn, dans les petits papiers de qn ‖ *tr* orner; honorer

graceful [ˈgresfəl] *adj* gracieux

grace' note' *s* note *f* d'agrément, appogiature *f*

gracious [ˈgreʃəs] *adj* gracieux; (*compassionate*) miséricordieux

grackle [ˈgrækəl] *s* (myna) mainate *m*; (*purple grackle*) quiscale *m*

gradation [greˈdeʃən] *s* gradation *f*

grade [gred] *s* (*rank*) grade *m*; (*of oil*) grade; qualité *f*; (*school class*) classe *f*, année *f*; (*mark in school*) note *f*; (*slope*) pente *f*; **to make the grade** réussir ‖ *tr* classer; (*a school paper*) noter; (*land*) niveler

grade' cross'ing *s* (rr) passage *m* à niveau

grade' school' *s* école *f* primaire

gradient [ˈgredɪ·ənt] *adj* montant ‖ *s* pente *f*; (phys) gradient *m*

gradual [ˈgrædʒʊ·əl] *adj & s* graduel *m*

gradually [ˈgrædʒʊ·əli] *adv* graduellement, peu à peu, par paliers

graduate [ˈgrædʒʊ·ɪt] *s* diplômé *m* ‖ [ˈgrædʒʊ,et] *tr* conférer un diplôme à, décerner des diplômes à; (*to mark with degrees*) graduer ‖ *intr* recevoir son diplôme

grad'uate school' *s* faculté *f* des hautes études

grad'uate stu'dent *s* étudiant *m* avancé, étudiant de maîtrise, de doctorat

grad'uate work' *s* études *fpl* avancées

grad'uat'ing class' *s* classe *f* sortante

graduation [ˌgrædʒʊˈeʃən] *s* collation *f* des grades; (*e.g., marking on beaker*) graduation *f*

graft [græft] *s* (hort, surg) greffe *f*; (*stealing*) (coll) gratte *f*, grattage *m*, magouille *f* ‖ *tr & intr* (hort, surg) greffer; (coll) gratter

grafter [ˈgræftər] *s* (hort) greffeur *m*; (coll) homme *m* véreux, concussionnaire *mf*

gra'ham bread' [ˈgre·əm] *s* pain *m* entier

gra'ham flour' *s* farine *f* entière

grain [gren] *s* (*small seed; tiny particle of sand, etc.; small unit of weight; small amount*) grain *m*; (*cereal seeds*) grains *mpl*, céréales *fpl*; (*in stone*) fil *m*; (*in wood*) fibres *fpl*; **against the grain** à rebours, à contre-fil, à rebrousse-poil ‖ *tr* grener; (*wood, etc.*) veiner

grain' el'evator *s* dépôt *m* et élévateur *m* à grains

grain' field' *s* champ *m* de blé

graining [ˈgrenɪŋ] *s* grenage *m*; (*of painting*) veinage *m*

gram [græm] *s* gramme *m*

grammar [ˈgræmər] *s* grammaire *f*

grammarian [grəˈmɛrɪ·ən] *s* grammairien *m*

gram'mar school' *s* école *f* primaire

grammatical [grəˈmætɪkəl] *adj* grammatical

grana·ry [ˈgrænəri] *s* (*pl* **-ries**) grenier *m*

grand [grænd] *adj* magnifique; (*person*) grand; (coll) formidable

grand' aunt' *s* grand-tante *f*

grand'child' *s* (*pl* **-chil'dren**) petit-fils *m*; petite-fille *f*; **grandchildren** petits-enfants *mpl*

grand'daugh'ter *s* petite-fille *f*

grand' duch'ess *s* grande-duchesse *f*

grand' duch'y *s* grand-duché *m*

grand' duke' *s* grand-duc *m*

grandee [grænˈdi] *s* grand *m* d'Espagne

grand'fa'ther *s* grand-père *m*

grand'father clause' *s* clause *f* des droits aquis

grand'father's clock' *s* pendule *f* à gaine, horloge *f* comtoise, horloge normande

grandiose [ˈgrændɪ,os] *adj* grandiose; pompeux

grand' ju'ry *s* jury *m* d'accusation

grand' lar'ceny *s* grand larcin *m*

grand' lodge' *s* grand orient *m*

grandma [ˈgrænd,mɑ], [ˈgræmə] *s* (coll) grand-maman *f*

grand'moth'er *s* grand-mère *f*

grand'neph'ew *s* petit-neveu *m*

grand'niece' *s* petite-nièce *f*

grand' op'era *s* grand opéra *m*

grandpa [ˈgrænd,pɑ], [ˈgræmpə] *s* (coll) grand-papa *m*; (*gramps*) pépé *m*

grand'par'ent *s* grand-père *m*; grand-mère *f*; **grandparents** grands-parents *mpl*

grand′ pian′o s piano m à queue
grand′ slam′ s grand chelem m
grand′son′ s petit-fils m
grand′stand′ s tribune f, gradins mpl
grand′ to′tal s total m global
grand′un′cle s grand-oncle m
grand′ vizier′ s grand vizir m
grange [grendʒ] s ferme f; syndicat m d'agriculteurs
granite [′grænɪt] s granite m, granit m
gran·ny [′græni] s (pl -nies) (coll) grand-mère f, mémé f
gran′ny knot′ s nœud m de vache
grant [grænt] s (of land) concession f; (subsidy) subvention f; (scholarship) bourse f ‖ tr concéder, accorder; (a wish) exaucer; (e.g., a charter) octroyer; (a degree) décerner; **to take for granted** escompter, tenir pour évident; traiter avec indifférence
grantee [græn′ti] s donataire mf
grantor [græn′tɔr] s donateur m
granular [′grænjələr] adj granulaire
granulate [′grænjə,let] tr granuler ‖ intr se granuler
gran′ulated sug′ar s sucre m cristallisé
granule [′grænjul] s granule m, granulé m
grape [grep] s (fruit) raisin m; (vine) vigne f; (single grape) grain m de raisin
grape′ ar′bor s treille f
grape′fruit′ s (fruit) pamplemousse m & f; (tree) pamplemoussier m
grape′ juice′ s jus m de raisin
grape′shot′ s mitraille f
grape′vine′ s vigne f; (chain of gossip) source f de canards; téléphone m arabe, téléphone m chinois
graph [græf] s graphique m; (gram) graphie f
graphic(al) [′græfɪk(əl)] adj graphique; (fig) vivant, net
graphite [′græfaɪt] s graphite m
graph′ pa′per s papier m quadrillé
grapnel [′græpnəl] s grappin m
grapple [′græpəl] s (tool) grappin m; (fight) corps à corps m ‖ tr (with a grappling iron) saisir au grappin; (a person) empoigner à bras le corps ‖ intr (to fight) lutter corps à corps; **to grapple with** en venir aux prises avec, s'attaquer à
grap′pling i′ron s grappin m
grasp [græsp] s prise f; **to have a good grasp of** avoir une profonde connaissance de; **within one's grasp** à sa portée ‖ tr saisir ‖ intr—**to grasp at** tâcher de saisir; saisir avidement
grasping [′græspɪŋ] adj avide, rapace
grass [græs] s herbe f; (pasture) herbage m; (lawn) gazon m; **keep off the grass** (public sign) ne marchez pas sur le gazon; **to go to grass** (fig) s'étaler par terre
grass′hop′per s sauterelle f
grass′-roots′ adj populaire, du peuple
grass′ seed′ s graine f fourragère; (for lawns) graine f pour gazon
grass′ snake′ s (Tropidonotus natrix) couleuvre f à collier
grass′ wid′ow s demi-veuve f

grass·y [′græsi] adj (comp -ier; super -iest) herbeux
grate [gret] s grille f, grillage m ‖ tr (to put a grate on) griller; (e.g., cheese) râper; **grate the teeth** grincer des dents ‖ intr grincer; **to grate on** écorcher
grateful [′gretfəl] adj reconnaissant; **to be grateful for** être reconnaissant de or pour
grater [′gretər] s râpe f
grati·fy [′grætɪ,faɪ] v (pret & pp -fied) tr faire plaisir à, satisfaire
gratifying [′grætɪ,faɪ·ɪŋ] adj agréable, satisfaisant
grating [′gretɪŋ] adj grinçant ‖ s grillage m, grille f
gratis [′grætɪs] adj gratuit, gracieux ‖ adv gratis, gratuitement
gratitude [′grætɪ,t(j)ud] s gratitude f, reconnaissance f; **gratitude for** reconnaissance de or pour
gratuitous [grə′t(j)u·ɪtəs] adj gratuit
gratui·ty [grə′t(j)u·ɪti] s (pl -ties) gratification f, pourboire m
grave [grev] adj grave ‖ s fosse f, tombe f
gravedigger [′grev,dɪgər] s fossoyeur m
gravel [′grævəl] s (on roadway) gravier m, gravillons mpl; (geol) gravier, (pathol) gravelle f
grav′en im′age [′grevən] s image f taillée
grave′stone′ s pierre f tombale
grave′yard′ s cimetière m
gravitate [′grævɪ,tet] intr graviter
gravitation [,grævɪ′teʃən] s gravitation f
gravi·ty [′grævɪti] s (pl -ties) gravité f; (phys) pesanteur f, gravité
gra·vy [′grevi] s (pl -vies) (juice from cooking meat) jus m; (sauce made with this juice) sauce f; (slang) profit m facile, profit supplémentaire
gra′vy boat′ s saucière f
gra′vy train′ s (slang) assiette f au beurre
gray [gre] adj gris; (gray-haired) gris, chenu; **to turn gray** grisonner ‖ s gris m ‖ intr grisonner
gray′beard′ s barbon m, ancien m
gray′-haired′ adj gris, chenu
gray′hound′ s lévrier m; (female) levrette f
grayish [′gre·ɪʃ] adj grisâtre
gray′ mat′ter s substance f grise
graze [grez] tr (to touch lightly) frôler, effleurer; (to scratch lightly in passing) érafler; (to pasture) faire paître ‖ intr paître
grease [gris] s graisse f ‖ [griz] tr graisser
grease′ cup′ [gris] s godet m graisseur
grease′ gun′ [gris] s graisseur m, seringue f à graisse
grease′ paint′ [gris] s fard m, grimage m
greas·y [′grisi] adj (comp -ier; super -iest) graisseux, gras
great [gret] adj grand; (coll) excellent, formidable; **a great deal, a great many** beaucoup
great′-aunt′ s grand-tante f
Great′ Bear′ s Grande Ourse f
Great′ Brit′ain s Grande Bretagne f; la Grande Bretagne

great'coat' s capote f
Great' Dane' s danois m
Great'er New' York' s le Grand New York
great'-grand'child' s (pl **-chil'dren**) arrière-petit-fils m; arrière-petite-fille f; **great-grandchildren** arrière-petits-enfants mpl
great'-grand'daugh'ter s arrière-petite-fille f
great'-grand'fa'ther s arrière-grand-père m, bisaïeul m
great'-grand'moth'er s arrière-grand-mère f, bisaïeule f
great'-grand'par'ents spl arrière-grands-parents mpl
great'-grand'son s arrière-petit-fils m
greatly ['gretli] adv grandement, fort, beaucoup
great'-neph'ew s petit-neveu m
greatness ['gretnis] s grandeur f
great'-niece' s petite-nièce f
great'-un'cle s grand-oncle m
Grecian ['griʃən] adj grec ‖ s (person) Grec m
Greece [gris] s Grèce f; **la Grèce**
greed [grid] s avidité f
greed·y ['gridi] adj (comp **-ier**; super **-iest**) avide
Greek [grik] adj grec ‖ s (language) grec m; (unintelligible language) (coll) hébreu m, e.g., **it's Greek to me** (coll) c'est de l'hébreu pour moi; (person) Grec m
Greek' fire' s feu m grégeois
green [grin] adj vert; inexpérimenté, novice ‖ s vert m; (lawn) gazon m; (golf) pelouse f d'arrivée; **greens** légumes mpl verts
green'back' s (U.S.A.) billet m de banque
greener·y ['grinəri] s (pl **-ies**) verdure f
green'-eyed' adj aux yeux verts; (envious) jaloux
green'gage' s (bot) reine-claude f
green'gro'cer·y s (pl **-ies**) fruiterie f
green'horn' s blanc-bec m, bleu m
green'house' s serre f
green'house effect' s effet m de serre
greenish ['griniʃ] adj verdâtre
Greenland ['grinlənd] s le Groënland
green' light' s feu m vert, voie f libre
greenness ['grinnis] s verdure f; (unripeness) verdeur f; inexpérience f, naïveté f
green' pep'per s poivron m vert
green'room' s (theat) foyer m
greensward ['grin,swɔrd] s pelouse f
green' thumb' s—**to have a green thumb** avoir la main verte
greet [grit] tr saluer; (to welcome) accueillir
greeting ['gritiŋ] s salutation f; (welcome) accueil m; **greetings** (on greeting card) vœux mpl ‖ **greetings** interj salut!
greet'ing card' s carte f de vœux
gregarious [gri'gɛri·əs] adj grégaire
Gregorian [gri'gori·ən] adj grégorien
grenade [gri'ned] s grenade f
grey [gre] adj, s, & intr var of **gray**
grey'hound' s var of **grayhound**
grid [grid] s (of storage battery and vacuum tube) grille f; (on map) quadrillage m; (culin) gril m

griddle ['gridəl] s plaque f chauffante
grid'dle·cake' s crêpe f
grid'i'ron s gril m; (sports) terrain m de football
grid' leak' s résistance f de fuite de la grille
grid' line' s ligne f de quadrillage
grief [grif] s chagrin m, affliction f; **to come to grief** finir mal
grief'-strick'en adj affligé, navré
grievance ['grivəns] s grief m
grieve [griv] tr chagriner, affliger ‖ intr se chagriner, s'affliger
grievous ['grivəs] adj grave, douloureux
griffin ['grifin] s griffon m
grill [gril] s gril m; (grating) grille f ‖ tr griller; (an accused person) (coll) cuisiner
grille [gril] s grille f; (aut) calandre f
grilled' beef'steak' s châteaubriand m
grill'room' s grill-room m
grim [grim] adj (comp **grimmer**; super **grimmest**) (fierce) menaçant; (repellent) macabre; (unyielding) implacable; (stern-looking) lugubre
grimace ['griməs] s grimace f ‖ intr grimacer
grime [graim] s crasse f, saleté f
grim·y ['graimi] adj (comp **-ier**; super **-iest**) crasseux, sale
grin [grin] s (smile) large sourire m ‖ v (pret & pp **grinned**; ger **grinning**) intr avoir un large sourire, rire à belles dents; (in pain) grimacer
grind [graind] s (of coffee) moulure f; (job) (coll) boulot m, collier m; (student) (coll) bûcheur m, fort-en-thème m; **daily grind** (coll) train-train m quotidien ‖ v (pret & pp **ground** [graund]) tr (coffee, flour) moudre; (food) broyer; (meat) hacher; (a knife) aiguiser; (the teeth) grincer; (valves) roder ‖ intr grincer; **to grind away at** (coll) bûcher
grinder ['graindər] s (for coffee, pepper, etc.) moulin m, broyeur m; (for meat) hachoir m; (for tools) repasseur m; (back tooth) molaire f
grind'stone' s meule f, pierre f à aiguiser
grip [grip] s (hold) prise f; (with hand) poigne f; (handle) poignée f; (handbag) sac m de voyage; (understanding) compréhension f; **to come to grips** en venir aux prises; **to lose one's grip** lâcher prise ‖ v (pret & pp **gripped**; ger **gripping**) tr serrer, saisir fortement; (e.g., a theater audience) empoigner
gripe [graip] s (coll) rouspétance f ‖ intr (coll) rouspéter, ronchonner
grippe [grip] s grippe f
gripping ['gripiŋ] adj passionnant
gris·ly ['grizli] adj (comp **-lier**; super **-liest**) horrible, macabre
grist [grist] s blé m à moudre
gristle ['grisəl] s cartilage m
gris·tly ['grisli] adj (comp **-tlier**; super **-tliest**) cartilagineux
grist'mill' s moulin m à blé
grit [grit] s (sand) grès m, sable m; (courage) cran m; **grits** gruau m ‖ v (pret

& *pp* **gritted**; *ger* **gritting**) *tr* (*one's teeth*) grincer

grit·ty [ˈgrɪti] *adj* (*comp* **-tier**; *super* **-tiest**) sablonneux; (*fig*) plein de cran

griz·zly [ˈgrɪzli] *adj* (*comp* **-zlier**; *super* **-zliest**) grisonnant ‖ *s* (*pl* **-zlies**) ours *m* gris

griz′zly bear′ *s* ours *m* gris

groan [gron] *s* gémissement *m* ‖ *intr* gémir

grocer [ˈgrosər] *s* épicier *m*

grocer·y [ˈgrosəri] *s* (*pl* **-ies**) épicerie *f*; **groceries** denrées *fpl*

gro′cery store′ *s* épicerie *f*

grog [grɑg] *s* grog *m*

grog·gy [ˈgrɑgi] *adj* (*comp* **-gier**; *super* **-giest**) (coll) vacillant; (*shaky, e.g., from a blow*) (coll) étourdi; (*drunk*) (coll) gris, ivre

groin [grɔɪn] *s* (anat) aine *f*; (archit) arête *f*

groom [grum] *s* (*bridegroom*) marié *m*; (*stableboy*) palefrenier *m* ‖ *tr* soigner, astiquer; (*horses*) panser; (*a politician, a starlet, etc.*) dresser, préparer

grooms′man *s* (*pl* **-men**) garçon *m* d'honneur

groove [gruv] *s* (*for sliding door, etc.*) rainure *f*; (*of pulley*) gorge *f*; (*of phonograph record*) sillon *m*; (*mark left by wheel*) ornière *f*; (*of window, door, etc.*) feuillure *f*; **in the groove** (coll) comme sur des roulettes; **to get into a groove** (coll) devenir routinier ‖ *tr* rainer, canneler

grope [grop] *intr* tâtonner; **to grope for** chercher à tâtons

gropingly [ˈgropɪŋli] *adv* à tâtons

grosbeak [ˈgros,bik] *s* gros-bec *m*

gross [gros] *adj* (*flagrant*) flagrant, choquant; (*error*) gros, lourd; (*fat, burly*) gras, épais; (*crass, vulgar*) grossier; (*weight; receipts*) brut; (*displacement*) global ‖ *s invar* recette *f* brute; (*twelve dozen*) grosse *f* ‖ *tr* produire en recette brute, produire brut, e.g., **the business grossed a million dollars** l'entreprise a produit un million de dollars, brut

gross′ na′tional prod′uct *s* revenu *m* national brut (R.N.B.), produit *m* national brut

gross′ weight′ *s* poids *m* brut, poids total

grotesque [groˈtɛsk] *adj* grotesque ‖ *s* grotesque *m*; (*ornament*) grotesque *f*

grot·to [ˈgrɑto] *s* (*pl* **-toes** or **-tos**) grotte *f*

grouch [graʊtʃ] *s* (coll) humeur *f* grognon; (*person*) (coll) grognon *m* ‖ *intr* (coll) grogner

grouch·y [ˈgraʊtʃi] *adj* (*comp* **-ier**; *super* **-iest**) (coll) grognon, maussade

ground [graʊnd] *s* terre *f*; (*piece of land*) terrain *m*; (*basis, foundation*) fondement *m*, base *f*; (*reason*) motif *m*, cause *f*; (elec) terre *f*; (*body of automobile corresponding to ground*) (elec) masse *f*; **ground for complaint** grief *m*; **grounds** parc *m*, terrain; fondement, cause; (*of coffee*) marc *m*; **on the ground of** pour raison de, sous prétexte de; **to be losing**

ground être en recul; **to break ground** donner le premier coup de pioche; **to have grounds for** avoir matière à; **to stand one's ground** tenir bon or ferme; **to yield ground** lâcher pied ‖ *tr* fonder, baser; (elec) mettre à terre; **grounded** (aer) interdit de vol, gardé au sol; **to ground s.o. in s.th.** enseigner à fond q.ch. à qn

ground′ connec′tion *s* prise *f* de terre

ground′ crew′ *s* équipe *f* au sol, personnel *m* rampant

ground′ floor′ *s* rez-de-chaussée *m*

ground′ glass′ *s* verre *m* dépoli

ground′ hog′ *s* marmotte *f* d'Amérique

grounding [ˈgraʊndɪŋ] *s* (aer) interdiction *f* de vol; (elec) mise *f* à la masse

ground′ installa′tions *spl* (aer) infrastructure *f*

ground′ lead′ [lid] *s* (elec) conduite *f* à terre

groundless [ˈgraʊndlɪs] *adj* sans fondement

ground′ meat′ *s* viande *f* hachée

ground′ plan′ *s* plan *m* de base; (archit) plan horizontal

ground′ speed′ *s* (aer) vitesse *f* par rapport au sol

ground′ swell′ *s* lame *f* de fond

ground′ troops′ *spl* (mil) effectifs *mpl* terrestres

ground′ wire′ *s* (elec) fil *m* de terre, fil de masse

ground′work′ *s* fondement *m*, fond *m*

group [grup] *s* groupe *m* ‖ *tr* grouper ‖ *intr* se grouper

grouse [graʊs] *s* coq *m* de bruyère ‖ *intr* (slang) grogner

grove [grov] *s* bocage *m*, bosquet *m*

grov·el [ˈgrʌvəl] *v* (*pret & pp* **-eled** or **-elled**; *ger* **-eling** or **-elling**) *intr* se vautrer; (*before s.o.*) ramper

grow [gro] *v* (*pret* **grew** [gru]; *pp* **grown** [gron]) *tr* cultiver, faire pousser; (*a beard*) laisser pousser ‖ *intr* croître; (*said of plants*) pousser; (*said of seeds*) germer; (*to become*) devenir; **to grow angry** se mettre en colère; **to grow old** vieillir; **to grow out of** se développer de; (*e.g., a suit of clothes*) devenir trop grand pour; **to grow up** grandir, profiter

growl [graʊl] *s* grondement *m*, grognement *m* ‖ *tr & intr* gronder, grogner

grown′-up′ *adj* adulte ‖ *s* (*pl* **grown-ups**) adulte *mf*; **grown-ups** grandes personnes *fpl*

growth [groθ] *s* croissance *f*, développement *m*; (*increase*) accroissement *m*; (*of trees, grass, etc.*) pousse *f*; (pathol) excroissance *f*, grosseur *f*

growth′ stock′ *s* valeur *f* d'avenir

grub [grʌb] *s* asticot *m*; (*person*) homme *m* de peine; (*food*) (coll) boustifaille *f* ‖ *v* (*pret & pp* **grubbed**; *ger* **grubbing**) *tr* défricher ‖ *intr* fouiller

grub·by [ˈgrʌbi] *adj* (*comp* **-bier**; *super* **-biest**) sale, malpropre

grudge [grʌdʒ] *s* rancune *f*; **to have a grudge against** garder rancune à ǁ *tr* donner à contre-cœur

grudgingly [ˈgrʌdʒɪŋli] *adv* à contre-cœur

gruel [ˈgru·əl] *s* gruau *m*, bouillie *f*

grueling [ˈgru·əlɪŋ] *adj* éreintant

gruesome [ˈgrusəm] *adj* macabre

gruff [grʌf] *adj* bourru, brusque; (*voice*) rauque, gros

grumble [ˈgrʌmbəl] *s* grognement *m* ǁ *intr* grogner, grommeler

grump·y [ˈgrʌmpi] *adj* (*comp* -**ier**; *super* -**iest**) maussade, grognon

grunt [grʌnt] *s* grognement *m* ǁ *intr* grogner

G′-string′ *s* (*loincloth*) pagne *m*; (*worn by women entertainers*) cache-sexe *m*; (mus) corde *f* de sol

guarantee [ˌgærənˈti] *s* garantie *f*; (*guarantor*) garant *m*, répondant *m*; (*security*) caution *f* ǁ *tr* garantir

guarantor [ˈgærənˌtɔr] *s* garant *m*

guaran·ty [ˈgærənti] *s* (*pl* -**ties**) garantie *f* ǁ *v* (*pret* & *pp* -**tied**) *tr* garantir

guard [gɑrd] *s* garde *f*; (*person*) garde *m*; **on guard** en garde; (*on duty*) de garde; (mil) en faction, de faction; **on one's guard** sur ses gardes; **to mount guard** monter la garde; **under guard** gardé à vue ǁ *tr* garder ǁ *intr* être de faction; **to guard against** se garder de

guard′ du′ty *s* service *m* de garde

guarded *adj* (*remark*) prudent

guard′house′ *s* guérite *f*, corps-de-garde *m*; (mil) salle *f* de police, prison *f* militaire

guardian [ˈgɑrdɪ·ən] *adj* gardien ǁ *s* gardien *m*; (*of a ward*) tuteur *m*

guard′ian an′gel *s* ange *m* gardien, ange tutélaire

guard′ian·ship′ *s* garde *f*; (law) tutelle *f*

guard′rail′ *s* garde-fou *m*, parapet *m*, glissière *f* de sécurité

guard′room′ *s* corps-de-garde *m*, salle *f* de police; (*prison*) tôle *f*

guards′man *s* (*pl* -**men**) garde *m*

Guatemalan [ˌgwɑtɪˈmɑlən] *adj* guatémaltèque ǁ *s* Guatemaltèque *mf*

guava [ˈgwɑvə] *s* goyave *f*; (*tree*) goyavier *m*

guerrilla [gəˈrɪlə] *s* guérillero *m*; **guerrillas** (*band*) guérilla *f*

guerril′la war′fare *s* guérilla *f*

guess [gɛs] *s* conjecture *f* ǁ *tr* & *intr* conjecturer; (*a secret, riddle, etc.*) deviner; (coll) supposer, penser; **I guess so** je crois que oui; **to guess right** bien deviner

guess′work′ *s* supposition *f*; **by guesswork** au jugé

guest [gɛst] *s* invité *m*, hôte *mf*; (*in a hotel*) client *m*, hôte

guest′ book′ *s* livre *m* d'or

guest′ room′ *s* chambre *f* d'ami

guest′ speak′er *s* orateur *m* de circonstance

guffaw [gəˈfɔ] *s* gros rire *m* ǁ *tr* dire avec un gros rire ǁ *intr* rire bruyamment

guidance [ˈgaɪdəns] *s* (*advice*) conseils *mpl*; (*guiding*) conduite *f*; (*in choosing a career*) orientation *f*; (*of rocket*) guidage *m*;

for your guidance pour votre gouverne

guid′ance coun′selor *s* orienteur *m*

guide [gaɪd] *s* guide *m* ǁ *tr* guider

guide′book′ *s* guide *m*

guid′ed mis′sile *s* engin *m* téléguidé

guide′ dog′ *s* chien *m* d'aveugle

guid′ed tour′ *s* visite *f* commentée, visite guidée

guide′ line′ *s* (fig) norme *f*, règle *f*; **guide lines** (*for writing straight lines*) transparent *m*, guide-âne *m*

guide′post′ *s* poteau *m* indicateur

guide′ word′ *s* lettrine *f*

guild [gɪld] *s* association *f*, corporation *f*; (eccl) confrérie *f*; (hist) guilde *f*

guild′hall′ *s* hôtel *m* de ville

guile [gaɪl] *s* astuce *f*, artifice *m*

guileful [ˈgaɪlfəl] *adj* astucieux, artificieux

guileless [ˈgaɪllɪs] *adj* candide, innocent

guillotine [ˈgɪləˌtin] *s* guillotine *f* ǁ *tr* guillotiner

guilt [gɪlt] *s* culpabilité *f*

guiltless [ˈgɪltlɪs] *adj* innocent

guilt·y [ˈgɪlti] *adj* (*comp* -**ier**; *super* -**iest**) coupable; **found guilty** reconnu coupable

guinea [ˈgɪni] *s* guinée *f*; **Guinea** Guinée; **la Guinée**

guin′ea fowl′ or **hen′** *s* poule *f* de Guinée, pintade *f*

guin′ea pig′ *s* cobaye *m*

guise [gaɪz] *s* apparences *fpl*, déguisement *m*; **under the guise of** sous un semblant de, sous le masque de

guitar [gɪˈtɑr] *s* guitare *f*

guitarist [gɪˈtɑrɪst] *s* guitariste *mf*

gulch [gʌltʃ] *s* ravin *m*

gulf [gʌlf] *s* golfe *m*; (fig) gouffre *m*

Gulf′ of Mex′ico *s* Golfe *m* du Mexique

Gulf′ Stream′ *s* Courant *m* du Golfe

gull [gʌl] *s* mouette *f*, goéland *m*; (coll) gogo *m*, jobard *m* ǁ *tr* escroquer, duper

gullet [ˈgʌlɪt] *s* gosier *m*

gullible [ˈgʌlɪbəl] *adj* crédule, naïf

gul·ly [ˈgʌli] *s* (*pl* -**lies**) ravin *m*; (*channel*) rigole *f*

gulp [gʌlp] *s* gorgée *f*, lampée *f*; **at one gulp** d'un trait ǁ *tr*—**to gulp down** avaler à grandes bouchées, lamper; (*e.g., tears*) ravaler, refouler ǁ *intr* avoir la gorge serrée

gum [gʌm] *s* gomme *f*; (*on eyelids*) chassie *f*; (anat) gencive *f* ǁ *v* (*pret* & *pp* **gummed**; *ger* **gumming**) *tr* gommer; **to gum up** encrasser; (coll) bousiller

gum′ ar′abic *s* gomme *f* arabique

gum′boil′ *s* phlegmon *m*, fluxion *f*

gum′ boot′ *s* botte *f* de caoutchouc

gum′drop′ *s* boule *f* de gomme, pâte *f* de fruits

gum·my [ˈgʌmi] *adj* (*comp* -**mier**; *super* -**miest**) gommeux; (*eyelids*) chassieux

gumption [ˈgʌmpʃən] *s* (coll) initiative *f*, cran *m*

gum′shoe′ *s* caoutchouc *m*; (coll) détective *m* ǁ *intr* rôder en tapinois, marcher furtivement

gun [gʌn] *s* fusil *m*; (*for spraying*) pistolet *m*; **to stick to one's guns** (coll) ne pas en démordre ‖ *v* (*pret & pp* **gunned**; *ger* **gunning**) *tr*—**to gun down** tuer d'un coup de fusil; **to gun the engine** (slang) appuyer sur le champignon ‖ *intr*—**to gun for** (*game*) chasser; (*an enemy*) pourchasser

gun′ bar′rel *s* canon *m*

gun′boat′ *s* cannonière *f*

gun′ car′riage *s* affût *m* de canon

gun′cot′ton *s* fulmicoton *m*

gun′ crew′ *s* peloton *m* de pièce, servants *mpl* de canon

gun′fire′ *s* canonnade *f*, coups *mpl* de feu

gun′ laws′ *spl* réglementation *f* du port d'armes

gun′ lob′by *s* lobby *m* des marchands de revolvers

gun′man *s* (*pl* **-men**) *s* bandit *m*

gun′ met′al *s* métal *m* bleui

gunner [ˈgʌnər] *s* canonnier *m*, artilleur *m*; (aer) mitrailleur *m*

gunnery [ˈgʌnəri] *s* tir *m*, canonnage *m*

gunnysack [ˈgʌni,sæk] *s* sac *m* de serpillière

gun′point′ *s*—**at gunpoint** à main armée

gun′pow′der *s* poudre *f* à canon

gun′run′ning *s* contrebande *f* d'armes

gun′shot′ *s* coup *m* de feu, coup de fusil

gun′shot wound′ *s* blessure *f* par balle

gun′smith′ *s* armurier *m*

gun′stock′ *s* fût *m*

gunwale [ˈgʌnəl] *s* (naut) plat-bord *m*

gup·py [ˈgʌpi] *s* (*pl* **-pies**) guppy *m*

gurgle [ˈgʌrgəl] *s* glouglou *m*, gargouillement *m* ‖ *intr* glouglouter, gargouiller

gush [gʌʃ] *s* jaillissement *m* ‖ *intr* jaillir; **to gush over** (coll) s'attendrir sur

gusher [ˈgʌʃər] *s* puits *m* jaillissant

gush·y [ˈgʌʃi] *adj* (*comp* **-ier**; *super* **-iest**) (coll) démonstratif, expansif

gusset [ˈgʌsɪt] *s* (*in garment*) soufflet *m*; (mach) gousset *m*

gust [gʌst] *s* bouffée *f*, coup *m*

gusto [ˈgʌsto] *s* goût *m*, entrain *m*

gust·y [ˈgʌsti] *adj* (*comp* **-ier**; *super* **-iest**) venteux; (*wind*) à rafales

gut [gʌt] *s* boyau *m*; **guts** (coll) cran *m*; **he has a lot of guts** (pej) il est vachement gonflé ‖ *v* (*pret & pp* **gutted**; *ger* **gutting**) *tr* raser à l'intérieur; (*to take out the guts of*) vider

gutter [ˈgʌtər] *s* (*on side of road*) caniveau *m*; (*in street*) ruisseau *m*; (*of roof*) gouttière *f*; (*ditch formed by rain water*) rigole *f*

gut′ter·snipe′ *s* (coll) voyou *m*

guttural [ˈgʌtərəl] *adj* guttural ‖ *s* gutturale *f*

guy [gaɪ] *s* (*supporting cable*) câble *m* tenseur; (naut) hauban *m*; (coll) type *m*, gars *m* ‖ *tr* haubaner; (coll) se moquer de

Guyana [gaɪˈænə] *s* Guyane *f*; la Guyane

guy′ rope′ *s* corde *f* de tente

guy′ wire′ *s* câble *m* tenseur, (naut) hauban *m*

guzzle [ˈgʌzəl] *tr & intr* boire avidement

guzzler [ˈgʌzlər] *s* soiffard *m*

gym [dʒɪm] *s* (coll) gymnase *m*

gymnasi·um [dʒɪmˈnezɪ·əm] *s* (*pl* **-ums** or **-a** [ə]) gymnase *m*

gymnast [ˈdʒɪmnæst] *s* gymnaste *mf*

gynecology [,gaɪnəˈkɑlədʒi] *s* gynécologie *f*

gyp [dʒɪp] *s* (slang) escroquerie *f*; (*person*) (slang) aigrefin *m* ‖ *v* (*pret & pp* **gypped**; *ger* **gypping**) *tr* (slang) tirer une carotte à, refaire, gruger, chiper, chaparder

gypsum [ˈdʒɪpsəm] *s* gypse *m*

gyp·sy [ˈdʒɪpsi] *adj* bohémien ‖ *s* (*pl* **-sies**) bohémien *m*; **Gypsy** (*language*) tsigane *m*, romanichel *m*; (*person*) gitan *m*, tsigane *mf*, romanichel *m*

gyp′sy moth′ *s* zigzag *m*

gyrate [ˈdʒaɪret] *intr* tournoyer

gyrocompass [ˈdʒaɪro,kʌmpəs] *s* gyrocompas *m*

gyroscope [ˈdʒaɪrə,skop] *s* gyroscope *m*

H

H, h [etʃ] *s* VIIIe lettre de l'alphabet

haberdasher [ˈhæbər,dæʃər] *s* chemisier *m*

haberdasher·y [ˈhæbər,dæʃəri] *s* (*pl* **-ies**) chemiserie *f*, confection *f* pour hommes

habit [ˈhæbɪt] *s* habitude *f*; (*dress*) habit *m*, costume *m*; **to get into the habit of** s'habituer à

habitual [həˈbɪtʃʊ·əl] *adj* habituel

habituate [həˈbɪtʃʊ,et] *tr* habituer

hack [hæk] *s* (*notch*) entaille *f*; (*cough*) toux *f* sèche; (*hackney*) voiture *f* de louage; (*old nag*) rosse *f*; (*writer*) écrivassier *m* ‖ *tr* hacher

hackney [ˈhækni] *s* voiture *f* de louage

hackneyed [ˈhæknid] *adj* banal, battu

hack′saw′ *s* scie *f* à métaux

haddock [ˈhædək] *s* églefin *m*

hag [hæg] *s* (*ugly woman*) guenon *f*; (*witch*) sorcière *f*; **old hag** vieille fée *f*

haggard [ˈhægərd] *adj* décharné, hâve; (*wild-looking*) hagard, farouche

haggle [ˈhægəl] *intr* marchander; **to haggle over** marchander

Hague [heg] *s*—**The Hague** La Haye

hail [hel] *s* (*frozen rain*) grêle *f*; **within hail** à portée de la voix ‖ *tr* saluer; (*a ship, taxi, etc.*) héler ‖ *intr* grêler; **to hail from** venir de ‖ *interj* salut!

Hail′ Mar′y *s* Ave Maria *m*

hail′stone′ *s* grêlon *m*

hail'storm' s tempête f de grêle
hair [hɛr] s poil m; (of person) cheveu m; (head of human hair) cheveux mpl; **against the hair** à rebrousse-poil, à contre-poil; **hairs** cheveux; **to a hair** à un cheveu près; **to get in s.o.'s hair** (slang) porter sur les nerfs à qn; **to let one's hair down** (slang) en prendre à son aise; **to make s.o.'s hair stand on end** faire dresser les cheveux à qn; **to not turn a hair** ne pas tiquer; **to split hairs** fendre or couper les cheveux en quatre
hair'breadth' s épaisseur f d'un cheveu; **to escape by a hairbreadth** l'échapper belle
hair'brush' s brosse f à cheveux
hair'cloth' s thibaude f; (for furniture) tissu-crin m
hair'cream' s fixateur m
hair'curl'er [,kʌrlər] s frisoir m; (pin) bigoudi m
hair'cut' s coupe f de cheveux; **to get a haircut** se faire couper les cheveux
hair'do' s (pl -dos) coiffure f
hair'dress'er s coiffeur m pour dames; coiffeuse f
hair'dress'ing s cosmétique m
hair'dri'er s sèche-cheveux m, séchoir m à cheveux
hair' dye' s teinture f des cheveux
hair'line' s (on face of type) délié m; (along the upper forehead) naissance f des cheveux, plantation f des cheveux
hair'net' s résille f
hair'pin' s épingle f à cheveux
hair'pin turn' s lacet m
hair'-rais'ing adj (coll) horripilant
hair' rib'bon s ruban m à cheveux
hair' set' s mise f en plis
hair' shirt' s haire f, cilice m
hair'split'ting adj vétilleux, trop subtil ‖ s ergotage m
hair' spray' s (for setting hair) laque f, fixatif m
hair'spring' s spiral m
hair' style' s coiffure f
hair' ton'ic s lotion f capillaire
hair' trig'ger s détente f douce
hair·y [`hɛri] adj (comp -ier; super -iest) poilu, velu; (on head) chevelu
Haiti [`heti] s Haïti f; **the Republic of Haiti** la république d'Haïti
Haitian [`heʃən] adj haïtien ‖ s Haïtien m
halberd [`hælbərd] s hallebarde f
hal'cyon days' [`hælsɪ-ən] spl jours mpl alcyoniens, jours sereins
hale [hel] adj vigoureux, sain; **hale and hearty** frais et gaillard ‖ tr haler
half [hæf] adj demi ‖ s (pl **halves** [hævz]) moitié f, la moitié; (of the hour) demi m; **by half** de moitié, à demi; **half an hour** une demi-heure; **in half** en deux; **to go halves** être de moitié ‖ adv moitié, à moitié; **half . . . half** moitié . . . moitié; **half past** et demie, e.g., **half past three** trois heures et demie
half'-and-half' adj & adv moitié l'un moitié l'autre, en parties égales ‖ s (for coffee) mélange m de lait et de crème; (beer) mélange de bière et de porter
half'back' s (football) demi-arrière m, demi m
half'-baked' adj à moitié cuit; (person) inexpérimenté; (plan) prématuré, incomplet
half' bind'ing s (bb) demi-reliure f à petits coins
half'-blood' s métis m; demi-frère m
half' boot' s demi-botte f
half'-bound' adj (bb) en demi-reliure à coins
half'-breed' s métis m, sang-mêlé m; (e.g., horse) demi-sang m
half' broth'er s demi-frère m
half'-cocked' adv (coll) avec trop de hâte
half'-day' s demi-journée f
half'-doz'en s demi-douzaine f
half' fare' s demi-tarif m, demi-place f
half'-full' adj à moitié plein
half'-heart'ed adj sans entrain, hésitant
half'-hol'iday s demi-congé m
half' hose' s chaussettes fpl
half'-hour' s demi-heure f; **every half-hour on the half-hour** toutes les demi-heures à la demi-heure juste; **on the half-hour** à la demie
half' leath'er s (bb) demi-reliure f à petits coins
half'-length' s demi-longueur f
half'-length por'trait s portrait m en buste
half'-life' s (phys) période f
half'-light' s demi-jour m
half'-line space' s (on typewriter) demi-interligne m de base
half'-mast' s—**at half-mast** en berne, à mi-mât
half'-moon' s demi-lune f
half' mourn'ing s demi-deuil m
half' note' s (mus) blanche f
half' pay' s demi-solde f
halfpen·ny [`hepəni], [`hepni] s (pl -nies) demi-penny m; (fig) sou m
half' pint' s demi-pinte f; (little runt) (slang) petit culot m
half'-seas o'ver adj—**to be half-seas over** avoir du vent dans les voiles
half' shell' s (either half of a bivalve) écaille f; **on the half shell** dans sa coquille
half' sis'ter s demi-sœur f
half' sole' s demi-semelle f
half'-staff' s—**at half-staff** à mi-mât
half'-tim'bered adj à demi-boisage
half' time' s (sports) mi-temps m
half'-time' adj à demi-journée
half' ti'tle s faux titre m, avant-titre m
half'tone' s (painting, phot) demi-teinte f; (typ) similigravure f
half' tone' s (mus) demi-ton m
half'-track' s semi-chenillé m
half'-truth' s demi-vérité f
half'turn' s demi-tour m; (of wheel) demi-révolution f
half'way' adj & adv à mi-chemin; **halfway through** à moitié de; **halfway up** à mi-

côte; **to meet s.o. halfway** couper la poire en deux avec qn

half′-wit′ted adj à moitié idiot

halibut [ˈhælɪbət] s flétan m

halitosis [ˌhælɪˈtosɪs] s mauvaise haleine f

hall [hɔl] s (*passageway*) corridor m, couloir m; (*entranceway*) entrée f, vestibule m; (*large meeting room*) salle f, hall m, salle des fêtes; (*assembly room of a university*) amphithéâtre m; (*building of a university*) bâtiment m

halleluiah or **hallelujah** [ˌhælɪˈlujə] s alléluia m ‖ interj alléluia!

hall′mark′ s estampille f, poinçon m; (fig) cachet m, marque f

hal·lo [həˈlo] s (pl **-los**) holà m ‖ intr huer ‖ interj holà!, ohé!; (hunting) taïaut!

hallow [ˈhælo] tr sanctifier

hallowed adj sanctifié, saint

Halloween or **Hallowe'en** [ˌhæloˈin] s la veille de la Toussaint

hallucinate [həˈlusɪnet] intr avoir des hallucinations

hallucination [həˌlusɪˈneʃən] s hallucination f

hallucinogenic [həˌlusənoˈdʒɛnɪk] adj hallucinogène

hall′way′ s corridor m, couloir m

ha·lo [ˈhelo] s (pl **-los** or **-loes**) (meteo) auréole f, halo m; (*around a head*) auréole f

halogen [ˈhælədʒən] s halogène m

halt [hɔlt] adj boiteux, estropié ‖ s halte f, arrêt m; **to come to a halt** faire halte ‖ tr faire faire halte à ‖ intr faire halte ‖ interj halte!; (mil) halte-là!

halter [ˈhɔltər] s licou m; (*noose*) corde f

halting [ˈhɔltɪŋ] adj boiteux; hésitant

halve [hæv] tr diviser or partager en deux; réduire de moitié

halyard [ˈhæljərd] s (naut) drisse f

ham [hæm] s (*part of leg behind knee*) jarret m; (*thigh and buttock*) fesse f; (culin) cuisse f; (*cured*) (culin) jambon m; (rad) radio amateur m; (theat) cabotin m; **hams** fesses

hamburger [ˈhæmˌbʌrgər] s sandwich m à la hambourgeoise, hamburger m; (*Hamburg steak*) biftek m haché

hamlet [ˈhæmlɪt] s hameau m

hammer [ˈhæmər] s marteau m; (*of gun*) chien m, percuteur m ‖ tr marteler; **to hammer out** étendre au marteau; (*to resolve*) résoudre ‖ intr—**to hammer away at** (*e.g., a job*) travailler d'arrache-pied à

hammock [ˈhæmək] s hamac m

hamper [ˈhæmpər] s manne f ‖ tr embarrasser, gêner, empêcher

hamster [ˈhæmstər] s hamster m

ham′string′ v (pret & pp **-strung**) tr couper le jarret à; (fig) couper les moyens à

hand [hænd] adj à main, à la main, manuel ‖ s main f; (*workman*) manœuvre m, ouvrier m; (*way of writing*) écriture f; (*clapping of hands*) applaudissements mpl; (*of clock or watch*) aiguille f; (*a round of play*) coup m, partie f, main; (*of God*) doigt m; (*measure*) palme m; (cards)

jeu m; **at hand** sous la main; (*said of approaching event*) proche, prochain; **by hand** à la main; **hand in hand** main dans la main; **hand off!** n'y touchez pas!; **hands up!** haut les mains!; **hand to hand** corps à corps; **on every hand** de toutes parts, de tous côtés; **on the one hand . . . on the other hand** d'une part . . . d'autre part; **to live from hand to mouth** vivre au jour le jour; **to rule with a firm hand** avoir de la poigne; **to shake hands with** serrer la main à; **to wait on hand and foot** être aux petits soins pour; **to win hands down** gagner dans un fauteuil; **under the hand and seal of** signé et scellé de ‖ tr donner, présenter; (*e.g., food at table*) passer; **to hand down** (*e.g., property*) léguer; (*a verdict*) prononcer; **to hand in** remettre; **to hand on** transmettre; **to hand out** distribuer; **to hand over** céder, livrer

hand′bag′ s sac m à main

hand′ bag′gage s menus bagages mpl, bagages à main

hand′ball′ s pelote f; (*game*) handball m

hand′bill′ s prospectus m

hand′book′ s manuel m

hand′ brake′ s frein m à main

hand′car′ s (rr) draisine f

hand′cart′ s voiture f à bras

hand′clasp′ s poignée f de main

hand′ control′ s commande f à la main

hand′cuff′ s menotte f ‖ tr mettre les menottes à

handful [ˈhændˌful] s poignée f

hand′ glass′ s miroir m à main; (*magnifying glass*) loupe f à main

hand′ grenade′ s grenade f à main

handi·cap [ˈhændɪˌkæp] s handicap m ‖ v (pret & pp **-capped**; ger **-capping**) tr handicaper

handicraft [ˈhændɪˌkræft] s habileté f manuelle; métier m; **handicrafts** produits mpl d'artisanat

handiwork [ˈhændɪˌwʌrk] s ouvrage m, travail m manuel; (fig) œuvre f

handkerchief [ˈhæŋkərtʃɪf] s mouchoir m

handle [ˈhændəl] s (*of basket, crock, pitcher*) anse f; (*of shovel, broom, knife*) manche m; (*of umbrella, sword, door*) poignée f; (*of frying pan*) queue f; (*of pump*) brimbale f; (*of handcart*) brancard m; (*of wheelbarrow*) bras m; (*opportunity, pretext*) prétexte m; (mach) manivelle f, manette f; **to fly off the handle** (coll) sortir de ses gonds ‖ tr manier; (*with one's hands*) palper, tâter; **handle with care** (*shipping label*) fragile; **to handle roughly** malmener ‖ intr—**to handle well** (mach) avoir de bonnes réactions

han′dle·bars′ spl guidon m

handler [ˈhændlər] s (sports) entraîneur m

handling [ˈhændlɪŋ] s (*e.g., of tool*) maniement m; (*e.g., of person*) traitement m; (*of merchandise*) manutention f

hand′made′ adj fait à la main

hand′maid′ or **hand′maid′en** s servante f; (fig) auxiliaire mf

hand′-me-down′ s (coll) décrochez-moi-ça m

hand′ or′gan s orgue m de Barbarie

hand′out′ s (notes) (coll) documentation f; (slang) aumône f

hand′-picked′ adj trié sur le volet

hand′rail′ s main f courante, rampe f

hand′saw′ s égoïne f, scie f à main

hand′set′ s combiné m

hand′shake′ s poignée f de main

handsome [′hænsəm] adj beau; (e.g., fortune) considérable

hand′spring′ s—**to do a handspring** prendre appui sur les mains pour faire la culbute

hand′-to-hand′ adj corps-à-corps

hand′-to-mouth′ adj—**to lead a hand-to-mouth existence** vivre au jour le jour

hand′ truck′ s bard m, diable m

hand′work′ s travail m à la main

hand′writ′ing s écriture f

handwritten [′hænd,rɪtən] adj manuscrit, autographe

hand·y [′hændi] adj (comp -ier; super -iest) (easy to handle) maniable; (within easy reach) accessible, sous la main; (skillful) adroit, habile; **to come in handy** être très à propos

hand′y·man s (pl -men′) homme m à tout faire, bricoleur m

hang [hæŋ] s (of dress, curtain, etc.) retombée f, drapé m; (skill; insight) adresse f, sens m; **I don't give a hang!** (coll) je m'en moque pas mal!; **to get the hang** (coll) saisir le truc, attraper le chic ‖ v (pret & pp **hung** [hʌŋ]) tr pendre; (laundry) étendre; (wallpaper) coller; (one's head) baisser; **hang it all!** zut alors!; **to hang up** suspendre, accrocher; (telp) raccrocher ‖ intr pendre, être accroché; **to hang around** flâner, rôder; **hang on** se cramponner à, s'accrocher à; (to depend on) dépendre de; (to stay put) tenir bon; **to hang out** pendre dehors; (slang) percher, loger; **to hang over** (to threaten) peser sur, menacer; **to hang together** rester unis; **to hang up** (telp) raccrocher ‖ v (pret & pp **hung** or **hanged**) tr (to execute by hanging) pendre ‖ intr se pendre

hangar [′hæŋər], [′hæŋɡɑr] s hangar m

hang′dog′ adj (look) patibulaire

hanger [′hæŋər] s crochet m; (coathanger) cintre m, portemanteau m

hang′er-on′ s (pl **hangers-on**) parasite m, pique-assiette m

hang′ glid′er s deltaplane m

hang′ glid′ing s vol m à libre, vol sur aile delta

hanging [′hæŋɪŋ] adj pendant, suspendu ‖ s pendaison f; **hangings** tentures fpl

hang′man s (pl -men) bourreau m

hang′nail′ s envie f

hang′out′ s (coll) repaire m

hang′o′ver s (coll) gueule f de bois

hank [hæŋk] s écheveau m

hanker [′hæŋkər] intr—**to hanker after** or **for** désirer vivement, être affamé de

Hannibal [′hænɪbəl] s Annibal m

haphazard [,hæp′hæzərd] adj fortuit, imprévu; au petit bonheur ‖ adv à l'aventure, au hasard

hapless [′hæplɪs] adj malheureux, malchanceux

happen [′hæpən] intr arriver, se passer; (to be the case by chance) survenir; **happen what may** advienne que pourra; **how does it happen that . . . ?** comment se fait-il que . . . ?, d'où vient-il que . . . ?; **to happen at the right moment** tomber pile; **to happen on** tomber sur; **to happen to** + inf se trouver + inf, venir à + inf

happening [′hæpənɪŋ] s événement m

happily [′hæpɪli] adv heureusement

happiness [′hæpɪnɪs] s bonheur m

hap·py [′hæpi] adj (comp **-pier**; super **-piest**) heureux; (pleased) content; (hour) propice; **to be happy to** être heureux or content de

hap′py-go-luck′y adj sans souci, insouciant ‖ adv (archaic) à l'aventure

hap′py me′dium s juste-milieu m

Hap′py New′ Year′ interj bonne année!

harangue [hə′ræŋ] s harangue f ‖ tr & intr haranguer

harass [hə′ræs] tr harceler; tourmenter

harbinger [′hɑrbɪndʒər] s avant-coureur m, précurseur m

harbor [′hɑrbər] s port m ‖ tr héberger, donner asile à; (a criminal, stolen goods, etc.) receler; (suspicions; a hope) entretenir, nourrir; (a grudge) garder

har′bor mas′ter s capitaine m de port

hard [hɑrd] adj dur; (difficult) difficile; (water) cru, calcaire; (work) assidu, dur; **to be hard on** (to treat severely) être dur or sévère envers; (to wear out fast) user ‖ adv dur, fort; (firmly) ferme; **hard upon** de près, tout contre; **to rain hard** pleuvoir fort; **to try hard** bien essayer

hard′-and-fast′ adj strict, inflexible, établi

hard-bitten [′hɑrd′bɪtən] adj tenace, dur à cuire

hard′-boiled′ adj (egg) dur; (coll) dur, inflexible

hard′bound edi′tion s édition f reliée

hard′ can′dy s bonbons mpl; **piece of hard candy** bonbon m

hard′ cash′ s espèces fpl sonnantes

hard′ ci′der s cidre m

hard′ coal′ s houille f éclatante, anthracite m

hard′ cop′y s (comp) fac-sim m

hard′ core′ s (of supporters, opponents, resistance) noyau m, cercle m, centre m

hard′-core′ adj (support, opposition) inconditionnel

hard′-core′ pornog′raphy s pornographie f (dite) dure

hard′cov′er adj (hardbound) relié ‖ s livre m relié

hard' drink' s boissons fpl alcooliques, liqueurs fpl fortes

hard' drink'er s grand buveur m

hard'-earned' adj péniblement gagné

harden [ˈhɑrdən] tr durcir, endurcir ‖ intr se durcir, s'endurcir

hardening [ˈhɑrdənɪŋ] s durcissement m; (fig) endurcissement m

hard' fact' s fait m brutal; **hard facts** réalités fpl

hard-fought [ˈhɑrdˈfɔt] adj acharné, chaudement disputé

hard'-head'ed adj positif, à la tête froide

hard'-heart'ed adj dur, sans compassion

hardihood [ˈhɑrdɪˌhʊd] s endurance f; courage m; audace f

hardiness [ˈhɑrdɪnɪs] s vigueur f

hard' la'bor s travaux mpl forcés

hard' land'ing s atterrissage m dur

hard' luck' s guigne f, malchance f

hardly [ˈhɑrdli] adv guère, à peine, ne . . . guère, e.g., **he hardly thinks of anything else** à peine pense-t-il à autre chose, il ne pense guère à autre chose; **hardly ever** presque jamais

hardness [ˈhɑrdnɪs] s dureté f

hard' of hear'ing adj dur d'oreille; **the hard of hearing** les malentendants

hard'-pressed' adj aux abois, gêné

hard' rub'ber s caoutchouc m durci, ébonite f

hard' sell' s (coll) vente f à l'arraché

hard'-shell' adj (clam) à carapace dure; (coll) opiniâtre

hard'ship' s peine f; **hardships** privations fpl; fatigues fpl

hard'tack' s biscuit m, biscotin m

hard' times' spl difficultés fpl, temps mpl difficiles

hard' to please' adj difficile à contenter, exigeant

hard' up' adj (coll) à court d'argent; **to be hard up for** (coll) être à court de

hard'ware' s quincaillerie f; (trimmings) ferrure f; (comp) matériel m

hard'ware'man s (pl -men) quincaillier m

hard'ware store' s quincaillerie f

hard-won [ˈhɑrd,wʌn] adj chèrement disputé, conquis de haute lutte

hard'wood' s bois m dur; arbre m de bois dur

hard'wood floor' s parquet m

har·dy [ˈhɑrdi] adj (comp -dier; super -diest) vigoureux, robuste; (rash) hardi; (hort) résistant

hare [hɛr] s lièvre m

hare'brained' adj écervelé, farfelu

hare'lip' s bec-de-lièvre m

harem [ˈhɛrəm] s harem m

hark [hɑrk] intr écouter; **to hark back to** en revenir à ‖ interj écoutez!

harken [ˈhɑrkən] intr—**to harken to** écouter

harlequin [ˈhɑrləkwɪn] s arlequin m

harlot [ˈhɑrlət] s prostituée f, fille f publique

harm [hɑrm] s mal m, dommage m ‖ tr nuire à, faire du mal à

harmful [ˈhɑrmfəl] adj nuisible

harmless [ˈhɑrmlɪs] adj inoffensif

harmonic [hɑrˈmɑnɪk] adj harmonique

harmonica [hɑrˈmɑnɪkə] s harmonica m

harmonious [hɑrˈmoni·əs] adj harmonieux

harmonize [ˈhɑrmə,naɪz] tr harmoniser ‖ intr s'harmoniser

harmo·ny [ˈhɑrməni] s (pl -nies) harmonie f

harness [ˈhɑrnɪs] s harnais m, harnachement m; **to die in the harness** (coll) mourir sous le harnais, mourir debout; **to get back in the harness** (coll) reprendre le collier ‖ tr harnacher; (e.g., a river) aménager, capter

har'ness mak'er s bourrelier m, harnacheur m

har'ness race' s course f attelée

harp [hɑrp] s harpe f ‖ intr—**to harp on** rabâcher

harpist [ˈhɑrpɪst] s harpiste mf

harpoon [hɑrˈpun] s harpon m ‖ tr harponner

harpsichord [ˈhɑrpsɪˌkɔrd] s clavecin m

har·py [ˈhɑrpi] s (pl -pies) harpie f

harrow [ˈhæro] s (agr) herse f ‖ tr tourmenter; (agr) herser

harrowing [ˈhæro·ɪŋ] adj horripilant

har·ry [ˈhæri] v (pret & pp -ried) tr harceler; (to devastate) ravager

harsh [hɑrʃ] adj (life, treatment, etc.) sévère, dur; (to the touch) rude; (to the taste) âpre; (to the ear) discordant

harshness [ˈhɑrʃnɪs] s dureté f, rudesse f; âpreté f

hart [hɑrt] s cerf m

harum-scarum [ˈhɛrəmˈskɛrəm] adj & s écervelé ‖ adv en casse-cou

harvest [ˈhɑrvɪst] s récolte f; (of grain) moisson f ‖ tr récolter, moissonner ‖ intr faire la récolte or moisson

harvester [ˈhɑrvɪstər] s moissonneur m; (mach) moissonneuse f

har'vest home' s fin f de la moisson; fête f de la moisson

har'vest moon' s lune f des moissons

has-been [ˈhæz,bɪn] s (coll) vieille croûte f

hash [hæʃ] s hachis m ‖ tr hacher

hash'house' s (slang) gargote f

hashish [ˈhæʃɪʃ] s hachisch m

hasp [hæsp], [hɑsp] s moraillon m

hassle [ˈhæsəl] s (coll) querelle f, accrochage m

hassock [ˈhæsək] s pouf m

haste [hest] s hâte f; **in haste** à la hâte; **to make haste** se hâter

hasten [ˈhesən] tr hâter ‖ intr se hâter

hast·y [ˈhesti] adj (comp -ier; super -iest) hâtif, précipité; (rash) inconsidéré, emporté

hat [hæt] s chapeau m; **hat in hand** chapeau bas; **hats off to . . . !** chapeau bas devant . . . !; **to keep under one's hat** (coll) garder strictement pour soi; **to talk through one's hat** (coll) parler à tort et à travers; **to throw one's hat in the ring** (coll) descendre dans l'arène

hat′band′ s ruban m de chapeau

hat′ block′ s forme f à chapeaux

hat′box′ s carton m à chapeaux

hatch [hætʃ] s (brood) éclosion f; (trap door) trappe f; (lower half of door) demi-porte f; (opening in ship's deck) écoutille f; (hood over hatchway) capot m; (lid for opening in ship's deck) panneau m de descente; **down the hatch!** (bottoms up!) derrière la cravate! ‖ tr (eggs) couver, faire éclore; (a plot) ourdir, manigancer; (to hachure) hachurer ‖ intr éclore; (said of chicks) sortir de la coquille

hatch′back′ s (aut) hayon m

hat′check girl′ s préposée f au vestiaire

hatchet [ˋhætʃɪt] s hachette f; **to bury the hatchet** faire la paix

hatch′way′ s écoutille f

hate [het] s haine f ‖ tr haïr, détester; **to hate to** haïr de

hateful [ˋhetfəl] adj haïssable

hat′pin′ s épingle f à chapeau

hat′rack′ s porte-chapeaux m

hatred [ˋhetrɪd] s haine f

hat′shop′ s chapellerie f

hatter [ˋhætər] s chapelier m

haughtiness [ˋhɔtɪnɪs] s hauteur f

haugh·ty [ˋhɔti] adj (comp -tier; super -tiest) hautain, altier

haul [hɔl] s (pull, tug) effort m; (amount caught) coup m de filet, prise f; (distance covered) parcours m, distance f de transport ‖ tr (to tug) tirer; (com) transporter

haulage [ˋhɔlɪdʒ] s transport m; (cost) frais m de transport

haunch [hɔntʃ] s (hip) hanche f; (hind quarter of an animal) quartier m; (leg of animal used for food) cuissot m

haunt [hɔnt], [hɑnt] s lieu m fréquenté, rendez-vous m; (e.g., of criminals) repaire m ‖ tr (to obsess) hanter; (to frequent) fréquenter

haunt′ed house′ s maison f hantée par les fantômes

Havana [həˋvænə] s La Havane

have [hæv] s—**the haves and the have-nots** les riches et les pauvres ‖ v (3d pers **has** [hæz]; pret & pp **had** [hæd]) tr avoir; **to have** + inf faire + inf, e.g., **I shall have him go** je le ferai aller; **to have** + pp faire + inf, e.g., **I am going to have a suit made** je vais faire faire un complet; **to have it in for someone** garder un chien de sa chienne; **to have nothing to do with** n'avoir rien à voir avec; **to have on** (clothing) porter; **to have s.th. to** + inf avoir q.ch. à + inf, e.g., **I have a lot of work to do** j'ai beaucoup de travail à faire ‖ intr—**to have to** avoir à; devoir; falloir, e.g., **I have to go** il me faut aller; falloir que, e.g., **I have to read him the letter** il faut que je lui lise la lettre ‖ aux (to form compound past tenses) avoir, e.g., **I have run too fast** j'ai couru trop vite; (to form compound past tenses with

some intransitive verbs and all reflexive verbs) être, e.g., **they have arrived** elles sont arrivées; **to have just** + pp venir de + inf, e.g., **they have just returned** ils viennent de rentrer; e.g., **they had just returned** ils venaient de rentrer

have′lock′ s couvre-nuque m

haven [ˋhevən] s havre m, asile m

haversack [ˋhævər,sæk] s havresac m

havoc [ˋhævək] s ravage m; **to play havoc with** causer des dégâts à

haw [hɔ] s (bot) cenelle f ‖ tr & intr tourner à gauche ‖ interj dia!, à gauche!

Hawaiian [həˋwaɪjən] adj hawaïen ‖ s Hawaïen m

Hawai′ian Is′lands spl îles fpl Hawaii

haw′-haw′ s rire m bête ‖ intr rire bêtement ‖ interj heu!

hawk [hɔk] s faucon m; (mortarboard) taloche f; (pol & fig) épervier m; (sharper) (coll) vautour m ‖ tr colporter; **to hawk up** expectorer ‖ intr chasser au faucon; (to hawk up phlegm) graillonner

hawker [ˋhɔkər] s colporteur m

hawk′ owl′ s chouette f épervière

hawks′bill tur′tle s caret m, caouane f

hawse [hɔz] s (hole) écubier m; (prow) nez m; (distance) évitage m

hawse′hole′ s écubier m

hawser [ˋhɔzər] s haussière f

haw′thorn′ s aubépine f

hay [he] s foin m; **to hit the hay** (slang) aller au plumard; **to make hay** faire les foins

hay′ fe′ver s rhume m des foins

hay′field′ s pré m à foin

hay′fork′ s fourche f à foin

hay′loft′ s fenil m, grenier m à foin

hay′mak′er s (boxing) coup m de poing en assommoir

haymow [ˋhe,maʊ] s fenil m; approvisionnement m de foin

hay′rack′ s râtelier m

hay′ride′ s promenade f en charrette de foin

hay′seed′ s graine f de foin; (coll) culterreux m

hay′stack′ s meule f de foin

hay′wire′ adj (slang) en pagaille; **to go haywire** (slang) perdre la boussole ‖ s fil m de fer à lier le foin

hazard [ˋhæzərd] s risque m, danger m; (golf) obstacle m; **at all hazards** à tout hasard ‖ tr hasarder, risquer

hazardous [ˋhæzərdəs] adj hasardé

haze [hez] s brume f; (fig) obscurité f ‖ tr brimer

hazel [ˋhezəl] adj couleur de noisette, brun clair ‖ s (tree) noisetier m, avelinier m

ha′zel·nut′ s noisette f, aveline f

hazing [ˋhezɪŋ] s brimade f; (of university freshmen) bizutage m

ha·zy [ˋhezi] adj (comp -zier; super -ziest) brumeux; (notion) nébuleux, vague

H′-bomb′ s bombe f H

he [hi] pron pers il §87; lui §85; ce §82B; **he who** celui qui §83

head [hɛd] *s* tête *f*; (*of bed*) chevet *m*; (*of boil*) tête; (*on glass of beer*) mousse *f*; (*of drum*) peau *f*; (*of cane*) pomme *f*; (*of coin*) face *f*; (*of barrel, cylinder, etc.*) fond *m*; (*of cylinder of automobile engine*) culasse *f*; (*of celery*) pied *m*; (*of ship*) avant *m*; (*of spear, ax, etc.*) fer *m*; (*of arrow*) pointe *f*; (*of business, department, etc.*) chef *m*, directeur *m*; (*of school*) directeur, principal *m*; (*of stream*) source *f*; (*of lake; of the table*) haut bout *m*, haut bout; (*of a match*) bout; (*caption*) titre *m*; (*decisive point*) point *m* culminant, crise *f*; **at the head of** à la tête de; **from head to foot** des pieds à la tête; **head downwards** la tête en bas; **head of a pin** tête d'épingle; **head of cattle** bœuf *m*; **head over heels in love (with)** éperdument amoureux (de); **heads or tails** pile ou face; **over one's head** (*beyond reach*) hors de la portée de qn; (*going to a higher authority*) sans tenir compte de qn; **to be out of one's head** (coll) être timbré ou fou; **to go to one's head** monter à la tête de qn; **to keep one's head** garder son sang-froid; **to keep one's head above water** se tenir à flot; **to not make head or tail of it** n'y comprendre rien; **to put heads together** prendre conseil; **to take it into one's head to** avoir l'idée de, se mettre en tête de; **to win by a head** gagner d'une tête ‖ *tr* (*to direct*) diriger; (*a procession*) conduire, mener; (*an organization; a class in school*) être en tête de; (*a list*) venir en tête de; **to head off** détourner ‖ *intr* (*said of grain*) épier; **to head for** or **toward** se diriger vers

head′ache′ *s* mal *m* de tête

head′band′ *s* bandeau *m*

head′board′ *s* panneau *m* de tête

head′cheese′ *s* fromage *m* de tête

head′ cold′ *s* rhume *m* de cerveau

head′dress′ *s* coiffure *f*

head′first′ *adv* la tête la première; (*impetuously*) précipitamment

head′frame′ *s* (min) chevalement *m*

head′gear′ *s* garniture *f* de tête, couvre-chef *m*; (*for protection*) casque *m*

head′hunt′er *s* chasseur *m* de têtes; (*for employment*) prospecteur-placier *m*

heading [′hɛdɪŋ] *s* titre *m*; (*of letter*) en-tête *m*; (*of chapter*) tête *f*

headland [′hɛdlənd] *s* promontoire *m*

headless [′hɛdlɪs] *adj* sans tête; (*leaderless*) sans chef

head′light′ *s* (aut) phare *m*; (naut) fanal *m*; (rr) feu *m* d'avant

head′line′ *s* (*of newspaper*) manchette *f*; (*of article*) titre *m*; **to make the headlines** apparaître aux premières pages des journaux ‖ *tr* mettre en vedette

head′lin′er *s* (slang) tête *f* d'affiche

head′long′ *adj* précipité ‖ *adv* précipitamment

head′man′ *s* (*pl* -men′) chef *m*

head′mas′ter *s* principal *m*, directeur *m*

head′most′ *adj* de tête, premier

head′ of′fice *s* bureau *m* central; (*director's office*) direction *f*; (*of a corporation*) siège *m* social

head′ of hair′ *s* chevelure *f*

head′-on′ *adj* & *adv* de front, face à face

head′phones′ *spl* écouteurs *mpl*, casque *m*

head′piece′ *s* (*any covering for head*) casque *m*; (*headset*) écouteur *m*; (*brains, judgment*) tête *f*, caboche *f*; (typ) vignette *f*, en-tête *m*

head′quar′ters *s* bureau *m* central, siège *m* principal; (*police station*) commissariat *m* de police; (mil) quartier *m* général; (*staff headquarters*) (mil) état-major *m*

head′rest′ *s* appui-tête *m*

head′set′ *s* casque *m*, écouteurs *mpl*

heads′man *s* (*pl* -men) bourreau *m*

head′stone′ *s* pierre *f* tumulaire (à la tête d'une tombe); (*cornerstone*) pierre angulaire

head′strong′ *adj* têtu, entêté

head′wait′er *s* maître *m* d'hôtel

head′wa′ters *spl* cours *m* supérieur d'une rivière

head′way′ *s* progrès *m*, marche *f* avant; (*between buses*) intervalle *m*; (naut) erre *f*; **to make headway** progresser, aller de l'avant

head′wear′ *s* garniture *f* de tête

headwind [′hɛd,wɪnd] *s* vent *m* contraire, vent debout

head′word′ *s* (*of a dictionary*) mot *m* d'entrée, mot-souche *m*, entrée *f*, adresse *f*

head′work′ *s* travail *m* mental, travail de tête

head·y [′hɛdi] *adj* (*comp* -ier; *super* -iest) (*wine*) capiteux; (*conduct*) emporté; (*news*) excitant; (*perfume*) entêtant

heal [hil] *tr* guérir; (*a wound*) cicatriser ‖ *intr* guérir

healer [′hilər] *s* guérisseur *m*

healing [′hilɪŋ] *s* guérison *f*

health [hɛlθ] *s* santé *f*; **to be in good health** se porter bien, être en bonne santé; **to be in poor health** se porter mal, être en mauvaise santé; **to drink to the health of** boire à la santé de; **to enjoy radiant health** avoir une santé florissante; **to your health!** à votre santé!

health′-food store′ *s* magasin *m* diététique

healthful [′hɛlfəl] *adj* sain; (*air, climate, etc.*) salubre; (*recreation, work, etc.*) salutaire

health′ insur′ance *s* assurance *f* maladie-sécurité

health·y [′hɛlθi] *adj* (*comp* -ier; *super* -iest) sain; (*air, climate, etc.*) salubre; (*person*) bien portant; (*appetite*) robuste

heap [hip] *s* tas *m*, amas *m* ‖ *tr* entasser, amasser; **to heap** (*honors, praise, etc.*) **on s.o.** combler qn de; **to heap** (insults) **on s.o.** accabler qn de

hear [hɪr] *v* (*pret* & *pp* **heard** [hʌrd]) *tr* entendre, ouïr; **to hear it said** l'entendre dire; **to hear s.o. sing, to hear s.o. singing** entendre chanter qn, entendre qn qui chante; **to hear s.th. sung** entendre chanter q.ch. || *intr* entendre; **hear! hear!** très bien!, bravo!; **hear ye!** oyez!; **to hear about** entendre parler de; **to hear from** avoir des nouvelles de; **to hear of** entendre parler de; **to hear tell of** (coll) entendre parler de; **to hear that** entendre dire que

hearer [`hɪrər] *s* auditeur *m*; **hearers** auditoire *m*

hearing [`hɪrɪŋ] *s* (*sense*) l'ouïe *f*; (*act; opportunity to be heard*) audition *f*; (law) audience *f*; **in the hearing of** en la présence de, devant; **within hearing** à portée de la voix

hear′ing aid′ *s* sonotone *m*, microvibrateur *m*, appareil *m* de correction auditive, appareil auditif; aide *f* auditive; (*fitted as part of eyeglasses*) lunettes *fpl* auditives

hear′say′ *s* ouï-dire *m*

hear′say ev′idence *s* simples ouï-dire *mpl*

hearse [hʌrs] *s* corbillard *m*, char *m* funèbre

heart [hɑrt] *s* cœur *m*; (cards) cœur; **after one's heart** selon son cœur; **at heart** au fond; **by heart** par cœur; **heart and soul** corps et âme; **lift up your hearts!** haut les cœurs!; **to break the heart of** fendre le cœur à; **to die of a broken heart** mourir de chagrin; **to eat one's heart out** se ronger le cœur; **to eat to one's heart's content** manger tout son soûl; **to get to the heart of the matter** entrer dans le vif de la question; **to have one's heart in one's work** avoir le cœur à l'ouvrage; **to have one's heart in the right place** avoir le cœur bien placé; **to lose heart** perdre courage; **to open one's heart to** épancher son cœur à; **to take heart** prendre courage; **to take to heart** prendre à cœur; **to wear one's heart on one's sleeve** avoir le cœur sur les lèvres; **with a heavy heart** le cœur gros; **with all one's heart** de tout son cœur; **with one's heart in one's mouth** le gosier serré

heart′ache′ *s* peine *f* de cœur

heart′ attack′ *s* crise *f* cardiaque

heart′beat′ *s* battement *m* du cœur

heart′break′ *s* crève-cœur *m*

heartbroken [`hɑrt,brokən] *adj* navré, chagriné

heart′burn′ *s* pyrosis *m*

heart′ cher′ry *s* guigne *f*

heart′ disease′ *s* maladie *f* de cœur

hearten [`hɑrtən] *tr* encourager

heart′ fail′ure *s* arrêt *m* du cœur

heartfelt [`hɑrt,fɛlt] *adj* sincère, cordial, bien senti

hearth [hɑrθ] *s* foyer *m*, âtre *m*

hearth′stone′ *s* pierre *f* de cheminée

heartily [`hɑrtɪli] *adv* de bon cœur, sincèrement

heartless [`hɑrtlɪs] *adj* sans cœur

heart′ of stone′ *s* (fig) cœur *m* de bronze

heart′-rend′ing *adj* désolant, navrant

heart′sick′ *adj* désolé, chagrin

heart′strings′ *spl* fibres *fpl*, replis *mpl* du cœur

heart′-to-heart′ *adj* franc, ouvert; sérieux || *adv* à cœur ouvert

heart′ trans′plant *s* greffe *f* du cœur, transplantation *f* cardiaque

heart′ trou′ble *s* maladie *f* de cœur

heart′wood′ *s* bois *m* de cœur

heart·y [`hɑrti] *adj* (*comp* **-ier**; *super* **-iest**) cordial, sincère; (*meal*) copieux; (*laugh*) sonore; (*eater*) gros

heat [hit] *s* chaleur *f*; (*heating*) chauffage *m*; (*rut of animals*) rut *m*; (*in horse racing*) éliminatoire *f*; **in heat** en rut || *tr* échauffer; (*e.g., a house*) chauffer || *intr* s'échauffer; **to heat up** chauffer

heated *adj* chauffé; (fig) chaud, échauffé

heater [`hitər] *s* (*for food*) réchaud *m*; (*for heating house*) calorifère *m*

heath [hiθ] *s* bruyère *f*

hea·then [`hiðən] *adj* païen || *s* (*pl* **-then** or **-thens**) païen *m*

heathendom [`hiðəndəm] *s* paganisme *m*

heather [`hɛðər] *s* bruyère *f*

heating [`hitɪŋ] *adj* échauffant || *s* chauffage *m*

heat′ing oil′ *s* fuel *m*

heat′ light′ning *s* éclairs *mpl* de chaleur

heat′ pump′ *s* pompe *f* de chaleur

heat′ shield′ *s* (rok) bouclier *m* contre la chaleur, bouclier antithermique

heat′stroke′ *s* insolation *f*, coup *m* de chaleur

heat′ wave′ *s* vague *f* de chaleur; (phys) onde *f* calorifique

heave [hiv] *s* soulèvement *m*; **heaves** (vet) pousse *f* || *v* (*pret & pp* **heaved** or **hove** [hov]) *tr* soulever; (*to throw*) lancer; (*a sigh*) pousser; (*the anchor*) lever || *intr* se soulever; faire des efforts pour vomir; (*said of bosom*) palpiter

heaven [`hɛvən] *s* ciel *m*; **for heaven's sake** pour l'amour de Dieu; **Heaven** le ciel; **heavens** cieux *mpl*, ciel

heavenly [`hɛvənli] *adj* céleste

heav′enly bod′y *s* céleste

heav·y [`hɛvi] *adj* (*comp* **-ier**; *super* **-iest**) lourd, pesant; (*heart; crop; eater; baggage; rain, sea, weather*) gros; (*meal*) copieux; (*sleep*) profond; (*work*) pénible; (*book, reading, etc.*) indigeste; (*parts*) (theat) tragique, sombre || *adv* lourd, lourdement; **to hang heavy on** peser sur

heav′y drink′er *s* fort buveur *m*

heav′y·du′ty *adj* extra-fort, à grand rendement

heav′y-heart′ed *adj* au cœur lourd

heav′y·set′ *adj* de forte carrure, costaud

heav′y wa′ter *s* eau *f* lourde

heav′y·weight′ *s* (boxing) poids *m* lourd

Hebraist [`hibre·ɪst] *s* hébraïsant *m*

Hebrew [`hibru] *adj* hébreu, hébraïque || *s* (*language*) hébreu *m*, langue *f* hébraïque; (*man*) Hébreu *m*, Juif *m*; (*woman*) Juive *f*

hecatomb [`hɛkə,tom] *s* hécatombe *f*

heckle [`hɛkəl] *tr* interrompre bruyamment, chahuter; (*on account of trifles*) asticoter, harceler

heckler [ˋhɛklər] *s* interrupteur *m* impertinent, interpellateur *m*

hectic [ˋhɛktɪk] *adj* fou, bouleversant

hedge [hɛdʒ] *s* haie *f* ‖ *tr* entourer d'une haie; **to hedge in** entourer de tous côtés ‖ *intr* chercher des échappatoires, hésiter; (com) faire la contrepartie

hedge′ cut′ter *s* taille-haies *m invar*

hedge′hog′ *s* hérisson *m*; (*porcupine*) porc-épic *m*

hedge′hop′ *v* (*pret & pp* **-hopped**; *ger* **-hopping**) *intr* (aer) voler en rasemottes

hedge′hop′per *s* rase-mottes *m invar*

hedgerow [ˋhɛdʒ,ro] *s* bordure *f* de haies, haie *f* vive

heed [hid] *s* attention *f*, soin *m*; **to take heed** prendre garde ‖ *tr* faire attention à, prendre garde à ‖ *intr* faire attention, prendre garde

heedful [ˋhidfəl] *adj* attentif

heedless [ˋhidlɪs] *adj* inattentif

heehaw [ˋhi,hɔ] *s* hi-han *m* ‖ *intr* pousser des hi-hans

heel [hil] *s* talon *m*; (slang) goujat *m*; **to be down at the heel** traîner la savate; **to cool one's heels** (coll) croquer le marmot, faire le pied de grue, faire le poireau

heft·y [ˋhɛfti] *adj* (*comp* **-ier**; *super* **-iest**) costaud; (*heavy*) pesant

hegira [hɪˋdʒaɪrə] *s* fuite *f* précipitée, hégire *f*; **Hegira** (rel) hégire

heifer [ˋhɛfər] *s* génisse *f*

height [haɪt] *s* hauteur *f*; (*e.g., of folly*) comble *m*

heighten [ˋhaɪtən] *tr* rehausser; (*to increase the amount of*) augmenter; (*to set off, bring out*) relever ‖ *intr* se rehausser; augmenter

heinous [ˋhenəs] *adj* odieux, atroce

heir [ɛr] *s* héritier *m*; **to become the heir of** hériter de

heir′ appar′ent *s* (*pl* **heirs apparent**) héritier *m* présomptif

heiress [ˋɛrɪs] *s* héritière *f*

heir′loom′ *s* meuble *m*, bijou *m*, or souvenir *m* de famille

Helen [ˋhɛlən] *s* Hélène *f*

helicopter [ˋhɛli,kɑptər] *s* hélicoptère *m*

hel′icopter land′ing *s* hélistation *f*

heliport [ˋhɛli,pɔrt] *s* héliport *m*

helium [ˋhili·əm] *s* hélium *m*

helix [ˋhiliks] *s* (*pl* **helixes** or **helices** [ˋhɛli,siz]) hélice *f*; (anat) hélix *m*

hell [hɛl] *s* enfer *m*; **a hell of a lot** tout un tas de; **come hell or high water** en dépit de tout, quoiqu'il arrive; **go to hell!** va te faire voir!, la barbe!; **to give s.o. hell** passer une engueulade à qn; **to raise hell** faire la foire

hell′bent′ *adj* (slang) hardi; **hellbent on** (slang) acharné en diable à

hell′cat′ *s* (*bad-tempered woman*) harpie *f*; (*witch*) sorcière *f*

Hellene [ˋhɛlin] *s* Hellène *mf*

Hellenic [hɛˋlɛnɪk], [hɛˋlinɪk] *adj* hellène

hell′fire′ *s* feu *m* de l'enfer

hellish [ˋhɛlɪʃ] *adj* infernal

hel·lo [hɛˋlo] *s* (*pl* **-los**) bonjour *m* ‖ *interj* bonjour!; (*on telephone*) allô!

helm [hɛlm] *s* gouvernail *m*

helmet [ˋhɛlmɪt] *s* casque *m*

helms′man *s* (*pl* **-men**) homme *m* de barre

help [hɛlp] *s* aide *f*, secours *m*; (*workers*) main-d'œuvre *f*; (*office workers*) employés *mpl*; (*domestic servants*) domestiques *mfpl*; **help wanted** (*public sign*) offres d'emploi, on embauche, recrutons; **there's no help for it** il n'y a pas de remède ‖ *tr* aider, secourir; **so help me God!** que Dieu me juge!; **to help down** aider à descendre; **to help oneself** se défendre; (*to food*) se servir; **to not be able to help** ne pouvoir s'empêcher de ‖ *intr* aider ‖ *interj* au secours!

helper [ˋhɛlpər] *s* aide *mf*, assistant *m*

helpful [ˋhɛlpfəl] *adj* utile; (*person*) serviable, secourable

helping [ˋhɛlpɪŋ] *s* (*of food*) portion *f*

helpless [ˋhɛlplɪs] *adj* (*weak*) faible; (*powerless*) impuissant; (*penniless*) sans ressource; (*confused*) désemparé; (*situation*) sans recours

helter-skelter [ˋhɛltərˋskɛltər] *adj* désordonné ‖ *s* débandade *f* ‖ *adv* pêle-mêle

hem [hɛm] *s* ourlet *m*, bord *m* ‖ *v* (*pret & pp* **hemmed**; *ger* **hemming**) *tr* ourler, border; **to hem in** entourer; cerner ‖ *intr* faire un ourlet; **to hem and haw** ânonner; (fig) tourner autour du pot ‖ *interj* hum!

hemisphere [ˋhɛmɪ,sfɪr] *s* hémisphère *m*

hemistich [ˋhɛmɪ,stɪk] *s* hémistiche *m*

hem′line′ *s* ourlet *m* de la jupe

hem′lock′ *s* (*Tsuga canadensis*) sapin *m* du Canada, pruche *f*; (*herb and poison*) ciguë *f*

hemoglobin [,hɛməˋglobɪn] *s* hémoglobine *f*

hemophilia [,hɛməˋfɪli·ə] *s* hémophilie *f*

hemophiliac [,hɛməˋfɪli·æk] *s* hémophile *mf*

hemorrhage [ˋhɛmərɪdʒ] *s* hémorragie *f*

hemorrhoids [ˋhɛmə,rɔɪdz] *spl* hémorroïdes *fpl*

hemostat [ˋhɛmə,stæt] *s* hémostatique *m*

hemp [hɛmp] *s* chanvre *m*

hem′stitch′ *s* ourlet *m* à jour ‖ *tr* ourler à jour ‖ *intr* faire un ourlet à jour

hen [hɛn] *s* poule *f*

hence [hɛns] *adv* d'ici; (*therefore*) d'où, donc

hence′forth′ *adv* désormais, dorénavant

hench·man [ˋhɛntʃmən] *s* (*pl* **-men**) partisan *m*, acolyte *m*, complice *m*

hen′coop′ *s* cage *f* à poules, épinette *f*

hen′house′ *s* poulailler *m*

henna [ˋhɛnə] *s* henné *m* ‖ *tr* teindre au henné

hen′peck′ *tr* mener par le bout du nez

hep [hɛp] *adj* (slang) à la page, dans le train; **to be hep to** (slang) être au courant de

hepatitis [,hɛpəˋtaɪtɪs] *s* (pathol) hépatite *f*

her [hʌr] *adj poss* son §88 ‖ *pron pers* elle §85; la §87; lui §87

herald [`hɛrəld] s héraut m; (fig) avant-coureur m ‖ tr annoncer; **to herald in** introduire

herald·ry [`hɛrəldri] s (pl **-ries**) héraldique f, blason m

herb [ʌrb], [hʌrb] s herbe f; (pharm) herbe médicinale or officinale; **herbs for seasoning** fines herbes

herbicide [`hʌrbɪ,saɪd] s herbicide m

herculean [hʌr`kjulɪ·ən] adj herculéen

herd [hʌrd] s troupeau m ‖ tr rassembler en troupeau ‖ intr—**to herd together** s'attrouper

herds′man s (pl **-men**) pâtre m; (of sheep) berger m; (of cattle) bouvier m

here [hɪr] adv ici; **from here to there** d'ici là; **here and there** çà et là, par-ci par-là; **here below** ici-bas; **here is** or **here are** voici; **here lies** ci-gît; **that′s neither here nor there** ça n'a rien à y voir ‖ interj tenez!; (answering roll call) présent!

hereabouts [`hɪrə,bauts] adv près d'ici

here·af′ter s—**the hereafter** l'autre monde ‖ adv désormais, à l'avenir; (farther along) ci-après

here·by′ adv par ce moyen, par ceci; (in legal language) par les présentes

hereditary [hɪ`rɛdɪ,tɛri] adj héréditaire

heredi·ty [hɪ`rɛdɪti] s (pl **-ties**) hérédité f

here·in′ adv ici; (on this point) en ceci; (in this writing) ci-inclus

here·of′ adv de ceci, à ce sujet

here·on′ adv là-dessus

here·sy [`hɛrəsi] s (pl **-sies**) hérésie f

heretic [`hɛrətɪk] adj & s hérétique mf

heretical [hɪ`rɛtɪkəl] adj hérétique

heretofore [,hɪrtu`for] adv jusqu'ici

here′upon′ adv là-dessus

here′with′ adv ci-joint, avec ceci

heritage [`hɛrɪtɪdʒ] s héritage m

hermetic(al) [hʌr`mɛtɪk(əl)] adj hermétique

hermit [`hʌrmɪt] s ermite m

hermitage [`hʌrmɪtɪdʒ] s ermitage m

herni·a [`hʌrnɪ·ə] s (pl **-as** or **-ae** [,i]) hernie f

he·ro [`hɪro] s (pl **-roes**) héros m

heroic [hɪ`ro·ɪk] adj héroïque ‖ **heroics** spl (verse) vers m héroïque; (language) grandiloquence f

heroin [`hɛro·ɪn] s héroïne f

her′oin ad′dict s héroïnomane mf

heroine [`hɛro·ɪn] s héroïne f

heroism [`hɛro,ɪzəm] s héroïsme m

heron [`hɛrən] s héron m

herpes [`hʌr,piz] s (pathol) herpès m

herring [`hɛrɪŋ] s hareng m

her′ring·bone′ s (in fabrics) point m de chausson; (in hardwood floors) parquet m à batons rompus; (in design) arête f de hareng

hers [hʌrz] pron poss le sien §89

her·self′ pron pers elle §85; soi §85; elle-même §86; se §87

hesitan·cy [`hɛzɪtənsi] s (pl **-cies**) hésitation f

hesitant [`hɛzɪtənt] adj hésitant

hesitate [`hɛzɪ,tet] intr hésiter

hesitation [,hɛzɪ`teʃən] s hésitation f

heterodox [`hɛtərə,dɑks] adj hétérodoxe

heterodyne [`hɛtərə,daɪn] adj hétérodyne

heterogeneous [,hɛtərə`dʒɪnɪ·əs] adj hétérogène

hew [hju] v (pret **hewed**; pp **hewed** or **hewn**) tr tailler, couper; **to hew down** abattre ‖ intr—**to hew close to the line** (coll) agir dans les règles, être très méticuleux

hex [hɛks] s porte-guigne m ‖ tr porter la guigne à

hey [he] interj hé!; attention!

hey′day′ s meilleure période f, fleur f

hi [haɪ] interj salut!

hia·tus [haɪ`etəs] s (pl **-tuses** or **-tus**) (gap) lacune f; (in a text; in verse) hiatus m

hibernate [`haɪbər,net] intr hiberner

hibiscus [hɪ`bɪskəs] s hibiscus m, ketmie f

hiccough or **hiccup** [`hɪkəp] s hoquet m ‖ intr hoqueter

hick [hɪk] adj (pej) péquenaud ‖ s (pej) péquenaud m, plouc m

hicko·ry [`hɪkəri] s (pl **-ries**) hickory m

hidden [`hɪdən] adj caché, dérobée; (mysterious) occulte

hide [haɪd] s peau f, cuir m ‖ v (pret **hid** [hɪd]; pp **hid** or **hidden** [`hɪdən]) tr cacher; **to hide s.th. from** cacher q.ch. à ‖ intr se cacher; **to hide from** se cacher à

hide′-and-seek′ s cache-cache m

hide′bound′ adj à l'esprit étroit

hideous [`hɪdɪ·əs] adj hideux

hide′-out′ s (coll) repaire m, planque f

hiding [`haɪdɪŋ] s dissimulation f; (punishment) (coll) raclée f, rossée f; **in hiding** caché

hid′ing place′ s cachette f

hierar·chy [`haɪ·ə,rɑrki] s (pl **-chies**) hiérarchie f

hieroglyphic [,haɪ·ərə`glɪfɪk] adj hiéroglyphique ‖ s hiéroglyphe m

hi-fi [`haɪ`faɪ] adj (coll) de haute fidélité ‖ s (coll) haute fidélité f

hi′-fi′ fan′ s (coll) fanatique mf de la haute fidélité

high [haɪ] adj haut; (river, price, rate, temperature, opinion) élevé; (fever, wind) fort; (sea, wind) gros; (cheekbones) saillant; (sound) aigu; (coll) gris; (culin) avancé; **high and dry** à sec; **high and mighty** prétentieux; **to be high** (coll) avoir son pompon ‖ s (aut) prise f directe; **on high** en haut, dans le ciel ‖ adv haut; à un prix élevé; **high and low** partout; **to aim high** viser haut; **to come high** se vendre cher

high′ al′tar s maître-autel m

high′ball′ s whisky m à l'eau

high′ blood′ pres′sure s hypertension f

high′born′ adj de haute naissance

high′boy′ s chiffonnier m semainier

high′brow′ adj & s (slang) intellectuel m

high′ chair′ s chaise f d'enfant

high′ command′ s haut commandement m

high′ cost of liv′ing s cherté f de la vie

high′er educa′tion [ˈhaɪ·ər] s enseignement m supérieur

high′er-up′ s (coll) supérieur m hiérarchique

high′est bid′der [ˈhaɪ·ɪst] s dernier enchérisseur m

high′ explo′sive s haut explosif m, explosif puissant

highfalutin [ˌhaɪfəˈlutən] adj (coll) pompeux, ampoulé

high′ fidel′ity s haute fidélité f

high′ fre′quency s haute fréquence f

high′ gear′ s (aut) prise f directe

high′-grade′ adj de qualité supérieure

high′-hand′ed adj autoritaire, arbitraire

high′ hat′ s chapeau m haut de forme

high′-hat′ adj (coll) snob, poseur ‖ **high′-hat′** v (pret & pp **-hatted**; ger **-hatting**) tr (coll) traiter de haut en bas

high′-heeled′ adj à talons hauts

high′ horse′ s raideur f hautaine; **to get up on one's high horse** monter sur ses grands chevaux

high′ jinks′ [ˌdʒɪŋks] s (slang) clownerie f, drôlerie f

high′ jump′ s saut m en hauteur

high′-key′ adj (phot) lumineux

highland [ˈhaɪlənd] s pays m de montagne; **highlands** hautes terres fpl

high′-level lan′guage s (comp) langage m évolué

high′ life′ s grand monde m

high′light′ s (big moment) clou m, instant m le plus marquant, point m culminant; (of a career) grand succès m; **highlights** (in a picture) clairs mpl ‖ tr mettre en vedette

highly [ˈhaɪli] adv hautement; (very) extrêmement, fort; haut, e.g., **highly colored** haut en couleur; **to think highly of** avoir une bonne opinion de

High′ Mass′ s grand-messe f

high′-mind′ed adj magnanime, noble

highness [ˈhaɪnɪs] s hauteur f; **Highness** Altesse f

high′ noon′ s plein midi m

high′-oc′tane adj à indice d'octane élevé

high′-pitched′ adj aigu; (roof) à forte pente

high′-powered′ adj de haute puissance

high′-pres′sure adj à haute pression; (fig) dynamique, persuasif ‖ tr (coll) gonfler à bloc

high′-priced′ adj de prix élevé

high′ priest′ s grand prêtre m; (fig) pontife m

high′ road′ s grand-route f; (fig) bonne voie f

high′ school′ s école f secondaire publique; (in France) lycée m

high′-school stu′dent s lycéen m; collégien m

high′ sea′ s houle f, grosse mer f; **high seas** haute mer

high′ soci′ety s la haute société, le beau monde

high′-sound′ing adj pompeux, prétentieux

high′-speed′ adj à grande vitesse, en accéléré

high′-spir′ited adj fougueux, plein d'entrain

high′ spir′its spl gaieté f, entrain m

high′ stakes′ spl—**to play for high stakes** jouer gros jeu

high-strung [ˈhaɪˈstrʌŋ] adj tendu, nerveux

high′-test′ gas′oline s supercarburant m

high′ tide′ s marée f haute, haute marée

high′ time′ s heure f, e.g., **it is high time for you to go** c'est certainement l'heure de votre départ; (slang) bombance f, bombe f

high′ trea′son s haute trahison f

high′ volt′age s haute tension f

high wa′ter s marée f haute, hautes eaux fpl

high′way′ s grand-route f

high′way commis′sion s administration f des ponts et chaussées

high′way′man s (pl **-men**) voleur m de grand chemin

high′way map′ s carte f routière

hijack [ˈhaɪˌdʒæk] tr (coll) arrêter et voler sur la route; (coll) saisir de force; (an airplane) (coll) détourner

hijacker [ˈhaɪˌdʒækər] s (coll) bandit m, bandit de grand chemin; (coll) pirate m de l'air, pirate aérien

hijacking [ˈhaɪˌdʒækɪŋ] s (coll) piraterie f aérienne, détournement m

hike [haɪk] s excursion f à pied, voyage m pédestre; (e.g., in rent) hausse f ‖ tr hausser, faire monter ‖ intr faire de longues promenades à pied

hiker [ˈhaɪkər] s excursionniste mf à pied, touriste mf pédestre

hilarious [hɪˈlɛrɪ·əs], [haɪˈlɛrɪ·əs] adj hilare, gai; (joke) hilarant

hill [hɪl] s colline f, coteau m; (incline) côte f; (mil) cote f; **over hill and dale** par monts et par vaux ‖ tr (a plant) butter, chausser

hill′bil′ly s (pl **-lies**) montagnard m rustique

hillock [ˈhɪlək] s tertre m, butte f

hill′side′ s versant m, coteau m

hill·y [ˈhɪli] adj (comp **-ier**; super **-iest**) montueux, accidenté; (steep) en pente, à fortes pentes

hilt [hɪlt] s poignée f; **up to the hilt** jusqu'à la garde

him [hɪm] pron pers lui §85, §87; le §87

him·self′ pron lui §85; soi §85; lui-même §86; se §87

hind [haɪnd] adj postérieur, de derrière ‖ s biche f

hind′ end′ s (slang) train m

hinder [ˈhɪndər] tr empêcher

hind′ legs′ spl pattes fpl de derrière

hind′most′ adj dernier, ultime

hind′quar′ter s arrière-train m, train m de derrière; (of horse) arrière-main m

hindrance [ˈhɪndrəns] s empêchement m

hind′sight′ s (of firearm) hausse f; compréhension f tardive

Hindu [ˈhɪndu] adj hindou ‖ s Hindou m

hinge [hɪndʒ] s charnière f, gond m; (of mollusk) charnière; (bb) onglet m ‖ intr—**to hinge on** axer sur, dépendre de

hin·ny [ˋhɪni] s (pl -nies) bardot m

hint [hɪnt] s insinuation f; (small quantity) soupçon m; **to take the hint** comprendre à demi-mot, accepter le conseil ‖ tr insinuer ‖ intr procéder par insinuation; **to hint at** laisser entendre

hinterland [ˋhɪntər,lænd] s arrière-pays m

hip [hɪp] adj (slang) à la page, dans le train; **to be hip to** (slang) être au courant de ‖ s hanche f; (of roof) arête f

hip′bone′ s os m coxal, os de la hanche

hip′ boots′ spl cuissardes fpl

hipped adj—**to be hipped on** (coll) avoir la manie de

hippety-hop [ˋhɪpɪtɪˋhɑp] adv (coll) en sautillant

hip·po [ˋhɪpo] s (pl -pos) (coll) hippopotame m

hippopota·mus [,hɪpəˋpɑtəməs] s (pl -muses or -mi [,maɪ]) hippopotame m

hip′ roof′ s toit m en croupe

hire [haɪr] s (salary) gages mpl; (renting) louage m; **for hire** à louer; (public sign) libre; **in the hire of** aux gages de ‖ tr (a person) engager, embaucher; (to rent) louer, prendre en location ‖ intr—**to hire out** (said of person) se louer, entrer en service

hired′ man′ s (pl men′) s (coll) valet m de ferme, garçon m de ferme

hireling [ˋhaɪrlɪŋ] adj & s mercenaire m

hiring [ˋhaɪrɪŋ] s embauchage m

his [hɪz] adj poss son §88 ‖ pron poss le sien §89

Hispanic [hɪsˋpænɪk] adj hispanique

hiss [hɪs] s sifflement m ‖ tr & intr siffler

hist [hɪst] interj psitt!, pst!

histology [hɪsˋtɑlədʒi] s histologie f

historian [hɪsˋtori·ən] s historien m

historic(al) [hɪsˋtɔrɪk(əl)] adj historique

histo·ry [ˋhɪstəri] s (pl -ries) histoire f

histrionic [,hɪstriˋɑnɪk] adj théâtral ‖ **histrionics** s art m du théâtre; (fig) attitude f spectaculaire

hit [hɪt] s coup m; (blow that hits its mark) coup au but, coup heureux; (sarcastic remark) coup de patte, trait m satirique; (on the hit parade) tube m; (baseball) coup de batte; (theat) succès m, spectacle m très couru; (coll) réussite f; **to make a hit** (coll) faire sensation ‖ v (pret & pp hit; ger hitting) tr frapper; (the mark) atteindre; (e.g., a car) heurter, heurter contre; (to move the emotions of) toucher; **to hit it off** (coll) s'entendre, se trouver d'accord ‖ intr frapper; **to hit on** tomber sur, trouver

hit′-and-run′ driv′er s chauffard m qui abandonne la scène d'un accident, qui prend la fuite

hitch [hɪtʃ] s saccade f, secousse f; obstacle m, difficulté f; (knot) nœud m, e.g., **timber hitch** nœud de bois; **without a hitch** sans accroc ‖ tr accrocher; (naut) nouer; **to hitch up** (e.g., a horse) atteler

hitch′hike′ intr (coll) faire de l'auto-stop

hitch′hik′er s auto-stoppeur m

hitch′hik′ing s auto-stop m

hitch′ing post′ s poteau m d'attache

hither [ˋhɪðər] adv ici; **hither and thither** çà et là

hith′er·to′ adv jusqu'ici, jusqu'à présent

hit′-or-miss′ adj capricieux, éventuel

hit′ parade′ s (coll) chansons fpl populaires du moment, palmarès m

hit′ rec′ord s (coll) disque m à succès

hive [haɪv] s ruche f; **hives** (pathol) urticaire f

hoard [hord] s entassement m, trésor m ‖ tr accumuler secrètement, thésauriser ‖ intr accumuler, entasser, thésauriser

hoarding [ˋhordɪŋ] s accumulation f secrète, thésaurisation f

hoarfrost [ˋhor,frɔst] s givre m, gelée f blanche

hoarse [hors] adj enroué, rauque

hoarseness [ˋhorsnɪs] s enrouement m

hoar·y [ˋhori] adj (comp -ier; super -iest) chenu, blanchi

hoax [hoks] s mystification f, canard m ‖ tr mystifier

hob [hɑb] s (of fireplace) plaque f; **to play hob** (coll) causer des ennuis; **to play hob with** (coll) bouleverser

hobble [ˋhɑbəl] s (limp) boitillement m; (rope used to tie legs of animal) entrave f ‖ tr faire boiter; (e.g., a horse) entraver ‖ intr boiter, clocher

hob·by [ˋhɑbi] s (pl -bies) distraction f, violon m d'Ingres; (orn) hobereau m; **to ride one's hobby** enfourcher son dada

hob′by·horse′ s cheval m de bois

hob′gob′lin s lutin m; (bogy) épouvantail m

hob′nail′ s caboche f

hob·nob [ˋhɑb,nɑb] v (pret & pp -nobbed; ger -nobbing) intr trinquer ensemble; **to hobnob with** être à tu et à toi avec

ho·bo [ˋhobo] s (pl -bos or -boes) chemineau m, vagabond m

hock [hɑk] s (of horse) jarret m; (wine) vin m du Rhin; (pawn) (coll) gage m; **in hock** (coll) au clou; (in prison) (coll) au bloc ‖ tr couper le jarret à; (to pawn) (coll) mettre en gage, mettre au clou

hockey [ˋhɑki] s hockey m

hock′ey play′er s hockeyeur m

hock′shop′ s (slang) mont-de-piété m, clou m

hocus-pocus [ˋhokəsˋpokəs] s tour m de passe-passe; (meaningless formula) abracadabra m

hod [hɑd] s oiseau m, auge f

hod′ car′rier s aide-maçon m

hodgepodge [ˋhɑdʒ,pɑdʒ] s salmigondis m, méli-mélo m

hoe [ho] s houe f, binette f ‖ tr houer, biner

hog [hɔg] s pourceau m, porc m; (pig) cochon ‖ v (pret & pp hogged; ger hogging) tr (slang) s'emparer de, saisir avidement

hog′back′ s dos m d'âne
hoggish [`hɒgɪʃ] adj glouton
hogs′head′ s barrique f
hog′wash′ s eaux fpl grasses; vinasse f; (fig) boniments mpl à la noix de coco
hoist [hɔɪst] s monte-charge m, grue f; (shove) poussée f vers le haut ‖ tr lever, guinder; (a flag, sail, boat, etc.) hisser
hoity-toity [`hɔɪti`tɔɪti] adj hautain; **to be hoity-toity** le prendre de haut
hokum [`hokəm] s (coll) boniments mpl, fumisterie f
hold [hold] s (grasp) prise f; (handle) poignée f, manche m; (domination) pouvoir m, autorité f; (mus) point m d'orgue; (naut) cale f; **hold for arrival** (formula on envelope) garder jusqu'à l'arrivée; **to be on hold** (telp) être en ligne, attendre; **to get hold of** (s.th.) trouver; (s.o.) contacter; **to take hold of** empoigner, saisir ‖ v (pret & pp held [hɛld]) tr tenir; (one's breath; s.o.'s attention) retenir; (to contain) contenir; (a job; a title) avoir, posséder; (e.g., a university chair) occuper; (a fort) défendre; (a note) (mus) tenir, prolonger; **to be held to be . . .** passer pour . . . ; **to hold** (telp) rester en ligne, attendre; **to hold back** or **in** retenir; **to hold one's own** rivaliser, se défendre; **to hold out** tendre, offrir; **to hold over** continuer, remettre; **to hold s.o. to be . . .** tenir qn pour . . . ; **to hold s.o. to his word** obliger qn à tenir sa promesse; **to hold up** (to delay) retarder; (to keep from falling) retenir, soutenir; (to rob) (coll) voler à main armée ‖ intr (to hold good) rester valable, rester en vigueur; **hold on!** (telp) restez en ligne!; **to hold back** se retenir, hésiter; **to hold forth** disserter; **to hold off** se tenir à distance; **to hold on** or **out** tenir bon; **to hold on to** s'accrocher à, se cramponner à; **to hold out for** insister pour
holder [`holdər] s possesseur m; (of stock) porteur m; (of stock; of a record) détenteur m; (of degree, fellowship, etc.) impétrant m; (for a cigarette) porte-cigarettes m; (of a post, a right, etc.) titulaire mf; (for holding, e.g., a hot dish) poignée f
holding [`holdɪŋ] s possession f; **holdings** valeurs fpl; (of an investor) portefeuille m; (of a landlord) propriétés fpl
hold′ing bay′ s (aer) aire f d'attente
hold′ing com′pany s holding trust m, holding m, société f d'unigestion
hold′ing pat′tern s (aer) trajectoire f d'attente
hold′up′ s (stop, delay) arrêt m; (coll) attaque f à main armée, hold-up m; **what's the holdup?** (coll) qu'est-ce qu'on attend?
hole [hol] s trou m; **in the hole** (coll) dans l'embarras; **to burn a hole in s.o.'s pocket** (coll) brûler la poche à qn; **to get s.o. out of a hole** (coll) tirer qn d'un mauvais pas; **to pick holes in** (coll)

trouver à redire à, démolir; **to wear holes in** (e.g., a garment) trouer ‖ intr—**to hole up** se terrer
holiday [`hɒlɪ,de] s jour m de fête, jour férié; (vacation) vacances fpl
holiness [`holɪnɪs] s sainteté f; **His Holiness** Sa Sainteté
holla [`hɒlə], [hə`lɑ] interj holà!
Holland [`hɒlənd] s Hollande f; la Hollande
Hollander [`hɒləndər] s Hollandais m
hollow [`hɒlo] adj & s creux m ‖ adv—**to beat all hollow** (coll) battre à plate couture ‖ tr creuser
hol·ly [`hɒli] s (pl -lies) houx m
hol′ly·hock′ s primerose f, rose f trémière
holm′ oak′ [hom] s yeuse f
holocaust [`hɒlə,kɔst] s (sacrifice) holocauste m; (disaster) sinistre m
holster [`holstər] s étui m; (on saddle) fonte f
ho·ly [`holi] adj (comp -lier; super -liest) saint; (e.g., water) bénit
Ho′ly Ghost′ s Saint-Esprit m
ho′ly or′ders spl ordres mpl sacrés
Ho′ly Scrip′ture s l'Écriture f Sainte
Ho′ly See′ s Saint-Siège m
Ho′ly Sep′ulcher s Saint Sépulcre m
Ho′ly Spir′it s Saint-Esprit m
ho′ly wa′ter s eau f bénite
Ho′ly Writ′ s l'Écriture f Sainte
homage [`hɒmɪdʒ] s hommage m
home [hom] adj (family) domestique, de famille; (econ, pol) national, du pays ‖ s foyer m, chez-soi m, domicile m; (house) maison f; (of the arts; native land) patrie f; (for the sick, poor, etc.) asile m, foyer, hospice m; **at home** à la maison; (at ease) à l'aise; **make yourself at home** faites comme chez vous ‖ adv à la maison; **to see s.o. home** raccompagner qn jusqu'à chez lui; **to strike home** frapper juste, toucher au vif
home′ address′ s adresse f personnelle; (on a form) domicile m (permanent)
home′-baked′ adj fait à la maison
home′bod′y s (pl -ies) casanier m, pantouflard m
homebred [`hom,brɛd] adj élevé à la maison; du pays, indigène
home′-brew′ s boisson f faite à la maison
home′-care nurs′ing s soins mpl à domicile
home′com′ing s retour m au foyer; (at university, church, etc.) journée f or semaine f des anciens
home′ comput′er s ordinateur m domestique, ordinateur familial, ordinateur maison
home′ coun′try s pays m natal
home′ deliv′ery s livraison f à domicile
home′ econom′ics s économie f domestique; (instruction) enseignement m ménager
home′ front′ s théâtre m d'opérations à l'intérieur du pays
home′ ground′ s domaine m, terrain m

home'-grown' *adj* (*e.g.*, *vegetables*) du jardin

home'land' *s* patrie *f*, pays *m* natal

homeless [ˈhomlɪs] *adj* sans foyer

home' life' *s* vie *f* familiale

home'like' *adj* familial, comme chez soi

home'-lov'ing *adj* casanier

home·ly [ˈhomli] *adj* (*comp* **-lier**; *super* **-liest**) (*not good-looking*) laid, vilain; (*not elegant*) sans façons

home'made' *adj* fait à la maison, de ménage

home'mak'er *s* maîtresse *f* de maison, ménagère *f*

home' of'fice *s* siège *m* social

homeopathy [ˌhomiˈɑpəθi] *s* homéopathie *f*

home'own'er *s* propriétaire *mf*

home' plate' *s* (baseball) marbre *m* (Canad)

home' port' *s* port *m* d'attache

home' rule' *s* autonomie *f*, gouvernement *m* autonome

home'sick' *adj* nostalgique; **to be homesick** avoir le mal du pays

home'sick'ness *s* mal *m* du pays, nostalgie *f*

homespun [ˈhomˌspʌn] *adj* filé à la maison; (fig) simple, sans apprêt

home'stead *s* bien *m* de famille, ferme *f*

home'stretch' *s* fin *f* de course, dernière étape *f*

home' team' *s* locaux *mpl*, équipe *f* qui reçoit

home'town' *s* ville *f* natale

homeward [ˈhomwərd] *adj* de retour ‖ *adv* vers la maison; vers son pays

home'work' *s* travail *m* à la maison; devoirs *mpl*

homey [ˈhomi] *adj* (*comp* **homier**; *super* **homiest**) (coll) familial, intime

homicidal [ˌhɑmɪˈsaɪdəl] *adj* homicide

homicide [ˈhɑmɪˌsaɪd] *s* (*act*) homicide *m*; (*person*) homicide *mf*

homi·ly [ˈhɑmɪli] *s* (*pl* **-lies**) homélie *f*

hom'ing head' *s* (*of missile*) tête *f* chercheuse

hom'ing pi'geon *s* pigeon *m* voyageur

hominy [ˈhɑmɪni] *s* semoule *f* de maïs

homo [ˈhomo] *s* (slang, pej) (*homosexual*) tapette *f*, tante *f*

homogeneous [ˌhoməˈdʒɪnɪ·əs], [ˌhɑməˈdʒɪnɪ·əs] *adj* homogène

homogenize [hɑˈmɑdʒəˌnaɪz] *tr* homogénéiser

homonym [ˈhɑmənɪm] *s* homonyme *m*

homonymous [həˈmɑnɪməs] *adj* homonyme

homosexual [ˌhoməˈsɛkʃʊ·əl] *adj & s* homosexuel *m*

homosexuality [ˌhoməˌsɛkʃʊˈælɪti] *s* homosexualité

hone [hon] *s* pierre *f* à aiguiser ‖ *tr* aiguiser, affiler

honest [ˈɑnɪst] *adj* honnête; (*money*) honnêtement acquis

honesty [ˈɑnɪsti] *s* honnêteté *f*; (bot) monnaie *f* du pape

hon·ey [ˈhʌni] *s* miel *m* ‖ *v* (*pret & pp* **-eyed** or **-ied**) *tr* emmieller

hon'ey·bee' *s* abeille *f* à miel

hon'ey·comb' *s* rayon *m*, gâteau *m* de cire; (*anything like a honeycomb*) nid *m* d'abeilles ‖ *tr* cribler

honeyed *adj* emmiellé

hon'ey·moon' *s* lune *f* de miel; voyage *m* de noces ‖ *intr* passer la lune de miel

hon'ey·suck'le *s* chèvrefeuille *m*

honk [hɔŋk] *s* (aut) klaxon *m* ‖ *tr* (*the horn*) sonner ‖ *intr* klaxonner

honkytonk [ˈhɔŋkiˌtɔŋk] *s* (slang) boui-boui *m*

honor [ˈɑnər] *s* honneur *m*; (*award*) distinction *f*; honneurs *m* ‖ *tr* honorer; **in honor of** en l'honneur de

honorable [ˈɑnərəbəl] *adj* honorable

hon'orable dis'charge *s* (mil) démobilisation *f* honorable

honorari·um [ˌɑnəˈrɛrɪ·əm] *s* (*pl* **-ums** or **-a** [ə]) *s* honoraires *mpl*

honorary [ˈɑnəˌrɛri] *adj* honoraire

honorific [ˌɑnəˈrɪfɪk] *adj* honorifique ‖ *s* formule *f* de politesse

hood [hʊd] *s* capuchon *m*, chaperon *m*; (*of chimney*) hotte *f*; (*academic hood*) capuce *m*; (aut) capot *m*; (slang) gangster *m*, loubard *m* ‖ *tr* capoter

hoodlum [ˈhudləm] *s* (coll) chenapan *m*

hoodoo [ˈhudu] *s* (*bad luck*) guigne *f*; (*rites*) vaudou *m* ‖ *tr* porter la guigne à

hood'wink' *tr* tromper, abuser, anarquer

hooey [ˈhu·i] *s* (slang) blague *f*

hoof [hʊf] *s* sabot *m*; **on the hoof** sur pied ‖ *tr*—**to hoof it** (coll) aller à pied

hoof'beat' *s* pas *m* de cheval

hook [hʊk] *s* crochet *m*; (*for fishing*) hameçon *m*; (*to join two things*) croc *m*; (*boxing*) crochet *m*; **by hook or by crook** (coll) de bric ou de broc, coûte que coûte; **hook line and sinker** (coll) tout à fait, avec tout le bataclan; **to get one's hooks on to** (coll) mettre le grappin sur; **to take off the hook** décrocher ‖ *tr* accrocher; (*e.g.*, *a dress*) agrafer; (*e.g.*, *a boat*) crocher, gaffer; (slang) amorcer, attraper; **to hook up** agrafer; (*e.g.*, *a loudspeaking system*) monter ‖ *intr* s'accrocher

hookah [ˈhukə] *s* narguilé *m*

hook' and eye' *s* agrafe *f* et porte *f*

hook' and lad'der *s* camion *m* équipé d'une échelle d'incendie

hooked' rug' *s* tapis *m* à points noués

hook' shot' *s* (sports) bras *m* roulé

hook'up' *s* (*diagram*) (rad, telv) montage *m*; (*network*) (rad, telv) chaîne *f*

hook'worm' *s* ankylostome *m*

hooky [ˈhuki] *s*—**to play hooky** (coll) faire l'école buissonnière

hooligan [ˈhulɪgən] *s* voyou *m*

hooliganism [ˈhulɪgənˌɪzəm] *s* voyouterie *f*

hoop [hup] *s* cerceau *m*; (*of cask*) cercle *m* ‖ *tr* cercler, entourer

hoop' skirt' *s* crinoline *f*

hoot [hut] *s* huée *f*; (*of owl*) ululement *m*; **I don't care a hoot** (slang) je m'en bats l'œil, je m'en fiche ‖ *tr* huer ‖ *intr* huer; (*said of owl*) ululer; **to hoot at** huer

hoot′ owl′ *s* chat-huant *m*, hulotte *f*

hop [hɑp] *s* saut *m*; (*dance*) (coll) sauterie *f*, surboum *m*; (coll) vol *m* en avion, étape *f*; **hops** (bot) houblon *m* ‖ *v* (*pret & pp* **hopped**; *ger* **hopping**) *tr* sauter, franchir; (*e.g., a taxi*) (coll) prendre ‖ *intr* sauter, sautiller; **to hop on one foot** sauter à cloche-pied; **to hop over** sauter

hope [hop] *s* (*feeling of hope*) espérance *f*; (*instance of hope*) espoir *m*; (*person or thing one puts one's hope in*) espérance, espoir ‖ *tr & intr* espérer; **to hope for** espérer; **to hope to** + *inf* espérer + *inf*

hope′ chest′ *s* trousseau *m*

hopeful [`hopfəl] *adj* (*feeling hope*) plein d'espoir; (*giving hope*) prometteur

hopeless [`hoplɪs] *adj* sans espoir

hopper [`hɑpər] *s* (*funnel-shaped container*) trémie *f*; (*of blast furnace*) gueulard *m*

hop′per car′ *s* wagon-trémie *m*

hop′scotch′ *s* marelle *f*

horde [hord] *s* horde *f*

horehound [`hor,haʊnd] *s* (bot) marrube *m*

horizon [hə`raɪzən] *s* horizon *m*

horizontal [,hɔrɪ`zɑntəl] *adj* horizontal ‖ *s* horizontale *f*

hor′izon′tal hold′ *s* (telv) commande *f* de stabilité horizontale, molette *f* horizontale

hormone [`hɔrmon] *s* hormone *f*

horn [hɔrn] *s* (*bony projection on head of certain animals*) corne *f*; (*of anvil*) bigorne *f*; (*of auto*) klaxon *m*; (*of snail; of insect*) antenne *f*; (mus) cor *m*; (*French horn*) (mus) cor d'harmonie; **horns** (*of deer*) bois *m*; **to blow one's own horn** (coll) se vanter, exalter son propre mérite; **to draw in one's horns** (fig) rentrer les cornes; **to toot the horn** corner ‖ *intr*—**to horn in** (slang) intervenir sans façon

horn′beam′ *s* (bot) charme *m*

horned *adj* cornu

horned′ owl′ *s* duc *m*

hornet [`hɔrnɪt] *s* frelon *m*; **to stir up a hornet's nest** mettre le feu aux poudres

hor′net's nest′ *s* guêpier *m*

horn′ of plen′ty *s* corne *f* d'abondance

horn′pipe′ *s* chalumeau *m*; (*dance*) matelote *f*

horn′rimmed glas′ses *spl* lunettes *fpl* à monture en corne

horn·y [`hɔrni] *adj* (*comp* -ier; *super* -iest) (*like horn*) corné; (*hands*) calleux; (*sexually aroused*) (slang) en rut, excité

horoscope [`hɔrə,skop] *s* horoscope *m*; **to cast s.o.'s horoscope** tirer l'horoscope de qn

horrible [`hɔrɪbəl] *adj* horrible; (coll) horrible, détestable

horrid [`hɔrɪd] *adj* affreux; (coll) affreux, très désagréable

horri·fy [`hɔrɪ,faɪ] *v* (*pret & pp* -fied) *tr* horrifier

horror [`hɔrər] *s* horreur *f*; **to have a horror of** avoir horreur de

hors d'oeuvre [ɔr`dʌrv] *s* (*pl* **hors d'oeuvres** [ɔr`dʌrvz]) hors-d'œuvre *m invar*

horse [hɔrs] *s* cheval *m*; (*of carpenter*) chevalet *m*; **hold your horses!** (coll) arrêtez un moment!; **to back the wrong horse** (coll) miser sur le mauvais cheval; **to be a horse of another color** (coll) être une autre paire de manches; **to eat like a horse** (coll) manger comme un ogre; **to ride a horse** monter à cheval ‖ *intr*—**to horse around** (slang) muser, se baguenauder

horse′back′ *s*—**on horseback** à cheval ‖ *adv*—**to ride horseback** monter à cheval

horse′back rid′ing *s* équitation *f*, exercice *m* à cheval

horse′ blan′ket *s* couverture *f* de cheval

horse′ break′er *s* dompteur *m* de chevaux

horse′car′ *s* tramway *m* à chevaux

horse′ chest′nut *s* (*tree*) marronnier *m* d'Inde; (*nut*) marron *m* d'Inde

horse′cloth′ *s* housse *f*

horse′ coll′ar *s* collier *m* de cheval

horse′ deal′er *s* marchand *m* de chevaux

horse′ doc′tor *s* (coll) vétérinaire *m*

horse′ fly′ *s* (*pl* **flies**) taon *m*

horse′hair′ *s* crin *m*

horse′hide′ *s* peau *f* or cuir *m* de cheval

horse′laugh′ *s* gros rire *m* bruyant

horse′less car′riage [`hɔrslɪs] *s* voiture *f* sans chevaux

horse′man *s* (*pl* **-men**) cavalier *m*; (*at race track*) turfiste *m*

horsemanship [`hɔrsmən,ʃɪp] *s* équitation *f*

horse′ meat′ *s* viande *f* de cheval

horse′ op′era *s* (coll) western *m*

horse′ pis′tol *s* pistolet *m* d'arçon

horse′play′ *s* jeu *m* de mains, clownerie *f*

horse′pow′er *s* (746 *watts*) cheval-vapeur *m* anglais

horse′ race′ *s* course *f* de chevaux

horse′rad′ish *s* raifort *m*

horse′ sense′ *s* (coll) gros bon sens *m*

horse′shoe′ *s* fer *m* à cheval

horse′shoe′ing *s* ferrure *f*, ferrage *m*

horse′shoe mag′net *s* aimant *m* en fer à cheval

horse′ show′ *s* exposition *f* de chevaux, concours *m* hippique

horse′tail′ *s* queue *f* de cheval; (bot) prèle *f*

horse′ thief′ *s* voleur *m* de chevaux

horse′ trad′er *s* maquignon *m*

horse′ trad′ing *s* maquignonnage *m*

horse′whip′ *s* cravache *f* ‖ *v* (*pret & pp* -whipped; *ger* -whipping) *tr* cravacher

horse′wom′an *s* (*pl* **-wom′en**) *s* cavalière *f*, amazone *f*

hors·y [`hɔrsi] *adj* (*comp* -ier; *super* -iest) chevalin; (coll) hippomane; (*awkward in appearance*) (coll) maladroit

horticultural [,hɔrtɪ`kʌltʃərəl] *adj* horticole

horticulture [`hɔrtɪ,kʌltʃər] *s* horticulture *f*

hose [hoz] *s* (*flexible tube*) tuyau *m* ‖ *s* (*pl* **hose**) (*stocking*) bas *m*; (*sock*) chaussette *f*

hosier [`hoʒər] *s* bonnetier *m*

hosiery [`hoʒəri] *s* la bonneterie; (*stockings*) les bas *mpl*

hospice [`hɑspɪs] *s* hospice *m*

hospitable [`hɑspɪtəbəl] *adj* hospitalier
hospital [`hɑspɪtəl] *s* hôpital *m*, clinique *f*, maison *f* de santé
hospitali·ty [,hɑspɪ`tælɪti] *s* (*pl* -ties) hospitalité *f*
hospitalize [`hɑspɪtə,laɪz] *tr* hospitaliser
hos′pital plane′ *s* avion *m* sanitaire
hos′pital ship′ *s* navire-hôpital *m*
hos′pital train′ *s* train *m* sanitaire
hos′pital ward′ *s* pavillon *m*
host [host] *s* hôte *m*; (*who entertains dinner guests*) amphitryon *m*; (*multitude*) foule *f*, légion *f*; (*army*) armée *f*; **Host** (eccl) hostie *f*
hostage [`hɑstɪdʒ] *s* otage *m*
hostel [`hɑstəl] *s* hôtellerie *f*, (*youth hostel*) auberge *f* de la jeunesse
hostel·ry [`hɑstəlri] *s* (*pl* -ries) hôtellerie *f*
hostess [`hostɪs] *s* hôtesse *f*; (*taxi dancer*) entraîneuse *f*
hostile [`hɑstɪl] *adj* hostile
hostili·ty [hɑs`tɪlɪti] *s* (*pl* -ties) hostilité *f*
hostler [`hɑslər], [`ɑslər] *s* palefrenier *m*, valet *m* d'écurie
hot [hɑt] *adj* (*comp* **hotter**; *super* **hottest**) chaud; (*spicy*) piquant; (*fight, pursuit, etc.*) acharné; (*in rut*) en chaleur; (*radioactive*) (coll) fortement radioactif; **hot off** (*e.g., the press*) (coll) sortant tout droit de; **to be hot** (*said of person*) avoir chaud; (*said of weather*) faire chaud; **to get hot under the collar** (coll) s'emporter; **to make it hot for** (coll) rendre la vie intenable à, harceler
hot′ air′ *s* (slang) hâblerie *f*, discours *mpl* vides
hot′-air′ fur′nace *s* calorifère *m* à air chaud
hot′ and cold′ run′ning wa′ter *s* eau *f* courante chaude et froide
hot′bed′ *s* (hort) couche *f*, couche de fumier; (*e.g., of vice*) foyer *m*; (*e.g., of intrigue*) officine *f*
hot′-blood′ed *adj* au sang fougueux
hot′box′ *s* (rr) coussinet *m* échauffé
hot′ cake′ *s* crêpe *f*; **to sell like hot cakes** (coll) se vendre comme des petits pains
hot′ dog′ *s* saucisse *f* de Francfort, saucisse chaude, hot-dog *m*
hotel [ho`tɛl] *adj* hôtelier ‖ *s* hôtel *m*
hotel′keep′er *s* hôtelier *m*
hot′foot′ *adv* (coll) à toute vitesse ‖ *tr*—**to hotfoot it after** (coll) s'élancer à la poursuite de
hot′head′ed *adj* exalté, fougueux
hot′house′ *s* serre *f* chaude
hot′ line′ *s* (pol) téléphone *m* rouge
hot′ mon′ey *s* (slang) capitaux *mpl* fébriles
hot′ pad′ *s* (*for plates at table*) garde-nappe *m*, dessous-de-plat *m*
hot′ pep′per *s* piment *m* rouge
hot′ plate′ *s* réchaud *m*
hot′ rod′ *s* (slang) bolide *m*
hot′ rod′der [,rɑdər] *s* (slang) bolide *m*, casse-cou *m*
hot′ springs′ *spl* sources *fpl* thermales
hot′-temp′ered *adj* coléreux, irascible

hot′ wa′ter *s* (coll) mauvaise passe *f*; **to be in hot water** (coll) être dans le pétrin
hot′-wa′ter boil′er *s* chaudière *f* à eau chaude
hot′-wa′ter bot′tle *s* bouillotte *f*
hot′-wa′ter heat′er *s* calorifère *m* à eau chaude; (*with instantaneous delivery of hot water*) chauffe-eau *m*
hot′-wa′ter heat′ing *s* chauffage *m* par eau chaude
hot′-wa′ter tank′ *s* réservoir *m* d'eau chaude, bâche *f*
hound [haund] *s* chien *m* de chasse, chien courant; **to follow the hounds** or **to ride to hounds** chasser à courre ‖ *tr* poursuivre avec ardeur, pourchasser
hound's′-tooth′ *adj* pied-de-poule
hour [aur] *s* heure *f*; **by the hour** à l'heure; **hours of credit** (educ) unités *fpl* de valeur; **on the hour** à l'heure sonnante; **to keep late hours** se coucher tard
hour′glass′ *s* sablier *m*, horloge *f* à sable
hour′-glass fig′ure *s* taille *f* de guêpe
hour′ hand′ *s* petite aiguille *f*, aiguille *f* des heures
hourly [`aurli] *adj* à l'heure, horaire ‖ *adv* toutes les heures; (*hour by hour*) d'heure en heure
house [haus] *s* (*pl* **houses** [`hauzɪz]) maison *f*; (*legislative body*) chambre *f*; (theat) salle *f*, e.g., **full house** salle comble; **to be on the house** (coll) être aux frais du patron; **to bring down the house** (theat) faire crouler la salle sous les applaudissements; **to keep house for** tenir la maison de; **to put one's house in order** (fig) mettre de l'ordre dans ses affaires ‖ [hauz] *tr* loger, abriter
house′ arrest′ *s*—**under house arrest** en résidence surveillée
house′boat′ *s* péniche *f*, bateau-maison *m*
house′boy′ *s* boy *m*
house′break′er *s* cambrioleur *m*
house′break′ing *s* effraction *f*, cambriolage *m*
housebroken [`haus,brokən] *adj* (*dog or cat*) dressé à la propreté
house′ clean′ing *s* grand nettoyage *m* de la maison
house′coat′ *s* peignoir *m*
house′ cur′rent *s* courant *m* de secteur, secteur *m*
house′fly′ *s* (*pl* -**flies**) mouche *f* domestique
houseful [`haus,ful] *s* pleine maison *f*
house′ fur′nishings *spl* ménage *m*
house′hold′ *adj* domestique, du ménage ‖ *s* ménage *m*, maisonnée *f*
house′hold′er *s* chef *m* de famille, maître *m* de maison
house′ hunt′ing *s* chasse *f* aux appartements
house′keep′er *s* ménagère *f*; (*employee*) femme *f* de charge; (*for a bachelor*) gouvernante *f*
house′keep′ing *s* le ménage, l'économie *f* domestique; **to set up housekeeping** se mettre en ménage

house′maid′ s bonne f
house′moth′er s maîtresse f d'internat
house′ of cards′ s château m de cartes
House′ of Com′mons s Chambre f des communes
house′ of ill′ repute′ s maison f mal famée, maison borgne
House′ of Represen′tatives s Chambre f des Représentants
house′ paint′er s peintre m en bâtiments
house′ physi′cian s (in hospital) interne m; (e.g., in hotel) médecin m
house′top′ s toit m; **to shout from the housetops** (coll) crier sur les toits
house′ trail′er s caravane f
house′warm′ing s—**to have a house-warming** pendre la crémaillère
house′wife′ s (pl -wives′) maîtresse f de maison, ménagère f
house′work′ s travaux mpl ménagers; **to do the housework** faire le ménage
housing [′hauzɪŋ] s logement m, habitation f; (horsecloth) housse f; (mach) enchâssure f, carter m
hous′ing devel′oper s promoteur m immobilier
hous′ing devel′opment s grand ensemble m, habitations fpl neuves, ensemble immobilier, lotissement m, complexe m résidentiel
hous′ing pro′ject s (apartments) projet m immobilier, cité f
hous′ing short′age s crise f du logement
hovel [′hʌvəl] s bicoque f, masure f; (shed for cattle, tools, etc.) appentis m, cabane f
hover [′hʌvər] intr planer, voltiger; (to move to and fro near a person) papillonner; (to hang around threateningly) rôder; (said of smile on lips) errer; hésiter
Hovercraft [′hʌvər,kræft] s (trademark) aéroglisseur m
how [hau] s comment m; **the how, the when, and the wherefore** (coll) tous les détails ‖ adv comment; **how + adj** quel + adj, e.g., **how beautiful a morning!** quelle belle matinée!; comme + c'est + adj, e.g., **how beautiful it is!** comme c'est beau!; que + c'est + adj, e.g., **how beautiful it is!** que c'est beau!; **how are you?** comment allez-vous?, ça va?' **how early** quand, à quelle heure; **how else** de quelle autre manière; **how far** jusqu'où; à quelle distance, e.g., **how far is it?** à quelle distance est-ce?; **how long** (in time) jusqu'à quand, combien de temps; **how long is the stick?** quelle est la longueur du bâton?; **how many** combien; **how much** combien; (at what price) à combien; **how often** combien de fois; **how old are you?** quel âge avez-vous?; **how soon** quand, à quelle heure; **how to** order mode m de commande; **to know how to** savoir
how-do-you-do [′haudəjə′du] s—**that's a fine how-do-you-do!** (coll) en voilà une affaire!

how·ev′er adv cependant, pourtant, toutefois; **however little it may be** si peu que ce soit; **however much** or **many it may be** autant que ce soit; **however pretty she may be** quelque jolie qu'elle soit; **however that may be** quoi qu'il en soit ‖ conj comme, e.g., **do it however you want** faites-le comme vous voudrez
howitzer [′hau·ɪtsər] s obusier m
howl [haul] s hurlement m ‖ tr hurler; **to howl down** faire taire en poussant des huées ‖ intr hurler; (said of wind) mugir
howler [′haulər] s hurleur m; (coll) grosse gaffe f, bourde f, bévue f
hoyden [′hɔɪdən] s petite coquine f
H.P. or **hp** abbr (horsepower) CV
hub [hʌb] s moyeu m; (fig) centre m
hubbub [′hʌbəb] s vacarme m, tumulte m
hub′cap′ s enjoliveur m, chapeau m de roue
huckster [′hʌkstər] s (peddler) camelot m; (adman) publicitaire mf
huddle [′hʌdəl] s (coll) conférence f secrète; **to go into a huddle** (coll) entrer en conclave ‖ intr s'entasser, se presser
hue [hju] s teinte f, nuance f
hue′ and cry′ s clameur f de haro; **with hue and cry** à cor et à cri
huff [hʌf] s accès m de colère; **in a huff** vexé, offensé
hug [hʌg] s étreinte f ‖ v (pret & pp hugged; ger hugging) tr étreindre; (e.g., the coast) serrer; (e.g., the wall) raser ‖ intr s'étreindre
huge [hjudʒ] adj énorme, immense
huh [hʌ] interj hein!, hé!
hulk [hʌlk] s (body of an old ship) carcasse f; (old ship used as warehouse, prison, etc.) ponton m; (heavy, unwieldy person) mastodonte m
hull [hʌl] s (of certain vegetables) cosse f; (of nuts) écale f; (of ship or hydroplane) coque f ‖ tr (e.g., peas) écosser; (e.g., almonds) écaler
hullabaloo [′hʌləbə,lu] s (coll) boucan m, brouhaha m
hum [hʌm] s (e.g., of bee) bourdonnement m; (e.g., of motor) vrombissement m; (of singer) fredonnement m ‖ v (pret & pp hummed; ger humming) tr (a melody) fredonner, chantonner ‖ intr (said of bee) bourdonner; (said of machine) vrombir; (said of singer) fredonner, chantonner; (to be active) (coll) aller rondement ‖ interj hum!
human [′hjumən] adj humain
hu′man be′ing s être m humain
humane [hju′men] adj humain, compatissant
humanist [′hjumənɪst] adj & s humaniste m
humanitarian [hju,mænɪ′tɛrɪ·ən] adj & s humanitaire mf
humani·ty [hju′mænɪti] s (pl -ties) humanité f; **humanities** (Greek and Latin classics) humanités classiques; (belles-lettres) humanités modernes
hu′man·kind′ s genre m humain

humble [ˈhʌmbəl], [ˈʌmbəl] *adj* humble ‖ *tr* humilier; **to humble oneself** s'humilier
hum′ble pie′ *s*—**to eat humble pie** faire amende honorable, s'humilier
hum′bug′ *s* blague *f*; (*person*) imposteur *m* ‖ *v* (*pret & pp* **-bugged**; *ger* **-bugging**) *tr* mystifier
hum′drum′ *adj* monotone, banal
humer·us [ˈhjumərəs] *s* (*pl* **-i** [ˌaɪ]) humérus *m*
humid [ˈhjumɪd] *adj* humide, moite
humidifier [hjuˈmɪdɪˌfaɪ·ər] *s* humidificateur *m*
humidi·fy [hjuˈmɪdɪˌfaɪ] *v* (*pret & pp* **-fied**) *tr* humidifier
humidity [hjuˈmɪdɪti] *s* humidité *f*
humiliate [hjuˈmɪlɪˌet] *tr* humilier
humiliating [hjuˈmɪlɪˌetɪŋ] *adj* humiliant
humili·ty [hjuˈmɪlɪti] *s* (*pl* **-ties**) humilité *f*
hum′ming·bird′ *s* oiseau-mouche *m*, colibri *m*
humor [ˈhjumər], [ˈjumər] *s* (*comic quality*) humour *m*; (*frame of mind; fluid*) humeur *f*; **out of humour** maussade, grognon; **to be in the humor to** être d'humeur à ‖ *tr* ménager, satisfaire; (*s.o.'s fancies*) se plier à, accéder à
humorist [ˈhjumərɪst], [ˈjumərɪst] *s* humoriste *mf*, comique *mf*
humorous [ˈhjumərəs], [ˈjumərəs] *adj* humoristique; (*writer*) humoriste
hump [hʌmp] *s* bosse *f*
hump′back′ *s* bossu *m*; (*whale*) mégaptère *m*
humus [ˈhjuməs] *s* humus *m*
hunch [hʌntʃ] *s* (*hump*) bosse *f*; (*premonition*) (coll) pressentiment *m* ‖ *tr* arrondir, voûter ‖ *intr* s'accroupir
hunch′back′ *s* bossu *m*
hundred [ˈhʌndrəd] *adj* cent ‖ *s* cent *m*, centaine *f*; **about a hundred** une centaine; **a hundred** or **one hundred** cent; une centaine; **by the hundreds** par centaines
hun′dred·fold′ *adj & s* centuple *m*; **to increase a hundredfold** centupler ‖ *adv* au centuple
hundredth [ˈhʌndrədθ] *adj, pron, & s* centième *m*
hun′dred·weight′ *s* quintal *m*
Hungarian [hʌŋˈgɛrɪ·ən] *adj* hongrois ‖ *s* (*language*) hongrois *m*; (*person*) Hongrois *m*
Hungary [ˈhʌŋgəri] *s* Hongrie *f*; la Hongrie
hunger [ˈhʌŋgər] *s* faim *f* ‖ *intr* avoir faim; **to hunger for** être affamé de
hun′ger march′ *s* marche *f* de la faim
hun′ger strike′ *s* grève *f* de la faim
hun·gry [ˈhʌŋgri] *adj* (*comp* **-grier**; *super* **-griest**) affamé; **to be hungry** avoir faim
hunk [hʌŋk] *s* gros morceau *m*
hunt [hʌnt] *s* (*act of hunting*) chasse *f*; (*hunting party*) équipage *m* de chasse; **on the hunt for** à la recherche de; **to use the hunt-and-peck system** taper à tâtons ‖ *tr* chasser; (*to seek, look for*) chercher; **to hunt down** donner la chasse à, traquer; **to**

hunt out faire la chasse à ‖ *intr* chasser; (*with dogs*) chasser à courre; **to go hunting** aller à la chasse; **to hunt for** chercher; **to take hunting** emmener à la chasse
hunter [ˈhʌntər] *s* chasseur *m*
hunting [ˈhʌntɪŋ] *adj* de chasse ‖ *s* chasse *f*
hunt′ing dog′ *s* chien *m* de chasse
hunt′ing ground′ *s* terrain *m* de chasse, chasse *f*
hunt′ing horn′ *s* cor *m* de chasse
hunt′ing jack′et *s* paletot *m* de chasse
hunt′ing knife′ *s* couteau *m* de chasse
hunt′ing li′cense *s* permis *m* de chasse
hunt′ing lodge′ *s* pavillon *m* de chasse
hunt′ing sea′son *s* saison *f* de la chasse
huntress [ˈhʌntrɪs] *s* chasseuse *f*
hunts′man *s* (*pl* **-men**) chasseur *m*
hurdle [ˈhʌrdəl] *s* (*hedge over which horses jump*) haie *f*; (*wooden frame over which runners jump*) barrière *f*; (fig) obstacle *m*; **hurdles** course *f* d'obstacles ‖ *tr* sauter
hur′dle race′ *s* course *f* d'obstacles; (turf) course de haies
hurdy-gur·dy [ˈhʌrdiˈgʌrdi] *s* (*pl* **-dies**) orgue *m* de Barbarie
hurl [hʌrl] *s* lancée *f* ‖ *tr* lancer; **to hurl back** repousser, refouler
hurrah [hʌˈrɑ] or **hurray** [huˈre] *s* hourra *m* ‖ *interj* hourra!; **hurrah for . . . !** vive . . . !
hurricane [ˈhʌrɪˌken] *s* ouragan *m*, hurricane *m*
hurried [ˈhʌrid] *adj* pressé, précipité; (*hasty*) hâtif, fait à la hâte
hur·ry [ˈhʌri] *s* (*pl* **-ries**) hâte *f*; **to be in a hurry** être pressé ‖ *v* (*pret & pp* **-ried**) *tr* hâter, presser ‖ *intr* se hâter, se presser; **to hurry after** courir après; **to hurry away** s'en aller bien vite; **to hurry back** revenir vite; **to hurry over** venir vite; **to hurry up** se dépêcher
hurt [hʌrt] *adj* blessé ‖ *s* blessure *f*; (*pain*) douleur *f* ‖ *v* (*pret & pp* **hurt**) *tr* faire mal à ‖ *intr* faire mal, e.g., **does that hurt?** ça fait mal?; avoir mal, e.g., **my head hurts** j'ai mal à la tête
hurtful [ˈhʌrtfəl] *adj* nuisible
hurtle [ˈhʌrtəl] *intr* se précipiter
husband [ˈhʌzbənd] *s* mari *m*, époux *m* ‖ *tr* ménager, économiser
hus′band·man *s* (*pl* **-men**) cultivateur *m*
husbandry [ˈhʌzbəndri] *s* agriculture *f*; (*raising of livestock*) élevage *m*
hush [hʌʃ] *s* silence *m*, calme *m* ‖ *tr* faire taire; **to hush up** (*e.g., a scandal*) étouffer ‖ *intr* se taire ‖ *interj* chut!
hushaby [ˈhʌʃəˌbaɪ] *interj* fais dodo!
hush′-hush′ *adj* très secret
hush′ mon′ey *s* prix *m* du silence
husk [hʌsk] *s* (*of certain vegetables*) cosse *f*, gousse *f*; (*of nuts*) écale *f*; (*of corn*) enveloppe *f*; (*of oats*) balle *f*; (*of onion*) pelure *f* ‖ *tr* (*grain*) vanner; (*vegetables*) éplucher; (*peas*) écosser; (*nuts*) écaler
husk′ing bee′ *s* réunion *f* pour l'épluchage du maïs

husk·y [ˈhʌski] *adj* (*comp* -ier; *super* -iest) (*burly*) costaud; (*hoarse*) enroué ‖ *s* (*pl* -ies) (*dog*) chien *m* esquimau

hus·sy [ˈhʌsi] *s* (*pl* -sies) (coll) coquine *f*, mâtine *f*; (pej) garce *f*, traînée *f*

hustle [ˈhʌsəl] *s* (coll) bousculade *f*, énergie *f*, allant *m* ‖ *tr* pousser, bousculer ‖ *intr* se dépêcher, se presser; (*to work hard*) (coll) se démener, s'activer

hustler [ˈhʌslər] *s* (*go-getter*) homme *m* d'action; (*swindler*) (slang) filou *m*; (*streetwalker*) (slang) traînée *f*, grue *f*

hut [hʌt] *s* hutte *f*, cabane *f*; (mil) baraque *f*

hutch [hʌtʃ] *s* (*for rabbits*) clapier *m*; (*used by baker*) huche *f*, pétrin *m*

hyacinth [ˈhaɪ·əsɪnθ] *s* (*stone*) hyacinthe *f*; (*flower*) jacinthe *f*

hybrid [ˈhaɪbrɪd] *adj & s* hybride *m*

hy·dra [ˈhaɪdrə] *s* (*pl* -dras or -drae [dri]) hydre *f*

hydrant [ˈhaɪdrənt] *s* prise *f* d'eau; (*faucet*) robinet *m*; (*fire hydrant*) bouche *f* d'incendie

hydrate [ˈhaɪdret] *s* hydrate *m* ‖ *tr* hydrater ‖ *intr* s'hydrater

hydraulic [haɪˈdrɔlɪk] *adj* hydraulique ‖ **hydraulics** *s* hydraulique *f*

hydrau'lic lift' *s* vérin *m* hydraulique

hydrau'lic ram' *s* bélier *m* hydraulique

hydrocarbon [ˌhaɪdrəˈkɑrbən] *s* hydrocarbure *m*

hy'drochlo'ric ac'id [ˌhaɪdrəˈklorɪk] *s* acide *m* chlorhydrique

hydroelectric [ˌhaɪdro·ɪˈlɛktrɪk] *adj* hydroélectrique

hydrofoil [ˈhaɪdrəˌfɔɪl] *s* hydrofoil *m*, hydroptère *m*

hydrogen [ˈhaɪdrədʒən] *s* hydrogène *m*

hy'drogen bomb' *s* bombe *f* à hydrogène

hy'drogen perox'ide *s* eau *f* oxygénée

hy'drogen sul'fide *s* hydrogène *m* sulfuré

hydrometer [haɪˈdrɑmɪtər] *s* aréomètre *m*, hydromètre *m*

hydrophobia [ˌhaɪdrəˈfobɪ·ə] *s* hydrophobie *f*

hydroplane [ˈhaɪdrəˌplen] *s* hydravion *m*

hydroxide [haɪˈdrɑksaɪd] *s* hydroxyde *m*

hyena [haɪˈinə] *s* hyène *f*

hygiene [ˈhaɪdʒin] *s* hygiène *f*

hygienic [ˌhaɪdʒɪˈɛnɪk] *adj* hygiénique

hymn [hɪm] *s* hymne *m*; (eccl) hymne *f*, cantique *m*

hymnal [ˈhɪmnəl] *s* livre *m* d'hymnes

hyperacidity [ˌhaɪpərəˈsɪdɪti] *s* hyperacidité *f*

hyperactivity [ˌhaɪpərækˈtɪvəti] *s* suractivité *f*

hyperbola [haɪˈpʌrbələ] *s* hyperbole *f*

hyperbole [haɪˈpʌrbəli] *s* hyperbole *f*

hypersensitive [ˌhaɪpərˈsɛnsɪtɪv] *adj* hypersensible, hypersensitif

hypertension [ˌhaɪpərˈtɛnʃən] *s* hypertension *f*

hyphen [ˈhaɪfən] *s* trait *m* d'union

hyphenate [ˈhaɪfəˌnet] *tr* joindre avec un trait d'union

hypno·sis [hɪpˈnosɪs] *s* (*pl* -ses [siz]) hypnose *f*

hypnotic [hɪpˈnɑtɪk] *adj & s* hypnotique *m*

hypnotism [ˈhɪpnəˌtɪzəm] *s* hypnotisme *m*

hypnotist [ˈhɪpnətɪst] *s* hypnotiseur *m*

hypnotize [ˈhɪpnəˌtaɪz] *tr* hypnotiser

hypochondriac [ˌhaɪpəˈkɑndrɪˌæk] *adj & s* hypocondriaque *mf*

hypocri·sy [hɪˈpɑkrəsi] *s* (*pl* -sies) hypocrisie *f*

hypocrite [ˈhɪpəkrɪt] *s* hypocrite *mf*

hypocritical [ˌhɪpəˈkrɪtɪkəl] *adj* hypocrite

hypodermic [ˌhaɪpəˈdʌrmɪk] *adj* hypodermique

hyposulfite [ˌhaɪpəˈsʌlfaɪt] *s* hyposulfite *m*

hypotenuse [haɪˈpɑtɪˌn(j)us] *s* hypoténuse *f*

hypothe·sis [haɪˈpɑθɪsɪs] *s* (*pl* -ses [ˌsiz]) hypothèse *f*

hypothetic(al) [ˌhaɪpəˈθɛtɪk(əl)] *adj* hypothétique

hysteria [hɪsˈtɪrɪ·ə] *s* agitation *f*, frénésie *f*; (pathol) hystérie *f*

hysteric [hɪsˈtɛrɪk] *adj* hystérique ‖ **hysterics** *spl* crise *f* de nerfs, crise de larmes, fou rire *m*

hysterical [hɪsˈtɛrɪkəl] *adj* hystérique

I

I, i [aɪ] *s* IXe lettre de l'alphabet

I *pron* je §87; moi §85

iambic [aɪˈæmbɪk] *adj* ïambique

Iberian [aɪˈbɪrɪ·ən] *adj* ibérien, ibérique ‖ *s* Ibérien *m*

ibex [ˈaɪbɛks] *s* (*pl* **ibexes** or **ibices** [ˈibɪˌsiz] bouquetin *m*

ice [aɪs] *s* glace *f*; **to break the ice** (fig) rompre la glace; **to cut no ice** (coll) ne rien casser, ne pas prendre; **to skate on thin ice** (coll) s'engager sur un terrain dangereux ‖ *tr* glacer; (*e.g., champagne*) frapper; (*e.g., melon*) rafraîchir ‖ *intr* geler; **to ice up** (*said of windshield, airplane wings, etc.*) se givrer

ice' age' *s* époque *f* glaciaire

ice' bag' *s* sac *m* à glace

ice' bank' *s* banquise *f*

iceberg [ˈaɪsˌbʌrg] *s* banquise *f*, iceberg *m*; (*person*) (coll) glaçon *m*

ice'boat' *s* (*icebreaker*) brise-glace *m*; (*for sport*) bateau *m* à patins

icebound [ˈaɪsˌbaʊnd] *adj* pris dans les glaces

ice′box′ s glacière f
ice′break′er s brise-glace m
ice′cap′ s calotte f glaciaire
ice′ cream′ s glace f
ice′-cream′ cone′ s cornet m de glace, glace f en cornet
ice′-cream′ freez′er s sorbetière f
ice′ crush′er s broyeur m de glace
ice′ cube′ s glaçon m
ice′-cube′ tray′ s bac m à glaçons
iced′ tea′ s thé m glacé
ice′ floe′ s banquise f
ice′ hock′ey s hockey m sur glace
ice′ jam′ s embâcle m
Iceland [ˈaɪslənd] s Islande f; l'Islande
Icelander [ˈaɪsˌlændər] s Islandais m
Icelandic [aɪsˈlændɪk] adj & s islandais m
ice′man′ s (pl -men′) glacier m
ice′ pack′ s (pack ice) embâcle m; (med) vessie f de glace
ice′ pail′ s seau m à glace
ice′ pick′ s poinçon m à glace; (of mountain climber) piolet m
ice′ skate′ s patin m à glace
ice′ wa′ter s eau f glacée f
ichthyology [ˌɪkθɪˈɑlədʒi] s ichtyologie f
icicle [ˈaɪsɪkəl] s glaçon m, chandelle f de glace
icing [ˈaɪsɪŋ] s (on cake) glaçage m; (aer) givrage m
icon [ˈaɪkɑn] s icône f
iconoclast [aɪˈkɑnəˌklæst] s iconoclaste mf
iconoclastic [aɪˌkɑnəˈklæstɪk] adj iconoclaste
Iconoscope [aɪˈkɑnəˌskop] s (trademark) iconoscope m
icy [ˈaɪsi] adj (comp icier; super iciest) glacé; (slippery) glissant; (fig) froid, glacial
idea [aɪˈdi·ə] s idée f; **the very idea!** par exemple!
ideal [aɪˈdi·əl] adj & s idéal m
idealist [aɪˈdi·əlɪst] adj & s idéaliste mf
idealistic [aɪˌdi·əlˈɪstɪk] adj idéaliste
idealize [aɪˈdi·əˌlaɪz] tr idéaliser
identic(al) [aɪˈdɛntɪk(əl)] adj identique
identification [aɪˌdɛntɪfɪˈkeʃən] s identification f
identifica′tion card′ s carte f d'identité
identifica′tion tag′ s plaque f d'identité
identi·fy [aɪˈdɛntɪˌfaɪ] v (pret & pp -fied) tr identifier
identi·ty [aɪˈdɛntɪti] s (pl -ties) identité f
ideolo·gy [ˌaɪdɪˈɑlədʒi] s (pl -gies) idéologie f
ides [aɪdz] spl ides fpl
idio·cy [ˈɪdɪ·əsi] s (pl -cies) idiotie f
idiom [ˈɪdɪ·əm] s (phrase, expression) idiotisme m; (language, style) idiome m
idiomatic [ˌɪdɪ·əˈmætɪk] adj idiomatique
idiosyncra·sy [ˌɪdɪ·əˈsɪnkrəsi] s (pl -sies) idiosyncrasie f
idiot [ˈɪdɪ·ət] s idiot m
idiotic [ˌɪdɪˈɑtɪk] adj idiot
idle [ˈaɪdəl] adj oisif, désœuvré; (futile) oiseux; **to run idle** marcher au ralenti || tr—**to idle away** (time) passer à ne rien

faire || intr fainéanter; (mach) tourner au ralenti
idleness [ˈaɪdəlnɪs] s oisiveté f
idler [ˈaɪdlər] s oisif m
idling [ˈaɪdlɪŋ] s (of motor) ralenti m
idol [ˈaɪdəl] s idole f
idola·try [aɪˈdɑlətri] s (pl -tries) idolâtrie f
idolize [ˈaɪdəˌlaɪz] tr idolâtrer
idyll [ˈaɪdəl] s idylle f
idyllic [aɪˈdɪlɪk] adj idyllique
i.e. abbr (Lat id est that is) c.-à-d., à savoir
if [ɪf] s—**ifs and buts** des si et des mais || conj si; **even if** quand même; **if it is true that** si tant est que; **if not** sinon; **if so** dans ce cas, s'il en est ainsi
ignis fatuus [ˈɪgnɪsˈfætʃu·əs] s (pl ignes fatui** [ˈɪgnizˈfætʃu·aɪ]) feu m follet
ignite [ɪgˈnaɪt] tr allumer || intr prendre feu
ignition [ɪgˈnɪʃən] s ignition f; (aut) allumage m; **to switch on the ignition** mettre le contact
igni′tion coil′ s (aut) bobine f d'allumage
igni′tion key′ s clef m de contact, clef d'allumage
igni′tion switch′ s (aut) contact m
ignoble [ɪgˈnobəl] adj ignoble
ignominious [ˌɪgnəˈmɪnɪ·əs] adj ignominieux
ignoramus [ˌɪgnəˈreməs] s ignorant m
ignorance [ˈɪgnərəns] s ignorance f
ignorant [ˈɪgnərənt] adj ignorant; **to be ignorant of** ignorer
ignore [ɪgˈnor] tr ne pas tenir compte de, ne pas faire attention à; (a suggestion) passer outre à; (to snub) faire semblant de ne pas voir, ignorer à dessein
ilk [ɪlk] s espèce f; **of that ilk** de cet acabit
ill [ɪl] adj (comp worse [wʌrs]; super worst [wʌrst] malade, souffrant || adv mal; **to take ill** prendre en mauvaise part; (to get sick) tomber malade
ill′-advised′ adj (person) malavisé; (action) peu judicieux
ill′ at ease′ adj mal à l'aise, gêné
ill-bred [ˈɪlˈbred] adj mal élevé
ill′-consid′ered adj peu réfléchi, hâtif
ill′-disposed′ adj mal disposé, malintentionné
illegal [ɪˈligəl] adj illégal
illegible [ɪˈledʒɪbəl] adj illisible
illegitimate [ˌɪlɪˈdʒɪtɪmɪt] adj illégitime
ill′-famed′ adj mal famé
ill′-fat′ed adj malheureux, infortuné
ill-gotten [ˈɪlˈgɑtən] adj mal acquis
ill′ health′ s mauvaise santé f
ill′-hu′mored adj de mauvaise humeur, maussade
illicit [ɪˈlɪsɪt] adj illicite
illitera·cy [ɪˈlɪtərəsi] s (pl -cies) ignorance f; analphabétisme m
illiterate [ɪˈlɪtərɪt] adj (uneducated) ignorant, illettré; (unable to read or write) analphabète || s analphabète mf
ill′-man′nered adj malappris, mal élevé
ill′-na′tured adj désagréable, méchant
illness [ˈɪlnɪs] s maladie f
illogical [ɪˈlɑdʒɪkəl] adj illogique

ill-spent [ˈɪlˈspɛnt] *adj* gaspillé

ill'-starred' *adj* néfaste, de mauvais augure

ill'-tem'pered *adj* désagréable, de mauvais caractère

ill'-timed' *adj* intempestif, mal à propos

ill'-treat' *tr* maltraiter, rudoyer

illuminate [ɪˈlumɪ,net] *tr* illuminer; (*a manuscript*) enluminer

illu'minating gas' *s* gaz *m* d'éclairage

illumination [ɪˈlumɪˈneʃən] *s* illumination *f*; (*in manuscript*) enluminure *f*

illusion [ɪˈluʒən] *s* illusion *f*

illusive [ɪˈlusɪv] *adj* illusoire, trompeur

illusory [ɪˈlusəri] *adj* illusoire

illustrate [ˈɪləs,tret] *tr* illustrer

illustration *s* [,ɪləsˈtreʃən] *s* illustration *f*; (*explanation*) explication *f*, éclaircissement *m*

illustrative [ɪˈlʌstrətɪv] *adj* explicatif, éclairant

illustrator [ˈɪləs,tretər] *s* illustrateur *m*, dessinateur *m*

illustrious [ɪˈlʌstrɪ·əs] *adj* illustre

ill' will' *s* rancune *f*

image [ˈɪmɪdʒ] *s* image *f*

image·ry [ˈɪmɪdʒri] *s* (*pl* **-ries**) images *fpl*

imaginary [ɪˈmædʒɪ,nɛri] *adj* imaginaire

imagination [ɪ,mædʒɪˈneʃən] *s* imagination *f*

imagine [ɪˈmædʒɪn] *tr* imaginer, s'imaginer || *intr* imaginer; **imagine!** figurez-vous!

imbecile [ˈɪmbɪsɪl] *adj & s* imbécile *mf*

imbecili·ty [,ɪmbɪˈsɪlɪti] *s* (*pl* **-ties**) imbécillité *f*

imbibe [ɪmˈbaɪb] *tr* absorber || *intr* boire, lever le coude

imbue [ɪmˈbju] *tr* imprégner, pénétrer; **imbued with** imbu de

imitate [ˈɪmɪ,tet] *tr* imiter

imitation [,ɪmɪˈteʃən] *adj* d'imitation || *s* imitation *f*

imitator [ˈɪmɪ,tetər] *s* imitateur *m*

immaculate [ɪˈmækjəlɪt] *adj* immaculé

Immac'ulate Concep'tion *s* (rel) Immaculée Conception *f*

immaterial [,ɪməˈtɪrɪ·əl] *adj* immatériel; (*pointless*) sans conséquence; **it's immaterial to me** cela m'est égal

immature [,ɪməˈtjʊr] *adj* pas mûr, peu mûr; pas adulte

immeasurable [ɪˈmɛʒərəbəl] *adj* immensurable

immediacy [ɪˈmidɪ·əsi] *s* caractère *m* immédiat, imminence *f*

immediate [ɪˈmidɪ·ɪt] *adj* immédiat

immediately [ɪˈmidɪ·ɪtli] *adv* immédiatement

immemorial [,ɪmɪˈmorɪ·əl] *adj* immémorial

immense [ɪˈmɛns] *adj* immense

immerse [ɪˈmʌrs] *tr* immerger, plonger

immersion [ɪˈmʌrʒən] *s* immersion *f*

immigrant [ˈɪmɪgrənt] *adj & s* immigrant *m*

immigrate [ˈɪmɪ,gret] *intr* immigrer

immigration [,ɪmɪˈgreʃən] *s* immigration *f*

imminent [ˈɪmɪnənt] *adj* imminent, très prochain

immobile [ɪˈmobɪl] *adj* immobile

immobilize [ɪˈmobɪ,laɪz] *tr* immobiliser

immoderate [ɪˈmɑdərɪt] *adj* immodéré

immodest [ɪˈmɑdɪst] *adj* impudique

immoral [ɪˈmɔrəl] *adj* immoral

immortal [ɪˈmɔrtəl] *adj & s* immortel *m*

immortalize [ɪˈmɔrtə,laɪz] *tr* immortaliser

immune [ɪˈmjun] *adj* dispensé, exempt; (med) immunisé

immune' sys'tem *s* système *m* immunitaire

immunize [ˈɪmjə,naɪz] *tr* immuniser

imp [ɪmp] *s* suppôt *m* du diable; (*child*) diablotin *m*, polisson *m*

impact [ˈɪmpækt] *s* impact *m*

impair [ɪmˈpɛr] *tr* endommager, affaiblir; (*health, digestion*) délabrer

impan·el [ɪmˈpænəl] *v* (*pret & pp* **-eled** or **-elled**; *ger* **-eling** or **-elling**) *tr* appeler à faire partie de; (*a jury*) dresser la liste de

impart [ɪmˈpart] *tr* imprimer, communiquer; (*to make known*) communiquer

impartial [ɪmˈparʃəl] *adj* impartial

impassable [ɪmˈpæsəbəl] *adj* (*road*) impraticable; (*mountain*) infranchissable

impassible [ɪmˈpæsɪbəl] *adj* impassible

impassioned [ɪmˈpæʃənd] *adj* passionné

impassive [ɪmˈpæsɪv] *adj* insensible; (*look, face*) impassible, composé

impatience [ɪmˈpeʃəns] *s* impatience *f*

impatient [ɪmˈpeʃənt] *adj* impatient

impeach [ɪmˈpitʃ] *tr* accuser; (*s.o.'s honor, veracity*) attaquer; (pol) entamer la procédure d'impeachment contre

impeachment [ɪmˈpitʃmənt] *s* accusation *f*; (*of honor, veracity*) attaque *f*; (pol) procédure *f* d'impeachment, mise *f* en accusation devant le Sénat, destitution *f*

impeccable [ɪmˈpɛkəbəl] *adj* impeccable

impecunious [,ɪmpɪˈkjunɪ·əs] *adj* besogneux, impécunieux

impede [ɪmˈpid] *tr* entraver, empêcher

impediment [ɪmˈpɛdɪmənt] *s* obstacle *m*, empêchement *m*

im·pel [ɪmˈpɛl] *v* (*pret & pp* **-pelled**; *ger* **-pelling**) *tr* pousser, forcer

impending [ɪmˈpɛndɪŋ] *adj* imminent

impenetrable [ɪmˈpɛnətrəbəl] *adj* impénétrable

impenitent [ɪmˈpɛnɪtənt] *adj* impénitent *m*

imperative [ɪmˈpɛrɪtɪv] *adj & s* impératif *m*

imperceptible [,ɪmpərˈsɛptɪbəl] *adj* imperceptible

imperfect [ɪmˈpʌrfɪkt] *adj & s* imparfait *m*

imperfection [,ɪmpərˈfɛkʃən] *s* imperfection *f*

imperial [ɪmˈpɪrɪ·əl] *adj* impérial

imperialist [ɪmˈpɪrɪ·əlɪst] *adj & s* impérialiste *mf*

imper·il [ɪmˈpɛrɪl] *v* (*pret & pp* **-iled** or **-illed**; *ger* **-iling** or **illing**) *tr* mettre en péril, exposer au danger

imperious [ɪmˈpɪrɪ·əs] *adj* impérieux

imperishable [ɪmˈpɛrɪʃəbəl] *adj* impérissable

impersonal [ɪmˈpʌrsənəl] *adj* impersonnel

impersonate [ɪmˈpʌrsə,net] *tr* contrefaire, singer; jouer le rôle de

impertinent [ɪmˈpʌrtɪnənt] *adj* impertinent

impetuous [ɪmˈpɛtʃu·əs] *adj* impétueux

impetus [ˈɪmpɪtəs] *s* impulsion *f*; (mech) force *f* impulsive; (fig) élan *m*

impie·ty [ɪmˈpaɪ·əti] *s* (*pl* **-ties**) impiété *f*

impinge [ɪmˈpɪndʒ] *intr*—**to impinge on** or **upon** empièter sur; (*to violate*) enfreindre

impious [ˈɪmpɪ·əs] *adj* impie

impish [ˈɪmpɪʃ] *adj* espiègle

implacable [ɪmˈplɛkəbəl] *adj* implacable

implant [ɪmˈplænt] *tr* implanter

implement [ˈɪmplɪmənt] *s* outil *m*, ustensile *m* ‖ *tr* mettre en œuvre, réaliser; (*to provide with implements*) outiller

implicate [ˈɪmplɪˌket] *tr* impliquer

implicit [ɪmˈplɪsɪt] *adj* implicite

implied [ɪmˈplaɪd] *adj* implicite, sous-entendu

implore [ɪmˈplor] *tr* implorer, supplier, solliciter

im·ply [ɪmˈplaɪ] *v* (*pret & pp* **-plied**) *tr* impliquer

impolite [ˌɪmpəˈlaɪt] *adj* impoli

import [ˈɪmport] *s* importance *f*; (*meaning*) sens *m*, signification *f*; (*extent*) portée *f*; (com) article *m* d'importation; **imports** importations *fpl* ‖ *tr* importer; (*to mean*) signifier, vouloir dire

importance [ɪmˈpɔrtəns] *s* importance *f*

important [ɪmˈpɔrtənt] *adj* important

importer [ɪmˈpɔrtər] *s* importateur *m*

importune [ˌɪmpɔrˈt(j)un] *tr* importuner, harceler

impose [ɪmˈpoz] *tr* imposer ‖ *intr*—**to impose on** or **upon** en imposer à, abuser de

imposing [ɪmˈpozɪŋ] *adj* imposant

imposition [ˌɪmpəˈzɪʃən] *s* (*laying on of a burden or obligation*) imposition *f*; (*rudeness, taking unfair advantage*) abus *m*

impossible [ɪmˈpɑsɪbəl] *adj* impossible

impostor [ɪmˈpɑstər] *s* imposteur *m*

imposture [ɪmˈpɑstʃər] *s* imposture *f*

impotence [ˈɪmpətəns] *s* impuissance *f*

impotent [ˈɪmpətənt] *adj* impuissant

impound [ɪmˈpaʊnd] *tr* confisquer, saisir; (*a dog, an auto, etc.*) mettre en fourrière

impoverish [ɪmˈpɑvərɪʃ] *tr* appauvrir

impracticable [ɪmˈpræktɪkəbəl] *adj* impraticable, inexécutable

impractical [ɪmˈpræktɪkəl] *adj* peu pratique; (*plan*) impraticable

impregnable [ɪmˈprɛgnəbəl] *adj* imprenable, inexpugnable

impregnate [ɪmˈprɛgnet] *tr* imprégner; (*to make pregnant*) féconder

impresari·o [ˌɪmprɪˈsɑri,o] *s* (*pl* **-os**) imprésario *m*

impress [ɪmˈprɛs] *tr* (*to have an effect on the mind or emotions of*) impressionner; (*to mark by using pressure*) imprimer; (*on the memory*) graver; (mil) enrôler de force; **to impress s.o. with** pénétrer qn de

impression [ɪmˈprɛʃən] *s* impression *f*

impressive [ɪmˈprɛsɪv] *adj* impressionnant

imprint [ˈɪmprɪnt] *s* empreinte *f*; (typ) rubrique *f*, griffe *f* ‖ [ɪmˈprɪnt] *tr* imprimer

imprison [ɪmˈprɪzən] *tr* emprisonner

imprisonment [ɪmˈprɪzənmənt] *s* emprisonnement *m*

improbable [ɪmˈprɑbəbəl] *adj* improbable

impromptu [ɪmˈprɑmpt(j)u] *adj & adv* impromptu ‖ *s* (mus) impromptu *m*

impromp′tu speech′ *s* improvisation *f*, discours *m* improvisé

improper [ɪmˈprɑpər] *adj* (*not the right*) impropre; (*contrary to good taste or decency*) inconvenant, incorrect

improve [ɪmˈpruv] *tr* améliorer, perfectionner ‖ *intr* s'améliorer, se perfectionner

improvement [ɪmˈpruvmənt] *s* amélioration *f*, perfectionnement *m*; (*of a building site*) viabilité *f*

improvident [ɪmˈprɑvɪdənt] *adj* imprévoyant

improvise [ˈɪmprə,vaɪz] *tr & intr* improviser

imprudent [ɪmˈprudənt] *adj* imprudent

impudent [ˈɪmpjədənt] *adj* impudent, effronté

impugn [ɪmˈpjun] *tr* contester, mettre en doute

impulse [ˈɪmpʌls] *s* impulsion *f*

impulsive [ɪmˈpʌlsɪv] *adj* impulsif

impunity [ɪmˈpjunɪti] *s* impunité *f*

impure [ɪmˈpjʊr] *adj* impur

impuri·ty [ɪmˈpjʊrɪti] *s* (*pl* **-ties**) impureté *f*

impute [ɪmˈpjut] *tr* imputer

in [ɪn] *adv* en dedans, à l'intérieur; (*at home*) à la maison, chez soi; (pol) au pouvoir; **all in** (*tired*) (coll) éreinté; **in here** ici, par ici; **in there** là-dedans, là ‖ *prep* dans; en; (*inside*) en dedans de, à l'intérieur de; (*in ratios*) sur, e.g., **one in a hundred** un sur cent; **in that** du fait que; **in one's life** de sa vie ‖ *s* (coll) entrée *f*, e.g., **to have an in with** avoir ses entrées chez

inability [ˌɪnəˈbɪlɪti] *s* incapacité *f*, impuissance *f*

inaccessible [ˌɪnækˈsɛsɪbəl] *adj* inaccessible, inabordable

inaccura·cy [ɪnˈækjərəsi] *s* (*pl* **-cies**) inexactitude *f*, infidélité *f*

inaccurate [ɪnˈækjərɪt] *adj* inexact, infidèle

inaction [ɪnˈækʃən] *s* inaction *f*

inactive [ɪnˈæktɪv] *adj* inactif

inactivity [ˌɪnækˈtɪvɪti] *s* inactivité *f*

inadequate [ɪnˈædɪkwɪt] *adj* insuffisant

inadvertent [ˌɪnədˈvʌrtənt] *adj* distrait, étourdi; commis par inadvertance

inadvisable [ˌɪnədˈvaɪzəbəl] *adj* imprudent, peu sage

inane [ɪnˈen] *adj* inepte, absurde

inanimate [ɪnˈænɪmɪt] *adj* inanimé

inappropriate [ˌɪnəˈpropri·ɪt] *adj* inapproprié; (*word*) impropre

inarticulate [ˌɪnɑrˈtɪkjəlɪt] *adj* inarticulé; (*person*) muet, incapable de s'exprimer

inartistic [ˌɪnɑrˈtɪstɪk] *adj* peu artistique; (*person*) peu artiste

inasmuch as [ˌɪnəzˈmʌtʃ ˌæz] *conj* attendu que, vu que

inattentive [ˌɪnəˈtɛntɪv] *adj* inattentif

inaudible [ɪnˈɔdɪbəl] *adj* inaudible

inaugural [ɪnˈɔgjərəl] *adj* inaugural ‖ *s* discours *m* d'inauguration

inaugurate [ɪnˈɔgjəˌret] *tr* inaugurer

inauguration [ɪnˌɔgjəˈreʃən] *s* inauguration *f*; (*investiture*) installation *f*

inborn [ˈɪnˌbɔrn] *adj* inné, infus

in'breed'ing *s* croisement *m* consanguin

Inc. *abbr* (**Incorporated**) S.A. (société anonyme)

incandescent [ˌɪnkənˈdɛsənt] *adj* incandescent

incapable [ɪnˈkepəbəl] *adj* incapable

incapacitate [ˌɪnkəˈpæsɪˌtet] *tr* rendre incapable

incarcerate [ɪnˈkɑrsəˌret] *tr* incarcérer

incarnate [ɪnˈkɑrnet] *adj* incarné ‖ *tr* incarner

incarnation [ˌɪnkɑrˈneʃən] *s* incarnation *f*

incendiar·y [ɪnˈsɛndɪˌɛri] *adj* incendiaire ‖ *s* (*pl* -**ies**) incendiaire *mf*

incense [ˈɪnsɛns] *s* encens *m* ‖ *tr* (*to burn incense before*) encenser ‖ [ɪnˈsɛns] *tr* exaspérer, irriter

in'cense burn'er *s* brûle-parfum *m*

incentive [ɪnˈsɛntɪv] *adj* & *s* stimulant *m*

inception [ɪnˈsɛpʃən] *s* début *m*

incessant [ɪnˈsɛsənt] *adj* incessant

incest [ˈɪnsɛst] *s* inceste *m*

incestuous [ɪnˈsɛstʃuˌəs] *adj* incestueux

inch [ɪntʃ] *s* pouce *m*; **by inches** peu à peu, petit à petit; **not to give way an inch** ne pas reculer d'une semelle; **within an inch of** à deux doigts de ‖ *intr*—**to inch along** se déplacer imperceptiblement; **to inch forward** avancer peu à peu

incidence [ˈɪnsɪdəns] *s* incidence *f*; (*range of occurrence*) portée *f*

incident [ˈɪnsɪdənt] *adj* & *s* incident *m*

incidental [ˌɪnsɪˈdɛntəl] *adj* accidentel, fortuit; (*expenses*) accessoire ‖ **incidentals** *spl* faux frais *mpl*

incidentally [ˌɪnsɪˈdɛntəli] *adv* incidemment, à propos

incinerate [ɪnˈsɪnəˌret] *tr* incinérer

incipient [ɪnˈsɪpɪ·ənt] *adj* naissant

incision [ɪnˈsɪʒən] *s* incision *f*

incisive [ɪnˈsaɪsɪv] *adj* incisif

incisor [ɪnˈsaɪzər] *s* incisive *f*

incite [ɪnˈsaɪt] *tr* inciter

inclement [ɪnˈklɛmənt] *adj* inclément

inclination [ˌɪnklɪˈneʃən] *s* inclination *f*; (*slope*) inclinaison *f*

incline [ˈɪnklaɪn] *s* inclinaison *f*, pente *f* ‖ [ɪnˈklaɪn] *tr* incliner ‖ *intr* s'incliner

include [ɪnˈklud] *tr* comprendre, comporter; (*to contain*) renfermer; (*e.g., in a letter*) inclure

including [ɪnˈkludɪŋ] *prep* y compris; **up to and including page ten** jusqu'à la page dix incluse

inclusive [ɪnˈklusɪv] *adj* global; (*including everything*) tout compris; **from Wednesday to Saturday inclusive** de mercredi à samedi inclus; **inclusive of . . .** qui comprend . . . ‖ *adv* inclusivement

incogni·to [ɪnˈkɑgnɪˌto] *adj* & *adv* incognito ‖ *s* (*pl* -**tos**) incognito *m*

incoherent [ˌɪnkoˈhɪrənt] *adj* incohérent

incombustible [ˌɪnkəmˈbʌstɪbəl] *adj* incombustible

income [ˈɪnkʌm] *s* revenu *m*, revenus; (*annual income*) rentes *fpl*, rentrée *f*

in'come tax' *s* impôt *m* sur le revenu

in'come-tax' blank' *s* feuille *f* d'impôt

in'come-tax return' *s* déclaration *f* de revenus

in'com'ing *adj* entrant, rentrant; (*tide*) montant ‖ *s* arrivée *f*

incomparable [ɪnˈkɑmpərəbəl] *adj* incomparable

incompatible [ˌɪnkəmˈpætɪbəl] *adj* incompatible

incompetent [ɪnˈkɑmpɪtənt] *adj* & *s* incompétent *m*, incapable *mf*

incomplete [ˌɪnkəmˈplit] *adj* incomplet

incomprehensible [ˌɪnkɑmprɪˈhɛnsɪbəl] *adj* incompréhensible

inconceivable [ˌɪnkənˈsivəbəl] *adj* inconcevable

inconclusive [ˌɪnkənˈklusɪv] *adj* peu concluant, non concluant

incongruous [ɪnˈkɑŋgru·əs] *adj* incongru, impropre; disparate

inconsequential [ɪnˌkɑnsɪˈkwɛnʃəl] *adj* sans importance

inconsiderate [ˌɪnkənˈsɪdərɪt] *adj* inconsidéré

inconsisten·cy [ˌɪnkənˈsɪstənsi] *s* (*pl* -**cies**) (*lack of coherence; instability*) inconsistance *f*; (*lack of logical connection or uniformity*) inconséquence *f*

inconsistent [ˌɪnkənˈsɪstənt] *adj* (*lacking coherence of parts; unstable*) inconsistant; (*not agreeing with itself or oneself*) inconséquent

inconspicuous [ˌɪnkənˈspɪkju·əs] *adj* peu apparent; peu impressionnant

inconstant [ɪnˈkɑnstənt] *adj* inconstant

incontinent [ɪnˈkɑntɪnənt] *adj* incontinent

incontrovertible [ˌɪnkɑntrəˈvʌtɪbəl] *adj* incontestable

inconvenience [ˌɪnkənˈvinɪ·əns] *s* incommodité *f* ‖ *tr* incommoder, gêner

inconvenient [ˌɪnkənˈvinɪ·ənt] *adj* incommode, gênant; (*time*) inopportun

incorporate [ɪnˈkɔrpəˌret] *tr* incorporer; (com) constituer en société anonyme ‖ *intr* s'incorporer; (com) se constituer en société anonyme

incorporation [ɪnˌkɔrpəˈreʃən] *s* incorporation *f*; (*of company*) constitution *f* en société anonyme; (*of town*) érection *f* en municipalité

incorrect [ˌɪnkəˈrɛkt] *adj* incorrect

increase [ˈɪnkris] *s* augmentation *f*; **on the increase** en voie d'accroissement ‖ [ɪnˈkris] *tr* & *intr* augmenter

increasingly [ɪnˈkrisɪŋli] *adv* de plus en plus

incredible [ɪnˈkrɛdɪbəl] *adj* incroyable

incredulous [ɪnˈkrɛdʒələs] *adj* incrédule

increment [ˈɪnkrɪmənt] *s* augmentation *f*; (comp, econ, math, pol) incrément *m* ‖ *tr* (comp) incrémenter

incriminate [ɪn'krɪmɪ,net] *tr* incriminer

incrust [ɪn'krʌst] *tr* incruster

incubate ['ɪnkjə,bet] *tr* incuber, couver ‖ *intr* couver

incubator ['ɪnkjə,betər] *s* incubateur *m*

inculcate [ɪn'kʌlket] *tr* inculquer

incumben·cy [ɪn'kʌmbənsi] *s* (*pl* -cies) charge *f*; période *f* d'exercice

incumbent [ɪn'kʌmbənt] *adj*—**to be incumbent on** incomber à ‖ *s* titulaire *mf*; (pol) sortant *m*

incunabula [,ɪnkju'næbjələ] *spl* origines *fpl*; (*books*) incunables *mpl*

in·cur [ɪn'kʌr] *v* (*pret & pp* -curred; *ger* -curring) *tr* encourir, s'attirer; (*a debt*) contracter

incurable [ɪn'kjʊrəbəl] *adj & s* incurable *mf*, inguérissable *mf*

incursion [ɪn'kʌrʒən] *s* incursion *f*

indebted [ɪn'dɛtɪd] *adj* endetté; **indebted to s.o. for** redevable à qn de

indecen·cy [ɪn'disənsi] *s* (*pl* -cies) indécence *f*, impudeur *f*, incorrection *f*

indecent [ɪn'disənt] *adj* indécent, impudique, incorrect

inde'cent expo'sure *s* attentat *m* à la pudeur

indecisive [,ɪndɪ'saɪsɪv] *adj* indécis

indeclinable [,ɪndɪ'klaɪnəbəl] *adj* (gram) indéclinable

indeed [ɪn'did] *adv* en effet, vraiment, en vérité; (as an intensifier) effectivement, extrêmement, infiniment; **is it indeed!** vraiment?, c'est vrai?; **yes indeed!** bien sûr!, certainement!

indefatigable [,ɪndɪ'fætɪgəbəl] *adj* infatigable

indefensible [,ɪndɪ'fɛnsɪbəl] *adj* indéfendable

indefinable [,ɪndɪ'faɪnəbəl] *adj* indéfinissable

indefinite [ɪn'dɛfɪnɪt] *adj* indéfini

indelible [ɪn'dɛlɪbəl] *adj* indélébile

indelicate [ɪn'dɛlɪkɪt] *adj* indélicat

indemnification [ɪn,dɛmnɪfɪ'keʃən] *s* indemnisation *f*

indemni·fy [ɪn'dɛmnɪ,faɪ] *v* (*pret & pp* -fied) *tr* indemniser

indemni·ty [ɪn'dɛmnɪti] *s* (*pl* -ties) indemnité *f*

indent [ɪn'dɛnt] *tr* denteler; (*to make a dent in*) laisser une empreinte sur; (*a sheet of metal*) bosseler; (*to recess*) renfoncer; (typ) mettre en alinéa, rentrer ‖ *intr* (typ) faire un alinéa

indentation [,ɪndɛn'teʃən] *s* (*notched edge*) dentelure *f*, découpure *f*; (*act*) découpage *m*; (*hollow mark*) empreinte *f*; (*in metal*) bosse *f*; (*recess*) renfoncement *m*; (typ) alinéa *m*

indented *adj* (typ) en alinéa

indenture [ɪn'dɛntʃər] *s* contrat *m* d'apprentissage ‖ *tr* mettre en apprentissage

independence [,ɪndɪ'pɛndəns] *s* indépendance *f*

independen·cy [,ɪndɪ'pɛndənsi] *s* (*pl* -cies) indépendance *f*; nation *f* indépendante

independent [,ɪndɪ'pɛndənt] *adj & s* indépendant *m*

indescribable [,ɪndɪ'skraɪbəbəl] *adj* indescriptible, indicible

indestructible [,ɪndɪ'strʌktɪbəl] *adj* indestructible

index ['ɪndɛks] *s* (*pl* **indexes** or **indices** ['ɪndɪ,siz]) index *m*; (*of prices*) indice *m*; (typ) main *f*; **Index** Index ‖ *tr* répertorier; (*a book*) faire un index à

in'dex card' *s* fiche *f*

in'dex fin'ger *s* index *m*

in'dex tab' *s* onglet *m*

India ['ɪndɪ·ə] *s* Inde *f*; l'Inde

In'dia ink' *s* encre *f* de Chine

Indian ['ɪndɪ·ən] *adj* indien ‖ *s* Indien *m*

In'dian club' *s* mil *m*, massue *f*

In'dian corn' *s* maïs *m*

In'dian file' *s* file *f* indienne ‖ *adv* en file indienne, à la queue leu leu

In'dian O'cean *s* mer *f* des Indes, océan *m* Indien

In'dian sum'mer *s* l'été *m* de la Saint-Martin

In'dia rub'ber *s* caoutchouc *m*, gomme *f*

indicate ['ɪndɪ,ket] *tr* indiquer

indication ['ɪndɪ'keʃən] *s* indication *f*

indicative [ɪn'dɪkətɪv] *adj & s* indicatif *m*

indicator ['ɪndɪ,ketər] *s* indicateur *m*

indict [ɪn'daɪt] *tr* (law) inculper

indictment [ɪn'daɪtmənt] *s* inculpation *f*, mise *f* en accusation

indifferent [ɪn'dɪfərənt] *adj* indifférent; (*poor*) médiocre

indigenous [ɪn'dɪdʒɪnəs] *adj* indigène

indigent ['ɪndɪdʒənt] *adj* indigent

indigestible [,ɪndɪ'dʒɛstɪbəl] *adj* indigeste

indigestion [,ɪndɪ'dʒɛstʃən] *s* indigestion *f*

indignant [ɪn'dɪgnənt] *adj* indigné

indignation [,ɪndɪg'neʃən] *s* indignation *f*

indigni·ty [ɪn'dɪgnɪti] *s* (*pl* -ties) indignité *f*

indi·go ['ɪndɪ,go] *adj* indigo ‖ *s* (*pl* -gos or -goes) indigo *m*

indirect [,ɪndɪ'rɛkt] *adj* indirect

in'direct dis'course *s* discours *m* indirect, style *m* indirect

indiscreet [,ɪndɪs'krit] *adj* indiscret

indispensable [,ɪndɪs'pɛnsəbəl] *adj* indispensable

indispose [,ɪndɪs'poz] *tr* indisposer

indisposed *adj* indisposé; (*disinclined*) peu enclin, peu disposé

indisputable [,ɪndɪs'pjutəbəl] *adj* incontestable, indiscutable

indissoluble [,ɪndɪ'saljəbəl] *adj* indissoluble

indistinct [,ɪndɪ'stɪŋkt] *adj* indistinct

individual [,ɪndɪ'vɪdʒʊ·əl] *adj* individuel ‖ *s* individu *m*

individuali·ty [,ɪndɪ,vɪdʒʊ'ælɪti] *s* (*pl* -ties) individualité *f*

indivisible [,ɪndɪ'vɪzɪbəl] *adj* indivisible

Indochina ['ɪndo't ʃaɪnə] *s* Indochine *f*; l'Indochine

indoctrinate [ɪn'dɑktrɪ,net] *tr* endoctriner, catéchiser

Indo-European [ˈɪndo͵jʊrəˈpiˑən] *adj* indo-européen ‖ *s* (*language*) indo-européen *m*; (*person*) Indo-Européen *m*
indolent [ˈɪndələnt] *adj* indolent
Indonesia [͵ɪndoˈniʒə] *s* Indonésie *f*; l'Indonésie
Indonesian [͵ɪndoˈniʒən] *adj* indonésien ‖ *s* (*language*) indonésien *m*; (*person*) Indonésien *m*
indoor [ˈɪn͵dor] *adj* d'intérieur; (*home-loving*) casanier; (*tennis*) couvert; (*swimming pool*) fermé
indoors [ˈɪnˈdorz] *adv* à l'intérieur
indubitable [ɪnˈd(j)ubɪtəbəl] *adj* indubitable
induce [ɪnˈd(j)us] *tr* induire; (*to bring about*) provoquer; **to induce s.o. to** porter qn à
induced *adj* provoqué; (elec) induit
inducement [ɪnˈd(j)usmənt] *s* encouragement *m*, mobile *m*, invite *f*
induct [ɪnˈdʌkt] *tr* installer; (mil) incorporer
inductee [͵ɪnˈdʌkti] *s* appelé *m*
induction [ɪnˈdʌkʃən] *s* installation *f*; (elec, logic) induction *f*; (mil) incorporation *f*
induc′tion coil′ *s* bobine *f* d'induction
indulge [ɪnˈdʌldʒ] *tr* favoriser; (*s.o.'s desires*) donner libre cours à; (*a child*) tout passer à ‖ *intr* (coll) boire; (coll) fumer; **to indulge in** se livrer à
indulgence [ɪnˈdʌldʒəns] *s* indulgence *f*; **indulgence in** jouissance de
indulgent [ɪnˈdʌldʒənt] *adj* indulgent
industrial [ɪnˈdʌstrɪˑəl] *adj* industriel
industrialist [ɪnˈdʌstrɪˈəlɪst] *s* industriel *m*
industrialize [ɪnˈdʌstrɪˑə͵laɪz] *tr* industrialiser
industrious [ɪnˈdʌstrɪˑəs] *adj* industrieux, appliqué, assidu
indus·try [ˈɪndəstri] *s* (*pl* **-tries**) industrie *f*; (*zeal*) assiduité *f*
inebriation [ɪn͵ibrɪˈeʃən] *s* ébriété *f*
inedible [ɪnˈɛdɪbəl] *adj* incomestible
ineffable [ɪnˈɛfəbəl] *adj* ineffable
ineffective [͵ɪnɪˈfɛktɪv] *adj* inefficace; (*person*) incapable
ineffectual [͵ɪnɪˈfɛktʃuˑəl] *adj* inefficace
inefficiency [͵ɪnəˈfɪʃənsi] *s* (*action, machine*) inefficacité *f*; (*person*) incapacité *f*, incompétence *f*
inefficient [͵ɪnɪˈfɪʃənt] *adj* (*action, machine*) inefficace; (*person*) incapable, incompétent
ineligible [ɪnˈɛlɪdʒɪbəl] *adj* inéligible
inept [ɪnˈɛpt] *adj* inepte
inequali·ty [͵ɪnɪˈkwɑlɪti] *s* (*pl* **-ties**) inégalité *f*
inequi·ty [ɪnˈɛkwɪti] *s* (*pl* **-ties**) injustice *f*
inertia [ɪnˈʌrʃə] *s* inertie *f*
inescapable [͵ɪnɛsˈkepəbəl] *adj* inéluctable
inevitable [ɪnˈɛvɪtəbəl] *adj* inévitable
inexact [͵ɪnɛgˈzækt] *adj* inexact
inexcusable [͵ɪnɛksˈkjuzəbəl] *adj* inexcusable
inexhaustible [͵ɪnɛgˈzɔstɪbəl] *adj* inexhaustible, inépuisable

inexorable [ɪnˈɛksərəbəl] *adj* inexorable
inexpedient [͵ɪnɛkˈspidɪˑənt] *adj* inopportun, peu expédient
inexpensive [͵ɪnɛkˈspɛnsɪv] *adj* pas cher, bon marché
inexperience [͵ɪnɛkˈspɪrɪˑəns] *s* inexpérience *f*
inexperienced *adj* inexpérimenté
inexplicable [ɪnˈɛksplɪkəbəl] *adj* inexplicable
inexpressible [͵ɪnɛkˈsprɛsɪbəl] *adj* inexprimable, indicible
I.N.F. [ˈaɪˈɛnˈɛf] *spl* (letterword) (**intermediate-range nuclear forces**) F.N.I. *fpl* (forces nucléaires intermédiaires)
infallible [ɪnˈfælɪbəl] *adj* infaillible
infamous [ˈɪnfəməs] *adj* infâme
infa·my [ˈɪnfəmi] *s* (*pl* **-mies**) infamie *f*
infan·cy [ˈɪnfənsi] *s* (*pl* **-cies**) première enfance *f*; (fig) enfance
infant [ˈɪnfənt] *adj* infantile; (*in the earliest stage*) (fig) débutant ‖ *s* nourrisson *m*, bébé *m*; enfant *mf* en bas âge
infantile [ˈɪnfən͵taɪl], [ˈɪnfəntɪl] *adj* infantile; (*childish*) enfantin
in′fantile paral′ysis *s* paralysie *f* infantile
infan·try [ˈɪnfəntri] *s* (*pl* **-tries**) infanterie *f*
in′fantry·man *s* (*pl* **-men**) militaire *m* de l'infanterie, fantassin *m*
infatuated [ɪnˈfætʃu͵etɪd] *adj* entiché, épris; **infatuated with oneself** infatué; **to be infatuated** s'engouer
infect [ɪnˈfɛkt] *tr* infecter
infection [ɪnˈfɛkʃən] *s* infection *f*
infectious [ɪnˈfɛkʃəs] *adj* infectieux; (*laughter*) communicatif, contagieux
in·fer [ɪnˈfʌr] *v* (*pret & pp* **-ferred**; *ger* **-ferring**) *tr* inférer
inferior [ɪnˈfɪrɪˑər] *adj & s* inférieur *m*
inferiority [ɪn͵fɪrɪˈɑrɪti] *s* infériorité *f*
inferior′ity com′plex *s* complexe *m* d'infériorité
infernal [ɪnˈfʌrnəl] *adj* infernal
infest [ɪnˈfɛst] *tr* infester
infidel [ˈɪnfɪdəl] *adj & s* infidèle *mf*
infideli·ty [͵ɪnfɪˈdɛlɪti] *s* (*pl* **-ties**) infidélité *f*
in′field′ *s* (baseball) petit champ *m*
infiltrate [ɪnˈfɪl͵tret] *tr* s'infiltrer dans, pénétrer; (*with conspirators*) noyauter ‖ *intr* s'infiltrer
infinite [ˈɪnfɪnɪt] *adj & s* infini *m*
infinitely [ˈɪnfɪnɪtli] *adv* infiniment
infinitive [ɪnˈfɪnɪtɪv] *adj & s* infinitif *m*
infini·ty [ɪnˈfɪnɪti] *s* (*pl* **-ties**) infinité *f*; (math) infini *m*
infirm [ɪnˈfʌrm] *adj* infirme, maladif
infirma·ry [ɪnˈfʌrməri] *s* (*pl* **-ries**) infirmerie *f*
infirmi·ty [ɪnˈfʌrmɪti] *s* (*pl* **-ties**) infirmité *f*
in′fix′ *s* infixe *m*
inflame [ɪnˈflem] *tr* enflammer ‖ *intr* s'enflammer
inflammable [ɪnˈflæməbəl] *adj* inflammable
inflammation [͵ɪnfləˈmeʃən] *s* inflammation *f*

inflammatory [ɪn'flæmə,tori] *adj* incendiaire, provocateur; (pathol) inflammatoire

inflate [ɪn'flet] *tr* gonfler ‖ *intr* se gonfler

inflation [ɪn'fleʃən] *s* gonflement *m*; (com) inflation *f*

inflationary [ɪn'fleʃən,ɛri] *adj* inflationniste

inflect [ɪn'flɛkt] *tr* infléchir; (*e.g., a noun*) décliner; (*a verb*) conjuguer; (*the voice*) moduler

inflection [ɪn'flɛkʃən] *s* inflexion *f*

inflexible [ɪn'flɛksɪbəl] *adj* inflexible

inflict [ɪn'flɪkt] *tr* infliger

influence ['ɪnflu·əns] *s* influence *f* ‖ *tr* influencer, influer sur

in'fluence ped'dling *s* trafic *m* d'influence

influential [,ɪnflu'ɛnʃəl] *adj* influent

influenza [,ɪnflu'ɛnzə] *s* influenza *f*

in'flux' *s* afflux *m*

inform [ɪn'fɔrm] *tr* informer, renseigner; **keep me informed** tenez-moi au courant ‖ *intr*—**to inform on** informer contre, dénoncer

informal [ɪn'fɔrməl] *adj* sans cérémonie; (*person; manners*) familier; (*unofficial*) officieux

infor'mal dance' *s* sauterie *f*

informant [ɪn'fɔrmənt] *s* informateur *m*; (*in, e.g., language study*) source *f* d'informations

information [,ɪnfər'meʃən] *s* information *f*, renseignements *mpl*; (telp) service *m* des renseignements téléphoniques; **piece of information** information, renseignement

informational [,ɪnfər'meʃənəl] *adj* instructif, documentaire; (comp) informatique

informa'tion bu'reau *s* bureau *m* de renseignements

informa'tion desk' *s* comptoir *m* informations

informa'tion proc'essing *s* (comp) traitement *m* des données, traitement de l'information

informative [ɪn'fɔrmətɪv] *adj* instructif, édifiant

informed' sour'ces *spl* sources *fpl* bien informées

informer [ɪn'fɔrmər] *s* délateur *m*, dénonciateur *m*; (*police spy*) indicateur *m*, mouchard *m*

infraction [ɪn'frækʃən] *s* infraction *f*

infrared [,ɪnfrə'rɛd] *adj & s* infrarouge *m*

infrastructure ['ɪnfrə,strʌktʃər] *s* infrastructure *f*

infrequent [ɪn'frikwənt] *adj* peu fréquent, rare

infringe [ɪn'frɪndʒ] *tr* enfreindre; (*a patent*) contrefaire ‖ *intr*—**to infringe on** empiéter sur, enfreindre

infringement [ɪn'frɪndʒmənt] *s* infraction *f*; (*on patent rights*) contrefaçon *f*

infuriate [ɪn'fjʊri,et] *tr* rendre furieux

infuse [ɪn'fjuz] *tr* infuser

infusion [ɪn'fjuʒən] *s* infusion *f*

ingenious [ɪn'dʒinjəs] *adj* ingénieux

ingenui·ty [,ɪndʒɪ'n(j)u·ɪti] *s* (*pl* **-ties**) ingéniosité *f*

ingenuous [ɪn'dʒɛnju·əs] *adj* ingénu, naïf

ingenuousness [ɪn'dʒɛnju·əsnɪs] *s* ingénuité *f*, naïveté *f*

ingest [ɪn'dʒɛst] *tr* ingérer

ingot ['ɪŋgət] *s* lingot *m*

in·grained' *adj* imprégné; (*habit*) invétéré; (*prejudice*) enraciné

ingrate ['ɪngret] *adj & s* ingrat *m*

ingratiate [ɪn'greʃi,et] *tr*—**to ingratiate oneself (with)** se faire bien voir (de)

ingratiating [ɪn'greʃi,etɪŋ] *adj* insinuant, persuasif

ingratitude [ɪn'græti,t(j)ud] *adj* ingratitude *f*

ingredient [ɪn'gridi·ənt] *s* ingrédient *m*

in'growing nail' *s* ongle *m* incarné

ingulf [ɪn'gʌlf] *tr* engouffrer

inhabit [ɪn'hæbɪt] *tr* habiter

inhabitant [ɪn'hæbɪtənt] *s* habitant *m*

inhale [ɪn'hel] *tr* inhaler, aspirer; (*smoke*) avaler ‖ *intr* (*while smoking*) avaler

inherent [ɪn'hɪrənt] *adj* inhérent

inherit [ɪn'hɛrɪt] *tr* (*e.g., money*) hériter; (*e.g., money to become the heir or successor of*) hériter de; **to inherit s.th. from s.o.** hériter q.ch. de qn

inheritance [ɪn'hɛrɪtəns] *s* héritage *m*

inher'itance tax' *s* droits *mpl* de succession

inheritor [ɪn'hɛrɪtər] *s* héritier *m*

inhibit [ɪn'hɪbɪt] *tr* inhiber

inhibition [,ɪnɪ'bɪʃən] *s* inhibition *f*

inhospitable [ɪn'hɑspɪtəbəl] *adj* inhospitalier

inhuman [ɪn'hjumən] *adj* inhumain

inhumane [,ɪnhju'men] *adj* inhumain, insensible

inhumani·ty [,ɪnhju'mænɪti] *s* (*pl* **-ties**) inhumanité *f*

inimical [ɪ'nɪmɪkəl] *adj* inamical

iniqui·ty [ɪ'nɪkwɪti] *s* (*pl* **-ties**) iniquité *f*; (*wickedness*) méchanceté *f*

ini·tial [ɪ'nɪʃəl] *adj* initial ‖ *s* initiale *f*; **initials** parafe *m*, initiales ‖ *v* (*pret* **-tialed** or **-tialled**; *ger* **-tialing** or **-tialling**) *tr* signer de ses initiales, parapher

initiate [ɪ'nɪʃi,et] *s* initié *m* ‖ *tr* initier; (*a project*) commencer

initiation [ɪ,nɪʃi'eʃən] *s* initiation *f*

initiative [ɪ'nɪʃi·ətɪv] *s* initiative *f*

inject [ɪn'dʒɛkt] *tr* injecter; (*a remark or suggestion*) introduire

injection [ɪn'dʒɛkʃən] *s* injection *f*

injudicious [,ɪndʒu'dɪʃəs] *adj* peu judicieux

injunction [ɪn'dʒʌŋkʃən] *s* injonction *f*; (law) mise *f* en demeure

injure ['ɪndʒər] *tr* (*to harm*) nuire à; (*to wound*) blesser; (*to offend*) faire tort à, léser

injurious [ɪn'dʒʊri·əs] *adj* nuisible, préjudiciable; (*offensive*) blessant, injurieux

inju·ry ['ɪndʒəri] *s* (*pl* **-ries**) blessure *f*, lésion *f*; (*harm*) tort *m*; injure *f*, offense *f*

injustice [ɪn'dʒʌstɪs] *s* injustice *f*

ink [ɪŋk] *s* encre *f* ‖ *tr* encrer

ink' blot' *s* pâté *m*, macule *f*

inkling [ˈɪŋklɪŋ] s soupçon m, pressentiment m

ink' pad' s tampon m encreur

ink'stand' s encrier m

ink'well' s encrier m de bureau

ink·y [ˈɪŋki] adj (comp **-ier;** super **-iest**) noir foncé; taché d'encre

inlaid [ˈɪnˌled], [ˌɪnˈled] adj incrusté

inland [ˈɪnlənd] adj & s intérieur m ‖ adv à l'intérieur, vers l'intérieur

in'-law' s (coll) parent m par alliance, pièce f rapportée; **the in-laws** (coll) la belle-famille, les beaux-parents mpl

in·lay [ˈɪnˌle] s incrustation f ‖ [ˈɪnˌle] v (pret & pp **-laid**) tr incruster

in'let s bras m de mer, crique f; (e.g., of air) arrivée f

in'mate s habitant m; (of an institution) pensionnaire mf

inn [ɪn] s auberge f

innate [ɪˈnet] adj inné, infus

inner [ˈɪnər] adj intérieur; (e.g., ear) interne; intime, secret

in'ner core' s noyau m (de la cité)

in'ner·spring' mat'tress s sommier m à ressorts internes

in'ner tube' s chambre f à air

inning [ˈɪnɪŋ] s manche f, tour m

inn'keep'er s aubergiste mf

innocence [ˈɪnəsəns] s innocence f

innocent [ˈɪnəsənt] adj & s innocent m

innocuous [ɪˈnɑkjʊ·əs] adj inoffensif

innovate [ˈɪnəˌvet] tr & intr innover

innovation [ˌɪnəˈveʃən] s innovation f

innuen·do [ˌɪnjʊˈɛndo] s (pl **-does**) allusion f, sous-entendu m

innumerable [ɪˈn(j)umərəbəl] adj innombrable

inoculate [ɪnˈɑkjəˌlet] tr inoculer

inoculation [ɪnˌɑkjəˈleʃən] s inoculation f

inoffensive [ˌɪnəˈfɛnsɪv] adj inoffensif

inoperative [ɪnˈɑpərətɪv] adj inopérant

inopportune [ɪnˌɑpərˈt(j)un] adj inopportun, mal choisi

inordinate [ɪnˈɔrdɪnɪt] adj désordonné, déréglé; (unrestrained) démesuré

inorganic [ˌɪnɔrˈgænɪk] adj inorganique

in'put' s (comp) information f fournie, données fpl; (elec) prise f, entrée f, énergie f; (mach) consommation f

inquest [ˈɪnkwɛst] s enquête f

inquire [ɪnˈkwaɪr] tr s'informer de, e.g., **to inquire the price of** s'informer du prix de ‖ intr s'enquérir; **to inquire about** s'enquérir de, se renseigner sur; **to inquire into** faire des recherches sur

inquir·y [ˈɪnkwɪri] s (pl **-ies**) investigation f, enquête f; (question) demande f; **to make inquiries** s'informer

inquisition [ˌɪnkwɪˈzɪʃən] s inquisition f

inquisitive [ɪnˈkwɪzɪtɪv] adj curieux, questionneur

in'road' s incursion f, empiètement m

ins' and outs' spl tours et détours mpl

insane [ɪnˈsen] adj dément, fou; (unreasonable) insensé, insane

insane' asy'lum s asile m d'aliénés

insani·ty [ɪnˈsænɪti] s (pl **-ties**) démence f, aliénation f

insatiable [ɪnˈseʃəbəl] adj insatiable

inscribe [ɪnˈskraɪb] tr inscrire; (a book) dédier

inscription [ɪnˈskrɪpʃən] s inscription f; (of a book) dédicace f; (on a medal) exergue m, inscription

inscrutable [ɪnˈskrutəbəl] adj impénétrable, fermé

insect [ˈɪnsɛkt] s insecte m

insecticide [ɪnˈsɛktɪˌsaɪd] adj & s insecticide m

insecure [ˌɪnsɪˈkjʊr] adj peu sûr; (nervous) inquiet

insensitive [ɪnˈsɛnsɪtɪv] adj insensible

inseparable [ɪnˈsɛpərəbəl] adj inséparable

insert [ˈɪnsʌrt] s (sewing) incrustation f; (typ) hors-texte m, encart m ‖ [ɪnˈsʌrt] tr insérer, introduire; (typ) encarter

insertion [ɪnˈsʌrʃən] s insertion f; (sewing) incrustation f

in·set [ˈɪnˌsɛt] s (map, picture, etc.) médaillon m, cartouche m; (sewing) incrustation f; (typ) hors-texte m, encart m ‖ [ɪnˈsɛt], [ˈɪnˌsɛt] v (pret & pp **-set**; ger **-setting**) tr insérer; (a page or pages) encarter

in'shore' adj côtier ‖ adv près de la côte

in'side' adj d'intérieur, interne; (information) secret, à la source ‖ s intérieur m, dedans m; **insides** (coll) entrailles fpl ‖ adv à l'intérieur; **inside and out** au-dedans et au-dehors; **inside of** à l'intérieur de; **inside out** à l'envers; **to turn inside out** (e.g., a coat) retourner ‖ prep à l'intérieur de, dans

in'side informa'tion s tuyau m, tuyaux

insider [ˌɪnˈsaɪdər] s initié m

in'side track' s—**to have the inside track** prendre à la corde; (fig) avoir un avantage

insidious [ɪnˈsɪdɪ·əs] adj insidieux

in'sight' s pénétration f; (psychol) défoulement m

insigni·a [ɪnˈsɪgnɪ·ə] s (pl **-a** or **-as**) insigne m

insignificant [ˌɪnsɪgˈnɪfɪkənt] adj insignifiant

insincere [ˌɪnsɪnˈsɪr] adj insincère, peu sincère

insinuate [ɪnˈsɪnjʊˌet] tr insinuer

insipid [ɪnˈsɪpɪd] adj insipide

insist [ɪnˈsɪst] intr insister; **to insist on** insister sur; **to insist on** + ger insister pour + inf

insofar as [ˌɪnsoˈfɑrəz] conj pour autant que, dans la mesure où

insolence [ˈɪnsələns] s insolence f

insolent [ˈɪnsələnt] adj insolent

insoluble [ɪnˈsɑljəbəl] adj insoluble

insolven·cy [ɪnˈsɑlvənsi] s (pl **-cies**) insolvabilité f

insolvent [ɪnˈsɑlvənt] adj insolvable

insomnia [ɪnˈsɑmnɪ·ə] s insomnie f

insomuch [ˌɪnsoˈmʌtʃ] adv—**insomuch as** vu que; **insomuch that** à tel point que

inspect [ɪnˈspɛkt] tr inspecter

inspection [ɪn'spɛkʃən] *s* inspection *f*
inspector [ɪn'spɛktər] *s* inspecteur *m*
inspiration [,ɪnspɪ'reʃən] *s* inspiration *f*
inspire [ɪn'spaɪr] *tr* inspirer
inspiring [ɪn'spaɪrɪŋ] *adj* inspirant
install [ɪn'stɔl] *tr* installer
installment [ɪn'stɔlmənt] *s* installation *f*; (*delivery*) livraison *f*; (*serial story*) feuilleton *m*; (*partial payment*) acompte *m*, versement *m*; **in installments** par acomptes, par tranches
install'ment buy'ing *s* achat *m* à tempérament
install'ment plan' *s* vente *f* à tempérament or à crédit; **on the installment plan** avec facilités de paiement
instance ['ɪnstəns] *s* cas *m*, exemple *m*; **for instance** par exemple
instant ['ɪnstənt] *adj* imminent, immédiat; **on the fifth instant** le cinq courant ‖ *s* instant *m*, moment *m*
instantaneous [,ɪnstən'teni·əs] *adj* instantané
in'stant cof'fee *s* café *m* en poudre, café instantané
instantly ['ɪnstəntli] *adv* à l'instant
instead [ɪn'stɛd] *adv* plutôt, au contraire; à ma (votre, sa, etc.) place; **instead of** au lieu de
in'step' *s* cou-de-pied *m*
instigate ['ɪnstɪ,get] *tr* inciter
instigation [,ɪnstɪ'geʃən] *s* instigation *f*
instill [ɪn'stɪl] *tr* instiller
instinct ['ɪnstɪŋkt] *s* instinct *m*
instinctive [ɪn'stɪŋktɪv] *adj* instinctif
institute ['ɪnstɪ,t(j)ut] *s* institut *m* ‖ *tr* instituer
institution [,ɪnstɪ't(j)uʃən] *s* institution *f*
instruct [ɪn'strʌkt] *tr* instruire
instruction [ɪn'strʌkʃən] *s* instruction *f*; (comp) instructions
instruc'tional soft'ware [ɪn'strʌkʃənəl] *s* (comp) didacticiel *m*
instruc'tion man'ual *s* livret *m* d'instruction
instructive [ɪn'strʌktɪv] *adj* instructif
instructor [ɪn'strʌktər] *s* instructeur *m*
instrument ['ɪnstrəmənt] *s* instrument *m* ‖ ['ɪnstrə,mɛnt] *tr* instrumenter
instrumental [,ɪnstrə'mɛntəl] *adj* instrumental; **to be instrumental in** contribuer à
instrumentalist [,ɪnstrə'mɛntəlɪst] *s* instrumentiste *mf*
instrumentali·ty [,ɪnstrəmən'tælɪti] *s* (*pl* **-ties**) intermédiaire *m*, intervention *f*
in'strument board' *s* tableau *m* de bord
in'strument fly'ing *s* radio-navigation *f*, vol *m* aux instruments
in'strument land'ing *s* atterrissage *m* aux instruments, aide *f* à la navigation
in'strument pan'el *s* tableau *m* de bord
insubordinate [,ɪnsə'bɔrdɪnɪt] *adj* insubordonné
insufferable [ɪn'sʌfərəbəl] *adj* insupportable, intolérable, imbuvable
insufficient [,ɪnsə'fɪʃənt] *adj* insuffisant

insuffi'cient ev'idence *s* insuffisance *f* de preuves
insular ['ɪnsələr], ['ɪnsjʊlər] *adj* insulaire
insulate ['ɪnsə,let] *tr* insoler
in'sulating tape' *s* ruban *m* isolant, chatterton *m*
insulation [,ɪnsə'leʃən] *s* isolation *f*
insulator ['ɪnsə,letər] *s* isolant *m*
insulin ['ɪnsəlɪn] *s* insuline *f*
insult ['ɪnsʌlt] *s* insulte *f* ‖ [ɪn'sʌlt] *tr* insulter
insulting [ɪn'sʌltɪŋ] *adj* insultant, injurieux
insurable [ɪn'ʃʊrəbəl] *adj* assurable
insurance [ɪn'ʃʊrəns] *s* assurance *f*
insure [ɪn'ʃʊr] *tr* assurer
insurer [ɪn'ʃʊrər] *s* assureur *m*
insurgent [ɪn'sʌrdʒənt] *adj* & *s* insurgé *m*
insurmountable [,ɪnsər'maʊntəbəl] *adj* insurmontable
insurrection [,ɪnsə'rɛkʃən] *s* insurrection *f*
intact [ɪn'tækt] *adj* intact
in'take' *s* (*place*) entrée *f*; (*act or amount*) prise *f*; (mach) admission *f*
in'take man'ifold *s* tubulure *f* d'admission, collecteur *m* d'admission
in'take valve' *s* soupape *f* d'admission
intangible [ɪn'tændʒɪbəl] *adj* intangible
intan'gible as'sets *spl* actif *m* incorporel
integer ['ɪntɪdʒər] *s* nombre *m* entier
integral ['ɪntɪgrəl] *adj* intégral (*part*) intégrant; **integral with** solidaire de ‖ *s* intégrale *f*
intergrate ['ɪntɪ,gret] *tr* intégrer
integration [,ɪntɪ'greʃən] *s* intégration *f*
integrity [ɪn'tɛgrɪti] *s* intégrité *f*
intellect ['ɪntə,lɛkt] *s* intellect *m*; (*person*) intelligence *f*
intellectual [,ɪntə'lɛktʃu·əl] *adj* & *s* intellectuel *m*
intelligence [ɪn'tɛlɪdʒəns] *s* intelligence *f*
intel'ligence bu'reau *s* deuxième bureau *m*, service *m* de renseignements
intel'ligence quo'tient *s* quotient *m* intellectuel
intel'ligence test' *s* test *m* d'habileté mentale, test de capacité intellectuelle
intelligent [ɪn'tɛlɪdʒənt] *adj* intelligent
intelligible [ɪn'tɛlɪdʒɪbəl] *adj* intelligible
intemperate [ɪn'tɛmpərɪt] *adj* intempérant
intend [ɪn'tɛnd] *tr* destiner; signifier; vouloir dire; **to intend to** avoir l'intention de, penser; **to intend to become** se destiner à
intended *adj* & *s* (coll) futur *m*
intense [ɪn'tɛns] *adj* intense
intensi·fy [ɪn'tɛnsɪ,faɪ] *v* (*pret* & *pp* **-fied**) *tr* intensifier ‖ *intr* s'intensifier
intensi·ty [ɪn'tɛnsɪti] *s* (*pl* **-ties**) intensité *f*
intensive [ɪn'tɛnsɪv] *adj* intensif
intent [ɪn'tɛnt] *adj* attentif; (*look, gaze*) fixe, intense; **intent on** résolu à ‖ *s* intention *f*; **to all intents and purposes** en fait, pratiquement
intention [ɪn'tɛnʃən] *s* intention *f*
intentional [ɪn'tɛnʃənəl] *adj* intentionnel, délibéré
intentionally [ɪn'tɛnʃənəli] *adv* exprès, à dessein

in·ter [ɪn'tʌr] v (pret & pp **-terred;** ger **-terring**) tr enterrer
interact [,ɪntər'ækt] intr agir réciproquement
interaction [,ɪntər'ækʃən] s interaction f
inter·breed [,ɪntər'brid] v (pret & pp **-bred**) tr croiser ‖ intr se croiser
intercalate [ɪn'tʌrkə,let] tr intercaler
intercede [,ɪntər'sid] intr intercéder
intercept [,ɪntər'sɛpt] tr intercepter
interceptor [,ɪntər'sɛptər] s intercepteur m
interchange ['ɪntər,tʃendʒ] s échange m, permutation f; (transfer point) correspondance f; (on highway) échangeur m ‖ [,ɪntər'tʃendʒ] tr échanger, permuter ‖ intr permuter
intercollegiate [,ɪntərkə'lidʒɪ·ɪt] adj interuniversitaire, entre universités
intercom ['ɪntər,kɑm] s (coll) interphone m, intervox m
intercourse ['ɪntər,kors] s relations fpl, rapports mpl; (copulation) copulation f, coït m
intercross [,ɪntər'krɔs], [,ɪntər'krɑs] tr entrecroiser ‖ intr s'entrecroiser
interdict ['ɪntər,dɪkt] s interdit m ‖ [,ɪntər'dɪkt] tr interdire; **to interdict s.o. from** + ger interdire à qn de + inf
interdisciplinary [,ɪntər'dɪsəplənɛri] adj interdisciplinaire
interest ['ɪntərɪst] s intérêt m ‖ ['ɪntə,rɛst] tr intéresser
interested adj intéressé; **to be interested in** s'intéresser à or dans
interesting ['ɪntrɪstɪŋ] adj intéressant
in'terest rate' s taux m d'intérêt
interface ['ɪntər,fes] s interface f
interfere [,ɪntər'fɪr] intr (to meddle) s'ingérer, s'immiscer; (phys) interférer; **to interfere with** intervenir dans, se mêler de; (e.g., one's plans) entraver, contrecarrer; **to interfere with each other** interférer (entre eux)
interference [,ɪntər'fɪrəns] s ingérence f, immixtion f; (phys) interférence f; (static) (rad) parasites mpl; (jamming) (rad) brouillage m; **interference with** immixtion dans
interim ['ɪntərɪm] adj provisoire, par intérim ‖ s intérim m
interior [ɪn'tɪrɪ·ər] adj & s intérieur m
inte'rior dec'orator s décorateur m d'intérieurs
interject [,ɪntər'dʒɛkt] tr interposer; (questions) lancer
interjection [,ɪntər'dʒɛkʃən] s intervention f; (gram) interjection f
interlard [,ɪntər'lɑrd] tr entrelarder
in'terli'brary loan' s le prêt interbibliothèque, le service des prêts entre bibliothèques
interline [,ɪntər'laɪn] tr interligner
interlining ['ɪntər,laɪnɪŋ] s doublure f intermédiaire
interlock [,ɪntər'lɑk] tr emboîter, engager ‖ intr s'emboîter, s'engager
interloper [,ɪntər'lopər] s intrus m

interlude ['ɪntər,lud] s (mov, mus, telv) interlude m; (theat, fig) intermède m
intermediar·y [,ɪntər'midɪ,ɛri] adj intermédiaire ‖ s (pl **-ies**) intermédiaire mf, interprète mf
intermediate [,ɪntər'midɪ·ɪt] adj intermédiaire
interme'diate-range' mis'sile s missile m à portée intermédiaire
interment [ɪn'tʌrmənt] s enterrement m, sépulture f
interminable [ɪn'tʌrmɪnəbəl] adj interminable
intermingle [,ɪntər'mɪŋgəl] tr entremêler ‖ intr s'entremêler
intermission [,ɪntər'mɪʃən] s relâche m, pause f; (theat) entracte m
intermittent [,ɪntər'mɪtənt] adj intermittent
intermix [,ɪntər'mɪks] tr entremêler ‖ intr s'entremêler
intern ['ɪntʌrn] s interne mf ‖ [ɪn'tʌrn] tr interner
internal [ɪn'tʌrnəl] adj interne
inter'nal-combus'tion en'gine s moteur m à explosion
inter'nal rev'enue s recettes fpl fiscales
international [,ɪntər'næʃənəl] adj international; (exposition) universel
in'terna'tional date' line' s ligne f de changement de date
in'terna'tional time' zone' s fuseau m horaire international
internecine [,ɪntər'nisɪn] adj domestique, intestin; (war) sanguinaire, d'extermination
internee [,ɪntʌr'ni] s interné m
internment [ɪn'tʌrnmənt] s internement m
in'tern·ship' s internat m
interpellate [,ɪntər'pɛlet] tr interpeller
interplanetary [,ɪntər'plænə,tɛri] adj interplanétaire
interplan'etary trav'el s voyages mpl interplanétaires
interplay ['ɪntər,ple] s interaction f
interpolate [ɪn'tʌrpə,let] tr interpoler
interpose [,ɪntər'poz] tr interposer
interpret [ɪn'tʌrprɪt] tr interpréter
interpretation [ɪn,tʌrprɪ'teʃən] s interprétation f
interpreter [ɪn'tʌrprɪtər] s interprète mf
interrogate [ɪn'tɛrə,get] tr interroger
interrogation [ɪn,tɛrə'geʃən] s interrogation f
interroga'tion mark' s point m d'interrogation
interrupt [,ɪntə'rʌpt] tr interrompre
interruption [,ɪntə'rʌpʃən] s interruption f
intersect [,ɪntər'sɛkt] tr entrecouper ‖ intr s'entrecouper
intersection [,ɪntər'sɛkʃən] s intersection f
intersperse [,ɪntər'spʌrs] tr entremêler
interstellar [,ɪntər'stɛlər] adj interstellaire
interstice [ɪn'tʌrstɪs] s interstice m
intertwine [,ɪntər'twaɪn] tr entrelacer ‖ intr s'entrelacer
interval ['ɪntərvəl] s intervalle m
intervene [,ɪntər'vin] intr intervenir

intervening [,ıntər'vinıŋ] *adj* (*period*) inter-médiaire; (*party*) intervenant
intervention [,ıntər'vɛnʃən] *s* intervention *f*
interview ['ıntər,vju] *s* entrevue *f*; (journ) interview *f* ‖ *tr* avoir une entrevue avec; (journ) interviewer
inter·weave [,ıntər'wiv] *v* (*pret* **-wove** or **-weaved**; *pp* **-wove, woven** or **weaved**) *tr* entrelacer; (*to intermingle*) entremêler
intestate [ın'tɛstet] *adj & s* intestat *m*
intestine [ın'tɛstın] *adj & s* intestin *m*
intima·cy ['ıntıməsi] *s* (*pl* **-cies**) intimité *f*; rapports *mpl* sexuels
intimate ['ıntımıt] *adj & s* intime *mf* ‖ ['ıntı,met] *tr* donner à entendre
intimation [,ıntı'meʃən] *s* suggestion *f*, insinuation *f*
intimidate [ın'tımı,det] *tr* intimider
into ['ıntu] *prep* dans, en
intolerant [ın'tɑlərənt] *adj* intolérant
intonation [,ıntə'neʃən] *s* intonation *f*
intone [ın'ton] *tr* (*to begin to sing*) entonner; (*to sing or recite in a monotone*) psalmodier ‖ *intr* psalmodier
intoxicant [ın'tɑksıkənt] *s* boisson *f* alcoolique
intoxicate [ın'tɑksı,ket] *tr* enivrer; (*to poison*) intoxiquer
intoxication [ın,tɑksı'keʃən] *s* ivresse *f*; (*poisoning*) intoxication *f*; (fig) enivrement *m*
intractable [ın'træktəbəl] *adj* intraitable
intransigent [ın'trænsıdʒənt] *adj* intransigeant
intransitive [ın'trænsıtıv] *adj* intransitif
intravenous [,ıntrə'vinəs] *adj* intraveineux
intrave'nous drip' *s* goutte-à-goutte *m* invar
intrepid [ın'trɛpıd] *adj* intrépide
intricate ['ıntrıkıt] *adj* compliqué
intrigue [ın'trig] *s* intrigue *f* ‖ *tr & intr* intriguer
intrinsic(al) [ın'trınsık(əl)] *adj* intrinsèque
introduce [,ıntrə'd(j)us] *tr* introduire; (*to make acquainted*) présenter
introduction [,ıntrə'dʌkʃən] *s* introduction *f*; (*the beginning part*) entrée en matière, exorde *m* (*of one person to another or others*) présentation *f*
introductory [,ıntrə'dʌktəri] *adj* préliminaire; (*text*) liminaire; (*speech, letter, etc.*) de présentation
introduc'tory of'fer *s* offre *f* de présentation, prix *m* de lancement
introspective [,ıntrə'spɛktıv] *adj* introspectif; (*person*) méditatif
introvert ['ıntrə,vʌrt] *adj & s* introverti *m*
intrude [ın'trud] *intr* s'ingérer, s'immiscer; **to intrude on s.o.** déranger qn
intruder [ın'trudər] *s* intrus *m*
intrusion [ın'truʒən] *s* intrusion; (*upon privacy*) immixtions *fpl*, ingérences *fpl*
intrusive [ın'trusıv] *adj* importun
intuition [,ınt(j)u'ıʃən] *s* intuition *f*
inundate ['ınən,det] *tr* inonder
inundation [,ınən'deʃən] *s* inondation *f*

inure [ın'jur] *tr* aguerrir, endurcir ‖ *intr* entrer en vigueur; **to inure to** rejaillir sur
invade [ın'ved] *tr* envahir
invader [ın'vedər] *s* envahisseur *m*
invalid [ın'vælıd] *adj* invalide, nul ‖ ['ınvəlıd] *adj & s* malade *mf*, invalide *mf*
invalidate [ın'vælı,det] *tr* invalider
invalidity [,ınvə'lıdıti] *s* invalidité *f*, nullité *f*
invaluable [ın'vælju·əbəl] *adj* inappréciable, inestimable
invariable [ın'vɛrı·əbəl] *adj* invariable
invasion [ın'veʒən] *s* invasion *f*
invective [ın'vɛktıv] *s* invective *f*
inveigh [ın've] *intr*—**to inveigh against** invectiver contre
inveigle [ın'vegəl] *tr* séduire, enjôler; **to inveigle s.o. into** + *ger* entraîner qn à + *inf*
invent [ın'vɛnt] *tr* inventer
invention [ın'vɛnʃən] *s* invention *f*
inventive [ın'vɛntıv] *adj* inventif
inventiveness [ın'vɛntıvnıs] *s* esprit *m* inventif
inventor [ın'vɛntər] *s* inventeur *m*
invento·ry ['ınvən,tori] *s* (*pl* **-ries**) inventaire *m*; **beginning inventory** (com) stock *m* d'ouverture; **ending inventory** (com) stock de fermeture ‖ *v* (*pret & pp* **-ried**) *tr* inventorier
inverse [ın'vʌrs] *adj & s* inverse *m*
inversion [ın'vʌrʒən] *s* interversion *f*, inversion *f*
invert ['ınvʌrt] *adj & s* inverti *m* ‖ [ın'vʌrt] *tr* inverser; (*an image*) invertir
invertebrate [ın'vʌrtı,bret] *adj & s* invertébré *m*
invest [ın'vɛst] *tr* investir; (*money*) investir, placer; **to invest with** investir de ‖ *intr* investir or placer de l'argent
investigate [ın'vɛstı,get] *tr* examiner, rechercher
investigation [ın,vɛstı'geʃən] *s* investigation *f*
investigator [ın'vɛstı,getər] *s* investigateur *m*, chercheur *m*
investment [ın'vɛstmənt] *s* investissement *m*, placement *m*; (*with an office or dignity*) investiture *f*; (*siege*) investissement
invest'ment trust' *s* fonds *m* de placement fermé
investor [ın'vɛstər] *s* capitaliste *mf*
inveterate [ın'vɛtərıt] *adj* invétéré
invidious [ın'vıdı·əs] *adj* odieux
invigorate [ın'vıgə,ret] *tr* vivifier, fortifier
invigorating [ın'vıgə,retıŋ] *adj* vivifiant, fortifiant
invincible [ın'vınsıbəl] *adj* invincible
invisible [ın'vızıbəl] *adj* invisible
invis'ible ink' *s* encre *f* sympathique
invitation [,ınvı'teʃən] *s* invitation *f*
invite [ın'vaıt] *tr* inviter
inviting [ın'vaıtıŋ] *adj* invitant
invoice ['ınvɔıs] *s* facture *f*; **as per invoice** suivant facture ‖ *tr* facturer
invoke [ın'vok] *tr* invoquer
involuntary [ın'vɑlən,tɛri] *adj* involontaire

involve [ɪn'vɑlv] *tr* impliquer, entraîner, engager
invulnerable [ɪn'vʌlnərəbəl] *adj* invulnérable
inward ['ɪnwərd] *adj* intérieur ‖ *adv* intérieurement, en dedans
iodide ['aɪ·ə,daɪd] *s* iodure *m*
iodine ['aɪ·ə,dɪn] *s* (chem) iode *m* ‖ ['aɪ·ə,daɪn] *s* (pharm) teinture *f* d'iode
ion ['aɪ·ən], ['aɪ·ɑn] *s* ion *m*
ionize [['aɪ·ə,naɪz] *tr* ioniser
ionosphere [aɪ'ɑnə,sfɪr] *s* ionosphère *f*
I.O.U. ['aɪ,o'ju] *s* (letterword) (**I owe you**) reconnaissance *f* de dette
I.Q. ['aɪ'kju] *s* (letterword) (**intelligence quotient**) quotient *m* intellectuel
Iran [ɪ'rɑn], [aɪ'ræn] *s* l'Iran *m*
Iranian [aɪ'renɪ·ən] *adj* iranien ‖ *s* (*language*) iranien *m*; (*person*) Iranien *m*
Iraq [ɪ'rɑk] *s* l'Irak *m*
Ira·qi [ɪ'rɑki] *adj* irakien ‖ *s* (*pl* **-qis**) Irakien *m*
irate ['aɪret], [aɪ'ret] *adj* irrité
ire [aɪr] *s* courroux *m*, colère *f*
Ireland ['aɪrlənd] *s* Irlande *f*; l'Irlande
iris ['aɪrɪs] *s* iris *m*
Irish ['aɪrɪʃ] *adj* irlandais ‖ *s* (*language*) irlandais *m*, **the Irish** les Irlandais
I'rish·man *s* (*pl* **-men**) Irlandais *m*
I'rish stew' *s* ragoût *m* irlandais
I'rish·wom'an *s* (*pl* **-wom'en**) Irlandaise *f*
irk [ʌrk] *tr* ennuyer, fâcher
irksome ['ʌrksəm] *adj* ennuyeux
iron ['aɪ·ərn] *s* fer *m*; (*for pressing clothes*) fer à repasser; **irons** (*fetters*) fers; **to have too many irons in the fire** courir deux lièvres à la fois; **to strike while the iron is hot** battre le fer tant qu'il est chaud ‖ *tr* (*clothes*) repasser; **to iron out** (*a difficulty*) aplanir
i'ron and steel' in'dustry *s* sidérurgie *f*
i'ron-bound' *adj* cerclé de fer; (*unyielding*) inflexible; (*rock-bound*) plein de récifs
ironclad ['aɪ·ərn,klæd] *adj* blindé, ferré, cuirassé; (*e.g., contract*) infrangible
i'ron cur'tain *s* rideau *m* de fer
i'ron diges'tion *s* estomac *m* d'autruche
i'ron gate' *s* grille *f* d'entrée
i'ron horse' *s* coursier *m* de fer
ironic(al) [aɪ'rɑnɪk(əl)] *adj* ironique
ironing ['aɪ,ərnɪŋ] *s* repassage *m*
i'roning board' *s* planche *f* à repasser
i'ron lung' *s* poumon *m* d'acier
i'ron ore' *s* minerai *m* de fer
i'ron-tipped' *adj* ferré
i'ron·ware' *s* quincaillerie *f*, ferblanterie *f*
i'ron will' *s* volonté *f* inflexible
i'ron·work' *s* ferrure *f*, ferronnerie *f*
i'ron·work'er *s* ferronnier *m*
iro·ny ['aɪrəni] *s* (*pl* **-nies**) ironie *f*
irradiate [ɪ'redɪ,et] *tr* & *intr* irradier
irrational [ɪ'ræʃənəl] *adj* irrationnel
irredeemable [,ɪrɪ'diməbəl] *adj* irrémédiable; (*bonds*) non remboursable
irrefutable [,ɪrɪ'fjutəbəl] *adj* irréfutable
irregular [ɪ'regjələr] *adj* & *s* irrégulier *m*

irrelevant [ɪ'rɛləvənt] *adj* non pertinent, hors de propos
irreligious [,ɪrɪ'lɪdʒəs] *adj* irréligieux
irremediable [,ɪrɪ'midɪ·əbəl] *adj* irrémédiable
irreparable [ɪ'rɛpərəbəl] *adj* irréparable
irreplaceable [,ɪrɪ'plesəbəl] *adj* irremplaçable
irrepressible [,ɪrɪ'prɛsɪbəl] *adj* irrépressible, irrésistible
irreproachable [,ɪrɪ'protʃəbəl] *adj* irréprochable
irresistible [,ɪrɪ'zɪstɪbəl] *adj* irrésistible
irrespective [,ɪrɪ'spɛktɪv] *adj*—**irrespective of** indépendant de
irresponsible [,ɪrɪ'spɑnsɪbəl] *adj* irresponsable
irretrievable [,ɪrɪ'trivəbəl] *adj* irréparable; (*lost*) irrécupérable
irreverent [ɪ'revərənt] *adj* irrévérencieux
irrevocable [ɪ'revəkəbəl] *adj* irrévocable
irrigate ['ɪrɪ,get] *tr* irriguer
irrigation [,ɪrɪ'geʃən] *s* irrigation *f*
irritant ['ɪrɪtənt] *adj* & *s* irritant *m*
irritate ['ɪrɪ,tet] *tr* irriter
irritation [,ɪrɪ'teʃən] *s* irritation *f*
irruption [ɪ'rʌpʃən] *s* irruption *f*
Isaiah [aɪ'ze·ə] *s* Isaïe *m*
isinglass ['aɪzɪŋ,glæs] *s* gélatine *f*, colle *f* de poisson; (mineral) mica *m*
Islam ['ɪsləm], [ɪs'lɑm] *s* l'Islam *m*
Islamic [ɪs'lɑmɪk] *adj* islamique
island ['aɪlənd] *s* île *f*
islander ['aɪləndər] *s* insulaire *mf*
isle [aɪl] *s* îlot *m*; (poetic) île *f*
isolate ['aɪsə,let] *tr* isoler
isolation [,aɪsə'leʃen] *s* isolement *m*
isolationist [,aɪsə'leʃənɪst] *adj* & *s* isolationniste *mf*
isosceles [aɪ'sɑsə,liz] *adj* isocèle
isotope ['aɪsə,top] *s* isotope *m*
Israel ['ɪzrɪ·əl] *s* Israël *m*; **in Israel** en Israël; **of Israel** d'Israël, e.g., **the state of Israel** l'état d'Israël; **to Israel** (*to give to*) à Israël; (*to go to*) en Israël
Israe·li [ɪz'reli] *adj* israélien ‖ *s* (*pl* **-lis** [liz]) Israélien *m*
Israelite ['ɪzrɪ·ə,laɪt] *adj* israélite ‖ *s* Israélite *mf*
issuance ['ɪʃu·əns] *s* émission *f*
issue ['ɪʃu] *s* (*way out*) sortie *f*, issue *f*; (*outcome*) issue; (*of a magazine*) numéro *m*; (*offspring*) descendance *f*; (*of banknotes, stamps, etc.*) émission *f*; (*under discussion*) point *m* à discuter; (pathol) écoulement *m*; **at issue** en jeu, en litige; **to take issue with** être en désaccord avec; **without issue** sans enfants ‖ *tr* (*a book, a magazine*) publier; (*banknotes, stamps, etc.*) émettre; (*a summons*) lancer; (*an order*) donner; (*a proclamation*) faire; (*a verdict*) rendre ‖ *intr* sortir, déboucher
isthmus ['ɪsməs] *s* isthme *m*
it [ɪt] *pron pers* ce §82B, §85; lui §85; il §87; le §87; y §87; en §87
Italian [ɪ'tæljən] *adj* italien ‖ *s* (*language*) italien *m*; (*person*) Italien *m*

italic [ɪˈtælɪk] *adj* (typ) italique; **Italic** italique ‖ **italics** *spl* caractères *mpl* penchés, italique *m*; **italics mine** c'est moi qui souligne
italicize [ɪˈtælɪˌsaɪz] *tr* mettre en italique
Italy [ˈɪtəli] *s* Italie *f*; l'Italie
itch [ɪtʃ] *s* démangeaison *f*; (pathol) gale *f* ‖ *tr* démanger à ‖ *intr* (*said of part of body*) démanger; (*said of person*) avoir une démangeaison; **to itch to** (fig) avoir une démangeaison de
itch·y [ˈɪtʃi] *adj* (*comp* -**ier**; *super* -**iest**) piquant; (pathol) galeux
item [ˈaɪtəm] *s* article *m*; (*in a list*) point *m*; (*piece of news*) nouvelle *f*
itemize [ˈaɪtəˌmaɪz] *tr* spécifier, énumérer
itinerant [aɪˈtɪnərənt] *adj & s* itinérant *m*

itinerar·y [aɪˈtɪnəˌrɛri] *adj* itinéraire ‖ *s* (*pl* -**ies**) itinéraire *m*
its [ɪts] *adj poss* son §88 ‖ *pron poss* le sien §89
it's = **it is** c'est; il est, elle est
it'self' *pron pers* soi §85; lui-même §86; se §87
ivied [ˈaɪvid] *adj* couvert de lierre
ivo·ry [ˈaɪvəri] *adj* d'ivoire, en ivoire ‖ *s* (*pl* -**ries**) ivoire *m*; **to tickle the ivories** (slang) taquiner l'ivoire
i'vory tow'er *s* (fig) tour *f* d'ivoire
I.V. stand [ˌaɪˈviˈstænd] *s* (med) goutte-à-goutte *m invar*
ivy [ˈaɪvi] *s* (*pl* **ivies**) lierre *m*

J

J, j [dʒe] *s* Xᵉ lettre de l'alphabet
jab [dʒæb] *s* (*with a sharp point; with a penknife; with the elbow*) coup m; (*with a needle*) piqûre *f*; (*with the fist*) coup sec ‖ *v* (*pret & pp* **jabbed**; *ger* **jabbing**) *tr* donner un coup de coude à; piquer; donner un coup sec à; (*a knife*) enfoncer
jabber [ˈdʒæbər] *tr & intr* jaboter
jack [dʒæk] *s* (aut) cric *m*, vérin *m*; (cards) valet *m*; (elec) jack *m*, prise *f*; (coll) fric *m*; **Jack** Jeannot *m* ‖ *tr*—**to jack up** soulever au cric; (*prices*) faire monter
jackal [ˈdʒækəl] *s* chacal *m*
jack'ass' *s* baudet *m*
jack'daw' *s* choucas *m*
jacket [ˈdʒækɪt] *s* (*of a woman; of a book*) jaquette *f*; (*of a man's suit*) veston *m*; (*metal casing*) chemise *f*
Jack' Frost' *s* le Bonhomme Hiver
jack'-in-the-box' *s* diable *m* à ressort, boîte *f* à surprise
jack'knife' *s* (*pl* -**knives**) couteau *m* de poche, couteau pliant; (*fancy dive*) saut *m* de carpe
jack'-of-all'-trades' *s* bricoleur *m*
jack-o'-lantern [ˈdʒækə ˌlæntərn] *s* potiron *m* lumineux
jack'pot' *s* gros lot *m*, poule *f*; **to hit the jackpot** décrocher la timbale
jack' rab'bit *s* lièvre *m* des prairies
Jacob [ˈdʒekəb] *s* Jacques *m*
jade [dʒed] *s* (*stone; color*) jade *m*; (*horse*) haridelle *f*; (*woman*) coquine *f*, friponne *f*
jaded *adj* éreinté, excédé; blasé
jag [dʒæg] *s* dentelure *f*; **to have a jag on** (slang) être paf
jagged [ˈdʒægɪd] *adj* dentelé
jaguar [ˈdʒægwɑr] *s* jaguar *m*
jail [dʒel] *s* prison *f* ‖ *tr* emprisonner
jail'bird' *s* cheval *m* de retour
jailer [ˈdʒelər] *s* geôlier *m*

jalop·y [dʒəˈlɑpi] *s* (*pl* -**ies**) bagnole *f*, tacot *m*, guimbarde *f*, clou *m*
jam [dʒæm] *s* confiture *f*; **to be in a jam** (coll) être dans le pétrin ‖ *v* (*pret & pp* **jammed**; *ger* **jamming**) *tr* coincer ‖ *intr* se coincer
jamboree [ˌdʒæmbəˈri] *s* (*of boy scouts*) jamboree *m*; (slang) bombance *f*
James [dʒemz] *s* Jacques *m*
jamming [ˈdʒæmɪŋ] *s* (rad) brouillage *m*
Jane [dʒen] *s* Jeanne *f*
jangle [ˈdʒæŋgəl] *s* cliquetis *m* ‖ *tr* faire cliqueter; (*nerves*) mettre en boule ‖ *intr* cliqueter
janitor [ˈdʒænitər] *s* concierge *m*
janitress [ˈdʒænitrɪs] *s* concierge *f*
January [ˈdʒænjuˌɛri] *s* janvier *m*
ja·pan [dʒəˈpæn] *s* laque *m* du Japon; **Ja-pan** le Japon ‖ *v* (*pret & pp* -**panned**; *ger* -**panning**) *tr* laquer
Japa·nese [ˌdʒæpəˈniz] *adj* japonais ‖ *s* (*language*) japonais *m* ‖ *s* (*pl* -**nese**) (*person*) Japonais *m*
Jap'anese bee'tle *s* cétoine *f*
Jap'anese lan'tern *s* lanterne *f* vénitienne
jar [dʒɑr] *s* (*container*) pot *m*, bocal *m*; (*jolt*) secousse *f* ‖ *v* (*pret & pp* **jarred**; *ger* **jarring**) *tr* ébranler, secouer ‖ *intr* trembler, vibrer; (*said of sounds, colors, opinions*) disorder; **to jar on the nerves** taper sur les nerfs
jargon [ˈdʒɑrgən] *s* jargon *m*
jasmine [ˈdʒæsmin] *s* jasmin *m*
jasper [ˈdʒæspər] *s* jaspe *m*
jaundice [ˈdʒɔndɪs] *s* jaunisse *f*, ictère *m*
jaundiced *adj* ictérique; (fig) amer
jaunt [dʒɔnt] *s* excursion *f*
jaun·ty [ˈdʒɔnti] *adj* (*comp* -**tier**; *super* -**tiest**) vif, dégagé; (*smart*) chic
javelin [ˈdʒævlɪn] *s* javelot *m*
jaw [dʒɔ] *s* mâchoire *f*; (*of animal*) gueule *f*; **jaws** (*e.g., of death*) griffes *fpl* ‖ *tr* (slang)

engueuler ‖ *intr* (*to gossip*) (slang) bavarder

jaw'bone' *s* mâchoire *f*, maxillaire *m*

jay [dʒe] *s* geai *m*

jay'walk' *intr* traverser la rue en dehors des clous

jaw'walk'er *s* piéton *m* distrait

jazz [dʒæz] *s* jazz *m* ‖ *tr*—**to jazz up** (coll) animer, égayer

jazz' band' *s* orchestre *m* de jazz

jazz' sing'er *s* chanteur *m* de rythme

jealous [ˈdʒɛləs] *adj* jaloux

jealous·y [ˈdʒɛləsi] *s* (*pl* **-ies**) jalousie *f*

jean [dʒin] *s* treillis *m*; **Jean** Jeanne *f*; **jeans** pantalon *m* de treillis

jeep [dʒip] *s* jeep *f*

jeer [dʒɪr] *s* raillerie *f* ‖ *intr* railler; **to jeer at** se moquer de

Jehovah [dʒɪˈhovə] *s* Jéhovah *m*

jell [dʒɛl] *s* gelée *f* ‖ *intr* se convertir en gelée; (*to take hold*) prendre forme, se préciser

jel·ly [ˈdʒɛli] *s* (*pl* **-lies**) gelée *f* ‖ *v* (*pret & pp* **-lied**) *tr* convertir en gelée ‖ *intr* se convertir en gelée

jel'ly·fish' *s* méduse *f*; (*person*) chiffe *f*

jeopardize [ˈdʒɛpər,daɪz] *tr* mettre en danger, compromettre

jeopardy [ˈdʒɛpərdi] *s* danger *m*

jerk [dʒʌrk] *s* saccade *f*, secousse *f*; (slang) mufle *m* ‖ *tr* tirer brusquement, secouer ‖ *intr* se mouvoir brusquement

jerk'water town' *s* trou *m*, petite ville *f* de province

jerk'water train' *s* tortillard *m*

jerk·y [ˈdʒʌrki] *adj* (*comp* **-ier;** *super* **-iest**) saccadé

Jerome [dʒəˈrom] *s* Jérôme *m*

jersey [ˈdʒʌrzi] *s* jersey *m*

Jerusalem [dʒɪˈrusələm] *s* Jérusalem *f*

jest [dʒɛst] *s* plaisanterie *f*; **in jest** en plaisantant ‖ *intr* plaisanter

jester [ˈdʒɛstər] plaisantin *m*; (*medieval clown*) bouffon *m*

Jesuit [ˈdʒɛʒʊ·ɪt] *adj* jésuite, jésuitique ‖ *s* Jésuite *m*

Jesus [ˈdʒizəs] *s* Jésus *m*

Je'sus Christ' *s* Jésus-Christ *m*

jet [dʒɛt] *s* (*color; mineral*) jais *m*; (*of water, gas, etc.*) jet *m*; avion *m* à réaction ‖ *v* (*pret & pp* **jetted;** *ger* **jetting**) *intr* gicler, jaillir; voyager en jet

jet'-black' *adj* noir de jais

jet' en'gine *s* moteur *m* à réaction

jet' fight'er *s* chasseur *m* à réaction

jet' fu'el *s* carburéacteur *m*, kérosène *m* aviation

jet' lag' *s* troubles *mpl* dûs au décalage horaire

jet' lin'er *s* avion *m* de ligne à réaction

jet' plane' *s* avion *m* à réaction

jet' propul'sion *s* propulsion *f* par réaction

jetsam [ˈdʒɛtsəm] *s* marchandise *f* jetée à la mer

jet' set' *s* monde *m* des playboys

jet' stream' *s* (meteo) courant-jet *m*

jettison [ˈdʒɛtɪsən] *s* jet *m* à la mer ‖ *tr* jeter à la mer; (fig) mettre au rebut, rejeter

jet·ty [ˈdʒɛti] *s* (*pl* **-ties**) (*wharf*) appontement *m*; (*breakwater*) jetée *f*

Jew [dʒu] *s* Juif *m*; (rel) juif *m*

jewel [ˈdʒu·əl] *s* joyau *m*, bijou *m*; (*of a watch*) rubis *m*; (*of a clock*) pierre *f*; (*person*) bijou

jew'el case' *s* écrin *m*

jeweler or **jeweller** [ˈdʒu·ələr] *s* horloger-bijoutier *m*, bijoutier *m*

jewelry [ˈdʒu·əlri] *s* joaillerie *f*

jew'elry store' *s* bijouterie *f*; (*for watches*) horlogerie *f*

Jewess [ˈdʒu·ɪs] *s* Juive *f*; (rel) juive *f*

Jewish [ˈdʒu·ɪʃ] *adj* juif, judaïque

jews'-harp or **jew's-harp** [ˈdʒuz,harp] *s* guimbarde *f*

jib [dʒɪb] *s* (mach) flèche *f*; (naut) foc *m*

jibe [dʒaɪb] *s* moquerie *f* ‖ *intr* (coll) concorder; **to jibe at** se moquer de

jif·fy [ˈdʒɪfi] *s* (*pl* **-fies**)—**in a jiffy** (coll) en un clin d'œil

jig [dʒɪg] *s* (*dance*) gigue *f*; **the jig is up** (slang) il n'y a pas mèche, tout est dans le lac

jigger [ˈdʒɪgər] *s* mesure *f* qui contient une once et demie; (*for fishing*) leurre *m*; (*tackle*) palan *m*; (*flea*) puce *f*; (*for separating ore*) crible *m*; (naut) tapecul *m*; (*gadget*) (coll) machin *m*

jiggle [ˈdʒɪgəl] *s* petite secousse *f* ‖ *tr* agiter, secouer ‖ *intr* se trémousser

jig'saw' *tr* chantourner, scie à découper, scie sauteuse

jig' saw' *s* scie *f* à chantourner

jig'saw puz'zle *s* casse-tête *m* chinois, puzzle *m*

jilt [dʒɪlt] *tr* lâcher, repousser

jim·my [ˈdʒɪmi] *s* (*pl* **-mies**) pince-monseigneur *f* ‖ *v* (*pret & pp* **-mied**) *tr* forcer à l'aide d'une pince-monseigneur

jingle [ˈdʒɪngəl] *s* (*small bell*) grelot *m*; (*sound*) grelottement *m*, tintement *m*, cliquetis *m*; (*poem*) rimes *fpl* enfantines; (*catchy verse*) petit couplet, slogan *m* à rimes; **advertising jingle** couplet *m* publicitaire, refrain *m* publicitaire, réclame *f* chantée, sonal *m* ‖ *tr* faire grelotter ‖ *intr* grelotter

jin·go [ˈdʒɪngo] *adj* chauvin ‖ *s* (*pl* **-goes**) chauvin *m*; **by jingo!** (coll) sapristi!

jingoism [ˈdʒɪngo,ɪzəm] *s* chauvinisme *m*

jinx [dʒɪŋks] *s* guigne *f* ‖ *tr* (coll) porter la guigne à

jitters [ˈdʒɪtərz] *spl* (coll) frousse *f*, trouille *f*; **to give the jitters to** (coll) flanquer la trouille à

jittery [ˈdʒɪtəri] *adj* froussard

Joan' of Arc' *s* Jeanne *f* d'Arc

job [dʒab] *s* (*piece of work*) travail *m*; (*chore*) besogne *f*, tâche *f*; (*employment*) emploi *m*; (*work done by contract*) travail à forfait; (slang) vol *m*; **bad job** (fig) mauvaise affaire *f*; **by the job** à la pièce; **on the job** faisant un stage; (slang) attentif; **soft job** (coll) filon *m*, fromage *m*; **to**

be out of a job être en chômage; **to lie down on the job** (slang) tirer au flanc
job′ ac′tion s grève f du zèle
jobber [ˈdʒɑbər] s grossiste m; *(pieceworker)* ouvrier m à la tâche; *(dishonest official)* agioteur m
job′ descrip′tion s définition f de fonction
job′ hold′er s employé m; *(in the government)* fonctionnaire m
job′ lot′ s solde m de marchandises
job′ print′ing s bilboquet m
job′ secur′ity s sécurité f de l'emploi
job′ va′cancy s poste m à pourvoir
jockey [ˈdʒɑki] s jockey m ‖ tr (coll) manœuvrer
jockstrap [ˈdʒɑk,stræp] s suspensoir m, slip m de soutien
jocose [dʒoˈkos] adj jovial, joyeux
jocular [ˈdʒɑkjələr] adj facétieux
jog [dʒɑg] s saccade f ‖ v *(pret & pp jogged; ger jogging)* tr secouer; *(the memory)* rafraîchir ‖ intr—**to jog along** aller au petit trot
jogging [ˈjɔgɪŋ] s jogging m
John [dʒɑn] s Jean m; **john** (slang) toilettes fpl; *(prostitute's customer)* (slang) micheton m
John′ Bull′ s l'Anglais m typique
John′ Doe′ s M. Dupont, M. Durand
Johnny [ˈdʒɑni] s (coll) Jeannot m
john′ny·cake′ s galette f de farine de maïs
John′ny-come′-late′ly s (coll) nouveau venu m
join [dʒɔɪn] tr joindre; *(to meet)* rejoindre; *(a club, a church)* se joindre à, entrer dans; *(a political party)* s'affilier à; *(the army)* s'engager dans; **to join s.o. in** + ger se joindre à qn pour + inf ‖ intr se joindre
joiner [ˈdʒɔɪnər] s menuisier m; (coll) clubiste mf
joint [dʒɔɪnt] adj commun, conjugué, joint, réuni ‖ s *(articulation)* joint m; *(culin)* rôti m; *(place)* (slang) boîte f; *(notorious drinking place)* (slang) bistrot m mal famé; *(gambling den)* (slang) tripot m; *(reefer)* (slang) joint m; **out of joint** disloqué; (fig) de travers
joint′ account′ s compte m indivis
joint′ commit′tee s commission f mixte
joint′ estate′ s *(of husband and wife)* communauté f
joint′ own′er s copropriétaire mf
joint′-stock′ com′pany s société f par actions
joist [dʒɔɪst] s solive f, poutre f
joke [dʒok] s plaisanterie f; **to play a joke on** faire une attrape à ‖ intr plaisanter
joker [ˈdʒokər] s farceur m, blagueur m; *(cards)* joker m, fou m; (coll) clause f ambiguë
jol·ly [ˈdʒɑli] adj *(comp* -lier; *super* -liest) joyeux, enjoué ‖ adv (coll) rudement
Jol′ly Rog′er [ˈrɑdʒər] s pavillon m noir
jolt [dʒolt] s cahot m, secousse f ‖ tr cahoter, secouer ‖ intr cahoter
Jonah [ˈdʒonə] s Jonas m

jonquil [ˈdʒɑŋkwɪl] s jonquille f
Jordan [ˈdʒɔrdən] s *(country)* Jordanie f; la Jordanie; *(river)* Jourdain m
josh [dʒɑʃ] tr & intr (coll) blaguer
jostle [ˈdʒɑsəl] tr bousculer ‖ intr se bousculer
jot [dʒɑt] s—**not a jot** pas un iota ‖ v *(pret & pp jotted; ger jotting)* tr—**to jot down** prendre note de
journal [ˈdʒʌrnəl] s journal m; *(magazine)* revue f; (mach) tourillon m; (naut) journal de bord
jour′nal box′ s boîte f d'essieu
journalism [ˈdʒʌrnə,lɪzəm] s journalisme m
journalist [ˈdʒʌrnəlɪst] s journaliste mf
journey [ˈdʒʌrni] s voyage m; trajet m, parcours m ‖ intr voyager
jour′ney·man s *(pl* -men) compagnon m
joust [dʒaʊst] s joute f ‖ intr jouter
Jove [dʒov] s Jupiter m; **by Jove!** parbleu!
jovial [ˈdʒovɪ·əl] adj jovial
jowl [dʒaʊl] s bajoue f
joy [dʒɔɪ] s joie f
joyful [ˈdʒɔɪfəl] adj joyeux
joyless [ˈdʒɔɪlɪs] adj sans joie
joyous [ˈdʒɔɪ·əs] adj joyeux
joy′ ride′ s (coll) balade f en auto
joy′ stick′ s manche m à balai
Jr. abbr *(junior)* fils, e.g., **Mr. Martin, Jr.** M. Martin fils
jubilant [ˈdʒubɪlənt] adj jubilant
jubilee [ˈdʒubɪ,li] s jubilé m
Judaism [ˈdʒude,ɪzəm] s judaïsme m
judge [dʒʌdʒ] s juge m ‖ tr & intr juger; **judging by** à en juger par
judge′ ad′vocate s commissaire m du gouvernement
judgment [ˈdʒʌdʒmənt] s jugement m
judg′ment day′ s jour m du jugement dernier
judicial [dʒuˈdɪʃəl] adj judiciaire; *(legal)* juridique
judiciar·y [dʒuˈdɪʃɪ,ɛri] adj judiciaire ‖ s *(pl* -ies) pouvoir m judiciaire; *(judges)* judicature f
judicious [dʒuˈdɪʃəs] s judicieux
jug [dʒʌg] s *(of earthenware)* cruche f; *(of metal)* broc m; *(jail)* (slang) bloc m, taule f
juggle [ˈdʒʌgəl] tr jongler avec; **to juggle away** escamoter ‖ intr jongler
juggler [ˈdʒʌglər] s jongleur m; imposteur m, mystificateur m
juggling [ˈdʒʌglɪŋ] s jonglerie f; *(trickery)* passe-passe m
Jugoslavia [ˈjugoˈslɑvɪ·ə] s Yougoslavie f; la Yougoslavie
jugular [ˈdʒʌgjələr] adj & s jugulaire f
juice [dʒus] s jus m; (coll) courant m électrique
juic·y [ˈdʒusi] adj *(comp* -ier; *super* -iest) juteux; (fig) savoureux
jukebox [ˈdʒuk,bɑks] s pick-up m électrique à sous, distributeur m de musique
July [dʒuˈlaɪ] s juillet m

jumble [ˈdʒʌmbəl] s fouillis m, enchevêtrement m ‖ tr brouiller
jumbo [ˈdʒʌmbo] adj (coll) géant
jum'bo jet' s avion-géant m, gros-porteur m
jump [dʒʌmp] s saut m, bond m; (nervous start) sursaut m; (sports) saut m; (sports) obstacle m ‖ tr sauter; **to jump ship** tirer une bordée; **to jump the gun** démarrer trop tôt; **to jump the track** dérailler ‖ intr sauter, bondir; **to jump at the chance** sauter sur l'occasion
jump' ball' s (sports) entre-deux m, chandelle f d'arbitre
jumper [ˈdʒʌmpər] s sauteur m, sauteuse f; (dress) robe-chasuble f
jump'er ca'ble s câble m de démarrage
jump'ing bean' s petit pois m sauteur
jump'ing jack' s pantin m
jump' rope' s corde f à sauter
jump' seat' s strapontin m
jump' suit' s (aer) combinaison f de saut
jump·y [ˈdʒʌmpi] adj (comp **-ier**; super **-iest**) nerveux
junction [ˈdʒʌŋkʃən] s jonction f; (of railroads, roads) embranchement m
juncture [ˈdʒʌŋktʃər] s jointure f; (occasion) conjoncture f; **at this juncture** en cette occasion
June [dʒun] s juin m
jungle [ˈdʒʌŋgəl] s jungle f
jun'gle war'fare s guerre f de la brousse
junior [ˈdʒunjər] adj cadet; **Bobby Watson, Junior** le jeune Bobby Watson; **Martin, Junior** Martin fils ‖ s cadet m; (educ) étudiant m de troisième année
jun'ior of'ficer s officier m subalterne
juniper [ˈdʒunɪpər] s genévrier m
ju'niper ber'ry s genièvre m
junk [dʒʌŋk] s (old metal) ferraille f; (worthless objects) bric-à-brac m; (cheap merchandise) camelote f, pacotille f; (coll) gnognote f; (naut) jonque f ‖ tr mettre au rebut
junk' deal'er s fripier m; marchand m de ferraille
junket [ˈdʒʌŋkɪt] s excursion f; voyage m officiel aux frais de la princesse
junk' food' s camelote f alimentaire
junkie [ˈdʒʌŋki] s (slang) camé m, drogué m
junk'man' s (pl **-men'**) ferrailleur m; chiffonnier m
junk' shop' s boutique f de bric-à-brac et friperie; bric-à-brac m
junk'yard' s cimetière m de ferraille
jurisdiction [ˌdʒʊrɪsˈdɪkʃən] s juridiction f; **within the jurisdiction of** du ressort de
jurist [ˈdʒʊrɪst] s légiste m
juror [ˈdʒʊrər] s juré m
ju·ry [ˈdʒʊri] s (pl **-ries**) jury m
just [dʒʌst] adj juste ‖ adv seulement; justement; **just as** à l'instant où; (in the same way that) de même que; **just as it is** tel quel; **just out** vient de paraître; **to have just** venir de
justice [ˈdʒʌstɪs] s justice f; (judge) juge m
jus'tice of the peace' s juge m de paix
justi·fy [ˈdʒʌstɪˌfaɪ] v (pret & pp **-fied**) tr justifier
justly [ˈdʒʌstli] adv justement
jut [dʒʌt] v (pret & pp **jutted**; ger **jutting**) intr—**to jut out** faire saillie
jute [dʒut] s jute m
juvenile [ˈdʒuvɛˌnaɪl] adj juvénile, adolescent; (e.g., books) pour la jeunesse ‖ s adolescent m
ju'venile delin'quency s délinquance f juvénile
ju'venile delin'quent s délinquant m juvénile; **juvenile delinquents** jeunes délinquants mpl
juxtapose [ˌdʒʌkstəˈpoz] tr juxtaposer

K

K, k [ke] s XIᵉ lettre de l'alphabet
kale [kel] s chou m frisé
kaleidoscope [kəˈlaɪdəˌskop] s kaléidoscope m
kamikaze [ˌkɑməˈkɑzi] s kamikaze m
kangaroo [ˌkæŋgəˈru] s kangourou m
kan'garoo court' s tribunal m bidon
karate [kəˈrɑti] s karaté m
Kashmir [ˈkæʃmɪr] s le Cachemire
kash'mir shawl' s châle m de cachemire
kayak [ˈkaɪæk] s kayak m
keel [kil] s quille f ‖ intr—**to keel over** (naut) chavirer; (coll) tomber dans les pommes
keen [kin] adj (having a sharp edge) aiguisé, affilé; (sharp, cutting) mordant, pénétrant; (sharp-witted) perçant, perspicace; (eager, much interested) enthousiaste, vif; (slang) formidable; **keen on** engoué de, passionné de
keep [kip] s (of medieval castle) donjon m; **for keeps** (for good) (coll) pour de bon; (forever) (coll) à tout jamais; **to earn one's keep** (coll) gagner sa nourriture, gagner sa vie; **to play for keeps** (coll) jouer le tout pour le tout ‖ v (pret & pp **kept** [kɛpt]) tr garder, conserver; (one's word or promise; accounts, a diary) tenir; (animals) élever; (a garden) cultiver; (a hotel, a school, etc.) diriger; (an appointment) ne pas manquer à; (a holiday) observer; (a person) avoir à sa charge, entretenir; **keep it up!** ne flanchez pas!, continuez!; **keep off the flowers** (public

sign) respecter les fleurs; **keep out of the bushes** (*public sign*) il est interdit de pénétrer dans le bosquet; **to keep away** éloigner; **to keep back** retenir; **to keep down** baisser; (*prices*) maintenir bas; (*a revolt*) réprimer; **to keep in** retenir; (*a student after school*) garder en retenue; (*dust, fire, etc.*) entretenir; **to keep off** éloigner; **to keep out** tenir éloigné, empêcher d'entrer; **to keep quiet** faire taire; **to keep running** laisser marcher; **to keep score** marquer les points; **to keep servants** avoir des domestiques; **to keep s.o. busy** occuper qn; **to keep s.o. clean (cool, warm, etc.)** tenir qn propre (au frais, au chaud, etc.); **to keep s.o. or s.th. from** + *ger* empêcher qn or q.ch. de + *inf*; **to keep s.o. informed about** mettre or tenir qn au courant de; **to keep s.o. waiting** faire attendre qn; **to keep up** maintenir; (*e.g., all night*) faire veiller ‖ *intr* rester, se tenir; (*in good shape*) demeurer, se conserver; (*e.g., from rotting*) se garder; **keep out** (public sign) entrée interdite; **that can keep** (coll) ça peut attendre; **to keep** + *ger* continuer à + *inf*; **to keep away** s'éloigner, se tenir à l'écart; **to keep from** + *ger* s'abstenir de + *inf*; **to keep in with** rester en bons termes avec; **to keep on** + *ger* continuer à + *inf*; **to keep out** rester dehors; **to keep out of** ne pas se mêler de; **to keep quiet** rester tranquille, se taire; **to keep to** (*e.g., the right*) garder (*e.g., la droite*); **to keep up** tenir bon, tenir ferme; **to keep up with** aller de pair avec

keeper [ˈkipər] *s* gardien *m*, garde *m*; (*of a game preserve*) garde forestier; (*of a horseshoe magnet*) armature *f*

keeping [ˈkipɪŋ] *s* garde *f*, surveillance *f*; (*of a holiday*) observance *f*; **in keeping with** en accord avec; **in safe keeping** sous bonne garde; **out of keeping with** en désaccord avec

keep′sake′ *s* souvenir *m*, gage *m* d'amitié

keg [kɛg] *s* tonnelet *m*; (*of herring*) caque *f*

ken [kɛn] *s*—**beyond the ken of** hors de la portée de

kennel [ˈkɛnəl] *s* chenil *m*

kep·i [ˈkɛpi] *s* (*pl* **-is**) képi *m*

kept′ wom′an [kɛpt] *s* (*pl* **wom′en**) femme *f* entretenue

kerchief [ˈkʌrtʃɪf] *s* fichu *m*

kernel [ˈkʌrnəl] *s* (*inner part of a nut or fruit stone*) amande *f*; (*of wheat or corn*) grain *m*; (fig) noyau *m*, cœur *m*

kerosene [ˈkɛrəˌsin] *s* kérosène *m*, pétrole *m* lampant

ker′osene lamp′ *s* lampe *f* à pétrole

kerplunk [ˌkʌrˈplʌŋk] *interj* patatras!

ketchup [ˈkɛtʃəp] *s* ketchup *m*

kettle [ˈkɛtəl] *s* chaudron *m*, marmite *f*; (*teakettle*) bouilloire *m*; **that's not my kettle of fish** (coll) ça n'est pas mes oignons

ket′tle·drum′ *s* timbale *f*

key [ki] *adj* clef, clé ‖ *s* clef *f*, clé *f*; (*of piano, typewriter, etc.*) touche *f*; (*wedge or cotter used to lock parts together*) cheville *f*, clavette *f*; (*reef or low island*) caye *f*; (*answer book*) livre *m* du maître; (*tone of voice*) ton *m*; (*to a map*) légende *f*; (bot) samare *f*; (mus) tonalité *f*; (telg) manipulateur *m*; **key to the city** droit *m* de cité; **off key** faux; **on key** juste ‖ *tr* claveter, coincer; **to be keyed up** être surexcité, être tendu

key′board′ *s* clavier *m*

key′hole′ *s* trou *m* de la serrure; (*of clock*) trou de clef

key′man′ *s* (*pl* **-men′**) pivot *m*, homme *m* indispensable

key′ mon′ey *s* pas *m* de porte

key′note′ *s* (mus) tonique *f*; (fig) dominante *f*

key′note speech′ *s* discours *m* d'ouverture

key′punch′ *s* (mach) perforatrice *f*

key′punch op′erator *s* perforeur *m*

key′ ring′ *s* porte-clefs *m*

key′ sig′nature *s* (mus) armature *f* de la clé

key′stone′ *s* clef *f* de voûte

key′ word′ *s* mot-clé *m*

kha·ki [ˈkɑki], [ˈkæki] *adj* kaki ‖ *s* (*pl* **-kis**) kaki *m*

khan [kɑn] *s* khan *m*

kibitz [ˈkɪbɪts] *intr* (coll) faire la mouche du coche

kibitzer [ˈkɪbɪtsər] *s* (coll) casse-pieds *mf*, curieux *m*

kick [kɪk] *s* coup *m* de pied; (*e.g., of a horse*) ruade *f*; (*of a gun*) recul *m*; (*complaint*) (slang) plainte *f*; (*thrill*) (slang) effet *m*, frisson *m*; **to get a kick out of** (slang) s'en payer une tranche de ‖ *tr* donner un coup de pied à; (*a ball*) botter; **to kick out** (coll) chasser à coups de pied; **to kick s.o. in the pants** (coll) botter le derrière à qn; **to kick the bucket** (coll) casser sa pipe, passer l'arme à gauche; **to kick up a row** (slang) déclencher un chahut ‖ *intr* donner un coup de pied; (*said of gun*) reculer; (*said of horse*) ruer; (sports) botter; **to kick against** regimber contre; **to kick off** (football) donner le coup d'envoi

kick′back′ *s* contrecoup *m*; (slang) ristourne *f*

kicker [ˈkɪkər] *s* (sports) botteur *m*

kick′off′ *s* (sports) coup *m* d'envoi

kid [kɪd] *s* chevreau *m*; (*child*) (coll) gosse *mf*; mioche *mf*; poulot *m* ‖ *v* (*pret & pp* **kidded**; *ger* **kidding**) *tr & intr* (slang) blaguer; **to kid oneself** (slang) se faire des illusions

kidder [ˈkɪdər] *s* (slang) blagueur *m*, plaisantin *m*

kidding [ˈkɪdɪŋ] *s* (slang) blague *f*; **no kidding!** (slang) sans blague!; **you're kidding!** (slang) tu galèges!

kid′ gloves′ *spl* gants *mpl* de chevreau; **to handle with kid gloves** traiter avec douceur, ménager

kid′nap v (pret & pp **-naped** or **-napped**; ger **-naping** or **-napping**) tr kidnapper
kidnaper or **kidnapper** [′kɪdnæpər] s kidnappeur m
kidnaping or **kidnapping** [′kɪdnæpɪŋ] s kidnappage m, enlèvement m
kidney [′kɪdni] s rein m; (culin) rognon m
kid′ney bean′ s haricot m de Soissons
kid′ney-shaped′ adj réniforme
kid′ney stone′ s calcul m rénal
kid′ney trans′plant s greffe f du rein
kill [kɪl] s mise f à mort; (bag of game) gibier m tué ‖ tr tuer; (an animal) abattre; (a bill, amendment, etc.) mettre son veto à, faire échouer
killer [′kɪlər] s assassin m
kill′er whale′ s épaulard m, orque f
killing [′kɪlɪŋ] adj meurtrier; (exhausting; ridiculous) crevant ‖ s tuerie f; **to make a killing** (coll) réussir un beau coup
kill′-joy′ s rabat-joie m, trouble-fête mf
kiln [kil], [kɪln] s four m
kil-o [′kilo] s (pl **-os**) kilo m, kilogramme m; kilomètre m
kilocycle [′kɪlə,saɪkəl] s kilocycle m
kilogram [′kɪlə,græm] s kilogramme m
kilometer [′kɪlə,mitər] s kilomètre m
kilowatt [′kɪlə,wɑt] s kilowatt m
kilowatt-hour [′kɪlə,wɑt′aʊr] s (pl **-hours**) kilowatt-heure m
kilt [kɪlt] s kilt m
kilter [′kɪltər] s—**to be out of kilter** (coll) être détraqué
kimo-no [kɪ′mono] s (pl **-nos**) kimono m
kin [kɪn] s (family relationship) parenté f; (relatives) les parents mpl; **of kin** apparenté; **the next of kin** le plus proche parent, les plus proches parents
kind [kaɪnd] adj bon, bienveillant; **kind to** bon pour; **to be so kind as to** être assez aimable que ‖ s espèce f, genre m, sorte f, classe f; **all kinds of** (coll) quantité de; **kind of** (coll) plutôt, en quelque sorte; **of a kind** semblable, de même nature; **to pay in kind** payer en nature
kindergarten [′kɪndər,gɑrtən] s jardin m d'enfants
kindergartner [′kɪndər,gɑrtnər] s élève mf de jardin d'enfants; (teacher) jardinière f
kind′-heart′ed adj bon, bienveillant
kindle [′kɪndəl] tr allumer ‖ intr s'allumer
kindling [′kɪndlɪŋ] s allumage m; (wood) bois m d'allumage
kin′dling wood′ s bois m d'allumage
kind·ly [′kaɪndli] adj (comp **-lier**; super **-liest**) (kind-hearted) bon, bienveillant; (e.g., climate) doux; (e.g., terrain) favorable ‖ adv avec bonté, avec bienveillance; **to take kindly** prendre en bonne part; **to take kindly to** prendre en amitié
kindness [′kaɪndnɪs] s bonté f, obligeance f
kindred [′kɪndrɪd] adj apparenté, de même nature ‖ s parenté f, famille f; parenté, ressemblance f
Kinescope [′kɪnɪ,skop] s (trademark) kinescope m

kinetic [kɪ′nɛtɪk] adj cinétique ‖ **kinetics** s cinétique f
kinet′ic en′ergy s énergie f cinétique
king [kɪŋ] s roi m; (cards, chess, & fig) roi; (checkers) pion m doublé, dame f ‖ tr (checkers) damer
king′bolt′ s cheville f maîtresse
kingdom [′kɪŋdəm] s royaume m; (one of three divisions of nature) règne m
king′fish′er s martin-pêcheur m
king·ly [′kɪŋli] adj (comp **-lier**; super **-liest**) royal, de roi, digne d'un roi ‖ adv en roi, de roi, comme un roi
king′pin′ s cheville f ouvrière; (bowling) quille f du milieu; (coll) ponte m, pontife m
king′ post′ s poinçon m
kingship [′kɪŋʃɪp] s royauté f
king′-size′ adj grand format, géant
king′s′ ran′som s rançon f de roi
kink [kɪŋk] s (twist, e.g., in a rope) nœud m; (in a wire) faux pli m; (in hair) frisette f, bouclette f; (soreness in neck) torticolis m; (flaw, difficulty) point m faible; (mental twist) lubie f; (naut) coque f ‖ tr nouer, entortiller ‖ intr se nouer, s'entortiller
kink·y [′kɪŋki] adj (comp **-ier**; super **-iest**) crépu, bouclé
kinsfolk [′kɪnz,fok] spl parents mpl
kin′ship s parenté f
kins·man [′kɪnzmən] s (pl **-men**) parent m
kins·woman [′kɪnz,wʊmən] s (pl **-wom′en**) parente f
kipper [′kɪpər] s kipper m ‖ tr saurer
kiss [kɪs] s baiser m ‖ tr embrasser, donner un baiser à ‖ intr s'embrasser
kit [kɪt] s nécessaire m; (tub) tonnelet m; (to put together) prêt-à-monter m; (of traveler) trousse f de voyage; (mil) équipement m, sac m; **the whole kit and caboodle** (coll) tout le saint-frusquin
kitchen [′kɪtʃən] s cuisine f
kitch′en cup′board s vaisselier m
kitchenette [,kɪtʃə′nɛt] s petite cuisine f, cuisinette f
kitch′en gar′den s jardin m potager
kitch′en·maid′ s fille f de cuisine
kitch′en police′ s (mil) corvée f de cuisine
kitch′en range′ s cuisinière f
kitch′en sink′ s évier m; **everything but the kitchen sink** tout sauf les murs
kitch′en·ware′ s ustensiles mpl de cuisine
kite [kaɪt] s cerf-volant m; (orn) milan m; **to fly a kite** lancer or enlever un cerf-volant
kith′ and kin′ [kɪθ] spl amis et parents mpl, cousinage m
kitten [′kɪtən] s chaton m, petit chat m
kittenish [′kɪtənɪʃ] adj enjoué, folâtre; (woman) coquette, chatte
kit·ty [′kɪti] s (pl **-ties**) minet m, minou m; (in card games) cagnotte f, poule f; **kitty, kitty, kitty!** minet, minet, minet!
kleptomaniac [,klɛptə′meni,æk] adj & s kleptomane mf
knack [næk] s adresse f, chic m
knapsack [′næp,sæk] s sac m à dos, havresac m

knave [nev] *s* fripon *m*; (cards) valet *m*

knaver·y [ˈnevəri] *s* (*pl* **-ies**) friponnerie *f*

knead [nid] *tr* pétrir; (*to massage*) masser

knee [ni] *s* genou *m*; **to bring s.o. to his knees** mettre qn à genoux; **to go down on one's knees** se mettre à genoux

knee′ breech′es *spl* culotte *f* courte

knee′cap′ *s* rotule *f*; (*protective covering*) genouillère *f*

knee′-deep′ *adj* jusqu'aux genoux

knee′-high′ *adj* à la hauteur du genou

knee′hole′ *s* trou *m*, évidement *m* pour l'entrée des genoux

knee′ jerk′ *s* réflexe *m* rotulien

kneel [nil] *v* (*pret & pp* **knelt** [nɛlt] or **kneeled**) *intr* s'agenouiller, se mettre à genoux

knee′pad′ *s* genouillère *f*

knee′pan′ *s* rotule *f*

knee′ swell′ *s* (*of organ*) genouillère *f*

knell [nɛl] *s* glas *m*; **to toll the knell of** sonner le glas de ‖ *intr* sonner le glas

knickers [ˈnɪkərz] *spl* pantalons *mpl* de golf, knickerbockers *mpl*

knickknack [ˈnɪk‚næk] *s* colifichet *m*

knife [naɪf] *s* (*pl* **knives** [naɪvz]) couteau *m*; (*of paper cutter or other instrument*) couperet *m*, lame *f*; **to go under the knife** (coll) monter or passer sur le billard ‖ *tr* poignarder

knife′ sharp′ener *s* fusil *m*, affiloir *m*

knife′ switch′ *s* (elect) interrupteur *m* à couteau

knight [naɪt] *s* chevalier *m*; (chess) cavalier *m* ‖ *tr* créer or faire chevalier

knight-errant [ˈnaɪtˈɛrənt] *s* (*pl* **knights-errant**) chevalier *m* errant

knighthood [ˈnaɪthʊd] *s* chevalerie *f*

knightly [ˈnaɪtli] *adj* chevaleresque

knit [nɪt] *v* (*pret & pp* **knitted** or **knit**; *ger* **knitting**) *tr* tricoter; (*one's brows*) froncer; **to knit together** lier, unir ‖ *intr* tricoter; (*said of bones*) se souder

knit′ goods′ *spl* tricot *m*, bonneterie *f*

knitting [ˈnɪtɪŋ] *s* (*action*) tricotage *m*; (*product*) tricot *m*

knit′ting machine′ *s* tricoteuse *f*

knit′ting nee′dle *s* aiguille *f* à tricoter

knit′wear′ *s* tricot *m*

knob [nɑb] *s* (*lump*) bosse *f*; (*of a door, drawer, etc.*) bouton *m*, poignée *f*; (*of a radio*) bouton

knock [nɑk] *s* coup *m*, heurt *m*; (*of an internal-combustion engine*) cognement *m*; (slang) éreintement *m*, dénigrement *m* ‖ *tr* frapper; (*repeatedly*) cogner à, contre, or sur; (slang) éreinter, dénigrer; **to knock about** bousculer; **to knock against** heurter contre; **to knock down** (*with a blow, punch, etc.*) renverser; (*to the highest bidder*) adjuger; **to knock in** enfoncer; **to knock off** faire tomber; **to knock out** faire sortir en cognant; (boxing) mettre knock-out; (*to fatigue*) (coll) claquer, fatiguer; **to knock up** (slang) engrosser ‖ *intr* frapper; (*said of internal-combustion engine*) cogner; **to knock about** vaga-

bonder, se balader; **to knock against** se heurter contre; **to knock at** or **on** (*e.g., a door*) heurter à, frapper à; **to knock off** (*to stop working*) (coll) débrayer

knock′down′ *adj* (*dismountable*) démontable ‖ *s* (*blow*) coup *m* d'assommoir; (*discount*) escompte *m*

knocked′ out′ *adj* éreinté, sonné; (boxing) knock-out

knocker [ˈnɑkər] *s* (*on a door*) heurtoir *m*, marteau *m*; (*critic*) (coll) éreinteur *m*

knock-kneed [ˈnɑk‚nid] *adj* cagneux

knock′out′ *s* (boxing) knock-out *m*; (*person*) (coll) type *m* renversant; (*thing*) (coll) chose *f* sensationnelle

knock′out drops′ *spl* (slang) narcotique *m*

knoll [nol] *s* mamelon *m*, tertre *m*

knot [nɑt] *s* nœud *m*; (*e.g. of people*) groupe *m*; (naut) nœud *m*, mille *m* marin à l'heure; (*loosely*) (naut) mille marin; **to tie a knot** faire un nœud; **to tie the knot** (coll) prononcer le conjungo ‖ *v* (*pret & pp* **knotted**; *ger* **knotting**) *tr* nouer; **to knot one's brow** froncer le sourcil ‖ *intr* se nouer

knot′hole′ *f* trou *m* de nœud

knot·ty [ˈnɑti] *adj* (*comp* **-tier**; *super* **-tiest**) noueux; (*e.g., question*) épineux

know [no] *s*—**to be in the know** (coll) être au courant, être à la page, être au parfum ‖ *v* (*pret* **knew** [n(j)u]; *pp* **known**) *tr & intr* (*by reasoning or learning*) savoir; (*by the senses or perception; through acquaintance or recognition*) connaître; **as far as I know** autant que je sache; **to know about** être informé de, savoir; **to know best** être le meilleur juge; **to know how to** + *inf* savoir + *inf*; **to let s.o. know about** faire part à qn de; **you ought to know better** vous devriez avoir honte; **you ought to know better than to . . .** vous devriez vous bien garder de . . .; **you wouldn't know s.o. from . . .** on prendrait qn pour . . .

knowable [ˈno·əbəl] *adj* connaissable

know′-how′ *s* technique *f*, savoir-faire *m*

knowing [ˈno·ɪŋ] *adj* avisé; (*look, smile*) entendu

knowingly [ˈno·ɪŋli] *adv* sciemment, en connaissance de cause; (*on purpose*) exprès

know′-it-all′ *adj* (coll) omniscient ‖ *s* (coll) Monsieur Je-sais-tout *m*

knowledge [ˈnɑlɪdʒ] *s* (*faculty*) science *f*, connaissances *fpl*, savoir *m*; (*awareness, familiarity*) connaissance *f*; **not to my knowledge** pas que je sache; **to have a thorough knowledge of** posséder une connaissance approfondie de; **to my knowledge, to the best of my knowledge** à ma connaissance, autant que je sache; **without my knowledge** à mon insu

knowledgeable [ˈnɑlɪdʒəbəl] *adj* (coll) intelligent, bien informé

know′-noth′ing *s* ignorant *m*

knuckle [ˈnʌkəl] *s* jointure *f* or articulation *f* du doigt; (*of a quadruped*) jarret *m*;

(mach) joint *m* en charnière; **knuckle of ham** jambonneau *m*; **to rap s.o. over the knuckles** donner sur les doigts or ongles à qn ‖ *intr*—**to knuckle down** se soumettre; (*to work hard*) s'y mettre sérieusement
knurl [nʌrl] *s* molette *f* ‖ *tr* moleter
k.o. [ˈkeˈo] (letterword) (**knockout**) *s* k.o. *m* ‖ *tr* mettre k.o.
Koran [koˈrɑn], [koˈræn] *s* Coran *m*
Korea [koˈriˑə] *s* Corée *f*; la Corée
Korean [koˈriˑən] *adj* coréen ‖ *s* (*language*) coréen; (*person*) Coréen *m*

kosher [ˈkoʃər] *adj* casher, kasher, kascher; (coll) convenable; **it's kosher** c'est kascher
kowtow [ˈkauˈtau] *intr* se prosterner à la chinoise; **to kowtow to** faire des courbettes à or devant
K.P. [ˈkeˈpi] *s* (letterword) (**kitchen police**) (mil) corvée *f* de cuisine; **to be on K.P. duty** (mil) être de soupe
Kremlin [ˈkrɛmlɪn] *s*—**the Kremlin** le Kremlin
kudos [ˈk(j)udɑs] *s* (coll) gloire *f*, éloges *mpl*, flatteries *fpl*

L

L, l [ɛl] *s* XIIᵉ lettre de l'alphabet
la·bel [ˈlebəl] *s* étiquette *f*; (*brand*) marque *f*; (*in a dictionary*) rubrique *f*, référence *f* ‖ *v* (*pret & pp* **-beled** or **-belled**; *ger* **-beling** or **-belling**) *tr* étiqueter
labeling [ˈlebəlɪŋ] *s* étiquetage *m*; **labeling and sealing** habillage *m*
labial [ˈlebɪˑəl] *adj* labial ‖ *s* labiale *f*
labor [ˈlebər] *adj* ouvrier ‖ *s* travail *m*; (*toil*) labeur *m*, peine *f*; (*job, task*) tâche *f*, besogne *f*; (*manual work involved in an undertaking; the wages for such work*) main-d'œuvre *f*; (*wage-earning worker as contrasted with capital and management*) le salariat, le travail; (*childbirth*) couches *fpl*, travail; **to be in labor** être en couches ‖ *tr* (*a point, subject, etc.*) insister sur; (*one's style*) travailler, élaborer ‖ *intr* travailler; (*to toil*) travailler dur, peiner; (*to exert oneself*) s'efforcer; (*said of ship*) fatiguer, bourlinguer; **to labor under** être victime de; **to labor up** (*a hill, slope, etc.*) gravir; **to labor uphill** peiner en côte; **to labor with child** être en travail d'enfant
la·bor and man·agement *spl* la classe ouvrière et le patronat
laborato·ry [ˈlæbərə‚tori] *s* (*pl* **-ries**) laboratoire *m*
lab·oratory class· *s* classe *f* de travaux pratiques
labored [ˈlebərd] *adj* travaillé, trop élaboré; (*e.g., breathing*) pénible
laborer [ˈlebərər] *s* travailleur *m*, ouvrier *m*; (*unskilled worker*) journalier *m*, manœuvre *m*
laborious [ləˈborɪˑəs] *adj* laborieux
la·bor move·ment *s* mouvement *m* syndicaliste
la·bor un·ion *s* syndicat *m*, syndicat ouvrier
Labourite [ˈlebə‚raɪt] *adj & s* (Brit) travailliste *mf*
La·bour Par·ty [ˈlebər] *adj* (Brit) travailliste ‖ *s* parti *m* travailliste
Labrador [ˈlæbrə‚dɔr] *s* le Labrador

laburnum [ləˈbʌrnəm] *s* cytise *m*
labyrinth [ˈlæbɪrɪnθ] *s* labyrinthe *m*
lace [les] *s* dentelle *f*; (*string to tie shoe, corset, etc.*) lacet *m*, cordon *m*; (*braid*) broderies *fpl* ‖ *tr* garnir or border de dentelles; (*shoes, corset, etc.*) lacer; (*to braid*) entrelacer; (coll) flanquer une rossée à rosser
lace· trim·ming *s* p. .ssementerie *f*
lace·work· *s* dentelles *fpl*, passementerie *f*
lachrymose [ˈlækrɪ‚mos] *adj* larmoyant
lacing [ˈlesɪŋ] *s* lacet *m*, cordon *m*; (*trimming*) galon *m*, passement *m*; (coll) rossée *f*
lack [læk] *s* manque *m*, défaut *m*; (*lack of necessities*) pénurie *f*; **for lack of** faute de ‖ *tr* manquer de, être dépourvu de ‖ *intr* (*to be lacking*) manquer, faire défaut
lackadaisical [‚lækəˈdezɪkəl] *adj* languissant, apathique
lackey [ˈlæki] *s* laquais *m*
lacking [ˈlækɪŋ] *prep* dépourvu de, dénué de
lack·lus·ter *adj* terne, fade
laconic [ləˈkɑnɪk] *adj* laconique
lacquer [ˈlækər] *s* laque *m & f* ‖ *tr* laquer
lac·quer ware· *s* laques *mpl*, objets *mpl* d'art en laque
lacrosse [ləˈkrɔs] *s* crosse *f*, jeu *m* de crosse; **to play lacrosse** jouer à la crosse
lacu·na [ləˈkjunə] *s* (*pl* **-nas** or **-nae** [ni]) lacune *f*
lac·y [ˈlesi] *adj* (*comp* **-ier**; *super* **-iest**) de dentelle; (fig) fin, léger
lad [læd] *s* garçon *m*, gars *m*
ladder [ˈlædər] *s* échelle *f*; (*stepping stone*) (fig) marchepied *m*, échelon *m*; (*stepladder*) marchepied, escabeau *m*; (*run in stocking*) (Brit) démaillage *m*; (*stairway*) (naut) escalier *m*
lad·der truck· *s* fourgon-pompe *m* à échelle
la·dies' room· *s* toilettes *fpl* pour dames, lavabos *mpl* pour dames
ladle [ˈledəl] *s* louche *f* ‖ *tr* servir à la louche

la·dy ['ledi] *s* (*pl* **-dies**) dame *f*; **ladies** (public sign) dames; **ladies and gentlemen!** (formula used in addressing an audience) mesdames, mesdemoiselles, messieurs!; messieurs dames! (coll)

la'dy·bird' or **la'dy·bug'** *s* cocinelle *f*, bête *f* à bon Dieu

la'dy·fin'ger *s* biscuit *m* à la cuiller

la'dy-in-wait'ing *s* (*pl* **ladies-in-waiting**) demoiselle *f* d'honneur

la'dy-kil'ler *s* bourreau *m* des cœurs, tombeur *m* de femmes

la'dy·like' *adj* de bon ton, de dame

la'dy·love' *s* bien-aimée *f*, dulcinée *f*

la'dy of the house' *s* maîtresse *f* de maison

la'dy's maid' *s* camériste *f*

la'dy's man' *s* homme *m* à succès

lag [læg] *s* retard *m* ‖ *v* (*pret* & *pp* **lagged**; *ger* **lagging**) *intr* traîner; **to lag behind** rester en arrière

la'ger beer' ['lɑgər] *s* bière *f* de fermentation basse, lager *m*

laggard ['lægərd] *adj* tardif ‖ *s* traînard *m*

lagoon [lə'gun] *s* lagune *f*

laid' pa'per [led] *s* papier *m* vergé

laid' up' *adj* mis en réserve; (naut) mis en rade; (coll) alité, au lit

lair [lɛr] *s* tanière *f*; (fig) repaire *m*

laity ['le·ɪti] *s* profanes *mfpl*; (eccl) laïques *mfpl*

lake [lek] *adj* lacustre ‖ *s* lac *m*

lamb [læm] *s* agneau *m*

lambaste [læm'best] *tr* (*to thrash*) (coll) flanquer une rossée à; (*to reprimand harshly*) (coll) passer un savon à

lamb' chop' *s* côtelette *f* d'agneau

lambkin ['læmkɪn] *s* agnelet *m*

lamb'skin' *s* peau *f* d'agneau; (*dressed with its wool*) mouton *m*, agnelin *m*

lame [lem] *adj* boiteux; (*sore*) endolori; (*e.g., excuse*) faible, piètre ‖ *tr* estropier, rendre boiteux

lament [lə'mɛnt] *s* lamentation *f*; (*dirge*) complainte *f* ‖ *tr* déplorer ‖ *intr* lamenter, se lamenter

lamentable ['læməntəbəl] *adj* lamentable

lamentation [,læmən'teʃən] *s* lamentation *f*

laminate ['læmɪ,net] *tr* laminer

lamp [læmp] *s* lampe *f*

lamp'black' *s* noir *m* de fumée

lamp' chim'ney *s* verre *m* de lampe

lamp'light' *s* lumière *f* de lampe

lamp'light'er *s* allumeur *m* de réverbères

lampoon [læm'pun] *s* libelle *m*, pasquinade *f* ‖ *tr* faire des libelles contre

lamp'post' *s* réverbère *m*, poteau *m* de réverbère

lamprey ['læmpri] *s* lamproie *f*

lamp'shade' *s* abat-jour *m*

lamp'wick' *s* mèche *f* de lampe

lance [læns] *s* lance *f*; (surg) lancette *f*, bistouri *m* ‖ *tr* percer d'un coup de lance; (surg) donner un coup de lancette or bistouri à

lancet ['lænsɪt] *s* (surg) lancette *f*, bistouri *m*

land [lænd] *adj* terrestre, de terre ‖ *s* terre *f*; **land of milk and honey** pays de cocagne;

to make land toucher terre; **to see how the land lies** sonder or tâter le terrain ‖ *tr* débarquer, mettre à terre; (*an airplane*) atterrir; (*a fish*) amener à terre; (*e.g., a job*) (coll) décrocher; (*a blow*) (coll) flanquer ‖ *intr* débarquer, descendre à terre; (*said of airplane*) atterrir; **to land on one's feet** retomber sur ses pieds; **to land on the moon** alunir; **to land on the water** amerrir

land' breeze' *s* brise *f* de terre

landed *adj* (*owning land*) terrien; (*real estate*) immobilier

land'ed prop'erty *s* propriété *f* foncière

land'fall' *s* (*sighting land*) abordage *m*; (*landing of ship or plane*) atterrissage *m*; (*landslide*) glissement *m* de terrain

land'fill' *s* dépotoir *m*

landing ['lændɪŋ] *s* (*of plane*) atterrissage *m*; (*of ship*) mise *f* à terre, débarquement *m*; (*place where passengers and goods are landed*) débarcadère *m*; (*of stairway*) palier *m*; (*on the moon*) alunissage *m*

land'ing bea'con *s* (aer) radiophare *m* d'atterissage

land'ing craft' *s* (nav) péniche *f* de débarquement

land'ing field' *s* (aer) terrain *m* d'atterrissage

land'ing force' *s* (nav) détachement *m* de débarquement

land'ing gear' *s* (aer) train *m* d'atterrissage

land'ing par'ty *s* (nav) détachement *m* de débarquement

land'ing stage' *s* débarcadère *m*

land'ing strip' *s* (aer) piste *f* d'atterrissage, aire *f* d'atterrissage

land'la'dy *s* (*pl* **-dies**) (*e.g., of an apartment*) logeuse *f*, propriétaire *f*; (*of a lodging house*) patronne *f*; (*of an inn*) aubergiste *f*

land'locked' *adj* entouré de terre

land'lord' *s* (*e.g., of an apartment*) logeur *m*, propriétaire *m*; (*of a lodging house*) patron *m*; (*of an inn*) aubergiste *m*

landlubber ['lænd,lʌbər] *s* marin *m* d'eau douce

land'mark' *s* point *m* de repère, borne *f*; (*important event*) étape *f* importante; (naut) amer *m*

land' of'fice *s* bureau *m* du cadastre

land'own'er *s* propriétaire *m* foncier

landscape ['lænd,skep] *s* paysage *m* ‖ *tr* aménager en jardins

land'scape ar'chitect *s* architecte *m* paysagiste

land'scape gar'dener *s* jardinier *m* paysagiste

land'scape paint'er *s* paysagiste *mf*

landscapist ['lænd,skepɪst]·*s* paysagiste *mf*

land'slide' *s* glissement *m* de terrain, éboulement *m*; (*in an election*) raz *m* de marée, majorité *f* écrasante

landward ['lændwərd] *adv* du côté de la terre, vers la terre

land' wind' [wɪnd] *s* vent *m* de terre

lane [len] s (*narrow street or passage*) ruelle f; (*in the country*) sentier m; (*of an automobile highway*) voie f; (*line of cars*) file f; (*of an air or ocean route*) route f de navigation

langsyne [ˈlæŋˈsaɪn] s (Scotch) le temps jadis ‖ adv (Scotch) au temps jadis

language [ˈlæŋgwɪdʒ] s langage m; (*e.g., of a nation*) langue f

lan'guage lab'oratory s laboratoire m de langues

languid [ˈlæŋgwɪd] adj languissant

languish [ˈlæŋgwɪʃ] intr languir

languor [ˈlæŋgər] s langueur f

languorous [ˈlæŋgərəs] adj langoureux

lank [læŋk] adj efflanqué, maigre; (*hair*) plat, e.g., **lank hair** cheveux plats

lank·y [ˈlæŋki] adj (comp **-ier**; super **-iest**) grand et maigre

lanolin [ˈlænəlɪn] s lanoline f

lantern [ˈlæntərn] s lanterne f

lan'tern slide' s diapositive f

lanyard [ˈlænjərd] s (*around the neck*) cordon m; (arti) tire-feu m; (naut) ride f

lap [læp] s (*of human body or clothing*) genoux mpl, giron m; (*of garment*) genoux, pan m; (*with the tongue*) coup m de langue; (*of the waves*) clapotis m; (*in a race*) (sports) tour m; **last lap** dernière étape f ‖ v (pret & pp **lapped**; ger **lapping**) tr (*with the tongue*) laper; **to lap up** laper; (coll) gober ‖ intr laper; (*said of waves*) clapoter; **to lap over** déborder

lap' dog' s bichon m, chien m de manchon

lapel [ləˈpɛl] s revers m

Lap'land' s Laponie f; la Laponie

Laplander [ˈlæp,lændər] s Lapon m

Lapp [læp] s (*language*) lapon m; (*person*) Lapon m

lap' robe' s couverture f de voyage

lapse [læps] s intervalle m; (*slipping into guilt or error*) faute f légère, écart m; (*fall, decline*) disparition f, oubli m, déchéance f; (*e.g., of an insurance policy*) expiration f, échéance f; (*of memory*) trou m, absence f; **a lapse of time** un laps de temps ‖ intr (*to elapse*) s'écouler, passer; (*to err*) manquer à ses devoirs; (*to decline*) déchoir; (*said, e.g., of a right*) périmer, tomber en désuétude; (*said, e.g., of a legacy*) devenir caduc; (*said, e.g., of an insurance policy*) cesser d'être en vigueur

lap'wing' s (orn) vanneau m huppé

larce·ny [ˈlɑrsəni] s (pl **-nies**) larcin m, vol m

larch [lɑrtʃ] s (bot) mélèze m

lard [lɑrd] s saindoux m ‖ tr larder

larder [ˈlɑrdər] s garde-manger m

large [lɑrdʒ] adj grand; **at large** en liberté

large' intes'tine s gros intestin m

largely [ˈlɑrdʒli] adv principalement

largeness [ˈlɑrdʒnɪs] s grandeur f

large'-scale' adj sur une large échelle, de grande envergure

lariat [ˈlærɪ·ət] s (*for catching animals*) lasso m; (*for tying grazing animals*) longe f

lark [lɑrk] s alouette f; (*prank*) espièglerie f; **to go on a lark** (coll) faire la bombe

lark'spur' s (*rocket larkspur*) pied-d'alouette m; (*field larkspur*) consoude f royale

lar·va [ˈlɑrvə] s (pl **-vae** [vi]) larve f

laryngeal [ˌlærɪnˈdʒi·əl] adj laryngé, laryngien

laryngitis [ˌlærɪnˈdʒaɪtɪs] s laryngite f

laryngoscope [ləˈrɪŋgə,skop] s laryngoscope m

larynx [ˈlærɪŋks] s (pl **larynxes** or **larynges** [ləˈrɪndʒiz]) larynx m

lascivious [ləˈsɪvɪ·əs] adj lascif

lasciviousness [ləˈsɪvɪ·əsnɪs] s lasciveté f

laser [ˈlezər] s (acronym) (**light amplification by stimulated emission of radiation**) laser m

lash [læʃ] s (*cord on end of whip*) mèche f; coup m; (*splatter of rain on window*) fouettement m; (*eyelash*) cil m ‖ tr fouetter, cingler; (*to bind, tie*) lier; (naut) amarrer ‖ intr fouetter; **to lash out at** cingler

lashing [ˈlæʃɪŋ] s fouettée f; (*rope*) amarre f; (naut) amarrage m

lass [læs] s jeune fille f, jeunesse f; bonne amie f

lassitude [ˈlæsɪ,t(j)ud] s lassitude f

las·so [ˈlæso] s (pl **-sos** or **-soes**) lasso m ‖ tr amarrer

last [læst] adj (*in a series*) dernier (before noun), e.g., **the last week of the war** la dernière semaine de la guerre; (*just elapsed*) dernier (after noun), e.g., **last week** la semaine dernière; **before last** avant-dernier, e.g., **the time before last** l'avant-dernière fois; **the last two** les deux derniers ‖ s dernier m; (*the end*) fin f, bout m; (*for holding shoe*) forme f; **at last** enfin, à la fin; **at long last** à la fin des fins; **the last of the month** la fin du mois; **to the last** jusqu'à la fin, jusqu'au bout ‖ intr durer; (*to hold out*) tenir

last' eve'ning adv hier soir

lasting [ˈlæstɪŋ] adj durable

lastly [ˈlæstli] adv pour finir, en dernier lieu, enfin

last'-minute news' s nouvelles fpl de dernière heure

last' name' s nom m, nom de famille

last' night' adv hier soir; cette nuit

last' quar'ter s dernier quartier m

last' sleep' s sommeil m de la mort

last' straw' s—**that's the last straw!** c'est le comble!

Last' Sup'per s (eccl) Cène f

last will' and tes'tament s testament m, acte m de dernière volonté

last' word' s dernier mot m; (*latest style*) (coll) dernier cri m

latch [lætʃ] s loquet m ‖ tr fermer au loquet

latch'key' s clef f de porte d'entrée

latch'string' s cordon m de loquet

late [let] *adj* (*happening after the usual time*) tardif; (*person; train, bus, etc.*) en retard; (*e.g., art*) de la dernière époque; (*events*) dernier, récent; (*news*) de la dernière heure; (*incumbent of an office*) ancien; (*deceased*) défunt, feu; **at a late hour in** (*the night, the day*) bien avant dans, à une heure avancée de; **in the late seventeenth century (eighteenth century, etc.)** vers la fin du dix-septième siècle (dix-huitième siècle, etc.); **it is late** il est tard; **of late** dernièrement, récemment, depuis peu; **to be late** être en retard; **to be late in** + *ger* tarder à + *inf* ‖ *adv* tard, tardivement; (*after the appointed time*) en retard; **better late than never** mieux vaut tard que jamais; **late in** (*the afternoon, the season, the week, the month*) vers la fin de; **late in life** sur le tard; **very late in** (*the night, the day*) bien avant dans, à une heure avancée de

late-comer [ˈletˌkʌmər] *s* (*newcomer*) nouveau venu *m*; (*one who arrives late*) retardataire *mf*

lateen′ sail′ [læˈtin] *s* voile *f* latine

lateen′ yard′ *s* antenne *f*

lately [ˈletli] *adv* dernièrement, récemment, depuis peu

latency [ˈletənsi] *s* latence *f*

latent [ˈletənt] *adj* latent

later [ˈletər] *adj comp* plus tard, plus tardif; (*event*) subséquent, plus récent; (*kings, luminaries, etc.*) derniers en date; **later than** postérieur à ‖ *adv comp* plus tard; **later on** plus tard, par la suite; **see you later** (coll) à tout à l'heure

lateral [ˈlætərəl] *adj* latéral

lath [læθ] *s* latte *f* ‖ *tr* latter

lathe [leð] *s* (mach) tour *m*; **to turn on a lathe** façonner au tour

lather [ˈlæðər] *s* (*of soap*) mousee *f*; (*of horse*) écume *f* ‖ *tr* savonner ‖ *intr* (*said of soap*) mousser; (*said of horse*) être couvert d'écume

lathing [ˈlæθɪŋ] *s* lattage *m*

Latin [ˈlætən] *adj* latin ‖ *s* (*language*) latin *m*; (*person*) Latin *m*

Lat′in Amer′ica *s* l'Amérique *f* latine

Lat′in-Amer′ican *adj* latino-américain ‖ *s* Latino-américain *m*

latitude [ˈlætɪˌt(j)ud] *s* latitude *f*

latrine [ləˈtrin] *s* latrines *fpl*

latter [ˈlætər] *adj* dernier; **the latter part of** (*e.g., a century*) la fin de ‖ *pron*—**the latter** celui-ci §84; le dernier

lattice [ˈlætɪs] *adj* treillissé ‖ *s* treillis *m* ‖ *tr* treillisser

lat′tice gird′er *s* poutre *f* à croisillons

lat′tice-work′ *s* treillis *m*, grillage *m*

laud [lɔd] *tr* louer

laudable [ˈlɔdəbəl] *adj* louable

laudanum [ˈlɔdənəm] *s* laudanum *m*

laudatory [ˈlɔdəˌtori] *adj* laudatif, élogieux

laugh [læf] *s* rire *m* ‖ *tr*—**to laugh away** chasser en riant; **to laugh off** tourner en plaisanterie ‖ *intr* rire; **to laugh at** rire de

laughable [ˈlæfəbəl] *adj* risible

laughing [ˈlæfɪŋ] *adj* riant, rieur; **it's no laughing matter** il n'y a pas de quoi rire ‖ *s* rire *m*

laugh′ing gas′ *s* gaz *m* hilarant

laugh′ing-stock′ *s* risée *f*, fable *f*

laughter [ˈlæftər] *s* rire *m*

launch [lɔntʃ] *s* (*open motorboat*) canot *m* automobile, vedette *f*; (naut) chaloupe *f* ‖ *tr* lancer; (*an attack*) déclencher ‖ *intr*—**to launch into, to launch out on** se lancer dans

launching [ˈlɔntʃɪŋ] *s* lancement *m*

launch′ing pad′ *s* rampe *f* de lancement, aire *f* de lancement

launder [ˈlɔndər] *tr* blanchir

launderer [ˈlɔndərər] *s* blanchisseur *m*, buandier *m*

laundering [ˈlɔndərɪŋ] *s* blanchissage *m*

laundress [ˈlɔndrɪs] *s* blanchisseuse *f*; buandière *f*

Laundromat [ˈlɔndrəˌmæt] *s* (trademark) laverie *f* automatique, laverie libre-service, lavromat *m*

laun·dry [ˈlɔndri] *s* (*pl* **-dries**) linge *m* à blanchir, lessive *f*; (*room*) buanderie *f*; (*business*) blanchisserie *f*

laun′dry·man *s* (*pl* **-men**) blanchisseur *m*, buandier *m*

laun′dry room′ *s* buanderie *f*

laun′dry·wom′an *s* (*pl* **-wom′en**) blanchisseuse *f*, buandière *f*

laureate [ˈlɔrɪ·ɪt] *adj & s* lauréat *m*

lau·rel [ˈlɔrəl] *s* laurier *m*; **to rest on one's laurels** s'endormir sur ses lauriers ‖ *v* (*pret & pp* **-reled** or **-relled**) *ger* **-reling** or **-relling**) *tr* couronner de lauriers

lava [ˈlɑvə] *s* lave *f*

lavaliere [ˌlævəˈlɪr] *s* pendentif *m*

lavato·ry [ˈlævəˌtori] *s* (*pl* **-ries**) (*room equipped for washing hands and face; bowl with running water*) lavabo *m*; (*toilet*) lavabos

lavender [ˈlævəndər] *s* lavande *f*

lav′ender wa′ter *s* eau *f* de lavande

lavish [ˈlævɪʃ] *adj* prodigue; (*reception, dinner, etc.*) somptueux, magnifique ‖ *tr* prodiguer

law [lɔ] *s* (*of man, of nature, of science*) loi *f*; (*branch of knowledge concerned with law; body of laws; study of law, profession of law*) droit *m*; **to go to law** recourir à la justice; **to go to law with s.o.** citer qn en justice; **to lay down the law** faire la loi; **to practice law** exercer le droit; **to read law** étudier le droit, faire son droit

law′-abid′ing *adj* soumis aux lois, respectueux des lois

law′ and or′der *s* ordre *m* public; **to maintain law and order** maintenir or faire régner l'ordre

law′break′er *s* transgresseur *m* de la loi

law′ court′ *s* cour *f* de justice, tribunal *m*

lawful [ˈlɔfəl] *adj* légal, légitime

lawless [ˈlɔlɪs] *adj* sans loi; (*unbridled*) sans frein, déréglé

law′mak′er *s* législateur *m*

lawn [lɔn] *s* pelouse *f*, gazon *m*; (*fabric*) batiste *f*, linon *m*
lawn′ mow′er *s* tondeuse *f* de gazon
law′ of′fice *s* étude *f* (d'avocat)
law′ of na′tions *s* loi *f* des nations
law′ of the jun′gle *s* loi *f* de la jungle
law′ stu′dent *s* étudiant *m* en droit
law′suit′ *s* procès *m*
lawyer [′lɔjər] *s* avocat *m*
lax [læks] *adj* (*in morals, discipline, etc.*) relâché, négligent; (*loose, not tense*) lâche; (*vague*) vague, flou
laxative [′læksətɪv] *adj* & *s* laxatif *m*
lay [le] *adj* (*not belonging to clergy*) laïc or laïque; (*not having special training*) profane ‖ *s* situation *f*; (*poem*) lai *m* ‖ *v* (*pret & pp* laid [led]) *tr* poser, mettre; (*a trap*) tendre; (*eggs*) pondre; (*e.g., bricks*) ranger; (*a foundation*) jeter, établir; (*a cable*) poser; (*a mine*) (naut) mouiller; **to be laid in Rome (in France, etc.)** (*said, e.g., of scene*) se passer à Rome (en France, etc.); **to lay aside, away,** or **by** mettre de côté; **to lay down** (*one's life*) sacrifier; (*one's weapons*) déposer; (*conditions*) imposer; **to lay down the law to s.o.** (coll) rappeler qn à l'ordre; **to lay in** (*supplies*) faire provision de; **to lay into s.o.** (coll) sauter dessus qn; **to lay it on thick** (coll) y aller fort; **to lay low** (*to overwhelm*) abattre, terrasser; **to lay off** (*an employee*) congédier; (*to mark the boundaries of*) tracer; (*to stop bothering*) (coll) laisser tranquille; **to lay on** (*paint*) appliquer; (*hands; taxes*) imposer; **to lay open** mettre à nu; **to lay out** arranger; (*to display*) étaler; (*to outline*) tracer; (*money*) débourser; (*a corpse*) faire la toilette de; (*a garden*) aménager; **to lay up** (*to stock up on*) amasser; (*to injure*) aliter; (*a boat*) mettre en rade ‖ *intr* (*said of hen*) pondre; **to lay about** frapper de tous côtés; **to lay for** être à l'affût de, guetter; **to lay into** (slang) rosser, battre; **to lay off** (coll) cesser; **to lay off smoking** (coll) renoncer au tabac; **to lay over** faire escale; **to lay to** (naut) se mettre à la cape
lay′ broth′er *s* frère *m* lai, frère convers
layer [′le·ər] *s* couche *f*; (*hen*) pondeuse *f* ‖ *tr* (hort) marcotter
lay′er cake′ *s* gâteau *m* sandwich
layette [le′ɛt] *s* layette *f*
lay′ fig′ure *s* mannequin *m*
laying [′le·ɪŋ] *s* (*of carpet*) pose *f*; (*of foundation*) assise *f*; (*of eggs*) ponte *f*
lay′man *s* (*pl* -**men**) (*person who is not a clergyman*) laïc *m* or laïque *mf*; (*person who has no special training*) profane *mf*
lay′off′ *s* (*discharge*) renvoi *m*; (*unemployment*) chômage *m*
lay′ of the land′ *s* configuration *f* du terrain; (fig) aspect *m* de l'affaire
lay′out′ *s* plan *m*, dessin *m*, tracé *m*; (*of tools*) montage *m*; (*organization*) disposition *f*; (*banquet*) (coll) festin *m*
lay′o′ver *s* arrêt *m* en cours de route
lay′ sis′ter *s* sœur *f* laie, sœur converse

laziness [′lezɪnɪs] *s* paresse *f*
la·zy [′lezi] *adj* (*comp* -**zier**; *super* -**ziest**) paresseux
la′zy-bones′ *s* (coll) flemmard *m*, fainéant *m*
la′zy Su′san *s* plateau *m* tournant
lb. *abbr* (**pound**) livre *f*
lea [li] *s* (*meadow*) pâturage *m*, prairie *f*
lead [lɛd] *adj* en plomb, de plomb ‖ [lɛd] *s* plomb *m*; (*of lead pencil*) mine *f* (de plombagine); (*for sounding depth*) (naut) sonde *f*; (typ) interligne *f* ‖ [lɛd] *v* (*pret & pp* **leaded**; *ger* **leading**) *tr* plomber; (typ) interligner ‖ [lid] *s* (*foremost place*) avance *f*; (*guidance*) direction *f*, conduite *f*; (*leash*) laisse *f*; (*of a newspaper article*) article *m* de fond; (*leading role*) premier rôle *m*; (*leading man*) jeune premier *m*; (elec) câble *m* de canalisation, conducteur *m*; (elec, mach) avance; (min) filon *m*; **to follow s.o.'s lead** suivre l'exemple de qn; **to have the lead** (cards) avoir la main; **to return the lead** (cards) rejouer la couleur; **to take the lead** prendre le pas ‖ [lid] *v* (*pret & pp* **led** [lɛd]) *tr* conduire, mener; (*to command*) commander, diriger; (*to be foremost in*) être à la tête de; (*e.g., an orchestra*) diriger; (*a good or bad life*) mener; (*a certain card*) attaquer de; (*a certain card suit*) attaquer; (elec, mach) canaliser; **to lead away** or **off** emmener; **to lead off** (*to start*) commencer; **to lead on** encourager; **to lead s.o. to believe** mener qn à croire ‖ *intr* aller devant, tenir la tête; (cards) avoir la main; **to lead to** conduire à, mener à; (*another street, a certain result, etc.*) aboutir à; **to lead up to** (*a great work*) préluder à (*un grand ouvrage*); (*a subject*) amener (*un sujet*)
leaden [′lɛdən] *adj* (*of lead; like lead*) de plomb, en plomb; (*heavy as lead*) pesant; (*sluggish*) alangui; (*complexion*) plombé
leader [′lidər] *s* chef *m*, guide *mf*; (*ringleader*) tête *f*; chef d'orchestre; (*in a dance; among animals*) meneur *m*; (*in a newspaper*) article *m* de fond; (*of a reel of tape or film*) amorce *f*; (*bargain*) article réclame; (*vein of ore*) filon *m*
leadership [′lidər‚ʃɪp] *s* direction *f*; don *m* de commandement
leading [′lidɪŋ] *adj* principal, premier
lead′ing edge′ *s* (aer) bord *m* d'attaque
lead′ing la′dy *s* vedette *f*, étoile *f*, jeune première *f*
lead′ing man′ *s* (*pl* **men′**) jeune premier *m*
lead′ing ques′tion *s* question *f* tendancieuse
lead′-in wire′ [′lid‚ɪn] *s* (rad, telv) fil *m* d'amenée
lead′ pen′cil [lɛd] *s* crayon *m* (à mine de graphite)
lead′ poi′soning [lɛd] *s* saturnisme *m*
leaf [lif] *s* (*pl* **leaves** [livz]) feuille *f*; (*inserted leaf of table*) rallonge *f*; (*hinged leaf of door or table top*) battant *m*; **to shake like a leaf** trembler comme une feuille; **to turn over a new leaf** tourner la page, faire peau neuve ‖ *intr*—**to leaf through** feuilleter

leafless ['liflɪs] *adj* sans feuilles, dénudé
leaflet ['liflɪt] *s* dépliant *m*, papillon *m*, feuillet *m*; (bot) foliole *f*
leaf'stalk' *s* (bot) pétiole *m*
leaf·y ['lifi] *adj* (*comp* **-ier**; *super* **-iest**) feuillu, touffu
league [lig] *s* (*unit of distance*) lieue *f*; (*association, alliance*) ligue *f* ‖ *tr* liguer ‖ *intr* se liguer
League' of Na'tions *s* Société *f* des Nations
leak [lik] *s* fuite *f*; (*in a ship*) voie *f* d'eau; (*of electricity, heat, etc.*) perte *f*, fuite; (*of news, secrets, money, etc.*) fuite; **to spring a leak** avoir une fuite; (naut) faire une voie d'eau ‖ *tr* faire couler; (*gas, steam; secrets, news*) laisser échapper ‖ *intr* fuire, s'écouler; (naut) faire eau; **to leak away** se perdre; **to leak out** (*said of news, secrets, etc.*) transpirer, s'ébruiter
leakage ['likɪdʒ] *s* fuite *f*; (elec) perte *f*
leak·y ['liki] *adj* (*comp* **-ier**; *super* **-iest**) percé, troué; qui a des fuites; (*shoes*) qui prennent l'eau; (coll) indiscret
lean [lin] *adj* maigre; (*gasoline mixture*) pauvre ‖ *s* (*leaning*) inclinaison *f*; (*of meat*) maigre *m* ‖ *v* (*pret & pp* **leaned** or **leant** [lɛnt]) *tr* incliner; **to lean s.th. against s.th.** appuyer q.ch. contre q.ch. ‖ *intr* s'incliner, pencher; **to lean against** s'appuyer contre; **to lean forward** s'incliner or se pencher en avant; **to lean out of** (*e.g., a window*) se pencher par; **to lean over** se pencher; (*e.g., s.o.'s shoulder*) se pencher sur; **to lean toward** (fig) incliner à or vers, pencher pour or vers
leaning ['linɪŋ] *adj* penché ‖ *s* inclinaison *f*; (fig) inclination *f*, penchant *m*
lean'-to' *s* (*pl* **-tos**) appentis *m*
lean' years' *spl* années *fpl* maigres
leap [lip] *s* saut *m*, bond *m*; **by leaps and bounds** par sauts et par bonds; **leap in the dark** saut *m* à l'aveuglette ‖ *v* (*pret & pp* **leaped** or **leapt** [lɛpt]) *tr* sauter, franchir ‖ *intr* sauter, bondir; **to leap across** or **over** sauter; **to leap up** sursauter; (*said, e.g., of flame*) jaillir
leap' day' *s* jour *m* intercalaire
leap'frog' *s* saute-mouton *m*
leap' year' *s* année *f* bissextile
learn [lʌrn] *v* (*pret & pp* **learned** [lʌrnd] or **learnt** [lʌrnt]) *tr* apprendre ‖ *intr* apprendre; **to learn to** apprendre à
learned ['lʌrnɪd] *adj* savant, érudit
learn'ed jour'nal *s* revue *f* d'une société savante
learn'ed profes'sion *s* profession *f* libérale
learn'ed soci'ety *s* société *f* savante
learn'ed word' *s* mot *m* savant
learner ['lʌrnər] *s* élève *mf*; (*beginner*) débutant *m*, apprenti *m*
learn'er's per'mit *s* (aut) permis *m* de conduire (*d'un élève chauffeur*)
learning ['lʌrnɪŋ] *s* (*act and time devoted*) étude *f*; (*scholarship*) savoir *m*, érudition *f*, science *f*
lease [lis] *s* bail *m*; **to give a new lease on life** donner un regain de vie ‖ *tr* (*in the*

role of landlord) donner or louer à bail; (*in the role of tenant*) prendre à bail
lease'hold' *adj* tenu à bail ‖ *s* tenure *f* à bail
leash [liʃ] *s* laisse *f*; **on the leash** en laisse, à l'attache; **to strain at the leash** (fig) ruer dans les brancards ‖ *tr* tenir en laisse
leasing ['lisɪŋ] *s* crédit-bail *m*
least [list] *adj super* (le) moindre §91 ‖ *s* (le) moins *m*; **at least** du moins; **at the very least** tout au moins; **it's the least of my worries** c'est le cadet de mes soucis; **not in the least** pas le moins du monde, nullement; **to say the least** pour ne pas dire plus ‖ *adv super* (le) moins §91
leather ['lɛðər] *s* cuir *m*
leath'er·back tur'tle *s* luth *m*
leath'er-bound' *adj* relié cuir
leath'er·neck' *s* (slang) fusilier *m* marin
leathery ['lɛðəri] *adj* (*e.g., steak*) (coll) coriace
leave [liv] *s* permission *f*; (mil) permission de détente; **by your leave** ne vous en déplaise; **on leave** en congé; (mil) en permission; **to give leave to s.o.** to permettre or accorder à qn de; **to take leave (of)** prendre congé (de), faire ses adieux (à) ‖ *v* (*pret & pp* **left** [lɛft]) *tr* (*to let stay; to stop, give up; to disregard*) laisser; (*to go away from*) partir de, quitter; (*to bequeath*) léguer, laisser; (*a wife*) quitter, abandonner; **to be left** rester, e.g., **the letter was left unanswered** la lettre est restée sans réponse; e.g., **there are three dollars left** il reste trois dollars; **to be left for s.o.** être à qn de; **to be left over** rester; **to leave about** (*without putting away*) laisser traîner; **to leave alone** laisser tranquille; **to leave it up to** s'en remettre à, s'en rapporter à; **to leave no stone unturned** faire flèche de tout bois, mettre tout en œuvre; **to leave off** (*a piece of clothing*) ne pas mettre; (*a passenger*) déposer; **to leave off** + *inf* cesser de + *inf*, renoncer à + *inf*; **to leave out** omettre ‖ *intr* partir, s'en aller; **where did we leave off?** où en sommes-nous restés?
leaven ['lɛvən] *s* levain *m* ‖ *tr* faire lever; (fig) transformer, modifier
leavening ['lɛvənɪŋ] *adj* transformateur ‖ *s* levain *m*
leave' of ab'sence *s* congé *m*
leave'-tak'ing *s* congé *m*, adieux *mpl*
leavings ['livɪŋz] *spl* restes *mpl*, reliefs *mpl*
Leba·nese [,lɛbə'niz] *adj* libanais ‖ *s* (*pl* **-nese**) Libanais *m*
Lebanon ['lɛbənən] *s* le Liban
lecher ['lɛtʃər] *s* débauché *m*, libertin *m* ‖ *intr* vivre dans la débauche
lecherous ['lɛtʃərəs] *adj* lubrique, lascif
lechery ['lɛtʃəri] *s* lubricité *f*, lasciveté *f*
lectern ['lɛktərn] *s* lutrin *m*
lecture ['lɛktʃər] *s* conférence *f*; (*tedious reprimand*) sermon *m* ‖ *tr* faire une conférence à; (*to rebuke*) sermonner ‖ *intr* faire une conférence or des conférences
lecturer ['lɛktʃərər] *s* conférencier *m*

ledge [lɛdʒ] saillie *f*, corniche *f*; (*projection in a wall*) corniche *f*

ledger ['lɛdʒər] *s* (*slab*) pierre *f* tombale; (com) grand livre *m*

ledg'er line' *s* (mus) ligne *f* supplémentaire

lee [li] *s* (*shelter*) (naut) abri *m*; (*quarter toward which wind blows*) côté *m* sous le vent; **lees** lie *f*

leech [litʃ] *s* sangsue *f*; **to stick like a leech to s.o.** s'accrocher à qn

leek [lik] *s* poireau *m*

leer [lɪr] *s* regard *m* lubrique, œillade *f* ‖ *intr* lancer or jeter une œillade; **to leer at** lorgner

leer·y ['lɪri] *adj* (*comp* **-ier**; *super* **-iest**) (coll) soupçonneux, méfiant

leeward ['liwərd], ['lu·ərd] *adj & adv* sous le vent ‖ *s* côté *m* sous le vent; **to pass to leeward of** passer sous le vent de

Lee'ward Is'lands ['liwərd] *spl* îles *fpl* Sous-le-Vent

lee'way' *s* (aer, naut) dérive *f*; (*of time, money*) (coll) marge *f*; (*for action*) (coll) champ *m*, liberté *f*

left [lɛft] *adj* gauche; (*left over*) de surplus ‖ *s* (*left hand*) gauche *f*; (boxing) gauche *m*; **on the left, to the left** à gauche; **the Left** (pol) la gauche; **to make a left** tourner à gauche ‖ *adv* à gauche

left' field' *s* (baseball) gauche *f* du grand champ

left'-hand' drive' *s* conduite *f* à gauche

left'-hand'ed *adj* gaucher; (*clumsy*) gauche; (*counterclockwise*) à gauche, en sens inverse des aiguilles d'une montre; (*e.g., compliment*) douteux, ambigu

leftish ['lɛftɪʃ] *adj* gauchisant

leftism ['lɛftɪzəm] *s* gauchisme *m*

leftist ['lɛftɪst] *adj & s* gauchiste *mf*

left'o'ver *adj* de surplus, restant ‖ **leftovers** *spl* restes *mpl*

left'-wing' *adj* gauchiste, gauchisant

left'-winger ['lɛft'wɪŋər] *s* (coll) gauchiste *mf*

left·y ['lɛfti] *adj* (coll) gaucher ‖ *s* (*pl* **-ies**) (coll) gaucher *m*

leg [lɛg] *s* jambe *f*; (*of boot or stocking*) tige *f*; (*of fowl; of frogs*) cuisse *f*; (*of journey*) étape *f*; **to be on one's last legs** n'avoir plus de jambes; **to pull the leg of** (coll) se payer la tête de, faire marcher

lega·cy ['lɛgəsi] *s* (*pl* **-cies**) legs *m*

legal ['ligəl] *adj* légal; (*practice*) juridique

le'gal flaw' *s* vice *m* de forme

le'gal hol'iday *s* jour *m* férié

legali·ty [lɪ'gælɪti] *s* (*pl* **-ties**) légalité *f*

legalize ['ligə,laɪz] *tr* légaliser

le'gal ten'der *s* cours *m* légal, monnaie *f* libératoire

legate ['lɛgɪt] *s* ambassadeur *m*, envoyé *m*; (eccl) légat *m*

legatee [,lɛgə'ti] *s* légataire *mf*

legation [lɪ'geʃən] *s* légation *f*

legend ['lɛdʒənd] *s* légende *f*

legendary ['lɛdʒən,dɛri] *adj* légendaire

legerdemain [,lɛdʒərdɪ'men] *s* escamotage *m*, passe-passe *m*

leggings ['lɛgɪŋz] *spl* jambières *fpl*, guêtres *fpl*, leggings *fpl*

leg·gy ['lɛgi] *adj* (*comp* **-gier**; *super* **-giest**) (*awkward*) dégingandé; (*attractive*) aux longues jambes élégantes

leg'horn' *s* (*hat*) chapeau *m* de paille d'Italie; (*chicken*) leghorn *f*; **Leghorn** Livourne *f*

legibility [,lɛdʒɪ'bɪlɪti] *s* lisibilité *f*

legible ['lɛdʒɪbəl] *adj* lisible

legion ['lidʒən] *s* légion *f*

le'gionnaire's' disease' ['lidʒə,nɛrz] *s* (pathol) maladie *f* du légionnaire

legislate ['lɛdʒɪs,let] *tr* imposer à force de loi ‖ *intr* faire des lois, légiférer

legislation [,lɛdʒɪs'leʃən] *s* législation *f*

legislative ['lɛdʒɪs,letɪv] *adj* législatif

legislator ['lɛdʒɪs,letər] *s* législateur *m*

legislature ['lɛdʒɪs,letʃər] *s* assemblée *f* législative, législature *f*

legitimacy [lɪ'dʒɪtɪməsi] *s* légitimité *f*

legitimate [lɪ'dʒɪtɪmɪt] *adj* légitime ‖ [lɪ'dʒɪtɪ,met] *tr* légitimer

legit'imate dra'ma *s* théâtre *m* régulier

legitimize [lɪ'dʒɪtɪ,maɪz] *tr* légitimer

leg' of lamb' *s* gigot *m* d'agneau

leg' of mut'ton *s* gigot *m*

leg'-of-mut'ton sleeve' *s* manche *f* gigot

legume ['lɛgjum], [lɪ'gjum] *s* (*pod*) légume *m*; (bot) légumineuse *f*

leisure ['liʒər], ['lɛʒər] *s* loisir *m*; **at leisure** à loisir; **in leisure moments** à temps perdu; **leisure activities** loisirs *mpl*

lei'sure class' *s* désœuvrés *mpl*, rentiers *mpl*

lei'sure hours' *spl* heures *fpl* de loisir

leisurely ['liʒərli] *adj* tranquille, posé ‖ *adv* posément, sans hâte

lemon ['lɛmən] *s* citron *m*; (*e.g., worthless car*) (coll) clou *m*

lemonade [,lɛmə'ned] *s* citronnade *f*

lem'on squeez'er *s* presse-citron *m*

lem'on tree' *s* citronnier *m*

lem'on verbe'na [vər'binə] *s* verveine *f* citronnelle

lend [lɛnd] *v* (*pret & pp* **lent** [lɛnt]) *tr* prêter

lender ['lɛndər] *s* prêteur *m*

lend'ing li'brary *s* bibliothèque *f* de prêt

length [lɛŋ θ] *s* longueur *f*; (*e.g., of string*) bout *m*, morceau *m*; (*of time*) durée *f*; **at length** longuement, en détail; (*finally*) enfin, à la fin; **in length** de longueur; **to go to any length** ne reculer devant rien pour; **to keep at arm's length** tenir à distance

lengthen ['lɛŋ θən] *tr* allonger, rallonger ‖ *intr* s'allonger

length'wise' *adj* longitudinal ‖ *adv* en longueur, dans le sens de la longueur

length·y ['lɛŋ θi] *adj* (*comp* **-ier**; *super* **-iest**) prolongé, assez long

leniency ['lini·ənsi] *s* douceur *f*, clémence *f*

lenient ['lini·ənt] *adj* doux, clément

lens [lɛnz] *s* lentille *f*; (anat) cristallin *m*

Lent [lɛnt] *s* le Carême

Lenten ['lɛntən] *adj* de carême

lentil ['lɛntəl] *s* lentille *f*

Leo [ˈli·o] *s* (astr, astrol) le Lion
leopard [ˈlɛpərd] *s* léopard *m*
leper [ˈlɛpər] *s* lépreux *m*
lep′er house′ *s* léproserie *f*
leprosy [ˈlɛprəsi] *s* lèpre *f*
leprous [ˈlɛprəs] *adj* lépreux
lesbian [ˈlɛzbɪ·ən] *adj* érotique; **Lesbian** lesbien ‖ *s* (*female homosexual*) lesbienne *f*; **Lesbian** Lesbien *m*
lesbianism [ˈlɛzbɪ·ə‚nɪzəm] *s* saphisme *m*
lese majesty [ˈlizˈmædʒɪsti] *s* crime *m* de lèse-majesté
lesion [ˈliʒən] *s* lésion *f*
less [lɛs] *adj comp* moindre §91 ‖ *s* moins *m* ‖ *adv comp* moins §91; **less and less** de moins en moins; **less than** moins que; (*followed by numeral*) moins de; **the less . . . the less** (or **the more**) moins . . . moins (or plus)
lessee [lɛsˈi] *s* preneur *m*; (*e.g., of house*) locataire *mf*; (*e.g., of gasoline station*) concessionnaire *mf*
lessen [ˈlɛsən] *tr* diminuer, amoindrir ‖ *intr* se diminuer, s'amoindrir
lesser [ˈlɛsər] *adj comp* moindre §91; **the lesser of two evils** le moindre de deux maux
lesson [ˈlɛsən] *s* leçon *f*
lessor [ˈlɛsər] *s* bailleur *m*
lest [lɛst] *conj* de peur que, de crainte que
let [lɛt] *v* (*pret & pp* **let**; *ger* **letting**) *tr* laisser; (*to rent*) louer; **let** + *inf* que + *subj*, e.g., **let him come in** qu'il entre; **let alone** sans parler de, sans compter; **let well enough alone** le mieux est souvent l'ennemi du bien; **let us eat, work, etc.** mangeons, travaillons, etc.; **to be let off with** en être quitte pour; **to let** à louer, e.g., **house to let** maison à louer; **to let alone, to let be** laisser tranquille; **to let by** laisser passer; **to let down** baisser, descendre; (*one's hair*) dénouer, défaire; (*e.g., a garment*) allonger; (*to leave in the lurch*) laisser en panne, faire faux bond à; **to let fly** décocher; **to let go** laisser partir; **to let have** laisser, e.g., **he let Robert have it for three dollars** il l'a laissé à Robert pour trois dollars; **to let in** laisser entrer; **to let in the clutch** (aut) embrayer; **to let into** admettre dans; **to let loose** lâcher; **to let off** laisser partir; (*e.g., steam from a boiler*) laisser échapper, lâcher; (*e.g., a culprit*) pardonner à; **to let oneself go** se laisser aller; **to let on that** (coll) faire croire que; **to let out** faire or laisser sortir; (*e.g., a dress*) élargir; (*a cry; a secret; a prisoner*) laisser échapper; (*to reveal*) révéler, divulguer; **to let out on bail** relâcher sous caution; **to let out the clutch** débrayer; **to let slip** laisser tomber; **to let s.o.** + *inf* permettre à qn de + *inf*; laisser qn + *inf*, e.g., **he let Mary go to the theater** il a laissé Marie aller au théâtre; **to let s.o. in on** (*a secret*) (coll) confier à qn; (*e.g., a racing tip*) (coll) tuyauter qn sur; **to let s.o. know s.th.** faire savoir q.ch. à qn, mettre qn au

courant de q.ch.; **to let s.o. off with** faire grâce à qn de; **to let stand** laisser, e.g., **he let the errors stand** il a laissé les fautes; **to let s.th. go for** (*a low price*) laisser q.ch. pour; **to let through** laisser passer; **to let up** laisser monter ‖ *intr* (*said of house, apartment, etc.*) se louer; **to let down** (coll) ralentir; **to let go of** lâcher prise de; **to let out** (*said of class, school, etc.*) finir, se terminer; **to let up** (coll) ralentir, diminuer; (*on discipline; on a person*) devenir moins sévère
let′down′ *s* diminution *f*; (*disappointment*) déception *f*
lethal [ˈliθəl] *adj* mortel; (*weapon*) meurtrier
lethargic [lɪˈθɑrdʒɪk] *adj* léthargique
lethar·gy [ˈlɛθərdʒi] *s* (*pl* **-gies**) léthargie *f*
letter [ˈlɛtər] *s* lettre *f*; **letters** (*literature*) lettres; **to the letter** à la lettre, au pied de la lettre ‖ *tr* marquer avec des lettres
let′ter box′ *s* boîte *f* aux lettres
let′ter car′rier *s* facteur *m*
let′ter drop′ *s* passe-lettres *m*, fente *f* (dans la porte pour le courrier)
lettered *adj* (*person*) lettré
let′ter file′ *s* classeur *m* de lettres
let′ter·head′ *s* en-tête *m*
lettering [ˈlɛtərɪŋ] *s* (*action*) lettrage *m*; (*title*) inscription *f*
let′ter of cred′it *s* lettre *f* de crédit
let′ter o′pener *s* coupe-papier *m*
let′ter pa′per *s* papier *m* à lettres
let′ter·per′fect *adj* correct; sûr
let′ter press′ *s* presse *f* à copier
let′ter·press′ *s* impression *f* typographique; (*in distinction to illustrations*) texte *m*
let′ter scales′ *spl* pèse-lettre *m*
let′ter·word′ *s* sigle *m*
lettuce [ˈlɛtɪs] *s* laitue *f*
let′up′ *s* accalmie *f*, pause *f*; **without letup** sans relâche
leucorrhea [‚lukəˈri·ə] *s* leucorrhée *f*
leukemia [luˈkimɪ·ə] *s* leucémie *f*
Levant [lɪˈvænt] *s* Levant *m*
Levantine [ˈlɛvən‚tin], [lɪˈvæntɪn] *adj* levantin ‖ *s* Levantin *m*
levee [ˈlɛvi] *s* (*embankment*) levée *f*, digue *f*; réception *f* royale
lev·el [ˈlɛvəl] *adj* de niveau; (*flat*) égal, uni; (*spoonful*) arasé; **level with** de niveau avec, à fleur de ‖ *s* niveau *m*; **on a level with** au niveau de; **to be on the level** (coll) être de bonne foi; **to find one's level** trouver son niveau ‖ *v* (*pret & pp* **-eled** or **-elled**; *ger* **-eling** or **-elling**) *tr* niveler; (*to smooth, flatten out*) aplanir, araser; (*to bring down*) raser; (*a gun*) braquer; (*accusations, sarcasm*) lancer, diriger; **to level out** égaliser; **to level up** (aer) redresser ‖ *intr* (aer) redresser; **to level with** (coll) parler franchement à
lev′el·head′ed *adj* équilibré, pondéré
lev′eling rod′ *s* (surv) jalon-mire *m*, jalon *m* d'arpentage
lever [ˈlivər] *s* levier *m* ‖ *tr* soulever or ouvrir au moyen d'un levier

leverage ['lɛvərɪdʒ] *s* puissance *f* or force *f* de levier; (fig) influence *f*, avantage *m*

leviathan [lɪ'vaɪ·əθən] *s* léviathan *m*

levitation [,lɛvɪ'teʃən] *s* lévitation *f*

levi·ty ['lɛvɪti] *s* (*pl* -ties) légèreté *f*

lev·y ['lɛvi] *s* (*pl* -ies) levée *f* ‖ *v* (*pret & pp* -ied) *tr* lever; (*a fine*) imposer

lewd [lud] *adj* luxurieux, lubrique

lewdness ['ludnɪs] *s* luxure *f*, lubricité *f*

lexical ['lɛksɪkəl] *adj* lexical

lexicographer [,lɛksɪ'kagrəfər] *s* lexicographe *mf*

lexicographic(al) [,lɛksɪkə'græfɪk(əl)] *adj* lexicographique

lexicography [,lɛksɪ'kagrəfi] *s* lexicographie *f*

lexicology [,lɛksɪ'kalədʒi] *s* lexicologie *f*

lexicon ['lɛksɪkən] *s* lexique *m*

liabili·ty [,laɪ·ə'bɪlɪti] *s* (*pl* -ties) responsabilité *f*; (*e.g., to disease*) prédisposition *f*; **liabilities** obligations *fpl*, dettes *fpl*

liabil'ity insur'ance *s* assurance *f* tous risques

liable ['laɪ·əbəl] *adj* sujet; **liable for** (*a debt, fine, etc.*) passible de, responsable de; **we (you, etc.) are liable to** + *inf* (coll) il se peut que nous (vous, etc.) + *pres subj*; (coll) il est probable que nous (vous, etc.) + *pres ind*

liaison [li'ezən] *s* liaison *f*

liar ['laɪ·ər] *s* menteur *m*

libation [laɪ'beʃən] *s* libation *f*

li·bel ['laɪbəl] *s* diffamation *f*, calomnie *f*; (*in writing*) écrit *m* diffamatoire ‖ *v* (*pret & pp* -beled or -belled) *ger* -beling or -belling) *tr* diffamer, calomnier

libelous ['laɪbələs] *adj* diffamatoire, calomnieux

liberal ['lɪbərəl] *adj* libéral; (*share, supply, etc.*) libéral, généreux, copieux; (*ideas*) large ‖ *s* libéral *m*

liberali·ty [,lɪbə'rælɪti] *s* (*pl* -ties) libéralité *f*; (*breadth of mind*) largeur *f* de vues

lib'eral·mind'ed *adj* tolérant

liberate ['lɪbə,ret] *tr* libérer

liberation [,lɪbə'reʃən] *s* libération *f*

liberator ['lɪbə,retər] *s* libérateur *m*

libertine ['lɪbər,tin] *adj & s* libertin *m*

liber·ty ['lɪbərti] *s* (*pl* -ties) liberté *f*; (mil) permission *f* exceptionnelle; **at liberty** en liberté; **at liberty to** libre de; **to take the liberty to** se permettre de, prendre la liberté de

libidinous [lɪ'bɪdɪnəs] *adj* libidineux

libido [lɪ'bido], [lɪ'baɪdo] *s* libido *f*

Libra ['librə] *s* (astr, astrol) la Balance

librarian [laɪ'brɛrɪ·ən] *s* bibliothécaire *mf*

librar·y ['laɪ,brɛri] *s* (*pl* -ies) bibliothèque *f*

li·brary num'ber *s* cote *f*

libret·to [lɪ'brɛto] *s* (*pl* -tos) livret *m*, libretto *m*

license ['laɪsəns] *s* permis *m*, licence *f*; (*to drive*) permis de conduire ‖ *tr* accorder un permis à, autoriser

li'cense num'ber *s* numéro *m* d'immatriculation; (aut) numéro minéralogique

li'cense plate' or **tag'** *s* plaque *f* d'immatriculation, plaque minéralogique

licentious [laɪ'sɛnʃəs] *adj* licencieux

lichen ['laɪkən] *s* lichen *m*

lick [lɪk] *s* (*with the tongue*) coup *m* de langue; (*salt lick*) terrain *m* salifère; (*blow*) (coll) coup *m*; **at full lick** (coll) à plein gaz; **to give a lick and a promise to** (coll) nettoyer à la six-quatre-deux; (coll) faire un brin de toilette à ‖ *tr* lécher; (*e.g., the fingers*) se lécher; (*to beat, thrash*) (coll) enfoncer les côtes à, rosser; (*to beat, surpass, e.g., in a sporting event*) (coll) battre, enfoncer; (*e.g., a problem*) (coll) venir à bout de; **to lick into shape** (coll) dégrossir; **to lick up** lécher

licking ['lɪkɪŋ] *s* léchage *m*; (*drubbing*) (coll) raclée *f*

licorice ['lɪkərɪs] *s* réglisse *f*

lid [lɪd] *s* (*on a dish, kettle, etc.*) couvercle *m*; (*eyelid*) paupière *f*; (*hat*) (slang) couvre-chef *m*

lie [laɪ] *s* mensonge *m*; **to give the lie to** donner le démenti à ‖ *v* (*pret & pp* **lied**; *ger* **lying**) *tr*—**to lie one's way out** se tirer d'affaire par des mensonges ‖ *intr* mentir ‖ *v* (*pret* **lay**; *pp* **lain** [lɛn]; *ger* **lying**) *intr* être couché; (*to be located*) se trouver; (*e.g., in the grave*) gésir, e.g., **here lies** ci-gît; **to lie down** se coucher

lie' detec'tor *s* détecteur *m* de mensonges, polygraphe *m*

lien [lin] *s* privilège *m*, droit *m* de rétention

lieu [lu] *s*—**in lieu of** au lieu de

lieutenant [lu'tɛnənt] *s* lieutenant *m*; (nav) lieutenant *m* de vaisseau

lieuten'ant colo'nel *s* lieutenant-colonel *m*

lieuten'ant comman'der *s* (nav) capitaine *m* de corvette

lieuten'ant gov'ernor *s* (U.S.A.) vice-gouverneur *m*; (Brit) lieutenant-gouverneur *m*

lieuten'ant jun'ior grade' *s* (nav) enseigne *m* de première classe

life [laɪf] *s* (*pl* **lives** [laɪvz]) vie *f*; (*of light bulb, lease, insurance policy*) durée *f*; **bigger than life** plus grand que nature; **for dear life** de toutes ses forces; **for life** à vie, pour la vie, à perpétuité; **for the life of me!** (coll) de ma vie!; **lives lost** morts *mpl*; **long life** longévité *f*; **never in my life!, not on your life!** jamais de la vie!; **run for your life!** sauve qui peut!; **such is life!** c'est la vie!; **taken from life** pris sur le vif; **to come to life** revenir à la vie; **to depart this life** quitter ce monde; **to risk life and limb** risquer sa peau

life' annu'ity *s* rente *f* viagère

life' belt' *s* ceinture *f* de sauvetage

life'blood' *s* sang *m*; (fig) vie *f*

life'boat' *s* chaloupe *f* de sauvetage; (*for shore-based rescue services*) canot *m* de sauvetage

life' buoy' *s* bouée *f* de sauvetage

life' expect'ancy *s* espérance *f* de vie

life' float' *s* radeau *m* de sauvetage

life′ guard′ s (mil) garde f du corps
life′guard′ s sauveteur m, maître nageur m
life′ impris′onment s emprisonnement m à vie, détention f perpétuelle
life′ insur′ance s assurance f sur la vie, assurance-vie f
life′ jack′et s gilet m de sauvetage
lifeless [′laɪflɪs] adj sans vie, inanimé; (colors) embu, terne
life′like′ adj vivant, ressemblant
life′ line′ s ligne f or corde f de sauvetage, planche f de salut
life′long′ adj de toute la vie, perpétuel
life′ mem′ber s membre m à vie, membre perpétuel
life′ of lei′sure s vie f de château
life′ of Ri′ley [′raɪli] s (slang) joyeuse vie f, vie oisive
life′ of the par′ty s (coll) boute-en-train m
life′ preserv′er [prɪˈzʌrvər] s appareil m de sauvetage
lifer [′laɪfər] s (slang) condamné m à perpétuité
life′ raft′ s radeau m de sauvetage
lifesaver [′laɪf,sevər] s sauveteur m; (fig) planche f de salut
life′sav′ing s sauvetage m
life′ sen′tence s condamnation f à perpétuité
life′-size′ adj de grandeur nature
life′ span′ s durée f de vie, espérance f de vie
life′time′ adj à vie ‖ s vie f, toute une vie; **in his lifetime** de son vivant
life′work′ s travail m de toute une vie
lift [lɪft] s haussement m, levée f; (aer) poussée f, portance f; (Brit) ascenseur m; (of dumbbell or weight) (sports) arraché m; **to give a lift to** (by offering a ride) conduire d'un coup de voiture, faire monter dans la voiture; (to aid) donner un coup de main à; (to raise the morale of) remonter le moral de, ranimer ‖ tr lever, soulever; (heart, mind, etc.) élever, ranimer; (a sail) soulager; (an embargo) lever; (e.g., passages from a book) démarquer, plagier; (to rob) (slang) dérober; **to lift up** (the hands) lever; (the head) relever; (the voice) élever ‖ intr se lever, se soulever; (said of clouds, fog, etc.) se lever, se dissiper
lift′ bridge′ s pont m levant, pont-levis m
lift′off′ s (rok) montée verticale, chandelle f
lift′ truck′ s chariot m élévateur
ligament [′lɪgəmənt] s ligament m
ligature [′lɪgətʃər] s ligature f
light [laɪt] adj léger; (having illumination) élairé; (color, complexion, hair) clair; (beer) blond; (wine) léger; **to make light of** faire peu de cas de ‖ s lumière f; (to control traffic) feu m; (window or other opening in a wall) jour m; (example, shining figure) lumière; (headlight of automobile) phare m; du feu, e.g., **do you have a light?** (e.g., to light a cigarette) avez-vous du feu?; **according to one's lights** selon ses lumières, dans la mesure

de son intelligence; **against the light** à contre-jour; **in a false light** sous un faux jour; **in a new light** sous un jour nouveau; **in the same light** sous le même aspect; **it is light (out)** il fait jour; **lights** (navigation lights; parking lights) feux mpl; (of sheep, calf, etc.) mou m; **lights out** (mil) l'extinction f des feux; **to bring to light** mettre au jour; **to come to light** se révéler; **to shed** or **throw light on** éclairer; **to strike a light** allumer ‖ adv à vide; **to run light** (said of engine) aller haut le pied ‖ v (pret & pp **lighted** or **lit** [lɪt]) tr (to furnish with illumination) éclairer, illuminer; (to set afire, ignite) allumer; **to light the way for** éclairer; **to light up** illuminer ‖ intr s'éclairer, s'illuminer; allumer; (to perch) se poser; **to light from** or **off** (an auto, carriage, etc.) descendre de; **to light into** (to attack; to berate) (slang) tomber sur; **to light out** (to skedaddle) (slang) décamper; **to light up** s'éclairer, s'illuminer; **to light upon** (by happenstance) tomber sur, trouver par hasard
light′ bulb′ s ampoule f électrique, lampe f électrique
light′ complex′ion s teint m clair
lighten [′laɪtən] tr (to make lighter in weight) alléger, soulager; (to provide more light) éclairer, illuminer; (to give a lighter or brighter hue to) éclaircir; (grief, punishment, etc.) adoucir ‖ intr (to become less dark or sorrowful) s'éclairer; (to give off flashes of lightning) faire des éclairs; (to become less weighty) s'alléger
lighter [′laɪtər] s (to light cigarette) briquet m; (flat-bottomed barge) chaland m, péniche f
light′-fin′gered adj à doigts agiles
light′-foot′ed adj au pied léger
light′-head′ed adj étourdi
light′-heart′ed adj joyeux, allègre, au cœur léger
light′house′ s phare m
lighting [′laɪtɪŋ] s allumage m, éclairage m
light′ing fix′tures spl appareils mpl d'éclairage
light′ me′ter s posemètre m
lightness [′laɪtnɪs] s (in weight) légèreté f; (in illumination; of complexion) clarté f
light′ning [′laɪtnɪŋ] s (electric discharge) foudre f; (light produced by this discharge) éclairs mpl ‖ v (ger **-ning**) intr faire des éclairs
light′ning arrest′er [ə,rɛstər] f parafoudre m
light′ning bug′ s luciole f
light′ning rod′ s paratonnerre m
light′ op′era s opérette f
light′ pen′ s (comp) photostyle m
light′ read′ing s livres mpl d'agrément; lecture f légère or amusante
light′ship′ s bateau-feu m
light-struck [′laɪt,strʌk] adj (phot) voilé
light′ wave′ s onde f lumineuse

light′weight′ *adj* léger ‖ *s* (sports) poids *m* léger

light′weight coat′ *s* surtout *m* de demisaison

light′-year′ *s* année-lumière *f*

likable [′laɪkəbəl] *adj* sympathique, agréable

like [laɪk] *adj* (*alike*) pareils, semblables; pareil à, semblable à; (*typical of*) caractéristique de; (*poles of a magnet*) (elec) de même nom; **like father like son** tel père tel fils; **that is like him** il n'en fait pas d'autres ‖ *s* pareil *m*, semblable *m*; **likes** (*desires*) goût *m*, inclinations *fpl*; **the likes of him** son pareil ‖ *adv*—**like enough** probablement; **like mad** comme un fou ‖ *prep* comme; **like that** de la sorte ‖ *conj* (coll) de la même manière que, comme ‖ *tr* aimer, aimer bien, trouver bon; plaire à, e.g., **I like milk** le lait me plaît; se plaire, e.g., **I like it in the country** je me plais à la campagne ‖ *intr* vouloir; **as you like** comme vous voudrez; **if you like** si vous voulez

likelihood [′laɪklɪ,hʊd] *s* probabilité *f*, vraisemblance *f*

like·ly [′laɪkli] *adj* (*comp* **-lier**; *super* **-liest**) probable, vraisemblable; **to be likely to** + *inf* être probable que + *ind*, e.g., **Mary is likely to come to see us tomorrow** il est probable que Marie viendra nous voir demain ‖ *adv* probablement, vraisemblablement

like′-mind′ed *adj* du même avis

liken [′laɪkən] *tr* comparer, assimiler

likeness [′laɪknɪs] *s* (*picture or image*) portrait *m*; (*similarity*) ressemblance *f*

like′wise′ *adv* également, de même; **to do likewise** en faire autant

liking [′laɪkɪŋ] *s* sympathie *f*, penchant *m*; **to one's liking** à souhait; **to take a liking to** (*a thing*) accueillir avec sympathie; (*a person*) montrer de la sympathie à, se prendre d'amitié pour

lilac [′laɪlək] *adj* & *s* lilas *m*

Lilliputian [,lɪlɪ′pjuʃən] *adj* & *s* lilliputien *m*

lilt [lɪlt] *s* cadence *f*

lil·y [′lɪli] *s* (*pl* **-ies**) lis *m*, lis blanc; (*royal arms of France*) fleur *f* de lis; **to gild the lily** orner la beauté même

lil′y of the val′ley *s* muguet *m*

lil′y pad′ *s* feuille *f* de nénuphar

lil′y-white′ *adj* blanc comme le lis, lilial

Li′ma bean′ [′laɪmə] *s* (*Phaseolus limensis*) haricot *m* de Lima

limb [lɪm] *s* (*arm or leg*) membre *m*; (*of a tree*) branche *f*; (*of a cross; of the sea*) bras *m*; (astr, bot) limbe *m*; **to be out on a limb** (coll) être sur la corde raide

limber [′lɪmbər] *adj* souple, flexible ‖ *intr*—**to limber up** se dégourdir

lim·bo [′lɪmbo] *s* (*pl* **-bos**) limbes *mpl*

lime [laɪm] *s* (*calcium oxide*) chaux *f*; (*linden tree*) tilleul *m*; (*Citrus aurantifolia*) citron *m*; **sweet lime** (*Citrus limetta*) lime *f*

lime′kiln′ *s* four *m* à chaux

lime′light′ *s*—**to be in the limelight** être sous les feux de la rampe

limerick [′lɪmərɪk] *s* poème *m* humoristique en cinq vers

lime′stone′ *adj* calcaire ‖ *s* calcaire *m*, pierre *f* à chaux

limit [′lɪmɪt] *s* limite *f*, borne *f*; **to be the limit** (*to be exasperating*) (coll) être le comble; (*to be bizarre*) (coll) être impayable; **to go the limit** aller jusqu'au bout ‖ *tr* limiter, borner

limitation [,lɪmɪ′teʃən] *s* limitation *f*

lim′ited-ac′cess high′way *s* autoroute *f*

lim′ited mon′archy *s* monarchie *f* constitutionnelle

limitless [′lɪmɪtlɪs] *adj* sans bornes, illimité

limousine [,lɪmə′zin] *s* (aut) limousine *f*

limp [lɪmp] *adj* mou, flasque, souple ‖ *s* boiterie *f* ‖ *intr* boiter

limpid [′lɪmpɪd] *adj* limpide

linchpin [′lɪntʃ,pɪn] *s* cheville *f* d'essieu, esse *f*

linden [′lɪndən] *s* tilleul *m*

line [laɪn] *s* ligne *f*; (*of poetry*) vers *m*; (*rope, string*) cordage *m*, corde *f*; (*wrinkle*) ride *f*; (*dash*) trait *m*; (*bar*) barre *f*; (*lineage*) lignée *f*; (*trade*) métier *m*; (*of merchandise*) article *m*; (*of traffic*) file *f*; (mil) rang *m*; (*of the spectrum*) (phys) raie *f*; **fault line** ligne de faille; **hold the line!** (telp) ne quittez pas!; **in line** aligné, en rang; **in line with** conforme à, d'accord avec; **off line** (comp) autonome; **on line** (comp) en ligne; **on the line** (telp) au bout du fil; **out of line** désaligné; en désaccord; **straight line** ligne droite; **the line is busy** (telp) la ligne est occupée; **to bring into line with** mettre d'accord avec; **to drop s.o. a line** envoyer un mot à qn; **to fall into line** se mettre en ligne, s'aligner; **to hand s.o. a line** (slang) faire du baratin à qn, bourrer le crâne de qn; **to have a line on** (coll) se tuyauter sur; **to learn one's lines** apprendre son texte *or* rôle; **to read between the lines** lire entre les lignes; **to stand** *or* **wait in line** faire la queue; **to toe the line** se mettre au pas ‖ *tr* aligner; (*a face*) rider; (*a suit, coat, etc.*) doubler; (*brakes*) fourrer; être bordé de (e.g., *trees*) être bordé de ‖ *intr*—**to line up** s'aligner, se mettre en ligne; faire la queue

lineage [′lɪnɪ·ɪdʒ] *s* lignée *f*, race *f*, lignage *m*

lineal [′lɪnɪ·əl] *adj* linéal; (*succession*) en ligne directe

lineaments [′lɪnɪ·əmənts] *spl* linéaments *mpl*

linear [′lɪnɪ·ər] *adj* linéaire

lined′ pa′per *s* papier *m* rayé

line′man *s* (*pl* **-men**) (elec) poseur *m* de lignes; (rr) garde-ligne *m*

linen [′lɪnən] *adj* de lin ‖ *s* (*fabric*) toile *f* de lin; (*yarn*) fil *m* de lin; (*sheets, tablecloths, underclothes, etc.*) linge *m*, lingerie *f*; **don't wash your dirty linen in public** il faut laver son linge sale en famille; il ne faut pas laver en public un linge sanglant; **pure linen** pur fil

lin'en clos'et *s* lingerie *f*

line' of fire' *s* (mil) ligne *f* de tir

line' of sight' *s* ligne *f* de mire, ligne de visée

liner ['laɪnər] *s* (naut) paquebot *m*

line'-up' *s* (*row*) file *f*, mise *f* en rang; (*arrangement*) disposition *f*; (*of suspects*) séance *f* d'identification d'un suspect; (pol) front *m*; (sports) composition *f* de l'équipe

linger ['lɪŋgər] *intr* s'attarder; (*said of hope, doubt, etc.*) persister; **to linger on** traîner; **to linger over** s'attarder sur

lingerie [,læŋʒə'ri] *s* lingerie *f* fine pour dames, lingerie de dame

lingering ['lɪŋgərɪŋ] *adj* prolongé, lent

lingual ['lɪŋgwəl] *adj* lingual ‖ *s* (*consonant*) linguale *f*

linguist ['lɪŋgwɪst] *s* (*person skilled in several languages*) polyglotte *mf*; (*specialist in linguistics*) linguiste *mf*

linguistic [lɪŋ'gwɪstɪk] *adj* linguistique ‖ **linguistics** *s* linguistique *f*

liniment ['lɪnɪmənt] *s* liniment *m*

lining ['laɪnɪŋ] *s* (*of a coat*) doublure *f*; (*of a hat*) coiffe *f*; (*of auto brake*) garniture *f*; (*of furnace, wall, etc.*) revêtement *m*

link [lɪŋk] *s* maillon *m*, chaînon *m*; (fig) lien *m*; **links** terrain *m* de golf ‖ *tr* enchaîner; lier ‖ *intr*—**to link in, on,** or **up** se lier

link'up *s* (rok) arrimage *m*

linnet ['lɪnɪt] *s* (orn) linotte *f*

linoleum [lɪ'nolɪ·əm] *s* linoléum *m*

linotype ['laɪnə,taɪp] (trademark) *s* linotype *f* ‖ *tr & intr* composer à la lino

lin'otype op'erator *s* linotypiste *mf*

lin'otype slug' *s* ligne-bloc *m*

linseed ['lɪn,sid] *s* linette *f*, graine *f* de lin

lin'seed oil' *s* huile *f* de lin

lint [lɪnt] *s* (*minute shreds*) petites parcelles *fpl* de fil; (*fluff*) peluches *fpl*; (*used to dress wounds*) charpie *f*; tissu *m* ouaté

lintel ['lɪntəl] *s* linteau *m*

lion ['laɪ·ən] *s* lion *m*; (fig) lion; **to put one's head in the lion's mouth** se fourrer dans la gueule du loup ou du lion

lioness ['laɪ·ənɪs] *s* lionne *f*

li'on-heart'ed *adj* au cœur de lion

lionize ['laɪ·ə,naɪz] *tr* faire une célébrité de, traiter en vedette

li'ons' den' *s* (Bib) fosse *f* aux lions

li'on's share' *s* part *f* du lion

lip [lɪp] *s* lèvre *f*; (*edge*) bord *m*; (slang) impertinence *f*; **to hang on the lips of** être suspendu aux lèvres de; **to smack one's lips** se lécher les babines

lip'read' *v* (*pret & pp* **-read** [,rɛd]) *tr & intr* lire sur les lèvres

lip' read'ing *s* lecture *f* sur les lèvres

lip' serv'ice *s* dévotion *f* des lèvres

lip'stick' *s* bâton *m* de rouge à lèvres

lique·fy ['lɪkwɪ,faɪ] *v* (*pret & pp* **-fied**) *tr* liquéfier

liqueur [lɪ'kʌr] *s* liqueur *f*

liquid ['lɪkwɪd] *adj* liquide *m*; (*consonant*) liquide *f*

liq'uid as'sets *spl* valeurs *fpl* disponibles

liquidate ['lɪkwɪ,det] *tr & intr* liquider

liquidity [lɪ'kwɪdɪti] *s* liquidité *f*

liquor ['lɪkər] *s* boisson *f* alcoolique, spiritueux *m*; (culin) jus *m*, bouillon *m*

Lisbon ['lɪzbən] *s* Lisbonne *f*

lisle [laɪl] *s* fil *m* d'Écosse, fil retors de coton

lisp [lɪsp] *s* zézayement *m*, blésement *m* ‖ *intr* zézayer, bléser

lissome ['lɪsəm] *adj* souple, flexible; (*nimble*) agile, leste

list [lɪst] *s* liste *f*; (*selvage*) lisière *f*; (naut) bande *f*, inclinaison *f*; **to enter the lists** entrer en lice; **to have a list** (naut) donner de la bande ‖ *tr* cataloguer, enregistrer; (comp) lister ‖ *intr* (naut) donner de la bande

listen ['lɪsən] *intr* écouter; **to listen in** rester à l'écoute; **to listen to** écouter; **to listen to reason** entendre raison

listener ['lɪsənər] *s* auditeur *m*; (educ) auditeur libre

listening ['lɪsənɪŋ] *s* écoute *f*

lis'tening post' *s* poste *m* d'écoute

listing ['lɪstɪŋ] *s* énumération *f*, compte *m*; (comp) listage *m*

listless ['lɪstlɪs] *adj* apathique, inattentif

list' price' *s* prix *m* courant, cote *f*

lita·ny ['lɪtəni] *s* (*pl* **-nies**) litanie *f*

liter ['litər] *s* litre *m*

literal ['lɪtərəl] *adj* littéral; (*person*) prosaïque

literally ['lɪtərəli] *adv* littéralement, mot à mot, au sens propre; (*without interpretation*) au pied de la lettre, à la lettre; (*really*) réellement; (*absolutely*) (coll) littéralement

literary ['lɪtə,rɛri] *adj* littéraire

literate ['lɪtərət] *adj* qui sait lire et écrire; (*well-read*) lettré ‖ *s* personne *f* qui sait lire et écrire; lettré *m*, érudit *m*

literati [,lɪtə'rati] *spl* littérateurs *mpl*

literature ['lɪtərətʃər] *s* littérature *f*; (com) documentation *f*

lithe [laɪð] *adj* souple, flexible

lithia ['lɪθɪ·ə] *s* (chem) lithine *f*

lithium ['lɪθɪ·əm] *s* (chem) lithium *m*

lithograph ['lɪθə,græf] *s* lithographie *f* ‖ *tr* lithographier

lithographer [lɪ'θɑgrəfər] *s* lithographe *mf*

lithography [lɪ'θɑgrəfi] *s* lithographie *f*

litigant ['lɪtɪgənt] *adj* plaidant ‖ *s* plaideur *m*

litigate ['lɪtɪ,get] *tr* mettre en litige ‖ *intr* plaider

litigation [,lɪtɪ'geʃən] *s* litige *m*

lit'mus pa'per ['lɪtməs] *s* papier *m* de tournesol

litter ['lɪtər] *s* (*disorder*) fouillis *m*; (*things strewn about*) jonchee *f*; (*scattered rubbish*) ordures *fpl*; (*young brought forth at one birth*) portée *f*; (*bedding for animals*) litière *f*; (*vehicle carried by men or animals*) palanquin *m*; (*stretcher*) civière *f* ‖ *tr* joncher ‖ *intr* (*to bring forth young*) mettre bas

lit′ter·bug′ s souillon m, malpropre m, personne f qui dépose des ordures et des papiers dans la rue

littering [′lɪtərɪŋ] s—**no littering** (public sign) défense de déposer des ordures

little [′lɪtəl] adj petit; (in amount) peu de, e.g., **little money** peu d′argent; **a little** un peu de, e.g., **a little money** un peu d′argent ‖ s peu m; **a little** un peu; **to make little of, to think little of** faire peu de cas de; **wait a little** attendez un petit moment, attendez quelques instants ‖ adv peu §91; ne . . . guère §90, e.g., **she little thinks that** elle ne se doute guère que; **little by little** peu à peu, petit à petit

Lit′tle Bear′ s Petite Ourse f

Lit′tle Dip′per s Petit Chariot m

lit′tle fin′ger s petit doigt m, auriculaire m; **to twist around one′s little finger** mener par le bout du nez

lit′tle·neck′ s coque f de Vénus

littleness [′lɪtəlnɪs] s petitesse f

lit′tle owl′ s (Athene noctua) chouette f chevêche, chevêche f

lit′tle peo′ple spl (fairies) fées fpl; (common people) menu peuple m

Lit′tle Red Rid′ing·hood′ s le Petit Chaperon rouge

lit′tle slam′ s (bridge) petit chelem m

liturgic(al) [lɪ′tʌrdʒɪk(əl)] adj liturgique

litur·gy [′lɪtərdʒi] s (pl **-gies**) liturgie f

livable [′lɪvəbəl] adj (house) habitable; (life, person) supportable

live [laɪv] adj vivant, vif; (coals; flame) ardent; (microphone) actif; (elec) sous tension; (telv) en direct ‖ [lɪv] tr vivre; **to live down** faire oublier ‖ intr vivre; (in a certain locality) demeurer, habiter; **live and learn** qui vivra verra; **to live high** mener grand train; **to live in** (e.g., a city) habiter; **to live on** continuer à vivre; (e.g., meat) vivre de; (a benefactor) vivre aux crochets de; (one′s capital) manger; **to live up to** (e.g., one′s reputation) faire honneur à

live′ coal′ [laɪv] s charbon m ardent

livelihood [′laɪvlɪ,hʊd] s vie f; **to earn one′s livelihood** gagner sa vie

livelong [′lɪv,lɔŋ] adj—**all the livelong day** toute la sainte journée

live·ly [′laɪvli] adj (comp **-lier;** super **-liest**) animé, vivant, plein d′entrain; (merry) enjoué, gai; (active, keen) vif; (resilient) élastique

liven [′laɪvən] tr animer ‖ intr s′animer

liver [′lɪvər] s vivant m; (e.g., in cities) habitant m; (anat) foie m

liver·y [′lɪvəri] s (pl **-ies**) livrée f

liv′ery·man s (pl **-men**) loueur m de chevaux

liv′ery sta′ble s écurie f de louage

live′ show′ [laɪv] s (telv) prise f de vues en direct

live′stock′ s bétail m, bestiaux mpl, cheptel m

live′ tel′evision broad′cast s prise f de vues en direct

live′ wire′ s fil m sous tension; (slang) type m dynamique, boute-en-train m invar

livid [′lɪvɪd] adj livide

living [′lɪvɪŋ] adj vivant, en vie ‖ s vie f; **to earn** or **to make a living** gagner sa vie

liv′ing quar′ters spl appartements mpl, habitations fpl

liv′ing room′ s salle f de séjour, salon m; (in a studio apartment) living m

liv′ing space′ s espace m vital

liv′ing wage′ s salaire m suffisant pour vivre, salaire de base

lizard [′lɪzərd] s lézard m

load [lod] s charge f; **loads (of)** (coll) énormément (de); **to get a load of** (slang) observer, écouter; **to have a load on** (slang) avoir son compte ‖ tr charger ‖ intr charger; se charger

loaded adj chargé; (very drunk) (slang) soûl; (very rich) (slang) huppé

load′ed dice′ spl dés mpl pipés

load′stone′ s pierre f d′aimant; (fig) aimant m

loaf [lof] s (pl **loaves** [lovz]) pain m ‖ intr flâner

loafer [′lofər] s flâneur m

loam [lom] s terre f franche, glaise f; (mixture used in making molds) potée f

loamy [′lomi] adj franc, glaiseux

loan [lon] s prêt m, emprunt m ‖ tr prêter

loan′ of′fice s entreprise f de prêt, caisse f de prévoyance

loan′ shark′ s usurier m

loan′ word′ s mot m d′emprunt

loath [loθ] adj—**loath to** peu enclin à

loathe [loð] tr détester

loathing [′loðɪŋ] s dégoût m

loathsome [′loðsəm] adj dégoûtant

lob [lɑb] s (tennis) lob m ‖ v (pret & pp **lobbed;** ger **lobbing**) tr frapper en hauteur, lober

lob·by [′lɑbi] s (pl **-bies**) vestibule m; (e.g., in a theater) foyer m; (pressure group) groupe m de pression, lobby m ‖ v (pret & pp **-bied**) intr faire les couloirs

lobbying [′lɑbɪ·ɪŋ] s intrigues fpl de couloir

lobbyist [′lɑbɪ·ɪst] s intrigant m de couloir

lobe [lob] s lobe m

lobster [′lɑbstər] s (spiny lobster) langouste f; (Homarus) homard m

lob′ster pot′ s casier m à homards

local [′lokəl] adj local ‖ s (of labor union) succursale f; (journ) informations fpl régionales; (rr) train m omnibus

locale [lo′kæl] s lieu m, milieu m; scène f

locali·ty [lo′kælɪti] s (pl **-ties**) localité f

localize [′lokə,laɪz] tr localiser

lo′cal supply′ cir′cuit s secteur m

locate [′loket] tr (to discover the location of) localiser; (to place, to settle) placer, installer; (to ascribe a particular location to) situer; **to be located** se trouver ‖ intr se fixer, s′établir

location [lo′keʃən] s (place, position) situation f, emplacement m; (act of placing) établissement m; (act of finding) localisation f, détermination f; (of a railroad line) tracé m; **on location** (mov) en extérieur

loca′tion shot′ s (mov) extérieur m

lock [lɑk] s serrure f; (of a canal) écluse f; (of hair) mèche f, boucle f; (of a firearm) platine f; (wrestling) clef f; **lock, stock, and barrel** tout le bataclan, tout le fourbi; **under lock and key** sous clé ‖ tr fermer à clef; (to key) caler, bloquer; (a boat) écluser, sasser; (a switch) (rr) verrouiller; **to be locked in each other's arms** être enlacés; **to lock in** enfermer à clef; **to lock out** fermer la porte à or sur; (workers) fermer les ateliers contre; **to lock up** fermer à clef, mettre sous clé; (e.g., a prisoner) boucler, enfermer; (a form) (typ) serrer ‖ intr (said of door) fermer à clef; (said of brake, wheel, etc.) se bloquer; **to lock into** s'engrener dans

locker [′lɑkər] s armoire f, coffre m de sûreté; (in a station or airport) casier m; (for keeping clothes) vestiaire m, placard m individuel; (locker room) vestiaire m

lock′er room′ s vestiaire m, vestiaire à placards individuels

locket [′lɑkɪt] s médaillon m

lock′jaw′ s trisme m

lock′ nut′ s contre-écrou m

lock′out′ s lock-out m

lock′smith′ s serrurier m

lock′ step′ **—to march in lock step** emboîter le pas

lock′ stitch′ s point m indécousable

lock′ten′der s éclusier m

lock′up′ s (prison) (coll) bloc m, violon m

lock′ wash′er s rondelle f à ressort

locomotive [,lokə′motɪv] s locomotive f

lo·cus [′lokəs] s (pl -ci) [saɪ] lieu m; (math) lieu géométrique

locust [′lokəst] s (Pachytylus) (ent) criquet m migrateur, locuste f; (Cicada) (ent) cigale f; (bot) faux acacia m

lode [lod] s filon m, veine f

lode′star′ s (astr) étoile f polaire; (fig) pôle m d'attraction

lodge [lɑdʒ] s (of gatekeeper; of animal; of Mason) loge f; (residence, e.g., for hunting) pavillon m; (hotel) relais m, hostellerie f ‖ tr loger; **to lodge a complaint with** porter plainte auprès de ‖ intr loger; (said of arrow, bullet) se loger

lodger [′lɑdʒər] s locataire mf, pensionnaire mf

lodging [′lɑdʒɪŋ] s logement m; (of a complaint) déposition f

loft [lɔft] s (attic) grenier m, soupente f; (hayloft) fenil m; (in theater or church) tribune f; (in store or office building) atelier m

loft·y [′lɔfti] adj (comp -ier; super -iest) (towering; sublime) élevé, exalté; (haughty) hautain

log [lɔg] s (of wood) bûche f, rondin m; (record book) registre m de travail; (aer) livre m de vol; (record book) (naut) journal m de bord; (chip log) (naut) loch m; (rad) carnet m d'écoute; **to sleep like a log** dormir comme une souche ‖ v (pret & pp **logged**; ger **logging**) tr (wood) tron-

çonner; (an event) porter au journal; (a certain distance) (naut) filer ‖ intr (to cut wood) couper des rondins

logarithm [′lɔgə,rɪðəm] s logarithme m

log′book′ s (aer) livre m de vol; (naut) journal m de bord, livre de loch

log′ cab′in s cabane f en rondins

log′ chip′ s (naut) flotteur m de loch

log′ driv′er s flotteur m

log′ driv′ing s flottage m

logger [′lɔgər] s bûcheron m; (loader) (mach) grue f de chargement; (mach) tracteur m

log′ger·head′ s tête f de bois; **at logger-heads** en bisbille, aux prises

logic [′lɑdʒɪk] s logique f

logical [′lɑdʒɪkəl] adj logique

logician [lo′dʒɪʃən] s logicien m

logistic(al) [lo′dʒɪstɪk(əl)] adj logistique

logistics [lo′dʒɪstɪks] s logistique f

log′jam′ s embâcle m de bûches; (fig) bouchon m, embouteillage m

log′ line′ s (naut) ligne f de loch

log′roll′ intr faire trafic de faveurs politiques

log′wood′ s bois m de campêche; (tree) campêche m

loin [lɔɪn] s (of beef) aloyau m; (of veal) longe f; (of pork) échine f; **to gird up one's loins** se ceindre les reins

loin′cloth′ s pagne m

loiter [′lɔɪtər] tr—**to loiter away** perdre en flânant ‖ intr flâner

loiterer [′lɔɪtərər] s flâneur m

loll [lɑll] intr se prélasser, s'allonger, s'affaler

lollipop [′lɑli,pɑp] s sucette f

Lom′bardy pop′lar [′lɑmbərdi] s peuplier m noir

London [′lʌndən] adj londonien ‖ s Londres m

Londoner [′lʌndənər] s Londonien m

lone [lon] adj (alone) solitaire, seul; (sole, single) unique

loneliness [′lonlinɪs] s solitude f

lone·ly [′lonli] adj (comp -lier; super -liest) solitaire, isolé

lonesome [′lonsəm] adj solitaire, seul

lone′ wolf′ s (fig) solitaire mf, ours m

long [lɔŋ] (comp **longer** [′lɔŋgər]; super **longest** [′lɔŋgɪst]) adj long; de long, de longueur, e.g., **two meters long** deux mètres de long or de longueur ‖ adv longtemps; **as long as** aussi longtemps que; (provided that) tant que; **before long** sous peu; **how long?** combien de temps?, depuis combien de temps?, depuis quand?; **long ago** il y a longtemps; **long before** longtemps avant; **longer** plus long; **long since** depuis longtemps; **no longer** ne . . . plus longtemps; ne . . . plus, e.g., **I could no longer see him** je ne pouvais plus le voir; **so long!** (coll) à bientôt!; **so long as** tant que; **to be long in** tarder à ‖ intr—**to long for** soupirer pour or après

long′boat′ s chaloupe f

long′ dis′tance s (telp) l'interurbain m; **to call s.o. long distance** appeler qn par l'interurbain

long′-dis′tance call′ s (telp) appel m interurbain

long′-dis′tance flight′ s (aer) vol m au long cours, raid m aérien

long′-drawn′-out′ adj prolongé; (story) délayé

longevity [lɑn'dʒɛvɪti] s longévité f

long′ face′ s (coll) triste figure f

long′ hair′ adj & s intellectuel m; fanatique mf de la musique classique

long′-haired′ adj à cheveux longs

long′ hand′ s écriture f ordinaire; **in long-hand** à la main

longing ['lɔŋɪŋ] adj ardent ‖ s désir m ardent

longitude ['lɑndʒɪ,t(j)ud] s longitude f

long′ jump′ s saut m en longueur

long-lived ['lɔŋ'laɪvd], ['lɔŋ'lɪvd] adj à longue vie; persistant

long′-play′ing rec′ord s disque m de longue durée

long′ prim′er ['prɪmər] s (typ) philosophie f

long′-range′ adj à longue portée; (e.g., plan) à long terme

long′-range plane′ s long-courrier m

long′shore′man s (pl **-men**) arrimeur m, débardeur m

long′ shot′ s (turf) outsider m

long′-stand′ing adj de longue date

long′-suf′fering adj patient, endurant

long′ suit′ s (cards) couleur f longue, longue f; (fig) fort m

long′-term′ adj à longue échéance

long′-wind′ed ['wɪndɪd] adj interminable; (person) intarissable

look [lʊk] s (appearance) aspect m; (glance) regard m; **looks** apparence f, mine f; **to take a look at** jeter un coup d'œil sur or à ‖ tr regarder; (e.g., one's age) paraître; **to look daggers at** lancer un regard furieux à; **to look the part** avoir le physique de l'emploi; **to look up** (e.g., in a dictionary) chercher, rechercher; (to visit) aller voir, venir voir ‖ intr regarder; (to seek) chercher; **it looks like rain** le temps est à la pluie; **look here!** dites donc!; **look out!** gare!, attention!; **to look after** s'occuper de; (e.g., an invalid) soigner; **to look at** regarder; **to look away** détourner les yeux; **to look back** regarder en arrière; **to look down on** mépriser; **to look for** chercher; (to expect) s'attendre à; **to look forward to** s'attendre à, attendre avec impatience; **to look ill** avoir mauvaise mine; **to look in on** passer voir; **to look into** examiner, vérifier; **to look like** (s.o. or s.th.) ressembler à; (to give promise of) avoir l'air de; **to look out** faire attention; (e.g., the window) regarder par; **to look out on** donner sur; **to look through** (a window) regarder par; (a telescope) regarder dans; (a book) feuilleter; **to look toward** regarder du côté de; **to look up** lever les yeux; **to look up to** respecter; **to look well** avoir bonne mine

looker-on [,lʊkər'ɑn] s (pl **lookers-on**) spectateur m, assistant m

look′ing glass′ s miroir m

look′ out′ s (observation) guet m, surveillance f; (person) guetteur m; (place) poste m d'observation; (person or place) (naut) vigie f; **that's his lookout** (coll) ça, c'est son affaire; **to be on the lookout for** être à l'affût de

loom [lum] s métier m ‖ intr (to appear) apparaître indistinctement; (to threaten) menacer, paraître imminent; **to loom up** surgir, s'élever

loon [lun] s lourdaud m, sot m; (orn) plongeon m

loon·y ['luni] adj (comp **-ier**; super **-iest**) (slang) toqué ‖ s (pl **-ies**) (slang) toqué m

loop [lup] s boucle f; (for fastening a button) bride f; (circular route) boulevard m périphérique; (in skating) croisé m; **to loop the loop** (aer) boucler la boucle ‖ tr & intr boucler

loop′hole′ s meurtrière f; (fig) échappatoire f

loop′-the-loop′ s looping m

loose [lus] adj lâche; (stone, tooth) branlant; (screw) desserré; (pulley, wheel) fou; (rope) mou, détendu; (coat, dress) vague, ample; (earth, soil) meuble, friable; (bowels) relâché; (style) décousu; (translation) libre, peu exact; (life, morals) relâché, dissolu; (woman) facile; (unpackaged) en vrac; (unbound, e.g., pages) détaché; **to become loose** se détacher; **to break loose** (from captivity) s'évader; (fig) se déchaîner; **to let loose** lâcher, lâcher la bride à ‖ s—**to be on the loose** (to debauch) (coll) courir la prétentaine; (to be out of work) (coll) être sans occupation ‖ tr lâcher; (to untie) détacher

loose′ end′ s (fig) affaire f pendante; **at loose ends** désœuvré, indécis

loose′-leaf note′book s cahier m à feuilles mobiles

loosen ['lusən] tr lâcher, relâcher; (a screw) desserrer ‖ intr se relâcher

looseness ['lusnɪs] s relâchement m; (of garment) ampleur f; (play of screw) jeu m, desserrage m

loose′strife′ s (common yellow type) chasse-bosse f, grande lysimaque f; (spiked-purple type) salicaire f

loose′-tongued′ adj—**to be loose-tongued** avoir la langue déliée

loot [lut] s butin m, pillage m ‖ tr piller, saccager

lop [lɑp] v (pret & pp **lopped**; ger **lopping**) tr—**to lop off** abattre, trancher; (a tree, a branch) élaguer ‖ intr pendre

lope [lop] s galop m lent ‖ intr—**to lope along** aller doucement

lop′sid′ed adj déjeté, bancal

loquacious [lo'kweʃəs] adj loquace

lord [lɔrd] s seigneur m; (hum & poetic) époux m; (Brit) lord m ‖ tr—**to lord it over** dominer despotiquement, traiter avec arrogance

lord·ly [ˈlɔrdli] *adj* (*comp* **-lier**; *super* **-liest**) de grand seigneur, majestueux; (*arrogant*) hautain, altier

Lord's' Day' *s* jour *m* du Seigneur

lordship [ˈlɔrdʃɪp] *s* seigneurie *f*

Lord's' Prayer' *s* oraison *f* dominicale

Lord's Sup'per *s* communion *f*, cène *f*; Cène

lore [lor] *s* savoir *m*, science *f*; tradition *f* populaire

lorgnette [lɔrnˈjɛt] *s* (*eyeglasses*) face-à-main *m*; (*opera glasses*) lorgnette *f*

lor·ry [ˈlɔri] *s* (*pl* **-ries**) lorry *m*, wagonnet *m*; (*truck*) (Brit) camion *m*; (*wagon*) (Brit) fardier *m*

lose [luz] *v* (*pret & pp* **lost** [lɔst]) *tr* perdre; (*a patient who dies*) ne pas réussir à sauver; (*several minutes, as a timepiece does*) retarder de; **to lose oneself in** s'absorber dans; **to lose one's way** s'égarer ‖ *intr* perdre; (*said of timepiece*) retarder

loser [ˈluzər] *s* perdant *m*

losing [ˈluzɪŋ] *adj* perdant ‖ **losings** *spl* pertes *fpl*

loss [lɔs] *s* perte *f*; **to be at a loss** ne savoir que faire; **to be at a loss** to avoir de la peine à, être bien embarrassé pour; **to sell at a loss** vendre à perte

loss' of face' *s* perte *f* de prestige

lost [lɔst] *adj* perdu; **lost in thought** perdu or absorbé dans ses pensées; **lost to** perdu pour

lost'-and-found' depart'ment *s* bureau *m* des objets trouvés

lost' sheep' *s* brebis *f* perdue, brebis égarée

lot [lɑt] *s* lot *m*; (*for building*) lotissement *m*, lot; (*fate*) sort *m*, lot; **a bad lot** (coll) un mauvais sujet, de la mauvaise graine; **a lot of** or **lots of** (coll) un tas de; **a queer lot** (coll) un drôle de numéro; **in a lot** en bloc; **to cast** or **to throw in one's lot with** tenter la fortune avec; **to draw** or **to cast lots** tirer au sort; **such a lot of**, tellement de; **what a lot of . . . !** que de . . . !

lotion [ˈloʃən] *s* lotion *f*

lotter·y [ˈlɑtəri] *s* (*pl* **-ies**) loterie *f*

lotto [ˈlɑto] *s* loto *m*

lotus [ˈlotəs] *s* lotus *m*

loud [lɑud] *adj* (*volume*) haut, fort; (*noisy*) bruyant; (*voice*) fort; (*showy*) voyant ‖ *adv* fort; (*noisily*) bruyamment; **out loud** à haute voix

loud·mouthed [ˈlɑud,mauθt] *adj* au verbe haut, gueulard

loud'speak'er *s* haut-parleur *m*

Louisiana [lu,izɪˈænə] *s* Louisiane *f*; la Louisiane

lounge [lɑundʒ] *s* divan *m*, sofa *m*; (*room*) petit salon *m*, salle *f* de repos; (*in a hotel*) hall *m* ‖ *intr* flâner; (*e.g., in a chair*) se vautrer

lounge' liz'ard *s* (slang) gigolo *m*

louse [lɑus] *s* (*pl* **lice** [lɑis]) pou *m*; (slang) salaud *m* ‖ *tr*—**to louse up** (slang) bâcler

lous·y [ˈlɑuzi] *adj* (*comp* **-ier**; *super* **-iest**) pouilleux; (*mean; ugly*) (coll) moche;

(*bungling*) (coll) maladroit, gauche; **lousy with** (slang) chargé de

lout [lɑut] *s* lourdaud *m*, balourd *m*

louver [ˈluvər] *s* abat-vent *m*; (aut) auvent *m*

lovable [ˈlʌvəbəl] *adj* aimable, sympathique

love [lʌv] *s* amour *m*; (*ending a letter*) affectueusement, bons baisers, je t'embrasse; passion *f*, e.g., **the theater was her great love** le théâtre était sa grande passion; (tennis) zéro *m*; **in love with** amoureux de; **love at first sight** le coup de foudre; **love to all!** vives amitiés à tous!; **not for love or money** pour rien au monde, à aucun prix; **to make love to** faire la cour à; **with much love!** avec mes affectueuses pensées! ‖ *tr & intr* aimer

love' affair' *s* affaire *f* de cœur

love'birds' *spl* (orn) perruches *fpl* inséparables; (*persons*) (fig) tourtereaux *mpl*

love' child' *s* enfant *mf* de l'amour

love' feast' *s* (eccl) agape *f*

love' game' *s* (tennis) jeu *m* blanc

love' knot' *s* lacs *m* d'amour

loveless [ˈlʌvlɪs] *adj* sans amour; (*feeling no love*) insensible à l'amour

love' let'ter *s* billet *m* doux

lovelorn [ˈlʌv,lɔrn] *adj* délaissé d'amour, éperdu d'amour

love·ly [ˈlʌvli] *adj* (*comp* **-lier**; *super* **-liest**) beau; (*adorable*) charmant, gracieux; (*enjoyable*) (coll) agréable, aimable

love' match' *s* mariage *m* d'amour

love' nest' *s* nid *m* d'amoureux

love' po'tion *s* philtre *m* d'amour

lover [ˈlʌvər] *s* amoureux *m*, amant *m*; (*of hunting, sports, music, etc.*) amateur *m*, fanatique *mf*

love' seat' *s* causeuse *f*

love'sick' *adj* féru d'amour

love'sick'ness *s* mal *m* d'amour

love' song' *s* romance *f*, chanson *f* d'amour

love' sto'ry *s* histoire *f* d'amour

loving [ˈlʌvɪŋ] *adj* aimant, affectueux; affectionné, e.g., **your loving daughter** votre fille affectionnée

lov'ing cup' *s* coupe *f* de l'amitié; trophée *m*

lov'ing-kind'ness *s* bonté *f* d'âme

low [lo] *adj* bas; (*speed; price*) bas; (*speed; price; number; light*) faible; (*opinion*) défavorable; (*dress*) décolleté; (*sound, note*) bas, grave; (*fever*) lent; (*bow*) profond; **to lay low** étendre, terrasser; **to lie low** se tenir coi ‖ *s* bas *m*; (*moo of cow*) meuglement *m*; (aut) première vitesse *f*; (meteo) dépression *f* ‖ *adv* bas; **to speak low** parler à voix basse ‖ *intr* (*said of cow*) meugler

low'born' *adj* de basse naissance

low'boy' *s* commode *f* basse

low'brow' *adj* (coll) peu intellectuel ‖ *s* (coll) ignorant *m*

low'-cost' hous'ing *s* habitations *fpl* à loyer modéré or à bon marché

Low' Coun'tries *spl* Pays-Bas *mpl*

low'-down' *adj* (coll) bas, vil ‖ **low'-down'** *s* (slang) faits *mpl* véritables; **to**

give s.o. the low-down on (slang) tuyauter qn sur

lower ['loˑər] *adj* inférieur, bas ‖ *tr & intr* baisser ‖ ['lauˑər] *intr* se renfrogner, regarder de travers

low′er berth′ *s* couchette *f* inférieure

low′er case′ *s* (typ) bas *m* de casse

low′er mid′dle class′ *s* petite bourgeoisie *f*

lowermost ['loˑər,most] *adj* (le) plus bas

low′-fre′quency *adj* à basse fréquence

low′ gear′ *s* première vitesse *f*

low′-in′come hous′ing *s* habitations *fpl* à bon marché (HBM)

lowland ['loland] *s* plaine *f* basse; **Lowlands** (*in Scotland*) Basse-Écosse *f*

low·ly ['loli] *adj* (*comp* **-lier**; *super* **-liest**) humble, modeste; (*in growth or position*) bas, infime

Low′ Mass′ *s* messe basse *f*, petite messe

low′-mind′ed *adj* d'esprit vulgaire

low′ neck′ *s* décolleté *m*

low′-necked *adj* décolleté

low′-pitched′ *adj* (*sound*) grave; (*roof*) à faible inclinaison

low′-pres′sure *adj* à basse pression

low′-priced′ *adj* à bas prix

low′ shoe′ *s* soulier *m* bas

low′-speed′ *adj* à petite vitesse

low′-spir′ited *adj* abattu

low′ spir′its *spl* abattement *m*, accablement *m*

low′ tide′ *s* marée *f* basse

low′ vis′ibil′ity *s* (aer) mauvaise visibilité *f*

low′-warp′ *adj* (tex) de basse lice

low′ wa′ter *s* (*of river*) étiage *m*; (*of sea*) niveau *m* des basses eaux; marée *f* basse

loyal ['lɔɪˑəl] *adj* loyal

loyalist ['lɔɪˑəlɪst] *s* loyaliste *mf*

loyal·ty ['lɔɪˑəlti] *s* (*pl* **-ties**) loyauté *f*

lozenge ['lazɪndʒ] *s* (*candy cough drop*) pastille *f*; (geom) losange *m*

LP ['ɛl'pi] *s* (letterword) (trademark) (**long-playing**) disque *m* de longue durée

lubricant ['lubrɪkənt] *adj & s* lubrifiant *m*

lubricate ['lubrɪ,ket] *tr* lubrifier

lubricous ['lubrɪkəs] *adj* (*slippery*) glissant, (*lewd*) lubrique; inconstant

lucerne [luˈsʌrn] *s* luzerne *f*

lucid ['lusɪd] *adj* lucide

luck [lʌk] *s* (*good or bad*) chance *f*; (*good*) chance, bonne chance; **to be down on one's luck, to be out of luck** avoir de la malchance, être dans la déveine; **to be in luck** avoir de la chance, avoir de la veine; **to bring luck** porter bonheur; **to try one's luck** tenter la fortune, tenter l'aventure; **worse luck!** tant pis!, pas de chance!

luckily ['lʌkɪli] *adv* heureusement, par bonheur

luckless ['lʌklɪs] *adj* malheureux, malchanceux

luck·y ['lʌki] *adj* (*comp* **-ier**; *super* **-iest**) heureux, fortuné; (*supposed to bring luck*) porte-bonheur; **how lucky!** quelle chance!; **to be lucky** avoir de la chance, être verni, avoir du pot

luck′y charm′ *s* porte-bonheur *m*

luck′y dog′ *s* (coll) veinard *m*

luck′y find′ *s* (coll) trouvaille *f*

luck′y hit′ *s* (coll) coup *m* de bonheur, coup de chance

lucrative ['lukrətɪv] *adj* lucratif

ludicrous ['ludɪkrəs] *adj* ridicule, risible

lug [lʌg] *s* oreille *f*; (*pull, tug*) saccade *f* ‖ *v* (*pret & pp* **lugged**; *ger* **lugging**) *tr* traîner, tirer; (*to bring up irrelevantly*) (coll) ressortir, amener de force

luggage ['lʌgɪdʒ] *s* bagages *mpl*

lug′gage car′rier *s* porte-bagages *m*

lugubrious [luˈg(j)ubrɪˑəs] *adj* lugubre

lukewarm ['luk′wɔrm] *adj* tiède

lull [lʌl] *s* accalmie *f* ‖ *tr* bercer, endormir, calmer

lulla·by ['lʌlə,baɪ] *s* (*pl* **-bies**) berceuse *f*

lumbago [lʌm′bego] *s* lumbago *m*

lumber ['lʌmbər] *s* bois *m* de charpente, bois de construction ‖ *intr* se traîner lourdement

lum′ber·jack′ *s* bûcheron *m*

lum′ber jack′et *s* canadienne *f*

lum′ber·man *s* (*pl* **-men**) (*dealer*) exploitant *m* forestier, propriétaire *m* forestier; (*man who cuts down lumber*) bûcheron *m*

lum′ber raft′ *s* train *m* de flottage

lum′ber room′ *s* fourre-tout *m*, débarras *m*

lum′ber·yard′ *s* chantier *m* de bois, dépôt *m* de bois de charpente

luminar·y ['lumɪ,nɛri] *s* (*pl* **-ies**) corps *m* lumineux; (astr) luminaire *m*; (*person*) (fig) lumière *f*

luminescent [,lumi′nɛsənt] *adj* luminescent

luminous ['lumɪnəs] *adj* lumineux

lummox ['lʌməks] *s* (coll) lourdaud *m*

lump [lʌmp] *s* masse *f*; (*of earth*) motte *f*; (*of sugar*) morceau *m*; (*of salt, flour, porridge, etc.*) grumeau *m*; (*swelling*) bosse *f*; (*of ice, stone, etc.*) bloc *m*; **in the lump** en bloc; **to get a lump in one's throat** avoir un serrement de gorge ‖ *tr* réunir; **to lump together** prendre en bloc, englober ‖ *intr*—**to lump along** marcher d'un pas lourd

lumpish ['lʌmpɪʃ] *adj* balourd

lump′ sug′ar *s* sucre *m* en morceaux

lump′ sum′ *s* somme *f* globale

lump·y ['lʌmpi] *adj* (*comp* **-ier**; *super* **-iest**) grumeleux; (*covered with lumps*) couvert de bosses; (sea) clapoteux

luna·cy ['lunəsi] *s* (*pl* **-cies**) folie *f*

lu′nar land′er ['lunər] *s* alunisseur *m*

lu′nar land′ing *s* alunissage *m*

lu′nar mod′ule *s* (rok) module *m* lunaire

lunatic ['lunətɪk] *adj & s* fou *m*

lu′natic asy′lum *s* maison *f* de fous

lu′natic fringe′ *s* minorité *f* fanatique, frange *f* des dingues

lunch [lʌntʃ] *s* (*midday meal*) déjeuner *m*; (*light meal*) collation *f*, petit repas *m* ‖ *intr* déjeuner; (*to snack*) casser la croûte, manger sur le pouce

lunch′ bas′ket *s* panier *m* à provisions

lunch′ cloth′ *s* nappe *f* à thé

lunch′ coun′ter *s* snack *m*, buffet *m*

luncheon ['lʌntʃən] *s* déjeuner *m*

luncheonette [,lʌntʃə'nɛt] s brasserie f, café-restaurant m
lunch' room' s brasserie f, café-restaurant m
lunch' time' s heure f du déjeuner
lung [lʌŋ] s poumon m
lung' can'cer s cancer m du poumon
lunge [lʌndʒ] s mouvement m en avant; (with a sword) botte f || intr se précipiter en avant; (with a sword) se fendre; **to lunge at** porter une botte à
lurch [lʌrtʃ] s embardée f; (of person) secousse f; **to leave in the lurch** laisser en plan || intr faire une embardée; (said of person) vaciller
lure [lʊr] s (decoy) leurre m, amorce f; (fig) attrait m || tr leurrer; **to lure away** détourner
lurid ['lʊrɪd] adj sensationnel; (gruesome) terrible, macabre; (fiery) rougeoyant; (livid) blafard
lurk [lʌrk] intr se cacher; (to prowl) rôder
luscious ['lʌʃəs] adj délicieux, succulent; luxueux, somptueux
lush [lʌʃ] adj plein de sève; (abundant) luxuriant; opulent, luxueux
lust [lʌst] f désir m ardent; (greed) convoitise f, soif f; (strong sexual appetite) luxure f
luster ['lʌstər] s lustre m
lus'ter·ware' s poterie f lustrée, poterie à reflets métalliques
lustful ['lʌstfəl] adj luxurieux, lascif, lubrique
lustrous ['lʌstrəs] adj lustré, chatoyant

lust·y ['lʌsti] adj (comp **-ier**; super **-iest**) robuste, vigoureux
lute [lut] s (mus) luth m; (substance used to close or seal a joint) (chem) lut m
Lutheran ['luθərən] adj luthérien || s Luthérien m
Luxemburg ['lʌksəm,bʌrg] s le Luxembourg
luxuriant [lʌg'ʒʊrɪ·ənt] adj luxuriant; (overornamented) surchargé
luxurious [lʌg'ʒʊrɪ·əs] adj luxueux, somptueux
luxu·ry ['lʌgʒəri] s (pl **-ries**) luxe m
lux'ury i'tem s produit m de luxe
lux'ury tax' s impôt m somptuaire
lyceum [laɪ'si·əm] s lycée m
lye [laɪ] s lessive f
lying ['laɪ·ɪŋ] adj menteur || s le mensonge
ly'ing-in' hos'pital s maternité f, clinique f d'accouchement
lymph [lɪmf] s lymphe f
lymphatic [lɪm'fætɪk] adj lymphatique
lynch [lɪntʃ] tr lyncher
lynching ['lɪntʃɪŋ] s lynchage m
lynx [lɪŋks] s lynx m
Lyons ['laɪ·ənz] s Lyon m
lyre [laɪr] s (mus) lyre f
lyric ['lɪrɪk] adj lyrique || s poème m lyrique; **lyrics** (of song) paroles fpl; (theat) chansons fpl du livret
lyrical ['lɪrɪkəl] adj lyrique
lyricism ['lɪrɪ,sɪzəm] s lyrisme m
lyricist ['lɪrɪsɪst] s poète m lyrique; (writer of words for songs) parolier m

M

M, m [ɛm] XIIIᵉ lettre de l'alphabet
ma'am [mæm], [mɑm] s (coll) madame f
macadam [mə'kædəm] s macadam m
macadamize [mə'kædə,maɪz] tr macadamiser
macaroon [,mækə'run] s macaron m
macaw [mə'kɔ] s (orn) ara m
mace [mes] s masse f
mace'bear'er s massier m
machination [,mækɪ'neʃən] s machination f
machine [mə'ʃin] s machine f; (of a political party) noyau m directeur, leviers mpl de commande || tr usiner, façonner
machine'gun' s mitrailleuse f
ma·chine'-gun' v (pret & pp **-gunned**; ger **-gunning**) tr mitrailler
ma·chine'-made' adj fait à la machine
machiner·y [mə'ʃinəri] s (pl **-ies**) machinerie f, machines fpl; (of a watch; of government) mécanisme m; (in literature) merveilleux m
machine' screw' s vis f à métaux; vis à tôle
machine' shop' s atelier m d'usinage

machine' tool' s machine-outil f
machine' transla'tion s traduction f automatique
machinist [mə'ʃinɪst] s mécanicien m
mackerel ['mækərəl] s maquereau m
mack'erel sky' s ciel m pommelé or moutonné
mad [mæd] adj (comp **madder**; super **maddest**) fou; (dog) enragé; (coll) fâché, irrité; **as mad as a hatter** fou à lier; **like mad** (coll) comme un fou, éperdument; **to be mad about** (coll) être fou or passionné de; **to drive mad** rendre fou
madam ['mædəm] s madame f; (of a brothel) (slang) tenancière f
mad'cap' adj & s écervelé m, étourdi m
madden ['mædən] tr rendre fou || intr devenir fou
made-to-order ['medtə'ɔrdər] adj fait sur demande; (clothing) fait sur mesure
made'-up' adj inventé; (artificial) postiche; (face) maquillé
mad'house' s maison f de fous

mad′man′ *s* (*pl* **-men′**) fou *m*
madness ['mædnɪs] *s* folie *f*; (*of dog*) rage *f*
Madonna [mə'dɑnə] *s* madone *f*; (eccl) Madone
maelstrom ['melstrəm] *s* maelstrom *m*, tourbillon *m*
Mafia or **Maffia** ['mɑfɪ·ə] *s* mafia *f*, maffia *f*
magazine ['mægə,zin], [,mægə'zin] *s* (*periodical*) revue *f*, magazine *m*; (*warehouse; for cartridges of gun or camera; for munitions or powder*) magasin *m*; (naut) soute *f*
mag′azine′ rack′ *s* casier *m* à revues
Magdalen ['mægdələn] *s* Madeleine *f*
Maggie ['mægi] *s* (coll) Margot *f*
maggot ['mægət] *s* asticot *m*
Magi ['medʒaɪ] *spl* mages *mpl*
magic ['mædʒɪk] *adj* magique ‖ *s* magie *f*; **as if by magic** comme par enchantement
magician [mə'dʒɪʃən] *s* magicien *m*
mag′ic mark′er pen′ *s* crayon-feutre *m*
magisterial [,mædʒɪs'tɪrɪ·əl] *adj* magistral
magistrate ['mædʒɪs,tret] *s* magistrat *m*
Magna Charta ['mægnə'kɑrtə] *s* la Grande Charte *f*
magnanimous [mæg'nænɪməs] *adj* magnanime
magnate ['mægnet] *s* magnat *m*
magnesium [mæg'niʃɪ·əm] *s* magnésium *m*
magnet ['mægnɪt] *s* aimant *m*
magnetic [mæg'nɛtɪk] *adj* magnétique; (fig) attrayant, séduisant
magnetism ['mægnɪ,tɪzəm] *s* magétisme *m*
magnetize ['mægnɪ,taɪz] *tr* aimanter
magne·to [mæg'nito] *s* (*pl* **-tos**) magnéto *f*
magnificent [mæg'nɪfɪsənt] *adj* magnifique
magni·fy ['mægnɪ,faɪ] *v* (*pret & pp* **-fied**) *tr* grossir; (opt) grossir
mag′nifying glass′ *s* loupe *f*
magnitude ['mægnɪ,t(j)ud] *s* grandeur *f*; (astr) magnitude *f*
magpie ['mæg,paɪ] *s* (orn, fig) pie *f*
mahlstick ['mɑl,stɪk] *s* appui-main *m*
mahoga·ny [mə'hɑgəni] *s* (*pl* **-nies**) acajou *m*
mahout [mə'haut] *s* cornac *m*
maid [med] *s* (*servant*) bonne *f*; (*young woman*) jeune fille *f*, demoiselle *f*
maiden ['medən] *s* jeune fille *f*, demoiselle *f*
maid′en·hair′ *s* (bot) capillaire *m*
maid′en·head′ *s* hymen *m*
maid′en·hood′ *s* virginité *f*
maid′en la′dy *s* demoiselle *f*, célibataire *f*
maidenly ['medənli] *adj* virginal, de jeune fille
maid′en name′ *s* nom *m* de jeune fille
maid′en voy′age *s* premier voyage *m*
maid′-in-wait′ing *s* (*pl* **maids-in-waiting**) fille *f* d'honneur, dame *f* d'honneur
maid′ of hon′or *s* demoiselle *f* d'honneur
maid′serv′ant *s* fille *f* de service, servante *f*
mail [mel] *adj* postal ‖ *s* courrier *m*; (*system*) poste *f*; (*armor*) mailles *fpl*, cotte *f* de mailles; **by return mail** par retour du courrier; **mails** poste ‖ *tr* mettre à la poste, envoyer par la poste

mail′bag′ *s* sac *m* postal
mail′boat′ *s* paquebot *m*, bateau-poste *m*
mail′box′ *s* boîte *f* aux lettres
mail′ car′ *s* fourgon *m* postal, bureau *m* ambulant, wagon-poste *m*
mail′ car′rier *s* facteur *m*, préposé *m*
mail′ clerk′ *s* postier *m*; (mil, nav) vaguemestre *m*; (rr) convoyeur *m* des postes
mailing ['melɪŋ] *s* envoi *m*; (*preparation*) adressage *m*
mail′ing list′ *s* liste *f* d'adresses, (*of subscribers*) liste d'abonnés
mail′ing per′mit *s* (label on envelopes) dispensé du timbrage
mail′man′ *s* (*pl* **-men′**) facteur *m*
mail′ or′der *s* commande *f* par la poste
mail′-order house′ *s* établissement *m* de vente par correspondance or de vente sur catalogue; comptoir *m* postal (Canad)
mail′-order sell′ing *s* vente *f* par correspondance
mail′plane′ *s* avion *m* postal
mail′ train′ *s* train-poste *m*
maim [mem] *tr* mutiler, estropier
main [men] *adj* principal ‖ *s* (*sewer*) égout *m* collecteur, canalisation *f* or conduite *f* principale; **in the main** en général, pour la plupart
main′ clause′ *s* proposition *f* principale
main′ course′ *s* (culin) plat *m* principal, pièce *f* de résistance
main′ deck′ *s* pont *m* principal
main′ en′trance *s* entrée *f* principale
main′ floor′ *s* rez-de-chaussée *m*
mainland ['men,lænd], ['menlənd] *s* terre *f* ferme, continent *m*
main′ line′ *s* (rr) grande ligne *f*
mainly ['menli] *adv* principalement
mainmast ['menmɑst] *s* grand mât *m*
mainsail ['mensəl] *s* grand-voile *f*
main′spring′ *s* (*of watch*) ressort *m* moteur, grand ressort; (fig) mobile *m* essentiel, principe *m*
main′stay′ *s* (naut) étai *m* de grand mât; (fig) point *m* d'appui
main′ street′ *s* rue *f* principale
maintain [men'ten] *tr* maintenir; (*e.g., a family*) entretenir, faire subsister
maintenance ['mentɪnəns] *s* entretien *m*, maintien *m*; (*department entrusted with upkeep*) services *mpl* d'entretien, maintenance *f*
maître d'hôtel [,metərdo'tɛl] *s* maître *m* d'hôtel
maize [mez] *s* maïs *m*
majestic [mə'dʒɛstɪk] *adj* majestueux
majes·ty ['mædʒɪsti] *s* (*pl* **-ties**) majesté *f*
major ['medʒər] *adj* majeur ‖ *s* (*person of full legal age*) majeur *m*; (educ) spécialisation *f*; (mil) commandant *m* ‖ *intr* (educ) se spécialiser
Majorca [mə'dʒɔrkə] *s* Majorque *f*; île *f* de Majorque
Majorcan [mə'dʒɔrkən] *adj* majorquin ‖ *s* Majorquin *m*
ma′jor gen′eral *s* général *m* de division

majori·ty [mə'dʒɑrɪti], [mə'dʒɔrɪti] *adj* majoritaire ‖ *s* (*pl* **-ties**) majorité *f*; (mil) grade *m* de commandant; **the majority of** la plupart de

major'ity vote' *s* scrutin *m* majoritaire

make [mek] *s* (*brand name*) marque *f*; (*production*) fabrication *f*; **on the make** (coll) prêt à tout pour faire fortune ‖ *v* (*pret & pp* **made** [med]) *tr* faire; rendre, e.g., **to make sick** rendre malade; (*money*) gagner; (*the cards*) battre; (*a train*) attraper; **to make into** transformer en; **to make known** faire savoir; **to make out** déchiffrer, distinguer; (*a bill, receipt, check*) écrire; (*a list*) dresser; **to make s.o.** + *inf* faire + *inf* + qn, e.g., **I will make my uncle talk** je ferai parler mon oncle ‖ *intr* être, e.g., **to make sure** être sûr; **to make believe** feindre; **to make good** réussir; **to make off** filer, décamper

make'-believe' *adj* simulé ‖ *s* faux-semblant *m*, feinte *f*

maker ['mekər] *s* fabricant *m*

make'shift' *adj* de fortune, de circonstance ‖ *s* expédient *m*; (*person*) bouche-trou *m*

make'-up' *s* arrangement *m*, composition *f*; (*cosmetic*) maquillage *m*; (typ) mise *f* en pages, imposition *f*

make'-up man' *s* (theat) maquilleur *m*; (typ) metteur *m* en pages, imposeur *m*

make'weight' *s* complément *m* de poids

making ['mekɪŋ] *s* fabrication *f*; (*of a dress; of a cooked dish*) confection *f*; **makings** éléments *mpl* constitutifs; (*money*) recettes *fpl*; **to have the makings of** avoir l'étoffe de

maladjusted [,mælə'dʒʌstɪd] *adj* inadapté

maladjustment [,mælə'dʒʌstmənt] *s* inadaptation *f*

mala·dy ['mælədi] *s* (*pl* **-dies**) maladie *f*

malaise [mæ'lez] *s* malaise *m*

malaria [mə'lɛrɪ·ə] *s* malaria *f*, paludisme *m*

Malay ['mele], [mə'le] *adj* malais ‖ *s* (*language*) malais *m*; (*person*) Malais *m*

Malaya [mə'le·ə] *s* Mallaisie *f*; la Malaisie

malcontent ['mælkən,tɛnt] *adj & s* mécontent *m*

male [mel] *adj & s* mâle *m*

malediction [,mælɪ'dɪkʃən] *s* malédiction *f*

malefactor ['mælɪ,fæktər] *s* malfaiteur *m*

male' nurse' *s* infirmier *m*

malevolent [mə'lɛvələnt] *adj* malveillant

malfeasance [,mæl'fizəns] *s* prévarication *f*, trafic *m*

malice ['mælɪs] *s* méchanceté *f*, malice *f*

malicious [mə'lɪʃəs] *adj* méchant

malign [mə'laɪn] *adj* pernicieux; malveillant ‖ *tr* calomnier

malignan·cy [mə'lɪgnənsi] *s* (*pl* **-cies**) malignité *f*

malignant [mə'lɪgnənt] *adj* méchant, malin

malinger [mə'lɪŋgər] *intr* faire le malade

malingerer [mə'lɪŋgərər] *s* simulateur *m*

mall [mɔl], [mæl] *s* (*tree-lined walk*) mail *m*, allée *f*; (*shopping mall*) galerie *f* marchande

mallard ['mælərd] *s* (orn) col-vert *m*

malleable ['mælɪ·əbəl] *adj* malléable

mallet ['mælɪt] *s* maillet *m*

mallow ['mælo] *s* (bot) mauve *f*

malnutrition [,mæln(j)u'trɪʃən] *s* sous-alimentation *f*, malnutrition *f*

malodorous [mæl'odərəs] *adj* malodorant

malpractice [mæl'præktɪs] *s* incurie *f*, méfait *m*; (med) incurie professionnelle, négligence *f*, faute *f* professionnelle

malt [mɔlt] *s* malt *m*

maltreat [mæl'trit] *tr* maltraiter

mamma ['mɑmə], [mə'mɑ] *s* maman *f*

mammal ['mæməl] *s* mammifère *m*

mammalian [mæ'melɪ·ən] *adj & s* mammifère *m*

mammoth ['mæməθ] *adj* énorme, colossal ‖ *s* mammouth *m*

man [mæn] *s* (*pl* **men** [mɛn]) *s* homme *m*; (*servant*) domestique *m*; (*worker*) ouvrier *m*, employé *m*; (checkers) pion *m*; (chess) pièce *f*; **a man** on, e.g., **what can a man do?** qu'est-ce qu'on peut faire?; **every man for himself!** sauve qui peut!; **man alive!** (coll) tiens!; fichtre!; **man and wife** mari et femme; **men at work** (public sign) travaux en cours ‖ *v* (*pret & pp* **manned**; *ger* **manning**) *tr* (*a ship*) équiper; (*a fort*) garnir; (*a cannon, the pumps, etc.*) armer; (*a battery*) servir

man' about town' *s* boulevardier *m*, coureur *m* de cabarets

manacle ['mænəkəl] *s* manilla *f*; **manacles** menottes *fpl* ‖ *tr* mettre les menottes à

manage ['mænɪdʒ] *tr* gérer, diriger; (*to handle*) manier ‖ *intr* se débrouiller; **how did you manage to . . . ?** comment avez-vous fait pour . . . ?; **to manage to** s'arranger pour

manageable ['mænɪdʒəbəl] *adj* maniable

management ['mænɪdʒmənt] *s* direction *f*, gérance *f*; (*group who manage*) direction, administration *f*; (*in contrast to labor*) patronat *m*; **under new management** (public sign) changement de propriétaire

manager [mænədʒər] *s* directeur *m*, gérant *m*; (*e.g., of a department*) chef *m*; (*impresario*) manager *m*

managerial [,mænə'dʒɪrɪ·əl] *adj* patronal

man'aging ed'itor *s* rédacteur *m* gérant

Manchuria [mæn'turɪə] *s* Mandchourie *f*; la Mandchourie

man'darin or'ange ['mændərɪn] *s* mandarine *f*

mandate ['mændet] *s* mandat *m* ‖ *tr* placer sous le mandat de

mandatory ['mændə,tori] *adj* obligatoire

mandolin ['mændəlɪn] *s* mandoline *f*

mandrake ['mændrek] *s* mandragore *f*

mane [men] *s* crinière *f*

maneuver [mə'nuvər] *s* manœuvre *m* ‖ *tr & intr* manœuvrer

manful ['mænfəl] *adj* viril, hardi

manganese ['mæŋgə,nis] *s* manganèse *m*

mange [mendʒ] *s* gale *f*

manger ['mendʒər] *s* mangeoire *f*, crèche *f*

mangle ['mæŋgəl] *s* calandre *f* ‖ *tr* lacérer, mutiler; (*to press*) calandrer

man·gy ['mendʒi] *adj* (*comp* **-gier;** *super* **-giest**) galeux; (*dirty, squalid*) miteux

man'han'dle *tr* malmener

man'hole' *s* trou *m* d'homme, regard *m*

manhood ['mænhʊd] *s* virilité *f*; humanité *f*

man'hunt' *s* chasse *f* à l'homme; chasse au mari

mania ['meni·ə] *s* manie *f*

maniac ['meni,æk] *adj & s* maniaque *mf*

maniacal [mə'naɪ·əkəl] *adj* maniaque

manicure [mænɪ,kjʊr] *s* soins *mpl* esthétiques des mains et des ongles; (*person*) manucure *mf* ‖ *tr* manucurer

manicurist ['mænɪ,kjʊrɪst] *s* manucure *mf*

manifest ['mænɪ,fɛst] *adj* manifeste ‖ *s* (naut) manifeste *m* ‖ *tr & intr* manifester

manifestation [,mænɪfɛs'teʃən] *s* manifestation *f*

manifes·to [,mænɪ'fɛsto] *s* (*pl* **-toes**) manifeste *m*

manifold ['mænɪ,fold] *adj* multiple, nombreux ‖ *s* (aut) tuyauterie *f*, collecteur *m*

manikin ['mænɪkɪn] *s* mannequin *m*; (*dwarf*) nabot *m*

man' in the moon' *s* homme *m* dans la lune

man' in the street' *s* homme *m* de la rue

manipulate [mə'nɪpjə,let] *tr* manipuler

man'kind' *s* le genre humain, l'humanité *f* ‖ **man'kind'** *s* le sexe fort, les hommes *mpl*

manliness ['mænlɪnɪs] *s* virilité *f*

man·ly ['mænli] *adj* (*comp* **-lier;** *super* **-liest**) viril, masculin

manna ['mænə] *s* manne *f*

manned' space'craft *s* vaisseau *m* spatial habité

mannequin ['mænɪkɪn] *s* mannequin *m*

manner ['mænər] *s* manière *f*; **by all manner of means** certainement; **by no manner of means** en aucune manière; **in a manner of speaking** pour ainsi dire; **in the manner of** à la, e.g., **in the manner of the French, in the French manner** à la manière française, à la française; **manners** manières; **manners of the time** mœurs *fpl* de l'époque; **to the manner born** créé et mis au monde pour ça

mannerism ['mænə,rɪzm] *s* maniérisme *m*

mannish ['mænɪʃ] *adj* hommasse

man' of let'ters *s* homme *m* de lettres, bel esprit *m*

man' of parts' *s* homme *m* de talent

man' of straw' *s* homme *m* de paille

man' of the world' *s* homme *m* du monde

man-of-war [,mænəv'wɔr] *s* (*pl* **men-of-war**) navire *m* de guerre

manor ['mænər] *s* seigneurie *f*

man'or house' *s* château *m*, manoir *m*

man' o'verboard' *interj* un homme à la mer!

man'pow'er *s* main-d'œuvre *f*; (mil) effectifs *mpl*

manse [mæns] *s* maison *f* du pasteur

man'serv'ant *s* (*pl* **-men'serv'ants**) valet *m*

mansion ['mænʃən] *s* hôtel *m* particulier; château *m*, manoir *m*

man'slaugh'ter *s* (law) homicide *m* involontaire

mantel ['mæntəl] *s* manteau *m* de cheminée

man'tel·piece' *s* manteau *m* de cheminée; dessus *m* de cheminée

mantilla [mæn'tɪlə] *s* mantille *f*

mantle ['mæntəl] *s* manteau *m*, mante *f*; (*of gaslight*) manchon *m* ‖ *tr* envelopper d'une mante; couvrir, revêtir; (*to hide*) voiler ‖ *intr* (*said of face*) rougir

manual ['mænjʊ·əl] *adj* manuel ‖ *s* (*book*) manuel *m*; (*of arms*) (mil) maniement *m*; (mus) clavier *m* d'orgue

man'ual dexter'ity *s* habileté *f* manuelle

man'ual train'ing *s* apprentissage *m* manuel

manufacture [,mænjə'fæktʃər] *s* fabrication *f*; (*thing manufactured*) produit *m* fabriqué ‖ *tr* fabriquer

manufacturer [,mænjə'fæktʃərər] *s* fabricant *m*

manure [mə'n(j)ʊr] *s* fumier *m* ‖ *tr* fumer

manuscript ['mænjə,skrɪpt] *adj & s* manuscrit *m*

many ['mɛni] *adj* beaucoup de; **a good many** bien des, maintes; **how many** combien de; **many another** bien d'autres; **many more** beaucoup d'autres; **so many** tant de; **too many** trop de; **twice as many** deux fois autant de ‖ *pron* beaucoup; **as many** as autant de; jusqu'à, e.g., **as many as twenty** jusqu'à vingt; **how many** combien; **many a** maint; **many another** bien d'autres; **many more** beaucoup d'autres; **so many** tant; **too many** trop; **twice as many** deux fois autant

man'y-sid'ed *adj* polygonal; (*having many interests or capabilities*) complexe

map [mæp] *s* carte *f*; (*of a city*) plan *m* ‖ *v* (*pret & pp* **mapped;** *ger* **mapping**) *tr* faire la carte de; **to map out** tracer le plan de; **to put on the map** (coll) faire connaître, mettre en vedette

maple ['mepəl] *s* érable *m*

ma'ple sug'ar *s* sucre *m* d'érable

mar [mɑr] *v* (*pret & pp* **marred;** *ger* **marring**) *tr* défigurer, gâcher

marathon ['mærə,θɑn] *s* marathon *m*

maraud [mə'rɔd] *tr* piller ‖ *intr* marauder

marauder [mə'rɔdər] *s* maraudeur *m*

marauding [mə'rɔdɪŋ] *adj* maraudeur ‖ *s* maraude *f*

marble ['mɑrbəl] *s* marbre *m*; (*little ball of glass*) bille *f*; **marbles** (game) jeu *m* de billes ‖ *tr* marbrer; (*the edge of a book*) jasper

march [mɑrtʃ] *s* marche *f*; **March** mars *m*; **to steal a march on** prendre de l'avance sur ‖ *tr* faire marcher ‖ *intr* marcher

marchioness ['mɑrʃənɪs] *s* marquise *f*

mare [mɛr] *s* (*female horse*) jument *m*; (*female donkey*) ânesse *f*

Margaret ['mɑrgərɪt] *s* Marguerite *f*

margarine ['mɑrdʒərɪn] *s* margarine *f*

margin [`mɑrdʒɪn] s marge f; (*border*) bord m; (com) acompte m

mar'gin account' s (com) compte m de couverture

marginal [`mɑrdʒɪnəl] adj marginal

mar'gin release' s déclenche-marge f, touche f marge libre, touche passe-marge

mar'gin set'ter s pose-marge f

mar'gin stop' s margeur m

marigold [`mærɪ,gold] s (*Calendula*) souci m; (*Tagetes*) illet m d'Inde

marihuana or **marijuana** [,mɑrɪ`hwɑnə] s marihuana f or marijuana f

marinate [`mærɪ,net] tr mariner

marine [mə`rin] adj marin, maritime ‖ s flotte f; (nav) fusilier m marin; **tell it to the marines!** (coll) à d'autres!

Marine' Corps' s infanterie f de marine

mariner [`mærɪnər] s marin m

marionette [,mærɪ·ə`nɛt] s marionette f

marital [`mærɪtəl] adj matrimonial

mar'ital sta'tus s état m civil

maritime [`mærɪ,taɪm] adj maritime

marjoram [`mɑrdʒərəm] s marjolaine f; origan m

mark [mɑrk] s marque f, signe m; (*of punctuation*) point m; (*in an examination*) note f; (*spot, stain*) tache f, marque; (*monetary unit*) mark m; (*starting point in a race*) ligne f de départ; **as a mark of** en témoignage de; **Mark** Marc m; **on your mark!** à vos marques!; **to hit the mark** mettre dans le mille, atteindre le but; **to leave one's mark** laisser son empreinte; **to make one's mark** se faire un nom, marquer; **to miss the mark** manquer le but; **to toe the mark** se conformer au mot d'ordre ‖ tr marquer; (*a student; an exam*) donner une note à; (*e.g., one's approval*) témoigner; **to mark down** noter; (com) démarquer; **to mark off** distinguer; **to mark up** (com) majorer

mark'down' s rabais m

marker [`mɑrkər] s marqueur m; (*of boundary*) borne f; (*landmark*) repère m

market [`mɑrkɪt] s marché m; **to bear the market** jouer à la baisse; **to bull the market** jouer à la hausse; **to play the market** jouer à la bourse; **to put on the market** lancer, vendre, or mettre sur le marché ‖ tr commercialiser

marketable [`mɑrkɪtəbəl] adj vendable

mar'ket bas'ket s panier m à provisions

marketing [`mɑrkɪtɪŋ] s marché m; (*of a product*) commercialisation f, exploitation f

mar'ket·place' s place f du marché

mar'ket price' s cours m du marché, prix m courant

mark'ing gauge' s trusquin m

marks·man [`mɑrksmən] s (*pl* -men) tireur m

marks'man·ship' s habileté f au tir, adresse f au tir

mark'up' s (*profit*) marge f bénéficiaire; (*price increase*) majoration f de prix

marl [mɑrl] s marne f ‖ tr marner

marmalade [`mɑrmə,led] s marmelade f

maroon [mə`run] adj & s (*color*) lie f de vin, rouge m violacé, bordeaux ‖ tr abandonner, isoler

marquee [mɑr`ki] s marquise f

marquis [`mɑrkwɪs] s marquis m

marquise [mɑr`kiz] s marquise f

marriage [`mærɪdʒ] s mariage m

marriageable [`mærɪdʒəbəl] adj mariable

mar'riage certif'icate s acte m de mariage

mar'riage por'tion s dot f

mar'riage rate' s taux m de nuptialité

mar'ried life' [`mærɪd] s vie f conjugale

marrow [`mæro] s moelle f

mar·ry [`mæri] v (*pret & pp* -ried) tr (*to join in wedlock*) marier; (*to take in marriage*) se marier avec; **to get married to** se marier avec; **to marry off** marier ‖ intr se marier

Mars [mɑrz] s Mars m

Marseilles [mɑr`selz] s Marseille f

marsh [mɑrʃ] s marais m, marécage m

mar·shal [`mɑrʃəl] s maître m des cérémonies; (*policeman*) shérif m; (mil) maréchal m ‖ v (*pret & pp* -shaled or -shalled; *ger* -shaling or -shalling) tr conduire; (*one's reasons, arguments, etc.*) ranger, rassembler

marsh' mal'low s (bot) guimauve f

marsh'mal'low s (*sweetened paste*) pâte f de guimauve; (*candy*) bonbon m à la guimauve

marsh·y [`mɑrʃi] adj (*comp* -ier; *super* -iest) marécageux

mart [mɑrt] s marché m, foire f

marten [`mɑrtən] s (*pine marten*) martre f; (*beech marten*) fouine f

Martha [`mɑrθə] s Marthe f

martial [`mɑrʃəl] adj martial

mar'tial law' s loi f martiale

martin [`mɑrtɪn] s (orn) martinet m

martinet [,mɑrtɪ`nɛt] s pètesec m

martyr [`mɑrtər] s martyr m ‖ tr martyriser

martyrdom [`mɑrtərdəm] s martyre m

mar·vel [`mɑrvəl] s merveille f ‖ v (*pret & pp* -veled or -velled; *ger* -veling or -velling) intr s'émerveiller; **to marvel at** s'émerveiller de

marvelous [`mɑrvələs] adj merveilleux

Marxist [`mɑrksɪst] adj & s marxiste mf

Maryland [`mɛrələnd] s le Maryland

marzipan [`mɑrzɪ,pæn] s massepain m

mascara [mæs`kærə] s rimmel m

mascot [`mæskɑt] s mascotte f

masculine [`mæskjəlɪn] adj & s masculin m

mash [mæʃ] s (*crushed mass*) bouillie f; (*to form wort*) fardeau m ‖ tr écraser; (*malt, in brewing*) brasser

mashed' pota'toes spl purée f de pommes de terre

masher [`mæʃər] s (*device*) broyeur m; (slang) tombeur m

mask [mæsk] s masque m; (phot) cache m ‖ tr masquer; (phot) poser un cache à ‖ intr se masquer

masked' ball' s bal m masqué

mask'ing tape' s ruban m cache

mason ['mesən] s maçon m; **Mason** Maçon

mason·ry ['mesənri] s (pl **-ries**) maçonnerie f; **Masonry** Maçonnerie

masquerade [,mæskə'red] s mascarade f || intr se déguiser; **to masquerade as** se faire passer pour

mass [mæs] s masse f; (eccl) messe f || tr masser || intr se masser

massacre ['mæsəkər] s massacre m || tr massacrer

massage [mə'sɑʒ] s massage m || tr masser

mass' arrest' s rafle f

masseur [mə'sʌr] s masseur m

masseuse [mə'suz] s masseuse f

massive ['mæsɪv] adj massif

mass' me'dia ['midɪ·ə] spl communication f de masse, media mpl; journalistes mfpl; presse f, radio f, télé f

mass' meet'ing s meeting m monstre, rassemblement m

mass' produc'tion s fabrication f en série

mast [mæst] s mât m; (food for swine) gland m, faîne f; **before the mast** comme simple matelot

master ['mæstər] s maître m; (employer) chef m, patron m; (male head of household) maître de maison; (title of respect) Monsieur m; (naut) commandant m || tr maîtriser; (a subject) connaître à fond, posséder

mas'ter bed'room s chambre f du maître

mas'ter build'er s entrepreneur m de bâtiments

masterful ['mæstərfəl] adj magistral, expert; impérieux, en maître

mas'ter key' s passe-partout m

masterly ['mæstərli] adj magistral, de maître || adv magistralement

mas'ter mechan'ic s maître m mécanicien

mas'ter·mind' s organisateur m, cerveau m || tr organiser, diriger

mas'ter of cer'emonies s maître m des cérémonies; (in a night club, on television, etc.) animateur m

mas'ter·piece' s chef-d'œuvre m

mas'ter stroke' s coup m de maître

mas'ter tape' s bande f génératrice, bande mère, bande souche

mas'ter·work' s chef-d'œuvre m

master·y ['mæstəri] s (pl **-ies**) maîtrise f

mast'head' s (of a newspaper) en-tête m; (naut) tête f de mât

masticate ['mæstɪ,ket] tr mastiquer

mastiff ['mæstɪf] s mâtin m

masturbate ['mæstər,bet] tr masturber || intr se masturber

mat [mæt] s (for floor) natte f; (for a cup, vase, etc.) dessous m de plat; (before a door) paillasson m || v (pret & pp **matted**; ger **matting**) tr (to cover with matting) couvrir de nattes; (hair) emmêler; (with blood) coller || intr s'emmêler

match [mætʃ] s (producing fire) allumette f; (wick) mèche f; (counterpart) égal m, pair m; (suitable partner in marriage) parti m; (suitably associated pair) assortiment m; (game, contest) match m, partie f; **to be a**

match for être de la force de, être à la hauteur de; **to meet one's match** trouver son pareil || tr égaler; (objects) faire pendant à, assortir || intr s'assortir

match'box' s boîte f d'allumettes, porte-allumettes m

matchless ['mætʃlɪs] adj incomparable, sans pareil

match'mak'er s marieur m

mate [met] s (husband) conjoint m; (wife) conjointe f; (to a female) mâle m; (to a male) femelle f; (fellow worker) camarade mf; (one of a pair) l'autre gant m, l'autre soulier m, l'autre chaussure f (etc.); (checkmate) mat m; (naut) officier m en second, second maître m || tr marier; (zool) accoupler || intr se marier; s'accoupler

material [mə'tɪrɪ·əl] adj matériel; important || s matériel m; (what a thing is made of) matière f; (cloth, fabric) étoffe f; (archit) matériau m; **materials** matériaux mpl

materialist [mə'tɪrɪ·əlɪst] s matérialiste mf

materialistic [mə,tɪrɪ·ə'lɪstɪk] adj matérialiste, matériel

materialize [mə'tɪrɪə,laɪz] intr se matérialiser; (to be realized) se réaliser

matériel [mə,tɪrɪ'ɛl] s matériel m

maternal [mə'tʌrnəl] adj maternel

maternity [mə'tʌrnɪti] s maternité f

mater'nity dress' s robe f de grossesse

mater'nity hos'pital s maternité f

mater'nity room' s salle f d'accouchement

mater'nity ward' s salle f des accouchées

math [mæθ] s (coll) math fpl

mathematical [,mæθɪ'mætɪkəl] adj mathématique

mathematician [,mæθɪmə'tɪʃən] s mathématicien m

mathematics [,mæθɪ'mætɪks] s mathématiques fpl

matinée [,mætɪ'ne] s matinée f

mat'ing sea'son s saison f des amours

matins ['mætɪnz] spl matines fpl

matriarch ['metrɪ,ɑrk] s matrone f

matriar·chy ['metrɪ,ɑrki] s (pl **-chies**) matriarcat m

matricide ['mætrɪ,saɪd] s (person) matricide mf; (action) matricide m

matriculate [mə'trɪkjə,let] tr immatriculer || intr s'inscrire à l'université, prendre ses inscriptions

matriculation [mə,trɪkjə'leʃən] s inscription f; immatriculation f

matrimonial [,mætrɪ'monɪ·əl] adj matrimonial

matrimo·ny ['mætrɪ,moni] s (pl **-nies**) mariage m, vie f conjugale

ma·trix ['metrɪks] s (pl **-trices** [trɪ,siz] or **-trixes**) matrice f

matron ['metrən] s (woman no longer young, and of good standing) matrone f; intendante f, surveillante f

matronly ['metrənli] adj de matrone, digne, respectable

matter ['mætər] *s* matière *f*; (pathol) pus *m*; **a matter of** affaire de, une question de; **for that matter** à vrai dire; **no matter** n'importe, pas d'importance; **no matter when** n'importe quand; **no matter where** n'importe où; **no matter who** n'importe qui; **what is the matter?** qu'y a-t-il?; **what is the matter with you?** qu'avez-vous? ‖ *intr* importer; **it doesn't matter** cela ne fait rien

mat′ter of course′ *s* chose *f* qui va de soi

mat′ter of fact′ *s*—**as a matter of fact** en réalité, effectivement, de fait

matter-of-fact ['mætərəv‚fækt] *adj* prosaïque, terre à terre

mattock ['mætək] *s* pioche *f*

mattress ['mætrɪs] *s* matelas *m*

mat′tress cov′er *s* alèze *f*

mature [mə'tʃʊr], [mə'tʊr] *adj* mûr; (*due*) échu ‖ *tr* faire mûrir ‖ *intr* mûrir; (*to become due*) échoir

maturity [mə'tʃʊrɪti], [mə'tʊrɪti] *s* maturité *f*; (com) échéance *f*

maudlin ['mɔdlɪn] *adj* larmoyant

maul [mɔl] *tr* malmener; (*to split*) fendre au coin

maulstick ['mɔl‚stɪk] *s* appui-main *m*

Maun′dy Thurs′day [mɔndi] *s* jeudi *m* saint

mausole·um [‚mɔsə'li·əm] *s* (*pl* **-ums** or **-a** [ə]) mausolée *m*

maw [mɔ] *s* (*of birds*) jabot *m*; (*of fish*) poche *f* d'air

mawkish ['mɔkɪʃ] *adj* à l'eau de rose; (*sickening*) écœurant

maxim ['mæksɪm] *s* maxime *f*

maximum ['mæksɪməm] *adj* & *s* maximum *m*

May [me] *s* mai *m* ‖ (*l.c.*) *v* (*pret* & *cond* **might** [maɪt]) *aux*—**it may be** il ne peut; **may I?** vous permettez?; **may I** + *inf* puis-je + *inf*, est-ce que je peux + *inf*; **may I** (**may we, etc.**) + *inf* peut-on + *inf*; **may you be happy!** puissiez-vous être heureux!

maybe ['mebi] *adv* peut-être

May′ Day′ *s* le premier mai *m*

mayhem ['mehɛm] *s* mutilation *f*

mayonnaise [‚me·ə'nez] *s* mayonnaise *f*

mayor ['me·ər], [mɛr] *s* maire *m*

May′pole′ *s* mai *m*

May′ queen′ *s* reine *f* du premier mai

maze [mez] *s* labyrinthe *m*, dédale *m*

me [mi] *pron* moi §85, §87; me §87

meadow ['mɛdo] *s* prairie *f*, pré *m*

mead′ow·land′ *s* herbage *m*, prairie *f*

meager ['migər] *adj* maigre

meal [mil] *s* (*dinner, lunch, etc.*) repas *m*; (*grain*) farine *f*; **to miss a meal** serrer la ceinture d'un cran

meal′ tick′et *s* ticket-repas *m*; (*job*) gagne-pain *m*

meal′time′ *s* heure *f* du repas

meal·y ['mili] *adj* (*comp* **-ier**; *super* **-iest**) farineux

mean [min] *adj* (*intermediate*) moyen; (*low in station or rank*) bas, humble; (*shabby*) vil, misérable; (*stingy*) mesquin; (*small-minded*) bas, vilain, méprisable; (*vicious*) sauvage, mal intentionné; **no mean** fameux, excellent ‖ *s* milieu *m*, moyen terme *m*; (math) moyenne *f*; **by all means** de toute façon, je vous en prie; **by means of** au moyen de; **by no means** en aucune façon; **means** ressources *fpl*, fortune *f*; (*agency*) moyen *m*; **means to an end** moyens d'arriver à ses fins; **not by any means!** jamais de la vie! ‖ *v* (*pret* & *pp* **meant** [mɛnt]) *tr* vouloir dire, signifier; (*to intend*) entendre; (*to entail*) entraîner; **to mean s.th. for s.o.** destiner q.ch à qn; **to mean to** avoir l'intention de, compter ‖ *intr*—**to mean well** avoir de bonnes intentions

meander [mɪ'ændər] *s* méandre *m* ‖ *intr* faire des méandres

meaning ['minɪŋ] *s* signification *f*, sens *m*; intention *f*

meaningful ['minɪŋfəl] *adj* significatif

meaningless ['minɪŋlɪs] *adj* sans signification, dénué de sens

meanness ['minnɪs] *s* bassesse *f*, vilenie *f*; (*stinginess*) mesquinerie *f*

mean′time′ *s*—**in the meantime** dans l'intervalle, sur ces entrefaites ‖ *adv* entre-temps, en attendant

mean′while′ *s* & *adv* var of **meantime**

measles ['mizəlz] *s* rougeole *f*; (*German measles*) rubéole *f*

mea·sly ['mizli] *adj* (*comp* **-slier**; *super* **-sliest**) rougeoleux; (slang) piètre, insignifiant

measurable ['mɛʒərəbəl] *adj* mesurable

measure ['mɛʒər] *s* mesure *f*; (*step, procedure*) mesure *f*, démarche *f*; (*legislative bill*) projet *m* de loi; (mus, poetic) mesure *f*; **in a large measure** en grande partie; **in a measure** dans une certaine mesure; **to take measures to** prendre des mesures pour; **to take s.o.'s measure** (fig) prendre la mesure de qn ‖ *tr* mesurer; **to measure out** mesurer, distribuer ‖ *intr* mesurer

measurement ['mɛʒərmənt] *s* mesure *f*; **to take s.o.'s measurements** prendre les mesures de qn

meas′uring cup′ *s* verre *m* gradué

meat [mit] *s* viande *f*; (*food in general*) nourriture *f*; (*gist*) moelle *f*, substance *f*

meat′ball′ *s* boulette *f* de viande

meat′hook′ *s* croc *m*, allonge *f*

meat′ mar′ket *s* boucherie *f*

meat′ pie′ *s* tourte *f* à la viande, pâté *m* en croûte

meat·y ['miti] *adj* (*comp* **-ier**; *super* **-iest**) charnu; (fig) plein de substance, étoffé

Mecca ['mɛkə] *s* La Mecque

mechanic [mə'kænɪk] *s* mécanicien *m*; **mechanics** mécanique *f*

mechanical [mə'kænɪkəl] *adj* mécanique; (fig) mécanique, machinal

mechan′ical draw′ing *s* dessin *m* industriel

mechan′ical engineer′ *s* ingénieur *m* mécanicien

mechan'ical toy' *s* jouet *m* mécanique

mechanics [mɪ'kænɪks] *s* mécanique *f*

mechanism ['mɛkə,nɪzəm] *s* mécanisme *m*

mechanize ['mɛkə,naɪz] *tr* mécaniser

medal ['mɛdəl] *s* médaille *f*

medallion [mɪ'dæljən] *s* médaillon *m*

meddle ['mɛdəl] *intr* s'ingérer; **to meddle in** or **with** se mêler de, s'immiscer dans

meddler ['mɛdlər] *s* intrigant *m*, touche-à-tout *m*

meddlesome ['mɛdəlsəm] *adj* intrigant

media ['midɪ·ə] *s* (journ, rad, telv) journalistes *mfpl*; presse *f*, radio *f*, télé *f*; **the media** les media *mpl*

median ['midɪ·ən] *adj* médian ‖ *s* médiane *f*

me'dian strip' *s* bande *f* médiane

mediate ['midɪ,et] *tr* procurer par médiation, négocier ‖ *intr* s'entremettre, s'interposer

mediation [,midɪ'eʃən] *s* médiation *f*

mediator ['midɪ,etər] *s* médiateur *m*

medical ['mɛdɪkəl] *adj* médical

med'ical stu'dent *s* étudiant *m* en médicine

medicinal [mə'dɪsɪnəl] *adj* médicinal

medicine ['mɛdɪsɪn] *s* (*science and art*) médicine *f*; (pharm) médicament *m*

med'icine cab'inet *s* armoire *f* à pharmacie, armoire de toilette

med'icine kit' *s* pharmacie *f* portative

med'icine man' *s* (*pl* **men'**) sorcier *m* indien; (*mountebank*) charlatan *m*

medi·co ['mɛdɪ,ko] *s* (*pl* **-cos**) (slang) carabin *m*, morticole *m*

medieval [,midɪ'ivəl], [,mɛdɪ'ivəl] *adj* médiéval, moyenâgeux; (pej) périmé, funeste

medievalist [,mɛdɪ'ivəlɪst] *s* médiéviste *mf*

mediocre [,midɪ'okər] *adj* médiocre

mediocri·ty [,midɪ'akrɪti] *s* (*pl* **-ties**) médiocrité *f*

meditate ['mɛdɪ,tet] *tr & intr* méditer

meditation [,mɛdɪ'teʃən] *s* méditation *f*

Mediterranean [,mɛdɪtə'renɪ·ən] *adj* méditerranéen ‖ *s* Méditerranée *f*

medi·um ['midɪ·əm] *adj* moyen; (culin) à point ‖ *s* (*pl* **-ums** or **-a** [ə]) milieu *m*; (*means*) moyen *m*; (*in spiritualism*) médium *m*; (journ) organe *m*; **through the medium of** par l'intermédiaire de

me'dium of exchange' *s* agent *m* monétaire

me'dium-range' *adj* à portée moyenne

me'dium-sized' *adj* de grandeur moyenne

medlar ['mɛdlər] *s* (*fruit*) nèfle *f*; (*tree*) néflier *m*

medley ['mɛdli] *s* mélange *m*; (mus) pot-pourri *m*

medul·la [mɪ'dʌlə] *s* (*pl* **-lae** [li]) moelle *f*

Medusa [mə'duzə] *s* Méduse *f*

meek [mik] *adj* doux, humble

meekness ['miknɪs] *s* douceur *f*, humilité *f*

meerschaum ['mɪrʃəm] *s* écume *f* de mer; pipe *f* d'écume de mer

meet [mit] *adj*—**it is meet that** il convient que ‖ *s* (sports) meeting *m* ‖ *v* (*pret & pp* **met** [mɛt]) *tr* rencontrer; (*to make the acquaintance of*) faire la connaissance de; (*to go to meet*) aller au-devant de; (*a car in the street; a person on the sidewalk*) croiser; (*by appointment*) retrouver, rejoindre; (*difficulties; expenses*) faire face à; (*one's debts*) honorer; (*one's death*) trouver; (*a need*) satisfaire à; (*an objection*) réfuter; (*the ear*) frapper; **meet my wife (my friend, etc.)** je vous présente ma femme (mon ami, etc.) ‖ *intr* se rencontrer; (*for an appointment*) se retrouver, se rejoindre; (*to assemble*) se réunir; (*to join, touch*) se joindre, se toucher; (*said of rivers*) confluer; (*said of roads; said of cars, persons, etc.*) croiser; **till we meet again** au revoir; **to meet with** se recontrer avec, recontrer; (*difficulties, an affront, etc.*) subir

meeting ['mitɪŋ] *s* rencontre *f*; (*session*) séance *f*; (*assemblage*) réunion *f*, assemblée *f*; (*of an association*) congrès *m*; (*of two rivers*) confluent *m*; (*of two cars; of two roads*) croisement *m*; (pol) meeting *m*

meet'ing of the minds' *s* bonne entente *f*

meet'ing place' *s* rendez-vous *m*

megacycle ['mɛgə,saɪkəl] *s* mégacycle *m*

megaphone ['mɛgə,fon] *s* mégaphone *m*, porte-voix *m*

megohm ['mɛg,om] *s* mégohm *m*

melancholia [,mɛlən'kolɪ·ə] *s* mélancolie *f*

melanchol·y ['mɛlən,kali] *adj* mélancolique ‖ *s* (*pl* **-ies**) mélancolie *f*

melee ['mele] *s* mêlée *f*

mellow ['mɛlo] *adj* moelleux; enjoué, débonnaire; (*ripe*) mûr ‖ *tr* rendre moelleux, mûrir

melodic [mɪ'ladɪk] *adj* mélodique

melodious [,mɪ'lodɪ·əs] *adj* mélodieux

melodramatic [,mɛlədrə'mætɪk] *adj* mélodramatique

melo·dy ['mɛlədi] *s* (*pl* **-dies**) mélodie *f*

melon ['mɛlən] *s* melon *m*

melt [mɛlt] *tr & intr* fondre; **to melt into** (*e.g., tears*) fondre en

melt'ing pot' *s* creuset *m*

member ['mɛmbər] *s* membre *m*

mem'ber·ship' *s* membres *mpl*; (*in a club, etc.*) association *f*; (*belonging*) appartenance *f*

mem'bership blank' *s* bulletin *m* d'adhésion

membrane ['mɛmbren] *s* membrane *f*

memen·to [mɪ'mɛnto] *s* (*pl* **-tos** or **-toes**) mémento *m*

mem·o ['mɛmo] *s* (*pl* **-os**) (coll) note *f*, rappel *m*

mem'o book' *s* calepin *m*, mémento *m*

memoir ['mɛmwar] *s* biographie *f*; **memoirs** mémoires *mpl*

mem'o pad' *s* bloc-notes *m*, bloc *m*

memoran·dum [,mɛmə'rændəm] *s* (*pl* **-dums** or **-da** [də]) memorandum *m*; note *f*, rappel *m*

memorial [mɪ'morɪ·əl] *adj* commémoratif ‖ *s* mémorial *m*; pétition *f*, mémoire *m*

memo'rial arch' *s* arc *m* de triomphe

Memo'rial Day' *s* la journée du Souvenir

memorialize [mɪ'morɪ·ə,laɪz] *tr* commémorer

memorize [ˈmɛmə,raɪz] *tr* apprendre par cœur

memo·ry [ˈmɛməri] *s* (*pl* **-ries**) mémoire *f*; **from memory** de mémoire; **in memory of** en souvenir de, à la mémoire de

menace [ˈmɛnɪs] *s* menace *f* ‖ *tr & intr* menacer

menagerie [məˈnæʒəri] *s* ménagerie *f*

mend [mɛnd] *s* raccommodage *m*, reprise *f* ‖ *tr* réparer; (*patch*) raccommoder; (*stockings*) repriser; (*to reform*) améliorer ‖ *intr* s'améliorer, s'amender

mendacious [mɛnˈdeʃəs] *adj* mensonger

mendicant [ˈmɛndɪkənt] *adj & s* mendiant *m*

mending [ˈmɛndɪŋ] *s* raccommodage *m*; (*of stockings*) reprisage *m*

menfolk [ˈmɛn,fok] *spl* hommes *mpl*

menial [ˈmini·əl] *adj* servile ‖ *s* domestique *mf*

menses [ˈmɛnsiz] *spl* menstrues *fpl*

men's' fur'nishings *spl* confection *f* pour hommes

men's' room' *s* toilettes *fpl* pour hommes, lavabos *mpl* pour messieurs

menstrual [ˈmɛnstrʊ·əl] *adj* menstruel

menstruate [ˈmɛnstrʊ,et] *intr* avoir ses règles

menstruation [,mɛnstrʊˈeʃən] *s* menstruation *f*

mental [ˈmɛntəl] *adj* mental

men'tal arith'metic *s* calcul *m* mental

men'tal case' *s* cas *m* mental

men'tal defec'tive *s* débile *mf*

men'tal ill'ness *s* maladie *f* mentale

mentali·ty [mɛnˈtælɪti] *s* (*pl* **-ties**) mentalité *f*

men'tal reserva'tion *s* arrière-pensée *f*, restriction *f* mentale

men'tal test' *s* test *m* psychologique

mention [ˈmɛnʃən] *s* mention *f* ‖ *tr* mentionner; **don't mention it** il n'y a pas de quoi, je vous en prie

menu [ˈmɛnju] *s* menu *m*, carte *f*

meow [mɪˈaʊ] *s* miaou *m* ‖ *intr* miauler

Mephistophelian [,mɛfɪstəˈfili·ən] *adj* méphistophélique

mercantile [ˈmʌrkən,taɪl] *adj* commercial, commerçant

mercenar·y [ˈmʌrsə,nɛri] *adj* mercenaire ‖ *s* (*pl* **-ies**) mercenaire *mf*

merchandise [ˈmʌrtʃən,daɪz] *s* marchandise *f*

merchandizing [ˈmʌrtʃən,daɪzɪŋ] marchandisage *m*

merchant [ˈmʌrtʃənt] *adj & s* marchand *m*

mer'chant·man *s* (*pl* **-men**) navire *m* marchand

mer'chant marine' *s* marine *f* marchande

mer'chant ves'sel *s* navire *m* marchand

merciful [ˈmʌrsɪfəl] *adj* miséricordieux

merciless [ˈmʌrsɪlɪs] *adj* impitoyable

mercurial [mɛrˈkjʊrɪ·əl] *adj* inconstant, versatile; (*lively*) vif

mercu·ry [ˈmʌrkjəri] *s* (*pl* **-ries**) mercure *m*

mer·cy [ˈmʌrsi] *s* (*pl* **-cies**) miséricorde *f*, pitié *f*; **at the mercy of** à la merci de

mere [mɪr] *adj* simple, pur; seul, e.g., **at the mere thought of it** à la seule pensée de cela; rien que, e.g., **to shudder at the mere thought of it** frissoner rien que d'y penser

meretricious [,mɛrɪˈtrɪʃəs] *adj* factice, postiche; de courtisane

merge [mʌrdʒ] *tr* fusionner ‖ *intr* fusionner; (*said of two roads*) converger; **to merge into** se fondre dans

merger [ˈmʌrdʒər] *s* fusion *f*

meridian [məˈrɪdɪ·ən] *adj & s* méridien *m*

meringue [məˈræŋ] *s* meringue *f*

merit [ˈmɛrɪt] *s* mérite *m* ‖ *tr* mériter

meritorious [,mɛrɪˈtorɪ·əs] *adj* méritoire; (*person*) méritant

merlin [ˈmʌrlɪn] *s* (orn) émerillon *m*

mermaid [ˈmʌr,med] *s* sirène *f*

merriment [ˈmɛrɪmənt] *s* gaieté *f*, réjouissance *f*

mer·ry [ˈmɛri] *adj* (*comp* **-rier;** *super* **-riest**) gai, joyeux; **to make merry** se divertir

Mer'ry Christ'mas *s* Joyeux Noël *m*

mer'ry-go-round' *s* chevaux *mpl* de bois, manège *m* forain

mer'ry·mak'er *s* noceur *m*, fêtard *m*

mesh [mɛʃ] *s* (*network*) réseau *m*; (*each open space of net*) maille *f*; (*net*) filet *m*; (*engagement of gears*) engrenage *m*; **meshes** rets *m*, filets *mpl* ‖ *tr* (mach) engrener ‖ *intr* s'engrener

mesmerize [ˈmɛsmə,raɪz] *tr* magnétiser

mess [mɛs] *s* (*disorder*) gâchis *m*; (*refuse*) saleté *f*; (*meal*) (mil) ordinaire *m*; (*for officers*) (mil) mess *m*; **to get into a mess** se mettre dans le pétrin; **to make a mess of** gâcher ‖ *tr*—**to mess up** (*to botch*) gâcher; (*to dirty*) salir ‖ *intr*—**to mess around** (*to putter*) (coll) bricoler; (*to waste time*) (coll) lambiner

message [ˈmɛsɪdʒ] *s* message *m*

messenger [ˈmɛsəndʒər] *s* messager *m*; (*one who goes on errands*) commissionnaire *m*

mess' hall' *s* cantine *f*; (*for officers*) mess *m*

Messiah [məˈsaɪ·ə] *s* Messie *m*

mess' kit' *s* gamelle *f*

mess'mate' *s* camarade *mf* de table; (nav) camarade de plat

mess' of pot'tage [ˈpɑtɪdʒ] *s* (Bib) plat *m* de lentilles

Messrs. [ˈmɛsərz] *pl* of **Mr.**

mess·y [ˈmɛsi] *adj* (*comp* **-ier;** *super* **-iest**) en désordre; (*dirty*) sale, poisseux

metal [ˈmɛtəl] *s* métal *m*

metallic [mɪˈtælɪk] *adj* métallique

metallurgy [ˈmɛtə,lʌrdʒi] *s* métallurgie *f*

met'al pol'ish *s* brilliant *m* à métaux

met'al·work' *s* serrurerie *f*, travail *m* des métaux

metamorpho·sis [,mɛtəˈmɔrfəsɪs] *s* (*pl* **-ses** [,siz]) métamorphose *f*

metaphony [məˈtæfəni] *s* métaphonie *f*, inflexion *f*

metaphor [ˈmɛtə,fɔr] *s* métaphore *f*

metaphorical [,mɛtəˈfɔrɪkəl] *adj* métaphorique

metathe·sis [mɪˈtæθɪsɪs] s (pl **-ses** [ˌsiz]) métathèse f

mete [mit] tr—**to mete out** distribuer

meteor [ˈmitɪ·ər] s étoile f filante; (atmospheric phenomenon) météore m

meteoric [ˌmitɪˈɔrɪk] adj météorique; (fig) fulgurant

meteorite [ˈmitɪ·əˌraɪt] s météorite m & f

meteorology [ˌmitɪ·əˈrɑlədʒi] s météorologie f

meter [ˈmitər] s (unit of measurement; verse) mètre m; (instrument for measuring gas, electricity, water) compteur m; (mus) mesure f

me′ter maid′ s contractuelle f, aubergine f

me′ter read′er s releveur m de compteurs

methane [ˈmɛθen] s méthane m

method [ˈmɛθəd] s méthode f

methodic(al) [mɪˈθɑdɪk(əl)] adj & s méthodique

Methodist [ˈmɛθədɪst] adj & s méthodiste mf

Methuselah [mɪˈθuzələ] s Mathusalem m

meticulous [mɪˈtɪkjələs] adj méticuleux

metric(al) [ˈmɛtrɪk(əl)] adj métrique

metrics [ˈmɛtrɪks] s métrique f

metronome [ˈmɛtrəˌnom] s métronome m

metropolis [mɪˈtrɑpəlɪs] s métropole f

metropolitan [ˌmɛtrəˈpɑlɪtən] adj & s métropolitain m

mettle [ˈmɛtəl] s ardeur f, fougue f; **to be on one′s mettle** se piquer au jeu

mettlesome [ˈmɛtəlsəm] adj ardent, vif, fougueux

mew [mju] s miaulement m ‖ intr miauler

Mexican [ˈmɛksɪkən] adj mexicain ‖ s Mexicain m

Mexico [ˈmɛksɪˌko] s le Mexique

Mex′ico Cit′y s Mexico

mezzanine [ˈmɛzəˌnin] s entresol m; (theat) mezzanine m & f, corbeille f

mica [ˈmaɪkə] s mica m

microbe [ˈmaɪkrob] s microbe m

microbiology [ˌmaɪkrəbaɪˈɑlədʒi] s microbiologie f

microcomputer [ˈmaɪkrəkəmˌpjutər] s micro-ordinateur m

microfilm [ˈmaɪkrəˌfɪlm] s microfilm m ‖ tr microfilmer

microgroove [ˈmaɪkrəˌgruv] adj & s microsillon m

mi′crogroove rec′ord s disque m à microsillons

microphone [ˈmaɪkrəˌfon] s microphone m

microprocesser [ˈmaɪkrəˈprɑsəsər] s microprocesseur m

microscope [ˈmaɪkrəˌskop] s microscope m

microscopic [ˌmaɪkrəˈskɑpɪk] adj microscopique

microwave [ˈmaɪkrəˌwev] s micro-onde f

mid [mɪd] adj—**in mid course** à mi-chemin

mid′day′ s midi m

middle [ˈmɪdəl] adj moyen, du milieu ‖ s milieu m; **in the middle of** au milieu de

mid′dle age′ s âge m moyen; **Middle Ages** moyen-âge m

middle-aged [ˈmɪdəlˌedʒd] adj d'un âge moyen

mid′dle class′ s classe f moyenne, bourgeoisie f

mid′dle-class′ adj bourgeois

Mid′dle East′ s Moyen-Orient m

Mid′dle Eng′lish s moyen anglais m

mid′dle fin′ger s majeur m, doigt m du milieu

mid′dle·man′ s (pl **-men′**) intermédiaire mf

mid′dle·weight′ s (boxing) poids m moyen

middling [ˈmɪdlɪŋ] adj moyen, assez bien, passable ‖ adv (coll) assez bien, passablement

mid·dy [ˈmɪdi] s (pl **-dies**) (coll) aspirant m

mid′dy blouse′ s marinière f

midget [ˈmɪdʒɪt] s nain m, nabot m

midland [ˈmɪdlənd] adj de l'intérieur ‖ s centre m du pays

mid′night′ adj de minuit; **to burn the midnight oil** pâlir sur les livres, se crever les yeux ‖ s minuit m

midriff [ˈmɪdrɪf] s diaphragme m

mid′ship′man s (pl **-men**) aspirant m

midst [mɪdst] s centre m; **in our (your, etc.) midst** parmi nous (vous, etc.); **in the midst of** au milieu de

mid′stream′ s—**in midstream** au milieu du courant

mid′sum′mer s milieu m de l'été

mid′way′ adj & adv à mi-chemin ‖ **mid′way′** s fête f foraine

mid′week′ s milieu m de la semaine

mid′wife′ s (pl **-wives′**) sage-femme f

mid′win′ter s milieu m de l'hiver

mid′year′ s mi-année f

mien [min] s mine f, aspect m

miff [mɪf] s (coll) fâcherie f ‖ tr (coll) fâcher

might [maɪt] s puissance f, force f; **with might and main, with all one′s might** de toute sa force ‖ aux used to form the potential mood, e.g., **she might not be able to come** il se pourrait qu'elle ne puisse pas venir

mightily [ˈmaɪtɪli] adv puissamment; (coll) énormément

might·y [ˈmaɪti] adj (comp **-ier**; super **-iest**) puissant; (of great size) grand, vaste ‖ adv (coll) rudement, diablement

mignonette [ˌmɪnjəˈnɛt] s réséda m

migraine [ˈmaɪgren] s migraine f

migrant [ˈmaɪgrənt] adj & s (animal) migrateur m; (person) nomade mf; **migrant worker** travailleur m, migrant m; (seasonal) travailleur saisonnier

migrate [ˈmaɪgret] intr émigrer

migratory [ˈmaɪgrəˌtori] adj migratoire

milch [mɪltʃ] adj laitier

mild [maɪld] adj doux

mildew [ˈmɪlˌd(j)u] s moisissure f; (on vine) mildiou m, blanc m

mildness [ˈmaɪldnɪs] s douceur f

mile [maɪl] s mille m

mileage [ˈmaɪlɪdʒ] s distance f en milles; (charge) tarif m au mille

mile′post′ s borne f milliaire

mile′stone′ s borne f milliaire; (fig) jalon m
militancy [ˈmɪlɪtənsi] s esprit m militant
militant [ˈmɪlɪtənt] adj & s militant m
militarism [ˈmɪlɪtə,rɪzəm] s militarisme m
militarize [ˈmɪlɪtə,raɪz] tr militariser
military [ˈmɪlɪ,tɛri] adj & s militaire m
mil′itary police′man s (pl -men) agent m de la police militaire
militate [ˈmɪlɪ,tet] intr militer
militia [mɪˈlɪʃə] s milice f
mili′tia·man s (pl -men) milicien m
milk [mɪlk] adj laitier ‖ s lait m ‖ tr traire; abuser de, exploiter; **to milk s.th. from s.o.** soutirer q.ch. à qn
milk′ can′ s pot m à lait, berthe f
milk′ car′ton s boîte f de lait, berlingot m
milk′ choc′olate s chocolat m au lait
milk′ di′et s régime m lacté
milk′maid′ s laitière f
milk′man′ s (pl -men′) laitier m, crémier m
milk′ pail′ s seau m à lait
milk′sop′ s poule f mouillée
milk′ tooth′ s dent f de lait
milk′weed′ s laiteron m
milk·y [ˈmɪlki] adj (comp **-ier;** super **-iest**) laiteux
Milk′y Way′ s Voie f Lactée
mill [mɪl] s moulin m; (factory) fabrique f, usine f; millième m de dollar; **to put through the mill** (coll) faire passer au laminoir ‖ tr moudre, broyer; (a coin) créneler; (gears) fraiser; (steel) laminer; (ore) bocarder; (chocolate) faire mousser ‖ intr—**to mill around** circuler
millennial [mɪˈlɛnɪ·əl] adj millénaire
millenni·um [mɪˈlɛnɪ·əm] s (pl **-ums** or **-a** [ə]) millénaire m
miller [ˈmɪlər] s meunier m
millet [ˈmɪlɪt] s millet m
milligram [ˈmɪlɪ,græm] s milligramme m
millimeter [ˈmɪlɪ,mitər] s millimètre m
milliner [ˈmɪlɪnər] s modiste f
mil′linery shop′ [ˈmɪlɪ,nɛri] s boutique f de modiste
milling [ˈmɪlɪŋ] s (of grain) mouture f
mill′ing machine′ s fraiseuse f
million [ˈmɪljən] adj million de ‖ s million m
millionaire [,mɪljənˈɛr] s millionnaire mf
millionth [ˈmɪljənθ] adj & pron millionième (masc, fem) ‖ s millionième m
mill′pond′ s retenue f, réservoir m
mill′race′ s bief m
mill′stone′ s meule f; (fig) boulet m
mill′ wheel′ s roue f de moulin
mill′work′ s ouvrage m de menuiserie
mime [maɪm] s mime mf ‖ tr & intr mimer
mimeograph [ˈmɪmɪ·ə,græf] s ronéo f ‖ tr ronéocopier, ronéotyper
mim·ic [ˈmɪmɪk] s mime mf, imitateur m ‖ v (pret & pp **-icked;** ger **-icking**) tr mimer, imiter
mimic·ry [ˈmɪmɪkri] s (pl **-ries**) mimique f, imitation f
minaret [,mɪnəˈrɛt] s minaret m
mince [mɪns] tr (meat) hacher menu ‖ intr minauder

mince′meat′ s hachis m de viande et de fruits aromatisés; **to make mincemeat of** (coll) mettre en marmelade
mind [maɪnd] s esprit m; **to be of one mind** être d'accord; **to change one's mind** changer d'avis; **to have a mind to** avoir envie de; **to have in mind** avoir en vue; **to lose one's mind** perdre la raison; **to make up one's mind to** prendre le parti de; **to slip one's mind** échapper à qn; **to speak one's mind** donner son avis ‖ tr (to take care of) garder; (to obey) obéir à; (to be troubled by) s'inquiéter de; (e.g., one's manners) faire attention à; (e.g., a dangerous step) prendre garde à; **mind your own business!** occupez-vous de vous affaires! ‖ intr—**do you mind?** cela ne vous ennuie pas?, cela ne vous gêne pas?; **if you don't mind** si cela ne vous fait rien, si cela vous est égal; **never mind!** n'importe!
mind′-bend′ing s renversant
mind′-blow′ing s hallucinant
mindful [ˈmaɪndfəl] adj attentif; **mindful of** attentif à, soigneux de
mind′ read′er s liseur m de la pensée
mind′ read′ing s lecture f de la pensée
mine [maɪn] s mine f ‖ pron poss le mien §89; à moi §85 A, 10 ‖ tr (coal, minerals, etc.) extraire; (to undermine; to lay mines in) miner
mine′field′ s champ m de mines
mine′lay′er s poseur m de mines
miner [ˈmaɪnər] s mineur m
mineral [ˈmɪnərəl] adj & s minéral m
mineralogy [,mɪnəˈralədʒi] s minéralogie f
min′eral wool′ s laine f minérale, laine de scories
mine′sweep′er s dragueur m de mines
mingle [ˈmɪŋgəl] tr mêler, mélanger ‖ intr se mêler, se mélanger
miniature [ˈmɪnɪ·ətʃər] s miniature f; **in miniature** en abrégé
miniaturization [,mɪnɪ·ətʃərɪˈzeʃən] s miniaturisation f
miniaturize [ˈmɪnɪ·ətʃə,raɪz] tr miniaturiser
minimal [ˈmɪnɪməl] adj minimum
minimize [ˈmɪnə,maɪz] tr minimiser
minimum [ˈmɪnɪməm] adj minimum; (temperature) minimal ‖ s minimum m
min′imum wage′ s salaire m minimum, minimum m vital
min′imum-wage′ earn′er s smicard m
mining [ˈmaɪnɪŋ] adj minier ‖ s exploitation f des mines; (nav) pose f de mines
minion [ˈmɪnjən] s favori m; (henchman) séide m
miniskirt [ˈmɪnɪ,skʌrt] s minijupe f
minister [ˈmɪnɪstər] s ministre m; (eccl) pasteur m ‖ intr—**to minister to** (the needs of) subvenir à; (a person) soigner; (a parish) desservir
ministerial [,mɪnɪsˈtɪrɪ·əl] adj ministériel
minis·try [ˈmɪnɪstri] s (pl **-tries**) ministère m; (eccl) clergé m; (eccl) pastorat m
mink [mɪŋk] s vision m

minnow [ˈmɪno] s vairon m

minor [ˈmaɪnər] adj & s mineur m

Minorca [mɪˈnɔrkə] s Minorque f; île f de Minorque

minori·ty [mɪˈnɔrɪti] adj minoritaire ‖ s (pl -ties) minorité f

minstrel [ˈmɪnstrəl] s (in a minstrel show) interprète m de chants nègres; (hist) ménestrel m

mint [mɪnt] s hôtel m des Monnaies, Monnaie f; (bot) menthe f; (fig) mine f ‖ tr frapper, monnayer; (fig) forger

minuet [ˌmɪnjuˈɛt] s menuet m

minus [ˈmaɪnəs] adj négatif ‖ s moins m ‖ prep moins; (coll) sans, dépourvu de

minute [maɪˈn(j)ut] adj (tiny) minime; (meticulous) minutieux ‖ [ˈmɪnɪt] s minute f; **minutes** compte m rendu, procès-verbal m de séance; (often omitted in expressions of time), e.g., **ten after two, ten minutes after two** deux heures dix; **up to the minute** de la dernière heure; à la dernière mode; au courant

min′ute hand′ [ˈmɪnɪt] s grande aiguille f

min′ute rice′ s riz m précuit

min′ute steak′ s entrecôte f minute

minutiae [mɪˈn(j)uʃɪ,i] spl minuties fpl

minx [mɪŋks] s effrontée f

miracle [ˈmɪrəkəl] s miracle m

mir′acle play′ s miracle m

miraculous [mɪˈrækjələs] adj miraculeux

mirage [mɪˈrɑʒ] s mirage m

mire [maɪr] s fange f

mirror [ˈmɪrər] s miroir m, glace f ‖ tr refléter

mirth [mʌrθ] s joie f, gaieté f

mir·y [ˈmaɪri] adj (comp -ier; super -iest) fangeux

misadventure [ˌmɪsədˈvɛntʃər] s mésaventure f

misanthrope [ˈmɪsən,θrop] s misanthrope mf

misapprehension [ˌmɪsæprɪˈhɛnʃən] s fausse idée f, malentendu m

misappropriation [ˌmɪsə,proprɪˈeʃən] s détournement m de fonds

misbehave [ˌmɪsbɪˈhev] intr se conduire mal

misbehavior [ˌmɪsbɪˈhevɪ·ər] s mauvaise conduite f

miscalculation [ˌmɪskælkjəˈleʃən] s mécompte m

miscarriage [mɪsˈkærɪdʒ] s fausse couche f; (e.g., of letter) perte f; (of justice) déni m, mal-jugé m; (fig) avortement m, insuccès m

miscar·ry [mɪsˈkæri] v (pret & pp -ried) intr faire une fausse couche; (said, e.g., of letter) s'égarer; (fig) avorter, échouer

miscellaneous [ˌmɪsəˈleni·əs] adj divers, mélangé

miscella·ny [ˈmɪsə,leni] s (pl -nies) miscellanées fpl

mischief [ˈmɪstʃɪf] s (harm) tort m; (disposition to annoy) méchanceté f; (prankishness) espièglerie f

mis′chief-mak′er s brandon m de discorde

mischievous [ˈmɪstʃɪvəs] adj (harmful) nuisible; (mean) méchant; (prankish) espiègle

misconception [ˌmɪskənˈsɛpʃən] s conception f erronée

misconduct [mɪsˈkɑndʌkt] s inconduite f; (e.g., of a business) mauvaise administration f ‖ [ˌmɪskənˈdʌkt] tr mal administrer; **to misconduct oneself** se conduire mal

misconstrue [ˌmɪskənˈstru], [mɪsˈkɑnstru] tr mal interpréter

miscount [mɪsˈkaunt] s erreur f de calcul ‖ tr & intr mal compter

miscue [mɪsˈkju] s fausse queue f; (blunder) bévue f ‖ intr faire fausse queue; (theat) se tromper de réplique

mis·deal [ˈmɪs,dil] s maldonne f, mauvaise donne f ‖ [mɪsˈdil] v (pret & pp -dealt) tr mal distribuer ‖ intr faire maldonne

misdeed [ˈmɪs,did] s méfait m

misdemeanor [ˌmɪsdɪˈminər] s mauvaise conduite f; (law) délit m correctionnel

misdirect [ˌmɪsdɪˈrɛkt] tr mal diriger

misdoing [mɪsˈdu·ɪŋ] s méfait m

miser [ˈmaɪzər] s avare mf

miserable [ˈmɪzərəbəl] adj misérable

miserly [ˈmaɪzərli] adj avare

miser·y [ˈmɪzəri] s (pl -ies) misère f, détresse f

misfeasance [mɪsˈfizəns] s (law) abus m de pouvoir

misfire [mɪsˈfaɪr] s raté m ‖ intr rater

mis·fit [ˈmɪs,fɪt] s (clothing) vêtement m manqué; (thing) laissé-pour-compte m; (person) (fig) inadapté m

misfortune [mɪsˈfɔrtʃən] s infortune f, malheur m; **misfortunes** misères fpl

misgiving [mɪsˈgɪvɪŋ] s pressentiment m, appréhension f, soupçon m

misgovern [mɪsˈgʌvərn] tr mal gouverner

misguidance [mɪsˈgaɪdəns] s mauvais conseils mpl

misguided [mɪsˈgaɪdɪd] adj mal placé, hors de propos; (e.g., youth) dévoyé

mishap [ˈmɪshæp] s contretemps m, mésaventure f

mishmash [ˈmɪʃ,mæʃ] s méli-mélo m

misinform [ˌmɪsɪnˈfɔrm] tr mal renseigner

misinterpret [ˌmɪsɪnˈtʌrprɪt] tr mal interpréter

misjudge [mɪsˈdʒʌdʒ] tr & intr mal juger

mis·lay [mɪsˈle] v (pret & pp -laid) tr égarer, perdre

mis·lead [mɪsˈlid] v (pret & pp -led) tr égarer; corrompre

misleading [mɪsˈlidɪŋ] adj trompeur

mismanagement [mɪsˈmænɪdʒmənt] s mauvaise administration f

misnomer [mɪsˈnomər] s faux nom m

misplace [mɪsˈples] tr mal placer; (to mislay) (coll) égarer, perdre

misprint [ˈmɪs,prɪnt] s erreur f typographique, coquille f ‖ [mɪsˈprɪnt] tr imprimer incorrectement

mispronounce [ˌmɪsprəˈnauns] tr mal prononcer

misquote [mɪs'kwot] *tr* citer à faux, citer inexactement

misrepresent [,mɪsrɛprɪ'zɛnt] *tr* représenter sous un faux jour; (*e.g., facts*) dénaturer, travestir

miss [mɪs] *s* coup *m* manqué; **a miss!** à côté!; **Miss** Mademoiselle *f*, Mlle; (*winner of beauty contest*) Miss *f* ‖ *tr* manquer; (*to feel the absence of*) regretter; (*not to run into*) ne pas voir, ne pas rencontrer; (*e.g., one's way*) se tromper de; **he misses you very much** vous lui manquez beaucoup ‖ *intr* manquer

missal ['mɪsəl] *s* missel *m*

misshapen [mɪs'ʃepən] *adj* difforme, contrefait

missile ['mɪsɪl] *s* projectile *m*; (*guided missile*) missile *m*

mis'sile gap' *s* déséquilibre *m* (de missiles)

mis'sile launch'er *s* lance-fusées *m*

missing [mɪsɪŋ] *adj* manquant, absent; perdu; **missing in action** (mil) porté disparu; **to be missing** manquer, e.g., **three are missing** il en manque trois

miss'ing per'sons *spl* disparus *mpl*

mission ['mɪʃən] *s* mission *f*

missionar·y ['mɪʃən,ɛrɪ] *adj* missionaire ‖ *s* (*pl* -ies) missionnaire *m*

missis ['mɪsɪz] *s*—**the missis** (coll) votre femme *f*

missive ['mɪsɪv] *adj & s* missive *f*

mis·spell [mɪs'spɛl] *v* (*pret & pp* -**spelled** or -**spelt**) *tr & intr* écrire incorrectement

misspelling [mɪs'spɛlɪŋ] *s* faute *f* d'orthographe

misspent [mɪs'spɛnt] *adj* gaspillé; dissipé

misstatement [mɪs'stetmənt] *s* rapport *m* inexact, erreur *f* de fait

misstep [mɪs'stɛp] *s* faux pas *m*

miss·y ['mɪsɪ] *s* (*pl* -ies) (coll) mademoiselle *f*

mist [mɪst] *s* brume *f*, buée *f*; (*fine spray*) vapeur *f*; (*of tears*) voile *m*

mis·take [mɪs'tek] *s* faute *f*; **by mistake** par erreur, par méprise; **to make a mistake** se tromper ‖ *v* (*pret* -**took**; *pp* -**taken**) *tr* (*to misunderstand*) mal comprendre; (*to be wrong about*) se tromper de; **to mistake s.o. for s.o. else** prendre qn pour qn d'autre

mistaken [mɪs'tekən] *adj* erroné, faux; (*person*) dans l'erreur

mistak'en iden'tity *s* erreur *f* d'identité, erreur sur la personne

mistakenly [mɪs'tekənli] *adv* par erreur

mister ['mɪstər] *s*—**the mister** (coll) votre mari *m* ‖ *interj* (slang & pej) Jules!, mon petit bonhomme!

mistletoe ['mɪsəl,to] *s* gui *m*

mistreat [mɪs'trit] *tr* maltraiter

mistreatment [mɪs'tritmənt] *s* mauvais traitement *m*

mistress ['mɪstrɪs] *s* maîtresse *f*

mistrial [mɪs'traɪ·əl] *s* (law) procès *m* entaché de nullité

mistrust [mɪs'trʌst] *s* méfiance *f* ‖ *tr* se méfier de ‖ *intr* se méfier

mistrustful [mɪs'trʌstfəl] *adj* méfiant

mist·y ['mɪsti] *adj* (*comp* -**ier;** *super* -**iest**) brumeux; vague, indistinct

misunder·stand [,mɪsʌndər'stænd] *v* (*pret & pp* -**stood**) *tr* mal comprendre

misunderstanding [,mɪsʌndər'stændɪŋ] *s* malentendu *m*

misuse [mɪs'jus] *s* mauvais usage *m*, abus *m*; (*of words*) emploi *m* abusif ‖ [mɪs'juz] *tr* faire mauvais usage de, abuser de; (*a person*) maltraiter

misword [mɪs'wʌrd] *tr* mal rédiger, mal exprimer

mite [maɪt] *s* (*small contribution*) obole *f*; (*small amount*) brin *m*, bagatelle *f*; (ent) mite *f*

miter ['maɪtər] *s* (*carpentry*) onglet *m*; (eccl) mitre *f* ‖ *tr* tailler à onglet

mi'ter box' *s* boîte *f* à onglets

mitigate ['mɪtɪ,get] *tr* adoucir, atténuer

mitt [mɪt] *s* (*fingerless glove*) mitaine *f*; (*mitten*) moufle *f*; (baseball) gant *m* de prise; (*hand*) (slang) main *f*

mitten ['mɪtən] *s* moufle *f*

mix [mɪks] *tr* mélanger, mêler; (*cement; a cake*) malaxer; (*the cards; the salad*) touiller; **to mix up** (*to confuse*) confondre ‖ *intr* se mélanger, se mêler; **to mix with** s'associer à or avec

mixed *adj* mélangé; (*races; style; colors*) mêlé; (*feelings; marriage; school; doubles*) mixte; (*candy*) assorti; (*salad, vegetables, etc.*) panaché; (*number*) fractionnaire; **to be all mixed up** (*facts, account*) être embrouillé; (*person*) être déboussolé, pédaler dans le choucroute

mixed' drink' *s* boisson *f* mélangée

mixer ['mɪksər] *s* (*device*) mélangeur *m*; (*for, e.g., concrete*) malaxeur *m*; **to be a good mixer** (coll) avoir le don de plaire

mix'ing fau'cet *s* robinet *m* mélangeur

mixture ['mɪkstʃər] *s* mélange *m*

mix'-up' *s* embrouillage *m*

mizzen ['mɪzən] *s* artimon *m*

moan [mon] *s* gémissement *m* ‖ *intr* gémir

moat [mot] *s* fossé *m*

mob [mɑb] *s* (*mass of common people*) foule *f*, masse *f*; (*crush of people*) cohue *f* grouillante; (*crowd bent on violence*) foule en colère; (*criminal gang*) bande *f*, gang *m*; (pej) populace *f* ‖ *v* (*pret & pp* **mobbed;** *ger* **mobbing**) *tr* s'attrouper autour de; (*to attack*) fondre sur, assaillir

mobile ['mobɪl], ['mobil] *adj & s* mobile *m*

mobility [mo'bɪlɪti] *s* mobilité *f*

mobilization [,mobɪlɪ'zefən] *s* mobilisation *f*

mobilize ['mobɪ,laɪz] *tr & intr* mobiliser

mob' rule' *s* loi *f* de la populace

mobster ['mɑbstər] *s* (slang) gangster *m*

moccasin ['mɑkəsɪn] *s* mocassin *m*

Mo'cha cof'fee ['mokə] *s* moka *m*

mock [mɑk] *adj* simulé, contrefait ‖ *s* moquerie *f* ‖ *tr* se moquer de, moquer; (*to imitate*) contrefaire, singer; (*to deceive*) tromper ‖ *intr* se moquer; **to mock at** se moquer de; **to mock up** construire une maquette de

mock′ elec′tion s élection f blanche

mocker·y [ˈmɑkəri] s (pl **-ies**) moquerie f; (subject of derision) objet m de risée; (poor imitation) parodie f; (e.g., of justice) simulacre m

mockingbird [ˈmɑkɪŋ ˌbʌrd] s moqueur m, oiseau m moqueur

mock′ or′ange s seringa m

mock′ tur′tle soup′ s potage m à la tête de veau

mock′-up′ s maquette f

mode [mod] s (kind) mode m; (fashion) mode f; (gram, mus) mode m

mod·el [ˈmɑdəl] adj modèle ‖ s modèle m; (for dressmaker or artist; at a fashion show) mannequin m; (of a statue) maquette f ‖ v (pret & pp **-eled** or **-elled**; ger **-eling** or **-elling**) tr modeler ‖ intr dessiner des modèles; servir de modèle, poser

mod′el air′plane s aéromodèle m

mod′el-air′plane build′er s aéromodéliste mf

mod′el-air′plane build′ing s aéromodélisme m

mod′el home′ s (sample home) maison f exposition, pavillon m témoin, villa f modèle

moderate [ˈmɑdərɪt] adj modéré ‖ [ˈmɑdəˌret] tr modérer; (a meeting) présider ‖ intr se modérer; présider

moderator [ˈmɑdəˌretər] s (over an assembly) président m; (mediator; substance used for slowing down neutrons) modérateur m

modern [ˈmɑdərn] adj moderne

modernize [ˈmɑdərˌnaɪz] tr moderniser

mod′ern lan′guages spl langues fpl vivantes

modest [ˈmɑdɪst] adj modeste

modes·ty [ˈmɑdɪsti] s (pl **-ties**) modestie f

modicum [ˈmɑdɪkəm] s petite quantité f

modifier [ˈmɑdɪˌfaɪ·ər] s (gram) modificateur m

modi·fy [ˈmɑdɪˌfaɪ] v (pret & pp **-fied**) tr modifier

modish [ˈmodɪʃ] adj à la mode, élégant

modulate [ˈmɑdʒə ˌlet] tr & intr moduler

modulation [ˌmɑdʒəˈleʃən] s modulation f

mohair [ˈmo ˌhɛr] s mohair m

Mohammad [moˈhæməd] s Mahomet m

Mohammedan [moˈhæmɪdən] adj mahométan ‖ s mahométan m

Mohammedanism [moˈhæmɪdəˌnɪzəm] s mahométisme m

moist [mɔɪst] adj humide; (e.g., skin) moite

moisten [ˈmɔɪsən] tr humecter ‖ intr s'humecter

moisture [ˈmɔɪstʃər] s humidité f

molar [ˈmolər] adj & s molaire f

molasses [məˈlæsɪz] s mélasse f

mold [mold] s moule m; (fungus) moisi m, moisissure f; (agr) humus m, terreau m; (fig) trempe f ‖ tr mouler; (to make moldy) moisir ‖ intr moisir, se moisir

molder [ˈmoldər] s mouleur m ‖ intr tomber en poussière

molding [ˈmoldɪŋ] s moulage m; (cornice, shaped strip of wood, etc.) moulure f

mold·y [ˈmoldi] adj (comp **-ier**; super **-iest**) moisi

mole [mol] s (breakwater) môle m; (inner harbor) bassin m; (spot on skin) grain m de beauté; (small mammal) taupe f

molec′ular phys′ics [məˈlɛkjələr] s physique f moléculaire

molecule [ˈmɑlɪ ˌkjul] s molécule f

mole′hill′ s taupinière f

mole′skin′ s (fur) taupe f; (fabric) moleskine f

molest [məˈlɛst] tr déranger, inquiéter; molester, rudoyer

moll [mɑl] s (slang) femme f du Milieu

molli·fy [ˈmɑlɪ ˌfaɪ] v (pret & pp **-fied**) tr apaiser, adoucir

mollusk [ˈmɑləsk] s mollusque m

mollycoddle [ˈmɑlɪ ˌkɑdəl] s poule f mouillée ‖ tr dorloter

molt [molt] s mue f ‖ intr muer

molten [ˈmoltən] adj fondu

molybdenum [məˈlɪbdɪnəm] s molybdène m

moment [ˈmomənt] s moment m; **at any moment** d'un moment à l'autre; **at that moment** à ce moment-là; **at this moment** en ce moment; **in a moment** dans un instant; **of great moment** d'une grande importance; **one moment please!** (telp) ne quittez pas!

momentary [ˈmomənˌtɛri] adj momentané

momentous [moˈmɛntəs] adj important, d'importance

momen·tum [moˈmɛntəm] s (pl **-tums** or **-ta** [tə]) élan m; (mech) force f d'impulsion, quantité f de mouvement

monarch [ˈmɑnərk] s monarque m

monarchic(al) [məˈnɑrkɪk(əl)] adj monarchique

monar·chy [ˈmɑnərki] s (pl **-chies**) monarchie f

monaster·y [ˈmɑnɛsˌtɛri] s (pl **-ies**) monastère m

monastic [məˈnæstɪk] adj monastique

monasticism [məˈnæstɪˌsɪzəm] s monachisme m

Monday [ˈmʌndi] s lundi m

monetary [ˈmɑnɪˌtɛri] adj (pertaining to coinage) monétaire; (pertaining to money) pécuniaire

money [ˈmʌni] s argent m; (legal tender of a country) monnaie f; **to get one's money's worth** en avoir pour son argent; **to make money** gagner de l'argent

mon′ey·bag′ s sacoche f; **moneybags** (wealth) (coll) sac m; (wealthy person) (coll) richard m

mon′ey belt′ s ceinture f porte-monnaie

moneychanger [ˈmʌni ˌtʃendʒər] s changeur m, cambiste m

moneyed [ˈmʌnid] adj possédant

mon′ey·lend′er s bailleur m de fonds

mon·ey·mak′er s amasseur m d'argent; (fig) source f de gain

mon′ey or′der s mandat m postal

Mongol [ˈmɑŋɡəl] adj mongol ‖ s (language) mongol m; (person) Mongol m

mon·goose [ˈmɑŋɡus] s (pl **-gooses**) mangouste f

mongrel [ˈmʌŋɡrəl] adj & s métis m

monitor [ˈmɑnɪtər] s contrôleur m; (at school) pion m, moniteur m; (comp) moniteur m ‖ tr contrôler; (rad) écouter

monk [mʌŋk] s moine m

monkey [ˈmʌŋki] s singe m; (female) guenon f; **to make a monkey of** tourner en ridicule ‖ intr—**to monkey around** tripoter; **to monkey around with** tripoter; **to monkey with** (to tamper with) tripatouiller

mon′key·shine′ s (slang) singerie f

mon′key wrench′ s clé f anglaise

monks′hood s (bot) napel m

monocle [ˈmɑnəkəl] s monocle m

monogamy [məˈnɑɡəmi] s monogamie f

monogram [ˈmɑnəˌɡræm] s monogramme m

monograph [ˈmɑnəˌɡræf] s monographie f

monolingual [ˌmɑnəˈlɪŋɡwəl] adj monolingue

monolithic [ˌmɑnəˈlɪθɪk] adj monolithique

monologue [ˈmɑnəˌlɔɡ] s monologue m

monomania [ˌmɑnəˈmenɪ·ə] s monomanie f

monomial [məˈnomɪ·əl] s monôme m

monoplane [ˈmɑnəˌplen] s monoplan m

monopolize [məˈnɑpəˌlaɪz] tr monopoliser

monopo·ly [məˈnɑpəli] s (pl **-lies**) monopole m

monorail [ˈmɑnəˌrel] s monorail m

monosyllable [ˈmɑnəˌsɪləbəl] s monosyllabe m

monotheist [ˈmɑnəˌθi·ɪst] adj & s monothéiste mf

monotonous [məˈnɑtənəs] adj monotone

monotony [məˈnɑtəni] s monotonie f

monotype [ˈmɑnəˌtaɪp] s monotype m; (machine to set type) monotype f

monoxide [məˈnɑksaɪd] s oxyde m, e.g., **carbon monoxide** oxyde m de carbone

monsignor [mɑnˈsinjər] s (pl **monsignors** or **monsignori**) [ˌmɑnsiˈnjori]) (eccl) monseigneur m

monsoon [mɑnˈsun] s mousson f

monster [ˈmɑnstər] adj & s monstre m

monstrance [ˈmɑnstrəns] s ostensoir m

monstrous [ˈmɑnstrəs] adj monstrueux

month [mʌnθ] s mois m

month·ly [ˈmʌnθli] adj mensuel ‖ s (pl **-lies**) revue f mensuelle; **monthlies** (coll) règles fpl ‖ adv mensuellement

monument [ˈmɑnjəmənt] s monument m

moo [mu] s meuglement m ‖ intr meugler ‖ interj meuh! meuh!

mood [mud] s humeur f, disposition f; (gram) mode m; **moods** accès mpl de mauvaise humeur

mood·y [ˈmudi] adj (comp **-ier**; super **-iest**) d'humeur changeante; (melancholy) maussade

moon [mun] s lune f ‖ intr—**to moon about** musarder; (to daydream about) rêver à

moon′beam′ s rayon m de lune

moon′light′ s clair m de lune ‖ intr cumuler

moon′light′ing s travail m noir

moon′lighting job′ s accessoire m, deuxième emploi m

moon′shine′ s clair m de lune; (idle talk) baliverne f; (coll) alcool m de contrebande

moon′ shot′ s tir m à la lune

moor [mur] s lande f, bruyère f; **Moor** Maure m ‖ tr amarrer ‖ intr s'amarrer

Moorish [ˈmurɪʃ] adj mauresque

moose [mus] s (pl **moose**) élan m du Canada, orignal m; (European elk) élan m

moot [mut] adj discutable

moot′ point′ question f discutable

mop [mɑp] s balai m à franges; (of hair) tignasse f ‖ v (pret & pp **mopped**; ger **mopping**) tr nettoyer avec un balai à franges; (e.g., one's brow) s'essuyer; **to mop up** (mil) nettoyer

mope [mop] intr avoir le cafard

moral [ˈmɔrəl] adj moral ‖ s (of a fable) morale f; **morals** mœurs fpl

morale [məˈræl] s moral m

morali·ty [məˈrælɪti] s (pl **-ties**) moralité f

morass [məˈræs] s marais m

moratori·um [ˌmɔrəˈtorɪ·əm] s (pl **-ums** or **-a** [ə]) moratoire m, moratorium m

morbid [ˈmɔrbɪd] adj morbide

mordacious [mɔrˈdeʃəs] adj mordant

mordant [ˈmɔrdənt] adj & s mordant m

more [mɔr] adj comp plus de §91; plus nombreux; de plus, e.g., **one minute more** une minute de plus; **more than** plus que; (followed by numeral) plus de ‖ s plus m; **all the more so** d'autant plus; **what is more** qui plus est; **what more do you need?** que vous faut-il de plus? ‖ pron indef plus, davantage ‖ adv comp plus §91; davantage; **more and more** de plus en plus; **more or less** plus ou moins; **more than** plus que, davantage que; (followed by numeral) plus de; **neither more nor less** ni plus ni moins; **never more** jamais plus, plus jamais; **no more ne** . . . plus §90; **once more** une fois de plus; **the more . . . the more** (or **the less**) plus . . . plus (or moins)

more·o′ver adv de plus, du reste

Moresk [moˈrɛsk] adj mauresque

morgue [mɔrɡ] s institut m médico-légal, morgue f; (journ) archives fpl

Mormon [ˈmɔrmən] adj & s mormon m

morning [ˈmɔrnɪŋ] adj matinal, du matin ‖ s matin m; (time between sunrise and noon) matinée f, matin; **in the morning** le matin; **the morning after** le lendemain matin; (coll) le lendemain de bombe

morn′ing coat′ s jaquette f

morn′ing-glo′ry s (pl **-ries**) belle-de-jour f

morn′ing sick′ness s des nausées fpl

morn′ing star′ s étoile f du matin

Moroccan [məˈrɑkən] adj marocain ‖ s Marocain m

morocco [mə'rako] s (*leather*) maroquin *m*; **Morocco** le Maroc

moron ['morɑn] s arriéré *m*; (coll) minus *mf*, minus habens *mf*

morose [mə'ros] adj morose

morphine ['mɔrfin] s morphine *f*

morphology [mɔr'fɑlədʒi] s morphologie *f*

morrow ['mɔro] s—**on the morrow (of)** le lendemain (de)

Morse' code' [mɔrs] s alphabet *m* morse

morsel ['mɔrsəl] s morceau *m*

mortal ['mɔrtəl] adj & s mortel *m*

mortality [mɔr'tælɪti] s mortalité *f*

mortar ['mɔrtər] s mortier *m*

mor'tar·board' s bonnet *m* carré; (*of mason*) taloche *f*

mortgage ['mɔrgɪdʒ] s hypothèque *f* ‖ tr hypothéquer

mortgagee [,mɔrgɪ'dʒi] s créancier *m* hypothécaire

mortgagor ['mɔrgɪdʒər] s débiteur *m* hypothécaire

mortician [mɔr'tɪʃən] s entrepreneur *m* de pompes funèbres

morti·fy ['mɔrtɪ,faɪ] v (*pret & pp* -**fied**) tr mortifier

mortise ['mɔrtɪs] s mortaise *f* ‖ tr mortaiser

mortuar·y ['mɔrtʃʊ,ɛri] adj mortuaire ‖ s (*pl* -**ies**) morgue *f*; chapelle *f* mortuaire

mosaic [mo'ze·ɪk] adj & s mosaïque *f*

Moscow ['maskaʊ] s Moscou *m*

Moses ['moziz] s Moïse *m*

Mos·lem ['mazləm] adj & s var of **Muslim**

mosque [mask] s mosquée *f*

mosqui·to [məs'kito] s (*pl* -**toes** or -**tos**) moustique *m*

mosqui'to control' s démoustication *f*

mosqui'to net' s moustiquaire *f*

moss [mɔs] s mousse *f*

moss·y ['mɔsi] adj (*comp* -**ier**; *super* -**iest**) moussu

most [most] adj super (le) plus de §91, (la) plupart de; **for the most part** pour la plupart ‖ s (le) plus, (la) plupart; **at the most** au plus, tout au plus; **most of** la plupart de; **to make the most of** tirer le meilleur parti possible de ‖ pron indef la plupart ‖ adv super (le) plus §91, e.g., **what I like (the) most** ce que j'aime le plus; **the** (or **his, etc.**) **most** + adj le (or son, etc.) plus + adj ‖ adv très, bien, fort, des plus

mostly ['mostli] adv pour la plupart, principalement

motel [mo'tɛl] s motel *m*

moth [mɔθ] s teigne *f*, papillon *m* nocturne; (*clothes moth*) mite *f*

moth'ball' s boule *f* antimite, boule de naphtaline

moth-eaten ['mɔθ,itən] adj mité

mother ['mʌðər] s mère *f* ‖ tr servir de mère à; (*to coddle*) dorloter

moth'er coun'try s mère patrie *f*

Moth'er Goos'e's Nurs'ery Rhymes' spl les Contes de ma mère l'oie

moth'er·hood' s maternité *f*

mothering ['mʌðərɪŋ] s maternage *m*

moth'er-in-law' s (*pl* **mothers-in-law**) belle-mère *f*

motherless ['mʌðərlɪs] adj orphelin de mère

motherly ['mʌðərli] adj maternel

mother-of-pearl ['mʌðərəv'pʌrl] adj de nacre, en nacre ‖ s nacre *f*

Moth'er's Day' s fête *f* des mères

moth'er supe'rior s mère *f* supérieure

moth'er tongue' s langue *f* maternelle

moth'er wit' s bon sens *m*, esprit *m*

moth' hole' s trou *m* de mite

moth'proof' adj antimite ‖ tr rendre antimite

moth·y ['mɔθi] adj (*comp* -**ier**; *super* -**iest**) mité, plein de mites

motif [mo'tif] s motif *m*

motion ['moʃən] s mouvement *m*; (*gesture*) geste *m*; (*in a deliberative assembly*) motion *f*, proposition *f* ‖ intr—**to motion to** faire signe à

motionless ['moʃənlɪs] adj immobile

mo'tion pic'ture s film *m*; **motion pictures** cinéma *m*

mo'tion-pic'ture adj cinématographique

mo'tion-pic'ture the'ater s cinéma *m*

motivate ['moti,vet] tr animer, inciter, pousser; (*to provide with a motive*) motiver

motive ['motɪv] adj moteur ‖ s mobile *m*, motif *m*

mo'tive pow'er s force *f* motrice

motley ['matli] adj bigarré; (*mixed*) mélangé

motor ['motər] adj & s moteur *m* ‖ intr aller en voiture

mo'tor·bike' s vélomoteur *m*

mo'tor·boat' s canot *m* automobile

mo'tor·bus' s autocar *m*

motorcade ['motər,ked] s défilé *m* de voitures

mo'tor·car' s automobile *f*

mo'tor·cy'cle s moto *f*

motorist ['motərɪst] s automobiliste *mf*

motorize ['motə,raɪz] tr motoriser

mo'tor launch' s chaloupe *f* à moteur

mo'tor·man s (*pl* -**men**) conducteur *m*, wattman *m*

mo'tor pool' s parc *m* automobile

mo'tor scoot'er s scooter *m*

mo'tor ship' s navire *m* à moteurs

mo'tor truck' s camion *m* automobile

mo'tor ve'hicle s véhicule *m* automobile

mottle ['matəl] tr marbrer, tacheter

mot·to ['mato] s (*pl* -**toes** or -**tos**) devise *f*

mound [maʊnd] s monticule *m*

mount [maʊnt] s montage *m*; (*hill, mountain*) mont *m*; (*horse for riding*) monture *f* ‖ tr & intr monter

mountain ['maʊntən] s montagne *f*

moun'tain climb'ing s alpinisme *m*

mountaineer [,maʊntə'nir] s montagnard *m*; (*climber*) alpiniste *m*

mountainous ['maʊntənəs] adj montagneux

moun'tain range' s chaîne *f* de montagnes

mountebank ['maʊntɪ,bæŋk] s saltimbanque *mf*

mounting ['maʊntɪŋ] s montage *m*

mourn [morn] *tr & intr* pleurer

mourner [ˈmornər] *s* affligé *m*; *(woman hired as mourner)* pleureuse *f*; pénitent *m*; **mourners** *(funeral procession)* cortège *m* funèbre, deuil *m*

mourn′er's bench′ *s* banc *m* des pénitents

mournful [ˈmornfəl] *adj* lugubre

mourning [ˈmornɪŋ] *s* deuil *m*

mouse [maʊs] *s* *(pl* **mice** [maɪs]*)* souris *f*

mouse′hole′ *s* trou *m* de souris

mouser [ˈmaʊzər] *s* souricier *m*

mouse′trap′ *s* souricière *f*

moustache [məsˈtæʃ] *s* moustache *f*

mouth [maʊθ] *s* *(pl* **mouths** [maʊðz]*)* bouche *f*; *(of gun; of, e.g., wolf)* gueule *f*; *(of river)* embouchure *f*; **by mouth** par voie buccale; **to make s.o.'s mouth water** faire venir l'eau à la bouche à qn

mouthful [ˈmaʊθ,fʊl] *s* bouchée *f*

mouth′ or′gan *s* harmonica *m*

mouth′piece′ *s* embouchure *f*; *(person)* porte-parole *m*

mouth′-to-mouth′ resus′cita′tion *s* méthode *f* insufflatoire bouche à bouche

mouth′wash′ *s* rince-bouche *m*, eau *f* dentifrice

movable [ˈmuvəbəl] *adj* mobile

move [muv] *s* mouvement *m*; *(from one house to another)* déménagement *m*; *(player's turn)* tour *m*; *(in chess and checkers)* coup *m*; *(maneuver)* démarche *f*; **knight's move** marche *f* du cavalier; **on the move** en mouvement ‖ *tr* remuer; *(to excite the feelings of)* émouvoir; **to move that** (parl) proposer que; **to move up** *(a date)* avancer ‖ *intr* remuer; *(to stir)* se remuer; *(said of traffic, crowd, etc.)* circuler; *(e.g., to another city)* déménager; **don't move!** ne bougez pas!; **to move away** or **off** s'éloigner; **to move back** reculer; **to move in** emménager

movement [ˈmuvmənt] *s* mouvement *m*

movie [ˈmuvi] *s* (coll) film *m*; **movies** (coll) cinéma *m*

mov′ie cam′era *s* caméra *f*

movie-goer [ˈmuvi,goˑər] *s* (coll) amateur *m* de cinéma

mov′ie house′ *s* (coll) cinéma *m*, salle *f* de spectacles

moving [ˈmuvɪŋ] *adj* mouvant, en marche; *(touching)* émouvant; *(force)* moteur ‖ *s* mouvement *m*; *(from one house to another)* déménagement *m*

mov′ing pic′ture *s* film *m*; **moving pictures** cinéma *m*

mov′ing-pic′ture the′ater *s* cinéma *m*

mov′ing side′walk *s* trottoir *m* roulant

mov′ing spir′it *s* âme *f*

mov′ing stair′way *s* escalier *m* mécanique, escalier roulant

mov′ing van′ *s* voiture *f* de déménagement, camion *m* de déménagement

mow [mo] *v* *(pret* **mowed;** *pp* **mowed** or **mown)** *tr* faucher; *(a lawn)* tondre; **to mow down** faucher

mower [ˈmoˑər] *s* faucheur *m*; (mach) faucheuse *f*; *(for lawns)* (mach) tondeuse *f*

m.p.h. [ˈɛmˈpiˈetʃ] *spl* (letterword) **(miles per hour**—*six tenths of a mile equaling approximately one kilometer)* km/h

Mr. [ˈmɪstər] *s* Monsieur *m*, M.

Mrs. [ˈmɪsɪz] *s* Madame *f*, Mme

much [mʌtʃ] *adj* beaucoup de, e.g., **much time** beaucoup de temps; bien de + *art*, e.g., **much trouble** bien du mal ‖ *pron indef* beaucoup; **too much** trop ‖ *adv* beaucoup, bien §91; **however much** pron autant que; **how much** combien; **much less** encore moins; **too much** trop; **very much** beaucoup

mucilage [ˈmjusɪlɪdʒ] *s* colle *f* de bureau; *(gummy secretion in plants)* mucilage *m*

muck [mʌk] *s* fange *f*

muck′rake′ *intr* (coll) dévoiler des scandales

mucous [ˈmjukəs] *adj* muqueux

mu′cous lin′ing *s* (anat) muqueuse *f*

mucus [ˈmjukəs] *s* mucus *m*, mucosité *f*

mud [mʌd] *s* boue *f*; **to sling mud at** couvrir de boue

muddle [ˈmʌdəl] *s* confusion *f*, fouillis *m* ‖ *tr* embrouiller ‖ *intr*—**to muddle through** se débrouiller

mud′dle·head′ *s* brouillon *m*

mud·dy [ˈmʌdi] *adj* *(comp* **-dier;** *super* **-diest)** boueux; *(clothes)* crotté ‖ *v* *(pret & pp* **-died)** *tr* salir; *(clothes)* crotter; *(a liquid)* troubler; (fig) embrouiller

mud′guard′ *s* garde-boue *m*

mud′hole′ *s* bourbier *m*

mudslinger [ˈmʌd,slɪŋər] *s* (fig) calomniateur *m*

muff [mʌf] *s* manchon *m*; *(failure)* coup *m* raté ‖ *tr* rater, louper

muffin [ˈmʌfɪn] *s* petit pain *m* rond, muffin *m*

muffle [ˈmʌfəl] *tr* *(a sound)* assourdir; *(the face)* emmitoufler

muffler [ˈmʌflər] *s* *(scarf)* cache-nez *m*; (aut) pot *m* d'échappement, silencieux *m*

mufti [ˈmʌfti] *s* vêtement *m* civil; **in mufti** en civil, en pékin, en bourgeois

mug [mʌg] *s* timbale *f*, gobelet *m*; *(tankard)* chope *f*; (slang) gueule *f*, museau *m* ‖ *v* *(pret & pp* **mugged;** *ger* **mugging)** *tr* *(e.g., a suspect)* (slang) photographier; *(a victim*) (slang) saisir à la gorge ‖ *intr* (slang) faire des grimaces

mugger [ˈmʌgər] *s* agresseur *m*

mug·gy [ˈmʌgi] *adj* *(comp* **-gier;** *super* **-giest)** lourd, étouffant

mulat·to [məˈlæto] *s* *(pl* **-toes)** mulâtre *m*

mulber·ry [ˈmʌl,bɛri] *s* *(pl* **-ries)** mûre *f*; *(tree)* mûrier *m*

mulct [mʌlkt] *tr* *(a person)* priver, dépouiller; *(money)* carotter, extorquer

mule [mjul] *s* *(female mule; slipper)* mule *f*; *(male mule)* mulet *m*

muleteer [,mjuləˈtɪr] *s* muletier *m*

mulish [ˈmjulɪʃ] *adj* têtu, entêté

mull [mʌl] *tr* chauffer avec des épices; *(to muddle)* embrouiller ‖ *intr*—**to mull over** réfléchir sur, remâcher

mullion [ˈmʌljən] *s* meneau *m*

multigraph [ˈmʌltɪˌgræf] s (trademark) ronéo f ‖ tr ronéotyper, polycopier

multilateral [ˌmʌltɪˈlætərəl] adj multilatéral

multinational [ˌmʌltɪˈnæʃənəl] adj multinational ‖ **multinationals** spl (corporations) mégagroupes mpl mondiaux

multiple [ˈmʌltɪpəl] adj & s multiple m

mul′tiple sclero′sis s (pathol) sclérose f en plaques

multiplici·ty [ˌmʌltɪˈplɪsɪti] s (pl -ties) multiplicité f

multi·ply [ˈmʌltɪˌplaɪ] v (pret & pp -plied) tr multiplier ‖ intr se multiplier

multiprocessing [ˌmʌltɪˈprɑsɛsɪŋ] s (comp) multitraitement m

multiprocessor [ˌmʌltɪˈprɑsɛsər] s (comp) multiprocesseur m

multitude [ˈmʌltɪˌt(j)ud] s multitude f

mum [mʌm] adj silencieux; **mum's the word!** motus!, bouche cousue!; **to keep mum about** ne souffler mot de

mumble [ˈmʌmbəl] tr & intr marmotter

mummer·y [ˈmʌməri] s (pl -ies) momerie f

mum·my [ˈmʌmi] s (pl -mies) momie f; (slang) maman f

mumps [mʌmps] s oreillons mpl

munch [mʌntʃ] tr mâchonner

mundane [ˈmʌnden] adj mondain

municipal [mjuˈnɪsɪpəl] adj municipal

municipali·ty [mjuˌnɪsɪˈpælɪti] s (pl -ties) municipalité f

munificent [mjuˈnɪfɪsənt] adj munificent

munition [mjuˈnɪʃən] s munition f ‖ tr approvisionner de munitions

muni′tion dump′ s dépôt m de munitions

mural [ˈmjʊrəl] adj mural ‖ s peinture f murale

murder [ˈmʌrdər] s assassinat m, meurtre m ‖ tr assassiner; (a language, proper names, etc.) (coll) estropier, écorcher

murderer [ˈmʌrdərər] s meurtrier f, assassin m

murderess [ˈmʌrdərɪs] s meurtrière f

murderous [ˈmʌrdərəs] adj meurtrier

murk·y [ˈmʌrki] adj (comp -ier; super -iest) ténébreux, nébuleux

murmur [ˈmʌrmər] s murmure m ‖ tr & intr murmurer

Mur′phy bed′ s (trademark) lit m escamotable

muscle [ˈmʌsəl] s muscle m

muscular [ˈmʌskjələr] adj musclé, musculeux; (system, tissue, etc.) musculaire

muse [mjuz] s muse f; the **Muses** les Muses ‖ intr méditer; **to muse on** méditer

museum [mjuˈzi·əm] s musée m

muse′um piece′ s pièce f de musée

mush [mʌʃ] s bouillie f; (coll) sentimentalité f de guimauve

mush′room′ s champignon m ‖ intr pousser comme un champignon

mush′room cloud′ s champignon m atomique

mush·y [ˈmʌʃi] adj (comp -ier; super -iest) mou; (ground) détrempé; (coll) à la guimauve, sentimental

music [ˈmjuzɪk] s musique f; **to face the music** (coll) affronter les opposants; **to set to music** mettre en musique

musical [ˈmjuzɪkəl] adj musical

mu′sical com′edy s comédie f musicale

musicale [ˌmjuzɪˈkæl] s soirée f musicale; matinée f musicale

mu′sic box′ s boîte f à musique

mu′sic cab′inet s casier m à musique

mu′sic hall′ s salle f de musique; (Brit) music-hall m

musician [mjuˈzɪʃən] s musicien m

mu′sic lov′er s mélomane mf

musicology [ˌmjuzɪˈkɑlədʒi] s musicologie f

mu′sic rack′ or **mu′sic stand′** s pupitre m à musique

musk [mʌsk] s musc m

musk′ deer′ s porte-musc m

musketeer [ˌmʌskɪˈtɪr] s mousquetaire m

musk′mel′on s melon m; cantaloup m

musk′rat′ s rat m musqué, ondatra m

mus·lim [ˈmʌzlɪm] adj musulman ‖ s (pl -lims or -lim) musulman m

muslin [ˈmʌzlɪn] s mousseline f

muss [mʌs] tr (the hair) ébouriffer; (the clothing) froisser

muss·y [ˈmʌsi] adj (comp -ier; super -iest) en désordre, froissé

must [mʌst] s moût m; nécessité f absolue ‖ aux used to express 1) necessity, e.g., **he must go away** il doit s'en aller; 2) conjecture, e.g., **he must be ill** il doit être malade; **he must have been ill** il a dû être malade

mustache [məsˈtæʃ] s moustache f

mustard [ˈmʌstərd] s moutarde f

mus′tard plas′ter s sinapisme m

muster [ˈmʌstər] s rassemblement m; (mil) revue f; **to pass muster** être porté à l'appel; (fig) être acceptable ‖ tr rassembler; **to muster in** enrôler; **to muster out** démobiliser; **to muster up courage** prendre son courage à deux mains

mus′ter roll′ s feuille f d'appel

mus·ty [ˈmʌsti] adj (comp -tier; super -tiest) (moldy) moist; (stale) renfermé; (antiquated) désuet

mutation [mjuˈteʃən] s mutation f

mute [mjut] adj muet ‖ s muet m; (mus) sourdine f ‖ tr amortir; (mus) mettre une sourdine à

mutilate [ˈmjutɪˌlet] tr mutiler

mutineer [ˌmjutɪˈnɪr] s mutin m

mutinous [ˈmjutɪnəs] adj mutiné

muti·ny [ˈmjutɪni] s (pl -nies) mutinerie f ‖ v (pret & pp -nied) intr se mutiner

mutt [mʌt] s (dog) (slang) cabot m, clebs m; (person) (slang) nigaud m

mutter [ˈmʌtər] tr & intr marmonner

mutton [ˈmʌtən] s mouton m

mut′ton·chop′ s côtelette f de mouton; **muttonchops** favoris mpl en côtelette

mutual [ˈmjutʃu·əl] adj mutuel

mu′tual aid′ s entraide f

mu′tual fund′ s société f d'investissement à capital variable

mu'tual insur'ance com'pany s mutuelle f
muzzle ['mʌzəl] s (projecting part of head of animal) museau m; (device to keep animal from biting) muselière f; (of firearm) gueule f ‖ tr museler
my [maɪ] adj poss mon §88
myriad ['mɪrɪ·əd] adj innombrable ‖ s myriade f
myrrh [mɪr] s myrrhe f
myrtle ['mʌrtəl] s myrte m; (periwinkle) pervenche f
my·self' pron pers moi §85; moi-même §86; me §87
mysterious [mɪs'tɪrɪ·əs] adj mystérieux
myster·y ['mɪstəri] s (pl -ies) mystère m

mystic ['mɪstɪk] adj & s mystique mf
mystical ['mɪstɪkəl] adj mystique
mysticism ['mɪstɪ,sɪzəm] s mysticisme m
mystification [,mɪstɪfɪ'keʃən] s mystification f
mysti·fy ['mɪstɪ,faɪ] v (pret & pp -fied) tr mystifier
myth [mɪθ] s mythe m
mythical ['mɪθɪkəl] adj mythique
mythological [,mɪθə'lɑdʒɪkəl] adj mythologique
mytholo·gy [mɪ'θɑlədʒi] s (pl -gies) mythologie f

N

N, n [ɛn] s XIVe lettre de l'alphabet
nab [næb] v (pret & pp nabbed; ger nabbing) tr (slang) happer; (to arrest) (slang) pincer, harponner
nag [næg] s bidet m ‖ v (pret & pp nagged; ger nagging) tr & intr gronder constamment; to nag at gronder constamment
nail [nel] s (of finger) ongle m; (to be hammered) clou m; to bite one's nails se ronger les ongles; to hit the nail on the head mettre le doigt dessus, frapper juste ‖ tr clouer; (a lie) mettre à découvert; (coll) saisir, attraper
nail' brush' s brosse f à ongles
nail' clip'pers spl coupe-ongles m
nail' file' s lime f à ongles
nail' pol'ish s vernis m à ongles
nail' scis'sors s & spl ciseaux mpl à ongles
nail' set' s chasse-clou m
naïve [nɑ'iv] adj naïf
naked ['nekɪd] adj nu; to be naked être au poil; to strip naked se mettre tout nu; mettre tout nu; with the naked eye à l'œil nu
namby-pamby ['næmbi'pæmbi] adj minaudier
name [nem] s nom m; (reputation) renom m; by name de nom; by the name of sous le nom de; to call names traiter de tous les noms; what is your name? comment vous appelez-vous? ‖ tr nommer; (a price) fixer, indiquer
name' brand' s image f de marque
name' day' s fête f
nameless ['nemlɪs] adj sans nom, anonyme; (horrid) odieux
namely ['nemli] adv à savoir, nommément
name'sake' s homonyme m
name' tag' s insigne m d'identité, barrette f
nan·ny ['næni] s (pl -nies) nounou f
nan'ny goat' s (coll) chèvre f, bique f
nap [næp] s (short sleep) somme m, sieste f; (of cloth) poil m, duvet m; to take a nap faire un petit somme ‖ v (pret & pp

napped; ger napping) intr faire un somme; manquer de vigilance; to catch napping prendre au dépourvu
napalm ['nepɑm] s (mil) napalm m
nape [nep] s nuque f
naphtha ['næfθə] s naphte m
napkin ['næpkɪn] s serviette f
nap'kin ring' s rond m de serviette
Napoleonic [nə,poli'ɑnɪk] adj napoléonien
narcissus [nɑr'sɪsəs] s narcisse m; **Narcissus** Narcisse
narcotic [nɑr'kɑtɪk] adj & s narcotique m
narrate [næ'ret] tr narrer, raconter
narration [næ'reʃən] s narration f
narrative ['nærətɪv] adj narratif ‖ s narration f, récit m
narrator [næ'retər] s narrateur m
narrow ['næro] adj étroit; (e.g., margin of votes) faible ‖ **narrows** spl détroit m, goulet m ‖ tr rétrécir ‖ intr se rétrécir
nar'row escape' s—it was a narrow escape il était moins une; to have a narrow escape l'échapper belle
nar'row gauge' s voie f étroite
nar'row-mind'ed adj à l'esprit étroit, intolérant
nasal ['nezəl] adj nasal; (sound, voice) nasillard ‖ s (phonet) nasale f
nasalize ['neza,laɪz] tr & intr nasaliser
nasturtium [nə'stɑrʃəm] s capucine f
nas·ty ['næsti] adj (comp -tier; super -tiest) mauvais, sale, dégoûtant; féroce, farouche; désagréable
nation ['neʃən] s nation f
national ['næʃənəl] adj national ‖ s national m, ressortissant m
na'tional an'them s hymne m national
nationalism ['næʃənə,lɪzəm] s nationalisme m
nationali·ty [,næʃən'ælɪti] s (pl -ties) nationalité f
nationalize ['næʃənə,laɪz] tr nationaliser, étatiser, fonctionnariser
na'tion·wide' adj de toute la nation

native [ˈnetɪv] *adj* natif; (*land, language*) natal; **native of** originaire de ‖ *s* natif *m*; (*original inhabitant*) naturel *m*, indigène *mf*, autochtone *mf*

na′tive land′ *s* pays *m* natal

nativi·ty [nəˈtɪvɪti] *s* (*pl* -ties) naissance *f*; (astrol) nativité *f*; **Nativity** Nativité *f*

NATO [ˈneto] *s* (acronym) (**North Atlantic Treaty Organization**) l′O.T.A.N. *f*, l′OTAN *f*

nat·ty [ˈnæti] *adj* (*comp* -tier; *super* -tiest) coquet, élégant, soigné

natural [ˈnætʃərəl] *adj* naturel ‖ *s* (mus) bécarre *m*; (mus) touche *f* blanche; **a natural** (coll) juste ce qu′il faut

naturalism [ˈnætʃərə͵lɪzəm] *s* naturalisme *m*

naturalist [ˈnætʃərəlɪst] *s* naturaliste *mf*

naturalization [͵nætʃərəlɪˈzeʃən] *s* naturalisation *f*

naturaliza′tion pa′pers *spl* déclaration *f* de naturalisation

naturalize [ˈnætʃərə͵laɪz] *tr* naturaliser

nature [ˈnetʃər] *s* nature *f*

naught [nɔt] *s* zéro *m*; rien *m*; **to come to naught** n′aboutir à rien

naugh·ty [ˈnɔti] *adj* (*comp* -tier; *super* -tiest) méchant, vilain; (*story*) risqué

nausea [ˈnɔʃɪ·ə], [ˈnɔsɪ·ə] *s* nausée *f*

nauseate [ˈnɔʃɪ͵et], [ˈnɔsɪ͵et] *tr* donner la nausée à ‖ *intr* avoir des nausées

nauseating [ˈnɔʃɪ͵etɪŋ], [ˈnɔsɪ͵etɪŋ] *adj* nauséabond

nauseous [ˈnɔʃɪ·əs], [ˈnɔsɪ·əs] *adj* nauséeux

nautical [ˈnɔtɪkəl] *adj* nautique; naval, marin

naval [ˈnevəl] *adj* naval

na′val acad′emy *s* école *f* navale

na′val of′ficer *s* officier *m* de marine

na′val sta′tion *s* station *f* navale

nave [nev] *s* (*of a church*) nef *f*, vaisseau *m*; (*of a wheel*) moyeu *m*

navel [ˈnevəl] *s* nombril *m*

na′vel or′ange *s* orange *f* navel

navigable [ˈnævɪgəbəl] *adj* (*river*) navigable; (*aircraft*) dirigeable; (*ship*) bon marcheur

navigate [ˈnævɪ͵get] *tr* gouverner, conduire; (*the sea*) naviguer sur ‖ *intr* naviguer

navigation [͵nævɪˈgeʃən] *s* navigation *f*

navigator [ˈnævɪ͵getər] *s* navigateur *m*

na·vy [ˈnevi] *adj* bleu marine ‖ *s* (*pl* -vies) marine *f* militaire, marine de guerre; (*color*) bleu *m* marine

na′vy bean′ *s* haricot *m* blanc

na′vy blue′ *s* bleu *m* marine

na′vy yard′ *s* chantier *m* naval

nay [ne] *adv* non; voire, même ‖ *s* non *m*; (parl) vote *m* négatif

Nazarene [͵næzəˈrin] *adj* nazaréen ‖ *s* (*person*) Nazaréen *m*

Nazi [ˈnɑtsi] *adj* & *s* nazi *m*

n.d. *abbr* (**no date**) s.d.

Ne′apol′itan ice′ cream′ [͵ni·əˈpɑlɪtən] *s* glace *f* panachée

neap′ tide′ [nip] *s* morte-eau *f*

near [nɪr] *adj* proche, prochain; **near at hand** tout près; **near side** (*of horse*) côté *m* de montoir ‖ *adv* près, de près; (*nearly*) presque; **to come near** s′approcher ‖ *prep* près de ‖ *tr* s′approcher de

near′by′ *adj* proche ‖ *adv* tout près

Near′ East′ *s*—**the Near East** le Proche Orient

nearly [ˈnɪrli] *adv* presque, de près; faillir, manquer de, e.g., **I nearly fell** j′ai failli tomber

near′ miss′ *s* (*near collision*) (aer) collision *f* manquée, quasi-collision *f*

near′-sight′ed *adj* myope

near′-sight′edness *s* myopie *f*

neat [nit] *adj* soigné, rangé; concis; (*clever*) adroit; (*liquor*) nature; (slang) chouette

neat′s′-foot oil′ *s* huile *f* de pied de bœuf

nebu·la [ˈnɛbjələ] *s* (*pl* -lae [͵li] or -las) nébuleuse *f*

nebulous [ˈnɛbjələs] *adj* nébuleux

necessarily [͵nɛsɪˈsɛrɪli] *adv* nécessairement, forcément

necessary [ˈnɛsɪ͵sɛri] *adj* nécessaire; **if necessary** si besoin est

necessitate [nɪˈsɛsɪ͵tet] *tr* nécessiter, exiger

necessi·ty [nɪˈsɛsɪti] *s* (*pl* -ties) nécessité *f*

neck [nɛk] *s* cou *m*; (*of bottle*) col *m*, goulot *m*; (*of land*) cap *m*; (*of tooth*) collet *m*; collet; (*of violin*) manche *m*, (*strait*) étroit *m*; **neck and neck** manche à manche; **to break one′s neck** (coll) se rompre le cou; **to stick one′s neck out** prêter le flanc; **to win by a neck** gagner par une encolure ‖ *intr* (slang) se peloter

neck′band′ *s* tour *m* de cou

neckerchief [ˈnɛkərtʃɪf] *s* foulard *m*

necking [ˈnɛkɪŋ] *s* (slang) pelotage *m*, bécotage *m*

necklace [ˈnɛklɪs] *s* collier *m*

neck′piece′ *s* col *m* de fourrure

neck′tie′ *s* cravate *f*

neck′tie pin′ *s* épingle *f* de cravate

necrolo·gy [nɛˈkrɑlədʒi] *s* (*pl* -gies) nécrologie *f*

nectar [ˈnɛktər] *s* nectar *m*

nectarine [͵nɛktəˈrin] *s* brugnon *m*

nee [ne] *adj* née

need [nid] *s* besoin *m*; (*want, poverty*) besoin, indigence *f*, nécessité *f*; **if need be** au besoin, s′il le faut ‖ *tr* avoir besoin de, falloir, e.g., **he needs money** il a besoin d′argent, il lui faut de l′argent; demander, e.g., **the motor needs oil** le moteur demande de l′huile ‖ *aux* devoir

needful [ˈnidfəl] *adj* nécessaire

needle [ˈnidəl] *s* aiguille *f*; **to look for a needle in a haystack** chercher une aiguille dans une botte de foin ‖ *tr* (*to prod*) aiguillonner; (coll) taquiner; (*a drink*) (coll) corser

nee′dle·point′ *s* broderie *f* sur canevas; (*lace*) dentelle *f* à l′aiguille

needless [ˈnidlɪs] *adj* inutile

nee′dle·work′ *s* ouvrage *m* à l′aiguille

need·y ['nidi] *adj* (*comp* **-ier;** *super* **-iest**) nécessiteux ‖ *s*—**the needy** les nécessiteux

ne'er-do-well ['nɛrdu,wɛl] *adj* propre à rien ‖ *s* vaurien *m*

nefarious [nɪ'fɛrɪ·əs] *adj* scélérat

negate [nɪ'get] *tr* invalider; nier

negation [nɪ'geʃən] *s* négation *f*

negative ['nɛgətɪv] *adj* négatif ‖ *s* (*opinion*) négative *f*; (gram) négation *f*; (phot) négatif *m*

neglect [nɪ'glɛkt] *s* négligence *f* ‖ *tr* négliger; **to neglect to** négliger de

négligée or **negligee** [,nɛglɪ'ʒe] *s* négligé *m*, robe *f* de chambre

negligence ['nɛglɪdʒəns] *s* négligence *f*

negligent ['nɛglɪdʒənt] *adj* négligent

negligible ['nɛglɪdʒɪbəl] *adj* négligeable

negotiable [nɪ'goʃɪ·əbəl] *adj* négociable

negotiate [nɪ'goʃɪ·et] *tr* & *intr* négocier

negotiation [nɪ,goʃɪ'eʃən] *s* négociation *f*

negotiator [nɪ,goʃɪ,etər] *s* négociateur *m*

Ne·gro ['nigro] *adj* (usually offensive) noir, nègre ‖ *s* (*pl* **-groes**) (usually offensive) noir *m*, nègre *m*

neigh [ne] *s* hennissement *m* ‖ *intr* hennir

neighbor ['nebər] *adj* voisin ‖ *s* voisin *m*; (fig) prochain *m* ‖ *tr* avoisiner ‖ *intr* être voisin

neigh'bor·hood' *s* voisinage *m*; **in the neighborhood of** aux environs de; (*approximately, about*) (coll) environ

neighborliness ['nebərlɪnɪs] *s* bon voisinage *m*

neighborly ['nebərli] *adj* bon voisin

neither ['niðər], ['naɪðər] *adj indef* ni, e.g., **neither one of us** ni l'un ni l'autre ‖ *pron indef* ni, e.g., **neither** ni l'un ni l'autre ‖ *conj* ni; ni . . . non plus, e.g., **neither do I** ni moi non plus; **neither . . . nor** ni . . . ni

neme·sis ['nɛmɪsɪs] *s* (*pl* **-ses** [,sɪz]) juste châtiment *m*; **Nemesis** Némésis *f*

neologism [ni'alə,dʒɪzəm] *s* néologisme *m*

neon ['ni·ɑn] *s* néon *m*

ne'on lamp' *s* lampe *f* au néon

ne'on sign' *s* réclame *f* lumineuse

neophyte ['ni·ə,faɪt] *s* néophyte *mf*

nephew ['nɛfju], ['nɛvju] *s* neveu *m*

neptunium [nɛp't(j)unɪ·əm] *s* neptunium *m*

Nero ['nɪro] *s* Néron *m*

nerve [nʌrv] *adj* nerveux ‖ *s* nerf *m*; (*self-confidence*) assurance *f*, courage *m*; **to get on s.o.'s nerves** porter sur les nerfs à qn; **to have a lot of nerve** (*to have a lot of cheek*) avoir du toupet; **to have nerves of steel** avoir du nerf; **to lose one's nerve** avoir le trac

nerve' cen'ter *s* (anat) centre *m* nerveux; (fig) centre *m* opérations, nœud *m* vital

nerve' end'ing *s* terminaison *f* nerveuse

nerve' gas' *s* gaz *m* asphyxiant

nerve'-rack'ing ['rækɪŋ] *adj* énervant, agaçant

nervous ['nʌrvəs] *adj* nerveux

ner'vous break'down *s* épuisement *m* nerveux, dépression *f* nerveuse

nerv·y ['nʌrvi] *adj* (*comp* **-ier;** *super* **-iest**) nerveux, musclé; (coll) audacieux, culotté; (slang) dévergondé

nest [nɛst] *s* nid *m*; (*set of things fitting together*) jeu *m* ‖ *intr* se nicher

nest' egg' *s* nichet *m*; (fig) boursicot *m*, bas *m* de laine

nestle ['nɛsəl] *intr* se blottir, se nicher

nest' of ta'bles *s* table *f* gigogne

net [nɛt] *adj* net ‖ *s* filet *m*; (*for fishing; for catching birds*) nappe *f*; (tex) tulle *m* ‖ *v* (*pret* & *pp* **netted;** *ger* **netting**) *tr* (*a profit*) réaliser

Netherlander ['nɛðər,lændər] *s* Néerlandais *m*

Netherlands ['nɛðərləndz] *s*—**The Netherlands** les Pays-Bas *mpl*

net' prof'it *s* bénéfice *m* net

nettle ['nɛtəl] *s* ortie *f* ‖ *tr* piquer au vif

net' weight' *s* poids *m* net

net'work' *s* réseau *m*; (rad, telv) chaîne *f*, réseau

neuralgia [n(j)ʊ'rældʒə] *s* névralgie *f*

neuron ['n(j)ʊrɑn] *s* neurone *m*

neuro·sis [n(j)ʊ'rosɪs] *s* (*pl* **-ses** [siz]) névrose *f*

neurotic [n(j)ʊ'rɑtɪk] *adj* & *s* névrosé *m*

neuter ['n(j)utər] *adj* & *s* neutre *m*

neutral ['n(j)utrəl] *adj* neutre ‖ *s* neutre *m*; (*gear*) point *m* mort

neutrality [n(j)u'trælɪti] *s* neutralité *f*

neutralize ['n(j)utrə,laɪz] *tr* neutraliser

neutron ['n(j)utrɑn] *s* neutron *m*

neu'tron bomb' *s* bombe *f* à neutrons

never ['nɛvər] *adv* jamais **§90B**; ne . . . jamais **§90**, e.g., **he never talks** il ne parle jamais

nev'er·more' *adv* ne . . . plus jamais ‖ *interj* jamais plus!, plus jamais!

nev'er·the·less' *adv* néanmoins

new [n(j)u] *adj* (*unused*) neuf; (*other, additional, different*) nouveau (before noun); (*recent*) nouveau (after noun); (*inexperienced*) novice; (*wine*) jeune; **what's new?** quoi de nouveau?, quoi de neuf?

new'born' *adj* nouveau-né

new'born child' *s* nouveau-né *m*

New'cas'tle *s*—**to carry coals to Newcastle** porter de l'eau à la rivière

newcomer ['n(j)u,kʌmər] *s* nouveau venu *m*

New' Cov'enant *s* (Bib) nouvelle alliance *f*

newel ['n(j)u·əl] *s* (*of winding stairs*) noyau *m*; (*post at end of stair rail*) pilastre *m*

New' Eng'land *s* Nouvelle-Angleterre *f*; la Nouvelle-Angleterre

newfangled ['n(j)u,fæŋgəld] *adj* à la dernière mode, du dernier cri

Newfoundland ['n(j)ufənd,lænd] *s* Terre-Neuve *f*; **in** or **to Newfoundland** à Terre-Neuve ‖ [n(j)u'faʊndlənd] *s* (*dog*) terre-neuve *m*

newly ['n(j)uli] *adv* nouvellement

new'ly·wed' *s* nouveau marié *m*

new' moon' *s* nouvelle lune *f*

newness ['n(j)unɪs] *s* nouveauté *f*

New' Or'leans ['ɔrlɪ·ənz] *s* la Nouvelle-Orléans

news [n(j)uz] *s* nouvelles *fpl;* **a news item** un fait-divers; **a piece of news** une nouvelle

news′ a′gency *s* agence *f* d'information, agence de presse; (com) agence à journaux

news′beat′ *s* exclusivité *f*

news′boy′ *s* vendeur *m* de journaux

news′ bul′letin *s* bulletin *m* d'actualités

news′ cam′era·man *s* reporter *m* d'images

news′cast′ *s* journal *m* parlé; journal télévisé

news′cast′er *s* reporter *m* de la radio

news′ con′ference *s* conférence *f* de presse

news′ cov′erage *s* reportage *m*

news′deal′er *s* marchand *m* de journaux

news′ ed′itor *s* rédacteur *m* des actualités, rédacteur de la chronique du jour

news′let′ter *s* (*of a company, organization, etc.*) bulletin *m* (de . . .) (*de la compagnie, etc.*)

news′man′ *s* (*pl* -men′) journaliste *m*; (*dealer*) marchand *m* de journaux

New′ South′ Wales′ *s* la Nouvelle-Galles du Sud

news′pa′per *adj* journalistique ‖ *s* journal *m*

news′paper clip′ping *s* coupure *f* de presse

news′paper·man′ *s* (*pl* -men′) journaliste *m*; (*dealer*) marchand *m* de journaux

news′paper rack′ *s* casier *m* à journaux

news′paper route′ *s* tournée *f* de distribution de journaux

news′paper se′rial *s* feuilleton *m*

news′print′ *s* papier *m* journal

news′reel′ *s* actualités *fpl* (filmées)

news′room′ *s* salle *f* de rédaction

news′stand′ *s* kiosque *m*

news′week′ly *s* (*pl* -lies) hebdomadaire *m*

news′wor′thy *adj* d'actualité

New′ Tes′tament *s* Nouveau Testament *m*

New′ Year′s′ Day′ *s* le jour de l'an, le nouvel an

New′ Year′s′ Eve′ *s* la Saint-Sylvestre

New′ Year′s′ greet′ings *spl* souhaits *mpl* de nouvel An

New′ Year′s′ resolu′tion *s* résolution *f* de nouvel An

New′ York′ [jɔrk] *adj* newyorkais ‖ *s* New York *m*

New′ York′er [′jɔrkər] *s* newyorkais *m*

next [nɛkst] *adj* (*in time*) prochain, suivant; (*in place*) voisin; (*first in the period which follows*) prochain (before noun), e.g., **the next time** la prochaine fois; (*following the present time*) prochain (after noun), e.g., **next week** la semaine prochaine; **next to** à côté de ‖ *adv* après, ensuite; la prochaine fois; **who comes next?** à qui le tour? ‖ *interj* au premier de ces messieurs!, au suivant!

next′-door′ *adj* d'à côté, voisin ‖ **next′-door′** *adv* à côté de; **next-door to** à côté de; à côté de chez

next′ of kin′ *s* (*pl* next of kin) proche parent *m*

Niag′ara Falls′ [naɪ′ægərə] *s* les chutes *fpl* du Niagara

nib [nɪb] *s* pointe *f*; (*of pen*) bec *m*

nibble [′nɪbəl] *s* grignotement *m*; (*on fish line*) touche *f*; (fig) morceau *m* ‖ *tr* & *intr* grignoter

nice [naɪs] *adj* agréable, gentil, aimable; (*distinction*) subtil, fin; (*weather*) beau; **nice and . . .** (coll) très; **not nice** (coll) vilain

nicely [′naɪsli] *adv* bien; avec délicatesse

nice·ty [′naɪsəti] *s* (*pl* -ties) précision *f*; (*subtlety*) finesse *f*

niche [nɪtʃ] *s* niche *f*; (*job, position*) place *f*, poste *m*

nick [nɪk] *s* (*e.g., on china*) brèche *f*; **in the nick of time** à point nommé, à pic ‖ *tr* ébrécher; (*for money, favors*) (slang) cramponner

nickel [′nɪkəl] *s* (*metal*) nickel *m*; (*coin*) pièce *f* de cinq sous ‖ *tr* nickeler

nick′el plate′ *s* nickelure *f*

nick′el-plate′ *tr* nickeler

nicknack [′nɪk,næk] *s* colifichet *m*

nick′name′ *s* sobriquet *m*, surnom *m* ‖ *tr* donner un sobriquet à, surnommer

nicotine [′nɪkə,tin] *s* nicotine *f*

niece [nis] *s* nièce *f*

nif·ty [′nɪfti] *adj* (*comp* -tier; *super* -tiest) (slang) coquet, pimpant

niggard [′nɪgərd] *adj* & *s* avare *mf*

night [naɪt] *s* nuit *f*; (*evening*) soir *m*; **last night** (*night that has just passed*) cette nuit; (*last evening*) hier soir; **night before last** avant-hier soir

night′cap′ *s* bonnet *m* de nuit, casque *m* à mèche; (*drink*) posset *m*

night′ club′ *s* boîte *f* de nuit

night′fall′ *s* tombée *f* de la nuit

night′gown′ *s* chemise *f* de nuit

night′hawk′ *s* noctambule *mf*; (orn) engoulevent *m*

nightingale [′naɪtən,gel] *s* rossignol *m*

night′latch′ *s* serrure *f* à ressort

night′ light′ *s* veilleuse *f*

night′long′ *adj* de toute la nuit ‖ *adv* pendant toute la nuit

nightly [′naɪtli] *adj* nocturne; de chaque nuit ‖ *adv* nocturnement; chaque nuit

night′mare′ *s* cauchemar *m*

nightmarish [′naɪt,mɛrɪʃ] *adj* (coll) cauchemardesque, cauchemardeux

night′owl′ *s* (coll) noctambule *mf*

night′ school′ *s* cours *mpl* du soir

night′shade′ *s* morelle *f*

night′ shift′ *s* équipe *f* de nuit

night′ ta′ble *s* table *f* de chevet

night′ watch′man *s* (*pl* -men) veilleur *m* de nuit

nihilism [′naɪ·ɪ,lɪzəm] *s* nihilisme *m*

nil [nɪl] *s* rien *m*

Nile [naɪl] *s* Nil *m*

nimble [′nɪmbəl] *adj* agile, leste; (*mind*) délié

nim·bus [′nɪmbəs] *s* (*pl* -buses or -bi [baɪ]) nimbe *m*, auréole *f*; (meteo) nimbus *m*

nincompoop [′nɪnkəm,pup] *s* nigaud *m*

nine [naɪn] *adj & pron* neuf ‖ *s* neuf *m*; **nine o'clock** neuf heures

nine'pins' *s* quilles *fpl*

nineteen [ˈnaɪnˈtin] *adj, pron, & s* dix-neuf *m*

nineteenth [ˈnaɪnˈtinθ] *adj & pron* dix-neuvième (*masc, fem*); **the Nineteenth** dix-neuf, e.g., **John the Nineteenth** Jean dix-neuf ‖ *s* dix-neuvième *m*; **the nineteenth** (*in dates*) le dix-neuf

ninetieth [ˈnaɪntɪ·ɪθ] *adj & pron* quatre-vingt-dixième (*masc, fem*) ‖ *s* quatre-vingt-dixième *m*

nine·ty [ˈnaɪntɪ] *adj & pron* quatre-vingt-dix ‖ *s* (*pl* -ties) quatre-vingt-dix *m*

nine'ty-first' *adj & pron* quatre-vingt-onzième (*masc, fem*) ‖ *s* quatre-vingt-onzième *m*

nine'ty-one' *adj, pron, & s* quatre-vingt-onze *m*

ninth [naɪnθ] *adj & pron* neuvième (*masc, fem*); **the Ninth** neuf, e.g., **John the Ninth** Jean neuf ‖ *s* neuvième *m*; **the ninth** (*in dates*) le neuf

nip [nɪp] *s* pincement *m*, petite morsure *f*; (*of cold weather*) morsure; (*of liquor*) goutte *f* ‖ *v* (*pret & pp* **nipped;** *ger* **nipping**) *tr* pincer, donner une petite morsure à; **to nip in the bud** tuer dans l'œuf ‖ *intr* (coll) biberonner, picoler

nipple [ˈnɪpəl] *s* mamelon *m*; (*of nursing bottle*) tétine *f*; (mach) raccord *m*

nip·py [ˈnɪpi] *adj* (*comp* -pier; *super* -piest) piquant; (*cold*) vif; (Brit) leste, rapide

nirvana [nɪrˈvɑnə] *s* le nirvâna

nit [nɪt] *s* pou *m*; (*egg*) lente *f*

nit'pick' *intr* chercher la petite bête

niter [ˈnaɪtər] *s* nitrate *m* de potasse; nitrate de soude

nitrate [ˈnaɪtret] *s* azotate *m*, nitrate *m*; (*fertilizer*) engrais *m* nitraté ‖ *tr* nitrater

nitric [ˈnaɪtrɪk] *adj* azotique, nitrique

nitrogen [ˈnaɪtrədʒən] *s* azote *m*

nitroglycerin [ˌnaɪtrəˈglɪsərɪn] *s* nitroglycérine *f*

nitrous [ˈnaɪtrəs] *adj* azoteux

ni'trous ox'ide *s* oxyde *m* azoteux, protoxyde *m* d'azote

nit'wit' *s* (coll) imbécile *mf*

no [no] *adj indef* aucun, nul, pas de §90B; **no admittance** entrée *f* interdite; **no answer** pas de réponse; **no comment!** rien à dire!; **no go** or **no soap** (coll) pas mèche *f*; **no kidding** (coll) blague *f* à part; **no littering** défense *f* de déposer des ordures; **no loitering** vagabondage *m* interdit; **no parking** stationnement *m* interdit; **no place** nulle part; **no place else** nulle part ailleurs; **no shooting** chasse *f* réservée; **no smoking** défense de fumer; **no thoroughfare** circulation *f* interdite, passage *m* interdit; **no use** inutile; **with no** sans ‖ *s* non *m* ‖ *adv* non; **no good** vil; **no longer** ne . . . plus §90, e.g., **he no longer works here** il travaille plus ici; **no more** ne . . . plus §90, e.g., **he has no more** il n'en a plus; **no more . . .** (or *comp* in **-er**) **than** ne . . . pas plus . . . que, e.g.,

she is no happier than he elle n'est pas plus heureuse que lui

No'ah's Ark' [ˈno·əz] *s* l'arche *f* de Noé

nobili·ty [noˈbɪlɪti] *s* (*pl* -ties) noblesse *f*

noble [ˈnobəl] *adj & s* noble *mf*

no'ble·man *s* (*pl* -men) noble *m*

nobleness [ˈnobəlnɪs] *s* noblesse *f*

nobod·y [ˈnoˌbɑdi] *s* (*pl* -ies) nullité *f* ‖ *pron indef* personne; ne . . . personne §90, e.g., **I see nobody there** je n'y vois personne; personne ne, nul ne §90, e.g., **nobody knows it** personne ne le sait, nul ne le sait

nocturnal [nɑkˈtʌrnəl] *adj* nocturne

nocturne [ˈnɑktʌrn] *s* nocturne *m*

nod [nɑd] *s* signe *m* de tête; (*greeting*) inclination *f* de tête ‖ *v* (*pret & pp* **nodded;** *ger* **nodding**) *tr* (*the head*) incliner; **to nod assent** faire un signe d'assentiment ‖ *intr* (*with sleep*) dodeliner de la tête; (*to greet*) incliner la tête

node [nod] *s* nœud *m*

noise [nɔɪz] *s* bruit *m* ‖ *tr* (*a rumor*) ébruiter

noiseless [ˈnɔɪzlɪs] *adj* silencieux

nois·y [ˈnɔɪzi] *adj* (*comp* -ier; *super* -iest) bruyant

nomad [ˈnomæd] *adj & s* nomade *mf*

no' man's' land' *s* région *f* désolée; (mil) zone *f* neutre

nominal [ˈnɑmɪnəl] *adj* nominal

nominate [ˈnɑmɪˌnet] *tr* désigner; (*to appoint*) nommer

nomination [ˌnɑmɪˈneʃən] *s* désignation *f*, investiture *f*

nominative [ˈnɑmɪnətɪv] *adj & s* nominatif *m*

nominee [ˌnɑmɪˈni] *s* désigné *m*, candidat *m*

nonbelligerent [ˌnɑnbəˈlɪdʒərənt] *adj & s* non-belligérant *m*

nonbreakable [nɑnˈbrekəbəl] *adj* incassable

nonchalant [ˈnɑnʃələnt] *adj* nonchalant

noncom [ˈnɑnˌkɑm] *s* (coll) sous-off *m*

noncombatant [nɑnˈkɑmbətənt] *adj & s* non-combattant *m*

noncommissioned [ˌnɑnkəˈmɪʃənd] *adj* non-breveté

non'commis'sioned of'ficer *s* sous-officier *m*

noncommittal [ˌnɑnkəˈmɪtəl] *adj* évasif, réticent

nonconductor [ˌnɑnkənˈdʌktər] *s* non-conducteur *m*, mauvais conducteur *m*

nonconformist [ˌnɑnkənˈfɔrmɪst] *adj & s* non-conformiste *mf*

nondenominational [ˌnɑndɪˌnɑmɪˈneʃənəl] *adj* indépendant, qui ne fait partie d'aucune secte religieuse; (*school*) laïque

nondescript [ˈnɑndɪˌskrɪpt] *adj* indéfinissable, inclassable

nondiscriminating [ˌnɑndɪsˈkrɪmɪˌnetɪŋ] *adj* (*employment, etc.*) égalitaire

none [nʌn] *pron indef* aucun §90B; (*nobody*) personne, nul §90B; ne . . . aucun, ne . . . nul §90; n'en . . . pas, e.g., **I have none** je n'en ai pas; (*as a response on the blank of an official form*) néant ‖

adv—**to be none the wiser** ne pas en être plus sage

nonenti·ty [nɑn'ɛntɪti] *s* (*pl* **-ties**) nullité *f*

none'such' *s* nonpareil *m*; (*apple*) nonpareille *f*; (bot) lupuline *f*, minette *f*

nonfiction [nɑn'fɪkʃən] *s* littérature *f* autre que le roman

nonfulfillment [,nɑnfʊl'fɪlmənt] *s* inaccomplissement *m*

nonintervention [,nɑnɪntər'vɛnʃən] *s* nonintervention *f*, non-ingérence *f*

nonmetal ['nɑn,mɛtəl] *s* métalloïde *m*

nonpartisan [nɑn'pɑrtɪzən] *adj* neutre, indépendant

nonpayment [nɑn'pemənt] *s* non-paiement *m*

non·plus [nɑn'plʌs] *s* perplexité *f* ‖ *v* (*pret* & *pp* **-plused** or **-plussed**; *ger* **-plusing** or **-plussing**) *tr* déconcerter, dérouter

nonprof'it or'ganization *s* organisation *f* sans but lucratif

nonresident [nɑn'rɛzɪdənt] *adj* & *s* nonrésident *m*

nonresidential [nɑn,rɛzɪ'dɛnʃəl] *adj* commercial

nonreturnable [,nɑnrɪ'tʌrnəbəl] *adj* (*bottle*) perdu

nonscientific [nɑn,saɪ·ən'tɪfɪk] *adj* antiscientifique

nonsectarian [,nɑnsək'tɛrɪ·ən] *adj* nonsectaire; qui ne fait partie d'aucune secte religieuse; (*education*) laïque

nonsense ['nɑnsɛns] *s* bêtise *f*, nonsens *m*

nonskid ['nɑn'skɪd] *adj* antidérapant

nonstop ['nɑn'stɑp] *adj* & *adv* sans arrêt, continu; (*without landing*) sans escale

nonviolence [nɑn'vaɪ·ələns] *s* nonviolence *f*

noodle ['nudəl] *s* nouille *f*; (*fool*) (slang) niais *m*; (*head*) (slang) tronche *f*

nook [nʊk] *s* coin *m*, recoin *m*

noon [nun] *s* midi *m*

no' one' or **no'-one'** *pron indef* personne §90B; ne . . . personne §90, e.g., **I see no one there** je n'y vois personne; personne ne, nul ne §90B, e.g., **no one knows it** personne ne le sait, nul ne le sait; **no one else** personne d'autre

noon'time' *s* midi *m*

noose [nus] *s* nœud *m* coulant; (*for hanging*) corde *f*, hart *f*

nor [nɔr] *conj* ni

norm [nɔrm] *s* norme *f*

normal ['nɔrməl] *adj* normal

Norman ['nɔrmən] *adj* normand ‖ *s* (*dialect*) normand *m*; (*person*) Normand *m*

Normandy ['nɔrməndi] *s* Normandie *f*; la Normandie

Norse [nɔrs] *adj* & *s* norrois *m*

Norse'man *s* (*pl* **-men**) Norrois *m*

north [nɔrθ] *adj* & *s* nord *m* ‖ *adv* au nord, vers le nord

North' Af'rican *adj* nord-africain ‖ *s* Nord-Africain *m*

north'east' *adj* & *s* nord-est *m*

north'east'er *s* vent *m* du nord-est

northern ['nɔrðərn] *adj* septentrional, du nord

North' Kore'a *s* Corée *f* du Nord; la Corée du Nord

North' Kore'an *adj* nord-coréen ‖ *s* (*person*) Nord-Coréen *m*

North' Pole' *s* pôle *m* Nord

northward ['nɔrθwərd] *adv* vers le nord

north'west' *adj* & *s* nord-ouest *m*

north' wind' *s* bise *f*

Norway ['nɔrwe] *s* Norvège *f*; la Norvège

Norwegian [nɔr'widʒən] *adj* norvégien ‖ *s* (*language*) norvégien *m*; (*person*) Norvégien *m*

nose [noz] *s* nez *m*; (*of certain animals*) museau *m*; **to blow one's nose** se moucher; **to have a nose for** avoir le flair de; **to keep one's nose to the grindstone** travailler sans relâche, buriner; **to lead by the nose** mener par le bout du nez; **to look down one's nose at** faire un nez à; **to talk through one's nose** parler du nez; **to thumb one's nose at** faire un pied de nez à; **to turn up one's nose at** faire la nique à; **under the nose of** à la barbe de ‖ *tr* flairer, sentir; **to nose out** flairer, dépister ‖ *intr*—**to nose about** fouiner; **to nose over** capoter

nose'bag' *s* musette *f*

nose'bleed' *s* saignement *m* de nez

nose' cone' *s* ogive *f*

nose' dive' *s* piqué *m*

nose'-dive' *intr* descendre en piqué

nose' drops' *spl* instillations *fpl* nasales

nose'gay' *s* bouquet *m*

nose' glass'es *spl* pince-nez *m*, binocle *m*

nostalgia [nɑ'stældʒə] *s* nostalgie *f*

nostalgic [nɑ'stældʒɪk] *adj* nostalgique

nostril ['nɑstrɪl] *s* narine *f*; (*of horse, cow, etc.*) naseau *m*

nostrum ['nɑstrəm] *s* (*quack and his medicine*) orviétan *m*; panacée *f*

nos·y ['nozi] *adj* (*comp* **-ier**; *super* **-iest**) fureteur, indiscret

not [nɑt] *adv* ne §87, §90C; ne . . . pas §90, e.g., **he is not here** il n'est pas ici; non, non pas; **not at all** pas du tout; **not much** peu de chose; **not one** pas un; **not that** non pas que; **not yet** pas encore; **to think not** croire que non

notable ['notəbəl] *adj* & *s* notable *m*

notarize ['notə,raɪz] *tr* authentiquer

notarized *adj* authentique

nota·ry ['notəri] *s* (*pl* **-ries**) notaire *m*

notation [no'teʃən] *s* notation *f*

notch [nɑtʃ] *s* coche *f*, entaille *f*; (*of a belt*) cran *m*; (*of a wheel*) dent *f*; (*gap in a mountain*) brèche *f* ‖ *tr* encocher, entailler

note [not] *s* note *f*; (*short letter*) billet *m*; **notes** commentaires *mpl*; (*of a speech*) feuillets *mpl*; **note to the reader** avis *m* au lecteur; **to hit a wrong note** faire un canard ‖ *tr* noter; **to note down** prendre note de

note'book' *s* cahier *m*; (*bill book, memo pad, etc.*) carnet *m*, calepin *m*

note'book cov'er *s* protège-cahier *m*

noted ['notɪd] *adj* éminent, distingué, connu

note' pad' *s* bloc-notes *m*

note'wor'thy s notable, remarquable

nothing ['nʌθɪŋ] s rien m; **nothing of importance** rien à signaler; **to count for nothing** compter pour du beurre ‖ pron indef rien §90B; ne . . . rien §90, e.g., **I have nothing** je n'ai rien; **nothing at all** rien du tout; **nothing doing!** (slang) pas mèche! ‖ adv—**nothing less than** rien moins que

nothingness ['nʌθɪŋnɪs] s néant m

notice ['notɪs] s (warning; advertisement) avis m; (in a newspaper) annonce f; (observation) attention f; (of dismissal) congé m; **at short notice** à bref délai; **to take notice of** faire attention à; **until further notice** jusqu'à nouvel ordre ‖ tr s'apercevoir de, remarquer

noticeable ['notɪsəbəl] adj apparent, perceptible

notification [,notɪfɪ'keʃən] s notification f, avertissement m

noti·fy ['notɪ,faɪ] v (pret & pp -fied) tr aviser, avertir

notion ['noʃən] s notion f; intention f; **notions** mercerie f; **to have a notion to** avoir dans l'idée, avoir envie de

notorie·ty [,notə'raɪ·ɪti] s (pl -ties) renom m déshonorant, triste notoriété f

notorious [no'torɪ·əs] adj insigne, mal famé; (person) d'une triste notoriété

no'-trump' adj & s sans-atout m

notwithstanding [,natwɪθ'stændɪŋ] adv nonobstant, néanmoins ‖ prep malgré ‖ conj quoique

nought [nɔt] s var of **naught**

noun [naʊn] s nom m

nourish ['nʌrɪʃ] tr nourrir

nourishment ['nʌrɪʃmənt] s nourriture f, alimentation f

Nova Scotia ['novə'skoʃə] s Nouvelle-Écosse f; **la Nouvelle-Écosse**

novel ['navəl] adj nouveau; original, bizarre ‖ s roman m

novelette [,navəl'ɛt] s nouvelle f, bluette f

novelist ['navəlɪst] s romancier m

novel·ty ['navəlti] s (pl -ties) nouveauté f; **novelties** bibelots, mpl, souvenirs mpl

November [no'vɛmbər] s novembre m

novice ['navɪs] s novice mf

novitiate [no'vɪʃɪ·ɪt] s noviciat m

novocaine ['novə,ken] s novocaïne f

now [naʊ] adv maintenant; **just now** tout à l'heure, naguère; **now and again** de temps en temps ‖ interj allez-y!

nowadays ['naʊ·ə,dez] adv de nos jours

no'way' or **no'ways'** adv en aucune façon

no'where' adv nulle part; ne . . . nulle part; **nowhere else** nulle autre part, nulle part ailleurs

noxious ['nakʃəs] adj nocif

nozzle ['nazəl] s (of hose) ajutage m; (of fire hose) lance f; (of sprinkling can) pomme f; (of candlestick) douille f; (of pitcher; of gas burner) bec m; (of carburetor) buse f; (of vacuum cleaner) suceur m; (nose) (slang) museau m

nth [ɛnθ] adj énième, nième; **for the nth time** pour la énième fois; **the nth power** la énième puissance

nuance [nju'ɑns], ['nju·ɑns] s nuance f

nub [nʌb] s protubérance f; (piece) petit morceau m; (slang) nœud m

nuclear ['n(j)uklɪ·ər] adj nucléaire

nu'clear ac'cident s accident m nucléaire

nu'clear pow'er plant' s centrale f nucléaire

nu'clear reac'tor s réacteur m nucléaire

nu'clear re'search lab'oratory m laboratoire m nucléaire

nu'clear test' s test m nucléaire, essai m nucléaire

nu'clear test' ban' s interdiction f des essais nucléaires

nucleolus [n(j)u'kli·ələs] s nucléole m

nucleon ['n(j)ukli·an] s nucléon m

nucle·us ['n(j)ukli·əs] s (pl -i [,aɪ] or -uses) noyau m

nude [n(j)ud] adj nu ‖ s nu m; **in the nude** nu, sans vêtements

nudge [nʌdʒ] s coup m de coude ‖ tr pousser du coude

nudist ['n(j)udɪst] adj & s nudiste mf

nudity ['n(j)udɪti] s nudité f

nugget ['nʌgɪt] s pépite f

nuisance ['n(j)usəns] s ennui m; (person) peste f

null [nʌl] adj indef nul

null' and void' adj nul et non avenu

nulli·fy ['nʌlɪ,faɪ] v (pret & pp -fied) tr annuler

numb [nʌm] adj engourdi; **to grow numb** s'engourdir ‖ tr engourdir

number ['nʌmbər] s (quantity) nombre m; (figure, numeral, digit) chiffre m; (house, page, registration, telephone, magazine) numéro m; (circus or vaudeville act) numéro; (car, manufactured goods, clothes) modèle m; **even (odd, whole, cardinal, ordinal) number** nombre pair (impair, entier, cardinal, ordinal); **round number** chiffre rond; **wrong number** faux numéro ‖ tr numéroter; nombrer; (to amount to) s'élever à, compter; **to number among** compter parmi

numberless ['nʌmbərlɪs] adj innombrable

numbness ['nʌmnɪs] s engourdissement m

numeral ['n(j)umərəl] adj numéral ‖ s numéro m, chiffre m; **Arabic numeral** chiffre m, chiffre arabe; **Roman numeral** chiffre romain

numeration [,n(j)umə'reʃən] s numération f

numerical [n(j)u'mɛrɪkəl] adj numérique

numerous ['n(j)umərəs] adj nombreux

numismatic [,n(j)umɪz'mætɪk] adj numismatique ‖ **numismatics** s numismatique f

numskull ['nʌm,skʌl] s (coll) sot m

nun [nʌn] s religieuse f, nonne f

nunci·o ['nʌnʃɪ,o] s (pl -os) nonce m

nuptial ['nʌpʃəl] adj nuptial ‖ **nuptials** spl noces fpl

nurse [nʌrs] s (female nurse) infirmière f; (male nurse) infirmier m; (wet nurse) nourrice f; (practical nurse) garde-malade mf; (*children's nurse*) bonne *f* d'enfant, nurse *f* ‖ *tr* soigner; (*hopes; plants; a baby*) nourrir

nurse′maid′ *s* bonne *f* d'enfant

nurser·y [ˈnʌrsəri] *s* (*pl* **-ies**) chambre *f* des enfants; (*for day care*) crèche *f*, pouponnière *f*; (*hort*) pépinière *f*

nurs′ery·man *s* (*pl* **-men**) pépiniériste *m*

nurs′ery school′ *s* maternelle *f*, école *f* maternelle

nurs′e's aid′ *s* aide-soignante *f*

nursing [ˈnʌrsɪŋ] *s* (*care of invalids*) soins *mpl* infirmière; (*profession*) métier *m* or profession *f* d'infirmière; (*suckling*) allaitement *m*; (*mothering*) maternage *m*

nurs′ing bot′tle *s* biberon *m*

nurs′ing home′ *s* maison *f* de repos, maison de santé

nursling [ˈnʌrslɪŋ] *s* nourrisson *m*

nurture [ˈnʌrtʃər] *s* (*training*) éducation *f*; (*food*) nourriture *f* ‖ *tr* élever; (*to nurse*) nourrir

nut [nʌt] *s* noix *f*, e.g., **Brazil nut** noix du Brésil; (*of walnut tree*) noix; (*of filbert*) noisette *f*; (*to screw on a bolt*) écrou *m*; (slang) extravagant *m*; **to be nuts about** (slang) être follement épris de

nut′crack′er *s* casse-noisettes *m*, casse-noix *m*; (orn) casse-noix

nut′hatch′ *s* sittelle *f*

nut′meat′ *s* graine *f* de fruit sec, graine de noix

nutmeg [ˈnʌt,mɛg] *s* (*seed or spice*) noix *f* muscade, muscade *f*; (*tree*) muscadier *m*

nutriment [ˈn(j)utrɪmənt] *s* nourriture *f*

nutrition [n(j)uˈtrɪʃən] *s* nutrition *f*

nutritious [n(j)uˈtrɪʃəs] *adj* nutritif

nuts [nʌts] *adj* (coll) dingue, cinglé, toqué; **to be nuts about** être emballé par ‖ *interj* la barbe!, je m'en fiche!

nut′shell′ *s* coquille *f* de noix; **in a nutshell** en un mot

nut·ty [ˈnʌti] *adj* (*comp* **-tier**; *super* **-tiest**) à goût de noisette, à goût de noix; (slang) cinglé, dingue

nuzzle [ˈnʌzəl] *tr* fouiller du groin ‖ *intr* fouiller du groin; s'envelopper chaudement; **to nuzzle up to** se pelotonner contre

nylon [ˈnaɪlɑn] *s* nylon *m*; **nylons** bas *mpl* de nylon, bas nylon

nymph [nɪmf] *s* nymphe *f*

O

O, o [o] *s* XVe lettre de l'alphabet

oaf [of] *s* lourdaud *m*, rustre *m*

oak [ok] *s* chêne *m*

oaken [ˈokən] *adj* de chêne, en chêne

oakum [ˈokəm] *s* étoupe *f*

oar [or], [ɔr] *s* rame *f*, aviron *m*

oar′lock′ *s* tolet *m*

oars′man′ *s* (*pl* **-men′**) rameur *m*

oa·sis [oˈesɪs] *s* (*pl* **-ses** [siz]) oasis *f*

oat [ot] *s* avoine *f*; **oats** (*edible grain*) avoine; **to feel one's oats** être imbu de sa personne; **to sow one's wild oats** (coll) jeter sa gourme

oath [oθ] *s* (*pl* **oaths** [oðz]) serment *m*; (*swearword*) juron *m*; **to administer an oath to** (law) faire prêter serment à; **to take an oath** prêter serment

oat′meal′ *s* farine *f* d'avoine; (*breakfast food*) flocons *mpl* d'avoine

obbligato [ˌɑblɪˈgato] *s* accompagnement *m* à volonté

obdurate [ˈɑbdjərɪt] *adj* obstiné, endurci

obedience [oˈbidɪ·əns] *s* obéissance *f*

obedient [oˈbidɪ·ənt] *adj* obéissant

obeisance [oˈbesəns] *s* hommage *m*; (*greeting*) révérance *f*

obelisk [ˈɑbəlɪsk] *s* obélisque *m*

obese [oˈbis] *adj* obèse

obesity [oˈbisɪti] *s* obésité *f*

obey [əˈbe] *tr* obéir à; **to be obeyed** être obéi ‖ *intr* obéir

obfuscate [ˈɑbfəs,ket] *tr* offusquer

obituar·y [oˈbɪtʃu,ɛri] *adj* nécrologique ‖ *s* (*pl* **-ies**) nécrologie *f*

object [ˈɑbdʒɪkt] *s* objet *m* ‖ [abˈdʒɛkt] *tr* objecter, rétorquer ‖ *intr* faire des objections; **to object to** s'opposer à, avoir des objections contre

objection [abˈdʒɛkʃən] *s* objection *f*

objectionable [abˈdʒɛkʃənəbəl] *adj* répréhensible; répugnant, désagréable

objective [abˈdʒɛktɪv] *adj* & *s* objectif *m*

obligate [ˈɑblɪ,get] *tr* obliger

obligation [ˌɑblɪˈgeʃən] *s* obligation *f*

obligatory [əˈblɪgə,tori] *adj* obligatoire

oblige [əˈblaɪdʒ] *tr* obliger; **much obliged** bien obligé, très reconnaissant; **to be obliged to** être obligé de

obliging [əˈblaɪdʒɪŋ] *adj* accommodant, obligeant

oblique [əˈblik] *adj* oblique

obliterate [əˈblɪtə,ret] *tr* effacer, oblitérer

oblivion [əˈblɪvɪ·ən] *s* oubli *m*

oblivious [əˈblɪvɪ·əs] *adj* oublieux

oblong [ˈɑblɔŋ] *adj* oblong

obnoxious [əbˈnɑkʃəs] *adj* odieux, désagréable

oboe [ˈobo] *s* hautbois *m*

oboist [ˈobo·ɪst] *s* hautboïste *mf*

obscene [abˈsin] *adj* obscène

obsceni·ty [abˈsɛnɪti] *s* (*pl* **-ties**) obscénité *f*

obscure [əbˈskjur] *adj* obscur; (*vowel*) relâché, neutre

obscuri·ty [əb'skjυrɪti] *s* (*pl* -**ties**) obscurité *f*

obsequies ['absɪkwiz] *spl* obsèques *fpl*

obsequious [əb'sikwɪ·əs] *adj* obséquieux

observance [əb'zʌrvəns] *s* observance *f*

observant [əb'zʌrvənt] *adj* observateur

observation [,ɑbzər've∫ən] *s* observation *f*

observato·ry [əb'zʌrvə,tori] *s* (*pl* -**ries**) observatoire *m*

observe [əb'zʌrv] *tr* observer; (*silence*) garder; (*a holiday*) célébrer; dire, remarquer

observer [əb'zʌrvər] *s* observateur *m*

obsess [əb'sɛs] *tr* obséder

obsession [əb'sɛ∫ən] *s* obsession *f*

obsolescent [,absə'lɛsənt] *adj* vieillissant

obsolete ['absəlit] *adj* désuet, vieilli; (*gram*) obsolète

obstacle ['abstəkəl] *s* obstacle *m*

ob'stacle course' *s* champ *m* d'obstacles, piste *f* d'obstacles

obstetrical [ab'stɛtrɪkəl] *adj* obstétrique

obstetrics [ab'stɛtrɪks] *spl* obstétrique *f*

obstina·cy ['abstɪnəsi] *s* (*pl* -**cies**) obstination *f*, entêtement *m*

obstinate ['abstɪnɪt] *adj* obstiné

obstreperous [əb'strɛpərəs] *adj* turbulent

obstruct [əb'strʌkt] *tr* obstruer; (*movements*) empêcher, entraver

obstruction [əb'strʌk∫ən] *s* obstruction *f*; (*on railroad tracks*) obstacle *m*; (*to movement*) empêchement *m*, entrave *f*

obtain [əb'ten] *tr* obtenir, se procurer ‖ *intr* prévaloir

obtrusive [əb'trusɪv] *adj* importun, intrus

obtuse [əb't(j)us] *adj* obtus

obviate ['abvɪ,et] *tr* obvier à

obvious ['abvɪ·əs] *adj* évident

occasion [ə'keʒən] *s* occasion *f*; **on occasion** en de différentes occasions ‖ *tr* occasionner

occasional [ə'keʒənəl] *adj* fortuit, occasionnel; (*verses*) de circonstance; (*showers*) épars; (*chair*) volant

occasionally [ə'keʒənəli] *adv* de temps en temps, occasionnellement

occident ['aksɪdənt] *s* occident *m*

occidental [,aksə'dɛntəl] *adj* & *s* occidental *m*

occlusion [ə'kluʒən] *s* occlusion *f*

occlusive [ə'klusɪv] *adj* occlusif ‖ *s* occlusive *f*

occult [ə'kʌlt], ['akʌlt] *adj* occulte

occupancy ['akjəpənsi] *s* occupation *f*, habitation *f*

occupant ['akjəpənt] *s* occupant *m*

occupation [,akjə'pe∫ən] *s* occupation *f*

occupational [,akjə'pe∫ənəl] *adj* professionnel; de métier

oc'cupa'tional ther'apy *s* thérapie *f* rééducative, réadaptation *f* fonctionnelle

occu·py ['akjə,paɪ] *v* (*pret* & *pp* -**pied**) *tr* occuper; **to be occupied with** s'occuper de

oc·cur [ə'kʌr] *v* (*pret* & *pp* -**curred**; *ger* -**curring**) *intr* arriver, avoir lieu; (*to be found; to come to mind*) se présenter; **it**

occurs to me that il me vient à l'esprit que

occurrence [ə'kʌrəns] *s* événement *m*; cas *m*, exemple *m*; **everyday occurrence** fait *m* journalier

ocean ['o∫ən] *s* océan *m*

oceanic [,o∫ɪ'ænɪk] *adj* océanique

o'cean lin'er *s* paquebot *m* transocéanique

ocher ['okər] *s* ocre *f*

o'clock [ə'klak] *adv*—**it is one o'clock** il est une heure; **it is two o'clock** il est deux heures

octane ['akten] *s* octane *m*

oc'tane num'ber *s* indice *m* d'octane

octave ['aktɪv], ['aktev] *s* octave *f*

October [ak'tobər] *s* octobre *m*

octo·pus ['aktəpəs] *s* (*pl* -**puses** or -**pi** [,paɪ]) pieuvre *f*, poulpe *m*

octoroon ['aktə'run] *s* octavon *m*

ocular ['akjələr] *adj* & *s* oculaire *m*

oculist ['akjəlɪst] *s* oculiste *mf*

odd [ad] *adj* (*number*) impair; (*that doesn't match*) dépareillé, déparié; (*queer*) bizarre, étrange; (*occasional*) divers; quelque, e.g., **three hundred odd horses** quelque trois cents chevaux; et quelques ‖ **odds** *spl* chances *fpl*; (*disparity*) inégalité *f*; (*on a horse*) cote *f*; **at odds** en désaccord, en bisbille; **by all odds** sans aucun doute; **to be at odds with** être mal avec; **to give odds to** donner de l'avance à; **to set at odds** brouiller

oddi·ty ['adɪti] *s* (*pl* -**ties**) bizarrerie *f*

odd' jobs' *spl* bricolage *m*, petits travaux *mpl*

odd' man' out' *s*—**to be odd man out** être en trop

odds' and ends' *spl* petits bouts *mpl*, bribes *fpl*; (*trinkets*) bibelots *mpl*; (*food*) restes *mpl*

ode [od] *s* ode *f*

odious ['odɪ·əs] *adj* odieux

odor ['odər] *s* odeur *f*; **to be in bad odor** être mal vu

odorless ['odərlɪs] *adj* inodore

Odyssey ['adɪsi] *s* Odyssée *f*

Œdipus ['ɛdɪpəs], ['idəpəs] *s* Œdipe *m*

of [av], [ʌv], [əv] *prep* de; à, e.g., **to think of** penser à; e.g., **to ask s.th. of s.o.** demander q.ch. à qn; en, e.g., **a doctor of medicine** un docteur en médecine; moins, e.g., **a quarter of two** deux heures moins le quart; entre, e.g., **he of all people** lui entre tous; d'entre, e.g., **five of them** cinq d'entre eux; par, e.g., **of necessity** par nécessité; (*made of*) en, de, e.g., **made of wood** en bois, de bois; (*not translated*), e.g., **the fifth of March** le cinq mars; e.g., **we often see her of a morning** nous la voyons le matin

off [ɔf], [af] *adj* mauvais, e.g., **off day** (*bad day*) mauvaise journée; libre, e.g., **off day** journée libre; de congé, e.g., **off day** jour de congé; (*account, sum*) inexact; (*meat*) avancé; (*electric current*) coupé; (*light*) éteint; (*radio; faucet*) fermé; (*street*) secondaire, transversal; (*distant*) éloigné, écarté ‖ *adv* loin; à . . . de distance, e.g., **three kilometers off** à trois kilomètres de distance; parti, e.g., **they're off**! les voilà partis!; bas, e.g., **hats off**! chapeaux bas!; (naut) au large; (theat) à la cantonade ‖ *prep* de; (*at a distance from*) éloigné de, écarté de; (naut) au large de, à la hauteur de; **from off** de dessous de; **off line** (comp) autonome

offal [ˈɔfəl] *s* (*of butchered meat*) abats *mpl*; (*refuse*) ordures *fpl*

off′ and on′ *adv* de temps en temps, par intervalles

off′beat′ *adj* (slang) insolite, rare

off′ chance′ *s* chance *f* improbable

off′-col′or *adj* décoloré; (*e.g., story*) grivois, vert

offend [əˈfɛnd] *tr* offenser; **to be offended** s'offenser ‖ *intr*—**to offend against** enfreindre

offender [əˈfɛndər] *s* offenseur *m*; (*criminal*) délinquant *m*, coupable *mf*

offense [əˈfɛns] *s* offense *f*; (law) délit *m*; **to take offense (at)** s'offenser (de)

offensive [əˈfɛnsɪv] *adj* offensant, blessant; (mil) offensif ‖ *s* offensive *f*

offer [ˈɔfər] *s* offre *f* ‖ *tr* offrir; (*excuses; best wishes*) présenter; (*prayers*) adresser ‖ *intr*—**to offer to** faire l'offre de; faire mine de, e.g., **he offered to fight** il a fait mine de se battre

offering [ˈɔfərɪŋ] *s* offre *f*; (eccl) offrande *f*

off′hand′ *adj* improvisé; brusque ‖ *adv* au pied levé; brusquement

office [ˈɔfɪs] *s* (*function*) charge *f*, fonction *f*, office *m*; (*in business, school, government*) bureau *m*; (*national agency*) office *m*; (*of lawyer*) étude *f*; (*of doctor*) cabinet *m*; **elective office** poste *m* électif; **good offices** bons offices; **to run for office** se présenter aux élections

of′fice boy′ *s* coursier *m*, commissionaire *m* de bureau

of′fice desk′ *s* bureau *m* ministre

of′fice-hold′er *s* fonctionnaire *mf*

of′fice hours′ *spl* heures *fpl* de bureau; (*of doctor, counselor, etc.*) heures de consultation

officer [ˈɔfɪsər] *s* (*of a company*) administrateur *m*, dirigeant *m*; (*of army, an order, a society, etc.*) officier *m*; (*police officer*) agent *m* de police, officier de police; **officer of the day** (mil) officier de service

of′ficer can′didate *s* élève-officier *m*

of′fice seek′er *s* solliciteur *m*

of′fice supplies′ *spl* fournitures *fpl* de bureau, articles *mpl* de bureau

of′fice-supply′ store′ *s* papeterie *f*

of′fice work′ *s* travail *m* de bureau

official [əˈfɪʃəl] *adj* officiel; (*e.g., stationery*) réglementaire ‖ *s* fonctionnaire *mf*, officiel *m*; **officials** cadres *mpl*; (*executives*) dirigeants *mpl*

offi′cial board′ *s* comité *m* directeur

offi′cial chan′nels *spl* filière *f* administrative

officialese [əˌfɪʃəˈliz] *s* jargon *m* administratif

officiate [əˈfɪʃɪˌet] *intr* (eccl) officier; **to officiate as** exercer les fonctions de

officious [əˈfɪʃəs] *adj* trop empressé; **to be officious** faire l'officieux

offing [ˈɔfɪŋ] *s*—**in the offing** au large; (fig) en perspective

off′-lim′its *adj* défendu; (public sign) défense d'entrer, entrée interdite; (mil) interdit aux troupes

off′-peak heat′er *s* thermosiphon *m* à accumulation

off′print′ *s* tiré *m* à part

off′-sea′son *s adj* hors-saison ‖ *s* morte-saison *f*; **in the off season** à la morte-saison

off′set′ *s* compensation *f*; (typ) offset *m* ‖ **off′set′** *v* (*pret & pp* **-set**; *ger* **-setting**) *tr* compenser

off′shoot′ *s* rejeton *m*

off′shore′ *adj* éloigné de la côte, du côté de la terre; (*wind*) de terre ‖ *adv* au large, vers la haute mer

off′side′ *adv* (sports) hors jeu

off′spring′ *s* descendance *f*; (*descendant*) rejeton *m*, enfant *mf*; (*result*) conséquence *f*

off′stage′ *adj* dans les coulisses ‖ *adv* à la cantonade

off′-the-cuff′ *adj* (coll) impromptu

off′-the-rec′ord *adj* confidentiel

off′-white′ *adj* blanc cassé

often [ˈɔfən], [ˈafən] *adv* souvent; **how often?** combien de fois?; **tous les combien?**; **not often** rarement; **once too often** une fois de trop

ogive [ˈodʒaɪv], [oˈdʒaɪv] *s* ogive *f*

ogle [ˈogəl] *tr* lancer une œillade à; (*to stare at*) dévisager

ogre [ˈogər] *s* ogre *m*

ohm [om] *s* ohm *m*

oil [ɔɪl] *s* huile *f*; (*painting*) huile, peinture *f* à l'huile; **holy oil** huile sainte, saintes huiles; **to pour oil on troubled waters** calmer la tempête, verser de l'huile sur les plaies de qn; **to smell of midnight oil** sentir l'huile; **to strike oil** atteindre une nappe pétrolifère; (fig) trouver le filon ‖ *tr* huiler; (*to bribe*) graisser la patte à ‖ *intr* (naut) faire le plein de mazout

oil′-and-vin′egar cru′et *s* huilier *m*

oil′ burn′er *s* réchaud *m* à pétrole

oil′can′ *s* bidon *m* d'huile, burette *f* d'huile

oil′cloth′ *s* toile *f* cirée

oil′ com′pany *s* société *f* pétrolière

oil′cup′ *s* (mach) godet *m* graisseur

oil′ drum′ *s* bidon *m* d'huile

oil′ field′ *s* gisement *m* pétrolifère

oil′ gauge′ *s* jauge *f* de niveau d'huile

oil′ lamp′ *s* lampe *f* à huile, lampe à pétrole

oil′man′ *s* (*pl* **-men′**) (*retailer*) huilier *m*; (*operator*) pétrolier *m*

oil′ pipe′line *s* oléoduc *m*

oil′ pump′ *s* pompe *f* à huile

oil′ rig′ s derrick m, tour f de forage; (*in water*) plate-forme f pétrolière

oil′ short′age s pénurie f de pétrole

oil′ stove′ s poêle m à mazout, fourneau m à pétrole

oil′ tank′er s pétrolier m, tanker m

oil′ well′ s puits m à pétrole

oil·y [′ɔɪli] adj (*comp* **-ier**; *super* **-iest**) huileux, oléagineux; (fig) onctueux

ointment [′ɔɪntmənt] s onguent m, pommade f

O.K. [′o′ke] (letterword) adj (coll) très bien, parfait ‖ s (coll) approbation f ‖ adv (coll) très bien ‖ v (*pret & pp* **O.K.'d**; *ger* **O.K.'ing**) tr (coll) approuver ‖ interj **O.K.!** ça colle!, d'accord!

okra [′okrə] s gombo m, ketmie f comestible

old [old] adj vieux; (*of former times*) ancien; (*wine*) vieux; **any old** n'importe, e.g., **any old time** n'importe quand; quelconque, e.g., **any old book** un livre quelconque; **at . . . years old** à l'âge de . . . ans; **how old is . . . ?** quel âge a . . . ?; **of old** d'autrefois, de jadis; **to be . . . years old** avoir . . . ans

old′ age′ s vieillesse f, âge m avancé

old′-clothes′man′ s (*pl* **-men′**) fripier m

old′ coun′try s mère patrie f

Old′ Cov′enant s (Bib) ancienne alliance f

old′-fash′ioned adj démodé, suranné, vieux jeu; (*literary style*) vieillot

old′ fo′gey or **old′ fo′gy** [′fogi] s (*pl* **-gies**) vieux bonhomme m, grime m

Old′ French′ s ancien français m

Old′ Glo′ry s le drapeau des États-Unis

old′ hag′ s vieille fée f

old′ hand′ s vieux routier m

old′ lad′y s vieille dame f; (coll) grandmère f

old′ maid′ s vieille fille f

old′ mas′ter s grand maître m; œuvre f d'un grand maître

old′ moon′ s lune f à son décours

old′ peo′ple's home′ s hospice m de vieillards

old′ salt′ s loup m de mer

old′ school′ s vieille école f, vieille roche f

oldster [′oldstər] s vieillard m, vieux m

Old′ Tes′tament s Ancien Testament m

old′-time′ adj du temps jadis, d'autrefois

old′-tim′er s (coll) vieux m de la vieille, vieux routier m

old′ wives′′ tale′ s conte m de bonne femme

Old Wom′an who lived′ in a shoe′ s mère f Gigogne

Old′ World′ s vieux monde m

old′-world′ adj de l'ancien monde; du vieux monde

oleander [,olɪ′ændər] s laurier-rose m

olfactory [ɑl′fæktəri] adj olfactif

oligar·chy [′ɑlɪ,gɑrki] s (*pl* **-chies**) oligarchie f

olive [′ɑlɪv] adj olive; (*complexion*) olivâtre ‖ s olive f; (*tree*) olivier m

ol′ive branch′ s rameau m d'olivier

ol′ive grove′ s olivaie f

ol′ive oil′ s huile f d'olive

Oliver [′ɑlɪvər] s Olivier m

ol′ive tree′ s olivier m

olympiad [o′lɪmpɪ,æd] s olympiade f

Olympian [o′lɪmpɪ·ən] adj olympien

Olympic [o′lɪmpɪk] adj olympique ‖ **Olympics** spl jeux mpl olympiques

ombudsman [′ɑmbʌdz,mæn] s intercesseur m, médiateur m

omelet [′ɑmlɪt] s omelette f

omen [′omən] s augure m, présage m

ominous [′ɑmɪnəs] adj de mauvais augure

omission [o′mɪʃən] s omission f

omit [o′mɪt] v (*pret & pp* **omitted**; *ger* **omitting**) tr omettre

omnibus [′ɑmnɪbəs] adj & s omnibus m

omnipotent [ɑm′nɪpətənt] adj omnipotent

omniscient [ɑm′nɪʃənt] adj omniscient

omnivorous [ɑm′nɪvərəs] adj omnivore

on [ɑn], [ɔn] adj (*light, radio*) allumé; (*faucet*) ouvert; (*machine, motor*) en marche; (*electrical appliance*) branché; (*brake*) serré; (*steak, chops, etc.*) dans la poêle; (*game, program, etc.*) commencé ‖ adv—**and so on** et ainsi de suite; **come on!** (coll) allons donc!; **farther on** plus loin; **from this day on** à dater de ce jour; **later on** plus tard; **move on!** circulez!; **to be on** (theat) être en scène; **to be on to s.o.** (coll) voir clair dans le jeu de qn; **to have on** être vêtu de, porter; **to . . . on** continuer à + *inf*, e.g., **to sing on** continuer à chanter; **well on** avancé, e.g., **well on in years** d'un âge avancé ‖ prep sur; (*at the time of*) lors de; à, e.g., **on foot** à pied; e.g., **on my arrival** à mon arrivée; e.g., **on page three** à la page trois; e.g., **on the first floor** au rez-de-chaussée; e.g., **on the right** à droite; en, à, e.g., **on a journey** en voyage; e.g., **on arriving** en arrivant; e.g., **on fire** en feu; e.g., **on sale** en vente; e.g., **on the** or **an average** en moyenne; e.g., **on the top of** en dessus de; dans, e.g., **on a farm** dans une ferme; e.g., **on the jury** dans le jury; e.g., **on the street** dans la rue; e.g., **on the train** dans le train; par, e.g., **he came on the train** il est venu par le train; e.g., **on a fine day** par un beau jour; de, e.g., **on good authority** de source certaine, de bonne part; e.g., **on the north** du côté du nord; e.g., **on the one hand . . . on the other hand** d'une part . . . d'autre part; e.g., **on this side** de ce côté-ci; e.g., **to have pity on** avoir pitié de; **to live on bread and water** vivre de pain et d'eau; sous, e.g., **on a charge of** sous l'inculpation de; e.g., **on pain of death** sous peine de mort; (not translated), e.g., **on Tuesday** mardi; e.g., **on Tuesdays** le mardi, tous les mardis; e.g., **on July fourteenth** le quatorze juillet; contre, e.g., **an attack on** une attaque contre; **it's on me** (*it's my turn to pay*) (coll) c'est ma tournée; **it's on the house** (coll) c'est la tournée du patron; **on examination** après examen; **on it** y, e.g., **there is the shelf; put the book on it** voilà l'étagère; mettez-y le livre; **on line** (comp) en ligne; **on or about** (*a certain date*) aux environs de; **on or after** (*a certain date*) à partir de; **on tap** en perce, à la pression; **on the spot** (*immediately*) sur-le-champ; (*there*) sur place; (slang) en danger imminent; **to be on the committee** faire partie du comité; **to march on a city** marcher sur une ville

on' and on' *adv* continuellement, sans fin

on'-board comput'er *s* ordinateur *m* à bord

once [wʌns] *s*—**this once** pour cette fois-ci ‖ *adv* une fois; (*formerly*) autrefois; **all at once** (*all together*) tous à la fois; (*suddenly*) tout à coup; **at once** tout de suite, sur-le-champ; (*at the same time*) à la fois, en même temps; **for once** pour une fois; **once and for all** une bonne fois, une fois pour toutes; **once in a while** de temps en temps; **once more** encore une fois; **once or twice** une ou deux fois; **once upon a time there was** il était une fois ‖ *conj* une fois que, dès que

once'-o'ver *s* (slang) examen *m* rapide; travail *m* hâtif; **to give the once-over to** (slang) jeter un coup d'œil à

one [wʌn] *adj & pron* un §77; un certain, e.g., **one Dupont** un certain Dupont; un seul, e.g., **with one voice** d'une seule voix; unique, e.g., **one price** prix unique; (not translated when preceded by an adjective), e.g., **the red pencil and the blue one** le crayon rouge et le bleu; **not one** pas un; **one and all** tous; **one and only** unique, e.g., **the one and only closet in the house** l'armoire unique de la maison; seul et unique, e.g., **my one and only umbrella** mon seul et unique parapluie; **one another** l'un l'autre; les uns les autres; **one by one** un à un; **one on one** en tête-à-tête; discussion *f* en tête-à-tête; **that one** celui-là; **the one that** celui que, celui qui; **this one** celui-ci; **to become one** s'unir, se marier ‖ *s* un *m*; **one o'clock** une heure ‖ *pron indef* on §87, e.g., **one cannot go there alone** on ne peut pas y aller seul; **one's** son, e.g., **one's son** son fils

one'-horse *adj* à un cheval; (coll) provincial, insignifiant

one'-horse town' *s* (coll) trou *m*

one'-man band' *s* homme-orchestre *m*

one'-man show' *s* spectacle *m* solo

onerous ['anərəs] *adj* onéreux

one·self' *pron* soi §85; soi-même §86; se §87, e.g., **to cut oneself** se couper; **to be oneself** se conduire sans affectation

one'-sid'ed *adj* à un côté, à une face; (*e.g., decision*) unilatéral; (*unfair*) partial, injuste

one'-track' *adj* à une voie; (coll) routinier

one'-way' *adj* à sens unique

one'-way tick'et *s* billet *m* d'aller, billet simple

onion ['ʌnjən] *s* oignon *m*; **to know one's onions** (coll) connaître son affaire

on'ion·skin' *s* papier *m* pelure

on'look'er *s* assistant *m*, spectateur *m*

only ['onli] *adj* seul, unique; (*child*) unique ‖ *adv* seulement; ne . . . que, e.g., **I have only two** je n'en ai que deux; réservé, e.g., **staff only** (public sign) réservé au personnel ‖ *conj* mais, si ce n'était que

on'rush' *s* ruée *f*

on'set' *s* attaque *f*; **at the onset** de prime abord, au premier abord

onslaught ['an,slɔt] *s* assaut *m*

on'-the-job' *adj* (*training*) en stage; (coll) alerte

onus ['onəs] *s* charge *f*, fardeau *m*

onward ['anwərd] or **onwards** ['anwərdz] *adv* en avant

onyx ['aniks] *s* onyx *m*

ooze [uz] *s* suintement *m*; (*mud*) vase *f*, limon *m* ‖ *tr* filtrer ‖ *intr* suinter, filtrer; **to ooze out** s'écouler

opal ['opəl] *s* opale *f*

opaque [o'pek] *adj* opaque; (*style*) obscur

OPEC ['opɛk] *s* (acronym) (**organization of petroleum-exporting countries**) OPEP (organisation des pays exportateurs de pétrole)

open ['opən] *adj* ouvert; (*personality*) franc, sincère; (*job, position*) vacant; (*hour*) libre; (*automobile*) découvert; (*market, trial*) public; (*question*) pendant, indécis; (*wound*) béant; (*to attack, to criticism, etc.*) exposé; (sports) international; **to break** or **crack open** éventrer; **to throw open the door** ouvrir la porte toute grande ‖ *s* ouverture *f*; (*in the woods*) clairière *f*; **in the open** au grand air, à ciel ouvert; (*in the open country*) en rase campagne; (*in the open sea*) en pleine mer; (*without being hidden*) découvert; (*openly*) ouvertement ‖ *tr* ouvrir; (*a canal lock*) lâcher; **to open fire** déclencher le feu ‖ *intr* ouvrir, s'ouvrir; (*said, e.g., of a play*) commencer, débuter; **to open into** aboutir à, déboucher sur; **to open on** donner sur; **to open up** s'épanouir, s'ouvrir

o'pen-air' *adj* en plein air, au grand air

o'pen-eyed' *adj* les yeux écarquillés

o'pen-hand'ed *adj* libéral, la main ouverte

o'pen-heart'ed *adj* ouvert, franc

o'pen-heart' sur'gery *s* chirurgie *f* à cœur ouvert

o'pen house' *s* journée *f* d'accueil; **to keep open house** tenir table ouverte

opening ['opənɪŋ] *s* ouverture *f*; (*in the woods*) clairière *f*, percée *f*; (*vacancy*) vacance *f*, poste *m* vacant; (*chance to say something*) occasion *f* favorable

o'pening night' *s* première *f*

o'pening num'ber *s* ouverture *f*

o'pening price' *s* cours *m* de début

o'pen-mind'ed *adj* à l'esprit ouvert, sans parti pris

o'pen se'cret *s* secret *m* de Polichinelle

o'pen shop' *s* atelier *m* ouvert aux nonsyndiqués

o'pen tick'et *s* coupon *m* date libre

o'pen·work' *s* ouvrage *m* à jour, ajours *mpl*

opera [`ɑpərə] *s* opéra *m*

op′era glass′es *spl* jumelles *fpl* de spectacle

op′era hat′ *s* claque *m*, gibus *m*

op′era house′ *s* opéra *m*

operate [`ɑpə,ret] *tr* actionner, faire marcher; exploiter ‖ *intr* fonctionner; s'opérer; (surg) opérer; **to operate on** (surg) opérer

operatic [,ɑpə`rætɪk] *adj* d'opéra

opera′ting expen′ses *spl* (*overhead*) frais *mpl* généraux, frais d'exploitation

op′erating room′ *s* salle *f* d'opération

opera′ting sys′tem *s* (comp) système *m* d'exploitation

op′erating ta′ble *s* table *f* d'opération, billard *m*

operation [,ɑpə`reʃən] *s* opération *f*; (*of a business, of a machine, etc.*) fonctionnement *m*; (med) intervention *f* chirurgicale, opération; **to have an operation (for)** se faire opérer (de); passer sur le billard (coll)

operative [`ɑpərətɪv] *adj* opératif; (surg) opératoire ‖ *s* (*workman*) ouvrier *m*; (*spy*) agent *m*, espion *m*

operator [`ɑpə,retər] *s* opérateur *m*; (*e.g., of a mine*) propriétaire *m* exploitant; (*of an automobile*) conducteur *m*; (telp) téléphoniste *mf*, standardiste *mf*; (slang) chevalier *m* d'industrie, aigrefin *m*; **operator on duty** opérateur de permanence

operetta [,ɑpə`rɛtə] *s* opérette *f*

opiate [`opɪ·et] *adj* opiacé ‖ *s* médicament *m* opiacé; (coll) narcotique *m*

opinion [ə`pɪnjən] *s* opinion *f*; **in my opinion** à mon avis

opinionated [ə`pɪnjə,netɪd] *adj* fier de ses opinions, dogmatique

opin′ion poll′ *s* sondage *m* d'opinion

opium [`opɪ·əm] *s* opium *m*

o′pium den′ *s* fumerie *f*

o′pium pop′py *s* œillette *f*

opossum [ə`pɑsəm] *s* opossum *m*, sarigue *f*

opponent [ə`ponənt] *s* adversaire *mf*, opposant *m*

opportune [,ɑpər`t(j)un] *adj* opportun, convenable

opportunist [,ɑpər`t(j)unɪst] *s* opportuniste *mf*

opportuni·ty [,ɑpər`t(j)unɪti] *s* (*pl* **-ties**) (*appropriate time*) occasion *f*; (*favorable condition or good chance for advancement*) chance *f*; **at your first** (or **earliest**) **opportunity** à votre première occasion

oppose [ə`poz] *tr* s'opposer à

opposite [`ɑpəsɪt] *adj* opposé, contraire; d'en face, e.g., **the house opposite** la maison d'en face ‖ *s* opposé *m*, contraire *m* ‖ *adv* en face, vis-à-vis ‖ *prep* en face de, à l'opposite de

op′posite num′ber *s* (fig) homologue *mf*

opposition [,ɑpə`zɪʃən] *s* opposition *f*

oppress [ə`prɛs] *tr* opprimer; (*to weigh heavily upon*) oppresser

oppression [ə`prɛʃən] *s* oppression *f*

oppressive [ə`prɛsɪv] *adj* oppressif; (*stifling*) étouffant, accablant

oppressor [ə`prɛsər] *s* oppresseur *m*

opprobrious [ə`probrɪ·əs] *adj* infamant, injurieux, honteux

opprobrium [ə`probrɪ·əm] *s* opprobre *m*

optic [`ɑptɪk] *adj* optique ‖ **optics** *s* optique *f*

optical [`ɑptɪkəl] *adj* optique

op′tical illu′sion *s* illusion *f* d'optique

optician [ɑp`tɪʃən] *s* opticien *m*

optimism [`ɑptɪ,mɪzəm] *s* optimisme *m*

optimist [`ɑptɪmɪst] *s* optimiste *mf*

optimistic [,ɑptɪ`mɪstɪk] *adj* optimiste

optimize [`ɑptɪ,maɪz] *tr* optimiser

option [`ɑpʃən] *s* option *f*

optional [`ɑpʃənəl] *adj* facultatif

optometrist [ɑp`tɑmɪtrɪst] *s* opticien *m*; optométriste *mf* (Canad)

opulent [`ɑpjələnt] *adj* opulent

or [ɔr] *conj* ou

oracle [`ɔrəkəl] *s* oracle *m*

oracular [o`rækjələr] *adj* d'oracle; dogmatique, sentencieux; (*ambiguous*) équivoque

oral [`orəl] *adj* oral

orange [`ɔrɪndʒ] *adj* orangé, orange ‖ *s* (*color*) orangé *m*, orange *m*; (*fruit*) orange *f*

orangeade [,ɔrɪndʒ`ed] *s* orangeade *f*

or′ange blos′som *s* fleur *f* d'oranger

or′ange grove′ *s* orangeraie *f*

or′ange juice′ *s* jus *m* d'orange

or′ange squeez′er *s* presse-fruits *m*

or′ange tree′ *s* oranger *m*

orang-outang [o`ræŋu,tæŋ] *s* orang-outan *m*

oration [o`reʃən] *s* discours *m*

orator [`ɔrətər] *s* orateur *m*

oratorical [,ɔrə`tɔrɪkəl] *adj* oratoire

oratori·o [,ɔrə`tori,o] *s* (*pl* **-os**) oratorio *m*

orato·ry [`ɔrə,tori] *s* (*pl* **-ries**) art *m* oratoire; (eccl) oratoire *m*

orb [ɔrb] *s* orbe *m*

orbit [`ɔrbɪt] *s* orbite *f*; **in orbit** sur orbite ‖ *tr* (*e.g., the sun*) tourner autour de; (*e.g., a rocket*) mettre en orbite, satelliser ‖ *intr* se mettre en orbite

orchard [`ɔrtʃərd] *s* verger *m*

orchestra [`ɔrkɪstrə] *s* orchestre *m*; (*pit for musicians*) fosse *f* d'orchestre; (*for spectators*) fauteuils *mpl* d'orchestre

orchestrate [`ɔrkɪ,stret] *tr* orchestrer

orchid [`ɔrkɪd] *s* orchidée *f*

ordain [ɔr`den] *tr* destiner; (eccl) ordonner; **to be ordained** (eccl) recevoir les ordres

ordeal [ɔr`di·əl] *s* épreuve *f*; (hist) ordalie *f*

order [`ɔrdər] *s* ordre *m*; (*of words*) ordonnance *f*; (*for merchandise, a meal, etc.*) commande *f*; (*military formation*) ordre; (law) arrêt *m*, arrêté *m*; **in order** en ordre; **in order of appearance** (theat) dans l'ordre d'entrée en scène; **in order that** pour que, afin que; **in order to** + *inf* pour + *inf*, afin de + *inf;* **on order** en commande, commandé; **order!** ordre!; **orders** (eccl) les ordres; (mil) la consigne; **pay to the order of** (com) payez à l'ordre de; **to get s.th. out of order** détraquer q.ch.; **to put in order** mettre en règle ‖ *tr* ordonner; (com) commander; **to order**

around faire aller et venir; **to order s.o. to** + *inf* ordonner à qn de + *inf*

or'der blank' *s* bon *m* de commande, bulletin *m* de commande

order·ly ['ɔrdərli] *adj* ordonné; (*life*) réglé; **to be orderly** avoir de l'ordre ‖ *s* (*pl* **-lies**) (med) ambulancier *m*, infirmier *m*; (mil) planton *m*

ordinal ['ɔrdɪnəl] *adj & s* ordinal *m*

ordinance ['ɔrdɪnəns] *s* ordonnance *f*

ordinary ['ɔrdɪn,ɛri] *adj* ordinaire; **out of the ordinary** exceptionnel

ordination [,ɔrdɪ'eʃən] *s* ordination *f*

ordnance ['ɔrdnəns] *s* artillerie *f*; (*branch of an army*) service *m* du matériel

ore [or] *s* minerai *m*

oregano [ə'rɛgə,no] *s* origan *m*

organ ['ɔrgən] *s* (anat, journ) organe *m*; (mus) orgue *m*

organdy ['ɔrgəndi] *s* organdi *m*

or'gan grind'er *s* joueur *m* d'orgue

organic [ɔr'gænɪk] *adj* organique

organism ['ɔrgə,nɪzəm] *s* organisme *m*

organist ['ɔrgənɪst] *s* organiste *mf*

organization [,ɔrgənɪ'zeʃən] *s* organisation *f*

organize ['ɔrgə,naɪz] *tr* organiser

organizer ['ɔrgə,naɪzər] *s* organisateur *m*

or'gan loft' *s* tribune *f* d'orgue

orgasm ['ɔrgæzəm] *s* orgasme *m*

or·gy ['ɔrdʒi] *s* (*pl* **-gies**) orgie *f*

orient ['ɔri·ənt] *s* orient *m*; **Orient** Orient ‖ ['ɔri,ɛnt] *tr* orienter

oriental [,ɔri'ɛntəl] *adj* oriental ‖ (*cap*) *s* Oriental *m*

orien'tal rug' *s* tapis *m* d'orient

orientate ['ɔri·ɛn,tet] *tr* orienter

orientation [,ɔri·ɛn'teʃən] *s* orientation *f*

orifice ['ɔrɪfɪs] *s* orifice *m*

origin ['ɔfədʒɪn] *s* origine *f*

original [ə'rɪdʒɪnəl] *adj* (*new, not copied; inventive*) original; (*earliest*) originel, primitif; (*first*) originaire, premier ‖ *s* original *m*

originality [ə,rɪdʒɪ'nælɪti] *s* originalité *f*

originate [ə'rɪdʒə,net] *tr* faire naître, créer ‖ *intr* prendre naissance; **to originate from** provenir de

oriole ['ɔri,ol] *s* loriot *m*

ormolu ['ɔrmə,lu] *s* bronze *m* doré; (*powdered gold for gilding*) or *m* moulu; (*alloy of zinc and copper*) similor *m*

ornament ['ɔrnəmənt] *s* ornement *m* ‖ ['ɔrnə,mɛnt] *tr* ornementer, orner

ornamental [,ɔrnə'mɛntəl] *adj* ornemental

ornate [ɔr'net], ['ɔrnet] *adj* orné, fleuri

ornery ['ɔrnəri] *adj* (coll) acariâtre, intraitable

ornithology [,ɔrnɪ'θalədʒi] *s* ornithologie *f*

orphan ['ɔrfən] *adj & s* orphelin *m*

orphanage ['ɔrfənɪdʒ] *s* (*asylum*) orphelinat *m*; (*orphanhood*) orphelinage *m*

Orpheus ['ɔrfi·əs] *s* Orphée *m*

orthodontics [,ɔrθə'dantɪks] *s* orthodontie *f*

orthodox ['ɔrθə,daks] *adj* orthodoxe

orthogra·phy [ɔr'θagrəfi] *s* (*pl* **-phies**) orthographe *f*

oscillate ['asɪ,let] *intr* osciller

osier ['oʒər] *s* osier *m*

osmosis [az'mosɪs] *s* osmose *f*

osprey ['aspri] *s* aigle *m* pêcheur

ossi·fy ['asɪ,faɪ] *v* (*pret & pp* **-fied**) *tr* ossifier ‖ *intr* s'ossifier

ostensible [as'tɛnsɪbəl] *adj* prétendu, apparent, soi-disant

ostentatious [,astɛn'teʃəs] *adj* ostentatoire, fastueux

osteopathy [,astɪ'apəθi] *s* ostéopathie *f*

ostracism ['astrə,sɪzəm] *s* ostracisme *m*

ostracize ['astrə,saɪz] *tr* frapper d'ostracisme

ostrich ['astrɪtʃ] *s* autruche *f*

other ['ʌðər] *adj* autre; **every other day** tous les deux jours; **every other one** un sur deux ‖ *pron indef* autre ‖ *adv*—**other than** autrement que

otherwise ['ʌðər,waɪz] *adv* autrement, à part cela ‖ *conj* sinon, e.g., **come at once, otherwise it will be too late** venez tout de suite, sinon il sera trop tard; sans cela, e.g., **thanks, otherwise I'd have forgotten** merci, sans cela j'aurais oublié

oth'er·world'ly *adj* détaché des contingences de ce monde

otter ['atər] *s* loutre *f*

Ottoman ['atəmən] *adj* ottoman ‖ (*l.c.*) *s* (*corded fabric*) ottoman *m*; (*divan*) ottomane *f*; (*footstool*) pouf *m*; **Ottoman** (*person*) Ottoman *m*

ouch [autʃ] *interj* aïe!

ought [ɔt] *s* zéro *m*; **for ought I know** pour autant que je sache ‖ *aux* used to express obligation, e.g., **he ought to go away** il devrait s'en aller; e.g., **he ought to have gone away** il aurait dû s'en aller

ounce [auns] *s* once *f*

our [aur] *adj poss* notre §88

ours [aurz] *pron poss* le nôtre §89

our·selves' *pron pers* nous-mêmes §86; nous §85, §87

oust [aust] *tr* évincer, chasser

out [aut] *adj* extérieur; absent; (*fire*) éteint; (*secret*) divulgé; (*tide*) bas; (*flower*) épanoui; (*rope*) filé; (*lease*) expiré; (*gear*) débrayé; (*unconscious person*) évanoui; (*boxer*) knockouté; (*book, magazine, etc.*) paru, publié; (*out of print, out of stock*) épuisé; (*a ball*) (sports) hors jeu; (*a player*) (sports) éliminé ‖ *s* (*pretext*) échappatoire *f*; **to be on the outs with** être brouillé avec ‖ *adv* dehors, au dehors; (*outdoors*) en plein air; **out and out** complètement; **out for** en quête de; **out for lunch** parti déjeuner; **out of** (*cash*) démuni de; (*a glass, cup, etc.*) dans; (*a bottle*) à; (*the window; curiosity, friendship, respect, etc.*) par; (*range, sight*) hors de; de, e.g., **to cry out of joy** pleurer de joie; e.g., **made out of** fait de; sur, e.g., **nine times out of ten** neuf fois sur dix; **out of sight, out of mind** loin des yeux, loin du cœur; **out with it!** allez, dites-le!; **to be out** (*to be absent*) être sorti; faire, e.g., **the sun is out** il fait du soleil;

to be out of bounds (sports) être hors jeu ‖ *prep* par ‖ *interj* hors d'ici!, ouste!

out′ and away′ *adv* de beaucoup, de loin

out′-and-out′ *adj* vrai; (*fanatic*) intransigeant; (*liar*) achevé

out′-and-out′er *s* (coll) intransigeant *m*

out′bid′ *v* (*pret* **-bid**; *pp* **-bid** or **-bidden**; *ger* **-bidding**) *tr* enchérir sur; (fig) renchérir sur ‖ *intr* surenchérir

out′board mo′tor *s* moteur *m* hors-bord, motogodille *f*

out′break′ *s* déchaînement *m*; (*of hives; of anger; etc.*) éruption *f*; (*of epidemic*) manifestation *f*; (*insurrection*) révolte *f*

out′build′ing *s* annexe *f*, dépendance *f*

out′burst′ *s* explosion *f*; (*of anger*) accès *m*; (*of laughter*) éclat *m*; (*e.g., of generosity*) élan *m*

out′cast′ *adj* & *s* banni *m*, proscrit *m*

out′caste′ *adj* hors caste; *s* hors-caste *mf*

out′come′ *s* résultat *m*, dénouement *m*

out′cry′ *s* (*pl* **-cries**) clameur *f*; (*of indignation*) levée *f* de boucliers, tollé *m*

out·dat′ed *adj* démodé, suranné

out′dis′tance *tr* dépasser; (sports) distancer

out′do′ *v* (*pret* **-did**; *pp* **-done**) *tr* surpasser, l'emporter sur; **to outdo oneself** se surpasser

out′door′ *adj* au grand air; (sports) de plein air

out′door grill′ *s* rôtisserie *f* en plein air

out′doors′ *s* rase campagne *f*, plein air *m* ‖ *adv* au grand air, en plein air; (*outside of the house*) hors de la maison; (*at night*) à la belle étoile

out′door swim′ming pool′ *s* piscine *f* à ciel ouvert

outer [′aʊtər] *adj* extérieur, externe

out′er space′ *s* cosmos *m*, espace *m* cosmique

out′field′ *s* (*baseball*) grand champ *m*

out′fit′ *s* équipement *m*, attirail *m*; (*caseful of implements*) trousse *f*, nécessaire *m*; (*ensemble*) costume et accessoires *mpl*; (*of a bride*) trousseau *m*; (*team*) équipe *f*; (*group of soldiers*) unité *f*; (com) compagnie *f* ‖ *v* (*pret* & *pp* **-fitted**; *ger* **-fitting**) *tr* équiper

out′go′ing *adj* en partance, partant; (*officeholder*) sortant; (*friendly*) communicatif, sympathique

out′grow′ *v* (*pret* **-grew**; *pp* **-grown**) *tr* devenir plus grand que; (*e.g., childhood clothes, activities, etc.*) devenir trop grand pour; abandonner, se défaire de

out′growth′ *s* excroissance *f*; (fig) résultat *m*, conséquence *f*

outing [′aʊtɪŋ] *s* excursion *f*, sortie *f*

outlandish [aʊt′lændɪʃ] *adj* bizarre, baroque

out′last′ *tr* durer plus longtemps que; survivre (with *dat*)

out′law′ *s* hors-la-loi *m*, proscrit *m* ‖ *tr* mettre hors la loi, proscrire

out′lay′ *s* débours *mpl*, dépenses *fpl* ‖ **out′lay′** *v* (*pret* & *pp* **-laid**) *tr* débourser, dépenser

out′let′ *s* (*for water, etc.*) sortie *f*, issue *f*; (*escape valve*) deversoir *m*; (*for, e.g., pent-up emotions*) exutoire *m*; (com) débouché *m*; (elec) prise *f* de courant, prise électrique; **no outlet** (public sign) rue sans issue

out′line′ *s* (*profile*) contour *m*; (*sketch*) esquisse *f*; (*summary*) aperçu *m*; (*of a work in preparation*) plan *m*; (*main points*) grandes lignes *fpl* ‖ *tr* esquisser; (*a work in preparation*) ébaucher

out′live′ *tr* survivre (with *dat*)

out′lived′ *adj* caduc, désuet

out′look′ *s* perspective *f*, point *m* de vue

out′ly′ing *adj* éloigné, écarté, isolé

outmoded [,aʊt′modɪd] *adj* démodé

out′num′ber *tr* surpasser en nombre

out′ of bounds′ *adj* hors jeu

out′-of-date′ *adj* démodé, suranné; (*document*) périmé

out′-of-door′ *adj* au grand air

out′-of-doors′ *adj* au grand air ‖ *s* rase campagne *f*, plein air *m* ‖ *adv* au grand air, hors de la maison

out′ of or′der *adj* en panne, en dérangement; **to be out of order** (*to be out of sequence*) ne pas être dans l'ordre

out′ of print′ *adj* épuisé

out′ of step′ *s*—**to be out of step** ne pas être au pas; **to be out of step with** marcher à contre-pas de; **to get out of step** perdre le pas

out′ of tune′ *adj* désaccordé ‖ *adv* faux, e.g., **to sing out of tune** chanter faux

out′ of work′ *adj* en chômage

out′pa′tient *s* malade *mf* de consultation externe

out′patient clin′ic *s* consultation *f* externe

out′post′ *s* avant-poste *m*, antenne *f*

out′put′ *s* rendement *m*, débit *m*; (*of a mine; of a worker*) production *f*

out′rage *s* outrage *m*; (*wanton violence*) atrocité *f*, attentat *m* honteux ‖ *tr* faire outrage à, outrager; (*a woman*) violer

outrageous [aʊt′redʒəs] *adj* outrageux; (*intolerable*) insupportable

out′rank′ *tr* dépasser en grade, dépasser en rang

out′rid′er *s* explorateur *m*; cow-boy *m*; (*mounted attendant*) piqueur *m*

outrigger [′aʊt,rɪgər] *s* (*outboard framework*) balancier *m*; (*oar support*) porte-en-dehors *m*

out′right′ *adj* pur, absolu; (*e.g., manner*) franc, direct ‖ **out′right′** *adv* complètement; (*frankly*) franchement; (*at once*) sur le coup

out′set′ *s* début *m*, commencement *m*

out′side′ *adj* du dehors, d'extérieur ‖ **out′side′s** dehors *m*, extérieur *m*; surface *f*; **at the outside** tout au plus, au maximum ‖ **out′side′** *adv* dehors, à l'extérieur; (*outdoors*) en plein air; **outside of** en dehors de, à l'extérieur de; (*except for*) sauf ‖ **out′side′** or **out′side′** *prep* en dehors de, à l'extérieur de

outsider [,aʊt'saɪdər] *s* étranger *m*; (*intruder*) intrus *m*; (*uninitiated*) profane *mf*; (*dark horse*) outsider *m*

out′size′ *adj* hors série

out′skirts′ *spl* approches *fpl*, périphérie *f*

out′spo′ken *adj* franc; **to be outspoken** avoir son franc-parler

out′stand′ing *adj* saillant; (*eminent*) hors pair, hors ligne; (*debts*) à recouvrer, impayé

outward ['aʊtwərd] *adj* extérieur; (*apparent*) superficiel; (*direction*) en dehors ‖ *adv* au dehors, vers le dehors

out′weigh′ *tr* peser plus que; (*in value*) l'emporter en valeur sur

out′wit′ *v* (*pret & pp* **-witted;** *ger* **-witting**) *tr* duper, déjouer; (*a pursuer*) dépister

oval ['ovəl] *adj & s* ovale *m*

ova·ry ['ovəri] *s* (*pl* **-ries**) ovaire *m*

ovation [o've∫ən] *s* ovation *f*

oven ['ʌvən] *s* four *m*; (*fig*) fournaise *f*

over ['ovər] *adj* fini, passé; (*additional*) en plus; (*excessive*) en excès; plus, e.g., **eight and over** huit et plus ‖ *adv* au-dessus, dessus; (*on the other side*) de l'autre côté; (*again*) de nouveau; (*on the reverse side of sheet of paper*) au verso; (*finished*) passé, achevé; **all over** (*everywhere*) partout; (*finished*) fini; (*completely*) jusqu'au bout des ongles; **I'll be right over** (coll) j'arrive tout de suite; **over!** (*turn the page!*) voir au verso!, tournez!; (rad) à vous!; **over again** de nouveau, encore une fois; **over against** en face de; (*compared to*) auprès de; **over and above** en plus de; **over and out!** (rad) terminé!; **over and over** à coups répétés, à plusieurs reprises; **over here** ici, de ce côté; **over there** là-bas; **to be over** (*an illness*) s'être remis de; **to hand over** remettre ‖ *prep* au-dessus de; (*on top of*) sur, par-dessus; (*with motion*) par-dessus, e.g., **to jump over a fence** sauter par-dessus une barrière; (*a period of time*) pendant, au cours de; (*near*) près de; (*a certain number or amount*) plus de, au-dessus de; (*concerning*) à propos de, au sujet de; (*on the other side of*) au delà de, de l'autre côté de; à, e.g., **over the telephone** au téléphone; (*while doing s.th.*) tout en prenant, e.g., **over a cup of coffee** tout en prenant une tasse de café; **all over** répandu sur; **over and above** en sus de, en plus de; **to fall over** (*e.g., a cliff*) tomber du haut de; **to reign over** régner sur ‖ *interj* (*CB language*) terminé!

o′ver·all′ *adj* hors tout, complet; général, total ‖ **overalls** *spl* combinaison *f* d'homme, cotte *f*, salopette *f*

o′ver·awe′ *tr* impressionner, intimider

o′ver·bear′ing *adj* impérieux, tranchant, autoritaire

o′ver·board′ *adv* par-dessus bord; **man overboard!** un homme à la mer!; **to throw overboard** jeter par-dessus le bord; (fig) abandonner

o′ver·book′ing *s* surréservation *f*

o′ver·cast′ *adj* obscurci, nuageux ‖ *s* ciel *m* couvert ‖ *v* (*pret & pp* **-cast**) *tr* obscurcir, couvrir

o′ver·charge′ *s* prix *m* excessif, majoration *f* excessive; (elec) surcharge *f* ‖ **o′ver·charge′** *tr* (*a customer*) rançonner; (elec) surcharger; **to overcharge s.o. for s.th.** faire payer trop cher q.ch. à qn ‖ *intr* demander un prix excessif

o′ver·coat′ *s* pardessus *m*

o′ver·come′ *v* (*pret* **-came;** *pp* **-come**) *tr* vaincre; (*difficulties*) surmonter

o′ver·con′fidence *s* témérité *f*, confiance *f* exagérée

o′ver·con′fident *adj* téméraire, excessivement confiant

o′ver·cooked′ *adj* trop cuit

o′ver·crowd′ *tr* bonder; (*a town, region, etc.*) surpeupler

o′ver·do′ *v* (*pret* **-did;** *pp* **-done**) *tr* exagérer; **overdone** (culin) trop cuit ‖ *intr* se surmener

o′ver·dose′ *s* dose *f* excessive, surdosage *m*

o′ver·draft′ *s* découvert *m*, solde *m* débiteur

o′ver·draw′ *v* (*pret* **-drew;** *pp* **-drawn**) *tr* tirer à découvert ‖ *intr* excéder son crédit

o′ver·drive′ *s* (aut) surmultiplication *f*

o′ver·due′ *adj* en retard; (com) échu, arriéré

o′ver·eat′ *v* (*pret* **-ate;** *pp* **-eaten**) *tr & intr* trop manger

o′ver·exer′tion *s* surmenage *m*

o′ver·expose′ *tr* surexposer

o′ver·expo′sure *s* surexposition *f*

o′ver·flow′ *s* débordement *m*; (*pipe*) trop-plein *m* ‖ **o′ver·flow′** *tr & intr* déborder

o′ver·fly′ *v* (*pret* **-flew;** *pp* **-flown**) *tr* survoler

o′ver·grown′ *adj* démesuré; (*e.g., child*) trop grand pour son âge; **overgrown with** (*e.g., weeds*) envahi par, recouvert de

o′ver·hang′ *v* (*pret & pp* **-hung**) *tr* surplomber, faire saillie au-dessus de; (*to threaten*) menacer ‖ *intr* (*to jut out*) faire saillie

o′ver·haul′ *s* remise *f* en état ‖ **o′ver·haul′** *tr* remettre en état; (*to catch up to*) rattraper

o′ver·head′ *adj* élevé; aérien, surélevé ‖ *s* (*overpass*) pont-route *m*; (com) frais *mpl* généraux ‖ **o′ver·head′** *adv* au-dessus de la tête, en haut

o′ver·head projec′tor *s* rétroprojecteur *m*

o′ver·head valve′ *s* soupape *f* en tête

o′ver·hear′ *v* (*pret & pp* **-heard**) *tr* entendre par hasard; (*a conversation*) surprendre

o′ver·heat′ *tr* surchauffer

overjoyed [,ovər'dʒɔɪd] *adj* ravi, transporté de joie

overland ['ovər,lænd] *adj & adv* par terre, par voie de terre

o′ver·lap′ *v* (*pret & pp* **-lapped;** *ger* **-lapping**) *tr* enchevaucher, imbriquer ‖ *intr* chevaucher

o′ver·lap′ping *s* recouvrement *m*, chevauchement *m*, imbrication *f*; (*of functions, offices, etc.*) double emploi *m*

o′ver·load′ *s* surcharge *f*; (comp) surcharge; **sudden overload** (elec) coup *m* de collier ‖ **o′ver·load′** *tr* surcharger

o′ver·look′ *tr* (*to survey*) donner sur, avoir vue sur; (*to ignore*) fermer les yeux sur, passer sous silence; (*to neglect*) oublier, négliger

o′ver·lord′ *s* suzerain *m* ‖ **o′ver·lord′** *tr* dominer, tyranniser

overly [′ovərli] *adv* (coll) trop, à l'excès

o′ver·med′icate *intr* (med) surmédicaliser

o′ver·night′ *adv* toute la nuit; du jour au lendemain; **to stay overnight** passer la nuit

o′ver·night′ bag′ *s* sac *m* de nuit

o′ver·pass′ *s* passage *m* supérieur, pontroute *m*, saut-de-mouton *m*

o′ver·pay′ment *s* surpaye *f*, rétribution *f* excessive

o′ver·pop′ula′tion *s* surpeuplement *m*, surpopulation *f*

o′ver·pow′er *tr* maîtriser; **overpowered with grief** accablé de douleur

o′ver·pow′ering *adj* accablant, irrésistible

o′ver·produc′tion *s* surproduction *f*

o′ver·rate′ *tr* surestimer

o′ver·reach′ *tr* dépasser

o′ver·ripe′ *adj* blet, trop mûr

o′ver·rule′ *tr* décider contre; (*to set aside*) annuler, casser

o′ver·run′ *v* (*pret* -ran; *pp* -run; *ger* -running) *tr* envahir; (*to flood*) inonder; (*limits, boundaries, etc.*) dépasser ‖ *intr* déborder

o′ver·sea′ or **o′ver·seas′** *adj* d'outre-mer ‖ **o′ver·sea′** or **o′ver·seas′** *adv* outre-mer

o′ver·see′ *v* (*pret* -saw; *pp* -seen) *tr* surveiller

o′ver·se′er *s* surveillant *m*, inspecteur *m*

o′ver·sexed′ *adj* hypersexué

o′ver·shad′ow *tr* ombrager; (fig) éclipser

o′ver·shoes′ *spl* caoutchoucs *mpl*

o′ver·sight′ *s* inadvertance *f*, étourderie *f*

o′ver·sleep′ *v* (*pret* & *pp* -slept) *intr* dormir trop longtemps

o′ver·step′ *v* (*pret* & *pp* -stepped; *ger* -stepping) *tr* dépasser, outrepasser

o′ver·stock′ *tr* surapprovisionner

o′ver·stuffed′ *adj* rembourré

o′ver·sup·ply′ *s* (*pl* -plies) excédent *m*, abondance *f* ‖ **o′ver·sup·ply′** *v* (*pret* & *pp* -plied) *tr* approvisionner avec excès

overt [′ovərt], [o′vʌrt] *adj* ouvert, manifeste; (*intentional*) prémédité

o′ver·take′ *v* (*pret* -took; *pp* -taken) *tr* rattraper; (*a runner*) dépasser; (*an automobile*) doubler; (*to surprise*) surprendre

o′ver·tax′ *tr* surtaxer; (*to tire*) surmener, excéder

o′ver-the-coun′ter *adj* vendu directement à l'acheteur

o′ver·throw′ *s* renversement *m* ‖ **o′ver·throw′** *v* (*pret* -threw; *pp* -thrown) *tr* renverser

o′ver·time′ *adj* & *adv* en heures supplémentaires ‖ *s* heures *fpl* supplémentaires

o′ver·time pe′riod *s* prolongation *f*

o′ver·tone′ *s* (mus) harmonique *m*; (fig) signification *f*, sous-entendu *m*

o′ver·trump′ *tr* surcouper

overture [′ovərtʃər] *s* ouverture *f*

o′ver·turn′ *tr* renverser, chavirer ‖ *intr* chavirer; (aer, aut) capoter

overweening [,ovər′winɪŋ] *adj* arrogant, outrecuidant

o′ver·weight′ *adj* au-dessus du poids normal; (*fat*) obèse ‖ *s* excédent *m* de poids

overwhelm [,ovər′hwɛlm] *tr* accabler, écraser; (*with favors, gifts, etc.*) combler

o′ver·work′ *s* surmenage *m*, excès *m* de travail ‖ **o′ver·work′** *tr* surmener, surcharger; abuser de, trop employer ‖ *intr* se surmener

Ovid [′ovɪd] *s* Ovide *m*

ow [aʊ] *interj* aïe!

owe [o] *tr* devoir ‖ *intr* avoir des dettes; **to owe for** avoir à payer, devoir

owing [′o·ɪŋ] *adj* dû, redû; **owing to** à cause de, en raison de

owl [aʊl] *s* (*Asio*) hibou *m*; (*Strix*) chouette *f*, hulotte *f*; (*Tyto alba*) effraie *f*

own [on] *adj* propre, e.g., **my own brother** mon propre frère ‖ *s*—**all its own** spécial, authentique, e.g., **an aroma all its own** un parfum spécial, un parfum authentique; **my own (your own, etc.)** le mien (le vôtre, etc.) §89; **of my own (of their own, etc.)** bien à moi (bien à eux, etc.); **on one's own** à son propre compte, de son propre chef; **to come into one's own** entrer en possession de son bien; (*to win out*) obtenir de succès; (*to receive due praise*) recevoir les honneurs qu'on mérite; **to hold one's own** se maintenir, se défendre ‖ *tr* posséder; être propriétaire de; (*to acknowledge*) reconnaître ‖ *intr*—**to own to** convenir de, reconnaître; **to own up** (coll) faire des aveux; **to own up to** (coll) faire l'aveu de, avouer

owner [′onər] *s* propriétaire *mf*, possesseur *m*

ownership [′onər,ʃɪp] *s* propriété *f*, possession *f*

own′er's li′cense *s* carte *f* grise

ox [aks] *s* (*pl* oxen [′aksən]) bœuf *m*

ox′cart′ *s* char *m* à bœufs

oxfords [′aksfərdz] *spl* richelieus *mpl*

oxide [′aksaɪd] *s* oxyde *m*

oxidize [′aksɪ,daɪz] *tr* oxyder ‖ *intr* s'oxyder

oxygen [′aksɪdʒən] *s* oxygène *m*

oxygenate [′aksɪdʒə,net] *tr* oxygéner

ox′ygen tent′ *s* tente *f* à oxygène

oxytone [′aksɪ,ton] *adj* & *s* oxyton *m*

oyster [′ɔɪstər] *adj* huîtrier ‖ *s* huître *f*

oys′ter bed′ *s* huîtrière *f*, banc *m* d'huîtres

oys′ter cock′tail *s* huîtres *fpl* écaillées aux condiments

oys′ter farm′ *s* parc *m* à huîtres, clayère *f*

oys′ter fork′ *s* fourchette *f* à huîtres

oys′ter knife′ *s* couteau *m* à huîtres

oys′ter·man *s* (*pl* -men) écailler *m*

oys'ter o'pener s (*person*) écailler m; (*implement*) ouvre-huîtres m
oys'ter plant' s salsifis m

oys'ter shell' s coquille f d'huître
oys'ter stew' s soupe f à huîtres
ozone [`ozon] s ozone m; (coll) air m frais

P

P, p [pi] s XVIe lettre de l'alphabet
pace [pes] s pas m; **to keep pace with** marcher de pair avec; **to put through one's paces** mettre à l'épreuve; **to set the pace** mener le train ‖ tr arpenter; **to pace off** mesurer au pas ‖ intr aller au pas; (equit) ambler
pace'mak'er s meneur m de train; (med) stimulateur m (cardiaque)
pacific [pə`sɪfɪk] adj pacifique ‖ **Pacific** adj & s Pacifique m
pacifier [`pæsɪ,faɪər] s pacificateur m; (*teething ring*) sucette f
pacifism [`pæsɪ,fɪzəm] s pacifisme m
pacifist [`pæsɪfɪst] adj & s pacifiste mf
paci-fy [`pæsɪ,faɪ] v (*pret & pp* -**fied**) tr pacifier
pack [pæk] s (*of peddler*) ballot m; (*of soldier*) paquetage m, sac m; (*of beast of burden*) bât m; (*of hounds*) meute f; (*of evildoers, of wolves*) bande f; (*of lies*) tissu m; (*of playing cards*) jeu m; (*of cigarettes*) paquet m; (*of floating ice*) banquise f; (*of troubles*) foule f; (*of fools*) tas m; (med) enveloppement m ‖ tr emballer, empaqueter; mettre en boîte; (*e.g., earth*) tasser; (*to stuff*) bourrer; **to send packing** (coll) envoyer promener ‖ intr faire ses bagages
package [`pækɪdʒ] s paquet m ‖ tr empaqueter
pack'age deal' s accord m global, achat m forfaitaire
pack'age plan' s voyage m à forfait
pack'aging s conditionnement m
pack'aging and prepara'tion s habillage m
pack' an'imal s bête f de somme
packet [`pækɪt] s paquet m; (naut) paquebot m; (pharm) sachet m
pack' horse' s cheval m de bât
pack'ing box' or **case'** s caisse f d'emballage
pack'ing house' s conserverie f
pack'sad'dle s bât m
pack'thread' s ficelle f
pack'train' s convoi m de bêtes de somme
pact [pækt] s pacte m
pad [pæd] s (*to prevent friction or damage*) bourrelet m; (*of writing paper*) bloc m; (*for inking*) tampon m; (*of an aquatic plant*) feuille f; (*for launching a rocket*) rampe f; (*sound of footsteps*) pas m; (*one's home*) (slang) piaule f, turne f, baraque f ‖ v (*pret & pp* **padded**; *ger* **padding**) tr rembourrer; (*to expand unnecessarily*) délayer ‖ intr aller à pied

pad'ded cell' s cellule f matelassée, cabanon m
paddle [`pædəl] s (*of a canoe*) pagaie f; (*for table tennis*) raquette f; (*of a wheel*) aube f; (*for beating*) palette f ‖ tr pagayer; (*to spank*) fesser ‖ intr pagayer; (*to splash*) barboter
pad'dle wheel' s roue f à aubes
paddock [`pædək] s enclos m; (*at race track*) paddock m
pad'dy wag'on [`pædi] s (slang) panier m à salade
pad'lock' s cadenas m ‖ tr cadenasser
pagan [`pagən] adj & s païen m
paganism [`pegə,nɪzəm] s paganisme m
page [pedʒ] s (*of a book*) page f; (*boy attendant*) page m; (*in a hotel or club*) chasseur m ‖ tr (*a book*) paginer; appeler, demander, e.g., **you are being paged** on vous demande
pageant [`pædʒənt] s parade f à grand spectacle
pageant·ry [`pædʒəntri] s (*pl* -**ries**) grand apparat m; vaines pompes fpl
page' proof' s épreuve f de pages, seconde épreuve f; (journ) morasse f
paginate [`pædʒɪ,net] tr paginer
paging [`pedʒɪŋ] s mise f en pages
paid' in full' [ped] adj (*formula stamped on bill*) pour acquit
paid' vaca'tion s congé m payé
pail [pel] s seau m
pain [pen] s douleur f; **on pain of** sous peine de; **pain in the neck** (fig) casse-pieds m; **to take pains** se donner de la peine ‖ tr faire mal à; **it pains me to** il me coûte de ‖ intr faire mal
painful [`penfəl] adj douloureux
pain'kil'ler s (coll) calmant m
painless [`penlɪs] adj sans douleur
pains'tak'ing adj soigneux; (*work*) soigné
paint [pent] s peinture f; **wet paint** peinture fraîche; (*public sign*) attention à la peinture! ‖ tr & intr peindre
paint'box' s boîte f de couleurs
paint'brush' s pinceau m
paint' buck'et s camion m
painter [`pentər] s peintre mf
painting [`pentɪŋ] s peinture f
paint' remov'er s décapant m
pair [pɛr] s paire f; (*of people*) couple m ‖ tr accoupler ‖ intr s'accoupler
pair' of scis'sors s ciseaux mpl
pair' of trou'sers s pantalon m
pajam'a par'ty [pə`dʒamə] s soirée-hébergement f

pajamas *spl* pyjama *m*, pyjamas

Pakistan [‚pɑkɪˈstɑn] *s* le Pakistan

Pakista·ni [‚pɑkɪˈstɑni] *adj* pakistanais ‖ *s* (*pl* **-nis**) Pakistanais *m*

pal [pæl] *s* copain *m* ‖ *v* (*pret & pp* **palled**; *ger* **palling**) *intr* (coll) être de bons copains; **to pal with** être copain de

palace [ˈpælɪs] *s* palais *m*

palatable [ˈpælətəbəl] *adj* savoureux; (*acceptable*) agréable

palatal [ˈpælətəl] *adj* palatal ‖ *s* palatale *f*

palate [ˈpælɪt] *s* palais *m*

pale [pel] *adj* pâle ‖ *s* (*stake*) pieu *m*; **beyond the pale** au-delà de la limite permise ‖ *intr* pâlir

pale′face′ *s* visage *m* pâle

palette [ˈpælɪt] *s* palette *f*

palfrey [ˈpɔlfri] *s* palefroi *m*

palisade [‚pælɪˈsed] *s* palissade *f*; (*line of cliffs*) falaise *f*

pall [pɔl] *s* (*over a casket*) poêle *m*, drap *m* mortuaire; (*coffin*) cercueil *m*, poêle; (*to cover chalice*) pale *f*; (*vestment*) pallium *m* ‖ *intr* devenir fade; **to pall on** rassasier

pall′bear′er *s* porteur *m* d'un cordon du poêle; **to be a pallbearer** tenir les cordons du poêle

pallet [ˈpælɪt] *s* grabat *m*

palliate [ˈpælɪ‚et] *tr* pallier

pallid [ˈpælɪd] *adj* pâle, blême

pallor [ˈpælər] *s* pâleur *f*

palm [pɑm] *s* (*of the hand*) paume *f*; (*measure*) palme *m*; (*leaf*) palme *f*; (*tree*) palmier *m*; **to carry off the palm** remporter la palme; **to grease the palm of** (slang) graisser la patte à ‖ *tr* (*a card*) escamoter; **to palm off s.th. on s.o.** refiler q.ch. à qn

palmet·to [pælˈmɛto] *s* (*pl* **-tos** or **-toes**) palmier *m* nain

palmist [ˈpɑmɪst] *s* chiromancien *m*

palmistry [ˈpɑmɪstri] *s* chiromancie *f*

palm′ leaf′ *s* palme *f*

palm′ oil′ *s* huile *f* de palme

Palm′ Sun′day *s* le dimanche des Rameaux

palm′ tree′ *s* palmier *m*

palpable [ˈpælpəbəl] *adj* palpable

palpitate [ˈpælpɪ‚tet] *intr* palpiter

pal·sy [ˈpɔlzi] *s* (*pl* **-sies**) paralysie *f* ‖ *v* (*pret & pp* **-sied**) *tr* paralyser

pal·try [ˈpɔltri] *adj* (*comp* **-trier**; *super* **-triest**) misérable

pamper [ˈpæmpər] *tr* choyer, gâter

pamphlet [ˈpæmflɪt] *s* brochure *f*

pan [pæn] *s* (*for cooking*) casserole *f*; (*basin; scale of a balance*) bassin *m*; (slang) binette *f*; **Pan** Pan *m* ‖ *v* (*pret & pp* **panned**; *ger* **panning**) *tr* (*gold*) laver à la batée; (coll) débiner, éreinter ‖ *intr* laver à la batée; (mov) panoramiquer; **to pan out well** (coll) réussir

panacea [‚pænəˈsi‚ə] *s* panacée *f*

Panama [ˈpænə‚mɑ] *s* le Panama

Pan′ama Canal′ *s* canal *m* de Panama

Pan′ama Canal′ Zone′ *s* zone *f* canal du Panama

Pan′ama hat′ *s* panama *m*

Pan-American [‚pænəˈmɛrɪkən] *adj* panaméricain

pan′cake′ *s* crêpe *f* ‖ *intr* (aer) descendre à plat, se plaquer

pan′cake land′ing *s* atterrissage *m* plaque, sur le ventre, or à plat

panchromatic [‚pænkroˈmætɪk] *adj* panchromatique

pancreas [ˈpænkrɪ‚əs] *s* pancréas *m*

panda [ˈpændə] *s* panda *m*

pander [ˈpændər] *s* entremetteur *m* ‖ *intr* servir d'entremetteur; **to pander to** se prêter à; encourager

pane [pen] *s* carreau *m*, vitre *f*

pan·el [ˈpænəl] *s* panneau *m*; (*on wall*) lambris *m*; (*door, wall*) panneau *m*; (*ceiling*) caisson *m*; (*discussion group*) groupe *m* de discussion; (law) liste *f*, tableau *m* ‖ *v* (*pret & pp* **-eled** or **-elled**; *ger* **-eling** or **-elling**) *tr* (*a room*) garnir de boiseries; (*a wall*) lambrisser

pan′el discus′sion *s* colloque *m*

panelist [ˈpænəlɪst] *s* membre *m* d'un groupe de discussion

pang [pæŋ] *s* élancement *m*, angoisse *f*

pan′han′dle *s* queue *f* de la poêle; (geog) projection *f* d'un territoire dans un autre ‖ *intr* (slang) mendigoter

pan′han′dler *s* (slang) mendigot *m*

pan·ic [ˈpænɪk] *adj & s* panique *f* ‖ *v* (*pret & pp* **-icked**; *ger* **-icking**) *tr* semer la panique dans ‖ *intr* être pris de panique

pan′ic-strick′en *adj* pris de panique

pano·ply [ˈpænəpli] *s* (*pl* **-plies**) panoplie *f*

panorama [‚pænəˈrɑmə] *s* panorama *m*

pan·sy [ˈpænzi] *s* (*pl* **-sies**) pensée *f*; (slang) tapette *f*

pant [pænt] *s* halètement *m*; **pants** pantalon *m*; **to wear the pants** (coll) porter la culotte ‖ *intr* haleter, panteler

pantheism [ˈpænθi‚ɪzəm] *s* panthéisme *m*

pantheon [ˈpænθi‚ɑn] *s* panthéon *m*

panther [ˈpænθər] *s* panthère *f*

panties [ˈpæntiz] *spl* culotte *f*, slip *m* de femme

pantomime [ˈpæntə‚maɪm] *s* pantomime *f*

pan·try [ˈpæntri] *s* (*pl* **-tries**) office *m & f*, dépense *f*

pant′y hose′ [ˈpænti] *s* collant *m*

pant′y lin′er *s* protège-slip *m*

pap [pæp] *s* bouillie *f*

papa [ˈpɑpə], [pəˈpɑ] *s* papa *m*

papa·cy [ˈpepəsi] *s* (*pl* **-cies**) papauté *f*

paper [ˈpepər] *s* papier *m*; (*newspaper*) journal *m*; (*of needles*) carte *f* ‖ *tr* tapisser

pa′per·back′ *s* livre *m* broché; (*pocketbook*) livre de poche

pa′per·boy′ *s* vendeur *m* de journaux

pa′per clip′ *s* attache *f*, trombone *m*

pa′per cone′ *s* cornet *m* de papier

pa′per cup′ *s* verre *m* en carton, gobelet *m* de papier

pa′per cut′ter *s* coupe-papier *m*

pa′per hand′kerchief *s* mouchoir *m* à jeter, mouchoir en papier

pa′per·hang′er *s* tapissier *m*

pa′per knife′ *s* coupe-papier *m*

pa′per mill′ s papeterie f
pa′per mon′ey s papier-monnaie m
pa′per nap′kin s serviette f en papier
pa′per plate′ s assiette f en carton, assiette de papier
pa′per tape′ s bande f de papier
pa′per tow′el s serviette f de toilette en papier
pa′per tow′eling s essuie-mains m invar en papier
pa′per·weight′ s presse-papiers m
pa′per work′ s travail m de bureau
papier-mâché [,pepərmə`ʃe] s papier-pierre m, papier m mâché
paprika [pæ`prikə] s paprika m
papy·rus [pə`paɪrəs] s (pl ri [raɪ]) papyrus m
par [pɑr] s pair m; (golf) normale f du parcours; **at par** au pair; **to be on a par with** aller de pair avec
parable [`pærəbəl] s parabole f
parabola [pə`ræbələ] s parabole f
parachute [`pærə,ʃut] s parachute m ‖ tr & intr parachuter
par′achute jump′ s saut m en parachute
parachutist [`pærə,ʃutɪst] s parachutiste mf
parade [pə`red] s défilé m; (ostentation) parade f; (mil) parade ‖ tr faire parade de ‖ intr défiler; parader
paradise [`pærə,daɪs] s paradis m
paradox [`pærə,dɑks] s paradoxe m
paradoxical [,pærə`dɑksɪkəl] adj paradoxal
paraffin [`pærəfɪn] s paraffine f ‖ tr paraffiner
paragon [`pærə,gɑn] s parangon m
paragraph [`pærə,græf] s paragraphe m
Paraguay [`pærə,gwaɪ] s le Paraguay
Paraguayan [,pærə`gwaɪ·ən] adj paraguayen ‖ s Paraguayen m
parakeet [`pærə,kit] s perruche f
paral·lel [`pærə,lɛl] adj parallèle ‖ s (line) parallèle f; (latitude; declination; comparison) parallèle m; **parallels** (typ) barres fpl; **without parallel** sans pareil ‖ v (pret & pp -leled or -lelled; ger -leling or -lelling) tr mettre en parallèle; entrer en parallèle avec, égaler
par′allel bars′ spl barres fpl parallèles
paraly·sis [pə`rælɪsɪs] s (pl -ses [,siz]) paralysie f
paralytic [,pærə`lɪtɪk] adj & s paralytique mf
paralyze [`pærə,laɪz] tr paralyser
paramount [`pærə,maunt] adj suprême, capital
paranoiac [,pærə`nɔɪ·æk] adj & s paranoïaque mf
parapet [`pærə,pɛt] s parapet m
paraphernalia [,pærəfər`nelɪ·ə] spl effets mpl personnels; attirail m
paraphrase [`pærə,frez] s remaniement m ‖ tr remanier
paraplegic [,pærə`plidʒɪk] adj & s paraplégique mf
parasite [`pærə,saɪt] s parasite m
parasitic(al) [,pærə`sɪtɪk(əl)] adj parasite
parasol [`pærə,sɔl] s parasol m, ombrelle f

paratrooper [`pærə,trupər] s parachutiste m
parboil [`pɑr,bɔɪl] tr faire cuire légèrement; (vegetables) blanchir
par·cel [`pɑrsəl] s colis m, paquet m ‖ v (pret & pp -celed or -celled; ger -celing or -celling) tr morceler; **to parcel out** répartir
par′cel post′ s colis mpl postaux
parch [pɑrtʃ] tr dessécher; (beans, grain, etc.) griller
parchment [`pɑrtʃmənt] s parchemin m
pardon [`pɑrdən] s pardon m; (remission of penalty by the state) grâce f; **I beg your pardon** je vous demande pardon ‖ tr pardonner; pardonner à; (a criminal) grâcier; **to pardon s.o. for s.th.** pardonner q.ch. à qn
pardonable [`pɑrdənəbəl] adj pardonnable
pare [pɛr] tr (potatoes, fruit, etc.) éplucher; (the nails) rogner; (costs) réduire
parent [`pɛrənt] s père m or mère f; origine f, base f; **parents** parents mpl, père et mère
parentage [`pɛrəntɪdʒ] s paternité f or maternité f; naissance f, origine f
parenthe·sis [pə`rɛnθɪsɪs] s (pl -ses [,siz]) parenthèse f; **in parentheses** entre parenthèses
parenthood [`pɛrənt,hud] s paternité f or maternité f
pariah [pə`raɪ·ə], [`pɑrɪ·ə] s paria m
par′ing knife′ s couteau m à éplucher
Paris [`pærɪs] s Paris m
parish [`pærɪʃ] adj paroissien ‖ s paroisse f
parishioner [pə`rɪʃənər] s paroissien m
Parisian [pə`riʒən] adj & s parisien m
parity [`pærɪti] s parité f
park [pɑrk] s parc m ‖ tr garer, parquer ‖ intr stationner
parked adj en stationnement
parking [`pɑrkɪŋ] s parcage m; (e.g., in a city street) stationnement m; **no parking** (public sign) stationnement interdit
park′ing ar′ea s aire f de stationnement
park′ing lights′ spl (aut) feux mpl de stationnement, feux de position
park′ing lot′ s parking m, parc m à autos
park′ing me′ter s parcomètre m, compteur m de stationnement
park′ing spot′ s stalle f
park′ing tick′et s contravention f, papillon m
park′way′ s route f panoramique; (turnpike) autoroute f
parley [`pɑrli] s pourparlers mpl ‖ intr parlementer
parliament [`pɑrlɪmənt] s parlement m
parliamentarian [,pɑrlɪmɛn`tɛrɪ·ən] s expert m en usages parlementaires
parlor [`pɑrlər] s salon m; (in an institution) parloir m
par′lor car′ s (rr) wagon-salon m
par′lor game′ s jeu m de société
Parnassus [pɑr`næsəs] s le Parnasse
parochial [pə`roki·əl] adj paroissial; (attitude) provincial

paro'chial school' s école f confessionnelle, école libre

paro·dy ['pærədi] s (pl **-dies**) parodie f || v (pret & pp **-died**) tr parodier

parole [pə'rol] s parole f d'honneur; liberté f sur parole || tr libérer sur parole

par·quet [par'ke], [par'kɛt] s parquet m; (theat) premiers rangs mpl du parterre || v (pret & pp **-queted** ['ked], ['kɛtɪd]; ger **-queting** ['ke·ɪŋ], ['kɛtɪŋ]) tr parqueter

parricide ['pærɪ,saɪd] s (act) parricide m; (person) parricide mf

parrot ['pærət] s perroquet m || tr répéter or imiter comme un perroquet

par·ry ['pæri] s (pl **-ries**) parade f || v (pret & pp **-ried**) tr parer; (a question) éluder

parse [pars] tr faire l'analyse grammaticale de

parsimonious [,parsɪ'moni·əs] adj parcimonieux, regardant

parsley ['parsli] s persil m

parsnip ['parsnɪp] s panais m

parson ['parsən] s curé m; pasteur m protestant

parsonage ['parsənɪdʒ] s presbytère m

part [part] s (section, division) partie f; (share) part f; (of a machine) organe m, pièce f; (of the hair) raie f; (theat) rôle m; **for my part** pour ma part; **for the most part** pour la plupart; **in part** en partie; **in these parts** dans ces parages; **on the part of** de la part de; **parts** (personal qualities) talent m; (anat) parties (génitales); (geog) région(s) f(pl); **to be** or **form part of** faire partie de; **to be part and parcel of** faire partie intégrante de; **to do one's part** faire son devoir; **to live a part** (theat) entrer dans la peau d'un personnage; **to look the part** avoir le physique de l'emploi; **to take part in** prendre part à; **to take the part of** prendre parti pour; jouer le rôle de || adv partiellement, en partie; **part . . . part** moitié . . . moitié || tr séparer; **to part the hair** se faire une raie || intr se séparer; (said, e.g., of road) diverger; (to break) rompre; **to part with** se défaire de; se dessaisir de

par·take [par'tek] v (pret **-took**; pp **-taken**) intr—**to partake in** participer à; **to partake of** (e.g., a meal) prendre; (e.g., joy) participer de

partial ['parʃəl] adj partiel; (prejudiced) partial

participant [par'tɪsɪpənt] adj & s participant m

participate [par'tɪsɪ,pet] intr participer

participation [par,tɪsɪ'peʃən] s participation f

participle ['partɪ,sɪpəl] s participe m

particle ['partɪkəl] s particule f; **a particle of truth** un grain de vérité; **not a particle of evidence** pas l'ombre d'une preuve

particular [pər'tɪkjələr] adj particulier; difficile, exigeant; méticuleux; **a particular . . .** un certain . . . || s détail m

particularize [pər'tɪkjələ,raɪz] tr & intr individualiser, particulariser

parting ['partɪŋ] s séparation f

partisan ['partɪzən] adj & s partisan m

partition [par'tɪʃən] s (dividing) partage m, division f; (of land) morcellement m; (wall) paroi f, cloison f || tr partager; **to partition off** séparer par des cloisons

partner ['partnər] s partenaire mf; (husband) conjoint m; (wife) conjointe f; (in a dance) cavalier m; (in business) associé m

part'ner·ship' s association f; (com) société f

part' of speech' s partie f du discours

part' own'er s copropriétaire mf

partridge ['partrɪdʒ] s perdrix m

part'-time' adj & adv à mi-temps

par·ty ['parti] adj de gala || s (pl **-ties**) fête f, soirée f; (diversion of a group of persons; individual named in contract or lawsuit) partie f; (with whom one is conversing) interlocuteur m; (mil) détachement m, peloton m; (pol) parti m; (telp) correspondant m; (coll) individu m; **to be a party to** être complice de

party-goer ['parti,go·ər] s invité m; (nightlifer) noceur m

par'ty hack' s politicien m à la petite semaine

par'ty line' s (between two properties) limite f; (telp) ligne f à postes groupés || **par'ty line'** s ligne du parti; (of communist party) directives fpl du parti

par'ty pol'itics s politique f de parti

par'ty wall' s mur m mitoyen

pass [pæs] s (navigable channel; movement of hands of magician; in sports) passe f; (straits) pas m; (in mountains) col m, passage m; (document) laissez-passer m, difficulté f; (mil) permission f; (rr) permis m de circulation; (theat) billet m de faveur || tr passer; (an exam) réussir à; (e.g., a student) recevoir; (a law) adopter, voter; (a red light) brûler; (to get ahead of) dépasser; (a car going in the same direction) doubler; (s.o. or s.th. coming toward one) croiser; (a certain place) passer devant; **to pass around** faire circuler; **to pass oneself off as** se faire passer pour; **to pass out** distribuer; **to pass over** passer sous silence; (to hand over) transmettre; **to pass s.th. off on s.o.** repasser or refiler q.ch. à qn || intr passer; (educ) être reçu; **to bring to pass** réaliser; **to come to pass** se passer; **to pass as** or **for** passer pour; **to pass away** disparaître; (to die out) s'éteindre; (to die) mourir; **to pass by** passer devant; **to pass out** sortir; (slang) s'évanouir; **to pass over** passer sur; (an obstacle) franchir; (said of storm) s'éloigner; (to pass through) traverser; **to pass over to** (e.g., the enemy) passer à

passable ['pæsəbəl] adj passable; (road, river, etc.) franchissable

passage ['pæsɪdʒ] s passage m; (of time) cours m; (of a law) adoption f

pass'book' s carnet m de banque

passenger [ˈpæsəndʒər] *adj* (*e.g.*, *train*) de voyageurs; (*e.g.*, *pigeon*) de passage ‖ *s* voyageur *m*, passager *m*

passer-by [ˈpæsərˈbaɪ] *s* (*pl* **passers-by**) passant *m*

passing [ˈpæsɪŋ] *adj* passager ‖ *s* passage *m* (*act of passing*) dépassement *m*; (*death*) trépas *m*; (*of time*) écoulement *m*; (*of a law*) adoption *f*; (*in an examination*) la moyenne; une mention passable; **in passing** (*in parenthesis*) du passage

passion [ˈpæʃən] *s* passion *f*

passionate [ˈpæʃənɪt] *adj* passionné

passive [ˈpæsɪv] *adj* & *s* passif *m*

pass′key′ *s* passe-partout *m*

pass′-out′ check′ *s* contremarque *f*

Pass′o′ver *s* Pâque *f*

pass′port′ *s* passeport *m*

pass′word′ *s* mot *m* de passe

past [pæst] *adj* passé, dernier; (*e.g.*, *president*) ancien ‖ *s* passé *m* ‖ *prep* au-delà de, passé, plus de; hors de, e.g., **past all understanding** hors de toute compréhension; **it's twenty past five** il est cinq heures vingt; **it's past three o'clock** il est trois heures passées

paste [pest] *s* (*glue*) colle *f* de pâte; (*jewelry*) strass *m*; (culin) pâte *f* ‖ *tr* coller

paste′board′ *s* carton *m*

pastel [pæsˈtɛl] *adj* & *s* pastel *m*

pasteurize [ˈpæstəˌraɪz] *tr* pasteuriser

pastime [ˈpæsˌtaɪm] *s* passe-temps *m*

past′ mas′ter *s* expert *m* en la matière, passé maître

pastor [ˈpæstər] *s* pasteur *m*

pastoral [ˈpæstərəl] *adj* pastoral ‖ *s* pastorale *f*

pastorate [ˈpæstərɪt] *s* pastorat *m*

pas·try [ˈpestri] *s* (*pl* **-tries**) pâtisserie *f*

pas′try cook′ *s* pâtissier *m*

pas′try shop′ *s* pâtisserie *f*

pasture [ˈpæstʃər] *s* pâturage *m*, pâture *f* ‖ *tr* faire paître ‖ *intr* paître

past·y [ˈpesti] *adj* (*comp* **-ier**; *super* **-iest**) pâteux; (*face*) terreux

pat [pæt] *adj* à propos; (*e.g.*, *excuse*) tout prêt ‖ *s* (*light stroke*) petite tape *f*; (*on an animal*) caresse *f*; (*of butter*) coquille *f* ‖ *v* (*pret & pp* **patted**; *ger* **patting**) *tr* tapoter; caresser; **to pat on the back** encourager, complimenter

patch [pætʃ] *s* (*e.g.*, *of cloth*) pièce *f*, raccommodage *m*; (*of land*) parcelle *f*; (*of ice*) plaque *f*; (*of inner tube*) rustine *f*; (*e.g.*, *of color*) tache *f*; (*beauty spot*) mouche *f* ‖ *tr* rapiécer; **to patch up** rapetasser; (*e.g.*, *a quarrel*) arranger, raccommoder

patent [ˈpetənt] *adj* patent ‖ [ˈpætənt] *adj* breveté ‖ *s* brevet *m* d'invention; **patent applied for** une demande de brevet a été déposée ‖ *tr* breveter

pat′ent leath′er [ˈpætənt] *s* cuir *m* verni

pat′ent med′icine *s* specialité *f* pharmaceutique

pat′ent rights′ *spl* propriété *f* industrielle

paternal [pəˈtʌrnəl] *adj* paternel

paternity [pəˈtʌrnɪti] *s* paternité *f*

path [pæθ] *s* (*way*) sentier *m*; (*in garden*) allée *f*; (*of bullet, heavenly body, etc.*) trajectoire *f*; (*for, e.g., riding horses*) piste *f*; (*course*) route *f*; **to beat a path** frayer un chemin

pathetic [pəˈθɛtɪk] *adj* pathétique

path′find′er *s* pionnier *m*

pathology [pəˈθɑlədʒi] *s* pathologie *f*

pathol′ogy lab′oratory *s* laboratoire *m* d'analyses

pathos [ˈpeθɑs] *s* pathétique *m*

path′way′ *s* sentier *m*; (fig) voie *f*

patience [ˈpeʃəns] *s* patience *f*

patient [ˈpeʃənt] *adj* patient ‖ *s* malade *mf*; (*undergoing surgery*) patient *m*

pati·o [ˈpɑtɪˌo] *s* (*pl* **-os**) patio *m*

patriarch [ˈpetrɪˌɑrk] *s* patriarche *m*

patrician [pəˈtrɪʃən] *adj* & *s* patricien *m*

patricide [ˈpætrɪˌsaɪd] *s* (*act*) parricide *m*; (*person*) parricide *mf*

patrimo·ny [ˈpætrɪˌmoni] *s* (*pl* **-nies**) patrimoine *m*

patriot [ˈpetrɪ·ət] *s* patriote *mf*

patriotic [ˌpetrɪˈɑtɪk] *adj* patriotique, patriote

patriotism [ˈpetrɪ·əˌtɪzəm] *s* patriotisme *m*

pa·trol [pəˈtrol] *s* patrouille *f* ‖ *v* (*pret & pp* **-trolled**; *ger* **-trolling**) *tr* faire la patrouille dans ‖ *intr* patrouiller

patrol′ car′ *s* voiture *f* de ronde

patrol′man *s* (*pl* **-men**) *s* agent *m* de police

patrol′ wag′on *s* voiture *f* cellulaire

patron [ˈpetrən] *adj* patron ‖ *s* protecteur *m*; (com) client *m*

patronage [ˈpetrənɪdʒ] *s* patronage *m*, clientèle *f*; (pol) politique *f* du place-sous

patronize [ˈpetrəˌnaɪz] *tr* patronner, protéger; traiter avec condescendance; (com) acheter chez

pa′tron saint′ *s* patron *m*

patter [ˈpætər] *s* (*sounds*) petit bruit *m*; (*of rain*) fouettement *m*; (*of magician, peddler, etc.*) boniment *m* ‖ *intr* (*said of rain*) fouetter; (*said of little feet*) trottiner

pattern [ˈpætərn] *s* (*design*) dessin *m*, motif *m*; (*salient characteristics*) profil *m*; (*model*) modèle *m*, exemple *m*; (sewing) patron *m*; **behavior pattern** type *m* de comportement ‖ *tr* (*to decorate*) orner de motifs; **to pattern s.th. on** modeler q.ch. sur

pat′tern book′ *s* album *m* d'échantillons; (sewing) album de modes

pat·ty [ˈpæti] *s* (*pl* **-ties**) petit pâté *m*

paucity [ˈpɔsɪti] *s* rareté *f*; manque *m*, disette *f*

paunch [pɔntʃ] *s* panse *f*

paunch·y [ˈpɔntʃi] *adj* (*comp* **-ier**; *super* **-iest**) ventru

pauper [ˈpɔpər] *s* indigent *m*

pause [pɔz] *s* pause *f*; (mus) point *m* d'orgue; **to give pause to** faire hésiter ‖ *intr* faire une pause; hésiter

pave [pev] *tr* paver

pavement [ˈpevmənt] *s* pavé *m*; (*surface*) chaussée *f*

pavilion [pə'vɪljən] *s* pavillon *m*

paw [pɔ] *s* patte *f*; (coll) main *f* ‖ *tr* donner un coup de patte à ‖ *intr* (*said of horse*) piaffer

pawl [pɔl] *s* cliquet *m* d'arrêt

pawn [pɔn] *s* (*in chess*) pion *m*; (*security, pledge*) gage *m*; (*tool of another person*) jouet *m* ‖ *tr* mettre en gage; **to pawn s.th. off on s.o.** (coll) refiler q.ch. à qn

pawn'bro'ker *s* prêteur *m* sur gages

pawn'shop' *s* mont-de-piété *m*, crédit *m* municipal

pawn' tick'et *s* reconnaissance *f* du mont-de-piété

pay [pe] *s* paye *f*; (mil) solde *f* ‖ *v* (*pret & pp* **paid** [ped]) *tr* payer; (mil) solder; (*a compliment; a visit; attention*) faire; **to pay back** payer de retour; **to pay down** payer comptant; **to pay off** (*a debt*) acquitter; (*a mortgage*) purger; (*a creditor*) rembourser; **to pay s.o. for s.th.** payer qn de q.ch., payer q.ch. à qn ‖ *intr* payer, rapporter; **to pay for** payer; **to pay off** (coll) avoir du succès; **to pay up** se libérer par un paiement

payable ['pe·əbəl] *adj* payable

pay' boost' *s* augmentation *f*

pay'check' *s* paye *f*

pay'day' *s* jour *m* de paye

pay'dirt' *s* alluvion *f* exploitable; (coll) source *f* d'argent

payee [pe'i] *s* bénéficiaire *mf*

pay' en'velope *s* sachet *m* de paye; paye *f*

payer ['pe·ər] *s* payeur *m*

pay'load' *s* charge *f* payante, charge utile; (aer) poids *m* utile

pay'mas'ter *s* payeur *m*

payment ['pemənt] *m* paiement *m*; (*install-ment, deposit, etc.*) versement *m*

pay' phone' *s* taxiphone *m*

pay'roll' *s* bulletin *m* de paye; (*for officers*) état *m* de solde; (*for enlisted men*) feuille *f* de prêt

pay' sta'tion *s* téléphone *m* public

pay' tel'evision *s* télévision *f* payante

pea [pi] *s* pois *m*; **green peas** petits pois

peace [pis] *s* paix *f*

peaceable ['pisəbəl] *adj* pacifique

peaceful ['pisfəl] *adj* paisible, pacifique

peace'mak'er *s* pacificateur *m*

peace' of mind' *s* tranquillité *f* d'esprit

peace' pipe' *s* calumet *m* de paix

peach [pitʃ] *s* pêche *f*; (slang) bijou *m*

peach' tree' *s* pêcher *m*

peach·y ['pitʃi] *adj* (*comp* **-ier**; *super* **-iest**) (slang) chouette

pea'coat' *s* (naut) caban *m*

pea'cock' *s* paon *m*

pea'hen' *s* paonne *f*

peak [pik] *s* cime *f*, sommet *m*; (*mountain; mountain top*) pic *m*; (*of beard*) pointe *f*; (*of a cap*) visière *f*; (elec) pointe

peak' hour' *s* heure *f* de pointe

peak' load' *s* (elec) charge *f* de point

peak' vol'tage *s* tension *f* de crête

peal [pil] *s* retentissement *m*; (*of bells*) ca-rillon *m* ‖ *intr* carillonner

peal' of laugh'ter *s* éclat *m* de rire

peal' of thun'der *s* coup *m* de tonnerre

pea'nut' *s* cacahuète *f*; (bot) arachide *f*

pea'nut but'ter *s* beurre *m* de cacahuètes ou d'arachide

pear [pɛr] *s* poire *f*

pearl [pʌrl] *s* perle *f*

pearl' oys'ter *s* huître *f* perlière

pear' tree' *s* poirier *m*

peasant ['pɛzənt] *adj & s* paysan *m*

pea'shoot'er *s* sarbacane *f*

pea' soup' *s* (culin, fig) purée *f* de pois

peat [pit] *s* tourbe *f*

pebble ['pɛbəl] *s* caillou *m*; (*on seashore*) galet *m*

pebbled *adj* (*leather*) grenu

peck [pɛk] *s* (*pecking*) coup *m* de bec; (*eight quarts*) picotin *m*; (*kiss*) (coll) baiser *m* d'oiseau, bécot *m*; (coll) tas *m* ‖ *tr* bec-queter ‖ *intr* picorer; **to peck at** picorer; (*food*) pignocher

peculation [,pɛkjə'leʃən] *s* péculat *m*, dé-tournement *m* de fonds

peculiar [pɪ'kjuljər] *adj* particulier; (*strange*) bizarre

pedagogue ['pɛdə,gɑg] *s* pédagogue *mf*

pedagogy ['pɛdə,gɑdʒi] *s* pédagogie *f*

ped·al ['pɛdəl] *s* pédale *f* ‖ *v* (*pret & pp* **-aled** ou **-alled**; *ger* **-aling** ou **-alling**) *tr* actionner les pédales de ‖ *intr* pédaler

pe'dal push'ers *spl* pantalon *m* corsaire

pedant ['pɛdənt] *s* pédant *m*

pedantic [pɪ'dæntɪk] *adj* pédant

pedant·ry ['pɛdəntri] *s* (*pl* **-ries**) pédanterie *f*

peddle ['pɛdəl] *tr & intr* colporter

peddler ['pɛdlər] *s* colporteur *m*

pederast ['pɛdə,ræst] *s* pédéraste *m*

pedestal ['pɛdɪstəl] *s* piédestal *m*

pedestrian [pɪ'dɛstrɪ·ən] *adj* (*style*) pro-saïque ‖ *s* piéton *m*; **pedestrian right of way** (*public sign*) priorité piétons

pedes'trian mall' *s* rue *f* piétonne

pediatrics [,pidɪ'ætrɪks] *s* pédiatrie *f*

pedigree ['pɛdɪ,gri] *s* généalogie *f*; (*table*) arbre *m* généalogique; (*of animal*) pedi-gree *m*

pediment ['pɛdɪmənt] *s* fronton *m*

peek [pik] *s* coup *m* d'œil furtif ‖ *intr*—**to peek at** regarder furtivement

peel [pil] *s* pelure *f*; (*of lemon*) zeste *m* ‖ *tr* peler; **to peel off** enlever ‖ *intr* se peler; (*said of paint*) s'écailler

peep [pip] *s* regard *m* furtif; (*of, e.g., chick-ens*) piaulement *m* ‖ *intr* piauler; **to peep at** regarder furtivement

peep'hole' *s* judas *m*

peer [pɪr] *s* pair *m* ‖ *intr* regarder avec attention; **to peer at** ou **into** scruter

peerless ['pɪrlɪs] *adj* sans pareil

peeve [piv] *s* (coll) embêtement *m* ‖ *tr* (coll) irriter, embêter, fâcher

peevish ['pivɪʃ] *adj* maussade

peg [pɛg] *s* (*of wood*) cheville *f*; (*of metal*) fiche *f*; (*for coat and hat*) patère *f*; (*for tent*) piquet *m*; **to take down a peg** (coll) rabattre le caquet de ‖ *v* (*pret & pp*

pegged; *ger* **pegging**) *tr* cheviller; (*e.g., prices*) indexer, fixer; (*points*) marquer ‖ *intr* piocher; **to peg away at** travailler ferme à

Pegasus [ˈpɛgəsəs] *s* Pégase *m*

peg' leg' *s* jambe *f* de bois

peg' top' *s* toupie *f*; **peg tops** pantalon *m* fuseau

Pekin·ese [ˌpikɪˈniz] *adj* pékinois ‖ *s* (*pl* **-ese**) Pékinois *m*

Peking [ˈpiˈkɪŋ] *s* Pékin *m*

pelf [pɛlf] *s* (pej) lucre *m*

pelican [ˈpɛlɪkən] *s* pélican *m*

pellet [ˈpɛlɪt] *s* (*of paper or bread*) boulette *f*; (*bullet*) grain *m* de plomb; (pharm) pilule *f*

pell-mell [ˈpɛlˈmɛl] *adj* confus ‖ *adv* pêle-mêle

pelt [pɛlt] *s* (*hide*) peau *m*; (*whack*) coup *m* violent; (*of stones, insults, etc.*) grêle *f* ‖ *tr* cribler; (*e.g., stones*) lancer ‖ *intr* tomber à verse

pen [pɛn] *s* (*for writing*) plume *f*; (*fountain pen*) stylo *m*; (*corral*) enclos *m*; (fig) plume; (*prison*) (slang) bloc *m* ‖ *v* (*pret & pp* **penned;** *ger* **penning**) *tr* écrire ‖ *v* (*pret & pp* **penned** or **pent** [pɛnt]; *ger* **penning**) *tr* parquer

penalize [ˈpinəˌlaɪz] *tr* (*an action*) sanctionner; (*a person*) punir; (sports) pénaliser

penal·ty [ˈpɛnəlti] *s* (*pl* **-ties**) peine *f*; (*for late payment; in a game*) pénalité *f*; **under penalty of** sous peine de

penance [ˈpɛnəns] *s* pénitence *f*

penchant [ˈpɛnʃənt] *s* penchant *m*

pen·cil [ˈpɛnsəl] *s* crayon *m*; (*of light*) faisceau *m* ‖ *v* (*pret & pp* **-ciled** or **-cilled;** *ger* **-ciling** or **-cilling**) *tr* crayonner

pen'cil sharp'ener *s* taille-crayon *m*

pendent [ˈpɛndɛnt] *adj* pendant ‖ *s* pendant *m*, pendentif *m*; (*of chandelier*) pendeloque *f*

pending [ˈpɛndɪŋ] *adj* pendant ‖ *prep* en attendant

pendulum [ˈpɛndʒələm] *s* pendule *m*

pen'dulum bob' *s* lentille *f*

penetrate [ˈpɛnɪˌtret] *tr & intr* pénétrer

penguin [ˈpɛŋgwɪn] *s* manchot *m*

pen'hold'er *s* porte-plume *m*; (*rack*) pose-plumes *m*

penicillin [ˌpɛnɪˈsɪlɪn] *s* pénicilline *f*

peninsula [pəˈnɪnsələ] *s* presqu'île *f*; (*large peninsula like Spain or Italy*) péninsule *f*

peninsular [pəˈnɪnsələr] *adj* péninsulaire

penis [ˈpinɪs] *s* pénis *m*

penitence [ˈpɛnɪtəns] *s* pénitence *f*

penitent [ˈpɛnɪtənt] *adj & s* pénitent *m*

pen'knife' *s* (*pl* **-knives**) canif *m*

penmanship [ˈpɛnmənˌʃɪp] *s* calligraphie *f*; (*person's handwriting*) écriture *f*

pen' name' *s* pseudonyme *m*

pennant [ˈpɛnənt] *s* flamme *f*; (sports) banderole *f* du championnat

penniless [ˈpɛnɪlɪs] *adj* sans le sou

pen·ny [ˈpɛni] *s* (*pl* **-nies**) (U.S.A.) centime *m*; **not a penny** pas un sou ‖ *s* (*pl* **pence** [pɛns]) (Brit) penny *m*

pen'ny-(pinch'ing *adj* regardant

pen'ny·weight' *s* poids *m* de 24 grains

pen' pal' *s* (coll) correspondant *m*

pen'point' *s* bec *m* de plume

pension [ˈpɛnʃən] *s* pension *f* ‖ *tr* pensionner

pensioner [ˈpɛnʃənər] *s* pensionné *m*

pensive [ˈpɛnsɪv] *adj* pensif

Pentagon [ˈpɛntəˌgɑn] *s* Pentagone *m*

Pentecost [ˈpɛntɪˌkɔst] *s* la Pentecôte

penthouse [ˈpɛntˌhaʊs] *s* toit *m* en auvent, appentis *m*; appartement *m* sur toit, maison *f* à terrasse

pent-up [ˈpɛntˈʌp] *adj* renfermé, refoulé

penult [ˈpinʌlt] *s* pénultième *f*

penum·bra [pɪˈnʌmbrə] *s* (*pl* **-brae** [bri] or **-bras**) pénombre *f*

penurious [pɪˈnʊrɪˌəs] *adj* (*stingy*) mesquin, parcimonieux; (*poor*) pauvre

penury [ˈpɛnjəri] *s* indigence *f*, misère *f*

pen'wip'er *s* essuie-plume *m*

peo·ny [ˈpiˌəni] *s* (*pl* **-nies**) pivoine *f*

people [ˈpipəl] *spl* gens *mpl*, personnes *fpl*; **many people** beaucoup de monde; **my people** ma famille, mes parents; **people say** on dit ‖ *s* (*pl* **peoples**) peuple *m*, nation *f* ‖ *tr* peupler

pep [pɛp] *s* (coll) allant *m* ‖ *v* (*pret & pp* **pepped;** *ger* **pepping**) *tr*—**to pep up** (coll) animer

pepper [ˈpɛpər] *s* (*spice*) poivre *m*; (*fruit*) grain *m* de poivre; (*plant*) poivrier *m*; (*plant or fruit of the hot or red pepper*) piment *m* rouge; (*plant or fruit of the sweet or green pepper*) piment doux, poivron *m* vert ‖ *tr* poivrer; (*e.g., with bullets*) cribler

pep'per·box' *s* poivrière *f*

pep'per mill' *s* moulin *m* à poivre

pep'per·mint' *s* menthe *f* poivrée; (*lozenge*) pastille *f* de menthe

per [pʌr] *prep* par; **as per** suivant

perambulator [pərˈæmbjəˌletər] *s* voiture *f* d'enfant

per capita [pərˈkæpɪtə] par tête, par personne

perceive [pərˈsiv] *tr* (*by the senses*) apercevoir; (*by understanding*) percevoir

per cent or **percent** [pərˈsɛnt] pour cent

percentage [pərˈsɛntɪdʒ] *s* pourcentage *m*; **to get a percentage** (slang) avoir part au gâteau

perceptible [pərˈsɛptəbəl] *adj* perceptible, sensible, appréciable

perception [pərˈsɛpʃən] *s* perception *f*; compréhension *f*, pénétration *f*

perch [pʌrtʃ] *s* (*vantage point*) perchoir *m*; (ichth) perche *f* ‖ *tr* percher ‖ *intr* percher, se percher

percolate [ˈpʌrkəˌlet] *tr & intr* filtrer

percolator [ˈpʌrkəˌletər] *s* cafetière *f* à filtre

percussion [pərˈkʌʃən] *s* percussion *f*

percus'sion cap' *s* capsule *f* fulminante

per diem [pərˈdaɪˌəm] par jour

perdition [pər'dıʃən] s perdition f
peremptory [pə'rɛmptəri] adj péremptoire
perennial [pə'rɛnɪ·əl] adj perpétuel; (bot) vivace ‖ s plante f vivace
perfect ['pʌrfıkt] adj & s parfait m ‖ [pər'fɛkt] tr perfectionner
perfidious [pər'fıdı·əs] adj perfide
perfi‧dy ['pʌrfıdi] s (pl -dies) perfidie f
perforate ['pʌrfə,ret] tr perforer
per'forated line' s pointillé m
perforation [,pʌrfə'reʃən] s perforation f; (of postage stamp) dentelure f
perforce [pər'fors] adv forcément
perform [pər'form] tr exécuter; (surg) faire; (theat) représenter ‖ intr jouer; (said of machine) fonctionner
performance [pər'forməns] s (accomplishing) exécution f; (production) rendement m; (of a machine) fonctionnement m; (of actor, singer, dancer) interprétation f; (sports) performance f; (theat) représentation f; **in the performance of his duties** dans l'exercice de ses fonctions
performer [pər'formər] s artiste mf, interprète mf
perform'ing arts' spl arts mpl du spectacle
perfume ['pʌrfjum] s parfum m ‖ [pər'fjum] tr parfumer
perfunctory [pər'fʌŋktəri] adj superficiel; négligent
perhaps [pər'hæps] adv peut-être; **perhaps not** peut-être que non
per hour' à l'heure
peril ['pɛrəl] s péril m
perilous ['pɛrıləs] adj périlleux
period ['pırı·əd] s période f; (in school) heure f de cours; (gram) point m; (sports) division f
pe'riod cos'tume s costume m d'époque
pe'riod fur'niture s meubles m d'époque
periodic [,pırı'adık] adj périodique
periodical [,pırı'adıkəl] adj périodique ‖ s publication f périodique
period'ical room' s (in a library) salle f des imprimés
peripheral [pə'rıfərəl] adj périphérique
peripher‧y [pə'rıfəri] s (pl -ies) périphérie f
periscope ['pɛrı,skop] s périscope m; (of a tank) épiscope m
perish ['pɛrıʃ] intr périr
perishable ['pɛrıʃəbəl] adj périssable
perjure ['pʌrdʒər] tr—**to perjure oneself** se parjurer
perju‧ry ['pʌrdʒəri] s (pl -ries) parjure m
perk [pʌrk] tr—**to perk up** (the head) redresser; (the ears) dresser; (the appetite) ravigoter ‖ intr—**to perk up** se ranimer
permafrost ['pərmə,frost] s pergélisol m
permanence ['pʌrmənəns] s permanence f
permanent ['pʌrmənənt] adj permanent ‖ s permanente f
per'manent address' s domicile m fixe
per'manent ten'ure s inamovibilité f
per'manent wave' s ondulation f permanente
permeate ['pʌrmı,et] tr & intr pénétrer
permissible [pər'mısıbəl] adj permis

permission [pər'mıʃən] s permission f
permissive [pər'mısıv] adj tolérant; (morals, law) laxiste; (society) de tolérance; (pej) trop tolérant
permissiveness [pər'mısıvnıs] s tolérance f; (pej) excès m de tolérance, mollesse f, laxisme m
per‧mit ['pʌrmıt] s permis m; (com) passavant m ‖ [pər'mıt] v (pret & pp -mitted; ger -mitting) tr permettre; **to permit s.o. to** permettre à qn de
permute [pər'mjut] tr permuter
pernicious [pər'nıʃəs] adj pernicieux
pernickety [pər'nıkıti] adj (coll) pointilleux
perox'ide blonde' [pər'aksaıd] s blonde f décolorée
perpendicular [,pʌrpən'dıkjələr] adj & s perpendiculaire f
perpetrate ['pʌrpı,tret] tr perpétrer
perpetual [pər'pɛtʃu·əl] adj perpétuel
perpetuate [pər'pɛtʃu,et] tr perpétuer
perplex [pər'plɛks] tr rendre perplexe
perplexed [pər'plɛkst] adj perplexe
perplexi‧ty [pər'plɛksıti] s (pl -ties) perplexité f
persecute ['pʌrsı,kjut] tr persécuter
persecution [,pʌrsı'kjuʃən] s persécution f
persevere [,pʌrsı'vır] intr persévérer
Persian ['pʌrʒən] adj persan ‖ s (language) persan m; (person) Persan m
Per'sian blind' s persienne f
Per'sian Gulf' s Golfe m Persique
Per'sian rug' s tapis m de Perse
persimmon [pər'sımən] s plaquemine f; (tree) plaqueminier m
persist [pər'sıst] intr persister; **to persist in** persister dans; + ger persister à + inf
persistent [pər'sıstənt] adj persistant
person ['pʌrsən] s personne f; **no person** personne; **per person** par personne, chacun
personage ['pʌrsənıdʒ] s personnage m
personal ['pʌrsənəl] adj personnel ‖ s (journ) note f dans la chronique mondaine
personali‧ty [,pʌrsə'nælıti] s (pl -ties) personnalité f
per'sonal prop'erty s biens mpl mobiliers
personi‧fy [pər'sanı,faı] v (pret & pp -fied) tr personnifier
personnel [,pʌrsə'nɛl] s personnel m
per'son-to-per'son tel'ephone call' s communication f avec préavis
perspective [pər'spɛktıv] s perspective f
perspicacious [,pʌrspı'keʃəs] adj perspicace
perspiration [,pʌrspı'reʃən] s transpiration f
perspire [pər'spaır] intr transpirer
persuade [pər'swed] tr persuader; **to persuade s.o. of s.th.** persuader q.ch. à qn, persuader qn de q.ch.; **to persuade s.o. to** persuader à qn de
persuasion [pər'sweʒən] s persuasion f; (faith) (coll) croyance f
pert [pʌrt] adj effronté; (sprightly) animé
pertain [pər'ten] intr—**to pertain to** avoir rapport à

pertinacious [,pʌrtɪ'neʃəs] *adj* obstiné, persévérant

pertinent ['pʌrtɪnənt] *adj* pertinent

perturb [pər'tʌrb] *tr* perturber

Peru [pə'ru] *s* le Pérou

peruse [pə'ruz] *tr* lire; lire attentivement

Peruvian [pə'ruvɪ·ən] *adj* péruvien ‖ *s* Péruvien *m*

pervade [pər'ved] *tr* pénétrer, s'infiltrer dans

perverse [pər'vʌrs] *adj* pervers; obstiné; capricieux

perversion [pər'vʌrʒən] *s* perversion *f*

perversi·ty [pər'vʌrsɪti] *s* (*pl* **-ties**) perversité *f*; obstination *f*

pervert ['pʌrvərt] *s* pervers *m*, perverti *m* ‖ [pər'vʌrt] *tr* pervertir

pes·ky ['pɛski] *adj* (*comp* **-kier;** *super* **-kiest**) (coll) importun

pessimism ['pɛsɪ,mɪzəm] *s* pessimisme *m*

pessimist ['pɛsɪmɪst] *s* pessimiste *mf*

pessimistic [,pɛsɪ'mɪstɪk] *adj* pessimiste

pest [pɛst] *s* insecte *m* nuisible; (*pestilence*) peste *f*; (*annoying person*) raseur *m*

pester ['pɛstər] *tr* casser la tête à, importuner

pest′house′ *s* lazaret *m*

pesticide ['pɛstɪ,saɪd] *s* pesticide *m*

pestiferous [pɛs'tɪfərəs] *adj* pestiféré; (coll) ennuyeux

pestilence ['pɛstɪləns] *s* pestilence *f*

pestle ['pɛsəl] *s* pilon *m*

pet [pɛt] *s* animal *m* favori, animal familial; (*child*) enfant *m* gâté; (*anger*) accès *m* de mauvaise humeur; **teacher's pet** chouchou *m* (*or* chouchoute *f*) du professeur ‖ *v* (*pret* & *pp* **petted;** *ger* **petting**) *tr* choyer; (*e.g., an animal's fur*) caresser ‖ *intr* (slang) se bécoter

petal ['pɛtəl] *s* pétale *m*

pet′cock′ *s* robinet *m* de purge

Peter ['pitər] *s* Pierre *m*; **to rob Peter to pay Paul** découvrir saint Pierre pour habiller saint Paul ‖ (*l.c.*) *intr*—**to peter out** (coll) s'épuiser, s'en aller en fumée

petition [pɪ'tɪʃən] *s* pétition *f* ‖ *tr* adresser or présenter une pétition à

pet′ name′ *s* mot *m* doux, nom *m* d'amitié

Petrarch ['pitrɑrk] *s* Pétrarque *m*

petri·fy ['pɛtrɪ,faɪ] *v* (*pret* & *pp* **-fied**) *tr* pétrifier ‖ *intr* se pétrifier

petrochemical [,pɛtro'kɛmɪkəl] *adj* pétrochimique

petrol ['pɛtrəl] *s* (Brit) essence *f*

petroleum [pɪ'trolɪ·əm] *s* pétrole *m*

pet′ shop′ *s* boutique *f* aux petites bêtes; (*for birds*) oisellerie *f*

petticoat ['pɛtɪ,kot] *s* jupon *m*

pet·ty ['pɛti] *adj* (*comp* **-tier;** *super* **-tiest**) insignifiant, petit; (*narrow*) mesquin; intolérant

pet′ty cash′ *s* petite caisse *f*

pet′ty expen′ses *s* menus frais *mpl*

pet′ty lar′ceny *s* vol *m* simple

pet′ty of′ficer *s* (naut) officier *m* marinier

petulant ['pɛtʃələnt] *adj* irritable, boudeur

pew [pju] *s* banc *m* d'église

pewter ['pjutər] *s* étain *m*

Pfc. ['pi'ɛf'si] *s* (letterword) (**private first class**) soldat *m* de première

phalanx ['felæŋks] *s* phalange *f*

phallic ['fælɪk] *adj* phallique

phallus ['fæləs] *s* phallus *m*, pénis *m*

phantasm ['fæntæzəm] *s* fantasme *m*

phantom ['fæntəm] *s* fantôme *m*

Pharaoh ['fɛro] *s* Pharaon *m*

pharisee ['færɪ,si] *s* pharisien *m*; **Pharisee** Pharisien *m*

pharmaceutical [,fɑrmə'sutɪkəl] *adj* pharmaceutique

pharmacist ['fɑrməsɪst] *s* pharmacien *m*

pharma·cy ['fɑrməsi] *s* (*pl* **-cies**) pharmacie *f*

pharynx ['færɪŋks] *s* pharynx *m*

phase [fez] *s* phase *f*; **out of phase** (*said of motor*) décalé ‖ *tr* mettre en phase; développer en phases successives; (coll) inquiéter; **to phase out** faire disparaître peu à peu

pheasant ['fɛzənt] *s* faisan *m*

phenobarbital [,fino'bɑrbɪ,tæl] *s* phénobarbital *m*

phenomenal [fɪ'nɑmɪ,nəl] *adj* phénoménal

phenome·non [fɪ'nɑmɪ,nɑn] *s* (*pl* **-na** [nə]) phénomène *m*

phial ['faɪ·əl] *s* fiole *f*

philanderer [fɪ'lændərər] *s* coureur *m*, galant *m*

philanthropist [fɪ'lænθrəpɪst] *s* philanthrope *mf*

philanthro·py [fɪ'lænθrəpi] *s* (*pl* **-pies**) philanthropie *f*

philatelist [fɪ'lætəlɪst] *s* philatéliste *mf*

philately [fɪ'lætəli] *s* philatélie *f*

Philippine ['fɪlɪ,pin] *adj* philippin ‖ **Philippines** *spl* Philippines *fpl*

Philistine ['fɪlɪ,stin] *adj* & *s* philistin *m*

philologist [fɪ'lɑlədʒɪst] *s* philologue *mf*

philology [fɪ'lɑlədʒi] *s* philologie *f*

philosopher [fɪ'lɑsəfər] *s* philosophe *mf*

philosophic(al) [,fɪlə'sɑfɪk(əl)] *adj* philosophique

philoso·phy [fɪ'lɑsəfi] *s* (*pl* **-phies**) philosophie *f*

philter ['fɪltər] *s* philtre *m*

phlebitis [flɪ'baɪtɪs] *s* phlébite *f*

phlegm [flɛm] *s* flegme *m*; **to cough up phlegm** cracher des glaires, tousser gras

phlegmatic(al) [flɛg'mætɪk(əl)] *adj* flegmatique

phobia ['fobɪ·ə] *s* phobie *f*

Phoebe ['fibi] *s* Phébé *f*

Phoenicia [fɪ'nɪʃə] *s* Phénicie *f*; la Phénicie

Phoenician [fɪ'nɪʃən] *adj* phénicien ‖ *s* Phénicien *m*

phoenix ['finɪks] *s* phénix *m*

phone [fon] *s* (coll) téléphone *m* ‖ *tr* & *intr* (coll) téléphoner

phone′ call′ *s* coup *m* de téléphone, coup de fil

phonetic [fo'nɛtɪk] *adj* phonétique ‖ **phonetics** *s* phonétique *f*

phone-in′ show′ *s* (rad, telv) tribune *f* téléphonique

phonograph ['fonə,græf] *s* phonographe *m*

phonology [fə'nɑlədʒi] *s* phonologie *f*

pho·ny ['foni] *adj* (*comp* **-nier;** *super* **-niest**) faux, truqué ‖ *s* (*pl* **-nies**) charlatan *m*

pho'ny war' *s* drôle *f* de guerre

phosphate ['fɑsfet] *s* phosphate *m*

phosphorescent [,fɑsfə'rɛsənt] *adj* phosphorescent

phospho·rus ['fɑsfərəs] *s* (*pl* **-ri** [,raɪ]) phosphore *m*

pho·to [foto] *s* (*pl* **-tos**) (coll) photo *f*

pho'to·cop'ier *s* photocopieur *m*

pho'to·cop'y *s* photocopie *f*

pho'to·engrav'ing *s* photogravure *f*

pho'to fin'ish *s* photo-finish *f*

photogenic [,foto'dʒɛnɪk] *adj* photogénique

pho'to·graph' *s* photographie *f* ‖ *tr* photographier ‖ *intr*—**to photograph well** être photogénique

photographer [fə'tɑgrəfər] *s* photographe *mf*

pho'to·graph li'brary *s* photothèque *f*

photography [fə'tɑgrəfi] *s* photographie *f*

Photostat ['fotə,stæt] *s* (trademark) photostat *m* ‖ *tr & intr* photocopier

phrase [frez] *s* locution *f*, expression *f*; (mus) phrase *f* ‖ *tr* exprimer, rédiger; (mus) phraser

phrenology [frɪ'nɑlədʒi] *s* phrénologie *f*

phys·ic ['fizɪk] *s* médicament *m*; (*laxative*) purgatif *m* ‖ *v* (*pret & pp* **-icked;** *ger* **-icking**) *tr* purger

physical ['fizɪkəl] *adj* physique

phys'ical de'fect *s* vice *m* de conformation

physician [fɪ'zɪʃən] *s* médecin *m*

physicist ['fizɪsɪst] *s* physicien *m*

physics ['fizɪks] *s* physique *f*

physiogno·my [,fizɪ'ɑgnəmi] *s* (*pl* **-mies**) physionomie *f*

physiological [,fizɪ·ə'ladʒɪkəl] *adj* physiologique

physiology [,fizɪ'ɑlədʒi] *s* physiologie *f*

physique [fɪ'zik] *s* physique *m*

pi [paɪ] *s* (math) pi *m*; (typ) pâté *m* ‖ *v* (*pret & pp* **pied;** *ger* **piing**) *tr* (typ) mettre en pâte

pianist ['pi·ənɪst] *s* pianiste *mf*

pian·o [pɪ'æno] *s* (*pl* **-os**) piano *m*

pian'o stool' *s* tabouret *m* de piano

pian'o tun'er *s* accordeur *m* (de piano)

pian'o wire' *s* corde *f* à piano

picayune [,pɪkə'jun] *adj* mesquin

picco·lo ['pɪkəlo] *s* (*pl* **-los**) piccolo *m*

pick [pɪk] *s* (*tool*) pic *m*, pioche *f*; (*choice*) choix *m*; (*choicest*) élite *f*, fleur *f* ‖ *tr* choisir; (*flowers*) cueillir; (*fibers*) effiler; (*one's teeth, nose, etc.*) se curer; (*a scab*) gratter; (*a fowl*) plumer; (*a bone*) ronger; (*a lock*) crocheter; (*the ground*) piocher; (*e.g., guitar strings*) toucher; (*a quarrel; flaws*) chercher; **to pick off** enlever; (*to shoot*) descendre; **to pick out** trier; **to pick pockets** voler à la tire; **to pick to pieces** (coll) éplucher; **to pick up** ramasser; (*one's strength*) reprendre; (*speed*) accroître; (*a passenger*) prendre; (*a man overboard*) recueillir; (*an anchor;*

a stitch; a fallen child) relever; (*information; a language*) apprendre; (*the scent*) retrouver; (rad) capter ‖ *intr* (*said of birds*) picorer; **to pick at** (*to scold*) (coll) gronder; **to pick at one's food** manger du bout des dents; **to pick on** choisir; (coll) gronder; **to pick up** (coll) se rétablir

pick'ax' *s* pioche *f*

picket ['pɪkɪt] *s* (*stake, pale*) pieu *m*; (*of strikers; of soldiers*) piquet *m* ‖ *tr* entourer de piquets de grève ‖ *intr* faire le piquet

pick'et fence' *s* palis *m*

pick'et line' *s* piquet *m* de grève

pickle ['pɪkəl] *s* (*gherkin*) cornichon *m*; (*brine*) marinade *f*, saumure *f*; (coll) gâchis *m* ‖ *tr* conserver dans du vinaigre

pick'lock' *s* crochet *m*; (*person*) crocheteur *m*

pick'-me-up' *s* (coll) remontant *m*

pick'pock'et *s* voleur *m* à la tire

pick'up' *s* (*passenger*) passager *m*; (*of a motor*) reprise *f*; (*truck; phonograph cartridge*) pick-up *m*; (*restorative*) remontant *m*; (*casual lover*) partenaire *mf* de rencontre

pick'up arm' *s* bras *m* de pick-up

pick'up truck' *s* camionnette *f*; pick-up *m invar*

pic·nic ['pɪknɪk] *s* pique-nique *m* ‖ *v* (*pret & pp* **-nicked;** *ger* **-nicking**) *intr* pique-niquer

pictorial [pɪk'torɪ·əl] *adj & s* illustré *m*

picture ['pɪktʃər] *s* tableau *m*, image *f*; (*photograph*) photographie *f*; (*painting*) peinture *f*; (*engraving*) gravure *f*; (mov) film *m*; (*screen*) (mov, telv) écran *m*; **a picture is worth a thousand words** une image vaut mieux que dix mille mots; **the very picture of** le portrait de, l'image de; **to receive the picture** (telv) capter l'image ‖ *tr* dépeindre, représenter; **to picture to oneself** s'imaginer

pic'ture gal'lery *s* musée *m* de peinture

pic'ture post' card' *s* carte *f* postale illustrée

pic'ture show' *s* exhibition *f* de peinture; (mov) cinéma *m*

pic'ture sig'nal *s* signal *m* vidéo

picturesque [,pɪktʃə'rɛsk] *adj* pittoresque

pic'ture tube' *s* tube *m* de l'image

pic'ture win'dow *s* fenêtre *f* panoramique

piddling ['pɪdlɪŋ] *adj* insignifiant

pie [paɪ] *s* pâté *m*; (*dessert*) tarte *f*; (*bird*) pie *f*

piece [pis] *s* (*of music; of bread*) morceau *m*; (*cannon, coin, chessman, pastry, clothing*) pièce *f*; (*of land*) parcelle *f*; (*e.g., of glass*) éclat *m*; **a piece of advice** un conseil; **a piece of furniture** un meuble; **to break into pieces** mettre en pièces, mettre en morceaux; **to give s.o. a piece of one's mind** (coll) dire son fait à qn; **to go to pieces** se désagréger; (*to be hysterical*) avoir ses nerfs; **to pick to**

pieces (coll) éplucher ‖ *tr* rapiécer; **to piece together** rassembler, coordonner
piece′meal′ *adv* pièce à pièce
piece′work′ *s* travail *m* à la tâche
piece′work′er *s* ouvrier *m* à la tâche
pied [paɪd] *adj* bigarré, panaché; (typ) tombé en pâté
pier [pɪr] *s* (*with amusements*) jetée *f*; (*breakwater*) brise-lames *m*; (*of a bridge*) pile *f*; (*of a harbor*) jetée *f*; (*wall between two openings*) (archit) trumeau *m*
pierce [pɪrs] *tr & intr* percer
piercing [′pɪrsɪŋ] *adj* perçant; (*sharp*) aigu
pier′ glass′ *s* grand miroir *m*
pie·ty [′paɪ·əti] *s* (*pl* -ties) piété *f*
piffle [′pɪfəl] *s* (coll) futilités *fpl*, sottises *fpl*
pig [pɪg] *s* cochon *m*, porc *m*
pigeon [′pɪdʒən] *s* pigeon *m*
pi′geon·hole′ *s* boulin *m*; (*in desk*) case *f* ‖ *tr* caser; mettre au rancart
pi′geon house′ *s* pigeonnier *m*
piggish [′pɪgɪʃ] *adj* goinfre
piggyback [′pɪgi,bæk] *adv* sur le dos, sur les epaules; (rr) en auto-couchette
pig′gy bank′ [′pɪgi] *s* tirelire *f*, grenouille *f*
pig′-head′ed *adj* cabochard, têtu
pig′ i′ron *s* gueuse *f*
piglet [′pɪglɪt] *s* cochonnet *m*
pigment [′pɪgmənt] *s* pigment *m*
pig′pen′ *s* porcherie *f*
pig′skin′ *s* peau *f* de porc; (coll) ballon *m* du football
pig′sty′ *s* (*pl* -sties) porcherie *f*
pig′tail′ *s* queue *f*, natte *f*; (*of tobacco*) carotte *f*
pike [paɪk] *s* pique *f*; autoroute *f* à péage; (*fish*) brochet *m*
piker [′paɪkər] *s* (slang) rat *m*
pile [paɪl] *s* (*heap*) tas *m*; (*stake*) pieu *m*; (*of rug*) poil *m*; (*of building*) masse *f*; (elec, phys) pile *f*; (coll) fortune *f*; **piles** (pathol) hémorroïdes *fpl* ‖ *tr* empiler ‖ *intr* s'empiler
pile′ dri′ver *s* batteur *m* de pieux; sonnette *f*
pile′ up′ *s* (aut) carambolage *m*
pilfer [′pɪlfər] *tr & intr* chaparder
pilgrim [′pɪlgrɪm] *s* pèlerin *m*
pilgrimage [′pɪlgrɪmɪdʒ] *s* pèlerinage *m*
pill [pɪl] *s* pilule *f*; (*something unpleasant*) pilule; (coll) casse-pieds *m*
pillage [′pɪlɪdʒ] *s* pillage *m* ‖ *tr & intr* piller
pillar [′pɪlər] *s* pilier *m*
pillo·ry [′pɪləri] *s* (*pl* -ries) pilori *m* ‖ *v* (*pret & pp* -ried) *tr* clouer au pilori
pillow [′pɪlo] *s* oreiller *m*
pil′low·case′ or **pil′low·slip′** *s* taie *f* d'oreiller
pilot [′paɪlət] *s* pilote *m*; (*of gas range*) veilleuse *f* ‖ *tr* piloter
pi′lot en′gine *s* locomotive-pilote *f*
pi′lot light′ *s* veilleuse *f*
pimp [pɪmp] *s* entremetteur *m*
pimple [′pɪmpəl] *s* bouton *m*
pim·ply [′pɪmpli] *adj* (*comp* -plier; *super* -pliest) boutonneux
pin [pɪn] *s* épingle *f*; (*of wearing apparel*) agrafe *f*; (*bowling*) quille *f*; (mach) cla-

vette *f*, cheville *f*, goupille *f*; **to be on pins and needles** être sur les chardons ardents ‖ *v* (*pret & pp* pinned; *ger* pinning) *tr* épingler; (mach) cheviller, goupiller; **to pin down** fixer, clouer
pinafore [′pɪnə,for] *s* tablier *m* d'enfant
pin′ball′ *s* billard *m* américain
pin′ball machine′ *s* flipper *m*
pincers [′pɪnsərz] *s & spl* pinces *fpl*
pinch [pɪntʃ] *s* (*pinching*) pincement *m*; (*of salt*) pincée *f*; (*of tobacco*) prise *f*; (*of hunger*) morsure *f*; (*trying time*) moment *m* critique; (slang) arrestation *f*; **in a pinch** au besoin ‖ *tr* pincer; (*to press tightly on*) serrer; (*e.g., one's finger in a door*) se prendre; (*to arrest*) (slang) pincer; (*to steal*) (slang) chiper ‖ *intr* (said, *e.g., of shoe*) gêner; (*to save*) lésiner
pinchers [′pɪntʃərz] *s & spl* pinces *fpl*
pin′cush′ion *s* pelote *f* d'épingles
pine [paɪn] *s* pin *m* ‖ *intr* languire; **to pine for** soupirer après
pine′ap′ple *s* ananas *m*
pine′ cone′ *s* pomme *f* de pin
pine′ nee′dle *s* aiguille *f* de pin
ping [pɪŋ] *s* sifflement *m*; (*in a motor*) cognement *m* ‖ *intr* siffler; cogner
Ping-Pong [′pɪŋ,pɔŋ] *s* (trademark) ping-pong *m*, tennis *m* de table
Ping′-Pong play′er *s* pongiste *mf*
pin′head′ *s* tête *f* d'épingle; (pej) crétin *m*
pink [pɪŋk] *adj* rose ‖ *s* rose *m*; (bot) œillet *m*; **to be in the pink** se porter à merveille
pin′ mon′ey *s* argent *m* de poche
pinnacle [′pɪnəkəl] *s* pinacle *m*
pin′point′ *adj* exact ‖ *s* (fig) point *m* critique ‖ *tr* situer avec précision
pin′prick′ *s* piqûre *f* d'épingle
pin′-striped′ *adj* rayé
pint [paɪnt] *s* chopine *f*
pin′up girl′ *s* pin up *f*
pin′wheel′ *s* (*fireworks*) soleil *m*; (*child's toy*) moulinet *m*
pioneer [,paɪ·ə′nɪr] *s* pionnier *m* ‖ *tr* défricher ‖ *intr* faire œuvre de pionnier
pious [′paɪ·əs] *adj* pieux, dévot
pip [pɪp] *s* (*in fruit*) pépin *m*; (*on cards, dice, etc.*) point *m*; (rad) top *m*; (vet) pépie *f*
pipe [paɪp] *s* tuyau *m*, tube *m*, conduit *m*; (*to smoke tobacco*) pipe *f*; (*of an organ*) tuyau; (mus) chalumeau *m* ‖ *tr* canaliser ‖ *intr* jouer du chalumeau; **pipe down!** (slang) boucle-la!
pipe′ clean′er *s* cure-pipe *m*
pipe′ dream′ *s* rêve *m*, projet *m* illusoire
pipe′ line′ *s* pipe-line *m*; (*of information*) tuyau *m*
pipe′ or′gan *s* grandes orgues *fpl*
piper [′paɪpər] *s* joueur *m* de chalumeau; (*bagpiper*) cornemuseur *m*; **to pay the piper** payer les violons
pipe′ wrench′ *s* clef *f* à tubes
piping [′paɪpɪŋ] *s* tuyauterie *f*; (sewing) passepoil *m*
pippin [′pɪpɪn] *s* (*apple*) reinette *f*; (*highly admired person or thing*) bijou *m*

piquancy [ˈpikənsi] s piquant m
piquant [ˈpikənt] adj piquant
pique [pik] s pique f ‖ tr piquer; **to pique oneself on** se piquer de
pira·cy [ˈpairəsi] s (pl -cies) piraterie f
Piraeus [paiˈriˑəs] s Le Pirée
pirate [ˈpairit] s pirate m ‖ tr piller ‖ intr pirater
pirouette [ˌpiruˈɛt] s pirouette f ‖ intr pirouetter
Pisces [ˈpaisiz] s (astr, astrol) les Poissons mpl
pistol [ˈpistəl] s pistolet m
piston [ˈpistən] s piston m
pis'ton ring' s segment m de piston
pis'ton rod' s tige f de piston
pis'ton stroke' s course f de piston
pit [pit] s fosse f, trou m; (in the skin) marque f; (of certain fruit) noyau m; (for cockfights, etc.) arène f; (of the stomach) creux m; (min) puits m; (theat) fauteuils mpl d'orchestre derrière les musiciens ‖ v (pret & pp **pitted**; ger **pitting**) tr trouer; (the face) grêler; (fruit) dénoyauter; **to pit oneself against** se mesurer contre
pitch [pitʃ] s (black sticky substance) poix f; (throw) lancement m, jet m; (of a boat) tangage m; (of a roof) degré m de pente; (of, e.g., a screw) pas m; (of a tone, of the voice, etc.) hauteur f; (coll) boniment m, tamtam m; **to such a pitch that** à tel point que ‖ tr lancer, jeter; (hay) fourcher; (a tent) dresser; enduire de poix; (mus) donner le ton de ‖ intr (said of boat) tanguer; **to pitch in** (coll) se mettre à la besogne; (coll) commencer à manger; **to pitch into** s'attaquer à
pitch' ac'cent s accent m de hauteur
pitcher [ˈpitʃər] s broc m, cruche f; (baseball) lanceur m
pitch'fork' s fourche f; **to rain pitchforks** pleuvoir à torrents
pitch' pipe' s diapason m de bouche
pit'fall' s trappe f; (fig) écueil m, pierre f d'écueil
pith [piθ] s moelle f; (fig) suc m
pith·y [ˈpiθi] adj (comp -ier; super -iest) moelleux; (fig) plein de suc
pitiful [ˈpitifəl] adj pitoyable
pitiless [ˈpitilis] adj impitoyable
pit·y [ˈpiti] s (pl -ies) pitié f; **for pity's sake!** par pitié!; **what a pity!** quel dommage! ‖ v (pret & pp -ied) tr avoir pitié de, plaindre
pivot [ˈpivət] s pivot m ‖ tr faire pivoter ‖ intr pivoter
placard [ˈplækɑrd] s placard m, affiche f ‖ tr placarder
placate [ˈpleket] tr apaiser
place [ples] s (location) endroit m, lieu m; (job) poste m, emploi m; (seat) place f; (rank) rang m; **everything in its place** chaque chose à sa place; **in no place** nulle part; **in place of** au lieu de; **in your place** à votre place; **out of place** déplacé; **to change places** changer de place; **to keep one's place** (fig) tenir ses distances; **to**

take place avoir lieu ‖ tr mettre, placer; (to find a job for; to invest) placer; (to recall) remettre, se rappeler; (to set down) poser ‖ intr (turf) finir placé
place·bo [pləˈsibo] s (pl -bos or -boes) remède m factice
place' card' s marque-place f, carton m marque-place
place' mat' s garde-nappe m
placement [ˈplesmənt] s placement m; (location) emplacement m
place'ment exam' s examen m probatoire
place'-name' s nom m de lieu, toponyme m
placid [ˈplæsid] adj placide
plagiarism [ˈpledʒəˌrizəm] s plagiat m
plagiarist [ˈpledʒərist] s plagiaire mf
plagiarize [ˈpledʒəˌraiz] tr plagier
plague [pleg] s peste f; (great public calamity) fléau m ‖ tr tourmenter
plaid [plæd] s plaid m
plain [plen] adj (manifest) clair, évident; (unambiguous) clair, franc; (talk) sans équivoque; (dress, style, diet, food) simple; (sheer, utter) pur, tout pur; (color) uni; (ugly) sans attraits ‖ s plaine f
plain' clothes' spl—**in plain clothes** en civil, en bourgeois
plain'clothes'man' s (pl -men') agent m en civil
plain' cook'ing s cuisine f bourgeoise
plain' om'elet s omelette f nature
plain' speech' s franc-parler m
plaintiff [ˈplentif] s (law) demandeur m, plaignant m
plaintive [ˈplentiv] adj plaintif
plan [plæn] s plan m, projet m; (drawing, diagram) plan, dessein m ‖ v (pret & pp **planned**; ger **planning**) tr projeter; **to plan to** se proposer de ‖ intr faire des projets
plane [plen] adj plan, plat ‖ s (aer) avion m; (bot) platane m; (carpentry) rabot m; (geom) plan m ‖ tr raboter
plane' sick'ness s mal m de l'air
planet [ˈplænit] s planète f
plane' tree' s platane m
plan'ing mill' s atelier m de rabotage
plank [plæŋk] s planche f; (pol) article m d'une plate-forme électorale
planning [ˈplæniŋ] s planification f, planning m
plant [plænt] s (factory) usine f; (building and equipment) installation f; (bot) plante f ‖ tr planter
plantation [plænˈteʃən] s plantation f
planter [ˈplæntər] s planteur m
plant' louse' s puceron m
plasma [ˈplæzmə] s plasma m
plaster [ˈplæstər] s plâtre m; (poultice) emplâtre m ‖ tr plâtrer; (a bill, poster) coller; (slang) griser
plas'ter·board' s placoplâtre m
plas'ter cast' s plâtre m
plas'ter of Par'is s plâtre m à mouler
plastic [ˈplæstik] adj & s plastique m
plas'tic bomb' s plastic m

plas′tic sur′gery s chirurgie f esthétique, chirurgie plastique

plate [plet] s (dish) assiette f; (platter) plateau m; (sheet of metal) tôle f, plaque f; vaisselle f d'or or d'argent; (anat, elec, phot, rad, zool) plaque; (typ) planche f ‖ tr plaquer; (elec) galvaniser; (typ) clicher

plateau [plæ′to] s plateau m, massif m

plate′ glass′ s verre m cylindré

platen [′plætən] s rouleau m

platform [′plæt,fɔrm] s plate-forme f; (for arrivals and departures) quai m; (of a speaker) estrade f; (political program) plate-forme

plat′form car′ s (rr) plate-forme f

platinum [′plætɪnəm] s platine m

plat′inum blonde′ s blonde f platinée

platitude [′plætɪ,t(j)ud] s platitude f

Plato [′pleto] s Platon m

platoon [plə′tun] s section f

platter [′plætər] s plat m; (slang) disque m

plausible [′plɔzɪbəl] adj plausible

play [ple] s jeu m; (drama) pièce f; (mach) jeu; **to give full play to** donner libre cours à ‖ tr jouer; (e.g., the fool) faire; (cards; e.g., football) jouer à; (an instrument) jouer de; **to play back** (a tape) faire repasser; **to play down** diminuer; **to play hooky** faire l'école buissonnière; **to play off** (sports) rejouer; **to play up** accentuer ‖ intr jouer; **to play out** s'épuiser; **to play safe** prendre des précautions; **to play sick** faire semblant d'être malade; **to play up to** passer de la pommade à

play′back′ s (device) lecteur m; (reproduction) lecture f, réécoute f, surjeu m; (act) présonorisation f

play′back head′ s tête f de lecture

play′bill′ s programme m; (poster) affiche f

player [′ple·ər] s joueur m; (mus) musicien m, joueur, exécutant m; (theat) acteur m, interprète mf

play′er pian′o s piano m mécanique

playful [′plefəl] adj enjoué, badin

playgoer [′ple,go·ər] s amateur m de théâtre

play′ground′ s terrain m de jeu

play′house′ s théâtre m; (dollhouse) maison f de poupée

play′ing card′ s carte f à jouer

play′ing field′ s terrain m de sports

play′mate′ s compagnon m de jeu

play′-off′ s finale f, match m d'appui

play′ on words′ s jeu m de mots

play′pen′ s parc m d'enfants

play′room′ s salle f de jeux

play′thing′ s jouet m

play′time′ s recréation f

playwright [′ple,raɪt] s auteur m dramatique, dramaturge mf

play′writ′ing s dramaturgie f

plea [pli] s requête f, appel m; prétexte m; (law) défense f

plead [plid] v (pret & pp **pleaded** or **pled** [pled]) tr & intr plaider; **to plead not guilty** plaider non coupable

pleasant [′plɛzənt] adj agréable

pleasant·ry [′plɛzəntri] s (pl **-ries**) plaisanterie f

please [pliz] tr plaire à; **it pleases him to** il lui plaît de; **please** + inf veuillez + inf; **to be pleased with** être content or satisfait de ‖ intr plaire; **as you please** comme vous voulez; **if you please** s'il vous plaît

pleasing [′plizɪŋ] adj agréable

pleasure [′plɛʒər] s plaisir m; **at the pleasure of** au gré de; **what is your pleasure?** qu'y a-t-il pour votre service?, que puis-je faire pour vous?

pleas′ure car′ s voiture f de tourisme

pleas′ure trip′ s voyage m d'agrément

pleat [plit] s pli m ‖ tr plisser

plebe [plib] s élève m de première année

plebeian [plɪ′bi·ən] adj & s plébéien m

plebiscite [′plɛbɪ,saɪt] s plébiscite m

pledge [plɛdʒ] s (security) gage m; (promise) engagement m d'honneur, promesse f ‖ tr mettre en gage; (one's word) engager

plentiful [′plɛntɪfəl] adj abondant

plenty [′plɛnti] s abondance f; **plenty of** beaucoup de ‖ adv (coll) largement

pleurisy [′plurɪsi] s pleurésie f

pliable [′plaɪ·əbəl] adj (substance) pliable, flexible; (character) docile, souple, malléable

pliers [′plaɪ·ərz] s & spl pinces fpl, tenailles fpl

plight [plaɪt] s embarras m; (promise) engagement m ‖ tr engager; **to plight one's troth** promettre fidélité

PLO [′pi′ɛl′o] s (letterword) (Palestine Liberation Organization) O.L.P. (Organisation de la libération de la Palestine)

plod [plɑd] v (pret & pp **plodded;** ger **plodding**) tr parcourir lourdement et péniblement ‖ intr cheminer; travailler laborieusement

plot [plɑt] s (conspiracy) complot m; (of a play or novel) intrigue f; (of ground) lopin m, parcelle f; (map) tracé m, plan m; (of vegetables) caré m ‖ v (pret & pp **plotted;** ger **plotting**) tr comploter, tramer; (a tract of land) faire le plan de; (a point) relever; (lines) tracer ‖ intr comploter; **to plot to** + inf comploter de + inf

plough [plaʊ] s, tr, & intr var of **plow**

plover [′plʌvər], [′plovər] s pluvier m

plow [plaʊ] s charrue f; (for snow) chasseneige m ‖ tr labourer; (the sea; the forehead) sillonner; (snow) déblayer; **to plow back** (com) affecter aux investissements ‖ intr labourer; **to plow through** avancer péniblement dans

plow′man s (pl **-men**) laboureur m

plow′share′ s soc m de charrue

pluck [plʌk] s courage m, cran m; (tug) petit coup m ‖ tr arracher; (flowers) cueillir; (a fowl) plumer; (one's eyebrows) épiler; (e.g., the strings of a guitar) pincer; **to pluck off** or **out** arracher; **to pluck up the courage** to trouver le courage de ‖ intr—**to pluck at** arracher d'un coup sec; **to pluck up** reprendre courage

pluck·y [ˈplʌki] *adj* (*comp* **-ier;** *super* **-iest**) courageux, crâne

plug [plʌg] *s* (*stopper*) tampon *m*, bouchon *m*; (*of sink, bathtub, etc.*) bonde *f*; (*of tobacco*) chique *f*; (aut) bougie *f*; (*on wall*) (elec) prise *f*; (*prongs*) (elec) fiche *f*, prise; (*old horse*) (coll) rosse *f*; (*hat*) (slang) haut-de-forme *m*; (slang) annonce *f* publicitaire ‖ *v* (*pret & pp* **plugged;** *ger* **plugging**) *tr* boucher; (*a melon*) entamer; **to plug in** (elec) brancher ‖ *intr*—**to plug away** (coll) persévérer

plum [plʌm] *s* prune *f*; (*tree*) prunier *m*; (slang) fromage *m*

plumage [ˈplumɪdʒ] *s* plumage *m*

plumb [plʌm] *adj* d'aplomb; (coll) pur ‖ *s* plomb *m*; **out of plumb** hors d'aplomb ‖ *adv* d'aplomb; (coll) en plein; (coll) complètement ‖ *tr* sonder

plumb′ bob′ *s* plomb *m*

plumber [ˈplʌmər] *s* plombier *m*

plumbing [ˈplʌmɪŋ] *s* plomberie *f*

plumb′ line′ *s* fil *m* à plomb

plume [plum] *s* (*cluster of feathers*) plumes *fpl*; (*small plume on hat*) plumet *m*; (*of a hat, of smoke, etc.*) panache *m* ‖ *tr* orner de plumes; (*feathers*) lisser; **to plume oneself on** se piquer de

plummet [ˈplʌmɪt] *s* plomb *m* ‖ *intr* tomber d'aplomb, se précipiter

plump [plʌmp] *adj* grassouillet, potelé, dodu ‖ *s* (coll) chute *f* lourde; (coll) bruit *m* sourd ‖ *adv* en plein; brusquement ‖ *tr* jeter brusquement; **to plump oneself down** s'affaler ‖ *intr* tomber lourdement

plum′ toma′to *s* olivette *f*

plunder [ˈplʌndər] *s* pillage *m*; (*booty*) butin *m* ‖ *tr* piller

plunge [plʌndʒ] *s* (*dive*) plongeon *m*; (*steep fall*) chute *f*; (*pitching movement*) tangage *m* ‖ *tr* plonger ‖ *intr* plonger; se précipiter; (fig) se plonger; (naut) tanguer; (slang) risquer de grosses sommes

plunger [ˈplʌndʒər] *s* (*for blocked drain*) ventouse *f*, débouchoir *m*; (*gambler*) (slang) risque-tout *m*

plunk [plʌŋk] *adv* d'un coup sec; (*squarely*) carrément ‖ *tr* jeter bruyamment ‖ *intr* tomber raide

plural [ˈplʊrəl] *adj & s* pluriel *m*

plus [plʌs] *adj* positif ‖ *s* (*sign*) plus *m*; quantité *f* positive ‖ *prep* plus

plush [plʌʃ] *adj* en peluche; (coll) rupin ‖ *s* peluche *f*

plush·y [ˈplʌʃi] *adj* (*comp* **-ier;** *super* **-iest**) pelucheux; (coll) rupin

plus′ sign′ *s* signe *m* plus

Plutarch [ˈplutark] *s* Plutarque *m*

Pluto [ˈpluto] *s* Pluton *m*

plutonium [pluˈtoni·əm] *s* plutonium *m*

ply [plaɪ] *s* (*pl* **plies**) (*e.g., of a cloth*) pli *m*; (*of rope, wool, etc.*) brin *m* ‖ *v* (*pret & pp* **plied**) *tr* manier; (*a trade*) exercer; **to ply s.o. with** presser qn de ‖ *intr* faire la navette

ply′wood′ *s* bois *m* de placage, contre-plaqué *m*

P.M. [ˈpiˈɛm] *adv* (letterword) (**post meridiem**) de l'après-midi, du soir

pneumatic [n(j)uˈmætɪk] *adj* pneumatique

pneumat′ic drill′ *s* foreuse *f* à air comprimé, marteau-piqueur *m*

pneumonia [n(j)uˈmoni·ə] *s* pneumonie *f*

P.O. [ˈpiˈo] *s* (letterword) (**post office**) poste *f*

poach [potʃ] *tr* (*eggs*) pocher ‖ *intr* (hunting) braconner

poached′ egg′ *s* œuf *m* poché

poacher [ˈpotʃər] *s* braconnier *m*

pock [pak] *s* pustule *f*

pocket [ˈpakɪt] *s* poche *f*; (billiards) blouse *f*; (aer) trou *m* d'air ‖ *tr* empocher; (*a billiard ball*) blouser; (*insults*) avaler

pock′et-book′ *s* portefeuille *m*; (*small book*) livre *m* de poche

pock′et cal′culator *s* calculatrice *f* de poche, calculette *f*

pock′et comput′er *s* ordinateur *m* de poche

pock′et hand′kerchief *s* mouchoir *m* de poche

pock′et-knife′ *s* (*pl* **-knives**) couteau *m* de poche, canif *m*

pock′et mon′ey *s* argent *m* de poche

pock′mark′ *s* marque *f* de la petite vérole

pock′marked′ *adj* grêlé

pod [pad] *s* cosse *f*, gousse *f*

poem [ˈpo·ɪm] *s* poème *m*

poet [ˈpo·ɪt] *s* poète *m*, poétesse *f*

poetess [ˈpo·ɪtɪs] *s* poétesse *f*

poetic [poˈɛtɪk] *adj* poétique ‖ **poetics** *s* poétique *f*

poetry [ˈpo·ɪtri] *s* poésie *f*

pogrom [ˈpogrəm] *s* pogrom *m*

poignancy [ˈpɔɪnənsi] *s* piquant *m*

poignant [ˈpɔɪnənt] *adj* poignant

point [pɔɪnt] *s* (*spot, dot, score, etc.*) point *m*; (*tip*) pointe *f*; (*of pen*) bec *m*; (*of conscience*) cas *m*; (*of a star*) rayon *m*; (*of a joke*) piquant *m*; (*of, e.g., grammar*) question *f*; (geog, naut) pointe; (typ) point; **beside the point, off the point** hors de propos; **on the point of** sur le point de; (*death*) à l'article de; **on this point** à cet égard, à ce propos; **point of a compass** aire *f* de vent; **point of order** rappel *m* au règlement; **point of view** point de vue; **points** (aut) vis *f* platinées; **to carry one's point** avoir gain de cause; **to come to the point** venir au fait; **to have one's good points** avoir ses qualités; **to make a point of** se faire un devoir de ‖ *tr* (*a gun, telescope, etc.*) braquer, pointer; (*a finger*) tendre; (*the way*) indiquer; (*a wall*) jointoyer; (*to sharpen*) tailler en point; **to point out** signaler, faire remarquer ‖ *intr* pointer; (*said of hunting dog*) tomber en arrêt; **to point at** montrer du doigt

point′-blank′ *adj & adv* (*fired straight at the mark*) à bout portant; (*straight forward*) à brûle-pourpoint

pointed *adj* pointu; (*remark*) mordant

pointer [ˈpɔɪntər] *s* (*stick*) baguette *f*; (*of a dial*) aiguille *f*; (*dog*) chien *m* d'arrêt, pointeur *m*

poise [pɔɪz] s équilibre m; (assurance) aplomb m ‖ tr tenir en équilibre ‖ intr être en équilibre; (in the air) planer

poison [ˈpɔɪzən] s poison m ‖ tr empoisonner

poi'son gas' s gaz m asphyxiant

poi'son i'vy s sumac m vénéneux

poisonous [ˈpɔɪzənəs] adj toxique; (plant) vénéneux; (snake) venimeux

poke [pok] s poussée f; (with elbow) coup m de coude; (coll) traînard m ‖ tr pousser; (the fire) tisonner; **to poke fun at** se moquer de; **to poke one's nose into** (coll) fourrer son nez dans; **to poke s.th. into** fourrer q.ch. dans ‖ intr aller sans se presser; **to poke about** fureter

poker [ˈpokər] s tisonnier m; (cards) poker m

pok'er face' s visage m impassible

pok·y [ˈpoki] adj (comp **-ier;** super **-iest)** (coll) lambin, lent

Poland [ˈpolənd] s Pologne f; la Pologne

polar [ˈpolər] adj polaire

po'lar bear' s ours m blanc

polarize [ˈpoləˌraɪz] tr polariser

pole [pol] s (long rod or staff) perche f; (of flag) hampe f; (upright support) poteau m; (astr, biol, elec, geog, math) pôle m; **Pole** (person) Polonais m ‖ tr pousser à la perche

pole'cat' s putois m

pole'star' s étoile f polaire

pole' vault' s saut m à la perche

police [pəˈlis] s police f ‖ tr maintenir l'ordre dans

police' brutal'ity s brutalité f policière

police' commis'sioner s préfet m de police

police'man s (pl **-men)** agent m de police

police' pre'cinct s commissariat m de police

police' state' s régime m policier

police' sta'tion s poste m de police, commissariat m

police'wom'an s (pl **-wom'en)** femme f agent

poli·cy [ˈpalɪsi] s (pl **-cies)** politique f; (ins) police f

polio [ˈpolɪˌo] s (coll) polio f

polish [ˈpalɪʃ] s (shine) poli m; (for household uses) cire f; (for shoes) cirage m; (fig) politesse f, vernis m ‖ tr polir; (shoes, floor, etc.) cirer; (one's nails) vernir; **to polish off** (coll) expédier; (e.g., a meal) (slang) engloutir ‖ **Polish** [ˈpolɪʃ] adj & s polonais m

polite [pəˈlaɪt] adj poli

politeness [pəˈlaɪtnɪs] s politesse f

politic [ˈpalɪtɪk] adj (prudent) diplomatique, politique; (shrewd) rusé

political [pəˈlɪtɪkəl] adj politique

politician [ˌpalɪˈtɪʃən] s politicien m

politics [ˈpalɪtɪks] s & spl politique f

poll [pol] s (list of voters) liste f électorale; (vote) scrutin m; (head) tête f; (opinion survey) sondage m d'opinion; **to go to the polls** aller aux urnes; **to take a poll** faire une enquête par sondage ‖ tr (e.g., a

delegation) dépouiller le scrutin de; (a certain number of votes) recevoir

pollen [ˈpalən] s pollen m

poll'ing booth' [ˈpolɪŋ] s isoloir m

polliwog [ˈpalɪˌwag] s têtard m

pol'liwog initia'tion s baptême m de la ligne

pollster [ˈpolstər] s sondeur m, enquêteur m

poll' tax' s taxe f par tête

pollute [pəˈlut] tr polluer

polluting [pəˈlutɪŋ] adj polluant

pollution [pəˈluʃən] s pollution f

polo [ˈpolo] s polo m

polonium [pəˈlonɪ·əm] s polonium m

polo shirt' s chemise f polo

polygamist [pəˈlɪgəmɪst] s polygame mf

polygamous [pəˈlɪgəməs] adj polygame

polyglot [ˈpalɪˌglat] adj & s polyglotte mf

polygon [ˈpalɪˌgan] s polygone m

polynomial [ˌpalɪˈnomɪ·əl] s polynôme m

polyp [ˈpalɪp] s polype m

polytheist [ˈpalɪˌθi·ɪst] s polythéiste mf

polytheistic [ˌpalɪθɪˈɪstɪk] adj polythéiste

polyvalent [palɪˈvelənt] adj polyvalent

pomade [pəˈmed] s pommade f

pomegranate [ˈpamˌgrænɪt] s (shrub) grenadier m; (fruit) grenade f

pom·mel [ˈpʌməl] s pommeau m ‖ v (pret & pp **-meled** or **-melled;** ger **-meling** or **-melling)** tr rosser

pomp [pamp] s pompe f

pompous [ˈpampəs] adj pompeux

pon·cho [ˈpantʃo] s (pl **-chos)** poncho m

pond [pand] s étang m, mare f

ponder [ˈpandər] tr peser ‖ intr méditer; **to ponder over** réfléchir sur

ponderous [ˈpandərəs] adj pesant

poniard [ˈpanjərd] s poignard m ‖ tr poignarder

pontiff [ˈpantɪf] s pontife m

pontifical [panˈtɪfɪkəl] adj (e.g., air) de pontife

pontoon [panˈtun] s ponton m

po·ny [ˈponi] s (pl **-nies)** poney m; (for drinking liquor) petit verre m; (coll) aide-mémoire m illicite

po'ny·tail' s queue-de-cheval f

poodle [ˈpudəl] s caniche m

pool [pul] s (small puddle) mare f; (for swimming) piscine f; (game) billard m; (in certain games) poule f; (of workers) équipe f; (combine) pool m; (com) fonds m commun ‖ tr mettre en commun

pool'room' s salle f de billard

pool' ta'ble s table f de billard

poop [pup] s poupe f; (deck) dunette f ‖ tr (slang) casser la tête à

pooped adj (slang) vanné, à plat, flagada

poor [pur] adj pauvre; (mediocre) piètre; (unfortunate) pauvre (before noun); (without money) pauvre (after noun)

poor' box' s tronc m des pauvres

poor'house' s asile m des indigents

poorly [ˈpurli] adj souffrant ‖ adv mal

pop [pap] s bruit m sec; (soda) boisson f gazeuse ‖ v (pret & pp **popped;** ger **popping)** tr (corn) faire éclater ‖ intr (*said, e.g., of balloon*) crever; (*said of cork*) sauter

pop'corn' *s* maïs *m* éclaté, maïs explosé; grains *mpl* de maïs soufflés, pop-corn *m*

pope [pop] *s* pape *m*

pop'eyed' *adj* aux yeux saillants

pop'gun' *s* canonnière *f*

poplar ['pɑplər] *s* peuplier *m*

pop·py ['pɑpi] *s* (*pl* **-pies**) pavot *m*; (*corn poppy*) coquelicot *m*

pop'py·cock' *s* (coll) fadaises *fpl*

populace ['pɑpjəlɪs] *s* peuple *m*, populace *f*

popular ['pɑpjələr] *adj* populaire

popularize ['pɑpjələ,raɪz] *tr* populariser, vulgariser

populate ['pɑpjə,let] *tr* peupler

population [,pɑpjə'leʃən] *s* population *f*

populous ['pɑpjələs] *adj* populeux

porcelain ['pɔrslɪn] *s* porcelaine *f*

porch [pɔrtʃ] *s* (*portico*) porche *m*; (*enclosed*) véranda *f*

porcupine ['pɔrkjə,paɪn] *s* porc-épic *m*

pore [pɔr] *s* pore *m* ‖ *intr*—**to pore over** examiner avec attention, s'absorber dans

pork [pɔrk] *s* porc *m*

pork' and beans' *spl* fèves *fpl* au lard

pork'chop' *s* côtelette *f* de porc

porn [pɔrn] *s* (coll) porno *m* & *f*

pornography [pɔr'nɑgrəfi] *s* pornographie *f*

porous ['pɔrəs] *adj* poreux

porphy·ry ['pɔrfɪri] *s* (*pl* **-ries**) porphyre *m*

porpoise ['pɔrpəs] *s* marsouin *m*

porridge ['pɔrɪdʒ] *s* bouillie *f*, porridge *m*

port [pɔrt] *s* port *m*; (*opening in ship's side*) hublot *m*, sabord *m*; (*left side of ship or airplane*) bâbord *m*; (*wine*) porto *m*; (mach) orifice *m*

portable ['pɔrtəbəl] *adj* portatif

port'able stand' *s* (*for a television set*) socle *m* roulant

port'able type'writer *s* machine *f* à écrire portative

portage ['pɔrtɪdʒ] *s* transport *m*; portage *m*

portal ['pɔrtəl] *s* portail *m*

portcullis [pɔrt'kʌlɪs] *s* herse *f*

portend [pɔr'tɛnd] *tr* présager

portent ['pɔrtɛnt] *s* présage *m*

portentous [pɔr'tɛntəs] *adj* extraordinaire; de mauvais augure

porter ['pɔrtər] *s* (*doorkeeper*) portier *m*, concierge *m*; (*in hotels and trains*) porteur *m*

portfoli·o [pɔrt'foli,o] *s* (*pl* **-os**) portefeuille *m*

port'hole' *s* hublot *m*

porti·co ['pɔrtɪ,ko] *s* (*pl* **-coes** or **-cos**) portique *m*

portion ['pɔrʃən] *s* portion *f*; (*dowry*) dot *f* ‖ *tr*—**to portion out** partager, répartir

port·ly ['pɔrtli] *adj* (*comp* **-lier**; *super* **-liest**) corpulent

port' of call' *s* port *m* d'escale

portrait ['pɔrtret] *s* portrait *m*; **to sit for one's portrait** se faire faire son portrait

portray [pɔr'tre] *tr* faire le portrait de; dépeindre, décrire; (theat) jouer le rôle de

portrayal [pɔr'tre·əl] *s* représentation *f*; description *f*

Portugal ['pɔrtʃəgəl] *s* le Portugal

Portu·guese ['pɔrtʃə,giz] *adj* portugais ‖ *s* (*language*) portugais *m* ‖ *s* (*pl* **-guese**) (*person*) Portugais *m*

port' wine' *s* porto *m*

pose [poz] *s* pose *f* ‖ *tr* & *intr* poser; **to pose as** se poser comme

posh [pɑʃ] *adj* (slang) chic, élégant

position [pə'zɪʃən] *s* position *f*; (*job*) poste *m*; **in position** en place; **in your position** à votre place

positive ['pɑzɪtɪv] *adj* & *s* positif *m*

possess [pə'zɛs] *tr* posséder

possession [pə'zɛʃən] *s* possession *f*; **to take possession of** s'emparer de

possible ['pɑsɪbəl] *adj* possible

possum ['pɑsəm] *s* opossum *m*; **to play possum** (coll) faire le mort

post [post] *s* (*upright*) poteau *m*; (*job, position*) poste *m*; (*post office*) poste *f*; (mil) poste *m* ‖ *tr* (*a notice, placard, etc.*) afficher, placarder; (*a letter*) poster, mettre à la poste; (*a sentinel*) poster; (*with news*) tenir au courant; **post no bills** (*public sign*) défense d'afficher

postage ['postɪdʒ] *s* port *m*, affranchissement *m*

post'age due' *s* port *m* dû, affranchissement *m* insuffisant

post'age me'ter *s* affranchisseuse *f* à compteur

post'age stamp' *s* timbre-poste *m*

postal ['postəl] *adj* postal

post'al card' *s* carte *f* postale

post'al clerk' *s* postier *m*

post'al mon'ey or'der *s* mandat-poste *m*

post'al per'mit *s* franchise *f* postale, dispensé *m* du timbrage

post'al sav'ings bank' *s* caisse *f* d'épargne postale

post' card' *s* carte *f* postale

post'date' *s* postdate *f* ‖ **post'date'** *tr* postdater

poster ['postər] *s* affiche *f*

posterity [pɑs'tɛrɪti] *s* postérité *f*

postern ['postərn] *s* poterne *f*

post'haste' *adv* en toute hâte

posthumous ['pɑstʃuməs] *adj* posthume

post'man *s* (*pl* **-men**) facteur *m*, préposé *m*

post'mark' *s* cachet *m* d'oblitération, timbre *m* ‖ *tr* timbrer

post'mas'ter *s* receveur *m* des postes, administrateur *m* du bureau de postes

post'master gen'eral *s* ministre *m* des Postes et Télécommunications

post-mortem [,post'mɔrtəm] *adj* après décès; (fig) après le fait ‖ *s* autopsie *f*; discussion *f* après le fait

post' of'fice *s* bureau *m* de poste

post'-office box' *s* case *f* postale, boîte *f* postale

post'paid' *adv* port payé, franc de port, franco de port

postpone [post'pon] *tr* remettre, différer; (*a meeting*) ajourner

postponement [post'ponmənt] s remise f, ajournement m

postscript ['post,skrɪpt] s post-scriptum m

posture ['pastʃər] s posture f ‖ intr prendre une posture

post'war' adj d'après-guerre

po·sy ['pozi] s (pl -sies) fleur f; bouquet m

pot [pat] s pot m; (in gambling) mise f; (culin) marmite f, pot; (marijuana) (slang) kif m, marie-jeanne f; **to go to pot** (slang) s'en aller à vau-l'eau

potash ['pat,æʃ] s potasse f

potassium [pə'tæsɪ·əm] s potassium m

pota·to [pə'teto] s (pl -toes) pomme f de terre; (sweet potato) patate f

pota'to chips' spl pommes fpl chips; croustelle f (Canad)

potbellied ['pat,bɛlid] adj ventru

poten·cy ['potənsi] s (pl -cies) puissance f; virilité f

potent ['potənt] adj puissant, fort; (effective) efficace

potentate ['potən,tet] s potentat m

potential [pə'tɛnʃəl] adj & s potentiel m

pot'hang'er s crémaillère f

pot'herb' s herbe f potagère

pot'hold'er s poignée f

pot'hole' s nid m de poule

pot'hook' s croc m

potion ['poʃən] s potion f

pot'luck' s—**to take potluck** manger à la fortune du pot

pot' shot' s coup m tiré à courte distance

potter ['patər] s potier m ‖ intr—**to potter around** s'occuper de bagatelles, bricoler

pot'ter's clay' s terre f à potier

pot'ter's field' s fosse f commune

pot'ter's wheel' s roue f or tour m de potier

potter·y ['patəri] s (pl -ies) poterie f

pouch [pautʃ] s poche f, petit sac m; (of kangaroo) poche f ventrale; (for tobacco) blague f

poultice ['poltɪs] s cataplasme m

poultry ['poltri] s volaille f

poul'try·man s (pl -men) éleveur m de volailles; (dealer) volailleur m

pounce [pauns] intr—**to pounce on** fondre sur, s'abattre sur

pound [paund] s (weight) livre f; (for automobiles, stray animals, etc.) fourrière f ‖ tr battre; (to pulverize) piler, broyer; (to bombard) pilonner; (e.g., an animal) mettre en fourrière; (e.g., the sidewalk) (fig) battre ‖ intr battre

pound' ster'ling s livre f sterling

pour [por] tr verser; **to pour off** décanter ‖ intr écouler; (said of rain) tomber à verse; **to pour out of** sortir à flots

pout [paut] s moue f ‖ intr faire la moue

poverty ['pavərti] s pauvreté f

POW ['pi'o'dʌbl,ju] s (letterword) (prisoner of war) P.G.

powder ['paudər] s poudre f ‖ tr réduire en poudre; (to sprinkle with powder) poudrer ‖ intr se poudrer

pow'dered cof'fee s café m soluble

pow'dered sug'ar s sucre m de confiseur, sucre en poudre, sucre glace

pow'der puff' s houppe f

pow'der room' s toilettes fpl pour dames

powdery ['paudəri] adj (like powder) poudreux; (sprinkled with powder) poussiéreux; (crumbly) friable

power ['pau·ər] s (authority; capacity) pourvoir m; (influential nation; energy, force, strength; of a machine, microscope, number) puissance f; (talent, capacity, etc.) faculté f; **the powers that be** les autorités fpl; **to seize power** saisir le pouvoir ‖ tr actionner

pow'er brake' s (aut) servo-frein m

pow'er dive' s piqué m à plein gaz

pow'er-dive' intr piquer à plein gaz

powerful ['pau·ərfəl] adj puissant

pow'er·house' s usine f centrale; (coll) foyer m d'énergie

pow'er lawn' mower s tondeuse f à gazon à moteur

powerless ['pau·ərlɪs] adj impuissant

pow'er line' s secteur m de distribution

pow'er mow'er s tondeuse f à gazon à moteur; motofaucheuse f

pow'er of attor'ney s procuration f, mandat m

pow'er pack' s (rad) unité f d'alimentation

pow'er plant' s (powerhouse) centrale f électrique; (aer, aut) groupe m motopropulseur

pow'er saw' s tronçonneuse f

pow'er steer'ing s (aut) servo-direction f

practicable ['præktɪkəbəl] adj praticable

practical ['præktɪkəl] adj pratique

prac'tical joke' s farce f, attrape f

prac'tical jok'er s fumiste m

practically ['præktɪkəli] adv pratiquement; (more or less) à peu près

prac'tical nurse' s garde-malade mf

practice ['præktɪs] s (habit, usage) pratique f; (of a profession) exercice m; (of a doctor) clientèle f; (exercise, training) entraînement m; (rehearsal) répétition f; **in practice** en pratique, pratiquement; (well-trained) en forme; **out of practice** rouillé ‖ tr pratiquer; (a profession) exercer, pratiquer; (e.g., the violin) s'exercer à; **to practice what one preaches** prêcher d'exemple ‖ intr faire des exercices, s'exercer; (said of doctor, lawyer, etc.) exercer

practiced adj expert

practitioner [præk'tɪʃənər] s praticien m

prairie ['prɛri] s steppes fpl; **the prairie** les Prairies fpl

praise [prez] s louange f ‖ tr louer

praise'wor'thy adj louable, digne d'éloges

pram [præm] s voiture f d'enfant

prance [præns] intr caracoler, cabrioler

prank [præŋk] s espièglerie f

prate [pret] intr bavarder, papoter

prattle ['prætəl] s bavardage m, papotage m ‖ intr bavarder, papoter; (said of children) babiller

prawn [prɔn] s crevette f rose, bouquet m

pray [pre] *tr* & *intr* prier
prayer [prɛr] *s* prière *f*
prayer' book' *s* livre *m* de prières
pray'ing man'tis [ˈmæntɪs] *s* mante *f* religieuse
preach [pritʃ] *tr* & *intr* prêcher
preacher [ˈpritʃər] *s* prédicateur *m*
preamble [ˈpri,æmbəl] *s* préambule *m*
precarious [prɪˈkɛrɪ·əs] *adj* précaire
precaution [prɪˈkɔʃən] *s* précaution *f*
precede [prɪˈsid] *tr* & *intr* précéder
precedent [ˈprɛsɪdənt] *s* précédent *m*
precept [ˈprisɛpt] *s* précepte *m*
precinct [ˈprisɪŋkt] *s* enceinte *f*; circonscription *f* électorale
precious [ˈprɛʃəs] *adj* précieux ‖ *adv*—**precious little** (coll) très peu
precipice [ˈprɛsɪpɪs] *s* précipice *m*
precipitate [prɪˈsɪpɪ,tet] *adj* & *s* précipité *m* ‖ *tr* précipiter ‖ *intr* se précipiter
precipitous [prɪˈsɪpɪtəs] *adj* escarpé; (*hurried*) précipité
precise [prɪˈsais] *adj* précis
precision [prɪˈsɪʒən] *s* précision *f*
preclude [prɪˈklud] *tr* empêcher
precocious [prɪˈkoʃəs] *adj* précoce
preconceived [,prikənˈsivd] *adj* préconçu
predatory [ˈprɛdə,tori] *adj* rapace; (zool) prédateur
predecessor [,prɛdɪˈsɛsər] *s* prédécesseur *m*, devancier *m*
predicament [prɪˈdɪkəmənt] *s* situation *f* difficile
predict [prɪˈdɪkt] *tr* prédire
prediction [prɪˈdɪkʃən] *s* prédiction *f*
predispose [,pridɪsˈpoz] *tr* prédisposer
predominant [prɪˈdɑmɪnənt] *adj* prédominant
preeminent [prɪˈɛmɪnənt] *adj* prééminent
preempt [prɪˈɛmpt] *tr* s'approprier
preen [prin] *tr* lisser; **to preen oneself** se bichonner; être fier, se piquer
prefabricated [priˈfæbrɪ,ketɪd] *adj* préfabriqué
preface [ˈprɛfɪs] *s* préface *f* ‖ *tr* préfacer
pre·fer [prɪˈfʌr] *v* (*pret* & *pp* **-ferred**; *ger* **-ferring**) *tr* préférer
preferable [ˈprɛfərəbəl] *adj* préférable
preference [ˈprɛfərəns] *s* préférence *f*
preferred' stock' *s* action *f* privilégiée, actions privilégiées
prefix [ˈprifɪks] *s* préfixe *m* ‖ *tr* préfixer
pregnan·cy [ˈprɛgnənsi] *s* (*pl* **-cies**) grossesse *f*
pregnant [ˈprɛgnənt] *adj* enceinte, grosse; (fig) gros
prehistoric [,prihɪsˈtɔrɪk] *adj* préhistorique
prejudice [ˈprɛdʒədɪs] *s* préjugé *m*; (*detriment*) préjudice *m* ‖ *tr* prévenir, prédisposer; (*to harm*) porter préjudice à
prejudicial [,prɛdʒəˈdɪʃəl] *adj* préjudiciable
prelate [ˈprɛlɪt] *s* prélat *m*
prelim [ˈprilɪm] *s* (educ) examen *m* préliminaire; (sports) épreuve *f* éliminatoire
preliminar·y [prɪˈlɪmɪ,nɛri] *adj* préliminaire ‖ *s* (*pl* **-ies**) préliminaire *m*

prelude [ˈprɛljud] *s* prélude *m* ‖ *tr* introduire; préluder à; (*a piece of music*) préluder par
premature [,priməˈt(j)ʊr] *adj* prématuré; (*plant*) hâtif
premeditate [priˈmɛdɪ,tet] *tr* préméditer
premier [prɪˈmɪr] *s* premier ministre *m*
première [prəˈmjɛr], [prɪˈmɪr] *s* première *f*; (*actress*) vedette *f*
premise [ˈprɛmɪs] *s* prémisse *f*; **on the premises** sur les lieux; **premises** local *m*, locaux *mpl*
premium [ˈprimɪ·əm] *s* prime *f*; **to be at a premium** faire prime
premonition [,priməˈnɪʃən] *s* prémonition *f*
preoccupation [pri,ɑkjəˈpeʃən] *s* préoccupation *f*
preoccu·py [priˈɑkjə,pai] *v* (*pret* & *pp* **-pied**) *tr* préoccuper
prepaid [priˈped] *adj* payé d'avance; (*letter*) affranchi
preparation [,prɛpəˈreʃən] *s* préparation *f*; **preparations** (*for a trip; for war*) préparatifs *mpl*
preparatory [prɪˈpærə,tori] *adj* préparatoire
prepare [prɪˈpɛr] *tr* préparer ‖ *intr* se préparer
preparedness [prɪˈpɛrdnɪs] *s* préparation *f*; armement *m* préventif
pre·pay [priˈpe] *v* (*pret* & *pp* **-paid**) *tr* payer d'avance
preponderant [prɪˈpɑndərənt] *adj* prépondérant
preposition [,prɛpəˈzɪʃən] *s* préposition *f*
prepossessing [,pripəˈzɛsɪŋ] *adj* avenant, agréable
preposterous [prɪˈpɑstərəs] *adj* absurde, extravagant
preppie [ˈprɛpi] *s* (slang) bon chic bon genre *m* (B.C.B.G.)
prep' school' [prɛp] *s* école *f* préparatoire
prerecorded [,prirɪˈkɔrdɪd] *adj* (rad, telv) différé, en différé
prerequisite [priˈrɛkwɪzɪt] *s* préalable *m*; (educ) cours *m* préalable
prerogative [prɪˈrɑgətɪv] *s* prérogative *f*
presage [ˈprɛsɪdʒ] *s* présage *m*; (*foreboding*) pressentiment *m* ‖ [prɪˈsedʒ] *tr* présager; pressentir
Presbyterian [,prɛzbɪˈtɪrɪ·ən] *adj* & *s* presbytérien *m*
prescribe [prɪˈskraib] *tr* prescrire ‖ *intr* faire une ordonnance
prescription [prɪˈskrɪpʃən] *s* prescription *f*; (*pharm*) ordonnance *f*
presence [ˈprɛzəns] *s* présence *f*
present [ˈprɛzənt] *adj* (*at this time*) actuel; (*at this place or time*) présent; **to be present at** assister à ‖ *s* cadeau *m*, présent *m*; (*present time or tense*) présent; **at present** à présent ‖ [prɪˈzɛnt] *tr* présenter
presentable [prɪˈzɛntəbəl] *adj* présentable, sortable
presentation [,prɛzənˈteʃən] *s* présentation *f*
presenta'tion cop'y *s* exemplaire *m* offert à titre d'hommage

presentiment [prɪ'zɛntɪmənt] s pressentiment m
presently ['prɛzəntli] adv tout à l'heure; (now) à présent
preserve [prɪ'zʌrv] s confiture f; (for game) chasse f gardée ‖ tr préserver, conserver; (to can) conserver
pre-shrunk [pri'ʃʌŋk] adj irrétrécissable
preside [prɪ'zaɪd] intr présider; **to preside over** présider
presiden·cy ['prɛzɪdənsi] s (pl -cies) présidence f
president ['prɛzɪdənt] s président m; (of a university) recteur m
pres'ident-elect' s président m désigné
presidential [,prɛzɪ'dɛnʃəl] adj présidentiel
press [prɛs] s presse f; (e.g., for wine) pressoir m; (pressure) pression f; (for clothes) armoire f; (in weight lifting) développé m; **in press** (said of clothes) lisse et net; (said of book being published) sous presse; **to go to press** être mis sous presse ‖ tr presser; (e.g., a button) appuyer sur, presser; (clothes) donner un coup de fer à, repasser ‖ intr presser; **to press against** se serrer contre; **to press forward, to press on** presser le pas
press' a'gent s agent m de publicité
press' box' s tribune f des journalistes
press' card' s coupe-file m d'un journaliste
press' con'ference s conférence f de presse
press' gal'lery s tribune f de la presse
pressing ['prɛsɪŋ] adj pressé, pressant
press' pass' s placard m de presse
press' release' s communiqué m de presse
pressure ['prɛʃər] s pression f
pres'sure cook'er s autocuiseur m, cocotte f minute
pressurize ['prɛʃə,raɪz] tr pressuriser
prestige [prɛs'tiʒ] s prestige m
pre'stressed con'crete ['pri,strɛst] s béton m précontraint
presumably [prɪ'z(j)uməbli] adv probablement
presume [prɪ'z(j)um] tr présumer; **to presume to** présumer ‖ intr présumer; **to presume on** or **upon** abuser de
presumption [prɪ'zʌmpʃən] s présomption f
presumptuous [prɪ'zʌmptʃu·əs] adj présomptueux
presuppose [,prisə'poz] tr présupposer
pretend [prɪ'tɛnd] tr feindre; **to pretend to** + inf feindre de + inf; (to claim) prétendre, e.g., **I don't pretend to know everything** je ne prétends pas tout savoir; (to imagine) se dire, e.g., **I am going to pretend to be sitting at an outdoor café** je vais me dire que je m'assieds à une terrasse de café ‖ intr feindre; **let's pretend!** (let's imagine that it's true) imaginons-nous!; **to pretend to** (e.g., the throne) prétendre à
pretender [prɪ'tɛndər] s prétendant m; (impostor) simulateur m
pretense [prɪ'tɛns], ['pritɛns] s prétention f; feinte f; **under false pretenses** par des

moyens frauduleux; **under pretense of** sous prétexte de
pretension [prɪ'tɛnʃən] s prétention f
pretentious [prɪ'tɛnʃəs] adj prétentieux
pretext ['pritɛkst] s prétexte m
pretonic [prɪ'tɑnɪk] adj prétonique
pret·ty ['prɪti] adj (comp -tier; super -tiest) joli; (coll) considérable ‖ adv assez; très
prevail [prɪ'vel] intr prévaloir, régner; **to prevail on** or **upon** persuader
prevailing [prɪ'velɪŋ] adj (opinion) prédominant, courant; (conditions) actuel; (wind) dominant; (fashion) en vogue
prevalent ['prɛvələnt] adj commun, courant, regnant
prevaricate [prɪ'væri,ket] intr mentir
prevent [prɪ'vɛnt] tr empêcher
prevention [prɪ'vɛnʃən] s empêchement m; (e.g., of accidents) prévention f
preventive [prɪ'vɛntɪv] adj & s préventif m
preview ['pri,vju] s (of something to come) amorce f; (private showing) (mov) avant-première f; (show of brief scenes for advertising) film m annonce
previous ['privi·əs] adj précédent, antérieur; (notice) préalable; (coll) pressé ‖ adv—**previous to** antérieurement à
prewar ['pri,wɔr] adj d'avant-guerre
prey [pre] s proie f; **to be a prey to** être en proie à ‖ intr—**to prey on** or **upon** faire sa proie de; (e.g., a seacoast) piller; (e.g., the mind) ronger, miner
price [praɪs] s prix m ‖ tr mettre un prix à, tarifer; s'informer du prix de
price' control' s contrôle m des prix
price' cut'ting s rabais m, remise f
price'-earn'ings ra'tio s quotient m cours-bénéficie
price' fix'ing s stabilisation f des prix
price' freez'ing s blocage m des prix
priceless ['praɪslɪs] adj sans prix, inestimable; (very funny) (coll) impayable, absurde
price' list' s liste f de prix, tarif m
price' war' s guerre f des prix
prick [prɪk] s piqûre f; (spur; sting of conscience) aiguillon m ‖ tr piquer; **to prick up** (the ears) dresser
prick·ly ['prɪkli] adj (comp -lier; super -liest) épineux
prick'ly heat' s lichen m vésiculaire, miliaire f
prick'ly pear' s figue f de Barbarie; (plant) figuier m de Barbarie
pride [praɪd] s (self-respect) orgueil m; (satisfaction) fierté f; (pej) arrogance f, orgueil; **to take pride in** être fier de ‖ tr—**to pride oneself on** or **upon** s'enorgueillir de
priest [prist] s prêtre m
priestess ['pristɪs] s prêtresse f
priesthood ['prist,hud] s sacerdoce m
priest·ly ['pristli] adj (comp -lier; super -liest) sacerdotal
prig [prɪg] s poseur m, pédant m
prim [prɪm] adj (comp **primmer**; super **primmest**) compassé, guindé

prima·ry [ˈpraɪməri] *adj* primaire ‖ *s* (*pl* -ries) élection *f* primaire; (elec) primaire *m*

primate [ˈpraɪmet] *s* (eccl) primat *m*; (zool) primate *m*

prime [praɪm] *adj* (*first*) premier, principal; (*of the best quality*) de première qualité, (le) meilleur; (math) prime ‖ *s* fleur *f*, perfection *f*; commencement *m*, premiers jours *mpl;* **prime of life** fleur or force de l'âge ‖ *tr* amorcer; (*a surface to be painted*) appliquer une couche de fond à; (*to supply with information*) mettre au courant

prime' min'ister *s* premier ministre *m*

primer [ˈprɪmər] *s* premier livre *m* de lecture, manuel *m* élémentaire ‖ [ˈpraɪmər] *s* (*for paint*) couche *f* de fond, impression, *f*; (mach) amorce *f*

prime' rate' *s* (com) taux *m* de base

primeval [praɪˈmivəl] *adj* primitif

primitive [ˈprɪmɪtɪv] *adj* & *s* primitif *m*

primordial [praɪˈmɔrdɪ·əl] *adj* primordial

primp [prɪmp] *tr* bichonner, pomponner ‖ *intr* se bichonner, se pomponner

prim'rose' *s* primevère *f*

prim'rose path' *s* chemin *m* de velours

prince [prɪns] *s* prince *m*

prince·ly [ˈprɪnsli] *adj* (*comp* -lier; *super* -liest) princier

Prince' of Wales' *s* prince *m* de Galles

princess [ˈprɪnsɪs] *s* princesse *f*

principal [ˈprɪnsɪpəl] *adj* & *s* principal *m*

principali·ty [ˌprɪnsɪˈpælɪti] *s* (*pl* -ties) principauté *f*

principle [ˈprɪnsɪpəl] *s* principe *m*

print [prɪnt] *s* (*mark*) empreinte *f*; (*printed cloth*) imprimé *m*; (*design in printed cloth*) estampe *f*; (*lettering*) lettres *fpl* moulées; (*act of printing*) impression *f*; (phot) épreuve *f*; **out of print** épuisé; **small print** petits caractères *mpl* ‖ *tr* imprimer; écrire en lettres moulées; publier; (*an edition; a photographic negative*) tirer; **to print out** (comp) imprimer, restituer

print'ed cir'cuit *s* circuit *m* imprimé

print'ed mat'ter *s* imprimés *mpl*

printer [ˈprɪntər] *s* imprimeur *m*; (comp) imprimante *f*

prin'ter's dev'il *s* apprenti *m* imprimeur

prin'ter's er'ror *s* faute *f* d'impression, coquille *f*

prin'ter's ink' *s* encre *f* d'imprimerie

prin'ter's mark' *s* nom *m* de l'imprimeur

printing [ˈprɪntɪŋ] *s* imprimerie *f*; (*act*) impression *f*; (*by hand*) écriture *f* en caractères d'imprimerie; édition *f*; tirage *m*; (phot) tirage

print'ing frame' *s* (phot) châssis-presse *m*

print'ing of'fice *s* imprimerie *f*

print'out' *s* (comp) tapuscrit *m*, listage *m*

prior [ˈpraɪ·ər] *adj* antérieur ‖ *s* prieur *m* ‖ *adv* antérieurement; **prior to** avant; avant de

priori·ty [praɪˈɔrɪti] *s* (*pl* -ties) priorité *f*

prism [ˈprɪzəm] *s* prisme *m*

prison [ˈprɪzən] *s* prison *f* ‖ *tr* emprisonner

prisoner [ˈprɪznər] *s* prisonnier *m*

pris'on van' *s* voiture *f* cellulaire

pris·sy [ˈprɪsi] *adj* (*comp* -sier; *super* -siest) (coll) bégueule

priva·cy [ˈpraɪvəsi] *s* (*pl* -cies) intimité *f*, secret *m*

private [ˈpraɪvɪt] *adj* privé, particulier; confidentiel, secret; (*public sign*) défense d'entrer ‖ *s* simple soldat *m*; **in private** dans l'intimité, en particulier; **privates** parties *fpl*

pri'vate cit'izen *s* simple particulier *m*, simple citoyen *m*

pri'vate first' class' *s* soldat *m* de première

pri'vate hos'pital *s* clinique *f*

pri'vate sec'retary *s* secrétaire *m* particulier

pri'vate sid'ing *s* embranchement *m* particulier

privet [ˈprɪvɪt] *s* troène *m*

privilege [ˈprɪvɪlɪdʒ] *s* privilège *m*

priv·y [ˈprɪvi] *adj* privé; **privy to** averti de ‖ *s* (*pl* -ies) cabinets *mpl* au fond du jardin

prize [praɪz] *s* prix *m*; (*something captured*) prise *f* ‖ *tr* faire cas de, estimer

prize' fight' *s* match *m* de boxe

prize' fight'er *s* boxeur *m* professionnel

prize' ring' *s* ring *m*

prize'win'ner *s* lauréat *m*; **prizewinners** (*list*) palmarès *m*

pro [pro] *s* (*pl* **pros**) vote *m* affirmatif; (*professional*) (coll) pro *m*; **the pros and the cons** le pour et le contre ‖ *prep* en faveur de

probabili·ty [ˌprɑbəˈbɪlɪti] *s* (*pl* -ties) probabilité *f*

probable [ˈprɑbəbəl] *adj* probable

probably [ˈprɑbəbli] *adv* probablement

probate [ˈprobet] *s* homologation *f* ‖ *tr* homologuer

probation [proˈbeʃən] *s* liberté *f* surveillée; (*on a job*) stage *m*

probe [prob] *s* sondage *m*; (*instrument*) sonde *f*; (rok) échos *mpl*; (rok) engin *m* exploratoire ‖ *tr* sonder

problem [ˈprɑbləm] *s* problème *m*

probl'em child' *s* enfant *mf* terrible

procedure [proˈsidʒər] *s* procédé *m*

proceed [ˈprosid] *s*—**proceeds** produit *m*, bénéfices *mpl* ‖ [proˈsid] *intr* avancer, continuer; continuer à parler; **to proceed from** procéder de; **to proceed to** se mettre à; (*to go to*) se diriger à

proceeding [proˈsidɪŋ] *s* procédé *m*; **proceedings** actes *mpl*

process [ˈprɑsɛs] *s* (*technique*) procédé *m*; (*development*) processus *m*; **in the process of** en train de ‖ *tr* soumettre à un procédé, traiter

processing [ˈprɑsɛsɪŋ] *s* (comp) traitement *m*, façonnage *m*; **processing by modem** (comp) télétraitement *m*

procession [proˈsɛʃən] *s* cortège *m*, défilé *m*, procession *f*

pro'cess serv'er *s* huissier *m* exploitant

proclaim [proˈklem] *tr* proclamer

proclitic [proˈklɪtɪk] *adj* & *s* proclitique *m*

procrastinate [proˈkræstɪˌnet] *tr* différer ‖ *intr* remettre les affaires à plus tard

proctor [ˈprɑktər] *s* surveillant *m*

procure [proˈkjʊr] *tr* obtenir, se procurer; (*a woman*) entraîner à la prostitution ‖ *intr* faire du proxénétisme

procurement [proˈkjʊrmənt] *s* obtention *f*, acquisition *f*

procurer [proˈkjʊrər] *s* proxénète *mf*

prod [prɑd] *s* poussée *f*; (*stick*) aiguillon *m* ‖ *v* (*pret & pp* **prodded**; *ger* **prodding**) *tr* aiguillonner

prodigal [ˈprɑdɪgəl] *adj & s* prodigue *mf*

prodigious [proˈdɪdʒəs] *adj* prodigieux

prodi·gy [ˈprɑdɪdʒi] *s* (*pl* **-gies**) prodige *m*

produce [ˈprɑd(j)us] *s* produit *m*; (*eatables*) denrées *fpl* ‖ [proˈd(j)us] *tr* produire; (*a play*) mettre en scène; (geom) prolonger

producer [proˈd(j)usər] *s* producteur *m*

product [ˈprɑdəkt] *s* produit *m*

production [proˈdʌkʃən] *s* production *f*

profane [proˈfen] *adj* profane; (*language*) impie, blasphématoire ‖ *s* profane *mf*; impie *mf* ‖ *tr* profaner

profani·ty [proˈfænɪti] *s* (*pl* **-ties**) blasphème *m*

profess [proˈfɛs] *tr* professer

profession [proˈfɛʃən] *s* profession *f*

professor [proˈfɛsər] *s* professeur *m*

proffer [ˈprɑfər] *s* offre *f* ‖ *tr* offrir, tendre

proficient [proˈfɪʃənt] *adj* compétent, expert

profile [ˈprofaɪl] *s* profil *m*; courte biographie *f* ‖ *tr* profiler; **to be profiled against** se profiler sur

profit [ˈprɑfɪt] *s* bénéfice *m*, profit *m* ‖ *tr* profiter à ‖ *intr* profiter; **to profit from** profiter à, de, or en

profitable [ˈprɑfɪtəbəl] *adj* profitable

prof′it-and-loss′ account′ *s* compte *m* de profits et pertes

profiteer [ˌprɑfɪˈtɪr] *s* profiteur *m* ‖ *intr* faire des bénéfices excessifs

prof′it mar′gin *s* marge *f* bénéficiaire

prof′it tak′ing *s* prise *f* de bénéfices

profligate [ˈprɑflɪgɪt] *adj & s* débauché *m*

pro′ for′ma in′voice [ˌproˈfɔrmə] *s* facture *f* simulée

profound [proˈfaʊnd] *adj* profond

pro-French′ *adj* francophile

profuse [proˈfjuz] *adj* abondant; (*extravagant*) prodigue

proge·ny [ˈprɑdʒəni] *s* (*pl* **-nies**) progéniture *f*

progno·sis [prɑgˈnosɪs] *s* (*pl* **-ses** [siz]) pronostic *m*

prognosticate [prɑgˈnɑstɪˌket] *tr* pronostiquer

pro·gram [ˈprogræm] *s* programme *m* ‖ *v* (*pret & pp* **-gramed**; *ger* **-graming**) *tr* programmer

pro′gramed learn′ing *s* enseignement *m* séquentiel

programer [ˈprogræmər] *s* (comp) programmeur *m*; (mov, rad, telv) programmateur *m*

programing [ˈprogræmɪŋ] *s* programmation

pro′gram pack′aging *s* (rad, telv) groupage *m* d'émissions

progress [ˈprɑgrɛs] *s* progrès *m*; cours *m*, e.g., **work in progress** travaux en cours; **to make progress** faire des progrès ‖ [prəˈgrɛs] *intr* progresser

progressive [prəˈgrɛsɪv] *adj* progressif; (pol) progressiste ‖ *s* (pol) progressiste *mf*

prohibit [proˈhɪbɪt] *tr* prohiber, interdire

prohibition [ˌproˈəˈbɪʃən] *s* prohibition *f*

project [ˈprɑdʒɛkt] *s* projet *m* ‖ [prəˈdʒɛkt] *tr* projeter ‖ *intr* (*to jut out*) saillir; (theat) passer la rampe

projectile [prəˈdʒɛktɪl] *s* projectile *m*

projection [prəˈdʒɛkʃən] *s* projection *f*; (*something jutting out*) saillie *f*

projec′tion booth′ *s* (mov) cabine *f* de projection

projector [prəˈdʒɛktər] *s* projecteur *m*; (mov, telv) sunlight *m invar*

proletarian [ˌproliˈtɛri·ən] *adj* prolétarien ‖ *s* prolétaire *m*

proletariat [ˌproliˈtɛri·ət] *s* prolétariat *m*

proliferate [prəˈlifəˌret] *intr* proliférer

prolific [prəˈlɪfɪk] *adj* prolifique

prolix [ˈproliks] *adj* prolixe

prologue [ˈprolɔg] *s* prologue *m*

prolong [proˈlɔŋ] *tr* prolonger

promenade [ˌprɑmɪˈned] *s* promenade *f*; bal *m* d'apparat; (theat) promenoir *m* ‖ *intr* se promener

prom′enade′ deck′ *s* (naut) pont-promenade *m*

prominent [ˈprɑmɪnənt] *adj* proéminent; (*well-known*) éminent

promiscuity [ˌprɑmɪsˈkju·əti] *s* promiscuité *f* sexuelle

promiscuous [prəˈmɪskju,as] *adj* (*in sexual matters*) de mœurs faciles, de mœurs légères, immoral; (*disorderly*) confus

promise [ˈprɑmɪs] *s* promesse *f* ‖ *tr & intr* promettre; **to promise s.o. to** promettre à qn de; **to promise s.th. to s.o.** promettre q.ch. à qn

prom′issory note′ [ˈprɑmɪˌsori] *m* billet *m* à ordre

promonto·ry [ˈprɑmənˌtori] *s* (*pl* **-ries**) promontoire *m*

promote [prəˈmot] *tr* promouvoir

promoter [prəˈmotər] *s* promoteur *m*

promotion [prəˈmoʃən] *s* promotion *f*

prompt [prɑmpt] *adj* prompt; ponctuel ‖ *tr* inciter; (theat) souffler son rôle à

prompter [ˈprɑmptər] *s* (theat) souffleur *m*

promp′ter's box′ *s* (theat) trou *m* du souffleur

promptness [ˈprɑmptnɪs] *s* promptitude *f*

promulgate [ˈprɑməlˌget] *tr* promulguer

prone [pron] *adj* à plat ventre, prostré; **prone to** enclin à

prong [prɔŋ], [prɑŋ] *s* dent *f*

pronoun [ˈpronaʊn] *s* pronom *m*

pronounce [prəˈnaʊns] *tr* prononcer

pronouncement [prəˈnaʊnsmənt] *s* déclaration *f*

pronunciation [prəˌnʌnsiˈeʃən] *s* prononciation *f*

proof [pruf] *adj*—**proof against** à l'épreuve de, résistant à ‖ *s* preuve *f*; (phot, typ) épreuve *f*; **to read proof** corriger les épreuves

proof′read′er *s* correcteur *m*

prop [prɑp] *s* appui *m*; (*to hold up a plant*) tuteur *m*; **props** (theat) accessoires *mpl* ‖ *v* (*pret* & *pp* **propped;** *ger* **propping**) *tr* appuyer; (hort) tuteurer

propaganda [,prɑpə'gændə] *s* propagande *f*

propagate ['prɑpə,get] *tr* propager

pro·pel [prə'pɛl] *s* (*pret* & *pp* **-pelled;** *ger* **-pelling**) *tr* propulser

propellant [prə'pɛlənt] *s* (rok) ergol *m*

propeller [prə'pɛlər] *s* hélice *f*

propensi·ty [prə'pɛnsɪti] *s* (*pl* **-ties**) propension *f*

proper ['prɑpər] *adj* (*fitting, correct*) convenable, correct; (*person*) comme il faut; (*name*) propre

proper·ty ['prɑpərti] *s* (*pl* **-ties**) propriété *f*; **properties** (theat) accessoires *mpl*

prop′erty own′er *s* propriétaire *mf*

prop′erty tax′ *s* impôt *m* foncier

prophe·cy ['prɑfɪsi] *s* (*pl* **-cies**) prophétie *f*

prophe·sy ['prɑfɪ,saɪ] *v* (*pret* & *pp* **-sied**) *tr* prophétiser

prophet ['prɑfɪt] *s* prophète *m*

prophetess ['prɑfɪtɪs] *s* prophétesse *f*

prophylactic [,prɑfɪ'læktɪk] *adj* prophylactique ‖ *s* (*preventive*) prophylactique *m*; (*contraceptive*) préservatif *m*, capote *f* anglaise

propitiate [prə'pɪʃɪ,et] *tr* apaiser

propitious [prə'pɪʃəs] *adj* propice

prop′jet′ *s* turbopropulseur *m*

proportion [prə'porʃən] *s* proportion *f*; **in proportion as** à mesure que; **in proportion to** en proportion de, en raison de; **out of proportion** hors de proportion ‖ *tr* proportionner

proportionate [prə'porʃənɪt] *adj* proportionné

proposal [prə'pozəl] *s* proposition *f*; demande *f* en mariage

propose [prə'poz] *tr* proposer ‖ *intr* faire sa déclaration; **to propose to** demander sa main à; (*to decide to*) se proposer de

proposition ['prɑpə'zɪʃən] *s* proposition *f* ‖ *tr* faire des propositions malhonnêtes à

propound [prə'paʊnd] *tr* proposer

proprietor [prə'praɪ·ətər] *s* propriétaire *mf*

proprietress [prə'praɪ·ətrɪs] *s* propriétaire *f*

proprie·ty [prə'praɪ·əti] *s* (*pl* **-ties**) propriété *f*; (*of conduct*) bienséance *f*; **proprieties** convenances *fpl*

propulsion [prə'pʌlʃən] *s* propulsion *f*

prorate [pro'ret] *tr* partager au prorata

prosaic [pro'ze·ɪk] *adj* prosaïque

proscenium [pro'sinɪ·əm] *s* avant-scène *f*

proscribe [pro'skraɪb] *tr* proscrire

prose [proz] *adj* en prose ‖ *s* prose *f*

prosecute ['prɑsɪ,kjut] *tr* poursuivre

prosecutor ['prɑsɪ,kjutər] *s* (*lawyer*) procureur *m*; (*plaintiff*) plaignant *m*

proselyte ['prɑsɪ,laɪt] *s* prosélyte *mf*

prose′ writ′er *s* prosateur *m*

prosody ['prɑsədi] *s* prosodie *f*

prospect ['prɑspɛkt] *s* (*outlook*) perspective *f*; (*future*) avenir *m*; (com) client *m* éventuel ‖ *tr* & *intr* prospecter; **to prospect for** (*e.g., gold*) chercher

prospector ['prɑspɛktər] *s* prospecteur *m*

prospectus [prə'spɛktəs] *s* prospectus *m*

prosper ['prɑspər] *intr* prospérer

prosperity [prɑs'pɛrɪti] *s* prospérité *f*

prosperous ['prɑspərəs] *adj* prospère

prostate (gland′) ['prɑstet] *s* prostate *f*

prostitute ['prɑstɪ,t(j)ut] *s* prostituée *f* ‖ *tr* prostituer

prostrate ['prɑstret] *adj* prosterné; (*exhausted*) prostré ‖ *tr* abattre; **to prostrate oneself** se prosterner

prostration [prɑs'treʃən] *s* prostration *f*; (*abasement*) prosternation *f*

protagonist [pro'tægənɪst] *s* protagoniste *m*

protect [prə'tɛkt] *tr* protéger

protection [prə'tɛkʃən] *s* protection *f*

protein ['proti·ɪn] *s* protéine *f*

pro-tempore [pro'tɛmpə,ri] *adj* intérimaire, par intérim

protest ['protɛst] *s* protestation *f* ‖ [pro'tɛst] *tr* protester de; protester ‖ *intr* protester

Protestant ['prɑtɪstənt] *adj* & *s* protestant *m*

protocol ['protə,kɑl] *s* protocole *m*

proton ['protɑn] *s* proton *m*

protoplasm ['protə,plæzəm] *s* protoplasme *m*

prototype ['protə,taɪp] *s* prototype *m*

protozoan [,protə'zo·ən] *s* protozoaire *m*

protract [pro'trækt] *tr* prolonger

protrude [pro'trud] *intr* saillir

protuberance [pro't(j)ubərəns] *s* protubérance *f*

proud [praʊd] *adj* fier; (*vain*) orgueilleux

proud′ flesh′ *s* chair *f* fongueuse

prove [pruv] *v* (*pret* **proved;** *pp* **proved** or **proven** ['pruvən]) *tr* prouver; (*to put to the test*) éprouver ‖ *intr* se montrer, se trouver; **to prove to be** se révéler, s'avérer

proverb ['prɑvərb] *s* proverbe *m*

provide [prə'vaɪd] *tr* pourvoir, fournir; **to provide s.th. for s.o.** fournir q.ch. à qn ‖ *intr*—**to provide for** pourvoir à; (*e.g., future needs*) prévoir

provided *conj* pourvu que, à condition que

providence ['prɑvɪdəns] *s* providence *f*; (*prudence*) prévoyance *f*

providential [,prɑvɪ'dɛnʃəl] *adj* providentiel

providing [prə'vaɪdɪŋ] *conj* pourvu que, à condition que

province ['prɑvɪns] *s* province *f*; (*sphere*) compétence *f*

prov′ing ground′ *s* terrain *m* d'essai

provision [prə'vɪʒən] *s* (*supplying*) fourniture *f*; clause *f*; **provisions** provisions *fpl*

provi·so [prə'vaɪzo] *s* (*pl* **-sos** or **-soes**) condition *f*, stipulation *f*

provocative [prə'vɑkətɪv] *adj* provocant

provoke [prə'vok] *tr* provoquer; fâcher, contrarier

provoking [prə'vokɪŋ] *adj* contrariant

prow [praʊ] *s* proue *f*
prowess [ˈpraʊ·ɪs] *s* prouesse *f*
prowl [praʊl] *intr* rôder
prowler [ˈpraʊlər] *s* rôdeur *m*
proximity [prɑkˈsɪmɪti] *s* proximité *f*
prox·y [ˈprɑksi] *s* (*pl* **-ies**) mandat *m*; (*agent*) mandataire *mf;* **by proxy** par procuration
prude [prud] *s* prude *mf*
prudence [ˈprudəns] *s* prudence *f*
prudent [ˈprudənt] *adj* prudent
pruder·y [ˈprudəri] *s* (*pl* **-ies**) pruderie *f*
prudish [ˈprudɪʃ] *adj* prude
prune [prun] *s* pruneau *m* ‖ *tr* élaguer
pruning [ˈprunɪŋ] *s* taille *f*, émondage *m*, cisaillement *m*
prun'ing shears' *spl* cisailles *fpl*
Prussian [ˈprʌʃən] *adj* prussien ‖ *s* Prussien *m*
pry [praɪ] *v* (*pret* & *pp* **pried**) *tr*—**to pry open** forcer avec un levier; **to pry s.th. out of s.o.** extorquer, soutirer q.ch. à qn ‖ *intr* fureter; **to pry into** fourrer son nez dans
P.S. [ˈpiˈɛs] *s* (letterword) (**postscript**) P.-S.
psalm [sɑm] *s* psaume *m*
Psalter [ˈsɔltər] *s* psautier *m*
pseudo [ˈs(j)udo] *adj* faux, supposé, feint, factice
pseudonym [ˈs(j)udənɪm] *s* pseudonyme *m*
psyche [ˈsaɪki] *s* psyché *f*
psychedelic [ˌsaɪkɪˈdɛlɪk] *adj* psychédélique
psychiatrist [saɪˈkaɪ·ətrɪst] *s* psychiatre *mf*
psychiatry [saɪˈkaɪ·ətri] *s* psychiatrie *f*
psychic [ˈsaɪkɪk] *adj* psychique; médiumnique ‖ *s* médium *m*
psycho [ˈsaɪko] *adj* & *s* (slang) fou *m*, dingue *mf*, cinglé *m*, agité *m*
psychoanalysis [ˌsaɪko·əˈnælɪsɪs] *s* psychanalyse *f*
psychoanalyze [ˌsaɪkoˈænəˌlaɪz] *tr* psychanalyser
psychologic(al) [ˌsaɪkoˈlɑdʒɪk(əl)] *adj* psychologique
psychologist [saɪˈkɑlədʒɪst] *s* psychologue *mf*
psychology [saɪˈkɑlədʒi] *s* psychologie *f*
psychopath [ˈsaɪkəˌpæθ] *s* psychopathe *mf*
psycho·sis [saɪˈkosɪs] *s* (*pl* **-ses** [siz]) psychose *f*
psy'cho·ther'apy *s* psychothérapie *f*
psychotic [saɪˈkɑtɪk] *adj* & *s* psychotique *mf*
ptomaine [ˈtomen] *s* ptomaïne *f*
pub [pʌb] *s* (Brit) bistrot *m*, café *m*
puberty [ˈpjubərti] *s* puberté *f*
public [ˈpʌblɪk] *adj* & *s* public *m*
pub'lic-address' sys'tem *s* sonorisation *f*
publication [ˌpʌblɪˈkeʃən] *s* publication *f*
pub'lic educa'tion *s* enseignement *m* public
publicity [pʌbˈlɪsɪti] *s* publicité *f*
public'ity stunt' *s* canard *m* publicitaire
publicize [ˈpʌblɪˌsaɪz] *tr* publier
pub'lic li'brary *s* bibliothèque *f* municipale

pub'lic-opin'ion poll' *s* sondage *m* de l'opinion, enquête *f* par sondage
pub'lic rela'tions *spl* relations *fmpl* publiques
pub'lic-rela'tions ex'pert *s* publiciste *mf*, publicitaire *mf*
pub'lic school' *s* (U.S.A.) école *f* primaire; (Brit) école privée
pub'lic serv'ant *s* fonctionnaire *mf*
pub'lic speak'ing *s* art *m* oratoire, éloquence *f*
pub'lic tel'ephone *s* téléphone *m* public
pub'lic toi'let *s* chalet *m* de nécessité
pub'lic transporta'tion *s* transport *m* en commun
pub'lic util'ity *s* entreprise *f* de service public; **public utilities** actions *fpl* émises par les entreprises de service public
publish [ˈpʌblɪʃ] *tr* publier
publisher [ˈpʌblɪʃər] *s* éditeur *m*
pub'lishing house' *s* maison *f* d'édition
puck [pʌk] *s* palet *m*
pucker [ˈpʌkər] *s* fronce *m*, faux pli *m* ‖ *tr* froncer ‖ *intr* se froncer
pudding [ˈpʊdɪŋ] *s* entremets *m* sucré au lait, crème *f*
puddle [ˈpʌdəl] *s* flaque *f* ‖ *tr* puddler
pudg·y [ˈpʌdʒi] *adj* (*comp* **-ier;** *super* **-iest**) bouffi, rondouillard
puerile [ˈpju·ərɪl] *adj* puéril
puerili·ty [ˌpju·əˈrɪlɪti] *s* (*pl* **-ties**) puérilité *f*
Puerto Rican [ˈpwɛrtoˈrikən] *adj* portoricain ‖ *s* Portoricain *m*
puff [pʌf] *s* (*of air*) souffle *m*; (*of smoke*) bouffée *f*; (*in clothing*) bouillon *m*; (*in sleeve*) bouffant *m*; (*for powder*) houppette *f*; (*swelling*) bouffissure *f*; (*praise*) battage *m*; (culin) moule *m* de pâte feuilletée fourré à la crème, à la confiture, etc. ‖ *tr* lancer des bouffées de; **to puff oneself up** se rengorger; **to puff out** souffler; **to puff up** gonfler ‖ *intr* souffler; (*to swell*) gonfler, se gonfler; **to puff at** or **on** (*a pipe*) tirer sur
puff' paste' *s* pâte *f* feuilletée
pugilism [ˈpjudʒɪˌlɪzəm] *s* science *f* pugilistique, boxe *f*
pugilist [ˈpjudʒɪlɪst] *s* pugiliste *m*
pugnacious [pʌgˈneʃəs] *adj* pugnance
pug'-nosed' *adj* camus
puke [pjuk] *s* (slang) dégobillage *m* ‖ *tr* & *intr* (slang) dégobiller
pull [pʊl] *s* (*tug*) traction *f*, secousse *f*, coup *m*; (*handle of door*) poignée *f*; (*of the moon*) attraction *f*; (slang) piston *m*, appuis *mpl* ‖ *tr* tirer; (*a muscle*) tordre; (*the trigger*) appuyer sur; (*a proof*) (typ) tirer; **to pull about** tirailler; **to pull away** arracher; **to pull down** baisser; (*e.g.*, *a house*) abattre; (*to degrade*) abaisser; **to pull in** rentrer; **to pull off** enlever; (fig) réussir; **to pull on** (*a garment*) mettre; **to pull oneself together** se ressaisir; **to pull out** sortir; (*a tooth*) arracher ‖ *intr* tirer; bouger lentement, bouger avec effort; **to pull at** tirer sur; **to pull for** (slang) plaider en faveur de; **to pull in** rentrer; (*said of*

train) entrer en gare; **to pull out** partir; (*said of train*) sortir de la gare; **to pull through** se tirer d'affaire; (*to get well*) se remettre

pull′ chain′ *s* chasse *f* d'eau

pullet [′pʊlɪt] *s* poulette *f*

pulley [′pʊli] *s* poulie *f*

pulmonary [′pʌlmə,nɛri] *adj* pulmonaire

pulp [pʌlp] *s* pulpe *f*; (*to make paper*) pâte *f*; (*of tooth*) bulbe *m*; **to beat to a pulp** (coll) mettre en bouillie

pulp′ fic′tion *s* romans *mpl* à sensation; le roman de la concierge

pulpit [′pʊlpɪt] *s* chaire *f*

pulsate [′pʌlset] *intr* palpiter; vibrer

pulsation pʌl′se∫ən] *s* pulsation *f*

pulse [pʌls] *s* pouls *m*; **to feel** or **take the pulse of** tâter le pouls à

pulverize [′pʌlvə,raɪz] *tr* pulvériser

pu′mice stone′ [′pʌmɪs] *s* pierre *f* ponce

pum·mel [′pʌməl] *v* (*pret & pp* **-meled** or **-melled;** *ger* **-meling** or **-melling**) *tr* bourrer de coups

pump [pʌmp] *s* pompe *f*; (*slipperlike shoe*) escarpin *m* ‖ *tr* pomper; (coll) tirer les vers du nez à; **to pump up** pomper; (*a tire*) gonfler ‖ *intr* pomper

pump′han′dle *s* bras *m* de pompe

pumpkin [′pʌmpkɪn] *s* citrouille *f*, potiron *m*

pun [pʌn] *s* calembour *m*, jeu *m* de mots ‖ *v* (*pret & pp* **punned;** *ger* **punning**) *intr* faire des jeux de mots

punch [pʌnt∫] *s* (*blow*) coup *m* de poing; (*to pierce metal*) mandrin *m*; (*to drive a nail or bolt*) poinçon *m*; (*for tickets*) pince *f*, emporte-pièce *m*; (*drink; blow*) punch *m*; (*mach*) poinçonneuse *f*; (*energy*) (coll) allant *m*, punch; **to pull no punches** parler carrément ‖ *tr* donner un coup de poing à; poinçonner

punch′ bowl′ *s* bol *m* à punch

punch′ card′ *s* carte *f* perforée

punch′ clock′ *s* horloge *f* de pointage

punch′-drunk′ *adj* abruti de coups; (coll) abruti, étourdi

punched′ tape′ *s* bande *f* enregistreuse perforée

punch′ing bag′ *s* punching-ball *m*; (fig) tête *f* de Turc, souffre-douleur *m invar*

punch′ line′ *s* point *m* final, phrase *f* clé

punctilious [pʌŋk′tɪli·əs] *adj* pointilleux, minutieux

punctual [′pʌŋkt∫u·əl] *adj* ponctuel

punctuate [′pʌŋkt∫u,et] *tr & intr* ponctuer

punctuation [,pʌŋkt∫u′e∫ən] *s* ponctuation *f*

punctua′tion mark′ *s* signe *m* de ponctuation

puncture [′pʌŋkt∫ər] *s* (*in skin, paper, leather*) piqûre *f*; (*of a tire*) crevaison *f*; (med) ponction *f* ‖ *tr* perforer; (*a tire*) crever; (med) ponctionner

punc′ture-proof′ *adj* increvable

pundit [′pʌndɪt] *s* pandit *m*; (*savant*) mandarin *m*; (pej) pontife *m*

pungent [′pʌndʒənt] *adj* piquant

punish [′pʌnɪ∫] *tr & intr* punir

punishment [′pʌnɪ∫mənt] *s* punition *f*; (*for a crime*) peine *f*; (*severe handling*) mauvais traitements *mpl*

punk [pʌŋk] *adj* (slang) moche, fichu; **to feel punk** (slang) être mal fichu ‖ *s* amadou *m*; mèche *f* d'amadou; (*decayed wood*) bois *m* pourri; (slang) voyou *m*, mauvais sujet *m*, loubard *m*

punster [′pʌnstər] *s* faiseur *m* de calembours

pu·ny [′pjuni] *adj* (*comp* **-nier;** *super* **-niest**) chétif, malingre

pup [pʌp] *s* chiot *m*

pupil [′pjupəl] *s* élève *mf*; (*of the eye*) pupille *f*, prunelle *f*

puppet [′pʌpɪt] *s* marionnette *f*; (*person controlled by another*) fantoche *m*, pantin *m*

pup′pet gov′ernment *s* gouvernement *m* fantoche

pup′pet show′ *s* spectacle *m* de marionnettes, marionnettes *fpl*

pup·py [′pʌpi] *s* (*pl* **-pies**) petit chien *m*

pup′py love′ *s* premières amours *fpl*

pup′ tent′ *s* tente-abri *f*

purchase [′pʌrt∫əs] *s* achat *m*; (*leverage*) point *m* d'appui, prise *f* ‖ *tr* acheter

pur′chasing pow′er *s* pouvoir *m* d'achat

pure [pjʊr] *adj* pur

purgative [′pʌrgətɪv] *adj & s* purgatif *m*

purgato·ry [′pʌrgə,tori] *s* (*pl* **-ries**) purgatoire *m*

purge [pʌrdʒ] *s* purge *f* ‖ *tr* purger

puri·fy [′pjʊrɪ,faɪ] *v* (*pret & pp* **-fied**) *tr* purifier

puritan [′pjʊrɪtən] *adj & s* puritain *m*; **Puritan** puritain

purity [′pjʊrɪti] *s* pureté *f*

purloin [pər′lɔɪn] *tr & intr* voler

purple [′pʌrpəl] *adj* pourpre ‖ *s* (*violescent*) pourpre *m*; (*deep red, crimson*) pourpre *f*; **born to the purple** né dans la pourpre

purport [′pʌrport] *s* sens *m*, teneur *f*; (*intention*) but *m*, objet *m* ‖ [pər′port] *tr* signifier, vouloir dire

purpose [′pʌrpəs] *s* intention *f*, dessein *m*; (*goal*) but *m*, objet *m*, fin *f*; **for all purposes** à tous usages; pratiquement; **for the purpose of, with the purpose of** dans le dessein de, dans le but de; **for this purpose** à cet effet; **for what purpose?** à quoi bon? à quelle fin?; **on purpose** exprès, à dessein; **to good purpose, to some purpose** utilement; **to no purpose** vainement; **to serve the purpose** faire l'affaire

purposely [′pʌrpəsli] *adv* exprès, à dessein, de propos délibéré

purr [pʌr] *s* ronron *m* ‖ *intr* ronronner ‖ *interj* miam! miam!

purse [pʌrs] *s* bourse *f*, porte-monnaie *m*; (*handbag*) sac *m* à main ‖ *tr* (*one's lips*) pincer

purser [′pʌrsər] *s* commissaire *m*

purse′ snatch′er [′snæt∫ər] *s* voleur *m* à la tire

purse′ strings′ *spl* cordons *mpl* de bourse

pursue [pər's(j)u] *tr* poursuivre; (*a profession*) suivre

pursuit [pər's(j)ut] *s* poursuite *f*; profession *f*

pursuit' plane' *s* chasseur *m*, avion *m* de chasse

purvey [pər've] *tr* fournir

pus [pʌs] *s* pus *m*

push [pʊʃ] *s* poussée *f* ‖ *tr* pousser; (*a button*) appuyer sur, presser; **to push around** (coll) rudoyer; **to push aside** écarter; **to push away** or **back** repousser; **to push in** enfoncer; **to push over** faire tomber; **to push through** amener à bonne fin; (*a resolution, bill, etc.*) faire adopter ‖ *intr* pousser; **to push forward** or **on** avancer; **to push off** se mettre en route; (naut) pousser au large

push' but'ton *s* bouton *m* électrique, poussoir *m*

push'-button tel'ephone *s* téléphone *m* à clavier

push'-but'ton war'fare *s* guerre *f* presse-bouton

push'cart' *s* voiture *f* à bras

pusher ['pʊʃər] *s* (*drug dealer*) revendeur *m* (de drogues); (slang) dealer *m*, vendeur *m* de mort, fourmi *f*

pushing ['pʊʃɪŋ] *adj* entreprenant; indiscret; agressif

pusillanimous [,pjusɪ'lænɪməs] *adj* pusillanime

puss [pʊs] *s* minet *m*; (slang) gueule *f*; **sly puss** (*girl*) (coll) futée *f* ‖ *interj* minet!

Puss' in Boots' *s* Chat *m* botté

puss' in the cor'ner *s* les quatre coins *mpl*

puss·y ['pʊsi] *s* (*pl* **-ies**) *s* minet *m* ‖ *interj* minet!

puss'y wil'low *s* saule *m* nord-américain aux chatons très soyeux

put [pʊt] *v* (*pret* & *pp* **put**; *ger* **putting**) *tr* mettre, placer; (*to throw*) lancer; (*a question*) poser; **to put across** passer; faire accepter; **to put aside** mettre de côté; **to put away** ranger; (*to jail*) mettre en prison; **to put back** remettre; retarder; **to put down** poser; (*e.g., a name*) noter; (*a revolution*) réprimer; (*to lower*) baisser; **to put off** renvoyer; (*to mislead*) dérouter; **to put on** (*clothes*) mettre; (*a play*) mettre en scène, monter; (*a brake*) serrer; (*a light, radio, etc.*) allumer; (*to feign*) feindre, simuler; **to put oneself out** se déranger; **to put on sale** mettre en vente; mettre en solde; **to put out** (*the hand*) étendre; (*the fire, light, etc.*) éteindre; (*s.o.'s eyes*) crever; (*e.g., a book*) publier; (*to show to the door*) mettre dehors; (*to vex*) contrarier; **to put over** (coll) faire accepter; **to put s.o. through s.th.** faire subir q.ch. à qn; **to put through** passer; (*a resolution, bill, etc.*) faire adopter; **to put up** lever; (*a house*) construire, faire construire; (*one's collar, hair, etc.*) relever; (*a picture*) accrocher; (*a notice*) afficher; (*a tent*) dresser; (*an umbrella*) ouvrir; (*the price*) augmenter; (*money as an investment*) fournir; (*resistance*) offrir; (*an overnight guest*) loger; (*fruit, vegetables, etc.*) conserver; (coll) pousser, inciter ‖ *intr* se diriger; **to put on** feindre; **to put up** loger; **to put up with** tolérer, s'accommoder de

put'-out' *adj* ennuyeux, fâcheux

putrid ['pjutrɪd] *adj* putride

putter ['pʌtər] *intr*—**to putter around** s'occuper de bagatelles

put·ty ['pʌti] *s* (*pl* **-ties**) mastic *m* ‖ *v* (*pret* & *pp* **-tied**) *tr* mastiquer

put'ty knife' *s* (*pl* **knives**) couteau *m* à mastiquer

put'-up' *adj* (coll) machiné à l'avance, monté

put'-up job' *s* (slang) coup *m* monté, micmac *m*

puzzle ['pʌzəl] *s* énigme *f* ‖ *tr* intriguer; **to puzzle out** déchiffrer ‖ *intr*—**to puzzle over** se creuser la tête pour comprendre

puzzler ['pʌzlər] *s* énigme *f*, colle *f*

puzzling ['pʌzlɪŋ] *adj* énigmatique

PW ['pi'dʌbəl,ju] *s* (letterword) (**prisoner of war**) P.G.

pyg·my ['pɪgmi] *adj* pygméen ‖ *s* (*pl* **-mies**) pygmée *m*

pylon ['paɪlɑn] *s* pylône *m*

pyramid ['pɪrəmɪd] *s* pyramide *f* ‖ *tr* augmenter graduellement ‖ *intr* pyramider

pyre [paɪr] *s* bûcher *m* funéraire

Pyrenees ['pɪrɪ,niz] *spl* Pyrénées *fpl*

pyrites ['paɪraɪts] *s* pyrite *f*

pyrotechnical [,paɪrə'tɛknɪkəl] *adj* pyrotechnique

pyrotechnics [,paɪrə'tɛknɪks] *spl* pyrotechnie *f*

python ['paɪθɑn] *s* python *m*

pythoness ['paɪθənɪs] *s* pythonisse *f*

pyx [pɪks] *s* (eccl) ciboire *m*; (*for carrying Eucharist to sick*) (eccl) pyxide *f*; (*at a mint*) boîte *f* des monnaies

Q

Q,q [kju] *s* XVIIe lettre de l'alphabet

quack [kwæk] *adj* frauduleux, de charlatan ‖ *s* charlatan *m* ‖ *intr* cancaner, faire couin-couin

quacker·y ['kwækəri] *s* (*pl* **-ies**) charlatanisme *m*

quadrangle ['kwɑd,ræŋgəl] *s* plan *m* quadrangulaire; cour *f* carrée

quadrant ['kwɑdrənt] *s* (*instrument*) quart *m* de cercle, secteur *m*; (math) quadrant *m*

quadroon [kwɑd'run] *s* quarteron *m*

quadruped ['kwɑdrə‚pɛd] *adj & s* quadrupède *m*

quadruple ['kwɑdrupəl] *adj & s* quadruple *m* ‖ *tr & intr* quadrupler

quadruplets ['kwɑdrʊ‚plɛts] *spl* quadruplés *mpl*

quaff [kwɑf], [kwæf] *s* lampée *f* ‖ *tr & intr* boire à longs traits

quagmire ['kwæg‚maɪr] *s* bourbier *m*, fondrière *f*

quail [kwel] *s* caille *f* ‖ *intr* fléchir

quaint [kwent] *adj* pittoresque, bizarre

quake [kwek] *s* tremblement *m*; (*earthquake*) tremblement de terre ‖ *intr* trembler

Quaker ['kwekər] *adj & s* quaker *m*

Quak'er meet'ing *s* réunion *f* de quakers; (coll) réunion où il y a très peu de conversation

quali·fy [kwɑlɪ‚faɪ] *v* (*pret & pp* **-fied**) *tr* qualifier; (*e.g., a recommendation*) apporter des réserves à, modifier; **to qualify oneself for** se préparer à, se rendre apte à ‖ *intr* se qualifier

quali·ty ['kwɑlɪti] *s* (*pl* **-ties**) qualité *f*; (*of a sound*) timbre *m*; **of good quality** de bonne facture; **quality of life** qualité de la vie

qualm [kwɑm] *s* scrupule *m*; (*remorse*) remords *m*; (*nausea*) soulèvement *m* de cœur

quanda·ry ['kwɑndəri] *s* (*pl* **-ries**) incertitude *f*, impasse *f*

quanti·ty ['kwɑntɪti] *s* (*pl* **-ties**) quantité *f*

quan·tum ['kwɑntəm] *adj* quantique ‖ *s* (*pl* **-ta** [tə]) quantum *m*

quan'tum the'ory *s* théorie *f* des quanta

quarantine ['kwɑrən‚tin] *s* quarantaine *f* ‖ *tr* mettre en quarantaine

quar·rel ['kwɑrəl] *s* querelle *f*, dispute *f*; **to have no quarrel with** n'avoir rien à redire à; **to pick a quarrel with** chercher querelle à ‖ *v* (*pret & pp* **-reled** or **-relled**; *ger* **-reling** or **-relling**) *intr* se quereller, se disputer; **to quarrel over** contester sur, se disputer

quarrelsome ['kwɑrəlsəm] *adj* querelleur

quar·ry ['kwɑri] *s* (*pl* **-ries**) carrière *f*; (*hunted animal*) proie *f* ‖ *v* (*pret & pp* **-ried**) *tr* extraire ‖ *intr* exploiter une carrière

quart [kwɔrt] *s* quart *m* de gallon, pinte *f*

quarter ['kwɔrtər] *s* quart *m*; (*American coin*) vingt-cinq cents *mpl*; (*of a year*) trimestre *m*; (*of town; of beef; of moon; of shield*) quartier *m*; **a quarter after one** une heure et quart; **a quarter of an hour** un quart d'heure; **a quarter to one** une heure moins le quart; **at close quarters** corps à corps; **quarters** (mil) quartiers *mpl*, cantonnement *m* ‖ *tr & intr* (mil) loger, cantonner

quar'ter·deck' *s* gaillard *m* d'arrière

quar'ter-hour' *s* quart *m* d'heure; **every quarter-hour on the quarter-hour** tous les quarts d'heure au quart d'heure juste

quarter·ly ['kwɔrtərli] *adj* trimestriel ‖ *s* (*pl* **-lies**) publication *f* or revue *f* trimestrielle ‖ *adv* trimestriellement, par trimestre

quar'ter·mas'ter *s* (mil) quartier-maître *m*, intendant *m* militaire

Quar'ter·master Corps' *s* Intendance *f*, service *m* d l'Intendance

quar'ter note' *s* (mus) noire *f*

quar'ter rest' *s* (mus) soupir *m*

quar'ter tone' *s* (mus) quart *m* de ton

quartet [kwɔr'tɛt] *s* quatuor *m*

quartz [kwɔrts] *s* quartz *m*

quartz' watch' *s* montre *f* à quartz

quasar ['kwesɑr] *s* (astr) quasar *m*

quash [kwɑʃ] *tr* étouffer; (*to set aside*) annuler, invalider

quatrain ['kwɑtren] *s* quatrain *m*

quaver ['kwevər] *s* tremblement *m*; (*in the singing voice*) trémolo *m*; (mus) croche *f* ‖ *intr* trembloter

quay [ki] *s* quai *m*, débarcadère *m*

queen [kwin] *s* reine *f*; (cards, chess) reine *f*

queen' bee' *s* reine *f* des abeilles

queen' dow'ager *s* reine *f* douairière

queen·ly ['kwinli] *adj* (*comp* **-lier**; *super* **-liest**) de reine, digne d'une reine

queen' moth'er *s* reine *f* mère

queen' post' *s* faux poinçon *m*

queer [kwɪr] *adj* bizarre, drôle; (*suspicious*) (coll) suspect; (*perverted*) pervers, inverti; (*homosexual*) (pej) de la pédale; **to feel queer** (coll) se sentir indisposé ‖ *s* excentrique *mf*; (*pervert*) pervers *m*, inverti *m*; (*homosexual male*) (pej) pédale *f*, pédé *m*; (*homosexual female*) (pej) gouine *f*, lesbienne *f* ‖ *tr* (slang) faire échouer, déranger

quell [kwɛl] *tr* étouffer, réprimer; (*pain, sorrow, etc.*) calmer

quench [kwɛntʃ] *tr* (*the thirst*) étancher; (*a rebellion*) étouffer; (*a fire*) éteindre

que·ry ['kwɪri] *s* (*pl* **-ries**) question *f*; doute *m*; (*question mark*) point *m* d'interrogation ‖ *v* (*pret & pp* **-ried**) *tr* questionner; mettre en doute; (*to affix a question mark*) marquer d'un point d'interrogation

quest [kwɛst] *s* quête *f*; **in quest of** en quête de

question ['kwɛstʃən] *s* question *f*; (*doubt*) doute *m*; **beyond question** indiscutable, incontestable; **it is a question of** il s'agit de; **out of the question** impossible, impensable; **to ask s.o. a question** poser une question à qn; **to beg the question** faire une pétition de principe; **to call into question** mettre en question; **to move the previous question** (parl) demander la question préalable; **without question** sans aucun doute ‖ *tr* interroger, questionner; (*to cast doubt upon*) douter de, contester

questionable ['kwɛstʃənəbəl] *adj* discutable, douteux

ques'tion mark' *s* point *m* d'interrogation

questionnaire [‚kwɛstʃən'ɛr] *s* questionnaire *m*

queue

queue [kju] *s* queue *f* ‖ *intr*—**to queue up** faire la queue
quibble ['kwɪbəl] *intr* chicaner, ergoter
quibbling ['kwɪblɪŋ] *s* chicane *f*
quick [kwɪk] *adj* rapide, vif ‖ *s*—**the quick and the dead** les vivants et les morts; **to cut to the quick** piquer au vif
quicken ['kwɪkən] *tr* accélérer; (*e.g., the imagination*) animer ‖ *intr* s'accélérer; s'animer
quick′ lime′ *s* chaux *f* vive
quick′ lunch′ *s* casse-croûte *m*, repas *m* léger
quickly ['kwɪkli] *adv* vite, rapidement
quick′ sand′ *s* sable *m* mouvant
quick′ sil′ ver *s* vif-argent *m*, mercure *m*
quick′ -tem′ pered *adj* coléreux
quiet ['kwaɪ·ət] *adj* (*still*) tranquille, silencieux; (*person*) modeste, discret; (*market*) (com) calme; **be quiet!** taisez-vous!; **to keep quiet** rester tranquille; (*to not speak*) se taire ‖ *s* tranquillité *f*; (*rest*) repos *m*; **on the quiet** en douce, à la dérobée ‖ *tr* calmer, tranquilliser; (*a child*) faire taire ‖ *intr*—**to quiet down** se calmer
quill [kwɪl] *s* plume *f* d'oie; (*hollow part*) tuyau *m* (de plume); (*of hedgehog, porcupine*) piquant *m*
quilt [kwɪlt] *s* courtepointe *f* ‖ *tr* piquer
quince [kwɪns] *s* coing *m*; (*tree*) cognassier *m*
quinine ['kwaɪnaɪn] *s* quinine *f*
quinsy ['kwɪnzi] *s* angine *f*
quintessence [kwɪn'tɛsəns] *s* quintessence *f*
quintet [kwɪn'tɛt] *s* quintette *m*
quintuplets [kwɪn'tʌplɛts] *spl* quintuplés *mpl*
quip [kwɪp] *s* raillerie *f*, quolibet *m* ‖ *v* (*pret & pp* **quipped;** *ger* **quipping**) *tr* dire sur un ton railleur ‖ *intr* railler
quire [kwaɪr] *s* main *f*
quirk [kwʌrk] *s* excentricité *f*; (*subterfuge*) faux-fuyant *m*; **quirk of fate** caprice *m* du sort

quit [kwɪt] *adj* quitte; **to be quits** être quitte; **to call it quits** cesser, s'y renoncer; **we are quits** nous voilà quittes ‖ *v* (*pret & pp* **quit** or **quitted;** *ger* **quitting**) *tr* (*e.g., a city*) quitter; (*one's work, a pursuit, etc.*) cesser, **I quit!** j'abandonne!; **to quit** + *ger* s'arrêter de + *inf* ‖ *intr* partir; (coll) lâcher la partie
quite [kwaɪt] *adv* tout à fait; **quite a story** (coll) toute une histoire
quitter ['kwɪtər] *s* défaitiste *m*, lâcheur *m*
quiver ['kwɪvər] *s* tremblement *m*; (*to hold arrows*) carquois *m* ‖ *intr* trembler
quixotic [kwɪks'ɑtɪk] *adj* de don Quichotte; visionnaire, exalté
quiz [kwɪz] *s* (*pl* **quizzes**) interrogation *f*, colle *f* ‖ *v* (*pret & pp* **quizzed;** *ger* **quizzing**) *tr* examiner, interroger
quiz′ sec′ tion *s* classe *f* d'exercices
quiz′ show′ *s* émission-questionnaire *f*
quizzical ['kwɪzɪkəl] *adj* curieux; (*laughable*) risible; (*mocking*) railleur
quoin [kɔɪn] *s* angle *m*; (*cornerstone*) pierre *f* d'angle; (*wedge*) coin *m*, cale *f* ‖ *tr* coincer, caler
quoit [kwɔɪt] *s* palet *m*; **to play quoits** jouer au palet
quondam ['kwɑndæm] *adj* ci-devant, d'autre-fois
quorum ['kworəm] *s* quorum *m*
quota ['kwotə] *s* quote-part *f*; (*e.g., of immigration*) quota *m*, contingent *m*
quotation [kwo'teʃən] *s* (*from a book*) citation *f*; (*of prices*) cours *m*, cote *f*
quota′ tion marks′ *spl* guillemets *mpl*
quote [kwot] *s* (*from a book*) citation *f*; (*of prices*) cours *m*, cote *f*; **in quotes** (coll) entre guillemets ‖ *tr* (*from a book*) citer; (*values*) coter ‖ *intr* tirer des citations; **to quote out of context** citer hors contexte ‖ *interj* je cite
quotient ['kwoʃənt] *s* quotient *m*

R

R, r [ɑr] *s* XVIIIᵉ lettre de l'alphabet
rabbet ['ræbɪt] *s* feuillure *f* ‖ *tr* feuiller
rab·bi ['ræbaɪ] *s* (*pl* -**bis** or -**bies**) rabbin *m*
rabbit ['ræbɪt] *s* lapin *m*
rab′ bit stew′ *s* lapin *m* en civet
rabble ['ræbəl] *s* canaille *f*
rab′ ble-rous′ er *s* fomentateur *m*, agitateur *m*
rabies ['rebiz] *s* rage *f*
raccoon [ræ'kun] *s* raton *m* laveur
race [res] *s* (*ethnic background*) race *f*; (*contest*) course *f*; (*channel to lead water*) bief *m*; (*rapid current*) raz *m* ‖ *tr* lutter de vitesse avec; (*e.g., a horse*) faire courir;

(*a motor*) emballer ‖ *intr* faire une course, courir; (*said of motor*) s'emballer
race′ horse′ *s* cheval *m* de course
race′ ri′ ot *s* émeute *f* raciale
race′ track′ *s* champ *m* de courses, hippodrome *m*
racial ['reʃəl] *adj* racial
rac′ ing car′ *s* automobile *f* de course
rac′ ing odds′ *spl* cote *f*
racism ['resɪzəm] *s* racisme *m*
racist ['resɪst] *s* raciste *mf*
rack [ræk] *s* (*shelf*) étagère *f*; (*to hang clothes*) portemanteau *m*; (*for baggage*) porte-bagages *m*; (*for guns; for fodder*)

râtelier *m*; (*for torture*) chevalet *m*; (*bar made to gear with a pinion*) crémaillère *f*; **to go to rack and ruin** aller à vau-l'eau ‖ *tr* (*with hunger, remorse, etc.*) tenailler; (*one's brains*) se creuser

racket ['rækɪt] *s* (*noise*) vacarme *m*; (sports) raquette *f*; (slang) racket *m*; **to make a racket** faire du tapage

racketeer [,rækɪ'tɪr] *s* racketter *m* ‖ *intr* pratiquer l'escroquerie

rack' rail'way *s* chemin *m* de fer à crémaillère

rac·y ['resɪ] *adj* (*comp* **-ier;** *super* **-iest**) plein de verve, vigoureux; parfumé; (*off-color*) sale, grivois

radar ['redɑr] *s* (acronym) (**radio detecting and ranging**) radar *m*

ra'dar sta'tion *s* poste *m* radar

ra'dial tire' ['redɪ·əl] *s* pneu *m* radial, pneumatique *m* à carcasse radiale

radiant ['redɪ·ənt] *adj* radieux, rayonnant; (*astr, phys*) radiant

radiate ['redɪ,et] *tr* rayonner; (*e.g., happiness*) répandre ‖ *intr* rayonner

radiation [,redɪ'eʃən] *s* rayonnement *m*, radiation *f*

radia'tion sick'ness *s* mal *m* des rayons

radiator ['redɪ,etər] *s* radiateur *m*

ra'diator cap' *s* bouchon *m* de radiateur

radical ['rædɪkəl] *adj* & *s* radical *m*

radi·o ['redɪ,o] (*pl* **-os**) radio *f* ‖ *tr* radiodiffuser

ra·dio·ac'tive *adj* radioactif

ra'dio·ac'tive fall'out *s* retombées *fpl* radioactives

ra'dio·ac'tive waste' *s* déchets *mpl* radioactifs

ra'dio am'ateur *s* sans-filiste *mf*

ra'dio announ'cer *s* speaker *m*

ra'dio·broad'cast'ing *s* radiodiffusion *f*

ra'dio control' *s* (rok) radioguidage *m*

ra'dio·fre'quency *s* radiofréquence *f*

ra'dio·gram' *s* radiogramme *m*

ra'dio lis'tener *s* auditeur *m* de la radio

radiology [,redɪ'ɑlədʒɪ] *s* radiologie *f*

ra'dio net'work *s* chaîne *f* de radiodiffusion

ra'dio news'cast *s* journal *m* parlé, radio-journal *m*

ra'dio·phone' *s* radiotéléphone *m*

ra'dio receiv'er *s* récepteur *m* de radio

radioscopy [,redɪ'ɑskəpɪ] *s* radioscopie *f*

ra'dio set' *s* poste *m* de radio

ra'dio sta'tion *s* poste *m* émetteur

ra'dio tax'i *s* radio-taxi *m*

ra'dio·ther'apy *s* radiothérapie *f*

ra'dio tube' *s* lampe *f* de radio

radish ['rædɪʃ] *s* radis *m*

radium ['redɪ·əm] *s* radium *m*

radi·us ['redɪ·əs] *s* (*pl* **-i** [,aɪ] or **-uses**) rayon *m*; (anat) radius *m*; **within a radius of** dans un rayon de, à . . . à la ronde

raffish ['ræfɪʃ] *adj* bravache; (*flashy*) criard

raffle ['ræfəl] *s* tombola *f* ‖ *tr* mettre en tombola

raft [ræft] *s* (*floating on water*) radeau *m*; **a raft of** (*a lot of*) (coll) un tas de

rafter ['ræftər] *s* chevron *m*

rag [ræg] *s* chiffon *m*; **in rags** en haillons; **to chew the rag** (slang) tailler une bavette

ragamuffin ['rægə,mʌfɪn] *s* gueux *m*, va-nu-pieds *m*; (*urchin*) gamin *m*

rag' doll' *s* poupée *f* de chiffon

rage [redʒ] *s* rage *f*; **to be all the rage** faire fureur; **to fly into a rage** entrer en fureur ‖ *intr* faire rage

rag' fair' *s* marché *m* aux puces

ragged ['rægɪd] *adj* en haillons; (*edge*) hérissé

ragpicker ['ræg,pɪkər] *s* chiffonnier *m*

rag'time' *s* rythme *m* syncopé du jazz; musique *f* syncopée du jazz

rag'weed' *s* ambroisie *f*

ragwort ['ræg,wʌrt] *s* (*Senecio vulgaris*) séneçon *m*; (*S. jacobaea*) jacobée *f*

raid [red] *s* incursion *f*, razzia *f*; (*by police*) descente *f*; (mil) raid *m* ‖ *tr* razzier; faire une descente dans

rail [rel] *s* rail *m*; (*railing*) balustrade *f*; (*of stairway*) rampe *f*; (*of, e.g., a bridge*) garde-fou *m*; (orn) râle *m*; **by rail** par chemin de fer ‖ *intr* invectiver; **to rail at** invectiver

rail' fence' *s* palissade *f* à claire-voie

rail'head' *s* tête *f* de ligne

railing ['relɪŋ] *s* balustrade *f*

rail'road' *adj* ferroviaire ‖ *s* chemin *m* de fer ‖ *tr* (*a bill*) faire voter en vitesse; (coll) emprisonner à tort

rail'road cros'sing *s* passage *m* à niveau

railroader ['rel,rodər] *s* cheminot *m*

rail'road sta'tion *s* gare *f*

rail'way' *adj* ferroviaire ‖ *s* chemin *m* de fer

raiment ['remənt] *s* habillement *m*

rain [ren] *s* pluie *f*; **in the rain** sous la pluie ‖ *tr* faire pleuvoir ‖ *intr* pleuvoir; **it is raining cats and dogs** il pleut à seaux

rainbow ['ren,bo] *s* arc-en-ciel *m*

rain'bow trout' *s* truite *f* arc-en-ciel

rain'coat' *s* imperméable *m*

rain'fall' *s* chute *f* de pluie

rain'proof' *adj* imperméable

rain' wa'ter *s* eau *f* de pluie

rain·y ['renɪ] *adj* (*comp* **-ier;** *super* **-iest**) pluvieux

raise [rez] *s* augmentation *f*, rallonge *f*; (*in poker*) relance *f* ‖ *tr* augmenter; (*plants, animals, children; one's voice; a number to a certain power*) élever; (*an army, a camp, a siege; anchor; game*) lever; (*an objection, questions, etc.*) soulever; (*doubts; a hope; a storm*) faire naître; (*a window*) relever; (*one's head, one's voice; prices; the land*) hausser; (*a flag*) arborer; (*the dead*) ressusciter; (*money*) se procurer; (*the ante*) relancer; **to raise up** soulever, dresser

raisin ['rezən] *s* raisin *m* sec, grain *m* de raisin sec

rake [rek] *s* râteau *m*; (*person*) débauché *m* ‖ *tr* ratisser; **to rake together** râteler

rake'-off' *s* (coll) gratte *f*

rakish ['rekɪʃ] *adj* gaillard; dissolu

ral·ly ['ræli] s (pl -lies) ralliement m; (pol) réunion f politique; (in a game) reprise f; (auto race) rallye m ‖ v (pret & pp -lied) tr rallier ‖ intr se rallier; (from illness) se remettre; (sports) se reprendre; **to rally to the side of** se rallier à

ram [ræm] s bélier m ‖ v (pret & pp **rammed**; ger **ramming**) tr tamponner; **to ram down** or **in** enfoncer ‖ intr se tamponner; **to ram into** tamponner

RAM ['ɑr'ɛ'ɛm] s (letterword) (**random access memory**) mémoire f vive

ramble ['ræmbəl] s flânerie f ‖ intr flâner, errer à l'aventure; (to talk aimlessly) divaguer

rami·fy ['ræmɪ,faɪ] v (pret & pp -**fied**) tr ramifier ‖ intr se ramifier

ramp [ræmp] s rampe f, bretelle f

rampage ['ræmpedʒ] s tempête f; **to go on a rampage** se déchaîner

rampart ['ræmpɑrt] s rempart m

ram'rod' s écouvillon m

ram'shack'le adj délabré

ranch [ræntʃ] s ranch m, rancho m

rancid ['rænsɪd] adj rance

rancor ['ræŋkər] s rancœur f

random ['rændəm] adj fortuit; **at random** au hasard

ran'dom ac'cess s (comp) accès m aléatoire, accès direct

ran'dom-ac'cess mem'ory s (comp) mémoire f vive, mémoire à accès sélectif

range [rendʒ] s (row) rangée f; (scope) portée f; (mountains) chaîne f; (stove) cuisinière f; (for rifle practice) champ m de tir; (of colors, musical notes, prices, speeds, etc.) gamme f; (or words) répartition f; (of voice) tessiture f; (of vision, of activity, etc.) champ m; (for pasture) grand pâturage m; **within range of** à portée de ‖ tr ranger ‖ intr se ranger; **to range from** s'échelonner entre, varier entre; **to range over** parcourir

range'find'er s télémètre m

rank [ræŋk] adj fétide, rance; (injustice) criant; (vegetation) luxuriant ‖ s rang m ‖ tr r, intr occuper le premier rang; **to rank above** être supérieur à; **to rank with** aller de pair avec

rank' and file' s hommes mpl de troupe; commun m des mortels; (of the party, union, etc.) commun m

rankle ['ræŋkəl] tr ulcérer; irriter ‖ intr s'ulcérer

ransack ['rænsæk] tr fouiller, fouiller dans; mettre à sac

ransom ['rænsəm] s rançon f; **to hold for ransom** mettre à rançon ‖ tr rançonner

rant [rænt] intr tempêter

rap [ræp] s (blow) tape f; (noise) petit coup m sec; (slang) éreintement m; **to not care a rap** (slang) s'en ficher; **to take the rap** (slang) se laisser châtier ‖ v (pret & pp **rapped**; ger **rapping**) tr & intr frapper d'un coup sec

rapacious [rə'peʃəs] adj rapace

rape [rep] s viol m ‖ tr violer

rapid ['ræpɪd] adj rapide ‖ **rapids** spl rapides mpl

rap'id-fire' adj à tir rapide

rapidity [rə'pɪdəti] s rapidité f

rapier ['repɪ·ər] s rapière f

rapt [ræpt] adj ravi; absorbé

rapture ['ræptʃər] s ravissement m

rare [rɛr] adj rare; (meat) saignant; (amusing) (coll) impayable

rare' bird' s merle m blanc

rare'-book' room' s salle f de la réserve

rarely ['rɛrli] adv rarement

rascal ['ræskəl] s coquin m

rash [ræʃ] adj téméraire ‖ s éruption f

rasp [ræsp] s crissement m; (tool) râpe f ‖ tr râper ‖ intr crisser

raspber·ry ['ræz,bɛri] s (pl -ries) framboise f

rasp'berry bush' s framboisier m

rat [ræt] s rat m; (false hair) (coll) postiche m; (deserter) (slang) lâcheur m; (informer) (slang) mouchard m; (scoundrel) (slang) cochon m; **rats!** zut!; **to smell a rat** (coll) soupçonner anguille sous roche

ratchet ['rætʃɪt] s encliquetage m

rate [ret] s taux m; (for freight, mail, a subscription) tarif m; **at any rate** en tout cas; **at the rate of** à raison de ‖ tr évaluer; mériter ‖ intr (coll) être favori

rate' of exchange' s cours m

rather ['ræðər], ['rɑðər] adv plutôt; (fairly) assez; **rather than** plutôt que ‖ interj je vous crois!

rathskeller ['ræts,kɛlər] s caveau m

rati·fy ['rætɪ,faɪ] v (pret & pp -**fied**) tr ratifier

rating ['retɪŋ] s classement m, cote f

ra·tio ['reʃo] s (pl -tios) raison f, rapport m

ration ['ræʃən] s ration f ‖ tr rationner

rational ['ræʃənəl] adj rationnel

ra'tion book' s tickets mpl de rationnement

ra'tion card' s carte f de ravitaillement

rat' poi'son s mort m aux rats

rat' race' s foire f d'empoigne

rat'-tail file' s queue-de-rat f

rattan [ræ'tæn] s rotin m

rattle ['rætəl] s (number of short, sharp sounds) bruit m de ferraille, cliquetis m; (noisemaking device) crécelle f; (child's toy) hochet m; (in the throat) râle m ‖ tr agiter; (to confuse) (coll) affoler; **to rattle off** débiter comme un moulin ‖ intr cliqueter; (said of windows) trembler

rat'tle·snake' s serpent m à sonnettes

rat'trap' s ratière f

raucous ['rɔkəs] adj rauque

ravage ['rævɪdʒ] s ravage m; **ravages** (of time) injure f ‖ tr ravager

rave [rev] s (coll) éloge m enthousiaste ‖ intr délirer; **to rave about** or **over** s'extasier devant or sur

raven ['revən] s corbeau m

ravenous ['rævənəs] adj vorace

rave' review' s article m dithyrambique

ravine [rə'vin] s ravin m

ravish ['rævɪʃ] tr ravir

ravishing ['rævɪʃɪŋ] adj ravissant

raw [rɔ] *adj* (*uncooked*) cru; (*sugar, metal*) brut; (*silk*) grège; (*wound*) vif; (*wind*) aigre; (*weather*) humide et froid; novice, inexpérimenté
raw'boned' *adj* décharné
raw' deal' *s* (slang) mauvais tour *m*
raw'hide' *s* cuir *m* vert
raw' mate'rial *s* matière *f* première, matières premières, matière brute
ray [re] *s* (*of light*) rayon *m*; (*fish*) raie *f*
rayon [ˈre·ɑn] *s* rayonne *f*
raze [rez] *tr* raser
razor [ˈrezər] *s* rasoir *m*
ra'zor blade' *s* lame *f* de rasoir
ra'zor strop' *s* cuir *m* à rasoir
razz [ræz] *tr* (slang) mettre en boîte
reach [ritʃ] *s* portée *f*; (*of a boxer*) allonge *f*; **out of reach (of)** hors d'atteinte (de), hors de portée (de); **within reach of** à portée de ‖ *tr* atteindre; arriver à; **to reach out** (*a hand*) tendre; (*an arm*) allonger ‖ *intr* s'étendre
react [rɪˈækt] *intr* réagir
reaction [rɪˈækʃən] *s* réaction *f*
reactionar·y [rɪˈækʃənˌɛri] *adj* réactionnaire ‖ *s* (*pl* **-ies**) réactionnaire *mf*
reactivate [riˈæktəˌvet] *tr* réactiver
reactor [rɪˈæktər] *s* réacteur *m*
read [rid] *v* (*pret & pp* **read** [rɛd]) *tr* lire; **to read over** parcourir ‖ *intr* lire; (*said of passage, description, etc.*) se lire; (*said, e.g., of thermometer*) marquer; **to read on** continuer à lire; **to read up on** étudier
reader [ˈridər] *s* lecteur *m*; livre *m* de lecture
read'head' *s* (comp) lecteur *m* de disquette
readily [ˈrɛdɪli] *adv* (*willingly*) volontiers; (*easily*) facilement
reading [ˈridɪŋ] *s* lecture *f*
read'ing desk' *s* pupitre *m*
read'ing glass' *s* loupe *f*; **reading glasses** lunettes *fpl* pour lire
read'ing lamp' *s* lampe *f* de bureau
read'ing room' *s* salle *f* de lecture
readjust [ˌri·əˈdʒʌst] *tr* réadapter; (*to correct*) rectifier; (*salaries*) rajuster
read'-on'ly mem'ory *s* (comp) mémoire *f* morte
read·y [ˈrɛdi] *adj* (*comp* **-ier;** *super* **-iest**) prêt; (*quick*) vif; (*money*) comptant ‖ *v* (*pret & pp* **-ied**) *tr* préparer ‖ *intr* se préparer
read'y cash' *s* argent *m* comptant
read'y-made' suit' *s* (*for men*) complet *m* de confection; (*for women*) costume *m* de confection
ready-to-eat [ˈrɛditəˈit] *adj* prêt à servir
ready-to-wear [ˈrɛditəˈwɛr] *adj* prêt à porter ‖ *s* prêt-à-porter *m*
reaffirm [ˌri·əˈfʌrm] *tr* réaffirmer
reagent [rɪˈedʒənt] *s* (chem) réactif *m*
real [ˈri·əl] *adj* vrai, réel
re'al estate' *s* biens *mpl* immobiliers
re'al-estate' *adj* immobilier
re'al-estate a'gent *s* agent *m* immobilier, agent de location
realism [ˈri·əˌlɪzəm] *s* réalisme *m*

realist [ˈri·əlɪst] *s* réaliste *mf*
realistic [ˌri·əˈlɪstɪk] *adj* réaliste
reali·ty [rɪˈælɪti] *s* (*pl* **-ties**) réalité *f*
realize [ˈri·əˌlaɪz] *tr* se rendre compte de, s'apercevoir de; (*hopes, profits, etc.*) réaliser
really [ˈri·əli] *adv* vraiment réellement, en réalité
realm [rɛlm] *s* royaume *m*; (*field*) domaine *m*
re'al time' *s* (comp) temps *m* réel
Realtor [ˈri·əltər] *s* (*official member*) (U.S.A.) agent *m* immobilier, agent de location
ream [rim] *s* rame *f*; **reams** (coll) masses *fpl* ‖ *tr* aléser
reap [rip] *tr* moissonner; (*to gather*) recueillir
reaper [ˈripər] *s* moissonneur *m*; (mach) moissonneuse *f*
reappear [ˌri·əˈpɪr] *intr* réapparaître
reappearance [ˌri·əˈpɪrəns] *s* réapparition *f*
reapportionment [ˌri·əˈporʃənmənt] *s* nouvelle répartition *f*
rear [rɪr] *adj* arrière, d'arrière, de derrière ‖ *s* derrière *m*; (*of a car, ship, etc.; of an army*) arrière *m*; (*of a row*) queue *f*; **to the rear!** (mil) demitour à droite! ‖ *tr* élever ‖ *intr* (*said of animal*) se cabrer
rear' ad'miral *s* contre-amiral *m*
rear'-axle assem'bly *s* (*pl* **-blies**) pont *m* arrière
rear' drive' *s* traction *f* arrière
rearmament [rɪˈɑrməmənt] *s* réarmement *m*
rearrange [ˌri·əˈrendʒ] *tr* arranger de nouveau
rear'-view mir'ror *s* rétroviseur *m*
rear' win'dow *s* (aut) lunette *f* arrière
reason [ˈrizən] *s* raison *f*; **by reason of** à cause de; **for good reason** pour cause; **to listen to reason** entendre raison; **to stand to reason** être de toute évidence ‖ *tr & intr* raisonner
reasonable [ˈrizənəbəl] *adj* raisonnable
reassessment [ˌri·əˈsɛsmənt] *s* réévaluation *f*
reassure [ˌri·əˈʃʊr] *tr* rassurer
reawaken [ˌri·əˈwekən] *tr* réveiller ‖ *intr* se réveiller
rebate [ˈribet] *s* (*discount*) rabais *m*, escompte *m*, ristourne *f*; (*money back*) remboursement *m*, ristourne *f* ‖ [rɪˈbet] *tr* faire un rabais sur
rebel [ˈrɛbəl] *adj & s* rebelle *mf* ‖ **re·bel** [rɪˈbɛl] *v* (*pret & pp* **-belled;** *ger* **-belling**) *intr* se rebeller
rebellion [rɪˈbɛljən] *s* rébellion *f*
rebellious [rɪˈbɛljəs] *adj* rebelle
re·bind [riˈbaɪnd] *v* (*pret & pp* **-bound**) *tr* (bb) relier à neuf
rebirth [ˈribʌrθ] *s* renaissance *f*
rebore [riˈbor] *tr* rectifier
rebound [ˈriˌbaʊnd] *s* rebondissement *m* ‖ [rɪˈbaʊnd] *intr* rebondir
rebroad·cast [riˈbrɔdˌkæst] *s* retransmission *f* ‖ *v* (*pret & pp* **-cast** or **-casted**) *tr* retransmettre
rebuff [rɪˈbʌf] *s* rebuffade *f* ‖ *tr* mal accueillir

re·build [rɪˈbɪld] v (pret & pp **-built**) tr reconstruire

rebuke [rɪˈbjuk] s réprimande f ‖ tr réprimander

re·but [rɪˈbʌt] v (pret & pp **-butted;** ger **-butting**) tr réfuter, repousser

rebuttal [rɪˈbʌtəl] s réfutation f

recall [ˈrikɔl] s rappel m ‖ [rɪˈkɔl] tr rappeler; se rappeler de

recant [rɪˈkænt] tr rétracter ‖ intr se rétracter

re·cap [ˈriˌkæp] v (pret & pp **-capped;** ger **-capping**) tr rechaper

recapitulation [ˌrikəˌpɪtʃəˈleʃən] s récapitulation f

re·cast [ˈriˌkæst] s refonte f ‖ [riˈkæst] v (pret & pp **-cast**) tr (metal; a play, novel, etc.) refondre; (the actors of a play) redistribuer

recede [rɪˈsid] intr reculer; (said of forehead, chin, etc.) fuir; (said of sea) se retirer

receipt [rɪˈsit] s (for goods) récépissé m; (for money) récépissé, reçu m; (recipe) recette f; **receipts** recettes; **to acknowledge receipt of** accuser réception de ‖ tr acquitter

receive [rɪˈsiv] tr recevoir; (stolen goods) recéler; (a station) (rad) capter; **received payment** pour acquit ‖ intr recevoir

receiver [rɪˈsivər] s (of letter) destinataire mf; (in bankruptcy) syndic m, liquidateur m; (telp) récepteur m

receiv'ing set' s poste m récepteur

recent [ˈrisənt] adj récent

recently [ˈrisəntli] adv récemment

receptacle [rɪˈsɛptəkəl] s récipient m; (in a coin phone) sébile f; (elec) prise f femelle

reception [rɪˈsɛpʃən] s réception f; (welcome) accueil m

recep'tion desk' s réception f

receptionist [rɪˈsɛpʃənɪst] s préposé m à la réception

receptive [rɪˈsɛptɪv] adj réceptif

recess [ˈrisɛs] s (of court, legislature, etc.) ajournement m; (at school) récréation f; (in a wall) niche f ‖ [rɪˈsɛs] tr ajourner; (s.th., e.g., in a wall) encastrer ‖ intr s'adjourner

recession [rɪˈsɛʃən] s récession f

rechargeable [riˈtʃardʒəbəl] adj rechargeable

recipe [ˈrɛsɪˌpi] s recette f

recipient [rɪˈsɪpɪ·ənt] s (person) bénéficiaire mf; (of a degree, honor, etc.) récipiendaire m; (of blood) receveur m; (container) récipient m

reciprocal [rɪˈsɪprəkəl] adj réciproque

reciprocity [ˌrɛsɪˈprasɪti] s réciprocité f

recital [rɪˈsaɪtəl] s récit m; (of music or poetry) récital m

recite [rɪˈsaɪt] tr réciter; narrer

reckless [ˈrɛklɪs] adj téméraire, imprudent, insouciant

reckon [ˈrɛkən] tr calculer; considérer; (coll) supposer, imaginer ‖ intr calculer;

to reckon on compter sur; **to reckon with** tenir compte de

reclaim [rɪˈklem] tr récupérer; (e.g., waste land) mettre en valeur; (a person) réformer

reclamation [ˌrɛkləˈmeʃən] s récupération f; (e.g., of waste land) mise f en valeur; (of a person) réforme f

recline [rɪˈklaɪn] tr appuyer, reposer ‖ intr s'appuyer, se reposer

reclin'ing seat' s siège m à dossier réglable

recluse [ˈrɛklus] adj & s reclus m

recognition [ˌrɛkəgˈnɪʃən] s reconnaissance f

recognize [ˈrɛkəgˌnaɪz] tr reconnaître; (parl) donner la parole à

recoil [rɪˈkɔɪl] s répugnance f; (of, e.g., firearm) recul m ‖ intr reculer

recollect [ˌrɛkəˈlɛkt] tr se rappeler

recollection [ˌrɛkəˈlɛkʃən] s souvenir m

recommend [ˌrɛkəˈmɛnd] tr recommander

recommendation [ˌrɛkəmɛnˈdaʃən] s recommandation f; (written) certificat m

recompense [ˈrɛkəmˌpɛns] s récompense f ‖ tr récompenser

reconcile [ˈrɛkənˌsaɪl] tr réconcilier; **to reconcile oneself to** se résigner à

reconnaissance [rɪˈkanɪsəns] s reconnaissance f

reconnoiter [ˌrɛkəˈnɔɪtər] tr & intr reconnaître

reconquer [riˈkaŋkər] tr reconquérir

reconquest [riˈkaŋkwɛst] s reconquête f

reconsider [ˌrikənˈsɪdər] tr reconsidérer

reconstruct [ˌrikənˈstrʌkt] tr reconstruire; (a crime) reconstituer

reconversion [ˌrikənˈvʌrʒən] s reconversion f

record [ˈrɛkərd] s enregistrement m, registre m; (to play on the phonograph) disque m; (mil) état m de service; (sports) record m; **off the record** en confidence; **records** archives fpl; **to break the record** battre le record; **to have a good record** être bien noté; (at school) avoir de bonnes notes ‖ [rɪˈkɔrd] tr enregistrer

rec'ord chang'er s tourne-disque m automatique

recorder [rɪˈkɔrdər] s (electron) appareil m enregistreur; (law) greffier m; (mus) flûte f à bec

rec'ord hold'er s recordman m

recording [rɪˈkɔrdɪŋ] adj enregistreur ‖ s enregistrement m

record'ing tape' s ruban m magnétique

rec'ord li'brary s discothèque m

rec'ord play'er s électrophone m

recount [ˈriˌkaʊnt] s nouveau dépouillement m du scrutin ‖ [riˈkaʊnt] tr (to count again) recompter ‖ [rɪˈkaʊnt] tr (to tell) raconter

recoup [rɪˈkup] tr recouvrer; **to recoup s.o. for** dédommager qn de

recourse [riˈkors], [ˈrikors] s recours m; **to have recourse to** recourir à

recover [rɪˈkʌvər] *tr (to get back)* recouvrer; *(to cover again)* recouvrir ‖ *intr (to get well)* se rétablir

recov'er·y [rɪˈkʌvəri] *s (pl* **-ies)** récupération *f,* recouvrement *m;* (*e.g., of health)* rétablissement *m*

recov'ery room' *s* (med) salle *f* de reveil, salle de réanimation

recreant [ˈrɛkrɪ·ənt] *adj & s* lâche *mf;* traître *m;* apostat *m*

recreation [ˌrɛkrɪˈeʃən] *s* récréation *f*

rec' room' [rɛk] *s* salle *f* de détente

recruit [rɪˈkrut] *s* recrue *f* ‖ *tr* recruter; **to be recuited** se recruter

rectangle [ˈrɛkˌtæŋgəl] *s* rectangle *m*

rectifier [ˈrɛktəˌfaɪ·ər] *s* rectificateur *m;* (elec) redresseur *m*

recti·fy [ˈrɛktɪˌfaɪ] *v (pret & pp* **-fied)** *tr* rectifier; (elec) redresser

rec·tum [ˈrɛktəm] *s (pl* **-ta** [tə]) rectum *m*

recumbent [rɪˈkʌmbənt] *adj* couché

recuperate [rɪˈkjupəˌret] *tr & intr* récupérer

re·cur [rɪˈkʌr] *v (pret & pp* **-curred;** *ger* **-curring)** *intr* revenir, se reproduire; revenir à la mémoire de

recurrent [rɪˈkʌrənt] *adj* récurrent

recycle [riˈsaɪkəl] *tr* recycler

recycling [riˈsaɪklɪŋ] *s* recyclage *m*

red [rɛd] *adj (comp* **redder;** *super* **reddest)** rouge ‖ *s (color)* rouge *m;* **in the red** en déficit; **Red** *(communist)* rouge *mf;* (*nickname)* Rouquin *m;* **to glow** or **turn red** rougeoyer

red'bait' *tr* taxer de communiste

red'bird' *s* cardinal *m* d'Amérique, tangara *m*

red'-blood'ed *adj* vigoureux

red'breast' *s* rouge-gorge *m*

red'cap' porteur *m;* (Brit) soldat *m* de la police militaire

red' cell' *s* globule *m* rouge

Red' Cross' *s* Croix-Rouge *f*

redden [ˈrɛdən] *tr & intr* rougir

redeem [rɪˈdim] *tr* racheter; *(a pawned article)* dégager; *(a promise)* remplir; *(a debt)* s'acquitter de, acquitter

redeemer [rɪˈdimər] *s* rédempteur *m*

redemption [rɪˈdɛmpʃən] *s* rachat *m;* (rel) rédemption *f*

red'-haired' *adj* roux

red'hand'ed *adj & adv* sur le fait, en flagrant délit

red'head' *s (woman)* rousse *f*

red' her'ring *s* hareng *m* saur; (fig) faux-fuyant *m*

red'-hot' *adj* chauffé au rouge; ardent; *(news)* tout frais

rediscount [riˈdɪskaʊnt] *s* réescompte *m;* ‖ *tr* réescompter

rediscover [ˌridɪsˈkʌvər] *tr* redécouvrir

red'-let'ter day' *s* jour *m* mémorable

red' light' *s* feu *m* rouge; **to go through a red light** brûler feu rouge

red'-light' dis'trict *s* quartier *m* réservé

red' man' *s (pl* **men')** Peau-Rouge *m*

re·do [ˈriˈdu] *v (pret* **-did;** *pp* **-done)** *tr* refaire

redolent [ˈrɛdələnt] *adj* parfumé; **redolent of** exhalant une senteur de; qui fait penser à

redouble [riˈdʌbəl] *s* (bridge) surcontre *m* ‖ *tr & intr* redoubler; (bridge) surcontrer

redoubt [rɪˈdaut] *s* redoute *f*

redound [rɪˈdaund] *intr* contribuer; **to redound to** tourner à

red' pep'per *s* piment *m* rouge

redress [ˈridrəs] *s* redressement *m* ‖ [rɪˈdrɛs] *tr* redresser

Red' Rid'ing·hood' *s* Chaperon rouge *m*

red'skin' *s* Peau-Rouge *mf*

red' tape' *s* paperasserie *f,* chinoiseries *fpl* administratives

reduce [rɪˈd(j)us] *tr* réduire, diminuer ‖ *intr* maigrir

reduc'ing ex'ercises *spl* exercises *mpl* amaigrissants

reduction [rɪˈdʌkʃən] *s* réduction *f,* diminution *f*

redundant [rɪˈdʌndənt] *adj* redondant

red' wine' *s* vin *m* rouge

red'wing' *s* (orn) mauvis *m*

red'wood' *s* séquoia *m*

reed [rid] *s (of instrument)* anche *f;* (bot) roseau *m;* **reeds** (mus) instruments *mpl* à anche

reedit [riˈɛdɪt] *tr* rééditer

reef [rif] *s* récif *m;* *(of sail)* ris *m* ‖ *tr* (náut) prendre un ris dans

reefer [ˈrifər] *s* (slang) joint *m,* cigarette *f* de marijuana

reek [rik] *intr* fumer; **to reek of** or **with** empester, puer

reel [ril] *s (cylinder)* bobine *f;* *(of film)* rouleau *m,* bobine, bande *f;* *(of fishing rod)* moulinet *m;* *(sway)* balancement *m;* **off the reel** (coll) d'affilée ‖ *tr* bobiner; **to reel off** dévider; (coll) réciter d'un trait ‖ *intr* chanceler

reelection [ˌri·ɪˈlɛkʃən] *s* réélection *f*

reenlist [ˌri·ɛnˈlɪst] *tr* rengager ‖ *intr* rengager, se rengager

reenlistment [ˌri·ɛnˈlɪstmənt] *s* rengagement *m;* *(person)* rengagé *m*

reen·try [riˈɛntri] *s (pl* **-tries)** rentrée *f;* (rok) retour *m* à la terre

reexamination [ˌri·ɛgˌzæmɪˈneʃən] *s* réexamen *m*

re·fer [rɪˈfʌr] *v (pret & pp* **-ferred;** *ger* **-ferring)** *tr* renvoyer ‖ *intr*—**to refer to** se référer à

referee [ˌrɛfəˈri] *s* arbitre *m,* directeur *m* de jeu ‖ *tr & intr* arbitrer

reference [ˈrɛfərəns] *s* référence *f*

ref'erence room' *s* bibliothèque *f* de consultation

referen·dum [ˌrɛfəˈrɛndəm] *s (pl* **-da** [də]) référendum *m*

refill [ˈrifɪl] *s* recharge *f* ‖ [riˈfɪl] *tr* remplir à nouveau

refine [rɪˈfaɪn] *tr* raffiner

refinement [rɪˈfaɪnmənt] *s* raffinage *m;* (*e.g., of manners)* raffinement *m*

refiner·y [rɪˈfaɪnəri] *s (pl* **-ies)** raffinerie *f*

reflect [rɪˈflɛkt] *tr* réfléchir, refléter ‖ *intr* (*to be reflected*) se refléter; (*to meditate*) réfléchir; **to reflect on** or **upon** réfléchir à or sur; (*to harm*) nuire à la réputation de
reflection [rɪˈflɛkʃən] *s* (*e.g.*, *of light*; *thought*) réflexion *f*; (*reflected light*; *image*) reflet *m*; **to cast reflections on** faire des réflexions à
reflector [rɪˈflɛktər] *s* réflecteur *m*
reflex [ˈriflɛks] *adj & s* réflexe *m*
reflexive [rɪˈflɛksɪv] *adj & s* réflechi *m*
reforestation [ˌrifɔrɪsˈteʃən] *s* reboisement *m*
reform [rɪˈfɔrm] *s* réforme *f* ‖ *tr* réformer ‖ *intr* se réformer
reformation [ˌrɛfərˈmeʃən] *s* réformation *f*; **the Reformation** la Réforme
reformato·ry [rɪˈfɔrməˌtori] *s* (*pl* **-ries**) maison *f* de correction
reformer [rɪˈfɔrmər] *s* réformateur *m*
reform′ school′ *s* maison *f* de correction
refraction [rɪˈfrækʃən] *s* réfraction *f*
refrain [rɪˈfren] *s* refrain *m* ‖ *intr* s'abstenir
refresh [rɪˈfrɛʃ] *tr* rafraîchir ‖ *intr* se rafraîchir
refreshing [rɪˈfrɛʃɪŋ] *adj* rafraîchissant
refreshment [rɪˈfrɛʃmənt] *s* rafraîchissement *m*
refresh′ment bar′ *s* buvette *f*
refrigerate [rɪˈfrɪdʒəˌret] *tr* réfrigérer
refrigerator [rɪˈfrɪdʒəˌretər] *s* (*icebox*) glacière; réfrigérateur *m*; (*condenser*) congélateur *m*
refrig′erator car′ *s* (rr) wagon *m* frigorifique
re·fuel [riˈfjul] *v* (*pret & pp* **-fueled** or **-fuelled**; *ger* **-fueling** or **-fuelling**) *tr* ravitailler en carburant ‖ *intr* se ravitailler en carburant
refuge [ˈrɛfjudʒ] *s* refuge *m*; **to take refuge (in)** se réfugier (dans)
refugee [ˌrɛfjuˈdʒi] *s* réfugié *m*
refund [ˈrifʌnd] *s* remboursement *m* ‖ [ˈrifʌnd] *tr* (*to pay back*) rembourser ‖ [riˈfʌnd] *tr* (*to fund again*) consolider
refurnish [riˈfʌrnɪʃ] *tr* remeubler
refusal [rɪˈfjuzəl] *s* refus *m*
refuse [ˈrɛfjus] *s* ordures *fpl*, détritus *mpl* ‖ [rɪˈfjuz] *tr & intr* refuser
refute [rɪˈfjut] *tr* réfuter
regain [rɪˈgen] *tr* regagner; (*consciousness*) reprendre
regal [ˈrigəl] *adj* royal
regale [rɪˈgel] *tr* régaler
regalia [rɪˈgelɪ·ə] *spl* atours *mpl*, ornements *mpl*; (*of an office*) insignes *mpl*
regard [rɪˈgɑrd] *s* considération *f*; (*esteem*) respect *m*; (*look*) regard *m*; **in** or **with regard to** à l'égard de; **regards** sincères amitiés *fpl* ‖ *tr* considérer, estimer; **as regards** quant à
regarding [rɪˈgɑrdɪŋ] *prep* au sujet de, touchant
regardless [rɪˈgɑrdlɪs] *adj* inattentif ‖ *adv* (coll) coûte que coûte; **regardless of** sans tenir compte de
regatta [rɪˈgætə] *s* régates *fpl*

regen·cy [ˈridʒənsi] *s* (*pl* **-cies**) régence *f*
regenerate [rɪˈdʒɛnəˌret] *tr* régénérer ‖ *intr* se régénérer
regent [ˈridʒənt] *s* régent *m*
regicide [ˈrɛdʒɪˌsaɪd] *s* (*act*) régicide *m*; (*person*) régicide *mf*
regime [reˈʒim] *s* régime *m*
regiment [ˈrɛdʒɪmənt] *s* régiment *m* ‖ [ˈrɛdʒɪˌmɛnt] *tr* enrégimenter, régenter
regimental [ˌrɛdʒɪˈmɛntəl] *adj* régimentaire ‖ **regimentals** *spl* tenue *f* militaire
region [ˈridʒən] *s* région *f*
register [ˈrɛdʒɪstər] *s* registre *m* ‖ *tr* enregistrer; (*a student*; *an automobile*) immatriculer; (*a letter*) recommander ‖ *intr* s'inscrire
reg′istered let′ter *s* lettre *f* recommandée
reg′istered mail′ *s* envoi *m* en recommandé
reg′istered nurse′ *s* infirmière *f* diplômée
registrar [ˈrɛdʒɪsˌtrɑr] *s* archiviste *mf*, secrétaire *mf*
registration [ˌrɛdʒɪsˈtreʃən] *s* enregistrement *m*; immatriculation *f*, inscription *f*; (*of mail*) recommandation *f*
registra′tion blank′ *s* fiche *f* d'inscription
registra′tion fee′ *s* frais *mpl* d'inscription, droit *m* d'inscription
registra′tion num′ber *s* (*of soldier or student*) numéro *m* matricule
re·gret [rɪˈgrɛt] *s* regret *m*; **regrets** excuses *fpl* ‖ *v* (*pret & pp* **-gretted;** *ger* **-gretting**) *tr* regretter
regrettable [rɪˈgrɛtəbəl] *adj* regrettable
regular [ˈrɛgjələr] *adj & s* régulier *m*
reg′ular fel′low *s* (coll) chic type *m*
regularity [ˌrɛgjəˈlærɪti] *s* régularité *f*
regularize [ˈrɛgjələˌraɪz] *tr* régulariser
regulate [ˈrɛgjəˌlet] *tr* régler; (*to control*) réglementer
regulation [ˌrɛgjəˈleʃən] *s* régulation *f*; (*rule*) règlement *m*
rehabilitate [ˌrihəˈbɪlɪˌtet] *tr* réadapter; (*in reputation, standing, etc.*) réhabiliter
rehearsal [rɪˈhɑrsəl] *s* répétition *f*
rehearse [rɪˈhɑrs] *tr & intr* répéter
reign [ren] *s* règne *m* ‖ *intr* régner
reimburse [ˌri·ɪmˈbʌrs] *tr* rembourser
rein [ren] *s* rêne *f*; **to give free rein to** donner libre cours à ‖ *tr* contenir, freiner
reincarnation [ˌri·ɪnkɑrˈneʃən] *s* réincarnation *f*
rein′deer′ *s* renne *m*
reinforce [ˌri·ɪnˈfors] *tr* renforcer; (*concrete*) armer
reinforcement [ˌri·ɪnˈforsmənt] *s* renforcement *m*
reinstate [ˌri·ɪnˈstet] *tr* rétablir
reiterate [riˈɪtəˌret] *tr* réitérer
reject [ˈridʒɛkt] *s* pièce *f* or article *m* de rebut; **rejects** rebuts *mpl* ‖ [rɪˈdʒɛkt] *tr* rejeter
rejection [rɪˈdʒɛkʃən] *s* rejet *m*, refus *m*
rejoice [rɪˈdʒɔɪs] *intr* se réjouir
rejoin [riˈdʒɔɪn] *tr* rejoindre
rejoinder [rɪˈdʒɔɪndər] *s* réplique *f*; (law) réponse *f* à une réplique

rejuvenation [rɪˌdʒuvɪˈneʃən] s rajeunisse-ment m
rekindle [riˈkɪndəl] tr rallumer
relapse [rɪˈlæps] s rechute f ‖ intr rechuter
relate [rɪˈlet] tr (to narrate) relater; (e.g., two events) établir un rapport entre; **to be related** être apparenté
relation [rɪˈleʃən] s (relationship) relation f, rapport m; (telling) récit m, relation; (relative) parent m; (kinship) parenté f; **in relation to or with** par rapport à; **relations** (of a sexual nature) rapports mpl; (diplomatic) relations fpl
relationship [rɪˈleʃənˌʃɪp] s (connection) rapport m; (kinship) parenté f
relative [ˈrɛlətɪv] adj relatif ‖ s parent m
relativity [ˌrɛləˈtɪvəti] s relativité f
relax [rɪˈlæks] tr détendre; **to be relaxed** être décontracté or détendu ‖ intr se détendre, décompresser
relaxation [ˌrilæksˈeʃən] s détente f, délasse-ment m
relaxing [rɪˈlæksɪŋ] adj tranquillisant, apai-sant; (diverting) délassant
relay [ˈrile] s relais m ‖ v (pret & pp -layed) tr relayer; (rad, telg, telp, telv) retrans-mettre ‖ [riˈle] v (pret & pp -laid) tr tendre de nouveau
re'lay race' s course f de relais
re'lay sat'ellite s satellite m de relais
re'lay transmit'ter s (electron) réémetteur m
release [rɪˈlis] s (from jail) mise f en liberté, libération f; (permission) autorisation f; (exemption) dérogation f; (aer) lâchage m; (mach) déclenchement m; **release on bail** libération f sous caution; **release on pa-role** libération conditionnelle ‖ tr délivrer; (from jail) mettre en liberté; autoriser; (a bomb) lâcher
relegate [ˈrɛlɪˌget] tr reléguer
relent [rɪˈlɛnt] intr se laisser attendrir, s'a-doucir
relentless [rɪˈlɛntlɪs] adj implacable
relevant [ˈrɛlɪvənt] adj pertinent
reliable [rɪˈlaɪ·əbəl] adj digne de confiance, digne de foi, fiable
reliance [rɪˈlaɪ·əns] s confiance f
relic [ˈrɛlɪk] s (rel) relique f; (fig) vestige m
relief [rɪˈlif] s (from pain, anxiety) soulage-ment m; (projection of figures; elevation) relief m; (aid) secours m; (welfare pro-gram) aide f sociale; (mil) relève f; **in relief** en relief
relieve [rɪˈliv] tr soulager; (to aid) secourir; (to release from a post; to give variety to) relever; (mil) relever
religion [rɪˈlɪdʒən] s religion f
religious [rɪˈlɪdʒəs] adj religieux
relinquish [rɪˈlɪŋkwɪʃ] tr abandonner
relish [ˈrɛlɪʃ] s (enjoyment) goût m; (condi-ment) assaisonnement m; **relish for** pen-chant pour ‖ tr goûter, apprécier
reluctance [rɪˈlʌktəns] s répugnance f; **with reluctance** à contrecœur
reluctant [rɪˈlʌktənt] adj hésitant, peu dis-posé

re·ly [rɪˈlaɪ] v (pret & pp -lied) intr—**to rely on** compter sur, se fier à
remain [rɪˈmen] s—**remains** restes mpl; (œuvres fpl posthumes ‖ intr rester
remainder [rɪˈmendər] s reste m; **remain-ders** bouillons mpl ‖ tr solder
re·make [riˈmek] v (pret & pp -made) tr refaire
remark [rɪˈmɑrk] s remarque f, observation f ‖ tr & intr remarquer, observer; **to remark on** faire des remarques sur
remarkable [rɪˈmɑrkəbəl] adj remarquable
remar·ry [rɪˈmæri] v (pret & pp -ried) tr remarier; se remarier avec ‖ intr se rema-rier
reme·dy [ˈrɛmɪdi] s (pl -dies) remède m ‖ v (pret & pp -died) tr remédier à
remember [rɪˈmɛmbər] tr se souvenir de, se rappeler; **remember me to** rappelez-moi au bon souvenir de ‖ intr se souvenir, se rappeler
remembrance [rɪˈmɛmbrəns] s souvenir m; **in remembrance of** en souvenir de
remind [rɪˈmaɪnd] tr rappeler
reminder [rɪˈmaɪndər] s note f de rappel, mémento m, pense-bête f
reminisce [ˌrɛmɪˈnɪs] intr se livrer au sou-venirs, raconter ses souvenirs
remiss [rɪˈmɪs] adj négligent
remission [rɪˈmɪʃən] s rémission f
re·mit [rɪˈmɪt] v (pret & pp -mitted; ger -mitting) tr remettre ‖ intr se calmer
remittance [rɪˈmɪtəns] s remise f, envoi m
remnant [ˈrɛmnənt] s (remainder) reste m; (of cloth) coupon m; (at reduced price) solde m
remod·el [riˈmɑdəl] v (pret & pp -eled or -elled; ger -eling or -elling) tr modeler de nouveau, remanier; (a house) transformer
remonstrance [rɪˈmɑnstrəns] s remon-trance f
remonstrate [rɪˈmɑnstret] intr protester; **to remonstrate with** faire des remontrances à
remorse [rɪˈmɔrs] s remords m
remorseful [rɪˈmɔrsfəl] adj contrit, repen-tant, plein de remords
remote' [rɪˈmot] adj loigné, retiré
remote' control' s commande f à distance, télécommande f
removable [rɪˈmuvəbəl] adj amovible
removal [rɪˈmuvəl] s enlèvement m; (from house) déménagement m; (dismissal) ré-vocation f
remove [rɪˈmuv] tr enlever, ôter; éloigner; (furniture) déménager; (to dismiss) ré-voquer ‖ intr se déplacer; déménager
remuneration [rɪˌmjunəˈreʃən] s rému-nération f
renaissance [ˌrɛnəˈsɑns] s renaissance f
rend [rɛnd] v (pret & pp -rent [rɛnt]) tr déchirer; (to split) fendre; (the air; the heart) fendre
render [ˈrɛndər] tr rendre; (a piece of mu-sic) interpréter; (lard) fondre
rendez·vous [ˈrɑndəˌvu] s (pl -vous [ˌvuz]) rendez-vous m ‖ v (pret & pp -voused

[,vud]; *ger* **-vousing** [,vuɪŋ]) *intr* se rencontrer

rendition [rɛnˈdɪʃən] *s* (*translation*) traduction *f*; (mus) interprétation *f*

renegade [ˈrɛnɪˌged] *s* renégat *m*

renege [rɪˈnɪg] *s* renonce *f* ‖ *intr* renoncer; (coll) se dédire, ne pas tenir sa parole

renew [rɪˈn(j)u] *tr* renouveler ‖ *intr* se renouveler

renewable [rɪˈn(j)u·əbəl] *adj* renouvelable

renewal [rɪˈn(j)u·əl] *s* renouvellement *m*; (*of strength*) regain *m*; (*of a lease*) reconduction *f*

renounce [rɪˈnaʊns] *s* renonce *f* ‖ *tr* renoncer à ‖ *intr* renoncer

renovate [ˈrɛnəˌvet] *tr* renouveler; (*a room, a house, etc.*) mettre à neuf, rénover, transformer

renown [rɪˈnaʊn] *s* renom *m*

renowned [rɪˈnaʊnd] *adj* renommé

rent [rɛnt] *adj* déchiré ‖ *s* loyer *m*, location *f*; (*tear, slit*) déchirure *f*; **for rent** à louer ‖ *tr* louer ‖ *intr* se louer

rental [ˈrɛntəl] *s* loyer *m*, location *f*

rent'al a'gen·cy *s* (*pl* **-cies**) agence *f* de location

rent'ed car' *s* voiture *f* de louage, voiture de location; (*chauffeur-driven limousine*) voiture de grande remise

renter [ˈrɛntər] *s* locataire *mf*

renunciation [rɪˌnʌnsɪˈeʃən] *s* renonciation *f*

reopen [riˈopən] *tr & intr* rouvrir

reopening [riˈopənɪŋ] *s* réouverture *f*; (*of school*) rentrée *f*

reorganize [riˈɔrgəˌnaɪz] *tr* réorganiser ‖ *intr* se réorganiser

repair [rɪˈpɛr] *s* réparation *f*; **in good repair** en bon état ‖ *tr* réparer ‖ *intr* se rendre

repair'man' *s* (rad, telv) agent *m* de dépannage

repaper [riˈpepər] *tr* retapisser

reparation [ˌrɛpəˈreʃən] *s* réparation *f*

repartee [ˌrɛparˈti] *s* repartie *f*

repast [rɪˈpæst] *s* repas *m*

repatriate [riˈpetrɪˌet] *tr* rapatrier

re·pay [rɪˈpe] *v* (*pret & pp* **-paid**) *tr* rembourser; récompenser

repayment [rɪˈpemənt] *s* remboursement *m*; récompense *f*

repeal [rɪˈpil] *s* révocation *f*, abrogation *f* ‖ *tr* révoquer, abroger

repeat [rɪˈpit] *s* répétition *f* ‖ *tr & intr* répéter

re·pel [rɪˈpɛl] *v* (*pret & pp* **-pelled;** *ger* **-pelling**) *tr* repousser; dégoûter

repent [rɪˈpɛnt] *tr* se repentir de ‖ *intr* se repentir

repentance [rɪˈpɛntəns] *s* repentir *m*

repentant [rɪˈpɛntənt] *adj* repentant

repercussion [ˌripərˈkʌʃən] *s* répercussion *f*, contrecoup *m*

reperto·ry [ˈrɛpərˌtori] *s* (*pl* **-ries**) répertoire *m*

repetition [ˌrɛpɪˈtɪʃən] *s* répétition *f*

replace [rɪˈples] *tr* (*to put back*) remettre en place; (*to take the place of*) remplacer

replaceable [rɪˈplesəbəl] *adj* remplaçable, amovible

replacement [rɪˈplesmənt] *s* (*putting back*) remise *f* en place, replacement *m*; (*substitution*) remplacement *m*; (*substitute part*) pièce *f* de rechange; (*person*) remplaçant *m*

replay [ˈriple] *s* match *m* rejoué; (telv) action *f* replay ‖ [riˈple] *tr* rejouer

replenish [rɪˈplɛnɪʃ] *tr* réapprovisionner; remplir

replete [rɪˈplit] *adj* rempli, plein

replica [ˈrɛplɪkə] *s* reproduction *f*, réplique *f*

re·ply [rɪˈplaɪ] *s* (*pl* **-plies**) réponse *f*, réplique *f* ‖ *v* (*pret & pp* **-plied**) *tr & intr* répondre, répliquer

reply' cou'pon *s* coupon-réponse *m*

report [rɪˈport] *s* (*account, statement*) rapport *m*; (*rumor*) bruit *m*; (*e.g., of firearm*) détonation *f* ‖ *tr* rapporter; dénoncer; **it is reported that** le bruit court que; **reported missing** porté manquant ‖ *intr* faire un rapport; (*to show up*) se présenter

report' card' *s* bulletin *m* scolaire

reportedly [rɪˈportɪdli] *adv* au dire de tout le monde

reporter [rɪˈportər] *s* reporter *m*

reporting [rɪˈportɪŋ] *s* reportage *m*

repose [rɪˈpoz] *s* repos *m* ‖ *tr* reposer; (*confidence*) placer ‖ *intr* reposer

reprehend [ˌrɛprɪˈhɛnd] *tr* reprendre

represent [ˌrɛprɪˈzɛnt] *tr* représenter

representation [ˌrɛprɪzɛnˈteʃən] *s* représentation *f*

representative [ˌrɛprɪˈzɛntətɪv] *adj* représentatif ‖ *s* représentant *m*

repress [rɪˈprɛs] *tr* réprimer; (psychoanal) refouler

repression [rɪˈprɛʃən] *s* répression *f*; (psychoanal) refoulement *m*

reprieve [rɪˈpriv] *s* sursis *m* ‖ *tr* surseoir à l'exécution de

reprimand [ˈrɛprɪˌmænd] *s* réprimande *f* ‖ *tr* réprimander

reprint [ˈriˌprɪnt] *s* (*book*) réimpression *f*; (*offprint*) tiré *m* à part ‖ [riˈprɪnt] *tr* réimprimer

reprisal [rɪˈpraɪzəl] *s* représailles *fpl*

reproach [rɪˈprotʃ] *s* (*rebuke*) reproche *m*; (*discredit*) honte *f*, opprobre *m* ‖ *tr* reprocher; couvrir d'opprobre; **to reproach s.o. for s.th.** reprocher q.ch. à qn

reproduce [ˌriprəˈd(j)us] *tr* reproduire ‖ *intr* se reproduire

reproduction [ˌriprəˈdʌkʃən] *s* reproduction *f*

reproof [rɪˈpruf] *s* reproche *m*

reprove [rɪˈpruv] *tr* réprimander

reptile [ˈrɛtɪl] *s* reptile *m*

republic [rɪˈpʌblɪk] *s* république *f*

republican [rɪˈpʌblɪkən] *adj & s* républicain *m*

repudiate [rɪˈpjudɪˌet] *tr* répudier

repugnant [rɪˈpʌgnənt] *adj* répugnant

repulse [rɪˈpʌls] *s* refus *m*; (*setback*) échec *m* ‖ *tr* repousser

repulsive [rɪˈpʌlsɪv] *adj* répulsif

reputation [ˌrɛpjəˈteʃən] *s* réputation *f*

repute [rɪ'pjut] s réputation f; **of ill repute** mal famé ‖ tr—**to be reputed to be** être réputé

reputedly [rɪ'pjutɪdli] adv suivant l'opinion commune

request [rɪ'kwɛst] s demande f; **on request** sur demande ‖ tr demander

Requiem ['rɛkwɪˌɛm] s Requiem m

require [rɪ'kwaɪr] tr exiger

requirement [rɪ'kwaɪrmənt] s exigence f; besoin m

requisite ['rɛkwɪzɪt] adj requis ‖ s chose f nécessaire; condition f nécessaire

requisition [ˌrɛkwɪ'zɪʃən] s réquisition f ‖ tr réquisitionner

requital [rɪ'kwaɪtəl] s récompense f; (retaliation) revanche f

requite [rɪ'kwaɪt] tr récompenser; (to avenge) venger

re·read [ri'rid] v (pret & pp -read ['rɛd]) tr relire

rerun ['riˌrʌn] s reprise f ‖ [ri'rʌn] tr (film, tape) passer de nouveau; (race) courir de nouveau

resale ['riˌsel], [ri'sel] s revente f

rescind [rɪ'sɪnd] tr abroger

rescue ['rɛskju] s sauvetage m; **to the rescue** au secours, à la rescousse ‖ tr sauver, secourir

res'cue par'ty s équipe f de secours

research [rɪ'sʌrtʃ], ['risʌrtʃ] s recherche f ‖ intr faire des recherches

re·sell [ri'sɛl] v (pret & pp -sold) tr revendre; (to sell back) recéder

resemblance [rɪ'zɛmbləns] s ressemblance f

resemble [rɪ'zɛmbəl] tr ressembler à; **to resemble one another** se ressembler

resent [rɪ'zɛnt] tr s'offenser de

resentful [rɪ'zɛntfəl] adj offensé

resentment [rɪ'zɛntmənt] s ressentiment m

reservation [ˌrɛzər'veʃən] s (booking) location f, réservation f; (Indian land) réserve f; **without reservation** sans réserve

reserve [rɪ'zʌrv] s réserve f ‖ tr réserver

reserve' room' s (in a library) réserve f, salle f de services du prêt

reservist [rɪ'zʌrvɪst] s réserviste m

reservoir ['rɛzərˌvwɑr] s réservoir m

re·set [ri'sɛt] v (pret & pp -set; ger -setting) tr remettre; (a gem) remonter

re·ship [ri'ʃɪp] v (pret & pp -shipped; ger -shipping) tr réexpédier; (on a ship) rembarquer ‖ intr se rembarquer

reshipment [ri'ʃɪpmənt] s réexpédition f; (on a ship) rembarquement m

reside [rɪ'zaɪd] intr résider, demeurer

residence ['rɛzɪdəns] s résidence f, domicile m

residency ['rɛzɪdənsi] s (med) résidanat m

resident ['rɛzɪdənt] adj & s habitant m

residential [ˌrɛzɪ'dɛnʃəl] adj résidentiel

residue ['rɛzɪˌd(j)u] s résidu m

resign [rɪ'zaɪn] tr démissionner de, résigner; **to resign oneself to** se résigner à ‖ intr démissionner; se résigner; **to resign from** démissionner de

resignation [ˌrɛzɪg'neʃən] s (from a job, etc.) démission f; (submissive state) résignation f

resin ['rɛzɪn] s résine f

resist [rɪ'zɪst] tr résister à; **to resist** + ger s'empêcher de + inf ‖ intr résister

resistance [rɪ'zɪstəns] s résistance f

resole [ri'sol] tr ressemeler

resolute ['rɛzəˌlut] adj résolu

resolution [ˌrɛzə'luʃən] s résolution f

resolve [rɪ'zɔlv] s résolution f ‖ tr résoudre ‖ intr résoudre, se résoudre

resonance ['rɛzənəns] s résonance f

resort [rɪ'zɔrt] s station f, e.g., **health resort** station climatique; (summer resort) camp m de vacances; (for help or support) recours m; **as a last resort** en dernier ressort ‖ intr—**to resort to** recourir à, avoir recours à

resound [rɪ'zaʊnd] intr résonner

resource [rɪ'sors], ['risors] s ressource f

resourceful [rɪ'sorsfəl] adj débrouillard, de ressource

respect [rɪ'spɛkt] s respect m; **in many respects** à bien des égards; **in this respect** sous ce rapport; **to pay one's respects (to)** présenter ses respects (à); **with respect to** par rapport à ‖ tr respecter

respectable [rɪ'spɛktəbəl] adj respectable; considérable

respectful [rɪ'spɛktfəl] adj respectueux

respectfully [rɪ'spɛktfəli] adv respectueusement; **respectfully yours** (complimentary close) veuillez agréer l'assurance de mes sentiments très respectueux

respective [rɪ'spɛktɪv] adj respectif

res'piratory tract' ['rɛspɪrəˌtori] s appareil m respiratoire

respite ['rɛspɪt] s répit m; **without respite** sans relâche

resplendent [rɪ'splɛndənt] adj resplendissant

respond [rɪ'spɑnd] intr répondre

response [rɪ'spɑns] s réponse f

responsibili·ty [rɪˌspɑnsɪ'bɪlɪti] s (pl -ties) responsabilité f

responsible [rɪ'spɑnsɪbəl] adj responsable; (person) digne de confiance; (job, position) de confiance; **responsible for** responsable de; **responsible to** responsable envers

responsive [rɪ'spɑnsɪv] adj sensible, réceptif; prompt à sympathiser

rest [rɛst] s (repose) repos m; (lack of motion) pause f; (what remains) reste m; (mus) silence m; **at rest** en repos; (dead) mort; **the rest** les autres; (the remainder) le restant; **the rest of us** nous autres; **to come to rest** s'immobiliser; **to lay to rest** enterrer ‖ tr reposer ‖ intr reposer, se reposer; **to rest on** reposer sur, s'appuyer sur

restaurant ['rɛstərənt] s restaurant m

rest' cure' s cure f de repos

restful ['rɛstfəl] adj reposant; (calm) tranquille, paisible

rest' home' s maison f de repos

rest′ing place′ s lieu m de repos, gîte m; (*of the dead*) dernière demeure f

restitution [ˌrɛstɪˈt(j)uʃən] s restitution f

restive [ˈrɛstɪv] *adj* rétif

restless [ˈrɛstlɪs] *adj* agité, inquiet; sans repos

restock [riˈstɑk] *tr* réapprovisionner; (*with fish or game*) repeupler

restoration [ˌrɛstəˈreʃən] s restauration f

restore [rɪˈstor] *tr* restaurer; (*health*) rétablir; (*to give back*) restituer

restrain [rɪˈstren] *tr* retenir, contenir

restraint [rɪˈstrent] s restriction f, contrainte f

restrict [rɪˈstrɪkt] *tr* restreindre

restriction [rɪˈstrɪkʃən] s restriction f

rest′ room′ s cabinet m d'aisance

rest′ stop′ s (*turnpike restaurant*) restoroute m

result [rɪˈzʌlt] s résultat m; **as a result of** par suite de ‖ *intr* résulter; **to result in** aboutir à

resume [rɪˈz(j)um] *tr & intr* reprendre

résumé [ˌrez(j)ʊˈme] s résumé m

resumption [rɪˈzʌmpʃən] s reprise f

resurface [riˈsʌrfɪs] *tr* refaire le revêtement de ‖ *intr* (*said of submarine*) faire surface

resurrect [ˌrɛzəˈrɛkt] *tr & intr* ressusciter

resurrection [ˌrɛzəˈrɛkʃən] s résurrection f

resuscitate [rɪˈsʌsɪˌtet] *tr & intr* ressusciter

retail [ˈritel] *adj & adv* au détail ‖ s vente f au détail ‖ *tr* vendre au détail, détailler ‖ *intr* se vendre au détail

retailer [ˈritelər] s détaillant m

retain [rɪˈten] *tr* retenir; engager

retaliate [rɪˈtælɪˌet] *intr* prendre sa revanche, user de représailles

retaliation [rɪˌtælɪˈeʃən] s représailles fpl

retard [rɪˈtɑrd] s retard m ‖ *tr* retarder

retarded *adj* (pathol) retardé, ariéré; (pej) demeuré

retch [rɛtʃ] *tr* vomir ‖ *intr* avoir un haut-le-cœur

retching [ˈrɛtʃɪŋ] s haut-le-cœur m

reticence [ˈrɛtɪsəns] s réserve f

reticent [ˈrɛtɪsənt] *adj* réservé

retina [ˈrɛtɪnə] s rétine f

retinue [ˈrɛtɪˌn(j)u] s suite f, cortège m

retire [rɪˈtaɪr] *tr* mettre à la retraite ‖ *intr* se retirer

retired *adj* en retraite, retiré

retirement [rɪˈtaɪrmənt] s retraite f

retire′ment pro′gram s programme m de prévoyance

retire′ment vil′lage s cité f retraite

retiring [rɪˈtaɪrɪŋ] *adj* (*shy*) effacé; (*e.g., congressman*) sortant

retort [rɪˈtɔrt] s riposte f, réplique f; (chem) cornue f ‖ *tr & intr* riposter

retouch [riˈtʌtʃ] *tr* retoucher

retrace [rɪˈtres] *tr* retracer; (*one's steps*) revenir sur

retract [rɪˈtrækt] *tr* rétracter ‖ *intr* se rétracter

retractable [rɪˈtræktəbəl] *adj* (aer) escamotable

retraining [riˈtrenɪŋ] s recyclage m

re·tread [ˈriˌtrɛd] s pneu m rechapé ‖ [riˈtrɛd] v (*pret & pp* **-treaded**) *tr* rechaper ‖ v (*pret* **-trod**; *pp* **-trod** or **-trodden**) *tr & intr* repasser

retreat [rɪˈtrit] s retraite f; **to beat a retreat** battre en retraite ‖ *intr* se retirer

retrench [rɪˈtrɛntʃ] *tr* restreindre ‖ *intr* faire des économies

retribution [ˌrɛtrɪˈbjuʃən] s rétribution f

retrieval [rɪˈtrivəl] s récupération f; (comp) retrouve f

retrieve [rɪˈtriv] *tr* retrouver, recouvrer; (*a fortune, a reputation, etc.*) rétablir; (*game*) rapporter ‖ *intr* (*said of hunting dog*) rapporter

retriever [rɪˈtrivər] s retriever m

retroactive [ˌrɛtroˈæktɪv] *adj* rétroactif

retrogress [ˈrɛtrəˌgrɛs] *intr* rétrograder

retrorocket [ˈrɛtroˌrɑkɪt] s rétrofusée f

retrospect [ˈrɛtrəˌspɛkt] s—**to consider in retrospect** jeter un coup d'œil rétrospectif à

retrospective [ˌrɛtrəˈspɛktɪv] *adj* rétrospectif

re·try [riˈtraɪ] v (*pret & pp* **-tried**) *tr* essayer de nouveau; (law) juger à nouveau

return [rɪˈtʌrn] *adj* de retour; **by return mail** par retour du courrier ‖ s retour m; (*profit*) bénéfice m; (*yield*) rendement m; (*unwanted merchandise*) rendu m; (*of ball*) renvoi m; (*of income tax*) déclaration f; (*typewriter key*) touche f de rappel de chariot, touche retour arrière; **in return** de retour; **in return for** en récompense de; **returns** (*profits*) recettes fpl; (*of an election*) résultats mpl; **many happy returns of the day!** bon anniversaire! ‖ *tr* rendre; (*to put back*) remettre; (*to bring back*) rapporter; (*e.g., a letter*) retourner ‖ *intr* (*to go back*) retourner; (*to come back*) revenir; (*to get back home*) rentrer; **return to sender** (*on letter*) retour à l'expéditeur; **to return empty-handed** revenir bredouille

return′able bot′tle s [rɪˈtɜrnəbəl] emballage m consigné

return′ address′ s adresse f de l'expéditeur

return′ bout′ s revanche f

return′ game′ or **match′** s match m retour

return′ tick′et s aller et retour m

return′ trip′ s voyage m de retour

reunification [riˌjunɪfɪˈkeʃən] s réunification f

reunion [riˈjunjən] s réunion f

reunite [ˌrijuˈnaɪt] *tr* réunir ‖ *intr* se réunir

reusable [riˈjuzəbəl] *adj* réutilisable

rev [rɛv] s (coll) tour m ‖ v (*pret & pp* **revved**; *ger* **revving**) *tr* (coll) accélérer; (*to race*) (coll) emballer ‖ *intr* (coll) s'accélérer

revalue [riˈvælju] *tr* révaloriser

revamp [riˈvæmp] *tr* refaire

reveal [rɪˈvil] *tr* révéler

reveille [ˈrɛvəli] s réveil m

rev·el [ˈrɛvəl] s fête f; **revels** ébats mpl, orgie f ‖ v (*pret & pp* **-eled** or **-elled**; *ger*

-eling or **-elling**) *intr* faire la fête, faire la bombe; **to revel in** se délecter à

revelation [ˌrɛvəˈleʃən] *s* révélation *f*; **Revelation** (Bib) Apocalypse *f*

revel·ry [ˈrɛvəlri] *s* (*pl* **-ries**) réjouissances *fpl*, orgie *f*

revenge [rɪˈvɛndʒ] *s* vengeance *f*; **to take revenge on s.o. for s.th.** se venger de q.ch. sur qn ‖ *tr* venger

revengeful [rɪˈvɛndʒfəl] *adj* vindicatif

revenue [ˈrɛvəˌn(j)u] *s* revenu *m*

rev′enue cut′ter *s* garde-côte *m*, vedette *f*

rev′enue stamp′ *s* timbre *m* fiscal

reverberate [rɪˈvʌrbəˌret] *intr* résonner, réverbérer

revere [rɪˈvɪr] *tr* révérer

reverence [ˈrɛvərəns] *s* révérence *f* ‖ *tr* révérer

reverend [ˈrɛvərənd] *adj* & *s* révérend *m*

reverent [ˈrɛvərənt] *adj* révérenciel

reverie [ˈrɛvəri] *s* rêverie *f*

reversal [rɪˈvʌrsəl] *s* renversement *m*

reverse [rɪˈvʌrs] *adj* contraire ‖ *s* (*opposite*) contraire *m*; (*of medal; of fortune*) revers *m*; (*of page*) verso *m*; (aut) marche *f* arrière ‖ *tr* renverser; (*a sentence*) (law) révoquer ‖ *intr* renverser; (*said of motor*) faire machine arrière; (aut) faire marche arrière

reverse′ lev′er *s* levier *m* de renvoi

reverse′ side′ *s* revers *m*, dos *m*

reversible [rɪˈvʌrsɪbəl] *adj* réversible

revert [rɪˈvʌrt] *intr* revenir, faire retour

review [rɪˈvju] *s* (*inspection*) revue *f*; (*of a book*) compte *m* rendu; (*of a lesson*) révision *f* ‖ *tr* revoir; (*a book*) faire la critique de; (*a lesson*) réviser, revoir; (*past events; troops*) passer en revue ‖ *intr* faire des révisions

revile [rɪˈvaɪl] *tr* injurier, outrager

revise [rɪˈvaɪz] *s* (typ) épreuve *f* de révision ‖ *tr* réviser, revoir

revised′ edi′tion *s* édition *f* revue et corrigée

revision [rɪˈvɪʒən] *s* révision *f*

revisionist [rɪˈvɪʒənɪst] *adj* & *s* révisionniste *mf*

revival [rɪˈvaɪvəl] *s* retour *m* à la vie; (*of learning*) renaissance *f*; (rel) réveil *m*; (theat) reprise *f*

reviv′al meet′ings *spl* (rel) réveils *mpl*

revive [rɪˈvaɪv] *tr* ranimer; (*a victim*) ressusciter; (*a memory*) réveiller; (*a play*) reprendre; (*hopes*) faire renaître; ‖ *intr* reprendre; se ranimer

revoke [rɪˈvok] *tr* révoquer

revolt [rɪˈvolt] *s* révolte *f* ‖ *tr* révolter ‖ *intr* se révolter

revolting [rɪˈvoltɪŋ] *adj* dégoûtant, repoussant; rebelle, révolté

revolution [ˌrɛvəˈluʃən] *s* révolution *f*

revolutionar·y [ˌrɛvəˈluʃəˌnɛri] *adj* révolutionnaire ‖ *s* (*pl* **-ies**) révolutionnaire *mf*

revolve [rɪˈvalv] *tr* faire tourner; (*in one's mind*) retourner ‖ *intr* tourner

revolver [rɪˈvalvər] *s* revolver *m*

revolv′ing book′case *s* bibliothèque *f* tournante

revolv′ing door′ *s* porte *f* à tambour, tambour *m* cylindrique

revolv′ing fund′ *s* fonds *m* de roulement

revolv′ing stage′ *s* scène *f* tournante

revue [rɪˈvju] *s* (theat) revue *f*

revulsion [rɪˈvʌlʃən] *s* aversion *f*, répugnance *f*; (*change of feeling*) revirement *m*

reward [rɪˈwɔrd] *s* récompense *f* ‖ *tr* récompenser

rewarding [rɪˈwɔrdɪŋ] *adj* rémunérateur; (*experience*) enrichissant

re·wind [riˈwaɪnd] *v* (*pret* & *pp* **-wound**) *tr* (*film, tape, etc.*) renverser la marche de; (*a typewriter ribbon*) embobiner de nouveau; (*a clock*) remonter

rewire [riˈwaɪr] *tr* (*a building*) refaire l'installation électrique dans

re·write [riˈraɪt] *v* (*pret* **-wrote;** *pp* **-written**) *tr* récrire

rhapso·dy [ˈræpsədi] *s* (*pl* **-dies**) *s* rhapsodie *f*

rheostat [ˈri·əˌstæt] *s* rhéostat *m*

rhetoric [ˈrɛtərɪk] *s* rhétorique *f*

rhetorical [rɪˈtɔrɪkəl] *adj* rhétorique

rheumatic [ruˈmætɪk] *adj* rhumatismal; (*person*) rhumatisant ‖ *s* rhumatisant *m*

rheumatism [ˈruməˌtɪzəm] *s* rhumatisme *m*

Rhine [raɪn] *s* Rhin *m*

Rhineland [ˈraɪnˌlænd] *s* Rhénanie *f*

rhine′stone′ *s* faux diamant *m*

rhinoceros [raɪˈnɑsərəs] *s* rhinocéros *m*

rhubarb [ˈrubarb] *s* rhubarbe *f*

rhyme [raɪm] *s* rime *f*; **in rhyme** en vers ‖ *tr* & *intr* rimer

rhythm [ˈrɪðəm] *s* rythme *m*

rhythmic(al) [ˈrɪðmɪk(əl)] *adj* rythmique

rib [rɪb] *s* côte *f*; (*of umbrella*) baleine *f*; (*archit, biol, mach*) nervure *f* ‖ *v* (*pret* & *pp* **ribbed;** *ger* **ribbing**) *tr* garnir de nervures; (slang) taquiner

ribald [ˈrɪbəld] *adj* grivois

ribbon [ˈrɪbən] *s* ruban *m*

rice [raɪs] *s* riz *m*

rice′ field′ *s* rizière *f*

rice′ pud′ding *s* riz *m* au lait

rich [rɪtʃ] *adj* riche; (*voice*) sonore; (*wine*) généreux; (*funny*) impayable; (coll) ridicule; **to get rich** s'enrichir; **to strike it rich** trouver le bon filon ‖ **riches** *spl* richesses *fpl*

rickets [ˈrɪkɪts] *s* rachitisme *m*

rickety [ˈrɪkɪti] *adj* (*object*) boiteux, délabré; (*person*) chancelant: (*suffering from rickets*) rachitique

rickshaw [ˈrɪkˌʃɔ] *s* pousse-pousse *m*

rid [rɪd] *v* (*pret* & *pp* **rid;** *ger* **ridding**) *tr* débarrasser; **to get rid of** se débarrasser de, débarquer

riddance [ˈrɪdəns] *s* débarras *m*; **good riddance!** bon débarras!

riddle [ˈrɪdəl] *s* devinette *f*, énigme *f* ‖ *tr*—**to riddle with** cribler de

ride [raɪd] *s* promenade *f*; **to take a ride** faire une promenade (en auto, à cheval, à motocyclette, etc.); **to take s.o. for a**

ride (*to dupe s.o.*) (slang) faire marcher qn; (*to murder s.o.*) (slang) descendre qn ‖ *v* (*pret* **rode** [rod]; *pp* **ridden** [ˈrɪdən]) *tr* monter à; (coll) se moquer de; **ridden** dominé; **to ride out** (*e.g., a storm*) étaler ‖ *intr* monter à cheval (à bicyclette, etc.); **to let ride** (coll) laisser courir

rider [ˈraɪdər] *s* (*on horseback*) cavalier *m*; (*on a bicycle*) cycliste *mf*; (*in a vehicle*) voyageur *m*; (*to a document*) annexe *f*

ridge [rɪdʒ] *s* arête *f*, crête *f*; (*of a fabric*) grain *m*

ridge′pole′ *s* faîtage *m*

ridicule [ˈrɪdɪˌkjul] *s* ridicule *m* ‖ *tr* ridiculiser

ridiculous [rɪˈdɪkjələs] *adj* ridicule

rid′ing acad′emy *s* école *f* d'équitation

rid′ing boot′ *s* botte *f* de cheval, botte à l'écuyère

rid′ing hab′it *s* habit *m* d'amazone

rid′ing mow′er *s* tondeuse *f* auto-portée

rife [raɪf] *adj* répandu; **rife with** abondant en

riffraff [ˈrɪfˌræf] *s* racaille *f*

rifle [ˈraɪfəl] *s* fusil *m*; (*spiral groove*) rayure *f* ‖ *tr* piller, mettre à sac; (*a gun barrel*) rayer

rift [rɪft] *s* fente *f*, crevasse *f*; (*disagreement*) désaccord *m*

rig [rɪg] *s* équipement *m*; (*carriage*) équipage *m*; (naut) gréement *m*; (*getup*) (coll) accoutrement *m* ‖ *v* (*pret & pp* **rigged**; *ger* **rigging**) *tr* équiper; (*to falsify*) truquer; (naut) gréer; **to rig out with** (coll) accoutrer de

rigging [ˈrɪgɪŋ] *s* gréement *m*; (*fraud*) truquage *m*

right [raɪt] *adj* droit; (*change, time, etc.*) exact; (*statement, answer, etc.*) correct; (*conclusion, word, etc.*) juste; (*name*) vrai; (*moment, house, road, etc.*) bon, e.g., **it's not the right road** ce n'est pas la bonne route; qu'il faut, e.g., **it's not the right village** (**spot, boy,** etc.) ce n'est pas le village (endroit, garçon, etc.) qu'il faut; **to be all right** aller très bien; **to be right** avoir raison ‖ *s* (*justice*) droit *m*; (*reason*) raison *f*; (*right hand*) droite *f*; (*fist or blow in boxing*) droit; **all rights reserved** tous droits réservés; **by right of** à titre de; **by rights** de plein droit; **by the right!** (mil) guide à droite!; **on the right** à droite; **right and wrong** le bien et le mal; **rights** droits; **to be in the right** avoir raison ‖ *adv* directement; correctement; complément; bien, en bon état; (*to the right*) à droite; (coll) très, même, e.g., **right here** ici même; **all right!** d'accord!; **right and left** à droite et à gauche; **right away** tout de suite; **to put right** mettre bon ordre à, mettre en état ‖ *tr* faire droit à; (*to correct*) corriger; (*to set upright*) redresser ‖ *intr* se redresser ‖ *interj* parfait!

right′ about′ face′ *s* volte-face *f* ‖ *interj* (mil) demi-tour à droite!

righteous [ˈraɪtʃəs] *adj* juste; vertueux

right′ field′ *s* (baseball) champ *m* droit

rightful [ˈraɪtfəl] *adj* légitime

right′-hand drive′ *s* conduite *f* à droite

right-hander [ˈraɪtˈhændər] *s* droitier *m*

right′-hand man′ *s* bras *m* droit

rightist [ˈraɪtɪst] *adj & s* droitier *m*

rightly [ˈraɪtli] *adv* à bon droit, à juste titre; correctement, avec sagesse; **rightly or wrongly** à tort ou à raison

right′ of assem′bly *s* liberté *f* de réunion

right′ of way′ *s* droit *m* de passage; **to yield the right of way** céder le pas

rights′ of man′ *spl* droits *mpl* de l'homme

right′-to-lif′er *s* (coll) nataliste *mf*

right to work [ˈraɪtəˈwʌrk] *s* liberté *f* du travail des ouvriers non syndiqués

right′-wing *adj* de droite

right-winger [ˈraɪtˈwɪŋər] *s* (coll) droitier *m*

rigid [ˈrɪdʒɪd] *adj* rigide

rigmarole [ˈrɪgməˌrol] *s* galimatias *m*

rigor [ˈrɪgər] *s* rigueur *f*; (pathol) rigidité *f*

rigorous [ˈrɪgərəs] *adj* rigoureux

rile [raɪl] *tr* (coll) exaspérer

rill [rɪl] *s* ruisselet *m*

rim [rɪm] *s* bord *m*, rebord *m*; (*of spectacles*) monture *f*; (*of wheel*) jante *f*

rind [raɪnd] *s* écorce *f*; (*of cheese*) croûte *f*; (*of bacon*) couenne *f*

ring [rɪŋ] *s* anneau *m*; (*for the finger*) bague *f*, anneau *m*; (*for some sport or exhibition*) piste *f*; (*for boxing*) ring *m*; (*for bullfight*) arène *f*; (*of a group of people*) cercle *m*; (*of evildoers*) gang *m*; (*under the eyes*) cerne *m*; (*sound*) son *m*; (*of bell, clock, telephone, etc.*) sonnerie *f*; (*of a small bell; in the ears; of the glass of glassware*) tintement *m*; (*to summon a person*) coup *m* de sonnette; (*quality*) timbre *m*; (telp) coup de téléphone ‖ *v* (*pret & pp* **ringed**) *tr* cerner ‖ *intr* décrire des cercles ‖ *v* (*pret* **rang** [ræŋ]; *pp*; **rung** [rʌŋ]) *tr* sonner; **to ring up** (telp) donner un coup de téléphone à ‖ *intr* sonner; (*said, e.g., of ears*) tinter; **to ring out** résonner

ring′bolt′ *s* piton *m*

ring′dove′ *s* (orn) ramier *m*

ring′ fin′ger *s* annulaire *m*

ringing [ˈrɪŋɪŋ] *adj* résonnant, retentissant ‖ *s* sonnerie *f*; (*in the ears*) tintement *m*

ring′lead′er *s* meneur *m*

ringlet [ˈrɪŋlɪt] *s* bouclette *f*

ring′mas′ter *s* maître *m* de manège, chef *m* de piste

ring′side′ *s* premier rang *m*

ring′snake′ *s* (*Tropidonotus natrix*) couleuvre *f* à collier

ring′worm′ *s* teigne *f*

rink [rɪŋk] *s* patinoire *f*

rinse [rɪns] *s* rinçage *m* ‖ *tr* rincer

riot [ˈraɪət] *s* émeute *f*; (*of colors*) orgie *f*; **to run riot** se déchaîner; (*said of plants or vines*) pulluler ‖ *intr* émeuter

rioter [ˈraɪətər] *s* émeutier *m*

ri′ot squad′ *s* unité *f* antimanifestation

rip [rɪp] *s* déchirure *f* ‖ *v* (*pret & pp* **ripped**; *ger* **ripping**) *tr* déchirer; **to rip away or off** arracher; **to rip off** (slang) arnaquer, braquer; **to rip open** or **up** découdre; (*a letter, package, etc.*) ouvrir en le déchirant ‖ *intr* se déchirer

rip′ cord′ *s* (*of parachute*) cordelette *f* de déclenchement

ripe [raɪp] *adj* mûr; (*cheese*) fait; (*olive*) noir

ripen [′raɪpən] *tr* & *intr* mûrir

rip′off *s* (slang) arnaque *f*, vol *m* à main armée

ripple [′rɪpəl] *s* ride *f*; (*sound*) murmure *m* ‖ *tr* rider ‖ *intr* se rider; murmurer

rise [raɪz] *s* hausse *f*, augmentation *f*; (*of ground; of the voice*) élévation *f*; (*of a heavenly body; of the curtain*) lever *m*; (*in one's employment, in one's fortunes*) ascension *f*; (*of water*) montée *f*; (*of a source of water*) naissance *f*; **to get a rise out of** (slang) se payer la tête de; **give rise to** donner naissance à ‖ *v* (*pret* **rose** [roz]; *pp* **risen** [′rɪzən] *intr* s'élever, monter; (*to get out of bed; to stand up; to ascend in the heavens*) se lever; (*to revolt*) se soulever; (*said, e.g., of a danger*) se montrer; (*said of a fluid*) jaillir; (*in someone's esteem*) grandir; (*said of river*) prendre sa source; **to rise above** dépasser; (*unfortunate events, insults, etc.*) se montrer supérieur à; **to rise to** (*e.g., the occasion*) se montrer à la hauteur de

riser [′raɪzər] *s* (*of staircase*) contremarche *f*; (*of gas or water*) colonne montante; **to be a late riser** faire la grasse matinée; **to be an early riser** être matinal

risk [rɪsk] *s* risque *m* ‖ *tr* risquer

risk·y [′rɪski] *adj* (*comp* **-ier**; *super* **-iest**) dangereux, hasardeux, risqué

risqué [rɪs′ke] *adj* risqué, osé

rite [raɪt] *s* rite *m*; **last rites** derniers sacrements *mpl*

ritual [′rɪtʃu·əl] *adj* & *s* rituel *m*

ri·val [′raɪvəl] *adj* & *s* rival *m* ‖ *v* (*pret* & *pp* **-valed** or **-valled**; *ger* **-valing** or **-valling**) *tr* rivaliser avec

rival·ry [′raɪvəlri] *s* (*pl* **-ries**) rivalité *f*

river [′rɪvər] *adj* fluvial ‖ *s* fleuve *m*; (*tributary*) rivière *f*; (*stream*) cours *m* d'eau; **down the river** en aval; **up the river** en amont

riv′er bas′in *s* bassin *m* fluvial

riv′er·bed′ *s* lit *m* de rivière

riv′er·front′ *s* rive *f* d'un fleuve

riv′er·side′ *adj* riverain ‖ *s* rive *f*

rivet [′rɪvɪt] *s* rivet *m* ‖ *tr* river

riv′et gun′ *s* riveuse *f* pneumatique

rivulet [′rɪvjəlɪt] *s* ruisselet *m*

R.N. [′ɑr′ɛn] *s* (letterword) (**registered nurse**) infirmière *f* diplômée

roach [rotʃ] *s* (ent) blatte *f*, cafard *m*; (ichth) gardon *m*

road [rod] *s* route *f*, chemin *m*; (naut) rade *f*; **road under construction** (*public sign*) travaux

road′bed′ *s* assiette *f*; (rr) infrastructure *f*

road′block′ *s* barrage *m*

road′ divid′er *s* séparateur *m*

road′ hog′ *s* écraseur *m*, chauffard *m*

road′house′ *s* guinguette *f* au bord de la route

road′ map′ *s* carte *f* routière

road′-salt′ing truck′ *s* saleuse *f*

road′ ser′vice *s* secours *m* routier

road′side′ *s* bord *m* de la route

road′ sign′ *s* poteau *m* indicateur

road′stead′ *s* rade *f*

road′way′ *s* chaussée *f*

roam [rom] *tr* parcourir; (*the seas*) sillonner ‖ *intr* errer, rôder

roar [ror] *s* (*of a lion*) rugissement *m*; (*of cannon, engine, etc.*) grondement *m*; (*of crowd*) hurlement *m*; (*of laughter*) éclat *m* ‖ *intr* rugir; gronder; hurler

roast [rost] *s* rôti *m*; (*of coffee*) torréfaction *f* ‖ *tr* rôtir; (*coffee*) torréfier; (*chestnuts*) griller ‖ *intr* se rôtir; se torréfier

roast′ beef′ *s* rosbif *m*, rôti *m* de bœuf

roaster [′rostər] *s* (*appliance*) rôtissoire *f*; (*for coffee*) brûloir *m*; (*fowl*) volaille *f* à rôtir

roast′ pork′ *s* porc *m* rôti

rob [rɑb] *v* (*pret* & *pp* **robbed**; *ger* **robbing**) *tr* & *intr* voler; **to rob s.o. of s.th.** voler q.ch. à qn

robber [′rɑbər] *s* voleur *m*

robber·y [′rɑbəri] *s* (*pl* **-ies**) vol *m*

robe [rob] *s* (*of a judge*) robe *f*; (*of a professor, judge, etc.*) toge *f*; (*dressing gown*) robe *f* de chambre; (*for lap in a carriage*) couverture *f* ‖ *tr* revêtir d'une robe ‖ *intr* revêtir sa robe

robin [′rɑbɪn] *s* (*Erithacus rubecula*) rougegorge *m*; (*Turdus migratorius*) grive *f* migratoire

robot [′robɑt] *s* robot *m*

robotize [′robɑtaɪz] *tr* robotiser

robust [ro′bʌst] *adj* robuste

rock [rɑk] *s* roche *f*; (*eminence*) roc *m*, rocher *m*; (*sticking out of water*) rocher; (*one that is thrown*) pierre *f*; (slang) diamant *m*; **on the rocks** (coll) fauché, à sec; (*said of liquor*) (coll) sur glace ‖ *tr* balancer; (*to rock to sleep*) bercer ‖ *intr* se balancer; se bercer

rock′-bot′tom *adj* (le) plus bas ‖ *s* (le) fin fond *m*

rock′ can′dy *s* candi *m*

rock′ crys′tal *s* cristal *m* de roche

rocker [′rɑkər] *s* bascule *f*; (*chair*) chaise *f* à bascule; **to go off one's rocker** (slang) perdre la boussole

rock′er arm′ *s* culbuteur *m*

rocket [′rɑkɪt] *s* fusée *f*; (arti, bot) roquette *f* ‖ *intr* monter en chandelle; (*said of prices*) monter en flèche

rock′et bomb′ *s* bombe *f* volante, fusée *f*

rock′et fu′el *s* kérosène *m* aviation

rock′et launch′er *s* lance-fuses *m*; (arti) lance-roquettes *m*

rock′et ship′ *s* fusée *f* interplanétaire, fusée interstellaire

rock′ gar′den *s* jardin *m* de rocaille

rock′ing chair′ *s* fauteuil *m* à bascule

rock′ing horse′ *s* cheval *m* à bascule

Rock′ of Gibral′tar [dʒɪ'brɔltər] *s* rocher *m* de Gibraltar

rock′ salt′ *s* sel *m* gemme

rock′ sing′er *s* chanteur *m* de rock

rock′ wool′ *s* laine *f* minérale, laine de verre

rock·y ['rɑki] *adj* (*comp* **-ier;** *super* **-iest**) rocheux, rocailleux

Rock′y Moun′tains *spl* Montagnes *fpl* Rocheuses

rod [rɑd] *s* (*wooden stick*) baguette *f*; (*for punishment*) verge *f*; (*of the retina; elongated microorganism*) bâtonnet *m*; (*of authority*) main *f*; (*of curtain*) tringle *f*; (*for fishing*) canne *f*; (Bib) lignée *f*, race *f*; (mach) bielle *f*; (surv) jalon *m*; (*revolver*) (slang) pétard *m*, flingot *m*, flingue *m*; **rod and gun** la chasse et la pêche

rodent ['rodənt] *adj* & *s* rongeur *m*

roe [ro] *s* (*deer*) chevreuil *m*; (*of fish*) œufs *mpl*

roger ['rɑdʒər] *interj* O.K.!; (rad) message reçu!

rogue [rog] *s* coquin *m*

rogues′′ gal′lery *s* fichier *m* de la police de portraits de criminels

roguish ['rogɪʃ] *adj* espiègle, coquin

roister ['rɔɪstər] *intr* faire du tapage

role or **rôle** [rol] *s* rôle *m*

roll [rol] *s* (*of paper, cloth, netting, wire, hair, etc.*) rouleau *m*; (*of thunder, drums, etc.*) roulement *m*; (*roll call*) appel *m*; (*list*) rôle *m*; (*of film*) rouleau; (*of paper money*) liasse *f*; (*of dice*) coup *m*; (*of a boat*) roulis *m*; (*of fat*) bourrelet *m*; (culin) petit pain *m*; **to call the roll** faire l'appel ‖ *tr* rouler; (*to rob*) (slang) entôler; **to roll over** retourner; **to roll up** enrouler ‖ *intr* rouler; (*said of thunder*) gronder; (*to sway*) se balancer; (*to overturn*) faire panache; (*said of ship*) rouler; **to roll over** se retourner; **to roll up** se rouler

roll′back′ *s* repoussement *m*; (com) baisse *f* de prix

roll′ call′ *s* appel *m*; (*vote*) appel nominal

roller ['rolər] *s* rouleau *m*; (*of a skate*) roulette *f*; (*wave*) lame *f* de houle

roll′er bear′ing *s* coussinet *m* à rouleaux

roll′er coast′er *s* montagnes *fpl* russes

roll′er skate′ *s* patin *m* à roulettes

roll′er-skate′ *intr* patiner sur des roulettes

roll′er-skating rink′ *s* skating *m*

roll′er tow′el *s* essuie-mains *m* à rouleau, serviette *f* sans fin

roll′ing mill′ *s* usine *f* de laminage; (*set of rollers*) laminoir *m*

roll′ing pin′ *s* rouleau *m*

roll′ing stock′ *s* (rr) matériel *m* roulant

roll′-top desk′ *s* bureau *m* à cylindre

roly-poly ['roli'poli] *adj* rondelet

ROM ['ɑr'o'ɛm] *s* (letterword) (**read-only memory**) mémoire *f* morte

romaine [ro'men] *s* romaine *f*

roman ['romən] *adj* & *s* (typ) romain *m*; **Roman** Romain *m*

Ro′man can′dle *s* chandelle *f* romaine

Ro′man Cath′olic *adj* & *s* catholique *mf*

Romance ['romæns], [ro'mæns] *adj* roman ‖ (*l.c.*) [ro'mæns], ['romæns] *s* (*chivalric narrative*) roman *m* de chevalerie; (*love story*) roman à l'eau de rose; (*made-up story*) conte *m* bleu; (*love affair*) idylle *f*; (mus) romance *f* ‖ (*l.c.*) [ro'mæns] *intr* exagérer, broder

Romanesque [,romən'ɛsk] *adj* & *s* roman *m*

Ro′man nose′ *s* nez *m* aguilin

Ro′man nu′meral *s* chiffre *m* romain

romantic [ro'mæntɪk] *adj* (*genre; literature; scenery*) romantique; (*imagination*) romanesque

romanticism [ro'mæntɪ,sɪzəm] *s* romantisme *m*

romanticist [ro'mæntɪsɪst] *s* romantique *mf*

romp [rɑmp] *intr* s'ébattre

rompers ['rɑmpərz] *spl* barboteuse *f*

roof [ruf] *s* toit *m*; (*of the mouth*) palais *m*; **to raise the roof** (slang) faire un boucan de tous les diables

roofer ['rufər] *s* couvreur *m*

roof′ gar′den *s* terrasse *f* avec jardin, pergola *f*

rook [ruk] *s* (chess) tour *f*; (orn) freux *m*, corneille *f* ‖ *tr* (coll) rouler; **to rook s.o. out of s.th.** (coll) filouter q.ch. à qn

rookie ['ruki] *s* (slang) bleu *m*

room [rum], [rʊm] *s* pièce *f*; (*especially bedroom*) chambre *f*; (*where people congregate*) salle *f*; (*space*) place *f*; **rooms** appartement *m*; **to make room for** faire place à ‖ *intr* vivre en garni; **to room with** partager une chambre avec

room′ and board′ *s* le vivre et le couvert, pension *f*; **for room and board** au pair

room′ clerk′ *s* employé *m* à la réception

roomer ['rumər] *s* locataire *mf*

roomette [ru'mɛt] *s* chambrette *f* de sleeping

room′ing house′ *s* maison *f* de rapport, immeuble *m* de rapport

room′mate′ *s* camarade *mf* de chambre

room·y ['rumi] *adj* (*comp* **-ier;** *super* **-iest**) spacieux, ample; (*clothes*) large, ample

roost [rust] *s* perchoir *m*; (coll) logis *m*, demeure *f*; **to rule the roost** (coll) faire la loi ‖ *intr* se percher, percher

rooster ['rustər] *s* coq *m*

root [rut] *s* racine *f*; **to get to the root of** approfondir; **to take root** prendre racine ‖ *tr* fouiller; **to root out** déraciner ‖ *intr* s'enraciner; **to root around in** fouiller dans; **to root for** (coll) applaudir, encourager

rooter ['rutər] *s* (coll) fanatique *mf*, fana *mf*

rope [rop] *s* corde *f*; (*lasso*) corde à nœud coulant; **to jump rope** sauter à la corde; **to know the ropes** (slang) connaître les ficelles ‖ *tr* corder; (*cattle*) prendre au lasso; **to rope in** (slang) entraîner

rope′ lad′der *s* échelle *f* de corde

rope′ walk′er *s* funambule *mf*, danseur *m* de corde

rosa·ry ['rozəri] *s* (*pl* **-ries**) rosaire *m*

rose [roz] *adj* rose ‖ *s* (*color*) rose *m*; (bot) rose *f*

rose′ bee′tle s cétoine f dorée

rose′bud′ s bouton m de rose

rose′bush′ s rosier m

rose′-col′ored adj rosé, couleur de rose; **to see everything through rose-colored glasses** voir tout en rose

rose′ gar′den s roseraie f

rosemar·y [`roz,mɛri] s (pl **-ies**) romarin m

rose′ of Shar′on [`ʃɛrən] s rose f de Saron

rosette [ro`zɛt] s rosette f; (archit, elec) rosace f

rose′ win′dow s rosace f, rose f

rose′wood′ s bois m de rose, palissandre m

rosin [`razɪn] s colophane f

roster [`rɑstər] s liste f, appel m; (educ) heures fpl de classe; (mil) tableau m de service; (naut) ôle m

rostrum [`rɑstrəm] s tribune f

ros·y [`rozi] adj (comp **-ier**; super **-iest**) rosé; (complexion) vermeil; (fig) riant

rot [rɑt] s pourriture f; (slang) sottise f ‖ v (pret & pp **rotted**; ger **rotting**) tr & intr pourrir

ro′tary press′ [`rotəri] s rotative f

rotate [`rotet] tr & intr tourner; (agr) alterner

rotation [ro`teʃən] s rotation f; **in rotation** à tour de rôle

rote [rot] s routine f; **by rote** par cœur, machinalement

rot′gut′ s (slang) tord-boyaux m

rotisserie [ro`tɪsəri] s rôtissoire f

rotogravure [,rotəgrə`vjʊr] s rotogravure f

rotten [`rɑtən] adj pourri

rotund [ro`tʌnd] adj rond, arrondi; (e.g., language) ampoulé

rotunda [ro`tʌndə] s rotonde f

rouge [ruʒ] s fard m, rouge m ‖ tr farder ‖ intr se farder, se mettre du rouge

rough [rʌf] adj (sound, voice, speech) rude; (uneven) inégal; (coarse) grossier; (unfinished) brut; (road) raboteux; (game) brutal; (sea) agité; (guess) approximatif ‖ tr—**to rough it** faire du camping, coucher sur la dure; **to rough up** malmener

roughage [`rʌfɪdʒ] s fibres fpl alimentaires

rough′ draft′ s ébauche f, avant-projet m, brouillon m

rough′house′ s boucan m, chahut m ‖ intr faire du boucan, chahuter

rough′ ide′a s aperçu m

roughly [`rʌfli] adv grossièrement; brutalement; approximativement

rough′neck′ s (coll) canaille f

roulette [ru`lɛt] s roulette f

round [raund] adj rond; (rounded) arrondi, rond; (e.g., shoulders) voûté; **three (four, etc.) feet round** trois (quatre, etc.) pieds de tour ‖ s rond m; (inspection) ronde f; (of golf; of drinks; of postman, doctor, etc.) tournée f; (of applause) salve f; (of ammunition) cartouche f; (of veal) noix f; (in a game) manche f; (boxing) round m; **to go the rounds** faire le tour ‖ adv à la ronde; **round about** aux alentours; **the year round** pendant toute l'année; **to pass round** faire circuler, passer à la

ronde ‖ prep autour de ‖ tr (to make round) arrondir; (e.g., a corner) tourner, prendre; (a cape) doubler; **to round off** or **out** arrondir; (to finish) achever; **to round up** rassembler; (suspects) cueillir ‖ intr s'arrondir

roundabout [`raundə,baut] adj indirect ‖ s détour m; (carrousel) (Brit) manège m; (traffic circle) (Brit) rond-point m

rounder [`raundər] s (coll) fêtard m

round′-headed screw′ s vis f à tête ronde

round′house′ s (rr) rotonde f

round′-shoul′dered adj voûté

round′ steak′ s gîte m à la noix

round′ ta′ble s table f ronde; **Round Table** Table ronde

round′-trip′ tick′et s billet m d'aller et retour

round′up′ s (of cattle) rassemblement m; (of suspects) rafle f

rouse [rauz] tr réveiller ‖ intr se réveiller

rout [raut] s déroute f ‖ tr mettre en déroute

route [rut] s route f; (of, e.g., bus) ligne f, parcours m ‖ tr acheminer

routine [ru`tin] adj routinier, systématique ‖ s routine f

routine′ examina′tion s examen m de routine

rove [rov] intr errer, vagabonder

rover [`rovər] s vagabond m

row [rau] s (coll) altercation f, prise f de bec; **to raise a row** (coll) faire du boucan ‖ [ro] s rang m; (of, e.g., houses) rangée f; (boat ride) promenade f en barque; **in a row** à la file; (without interruption) de suite; **in rows** par rangs ‖ intr ramer

rowboat [`ro,bot] s bateau m à rames, canot m

row·dy [`raudi] adj (comp **-dier**; super **-diest**) tapageur ‖ s (pl **-dies**) tapageur m

rower [`roər] s rameur m

rowing [`ro·ɪŋ] s nage f, canotage m, sport m de l'aviron

royal [`rɔɪ·əl] adj royal

royalist [`rɔɪ·əlɪst] adj & s royaliste mf

royal·ty [`rɔɪ·əlti] s (pl **-ties**) royauté f; (remuneration) droit m d'auteur; redevance f, droit d'inventeur

r.p.m. [`ar`pi`ɛm] spl (letterword) (**revolutions per minute**) tr/mn, tours mpl à la minute

rub [rʌb] s frottement m; **there's the rub** (coll) voilà le hic ‖ v (pret & pp **rubbed**; ger **rubbing**) tr frotter; **to rub elbows with** coudoyer; **to rub out** effacer; (slang) descendre, liquider ‖ intr se frotter; (said, e.g., of moving parts) frotter; **to rub off** s'enlever, disparaître

rubber [`rʌbər] s caoutchouc m; (eraser) gomme f à effacer; (in bridge) robre m; (condom) préservatif m; **rubbers** (overshoes) caoutchoucs

rub′ber band′ s bande f élastique

rub′ber band′ s élastique m

rubberize [`rʌbə,raɪz] tr caoutchouter

rub′ber·neck′ s (coll) badaud m ‖ intr (coll) badauder

rub′ber plant′ s figuier m élastique, caoutchoutier m; (*tree*) arbre m à caoutchouc, hévéa m

rub′ber stamp′ s tampon m; (coll) béni-oui-oui m

rub′ber-stamp′ tr apposer le tampon sur; (*with a person's signature*) estampiller; (coll) approuver à tort et à travers

rub′bing al′cohol s alcool m pour les frictions

rubbish [ˈrʌbɪʃ] s détritus m, rebut m; (coll) imbécillités fpl

rubble [ˈrʌbəl] s (*broken stone*) décombres mpl; (*used in masonry*) moellons mpl

rub′down′ s friction f

rubric [ˈrubrɪk] s rubrique f

ru·by [ˈrubi] adj (*lips*) vermeil ‖ s (pl -bies) rubis m

rucksack [ˈrʌk,sæk] s sac-à-dos m

rudder [ˈrʌdər] s gouvernail m

rud·dy [ˈrʌdi] adj (comp -dier; super -diest) rougeaud, coloré

rude [rud] adj (*rough, rugged*) rude; (*discourteous*) impoli, grossier

rudeness [ˈrudnɪs] s rudesse f; impolitesse f

rudiment [ˈrudɪmənt] s rudiment m

rue [ru] tr regretter amèrement

rueful [ˈrufəl] adj lamentable; triste

ruffian [ˈrʌfɪən] s brute f

ruffle [ˈrʌfəl] s (*in water*) rides fpl; (*of drum*) roulement m; (sewing) jabot m plissé ‖ tr (*to tousle; to vex*) froisser; (*the water*) rider; (*its feathers*) hérisser; (*one's hair*) ébouriffer

rug [rʌg] s tapis m, carpette f

rugged [ˈrʌgɪd] adj (*manners, person, features*) rude, sévère; (*ground, landscape*) accidenté; (*coast*) déchiqueté; (*road, country, etc.*) raboteux; (*husky*) robuste; (*e.g., machine*) résistant à toute épreuve

ruin [ˈru·ɪn] s ruine f; **to fall into ruins** se ruiner ‖ tr ruiner

rule [rul] s règle f; (*regulation*) règlement m; (*custom*) coutume f, habitude f; (*authority*) autorité f; (*reign*) règne m; (law) décision f; **as a rule** en général; **by rule of thumb** empiriquement, à vue de nez ‖ tr gouverner; (*to lead*) diriger, guider; (*one's passions*) contenir; (*with lines*) régler; (law) décider; **to rule out** écarter, éliminer ‖ intr gouverner; (*to be the rule*) prévaloir; **to rule over** régner sur

ruler [ˈrulər] s dirigeant m; sourverain m; (*for ruling lines*) règle f

ruling [ˈrulɪŋ] adj actuel; (*e.g., classes*) dirigeant; (*quality, trait, etc.*) dominant ‖ s (*of paper*) réglage m; (law) décision f

rum [rʌm] s rhum m

Rumanian [ruˈmenɪ·ən] adj roumain ‖ s (*language*) roumain m; (*person*) Roumain m

rumble [ˈrʌmbəl] s (*of thunder*) grondement m; (*of a cart*) roulement m; (*of intestines*) gargouillement m; (*gang war*) (slang) baroud m, rixe f entre gangs ‖ intr gronder, rouler

ruminate [ˈrumɪ,net] tr & intr ruminer

rummage [ˈrʌmɪdʒ] intr fouiller

rum′mage sale′ s vente f d'objets usagés

rumor [ˈrumər] s rumeur f ‖ tr—**it is rumored that** le bruit court que

rump [rʌmp] s (*of animal*) croupe f; (*of bird*) croupion m; (*cut of meat*) culotte f; (*buttocks*) postérieur m

rumple [ˈrʌmpəl] s faux pli m ‖ tr (*paper, cloth, etc.*) froisser, chiffonner; (*one's hair*) ébouriffer

rump′ steak′ s romsteck m

rumpus [ˈrʌmpəs] s (coll) chalut m; (*argument*) (coll) prise f de bec; **to raise a rumpus** (coll) déclencher un chahut; faire une scène violente

rum′pus room′ s salle f de jeux

run [rʌn] s (*act of running*) course f; (*e.g., of good or bad luck*) suite f; (*on a bank by depositors*) descente f; (*of salmon*) remonte f; (*of, e.g., a bus*) parcours m; (*in a stocking*) échelle f, démaillage m; (cards) séquence f; (mus) roulade f; **in the long run** à la longue; **on the run** à la débandade, en fuite; **run of bad luck** série f noire; **the general run** la généralité; **to give free run to** donner libre carrière à; **to give s.o. a run for his money** en donner à qn pour son argent; **to have a long run** (theat) tenir longtemps l'affiche; **to have the run of** avoir libre accès à or dans; **to keep s.o. on the run** ne laisser aucun répit à qn; **to make a run in** (a stocking) démailler ‖ v (pret **ran** [ræn]; pp **run**; ger **running**) tr (*the streets; a race; a risk*) courir; (*a motor, machine, etc.*) faire marcher; (*an organization, project, etc.*) diriger; (*a business, factory, etc.*) exploiter; (*a blockade*) forcer; (*a line*) tracer; (turf) faire courir; **to run aground** échouer; **to run down** (*to knock down*) renverser; (*to find*) dépister; (*game*) mettre aux abois; (*to disparage*) (coll) dénigrer; **to run in** (*a motor*) roder; **to run off** (*a liquid*) faire écouler; (*copies, pages, etc.*) tirer; **to run through** (*e.g., with a sword*) transpercer; **to run up** (*a flag*) hisser; (*a debt*) (coll) laisser accumuler ‖ intr courir; (*said, e.g., of water; said of fountain pen, nose, etc.*) couler; (*said of stockings*) se démailler; (*said of salmon*) faire la montaison; (*said of colors*) s'étaler, se déteindre; (*said of sore*) suppurer; (*said of rumor, news, etc.*) circuler, courir; (*for office*) se présenter; (mach) fonctionner, marcher; (theat) rester à l'affiche, se jouer; **run along!** filez!; **to run across** (*to meet by chance*) rencontrer par hasard; **to run along** border, longer; (*to go*) s'en aller; **to run at** se jeter sur; **to run away** se sauver, s'enfuir; (*said of horse*) s'emballer, s'emporter; **to run away with** enlever; **to run down** (*e.g., a hill*) descendre en courant; (*said of spring*) se détendre; (*said of watch*) s'arrêter (faute d'être remonté); (*said of storage battery*) se décharger, s'épuiser; **to run for** (*an office*) poser sa candidature pour; **to run in the family** tenir de famille; **to run into** heurter; (*to meet*) (coll) rencontrer; **to run off** se sauver, s'enfuir; (*said of liquid*) s'écouler; **to run out** (*said of passport, lease, etc.*) expirer; **to run out of** être à court de; **to run over** (*said of a liquid*) déborder; (*an article, a text, etc.*) parcourir; (*s.th. in the road*) passer sur; (*e.g., a pedestrian*) écraser; **to run through** (*an article, text, etc.*) parcourir; (*a fortune*) gaspiller

run′away′ *adj* fugitif; (*horse*) emballé ‖ *s* fugitif *m*; cheval *m* emballé

run′down′ *s* compte rendu *m*, récit *m*

run′-down′ *adj* délabré; (*person; battery*) épuisé, à plat; (*clock spring*) détendu

rung [rʌŋ] *s* (*of ladder or chair*) barreau *m*; (*of wheel*) rayon *m*

runner [′rʌnər] *s* (*person*) coureur *m*; (*messenger*) courrier *m*; (*of ice skate or sleigh*) patin *m*; (*narrow rug*) rampe *f* d'escalier; (*strip of cloth for table top*) chemin *m* de table; (*in stockings*) démaillage *m*; (bot) coulant *m*

run′ner-up′ *s* (*pl* **runners-up**) bon second *m*, premier accessit *m*

running [′rʌnɪŋ] *adj* (*person; water; expenses*) courant; (*stream; knot; style*) coulant; (*sore*) suppurant; (*e.g., motor*) en marche ‖ *s* (*of man or animal*) course *f*; (*of water*) écoulement *m*; (*of machine*) fonctionnement *m*, marche *f*; (*of business*) direction *f*

run′ning board′ *s* marchepied *m*

run′ning com′mentar′y *s* (*pl* **-ies**) (rad, telv) reportage *m* en direct

run′ning head′ *s* titre *m* courant

run′ning mate′ *s* (pol) coéquipier *m*, colistier *m*

run′ning start′ *s* départ *m* lancé

run′off′ elec′tion *s* scrutin *m* de ballottage

run′proof′ *adj* indémaillable

runt [rʌnt] *s* avorton *m*

run′way′ *s* piste *f*, rampe *f*

rupture [′rʌptʃər] *s* rupture *f*; (pathol) hernie *f* ‖ *tr* rompre; (*a ligament, blood vessel, etc.*) se rompre ‖ *intr* se rompre

rural [′rʊrəl] *adj* rural

ru′ral free′ deliv′ery *s* distribution *f* gratuite par le facteur rural

ru′ral police′man *s* garde *m* champêtre

ruse [ruz] *s* ruse *f*

rush [rʌʃ] *adj* urgent ‖ *s* (*rapid movement*) course *f* précipitée, ruée *f*; (*haste*) hâte *f*, précipitation *f*; (bot) jonc *m*; (*formula on envelope or letterhead*) urgent; **rushes** (mov) épreuves *fpl;* **to be in a rush to** être pressé de ‖ *tr* pousser vivement; (*e.g., to the hospital*) transporter d'urgence; (*a piece of work*) exécuter d'urgence; (*e.g., a girl*) (slang) insister auprès de; **to rush through** (*e.g., a law*) faire passer à la hâte ‖ *intr* se précipiter, se ruer; **to rush about** courir çà et là; **to rush headlong** foncer tête baissée; **to rush into** (*e.g., a room*) faire irruption dans; (*an affair*) se jeter dans; **to rush out** sortir précipitamment; **to rush through** (*one's lessons, prayers, etc.*) expédier; (*e.g., a town*) traverser à toute vitesse; (*a tourist attraction*) visiter au pas de course; (*a book*) lire à la hâte; **to rush to** s'empresser de; **to rush to one's face** (*said of blood*) monter au visage à qn; **to rush up to** accourir à *or* vers

rush′-bot′tomed chair′ *s* chaise *f* à fond de paille

rush′ hours′ *spl* heures *fpl* d'affluence or de pointe

rush′ or′der *s* commande *f* urgente

russet [′rʌsɪt] *adj* roussâtre, roux

Russia [′rʌʃə] *s* Russie *f*; la Russie

Russian [′rʌʃən] *adj* russe ‖ *s* (*language*) russe *m*; (*person*) Russe *mf*

rust [rʌst] *s* rouille *f* ‖ *tr* rouiller ‖ *intr* se rouiller

rustic [′rʌstɪk] *adj* rustique; simple, net; (pej) rustaud ‖ *s* paysan *m*, villageois *m*

rustle [′rʌsəl] *s* (*of leaves*) bruissement *m*; (*of a dress*) froufrou *m*, bruissement; (*of papers*) froissement *m* ‖ *tr* faire bruire; (*cattle*) (coll) voler ‖ *intr* bruire; (*said, e.g., of a dress*) froufrouter; **to rustle around** (coll) se démener

rust′proof′ *adj* inoxydable

rust·y [′rʌsti] *adj* (*comp* **-ier**; *super* **-iest**) rouillé

rut [rʌt] *s* ornière *f*; (zool) rut *m*

ruthless [′ruθlɪs] *adj* impitoyable

rye [raɪ] *s* seigle *m*; whisky *m* de seigle

S

S, s [ɛs] *s* XIVᵉ lettre de l'alphabet

Sabbath [′sæbəθ] *s* sabbat *m;* dimanche *m*

sabbat′ical year′ [sə′bætɪkəl] *s* année *f* de congé

saber [′sebər] *s* sabre *m* ‖ *tr* sabrer

sable [′sebəl] *adj* noir ‖ *s* (*animal, fur*) zibeline *f*; noir *m*; **sables** vêtements *mpl* de deuil

sabotage [′sæbə,taʒ] *s* sabotage *m* ‖ *tr* & *intr* saboter

saccharin [′sækərɪn] *s* saccharine *f*

sachet [sæ′ʃe] *s* sachet *m* (à parfums)

sack [sæk] *s* sac *m*; (*wine*) xérès *m* ‖ *tr* mettre en sac; (mil) saccager; (coll) saquer, congédier

sack′cloth′ *s* grosse toile *f* d'emballage,

serpillière *f*; (*worn for penitence*) cilice *m*; **in sackcloth and ashes** sous le sac et la cendre

sacrament ['sækrəmənt] *s* sacrement *m*

sacramental [,sækrə'mɛntəl] *adj* sacramentel

sacred ['sekrəd] *adj* sacré

sa′cred cow′ *s* (fig) monstre *m* sacré

sacrifice ['sækrɪ,faɪs] *s* sacrifice *m*; **at a sacrifice** à perte ‖ *tr & intr* sacrifier

sacrilege ['sækrəlɪdʒ] *s* sacrilège *m*

sacrilegious [,sækrɪ'lɪdʒəs] *adj* sacrilège

sacristan ['sækrɪstən] *s* sacristain *m*

sad [sæd] *adj* (*comp* **sadder**; *super* **saddest**) triste

sadden ['sædən] *tr* attrister ‖ *intr* s'attrister

saddle ['sædəl] *s* selle *f* ‖ *tr* seller; **to saddle with** charger de, encombrer de

sad′dle·bag′ *s* sacoche *f* (de selle)

saddlebow ['sædəl,bo] *s* arçon *m* de devant

saddler ['sædlər] *s* sellier *m*

sad′dle·tree′ *s* arçon *m*

sadist ['sedɪst] *s* sadique *mf*

sadistic [sæ'dɪstɪk] *adj* sadique

sadness ['sædnɪs] *s* tristesse *f*

sad′ sack′ *s* (slang) bidasse *mf*

safe [sef] *adj* (*from danger*) sûr; (*unhurt*) sauf; (*margin*) certain; **safe and sound** sain et sauf; **safe from** à l'abri de ‖ *s* coffre-fort *m*, caisse *f*

safe′-con′duct *s* sauf-conduit *m*

safe′-depos′it box′ *s* coffre *m* à la banque; coffret de sûreté (Canad)

safe′guard′ *s* sauvegarde *f* ‖ *tr* sauvegarder

safe′keep′ing *s* bonne garde *f*

safe·ty ['sefti] *adj* de sûreté ‖ *s* (*pl* **-ties**) (*state of being safe*) sécurité *f*, sûreté *f*; (*avoidance of danger*) salut *m*

safe′ty belt′ *s* ceinture *f* de sécurité

safe′ty fac′tor *s* (aer) coefficient *m* de sécurité

safe′ty match′ *s* allumette *f* de sûreté

safe′ty pin′ *s* épingle *f* de sûreté

saf′ty ra′zor *s* rasoir *m* de sûreté

safe′ty valve′ *s* soupape *f* de sûreté

safe′ty zone′ *s* zone *f* protégée pour piétons

saffron ['sæfrən] *adj* safrane ‖ *s* safran *m*

sag [sæg] *s* affaissement *m* ‖ *v* (*pret & pp* **sagged**; *ger* **sagging**) *intr* s'affaisser

sagacious [sə'geʃəs] *adj* sagace

sage [sedʒ] *adj* sage ‖ *s* sage *mf*; (*plant*) sauge *f*

sage′brush′ *s* armoise *f*

Sagittarius [,sædʒɪ'tɛrɪ·əs] *s* (astr, astrol) le Sagittaire

sail [sel] *s* voile *f*; (*sails*) voilure *f*; (*of windmill*) aile *f*; **full sail** toutes voiles dehors; **to set sail** mettre les voiles; **to take a sail** faire une promenade à la voile; **to take in sail** baisser pavillon ‖ *tr* (*a ship*) gouverner, commander; (*to travel over*) naviguer sur ‖ *intr* naviguer; **to sail along the coast** côtoyer; **to sail into** (coll) assaillir

sail′boat′ *s* bateau *m* à voiles

sail′cloth′ *s* toile *f* à voile

sailing ['selɪŋ] *s* navigation *f*; (*working of ship*) manœuvre *f*; (*of pleasure craft*) voile *f*

sail′ing ves′sel *s* voilier *m*

sail′mak′er *s* voilier *m*

sailor ['selər] *s* marin *m*; (*simple crewman*) matelot *m*

saint [sent] *adj & s* saint *m*

saint′hood *s* sainteté *f*

saintliness ['sentlɪnɪs] *s* sainteté *f*

Saint′ Vi′tus's dance′ ['vaɪtəsəz] *s* (pathol) danse *f* de Saint-Guy

sake [sek] *s*—**for the sake of** pour l'amour de, dans l'intérêt de; **for your sake** pour vous

salable ['seləbəl] *adj* vendable

salacious [sə'leʃəs] *adj* lubrique

salad ['sæləd] *s* salade *f*

sal′ad bar′ *s* buffet *m* de salades, table *f* à salade

sal′ad bowl′ *s* saladier *m*

sala·ry ['sæləri] *s* (*pl* **-ries**) salaire *m*

sale [sel] *s* vente *f*; **for sale** en vente; **on sale** en solde, en réclame

sales′ clerk′ *s* vendeur *m*

sales′la′dy *s* (*pl* **-dies**) vendeuse *f*, demoiselle *f* de magasin

sales′man *s* (*pl* **-men**) vendeur *m*, commis *m*

sales′man·ship′ *s* l'art *m* de vendre

sales′ promo′tion *s* stimulation *f* de la vente

sales′room′ *s* salle *f* de vente

sales′ talk′ *s* raisonnements *mpl* destinés à convaincre le client

sales′ tax′ *s* taxe *f* sur les ventes, impôt *m* indirect

saliva [sə'laɪvə] *s* salive *f*

sallow ['sælo] *adj* olivâtre

sal·ly ['sæli] *s* (*pl* **-lies**) saillie *f*; (mil) sortie *f* ‖ *v* (*pret & pp* **-lied**) *intr* faire une sortie

salmon ['sæmən] *adj & s* saumon *m*

salm′on trout′ *s* truite *f* saumonée

saloon [sə'lun] *s* cabaret *m*, estaminet *m*, bistrot *m*; (naut) salon *m*

salt [sɔlt] *s* sel *m* ‖ *tr* saler; **to salt away** (coll) économiser, mettre de côté

salt′cel′lar *s* salière *f*

salt′ lick′ *s* terrain *m* salifère

salt′pe′ter *s* (*potassium nitrate*) salpêtre *m*; (*sodium nitrate*) nitrate *m* du Chili

salt′ pork′ *s* salé *m*

salt′sha′ker *s* salière *f*

salt·y ['sɔlti] *adj* (*comp* **-ier**; *super* **-iest**) salé

salute [sə'lut] *s* salut *m* ‖ *tr* saluer

salvage ['sælvɪdʒ] *s* sauvetage *m*; biens *mpl* sauvés ‖ *tr* sauver; récupérer

salvation [sæl'veʃən] *s* salut *m*

Salva′tion Ar′my *s* Armée *f* du Salut

salve [sæv] *s* onguent *m*, pommade *f*; (fig) baume *m* ‖ *tr* appliquer un onguent sur; (fig) apaiser

sal·vo ['sælvo] *s* (*pl* **-vos** or **-voes**) salve *f*

Samaritan [sə'mærɪtən] *adj* samaritain ‖ *s* Samaritain *m*

same [sem] *adj & pron indef* même (before noun); **at the same time** en même temps, au même moment, à la fois; **it's all the**

same to me ça m'est égal; **just the same, all the same** malgré tout, quand même; **the same . . . as** le même . . . que

sameness ['semnɪs] s monotonie f

sample ['sæmpəl] s échantillon m ‖ tr échantillonner; essayer

sam'ple cop'y s (pl **-ies**) numéro m spécimen, spécimen m

sam'ple home' s villa f modèle, maison f exposition, pavillon m témoin

sancti·fy ['sæŋktɪ,faɪ] v (pret & pp **-fied**) tr sanctifier

sanctimonious [,sæŋktɪ'monɪ·əs] adj papelard, bigot

sanction ['sæŋkʃən] s sanction f ‖ tr sanctionner

sanctuar·y ['sæŋktʃu,ɛri] s (pl **-ies**) sanctuaire m; refuge m, asile m

sand [sænd] s sable m ‖ tr sablonner

sandal ['sændəl] s sandale f

san'dal·wood' s santal m

sand'bag' s sac m de sable

sand'bar' s banc m de sable

sand'blast' s jet m de sable; (apparatus) sableuse f ‖ tr sabler

sand'box' s (rr) sablière f

sander ['sændər] s (mach) ponceuse f

sand'glass' s sablier m

sand'pa'per s papier m de verre ‖ tr polir au papier de verre

sand'pi'per s bécasseau m

sand'stone' s grès m

sand'storm' s tempête f de sable

sandwich ['sændwɪtʃ] s sandwich m ‖ tr intercaler

sand'wich man' s homme-affiche m

sand·y ['sændi] adj (comp **-ier**; super **-iest**) sablonneux; (hair) blond roux

sane [sen] adj sain, équilibré; (principles) raisonnable

sanguine ['sæŋgwɪn] adj confiant, optimiste; (countenance) sanguin

sanitary ['sænɪ,tɛri] adj sanitaire

san'itary nap'kin s serviette f hygiénique

sanitation [,sænɪ'teʃən] s hygiène f, salubrité f; (drainage) assainissement m

sanity ['sænɪti] s santé f mentale; bon sens m

Santa Claus ['sæntə,klɔz] s le père Noël

sap [sæp] s sève f; (mil) sape f; (coll) poire f, nigaud m ‖ v (pret & pp **sapped**; ger **sapping**) tr tirer la sève de; (to weaken) affaiblir; (mil) saper

sapling ['sæplɪŋ] s jeune arbre m; jeune homme m

sapphire ['sæfaɪr] s saphir m

Saracen ['særəsən] adj sarrasin ‖ s Sarrasin m

sarcasm ['sɑrkæzəm] s sarcasme m

sardine [sɑr'din] s sardine f; **packed in like sardines** serrés comme des harengs

Sardinia [sɑr'dɪnɪ·ə] s Sardaigne; la Sardaigne

Sardinian [sɑr'dɪnɪ·ən] adj sarde ‖ s (language) sarde m; (person) Sarde mf

sarsaparilla [,sɑrsəpə'rɪlə] s salsepareille f

sash [sæʃ] s ceinture f; (of window) châssis m

sash' win'dow s fenêtre f à guillotine

sas·sy ['sæsi] adj (comp **-sier**; super **-siest**) (coll) impudent, effronté

satchel ['sætʃəl] sacoche f; (of schoolboy) carton m

sate [set] tr soûler

sateen [sæ'tin] s satinette f

satellite ['sætə,laɪt] adj & s satellite m

sat'ellite coun'try s pays m satellite

sat'ellite dish' s (telv) disque m de satellite

satiate ['seʃɪ,et] adj rassasié ‖ tr rassasier

satin ['sætɪn] s satin m

satire ['sætaɪr] s satire f

satiric(al) [sə'tɪrɪk(əl)] adj satirique

satirize ['sætɪ,raɪz] tr satiriser

satisfaction [,sætɪs'fækʃən] s satisfaction f

satisfactory [,sætɪs'fæktəri] adj satisfaisant

satis·fy ['sætɪs,faɪ] v (pret & pp **-fied**) tr satisfaire; (a requirement, need, etc.) satisfaire à ‖ intr satisfaire

saturate ['sætʃə,ret] tr saturer

satura'tion bom'bing [,sætʃə'reʃən] s bombardement m en tapis, tactique f de saturation

Saturday ['sætərdi] s samedi m

Saturn ['sætərn] s Saturne m

sauce [sɔs] s sauce f; (coll) insolence f, toupet m ‖ tr assaisonner ‖ tr (coll) parler avec impudence à

sauce'pan' s casserole f

saucer ['sɔsər] s soucoupe f

sau·cy ['sɔsi] adj (comp **-cier**; super **-ciest**) impudent, effronté

sauerkraut ['saur,kraut] s choucroute f

saunter ['sɔntər] s flânerie f ‖ intr flâner

sausage ['sɔsɪdʒ] s saucisse f, saucisson m

sauté [so'te] tr sauter, faire sauter

savage ['sævɪdʒ] adj & s sauvage mf

savant ['sævənt] s savant m, érudit m

save [sev] prep sauf, excepté ‖ tr sauver; (money) épargner; (time) gagner ‖ intr économiser

saving ['sevɪŋ] adj économe ‖ **savings** spl épargne f, économies fpl

sav'ings account' s dépôt m d'épargne

sav'ings and loan' associa'tion s caisse f d'épargne et de prêt

sav'ings bank' s caisse f d'épargne

sav'ings book' s livret m de caisse d'épargne

savior ['sevjər] s sauveur m

Saviour ['sevjər] s Sauveur m

savor ['sevər] s saveur f ‖ tr savourer ‖ intr—**to savor of** avoir un goût de

savor·y ['sevəri] adj (comp **-ier**; super **-iest**) (taste) savoureux; (smell) odorant ‖ s (pl **-ies**) (bot) sariette f

saw [sɔ] s scie f; (proverb) dicton m ‖ tr scier

saw'dust' s sciure f de bois

sawed'-off shot'gun s fusil m à canon scié

saw'horse' s chevalet m

saw'mill' s scierie f

Saxon ['sæksən] adj saxon ‖ s (language) saxon m; (person) Saxon m

saxophone ['sæksə,fon] s saxophone m

say [se] *s*—**to have one's say** avoir son mot à dire, avoir voix au chapitre ‖ *v* (*pret & pp* **said** [sɛd]) *tr* dire; **I should say not!** absolument pas!; **I should say so!** je crois bien!; **it is said** on dit; **no sooner said than done** sitôt dit, sitôt fait; **that is to say** c'est-à-dire; **to go without saying** aller sans dire; **what will the neighbors say?** qu'en dira-t-on?; **you don't say!** tu parles Charles!; **you said it!** (coll) et comment!, tu parles!

saying ['se·ɪŋ] *s* proverbe *m*

scab [skæb] *s* croûte *f*; (*strikebreaker*) jaune *m*; canaille *f*

scabbard ['skæbərd] *s* fourreau *m*

scab·by ['skæbi] *adj* (*comp* **-bier;** *super* **-biest**) croûteux; (coll) vil

scabrous ['skæbrəs] *adj* scabreux; (*uneven*) rugueux

scads [skædz] *spl* (slang) des tas *mpl*

scaffold ['skæfəld] *s* échafaud *m*; (*used in construction*) échafaudage *m*

scaffolding ['skæfəldɪŋ] *s* échafaudage *m*

scald [skɔld] *tr* échauder

scale [skel] *s* (*of thermometer, map, salaries, etc.*) échelle *f*; (*for weighing*) plateau *m*; (*incrustation*) tartre *m*; (bot, zool) écaille *f*; (mus) échelle *f*; **on a large scale** sur une grande échelle; **scales** balance *f*; **to tip the scales** faire pencher la balance ‖ *tr* escalader; **to scale down** réduire l'échelle de

scallion ['skæli·ən] *s* échalote *f*, ciboule *f*

scallop ['skæləp] *s* (*seafood*) coquille *f* Saint-Jacques, peigne *m*, pétoncle *m*; (*thin slice of meat*) escalope *f*; (*on edge of cloth*) feston *m* ‖ *tr* (*the edges*) denteler, découper; (culin) gratiner et cuire au four et à la crème

scalp [skælp] *s* cuir *m* chevelu; (*trophy*) scalp *m* ‖ *tr* scalper; (*tickets*) (coll) faire le trafic de; (*too hoodwink*) (slang) abuser de

scalpel ['skælpəl] *s* scalpel *m*

scal·y ['skeli] *adj* (*comp* **-ier;** *super* **-iest**) écailleux

scamp [skæmp] *s* garnement *m*

scamper ['skæmpər] *intr* courir allégrement; **to scamper away** or **off** détaler

scan [skæn] *v* (*pret & pp* **scanned;** *ger* **scanning**) *tr* scruter; (*e.g., a page*) jeter un coup d'œil sur; (*verses*) scander; (telv) balayer

scandal ['skændəl] *s* scandale *m*

scandalize ['skændə,laɪz] *tr* scandaliser

scandalous ['skændələs] *adj* scandaleux

Scandinavian [,skændɪ'nevɪ·ən] *adj* scandinave ‖ *s* (*language*) scandinave *m*; (*person*) Scandinave *mf*

scanning ['skænɪŋ] *s* (telv) balayage *m*

scant [skænt] *adj* maigre; (*attire*) léger, sommaire ‖ *tr* réduire; lésiner sur

scant·y ['skænti] *adj* (*comp* **-ier;** *super* **-iest**) rare, maigre; léger

scapegoat ['skep,got] *s* bouc *m* émissaire, tête *f* de Turc

scar [skɑr] *s* cicatrice *f*; (*on face*) balafre *f* ‖ *v* (*pret & pp* **scarred;** *ger* **scarring**) *tr* balafrer

scarce [skɛrs] *adj* rare, peu abondant

scarcely ['skɛrsli] *adv* à peine, presque pas; ne . . . guère §90; **scarcely ever** rarement

scarci·ty ['skɛrsɪti] *s* (*pl* **-ties**) manque *m*, pénurie *f*

scare [skɛr] *s* panique *f*, effroi *m* ‖ *tr* épouvanter, effrayer; **to scare away** or **off** effaroucher; **to scare up** (coll) procurer ‖ *intr* s'effaroucher

scare'crow' *s* épouvantail *m*

scarf [skɑrf] *s* (*pl* **scarfs** or **scarves** [skɑrvz]) foulard *m*, écharpe *f*

scarlet ['skɑrlɪt] *adj & s* écarlate *f*

scar'let fe'ver *s* scarlatine *f*

scar·y ['skɛri] *adj* (*comp* **-ier;** *super* **-iest**) (*easily frightened*) (coll) peureux, ombrageux; (*causing fright*) (coll) effrayant

scathing ['skeðɪŋ] *adj* cinglant

scatter ['skætər] *tr* éparpiller; (*a mob*) disperser ‖ *intr* se disperser

scat'ter·brained' *adj* (coll) étourdi

scenari·o [sɪ'nɛrɪ,o] *s* (*pl* **-os**) scénario *m*

scene [sin] *s* scène *f*; (*landscape*) paysage *m*; **behind the scenes** dans les coulisses; **to make a scene** faire une scène

scener·y ['sinəri] *s* (*pl* **-ies**) paysage *m*; (theat) décor *m*, décors

sceneshifter ['sin,ʃɪftər] *s* (theat) machiniste *m*

scenic ['sinɪk] *adj* pittoresque; spectaculaire; (theat) scénique

sce'nic rail'way *s* chemin *m* de fer en miniature des parcs d'attraction

scent [sɛnt] *s* odeur *f*; parfum *m*; (*trail*) piste *f* ‖ *tr* parfumer; (*an odor*) renifler; (*game as a dog does; a trap*) flairer

scepter ['sɛptər] *s* sceptre *m*

sceptio ['skɛptɪk] *adj & s* sceptique *mf*

sceptical ['skɛptɪkəl] *adj* sceptique

scepticism ['skɛptɪ,sɪzəm] *s* scepticisme *m*

schedule ['skɛdʒul] *s* (*of work*) plan *m*, programme *m*; (*of things to do*) emploi *m* du temps; (*of prices*) barème *m*; (rr) horaire *m*; **on schedule** selon l'horaire; selon les prévisions ‖ *tr* classer; inscrire au programme, à l'horaire, etc.; **scheduled to speak** prévu comme orateur

scheduled *adj* prévu, indiqué; (*train, bus, plane*) régulier

sched'uled air'line *s* compagnie *f* aérienne de transport régulier

scheme [skim] *s* projet *m*; machination *f*, truc *m* ‖ *tr* projeter ‖ *intr* ruser

schemer ['skimər] *s* faiseur *m* de projets; intrigant *m*

schism ['sɪzəm] *s* schisme *m*, scisson *f*

schizophrenia [,skɪtsə'frini·ə] *s* schizophrénie *f*

scholar ['skɑlər] *s* (*pupil*) écolier *m*; (*learned person*) érudit *m*, savant *m*; (*holder of scholarship*) boursier *m*

scholarly ['skɑlərli] *adj* érudit, savant ‖ *adv* savamment

schol'ar·ship' *s* érudition *f*; (*award*) bourse *f*

scholasticism [skə'læstɪ,sɪzəm] *s* scolastique *f*

school [skul] *adj* scolaire ‖ *s* école *f*; (*of a university*) faculté *f*; (*of fish*) banc *m* ‖ *tr* instruire, discipliner

school' board' *s* conseil *m* de l'instruction publique

school'book' *s* livre *m* de classe, livre scolaire

school'boy' *s* écolier *m*

school' bus' *s* voiture *f* école

school'girl' *s* écolière *f*

school'house' *s* maison *f* d'école

schooling ['skulɪŋ] *s* instruction *f*, études *fpl*; (teaching) enseignement *m*

schoolmarm ['skul,mɑrm] *s* maîtresse *f* d'école, institutrice *f*

school'mas'ter *s* maître *m* d'école, instituteur *m*

school'mate' *s* camarade *mf* d'école, condisciple *m*

school'room' *s* classe *f*, salle *f* de classe

school'teach'er *s* enseignant *m*, instituteur *m*

school'yard' *s* cour *f* de récréation

school' year' *s* année *f* scolaire

school' zone' *s* (*public sign*) ralentir école

schooner ['skunər] *s* schooner *m*, goélette *f*

sciatica [saɪ'ætɪkə] *s* (pathol) sciatique *f*

science ['saɪ·əns] *s* science *f*

sci'ence fic'tion *s* science-fiction *f*

scientific [,saɪ·ən'tɪfɪk] *adj* scientifique

scientist ['saɪ·əntɪst] *s* homme *m* de science, savant *m*

scimitar ['sɪmɪtər] *s* cimeterre *m*

scintillate ['sɪntɪ,let] *intr* scintiller, étinceler

scion ['saɪ·ən] *s* héritier *m*; (hort) scion *m*

scissors ['sɪzərz] *s & spl* ciseaux *mpl*

scis'sors-grind'er *s* rémouleur *m*; (orn) engoulevent *m*

scoff [skɔf] *s* raillerie *f* ‖ *intr*—**to scoff at** se moquer de

scold [skold] *s* harpie *f* ‖ *tr & intr* gronder

scolding ['skoldɪŋ] *s* gronderie *f*

scoop [skup] *s* (*for flour, sugar, etc.*) pelle *f* à main; (*for ice cream*) cuiller *f* à glace; (*kitchen utensil*) louche *f*; (*of dredge*) godet *m*; (*for coal*) seau *m*; (journ) nouvelle *f* à sensation, nouvelle en exclusivité, scoop *m*; (mach) benne *f* preneuse; (naut) écope *f* ‖ *tr* creuser; **to scoop out** excaver à la pelle; (*water*) écoper

scoot [skut] *intr* (coll) détaler

scooter ['skutər] *s* trottinette *f*, patinette *f*

scope [skop] *s* (*field*) domaine *m*, étendue *f*; (*reach*) portée *f*, envergure *f*; **to give free scope to** donner libre carrière à

scorch [skɔrtʃ] *tr* roussir; flétrir, dessécher

scorched'-earth' pol'icy *s* politique *f* de la terre brûlée

scorching ['skɔrtʃɪŋ] *adj* brûlant; caustique, mordant

score [skor] *s* (*debt*) compte *m*; (*twenty*) vingtaine *f*; (*notch*) entaille *f*; (*on metal*) rayure *f*, éraflure *f*; (mus) partition *f*; (sports) score *m*, marque *f*; **on that score** à cet égard; **to keep score** compter les points; **to settle a score with s.o.** régler son compte à qn ‖ *tr* (*to notch*) entailler; (*to criticize*) blâmer; (*metal*) rayer, érafler; (*a success*) remporter; (*e.g., a goal*) marquer; (mus) orchestrer

score'board' *s* tableau *m*

score'keep'er *s* marqueur *m*

scorn [skɔrn] *s* mépris *m*, dédain *m* ‖ *tr* mépriser, dédaigner ‖ *intr*—**to scorn to** dédaigner de

Scorpio ['skɔrpɪ,o] *s* (astr, astrol) le Scorpion

scorpion ['skɔrpɪ·ən] *s* scorpion *m*

Scot [skɑt] *s* Écossais *m*

Scotch [skɑtʃ] *adj* écossais; (slang) avare, chiche ‖ *s* (*dialect*) écossais *m*; whiskey *m* écossais; **the Scotch** les Écossais ‖ (*l.c.*) *s* (*wedge*) cale *f*; (*notch*) entaille *f* ‖ *tr* caler; entailler; (*a rumor*) étouffer

Scotch'man *s* (*pl* **-men**) Écossais *m*

Scotch' pine' *s* pin *m* sylvestre

Scotch' tape' *s* (trademark) ruban *m* cellulosique, adhésif *m* scotch

Scotland ['skɑtlənd] *s* Écosse *f*; l'Écosse

Scottish ['skɑtɪʃ] *adj* écossais ‖ *s* (*dialect*) écossais *m*; **the Scottish** les Écossais

scoundrel ['skaundrəl] *s* coquin *m*, fripon *m*, canaille *f*

scour [skaur] *tr* récurer; (*e.g., the countryside*) parcourir

scourge [skʌrʒ] *s* nerf *m* de bœuf, discipline *f*; (fig) fléau *m* ‖ *tr* fouetter, flageller

scout [skaut] *adj* scout ‖ *s* éclaireur *m*; (*boy scout*) scout *m*, éclaireur; **a good scout** (coll) un brave gars ‖ *tr* reconnaître; (*to scoff at*) repousser avec dédain ‖ *intr* aller en reconnaissance

scouting ['skautɪŋ] *s* scoutisme *m*

scout'ing par'ty *s* (*pl* **-ties**) (mil) détachement *m* de reconnaissance

scout'mas'ter *s* chef *m* de troupe

scowl [skaul] *s* renfrognement *m* ‖ *intr* se renfrogner

scram [skræm] *v* (*pret & pp* **scrammed;** *ger* **scramming**) *intr* (coll) ficher le camp; **scram!** (coll) fiche-moi le camp!

scramble ['skræmbəl] *s* bousculade *f* ‖ *tr* brouiller ‖ *intr* se disputer; grimper à quatre pattes

scram'bled eggs' *spl* œufs *mpl* brouillés

scrambling ['skræmblɪŋ] *s* (electron) embrouillage *m*

scrap [skræp] *s* (*metal*) ferraille *f*; (*little bit*) bout *m*, petit morceau *m*; (*fight*) (coll) chamaillerie *f* ‖ *v* (*pret & pp* **scrapped;** *ger* **scrapping**) *tr* mettre au rebut ‖ *intr* (coll) se chamailler

scrap'book' *s* album *m* de découpures

scrape [skrep] *s* grincement *m*; (coll) mauvaise affaire *f* ‖ *tr* gratter, râcler

scrap' heap' *s* tas *m* de rebut

scrap' i'ron *s* ferraille *f*

scrap' pa'per *s* bloc-notes *m*; (*refuse*) papier *m* de rebut

scratch [skrætʃ] *s* égratignure *f*; **to start from scratch** partir de rien ‖ *tr* gratter, égratigner; *(to eliminate from an event)* déclarer forfait

scratch′ pad′ *s* bloc-notes *m*, brouillon *m*

scratch′ pa′per *s* bloc-notes *m*

scrawl [skrɔl] *s* griffonnage *m* ‖ *tr & intr* griffonner

scraw·ny [ˈskrɔni] *adj (comp* **-nier;** *super* **-niest)** décharné, mince

scream [skrim] *s* cri *m* perçant; (slang) personne *f* ridicule; (slang) chose *f* ridicule ‖ *tr & intr* pousser des cris, crier

screech [skritʃ] *s* cri *m* perçant ‖ *intr* jeter des cris perçants

screech′ owl′ *s* chat-huant *m*; *(barn owl)* effraie *f*

screen [skrin] *s* écran *m*; grillage *m* en fil de fer, treillis *m* métallique; *(for sifting)* crible *m* ‖ *tr* abriter; *(candidates)* trier; (mov) porter à l'écran

screen′ grid′ *s* (electron) grille *f* blindée

screening [ˈskriniŋ] *s* présélection *f*; (med) dépistage *m*

screen′play′ *s* scénario *m*; drame *m* filmé

screen′ test′ *s* bout *m* d'essai

screw [skru] *s* vis *f*; (naut) hélice *f*; **to have a screw loose** (coll) être toqué ‖ *tr* visser; **to screw off** dévisser; **to screw tight** visser à bloc; **to screw up** *(one's courage)* rassembler ‖ *intr* se visser

screw′ball′ *adj & s* (slang) extravagant *m*, loufoque *m*

screw′driv′er *s* tournevis *m*

screw′ eye′ *s* vis *f* à œil

screw′ press′ *s* cric *m* à vis

screw′ propel′ler *s* hélice *f*

screw·y [ˈskru·i] *adj (comp* **-ier;** *super* **-iest)** (slang) loufoque

scrib′al er′ror [ˈskraɪbəl] *s* faute *f* de copiste

scribble [ˈskrɪbəl] *s* griffonnage *m* ‖ *tr & intr* griffonner

scribe [skraɪb] *s* scribe *m*

scrimmage [ˈskrɪmɪdʒ] *s* mêlée *f*

scrimp [skrɪmp] *tr* lésiner sur ‖ *intr* lésiner

scrip [skrɪp] *s* monnaie *f* scriptural, script *m*

script [skrɪpt] *s* manuscrit *m*, original *m*; *(handwriting)* écriture *f*; (mov) scénario *m*; (typ) script *m*; (mov, telv) texte *m*

scriptural [ˈskrɪptʃərəl] *adj* biblique

scripture [ˈskrɪptʃər] *s* citation *f* tirée de l'Écriture; **Scripture** l'Écriture *f*; **the Scriptures** les Écritures

script′writ′er *s* scénariste *mf*

scrofula [ˈskrɑfjələ] *s* scrofule *f*

scroll [skrol] *s* rouleau *m*; (archit) volute *f*

scroll′work′ *s* ornementation *f* en volute

scro·tum [ˈskrotəm] *s (pl* **-ta** [tə] or **-tums)** scrotum *m*, bourses *fpl*

scrub [skrʌb] *adj* rabougri ‖ *s (scrubbing)* nettoyage *m* à la brosse; *(underbrush)* broussailles *fpl;* (rok) vol *m* annulé; (sports) joueur *m* novice ‖ *v (pret & pp* **scrubbed;** *ger* **scrubbing)** *tr* frotter, nettoyer, récurer; *(to cancel)* (rok) annuler

scrub′bing brush′ *s* brosse *f* de chiendent

scrub′wom′an *s (pl* **-wom′en)** nettoyeuse *f*

scruff [skrʌf] *s* nuque *f*

scruple [ˈskrupəl] *s* scrupule *f*

scrupulous [ˈskrupjələs] *adj* scrupuleux

scrutinize [ˈskrutɪˌnaɪz] *tr* scruter

scruti·ny [ˈskrutɪni] *s (pl* **-nies)** examen *m* minutieux

scuff [skʌf] *s* usure *f* ‖ *tr* érafler

scuffle [ˈskʌfəl] *s* bagarre *f* ‖ *intr* se bagarrer

scull [skʌl] *s (stern oar)* godille *f*; aviron *m* de couple ‖ *tr* godiller ‖ *intr* ramer en couple

sculler·y [ˈskʌləri] *s (pl* **-ies)** arrière-cuisine *f*

scul′lery maid′ *s* laveuse *f* de vaisselle

scullion [ˈskʌljən] *s* marmiton *m*

sculptor [ˈskʌlptər] *s* sculpteur *m*

sculptress [ˈskʌlptrɪs] *s* femme *f* sculpteur

sculpture [ˈskʌlptʃər] *s* sculpture *f* ‖ *tr & intr* sculpter

scum [skʌm] *s* écume *f*; *(of society)* canaille *f* ‖ *v (pret & pp* **scummed;** *ger* **scumming)** *tr & intr* écumer

scum·my [ˈskʌmi] *adj (comp* **-mier;** *super* **-miest)** écumeux; (fig) vil

scurrilous [ˈskʌrɪləs] *adj* injurieux, grossier, outrageant

scur·ry [ˈskʌri] *v (pret & pp* **-ried)** *intr*—**to scurry around** galoper; **to scurry away** or **off** déguerpir

scur·vy [ˈskʌrvi] *adj (comp* **-vier;** *super* **-viest)** méprisable, vil ‖ *s* scorbut *m*

scuttle [ˈskʌtəl] *s (bucket for coal)* seau *m* à charbon; *(trap door)* trappe *f*; *(run)* course *f* précipitée; (naut) écoutillon *m* ‖ *tr* saborder ‖ *intr* filer, déguerpir

scut′tle·butt′ *s* (coll) on-dit *m*

scythe [saɪð] *s* faux *f*

sea [si] *s* mer *f*; **at sea** en mer; (fig) désorienté; **by the sea** au bord de la mer; **to put to sea** prendre le large

sea′board′ *s* littoral *m*

sea′ breeze′ *s* brise *f* de mer

sea′coast′ *s* côté *f*, littoral *m*

seafarer [ˈsiˌfɛrər] *s* marin *m*; voyageur *m* par mer

sea′food′ *s* fruits *mpl* de mer, marée *f*

seagoing [ˈsiˌgo·ɪŋ] *adj* de haute mer, au long cours

sea′ gull′ *s* mouette *f*, goéland *m*

seal [sil] *s (on a document)* sceau *m*; (zool) phoque *m* ‖ *tr* sceller; **in a sealed envelope** sous pli fermé

sea′ legs′ *spl* pied *m* marin

sea′ lev′el *s* niveau *m* de la mer

seal′ing wax′ *s* cire *f* à cacheter

sea′ li′on *s* otarie *f*

seal′skin′ *s* peau *f* de phoque

seam [sim] *s* couture *f*; *(of metal)* joint *m*; (geol) fissure *f*; (min) couche *f*

sea′man *s (pl* **-men)** marin *m*

sea′ mile′ *s* mille *m* marin

seamless [ˈsimlɪs] *adj* sans couture; (mach) sans soudure

seamstress [ˈsimstrɪs] *s* couturière *f*

seam·y [ˈsimi] *adj (comp* **-ier;** *super* **-iest)** plein de coutures; vil, vilain

séance [ˈse·ɑns] *s* séance *f* de spiritisme

sea′plane′ *s* hydravion *m*

sea′port′ s port m de mer

sea′ pow′er s puissance f maritime

sear [sɪr] adj desséché ‖ s cicatrice f de brûlure ‖ tr dessécher; marquer au fer rouge

search [sʌrtʃ] s recherche f; **in search of** à la recherche de ‖ tr & intr fouiller; **to search for** chercher

searching [′sʌrtʃɪŋ] adj pénétrant, scrutateur

search′light′ s projecteur m

search′ war′rant s mandat m de perquisition

seascape [′si,skep] s panorama m marin; (painting) marine f

sea′ shell′ s coquille f de mer

sea′shore′ s bord m de la mer

sea′sick′ adj—**to be seasick** avoir le mal de mer

sea′sick′ness s mal m de mer

season [′sizən] s saison f ‖ tr assaisonner; (troops) aguerrir; (wood) sécher

seasonal [′sizənəl] adj saisonnier

seasoning [′sizənɪŋ] s assaisonnement m

sea′son's greet′ings spl meilleurs souhaits mpl, tous mes vœux mpl

sea′son tick′et s carte f d'abonnement

seat [sit] s siège m; (place or right) place f; (in theater) fauteuil m; (on bus or train) banquette f; (on cycle) selle f; (of trousers) fond m; **have a seat** asseyez-vous donc; **keep your seat** restez assis; **to have a good seat** (equit) avoir une bonne assiette ‖ tr asseoir; (a number of persons) contenir; **to be seated** (to sit down) s'asseoir; (to be in sitting posture) être assis

seat′ belt′ s ceinture f de sécurité

seat′ cov′er s (aut) housse f

SEATO [′sito] s (acronym) (Southeast Asia Treaty Organization) OTASE f

sea′ wall′ s digue f

sea′way′ s voie f maritime; (of ship) sillage m; (rough sea) mer f dure

sea′weed′ s algue f marine; plante f marine

sea′wor′thy adj en état de naviguer

secede [sɪ′sid] intr se séparer, faire sécession

secession [sɪ′sɛʃən] s sécession f

seclude [sɪ′klud] tr tenir éloigné; (to shut up) enfermer

secluded adj retiré, écarté

seclusion [sɪ′kluʒən] s retraite f

second [′sɛkənd] adj & pron deuxième (masc, fem), second; **the Second** deux, e.g., **John the Second** Jean deux; **to be second in command** commander en second; **to be second to none** ne le céder à personne ‖ s deuxième m, second m; (in time; musical interval; of angle) seconde f; (in a duel) témoin m, second m; (com) article m de deuxième qualité; **the second** (in dates) le deux ‖ adv en second lieu ‖ tr affirmer; (to back up) seconder

secondar·y [′sɛkən,dɛri] adj secondaire ‖ s (pl -ies) (elec) secondaire m

sec′ondary educa′tion s enseignement m secondaire

sec′ond best′ s pis-aller m

sec′ond-best′ adj (everyday) de tous les jours; **to come off second-best** être battu

sec′ond-class′ adj de second ordre; (rr) de seconde classe

sec′ond floor′ s premier étage m; (second floor above the ground floor = American third floor) (Brit) deuxième étage

sec′ond hand′ s trotteuse f

sec′ond·hand′ adj d'occasion, de seconde main

sec′ond·hand book′dealer s bouquiniste mf

sec′ond lieuten′ant s sous-lieutenant m

sec′ond mate′ s (naut) second maître m

sec′ond-rate′ adj de second ordre

sec′ond sight′ s seconde vue f

sec′ond wind′ s second souffle m; **to get one's second wind** reprendre haleine

secre·cy [′sikrəsi] s (pl -cies) secret m; **in secrecy** en secret

secret [′sikrɪt] adj & s secret m; **in secret** en secret

secretar·y [′sɛkrɪ,tɛri] s (pl -ies) secrétaire mf; (desk) secrétaire m

se′cret bal′lot s scrutin m secret

secrete [sɪ′krit] tr cacher; (physiol) sécréter

secretive [sɪ′kritɪv] adj cachottier

se′cret serv′ice s deuxième bureau m

sect [sɛkt] s secte f

sectarian [sɛk′tɛri·ən] adj sectaire; (school) confessionnel ‖ sectaire mf

section [′sɛkʃən] s section f

sectionalism [′sɛkʃənə,lɪzəm] s régionalisme m

sec′tion hand′ s cantonnier m

sector [′sɛktər] s secteur m; (instrument) compas m de proportion

secular [′sɛkjələr] adj (worldly, of this world) séculier; (century-old) séculaire ‖ s séculier m

secularism [′sɛkjələ,rɪzəm] s laïcisme m, mondanité f

secure [sɪ′kjʊr] adj sûr ‖ tr obtenir; (to make fast) fixer

securi·ty [sɪ′kjʊrɪti] s (pl -ties) sécurité f; (pledge) garantie f; (person) garant m; **securities** valeurs fpl

secu′rity-sys′tems com′pany s société f de gardiennage

sedan [sɪ′dæn] s (aut) conduite f intérieure

sedan′ chair′ s chaise f à porteurs

sedate [sɪ′det] adj calme, discret

sedation [sɪ′deʃən] s sédation f

sedative [′sɛdətɪv] adj & s sédatif m

sedentary [′sɛdən,tɛri] adj sédentaire

sedge [sɛdʒ] s (Carex) laîche f

sediment [′sɛdɪmənt] s sédiment m

sedition [sɪ′dɪʃən] s sédition f

seditious [sɪ′dɪʃəs] adj séditieux

seduce [sɪ′d(j)us] tr séduire

seducer [sɪ′d(j)usər] s séducteur m

seduction [sɪ′dʌkʃən] s séduction f

seductive [sɪ′dʌktɪv] adj séduisant

sedulous [′sɛdʒələs] adj assidu

see [si] s (eccl) siège m ‖ v (pret **saw** [sɔ]; pp **seen** [sin]) tr voir; **see other side** (turn the page) voir au dos; **to see s.o. play, to**

see s.o. playing voir jouer qn, voir qn qui joue; **to see s.th. played** voir jouer q.ch. ‖ *intr* voir; **to see through s.o.** (fig) voir venir qn

seed [sid] *s* graine *f*, semence *f*; sperme *m*; (*in fruit*) pépin *m*; (fig) germe *m*; **to go to seed** monter en graine ‖ *intr* semer, ensemencer

seed'bed' *s* semis *m*

seeder ['sidər] *s* (mach) semeuse *f*

seedling ['sidlɪŋ] *s* semis *m*

seed·y ['sidi] *adj* (*comp* **-ier**; *super* **-iest**) (coll) râpé, miteux

seeing ['si·ɪŋ] *adj* voyant ‖ *s* vue *f* ‖ *conj* vu que

See'ing Eye' dog' *s* (trademark) chien *m* d'aveugle

seek [sik] *v* (*pret* & *pp* **sought** [sɔt]) *tr* chercher ‖ *intr* chercher; **to seek after** rechercher; **to seek to** chercher à

seem [sim] *intr* sembler

seemingly ['simɪŋli] *adv* en apparence

seem·ly ['simli] *adj* (*comp* **-lier**; *super* **-liest**) gracieux; (*correct*) bienséant

seep [sip] *intr* suinter

seer [sɪr] *s* prophète *m*, voyant *m*

see'saw' *s* balançoire *f*, bascule *f*; (*motion*) va-et-vient *m* ‖ *intr* basculer, balancer

seethe [sið] *intr* bouillonner

segment ['sɛgmənt] *s* segment *m*

segregate ['sɛgrɪ,get] *tr* mettre à part, isoler

segregation [,sɛgrɪ'geʃən] *s* ségrégation *f*

segregationist [,sɛgrɪ'geʃənɪst] *s* ségrégationniste *mf*

seismic ['saɪzmɪk] *adj* sismique

seismograph ['saɪzmə,græf] *s* sismographe *m*

seismology [saɪz'mɑlədʒi] *s* sismologie *f*

seize [siz] *tr* saisir

seizure ['siʒər] *s* prise *f*; (law) saisie *f*; (pathol) attaque *f*

seldom ['sɛldəm] *adv* rarement

select [sɪ'lɛkt] *adj* choisi ‖ *tr* choisir, sélectionner

selection [sɪ'lɛkʃən] *s* sélection *f*

selective [sɪ'lɛktɪv] *adj* sélectif

self [sɛlf] *adj* de même ‖ *s* (*pl* **selves** [sɛlvz]) moi *m*, être *m*; **all by one's self** tout seul; **one's better self** notre meilleur côté ‖ *pron*—**payable to self** payable à moi-même

self'-addressed en'velope *s* enveloppe *f* adressée à l'envoyeur

self'-cen'tered *adj* égocentrique

self'-clean'ing ov'en *s* four *m* auto-nettoyant

self'-con'fidence *s* confiance *f* en soi

self'-con'fident *adj* sûr de soi

self'-con'scious *adj* gêné, embarrassé, emprunté

self'-control' *s* sang-froid *m*, maîtrise *f* de soi

self'-defense' *s* autodéfense *f*; **in self-defense** en légitime défense

self'-deni'al *s* abnégation *f*

self'-deter'mina'tion *s* autodétermination *f*

self'-dis'cipline *s* discipline *f* personnelle

self'-ed'ucated *adj* autodidacte

self'-employed' *adj* indépendant

self'-esteem' *s* amour-propre *m*

self'-ev'ident *adj* évident aux yeux de tout le monde

self'-explan'ator'y *adj* qui s'explique de soi-même

self'-gov'ernment *s* autonomie *f*; maîtrise *f* de soi

self'-impor'tant *adj* suffisant, présomptueux

self'-indul'gence *s* faiblesse *f* envers soi-même, intempérance *f*

self'-in'terest *s* intérêt *m* personnel

selfish ['sɛlfɪʃ] *adj* égoïste

selfishness ['sɛlfɪʃnɪs] *s* égoïsme *m*

selfless ['sɛlflɪs] *adj* désintéressé

self'-love' *s* égoïsme *m*

self'-made man' *s* (*pl* **-men'**) fils *m* de ses œuvres

self'-por'trait *s* autoportrait *m*

self'-possessed' *adj* maître de soi

self'-preserva'tion *s* conservation *f* de soi-même

self'-reli'ant *adj* sûr de soi, assuré

self'-respect'ing *adj* correct, honorable

self'-right'eous *adj* pharisaïque

self'-sac'rifice' *s* abnégation *f*

self'same' *adj* identique

self'-sat'isfied *adj* content de soi

self'-seal'ing *adj* (*envelope*) autocollant, auto-adhésif; (*container*) à obturation automatique

self'-seek'ing *adj* égoïste, intéressé

self'-serv'ice *s* libre-service *m*

self'-serv'ice laun'dry *s* (*pl* **-dries**) laverie *f* libre-service, laverie automatique, lavromat *m*

self'-serv'ice sta'tion *s* station *f* libre-service

self'-start'er *s* démarreur *m* automatique

self'-styled' *adj* soi-disant

self'-taught' *adj* autodidacte

self'-tim'er *s* (phot) retardateur *m*

self'-willed' *adj* obstiné, entêté

self'-wind'ing *adj* à remontage automatique

sell [sɛl] *v* (*pret* & *pp* **sold** [sold]) *tr* vendre; **to sell back** réceder; **to sell out** solder; (*to betray*) vendre ‖ *intr* vendre; **to sell for** (*e.g., ten dollars*) se vendre à

seller ['sɛlər] *s* vendeur *m*

selling ['sɛlɪŋ] *s* vente *f*; **selling by mail** postalage *m*; **selling price** prix *m* de vente

Selt'zer wa'ter ['sɛltsər] *s* eau *f* de Seltz

selvage ['sɛlvɪdʒ] *s* (*of fabric*) lisière *f*; (*of lock*) gâche *f*

semantic [sɪ'mæntɪk] *adj* sémantique ‖ **semantics** *s* sémantique *f*

semaphore ['sɛmə,for] *s* sémaphore *m*

semblance ['sɛmbləns] *s* semblant *m*

semen ['simɛn] *s* sperme *m*, semence *f*

semester [sɪ'mɛstər] *adj* semstriel ‖ *s* semestre *m*

semes'ter hour' *s* (educ) heure *f* semestrielle

semicircle ['sɛmɪ,sʌrkəl] *s* demi-cercle *m*

semicolon ['sɛmɪ,kolən] *s* point-virgule *m*

semiconductor [,sɛmɪkən'dʌktər] *s* semiconducteur *m*

semiconscious [,sɛmɪ'kɑnʃəs] *adj* à demi conscient

semifinal [,sɛmɪ'faɪnəl] *adj* avant-dernière ‖ *s* demi-finale *f*

semilearned [,sɛmɪ'lʌrnɪd] *adj* à moitié savant

seminar ['sɛmɪ,nɑr] *s* séminaire *m*

seminar·y ['sɛmɪ,nəri] *s* (*pl* **-ies**) séminaire *m*

semiprecious [,sɛmɪ'prɛʃəs] *adj* fin, semiprécieux

Semite ['sɛmaɪt] *s* Sémite *mf*

Semitic [sɪ'mɪtɪk] *adj* (*e.g., language*) sémitique; (*person*) sémite

semitrailer ['sɛmɪ,trelər] *s* semi-remorque *f*

senate ['sɛnɪt] *s* sénat *m*

senator ['sɛnətər] *s* sénateur *m*

send [sɛnd] *v* (*pret & pp* **sent** [sɛnt]) *tr* envoyer; (rad, telv) émettre; **to send back** renvoyer; **to send out** envoyer; **to send s.o. for s.th.** or **s.o.** envoyer qn chercher q.ch. or qn; **to send s.o. to** + *inf* envoyer qn + *inf* ‖ *intr* (rad, telv) émettre; **to send for** envoyer chercher

sender ['sɛndər] *s* expéditeur *m*; (telg) transmetteur *m*

send'-off' *s* manifestation *f* d'adieu

senile ['sinaɪl] *adj* sénile

senility [sɪ'nɪlɪti] *s* sénilité *f*

senior ['sinjər] *adj* aîné; (*clerk, partner, etc.*) principal; (*rank*) supérieur; père, e.g., **Maurice Laporte, Senior** Maurice Laporte père ‖ *s* aîné *m*, doyen *m*; (*U.S. upperclassman*) étudiant *m* de dernière année

sen'ior cit'izens *spl* les vieilles gens *fpl*

seniority [sin'jɔrɪti] *s* ancienneté *f*, doyenneté *f*

sen'ior staff' *s* personnel *m* hors classe

sensation [sɛn'seʃən] *s* sensation *f*

sensational [sɛn'seʃənəl] *adj* sensationnel

sense [sɛns] *s* sens *m*; (*wisdom*) bon sens; (*e.g., of pain*) sensation *f*; **to make sense out of** arriver à comprendre ‖ *tr* percevoir, sentir

senseless ['sɛnslɪs] *adj* (*lacking perception*) insensible; (*unconscious*) sans connaissance; (*unreasonable*) insensé

sense' of guilt' *s* remords *m*

sense' or'gans *spl* organes *mpl* des sens

sensibili·ty [,sɛnsɪ'bɪlɪti] *s* (*pl* **-ties**) sensibilité *f*; susceptibilité *f*

sensible ['sɛnsɪbəl] *adj* sensible; (*endowed with good sense*) sensé, raisonnable

sensitive ['sɛnsɪtɪv] *adj* sensible; (*touchy*) susceptible, sensitif

sensitize ['sɛnsɪ,taɪz] *tr* sensibiliser

sensor ['sɛn,sɔr] *s* (rok) capteur *m*

sensory ['sɛnsəri] *adj* sensoriel

sensual ['sɛnʃu·əl] *adj* sensuel

sensuous ['sɛnʃu·əs] *adj* sensuel

sentence ['sɛntəns] *s* (gram) phrase *f*; (law) sentence *f* ‖ *tr* condamner

sentiment ['sɛntɪmənt] *s* sentiment *m*

sentimental [,sɛntɪ'mɛntəl] *adj* sentimental

sentinel ['sɛntɪnəl] *s* sentinelle *f*; **to stand sentinel** être en sentinelle

sen·try ['sɛntri] *s* (*pl* **-tries**) sentinelle *f*

sen'try box' *s* guérite *f*

separate ['sɛpərɪt] *adj* séparé ‖ ['sɛpə,ret] *tr* séparer ‖ *intr* se séparer

separation [,sɛpə'reʃən] *s* séparation *f*

September [sɛp'tɛmbər] *s* septembre *m*

septic ['sɛptɪk] *adj* septique

sepulcher ['sɛpəlkər] *s* sépulcre *m*

sequel ['sikwəl] *s* conséquence *f*; (*something following*) suite *f*

sequence ['sikwəns] *s* succession *f*, ordre *m*; (cards, mov) séquence *f*; (*of tenses*) (gram) concordance *f*

sequester [sɪ'kwɛstər] *tr* séquestrer

sequin ['sikwɪn] *s* paillette *f*

ser·aph ['sɛrəf] *s* (*pl* **-aphs** or **-aphim** [əfɪm]) séraphin *m*

Serb [sʌrb] *adj* serbe ‖ *s* Serbe *mf*

sere [sɪr] *adj* sec, desséché

serenade [,sɛrə'ned] *s* sérénade *f* ‖ *tr* donner une sérénade à ‖ *intr* donner des sérénades

serene [sɪ'rin] *adj* serein

serenity [sɪ'rɛnɪti] *s* sérénité *f*

serf [sʌrf] *s* serf *m*

serfdom ['sʌrfdəm] *s* servage *m*

serge [sʌrdʒ] *s* serge *f*

sergeant ['sɑrdʒənt] *s* sergent *m*

ser'geant-at-arms' *s* (*pl* **sergeants-at-arms**) huissier *m*, sergent *m* d'armes

ser'geant ma'jor *s* (*pl* **sergeant majors**) sergent-major *m*

serial ['sɪrɪ·əl] *adj* de série ‖ *s* roman-feuilleton *m*

serially ['sɪrɪ·əli] *adv* en série; (*in installments*) en feuilleton

se'rial num'ber *s* numéro *m* d'ordre; (mil) numéro *m* matricule

se·ries ['sɪriz] *s* (*pl* **-ries**) série *f*; **in series** en série

serious ['sɪrɪ·əs] *adj* (*illness, injury, mistake, tone, attitude, smile, look*) grave, sérieux; (*damage*) important, considérable

seriousness ['sɪrɪ·əsnɪs] *s* sérieux *m*, gravité *f*

sermon ['sʌrmən] *s* sermon *m*

sermonize ['sʌrmə,naɪz] *tr & intr* sermonner

serpent ['sʌrpənt] *s* serpent *m*

se·rum ['sɪrəm] *s* (*pl* **-rums** or **-ra** [rə]) sérum *m*

servant ['sʌrvənt] *s* domestique *mf*; (*civil servant*) fonctionnaire *mf*; (*housemaid*) bonne *f*; (*humble servant*) (fig) serviteur *m*

serv'ant girl' *s* servante *f*

serv'ant prob'lem *s* crise *f* domestique

serve [sʌrv] *tr* servir; **to serve s.o. as** servir à qn de; **to serve time** purger une peine ‖ *intr* servir; **to serve as** (*to function as*) servir de; (*to be useful for*) servir à

service ['sʌrvɪs] *s* service *m*; (eccl) office *m*; **the services** (mil) les forces *fpl* armées ‖ *tr* entretenir, réparer

serviceable ['sʌrvɪsəbəl] *adj* utile, pratique; résistant

serv′ice club′ *s* foyer *m* du soldat

serv′ice·man′ *s* (*pl* **-men′**) réparateur *m*; (mil) militaire *m*

serv′ice rec′ord *s* état *m* de service

serv′ice sta′tion *s* station-service *f*

ser′vice stop′ *s* (*on a superhighway*) relais *m* routier

serv′ice stripe′ *s* chevron *m*, galon *m*

servicing [′sʌrvɪsɪŋ] *s* entretien *m* courant

servile [′sʌrvɪl] *adj* servile

servitude [′sʌrvɪ,t(j)ud] *s* servitude *f*

sesame [′sɛsəmi] *s* sésame *m*; **open sesame!** sésame, ouvre-toi!

session [′sɛʃən] *s* session *f*; **to be in session** siéger

set [sɛt] *adj* (*rule*) établi; (*price*) fixe; (*time*) fixé; (*smile; locution*) figé ‖ *s* ensemble *m*; (*of dishes, linen, etc.*) assortiment *m*; (*of dishes*) service *m*; (*of kitchen utensils*) batterie *f*; (*of pans; of weights; of tickets*) série *f*; (*of tools, chessmen, oars, etc.*) jeu *m*; (*of books*) collection *f*; (*of diamonds*) parure *f*; (*of tennis*) set *m*; (*of cement*) prise *f*; (*of a garment*) tournure *f*; (*group of persons*) coterie *f*; (mov) plateau *m*; (rad) poste *m*; (theat) mise *f* en scène; **set of false teeth** dentier *m*; **set of teeth** denture *f* ‖ *v* (*pret & pp* **set;** *ger* **setting**) *tr* mettre, placer, poser; (*a date, price, etc.*) fixer; (*a gem*) monter; (*a trap*) tendre; (*a timepiece*) mettre à l'heure, régler; (*the hair*) mettre en plis; (*a bone*) remettre; **to set aside** mettre de côté; annuler; **to set going** mettre en marche; **to set off** mettre en valeur; (*e.g., a rocket*) lancer, tirer ‖ *intr* se figer; (*said of sun, moon, etc.*) se coucher; (*said of hen*) couver; (*said of garment*) tomber; **to set about, to set out to** se mettre à; **to set upon** attaquer

set′back′ *s* revers *m*, échec *m*

set′screw′ *s* vis *f* de pression

settee [sɛ′ti] *s* canapé *m*; (*for two*) canapé à deux places, causeuse *f*

setting [′sɛtɪŋ] *s* (*surroundings*) cadre *m*; (*of a gem*) monture *f*; (*of cement*) prise *f*; (*of sun*) coucher *m*; (*of a bone*) recollement *m*; (*of a watch*) réglage *m*; (*adjustment*) ajustage *m*; (theat) mise *f* en scène

set′ting-up′ ex′ercises *spl* gymnastique *f* rhythmique, gymnastique suédoise

settle [′sɛtəl] *tr* (*a region*) coloniser; (*a dispute, account, debt, etc.*) régler; (*a problem*) résoudre; (*doubts, fears, etc.*) calmer; (*to stop wobbling*) stabiliser ‖ *intr* se coloniser; se calmer; (*said of weather*) se mettre au beau; (*said of building*) se tasser; (*said of sediment, dust, etc.*) se déposer; (*said of liquid*) se clarifier; **to settle down** s'établir; (*to be less wild*) se ranger; **to settle down to** (*a task*) s'appliquer à; **to settle on** se décider pour

settlement [′sɛtəlmənt] *s* établissement *m*, colonie *f*; (*of an account, dispute, etc.*) règlement *m*; (*of a debt*) liquidation *f*; (*settlement house*) œuvre *f* sociale

settler [′sɛtlər] *s* colon *m*

set′up′ *s* port *m*, maintien *m*; (*of the parts of a machine*) installation *f*; (coll) organisation *f*

seven [′sɛvən] *adj & pron* sept ‖ *s* sept *m*; **seven o'clock** sept heures

seventeen [′sɛvən′tin] *adj, pron, & s* dix-sept *m*

seventeenth [′sɛvən′tinθ] *adj & pron* dix-septième (*masc, fem*); **the Seventeenth** dix-sept, e.g., **John the Seventeenth** Jean dix-sept ‖ *s* dix-septième *m*; **the seventeenth** (*in dates*) le dix-sept

seventh [′sɛvənθ] *adj & pron* septième (*masc, fem*); **the Seventh** sept, e.g., **John the Seventh** Jean sept ‖ *s* septième *m*; **the seventh** (*in dates*) le sept

seventieth [′sɛvəntɪ·ɪθ] *adj & pron* soixante-dixième (*masc, fem*) ‖ *s* soixante-dixième *m*

seven·ty [′sɛvənti] *adj & pron* soixante-dix ‖ *s* (*pl* **-ties**) soixante-dix *m*

sev′enty-first′ *adj & pron* soixante et onzième (*masc, fem*) ‖ *s* soixante et onzième *m*

sev′enty-one′ *adj, pron, & s* soixante et onze *m*

sever [′sɛvər] *tr* séparer; (*relations*) rompre ‖ *intr* se séparer

several [′sɛvərəl] *adj & pron indef* plusieurs

severance [′sɛvərəns] *s* séparation *f*; (*of relations*) rupture *f*; (*of communications*) interruption *f*

sev′erance pay′ *s* indemnité *f* pour cause de renvoi

severe [sɪ′vɪr] *adj* sévère; (*weather*) rigoureux; (*pain*) aigu; (*illness*) grave

sew [so] *v* (*pret* **sewed;** *pp* **sewed** or **sewn**) *tr & intr* coudre

sewer [′s(j)u·ɪdʒ] *s* eaux *fpl* d'égouts

sewer [′s(j)u·ər] *s* égout *m* ‖ [′so·ər] *s* (*one who sews*) couseur *m*

sewerage [′s(j)u·ərɪdʒ] *s* (*removal*) vidange *f*; (*system*) système *m* d'égouts; (*sewage*) eaux *fpl* d'égouts

sew′ing bas′ket *s* nécessaire *m* de couture

sew′ing machine′ *s* machine *f* à coudre

sew′ing ta′ble *s* chiffonnière *f*

sex [sɛks] *s* sexe *m*; **the fair sex** le beau sexe; **the sterner sex** le sexe fort; **to have sex with** (coll) avoir des rapport avec

sex′ appeal′ *s* sex-appeal *m*

sexism [′sɛksɪzəm] *s* sexisme *m*

sexist [′sɛksɪst] *adj & s* sexiste *mf*

sextant [′sɛkstənt] *s* sextant *m*

sextet [sɛks′tɛt] *s* sextuor *m*

sexton [′sɛkstən] *s* sacristain *m*

sexual [′sɛkʃu·əl] *adj* sexuel

sex·y [′sɛksi] *adj* (*comp* **-ier;** *super* **-iest**) (slang) aguichant, grivois; (*story*) érotique; **to be sexy** avoir du chien

sh [ʃ] *interj* chut!

shab·by [′ʃæbi] *adj* (*comp* **-bier;** *super* **-biest**) râpé, usé; (*mean*) mesquin; (*house*) délabré

shack [ʃæk] *s* cabane *f*, case *f*

shackle [′ʃækəl] *s* boucle *f*; **shackles** entraves *fpl* ‖ *tr* entraver

shad [ʃæd] *s* alose *f*

shade [ʃed] *s* (*shadow*) ombre *f*; (*of lamp*) abat-jour *m*; (*of window*) store *m*; (*hue; slight difference*) nuance *f*; (*little bit*) soupçon *m* ‖ *tr* ombrager; (*to make gradual changes in*) nuancer

shadow [ʃædo] *s* ombre *f* ‖ *tr* ombrager; (*to spy on*) filer, pister

shad′ow gov′ernment *s* gouvernement *m* fantôme

shadowy [ʃædo·i] *adj* ombreux, sombre; (*fig*) vague, obscur

shad·y [ʃedi] *adj* (*comp* **-ier;** *super* **-iest**) ombreux, ombragé; (*coll*) louche

shaft [ʃæft] *s* (*of mine; of elevator*) puits *m*; (*of feather*) tige *f*; (*of arrow*) bois *m*; (*of column*) fût *m*, tige; (*of flag*) mât *m*; (*of wagon*) brancard *m*, limon *m*; (*of motor*) arbre *m*; (*of light*) rayon *m*; (*to make fun of s.o.*) trait *m*

shag·gy [ʃægi] *adj* (*comp* **-gier;** *super* **-giest**) poilu, à longs poils

shag′gy dog′ sto′ry *s* (*pl* **-ries**) histoire *f* sans queue ni tête

shagreen [ʃəˈgrin] *s* peau *f* de chagrin

shake [ʃek] *s* secousse *f* ‖ *v* (*pret* **shook** [ʃʊk]; *pp* **shaken**) *tr* secouer; (*the head*) hocher, secouer; (*one′s hand*) serrer; **to shake down** faire tomber; (*a thermometer*) secouer; (*slang*) escroquer; **to shake off** secouer; (*to get rid of*) se débarrasser de; **to shake up** (*a liquid*) agiter; (*fig*) ébranler ‖ *intr* trembler

shake′down′ *adj* (*cruise*) préparatoire, préliminaire ‖ *s* (*search*) fouille *f*; (*extortion*) extorsion *f*, chantage *m*

shaker [ʃekər] *s* (*for salt*) salière *f*; (*for cocktails*) shaker *m*

shake′up′ *s* bouleversement *m*; (*reorganization*) remaniement *m*

shak·y [ʃeki] *adj* (*comp* **-ier;** *super* **-iest**) tremblant, chancelant; (*hand; writing*) tremblé; (*voice*) tremblotant

shale [ʃel] *s* schiste *m* (argileux)

shall [ʃæl] *v* (*cond* **should** [ʃʊd]) *aux* used to express 1) the future indicative, e.g., **I shall arrive** j′arriverai; 2) the future perfect indicative, e.g., **I shall have arrived** je serai arrivé; 3) the potential mood, e.g., **what shall he do?** que doit-il faire?

shallow [ʃælo] *adj* peu profond; (*dish*) plat; (*fig*) creux, superficiel ‖ **shallows** *spl* haut-fond *m*

sham [ʃæm] *adj* feint, simulé ‖ *s* feinte *f*, simulacre *m*; (*person*) imposteur *m* ‖ *v* (*pret* & *pp* **shammed;** *ger* **shamming**) *tr* & *intr* feindre, simuler

sham′ bat′tle *s* combat *m* simulé

shambles [ʃæmbəlz] *spl* boucherie *f*; ravage *m*, ruine *f*; (*disorder*) pagaille *f*

shame [ʃem] *s* honte *f*; **shame on you!, for shame!** quelle honte!; **what a shame!** quel dommage! ‖ *tr* faire honte à

shame′faced′ *adj* penaud, honteux

shameful [ʃemfəl] *adj* honteux

shameless [ʃemlɪs] *adj* éhonté

shampoo [ʃæmˈpu] *s* shampooing *m* ‖ *tr* (*the hair*) laver; (*a person*) faire un shampooing à

shamrock [ʃæmrɑk] *s* trèfle *m* d′Irlande

Shanghai [ʃæŋhaɪ] *s* Changhaï ‖ (*l.c.*) *tr* (coll) racoler

Shangri-la [ˌʃæŋɡrɪˈlɑ] *s* le pays de Cocagne

shank [ʃæŋk] *s* jambe *f*, tibia *m*; (*of horse*) canon *m*; (*of anchor*) verge *f*; (culin) manche *m*; (*of a column*) fût *m*

shan·ty [ʃænti] *s* (*pl* **-ties**) masure *f*, bicoque *f*

shan′ty·town′ *s* bidonville *m*

shape [ʃep] *s* forme *f*; **in bad shape** (coll) mal en point; **in good shape** (*physically*) en bonne tenue; **out of shape** déformé; **to take shape** prendre tournure; ‖ *tr* former ‖ *intr* se former; **to shape up** prendre forme; avancer

shapeless [ʃeplɪs] *adj* informe

shape·ly [ʃepli] *adj* (*comp* **-lier;** *super* **-liest**) bien proportionné, bien fait, svelte

share [ʃɛr] *s* part *f*; (*of stock in a company*) action *f* ‖ *tr* partager ‖ *intr*—**to share in** prendre part à, participer à

sharecropper [ʃɛr,krɑpər] *s* métayer *m*

share′hold′er *s* actionnaire *mf*

shark [ʃɑrk] *s* requin *m*; (*swindler*) escroc *m*; (*slang*) as *m*, expert *m*

sharp [ʃɑrp] *adj* (*point; pain; intelligence; voice, sound*) aigu; (*wind, cold, pain, fight, criticism, edge, trot; person, mind*) vif; (*knife*) tranchant; (*point; needle, pin, nail; tongue*) acéré; (*slope*) raide; (*curve*) prononcé; (*turn*) brusque; (*photograph*) net; (*hearing*) fin; (*step, gait*) rapide; (*eyesight*) perçant; (*taste*) piquant; (*reprimand*) vert; (*keen; cunning*) rusé, fin; (mus) dièse; (*stylish*) (coll) chic; **sharp features** traits *mpl* accentués ‖ *adv* vivement; brusquement; précis, sonnant, tapant, e.g., **at four o′clock sharp** à quatre heures précises, sonnantes, or tapantes; **to stop short** s′arrêter net or pile ‖ *s* (mus) dièse *m* ‖ *tr* (mus) diéser

sharpen [ʃɑrpən] *tr* aiguiser; (*a pencil*) tailler ‖ *intr* s′aiguiser

sharpener [ʃɑrpənər] *s* aiguisoir *m*

sharper [ʃɑrpər] *s* filou *m*, tricheur *m*

sharp′shoot′er *s* tireur *m* d′élite

shatter [ʃætər] *tr* fracasser, briser ‖ *intr* se fracasser, se briser

shat′ter·proof′ *adj* de sécurité

shave [ʃev] *s*—**to get a shave** se faire raser, se faire faire la barbe; **to have a close shave** (coll) l′échapper belle ‖ *tr* (*hair, beard, etc.*) raser; (*a person*) faire la barbe à, raser; (*e.g., wood*) doler; (*e.g., expenses*) rogner ‖ *intr* se raser, se faire la barbe

shaving [ʃevɪŋ] *s* rasage *m*; **shavings** rognures *fpl*, copeaux *mpl*

shav′ing brush′ *s* blaireau *m*

shav′ing soap′ *s* savon *m* à barbe, savonnade *f*

shawl [ʃɔl] *s* châle *m*, fichu *m*

she [ʃi] *s* femelle *f* ‖ *pron pers* elle §85, §87; ce §82B; **she who** celle qui §83

sheaf [ʃif] *s* (*pl* **sheaves** [ʃivz]) gerbe *f*; (*of papers*) liasse *f*

shear [ʃɪr] *s* lame *f* de ciseau; **shears** ciseaux *mpl*; (*to cut metal*) cisaille *f* ‖ *v* (*pret* **sheared**; *pp* **sheared** or **shorn** [ʃorn]) *tr* (*sheep*) tondre; (*velvet*) ciseler; (*metal*) cisailler; **to shear off** couper

sheath [ʃiθ] *s* (*pl* **sheaths** [ʃiðz]) gaine *f*, fourreau *m*

sheathe [ʃið] *tr* envelopper; (*a sword*) rengainer

shed [ʃɛd] *s* (*warehouse; engine shed; barn*) hangar *m*; (*for, e.g., tools*) remise *f*; (*rough shelter*) hutte *f*, cabane *f*; (*for cattle*) étable *f*; (*line from which water flows in two directions*) ligne *f* de faîte ‖ *v* (*pret & pp* **shed**; *ger* **shedding**) *tr* répandre, verser; (*e.g., leaves*) perdre; (*e.g., light; skin*) jeter

sheen [ʃin] *s* lustre *m*, brilliant *m*

sheep [ʃip] *s* (*pl* **sheep**) mouton *m*; (*ewe*) brebis *f*

sheep'dog' *s* chien *m* de berger

sheep'fold' *s* bergerie *f*

sheepish [ʃipɪʃ] *adj* penaud, honteux

sheep'skin' *s* (*undressed*) peau *f* de mouton; (*dressed*) basane *f*; (*diploma*) (coll) peau d'âne

sheep'skin jack'et *s* canadienne *f*

sheer [ʃɪr] *adj* (*stocking*) extra-fin; (*steep*) à pic; (*impossibility; necessity; waste of time*) absolu; (*utter*) pur; (fig) vif, e.g., **by sheer force** de vive force ‖ *intr* faire une embardée

sheet [ʃit] *s* (*e.g., for the bed*) drap *m*; (*of paper*) feuille *f*; (*of metal*) tôle *f*, lame *f*; (*of water*) nappe *f*; (*of ice*) couche *f*; (naut) écoute *f*; **white as a sheet** blanc comme un linge

sheet' light'ning *s* fulguration *f*, éclairs *mpl* en nappe

sheet' met'al *s* tôle *f*

sheet' mu'sic *s* morceaux *mpl* de musique

sheik [ʃik] *s* cheik *m*; (coll) tombeur *m* de femmes

shelf [ʃɛlf] *s* (*pl* **shelves** [ʃɛlvz]) tablette *f*, planche *f*; (*of cupboard; of library*) rayon *m*; (geog) plateau *m*; **on the shelf** (*inactive*) (coll) au rancart, laissé à l'écart; **shelves** rayonnages *mpl*

shell [ʃɛl] *s* (*of egg, nut, oyster, snail, etc.*) coque *f*, coquille *f*; (*of nut*) écale *f*, coque; (*of pea*) cosse *f*; (*of oyster, clam, etc.*) écaille *f*; (*of tortoise, lobster, crab*) carapace *f*; (*of building, ship, etc.*) carcasse *f*; (*cartridge*) cartouche *f*; (*projectile*) obus *m*; (*long, narrow racing boat*) yole *f*, outrigger *m* ‖ *tr* écaler, écosser; (mil) bombarder, pilonner; **to shell out** (coll) débourser ‖ *intr*—**to shell out** (coll) casquer

shel·lac [ʃə'læk] *s* laque *f*, gomme *f* laque ‖ *v* (*pret & pp* **-lacked**; *ger* **-lacking**) *tr* laquer; (slang) tabasser

shell'fish' *s* fruits *mpl* de mer, coquillages *mpl*

shell' hole' *s* entonnoir *m*, trou *m* d'obus

shell' shock' *s* commotion *f* cérébrale

shelter ['ʃɛltər] *s* abri *m* ‖ *tr* abriter

shelve [ʃɛlv] *tr* (*a book*) ranger; (*merchandise*) entreposer; (*a project, a question, etc., by putting it aside*) enterrer, classer; (*to provide with shelves*) garnir de tablettes, rayons, or planches

shelving ['ʃɛlvɪŋ] *s* rayonnage *m*, étagères *fpl*

shepherd ['ʃɛpərd] *s* berger *m*; (fig) pasteur *m* ‖ *tr* veiller sur, guider

shep'herd dog' *s* berger *m*, chien *m* de berger

shepherdess ['ʃɛpərdɪs] *s* bergère *f*

sherbet ['ʃʌrbət] *s* sorbet *m*

sheriff ['ʃɛrɪf] *s* shérif *m*

sher·ry ['ʃɛri] *s* (*pl* **-ries**) xérès *m*

shield [ʃild] *s* bouclier *m*; (elec) blindage *m*; (heral, hist) écu *m*, écusson *m* ‖ *tr* protéger; (elec) blinder

shift [ʃɪft] *s* (*change*) changement *m*; (*in wind, temperature, etc.*) saute *f*; (*group of workmen*) équipe *f* de relais; (fig) expédient *m* ‖ *tr* changer; (*the blame, the guilt, etc.*) rejeter; **to shift gears** changer de vitesse ‖ *intr* changer; changer de place; changer de direction; **to shift for oneself** se débrouiller tout seul

shift' key' *s* touche *f* majuscules

shiftless ['ʃɪftlɪs] *adj* mollasse, peu débrouillard

shift'-lock' key' *s* fixe-majuscules *m*

shift·y ['ʃɪfti] *adj* (*comp* **-ier**; *super* **-iest**) roublard; (*look*) chafouin; (*eye*) fuyant

shimmer ['ʃɪmər] *s* chatoiement *m*, miroitement *m* ‖ *intr* chatoyer, miroiter

shin [ʃɪn] *s* tibia *m*; (culin) jarret *m* ‖ *v* (*pret & pp* **shinned**; *ger* **shinning**) *intr*—**to shin up** grimper

shin'bone' *s* tibia *m*

shine [ʃaɪn] *s* (*shining*) éclat *m*, brillant *m*; (*of cloth, clothing, etc.*) luisant *m*; (*on shoes*) coup *m* de cirage; **to take a shine to** (slang) s'enticher de ‖ *v* (*pret & pp* **shined**) *tr* faire briller, faire reluire; (*shoes*) cirer ‖ *v* (*pret & pp* **shone** [ʃon]) *intr* briller, reluire

shiner ['ʃaɪnər] *s* (slang) œil *m* poché

shingle ['ʃɪŋgəl] *s* bardeau *m*; (*of doctor, laywer, etc.*) (coll) enseigne *f*; **shingles** (pathol) zona *m*

shining ['ʃaɪnɪŋ] *adj* brillant, luisant

shin·y ['ʃaɪni] *adj* (*comp* **-ier**; *super* **-iest**) brillant, reluisant; (*from much wear*) lustré

ship [ʃɪp] *s* navire *m*; (*steamer, liner*) paquebot *m*; (aer) appareil *m*; (nav) bâtiment *m* ‖ *v* (*pret & pp* **shipped**; *ger* **shipping**) *tr* expédier; (*a cargo; water*) embarquer; (*oars*) armer, rentrer ‖ *intr* s'embarquer

ship'board' *s* bord *m*; **on shipboard** à bord

ship'build'er *s* constructeur *m* de navires

ship'build'ing *s* construction *f* navale

ship'mate' *s* compagnon *m* de bord

shipment ['ʃɪpmənt] *s* expédition *f*; (*goods shipped*) chargement *m*
ship′own′er *s* armateur *m*
shipper ['ʃɪpər] *s* expéditeur *m*
shipping ['ʃɪpɪŋ] *s* embarquement *m*, expédition *f*; (naut) transport *m* maritime
ship′ping clerk′ *s* expéditionnaire *mf*
ship′ping mem′o *s* connaissement *m*
ship′ping room′ *s* salle *f* d'expédition
ship′shape′ *adj & adv* en bon ordre
ship′s′ pa′pers *spl* papiers *mpl* de bord
ship′s′ time′ *s* heure *f* locale du navire
ship′-to-shore′ ra′di·o ['ʃɪptə ʃor] *s* (*pl* -os) liaison *f* radio maritime
ship′wreck′ *s* naufrage *m* ‖ *tr* faire naufrager ‖ *intr* faire naufrage
ship′yard′ *s* chantier *m* de construction navale or maritime
shirk [ʃʌrk] *tr* manquer à, esquiver ‖ *intr* négliger son devoir
shirred′ eggs′ [ʃʌrd] *spl* œufs *mpl* pochés à la crème
shirt [ʃʌrt] *s* chemise *f*; **keep your shirt on!** (slang) ne vous emballez pas!; **to lose one's shirt** perdre jusqu'à son dernier sou
shirt′band′ *s* encolure *f*
shirt′ front′ *s* plastron *m* de chemise
shirt′ sleeve′ *s* manche *f* de chemise; **in shirt sleeves** en bras de chemise
shirt′tails′ *spl* pans *mpl* de chemise
shirt′waist′ *s* chemisier *m*
shiver ['ʃɪvər] *s* frisson *m* ‖ *intr* frissonner
shoal [ʃol] *s* banc *m*, bas-fond *m*
shock [ʃɑk] *s* (*bump, clash*) choc *m*, heurt *m*; (*upset, misfortune; earthquake tremor*) secousse *f*; (*of grain*) gerbe *f*, moyette *f*; (*of hair*) tignasse *f*; (elec) commotion *f*, choc; **to die of shock** mourir de saisissement ‖ *tr* choquer; (elec) commotionner, choquer
shock′ absorb′er [æb,sɔrbər] *s* amortisseur *m*
shocking ['ʃɑkɪŋ] *adj* choquant, scandaleux
shock′ troops′ *spl* troupes *fpl* de choc
shod·dy ['ʃɑdi] *adj* (*comp* -dier; *super* -diest) inférieur, de pacotille
shoe [ʃu] *s* soulier *m*; **to be in the shoes of** être dans la peau de; **to put one's shoes on** se chausser; **to take one's shoes off** se déchausser ‖ *v* (*pret & pp* shod [ʃɑd]) *tr* chausser; (*a horse*) ferrer
shoe′black′ *s* cireur *m* de bottes
shoe′horn′ *s* chausse-pied *m*
shoe′lace′ *s* lacet *m*, cordon *m* de soulier
shoe′mak′er *s* cordonnier *m*
shoe′ pol′ish *s* cirage *m* de chaussures
shoe′shine′ *s* cirage *m*
shoe′ store′ *s* magasin *m* de chaussures
shoe′string′ *s* lacet *m*, cordon *m* de soulier; **on a shoestring** avec de minces capitaux
shoe′tree′ *s* embauchoir *m*, forme *f*
shoo [ʃu] *tr* chasser ‖ *interj* ch!, filez!
shoot [ʃut] *s* (*sprout, twig*) rejeton *m*, pousse *f*; (*for grain, sand, etc.*) goulotte *f*; (*contest*) concours *m* de tir; (*hunting party*) partie *f* de chasse ‖ *v* (*pret & pp* shot [ʃɑt]) *tr* tirer; (*a person*) tuer d'un coup

de fusil; (*to execute with a discharge of rifles*) fusiller; (*with a camera*) photographier; (*a scene; a motion picture*) tourner, roder; (*the sun*) prendre la hauteur de; (*dice*) jeter; **to shoot down** abattre; **to shoot up** (slang) cribler de balles ‖ *intr* tirer; s'élancer, se précipiter; (*said of pain*) lanciner; (*said of star*) filer; **to shoot at** faire feu sur; (*to strive for*) viser; **to shoot up** (*said of plant*) pousser; (*said of flame*) jaillir; (*said of prices*) augmenter; (*intravenously*) (slang) se shooter
shooting ['ʃutɪŋ] *s* tir *m*; (phot) prise *f* de vues
shoot′ing gal′ler·y *s* (*pl* -ies) stand *m* de tir, tir *m*
shoot′ing match′ *s* concours *m* de tir
shoot′ing script′ *s* découpage *m*
shoot′ing star′ *s* étoile *f* filante
shop [ʃɑp] *s* (*store*) boutique *f*; (*workshop*) atelier *m*; **to talk shop** parler boutique, parler affaires ‖ *v* (*pret & pp* shopped; *ger* shopping) *intr* faire des emplettes, faire des courses; magasiner (Canad); **to go shopping** faire des emplettes, faire des courses; **to shop around** être à l'affût de bonnes occasions; **to shop for** chercher à acheter
shop′girl′ *s* vendeuse *f*
shop′keep′er *s* boutiquier *m*
shoplifter ['ʃɑp,lɪftər] *s* voleur *m* à l'étalage
shopper ['ʃɑpər] *s* acheteur *m*
shopping ['ʃɑpɪŋ] *s* achat *m*; (*purchases*) achats *mpl*, emplettes *fpl*
shop′ping bag′ *s* sac *m* à provisions, cabas *m*
shop′ping cen′ter *s* centre *m* commercial
shop′ping dis′trict *s* quartier *m* commerçant
shop′ping mall′ *s* galerie *f* marchande
shop′ stew′ard *s* délégué *m* d'atelier
shop′win′dow *s* vitrine *f*, devanture *f*
shop′worn′ *adj* défraîchi
shore [ʃor] *s* rivage *m*, rive *f*, bord *m*; (*sandy beach*) plage *f*; **shores** (poetic) pays *m* ‖ *tr*—**to shore up** étayer
shore′ din′ner *s* dîner *m* de marée
shore′ leave′ *s* (nav) descente *f* à terre
shore′line′ *s* ligne *f* de côte
shore′ patrol′ *s* patrouille *f* de garde-côte; (*police*) (nav) police *f* militaire de la marine
short [ʃɔrt] *adj* court; (*person*) petit; (*temper*) brusque; (phonet) bref; **in short** en somme; **short of breath** poussif; **to be short for** (coll) être le diminutif de; **to be short of** être à court de ‖ *s* (elec) court-circuit *m*; (mov) court-métrage *m*; **shorts** culotte *f* courte, culotte de sport ‖ *adv* court, de court; **to run short of** être à court de, manquer de; **to sell short** (com) vendre à découvert; **to stop short** s'arrêter net ‖ *tr* (elec) court-circuiter ‖ *intr* (elec) se mettre en court-circuit
shortage ['ʃɔrtɪʤ] *s* manque *m*, pénurie *f*; crise *f*, e.g., **housing shortage** crise du logement; (com) déficit *m*; **shortages** manquants *mpl*

short′cake′ s gâteau m recouvert de fruits frais m

short′-change′ tr ne pas rendre assez de monnaie à; (to cheat) (coll) rouler

short′ cir′cuit s court-circuit m

short′-cir′cuit tr court-circuiter

short′com′ing s défaut m

short′cut′ s raccourci m

shorten [′ʃɔrtən] tr raccourcir ‖ intr se raccourcir

shortening [′ʃɔrtənɪŋ] s raccourcissement m; (culin) saindoux m

short′hand′ adj sténographique ‖ s sténographie f; **to take down in shorthand** sténographier

short′hand notes′ spl sténogramme m

short′hand typ′ist s sténodactylo mf

short-lived [′ʃɔrt′laɪvd], [′ʃɔrt′lɪvd] adj de courte durée, bref

shortly [′ʃɔrtli] adv tantôt, sous peu; brièvement; (curtly) sèchement; **shortly after** peu après

short′-range′ adj à courte portée

short′-range plane′ s court-courrier m

short′ sale′ s vente f à découvert

short′-sight′ed adj myope; **to be short-sighted** (fig) avoir la vue courte

short′ sto′ry s nouvelle f, conte m

short′-tem′pered adj vif, emporté

short′-term′ adj à court terme

short′wave′ adj aux petites ondes, aux ondes courtes ‖ s petite onde f, onde courte

short′ weight′ s poids m insuffisant

shot [ʃɑt] adj (silk) changeant; (e.g., chances) (coll) réduit à zéro; (drunk) (slang) paf ‖ s coup m de feu, décharge f; (marksman) tireur m; (pellets) petits plombs mpl; (of a rocket into space) lancement m, tir m; (in certain games) shoot m; (snapshot) instantané m; (mov) plan m; (hypodermic injection) (coll) piqûre f; (drink of liquor) (slang) verre m d'alcool; **a long shot** un gros risque, une chance sur mille; **to fire a shot at** tirer sur; **to start like a shot** partir comme un trait

shot′gun′ s fusil m de chasse

shot′-put′ s (sports) lancement m du poids

should [ʃud] aux used to express 1) the present conditional, e.g., **if I waited for him, I should miss the train** si je l'attendais, je manquerais le train; 2) the past conditional, e.g., **if I had waited for him, I should have missed the train** si je l'avais attendu, j'aurais manqué le train; 3) the potential mood, e.g., **he should go at once** il devrait aller aussitôt; e.g., **he should have gone at once** il aurait dû aller aussitôt; 4) a softened affirmation, e.g., **I should like a drink** je prendrais bien quelque chose à boire; e.g., **I should have thought that you would have known better** j'aurais cru que vous auriez été plus avisé

shoulder [′ʃoldər] s épaule f; (of a road) accotement m; **across the shoulder** en bandoulière, en écharpe; **shoulders** (of a garment) carrure f; **to cry on someone's shoulder** pleurer dans le gilet de qn ‖ tr (a gun) mettre sur l'épaule; **to shoulder aside** pousser de l'épaule

shoul′der blade′ s omoplate f

shoul′der strap′ s (of underwear) épaulette f; (mil) bandoulière f

shout [ʃaut] s cri m ‖ tr crier; **to shout down** huer ‖ intr crier

shove [ʃʌv] s poussée f, bourrade f ‖ tr pousser, bousculer ‖ intr pousser; **to shove off** pousser au large; (slang) filer, décamper

shov·el [′ʃʌvəl] s pelle f ‖ v (pret & pp -eled or -elled; ger -eling or -elling) tr pelleter; (e.g., snow) balayer

show [ʃo] s (of hatred or affection) démonstration f; (semblance) apparence f; (exhibition) exposition f; (display) étalage m, parade f; (of hands) levée f; (each performance) séance f; (mov) film m; (theat) spectacle m; **by show of hands** à main levée; **to make a show of** faire parade de ‖ v (pret **showed;** pp **shown** [ʃon] or **showed**) tr montrer; (one's passport) présenter; (a film) projeter; (e.g., to the door) conduire; **to show off** faire étalage de; **to show up** (coll) démasquer ‖ intr se montrer; **to show through** transparaître; **to show up** (against a background) ressortir; (coll) faire son apparition

show′ bill′ s affiche f

show′boat′ s bateau-théâtre m

show′ busi′ness s l'industrie f du spectacle

show′case′ s vitrine f

show′down′ s cartes fpl sur table, moment m critique; **to come to a showdown** en venir au fait; **to force a showdown** mettre au pied du mur

shower [′ʃau·ər] s averse f, ondée f; (of blows, bullets, kisses, etc.) pluie f; (bath) douche f ‖ tr faire pleuvoir; **to shower with** combler de ‖ intr pleuvoir à verse

show′ girl′ s girl f

show′man s (pl -men) impresario m; **he's a great showman** c'est un as pour la mise en scène

show′-off′ s (coll) m'as-tu-vu m

show′piece′ s pièce f maîtresse

show′place′ s lieu m célèbre

show′room′ s salon m d'exposition

show′ win′dow s vitrine f

show·y [′ʃo·i] adj (comp -ier; super -iest) fastueux; (gaudy) voyant

shrapnel [′ʃræpnəl] s shrapnel m, obus m à mitraille; éclat m d'obus

shred [ʃrɛd] s morceau m, lambeau m; **not a shred of** pas l'ombre de; **to tear to shreds** mettre en lambeaux ‖ v (pret & pp **shredded** or **shred;** ger **shredding**) tr mettre en lambeaux, déchiqueter

shrew [ʃru] s (nagging woman) mégère f; (zool) musaraigne f

shrewd [ʃrud] adj sagace, fin

shriek [ʃrik] s cri m perçant ‖ intr pousser un cri perçant

shrike [ʃraɪk] *s* pie-grièche *f*

shrill [ʃrɪl] *adj* aigu, perçant

shrimp [ʃrɪmp] *s* crevette *f*; (*insignificant person*) gringalet *m*

shrine [ʃraɪn] *s* tombeau *m* de saint; (*reliquary*) châsse *f*; (*holy place*) lieu *m* saint, sanctuaire *m*

shrink [ʃrɪŋk] *v* (*pret* **shrank** [ʃræŋk] or **shrunk** [ʃrʌŋk]; *pp* **shrunk** or **shrunken**) *tr* rétrécir ‖ *intr* se rétrécir; **to shrink away** or **back from** reculer devant

shrinkage [ʃrɪŋkɪdʒ] *s* rétrécissement *m*

shriv·el [ʃrɪvəl] *v* (*pret & pp* **-eled** or **-elled**; *ger* **-eling** or **-elling**) *tr* ratatiner, recroqueviller ‖ *intr* se ratatiner, se recroqueviller

shroud [ʃraʊd] *s* linceul *m*; (*veil*) voile *m*; **shrouds** (naut) haubans *mpl* ‖ *tr* ensevelir; voiler

Shrove' Tues'day [ʃrov] *s* mardi *m* gras

shrub [ʃrʌb] *s* arbuste *m*

shrubber·y [ʃrʌbəri] *s* (*pl* **-ies**) bosquet *m*

shrug [ʃrʌg] *s* haussement *m* d'épaules ‖ *v* (*pret & pp* **shrugged**; *ger* **shrugging**) *tr* (*one's shoulders*) hausser; **to shrug off** minimiser; ne tenir aucun compte de ‖ *intr* hausser les épaules

shudder [ʃʌdər] *s* frisson *m*, frémissement *m* ‖ *intr* frissonner, frémir

shuffle [ʃʌfəl] *s* (*of cards*) battement *m*, mélange *m*; (*of feet*) frottement *m*; (*change of place*) déplacement *m* ‖ *tr* (*cards*) battre; (*the feet*) traîner; (*to mix up*) mêler, brouiller ‖ *intr* battre les cartes; traîner les pieds

shuf·fle·board' *s* jeu *m* de palets

shun [ʃʌn] *v* (*pret & pp* **shunned**; *ger* **shunning**) *tr* éviter, fuir

shunt [ʃʌnt] *tr* garer, manœuvrer; (elec) shunter, dériver

shut [ʃʌt] *adj* fermé ‖ *v* (*pret & pp* **shut**; *ger* **shutting**) *tr* fermer; **to shut in** enfermer; **to shut off** couper; **to shut up** enfermer; (coll) faire taire, clouer le bec à ‖ *intr* se fermer; **shut up!** (slang) tais-toi!, ferme-la!

shut'down' *s* fermeture *f*

shutter [ʃʌtər] *s* volet *m*, contrevent *m*; (*over store window*) rideau *m*; (phot) obturateur *m*

shuttle [ʃʌtəl] *s* navette *f* ‖ *intr* faire la navette

shut'tle train' *s* navette *f*

shy [ʃaɪ] *adj* (*comp* **shyer** or **shier**; *super* **shyest** or **shiest**) timide, sauvage; (*said of horse*) ombrageux; **I am shy a dollar** il me faut un dollar; **to be shy of** se méfier de ‖ *v* (*pret & pp* **shied**) *intr* (*said of horse*) faire un écart; **to shy away from** éviter

shyster [ʃaɪstər] *s* (coll) avocat *m* marron

Sia·mese [ˌsaɪ·ə'miz] *adj* siamois ‖ *s* (*pl* **-mese**) Siamois *m*

Si'amese twins' *spl* frères *mpl* siamois

Siberian [saɪ'bɪrɪ·ən] *adj* sibérien ‖ *s* Sibérien *m*

sibyl [ˈsɪbɪl] *s* sibylle *f*

sic [sɪk] *adv* sic ‖ [sɪk] *v* (*pret & pp* **sicked; ger sicking**) *tr*—**sic 'em!** (coll) pille!; **to sic on** lancer après

Sicilian [sɪ'sɪljən] *adj* sicilien ‖ *s* Sicilien *m*

Sicily [ˈsɪsɪli] *s* Sicile *f*; la Sicile

sick [sɪk] *adj* malade; **to be sick and tired of** (coll) en avoir plein le dos de, en avoir marre de; **to be sick at** or **to one's stomach** avoir mal au cœur, avoir des nausées; **to take sick** tomber malade

sick'bed' *s* lit *m* de malade

sicken [ˈsɪkən] *tr* rendre malade ‖ *intr* tomber malade; (*to be disgusted*) être écœuré

sickening [ˈsɪkənɪŋ] *adj* écœurant, dégoûtant

sick' head'ache *s* migraine *f* avec nausées

sickle [ˈsɪkəl] *s* faucille *f*

sick' leave' *s* congé *m* de maladie

sick'le cell' ane'mia *s* (pathol) drépanocytose *f*

sick·ly [ˈsɪkli] *adj* (*comp* **-lier**; *super* **-liest**) maladif, débile

sickness [ˈsɪknɪs] *s* maladie *f*; nausée *f*

side [saɪd] *adj* latéral, de côté ‖ *s* côté *m*; (*of phonograph*) face *f*; (*of team, government, etc.*) camp *m*, parti *m*, côté; **this side up** (*on package*) haut ‖ *intr*—**to side with** prendre le parti de

side' arms' *spl* armes *fpl* de ceinturon

side'board' *s* buffet *m*, desserte *f*

side'burns' *spl* favoris *mpl*

side' dish' *s* plat *m* d'accompagnement

side' door' *s* porte *f* latérale, porte *f* de service

side' effect' *s* effet *m* secondaire

side' en'trance *s* entrée *f* latérale

side' glance' *s* regard *m* de côté

side' is'sue *s* question *f* d'intérêt secondaire

side'line' *s* occupation *f* secondaire; **on the sidelines** sans y prendre part

sidereal [saɪ'dɪrɪ·əl] *adj* sidéral

side' road' *s* chemin *m* de traverse

side'sad'dle *adv* en amazone

side' show' *s* spectacle *m* forain; (fig) événement *m* secondaire

side'slip' *s* glissade *f* sur l'aile

side' split'ting *adj* désopilant

side' step' *s* écart *m*

side'-step' *v* (*pret & pp* **-stepped**; *ger* **-stepping**) *tr* éviter ‖ *intr* faire un pas de côté

side'stroke' *s* nage *f* sur le côté

side' ta'ble *s* console *f*

side'track' *s* voie *f* de garage ‖ *tr* écarter, dévier; (rr) aiguiller sur une voie de garage

side' view' *s* vue *f* de profil

side'walk' *s* trottoir *m*

side'walk café' *s* terrasse *f* de café

side'walk sale' *s* vente *f* à l'éventaire

sideward [ˈsaɪdwərd] *adj* latéral ‖ *adv* latéralement, de côté

side'ways' *adj* latéral ‖ *adv* latéralement, de côté

side' whisk'ers *spl* favoris *mpl*

side′wise′ *adj* latéral ‖ *adv* latéralement, de côté

siding [′saɪdɪŋ] *s* (*on a house*) bardage *m*; (rr) voie *f* d'évitement, voie de garage

sidle [′saɪdəl] *intr* avancer de biais; **to sidle up to** se couler auprès de

siege [sidʒ] *s* siège *m*; **to lay siege to** mettre le siège devant

siesta [si′estə] *s* sieste *f*; **to take a siesta** faire la sieste

sieve [sɪv] *s* crible *m*, tamis *m* ‖ *tr* passer au crible, passer au tamis

sift [sɪft] *tr* passer au crible, passer au tamis; (*flour*) tamiser; (fig) examiner soigneusement

sigh [saɪ] *s* soupir *m* ‖ *intr* soupirer

sight [saɪt] *s* vue *f*; (*of firearm*) mire *f*; (*of telescope, camera, etc.*) viseur *m*; chose *f* digne d'être vue; **a sight of** (coll) énormément de; **at sight** à vue; **à livre ouvert**; **by sight** de vue; **in sight of** à la vue de; **sad sight** spectacle *m* navrant; **sights** curiosités *fpl*; **to catch sight of** apercevoir; **what a sight you are!** comme vous voilà fait! ‖ *tr & intr* viser

sight′ draft′ *s* (com) effet *m* à vue

sight′-read′ *v* (*pret & pp* **read** [,rɛd]) *tr & intr* lire à livre ouvert; (mus) déchiffrer

sight′ read′er *s* déchiffreur *m*

sight′see′ing *s* tourisme *m*; **to go sightseeing** visiter les curiosités

sightseer [′saɪt,si·ər] *s* touriste *mf*, excursionniste *mf*

sign [saɪn] *s* signe *m*; (*on a store*) enseigne *f* ‖ *tr* signer; **to sign up** engager, embaucher ‖ *intr* signer; **to sign off** (rad) terminer l'émission; **to sign up for** (coll) s'inscrire à

sig·nal [′sɪgnəl] *adj* signalé, insigne ‖ *s* signal *m* ‖ *v* (*pret & pp* **-naled** or **-nalled**; *ger* **-naling** or **-nalling**) *tr* faire signe à, signaler ‖ *intr* faire des signaux

sig′nal tow′er *s* tour *f* de signalisation

signature [′sɪgnətʃər] *s* signature *f*; (bb) cahier *m* (d'imprimerie); (mus) armature *f*; (rad) indicatif *m*

sign′board′ *s* panneau *m* d'affichage

signer [′saɪnər] *s* signataire *mf*

sig′net ring′ [′sɪgnɪt] *s* chevalière *f*

significance [sɪg′nɪfɪkəns] *s* importance *f*; (*meaning*) signification *f*

significant [sɪg′nɪfəkənt] *adj* important; significatif

signi·fy [′sɪgnɪ,faɪ] *v* (*pret & pp* **-fied**) *tr* signifier

sign′post′ *s* poteau *m* indicateur

silence [′saɪləns] *s* silence *m* ‖ *tr* faire taire, réduire au silence

silencer [′saɪlənsər] *s* (*of a gun*) silencieux *m*

silent [′saɪlənt] *adj* silencieux

si′lent major′ity *s* majorité *f* silencieuse

si′lent mov′ie *s* film *m* muet

silhouette [,sɪlu′ɛt] *s* silhouette *f* ‖ *tr* silhouetter

silicon [′sɪlɪkən] *s* silicium *m*

silicone [′sɪlɪ,kon] *s* silicone *f*

silk [sɪlk] *s* soie *f*

silk′-cotton tree′ *s* fromager *m*

silken [′sɪlkən] *adj* soyeux

silk′ hat′ *s* haut-de-forme *m*

silk′-stock′ing *adj* aristocratique ‖ *s* aristocrate *mf*

silk′worm′ *s* ver *m* à soie

silk·y [′sɪlki] *adj* (*comp* **-ier**; *super* **-iest**) soyeux

sill [sɪl] *s* (*of window*) rebord *m*; (*of door*) seuil *m*; (*of walls*) sablière *f*

sil·ly [′sɪli] *adj* (*comp* **-lier**; *super* **-liest**) sot, niais

si·lo [′saɪlo] *s* (*pl* **-los**) silo *m* ‖ *tr* ensiler

silt [sɪlt] *s* vase *f*

silver [′sɪlvər] *s* argent *m* ‖ *tr* argenter; (*a mirror*) étamer

sil′ver·fish′ *s* (ent) poisson *m* d'argent

sil′ver foil′ *s* feuille *f* d'argent

sil′ver lin′ing *s* beau côté *m*, côté brillant

sil′ver plate′ *s* argenterie *f*

sil′ver screen′ *s* écran *m*

sil′ver·smith′ *s* orfèvre *m*

sil′ver spoon′ *s*—**born with a silver spoon in one's mouth** né coiffé

sil′ver-tongued′ *adj* à la langue dorée, éloquent

sil′ver·ware′ *s* argenterie *f*

similar [′sɪmɪlər] *adj* semblable

similari·ty [,sɪmɪ′lærɪti] *s* (*pl* **-ties**) ressemblance *f*, similitude *f*

simile [′sɪmɪli] *s* comparaison *f*

simmer [′sɪmər] *tr* mijoter ‖ *intr* mijoter; **to simmer down** s'apaiser

Simon [′saɪmən] *s* Simon *m*; **Simon says . . .** (game) Caporal a dit . . .

simper [′sɪmpər] *s* sourire *m* niais ‖ *intr* sourire bêtement

simple [′sɪmpəl] *adj & s* simple *m*

sim′ple-mind′ed *adj* simple, naïf; niais

simpleton [′sɪmpəltən] *s* niais *m*

simpli·fy [′sɪmplɪ,faɪ] *v* (*pret & pp* **-fied**) *tr* simplifier

simulate [′sɪmjə,let] *tr* simuler

simultaneous [,saɪməl′teni·əs] *adj* simultané

si′multa′neous transla′tion *s* traduction *f* en simultanée

sin [sɪn] *s* péché *m* ‖ *v* (*pret & pp* **sinned**; *ger* **sinning**) *intr* pécher

since [sɪns] *adv & prep* depuis ‖ *conj* depuis que; (*inasmuch as*) puisque

sincere [sɪn′sɪr] *adj* sincère

sincerity [sɪn′sɛrɪti] *s* sincérité *f*

sine [saɪn] *s* (trig) sinus *m*

sinecure [′saɪnɪ,kjur] *s* sinécure *f*

sinew [′sɪnju] *s* tendon *m*; (fig) nerf *m*, force *f*

sinful [′sɪnfəl] *adj* (*person*) pécheur; (*act, intention*) coupable

sing [sɪŋ] *v* (*pret* **sang** [sæŋ] or **sung** [sʌŋ]; *pp* **sung**) *tr & intr* chanter

singe [sɪndʒ] *v* (*ger* **singeing**) *tr* roussir; (*poultry*) flamber

singer [′sɪŋər] *s* chanteur *m*

single [′sɪŋgəl] *adj* seul, unique; (*unmarried*) célibataire; (*e.g., room in a hotel*) à un lit; (*bed*) à une place; (*e.g., devotion*) simple, honnête ‖ *tr*—**to single out** distinguer, choisir

sin'gle bless'edness ['blɛsɪdnɪs] *s* le bonheur *m* du célibat

sin'gle·breast'ed *adj* droit

sin'gle-en'try *adj* (bk) en partie simple

sin'gle-en'try book'keeping *s* comptabilité *f* simple

sin'gle file' *s*—**in single file** en file indienne, à la file

sin'gle-hand'ed *adj* sans aide, tout seul

sin'gle life' *s* vie *f* de célibataire

sin'gle room' *s* chambre *f* à un lit

sin'gle-spaced' *s* à simple interligne

sin'gle-track' *adj* (rr) à voie unique; (coll) d'une portée limitée

sing'song' *adj* monotone ‖ *s* mélopée *f*

singular ['sɪŋgjələr] *adj & s* singulier *m*

sinister ['sɪnɪstər] *adj* sinistre

sink [sɪŋk] *s* (*in kitchen or laundry*) évier *m*; (*in bathroom*) lavabo *m*; (*drain*) égout *m* ‖ *v* (*pret* **sank** [sæŋk] or **sunk** [sʌŋk]; *pp* **sunk**) *tr* enfoncer; (*a ship*) couler, faire sombrer; (*a well*) creuser; (*money*) immobiliser ‖ *intr* s'enfoncer, s'affaisser; (*under the water*) couler, sombrer; (*said of heart*) se serrer; (*said of health, prices, sun, etc.*) baisser; **to sink into** plonger dans; (*an armchair*) s'effondrer dans

sink'ing fund' *s* caisse *f* d'amortissement

sink'hole' *s* (fig) cloaque *m* de vice

sinless ['sɪnlɪs] *adj* sans péché

sinner ['sɪnər] *s* pécheur *m*

sintering ['sɪntərɪŋ] *s* (metallurgy) frittage *m*

sinuous ['sɪnjʊ·əs] *adj* sinueux

sinus ['saɪnəs] *s* sinus *m*

sip [sɪp] *s* petite gorgée *f*, petit coup *m* ‖ *v* (*pret & pp* **sipped**; *ger* **sipping**) *tr* boire à petit coups, siroter

siphon ['saɪfən] *s* siphon *m* ‖ *tr* siphonner

si'phon bot'tle *s* siphon *m*

sir [sʌr] *s* monsieur *m*; (*British title*) Sir *m*; **Dear Sir** Monsieur

sire [saɪr] *s* sire *m*; (*of a quadruped*) père *m* ‖ *tr* engendrer

siren ['saɪrən] *s* sirène *f*

sirloin ['sʌrlɔɪn] *s* aloyau *m*

sirup ['sɪrəp], ['sʌrəp] *s* sirop *m*

sis·sy ['sɪsi] *s* (*pl* **-sies**) efféminé *m*; fillette *f*; (*cowardly fellow*) poule *f* mouillée

sister ['sɪstər] *adj* (fig) jumeau ‖ *s* sœur *f*

sis'ter-in-law' *s* (*pl* **sisters-in-law**) belle-sœur *f*

sit [sɪt] *v* (*pret & pp* **sat** [sæt]; *ger* **sitting**) *intr* s'asseoir; être assis; (*said of hen on eggs*) couver; (*for a portrait*) poser; (*said of legislature, court, etc.*) siéger; **to sit down** s'asseoir; **to sit still** ne pas bouger; **to sit up** se redresser; se tenir droit; **to sit up and beg** (*said of dog*) faire le beau

sitcom ['sɪt,kɑm] *s* (rad, telv) comédie *f* de situation

sit'-down strike' *s* grève *f* sur le tas

site [saɪt] *s* site *m*

sit'-in' *s* occupation *f* sauvage

sitting ['sɪtɪŋ] *s* séance *f*

sit'ting duck' *s* (coll) cible *f* facile

sit'ting room' *s* salon *m*

situate ['sɪtʃʊ,et] *tr* situer

situation [,sɪtʃʊ'eʃən] *s* situation *f*; poste *m*, emploi *m*

sit'up' *s* (*exercise*) redressement *m* assis

sitz' bath' [sɪts] *s* bain *m* de siège

six [sɪks] *adj & pron* six ‖ *s* six *m*; **at sixes and sevens** de travers, en désaccord; **six o'clock** six heures

sixteen ['sɪks'tin] *adj, pron, & s* seize *m*

sixteenth ['sɪks'tinθ] *adj & pron* seizième (*masc, fem*); **the Sixteenth** seize, e.g., **John the Sixteenth** Jean seize ‖ *s* seizième *m*; (*in dates*) le seize

sixth [sɪksθ] *adj & pron* sixième (*masc, fem*); **the Sixth** six, e.g., **John the Sixth** Jean six ‖ *s* sixième *m*; **the sixth** (*in dates*) le six

sixtieth ['sɪkstɪ·ɪθ] *adj & pron* soixantième (*masc, fem*) ‖ *s* soixantième *m*

six·ty ['sɪksti] *adj & pron* soixante; **about sixty** une soixantaine de ‖ *s* (*pl* **-ties**) soixante *m*; (*age of*) soixantaine *f*

sizable ['saɪzəbəl] *adj* assez grand, considérable

size [saɪz] *s* grandeur *f*, dimensions *fpl*; (*of a person or garment*) taille *f*; (*of a shoe, glove, or hat*) pointure *f*; (*of a shirt collar*) encolure *f*; (*of a book or box*) format *m*; (*to fill a porous surface*) apprêt *m*; **what size hat do you wear?** du combien coiffez-vous?; **what size shoes do you wear?** du combien chaussez-vous? ‖ *tr* classer; (*wood to be painted*) coller; **to size up** juger

sizzle ['sɪzəl] *s* grésillement *m* ‖ *intr* grésiller

skate [sket] *s* patin *m*; (ichth) raie *f*; **good skate** (slang) brave homme *m* ‖ *intr* patiner; **to go skating** faire du patin

skate'board' *s* planche *f* à roulettes

skat'ing rink' *s* patinoire *f*

skein [sken] *s* écheveau *m*

skeleton ['skɛlɪtən] *s* squelette *m*; **skeleton in the closet** squelette *m* dans un placard

skel'eton key' *s* fausse clé *f*, passe-partout *m*

skeptic ['skɛptɪk] *adj & s* sceptique *mf*

skeptical ['skɛptɪkəl] *adj* sceptique

skepticism ['skɛptɪ,sɪzəm] *s* scepticisme *m*

sketch [skɛtʃ] *s* esquisse *f*; (*pen or pencil drawing*) croquis *m*, esquisse; (lit) aperçu *m*; (theat) sketch *m* ‖ *tr* esquisser ‖ *intr* croquer

sketch'book' *s* album *m* de croquis

skew [skju] *adj & s* biais *m* ‖ *intr* biaiser

skewer ['skju·ər] *s* brochette *f* ‖ *tr* embrocher

ski [ski] *s* ski *m* ‖ *intr* skier; **to go skiing** faire du ski

ski' boots' *spl* chaussures *fpl* de ski

skid [skɪd] *s* (*sidewise*) dérapage *m*; (*forward*) patinage *m*; (*of wheel*) sabot *m*, patin *m* ‖ *v* (*pret & pp* **skidded**; *ger* **skidding**) *tr* enrayer, bloquer ‖ *intr* (*side wise*) déraper; (*forward*) patiner

skid' row' [ro] *s* quartier *m* mal famé

skier ['ski·ər] *s* skieur *m*

skiff [skɪf] *s* skiff *m*, esquif *m*

skiing ['ski·ɪŋ] *s* ski *m*

ski' jack'et *s* anorak *m*

ski' jump' *s* (*place to jump*) tremplin *m*; (*act of jumping*) saut *m* en skis

ski' lift' *s* remonte-pente *m*, téléski *m*

skill [skɪl] *s* habilité *f*, adresse *f*; (*job*) métier *m*

skilled *adj* habile, adroit

skillet ['skɪlɪt] *s* casserole *f*; (*frying pan*) poêle *f*

skillful ['skɪlfəl] *adj* habile, expert

skim [skɪm] *v* (*pret & pp* **skimmed;** *ger* **skimming**) *tr* (*milk*) écrémer; (*molten metal*) écumer; (*to graze*) raser ‖ *intr*—**to skim over** passer légèrement sur

ski' mask' *s* passe-montagne *m*

skimmer ['skɪmər] *s* écumoire *f*; (*straw hat*) canotier *m*

skim' milk' *s* lait *m* écrémé

skimp [skɪmp] *tr* bâcler ‖ *intr* lésiner; **to skimp on** lésiner sur

skimp·y ['skɪmpi] *adj* (*comp* -**ier;** *super* -**iest**) maigre; (*garment*) étriqué; avare, mesquin

skin [skɪn] *s* peau *f*; **by the skin of one's teeth** de justesse, par un cheveu; **soaked to the skin** trempé jusqu'aux os; **to strip to the skin** se mettre à poil ‖ *v* (*pret & pp* **skinned;** *ger* **skinning**) *tr* écorcher, dépouiller; (*e.g., an elbow*) s'écorcher; **to skin alive** (coll) écorcher vif

skin'-deep' *adj* superficiel; (*beauty*) à fleur de peau

skin' div'er *s* plongeur *m* autonome

skin'flint' *s* grippe-sou *m*

skin' game' *s* (slang) escroquerie *f*

skin' graft'ing *s* greffe *f* cutanée, autoplastie *f*

skin·ny ['skɪni] *adj* (*comp* -**nier;** *super* -**niest**) maigre, décharné

skin' test' *s* (med) cuti-réaction *f*

skin'tight' *adj* collant, ajusté

skip [skɪp] *s* saut *m* ‖ *v* (*pret & pp* **skipped;** *ger* **skipping**) *tr* sauter; **skip it!** ça suffit!, laisse tomber!; **to skip rope** sauter à la corde ‖ *intr* sauter; **to skip out** or **off** filer

ski' pole' *s* bâton *m* de skis

skipper ['skɪpər] *s* patron *m* ‖ *tr* commander, conduire

skirmish ['skʌrmɪʃ] *s* escarmouche *f* ‖ *intr* escarmoucher

skirt [skʌrt] *s* jupe *f*; (*woman*) (slang) jupe ‖ *tr* côtoyer, longer; éviter

ski' run' *s* descente *f* en skis

ski' stick' *s* bâton *m* de skis

skit [skɪt] *s* sketch *m*

skittish ['skɪtɪʃ] *adj* capricieux; timide; (*e.g., horse*) ombrageux

ski' wax' *s* fart *m*

skulduggery [skʌl'dʌgəri] *s* (coll) fourberie *f*, ruse *f*, cuisine *f*

skull [skʌl] *s* crâne *m*

skull' and cross'bones *s* tibias *mpl* croisés et tête *f* de mort

skull'cap' *s* calotte *f*

skunk [skʌŋk] *s* mouffette *f*; (*person*) (coll) salaud *m*

sky [skaɪ] *s* (*pl* **skies**) ciel *m*; **to praise to the skies** porter aux nues

sky'div'er *s* parachutiste *mf*

sky'div'ing *s* parachutisme *m*, saut *m* en chute libre

Sky'lab' *s* laboratoire *m* du ciel

sky'lark' *s* (*Alauda arvensis*) alouette *f*, alouette des champs ‖ *intr* (coll) batifoler

sky'light' *s* lucarne *f*

sky'line' *s* ligne *m* d'horizon; (*of city*) profil *m*

sky'rock'et *s* fusée *f* volante ‖ *intr* monter en flèche

sky'scrap'er *s* gratte-ciel *m*

slab [slæb] *s* (*of stone*) dalle *f*; (*slice*) tranche *f*

slack [slæk] *adj* (*loose*) lâche, mou; (*careless*) négligent ‖ *s* mou *m*; (*slowdown*) ralentissement *m*; **slacks** pantalon *m*; **to take up the slack** (coll) prendre le relais ‖ *tr* relâcher; (*lime*) éteindre; **to slack off** larguer ‖ *intr*—**to slack off** or **up** se relâcher

slacken ['slækən] *tr* relâcher; (*to slow down*) ralentir ‖ *intr* se relâcher; se ralentir

slacker ['slækər] *s* flemmard *m*; (mil) tireau-flanc *m*, embusqué *m*

slack' hours' *spl* heures *fpl* creuses

slag [slæg] *s* scorie *f*

slake [slek] *tr* apaiser, étancher; (*lime*) éteindre

slalom ['slɑləm] *s* slalom *m*

slam [slæm] *s* claquement *m*; (cards) chelem *m*; (coll) critique *f* sévère ‖ *v* (*pret & pp* **slammed;** *ger* **slamming**) *tr* claquer; (coll) éreinter; **to slam down on** flanquer sur ‖ *intr* claquer

slander ['slændər] *s* calomnie *f* ‖ *tr* calomnier

slanderous ['slændərəs] *adj* calomnieux

slang [slæŋ] *s* argot *m*; (*e.g., of the underworld*) langue *f* verte

slant [slænt] *s* pente *f*; (*bias*) point *m* de vue ‖ *tr* mettre en pente, incliner; donner un biais spécial à ‖ *intr* être en pente, s'incliner

slap [slæp] *s* tape *f*, claque *f*; (*in the face*) soufflet *m*, gifle *f* ‖ *v* (*pret & pp* **slapped;** *ger* **slapping**) *tr* taper, gifler

slap'dash' *adj*—**in a slapdash manner** à la va-comme-je-te-pousse ‖ *adv* à la six-quatre-deux

slap'stick' *adj* bouffon ‖ *s* bouffonnerie *f*

slash [slæʃ] *s* entaille *f* ‖ *tr* taillader; (*e.g., prices*) réduire beaucoup

slat [slæt] *s* latte *f*

slate [slet] *s* ardoise *f*; (*of candidates*) liste *f* ‖ *tr* couvrir d'ardoises; inscrire sur la liste, désigner

slate' pen'cil *s* crayon *m* d'ardoise

slate' roof' *s* toit *m* d'ardoises

slattern ['slætərn] *s* (*slovenly woman*) marie-salope *f*; (*slut*) voyoute *f*, gueuse *f*

slaughter ['slɔtər] *s* boucherie *f* ‖ *tr* abattre; massacrer

slaught′er·house′ s abattoir m

Slav [slɑv], [slæv] adj slave || s (language) slave m; (person) Slave mf

slave [slev] adj & s esclave mf || intr besogner, trimer

slave′ driv′er s (hist, fig) négrier m

slavery [ˈslevəri] s esclavage m; (institution of keeping slaves) esclavagisme m

slave′ ship′ s négrier m

slave′ trade′ s traite f des noirs

Slavic [ˈslævɪk] adj & s slave m

slavish [ˈslevɪʃ] adj servile

slay [sle] v (pret **slew** [slu]; pp **slain** [slen]) tr tuer, massacrer

slayer [ˈsle·ər] s meurtrier m

sled [slɛd] s luge f || v (pret & pp **sledded**; ger **sledding**) intr faire de la luge, luger

sled′ dog′ s chien m de traîneau

sledge′ ham′mer [slɛdʒ] s massette f, masse f

sleek [slik] adj lisse, luisant || tr lisser

sleep [slip] s sommeil m; **to go to sleep** s'endormir; **to put to sleep** endormir || v (pret & pp **slept** [slɛpt]) tr—**to sleep it over, to sleep on it** prendre conseil de son oreiller; **to sleep off** (a hangover, headache, etc.) faire passer en dormant || intr dormir; (e.g., with a woman) coucher; **to sleep late** faire la grasse matinée; **to sleep like a log** dormir comme un loir

sleeper [ˈslipər] s dormeur m; (girder) poutre f horizontale; (tie) (rr) traverse f

sleep′ing bag′ s sac m de couchage

sleep′ing car′ s wagon-lit m

sleep′ing pill′ s somnifère m

sleepless [ˈsliplɪs] adj sans sommeil

sleep′less night′ s nuit f blanche

sleep′walk′er s somnambule mf

sleep·y [ˈslipi] adj (comp **-ier**; super **-iest**) endormi, somnolent; **to be sleepy** avoir sommeil

sleep′y·head′ s endormi m, grand dormeur m

sleet [slit] s grésil m; (frozen coating on ground) verglas m || intr grésiller

sleet·y [ˈsliti] adj (comp **-tier**; super **-tiest**) de grésil; (iced-over) verglacé

sleeve [sliv] s manche f; (mach) manchon m, douille f; **to laugh in** or **up one's sleeve** rire sous cape

sleigh [sle] s traîneau m || intr aller en traîneau

sleigh′ bell′ s grelot m

sleigh′ ride′ s promenade f en traîneau

sleight′ of hand′ [slaɪt] s prestidigitation f, tours mpl de passe-passe

slender [ˈslɛndər] adj svelte, mince, élancé; (resources) maigre

sleuth [sluθ] s limier m, détective m

slew [slu] s (coll) tas m, floppée f

slice [slaɪs] s tranche f || tr trancher

slick [slɪk] adj lisse; (appearance) élégant; (coll) rusé || s tache f, e.g., **oil slick** tache d'huile || tr lisser; **to slick up** (coll) mettre en ordre

slicker [ˈslɪkər] s ciré m, imper m; (coll) enjôleur m

slide [slaɪd] s (sliding) glissade f, glissement m; (sliding place) glissoire m; (of microscope) plaque f; (of trombone) coulisse f; (on a slide rule) curseur m; (piece that slides) glissière f; (phot) diapositive f, diapo f || v (pret & pp **slid** [slɪd]) tr glisser || intr glisser; **to let slide** ne faire aucun cas de, laisser aller

slide′ fas′tener s fermeture f éclair

slide′ projec′tor s projecteur m de diapositives

slide′ rule′ s règle f à calcul

slide′ valve′ s soupape f à tiroir

slid′ing con′tact s curseur m

slid′ing door′ s porte f à coulisse

slid′ing scale′ s échelle f mobile

slight [slaɪt] adj (small) léger; (slender) mince; (insignificant) faible; (e.g., effort) faible || s affront m || tr faire peu de cas de, dédaigner; (a person) méconnaître

slim [slɪm] adj (comp **slimmer**; super **slimmest**) mince, svelte; (chance, excuse) mauvais; (resources) maigre

slime [slaɪm] s limon m, vase f; (of snakes, fish, etc.) bave f

slim·y [ˈslaɪmi] adj (comp **-ier**; super **-iest**) limoneux, vaseux

sling [slɪŋ] s (to shoot stones) fronde f; (to hold up a broken arm) écharpe f; (shoulder strap) bretelle f, bandoulière f || v (pret & pp **slung** [slʌŋ]) tr lancer; passer en bandoulière

sling′shot′ s fronde f

slink [slɪŋk] v (pret & pp **slunk** [slʌŋk]) intr—**to slink away** s'esquiver

slip [slɪp] s (slide) dérapage m, glissade f, glissement m; (small sheet) bout m de papier; (for indexing, filing, etc.) fiche f; (cutting from plant) bouture f; (piece of underclothing) combinaison f; (blunder) faux pas m, bévue f; (naut) cale f; **to give the slip to** échapper à || v (pret & pp **slipped**; ger **slipping**) tr glisser; **to slip off** (a garment) enlever, ôter; **to slip on** (a garment, shoes, etc.) enfiler; **to slip one's mind** sortir de l'esprit, échapper à qn || intr glisser; (to blunder) faire un faux pas; **to let slip** laisser échapper; **to slip away** or **off** s'échapper, se dérober; **to slip by** s'échapper; (said of time) s'écouler; **to slip up** se tromper

slip′cov′er s housse f

slipper [ˈslɪpər] s pantoufle f

slippery [ˈslɪpəri] adj glissant; (deceitful) rusé

slip′-up′ s (coll) erreur f, bévue f

slit [slɪt] s fente f, fissure f || v (pret & pp **slit**; ger **slitting**) tr fendre; (e.g., pages) couper; **to slit the throat of** égorger

sliver [ˈslɪvər] s écharde f, éclat m

slob [slɑb] s (slang) rustaud m

slobber [ˈslɑbər] s bave f; (fig) sentimentalité f || intr baver

sloe [slo] s (shrub) prunellier m; (fruit) prunelle f

slogan [ˈslogən] s mot m d'ordre, devise f; (com) slogan m

sloop [slup] *s* sloop *m*

slop [slɑp] *s* lavure *f*, rinçure *f* ‖ *v* (*pret* & *pp* **slopped;** *ger* **slopping**) *tr* répandre ‖ *intr* se répandre; **to slop over** déborder

slope [slop] *s* pente *f*; (*of a roof*) inclinaison *f*; (*of a region, mountain, etc.*) versant *m* ‖ *tr* pencher, incliner ‖ *intr* se pencher, s'incliner

slop·py [slɑpi] *adj* (*comp* **-pier;** *super* **-piest**) mouillé; (*dress*) négligé, mal ajusté; (*work*) bâclé

slot [slɑt] *s* entaille *f*, rainure *f*; (*e.g., in a coin telephone*) fente *f*

sloth [sloθ] *s* paresse *f*; (zool) paresseux *m*

slot′ machine′ *s* (*for gambling*) appareil *m* à sous; (*for vending*) distributeur *m* automatique

slouch [slautʃ] *s* démarche *f* lourde; (*person*) lourdaud *m* ‖ *intr* ne pas se tenir droit; (*e.g., in a chair*) se vautrer; **to slouch along** traîner le pas

slouch′ hat′ *s* chapeau *m* mou

slough [slau] *s* bourbier *m* ‖ [slʌf] *s* (*of snake*) dépouille *f*; (pathol) escarre *f* ‖ *tr*—**to slough off** se débarrasser de ‖ *intr* muer, se dépouiller

Slovak ['slovæk] *adj* slovaque ‖ *s* (*language*) slovaque *m*; (*person*) Slovaque *mf*

sloven·ly ['slʌvənli] *adj* (*comp* **-lier;** *super* **-liest**) négligé, malpropre

slow [slo] *adj* lent; (*sluggish*) traînard; (*clock, watch*) en retard; (*in understanding*) lourdaud ‖ *adv* lentement ‖ *tr* & *intr* ralentir; **SLOW** (*public sign*) ralentir; **to slow down** ralentir

slow′down′ *s* grève *f* perlée

slow′ mo′tion *s* ralenti *m*; **in slow motion** au ralenti, en ralenti

slow′poke′ *s* (coll) lambin *m*, traînard *m*

slug [slʌg] *s* (*used as coin*) jeton *m*; (*of linotype*) ligne-bloc *f*; (zool) limace *f*; (*blow*) (coll) bon coup *m*; (*drink*) (coll) gorgée *f* ‖ *v* (*pret* & *pp* **slugged;** *ger* **slugging**) *tr* (coll) flanquer un coup à

sluggard ['slʌgərd] *s* paresseux *m*

sluggish ['slʌgɪʃ] *adj* traînard

sluice [slus] *s* canal *m*; (*floodgate*) écluse *f*; (*dam; flume*) bief *m*

sluice′ gate′ *s* vanne *f*

slum [slʌm] *s* bas quartiers *mpl* ‖ *v* (*pret* & *pp* **slummed;** *ger* **slumming**) *intr*—**to go slumming** aller visiter les taudis

slumber ['slʌmbər] *s* sommeil *m*, assoupissement *m* ‖ *intr* sommeiller

slum′ber par′ty *s* soirée-hébergement *f*

slum′ dwell′ing *s* taudis *m*

slump [slʌmp] *s* affaissement *m*; (com) crise *f*, baisse *f* ‖ *intr* s'affaisser; (*said of prices, stocks, etc.*) dégringoler, s'effondrer

slur [slʌr] *s* (*in pronunciation*) mauvaise articulation *f*; (*insult*) affront *m*; (mus) liaison *f*; **to cast a slur on** porter atteinte à ‖ *v* (*pret* & *pp* **slurred;** *ger* **slurring**) *tr* (*a sound, a syllable, etc.*) mal articuler; (*a person*) déprécier; (mus) lier; **to slur over** glisser sur

slush [slʌʃ] *s* névasse *f*, fange *f*, boue *f* liquide; (*gush*) sensiblerie *f*

slut [slʌt] *s* chienne *f*; (*slovenly woman*) marie-salope *f*

sly [slai] *adj* (*comp* **slyer** or **slier;** *super* **slyest** or **sliest**) rusé, sournois; (*mischievous*) espiègle, futé; **on the sly** furtivement, en cachette

smack [smæk] *s* (*sound*) claquement *m*; (*with the hand*) gifle *f*, claque *f*; (*trace, touch*) soupçon *m*; (*kiss*) (coll) gros baiser *m* ‖ *adv* en plein ‖ *tr* claquer ‖ *intr*—**to smack of** sentir; avoir un goût de

small [smɔl] *adj* petit §91; (*income*) modique; (*short in stature*) court; (*petty*) mesquin; (*typ*) minuscule

small′ arms′ *spl* armes *fpl* portatives

small′ beer′ *s* petite bière *f*; (slang) petite bière

small′ busi′ness *s* petite industrie *f*

small′ cap′ital *s* (typ) petite capitale *f*

small′ change′ *s* petite monnaie *f*, menue monnaie

small′ fry′ *s* menu fretin *m*

small′ intes′tine *s* intestin *m* grêle

small′-mind′ed *adj* mesquin, étriqué, étroit

small′ of the back′ *s* chute *f* des reins, bas *m* du dos

smallpox ['smɔl,pɑks] *s* variole *f*

small′ print′ *s* petits caractères *mpl*

small′ talk′ *s* ragots *mpl*, papotage *m*

small′-time′ *adj* de troisième ordre, insignifiant, petit

small′-town′ *adj* provincial

smart [smɑrt] *adj* intelligent, éveillé; (*pace*) vif; (*person, clothes*) élégant, chic; (*pain*) cuisant; (*saucy*) impertinent ‖ *s* douleur *f* cuisante ‖ *intr* brûler, cuire; (*said of person with hurt feelings*) être cinglé

smart′ al′eck [,ælɪk] *s* (coll) fat *m*, présomptueux *m*

smart′ set′ *s* monde *m* élégant, gens *mpl* chic

smash [smæʃ] *s* fracassement *m*, fracas *m*; (coll) succès *m* ‖ *tr* fracasser ‖ *intr* se fracasser; **to smash into** emboutir, écraser

smash′ hit′ *s* (coll) succès *m*, succès fou; (coll) pièce *f* à succès

smash′-up′ *s* collision *f*; débâcle *f*, culbute *f*

smattering ['smætərɪŋ] *s* légère connaissance *f*, teinture *f*

smear [smɪr] *s* tache *f*; (*vilification*) calomnie *f*; (med) frottis *m* ‖ *tr* tacher; calomnier; (*to coat*) enduire

smear′ campaign′ *s* campagne *f* de calomnies

smell [smɛl] *s* odeur *f*; (*aroma*) parfum *m*, senteur *f*; (*sense*) odorat *m* ‖ *v* (*pret* & *pp* **smelled** or **smelt** [smɛlt]) *tr* & *intr* sentir; **to smell of** sentir

smell′ing salts′ *spl* sels *mpl* volatils

smell·y ['smɛli] *adj* (*comp* **-ier;** *super* **-iest**) malodorant, puant

smelt [smɛlt] *s* (*fish*) éperlan *m* ‖ *tr* & *intr* fondre

smile [smail] *s* sourire *m* ‖ *intr* sourire; **to smile at** sourire à

smirk [smʌrk] s minauderie f ‖ intr minauder

smite [smaɪt] v (pret **smote** [smot]; pp **smitten** ['smɪtən] or **smit** [smɪt]) tr frapper; **to smite down** abattre

smith [smɪθ] s forgeron m

smith·y ['smɪθi] s (pl -ies) forge f

smitten ['smɪtən] adj frappé, affligé; (coll) épris, amoureux

smock [smak] s blouse f; (of artists) sarrau m; (buttoned in back) tablier m

smock' frock' s sarrau m

smog [smɑg] s (coll) brouillard m fumeux, fumillard m

smoke [smok] s fumée f; (coll) cigarette f; **to go up in smoke** s'en aller en fumée ‖ tr & intr fumer

smoked' glass'es spl verres mpl fumés

smoke'-filled room' s tabagie f

smoke'less pow'der ['smoklɪs] s poudre f sans fumée

smoker ['smokər] s fumeur m; (room) fumoir m; (meeting) réunion f de fumeurs; (rr) compartiment m pour fumeurs

smoke' rings' spl ronds mpl de fumée

smoke' screen' s rideau m de fumée

smoke'stack' s cheminée f

smoking ['smokɪŋ] s le fumer m; **no smoking** (public sign) défense de fumer

smok'ing car' s voiture f de fumeurs

smok'ing jack'et s veston m d'intérieur

smok'ing room' s fumoir m

smok·y ['smoki] adj (comp -ier; super -iest) fumeux, enfumé

smolder ['smoldər] s (dense smoke) fumée f épaisse; (smoldering fire) feu m qui couve ‖ intr brûler sans flamme; (said of fire, anger, rebellion, etc.) couver

smooch [smutʃ] intr (coll) se bécoter

smooth [smuð] adj uni, lisse; (gentle, mellow) doux, moelleux; (operation) doux, régulier; (style) facile ‖ tr unir, lisser; **to smooth away** (e.g., obstacles) aplanir, enlever; **to smooth down** (to calm) apaiser, calmer; **to smooth out** défroisser

smooth'-faced' adj imberbe

smooth-shaven ['smuð'ʃevən] adj rasé de près

smooth·y ['smuði] s (pl -ies) (coll) chattemite f, flagorneur m

smother ['smʌðər] tr suffoquer, étouffer; (culin) recouvrir

smudge [smʌdʒ] s tache f; (smoke) fumée f épaisse ‖ tr tacher; (agr) fumiger

smudge' pot' s fumigène m

smug [smʌg] adj (comp **smugger**; super **smuggest**) fat, suffisant

smuggle ['smʌgəl] tr introduire en contrebande, faire la contrebande de ‖ intr faire la contrebande

smuggler ['smʌglər] s contrebandier m

smuggling ['smʌglɪŋ] s contrebande f

smut [smʌt] s tache f de suie; (obscenity) ordure f; (agr) nielle f

smut·ty ['smʌti] adj (comp -tier; super -tiest) taché de suie, noirci; (obscene) ordurier; (agr) niellé

snack [snæk] s casse-croûte m; **to have a snack** casser la croûte

snack' bar' s snack-bar m, snack m

snag [snæg] s (of tree; of tooth) chicot m; **to hit a snag** se heurter à un obstacle, tomber sur un bec ‖ v (pret & pp **snagged**; ger **snagging**) tr (a stocking) faire un accroc à

snail [snel] s escargot m; **at a snail's pace** à pas de tortue, comme un escargot

snake [snek] s serpent m ‖ intr serpenter

snake' in the grass' s serpent m caché sous les fleurs; ami m perfide, traître m, individu m louche

snap [snæp] s (breaking) cassure f; (crackling sound) bruit m sec; (of the fingers) chiquenaude f; (bite) coup m de dents; (cookie) biscuit m croquant; (catch or fastener) bouton-pression m, fermoir m; (phot) instantané m; (slang) jeu m d'enfant, coup facile; **cold snap** coup m de froid; **it's a snap!** (slang) c'est du tout cuit! ‖ v (pret & pp **snapped**; ger **snapping**) tr casser net; (one's fingers, a whip, etc.) faire claquer; (a picture, a scene) prendre un instantané de; **snap it up!** (hurry!) (slang) grouille-toi!; **to snap up** happer, saisir ‖ intr casser net; faire un bruit sec; (from fatigue) s'effondrer; **to snap at** donner un coup de dents à; (to speak sharply to) rembarrer; (an opportunity) saisir; **to snap out of it** (slang) se secouer; **to snap shut** se fermer avec un bruit sec

snap' course' s (slang) cours m tout mâché

snap'drag'on s (bot) gueule-de-loup f

snap' fas'tener s bouton-pression m

snap' judg'ment s décision f prise sans réflexion

snap·py ['snæpi] adj (comp -pier; super -piest) mordant, acariâtre; (quick, sudden) vif; **make it snappy!** (slang) grouillez-vous!

snap'shot' s instantané m

snare [snɛr] s collet m; (trap) piège m; (of a drum) timbre m, corde f de timbre ‖ tr prendre au collet, prendre au piège

snare' drum' s caisse f claire

snarl [snɑrl] s (sound) grognement m; (intertwining) enchevêtrement m ‖ tr dire en grognant; enchevêtrer ‖ intr grogner; s'enchevêtrer

snatch [snætʃ] s (action) geste m vif (pour saisir), arrachement m; (theft) vol m (à l'arraché); (bit, scrap) bribe f, fragment m; (in weight lifting) arraché m ‖ tr saisir brusquement, arracher; **to snatch from** arracher à; **to snatch up** ramasser vivement ‖ intr—**to snatch at** saisir au vol

sneak [snik] adj furtif ‖ s chipeur m, mauvais type m ‖ tr (e.g., a drink) prendre à la dérobée; glisser furtivement; (coll) chiper ‖ intr se glisser furtivement; **to sneak into** se faufiler dans; **to sneak out** s'esquiver

sneaker ['snikər] s espadrille f

sneak' thief' s chipeur m, voleur m à la tire

sneak·y ['sniki] *adj* (*comp* **-ier;** *super* **-iest**) furtif, sournois

sneer [snɪr] *s* ricanement *m* ‖ *intr* ricaner; **to sneer at** se moquer de

sneeze [sniz] *s* éternuement *m* ‖ *intr* éternuer; **it's not to be sneezed at** (coll) il ne faut pas cracher dessus

snicker ['snɪkər] *s* rire *m* bête; (*sneer*) rire narquois; (*in response to smut*) petit rire grivois ‖ *intr* rire bêtement; **to snicker at** se moquer de

sniff [snɪf] *s* reniflement *m*; (*odor*) parfum *m*; (*e.g., of air*) bouffée *f* ‖ *tr* renifler; (*e.g., fresh air*) humer; (*e.g., a scandal*) flairer; **to sniff up** renifler ‖ *intr* renifler; **to sniff at** flairer; (*to disdain*) cracher sur

sniffle ['snɪfəl] *s* reniflement *m*; **to have the sniffles** être enchifrené ‖ *intr* renifler

snip [snɪp] *s* (*e.g., of cloth*) petit bout *m*; (*cut*) coup *m* de ciseaux; (coll) personne *f* insignifiante ‖ *v* (*pret & pp* **snipped;** *ger* **snipping**) *tr* couper; **to snip off** enlever, détacher

snipe [snaɪp] *s* (orn) bécassine *f* ‖ *intr*—**to snipe at** canarder

sniper ['snaɪpər] *s* tireur *m* embusqué, tireur isolé

snippet ['snɪpɪt] *s* petit bout *m*, bribe *f*; personne *f* insignifiante

snip·py ['snɪpi] *adj* (*comp* **-pier;** *super* **-piest**) hautain, brusque

snitch [snɪtʃ] *tr* (coll) chaparder ‖ *intr* (coll) moucharder; **to snitch on** (coll) moucharder

sniv·el ['snɪvəl] *s* pleurnicherie *f*; (*mucus*) morve *f* ‖ *v* (*pret & pp* **-eled** or **-elled;** *ger* **-eling** or **-elling**) *intr* pleurnicher; (*to have a runny nose*) être morveux

snob [snɑb] *s* snob *m*

snobbery ['snɑbəri] *s* snobisme *m*

snobbish ['snɑbɪʃ] *adj* snob

snoop [snup] *s* (coll) curieux *m* ‖ *intr* (coll) fouiner, fureter

snoop·y ['snupi] *adj* (*comp* **-ier;** *super* **-iest**) (coll) curieux

snoot [snut] *s* (slang) nez *m*

snoot·y ['snuti] *adj* (*comp* **-ier;** *super* **-iest**) (slang) snob, hautain

snooze [snuz] *s* (coll) petit somme *m* ‖ *intr* (coll) sommeiller

snore [snor] *s* ronflement *m* ‖ *intr* ronfler

snort [snɔrt] *s* ébrouement *m*; (*of person, horse, etc.*) reniflement *m* ‖ *tr* dire en reniflant, grogner ‖ *intr* s'ébrouer, renifler bruyamment

snot [snɑt] *s* (slang) morve *f*

snot·ty ['snɑti] *adj* (*comp* **-tier;** *super* **-tiest**) (coll) morveux; (slang) snob, hautain

snout [snaut] *s* museau *m*; (*of pig*) groin *m*; (*of bull*) mufle *m*; (*something shaped like the snout of an animal*) bec *m*, tuyère *f*

snow [sno] *s* neige *f* ‖ *intr* neiger; **it is snowing** il neige; **to shovel snow** balayer la neige

snow'ball' *s* boule *f* de neige ‖ *tr* lancer des boules de neige à ‖ *intr* faire boule de neige

snow'bank' *s* talus *m* de neige, banc *m* de neige

snow' blind'ness *s* cécité *f* des neiges

snow' blow'er *s* chasse-neige *m*

snow'-capped' *adj* couronné de neige

snow'-clad' *adj* enneigé

snow'drift' *s* congère *f*

snow'fall' *s* chute *f* de neige; (*amount*) enneigement *m*

snow'flake' *s* flocon *m* de neige

snow' flur'ry *s* (*pl* **-ries**) bouffée *f* de neige

snow' line' *s* limite *f* des neiges éternelles

snow'mak'ing *s* enneigement *m* artificiel

snow'man' *s* (*pl* **-men'**) bonhomme *m* de neige

snowmobile ['snomə,bil] *s* motoneige *f*

snow'plow' *s* chasse-neige *m*

snow' remov'al *s* déneigement *m*

snow'shoe' *s* raquette *f*

snow'slide' *s* avalanche *f*

snow'storm' *s* tempête *f* de neige

snow' tire' *s* pneu *m* à neige

snow'white' *adj* blanc comme la neige ‖ **Snowwhite** *s* Blanche-Neige *f*

snow·y ['sno·i] *adj* (*comp* **-ier;** *super* **-iest**) neigeux

snow'y owl' *s* chouette *f* blanche

snub [snʌb] *s* affront *m*, rebuffade *f* ‖ *v* (*pret & pp* **snubbed;** *ger* **snubbing**) *tr* traiter avec froideur, rabrouer

snub·by ['snʌbi] *adj* (*comp* **-bier;** *super* **-biest**) trapu; (*nose*) camus

snub'-nosed' *adj* camard

snuff [snʌf] *s* tabac *m* à priser; (*of a candlewick*) mouchure *f*; **to be up to snuff** (*to be shrewd*) (slang) être dessalé; (*to be up to par*) (slang) être dégourdi ‖ *tr* priser; (*a candle*) moucher; **to snuff out** éteindre

snuff'box' *s* tabatière *f*

snuffers ['snʌfərs] *spl* mouchettes *fpl*

snug [snʌg] *adj* (*comp* **snugger;** *super* **snuggest**) confortable; (*garment*) bien ajusté; (*bed*) douillet; (*sheltered*) abrité; (*hidden*) caché; **snug and warm** bien au chaud; **snug as a bug in a rug** comme un poisson dans l'eau

snuggle ['snʌgəl] *tr* serrer dans ses bras ‖ *intr* se pelotonner; **to snuggle up to** se serrer tout près de

so [so] *adv* si, tellement; ainsi; donc, par conséquent, aussi; **or so** plus ou moins; **so as to** afin de, pour; **so far** jusqu'ici; **so long!** (coll) à bientôt!; **so many** tant; tant de; **so much** tant; tant de; **so that** pour que, afin que; de sorte que; **so to speak** pour ainsi dire; **so what?** (slang) et alors?; **to hope so** espérer bien; **to think so** croire que oui ‖ *conj* (coll) de sorte que

soak [sok] *s* trempage *m*; (slang) sac *m* à vin, soûlard *m* ‖ *tr* tremper; (*to swindle*) (slang) estamper; **to soak to the skin** tremper jusqu'aux os ‖ *intr* tremper

so'-and-so' *s* (*pl* **-sos**) (pej) triste individu *m*, mauvais sujet *m*; **Mr. So-and-so** Monsieur Untel

soap [sop] *s* savon *m* ‖ *tr* savonner

soap'box' *s* caisse *f* à savon; (fig) plateforme *f*

soap'box or'ator *s* orateur *m* de carrefour

soap' bub'ble *s* bulle *f* de savon

soap' dish' *s* plateau *m* à savon

soap' fac'to·ry *s* (*pl* **-ries**) savonnerie *f*

soap' flakes' *spl* savon *m* en paillettes

soap' op'era *s* mélo *m*

soap' pow'der *s* savon *m* en poudre

soap'stone' *s* pierre *f* de savon; craie *f* de tailleur

soap'suds' *spl* mousse *f* de savon, eau *f* de savon

soap·y ['sopi] *adj* (*comp* **-ier**; *super* **-iest**) savonneux

soar [sor] *intr* planer dans les airs; prendre l'essor, monter subitement

sob [sab] *s* sanglot *m* ‖ *v* (*pret* & *pp* **sobbed**; *ger* **sobbing**) *intr* sangloter

sober ['sobər] *adj* sobre; (*expression*) grave; (*truth*) simple; (*not drunk*) pas ivre; (*no longer drunk*) dégrisé ‖ *tr* calmer; **to sober up** dégriser ‖ *intr*—**to sober up** se dégriser

sobriety [so'braɪ·əti] *s* sobriété *f*

sob' sis'ter *s* (slang) journaliste *f* larmoyante

sob' sto'ry *s* (*pl* **-ries**) histoire *f* larmoyante, histoire d'un pathétique facile, histoire à vous fendre la cœur

so'-called' *adj* dit; soi-disant, prétendu; ainsi nommé

soccer ['sakər] *s* football *m*

sociable ['soʃəbəl] *adj* sociable

social ['soʃəl] *adj* social ‖ *s* réunion *f* sans cérémonie

so'cial climb'er *s* parvenu *m*, arriviste *mf*

so'cial events' *spl* mondanités *fpl*

socialism ['soʃə,lɪzəm] *s* socialisme *m*

socialist ['soʃəlɪst] *s* socialiste *mf*

socialite ['soʃə,laɪt] *s* (coll) membre *m* de la haute société

so'cial reg'ister *s* annuaire *m* de la haute société

so'cial secu'rity *s* sécurité *f* sociale, assistance *f* familiale

so'cial serv'ice *s* assistance *f* sociale, aide *f* sociale, aide familiale

so'cial stra'ta [,strætə] *spl* couches *fpl* sociales

so'cial work'er *s* assistant *m* social, travailleuse *f* familiale

socie·ty [sə'saɪ·əti] *s* (*pl* **-ties**) société *f*

soci'ety col'umn *s* carnet *m* mondain

soci'ety ed'itor *s* chroniqueur *m* mondain

sociology [,sosɪ'alədʒi] *s* sociologie *f*

sock [sak] *s* chaussette *f*; (slang) coup *m* de poing ‖ *tr* (slang) donner un coup de poing à

socket ['sakɪt] *s* (*of bone*) cavité *f*, glène *f*; (*of candlestick*) tube *m*; (*of caster*) sabot *m*; (*of eye*) orbite *f*; (*of tooth*) alvéole *m*; (elec) douille *f*

sock'et joint' *s* joint *m* à rotule

sock'et wrench' *s* clé *f* à tube

sod [sad] *s* gazon *m*; motte *f* de gazon ‖ *v* (*pret* & *pp* **sodded**; *ger* **sodding**) *tr* gazonner

soda ['sodə] *s* (*soda water*) soda *m*; (chem) soude *f*

so'da crack'er *s* biscuit *m* soda

so'da wa'ter *s* soda *m*

sodium ['sodɪ·əm] *s* sodium *m*

sodomy ['sadəmi] *s* sodomie *f*

sofa ['sofə] *s* canapé *m*, sofa *m*

so'fa bed' *s* lit-canapé *m*

soft [saft] *adj* (*yielding*) mou; (*mild*) doux; (*weak in character*) faible; **to go soft** (coll) perdre la boule

soft'-boiled egg' *s* œuf *m* à la coque

soft' coal' *s* houille *f* grasse

soft' drink' *s* boisson *f* non-alcoolisée

soften ['safən] *tr* amollir; (*e.g., noise*) atténuer; (*one's voice*) adoucir; (*one's moral fiber*) affaiblir; **to soften up** amollir ‖ *intr* s'amollir; s'adoucir; s'affaiblir

soft' land'ing *s* (rok) arrivée *f* en douceur

soft' ped'al *s* (mus) pédale *f* sourde

soft'-ped'al *v* (*pret* & *pp* **-aled** or **-alled**; *ger* **-aling** or **-alling**) *tr* (coll) atténuer, modérer

soft' shoul'der *s* (aut) accotement *m* non-stabilisé

soft' soap' *s* savon *m* mou, savon noir; (coll) pommade *f*

soft'-soap' *tr* (coll) passer de la pommade à

soft'ware' *s* (comp) logiciel *m*, programme-rie *f*

soft'ware engineer'ing *s* genie *m* logiciel

sog·gy ['sagi] *adj* (*comp* **-gier**; *super* **-giest**) saturé, détrempé

soil [saɪl] *s* sol *m*, terroir *m* ‖ *tr* salir, souiller ‖ *intr* se salir

soil' pipe' *s* tuyau *m* de descente

sojourn ['sodʒʌrn] *s* séjour *m* ‖ *intr* séjourner

solace ['salɪs] *s* consolation *f* ‖ *tr* consoler

solar ['solər] *adj* solaire

so'lar bat'tery *s* photopile *f*

so'lar heat'er *s* insolateur *m*

so'lar radia'tion *s* rayonnement *m* solaire

sold [sold] *adj*—**sold out** (*no more room*) complet; (*no more merchandise*) épuisé; **to be sold on** (coll) raffoler de ‖ *interj* (*to the highest bidder*) adjugé!

solder ['sadər] *s* soudure *f* ‖ *tr* souder

sol'dering i'ron *s* fer *m* à souder

soldier ['soldʒər] *s* soldat *m*

sole [sol] *adj* seul, unique ‖ *s* (*of shoe*) semelle *f*; (*of foot*) plante *f*; (*fish*) sole *f* ‖ *tr* ressemeler

solemn ['saləm] *adj* sérieux, grave; (*ceremony*) solennel

solemnize ['salɛm,naɪz] *tr* solenniser

solenoid ['solə,nɔɪd] *s* solénoïde *m*

solicit [sə'lɪsɪt] *tr* solliciter ‖ *intr* quêter; (*with immoral intentions*) racoler

solicitor [sə'lɪsɪtər] *s* (*for contributions*) solliciteur *m*; (*for trade*) agent *m*, représentant *m*; (com) démarcheur *m*; (law) procureur *m*; (Brit) avoué *m*

solicitous [sə'lɪsɪtəs] *adj* soucieux

solid ['salɪd] *adj* solide; (*clouds*) dense; (*gold*) massif; (*opinion*) unanime; (*color*) uni; (*hour, day, week*) entier; (*e.g., three days*) d'affilée ‖ *s* solide *m*

sol'id geom'etry *s* géométrie *f* dans l'espace

solidity [sə'lɪdɪti] *s* solidité *f*, consistance *f*

sol'id-state' *adj* (electron) en état solide

solilo·quy [sə'lɪləkwi] *s* (*pl* **-quies**) soliloque *m*

solitaire ['salɪ,tɛr] *s* solitaire *m*; (cards) patience *f*, réussite *f*; **to play solitaire** faire une réussite

solitar·y ['salɪ,tɛri] *adj* solitaire ‖ *s* (*pl* **-ies**) solitaire *m*

sol'itary confine'ment *s* régime *m* cellulaire

solitude ['salɪ,t(j)ud] *s* solitude *f*

so·lo ['solo] *adj* solo ‖ *s* (*pl* **-los**) solo *m*

soloist ['solo·ɪst] *s* soliste *mf*

solstice ['salstɪs] *s* solstice *m*

soluble ['saljəbəl] *adj* soluble

solution [sə'luʃən] *s* solution *f*

solvable ['salvəbəl] *adj* soluble

solve [salv] *tr* résoudre

solvency ['salvənsi] *s* solvabilité *f*

solvent ['salvənt] *adj* (*substance*) solubilisant; (*person or business*) solvable ‖ *s* (*of a substance*) solvant *m*

somber ['sambər] *adj* sombre

some [sʌm] *adj indef* quelque, du; **some way or other** d'une manière ou d'une autre ‖ *pron indef* certains, quelques-uns §81; en §87 ‖ *adv* un peu, passablement, assez; environ; quelque, e.g., **some two hundred soldiers** quelque deux cents soldats

some'bod'y *pron indef* quelqu'un §81; **somebody else** quelqu'un d'autre ‖ *s* (*pl* **-ies**) (coll) quelqu'un *m*

some'day' *adv* un jour

some'how' *adv* dans un sens, je ne sais comment; **somehow or other** d'une manière ou d'une autre, vaille que vaille

some'one' *pron indef* quelqu'un §81; **someone else** quelqu'un d'autre

somersault ['sʌmər,sɔlt] *s* saut *m* périlleux

some'thing *s* (coll) quelque chose *m* ‖ *pron indef* quelque chose (*masc*) ‖ *adv* quelque peu, un peu

some'time' *adj* ancien, ci-devant ‖ *adv* un jour; un de ces jours

some'times' *adv* quelquefois, de temps en temps; **sometimes . . . sometimes** tantôt . . . tantôt

some'way' *adv* d'une manière ou d'une autre

some'what' *adv* un peu, assez

some'where' *adv* quelque part; **somewhere else** ailleurs, autre part

somnambulist [sam'næmbjəlɪst] *s* somnambule *mf*

somnolent ['samnələnt] *adj* somnolent

son [sʌn] *s* fils *m*

sonata [sə'natə] *s* sonate *f*

song [sɔŋ] *s* chanson *f*; (*of praise*) hymne *m*; **to buy for a song** (coll) acheter pour une bouchée de pain

song'bird' *s* oiseau *m* chanteur

song' book' *s* recueil *m* de chansons

Song' of Songs' *s* (Bib) Cantique *m* des Cantiques

song'thrush' *s* grive *f* musicienne

song'writ'er *s* chansonnier *m*

sonic ['sanɪk] *adj* sonique

son'ic boom' *s* double bang *m*

son'-in-law' *s* (*pl* **sons-in-law**) gendre *m*, beau fils *m*

sonnet ['sanɪt] *s* sonnet *m*

son·ny ['sʌni] *s* (*pl* **-nies**) fiston *m*

soon [sun] *adv* bientôt; (*early*) tôt; **as soon as** aussitôt que, dès que, sitôt que; **as soon as possible** le plus tôt possible; **how soon** quand; **no sooner said than done** sitôt dit sitôt fait; **soon after** tôt après; **sooner** plus tôt; (*rather*) (coll) plutôt; **sooner or later** tôt ou tard; **so soon** si tôt; **too soon** trop tôt

soot [sʊt] *s* suie *f* ‖ *tr*—**to soot up** encrasser de suie ‖ *intr* s'encrasser

soothe [suð] *tr* calmer, apaiser; flatter

soothsayer ['suθ,se·ər] *s* devin *m*

soot·y ['sʊti] *adj* (*comp* **-ier**; *super* **-iest**) (*color; flame*) fuligineux; couvert de suie

sop [sap] *s* morceaux *m* trempé; (fig) os *m* à ronger, cadeau *m* ‖ *v* (*pret & pp* **sopped**), ger **sopping**) *tr* tremper, faire tremper; **to sop up** absorber

sophisticated [sə'fɪstɪ,ketɪd] *adj* mondain, sceptique; complexe; (comp) sophistiqué

sophistication [sə,fɪstɪ'keʃən] *s* mondanité *f*

sophomore ['safə,mor] *s* étudiant *m* de deuxième année

sophomoric [,safə'mɔrɪk] *adj* naïf, suffisant, présomptueux

sopping ['sapɪŋ] *adj* détrempé, trempé ‖ *adv*—**sopping wet** trempé comme une soupe

sopran·o [sə'præno] *adj* de soprano ‖ *s* (*pl* **-os**) soprano *f*; (*boy*) soprano *m*

sorcerer ['sɔrsərər] *s* sorcier *m*

sorceress ['sɔrsərɪs] *s* sorcière *f*

sorcer·y ['sɔrsəri] *s* (*pl* **-ies**) sorcellerie *f*

sordid ['sɔrdɪd] *adj* sordide

sore [sor] *adj* douloureux, enflammé; (coll) fâché ‖ *s* plaie *f*, ulcère *m*

sore'head' *s* (coll) rouspéteur *m*, grincheux *m*

sorely ['sorli] *adv* gravement, grièvement; cruellement

soreness ['sornɪs] *s* douleur *f*, sensibilité *f*

sore' throat' *s*—**to have a sore throat** avoir mal à la gorge

sorori·ty [sə'rɔriti] *s* (*pl* **-ties**) club *m* d'étudiantes universitaires

sorrow ['sɔro] *s* chagrin *m*, peine *f*, affliction *f*, tristesse *f* ‖ *intr* s'affliger, avoir du chagrin; être en deuil; **to sorrow for** s'affliger de

sorrowful ['sɔrəfəl] *adj* (*person*) affligé, attristé; (*news*) affligeant

sor·ry [ˈsɔri] *adj* (*comp* **-rier**; *super* **-riest**) désolé, navré, fâché; (*appearance*) piteux, misérable; (*situation*) triste; **to be** or **feel sorry** regretter; **to be** or **feel sorry for** regretter (*q.ch.*); plaindre (*qn*); **to be sorry to** + *inf* regretter de + *inf* ‖ *interj* pardon!

sort [sɔrt] *s* sorte *f*, espèce *f*, genre *m*; **a sort of** une espèce de; **to be out of sorts** être de mauvaise humeur, ne pas être dans son assiette ‖ *tr* classer; **to sort out** trier

so′-so′ *adj* (coll) assez bon, passable, supportable ‖ *adv* assez bien, comme ci comme ça

sot [sɑt] *s* ivrogne *mf*

soul [sol] *s* âme *f*; **not a soul** (coll) pas un chat; **upon my soul!** par ma foi!

sound [saʊnd] *adj* (*body, fruit, tree*) sain; (*structure, floor, bridge*) solide, en bon état; (*healthy, robust*) en bonne santé, bien portant; (*sleep*) profond ‖ *s* son *m*; (*probe*) sonde *f*; (geog) goulet *m*, détroit *m*, bras *m* de mer ‖ *adv* (*asleep*) profondément ‖ *tr* sonner; (*to take a sounding of*) sonder; **to sound out** sonder; **to sound the horn** klaxonner, corner ‖ *intr* sonner; **to sound off** parler haut; **to sound strange** sembler bizarre

sound′ bar′rier *s* mur *m* du son

sound′ film′ *s* film *m* sonore

sound′ hole′ *s* (*of a violin*) ouïe *f*

soundly [ˈsaʊndli] *adj* sainement; profondément; (*hard*) bien

sound′ post′ *s* (*of a violin*) âme *f*

sound′proof′ *adj* insonorisé, insonore ‖ *tr* insonoriser

sound′proof(ed) room′ *s* chambre *f* sourde

sound′ track′ *s* piste *f* sonore, sonorisation *f*

sound′ wave′ *s* onde *f* sonore

soup [sup] *s* potage *m*, bouillon *m*; (*with vegetables*) soupe *f*; **in the soup** (coll) dans le pétrin or la mélasse

soup′ kitch′en *s* soupe *f* populaire

soup′ spoon′ *s* cuiller *f* à soupe

soup′ tureen′ *s* soupière *f*

sour [saʊr] *adj* aigre; (*grapes*) vert; (*apples*) sur; (*milk*) tourné ‖ *tr* rendre aigre ‖ *intr* tourner, s'aigrir

source [sors] *s* source *f*

source′ lan′guage *s* langue *f* source, langue de départ

source′ mate′rial *s* sources *fpl* originales

sour′ cher′ry *s* (*pl* **-ries**) griotte *f*; (*tree*) griottier *m*

sour′ grapes′ *interj* ils sont trop verts!

sour′puss′ *s* (slang) grincheux *m*

south [saʊθ] *adj* & *s* sud *m*; **the South** (*of France, Italy, etc.*) le Midi; (*of U.S.A.*) le Sud ‖ *adv* au sud, vers le sud

South′ Af′rica *s* la République sud-africaine

South′ Amer′ica *s* Amérique *f* du Sud; l'Amérique du Sud

South′ Amer′ican *adj* sud-américain ‖ *s* (*person*) Sud-Américain *m*

south′east′ *adj* & *s* sud-est *m*

southern [ˈsʌðərn] *adj* du sud, méridional

southerner [ˈsʌðərnər] *s* Méridional *m*; (U.S.A.) sudiste *mf*

South′ Kore′a *s* Corée *f* du Sud; la Corée du Sud

South′ Kore′an *adj* sud-coréen ‖ *s* (*person*) Sud-Coréen *m*

south′paw′ *adj* & *s* (coll) gaucher *m*

South′ Pole′ *s* pôle *m* Sud

southward [ˈsaʊθwərd] *adv* vers le sud

south′west′ *adj* & *s* sud-ouest *m*

souvenir [ˌsuvəˈnɪr] *s* souvenir *m*

sovereign [ˈsɑvrɪn] *adj* souverain ‖ *s* (*king*) souverain *m*; (*queen*) souveraine *f*; (*coin*) souverain *m*

sovereign·ty [ˈsɑvrɪnti], *s* (*pl* **-ties**) souveraineté *f*

soviet [ˈsovɪˌɛt] *adj* soviétique ‖ *s* soviet *m*; **Soviet** (*person*) Soviétique *mf*

So′viet Rus′sia *s* la Russie *f* soviétique

So′viet Un′ion *s* Union *f* soviétique

sow [saʊ] *s* truie *f* ‖ [so] *v* (*pret* **sowed**; *pp* **sown** or **sowed**) *tr* (*seed; a field*) semer; (*a field*) ensemencer

soybean [ˈsɔɪˌbin] *s* soya *m*, soja *m*

spa [spɑ] *s* ville *f* d'eau, station *f* thermale, bains *mpl*

space [spes] *s* espace *m*; (*in typing*) frappe *f*; (typ) espace *f* ‖ *tr* espacer

space′ age′ *s* âge *m* de l'exploration spatiale

space′ bar′ *s* barre *f* d'espacement

space′ cap′sule *s* capsule *f* spatiale

space′craft′ *s* astronef *m*

space′ flight′ *s* voyage *m* spatial, vol *m* spatial

space′ heat′er *s* chaufferette *f*

space′ hel′met *s* casque *m* de cosmonaute

space′man or **space′man** *s* (*pl* **-men**) or **-men**) homme *m* de l'espace, astronaute *m*, cosmonaute *m*

space′ probe′ *s* sonde *m* spatiale, coup *m* de sonde dans l'espace; (*rocket*) fusée *f* sonde

spacer [ˈspesər] *s* (*of typewriter*) barre *f* d'espacement

space′ship′ *s* vaisseau *m* spatial, astronef *m*

space′ shut′tle *s* navette *f* spatiale

space′ sta′tion *s* station *f* orbitale

space′ suit′ *s* (rok) scaphandre *m* des cosmonautes, scaphandre spatial, combinaison *f* spatiale

space′ ve′hicle *s* spationef *m*

space′ walk′ *s* promenade *f* dans l'espace

spacious [ˈspeʃəs] *adj* spacieux

spade [sped] *s* bêche *f*; (cards) pique *m*; **to call a spade a spade** (coll) appeler un chat un chat

spade′work′ *s* gros travail *m*, défrichage *m*

spaghetti [spəˈgɛti] *s* spaghetti *mpl*

Spain [spen] *s* Espagne *f*; l'Espagne

span [spæn] *s* portée *f*; (*of time*) durée *f*; (*of hand*) empan *m*; (*of wing*) envergure *f*; (*of bridge*) travée *f* ‖ *v* (*pret* & *pp* **spanned**; *ger* **spanning**) *tr* couvrir, traverser

spangle [ˈspæŋgəl] *s* paillette *f* ‖ *tr* orner de paillettes

Spaniard [ˈspænjərd] *s* Espagnol *m*

spaniel [ˈspænjəl] *s* épagneul *m*

Spanish ['spænɪʃ] *adj* espagnol ‖ *s* (*language*) espagnol *m*; **the Spanish** (*persons*) les Espagnols *mpl*

Span'ish-Amer'ican *adj* hispano-américain ‖ *s* Hispano-Américain *m*

Span'ish broom' *s* genêt *m* d'Espagne

Span'ish fly' *s* cantharide *f*

Span'ish Main' *s* Terre *f* ferme; mer *f* des Antilles

Span'ish moss' *s* tillandsie *f*

spank [spæŋk] *tr* fesser

spanking ['spæŋkɪŋ] *adj* (Brit) de premier ordre; **at a spanking pace** à toute vitesse ‖ *s* fessée *f*

spar [spɑr] *s* (mineral) spath *m*; (naut) espar *m* ‖ *v* (*pret & pp* **sparred;** *ger* **sparring**) *intr* s'entraîner à la boxe; se battre

spare [spɛr] *adj* (*thin*) maigre; (*available*) disponible; (*interchangeable*) de rechange; (*left over*) en surnombre ‖ *tr* (*to save*) épargner, économiser; (*one's efforts*) ménager; (*a person*) faire grâce à, traiter avec indulgence; (*time, money, etc.*) disposer de; (*something*) se passer de

spare' parts' *spl* pièces *fpl* détachées, pièces de rechange

spare'rib' *s* côte *f* découverte de porc, plat *m* de côtes

spare' room' *s* chambre *f* d'ami

spare' tire' *s* pneu *m* de rechange

spare' wheel' *s* roue *f* de secours

sparing ['spɛrɪŋ] *adj* économe, frugal

spark [spɑrk] *s* étincelle *f*

spark' coil' *s* bobine *f* d'allumage

spark' gap' *s* (*of induction coil*) éclateur *m*; (*of spark plug*) entrefer *m*

sparkle ['spɑrkəl] *s* étincellement *m*, éclat *m* ‖ *intr* étinceler

sparkling ['spɑrklɪŋ] *adj* étincelant; (*wine*) mousseux; (*soft drink*) gazeux

spark' plug' *s* bougie *f*

sparrow ['spæro] *s* moineau *m*

spar'row hawk' *s* épervier *m*

sparse [spɑrs] *adj* clairsemé, rare; peu nombreux

Spartan ['spɑrtən] *adj* spartiate ‖ *s* Spartiate *mf*

spasm ['spæzəm] *s* spasme *m*

spasmodic [spæz'mɑdɪk] *adj* intermittent, irrégulier; (pathol) spasmodique

spastic ['spæstɪk] *adj* spasmodique

spat [spæt] *s* (coll) dispute *f*, prise *f* de bec; **spats** demi-guêtres *fpl* ‖ *v* (*pret & pp* **spatted;** *ger* **spatting**) *intr* se disputer

spatial ['speʃəl] *adj* spatial, de l'espace

spatter ['spætər] *s* éclaboussure *f* ‖ *tr* éclabousser

spatula ['spætʃələ] *s* spatule *f*

spawn [spɔn] *s* frai *m* ‖ *tr* engendrer ‖ *intr* frayer

spay [spe] *tr* châtrer

speak [spik] *v* (*pret* **spoke** [spok]; *pp* **spoken**) *tr* (*a word, one's mind, the truth*) dire; (*a language*) parler ‖ *intr* parler; **so to speak** pour ainsi dire; **speaking!** à l'appareil!; **to speak out** or **up** parler plus haut, élever la voix; (fig) parler franc

speak'-eas'y *s* (*pl* **-ies**) bar *m* clandestin

speaker ['spikər] *s* parleur *m*; (*person addressing a group*) conférencier *m*; (*presiding officer*) speaker *m*, président *m*; (rad) haut-parleur *m*

spear [spɪr] *s* lance *f* ‖ *tr* percer d'un coup de lance

spear'head' *s* fer *m* de lance; (mil) pointe *f*, avancée *f* ‖ *tr* (*e.g., a campaign*) diriger

spear'mint' *s* menthe *f* verte

special ['spɛʃəl] *adj* spécial, particulier ‖ *s* train *m* spécial

spe'cial-deliv'ery let'ter *s* lettre *f* exprès

specialist ['spɛʃəlɪst] *s* spécialiste *mf*

specialize ['spɛʃə,laɪz] *tr* spécialiser ‖ *intr* se spécialiser

special·ty ['spɛʃəlti] *s* (*pl* **-ties**) spécialité *f*

specie ['spisi] *s*—**in specie** en espèces, en numéraire

spe·cies ['spisiz] *s* (*pl* **-cies**) espèce *f*

specific [spɪ'sɪfɪk] *adj & s* spécifique *m*

specif'ic grav'ity *s* poids *m* spécifique

speci·fy ['spɛsɪ,faɪ] *v* (*pret & pp* **-fied**) *tr* spécifier

specimen ['spɛsɪmən] *s* spécimen *m*; (coll) drôle *m* de type

specious ['spiʃəs] *adj* spécieux

speck [spɛk] *s* (*on fruit, face, etc.*) tache *f*; (*in the distance*) point *m*; (*small quantity*) brin *m*, grain *m*, atome *m* ‖ *tr* tacheter

speckle ['spɛkəl] *s* petite tache *f* ‖ *tr* tacheter, moucheter

spectacle ['spɛktəkəl] *s* spectacle *m*; **spectacles** lunettes *fpl*

spec'tacle case' *s* étui *m* à lunettes

spectator ['spɛktetər] *s* spectateur *m*

specter ['spɛktər] *s* spectre *m*

spec·trum ['spɛktrəm] *s* (*pl* **-tra** [trə] or **-trums**) spectre *m*

speculate ['spɛkjə,let] *intr* spéculer

speculator ['spɛkjə,letər] *s* spéculateur *m*, boursicotier *m*

speech [spitʃ] *s* (*faculty*) parole *f*; (*language*) langage *m*; (*of a people or region*) parler *m*; (*manner of speaking*) façon *f* de parler; (*enunciation*) articulation *f*, élocution *f*; (*formal address*) discours *m*; (theat) tirade *f*; **to make a speech** prononcer un discours

speech' clin'ic *s* centre *m* de rééducation de la parole

speech' correc'tion *s* rééducation *f* de la parole

speech' de'fect *s* défaut *m* d'élocution

speechless ['spitʃlɪs] *adj* sans parole, muet; (fig) sidéré, stupéfié

speech' ther'apy *s* phoniatrie *f*

speed [spid] *s* vitesse *f*; **at full speed** à toute vitesse ‖ *v* (*pret & pp* **speeded** or **sped** [spɛd]) *tr* dépêcher, hâter ‖ *intr* se dépêcher; **to speed up** aller plus vite

speed' bump' *s* dos *m* d'âne

speeding ['spidɪŋ] *s* excès *m* de vitesse

speed' king' *s* as *m* du volant

speed' lim'it *s* vitesse *f* maximum

speedometer [spi'dɑmɪtər] *s* indicateur *m* de vitesse

speed′ rec′ord s record m de vitesse
speed′-up′ s accélération f
speed′way′ s (racetrack) piste f d'autos; (highway) autoroute f
speed·y [′spidi] adj (comp **-ier;** super **-iest**) rapide, vite, prompt
speed′ zone′ s zone f de vitesse surveillée
spell [spɛl] s (magic power) sortilège m, charme m; (brief period) intervalle m; (turn) tour m; (magic words) formule f magique; (attack) accès m ‖ v (pret & pp **spelled** or **spelt** [spɛlt]) tr (orally) épeler; (in writing) orthographier, écrire; **to spell out** (coll) expliquer en détail ‖ v (pret & pp **spelled**) tr (to relieve) remplacer, relever, relayer
spell′bind′er s orateur m fascinant, orateur entraînant
spell′bound′ adj fasciné
spelling [′spɛlɪŋ] s orthographe f
spell′ing bee′ s concours m d'orthographe
spelunker [spɪ′lʌŋkər] s spéléo m
spend [spɛnd] v (pret & pp **spent** [spɛnt]) tr dépenser; (a period of time) passer
spender [′spɛndər] s dépensier m
spend′ing mon′ey s argent m de poche pour les menues dépenses
spend′thrift′ s prodigue mf, grand dépensier m
sperm [spʌrm] s sperme m
sperm′ bank′ s banque f de sperme
sperm′ whale′ s cachalot m
spew [spju] tr & intr vomir
sphere [sfɪr] s sphère f; corps m céleste
spherical [′sfɛrɪkəl] adj sphérique
sphinx [sfɪŋks] s (pl **sphinxes** or **sphinges** [′sfɪndʒiz]) sphinx m
spice [spaɪs] s épice f; (fig) sel m, piquant m ‖ tr épicer
spick-and-span [′spɪkənd′spæn] adj (room) brillant comme un sou neuf; (person) tiré à quatre épingles
spic·y [′spaɪsi] adj (comp **-ier;** super **-iest**) épicé, aromatique; (e.g., gravy) relevé; (conversation, story, etc.) épicé, salé, piquant, grivois
spider [′spaɪdər] s araignée f
spi′der·web′ s toile f d'araignée
spiff·y [′spɪfi] adj (comp **-ier;** super **-iest**) (slang) épatant, élégant
spigot [′spɪgət] s robinet m
spike [spaɪk] s pointe f; (nail) clou m à large tête; (bot) épi m; (rr) crampon m ‖ tr clouer; ruiner, supprimer; (a drink) (coll) corser à l'alcool ‖ intr (bot) former des épis
spill [spɪl] s chute f, culbute f ‖ v (pret & pp **spilled** or **spilt** [spɪlt]) tr renverser; (a liquid) répandre; (a rider) désarçonner; (passengers) verser ‖ intr se répandre, s'écouler
spill′way′ s déversoir m
spin [spɪn] s (turning motion) tournoiement m, rotation f; (on a ball) effet m; (aer) vrille f; **to go for a spin** (coll) se balader en voiture; **to go into a spin** (aer) descendre en vrille ‖ v (pret & pp **spun** [spʌn];

ger **spinning**) tr filer; faire tournoyer ‖ intr filer; tournoyer
spinach [′spɪnɪtʃ] s épinard m; (leaves used as food) des épinards
spinal [′spaɪnəl] adj spinal
spi′nal col′umn s colonne f vertébrale
spi′nal cord′ s moelle f épinière
spindle [′spɪndəl] s fuseau m
spin′-dri′er s essoreuse f
spin′-dry′ v (pret & pp **-dried**) tr essorer
spine [spaɪn] s (in body) épine f dorsale, échine f; (quill, fin) épine; (ridge) arête f; (of book) dos m; (fig) courage m
spineless [′spaɪnlɪs] adj sans épines; (weak) mou; **to be spineless** (fig) avoir l'échine souple
spinet [′spɪnɪt] s épinette f
spinner [′spɪnər] s fileur m; machine f à filer
spinning [′spɪnɪŋ] adj tournoyant ‖ s (act) filage m; (art) filature f
spin′ning wheel′ s rouet m
spin′-off′ s avantage m inattendu; (com) sous-produit m, application f secondaire; **to be a spin-off from** (telv) être tiré de, être issu de
spinster [′spɪnstər] s (usually offensive) célibataire f, vieille fille f
spiraea [spaɪ′ri·ə] s spirée f
spi·ral [′spaɪrəl] adj spiral, en spirale ‖ s spirale f ‖ v (pret & pp **-raled** or **-ralled;** ger **-raling** or **-ralling**) intr tourner en spirale; (aer) vriller
spi′ral stair′case s escalier m en colimaçon
spire [spaɪr] s aiguille f; (of clock tower) flèche f
spirit [′spɪrɪt] s esprit m; (enthusiasm) feu m; (temper, genius) génie m; (ghost) esprit, revenant m; **high spirits** joie f, abandon m; **spirits** (alcoholic liquor) esprit m, spiritueux m; **to raise the spirits of** remonter le courage de ‖ tr—**to spirit away** enlever, faire disparaître mystérieusement
spirited adj animé, vigoureux
spiritless [′spɪrɪtlɪs] adj sans force, abattu, déprimé
spir′it lev′el s niveau m à bulle
spiritual [′spɪrɪtʃu·əl] adj spirituel ‖ s chant m religieux populaire
spiritualism [′spɪrɪtʃu·ə,lɪzəm] s spiritisme m
spiritualist [′spɪrɪtʃu·əlɪst] s spirite mf; (philos) spiritualiste mf
spir′ituous bev′erages [′spɪrɪtʃu·əs] spl boissons fpl spiritueuses
spit [spɪt] s salive f; (culin) broche f ‖ v (pret & pp **spat** [spæt] or **spit;** ger **spitting**) tr & intr cracher
spit′ curl′ s rouflaquette f
spite [spaɪt] s dépit m, rancune f; **in spite of** en dépit de, malgré ‖ tr dépiter, contrarier
spiteful [′spaɪtfəl] adj rancunier
spit′fire′ s mégère f
spit′ting im′age s (coll) portrait m craché
spittoon [spɪ′tun] s crachoir m
splash [splæʃ] s éclaboussure f; (of waves) clapotis m; **to make a splash** (coll) faire

sensation ‖ *tr* & *intr* éclabousser ‖ *interj* flic flac!

splash′down′ *s* (rok) amerrissage *m*

spleen [splin] *s* (anat) rate *f*; (fig) maussaderie *f*, mauvaise humeur *f*; **to vent one's spleen on** décharger sa bile sur

splendid [′splɛndɪd] *adj* splendide; (coll) admirable, superbe

splendor [′splɛndər] *s* splendeur *f*

splice [splaɪs] *s* (*in rope*) épissure *f*; (*in wood*) enture *f* ‖ *tr* (*rope*) épisser; (*wood*) enter; (*film*) réparer, coller; (slang) marier

splint [splɪnt] *s* éclisse *f* ‖ *tr* éclisser

splinter [′splɪntər] *s* éclat *m*, éclisse *f*; (*lodged under the skin*) écharde *f* ‖ *tr* briser en éclats ‖ *intr* voler en éclats

splin′ter group′ *s* minorité *f* dissidente, groupe *m* fragmentaire

split [splɪt] *adj* fendu; (*pea*) cassé; (*skirt*) déchiré ‖ *s* fente *f*, fissure *f*; (*quarrel*) rupture *f*; (*one's share*) part *f*; (*bottle*) quart *m*, demi *m*; (gymnastics) grand écart *m* ‖ *v* (*pret* & *pp* **split**; *ger* **splitting**) *tr* fendre; (*money; work; ticket*) partager; (*in two*) couper; (*a hide*) dédoubler; **to split hairs** couper les cheveux en quatre; **to split one's sides laughing** se tenir les côtes de rire; **to split the difference** couper la poire en deux ‖ *intr* se fendre; **to split away (from)** se séparer (de)

split′ fee′ *s* (*between doctors*) dichotomie *f*

split′ personal′ity *s* personnalité *f* dédoublée

split′ skirt′ *s* jupe-culotte *f*

split′ tick′et *s* (pol) panachage *m*

splitting [′splɪtɪŋ] *adj* violent; (*headache*) atroce ‖ *s* fendage *m*; (*of the atom*) désintégration *f*; (*of the personality*) dédoublement *m*

splotch [splɑtʃ] *s* tache *f* ‖ *tr* tacher, barbouiller

splurge [splʌrdʒ] *s* (coll) épate *f* ‖ *intr* (coll) se payer une fête; (*to show off*) (coll) faire de l'épate

splutter [′splʌtər] *s* crachement *m* ‖ *tr*—**to splutter out** bredouiller ‖ *intr* crachoter; (*said of candle, grease, etc.*) grésiller

spoil [spɔɪl] *s* (*object of plunder*) prise *f*, proie *f*; **spoils** (*booty*) butin *m*, dépouilles *fpl*; (*emoluments, especially of public office*) assiette *f* au beurre, part *f* du gâteau ‖ *v* (*pret* & *pp* **spoiled** *or* **spoilt** [spɔɪlt]) *tr* gâter, abîmer ‖ *intr* se gâter, s'abîmer; **to be spoiling for** (coll) brûler du désir de

spoilage [′spɔɪlɪdʒ] *s* déchet *m*

spoiled *adj* gâté

spoil′sport′ *s* rabat-joie *m*

spoils′ sys′tem *s* système *m* des postes aux petits copains

spoke [spok] *s* rai *m*, rayon *m*; (*of a ladder*) échelon *m*; (*of an umbrella*) baleine *f*

spokes′man *s* (*pl* **-men**) porte-parole *m*, interprète *mf*

sponge [spʌndʒ] *s* éponge *f* ‖ *tr* éponger; (*a meal*) (coll) écornifler ‖ *intr* (coll) écornifler; **to sponge on** (coll) vivre aux crochets de

sponge′ cake′ *s* gâteau *m* de Savoie, gâteau mousseline, génoise *f*

sponger [′spʌndʒər] *s* écornifleur *m*, pique assiette *mf*

sponge′ rub′ber *s* caoutchouc *m* mousse

spon·gy [′spʌndʒi] *adj* (*comp* **-gier**, *supe,* **-giest**) spongieux

sponsor [′spɑnsər] *s* patron *m*; (*godfather*) parrain *m*; (*godmother*) marraine *f*; (law) garant *m*; (rad, telv) commanditaire *m* ‖ *tr* patronner, parrainer; (law) se porter garant de; (rad, telv) commanditer

spon′sor·ship′ *s* patronnage *m*

spontaneous [spɑn′teni·əs] *adj* spontané

spoof [spuf] *s* (slang) mystification *f*; (slang) parodie *f* ‖ *tr* (slang) mystifier; (slang) blaguer ‖ *intr* (slang) blaguer

spook [spuk] *s* (coll) revenant *m*, spectre *m*

spool [spul] *s* bobine *f*

spoon [spun] *s* cuiller *f*; **to be born with a silver spoon in one's mouth** (coll) être né coiffé ‖ *tr* prendre dans une cuiller; **to spoon off** enlever avec la cuiller ‖ *intr* (coll) se faire des mamours

spooner [′spunər] *s* (coll) peloteur *m*

spoonerism [′spunə,rɪzəm] *s* contrepèterie *f*

spoon′-feed′ *v* (*pret* & *pp* **-fed**) *tr* nourrir à la cuiller; (*an industry*) subventionner; (coll) mâcher la besogne à

spoonful [′spunˌful] *s* cuillerée *f*

spoon·y [′spuni] *adj* (*comp* **-ier**; *super* **-iest**) (coll) peloteur

sporadic(al) [spə′rædɪk(əl)] *adj* sporadique

spore [spɔr] *s* spore *f*

sport [spɔrt] *adj* sportif, de sport ‖ *s* sport *m*; amusement *m*, jeu *m*; (biol) mutation *f*; (coll) chic type *m*; **a good sport** un bon copain; (*a good loser*) un beau joueur; **in sport** par plaisanterie; **to make sport of** tourner en ridicule ‖ *tr* faire parade de, arborer ‖ *intr* s'amuser, jouer

sport′ clothes′ *spl* vêtements *mpl* de sport

sport′ing goods′ *spl* articles *mpl* de sport

sports′cast′er *s* radioreporteur *m* sportif

sports′ ed′itor *s* rédacteur *m* sportif

sports′ fan′ *s* fanatique *mf*, enragé *m* des sports

sports′man *s* (*pl* **-men**) sportif *m*

sports′man·like′ *adj* sportif

sports′man·ship′ *s* sportivité *f*

sports′wear′ *s* vêtements *mpl* sport

sports′writ′er *s* reporter *m* sportif

sport·y [′sporti] *adj* (*comp* **-ier**; *super* **-iest**) (coll) sportif; (*smart in dress*) (coll) chic; (*flashy*) (coll) criard, voyant; (coll) dissolu, libertin

spot [spɑt] *s* (*stain*) tache *f*; (*place*) endroit *m*, lieu *m*; **on the spot** sur place, à pied d'œuvre; (slang) dans le pétrin; **spots** (*before eyes*) mouches *fpl* ‖ *v* (*pret* & *pp* **spotted**; *ger* **spotting**) *tr* tacher; (coll) repérer, détecter ‖ *intr* se tacher

spot′ cash′ *s* argent *m* comptant

spot′ check′ *s* échantillonnage *m*

spot′-check′ *tr* échantillonner

spotless [′spɑtlɪs] *adj* sans tache

spot'light' s spot m; (aut) projecteur m auxiliaire orientable; **to hold the spotlight** (fig) être en vedette ‖ tr diriger les projecteurs sur; (fig) mettre en vedette

spot' remov'er [rɪ,muvər] s détachant m

spot' weld'ing s soudage m par points

spouse [spaʊz], [spaʊs] s (man) époux m, conjoint m; (woman) épouse f, conjointe f

spout [spaʊt] s (discharge pipe or tube) tuyau m de décharge; (e.g., of teapot) bec m; (of sprinkling can) col m, queue f; (of water) jet m ‖ tr faire jaillir; (e.g., insults) (coll) déclamer ‖ intr jaillir; **to spout off** (coll) déclamer

sprain [spren] s foulure f, entorse f ‖ tr fouler, se fouler

sprawl [sprɔl] intr s'étaler, se carrer

spray [spre] s (of ocean) embruns mpl; (branch) rameau m; (for insects) liquide m insecticide; (for weeds) produit m herbicide; (for spraying insects or weeds) pulvérisateur m; (for spraying perfume) vaporisateur m, atomiseur m; (med) pulvérisation f ‖ tr pulvériser; (with a vaporizer) vaporiser; (hort) désinfecter par pulvérisation d'insecticide; **to spray paint on** peindre au pistolet ‖ intr—**to spray out** gicler

sprayer ['spre·ər] s vaporisateur m, pulvérisateur m

spray' gun' s pulvérisateur m; (for paint) pistolet m; (hort) seringue f

spread [sprɛd] adj étendu, écarté, ouvert ‖ s (extent, expanse) étendue f, rayonnement m; (of disease, fire) propagation f, progression f; (of wings) envergure f; (on bed) dessus-de-lit m, couvre-lit m; (on sandwich) pâte f; (buffet lunch) collation f ‖ v (pret & pp spread) tr étendre, étaler; (news) répandre; (disease) propager; (the wings) déployer; (a piece of bread) tartiner ‖ intr s'étendre, s'étaler; se répandre, rayonner

spree [spri] s bombance f, orgie f; **to go on a spree** (coll) faire la bombe

sprig [sprɪg] s brin m, brindille f

spright·ly ['spraɪtli] adj (comp -lier; super -liest) vif, enjoué

spring [sprɪŋ] adj printanier ‖ s (of water) source f; (season) printemps m; (jump) saut m, bond m; (elastic device) ressort m; (quality) élasticité f ‖ v (pret sprang [spræŋ] or sprung [sprʌŋ]; pp sprung) tr (the frame of a car) faire déjeter; (a lock) faire jouer; (a leak) contracter; (a question) proposer à l'improviste; (a prisoner) (coll) faire sortir de prison ‖ intr sauter, bondir; (said of oil, water, etc.) jaillir; **to spring up** se lever, naître

spring'-and-fall' adj (coat) de demi-saison

spring'board' s tremplin m

spring' fe'ver s (hum) malaise m des premières chaleurs, flemme f

spring'like' adj printanier

spring'time' s printemps m

sprinkle ['sprɪŋkəl] s pluie f fine; (culin) pincée f ‖ tr (with water) asperger, ar-

roser; (with powder) saupoudrer; (to strew) parsemer ‖ intr tomber en pluie fine

sprinkler ['sprɪŋklər] s arrosoir m

sprinkling ['sprɪŋklɪŋ] s aspersion f, arrosage m; (with holy water) aspersion; (with powder) saupoudrage m; (of knowledge) bribes fpl, notions fpl; (of persons) petit nombre m

sprin'kling can' s arrosoir m

sprint [sprɪnt] s course f de vitesse, sprint m ‖ intr faire une course de vitesse, courir à toute vitesse

sprite [spraɪt] s lutin m

sprocket ['sprɑkɪt] s dent f de pignon; (wheel) pignon m de chaîne

sprock'et wheel' s pignon m de chaîne

sprout [spraʊt] s pousse f, rejeton m; (of seed) germe m ‖ intr (said of plant) pousser, pointer; (said of seed) germer

spruce [sprus] adj pimpant, tiré à quatre épingles ‖ s sapin m; (Norway spruce) épicéa m commun ‖ intr—**to spruce up** se faire beau, se pomponner

spry [spraɪ] adj (comp spry'er or sprier; super spryest or spriest) vif, alerte

spud [spʌd] s (chisel) bédane f; (agr) arrache-racines m; (coll) pomme f de terre, patate f

spun' glass' [spʌn] s coton m de verre

spunk [spʌŋk] s (coll) cran m, courage m

spur [spʌr] s éperon m; (of rooster) ergot m; (stimulant) aiguillon m, stimulant m; (rr) embranchement m; **on the spur of the moment** sous l'impulsion du moment ‖ v (pret & pp spurred; ger spurring) tr éperonner; **to spur on** aiguillonner, stimuler

spurious ['spjʊrɪ·əs] adj faux; (sentiments) simulé, feint; (document) apocryphe

spurn [spʌrn] tr repousser avec mépris, faire fi de

spurt [spʌrt] s jaillissement m, giclée f, jet m; (of enthusiasm) élan m; effort m soudain ‖ intr jaillir; **to spurt out** gicler

sputnik ['sputnɪk] s spoutnik m

sputter ['spʌtər] s (manner of speaking) bredouillement m; (of candle) grésillement m; (of fire) crachement m ‖ tr (words) débiter en lançant des postillons ‖ intr postillonner; (said of candle) grésiller; (said of fire) cracher, pétiller

spu·tum ['spjutəm] s (pl -ta [tə]) crachat m

spy [spaɪ] s (pl spies) espion m ‖ v (pret & pp spied) tr (to catch sight of) entrevoir; **to spy out** découvrir par ruse ‖ intr espionner; **to spy on** épier, guetter

spy'glass' s longue-vue f

spying ['spaɪ·ɪŋ] s espionnage m

spy' plane' s avion m fugitif

spy' ring' s réseau m d'espionnage

spy' sat'ellite s satellite m d'espionnage

squabble ['skwɑbəl] s chamaillerie f ‖ intr se chamailler

squad [skwɑd] s escouade f, peloton m; (of detectives) brigade f

squadron ['skwɑdrən] *s* (aer) escadrille *f*; (mil) escadron *m*; (nav) escadre *f*

squalid ['skwɑlɪd] *adj* sordide

squall [skwɑl] *s* (*of rain*) bourrasque *f*, rafale *f*; (*cry*) braillement *m* ; (coll) grabuge *m* ‖ *intr* souffler en bourrasque; brailler

squalor ['skwɑlər] *s* saleté *f*; misère *f*

squander ['skwɑndər] *tr* gaspiller

square [skwɛr] *adj* carré; (*honest*) loyal, franc; (*real*) véritable; (*conventional*) (slang) formaliste; **nine (ten, etc.) inches square** de neuf (dix, etc.) pouces en carré; **nine (ten, etc.) square inches** neuf (dix, etc.) pouces carrés; **to get square with** (coll) régler ses comptes avec; **we'll call it square** (coll) nous sommes quittes ‖ *s* carré *m*; (*of checkerboard or chessboard*) case *f*; (*city block*) pâté *m* de maisons; (*open area in town or city*) place *f*; (*of carpenter*) équerre *f*; **to be on the square** (coll) jouer franc jeu; **to go back to square one** (slang) se retrouver à la case départ, repartir à zéro ‖ *adv* carrément ‖ *tr* carrer; (*a number*) élever au carré; (*wood, marble, etc.*) équarrir; (*a debt*) régler; (bk) balancer ‖ *intr*—**to square off** (coll) se mettre en posture de combat; **to square with** (*to tally with*) s'accorder avec; régler ses comptes avec

square' dance' *s* quadrille *m* américain

square' deal' *s* (coll) procédé *m* loyal

square' meal' *s* repas *m* copieux

square' root' *s* racine *f* carrée

squash [skwɑʃ] *s* écrasement *m*; (bot) courge *f*; (sports) squash *m* ‖ *tr* écraser ‖ *intr* s'écraser

squash·y ['skwɑʃi] *adj* (*comp* **-ier**; *super* **-iest**) mou et humide; (*fruit*) à pulpe molle

squat [skwɑt] *adj* (*heavyset*) tassé, trapu, ramassé ‖ *s* position *f* accroupie ‖ *v* (*pret & pp* **squatted**; *ger* **squatting**) *intr* s'accroupir; (*to settle*) s'installer sans titre légal

squatter ['skwɑtər] *s* squatter *m*

squatting ['skwɑtɪŋ] *adj* (*person*) accroupi; (*animal*) tapi, ramassé

squaw [skwɔ] *s* femme *f* peau-rouge

squawk [skwɔk] *s* cri *m* rauque; (slang) protestation *f*, piaillerie *f* ‖ *intr* pousser un cri rauque; (slang) protester, piailler

squeak [skwik] *s* grincement *m*; (*of living being*) couic *m*, petit cri *m* ‖ *intr* grincer; pousser des petits cris, couiner

squeal [skwil] *s* cri *m* aigu ‖ *intr* piailler; (slang) manger le morceau; **to squeal on** (slang) moucharder

squealer ['skwilər] *s* (coll) cafard *m*

squeamish ['skwimɪʃ] *adj* trop scrupuleux, prude; sujet aux nausées

squeeze [skwiz] *s* pression *f*; (coll) extorsion *f*; **it's a tight squeeze** (coll) ça tient tout juste ‖ *tr* serrer; (*fruit*) presser; **to squeeze from** (coll) extorquer à; **to squeeze into** faire entrer de force dans ‖ *intr* se blottir; **to squeeze through** se frayer un passage à travers

squeezer ['skwizər] *s* presse *f*, presse-fruits *m*

squelch [skwɛltʃ] *s* (coll) remarque *f* écrasante ‖ *tr* écraser, réprimer

squid [skwɪd] *s* calmar *m*

squill [skwɪl] *s* (bot) scille *f*; (zool) squille *f*

squint [skwɪnt] *s* coup *m* d'œil furtif; (pathol) strabisme *m* ‖ *tr* fermer à moitié ‖ *intr* loucher; **to squint at** regarder furtivement

squint'-eyed' *adj* bigle, strabique; malveillant

squire [skwaɪr] *s* (*knight's attendant*) écuyer *m*; (*lady's escort*) cavalier *m* servant; (*property owner*) propriétaire *m* terrien; (law) juge *m* de paix ‖ *tr* escorter

squirm [skwʌrm] *s* tortillement *m* ‖ *intr* se tortiller; **to squirm out of** se tirer de

squirrel ['skwʌrəl] *s* écureuil *m*

squirt [skwʌrt] *s* giclée *f*, jet *m*; (*syringe*) seringue *f*; (coll) morveux *m* ‖ *tr* faire gicler ‖ *intr* gicler, jaillir

stab [stæb] *s* coup *m* de poignard, de couteau; (*wound*) estafilade *f*; (coll) coup d'essai; **to make a stab at** (coll) s'essayer à ‖ *v* (*pret & pp* **stabbed**; *ger* **stabbing**) *tr* poignarder

stabilize ['stebəl,aɪz] *tr* stabiliser

stab' in the back' *s* coup *m* de Jarnac, coup de traître

stable ['stebəl] *adj* stable ‖ *s* (*for cows*) étable *f*; (*for horses*) écurie *f*

stack [stæk] *s* (*of wood, books, papers*) tas *m*, pile *f*; (*of hay, straw, etc.*) meule *f*; (*of sheaves*) gerbier *m*; (*e.g., of rifles*) faisceau *m*; (*of ship or locomotive*) cheminée *f*; (*of fireplace*) souche *f*; (*airplanes in a holding pattern*) pile *f* d'attente, pile *f* d'attente, manège *m* d'avions; **stacks** (*in library*) rayons *mpl* ‖ *tr* entasser, empiler; mettre en meule, en gerbier, or en faisceau; (*a deck of cards*) truquer, donner un coup de pouce à; (aer) faire attendre (sur niveaux différents); **to be stacked** (aer) s'échelonner; **to stack arms** former les faisceaux

stadi·um ['stedɪ·əm] *s* (*pl* **-ums** or **-a** [ə]) stade *m*

staff [stæf] *s* (*rod, pole*) bâton *m*; (*of pilgrim*) bourdon *m*; (*of flag*) hampe *f*; (*of newspaper*) rédaction *f*; (*employees*) personnel *m*; (*servants*) domestiques *mfpl*; (*support*) soutien *m*; (mil) état-major *m*; (mus) portée *f* ‖ *tr* fournir, pourvoir de personnel; nommer le personnel pour

staff' head'quarters *spl* (mil) état-major *m*

staff' meet'ing *s* réunion *f* de service

staff' of'ficer *s* officier *m* d'état-major

stag [stæg] *adj* exclusivement masculin; **to go stag** aller sans compagne ‖ *s* homme *m*; (*male deer*) cerf *m*

stage [stedʒ] *s* (*point in time, section, process*) stade *m*, étape *f*, phase *f*; (*of rocket*) étage *m*; (*stagecoach*) diligence *f*; (*scene*) champ *m* d'action, scène *f*; (*staging*) échafaudage *m*; (*platform*) estrade *f*; (*of microscope*) platine *f*; (theat) scène *f*; **by**

easy stages par petites étapes; **by successive stages** par échelons; **to go on the stage** monter sur les planches ‖ *tr* (*a play, demonstration, riot, etc.*) monter; (*a play*) mettre en scène

stage'coach' *s* diligence *f*, coche *m*

stage'craft' *s* technique *f* de la scène

stage' door' *s* entrée *f* des artistes

stage'-door John'ny *s* (*pl* **-nies**) coureur *m* de girls

stage' effect' *s* effet *m* scénique

stage' fright' *s* trac *m*

stage' hand' *s* machiniste *m*

stage' left' *s* côté *m* jardin

stage' man'ager *s* régisseur *m*

stage' name' *s* nom *m* de théâtre

stage' prop'erties *spl* accessoires *mpl*

stage' right' *s* côté *m* cour

stage'-struck' [strʌk] *adj* entiché de théâtre

stage' whis'per *s* aparté *m*

stagger ['stægər] *tr* faire chanceler, faire tituber; (*to upset*) atterrer, bouleverser; (*to surprise*) étonner; (*to arrange*) disposer en chicane, en zigzag; (*hours of work, train schedules, etc.*) échelonner ‖ *intr* chanceler, tituber

staggering ['stægərɪŋ] *adj* (*swaying*) chancelant; (*amazing*) étonnant, faramineux, hallucinant

staging ['stedʒɪŋ] *s* échafaudage *m*; (theat) mise *f* en scène

stagnant ['stægnənt] *adj* stagnant

stag' par'ty *s* (*pl* **-ties**) (coll) réunion *f* entre hommes, réunion d'hommes seuls

staid [sted] *adj* posé, sérieux

stain [sten] *s* tache *f*, souillure *f* ‖ *tr* tacher, souiller; (*to tint*) teindre ‖ *intr* se tacher

stained' glass' *s* vitre *f* de couleur

stained'-glass win'dow *s* vitrail *m*

stain'less steel' ['stenlɪs] *s* acier *m* inoxydable

stair [stɛr] *s* escalier *m*; (*step of a series*) marche *f*, degré *m*; **stairs** escalier *m*

stair'case' or **stair'way'** *s* escalier *m*

stair'well' *s* cage *f* d'escalier

stake [stek] *s* (*hammered in the ground*) pieu *m*, poteau *m*; (*of tent*) piquet *m*; (*marker*) jalon *m*; (*for burning condemned persons*) bûcher *m*; (*in a game of chance*) mise *f*, enjeu *m*; **at stake** en jeu; **to pull up stakes** (coll) déménager ‖ *tr* (*a road*) bornoyer; (*plants*) échalasser, ramer; (*money*) risquer; (*to back financially*) (slang) fournir aux besoins de; **to stake all** mettre tout en jeu; **to stake off** or **out** jalonner, piqueter

stale [stel] *adj* (*bread*) rassis; (*wine or beer*) éventé; (*air*) confiné; (*joke*) vieux; (*check*) proscrit; (*subject*) rabattu; (*news*) défloré, défraîchi; **to smell stale** (*said of room*) sentir le renfermé

stale'mate' *s* (chess) pat *m*; (fig) impasse *f*; **in stalemate** pat ‖ *tr* (chess) faire pat; (fig) paralyser

stalk [stɔk] *s* tige *f*; (*of flower or leaf*) queue *f* ‖ *tr* traquer, suivre à la piste ‖ *intr*

marcher fièrement, marcher à grandes enjambées

stall [stɔl] *s* (*for a horse*) stalle *f*; (*at a market*) étal *m*, échoppe *f*; (aer) décrochage *m*; (sports) anti-jeu *m*; (slang) prétexte *m* ‖ *tr* mettre dans une stalle; (*a car*) caler; (*an airplane*) mettre en perte de vitesse; **to stall off** (coll) différer sous prétexte ‖ *intr* (*said of motor*) se bloquer; **to stall for time** (slang) temporiser

stallion ['stæljən] *s* étalon *m*

stalwart ['stɔlwərt] *adj* robuste; vaillant ‖ *s* partisan *m* loyal

stamen ['stemən] *s* étamine *f*

stamina ['stæmɪnə] *s* vigueur *f*, résistance *f*

stammer ['stæmər] *s* bégaiement *m*, balbutiement *m* ‖ *tr* & *intr* bégayer, balbutier

stammerer ['stæmərər] *s* bègue *mf*

stamp [stæmp] *s* (*mark, impression*) empreinte *f*; (*for postage*) timbre *m*; (*for stamping*) poinçon *m* ‖ *tr* (*mail*) affranchir; (*money; leather; a medal*) frapper, estamper; (*a document*) timbrer; (*a passport*) viser; **to stamp one's feet** trépigner; **to stamp one's foot** frapper du pied; **to stamp out** (*e.g., a rebellion*) écraser, étouffer

stampede [stæm'pid] *s* (*of animals or people*) débandade *f*; (*rush*) ruée *f*; (*of people*) sauve-qui-peut *m* ‖ *tr* provoquer la ruée de ‖ *intr* se débander

stamped' self'-addressed' en'velope *s* enveloppe *f* timbrée par l'expéditeur

stamp'ing grounds' *spl*—**to be on one's stamping grounds** (slang) être sur son terrain, être dans son domaine

stamp' pad' *s* tampon *m* encreur

stamp'-vend'ing machine' *s* distributeur *m* automatique de timbres-poste

stance [stæns] *s* attitude *f*, posture *f*

stanch [stantʃ] *adj* ferme, solide; vrai, loyal; (*watertight*) étanche ‖ *tr* étancher

stand [stænd] *s* (*place, attitude*) position *f*; (*opposition*) résistance *f*; (*of a merchant*) étal *m*, éventaire *m*; (*of a speaker*) tribune *f*, estrade *f*; (*of a horse*) aplombs *mpl*; (*piece of furniture*) guéridon *m*, console *f*; (*to hold music, papers*) pupitre *m*; **stands** tribune *f*, stand *m* ‖ *v* (*pret & pp* **stood** [stud]) *tr* mettre, placer, poser; (*the cold*) supporter; (*a shock; an attack*) soutenir; (*a round of drinks*) (coll) payer; **to stand off** repousser; **to stand up** (*to keep waiting*) (coll) poser un lapin à ‖ *intr* se lever, se mettre debout; se tenir debout, être debout; en être, e.g., **how does it stand?** où en est-il? **stand by!** en attente!; **to stand aloof** or **aside** se tenir à l'écart; **to stand by** se tenir prêt; (*e.g., a friend*) rester fidèle à; **to stand fast** tenir bon; **to stand for** (*to mean*) signifier; (*to affirm*) soutenir; (*to allow*) tolérer; **to stand in for** doubler, remplacer; **to stand in line** faire la queue; **to stand out** sortir, saillir; **to stand up** se lever, se mettre debout; se tenir debout, être debout; **to stand up**

against or **to** tenir tête à; **to stand up for** prendre fait et cause pour

standard ['stændərd] *adj* (*product, part, unit*) standard, de série, normal; (*current*) courant; (*author, book, work*) classique; (*edition*) définitif; (*keyboard of typewriter*) universel; (*coinage*) au titre ‖ *s* norme *f*, mesure *f*, règle *f*, pratique *f*; (*of quantity, weight, value*) standard *m*; (*banner*) étendard *m*; (*of lamp*) support *m*; (*of wires*) pylône *m*; (*of coinage*) titre *m*; (*for a monetary system*) étalon *m*; (fig) degré *m*, niveau *m*; **standards** critères *mpl*; **up to standard** suivant la norme

stand′ard·bear′er *s* porte-drapeau *m*

stand′ard gauge′ *s* voie *f* normale

standardize ['stændər,daɪz] *tr* standardiser

stand′ard of liv′ing *s* niveau *m* de vie

stand′ard time′ *s* heure *f* légale

standee [stæn'di] *s* voyageur *m* debout; (theat) spectateur *m* debout

stand′-in′ *s* (mov., theat) doublure *f*, remplaçant *m*; (coll) appuis *mpl*, piston *m*

standing ['stændɪŋ] *adj* (*upright*) debout; (*statue*) en pied; (*water*) stagnant; (*army; committee*) permanent; (*price; rule; rope*) fixe; (*custom*) établi, courant; (*jump*) à pieds joints ‖ *s* standing *m*, position *f*, importance *f*; **in good standing** estimé, accrédité; **of long standing** de longue date

stand′ing ar′my *s* armée *f* permanente

stand′ing room′ *s* places *fpl* debout

stand′ing vote′ *s* vote *m* par assis et levé

stand′pat′ *adj* & *s* (coll) immobiliste *mf*

stand′pat′ter *s* (coll) immobiliste *mf*

stand′point′ *s* point *m* de vue; **from the standpoint of** sous le rapport de

stand′still′ *s* arrêt *m*, immobilisation *f*; **at a standstill** au point mort; **to come to a standstill** s'arrêter court

stand′-up come′dian *s* monologuiste *mf* comique

stanza ['stænzə] *s* strophe *f*

staple ['stepəl] *adj* principal ‖ *s* (*product*) produit *m* principal; (*for holding papers together*) agrafe *f*; (bb) broche *f*; **staples** denrées *fpl* principales ‖ *tr* agrafer; (*books*) brocher

stapler ['steplər] *s* agrafeuse *f*; (bb) brocheuse *f*

star [stɑr] *s* astre *m*; (*heavenly body except sun and moon; figure that represents a star*) étoile *f*; (*of stage or screen*) vedette *f* ‖ *v* (*pret* & *pp* **starred**; *ger* **starring**) *tr* étoiler, consteller; (mov, rad, telv, theat) mettre en vedette; (typ) marquer d'un astérisque ‖ *intr* apparaître comme vedette

starboard ['stɑr,bord] *adj* de tribord ‖ *s* tribord *m* ‖ *adv* à tribord

star′ board′er *s* (coll) pensionnaire *mf* de prédilection

starch [stɑrtʃ] *s* amidon *m*; (*for fabrics*) empois *m*; (*formality*) raideur *f*; (bot, culin) fécule *f*; (coll) force *f*, vigueur *f* ‖ *tr* empeser

starch·y ['stɑrtʃi] *adj* (*comp* **-ier**; *super* **-iest**) empesé; (*foods*) féculent; (*manner*) raide, guindé

stare [stɛr] *s* regard *m* fixe ‖ *tr*—**to stare s.o. in the face** dévisager qn; (*to be obvious to s.o.*) sauter aux yeux de qn ‖ *intr* regarder fixement; **to stare at** regarder fixement, dévisager

star′fish′ *s* étoile *f* de mer

star′gaze′ *intr* regarder les étoiles; rêvasser, être dans la lune

stark [stɑrk] *adj* pur; rigide; désert, solitaire ‖ *adv* entièrement

stark′-na′ked *adj* tout nu

star′light′ *s* lumière *f* des étoiles

starling ['stɑrlɪŋ] *s* étourneau *m*

star·ry ['stɑri] *adj* (*comp* **-rier**; *super* **-riest**) étoilé

Stars′ and Stripes′ *spl* or **Star′-Spangled Ban′ner** *s* bannière *f* étoilée

start [stɑrt] *s* (*beginning*) commencement *m*, début *m*; (*sudden start*) sursaut *m*, haut-le-corps *m* ‖ *tr* commencer; (*a car, a motor, etc.*) mettre en marche, démarrer; (*a conversation*) entamer; (*a hare*) lever; (*a deer*) lancer; **to start** + *ger* se mettre à + *inf* ‖ *intr* commencer, débuter; démarrer; (*to be startled*) sursauter; **starting from** or **with** à partir de; **to start after** sortir à la recherche de; **to start out** se mettre en route

starter ['stɑrtər] *s* initiateur *m*; (aut) démarreur *m*; (sports) starter *m*

start′ing point′ *s* point *m* de départ

startle ['stɑrtəl] *tr* faire tressaillir ‖ *intr* tressaillir

startling ['stɑrtlɪŋ] *adj* effrayant; (*event*) sensationnel; (*resemblance*) saisissant

starvation [stɑr've ʃən] *s* inanition *f*, famine *f*

starva′tion di′et *s* diète *f* absolue

starva′tion wag′es *spl* salaire *m* de famine

starve [stɑrv] *tr* affamer; faire mourir de faim; **to starve out** réduire par la faim ‖ *intr* être affamé; être dans la misère; mourir de faim; (coll) mourir de faim

state [stet] *s* état *m*; (*pomp*) apparat *m*; **to lie in state** être exposé solennellement ‖ *tr* affirmer, déclarer; (*an hour or date*) régler, fixer; (*a problem*) poser

stateless ['stetlɪs] *adj* apatride

state·ly ['stetli] *adj* (*comp* **-lier**; *super* **-liest**) majestueux, imposant

statement ['stetmənt] *s* énoncé *m*, exposé *m*; (*account, report*) compte rendu *m*, rapport *m*; (*of an account*) (com) relevé *m*; (comp) instruction *f*

state′ of mind′ *s* état *m* d'esprit, état d'âme

state′ of the art′ *s* état *m* or dernier cri *m* de la technique, état présent

state′room′ *s* (naut) cabine *f*; (rr) compartiment *m*

states′man *s* (*pl* **-men**) homme *m* d'État

static ['stætɪk] *adj* statique; (rad) parasite ‖ *s* (rad) parasites *mpl*

station ['steʃən] *s* station *f*; (*for police; for selling gasoline; for broadcasting*) poste *m*; (*of bus, subway, rail line, taxi; for observation*) station; (rr) gare *f* ‖ *tr* poster, placer

sta′tion a′gent *s* chef *m* de gare

stationary [′steʃən,ɛri] *adj* stationnaire

sta′tion break′ *s* (rad) pause *f*

stationer [′steʃənər] *s* papetier *m*

stationery [′steʃən,ɛri] *s* papeterie *f*, fournitures *fpl* de bureau

sta′tionery store′ *s* papeterie *f*

sta′tion house′ *s* commissariat *m* de police

sta′tion identifica′tion *s* (rad) indicatif *m*

sta′tion·mas′ter *s* chef *m* de gare

Sta′tions of the Cross′ *s* (rel) stations *fpl* de la Croix

sta′tion wag′on *s* familiale *f*, break *m*

statistical [stə′tɪstɪkəl] *adj* statistique

statistician [,stætɪs′tɪʃən] *s* statisticien *m*

statistics [stə′tɪstɪks] *s* (*science*) statistique *f* ‖ *spl* (*data*) statistique, statistiques

statue [′stætʃʊ] *s* statue *f*

Stat′ue of Lib′erty *s* Liberté *f* éclairant le monde, Statue *f* de la Liberté

statuesque [,stætʃʊ′ɛsk] *adj* sculptural

stature [′stætʃər] *s* stature *f*, taille *f*; caractère *m*, stature

status [′stetəs] *s* condition *f*; rang *m*, standing *m*; **the status of** le statut de

sta′tus quo′ [kwo] *s* statu quo *m*

sta′tus seek′er *s* obsédé *m* du standing

sta′tus sym′bol *s* symbole *m* du rang social

statute [′stætʃʊt] *s* statut *m*

stat′ute of limita′tions *s* loi *f* concernant la prescription

statutory [′stætʃʊ,tori] *adj* statutaire

staunch [stɔntʃ] *adj* & *tr* var of **stanch**

stave [stev] *s* (*of barrel*) douve *f*; (*of ladder*) échelon *m*; (mus) portée *f* ‖ *v* (*pret* & *pp* **staved** or **stove** [stov]) *tr*—**to stave in** défoncer, crever; **to stave off** détourner, éloigner

stay [ste] *s* (*visit*) séjour *m*; (*prop*) étai *m*; (*of a corset*) baleine *f*; (*of execution*) sursis *m*; (fig) soutien *m* ‖ *tr* arrêter ‖ *intr* rester; séjourner; (*at a hotel*) descendre; **to stay put** ne pas bouger; **to stay up** veiller

stay′-at-home′ *adj* & *s* casanier *m*

STD [′ɛs′ti′di] *s* (letterword) (**sexually transmitted disease**) MST (maladie sexuellement transmissible)

stead [stɛd] *s*—**in s.o.'s stead** à la place de qn; **to stand s.o. in good stead** être fort utile à qn

stead′fast′ *adj* ferme; constant

stead·y [′stɛdi] *adj* (*comp* **-ier**; *super* **-iest**) ferme, solide; régulier; (*market*) soutenu ‖ *v* (*pret* & *pp* **-ied**) *tr* raffermir ‖ *intr* se raffermir

steak [stek] *s* (*slice*) tranche *f*; bifteck *m*

steal [stil] *s* (coll) vol *m*; (*bargain*) (coll) occasion *f* ‖ *v* (*pret* **stole** [stol]; *pp* **stolen**) *tr* voler; **to steal s.th. from s.o.** voler q.ch. à qn ‖ *intr* voler; **to steal away** se dérober; **to steal into** se glisser dans; **to steal upon** s'approcher en tapinois de

stealth [stɛlθ] *s*—**by stealth** en tapinois, à la dérobée

steam [stim] *s* vapeur *f*; (*e.g., on a window*) buée *f*; **full steam ahead!** en avant à toute vapeur!; **to get up steam** faire monter la pression; **to let off steam** lâcher la vapeur; (fig) s'épancher ‖ *tr* passer à la vapeur; (culin) cuire à la vapeur; **to steam up** (*e.g., a window*) embuer ‖ *intr* dégager de la vapeur, fumer; s'évaporer; **to steam ahead** avancer à la vapeur; (fig) faire des progrès rapides; **to steam up** s'embuer

steam′boat′ *s* vapeur *m*

steam′ chest′ *s* boîte *f* à vapeur

steam′ en′gine *s* machine *f* à vapeur

steamer [′stimər] *s* vapeur *m*

steam′ heat′ *s* chauffage *m* à la vapeur

steam′ roll′er *s* rouleau *m* compresseur; (fig) force *f* irrésistible

steam′ship′ *s* vapeur *m*

steam′ shov′el *s* pelle *f* à vapeur

steam′ ta′ble *s* table *f* à compartiments chauffés à la vapeur

steed [stid] *s* coursier *m*

steel [stil] *adj* (*industry*) sidérurgique ‖ *s* acier *m*; (*for striking fire from flint*) briquet *m*; (*for sharpening knives*) fusil *m* ‖ *tr* aciérer; **to steel oneself against** se cuirasser contre

steel′ wool′ *s* laine *f* d'acier, paille *f* de fer, jex *m*

steel′works′ *spl* aciérie *f*

steelyard [′stil,jɑrd] *s* romaine *f*

steep [stip] *adj* raide, abrupt; (*cliff*) escarpé; (*price*) (coll) exorbitant ‖ *tr* tremper; (*e.g., tea*) infuser; **steeped in** saturé de; (*ignorance*) pétri de; (*the classics*) nourri de

steeple [′stipəl] *s* clocher *m*; (*spire*) flèche *f*

stee′ple·chase′ *s* course *f* d'obstacles

steer [stɪr] *s* bouvillon *m* ‖ *tr* diriger, conduire; (naut) gouverner ‖ *intr* se diriger; (naut) se gouverner; **to steer clear of** (coll) éviter

steerage [′stɪrɪdʒ] *s* entrepont *m*

steer′age pas′senger *s* passager *m* d'entrepont

steer′ing commit′tee *s* comité *m* d'organisation

steer′ing wheel′ *s* volant *m*; (naut) roue *f* de gouvernail

stellar [′stɛlər] *adj* stellaire; (*rôle*) de vedette

stem [stɛm] *s* (*of plant; of key*) tige *f*; (*of column; of tree*) fût *m*, tige; (*of fruit*) queue *f*; (*of pipe; of feather*) tuyau *m*; (*of goblet*) pied *m*; (*of watch*) remontoir *m*; (*of word*) radical *m*, thème *m*; (naut) étrave *f*; **from stem to stern** de l'étrave à l'étambot, d'un bout à l'autre ‖ *v* (*pret* & *pp* **stemmed**; *ger* **stemming**) *tr* (*e.g., grapes*) égrapper; (*e.g., the flow of blood*) étancher; (*the tide*) lutter contre, refouler; (*to check*) arrêter, endiguer ‖ *intr*—**to stem from** provenir de

stem′-wind′er *s* montre *f* à remontoir

stench [stɛntʃ] s puanteur f
sten·cil ['stɛnsəl] s (of metal, cardboard) pochoir m; (of paper) poncif m; (work produced by it) travail m au pochoir; (for reproducing typewriting) stencil m ‖ v (pret & pp **-ciled** or **-cilled**; ger **-ciling** or **-cilling**) tr passer au pochoir; tirer au stencil
stenographer [stə'nɑgrəfər] s sténo f, sténographe mf
stenography [stə'nɑgrəfi] s sténographie f
step [stɛp] s pas m; (of staircase) marche f, degré m; (footprint) trace f; (of carriage) marchepied m; (of ladder) échelon m; (procedure) démarche f; **in step with** au pas avec; **step by step** pas à pas; **to march in step** marcher en cadence; **watch your step!** prenez garde de tomber!; (fig) évitez tout faux pas! ‖ v (pret & pp **stepped**; ger **stepping**) tr échelonner; **to step off** mesurer au pas ‖ intr faire un pas; marcher; (coll) aller en toute hâte; **to step aside** s'écarter; **to step back** reculer; **to step in** entrer; **to step on it** (coll) mettre tous les gaz; **to step on the starter** appuyer sur le démarreur
step'broth'er s demi-frère m
step'child' s (pl **-child'ren**) beau-fils m; belle-fille f
step'daugh'ter s belle-fille f
step'fa'ther s beau-père m
step'lad'der s échelle f double, marche-pied m, escabeau m
step'moth'er s belle-mère f
steppe [stɛp] s steppe f
step'ping stone' s pierre f de passage; (fig) marchepied m
step'sis'ter s demi-sœur f
step'son' s beau-fils m
stere·o ['stɛri,o] adj (coll) stéréo, stéréophonique; (coll) stéréoscopique ‖ s (pl **-os**) (coll) disque m stéréo; (coll) émission f en stéréophonique; (coll) photographie f stéréoscopique
stereotyped ['stɛri·ə,taɪpt] adj stéréotypé
sterile ['stɛrɪl] adj stérile
sterilize ['stɛrɪ,laɪz] tr stériliser
sterling ['stʌrlɪŋ] adj de bon aloi ‖ s livres fpl sterling; (sterling silver) argent m fin, argent de bon aloi
stern [stʌrn] adj sévère, austère; (look) rébarbatif ‖ s poupe f
stethoscope ['stɛθə,skop] s stéthoscope m
stevedore ['stivə,dor] s arrimeur m
stew [st(j)u] s ragoût m ‖ tr mettre en ragoût ‖ intr (coll) être dans tous ses états
steward ['st(j)u·ərd] s (on estate, etc.) régisseur m, intendant m; (in a restaurant) maître m d'hôtel; (aer) flight attendant; (naut) steward m
stewardess ['st(j)u·ərdɪs] s (aer) hôtesse f de l'air; (naut) stewardess f
stewed' fruit' s compote f
stewed' toma'toes spl purée f de tomates
stick [stɪk] s bâtonnet m, bâton m; (rod) verge f; (wand; drumstick) baguette f; (of chewing gum; of dynamite) bâton;

(firewood) bois m sec; (walking stick) canne f; (naut) mât m; (typ) composteur m ‖ v (pret & pp **stuck** [stʌk]) tr piquer, enfoncer; (to fasten in position) clouer, ficher, planter; (to glue) coller; (a pig) saigner; (coll) confondre; **stick 'em up!** (slang) haut les mains!; **to be stuck** être pris; (e.g., in the mud) s'enliser; (to be unable to continue) (coll) être en panne; **to stick it out** (coll) tenir jusqu'au bout; **to stick out** (one's tongue) tirer; (one's head) passer; (one's chest) bomber; **to stick up** (in order to rob) (slang) voler à main armée ‖ intr se piquer, s'enfoncer; se ficher, se planter; (to be jammed) être pris, se coincer; (to adhere) coller; (to remain) continuer, rester; **to stick out** saillir, dépasser; (to be evident) sauter aux yeux; **to stick up for** (coll) prendre la défense de
sticker ['stɪkər] s (label) étiquette f gommée; (difficult question) (coll) colle f
stick'pin' s épingle f de cravate
stick'-up' s (slang) attaque f à main armée, hold-up m
stick·y ['stɪki] adj (comp **-ier**; super **-iest**) gluant, collant; (hands) poisseux; (weather) étouffant; (question) épineux; (unaccommodating) tatillon
stiff [stɪf] adj raide, difficile, ardu; (joint) ankylosé; (brush; batter) dur; (style, manner) guindé, empesé; (drink) fort; (price) (coll) salé, exagéré; **to be scared stiff** (slang) les avoir à zéro ‖ s (corpse) (slang) macchabée m
stiff' col'lar s col m empesé
stiffen ['stɪfən] tr raidir, tendre; (culin) épaisser ‖ intr se raidir
stiff' neck' s torticolis m
stiff'-necked' adj obstiné, entêté
stiff' shirt' s chemise f empesée, chemise à plastron
stifle ['staɪfəl] tr & intr étouffer
stig·ma ['stɪgmə] s (pl **-mas** or **-mata** [mətə]) stigmate m
stigmatize ['stɪgmə,taɪz] tr stigmatiser
stilet·to [stɪ'lɛto] s (pl **-tos**) stylet m
still [stɪl] adj (peaceful, quiet) tranquille, calme, silencieux; (motionless) immobile; (water) dormant; (wine) non mousseux ‖ s (for distilling) alambic m; (phot) image f; (mov) photogramme m; (poetic) silence m ‖ adv (yet) encore, toujours ‖ conj cependant, pourtant ‖ tr calmer, apaiser; (to silence) faire taire ‖ intr se calmer, s'apaiser; se taire
still'born' adj mort-né
still' life' s (pl **still lifes** or **still lives**) nature f morte
stilt [stɪlt] s échasse f; (in the water) pilotis m
stilted adj guindé; (archit) surhaussé
stimulant ['stɪmjələnt] adj & s stimulant m
stimulate ['stɪmjə,let] tr stimuler
stimu·lus ['stɪmjələs] s (pl **-li** [,laɪ]) stimulant m, aiguillon m; (physiol) stimulus m

sting [stɪŋ] s piqûre f; (*stinging organ*) aiguillon m, dard m ‖ v (*pret & pp* **stung** [stʌŋ]) tr & intr piquer

stin·gy ['stɪndʒi] adj (*comp* **-gier;** *super* **-giest**) avare, pingre

stink [stɪŋk] s puanteur f ‖ v (*pret* **stank** [stæŋk]; *pp* **stunk** [stʌŋk]); **to stink up** empester, empuantir ‖ intr puer, empester; **to stink of** puer, empester

stinker ['stɪŋkər] s (slang) peau f de vache, chameau m

stint [stɪnt] s tâche f, besogne f; **without stint** sans réserve, sans limite ‖ tr limiter, réduire; **to stint oneself** se priver ‖ intr lésiner, être chiche

stipend ['staɪpənd] s traitement m, honoraires mpl

stipulate ['stɪpjə,let] tr stipuler

stir [stʌr] s remuement m, agitation f; (*prison*) (slang) bloc m; **to create a stir** faire sensation ‖ v (*pret & pp* **stirred;** *ger* **stirring**) tr remuer, agiter; **to stir up** (*trouble*) fomenter ‖ intr remuer, s'agiter, bouger

stirring ['stʌrɪŋ] adj entraînant

stirrup ['stʌrəp], ['stɪrəp] s étrier m

stitch [stɪtʃ] s (*in sewing*) point m; (*in knitting*) maille f; (surg) point de suture; **not a stitch of** (coll) pas un brin de; **stitch in the side** point de côté; **to be in stitches** (coll) se tenir les côtes ‖ tr coudre; (bb) brocher; (surg) suturer ‖ intr coudre

stock [stɑk] s (*supply*) réserve f, provision f, stock m; (*assortment*) assortiment m; capital m, fonds m; (*shares*) valeurs fpl, actions fpl; (*of meat*) bouillon m; (*of a tree*) tronc m; (*of an anvil*) billot m; (*of a rifle*) crosse f; (*of a tree; of a family*) souche f; (*livestock*) bétail m, bestiaux mpl; (*handle*) poignée f; (*for dies*) tourne-à-gauche m; (hort) ente f; **in stock** en magasin; **on the stocks** (fig) sur le métier; **out of stock** épuisé; **stocks** (*for punishment*) pilori m; (naut) chantier m; **to take stock** (com) faire l'inventaire; (fig) faire le point; **to take stock in** (coll) faire grand cas de; **to take stock of** faire l'inventaire de ‖ tr approvisionner; garder en magasin; (*a forest or lake*) peupler; (*a farm*) monter en bétail; (*a pool*) empoissonner

stockade [stɑ'ked] s palanque f, palissade f ‖ tr palissader

stock'breed'er s éleveur m de bestiaux

stock'breed'ing s élevage m

stock'bro'ker s agent m de change, courtier m de bourse

stock' car' s (aut) voiture f de série; (rr) wagon m à bestiaux

stock'-car race' s course f de bolides

stock' com'pany s (com) société f anonyme; (theat) troupe f à demeure

stock' div'idend s action f gratuite

stock' exchange' s bourse f

stock'hold'er s actionnaire mf

stocking ['stɑkɪŋ] s bas m

stock' mar'ket s bourse f, marché m des valeurs; **to play the stock market** jouer à la bourse

stock'pile' s stocks mpl de réserve ‖ tr & intr stocker

stock' rais'ing s élevage m

stock'room' s magasin m

stock·y ['stɑki] adj (*comp* **-ier;** *super* **-iest**) trapu, costaud

stock'yard' s parc m à bétail

stoic ['sto·ɪk] adj & s stoïque; **Stoic** stoïcien m

stoke [stok] tr (*a fire*) attiser; (*a furnace*) alimenter, charger

stoker ['stokər] s chauffeur m; (mach) stoker m

stolid ['stɑlɪd] adj flegmatique, impassible, lourd

stomach ['stʌmək] s estomac m ‖ tr digérer; (coll) digérer, avaler

stom'ach ache' s mal m d'estomac

stom'ach pump' s pompe f stomacale

stone [ston] s pierre f; (*of fruit*) noyau m; (pathol) calcul m; (typ) marbre m ‖ tr lapider; (*fruit*) dénoyauter

stone'-broke' adj (coll) complètement fauché, raide

stone'-deaf' adj sourd comme un pot

stone'ma'son s maçon m

stone' quar'ry s (*pl* **-ries**) carrière f

stone's' throw' s—**within a stone's throw** à un jet de pierre

stone'wall' intr donner des réponses évasives

ston·y ['stoni] adj (*comp* **-ier;** *super* **-iest**) pierreux; (fig) dur, endurci

stooge [studʒ] s (theat) compère m; (slang) homme f de paille, acolyte m

stool [stul] s tabouret m, escabeau m; (*bowel movement*) selles fpl

stool' pi'geon s appeau m; (slang) mouchard m, mouton m

stoop [stup] s courbure f, inclinaison f; (*porch*) véranda f ‖ intr se pencher; se tenir voûté; (*to debase oneself*) s'abaisser

stoop'-shoul'dered adj voûté

stop [stɑp] s arrêt m; (*in telegrams*) stop m; (*full stop*) point m; (*of a guitar*) touche f; (mus) jeu m d'orgue; (*public sign*) stop; **to pull out all the stops** (coll) mettre le paquet; **to put a stop to** mettre fin à ‖ v (*pret & pp* **stopped;** *ger* **stopping**) tr arrêter; (*a check*) faire opposition à; **to stop up** boucher ‖ intr s'arrêter, arrêter; **to stop** + *ger*, cesser de + *inf*, s'arrêter de + *inf*; **to stop off** descendre en passant; **to stop off at** s'arrêter un moment à; **to stop over** (aer, naut) faire escale

stop'cock' s robinet m d'arrêt

stop'gap' adj provisoire ‖ s bouche-trou m

stop'light' s signal m lumineux; (aut) feu m stop, stop m

stop'o'ver s arrêt m en cours de route, étape f

stoppage ['stɑpɪdʒ] s arrêt m; (*of payments*) suspension f; (*of wages*) retenue f; obstruction f; (pathol) occlusion f

stopper ['stɑpər] *s* bouchon *m*, tampon *m*
stop'ping for unload'ing *s* manutention *f*
stop' sign' *s* signal *m* d'arrêt
stop' thief' *interj* au voleur!
stop'watch' *s* chronomètre *m* à déclic, compte-secondes *m*
storage ['storɪdʒ] *s* emmagasinage *m*, entreposage *m*; **to put in storage** entreposer
stor'age bat'ter·y *s* (*pl* **-ies**) (elec) accumulateur *m*, accu *m*
store [stor] *s* (*where goods are sold*) magasin *m*; (*shop*) boutique *f*; (*supply*) provision *f*, réserve *f*, stock *m*; (*of learning, information*) fonds *m*; (*warehouse*) (Brit) entrepôt *m*; **stores** (*materials*) matériel *m*; (*provisions*) vivres *mpl*; **to set great store by** faire grand cas de ‖ *tr* emmagasiner; (*to warehouse*) entreposer; (*to supply or stock*) approvisionner; **to store away** or **up** accumuler
store'house' *s* magasin *m*, entrepôt *m*; (*of information*) mine *f*
store'keep'er *s* boutiquier *m*
store'room' *s* dépense *f*, office *f*; (*for furniture*) garde-meuble *m*; (naut) soute *f*
stork [stork] *s* cigogne *f*
storm [storm] *s* orage *m*; (mil) assaut *m*; (fig) tempête *f*; **to take by storm** prendre d'assaut ‖ *tr* livrer l'assaut à ‖ *intr* faire de l'orage; (fig) tempêter
storm' cloud' *s* nuage *m* orageux; (fig) nuage noir
storm' door' *s* contre-porte *f*
storm' pet'rel ['pɛtrəl] *s* oiseau *m* des tempêtes
storm' sash' *s* contre-fenêtre *f*
storm' sew'er *s* évacuateur *m* pluvial
storm' troops' *spl* troupes *fpl* d'assaut
storm' win'dow *s* contre-fenêtre *f*, double fenêtre *f*
storm·y ['stormi] *adj* (*comp* **-ier**; *super* **-iest**) orageux
sto·ry ['stori] *s* (*pl* **-ries**) (*narration*) histoire *f*; (*tale*) conte *m*; (*plot*) intrigue *f*; (*floor*) étage *m*; (coll) mensonge *m*, histoire
sto'ry·tel'ler *s* conteur *m*; (*fibber*) menteur *m*
stout [staut] *adj* (*fat*) corpulent, gros; (*courageous*) vaillant; (*determined*) ferme, résolu; (*strong*) fort ‖ *s* stout *m*
stout'-heart'ed *adj* au cœur vaillant
stove [stov] *s* (*for heating a house or room*) poêle *m*; (*for cooking*) fourneau *m* de cuisine, cuisinière *f*
stove'pipe' *s* tuyau *m* de poêle; (*hat*) (coll) huit-reflets *m*, tuyau *m* de poêle
stow [sto] *tr* mettre en place, ranger; (naut) arrimer; **to stow with** remplir de ‖ *intr*—**to stow away** s'embarquer clandestinement
stowage ['sto·ɪdʒ] *s* arrimage *m*; (*costs*) frais *mpl* d'arrimage
stow'away' *s* passager *m* clandestin
straddle ['strædəl] *tr* enfourcher, chevaucher ‖ *intr* se mettre à califourchon; (coll) répondre en normand

strafe [strɑf], [stref] *s* (slang) bombardement *m*, marmitage *m* ‖ *tr* (slang) bombarder, marmiter
straggle ['strægəl] *intr* traîner; (*to be scattered*) s'éparpiller; **to straggle along** marcher sans ordre
straggler ['stræglər] *s* traînard *m*
straight [stret] *adj* (*not curved*) droit; (*shortest route*) direct; (*honest*) loyal, honnête; (*in order*) correct, en ordre; (*chair*) à dossier droit; (*hair*) raide; (*whiskey*) sec; (*candid*) franc; (*hanging straight*) d'aplomb; (*part in a play*) sérieux; (*not homosexual*) qui n'est pas homosexuel; (*not a drug addict*) qui ne se drogue pas; (*not a criminal*) qui n'est pas véreux; **to set s.o. straight** faire la leçon à qn ‖ *s* (poker) séquence *f* ‖ *adv* droit; directement; loyalement, honnêtement; (*without interruption*) de suite; **straight ahead** tout droit; **straight out** franchement, sans détours; **straight through** de part en part; d'un bout à l'autre; **to go straight** (coll) vivre honnêtement
straighten ['stretən] *tr* redresser; mettre en ordre ‖ *intr* se redresser
straight' face' *s*—**to keep a straight face** montrer un front sérieux
straight'for'ward *adj* franc, direct; loyal
straight' off' *adv* sur-le-champ, d'emblée
straight' ra'zor *s* rasoir *m* à main
straight'way' *adv* sur-le-champ, d'emblée
strain [stren] *s* tension *f*, effort *m*, pression *f*; (*of a muscle*) foulure *f*; (*descendants*) lignée *f*; (*ancestry; type of virus*) souche *f*; (*trait*) héritage *m*, tendance *f*; (*vein*) ton *m*, sens *m*; (*bit*) trace *f*; (coll) grand effort *m*; **mental strain** surmenage *m* intellectuel; **strains** (*of, e.g., the Marseillaise*) accents *mpl*; **sweet strains** doux accords *mpl* ‖ *tr* forcer; (*e.g., a wrist*) se fouler; (*e.g., one's eyes*) se fatiguer; (*e.g., part of a machine*) déformer; (*e.g., a liquid*) filtrer, tamiser; **to strain oneself** se surmener ‖ *intr* s'efforcer; filtrer, tamiser; (*to trickle*) suinter; (*said of beam, ship, motor, etc.*) fatiguer; **to strain at** (*a leash, rope, etc.*) tirer sur; (*to balk at*) reculer devant
strained *adj* (*smile*) forcé; (*friendship*) tendu; (*nervous*) crispé
strainer ['strenər] *s* passoire *f*, filtre *m*
strait [stret] *s* détroit *m*; **straits** détroit *m*; **to be in dire straits** être dans la plus grande gêne
strait' jack'et *s* camisole de force
strait'-laced' *adj* prude, collet monté, puritain
Straits' of Do'ver *spl* Pas *m* de Calais
strand [strænd] *s* (*beach*) plage *f*, grève *f*; (*of rope or cable*) toron *m*; (*of thread*) brin *m*; (*of pearls*) collier *m*; (*of hair*) cheveu *m* ‖ *tr* toronner; (*to undo strands of*) décorder; (*a ship*) échouer
stranded *adj* abandonné; (*lost*) égaré; (*ship*) échoué; (*rope or cable*) à torons; **to leave s.o. stranded** laisser qn en plan

strange [strendʒ] *adj* étrange; (*unfamiliar*) inconnu, étranger; (*unaccustomed*) inhabituel

stranger ['strendʒər] *s* étranger *m*; visiteur *m*

strangle ['stræŋgəl] *tr* étrangler, étouffer ‖ *intr* s'étrangler

strap [stræp] *s* (*of leather, rubber, etc.*) courroie *f*; (*of cloth, metal, leather, etc.*) bande *f*; (*to sharpen a razor*) cuir *m* à rasoir; (*of, e.g., a harness*) sangle *f* ‖ *v* (*pret & pp* **strapped**; *ger* **strapping**) *tr* attacher avec une courroie, sangler; (*a razor*) repasser sur le cuir

strap'hang'er *s* (coll) voyageur *m* debout

strapping ['stræpɪŋ] *adj* bien découplé, robuste; (coll) énorme, gros

stratagem ['strætədʒəm] *s* stratagème *m*

strategic(al) [strə'tidʒɪk(əl)] *adj* stratégique

strategist ['strætɪdʒɪst] *s* stratège *m*

strate·gy ['strætɪdʒi] *s* (*pl* **-gies**) stratégie *f*

strati·fy ['strætɪ,faɪ] *v* (*pret & pp* **-fied**) *tr* stratifier ‖ *intr* se stratifier

stratosphere ['strætə,sfɪr] *s* stratosphère *f*

stra·tum ['strætəm] *s* (*pl* **-ta** [tə] or **-tums**) couche *f*; (*e.g., of society*) classe *f*, couche

straw [strɔ] *s* paille *f*; (*for drinking*) chalumeau *m*, paille; **it's the last straw!** c'est le bouquet!, il ne manquait plus que cela!, c'est la fin des haricots!

straw'ber'ry *s* (*pl* **-ries**) fraise *f*; (*plant*) fraisier *m*

straw'hat' *s* chapeau *m* de paille; (*skimmer*) canotier *m*

straw' man' *s* (*pl* **-men'**) (*figurehead*) homme *m* de paille, sanglier *m* de carton; (*scarecrow*) épouvantail *m*; (*red herring*) canard *m*, diversion *f*

straw' mat'tress *s* paillasse *f*

straw' vote' *s* vote *m* d'essai

stray [stre] *adj* égaré; (*bullet*) perdu; (*scattered*) épars ‖ *s* animal *m* égaré ‖ *intr* s'égarer

streak [strik] *s* raie *f*, rayure *f*, bande *f*; (*of light*) trait *m*, filet *m*; (*of lightning*) éclair *m*; (*layer*) veine *f*; (*bit*) trace *f*; **like a streak** comme un éclair; **streak of luck** filon *m* ‖ *tr* rayer, strier, zébrer ‖ *intr* faire des raies; passer comme un éclair

stream [strim] *s* (*brook*) ruisseau *m*; (*steady flow of current*) courant *m*; (*of people, abuse, light, etc.*) flot *m*; (*of, e.g., automobiles*) défilé *m* ‖ *intr* couler; (*said of blood*) ruisseler; (*said of light*) jaillir; (*said of flag*) flotter; **to stream out** sortir à flots

streamer ['strimər] *s* banderole *f*

stream'lined' *adj* aérodynamique, caréné; (fig) abrégé, concis

stream'lin'er *s* train *m* caréné de luxe

street [strit] *s* rue *f*; (*surface of the street*) chaussée *f*

street'car' *s* tramway *m*

street' clean'er *s* balayeur *m*; (mach) balayeuse *f*

street' clothes' *spl* vêtements *mpl* de ville

street' floor' *s* rez-de-chaussée *m*

street'light' *s* réverbère *m*

street' sprink'ler *s* arroseuse *f*

street' u'rinal *s* vespasienne *f*, édicule *m*, urinoir *m*

street'walk'er *s* racoleuse *f*, fille *f* des rues

street'wise' *adj* démerdard

strength [strɛŋθ] *s* force *f*, puissance *f*; (*of a fabric*) solidité *f*; (*of spirituous liquors*) degré *m*, titre *m*; (com) tendance *f* à la hausse; (mil) effectif(s) *m*(*pl*); **on the strength of** sur la foi de

strengthen ['strɛŋθən] *tr* fortifier, renforcer ‖ *intr* se fortifier, se renforcer

strenuous ['strɛnjʊ·əs] *adj* actif, énergique; (*work*) ardu; (*effort*) acharné; (*objection*) vigoureux

stress [strɛs] *s* tension *f*, force *f*; (mach) stress *m*, tension; (phonet) accent *m* d'intensité; **to lay stress on** insister sur ‖ *tr* (*e.g., a beam*) charger; (*a syllable*) accentuer; (*a point*) insister sur, appuyer sur

stress' ac'cent *s* accent *m* d'intensité

stretch [strɛtʃ] *s* (*act, gesture*) étirement *m*; (*span*) envergure *f*; (*of the arm; of the meaning*) extension *f*; (*of the imagination*) effort *m*; (*distance in time or space*) intervalle *m*, période *f*; (*section of road*) section *f*; (*section of country, water, etc.*) étendue *f*; **at a stretch** d'un trait; **in one stretch** d'une seule traite; **to do a stretch** (slang) faire de la taule ‖ *tr* tendre; (*the sense of a word*) forcer; (*a sauce*) allonger; **to stretch oneself** s'étirer; **to stretch out** allonger, étendre; (*the hand*) tendre ‖ *intr* s'étirer; (*said of shoes, gloves, etc.*) s'élargir; **to stretch out** s'allonger, s'étendre

stretcher ['strɛtʃər] *s* (*for gloves, trousers, etc.*) tendeur *m*; (*for a painting*) châssis *m*; (*to carry sick or wounded*) civière *f*, brancard *m*

stretch'er-bear'er *s* brancardier *m*

strew [stru] *v* (*pret* **strewed**; *pp* **strewed** or **strewn**) *tr* semer, éparpiller; (*e.g., with flowers*) joncher, parsemer

stricken ['strɪkən] *adj* frappé; (*e.g., with grief*) affligé; (*crossed out*) rayé; **stricken with** atteint de

strict [strɪkt] *adj* strict; (*exacting*) sévère

stricture ['strɪktʃər] *s* critique *f* sévère; (pathol) rétrécissement *m*

stride [straɪd] *s* enjambée *f*; **to hit one's stride** attraper la cadence; **to make great** (or **rapid**) **strides** avancer à grands pas; **to take in one's stride** faire sans le moindre effort ‖ *v* (*pret* **strode** [strod]; *pp* **stridden** ['strɪdən]) *tr* parcourir à grandes enjambées; (*to straddle*) enfourcher ‖ *intr*—**to stride across** or **over** enjamber; **to stride along** marcher à grandes enjambées

strident ['straɪdənt] *adj* strident

strife [straɪf] *s* lutte *f*

strike [straɪk] *s* (*blow*) coup *m*; (*stopping of work*) grève *f*; (*discovery of ore, oil, etc.*) rencontre *f*; (baseball) coup du batteur; **to go on strike** se mettre en grève ‖ *v* (*pret & pp* **struck** [strʌk]) *tr* frapper; (*coins*)

frapper; (*a match*) frotter; (*a bargain*) conclure; (*camp*) lever; (*the sails; the colors*) amener; (*the hour*) sonner; (*root; a pose*) prendre; **how does he strike you?** quelle impression vous fait-il?; **to strike it rich** trouver le filon; **to strike out** or **off** rayer; **to strike up** (*a song, piece of music, etc.*) attaquer, entonner; (*an acquaintance, conversation, etc.*) lier ‖ *intr* frapper; (*said of clock*) sonner; (*said of workers*) faire la grève; (mil) donner l'assaut; **to strike out** se mettre en route
strike′break′er *s* briseur *m* de grève, jaune *m*
strike′ pay′ *s* salaire *m* de gréviste
striker ['straɪkər] *s* frappeur *m*; (*on door*) marteau *m*; (*worker on strike*) gréviste *mf*
striking ['straɪkɪŋ] *adj* frappant, saisissant; (*workers*) en grève
strik′ing pow′er *s* force *f* de frappe
string [strɪŋ] *s* ficelle *f*; (*of onions or garlic; of islands; of pearls; of abuse*) chapelet *m*; (*of words, insults*) enfilade *f*, kyrielle *f*; (*e.g., of cars*) file *f*; (*of beans*) fil *m*; (*for shoes*) lacet *m*; (mus) corde *f*; **strings** instruments *mpl* à cordes; **to pull strings** (fig) tirer les ficelles; **with no strings attached** (coll) sans restriction ‖ *v* (*pret & pp* **strung** [strʌŋ]) *tr* mettre une ficelle à, garnir de cordes; (*e.g., a violin*) mettre les cordes à; (*a bow*) bander; (*a tennis racket*) corder; (*beads, sentences, etc.*) enfiler; (*a cord, a thread, a wire, etc.*) tendre; (*to tune*) moner; **to string along** (slang) lanterner, faire marcher; **to string up** (coll) pendre ‖ *intr*—**to string along with** (slang) collaborer avec, suivre
string′ bean′ *s* haricot *m* vert
stringed′ in′strument *s* instrument *m* à cordes
stringent ['strɪndʒənt] *adj* rigoureux; (*tight*) tendu; (*convincing*) convaincant
string′ quartet′ *s* quatuor *m* à cordes
string·y ['strɪŋi] *adj* (*comp* **-ier**; *super* **-iest**) fibreux, filandreux
strip [strɪp] *s* (*of paper, cloth, land, stamps*) bande *f*; (*of metal*) lame *f*, ruban *m* ‖ *v* (*pret & pp* **stripped**; *ger* **stripping**) *tr* dépouiller; (*to strip bare*) mettre à nu; (*the bed*) défaire; (*a screw*) arracher le filet de, faire foirer; (*tobacco*) écoter; **to strip down** (*e.g., a motor*) démonter; **to strip off** enlever; (*e.g., bark*) écorcer ‖ *intr* se déshabiller
stripe [straɪp] *s* raie *f*, bande *f*; (*on cloth*) rayure *f*; (*flesh wound*) marque *f*; (mil, nav) chevron *m*, galon *m*; **of any stripe** de tous poils; **to win one's stripes** gagner ses galons ‖ *tr* rayer
strip′ min′ing *s* exploitation *f* minière à ciel ouvert
strip′tease′ *s* strip-tease *m*, déshabillage *m* suggestif
stripteaser ['strɪp,tizər] *s* effeuilleuse *f*, strip-teaseuse *f*
strive [straɪv] *v* (*pret* **strove** [strov]; *pp* **striven** ['strɪvən]) *intr* s'efforcer; **to strive after** rechercher; **to strive against** lutter

contre; **to strive to** s'efforcer à, s'évertuer à
stroke [strok] *s* coup *m*; (*of pen; of wit*) trait *m*; (*of arms in swimming*) brassée *f*; (*caress with hand*) caresse *f* de la main; (*of a piston*) course *f*; (*of lightning*) foudre *f*; (pathol) attaque *f* d'apoplexie; **at the stroke of** sonnant, e.g., **at the stroke of five** à cinq heures sonnantes; **to not do a stroke of work** ne pas en ficher une ramée ‖ *tr* caresser de la main
stroll [strol] *s* promenade *f*; **to take a stroll** aller faire un tour ‖ *intr* se promener
stroller ['strolər] *s* promeneur *m*; (*for babies*) poussette *f*
strong [strɔŋ] *adj* (*comp* **stronger** ['strɔŋgər]; *super* **strongest** ['strɔŋgɪst]) fort; (*stock market*) ferme; (*musical beat*) marqué; (*spicy*) piquant; (*rancid*) rance
strong′box′ *s* coffre-fort *m*
strong′ drink′ *s* boissons *fpl* spiritueuses
strong′hold′ *s* place *f* forte
strong′ man′ *s* (*pl* **-men′**) (*e.g., in a circus*) hercule *m* forain; (*leader, good planner*) animateur *m*; (*dictator*) chef *m* autoritaire
strong′-mind′ed *adj* résolu, décidé; (*woman*) hommasse
strontium ['strɑnʃɪ·əm] *s* strontium *m*
strop [strɑp] *s* cuir *m* à rasoir ‖ *v* (*pret & pp* **stropped**; *ger* **stropping**) *tr* repasser sur le cuir
strophe ['strofi] *s* strophe *f*
structure ['strʌktʃər] *s* structure *f*, (*building*) édifice *m*
struggle ['strʌgəl] *s* lutte *f* ‖ *intr* lutter; **to struggle along** avancer péniblement
strug′gle for exist′ence *s* lutte *f* pour la vie
strum [strʌm] *v* (*pret & pp* **strummed**; *ger* **strumming**) *tr* (*an instrument*) gratter de; (*a tune*) tapoter ‖ *intr* jouailler; **to strum on** plaquer des arpèges sur
strumpet ['strʌmpɪt] *s* putain *f*
strut [strʌt] *s* (*brace, prop*) étai *m*, support *m*, entretoise *f*; démarche *f* orgueilleuse ‖ *v* (*pret & pp* **strutted**; *ger* **strutting**) *intr* se pavaner
strychnine ['strɪknaɪn] *s* strychnine *f*
stub [stʌb] *s* (*fragment*) tronçon *m*; (*of a tree*) souche *f*; (*of a pencil; of a cigar, cigarette*) bout *m*; (*of a check*) talon *m*, souche *f* ‖ *v* (*pret & pp* **stubbed**; *ger* **stubbing**) *tr*—**to stub one's toe** se cogner le bout du pied
stubble ['stʌbəl] *s* éteule *f*, chaume *m*; (*of beard*) poil *m* court et raide
stubborn ['stʌbərn] *adj* obstiné; (*headstrong*) têtu; (*resolute*) acharné; (*fever*) rebelle; (*soil*) ingrat
stuc·co ['stʌko] *s* (*pl* **-coes** or **-cos**) stuc *m* ‖ *tr* stuquer
stuck [stʌk] *adj* coincé, pris; (*glued*) collé; (*unable to continue*) en panne; **stuck on** (coll) entiché de
stuck′-up′ *adj* (coll) hautain, prétentieux
stud [stʌd] *s* (*nail, knob*) clou *m* à grosse tête; (*ornament*) clou doré; (*on shirt*) bouton *m*; (*studhorse*) étalon *m*; (*horse farm*)

haras *m*; (*bolt*) goujon *m*; (*archit*) montant *m* ‖ *v* (*pret & pp* **studded;** *ger* **studding**) *tr* clouter; **studded with** jonché de, parsemé de

stud' bolt' *s* goujon *m*

stud'ded tire' *s* pneu *m* à clou

student ['st(j)udənt] *adj* estudiantin ‖ *s* étudiant *m*; (*researcher*) chercheur *m*

stu'dent bod'y *s* étudiants *mpl*

stu'dent cen'ter *s* foyer *m* d'étudiants, centre *m* social des étudiants

stu'dent nurse' *s* élève *f* infirmière

stu'dent teach'er *s* stagiaire *mf*

stud' farm' *s* haras *m*

stud'horse' *s* étalon *m*

studied ['stʌdɪd] *adj* prémédité; recherché

studi·o ['st(j)udɪ,o] *s* (*pl* **-os**) studio *m*, atelier *m*

studious ['st(j)udɪ·əs] *adj* studieux, appliqué

stud·y ['stʌdi] *s* (*pl* **-ies**) étude *f*; rêverie *f*; cabinet *m* ‖ *v* (*pret & pp* **-ied**) *tr & intr* étudier

stuff [stʌf] *s* chose *f*, truc *m*; (*miscellaneous objects*) choses *fpl*, fatras *m*; (*possessions*) affaires *fpl*; **to know one's stuff** (coll) s'y connaître ‖ *tr* bourrer; (*with food*) gaver; (*furniture*) rembourrer; (*an animal*) empailler; (culin) farcir; **to stuff up** boucher ‖ *intr* se gaver

stuffed' shirt' *s* collet *m* monté

stuffing ['stʌfɪŋ] *s* rembourrage *m*; (culin) farce *f*

stuff·y ['stʌfi] *adj* (*comp* **-ier;** *super* **-iest**) (*room*) mal ventilé; (*tedious*) ennuyeux; (*pompous*) collet monté; **to smell stuffy** sentir le renfermé

stumble ['stʌmbəl] *intr* trébucher; (*in speaking*) hésiter

stum'bling block' *s* pierre *f* d'achoppement

stump [stʌmp] *s* (*of tree*) souche *f*; (*e.g., of arm*) moignon *m*; (*of tooth*) chicot *m* ‖ *tr* (*a design*) estomper; (coll) embarrasser, coller; (*a state, district, region*) (coll) faire une tournée électorale en, dans, or à ‖ *intr* clopiner

stump' speak'er *s* orateur *m* de carrefour

stump' speech' *s* harangue *f* électorale improvisée

stun [stʌn] *v* (*pret & pp* **stunned;** *ger* **stunning**) *tr* étourdir

stunning ['stʌnɪŋ] *adj* (coll) étourdissant, épatant

stunt [stʌnt] *s* (*underdeveloped creature*) avorton *m*; (*feat*) tour *m* de force, acrobatie *f*; (*trick*) truc *m*; **to do a stunt** (mov) faire une cascade ‖ *tr* atrophier ‖ *intr* (coll) faire des acrobaties

stunted ['stʌntɪd] *adj* rabougri

stunt' fly'ing *s* vol *m* de virtuosité, acrobatie *f* aérienne

stunt' man' *s* (*pl* **men'**) cascadeur *m*, doublure *f*

stupe·fy ['st(j)upɪ,faɪ] *v* (*pret & pp* **-fied**) *tr* stupéfier

stupendous [st(j)u'pɛndəs] *adj* prodigieux, formidable

stupid ['st(j)upɪd] *adj* stupide

stupor ['st(j)upər] *s* stupeur *f*

stur·dy ['stʌrdi] *adj* (*comp* **-dier;** *super* **-diest**) robuste, vigoureux; (*resolute*) ferme, hardi

sturgeon ['stʌrdʒən] *s* esturgeon *m*

stutter ['stʌtər] *s* bégaiement *m* ‖ *tr & intr* bégayer

sty [staɪ] *s* (*pl* **sties**) porcherie *f*; (pathol) orgelet *m*

style [staɪl] *s* style *m*; (*fashion*) mode *f*; (*elegance*) ton *m*, chic *m*; **to live in great style** mener grand train ‖ *tr* appeler, dénommer; **to style oneself** s'intituler

stylish ['staɪlɪʃ] *adj* à la mode, élégant, chic

sty·mie ['staɪmi] *v* (*pret & pp* **-mied;** *ger* **-mieing**) *tr* contrecarrer

styp'tic pen'cil ['stɪptɪk] *s* crayon *m* styptique

suave [swɑv] *adj* suave; (*person*) affable; (*manners*) doucereux

sub [sʌb] *s* (coll) sous-marin *m*

subconscious [səb'kɑnʃəs] *adj & s* subconscient *m*

sub'contrac'tor *s* sous-traitant *m*

sub'divide' or **sub'divide'** *tr* subdiviser ‖ *intr* se subdiviser

subdue [səb'd(j)u] *tr* subjuguer, vaincre, asservir; (*color, light, sound*) adoucir, amortir; (*passions, feelings*) dompter

sub'head' *s* sous-titre *m*

subject ['sʌbdʒɪkt] *adj* sujet, assujetti, soumis ‖ *s* sujet *m*; (*e.g., in school*) matière *f* ‖ [səb'dʒɛkt] *tr* assujettir, soumettre

subjection [səb'dʒɛkʃən] *s* sujétion *f*, soumission *f*

subjective [səb'dʒɛktɪv] *adj* subjectif

sub'ject mat'ter *s* matière *f*

subjugate ['sʌbdʒə,get] *tr* subjuguer

subjunctive [səb'dʒʌŋktɪv] *adj & s* subjonctif *m*

sub'lease' *s* sous-location *f* ‖ **sub'lease'** *tr* sous-louer

sub·let [səb'lɛt], ['sʌb,lɛt] *v* (*pret & pp* **-let;** *ger* **-letting**) *tr* sous-louer

sub'machine' gun' *s* mitraillette *f*

sub'marine' *adj & s* sous-marin *m*

sub'marine chas'er *s* chasseur *m* de sous-marins

submerge [səb'mʌrdʒ] *tr* submerger ‖ *intr* (*said of submarine*) plonger

submersion [səb'mʌrʒən] *s* submersion *f*

submission [səb'mɪʃən] *s* soumission *f*; (*delivery*) présentation *f*

submissive [səb'mɪsɪv] *adj* soumis

sub·mit [səb'mɪt] *v* (*pret & pp* **-mitted;** *ger* **-mitting**) *tr* soumettre ‖ *intr* se soumettre

subordinate [səb'ɔrdɪnɪt] *adj & s* subordonné *m* ‖ [səb'ɔrdɪ,net] *tr* subordonner

subpoena [sə'pinə] *s* assignation *f*, citation *f* ‖ *tr* citer

subscribe [səb'skraɪb] *tr* souscrire ‖ *intr*—**to subscribe to** (*an opinion; a charity; a loan; a newspaper*) souscrire à; (*a newspaper*) s'abonner à

subscriber [səb'skraɪbər] *s* abonné *m*

subscription [səb'skrɪpʃən] s souscription f; (to newspaper or magazine) abonnement m; (to club) cotisation f; **to take out a subscription for** s.o. abonner qn; **to take out a subscription to** s'abonner à

subsequent ['sʌbsɪkwənt] adj subséquent, suivant

subservient [səb'sʌrvɪ·ənt] adj asservi, subordonné

subside [səb'saɪd] intr (said of water, ground, etc.) s'abaisser; (said of storm, excitement, etc.) s'apaiser

subsidiar·y [səb'sɪdɪˌɛri] adj subsidiaire ‖ s (pl -ies) filiale f

subsidize ['sʌbsɪˌdaɪz] tr subventionner; suborner

subsi·dy ['sʌbsɪdi] s (pl -dies) subside m, subvention f

subsist [səb'sɪst] intr subsister

subsistence [səb'sɪstəns] s (supplies) subsistance f; existence f

sub'soil' s sous-sol m

subsonic [ˌsʌb'sɑnɪk] adj subsonique

substance ['sʌbstəns] s substance f

sub·stand'ard adj inférieur au niveau normal

substantial [səb'stænʃəl] adj substantiel; (wealthy) aisé, cossu

substantiate [səb'stænʃɪˌet] tr établir, vérifier

substantive ['sʌbstəntɪv] adj & s substantif m

sub'sta'tion s (of post office) bureau m auxiliaire; (elec) sous-station f

substitute ['sʌbstɪˌt(j)ut] s (person) remplaçant m, suppléant m, substitut m; (for coffee) succédané m ‖ tr remplacer, e.g., they substituted copper for silver ils ont remplacé l'argent par le cuivre; substituer, e.g., a hind was substituted for Iphigenia une biche fut substituée à Iphigénie ‖ intr servir de remplaçant; **to substitute for** remplacer, suppléer

substitution [ˌsʌbstɪ't(j)uʃən] s substitution f

sub'stra'tum s (pl -ta [tə] or -tums) substrat m

subterfuge ['sʌbtər'fjudʒ] s subterfuge m, faux-fuyant m

subterranean [ˌsʌbtə'renɪ·ən] adj souterrain

sub'ti'tle s sous-titre m

subtle ['sʌtəl] adj subtil

subtle·ty ['sʌtəlti] s (pl -ties) subtilité f

subtract [səb'trækt] tr soustraire

subtraction [səb'trækʃən] s soustraction f

suburb ['sʌbʌrb] s ville f de la banlieue; **the suburbs** la banlieue

suburban [sə'bʌrbən] adj suburbain

suburbanite [sə'bʌrbəˌnaɪt] s banlieusard m

subvention [səb'vɛnʃən] s subvention f ‖ tr subventionner

subversive [səb'vʌrsɪv] adj subversif ‖ s factieux m

subvert [səb'vʌrt] tr corrompre; renverser

sub'way' s métro m; (tunnel for pedestrians) souterrain m

sub'way car' s voiture f de métro

sub'way sta'tion s station f de métro

succeed [sək'sid] tr succéder à; **to succeed one another** se succéder ‖ intr réussir; **to succeed in** + ger réussir à + inf; **to succeed to** (the throne; a fortune) succéder à

success [sək'sɛs] s succès m, réussite f; **to be a howling success** (theat) faire un malheur; **to be a success** avoir du succès

successful [sək'sɛsfəl] adj réussi; heureux, prospère

succession [sək'sɛʃən] s succession f; **in succession** de suite

successive [sək'sɛsɪv] adj successif

succor ['sʌkər] s secours m ‖ tr secourir

succotash ['sʌkəˌtæʃ] s plat m de fèves et de maïs

succumb [sə'kʌm] intr succomber

such [sʌtʃ] adj & pron indef tel, pareil, semblable; **such a** un tel; **such and such** tel et tel; **such as** tel que

suck [sʌk] s—**to give suck to** allaiter ‖ tr sucer; (a nipple) téter; **to suck in** aspirer; (to absorb) sucer ‖ intr sucer; téter

sucker ['sʌkər] s suceur m; (sucking organ) suçoir m, ventouse f; (bot) drageon m; (ichth) rémora m; (gullible person) (coll) gogo m; (lollipop) (coll) sucette f

suckle ['sʌkəl] tr allaiter

suck'ling pig' s cochon m de lait

suction ['sʌkʃən] s succion f

suc'tion cup' s ventouse f

suc'tion pump' s pompe f aspirante

sudden ['sʌdən] adj brusque, soudain; **all of a sudden** tout à coup

suddenly ['sʌdənli] adv tout à coup

suds [sʌdz] spl eau f savonneuse; mousse f de savon

sue [s(j)u] tr poursuivre en justice ‖ intr intenter un procès

suede [swed] s suède m; (for shoes) daim m

suet ['s(j)u·ɪt] s graisse f de rognon

suffer ['sʌfər] tr souffrir; (to allow) permettre; (a defeat) essuyer, subir ‖ intr souffrir

sufferance ['sʌfərəns] s tolérance f

suffering ['sʌfərɪŋ] adj souffrant ‖ s souffrance f

suffice [sə'faɪs] tr suffire à ‖ intr suffire; **it suffices to** + inf il suffit de + inf

sufficient [sə'fɪʃənt] adj suffisant

suffix ['sʌfɪks] s suffixe m

suffocate ['sʌfəˌket] tr & intr suffoquer, étouffer

suffrage ['sʌfrɪdʒ] s suffrage m

suffragist ['sʌfrədʒɪst] s partisan m du droit de vote des femmes

suffuse [sə'fjuz] tr baigner, saturer

sugar ['ʃʊgər] s sucre m ‖ tr sucrer; (a cake) saupoudrer de sucre; (a pill) recouvrir de sucre ‖ intr former du sucre

sug'ar beet' s betterave f sucrière, betterave à sucre

sug'ar bowl' s sucrier m

sug'ar cane' s canne f à sucre

sug'ar-coat' tr dragéifier; (fig) dorer

sug'ar dad'dy s (pl -dies) papa m gâteau

sug'ar ma'ple s érable m à sucre

sug'ar pea' *s* mange-tout *m*
sug'ar tongs' *spl* pince *f* à sucre
sugary ['ʃugəri] *adj* sucré; (fig) doucereux
suggest [səg'dʒɛst] *tr* suggérer
suggestion [səg'dʒɛstʃən] *s* suggestion *f*; nuance *f*, pointe *f*, soupçon *m*
suggestive [səg'dʒɛstɪv] *adj* suggestif
suicidal [ˌs(j)uˈɪˈsaɪdəl] *adj* suicidaire
suicide ['s(j)uˈɪˌsaɪd] *s* (*act*) suicide *m*; (*person*) suicidé *m*; **to commit suicide** se suicider
suit [s(j)ut] *s* (*men's*) complet *m*, costume *m*; (*women's*) costume tailleur, tailleur *m*; (*lawsuit*) procès *m*; (*plea*) requête *f*; (*cards*) couleur *f*; **to follow suit** jouer la couleur; (fig) en faire autant ‖ *tr* adapter; convenir à, e.g., **does that suit him?** cela lui convient?; aller à, seoir à, e.g., **the dress suits her well** la robe lui va bien, la robe lui sied bien ‖ *intr* convenir, aller
suitable ['s(j)utəbəl] *adj* convenable, à propos; compétent
suit'case' *s* valise *f*
suite [swit] *s* suite *f* ‖ [s(j)ut] *s* (*of furniture*) ameublement *m*, mobilier *m*
suiting ['s(j)utɪŋ] *s* étoffe *f* pour complets
suit' of clothes' *s* complet-veston *m*
suitor ['s(j)utər] *s* prétendant *m*, soupirant *m*
sul'fa drugs' ['sʌlfə] *spl* sulfamides *mpl*
sulfide ['sʌlfaɪd] *s* sulfure *m*
sulfur ['sʌlfər] *adj* soufré ‖ *s* soufre *m* ‖ *tr* soufrer
sulfuric [sʌl'fjurɪk] *adj* sulfurique
sul'fur mine' *s* soufrière *f*
sulk [sʌlk] *s* bouderie *f* ‖ *intr* bouder
sulk·y ['sʌlki] *adj* (*comp* -**ier**; *super* -**iest**) boudeur, maussade
sullen ['sʌlən] *adj* maussade, rébarbatif
sul·ly ['sʌli] *v* (*pret & pp* -**lied**) *tr* souiller
sulphate ['sʌlfet] *s* sulfate *m*
sulphur ['sʌlfər] *adj*, *s & tr* var of **sulfur**
sultan ['sʌltən] *s* sultan *m*
sul·try ['sʌltri] *adj* (*comp* -**trier**; *super* -**triest**) étouffant, suffocant
sum [sʌm] *s* somme *f*; tout *m*, total *m*; **in sum** somme toute ‖ *v* (*pret & pp* **summed**; *ger* **summing**) *tr*—**to sum up** résumer
sumac or **sumach** ['sumæk] *s* sumac *m*
summarize ['sʌməˌraɪz] *tr* résumer
summa·ry ['sʌməri] *adj* sommaire ‖ *s* (*pl* -**ries**) sommaire *m*
summer ['sʌmər] *adj* estival ‖ *s* été *m* ‖ *intr* passer l'été
sum'mer resort' *s* station *f* estivale
sum'mer school' *s* cours *m* d'été, cours de vacances
summery ['sʌməri] *adj* estival, d'été
summit ['sʌmɪt] *s* sommet *m*
sum'mit con'ference *s* conférence *f* au sommet
summon ['sʌmən] *tr* appeler, convoquer; (law) sommer, citer, assigner
summons ['sʌmənz] *s* appel *m*; (law) mandat *m* d'amener, citation *f*, assignation *f*, exploit *m*
sumptuous ['sʌmptʃuˈəs] *adj* somptueux

sun [sʌn] *s* soleil *m* ‖ *v* (*pret & pp* **sunned**; *ger* **sunning**) *tr* exposer au soleil ‖ *intr* prendre le soleil
sun' bath' *s* bain *m* de soleil
sun'beam' *s* rayon *m* de soleil
sun'bon'net *s* capeline *f*
sun'burn' *s* coup *m* de soleil ‖ *v* (*pret & pp* -**burned** or -**burnt**) *tr* hâler, basaner ‖ *intr* se basaner
sun'burned' *adj* brûlé par le soleil
sundae ['sʌndi] *s* coupe *f* de glace garnie de fruits, sundae *m*
Sunday ['sʌndi] *adj* dominical ‖ *s* dimanche *m*
Sun'day best' *s* (coll) habits *mpl* du dimanche
Sun'day driv'er *s* chauffeur *m* du dimanche
Sun'day school' *s* école *f* du dimanche
sunder ['sʌndər] *tr* séparer, rompre
sun'di'al *s* cadran *m* solaire, gnomon *m*, horloge *f* solaire
sun'down' *s* coucher *m* du soleil
sundries ['sʌndriz] *spl* articles *mpl* divers
sundry ['sʌndri] *adj* divers
sun'fish' *s* poisson-lune *m*
sun'flow'er *s* soleil *m*, tournesol *m*
sun'glass'es *spl* lunettes *fpl* de soleil, verres *mpl* fumés
sunken ['sʌŋkən] *adj* creux, enfoncé; (*rock*) noyé; (*ship*) sous-marin
sun' lamp' *s* lampe *f* à rayons ultraviolets
sun'light' *s* lumière *f* du soleil
sun·ny ['sʌni] *adj* (*comp* -**nier**; *super* -**niest**) ensoleillé; (*happy*) enjoué; **it is sunny** il fait du soleil
sun'ny side' *s* côté *m* exposé au soleil; (fig) bon côté
sun' par'lor *s* véranda *f*
sun'rise' *s* lever *m* du soleil
sun'set' *s* coucher *m* du soleil
sun'shade' *s* (*over door*) banne *f*; parasol *m*; abat-jour *m*, visière *f*
sun'shine' *s* clarté *f* du soleil, soleil *m*; (fig) gaieté *f* rayonnante; **in the sunshine** en plein soleil
sun'spot' *s* tache *f* solaire
sun'stroke' *s* insolation *f*
sun' tan' *s* hâle *m*
sun'-tan oil' *s* huile *f* solaire
sun'up' *s* lever *m* du soleil
sun' vi'sor *s* abat-jour *m*
sup [sʌp] *v* (*pret & pp* **supped**; *ger* **supping**) *intr* souper
super ['supər] *adj* (slang) superbe, formidable ‖ *s* (theat) figurant *m*; (slang) concierge *mf*
su'per·abun'dant *adj* surabondant
superannuated [ˌsupərˈænjuˌetɪd] *adj* (*person*) retraité; (*thing*) suranné
superb [suˈpʌrb] *adj* superbe
su'per·car'go *s* (*pl* -**goes** or -**gos**) subrécargue *m*
su'per·charge' *s* surcompression *f* ‖ *tr* surcomprimer
supercilious [ˌsupərˈsɪlɪˈəs] *adj* sourcilleux, hautain, arrogant

superficial [,supər'fɪʃəl] *adj* superficiel
superfluous [sU'pʌrflu·əs] *adj* superflu
su′per·high′way′ *s* autoroute *f*
su′per·hu′man *adj* surhumain
su′per·impose′ *tr* superposer
su′per·intend′ *tr* surveiller; diriger
superintendent [,supərɪn'tɛndənt] *s* directeur *m*, directeur en chef; (*of a building*) concierge *mf*
superior [sə'pɪrɪ·ər] *adj & s* supérieur *m*
superiority [sə,pɪrɪ'arɪti] *s* supériorité *f*
superlative [sə'pʌrlətɪv] *adj & s* superlatif *m*
su′per·man′ *s* (*pl* -men′) surhomme *m*
su′per·mar′ket *s* supermarché *m*
su′per·nat′ural *adj & s* surnaturel *m*
supersede [,supər'sid] *tr* remplacer
su′per·sen′sitive *adj* hypersensible
su′per·son′ic *adj* supersonique
superstition [,supər'stɪʃən] *s* superstition *f*
superstitious [,supər'stɪʃəs] *adj* superstitieux
su′per·tank′er *s* pétrolier *m* géant, tanker *m* géant
supervene [,supər'vin] *intr* survenir
supervise ['supər,vaɪz] *tr* surveiller; diriger
su′per·vi′sion *s* surveillance *f*; direction *f*
su′per·vi′sor *s* surveillant *m*, inspecteur *m*; directeur *m*
supper ['sʌpər] *s* souper *m*
sup′per·time′ *s* heure *f* du souper
supplant [sə'plænt] *tr* supplanter
supple ['sʌpəl] *adj* souple, flexible
supplement ['sʌplɪmənt] *s* supplément *m* || *tr* ajouter à
supplementary [,sʌplə'mɛntəri] *adj* supplémentaire
suppliant ['sʌplɪ·ənt] *adj & s* suppliant *m*
supplicant ['sʌplɪkənt] *s* suppliant *m*
supplicate ['sʌplɪ,ket] *tr* supplier
supplier [sə'plaɪ·ər] *s* fournisseur *m*, pourvoyeur *m*
sup·ply [sə'plaɪ] *s* (*pl* -plies) (*action*) fourniture *f*, provision *f*, approvisionnement *m*; (*store*) provision *f*, réserve *f*, stock *m*; **supplies** fournitures, approvisionnements; (*of food*) vivres *mpl* || *v* (*pret & pp* -plied) *tr* fournir; (*a person, a city, a fort*) pourvoir, munir; (*a need*) répondre à; (*what is lacking*) suppléer; (*mil*) approvisionner
supply′ and demand′ *spl* l'offre *f* et la demande
support [sə'port] *s* soutien *m*, appui *m*; (*living expenses*) ressources *fpl*, de quoi vivre *m*; (*pillar*) support *m* || *tr* soutenir, appuyer; (*e.g., a wife*) entretenir, soutenir; (*to hold up; to corroborate; to tolerate*) supporter; **to support oneself** gagner sa vie
supporter [sə'portər] *s* partisan *m*, supporter *m*; (*for part of body*) suspensoir *m*, slip *m* de soutien
suppose [sə'poz] *tr* supposer; **I suppose so** probablement; **suppose that . . .** à supposer que . . . ; **suppose we take a walk?** si nous faisions une promenade?; **to be supposed to** + *inf* devoir + *inf*; (*to be considered to be*) être censé + *inf*

supposedly [sə'pozɪdli] *adv* censément
supposition [,sʌpə'zɪʃən] *s* supposition *f*
supposito·ry [sə'pazɪ,tori] *s* (*pl* -ries) suppositoire *m*
suppress [sə'prɛs] *tr* supprimer; (*rebellion; anger*) réprimer, contenir; (*a yawn*) étouffer, empêcher
suppression [sə'prɛʃən] *s* suppression *f*; (*of a rebellion*) subjugation *f*, répression *f*; (*of a yawn*) empêchement *m*
suppurate ['sʌpjə,ret] *intr* suppurer
supremacy [sə'prɛməsi] *s* suprématie *f*
supreme [sə'prim], [sU'prim] *adj* suprême
supreme′ court′ *s* cour *f* de cassation
surcharge ['sʌr,tʃardʒ] *s* surcharge *f* || *tr* surcharger
sure [ʃUr] *adj* sûr, certain; (*e.g., hand*) ferme; **for sure** à coup sûr, pour sûr; **to be sure to** + *inf* ne pas manquer de + *inf*; **to make sure** s'assurer || *adv* (coll) certainement; **sure enough** (coll) effectivement, assurément || *interj* (slang) mais oui!, bien sûr!, entendu!
sure′-foot′ed *adj* au pied sûr
sure·ty ['ʃUrti] *s* (*pl* -ties) sûreté *f*
surf [sʌrf] *s* barre *f*, ressac *m*, brisants *mpl*
surface ['sʌrfɪs] *adj* superficiel || *s* surface *f*; (*area*) superficie *f*; **on the surface** à la surface, en apparence; **to float under the surface** nager entre deux eaux || *tr* polir la surface de; (*a road*) recouvrir, revêtir || *intr* (*said of submarine*) faire surface
sur′face mail′ *s* courrier *m* par voie ordinaire
surf′ and turf′ *s* (culin) pré *m* et marée
surf′board′ *s* planche *f* pour le surf, surfboard *m*
surfeit ['sʌrfɪt] *s* satiété *f* || *tr* rassasier || *intr* se rassasier
surf′rid′ing *s* surfing *m*, planking *m*
surge [sʌrdʒ] *s* houle *f*; (elec) surtension *f* || *intr* être houleux; se répandre; **to surge up** s'enfler, s'élever
surgeon ['sʌrdʒən] *s* chirurgien *m*
surger·y ['sʌrdʒəri] *s* (*pl* -ies) chirurgie *f*; salle *f* d'opération
surgical ['sʌrdʒɪkəl] *adj* chirurgical
sur·ly ['sʌrli] *adj* (*comp* -lier; *super* -liest) hargneux, maussade, bourru
surmise [sər'maɪz] *s* conjecture *f* || *tr & intr* conjecturer
surmount [sər'maUnt] *tr* surmonter
surname ['sʌr,nem] *s* nom *m* de famille; surnom *m* || *tr* donner un nom de famille à; surnommer
surpass [sər'pæs], [sər'pas] *tr* surpasser
surplice ['sʌrplɪs] *s* surplis *m*
surplus ['sʌrplʌs] *adj* excédent, excédentaire, en excédent || *s* surplus *m*, excédent *m*
sur′plus bag′gage *s* excédent *m* de bagages
surprise [sər'praɪz] *adj* à l'improviste, brusqué, inopiné || *s* surprise *f*; **to take by surprise** prendre à l'improviste, prendre au dépourvu || *tr* surprendre; **to be surprised at** être surpris de
surprise′ attack′ *s* attaque *f* brusquée

surprise′ pack′age *s* surprise *f*, pochette *f* surprise

surprise′ par′ty *s* (*pl* **-ties**) réunion *f* à l'improviste

surprising [sər′praɪzɪŋ] *adj* surprenant

surrealism [sə′ri·ə,lɪzəm] *s* surréalisme *m*

surrender [sə′rɛndər] *s* reddition *f*, soumission *f*; (*e.g., of prisoners, goods*) remise *f*; (*e.g., of rights, property*) cession *f* ‖ *tr* rendre, céder ‖ *intr* se rendre

surren′der val′ue *s* valeur *f* de rachat

surreptitious [,sʌrɛp′tɪʃəs] *adj* subreptice

surrogate [′sʌrə,get] *s* substitut *m*

sur′rogate moth′er *s* femme *f* porteuse

surround [sə′raʊnd] *tr* entourer

surrounding [sə′raʊndɪŋ] *adj* entourant, environnant ‖ **surroundings** *spl* environs *mpl*, alentours *mpl*; entourage *m*, milieu *m*

surtax [′sʌr,tæks] *s* surtaxe *f* ‖ *tr* surtaxer

surveillance [sər′vel(j)əns] *s* surveillance *f*

survey [′sʌrve] *s* (*for verification*) contrôle *m*; (*for evaluation*) appréciation *f*, évaluation *f*; (*report*) expertise *f*, aperçu *m*; (*of a whole*) vue *f* d'ensemble, tour *m* d'horizon; (*measured plan or drawing*) levé *m*, plan *m*; (surv) lever *m* or levé des plans; **to make a survey** (*to map out*) lever un plan; (*to poll*) effectuer un contrôle par sondage ‖ [sʌr′ve], [′sʌrve] *tr* contrôler; apprécier, évaluer, faire l'expertise de; (*as a whole*) jeter un coup d'œil sur; (*to poll*) sonder; (*e.g., a farm*) arpenter, faire l'arpentage de; (*e.g., a city*) faire le levé de

sur′vey course′ *s* cours *m* général

surveying [sʌr′ve·ɪŋ] *s* arpentage *m*, géodésie *f*, levé *m* des plans

surveyor [sər′ve·ər] *s* arpenteur *m*

survival [sər′vaɪvəl] *s* survivance *f*; (*after death*) survie *f*; **survival of the fittest** loi *f* sélective du plus fort, survie *f* du plus apte

surviv′al kit′ *s* équipement *m* de survie

survive [sər′vaɪv] *tr* survivre à ‖ *intr* survivre

surviving [sər′vaɪvɪŋ] *adj* survivant

survivor [sər′vaɪvər] *s* survivant *m*

survivorship [sər′vaɪvər,ʃɪp] *s* (law) survie *f*

susceptible [sə′sɛptɪbəl] *adj* (*capable*) susceptible; (*liable, subject*) sensible; (*to love*) facilement amoureux

suspect [′sʌspɛkt], [səs′pɛkt] *adj & s* suspect *m* ‖ [səs′pɛkt] *tr* soupçonner ‖ *intr* s'en douter

suspend [səs′pɛnd] *tr* suspendre

suspenders [səs′pɛndərz] *spl* bretelles *fpl*

suspense [səs′pɛns] *s* suspens *m*

suspension [səs′pɛnʃən] *s* suspension *f*; **suspension of driver's license** retrait *m* de permis

suspen′sion bridge′ *s* pont *m* suspendu

suspicion [səs′pɪʃən] *s* soupçon *m*

suspicious [səs′pɪʃəs] *adj* (*inclined to suspect*) soupçonneux; (*subject to suspicion*) suspect

sustain [səs′ten] *tr* soutenir; (*a loss, injury, etc.*) éprouver

sustenance [′sʌstɪnəns] *s* subsistance *f*; (*food*) nourriture *f*

sustain′ing mem′ber [səs′tenɪŋ] *s* membre *m* bienfaiteur

swab [swɑb] *s* écouvillon *m*; (naut) faubert *m*; (surg) tampon *m* ‖ *v* (*pret & pp* **swabbed;** *ger* **swabbing**) *tr* écouvillonner

swaddle [′swɑdəl] *tr* emmailloter

swad′dling clothes′ *spl* maillot *m*

swagger [′swægər] *s* fanfaronnade *f* ‖ *intr* faire des fanfaronnades

swain [swen] *s* garçon *m*; jeune berger *m*; soupirant *m*

swallow [′swɑlo] *s* gorgée *f*; (orn) hirondelle *f* ‖ *tr & intr* avaler

swal′low-tailed coat′ *s* frac *m*

swamp [swɑmp] *s* marécage *m* ‖ *tr* submerger, inonder

swamp·y [′swɑmpi] *adj* (*comp* **-ier;** *super* **-iest**) marécageux

swan [swɑn] *s* cygne *m*

swan′ dive′ *s* saut *m* de l'ange

swank [swæŋk] *adj* (slang) élégant, chic

swan′ knight′ *s* chevalier *m* au cygne

swan's′-down′ *s* cygne *m*, duvet *m* de cygne

swan′ song′ *s* chant *m* du cygne

swap [swɑp] *s* (coll) troc *m* ‖ *v* (*pret & pp* **swapped;** *ger* **swapping**) *tr & intr* troquer

swarm [swɔrm] *s* essaim *m* ‖ *intr* essaimer; (fig) fourmiller

swarth·y [′swɔrði] *adj* (*comp* **-ier;** *super* **-iest**) basané, brun, noiraud

swashbuckler [′swɑʃ,bʌklər] *s* rodomont *m*, bretteur *m*

swat [swɑt] *s* (coll) coup *m* violent ‖ *v* (*pret & pp* **swatted;** *ger* **swatting**) *tr* (coll) frapper; (*a fly*) (coll) écraser

sway [swe] *s* balancement *m*; (*domination*) empire *m* ‖ *tr* balancer ‖ *intr* se balancer; (*to hesitate*) balancer

swear [swɛr] *v* (*pret* **swore** [swor]; *pp* **sworn** [sworn]) *tr* jurer; **to swear in** faire prêter serment à; **to swear off** jurer de renoncer à ‖ *intr* jurer; **to swear at** injurier; **to swear by** (*e.g., a remedy*) préconiser; **to swear to** déclarer sous serment; jurer de + *inf*

swear′ words′ *spl* gros mots *mpl*

sweat [swɛt] *s* sueur *f* ‖ *v* (*pret & pp* **sweat** or **sweated**) *tr* (*e.g., blood*) suer; (slang) faire suer; **to sweat it out** (slang) en baver jusqu'à la fin ‖ *intr* suer

sweater [′swɛtər] *s* chandail *m*

sweat′ shirt′ *s* maillot *m* de sport

sweat·y [′swɛti] *adj* (*comp* **-ier;** *super* **-iest**) suant

Swede [swid] *s* Suédois *m*

Sweden [′swidən] *s* Suède *f*; la Suède

Swedish [′swidɪʃ] *adj & s* suédois *m*

sweep [swip] *s* (*sweeping*) balayage *m*; (*range*) champ *m*, étendue *f*; (*movement of the arm*) grand geste *m*; (*curve*) courbe *f*; (*of wind*) souffle *m*; (*of well*) chadouf *m*; **at one sweep** d'un seul coup; **to make a clean sweep of** faire table rase de; (*to win all of*) rafler ‖ *v* (*pret & pp* **swept** [swɛpt]) *tr* balayer; (*the chimney*) ramoner; (*for* *mines*) draguer ‖ *intr* balayer; s'étendre

sweeper ['swipər] *s* balayeur *m*; (mach) balai *m* mécanique

sweeping ['swipɪŋ] *adj* (*movement*) vigoureux; (*statement*) catégorique ‖ *s* balayage *m*; **sweepings** balayures *fpl*

sweep'-sec'ond *s* trotteuse *f* centrale

sweep'stakes *s* or *spl* loterie *f*; (turf) sweepstake *m*

sweet [swit] *adj* doux; (*sugared*) sucré; (*perfume, music, etc.*) suave; (*sound*) mélodieux; (*milk*) frais; (*person*) charmant, gentil; (*dear*) cher; **to be sweet on** (coll) avoir un béguin pour; **to smell sweet** sentir bon ‖ **sweets** *spl* sucreries *fpl*

sweet'bread' *s* ris *m* de veau

sweet'bri'er *s* églantier *m*

sweeten ['switən] *tr* sucrer; purifier; (fig) adoucir ‖ *intr* s'adoucir

sweet'heart' *s* petite amie *f*, chérie *f*; **sweethearts** amoureux *mpl*

sweet' mar'joram *s* marjolaine *f*

sweet'meats *spl* sucreries *fpl*

sweet' pea' *s* gesse *f* odorante, pois *m* de senteur

sweet' pep'per *s* piment *m* doux, poivron *m*

sweet' pota'to *s* patate *f* douce

sweet'-scent'ed *adj* parfumé

sweet'-talk' *tr* (coll) baratiner

sweet'-toothed' *adj* friand de sucreries

sweet' wil'liam *s* œillet *m* de poète

swell [swɛl] *adj* (coll) élégant; (slang) épatant ‖ *s* (*swelling*) gonflement *m*; (*of sea*) houle *f*; (mus) crescendo *m*; (pathol) enflure *f*; (*dandy*) (coll) rupin *m* ‖ *v* (*pret* **swelled;** *pp* **swelled** or **swollen** ['swolən]) *tr* gonfler, enfler ‖ *intr* se gonfler, s'enfler; (*said of sea*) se soulever; (fig) augmenter

swell'head'ed *adj* suffisant, vaniteux

swelter ['swɛltər] *intr* étouffer de chaleur

swept'back wing' *s* aile *f* en flèche

swerve [swʌrv] *s* écart *m*, déviation *f*; (aut) embardée *f* ‖ *tr* faire dévier ‖ *intr* écarter, dévier; (aut) faire une embardée

swift [swɪft] *adj* rapide ‖ *adv* vite ‖ *s* (orn) martinet *m*

swig [swɪg] *s* (coll) lampée *f*, trait *m* ‖ *v* (*pret* & *pp* **swigged;** *ger* **swigging**) *tr* & *intr* lamper

swill [swɪl] *s* eaux *fpl* grasses, ordures *fpl*; (*drink*) lampée *f* ‖ *tr* & *intr* lamper

swim [swɪm] *s* nage *f*; **to be in the swim** (coll) être dans le train ‖ *v* (*pret* **swam** [swæm]; *pp* **swum** [swʌm]; *ger* **swimming**) *tr* nager ‖ *intr* nager; (*said of head*) tourner; **to swim across** traverser à la nage; **to swim under water** nager entre deux eaux

swimmer ['swɪmər] *s* nageur *m*

swimming ['swɪmɪŋ] *s* natation *f*, nage *f*

swim'ming pool' *s* piscine *f*

swim'ming suit' *s* maillot *m* de bain

swim'ming trunks' *spl* slip *m* de bain

swindle ['swɪndəl] *s* escroquerie *f* ‖ *tr* escroquer

swine [swaɪn] *s* (*pl* **swine**) cochon *m*, pourceau *m*, porc *m*

swing [swɪŋ] *s* balancement *m*, oscillation *f*; (*device used for recreation*) escarpolette *f*; (*trip*) tournée *f*; (boxing, mus) swing *m*; **in full swing** en pleine marche ‖ *v* (*pret* & *pp* **swung** [swʌŋ]) *tr* balancer, faire osciller; (*the arms*) agiter; (*a sword*) brandir; (*e.g., an election*) mener à bien ‖ *intr* se balancer; (*said of pendulum*) osciller; (*said of door*) pivoter; (*said of bell*) branler; **to swing open** s'ouvrir tout d'un coup

swing'ing door' *s* porte *f* va-et-vient

swinish ['swaɪnɪʃ] *adj* cochon

swipe [swaɪp] *s* (coll) coup *m* à toute volée ‖ *tr* (coll) frapper à toute volée; (*to steal*) (slang) chiper

swirl [swʌrl] *s* remous *m*, tourbillon *m* ‖ *tr* faire tourbillonner ‖ *intr* tourbillonner

swish [swɪʃ] *s* (*e.g., of a whip*) sifflement *m*; (*of a dress*) froufrou *m*; (*e.g., of water*) susurrement *m* ‖ *tr* (*a whip*) faire siffler; (*its tail*) battre ‖ *intr* siffler; froufrouter; susurrer

Swiss [swɪs] *adj* suisse ‖ *s* Suisse *m*; **the Swiss** les Suisses *mpl*

Swiss' chard' [tʃard] *s* bette *f*, poirée *f*

Swiss' cheese' *s* emmenthal *m*, gruyère *m*

Swiss' Guard' *s* suisse *m*

switch [swɪtʃ] *s* (*stick*) badine *f*; (*exchange*) échange *m*; (*hairpiece*) postiche *m*; (elec) interrupteur *m*; (rr) aiguille *f* ‖ *tr* cingler; (*places*) échanger; (rr) aiguiller; **to switch off** couper; (*a light*) éteindre; **to switch on** mettre en circuit; (*a light*) allumer ‖ *intr* changer de place

switch'back' *s* chemin *m* en lacet

switch'blade knife' *s* couteau *m* à cran d'arrêt

switch'board' *s* tableau *m* de distribution; standard *m* téléphonique

switch'board op'erator *s* standardiste *mf*

switch'ing en'gine *s* locomotive *f* de manœuvre

switch'man *s* (*pl* **-men**) aiguilleur *m*

switch' tow'er *s* poste *m* d'aiguillage

switch'yard' *s* gare *f* de triage

Switzerland ['swɪtsərlənd] *s* Suisse *f*; la Suisse

swiv·el ['swɪvəl] *s* pivot *m*; (*link*) émerillon *m* ‖ *v* (*pret* & *pp* **-eled** or **-elled;** *ger* **-eling** or **-elling**) *tr* faire pivoter ‖ *intr* pivoter

swiv'el chair' *s* fauteuil *m* tournant, chaise *f* pivotante

swiz'zle stick *s* agitateur *m*

swoon [swun] *s* évanouissement *m* ‖ *intr* s'évanouir

swoop [swup] *s* attaque *f* brusque; **at one fell swoop** d'un seul coup ‖ *intr* foncer, fondre; **to swoop down on** s'abattre sur

sword [sord] *s* épée *f*; **to cross swords with** croiser le fer avec; **to put to the sword** passer au fil de l'épée

sword' belt' *s* ceinturon *m*

sword'fish' *s* espadon *m*

swords'man *s* (*pl* **-men**) épéiste *m*

sword' swal'lower [ˈswɑlo·ər] s avaleur m de sabres

sword' thrust' s coup m de pointe, coup d'épée

sworn [sworn] adj (enemy) juré; **sworn in** assermenté

sycophant [ˈsɪkəfənt] s flagorneur m

syllable [ˈsɪləbəl] s syllabe f

sylla·bus [ˈsɪləbəs] s (pl -bi [ˌbaɪ] or -buses) programme m

syllogism [ˈsɪləˌdʒɪzəm] s syllogisme m

sylph [sɪlf] s sylphe m

sylvan [ˈsɪlvən] adj sylvestre

symbol [ˈsɪmbəl] s symbole m

symbolic(al) [sɪmˈbɑlɪk(əl)] adj symbolique

symbolism [ˈsɪmbəˌlɪzm] s symbolisme m

symbolize [ˈsɪmbəˌlaɪz] tr symboliser

symmetric(al) [sɪˈmetrɪk(əl)] adj symétrique

symme·try [ˈsɪmɪtri] s (pl -tries) symétrie f

sympathetic [ˌsɪmpəˈθetɪk] adj (kind) compatissant; (favoring) bien disposé; (anat, physiol) sympathique

sympathize [ˈsɪmpəˌθaɪz] intr—**to sympathize with** compatir à; comprendre

sympa·thy [ˈsɪmpəθi] s (pl -thies) (pity) compassion f; (fellow feeling) solidarité f; sympathie f, e.g., **expressions of sympathy** témoignages de sympathie; **to be in sympathy with** être en sympathie avec; **to extend one's sympathy to** offrir ses condoléances à

sym'pathy strike' s grève f de solidarité

sympho·ny [ˈsɪmfəni] s (pl -nies) symphonie f

symposi·um [sɪmˈpozɪ·əm] s (pl -a [ə]) colloque m, symposium m

symptom [ˈsɪmptəm] s symptôme m

synagogue [ˈsɪnəˌgɔg] s synagogue f

synchronize [ˈsɪŋkrəˌnaɪz] tr synchroniser

synchronous [ˈsɪŋkrənəs] adj synchrone

syncopation [ˌsɪŋkəˈpeʃən] s syncope f

syncope [ˈsɪŋkəˌpi] s syncope f

syndicate [ˈsɪndɪkɪt] s (journ) syndicat m (de distribution) ‖ [ˈsɪndɪˌket] tr syndiquer ‖ intr se syndiquer

syndrome [ˈsɪndrom] s syndrome m

synonym [ˈsɪnənɪm] s synonyme m

synonymous [sɪˈnɑnɪməs] adj synonyme

synop·sis [sɪˈnɑpsɪs] s (pl -ses [siz]) abrégé m, résumé m; (mov) synopsis m & f

syntax [ˈsɪntæks] s syntaxe f

synthe·sis [ˈsɪnθɪsɪs] s (pl -ses [ˌsiz]) synthèse f

synthesize [ˈsɪnθɪˌsaɪz] tr synthétiser

synthetic(al) [sɪnˈθetɪk(əl)] adj synthétique

syphilis [ˈsɪfɪlɪs] s syphilis f

Syria [ˈsɪrɪ·ə] s Syrie f; la Syrie

Syrian [ˈsɪrɪ·ən] adj syrien ‖ s (language) syrien m; (person) Syrien m

syringe [ˈsɪrɪndʒ] s seringue f ‖ tr seringuer

syrup [ˈsɪrəp], [ˈsʌrəp] s sirop m

system [ˈsɪstəm] s système m; (of lines, wires, pipes, roads) réseau m

systematic(al) [ˌsɪstəˈmætɪk(əl)] adj systématique

systematize [ˈsɪstəməˌtaɪz] tr systématiser

systole [ˈsɪstəli] s systole f

T

T, t [ti] s XXᵉ lettre de l'alphabet

tab [tæb] s patte f; (label) étiquette f; (dinner check) (coll) note f; **to keep tab on** (coll) garder à l'œil; **to pick up the tab** (coll) payer l'addition

tab·by [ˈtæbi] s (pl -bies) chat m moucheté; (female cat) chatte f; (old maid) vieille fille f; (spiteful female) vieille chipie f

tabernacle [ˈtæbərˌnækəl] s tabernacle m

table [ˈtebəl] s table f; (tableland) plateau m; (list, chart) tableau m, table; **to clear the table** ôter le couvert; **to set the table** mettre le couvert ‖ tr ajourner la discussion de

tab·leau [ˈtæblo] s (pl -leaus or -leaux [loz]) tableau m vivant

ta'ble·cloth' s nappe f

table d'hôte [ˈtɑbəlˈdot] s repas m à prix fixe

ta'ble·land' s plateau m

ta'ble lin'en s nappage m, linge m de table

ta'ble man'ners spl—**to have good table manners** bien se tenir à table

tab'le·mate' s commensal m

ta'ble nap'kin s serviette f de table

ta'ble of con'tents s table f des matières

ta'ble salt' s sel m fin, sel de table

ta'ble·spoon' s cuiller f à soupe

tablespoonful [ˈtebəlˌspunˌful] s cuillerée f à soupe or à bouche

tablet [ˈtæblɪt] s (writing pad) bloc-notes m, bloc m; (lozenge) pastille f, comprimé m; plaque f commémorative

ta'ble talk' s propos mpl de table

ta'ble ten'nis s ping-pong m, tennis m de table

ta'ble-ten'nis play'er s pongiste mf

ta'ble-top' s dessus m de table

ta'ble·ware' s ustensiles mpl de table

ta'ble wine' s vin m ordinaire

tabloid [ˈtæblɔɪd] adj (press, article, etc.) à sensation ‖ s journal m de petit format à l'affût du sensationnel, tableautier m

taboo [təˈbu] adj & s tabou m ‖ tr déclarer tabou

tabular [ˈtæbjələr] adj tabulaire

tabulate ['tæbjə,let] *tr* disposer en forme de table or en tableaux, dresser un tableau de, aligner en colonnes

tabulator ['tæbjə,letər] *s* tabulateur *m*

tab′ulator set′ting *s* arrêt *m* de tabulateur

tacit ['tæsɪt] *adj* tacite

taciturn ['tæsɪtərn] *adj* taciturne

tack [tæk] *s* (*nail*) semence *f*; (*plan*) voie *f*, tactique *f*; (*of sail*) amure *f*; (naut) bordée *f*; (sewing) point *m* de bâti ‖ *tr* clouer; (sewing) bâtir ‖ *intr* louvoyer

tackle ['tækəl] *s* (*for lifting*) treuil *m*; (football) plaquage *m*; (naut) palan *m* ‖ *tr* empoigner, saisir; (*a problem, job, etc.*) chercher à résoudre, attaquer; (football) plaquer

tack·y ['tæki] *adj* (*comp* -ier; *super* -iest) collant; (coll) râpé, minable

tact [tækt] *s* tact *m*

tactful ['tæktfəl] *adj* plein de tact; **to be tactful** avoir du tact

tactical ['tæktɪkəl] *adj* tactique

tactician [tæk'tɪʃən] *s* tacticien *m*

tactics ['tæktɪks] *spl* tactique *f*

tactless ['tæktlɪs] *adj* sans tact

tadpole ['tæd,pol] *s* têtard *m*

taffeta ['tæfɪtə] *s* taffetas *m*

taffy ['tæfi] *s* pâte *f* à berlingots; (coll) flagornerie *f*

tag [tæg] *s* (*label*) étiquette *f*; (*of shoelace*) ferret *m*; (*game*) chat *m* perché ‖ *v* (*pret & pp* **tagged**; *ger* **tagging**) *tr* étiqueter; (*in the game of tag*) attraper ‖ *intr* (coll) suivre de près; **to tag along behind s.o.** (coll) traîner derrière qn

tag′ day′ *s* jour *m* de collecte publique

tag′ end′ *s* queue *f*; (*remnant*) coupon *m*

Tagus ['tegəs] *s* Tage *m*

tail [tel] *s* queue *f*; (*of shirt*) pan *m*; **tails** (*of a coin*) pile *f*; (*formal dress*) (coll) frac *m*, queue-de-morue *f*; **to turn tail** tourner les talons ‖ *tr* (coll) suivre de tout près ‖ *intr*—**to tail after** marcher sur les talons de; **to tail off** s'éteindre, disparaître

tail′ assem′bly *s* (*pl* **-blies**) (aer) empennage *m*

tail′ end′ *s* queue *f*, fin *f*

tail′ gate′ *tr & intr* (aut) talonner

tail′gat′ing *s* (aut) talonnage *m*; (sports) pique-nique *m* à l'occasion d'un match

tail′ light′ *s* feu *m* arrière

tailor ['telər] *s* tailleur *m* ‖ *tr* (*a suit*) faire ‖ *intr* être tailleur

tailoring ['telərɪŋ] *s* métier *m* de tailleur

tai′lor-made suit′ *s* (*men's*) costume *m* sur mesure, complet *m* sur mesure; (*women's*) costume tailleur, tailleur *m*

tai′lor shop′ *s* boutique *f* de tailleur

tail′piece′ *s* queue *f*; (*of stringed instrument*) cordier *m*

tail′race′ *s* canal *m* du fuite

tail′spin′ *s* chute *f* en vrille

tail′wind′ *s* (aer) vent *m* arrière; (naut) vent en poupe

taint [tent] *s* tache *f* ‖ *tr* tacher; (*food*) gâter

take [tek] *s* prise *f*; (mov) prise de vues; (slang) recette *f* ‖ *v* (*pret* **took** [tʊk]; *pp* **taken**) *tr* prendre; (*a walk; a trip*) faire; (*a course; advice*) suivre; (*an examination*) passer; (*a person on a trip*) emmener; (*the occasion*) profiter de; (*a photograph*) prendre; (*a newspaper*) être abonné à; (*a purchase*) garder; (*a certain amount of time*) falloir, e.g., **it takes an hour to walk there** il faut une heure pour y aller à pied; (*to lead*) conduire, mener; (*to tolerate, stand*) supporter; (*a seat*) prendre, occuper, e.g., **this seat is taken** cette place est prise or occupée; **do you take that to be important?** tenez-vous cela pour important?; **I take it that** je suppose que; **take it easy!** (coll) allez-y doucement!; **to be taken ill** tomber malade; **to take amiss** prendre mal; **to take away** enlever; emmener; (*to subtract*) soustraire, retrancher; **to take down** descendre; (*a building*) démolir; (*in writing*) noter; **to take in** (*a roomer*) recevoir; (*laundry*) prendre à faire à la maison; (*the harvest*) rentrer; (*a seam*) reprendre; (*to include*) embrasser; (*to deceive*) (coll) duper; **to take off** ôter, enlever; (*from the price*) rabattre; (*to imitate*) (coll) singer; **to take on** (*passengers*) prendre; (*a responsibility*) prendre sur soi; (*workers*) embaucher, prendre; **to take out** sortir; (*a bullet from a wound; a passage from a text; an element from a compound*) extraire; (public sign) à emporter; **to take over** (*to escort across*) transporter; (*to assume responsibility for*) reprendre, prendre à sa charge; **to take place** avoir lieu; **to take s.th. from s.o.** enlever, ôter, or prendre q.ch. à qn; **to take up** (*to carry up*) monter; (*to remove*) enlever; (*a dress*) raccourcir; (*an idea, method, etc.*) adopter; (*a profession*) embrasser, prendre; (*a question, a study, etc.*) aborder ‖ *intr* prendre; **to not take to** (*a person*) prendre en grippe; **to take after** ressembler à; (*to chase*) poursuivre; **to take off** s'en aller; (aer) décoller; **to take over** (pol) prendre le pouvoir; **to take over from s.o.** prendre le relève (*or* le relais) de qn; **to take to** (*flight; the woods*) prendre; (*a bad habit*) se livrer à; (*a person*) se prendre d'amitié avec; (*to like*) s'adonner à; **to take to** + *ger* se mettre à + *inf*; **to take up with s.o.** (coll) se lier avec qn

take′-home pay′ *s* salaire *m* net

take′-off′ *s* (aer) décollage *m*; (coll) caricature *f*

take′o′ver *s* (*of a corporation*) rachat *m*

take′over bid′ *s* offre *f* publique d'achat (O.P.A.)

tal′cum pow′der ['tælkəm] *s* poudre *f* de talc

tale [tel] *s* conte *m*; mensonge *m*; (*gossip*) raconter *m*, histoire *f*

tale′bear′er *s* rapporteur *m*

talent ['tælənt] *s* (*ability*) talent *m*; (*persons*) gens *mpl* de talent

talented ['tæləntɪd] *adj* doué, talentueux

tal′ent scout′ s dénicheur m de vedettes

tal′ent show′ s crochet m radiophonique, radio-crochet m

talk [tɔk] s paroles fpl; (*gossip*) racontars mpl, dires mpl; (*lecture*) conférence f, causerie f; **to cause talk** défrayer la chronique; **to have a talk with** s'entretenir avec ‖ tr parler; **to talk over** discuter; **to talk up** vanter ‖ intr parler; (*to chatter, gossip, etc.*) bavarder, jaser; **to talk back** répliquer; **to talk on** continuer à parler

talkative [′tɔkətɪv] adj bavard

talker [′tɔkər] s parleur m; **a great talker** (coll) un causeur, un hâbleur

talkie [′tɔki] s (coll) film m parlant

talk′ing doll′ [′tɔkɪŋ] s poupée f parlante

talk′ show′ s (rad, telv) causerie f (radiodiffusée or télévisée), tête-à-tête m invar or entretien m (radiodiffusé or télévisé)

tall [tɔl] adj haut, élevé; (*person*) grand; (coll) exagéré

tallow [′tælo] s suif m

tal·ly [′tæli] s (pl **-lies**) compte m, pointage m ‖ v (pret & pp **-lied**) tr pointer, contrôler ‖ intr s'accorder

tallyho [′tælɪ,ho] interj taïaut!

tal′ly sheet′ s feuille f de pointage, bordereau m

talon [′tælən] s serre f

tamarack [′tæmə,ræk] s mélèze m d'Amérique

tambourine [,tæmbə′rin] s tambour m de basque

tame [tem] adj apprivoisé; (*e.g., lion*) dompté; (*e.g., style*) fade, terne ‖ tr apprivoiser; (*e.g., a lion*) dompter

tamp [tæmp] tr bourrer; (*e.g., a hole in the ground*) damer

tamper [′tæmpər] intr—**to tamper with** se mêler de; (*a lock*) fausser; (*a document*) falsifier; (*a witness*) suborner

tampon [′tæmpɑn] s (surg) tampon m ‖ tr (surg) tamponner

tan [tæn] adj jaune; (*e.g., skin*) bronzé, hâlé ‖ v (pret & pp **tanned**; ger **tanning**) tr tanner; (*e.g., the skin*) bronzer, hâler ‖ intr se hâler

tandem [′tændəm] adj & adv en tandem, en flèche ‖ s tandem m

tang [tæŋ] s goût m vif, saveur f; (*ringing sound*) tintement m

tangent [′tændʒənt] adj tangent ‖ s tangente f; **to fly off at** or **on a tangent** changer brusquement de sujet

tangerine [,tændʒə′rin] s mandarine f

tangible [′tændʒɪbəl] adj tangible

Tangier [tæn′dʒɪr] s Tanger m

tangle [′tæŋgəl] s enchevêtrement m ‖ tr enchevêtrer ‖ intr s'enchevêtrer

tank [tæŋk] s réservoir m; (mil) char m

tank′ car′ s (rr) wagon-citerne m

tanker [′tæŋkər] s (*ship*) bateau-citerne m, pétrolier m; (*truck*) camion-citerne m; (*plane*) ravitailleur m

tank′ truck′ s camion-citerne m

tanner [′tænər] s tanneur m

tanner·y [′tænəri] s (pl **-ies**) tannerie f

tantalize [′tæntə,laɪz] tr tenter, allécher

tantamount [′tæntə,maʊnt] adj équivalent

tantrum [′tæntrəm] s accès m de colère; **in a tantrum** en rogne

tap [tæp] s (*light blow*) petit coup m; (*faucet*) robinet m; (elec) prise f; (mach) taraud m; **on tap** au tonneau, en perce; (*available*) (coll) disponible; **taps** (mil) l'extinction f des feux ‖ v (pret & pp **tapped**; ger **tapping**) tr taper; (*a cask*) mettre en perce; (*a tree*) entailler; (*a telephone*) passer à la table d'écoute; (*a nut*) tarauder; (*resources, talent, etc.*) drainer; (elec) brancher sur ‖ intr taper

tap′ dance′ s danse f à claquettes

tap′-dance′ intr danser les claquettes, faire les claquettes

tap′ dan′cer s danseur m à claquettes

tape [tep] s ruban m ‖ tr (*an electric wire*) guiper; (*land*) mesurer au cordeau; (*to tape-record*) enregistrer sur ruban

tape′ meas′ure s mètre-ruban m, centimètre m

taper [′tepər] s (*for lighting candles*) allumette-bougie f; (eccl) cierge m ‖ tr effiler ‖ intr s'effiler

tape′-record′ tr enregistrer sur ruban magnétique or au magnétophone

tape′ record′er s magnétophone m

tapes·try [′tæpɪstri] s (pl **-tries**) tapisserie f ‖ v (pret & pp **-tried**) tr tapisser

tape′worm′ s ver m solitaire

tappet [′tæpɪt] s (mach) taquet m

tap′room′ s débit m de boissons, buvette f

tap′ wa′ter s eau f du robinet

tap′ wrench′ s taraudeuse f

tar [tɑr] s goudron m; (coll) marin m ‖ v (pret & pp **tarred**; ger **tarring**) tr goudronner; **to tar and feather** enduire de goudron et de plumes

tar·dy [′tɑrdi] adj (comp **-dier**; super **-diest**) lent; retardataire, en retard

tare [tɛr] s (*weight*) tare f; (Bib) ivraie f ‖ tr tarer

target [′tɑrgɪt] s cible f, point m de mire; (*goal*) but m; (mil) objectif m; (*butt*) (fig) cible

tar′get ar′ea s zone f de tir

tar′get lan′guage s langue f cible, langue d'arrivée

tar′get prac′tice s tir m à la cible

tariff [′tærɪf] s (*duties*) droits mpl de douane; (*rates in general*) tarif m

tarnish [′tɑrnɪʃ] s ternissure f ‖ tr ternir ‖ intr se ternir

tar′ pa′per s papier m goudronné

tarpaulin [tɑr′pɔlɪn] s bâche f, prélart m

tarragon [′tærəgən] s estragon m

tar·ry [′tɑri] adj (comp **-rier**; super **-riest**) goudronneux ‖ [′tæri] v (pret & pp **-ried**) intr tarder; (*to stay*) rester, demeurer

tart [tɑrt] adj (*taste*) aigrelet; (*reply*) mordant ‖ s tarte f; (slang) grue f, poule f

tartar [′tɑrtər] adj (*sauce*) tartare; **Tartar** tartare ‖ s (*on teeth*) tartre m; **Tartar** Tartare mf

task [tæsk] s tâche f; **to bring** or **take to task** prendre à partie

task' force' s (mil) groupement m stratégique mixte

task'mas'ter s chef m de corvée; (fig) tyran m

tassel ['tæsəl] s gland m; (on corn) barbe f; (on nightcap) mèche f; (bot) aigrette f

taste [test] s goût m, saveur f; (sense of what is fitting) goût, bon goût ‖ tr goûter; (to sample) goûter à; (to try out) goûter de ‖ intr goûter; **to taste like** avoir le goût de; **to taste of** avoir un goût de

taste' bud' s papille f gustative

tasteless ['testlɪs] adj sans saveur, fade; (in bad taste) de mauvais goût

tast·y ['testi] adj (comp **-ier**; super **-iest**) (coll) savoureux; (coll) de bon goût

tatter ['tætər] s lambeau m ‖ tr mettre en lambeaux

tatterdemalion [,tætərdɪ'meljen] s loqueteux m

tattered adj en lambeaux, en loques

tattle ['tætəl] s bavardage m; (gossip) cancan m ‖ intr bavarder; cancaner

tat'tle·tale' adj révélateur ‖ s rapporteur m, cancanier m

tattoo [tæ'tu] s tatouage m; (mil) retraite f ‖ tr tatouer

taunt [tɔnt] s sarcasme m ‖ tr bafouer

Taurus ['tɔrəs] s (astr, astrol) le Taureau

taut [tɔt] adj tendu

tavern ['tævərn] s café m, bar m, bistrot m; (inn) taverne f

taw·dry ['tɔdri] adj (comp **-drier**; super **-driest**) criard, voyant

taw·ny ['tɔni] adj (comp **-nier**; super **-niest**) fauve; (skin) basané

tax [tæks] s impôt m; **to reduce the tax on** dégrever ‖ tr imposer; (e.g., one's patience) mettre à l'épreuve; **to tax s.o. with** (e.g., laziness) taxer qn de

taxable ['tæksəbəl] adj imposable

taxation [tæk'seʃən] s imposition f; charges fpl fiscales, impôts mpl

tax' ba'sis m assiette f fiscale

tax' brack'et s niveau m d'imposition, tranche f

tax' collec'tor s percepteur m

tax' cut' s dégrèvement m d'impôt

tax' deduc'tion s dégrèvement m

tax' eva'sion s fraude f fiscale

tax'-exempt' adj net d'impôt, exempt d'impôts

tax' ha'ven s refuge m fiscal

tax·i ['tæksi] s (pl **-is**) taxi m ‖ v (pret & pp **-ied**; ger **-iing** or **-ying**) tr (aer) rouler au sol ‖ intr aller en taxi; (aer) rouler au sol ‖ interj hep taxi!

tax'i·cab' s taxi m

tax'i danc'er s taxi-girl f

taxidermy ['tæksɪ,dʌrmi] s taxidermie f

tax'i driv'er s chauffeur m de taxi

tax'i·plane' s avion-taxi m

tax'i stand' s station f de taxis

tax'i·way' s (aer) chemin m de roulement

tax'pay'er s contribuable mf

tax' rate' s taux m de l'impôt

tax' return' s déclaration f de revenus, déclaration d'impôts; (blank) feuille f de déclaration de revenus

tea [ti] s thé m; (medicinal infusion) tisane f

tea' bag' s sachet m de thé

tea' ball' s boule f à thé

tea'cart' s table f roulante

teach [titʃ] v (pret & pp **-taught** [tɔt]) tr enseigner; **to teach s.o. s.th.** enseigner q.ch à qn; **to teach s.o. to** + inf enseigner à qn à + inf ‖ intr enseigner

teacher ['titʃər] s instituteur m, enseignant m; (such as adversity) (fig) maître m

teach'er's pet' s élève m gâté

teaching ['titʃɪŋ] s enseignement m

teach'ing aids' spl matériel m auxiliaire d'enseignement

teach'ing staff' s corps m enseignant

tea'cup' s tasse f à thé

tea' dance' s thé m dansant

teak [tik] s teck m

tea'ket'tle s bouilloire f

team [tim] s (of horses, oxen, etc.) attelage m; (sports) équipe f ‖ tr atteler ‖ intr—**to team up with** faire équipe avec

team'mate' s équipier m

teamster ['timstər] s (of horses) charretier m; (of a truck) camionneur m

team'work' s travail m en équipe; (spirit) esprit m d'équipe

tea'pot' s théière f

tear [tɪr] s larme f; **to burst into tears** fondre en larmes ‖ [tɛr] s déchirure f ‖ [tɛr] v (pret **tore** [tor]; pp **torn** [tɔrn] tr déchirer; **to tear away, down, off** or **out** arracher; **to tear up** (e.g., a letter) déchirer ‖ intr se déchirer; **to tear along** filer précipitamment, aller à fond de train

tear' bomb' [tɪr] s bombe f lacrymogène

tear' duct' [tɪr] s conduit m lacrymal

tearful ['tɪrfəl] adj larmoyant, éploré

tear' gas' [tɪr] s gaz m lacrymogène

tear·jerker ['tɪr,dʒʌrkər] s (slang) comédie f larmoyante

tea'room' s salon m de thé

tease [tiz] tr taquiner

tea'spoon' s cuiller f à café

teaspoonful ['ti,spun,fʊl] s cuillerée f à café

teat [tit] s tétine f

tea'time' s l'heure f du thé

technical ['tɛknɪkəl] adj technique

technicali·ty [,tɛknɪ'kælɪti] s (pl **-ties**) technicité f; (fine point) subtilité f

technician [tɛk'nɪʃən] s technicien m

technique [tɛk'nik] s technique f

ted'dy bear' ['tɛdi] s ours m en peluche

tedious ['tidɪ·əs] adj ennuyeux, fatigant

teem [tim] intr fourmiller; **to teem with** abonder en, fourmiller de

teeming ['timɪŋ] adj fourmillant; (rain) torrentiel

teen·ager ['tin,edʒər] s adolescent m de 13 à 19 ans

teens [tinz] spl numéros anglais qui se terminent en **-teen** (de 13 à 19); adolescence *f* de 13 à 19 ans; **to be in one's teens** être adolescent

tee·ny ['tini] *adj* (*comp* **-nier**; *super* **-niest**) (coll) minuscule, tout petit

teeter ['titər] *s* branlement *m*; balançoire *f* ‖ *intr* se balancer, chanceler

teethe [tið] *intr* faire ses dents

teething ['tiðɪŋ] *s* dentition *f*

teeth'ing ring' *s* sucette *f*

teetotaler [ti'totələr] *s* antialcoolique *mf* (*qui s'abstient totalement de boissons alcooliques*)

tele·cast ['tɛlɪ,kæst] *s* émission *f* télévisée ‖ *v* (*pret* & *pp* **-cast** or **-casted**) *tr* & *intr* téléviser

telecommunications ['tɛləkə,mjunə'keʃənz] *s* télécommunications *fpl*

telegram ['tɛlɪ,græm] *s* télégramme *m*

telegraph ['tɛlɪ,græf] *s* télégraphe *m* ‖ *tr* & *intr* télégraphier

telegrapher [tɪ'lɛgrəfər] *s* télégraphiste *mf*

tel'egraph pole' *s* poteau *m* télégraphique

telemeter [tɪ'lɛmɪtər] *s* télémètre *m*

telepathy [tɪ'lɛpəθi] *s* télépathie *f*

telephone ['tɛlɪ,fon] *s* téléphone *m* ‖ *tr* & *intr* téléphoner

tel'ephone booth' *s* cabine *f* téléphonique

tel'ephone call' *s* appel *m* téléphonique

tel'ephone direc'tory *s* annuaire *m* du téléphone

tel'ephone exchange' *s* central *m* téléphonique

tel'ephone num'ber *s* numéro *m* d'appel

tel'ephone op'erator *s* standardiste *mf*, téléphoniste *mf*

tel'ephone receiv'er *s* récepteur *m* de téléphone

tel'ephone ta'ble *s* table *f* du téléphone

tel'ephoto lens' ['tɛlɪ,foto] *s* téléobjectif *m*

teleprinter ['tɛlɪ,prɪntər] *s* téléimprimeur *m*

teleprocessing ['tɛlə,prɑsɛsɪŋ] *s* télétraitement *m*

teleprompter ['tɛlə,prɑmptər] *s* télésouffleur *m*

telescope ['tɛlɪ,skop] *s* télescope *m* ‖ *tr* télescoper ‖ *intr* se télescoper

telescopic [,tɛlɪ,skɑpɪk] *adj* télescopique

Teletype ['tɛlɪ,taɪp] *s* (trademark) télétype *m*

tel'etype'writ'er *s* téléscripteur *m*

televangelism ['tɛlɪ'vændʒəlɪzəm] *s* télévangélisme *m*

televangelist ['tɛlɪ'vændʒəlɪst] *s* télévangéliste *m*

teleview ['tɛlɪ,vju] *tr* & *intr* voir à la télévision

televiewer ['tɛlɪ,vju·ər] *s* téléspectateur *m*

televise ['tɛlɪ,vaɪz] *tr* téléviser

television ['tɛlɪ,vɪʒən] *adj* télévisuel ‖ *s* télévision *f*

tel'evision screen' *s* écran *m* de télévision, petit écran

tel'evision set' *s* téléviseur *m*

telex ['tɛlɛks] *s* télex *m* ‖ *tr* envoyer par télex

tell [tɛl] *v* (*pret* & *pp* **told** [told]) *tr* dire; (*a story*) raconter; (*to count*) compter; (*to recognize as distinct*) distinguer; **tell me another!** (coll) à d'autres!; **to tell off** compter; (coll) dire son fait à; **to tell s.o. to** + *inf* dire à qn de + *inf* ‖ *intr* produire un effet; **do tell!** (coll) vraiment!; **to tell on** influer sur; (coll) dénoncer; **who can tell?** qui sait?

teller ['tɛlər] *s* narrateur *m*; (*of a bank*) caissier *m*; (*of votes*) scrutateur *m*

temper ['tɛmpər] *s* humeur *f*, caractère *m*; (*of steel, glass, etc.*) trempe *f*; **to keep one's temper** retenir sa colère; **to lose one's temper** se mettre en colère ‖ *tr* tremper ‖ *intr* se tremper

temperament ['tɛmpərəmənt] *s* tempérament *m*

temperamental [,tɛmpərə'mɛntəl] *adj* constitutionnel; capricieux, instable

temperance ['tɛmpərəns] *s* tempérance *f*

temperate ['tɛmpərɪt] *adj* tempéré; (*in food or drink*) tempérant

temperature ['tɛmpərətʃər] *s* température *f*

tempest ['tɛmpɪst] *s* tempête *f*; **tempest in a teapot** tempête dans un verre d'eau

tempestuous [tɛm'pɛstʃu·əs] *adj* tempétueux

temple ['tɛmpəl] *s* temple *m*; (*side of forehead*) tempe *f*; (*of spectacles*) branche *f*

templet ['tɛmplɪt] *s* gabarit *m*

tem·po ['tɛmpo] *s* (*pl* **-pos** or **-pi** [pi]) tempo *m*

temporal ['tɛmpərəl] *adj* temporel; (anat) temporal

temporary ['tɛmpə,rɛri] *adj* temporaire

temporize ['tɛmpə,raɪz] *intr* temporiser

tempt [tɛmpt] *tr* tenter

temptation [tɛmp'teʃən] *s* tentation *f*

tempter ['tɛmptər] *s* tentateur *m*

tempting ['tɛmptɪŋ] *adj* tentant

ten [tɛn] *adj* & *pron* dix; **about ten** une dizaine de ‖ *s* dix *m*; **ten o'clock** dix heures

tenable ['tɛnəbəl] *adj* soutenable

tenacious [tɪ'neʃəs] *adj* tenace

tenacity [tɪ'næsɪti] *s* ténacité *f*

tenant ['tɛnənt] *s* locataire *mf*

ten'ant farm'er *s* métayer *m*

tend [tɛnd] *tr* soigner; (*sheep*) garder; (*a machine*) surveiller ‖ *intr*—**to tend to** (*to be disposed to*) tendre à; (*to attend to*) vaquer à; **to tend towards** tendre vers or à

tenden·cy ['tɛndənsi] *s* (*pl* **-cies**) tendance *f*

tender ['tɛndər] *adj* tendre ‖ *s* offre *f*; (aer, naut) ravitailleur *m*; (rr) tender *m* ‖ *tr* offrir

ten'der-heart'ed *adj* au cœur tendre

ten'der·loin *s* filet *m*

tenderness ['tɛndərnɪs] *s* tendresse *f*; (*of, e.g., the skin*) sensibilité *f*; (*of, e.g., meat*) tendreté *f*

tendon ['tɛndən] *s* tendon *m*

tendril ['tɛndrɪl] *s* vrille *f*

tenement ['tɛnɪmənt] *s* maison *f* d'habitation; (*slum tenement house*) taudis *m*

ten'ement house' *s* maison *f* de rapport; (*in the slums*) taudis *m*

tenet ['tɛnɪt] *s* doctrine *f*, principe *m*

tennis ['tɛnɪs] *s* tennis *m*
ten'nis ball' *s* balle *f* de tennis
ten'nis court' *s* court *m* de tennis
tenor ['tɛnər] *s* teneur *f*, cours *m*; (mus) ténor *m*
ten'or clef' *s* clef *f* d'ut
tense [tɛns] *adj* tendu ‖ *s* (gram) temps *m*
tension ['tɛnʃən] *s* tension *f*
tent [tɛnt] *s* tente *f*
tentacle ['tɛntəkəl] *s* tentacule *m*
tentative ['tɛntətɪv] *adj* provisoire; (*hesitant*) timide
tenth [tɛnθ] *adj & pron* dixième (*masc, fem*); **the Tenth** dix, e.g., **John the Tenth** Jean dix ‖ *s* dixième *m*; **the tenth** (*in dates*) le dix
tent' pole' *s* montant *m* de tente
tenuous ['tɛnju·əs] *adj* ténu
tenure ['tɛnjər] *s* (*possession*) tenure *f*; (*of an office*) occupation *f*; (*protection from dismissal*) inamovibilité *f*
tepid ['tɛpɪd] *adj* tiède
term [tʌrm] *s* terme *m*; (*of imprisonment*) temps *m*; (*of office*) mandat *m*; (*of the school year*) semestre *m*; **terms** conditions *fpl*; **to be on good terms with** avoir de bons rapports avec ‖ *tr* appeler, qualifier
termagant ['tʌrməgənt] *s* mégère *f*
terminal ['tʌrmɪnəl] *adj* terminal ‖ *s* (comp) terminal *m*; (elec) borne *f*; (rr) terminus *m*
terminate ['tʌrmɪ,net] *tr* terminer ‖ *intr* se terminer
termination [,tʌrmɪ'neʃən] *s* conclusion *f*; (*extremity*) bout *m*; (*of word*) désinence *f*; (*of a treaty*) extinction *f*
terminus ['tʌrmɪnəs] *s* bout *m*, extrémité *f*; (*boundary*) borne *f*; (rr) terminus *m*
termite ['tʌrmaɪt] *s* termite *m*
term' pa'per *s* dissertation *f*
terrace ['tɛrəs] *s* terrasse *f* ‖ *tr* disposer en terrasse
terra firma ['tɛrə'fʌrmə] *s* terre *f* ferme
terrain [tɛ'ren] *s* terrain *m*
terrestrial [tə'rɛstrɪ·əl] *adj* terrestre
terrible ['tɛrɪbəl] *adj* terrible; (*extremely bad*) atroce
terrific [tə'rɪfɪk] *adj* terrible, terrifiant; (coll) formidable, dynamite
terri·fy ['tɛrɪ,faɪ] *v* (*pret & pp* **-fied**) *tr* terrifier
territo·ry ['tɛrɪ,tori] *s* (*pl* **-ries**) territoire *m*
terror ['tɛrər] *s* terreur *f*
terrorize ['tɛrə,raɪz] *tr* terroriser
ter'ry cloth' ['tɛri] *s* tissu-éponge *m*
terse [tʌrs] *adj* concis, succinct
tertiary ['tʌrʃəri] *adj* tertiaire
test [tɛst] *s* (*physical, mental, moral*) épreuve *f*; (*exam*) examen *m*; (*trial*) essai *m*; (*e.g., of intelligence*) test *m* ‖ *tr* éprouver, mettre à l'épreuve; examiner, tester
testament ['tɛstəmənt] *s* testament *m*
test' ban' *s* interdiction *f* des essais nucléaires
test' flight' *s* vol *m* d'essai
testicle ['tɛstɪkəl] *s* testicule *m*

testi·fy ['tɛstɪ,faɪ] *v* (*pret & pp* **-fied**) *tr* déclarer ‖ *intr* déposer; **to testify to** témoigner de
testimonial [,tɛstɪ'moni·əl] *s* attestation *m*
testimo·ny ['tɛstɪ,moni] *s* (*pl* **-nies**) témoignage *m*
test'ing ground' *s* terrain *m* d'essai
test' pat'tern *s* (telv) mire *f*
test' pi'lot *s* pilote *m* d'essai
test' tube' *s* éprouvette *f*
test'-tube ba'by *s* bébé *m* éprouvette
tes·ty ['tɛsti] *adj* (*comp* **-tier**; *super* **-tiest**) susceptible
tetanus ['tɛtənəs] *s* tétanos *m*
tether ['tɛðər] *s* attache *f*; **at the end of one's tether** à bout de ressources ‖ *tr* mettre à l'attache
tetter ['tɛtər] *s* (pathol) dartre *f*
text [tɛkst] *s* texte *m*
text'book' *s* manuel *m* scolaire, livre *m* de classe
textile ['tɛkstaɪl] *adj & s* textile *m*
textual ['tɛkstʃu·əl] *adj* textuel
texture ['tɛkstʃər] *s* texture *f*; (*woven fabric*) tissu *m*
Thai ['tɑ·i], [taɪ] *adj* thaï, thaïlandais ‖ *s* (*language*) thaï *m*; (*person*) Thaïlandais *m*; **the Thai** les Thaïlandais
Thailand ['taɪlənd] *s* Thaïlande *f*; la Thaïlande
Thames [tɛmz] *s* Tamise *f*
than [ðæn] *conj* que; (*before a numeral*) de, e.g., **more than three** plus de trois
thank [θæŋk] *adj* (e.g., *offering*) de reconnaissance ‖ **thanks** *spl* remerciements *mpl*; **thanks to** grâce à ‖ **thanks** *interj* merci!; **no thanks!** merci! ‖ **thank** *tr* remercier; **thank you** je vous remercie; **thank you for** merci de or pour; **thank you for** + *ger* merci de + *inf*; **to thank s.o. for** remercier qn de or pour; **to thank s.o. for** + *ger* remercier qn de + *inf*
thankful ['θæŋkfəl] *adj* reconnaissant
thankless ['θæŋklɪs] *adj* ingrat
Thanksgiv'ing Day' *s* le jour d'action de grâces
that [ðæt] *adj dem* (*pl* **those**) ce §82; **that one** celui-là §84 ‖ *pron dem* (*pl* **those**) celui §83; celui-là §84 ‖ *pron rel* qui; que ‖ *pron neut* cela, ça; **that is** c'est-à-dire; **that's all** voilà tout; **that will do** cela suffit ‖ *adv* tellement, si, aussi; **that far** si loin, aussi loin; **that much, that many** tant ‖ *conj* que; (*in order that*) pour que, afin que; **it is** ce que
thatch [θætʃ] *s* chaume *m* ‖ *tr* couvrir de chaume
thatched' cot'tage *s* chaumière *f*
thaw [θɔ] *s* dégel *m* ‖ *tr & intr* dégeler
the [ðə], [ðɪ], [ði] *art def* le §77 ‖ *adv* d'autant plus, e.g., **she will be the happier for it** elle en sera d'autant plus heureuse; **the more . . . the more** plus . . . plus
theater ['θi·ətər] *s* théâtre *m*
the'ater club' *s* association *f* des spectateurs
the'ater·go'er *s* habitué *m* du théâtre

the′ater page′ s chronique f théâtrale

theatrical [θɪˈætrɪkəl] adj théâtral

thee [ði] pron pers (archaic, poetic, Bib) toi §85; te §87

theft [θɛft] s vol m

their [ðɛr] adj poss leur §88

theirs [ðɛrz] pron poss le leur §89

them [ðɛm] pron pers eux §85; les §87; leur §87; **of them** en §87; **to them** leur §87; y §87

theme [θim] s thème m; (essay) composition f; (mus) thème

theme′ song′ s leitmotiv m; (rad) indicatif m

them·selves′ pron pers soi §85; eux-mêmes §86; se §87; eux §85

then [ðɛn] adv alors; (next) ensuite, puis; (therefore) donc; **by then** d'ici là; **from then on, since then** depuis lors, dès lors; **then and there** séance tenante; **till then** jusque-là; **what then?** et après?

thence [ðɛns] adv de là; (from that fact) pour cette raison

thence′forth′ adv dès lors

theolo·gy [θiˈɑlədʒi] s (pl -gies) théologie f

theorem [ˈθiərəm] s théorème m

theoretical [ˌθiəˈrɛtɪkəl] adj théorique

theo·ry [ˈθiəri] s (pl -ries) théorie f

therapeutic [ˌθɛrəˈpjutɪk] adj thérapeutique ‖ **therapeutics** spl thérapeutique f

thera·py [ˈθɛrəpi] s (pl -pies) thérapie f

there [ðɛr] adv là; y §87; **down there, over there** là-bas; **from there** de là; en §87; **in there** là-dedans; **on there** là-dessus; **there is** or **there are** il y a; (pointing out) voilà; **under there** là-dessous; **up there** là-haut

there′abouts′ adv aux environs, près de là; (approximately) à peu près

there′af′ter adv par la suite

there′by′ adv par là; de cette manière

therefore [ˈðɛrˌfor] adv par conséquent, donc

there′in′ adv dedans, là-dedans

there′of′ adv de cela; en §87

there′upon′ adv là-dessus §85A; sur ce

there′with′ adv avec cela

thermal [ˈθʌrməl] adj (waters) thermal; (capacity) thermique

ther′mal cone′ s bouclier m thermique

thermocouple [ˈθʌrmoˌkʌpəl] s thermocouple m

thermodynamic [ˌθʌrmodaɪˈnæmɪk] adj thermodynamique ‖ **thermodynamics** spl thermodynamique f

thermometer [θərˈmɑmɪtər] s thermomètre m

thermonuclear [ˌθʌrmoˈn(j)ukliˌər] adj thermonucléaire

Thermopylae [θərˈmɑpɪˌli] s les Thermopyles fpl

ther′mos bot′tle [ˈθʌrməs] s thermos m & f, bouteille f thermos

thermostat [ˈθʌrməˌstæt] s thermostat m

thesau·rus [θɪˈsɔrəs] s (pl -ruses [rəsəs] or -ri [raɪ]) trésor m; (dictionary) dictionnaire m analogique; (treasury) trésor m; (comp) thesaurus m

these [ðiz] adj dem pl ces §82 ‖ pron dem pl ceux §83; ceux-ci §84

the·sis [ˈθisɪs] s (pl -ses [siz]) thèse f

they [ðe] pron pers ils §87; eux §85; on §87, e.g., **they say** on dit; ce §82B

thick [θɪk] adj épais; (pipe, rod, etc.) gros; (forest, eyebrows, etc.) touffu; (grass, grain, etc.) dru; (voice) pâteux; (gravy) court; (coll) stupide, obtus; (coll) intime ‖ s (of thumb, leg, etc.) gras m; **the thick of** (e.g., a crowd) le milieu de; (e.g., a battle) le fort de; **through thick and thin** contre vents et marées

thicken [ˈθɪkən] tr épaissir ‖ intr s'épaissir; (said, e.g., of plot) se corser

thicket [ˈθɪkɪt] s fourré m, maquis m

thick′-head′ed adj à la tête dure

thick′-lipped′ adj lippu

thick′-set′ adj trapu

thief [θif] s (pl thieves [θivz]) voleur m

thieve [θiv] intr voler

thiever·y [ˈθivəri] s (pl -ies) volerie f

thigh [θaɪ] s cuisse f

thigh′bone′ s fémur m

thimble [ˈθɪmbəl] s dé m

thin [θɪn] adj (comp **thinner**; super **thinnest**) mince; (person) élancé, maigre; (hair) rare; (soup) clair; (gravy) long; (voice) grêle; (excuse) faible ‖ v (pret & pp **thinned**; ger **thinning**) tr amincir; (colors) délayer; **to thin out** éclaircir ‖ intr s'amincir; **to thin out** s'éclaircir

thine [ðaɪn] adj poss (archaic, poetic, Bib) ton §88 ‖ pron poss (archaic, poetic, Bib) le tien §89

thing [θɪŋ] s chose f; **for another thing** d'autre part; **for one thing** en premier lieu; **of all things!** par exemple!; **to be the thing** être le dernier cri; **to see things** avoir des hallucinations

thingamajig [ˈθɪŋəməˌdʒɪg] s (coll) truc m, machin m, bidule f

think [θɪŋk] v (pret & pp **thought** [θɔt]) tr penser; (to deem, consider) estimer; **to think of** (to have an opinion of) penser de, e.g., **what do you think of your uncle?** que pensez-vous de votre oncle? ‖ intr penser, songer; **to think fast** avoir l'esprit alerte; **to think of** (to direct one's thoughts toward) penser à, songer à, e.g., **do you ever think of your uncle?** pensez-vous jamais à votre oncle?; **to think of it** or **them** y penser, y songer; **to think so** croire que oui

thinker [ˈθɪŋkər] s penseur m

third [θʌrd] adj & pron troisième (masc, fem); **the Third** trois, e.g., **John the Third** Jean trois ‖ s troisième m; (in fractions) tiers m; **the third** (in dates) le trois

third′ degree′ s (coll) passage m à tabac, cuisinage m

third′ fin′ger s annulaire m

third′ rail′ s (rr) rail m de contact; rail conducteur

third′-rate′ adj de troisième ordre

Third′ World′ s Tiers Monde m

thirst [θʌrst] *s* soif *f* ‖ *intr* avoir soif; **to thirst for** avoir soif de

thirst'-quench'ing *adj* désaltérant

thirst·y ['θʌrsti] *adj* (*comp* **-ier**; *super* **-iest**) altéré, assoiffé; **to be thirsty** avoir soif

thirteen ['θʌr'tin] *adj, pron,* & *s* treize *m*

thirteenth ['θʌr'tinθ] *adj & pron* treizième (*masc, fem*); **the Thirteenth** treize, e.g., **John the Thirteenth** Jean treize ‖ *s* treizième *m*; **the thirteenth** (*in dates*) le treize

thirtieth ['θʌrtɪ·ɪθ] *adj & pron* trentième (*masc, fem*) ‖ *s* trentième *m*; **the thirtieth** (*in dates*) trente

thir·ty ['θʌrti] *adj & pron* trente; **about thirty** une trentaine de ‖ *s* (*pl* **-ties**) trente *m*; **the thirties** les années *fpl* trente

this [ðɪs] *adj dem* (*pl* **these**) ce §82; **this one** celui-ci §84 ‖ *pron dem* (*pl* **these**) celui §83; celui-ci §84 ‖ *pron neut* ceci ‖ *adv* tellement, si, aussi; **this far** si loin, aussi loin; **this much, this many** tant

thistle ['θɪsəl] *s* chardon *m*

thither ['θɪðər] *adv* là, de ce côté là

thong [θɔŋ] *s* courroie *f*

tho·rax ['θoræks] *s* (*pl* **-raxes** or **-races** [rə,siz]) thorax *m*

thorn [θɔrn] *s* épine *f*

thorn·y ['θɔrni] *adj* (*comp* **-ier**; *super* **-iest**) épineux

thorough ['θʌro] *adj* approfondi, complet; consciencieux, minutieux

thor'ough-bred' *adj* de race, racé; (*horse*) pur sang ‖ *s* personne *f* racée; (*horse*) pur-sang *m*

thor'ough-fare' *s* voie *f* de communication; **no thoroughfare** (*public sign*) rue barrée

thor'ough-go'ing *adj* parfait; consciencieux

thoroughly ['θʌroli] *adv* à fond

those [ðoz] *adj dem pl* ces §82 ‖ *pron dem pl* ceux §83; ceux-là §84

thou [ðaʊ] *pron pers* (archaic, poetic, Bib) tu §87 ‖ *tr & intr* tutoyer

though [ðo] *adv* cependant ‖ *conj* (*although*) bien que, quoique; (*even if*) même si; **as though** comme si

thought [θɔt] *s* pensée *f*

thought' control' *s* asservissement *m* des consciences

thoughtful ['θɔtfəl] *adj* pensif; (*considerate*) prévenant, attentif; (*serious*) profond

thoughtless ['θɔtlɪs] *adj* étourdi, négligent; inconsidéré

thousand ['θaʊzənd] *adj & pron* mille; mil, e.g., **the year one thousand nineteen hundred and eighty-one** l'an mil neuf cent quatre-vingt-un ‖ *s* mille *m*; **a thousand** un millier de, mille

thousandth ['θaʊzəndθ] *adj & pron* millième (*masc, fem*) ‖ *s* millième *m*

thrash [θræʃ] *tr* rosser; (agr) battre; **to thrash out** débattre ‖ *intr* s'agiter; (agr) battre le blé

thread [θred] *s* fil *m*; (bot) filament *m*; (mach) filet *m*; **to hang by a thread** ne tenir qu'à un fil; **to lose the thread of** perdre le fil de ‖ *tr* enfiler; (mach) fileter

thread'bare' *adj* élimé, râpé; (*tire*) usé jusqu'à la corde

threat [θrɛt] *s* menace *f*

threaten ['θrɛtən] *tr* & *intr* menacer

threatening ['θrɛtənɪŋ] *adj* menaçant

three [θri] *adj & pron* trois ‖ *s* trois *m*; **three o'clock** trois heures; **three of a kind** (cards) un fredon

three'-cor'nered *adj* triangulaire; (*hat*) tricorne

three'-ply' *adj* à trois épaisseurs; (*e.g., wool*) à trois fils

three' R's' [ɑrz] *spl* la lecture, l'écriture et l'arithmétique, premières notions *fpl*

three'score' *adj* soixante

threno·dy ['θrɛnədi] *s* (*pl* **-dies**) thrène *m*

thresh [θrɛʃ] *tr* (agr) battre; **to thresh out** (*a problem*) débattre ‖ *intr* s'agiter; (agr) battre le blé

thresh'ing floor' *s* aire *f*

thresh'ing machine' *s* batteuse *f*

threshold ['θrɛʃold] *s* seuil *m*; **to cross the threshold** franchir le seuil

thrice [θraɪs] *adv* trois fois

thrift [θrɪft] *s* économie *f*, épargne *f*

thrift·y ['θrɪfti] *adj* (*comp* **-ier**; *super* **-iest**) économe, ménager, frugal; prospère

thrill [θrɪl] *s* frisson *m* ‖ *tr* faire frémir ‖ *intr* frémir

thriller ['θrɪlər] *s* roman *m*, film *m*, or pièce *f* à sensation; (*novel*) roman de série noire

thrilling ['θrɪlɪŋ] *adj* émouvant, passionnant

thrive [θraɪv] *v* (*pret* **thrived** or **throve** [θrov]; *pp* **thrived** or **thriven** ['θrɪvən]) *intr* prospérer; (*said of child, plant, etc.*) croître, se développer

throat [θrot] *s* gorge *f*; **to clear one's throat** s'éclaircir le gosier; **to have a sore throat** avoir mal à la gorge

throb [θrɑb] *s* palpitation *f*, battement *m*; (*of motor*) vrombissement *m* ‖ *v* (*pret & pp* **throbbed**; *ger* **throbbing**) *intr* palpiter, battre fort; (*said of motor*) vrombir

throes [θroz] *spl* (*of childbirth*) douleurs *fpl*; (*of death*) affres *fpl*; **in the throes of** luttant avec

throne [θron] *s* trône *m*

throng [θrɔŋ] *s* foule *f*, affluence *f* ‖ *intr* affluer

throttle ['θrɑtəl] *s* (*of steam engine*) régulateur *m*; (aut) étrangleur *m* ‖ *tr* régler; étrangler

through [θru] *adj* direct; (*finished*) fini; (*traffic*) prioritaire ‖ *adv* à travers; complètement ‖ *prep* au travers de, par; grâce à, par le canal de

through·out' *adv* d'un bout à l'autre ‖ *prep* d'un bout à l'autre de; (*during*) pendant tout

through' street' *s* rue *f* à circulation prioritaire

through'way' *s* autoroute *f*

throw [θro] *s* jet *m*, lancement *m*; (*scarf*) châle *m* ‖ *v* (*pret* **threw** [θru]; *pp* **thrown**) *tr* jeter, lancer; (*a glance; the dice*) jeter; (*e.g., a baseball*) lancer; (*e.g., a shadow*) projeter; (*blame; responsibility*) rejeter; (*a rider*) désarçonner; (*a game, career, etc.*) perdre à dessein; **to throw away** jeter; **to throw back** renvoyer; **to throw in** ajouter; **to throw out** expulser, chasser; (*e.g., an odor*) répandre; (*one's chest*) bomber; **to throw over** abandonner; **to throw up** jeter en l'air; vomir; (*one's hands*) lever; (*e.g., one's claims*) renoncer à ‖ *intr* jeter, lancer; jeter des dés; **to throw up** vomir

throw′back′ *s* recul *m*; (*setback*) échec *m*; (*reversion*) retour *m* atavique

thrum [θrʌm] *v* (*pret & pp* **thrummed**; *ger* **thrumming**) *intr* pianoter

thrush [θrʌʃ] *s* grive *f*

thrust [θrʌst] *s* poussée *f*; (*with a weapon*) coup *m* de pointe; (*with a sword*) coup d'estoc; (*jibe*) trait *m*; (rok) poussée *f*; **thrust and parry** la botte et la parade ‖ *v* (*pret & pp* **thrust**) *tr* pousser; (*e.g., a dagger*) enfoncer; **to thrust oneself on** s'imposer à

thud [θʌd] *s* bruit *m* sourd ‖ *v* (*pret & pp* **thudded**; *ger* **thudding**) *tr & intr* frapper avec un son mat

thug [θʌg] *s* bandit *m*, assassin *m*

thumb [θʌm] *s* pouce *m*; **all thumbs** (coll) maladroit; **to twiddle one's thumbs** se tourner les pouces; **under the thumb of** sous la coupe de ‖ *tr* tripoter; (*a book*) feuilleter; **to thumb a ride** faire de l'auto-stop; **to thumb one's nose at** (coll) faire un pied de nez à

thumb′ in′dex *s* onglet *m*, encoche *f*

thumb′print′ *s* marque *f* de pouce

thumb′screw′ *s* papillon *m*, vis *f* à ailettes

thumb′tack′ *s* punaise *f* ‖ *tr* punaiser

thump [θʌmp] *s* coup *m* violent ‖ *tr* cogner ‖ *intr* tomber avec un bruit sourd; (*said, e.g., of marching feet*) sonner lourdement; (*said of heart*) battre fort

thumping [′θʌmpɪŋ] *adj* (coll) énorme

thunder [′θʌndər] *s* tonnerre *m* ‖ *tr* fulminer ‖ *intr* tonner; **to thunder at** tonner contre, tempêter contre

thun′der·bolt′ *s* foudre *f*; (*disaster*) coup *m* de foudre

thun′der·clap′ *s* coup *m* de tonnerre

thunderous [′θʌndərəs] *adj* orageux; (*voice; applause*) tonnant

thun′der·show′er *s* pluie *f* d'orage

thun′der·storm′ *s* orage *m*

thunderstruck [′θʌndər,strʌk] *adj* foudroyé, pantois

Thursday [′θʌrzdi] *s* jeudi *m*

thus [ðʌs] *adv* ainsi; (*therefore*) donc; **thus far** jusqu'ici

thwack [θwæk] *s* coup *m* ‖ *tr* flanquer un coup à

thwart [θwɔrt] *adj* transversal ‖ *adv* en travers ‖ *tr* déjouer, frustrer

thy [ðaɪ] *adj poss* (archaic, poetic, Bib) ton §88

thyme [taɪm] *s* thym *m*

thyroid [′θaɪrɔɪd] *s* thyroïde *f*; (pharm) extrait *m* thyroïde

thyself [ðaɪ′sɛlf] *pron* (archaic, poetic, Bib) toi-même §86; te §87

tiara [taɪ′ɑrə], [taɪ′ɛrə] *s* tiare *f*; (*woman's headdress*) diadème *m*

tic [tɪk] *s* (pathol) tic *m*

tick [tɪk] *s* (*ticking*) tic-tac *m*; (*e.g., of pillow*) taie *f*; (*e.g., of mattress*) housse *f* de coutil; (ent) tique *f*; **on tick** à crédit ‖ *tr*—**to tick off** (*to check off*) pointer ‖ *intr* tictaquer; (*said of heart*) battre

ticker [′tɪkər] *s* téléimprimeur *m*; (*watch*) (slang) toquante *f*; (*heart*) (slang) cœur *m*

tick′er tape′ *s* bande *f* de téléimprimeur

ticket [′tɪkɪt] *s* billet *m*; (*of bus, subway, etc.*) ticket *m*; (*of baggage, checkroom*) bulletin *m*; (*of cloakroom*) numéro *m*; (*for boat trip*) passage *m*; (*of a political party*) liste *f* électorale; (*for violation*) (coll) papillon *m* de procès-verbal, contravention *f*; **that's the ticket** (coll) c'est bien ça, à la bonne heure; **tickets, please!** vos places, s'il vous plaît!

tick′et a′gent *s* guichetier *m*

tick′et collec′tor *s* contrôleur *m*

ticketing [′tɪkɪtɪŋ] *s* billetterie *f*

tick′et of′fice *s* guichet *m*; (theat) bureau *m* de location

tick′et scalp′er [,skælpər] *s* trafiquant *m* de billets de théâtre

tick′et win′dow *s* guichet *m*

ticking [′tɪkɪŋ] *s* (*of a clock*) tic-tac *m*; (tex) coutil *m*

tickle [′tɪkəl] *s* chatouillement *m* ‖ *tr* chatouiller; (*to amuse*) amuser; (*to please*) plaire à ‖ *intr* chatouiller

ticklish [′tɪklɪʃ] *adj* chatouilleux; (*touchy*) susceptible; (*subject, question*) épineux, délicat

tick′-tack-toe′ *s* morpion *m*

ticktock [′tɪk,tɑk] *s* tic-tac *m* ‖ *intr* faire tic-tac

tid′al ba′sin *s* bassin *m* à flot

tid′al wave′ [′taɪdəl] *s* raz *m* de marée; (*e.g., of popular indignation*) vague *f*

tidbit [′tɪd,bɪt] *s* bon morceau *m*

tiddlywinks [′tɪdli,wɪŋks] *s* jeu *m* de puce

tide [taɪd] *s* marée *f*; **against the tide** à contre-marée; **to go with the tide** suivre le courant ‖ *tr*—**to tide over** dépanner, remettre à flot; (*a difficulty*) venir à bout de

tide′land′ *s* terres *fpl* inondées aux grandes marées

tide′wa′ter *s* eaux *fpl* de marée; bord *m* de la mer

tide′water pow′er plant′ *s* usine *f* marémotrice

tidings [′taɪdɪŋz] *spl* nouvelles *fpl*

ti·dy [′taɪdi] *adj* (*comp* **-dier**; *super* **-diest**) propre, net, bien tenu; (*considerable*) (coll) joli, fameux ‖ *s* (*pl* **-dies**) voile *m* de fauteuil ‖ *v* (*pret & pp* **-died**) *tr* mettre en ordre, nettoyer ‖ *intr*—**to tidy up** faire un brin de toilette

tie [taɪ] *s* (*connection*) lien *m*, attache *f*; (*knot*) nœud *m*; (*necktie*) cravate *f*; (*in games*) match *m* nul; (mus) liaison *f*; (rr) traverse *f* ‖ *v* (*pret & pp* **tied**; *ger* **tying**) *tr* lier; (*a knot, a necktie, etc.*) nouer; (*shoelaces; a knot; one's apron*) attacher; (*an artery*) ligaturer; (*a competitor*) être à égalité avec; (mus) lier; **tied up** (*busy*) occupé; **to tie down** assujettir; **to tie up** attacher; (*a package*) ficeler; (*a person*) ligoter; (*a wound*) bander; (*funds*) immobiliser; (*traffic, a telephone line*) embouteiller ‖ *intr* (sports) faire match nul, égaliser

tie′back′ *s* embrasse *f*

tie′ game′ *s* match *m* nul

tie′pin′ *s* épingle *f* de cravate

tier [tɪr] *s* étage *m*; (*of stadium*) gradin *m*

tiger [′taɪgər] *s* tigre *m*

ti′ger lil′y *s* lis *m* tigré

tight [taɪt] *adj* serré, juste; (*e.g., rope*) tendu; (*clothes*) ajusté; (*container*) étanche; (*game*) serré; (*money*) rare; (*miserly*) (coll) chiche; (*drunk*) (coll) rond, noir ‖ **tights** *spl* collant *m*, maillot *m* ‖ *adv* fermement, bien; **to hold tight** tenir serré; se tenir, se cramponner; **to sit tight** (coll) tenir bon

tighten [′taɪtən] *tr* (*a knot, a bolt*) serrer, resserrer; (*e.g., a rope*) tendre ‖ *intr* se serrer; se tendre

tight-fisted [′taɪt′fɪstɪd] *adj* dur à la détente, serré

tight′-fit′ting *adj* collant, ajusté

tight′rope′ *s* corde *f* raide

tight′rope walk′er *s* funambule *mf*

tight′ squeeze′ *s* (coll) situation *f* difficile, embarras *m*

tight′wad′ *s* (coll) grippe-sou *m*

tigress [′taɪgrɪs] *s* tigresse *f*

tile [taɪl] *s* (*for roof*) tuile *f*; (*for floor*) carreau *m* ‖ *tr* (*e.g., a house*) couvrir de tuiles; (*a floor*) carreler

tile′ roof′ *s* toit *m* de tuiles

till [tɪl] *s* tiroir-caisse m ‖ *prep* jusqu'à ‖ *conj* jusqu'à ce que ‖ *tr* labourer

tilt [tɪlt] *s* (*slant*) pente *f*, inclinaison *f*; (*contest*) joute *f*; **full tilt** à fond de train ‖ *tr* pencher, incliner; **to tilt back** renverser en arrière; **to tilt up** redresser ‖ *intr* se pencher, s'incliner; (*with lance*) jouter; (naut) donner de la bande; **to tilt at** attaquer, critiquer; **to tilt back** se renverser en arrière

timber [′tɪmbər] *s* bois *m* de construction; (*trees*) bois de haute futaie; (*rafter*) poutre *f*

tim′ber·land′ *s* bois *m* pour exploitation forestière

tim′ber line′ *s* limite *f* de la végétation forestière, ligne *f* des arbres

timbre [′tɪmbər] *s* (phonet, phys) timbre *m*

time [taɪm] *s* temps *m*; heure *f*, e.g., **what time is it?** quelle heure est-il?; fois, e.g., **five times** cinq fois; e.g., **five times two is ten** cinq fois deux font dix; (*period of payment*) délai *m*; (phot) temps d'exposition; **at that time** à ce moment-là; à cette époque; **at the present time** à l'heure actuelle; **at the same time** en même

temps; **at times** parfois; **behind the times** en retard sur son époque; **between times** entre-temps; **full time** plein temps; **in due time** en temps et lieu; **in no time** en moins de rien; **in the time of** au temps de; **on time** à l'heure, à temps; **several times** à plusieurs reprises; **time and time again** maintes fois; **to beat time** (mus) battre la mesure; **to do time** (coll) faire son temps; **to have a good time** s'amuser bien, se divertir; **to lose time** (*said of timepiece*) retarder; **to mark time** marquer le pas; **to play for time** (coll) chercher à gagner du temps ‖ *tr* mesurer la durée de; (sports) chronométrer

time′ bomb′ *s* bombe *f* à retardement

time′card′ *s* registre *m* de présence

time′ clock′ *s* horloge *f* enregistreuse

time′ expo′sure *s* (phot) pose *f*

time′ fuse′ *s* fusée *f* fusante

time′-hon′ored *adj* consacré par l'usage

time′keep′er *s* pointeur *m*, chronométreur *m*; (*clock*) pendule *f*; (*watch*) montre *f*

timeless [′taɪmlɪs] *adj* sans fin, éternel

time·ly [′taɪmli] *adj* (*comp* **-lier**; *super* **-liest**) opportun, à propos

time′-out′ *s* (sports) temps *m* mort

time′piece′ *s* (*clock*) pendule *f*; (*watch*) montre *f*

timer [′taɪmər] *s* (*person*) chronométreur *m*; (*of an electrical appliance*) minuterie *f*, compte-minutes *m invar*

time′-release medica′tion *s* médicament *m* à action prolongée, médication *f* retard

time′-shar′ing *adj* (comp) en temps partagé

time′ shar′ing *s* (comp) temps *m* partagé, partage *m* du temps

time′ sheet′ *s* feuille *f* de présence

time′ sig′nal *s* signal *m* horaire

time′ slot′ *s* créneau *m* temporel

time′ta′ble *s* horaire *m*; (rr) indicateur *m*

time′work′ *s* travail *m* à l'heure

time′worn′ *adj* usé par le temps; (*venerable*) séculaire

time′ zone′ *s* fuseau *m* horaire

timid [′tɪmɪd] *adj* timide

timing [′taɪmɪŋ] *s* (*recording of time*) chronométrage *m*; (*selecting the right time*) choix *m* du moment propice; (*of an electrical appliance*) minuterie *f*; (aut, mach) réglage *m*; (sports) chronométrage; (theat) tempo *m*, minutage *m*

tim′ing gears′ *spl* engrenage *m* de distribution

timorous [′tɪmərəs] *adj* timoré, peureux

tin [tɪn] *s* (*element*) étain *m*; (*tin plate*) fer-blanc *m*; (*cup, box, etc.*) boîte *f* ‖ *v* (*pret & pp* **tinned**; *ger* **tinning**) *tr* étamer; (*to can*) (Brit) mettre en boîte

tin′can′ *s* boîte *f* en fer-blanc, boîte de conserve

tincture [′tɪŋktʃər] *s* teinture *f*

tin′ cup′ *s* timbale *f*

tinder [′tɪndər] *s* amadou *m*

tin′der·box′ *s* briquet *m* à amadou; (fig) foyer *m* de l'effervescence

tin′ foil′ *s* feuille *f* d'étain, papier *m* d'argent

ting-a-ling [ˈtɪŋəˌlɪŋ] *s* drelin *m*

tinge [tɪndʒ] *s* teinte *f*, nuance *f* ‖ *v* (*ger* **tingeing** or **tinging**) *tr* teinter, nuancer

tingle [ˈtɪŋɡəl] *s* picotement *m*, fourmillement *m* ‖ *intr* picoter, fourmiller; (*e.g.*, *with enthusiasm*) tressaillir

tin' hat' *s* (coll) casque *m* en acier

tinker [ˈtɪŋkər] *s* chaudronnier *m* ambulant; (*bungler*) bousilleur *m* ‖ *intr* bricoler; **to tinker with** tripatouiller

tinkle [ˈtɪŋkəl] *s* tintement *m* ‖ *tr* faire tinter ‖ *intr* tinter

tin' plate' *s* fer-blanc *m*

tin'-plate' *tr* étamer

tin' roof' *s* toit *m* de fer-blanc

tinsel [ˈtɪnsəl] *s* clinquant *m*; (*for a Christmas tree*) paillettes *fpl*, guirlandes *fpl* clinquantes

tin'smith' *s* ferblantier *m*

tin' sol'dier *s* soldat *m* de plomb

tint [tɪnt] *s* teinte *f* ‖ *tr* teinter

tin'type' *s* ferrotypie *f*

tin'ware' *s* ferblanterie *f*

ti·ny [ˈtaɪni] *adj* (*comp* **-nier**; *super* **-niest**) minuscule

tip [tɪp] *s* (*end*) bout *m*, pointe *f*; (*slant*) inclinaison *f*; (*fee to a waiter*) pourboire *m*; (*secret information*) (slang) tuyau *m* ‖ *v* (*pret & pp* **tipped**; *ger* **tipping**) *tr* incliner; (*the scales*) faire pencher; (*a waiter*) donner un pourboire à, donner la pièce à; **to tip off** (slang) tuyauter; **to tip over** renverser ‖ *intr* se renverser; donner un pourboire

tip'cart' *s* tombereau *m*

tip'-in' *s* (bb) hors-texte *m*

tip'-off' *s* (coll) tuyau *m*

tipped'-in' *adj* (bb) hors texte

tipple [ˈtɪpəl] *intr* biberonner

tip'staff' *s* verge *f* d'huissier; huissier *m* à verge

tip·sy [ˈtɪpsi] *adj* (*comp* **-sier**; *super* **-siest**) gris, grisé

tip'toe' *s* pointe *f* des pieds ‖ *v* (*pret & pp* **-toed**; *ger* **toeing**) *intr* marcher sur la pointe des pieds

tirade [ˈtaɪred] *s* diatribe *f*

tire [taɪr] *s* pneu *m* ‖ *tr* fatiguer ‖ *intr* se fatiguer

tire' chain' *s* chaîne *f* antidérapante

tired [taɪrd] *adj* fatigué, las

tire' gauge' *s* manomètre *m*

tire' i'ron *s* démonte-pneu *m*

tireless [ˈtaɪrlɪs] *adj* infatigable

tire' pres'sure *s* pression *f* des pneus

tire' pump' *s* gonfleur *m* pour pneus

tiresome [ˈtaɪrsəm] *adj* fatigant, ennuyeux

tissue [ˈtɪsju] *s* (*thin paper*) papier *m* de soie; (*toilet tissue*) papier hygiénique; (*paper handkerchief*) mouchoir *m* en papier; (tex) tissu *m*, étoffe *f*; (*web, mesh*) (fig) tissu, enchevêtrement *m*

tis'sue pa'per *s* papier *m* de soie

tit [tɪt] *s* téton *m*; (orn) mésange *f*; **tit for tat** à bon chat bon rat

titanium [taɪˈteni·əm] *s* titane *m*

tithe [taɪð] *s* dixième *m*; (rel) dîme *f* ‖ *tr* soumettre à la dîme; payer la dîme sur

Titian [ˈtɪʃən] *s* le Titien *m*

Ti'tian red' *s* blond *m* vénitien

title [ˈtaɪtəl] *s* titre *m*; (*of an automobile*) carte *f* grise ‖ *tr* intituler

ti'tle deed' *s* titre *m* de propriété

ti'tle·hold'er *s* tenant *m* du titre

ti'tle page' *s* page *f* de titre

ti'tle role' *s* rôle *m* principal

tit'mouse' *s* (*pl* **-mice**) (orn) mésange *f*

titter [ˈtɪtər] *s* rire *m* étouffé ‖ *intr* rire en catimini

titular [ˈtɪtʃələr] *adj* titulaire

to [tu], [tʊ], [tə] *adv*—**to and fro** de long en large ‖ *prep* à; (*towards*) vers; (*in order to*) afin de, pour; envers, pour, e.g., **good to her** bon envers elle, bon pour elle; jusqu'à, e.g., **to this day** jusqu'à ce jour; e.g., **to count to a hundred** compter jusqu'à cent; moins, e.g., **a quarter to eight** huit heures moins le quart; contre, e.g., **seven to one** sept contre un; dans, e.g., **to a certain extent** dans une certaine mesure; en, e.g., **from door to door** de porte en porte; de, e.g., **I am going to France** je vais en France; de, e.g., **to try to** + *inf* essayer de + *inf*; **to him** lui §87

toad [tod] *s* crapaud *m*

toad'stool' *s* agaric *m*; champignon *m* vénéneux

to-and-fro [ˈtu·əndˈfro] *adj* de va-et-vient

toast [tost] *s* pain *m* grillé; (*with a drink*) toast *m* ‖ *tr* griller; porter un toast à, boire à la santé de

toaster [ˈtostər] *s* grille-pain *m*

toast'er ov'en *s* grille-pain-four *m*

toast'mas'ter *s* préposé *m* aux toasts

tobac·co [təˈbæko] *s* (*pl* **-cos**) tabac *m*

tobac'co pouch' *s* blague *f*

toboggan [təˈbɑɡən] *s* toboggan *m*

tocsin [ˈtɑksɪn] *s* tocsin *m*; (*bell*) cloche *f* qui sonne le tocsin

today [tuˈde] *s & adv* aujourd'hui *m*

toddle [ˈtɑdəl] *s* allure *f* chancelante ‖ *intr* marcher à petits pas chancelants

toddler [ˈtɑdlər] *s* tout-petit *m*

tod·dy [ˈtɑdi] *s* (*pl* **-dies**) grog *m*

to-do [təˈdu] *s* (*pl* **-dos**) embarras *mpl*, chichis *mpl*, façons *fpl*

toe [to] *s* doigt *m* du pied, orteil *m*; (*of shoe, of stocking*) bout *m* ‖ *v* (*pret & pp* **toed**; *ger* **toeing**) *tr*—**to toe the line** or **the mark** s'aligner, se mettre au pas

toe'nail' *s* ongle *m* du pied

tog [tɑg] *v* (*pret & pp* **togged**; *ger* **togging**) *tr*—**to tog out** or **up** attifer, fringuer ‖ **togs** *spl* fringues *fpl*

together [tuˈɡɛðər] *adv* ensemble; (*at the same time*) en même temps, à la fois

tog'gle switch' [ˈtɑgəl] *s* (elec) interrupteur *m* à culbuteur or à bascule

toil [tɔɪl] *s* travail *m* dur; **toils** filet *m*, piège *m* ‖ *intr* travailler dur

toilet [ˈtɔɪlɪt] *s* toilette *f*; (*rest room*) cabinet *m* de toilette

toi′let ar′ticles *spl* objets *mpl* de toilette

toi′let bowl′ *s* cuvette *f*

toi′let pa′per *s* papier *m* hygiénique

toi′let seat′ *s* siège *m* des toilettes, abattant *m*

toi′let set′ *s* nécessaire *m* de toilette

toi′let soap′ *s* savonnette *f*

toi′let wa′ter *s* eaux *fpl* de toilette

token [′tokən] *adj* symbolique ‖ *s* (*symbol*) signe *m*, marque *f*; (*keepsake*) souvenir *m*; (*used as money*) jeton *m*; **by the same token** de plus; **in token of** en témoignage de

tolerance [′talərəns] *s* tolérance *f*

tolerate [′talə,ret] *tr* tolérer

toll [tol] *s* (*of bells*) glas *m*; (*payment*) droit *m* de passage, péage *m*; (*number of victims*) mortalité *f*; (telp) tarif *m* ‖ *tr* tinter; (*to ring the knell for*) sonner le glas de ‖ *intr* sonner le glas

toll′ bridge′ *s* pont *m* à péage

toll′ call′ *s* appel *m* interurbain

toll′ gate′ *s* barrière *f* à péage

toll′ road′ *s* autoroute *f* à péage

toma·to [tə′meto], [tə′mato] *s* (*pl* **-toes**) tomate *f*

tomb [tum] *s* tombeau *m*

tomboy [′tam,bɔɪ] *s* garçon *m* manqué

tomb′stone′ *s* pierre *f* tombale

tomcat [′tam,kæt] *s* matou *m*

tome [tom] *s* tome *m*

tomorrow [tʊ′mɔro] *adj*, *s*, & *adv* demain *m*; **tomorrow morning** demain matin; **until tomorrow** à demain

tom-tom [′tam,tam] *s* tam-tam *m*

ton [tʌv] *s* tonne *f*

tone [ton] *s* ton *m* ‖ *tr* accorder; **to tone down** atténuer; **to tone up** renforcer; (*e.g., the muscles*) tonifier ‖ *intr*—**to tone down** se modérer

tone′ po′em *s* poème *m* symphonique

tone′ tel′ephone *s* téléphone *m* à clavier

tongs [tɔŋz] *spl* pincettes *fpl*; (*e.g., for sugar*) pince *f*; (*of blacksmith*) tenailles *fpl*

tongue [tʌŋ] *s* (*language; part of body*) langue *f*; (*of wagon*) timon *m*; (*of buckle*) ardillon *m*; (*of shoe*) languette *f*; (*neck or narrow strip of land*) langue de terre; **to hold one's tongue** se mordre la langue

tongue-tied [′tʌŋ,taɪd] *adj* bouche cousue

tongue′ twist′er *s* phrase *f* à décrocher la mâchoire, casse-langue *m invar*

tonic [′tanɪk] *adj* & *s* tonique *m*

tonight [tʊ′naɪt] *adj* & *s* ce soir

tonsil [′tansəl] *s* amygdale *f*

tonsillitis [,tansɪ′laɪtɪs] *s* amygdalite *f*

ton·y [′toni] *adj* (*comp* **-ier**; *super* **-iest**) (slang) élégant, chic

too [tu] *adv* (*also*) aussi; (*more than enough*) trop; (*moreover*) d'ailleurs; **I did too!** mais si!; **too bad!** c'est dommage!; **too many, too much** trop, trop de

tool [tul] *s* outil *m* ‖ *tr* (*a piece of metal*) usiner; (*leather*) repousser; (bb) dorer ‖ *intr*—**to tool along** rouler; **to tool up** s'outiller

tool′box′ *s* trousse *f* à outils

tool′mak′er *s* taillandier *m*

toot [tut] *s* (*sound of tooting*) son *m* du cor; (*of auto*) coup *m* de klaxon; (*of locomotive*) coup de sifflet ‖ *tr* sonner ‖ *intr* corner; (aut) klaxonner

tooth [tuθ] *s* (*pl* **teeth** [tiθ]) dent *f*; **to grit, grind,** or **gnash the teeth** grincer des dents, crisser des dents

tooth′ache′ *s* mal *m* de dents

tooth′brush′ *s* brosse *f* à dents

toothless [′tuθlɪs] *adj* édenté

tooth′paste′ *s* pâte *f* dentifrice

tooth′pick′ *s* cure-dent *m*

tooth′ pow′der *s* poudre *f* dentifrice

top [tap] *adj* premier, de tête ‖ *s* sommet *m*, cime *f*, faîte *m*; (*of a barrel, table, etc.*) dessus *m*; (*of a page*) haut *m*; (*of a box*) couvercle *m*; (*of a carriage or auto*) capote *f*; (*toy*) toupie *f*; (naut) hune *f*; **at the top of** en haut de; (*e.g., one's class*) à la tête de; **at the top of one's voice** à tue-tête; **from top to bottom** de haut en bas, de fond en comble; **on top of** sur; (*in addition to*) en plus de; **top** (*e.g., of carrots*) fanes *fpl*; **to sleep like a top** dormir comme un sabot ‖ *v* (*pret & pp* **topped**; *ger* **topping**) *tr* couronner, surmonter; (*to surpass*) dépasser; (*a tree, plant, etc.*) écimer

topaz [′topæz] *s* topaze *f*

top′ bill′ing *s* tête *f* d'affiche

top′coat′ *s* surtout *m* de demi-saison

toper [′topər] *s* soiffard *m*

top′ hat′ *s* haut-de-forme *m*

top′-heav′y *adj* trop lourd du haut

topic [′tapɪk] *s* sujet *m*

top′knot′ *s* chignon *m*

top′less swim′suit *s* monokini *m*

top′mast′ *s* mât *m* de hune

top′most′ *adj* (le) plus haut

top′notch′ *adj* (coll) d'élite

top′-of-the-line′ *adj* haut de gamme

topography [tə′pagrəfi] *s* (*pl* **-phies**) topographie *f*

topple [′tapəl] *tr* & *intr* culbuter

top′ prior′ity *s* priorité *f* absolue, priorité numéro un

topsail [′tapsəl], [′tap,sel] *s* (naut) hunier *m*

top′-se′cret *adj* ultra-secret

top′soil′ *s* couche *f* arable

topsy-turvy [′tapsi′tʌrvi] *adj* & *adv* sens dessus dessous

torch [tɔrtʃ] *s* torche *f*, flambeau *m*; (Brit) lampe *f* torche; **to carry the torch for** (slang) avoir un amour sans retour pour

torch′bear′er *s* porte-flambeau *m*; (fig) défenseur *m*

torch′light′ *s* lueur *f* des flambeaux

torch′light proces′sion *s* défilé *m* aux flambeaux

torch′ song′ *s* chanson *f* de l'amour non partagé

torment [′tɔrmɛnt] *s* tourment *m* ‖ [tɔr′mɛnt] *tr* tourmenter

torna·do [tɔr′nedo] *s* (*pl* **-does** or **-dos**) tornade *f*

torpe·do [tɔr′pido] *s* (*pl* **-does**) torpille *f* ‖ *tr* torpiller

torpe'do-boat destroy'er *s* contre-torpil-leur *m*

torpid ['tɔrpɪd] *adj* engourdi

torque [tɔrk] *s* effort *m* de torsion, couple *m* de torsion

torrent ['tɔrənt] *s* torrent *m*

torrid ['tɔrɪd] *adj* torride

tor·so ['tɔrso] *s* (*pl* **-sos**) torse *m*

tort [tɔrt] *s* (law) acte *m* dommageable sauf rupture de contrat ou abus de confiance

tortoise ['tɔrtəs] *s* tortue *f*

tor'toise shell' *s* écaille *f*

torture ['tɔrʃər] *s* torture *f* ‖ *tr* torturer

toss [tɔs] *s* (*throw*) lancement *m*; (*of the head*) mouvement *m* dédaigneux ‖ *tr* lancer; (*one's head*) relever dédaigneusement; (*a rider*) démonter; (*a coin*) jouer à pile et face avec; **to toss about** agiter, ballotter; **to toss off** (*e.g., work*) expédier; (*in one gulp*) lamper; **to toss up** jeter en l'air ‖ *intr* s'agiter; **to toss and turn** se tourner et retourner

toss'up' *s* (*flip of a coin*) (coll) coup *m* de pile ou face; (*fifty-fifty chance*) (coll) chances *fpl* égales

tot [tɑt] *s* bambin *m*, tout petit *m* ‖ *v* (*pret & pp* **totted**; *ger* **totting**) *tr*—**to tot up** additionner

to·tal ['totəl] *adj & s* total *m*; **as a total** au total ‖ *v* (*pret & pp* **-taled** or **-talled**; *ger* **-taling** or **-talling**) *tr* additionner, totaliser; (*to amount to*) s'élever à

totalitarian [to,tælɪ'tɛrɪ·ən] *adj & mf* totalitaire

totem ['totəm] *s* totem *m*

totter ['tɑtər] *intr* chanceler

touch [tʌtʃ] *s* (*act*) attouchement *m*; (*e.g., of color; with a brush*) touche *f*; (*sense; of pianist*) toucher *m*; (*of typist*) frappe *f*; (*little bit*) pointe *f*, brin *m*; **in touch** in communication; **to get in touch with** prendre contact avec ‖ *tr* toucher; (*for a loan*) (slang) taper; **to touch off** déclencher; **to touch up** retoucher ‖ *intr* se toucher; **to touch on** toucher à

touched *adj* touché; (*crazy*) timbré

touching ['tʌtʃɪŋ] *adj* touchant, émouvant ‖ *prep* touchant, concernant

touch·y ['tʌtʃi] *adj* (*comp* **-ier**; *super* **-iest**) susceptible, irritable

tough [tʌf] *adj* dur, coriace; (*tenacious*) résistant; (*task*) difficile ‖ *s* voyou *m*

toughen ['tʌfən] *tr* endurcir ‖ *intr* s'endurcir

tough' luck' *s* déveine *f*

tour [tur] *s* tour *m*; (*e.g., of inspection*) tournée *f*; **on tour** en tournée ‖ *tr* faire le tour de; (*e.g., a country*) voyager en; (theat) faire une tournée de, en, or dans ‖ *intr* voyager

tour'ing car' *s* voiture *f* de tourisme

tourist ['turɪst] *adj & s* touriste *mf*

tour'ist in'dustry *s* tourisme *m*

tournament ['turnəmənt], ['tʌrnəmənt] *s* tournoi *m*

tourney ['turni] *s* tournoi *m* ‖ *intr* tournoyer

tourniquet ['turnɪ,kɛt] *s* (surg) garrot *m*, tourniquet *m*

tousle ['tauzəl] *tr* (*to dishevel*) ébouriffer; (*to handle roughly*) tirailler, maltraiter

tow [to] *s* (*towing*) remorque *f*; (*e.g., of hemp*) filasse *f*; **to take in tow** prendre en remorque; (fig) se charger de ‖ *tr* remorquer

towage ['to·ɪdʒ] *s* remorquage *m*; (*fee*) droits *mpl* de remorquage

toward(s) [tord(z)], [tə'wɔrd(z)] *prep* vers; (*in regard to*) envers

tow'boat' *s* remorqueur *m*

tow·el ['tau·əl] *s* serviette *f*, essuie-main *m* ‖ *v* (*pret & pp* **-eled** or **-elled**; *ger* **-eling** or **elling**) *tr* essuyer avec une serviette

tow'el rack' *s* porte-serviettes *m*

tower ['tau·ər] *s* tour *f* ‖ *intr* s'élever

towering ['tau·ərɪŋ] *adj* élevé, géant; (*e.g., ambition*) sans bornes

tow'er·man *s* (*pl* **-men**) (aer, rr) aiguilleur *m*

tow'ing serv'ice ['to·ɪŋ] *s* service *m* de dépannage

tow'line' *s* câble *m* de remorque

town [taun] *s* ville *f*; **in town** en ville

town' clerk' *s* secrétaire *m* de mairie

town' coun'cil *s* conseil *m* municipal

town' cri'er *s* crieur *m* public

town' hall' *s* hôtel *m* de ville

town' plan'ning *s* urbanisme *m*

towns'folk' *spl* citadins *mpl*

town'ship *s* commune *f*; (U.S.A.) circonscription *f* administrative de six milles carrée

towns'man ['taunzmən] *s* (*pl* **-men**) citadin *m*

towns'peo'ple *spl* citadins *mpl*

town' talk' *s* sujet *m* du jour

tow'path' *s* chemin *m* de halage

tow'rope' *s* corde *f* de remorque

tow' truck' *s* dépanneuse *f*, voiture *f* de dépannage, camion *m* de remorquage

toxic ['tɑksɪk] *adj & s* toxique *m*

toy [tɔɪ] *adj* (*small*) petit; (*child's*) d'enfant ‖ *s* jouet *m*; (*trifle*) bagatelle *f* ‖ *intr* jouer, s'amuser; **to toy with** (*a person*) badiner avec; (*an idea*) caresser

toy' dog' *s* chien *m* de manchon

toy' sol'dier *s* soldat *m* de plomb

trace [tres] *s* trace *f*; (*of harness*) trait *m* ‖ *tr* tracer; (*the whereabouts of s.o. or s.th.*) pister; (*e.g., an influence*) retrouver les traces de; (*a design seen through thin paper*) calquer; **to trace back** remonter jusqu'à l'origine de

trace' el'ement *s* oligo-élément *m*

tracer ['tresər] *s* traceur *m*

trac'er bul'let *s* balle *f* traçante

trache·a ['trekɪ·ə] *s* (*pl* **-ae** [,i]) trachée *f*

tracing ['tresɪŋ] *s* tracé *m*

trac'ing tape' *s* cordeau *m*

track [træk] *s* (*of foot or vehicle*) trace *f*; (*of an animal; in a stadium*) piste *f*; (*of a boat*) sillage *m*; (*of a railroad*) voie *f*; (*of an airplane, of a hurricane*) trajet *m*; (*of a tractor*) chenille *f*; (*course followed*) chemin *m* tracé; (sports) la course et le saut de barrières; (sports) athlétisme *m*; **off the beaten track** hors des sentiers battus; **on the right track** sur la bonne voie; **to be on the wrong track** faire fausse route; **to have an inside track** tenir la corde; **to keep track of** ne pas perdre de vue; **to make tracks** (coll) filer ‖ *tr* traquer; laisser des traces de pas dans; **to track down** dépister

tracking [ˈtrækɪŋ] *s* pistage *m*; (*of spaceship*) repérage *m*; (aer) poursuite *f*

track'ing sta'tion *s* poste *m* de repérage

track'less trol'ley *s* trolleybus *m*

track' meet' *s* concours *m* de courses et de sauts, épreuve *f* d'athlétisme

track'walk'er *s* garde-voie *m*

tract [trækt] *s* (*of land*) étendue *f*; (*leaflet*) tract *m*; (anat) voie *f*

traction [ˈtrækʃən] *s* traction *f*

trac'tion com'pany *s* entreprise *f* de transports urbains

tractor [ˈtræktər] *s* tracteur *m*

trade [tred] *s* (*business*) commerce *m*, négoce *m*; (*customers*) clientèle *f*; (*calling, job*) métier *m*; (*exchange*) échange *m*; (*in slaves*) traite *f*; **to take in trade** reprendre en compte ‖ *tr* échanger; **to trade in** (*e.g., a used car*) donner en reprise ‖ *intr* commercer; **to trade in** faire le commerce de; **to trade on** exploiter

trade'-in' *s* reprise *f*

trade'mark *s* marque *f* déposée

trade' name' *s* raison *f* sociale

trader [ˈtredər] *s* commerçant *m*

trade' school' *s* école *f* des arts et métiers

trade' show' *s* exposition *f* interprofessionnelle

trades'man *s* (*pl* **-men**) commerçant *m*; (*shopkeeper*) boutiquier *m*; (Brit) artisan *m*

trades' un'ion or **trade' un'ion** *s* syndicat *m* ouvrier

trade' winds' *spl* vents *mpl* alizés

trad'ing post' [ˈtredɪŋ] *s* factorerie *f*

trad'ing stamp' *s* timbre-prime *m*

tradition [trəˈdɪʃən] *s* tradition *f*

traditional [trəˈdɪʃənəl] *adj* traditionnel

traf-fic [ˈtræfɪk] *s* (*commerce*) négoce *m*; (*in the street*) circulation *f*; (*illegal*) trafic *m*; (*in, e.g, slaves*) traite *f*; (naut, rr) trafic ‖ *v* (*pret & pp* **-ficked**; *ger* **-ficking**) *intr* trafiquer

traf'fic cir'cle *s* rond-point *m*

traf'fic cop' *s* agent *m* de la circulation

traf'fic court' *s* tribunal *m* de simple police (pour les contraventions au code de la route)

traf'fic jam' *s* embouteillage *m*

traf'fic light' *s* feu *m* de circulation

traf'fic sign' *s* panneau *m* de signalisation, poteau *m* indicateur

traf'fic sig'nal *s* signal *m* routier

traf'fic tick'et *s* contravention *f*

traf'fic vi'olator *s* contrevenant *m*

tragedian [trəˈdʒidɪ·ən] *s* tragédien *m*

trage·dy [ˈtrædʒɪdi] *s* (*pl* **-dies**) tragédie *f*

tragic [ˈtrædʒɪk] *adj* tragique

trail [trel] *s* trace *f*, piste *f*; (*e.g., of smoke*) traînée *f* ‖ *tr* traîner; (*to look for*) pister ‖ *intr* traîner; (*said of a plant*) grimper; **to trail off** se perdre

trailer [ˈtrelər] *s* remorque *f*; (*for vacationing*) remorque de plaisance, caravane *f*; (mov) film-annonce *m*

trail'er court' *s* camp *m* pour caravanes

trail'er home' *s* caravane *f*

train [tren] *s* (*of railway cars*) train *m*; (*of dress*) traîne *f*; (*of thought*) enchaînement *m*; (*streak*) traînée *f* ‖ *tr* entraîner, former; (*plants*) palisser; (*a gun; a telescope*) pointer ‖ *intr* s'entraîner

train' crew' *s* (rr) personnel de route

trained' an'imals *spl* animaux *mpl* savants

trained' nurse' *s* infirmière *f* diplômée

trainee [treˈni] *s* stagiaire *mf*, apprenti *m*

trainer [ˈtrenər] *s* (*of animals*) dresseur *m*; (sports) entraîneur *m*

training [ˈtrenɪŋ] *s* entraînement *m*, formation *f*, instruction *f*; (*of animals*) dressage *m*

train'ing school' *s* école *f* technique; (*reformatory*) maison *f* de correction

train'ing ship' *s* navire-école *m*

trait [tret] *s* trait *m*

traitor [ˈtretər] *s* traître *m*

traitress [ˈtretrɪs] *s* traîtresse *f*

trajecto·ry [trəˈdʒɛktəri] *s* (*pl* **-ries**) trajectoire *f*

tramp [træmp] *s* (*hobo*) vagabond *m*; (*sound of steps*) bruit *m* de pas lourds ‖ *tr* parcourir à pied; (*the street*) battre ‖ *intr* vagabonder; marcher lourdement; **to tramp on** marcher sur

trample [ˈtræmpəl] *tr* fouler, piétiner ‖ *intr*—**to trample on** or **upon** fouler, piétiner

trampoline [ˈtræmpə,lin] *s* tremplin *m* de gymnase

tramp' steam'er *s* tramp *m*

trance [træns] *s* transe *f*; **in a trance** en transe

tranquil [ˈtræŋkwɪl] *adj* tranquille

tranquilize [ˈtræŋkwɪ,laɪz] *tr* tranquilliser

tranquilizer [ˈtræŋkwɪ,laɪzər] *s* tranquillisant *m*

tranquillity [trænˈkwɪlɪti] *s* tranquillité *f*

transact [trænˈzækt] *tr* traiter, négocier ‖ *intr* faire des affaires

transaction [trænˈzækʃən] *s* transaction *f*; (*of business*) conduite *f*; **transactions** (*of a society*) actes *mpl*

transatlantic [,trænsətˈlæntɪk] *adj & s* transatlantique *m*

transcend [trænˈsɛnd] *tr* transcender ‖ *intr* se transcender

transcribe [trænˈskraɪb] *tr* transcrire

transcript [ˈtrænskrɪpt] *s* copie *f*; (*of a meeting*) procès-verbal *m*; (educ) livret *m* scolaire

transcription [trænˈskrɪpʃən] *s* transcription *f*

transept [ˈtrænsɛpt] *s* transept *m*

trans·fer [ˈtrænsfər] *s* (*e.g., of stock, property, etc.*) transfert *m*; (*from one place to the other*) translation *f*; (*from one job to* *the other*) mutation *f*; (*of a design*) décalque *m*; (*for bus or subway*) billet *m* de correspondance; (*public sign*) correspondance ‖ [træns'fʌr], ['trænsfər] *v* (*pret & pp* **-ferred**; *ger* **-ferring**) *tr* transférer; transporter; (*e.g., a civil servant*) déplacer; (*a design*) décalquer ‖ *intr* se déplacer; changer de train (de l'autobus, etc.)

transfix [træns'fɪks] *tr* transpercer

transform [træns'fɔrm] *tr* transformer ‖ *intr* se transformer

transformer [træns'fɔrmər] *s* transformateur *m*

transfusion [træns'fjuʒən] *s* transfusion *f*

transgress [træns'grɛs] *tr & intr* transgresser

transgression [træns'grɛʃən] *s* transgression *f*

transient ['trænʃənt] *adj* transitoire, passager; (*e.g., guest*) de passage ‖ *s* hôte *mf* de passage

transistor [træn'sɪstər] *s* transistor *m*

transistorize [træn'zɪstə,raɪz] *tr* transistoriser

transistorized *adj* transistorisé, à transistors

transit ['trænsɪt], ['trænzɪt] *s* transit *m*

transition [træn'zɪʃən] *s* transition *f*

transitional [træn'zɪʃənəl] *adj* transitoire, de transition

transitive ['trænsɪtɪv] *adj* transitif ‖ *s* verbe *m* transitif

transitory ['trænsɪ,tori] *adj* transitoire

translate ['trænslet] *tr* traduire

translation [træns'leʃən] *s* traduction *f*; (*transfer*) translation *f*

translator [træns'letər] *s* traducteur *m*

transliterate [træns'lɪtə,ret] *tr* translitérer

translucent [træns'lusənt] *adj* translucide, diaphane

transmission [træns'mɪʃən] *s* transmission *f*; (*gear change*) changement *m* de vitesse; (*housing for gears*) boîte *f* de vitesses

transmis'sion-gear' box' *s* boîte *f* de vitesses

trans·mit [træns'mɪt] *v* (*pret & pp* **-mitted**; *ger* **-mitting**) *tr & intr* transmettre; (*rad*) émettre

transmitter [træns'mɪtər] *s* (telg, telp) transmetteur *m*; (rad) émetteur *m*

transmit'ting sta'tion *s* poste *m* émetteur

transmute [træns'mjut] *tr* transmuer

transom ['trænsəm] *s* (*crosspiece*) linteau *m*; (*window over door*) imposte *f*, vasistas *m*; (*of ship*) barre *f* d'arcasse

transparen·cy [træns'pɛrənsi] *s* (*pl* **-cies**) transparence *f*; (phot) diapositive *f*

transparent [træns'pɛrənt] *adj* transparent

transpire [træns'paɪr] *intr* se passer; (*to leak out*) transpirer

transplant ['træns,plænt] *s* (*organ or tissue*) greffon *m*; (*operation*) greffe *f* ‖ [træns'plænt] *tr* transplanter; (*e.g., a heart*) greffer

transport ['trænsport] *s* transport *m* ‖ [træns'port] *tr* transporter

transportation [,trænspor'teʃən] *s* transport *m*; billet *m* de train, de bateau, or d'avion; (*deportation*) transportation *f*

transport'er bridge' [træns'portər] *s* transbordeur *m*

trans'port work'er *s* employé *m* des entreprises de transport

transpose [træns'poz] *tr* transposer

trans·ship [træns'ʃɪp] *v* (*pret & pp* **-shipped**; *ger* **-shipping**) *tr* transborder

transshipment [træns'ʃɪpmənt] *s* transbordement *m*

transvestism [træns'vɛstɪzəm] *s* travestisme *m*

transvestite [træns'vɛstaɪt] *s* travesti *m*, travestie *f*

trap [træp] *s* piège *m*; (*pitfall*) trappe *f*; (*double-curved pipe*) siphon *m*; **traps** (mus) batterie *f* de jazz ‖ *v* (*pret & pp* **trapped**; *ger* **trapping**) *tr* prendre au piège, attraper

trap' door' *s* trappe *f*

trapeze [trə'piz] *s* trapèze *m*

trapezoid ['træpɪ,zɔɪd] *s* trapèze *m*

trapper ['træpər] *s* trappeur *m*

trappings ['træpɪŋz] *spl* (*adornments*) atours *mpl*; (*of horse's harness*) harnachement *m*

trap'shoot'ing *s* tir *m* au pigeon

trash [træʃ] *s* déchets *mpl*, rebuts *mpl*; (*junk*) camelote *f*; (*nonsense*) ineptie *f*; (*worthless people*) racaille *f*

trash' bag' *s* sac *m* poubelle

trash' can' *s* poubelle *f*

travail [trə'vel] *s* labeur *m*; douleur *f* de l'enfantement

trav·el ['trævəl] *s* voyages *mpl*; (mach) course *f* ‖ *v* (*pret & pp* **-eled** or **-elled**; *ger* **-eling** or **-elling**) *tr* parcourir ‖ *intr* voyager; (mach) se déplacer

trav'el bur'eau *s* agence *f* de voyages

traveler ['trævələr] *s* voyageur *m*

trav'eler's check' *s* chèque *m* de voyage

trav'eling bag' *s* sac *m* de voyage

trav'eling expen'ses *spl* frais *mpl* de voyage

trav'eling sales'man *s* (*pl* **-men**) commis *m* voyageur

traverse [trə'vʌrs] *tr* parcourir, traverser

traves·ty ['trævɪsti] *s* (*pl* **-ties**) travestissement *m* ‖ *v* (*pret & pp* **-tied**) *tr* travestir

trawl [trɔl] *s* chalut *m* ‖ *tr* traîner ‖ *intr* pêcher au chalut

trawler ['trɔlər] *s* chalutier *m*

tray [tre] *s* plateau *m*; (*of refrigerator*) bac *f*; (chem, phot) cuvette *f*

treacherous ['trɛtʃərəs] *adj* traître

treacher·y ['trɛtʃəri] *s* (*pl* **-ies**) trahison *f*

tread [trɛd] *s* (*step; sound of steps*) pas *m*; (*gait*) allure *f*; (*of stairs*) giron *m*; (*of tire*) chape *f*; (*of shoe*) semelle *f*; (*of egg*) cicatricule *f* ‖ *v* (*pret* **trod** [trɑd]; *pp* **trodden** ['trɑdən] or **trod**) *tr* marcher sur, piétiner ‖ *intr* marcher

treadle ['trɛdəl] *s* pédale *f*

tread'mill' *s* trépigneuse *f*; (*futile drudgery*) besogne *f* ingrate

treason ['trizən] *s* trahison *f*

treasonable ['trizənəbəl] *adj* traître

treasure ['trɛʒər] *s* trésor *m* ‖ *tr* garder soigneusement; (*to prize*) tenir beaucoup à

treasurer ['trɛʒərər] *s* trésorier *m*

treasur·y ['trɛʒəri] *s* (*pl* **-ies**) trésorerie *f;* trésor *m*

treat [trit] *s* régal *m*, plaisir *m* ‖ *tr* traiter; régaler; (*to a drink*) payer à boire à; **to treat everyone to a round of drinks** offrir la tournée générale ‖ *intr* traiter

treatise ['tritɪs] *s* traité *m*

treatment ['tritmənt] *s* traitement *m*

trea·ty ['triti] *s* (*pl* **-ties**) traité *m*

treble ['trɛbəl] *adj* (*threefold*) triple; (mus) de soprano ‖ *s* soprano *mf;* (*voice*) soprano *m* ‖ *tr & intr* tripler

tre′ble clef′ [klɛf] *s* clef *f* de sol

tree [tri] *s* arbre *m*

tree′ farm′ *s* taillis *m*

treeless ['trilɪs] *adj* sans arbres

tree′top′ *s* cime *f* d'un arbre

trellis ['trɛlɪs] *s* treillis *m*, treillage *m;* (*summerhouse*) tonnelle *f* ‖ *tr* treillager

tremble ['trɛmbəl] *s* tremblement *m* ‖ *intr* trembler

tremendous [trɪ'mɛndəs] *adj* terrible; (coll) formidable

tremolo ['trɛmə,lo] *s* trémolo *m*

tremor ['trɛmər] *s* tremblement *m*

trench [trɛntʃ] *s* tranché *f*

trenchant ['trɛntʃənt] *adj* tranchant

trench′ mor′tar *s* lance-bombes *m*

trend [trɛnd] *s* tendance *f*, cours *m*

trendy ['trɛndi] *adj* dernier cri, dans le vent, à la dernière mode

trespass ['trɛspəs] *s* (*illegal entry*) entrée *f* sans permission; (rel) offense *f* ‖ *intr* entrer sans permission; **no trespassing** (*public sign*) défense d'entrer; **to trespass against** offenser; **to trespass on** empiéter sur; (*s.o.'s patience*) abuser de

trespasser ['trɛspəsər] *s* intrus *m*

tress [trɛs] *s* tresse *f;* **tresses** chevelure *f*

trestle ['trɛsəl] *s* tréteau *m;* (*bridge*) pont *m* en treillis

trial ['traɪ·əl] *s* essai *m;* (*difficulty*) épreuve *f;* (law) procès *m;* **on trial** à titre d'essai; (law) en jugement; **to bring to trial** faire passer en jugement

tri′al and er′ror *s*—**by trial and error** par tâtonnements

tri′al balloon′ *s* ballon *m* d'essai

tri′al by jur′y *s* jugement *m* par jury

tri′al ju′ry *s* jury *m* de jugement

tri′al or′der *s* commande *f* d'essai

tri′al run′ *s* course *f* d'essai

triangle ['traɪ,æŋgəl] *s* triangle *m*

tribe [traɪb] *s* tribu *f*

tribunal [trɪ'bjunəl] *s* tribunal *m*

tribune ['trɪbjun] *s* tribune *f*

tributar·y ['trɪbjə,tɛri] *adj* tributaire ‖ *s* (*pl* **-ies**) tributaire *m*

tribute ['trɪbjut] *s* (*homage; payment*) tribut *m;* **to pay tribute to** (*e.g., merit*) rendre hommage à

trice [traɪs] *s*—**in a trice** en un clin d'œil

trichinosis [,trɪkə'nosɪs] *s* (pathol) trichinose *f*

trick [trɪk] *s* (*prank, joke*) tour *m*, farce *f*, blague *f;* (*artifice*) ruse *f;* (*cards in one round*) levée *f;* (*habit*) manie *f;* (*girl*) (coll) belle *f;* **to be up to one's old tricks again** faire encore des siennes; **to play a dirty trick on** faire un vilain tour à, faire un tour de cochon à; **tricks of the trade** trucs *mpl* du métier ‖ *tr* duper

tricker·y ['trɪkəri] *s* (*pl* **-ies**) tromperie *f*

trickle ['trɪkəl] *s* filet *m* ‖ *intr* dégoutter

trickster ['trɪkstər] *s* fourbe *mf*

trick·y ['trɪki] *adj* (*comp* **-ier;** *super* **-iest**) rusé; (*difficult*) compliqué, délicat

tricolor ['traɪ,kʌlər] *adj & s* tricolore *m*

tried [traɪd] *adj* loyal, éprouvé

trifle ['traɪfəl] *s* bagatelle *f,* (*article of little value*) bricole *f* ‖ *tr*—**to trifle away** gaspiller ‖ *intr* badiner

trifling ['traɪflɪŋ] *adj* frivole; insignifiant

trifocals [traɪ'fokəlz] *spl* lunettes *fpl* à trois foyers

trigger ['trɪgər] *s* (*of gun*) détente *f;* (*of any device*) déclencheur *m;* **to pull the trigger** appuyer sur la détente ‖ *tr* déclencher

trig′ger-hap′py *adj*—**to be trigger-happy** (coll) avoir la gâchette facile

trigonometry [,trɪgə'nɑmɪtri] *s* trigonométrie *f*

trill [trɪl] *s* trille *m* ‖ *tr & intr* triller

trillion ['trɪljən] *s* (U.S.A.) billion *m;* (Brit) trillion *m*

trilo·gy ['trɪlədʒi] *s* (*pl* **-gies**) trilogie *f*

trim [trɪm] *adj* (*comp* **trimmer;** *super* **trimmest**) ordonné, coquet ‖ *s* (*condition*) état *m;* (*adornment*) ornement *m;* (*of sails*) orientation *f;* (*around doors and windows*) moulures *fpl;* **in good trim** (sports) en bonne forme ‖ *v* (*pret & pp* **trimmed;** *ger* **trimming**) *tr* enguirlander; (*a Christmas tree*) orner; (*hat, dress, etc.*) garnir; (*the hair*) rafraîchir; (*a candle or lamp*) moucher; (*trees, plants*) tailler; (*the edges of a book*) rogner; (*the sails*) orienter; (coll) battre

trimming ['trɪmɪŋ] *s* (*of clothes, hat, etc.*) garniture *f;* (*of hedges*) taille *f;* (*of sails*) orientation *f;* **to get a trimming** (coll) essuyer une défaite

trini·ty ['trɪnɪti] *s* (*pl* **-ties**) trinité *f;* **Trinity** Trinité

trinket ['trɪŋkɪt] *s* colifichet *m;* (*trifle*) babiole *f*

tri·o ['tri·o] *s* (*pl* **-os**) trio *m*

trip [trɪp] *s* (*journey*) voyage *m;* (*distance covered*) trajet *m*, parcours *m;* (*stumble; blunder*) faux pas *m;* (*act of causing a person to stumble*) croc-en-jambe *m;* (*on drugs*) (slang) trip *m*, défonce *f* ‖ *v* (*pret & pp* **tripped;** *ger* **tripping**) *tr* faire trébucher; **to trip up** donner un croc-en-jambe à; prendre en défaut ‖ *intr* trébucher

tripartite [traɪ'partaɪt] *adj* tripartite

tripe [traɪp] *s* tripe *f;* (slang) fatras *m*

trip′ham′mer *s* marteau *m* à bascule

triple ['trɪpəl] *adj* & *s* triple *m* ‖ *tr* & *intr* tripler

triplet ['trɪplɪt] *s* (*offspring*) triplet *m*; (*stanza*) tercet *m*; (*mus*) triolet *m*; **triplets** (*offspring*) triplés *mpl*

triplicate ['trɪplɪkɪt] *adj* triple ‖ *s* triplicata *m*; **in triplicate** en trois exemplaires

tripod ['traɪpɑd] *s* trépied *m*

triptych ['trɪptɪk] *s* triptyque *m*

trite [traɪt] *adj* banal, rebattu

triumph ['traɪ·əmf] *s* triomphe *m* ‖ *intr* triompher; **to triumph over** triompher de

trium'phal arch' [traɪ'ʌmfəl] *s* arc *m* de triomphe

triumphant [traɪ'ʌmfənt] *adj* triomphant

trivia ['trɪvɪ·ə] *spl* vétilles *fpl*

trivial ['trɪvɪ·əl] *adj* trivial, insignifiant

triviali·ty [,trɪvɪ'ælɪti] *s* (*pl* -**ties**) trivialité *f*, insignifiance *f*

Trojan ['trodʒən] *adj* troyen ‖ *s* Troyen *m*

Tro'jan Horse' *s* cheval *m* de Troie

Tro'jan war' *s* guerre *f* de Troie

troll [trol] *tr* & *intr* pêcher à la cuiller

trolley ['trɑli] *s* trolley *m*; (*streetcar*) tramway *m*

trol'ley car' *s* tramway *m*

trol'ley pole' *s* perche *f*

trolling ['trolɪŋ] *s* pêche *f* à la cuiller

trollop ['trɑləp] *s* souillon *f*; (*prostitute*) traînée *f*

trombone ['trɑmbon] *s* trombone *m*

troop [trup] *s* troupe *f*; **troops** (mil) troupes *fpl* ‖ *tr* (*the colors*) présenter ‖ *intr* s'attrouper

trooper ['trupər] *s* membre *m* de la police montée; (*state trooper*) agent *m* de police; (mil) soldat *m* de cavalerie; **to swear like a trooper** jurer comme un charretier

tro·phy ['trofi] *s* (*pl* -**phies**) trophée *m*; (sports) coupe *f*

tropic ['trɑpɪk] *adj* & *s* tropique *m*; **tropics** tropiques, zone *f* tropicale

tropical ['trɑpɪkəl] *adj* tropical

trot [trɑt] *s* trot *m* ‖ *v* (*pret* & *pp* **trotted**; *ger* **trotting**) *tr* faire trotter; **to trot out** (slang) exhiber ‖ *intr* trotter

troth [troθ] *s* foi *f*; **in troth** en vérité; **to plight one's troth** promettre fidélité; donner sa promesse de mariage

trouble ['trʌbəl] *s* (*unpleasantness*) ennuis *mpl*, dérangement *m*; (*problem*) difficulté *f*, problème *m*; (*bother*, *effort*) mal *m*, peine *f*; (*social unrest*) troubles *mpl*; **that's not worth the trouble** cela ne vaut pas la peine; **that's the trouble** voilà le hic; **the trouble is that . . .** la difficulté c'est que . . . ; **to be in trouble** avoir des ennuis; (*said of a woman*) (coll) faire Pâques avant les Rameaux; **to be looking for trouble** chercher querelle; **to get into trouble** se créer des ennuis, s'attirer une mauvaise affaire; **to take the trouble to** se donner la peine de; **with very little trouble** à peu de frais ‖ *tr* (*to disturb*) déranger; (*to grieve*) affliger; **to be troubled about** se tourmenter au sujet de; **to trouble oneself** s'inquiéter ‖ *intr* se dé-

ranger; **to trouble to** se donner la peine de

trou'ble light' *s* lampe *f* de secours

trou'ble·mak'er *s* fomentateur *m*, perturbateur *m*

troubleshooter ['trʌbəl,ʃutər] *s* dépanneur *m*; (*in disputes*) arbitre *m*

trou'ble·shoot'ing *s* dépannage *m*; (*of disputes*) composition *f*, arbitrage *m*

troublesome ['trʌbəlsəm] *adj* ennuyeux

trou'ble spot' *s* foyer *m* de conflit

trough [trɔf] *s* (*e.g.*, *to knead bread*) pétrin *m*; (*for water for animals*) abreuvoir *m*; (*for feeding animals*) auge *f*; (*under the eaves*) chéneau *m*; (*between two waves*) creux *m*

troupe [trup] *s* troupe *f*

trouper ['trupər] *s* membre *m* de la troupe; vieil acteur *m*; vieux routier *m*

trousers ['trauzərz] *spl* pantalon *m*

trous·seau [tru'so], ['truso] *s* (*pl* -**seaux** or -**seaus**) trousseau *m*

trout [traut] *s* truite *f*

trowel ['trau·əl] *s* truelle *f*; (*for gardening*) déplantoir *m*

Troy [trɔɪ] *s* Troie *f*

truant ['tru·ənt] *s*—**to play truant** faire l'école buissonnière

truce [trus] *s* trêve *f*

truck [trʌk] *s* camion *m*, poids *m* lourd; (*for baggage*) diable *m*; (*vegetables*) produits *mpl* maraîchers; **to have no truck with** (coll) refuser d'avoir affaire à ‖ *tr* camionner

truck'driv'er *s* camionneur *m*

truck' farm'ing *s* culture *f* maraîchère

truck' gar'den *s* jardin *m* maraîcher

trucking ['trʌkɪŋ] *s* camionnage *m*

truculent ['trʌkjələnt] *adj* truculent

trudge [trʌdʒ] *intr* cheminer

true [tru] *adj* vrai; loyal; (*exact*) juste; (*copy*) conforme; **to come true** se réaliser ‖ *tr* rectifier, dégauchir

true' cop'y *s* (*pl* -**ies**) copie *f* conforme

true'-heart'ed *adj* au cœur sincère

true'love *s* bien-aimé *m*

truffle ['trʌfəl] *s* truffe *f*

truism ['tru·ɪzm] *s* truisme *m*

truly ['truli] *adv* vraiment; sincèrement; **yours truly** (complimentary close) veuillez agréer, Monsieur (Madame, etc.), l'assurance de mes sentiments distingués

trump [trʌmp] *s* atout *m*; brave garçon *m*, brave fille *f*; **no trump** sans atout ‖ *tr* couper; **to trump up** inventer ‖ *intr* couper

trumpet ['trʌmpɪt] *s* trompette *f* ‖ *tr* & *intr* trompeter

trumpeter ['trʌmpətər] *s* trompette *m*

truncheon ['trʌntʃən] *s* matraque *f*; (*of policeman*) bâton *m*

trunk [trʌŋk] *s* (*chest for clothes*) malle *f*; (*of elephant*) trompe *f*; (anat, bot) tronc *m*; (aut) coffre *m*; **trunks** slip *m*

truss [trʌs] *s* (*framework*) armature *f*; (med) bandage *m* herniaire ‖ *tr* armer; (culin) trousser

trust [trʌst] s confiance f; (*hope*) espoir m; (*duty*) charge f; (*safekeeping*) dépôt m; (com) trust m, cartel m ‖ tr se fier à; (*to entrust*) confier; (com) faire crédit à ‖ intr espérer; **to trust in** avoir confiance en
trust′ com′pany s crédit m, société f de banque
trustee [trʌs′ti] s administrateur m; (*of a university*) régent m; (*of an estate*) fidéicommissaire mf
trusteeship [trʌs′tiʃɪp] s tutelle f
trustful [′trʌstfəl] adj confiant
trust′wor′thy adj digne de confiance
trust·y [′trʌsti] adj (comp **-ier**; super **-iest**) sûr, loyal ‖ s (pl **-ies**) forçat m bien noté
truth [truθ] s vérité f; **in truth** en vérité
truthful [′truθfəl] adj véridique
try [traɪ] s (pl **tries**) essai m ‖ v (pret & pp **tried**) tr mettre à l'épreuve; (law) juger; **to try on** or **out** essayer ‖ intr essayer; **to try to** essayer de
trying [′traɪ·ɪŋ] adj pénible
tryst [trɪst], [traɪst] s rendez-vous m
T′-shirt′ s gilet m de peau avec manches
tub [tʌb] s cuvier m, baquet m; (*clumsy boat*) (coll) rafiot m
tube [t(j)ub] s tube m; (aut) chambre f à air; (*subway*) (Brit) métro m
tuber [′t(j)ubər] s tubercule m
tubercle [′t(j)ubərkəl] s tubercule m
tuberculosis [t(j)u,bʌrkjə′losɪs] s tuberculose f
tuck [tʌk] s pli m, rempli m ‖ tr plisser, remplier; **to tuck away** reléguer; **to tuck in** rentrer; **to tuck in bed** border; **to tuck up** retrousser
tucker [′tʌkər] tr—**to tucker out** (coll) fatiguer
Tuesday [′t(j)uzdi] s mardi m
tuft [tʌft] s touffe f ‖ tr garnir de touffes ‖ intr former une touffe
tug [tʌg] s tiraillement m, effort m; (*boat*) remorqueur m ‖ v (pret & pp **tugged**; ger **tugging**) tr tirer fort; (*a boat*) remorquer ‖ intr tirer fort
tug′boat′ s remorqueur m
tug′ of war′ s lutte f à la corde (de traction)
tuition [t(j)u′ɪʃən] s enseignement m; (*fees*) frais mpl de scolarité
tulip [′t(j)ulɪp] s tulipe f
tumble [′tʌmbəl] s chute f; (sports) culbute f ‖ tr culbuter ‖ intr tomber, culbuter; (sports) faire des culbutes; (*to catch on*) (slang) comprendre; **to tumble down** dégringoler
tum·ble·down′ adj croulant, délabré
tumbler [′tʌmblər] s gobelet m, verre m; acrobate m; (*self-righting toy*) poussah m, ramponneau m
tummy [′tʌmi] s (coll) bide f
tumor [′t(j)umər] s tumeur f
tumult [′t(j)umʌlt] s tumulte m
tun [tʌn] s tonne f
tuna [′tunə] s thon m
tune [t(j)un] s air m; (*manner of acting or speaking*) ton m; **in tune** (mus) accordé; (rad) en syntonie; **out of tune** (mus) dés-

accordé; **to change one's tune** (coll) changer de disque ‖ tr accorder; (*a radio or television set*) régler; **to tune in** (rad) syntoniser; **to tune up** régler
tungsten [′tʌŋstən] s tungstène m
tunic [′t(j)unɪk] s tunique f
tuning [′t(j)unɪŋ] s réglage m; (rad) syntonisation f
tun′ing coil′ s bobine f de syntonisation
tun′ing fork′ s diapason m
tun·nel [′tʌnəl] s tunnel m; (min) galerie f ‖ v (pret & pp **-neled** or **nelled**; ger **-neling** or **-nelling**) tr percer un tunnel dans or sous
turban [′tʌrbən] s turban m
turbid [′tʌrbɪd] adj trouble
turbine [′tʌrbɪn] s turbine f
turbojet [′tʌrbo,dʒɛt] s turboréacteur m; avion m à turboréacteur
turboprop [′tʌrbo,prɑp] s turbopropulseur m; avion m à turbopropulseur
turbosupercharger [′tʌrbo′supər′tʃɑrdʒər] s turbocompresseur m de suralimentation
turbulent [′tʌrbjələnt] adj turbulent
tureen [t(j)u′rin] s soupière f
turf [tʌrf] s gazon m; (*sod*) motte f de gazon; (*peat*) tourbe f; **the turf** le turf
turf′man s (pl **-men**) turfiste mf
Turk [tʌrk] s Turc m
turkey [′tʌrki] s dindon m; (culin) dinde f; (*flop*) (slang) four m; **Turkey** Turquie f, la Turquie
tur′key vul′ture s urubu m
Turkish [′tʌrkɪʃ] adj & s turc m
Turk′ish delight′ s loukoum m
Turk′ish tow′el s serviette f éponge
turmoil [′tʌrmɔɪl] s agitation f
turn [tʌrn] s tour m; (*change of direction*) virage m; (*bend*) tournant m; (*of events; of an expression*) tournure f; (*in a wire*) spire f; (coll) coup m, choc m; **at every turn** à tout propos; **by turns** tour à tour; **in turn** à tour de rôle; **to a turn** (culin) à point; **to do a good turn** rendre un service; **to take turns** alterner; **to wait one's turn** prendre son tour; **whose turn is it?** à qui le tour? ‖ tr tourner; **to turn about** or **around** retourner; **to turn aside** or **away** détourner; **to turn back** renvoyer; (*an attack*) repousser; (*a clock*) retarder; **to turn down** (*a collar*) rabattre; (*e.g., the gas*) baisser; (*an offer*) refuser; **to turn from** détourner de; **to turn in** replier; (*a wrongdoer*) dénoncer; **to turn into** changer en; **to turn off** (*the water, the gas, etc.*) fermer; (*the light, the radio, etc.*) éteindre; (*a road*) quitter; **to turn on** (*the water, the gas, etc.*) ouvrir; (*the light, the radio, the gas, etc.*) allumer; **to turn out** mettre dehors; (*to manufacture*) produire; (*e.g., the light*) éteindre; **to turn over and over** tourner et retourner; **to turn up** (*a collar*) relever; (*one's sleeves*) retrousser; (*to unearth*) déterrer ‖ intr tourner, se tourner; (*said of milk*) tourner; (*to toss and turn*) se retourner; (*to be dizzy*) tourner, e.g., **his head is turning**

la tête lui tourne; **to turn about** or **around** se retourner, se tourner; **to turn aside** or **away** se détourner; **to turn back** rebrousser chemin; **to turn down** se rabattre; **to turn in** (coll) aller se coucher; **to turn into** tourner à or en; **to turn on** se jeter sur; (*to depend on*) dépendre de; **to turn out to be** se trouver être; **to turn out well** tourner bien; **to turn over** se retourner; (*said of auto*) capoter; **to turn up** (*to increase*) se relever; (*to appear*) se présenter, arriver

turn′coat′ *s* transfuge *m*

turn′down′ *adj* rabattu || *s* refus *m*

turn′ing point′ *s* moment *m* décisif

turnip [′tʌrnɪp] *s* navet *m*; (*big watch*) (slang) bassinoire *f*; (slang) tête *f* de bois

turn′key′ *s* geôlier *m*

turn′ of life′ *s* retour *m* d'âge

turn′ of mind′ *s* inclination *f* naturelle

turn′out′ *s* (*gathering*) assistance *f*; (*output*) rendement *m*; (*equipment*) attelage *m*

turn′o′ver *s* renversement *m*; (com) chiffre *m* d'affaires

turn′pike′ *s* autoroute *f* à péage

turn′pike res′taurants *spl* ponts *mpl* restaurants

turn′spit′ *s* tournebroche *m*

turnstile [′tʌrn‚staɪl] *s* tourniquet *m*

turn′stone′ *s* (orn) tourne-pierre *m*

turn′ta′ble *s* (*of phonograph*) plateau *m* porte-disque; (rr) plaque *f* tournante

turpentine [′tʌrpən‚taɪn] *s* térébenthine *f*

turpitude [′tʌrpɪ‚t(j)ud] *s* turpitude *f*

turquoise [′tʌrkɔɪz] *s* turquoise *f*

turret [′tʌrɪt] *s* tourelle *f*

turreted *adj* en poivrière

turtle [′tʌrtəl] *s* tortue *f*

tur′tle·dove′ *s* tourterelle *f*

tur′tle·neck′ *s* col *m* roulé

tur′tle·neck sweat′er *s* sweater *m* or chandail *m* à col roulé

Tuscan [′tʌskən] *adj* & *s* toscan *m*

Tuscany [′tʌskəni] *s* Toscane *f*; la Toscane

tusk [tʌsk] *s* défense *f*

tussle [′tʌsəl] *s* bagarre *f* || *intr* se bagarrer

tutor [′t(j)utər] *s* précepteur *m*, répétiteur *m* || *tr* donner des leçons particulières à || *intr* donner des leçons particulières

tuxe·do [tʌk′sido] *s* (*pl* **-dos**) smoking *m*

TV [′ti′vi] *s* (letterword) (**television**) tévé *f*, télé *f*

T′V′ din′ner *s* plateau-repas *m* congelé

twaddle [′twɑdəl] *s* fadaises *fpl* || *intr* dire des fadaises

twang [twæŋ] *s* (*of musical instrument*) son *m* vibrant; (*of voice*) ton *m* nasillard || *tr* faire résonner; dire en nasillant || *intr* nasiller

twang·y [′twæŋi] *adj* (*comp* **-ier**; *super* **-iest**) (*nasal*) nasillard; (*resonant*) vibrant

tweed [twid] *s* tweed *m*

tweet [twit] *s* pépiement *m* || *intr* pépier

tweeter [′twitər] *s* (rad) tweeter *m*

tweezers [′twizərz] *spl* brucelles *fpl*; pince *f* à épiler

twelfth [twɛlfθ] *adj* & *pron* douzième (*masc, fem*); **the Twelfth** douze, e.g., **John the Twelfth** Jean douze || *s* douzième *m*; **the twelfth** (*in dates*) le douze

twelve [twɛlv] *adj* & *pron* douze; **about twelve** une douzaine de || *s* douze *m*; **twelve o'clock** (*noon*) midi *m*; (*midnight*) minuit *m*

twentieth [′twɛntɪ·ɪθ] *adj* & *pron* vingtième (*masc, fem*); **the Twentieth** vingt, e.g., **John the Twentieth** Jean vingt || *s* vingt *m*; **the twentieth** (*in dates*) le vingt

twen·ty [′twɛnti] *adj* & *pron* vingt; **about twenty** une vingtaine de || *s* (*pl* **-ties**) vingt *m*; **the twenties** les années *fpl* vingt

twen′ty-first′ *adj* & *pron* vingt et unième (*masc, fem*); **the Twenty-first** vingt et un, e.g., **John the Twenty-first** Jean vingt et un || *s* vingt et unième *m*; **the twenty-first** (*in dates*) le vingt et un

twen′ty-one′ *adj* & *pron* vingt et un || *s* vingt et un *m*; (cards) vingt-et-un

twen′ty-sec′ond *adj* & *pron* vingt-deuxième (*masc, fem*); **the Twenty-second** vingt-deux, e.g., **John the Twenty-second** Jean vingt-deux || *s* vingt-deuxième *m*; **the twenty-second** (*in dates*) le vingt-deux

twen′ty-two′ *adj, pron,* & *s* vingt-deux *m*

twice [twaɪs] *adv* deux fois; **twice over** à deux reprises

twiddle [′twɪdəl] *tr* tourner, jouer avec; (*e.g., one's moustache*) tortiller

twig [twɪg] *s* brindille *f*

twilight [′twaɪ‚laɪt] *adj* crépusculaire || *s* crépuscule *m*

twill [twɪl] *s* croisé *m* || *tr* croiser

twin [twɪn] *adj* & *s* jumeau *m* || *v* (*pret & pp* **twinned**; *ger* **twinning**) *tr* jumeler

twin′ beds′ *spl* lits *mpl* jumeaux

twine [twaɪn] *s* ficelle *f* || *tr* enrouler || *intr* s'enrouler

twinge [twɪndʒ] *s* élancement *m* || *intr* élancer

twin′jet′ plane′ *s* biréacteur *m*

twinkle [′twɪŋkəl] *s* scintillement *m*; (*of the eye*) clignotement *m* || *intr* scintiller; clignoter

twin′-screw′ *adj* à hélices jumelles

twirl [twʌrl] *s* tournoiement *m* || *tr* faire tournoyer; (*e.g., a cane*) faire des moulinets avec || *intr* tournoyer

twist [twɪst] *s* (*action*) torsion *f*; (*strand*) cordon *m*; (*of the wrist, of rope, etc.*) tour *m*; (*of the road, river, etc.*) coude *m*; (*of tobacco*) rouleau *m*; (*of the ankle*) entorse *f*; (*of mind or disposition*) prédisposition *f* || *tr* tordre, tortiller || *intr* se tordre, se tortiller; **to twist and turn** (*said, e.g., of road*) serpenter; (*said of sleeper*) se tourner et se retourner

twister [′twɪstər] *s* (coll) tornade *f*

twit [twɪt] *v* (*pret & pp* **twitted**; *ger* **twitting**) *tr* taquiner

twitch [twɪtʃ] *s* crispation *f* || *intr* se crisper

twitter [′twɪtər] *s* gazouillement *m* || *intr* gazouiller

two [tu] *adj & pron* deux ‖ *s* deux *m*; **to put two and two together** raisonner juste; **two o'clock** deux heures
two'-cy'cle *adj* (mach) à deux temps
two'-cyl'inder *adj* (mach) à deux cylindres
two'-edged' *adj* à deux tranchants
two' hun'dred *adj, pron, & s* deux cents *m*
twosome ['tusəm] *s* paire *f*; jeu *m* à deux joueurs
two'-time' *tr* (slang) tromper
tycoon [taɪ'kun] *s* (coll) magnat *m*
type [taɪp] *s* type *m* ‖ *tr* typer; (*to typewrite*) taper; (*a sample of blood*) chercher le groupe sanguin sur ‖ *intr* taper
type'face' *s* œil *m*
type'script' *s* manuscrit *m* dactylographié
typesetter ['taɪp,sɛtər] *s* compositeur *m*, typographe *mf*; machine *f* à composer
type'write' *v* (*pret* -**wrote**; *pp* -**written**) *tr & intr* taper à la machine

type'writ'er *s* machine *f* à écrire
type'writer rib'bon *s* ruban *m* encreur
type'writ'ing *s* dactylographie *f*
ty'phoid fe'ver ['taɪfɔɪd] *s* fièvre *f* typhoïde
typhoon [taɪ'fun] *s* typhon *m*
typical ['tɪpɪkəl] *adj* typique
typi-fy ['tɪpɪ,faɪ] *v* (*pret & pp* -**fied**) *tr* symboliser; être le type de
typ'ing er'ror *s* faute *f* de frappe
typist ['taɪpɪst] *s* dactylo *f*
typographic(al) [,taɪpə'græfɪk(əl)] *adj* typographique
typograph'ical er'ror *s* erreur *f* typographique
typography [taɪ'pɑgrəfi] *s* typographie *f*
tyrannic(al) [tɪ'rænɪk(əl)] *adj* tyrannique
tyran-ny ['tɪrəni] *s* (*pl* -**nies**) tyrannie *f*
tyrant ['taɪrənt] *s* tyran *m*
ty-ro ['taɪro] *s* (*pl* -**ros**) novice *mf*

U

U, u [ju] *s* XXIᵉ lettre de l'alphabet
ubiquitous [ju'bɪkwɪtəs] *adj* ubiquiste, omniprésent
udder ['ʌdər] *s* pis *m*
UFO ['ju'ɛf'o] *s* (letterword) (**unidentified flying object**) O.V.N.I. (objet volant nonidentifié)
UFOlogy [ju'fɑlədzi] *s* étude *f* des ovnis
ugliness ['ʌglɪnɪs] *s* laideur *f*
ug-ly ['ʌgli] *adj* (*comp* -**lier**; *super* -**liest**) laid; (*disagreeable; mean*) vilain
Ukraine ['jukren], [ju'kren] *s* Ukraine *f*; l'Ukraine
Ukrainian [ju'kreni·ən] *adj* ukrainien ‖ *s* (*language*) ukrainien *m*; (*person*) Ukrainien *m*
ulcer ['ʌlsər] *s* ulcère *m*
ulcerate ['ʌlsə,ret] *tr* ulcérer ‖ *intr* s'ulcérer
ulterior [ʌl'tɪrɪ·ər] *adj* ultérieur; secret, inavoué
ultimate ['ʌltɪmɪt] *adj* ultime, final, définitif
ultima·tum [,ʌltɪ'metəm] *s* (*pl* -**tums** or -**ta** [tə]) ultimatum *m*
ultrashort [,ʌltrə'ʃɔrt] *adj* (electron) ultracourt
ultraviolet [,ʌltrə'vaɪ·əlɪt] *adj & s* ultraviolet *m*
ul'travi'olet light' *s* lumière *f* ultraviolette
umbil'ical cord' [ʌm'bɪlɪkəl] *s* cordon *m* ombilical
umbrage ['ʌmbrɪdʒ] *s*—**to take umbrage at** prendre ombrage de
umbrella [ʌm'brɛlə] *s* parapluie *m*; (mil) ombrelle *f* de protection
umbrel'la stand' *s* porte-parapluies *m*
umlaut ['umlaut] *s* métaphonie *f*, inflexion *f* vocalique; (*mark*) tréma *m* ‖ *tr* changer le timbre de; écrire avec un tréma

umpire ['ʌmpaɪr] *s* arbitre *m*, juge *m* arbitre ‖ *tr & intr* arbitrer
UN ['ju'ɛn] (letterword) (**United Nations**) ONU *f*
unable [ʌn'ebəl] *adj* incapable; **to be unable to** être incapable de
unabridged [,ʌnə'brɪdʒd] *adj* intégral
unaccented [,ʌnæk'sɛntɪd] *adj* inaccentué
unacceptable [,ʌnək'sɛptəbəl] *adj* inacceptable, irrecevable
unaccountable [,ʌnə'kaʊntəbəl] *adj* inexplicable; irresponsable
unaccounted-for [,ʌnə'kaʊntɪd,fɔr] *adj* inexpliqué, pas retrouvé
unaccustomed [,ʌnə'kʌstəmd] *adj* inaccoutumé
unafraid [,ʌnə'fred] *adj* sans peur
unaligned [,ʌnə'laɪnd] *adj* non-engagé
unanimity [,junə'nɪmɪti] *s* unanimité *f*
unanimous [ju'nænɪməs] *adj* unanime
unanswerable [ʌn'ænsərəbəl] *adj* incontestable, sans réplique; (*argument*) irréfutable
unappreciative [,ʌnə'priʃɪ,etɪv] *adj* ingrat, peu reconnaissant
unapproachable [,ʌnə'protʃəbəl] *adj* inabordable; (fig) incomparable
unarmed [ʌn'ɑrmd] *adj* sans armes
unascertainable [ʌn,æsər'tenəbəl] *adj* non vérifiable
unasked [ʌn'æskt] *adj* non invité; **to do s.th. unasked** faire q.ch. spontanément
unassembled [,ʌnə'sɛmbəld] *adj* démonté
unassuming [,ʌnə's(j)umɪŋ] *adj* modeste, sans prétentions
unattached [,ʌnə'tætʃt] *adj* indépendant; (*loose*) détaché; (*not engaged to be married*) seul; (mil, nav) en disponibilité

unattainable [‚ʌnə'tenəbəl] *adj* inaccessible

unattractive [‚ʌnə'træktıv] *adj* peu attrayant, peu séduisant

unavailable [‚ʌnə'veləbəl] *adj* non disponible

unavailing [‚ʌnə'velıŋ] *adj* inutile

unavoidable [‚ʌnə'vɔıdəbəl] *adj* inévitable

unaware [‚ʌnə'wɛr] *adj* ignorant; **to be unaware of** ignorer ‖ *adv* à l'improviste; à mon (son, etc.) insu

unawares [‚ʌnə'wɛrz] *adv* (*unexpectedly*) à l'improviste; (*unknowingly*) à mon (son, etc.) insu

unbalanced [ʌn'bælənst] *adj* non équilibré; (*mind*) déséquilibré; (*bank account*) non soldé

unbandage [ʌn'bændıdʒ] *tr* débander

un·bar [ʌn'bar] *v* (*pret & pp* **-barred;** *ger* **-barring**) *tr* débarrer

unbearable [ʌn'bɛrəbəl] *adj* insupportable, imbuvable

unbeatable [ʌn'bitəbəl] *adj* imbattable

unbecoming [‚ʌnbı'kʌmıŋ] *adj* déplacé, inconvenant; (*dress*) peu seyant

unbelievable [‚ʌnbı'livəbəl] *adj* incroyable

unbeliever [‚ʌbnı'livər] *s* incroyant *m*

unbending [ʌn'bɛndıŋ] *adj* inflexible

unbiased [ʌn'baı·əst] *adj* impartial

un·bind [ʌn'baınd] *v* (*pret & pp* **-bound**) *tr* délier

unbleached [ʌn'blitʃt] *adj* écru

unbolt [ʌn'bolt] *tr* (*a gun; a door*) déverrouiller; (*a machine*) déboulonner

unborn [ʌn'bɔrn] *adj* à naître, futur

unbosom [ʌn'buzəm] *tr* découvrir; **to unbosom oneself** ouvrir son cœur

unbound [ʌn'baund] *adj* non relié

unbreakable [ʌn'brekəbəl] *adj* incassable; (*e.g., glasses*) impact résistant

unbroken [ʌn'brokən] *adj* intact; ininterrompu; (*spirit*) indompté; (*horse*) non rompu

unbuckle [ʌn'bʌkəl] *tr* déboucler

unburden [ʌn'bʌrdən] *tr* alléger; **to unburden oneself of** se soulager de

unburied [ʌn'bɛrid] *adj* non enseveli

unbutton [ʌn'bʌtən] *tr* déboutonner

uncalled-for [ʌn'kɔld‚fɔr] *adj* déplacé; (*e.g., insult*) gratuit

uncanny [ʌn'kæni] *adj* inquiétant, mystérieux; rare, remarquable

uncared-for [ʌn'kɛrd‚fɔr] *adj* négligé; peu soignée

unceasing [ʌn'sisıŋ] *adj* incessant

unceremonious [‚ʌnsɛrı'moni·əs] *adj* sans façon

uncertain [ʌn'sʌrtən] *adj* incertain

uncertain·ty [ʌn'sʌrtənti] *s* (*pl* **-ties**) incertitude *f*

unchain [ʌn'tʃen] *tr* désenchaîner

unchangeable [ʌn'tʃendʒəbəl] *adj* immuable

uncharted [ʌn'tʃartıd] *adj* inexploré

unchecked [ʌn'tʃɛkt] *adj* sans frein, non contenu; non vérifié

uncivilized [ʌn'sıvı‚laızd] *adj* incivilisé

unclad [ʌn'klæd] *adj* déshabillé

unclaimed [ʌn'klemd] *adj* non réclamé; (*mail*) au rebut

unclasp [ʌn'klæsp] *tr* dégrafer; (*one's hands*) desserrer

unclassified [ʌn'klæsı‚faıd] *adj* non classé; (*documents, information, etc.*) pas secret

uncle ['ʌŋkəl] *s* oncle *m*

unclean [ʌn'klin] *adj* sale, immonde

un·clog [ʌn'klag] *v* (*pret & pp* **-clogged;** *ger* **-clogging**) *tr* dégager, désobstruer

unclouded [ʌn'klaudıd] *adj* clair, dégagé

uncollectible [‚ʌnkə'lɛktıbəl] *adj* irrécouvrable

uncomfortable [ʌn'kʌmfərtəbəl] *adj* (*causing discomfort*) inconfortable; (*feeling discomfort*) mal à l'aise

uncommitted [‚ʌnkə'mıtıd] *adj* non-engagé

uncommon [ʌn'kamən] *adj* peu commun

uncompromising [ʌn'kamprə‚maızıŋ] *adj* intransigeant

unconcerned [‚ʌnkən'sʌrnd] *adj* indifférent

unconditional [‚ʌnkən'dıʃənəl] *adj* inconditionnel

uncongenial [‚ʌnkən'dʒini·əl] *adj* peu sympathique; incompatible; désagréable

unconquerable [ʌn'kaŋkərəbəl] *adj* invincible

unconquered [ʌn'kaŋkərd] *adj* invaincu, indompté

unconscious [ʌn'kanʃəs] *adj* inconscient; (*temporarily deprived of consciousness*) sans connaissance ‖ *s*—**the unconscious** l'inconscient *m*

unconsciousness [ʌn'kanʃəsnıs] *s* inconscience *f*; perte *f* de connaissance, évanouissement *m*

unconstitutional [‚ʌnkanstı't(j)uʃənəl] *adj* inconstitutionnel

uncontrollable [‚ʌnkən'troləbəl] *adj* ingouvernable; (*e.g., desires*) irrésistible; (*e.g., laughter*) inextinguible

unconventional [‚ʌnkən'vɛnʃənəl] *adj* original, peu conventionnel; (*person*) non-conformiste

uncork [ʌn'kɔrk] *tr* déboucher

uncouple [ʌn'kʌpəl] *tr* désaccoupler

uncouth [ʌn'kuθ] *adj* gauche, sauvage; (*language*) grossier

uncover [ʌn'kʌvər] *tr* découvrir

unction ['ʌŋkʃən] *s* onction *f*

unctuous ['ʌŋktʃu·əs] *adj* onctueux

uncultivated [ʌn'kʌltı‚vetıd] *adj* inculte

uncultured [ʌn'kʌltʃərd] *adj* inculte, sans culture

uncut [ʌn'kʌt] *adj* non coupé; (*stone, diamond*) brut; (*crops*) sur pied; (*book*) non rogné

undamaged [ʌn'dæmıdʒd] *adj* indemne

undaunted [ʌn'dɔntıd] *adj* pas découragé; sans peur

undecided [‚ʌndı'saıdıd] *adj* indécis

undefeated [‚ʌndı'fitıd] *adj* invaincu

undefended [‚ʌndı'fɛndıd] *adj* sans défense

undefiled [‚ʌndı'faıld] *adj* sans tache

undeniable [‚ʌndı'naı·əbəl] *adj* indéniable

under [`ʌndər] *adj* (*lower*) inférieur; (*underneath*) de dessous ‖ *adv* dessous; **to go under** sombrer; **to keep under** tenir dans la soumission ‖ *prep* sous, au-dessous de, dessous; moins de, e.g., **under forty** moins de quarante ans; dans, e.g., **under the circumstances** dans les circonstances; en, e.g., **under treatment** en traitement; e.g., **under repair** en voie de réparation; à, e.g., **under the microscope** au microscope; e.g., **under examination** à l'examen; e.g., **under the terms of** aux termes de; e.g., **under the word** (*in dictionary*) au mot; **to serve under** servir sous les ordres de

un'der·age' *adj* mineur

un'der·arm pad' *s* dessous-de-bras *m*

un'der·bid' *v* (*pret & pp* -bid; *ger* -bidding) *tr* offrir moins que

un'der·brush' *s* broussailles *fpl*

un'der·car'riage *s* (aer) train *m* d'atterrissage; (aut) dessous *m*

un'der·clothes' *spl* sous-vêtements *mpl*

un'der·consump'tion *s* sous-consommation *f*

un'der·cov'er *adj* secret

un'der·cur'rent *s* courant *m* de fond; (fig) vague *f* de fond

un'der·devel'oped *adj* sous-développé

un'der·dog' *s* opprimé *m*; (sports) parti *m* non favori, outsider *m*

underdone [`ʌndər,dʌn] *adj* pas assez cuit

un'der·es'timate *tr* sous-estimer

un'der·gar'ment *s* sous-vêtement *m*

un'der·go' *v* (*pret* -went; *pp* -gone) *tr* subir, éprouver, souffrir

un'der·grad'uate *adj & s* non diplômé *m*

un'der·ground' *adj* souterrain; (fig) clandestin ‖ *s* (*subway*) métro *m*; (pol) résistance *f*, maquis *m* ‖ *adv* sous terre; **to go underground** (fig) entrer dans la clandestinité, prendre le maquis

un'der·growth' *s* sous-bois *m*; (*underbrush*) broussailles *fpl*

un'der·hand'ed *adj* sournois, dissimulé

un'der·line' or un'der·line' *tr* souligner

underling [`ʌndərlɪŋ] *s* sous-ordre *m*, sous-fifre *m*

un'der·mine' *tr* miner, saper

underneath [,ʌndər`niθ] *adj* de dessous; (*lower*) inférieur ‖ *s* dessous *m* ‖ *adv* dessous, en dessous ‖ *prep* sous, au-dessous de

un'der·nour'ished *adj* sous-alimenté

un'der·nour'ishment *s* sous-alimentation *f*

underpaid [,ʌndər`ped] *adj* mal rétribué

un'der·pass' *s* passage *m* souterrain

un'der·pin' *v* (*pret & pp* -pinned; *ger* -pinning) *tr* étayer

un'der·priv'ileged *adj* déshérité, défavorisé, déshérité; (econ) économiquement faible

un'der·rate' *tr* sous-estimer

un'der·score' *tr* souligner

un'der·sea' *adj* sous-marin ‖ un'der·sea' *adv* sous la surface de la mer

un'der·sec'retar'y *s* (*pl* -ies) sous-secrétaire *m*

un'der·sell' *v* (*pret & pp* -sold) *tr* vendre à meilleur marché que; (*for less than the actual value*) solder

un'der·shirt' *s* gilet *m*, maillot *m* de corps, tricot *m* de corps, tricot de peau

un'der·signed' *adj* soussigné

un'der·skirt' *s* jupon *m*

un'der·stand' *v* (*pret & pp* -stood) *tr & intr* comprendre, entendre

understandable [,ʌndər`stændəbəl] *adj* compréhensible; **that's understandable** cela se comprend

un'der·stand'ing *adj* compréhensif ‖ *s* compréhension *f*; (*intellectual faculty, mind*) entendement *m*; (*agreement*) accord *m*, entente *f*; **on the understanding that** à condition que; **to come to an understanding** arriver à un accord

un'der·stud'y *s* (*pl* -ies) doublure *f* ‖ *v* (*pret & pp* -ied) *tr* (*an actor*) doubler

un'der·take' *v* (*pret* -took; *pp* -taken) *tr* entreprendre; (*to agree to perform*) s'engager à faire; **to undertake to** s'engager à

undertaker [`ʌndər,tekər] *s* (*mortician*) entrepreneur *m* de pompes funèbres

undertaking [,ʌndər`tekɪŋ] *s* entreprise *f*; (*commitment*) engagement *m* ‖ [`ʌndər,tekɪŋ] *s* service *m* des pompes funèbres

un'der·tone' *s* ton *m* atténué; (*background sound*) fond *m* obscur; **in an undertone** à voix basse

un'der·tow' *s* (*countercurrent below surface*) courant *m* de fond; (*on beach*) ressac *m*

un'der·wear' *s* sous-vêtements *mpl*

un'der·world' *s* (*criminal world*) bas-fonds *mpl*, pègre *f*; (*pagan world of the dead*) enfers *mpl*

un'der·write' or un'der·write' *v* (*pret* -wrote; *pp* -written) *tr* souscrire; (ins) assurer

un'der·writ'er *s* souscripteur *m*; (ins) assureur *m*

undeserved [,ʌndɪ`zʌrvd] *adj* immérité

undesirable [,ʌndɪ`zaɪrəbəl] *adj* peu désirable; (*e.g., alien*) indésirable ‖ *s* indésirable *mf*

undetachable [,ʌndɪ`tætʃəbəl] *adj* inséparable

undeveloped [,ʌndɪ`vɛləpt] *adj* (*land*) inexploité; (*country*) sous-développé

undigested [,ʌndɪ`dʒɛstɪd] *adj* indigeste

undignified [ʌn`dɪgnɪ,faɪd] *adj* sans dignité, peu digne

undiscernible [,ʌndɪ`zʌrnɪbəl], [,ʌndɪ`sʌrnəbəl] *adj* imperceptible

undisputed [,ʌndɪs`pjutɪd] *adj* incontesté

undo [ʌn`du] *v* (*pret* -did; *pp* -done) *tr* défaire; (fig) ruiner

undoing [ʌn`duɪŋ] *s* perte *f*, ruine *f*

undone [ʌn`dʌn] *adj* (*omitted*) inaccompli; **to come undone** se défaire; **to leave nothing undone** ne rien négliger

undoubtedly [ʌn'dautɪdli] *adv* sans aucun doute, incontestablement

undramatic [ˌʌndrə'mætɪk] *adj* peu dramatique

undress [ʌn'drɛs] *s* déshabillé *m*; (*scanty dress*) petite tenue *f* ‖ *tr* déshabiller ‖ *intr* se déshabiller

undressing [ʌn'drɛsɪŋ] *s* déshabillage *m*, déculottage *m*

undrinkable [ʌn'drɪŋkəbəl] *adj* imbuvable

undue [ʌn'd(j)u] *adj* indu

undulate ['ʌndjə,let] *intr* onduler

unduly [ʌn'd(j)uli] *adv* indûment

undying [ʌn'daɪ·ɪŋ] *adj* impérissable

un'earned in'come ['ʌnʌrnd] *s* rente *f*, revenu *m* d'un bien

un'earned in'crement *s* plus-value *f*

unearth [ʌn'ʌrθ] *tr* déterrer

unearthly [ʌn'ʌrθli] *adj* surnaturel, spectral; bizarre; (*hour*) indu

uneasy [ʌn'izi] *adj* inquiet; contraint, gêné

uneatable [ʌn'itəbəl] *adj* immangeable

uneconomic(al) [ˌʌnikə'namɪk'əl)] *adj* peu économique; (*person*) peu économe

uneducated [ʌn'ɛdjə,ketɪd] *adj* ignorant, sans instruction

unemployed [ˌʌnɛm'plɔɪd] *adj* en chômage, sans travail ‖ *spl* chômeurs *mpl*, sans-travail *mfpl*

unemployment [ˌʌnɛm'plɔɪmənt] *s* chômage *m*

un'employ'ment insur'ance *s* assurance-chômage *f*, allocation *f* de chômage

unending [ʌn'ɛndɪŋ] *adj* interminable

unequal [ʌn'ikwəl] *adj* inégal; **to be unequal to** (*a task*) ne pas être à la hauteur de

unequaled or **unequalled** [ʌn'ikwəld] *adj* sans égal, sans pareil

unerring [ʌn'ʌrɪŋ] *adj* infaillible

UNESCO [ju'nɛsko] *s* (acronym) (**United Nations Educational, Scientific, and Cultural Organization**) l'Unesco *f*

unessential [ˌʌnɛ'sɛnʃəl] *adj* non essentiel

uneven [ʌn'ivən] *adj* inégal; (*number*) impair

uneventful [ˌʌnɪ'vɛntfəl] *adj* sans incident, peu mouvementé

unexceptionable [ˌʌnɛk'sɛpʃənəbəl] *adj* irréprochable

unexpected [ˌʌnɛk'spɛktɪd] *adj* inattendu, imprévu

unexplained [ˌʌnɛk'splend] *adj* inexpliqué

unexplored [ˌʌnɛk'splord] *adj* inexploré

unexposed [ˌʌnɛk'spozd] *adj* (phot) vierge

unfading [ʌn'fedɪŋ] *adj* immarcescible

unfailing [ʌn'felɪŋ] *adj* infaillible; (*inexhaustible*) intarissable

unfair [ʌn'fɛr] *adj* injuste, déloyal

unfaithful [ʌn'feθfəl] *adj* infidèle

unfamiliar [ˌʌnfə'mɪljər] *adj* étranger, peu familier

unfasten [ʌn'fæsən] *tr* défaire, détacher

unfathomable [ʌn'fæðəməbəl] *adj* insondable

unfavorable [ʌn'fevərəbəl] *adj* défavorable

unfeeling [ʌn'filɪŋ] *adj* insensible

unfilled [ʌn'fɪld] *adj* vide; (*post*) vacant

unfinished [ʌn'fɪnɪʃt] *adj* inachevé

unfit [ʌn'fɪt] *adj* impropre, inapte

unfitted *adj* inapte, inhabile

unfold [ʌn'fold] *tr* déplier ‖ *intr* se déplier

unforeseeable [ˌʌnfor'si·əbəl] *adj* imprévisible

unforeseen [ˌʌnfor'sin] *adj* imprévu

unforgettable [ˌʌnfər'gɛtəbəl] *adj* inoubliable

unforgivable [ˌʌnfər'gɪvəbəl] *adj* impardonnable

unfortunate [ʌn'fɔrtjənɪt] *adj & s* malheureux *m*

un·freeze [ʌn'friz] *v* (*pret* **-froze**; *pp* **-frozen**) *tr* dégeler

unfriend·ly [ʌn'frɛndli] *adj* (*comp* **-lier**; *super* **-liest**) inamical

unfruitful [ʌn'frutfəl] *adj* infructueux

unfulfilled [ˌʌnfəl'fɪld] *adj* inaccompli

unfurl [ʌn'fʌrl] *tr* déployer

unfurnished [ʌn'fʌrnɪʃt] *adj* non meublé

ungain·ly [ʌn'genli] *adj* gauche, disgracieux

ungentlemanly [ʌn'dʒɛntəlmənli] *adj* mal élevé, impoli

ungird [ʌn'gʌrd] *tr* déceindre

ungodly [ʌn'gadli] *adj* impie; (*dreadful*) (coll) atroce

ungracious [ʌn'greʃəs] *adj* malgracieux

ungrammatical [ˌʌngrə'mætɪkəl] *adj* peu grammatical

ungrateful [ʌn'gretfəl] *adj* ingrat

ungrudgingly [ʌn'grʌdʒɪŋli] *adj* de bon cœur, libéralement

unguarded [ʌn'gardɪd] *adj* sans défense; (*moment*) d'inattention; (*card*) sec

unguent ['ʌŋgwənt] *s* onguent *m*

unhandy [ʌn'hændi] *adj* maladroit; (*e.g., tool*) incommode, pas maniable

unhap·py [ʌn'hæpi] *adj* (*comp* **-pier**; *super* **-piest**) malheureux, triste; (*unlucky*) malheureux, malencontreux; (*fateful*) funeste

unharmed [ʌn'harmd] *adj* indemne

unharness [ʌn'harnɪs] *tr* dételer

unheal·thy [ʌn'hɛlθi] *adj* (*comp* **-thier**, *super* **-thiest**) malsain; (*person*) maladif

unheard-of [ʌn'hʌrd,av] *adj* inouï

unhinge [ʌn'hɪndʒ] *tr* (fig) détraquer

unhitch [ʌn'hɪtʃ] *tr* décrocher; (*e.g., a horse*) dételer

unho·ly [ʌn'holi] *adj* (*comp* **-lier**; *super* **-liest**) profane; (coll) affreux

unhook [ʌn'huk] *tr* décrocher; (*e.g., a dress*) dégrafer

unhoped-for [ʌn'hopt,for] *adj* inespéré

unhorse [ʌn'hors] *tr* désarçonner

unhurt [ʌn'hʌrt] *adj* indemne

unicorn ['junɪ,kɔrn] *s* unicorne *m*

un'iden'tified fly'ing ob'ject [ˌʌnaɪ'dɛntə,faɪd] *s* objet *m* volant non identifié (O.V.N.I.)

unification [ˌjunɪfɪ'keʃən] *s* unification *f*

uniform ['junɪ,fɔrm] *adj & s* uniforme *m* ‖ *tr* uniformiser; vêtir d'un uniforme

uniformi·ty [ˌjunɪ'fɔrmɪti] *s* (*pl* **-ties**) uniformité *f*

uni·fy [ˋjunɪ,faɪ] *v* (*pret & pp* **-fied**) unifier
unilateral [,junɪˋlætərəl] *adj* unilatéral
unimpeachable [,ʌnɪmˋpitʃəbəl] *adj* irrécusable
unimportant [,ʌnɪmˋpɔrtənt] *adj* peu important, sans importance
uninhabited [,ʌnɪnˋhæbɪtɪd] *adj* inhabité
uninspired [,ʌnɪnˋspaɪrd] *adj* sans inspiration, sans vigueur
unintelligent [,ʌnɪnˋtɛlɪdʒənt] *adj* inintelligent
unintelligible [,ʌnɪnˋtɛlɪdʒɪbəl] *adj* inintelligible
uninterested [ʌnˋɪntrɪstɪd], [ʌnˋɪntə,rɛstɪd] *adj* indifférent
uninteresting [ʌnˋɪntrɪstɪŋ], [ʌnˋɪntə,rɛstɪŋ] *adj* peu intéressant
uninterrupted [,ʌnɪntəˋrʌptɪd] *adj* ininterrompu
union [ˋjunjən] *adj* (*leader, scale, card, etc.*) syndical ‖ *s* union *f*; (*of workmen*) syndicat *m*
unionize [ˋjunjə,naɪz] *tr* syndiquer ‖ *intr* se syndiquer
un′ion shop′ *s* atelier *m* syndical
un′ion suit′ *s* sous-vêtement *m* d'une seule pièce
unique [jʊˋnik] *adj* unique
unisex [ˋjuni,sɛks] *adj* unisex, unisexué
unison [ˋjunɪsən] *s* unisson *m*; **in unison (with)** à l'unisson (de)
unit [ˋjunɪt] *adj* unitaire ‖ *s* unité *f*; (elec, mach) groupe *m*
unite [jʊˋnaɪt] *tr* unir ‖ *intr* s'unir
united [jʊˋnaɪtɪd] *adj* uni
Unit′ed King′dom *s* Royaume-Uni *m*
Unit′ed Na′tions *spl* Nations *fpl* Unies
Unit′ed States′ *adj* des États-Unis, américain ‖ *s*—**the United States** les États-Unis *mpl*
uni·ty [ˋjunɪti] *s* (*pl* **-ties**) unité *f*
universal [,junɪˋvʌrsəl] *adj & s* universel *m*
u′niversal joint′ *s* joint *m* articulé, cardan *m*
universe [ˋjunɪ,vʌrs] *s* univers *m*
universi·ty [,junɪˋvʌrsɪti] *adj* universitaire ‖ *s* (*pl* **-ties**) université *f*
unjust [ʌnˋdʒʌst] *adj* injuste
unjustified [ʌnˋdʒʌstɪ,faɪd] *adj* injustifié
unkempt [ʌnˋkɛmpt] *adj* dépeigné; mal tenu, négligé
unkind [ʌnˋkaɪnd] *adj* désobligeant; (*pitiless*) impitoyable, dur
unknowable [ʌnˋno·əbəl] *adj* inconnaissable
unknowingly [ʌnˋno·ɪŋli] *adv* inconsciemment
unknown [ʌnˋnon] *adj* inconnu; (*not yet revealed*) inédit; **unknown to** à l'insu de ‖ *s* inconnu *m*; (*math*) inconnue *f*
un′known quan′tity *s* (math, fig) inconnue *f*
Un′known Sol′dier *s* Soldat *m* inconnu
unlace [ʌnˋles] *tr* délacer
unlatch [ʌnˋlætʃ] *tr* lever le loquet de
unlawful [ʌnˋlɔfəl] *adj* illégal, illicite
unleash [ʌnˋliʃ] *tr* lâcher
unleavened [ʌnˋlɛvənd] *adj* azyme
unless [ʌnˋlɛs] *prep* sauf ‖ *conj* à moins que
unlettered [ʌnˋlɛtərd] *adj* illettré
unlike [ʌnˋlaɪk] *adj* (*not alike*) dissemblables; différent de; (*not typical of*) pas caractéristique de; (*poles of a magnet*) (elec) de noms contraires ‖ *prep* (*contrary to*) à la différence de
unlikely [ʌnˋlaɪkli] *adj* peu probable
unlimited [ʌnˋlɪmɪtɪd] *adj* illimité
unlined [ʌnˋlaɪnd] *adj* (*coat*) non fourré; (*paper*) non rayé; (*face*) sans rides
unlist′ed tel′ephone num′ber [ʌnˋlɪstɪd] *s* téléphone *m* non sur la liste rouge
unload [ʌnˋlod] *tr* décharger; (*a gun*) désarmer; (coll) se décharger de ‖ *intr* décharger
unloading [ʌnˋlodɪŋ] *s* déchargement *m*; (*stopping for unloading*) manutention *f*
unlock [ʌnˋlɑk] *tr* ouvrir; (*a bolted door*) déverrouiller; (*the jaws*) desserrer
unloose [ʌnˋlus] *tr* lâcher; (*to undo*) délier; (*a mighty force*) déchaîner
unloved [ʌnˋlʌvd] *adj* peu aimé, haï
unlovely [ʌnˋlʌvli] *adj* disgracieux
unluck·y [ʌnˋlʌki] *adj* (*comp* **-ier;** *super* **-iest**) malchanceux, malheureux
un·make [ʌnˋmek] *v* (*pret & pp* **-made**) *tr* défaire
unmanageable [ʌnˋmænɪdʒəbəl] *adj* difficile à manier, ingouvernable
unmanly [ʌnˋmænli] *adj* indigne d'un homme, poltron; efféminé
unmannerly [ʌnˋmænərli] *adj* impoli, mal élevé
unmarketable [ʌnˋmɑrkɪtəbəl] *adj* invendable
unmarriageable [ʌnˋmærɪdʒəbəl] *adj* non mariable
unmarried [ʌnˋmærid] *adj* célibataire
unmask [ʌnˋmæsk] *tr* démasquer ‖ *intr* se démasquer
unmatched [ʌnˋmætʃt] *adj* sans égal, incomparable; (*unpaired*) désassorti, dépareillé
unmerciful [ʌnˋmʌrsɪfəl] *adj* impitoyable
unmesh [ʌnˋmɛʃ] *tr* (mach) désengrener ‖ *intr* (mach) se désengrener
unmindful [ʌnˋmaɪndfəl] *adj* oublieux
unmistakable [,ʌnmɪsˋtekəbəl] *adj* évident, facilement reconnaissable
unmitigated [ʌnˋmɪtɪ,getɪd] *adj* parfait, fieffé
unmixed [ʌnˋmɪkst] *adj* sans mélange
unmoor [ʌnˋmʊr] *tr* désamarrer
unmovable [ʌnˋmuvəbəl] *adj* inamovible
unmoved [ʌnˋmuvd] *adj* impassible
unmuzzle [ʌnˋmʌzəl] *tr* démuseler
unnatural [ʌnˋnætʃərəl] *adj* anormal, dénaturé; maniéré; artificiel
unnecessary [ʌnˋnɛsə,sɛri] *adj* inutile
unnerve [ʌnˋnʌrv] *tr* démonter, décontenancer, bouleverser
unnoticeable [ʌnˋnotisəbəl] *adj* imperceptible
unnoticed [ʌnˋnotɪst] *adj* inaperçu
unobserved [,ʌnəbˋzʌrvd] *adj* inobservé, inaperçu

unobtainable [,ʌnəb'tenəbəl] *adj* introuvable

unobtrusive [,ʌnəb'trusɪv] *adj* discret, effacé

unoccupied [ʌn'akjə,paɪd] *adj* libre, inoccupé

unofficial [,ʌnə'fɪʃəl] *adj* officieux, non officiel

unopened [ʌn'opənd] *adj* fermé; (*letter*) non décacheté

unopposed [,ʌnə'pozd] *adj* sans opposition; (*candidate*) unique

unorthodox [ʌn'ɔrθə,daks] *adj* peu orthodox

unpack [ʌn'pæk] *tr* déballer

unpaid [ʌn'ped] *adj* impayé

unpalatable [ʌn'pælətəbəl] *adj* fade, insipide

unparalleled [ʌn'pærə,lɛld] *adj* sans précédent, sans pareil

unpardonable [ʌn'pardənəbəl] *adj* impardonnable

unpatriotic [,ʌnpetrɪ'atɪk] *adj* antipatriotique

unperceived [,ʌnpər'sivd] *adj* inaperçu

unperturbable [,ʌnpər'tʌrbəbəl] *adj* imperturbable

unpleasant [ʌn'plɛzənt] *adj* désagréable, déplaisant

unpopular [ʌn'papjələr] *adj* impopulaire

unpopularity [ʌn,papjə'lærɪti] *s* impopularité *f*

unprecedented [ʌn'prɛsɪ,dɛntɪd] *adj* sans précédent, inédit

unprejudiced [ʌn'prɛdʒədɪst] *adj* sans préjugés, impartial

unpremeditated [,ʌnprɪ'mɛdɪ,tetɪd] *adj* non prémédité

unprepared [,ʌnprɪ'pɛrd] *adj* sans préparation; (*e.g., speech*) improvisé

unprepossessing [,ʌnpripə'zɛsɪŋ] *adj* peu engageant

unpresentable [,ʌnprɪ'zɛntəbəl] *adj* peu présentable

unpretentious [,ʌnprɪ'tɛnʃəs] *adj* sans prétentions, modeste

unprincipled [ʌn'prɪnsɪpəld] *adj* sans principes, sans scrupules

unproductive [,ʌnprə'dʌktɪv] *adj* improductif

unprofitable [ʌn'prafɪtəbəl] *adj* peu profitable, inutile

unpronounceable [,ʌnprə'naʊnsəbəl] *adj* imprononçable

unpropitious [,ʌnprə'pɪʃəs] *adj* défavorable

unpublished [ʌn'pʌblɪʃt] *adj* inédit

unpunished [ʌn'pʌnɪʃt] *adj* impuni

unqualified [ʌn'kwalə,faɪd] *adj* incompétent; parfait, fieffé

unquenchable [ʌn'kwɛntʃəbəl] *adj* inextinguible

unquestionable [ʌn'kwɛstʃənəbəl] *adj* indiscutable

unrav·el [ʌn'rævəl] *v* (*pret & pp* **-eled** or **-elled**; *ger* **-eling** or **-elling**) *tr* effiler; (fig)

débrouiller ‖ *intr* s'effiler; (fig) se débrouiller

unreachable [ʌn'ritʃəbəl] *adj* inaccessible

unreal [ʌn'ri-əl] *adj* irréel

unreali·ty [,ʌnri'ælɪti] *s* (*pl* **-ties**) irréalité *f*

unreasonable [ʌn'rizənəbəl] *adj* déraisonnable

unrecognizable [ʌn'rɛkəg,naɪzəbəl] *adj* méconnaissable

unreel [ʌn'ril] *tr* dérouler ‖ *intr* se dérouler

unrelenting [,ʌnrɪ'lɛntɪŋ] *adj* implacable

unreliable [,ʌnrɪ'laɪ·əbəl] *adj* peu fidéle, instable, sujet à caution

unremitting [,ʌnrɪ'mɪtɪŋ] *adj* incessant, infatigable

unrented [ʌn'rɛntɪd] *adj* libre, sans locataires

unrepentant [,ʌnrɪ'pɛntənt] *adj* impénitent

un'requit'ed love' [,ʌnrɪ'kwaɪtɪd] *s* amour *m* non partagé

unresponsive [,ʌnrɪ'spansɪv] *adj* peu sensible, froid, détaché

unrest [ʌn'rɛst] *s* agitation *f*, trouble *m*; inquiétude *f*

un·rig [ʌn'rɪg] *v* (*pret & pp* **-rigged;** *ger* **-rigging**) *tr* (naut) dégréer

unrighteous [ʌn'raɪtʃəs] *adj* inique, injuste

unripe [ʌn'raɪp] *adj* vert, pas mûr; précoce

unrivaled or **unrivalled** [ʌn'raɪvəld] *adj* sans rival

unroll [ʌn'rol] *tr* dérouler ‖ *intr* se dérouler

unromantic [,ʌnro'mæntɪk] *adj* peu romanesque, terre à terre

unruffled [ʌn'rʌfəld] *adj* calme, serein

unruly [ʌn'ruli] *adj* indiscipliné, ingouvernable

unsaddle [ʌn'sædəl] *tr* (*a horse*) desseller; (*a horseman*) désarçonner

unsafe [ʌn'sef] *adj* dangereux

unsaid [ʌn'sɛd] *adj*—**to leave unsaid** passer sous silence

unsalable [ʌn'seləbəl] *adj* invendable

unsanitary [ʌn'sænɪ,tɛri] *adj* peu hygiénique

unsatisfactory [ʌn,sætɪs'fæktəri] *adj* peu satisfaisant

unsatisfied [ʌn'sætɪs,faɪd] *adj* insatisfait, inassouvi

unsavory [ʌn'sevəri] *adj* désagréable; (fig) équivoque, louche

unscathed [ʌn'skeðd] *adj* indemne

unscientific [,ʌnsaɪ·ən'tɪfɪk] *adj* antiscientifique

unscrew [ʌn'skru] *tr* dévisser

unscrupulous [ʌn'skrupjələs] *adj* sans scrupules

unseal [ʌn'sil] *tr* desceller

unsealed *adj* (*mail*) non clos

unseasonable [ʌn'sizənəbəl] *adj* hors de saison; (*untimely*) inopportun

unseemly [ʌn'simli] *adj* inconvenant

unseen [ʌn'sin] *adj* invisible

unselfish [ʌn'sɛlfɪʃ] *adj* désintéressé

unsettled [ʌn'sɛtəld] *adj* instable; (*region*) non colonisé; (*question*) en suspens; (*weather*) variable; (*bills*) non réglé; **to be**

unsettled (*to be uneasy*) avoir du vague à l'âme

unshackle [ʌnˈʃækəl] *tr* désentraver

unshaken [ʌnˈʃekən] *adj* inébranlé

unshapely [ʌnˈʃepli] *adj* difforme, informe

unshaven [ʌnˈʃevən] *adj* non rasé

unsheathe [ʌnˈʃið] *tr* dégainer

unshod [ʌnˈʃɑd] *adj* déchaussé; (*horse*) déferré

unshrinkable [ʌnˈʃrɪŋkəbəl] *adj* irrétrécissable

unsightly [ʌnˈsaɪtli] *adj* laid, hideux

unsinkable [ʌnˈsɪŋkəbəl] *adj* insubmersible

unskilled [ʌnˈskɪld] *adj* inexpérimenté; de manœuvre

un′skilled la′borer *s* manœuvre *m*

unskillful [ʌnˈskɪlfəl] *adj* maladroit

unsnarl [ʌnˈsnɑrl] *tr* débrouiller

unsociable [ʌnˈsoʃəbəl] *adj* insociable

unsold [ʌnˈsold] *adj* invendu

unsolder [ʌnˈsɑdər] *tr* dessouder

unsophisticated [ˌʌnsəˈfɪstɪˌketɪd] *adj* ingénu, naïf, simple

unsound [ʌnˈsaʊnd] *adj* peu solide; (*false*) faux; (*decayed*) gâté; (*mind*) dérangé; (*sleep*) léger

unspeakable [ʌnˈspikəbəl] *adj* indicible; (*disgusting*) sans nom

unsportsmanlike [ʌnˈsportsmənˌlaɪk] *adj* antisportif

unstable [ʌnˈstebəl] *adj* instable

unsteady [ʌnˈstɛdi] *adj* chancelant, tremblant, vacillant

unstinted [ʌnˈstɪntɪd] *adj* abondant, sans bornes

unstitch [ʌnˈstɪtʃ] *tr* découdre

un·stop [ʌnˈstɑp] *v* (*pret & pp* **-stopped**; *ger* **-stopping**) *tr* déboucher

unstressed [ʌnˈstrɛst] *adj* inaccentué

unstrung [ʌnˈstrʌŋ] *adj* détraqué; (*necklace*) défilé; (*mus*) sans cordes

unsuccessful [ˌʌnsəkˈsɛsfəl] *adj* non réussi; **to be unsuccessful** ne pas réussir

unsuitable [ʌnˈs(j)utəbəl] *adj* impropre; (*time*) inopportun; **unsuitable for** peu fait pour, inapte à

unsuspected [ˌʌnsəsˈpɛktɪd] *adj* insoupçonné

unswerving [ʌnˈswʌrvɪŋ] *adj* ferme, inébranlable

unsympathetic [ˌʌnsɪmpəˈθɛtɪk] *adj* peu compatissant

unsystematic(al) [ˌʌnsɪstəˈmætɪk(əl)] *adj* non systématique, sans méthode

untactful [ʌnˈtæktfəl] *adj* indiscret, indélicat

untamed [ʌnˈtemd] *adj* indompté

untangle [ʌnˈtæŋgəl] *tr* démêler, débrouiller

untenable [ʌnˈtɛnəbəl] *adj* insoutenable

unthankful [ʌnˈθæŋkfəl] *adj* ingrat

unthinkable [ʌnˈθɪŋkəbəl] *adj* impensable

unthinking [ʌnˈθɪŋkɪŋ] *adj* irréfléchi

untidy [ʌnˈtaɪdi] *adj* désordonné, débraillé

un·tie [ʌnˈtaɪ] *v* (*pret & pp* **-tied**; *ger* **-tying**) *tr* délier, dénouer

until [ʌnˈtɪl] *prep* jusqu'à || *conj* jusqu'à ce que, en attendant que

untimely [ʌnˈtaɪmli] *adj* inopportun; (*premature*) prématuré; (*excessive*) intempestif

untiring [ʌnˈtaɪrɪŋ] *adj* infatigable

untold [ʌnˈtold] *adj* incalculable; (*suffering*) inouï; (*joy*) indicible; (*tale*) non raconté

untouchable [ʌnˈtʌtʃəbəl] *adj & s* intouchable *mf*

untouched [ʌnˈtʌtʃt] *adj* intact; indifférent; non mentionné

untoward [ʌnˈtord] *adj* malencontreux

untrained [ʌnˈtrend] *adj* inexpérimenté; (*animal*) non dressé

untrammeled or **untrammelled** [ʌnˈtræməld] *adj* sans entraves

untried [ʌnˈtraɪd] *adj* inéprouvé

untroubled [ʌnˈtrʌbəld] *adj* calme, insoucieux

untrue [ʌnˈtru] *adj* faux; infidèle

untrustworthy [ʌnˈtrʌst,wʌrði] *adj* indigne de confiance

untruth [ʌnˈtruθ] *s* mensonge *m*

untruthful [ʌnˈtruθfəl] *adj* mensonger

untwist [ʌnˈtwɪst] *tr* détordre || *intr* se détordre

unused [ʌnˈjuzd] *adj* inutilisé, inemployé; **unused to** peu accoutumé à, inaccoutumé à

unusual [ʌnˈjuʒʊ·əl] *adj* insolite, inusité, inhabituel

unutterable [ʌnˈʌtərəbəl] *adj* indicible, inexprimable

unvanquished [ʌnˈvæŋkwɪʃt] *adj* invaincu

unvarnished [ʌnˈvɑrnɪʃt] *adj* non verni; (fig) sans fard, simple

unveil [ʌnˈvel] *tr* dévoiler; (*e.g., a statue*) inaugurer || *intr* se dévoiler

unveiling [ʌnˈvelɪŋ] *s* dévoilement *m*

unventilated [ʌnˈvɛntɪˌletɪd] *adj* sans aération

unvoice [ʌnˈvɔɪs] *tr* dévoiser, assourdir

unwanted [ʌnˈwɑntɪd] *adj* non voulu

unwarranted [ʌnˈwɑrəntɪd] *adj* injustifié; sans garantie

unwary [ʌnˈwɛri] *adj* imprudent

unwavering [ʌnˈwevərɪŋ] *adj* constant, ferme, résolu

unwelcome [ʌnˈwɛlkəm] *adj* (*e.g., visitor*) importun; (*e.g., news*) fâcheux

unwell [ʌnˈwɛl] *adj* indisposé, souffrant; (*menstruating*) indisposée

unwholesome [ʌnˈholsəm] *adj* malsain, insalubre

unwieldy [ʌnˈwildi] *adj* peu maniable

unwilling [ʌnˈwɪlɪŋ] *adj* peu disposé

unwillingly [ʌnˈwɪlɪŋli] *adv* à contrecœur

un·wind [ʌnˈwaɪnd] *v* (*pret & pp* **-wound**) *tr* dérouler || *intr* se dérouler

unwise [ʌnˈwaɪz] *adj* peu judicieux, malavisé

unwished-for [ʌnˈwɪʃt,fɔr] *adj* non souhaité

unwittingly [ʌnˈwɪtɪŋli] *adv* inconsciemment, sans le savoir

unwonted [ʌn'wʌntɪd] *adj* inaccoutumé, peu commun

unworldly [ʌn'wʌrldli] *adj* peu mondain; simple, naïf

unworthy [ʌn'wʌrði] *adj* indigne

un·wrap [ʌn'ræp] *v* (*pret* & *pp* **-wrapped**; *ger* **-wrapping**) *tr* dépaqueter, désenvelopper

unwrinkled [ʌn'rɪŋkəld] *adj* uni, lisse, sans rides

unwritten [ʌn'rɪtən] *adj* non écrit; oral; (*blank*) vierge, blanc

unwrit'ten law' *s* droit *m* coutumier

unyielding [ʌn'jildɪŋ] *adj* ferme, solide; inébranlable

unyoke [ʌn'jok] *tr* dételer

up [ʌp] *adj* montant, ascendant; (*raised*) levé; (*standing*) debout; (*time*) expiré; (*blinds*) relevé; **up in arms** soulevé, indigné ‖ *adv* haut, en haut; **to be up against** se heurter à; **to be up against it** avoir la déveine; **to be up to** être capable de, être à la hauteur de; être à, e.g., **to be up to you (me, etc.)** être à vous (moi, etc.); **up and down** de haut en bas; (*back and forth*) de long en large; **up there** là-haut; **up to** jusqu'à; (*at the level of*) au niveau de, à la hauteur de; **up to and including** jusques et y compris; **what's up?** qu'est-ce qui se passe?; for expressions like **to go up** monter and **to get up** se lever, see the verb ‖ *prep* en haut de, vers le haut de; (*a stream*) en montant ‖ *v* (*pret* & *pp* **-upped**; *ger* **upping**) *tr* (coll) faire monter; (*prices, wages*) (coll) élever ‖ *interj* debout!

up-and-coming ['ʌpən'kʌmɪŋ] *adj* (coll) entreprenant

up-and-doing ['ʌpən'du·ɪŋ] *adj* (coll) entreprenant, alerte, énergique

up-and-up ['ʌpən'ʌp] *s*—**to be on the up-and-up** (coll) être en bonne voie; (coll) être honnête

up·braid' *tr* réprimander, reprendre

upbringing ['ʌp,brɪŋɪŋ] *s* éducation *f*

up'coun'try *adv* (coll) à l'intérieur du pays ‖ *s* (coll) intérieur *m* du pays

up·date' *tr* mettre à jour

upheaval [ʌp'hivəl] *s* soulèvement *m*

up'hill' *adj* montant; difficile, pénible ‖ **up'hill'** *adv* en montant

up·hold' *v* (*pret* & *pp* **-held**) *tr* soutenir, maintenir

upholster [ʌp'holstər] *tr* tapisser

upholsterer [ʌp'holstərər] *s* tapissier *m*

upholster·y [ʌp'holstəri] *s* (*pl* **-ies**) tapisserie *f*

up'keep' *s* entretien *m*; (*expenses*) frais *mpl* d'entretien

upland ['ʌp,lænd] *adj* élevé ‖ *s* région *f* montagneuse; **uplands** hautes terres *fpl*

up'lift' *s* élévation *f*; (*moral improvement*) édification *f* ‖ **up·lift'** *tr* soulever, élever

upon [ə'pɑn] *prep* sur; à, e.g., **upon my arrival** à mon arrivée; **upon** + *ger* en + *ger*, e.g., **upon arriving** en arrivant

upper ['ʌpər] *adj* supérieur; haut; (*first*) premier ‖ *s* (*of shoe*) empeigne *f*

up'per berth' *s* couchette *f* du haut, couchette supérieure

up'per-case' *adj* (typ) du haut de casse

up'per clas'ses *spl* hautes classes *fpl*

up'per hand' *s* dessus *m*, haute main *f*

up'per mid'dle class' *s* haute bourgeoisie *f*

up'per·most' *adj* (le) plus haut, (le) plus élevé; (le) premier ‖ *adv* en dessus

Up'per Room' *s* (eccl) cénacle *m*

uppish ['ʌpɪʃ] *adj* (coll) suffisant, arrogant

up·raise' *tr* lever

up'right' *adj* & *adv* droit ‖ *s* montant *m*

uprising ['ʌp,raɪzɪŋ] *s* soulèvement *m*, insurrection *f*

up'roar' *s* tumulte *m*, vacarme *m*

uproarious [ʌp'rorɪ·əs] *adj* tumultueux; (*funny*) comique, impayable

up·root' *tr* déraciner

ups' and downs' *spl* vicissitudes *fpl*

up·set' or **up'set'** *adj* (*overturned*) renversé; (*disturbed*) bouleversé; (*stomach*) dérangé ‖ **up'set'** *s* (*overturn*) renversement *m*; (*of emotions*) bouleversement *m* ‖ **up·set'** *v* (*pret* & *pp* **-set**; *ger* **-setting**) *tr* renverser; bouleverser ‖ *intr* se renverser

up'set price' *s* prix *m* de départ

upsetting [ʌp'sɛtɪŋ] *adj* bouleversant, inquiétant

up'shot' *s* résultat *m*; point *m* essentiel

up'side down' *adv* sense dessus dessous; **to turn upside down** renverser; se renverser; (*said of carriage*) verser

up'stage' *adj* & *adv* au second plan, à l'arrière-plan; **to go upstage** remonter ‖ *s* arrière-plan *m* ‖ **up'stage'** *tr* (coll) prendre un air dédaigneux envers

up'stairs' *adj* d'en haut ‖ *s* l'étage *m* supérieur ‖ *adv* en haut; **to go upstairs** monter, monter en haut

up·stand'ing *adj* droit; (*vigorous*) gaillard; (*sincere*) honnête, probe

up'start' *adj* & *s* parvenu *m*

up'stream' *adj* d'amont ‖ *adv* en amont

up'stroke' *s* (*in writing*) délié *m*; (mach) course *f* ascendante

up'surge' *s* poussée *f*

up'swing' *s* mouvement *m* de montée; (com) amélioration *f*

up'tight' *adj* (coll) inquiet, soucieux

up-to-date ['ʌptə'det] *adj* à la page; (*e.g., account books*) mis à jour

up-to-the-minute ['ʌptəðə'mɪnɪt] *adj* de la dernière heure

up'trend' *s* tendance *f* à la hausse

up'turn' *s* hausse *f*, amélioration *f*

up·turned' *adj* (*e.g., eyes*) levé; (*part of clothing*) relevé; (*nose*) retroussé

upward ['ʌpwərd] *adj* ascendant ‖ *adv* vers le haut; **upward of** plus de

Ural ['jurəl] *adj* Ouralien ‖ *s* Oural *m*; **Urals** Oural

uranium [ju'renɪ·əm] *s* uranium *m*

urban ['ʌrbən] *adj* urbain

urbane [ʌr'ben] *adj* urbain, courtois

ur'ban guer'rilla *s* guérillero *m* urbain

urbanite [`ʌrbə,naɪt`] *s* citadin *m*, habitant *m* d'une ville

urbanity [ʌr`bæniti`] *s* urbanité *f*

urbanize [`ʌrbə,naɪz`] *tr* urbaniser

ur'ban renew'al *s* renouveau *m* urbain

urchin [`ʌrtʃɪn`] *s* gamin *m*, galopin *m*

ure·thra [jʊ`riθrə`] *s* (*pl* **-thras** or **-thrae** [θri]) urètre *m*

urge [ʌrdʒ] *s* impulsion *f* ‖ *tr* & *intr* presser

urgen·cy [`ʌrdʒənsi`] *s* (*pl* **-cies**) urgence *f*; insistance *f*, sollicitation *f*

urgent [`ʌrdʒənt`] *adj* urgent, pressant; (*insistent*) pressant, importun

urinal [`jʊrɪnəl`] *s* (*small building or convenience for men*) urinoir *m*, vespasienne *f*; (*for bed*) urinal *m*

urinary [`jʊrɪ,nɛri`] *adj* urinaire

urinate [`jʊrɪ,net`] *tr* & *intr* uriner; pisser (coll)

urine [`jʊrɪn`] *s* urine *f*

urn [ʌrn] *s* urne *f*; (*for tea, coffee, etc.*) fontaine *f*

urology [jʊ`rɑlədʒi`] *s* urologie *f*

us [ʌs] *pron pers* nous §85, §87

U.S.A. [`ju`ɛs`e`] *s* (letterword) (**United States of America**) E.-U.A. *mpl* or U.S.A. *mpl*

usable [`juzəbəl`] *adj* utilisable

usage [`juzɪdʒ`] *s* usage *m*

use [jus] *s* emploi *m*, usage *m*; (*usefulness*) utilité *f*; **in use** occupé; **of what use is it?** à quoi cela sert-il?; **not in use** libre; **out of use** hors de service; **to be of no use** ne servir à rien; **to have no use for s.o.** tenir qn en mauvaise estime; **to make use of** se servir de; **what's the use?** à quoi bon? ‖ [juz] *tr* employer, se servir de, user de; **to use up** épuiser, user ‖ *intr*—**I used to visit my friend every evening** je visitais mon ami tous les soirs

used [juzd] *adj* usagé, usé; d'occasion, e.g., **used car** voiture *f* d'occasion; **to be used** (*to be put into use*) être usité, être

employé; **to be used as** servir de; **to be used to** (*to be useful for*) servir à; **used to** [`justʊ`] accoutumé à; **used up** épuisé

useful [`jusfəl`] *adj* utile

usefulness [`jusfəlnɪs`] *s* utilité *f*

useless [`juslɪs`] *adj* inutile

user [`juzər`] *s* usager *m*; (*of a machine, of a computer, of gas, etc.*) utilisateur *m*

usher [`ʌʃər`] *s* placeur *m*; ouvreuse *f*; (*doorkeeper*) huissier *m* ‖ *tr*—**to usher in** inaugurer; (*a person*) introduire

U.S.S.R. [`ju`ɛs`ɛs`ɑr`] *s* (letterword) (**Union of Soviet Socialist Republics**) U.R.S.S. *f*

usual [`juʒʊ·əl`] *adj* usuel; **as usual** comme d'habitude

usually [`juʒʊ·əli`] *adv* usuellement, d'habitude, d'ordinaire

usurp [ju`zʌrp`] *tr* usurper

usu·ry [`juʒəri`] *s* (*pl* **-ries**) usure *f*

utensil [jʊ`tɛnsɪl`] *s* ustensile *m*

uter·us [`jutərəs`] *s* (*pl* **-i** [,aɪ]) utérus *m*

utilitarian [,jutɪlɪ`tɛrɪ·ən`] *adj* utilitaire

utili·ty [ju`tɪlɪti`] *s* (*pl* **-ties**) utilité *f*; service *m* public; **utilities** services en commun (*gaz, transports, etc.*)

utilize [`jutɪ,laɪz`] *tr* utiliser

utmost [`ʌt,most`] *adj* extrême; (*larger*) plus grand; (*further away*) plus éloigné ‖ *s*—**the utmost** l'extrême *m*, le comble *m*; **to do one's utmost** faire tout son possible; **to the utmost** jusqu'au dernier point

utopia [ju`topɪ·ə`] *s* utopie *f*

utopian [ju`topɪ·ən`] *adj* utopique ‖ *s* utopiste *mf*

utter [`ʌtər`] *adj* complet, total, absolu ‖ *tr* proférer, émettre; (*a cry*) pousser

utterance [`ʌtərəns`] *s* expression *f*, émission *f*; (gram) énoncé *m*; **to give utterance to** exprimer

utterly [`ʌtərli`] *adj* complètement, tout à fait, totalement

U-turn [`ju,tərn`] *s* demi-volte *f*

V

V, v [vi] *s* XXIIe lettre de l'alphabet

vacan·cy [`vekənsi`] *s* (*pl* **-cies**) (*emptiness; gap, opening*) vide *m*; (*unfilled position or job*) vacance *f*; (*in a building*) appartement *m* disponible; (*in a hotel*) chambre *f* de libre; **no vacancy** (public sign) complet

vacant [`vekənt`] *adj* (*empty*) vide; (*having no occupant; untenanted*) vacant, libre, disponible; (*expression, look*) distrait, vague

va'cant lot' *s* terrain *m* vague

vacate [`veket`] *tr* quitter, évacuer ‖ *intr* (*to move out*) déménager

vacation [ve`keʃən`] *s* vacances *fpl*; **on va-**

cation en vacances ‖ *intr* prendre ses vacances, passer les vacances

vacationist [ve`keʃənɪst`] *s* vacancier *m*

vaca'tion with pay' *s* congé *m* payé

vaccinate [`væksɪ,net`] *tr* vacciner

vaccination [,væksɪ`neʃən`] *s* vaccination *f*

vaccine [væk`sin`] *s* vaccin *m*

vacillate [`væsɪ,let`] *intr* vaciller

vacui·ty [væ`kju·ɪti`] *s* (*pl* **-ties**) vacuité *f*

vacu·um [`vækjʊ·əm`] *s* (*pl* **-ums** or **-a** [ə]) vacuum *m*, vide *m* ‖ *tr* passer à l'aspirateur, dépoussiérer

vac'uum clean'er *s* aspirateur *m*

vac'uum pump' *s* pompe *f* à vide

vac'uum tube' *s* tube *m* à vide

vagabond [ˈvægəˌbɑnd] *adj & s* vagabond *m*

vagar·y [vəˈgɛri] *s* (*pl* **-ies**) caprice *m*

vagina [vəˈdʒaɪnə] *s* vagin *m*

vagran·cy [ˈvegrənsi] *s* (*pl* **-cies**) vagabondage *m*

vague [veg] *adj* vague

vain [ven] *adj* vain; **in vain** en vain

vainglorious [venˈgloriˌəs] *adj* vaniteux

valance [ˈvæləns] *s* cantonnière *f*, lambrequin *m*

vale [vel] *s* vallon *m*

valedicto·ry [ˌvælɪˈdɪktəri] *s* (*pl* **-ries**) discours *m* d'adieu

valence [ˈveləns] *s* (chem) valence *f*

valentine [ˈvælənˌtaɪn] *s* (*sweetheart*) valentin *m*; (*card*) carte *f* de la Saint-Valentin

Val'entine Day' *s* la Saint-Valentin

vale' of tears' *s* vallée *f* de larmes

valet [ˈvælɪt], [ˈvæle] *s* valet *m*

valiant [ˈvæljənt] *adj* vaillant

valid [ˈvælɪd] *adj* valable, valide

validate [ˈvælɪˌdet] *tr* valider; (sports) homologuer

validation [ˌvælɪˈdeʃən] *s* validation *f*; (sports) homologation *f*

validi·ty [vəˈlɪdɪti] *s* (*pl* **-ties**) validité *f*

valise [vəˈlis] *s* mallette *f*

valley [ˈvæli] *s* vallée *f*, vallon *m*; (*of roof*) cornière *f*

valor [ˈvælər] *s* valeur *f*, vaillance *f*

valorous [ˈvælərəs] *adj* valeureux

valuable [ˈvæljuˌəbəl], [ˈvæljəbəl] *adj* précieux, de valeur ‖ **valuables** *spl* objets *mpl* de valeur

value [ˈvælju] *s* valeur *f*; (*bargain*) affaire *f*, occasion *f*; **to set a value on** estimer, évaluer ‖ *tr* (*to think highly of*) priser, estimer; (*to set a price for*) estimer, évaluer; **if you value your life** si vous tenez à la vie

val'ue-added tax' *s* taxe *f* à la valeur ajoutée, T.V.A.

valueless [ˈvæljulɪs] *adj* sans valeur

valve [vælv] *s* soupape *f*; (*of mollusk; of fruit; of tire*) valve *f*; (*of heart*) valvule *f*; (mus) clé *f*

valve' cap' *s* chapeau *m*, bouchon *m*

valve' gears' *spl* (*of gas engine*) engrenages *mpl* de distribution; (*of steam engine*) mécanisme *m* de distribution

valve'-in-head' en'gine *s* moteur *m* à soupapes en tête, moteur à culbuteurs

valve' seat' *s* siège *m* de soupape

valve' spring' *s* ressort *m* de soupape

valve' stem' *s* tige *f* de soupape

vamp [væmp] *s* (*of shoe*) empeigne *f*; (*patchwork*) rapiéçage *m*; (*woman who preys on man*) (coll) femme *f* fatale, vamp *f* ‖ *tr* (*a shoe*) mettre une empeigne à; (*to piece together*) rapiécer; (*a susceptible man*) (coll) vamper; (*an accompaniment*) (coll) improviser

vampire [ˈvæmpaɪr] *s* vampire *m*; femme *f* fatale, vamp *f*

van [væn] *s* camion *m*, voiture *f* de déménagement; (mil, fig) avant-garde *f*; (*railway car*) (Brit) fourgon *m*

vandal [ˈvændəl] *adj & s* vandale *m* ‖ (*cap*) *adj* vandale ‖ (*cap*) *s* Vandale *mf*

vandalism [ˈvændəˌlɪzəm] *s* vandalisme *m*

vane [ven] *s* (*weathervane*) girouette *f*; (*of windmill*) aile *f*; (*of propeller or turbine*) ailette *f*; (*of feather*) lame *f*; (*of a wheel*) aube *f*

vanguard [ˈvænˌgɑrd] *s* (mil, fig) avant-garde *f*; **in the vanguard** à l'avant-garde

vanilla [vəˈnɪlə] *s* vanille *f*

vanish [ˈvænɪʃ] *intr* s'évanouir, disparaître

van'ishing cream' *s* crème *f* de jour

vani·ty [ˈvænɪti] *s* (*pl* **-ties**) vanité *f*; (*dressing table*) table *f* de toilette, coiffeuse *f*; (*vanity case*) poudrier *m*

van'ity case' *s* poudrier *m*, nécessaire *m* de toilette

vanquish [ˈvæŋkwɪʃ] *tr* vaincre

van'tage point' [ˈvæntɪdʒ] *s* position *f* avantageuse

vapid [ˈvæpɪd] *adj* insipide

vapor [ˈvepər] *s* vapeur *f*

vaporize [ˈvepəˌraɪz] *tr* vaporiser ‖ *intr* se vaporiser

va'por lock' *s* bouchon *m* de vapeur

va'por trail' *s* (aer) sillage *m* de fumée

variable [ˈvɛrɪ·əbl] *adj & s* variable *f*

variance [ˈvɛrɪ·əns] *s* différence *f*, variation *f*; **at variance with** en désaccord avec

variant [ˈvɛrɪ·ənt] *adj* variant ‖ *s* variante *f*

variation [ˌvɛrɪˈeʃən] *s* variation *f*

varicose [ˈværɪˌkos] *adj* variqueux

var'icose veins' *spl* (pathol) varice *f*

varied [ˈvɛrid] *adj* varié

variegated [ˈvɛrɪ·əˌgetɪd] *adj* varié; (*spotted*) bigarré, bariolé

varie·ty [vəˈraɪ·ɪti] *s* (*pl* **-ties**) variété *f*

vari'ety show' *s* spectacle *m* de variétés

vari'ety store' *s* magasin *m* à prix unique

various [ˈvɛrɪ·əs] *adj* divers, différent; (*several*) plusieurs; (*variegated*) bigarré

varnish [ˈvɑrnɪʃ] *s* vernis *m* ‖ *tr* vernir; (*e.g., the truth*) farder, embellir

varsi·ty [ˈvɑrsɪti] *adj* (sports) universitaire ‖ *s* (*pl* **-ties**) (sports) équipe *f* universitaire principale

var·y [ˈvɛri] *v* (*pret & pp* **-ied**) *tr & intr* varier

vase [ves], [vez] *s* vase *m*

Vaseline [ˈvæsəˌlin] *s* (trademark) vaseline *f*

vassal [ˈvæsəl] *adj & s* vassal *m*

vast [væst] *adj* vaste

vastness [ˈvæstnɪs] *s* vaste étendue *f*, immensité *f*

vat [væt] *s* cuve *f*, bac *m*

Vatican [ˈvætɪkən] *adj* vaticane ‖ *s* Vatican *m*

vaudeville [ˈvodvɪl] *s* spectacle *m* de variétés, music-hall *m*; (*light theatrical piece interspersed with songs*) vaudeville *m*

vault [vɔlt] *s* (*underground chamber*) souterrain *m*; (*of a bank*) chambre *f* forte;

(*burial chamber*) caveau *m*; (*leap*) saut *m*; (anat, archit) voûte *f* || *tr & intr* sauter
vaunt [vɔnt], [vɑnt] *s* vantardise *f* || *tr* vanter || *intr* se vanter
VCR [ˈviˈsiˈɑr] *s* (letterword) (**videocassette recorder**) magnétoscope *m*
VD [ˈviˈdi] *s* (letterword) (**venereal disease**) maladie *f* vénérienne
veal [vil] *s* veau *m*
veal' chop' *s* côtelette *f* de veau
veal' cut'let *s* escalope *f* de veau
veer [vɪr] *s* virage *m* || *tr* faire virer || *intr* virer
vegetable [ˈvɛdʒɪtəbəl] *adj* végétal || *s* (*plant*) végétal *m*; (*edible part of plant*) légume *m*
veg'etable gar'den *s* potager *m*
veg'etable soup' *s* potage *m* aux légumes
vegetarian [ˌvɛdʒɪˈtɛriˈən] *adj & s* végétarien *m*
vegetate [ˈvɛdʒɪˌtet] *intr* végéter
vehemence [ˈviˈɪməns] *s* véhémence *f*
vehement [ˈviˈɪmənt] *adj* véhément
vehicle [ˈviˈɪkəl] *s* véhicule *m*
veil [vel] *s* voile *m*; **to take the veil** prendre le voile || *tr* voiler || *intr* se voiler
vein [ven] *s* veine *f* || *tr* veiner
velar [ˈvilər] *adj & s* vélaire *f*
vellum [ˈvɛləm] *s* vélin *m*; papier *m* vélin
veloci·ty [vɪˈlɑsɪti] *s* (*pl* **-ties**) vitesse *f*
velvet [ˈvɛlvɪt] *s* velours *m*
velveteen [ˌvɛlvɪˈtin] *s* velvet *m*
velvety [ˈvɛlvɪti] *adj* velouté
vend [vɛnd] *tr* vendre, colporter
vend'ing machine' *s* distributeur *m* automatique
vendor [ˈvɛndər] *s* vendeur *m*
veneer [vəˈnɪr] *s* placage *m*; (fig) vernis *m* || *tr* plaquer
venerable [ˈvɛnərəbəl] *adj* vénérable
venerate [ˈvɛnəˌret] *tr* vénérer
venereal [vɪˈnɪriˈəl] *adj* vénérien
Venetian [vɪˈniʃən] *adj* vénitien || *s* Vénitien *m*
Vene'tian blind' *s* jalousie *f*, store *m* vénitien
vengeance [ˈvɛndʒəns] *s* vengeance *f*; **with a vengeance** furieusement, à outrance; (*to the utmost limit*) tant que ça peut
vengeful [ˈvɛndʒfəl] *adj* vengeur
Venice [ˈvɛnɪs] *s* Venise *f*
venison [ˈvɛnɪsən] *s* venaison *f*
venom [ˈvɛnəm] *s* venin *m*
venomous [ˈvɛnəməs] *adj* venimeux
vent [vɛnt] *s* orifice *m*; (*for air*) ventouse *f*; **to give vent to** donner libre cours à || *tr* décharger
ventilate [ˈvɛntɪˌlet] *tr* ventiler
ventilator [ˈvɛntɪˌletər] *s* ventilateur *m*
ventricle [ˈvɛntrɪkəl] *s* ventricule *m*
ventriloquism [vɛnˈtrɪləˌkwɪzəm] *s* ventriloquie *f*
ventriloquist [vɛnˈtrɪləkwɪst] *s* ventriloque *mf*
venture [ˈvɛntʃər] *s* entreprise *f* risquée; **at a venture** à l'aventure || *tr* aventurer || *intr* s'aventurer; **to venture on** hasarder

venturesome [ˈvɛntʃərsəm] *adj* aventureux
venturous [ˈvɛntʃərəs] *adj* aventureux
vent' win'dow *s* (aut) déflecteur *m*
venue [ˈvɛnju] *s* (law) lieu *m* du jugement; **change of venue** (law) renvoi *m*
Venus [ˈvinəs] *s* Vénus *f*
veracious [vɪˈreʃəs] *adj* véridique
veraci·ty [vɪˈræsɪti] *s* (*pl* **-ties**) véracité *f*
veranda or **verandah** [vəˈrændə] *s* véranda *f*
verb [vʌrb] *adj* verbal || *s* verbe *m*
verbalize [ˈvʌrbəˌlaɪz] *tr* exprimer par des mots; (gram) changer en verbe || *intr* être verbeux
verbatim [vərˈbetɪm] *adj* textuel || *adv* textuellement
verbiage [ˈvʌrbɪˌɪdʒ] *s* verbiage *m*
verbose [vərˈbos] *adj* verbeux
verdant [ˈvʌrdənt] *adj* vert; naïf, candide
verdict [ˈvʌrdɪkt] *s* verdict *m*
verdigris [ˈvʌrdɪˌgris] *s* vert-de-gris *m*
verdure [ˈvʌrdʒər] *s* verdure *f*
verge [vʌrdʒ] *s* bord *m*, limite *f*; **on the verge of** sur le point de || *intr*—**to verge on** or **upon** toucher à; (*bad faith; the age of forty; etc.*) friser
verification [ˌvɛrɪfɪˈkeʃən] *s* vérification *f*
veri·fy [ˈvɛrɪˌfaɪ] *v* (*pret & pp* **-fied**) *tr* vérifier
verily [ˈvɛrɪli] *adv* en vérité
veritable [ˈvɛrɪtəbəl] *adj* véritable
vermilion [vərˈmɪljən] *adj & s* vermillon *m*
vermin [ˈvʌrmɪn] *s* (*objectionable person*) vermine *f* || *spl* (*objectionable animals or persons*) vermine
vermouth [vərˈmuθ], [ˈvʌrmuθ] *s* vermout *m*
vernacular [vərˈnækjələr] *adj* vernaculaire || *s* langue *f* vernaculaire; (*everyday language*) langage *m* vulgaire; (*language peculiar to a class or profession*) jargon *m*
versatile [ˈvʌrsətɪl] *adj* aux talents variés; (*e.g., mind*) universel, souple
verse [vʌrs] *s* vers *mpl*; (*stanza*) strophe *f*; (Bib) verset *m*
versed [vʌrst] *adj*—**versed in** versé dans; spécialiste de
versification [ˌvʌrsɪfɪˈkeʃən] *s* versification *f*
versi·fy [ˈvʌrsɪˌfaɪ] *v* (*pret & pp* **-fied**) *tr & intr* versifier
version [ˈvʌrʒən] *s* version *f*
ver·so [ˈvʌrso] *s* (*pl* **-sos**) (*e.g., of a coin*) revers *m*; (typ) verso *m*
versus [ˈvʌrsəs] *prep* contre
verte·bra [ˈvʌrtɪbrə] *s* (*pl* **-brae** [ˌbri] or **-bras**) vertèbre *f*
vertebrate [ˈvʌrtɪˌbret] *adj & s* vertébré *m*
ver·tex [ˈvʌrtɛks] *s* (*pl* **-texes** or **-tices** [tɪˌsiz]) sommet *m*
vertical [ˈvʌrtɪkəl] *adj* vertical || *s* verticale *f*
ver'tical hold' *s* (telv) commande *f* de stabilité verticale
ver'tical rud'der *s* gouvernail *m* de direction
ver'tical take'-off *s* décollage *m* vertical

verti·go [ˈvʌrtɪˌgo] s (pl -gos or -goes) vertige m

very [ˈvɛri] adj véritable; même, e.g., **at this very moment** à cet instant même ‖ adv très, e.g., **I am very hungry** j'ai très faim; bien, e.g., **you are very nice** vous êtes bien gentil; tout, e.g., **the very first** le tout premier; e.g., **my very best** tout mon possible; **for my very own** pour moi tout seul; **very much** beaucoup

vesicle [ˈvɛsɪkəl] s vésicule f

vespers [ˈvɛspərz] spl vêpres fpl

vessel [ˈvɛsəl] s bâtiment m, navire m; (container) vase m; (anat, bot, zool) vaisseau m

vest [vɛst] s gilet m; **to play it close to the vest** (coll) jouer serré ‖ tr revêtir; **to vest with** investir de, revêtir de

vest'ed in'terests spl classes fpl dirigeantes

vestibule [ˈvɛstɪˌbjul] s vestibule m

ves'tibule car' s (rr) wagon m à soufflets

vestige [ˈvɛstɪdʒ] s vestige m

vestment [ˈvɛstmənt] s vêtement m sacerdotal

vest'-pock'et adj de poche, de petit format

ves·try [ˈvɛstri] s (pl -tries) sacristie f; (committee) conseil m paroissial

ves'try·man s (pl -men) marguillier m

Vesuvius [vɪˈs(j)uvɪ·əs] s le Vésuve

vetch [vɛtʃ] s vesce f; (Lathyrus sativus) gesse f

veteran [ˈvɛtərən] s vétéran m

veterinarian [ˌvɛtərɪˈnɛrɪ·ən] s vétérinaire mf

veterinar·y [ˈvɛtərɪˌnɛri] adj vétérinaire ‖ s (pl -ies) vétérinaire mf

ve·to [ˈvito] s (pl -toes) veto m ‖ tr mettre son veto à

vex [vɛks] tr vexer, contrarier

vexation [vɛkˈseʃən] s vexation f

via [ˈvaɪ·ə] prep via

viaduct [ˈvaɪ·əˌdʌkt] s viaduc m

vial [ˈvaɪ·əl] s fiole f

viand [ˈvaɪ·ənd] s mets m

vibrate [ˈvaɪbret] intr vibrer

vibration [vaɪˈbreʃən] s vibration f

vicar [ˈvɪkər] s vicaire m; (in Church of England) curé m

vicarage [ˈvɪkərɪdʒ] s presbytère m; (duties of vicar) cure f

vicarious [vaɪˈkɛrɪ·əs] adj substitut; (punishment) souffert pour autrui; (power, authority) délégué; (enjoyment) partagé

vice [vaɪs] s vice m; (device) étau m

vice'-ad'miral s vice-amiral m

vice'-pres'ident s vice-président m

viceroy [ˈvaɪsrɔɪ] s vice-roi m

vice' squad' s brigade f des mœurs

vice versa [ˈvaɪsəˈvʌrsə] adv vice versa

vicini·ty [vɪˈsɪnɪti] s (pl -ties) voisinage m; environs mpl, e.g., **New York and vicinity** New York et ses environs

vicious [ˈvɪʃəs] adj vicieux; (mean) méchant; (ferocious) féroce

vicissitude [vɪˈsɪsɪˌt(j)ud] s vicissitude f

victim [ˈvɪktɪm] s victime f; (e.g., of a collision, fire) accidenté m

victimize [ˈvɪktɪˌmaɪz] tr prendre pour victime; (to swindle) duper

victor [ˈvɪktər] s vainqueur m

victorious [vɪkˈtorɪ·əs] adj victorieux

victo·ry [ˈvɪktəri] s (pl -ries) victoire f

victuals [ˈvɪtəlz] spl victuailles fpl

video [ˈvɪdɪ·o] s télévision f

vid'eo-cassette' s vidéocassette f

vid'eo-cassette' record'er s magnétoscope m

vid'eo-cassette' record'ing s magnétoscopie f

vid'eo-record'er s magnétoscope m

vid'eo-record'ing s vidéogramme m, magnétoscopie f

vid'eo-sig'nal s signal m d'image

vid'eo-tape' s bande f vidéo; (in a cassette) vidéocassette f, vidéogramme m

vid'eo-tape' record'er s magnétoscope m

vid'eo-tape' record'ing s magnétoscopie f

vie [vaɪ] v (pret & pp **vied**; ger **vying**) intr rivaliser, lutter

Vienna [vɪˈɛnə] s Vienne f

Vien·nese [ˌvi·əˈniz] adj viennois ‖ s (pl -nese) Viennois m

Vietnam [ˌvɪ·ɛtˈnɑm] s le Vietnam

Vietnam·ese [vɪˌɛtnəˈmiz] adj vietnamien ‖ s (pl -ese) Vietnamien m

view [vju] s vue f; **in my view** à mon avis, selon mon opinion; **in view** en vue; **in view of** étant donné, vu; **on view** exposé; **with a view to** en vue de ‖ tr voir, regarder; considérer, examiner

viewer [ˈvju·ər] s spectateur m; (for film, slides, etc.) visionneuse f; (telv) téléspectateur m

view'find'er s viseur m

view'point' s point m de vue

vigil [ˈvɪdʒɪl] s veille f; (eccl) vigile f; **to keep a vigil** veiller

vigilance [ˈvɪdʒɪləns] s vigilance f

vigilant [ˈvɪdʒɪlənt] adj vigilant

vignette [vɪnˈjɛt] s vignette f

vigor [ˈvɪgər] s vigueur f

vigorous [ˈvɪgərəs] adj vigoureux

vile [vaɪl] adj vil; (smell) infect; (weather) sale; (disgusting) détestable

vili·fy [ˈvɪlɪˌfaɪ] v (pret & pp -fied) tr diffamer, dénigrer

villa [ˈvɪlə] s villa f

village [ˈvɪlɪdʒ] s village m

villager [ˈvɪlɪdʒər] s villageois m

villain [ˈvɪlən] s scélérat m; (of a play) traître m

villainous [ˈvɪlənəs] adj vil, infame

villain·y [ˈvɪləni] s (pl -ies) vilenie f, infamie f

vim [vɪm] s énergie f, vigueur f

vinaigrette' sauce' [ˌvɪnəˈgrɛt] s vinaigrette f

vindicate [ˈvɪndɪˌket] tr justifier, défendre

vindictive [vɪnˈdɪktɪv] adj vindicatif

vine [vaɪn] s plante f grimpante; (grape plant) vigne f

vinegar [ˈvɪnɪgər] s vinaigre m

vinegary [ˈvɪnɪgəri] adj aigre, acide; (ill-tempered) acariâtre

vine' stock' *s* cep *m*

vineyard ['vɪnjərd] *s* vignoble *m*, vigne *f*

vintage ['vɪntɪdʒ] *s* vendange *f*; (*year*) année *f*, cru *m*; (coll) classe *f*, catégorie *f*

vin'tage wine' *s* bon cru *m*

vin'tage year' *s* grande année *f*

vintner ['vɪntnər] *s* négociant *m* en vins; (*person who makes wine*) vigneron *m*

vinyl ['vaɪnɪl] *s* vinyle *m*

viola [vaɪ'olə], [vɪ'olə] *s* alto *m*

violate ['vaɪ·ə,let] *tr* violer

violation [,vaɪ·ə'leʃən] *s* violation *f*

violence ['vaɪ·ələns] *s* violence *f*

violent ['vaɪ·ələnt] *adj* violent

violet ['vaɪ·əlɪt] *adj* violet || *s* (*color*) violet *m*; (bot) violette *f*

violin [,vaɪ·ə'lɪn] *s* violon *m*

violinist [,vaɪ·ə'lɪnɪst] *s* violoniste *mf*

violoncel·lo [,vaɪ·ələn'tʃɛlo] *s* (*pl* -los) violoncelle *m*

viper ['vaɪpər] *s* vipère *f*

vira·go [vɪ'rego] *s* (*pl* -goes or -gos) mégère *f*

virgin ['vɜrdʒɪn] *adj* vierge || *s* vierge *f*; (*male virgin*) puceau *m*

Virgin'ia creep'er [vər'dʒɪnɪ·ə] *s* vigne *f* vierge

virginity [vər'dʒɪnɪti] *s* virginité *f*

Virgo ['vɜrgo] *s* (astr, astrol) la Vièrge

virility [vɪ'rɪlɪti] *s* virilité *f*

virology [vaɪ'ralədʒi] *s* virologie *f*

virtual ['vɜrtʃu·əl] *adj* véritable, effectif; (mech, opt, phys) virtuel

virtue ['vɜrtʃu] *s* vertu *f*; mérite *m*, avantage *m*

virtuosi·ty [,vɜrtʃu'asɪti] *s* (*pl* -ties) virtuosité *f*

virtuo·so [,vɜrtʃu'oso] *s* (*pl* -sos or -si [si]) virtuose *mf*

virtuous ['vɜrtʃu·əs] *adj* vertueux

virulence ['vɪrjələns] *s* virulence *f*

virulent ['vɪrjələnt] *adj* virulent

virus ['vaɪrəs] *s* virus *m*

visa ['vizə] *s* visa *m* || *tr* viser

visage ['vɪzɪdʒ] *s* visage *m*

vis-à-vis [,vizə'vi] *adj* face à face || *s & adv* vis-à-vis *m* || *prep* vis-à-vis de

viscera ['vɪsərə] *spl* viscères *mpl*

viscount ['vaɪkaunt] *s* vicomte *m*

viscountess ['vaɪkauntɪs] *s* vicomtesse *f*

viscous ['vɪskəs] *adj* visqueux

vise [vaɪs] *s* étau *m*

visible ['vɪzɪbəl] *adj* visible

vision ['vɪʒən] *s* vision *f*

visionar·y ['vɪʒə,nɛri] *adj* visionnaire || *s* (*pl* -ies) visionnaire *mf*

visit ['vɪzɪt] *s* visite *f* || *tr* visiter; (*e.g., a person*) rendre visite à || *intr* faire des visites

visitation [,vɪzɪ'teʃən] *s* visite *f*; justice *f* du ciel; clémence *f* du ciel; (*e.g., in a séance*) apparition *f*; **Visitation** (eccl) Visitation *f*

vis'iting card' *s* carte *f* de visite

vis'iting hours' *spl* heures *fpl* de visite

vis'iting nurse' *s* infirmière *f* visiteuse

vis'iting profes'sor *s* visiting *m*

visitor ['vɪzɪtər] *s* visiteur *m*

visor ['vaɪzər] *s* visière *f*

vista ['vɪstə] *s* perspective *f*

visual ['vɪʒu·əl] *adj* visuel

visualize ['vɪʒu·ə,laɪz] *tr* (*in one's mind*) se faire une image mentale de, se représenter; (*to make visible*) visualiser

vital ['vaɪtəl] *adj* vital || **vitals** *spl* organes *mpl* vitaux

vitality [vaɪ'tælɪti] *s* vitalité *f*

vitalize ['vaɪtə,laɪz] *tr* vitaliser

vitamin ['vaɪtəmɪn] *s* vitamine *f*

vitiate ['vɪʃɪ,et] *tr* vicier

vitreous ['vɪtrɪ·əs] *adj* vitreux

vitriolic [,vɪtrɪ'alɪk] *adj* (chem) vitriolique; (fig) trempé dans du vitriol

vituperate [vaɪ't(j)upə,ret] *tr* vitupérer

viva ['vivə] *s* vivat *m* || *interj* vive!

vivacious [vaɪ'veʃəs] *adj* vif, animé

vivaci·ty [vaɪ'væsɪti] *s* (*pl* -ties) vivacité *f*

viva voce ['vaɪvə'vosi] *adv* de vive voix

vivid ['vɪvɪd] *adj* vif; (*description*) vivant; (*recollection*) vivace

vivi·fy ['vɪvɪ,faɪ] *v* (*pret & pp* -fied) *tr* vivifier

vivisection [,vɪvɪ'sɛkʃən] *s* vivisection *f*

vixen ['vɪksən] *s* mégère *f*; (zool) renarde *f*

viz. *abbr* (Lat: **videlicet** namely, to wit) c.-à-d., à savoir

vizier [vɪ'zɪr], ['vɪzjər] *s* vizir *m*

vocabular·y [vo'kæbjə,lɛri] *s* (*pl* -ies) vocabulaire *m*

vocal ['vokəl] *adj* vocal; (*inclined to express oneself freely*) communicatif, démonstratif

vocalist ['vokəlɪst] *s* chanteur *m*

vocalize ['vokə,laɪz] *tr* vocaliser || *intr* vocaliser; (phonet) se vocaliser

vocation [vo'keʃən] *s* vocation *f*; profession *f*, métier *m*

voca'tional guid'ance [vo'keʃənəl] *s* orientation *f* professionnelle

voca'tional school' *s* école *f* professionnelle

vocative ['vokətɪv] *s* vocatif *m*

vociferate [vo'sɪfə,ret] *intr* vociférer

vociferous [vo'sɪfərəs] *adj* vociférant, criard

vogue [vog] *s* vogue *f*; **in vogue** en vogue

voice [vɔɪs] *s* voix *f*; **in a loud voice** à voix haute; **in a low voice** à voix basse; **with one voice** unanimement || *tr* exprimer; (*a consonant*) voiser, sonoriser || *intr* se voiser

voiced *adj* (phonet) voisé, sonore

voiceless ['vɔɪslɪs] *adj* sans voix, aphone; (*consonant*) dévoisée, sourde

void [vɔɪd] *adj* vide; (law) nul; **void of** dénué de || *s* vide *m* || *tr* vider; (*the bowels*) évacuer; (law) rendre nul || *intr* évacuer, excréter

voile [vɔɪl] *s* voile *m*

volatile ['valətɪl] *adj* (*solvent*) volatil; (*disposition*) volage; (*temper*) vif

volatilize ['valətə,laɪz] *tr* volatiliser || *intr* se volatiliser

volcanic [val'kænɪk] *adj* volcanique

volca·no [val'keno] *s* (*pl* -noes or -nos) volcan *m*

volition [vəˈlɪʃən] s volition f, volonté f; **of one's own volition** de son propre gré
volley [ˈvɑli] s volée f ‖ tr lancer à la volée; (sports) reprendre de volée ‖ intr lancer une volée
vol´ley·ball´ s volley-ball m
volplane [ˈvɑl,plen] s vol m plané ‖ intr descendre en vol plané
volt [volt] s volt m
voltage [ˈvoltɪdʒ] s voltage m, tension f; **high voltage** haute tension f
volt´age drop´ s perte f de charge
volte-face [ˈvɔltˈfɑs] s volte-face f
volt´me´ter s voltmètre m
voluble [ˈvɑljəbəl] adj volubile
volume [ˈvɑljəm] s volume m; **to speak volumes** en dire long
vol´ume num´ber s tomaison f
voluminous [vəˈlumɪnəs] adj volumineux
voluntar·y [ˈvɑlən,tɛri] adj volontaire ‖ s (pl -ies) (mus) morceau m d'orgue improvisé
volunteer [,vɑlənˈtɪr] adj & s volontaire mf ‖ tr offrir volontairement ‖ intr (mil) s'engager; **to volunteer to** + inf s'offrir à + inf
voluptuar·y [vəˈlʌptʃu,ɛri] adj voluptuaire ‖ s (pl -ies) voluptueux m
voluptuous [vəˈlʌptʃu·əs] adj voluptueux
vomit [ˈvɑmɪt] s vomissure f ‖ tr & intr vomir
voodoo [ˈvudu] adj & s vaudou m
voracious [vəˈreʃəs] adj vorace
voraci·ty [vəˈræsɪti] s (pl -ties) voracité f
vor·tex [ˈvɔrtɛks] s (pl -texes or -tices [tɪ,siz]) vortex m, tourbillon m
vota·ry [ˈvotəri] s (pl -ries) fidèle mf

vote [vot] s vote m; **by popular vote** au suffrage universel; **to put to the vote** mettre aux voix; **to tally the votes** dépouiller le scrutin; **vote by show of hands** vote à main levée ‖ tr voter; **to vote down** repousser; **to vote in** élire ‖ intr voter; **to vote for** voter; **to vote on** passer au vote
voter [ˈvotər] s votant m, électeur m
vot´ing booth´ s isoloir m
vot´ing machine´ s machine f électorale
votive [ˈvotɪv] adj votif
vouch [vautʃ] tr affirmer, garantir ‖ intr—**to vouch for** répondre de
voucher [ˈvautʃər] s garant m; (certificate) récépissé m, pièce f comptable, bon m de change
vouch·safe´ tr octroyer ‖ intr—**to vouch-safe to** + inf daigner + inf
vow [vau] s vœu m; **to take vows** entrer en religion ‖ tr (e.g., revenge) jurer ‖ intr faire un vœu; **to vow to** faire vœu de
vowel [ˈvau·əl] s voyelle f
voyage [ˈvɔɪ·ɪdʒ] s (by air or sea) traversée f; (any journey) voyage m ‖ tr traverser ‖ intr voyager
voyager [ˈvɔɪ·ɪdʒər] s voyageur m
vs. abbr (**versus**) contre
vulcanize [ˈvʌlkə,naɪz] tr vulcaniser
vulgar [ˈvʌlgər] adj grossier; (popular, common; vernacular) vulgaire
vulgari·ty [vʌlˈgærɪti] s (pl -ties) grossièreté f, vulgarité f
Vul´gar Lat´in s latin m vulgaire
vulnerable [ˈvʌlnərəbəl] adj vulnérable
vulture [ˈvʌltʃər] s vautour m

W

W, w [ˈdʌbəl,ju] s XXIIIᵉ lettre de l'alphabet
wad [wɑd] s (of cotton) tampon m; (of papers) liasse f; (in a gun) bourre f ‖ v (pret & pp **wadded;** ger **wadding**) tr bourrer
waddle [ˈwɑdəl] s dandinement m ‖ intr se dandiner
wade [wed] tr traverser à gué ‖ intr marcher dans l'eau, patauger; **to wade into** (coll) s'attaquer à; **to wade through** (coll) avancer péniblement dans
wad´ing bird´ s (orn) échassier m
wad´ing pool´ s pataugeoire f
wafer [ˈwefər] s (thin, crisp cake) gaufrette f; (pill) cachet m; (for sealing letters) pain m à cacheter; (eccl) hostie f
waffle [ˈwɑfəl] s gaufre f
waf´fle i´ron s gaufrier m, moule m à gaufre
waft [wæt], [wɑft] tr porter; (a kiss) envoyer ‖ intr flotter

wag [wæg] s (of head) hochement m; (of tail) frétillement m; (jester) farceur m ‖ v (pret & pp **wagged;** ger **wagging**) tr (the head) hocher; (the tail) remuer ‖ intr frétiller
wage [wedʒ] s salaire m; **wages** gages mpl, salaire m; (fig) salaire, récompense f ‖ tr—**to wage war** faire la guerre
wage´ earn´er [,ʌrnər] s salarié m
wage´-price´ freeze´ s blocage m des prix et des salaires
wager [ˈwedʒər] s pari m; **to lay a wager** faire un pari ‖ tr & intr parier
wage´work´er s salarié m
waggish [ˈwægɪʃ] adj plaisant, facétieux
wagon [ˈwægən] s charrette f; (Conestoga wagon; plaything) chariot m; (mil) fourgon m; **to be on the wagon** (slang) s'abstenir de boissons alcooliques
wag´tail´ s hochequeue m, bergeronnette f
waif [wef] s (founding) enfant m trouvé;

animal *m* égaré or abandonné; (*stray child*) voyou *m*

wail [wel] *s* lamentation *f*, plainte *f* ‖ *intr* se lamenter, gémir

wain·scot [ˈwenskət] *s* lambris *m* ‖ *v* (*pret & pp* **-scoted** or **-scotted**; *ger* **-scoting or -scotting**) *tr* lambrisser

waist [west] *s* (*of human body; corresponding part of garment*) taille *f*, ceinture *f*; (*garment*) corsage *m*, blouse *f*

waist′band′ *s* ceinture *f*

waist′cloth′ *s* pagne *m*

waistcoat [ˈwest,kot] *s* gilet *m*

waist′-deep′ *adj* jusqu'à la ceinture

waist′line′ *s* taille *f*, ceinture *f*; **to keep or watch one's waistline** garder or soigner sa ligne

wait [wet] *s* attente *f*; **to lie in wait for** guetter ‖ *tr*—**to wait one's turn** attendre son tour ‖ *intr* attendre; **to wait for** attendre; **to wait on** (*customers; dinner guests*) servir

wait′-and-see′ pol′icy *s* attentisme *m*

waiter [ˈwetər] *s* garçon *m*; (*tray*) plateau *m*

wait′ing list′ *s* liste *f* d'attente

wait′ing room′ *s* salle *f* d'attente; (*of a doctor*) antichambre *f*

waitress [ˈwetrɪs] *s* serveuse *f*; **waitress!** mademoiselle!

waive [wev] *tr* renoncer à; (*to defer*) différer

waiver [ˈwevər] *s* renonciation *f*, abandon *m*

wake [wek] *s* (*watch by the body of a dead person*) veillée *f* mortuaire; (*of a boat or other moving object*) silage *m*; **in the wake of** dans le sillage de, à la suite de ‖ *v* (*pret* **waked** or **woke** [wok]; *pp* **waked**) *tr* réveiller ‖ *intr*—**to wake to** se rendre compte de; **to wake up** se réveiller

wakeful [ˈwekfəl] *adj* éveillé

wakefulness [ˈwekfəlnɪs] *s* veille *f*

waken [ˈwekən] *tr* éveiller, réveiller ‖ *intr* s'éveiller, se réveiller

wale [wel] *s* zébrure *f* ‖ *tr* zébrer

Wales [welz] *s* le pays de Galles

walk [wɔk] *s* (*act*) promenade *f*; (*distance*) marche *f*; (*way of walking, bearing*) démarche *f*; (*of a garden*) allée *f*; (*calling*) métier *m*; **to fall into a walk** (*said of horse*) se mettre au pas; **to go for a walk** faire une promenade ‖ *tr* promener; (*a horse*) promener au pas ‖ *intr* aller à pied, marcher; (*to stroll*) se promener; **to walk away** s'en aller à pied; **to walk off with** (*a prize*) gagner; (*a stolen object*) décamper avec; **to walk out** sortir, partir subitement; (*to go on strike*) se mettre en grève; **to walk out on** abandonner; quitter en colère

walk′away′ *s* (coll) victoire *f* facile

walker [ˈwɔkər] *s* marcheur *m*, promeneur *m*; (*pedestrian*) piéton *m*; (*go-cart*) chariot *m* d'enfant; (*used by an infirm person*) déambulateur *m*

walkie-talkie [ˈwɔkiˈtɔki] *s* (rad) talkie-walkie *m*, émetteur-récepteur *m* portatif, parle-en-marche *m*

walk′ing pa′pers *spl*—**to give s.o. his walking papers** (coll) congédier qn

walk′ing shoes′ *spl* souliers *mpl* de marche

walk′ing stick′ *s* canne *f*

walk′man′ *s* (rad) baladeur *m*, walkman *m*, somnambule *m*

walk′-on′ *s* (*actor*) figurant *m*, comparse *mf*; (*role*) figuration *f*

walk′out′ *s* (coll) grève *f* improvisée

walk′o′ver *s* (coll) victoire *f* dans un fauteuil

walk′-up′ *s* appartement *m* sans ascenseur

wall [wɔl] *s* mur *m*; (*between rooms; of a pipe, boiler, etc.*) paroi *f*; (*of a fortification*) muraille *f*; **to go to the wall** succomber; perdre la partie ‖ *tr* entourer de murs; **to wall up** murer

wall′board′ *s* panneau *m* or carreau *m* de revêtement

wall′ clock′ *s* pendule *f* murale

wallet [ˈwɑlɪt] *s* portefeuille *m*

wall′flow′er *s* (bot) ravenelle *f*, giroflée *f*; **to be a wallflower** (coll) faire tapisserie

wall′ lamp′ *s* applique *f*

wall′ map′ *s* carte *f* murale

Walloon [wɑˈlun] *adj* wallon ‖ *s* (*dialect*) wallon *m*; (*person*) Wallon *m*

wallop [ˈwɑləp] *s* (coll) coup *m*, gnon *m*; **with a wallop** (fig) à grand fracas ‖ *tr* (coll) tanner le cuir à, rosser; (*a ball*) (coll) frapper raide; (*to defeat*) (coll) battre

wallow [ˈwɑlo] *s* souille *f* ‖ *intr* se vautrer; (*e.g., in wealth*) nager

wall′pa′per *s* papier *m* peint ‖ *tr* tapisser

wall′-to-wall′ car′peting *s* tapis *m* mur à mur

walnut [ˈwɔlnət] *s* noix *f*; (*tree and wood*) noyer *m*

walrus [ˈwɔlrəs], [ˈwɑlrəs] *s* morse *m*

Walter [ˈwɔltər] *s* Gautier *m*

waltz [wɔlts] *s* valse *f* ‖ *tr & intr* valser

wan [wɑn] *adj* (*comp* **wanner**; *super* **wannest**) pâle blême; (*weak*) faible

wand [wɑnd] *s* baguette *f*; (*emblem of authority*) bâton *m*, verge *f*

wander [ˈwɑndər] *tr* vagabonder sur, parcourir ‖ *intr* errer, vaguer; (*said of one's mind*) vagabonder

wanderer [ˈwɑndərər] *s* vagabond *m*

wan′der·lust′ *s* manie *f* des voyages, bougeotte *f*

wane [wen] *s* déclin *m*; (*of moon*) décours *m* ‖ *intr* décliner; (*said of moon*) décroître

wangle [ˈwæŋɡəl] *tr* (*to obtain by scheming*) (coll) resquiller; (*accounts*) (coll) cuisiner; (*e.g., a leave of absence*) (coll) carotter; **to wangle one's way out of** (coll) se débrouiller de ‖ *intr* (coll) pratiquer le système D

want [wɔnt] *s* (*need; misery*) besoin *m*; (*lack*) manque *m*; **for want of** faute de, à défaut de; **to be in want** être dans la gêne ‖ *tr* (*to need*) avoir besoin de; **to want s.o. to** + *inf* vouloir que qn + *subj*; **to want to** + *inf* avoir envie de + *inf*, vouloir + *inf* ‖ *intr* être dans le besoin; **to be wanting** manquer

want' ads' *spl* petites annonces *fpl*

wanton ['wɑntən] *adj* déréglé; (*e.g., cruelty*) gratuit; (*e.g., child*) espiègle; (*e.g., woman*) impudique

war [wɔr] *s* guerre *f*; **to go to war** se mettre en guerre; (*as a soldier*) aller à la guerre; **to wage war** faire la guerre ‖ *v* (*pret & pp* **warred**; *ger* **warring**) *intr* faire la guerre; **to war on** faire la guerre contre

warble ['wɔrbəl] *s* gazouillement *m* ‖ *intr* gazouiller

warbler ['wɔrblər] *s* (orn) fauvette *f*

war' cloud' *s* menace *f* de guerre

war' correspon'dent *s* correspondant *m* de guerre

war' cry' *s* (*pl* **cries**) cri *m* de guerre

ward [wɔrd] *s* (*person, usually a minor under protection of another*) pupille *mf*; (*guardianship*) tutelle *f*; (*of a city*) circonscription *f* électorale, quartier *m*; (*of a hospital*) salle *f*; (*of a lock*) gardes *fpl* ‖ *tr*—**to ward off** parer

war' dance' *s* danse *f* guerrière

warden ['wɔrdən] *s* gardien *m*; (*of a jail*) directeur *m*; (*of a church*) marguillier *m*; (*gamekeeper*) garde-chasse *m*

ward' heel'er *s* politicailleur *m* servile

ward'robe' *s* garde-robe *f*

ward'robe trunk' *s* malle-armoire *f*

ward'room' *s* (nav) carré *m* des officiers

ware [wɛr] *s* faïence *f*; **wares** articles *mpl* de vente, marchandises *fpl*

ware'house' *s* entrepôt *m*

ware'house'man *s* (*pl* **-men**) garde-magasin *m*, magasinier *m*

war'fare' *s* guerre *f*

war'head' *s* charge *f* creuse

war'-horse' *s* cheval *m* de bataille; (coll) vétéran *m*

warily ['wɛrɪli] *adv* prudemment

war'like' *adj* guerrier

war' loan' *s* emprunt *m* de guerre

war' lord' *s* seigneur *m* de la guerre

warm [wɔrm] *adj* chaud; (*welcome, thanks, friend, etc.*) chaleureux; (*heart*) généreux; **it is warm** (*said of weather*) il fait chaud; **to be warm** (*said of person*) avoir chaud; **to keep s.th. warm** tenir q.ch. au chaud; **you're getting warm!** (*you've almost found it!*) vous brûlez! ‖ *tr* chauffer, faire chauffer; **to warm up** réchauffer ‖ *intr* se réchauffer; **to warm up** se réchauffer, chauffer, se chauffer; (*said of speaker, discussion, etc.*) s'animer s'échauffer

warm'-blood'ed *adj* passionné, ardent; (*animals*) à sang chaud

war' memor'ial *s* monument *m* aux morts de la guerre

warmer ['wɔrmər] *s* (culin) réchaud *m*

warm'-heart'ed *adj* au cœur généreux

warm'ing pan' *s* bassinoire *f*

warmonger ['wɔr,mʌŋgər] *s* belliciste *mf*

war' moth'er *s* marraine *f* de guerre

warmth [wɔrmθ] *s* chaleur *f*

warm'-up' *s* exercises *mpl* d'assouplissement; mise *f* en condition

warn [wɔrn] *tr* prévenir; **to warn s.o. to** avertir qn de

warning ['wɔrnɪŋ] *s* avertissement *m*; **without warning** par surprise

warn'ing shot' *s* coup *m* de semonce

war' of attri'tion *s* guerre *f* d'usure

warp [wɔrp] *s* (*of a fabric*) chaîne *f*; (*of a board*) gauchissement *m*; (naut) touée *f* ‖ *tr* gauchir; (*the mind, judgment, etc.*) fausser; (naut) touer ‖ *intr* se gauchir; (naut) se touer

war'path' *s*—**to be on the warpath** être sur le sentier de la guerre; (*to be out of sorts*) (coll) être d'une humeur de dogue

war' plane' *s* avion *m* de guerre

warrant ['wɔrənt] *s* (*guarantee*) garantie *f*; (*attestation*) certificat *m*; (*right*) justification *f*; (*for arrest*) mandat *m* d'arrêt ‖ *tr* garantir; certifier; justifier

war'rant of'ficer *s* (mil) sous-officier *m* breveté; (nav) premier maître *m*

warran·ty ['wɔrənti] *s* (*pl* **-ties**) garantie *f*; autorisation *f*

war' ranty ser'vice *s* service *m* après vente

warren ['wɔrən] *s* garenne *f*

warrior ['wɔrjər] *s* guerrier *m*

Warsaw ['wɔrsɔ] *s* Varsovie *f*

war'ship' *s* navire *m* de guerre

wart [wɔrt] *s* verrue *f*

war'time' *s* temps *m* de guerre

war'-torn' *adj* dévasté par la guerre

war·y ['wɛri] *adj* (*comp* **-ier**; *super* **-iest**) prudent, avisé

wash [wɔʃ] *s* (*washing*) lavage *m*; (*clothes washed or to be washed*) lessive *f*; (*dirty water*) lavure *f*; (*place where the surf breaks; broken water behind a moving ship*) remous *m*; (aer) souffle *m* ‖ *tr* laver; (*one's hands, face, etc.*) se laver; (*dishes, laundry, etc.*) faire; (*e.g., a seacoast*) baigner; **to wash away** enlever; (*e.g., a bank*) affouiller, ronger ‖ *intr* se laver; (*to do the laundry*) faire la lessive

washable ['wɔʃəbəl] *adj* lavable

wash'-and-wear' *adj* de repassage superflu de séchage rapide

wash'ba'sin *s* (*basin*) cuvette *f*; (*fixture*) lavabo *m*

wash'bas'ket *s* corbeille *f* à linge

wash'board' *s* planche *f* à laver

wash'bowl' *s* (*basin*) cuvette *f*; (*fixture*) lavabo *m*

wash'cloth' *s* gant *m* de toilette

wash'day' *s* jour *m* de lessive

washed'-out' *adj* délavé, déteint; (coll) flapi, vanné, à plat, vaseux

washed'-up' *adj* (coll) hors de combat, ruiné

washer ['wɔʃər] *s* (*person*) laveur *m*; (*machine*) laveuse *f*, lessiveuse *f*; (*ring of metal*) rondelle *f*; (*ring of rubber*) rondelle de robinet

wash'er·wom'an *s* (*pl* **-wom'en**) blanchisseuse *f*

wash' goods' *spl* tissus *mpl* grand teint

washing ['wɔʃɪŋ] s lavage m; (*act of washing clothes*) blanchissage m; (*clothes washed or to be washed*) lessive f; **washings** lavures fpl

wash'ing machine' s machine f à laver, laveuse f automatique

wash'ing so'da s cristaux mpl de soude

wash'out' s affouillement m; (*person*) (coll) raté m; **to be a washout** (coll) faire fiasco, faire four

wash'rag' s gant m de toilette, torchon m

wash'room' s cabinet m de toilette, lavabo m

wash' sale' s (com) lavage m des titres

wash'stand' s lavabo m

wash'tub' s baquet m, cuvier m

wash' wa'ter s lavure f

wasp [wɑsp] s guêpe f

wasp' waist' s taille f de guêpe

waste [west] adj (*land*) inculte; (*material*) de rebut ‖ s (*loss*) gaspillage m; (*garbage*) déchets mpl; (*wild region*) région f inculte; (*of time*) perte f; (*for wiping machinery*) chiffons mpl de nettoyage, effiloche f de coton; **to lay waste** dévaster; **wastes** déchets; excrément m ‖ tr gaspiller, perdre ‖ intr—**to waste away** dépérir, maigrir

waste'bas'ket s corbeille f à papier

wasteful ['westfəl] adj gaspilleur

waste'pa'per s papier m de rebut; (*public sign*) papers

waste' pipe' s tuyau m d'écoulement, vidange f

waste' prod'ucts spl déchets mpl

wastrel ['westrəl] s gaspilleur m, prodigue mf

watch [wɑtʃ] s (*for telling time*) montre f; (*lookout*) garde f, guet m; (naut) quart m; **to be on the watch for** guetter; **to be on watch** (naut) être de quart; **to keep watch over** surveiller ‖ tr (*to look at*) observer; (*to oversee*) surveiller ‖ intr être aux aguets; (*to keep awake*) veiller; **to watch for** guetter; **to watch out** faire attention; **to watch over** surveiller; **watch out!** attention! gare!

watch'case' s boîtier m de montre

watch' chain' s chaîne f de montre

watch' charm' s breloque f

watch' crys'tal s verre m de montre

watch'dog' s chien m de garde; gardien m vigilant

watch'dog' commit'tee s comité m de surveillance

watchful ['wɑtʃfəl] adj vigilant

watchfulness ['wɑtʃfəlnɪs] s vigilance f

watch'mak'er s horloger m

watch'man s (pl -men) gardien m

watch' night' s réveillon m du jour de l'an

watch' pock'et s gousset m

watch' strap' s bracelet m d'une montre

watch'tow'er s tour f de guet

watch'word' s (*password*) mot m d'ordre, mot de passe; (*slogan*) devise f

water ['wɔtər] s eau f; **of the first water** de premier ordre; (*diamond*) de première eau; **to back water** (naut) culer; reculer; **to be** in hot water (coll) être dans le pétrin; **to fish in troubled waters** pêcher en eau trouble; **to hold water** (coll) tenir debout, être bien fondé; **to make water** (*to urinate*) uriner; (naut) faire eau; **to pour** or **throw cold water on** (fig) jeter une douche froide sur, refroidir; **to swim under water** nager entre deux eaux; **to tread water** nager debout ‖ tr (*e.g., plants*) arroser; (*horses, cattle, etc.*) abreuver; (*wine*) couper; **to water down** atténuer ‖ intr (*said of horses, cattle, etc.*) s'abreuver; (*said of locomotive, ship, etc.*) faire de l'eau; (*said of eyes*) se mouiller, larmoyer

wa'ter bed' s matelas m à eau

wa'ter buf'fa·lo s (pl -loes or -los) buffle m

wa'ter car'rier s porteur m d'eau

wa'ter clock' s horloge f à eau, horloge d'eau

wa'ter clos'et s water-closet m, waters mpl

wa'ter·col'or s aquarelle f

wa'ter-cooled' adj à refroidissement d'eau

wa'ter·course' s cours m d'eau; (*of a stream*) lit m

wa'ter·cress' s cresson m de fontaine

wa'ter cure' s cure f des eaux

wa'ter·fall' s chute f d'eau

wa'ter·front' s terrain m sur la rive

wa'ter gap' s percée f, trouée f, gorge f

wa'ter ham'mer s (*in pipe*) coup m de bélier

wa'ter heat'er s chauffe-eau m, chauffe-bain m

wa'ter ice' s boisson f à demi glacée

wa'tering can' s arrosoir m

wa'tering place' s (*for cattle*) abreuvoir m; (*for tourists*) ville f d'eau

wa'tering pot' s arrosoir m

wa'tering trough' s abreuvoir m

wa'ter jack'et s chemise f d'eau

wa'ter lil'y s nénuphar m

wa'ter line' s ligne f de flottaison; niveau m d'eau

wa'ter·logged' adj détrempé

wa'ter main' s conduite f principale

wa'ter·mark' s (*in paper*) filigrane m; (naut) laisse f

wa'ter·mel'on s pastèque f, melon m d'eau

wa'ter me'ter s compteur m à eau

wa'ter pick' s (dentistry) jet m dentaire

wa'ter pipe' s conduite f d'eau

wa'ter po'lo s water-polo m

wa'ter pow'er s force f hydraulique, houille f blanche

wa'ter·proof' adj & s imperméable m

wa'ter·proof'ing s imperméabilisation f

wa'ter rights' spl droits mpl de captation d'eau, droits d'irrigation

wa'ter·shed' s ligne f de partage des eaux, ligne de faîte

wa'ter ski'er s skieur m nautique

wa'ter ski'ing s ski m nautique

wa'ter sof'tener s assouplisseur m

wa'ter span'iel s (zool) barbet m

wa'ter·spout' s descente f d'eau, gouttière f; (*funnel of wet air*) trombe f

wa'ter-supply sys'tem *s* service *m* des eaux; réseau *m* de conduites d'eau

wa'ter ta'ble *s* (geol) nappe *f* phréatique

wa'ter-tight' *adj* étanche; (*argument*) inattaquable; (law) sans clause échappatoire

wa'ter tow'er *s* château *m* d'eau

wa'ter va'por *s* vapeur *m* d'eau

wa'ter wag'on *s*—**to be on the water wagon** (coll) s'abstenir de boissons alcooliques

wa'ter-way' *s* voie *f* navigable

wa'ter wheel' *s* roue *f* hydraulique; roue à aubes *or* à palettes; roue-turbine *f*

wa'ter wings' *spl* flotteur *m* de natation

wa'ter-works' *s* (*system*) canalisations *fpl* d'eau; (*pumping station*) usine *f* de distribution des eaux

watery ['wɔtəri] *adj* aqueux; (*eyes*) larmoyant; (*food*) insipide, fade

watt [wɑt] *s* watt *m*

wattage ['wɑtɪdʒ] *s* puissance *f* en watts

watt'-hour' *s* (*pl* **watt-hours**) watt-heure *m*

wattle ['wɑtəl] *s* (*of bird*) caroncule *f*; (*of fish*) barbillon *m*

watt'me'ter *s* wattmètre *m*

wave [wev] *s* onde *f*, vague *f*; (*in hair*) ondulation *f*; geste *m* de la main; (*of heat or cold*; *of people*; *of the future*) vague *f*; (phys) onde ‖ *tr* (*a handkerchief*) agiter; (*the hair*) onduler; (*a hat, newspaper, cane*) brandir; **to wave aside** écarter d'un geste; **to wave good-bye** faire un signe d'adieu; **to wave one's hand** faire un geste de la main ‖ *intr* s'agiter; (*said of a flag*) ondoyer; **to wave to** faire signe à

wave'length' *s* longueur *f* d'onde

wave' mo'tion *s* mouvement *m* ondulatoire

waver ['wevər] *intr* vaciller

wav·y ['wevi] *adj* (*comp* **-ier**; *super* **-iest**) onduleux, ondoyant; (*hair*; *road surface*) ondulé; (*line*) tremblé, onduleux

wax [wæks] *s* cire *f* ‖ *tr* cirer ‖ *intr*—**to wax and wane** croître et décroître; **to wax indignant** s'indigner

wax' bean' *s* haricot *m* beurre

wax' pa'per *s* papier *m* paraffiné

wax' ta'per *s* allumette-bougie *f*

wax'wing' *s* (orn) jaseur *m*

wax'works' *s* musée *m* de cire

way [we] *s* voie *f*; (*road*) chemin *m*; (*direction*) côté *m*, sens *m*; (*manner*) façon *f*, manière *f*; (*means*) moyen *m*; (*habit, custom*) manière *f*, habitude *f*, usage *m*; **across the way** en face; **all the way** jusqu'au bout; **by the way** à propos; **by way of** par; comme; **get out of the way!** ôtez-vous de là!; **in a way** en un certain sens; **in every way** à tous les égards; **in my (his, etc.) own way** à ma (sa, etc.) façon *or* manière; **in no way** en aucune façon; **in some ways** par certains côtés; **in such a way that** de sorte que; **in that way** de la sorte; **in this way** de cette façon; **on the way** chemin faisant; **on the way to** en route pour; **out of the way** écarté **that way** par là; **the wrong way** le mauvais sens, la mauvaise route; (*the wrong man-*

ner) la mauvaise façon; (*when brushing hair*) à contre-poil; **this way** par ici; **to be in the way** être encombrant; **to feel one's way** avancer à tâtons; **to get out of the way** s'écarter; **to get** (*s.th. or s.o.*) **out of the way** se débarrasser de (*q.ch. or qn*); **to give way** céder; **to go one's own way** faire bande à part; **to go one's way** passer son chemin; **to go out of one's way** faire un détour; (fig) se déranger; **to have one's way** avoir le dernier mot, l'emporter; **to keep out of s.o.'s way** se tenir à l'écart de qn; **to know one's way around** connaître son affaire, être à la coule; **to lead the way** montrer le chemin; **to make one's way** se frayer un chemin; **to make way for** faire place à; **to mend one's ways** s'amender; **to see one's way to** trouver moyen de; **to stand in the way of** barrer le chemin à; **under way** en marche, en cours; **way down** descente *f*; **way in** entrée *f*; **way out** sortie *f*; **ways** (*for launching a ship*) couette *f*, anguilles *fpl*; **way through** passage *m*; **way up** montée *f*; **which way?** par où?

way'bill' *s* feuille *f* de route, lettre *f* de voiture

wayfarer ['we,fɛrər] *s* voyageur *m*, vagabond *m*

way'lay' *v* (*pret & pp* **-laid**) *tr* embusquer; (*to buttonhole*) arrêter au passage

way' of life' *s* manière *f* de vivre, genre *m* de vie, train *m* de vie

way'side' *s* bord *m* de la route; **to fall by the wayside** rester en chemin

wayward ['wewərd] *adj* capricieux; rebelle

we [wi] *pron pers* nous §85, §87; nous autres, e.g., **we Americans** nous autres américains

weak [wik] *adj* faible

weaken ['wikən] *tr* affaiblir ‖ *intr* faiblir, s'affaiblir

weakling ['wiklɪŋ] *s* chétif *m*, malingre *mf*; (*in character*) mou *m*

weak'-mind'ed *adj* irrésolu, d'esprit faible; (*feeble-minded*) débile

weakness ['wiknɪs] *s* faiblesse *f*

weal [wil] *s* papule *f*; (archaic) bien *m*

wealth [wɛlθ] *s* richesse *f*

wealth·y ['wɛlθi] *adj* (*comp* **-ier**; *super* **-iest**) riche, opulent

wean [win] *tr* sevrer; **to wean away from** détacher de

weapon ['wɛpən] *s* arme *f*

weaponry ['wɛpənri] *s* armement *m*

wear [wɛr] *s* (*use*) usage *m*; (*wasting away from use*) usure *f*; (*clothing*) vêtements *mpl*, articles *mpl* d'habillement; **for evening wear** pour le soir; **for everyday wear** pour tous les jours ‖ *v* (*pret* **wore** [wor]; *pp* **worn** [worn]) *tr* porter; (*to put on*) mettre; **to wear down** *or* **out** user; (*e.g., one's patience*) épuiser ‖ *intr* s'user; **to wear off** s'effacer; **to wear on** s'écouler, s'avancer; **to wear out** s'user; **to wear well** durer

wearable ['wɛrəbəl] *adj* mettable

wear′ and tear′ [tɛr] s usure f

weariness [ˈwɪrɪnɪs] s lassitude f, fatigue f; (boredom) ennui m

wear′ing appar′el [ˈwɛrɪŋ] s vêtements mpl, habits mpl

wearisome [ˈwɪrɪsəm] adj lassant, ennuyeux

wea·ry [ˈwɪri] adj (comp -rier; super -riest) las ‖ v (pret & pp -ried) tr lasser ‖ intr se lasser

weasel [ˈwizəl] s (zool) belette f; (slang) mouchard m

wea′sel words′ spl mots mpl ambigus

weather [ˈwɛðər] s temps m; **to be under the weather** (coll) se sentir patraque; (from drinking) (coll) avoir mal aux cheveux; **what′s the weather like?** quel temps fait-il? ‖ tr altérer; (e.g., difficulties) survivre à, étaler ‖ intr s′altérer

weath′er balloon′ s ballon m atmosphérique

weath′er-beat′en adj usé par les intempéries

weath′er bu′reau s bureau m météorologique, météo f

weath′er·cock′ s girouette f; (fig) girouette, caméléon m

weath′er fore′cast s bulletin m météorologique

weath′er fore′casting s prévision f du temps

weath′er·man′ s (pl -men′) météorologue mf, météorologiste mf

weath′er report′ s bulletin m de la météo

weath′er strip′ping s bourrelet m

weath′er vane′ s girouette f

weave [wiv] s armure f ‖ v (pret wove [wov] or weaved; pp wove or woven [ˈwovən]) tr tisser; **to weave one′s way through** se faufiler à travers, se faufiler entre ‖ intr tisser; serpenter, zigzaguer

weaver [ˈwivər] s tisserand m

web [wɛb] s (piece of cloth) tissu m; (roll of newsprint) rouleau m; (of spider) toile f; (between toes of birds and other animals) palmure f; (of an iron rail) âme f; (fig) trame f

web′-foot′ed adj palmé, palmipède

wed [wɛd] v (pret & pp wed or wedded; ger wedding) tr (to join in wedlock) marier; (to take in marriage) épouser ‖ intr épouser, se marier

wedding [ˈwɛdɪŋ] adj nuptial ‖ s mariage m, noces fpl

wed′ding ban′quet s repas m de noce

wed′ding cake′ s gâteau m de mariage

wed′ding cer′emo·ny s (pl -nies) cérémonie f nuptiale

wed′ding day′ s jour m des noces; (anniversry) anniversaire m du mariage

wed′ding dress′ s robe f nuptiale, robe de noce, robe de mariée

wed′ding march′ s marche f nuptiale

wed′ding night′ s nuit f de noces

wed′ding pres′ent s cadeau m de mariage; **wedding presents** corbeille f de mariage

wed′ding ring′ s anneau m nuptial, alliance f

wedge [wɛdʒ] s coin m ‖ tr coincer

wedlock [ˈwɛdlɑk] s mariage m

Wednesday [ˈwɛnzdi] s mercredi m

wee [wi] adj tout petit

weed [wid] s mauvaise herbe f; **the weed** (coll) le tabac; **weeds** vêtements mpl de deuil ‖ tr & intr désherber, sarcler; **to weed out** éliminer, extirper

weed′ing hoe′ s sarcloir m

weed′ kill′er s herbicide m

weed′ whack′er [ˌhwækər] s taille-herbe m

week [wik] s semaine f; **a week from today** d′aujourd′hui en huit; **week in week out** d′un bout de la semaine à l′autre

week′day′ s jour m de semaine, jour ouvrable

week′end′ s fin f de semaine, week-end m ‖ intr passer le week-end

week·ly [ˈwikli] adj hebdomadaire ‖ s (pl -lies) hebdomadaire m ‖ adv tous les huit jours

weep [wip] v (pret & pp wept [wɛpt]) tr pleurer ‖ intr pleurer; (to drip) suinter; **to weep for** pleurer; (joy) pleurer de

weep′ing wil′low s saule m pleureur

weep·y [ˈwipi] adj (comp -ier; super -iest) (coll) pleurnicheur

weevil [ˈwivəl] s charançon m

weft [wɛft] s (yarns running across warp) trame f; (fabric) tissu m

weigh [we] tr peser; (anchor) lever; **to weigh down** faire pencher; **to weigh in one′s hand** soupeser ‖ intr peser; **to weigh heavily with** avoir du poids auprès de; **to weigh in** (sports) se faire peser

weight [wet] s poids m; **to gain weight** prendre du poids; **to lift weights** faire des haltères; **to lose weight** perdre du poids; **to throw one′s weight around** (coll) s′imposer ‖ tr charger; (statistically) pondérer; **to weight down** alourdir

weightless [ˈwetlɪs] adj sans pesanteur

weightlessness [ˈwetlɪsnɪs] s apesanteur f, impesanteur f

weight′ lift′er [ˌlɪftər] s (sports) haltérophile m

weight′ lift′ing s poids et haltères mpl

weight·y [ˈweti] adj (comp -ier; super -iest) pesant, lourd; (troublesome) grave; important, puissant

weir [wɪr] s (dam) barrage m; (trap) filet m à poissons

weird [wɪrd] adj surnaturel; étrange

welcome [ˈwɛlkəm] adj bienvenu; (change, news, etc.) agréable; **to be welcome to** + inf être libre de + inf; **you are welcome!** (i.e., gladly received) soyez le bienvenu!; (in response to thanks) de rien!, je vous en prie!, il n′y a pas de quoi!; **you are welcome to it** c′est à votre disposition; (ironically) je ne vous envie pas ‖ s bienvenue f, bon accueil m ‖ tr souhaiter la bienvenue à, faire bon accueil à, accueillir; **to welcome coldly** faire mauvais accueil à, accueillir froidement

welcoming ['wɛlkəmɪŋ] *adj* (*friendly*) accueillant; (*party, speeches*) d'accueil

weld [wɛld] *s* soudure *f* autogène; (bot) gaude *f*, réséda *m* ‖ *tr* souder à l'autogène

welder ['wɛldər] *s* soudeur *m*; (mach) soudeuse *f*

welding ['wɛldɪŋ] *s* soudure *f* autogène

weld'ing gun' *s* pistolet *m* à souder

welfare ['wɛl,fɛr] *s* bien-être *m*; (*for underprivileged*) aide *f* sociale

wel'fare state' *s* état-providence *m*

wel'fare work' *s* assistance *f* sociale

well [wɛl] *adj* bien (*enjoying good health*) bien, bien portant; **all's well** tout est bien; **it would be just as well to** il serait bon de; **to be well** aller bien ‖ *s* (*drilled hole*) puits *m*; (*natural source of water*) source *f*, fontaine *f*; (*of stairway*) cage *f* ‖ *adv* bien; **as well** aussi; **as well as** aussi bien que; **well and good!** à la bonne heure! ‖ *intr*—**to well up** jaillir ‖ *interj* alors!, tiens!

well'-behaved' *adj* de bonne conduite; (*child*) sage

well'-be'ing *s* bien-être *m*

well'born' *adj* bien né

well-bred ['wɛl'brɛd] *adj* bien élevé

well'-built' *adj* (*building*) bien construit, solide; (*person*) bien bâti, solide, costaud

well'-disposed' *adj* bien dispose

well-done ['wɛl'dʌn] *adj* bien fait; (culin) bien cuit

well'-dressed' *adj* bien vêtu

well'-fixed' *adj* (coll) bien renté, riche

well'-formed' *adj* bien conformé

well'-found'ed *adj* bien fondé

well'-groomed' *adj* paré, soigné

well'-heeled' *adj* (coll) huppé, riche

well'-informed' *adj* bien informé

well'-inten'tioned *adj* bien intentionné

well-kept ['wɛl'kɛpt] *adj* bien tenu; (*secret*) bien gardé

well-known ['wɛl'non] *adj* bien connu, notoire

well'-matched' *adj* bien assortis

well'-mean'ing *adj* bien intentionné

well'-nigh' *adv* presque

well'-off' *adj* fortuné, prospère

well'-preserved' *adj* bien conservé

well-read ['wɛl'rɛd] *adj* qui a beaucoup de lecture

well-spent ['wɛl'spɛnt] *adj* bien employé

well'spring' *s* source *f*, source intarissable

well' sweep' *s* chadouf *m*

well'-thought'-of' *adj* de bonne réputation

well'-timed' *adj* opportun

well-to-do ['wɛltə'du] *adj* aisé, cossu

well-wisher ['wɛl'wɪʃər] *s* partisan *m*, ami *m* fidèle

well'-worn' *adj* usé; (*subject*) rebattu

Welsh [wɛlʃ] *adj* gallois ‖ *s* (*language*) gallois *m*; **the Welsh** les Gallois *mpl* ‖ (*l.c.*) *intr* (slang) manquer à sa parole, manquer à ses obligations; **to welsh on s.o.** (slang) manquer à qn

Welsh'man *s* (*pl* -**men**) Gallois *m*

Welsh' rab'bit or **rare'bit** ['rɛrbɪt] *s* fondue *f* au fromage et à la bière sur canapé

welt [wɛlt] *s* zébrure *f*; (*border*) bordure *f*; (*of shoe*) trépointe *f*

welter ['wɛltər] *s* confusion *f*, fouillis *m* ‖ *intr* se vautrer

wel'ter·weight' *s* (*boxing*) poids *m* mi-moyen, poids welter, mi-moyen *m*

wen [wɛn] *s* kyste *m* sébacé, loupe *f*

wench [wɛntʃ] *s* jeune fille *f*, jeune femme *f*

wend [wɛnd] *tr*—**to wend one's way (to)** diriger ses pas (vers)

west [wɛst] *adj* & *s* ouest *m* ‖ *adv* à l'ouest, vers l'ouest

western ['wɛstərn] *adj* occidental, de l'ouest ‖ *s* (mov) western *m*

westerner ['wɛstərnər] *s* habitant *m* de l'ouest, Occidental *m*

West' Ger'many *s* Allemagne *f* de l'Ouest; l'Allemagne de l'Ouest

West' In'dies ['ɪndɪz] *spl* Indes *fpl* occidentales, Antilles *fpl*

westward ['wɛstwərd] *adv* vers l'ouest

wet [wɛt] *adj* (*comp* **wetter**; *super* **wettest**) mouillé; (*damp*) humide; (*rainy*) pluvieux; (*paint*) frais, (coll) antiprohibitionniste; **all wet** (slang) fichu, erroné ‖ *s* antiprohibitionniste *mf* ‖ *v* (*pret & p* **wet** or **wetted**; *ger* **wetting**) *tr* mouiller ‖ *intr* se mouiller

wet' bat'ter·y *s* (*pl* -**ies**) pile *f* à liquide

wet' blan'ket *s* trouble-fête *mf*, rabat-joie *m*

wet' dream' *s* pollution f nocturne

wet' nurse' *s* nourrice *f*

wet' paint' *s* peinture *f* fraîche; (*public sign*) attention à la peinture

whack [hwæk] *s* (coll) coup *m*, gnon *m*; (*try*) (coll) tentative *f*; **to have a whack at** (coll) s'attaquer à ‖ *tr* (coll) cogner

whale [hwel] *s* baleine *f*; (*sperm whale*) cachalot *m*; **to have a whale of a time** (coll) s'amuser follement ‖ *tr* (coll) rosser

whale'bone' *s* baleine *f*, fanon *m* de baleine

whaler ['hwelər] *s* baleinier *m*

wharf [hwɔrf] *s* (*pl* **wharves** [hwɔrvz] or **wharfs**) quai *m*, débarcadère *m*

what [hwɑt] *adj interr* quel §80, e.g., **what time is it?** quelle heure est-il?; e.g., **what is his occupation?** quel est son métier? ‖ *adj rel* ce qui, e.g., **I'll give you what water I have left** je vous donnerai ce qui me reste d'eau; ce que, e.g., **I know what drink you want** je sais ce que vous voulez comme boisson ‖ *pron interr* qu'est-ce qui, e.g., **what happened?** qu'est-ce qui s'est passé?; que, e.g., **what are you doing?** que faites-vous?; qu'est-ce que, e.g., **what are you doing?** qu'est-ce que vous faites?; comment, e.g., **what is he like?** comment est-il?; combien, e.g., **what is two and two?** combien font deux et deux?; **what** (*did you say*)? comment?; **what else?** quoi d'autre?, quoi encore; **what for?** pourquoi donc?; **what if** si, e.g, **what if I were to die?** si je venais à mourir?; **what if I did?**, **what of it?**, **so what?** qu'importe?; **what is it?** qu'est-ce que c'est?, qu'est-ce qu'il y a?; **what now?** alors?; **what's that?** qu'est-ce que c'est que cela?; **what then?** et après? ‖ *pron rel* ce qui, ce que; ce dont §79, e.g., **I have what you need** j'ai ce dont vous avez besoin; ce à quoi, e.g., **I know what you are thinking of** je sais ce à quoi vous pensez; (sometimes untranslated), e.g, **he asked them what time it was** il leur a demandé l'heure; **to know what's what** (coll) s'y connaître, être au courant ‖ *interj* comment!; **what a** que de, e.g., **what a lot of people!** que de monde!; **quel §80,** e.g., **what a pity!** quel dommage!

what·ev′er *adj* quel que §80; moindre or quelconque, e.g., **is there any hope whatever?** y a-t-il le moindre espoir?, a-t-il un espoir quelconque? ‖ *pron* tout ce qui; tout ce que, e.g., **tell him whatever you like** dites-lui tout ce que vous voudrez; quoi que, e.g., **whatever you do** quoi que vous fassiez; **whatever comes** à tout hasard

what′not′ *s* étagère *f*

what's′-his-name′ *s* (coll) Monsieur un tel

wheal [wil] *s* papule *f*

wheat [hwit] *s* blé *m*

wheedle [ˈhwidəl] *tr* enjôler

wheel [hwil] *s* roue *f*; **at the wheel** au volant ‖ *tr* (*to turn*) faire pivoter; (*a wheelbarrow, table, etc.*) rouler ‖ *intr* pivoter; (*said, e.g., of birds in the sky*) tournoyer; **to wheel about** or **around** faire demi-tour

wheelbarrow [ˈhwil,bæro] *s* brouette *f*

wheel′base′ *s* (aut) empattement *m*

wheel′chair′ *s* fauteuil *m* roulant pour malade, voiture *f* d'infirme, chaise *f* roulante

wheel′ horse′ *s* (*horse*) timonier *m*; (*person*) bûcheur *m*

wheelwright [ˈhwil,raɪt] *s* charron *m*

wheeze [hwiz] *s* respiration *f* sifflante; (pathol) cornage *m* ‖ *intr* respirer avec peine, souffler

whelp [hwɛlp] *s* petit *m* ‖ *tr* & *intr* mettre bas

when [hwɛn] *adv* quand ‖ *conj* quand, lorsque; (*on which, in which*) où; (*whereas*) alors que

whence [hwɛns] *adv* & *conj* d'où

when·ev′er *conj* chaque fois que, quand

where [hwɛr] *adv* & *conj* où; **from where** d'où

whereabouts [ˈhwɛrə,baʊts] *s*—**the whereabouts of** l'endroit où se trouve ‖ *adv* & *conj* où donc

whereas [hwɛrˈæz] *conj* tandis que, attendu que ‖ *s* considérant *m*

where·by′ *conj* par lequel

wherefore [ˈhwɛrfor] *s* & *adv* pourquoi *m* ‖ *conj* à cause de quoi

where·from′ *adv* d'où

where·in′ *adv* d'où; en quoi ‖ *conj* où

where·of′ *adv* de quoi ‖ *conj* dont §79

where·up·on′ *adv* sur quoi, sur ce

wherever [hwɛrˈɛvər] *conj* partout où; où que, n'importe où

wherewithal [ˈhwɛrwɪð,ɔl] *s* ressources *fpl*, moyens *mpl*

whet [hwɛt] *v* (*pret* & *pp* **whetted;** *ger* **whetting**) *tr* aiguiser

whether [ˈwɛðər] *conj* si; que, e.g., **it is doubtful whether you can finish** il est douteux que vous puissiez finir; e.g., **whether he is rich or poor** qu'il soit riche ou qu'il soit pauvre; **whether or no** de toute façon; **whether or not** qu'il en soit ainsi ou non

whet′stone′ *s* pierre *f* à aiguiser

whew [hwju] *interj* ouf!

whey [hwe] *s* petit lait *m*

which [hwɪtʃ] *adj interr* quel §80, e.g., **which university do you prefer?** quelle université préférez-vous?; **which one?** lequel? ‖ *adj rel* le . . . que, e.g., **choose which road you prefer** choisissez le chemin que vous préférez ‖ *pron interr* lequel §78; **which is which?** lequel des deux est-ce?; **which of them?** lequel d'entre eux? ‖ *pron rel* qui; que; dont §79

which·ev′er *adj rel* n'importe quel ‖ *pron rel* n'importe lequel

whiff [hwɪf] *s* bouffée *f*; **to get a whiff of** flairer

while [hwaɪl] *s* temps *m*, moment *m*; **a long while** longtemps; **a (little) while ago** tout à l'heure; **in a little while** sous peu, tout à l'heure ‖ *conj* pendant que; (*as long as*) tant que; (*although*) quoique ‖ *tr—to* **while away** tuer, faire passer

whim [hwɪm] *s* caprice *m*, lubie *f*

whimper [ˈhwɪmpər] *s* pleurnicherie *f* ‖ *tr* dire en pleurnichant ‖ *intr* pleurnicher

whimsical [ˈhwɪmzɪkəl] *adj* capricieux, lunatique

whine [hwaɪn] *s* geignement *m*; (*of siren*) hurlement *m* ‖ *intr* geindre; (*said of siren*) hurler

whin·ny [ˈhwɪni] *s* (*pl* **-nies**) hennissement *m* ‖ *v* (*pret* & *pp* **-nied**) *intr* hennir

whip [hwɪp] *s* fouet *m* ‖ *v* (*pret* & *pp* **whipped** or **whipt;** *ger* **whipping**) *tr* fouetter; (*to defeat*) battre; (*the end of a rope*) surlier; **to whip out** (*e.g., a gun*) sortir brusquement; **to whip up** (*e.g., a supper*) (coll) préparer à l'improviste; (*e.g., enthusiasm*) (coll) stimuler

whip′cord′ *s* corde *f* à fouet

whip′ hand′ *s* main *f* du fouet; (*upper hand*) avantage *m*, dessus *m*

whip′lash′ *s* mèche *f* de fouet

whipped′ cream′ *s* crème *f* fouettée, chantilly *m*

whipper-snapper [ˈhwɪpər,snæpər] *s* freluquet *m*, paltoquet *m*

whipping [ˈhwɪpɪŋ] *s* (*punishment*) correction *f*; (*of rope*) surliure *f*; **to give s.o. a whipping** fouetter qn

whip′ping boy′ *s* tête *f* de Turc

whip′ping post′ *s* poteau *m* des condamnés au fouet

whippoorwill [,hwɪpərˈwɪl] *s* (*Caprimulgus vociferus*) engoulevent *m* américain

whir [hwʌr] s ronflement m ‖ v (pret & pp **whirred;** ger **whipping**) intr ronfler

whirl [hwʌrl] s tourbillon m; (of events, parties, etc.) succession f ininterrompue ‖ tr faire tourbillonner ‖ intr tourbillonner; **his head whirls** la tête lui tourne

whirligig ['hwʌrlɪ,gɪg] s tourniquet m; (ent) gyrin m, tourniquet

whirl′pool′ s tourbillon m, remous m

whirl′wind′ s tourbillon m

whirlybird ['hwʌrlɪ,bʌrd] s (coll) hélicoptère m

whisk [hwɪsk] s (rapid, sweeping stroke) coup m léger; (broom) époussette f; (culin) fouet m ‖ tr balayer; (culin) fouetter; **to whisk out of sight** escamoter ‖ intr aller comme un trait

whisk′ broom′ s époussette f

whiskers ['hwɪskərz] spl barbe f, poils mpl de barbe; (on side of face) favoris mpl; (of cat) moustaches fpl

whiskey ['hwɪskɪ] s whisky m

whisper ['hwɪspər] s chuchotement m ‖ tr chuchoter, dire à l'oreille ‖ intr chuchoter

whispering ['hwɪspərɪŋ] s chuchotement m

whist [hwɪst] s whist m

whistle ['hwɪsəl] s (sound) sifflement m; (device) sifflet m; **to wet one's whistle** (coll) s'humecter le gosier ‖ tr siffler, souffloter ‖ intr siffler; **to whistle for** siffler; attendre en vain, se voir obligé de se passer de

whis′tle stop′ s arrêt m facultatif

whit [hwɪt] s—**not a whit** pas un brin; **to not care a whit** s'en moquer

white [hwaɪt] adj blanc ‖ s blanc m; blanc d'œuf; **whites** (pathol) pertes fpl blanches

white′caps′ spl moutons mpl

white′ coal′ s houille f blanche

white′ cof′fee s càfé m crème

white′-col′lar adj de bureau

white′-col′lar work′er s col m blanc

white′ feath′er s—**to show the white feather** lâcher pied, flancher, caner

white′fish′ s poisson m blanc, merlan m

white′ goods′ spl vêtements mpl blancs; tissus mpl de coton, cotonnade f; (appliances) appareils mpl électroménagers

white′-haired′ adj aux cheveux blancs, chenu; (coll) favori

white′-hot′ adj chauffé à blanc

White′ House′ s—**the White House** la Maison Blanche

white′ lead′ [lɛd] s céruse f, blanc m de céruse

white′ lie′ s mensonge m pieux

white′ meat′ s blanc m

whiten ['hwaɪtən] tr & intr blanchir

whiteness ['hwaɪtnɪs] s blancheur f

white′ slav′ery s traite f des blanches

white′ tie′ s cravate f blanche; tenue f de soirée

white′wash′ s blanc m de chaux, badigeon m; (cover-up) couverture f ‖ tr blanchir à la chaux; (e.g., a guilty person, a scandal) blanchir

whither ['hwɪðər] adv & conj où, là où

whitish ['hwaɪtɪʃ] adj blanchâtre

whitlow ['hwɪtlo] s panaris m

Whitsuntide ['hwɪtsən,taɪd] s saison f de la Pentecôte

whittle ['hwɪtəl] tr tailler au couteau; **to whittle away** or **down** amenuiser

whiz or **whizz** [hwɪz] s sifflement m; (slang) prodige m ‖ v (pret & pp **whizzed;** ger **whizzing**) intr—**to whiz by** passer en sifflant, passer comme le vent

who [hu] pron interr qui; quel §80; **who else?** qui d'autre?; qui encore?; **who is there?** (mil) qui vive? ‖ pron rel qui; celui qui §83

whoa [hwo] interj holà!, doucement!

whodunit [hu'dʌnɪt] s roman m noir

who·ev′er pron rel quiconque; celui qui §83; qui que, e.g., **whoever you are** qui que vous soyez

whole [hol] adj entier ‖ s tout m, totalité f, ensemble m; **on the whole** somme toute, à tout prendre

whole′heart′ed adj sincère, de bon cœur

whole′ note′ s (mus) ronde f

whole′ rest′ s (mus) pause f

whole′sale′ adj & adv en gros; (e.g., slaughter) en masse ‖ s gros m, vente f en gros ‖ tr & intr vendre en gros

whole′sale price′ s prix m de gros

wholesaler ['hol,selər] s commerçant m en gros, grossiste mf

whole′sale trade′ s commerce m de gros

wholesome ['holsəm] adj sain

wholly ['holɪ] adv entièrement

whom [hum] pron interr qui ‖ pron rel que; lequel §78; celui que §83; **of whom** dont, de qui §79

whom·ev′er pron rel celui que §83; tous ceux que; (with a preposition) quiconque

whoop [hup], [hwup] s huée f; (cough) quinte f ‖ tr—**to whoop it up** (slang) pousser des cris ‖ intr huer

whoop′ing cough′ ['hupɪŋ] s coqueluche f

whopper ['hwapər] s (coll) chose f énorme; (lie) (coll) gros mensonge m

whopping ['hwapɪŋ] adj (coll) énorme

whore [hor] s putain f ‖ intr—**to whore around** courir la gueuse

whore′house′ s maison f de débauche, maison publique, maison borgne, boxon m

whose [huz] pron interr à qui, e.g., **whose pen is that?** à qui est ce stylo? ‖ pron rel dont, de qui §79; duquel §78

why [hwaɪ] s (pl **whys** [hwaɪz]) pourquoi m; **the why and the wherefore** le pourquoi et le comment ‖ adv pourquoi; **why not?** pourquoi pas? ‖ interj tiens!; **why, certainly!** mais bien sûr!; **why, yes!** mais oui!

wick [wɪk] s mèche f

wicked ['wɪkɪd] adj méchant, mauvais

wicker ['wɪkər] adj en osier ‖ s osier m

wicket ['wɪkɪt] s guichet m; (croquet) arceau m

wide [waɪd] adj large; (range) vaste, étendu; (spread, angle, etc.) grand; large de, e.g.,

eight feet wide large de huit pieds ‖ *adv* loin, partout; **open wide!** ouvrez bien!

wide'-an'gle *adj* grand-angulaire

wide'-awake' *adj* bien éveillé

widen ['waɪdən] *tr* élargir ‖ *intr* s'élargir

wide'-o'pen *adj* grand ouvert

wide'spread' *adj* (*arms, wings*) étendu; répandu, universel

widow ['wɪdo] *s* veuve *f* ‖ *tr*—**to be widowed** devenir veuf

widower ['wɪdo·ər] *s* veuf *m*

widowhood ['wɪdo,hʊd] *s* veuvage *m*

wid'ow's mite' *s* obole *f*

wid'ow's weeds' *spl* deuil *m* de veuve

width [wɪdθ] *s* largeur *f*; (*of cloth*) lé *m*

wield [wild] *tr* (*sword, pen*) manier; (*power*) exercer

wife [waɪf] *s* (*pl* **wives** [waɪvz]) femme *f*, épouse *f*

wig [wɪg] *s* perruque *f*

wiggle ['wɪgəl] *s* tortillement *m* ‖ *tr* agiter ‖ *intr* tortiller, se tortiller

wig'wag' *s* télégraphie *f* optique ‖ *v* (*pret & pp* **-wagged;** *ger* **-wagging**) *tr* transmettre à bras avec fanions ‖ *intr* signaler à bras avec fanions

wigwam ['wɪgwɑm] *s* wigwam *m*

wild [waɪld] *adj* sauvage; (*untamed*) sauvage, fauve; (*frantic, mad*) frénétique; (*hair; dance; dream*) échevelé; (*passion; torrent; night*) tumultueux; (*idea, plan*) insensé, extravagant; (*life*) déréglé; (*blows, bullet, shot*) perdu; **wild about or for** fou de ‖ **wilds** *spl* régions *fpl* sauvages ‖ *adv*—**to run wild** dépasser toutes les bornes; (*said of plants*) pousser librement

wild' boar' *s* sanglier *m*

wild' card' *s* mistigri *m*

wild'cat' *s* chat *m* sauvage; lynx *m*, (*well*) sondage *m* d'exploration

wild'cat strike' *s* grève *f* sauvage, grève spontanée

wild' cher'ry *s* (*pl* **-ries**) merise *f*; (*tree*) merisier *m*

wilderness ['wɪldərnɪs] *s* désert *m*

wil'derness camp'ing *s* camping *m* sauvage

wild'fire' *s* feu *m* grégeois; feu *m* follet; éclairs *mpl* en nappe; **like wildfire** comme une traînée de poudre

wild' flow'er *s* fleur *f* des champs

wild' goose' *s* oie *f* sauvage

wild'-goose' chase' *s*—**to go on a wild-goose chase** faire buisson creux

wild'life' *s* animaux *mpl* sauvages

wild' oats' *spl*—**to sow one's wild oats** jeter sa gourme

wile [waɪl] *s* ruse *f* ‖ *tr*—**to while away** tuer, faire passer

will [wɪl] *s* volonté *f*; (law) testament *m*; **against one's will** à contre-cœur; **at will** à volonté; **to put s.o. in one's will** porter qn sur son testament; **with a will** de bon cœur ‖ *tr* vouloir; (*to bequeath*) léguer ‖ *intr* vouloir; **do as you will** faites comme vous voudrez ‖ (*pret & cond* **would** [wʊd]) *aux* used to express 1) the future

indicative, e.g., **he will arrive early** il arrivera de bonne heure; 2) the future perfect indicative, e.g., **he will have arrived before I leave** il sera arrivé avant que je parte; 3) the present indicative denoting habit or custom, e.g., **after breakfast he will go out for a walk every morning** après le petit déjeuner il fait une promenade tous les matins

willful ['wɪlfəl] *adj* volontaire; (*stubborn*) obstiné

willfulness ['wɪlfəlnɪs] *s* entêtement *m*

William ['wɪljəm] *s* Guillaume *m*

willing ['wɪlɪŋ] *adj* disposé, prêt; **to be willing to** vouloir bien; **willing or unwilling** bon gré mal gré

willingly ['wɪlɪŋli] *adv* volontiers

willingness ['wɪlɪŋnɪs] *s* bonne volonté *f*, consentement *m*

will-o'-the-wisp ['wɪləðə'wɪsp] *s* feu *m* follet; (fig) chimère *f*

willow ['wɪlo] *s* saule *m*

willowy ['wɪlo·i] *adj* souple, agile; svelte, élancé; couvert de saules

will' pow'er *s* force *f* de volonté

willy-nilly ['wɪli'nɪli] *adv* bon gré mal gré

wilt [wɪlt] *tr* flétrir ‖ *intr* se flétrir

wil·y ['waɪli] *adj* (*comp* **-ier;** *super* **-iest**) rusé, astucieux

wimp [wɪmp] *s* poule *f* mouillée

wimple ['wɪmpəl] *s* guimpe *f*

win [wɪn] *s* (coll) victoire *f* ‖ *v* (*pret & pp* **won** [wʌn];** *ger* **winning**) *tr* gagner; (*a victory, a prize*) remporter; **to win back** regagner; **to win over** gagner, convaincre ‖ *intr* gagner; convaincre; **to win out** (coll) réussir

wince [wɪns] *s*—**without a wince** sans sourciller ‖ *intr* tressaillir

winch [wɪntʃ] *s* treuil *m*; (*handle, crank*) manivelle *f*

wind [wɪnd] *s* vent *m*; (*breath*) haleine *f*, souffle *m*; **to break wind** lâcher un vent, faire un pet; **to get wind of** avoir vent de; **to sail close to the wind** courir au plus près; **to sail into the wind** aller au lof, venir au lof ‖ *tr* faire perdre le souffle à ‖ *intr* flairer le gibier ‖ [waɪnd] *v* (*pret & pp* **wound** [waʊnd]) *tr* enrouler; (*a timepiece*) remonter; (*yarn, thread, etc.*) pelotonner; **to wind up** enrouler; remonter; (*to finish*) (coll) terminer, régler ‖ *intr* serpenter

windbag ['wɪnd,bæg] *s* (*of bagpipe*) outre *f*; (coll) moulin *m* à paroles

wind'break' *s* abrivent *m*

wind'break'er *s* (*jacket*) blouson *m*

wind' -chill fac'tor *s* déperdition *f* de chaleur due au vent

wind' cone' *s* (aer) manche *f* à air

winded ['wɪndɪd] *adj* essoufflé

wind'fall *s* (fig) aubaine *f*

wind'ing road' ['waɪndɪŋ] *s* route *f* en lacet

wind'ing sheet' *s* linceul *m*

wind'ing stairs' *spl* escalier *m* en colimaçon

wind′ in′strument [wɪnd] *s* (mus) instrument *m* à vent

windlass [′wɪndləs] *s* treuil *m*

wind′mill′ *s* moulin *m* à vent; (*on a modern farm*) aéromoteur *m*; **to tilt at windmills** se battre contre des moulins à vent

window [′wɪndo] *s* fenêtre *f*; (*of ticket office*) guichet *m*; (*of store*) vitrine *f*; (aut) glace *f*

win′dow dress′er *s* étalagiste *mf*

win′dow dress′ing *s* art *m* de l'étalage; (coll) façade *f*

win′dow en′velope *s* enveloppe *f* à fenêtre

win′dow frame′ *s* châssis *m*, dormant *m*

win′dow·pane′ *s* vitre *f*, carreau *m*

win′dow screen′ *s* grillage *m*, écran *m* en fil de fer

win′dow shade′ *s* store *m*

win′dow-shop′ *v* (*pret & pp* **-shopped**; *ger* **-shopping**) *intr* faire du lèche-vitrines, lécher les vitrines

win′dow shut′ter *s* volet *m*

win′dow sill′ *s* rebord *m* de fenêtre

wind′pipe′ *s* trachée-artère *f*

wind′ shear′ *s* cisaillement *m* du vent

wind′shield′ *s* pare-brise *m*

wind′shield wash′er *s* lave-glace *m*

wind′shield wip′er *s* essuie-glace *m*

wind′sock′ *s* manche *f* à air

wind′storm′ *s* tempête *f* de vent

wind′ surf′ing *s* planche *f* à voile

wind′ tun′nel *s* tunnel *m* aérodynamique

wind-up [′waɪnd,ʌp] *s* conclusion *f*, fin *f*

windward [′wɪndwərd] *adj & adv* au vent ‖ *s* côté *m* du vent; **to turn to windward** louvoyer

wind·y [′wɪndi] *adj* (*comp* **-ier**; *super* **-iest**) venteux; (*verbose*) verbeux; **it is windy** il fait du vent

wine [waɪn] *s* vin *m* ‖ *tr*—**to wine and dine s.o.** fêter qn

wine′ cel′lar *s* cave *f*

wine′glass′ *s* verre *m* à vin

winegrower [′waɪn,gro·ər] *s* viticulteur *m*, vigneron *m*

winegrowing [′waɪn,gro·ɪŋ] *s* viticulture *f*

wine′ list′ *s* carte *f* des vins

wine′ press′ *s* pressoir *m*

winer·y [′waɪnəri] *s* (*pl* **-ies**) pressoir *m*

wine′skin′ *s* outre *f* à vin

wine′ stew′ard *s* sommelier *m*; (*of prince, king*) bouteiller *m*

winetaster [′waɪn,testər] *s* (*person*) dégustateur *m*; (*pipette*) taste-vin *m*

wing [wɪŋ] *s* aile *f*; (*e.g., of hospital*) pavillon *m*; (pol) parti *m*, faction *f*; **in the wings** (theat) dans la coulisse; **on the wing** au vol; **to take wing** prendre son essor ‖ *tr* (*to wound*) blesser; **to wing one's way** voler

wing′ chair′ *s* fauteuil *m* à oreilles

wing′ col′lar *s* col *m* rabattu

wing′ load′ *s* (aer) charge *f* alaire

wing′ nut′ *s* écrou *m* ailé, vis *f* à ailettes

wing′spread′ *s* envergure *f*

wink [wɪŋk] *s* clin *m* d'œil; **to not sleep a wink** ne pas fermer l'œil; **to take forty**

winks (coll) piquer un roupillon ‖ *tr* cligner ‖ *intr* cligner des yeux; **to wink at** cligner de l'œil à; (*e.g., an abuse*) fermer les yeux sur

winner [′wɪnər] *s* gagnant *m*, vainqueur *m*

winning [′wɪnɪŋ] *adj* gagnant; (*attractive*) séduisant ‖ **winnings** *spl* gains *mpl*

winnow [′wɪno] *tr* vanner, sasser; (*e.g., the evidence*) passer au crible

winsome [′wɪnsəm] *adj* séduisant, engageant

winter [′wɪntər] *s* hiver *m* ‖ *intr* passer l'hiver; (*said of animals, troops, etc.*) hiverner

win′ter·green′ *s* (*oil*) wintergreen *m*; (bot) gaulthérie *f*

winterize [′wɪntəraɪz] *tr* hivériser

win·try [′wɪntri] *adj* (*comp* **-trier**; *super* **-triest**) hivernal, froid

wipe [waɪp] *tr* essuyer; **to wipe away** essuyer; **to wipe off** or **out** effacer; (*to annihilate*) anéantir; **to wipe up** nettoyer

wiper [′waɪpər] *s* torchon *m*; (elec) contact *m* glissant; (mach) came *f*

wire [waɪr] *s* fil *m*; télégramme *m*; **hold the wire!** (telp) restez à l'écoute!; **on the wire** (telp) au bout du fil; **reply by wire** réponse *f* télégraphique; **to get in under the wire** arriver juste à temps; terminer juste à temps; **to pull wires** (coll) tirer les ficelles ‖ *tr* attacher avec du fil de fer; (*a message*) télégraphier; (*a house*) canaliser ‖ *intr* télégraphier

wire′ cut′ter *s* coupe-fil *m*

wire′draw′ *v* (*pret* **-drew**; *pp* **-drawn**) *tr* tréfiler

wire′ entan′glement *s* réseau *m* de barbelés

wire′ gauge′ *s* calibre *m* or jauge *f* pour fils métalliques

wire′-haired′ *adj* à poil dur

wireless [′waɪrlɪs] *adj* sans fil

wire′ nail′ *s* clou *m* de Paris

Wire′pho′to *s* (*pl* **-tos**) (trademark) (*device*) bélinographe *m*; (*photo*) bélinogramme *m*

wire′pull′ing *s* (coll) influences *fpl* secrètes, piston *m*

wire′ record′er *s* magnétophone *m* à fil d'acier

wire′tap′ *s* (*device*) table *f* d'écoute ‖ *v* (*pret & pp* **-tapped**; *ger* **-tapping**) *tr* passer à la table d'écoute

wiring [′waɪrɪŋ] *s* (*e.g., of house*) canalisation *f*; (*e.g., of radio*) montage *m*

wir·y [′waɪri] *adj* (*comp* **-ier**; *super* **-iest**) nerveux; (*hair*) raide

wisdom [′wɪzdəm] *s* sagesse *f*

wis′dom tooth′ *s* dent *f* de sagesse

wise [waɪz] *adj* sage; (*step, decision*) judicieux, prudent; **to be wise to** (slang) voir clair dans le jeu de, percer le jeu de; **to get wise** (coll) se mettre au courant ‖ *s*—**in no wise** en aucune manière ‖ *tr*—**to wise up** (slang) avertir, désabuser

wiseacre [′waɪz,ekər] *s* fat *m*, fierot *m*

wise′crack′ *s* (coll) blague *f*, plaisanterie *f* ‖ *intr* (coll) blaguer, plaisanter

wise′ guy′ s (slang) type m goguenard, fier-à-bras m

wish [wɪʃ] s souhait m, désir m; **best wishes** meilleurs vœux mpl; (formula used to close a letter) amitiés; **last wishes** dernières volontés fpl; **our best wishes** (formula in letter writing) nos meilleurs sentiments; **to make a wish** faire un vœu ‖ tr souhaiter, désirer; **to wish s.o. s.th.** souhaiter q.ch. à qn; **to wish s.o. to** + inf souhaiter que qn + subj; **to wish to** + inf vouloir + inf

wish′bone′ s fourchette f

wishful [ˈwɪʃfəl] adj désireux

wish′ful think′ing s optimisme m à outrance; **to indulge in wishful thinking** se forger des chimères

wish′ing well′ s puits m aux souhaits

wistful [ˈwɪstfəl] adj pensif, rêveur

wit [wɪt] s esprit m; (person) homme m d'esprit; **to be at one's wits' end** ne plus savoir que faire; **to keep one's wits about one** conserver toute sa présence d'esprit; **to live by one's wits** vivre d'expédients

witch [wɪtʃ] s sorcière f

witch′craft′ s sorcellerie f

witch′ doc′tor s sorcier m guérisseur

witch′es′ Sab′bath s sabbat m

witch′ ha′zel s teinture f d'hamamélis; (bot) hamamélis m

witch′ hunt′ s chasse f aux sorcières

with [wɪð], [wɪθ] prep avec; (at the home of; in the case of) chez; (in spite of) malgré; à, e.g., **the girl with the blue eyes** la jeune fille aux yeux bleus; e.g., **coffee with milk** café au lait; e.g., **with open arms** à bras ouverts; e.g., **with these words . . .** à ces mots . . . ; de, e.g., **with a loud voice** d'une voix forte; e.g., **with all his strength** de toutes ses forces; e.g., **to be satisfied with** être satisfait de; e.g., **to fill with** remplir de

with·draw′ v (pret **-drew**; pp **-drawn**) tr retirer ‖ intr se retirer

withdrawal [wɪðˈdrɔ·əl] s retrait m

withdraw′al symp′tom s symptôme m de l'état de manque

wither [ˈwɪðər] tr faner ‖ intr se faner

with·hold′ v (pret & pp **-held**) tr (money, taxes, etc.) retenir; (permission) refuser; (the truth) cacher

with·hold′ing tax′ s impôt m retenu à la source

with·in′ adv à l'intérieur; là-dedans §85A ‖ prep à l'intérieur de; (in less than) en moins de; (within the limits of) dans; (in the bosom of) au sein de; (not exceeding a margin of error of) à . . . près, e.g., **I can tell you what time it is within five minutes** je peux vous dire l'heure à cinq minutes près; à portée de, e.g., **within reach** à portée de la main

with·out′ adv au-dehors, dehors ‖ prep au dehors de; (lacking, not with) sans; **to do without** se passer de; **without** + ger sans + inf, e.g., **he left without seeing me** il est parti sans me voir; sans que + subj,

e.g., **he left without anyone seeing him** il est parti sans que personne ne le voie

with·stand′ v (pret & pp **-stood**) tr résister à

witness [ˈwɪtnɪs] s témoin m; **in witness whereof** en foi de quoi; **to bear witness** rendre témoignage ‖ tr (to be present at) être témoin de, assister à; (to attest) témoigner; (e.g., a contract) signer

wit′ness stand′ s barre f des témoins

witticism [ˈwɪtɪ‚sɪzəm] s trait m d'esprit

wittingly [ˈwɪtɪŋli] adv sciemment

wit·ty [ˈwɪti] adj (comp **-tier**; super **-tiest**) spirituel

wizard [ˈwɪzərd] s sorcier m

wizardry [ˈwɪzərdri] s sorcellerie f

wizened [ˈwɪzənd] adj desséché

woad [wod] s guède f

wobble [ˈwɑbəl] intr chanceler; (said of table) branler; (said of voice) chevroter; vaciller

wob·bly [ˈwɑbli] adj (comp **-blier**; super **-bliest**) vacillant

woe [wo] s malheur m, affliction f; **woe is me!** pauvre de moi!; **woes** misères fpl

woebegone [ˈwobɪ‚gɔn] adj navré, abattu, désolé

woeful [ˈwofəl] adj triste, désolé; très mauvais

wolf [wʊlf] s (pl **wolves** [wʊlvz]) loup m; galant m, tombeur m de femmes; **to cry wolf** crier au loup; **to keep the wolf from the door** se mettre à l'abri du besoin, joindre les deux bouts ‖ tr & intr engloutir

wolf′ cub′ s louveteau m

wolf′hound′ s chien-loup m

wolf′ pack′ s bande f de loups

wolfram [ˈwʊlfrəm] s (element) tungstène m; (mineral) wolfram m

wolf's′-bane′ or **wolfs′bane′** s tue-loup m, aconit m, napel m

woman [ˈwʊmən] s (pl **women** [ˈwɪmɪn]) femme f

wom′an doc′tor s femme f médecin, doctoresse f

womanhood [ˈwʊmən‚hʊd] s le sexe féminin; les femmes fpl

womanish [ˈwʊmənɪʃ] adj féminin; (effeminate) efféminé

wom′an·kind′ s le sexe féminin

wom′an la′borer s femme f manœuvre

woman·ly [ˈwʊmənli] adj (comp **-lier**; super **-liest**) féminin, femme

wom′an preach′er s femme f pasteur

womb [wum] s utérus m, matrice f; (fig) sein m

wom′en's libera′tion move′ment m mouvement m de la libération de la femme (M.L.F.)

wonder [ˈwʌndər] s merveille f; (feeling of surprise) émerveillement m; (something strange) miracle m; **for a wonder** chose étonnante; **no wonder that . . .** rien d'étonnant que . . . ; **to work wonders** faire des merveilles ‖ tr—**to wonder that** s'étonner que; **to wonder why, if, whether**

se demander pourquoi, si ‖ *intr*—**to won-der at** s'émerveiller de, s'étonner de

won′der drug′ *s* remède *m* miracle, médicament *m* miracle, drogue-miracle *f*

wonderful [′wʌndərfəl] *adj* merveilleux, étonnant

won′der·land′ *s* pays *m* des merveilles

wonderment [′wʌndərmənt] *s* étonnement *m*

wont [wɔnt] *adj*—**to be wont to** avoir l'habitude de ‖ *s*—**his wont** son habitude

wonted *adj* habituel, accoutumé

woo [wu] *tr* courtiser

wood [wud] *s* bois *m*; (*for wine*) fût *m*; **out of the woods** (coll) hors de danger, hors d'affaire; **to take to the woods** se sauver dans la nature; **woods** bois *m* or *mpl*

woodbine [′wud‚baɪn] *s* (*honeysuckle*) chèvrefeuille *m*; (*Virginia creeper*) vigne *f* vierge

wood′ carv′ing *s* sculpture *f* sur bois

wood′chuck′ *s* marmotte *f* d'Amérique

wood′cock′ *s* bécasse *f*

wood′cut′ *s* (typ) gravure *f* sur bois

wood′cut′ter *s* bûcheron *m*

wooded [′wudɪd] *adj* boisé

wooden [′wudən] *adj* en bois; (*style, manners*) guindé, raide

wood′ engrav′ing *s* (typ) gravure *f* sur bois

wood′en-head′ed *adj* (coll) stupide, obtus

wood′en leg′ *s* jambe *f* en bois

wood′en shoe′ *s* sabot *m*

wood′ grouse′ *s* grand tétras *m*, grand coq *m* de bruyère

woodland [′wudlənd] *adj* sylvestre ‖ *s* pays *m* boisé

wood′land scene′ *s* (painting) paysage *m* boisé

wood′man *s* (*pl* **-men**) bûcheron *m*

woodpecker [′wud‚pɛkər] *s* pic *m*; (*green woodpecker*) pivert *m*, pic-vert *m*

wood′ pig′eon *s* (orn) ramier *m*

wood′pile′ *s* tas *m* de bois

wood′ screw′ *s* vis *f* à bois

wood′shed′ *s* bûcher *m*

woods′man *s* (*pl* **-men**) bûcheron *m*; (*trapper*) trappeur *m*, chasseur *m*

wood′ tick′ *s* vrillette *f*

wood′winds′ *spl* (mus) bois *mpl*

wood′work′ *s* (*working in wood*) menuiserie *f*; (*things made of wood*) boiseries *fpl*

wood′work′er *s* menuisier *m*

wood′worm′ *s* (ent) artison *m*

wood·y [′wudi] *adj* (*comp* **-ier;** *super* **-iest**) boisé; (*like wood*) ligneux

wooer [′wu·ər] *s* prétendant *m*

woof [wuf] *s* trame *f*; (*fabric*) tissu *m*

woofer [′wufər] *s* (rad) boomer *m*, woofer *m*

wool [wul] *s* laine *f*

woolen [′wulən] *adj* de laine ‖ *s* tissu *m* de laine; **woolens** lainage *m*

wool′gath′ering *s* rêvasserie *f*

woolgrower [′wul‚gro·ər] *s* éleveur *m* des bêtes à laine

wool·ly [′wuli] *adj* (*comp* **-lier;** *super* **-liest**) laineux

word [wʌrd] *s* mot *m*; (*promise, assurance*) parole *f*; **in other words** autrement dit; **in your own words** en vous propres termes; **my word!** ça alors!; **not a word!** motus!; **the Word** (eccl) le Verbe; **to break one's word** manquer à sa parole; **to have words with** échanger des propos désagréables avec; **to make s.o. eat his words** faire ravaler ses paroles à qn; **to put in a word** placer un mot; **to take s.o. at his word** prendre qn au mot, croire qn sur parole; **upon my word!** ma foi!; **without a word** sans mot dire; **words** (*e.g., of song*) paroles ‖ *tr* formuler, rédiger

word′ forma′tion *s* formation *f* des mots

wording [′wʌrdɪŋ] *s* langage *m*

word′ or′der *s* ordre *m* des mots

word′ proc′essing *s* traitement *m* des mots

word′-stock′ *s* vocabulaire *m*

word·y [′wʌrdi] *adj* (*comp* **-ier;** *super* **-iest**) verbeux

work [wʌrk] *s* travail *m*; (*production, book*) œuvre *f*, ouvrage *m*; **at work** en œuvre; (*not at home*) au travail, au bureau, à l'usine; **out of work** sans travail, en chômage; **to shoot the works** (slang) mettre le paquet, jouer le tout pour le tout; **works** œuvres; mécanisme *m*; (*of clock*) mouvement *m* ‖ *tr* faire travailler; (*to operate*) faire fonctionner, faire marcher; (*wood, iron*) travailler; (*mine*) exploiter; **to work out** élaborer, résoudre; **to work up** préparer; stimuler ‖ *intr* travailler; (*said of motor, machine, etc.*) fonctionner, marcher; (*said of remedy*) faire de l'effet; (*said of wine, beer*) fermenter; **how will things work out!** à quoi tout cela aboutira-t-il?; **to work hard** travailler dur; **to work loose** se desserrer; **to work out** (sports) s'entraîner; **to work too hard** se surmener

workable [′wʌrkəbəl] *adj* (*feasible*) réalisable; (*that can be worked*) ouvrable

workaholic [′wʌrkə′hɔlɪk] *s* bourreau *m* de travail, drogué *m* du travail, travaillomane *mf*

work′bas′ket *s* corbeille *f* à ouvrage

work′bench′ *s* établi *m*

work′book′ *s* manuel *m*; (*notebook*) carnet *m*; (*for student*) cahier *m* de devoirs

work′box′ *s* boîte *f* à ouvrage; (*for needlework*) coffret *m* de travail

work′day′ *adj* de tous les jours; prosaïque, ordinaire ‖ *s* jour *m* ouvrable; (*part of day devoted to work*) journée *f*

worked′-up′ *adj* préparé, ouvré; (*excited*) agité, emballé

worker [′wʌrkər] *s* travailleur *m*, ouvrier *m*, employé *m*

work′ flow′ *s* déroulement *m* des opérations

work′ force′ *s* main-d'œuvre *f*; personnel *m*

work′horse′ *s* cheval *m* de charge; (*tireless worker*) vrai cheval *m* de labour

work′house′ *s* maison *f* de correction; (Brit) asile *m* des pauvres

work′ing class′ *s* classe *f* ouvrière

work′ing day′ *s* jour *m* ouvrable; (*daily hours for work*) journée *f*

work′ing hours′ *spl* heures *fpl* de travail

work′ing·man′ *s* (*pl* **-men′**) travailleur *m*

work′ing·wom′an *s* (*pl* **-wom′en**) ouvrière *f*

work′man *s* (*pl* **-men**) ouvrier *m*

workmanship [′wʌrkmən,ʃɪp] *s* habileté *f* professionnelle, facture *f*; (*work executed*) travail *m*

work′ of art′ *s* œuvre *f* d'art

work′ or′der *s* bon *m* de travail

work′out′ *s* essai *m*, épreuve *f*; (*physical exercise*) séance *f* d'entraînement

work′room′ *s* atelier *m*; (*for study*) cabinet *m* de travail, cabinet d'études

work′shop′ *s* atelier *m*

work′ stop′page *s* arrêt *m* du travail

world [wʌrld] *adj* mondial ‖ *s* monde *m*; **a world of** énormément de; **for all the world** à tous les égards, exactement; **not for all the world** pour rien au monde; **since the world began** depuis que le monde est monde; **the other world** l'autre monde; **to bring into the world** mettre au monde; **to go around the world** faire le tour du monde; **to see the world** voir du pays; **to think the world of** estimer énormément, avoir une très haute opinion de

world′ affairs′ *spl* affaires *fpl* internationales

world′-fa′mous *adj* de renommée mondiale

world′ his′tory *s* histoire *f* universelle

world′ly [′wʌrldli] *adj* (*comp* **-lier**; *super* **-liest**) mondain

world′ly-wise′ *adj*—**to be worldy-wise** savoir ce que c'est que la vie

world′ map′ *s* mappemonde *f*

World′ Se′ries *s* championnat *m* mondial

world′s′ fair′ *s* exposition *f* universelle

world′ war′ *s* guerre *f* mondiale

world′-wide′ *adj* mondial, universel

worm [wʌrm] *s* ver *m* ‖ *tr* enlever les vers de; (*a secret, money, etc.*) soutirer; **to worm it out of him** lui tirer les vers du nez ‖ *intr* se faufiler

worm-eaten [′wʌrm,itən] *adj* vermoulu

worm′ gear′ *s* engrenage *m* à vis sans fin

worm′wood′ *s* (*Artemisia*) armoise *f*; (*Artemisia absinthium*) armoise absinthe; (*something grievous*) (fig) absinthe *f*

worm·y [′wʌrmi] *adj* (*comp* **-ier**; *super* **-iest**) véreux

worn [worn] *adj* usé, fatigué

worn′-out′ *adj* épuisé, usé; éreinté

worrisome [′wʌrisəm] *adj* inquiétant; inquiet, anxieux

wor·ry [′wʌri] *s* (*pl* **-ries**) souci *m*, inquiétude *f*; (*cause of anxiety*) ennui *m*, tracas *m* ‖ *v* (*pret & pp* **-ried**) *tr* inquiéter; (*to harass, pester*) ennuyer, tracasser; **to be worried** s'inquiéter ‖ *intr* s'inquiéter; **don't worry!** ne vous en faites pas!

worse [wʌrs] *adj comp* pire, plus mauvais **§91; and to make matters worse** et par surcroît de malheur; **so much the worse** tant pis; **to make** or **get worse** empirer; **what's worse** qui pis est; **worse and**

worse de pis en pis ‖ *adv comp* pis, plus mal **§91**

worsen [′wʌrsən] *tr & intr* empirer

wor·ship [′wʌrʃɪp] *s* culte *m*, adoration *f* ‖ *v* (*pret & pp* **-shiped** or **-shipped**; *ger* **-shiping** or **-shipping**) *tr* adorer ‖ *intr* prier; (*to go to church*) aller au culte

worshiper or **worshipper** [′wʌrʃɪpər] *s* adorateur *m*, fidèle *mf*

worst [wʌrst] *adj super* pire **§91**; pis ‖ *s* (le) pire, (le) pis; **to be hurt the worst** être le plus gravement atteint (blessé, etc.); **to get the worst of it** avoir le dessous ‖ *adv super* pis **§91**

worsted [′wʊstɪd] *adj* de laine peignée ‖ *s* peigné *m*, tissu *m* de laine peignée

wort [wʌrt] *s* (*of beer*) moût *m*

worth [wʌrθ] *adj* digne de; valant, e.g., **book worth three dollars** livre valant trois dollars; **to be worth** valoir une fortune de; **to be worth** + *ger* valoir la peine de + *inf*; **to be worth while** valoir la peine ‖ *s* valeur *f*; **a dollar's worth of** pour un dollar de

worthless [′wʌrθlɪs] *adj* sans valeur; (*person*) bon à rien, indigne

worth′while′ *adj* utile, de valeur

wor·thy [′wʌrði] *adj* (*comp* **-thier**; *super* **-thiest**) digne ‖ *s* (*pl* **-thies**) notable *mf*; (hum, ironical) personnage *m*

would [wʊd] *aux* used to express 1) the past future, e.g., **he said he would come** il a dit qu'il viendrait; 2) the present conditional, e.g., **he would come if he could** il viendrait s'il pouvait; 3) the past conditional, e.g., **he would have come if he had been able (to)** il serait venu s'il avait pu; 4) the potential mood, e.g., **would that I knew it!** plût à Dieu que je le sache!, je voudrais le savoir!; 5) the past indicative denoting habit or custom in the past, e.g., **he would visit us every day** il nous visitait tous les jours

would′-be′ *adj* prétendu

wound [wʊnd] *s* blessure *f* ‖ *tr* blesser

wounded [′wʊndɪd] *adj* blessé ‖ *s*—**the wounded** les blessés *mpl*

wow [waʊ] *s* (*e.g., of phonograph record*) distorsion *f*; (slang) succès *m* formidable ‖ *tr* (slang) enthousiasmer ‖ *interj* (slang) formidable!

wrack [ræk] *s* vestige *m*; (*ruin*) naufrage *m*; (bot) varech *m*

wraith [reθ] *s* apparition *f*

wrangle [′ræŋgəl] *s* querelle *f* ‖ *intr* se quereller

wrap [ræp] *s* couverture *f*; (*coat*) manteau *m* ‖ *v* (*pret & pp* **wrapped**; *ger* **wrapping**) *tr* envelopper, emballer

wrap′around skirt′ *s* jupe *f* portefeuille

wrap′around wind′shield *s* pare-brise *m* panoramique

wrapper [′ræpər] *s* saut-de-lit *m*; (*of newspaper or magazine*) bande *f*; (*of tobacco*) robe *f*

wrap′ping pa′per *s* papier *m* d'emballage

wrath [ræθ] *s* colère *f*

wrathful [ˈræθfəl] adj courroucé, en colère
wreak [rik] tr assouvir
wreath [riθ] s (pl **wreaths** [riðz]) couronne f; (of smoke) volute f, panache m
wreathe [rið] tr enguirlander; (e.g., flowers) entrelacer ‖ intr (said of smoke) s'élever en volutes
wreck [rɛk] s (shipwreck) naufrage m; (debris at sea or elsewhere) épave f; (of train) déraillement m; (of airplane) écrasement m; (of auto) accident m; (of one's hopes) naufrage; **to be a wreck** être une ruine ‖ tr (a ship, one's hopes) faire échouer; (a train) faire dérailler; (one's health) ruiner
wreckage [ˈrɛkɪdʒ] s débris mpl, décombres mpl, ruines fpl
wrecker [ˈrɛkər] s (tow truck) dépanneuse f; (person) dépanneur m
wreck′ing car′ s voiture f de dépannage
wreck′ing crane′ s grue f de dépannage
wren [rɛn] s (orn) troglodyte m; (kinglet) (orn) roitelet m
wrench [rɛntʃ] s (tool) clef f; (pull) secousse f; (twist of a joint) foulure f ‖ tr (e.g., one's ankle) se fouler; (to twist) tordre
wrest [rɛst] tr arracher violemment
wrestle [ˈrɛsəl] s lutte f ‖ intr lutter
wrestling [ˈrɛslɪŋ] s (sports) lutte f, catch m
wres′tling match′ s rencontre f de catch
wretch [rɛtʃ] s misérable mf
wretched [ˈrɛtʃɪd] adj misérable
wriggle [ˈrɪgəl] s tortillement m ‖ tr tortiller ‖ intr se tortiller; **to wriggle out of** esquiver adroitement
wrig·gly [ˈrɪgli] adj (comp **-glier**; super **-gliest**) frétillant; évasif
wring [rɪŋ] v (pret & pp **wrung** [rʌŋ]) tr tordre; (one's hands) se tordre; (s.o.'s hand) serrer fortement; **to wring out** (clothes) essorer; (money, a secret, etc.) arracher
wringer [ˈrɪŋər] s essoreuse f
wrinkle [ˈrɪŋkəl] s (in skin) ride f; (in clothes) pli m, faux pli; (clever idea or trick) (coll) truc m ‖ tr plisser ‖ intr se plisser
wrin·kly [ˈrɪŋkli] adj (comp **-klier**; super **-kliest**) ridé, chiffonné
wrist [rɪst] s poignet m
wrist′band′ s poignet m
wrist′ watch′ s montre-bracelet f
writ [rɪt] s (eccl) écriture f; (law) acte m judiciaire
write [raɪt] v (pret **wrote** [rot]; pp **written** [ˈrɪtən]) tr écrire; **to write down** con-

signer par écrit; baisser le prix de; **to write in** insérer; **to write off** (a debt) passer aux profits et pertes; **to write up** rédiger un compte rendu de; (to ballyhoo) faire l'éloge de ‖ intr écrire; **to write back** répondre par écrit
writer [ˈraɪtər] s écrivain m
writ′er's cramp′ s crampe f des écrivains
write′-up′ s compte m rendu; (ballyhoo) battage m; (com) surestimation f
writhe [raɪð] intr se tordre
writing [ˈraɪtɪŋ] s l'écriture f; (something written) écrit m, œuvre f; (profession) métier m d'écrivain; **at this writing** au moment où j'écris; **to put in writing** mettre par écrit
writ′ing desk′ s bureau m, écritoire f; (in schoolroom) pupitre m
writ′ing pa′per s papier m à lettres
wrong [rɔŋ] adj (unjust) injuste; (incorrect) erroné; (road, address, side, place, etc.) mauvais; ne pas . . . qu'il faut, e.g., **I arrived at the wrong city** je ne suis pas arrivé à la ville qu'il fallait; (word) impropre; qui ne marche pas, e.g., **something is wrong with the motor** il y a quelque chose qui ne marche pas dans le moteur; **to be wrong** (i.e., in error) avoir tort; (i.e., to blame) être le coupable ‖ s mal m; injustice f; **to be in the wrong** être dans son tort, avoir tort; **to do wrong** faire du mal, faire du tort ‖ adv mal; **to go wrong** faire fausse route; (said, e.g., of a plan) ne pas marcher; (said of one falling into evil ways) se dévoyer; **to guess wrong** se tromper ‖ tr faire du tort à, être injuste envers
wrongdoer [ˈrɔŋˌduˌər] s malfaiteur m
wrong′do′ing s mal m, tort m; (misdeeds) méfaits mpl
wrong′ num′ber s (telp) mauvais numéro m; **you have the wrong number** vous vous trompez de numéro
wrong′ side′ s (e.g., of material) revers m, envers m; (of the street) mauvais côté m; **to drive on the wrong side** circuler à contre-voie; **to get out of bed on the wrong side** se lever du pied gauche; **wrong side out** à l'envers; **wrong side up** sens dessus dessous
wrought′ i′ron [rɔt] s fer m forgé
wrought′-up′ adj excité, agité
wry [raɪ] adj (comp **wrier**; super **wriest**) tordu, de travers; forcé, ironique
wry′neck′ s (orn) torcol m; (pathol) torticolis m

X

X, x [ɛks] *s* XXIVe lettre de l'alphabet
Xavier [`zevɪ-ər] *s* Xavier *m*
xenophobe [`zɛnə,fob] *s* xénophobe *mf*
xerography [zɪ `rɑgrəfi] *s* xérographie *f*
Xerxes [`zʌrksiz] *s* Xerxès *m*
Xmas [`krɪsməs] *adj* de Noël ‖ *s* Noël *m*

X' ray' *s* (*photograph*) radiographie *f*; **to have an X ray** passer à la radio; **X rays** rayons *mpl* X
X'-ray *adj* radiographique ‖ **X'-ray'** *tr* radiographier
X'-ray treat'ment *s* radiothérapie *f*
xylophone [`zaɪlə,fon] *s* xylophone *m*

Y

Y, y [waɪ] *s* XXVe lettre de l'alphabet
yacht [jɑt] *s* yacht *m*
yacht'club' *s* yacht-club *m*
yah [jɑ] *interj* (*in disgust*) pouah!; (*in derision*) oh là là!
yam [jæm] *s* igname *f*; (*sweet potato*) patate *f* douce
yank [jæŋk] *s* (coll) secousse *f* ‖ *tr* (coll) tirer d'un coup sec
Yankee [`jænki] *adj & s* yankee *mf*
yap [jæp] *s* jappement *m*; (slang) criaillerie *f* ‖ *v* (*pret & pp* **yapped**; *ger* **yapping**) *intr* japper; (slang) criailler; (slang) dégoiser
yard [jɑrd] *s* cour *f*; (*for lumber, for repairs, etc.*) chantier *m*; (*measure*) yard *m*; (naut) vergue *f*; (rr) gare *f* de triage
yard'arm' *s* (naut) bout *m* de vergue
yard'mas'ter *s* (rr) chef *m* de dépôt
yard'stick' *s* yard *m* en bois (en métal, etc.); (fig) unité *f* de comparaison
yarn [jɑrn] *s* fil *m*, filé *m*; (coll) histoire *f*
yarrow [`jæro] *s* mille-feuille *f*
yaw [jɔ] *s* (naut) embardée *f*; **yaws** (pathol) pian *m* ‖ *intr* faire des embardées
yawl [jɔl] *s* yole *f*
yawn [jɔn] *s* bâillement *m* ‖ *intr* bâiller; être béant
ye (old spelling of **the** [ðə]) *art* le, e.g., **ye olde shoppe** la vieille boutique ‖ [ji] *pron pl* (obs) vous (*pl*)
yea [je] *s* oui *m*; vote *m* affirmatif ‖ *adv* oui, voire
yeah [je] *adv* (coll) oui; **oh yeah?** (coll) de quoi?; **oh yeah!** (coll) ouais!
yean [jin] *intr* (*said of ewe*) agneler; (*said of goat*) chevreter
year [jɪr] *s* an *m*, année *f*;(*of issue; vintage*) millésime *m*; **six-year-old, seven-year-old,** etc. de six ans, de sept ans, etc.; **to be . . . years old** avoir . . . ans; **year in year out** bon an mal an
year'book' *s* annuaire *m*
yearling [`jɪrlɪŋ] *s* animal *m* d'un an; (*horse*) yearling *m*
yearly [`jɪrli] *adj* annuel ‖ *adv* annuellement
yearn [jʌrn] *intr*—**to yearn for** soupirer après; **to yearn to** brûler de
yearning [`jʌrnɪŋ] *s* désir *m* ardent
yeast [jist] *s* levure *f*

yell [jɛl] *s* hurlement *m*; (*school yell*) cri *m* de ralliement ‖ *tr & intr* hurler
yellow [`jɛlo] *adj* jaune; (*cowardly*) (coll) froussard; (*e.g., press*) à sensation; **to turn yellow** jaunir; (coll) avoir la frousse ‖ *s* jaune *m* ‖ *tr & intr* jaunir
yel'low fe'ver *s* fièvre *f* jaune
yel'low·ham'mer *s* (orn) bruant *m* jaune
yellowish [`jɛlo·ɪʃ] *adj* jaunâtre
yel'low·jack'et *s* (ent) frelon *m*
yel'low streak' *s* (coll) trait *m* de lâcheté
yelp [jɛlp] *s* glapissement *m*, jappement *m* ‖ *intr* glapir, japper
yen [jɛn] *s*—**to have a yen to** or **for** (coll) avoir envie de
yeo·man [`jomən] *s* (*pl* **-men**) yeoman *m*; (*clerical worker*) (nav) commis *m* aux écritures
yeo'man of the guard' *s* (Brit) hallebardier *m* de la garde du corps
yeo'man's serv'ice *s* effort *m* précieux
yes [jɛs] *s* oui *m* ‖ *adv* oui; (to contradict a negative statement or question) si or pardon, e.g., **"You didn't know." "Yes, I did!"** "Vous ne le saviez pas." "Si!" ‖ *v* (*pret & pp* **yessed**; *ger* **yessing**) *tr* dire oui à ‖ *intr* dire oui
yes' man' *s* (*pl* **yes men'**) (coll) M. Toujours; **to be a yes man** opiner du bonnet; **yes men** (coll) béni-oui-oui *mpl*
yesterday [`jɛstər,de] *adj, s, & adv* hier *m*; **yesterday morning** hier matin
yet [jɛt] *adv* encore; déjà, e.g., **has he arrived yet?** est-il déjà arrivé?; **as yet** jusqu'à présent; **not yet** pas encore ‖ *conj* cependant
yew'tree' [ju] *s* if *m*
Yiddish [`jɪdɪʃ] *adj & s* yiddish *m invar*, yidich *m*
yield [jild] *s* rendement *m*; (*crop*) produit *m*; (*income produced*) rapport *m*, revenu *m* ‖ *tr* rendre, produire; (*a profit; a crop*) rapporter; (*to surrender*) céder ‖ *intr* (*to produce*) produire, rapporter; (*to give way*) céder, se rendre; (*public sign*) priorité (à droite; à gauche)
yo·del [`jodəl] *s* tyrolienne *f* ‖ *v* (*pret & pp* **-deled** or **-delled**; *ger* **-deling** or **-delling**) *tr & intr* jodler
yogurt [`jogʊrt] *s* yogourt *m*

yoke [jok] *s* (*pair of draft animals*) paire *f*; (*device to join a pair of draft animals*) joug *m*; (*of a shirt*) empiècement *m*; (elec) culasse *f*; (fig) joug; **to throw off the yoke** secouer le joug ‖ *tr* accoupler

yokel ['jokəl] *s* rustaud *m*, manant *m*

yolk [jok] *s* jaune *m* d'œuf

yonder ['jɑndər] *adj* ce . . . -là là-bas, e.g., **that tree yonder** cet arbre-là là-bas ‖ *adv* là-bas

yore [jor] *s*—**of yore** d'antan

you [ju] *pron pers* vous, toi §85; vous, tu §87; vous, te §87 ‖ *pron indef* (coll) on §87, e.g., **you go in this way** on entre par ici

young [jʌŋ] *adj* (*comp* **younger** ['jʌŋgər]; *super* **youngest** ['jʌŋgɪst]) jeune ‖ **the young** les jeunes; (*of animal*) les petits *mpl*; **to be with young** (*said of animal*) être pleine; **young and old** les grands et les petits

young' la'dy *s* (*pl* **-dies**) jeune fille *f*; (*married*) jeune femme *f*; **young ladies** jeunes personnes *fpl*

young' man' *s* (*pl* **men'**) jeune homme *m*; **young men** jeunes gens *mpl*

young' peo'ple *spl* jeunes gens *mpl*

youngster ['jʌŋstər] *s* gosse *mf*

your [jʊr] *adj poss* votre, ton §88

yours [jʊrz] *pron poss* le vôtre, le tien §89; **a friend of yours** un de vos amis; **cordially yours** (complimentary close) amitiés; **yours truly** or **sincerely yours** (complimentary close) veuillez agréer, Monsieur, l'expression de mes sentiments distingués

your·self [jʊr'sɛlf] *pron pers* (*pl* **-selves** ['sɛlvz]) vous-même, toi-même §86; vous, te §87; vous, toi §85

youth [juθ] *s* (*pl* **youths** [juθs], [juðz]) jeunesse *f*; (*person*) jeune homme *m*; **youths** jeunes *mpl*

youthful ['juθfəl] *adj* jeune, juvénile

youth' hos'tel *s* auberge *f* de jeunesse

yowl [jaʊl] *s* hurlement *m* ‖ *intr* hurler

Yugoslav ['jugo'slɑv] *adj* yougoslave ‖ *s* Yougoslave *mf*

Yugoslavia ['jugo'slɑvɪ·ə] *s* Yougoslavie *f*; la Yougoslavie

Yule'log' [jul] *s* bûche *f* de Noël

Yule'tide' *s* les fêtes *fpl* de Noël

yummy ['jʌmi] *adj* délicieux

yum yum ['jʌm 'jʌm] *interj* miam! miam!

Z

Z, z [zi] or [zɛd] (Brit) *s* XXVIᵉ lettre de l'alphabet

za·ny ['zeni] *adj* (*comp* **-nier**; *super* **-niest**) bouffon, toqué ‖ *s* (*pl* **-nies**) bouffon *m*

zeal [zil] *s* zèle *m*

zealot ['zɛlət] *s* zélateur *m*, adepte *mf*

zealotry ['zɛlətri] *s* fanatisme *m*

zealous ['zɛləs] *adj* zélé

zebra ['zibrə] *s* zèbre *m*

zenith ['zinɪθ] *s* zénith *m*

zephyr ['zɛfər] *s* zéphyr *m*

zeppelin ['zɛpəlin] *s* zeppelin *m*

ze·ro ['zɪro] *s* (*pl* **-ros** or **-roes**) zéro *m* ‖ *intr*—**to zero in** (mil) régler la ligne de mire; **to zero in on** (coll) pointer sur

ze'ro grav'ity *s* apesanteur *f*

ze'ro growth' *s* croissance *f* zéro

ze'ro hour' *s* heure *f* H

ze'ro op'tion *s* option *f* nulle

zest [zɛst] *s* enthousiasme *m*; (*agreeable and piquant flavor*) saveur *f*, piquant *m*

Zeus [zus] *s* Zeus *m*

zig·zag ['zig,zæg] *adj & adv* en zigzag ‖ *s* zigzag *m* ‖ *v* (*pret & pp* **-zagged**; *ger* **-zagging**) *intr* zigzaguer

zinc [zɪŋk] *s* zinc *m*

Zionism ['zaɪ·ə,nɪzəm] *s* sionisme *m*

zip [zɪp] *s* (coll) sifflement *m*; (coll) énergie *f* ‖ *v* (*pret & pp* **zipped**; *ger* **zipping**) *tr* fermer à fermeture éclair ‖ *intr* siffler; **to zip by** (coll) passer comme un éclair

Zip' code' *s* indicatif *m* postal

zipper ['zɪpər] *s* fermeture *f* éclair, fermeture à glissière

zither ['zɪθər] *s* cithare *f*

zodiac ['zodɪ,æk] *s* zodiaque *m*

zone [zon] *s* zone *f*

zoning ['zonɪŋ] *s* zonage *m*, zoning *m*

zon'ing code' *s* plan *m* d'occupation des sols (P.O.S.)

zon'ing or'dinance *s* réglementation *f* urbaine

zon'ing per'mit *s* certificat *m* d'urbanisation

zoo [zu] *s* zoo *m*

zoologic(al) [,zo·ə'lɑdʒɪk(əl)] *adj* zoologique

zoology [zo'ɑlədʒi] *s* zoologie *f*

zoom [zum] *s* vrombissement *m*; (aer) montée *f* en chandelle ‖ *intr* vrombir; **to zoom up** monter en chandelle

zoom' lens' *s* zoom *m*

zoot' suit' [zut] *s* costume *m* zazou

Zu·lu ['zulu] *adj* zoulou ‖ *s* (*pl* **-lus**) Zoulou *m*

zygote ['zaɪgot] *s* zygote *m*

CONVERSION TABLES

American Measurements and the Metric System*

	AMERICAN UNIT	METRIC EQUIVA- LENT	METRIC UNIT	AMERICAN EQUIVA- LENT
Length	one mile (mi.)	1.6 kilometers	un kilomètre (km)	.6 mile
	one yard (yd.)	.9 meter	un mètre (m)	39.34 inches
	one foot (ft.)	30 centimeters	un centimètre (cm)	or 3.28 feet
				.39 inch
	one inch (in.)	25.4 millime- ters	un millimètre (mm)	.039 inch
Surface	one acre (a.)	.4 hectare	un hectare (ha)	2.5 acres
	one square mile (sq. mi.)	259 hectares	un kilomètre carré (km²)	.39 square mile
Volume	one cubic foot (cu. ft.)	.028 cubic meter	un mètre cube (m³)	35.314 cubic feet
Capacity	one liquid quart (qt.)	.95 liter	un litre (l)	1.057 quarts
	one gallon (gal.)	3.8 liters		or .26 gal- lon
Weight	one pound (lb.)	.45 kilogram	un kilogram (kg) (un kilo)	2.2 pounds
	one ounce (oz.)	28.35 grams	100 grammes	3.5 ounces
	one ton (2,000 pounds)	907.2 kilo- grams	un gramme (g)	15.432 grains

* International System of Units—Le système international d'unités (SI).

Approximate Comparison of Fahrenheit and Centigrade (Celsius) Temperatures

FAHRENHEIT			CENTIGRADE
Boiling point ►	212	100 ◄	Point d'ébullition
	140	60	
	104	40	
	100	38	
Normal body temperature ► (physiol)	98.6	37 ◄	Température normale (physiol)
	97	36	
	88	31	
	77	25	
	68	20	
	59	15	
	50	10	
	41	5	
Freezing point ►	32	0 ◄	Point de congélation
	23	−5	
	14	−10	
	5	−15	
	0	−18	
	−13	−25	
	−22	−30	
	−40	−40	

For exact conversion, use the following:
(a) To convert Fahrenheit into centigrade, subtract 32, multiply by 5, and divide by 9.
(b) To convert centigrade into Fahrenheit, multiply by 9, divide by 5, and add 32.

Tire Pressure

Pounds per square inch *Livres par pouce carré*	Kilograms per square centimeter *Kilogrammes par centimètre carré*	Pounds per square inch *Livres par pouce carré*	Kilograms per square centimeter *Kilogrammes par centimètre carré*
16	1,12	30	2,10
18	1,26	32	2,24
20	1,40	36	2,52
22	1,54	40	2,80
24	1,68	50	3,50
26	1,82	60	4,20
28	1,96	70	4,90

Sizes of Clothing in the United States and France

LADIES—*DAMES*

Size of coats, dresses—*Taille de manteaux, de robes*

American	8	10	12	14	16	18	20
French	38	40	42	44	46	48	50

Size of blouses, sweaters, and slips—*Taille de chemisiers (corsages), de chandails et de combinaisons*

American	32	34	36	38	40	42
French	38	40	42	44	46	48

Size of shoes, slippers—*Pointure de chaussures, de pantoufles*

American	4	5	6	7	8	9
French	36	37	38	39	40	41

MEN—*MESSIEURS*

Size of topcoats, suits—*Taille de pardessus, de costumes*

American	30	32	34	36	38	40	42	44	46
French	40	42	44	46	48	50	52	54	56

Size (neck size) of shirts—*Taille (encolure) de chemises*

American	14	14½	15	15½	16	16½
French	37	38	39	40	41	42

Size of shoes, slippers—*Pointure de chaussures, de pantoufles*

American	8	8½	9	9½	10	10½	11
French	41	42	43	44	45	46	47

Size of hats—*Pointure (tours de la tête en centimètres) de chapeaux*

American	6⅝	6¾	6⅞	7	7⅛	7¼	7⅜	7½	7⅝
French	53	54	55	56	57	58	59	60	61

ROGER J. STEINER is Senior Professor of Languages and Linguistics, University of Delaware. He is the author of numerous articles on lexicography and language.

Amsco School Publications, Inc.